THE ONE YEAR BIBLE
for New Believers

NEW LIVING TRANSLATION

The ONE YEAR® BIBLE

for NEW BELIEVERS

Arranged in 365 Daily Readings
with Notes for New Believers

New Living
Translation®

SECOND EDITION

Tyndale House Publishers, Inc.
Carol Stream, Illinois

Visit Tyndale's exciting Web site at www.tyndale.com

The One Year Bible for New Believers, copyright © 2006 by Tyndale House Publishers, Inc., Carol Stream, Illinois 60188. All rights reserved.

Produced with the assistance of The Livingstone Corporation (www.LivingstoneCorp.com). Project staff includes: Linda Taylor, Carol Fielding, Carol Smith, Maggie Rowe, Mary Horner Collins, Joan Guest, Anthony Charles, Jonathan Ziman, Bruce Barton.

Reading introductions and daily study notes copyright © 2006 by The Livingstone Corporation. All rights reserved.

Cover photograph copyright © by Edmond Van Hoorick/Getty Images. All rights reserved.

This Bible is typeset in the typeface *Lucerna,* designed by Brian Sooy & Co. exclusively for Tyndale House Publishers, Inc. All rights reserved.

ISBN-13: 978-1-4143-0073-3   ISBN-10: 1-4143-0073-5 Hardcover

ISBN-13: 978-1-4143-0074-0   ISBN-10: 1-4143-0074-3 Softcover

Printed in the United States of America

12   11   10   09   08   07   06

7   6   5   4   3   2   1

Tyndale House Publishers and Wycliffe Bible Translators share the vision for an understandable, accurate translation of the Bible for every person in the world. Each sale of the *Holy Bible,* New Living Translation, benefits Wycliffe Bible Translators. Wycliffe is working with partners around the world to accomplish Vision 2025—an initiative to start a Bible translation program in every language group that needs it by the year 2025.

CONTENTS

Alphabetical Listing of Bible Books

HOW TO USE THIS BIBLE

Dear new believer in Christ,

Welcome to the family! Your decision to follow Christ has joined you to a family of believers that stretches around the globe and back through the centuries. It is a decision that will make a difference for the rest of your life on this earth—and then on into eternity.

You hold in your hands the guidebook for your life in Christ—the Bible, God's Word to us. This book looks a bit different from other Bibles you've seen. We'd like to tell you a little about it.

(1) This Bible features the accurate and easy-to-read New Living Translation. Its clarity and precision will help you to understand God's Word.

(2) Because Bible reading needs to become a part of your daily life, this Bible is divided into 365 daily readings. Each day presents a portion of the Old Testament, a portion of the New Testament, a psalm from the book of Psalms, and a proverb from the book of Proverbs. If you follow this format, in one year's time you will read the entire Bible once and the book of Psalms twice. Many people set aside a short block of time each day to follow this format. However, there is more than one way to utilize the One Year Bible reading plan. Here are some popular variations:

The Revised One-Year Plan. Schedule some time in both the morning and evening. Then read the New Testament and Psalms selections in the morning and the Old Testament and Proverbs selections in the evening.

The Two-Year Plan. During the first year, just read the Old Testament and Proverbs selections. Then during the second year, read the selections from the New Testament and Psalms.

The Three-Year Plan. Read the Old Testament selection the first year, the New Testament selection the second year, and the Psalms and Proverbs selections during the third year.

You need not limit yourself to these suggestions. The arrangement of *The One Year Bible* makes it easy to devise any number of Bible reading plans to meet your particular needs.

(3) At the beginning of each Old and New Testament reading, you will find a brief introductory paragraph designed to help you understand the context of what you'll be reading.

(4) There are 365 study notes in this Bible—one for each day. These notes provide an opportunity for further reflection on a verse or verses from the day's readings. The notes fall into three basic categories:

WHO GOD IS
HOW WE LIVE
WHAT THE BIBLE SAYS

The notes are designed to help you learn the basics of the Christian life and offer guidance when a particular day's reading contains something that is difficult to understand. You can read one per day or use the index that begins on page 1493 to do a more systematic study of a particular topic.

(5) As you read the daily selections remember these basic facts:

Old Testament. The Old Testament gives much of the history of the Jewish people in ancient times. God is revealed in his interactions with his people. Our need for a Savior is revealed in the people's persistent unfaithfulness to the Lord.

New Testament. The New Testament tells the story of Jesus and his first followers. Jesus' death and resurrection is the basis for our salvation from sin and death. Through Jesus' teachings and in letters written by various church leaders, we find guidance for living the Christian life.

Psalms. The psalms are songs and poems focusing on praise and adoration, request for help, historical reflection, and lament. Through their powerful language we learn what it means to have a heart that is devoted to God.

Proverbs. The proverbs give nuggets of practical wisdom for every day living.

Beginning on page A53 you will find a more detailed introduction to the books of the Bible. There you'll find an overview of each book's content plus information about who wrote it, when it was written, and for what purpose.

(6) Finally, we've included the Tyndale Bible Verse Finder. This useful tool will help you find out what the Bible says about a variety of important doctrinal (the stuff Christians believe) and practical life issues. It starts on page A21.

Don't let all this overwhelm you. Reading God's Word is a life-long journey of discovery and devotion, and we've given you some tools and some options to get started. Go at your own pace. Dwell longer in some places, move quickly through others. If you miss a day or two, don't get discouraged. Everyone does. Catch up when you can, or jump ahead to the current day. The important thing is that you are reading God's Word daily and allowing him to speak to you through it. This is one of the most important keys to growth as a new believer.

We pray that you find *The One Year Bible for New Believers* helpful as you begin your journey with the Lord Jesus Christ.

The Editors

A NOTE TO READERS

The *Holy Bible*, New Living Translation, was first published in 1996. It quickly became one of the most popular Bible translations in the English-speaking world. While the NLT's influence was rapidly growing, the Bible Translation Committee determined that an additional investment in scholarly review and text refinement could make it even better. So shortly after its initial publication, the committee began an eight-year process with the purpose of increasing the level of the NLT's precision without sacrificing its easy-to-understand quality. This second-generation text was completed in 2004 and is reflected in this edition of the New Living Translation.

The goal of any Bible translation is to convey the meaning and content of the ancient Hebrew, Aramaic, and Greek texts as accurately as possible to contemporary readers. The challenge for our translators was to create a text that would communicate as clearly and powerfully to today's readers as the original texts did to readers and listeners in the ancient biblical world. The resulting translation is easy to read and understand, while also accurately communicating the meaning and content of the original biblical texts. The NLT is a general-purpose text especially good for study, devotional reading, and reading aloud in worship services.

We believe that the New Living Translation—which combines the latest biblical scholarship with a clear, dynamic writing style—will communicate God's word powerfully to all who read it. We publish it with the prayer that God will use it to speak his timeless truth to the church and the world in a fresh, new way.

The Publishers, July 2004

INTRODUCTION TO THE
NEW LIVING TRANSLATION

Translation Philosophy and Methodology.   English Bible translations tend to be governed by one of two general translation theories. The first theory has been called "formal-equivalence," "literal," or "word-for-word" translation. According to this theory, the translator attempts to render each word of the original language into English and seeks to preserve the original syntax and sentence structure as much as possible in translation. The second theory has been called "dynamic-equivalence," "functional-equivalence," or "thought-for-thought" translation. The goal of this translation theory is to produce in English the closest natural equivalent of the message expressed by the original-language text, both in meaning and in style.

Both of these translation theories have their strengths. A formal-equivalence translation preserves aspects of the original text—including ancient idioms, term consistency, and original-language syntax—that are valuable for scholars and professional study. It allows a reader to trace formal elements of the original-language text through the English translation. A dynamic-equivalence translation, on the other hand, focuses on translating the message of the original-language text. It ensures that the meaning of the text is readily apparent to the contemporary reader. This allows the message to come through with immediacy, without requiring the reader to struggle with foreign idioms and awkward syntax. It also facilitates serious study of the text's message and clarity in both devotional and public reading.

The pure application of either of these translation philosophies would create translations at opposite ends of the translation spectrum. But in reality, all translations contain a mixture of these two philosophies. A purely formal-equivalence translation would be unintelligible in English, and a purely dynamic-equivalence translation would risk being unfaithful to the original. That is why translations shaped by dynamic-equivalence theory are usually quite literal when the original text is relatively clear, and the translations shaped by formal-equivalence theory are sometimes quite dynamic when the original text is obscure.

The translators of the New Living Translation set out to render the message of the original texts of Scripture into clear, contemporary English. As they did so, they kept the concerns of both formal-equivalence and dynamic-equivalence in mind. On the one hand, they translated as simply and literally as possible when that approach yielded an accurate, clear, and natural English text. Many words and phrases were rendered literally and consistently into English, preserving essential literary and rhetorical devices, ancient metaphors, and word choices that give structure to the text and provide echoes of meaning from one passage to the next.

On the other hand, the translators rendered the message more dynamically when the literal rendering was hard to understand, was misleading, or yielded archaic or foreign wording. They clarified difficult metaphors and terms to aid in the reader's understanding. The translators first struggled with the meaning of the words and phrases in the ancient context; then they rendered the message into clear, natural English. Their goal was to be both faithful to the ancient texts and eminently readable. The result is a translation that is both exegetically accurate and idiomatically powerful.

Translation Process and Team.   To produce an accurate translation of the Bible into contemporary English, the translation team needed the skills necessary to enter into the thought patterns of the ancient authors and then to render their ideas, connotations, and effects into clear, contemporary English. To begin this process, qualified biblical scholars were needed to interpret the meaning of the original text and to check it against our base English translation. In order to guard against personal and theological biases, the scholars needed to represent a diverse group of Evangelicals who would employ the best exegetical tools. Then to work alongside the scholars, skilled English stylists were needed to shape the text into clear, contemporary English.

With these concerns in mind, the Bible Translation Committee recruited teams of scholars that represented a broad spectrum of denominations, theological perspectives, and backgrounds within the worldwide Evangelical community. (These scholars are listed at the end of this introduction.) Each book of the Bible was assigned to three different scholars with proven expertise in the book or group of books to be reviewed. Each of these scholars made a thorough review of a base translation and submitted suggested revisions to the appropriate Senior Translator. The Senior Translator then reviewed and summarized these suggestions and proposed a first-draft revision of the base text. This draft served as the basis for several additional phases of exegetical and stylistic committee review. Then the Bible Translation Committee jointly reviewed and approved every verse of the final translation.

Throughout the translation and editing process, the Senior Translators and their scholar teams were given a chance to review the editing done by the team of stylists. This ensured that exegetical errors would not be introduced late in the process and that the entire Bible Translation Committee was happy with the final result. By choosing a team of qualified scholars and skilled stylists and by setting up a process that allowed their interaction throughout the process, the New Living Translation has been refined to preserve the essential formal elements of the original biblical texts, while also creating a clear, understandable English text.

The New Living Translation was first published in 1996. Shortly after its initial publication, the Bible Translation Committee began a process of further committee review and translation refinement. The purpose of this continued revision was to increase the level of precision without sacrificing the text's easy-to-understand quality. This second-edition text was completed in 2004, and this printing of the New Living Translation reflects the updated text.

Written to Be Read Aloud. It is evident in Scripture that the biblical documents were written to be read aloud, often in public worship (see Nehemiah 8; Luke 4:16-20; 1 Timothy 4:13; Revelation 1:3). It is still the case today that more people will hear the Bible read aloud in church than are likely to read it for themselves. Therefore, a new translation must communicate with clarity and power when it is read publicly. Clarity was a primary goal for the NLT translators, not only to facilitate private reading and understanding, but also to ensure that it would be excellent for public reading and make an immediate and powerful impact on any listener.

The Texts behind the New Living Translation. The Old Testament translators used the Masoretic Text of the Hebrew Bible as represented in *Biblia Hebraica Stuttgartensia* (1977), with its extensive system of textual notes; this is an update of Rudolf Kittel's *Biblia Hebraica* (Stuttgart, 1937). The translators also further compared the Dead Sea Scrolls, the Septuagint and other Greek manuscripts, the Samaritan Pentateuch, the Syriac Peshitta, the Latin Vulgate, and any other versions or manuscripts that shed light on the meaning of difficult passages.

The New Testament translators used the two standard editions of the Greek New Testament: the *Greek New Testament,* published by the United Bible Societies (UBS, fourth revised edition, 1993), and *Novum Testamentum Graece,* edited by Nestle and Aland (NA, twenty-seventh edition, 1993). These two editions, which have the same text but differ in punctuation and textual notes, represent, for the most part, the best in modern textual scholarship. However, in cases where strong textual or other scholarly evidence supported the decision, the translators sometimes chose to differ from the UBS and NA Greek texts and followed variant readings found in other ancient witnesses. Significant textual variants of this sort are always noted in the textual notes of the New Living Translation.

Translation Issues. The translators have made a conscious effort to provide a text that can be easily understood by the typical reader of modern English. To this end, we sought to use only vocabulary and language structures in common use today. We avoided using language likely to become quickly dated or that reflects only a narrow sub-dialect of English, with the goal of making the New Living Translation as broadly useful and timeless as possible.

But our concern for readability goes beyond the concerns of vocabulary and sentence structure. We are also concerned about historical and cultural barriers to understanding the Bible, and we have sought to translate terms shrouded in history and culture in ways that can be immediately understood. To this end:

- We have converted ancient weights and measures (for example, "ephah" [a unit of dry volume] or "cubit" [a unit of length]) to modern English (American) equivalents, since the ancient measures are not generally meaningful to today's readers. Then in the textual footnotes we offer the literal Hebrew, Aramaic, or Greek measures, along with modern metric equivalents.
- Instead of translating ancient currency values literally, we have expressed them in common terms that communicate the message. For example, in the Old Testament, "ten shekels of silver" becomes "ten pieces of silver" to convey the intended message. In the New Testament, we have often translated the "denarius" as "the normal daily wage" to facilitate understanding. Then a footnote offers: "Greek *a denarius,* the payment for a full day's wage." In general, we give a clear English rendering and then state the literal Hebrew, Aramaic, or Greek in a textual footnote.
- Since the names of Hebrew months are unknown to most contemporary readers, and since the Hebrew lunar calendar fluctuates from year to year in relation to the solar calendar used today, we have looked for clear ways to communicate the time of year the Hebrew months (such as Abib) refer to. When an expanded or interpretive rendering is given in the text, a textual note gives the literal rendering. Where it is possible to define a specific ancient date in terms of our modern calendar, we use modern dates in the text. A textual footnote then gives the literal Hebrew date and states the rationale for our rendering. For example, Ezra 6:15 pinpoints the date when the post-exilic Temple was completed in Jerusalem: "the third day of the month Adar." This was during the sixth year of King Darius's reign (that is, 515 B.C.). We have translated that date as March 12, with a footnote giving the Hebrew and identifying the year as 515 B.C.
- Since ancient references to the time of day differ from our modern methods of denoting time, we have used renderings that are instantly understandable to the modern reader. Accordingly, we have rendered specific times of day by using approximate equivalents in terms of our common "o'clock" system. On occasion, translations such as "at dawn the next morning" or "as the sun began to set" have been used when the biblical reference is more general.
- When the meaning of a proper name (or a wordplay inherent in a proper name) is relevant to the message of the text, its meaning is often illuminated with a textual footnote. For example, in Exodus 2:10 the text reads: "The princess named him Moses, for she explained, 'I lifted him out of the water.' " The accompanying footnote reads: "*Moses* sounds like a Hebrew term that means 'to lift out.' "

  Sometimes, when the actual meaning of a name is clear, that meaning is included in parentheses within the text itself. For example, the text at Genesis 16:11 reads: "You are to name him Ishmael *(which means 'God hears'),* for the LORD has heard your cry of distress." Since the original hearers and readers would have instantly understood the meaning of the name "Ishmael," we have provided modern readers with the same information so they can experience the text in a similar way.
- Many words and phrases carry a great deal of cultural meaning that was obvious to the original readers but needs explanation in our own culture. For example, the phrase "they beat their breasts" (Luke 23:48) in ancient times meant that people were very upset, often in mourning. In our translation we chose to translate this phrase dynamically for clarity: "They went home *in deep sorrow.*" Then we included a footnote with the literal Greek, which reads: "Greek *went home beating their breasts.*" In other similar cases, however, we have sometimes chosen to illuminate the existing literal expression to make it immediately understandable. For example, here we might have expanded the literal Greek phrase to read: "They went home beating their breasts *in sorrow.*" If we had done this, we would not have included a textual footnote, since the literal Greek clearly appears in translation.
- Metaphorical language is sometimes difficult for contemporary readers to understand, so at times we have chosen to translate or illuminate the meaning of a metaphor. For example, the ancient poet writes, "Your neck is *like* the tower of David" (Song of Songs 4:4). We have rendered it "Your neck is *as beautiful as* the tower of David" to clarify the intended positive

meaning of the simile. Another example comes in Ecclesiastes 12:3, which can be literally rendered: "Remember him . . . when the grinding women cease because they are few, and the women who look through the windows see dimly." We have rendered it: "Remember him before your teeth—your few remaining servants—stop grinding; and before your eyes—the women looking through the windows—see dimly." We clarified such metaphors only when we believed a typical reader might be confused by the literal text.

- When the content of the original language text is poetic in character, we have rendered it in English poetic form. We sought to break lines in ways that clarify and highlight the relationships between phrases of the text. Hebrew poetry often uses parallelism, a literary form where a second phrase (or in some instances a third or fourth) echoes the initial phrase in some way. In Hebrew parallelism, the subsequent parallel phrases continue, while also furthering and sharpening, the thought expressed in the initial line or phrase. Whenever possible, we sought to represent these parallel phrases in natural poetic English.

- The Greek term *hoi Ioudaioi* is literally translated "the Jews" in many English translations. In the Gospel of John, however, this term doesn't always refer to the Jewish people generally. In some contexts, it refers more particularly to the Jewish religious leaders. We have attempted to capture the meaning in these different contexts by using terms such as "the people" (with a footnote: Greek *the Jewish people*) or "the religious leaders," where appropriate.

- One challenge we faced was how to translate accurately the ancient biblical text that was originally written in a context where male-oriented terms were used to refer to humanity generally. We needed to respect the nature of the ancient context while also trying to make the translation clear to a modern audience that tends to read male-oriented language as applying only to males. Often the original text, though using masculine nouns and pronouns, clearly intends that the message be applied to both men and women. A typical example is found in the New Testament letters, where the believers are called "brothers" (*adelphoi*). Yet it is clear from the content of these letters that they were addressed to all the believers—male and female. Thus, we have usually translated this Greek word as "brothers and sisters" in order to represent the historical situation more accurately.

We have also been sensitive to passages where the text applies generally to human beings or to the human condition. In some instances we have used plural pronouns (they, them) in place of the masculine singular (he, him). For example, a traditional rendering of Proverbs 22:6 is: "Train up a child in the way he should go, and when he is old he will not turn from it." We have rendered it: "Direct your children onto the right path, and when they are older, they will not leave it." At times, we have also replaced third person pronouns with the second person to ensure clarity. A traditional rendering of Proverbs 26:27 is: "He who digs a pit will fall into it, and he who rolls a stone, it will come back on him." We have rendered it: "If you set a trap for others, you will get caught in it yourself. If you roll a boulder down on others, it will crush you instead."

We should emphasize, however, that all masculine nouns and pronouns used to represent God (for example, "Father") have been maintained without exception. All decisions of this kind have been driven by the concern to reflect accurately the intended meaning of the original texts of Scripture.

Lexical Consistency in Terminology.   For the sake of clarity, we have translated certain original-language terms consistently, especially within synoptic passages and for commonly repeated rhetorical phrases, and within certain word categories such as divine names and non-theological technical terminology (e.g., liturgical, legal, cultural, zoological, and botanical terms). For theological terms, we have allowed a greater semantic range of acceptable English words or phrases for a single Hebrew or Greek word. We have avoided some theological terms that are not readily understood by many modern readers. For example, we avoided using words such as "justification," "sanctification," and "regeneration," which are carryovers from Latin translations. In place of these words, we have provided renderings such as "we are made right with God," "we are made holy," and "we are born anew."

The Spelling of Proper Names.   Many individuals in the Bible, especially the Old Testament, are known by more than one name (e.g., Uzziah/Azariah). For the sake of clarity, we have tried to use a single spelling for any one individual, footnoting the literal spelling whenever we differ from it. This is especially helpful in delineating the kings of Israel and Judah. King Joash/Jehoash of Israel has been consistently called Jehoash, while King Joash/Jehoash of Judah is called Joash. A similar distinction has been used to distinguish between Joram/Jehoram of Israel and Joram/Jehoram of Judah. All such decisions were made with the goal of clarifying the text for the reader. When the ancient biblical writers clearly had a theological purpose in their choice of a variant name (e.g., Eshbaal/Ishbosheth), the different names have been maintained with an explanatory footnote.

For the names Jacob and Israel, which are used interchangeably for both the individual patriarch and the nation, we generally render it "Israel" when it refers to the nation and "Jacob" when it refers to the individual. When our rendering of the name differs from the underlying Hebrew text, we provide a textual footnote, which includes this explanation: "The names 'Jacob' and 'Israel' are often interchanged throughout the Old Testament, referring sometimes to the individual patriarch and sometimes to the nation."

The Rendering of Divine Names. All appearances of *'el, 'elohim,* or *'eloah* have been translated "God," except where the context demands the translation "god(s)." We have generally rendered the tetragrammaton (*YHWH*) consistently as "the LORD," utilizing a form with small capitals that is common among English translations. This will distinguish it from the name *'adonai,* which we render "Lord." When *'adonai* and *YHWH* appear together, we have rendered it "Sovereign LORD." This also distinguishes *'adonai YHWH* from cases where *YHWH* appears with *'elohim,* which is rendered "LORD God." When *YH* (the short form of *YHWH*) and *YHWH* appear together, we have rendered it "LORD GOD." When *YHWH* appears with the term *tseba'oth,* we have rendered it "LORD of Heaven's Armies" to translate the meaning of the name. In a few cases, we have utilized the transliteration, *Yahweh,* when the personal character of the name is being invoked in contrast to another divine name or the name of some other god (for example, see Exod 3:15; 6:2-3).

In the New Testament, the Greek word *christos* has been translated as "Messiah" when the context assumes a Jewish audience. When a Gentile audience can be assumed, *christos* has been translated as "Christ." The Greek word *kurios* is consistently translated "Lord," except that it is translated "LORD" wherever the New Testament text explicitly quotes from the Old Testament, and the text there has it in small capitals.

Textual Footnotes. The New Living Translation provides several kinds of textual footnotes, all designated in the text with an asterisk:

- When for the sake of clarity the NLT renders a difficult or potentially confusing phrase dynamically, we generally give the literal rendering in a textual footnote. This allows the reader to see the literal source of our dynamic rendering and how our translation relates to other more literal translations. These notes are prefaced with "Hebrew," "Aramaic," or "Greek," identifying the language of the underlying source text. For example, in Acts 2:42 we translated the literal "breaking of bread" (from the Greek) as "the Lord's Supper" to clarify that this verse refers to the ceremonial practice of the church rather than just an ordinary meal. Then we attached a footnote to "the Lord's Supper," which reads: "Greek *the breaking of bread.*"
- Textual footnotes are also used to show alternative renderings, prefaced with the word "Or." These normally occur for passages where an aspect of the meaning is debated. On occasion, we also provide notes on words or phrases that represent a departure from long-standing tradition. These notes are prefaced with "Traditionally rendered." For example, the footnote to the translation "serious skin disease" at Leviticus 13:2 says: "Traditionally rendered *leprosy.* The Hebrew word used throughout this passage is used to describe various skin diseases."
- When our translators follow a textual variant that differs significantly from our standard Hebrew or Greek texts (listed earlier), we document that difference with a footnote. We also footnote cases when the NLT excludes a passage that is included in the Greek text known as the *Textus Receptus* (and familiar to readers through its translation in the King James Version). In such cases, we offer a translation of the excluded text in a footnote, even though it is generally recognized as a later addition to the Greek text and not part of the original Greek New Testament.

- All Old Testament passages that are quoted in the New Testament are identified by a textual footnote at the New Testament location. When the New Testament clearly quotes from the Greek translation of the Old Testament, and when it differs significantly in wording from the Hebrew text, we also place a textual footnote at the Old Testament location. This note includes a rendering of the Greek version, along with a cross-reference to the New Testament passage(s) where it is cited (for example, see notes on Proverbs 3:12; Psalms 8:2; 53:3).

- Some textual footnotes provide cultural and historical information on places, things, and people in the Bible that are probably obscure to modern readers. Such notes should aid the reader in understanding the message of the text. For example, in Acts 12:1, "King Herod" is named in this translation as "King Herod Agrippa" and is identified in a footnote as being "the nephew of Herod Antipas and a grandson of Herod the Great."

- When the meaning of a proper name (or a wordplay inherent in a proper name) is relevant to the meaning of the text, it is either illuminated with a textual footnote or included within parentheses in the text itself. For example, the footnote concerning the name "Eve" at Genesis 3:20 reads: "Eve sounds like a Hebrew term that means 'to give life.'" This wordplay in the Hebrew illuminates the meaning of the text, which goes on to say that Eve "would be the mother of all who live."

AS WE SUBMIT this translation for publication, we recognize that any translation of the Scriptures is subject to limitations and imperfections. Anyone who has attempted to communicate the richness of God's Word into another language will realize it is impossible to make a perfect translation. Recognizing these limitations, we sought God's guidance and wisdom throughout this project. Now we pray that he will accept our efforts and use this translation for the benefit of the church and of all people.

We pray that the New Living Translation will overcome some of the barriers of history, culture, and language that have kept people from reading and understanding God's Word. We hope that readers unfamiliar with the Bible will find the words clear and easy to understand and that readers well versed in the Scriptures will gain a fresh perspective. We pray that readers will gain insight and wisdom for living, but most of all that they will meet the God of the Bible and be forever changed by knowing him.

The Bible Translation Committee, July 2004

BIBLE TRANSLATION TEAM
HOLY BIBLE, NEW LIVING TRANSLATION

PENTATEUCH
Daniel I. Block, Senior Translator
The Southern Baptist Theological Seminary

GENESIS
Allen Ross, *Beeson Divinity School, Samford University*
Gordon Wenham, *University of Gloucester*

EXODUS
Robert Bergen, *Hannibal-LaGrange College*
Daniel I. Block, *The Southern Baptist Theological Seminary*
Eugene Carpenter, *Bethel College, Mishawaka, Indiana*

LEVITICUS
David Baker, *Ashland Theological Seminary*
Victor Hamilton, *Asbury College*
Kenneth Mathews, *Beeson Divinity School, Samford University*

NUMBERS
Dale A. Brueggemann, *Assemblies of God Division of Foreign Missions*
R. K. Harrison (deceased), *Wycliffe College*
Paul R. House, *Wheaton College*
Gerald L. Mattingly, *Johnson Bible College*

DEUTERONOMY
J. Gordon McConville, *University of Gloucester*
Eugene H. Merrill, *Dallas Theological Seminary*
John A. Thompson (deceased), *University of Melbourne*

HISTORICAL BOOKS
Barry J. Beitzel, Senior Translator
Trinity Evangelical Divinity School

JOSHUA, JUDGES
Carl E. Armerding, *Schloss Mittersill Study Centre*
Barry J. Beitzel, *Trinity Evangelical Divinity School*
Lawson Stone, *Asbury Theological Seminary*

1 & 2 SAMUEL
Robert Gordon, *Cambridge University*
V. Philips Long, *Regent College*
J. Robert Vannoy, *Biblical Theological Seminary*

1 & 2 KINGS
Bill T. Arnold, *Asbury Theological Seminary*
William H. Barnes, *North Central University*
Frederic W. Bush, *Fuller Theological Seminary*

1 & 2 CHRONICLES
Raymond B. Dillard (deceased), *Westminster Theological Seminary*
David A. Dorsey, *Evangelical School of Theology*
Terry Eves, *Erskine College*

RUTH, EZRA—ESTHER
William C. Williams, *Vanguard University*
H. G. M. Williamson, *Oxford University*

WISDOM BOOKS
Tremper Longman III, Senior Translator
Westmont College

JOB
August Konkel, *Providence Theological Seminary*
Tremper Longman III, *Westmont College*
Al Wolters, *Redeemer College*

PSALMS 1–75
Mark D. Futato, *Reformed Theological Seminary*
Douglas Green, *Westminster Theological Seminary*
Richard Pratt, *Reformed Theological Seminary*

PSALMS 76–150
David M. Howard Jr., *Bethel Theological Seminary*
Raymond C. Ortlund Jr., *Trinity Evangelical Divinity School*
Willem VanGemeren, *Trinity Evangelical Divinity School*

PROVERBS
Ted Hildebrandt, *Gordon College*
Richard Schultz, *Wheaton College*
Raymond C. Van Leeuwen, *Eastern College*

ECCLESIASTES, SONG OF SONGS
Daniel C. Fredericks, *Belhaven College*
David Hubbard (deceased), *Fuller Theological Seminary*
Tremper Longman III, *Westmont College*

PROPHETS
John N. Oswalt, Senior Translator
Wesley Biblical Seminary

ISAIAH
John N. Oswalt, *Wesley Biblical Seminary*
Gary Smith, *Midwestern Baptist Theological Seminary*
John Walton, *Wheaton College*

JEREMIAH, LAMENTATIONS
G. Herbert Livingston, *Asbury Theological Seminary*
Elmer A. Martens, *Mennonite Brethren Biblical Seminary*

EZEKIEL

Daniel I. Block, *The Southern Baptist Theological Seminary*
David H. Engelhard, *Calvin Theological Seminary*
David Thompson, *Asbury Theological Seminary*

DANIEL, HAGGAI—MALACHI

Joyce Baldwin Caine (deceased), *Trinity College, Bristol*
Douglas Gropp, *Catholic University of America*
Roy Hayden, *Oral Roberts School of Theology*
Andrew Hill, *Wheaton College*
Tremper Longman III, *Westmont College*

HOSEA—ZEPHANIAH

Joseph Coleson, *Nazarene Theological Seminary*
Roy Hayden, *Oral Roberts School of Theology*
Andrew Hill, *Wheaton College*
Richard Patterson, *Liberty University*

GOSPELS AND ACTS

Grant R. Osborne, Senior Translator
Trinity Evangelical Divinity School

MATTHEW

Craig Blomberg, *Denver Seminary*
Donald A. Hagner, *Fuller Theological Seminary*
David Turner, *Grand Rapids Baptist Seminary*

MARK

Robert Guelich (deceased), *Fuller Theological Seminary*
George Guthrie, *Union University*
Grant R. Osborne, *Trinity Evangelical Divinity School*

LUKE

Darrell Bock, *Dallas Theological Seminary*
Scot McKnight, *North Park University*
Robert Stein, *The Southern Baptist Theological Seminary*

JOHN

Gary M. Burge, *Wheaton College*
Philip W. Comfort, *Coastal Carolina University*
Marianne Meye Thompson, *Fuller Theological Seminary*

ACTS

D. A. Carson, *Trinity Evangelical Divinity School*
William J. Larkin, *Columbia International University*
Roger Mohrlang, *Whitworth College*

LETTERS AND REVELATION

Norman R. Ericson, Senior Translator
Wheaton College

ROMANS, GALATIANS

Gerald Borchert, *Northern Baptist Theological Seminary*
Douglas J. Moo, *Wheaton College*
Thomas R. Schreiner, *The Southern Baptist Theological Seminary*

1 & 2 CORINTHIANS

Joseph Alexanian, *Trinity International University*
Linda Belleville, *North Park Theological Seminary*
Douglas A. Oss, *Central Bible College*
Robert Sloan, *Baylor University*

EPHESIANS—PHILEMON

Harold W. Hoehner, *Dallas Theological Seminary*
Moises Silva, *Gordon-Conwell Theological Seminary*
Klyne Snodgrass, *North Park Theological Seminary*

HEBREWS, JAMES, 1 & 2 PETER, JUDE

Peter Davids, *Schloss Mittersill Study Centre*
Norman R. Ericson, *Wheaton College*
William Lane (deceased), *Seattle Pacific University*
J. Ramsey Michaels, *S. W. Missouri State University*

1—3 JOHN, REVELATION

Greg Beale, *Wheaton College*
Robert Mounce, *Whitworth College*
M. Robert Mulholland Jr., *Asbury Theological Seminary*

SPECIAL REVIEWERS

F. F. Bruce (deceased), *University of Manchester*
Kenneth N. Taylor (deceased), *Translator,* The Living Bible

COORDINATING TEAM

Mark D. Taylor, *Director and Chief Stylist*
Ronald A. Beers, *Executive Director and Stylist*
Mark R. Norton, *Managing Editor and O.T. Coordinating Editor*
Philip W. Comfort, *N.T. Coordinating Editor*
Daniel W. Taylor, *Bethel University, Senior Stylist*

TYNDALE BIBLE VERSE FINDER

ABORTION God cares for the unborn (Exodus 21:22-25, February 5)
We should protect the helpless (Psalm 82:3-4, April 13)
Children are from God (Psalm 127:3, June 9)
God forms every child (Psalm 139:13-16, June 21)
God plans the future of every child (Jeremiah 1:5, October 3)

ABUSE God cares about minorities (Exodus 22:21, February 5)
God protects those who are helpless (Psalm 12:5, January 14)
Jesus was abused (Matthew 26:67-68, February 10)
Abuse has no place in family relationships (Ephesians 5:21–6:4,
September 27)

ACCOUNTABILITY God will judge our work (2 Chronicles 19:5-10, July 27)
Sin has consequences (Ezekiel 18:20, November 8)
God will hold us accountable for our sin (Ezekiel 18:30,
November 8)
We are accountable for every word that we speak (Matthew 12:36,
January 18)
Confronting others with their sins should be done in private
(Matthew 18:15, January 27)
We should hold each other accountable (Luke 17:3, April 14)
We are accountable for what we believe (John 3:18, May 3)
God holds Christians accountable (Romans 14:11-12, July 31)
God will reward Christians for their good deeds (1 Corinthians 3:8,
August 7)
God will examine our actions (2 Corinthians 5:10, August 31)

ACCUSATIONS Satan accuses God's people of doing wrong (Zechariah 3:1,
December 22)
Jesus was falsely accused (Matthew 26:59-60, February 10)
Christians' sins are forgiven (Colossians 1:22, October 5)
Accusations against church leaders must come from more than one
person (1 Timothy 5:19, October 20)
Satan is known as the Accuser (Revelation 12:10, December 21)

ADOLESCENCE Young people should worship God (1 Kings 18:12, June 17)
God can give hope to young people (Psalm 71:5, March 30)
Young people should remember God (Ecclesiastes 12:1, September 5)
Young people should be an example to others (1 Timothy 4:12,
October 19)
Young people should run from their sinful desires (2 Timothy 2:22,
October 24)

ADOPTION, God's children should obey him (Deuteronomy 26:18, April 4)
SPIRITUAL God disciplines his children (2 Samuel 7:14, May 25)
Do not despise God's discipline (Proverbs 3:11-12, January 13)
God is our Father (Matthew 6:9, January 7)
Christians are God's children (John 1:12, April 30)
God's Spirit leads his children (Romans 8:14-17, July 23)

God's children act differently than the world (2 Corinthians 6:17-18, September 3)
All of God's children are equal in God's eyes (Galatians 3:28, September 18)
God's children will receive a spiritual inheritance (Galatians 4:4-7, September 18)
God chose us to be his children (Ephesians 1:4-5, September 22)
Jesus is our spiritual brother (Hebrews 2:11, October 31)

ADULTERY God forbids adultery (Exodus 20:14, February 4)
Adultery has consequences (Proverbs 6:26, February 2)
Adultery is foolish (Proverbs 6:32, February 3)
Adultery is disgusting to God (Jeremiah 7:9-10, October 6)
God considers lust as sinful as adultery (Matthew 5:27-28, January 6)
Divorce often yields adultery (Mark 10:11-12, February 28)
God can forgive the adulterer (John 8:1-11, May 14)

ADVICE Leaders should consider the advice of others (Exodus 18:13-26, February 3)
Older people often give wise advice (1 Kings 12:1-11, June 13)
Stay away from people who give wicked advice (Psalm 1:1, January 1)
God's advice is best (Psalm 73:24, April 1)
Wise people seek advice (Proverbs 1:5, January 1)
Advice helps provide success (Proverbs 11:14, March 16)
Foolish people do not listen to advice (Proverbs 12:15, April 4)
Give advice to those in need (1 Thessalonians 5:14, October 12)

ALCOHOL Being controlled by alcohol is foolish (Proverbs 20:1, July 25)
Becoming drunk is a sin (Romans 13:13-14, July 30)
God hates drunkenness (Galatians 5:19-21, September 20)
Church leaders should not be controlled by alcohol (Titus 1:7, October 26)

ANGELS Angels carry out God's judgment (2 Samuel 24:16-17, June 5)
Angels serve God (Psalm 103:21, May 2)
Angels praise God (Psalm 148:2, June 30)
Angels are messengers (Daniel 4:17, November 27)
Angels protect God's people (Daniel 6:22, November 29)
Angels do not marry (Matthew 22:30, February 2)
Angels do not die (Luke 20:36, April 21)
Angels will be judged by people (1 Corinthians 6:3, August 10)
Satan disguises himself as an angel of light (2 Corinthians 11:14, September 9)
Angels encourage Christians (Hebrews 1:14, October 30)
Angels who followed Satan were thrown out of heaven (2 Peter 2:4, November 28)
Angels are holy (Jude 1:14, December 8)
Angels are in the presence of God (Revelation 4:8, December 13)
Angels should not be worshiped (Revelation 22:8-9, December 31)

ANGER Anger can lead to murder (Genesis 4:3-8, January 2)
Anger leads to evil actions (Psalm 37:8, February 18)
Showing anger is foolish (Proverbs 12:16, April 4)
Gentle words can soothe anger (Proverbs 15:1, May 11)
Being quick-tempered is foolish (Ecclesiastes 7:9, September 4)
God becomes angry when we are ruled by anger (Amos 1:11, December 10)
Anger is like murdering someone (Matthew 5:21-22, January 5)

Jesus grew angry at sin (John 2:13-17, May 2)
Anger can give Satan a place in your life (Ephesians 4:26-27,
  September 26)
Christians should get rid of anger (Colossians 3:8, October 7)
Leaders in the church should not be quick-tempered (Titus 1:7,
  October 26)
Be slow to become angry (James 1:19, November 18)

ANTICHRIST Many will claim to be God's messengers (Matthew 24:5, February 5)
Many will have miraculous powers (Matthew 24:24, February 5)
Many will claim to be Christ (Luke 21:8, April 22)
The Antichrist will be lawless and deceitful (2 Thessalonians 2:1-10,
  October 14)
There are many Antichrists (1 John 2:18, December 2)
The Antichrist will oppose God (1 John 4:3, December 4)
The Antichrist will curse God (Revelation 13:1-8, December 22)
The Antichrist will be punished by God (Revelation 20:10,
  December 29)

APPEARANCE God is not impressed by someone's appearance (1 Samuel 16:70,
  May 14)
Physical beauty fades (Proverbs 31:30, December 31)
Do not worry about clothes (Matthew 6:25-34, January 8)
Appearances can be deceiving (Matthew 23:27, February 4)
Christians should care more for their spiritual status than their
  physical appearance (1 Timothy 2:9-10, October 17)
Do not judge others by their appearance (James 2:2-4, November 18)
Inner beauty is more important than physical beauty (1 Peter 3:1-6,
  November 24)

ARGUMENTS Arguments can be avoided by using gentle words (Proverbs 15:1,
  May 11)
Loving arguments is a sin (Proverbs 17:19, June 21)
A fool is quick to argue (Proverbs 20:3, July 26)
Avoid becoming entangled in others' arguments (Proverbs 26:17,
  October 27)
Avoid arguing with a new Christian (Romans 14:1, July 31)
We should avoid arguments (Philippians 2:14, September 30)
Arguments between Christians are useless (Titus 3:9, October 28)

ARMOR Armor for physical battle (1 Samuel 17:38, May 15)
Soldiers need armor (Jeremiah 46:3-4, October 24)
Weapons cannot stop God's power (Ezekiel 38:4, November 18)
Spiritual armor prepares us for life (Romans 13:12, July 30)
Righteousness is a spiritual weapon (2 Corinthians 6:7, September 2)
Spiritual armor defeats God's enemy (2 Corinthians 10:4,
  September 8)
The armor of God (Ephesians 6:11-18, September 28)

ASSURANCE God always holds his children (Psalm 37:23-24, February 19)
God will never abandon his people (Psalm 138:8, June 20)
God's promises last forever (Jeremiah 32:40, October 18)
False assurance is dangerous (Luke 18:18-30, April 17)
We can be assured of eternal life (John 5:24, May 8)
God will not refuse any who come to him (John 6:37-40, May 10)
Our place in God's family is secure (John 10:27-28, May 19)
Christians have peace with God (Romans 5:1-5, July 18)
Nothing can separate God's children from God (Romans 8:35-39, July 24)
Salvation cannot be canceled (Romans 11:29, July 28)

Accountability should help others (Galatians 6:1, September 21)
Our salvation was guaranteed before Creation (Ephesians 1:4-5, September 22)
Assurance comes from faith (Ephesians 3:12, September 24)
God will guard what has been entrusted to him (2 Timothy 1:12, October 22)

ATONEMENT God required a perfect sacrifice (Exodus 12:5, January 30)
God required blood for our atonement (Leviticus 17:11, February 25)
Jesus paid for all of our sins (Isaiah 53:3-12, September 27)
Atonement is good news (Luke 4:18-19, March 20)
Jesus willingly died for our sins (John 10:17, May 18)
Christ secured salvation through his blood (Acts 20:28, June 30)
Jesus provided the atonement for sins (Romans 3:23-25, July 16)
Jesus' death purchased forgiveness (1 Corinthians 7:23, August 11)
Jesus died for sins (1 Corinthians 15:3, August 23)
Our atonement allows us to know God (Ephesians 2:13, September 23)
Jesus' death rescues us from eternal punishment (Colossians 1:13, October 4)
Christ's death purifies God's people (Titus 2:14, October 27)
Sin requires that a sacrifice be made (Hebrews 9:22, November 9)
Jesus' sacrifice was perfect (1 Peter 1:18-19, November 23)
Jesus took our punishment (1 Peter 2:21-24, November 24)
We cannot improve Jesus' sacrifice (1 Peter 3:18, November 25)

ATTITUDE Bad attitudes hurt our relationship with God (Genesis 4:6-7, January 2)
Bad attitudes lead to poor decisions (Numbers 14:1-4, March 10)
Always trust God for your life (Proverbs 29:25, December 13)
Choose a positive attitude (Habakkuk 3:17-19, December 18)
God will reward the meek (Matthew 5:5, January 5)
God gives Christians a new attitude (Philippians 1:20-25, September 29)
We should imitate Jesus' attitude (Philippians 2:5, September 30)
Christians should always rejoice (Philippians 4:4, October 3)
Never be anxious (Philippians 4:6-7, October 3)

AUTHORITY (see also RESPECT)
God will hold people in authority accountable for their actions (Daniel 4:31, November 27)
Jesus is the highest authority (Matthew 28:18, February 14)
God gave government its authority (John 19:11, May 30)
Christians should obey the government (Romans 13:1-2, July 30)
Parents are authorities to their children (Ephesians 6:1, September 28)
The Bible is our authority (2 Timothy 3:16, October 24)
Church leaders are authoritative (Hebrews 13:17, November 16)

BAPTISM Baptism signifies repentance (Matthew 3:11, January 3)
All followers of Jesus should be baptized (Matthew 28:19, February 14)
Jesus was baptized (Mark 1:9, February 15)
The Holy Spirit baptizes Christians (John 1:32-33, May 1)
Baptism is closely linked with a changed life (Acts 2:38, June 4)
New Christians should be baptized (Acts 8:12-17, June 12)
Entire families of the early church were baptized (Acts 16:33-34, June 25)
Baptism initiates us into Christ (Romans 6:3-8, July 20)
Salvation is identified with baptism (1 Peter 3:21, November 25)

BELIEF Believing God makes us righteous (Genesis 15:6, January 6)
Belief in God should be accompanied by action (Deuteronomy 27:10, April 4)

Belief affects the way we live (Mark 1:15, February 15)
Beliefs should reflect the heart (Romans 10:9, July 26)
Believing is more than acknowledging (James 2:21, November 19)

BIBLE The Bible is perfect (Psalm 18:30, January 21)
The Bible is true (Psalm 33:4, February 11)
The Bible will last forever (Psalm 119:89, May 28)
The Bible gives us wisdom (Psalm 119:99, May 29)
The Bible can be trusted (Psalm 119:138, May 31)
The Bible reveals the truth (Acts 18:28, June 28)
The Bible is holy (Romans 1:2, July 12)
God's Holy Spirit helps us understand the Bible (1 Corinthians 2:12-16, August 6)
The Bible is authoritative (Galatians 3:10, September 17)
The Bible is a Christian's spiritual weapon (Ephesians 6:17, September 28)
The Bible is inspired by God (2 Timothy 3:16, October 24)
The Bible judges our lives (Hebrews 4:12, November 2)
The Bible helps us grow spiritually (1 Peter 2:2, November 23)

BIRTH God is the Life-Giver (Genesis 2:7, January 1)
Children are a blessing from God (Psalm 127:3-5, June 9)
God carefully creates each person (Psalm 139:13-14, June 21)
God's Son was born (Isaiah 9:6, September 11)
God plans the lives of people before they are born (Jeremiah 1:5, October 3)
Jesus' birth (Luke 2:7, March 16)
God's children are reborn spiritually (John 1:12-13, April 30)
People must be reborn spiritually to enter heaven (John 3:3, May 3)

BLESSING God blesses those who obey him (Leviticus 26:3-5, March 2)
God blesses godly people (Psalm 5:12, January 5)
We are blessed when we worship God (Psalm 24:3-6, January 29)
Christians bless God through praise (Psalm 103:1, May 2)
God will bless those who fear him (Psalm 112:1-3, May 16)
God blesses us when we seek to please him (Matthew 6:33, January 8)
Christians should bless their enemies (Luke 6:28, March 24)
Salvation is our greatest blessing (Ephesians 1:3, September 22)
The Bible brings us blessing (James 1:25, November 17)

BLOOD God hates the shedding of an innocent person's blood (Genesis 4:10, January 2)
Jesus' blood seals God's relationship with his people (Matthew 26:28, February 9)
Jesus' blood allows us to have access to God (Romans 5:8-9, July 19)
Christians are redeemed by Jesus' blood (Ephesians 1:5-7, September 22)
Blood is required for forgiveness (Hebrews 9:22, November 9)

BODY OF CHRIST The body of Christ has been given many gifts (Romans 12:3-6, July 29)
There are many parts, but one body (1 Corinthians 12:12-13, August 19)
Christians make up the body of Christ (1 Corinthians 12:27, August 20)
Christians of different nationalities form one body (Ephesians 3:6, September 24)
There is unity in the body of Christ (Ephesians 4:3, September 25)
Different members of the body help each other grow (Ephesians 4:11-12, September 25)
Jesus is the head of the body (Colossians 1:18, October 4)

BOOK OF LIFE God writes our names in his book (Psalm 87:6, April 18)

The names of Christians are in the Book of Life (Philippians 4:3, October 3)

Our names cannot be removed from the Book of Life (Revelation 3:5, December 11)

People whose names are not written in the Book of Life will experience God's wrath (Revelation 20:15, December 29)

Only those whose names are in God's Book will enter heaven (Revelation 21:27, December 30)

BRIDE God's children should be as pure as a bride (Isaiah 49:18, September 26)

We should be devoted to God as a bride is to her husband (Jeremiah 2:2, October 3)

The church is the bride of Christ (2 Corinthians 11:2-3, September 9)

The bride of Christ will be presented to Christ (Revelation 19:7, December 28)

BUSINESS God's people should be good workers (Genesis 31:42, January 15)

Work should not overrun your time with God (Exodus 16:23, February 2)

God gives you the ability to work (Exodus 35:30-31, February 13)

Workers should be trustworthy (Proverbs 25:13, October 13)

Do the best job you can (Ecclesiastes 9:10, September 4)

Work as though Jesus were your boss (Ephesians 6:6-7, September 28)

Christians should do their best at their job (Titus 2:9-10, October 27)

CARING God cares for his people (Deuteronomy 7:9, March 27)

God cares for underprivileged people (Psalm 68:5, March 25)

Protect the needy (Psalm 82:3, April 13)

God's people should help the oppressed (Isaiah 1:17, September 8)

Care for your enemies (Luke 6:27, March 24)

God's people should care for the needy (Luke 14:13-14, April 11)

God cares for his children (Romans 1:6-7, July 12)

Treat parents with care (Ephesians 6:2, September 28)

Treat co-workers with care (Colossians 4:1, October 8)

Care for the elderly (1 Timothy 5:1-4, October 20)

Christians need to care for the needy (James 1:27, November 18)

CHILDREN God tells children to honor their parents (Exodus 20:12, February 4)

Parents should teach their children to follow God (Deuteronomy 6:6-7, March 26)

Christians are children of God (John 1:12, April 30)

Children of God should imitate God (Ephesians 5:1, September 27)

Parents should nurture their children (Ephesians 6:4, September 28)

Children must obey their parents (Colossians 3:20, October 8)

CHURCH (*see also* WORSHIP)

Jesus is the capstone of the church (Psalm 118:22, May 22)

We should have joy going to God's house (Psalm 122:1, June 4)

Satan works against the church (Matthew 16:18, January 25)

Members of the church should take care of each other (Acts 2:44, June 4)

The church sends out missionaries (Acts 13:2, June 19)

The church is like a body (1 Corinthians 12:12-13, August 19)

The church is a family of Christians (Galatians 6:10, September 21)

God's children form the church (Ephesians 2:19-22, September 23)

The church should not allow immoral behavior by its members (Ephesians 5:3-4, September 27)

Christ is the head of the church (Colossians 1:18, October 4)

Many people groups form one universal church (Colossians 3:11, October 7)

Church leaders are qualified to lead by their character (Titus 1:6-9, October 26)

The church is made up of God's children (1 John 3:1, December 2)

The church is the bride of Christ (Revelation 19:7-8, December 28)

COMFORT Friends should comfort each other (Job 2:12-13, August 21)

God comforts us (Isaiah 40:1-11, September 22)

God promises to comfort those who mourn (Matthew 5:4, January 5)

God's Holy Spirit is our Comforter (John 14:16, May 25)

Jesus has overcome the world's troubles (John 16:33, May 27)

God comforts those who are hurting (2 Corinthians 1:3-11, August 26)

Christians should comfort each other (1 Thessalonians 4:18, October 11)

All pain will end (Revelation 21:3-4, December 30)

COMPLAIN Bring your complaints to God (Psalm 142:1-2, December 23)

Christians should not complain to each other (Philippians 2:14, September 30)

People complain because they want their own way (Jude 1:16, December 8)

COMPROMISE Do not compromise your convictions (1 Kings 11:4, June 13)

Compromise can be wise (Matthew 5:25, January 5)

Compromise can divide our loyalty (Matthew 6:24, January 7)

Compromise can keep us from doing what is right (Mark 15:15, March 11)

Compromise can weaken faith (2 Corinthians 6:14-18, September 3)

CONFESSION OF SIN Sin must be confessed (Leviticus 5:5, February 17)

God will restore those who turn away from evil (2 Chronicles 7:14, July 22)

Remorse accompanies confessing sin (Ezra 10:1, August 10)

God forgives confessed sins (Psalm 32:5, February 10)

Do not try to hide sin (Proverbs 28:13, November 24)

Confession of sin accompanies a changed lifestyle (2 Timothy 2:19, October 23)

God purifies those who confess their sin (1 John 1:9, November 30)

CONSCIENCE (see also REPENTANCE)

Conscience moves us to turn from our mistakes (Proverbs 28:13, November 24)

We can suppress our conscience (Jonah 1:5, December 14)

The Holy Spirit can speak through our conscience (Romans 9:1, July 25)

Keep your conscience clear (1 Timothy 1:18-19, October 16)

Church leaders must have clear consciences (1 Timothy 3:9, October 18)

Consciences can be destroyed (1 Timothy 4:2, October 19)

Jesus' forgiveness clears our conscience (Hebrews 9:14, November 9)

A clear conscience helps you live a God-honoring life (1 Peter 3:16, November 25)

COURAGE God gives us victory (Psalm 112:8, May 16)

Jesus' strength gives us courage (John 16:33, May 27)

Courage helps us boldly represent Christ (Acts 4:31, June 6)

Christians should be courageous (1 Corinthians 16:13, August 25)

Pray for courage (Ephesians 6:19-20, September 28)

Christians can pray to God with confidence (Hebrews 4:16, November 2)

COVENANT God's promise can be trusted (Genesis 9:17, January 4)
Jesus established a new covenant (Luke 22:20, April 24)
God's covenant brings life (2 Corinthians 3:6, August 29)
The new covenant is superior to the old covenant (Hebrews 8:6, November 7)
The old covenant foreshadowed the new covenant (Hebrews 10:1, November 10)

CREATION God the Holy Spirit was involved in Creation (Genesis 1:1-2, January 1)
God created people (Genesis 1:27, January 1)
God created the world good (Genesis 1:31, January 1)
God the Father was involved in Creation (Psalm 33:6, February 11)
God rules over his creation (Psalm 89:11, April 20)
God created every angel (Psalm 148:2-5, June 30)
God created everything (Jeremiah 10:16, October 8)
Creation reveals God's greatness (Amos 4:13, December 11)
Jesus was involved in Creation (Colossians 1:16, October 4)
God the Creator is worthy of worship (Revelation 4:11, December 13)
God will make a new heaven and new earth (Revelation 21:1-4, December 30)

CRITICISM Take care of your own problems before criticizing others (Matthew 7:3-5, January 8)
Criticism should help people deepen their relationship with God (Luke 17:3-5, April 14)
Criticism should be given with a loving attitude (1 Corinthians 13:4-5, August 20)
Harsh criticism can destroy rather than help (Galatians 5:15, September 20)

CROSS Jesus was crucified (Matthew 27:31-35, February 13)
Christians should pick up their own crosses (Mark 8:34-38, February 26)
Jesus' death was powerful (1 Corinthians 1:17-18, August 4)
Jesus' death unified all Christians (Ephesians 2:16, September 23)
Jesus' death was a sacrifice (Colossians 1:20-22, October 5)
Jesus' death defeated Satan (Colossians 2:14-15, October 6)
Jesus' cross is an example for us (Hebrews 12:2, November 14)

CULT God hates the occult (Leviticus 19:26, February 26)
God judges those who wrongly claim to speak for him (Deuteronomy 18:20-22, April 1)
God hates cultic practices (2 Kings 17:17, June 30)
God despises false prophets (Ezekiel 13:8-9, November 5)
False teachers will come (Matthew 7:15, January 9)
Only Jesus brings salvation (John 14:6, May 24)
Members of the occult will never enter God's kingdom (Galatians 5:19-21, September 20)
Be careful in your spiritual life (1 Thessalonians 5:21, October 12)

DARKNESS, God's Word enlightens us (Psalm 119:105, November 27)
SPIRITUAL The way of wicked people is darkness (Proverbs 4:19, January 23)
Jesus brings light to darkened lives (John 1:5, April 30)
Living without God is living in spiritual darkness (Acts 26:17-18, July 8)
Christians do not live in spiritual darkness (Ephesians 5:8, September 27)
God rescued us from eternal darkness (Colossians 1:13, October 4)
There is no darkness in Jesus (1 John 1:5, November 30)
Sinners' eternal punishment will be in darkness (Jude 1:4-13, December 8)

DEATH Death is a result of sin (Genesis 3:17-19, January 2)
Life is short (Job 7:6-7, August 22)
Every person will face death (Psalm 89:48, April 22)
Death of Christians is precious (Psalm 116:15, May 19)
Christians enter perfect peace at death (Isaiah 57:1-2, September 28)
God has power over death (John 14:19, May 25)
The death of Christians brings fellowship with Jesus (Acts 7:59,
June 11)
God provides eternal life (Romans 6:23, July 20)
Jesus will raise everyone who has died (1 Corinthians 15:20-23,
August 23)
Living in heaven is better than living on earth (2 Corinthians 5:6-7,
August 31)
Death is not the end of a person (1 Thessalonians 4:13-14, October 11)
Prepare your spiritual life for death (Hebrews 9:27-28, November 9)
We don't know how long we'll live (James 4:13-14, November 20)
God will destroy death (Revelation 21:4, December 30)

DECISIONS Pray before making decisions (Nehemiah 1:4, August 11)
Decide to do things that honor God (Job 1:8, August 21)
God's Word helps us makes decisions (Psalm 119:105, November 27)
Get good advice before making decisions (Proverbs 18:15, July 5)
Ask God for wisdom before making decisions (James 1:2-8,
November 17)

DEMONS (see also SATAN)
Worship in false religions honors demons (Psalm 106:37, May 10)
Demons try to hinder God's plan (Daniel 10:13, December 2)
Demons are no match for Jesus (Mark 1:34, February 16)
Demons want to destroy people (Mark 5:5, February 20)
Demons submit to the name of Jesus (Luke 10:17, April 3)
Demons can be driven out by Jesus' followers (Acts 16:16-18, June 25)
Demons are powerful (Acts 19:16, June 29)
Demons cannot separate people from God's love (Romans 8:38-39,
July 24)
Demons deceive people (2 Corinthians 11:13-15, September 9)
Christians fight against the plans of demons (Ephesians 6:12,
September 28)
Demons want to mislead people (1 Timothy 4:1-2, October 19)
Demons believe in God (James 2:19, November 19)
Demons are angels that have sinned (2 Peter 2:4, November 28)
God will judge demons (Jude 1:6, December 8)
Do not take demons lightly (Jude 1:8-9, December 8)
Demons can work miracles (Revelation 16:13-14, December 25)
In the last days, demons will be bound by God (Revelation 20:1-3,
December 29)

DEPRESSION Depression can follow exhausting times (Judges 15:18, May 2)
God can encourage hurting people (2 Samuel 22:29-31, June 4)
Depression can follow success (1 Kings 19:3-4, June 18)
God helps those who feel crushed (Psalm 34:18, February 14)
Abraham had hope when there was no reason to hope (Romans
4:18-22, July 18)
God will wipe away depression (Revelation 21:4, December 30)

DESIRES You should not desire something that belongs to someone else
(Exodus 20:17, February 4)
Wicked people desire evil (Psalm 36:1-4, February 17)

God gives those who fellowship with him what they desire (Psalm 37:4, February 18)

Desire to know God (Psalm 42:1, February 26)

Desire to worship God (Psalm 84:1-2, April 15)

Desire to honor God (Psalm 86:12, April 17)

Do not desire self-promotion (Psalm 119:36, May 25)

Money doesn't satisfy desires (Ecclesiastes 5:10, September 3)

Christians should not give in to sinful desires (Ephesians 4:22, September 26)

Sinful desires should not have a home with God's children (1 Peter 1:14, November 23)

Desire to do God's will (1 Peter 4:2, November 25)

God's children desire to obey God (1 John 2:3-6, December 1)

DETERMINATION Be determined to obey God (1 Samuel 7:3, May 9)

Determine not to sin (Job 31:1, August 29)

Determine to stand firm (Isaiah 7:9, September 10)

God helps us be determined (Isaiah 50:7, September 26)

Determine to follow Christ (Mark 8:34-38, February 26)

DEVOTION Be fully devoted to God (1 Chronicles 28:9, July 19)

Worship God with devotion (1 Chronicles 29:9, July 19)

Be devoted to prayer (Psalm 5:3, January 5)

Let your life be devoted to God (Romans 12:1-2, July 29)

DISCERNMENT The Bible will help you discern bad teaching (Acts 17:11, June 26)

God grants discernment (1 Corinthians 12:10, August 19)

Discern between right and wrong behavior (Hebrews 5:14, November 3)

Ask God for help in discerning his will (James 1:5, November 18)

DISCIPLESHIP Christians are to make disciples (Matthew 28:19-20, February 14)

Jesus' followers are known by their love (John 13:35, May 24)

Christians should help other Christians grow (Acts 14:21-22, June 22)

DISCIPLINE Punishment is a consequence of sinful actions (Genesis 3:6-19, January 2)

God's punishment does not change his love for us (Psalm 89:32-33, October 20)

The Lord disciplines those he loves (Proverbs 3:11-12, January 13)

Parents are responsible to discipline their children (Proverbs 13:24, April 23)

Punishment for sin may be swift and severe (Acts 5:1-11, June 7)

Paul commanded punishment for blatant sin in the church (1 Corinthians 5:1-5, August 9)

Punishment should lead to repentance (2 Corinthians 7:8-9, September 4)

Sometimes God punishes us to bring us back to himself (Hebrews 12:5-11, November 14)

DISCRIMINATION Be fair in your judgment of others (Leviticus 19:15, February 26)

Don't discriminate against someone who is not powerful (Deuteronomy 1:17, March 23)

Do not oppress the disadvantaged (Malachi 3:5, December 31)

God does not discriminate among his people (Acts 10:34, June 16)

All Christians are equal in God's eyes (Galatians 3:28, September 18)

God will judge those who discriminate (Colossians 3:25, October 8)

Do not discriminate against the poor (James 2:1-9, November 18)

DISHONESTY Dishonesty is listed in the Ten Commandments (Leviticus 19:11, February 26)
Be honest in your business dealings (Leviticus 19:35-36, February 26)
Do not lie for your own gain (Deuteronomy 19:14, April 1)
Dishonest people cannot know God (Psalm 101:7, April 30)
God hates deception (Proverbs 12:22, April 7)
God will punish those who take advantage of others (1 Thessalonians 4:6, October 11)

DOCTRINE Protect sound doctrine (2 Timothy 1:13-14, October 22)
Doctrine comes from the Bible (2 Timothy 3:16, October 24)
Leaders in the church must have sound doctrine (Titus 1:6-9, October 26)
Christians should teach correct beliefs (Titus 2:1, October 27)

DOUBT God will help us overcome doubts (Psalm 42:5-6, February 26)
God doesn't leave us during our time of doubt (Isaiah 40:27-28, September 22)
Help those who have spiritual doubts (Hebrews 3:12, November 1)
Doubt inhibits our prayers (James 1:5-7, November 17)

DRINKING People controlled by alcohol are fools (Proverbs 20:1, July 25)
Alcohol can cause you to become poor (Proverbs 21:17, August 17)
Alcohol can destroy you (Proverbs 23:29-35, September 23)
God will judge those who are controlled by alcohol (Isaiah 5:22, September 9)
Becoming drunk is dangerous (Luke 21:34, April 23)
Drunkenness is not fitting for a Christian (Romans 13:11-14, July 30)
Drunkenness can cause immoral behavior (Ephesians 5:18, September 27)

EARTH God created the earth (Genesis 1:1, January 1)
People are the caretakers of the earth (Genesis 1:28, January 1)
The earth was cursed because of sin (Genesis 3:17-19, January 2)
The earth belongs to God (Psalm 89:11, April 20)
The earth was created for God's glory (Colossians 1:16, October 4)
Jesus sustains the earth (Hebrews 1:3, October 30)

EDUCATION Parents are responsible to teach their children (Deuteronomy 6:1-9, March 26)
Train children to follow God (Proverbs 22:6, August 27)
Christians should always learn more about God (Ephesians 4:14-15, September 25)

EMBARRASSMENT Be careful not to embarrass others (Ruth 2:15, May 6)
Embarrassment can lead to rash actions (Matthew 14:1-12, January 21)
We should not be embarrassed about the gospel (Romans 1:16, July 12)
We should not be embarrassed by Jesus (Galatians 1:10, September 14)

EMOTIONS Emotions can lead us to sin (Genesis 4:2-6, January 2)
Emotions can lead to foolish promises (Judges 11:29-40, April 30)
Emotions are a part of worship (Ezra 3:1-13, August 6)
God heals those with broken hearts (Psalm 34:18, February 14)
Carefully guard your emotions (Proverbs 4:23, January 24)
Emotions can crush us (Proverbs 15:13, May 16)
Do not be led by emotions (Proverbs 19:2, July 11)
Jesus experienced emotions (John 11:35, May 20)
Emotions are not reliable guides (Galatians 5:1-17, September 19)
Some emotions can be sinful (Ephesians 4:31, September 26)

EMPLOYMENT God's people should be good workers (Genesis 31:42, January 15)
Work should not overrun your time with God (Exodus 16:23, February 2)
God gives you the ability to work (Exodus 35:30-31, February 13)
Workers should be trustworthy (Proverbs 25:13, October 13)
Do the best job you can (Ecclesiastes 9:10, September 4)
Work as though Jesus were your boss (Ephesians 6:6-7, September 28)
Christians should do their best at their job (Titus 2:9-10, October 27)

ENCOURAGEMENT Encourage the underprivileged (Isaiah 1:17, September 8)
God encourages us (Isaiah 40:31, September 22)
The Holy Spirit encourages us (Acts 9:31, June 14)
Encourage your neighbor (Romans 15:2, August 1)
The Bible encourages us (Romans 15:4, August 1)
Our position in Christ encourages us (Philippians 2:1, September 30)
We should encourage each other (1 Thessalonians 4:18, October 11)
Encourage those who are weak and afraid (1 Thessalonians 5:14, October 12)
Encourage elderly people (1 Timothy 5:1-4, October 20)
Encourage others not to sin (Hebrews 3:13, November 1)
Encourage others to love (Hebrews 10:24, November 11)

ENVY Envy can destroy someone (Job 5:2, August 22)
Do not envy those who do wrong (Psalm 37:1, February 18)
Do not envy the prosperity of wicked people (Psalm 73:2-3, April 1)
Envy steals your peace (Proverbs 14:30, May 8)
Envy is a powerful enemy (Proverbs 27:4, November 6)
Being envious is foolish (Ecclesiastes 4:4, September 3)
Envy can cause you to act rashly (Acts 7:9, June 9)
Envy characterizes sinful people (Romans 1:29, July 13)
We should not envy other Christians (Galatians 5:26, September 20)
Envy has no place in a Christian's life (Titus 3:3, October 28)
Do not harbor envy (James 3:14-15, November 19)
Get rid of envy (1 Peter 2:1, November 23)

ETERNAL LIFE Eternal life is only for those who do God's will (Matthew 7:21, January 9)
The righteous will receive eternal life (Matthew 25:46, February 8)
Belief in Jesus is required for eternal life (John 3:15-16, May 3)
Evil people will receive eternal punishment (John 5:28-29, May 8)
Jesus came to give life (John 10:10, May 18)
Jesus gives eternal life (John 11:25, May 20)
Jesus is eternal life (John 14:6, May 24)
Eternal life cannot be earned (Ephesians 2:8-9, September 23)
Eternal life comes from God (Titus 1:2, October 26)
Eternal life gives us hope (Titus 3:7, October 28)

EVANGELISM (*see also* WITNESSING)
We are God's messengers (Isaiah 43:10-11, September 23)
Christians bring light to a spiritually dark world (Matthew 5:14-16, January 5)
Jesus made salvation available to all people (Matthew 9:9-13, January 12)
Be bold in your evangelism (Matthew 10:33, January 15)
Jesus sent his followers to make disciples (Matthew 28:18-20, February 14)
The Holy Spirit gives us power to evangelize (Acts 1:8, June 3)

EVIL God will destroy evil people (Job 4:8, August 22)
God helps keep his people from sin (Psalm 19:13, January 23)

God hates people who do evil (Psalm 26:5, February 1)
God permits evil (Romans 1:24-28, July 13)
God cannot coexist with evil (Galatians 5:16-17, September 20)
Christians should put away evil from their lives (Ephesians 4:22,
    September 26)
There are spiritual forces behind evil (Ephesians 6:12, September 28)

FAITH Believing God takes faith (Genesis 15:6, January 6)
Only a small amount of faith is needed (Luke 17:6, April 14)
Faith is needed for salvation (Romans 3:28, July 16)
Faith puts us in a right relationship with God (Romans 5:1, July 18)
Faith comes from hearing the Word of God (Romans 10:17, July 27)
Accept the person who has weak faith (Romans 14:1, July 31)
Christianity is the only true faith (Ephesians 4:5, September 25)
Faith is hoping in what is not seen (Hebrews 11:1, November 12)
Faith accompanies obedience to God (Hebrews 11:7-12, November 12)

FAMILY The members of a family can teach each other about God
    (Deuteronomy 6:4-9, March 26)
Do not let sin affect your family life (Psalm 101:2, April 30)
Do not bring trouble to a family (Proverbs 11:29, March 26)
Christian faith is of greater importance than family (Luke 12:51-53,
    April 8)
Christians are members of God's family (Ephesians 2:19,
    September 23)
Husbands and wives should love each other (Ephesians 5:21-33,
    September 27)
Children should obey their parents (Ephesians 6:1, September 28)
Church leaders must have a good family life (1 Timothy 3:4-5,
    October 18)
Families should take care of each other (1 Timothy 5:3-5, October 20)

FEAR God will protect us (Genesis 15:1, January 6)
God will not forget us (Genesis 46:3, January 23)
We should fear God (Psalm 25:12, January 30)
Christians do not need to fear anyone (Psalm 27:1,
    February 2)
God strengthens us (Psalm 46:1-3, March 3)
We do not need to fear darkness or violence (Psalm 91:5, April 23)
We do not need to fear bad news (Psalm 112:7, May 16)
Love drives fear away (1 John 4:18, December 4)

FOOLISHNESS Being foolish is lacking discernment (Job 5:2, August 22)
Fools do not acknowledge God (Psalm 14:1, January 16)
Fools do not know God (Proverbs 1:7, January 2)
Fools invite their own destruction (Proverbs 10:14, February 24)
Fools enjoy evil (Proverbs 10:23, March 3)
Fools show their annoyance (Proverbs 12:16, April 4)
Stay away from foolish people (Proverbs 14:7, April 27)
A foolish person rejects discipline (Proverbs 15:5, May 13)
Fools return to their folly (Proverbs 26:11, October 25)
A foolish person gives in to anger (Proverbs 29:11, December 6)
A foolish person is lazy (Ecclesiastes 4:5, September 3)
The foolishness of God is wiser than man's wisdom
    (1 Corinthians 1:25, August 5)

FORGIVENESS God forgives our many sins (Psalm 65:3, March 22)
God forgives us because he loves us (Psalm 86:5, April 17)

God makes us as clean as freshly fallen snow (Isaiah 1:18, September 8)

God removes our impurities (Ezekiel 36:25, November 17)

We must forgive others (Matthew 6:14-15, January 7)

Don't keep track of how many times you forgive (Matthew 18:21-35, January 28)

Freely forgive others as God has forgiven you (Colossians 3:13, October 7)

God will forgive our sins if we confess them (1 John 1:8-9, November 30)

FOUL LANGUAGE Foul language is not fitting for a Christian (Ephesians 5:4, September 27)

Our speech reflects our relationship with God (Colossians 4:6, October 8)

Our speech should be an example to others (1 Timothy 4:12, October 19)

FREEDOM Christians are spiritually free (John 8:36, May 16)

Christians are free from sin's power (Romans 5:21, July 19)

Christians are free in order to serve others (Galatians 5:1, September 19)

FRIENDSHIP (see also RELATIONSHIPS)

Friends can cause great pain (Psalm 55:12-14, March 12)

Friends love during difficult times (Proverbs 17:17, June 20)

Faithful friends are not common (Proverbs 18:24, July 10)

Friends influence you (Proverbs 22:24-25, September 7)

Friendship is marked by sacrifice (John 15:13-15, May 26)

We can be friends with God (James 2:23, November 19)

FUTURE God has plans for our future (Genesis 12:1-4, January 5)

God will bless our future if we obey him (Deuteronomy 5:29, March 26)

Do not plan your future like evil people do (Jeremiah 10:2-3, October 8)

God gives us hope for our future (Jeremiah 31:17, October 17)

God prepares us for the future (1 Corinthians 2:9, August 6)

GIVING God is honored by our gifts (Exodus 35:22, February 13)

Generous giving honors God (Ezra 2:68-69, August 5)

God will reward us for giving to others (Mark 9:41, February 28)

Giving helps others live (Acts 2:44-45, June 4)

We should support Christian workers (Acts 28:10, July 11)

Wealthy people should give generously (1 Timothy 6:17-19, October 21)

God is pleased with our gifts (Hebrews 13:16, November 16)

Giving reflects God's love (1 John 3:17, December 3)

GOD God created everything (Genesis 1:1, January 1)

God is a warrior (Exodus 15:3, February 1)

God is one (Deuteronomy 6:4, March 26)

God is trustworthy (Deuteronomy 7:9, March 27)

God is too great to be described (1 Kings 8:27, June 11)

God is gracious and merciful (Nehemiah 9:31, August 15)

God is good (Psalm 34:8, February 13)

God helps his people when they are in trouble (Psalm 46:1, March 3)

God is mighty (Psalm 50:1, March 7)

God is our rock (Psalm 62:6, March 19)

God is our hope (Psalm 71:5, March 30)

God is near everyone (Psalm 75:1, April 3)
God is our salvation (Isaiah 12:2, September 13)
God is sovereign (Isaiah 25:8, September 17)
God is holy (Isaiah 29:23, September 18)
Only God is worthy of glory (Isaiah 42:8, September 23)
God is our father (Matthew 6:9, January 7)
God is all-powerful (Luke 1:37, March 14)
God is spirit (John 4:24, May 5)
God is all-knowing (Romans 11:33, July 28)
God is knowable (Ephesians 1:17, September 22)
God is living (1 Timothy 4:10, October 19)
God is King of kings (1 Timothy 6:15, October 21)
God is approachable (James 4:8, November 20)
God is judge (James 4:12, November 20)
God is love (1 John 4:16, December 4)
God is almighty (Revelation 1:8, December 9)

GOD'S WILL God guides us (Psalm 16:7, January 18)
Ask God for guidance (Psalm 25:4-7, January 30)
God will direct you (Psalm 48:14, March 5)
God works everything out for his plan (Proverbs 16:4, May 27)
God directs events in our lives (Acts 16:6-7, June 24)
God gives wisdom for making decisions (James 1:2-5, November 17)

GOSPEL Christians should tell others about the gospel (Matthew 28:18-19,
February 14)
The gospel's message is for everyone (Luke 24:46-47, April 29)
People should respond to the gospel with faith (John 1:12, April 30)
The gospel is powerful (Romans 1:16, July 12)
The gospel of Jesus (1 Corinthians 15:1-5, August 23)
Believing the gospel brings a change to life (1 Thessalonians 1:4-5,
October 9)

GOSSIP Do not gossip (Exodus 23:1, February 5)
Be careful not to slander (Leviticus 19:16, February 26)
Gossiping betrays confidence (Proverbs 11:13, March 15)
Gossip separates friends (Proverbs 16:28, June 9)
Gossip prolongs tension between people (Proverbs 26:20,
October 29)
Gossip is attractive (Proverbs 26:22, October 30)
People who gossip are wicked (Romans 1:29, July 13)
Gossip should have no place among Christians (1 Timothy 5:13,
October 20)

GOVERNMENT God holds those in government accountable (Deuteronomy 17:18-19,
March 31)
God gives authority to those in government (Romans 13:1, July 30)
Christians should obey the government (Titus 3:1, October 28)

GRACE God is full of grace (Exodus 34:6, February 12)
God is slow to become angry (Psalm 86:15, April 17)
God's grace makes salvation possible (Ephesians 1:7-8, September 22)
God accepts us by his grace (Ephesians 2:8-9, September 23)
God's grace gives us hope (1 Peter 1:13, November 23)

GREED Greed creates disagreement (Proverbs 28:25, December 1)
The Pharisees had greedy hearts (Matthew 23:25, February 4)
Christians should avoid being greedy (Ephesians 5:3, September 27)
People full of greed will not enter heaven (Ephesians 5:5, September 27)
Leaders of the church must not be greedy (Titus 1:7, October 26)

GRIEF (*see also* SORROW)
Friends should comfort each other (Job 2:12-13, August 21)
God comforts us in our darkest times (Job 35:9-10, August 30)
God comforts us (Isaiah 40, September 22)
God promises to comfort those who grieve (Matthew 5:4, January 5)
God's Holy Spirit is our Comforter (John 14:16, May 25)
Jesus has overcome the world's troubles (John 16:33, May 27)
The Holy Spirit comforts us (Acts 9:31, June 14)
The Bible comforts us (Romans 15:4, August 1)
God comforts those who grieve (2 Corinthians 1:3-11, August 26)
All grief will end (Revelation 21:3-4, December 30)

GUIDANCE Ask God to give you guidance (Psalm 25:4-5, January 30)
God will guide you (Psalm 32:8, February 10)
The Bible gives us guidance (Psalm 119:133, May 31)
God directs your path when you trust him (Proverbs 3:5-6, January 10)

GUILT Guilt causes us to hide from God (Genesis 3:7-11, January 2)
Ask God to forgive hidden sins (Psalm 19:12-13, January 23)
God forgives sins and removes guilt (Psalm 32:5, February 10)
God can cleanse us from all sin (Psalm 51:2, March 8)
All people are guilty of sin (Romans 3:9-12, July 16)
Jesus Christ takes away all guilt (Romans 3:23-24, July 16)

HATRED Hatred causes trouble (Proverbs 10:12, February 23)
Followers of Jesus will be hated (Matthew 10:22, January 14)
Many in the world hate Jesus (John 15:18, May 26)
Christians should hate evil (Romans 12:9, July 29)
All people are equal in Christ (Galatians 3:28-29, September 18)
Christians need to get rid of their own hatred (Colossians 3:8, October 7)

HEART Love God with all of your heart (Deuteronomy 6:5, March 26)
Our heart can have confidence (Psalm 27:3, February 2)
God will not despise a repentant heart (Psalm 51:17, March 8)
Guard your heart (Proverbs 4:23, January 24)
Those who have pure hearts will see God (Matthew 5:8, January 5)
Words and actions begin in the heart (Luke 6:45, March 25)

HEAVEN Death will not exist in heaven (Isaiah 25:8, September 17)
Only righteous people will enter heaven (Matthew 5:17-20, January 5)
Few people will enter heaven (Matthew 7:13-14, January 8)
Jesus is preparing heaven for his followers (John 14:2-3, May 24)
Our lives will not be complete until we enter heaven (2 Corinthians 5:2, August 31)
Heaven is much better than earth (Philippians 1:23, September 29)
Christians should look forward to heaven (Colossians 3:1-5, October 7)
Heaven is the home of righteousness (2 Peter 3:13, November 29)
God is the focus of attention in heaven (Revelation 7:17, December 16)
There will not be any sadness in heaven (Revelation 21:4, December 30)
People in heaven will walk with God (Revelation 22:5, December 31)

HELL God will deliver his children from hell (Psalm 86:13, April 17)
Hell is a place of weeping (Matthew 8:12, January 10)
Hell was prepared for Satan and demons (Matthew 25:41, February 8)
Wicked people will receive punishment (Romans 1:18-20, July 13)
God will punish those who do not turn from their sin (2 Peter 2:4-9, November 28)

Hell is a place of eternal fire (Jude 1:7, December 8)
God will send to hell those who do not believe in him (Revelation 21:8, December 30)

HOLY God is known for his holiness (Psalm 93:5, April 24)
God cannot tolerate sin (Isaiah 59:2, September 29)
God uses his Word to make us holy (John 17:17, May 28)
Christians should try to be holy (1 Peter 1:15, November 23)
God is worthy of praise because he is holy (Revelation 4:8, December 13)

HOLY SPIRIT The Holy Spirit was involved in Creation (Genesis 1:2, January 1)
The Holy Spirit empowers leaders (Judges 3:10, April 24)
The Holy Spirit teaches us (John 14:26, May 25)
The Holy Spirit guides us (John 16:13, May 27)
The Holy Spirit empowers us to be witnesses (Acts 1:8, June 3)
The Holy Spirit lives within us (Romans 8:11, July 23)
The Holy Spirit sanctifies us (Romans 15:16, August 1)
The Holy Spirit opens our spiritual eyes (1 Corinthians 2:10, August 6)
The Holy Spirit is involved in salvation (Titus 3:5, October 28)

HOMOSEXUALITY God finds homosexual behavior disgusting (Leviticus 18:22, February 25)
God will judge those who practice homosexual behavior (Romans 1:18-32, July 13)
Homosexual behavior has no place among Christians (1 Corinthians 6:9-10, August 10)

HONESTY Honesty is commanded by God (Exodus 20:16, February 4)
Only honest people can worship God (Psalm 24:3-4, January 29)
God is truth and desires truth (Psalm 51:6, March 8)
God hates lies (Proverbs 6:16-17, February 1)
Be honest (Proverbs 19:1, July 11)
Christians should be known by their honesty (Matthew 5:37, January 6)
Lies make someone unclean before God (Matthew 15:18-20, January 23)
Christians should put away dishonesty from their lives (Ephesians 4:25, September 26)

HOPE God gives hope to the needy (Psalm 9:18, January 10)
Hope gives us confidence (Psalm 25:3, January 30)
The Bible gives us hope (Psalm 119:43, May 25)
Christians always have hope (Romans 8:28, July 24)
Hope comes from the Holy Spirit (Romans 15:13, August 1)
Jesus' resurrection gives us hope (1 Corinthians 6:14, August 10)
We have hope in Jesus (1 Corinthians 15:19, August 23)
We have confidence of eternal life (Titus 1:1-2, October 26)

HOSPITALITY Christians should take care of those in need (Matthew 25:34-40, February 8)
Hospitality brings heavenly reward (Mark 9:41, February 28)
Christians should be hospitable (Romans 12:13, July 29)
Christians should be hospitable to people they do not know well (Hebrews 13:2, November 16)
Be cheerful about being hospitable (1 Peter 4:9-11, November 26)
Hospitality reflects God's love (3 John 1:5-8, December 7)

HUMILITY God humbles us for our own good (Deuteronomy 8:16, March 27)
God hears the prayers of the humble (2 Chronicles 7:14, July 22)

God saves those who are humble (Psalm 18:27, January 21)
God preserves the lives of humble people (Psalm 147:6, June 29)
Those who are humble become wise (Proverbs 11:2, March 9)
God cares for the humble (Isaiah 66:2, October 2)
God will exalt the humble (Luke 18:14, April 16)
Be humble in dealing with others (Philippians 2:1-11, September 30)
Humble yourself before God (James 4:10, November 20)

HYPOCRISY Do not associate with hypocrites (Psalm 26:4, February 1)
God hates hypocrisy in worship (Isaiah 29:13, September 18)
Hypocrites pretend to be devoted to God (Ezekiel 33:31-32, November 16)
God finds hypocrites repulsive (Matthew 23:27-28, February 4)
Beware of hypocrisy in your own life (Luke 12:1-2, April 6)
God will punish hypocrisy (Luke 20:46-47, April 21)
Hypocrites are worthless (Titus 1:16, October 26)
Get rid of hypocrisy (1 Peter 2:1, November 23)

IDOLATRY We should have no other gods (Exodus 20:3, February 4)
Do not be devoted to anyone or anything more than God (Deuteronomy 4:23, March 25)
Devote your heart to God (Joshua 24:14, April 22)
Look to God for your security (Judges 10:13-16, April 29)
We give in to idolatry when we forget God (Psalm 106:19-22, May 9)
God will not share his glory with anything else (Isaiah 42:8, September 23)
Christians cannot serve both God and the things of this world (Luke 16:13, April 13)

IMMORALITY Compromises can lead to immorality (Judges 3:1-11, April 24)
Stay away from immoral Christians (1 Corinthians 5:9-11, August 9)
Practicing immorality treats God lightly (1 Corinthians 6:19-20, August 10)
Immorality should have no place among Christians (Ephesians 4:17-19, September 26)

INSULT Respond properly to an insult (Proverbs 12:16, April 4)
God will bless Christians who are insulted because of their faith (Luke 6:22, March 24)
Do not insult others (1 Peter 3:9, November 25)

INTEGRITY Leaders should have integrity (Psalm 78:72, April 9)
Integrity takes effort (Psalm 101:3-8, April 30)
Leaders in the church should be full of integrity (Titus 1:7, October 26)
Maintain integrity in teaching others (Titus 2:7, October 27)

INTIMIDATION God can help us overcome intimidation (Genesis 15:1, January 6)
God does not forget us when we are intimidated (Genesis 46:3, January 23)
We do not need to fear anyone (Psalm 27:1, February 2)
God empowers us (Psalm 46:1-3, March 3)
We do not need to be intimidated (Psalm 112:7-8, May 16)
Jesus' strength can give us courage (John 16:33, May 27)
God will help us be bold (Acts 4:31, June 6)
Be on your guard against intimidation (1 Corinthians 16:13, August 25)
Pray for courage (Ephesians 6:19-20, September 28)
Christians can pray without being intimidated (Hebrews 4:16, November 2)

JEALOUSY God doesn't want to share our devotion (Deuteronomy 4:24, March 25)

Jealousy can destroy someone (Job 5:2, August 22)

Do not envy those who do wrong (Psalm 37:1, February 18)

Do not be jealous of wicked people (Psalm 73:2-3, April 1)

Jealousy steals away peace (Proverbs 14:30, May 8)

Jealousy is a powerful enemy (Proverbs 27:4, November 6)

Jealousy is foolish (Ecclesiastes 4:4, September 3)

Jealousy can cause rash behavior (Acts 7:9, June 9)

We should not be jealous of other Christians (Galatians 5:26, September 20)

Jealousy has no place in a Christian's life (Titus 3:3-5, October 28)

JESUS CHRIST Jesus is all-powerful (Isaiah 9:6, September 11)

Jesus has authority over demons (Mark 1:27, February 15)

Jesus is the Son of God (Luke 1:35, March 14)

Jesus is God (John 1:1-5, April 30)

Jesus is the Messiah (John 4:25-26, May 5)

Jesus is the judge (John 5:22, May 7)

Jesus gives life (John 10:10, May 18)

Jesus is the Good Shepherd (John 10:11, May 18)

Jesus is the only way to God (John 14:6, May 24)

Jesus is the author of life (Acts 3:15, June 5)

Jesus is the wisdom of God (1 Corinthians 1:21-24, August 5)

Jesus is the head of the church (Ephesians 5:23, September 27)

Jesus is the highest authority (Philippians 2:9-10, September 30)

Jesus is the Creator (Colossians 1:15-16, October 4)

Jesus is faithful (2 Timothy 2:13, October 23)

Jesus is coming again (Titus 2:13, October 27)

Jesus is sinless (Hebrews 4:15, November 2)

Jesus is holy (Hebrews 7:26, November 6)

Jesus is the King of the ages (Revelation 15:3, December 24)

Jesus is the Lamb of God (Revelation 21:22, December 30)

JUDGMENT God is able to judge (Job 34:23, August 30)

God is the ultimate authority (Psalm 9:7, January 9)

God will judge all people (Ecclesiastes 3:17, September 2)

God will judge people for their actions (Ecclesiastes 11:9, September 5)

God will judge everything done in secret (Ecclesiastes 12:14, September 5)

God will rule that wicked people are guilty (Malachi 3:5, December 31)

God will judge the words we speak (Matthew 12:36, January 18)

God does not judge by appearances (John 7:24, May 12)

God will judge Christians (Romans 14:10, July 31)

God will judge Christians for their actions (2 Corinthians 5:10, August 31)

God will judge all people (Hebrews 9:27, November 9)

People whose names are in God's Book of Life will enter heaven (Revelation 20:11-15, December 29)

JUSTICE Justice should not be influenced by a crowd (Exodus 23:2, February 5)

Protect the poor (Exodus 23:6, February 5)

Do not hold back justice (Deuteronomy 27:19, April 4)

God loves justice (Psalm 11:7, January 13)

Jesus' death was justice for sin (Romans 3:25-26, July 16)

KINDNESS Christians should be kind to each other (Ephesians 4:32, September 26)

Be kind to people who treat you wrongly (1 Thessalonians 5:15, October 12)

Choose to be kind rather than to argue (2 Timothy 2:24, October 24)

Being kind takes effort (2 Peter 1:5-7, November 27)

KINGDOM OF GOD/HEAVEN You must turn from sin before you can enter God's kingdom (Matthew 3:1-2, January 2)

Jesus describes members of God's kingdom (Matthew 5:1-19, January 5)

Obeying God's commands yields great rewards in his kingdom (Matthew 5:19, January 5)

Only righteous people will enter God's kingdom (Matthew 5:20, January 5)

God's kingdom is open to those who do his will (Matthew 7:21, January 9)

Healed lives are associated with God's kingdom (Matthew 9:35-36, January 13)

Entering God's kingdom costs someone everything (Matthew 13:44-45, January 20)

God's kingdom is reserved for the humble (Matthew 18:2-3, January 27)

No one deserves God's kingdom (Matthew 18:23-35, January 28)

God's kingdom is within our hearts (Luke 17:20-21, April 15)

God's kingdom will fully arrive in the future (Luke 21:25-31, April 22)

Only those who are spiritually reborn can enter God's kingdom (John 3:3, May 3)

Entering God's kingdom is not easy (Acts 14:22, June 22)

Christians should tell others about the Kingdom of God (Acts 28:31, July 11)

God's kingdom affects our lives (Romans 14:17, July 31)

God's kingdom is powerful (1 Corinthians 4:20, August 8)

No immoral person will be allowed into God's kingdom (Ephesians 5:5, September 27)

Christians are members of God's kingdom (Colossians 1:13, October 4)

Christians' lives should reflect their membership in God's kingdom (1 Thessalonians 2:12, October 10)

God calls people into his kingdom (1 Thessalonians 2:12, October 10)

God's kingdom cannot be shaken (Hebrews 12:28, November 15)

God's kingdom will one day be fully consummated (Revelation 11:15, December 20)

LAZINESS Laziness can ruin you (Proverbs 6:6-11, January 30)

Laziness can make you poor (Proverbs 10:4-5, February 18)

Lazy people work for others (Proverbs 12:24, April 8)

Lazy people make excuses (Proverbs 22:13, August 31)

Lazy people oversleep (Proverbs 26:14, October 26)

Encourage lazy people to work (1 Thessalonians 5:14, October 12)

Lazy people should not be allowed to be freeloaders (2 Thessalonians 3:10, October 15)

LEADERSHIP Leaders should be trustworthy (Exodus 18:21, February 3)

Leaders look out for the people's best interests (Numbers 27:16-17, March 18)

Leaders should represent God in their decisions (2 Chronicles 19:5-7, July 27)

Leaders should receive advice (Proverbs 11:14, March 16)

Leaders must serve others (Matthew 20:26-28, January 30)
Leaders should sacrifice for others (John 10:11, May 18)
Leaders should be obeyed (Romans 13:1-4, July 30)
Leaders give an account to God for their actions (Hebrews 13:17,
    November 16)

LIFE Life comes from God (Genesis 2:7, January 1)
God carefully creates each person (Psalm 139:13-14, June 21)
Life should be enjoyed (Ecclesiastes 9:9, September 4)
God plans the lives of people before they are born (Jeremiah 1:5,
    October 3)
People must be reborn spiritually to enter heaven (John 3:3, May 3)
Jesus came to give abundant life (John 10:10, May 18)
We should live lives worthy of our Christian calling (Ephesians 4:1,
    September 25)
Christ is the reason for life (Philippians 1:21, September 29)
Our lives should honor God (Colossians 3:17, October 7)

LIGHT Light comes from God (Genesis 1:3, January 1)
God is light (Psalm 27:1, February 2)
God's Word enlightens our path (Psalm 119:105, May 29)
God can turn darkness into light (Isaiah 42:16, September 23)
Christians are the light of the world (Matthew 5:14, January 5)
Jesus is the Light of the World (John 8:12, May 14)
Light shines in the hearts of Christians (2 Corinthians 4:6, August 30)
Christians are children of light (Ephesians 5:8, September 27)

LONELINESS God is concerned about our loneliness (Genesis 2:18, January 1)
God encourages the lonely (1 Kings 19:14-18, June 18)
God takes care of lonely people (Psalm 68:6, March 25)
Friends help in times of loneliness (Ecclesiastes 4:10-11,
    September 3)
God remains with us (Matthew 28:20, February 14)

LORD'S SUPPER Jesus celebrated the Lord's Supper with his disciples (Matthew
    26:26-29, February 9)
Christians should be thankful for the Lord's Supper
    (1 Corinthians 10:16, August 16)
Christians who celebrate the Lord's Supper together should be unified
    (1 Corinthians 11:20-34, August 18)

LOVE Love in marriage is strong (Song of Songs 8:6-7, September 7)
Love your enemies (Matthew 5:43-44, January 6)
Loving God is the most important command (Mark 12:29-30, March 5)
Christians must love each other (John 13:34, May 24)
We cannot be separated from Jesus' love (Romans 8:35-39, July 24)
Love must be genuine (Romans 12:9, July 29)
Love never quits (1 Corinthians 13:4-8, August 20)
God's love for us is beyond our understanding (Ephesians 3:18,
    September 24)
Love helps you look past offenses (1 Peter 4:8, November 26)
God is love (1 John 4:16, December 4)
We must be known for our love (2 John 1:5, December 6)

LOYALTY Friends are loyal (Proverbs 17:17, June 20)
We cannot divide our loyalty (Matthew 6:24, January 7)
There must be loyalty in marriage (Hebrews 13:4, November 16)

LUST Lustful thoughts are sinful (Matthew 5:28, January 6)
Christians should not give in to lust (Colossians 3:5, October 7)

Christians should avoid lust (1 Thessalonians 4:3-5, October 11)
Non-Christians are known for their lust (1 Peter 4:3, November 25)

LYING (*see* DISHONESTY)

MARRIAGE God hates divorce (Malachi 2:16, December 30)
Two people become one through marriage (Mark 10:2-12, February 28)
Angels do not get married (Mark 12:25, March 5)
Married partners should meet the needs of their own spouse
(1 Corinthians 7:2-5, August 11)
Married partners are united to each other for life (1 Corinthians 7:39,
August 12)
A Christian wife can witness to her non-Christian husband
(1 Peter 3:1-6, November 24)

MERCY God requires that we show mercy (Micah 6:8, December 16)
People who show mercy to others will be rewarded (Matthew 5:7,
January 5)
We should imitate God's mercy (Luke 6:36, March 24)
Jesus is merciful (1 Timothy 1:2, October 16)
Mercy is from God (2 Timothy 1:2, October 22)

MESSIAH The prophets prophesied about the Messiah (Genesis 3:15,
January 2)
The Messiah's mother would be a virgin (Isaiah 7:14, September 10)
The Messiah would be great (Isaiah 9:6-7, September 11)
The Messiah would suffer (Isaiah 53:2-12, September 27)
The Messiah would heal broken lives (Isaiah 61:1-3, September 30)
The Messiah would be born in Bethlehem (Micah 5:2, December 16)
Jesus' disciples knew he was the Messiah (Mark 8:27-29, February 26)
The Messiah will come again (Mark 14:61-62, March 10)
Jesus claimed to be the Messiah (John 4:25-42, May 5)
The Messiah brings salvation (Hebrews 2:10, October 31)

MIND Keep away from mental sins (Matthew 5:27-30, January 6)
A Christian's thoughts should be holy (Romans 12:2, July 29)
Our fellowship with God helps us make decisions (1 Corinthians
2:6-16, August 6)
Christians should please God with their thoughts (Philippians 4:8,
October 3)

MONEY Greed brings trouble (Proverbs 15:27, May 22)
Do not make money the most important part of your life
(Matthew 6:19, January 7)
Money can distract people from God (Mark 10:17-24, March 1)
You cannot serve both God and money (Luke 16:13, April 13)
Christians should share their resources with those in need (Acts
2:42-45, June 4)
Christians should not be lovers of money (1 Timothy 3:3, October 18)
We should look to God for security, not money (1 Timothy 6:17-19,
October 21)
Do not love money (Hebrews 13:5, November 16)
Be careful to treat rich and poor equally (James 2:1-9, November 18)

MURDER God has forbidden murder (Deuteronomy 5:17, March 26)
Hateful anger is the same in God's eyes as murder (Matthew 5:21-22,
January 5)

MUSIC Music can be used to worship God (Exodus 15:1, February 1)
Music is useful to focus our attention on God (Psalm 81:1-2, April 12)
We should make music for God's glory (Colossians 3:16, October 7)

OBEDIENCE Obeying is better than saying, "I'm sorry" (1 Samuel 15:22, May 14)
People who obey God's Word will be blessed (Luke 11:28, April 5)
Christians should obey the government (Romans 13:1-4, July 30)
Children should obey their parents (Ephesians 6:1, September 28)
Christians obey God (1 John 2:3, December 1)

PAIN God cares for his people (Deuteronomy 7:9, March 27)
Friends should comfort each other (Job 2:12-13, August 21)
God comforts us in our darkest times (Job 35:10, August 30)
God watches over the weak (Psalm 12:5, January 14)
God comforts us (Isaiah 40:9-11, September 22)
God promises to comfort those who mourn (Matthew 5:4, January 5)
God's Holy Spirit is our Comforter (John 14:16, May 25)
Christians should comfort each other (1 Thessalonians 4:18, October 11)
All pain will end (Revelation 21:3-4, December 30)

PARENTS Parents should teach children to follow God (Deuteronomy 6:6-7, March 26)
Parents should nurture their children (Ephesians 6:4, September 28)
Children must obey their parents (Colossians 3:20, October 8)

PATIENCE Be patient with God (Psalm 75:2, April 3)
Patience is valuable (Proverbs 25:15, October 14)
Patience is better than pride (Ecclesiastes 7:8, September 4)
Patience demonstrates love (1 Corinthians 13:4, August 20)
Patience is evidence of the Holy Spirit working in our lives (Galatians 5:22, September 20)
Be patient with each other (Ephesians 4:2, September 25)

PEACE Be full of peace (Psalm 34:14, February 14)
Jesus is known as the Prince of Peace (Isaiah 9:6-7, September 11)
Wicked people will not know peace (Isaiah 48:22, September 26)
We can have peace with God (Isaiah 53:5, September 27)
Make peace with others quickly (Matthew 5:23-26, January 5)
The peace Jesus gives is different than the world's peace (John 14:27, May 25)
Jesus gives us peace (Romans 5:1, July 18)
Peace is evidence of the Holy Spirit working in our lives (Galatians 5:22, September 20)
We can have peace through prayer (Philippians 4:4-7, October 3)

POWER Christians receive power from the Holy Spirit (Acts 1:8, June 3)
The Bible is a powerful weapon (Ephesians 6:17, September 28)
Jesus is the greatest power (Hebrews 1:1-4, October 30)
Prayer can be powerful (James 5:16, November 21)
Christians have power to overcome the world (1 John 5:4-5, December 5)

PRAISE (see WORSHIP)

PRAYER Ask God for help (Psalm 40:13, February 24)
God does not hear our prayers if we are purposely sinning (Micah 3:4, December 15)
Prayer should not be a show (Matthew 6:6, January 7)
Jesus taught his disciples how to pray (Matthew 6:9-13, January 7)
Pray with an attitude of humility (Luke 18:9-14, April 16)
Pray in Jesus' name (John 16:23-24, May 27)
Pray all the time (Ephesians 6:18, September 28)
Pray without doubting (James 1:6, November 17)
Pray with the right motives (James 4:3, November 20)
Pray according to God's will (1 John 5:14-15, December 5)

PRIDE (see also SELF-ESTEEM)
Pride leads to shame (Proverbs 11:2, March 9)
Pride leads to arguments (Proverbs 13:10, April 17)
Pride will be punished (Proverbs 16:5, May 27)
Pride ends in destruction (Proverbs 16:18, June 3)
Pride cuts us off from God and others (Luke 18:9-14, April 16)
There is no place for proud boasting in the Christian life
    (Romans 3:27, July 16)
God chose to reveal himself to the humble, not the proud
    (1 Corinthians 1:26-31, August 5)
Pride is not compatible with the fruit of the Spirit (Galatians 5:22-26,
    September 20)
God opposes the proud (James 4:6, November 20)

PROBLEMS (see STRESS, SUFFERING, TRIALS)

PROCRASTINATION We must not procrastinate in choosing to serve the Lord
    (Joshua 24:15, April 22)
God does not procrastinate (Habakkuk 2:3, December 18)
Those who procrastinate lose out (Luke 14:16-21, April 11)
Today is the day to be saved (2 Corinthians 6:2, September 2)
No one can procrastinate forever (Revelation 10:6, December 19)

PROPHECY (see also TEACHING)
Prophecy reveals a message from God (Deuteronomy 18:21-22,
    April 1)
False prophecy is not from God (Jeremiah 23:25-32, October 14)
Claiming to prophesy does not indicate salvation (Matthew 7:21-23,
    January 9)
The Holy Spirit allows believers to prophesy (Acts 2:17-18, June 4)
Prophecy is a spiritual gift (1 Corinthians 14:1-5, August 21)
We should listen to God's message (1 Thessalonians 5:20, October 12)
True prophets speak God's words (2 Peter 1:20-21, November 27)

PURITY Only God can make us pure (Psalm 51:1-10, March 8)
We can remain pure by following God's Word (Psalm 119:1-20, May 23)
We cannot claim purity apart from God (Proverbs 20:9, July 29)
The pure in heart will see God (Matthew 5:8, January 5)
Purity begins in the heart (Matthew 5:27-30, January 6)
Outward purity cannot substitute for inner purity (Matthew
    23:25-28, February 4)
Purity comes from God (John 17:17, May 28)
Purity ought to mark believers' lives (Ephesians 5:1-4, September 27)
Our minds should think about things that are pure (Philippians 4:8,
    October 3)
One day, our purity will be like Christ's (1 John 3:1-3, December 2)

QUESTIONS God may not always answer our questions (Job 42:1-3, September 1)
God welcomes our sincere questions (Luke 7:18-23, March 26)
We need not be afraid when questioned about our faith (Luke 21:12-
    15, April 22)
We should be ready with answers when questioned about our faith
    (1 Peter 3:15, November 25)

RAPTURE (see SECOND COMING OF CHRIST)

RELATIONSHIPS (see also FRIENDSHIP, MARRIAGE)
Our relationship with God is made possible through Jesus Christ
    (John 14:19-21, May 25)

Our relationships should not compromise our faith
(2 Corinthians 6:14-18, September 3)
We are unified with all believers in God's family (Ephesians 2:21-22,
September 23)
Our relationship with Christ is deep and abiding (2 Timothy 2:11-13,
October 23)
Our relationship with Christ makes us children of God (1 John 3:1-3,
December 2)

REPENTANCE (see also CONFESSION OF SIN)
Repentance of sin opens the way for a relationship with God
(Luke 3:7-8, March 18)
Without repenting of our sin, we would perish (Luke 13:3-5, April 9)
Angels rejoice when a sinner repents (Luke 15:7, April 12)
Forgive those who repent of wrongs done to you (Luke 17:4, April 14)
Repentance is essential for the Holy Spirit to work (Acts 2:38, June 4)
God can use difficulties to encourage us to repent (2 Corinthians
7:9-10, September 4)
God would like everyone to repent and believe (2 Peter 3:9,
November 29)

REPUTATION A good reputation can be built by obeying God's Word
(Deuteronomy 4:1-14, March 25)
Integrity builds a good reputation (Ruth 2:1-13, May 6)
A bad reputation will follow you (Proverbs 25:9-10, October 12)
The Christians in Rome had a reputation for obedience
(Romans 16:19, August 3)
Guard your reputation (2 Corinthians 8:18-24, September 6)
Maintain a good reputation among non-Christians (Colossians 4:5,
October 8)

RESPECT (see also AUTHORITY)
God is worthy of our respect (Exodus 3:5, January 26)
Our parents are worthy of respect (Leviticus 19:3, February 26)
Those in authority should have our respect (1 Samuel 24:1-6, May 19)
Husbands and wives should respect each other (Ephesians 5:33,
September 27)
Those in leadership should have respectful children (1 Timothy 3:4,
October 18)
Show respect to all people (1 Peter 2:17, November 24)

RESPONSIBILITY Responsible people admit their wrongs (1 Chronicles 21:8, July 15)
Responsible people are faithful with what they have been given
(Matthew 25:14-30, February 7)
People are responsible for their decision about Christ (John 3:18-19,
May 3)
Responsible people know their abilities and limitations (Acts 6:1-7,
June 8)
People are responsible for their own actions (James 1:13-15,
November 17)

REST God gave us an example of and a command to rest (Genesis 2:3,
January 1)
Rest is important for worship (Exodus 20:8, February 4)
God tells us to rest (Exodus 23:12, February 5)
Jesus promises to give us rest from our burdens (Matthew 11:28-30,
January 16)
Rest is a gift of God (Hebrews 4:9-11, November 2)
Heaven will be a place of rest (Revelation 14:13, December 23)

RESURRECTION Christ's resurrection is a historical fact (Matthew 28:5-10, February 14)
All people will be resurrected (John 5:24-30, May 8)
Jesus promised to raise his followers (John 6:38-40, May 10)
We know we will be resurrected (John 11:24-26, May 20)
We will experience resurrection (Romans 6:3-11, July 20)
Jesus' resurrection is the foundation of Christianity
(1 Corinthians 15:12-21, August 23)
Our resurrected bodies will be eternal bodies (1 Corinthians 15:51-53, August 24)

REVENGE God's people should not seek revenge (Leviticus 19:18, February 26)
Do not pay back evil for evil (Proverbs 24:29, October 8)
Believers ought to resist revenge (Matthew 5:38-42, January 6)
Leave revenge in God's hands (Romans 12:19, July 29)
Desire for revenge is not compatible with the Christian life
(1 Thessalonians 5:15, October 12)
Jesus is our example (1 Peter 2:21-23, November 24)

RIGHTEOUS/ God is completely righteous (Isaiah 45:21-24, September 25)
RIGHTEOUSNESS We cannot attain righteousness on our own (Isaiah 64:6, October 1)
Human nature is the opposite of righteousness (Romans 3:10-18, July 16)
Righteousness is not attained by works (Romans 4:18-25, July 18)
Strict legalism cannot make us righteous (Galatians 3:11-21, September 17)
Our God-given righteousness is armor against Satan's attacks
(Ephesians 6:14, September 28)
We become righteous through faith in Christ (Philippians 3:9, October 2)
Studying God's Word helps us grow in righteousness (2 Timothy 3:16, October 24)
Righteousness ought to characterize each believer's life (1 Peter 2:24, November 24)

SADNESS (see GRIEF, SORROW)

SALVATION Those who receive salvation become God's children (John 1:12-13, April 30)
Salvation is a work of the Holy Spirit in a person's life (John 3:1-16, May 3)
Belief and trust in Jesus Christ are the only way to be saved (John 14:6, May 24)
Salvation includes gaining a relationship with God (John 17:1-5, May 28)
Receiving salvation means we must turn from our sins (Acts 2:37-38, June 4)
Salvation cannot be earned; it is a gift of God (Romans 6:23, July 20)
Receiving salvation is simple and personal (Romans 10:8-10, July 26)
Salvation is by God's grace alone (Ephesians 2:1-9, September 23)
Salvation rescues us from Satan's dominion (Colossians 1:13-14, October 4)
Our salvation was obtained by Jesus' blood (1 Peter 1:18-19, November 23)

SATAN (see also DEMONS)
Satan is under God's authority (Job 1:6-12, August 21)
Satan will tempt Jesus' followers (Matthew 4:1-11, January 3)
Satan is completely evil (John 8:44, May 16)

Satan is the temporary ruler over this world (Ephesians 2:1-2, September 23)

Satan and his demons are spiritual (Ephesians 6:12, September 28)

Satan works through an army of demons (1 Timothy 4:1, October 19)

Believers have the authority to resist Satan (James 4:1-10, November 20)

Satan is an enemy to Christians (1 Peter 5:8, November 26)

Jesus destroyed Satan's work with his death on the cross (1 John 3:7-8, December 3)

Satan is a defeated enemy (Revelation 20:10, December 29)

SECOND COMING OF CHRIST We do not know when Jesus will return (Matthew 24:36, February 6)

Christ's return will be unmistakable (Mark 13:26-27, March 7)

Christ's return will be joyous for those who are ready (Luke 12:35-40, April 8)

The Second Coming will be a time of judgment on unbelievers (John 12:37-50, May 22)

At Christ's second coming we will be with him forever (John 14:1-3, May 24)

The promise of Christ's return (Acts 1:10-11, June 3)

Believers will be resurrected and given glorious bodies (1 Corinthians 15:51-57, August 24)

Christ's return will be visible and glorious (1 Thessalonians 4:16, October 11)

At Christ's return, Christians who are dead and alive will rise to meet him (1 Thessalonians 4:16-17, October 11)

Continue to serve God as you await the Second Coming (1 Peter 4:7-8, November 26)

Patiently await Christ's return (2 Peter 3:8-13, November 29)

Jesus is coming soon (Revelation 22:20-21, December 31)

SELF-ESTEEM (see also PRIDE)

We are made in God's image (Genesis 1:26-27, January 1)

We are a little lower than the angels (Psalm 8:3-5, January 8)

God took special care to create us (Psalm 139:1-18, June 21)

We have been formed by God's loving hands (Isaiah 64:8, October 1)

We are of great value to God (Luke 12:4-12, April 6)

God gave his Son for us (John 3:16, May 3)

Our self-esteem is affected by our relationship with Christ (Romans 12:1-8, July 29)

Our self-esteem is based on God's approval (2 Corinthians 10:12-18, September 8)

We should not overestimate ourselves (Galatians 6:3-5, September 21)

SEX Sex is God's gift to married people (Proverbs 5:15-21, January 27)

Sex outside of marriage is foolish (Proverbs 6:23-35, February 2)

Sex within marriage is meant to be a delight (Song of Songs 4:1-16, September 6)

Sexual sin begins in the mind (Matthew 5:27-30, January 6)

Sex is a powerful bond not meant to be taken lightly (1 Corinthians 6:13-20, August 10)

Sexual immorality is improper for Christians (Ephesians 5:1-3, September 27)

Believers get rid of any sexual immorality in their lives (Colossians 3:5, October 7)

Place sexual desires under Christ's control (1 Thessalonians 4:1-8, October 11)

Sex in marriage is honorable and pure (Hebrews 13:4, November 16)

SICKNESS God cares for the sick (Psalm 41:1-13, February 25)

A cheerful spirit can act as good medicine against sickness (Proverbs 17:22, June 22)

Jesus can heal sickness (Matthew 4:23-25, January 4)

Believers ought to have compassion on the sick (Matthew 25:34-40, February 8)

It is better to be physically crippled than spiritually crippled (Mark 9:43-48, February 28)

Paul had an infirmity that God would not remove (2 Corinthians 12:7-10, September 11)

SIN Sin has consequences (Genesis 3:1-19, January 2)

God must punish sin (Exodus 32:34, February 11)

Our consciences can identify sin (2 Samuel 24:10-15, June 5)

We should humbly confess our sins to God (Ezra 9:5-15, August 9)

We should ask God to forgive our sins (Psalm 51:1-10, March 8)

Stay away from people who lead you to sin (Proverbs 1:10-19, January 3)

Sin can begin in the mind (Matthew 5:27-28, January 6)

All people have sinned (Romans 3:23, July 16)

Sin leads to eternal death (Romans 6:23, July 20)

Jesus takes the penalty of our sin on himself (Romans 8:1-2, July 22)

Sin begins with temptation (James 1:15, November 17)

We can sin by avoiding something we should do (James 4:17, November 20)

God is willing to forgive our sins (1 John 1:8-9, November 30)

SINGLENESS Some people remain single to work for God's kingdom (Matthew 19:12, January 28)

Singleness is a gift from God (1 Corinthians 7:7-8, August 11)

Single people can serve God (1 Corinthians 7:25-31, August 12)

Singleness can help a person focus on service for God (1 Corinthians 7:32-35, August 12)

SORROW (see also GRIEF)

Sorrow is often a necessary part of repentance (Judges 2:4-5, April 23)

Weeping will be followed by joy (Psalm 30:5, February 6)

Jesus understands sorrow (Isaiah 53:3-9, September 27)

God promises comfort to those who experience sorrow (Matthew 5:4, January 5)

God may use sorrow to point out sin and draw us back to him (2 Corinthians 7:10-11, September 4)

We sorrow over believers who die, but one day we will meet again (1 Thessalonians 4:13-18, October 11)

Sorrow will not exist in God's kingdom (Revelation 21:3-4, December 30)

SOUL People cannot destroy your soul (Matthew 10:28, January 15)

We are to love God with our whole being—heart, soul, and mind (Matthew 22:36-40, February 3)

It is of no value to gain the world but lose your soul (Mark 8:34-38, February 26)

We can place our soul under Jesus' Christ's protection (John 10:27-29, May 19)

Believers are assured immortality (1 Corinthians 15:46-53, August 24)

SPIRITUAL GIFTS God expects us to use our gifts (Romans 12:3-8, July 29)

God gives us our spiritual gifts (1 Corinthians 12:4-11, August 19)

Spiritual gifts build up the body of Christ (Ephesians 4:11-13, September 25)

Spiritual gifts ought not be denied nor overemphasized (1 Thessalonians 5:19-22, October 12)

God distributes spiritual gifts according to his will (Hebrews 2:4, October 31)

STRESS Delegating work can alleviate stress (Exodus 18:13-26, February 3)

God is a refuge in times of stress (Psalm 62:1-8, March 19)

Pray to God in times of stress (Psalm 69:1-36, March 27)

Wait upon the Lord (Isaiah 40:30-31, September 22)

God is always with us (Romans 8:31-39, July 24)

God cares about our stress (2 Corinthians 4:8-12, August 30)

Don't let stress cause you to worry (Philippians 4:4-9, October 3)

SUBMISSION (see also OBEDIENCE)

Christ is our example of submission to the Father's will (Matthew 26:39, 42, February 9)

Following Christ requires submission to him (Luke 14:27, April 11)

God created lines of authority for harmonious relationships (1 Corinthians 11:2-16, August 17)

Marriage calls for mutual submission (Ephesians 5:21-33, September 27)

Submit to God (James 4:7-10, November 20)

SUFFERING (see also TRIALS)

Those who suffer need encouragement (Job 16:1-6, August 25)

Christ's followers will face suffering (Matthew 16:21-26, January 25)

Our suffering helps us comfort others who are suffering (2 Corinthians 1:3-7, August 26)

Our suffering will end in glory (2 Corinthians 4:17-18, August 31)

Jesus can help us through suffering (Hebrews 2:11-18, October 31)

Christ showed how to handle suffering (1 Peter 2:21-24, November 24)

There will be no suffering in Christ's kingdom (Revelation 21:4, December 30)

TEACHING (see also WITNESSING)

Parents must teach their children about the Lord (Deuteronomy 6:4-9, March 26)

Believers teach each other (2 Timothy 2:2, October 23)

Qualities of a good teacher (2 Timothy 2:22-26, October 24)

Instruction to those who teach God's Word (Titus 2:1-15, October 27)

TEMPTATION Temptation comes from Satan (Genesis 3:1-6, January 2)

How to avoid temptation (Proverbs 7:1-5, February 4)

How to respond when tempted (Matthew 4:1-11, January 3)

God will provide a way of escape from every temptation (1 Corinthians 10:13, August 15)

Run from temptation (2 Timothy 2:22, October 24)

Christ can help us, for he, too, has faced temptation (Hebrews 4:15-16, November 2)

God never tempts people to sin (James 1:13-15, November 17)

THANKFULNESS Thank the Lord because he is good (Psalm 107:1-3, May 11)

Be thankful for answers to prayer (Psalm 138:1-5, June 20)

Be thankful for salvation (Ephesians 2:4-10, September 23)

Our prayers should include words of thankfulness (Philippians 4:6,
　　October 3)
Our lives should be characterized by thankfulness to God
　　(Colossians 3:15-17, October 7)
We are called to give thanks in all circumstances
　　(1 Thessalonians 5:16-18, October 12)

TRIALS (*see also* SUFFERING)
Christ promises us rest from our trials (Matthew 11:28-30,
　　January 16)
Jesus understands our struggles (John 15:18, May 26)
Have peace in trials (John 16:33, May 27)
Trials help us develop patience (Romans 5:1-5, July 18)
God knows what he is doing with our lives (Romans 8:28, July 24)
Believers can expect to suffer for their faith (2 Corinthians 6:3-13,
　　September 2)
Present trials fade in comparison to the joy of our relationship with
　　Christ (Philippians 3:7-11, October 2)
God expects us to grow through our trials (James 1:2-4, November 17)

TRUST (*see* FAITH)

TRUTH God wants us to be true and righteous (Psalm 51:1-6, March 8)
Truth never changes (Proverbs 12:19, April 6)
Truth sets us free (John 8:31-32, May 16)
Truth is found in Jesus Christ (John 14:6, May 24)
God's Word is truth (John 17:17, May 28)
We must not only believe the truth but also live by it (1 John 1:5-7,
　　November 30)

UNBELIEVERS We must not imitate unbelievers (Psalm 26:5, February 1)
We must share the gospel with unbelievers (John 17:14-19, May 28)
Unbelievers do not belong to Christ (Romans 8:9, July 23)
We should avoid situations that force us to compromise our beliefs
　　(2 Corinthians 6:14-18, September 3)
Unbelievers will not enter heaven (1 John 5:10-12, December 5)

UNITY Unity among believers pleases God (Psalm 133:1, June 15)
Christians are not supposed to live in isolation (John 17:11, May 28)
Unity includes bearing one another's joys and burdens (Romans
　　12:9-16, July 29)
Believers must seek unity in all essentials (1 Corinthians 1:10,
　　August 4)
There can be great unity even in great diversity (Ephesians 4:3-13,
　　September 25)
The love Christ commanded should create unity among believers
　　(Philippians 1:3-11, September 29)
Unity ought to be a distinctive mark among Christians
　　(Philippians 2:1-2, September 30)

WISDOM The fear of God is the beginning of wisdom (Proverbs 1:7,
　　January 2)
To find wisdom, first find God (Proverbs 2:6-12, January 8)
Wise people accept advice (Proverbs 13:10, April 17)
Wise people boast not in their wisdom but in God (Jeremiah 9:23-24,
　　October 7)
The wise understand God's ways and follow his guidance (Hosea 14:9,
　　December 8)
Wise people build on the solid foundation of God and his Word
　　(Matthew 7:24-27, January 9)

God's wisdom is different from the world's wisdom
(1 Corinthians 2:1-16, August 5)
God will give us wisdom if we ask for it (James 1:5, November 17)

WITNESSING (*see also* EVANGELISM, TEACHING)
Bringing the good news of Christ is a wonderful privilege (Isaiah 52:7,
September 27)
God's message will accomplish what he desires wherever it is spoken
(Isaiah 55:10-11, September 28)
God holds us accountable for avoiding a chance to witness for him
(Ezekiel 3:18-19, November 2)
Let your light shine (Matthew 5:14-16, January 5)
Jesus commanded all believers to witness (Matthew 28:16-20,
February 14)
If we acknowledge our faith before people, God will acknowledge us
(Luke 12:8-9, April 7)
Christians are called to spread the gospel across the world (Acts 1:8,
June 3)
We plant or water the seed of faith, but only God makes it grow
(1 Corinthians 3:5-9, August 7)
God has entrusted us with the message we need to share with others
(2 Corinthians 5:18-21, September 1)
Always be ready to tell what God has done for you (1 Peter 3:15,
November 25)

WOMEN God's image is shared equally by women and men (Genesis 1:26-27,
January 1)
Women should fulfill their responsibilities well (Proverbs 31:10-31,
December 30)
Women and men are equal before God (Galatians 3:28,
September 18)
Advice for helping widows in the church (1 Timothy 5:3-16,
October 20)

WORK Hard work is honored by God (Genesis 31:38-42, January 15)
Use your skills to honor God (Exodus 36:1, February 13)
Hard work brings rewards (Proverbs 12:14, April 3)
Hard work helps supply basic needs (Proverbs 28:19,
November 28)
Our work for God is never wasted (1 Corinthians 15:58, August 24)
All work should be done as though we are working for God
(Ephesians 6:5-9, September 28)

WORRY (*see* STRESS)

WORSHIP (*see also* CHURCH)
Worship is an encounter with the living and holy God (Exodus 3:1-6,
January 26)
Worship is reserved for God alone (Exodus 34:14, February 12)
In worship, we ascribe to the Lord the glory due to him (Psalm 29:1-2,
February 5)
We can worship because of Christ's sacrifice on our behalf
(Hebrews 10:1-10, November 10)
We should worship with reverence for God (Hebrews 12:28,
November 15)
When we draw near to God, he draws near to us (James 4:8,
November 20)

YOUTH (*see* ADOLESCENCE)

God's wisdom is different from the world's wisdom
(1 Corinthians 2:1-16, August 5)
God will give us wisdom if we ask for it (James 1:5, November 17)

WITNESSING (see also EVANGELISM, TEACHING)
Bringing the good news of Christ is a wonderful privilege (Isaiah 52:7, September 27)
God's message will accomplish what he desires wherever it is spoken (Isaiah 55:10-11, September 28)
God holds us accountable for avoiding a chance to witness for him (Ezekiel 3:18-19, November 2)
Let your light shine (Matthew 5:14-16, January 5)
Jesus commanded all believers to witness (Matthew 28:16-20, February 14)
If we acknowledge our faith before people, God will acknowledge us (Luke 12:8-9, April 7)
Christians are called to spread the gospel across the world (Acts 1:8, June 5)
We plant or water the seed of faith, but only God makes it grow (1 Corinthians 3:5-9, August 7)
God has entrusted us with the message we need to share with others (2 Corinthians 5:18-21, September 1)
Always be ready to tell what God has done for you (1 Peter 3:15, November 25)

WOMEN God's image is shared equally by women and men (Genesis 1:26-27, January 1)
Women should fulfill their responsibilities well (Proverbs 31:10-31, December 30)
Women and men are equal before God (Galatians 3:28, September 18)
Advice for helping widows in the church (1 Timothy 5:3-16, October 20)

WORK Hard work is honored by God (Genesis 3:17-19, January 15)
Use your skills to honor God (Exodus 36:1, February 13)
Hard work brings rewards (Proverbs 12:14, April 3)
Hard work helps supply basic needs (Proverbs 28:19, November 24)
Our work for God is never wasted (1 Corinthians 15:58, August 24)
All work should be done as though we are working for God (Ephesians 6:5-9, September 28)

WORRY (see STRESS)

WORSHIP (see also CHURCH)
Worship is an encounter with the living and holy God (Exodus 3:1-6, January 26)
Worship is reserved for God alone (Exodus 34:14, February 12)
In worship, we ascribe to the Lord the glory due to him (Psalm 29:1-2, February 3)
We can worship because of Christ's sacrifice on our behalf (Hebrews 10:1-10, November 10)
We should worship with reverence for God (Hebrews 12:28, November 13)
When we draw near to God, he draws near to us (James 4:8, November 20)

YOUTH (see ADOLESCENCE)

INTRODUCTION TO THE BOOKS OF THE BIBLE

GENESIS
January 1-25

As its name implies, Genesis is the book of beginnings. It starts with the creation of the world and every living creature in it. It records the first marriage, the first sin, the first consequences of sin, and the first reference to God's future plan to redeem humanity. After recounting the stories of the Flood and the Tower of Babel, Genesis also tells the story of the birth of a nation—Israel. The story begins as God calls Abraham, the father of the Israelites, to leave his hometown, Ur (located in modern-day Iraq), and move to Canaan—the land God promised his descendants. Eventually, the Redeemer of the world would come from the descendants of Abraham. The story shifts to the exploits of Isaac, Abraham's son, and then to Jacob, Abraham's grandson. Genesis concludes with the remarkable experiences of Joseph.

OUTLINE
1:1–2:25 The creation of the world and humanity
3:1–3:24 The fall of Adam and Eve
4:1–9:29 The history of fallen humanity up to the Flood
10:1–11:32 The spread of people around the world
12:1–25:18 The life of Abraham
25:19–26:35 The life of Isaac
27:1–37:1 The lives of Jacob and Esau
37:2–50:26 The life of Joseph

AUTHOR Moses, according to tradition

DATE WRITTEN 1450–1410 BC

PURPOSE To show how the world and everything in it came about and to show God's desire to have a people set apart to worship him

THEMES Origin of the world, humanity, sin, and the nation of Israel; the sovereignty and trustworthiness of God; obedience and blessing

EXODUS
January 25–
February 15

Every country has its own national history—a record of the events leading to the nation's independence. The book of Exodus records Israel's national history, recounting the earliest years of the nation and of God's covenant with them. Exodus takes its name from the main event of the book: the Israelites' deliverance from slavery in Egypt. The book begins with a short account of how the Israelites became slaves in Egypt. The focus then shifts to the birth and life of Moses, God's chosen leader for Israel. From a burning bush in the Sinai Desert, God called Moses to return to his homeland of Egypt and lead the Israelites to freedom. But Pharaoh refused to free the Israelites, and so he set in motion God's ten devastating plagues upon Egypt. The final plague not only changed Pharaoh's mind—it became a memorial of God's deliverance, celebrated in the observance of Passover. Once set free, the Israelites traveled to the wilderness of Sinai to worship God. But Pharaoh chased the Israelites to the Red Sea, where God displayed his power by parting the sea for the Israelites to cross and then closing it over the pursuing Egyptians. The Israelites were then free to travel to Mount Sinai. There God established his covenant with them, giving them the Ten Commandments and plans for the Tabernacle. After the Israelites constructed the Tabernacle, God filled it with his glory, signifying his presence with them.

OUTLINE 1:1-22 Israel's bondage in Egypt
2:1-7:7 The birth and calling of Moses
7:8-15:21 The plagues, the Passover, and the Exodus
15:22-24:18 The trip to Sinai and the giving of the law
25:1-31:18 Instructions for the Tabernacle
32:1-35:3 Israel's sin and repentance
35:4-40:38 The building of the Tabernacle

AUTHOR Moses, according to tradition
DATE WRITTEN 1450-1410 BC
PURPOSE To record the events of Israel's deliverance from Egypt and development as a nation
THEMES God's sovereignty, guidance, redemption, and covenant with Israel; obedience

LEVITICUS Our entire lives should glorify God—from our religious worship to our
February 16– daily tasks. With this in mind, the book of Leviticus was written as a
March 3 handbook for the priests and Levites (religious servants) of Israel. Leviticus gives detailed rules concerning the daily lives of the Israelites and special procedures for the worship of the Lord. It provides instructions for offering sacrifices. Leviticus also describes the proper methods for the Israelites to observe major festivals and holidays and for the priests to carry out the duties of their office.

OUTLINE 1:1-15:33 The sacrificial system
16:1-34 The great Day of Atonement
17:1-20:27 Various regulations
21:1-22:33 Rules for the priests
23:1-25:55 Rules concerning the festivals
26:1-27:34 Obedience, vows, and tithes

AUTHOR Moses, according to tradition
DATE WRITTEN 1445-1444 BC
PURPOSE To outline the Levites' duties in worship and to teach the Israelites how to live holy lives
THEMES Sacrifice and offering, proper worship, healthy living, the importance of holiness

NUMBERS The discontented whining of a young child can be difficult to ignore.
March 3-23 Likewise, the childlike whining of the Israelites in the wilderness characterizes the book of Numbers. This book picks up where Exodus leaves off—with the Israelites camped at the base of Mount Sinai. From here the Israelites journeyed to the wilderness of Paran, south of the Promised Land. Scouts were sent to explore the Promised Land and give a report on its inhabitants. When they returned to the camp, their report was not favorable, and the people began to doubt God's ability to give them their inheritance, and they complained against him. Because of their sin, God condemned them to wander in the wilderness until the generation of complainers died off and a new generation took their place. Forty years later they slowly made their way back to Canaan—this time ready to obey God's commands. After winning some important battles east of the Jordan River, the Israelites prepared to enter the heart of the Promised Land they had waited so long to see.

OUTLINE 1:1–2:34 The census of the men for battle
3:1–10:10 Special regulations for the Israelites
10:11–14:45 The journey to Canaan and the great rebellion
15:1–19:22 Wandering in the wilderness
20:1–25:18 The journey to the plains of Moab and Balaam's oracles
26:1–36:13 Preparations in Moab for entry into Canaan

AUTHOR Moses, according to tradition
DATE WRITTEN 1450–1410 BC
PURPOSE To tell the story of how Israel prepared to enter the Promised Land, how they sinned and were punished, and how they returned again to enter the land
THEMES Rebellion, faith, God's justice and faithfulness

DEUTERONOMY The book of Deuteronomy records the covenant between God and Israel.
March 23–April 10 It calls each new generation of Israel to remember who God is and what he has done for them. Through a series of speeches, this fifth and final book of Moses summarizes the events that led up to this moment in Israel's history: the eve of Israel's entry into the Promised Land. Moses exhorted the Israelites to remain faithful and obedient and called them to rededicate their lives to the task God had given them. Then Moses led the people in worship. Finally, Moses appointed his successor, Joshua, and went off to a mountain by himself to view the Promised Land from a distance before he died.

OUTLINE 1:1–4:49 Moses' first address
5:1–26:19 Moses' second address
27:1–28:68 Summary of various laws
29:1–32:43 Moses' third address and the appointment of Joshua
32:44–34:12 Moses' final words and death

AUTHOR Moses, according to tradition (except for the final summary, possibly written by Joshua)
DATE WRITTEN 1407–1406 BC
PURPOSE To remind the people of what God had done for them and to encourage them to rededicate their lives to him
THEMES God's faithfulness, God's laws for his people, the consequences of sin, a call to obedience, God's love for his people

JOSHUA The book of Joshua is about leadership—more specifically, about Joshua's
April 10-22 leadership of the Israelites. At the opening of the book, Moses had already died, and Joshua had been appointed his successor. While the Israelites waited on the plains of Moab, Joshua prepared them for battle. Once they were ready, Joshua led them across the Jordan River to begin their conquest of the land God had promised them. The Israelites then fought three campaigns: (1) one in the central region, (2) one in the south, and (3) one in the north. After the initial victories, Joshua and his people divided the land among the tribes of Israel. As the book comes to an end, Joshua was old and close to death, and he urged the Israelites to follow the LORD their God.

OUTLINE 1:1–5:15 Mobilizing Israel and entering the Promised Land
6:1–8:35 The central campaign
9:1–10:43 The southern campaign
11:1-15 The northern campaign
11:16–22:34 Summary and division of the land
23:1–24:33 Joshua's final words and death

AUTHOR Joshua, according to Jewish tradition (except for the ending, possibly written by Phinehas the high priest)

DATE WRITTEN 1380 BC
PURPOSE To give the history of Israel's conquest of the Promised Land
THEMES Obedience, faith, guidance, godly leadership

JUDGES Often the greatest heroes appear in the midst of the worst chaos and
April 23–May 5 confusion. This is true in the book of Judges, where true heroes and
heroines repeatedly are called upon to save the day after the people have
fallen into sin. After Joshua's armies conquered Canaan, the twelve tribes
of Israel settled their allotted portions of land. They had no earthly king
because God was to serve as their king. But this required that the people
follow and obey God—a situation that rarely existed during this period.
The people soon became unfaithful to God and practiced the ways of
their pagan neighbors. To punish their disobedience, God allowed the
Israelites' neighbors to oppress them. The Israelites then repented and
asked God to rescue them, and so he raised up various leaders among
them to drive out the enemy. These leaders were known as judges. They
not only defeated their enemies and drove them from the land but they
turned the Israelites' hearts back to God. But time after time, soon after
the people were delivered from their oppressive neighbors, they lost their
zeal for God, and the whole cycle began again.

OUTLINE 1:1–3:4 Summary of current events
3:5–31 The first judges—Othniel, Ehud, and Shamgar
4:1–5:31 Deborah and Barak's victory
6:1–8:35 The story of Gideon
9:1-57 The story of Abimelech
10:1–12:15 The stories of Tola, Jair, Jephthah, Ibzan, Elon, and Abdon
13:1–16:31 The story of Samson
17:1–21:25 Anarchy in the land

AUTHOR Samuel, according to Jewish tradition
DATE WRITTEN Uncertain, perhaps around 1000 BC
PURPOSE To show the pitfalls of Israel's lack of central authority, the consequences
of sin, and God's willingness to rescue those who repent
THEMES Compromise, unfaithfulness, punishment of sin, repentance, deliverance

RUTH God often uses the most unlikely people to accomplish his plans and
May 5-6 purposes. In this book, Ruth, a Moabite widow, willingly leaves her
homeland to care for her mother-in-law, Naomi, who is also a widow. Being
a Moabite, Ruth was not a part of God's chosen people, Israel, but she chose
to follow God anyway. God rewarded her for her faithfulness and her
kindness to her mother-in-law. First, he provided for Ruth's physical needs.
As Ruth went out to get food, she came upon a field where the owner
allowed her to gather as much leftover grain as she needed. But God's
provision did not stop at Ruth's immediate physical needs. The owner of
the field, Boaz, also happened to be a relative of Naomi. Boaz took a sincere
interest in Ruth, and eventually they were married. God continued to show
his faithful love to Ruth and Boaz by honoring them through their
descendants—King David and, hundreds of years later, Jesus Christ.

OUTLINE 1:1-10 Naomi's tragedy
1:11-22 Ruth's loyalty to Naomi
2:1–3:18 The friendship of Naomi's relative Boaz
4:1-17 The marriage of Boaz and Ruth
4:18-22 The genealogy of King David

AUTHOR Samuel, according to Jewish tradition (although the genealogy suggests it
was written after his death)
DATE WRITTEN 1375–1050 BC

PURPOSE To show that God rewards those who trust in him
THEMES Faithfulness, kindness, integrity, God's protection and blessing

1 SAMUEL
May 7-21

The choices people make say a lot about their character. The book of 1 Samuel is full of choices—some good and some bad. The first significant choice in 1 Samuel is made by Hannah, a woman who was unable to have children. She chose to cry out to God for a child. God heard her prayer and granted her request. Grateful to God for his goodness, Hannah dedicated her child, Samuel, to the Lord from the time he was born. So Samuel grew up among the priests at the Tabernacle, and eventually he himself became the leading priest. Near the end of Samuel's life, the Israelites rejected Samuel's sons as judges over Israel and asked him to appoint a king over them. Samuel warned the Israelites that a king would oppress them, but they chose to have one anyway. Thus began the history of Israel's kings. Samuel chose a tall, handsome man named Saul to be Israel's first king. At first Saul appeared to make some good decisions. But soon he began to make some very bad choices, and God brought an end to his reign. David, a shepherd from Bethlehem, was chosen to take Saul's place. Saul made several attempts on David's life; but by the end of the book, Saul and his sons are dead, and David is in line to become the next king.

OUTLINE 1:1–7:17 Samuel's early ministry and the Philistine war
8:1–15:35 King Saul's early successes
16:1–20:42 Saul's decline and the rise of David
21:1–24:22 Saul's persecution of David
25:1–31:13 David's growing strength and the death of Saul

AUTHOR Uncertain; some have suggested Samuel and the prophets Nathan and Gad
DATE WRITTEN Uncertain; perhaps around 1000 BC
PURPOSE To record the life of Israel's last judge, Samuel, the reign and decline of Israel's first king, Saul, and the selection and preparation of Israel's greatest king, David
THEMES Israel's rejection of God as king, leadership, obedience, God's faithfulness

2 SAMUEL
May 22–June 5

Among the godly men and women mentioned in the Bible, King David stands as one of the most prominent. The prophet Samuel had said that God wanted "a man after his own heart," and David was that man. The book of 2 Samuel tells King David's story, covering a period of approximately forty years—the bulk of David's reign as king. It begins with David being proclaimed king of Israel. Soon after his inauguration, David consolidated his position against rivals to the throne. After conquering Jerusalem there, David made it his capital and brought the sacred Ark of the Covenant there. Then he defeated the Philistines—neighbors who had harassed the Israelites for hundreds of years. But 2 Samuel also describes the darker side of David's career as well, including his affair with Bathsheba and the rebellion led by his son Absalom. The book comes to a close near the end of David's long reign.

OUTLINE 1:1–6:23 David's first acts as king
7:1-29 God's covenant with David
8:1–10:19 David's victories over his enemies
11:1–12:25 David's sin with Bathsheba and Nathan's rebuke
12:26–21:22 David's troubled reign
22:1–23:7 David's final praise
23:8–24:25 Further problems in David's reign

AUTHOR Uncertain; some have suggested Nathan's son Zabud and the prophets
Nathan and Gad
DATE WRITTEN 930 BC, soon after David's reign (1050–970 BC)
PURPOSE To record the history of David's reign, to validate the Davidic dynasty, and
to depict David as the ideal example of good leadership
THEMES Prosperity under David, ideal leadership, justice, consequences of sin

1 KINGS Effective leadership often has more to do with character than with
June 6-20 accomplishments. At least that seems to be the case in the book
of 1 Kings. The books of 1 and 2 Kings form one book in the Hebrew
Bible, covering the period when kings ruled Israel after David's reign.
First Kings opens with the death of David, followed by the reign of
Solomon and the building of the Temple in Jerusalem. The book then
records Solomon's death and the division of the kingdom into northern
and southern halves (Israel and Judah). This division resulted from a
foolish decision by Solomon's heir, Rehoboam. Despite wise advice from
his older advisers, Rehoboam chose to follow a policy of harsh rule, and the
ten northern tribes rebelled. First Kings then begins a chronicle of each
king who ruled Israel or Judah, giving him a rating of either good or bad,
depending on his faithfulness to God and the covenant. The book closes
with a great conflict between Elijah the prophet and Ahab, king of Israel.

OUTLINE 1:1–2:11 The death of David
2:12–11:43 The reign of Solomon
12:1-24 The division of the kingdom
12:25–16:28 The rivalry between Israel and Judah up to Ahab
16:29–22:40 Elijah and Ahab
22:41-53 The reigns of Jehoshaphat and Ahaziah

AUTHOR Uncertain; some have suggested Jeremiah or a group of prophets
DATE WRITTEN Uncertain; possibly shortly after King Jehoiachin's release in 562 BC
PURPOSE To contrast the lives of the godly and ungodly kings throughout the
history of Israel and Judah and to demonstrate the consequences of
idolatry and wickedness
THEMES Idolatry, the Temple, good and bad kings, the rise of the prophet
movement, sin and its consequences

2 KINGS If you have ever seen a salmon struggling to swim upstream, you have an
June 21–July 4 idea of what it was like to be a good king in Israel or Judah. In 2 Kings,
most of the kings simply go along with the current of evil. Only a handful
of kings struggle to follow the God of Israel, rejecting the idolatry,
immorality, and complacency that surrounds them. In order to counter
this widespread wickedness, the prophets often take center stage
in 2 Kings, warning kings and others about the consequences of sin.
Ultimately, however, wickedness prevails, and 2 Kings describes two
tragedies that changed the face of Israel's history. In 722 BC the northern
kingdom of Israel was destroyed by the Assyrians, and in 586 BC the
southern kingdom of Judah was dismantled by the Babylonians. As in
the book of 1 Kings, all these events are interpreted as being the direct
result of the idolatry and wickedness that pervaded the nations of Israel
and Judah.

OUTLINE 1:1–2:11 The end of Elijah's ministry
2:12–8:15 The ministry of Elisha the prophet
8:16–17:41 The kings of Israel and Judah until the fall of Israel
18:1–25:30 The kingdom of Judah until the fall of Jerusalem

AUTHOR Uncertain; some have suggested Jeremiah or a group of prophets
DATE WRITTEN Uncertain, possibly shortly after King Jehoiachin's release in 562 BC

PURPOSE To contrast the lives of the godly and ungodly kings throughout the history of Israel and Judah and to demonstrate the consequences of idolatry and wickedness

THEMES Idolatry, the Temple, good and bad kings, the rise of the prophet movement, sin and its consequences

1 CHRONICLES
July 5-19

Understanding your family's history is important. Knowing where your ancestors came from and what they accomplished provides a sense of identity, heritage, and destiny. These are some of the reasons the writer of Chronicles penned this extensive account of Israel's family history. The book of 1 Chronicles begins with a series of genealogies that trace the roots of both King David and the Levites. This list represents more than just names; it represents the chosen people of God—the ancestors of God's covenant people. After the genealogies comes the account of Israel's first two kings, Saul and David. Their successes and failures are shown to stem largely from their spiritual choices. Special emphasis is given to the admirable accomplishments of David's reign. The book closes with David's vision for the Temple that is to be built.

OUTLINE 1:1–9:44 The genealogies
10:1-14 The death of Saul
11:1–23:1 The reign of David
23:2–27:34 The Temple, the Levites, and the tribal leaders
28:1–29:30 David's final years

AUTHOR Ezra, according to Jewish tradition

DATE WRITTEN About 430 BC; recording events that occurred from about 1000 to 960 BC

PURPOSE To unify God's people, to trace the roots of King David and of the twelve tribes, and to teach that genuine worship ought to be the center of individual and national life

THEMES Israel's history as God's chosen people, the accomplishments of King David, true worship, the Temple, and the priests

2 CHRONICLES
July 20–August 4

Christians often wonder at the ignorance of "primitive peoples" who worship idols. Meanwhile, we ourselves devotedly serve idols of wealth, prestige, and self-fulfillment. Second Chronicles, however, calls us back to wholehearted, single-minded devotion to God. Continuing the history of Israel and Judah that was begun in 1 Chronicles, this book recounts the glory of Solomon's reign, highlighting the construction and dedication of the Temple. It also records the actions of the kings of Judah who came after Solomon, taking special note of each one's attention to the religious affairs of their nation. Second Chronicles highlights the deeds of Hezekiah, under whose reign an extended revival took place. The writer also describes the destruction of Jerusalem and the exile of the people to Babylon. The book ends on a positive note, however, as King Cyrus of Persia decrees that the people of Judah are free to return home. As the writer of 2 Chronicles provides his readers with a history of Israel's past, he indirectly urges his readers to rededicate their lives to the one true God.

OUTLINE 1:1-17 The beginning of Solomon's reign
2:1–7:22 The building and dedication of the Temple
8:1–9:31 The glory of Solomon's reign
10:1–36:23 The remaining kings of Judah

AUTHOR Ezra, according to Jewish tradition

DATE WRITTEN About 430 BC; recording events from the beginning of Solomon's reign (970 BC) to the beginning of the Babylonian captivity (586 BC)

PURPOSE To unify the nation around true worship of God by showing the rewards of faithfulness and the consequences of sin

THEMES Rewards of faithfulness, consequences of sin, the Temple, reform, national collapse, restoration

EZRA
August 5-10 Many great men and women never gain celebrity status. They do their deeds in relative obscurity, yet their contributions profoundly impact the lives of those who come after them. Ezra was just such a person. The book of Ezra details the Israelites' return to the land of Palestine after their captivity in Babylon. The book opens with the return of a large group of exiles and the rebuilding of the Temple under Zerubbabel. Halfway through the book, we are introduced to Ezra, a scribe schooled in the laws of Moses. The book records how Ezra dealt with the problems that arose, such as marriages between Israelites and non-Israelites. After a great deal of struggle regarding the rebuilding of the Temple, the project was finally completed and dedicated to the glory of God.

OUTLINE 1:1-2:70 The return of the first group of exiles to Jerusalem
3:1-13 The rebuilding of the Temple begun
4:1-24 The work on the Temple halted
5:1-6:22 The completion and rededication of the Temple
7:1-10:44 The ministry of Ezra

AUTHOR Ezra, according to Jewish tradition
DATE WRITTEN About 430 BC, recording events from about 538 to 430 BC
PURPOSE To show God's faithfulness to restore his people to their land
THEMES The return of the exiles, the rebuilding of the Temple, faithfulness to Mosaic law

NEHEMIAH
August 11-17 It is easy to analyze, scrutinize, and talk about all the problems in the world, but we really need people who will do something about them. The book of Nehemiah shows what happens when such a person steps forward. The story begins as Nehemiah learns of a problem that greatly distresses him: The city walls of Jerusalem were broken down, and the city was defenseless. The small number of Jews who had returned to their homeland after decades of Babylonian captivity desperately needed the walls to be rebuilt. Nehemiah knew that the task could not wait, so he obtained permission from the king of Persia and traveled to Jerusalem. There he surveyed the situation and led the reconstruction of the walls. Despite several setbacks from the enemies of Jerusalem, the task was completed within a very short time, and the walls were dedicated to the glory of God. Ezra also led the people to recommit their lives to following God's laws.

OUTLINE 1:1-2:20 Nehemiah's arrival in Jerusalem
3:1-7:73 The work on the walls begun
8:1-10:39 The reading of the law and national repentance
11:1-13:31 The dedication of the walls and Nehemiah's reforms

AUTHOR Possibly Ezra, although Nehemiah's words are written in first person, suggesting that he contributed to the book
DATE WRITTEN About 430 BC
PURPOSE To chronicle the return of the exiles to Jerusalem and the rebuilding of Jerusalem's walls and to encourage the people to remain faithful to God's laws
THEMES Vision/leadership, prayer, repentance/revival

ESTHER
August 18-20 With drama, intrigue, romance, and murder, the book of Esther tells of the near destruction of the Jewish people. It tells how a Jewish woman named Esther risked her life to save her people. Esther and her cousin lived in the

land of Persia, where the Jews were in exile. After Vashti, queen of Persia, insulted her husband, the king, she was deposed, and the king began looking for a new queen. Esther was selected for her beauty, but she kept her Jewish nationality a secret. Meanwhile, a wicked man named Haman became the king's adviser and began plotting the extermination of all Jews in the empire. Esther's cousin learned of the plot and begged Esther to intervene, asking, "Who knows if perhaps you were made queen for just such a time as this?" (4:14). So Esther risked her life and approached the king about the matter. The king heard her plea and the Jews were saved, while Haman was impaled on a pole he had prepared especially for Esther's cousin. This remarkable deliverance of the Jews is celebrated by the Jewish feast of Purim.

OUTLINE 1:1–2:23 Esther becomes queen
3:1–4:3 Haman's plan to destroy the Jews
4:4–7:10 Esther's plan to save the Jews
8:1–10:3 The deliverance of the Jews and the feast of Purim

AUTHOR Mordecai, according to tradition (although some have suggested Ezra or Nehemiah based on similarities in writing style)
DATE WRITTEN About 470 BC
PURPOSE To demonstrate God's sovereignty and his loving care for his people
THEMES God's sovereignty, loyalty to Judaism

JOB The problem of human suffering is pondered by almost everyone at
August 21– some time or another. The book of Job addresses this ancient and
September 1 difficult problem. It tells the story of Job, a godly man who endured an enormous amount of suffering while remaining faithful to God. The story begins with Job losing his children, his vast wealth, and even his health—all within a very short period of time. Only Job and his wife survived the ruin that Satan inflicted upon him. Then Job's three friends came to comfort him and to reflect on the purpose for his suffering. They each considered the basic question: Why must we endure suffering when God is powerful enough to do something about it? Job's wife simply declared it all unfair, advising Job, "Curse God and die" (2:9). Each of Job's three friends—Eliphaz, Bildad, and Zophar—delivered speeches accounting for Job's misery. A fourth young man, Elihu, tried to summarize the situation with yet another explanation. But all of them failed to provide Job with a satisfactory answer. Finally, God himself spoke directly to Job, asking him questions that forced him to recognize his finite understanding of life. Job realized that ultimately God is in charge and knows what he is doing. So Job remained silent and stood in awe of God's sovereignty. In the end, God restored Job's health, possessions, and family.

OUTLINE 1:1–2:13 The onset of Job's misery
3:1–14:22 First set of speeches
15:1–21:34 Second set of speeches
22:1–31:40 Third set of speeches
32:1–37:24 Elihu's speech
38:1–41:34 The Lord's response to Job
42:1–17 The restoration of Job

AUTHOR Uncertain; Jewish tradition regards Moses as the author; others have suggested Job himself as the author
DATE WRITTEN Unknown. Some of the events recorded suggest it was written during the time of the patriarchs, about 2000–1800 BC

PURPOSE To demonstrate God's sovereignty and address the problem of innocent
suffering

THEMES Innocent suffering, God's sovereignty, God's goodness, human arrogance

PSALMS
January–December

Throughout our lives, we all experience a wide range of emotions, such as
joy, anger, peacefulness, frustration, despair, happiness, and anxiety. These
feelings don't typically obey carefully scripted creeds. Music and poetry
often seem to be the only way to express them fully. The book of Psalms
speaks to this part of human experience through the poetic words of
people who offered their feelings to God. Are you angry about something?
The book of Psalms includes several prayers that express this same
emotion (see Psalm 35). Are you afraid? So was David when he wrote
Psalm 2. Are you frustrated by injustice? Psalm 79 laments this same
situation. Likewise, Psalm 19 and Psalm 104 celebrate the incredible
power of God as it is revealed in his creation. This collection of hymns and
prayers touches every corner of the human soul. As with the psalm writers
themselves, these honest expressions of feeling will draw you closer to the
God who made you.

OUTLINE 1–41 The first book of Psalms
42–72 The second book of Psalms
73–89 The third book of Psalms
90–106 The fourth book of Psalms
107–150 The fifth book of Psalms

AUTHOR According to Jewish tradition, David wrote 73 psalms; Asaph wrote 12;
the sons of Korah wrote 9; Solomon wrote 2; Heman (with the sons of
Korah), Ethan, and Moses each wrote 1; and 51 psalms are anonymous.
The New Testament ascribes two of the anonymous psalms (Psalms 2
and 95) to David (see Acts 4:25; Hebrews 4:7).

DATE WRITTEN Between the time of Moses (about 1440 BC) and the Babylonian captivity
(586 BC)

PURPOSE To provide poetry for the expression of praise, worship, and confession to
God

THEMES Praise, forgiveness, thankfulness, trust, reverence for God and his creation

PROVERBS
January–December

Knowledge is good, but wisdom is even better. Knowledge can help you
pass tests and accomplish tasks, but wisdom will guide you through the
most important decisions in life. The book of Proverbs was written by
Solomon, the wisest man who ever lived. It contains hundreds of short,
simple statements about how to live wisely and an assortment of longer
passages that express wisdom with a bit more detail. These proverbs,
however, are more than just wise sayings of the sort we find in most
cultures. They are not a haphazard collection of commonsense directives.
These proverbs expressly state, "Fear of the LORD is the foundation of
true knowledge" (1:7). Respect for God is the foundation for these wise
sayings. They help the reader to distinguish between two paths: the way
of the wise and the way of the fool. They deal with almost all the major
areas of life, including growing up, parenting, social justice, wise speech,
work, marriage, sexuality, and money.

OUTLINE 1:1-7 Introduction and theme of Proverbs
1:8–9:18 Proverbs mainly for parents and children
10:1–22:16 The first collection of Solomon's wisdom
22:17–24:34 Two collections of wise sayings
25:1–29:27 The second collection of Solomon's wisdom
30:1–31:9 The wisdom of Agur and Lemuel
31:10-31 A portrait of a wife of good character

AUTHORS Solomon, Agur, and Lemuel, according to Jewish tradition
DATE WRITTEN Possibly about 960 BC
PURPOSE To apply divine wisdom to daily life and to provide moral instruction
THEMES Wisdom, relationships, speech, work, success

ECCLESIASTES There are few experiences in life that are more universal than
September 2-5 disappointment. It seems as if everyone has experienced a broken
promise, an unfulfilled expectation, or a shattered belief. The "Teacher"
in the book of Ecclesiastes recorded his own experiences with
disappointment as he tried to find peace apart from God. The Teacher
uses a series of examples—wealth, wisdom, popularity, pleasure—and
shows how each of them ultimately ends in disappointment if it becomes
the sole reason for one's existence. After pondering this for several
chapters, the author finally offers his conclusion: "Fear God and obey
his commands, for this is everyone's duty" (12:13). It appears that the
Teacher abandoned any hope in worldly pursuits and decided that
glorifying God provides the only lasting meaning in life.

OUTLINE 1:1-11 The pointless cycle of life
1:12–2:23 The futility of life
2:24–4:12 Weariness, oppression, and inhumanity
4:13–6:12 The futility of popularity, religiosity, and wealth
7:1–11:10 The futility of life
12:1-14 Conclusion: Fear God and obey his commands

AUTHOR Solomon, according to Jewish tradition
DATE WRITTEN Possibly about 935 BC, late in Solomon's life
PURPOSE To teach that life is meaningless apart from God
THEMES Searching, emptiness, injustice, work, death, wisdom

SONG OF SONGS Popular sexual behavior today is a sad distortion of the plan God
September 6-7 established in the Garden of Eden. Contrary to God's design, sex has
become a freely traded commodity rather than an exclusive, private
treasure shared between a committed husband and wife. God values
romantic love and sexual union, and the Song of Songs expresses the
beauty of this love as God intended it. This poetic book describes several
interactions between Solomon, a young woman, and possibly another
young man. It is a song that uses vivid metaphors to describe love,
courtship, and marriage. These poetic verses describe a couple's desire
for each other, the struggles they overcome, the tender feelings love
awakens in them, and the joy they find in being together. The "young
women of Jerusalem" also add some observations of their own. Many
scholars believe this poem should also be understood as an illustration
of Christ's love for the church.

OUTLINE 1:1–2:7 The bride describes herself and her feelings for her fiancé
2:8–3:11 The king invites his bride for a springtime trip; the bride
dreams of losing the king
4:1–5:1 Solomon describes his bride
5:2–6:3 The bride describes her husband
6:4–7:9 The king describes his wife
7:10–8:4 The desires of the woman
8:5-14 The power of love and the rewards of purity

AUTHOR Solomon, according to Jewish tradition
DATE WRITTEN Possibly about 960 BC, early in Solomon's reign
PURPOSE To celebrate romantic love as God intended it and to picture God's love for
his people
THEMES The joys of romantic love, commitment, beauty, intimacy

ISAIAH
September 8–
October 2

Isaiah's long ministry lasted almost sixty years and covered the reigns of four kings, including Hezekiah. The prophecies of Isaiah spoke primarily to the people of Judah, although his messages applied to the northern kingdom of Israel as well. Isaiah lived through the dark days of the civil war between Israel and Judah (734–732 BC) and saw the destruction of Israel by Assyria in 722 BC. Isaiah used the grim lesson of Israel's fall to teach King Hezekiah of Judah to trust in the Lord. Isaiah also spoke about events that would take place after his own time, including the coming exile of Judah to Babylon and the deliverance that God would provide afterward. Isaiah warned the nations surrounding Israel and Judah that they, too, would be judged for their actions. In the end, however, Isaiah offered a message of hope and comfort for the entire world, promising that God would restore the nations after their punishment was completed. Isaiah's messages, like those of most prophets, made him few friends during his lifetime. Nevertheless, he faithfully continued to bring God's message to the world.

OUTLINE 1:1–23:18 Prophecies concerning Judah and the nations
24:1–27:13 God's judgment upon the world's sin
28:1–35:10 Prophecies concerning Judah and Israel
36:1–39:8 Events during Hezekiah's reign
40:1–66:24 Judah's future comfort and God's salvation

AUTHOR Isaiah or his followers

DATE WRITTEN The events of chapters 1–39 occurred during Isaiah's ministry, so they were probably written about 700 BC. Chapters 40–66, however, may have been written near the end of his life, about 681 BC.

PURPOSE To call the nation of Judah back to God and to tell of God's plan of salvation through the Messiah

THEMES Holiness, punishment, salvation, the coming Messiah, hope

JEREMIAH
October 3-28

By any human measure of success, the prophet Jeremiah was a colossal failure. For most of his life he was poor, unpopular, isolated, and persecuted. Jeremiah lived in Judah for forty years just before the people were exiled to Babylon, and his prophecies were collected into the book that bears his name. The main message of his prophecies is simple: It is too late to avoid God's discipline, so accept it and turn from your sins. After a time of punishment, however, God will restore Israel and Judah. Jeremiah often used figurative actions to communicate this message, such as shattering a clay jar to show how God would shatter Jerusalem. Unfortunately, Jeremiah's messages were not well received. His audience discounted his warnings, locked him up in stocks, and even threatened his life. As a result, Jeremiah lived to see the invasions by the Babylonian armies, the deportations of his people, the slaughter of Jerusalem's inhabitants, and the destruction of the Temple. Because of his troubles, Jeremiah has often been called "the weeping prophet."

OUTLINE

1:1–25:38 Prophecies concerning Judah
26:1–42:22 Prophecies at the end of Judah's existence
43:1–45:5 Jeremiah's prophecies in Egypt
46:1–51:64 Prophecies concerning the nations
52:1-34 Historical appendix

AUTHOR Jeremiah or his followers

DATE WRITTEN During Jeremiah's ministry, about 627 to 586 BC

PURPOSE To urge people to repent of their sins and turn back to God

THEMES Consequences of sin, impending judgment, God's dominion, new hearts, restoration

LAMENTATIONS　A lamentation is a sad funeral song. Jeremiah recorded these lamentations
October 29-31　to express his grief over the tragic destruction of Jerusalem and the exile
of its inhabitants to Babylon. Through acrostic poetry, the book of
Lamentations graphically describes the destruction of Jerusalem and
the pillaging of its people. Jeremiah spared his readers little detail as he
recalled the horrible tragedy. There is very little comfort in Jeremiah's
lament, though in chapter 5 his prayer does look beyond the desolate
ashes of Jerusalem as he pleads to God, whose throne endures forever.

OUTLINE　1:1-22 Jerusalem's sorrow and desolation
2:1-22 God's anger at Jerusalem's sin
3:1-66 Jerusalem's only hope is God's mercy
4:1-22 Jerusalem's former glory and present humiliation
5:1-22 Jerusalem's prayer for deliverance

AUTHOR　Jeremiah, according to Jewish tradition
DATE WRITTEN　Soon after the fall of Jerusalem in 586 BC
PURPOSE　To record in graphic detail the consequences of sin and to show that God
suffers along with his people
THEMES　Destruction of Jerusalem, consequences of sin, God's mercy

EZEKIEL　Like stubborn children refusing to obey their father, the people of Israel
November 1-24　often refused to listen to God. And like a loving parent, God repeatedly
called his people back to obedience. He sent prophets, like Ezekiel, to
preach messages of judgment and restoration. According to his book,
Ezekiel was a priest who was among the captives taken to Babylon when
the Jews were deported in 597 BC. There in Babylon, God called Ezekiel
to be a prophet, and he began to forewarn his people that Jerusalem's
judgment was not yet complete. His preaching was not well received
by the Jews who were with him in captivity. They thought he should be
giving messages of comfort and hope, not judgment. But Ezekiel's dire
predictions came true as Jerusalem was destroyed in 586 BC. From
then on, the people listened carefully to his preaching. After Ezekiel's
predictions of doom had taken place, however, his message changed
from one of judgment to one of comfort and hope. The worst was past;
it was time to begin again.

OUTLINE　1:1-3:27 The call of Ezekiel
4:1-24:27 Prophecies against Israel and Jerusalem
25:1-32:32 Prophecies against the foreign nations
33:1-39:29 The promise of return and restoration
40:1-48:35 The renewed Temple in the New Jerusalem

AUTHOR　Ezekiel—a Zadokite priest
DATE WRITTEN　About 571 BC
PURPOSE　To announce God's judgment on Israel and other nations and to proclaim
restoration for God's people
THEMES　God's holiness, sin, restoration, worship, the new Temple

DANIEL　A stranger in a strange land, Daniel lived during a time when the Jewish
November 25-　people seemed to have little hope. They were living as captives in Babylon,
December 4　hundreds of miles from home, with only promises from God that they
would ever see their homeland again. As this book records, Daniel and
his friends were taken to Babylon as young men. Although they were
captives, they received an excellent education and rose to high positions in
the Babylonian and Persian governments. Because of their faith in the God
of Israel, they were persecuted and even sentenced to die. God rewarded
them for their faithfulness, however, and they were rescued from certain

death. Daniel had several encounters with King Nebuchadnezzar, and God revealed his sovereignty in each instance. The second half of the book records Daniel's visions of future events. These apocalyptic dreams and the stories of Daniel and his friends provided encouragement for the Jews to remain faithful to God in the midst of persecution.

OUTLINE 1:1–6:28 Daniel's life in Babylon
7:1–8:27 Daniel's visions of the beasts
9:1-27 Daniel's prayer and prophecies
10:1–12:13 Daniel's vision of God and the future

AUTHOR Daniel
DATE WRITTEN About 535 BC, recording events that occurred from about 605 to 535 BC
PURPOSE To demonstrate through Daniel's experiences that God is sovereign over the whole earth and to encourage the Jews to remain faithful to God despite persecution
THEMES God's sovereignty, God's faithfulness, perseverance

HOSEA The book of Hosea is a tragic love story with a happy ending. Hosea was a
December 5-8 prophet to the northern kingdom of Israel before its fall in 722 BC, and his ministry spanned some forty years. He was a contemporary of Amos, Isaiah, and Micah. In his book, Hosea was called by God to marry an unfaithful woman, and so he married Gomer. After bearing three children to Hosea, Gomer acted unfaithfully, and the marriage was shattered. In the end, however, Hosea urged Gomer to repent and receive forgiveness and restoration. Hosea used this experience with Gomer to illustrate God's experience with Israel. The first half of Hosea's book describes his marriage to Gomer, the birth of their children, and her unfaithfulness. The second half of the book draws lessons from the symbolic story. Hosea warned of stern judgment for Israel's unfaithfulness, for Israel had turned to other gods, just as Gomer had left Hosea for other men. Like Gomer, Israel would receive forgiveness and restoration if the people would return to God.

OUTLINE 1:1–3:5 Hosea's tragic home life
4:1–8:14 Israel's rebellion against God
9:1–13:16 The judgment to come
14:1-9 The promised restoration

AUTHOR Hosea
DATE WRITTEN About 715 BC, recording events from about 753 to 715 BC
PURPOSE To illustrate God's love for his sinful people
THEMES Israel's unfaithfulness, God's judgment, God's love, restoration

JOEL Displays of power can be impressive, but none will be more impressive
December 9 than the coming "day of the LORD." On that day God will call all to account for their rebellion and sin. For those who have forsaken God, it will be a terrible day of judgment. This great day is the focus of Joel's prophecies. Joel used a plague of locusts to figuratively illustrate the coming of this terrible judgment, and he urged God's people to listen— how much better to repent and live! But Joel's prophecies contain messages of hope as well as warning. If the people would respond to his warning, God would be merciful. God promised, "I will give you back what you lost to the swarming locusts" (2:25). God's desire was to bless his people, not to destroy them. That was the reason for the locusts—to make people see while there was still time.

OUTLINE 1:1–2:17 The plague of locusts and its meaning
2:18-27 Immediate blessing promised

2:28-32 Future blessing promised
3:1-21 The judgment of Israel's enemies

AUTHOR	Joel
DATE WRITTEN	During Joel's ministry, possibly from about 835 to 796 BC
PURPOSE	To warn people of God's impending judgment unless they turn from their sins
THEMES	Punishment, forgiveness, promise of the Spirit

AMOS
December 10-12

When we think of the first prophets God called to preach against the northern kingdom of Israel, Amos is not someone we would normally imagine as a candidate. Amos was a shepherd and a sycamore-fig farmer, not an educated priest or a religious servant. But Amos was faithful to his calling, and he delivered God's message to the people. Amos was a contemporary of the prophets Hosea, Isaiah, and Micah. Like Hosea, Amos's message was directed mainly to the northern kingdom of Israel, although he himself was from the southern kingdom of Judah. Amos's prophecy begins by pronouncing judgment upon the surrounding nations; then the prophecy focuses on Israel itself. Amos denounced the injustice, corruption, greed, and false worship that were rampant in Israel. Amos's prophecy continues with a series of visions, and the book ends with the hope that Israel will heed these warnings.

OUTLINE
1:1-2 Introduction
1:3–2:16 Judgment upon the nations and Israel
3:1–6:14 The prophet's message of judgment
7:1–9:10 Five visions of judgment
9:11-15 A future hope

AUTHOR	Amos
DATE WRITTEN	Probably during the reigns of Jeroboam II of Israel and Uzziah of Judah (about 760–750 BC)
PURPOSE	To pronounce God's judgment upon Israel for their complacency, idolatry, and oppression of the poor
THEMES	Complacency, social justice, superficial religion

OBADIAH
December 13

Often the most painful betrayals come from those who are closest to us. At least this was how Obadiah felt about the Edomites' attack on Jerusalem. In this short book, Obadiah foretold Edom's doom for treacherously plundering Jerusalem after its fall to the Babylonians in 586 BC. The Edomites were descendants of Esau, Jacob's brother, so they were related by blood to the Israelites who inhabited Jerusalem. Of all people, the Edomites should have come to Jerusalem's aid. Instead, they took part in the destruction and gloated over Jerusalem's demise. The Edomites had failed to realize that their survival depended upon their humility before almighty God and not upon their "invincible" mountain fortresses.

OUTLINE
1:1-9 Edom's destruction foretold
1:10-14 The sins of Edom
1:15-21 The day of the Lord and Judah's restoration

AUTHOR	Obadiah
DATE WRITTEN	Shortly after the fall of Jerusalem in 586 BC
PURPOSE	To condemn Edom for its cruel treachery upon Jerusalem
THEMES	Treachery, justice, pride

JONAH
December 14

If you were given an assignment to preach the gospel to a band of convicted killers, would you do it? This is similar to the assignment God gave Jonah. Jonah was a prophet born in Israel (see 2 Kings 14:25) and called by God to preach to the people of Nineveh, the capital city of Assyria. Not only was Assyria the most powerful empire in that day, it was also ruthlessly violent toward its conquered enemies. So it is unlikely that many Israelites would have accepted Jonah's task. The book of Jonah relates how Jonah first tried to flee his calling and travel by ship to another country. But God sent a storm to change his plans. Jonah was thrown overboard, and a giant fish swallowed him. The fish then spewed Jonah back onto the shore, and Jonah went to Assyria. To Jonah's dismay, the king and citizens of Nineveh heard his message and repented, and God spared them from their promised destruction. In disgust, Jonah went outside the city and wished it would be destroyed. God rebuked Jonah, however, and expressed his desire for all people, Jews and Gentiles alike, to come to know him.

OUTLINE 1:1-17 Jonah's fall and flight from God
2:1-10 Jonah's prayer in the fish's belly
3:1-10 Jonah's renewed commission and success
4:1-11 Jonah's reaction and God's concern

AUTHOR: Jonah, according to Jewish tradition
DATE WRITTEN About 785 to 760 BC
PURPOSE To show that God wants all people to come to know him
THEMES God's sovereignty, repentance, God's universal compassion

MICAH
December 15-16

Can a loving God hate sin? According to the prophet Micah, God most certainly can—and does. Micah was a contemporary of Isaiah who preached to Israel and Judah during the eighth century BC. He lived in a small town called Moresheth, which lies south of Jerusalem. Micah denounced the oppression, pride, greed, corruption, false piety, and arrogance of the two kingdoms. He summoned the priests and leaders to appear before God and plead their case, for they were about to be judged for their wickedness. God would indeed hold everyone accountable for his or her actions. But Micah also made it clear that God's love never dies. Judgment often comes after we have been given many opportunities to repent. And once God's punishment has been given, he will restore his people to himself again and will forgive their sins.

OUTLINE 1:1-16 The judgment of God
2:1-3:12 God's hatred of sin
4:1-5:1 Future blessings
5:2-15 The coming Messiah
6:1-7:20 God's judgment on Israel

AUTHOR: Micah
DATE WRITTEN Possibly during the reigns of Jotham, Ahaz, and Hezekiah (742-687 BC)
PURPOSE To warn God's people that judgment is coming and to offer pardon to all who repent
THEMES Wicked leaders, injustice, the coming Messiah, restoration

NAHUM
December 17

Be warned—God will indeed repay those who have inflicted terrible suffering on others. This was the message Nahum spoke against Nineveh, the capital of Assyria. The Assyrians had destroyed Samaria, the capital of the northern kingdom of Israel, in 722 BC and had exiled its inhabitants to distant lands throughout the empire. They were ruthlessly violent to their enemies and showed them no mercy. They were guilty of arrogance, cruelty, idolatry, murder, lying, treachery, superstition, and oppression. The book of Nahum rails against the people of Nineveh for this wickedness and pronounces God's judgment upon them.

OUTLINE 1:1-15 God and his punishment for evil
2:1-13 The destruction of Nineveh
3:1-19 The sin of Nineveh

AUTHOR Nahum
DATE WRITTEN Sometime during Nahum's prophetic ministry (probably between 663 and 654 BC)
PURPOSE To pronounce God's judgment upon Assyria
THEMES Judgment, vengeance, justice

HABAKKUK
December 18

"If God exists, why do the wicked so often prosper?" This question is commonly asked by those who are sensitive to social justice. The prophet Habakkuk was quite sympathetic to such concerns. Habakkuk preached during the last days of Judah before its fall to Babylon in 586 BC. He foresaw the impending doom and was troubled by two things—why God allowed the people of Judah to sin and how God could use a sinful nation like Babylon to punish Judah. Desperate for answers, Habakkuk boldly and confidently took his complaints directly to God. God answers Habakkuk's questions in this book, asserting that he will judge all people but that righteousness will ultimately prevail. It may not happen immediately, but it will happen. This assurance, along with his glimpse of God's sovereign rule, gave Habakkuk the courage and hope to trust in God's plans regarding the dark days ahead.

OUTLINE 1:1-11 Sin and punishment
1:12–2:20 Babylon and God's answer
3:1-19 Habakkuk's triumphant faith

AUTHOR Habakkuk
DATE WRITTEN Between 612 and 589 BC
PURPOSE To show that God is still sovereign despite the apparent triumph of evil
THEMES Questioning God, God's sovereignty, hope

ZEPHANIAH
December 19

Though dark days loom ahead, there is hope for the future. This is Zephaniah's basic message to the people of Judah. Zephaniah was a prophet in the last decades before Jerusalem was destroyed by the Babylonians. The opening stanzas of his prophecies bring bad news. The people of Judah had completely abandoned the Lord and had chosen to worship many false gods. In addition, they had dismissed obedience to God as irrelevant. They were materially prosperous and saw no need to repent of their sins in order to please God. Consequently, Zephaniah's message to them was harsh: When the "day of the LORD" comes, Judah will be completely destroyed. Even the animals will be killed as the Babylonian troops pillage the land. This dreadful day will also visit several nations surrounding Judah. But God will not leave them without hope. Judah will eventually be restored and will return to the Lord.

OUTLINE 1:1–2:3 The coming judgment of God
2:4–3:8 Judgment upon the nations and Jerusalem
3:9-20 Blessing promised to Judah

AUTHOR Zephaniah
DATE WRITTEN Probably near the end of Zephaniah's ministry (640–621 BC), when King Josiah's great reforms began
PURPOSE To shake the people of Judah out of their complacency and urge them to return to God
THEMES Day of the judgment, religious complacency, restoration

HAGGAI
December 20

Do you have trouble finishing the projects you start? This was a definite problem for the people of Haggai's day. Haggai lived in Jerusalem shortly after many Jews had returned from exile in Babylonia. Those who returned had begun to rebuild the Temple, but opposition from local enemies soon mounted. Eventually the Jews abandoned the project when it was only half finished. After several years, Haggai, along with a prophet/priest named Zechariah, began a campaign to continue work on the Temple. In this book, Haggai admonishes the governor, Zerubbabel, and the high priest, Jeshua, to finish building a house for the Lord. Apparently the combined efforts of Haggai and Zechariah worked, and the Temple was completed and rededicated in 516 BC.

OUTLINE
1:1-11 The prophet's rebuke for neglecting the Temple
1:12-15 The favor of God
2:1-9 Encouragement for the builders
2:10-19 Blessings to follow the work
2:20-23 God's judgment on the nations

AUTHOR Haggai
DATE WRITTEN 520 BC
PURPOSE To call the people to complete the rebuilding of the Temple
THEMES Right priorities, finishing the Temple

ZECHARIAH
December 21-29

From time to time God gives us glimpses of the future. Usually these glimpses come through the words of prophets like Zechariah. His book includes some of the most graphic images of the future found in the Bible. Zechariah was both a priest and a prophet to the Jews living in Palestine after their exile in Babylonia. He was a contemporary of the prophet Haggai and assisted him in campaigning to finish rebuilding the Temple. In his book, Zechariah explains that Israel was exiled for its sinful practices, but he promises that God himself will eventually transform his people and usher in a new age of holiness throughout the earth. The first half of Zechariah's book describes eight night visions and discusses the ritual of fasting. Several of the visions focus on the reconstruction of the Temple and the reinstitution of the priesthood. The second half of Zechariah's book describes the age to come when God will transform Israel into a truly holy society and the nations will come to worship God in Jerusalem. Zechariah saw the reconstruction of the Temple as the dawn of this new era. Zechariah also told of a great "shepherd," or Messiah, who would come to reign over a new kingdom of perfect harmony.

OUTLINE
1:1-6 Introduction
1:7-6:8 Eight prophetic visions
6:9-15 The prophetic coronation of Jeshua
7:1-10:12 Various messages of judgment and hope
11:1-13:9 The coming Messiah and his rejection
14:1-21 The ultimate triumph of the Messiah

AUTHOR Zechariah
DATE WRITTEN Chapters 1-8 were written about 520 to 518 BC. Chapters 9-14 were written about 480 BC.
PURPOSE To give hope to God's people by revealing God's future deliverance through the Messiah
THEMES Rebuilding the Temple, restoration, the coming Messiah

MALACHI
December 30-31

Spiritual health requires constant maintenance. Otherwise we quickly lapse into apathy and insincerity. This was a problem in the time of Malachi as well. After returning from exile in Babylonia, the Jews rebuilt the Temple and reinstated the priesthood. Everything seemed to be going well. But after a few generations passed, it appears that many Jews became complacent about their faith. Even the priests became corrupt and careless in carrying out their duties. So Malachi prophesied against the people's insincere worship, their refusal to tithe the full amount, and their lack of concern for God's commands. He did not just condemn them for their failures, however; he also promised them great blessings for their obedience. Malachi also foretold the coming of Elijah, who would prepare the way for the great "day of the LORD."

OUTLINE 1:1–2:9 God's love and Israel's shame
2:10-17 Israel's sins denounced
3:1-6 Future judgment predicted
3:7-18 The neglected tithe
4:1-6 The coming of Elijah foretold

AUTHOR Malachi
DATE WRITTEN About 430 BC
PURPOSE To confront the people with their sins of insincere worship and corruption and to restore their relationship with God
THEMES God's love, the corruption of the priests, the sins of the people, the day of the judgment

MATTHEW
January 1–
February 14
The birth of Jesus of Nazareth ushered in the long-awaited age of a new kingdom on earth—the Kingdom of Heaven. Matthew's Gospel records the advent of this new Kingdom through the teachings and actions of Jesus, the Messiah. Since the Kingdom of Heaven is a major theme throughout this Gospel, Matthew was careful to show how Jesus fulfilled the Old Testament passages that speak of the Messiah, the ruler of the Kingdom. He recounted Jesus' family history to show his royal lineage. After describing the Virgin Birth of Jesus, Matthew detailed Jesus' messianic baptism, his temptation in the wilderness, and the early days of his ministry. In the Sermon on the Mount, Jesus taught his disciples how life in the Kingdom should be lived. Jesus also performed many miracles and taught the people various parables, or stories, that further illustrated what the Kingdom of Heaven is like. Matthew was careful to point out that the Gentiles, as well as the Jews, would be included in the Kingdom of Heaven. Matthew's Gospel concludes with Jesus' death and resurrection and his command to make disciples from every nation.

OUTLINE 1:1–4:25 The early life and ministry of Jesus
5:1–7:29 The Sermon on the Mount
8:1–18:35 General teaching, parables, and discourses
19:1–23:39 Journey to Jerusalem and final warnings
24:1–25:46 Prophecies of things to come
26:1–28:20 Jesus' death and resurrection

AUTHOR Matthew (Levi)
DATE WRITTEN Probably between AD 60 and 65
PURPOSE To present Jesus as the Messiah, who has brought the Kingdom of Heaven to earth
THEMES Jesus the Messiah, the Kingdom of Heaven, Gentiles' inclusion in the Kingdom of Heaven

MARK
February 15–
March 12
Many passages of Scripture speak of Jesus as the exalted Lord; but Mark's Gospel presents another side of Jesus as well—his servanthood. Mark was not one of the twelve disciples, but it is traditionally believed that his Gospel is compiled from the sermons of the apostle Peter. Mark set the pace for his Gospel from the very start, forgoing the details of Jesus' birth

and moving straight into his baptism and ministry. Throughout this Gospel, Jesus is constantly on the move, healing the sick, confronting demons, feeding large crowds, giving time to "outsiders," and tirelessly responding to requests for help and guidance. Mark included several passages of teaching as well, but these are largely overshadowed by the accounts of Jesus' actions. Mark made it clear that Jesus is indeed the Son of God; no one else could have done what Jesus did. But Jesus' actions and teaching also point toward a core theme of the book: "For even the Son of Man came not to be served but to serve others and to give his life as a ransom for many" (10:45). The book closes with Jesus' death and resurrection, thus completing a basic outline of the life of Jesus Christ.

OUTLINE 1:1-13 John the Baptist and the baptism of Jesus
         1:14-9:50 The Galilean ministry of Jesus
         10:1-11:25 Trip to Jerusalem and entrance into the city
         11:27-12:44 Conflicts in the city
         13:1-37 Prophecies of things to come
         14:1-16:20 Jesus' death and resurrection

AUTHOR John Mark. He was not one of the twelve disciples, but it is traditionally believed that his Gospel is compiled from the sermons of the apostle Peter.

DATE WRITTEN Between AD 55 and 65

PURPOSE To present Jesus Christ as both servant and Son of God by recounting his ministry and teachings in a basic biographical outline

THEMES Jesus the Messiah, servanthood/ministry, miracles

LUKE Like an investigative journalist compiling a story from several informants,
March 13–April 29 Luke composed his Gospel from the accounts of several eyewitnesses of Jesus Christ. Luke, a Gentile physician who traveled extensively with the apostle Paul, wrote his Gospel for a man named Theophilus (1:1-4), most likely another Gentile believer. After consulting several eyewitnesses and accounts of Jesus' life, Luke wrote this fresh account of Jesus' life and ministry. Since both Luke and Theophilus were Gentiles, it is not surprising that this Gospel has a very universal flavor to its stories and teachings of Jesus. Luke also highlighted Jesus' concern for the oppressed and outcast, such as women and the poor, and there is a notable emphasis on the role of the Holy Spirit. Luke was careful to give precise dates to the events recorded in his Gospel, beginning with an extensive record of Jesus' birth and the only canonical story from Jesus' childhood years. Luke arranged his outline of Jesus' ministry in the same general order as the Gospels of Matthew and Mark, and he added a lengthy account of Jesus' trip to Jerusalem. After Jesus' death and resurrection, the book leaves the disciples rejoicing and waiting for the promised power of God to fill them.

OUTLINE 1:1-2:52 Jesus' birth and boyhood
         3:1-4:13 Jesus' baptism and temptation
         4:14-9:50 Jesus' Galilean ministry
         9:51-19:27 Jesus' ministry on the way to Jerusalem
         19:28-20:47 Jesus' ministry in Jerusalem
         21:1-38 Prophecies of things to come
         22:1-24:53 Jesus' death and resurrection

AUTHOR Luke, a Gentile physician and associate of Paul

DATE WRITTEN About AD 60

PURPOSE To present an accurate account of the life and ministry of Jesus Christ

THEMES Jesus Christ the Savior, the Holy Spirit, compassion for the oppressed, salvation for Gentiles

JOHN
April 30–June 2

Each Gospel was written with a theological agenda in mind, but only John, "the disciple Jesus loved" (21:20), made his agenda explicit: "But these are written so that you may continue to believe that Jesus is the Messiah, the Son of God, and that by believing in him you will have life by the power of his name" (20:31). Because of this goal, John's Gospel takes on a different flavor than the other three accounts. John was less concerned with Jesus' actions than with what his actions said about him. John spoke of Jesus' miracles as "signs," and he recorded lengthy theological monologues by Jesus, including seven "I am" statements about himself. John opened his Gospel with an account of the preexistent Christ—"the Word," the unique Son of God—who became human and made God the Father known to us. After recounting details of John the Baptist and his ministry, John described Jesus' baptism. At this point the general outline of John's narrative breaks sharply from those of the other three accounts, rearranging some of the events and including different material. For instance, John's Gospel records more than one trip to Jerusalem by Jesus, unlike the other Gospels. After describing in detail Jesus' last supper with his disciples, John recounts Jesus' crucifixion and resurrection. The book closes with some encounters between Jesus and his disciples.

OUTLINE
1:1-14 Prologue
1:15-4:54 Jesus' pre-Galilean ministry
5:1-10:42 Jesus' Galilean ministry and conflicts in Jerusalem
11:1-57 The raising of Lazarus from the dead and the plot to kill Jesus
12:1-17:26 Jesus' triumphal entry into Jerusalem and final teachings
18:1-20:10 Jesus' death and resurrection
20:11-21:25 Jesus' resurrection appearances

AUTHOR John the apostle, son of Zebedee and brother of James the apostle
DATE WRITTEN About AD 90
PURPOSE To show that Jesus is the Messiah, the Son of God, and that all who believe in him will have eternal life
THEMES Jesus as the unique Son of God, eternal life, the Holy Spirit, light vs. dark, Jesus' "I am" declarations

ACTS
June 3–July 11

Nearly two thousand years ago, a match was struck in Palestine that would eventually ignite the whole world. Soon after Jesus' ascension into heaven, the Holy Spirit descended at Jerusalem, and about three thousand people became followers of Jesus Christ. This marked the birth of the Christian church. The book of Acts chronicles the birth and spread of the church, highlighting the deeds of some of its most influential leaders, such as Peter and Paul. Acts continues the story begun in the Gospel of Luke, showing how the church continues the work that Jesus began. After recounting Peter's sermon and the birth of the church, Acts describes the life of the church in Jerusalem, the spread of the gospel to Samaria, the activities of Peter, and the early persecution of the believers. After describing the death of James, the focus of the book shifts to the apostle Paul and his missionary work throughout the Gentile world. His three missionary journeys are described in detail, and the first major council in Jerusalem is recorded as well. Acts concludes with Paul's trip to Rome, where the book abruptly ends.

OUTLINE
1:1-5:42 The early days of the church
6:1-9:31 Persecution and expansion
9:32-12:25 Peter's missionary activity
13:1-14:28 Paul's first missionary journey
15:1-35 The meeting in Jerusalem
15:36-18:22 Paul's second missionary journey

18:23–21:14 Paul's third missionary journey
21:15–28:31 Paul's arrest and trip to Rome

AUTHOR Luke

DATE WRITTEN Between AD 63 and 70

PURPOSE To record the birth and growth of the Christian church

THEMES The Holy Spirit, the growth of the church, opposition, inclusion of Gentile believers, the apostolic work of Peter and Paul

ROMANS
July 12–August 3

Like a skilled lawyer presenting his case, Paul established a solid framework for understanding the broad scope of the gospel in his letter to the Romans. Of all the epistles of Paul, this is the longest, the most elaborate, and the most systematic in design, reading more like a theological treatise than a personal letter. After a lofty introduction, Paul opened his discourse by discussing humanity's relationship to God. Once he established the basic concept that all human beings are violators of God's holy law, Paul offered a solution—the sacrifice of Jesus Christ. Those who believe in Jesus Christ receive forgiveness for sin and gain new life in the Holy Spirit. Paul also examined Israel's place in God's grand scheme of history and discussed the future roles of Israel and the Gentile nations in the Kingdom of God. Returning to his earlier train of thought, Paul discussed some practical applications of redemption through Jesus Christ. He concluded his letter with heartfelt salutations to several believers in Rome. Paul's epistle to the Roman church provides the Christian church with a systematic presentation of the gospel of Jesus Christ.

OUTLINE
1:1-17 Introduction
1:18–5:21 Humanity's sin and Christ's salvation
6:1–8:39 Victory over sin by the power of Christ
9:1–11:36 God's plan for the Jews
12:1–15:13 Principles of Christian living
15:14–16:27 Concluding remarks

AUTHOR Paul

DATE WRITTEN About AD 58

PURPOSE To present a systematic explanation of the gospel of Jesus Christ to the church at Rome

THEMES Sin, atonement, living according to the Holy Spirit, the place of Jews and Gentiles in God's plan

1 CORINTHIANS
August 4-25

Surrounded by corruption and flagrant sin, the Christians in Corinth felt pressure to adapt to the low standards around them. Many who had already compromised asserted that they were free in Christ, but what did this freedom mean? To resolve this confusion, Paul wrote this letter to the Corinthian church. The letter covers a wide variety of topics, including rival factions within the church, incest among believers, public lawsuits between fellow Christians, abuses of spiritual gifts, and disorderly conduct during church meetings and the Lord's Supper. Paul addressed each of these problems, pointing to Christ as the ultimate solution. Paul also answered specific questions asked by the Corinthians. Those questions related to marriage, eating food sacrificed to idols, and the resurrection of Christ and his followers. Throughout the letter, Paul emphasized that believers should be shaped by Christ, not by the world around them. First Corinthians provides the Christian church with an actual sample of how specific problems were addressed and corrected in the early church.

OUTLINE
1:1-9 Paul's greetings
1:10–4:21 The problem of divisions
5:1-13 The problem of sexual sin

6:1-11 The problem of lawsuits
6:12-20 The problem of sexual immorality
7:1-40 Problems related to marriage
8:1–11:1 Problems concerning idols
11:2–14:40 Problems at worship, and spiritual gifts
15:1-58 Thoughts concerning the resurrection
16:1-24 Concluding remarks

AUTHOR Paul

DATE WRITTEN About AD 56, near the end of Paul's three-year ministry in Ephesus during his third missionary journey

PURPOSE To identify problems in the Corinthian church, to offer solutions, and to teach believers how to live as Christians in a corrupt society

THEMES Divisions, sexual immorality, freedom in Christ, worship, resurrection

2 CORINTHIANS
August 26–
September 13

Following Christ is a constant struggle. The church at Corinth knew this all too well. Though the believers there were being renewed by the Holy Spirit, they still struggled against the immoral influences of the culture around them. Through personal visits and letters, Paul instructed the Corinthian believers in the faith and addressed several problems there. Most of the members received this instruction well, but a few false teachers slandered Paul and denied his authority over them. So Paul wrote this letter to defend his authority and denounce those who were twisting the truth. Paul's critics had attacked his motives, saying that he did not care for the Corinthians and used them only for his gain. So Paul pointed to evidence that showed how he had always been straightforward with the Corinthians and had worked tirelessly for their good. Paul also defended himself against charges of incompetence by comparing himself with the false teachers. Paul encouraged the Corinthians to continue following his example—to be holy, generous, and true to Christ.

OUTLINE 1:1-11 Paul's greetings
1:12–2:13 A summary of Paul's actions
2:14–6:10 A discourse on Paul's apostolic ministry
6:11–7:16 Paul's personal remarks
8:1–9:15 The collection for the poor in Jerusalem
10:1–13:10 Paul's defense of his apostolic authority
13:11-13 Concluding remarks

AUTHOR Paul

DATE WRITTEN About AD 57

PURPOSE To defend his apostolic authority and ministry and to refute the false teachers in Corinth

THEMES Apostolic authority and ministry, church discipline, hope, giving, sound doctrine

GALATIANS
September 14-21

Who, after being set free, would ever willingly submit themselves to slavery again? This was Paul's question to the Galatians, who were giving up their freedom in Christ to serve the law again. It was clear to the early church that the sacrifice of Jesus Christ achieved salvation for all who believed, but what did this mean for the law of Moses? Should Christians continue observing the law or not? The Galatian church was divided over this question. Paul wrote this letter to the Galatians to settle this dispute. He opened his letter with a very short introduction and then cut right to the heart of the matter: If believers are justified by grace through Christ, why were many Galatians insisting upon other requirements? Paul drew a lesson from Abraham, who lived more than four hundred years prior to the giving of the law. Paul showed that Abraham was justified by his faith, not his deeds. Likewise, the Galatians should see themselves as free from the law—free, that is, to serve Christ and be transformed by the Holy Spirit.

OUTLINE 1:1–2:21 Paul's defense of himself and the gospel
3:1-22 Freedom from the curse of the law
3:23–4:31 The gospel's superiority over the law
5:1-26 The freedom of the Christian
6:1-18 Practical exhortations

AUTHOR Paul
DATE WRITTEN About AD 49 from Antioch, prior to the Jerusalem council (AD 50)
PURPOSE To refute those who insisted that Christians must obey the law of Moses and to remind Christians of their freedom in Christ
THEMES Law, faith, freedom, work of the Holy Spirit

EPHESIANS Every once in a while, God grants his people a glimpse of their place in
September 22-28 the grand scheme of history—there is a brief moment when they can assess who they are, where they have come from, and where they are going. Paul's letter to the Ephesians provides the church with just such a vision. This letter, which was possibly intended to be circulated among several churches, was written while Paul was a prisoner in Rome. Paul began his lofty message with an overview of God's work in eternity past, where God worked out his plans for the world. Paul then moved to the present, where God is saving and transforming those who believe in Christ. Paul concluded this section with a vision of the future, when all evil will be overcome. He pointed out that in the present, however, we will continue to have conflicts because our battle is with the forces of evil. Paul ended the letter with directives for some practical matters of the Christian life, such as family life and work. The letter to the Ephesians provides the Christian church with a grand vision of itself toward which it can continually grow.

OUTLINE 1:1–2:22 God's plan and the believer's salvation
3:1-21 The mystery of the gospel
4:1–5:20 The Christian's life in the world
5:21–6:9 The Christian's relationships
6:10-24 The Christian's battle with evil

AUTHOR Paul
DATE WRITTEN About AD 61, during Paul's imprisonment in Rome
PURPOSE To strengthen believers by explaining the nature and purpose of the church, the body of Christ
THEMES The church, the body of Christ, God's grand purpose in history, unity in the church, Christian conduct

PHILIPPIANS Contentment. Paul had learned the secret of this attitude, and he revealed
September 29– it to the Philippians. While under house arrest, Paul wrote this letter to
October 3 the Philippians to thank some dear friends who had sent him money. In this letter he told them about a joy that does not depend upon external circumstances because it is rooted in Jesus Christ, who gives it freely. Paul began by expressing his thanks to the Philippians. After describing some problems he was facing in Rome, Paul revealed his uncertainty about his future—whether he would be executed or released. Despite his uncertainty, however, Paul remained confident in the face of death, for he trusted in Christ. Paul then painted a picture of Christ's humility and urged the Philippians to follow this example. Paul digressed for a bit and warned his readers against relying upon external qualifications for their

faith. After a few personal comments, Paul closed his letter by thanking the Philippians again for their generosity.

OUTLINE 1:1-30 Paul's joy despite the problems at Rome
2:1-30 The example of Christ's humility
3:1-21 Warnings and direction for Christian living
4:1-23 God's peace and his provisions for the believer

AUTHOR Paul

DATE WRITTEN About AD 61, during Paul's imprisonment in Rome

PURPOSE To thank the Philippians for the gift they had sent him and to encourage them by describing the contentment he had found in Jesus Christ

THEMES Contentment, humility, unity, generosity, joy

COLOSSIANS Who is Jesus? From the earliest days of Christianity, there has never been
October 4-8 a shortage of answers and theories regarding this question. Paul's letter to the Colossians addressed this question as well, as he combated pagan ideas that were creeping into the church. Paul had never visited the church at Colosse, but he was concerned about its members and warned them against those who were promoting theories about Jesus that mixed pagan and scriptural ideas. These false teachers had taken elements of astrology, magic, and Judaism and produced a doctrine that regarded Jesus as merely an angelic being. To correct this view, Paul emphasized the deity of Christ and listed several titles of Jesus that highlight his uniqueness: "the visible image of the invisible God," "through him God created everything," "the head of the church," and "supreme over all who rise from the dead." Then Paul instructed his readers in the new life they should lead in Christ. After several personal greetings, Paul concluded the letter.

OUTLINE 1:1-14 Paul's opening prayer
1:15-2:3 The glory of Christ
2:4-23 Warnings against false beliefs
3:1-4:1 Instructions for Christian living
4:2-18 Exhortations to prayer and concluding remarks

AUTHOR Paul

DATE WRITTEN About AD 61, during Paul's imprisonment in Rome

PURPOSE To combat false doctrines about Jesus Christ and to show the sufficiency of Jesus Christ for the Colossians

THEMES The person of Jesus Christ, false doctrines, new life in Christ

1 THESSALONIANS Like a father instructing his growing children, Paul urged the
October 9-12 Thessalonians to lead lives worthy of Christ's Kingdom, which would soon be established. This is one of Paul's first epistles, and he wrote it shortly after the church was founded at Thessalonica (2:17). Paul opened the letter by commending the Thessalonians for their faith and for their eagerness to spread the gospel throughout their region. He encouraged them to remain strong for the sake of the gospel despite persecution. After expressing his longing to see them, Paul also guided the church in a few practical matters, addressing adultery, revelry, disrespect, and obstruction of the Holy Spirit's work. Paul corrected these believers while affirming his love for them. Some believers whose relatives had died needed comfort and reassurance that their relatives would also be included in the Kingdom. Paul's discussion about Christ's return also encouraged the believers to live in constant hope.

OUTLINE 1:1-10 Paul's heartfelt thanks for the Thessalonians
2:1-16 Paul's personal defense

2:17–3:13 Description of events since leaving Thessalonica
4:1-12 Direction and encouragement to live a godly life
4:13–5:11 The return of Christ
5:12-28 Final admonitions

AUTHOR Paul
DATE WRITTEN About AD 51, one of Paul's earliest letters
PURPOSE To encourage the Thessalonian believers in their faith and assure them of Christ's return
THEMES Faith, persecution, hope in Christ's return, resurrection

2 THESSALONIANS
October 13-15
Good communication is essential for understanding one another's thoughts. Often the message we receive is not the message the other person intended to send. This is what happened with Paul's first letter to the Thessalonians. In his first letter, Paul had explained that Christ could return at any moment, but apparently some believers misunderstood this to mean that they should stop working and simply wait for Christ to come back. Paul meant to encourage them—not give them a detailed schedule for the future. So he wrote 2 Thessalonians to correct these misunderstandings. Paul began his second letter by encouraging those who were still enduring persecution for their faith. Moving quickly to the heart of the matter, Paul explained that no one knows the exact time of Christ's return, only that he will return. He explained that this great day of judgment will not take them by surprise but will be preceded by a series of recognizable events. Therefore, in the light of Christ's sure return, Christians should lead lives that are above reproach.

OUTLINE 1:1-12 Encouragement from Christ's promised return
2:1-12 The events before Christ returns
2:13–3:5 Further instructions and admonitions
3:6-18 Christian behavior and final greetings

AUTHOR Paul
DATE WRITTEN About AD 51 or 52, a few months after 1 Thessalonians
PURPOSE To clear up confusion about the day of Christ's return
THEMES Persecution, Christ's return, the man of lawlessness and the great rebellion, endurance

1 TIMOTHY
October 16-21
Timothy is the first "second-generation" Christian leader mentioned in the New Testament. He became Paul's protégé and a leader in the Ephesian church. As a young minister, Timothy faced all sorts of pressures, conflicts, and challenges from the church and the surrounding culture. Paul sent this personal letter to counsel and encourage Timothy. Paul spent the final years of his life in prison (see Acts 25–28), but many scholars believe he enjoyed a period of freedom between AD 62 and 64 before he was imprisoned again and executed. He probably wrote this letter during his period of freedom. In his letter, Paul warned against false teachers and encouraged Timothy to remain strong in the faith. Paul also gave several directives for worship and for the ordination of church officers. The letter tends to be fairly personal, but many of its instructions are still helpful for church leaders today.

OUTLINE 1:1-20 Warnings about false doctrine
2:1-15 Instructions regarding prayer and worship
3:1-16 Concerning the ordination of elders and deacons
4:1–5:25 Exhortations and ministry
6:1-21 The Christian ministry and Paul's charge to Timothy

AUTHOR Paul

DATE WRITTEN About AD 64, probably just prior to Paul's final imprisonment in Rome
PURPOSE To encourage and instruct Timothy, a young church leader
THEMES Sound doctrine, public worship, church leadership, personal discipline, a caring church

2 TIMOTHY
October 22-25

We tend to pay special attention to the words of a person who is very near death because we believe that those words will contain important wisdom, reflection, and advice. Paul's second letter to Timothy expresses Paul's thoughts and reflections shortly before his death. This letter is very personal and is probably the last letter Paul ever wrote. It expressed Paul's deepest feelings and his assurance that, though his earthly life might end soon, God has eternal life waiting for him in heaven (1:10-12). Paul also reflected upon the faithfulness of God and exhorted Timothy to remain faithful, though the days were coming when Christians would be persecuted and some would depart from the truth.

OUTLINE 1:1-5 Paul's thanksgiving for Timothy
1:6–2:2 Paul's charge to Timothy
2:3-26 A description of a faithful servant
3:1-17 The coming rebellion against God
4:1-22 Paul's final words

AUTHOR Paul
DATE WRITTEN About AD 66 or 67 from prison in Rome, shortly before his execution
PURPOSE To give final instructions and encouragement to Timothy, a young church leader
THEMES Faithfulness, boldness in preaching, the coming rebellion against God

TITUS
October 26-28

Like Timothy, Titus was one of Paul's trusted assistants who was commissioned to help lead a church. Paul wrote this letter to instruct Titus in his pastoral duties on the island of Crete. Paul advised Titus regarding the ordination of elders and the teaching of the basic doctrines of the faith. He went into some detail regarding the qualifications for the office of elder and gave instructions for others in the church as well. Paul directed Titus to encourage the people to be submissive to the governing authorities whenever possible. Paul also addressed problems that church leaders often faced and instructed Titus in how to solve them.

OUTLINE 1:1-4 Personal greeting
1:5-16 Concerning the ordination of elders
2:1-15 General remarks for church members
3:1-15 Exhortation to Christian living

AUTHOR Paul
DATE WRITTEN About AD 64, around the same time 1 Timothy was written
PURPOSE To instruct Titus in his duties as a leader of the church in Crete
THEMES Church leadership, godly behavior in the church and in society

PHILEMON
October 29

Forgiveness. All Christians have received forgiveness from God, so we should forgive others as well. That is why Paul wrote to Philemon, a believer in the church at Colosse. Philemon owned a slave named Onesimus, who had fled from his master. Paul had met Onesimus after he had fled, and Onesimus became a Christian. Paul then sent Onesimus back to his owner with this letter asking Philemon to forgive Onesimus and treat him like a brother in Christ. It is very likely that this letter was sent along with Paul's letter to the Colossians.

OUTLINE 1:1-3 Paul's greetings to Philemon
1:4-7 Paul's praise of Philemon
1:8-21 Paul's plea for Onesimus
1:22-25 Concluding remarks

AUTHOR Paul
DATE WRITTEN About AD 61, during Paul's imprisonment in Rome
PURPOSE To convince Philemon to forgive his runaway slave and accept him as a brother in Christ
THEME Forgiveness

HEBREWS Have you ever second-guessed yourself on a major decision and wondered
October 30– if you had made a big mistake? The letter to the Hebrews deals with
November 16 this concern among Jewish Christians. Apparently, after pressure and
persecution, some believers were having second thoughts about their
decision to leave Judaism to become Christians. So this letter shows how
Christianity is superior to Judaism. In every way, Christ is shown to be
better. As God, he is superior to angels, to Moses, and to the Old Testament
priests. At the same time, Jesus Christ is fully human, so he is able to
identify with our human struggles. Jesus Christ has sealed a new covenant
that is far superior to the old covenant of Judaism. So the author
admonished the believers to move beyond questions about the basics of
the faith. The believers were encouraged to follow the many examples
of faithful men and women of the past who followed God in the midst of
persecution. The author concluded with personal greetings and thoughts.

OUTLINE 1:1–3:19 The superiority of Christ
4:1-16 The better life of the believer
5:1–8:13 Christ's superior priestly work
9:1–10:39 The better covenant
11:1-40 Great believers of old
12:1–13:19 Practical instructions for believers
13:20-25 Concluding words

AUTHOR Uncertain; some have suggested Paul, Barnabas, Apollos, Priscilla, Luke, and others
DATE WRITTEN Probably a few years before the destruction of the Temple in Jerusalem (AD 70)
PURPOSE To present Christianity as superior to Judaism and to show the sufficiency of Jesus Christ's work
THEMES Superiority of Christianity over Judaism, Jesus as High Priest, Jesus as the ultimate sacrifice, rest, maturity, faith, endurance

JAMES Actions speak louder than words. That old adage comes through loud and
November 17-21 clear in the book of James. This book attacks the notion that becoming a
Christian is simply a matter of assenting to a few spiritual truths without
experiencing any real change in behavior or thought. James was a leader in
the church at Jerusalem, so his book has a very Jewish flavor. It contains
many short, proverbial sayings and resembles the teachings of Jesus—
especially the Sermon on the Mount. James addressed several matters
in which Christian behavior should reflect Christian faith. He discussed
pride, discrimination, greed, lust, hypocrisy, worldliness, and slander.
James used several analogies to show how true faith must evidence itself
in good works. He compared believers to fruit trees bearing only the kind
of fruit that belongs to them. Because of the book's emphasis on good
works, it is a very practical book regarding the Christian life.

OUTLINE 1:1-27 The true life of faith
2:1-13 The social implications of faith

2:14-26 Faith and works
3:1-18 A discourse on controlling the tongue
4:1-17 Practical exhortations
5:1-6 The rich rebuked
5:7-20 Concluding exhortations

AUTHOR James, the half brother of Jesus, a leader in the Jerusalem church
DATE WRITTEN Probably about AD 45, prior to the Jerusalem council held in AD 50
PURPOSE To correct the false belief that a person can have faith without a change of behavior and to give practical instruction regarding the Christian life
THEMES Faith and deeds, trials of faith, controlling the tongue, the dangers of wealth

1 PETER Abuse and persecution were par for the course for many who followed
November 22-26 Christ in the first century. To comfort and encourage these persecuted believers, the apostle Peter wrote them a letter near the end of his life. The letter was addressed to believers in five different regions of Asia Minor, so it was probably routed among them. Peter opened his letter by reminding his readers of their precious hope in Jesus Christ. This hope far outweighed any sufferings they would endure for their faith. In light of this hope, Peter urged all believers—husbands and wives, masters and slaves, elders and laypeople—to live holy lives among unbelievers, thereby giving testimony to Jesus Christ. He comforted them regarding the abuse they had endured, noting that Jesus Christ had also suffered. But Peter also prepared his readers for even harder times. These sufferings would perfect the believers' faith and purify their souls.

OUTLINE 1:1-25 The glory of salvation in Christ
2:1-10 Christians as God's chosen people
2:11-25 Suffering and the example of Christ
3:1-17 Christian living at home and in the world
3:18–4:19 Suffering and the example of Christ
5:1-14 Christian service and concluding words

AUTHOR Peter
DATE WRITTEN About AD 63
PURPOSE To offer encouragement to suffering Christians
THEMES Salvation, persecution, believers as living building stones, obedience

2 PETER Like a road sign warning of things ahead, Peter's second letter, written
November 27-29 shortly before his death, alerts readers to the coming return of the Lord. In light of the Lord's imminent return, Peter urged his readers to live lives that would glorify God. He also cautioned them to watch out for false teachers who would distort the gospel. These evil workers will receive their punishment when the Lord returns. Peter instructed his readers to pay no attention to scoffers who cast doubt into the minds of believers regarding the return of the Lord. He assured them that the Lord would indeed return and establish a new heaven and a new earth. The letter closes with a final comment about Paul's letters, noting that they are difficult to understand. Peter warned his readers about those who might twist Paul's words to justify their own lawless actions, and he encouraged believers to continually grow in their knowledge of Jesus Christ.

OUTLINE 1:1-21 Strategy for spiritual growth
2:1-22 Warnings about false teachers
3:1-18 Exhortations based on the Lord's return

AUTHOR Peter
DATE WRITTEN About AD 67, shortly before his execution

PURPOSE To warn believers about false teachers and to encourage them to grow in the grace and knowledge of Jesus Christ

THEMES Diligence, false teachers, the Lord's return

1 JOHN
November 30–
December 5

For the most part, seeing is believing. Learning something by word of mouth leaves room for misunderstanding, but witnessing an event firsthand gives a person's testimony special significance. John's first letter to the church makes it clear that he had indeed seen Jesus Christ with his own two eyes and that he really knew Jesus. This epistle was prompted by a heretical faction that had developed within the church. The faction had distorted the apostles' teachings about the person of Christ, denying that Jesus Christ had actually come in the flesh. In order to counter these false assertions, John reaffirmed that he and the other apostles had actually seen and touched Jesus Christ. He exhorted his readers to do several things: walk in the light with God and fellow Christians, confess their sins, love God and others, purify themselves from worldly lusts, follow the Spirit of truth, and esteem Jesus Christ as God. John stressed the importance of fellowship in order to safeguard against further division and heresy.

OUTLINE 1:1-10 The believers' fellowship with God
2:1-17 The new command to love
2:18-27 Warnings against the Antichrist and evil
2:28–3:24 Christian behavior
4:1-6 False teachers
4:7-21 The love of God
5:1-21 The victory of faith

AUTHOR John the apostle

DATE WRITTEN Probably between AD 85 and 90

PURPOSE To reaffirm Jesus Christ's humanity and divinity and to instruct believers in their Christian walk

THEMES Walking in the light, the family of God, truth and error, God is love, God is life

2 JOHN
December 6

John wrote this short letter "to the chosen lady and to her children," probably meaning a church and its members. It was written to encourage true Christian love and to warn against deceivers who might deny that Jesus Christ became truly human. John directed his readers to hold fast to the teachings of Jesus Christ and cautioned against hosting those who did not hold to these teachings. John closed his letter by telling them that he wished to see them soon.

OUTLINE 1:1-3 Introduction
1:4-6 The life of love
1:7-11 Rejecting the Antichrist
1:12-13 Closing remarks

AUTHOR John the apostle

DATE WRITTEN About AD 90, around the same time as 1 John

PURPOSE To emphasize truth and love among believers and to warn against false teachers

THEMES Truth, love, false teachers

3 JOHN
December 7

This short letter is a personal note from John the apostle to his friend Gaius. Apparently Gaius regularly welcomed traveling Christian workers into his home. John commended Gaius for his deeds and encouraged him to continue his ministry. John also denounced the actions of Diotrephes, who refused to acknowledge the authority of John and his associates, but he commended Demetrius, who followed the truth. John closed the letter by telling Gaius that he wanted to see him face-to-face.

OUTLINE	1:1-4 Introduction
	1:5-8 Christian hospitality
	1:9-11 The evil work of Diotrephes
	1:12 The good work of Demetrius
	1:13-15 Closing remarks
AUTHOR	John the apostle
DATE WRITTEN	About AD 90, around the same time as 2 John
PURPOSE	To commend Gaius for his hospitality and to denounce the actions of Diotrephes
THEMES	Hospitality, pride

JUDE
December 8

Why do lies tickle our ears so much more than the truth? Often we allow false information to be spread among us because it is interesting, and we are slow to put an end to it. Jude was concerned about this problem as he wrote this letter. We do not know where he sent his letter, but the message is very clear: Christians must stand firm against false teachers and their false doctrines. Jude warned his readers that intruders had slipped in among them and spread false teachings. He condemned these teachers and compared their fate to that of Cain, Balaam, and Sodom and Gomorrah. He described these teachers as lawless, lustful malcontents who schemed for their own gain. Jude challenged his readers to be faithful followers of Jesus Christ and to help others who were wavering in their faith.

OUTLINE	1:1-2 Introduction
	1:3-7 Warnings concerning false teachers
	1:8-19 The evil lives of false teachers
	1:20-23 Exhortation to Christians
	1:24-25 Doxology
AUTHOR	Jude, the half brother of Jesus
DATE WRITTEN	About AD 65
PURPOSE	To warn believers about false teachers and to encourage believers to remain faithful to Jesus Christ
THEMES	False teachers, rebellion against God

REVELATION
December 9-31

When faced with fierce persecution and even death, how could Christians of the first century remain faithful to their Lord? The answer is simple— hope. Though the world around them was hostile and often appeared to be winning the battle, these Christians could stand firm because they knew the end of the story: Jesus Christ and his saints would be victorious in the end. This is the message of the book of Revelation. The first three chapters of the book are written as letters to various churches in Asia Minor, warning them about their specific shortcomings. The rest of the book recounts John's fantastic vision involving bizarre creatures, divine beings, symbolic signs and numbers, and various plagues and curses. The meaning of this vision is related to the final judgment. At God's appointed time, Jesus Christ will come in glory and reveal himself to the entire world as the sovereign Lord. Those who love him will be glad, and those who do not will be afraid, for they will be allied with Satan in a battle doomed to failure. Ultimately, Jesus Christ will defeat them and usher in his eternal Kingdom. The book of Revelation provides a fitting end to the Bible's grand story about God and humanity.

OUTLINE 1:1-20 The opening vision
2:1–3:22 The letters to the seven churches
4:1–5:14 The vision of God and the Lamb
6:1–8:5 The seven seals of judgment
8:6–11:19 The seven trumpets of judgment
12:1–14:20 Visions of earthly and heavenly conflict
15:1–16:21 The seven bowls of judgment
17:1–19:21 The judgment of the prostitute and Babylon
20:1–22:21 The end of the age and the age to come

AUTHOR John the apostle
DATE WRITTEN About AD 95 from the island of Patmos
PURPOSE To encourage believers to remain faithful to Jesus Christ and to give them hope that they will ultimately be victorious
THEMES God's sovereignty, Christ's return, God's faithful people, judgment, hope

GENESIS 1:1–2:25

Plenty of ancient and modern sources try to explain how the world and humanity came to exist. The first chapters of the Bible give the definitive answer: the all-powerful God created the world and made humans to live, work, and have fellowship with him in it.

In the beginning God created the heavens and the earth.* ²The earth was formless and empty, and darkness covered the deep waters. And the Spirit of God was hovering over the surface of the waters.

³Then God said, "Let there be light," and there was light. ⁴And God saw that the light was good. Then he separated the light from the darkness. ⁵God called the light "day" and the darkness "night."

And evening passed and morning came, marking the first day.

⁶Then God said, "Let there be a space between the waters, to separate the waters of the heavens from the waters of the earth." ⁷And that is what happened. God made this space to separate the waters of the earth from the waters of the heavens. ⁸God called the space "sky."

And evening passed and morning came, marking the second day.

⁹Then God said, "Let the waters beneath the sky flow together into one place, so dry ground may appear." And that is what happened. ¹⁰God called the dry ground "land" and the waters "seas." And God saw that it was good. ¹¹Then God said, "Let the land sprout with vegetation—every sort of seed-bearing plant, and trees that grow seed-bearing fruit. These seeds will then produce the kinds of plants and trees from which they came." And that is what happened. ¹²The land produced vegetation—all sorts of seed-bearing plants, and trees with seed-bearing fruit. Their seeds produced plants and trees of the same kind. And God saw that it was good.

¹³And evening passed and morning came, marking the third day.

¹⁴Then God said, "Let lights appear in the sky to separate the day from the night. Let them mark off the seasons, days, and years. ¹⁵Let these lights in the sky shine down on the earth." And that is what happened. ¹⁶God made two great lights—the larger one to govern the day, and the smaller one to govern the night. He also made the stars. ¹⁷God set these lights in the sky to light the earth, ¹⁸to govern the day and night, and to separate the light from the darkness. And God saw that it was good.

¹⁹And evening passed and morning came, marking the fourth day.

²⁰Then God said, "Let the waters swarm with fish and other life. Let the skies be filled with birds of every kind." ²¹So God created great sea creatures and every living thing that scurries and swarms in the water, and every sort of bird—each producing offspring of the same kind. And God saw that it was good. ²²Then God blessed them, saying, "Be fruitful and multiply. Let the fish fill the seas, and let the birds multiply on the earth."

²³And evening passed and morning came, marking the fifth day.

²⁴Then God said, "Let the earth produce every sort of animal, each producing offspring of the same kind—livestock, small animals that scurry along the ground, and wild animals." And that is

what happened. [25]God made all sorts of wild animals, livestock, and small animals, each able to produce offspring of the same kind. And God saw that it was good.

[26]Then God said, "Let us make human beings* in our image, to be like us. They will reign over the fish in the sea, the birds in the sky, the livestock, all the wild animals on the earth, and the small animals that scurry along the ground."

[27] So God created human beings*
      in his own image.
  In the image of God he created
      them;
    male and female he created
      them.

[28]Then God blessed them and said, "Be fruitful and multiply. Fill the earth and govern it. Reign over the fish in the sea, the birds in the sky, and all the animals that scurry along the ground."

[29]Then God said, "Look! I have given you every seed-bearing plant throughout the earth and all the fruit trees for your food. [30]And I have given every green plant as food for all the wild animals, the birds in the sky, and the small animals that scurry along the ground—everything that has life." And that is what happened.

[31]Then God looked over all he had made, and he saw that it was very good!

And evening passed and morning came, marking the sixth day.

[2:1]So the creation of the heavens and the earth and everything in them was completed. [2]On the seventh day God had finished his work of creation, so he rested* from all his work. [3]And God blessed the seventh day and declared it holy, because it was the day when he rested from all his work of creation.

[4]This is the account of the creation of the heavens and the earth.

When the LORD God made the earth and the heavens, [5]neither wild plants nor grains were growing on the earth. For the LORD God had not yet sent rain to water the earth, and there were no people to cultivate the soil. [6]Instead, springs* came up from the ground and watered all the land. [7]Then the LORD God formed the man from the dust of the ground. He breathed the breath of life into the man's nostrils, and the man became a living person.

[8]Then the LORD God planted a garden in Eden in the east, and there he placed the man he had made. [9]The LORD God made all sorts of trees grow up from the ground—trees that were beautiful and that produced delicious fruit. In the middle of the garden he placed the tree of life and the tree of the knowledge of good and evil.

[10]A river flowed from the land of Eden, watering the garden and then dividing into four branches. [11]The first branch, called the Pishon, flowed around the entire land of Havilah, where gold is found. [12]The gold of that land is exceptionally pure; aromatic resin and onyx stone are also found there. [13]The second branch, called the Gihon, flowed around the entire land of Cush. [14]The third branch, called the Tigris, flowed east of the land of Asshur. The fourth branch is called the Euphrates.

[15]The LORD God placed the man in the Garden of Eden to tend and watch over it. [16]But the LORD God warned him, "You may freely eat the fruit of every tree in the garden—[17]except the tree of the knowledge of good and evil. If you eat its fruit, you are sure to die."

[18]Then the LORD God said, "It is not good for the man to be alone. I will make a helper who is just right for him." [19]So the LORD God formed from the ground all the wild animals and all the birds of the sky. He brought them to the man* to see what he would call them, and the man chose a name for each one. [20]He gave names to all the livestock, all the birds of the sky, and all the wild animals. But still there was no helper just right for him.

[21]So the LORD God caused the man to fall into a deep sleep. While the man slept, the LORD God took out one of the man's ribs* and closed up the opening. [22]Then the LORD God made a woman from the rib, and he brought her to the man.

[23]"At last!" the man exclaimed.

"This one is bone from my bone,
and flesh from my flesh!
She will be called 'woman,'
because she was taken from 'man.'"

24This explains why a man leaves his father and mother and is joined to his wife, and the two are united into one.

25Now the man and his wife were both naked, but they felt no shame.

1:1 Or *In the beginning when God created the heavens and the earth, . . .* Or *When God began to create the heavens and the earth, . . .* 1:26 Or *man;* Hebrew reads *adam.* 1:27 Or *the man;* Hebrew reads *ha-adam.* 2:2 Or *ceased;* also in 2:3. 2:6 Or *mist.* 2:19 Or *Adam,* and so throughout the chapter. 2:21 Or *took a part of the man's side.*

MATTHEW 1:1-2:12
In the New Testament we read of the fulfillment of the promises God made in the Old Testament to send the world a Savior. Matthew was a Jew who wrote this book to show that Jesus was the fulfillment of Old Testament prophecies.

This is a record of the ancestors of Jesus the Messiah, a descendant of David* and of Abraham:

2 Abraham was the father of Isaac.
Isaac was the father of Jacob.
Jacob was the father of Judah and his brothers.
3 Judah was the father of Perez and Zerah (whose mother was Tamar).
Perez was the father of Hezron.
Hezron was the father of Ram.*
4 Ram was the father of Amminadab.
Amminadab was the father of Nahshon.
Nahshon was the father of Salmon.
5 Salmon was the father of Boaz (whose mother was Rahab).
Boaz was the father of Obed (whose mother was Ruth).
Obed was the father of Jesse.
6 Jesse was the father of King David.
David was the father of Solomon (whose mother was Bathsheba, the widow of Uriah).
7 Solomon was the father of Rehoboam.
Rehoboam was the father of Abijah.
Abijah was the father of Asa.*
8 Asa was the father of Jehoshaphat.
Jehoshaphat was the father of Jehoram.*
Jehoram was the father* of Uzziah.
9 Uzziah was the father of Jotham.
Jotham was the father of Ahaz.
Ahaz was the father of Hezekiah.
10 Hezekiah was the father of Manasseh.
Manasseh was the father of Amon.*
Amon was the father of Josiah.
11 Josiah was the father of Jehoiachin* and his brothers (born at the time of the exile to Babylon).
12 After the Babylonian exile:
Jehoiachin was the father of Shealtiel.
Shealtiel was the father of Zerubbabel.
13 Zerubbabel was the father of Abiud.
Abiud was the father of Eliakim.
Eliakim was the father of Azor.

WHO GOD IS

God is the Creator

GENESIS 1:1 God is the Creator of all things. Not bound by time or space, God has always existed. That's difficult for us to grasp because, as creations of God, we are finite (limited), whereas he is infinite (unlimited). Understanding and explaining God fully—for example, how it is possible that he never had a beginning or how he formed the vast universe—is beyond our capacity. However, we can gaze upon the beauty of God's creation and marvel at his goodness and power in creating all things. He loved us enough to create us and to give us a world, not of black and white, but of vibrant color, sound, smell, and even taste! • You can choose to believe the theory that you came up out of the ooze over billions of years as basically an accident of chance. Or, you can accept the Bible's statement of fact that all people—including you—are created by a God who made you because he loves you and has a purpose and plan for your life. The choice is yours.

14 Azor was the father of Zadok.
Zadok was the father of Akim.
Akim was the father of Eliud.
15 Eliud was the father of Eleazar.
Eleazar was the father of Matthan.
Matthan was the father of Jacob.
16 Jacob was the father of Joseph, the
husband of Mary.
Mary gave birth to Jesus, who is called
the Messiah.

17All those listed above include fourteen generations from Abraham to David, fourteen from David to the Babylonian exile, and fourteen from the Babylonian exile to the Messiah.

18This is how Jesus the Messiah was born. His mother, Mary, was engaged to be married to Joseph. But before the marriage took place, while she was still a virgin, she became pregnant through the power of the Holy Spirit. 19Joseph, her fiancé, was a good man and did not want to disgrace her publicly, so he decided to break the engagement* quietly.

20As he considered this, an angel of the Lord appeared to him in a dream. "Joseph, son of David," the angel said, "do not be afraid to take Mary as your wife. For the child within her was conceived by the Holy Spirit. 21And she will have a son, and you are to name him Jesus,* for he will save his people from their sins."

22All of this occurred to fulfill the Lord's message through his prophet:

23 "Look! The virgin will conceive a child!
She will give birth to a son,
and they will call him Immanuel,*
which means 'God is with us.'"

24When Joseph woke up, he did as the angel of the Lord commanded and took Mary as his wife. 25But he did not have sexual relations with her until her son was born. And Joseph named him Jesus.

2:1JESUS was born in Bethlehem in Judea, during the reign of King Herod. About that time some wise men* from eastern lands arrived in Jerusalem, asking, 2"Where is the newborn king of the Jews? We saw his star as it rose,* and we have come to worship him."

3King Herod was deeply disturbed when he heard this, as was everyone in Jerusalem. 4He called a meeting of the leading priests and teachers of religious law and asked, "Where is the Messiah supposed to be born?"

5"In Bethlehem in Judea," they said, "for this is what the prophet wrote:

6 'And you, O Bethlehem in the land
of Judah,
are not least among the ruling
cities* of Judah,
for a ruler will come from you
who will be the shepherd for my
people Israel.'*"

7Then Herod called for a private meeting with the wise men, and he learned from them the time when the star first appeared. 8Then he told them, "Go to Bethlehem and search carefully for the child. And when you find him, come back and tell me so that I can go and worship him, too!"

9After this interview the wise men went their way. And the star they had seen in the east guided them to Bethlehem. It went ahead of them and stopped over the place where the child was. 10When they saw the star, they were filled with joy! 11They entered the house and saw the child with his mother, Mary, and they bowed down and worshiped him. Then they opened their treasure chests and gave him gifts of gold, frankincense, and myrrh.

12When it was time to leave, they returned to their own country by another route, for God had warned them in a dream not to return to Herod.

1:1 Greek *Jesus the Messiah, son of David.*   1:3 Greek *Aram,* a variant spelling of Ram; also in 1:4. See 1 Chr 2:9-10. 1:7 Greek *Asaph,* a variant spelling of Asa; also in 1:8. See 1 Chr 3:10.   1:8a Greek *Joram,* a variant spelling of Jehoram; also in 1:8b. See 1 Kgs 22:50 and note at 1 Chr 3:11. 1:8b Or *ancestor;* also in 1:11.   1:10 Greek *Amos,* a variant spelling of Amon; also in 1:10b. See 1 Chr 3:14.   1:11 Greek *Jeconiah,* a variant spelling of Jehoiachin; also in 1:12. See 2 Kgs 24:6 and note at 1 Chr 3:16.   1:19 Greek *to divorce her.*   1:21 *Jesus* means "The LORD saves."   1:23 Isa 7:14; 8:8, 10 (Greek version).   2:1 Or *royal astrologers;* Greek reads *magi;* also in 2:7, 16.   2:2 Or *star in the east.* 2:6a Greek *the rulers.*   2:6b Mic 5:2; 2 Sam 5:2.

PSALM 1:1-6
Oh, the joys of those who do not
follow the advice of the wicked,
or stand around with sinners,
or join in with mockers.
2 But they delight in the law of the LORD,
meditating on it day and night.

[3] They are like trees planted along
         the riverbank,
      bearing fruit each season.
      Their leaves never wither,
         and they prosper in all they do.

[4] But not the wicked!
      They are like worthless chaff,
         scattered by the wind.
[5] They will be condemned at the time
         of judgment.
      Sinners will have no place among
         the godly.
[6] For the LORD watches over the path
         of the godly,
      but the path of the wicked leads
         to destruction.

GENESIS 3:1–4:26
When God created people, he created them with
the ability to choose. He could have made robots,
but he didn't. He wanted to create people who
would obey him because they loved him and
chose to do so. But there was risk involved. Read
what Adam and Eve did with their opportunity to
choose.

The serpent was the shrewdest of all the
wild animals the LORD God had made.
One day he asked the woman, "Did God
really say you must not eat the fruit from
any of the trees in the garden?"

[2]"Of course we may eat fruit from the
trees in the garden," the woman replied.
[3]"It's only the fruit from the tree in the
middle of the garden that we are not
allowed to eat. God said, 'You must not
eat it or even touch it; if you do, you will
die.'"

[4]"You won't die!" the serpent replied to
the woman. [5]"God knows that your eyes
will be opened as soon as you eat it, and
you will be like God, knowing both good
and evil."

[6]The woman was convinced. She saw
that the tree was beautiful and its fruit
looked delicious, and she wanted the wisdom it would give her. So she took some
of the fruit and ate it. Then she gave some
to her husband, who was with her, and he

PROVERBS 1:1-6
These are the proverbs of Solomon, David's son, king of Israel. □ Their purpose is
to teach people wisdom and discipline, to
help them understand the insights of the
wise. Their purpose is to teach people to
live disciplined and successful lives, to
help them do what is right, just, and fair.
These proverbs will give insight to the
simple, knowledge and discernment to
the young. □ Let the wise listen to these
proverbs and become even wiser. Let
those with understanding receive guidance by exploring the meaning in these
proverbs and parables, the words of the
wise and their riddles.

JANUARY**2**

ate it, too. [7]At that moment their eyes were
opened, and they suddenly felt shame at
their nakedness. So they sewed fig leaves
together to cover themselves.

[8]When the cool evening breezes were
blowing, the man* and his wife heard the
LORD God walking about in the garden. So
they hid from the LORD God among the
trees. [9]Then the LORD God called to the
man, "Where are you?"

[10]He replied, "I heard you walking in
the garden, so I hid. I was afraid because I
was naked."

[11]"Who told you that you were naked?"
the LORD God asked. "Have you eaten
from the tree whose fruit I commanded
you not to eat?"

[12]The man replied, "It was the woman
you gave me who gave me the fruit, and I
ate it."

[13]Then the LORD God asked the woman, "What have you done?"

"The serpent deceived me," she replied.
"That's why I ate it."

[14]Then the LORD God said to the serpent,

"Because you have done this, you
         are cursed
      more than all animals, domestic
         and wild.
      You will crawl on your belly,

groveling in the dust as long as
you live.

15 And I will cause hostility between
you and the woman,
and between your offspring and
her offspring.
He will strike* your head,
and you will strike his heel."

16Then he said to the woman,

"I will sharpen the pain of your
pregnancy,
and in pain you will give birth.
And you will desire to control your
husband,
but he will rule over you.*"

17And to the man he said,

"Since you listened to your wife and
ate from the tree
whose fruit I commanded you not
to eat,
the ground is cursed because of you.
All your life you will struggle to
scratch a living from it.
18 It will grow thorns and thistles for you,
though you will eat of its grains.
19 By the sweat of your brow
will you have food to eat
until you return to the ground
from which you were made.
For you were made from dust,
and to dust you will return."

20Then the man—Adam—named his
wife Eve, because she would be the mother
of all who live.* 21And the LORD God made
clothing from animal skins for Adam and
his wife.

22Then the LORD God said, "Look, the
human beings* have become like us,
knowing both good and evil. What if they
reach out, take fruit from the tree of life,
and eat it? Then they will live forever!"
23So the LORD God banished them from
the Garden of Eden, and he sent Adam
out to cultivate the ground from which
he had been made. 24After sending them
out, the LORD God stationed mighty
cherubim to the east of the Garden of
Eden. And he placed a flaming sword
that flashed back and forth to guard the
way to the tree of life.

4:1Now Adam* had sexual relations with
his wife, Eve, and she became pregnant.
When she gave birth to Cain, she said,
"With the LORD's help, I have produced*
a man!" 2Later she gave birth to his brother and named him Abel.

When they grew up, Abel became a
shepherd, while Cain cultivated the
ground. 3When it was time for the harvest,
Cain presented some of his crops as a gift
to the LORD. 4Abel also brought a gift—the
best of the firstborn lambs from his flock.
The LORD accepted Abel and his gift, 5but
he did not accept Cain and his gift. This
made Cain very angry, and he looked
dejected.

6"Why are you so angry?" the LORD
asked Cain. "Why do you look so dejected? 7You will be accepted if you do
what is right. But if you refuse to do what
is right, then watch out! Sin is crouching
at the door, eager to control you. But you
must subdue it and be its master."

8One day Cain suggested to his brother,
"Let's go out into the fields."* And while
they were in the field, Cain attacked his
brother, Abel, and killed him.

9Afterward the LORD asked Cain,
"Where is your brother? Where is Abel?"

"I don't know," Cain responded. "Am I
my brother's guardian?"

10But the LORD said, "What have you
done? Listen! Your brother's blood cries
out to me from the ground! 11Now you
are cursed and banished from the ground,
which has swallowed your brother's blood.
12No longer will the ground yield good
crops for you, no matter how hard you
work! From now on you will be a homeless
wanderer on the earth."

13Cain replied to the LORD, "My punishment* is too great for me to bear! 14You
have banished me from the land and from
your presence; you have made me a homeless wanderer. Anyone who finds me will
kill me!"

15The LORD replied, "No, for I will give a
sevenfold punishment to anyone who kills
you." Then the LORD put a mark on Cain to
warn anyone who might try to kill him.
16So Cain left the LORD's presence and settled in the land of Nod,* east of Eden.

17Cain had sexual relations with his
wife, and she became pregnant and gave

birth to Enoch. Then Cain founded a city, which he named Enoch, after his son. [18]Enoch had a son named Irad. Irad became the father of* Mehujael. Mehujael became the father of Methushael. Methushael became the father of Lamech.

[19]Lamech married two women. The first was named Adah, and the second was Zillah. [20]Adah gave birth to Jabal, who was the first of those who raise livestock and live in tents. [21]His brother's name was Jubal, the first of all who play the harp and flute. [22]Lamech's other wife, Zillah, gave birth to a son named Tubalcain. He became an expert in forging tools of bronze and iron. Tubal-cain had a sister named Naamah. [23]One day Lamech said to his wives,

"Adah and Zillah, hear my voice;
    listen to me, you wives of Lamech.
I have killed a man who attacked me,
    a young man who wounded me.
[24] If someone who kills Cain is punished
        seven times,
    then the one who kills me will be
        punished seventy-seven times!"

[25]Adam had sexual relations with his wife again, and she gave birth to another son. She named him Seth,* for she said, "God has granted me another son in place of Abel, whom Cain killed." [26]When Seth grew up, he had a son and named him Enosh. At that time people first began to worship the LORD by name.

3:8 Or *Adam,* and so throughout the chapter.   **3:15** Or *bruise;* also in 3:15b.   **3:16** Or *And though you will have desire for your husband, / he will rule over you.*   **3:20** *Eve* sounds like a Hebrew term that means "to give life."   **3:22** Or *the man;* Hebrew reads *ha-adam.*   **4:1a** Or *the man;* also in 4:25.   **4:1b** Or *I have acquired. Cain* sounds like a Hebrew term that can mean "produce" or "acquire."   **4:8** As in Samaritan Pentateuch, Greek and Syriac versions, and Latin Vulgate; Masoretic Text lacks *"Let's go out into the fields."*   **4:13** Or *My sin.*   **4:16** *Nod* means "wandering."   **4:18** Or *the ancestor of,* and so throughout the verse.   **4:25** *Seth* probably means "granted"; the name may also mean "appointed."

MATTHEW 2:13–3:6

Satan has been making trouble ever since he first tempted Eve in the Garden. You'll find him again in today's reading. This time he tried to get rid of the baby Jesus. Why do you think Satan wanted to get rid of Jesus?

After the wise men were gone, an angel of the Lord appeared to Joseph in a dream. "Get up! Flee to Egypt with the child and his mother," the angel said. "Stay there until I tell you to return, because Herod is going to search for the child to kill him."

[14]That night Joseph left for Egypt with the child and Mary, his mother, [15]and they stayed there until Herod's death. This fulfilled what the Lord had spoken through the prophet: "I called my Son out of Egypt."*

WHAT THE BIBLE SAYS

Is the Bible reliable?

GENESIS 3:6 To some it might seem old-fashioned to take seriously stories like Noah's ark, David and Goliath, Jonah and the fish—and even Eve and the serpent. However, as a new believer you need to accept the reliability of God's Word. If you decide not to believe these stories, how can you then believe the Bible when it says you've been saved and that you're going to heaven? You can't pick and choose what parts of the Bible to accept and what parts to set aside.   • Why believe the Bible? Because it contains God's very own words. He spoke through human writers, but it was he who was speaking nonetheless. The Bible was written across thousands of years, yet the entire message holds together perfectly. Its overall plot tells us who God is, why the world is the way it is, why we are the way we are, what God did to rescue us, and what the future holds. The story of Eve's encounter with the serpent is a vital part of the plot. It explains how sin came into the world and who our enemy is (Satan). This was the tragic event that ultimately led to God's sending the Savior, Jesus Christ.

[16] Herod was furious when he realized that the wise men had outwitted him. He sent soldiers to kill all the boys in and around Bethlehem who were two years old and under, based on the wise men's report of the star's first appearance. [17] Herod's brutal action fulfilled what God had spoken through the prophet Jeremiah:

[18] "A cry was heard in Ramah—
weeping and great mourning.
Rachel weeps for her children,
refusing to be comforted,
for they are dead."*

[19] When Herod died, an angel of the Lord appeared in a dream to Joseph in Egypt. [20] "Get up!" the angel said. "Take the child and his mother back to the land of Israel, because those who were trying to kill the child are dead."

[21] So Joseph got up and returned to the land of Israel with Jesus and his mother. [22] But when he learned that the new ruler of Judea was Herod's son Archelaus, he was afraid to go there. Then, after being warned in a dream, he left for the region of Galilee. [23] So the family went and lived in a town called Nazareth. This fulfilled what the prophets had said: "He will be called a Nazarene."

[3:1] In those days John the Baptist came to the Judean wilderness and began preaching. His message was, [2] "Repent of your sins and turn to God, for the Kingdom of Heaven is near.*" [3] The prophet Isaiah was speaking about John when he said,

"He is a voice shouting in the
    wilderness,
'Prepare the way for the LORD's
    coming!
Clear the road for him!'"*

[4] John's clothes were woven from coarse camel hair, and he wore a leather belt around his waist. For food he ate locusts and wild honey. [5] People from Jerusalem and from all of Judea and all over the Jordan Valley went out to see and hear John. [6] And when they confessed their sins, he baptized them in the Jordan River.

2:15 Hos 11:1.   **2:18** Jer 31:15.   **3:2** Or *has come,* or *is coming soon.*   **3:3** Isa 40:3 (Greek version).

PSALM 2:1-12

Why are the nations so angry?
    Why do they waste their time with
        futile plans?
[2] The kings of the earth prepare for
        battle;
    the rulers plot together
against the LORD
    and against his anointed one.
[3] "Let us break their chains," they cry,
    "and free ourselves from slavery
        to God."

[4] But the one who rules in heaven
        laughs.
    The Lord scoffs at them.
[5] Then in anger he rebukes them,
    terrifying them with his fierce
        fury.
[6] For the Lord declares, "I have placed
    my chosen king on the throne
in Jerusalem,* on my holy
    mountain."

[7] The king proclaims the LORD's
        decree:
"The LORD said to me, 'You are my
        son.*
    Today I have become your
        Father.*
[8] Only ask, and I will give you the
        nations as your inheritance,
    the whole earth as your
        possession.
[9] You will break* them with an
        iron rod
    and smash them like clay pots.'"

[10] Now then, you kings, act wisely!
    Be warned, you rulers of the
        earth!
[11] Serve the LORD with reverent fear,
    and rejoice with trembling.
[12] Submit to God's royal son,* or he
        will become angry,
    and you will be destroyed
        in the midst of all your
        activities—
for his anger flares up in an
        instant.
    But what joy for all who take
        refuge in him!

2:6 Hebrew *on Zion.*   **2:7a** Or *Son;* also in 2:12.   **2:7b** Or *Today I reveal you as my son.*   **2:9** Greek version reads *rule.* Compare Rev 2:27.   **2:12** The meaning of the Hebrew is uncertain.

PROVERBS 1:7-9

Fear of the LORD is the foundation of true knowledge, but fools despise wisdom and discipline. □ My child,* listen when your father corrects you. Don't neglect your mother's instruction. What you learn from them will crown you with grace and be a chain of honor around your neck.

1:8 Hebrew *My son;* also in 1:10, 15.

JANUARY**3**

GENESIS 5:1–7:24

Yesterday you read how sin entered the human race; today you will begin to see how quickly sin spread and what devastation it caused. It got so bad, in fact, that God decided to basically start over with humanity.

This is the written account of the descendants of Adam. When God created human beings,* he made them to be like himself. ²He created them male and female, and he blessed them and called them "human."

³When Adam was 130 years old, he became the father of a son who was just like him—in his very image. He named his son Seth. ⁴After the birth of Seth, Adam lived another 800 years, and he had other sons and daughters. ⁵Adam lived 930 years, and then he died.

⁶When Seth was 105 years old, he became the father of* Enosh. ⁷After the birth of* Enosh, Seth lived another 807 years, and he had other sons and daughters. ⁸Seth lived 912 years, and then he died.

⁹When Enosh was 90 years old, he became the father of Kenan. ¹⁰After the birth of Kenan, Enosh lived another 815 years, and he had other sons and daughters. ¹¹Enosh lived 905 years, and then he died.

¹²When Kenan was 70 years old, he became the father of Mahalalel. ¹³After the birth of Mahalalel, Kenan lived another 840 years, and he had other sons and daughters. ¹⁴Kenan lived 910 years, and then he died.

¹⁵When Mahalalel was 65 years old, he became the father of Jared. ¹⁶After the birth of Jared, Mahalalel lived another 830 years, and he had other sons and daughters. ¹⁷Mahalalel lived 895 years, and then he died.

¹⁸When Jared was 162 years old, he became the father of Enoch. ¹⁹After the birth of Enoch, Jared lived another 800 years, and he had other sons and daughters. ²⁰Jared lived 962 years, and then he died.

²¹When Enoch was 65 years old, he became the father of Methuselah. ²²After the birth of Methuselah, Enoch lived in close fellowship with God for another 300 years, and he had other sons and daughters. ²³Enoch lived 365 years, ²⁴walking in close fellowship with God. Then one day he disappeared, because God took him.

²⁵When Methuselah was 187 years old, he became the father of Lamech. ²⁶After the birth of Lamech, Methuselah lived another 782 years, and he had other sons and daughters. ²⁷Methuselah lived 969 years, and then he died.

²⁸When Lamech was 182 years old, he became the father of a son. ²⁹Lamech named his son Noah, for he said, "May he bring us relief* from our work and the painful labor of farming this ground that the LORD has cursed." ³⁰After the birth of Noah, Lamech lived another 595 years, and he had other sons and daughters. ³¹Lamech lived 777 years, and then he died.

³²By the time Noah was 500 years old, he was the father of Shem, Ham, and Japheth.

6:1THEN the people began to multiply on the earth, and daughters were born to them. ²The sons of God saw the beautiful women* and took any they wanted as their wives. ³Then the LORD said, "My Spirit will not put up with* humans for such a long time, for they are only mortal flesh. In the future, their normal lifespan will be no more than 120 years."

⁴In those days, and for some time after, giant Nephilites lived on the earth, for whenever the sons of God had intercourse with women, they gave birth to children who became the heroes and famous warriors of ancient times.

⁵The LORD observed the extent of human wickedness on the earth, and he saw that everything they thought or imagined was consistently and totally evil. ⁶So the LORD was sorry he had ever made them and put them on the earth. It broke his heart. ⁷And the LORD said, "I will wipe this human race I have created from the face of the earth. Yes, and I will destroy every living thing—all the people, the large animals, the small animals that scurry along the ground, and even the birds of the sky. I am sorry I ever made them." ⁸But Noah found favor with the LORD.

⁹This is the account of Noah and his family. Noah was a righteous man, the only blameless person living on earth at the time, and he walked in close fellowship with God. ¹⁰Noah was the father of three sons: Shem, Ham, and Japheth.

¹¹Now God saw that the earth had become corrupt and was filled with violence. ¹²God observed all this corruption in the world, for everyone on earth was corrupt. ¹³So God said to Noah, "I have decided to destroy all living creatures, for they have filled the earth with violence. Yes, I will wipe them all out along with the earth!

¹⁴"Build a large boat* from cypress wood* and waterproof it with tar, inside and out. Then construct decks and stalls throughout its interior. ¹⁵Make the boat 450 feet long, 75 feet wide, and 45 feet high.* ¹⁶Leave an 18-inch opening* below the roof all the way around the boat. Put the door on the side, and build three decks inside the boat—lower, middle, and upper.

¹⁷"Look! I am about to cover the earth with a flood that will destroy every living thing that breathes. Everything on earth will die. ¹⁸But I will confirm my covenant with you. So enter the boat—you and your wife and your sons and their wives. ¹⁹Bring a pair of every kind of animal—a male and a female—into the boat with you to keep them alive during the flood. ²⁰Pairs of every kind of bird, and every kind of animal, and every kind of small animal that scurries along the ground, will come to you to be kept alive. ²¹And be sure to take on board enough food for your family and for all the animals."

²²So Noah did everything exactly as God had commanded him.

7:1WHEN everything was ready, the LORD said to Noah, "Go into the boat with all your family, for among all the people of the earth, I can see that you alone are righteous. ²Take with you seven pairs—male and female—of each animal I have approved for eating and for sacrifice,* and take one pair of each of the others. ³Also take seven pairs of every kind of bird. There must be a male and a female in each pair to ensure that all life will survive on the earth after the flood. ⁴Seven days from now I will make the rains pour down on the earth. And it will rain for forty days and forty nights, until I have wiped from the earth all the living things I have created."

⁵So Noah did everything as the LORD commanded him.

⁶Noah was 600 years old when the flood covered the earth. ⁷He went on board the boat to escape the flood—he and his wife and his sons and their wives. ⁸With them were all the various kinds of animals—those approved for eating and for sacrifice and those that were not—along with all the birds and the small animals that scurry along the ground. ⁹They entered the boat in pairs, male and female, just as God had commanded Noah. ¹⁰After seven days, the waters of the flood came and covered the earth.

¹¹When Noah was 600 years old, on the seventeenth day of the second month, all the underground waters erupted from the earth, and the rain fell in mighty torrents

from the sky. [12] The rain continued to fall for forty days and forty nights.

[13] That very day Noah had gone into the boat with his wife and his sons—Shem, Ham, and Japheth—and their wives. [14] With them in the boat were pairs of every kind of animal—domestic and wild, large and small—along with birds of every kind. [15] Two by two they came into the boat, representing every living thing that breathes. [16] A male and female of each kind entered, just as God had commanded Noah. Then the LORD closed the door behind them.

[17] For forty days the floodwaters grew deeper, covering the ground and lifting the boat high above the earth. [18] As the waters rose higher and higher above the ground, the boat floated safely on the surface. [19] Finally, the water covered even the highest mountains on the earth, [20] rising more than twenty-two feet* above the highest peaks. [21] All the living things on earth died—birds, domestic animals, wild animals, small animals that scurry along the ground, and all the people. [22] Everything that breathed and lived on dry land died. [23] God wiped out every living thing on the earth—people, livestock, small animals that scurry along the ground, and the birds of the sky. All

were destroyed. The only people who survived were Noah and those with him in the boat. [24] And the floodwaters covered the earth for 150 days.

5:1 Or *man;* Hebrew reads *adam;* similarly in 5:2.   **5:6** Or *the ancestor of;* also in 5:9, 12, 15, 18, 21, 25.   **5:7** Or *the birth of this ancestor of;* also in 5:10, 13, 16, 19, 22, 26.   **5:29** *Noah* sounds like a Hebrew term that can mean "relief" or "comfort."   **6:2** Hebrew *daughters of men;* also in 6:4.   **6:3** Greek version reads *will not remain in.*   **6:14a** Traditionally rendered *an ark.*   **6:14b** Or *gopher wood.*   **6:15** Hebrew *300 cubits* [138 meters] *long, 50 cubits* [23 meters] *wide, and 30 cubits* [13.8 meters] *high.*   **6:16** Hebrew *an opening of 1 cubit* [46 centimeters] *high.*   **7:2** Hebrew *of each clean animal;* similarly in 7:8.   **7:20** Hebrew *15 cubits* [6.9 meters].

MATTHEW 3:7-4:11
Jesus had John the Baptist baptize him—not in repentance for sin (Jesus was sinless), but in order for Jesus to identify with the people to whom he would be ministering. Before commencing his ministry, however, Jesus faced a period of temptation by Satan. Take note of the ways Satan tempted Jesus and the ways Jesus responded.

But when he [John] saw many Pharisees and Sadducees coming to watch him baptize,* he denounced them. "You brood of snakes!" he exclaimed. "Who warned you to flee God's coming wrath? [8] Prove by the way you live that you have repented of your sins and turned to God. [9] Don't just say to each other, 'We're safe, for we are descendants of Abraham.' That

HOW WE LIVE   **Resisting temptation**

MATTHEW 4:1-2 The same Satan who tempted Eve in the Garden of Eden and tried to kill the infant Jesus was at it again. Satan arrived after Jesus had not eaten for forty days, waiting until Jesus was the most vulnerable before he slithered in with his temptations. First temptation on the menu: bread. Second temptation: testing God. Third temptation: pride and power. Satan misquoted Scripture in order to back up his temptations! Unfortunately for him, Jesus understood the true intent of those verses and countered by quoting Scripture accurately and effectively.   • Now that you are a follower of Jesus Christ, Satan is going to try to draw you away by tempting you to disobey God's Word. He is going to hit you when and where you're most vulnerable. Remember that it's not a sin to be tempted—Jesus was tempted, and Jesus never sinned. The sin happens when you give in to temptation. You can avoid giving in by making up your mind ahead of time to do what you know is right. Keep reading the Bible; underline verses that show you what to do in areas where you are vulnerable. Use those verses to help you the next time Satan slithers your way.

means nothing, for I tell you, God can create children of Abraham from these very stones. [10]Even now the ax of God's judgment is poised, ready to sever the roots of the trees. Yes, every tree that does not produce good fruit will be chopped down and thrown into the fire.

[11]"I baptize with* water those who repent of their sins and turn to God. But someone is coming soon who is greater than I am—so much greater that I'm not worthy even to be his slave and carry his sandals. He will baptize you with the Holy Spirit and with fire.* [12]He is ready to separate the chaff from the wheat with his winnowing fork. Then he will clean up the threshing area, gathering the wheat into his barn but burning the chaff with never-ending fire."

[13]Then Jesus went from Galilee to the Jordan River to be baptized by John. [14]But John tried to talk him out of it. "I am the one who needs to be baptized by you," he said, "so why are you coming to me?"

[15]But Jesus said, "It should be done, for we must carry out all that God requires.*" So John agreed to baptize him.

[16]After his baptism, as Jesus came up out of the water, the heavens were opened* and he saw the Spirit of God descending like a dove and settling on him. [17]And a voice from heaven said, "This is my dearly loved Son, who brings me great joy."

[4:1]THEN Jesus was led by the Spirit into the wilderness to be tempted there by the devil. [2]For forty days and forty nights he fasted and became very hungry. [3]During that time the devil* came and said to him, "If you are the Son of God, tell these stones to become loaves of bread."

[4]But Jesus told him, "No! The Scriptures say,

'People do not live by bread alone,
　　but by every word that comes from
　　　　the mouth of God.'*"

[5]Then the devil took him to the holy city, Jerusalem, to the highest point of the Temple, [6]and said, "If you are the Son of God, jump off! For the Scriptures say,

'He will order his angels to
　　protect you.

And they will hold you up with their
　　hands
so you won't even hurt your foot
　　on a stone.'*"

[7]Jesus responded, "The Scriptures also say, 'You must not test the LORD your God.'*"

[8]Next the devil took him to the peak of a very high mountain and showed him all the kingdoms of the world and their glory. [9]"I will give it all to you," he said, "if you will kneel down and worship me."

[10]"Get out of here, Satan," Jesus told him. "For the Scriptures say,

'You must worship the LORD your God
　　and serve only him.'*"

[11]Then the devil went away, and angels came and took care of Jesus.

3:7 Or *coming to be baptized.* 3:11a Or *in.* 3:11b Or *in the Holy Spirit and in fire.* 3:15 Or *for we must fulfill all righteousness.* 3:16 Some manuscripts read *opened to him.* 4:3 Greek *the tempter.* 4:4 Deut 8:3. 4:6 Ps 91:11-12. 4:7 Deut 6:16. 4:10 Deut 6:13.

PSALM 3:1-8
A psalm of David, regarding the time David fled from his son Absalom.

[1] O LORD, I have so many enemies;
　　so many are against me.
[2] So many are saying,
　　"God will never rescue him!"

*Interlude**

[3] But you, O LORD, are a shield
　　around me;
　　you are my glory, the one who
　　　　holds my head high.
[4] I cried out to the LORD,
　　and he answered me from his
　　　　holy mountain. *Interlude*
[5] I lay down and slept,
　　yet I woke up in safety,
　　for the LORD was watching
　　　　over me.
[6] I am not afraid of ten thousand
　　enemies
　　who surround me on every side.

[7] Arise, O LORD!
　　Rescue me, my God!
　　Slap all my enemies in the face!
　　Shatter the teeth of the
　　　　wicked!

⁸ Victory comes from you, O LORD.
    May you bless your people.

Interlude

3:2 Hebrew *Selah*. The meaning of this word is uncertain,
though it is probably a musical or literary term. It is rendered
Interlude throughout the Psalms.

PROVERBS 1:10-19

My child, if sinners entice you, turn your
back on them! They may say, "Come and
join us. Let's hide and kill someone! Just
for fun, let's ambush the innocent! Let's
swallow them alive, like the grave*; let's
swallow them whole, like those who go
down to the pit of death. Think of the
great things we'll get! We'll fill our houses
with all the stuff we take. Come, throw in
your lot with us; we'll all share the loot."
☐ My child, don't go along with them! Stay
far away from their paths. They rush to
commit evil deeds. They hurry to commit
murder. If a bird sees a trap being set, it
knows to stay away. But these people set
an ambush for themselves; they are trying
to get themselves killed. Such is the fate
of all who are greedy for money; it robs
them of life.

1:12 Hebrew *like Sheol*.

JANUARY**4**

GENESIS 8:1-10:32

Noah obeyed God, built a boat, and began his year-
long voyage. When the flood ended, God made a
promise to Noah—and to us. That wonderful promise is in today's reading. Let it remind you that God
keeps all of his promises.

But God remembered Noah and all the
wild animals and livestock with him in
the boat. He sent a wind to blow across
the earth, and the floodwaters began
to recede. ²The underground waters
stopped flowing, and the torrential rains
from the sky were stopped. ³So the floodwaters gradually receded from the earth.
After 150 days, ⁴exactly five months
from the time the flood began,* the boat
came to rest on the mountains of Ararat.
⁵Two and a half months later,* as the
waters continued to go down, other
mountain peaks became visible.

⁶After another forty days, Noah opened
the window he had made in the boat ⁷and
released a raven. The bird flew back and
forth until the floodwaters on the earth
had dried up. ⁸He also released a dove to
see if the water had receded and it could
find dry ground. ⁹But the dove could find
no place to land because the water still
covered the ground. So it returned to the
boat, and Noah held out his hand and
drew the dove back inside. ¹⁰After waiting
another seven days, Noah released the
dove again. ¹¹This time the dove returned
to him in the evening with a fresh olive
leaf in its beak. Then Noah knew that the
floodwaters were almost gone. ¹²He
waited another seven days and then released the dove again. This time it did not
come back.

¹³Noah was now 601 years old. On the
first day of the new year, ten and a half
months after the flood began,* the
floodwaters had almost dried up from
the earth. Noah lifted back the covering
of the boat and saw that the surface of
the ground was drying. ¹⁴Two more
months went by,* and at last the earth
was dry!

¹⁵Then God said to Noah, ¹⁶"Leave the
boat, all of you—you and your wife, and
your sons and their wives. ¹⁷Release all
the animals—the birds, the livestock, and
the small animals that scurry along the
ground—so they can be fruitful and multiply throughout the earth."

¹⁸So Noah, his wife, and his sons and
their wives left the boat. ¹⁹And all of the
large and small animals and birds came
out of the boat, pair by pair.

²⁰Then Noah built an altar to the LORD,
and there he sacrificed as burnt offerings the animals and birds that had been

approved for that purpose.* ²¹And the LORD was pleased with the aroma of the sacrifice and said to himself, "I will never again curse the ground because of the human race, even though everything they think or imagine is bent toward evil from childhood. I will never again destroy all living things. ²²As long as the earth remains, there will be planting and harvest, cold and heat, summer and winter, day and night."

9:1THEN God blessed Noah and his sons and told them, "Be fruitful and multiply. Fill the earth. ²All the animals of the earth, all the birds of the sky, all the small animals that scurry along the ground, and all the fish in the sea will look on you with fear and terror. I have placed them in your power. ³I have given them to you for food, just as I have given you grain and vegetables. ⁴But you must never eat any meat that still has the lifeblood in it.

⁵"And I will require the blood of anyone who takes another person's life. If a wild animal kills a person, it must die. And anyone who murders a fellow human must die. ⁶If anyone takes a human life, that person's life will also be taken by human hands. For God made human beings* in his own image. ⁷Now be fruitful and multiply, and repopulate the earth."

⁸Then God told Noah and his sons, ⁹"I hereby confirm my covenant with you and your descendants, ¹⁰and with all the animals that were on the boat with you—the birds, the livestock, and all the wild animals—every living creature on earth. ¹¹Yes, I am confirming my covenant with you. Never again will floodwaters kill all living creatures; never again will a flood destroy the earth."

¹²Then God said, "I am giving you a sign of my covenant with you and with all living creatures, for all generations to come. ¹³I have placed my rainbow in the clouds. It is the sign of my covenant with you and with all the earth. ¹⁴When I send clouds over the earth, the rainbow will appear in the clouds, ¹⁵and I will remember my covenant with you and with all living creatures. Never again will the floodwaters destroy all life. ¹⁶When I see the rainbow in the clouds, I will remember the eternal covenant between God and every living creature on earth." ¹⁷Then God said to Noah, "Yes, this rainbow is the sign of the covenant I am confirming with all the creatures on earth."

¹⁸The sons of Noah who came out of the boat with their father were Shem, Ham, and Japheth. (Ham is the father of Canaan.) ¹⁹From these three sons of Noah came all the people who now populate the earth.

²⁰After the flood, Noah began to cultivate the ground, and he planted a vineyard. ²¹One day he drank some wine he had made, and he became drunk and lay naked inside his tent. ²²Ham, the father of Canaan, saw that his father was naked and went outside and told his brothers. ²³Then Shem and Japheth took a robe, held it over their shoulders, and backed into the tent to cover their father. As they did this, they looked the other way so they would not see him naked.

²⁴When Noah woke up from his stupor, he learned what Ham, his youngest son, had done. ²⁵Then he cursed Canaan, the son of Ham:

"May Canaan be cursed!
May he be the lowest of servants
to his relatives."

²⁶Then Noah said,

"May the LORD, the God of Shem,
be blessed,
and may Canaan be his servant!
²⁷ May God expand the territory of
Japheth!
May Japheth share the prosperity
of Shem,*
and may Canaan be his servant."

²⁸Noah lived another 350 years after the great flood. ²⁹He lived 950 years, and then he died.

10:1THIS is the account of the families of Shem, Ham, and Japheth, the three sons of Noah. Many children were born to them after the great flood.

²The descendants of Japheth were Gomer, Magog, Madai, Javan, Tubal, Meshech, and Tiras.
³The descendants of Gomer were Ashkenaz, Riphath, and Togarmah.
⁴The descendants of Javan were Elishah,

Tarshish, Kittim, and Rodanim.*
⁵Their descendants became the seafaring peoples that spread out to various lands, each identified by its own language, clan, and national identity.

⁶The descendants of Ham were Cush, Mizraim, Put, and Canaan.

⁷The descendants of Cush were Seba, Havilah, Sabtah, Raamah, and Sabteca. The descendants of Raamah were Sheba and Dedan.

⁸Cush was also the ancestor of Nimrod, who was the first heroic warrior on earth. ⁹Since he was the greatest hunter in the world,* his name became proverbial. People would say, "This man is like Nimrod, the greatest hunter in the world." ¹⁰He built his kingdom in the land of Babylonia,* with the cities of Babylon, Erech, Akkad, and Calneh. ¹¹From there he expanded his territory to Assyria,* building the cities of Nineveh, Rehoboth-ir, Calah, ¹²and Resen (the great city located between Nineveh and Calah).

¹³Mizraim was the ancestor of the Ludites, Anamites, Lehabites, Naphtuhites, ¹⁴Pathrusites, Casluhites, and the Caphtorites, from whom the Philistines came.*

¹⁵Canaan's oldest son was Sidon, the ancestor of the Sidonians. Canaan was also the ancestor of the Hittites, ¹⁶Jebusites, Amorites, Girgashites, ¹⁷Hivites, Arkites, Sinites, ¹⁸Arvadites, Zemarites, and Hamathites. The Canaanite clans eventually spread out, ¹⁹and the territory of Canaan extended from Sidon in the north to Gerar and Gaza in the south, and east as far as Sodom, Gomorrah, Admah, and Zeboiim, near Lasha.

²⁰These were the descendants of Ham, identified by clan, language, territory, and national identity.

²¹Sons were also born to Shem, the older brother of Japheth.* Shem was the ancestor of all the descendants of Eber.

²²The descendants of Shem were Elam, Asshur, Arphaxad, Lud, and Aram.

²³The descendants of Aram were Uz, Hul, Gether, and Mash.

²⁴Arphaxad was the father of Shelah,* and Shelah was the father of Eber.

²⁵Eber had two sons. The first was named Peleg (which means "division"), for during his lifetime the people of the world were divided into different language groups. His brother's name was Joktan.

HOW WE LIVE

Obeying God

MATTHEW 4:18-20 Today's first two readings include the topic of obedience. Noah obeyed God by building a boat long before rain had ever fallen; he obeyed God when he stayed in the boat; he obeyed God when he got off the boat and built an altar. His radical obedience saved his life and the lives of his family members. • Several hundred years later, fishermen standing beside the Sea of Galilee also acted with radical obedience. Jesus called them to follow him, and they did. For all of them, this was the change of a lifetime. They would never go back. Their radical obedience would change the world. • Obedience is a threatening word in today's culture, but it need not be that way. Obeying God means that your life is constantly changing for the better. You seek to do what you know God would want you to do. You still have freedom to make choices, and at times you will make the wrong choice—everybody does! But as you get to know God and his Word better, you'll learn how to live in a way that pleases him. The more you obey him, the more you'll find that doing so brings deep, long-lasting fulfillment and joy.

²⁶Joktan was the ancestor of Almodad, Sheleph, Hazarmaveth, Jerah, ²⁷Hadoram, Uzal, Diklah, ²⁸Obal, Abimael, Sheba, ²⁹Ophir, Havilah, and Jobab. All these were descendants of Joktan. ³⁰The territory they occupied extended from Mesha all the way to Sephar in the eastern mountains.

³¹These were the descendants of Shem, identified by clan, language, territory, and national identity.

³²These are the clans that descended from Noah's sons, arranged by nation according to their lines of descent. All the nations of the earth descended from these clans after the great flood.

8:4 Hebrew *on the seventeenth day of the seventh month;* see 7:11.   8:5 Hebrew *On the first day of the tenth month;* see 7:11 and note on 8:4.   8:13 Hebrew *On the first day of the first month;* see 7:11.   8:14 Hebrew *The twenty-seventh day of the second month arrived;* see note on 8:13. 8:20 Hebrew *every clean animal and every clean bird.* 9:6 Or *man;* Hebrew reads *ha-adam.*   9:27 Hebrew *May he live in the tents of Shem.*   10:4 As in some Hebrew manuscripts and Greek version (see also 1 Chr 1:7); most Hebrew manuscripts read *Dodanim.*   10:9 Hebrew *a great hunter before the LORD;* also in 10:9b.   10:10 Hebrew *Shinar.* 10:11 Or *From that land Assyria went out.*   10:14 Hebrew *Casluhites, from whom the Philistines came, and Caphtorites.* Compare Jer 47:4; Amos 9:7.   10:21 Or *Shem, whose older brother was Japheth.*   10:24 Greek version reads *Arphaxad was the father of Cainan, Cainan was the father of Shelah.* Compare Luke 3:36.

MATTHEW 4:12-25

Early in his ministry, Jesus preached the Good News, taught the Scriptures, and healed people all throughout the region of Galilee. In today's reading, Jesus chooses some of the men who would be his closest companions. Into them he would pour his time and teaching.

When Jesus heard that John had been arrested, he left Judea and returned to Galilee. ¹³He went first to Nazareth, then left there and moved to Capernaum, beside the Sea of Galilee, in the region of Zebulun and Naphtali. ¹⁴This fulfilled what God said through the prophet Isaiah:

¹⁵ "In the land of Zebulun and of Naphtali,
   beside the sea, beyond the Jordan River,
   in Galilee where so many Gentiles live,
¹⁶ the people who sat in darkness
   have seen a great light.

And for those who lived in the land
   where death casts its shadow,
   a light has shined."*

¹⁷From then on Jesus began to preach, "Repent of your sins and turn to God, for the Kingdom of Heaven is near.*"

¹⁸One day as Jesus was walking along the shore of the Sea of Galilee, he saw two brothers—Simon, also called Peter, and Andrew—throwing a net into the water, for they fished for a living. ¹⁹Jesus called out to them, "Come, follow me, and I will show you how to fish for people!" ²⁰And they left their nets at once and followed him.

²¹A little farther up the shore he saw two other brothers, James and John, sitting in a boat with their father, Zebedee, repairing their nets. And he called them to come, too. ²²They immediately followed him, leaving the boat and their father behind.

²³Jesus traveled throughout the region of Galilee, teaching in the synagogues and announcing the Good News about the Kingdom. And he healed every kind of disease and illness. ²⁴News about him spread as far as Syria, and people soon began bringing to him all who were sick. And whatever their sickness or disease, or if they were demon possessed or epileptic or paralyzed—he healed them all. ²⁵Large crowds followed him wherever he went—people from Galilee, the Ten Towns,* Jerusalem, from all over Judea, and from east of the Jordan River.

4:15-16 Isa 9:1-2 (Greek version).   4:17 Or *has come,* or *is coming soon.*   4:25 Greek *Decapolis.*

PSALM 4:1-8

For the choir director: A psalm of David, to be accompanied by stringed instruments.

¹ **A**nswer me when I call to you,
   O God who declares me innocent.
   Free me from my troubles.
   Have mercy on me and hear my prayer.

² How long will you people ruin my reputation?
   How long will you make groundless accusations?

How long will you continue your
lies?   *Interlude*
³ You can be sure of this:
  The LORD set apart the godly for
    himself.
  The LORD will answer when I call
    to him.

⁴ Don't sin by letting anger control you.
  Think about it overnight and
    remain silent.   *Interlude*
⁵ Offer sacrifices in the right spirit,
  and trust the LORD.

⁶ Many people say, "Who will show
    us better times?"
  Let your face smile on us, LORD.
⁷ You have given me greater joy

than those who have abundant
  harvests of grain and new wine.
⁸ In peace I will lie down and sleep,
  for you alone, O LORD, will keep
    me safe.

PROVERBS 1:20-23

Wisdom shouts in the streets. She cries
out in the public square. She calls to the
crowds along the main street, to those
gathered in front of the city gate: "How
long, you simpletons, will you insist on
being simpleminded? How long will you
mockers relish your mocking? How long
will you fools hate knowledge? Come and
listen to my counsel. I'll share my heart
with you and make you wise."

JANUARY5

GENESIS 11:1-13:4

At the outset of today's reading, humanity is still
challenging God rather than worshiping him. After
the judgment at the tower of Babel—the event
which led to the diversity of human languages and
cultures—God chose Abram to go to a new land and
build a new nation that would worship and follow
him alone.

At one time all the people of the world
spoke the same language and used the
same words. ²As the people migrated to
the east, they found a plain in the land of
Babylonia* and settled there.

³They began saying to each other, "Let's
make bricks and harden them with fire."
(In this region bricks were used instead of
stone, and tar was used for mortar.) ⁴Then
they said, "Come, let's build a great city for
ourselves with a tower that reaches into
the sky. This will make us famous and
keep us from being scattered all over the
world."

⁵But the LORD came down to look at
the city and the tower the people were
building. ⁶"Look!" he said. "The people
are united, and they all speak the same
language. After this, nothing they set out
to do will be impossible for them! ⁷Come,

let's go down and confuse the people with
different languages. Then they won't be
able to understand each other."

⁸In that way, the LORD scattered them
all over the world, and they stopped building the city. ⁹That is why the city was
called Babel,* because that is where the
LORD confused the people with different
languages. In this way he scattered them
all over the world.

¹⁰This is the account of Shem's family.

Two years after the great flood, when
  Shem was 100 years old, he became
  the father of* Arphaxad. ¹¹After the
  birth of* Arphaxad, Shem lived
  another 500 years and had other sons
  and daughters.
¹²When Arphaxad was 35 years old, he
  became the father of Shelah. ¹³After
  the birth of Shelah, Arphaxad lived
  another 403 years and had other sons
  and daughters.*
¹⁴When Shelah was 30 years old, he
  became the father of Eber. ¹⁵After
  the birth of Eber, Shelah lived another
  403 years and had other sons and
  daughters.

[16]When Eber was 34 years old, he became the father of Peleg. [17]After the birth of Peleg, Eber lived another 430 years and had other sons and daughters.

[18]When Peleg was 30 years old, he became the father of Reu. [19]After the birth of Reu, Peleg lived another 209 years and had other sons and daughters.

[20]When Reu was 32 years old, he became the father of Serug. [21]After the birth of Serug, Reu lived another 207 years and had other sons and daughters.

[22]When Serug was 30 years old, he became the father of Nahor. [23]After the birth of Nahor, Serug lived another 200 years and had other sons and daughters.

[24]When Nahor was 29 years old, he became the father of Terah. [25]After the birth of Terah, Nahor lived another 119 years and had other sons and daughters.

[26]When Terah was 70 years old, he had become the father of Abram, Nahor, and Haran.

[27]This is the account of Terah's family. Terah was the father of Abram, Nahor, and Haran; and Haran was the father of Lot. [28]But Haran died in Ur of the Chaldeans, the land of his birth, while his father, Terah, was still living. [29]Meanwhile, Abram and Nahor both married. The name of Abram's wife was Sarai, and the name of Nahor's wife was Milcah. (Milcah and her sister Iscah were daughters of Nahor's brother Haran.) [30]But Sarai was unable to become pregnant and had no children.

[31]One day Terah took his son Abram, his daughter-in-law Sarai (his son Abram's wife), and his grandson Lot (his son Haran's child) and moved away from Ur of the Chaldeans. He was headed for the land of Canaan, but they stopped at Haran and settled there. [32]Terah lived for 205 years* and died while still in Haran.

[12:1]THE LORD had said to Abram, "Leave your native country, your relatives, and your father's family, and go to the land that I will show you. [2]I will make you into a great nation. I will bless you and make you famous, and you will be a blessing to others. [3]I will bless those who bless you and curse those who treat you with contempt. All the families on earth will be blessed through you."

[4]So Abram departed as the LORD had instructed, and Lot went with him. Abram was seventy-five years old when he left Haran. [5]He took his wife, Sarai, his nephew Lot, and all his wealth—his livestock and all the people he had taken into his household at Haran—and headed for the land of Canaan. When they arrived in Canaan, [6]Abram traveled through the land as far as Shechem. There he set up camp beside the oak of Moreh. At that time, the area was inhabited by Canaanites.

[7]Then the LORD appeared to Abram and said, "I will give this land to your descendants.*" And Abram built an altar there and dedicated it to the LORD, who had appeared to him. [8]After that, Abram traveled south and set up camp in the hill country, with Bethel to the west and Ai to the east. There he built another altar and dedicated it to the LORD, and he worshiped the LORD. [9]Then Abram continued traveling south by stages toward the Negev.

[10]At that time a severe famine struck the land of Canaan, forcing Abram to go down to Egypt, where he lived as a foreigner. [11]As he was approaching the border of Egypt, Abram said to his wife, Sarai, "Look, you are a very beautiful woman. [12]When the Egyptians see you, they will say, 'This is his wife. Let's kill him; then we can have her!' [13]So please tell them you are my sister. Then they will spare my life and treat me well because of their interest in you."

[14]And sure enough, when Abram arrived in Egypt, everyone spoke of Sarai's beauty. [15]When the palace officials saw her, they sang her praises to Pharaoh, their king, and Sarai was taken into his palace. [16]Then Pharaoh gave Abram many gifts because of her—sheep, goats, cattle, male and female donkeys, male and female servants, and camels.

[17]But the LORD sent terrible plagues upon Pharaoh and his household because of Sarai, Abram's wife. [18]So Pharaoh summoned Abram and accused him

sharply. "What have you done to me?" he demanded. "Why didn't you tell me she was your wife? ¹⁹Why did you say, 'She is my sister,' and allow me to take her as my wife? Now then, here is your wife. Take her and get out of here!" ²⁰Pharaoh ordered some of his men to escort them, and he sent Abram out of the country, along with his wife and all his possessions.

13:1 So Abram left Egypt and traveled north into the Negev, along with his wife and Lot and all that they owned. ²(Abram was very rich in livestock, silver, and gold.) ³From the Negev, they continued traveling by stages toward Bethel, and they pitched their tents between Bethel and Ai, where they had camped before. ⁴This was the same place where Abram had built the altar, and there he worshiped the LORD again.

11:2 Hebrew *Shinar.*   **11:9** Or *Babylon. Babel* sounds like a Hebrew term that means "confusion."   **11:10** Or *the ancestor of;* also in 11:12, 14, 16, 18, 20, 22, 24.   **11:11** Or *the birth of this ancestor of;* also in 11:13, 15, 17, 19, 21, 23, 25.   **11:12-13** Greek version reads ¹²*When Arphaxad was 135 years old, he became the father of Cainan.* ¹³*After the birth of Cainan, Arphaxad lived another 430 years and had other sons and daughters, and then he died. When Cainan was 130 years old, he became the father of Shelah. After the birth of Shelah, Cainan lived another 330 years and had other sons and daughters, and then he died.* Compare Luke 3:35-36.   **11:32** Some ancient versions read *145 years;* compare 11:26 and 12:4.   **12:7** Hebrew *seed.*

MATTHEW 5:1-26
Jesus began his well-known Sermon on the Mount by showing the distinction between God's values and ours. His words remind us that God holds his people to a higher standard of living—the standard of heart obedience.

One day as he saw the crowds gathering, Jesus went up on the mountainside and sat down. His disciples gathered around him, ²and he began to teach them.

³ "God blesses those who are poor and
     realize their need for him,*
   for the Kingdom of Heaven is theirs.
⁴ God blesses those who mourn,
   for they will be comforted.
⁵ God blesses those who are humble,
   for they will inherit the whole earth.
⁶ God blesses those who hunger and
     thirst for justice,*
   for they will be satisfied.
⁷ God blesses those who are merciful,
   for they will be shown mercy.
⁸ God blesses those whose hearts are pure,
   for they will see God.
⁹ God blesses those who work for peace,
   for they will be called the children
     of God.
¹⁰ God blesses those who are persecuted
     for doing right,
   for the Kingdom of Heaven is theirs.

HOW WE LIVE

Following Jesus

MATTHEW 5:11-12 Every believer is called not only to believe in Jesus but to follow him as a disciple. A disciple is someone who lives in complete devotion to him and his teachings. That level of dedication is within every believer's reach, but it isn't necessarily easy. It requires a certain amount of discipline and sacrifice.   • In Matthew 5:11-12, Jesus tells his disciples to be happy when others mistreat them because they are his disciples. Why? Because there awaits a great reward in heaven. God does not forget about the hardships we sometimes face in this world because of loving and following him.   •The sacrifices you make as a follower of Jesus may be as small as spending more of your time in God's Word or devoting a greater amount of your income to supporting a ministry. In some places in the world, people give their very lives in order to be Jesus' disciples. Ask God to show you ways in which you can serve him. What God asks of you may look very different from what he asks of others. In whatever way he calls you, remember that you are the salt of the earth and the light of the world. What an awesome privilege!

11"God blesses you when people mock you and persecute you and lie about you* and say all sorts of evil things against you because you are my followers. 12Be happy about it! Be very glad! For a great reward awaits you in heaven. And remember, the ancient prophets were persecuted in the same way.

13"You are the salt of the earth. But what good is salt if it has lost its flavor? Can you make it salty again? It will be thrown out and trampled underfoot as worthless.

14"You are the light of the world—like a city on a hilltop that cannot be hidden. 15No one lights a lamp and then puts it under a basket. Instead, a lamp is placed on a stand, where it gives light to everyone in the house. 16In the same way, let your good deeds shine out for all to see, so that everyone will praise your heavenly Father.

17"Don't misunderstand why I have come. I did not come to abolish the law of Moses or the writings of the prophets. No, I came to accomplish their purpose. 18I tell you the truth, until heaven and earth disappear, not even the smallest detail of God's law will disappear until its purpose is achieved. 19So if you ignore the least commandment and teach others to do the same, you will be called the least in the Kingdom of Heaven. But anyone who obeys God's laws and teaches them will be called great in the Kingdom of Heaven.

20"But I warn you—unless your righteousness is better than the righteousness of the teachers of religious law and the Pharisees, you will never enter the Kingdom of Heaven!

21"You have heard that our ancestors were told, 'You must not murder. If you commit murder, you are subject to judgment.'* 22But I say, if you are even angry with someone,* you are subject to judgment! If you call someone an idiot,* you are in danger of being brought before the court. And if you curse someone,* you are in danger of the fires of hell.*

23"So if you are presenting a sacrifice* at the altar in the Temple and you suddenly remember that someone has something against you, 24leave your sacrifice there at the altar. Go and be reconciled to that person. Then come and offer your sacrifice to God.

25"When you are on the way to court with your adversary, settle your differences quickly. Otherwise, your accuser may hand you over to the judge, who will hand you over to an officer, and you will be thrown into prison. 26And if that happens, you surely won't be free again until you have paid the last penny.*"

5:3 Greek *poor in spirit.*   5:6 Or *for righteousness.*
5:11 Some manuscripts omit *and lie about you.*   5:21 Exod
20:13; Deut 5:17.   5:22a Some manuscripts add *without
cause.*   5:22b Greek uses an Aramaic term of contempt: *If you
say to your brother, 'Raca.'*   5:22c Greek *if you say, 'You fool.'*
5:22d Greek *Gehenna;* also in 5:29, 30.   5:23 Greek *gift;* also
in 5:24.   5:26 Greek *the last kodrantes* [i.e., quadrans].

PSALM 5:1-12
*For the choir director: A psalm of David,
to be accompanied by the flute.*

1 O LORD, hear me as I pray;
    pay attention to my groaning.
2 Listen to my cry for help, my King and
        my God,
    for I pray to no one but you.
3 Listen to my voice in the morning, LORD.
    Each morning I bring my requests
        to you and wait expectantly.

4 O God, you take no pleasure in
        wickedness;
    you cannot tolerate the sins of the
        wicked.
5 Therefore, the proud may not stand
        in your presence,
    for you hate all who do evil.
6 You will destroy those who tell lies.
    The LORD detests murderers and
        deceivers.

7 Because of your unfailing love, I can
        enter your house;
    I will worship at your Temple with
        deepest awe.
8 Lead me in the right path, O LORD,
    or my enemies will conquer me.
    Make your way plain for me to follow.

9 My enemies cannot speak a truthful
        word.
    Their deepest desire is to destroy
        others.
    Their talk is foul, like the stench from
        an open grave.
    Their tongues are filled with flattery.*

¹⁰ O God, declare them guilty.
  Let them be caught in their own
    traps.
Drive them away because of their
    many sins,
  for they have rebelled against you.

¹¹ But let all who take refuge in you rejoice;
  let them sing joyful praises forever.
Spread your protection over them,
  that all who love your name may be
    filled with joy.
¹² For you bless the godly, O LORD;
  you surround them with your shield
    of love.

5:9 Greek version reads *with lies.* Compare Rom 3:12.

GENESIS 13:5–15:21

*Abram and his family arrived in the land God had
promised to give to him and his descendants.
Abram began to grow in wealth and status, but his
wife, Sarai, was still unable to have a child. So God
came to Abram again and solidified his promise to
give him many descendants.*

Lot, who was traveling with Abram, had
also become very wealthy with flocks of
sheep and goats, herds of cattle, and
many tents. ⁶But the land could not support both Abram and Lot with all their
flocks and herds living so close together.
⁷So disputes broke out between the
herdsmen of Abram and Lot. (At that time
Canaanites and Perizzites were also living
in the land.)

⁸Finally Abram said to Lot, "Let's not
allow this conflict to come between us or
our herdsmen. After all, we are close
relatives! ⁹The whole countryside is
open to you. Take your choice of any section of the land you want, and we will
separate. If you want the land to the left,
then I'll take the land on the right. If you
prefer the land on the right, then I'll go to
the left."

¹⁰Lot took a long look at the fertile
plains of the Jordan Valley in the direc-

PROVERBS 1:24-28

"**I** [Wisdom] called you so often, but you
wouldn't come. I reached out to you, but
you paid no attention. You ignored my
advice and rejected the correction I offered. So I will laugh when you are in
trouble! I will mock you when disaster
overtakes you—when calamity overtakes
you like a storm, when disaster engulfs
you like a cyclone, and anguish and distress overwhelm you. ☐ "When they cry
for help, I will not answer. Though they
anxiously search for me, they will not
find me."

tion of Zoar. The whole area was well
watered everywhere, like the garden of
the LORD or the beautiful land of Egypt.
(This was before the LORD destroyed
Sodom and Gomorrah.) ¹¹Lot chose for
himself the whole Jordan Valley to the
east of them. He went there with his
flocks and servants and parted company
with his uncle Abram. ¹²So Abram settled in the land of Canaan, and Lot moved
his tents to a place near Sodom and settled among the cities of the plain. ¹³But
the people of this area were extremely
wicked and constantly sinned against the
LORD.

¹⁴After Lot had gone, the LORD said to
Abram, "Look as far as you can see in every
direction—north and south, east and west.
¹⁵I am giving all this land, as far as you can
see, to you and your descendants* as a permanent possession. ¹⁶And I will give you
so many descendants that, like the dust of
the earth, they cannot be counted! ¹⁷Go
and walk through the land in every direction, for I am giving it to you."

¹⁸So Abram moved his camp to Hebron
and settled near the oak grove belonging
to Mamre. There he built another altar to
the LORD.

¹⁴:¹ABOUT this time war broke out in the region. King Amraphel of Babylonia,* King Arioch of Ellasar, King Kedorlaomer of Elam, and King Tidal of Goiim ²fought against King Bera of Sodom, King Birsha of Gomorrah, King Shinab of Admah, King Shemeber of Zeboiim, and the king of Bela (also called Zoar).

³This second group of kings joined forces in Siddim Valley (that is, the valley of the Dead Sea*). ⁴For twelve years they had been subject to King Kedorlaomer, but in the thirteenth year they rebelled against him.

⁵One year later Kedorlaomer and his allies arrived and defeated the Rephaites at Ashteroth-karnaim, the Zuzites at Ham, the Emites at Shaveh-kiriathaim, ⁶and the Horites at Mount Seir, as far as El-paran at the edge of the wilderness. ⁷Then they turned back and came to En-mishpat (now called Kadesh) and conquered all the territory of the Amalekites, and also the Amorites living in Hazazon-tamar.

⁸Then the rebel kings of Sodom, Gomorrah, Admah, Zeboiim, and Bela (also called Zoar) prepared for battle in the valley of the Dead Sea.* ⁹They fought against King Kedorlaomer of Elam, King Tidal of Goiim, King Amraphel of Babylonia, and King Arioch of Ellasar—four kings against five. ¹⁰As it happened, the valley of the Dead Sea was filled with tar pits. And as the army of the kings of Sodom and Gomorrah fled, some fell into the tar pits, while the rest escaped into the mountains. ¹¹The victorious invaders then plundered Sodom and Gomorrah and headed for home, taking with them all the spoils of war and the food supplies. ¹²They also captured Lot— Abram's nephew who lived in Sodom—and carried off everything he owned.

¹³But one of Lot's men escaped and reported everything to Abram the Hebrew, who was living near the oak grove belonging to Mamre the Amorite. Mamre and his relatives, Eshcol and Aner, were Abram's allies.

¹⁴When Abram heard that his nephew Lot had been captured, he mobilized the 318 trained men who had been born into his household. Then he pursued

Kedorlaomer's army until he caught up with them at Dan. ¹⁵There he divided his men and attacked during the night. Kedorlaomer's army fled, but Abram chased them as far as Hobah, north of Damascus. ¹⁶Abram recovered all the goods that had been taken, and he brought back his nephew Lot with his possessions and all the women and other captives.

¹⁷After Abram returned from his victory over Kedorlaomer and all his allies, the king of Sodom went out to meet him in the valley of Shaveh (that is, the King's Valley).

¹⁸And Melchizedek, the king of Salem and a priest of God Most High,* brought Abram some bread and wine. ¹⁹Melchizedek blessed Abram with this blessing:

"Blessed be Abram by God
    Most High,
    Creator of heaven and earth.
²⁰ And blessed be God Most High,
    who has defeated your enemies
    for you."

Then Abram gave Melchizedek a tenth of all the goods he had recovered.

²¹The king of Sodom said to Abram, "Give back my people who were captured. But you may keep for yourself all the goods you have recovered."

²²Abram replied to the king of Sodom, "I solemnly swear to the LORD, God Most High, Creator of heaven and earth, ²³that I will not take so much as a single thread or sandal thong from what belongs to you. Otherwise you might say, 'I am the one who made Abram rich.' ²⁴I will accept only what my young warriors have already eaten, and I request that you give a fair share of the goods to my allies—Aner, Eshcol, and Mamre."

¹⁵:¹SOME time later, the LORD spoke to Abram in a vision and said to him, "Do not be afraid, Abram, for I will protect you, and your reward will be great."

²But Abram replied, "O Sovereign LORD, what good are all your blessings when I don't even have a son? Since you've given me no children, Eliezer of Damascus, a servant in my household, will inherit all my wealth. ³You have given

me no descendants of my own, so one of my servants will be my heir."

⁴Then the LORD said to him, "No, your servant will not be your heir, for you will have a son of your own who will be your heir." ⁵Then the LORD took Abram outside and said to him, "Look up into the sky and count the stars if you can. That's how many descendants you will have!"

⁶And Abram believed the LORD, and the LORD counted him as righteous because of his faith.

⁷Then the LORD told him, "I am the LORD who brought you out of Ur of the Chaldeans to give you this land as your possession."

⁸But Abram replied, "O Sovereign LORD, how can I be sure that I will actually possess it?"

⁹The LORD told him, "Bring me a three-year-old heifer, a three-year-old female goat, a three-year-old ram, a turtledove, and a young pigeon." ¹⁰So Abram presented all these to him and killed them. Then he cut each animal down the middle and laid the halves side by side; he did not, however, cut the birds in half. ¹¹Some vultures swooped down to eat the carcasses, but Abram chased them away.

¹²As the sun was going down, Abram fell into a deep sleep, and a terrifying darkness came down over him. ¹³Then the LORD said to Abram, "You can be sure that your descendants will be strangers in a foreign land, where they will be oppressed as slaves for 400 years. ¹⁴But I will punish the nation that enslaves them, and in the end they will come away with great wealth. ¹⁵(As for you, you will die in peace and be buried at a ripe old age.) ¹⁶After four generations your descendants will return here to this land, for the sins of the Amorites do not yet warrant their destruction."

¹⁷After the sun went down and darkness fell, Abram saw a smoking firepot and a flaming torch pass between the halves of the carcasses. ¹⁸So the LORD made a covenant with Abram that day and said, "I have given this land to your descendants, all the way from the border of Egypt* to the great Euphrates River— ¹⁹the land now occupied by the Kenites, Kenizzites, Kadmonites, ²⁰Hittites, Perizzites, Rephaites, ²¹Amorites, Canaanites, Girgashites, and Jebusites."

13:15 Hebrew *seed;* also in 13:16.   **14:1** Hebrew *Shinar;* also in 14:9.   **14:3** Hebrew *Salt Sea.*   **14:8** Hebrew *Siddim Valley* (see 14:3); also in 14:10.   **14:18** Hebrew *El-Elyon;* also in 14:19, 20, 22.   **15:18** Hebrew *the river of Egypt,* referring either to an eastern branch of the Nile River or to the Brook of Egypt in the Sinai (see Num 34:5).

WHAT THE BIBLE SAYS

Salvation and forgiveness

MATTHEW 5:43-45 Jesus teaches that we must love our enemies and pray for them. He's not talking so much about a feeling as he is about a decision. By praying for your enemies, you are extending to them the same love Christ has for you. That still doesn't make it easy, however. True forgiveness is impossible without the help of the Holy Spirit. We all fall short in the area of forgiveness in one way or another, but take heart. The Bible is full of examples of the divine nature of forgiveness: God's Spirit kept David from taking advantage of an opportunity to kill King Saul, a man who sought to murder David (1 Samuel 24, May 19); God's Spirit allowed Stephen to pray for the very people who were stoning him to death (Acts 7:59-60, June 11). The ultimate act of forgiveness was modeled by Jesus. While nailed to the cross, Jesus prayed, "Father, forgive them, for they don't know what they are doing" (Luke 23:34, April 27). • As a believer, you have God's Spirit within you. He will enable you to love, pray for, and forgive even those who hate or hurt you.

MATTHEW 5:27-48

Jesus' Sermon on the Mount calls us to go beyond what the world considers normal and right and to love others proactively. By being kind, even to those who are unkind, we manifest God's presence in the world.

"**Y**ou have heard the commandment that says, 'You must not commit adultery.'* [28]But I say, anyone who even looks at a woman with lust has already committed adultery with her in his heart. [29]So if your eye—even your good eye*—causes you to lust, gouge it out and throw it away. It is better for you to lose one part of your body than for your whole body to be thrown into hell. [30]And if your hand—even your stronger hand*—causes you to sin, cut it off and throw it away. It is better for you to lose one part of your body than for your whole body to be thrown into hell.

[31]"You have heard the law that says, 'A man can divorce his wife by merely giving her a written notice of divorce.'* [32]But I say that a man who divorces his wife, unless she has been unfaithful, causes her to commit adultery. And anyone who marries a divorced woman also commits adultery.

[33]"You have also heard that our ancestors were told, 'You must not break your vows; you must carry out the vows you make to the LORD.'* [34]But I say, do not make any vows! Do not say, 'By heaven!' because heaven is God's throne. [35]And do not say, 'By the earth!' because the earth is his footstool. And do not say, 'By Jerusalem!' for Jerusalem is the city of the great King. [36]Do not even say, 'By my head!' for you can't turn one hair white or black. [37]Just say a simple, 'Yes, I will,' or 'No, I won't.' Anything beyond this is from the evil one.

[38]"You have heard the law that says the punishment must match the injury: 'An eye for an eye, and a tooth for a tooth.'* [39]But I say, do not resist an evil person! If someone slaps you on the right cheek, offer the other cheek also. [40]If you are sued in court and your shirt is taken from you, give your coat, too. [41]If a soldier demands that you carry his gear for a mile,* carry it two miles. [42]Give to those who ask, and don't turn away from those who want to borrow.

[43]"You have heard the law that says, 'Love your neighbor'* and hate your enemy. [44]But I say, love your enemies!* Pray for those who persecute you! [45]In that way, you will be acting as true children of your Father in heaven. For he gives his sunlight to both the evil and the good, and he sends rain on the just and the unjust alike. [46]If you love only those who love you, what reward is there for that? Even corrupt tax collectors do that much. [47]If you are kind only to your friends,* how are you different from anyone else? Even pagans do that. [48]But you are to be perfect, even as your Father in heaven is perfect."

5:27 Exod 20:14; Deut 5:18. **5:29** Greek *your right eye.* **5:30** Greek *your right hand.* **5:31** Deut 24:1. **5:33** Num 30:2. **5:38** Greek *the law that says: 'An eye for an eye and a tooth for a tooth.'* Exod 21:24; Lev 24:20; Deut 19:21. **5:41** Greek *milion* [4,854 feet or 1,478 meters]. **5:43** Lev 19:18. **5:44** Some manuscripts add *Bless those who curse you. Do good to those who hate you.* Compare Luke 6:27-28. **5:47** Greek *your brothers.*

PSALM 6:1-10

*For the choir director: A psalm of David, to be accompanied by an eight-stringed instrument.**

[1] **O** LORD, don't rebuke me in your anger
  or discipline me in your rage.
[2] Have compassion on me, LORD, for I am weak.
  Heal me, LORD, for my bones are in agony.
[3] I am sick at heart.
  How long, O LORD, until you restore me?

[4] Return, O LORD, and rescue me.
  Save me because of your unfailing love.
[5] For the dead do not remember you.
  Who can praise you from the grave?*

[6] I am worn out from sobbing.
  All night I flood my bed with weeping,
  drenching it with my tears.
[7] My vision is blurred by grief;
  my eyes are worn out because of all my enemies.

⁸ Go away, all you who do evil,
  for the LORD has heard my
    weeping.
⁹ The LORD has heard my plea;
  the LORD will answer my prayer.
¹⁰ May all my enemies be disgraced and
    terrified.
  May they suddenly turn back in
    shame.

6:TITLE Hebrew *with stringed instruments; according to the sheminith.*   6:5 Hebrew *from Sheol?*

GENESIS 16:1–18:15

God had promised Abram and Sarai a son, but they became impatient as the years passed. They tried to meddle with God's promise and ended up with difficult consequences as a result.

Now Sarai, Abram's wife, had not been able to bear children for him. But she had an Egyptian servant named Hagar. ²So Sarai said to Abram, "The LORD has prevented me from having children. Go and sleep with my servant. Perhaps I can have children through her." And Abram agreed with Sarai's proposal. ³So Sarai, Abram's wife, took Hagar the Egyptian servant and gave her to Abram as a wife. (This happened ten years after Abram had settled in the land of Canaan.)

⁴So Abram had sexual relations with Hagar, and she became pregnant. But when Hagar knew she was pregnant, she began to treat her mistress, Sarai, with contempt. ⁵Then Sarai said to Abram, "This is all your fault! I put my servant into your arms, but now that she's pregnant she treats me with contempt. The LORD will show who's wrong—you or me!"

⁶Abram replied, "Look, she is your servant, so deal with her as you see fit." Then Sarai treated Hagar so harshly that she finally ran away.

⁷The angel of the LORD found Hagar beside a spring of water in the wilderness, along the road to Shur. ⁸The angel said to her, "Hagar, Sarai's servant, where have you come from, and where are you going?"

PROVERBS 1:29-33

"**F**or they hated knowledge and chose not to fear the LORD. They rejected my advice and paid no attention when I corrected them. Therefore, they must eat the bitter fruit of living their own way, choking on their own schemes. For simpletons turn away from me—to death. Fools are destroyed by their own complacency. But all who listen to me will live in peace, untroubled by fear of harm."

JANUARY**7**

"I'm running away from my mistress, Sarai," she replied.

⁹The angel of the LORD said to her, "Return to your mistress, and submit to her authority." ¹⁰Then he added, "I will give you more descendants than you can count."

¹¹And the angel also said, "You are now pregnant and will give birth to a son. You are to name him Ishmael (which means 'God hears'), for the LORD has heard your cry of distress. ¹²This son of yours will be a wild man, as untamed as a wild donkey! He will raise his fist against everyone, and everyone will be against him. Yes, he will live in open hostility against all his relatives."

¹³Thereafter, Hagar used another name to refer to the LORD, who had spoken to her. She said, "You are the God who sees me."* She also said, "Have I truly seen the One who sees me?" ¹⁴So that well was named Beer-lahai-roi (which means "well of the Living One who sees me"). It can still be found between Kadesh and Bered.

¹⁵So Hagar gave Abram a son, and Abram named him Ishmael. ¹⁶Abram was eighty-six years old when Ishmael was born.

^{17:1}WHEN Abram was ninety-nine years old, the LORD appeared to him and said, "I am El-Shaddai—'God Almighty.' Serve me faithfully and live a blameless life. ²I will make a covenant with you, by which

I will guarantee to give you countless descendants."

[3]At this, Abram fell face down on the ground. Then God said to him, [4]"This is my covenant with you: I will make you the father of a multitude of nations! [5]What's more, I am changing your name. It will no longer be Abram. Instead, you will be called Abraham,* for you will be the father of many nations. [6]I will make you extremely fruitful. Your descendants will become many nations, and kings will be among them!

[7]"I will confirm my covenant with you and your descendants* after you, from generation to generation. This is the everlasting covenant: I will always be your God and the God of your descendants after you. [8]And I will give the entire land of Canaan, where you now live as a foreigner, to you and your descendants. It will be their possession forever, and I will be their God."

[9]Then God said to Abraham, "Your responsibility is to obey the terms of the covenant. You and all your descendants have this continual responsibility. [10]This is the covenant that you and your descendants must keep: Each male among you must be circumcised. [11]You must cut off the flesh of your foreskin as a sign of the covenant between me and you. [12]From generation to generation, every male child must be circumcised on the eighth day after his birth. This applies not only to members of your family but also to the servants born in your household and the foreign-born servants whom you have purchased. [13]All must be circumcised. Your bodies will bear the mark of my everlasting covenant. [14]Any male who fails to be circumcised will be cut off from the covenant family for breaking the covenant."

[15]Then God said to Abraham, "Regarding Sarai, your wife—her name will no longer be Sarai. From now on her name will be Sarah.* [16]And I will bless her and give you a son from her! Yes, I will bless her richly, and she will become the mother of many nations. Kings of nations will be among her descendants."

[17]Then Abraham bowed down to the ground, but he laughed to himself in disbelief. "How could I become a father at the age of 100?" he thought. "And how can Sarah have a baby when she is ninety years old?" [18]So Abraham said to God, "May Ishmael live under your special blessing!"

[19]But God replied, "No—Sarah, your wife, will give birth to a son for you. You will name him Isaac,* and I will confirm my covenant with him and his descendants as an everlasting covenant. [20]As for Ishmael, I will bless him also, just as you have asked. I will make him extremely fruitful and multiply his descendants. He will become the father of twelve princes, and I will make him a great nation. [21]But my covenant will be confirmed with Isaac, who will be born to you and Sarah about this time next year." [22]When God had finished speaking, he left Abraham.

[23]On that very day Abraham took his son, Ishmael, and every male in his household, including those born there and those he had bought. Then he circumcised them, cutting off their foreskins, just as God had told him. [24]Abraham was ninety-nine years old when he was circumcised, [25]and Ishmael, his son, was thirteen. [26]Both Abraham and his son, Ishmael, were circumcised on that same day, [27]along with all the other men and boys of the household, whether they were born there or bought as servants. All were circumcised with him.

[18:1]THE LORD appeared again to Abraham near the oak grove belonging to Mamre. One day Abraham was sitting at the entrance to his tent during the hottest part of the day. [2]He looked up and noticed three men standing nearby. When he saw them, he ran to meet them and welcomed them, bowing low to the ground.

[3]"My lord," he said, "if it pleases you, stop here for a while. [4]Rest in the shade of this tree while water is brought to wash your feet. [5]And since you've honored your servant with this visit, let me prepare some food to refresh you before you continue on your journey."

"All right," they said. "Do as you have said."

[6]So Abraham ran back to the tent and said to Sarah, "Hurry! Get three large

measures* of your best flour, knead it into dough, and bake some bread." ⁷Then Abraham ran out to the herd and chose a tender calf and gave it to his servant, who quickly prepared it. ⁸When the food was ready, Abraham took some yogurt and milk and the roasted meat, and he served it to the men. As they ate, Abraham waited on them in the shade of the trees.

⁹"Where is Sarah, your wife?" the visitors asked.

"She's inside the tent," Abraham replied.

¹⁰Then one of them said, "I will return to you about this time next year, and your wife, Sarah, will have a son!"

Sarah was listening to this conversation from the tent. ¹¹Abraham and Sarah were both very old by this time, and Sarah was long past the age of having children. ¹²So she laughed silently to herself and said, "How could a worn-out woman like me enjoy such pleasure, especially when my master—my husband—is also so old?"

¹³Then the LORD said to Abraham, "Why did Sarah laugh? Why did she say, 'Can an old woman like me have a baby?' ¹⁴Is anything too hard for the LORD? I will return about this time next year, and Sarah will have a son."

¹⁵Sarah was afraid, so she denied it, saying, "I didn't laugh."

But the LORD said, "No, you did laugh."

16:13 Hebrew *El-roi*.   17:5 *Abram* means "exalted father"; *Abraham* sounds like a Hebrew term that means "father of many."   17:7 Hebrew *seed;* also in 17:7b, 8, 9, 10, 19.
17:15 *Sarai* and *Sarah* both mean "princess."   17:19 *Isaac* means "he laughs."   18:6 Hebrew *3 seahs,* about 15 quarts or 18 liters.

MATTHEW 6:1-24

In today's reading, Jesus exposes the futility of living merely for worldly recognition and wealth. He also gives his disciples a model prayer to guide their own personal praying to God.

"**W**atch out! Don't do your good deeds publicly, to be admired by others, for you will lose the reward from your Father in heaven. ²When you give to someone in need, don't do as the hypocrites do—blowing trumpets in the synagogues and streets to call attention to their acts of charity! I tell you the truth, they have received all the reward they will ever get. ³But when you give to someone in need, don't let your left hand know what your right hand is doing. ⁴Give your gifts in private, and your Father, who sees everything, will reward you.

⁵"When you pray, don't be like the hypocrites who love to pray publicly on street corners and in the synagogues

HOW WE LIVE

Prayer

MATTHEW 6:7-8 Some people repeat the prayer known as the Lord's Prayer (Matthew 6:9-13) over and over, as if it were an incantation that will give them whatever they ask. While Jesus does encourage us to be persistent in our prayers, we must remember that shallow repetition without sincerity will get us nowhere.   • In today's reading, Jesus provides us with a simple prayer as a model for our own prayers. This is why he said, "Pray *like* this" (Matthew 6:9). His example prayer puts the focus on God first and our own needs second. We begin by honoring God's name and anticipating his coming Kingdom. Then we ask that his will be done; that is, no matter what our following requests may be, we recognize that his will supercedes our own desires because he knows what is best for us. Next we make our requests known to God, acknowledging him as our provider. We know he will never tempt us, but we must pray for strength not to give in to temptation and to be delivered from evil influences.   • While repetition of the Lord's Prayer can be very meaningful, it is important to use it as a model prayer in which you praise him, pray for his continued work in the world, and pray for your daily needs, both physical and spiritual.

where everyone can see them. I tell you the truth, that is all the reward they will ever get. ⁶But when you pray, go away by yourself, shut the door behind you, and pray to your Father in private. Then your Father, who sees everything, will reward you.

⁷"When you pray, don't babble on and on as people of other religions do. They think their prayers are answered merely by repeating their words again and again. ⁸Don't be like them, for your Father knows exactly what you need even before you ask him! ⁹Pray like this:

Our Father in heaven,
    may your name be kept holy.
¹⁰ May your Kingdom come soon.
    May your will be done on earth,
        as it is in heaven.
¹¹ Give us today the food we need,*
¹² and forgive us our sins,
        as we have forgiven those who sin
            against us.
¹³ And don't let us yield to
        temptation,*
    but rescue us from the evil one.*

¹⁴"If you forgive those who sin against you, your heavenly Father will forgive you. ¹⁵But if you refuse to forgive others, your Father will not forgive your sins.

¹⁶"And when you fast, don't make it obvious, as the hypocrites do, for they try to look miserable and disheveled so people will admire them for their fasting. I tell you the truth, that is the only reward they will ever get. ¹⁷But when you fast, comb your hair and wash your face. ¹⁸Then no one will notice that you are fasting, except your Father, who knows what you do in private. And your Father, who sees everything, will reward you.

¹⁹"Don't store up treasures here on earth, where moths eat them and rust destroys them, and where thieves break in and steal. ²⁰Store your treasures in heaven, where moths and rust cannot destroy, and thieves do not break in and steal. ²¹Wherever your treasure is, there the desires of your heart will also be.

²²"Your eye is a lamp that provides light for your body. When your eye is good, your whole body is filled with light. ²³But when your eye is bad, your whole body is filled with darkness. And if the light you

think you have is actually darkness, how deep that darkness is!

²⁴"No one can serve two masters. For you will hate one and love the other; you will be devoted to one and despise the other. You cannot serve both God and money."

6:11 Or *Give us today our food for the day;* or *Give us today our food for tomorrow.* 6:13a Or *And keep us from being tested.* 6:13b Or *from evil.* Some manuscripts add *For yours is the kingdom and the power and the glory forever. Amen.*

PSALM 7:1-17

A psalm of David, which he sang to the LORD *concerning Cush of the tribe of Benjamin.*

¹ **I** come to you for protection, O LORD
        my God.
    Save me from my persecutors—
        rescue me!
² If you don't, they will maul me like
        a lion,
    tearing me to pieces with no one
        to rescue me.
³ O LORD my God, if I have done wrong
        or am guilty of injustice,
⁴ if I have betrayed a friend
    or plundered my enemy without
        cause,
⁵ then let my enemies capture me.
    Let them trample me into the
        ground
    and drag my honor in the dust.
                                Interlude

⁶ Arise, O LORD, in anger!
    Stand up against the fury of my
        enemies!
    Wake up, my God, and bring justice!
⁷ Gather the nations before you.
    Rule over them from on high.
⁸   The LORD judges the nations.
    Declare me righteous, O LORD,
        for I am innocent, O Most High!
⁹ End the evil of those who are wicked,
    and defend the righteous.
    For you look deep within the mind
        and heart,
    O righteous God.

¹⁰ God is my shield,
    saving those whose hearts are true
        and right.
¹¹ God is an honest judge.
    He is angry with the wicked every
        day.

¹² If a person does not repent,
    God* will sharpen his sword;
    he will bend and string his bow.
¹³ He will prepare his deadly weapons
    and shoot his flaming arrows.

¹⁴ The wicked conceive evil;
    they are pregnant with trouble
    and give birth to lies.
¹⁵ They dig a deep pit to trap others,
    then fall into it themselves.
¹⁶ The trouble they make for others
    backfires on them.
    The violence they plan falls on
    their own heads.

¹⁷ I will thank the LORD because he
    is just;

    I will sing praise to the name of the
    LORD Most High.

7:12 Hebrew *he.*

PROVERBS 2:1-5

My child,* listen to what I say, and treasure my commands. Tune your ears to
wisdom, and concentrate on understanding. Cry out for insight, and ask for
understanding. Search for them as you
would for silver; seek them like hidden
treasures. Then you will understand what
it means to fear the LORD, and you will
gain knowledge of God.

2:1 Hebrew *My son.*

JANUARY**8**

GENESIS 18:16–19:38

God confirmed Abraham's special status when he
revealed to Abraham his plans to destroy the hopelessly wicked Sodom and Gomorrah. Through Abraham's intervention, Lot was saved from the
destruction.

Then the men got up from their meal and
looked out toward Sodom. As they left,
Abraham went with them to send them on
their way.

¹⁷"Should I hide my plan from Abraham?" the LORD asked. ¹⁸"For Abraham
will certainly become a great and mighty
nation, and all the nations of the earth will
be blessed through him. ¹⁹I have singled
him out so that he will direct his sons and
their families to keep the way of the LORD
by doing what is right and just. Then I will
do for Abraham all that I have promised."

²⁰So the LORD told Abraham, "I have
heard a great outcry from Sodom and Gomorrah, because their sin is so flagrant.
²¹I am going down to see if their actions
are as wicked as I have heard. If not, I want
to know."

²²The other men turned and headed
toward Sodom, but the LORD remained
with Abraham. ²³Abraham approached

him and said, "Will you sweep away
both the righteous and the wicked?
²⁴Suppose you find fifty righteous people living there in the city—will you still
sweep it away and not spare it for their
sakes? ²⁵Surely you wouldn't do such a
thing, destroying the righteous along
with the wicked. Why, you would be
treating the righteous and the wicked
exactly the same! Surely you wouldn't do
that! Should not the Judge of all the
earth do what is right?"

²⁶And the LORD replied, "If I find fifty
righteous people in Sodom, I will spare
the entire city for their sake."

²⁷Then Abraham spoke again. "Since I
have begun, let me speak further to my
Lord, even though I am but dust and ashes.
²⁸Suppose there are only forty-five righteous people rather than fifty? Will you
destroy the whole city for lack of five?"

And the LORD said, "I will not destroy it
if I find forty-five righteous people there."

²⁹Then Abraham pressed his request
further. "Suppose there are only forty?"

And the LORD replied, "I will not destroy it for the sake of the forty."

³⁰"Please don't be angry, my Lord,"

Abraham pleaded. "Let me speak—suppose only thirty righteous people are found?"

And the LORD replied, "I will not destroy it if I find thirty."

³¹Then Abraham said, "Since I have dared to speak to the Lord, let me continue—suppose there are only twenty?"

And the LORD replied, "Then I will not destroy it for the sake of the twenty."

³²Finally, Abraham said, "Lord, please don't be angry with me if I speak one more time. Suppose only ten are found there?"

And the LORD replied, "Then I will not destroy it for the sake of the ten."

³³When the LORD had finished his conversation with Abraham, he went on his way, and Abraham returned to his tent.

¹⁹:¹THAT evening the two angels came to the entrance of the city of Sodom. Lot was sitting there, and when he saw them, he stood up to meet them. Then he welcomed them and bowed with his face to the ground. ²"My lords," he said, "come to my home to wash your feet, and be my guests for the night. You may then get up early in the morning and be on your way again."

"Oh no," they replied. "We'll just spend the night out here in the city square."

³But Lot insisted, so at last they went home with him. Lot prepared a feast for them, complete with fresh bread made without yeast, and they ate. ⁴But before they retired for the night, all the men of Sodom, young and old, came from all over the city and surrounded the house. ⁵They shouted to Lot, "Where are the men who came to spend the night with you? Bring them out to us so we can have sex with them!"

⁶So Lot stepped outside to talk to them, shutting the door behind him. ⁷"Please, my brothers," he begged, "don't do such a wicked thing. ⁸Look, I have two virgin daughters. Let me bring them out to you, and you can do with them as you wish. But please, leave these men alone, for they are my guests and are under my protection."

⁹"Stand back!" they shouted. "This fellow came to town as an outsider, and now he's acting like our judge! We'll treat you far worse than those other men!" And they lunged toward Lot to break down the door.

¹⁰But the two angels* reached out, pulled Lot into the house, and bolted the door. ¹¹Then they blinded all the men, young and old, who were at the door of the house, so they gave up trying to get inside.

¹²Meanwhile, the angels questioned Lot. "Do you have any other relatives here in the city?" they asked. "Get them out of this place—your sons-in-law, sons, daughters, or anyone else. ¹³For we are about to destroy this city completely. The outcry against this place is so great it has reached the LORD, and he has sent us to destroy it."

¹⁴So Lot rushed out to tell his daughters' fiancés, "Quick, get out of the city! The LORD is about to destroy it." But the young men thought he was only joking.

¹⁵At dawn the next morning the angels became insistent. "Hurry," they said to Lot. "Take your wife and your two daughters who are here. Get out right now, or you will be swept away in the destruction of the city!"

¹⁶When Lot still hesitated, the angels seized his hand and the hands of his wife and two daughters and rushed them to safety outside the city, for the LORD was merciful. ¹⁷When they were safely out of the city, one of the angels ordered, "Run for your lives! And don't look back or stop anywhere in the valley! Escape to the mountains, or you will be swept away!"

¹⁸"Oh no, my lord!" Lot begged. ¹⁹"You have been so gracious to me and saved my life, and you have shown such great kindness. But I cannot go to the mountains. Disaster would catch up to me there, and I would soon die. ²⁰See, there is a small village nearby. Please let me go there instead; don't you see how small it is? Then my life will be saved."

²¹"All right," the angel said, "I will grant your request. I will not destroy the little village. ²²But hurry! Escape to it, for I can do nothing until you arrive there." (This

explains why that village was known as Zoar, which means "little place.")

²³Lot reached the village just as the sun was rising over the horizon. ²⁴Then the LORD rained down fire and burning sulfur from the sky on Sodom and Gomorrah. ²⁵He utterly destroyed them, along with the other cities and villages of the plain, wiping out all the people and every bit of vegetation. ²⁶But Lot's wife looked back as she was following behind him, and she turned into a pillar of salt.

²⁷Abraham got up early that morning and hurried out to the place where he had stood in the LORD's presence. ²⁸He looked out across the plain toward Sodom and Gomorrah and watched as columns of smoke rose from the cities like smoke from a furnace.

²⁹But God had listened to Abraham's request and kept Lot safe, removing him from the disaster that engulfed the cities on the plain.

³⁰Afterward Lot left Zoar because he was afraid of the people there, and he went to live in a cave in the mountains with his two daughters. ³¹One day the older daughter said to her sister, "There are no men left anywhere in this entire area, so we can't get married like everyone else. And our father will soon be too old to have children. ³²Come, let's get him drunk with wine, and then we will have sex with him. That way we will preserve our family line through our father."

³³So that night they got him drunk with wine, and the older daughter went in and had intercourse with her father. He was unaware of her lying down or getting up again.

³⁴The next morning the older daughter said to her younger sister, "I had sex with our father last night. Let's get him drunk with wine again tonight, and you go in and have sex with him. That way we will preserve our family line through our father." ³⁵So that night they got him drunk with wine again, and the younger daughter went in and had intercourse with him. As before, he was unaware of her lying down or getting up again.

³⁶As a result, both of Lot's daughters became pregnant by their own father. ³⁷When the older daughter gave birth to a son, she named him Moab.* He became the ancestor of the nation now known as the Moabites. ³⁸When the younger daughter gave birth to a son, she named him Ben-ammi.* He became the ancestor of the nation now known as the Ammonites.

19:10 Hebrew *men;* also in 19:12, 16.   **19:37** *Moab* sounds like a Hebrew term that means "from father."
19:38 *Ben-ammi* means "son of my kinsman."

HOW WE LIVE

Seeking God's will

GENESIS 18:17-19 Have you ever wondered what is in store for you regarding a spouse, family, job, or where you will live? The world will tell you that whatever happens is fate, chance, or perhaps the results of "karma." The Bible says clearly that God is in control and has a plan for your life. •In today's reading in Genesis, the Lord revealed his will to Abraham. He decided to tell Abraham what would happen to Sodom and Gomorrah so that Abraham might use the lessons learned to teach his own descendants about obedience to God. Abraham attempted to change God's mind, but through God's kindness and patience, Abraham understood God's will. •Asking for God's will to be done in your life means that you want him to direct you, and that you will be willing to follow those directions. God isn't trying to hide his will; he *wants* to show you! In the end, finding God's will comes down to obeying what you read in God's Word. As you walk obediently, God will guide you step by step.

MATTHEW 6:25–7:14

Jesus challenged his listeners to trust God in a variety of ways. Do you trust God to care for your needs? Do you trust him to be a fair judge? Do you trust him to be a good Father? Do you trust him to show the way of eternal life?

"That is why I tell you not to worry about everyday life—whether you have enough food and drink, or enough clothes to wear. Isn't life more than food, and your body more than clothing? ²⁶Look at the birds. They don't plant or harvest or store food in barns, for your heavenly Father feeds them. And aren't you far more valuable to him than they are? ²⁷Can all your worries add a single moment to your life?

²⁸"And why worry about your clothing? Look at the lilies of the field and how they grow. They don't work or make their clothing, ²⁹yet Solomon in all his glory was not dressed as beautifully as they are. ³⁰And if God cares so wonderfully for wildflowers that are here today and thrown into the fire tomorrow, he will certainly care for you. Why do you have so little faith?

³¹"So don't worry about these things, saying, 'What will we eat? What will we drink? What will we wear?' ³²These things dominate the thoughts of unbelievers, but your heavenly Father already knows all your needs. ³³Seek the Kingdom of God* above all else, and live righteously, and he will give you everything you need.

³⁴"So don't worry about tomorrow, for tomorrow will bring its own worries. Today's trouble is enough for today.

7:1"Do not judge others, and you will not be judged. ²For you will be treated as you treat others.* The standard you use in judging is the standard by which you will be judged.*

³"And why worry about a speck in your friend's eye* when you have a log in your own? ⁴How can you think of saying to your friend,* 'Let me help you get rid of that speck in your eye,' when you can't see past the log in your own eye? ⁵Hypocrite! First get rid of the log in your own eye; then you will see well enough to deal with the speck in your friend's eye.

⁶"Don't waste what is holy on people who are unholy.* Don't throw your pearls to pigs! They will trample the pearls, then turn and attack you.

⁷"Keep on asking, and you will receive what you ask for. Keep on seeking, and you will find. Keep on knocking, and the door will be opened to you. ⁸For everyone who asks, receives. Everyone who seeks, finds. And to everyone who knocks, the door will be opened.

⁹"You parents—if your children ask for a loaf of bread, do you give them a stone instead? ¹⁰Or if they ask for a fish, do you give them a snake? Of course not! ¹¹So if you sinful people know how to give good gifts to your children, how much more will your heavenly Father give good gifts to those who ask him.

¹²"Do to others whatever you would like them to do to you. This is the essence of all that is taught in the law and the prophets.

¹³"You can enter God's Kingdom only through the narrow gate. The highway to hell* is broad, and its gate is wide for the many who choose that way. ¹⁴But the gateway to life is very narrow and the road is difficult, and only a few ever find it."

6:33 Some manuscripts do not include *of God.* 7:2a Or *For God will judge you as you judge others.* 7:2b Or *The measure you give will be the measure you get back.* 7:3 Greek *your brother's eye;* also in 7:5. 7:4 Greek *your brother.* 7:6 Greek *Don't give the sacred to dogs.* 7:13 Greek *The road that leads to destruction.*

PSALM 8:1–9

*For the choir director: A psalm of David, to be accompanied by a stringed instrument.**

¹ **O** LORD, our Lord, your majestic name
    fills the earth!
  Your glory is higher than the
    heavens.
² You have taught children and infants
    to tell of your strength,*
  silencing your enemies
    and all who oppose you.

³ When I look at the night sky and see
    the work of your fingers—
  the moon and the stars you set
    in place—
⁴ what are mere mortals that you should
    think about them,
  human beings that you should care
    for them?*

⁵ Yet you made them only a little lower
    than God*
    and crowned them* with glory and
    honor.
⁶ You gave them charge of everything
    you made,
    putting all things under their
    authority—
⁷ the flocks and the herds
    and all the wild animals,
⁸ the birds in the sky, the fish in the sea,
    and everything that swims the
    ocean currents.

⁹ O Lord, our Lord, your majestic name
    fills the earth!

8:TITLE Hebrew *according to the gittith.*   8:2 Greek version
reads *to give you praise.* Compare Matt 21:16.   8:4 Hebrew
*what is man that you should think of him, / the son of man
that you should care for him?*   8:5a Or *Yet you made them
only a little lower than the angels;* Hebrew reads *Yet you
made him* [i.e., man] *a little lower than Elohim.*
8:5b Hebrew *him* [i.e., man]; similarly in 8:6.

GENESIS 20:1–22:24
Abraham's trust in God was tested repeatedly—and
he didn't always pass the test with flying colors (as
the incidents with Hagar and here with Abimelech
reveal). Then came the ultimate test recorded in
your reading today. Read how Abraham responded.

Abraham moved south to the Negev and
lived for a while between Kadesh and
Shur, and then he moved on to Gerar.
While living there as a foreigner, ²Abra-
ham introduced his wife, Sarah, by saying,
"She is my sister." So King Abimelech of
Gerar sent for Sarah and had her brought
to him at his palace.

³But that night God came to Abimelech
in a dream and told him, "You are a dead
man, for that woman you have taken is already married!"

⁴But Abimelech had not slept with her
yet, so he said, "Lord, will you destroy an
innocent nation? ⁵Didn't Abraham tell me,
'She is my sister'? And she herself said,
'Yes, he is my brother.' I acted in complete
innocence! My hands are clean."

⁶In the dream God responded, "Yes, I

PROVERBS 2:6-15
For the Lord grants wisdom! From his
mouth come knowledge and understanding. He grants a treasure of common sense to the honest. He is a shield to
those who walk with integrity. He guards
the paths of the just and protects those
who are faithful to him. □ Then you will
understand what is right, just, and fair,
and you will find the right way to go. For
wisdom will enter your heart, and knowledge will fill you with joy. Wise choices
will watch over you. Understanding will
keep you safe. □ Wisdom will save you
from evil people, from those whose
words are twisted. These men turn from
the right way to walk down dark paths.
They take pleasure in doing wrong, and
they enjoy the twisted ways of evil. Their
actions are crooked, and their ways are
wrong.

JANUARY**9**

know you are innocent. That's why I kept
you from sinning against me, and why I
did not let you touch her. ⁷Now return the
woman to her husband, and he will pray
for you, for he is a prophet. Then you will
live. But if you don't return her to him, you
can be sure that you and all your people
will die."

⁸Abimelech got up early the next morning and quickly called all his servants together. When he told them what had
happened, his men were terrified. ⁹Then
Abimelech called for Abraham. "What
have you done to us?" he demanded.
"What crime have I committed that deserves treatment like this, making me and
my kingdom guilty of this great sin? No
one should ever do what you have done!
¹⁰Whatever possessed you to do such a
thing?"

¹¹Abraham replied, "I thought, 'This is a
godless place. They will want my wife and
will kill me to get her.' ¹²And she really is
my sister, for we both have the same father,

but different mothers. And I married her.
[13] When God called me to leave my father's home and to travel from place to place, I told her, 'Do me a favor. Wherever we go, tell the people that I am your brother.'"

[14] Then Abimelech took some of his sheep and goats, cattle, and male and female servants, and he presented them to Abraham. He also returned his wife, Sarah, to him. [15] Then Abimelech said, "Look over my land and choose any place where you would like to live." [16] And he said to Sarah, "Look, I am giving your 'brother' 1,000 pieces of silver* in the presence of all these witnesses. This is to compensate you for any wrong I may have done to you. This will settle any claim against me, and your reputation is cleared."

[17] Then Abraham prayed to God, and God healed Abimelech, his wife, and his female servants, so they could have children. [18] For the LORD had caused all the women to be infertile because of what happened with Abraham's wife, Sarah.

21:1 THE LORD kept his word and did for Sarah exactly what he had promised. [2] She became pregnant, and she gave birth to a son for Abraham in his old age. This happened at just the time God had said it would. [3] And Abraham named their son Isaac. [4] Eight days after Isaac was born, Abraham circumcised him as God had commanded. [5] Abraham was 100 years old when Isaac was born.

[6] And Sarah declared, "God has brought me laughter.* All who hear about this will laugh with me. [7] Who would have said to Abraham that Sarah would nurse a baby? Yet I have given Abraham a son in his old age!"

[8] When Isaac grew up and was about to be weaned, Abraham prepared a huge feast to celebrate the occasion. [9] But Sarah saw Ishmael—the son of Abraham and her Egyptian servant Hagar—making fun of her son, Isaac.* [10] So she turned to Abraham and demanded, "Get rid of that slave woman and her son. He is not going to share the inheritance with my son, Isaac. I won't have it!"

[11] This upset Abraham very much because Ishmael was his son. [12] But God told Abraham, "Do not be upset over the boy and your servant. Do whatever Sarah tells you, for Isaac is the son through whom your descendants will be counted. [13] But I will also make a nation of the descendants of Hagar's son because he is your son, too."

[14] So Abraham got up early the next morning, prepared food and a container of water, and strapped them on Hagar's shoulders. Then he sent her away with their son, and she wandered aimlessly in the wilderness of Beersheba.

[15] When the water was gone, she put the boy in the shade of a bush. [16] Then she went and sat down by herself about a hundred yards* away. "I don't want to watch the boy die," she said, as she burst into tears.

[17] But God heard the boy crying, and the angel of God called to Hagar from heaven, "Hagar, what's wrong? Do not be afraid! God has heard the boy crying as he lies there. [18] Go to him and comfort him, for I will make a great nation from his descendants."

[19] Then God opened Hagar's eyes, and she saw a well full of water. She quickly filled her water container and gave the boy a drink.

[20] And God was with the boy as he grew up in the wilderness. He became a skillful archer, [21] and he settled in the wilderness of Paran. His mother arranged for him to marry a woman from the land of Egypt.

[22] About this time, Abimelech came with Phicol, his army commander, to visit Abraham. "God is obviously with you, helping you in everything you do," Abimelech said. [23] "Swear to me in God's name that you will never deceive me, my children, or any of my descendants. I have been loyal to you, so now swear that you will be loyal to me and to this country where you are living as a foreigner."

[24] Abraham replied, "Yes, I swear to it!" [25] Then Abraham complained to Abimelech about a well that Abimelech's servants had taken by force from Abraham's servants.

[26] "This is the first I've heard of it," Abimelech answered. "I have no idea who is responsible. You have never complained about this before."

[27] Abraham then gave some of his sheep, goats, and cattle to Abimelech, and

they made a treaty. ²⁸But Abraham also took seven additional female lambs and set them off by themselves. ²⁹Abimelech asked, "Why have you set these seven apart from the others?"

³⁰Abraham replied, "Please accept these seven lambs to show your agreement that I dug this well." ³¹Then he named the place Beersheba (which means "well of the oath"), because that was where they had sworn the oath.

³²After making their covenant at Beersheba, Abimelech left with Phicol, the commander of his army, and they returned home to the land of the Philistines. ³³Then Abraham planted a tamarisk tree at Beersheba, and there he worshiped the LORD, the Eternal God.* ³⁴And Abraham lived as a foreigner in Philistine country for a long time.

22:1SOME time later, God tested Abraham's faith. "Abraham!" God called.

"Yes," he replied. "Here I am."

²"Take your son, your only son—yes, Isaac, whom you love so much—and go to the land of Moriah. Go and sacrifice him as a burnt offering on one of the mountains, which I will show you."

³The next morning Abraham got up early. He saddled his donkey and took two of his servants with him, along with his son, Isaac. Then he chopped wood for a fire for a burnt offering and set out for the place God had told him about. ⁴On the third day of their journey, Abraham looked up and saw the place in the distance. ⁵"Stay here with the donkey," Abraham told the servants. "The boy and I will travel a little farther. We will worship there, and then we will come right back."

⁶So Abraham placed the wood for the burnt offering on Isaac's shoulders, while he himself carried the fire and the knife. As the two of them walked on together, ⁷Isaac turned to Abraham and said, "Father?"

"Yes, my son?" Abraham replied.

"We have the fire and the wood," the boy said, "but where is the sheep for the burnt offering?"

⁸"God will provide a sheep for the burnt offering, my son," Abraham answered. And they both walked on together.

⁹When they arrived at the place where God had told him to go, Abraham built an altar and arranged the wood on it. Then he tied his son, Isaac, and laid him on the altar on top of the wood. ¹⁰And Abraham picked up the knife to kill his son as a sacrifice. ¹¹At that moment the angel of the LORD called to him from heaven, "Abraham! Abraham!"

"Yes," Abraham replied. "Here I am!"

¹²"Don't lay a hand on the boy!" the angel said. "Do not hurt him in any way, for now I know that you truly fear God. You

HOW WE LIVE — Faith and works

MATTHEW 7:21-23 Jesus sheds light on the difference between "going through the motions" of the Christian life and actually living out faith in him through obedience and prayer. Some people think they will get to heaven because they've sounded religious and lived good lives. However, on judgment day, Jesus will look at them and say, "I never knew you." On that day—the final day of reckoning when God will settle all accounts and judge sin—those who have a personal relationship with Jesus will get into heaven. Those who have tried to get by on their good works, their good reputations, or their good ideas will find themselves cast aside for all eternity.   • You can't be saved by your good works; however, the Bible makes it clear that your faith should reveal itself in good works. In other words, as a Christian, your life needs to begin to show that you are seeking to live by God's laws and principles. You cannot be perfect, and throughout your life you will inevitably make mistakes and continue to sin. However, true faith will always have a positive impact on the way you live, as you grow in your relationship with God.

have not withheld from me even your son, your only son."

¹³Then Abraham looked up and saw a ram caught by its horns in a thicket. So he took the ram and sacrificed it as a burnt offering in place of his son. ¹⁴Abraham named the place Yahweh-Yireh (which means "the LORD will provide"). To this day, people still use that name as a proverb: "On the mountain of the LORD it will be provided."

¹⁵Then the angel of the LORD called again to Abraham from heaven. ¹⁶"This is what the LORD says: Because you have obeyed me and have not withheld even your son, your only son, I swear by my own name that ¹⁷I will certainly bless you. I will multiply your descendants* beyond number, like the stars in the sky and the sand on the seashore. Your descendants will conquer the cities of their enemies. ¹⁸And through your descendants all the nations of the earth will be blessed—all because you have obeyed me."

¹⁹Then they returned to the servants and traveled back to Beersheba, where Abraham continued to live.

²⁰Soon after this, Abraham heard that Milcah, his brother Nahor's wife, had borne Nahor eight sons. ²¹The oldest was named Uz, the next oldest was Buz, followed by Kemuel (the ancestor of the Arameans), ²²Kesed, Hazo, Pildash, Jidlaph, and Bethuel. ²³(Bethuel became the father of Rebekah.) In addition to these eight sons from Milcah, ²⁴Nahor had four other children from his concubine Reumah. Their names were Tebah, Gaham, Tahash, and Maacah.

20:16 Hebrew *1,000 shekels of silver,* about 25 pounds or 11.4 kilograms in weight.   **21:6** The name *Isaac* means "he laughs."   **21:9** As in Greek version and Latin Vulgate; Hebrew omits *of her son, Isaac.*   **21:16** Hebrew *a bowshot.* **21:33** Hebrew *El-Olam.*   **22:17** Hebrew *seed;* also in 22:17b, 18.

MATTHEW 7:15-29

No one likes people who are fake—those who say one thing but act differently. In the final segment of his Sermon on the Mount, Jesus reminded believers that they must live what they believe. There is no place for hypocrites in God's Kingdom.

"**B**eware of false prophets who come disguised as harmless sheep but are really vicious wolves. ¹⁶You can identify them by their fruit, that is, by the way they act. Can you pick grapes from thornbushes, or figs from thistles? ¹⁷A good tree produces good fruit, and a bad tree produces bad fruit. ¹⁸A good tree can't produce bad fruit, and a bad tree can't produce good fruit. ¹⁹So every tree that does not produce good fruit is chopped down and thrown into the fire. ²⁰Yes, just as you can identify a tree by its fruit, so you can identify people by their actions.

²¹"Not everyone who calls out to me, 'Lord! Lord!' will enter the Kingdom of Heaven. Only those who actually do the will of my Father in heaven will enter. ²²On judgment day many will say to me, 'Lord! Lord! We prophesied in your name and cast out demons in your name and performed many miracles in your name.' ²³But I will reply, 'I never knew you. Get away from me, you who break God's laws.'

²⁴"Anyone who listens to my teaching and follows it is wise, like a person who builds a house on solid rock. ²⁵Though the rain comes in torrents and the floodwaters rise and the winds beat against that house, it won't collapse because it is built on bedrock. ²⁶But anyone who hears my teaching and doesn't obey it is foolish, like a person who builds a house on sand. ²⁷When the rains and floods come and the winds beat against that house, it will collapse with a mighty crash."

²⁸When Jesus had finished saying these things, the crowds were amazed at his teaching, ²⁹for he taught with real authority—quite unlike their teachers of religious law.

PSALM 9:1-12

For the choir director: A psalm of David, to be sung to the tune "Death of the Son."

¹ **I** will praise you, LORD, with all my heart;
   I will tell of all the marvelous things you have done.
² I will be filled with joy because of you.
   I will sing praises to your name,
   O Most High.

³ My enemies retreated;
   they staggered and died when you appeared.
⁴ For you have judged in my favor;

from your throne you have judged
　　with fairness.
[5] You have rebuked the nations and
　　destroyed the wicked;
　　you have erased their names
　　　forever.
[6] The enemy is finished, in endless ruins;
　　the cities you uprooted are now
　　　forgotten.

[7] But the LORD reigns forever,
　　executing judgment from his throne.
[8] He will judge the world with justice
　　and rule the nations with fairness.
[9] The LORD is a shelter for the
　　　oppressed,
　　a refuge in times of trouble.
[10] Those who know your name trust
　　　in you,
　　for you, O LORD, do not abandon
　　　those who search for you.

[11] Sing praises to the LORD who reigns
　　in Jerusalem.*

Tell the world about his
　　unforgettable deeds.
[12] For he who avenges murder cares for
　　the helpless.
　　He does not ignore the cries of
　　　those who suffer.

9:11 Hebrew *Zion;* also in 9:14.

PROVERBS 2:16-22

Wisdom will save you from the immoral
woman, from the seductive words of the
promiscuous woman. She has abandoned
her husband and ignores the covenant
she made before God. Entering her house
leads to death; it is the road to the grave.*
The man who visits her is doomed. He
will never reach the paths of life. □ Follow
the steps of good men instead, and stay
on the paths of the righteous. For only the
godly will live in the land, and those with
integrity will remain in it. But the wicked
will be removed from the land, and the
treacherous will be uprooted.

2:18 Hebrew *to the spirits of the dead.*

JANUARY**10**

GENESIS 23:1-24:51

Abraham and Sarah were already very old when Isaac
was born. Sarah died when Isaac was but a young
man. To ensure the family lineage, an aged Abraham
arranged for his servant to find an acceptable wife
for Isaac among relatives back in his homeland.

When Sarah was 127 years old, [2] she died
at Kiriath-arba (now called Hebron) in the
land of Canaan. There Abraham mourned
and wept for her.

[3] Then, leaving her body, he said to the
Hittite elders, [4]"Here I am, a stranger and
a foreigner among you. Please sell me a
piece of land so I can give my wife a proper
burial."

[5] The Hittites replied to Abraham, [6]"Listen, my lord, you are an honored prince
among us. Choose the finest of our tombs
and bury her there. No one here will refuse
to help you in this way."

[7] Then Abraham bowed low before the
Hittites and said, [8]"Since you are willing to

help me in this way, be so kind as to ask
Ephron son of Zohar [9] to let me buy his
cave at Machpelah, down at the end of his
field. I will pay the full price in the presence of witnesses, so I will have a permanent burial place for my family."

[10] Ephron was sitting there among the
others, and he answered Abraham as the
others listened, speaking publicly before
all the Hittite elders of the town. [11]"No, my
lord," he said to Abraham, "please listen to
me. I will give you the field and the cave.
Here in the presence of my people, I give it
to you. Go and bury your dead."

[12] Abraham again bowed low before the
citizens of the land, [13] and he replied to
Ephron as everyone listened. "No, listen to
me. I will buy it from you. Let me pay the
full price for the field so I can bury my
dead there."

[14] Ephron answered Abraham, [15]"My
lord, please listen to me. The land is

worth 400 pieces* of silver, but what is that between friends? Go ahead and bury your dead."

¹⁶So Abraham agreed to Ephron's price and paid the amount he had suggested—400 pieces of silver, weighed according to the market standard. The Hittite elders witnessed the transaction.

¹⁷So Abraham bought the plot of land belonging to Ephron at Machpelah, near Mamre. This included the field itself, the cave that was in it, and all the surrounding trees. ¹⁸It was transferred to Abraham as his permanent possession in the presence of the Hittite elders at the city gate. ¹⁹Then Abraham buried his wife, Sarah, there in Canaan, in the cave of Machpelah, near Mamre (also called Hebron). ²⁰So the field and the cave were transferred from the Hittites to Abraham for use as a permanent burial place.

²⁴:¹ABRAHAM was now a very old man, and the LORD had blessed him in every way. ²One day Abraham said to his oldest servant, the man in charge of his household, "Take an oath by putting your hand under my thigh. ³Swear by the LORD, the God of heaven and earth, that you will not allow my son to marry one of these local Canaanite women. ⁴Go instead to my homeland, to my relatives, and find a wife there for my son Isaac."

⁵The servant asked, "But what if I can't find a young woman who is willing to travel so far from home? Should I then take Isaac there to live among your relatives in the land you came from?"

⁶"No!" Abraham responded. "Be careful never to take my son there. ⁷For the LORD, the God of heaven, who took me from my father's house and my native land, solemnly promised to give this land to my descendants.* He will send his angel ahead of you, and he will see to it that you find a wife there for my son. ⁸If she is unwilling to come back with you, then you are free from this oath of mine. But under no circumstances are you to take my son there."

⁹So the servant took an oath by putting his hand under the thigh of his master, Abraham. He swore to follow Abraham's instructions. ¹⁰Then he loaded ten of Abraham's camels with all kinds of expensive gifts from his master, and he traveled to distant Aram-naharaim. There he went to the town where Abraham's brother Nahor had settled. ¹¹He made the camels kneel beside a well just outside the town. It was evening, and the women were coming out to draw water.

¹²"O LORD, God of my master, Abraham," he prayed. "Please give me success today, and show unfailing love to my master, Abraham. ¹³See, I am standing here beside this spring, and the young women of the town are coming out to draw water. ¹⁴This is my request. I will ask one of them, 'Please give me a drink from your jug.' If she says, 'Yes, have a drink, and I will water your camels, too!'—let her be the one you have selected as Isaac's wife. This is how I will know that you have shown unfailing love to my master."

¹⁵Before he had finished praying, he saw a young woman named Rebekah coming out with her water jug on her shoulder. She was the daughter of Bethuel, who was the son of Abraham's brother Nahor and his wife, Milcah. ¹⁶Rebekah was very beautiful and old enough to be married, but she was still a virgin. She went down to the spring, filled her jug, and came up again. ¹⁷Running over to her, the servant said, "Please give me a little drink of water from your jug."

¹⁸"Yes, my lord," she answered, "have a drink." And she quickly lowered her jug from her shoulder and gave him a drink. ¹⁹When she had given him a drink, she said, "I'll draw water for your camels, too, until they have had enough to drink." ²⁰So she quickly emptied her jug into the watering trough and ran back to the well to draw water for all his camels.

²¹The servant watched her in silence, wondering whether or not the LORD had given him success in his mission. ²²Then at last, when the camels had finished drinking, he took out a gold ring for her nose and two large gold bracelets* for her wrists.

²³"Whose daughter are you?" he asked. "And please tell me, would your father have any room to put us up for the night?"

²⁴"I am the daughter of Bethuel," she replied. "My grandparents are Nahor and Milcah. ²⁵Yes, we have plenty of straw and

feed for the camels, and we have room for guests."

²⁶The man bowed low and worshiped the LORD. ²⁷"Praise the LORD, the God of my master, Abraham," he said. "The LORD has shown unfailing love and faithfulness to my master, for he has led me straight to my master's relatives."

²⁸The young woman ran home to tell her family everything that had happened. ²⁹Now Rebekah had a brother named Laban, who ran out to meet the man at the spring. ³⁰He had seen the nose-ring and the bracelets on his sister's wrists, and had heard Rebekah tell what the man had said. So he rushed out to the spring, where the man was still standing beside his camels. Laban said to him, ³¹"Come and stay with us, you who are blessed by the LORD! Why are you standing here outside the town when I have a room all ready for you and a place prepared for the camels?"

³²So the man went home with Laban, and Laban unloaded the camels, gave him straw for their bedding, fed them, and provided water for the man and the camel drivers to wash their feet. ³³Then food was served. But Abraham's servant said, "I don't want to eat until I have told you why I have come."

"All right," Laban said, "tell us."

³⁴"I am Abraham's servant," he explained.

³⁵"And the LORD has greatly blessed my master; he has become a wealthy man. The LORD has given him flocks of sheep and goats, herds of cattle, a fortune in silver and gold, and many male and female servants and camels and donkeys.

³⁶"When Sarah, my master's wife, was very old, she gave birth to my master's son, and my master has given him everything he owns. ³⁷And my master made me take an oath. He said, 'Do not allow my son to marry one of these local Canaanite women. ³⁸Go instead to my father's house, to my relatives, and find a wife there for my son.'

³⁹"But I said to my master, 'What if I can't find a young woman who is willing to go back with me?' ⁴⁰He responded, 'The LORD, in whose presence I have lived, will send his angel with you and will make your mission successful. Yes, you must find a wife for my son from among my relatives, from my father's family. ⁴¹Then you will have fulfilled your obligation. But if you go to my relatives and they refuse to let her go with you, you will be free from my oath.'

⁴²"So today when I came to the spring, I prayed this prayer: 'O LORD, God of my master, Abraham, please give me success on this mission. ⁴³See, I am standing here beside this spring. This is my request. When a young woman comes to draw water, I will say to her, "Please give me a little

---

HOW WE LIVE — Seeking God's will

PROVERBS 3:5-6 When we are faced with important decisions, we sometimes wonder who we can trust for guidance. Friends and family won't always have the knowledge or the wisdom necessary to help us make the right decision. God knows all things, and he knows what is best for each one of us. This is why it is important to trust the Lord and not depend on our own understanding when we need direction.   • As a new believer, you must learn to put God at the center of your decision-making process. You do that by searching God's Word, praying for guidance, and seeking the advice of wise counselors. When you do those things, God's direction will become clear.   • The reading in Matthew 8 describes the reward given to those who place their full trust in Jesus. The man with leprosy says, "If you are willing . . ." He asked flat out for God's will to be done in his life. When you make Jesus and his will for your life your first priority, he promises to "show you which path to take." Nothing is more reassuring than entrusting an unknown future to a known God, who wants to be an integral part of every decision you make. Will you let him?

drink of water from your jug." ⁴⁴If she says, "Yes, have a drink, and I will draw water for your camels, too," let her be the one you have selected to be the wife of my master's son.'

⁴⁵"Before I had finished praying in my heart, I saw Rebekah coming out with her water jug on her shoulder. She went down to the spring and drew water. So I said to her, 'Please give me a drink.' ⁴⁶She quickly lowered her jug from her shoulder and said, 'Yes, have a drink, and I will water your camels, too!' So I drank, and then she watered the camels.

⁴⁷"Then I asked, 'Whose daughter are you?' She replied, 'I am the daughter of Bethuel, and my grandparents are Nahor and Milcah.' So I put the ring on her nose, and the bracelets on her wrists.

⁴⁸"Then I bowed low and worshiped the LORD. I praised the LORD, the God of my master, Abraham, because he had led me straight to my master's niece to be his son's wife. ⁴⁹So tell me—will you or won't you show unfailing love and faithfulness to my master? Please tell me yes or no, and then I'll know what to do next."

⁵⁰Then Laban and Bethuel replied, "The LORD has obviously brought you here, so there is nothing we can say. ⁵¹Here is Rebekah; take her and go. Yes, let her be the wife of your master's son, as the LORD has directed."

23:15 Hebrew *400 shekels*, about 10 pounds or 4.6 kilograms in weight; also in 23:16.   24:7 Hebrew *seed*; also in 24:60.
24:22 Hebrew *a gold nose-ring weighing a half shekel [0.2 ounces or 6 grams] and two gold bracelets weighing 10 shekels* [4 ounces or 114 grams].

MATTHEW 8:1-17

At present, the Kingdom of God is not an earthly place of civil government; it is God's rule in the hearts and minds of his people. The Kingdom of God is open to all people (Jews and non-Jews alike) who trust Jesus as their personal Savior and follow him each day.

Large crowds followed Jesus as he came down the mountainside. ²Suddenly, a man with leprosy approached him and knelt before him. "Lord," the man said, "if you are willing, you can heal me and make me clean."

³Jesus reached out and touched him. "I am willing," he said. "Be healed!" And instantly the leprosy disappeared. ⁴Then Jesus said to him, "Don't tell anyone about this. Instead, go to the priest and let him examine you. Take along the offering required in the law of Moses for those who have been healed of leprosy.* This will be a public testimony that you have been cleansed."

⁵When Jesus returned to Capernaum, a Roman officer* came and pleaded with him, ⁶"Lord, my young servant* lies in bed, paralyzed and in terrible pain."

⁷Jesus said, "I will come and heal him."

⁸But the officer said, "Lord, I am not worthy to have you come into my home. Just say the word from where you are, and my servant will be healed. ⁹I know this because I am under the authority of my superior officers, and I have authority over my soldiers. I only need to say, 'Go,' and they go, or 'Come,' and they come. And if I say to my slaves, 'Do this,' they do it."

¹⁰When Jesus heard this, he was amazed. Turning to those who were following him, he said, "I tell you the truth, I haven't seen faith like this in all Israel! ¹¹And I tell you this, that many Gentiles will come from all over the world—from east and west—and sit down with Abraham, Isaac, and Jacob at the feast in the Kingdom of Heaven. ¹²But many Israelites—those for whom the Kingdom was prepared—will be thrown into outer darkness, where there will be weeping and gnashing of teeth."

¹³Then Jesus said to the Roman officer, "Go back home. Because you believed, it has happened." And the young servant was healed that same hour.

¹⁴When Jesus arrived at Peter's house, Peter's mother-in-law was sick in bed with a high fever. ¹⁵But when Jesus touched her hand, the fever left her. Then she got up and prepared a meal for him.

¹⁶That evening many demon-possessed people were brought to Jesus. He cast out the evil spirits with a simple command, and he healed all the sick. ¹⁷This fulfilled the word of the Lord through the prophet Isaiah, who said,

"He took our sicknesses
  and removed our diseases."*

8:4 See Lev 14:2-32.   8:5 Greek *a centurion;* similarly in 8:8, 13.   8:6 Or *child;* also in 8:13.   8:17 Isa 53:4.

PSALM 9:13-20

LORD, have mercy on me.
See how my enemies torment me.
Snatch me back from the jaws of
death.
[14] Save me so I can praise you publicly
at Jerusalem's gates,
so I can rejoice that you have
rescued me.

[15] The nations have fallen into the pit
they dug for others.
Their own feet have been caught in
the trap they set.
[16] The LORD is known for his justice.
The wicked are trapped by their
own deeds.   *Quiet Interlude**

[17] The wicked will go down to the grave.*
This is the fate of all the nations
who ignore God.
[18] But the needy will not be ignored
forever;
the hopes of the poor will not
always be crushed.

[19] Arise, O LORD!
Do not let mere mortals defy you!
Judge the nations!
[20] Make them tremble in fear, O LORD.
Let the nations know they are
merely human.   *Interlude*

9:16 Hebrew *Higgaion Selah*. The meaning of this phrase is
uncertain.   **9:17** Hebrew *to Sheol*.

PROVERBS 3:1-6

My child,* never forget the things I have
taught you. Store my commands in your
heart. If you do this, you will live many
years, and your life will be satisfying.
Never let loyalty and kindness leave you!
Tie them around your neck as a reminder.
Write them deep within your heart. Then
you will find favor with both God and people, and you will earn a good reputation.
□ Trust in the LORD with all your heart; do
not depend on your own understanding.
Seek his will in all you do, and he will show
you which path to take.

3:1 Hebrew *My son*; also in 3:11, 21.

JANUARY**11**

GENESIS 24:52–26:16

Abraham, ancestor of the Jewish nation and
of Jesus Christ, found a wife for his son Isaac.
Isaac and Rebekah had twin boys, Esau and
Jacob. Through Jacob, God carried on his promises to Abraham. Jacob was far from perfect;
through the account of his life, we learn that
God continues to accomplish his will and keep
his promises even when his people make
mistakes.

When Abraham's servant heard their answer, he bowed down to the ground and
worshiped the LORD. [53] Then he brought
out silver and gold jewelry and clothing
and presented them to Rebekah. He also
gave expensive presents to her brother
and mother. [54] Then they ate their meal,
and the servant and the men with him
stayed there overnight.

But early the next morning, Abraham's
servant said, "Send me back to my master."
[55] "But we want Rebekah to stay with us

at least ten days," her brother and mother
said. "Then she can go."
[56] But he said, "Don't delay me. The
LORD has made my mission successful;
now send me back so I can return to my
master."
[57] "Well," they said, "we'll call Rebekah
and ask her what she thinks." [58] So they
called Rebekah. "Are you willing to go with
this man?" they asked her.
And she replied, "Yes, I will go."
[59] So they said good-bye to Rebekah
and sent her away with Abraham's servant
and his men. The woman who had been
Rebekah's childhood nurse went along
with her. [60] They gave her this blessing as
she parted:

"Our sister, may you become
the mother of many millions!
May your descendants be strong
and conquer the cities of their
enemies."

⁶¹Then Rebekah and her servant girls mounted the camels and followed the man. So Abraham's servant took Rebekah and went on his way.

⁶²Meanwhile, Isaac, whose home was in the Negev, had returned from Beer-lahai-roi. ⁶³One evening as he was walking and meditating in the fields, he looked up and saw the camels coming. ⁶⁴When Rebekah looked up and saw Isaac, she quickly dismounted from her camel. ⁶⁵"Who is that man walking through the fields to meet us?" she asked the servant.

And he replied, "It is my master." So Rebekah covered her face with her veil. ⁶⁶Then the servant told Isaac everything he had done.

⁶⁷And Isaac brought Rebekah into his mother Sarah's tent, and she became his wife. He loved her deeply, and she was a special comfort to him after the death of his mother.

²⁵:¹ABRAHAM married another wife, whose name was Keturah. ²She gave birth to Zimran, Jokshan, Medan, Midian, Ishbak, and Shuah. ³Jokshan was the father of Sheba and Dedan. Dedan's descendants were the Asshurites, Letushites, and Leummites. ⁴Midian's sons were Ephah, Epher, Hanoch, Abida, and Eldaah. These were all descendants of Abraham through Keturah.

⁵Abraham gave everything he owned to his son Isaac. ⁶But before he died, he gave gifts to the sons of his concubines and sent them off to a land in the east, away from Isaac.

⁷Abraham lived for 175 years, ⁸and he died at a ripe old age, having lived a long and satisfying life. He breathed his last and joined his ancestors in death. ⁹His sons Isaac and Ishmael buried him in the cave of Machpelah, near Mamre, in the field of Ephron son of Zohar the Hittite. ¹⁰This was the field Abraham had purchased from the Hittites and where he had buried his wife Sarah. ¹¹After Abraham's death, God blessed his son Isaac, who settled near Beer-lahai-roi in the Negev.

¹²This is the account of the family of Ishmael, the son of Abraham through Hagar, Sarah's Egyptian servant. ¹³Here is a list, by their names and clans, of Ishmael's descendants: The oldest was Nebaioth, followed by Kedar, Adbeel, Mibsam, ¹⁴Mishma, Dumah, Massa, ¹⁵Hadad, Tema, Jetur, Naphish, and Kedemah. ¹⁶These twelve sons of Ishmael became the founders of twelve tribes named after them, listed according to the places they settled and camped. ¹⁷Ishmael lived for 137 years. Then he breathed his last and joined his ancestors in death. ¹⁸Ishmael's descendants occupied the region from Havilah to Shur, which is east of Egypt in the direction of Asshur. There they lived in open hostility toward all their relatives.*

¹⁹This is the account of the family of Isaac, the son of Abraham. ²⁰When Isaac was forty years old, he married Rebekah, the daughter of Bethuel the Aramean from Paddan-aram and the sister of Laban the Aramean.

²¹Isaac pleaded with the LORD on behalf of his wife, because she was unable to have children. The LORD answered Isaac's prayer, and Rebekah became pregnant with twins. ²²But the two children struggled with each other in her womb. So she went to ask the LORD about it. "Why is this happening to me?" she asked.

²³And the LORD told her, "The sons in your womb will become two nations. From the very beginning, the two nations will be rivals. One nation will be stronger than the other; and your older son will serve your younger son."

²⁴And when the time came to give birth, Rebekah discovered that she did indeed have twins! ²⁵The first one was very red at birth and covered with thick hair like a fur coat. So they named him Esau.* ²⁶Then the other twin was born with his hand grasping Esau's heel. So they named him Jacob.* Isaac was sixty years old when the twins were born.

²⁷As the boys grew up, Esau became a skillful hunter. He was an outdoorsman, but Jacob had a quiet temperament, preferring to stay at home. ²⁸Isaac loved Esau because he enjoyed eating the wild game Esau brought home, but Rebekah loved Jacob.

²⁹One day when Jacob was cooking some stew, Esau arrived home from the wilderness exhausted and hungry. ³⁰Esau said to Jacob, "I'm starved! Give me some

of that red stew!" (This is how Esau got his other name, Edom, which means "red.")

³¹"All right," Jacob replied, "but trade me your rights as the firstborn son."

³²"Look, I'm dying of starvation!" said Esau. "What good is my birthright to me now?"

³³But Jacob said, "First you must swear that your birthright is mine." So Esau swore an oath, thereby selling all his rights as the firstborn to his brother, Jacob.

³⁴Then Jacob gave Esau some bread and lentil stew. Esau ate the meal, then got up and left. He showed contempt for his rights as the firstborn.

²⁶:¹A SEVERE famine now struck the land, as had happened before in Abraham's time. So Isaac moved to Gerar, where Abimelech, king of the Philistines, lived.

²The LORD appeared to Isaac and said, "Do not go down to Egypt, but do as I tell you. ³Live here as a foreigner in this land, and I will be with you and bless you. I hereby confirm that I will give all these lands to you and your descendants,* just as I solemnly promised Abraham, your father. ⁴I will cause your descendants to become as numerous as the stars of the sky, and I will give them all these lands. And through your descendants all the nations of the earth will be blessed. ⁵I will

do this because Abraham listened to me and obeyed all my requirements, commands, decrees, and instructions." ⁶So Isaac stayed in Gerar.

⁷When the men who lived there asked Isaac about his wife, Rebekah, he said, "She is my sister." He was afraid to say, "She is my wife." He thought, "They will kill me to get her, because she is so beautiful." ⁸But some time later, Abimelech, king of the Philistines, looked out his window and saw Isaac caressing Rebekah.

⁹Immediately, Abimelech called for Isaac and exclaimed, "She is obviously your wife! Why did you say, 'She is my sister'?"

"Because I was afraid someone would kill me to get her from me," Isaac replied.

¹⁰"How could you do this to us?" Abimelech exclaimed. "One of my people might easily have taken your wife and slept with her, and you would have made us guilty of great sin."

¹¹Then Abimelech issued a public proclamation: "Anyone who touches this man or his wife will be put to death!"

¹²When Isaac planted his crops that year, he harvested a hundred times more grain than he planted, for the LORD blessed him. ¹³He became a very rich man, and his wealth continued to grow. ¹⁴He acquired so many flocks of sheep

Demons

WHAT THE BIBLE SAYS

MATTHEW 8:28-29 Matthew 8:28 tells of two men possessed by demons who were "so violent" that people couldn't even walk past the cemetery where they lived. Demon-possessed people are under the control of one or more demons. Demons are fallen angels who joined Satan in his rebellion against God; they are now evil spirits under Satan's control. Wherever they show up, they seek to cause pain and ultimately to bring ruin. In this situation, the demons were taking a maniacal and destructive hold on two men who did not have a relationship with God. • It is interesting to note that demons themselves know that God is more powerful than they are and will one day send them to eternal torture (see James 2:19, November 19). Christ's authority is enough to drive them away. When Christ commanded the demons to leave the men, they were cast into a herd of pigs and—as a testament to the destructive nature of demons—the pigs ran down the steep hillside into the lake and died. •People who have a true relationship with Christ cannot be overcome by demons. Those who reject Christ will find themselves in the company of the demons at the time of judgment.

and goats, herds of cattle, and servants that the Philistines became jealous of him. [15]So the Philistines filled up all of Isaac's wells with dirt. These were the wells that had been dug by the servants of his father, Abraham.

[16]Finally, Abimelech ordered Isaac to leave the country. "Go somewhere else," he said, "for you have become too powerful for us."

25:18 The meaning of the Hebrew is uncertain. 25:25 *Esau* sounds like a Hebrew term that means "hair." 25:26 *Jacob* sounds like the Hebrew words for "heel" and "deceiver." 26:3 Hebrew *seed;* also in 26:4, 24.

MATTHEW 8:18-34

Jesus spoke with authority and power—to his followers, to a storm at sea, to the demons who had been ravaging two men's lives. Unfortunately, he was often met with fear, derision, or estrangement. Those who believed in him, however, "praised God for sending a man with such great authority" (Matthew 9:8).

When Jesus saw the crowd around him, he instructed his disciples to cross to the other side of the lake.

[19]Then one of the teachers of religious law said to him, "Teacher, I will follow you wherever you go."

[20]But Jesus replied, "Foxes have dens to live in, and birds have nests, but the Son of Man* has no place even to lay his head."

[21]Another of his disciples said, "Lord, first let me return home and bury my father."

[22]But Jesus told him, "Follow me now. Let the spiritually dead bury their own dead.*"

[23]Then Jesus got into the boat and started across the lake with his disciples. [24]Suddenly, a fierce storm struck the lake, with waves breaking into the boat. But Jesus was sleeping. [25]The disciples went and woke him up, shouting, "Lord, save us! We're going to drown!"

[26]Jesus responded, "Why are you afraid? You have so little faith!" Then he got up and rebuked the wind and waves, and suddenly there was a great calm.

[27]The disciples were amazed. "Who is this man?" they asked. "Even the winds and waves obey him!"

[28]When Jesus arrived on the other side of the lake, in the region of the Gadarenes,* two men who were possessed by demons met him. They lived in a cemetery and were so violent that no one could go through that area.

[29]They began screaming at him, "Why are you interfering with us, Son of God? Have you come here to torture us before God's appointed time?"

[30]There happened to be a large herd of pigs feeding in the distance. [31]So the demons begged, "If you cast us out, send us into that herd of pigs."

[32]"All right, go!" Jesus commanded them. So the demons came out of the men and entered the pigs, and the whole herd plunged down the steep hillside into the lake and drowned in the water.

[33]The herdsmen fled to the nearby town, telling everyone what happened to the demon-possessed men. [34]Then the entire town came out to meet Jesus, but they begged him to go away and leave them alone.

8:20 "Son of Man" is a title Jesus used for himself. 8:22 Greek *Let the dead bury their own dead.* 8:28 Other manuscripts read *Gerasenes;* still others read *Gergesenes.* Compare Mark 5:1; Luke 8:26.

PSALM 10:1-15

O LORD, why do you stand so far away?
　　Why do you hide when I am in
　　　　trouble?
[2] The wicked arrogantly hunt down the
　　　　poor.
　　Let them be caught in the evil they
　　　　plan for others.
[3] For they brag about their evil desires;
　　they praise the greedy and curse
　　　　the LORD.

[4] The wicked are too proud to seek God.
　　They seem to think that God is
　　　　dead.
[5] Yet they succeed in everything they do.
　　They do not see your punishment
　　　　awaiting them.
　　They sneer at all their enemies.
[6] They think, "Nothing bad will ever
　　　　happen to us!
　　We will be free of trouble forever!"

[7] Their mouths are full of cursing, lies,
　　　　and threats.*
　　Trouble and evil are on the tips of
　　　　their tongues.
[8] They lurk in ambush in the villages,

waiting to murder innocent
people.
They are always searching for
helpless victims.
⁹ Like lions crouched in hiding,
they wait to pounce on the
helpless.
Like hunters they capture the helpless
and drag them away in nets.
¹⁰ Their helpless victims are crushed;
they fall beneath the strength of
the wicked.
¹¹ The wicked think, "God isn't
watching us!
He has closed his eyes and won't
even see what we do!"

¹² Arise, O LORD!
Punish the wicked, O God!
Do not ignore the helpless!
¹³ Why do the wicked get away with
despising God?

They think, "God will never call us
to account."
¹⁴ But you see the trouble and grief they
cause.
You take note of it and punish
them.
The helpless put their trust in you.
You defend the orphans.

¹⁵ Break the arms of these wicked, evil
people!
Go after them until the last one
is destroyed.

10:7 Greek version reads *cursing and bitterness.* Compare
Rom 3:14.

PROVERBS 3:7-8
Don't be impressed with your own wisdom. Instead, fear the LORD and turn
away from evil. Then you will have healing for your body and strength for your
bones.

JANUARY**12**

GENESIS 26:17–27:46
Isaac had to deal with international disputes as
well as the dysfunction of his own family. Problems
arise when parents show favoritism to certain of
their children. Ultimately, things worked together to
bring about God's plan to carry out his promise to
Abraham through Jacob.

So Isaac moved away to the Gerar Valley,
where he set up their tents and settled
down. ¹⁸He reopened the wells his father
had dug, which the Philistines had filled
in after Abraham's death. Isaac also restored the names Abraham had given
them.

¹⁹Isaac's servants also dug in the Gerar
Valley and discovered a well of fresh water. ²⁰But then the shepherds from Gerar
came and claimed the spring. "This is our
water," they said, and they argued over it
with Isaac's herdsmen. So Isaac named
the well Esek (which means "argument").
²¹Isaac's men then dug another well, but
again there was a dispute over it. So Isaac
named it Sitnah (which means "hostil-

ity"). ²²Abandoning that one, Isaac moved
on and dug another well. This time there
was no dispute over it, so Isaac named the
place Rehoboth (which means "open
space"), for he said, "At last the LORD has
created enough space for us to prosper in
this land."

²³From there Isaac moved to Beersheba, ²⁴where the LORD appeared to him
on the night of his arrival. "I am the God of
your father, Abraham," he said. "Do not be
afraid, for I am with you and will bless
you. I will multiply your descendants, and
they will become a great nation. I will do
this because of my promise to Abraham,
my servant." ²⁵Then Isaac built an altar
there and worshiped the LORD. He set up
his camp at that place, and his servants
dug another well.

²⁶One day King Abimelech came from
Gerar with his adviser, Ahuzzath, and also
Phicol, his army commander. ²⁷"Why
have you come here?" Isaac asked. "You

obviously hate me, since you kicked me off your land."

28They replied, "We can plainly see that the LORD is with you. So we want to enter into a sworn treaty with you. Let's make a covenant. 29Swear that you will not harm us, just as we have never troubled you. We have always treated you well, and we sent you away from us in peace. And now look how the LORD has blessed you!"

30So Isaac prepared a covenant feast to celebrate the treaty, and they ate and drank together. 31Early the next morning, they each took a solemn oath not to interfere with each other. Then Isaac sent them home again, and they left him in peace.

32That very day Isaac's servants came and told him about a new well they had dug. "We've found water!" they exclaimed. 33So Isaac named the well Shibah (which means "oath"). And to this day the town that grew up there is called Beersheba (which means "well of the oath").

34At the age of forty, Esau married two Hittite wives: Judith, the daughter of Beeri, and Basemath, the daughter of Elon. 35But Esau's wives made life miserable for Isaac and Rebekah.

27:1ONE day when Isaac was old and turning blind, he called for Esau, his older son, and said, "My son."

"Yes, Father?" Esau replied.

2"I am an old man now," Isaac said, "and I don't know when I may die. 3Take your bow and a quiver full of arrows, and go out into the open country to hunt some wild game for me. 4Prepare my favorite dish, and bring it here for me to eat. Then I will pronounce the blessing that belongs to you, my firstborn son, before I die."

5But Rebekah overheard what Isaac had said to his son Esau. So when Esau left to hunt for the wild game, 6she said to her son Jacob, "Listen. I overheard your father say to Esau, 7'Bring me some wild game and prepare me a delicious meal. Then I will bless you in the LORD's presence before I die.' 8Now, my son, listen to me. Do exactly as I tell you. 9Go out to the flocks, and bring me two fine young goats. I'll use them to prepare your father's favorite

dish. 10Then take the food to your father so he can eat it and bless you before he dies."

11"But look," Jacob replied to Rebekah, "my brother, Esau, is a hairy man, and my skin is smooth. 12What if my father touches me? He'll see that I'm trying to trick him, and then he'll curse me instead of blessing me."

13But his mother replied, "Then let the curse fall on me, my son! Just do what I tell you. Go out and get the goats for me!"

14So Jacob went out and got the young goats for his mother. Rebekah took them and prepared a delicious meal, just the way Isaac liked it. 15Then she took Esau's favorite clothes, which were there in the house, and gave them to her younger son, Jacob. 16She covered his arms and the smooth part of his neck with the skin of the young goats. 17Then she gave Jacob the delicious meal, including freshly baked bread.

18So Jacob took the food to his father. "My father?" he said.

"Yes, my son," Isaac answered. "Who are you—Esau or Jacob?"

19Jacob replied, "It's Esau, your firstborn son. I've done as you told me. Here is the wild game. Now sit up and eat it so you can give me your blessing."

20Isaac asked, "How did you find it so quickly, my son?"

"The LORD your God put it in my path!" Jacob replied.

21Then Isaac said to Jacob, "Come closer so I can touch you and make sure that you really are Esau." 22So Jacob went closer to his father, and Isaac touched him. "The voice is Jacob's, but the hands are Esau's," Isaac said. 23But he did not recognize Jacob, because Jacob's hands felt hairy just like Esau's. So Isaac prepared to bless Jacob. 24"But are you really my son Esau?" he asked.

"Yes, I am," Jacob replied.

25Then Isaac said, "Now, my son, bring me the wild game. Let me eat it, and then I will give you my blessing." So Jacob took the food to his father, and Isaac ate it. He also drank the wine that Jacob served him. Then Isaac said to Jacob, 26"Please come a little closer and kiss me, my son."

²⁷So Jacob went over and kissed him. And when Isaac caught the smell of his clothes, he was finally convinced, and he blessed his son. He said, "Ah! The smell of my son is like the smell of the outdoors, which the LORD has blessed!

²⁸ "From the dew of heaven
and the richness of the earth,
may God always give you abundant
harvests of grain
and bountiful new wine.
²⁹ May many nations become your
servants,
and may they bow down to you.
May you be the master over your
brothers,
and may your mother's sons bow
down to you.
All who curse you will be cursed,
and all who bless you will be
blessed."

³⁰As soon as Isaac had finished blessing Jacob, and almost before Jacob had left his father, Esau returned from his hunt. ³¹Esau prepared a delicious meal and brought it to his father. Then he said, "Sit up, my father, and eat my wild game so you can give me your blessing."

³²But Isaac asked him, "Who are you?"

Esau replied, "It's your son, your first-born son, Esau."

³³Isaac began to tremble uncontrollably and said, "Then who just served me wild game? I have already eaten it, and I blessed him just before you came. And yes, that blessing must stand!"

³⁴When Esau heard his father's words, he let out a loud and bitter cry. "Oh my father, what about me? Bless me, too!" he begged.

³⁵But Isaac said, "Your brother was here, and he tricked me. He has taken away your blessing."

³⁶Esau exclaimed, "No wonder his name is Jacob, for now he has cheated me twice.* First he took my rights as the first-born, and now he has stolen my blessing. Oh, haven't you saved even one blessing for me?"

³⁷Isaac said to Esau, "I have made Jacob your master and have declared that all his brothers will be his servants. I have guaranteed him an abundance of grain and wine—what is left for me to give you, my son?"

³⁸Esau pleaded, "But do you have only one blessing? Oh my father, bless me, too!" Then Esau broke down and wept.

³⁹Finally, his father, Isaac, said to him,

HOW WE LIVE

Trusting God

GENESIS 27:8-10 "In God We Trust" has become a catch phrase—it is even imprinted on American currency. In day-to-day life we trust all kinds of people. When we lift off the ground in an airliner, we place our lives in the hands of a pilot. Why, then, is trusting in God sometimes so difficult? We're too often like Rebekah, choosing to take matters into our own hands instead of trusting in and waiting for God's timing. Even though God had already personally spoken to Rebekah (Genesis 25:22-26, January 11), telling her that Jacob would become a great leader, Rebekah resorted to deceit in order to bring about something that God had said would happen anyway! Her intervention caused great turmoil and pain in the family, which might have been avoided had she let God work. • Is there an area in your life where you need to trust in God's leading? Are you impatient for his plan for your life to be revealed? Don't be like Rebekah, becoming so wrapped up in achieving the end result that she degraded her own character along the way. Continue to read and study God's Word, growing in the knowledge of his life, his love, and his sacrifice for you. Trust him to work out his plans in his way in his time.

"You will live away from the richness
of the earth,
and away from the dew of the
heaven above.
40 You will live by your sword,
and you will serve your brother.
But when you decide to break free,
you will shake his yoke from your
neck."

41From that time on, Esau hated Jacob because their father had given Jacob the blessing. And Esau began to scheme: "I will soon be mourning my father's death. Then I will kill my brother, Jacob."

42But Rebekah heard about Esau's plans. So she sent for Jacob and told him, "Listen, Esau is consoling himself by plotting to kill you. 43So listen carefully, my son. Get ready and flee to my brother, Laban, in Haran. 44Stay there with him until your brother cools off. 45When he calms down and forgets what you have done to him, I will send for you to come back. Why should I lose both of you in one day?"

46Then Rebekah said to Isaac, "I'm sick and tired of these local Hittite women! I would rather die than see Jacob marry one of them."

27:36 *Jacob* sounds like the Hebrew words for "heel" and "deceiver."

MATTHEW 9:1-17

Jesus associated not with the religious leadership who thought they had a corner on righteousness, but with people who needed help to clean up their acts. He touched, he healed, and he forgave sins. He challenged the traditional views of righteousness and called his disciples to a new way of living.

Jesus climbed into a boat and went back across the lake to his own town. 2Some people brought to him a paralyzed man on a mat. Seeing their faith, Jesus said to the paralyzed man, "Be encouraged, my child! Your sins are forgiven."

3But some of the teachers of religious law said to themselves, "That's blasphemy! Does he think he's God?"

4Jesus knew* what they were thinking, so he asked them, "Why do you have such evil thoughts in your hearts? 5Is it easier to say 'Your sins are forgiven,' or 'Stand up and walk'? 6So I will prove to you that the Son of Man* has the authority on earth to forgive sins." Then Jesus turned to the paralyzed man and said, "Stand up, pick up your mat, and go home!"

7And the man jumped up and went home! 8Fear swept through the crowd as they saw this happen. And they praised God for sending a man with such great authority.*

9As Jesus was walking along, he saw a man named Matthew sitting at his tax collector's booth. "Follow me and be my disciple," Jesus said to him. So Matthew got up and followed him.

10Later, Matthew invited Jesus and his disciples to his home as dinner guests, along with many tax collectors and other disreputable sinners. 11But when the Pharisees saw this, they asked his disciples, "Why does your teacher eat with such scum?*"

12When Jesus heard this, he said, "Healthy people don't need a doctor—sick people do." 13Then he added, "Now go and learn the meaning of this Scripture: 'I want you to show mercy, not offer sacrifices.'* For I have come to call not those who think they are righteous, but those who know they are sinners."

14One day the disciples of John the Baptist came to Jesus and asked him, "Why don't your disciples fast* like we do and the Pharisees do?"

15Jesus replied, "Do wedding guests mourn while celebrating with the groom? Of course not. But someday the groom will be taken away from them, and then they will fast.

16"Besides, who would patch old clothing with new cloth? For the new patch would shrink and rip away from the old cloth, leaving an even bigger tear than before.

17"And no one puts new wine into old wineskins. For the old skins would burst from the pressure, spilling the wine and ruining the skins. New wine is stored in new wineskins so that both are preserved."

9:4 Some manuscripts read *saw.*   9:6 "Son of Man" is a title Jesus used for himself.   9:8 Greek *for giving such authority to human beings.*   9:11 Greek *with tax collectors and sinners?*   9:13 Hos 6:6 (Greek version).   9:14 Some manuscripts read *fast often.*

PSALM 10:16-18
The LORD is king forever and ever!
The godless nations will vanish
from the land.
[17] LORD, you know the hopes of the
helpless.
Surely you will hear their cries and
comfort them.
[18] You will bring justice to the orphans
and the oppressed,
so mere people can no longer
terrify them.

PROVERBS 3:9-10
Honor the LORD with your wealth and
with the best part of everything you produce. Then he will fill your barns with
grain, and your vats will overflow with
good wine.

JANUARY**13**

GENESIS 28:1-29:35
Whereas Jacob had tricked his brother out of the
family blessing, in today's passage the trick was on
him. Jacob fell in love with one of his uncle Laban's
daughters and asked for her as a wife. Through Laban's clever scheme, Jacob got two wives!

So Isaac called for Jacob, blessed him,
and said, "You must not marry any of
these Canaanite women. [2]Instead, go at
once to Paddan-aram, to the house of
your grandfather Bethuel, and marry one
of your uncle Laban's daughters. [3]May
God Almighty* bless you and give you
many children. And may your descendants multiply and become many nations! [4]May God pass on to you and your
descendants* the blessings he promised
to Abraham. May you own this land where
you are now living as a foreigner, for God
gave this land to Abraham."

[5]So Isaac sent Jacob away, and he went
to Paddan-aram to stay with his uncle Laban, his mother's brother, the son of Bethuel the Aramean.

[6]Esau knew that his father, Isaac, had
blessed Jacob and sent him to Paddan-
aram to find a wife, and that he had warned
Jacob, "You must not marry a Canaanite
woman." [7]He also knew that Jacob had
obeyed his parents and gone to Paddan-
aram. [8]It was now very clear to Esau that
his father did not like the local Canaanite
women. [9]So Esau visited his uncle Ishmael's family and married one of Ishmael's
daughters, in addition to the wives he already had. His new wife's name was Mahalath. She was the sister of Nebaioth and the
daughter of Ishmael, Abraham's son.

[10]Meanwhile, Jacob left Beersheba and
traveled toward Haran. [11]At sundown he
arrived at a good place to set up camp and
stopped there for the night. Jacob found a
stone to rest his head against and lay
down to sleep. [12]As he slept, he dreamed
of a stairway that reached from the earth
up to heaven. And he saw the angels of
God going up and down the stairway.

[13]At the top of the stairway stood the
LORD, and he said, "I am the LORD, the God
of your grandfather Abraham, and the
God of your father, Isaac. The ground you
are lying on belongs to you. I am giving it
to you and your descendants. [14]Your descendants will be as numerous as the dust
of the earth! They will spread out in all directions—to the west and the east, to the
north and the south. And all the families
of the earth will be blessed through you
and your descendants. [15]What's more, I
am with you, and I will protect you wherever you go. One day I will bring you back
to this land. I will not leave you until I have
finished giving you everything I have
promised you."

[16]Then Jacob awoke from his sleep and
said, "Surely the LORD is in this place, and I
wasn't even aware of it!" [17]But he was also
afraid and said, "What an awesome place
this is! It is none other than the house of
God, the very gateway to heaven!"

[18]The next morning Jacob got up very
early. He took the stone he had rested his

head against, and he set it upright as a memorial pillar. Then he poured olive oil over it. ¹⁹He named that place Bethel (which means "house of God"), although the name of the nearby village was Luz.

²⁰Then Jacob made this vow: "If God will indeed be with me and protect me on this journey, and if he will provide me with food and clothing, ²¹and if I return safely to my father's home, then the LORD will certainly be my God. ²²And this memorial pillar I have set up will become a place for worshiping God, and I will present to God a tenth of everything he gives me."

29:¹THEN Jacob hurried on, finally arriving in the land of the east. ²He saw a well in the distance. Three flocks of sheep and goats lay in an open field beside it, waiting to be watered. But a heavy stone covered the mouth of the well.

³It was the custom there to wait for all the flocks to arrive before removing the stone and watering the animals. Afterward the stone would be placed back over the mouth of the well. ⁴Jacob went over to the shepherds and asked, "Where are you from, my friends?"

"We are from Haran," they answered.

⁵"Do you know a man there named Laban, the grandson of Nahor?" he asked.

"Yes, we do," they replied.

⁶"Is he doing well?" Jacob asked.

"Yes, he's well," they answered. "Look, here comes his daughter Rachel with the flock now."

⁷Jacob said, "Look, it's still broad daylight—too early to round up the animals. Why don't you water the sheep and goats so they can get back out to pasture?"

⁸"We can't water the animals until all the flocks have arrived," they replied. "Then the shepherds move the stone from the mouth of the well, and we water all the sheep and goats."

⁹Jacob was still talking with them when Rachel arrived with her father's flock, for she was a shepherd. ¹⁰And because Rachel was his cousin—the daughter of Laban, his mother's brother—and because the sheep and goats belonged to his uncle Laban, Jacob went over to the well and moved the stone from its mouth and watered his uncle's flock. ¹¹Then Jacob kissed Rachel, and

he wept aloud. ¹²He explained to Rachel that he was her cousin on her father's side—the son of her aunt Rebekah. So Rachel quickly ran and told her father, Laban.

¹³As soon as Laban heard that his nephew Jacob had arrived, he ran out to meet him. He embraced and kissed him and brought him home. When Jacob had told him his story, ¹⁴Laban exclaimed, "You really are my own flesh and blood!"

After Jacob had stayed with Laban for about a month, ¹⁵Laban said to him, "You shouldn't work for me without pay just because we are relatives. Tell me how much your wages should be."

¹⁶Now Laban had two daughters. The older daughter was named Leah, and the younger one was Rachel. ¹⁷There was no sparkle in Leah's eyes,* but Rachel had a beautiful figure and a lovely face. ¹⁸Since Jacob was in love with Rachel, he told her father, "I'll work for you for seven years if you'll give me Rachel, your younger daughter, as my wife."

¹⁹"Agreed!" Laban replied. "I'd rather give her to you than to anyone else. Stay and work with me." ²⁰So Jacob worked seven years to pay for Rachel. But his love for her was so strong that it seemed to him but a few days.

²¹Finally, the time came for him to marry her. "I have fulfilled my agreement," Jacob said to Laban. "Now give me my wife so I can marry her."

²²So Laban invited everyone in the neighborhood and prepared a wedding feast. ²³But that night, when it was dark, Laban took Leah to Jacob, and he slept with her. ²⁴(Laban had given Leah a servant, Zilpah, to be her maid.)

²⁵But when Jacob woke up in the morning—it was Leah! "What have you done to me?" Jacob raged at Laban. "I worked seven years for Rachel! Why have you tricked me?"

²⁶"It's not our custom here to marry off a younger daughter ahead of the first-born," Laban replied. ²⁷"But wait until the bridal week is over, then we'll give you Rachel, too—provided you promise to work another seven years for me."

²⁸So Jacob agreed to work seven more years. A week after Jacob had married Leah, Laban gave him Rachel, too. ²⁹(Laban

gave Rachel a servant, Bilhah, to be her maid.) 30So Jacob slept with Rachel, too, and he loved her much more than Leah. He then stayed and worked for Laban the additional seven years.

31When the LORD saw that Leah was unloved, he enabled her to have children, but Rachel could not conceive. 32So Leah became pregnant and gave birth to a son. She named him Reuben,* for she said, "The LORD has noticed my misery, and now my husband will love me."

33She soon became pregnant again and gave birth to another son. She named him Simeon,* for she said, "The LORD heard that I was unloved and has given me another son."

34Then she became pregnant a third time and gave birth to another son. She named him Levi,* for she said, "Surely this time my husband will feel affection for me, since I have given him three sons!"

35Once again Leah became pregnant and gave birth to another son. She named him Judah,* for she said, "Now I will praise the LORD!" And then she stopped having children.

28:3 Hebrew *El-Shaddai.*   28:4 Hebrew *seed;* also in 28:13, 14.   29:17 Or *Leah had dull eyes,* or *Leah had soft eyes.* The meaning of the Hebrew is uncertain.   29:32 *Reuben* means "Look, a son!" It also sounds like the Hebrew for "He has seen my misery."   29:33 *Simeon* probably means "one who hears."   29:34 *Levi* sounds like a Hebrew term that means "being attached" or "feeling affection for."   29:35 *Judah* sounds like the Hebrew term for "praise."

MATTHEW 9:18-38
Jesus' power and healing poured out of him to people in need. He traveled the countryside teaching, healing, and being a shepherd to lost sheep. The harvest was great when Jesus walked the earth, and it is still so. Will you be one of the workers in his harvest?

As Jesus was saying this, the leader of a synagogue came and knelt before him. "My daughter has just died," he said, "but you can bring her back to life again if you just come and lay your hand on her."

19So Jesus and his disciples got up and went with him. 20Just then a woman who had suffered for twelve years with constant bleeding came up behind him. She touched the fringe of his robe, 21for she thought, "If I can just touch his robe, I will be healed."

22Jesus turned around, and when he saw her he said, "Daughter, be encouraged! Your faith has made you well." And the woman was healed at that moment.

23When Jesus arrived at the official's home, he saw the noisy crowd and heard the funeral music. 24"Get out!" he told them. "The girl isn't dead; she's only asleep." But the crowd laughed at him. 25After the crowd was put outside, however, Jesus went in and took the girl by the hand, and she stood up! 26The report of this miracle swept through the entire countryside.

WHO GOD IS | Jesus is our healer

MATTHEW 9:35 Through his miracles of healing, Jesus was fulfilling prophecy. Isaiah had written of the coming Messiah, "In that day the deaf will hear . . . the blind will see. . . . The lame will leap like a deer, and those who cannot speak will sing for joy!" (Isaiah 29:18; 35:6, September 18, 20). • In addition, Jesus was showing the authority of his words by his miracles. For example, in Luke 5:17-26 (March 22), Jesus healed a paralyzed man. He first forgave the lame man's sins, which upset the religious establishment: "Who does he think he is?" they said. Jesus responded to their criticism by saying that he would perform a miraculous healing in order to prove that he had the authority to forgive sins. He then told the lame man to get up and walk! •Jesus' compassion compelled him to heal, but in the encounters you read, you will discover that he also touched people's hearts and spirits as well as their bodies. Through these miracles, he showed himself to be the promised Messiah who came to bring ultimate healing and eternal life to all who would receive it—including you.

²⁷After Jesus left the girl's home, two blind men followed along behind him, shouting, "Son of David, have mercy on us!"

²⁸They went right into the house where he was staying, and Jesus asked them, "Do you believe I can make you see?"

"Yes, Lord," they told him, "we do."

²⁹Then he touched their eyes and said, "Because of your faith, it will happen." ³⁰Then their eyes were opened, and they could see! Jesus sternly warned them, "Don't tell anyone about this." ³¹But instead, they went out and spread his fame all over the region.

³²When they left, a demon-possessed man who couldn't speak was brought to Jesus. ³³So Jesus cast out the demon, and then the man began to speak. The crowds were amazed. "Nothing like this has ever happened in Israel!" they exclaimed.

³⁴But the Pharisees said, "He can cast out demons because he is empowered by the prince of demons."

³⁵Jesus traveled through all the towns and villages of that area, teaching in the synagogues and announcing the Good News about the Kingdom. And he healed every kind of disease and illness. ³⁶When he saw the crowds, he had compassion on them because they were confused and helpless, like sheep without a shepherd. ³⁷He said to his disciples, "The harvest is great, but the workers are few. ³⁸So pray to the Lord who is in charge of the harvest; ask him to send more workers into his fields."

PSALM 11:1-7
For the choir director: A psalm of David.

¹ I trust in the LORD for protection.
So why do you say to me,
"Fly like a bird to the mountains
for safety!
² The wicked are stringing their bows
and fitting their arrows on the
bowstrings.
They shoot from the shadows
at those whose hearts are right.
³ The foundations of law and order
have collapsed.
What can the righteous do?"

⁴ But the LORD is in his holy Temple;
the LORD still rules from heaven.
He watches everyone closely,
examining every person on earth.
⁵ The LORD examines both the
righteous and the wicked.
He hates those who love violence.
⁶ He will rain down blazing coals and
burning sulfur on the wicked,
punishing them with scorching
winds.
⁷ For the righteous LORD loves justice.
The virtuous will see his face.

PROVERBS 3:11-12
My child, don't reject the LORD's discipline, and don't be upset when he corrects you. For the LORD corrects those he loves, just as a father corrects a child in whom he delights.*

3:12 Greek version reads *And he punishes those he accepts as his children.* Compare Heb 12:6.

JANUARY**14**

GENESIS 30:1-31:16
Jacob's two wives began competing to win Jacob's preference by bearing him sons and heirs. They competed fiercely, using every means possible, including their own female servants. In the meantime, the schemer Jacob laid his own plans to return to his home with some of his father-in-law's fortune.

When Rachel saw that she wasn't having any children for Jacob, she became jeal-ous of her sister. She pleaded with Jacob, "Give me children, or I'll die!"

²Then Jacob became furious with Rachel. "Am I God?" he asked. "He's the one who has kept you from having children!"

³Then Rachel told him, "Take my maid, Bilhah, and sleep with her. She will bear children for me,* and through her I can have a family, too." ⁴So Rachel gave her servant, Bilhah, to Jacob as a wife, and he

slept with her. ⁵Bilhah became pregnant and presented him with a son. ⁶Rachel named him Dan,* for she said, "God has vindicated me! He has heard my request and given me a son." ⁷Then Bilhah became pregnant again and gave Jacob a second son. ⁸Rachel named him Naphtali,* for she said, "I have struggled hard with my sister, and I'm winning!"

⁹Meanwhile, Leah realized that she wasn't getting pregnant anymore, so she took her servant, Zilpah, and gave her to Jacob as a wife. ¹⁰Soon Zilpah presented him with a son. ¹¹Leah named him Gad,* for she said, "How fortunate I am!" ¹²Then Zilpah gave Jacob a second son. ¹³And Leah named him Asher,* for she said, "What joy is mine! Now the other women will celebrate with me."

¹⁴One day during the wheat harvest, Reuben found some mandrakes growing in a field and brought them to his mother, Leah. Rachel begged Leah, "Please give me some of your son's mandrakes."

¹⁵But Leah angrily replied, "Wasn't it enough that you stole my husband? Now will you steal my son's mandrakes, too?"

Rachel answered, "I will let Jacob sleep with you tonight if you give me some of the mandrakes."

¹⁶So that evening, as Jacob was coming home from the fields, Leah went out to meet him. "You must come and sleep with me tonight!" she said. "I have paid for you with some mandrakes that my son found." So that night he slept with Leah. ¹⁷And God answered Leah's prayers. She became pregnant again and gave birth to a fifth son for Jacob. ¹⁸She named him Issachar,* for she said, "God has rewarded me for giving my servant to my husband as a wife." ¹⁹Then Leah became pregnant again and gave birth to a sixth son for Jacob. ²⁰She named him Zebulun,* for she said, "God has given me a good reward. Now my husband will treat me with respect, for I have given him six sons." ²¹Later she gave birth to a daughter and named her Dinah.

²²Then God remembered Rachel's plight and answered her prayers by enabling her to have children. ²³She became pregnant and gave birth to a son. "God has removed my disgrace," she said. ²⁴And she named him Joseph,* for she said, "May the LORD add yet another son to my family."

²⁵Soon after Rachel had given birth to Joseph, Jacob said to Laban, "Please release me so I can go home to my own country. ²⁶Let me take my wives and children, for I have earned them by serving you, and let me be on my way. You certainly know how hard I have worked for you."

²⁷"Please listen to me," Laban replied. "I have become wealthy, for* the LORD has blessed me because of you. ²⁸Tell me how much I owe you. Whatever it is, I'll pay it."

²⁹Jacob replied, "You know how hard I've worked for you, and how your flocks and herds have grown under my care. ³⁰You had little indeed before I came, but your wealth has increased enormously. The LORD has blessed you through everything I've done. But now, what about me? When can I start providing for my own family?"

³¹"What wages do you want?" Laban asked again.

Jacob replied, "Don't give me anything. Just do this one thing, and I'll continue to tend and watch over your flocks. ³²Let me inspect your flocks today and remove all the sheep and goats that are speckled or spotted, along with all the black sheep. Give these to me as my wages. ³³In the future, when you check on the animals you have given me as my wages, you'll see that I have been honest. If you find in my flock any goats without speckles or spots, or any sheep that are not black, you will know that I have stolen them from you."

³⁴"All right," Laban replied. "It will be as you say." ³⁵But that very day Laban went out and removed the male goats that were streaked and spotted, all the female goats that were speckled and spotted or had white patches, and all the black sheep. He placed them in the care of his own sons, ³⁶who took them a three-days' journey from where Jacob was. Meanwhile, Jacob stayed and cared for the rest of Laban's flock.

³⁷Then Jacob took some fresh branches from poplar, almond, and plane trees and peeled off strips of bark, making white streaks on them. ³⁸Then he placed these

peeled branches in the watering troughs where the flocks came to drink, for that was where they mated. [39]And when they mated in front of the white-streaked branches, they gave birth to young that were streaked, speckled, and spotted. [40]Jacob separated those lambs from Laban's flock. And at mating time he turned the flock to face Laban's animals that were streaked or black. This is how he built his own flock instead of increasing Laban's.

[41]Whenever the stronger females were ready to mate, Jacob would place the peeled branches in the watering troughs in front of them. Then they would mate in front of the branches. [42]But he didn't do this with the weaker ones, so the weaker lambs belonged to Laban, and the stronger ones were Jacob's. [43]As a result, Jacob became very wealthy, with large flocks of sheep and goats, male and female servants, and many camels and donkeys.

[31:1]BUT Jacob soon learned that Laban's sons were grumbling about him. "Jacob has robbed our father of everything!" they said. "He has gained all his wealth at our father's expense." [2]And Jacob began to notice a change in Laban's attitude toward him.

[3]Then the LORD said to Jacob, "Return to the land of your father and grandfather and to your relatives there, and I will be with you."

[4]So Jacob called Rachel and Leah out to the field where he was watching his flock. [5]He said to them, "I have noticed that your father's attitude toward me has changed. But the God of my father has been with me. [6]You know how hard I have worked for your father, [7]but he has cheated me, changing my wages ten times. But God has not allowed him to do me any harm. [8]For if he said, 'The speckled animals will be your wages,' the whole flock began to produce speckled young. And when he changed his mind and said, 'The striped animals will be your wages,' then the whole flock produced striped young. [9]In this way, God has taken your father's animals and given them to me.

[10]"One time during the mating season, I had a dream and saw that the male goats mating with the females were streaked, speckled, and spotted. [11]Then in my dream, the angel of God said to me, 'Jacob!' And I replied, 'Yes, here I am.'

[12]"The angel said, 'Look up, and you will see that only the streaked, speckled, and spotted males are mating with the females of your flock. For I have seen how Laban has treated you. [13]I am the God who appeared to you at Bethel,* the place where you anointed the pillar of stone and made your vow to me. Now get ready and leave this country and return to the land of your birth.'"

[14]Rachel and Leah responded, "That's fine with us! We won't inherit any of our father's wealth anyway. [15]He has reduced our rights to those of foreign women. And after he sold us, he wasted the money you paid him for us. [16]All the wealth God has given you from our father legally belongs to us and our children. So go ahead and do whatever God has told you."

30:3 Hebrew *bear children on my knees.* 30:6 *Dan* means "he judged" or "he vindicated." 30:8 *Naphtali* means "my struggle." 30:11 *Gad* means "good fortune." 30:13 *Asher* means "happy." 30:18 *Issachar* sounds like a Hebrew term that means "reward." 30:20 *Zebulun* probably means "honor." 30:24 *Joseph* means "may he add." 30:27 Or *I have learned by divination that.* 31:13 As in Greek version and an Aramaic Targum; Hebrew reads *the God of Bethel.*

MATTHEW 10:1-23
Jesus sent his followers out to spread the news of the Kingdom of God. They could trust God to give them "the right words at the right time" (Matthew 10:19). You, too, are called to be a witness, and you can rely on God's presence and help to accomplish that mission.

Jesus called his twelve disciples together and gave them authority to cast out evil* spirits and to heal every kind of disease and illness. [2]Here are the names of the twelve apostles:

first, Simon (also called Peter),
then Andrew (Peter's brother),
James (son of Zebedee),
John (James's brother),
[3] Philip,
Bartholomew,
Thomas,
Matthew (the tax collector),
James (son of Alphaeus),
Thaddaeus,*

⁴ Simon (the zealot*),
   Judas Iscariot (who later betrayed
      him).

⁵Jesus sent out the twelve apostles with these instructions: "Don't go to the Gentiles or the Samaritans, ⁶but only to the people of Israel—God's lost sheep. ⁷Go and announce to them that the Kingdom of Heaven is near.* ⁸Heal the sick, raise the dead, cure those with leprosy, and cast out demons. Give as freely as you have received!

⁹"Don't take any money in your money belts—no gold, silver, or even copper coins. ¹⁰Don't carry a traveler's bag with a change of clothes and sandals or even a walking stick. Don't hesitate to accept hospitality, because those who work deserve to be fed.

¹¹"Whenever you enter a city or village, search for a worthy person and stay in his home until you leave town. ¹²When you enter the home, give it your blessing. ¹³If it turns out to be a worthy home, let your blessing stand; if it is not, take back the blessing. ¹⁴If any household or town refuses to welcome you or listen to your message, shake its dust from your feet as you leave. ¹⁵I tell you the truth, the wicked cities of Sodom and Gomorrah will be better off than such a town on the judgment day.

¹⁶"Look, I am sending you out as sheep among wolves. So be as shrewd as snakes and harmless as doves. ¹⁷But beware! For you will be handed over to the courts and will be flogged with whips in the synagogues. ¹⁸You will stand trial before governors and kings because you are my followers. But this will be your opportunity to tell the rulers and other unbelievers about me.* ¹⁹When you are arrested, don't worry about how to respond or what to say. God will give you the right words at the right time. ²⁰For it is not you who will be speaking—it will be the Spirit of your Father speaking through you.

²¹"A brother will betray his brother to death, a father will betray his own child, and children will rebel against their parents and cause them to be killed. ²²And all nations will hate you because you are my followers.* But everyone who endures to the end will be saved. ²³When you are persecuted in one town, flee to the next. I tell you the truth, the Son of Man* will return before you have reached all the towns of Israel."

10:1 Greek *unclean.*   10:3 Other manuscripts read *Lebbaeus;* still others read *Lebbaeus who is called Thaddaeus.* 10:4 Greek *the Cananean,* an Aramaic term for Jewish nationalists.   10:7 Or *has come,* or *is coming soon.* 10:18 Or *But this will be your testimony against the rulers and other unbelievers.*   10:22 Greek *on account of my name.*   10:23 "Son of Man" is a title Jesus used for himself.

WHO GOD IS

God keeps his promises

GENESIS 31:3 Jacob was not a sterling example of virtue. He manipulated his older brother to get his birthright and then lied to their father to get the family blessing as well. Sent away for his own safety to another land, Jacob began a long journey of faith. The manipulator was himself manipulated into marrying both of Laban's daughters—getting the one he didn't want first and having to strike another deal in order to marry the woman he loved. Jacob was definitely a work in progress. But when the time came, God spoke to Jacob and sent him back to his homeland, promising, "I will be with you" (Genesis 31:3). Why? Because God had promised that land to Abraham and to his descendants. God had made a promise, and God always keeps his promises. As he had been with Abraham, so he would be with Abraham's grandson Jacob. •Our faith is built on the fact that God always keeps his promises. The slightest doubt about God's ability or desire to do what he says would leave us floundering in hopelessness. We may wonder why God would care about us, as imperfect as we are, but he does. The promises he made to us, he will keep. You can bet on it.

PSALM 12:1-8

*For the choir director: A psalm of David,
to be accompanied by an eight-stringed
instrument.**

¹ **H**elp, O LORD, for the godly are fast
   disappearing!
   The faithful have vanished from
      the earth!
² Neighbors lie to each other,
   speaking with flattering lips and
      deceitful hearts.
³ May the LORD cut off their flattering
      lips
   and silence their boastful tongues.
⁴ They say, "We will lie to our hearts'
      content.
   Our lips are our own—who can
      stop us?"
⁵ The LORD replies, "I have seen
      violence done to the helpless,
   and I have heard the groans of the
      poor.

Now I will rise up to rescue them,
   as they have longed for me to do."
⁶ The LORD's promises are pure,
   like silver refined in a furnace,
      purified seven times over.
⁷ Therefore, LORD, we know you will
      protect the oppressed,
   preserving them forever from
      this lying generation,
⁸ even though the wicked strut
      about,
   and evil is praised throughout
      the land.

12:TITLE Hebrew *according to the sheminith.*

PROVERBS 3:13-15

Joyful is the person who finds wisdom,
the one who gains understanding. For
wisdom is more profitable than silver, and
her wages are better than gold. Wisdom is
more precious than rubies; nothing you
desire can compare with her.

JANUARY**15**

GENESIS 31:17–32:12

Conflict seemed to follow Jacob. He had left his
home to escape his own brother's revenge. He
planned to return home in the midst of a disagreement with his father-in-law, Laban. On the journey
described in this reading, both relationships were
revisited.

So Jacob put his wives and children on
camels, ¹⁸and he drove all his livestock in
front of him. He packed all the belongings
he had acquired in Paddan-aram and set
out for the land of Canaan, where his father, Isaac, lived. ¹⁹At the time they left,
Laban was some distance away, shearing
his sheep. Rachel stole her father's household idols and took them with her. ²⁰Jacob outwitted Laban the Aramean, for
they set out secretly and never told Laban
they were leaving. ²¹So Jacob took all his
possessions with him and crossed the Euphrates River,* heading for the hill country of Gilead.

²²Three days later, Laban was told that
Jacob had fled. ²³So he gathered a group

of his relatives and set out in hot pursuit.
He caught up with Jacob seven days later
in the hill country of Gilead. ²⁴But the previous night God had appeared to Laban
the Aramean in a dream and told him, "I'm
warning you—leave Jacob alone!"

²⁵Laban caught up with Jacob as he was
camped in the hill country of Gilead, and
he set up his camp not far from Jacob's.
²⁶"What do you mean by stealing away like
this?" Laban demanded. "How dare you
drag my daughters away like prisoners of
war? ²⁷Why did you slip away secretly?
Why did you steal away? And why didn't
you say you wanted to leave? I would have
given you a farewell feast, with singing and
music, accompanied by tambourines and
harps. ²⁸Why didn't you let me kiss my
daughters and grandchildren and tell
them good-bye? You have acted very foolishly! ²⁹I could destroy you, but the God of
your father appeared to me last night and
warned me, 'Leave Jacob alone!' ³⁰I can
understand your feeling that you must go,

and your intense longing for your father's home. But why have you stolen my gods?"

³¹"I rushed away because I was afraid," Jacob answered. "I thought you would take your daughters from me by force. ³²But as for your gods, see if you can find them, and let the person who has taken them die! And if you find anything else that belongs to you, identify it before all these relatives of ours, and I will give it back!" But Jacob did not know that Rachel had stolen the household idols.

³³Laban went first into Jacob's tent to search there, then into Leah's, and then the tents of the two servant wives—but he found nothing. Finally, he went into Rachel's tent. ³⁴But Rachel had taken the household idols and hidden them in her camel saddle, and now she was sitting on them. When Laban had thoroughly searched her tent without finding them, ³⁵she said to her father, "Please, sir, forgive me if I don't get up for you. I'm having my monthly period." So Laban continued his search, but he could not find the household idols.

³⁶Then Jacob became very angry, and he challenged Laban. "What's my crime?" he demanded. "What have I done wrong to make you chase after me as though I were a criminal? ³⁷You have rummaged through everything I own. Now show me what you found that belongs to you! Set it out here in front of us, before our relatives, for all to see. Let them judge between us!

³⁸"For twenty years I have been with you, caring for your flocks. In all that time your sheep and goats never miscarried. In all those years I never used a single ram of yours for food. ³⁹If any were attacked and killed by wild animals, I never showed you the carcass and asked you to reduce the count of your flock. No, I took the loss myself! You made me pay for every stolen animal, whether it was taken in broad daylight or in the dark of night.

⁴⁰"I worked for you through the scorching heat of the day and through cold and sleepless nights. ⁴¹Yes, for twenty years I slaved in your house! I worked for fourteen years earning your two daughters, and then six more years for your flock. And you changed my wages ten times!

⁴²In fact, if the God of my father had not been on my side—the God of Abraham and the fearsome God of Isaac*—you would have sent me away empty-handed. But God has seen your abuse and my hard work. That is why he appeared to you last night and rebuked you!"

⁴³Then Laban replied to Jacob, "These women are my daughters, these children are my grandchildren, and these flocks are my flocks—in fact, everything you see is mine. But what can I do now about my daughters and their children? ⁴⁴So come, let's make a covenant, you and I, and it will be a witness to our commitment."

⁴⁵So Jacob took a stone and set it up as a monument. ⁴⁶Then he told his family members, "Gather some stones." So they gathered stones and piled them in a heap. Then Jacob and Laban sat down beside the pile of stones to eat a covenant meal. ⁴⁷To commemorate the event, Laban called the place Jegar-sahadutha (which means "witness pile" in Aramaic), and Jacob called it Galeed (which means "witness pile" in Hebrew).

⁴⁸Then Laban declared, "This pile of stones will stand as a witness to remind us of the covenant we have made today." This explains why it was called Galeed—"Witness Pile." ⁴⁹But it was also called Mizpah (which means "watchtower"), for Laban said, "May the LORD keep watch between us to make sure that we keep this covenant when we are out of each other's sight. ⁵⁰If you mistreat my daughters or if you marry other wives, God will see it even if no one else does. He is a witness to this covenant between us.

⁵¹"See this pile of stones," Laban continued, "and see this monument I have set between us. ⁵²They stand between us as witnesses of our vows. I will never pass this pile of stones to harm you, and you must never pass these stones or this monument to harm me. ⁵³I call on the God of our ancestors—the God of your grandfather Abraham and the God of my grandfather Nahor—to serve as a judge between us."

So Jacob took an oath before the fearsome God of his father, Isaac,* to respect the boundary line. ⁵⁴Then Jacob offered a sacrifice to God there on the mountain and invited everyone to a covenant feast. After they had eaten, they spent the night on the mountain.

55*Laban got up early the next morning, and he kissed his grandchildren and his daughters and blessed them. Then he left and returned home.

32:1*As Jacob started on his way again, angels of God came to meet him. 2When Jacob saw them, he exclaimed, "This is God's camp!" So he named the place Mahanaim.*

3Then Jacob sent messengers ahead to his brother, Esau, who was living in the region of Seir in the land of Edom. 4He told them, "Give this message to my master Esau: 'Humble greetings from your servant Jacob. Until now I have been living with Uncle Laban, 5and now I own cattle, donkeys, flocks of sheep and goats, and many servants, both men and women. I have sent these messengers to inform my lord of my coming, hoping that you will be friendly to me.'"

6After delivering the message, the messengers returned to Jacob and reported, "We met your brother, Esau, and he is already on his way to meet you—with an army of 400 men!" 7Jacob was terrified at the news. He divided his household, along with the flocks and herds and camels, into two groups. 8He thought, "If Esau meets one group and attacks it, perhaps the other group can escape."

9Then Jacob prayed, "O God of my grandfather Abraham, and God of my father, Isaac—O LORD, you told me, 'Return to your own land and to your relatives.' And you promised me, 'I will treat you kindly.' 10I am not worthy of all the unfailing love and faithfulness you have shown to me, your servant. When I left home and crossed the Jordan River, I owned nothing except a walking stick. Now my household fills two large camps! 11O LORD, please rescue me from the hand of my brother, Esau. I am afraid that he is coming to attack me, along with my wives and children. 12But you promised me, 'I will surely treat you kindly, and I will multiply your descendants until they become as numerous as the sands along the seashore—too many to count.'"

31:21 Hebrew *the river.*   31:42 Or *and the Fear of Isaac.*
31:53 Or *the Fear of his father, Isaac.*   31:55 Verse 31:55 is numbered 32:1 in Hebrew text.   32:1 Verses 32:1-32 are numbered 32:2-33 in Hebrew text.   32:2 *Mahanaim* means "two camps."

MATTHEW 10:24-11:6

Both Jesus' life and his message were controversial. Even John the Baptist wondered about Jesus' revolutionary ways. Jesus responded by saying, in essence, "See how I fulfill the prophecies of what the Messiah would do. I am indeed the promised Messiah."

"**S**tudents* are not greater than their teacher, and slaves are not greater than their master. 25Students are to be like their teacher, and slaves are to be like their master. And since I, the master of the household, have been called the prince of demons,* the members of my household will be called by even worse names!

26"But don't be afraid of those who threaten you. For the time is coming when everything that is covered will be revealed, and all that is secret will be made known to all. 27What I tell you now in the darkness, shout abroad when daybreak comes. What I whisper in your ear, shout from the housetops for all to hear!

28"Don't be afraid of those who want to kill your body; they cannot touch your soul. Fear only God, who can destroy both soul and body in hell.* 29What is the price of two sparrows—one copper coin*? But not a single sparrow can fall to the ground without your Father knowing it. 30And the very hairs on your head are all numbered. 31So don't be afraid; you are more valuable to God than a whole flock of sparrows.

32"Everyone who acknowledges me publicly here on earth, I will also acknowledge before my Father in heaven. 33But everyone who denies me here on earth, I will also deny before my Father in heaven.

34"Don't imagine that I came to bring peace to the earth! I came not to bring peace, but a sword.

35 'I have come to set a man against
    his father,
  a daughter against her mother,
  and a daughter-in-law against her
    mother-in-law.
36 Your enemies will be right in your
    own household!'*

³⁷"If you love your father or mother more than you love me, you are not worthy of being mine; or if you love your son or daughter more than me, you are not worthy of being mine. ³⁸If you refuse to take up your cross and follow me, you are not worthy of being mine. ³⁹If you cling to your life, you will lose it; but if you give up your life for me, you will find it.

⁴⁰"Anyone who receives you receives me, and anyone who receives me receives the Father who sent me. ⁴¹If you receive a prophet as one who speaks for God,* you will be given the same reward as a prophet. And if you receive righteous people because of their righteousness, you will be given a reward like theirs. ⁴²And if you give even a cup of cold water to one of the least of my followers, you will surely be rewarded."

¹¹:¹WHEN Jesus had finished giving these instructions to his twelve disciples, he went out to teach and preach in towns throughout the region.

²John the Baptist, who was in prison, heard about all the things the Messiah was doing. So he sent his disciples to ask Jesus, ³"Are you the Messiah we've been expecting,* or should we keep looking for someone else?"

⁴Jesus told them, "Go back to John and tell him what you have heard and seen—

⁵the blind see, the lame walk, the lepers are cured, the deaf hear, the dead are raised to life, and the Good News is being preached to the poor. ⁶And tell him, 'God blesses those who do not turn away because of me.*'"

10:24 Or *Disciples.*   10:25 Greek *Beezeboul;* other manuscripts read *Beezeboul;* Latin version reads *Beelzebub.* 10:28 Greek *Gehenna.*   10:29 Greek *one assarion* [i.e., one "as," a Roman coin equal to ¹⁄₁₆ of a denarius].   10:35-36 Mic 7:6.   10:41 Greek *receive a prophet in the name of a prophet.*   11:3 Greek *Are you the one who is coming?* 11:6 Or *who are not offended by me.*

PSALM 13:1-6
For the choir director: A psalm of David.

¹ O LORD, how long will you forget me?
      Forever?
      How long will you look the other
         way?
² How long must I struggle with
      anguish in my soul,
      with sorrow in my heart
         every day?
      How long will my enemy have
         the upper hand?

³ Turn and answer me, O LORD
      my God!
      Restore the sparkle to my eyes,
         or I will die.
⁴ Don't let my enemies gloat, saying,
      "We have defeated him!"
      Don't let them rejoice at my
         downfall.

HOW WE LIVE Dealing with problems

GENESIS 32:11-12 Jacob had a problem: the brother from whom he had stolen both inheritance and blessing was soon to appear on his "doorstep" for the first time in twenty years. He would soon come face-to-face with a brother who definitely had reason to carry a big grudge! •Jacob could have done many things to spin the situation in his favor—he could have had his brother ambushed and killed; he could have run for another land; he could have prepared his men for battle. In his earlier days, Jacob might have chosen one of those options. Instead, after years of personal growth, Jacob dealt with this crisis by going to the ultimate problem-solver—God. He humbly confessed his unworthiness but then asked for rescue, claiming the promise God had made to him. •God desires such humility from his followers. When you turn to him with your problems, he delights to surprise you with an outcome or answer that you couldn't have imagined in your wildest dreams.

5 But I trust in your unfailing
    love.
  I will rejoice because you have
    rescued me.
6 I will sing to the LORD
    because he is good to me.

JANUARY**16**

GENESIS 32:13–34:31

What would you do the night before you faced
someone whose life you'd damaged irreparably?
Read about how Jacob faced Esau, the brother from
whom he had stolen a large portion of the family
inheritance.

Jacob stayed where he was for the night.
Then he selected these gifts from his possessions to present to his brother, Esau:
14200 female goats, 20 male goats,
200 ewes, 20 rams, 1530 female camels
with their young, 40 cows, 10 bulls, 20 female donkeys, and 10 male donkeys. 16He
divided these animals into herds and assigned each to different servants. Then he
told his servants, "Go ahead of me with the
animals, but keep some distance between
the herds."

17He gave these instructions to the
men leading the first group: "When my
brother, Esau, meets you, he will ask,
'Whose servants are you? Where are you
going? Who owns these animals?' 18You
must reply, 'They belong to your servant
Jacob, but they are a gift for his master
Esau. Look, he is coming right behind us.'"

19Jacob gave the same instructions to
the second and third herdsmen and to all
who followed behind the herds: "You must
say the same thing to Esau when you meet
him. 20And be sure to say, 'Look, your servant Jacob is right behind us.'"

Jacob thought, "I will try to appease
him by sending gifts ahead of me. When I
see him in person, perhaps he will be
friendly to me." 21So the gifts were sent on
ahead, while Jacob himself spent that
night in the camp.

22During the night Jacob got up and
took his two wives, his two servant wives,

PROVERBS 3:16-18

She [Wisdom] offers you long life in her
right hand, and riches and honor in her
left. She will guide you down delightful
paths; all her ways are satisfying. Wisdom
is a tree of life to those who embrace her;
happy are those who hold her tightly.

and his eleven sons and crossed the
Jabbok River with them. 23After taking
them to the other side, he sent over all his
possessions.

24This left Jacob all alone in the camp,
and a man came and wrestled with him until the dawn began to break. 25When the
man saw that he would not win the match,
he touched Jacob's hip and wrenched it out
of its socket. 26Then the man said, "Let me
go, for the dawn is breaking!"

But Jacob said, "I will not let you go unless you bless me."

27"What is your name?" the man asked.

He replied, "Jacob."

28"Your name will no longer be Jacob,"
the man told him. "From now on you will
be called Israel,* because you have fought
with God and with men and have won."

29"Please tell me your name," Jacob
said.

"Why do you want to know my name?"
the man replied. Then he blessed Jacob
there.

30Jacob named the place Peniel (which
means "face of God"), for he said, "I have
seen God face to face, yet my life has been
spared." 31The sun was rising as Jacob left
Peniel,* and he was limping because of
the injury to his hip. 32(Even today the
people of Israel don't eat the tendon near
the hip socket because of what happened
that night when the man strained the tendon of Jacob's hip.)

33:1THEN Jacob looked up and saw Esau
coming with his 400 men. So he divided
the children among Leah, Rachel, and his
two servant wives. 2He put the servant
wives and their children at the front, Leah

and her children next, and Rachel and Joseph last. [3]Then Jacob went on ahead. As he approached his brother, he bowed to the ground seven times before him. [4]Then Esau ran to meet him and embraced him, threw his arms around his neck, and kissed him. And they both wept.

[5]Then Esau looked at the women and children and asked, "Who are these people with you?"

"These are the children God has graciously given to me, your servant," Jacob replied. [6]Then the servant wives came forward with their children and bowed before him. [7]Next came Leah with her children, and they bowed before him. Finally, Joseph and Rachel came forward and bowed before him.

[8]"And what were all the flocks and herds I met as I came?" Esau asked.

Jacob replied, "They are a gift, my lord, to ensure your friendship."

[9]"My brother, I have plenty," Esau answered. "Keep what you have for yourself."

[10]But Jacob insisted, "No, if I have found favor with you, please accept this gift from me. And what a relief to see your friendly smile. It is like seeing the face of God! [11]Please take this gift I have brought you, for God has been very gracious to me. I have more than enough." And because Jacob insisted, Esau finally accepted the gift.

[12]"Well," Esau said, "let's be going. I will lead the way."

[13]But Jacob replied, "You can see, my lord, that some of the children are very young, and the flocks and herds have their young, too. If they are driven too hard, even for one day, all the animals could die. [14]Please, my lord, go ahead of your servant. We will follow slowly, at a pace that is comfortable for the livestock and the children. I will meet you at Seir."

[15]"All right," Esau said, "but at least let me assign some of my men to guide and protect you."

Jacob responded, "That's not necessary. It's enough that you've received me warmly, my lord!"

[16]So Esau turned around and started back to Seir that same day. [17]Jacob, on the other hand, traveled on to Succoth. There he built himself a house and made shelters for his livestock. That is why the place was named Succoth (which means "shelters").

[18]Later, having traveled all the way from Paddan-aram, Jacob arrived safely at the town of Shechem, in the land of Canaan. There he set up camp outside the town. [19]Jacob bought the plot of land where he camped from the family of Hamor, the father of Shechem, for 100 pieces of silver.* [20]And there he built an altar and named it El-Elohe-Israel.*

34:1ONE day Dinah, the daughter of Jacob and Leah, went to visit some of the young women who lived in the area. [2]But when the local prince, Shechem son of Hamor the Hivite, saw Dinah, he seized her and raped her. [3]But then he fell in love with her, and he tried to win her affection with tender words. [4]He said to his father, Hamor, "Get me this young girl. I want to marry her."

[5]Soon Jacob heard that Shechem had defiled his daughter, Dinah. But since his sons were out in the fields herding his livestock, he said nothing until they returned. [6]Hamor, Shechem's father, came to discuss the matter with Jacob. [7]Meanwhile, Jacob's sons had come in from the field as soon as they heard what had happened. They were shocked and furious that their sister had been raped. Shechem had done a disgraceful thing against Jacob's family,* something that should never be done.

[8]Hamor tried to speak with Jacob and his sons. "My son Shechem is truly in love with your daughter," he said. "Please let him marry her. [9]In fact, let's arrange other marriages, too. You give us your daughters for our sons, and we will give you our daughters for your sons. [10]And you may live among us; the land is open to you! Settle here and trade with us. And feel free to buy property in the area."

[11]Then Shechem himself spoke to Dinah's father and brothers. "Please be kind to me, and let me marry her," he begged. "I will give you whatever you ask. [12]No matter what dowry or gift you demand, I will gladly pay it—just give me the girl as my wife."

¹³But since Shechem had defiled their sister, Dinah, Jacob's sons responded deceitfully to Shechem and his father, Hamor. ¹⁴They said to them, "We couldn't possibly allow this, because you're not circumcised. It would be a disgrace for our sister to marry a man like you! ¹⁵But here is a solution. If every man among you will be circumcised like we are, ¹⁶then we will give you our daughters, and we'll take your daughters for ourselves. We will live among you and become one people. ¹⁷But if you don't agree to be circumcised, we will take her and be on our way."

¹⁸Hamor and his son Shechem agreed to their proposal. ¹⁹Shechem wasted no time in acting on this request, for he wanted Jacob's daughter desperately. Shechem was a highly respected member of his family, ²⁰and he went with his father, Hamor, to present this proposal to the leaders at the town gate.

²¹"These men are our friends," they said. "Let's invite them to live here among us and trade freely. Look, the land is large enough to hold them. We can take their daughters as wives and let them marry ours. ²²But they will consider staying here and becoming one people with us only if all of our men are circumcised, just as they are. ²³But if we do this, all their livestock and possessions will eventually be ours. Come, let's agree to their terms and let them settle here among us."

²⁴So all the men in the town council agreed with Hamor and Shechem, and every male in the town was circumcised. ²⁵But three days later, when their wounds were still sore, two of Jacob's sons, Simeon and Levi, who were Dinah's full brothers, took their swords and entered the town without opposition. Then they slaughtered every male there, ²⁶including Hamor and his son Shechem. They killed them with their swords, then took Dinah from Shechem's house and returned to their camp.

²⁷Meanwhile, the rest of Jacob's sons arrived. Finding the men slaughtered, they plundered the town because their sister had been defiled there. ²⁸They seized all the flocks and herds and donkeys—everything they could lay their hands on, both inside the town and outside in the fields. ²⁹They looted all their wealth and plundered their houses. They also took all their little children and wives and led them away as captives.

³⁰Afterward Jacob said to Simeon and Levi, "You have ruined me! You've made me stink among all the people of this land—among all the Canaanites and Perizzites. We are so few that they will join forces and crush us. I will be ruined, and my entire household will be wiped out!"

³¹"But why should we let him treat our sister like a prostitute?" they retorted angrily.

32:28 *Jacob* sounds like the Hebrew words for "heel" and "deceiver." *Israel* means "God fights."   32:31 Hebrew *Penuel,* a variant spelling of Peniel.   33:19 Hebrew *100 kesitahs;* the value or weight of the kesitah is no longer known.   33:20 *El-Elohe-Israel* means "God, the God of Israel."   34:7 Hebrew *a disgraceful thing in Israel.*

MATTHEW 11:7-30

Neither the piety and preaching of John the Baptist nor the miracles and compassion of Jesus satisfied those with hard hearts in Jesus' day. Jesus brought a new way of living and thinking, but who would hear him and believe?

As John's disciples were leaving, Jesus began talking about him to the crowds. "What kind of man did you go into the wilderness to see? Was he a weak reed, swayed by every breath of wind? ⁸Or were you expecting to see a man dressed in expensive clothes? No, people with expensive clothes live in palaces. ⁹Were you looking for a prophet? Yes, and he is more than a prophet. ¹⁰John is the man to whom the Scriptures refer when they say,

'Look, I am sending my messenger
  ahead of you,
    and he will prepare your way before
    you.'*

¹¹"I tell you the truth, of all who have ever lived, none is greater than John the Baptist. Yet even the least person in the Kingdom of Heaven is greater than he is! ¹²And from the time John the Baptist began preaching until now, the Kingdom of Heaven has been forcefully advancing,* and violent people are attacking it. ¹³For before John came, all the prophets and the law of Moses looked forward to this present time. ¹⁴And if you are willing to accept what I say, he is Elijah, the one the proph-

ets said would come.* [15]Anyone with ears to hear should listen and understand!

[16]"To what can I compare this generation? It is like children playing a game in the public square. They complain to their friends,

[17] 'We played wedding songs,
   and you didn't dance,
so we played funeral songs,
   and you didn't mourn.'

[18]For John didn't spend his time eating and drinking, and you say, 'He's possessed by a demon.' [19]The Son of Man,* on the other hand, feasts and drinks, and you say, 'He's a glutton and a drunkard, and a friend of tax collectors and other sinners!' But wisdom is shown to be right by its results."

[20]Then Jesus began to denounce the towns where he had done so many of his miracles, because they hadn't repented of their sins and turned to God. [21]"What sorrow awaits you, Korazin and Bethsaida! For if the miracles I did in you had been done in wicked Tyre and Sidon, their people would have repented of their sins long ago, clothing themselves in burlap and throwing ashes on their heads to show their remorse. [22]I tell you, Tyre and Sidon will be better off on judgment day than you.

[23]"And you people of Capernaum, will you be honored in heaven? No, you will go down to the place of the dead.* For if the miracles I did for you had been done in wicked Sodom, it would still be here today. [24]I tell you, even Sodom will be better off on judgment day than you."

[25]At that time Jesus prayed this prayer: "O Father, Lord of heaven and earth, thank you for hiding these things from those who think themselves wise and clever, and for revealing them to the childlike. [26]Yes, Father, it pleased you to do it this way!

[27]"My Father has entrusted everything to me. No one truly knows the Son except the Father, and no one truly knows the Father except the Son and those to whom the Son chooses to reveal him."

[28]Then Jesus said, "Come to me, all of you who are weary and carry heavy burdens, and I will give you rest. [29]Take my yoke upon you. Let me teach you, because I am humble and gentle at heart, and you will find rest for your souls. [30]For my yoke is easy to bear, and the burden I give you is light."

11:10 Mal 3:1.   **11:12** Or *the Kingdom of Heaven has suffered from violence.*   **11:14** See Mal 4:5.   **11:19** "Son of Man" is a title Jesus used for himself.   **11:23** Greek *to Hades.*

PSALM 14:1-7
For the choir director: A psalm of David.

[1] **O**nly fools say in their hearts,
   "There is no God."
They are corrupt, and their actions
   are evil;
      not one of them does good!

HOW WE LIVE

Knowing God's peace

MATTHEW 11:28-30 The pious religious leaders of Jesus' day had burdened the Jewish people with many rules and regulations. Jesus told the people to take off those burdens, which were only false attempts to earn God's favor, and pick up his yoke. There is still a yoke—following Jesus means commitment and sacrifice—but his yoke yields joy, fruitful service, and fulfillment.   • A couple of extremes exist in the world today. Some believers want to take away other believers' freedom in Christ and replace it with a list of rules for how to live acceptably. These people are modern-day Pharisees. Others claim to be Christians but throw out all of the Bible's clear commands. The first group ignores God's grace; the second abuses it. In between stands Jesus, who has set us free from bondage to false religion in order for us to take up his yoke of true righteousness. His yoke is not meant to drag us down into shame or guilt, but to make us contagious, thankful, peaceful, joyous believers!

2 The LORD looks down from heaven
　　on the entire human race;
　he looks to see if anyone is truly wise,
　　if anyone seeks God.
3 But no, all have turned away;
　　all have become corrupt.*
　No one does good,
　　not a single one!

4 Will those who do evil never learn?
　　They eat up my people like bread
　　and wouldn't think of praying to
　　　the LORD.
5 Terror will grip them,
　　for God is with those who
　　　obey him.
6 The wicked frustrate the plans of the
　　oppressed,

but the LORD will protect his
　　people.

7 Who will come from Mount Zion
　　to rescue Israel?
　When the LORD restores his
　　people,
　Jacob will shout with joy, and Israel
　　will rejoice.

14:3 Greek version reads *have become useless.* Compare
Rom 3:12.

PROVERBS 3:19-20

By wisdom the LORD founded the earth;
by understanding he created the heavens.
By his knowledge the deep fountains of
the earth burst forth, and the dew settles
beneath the night sky.

JANUARY**17**

GENESIS 35:1-36:43

Jacob's descendants would become the nation of
Israel. The descendants of his twin brother, Esau,
would become the nation of Edom. Though these
brothers seemed to have settled their differences,
the nations that grew from them were in conflict for
the rest of the Old Testament.

Then God said to Jacob, "Get ready and
move to Bethel and settle there. Build an
altar there to the God who appeared to
you when you fled from your brother,
Esau."

2 So Jacob told everyone in his household, "Get rid of all your pagan idols, purify
yourselves, and put on clean clothing. 3 We
are now going to Bethel, where I will build
an altar to the God who answered my
prayers when I was in distress. He has
been with me wherever I have gone."

4 So they gave Jacob all their pagan idols
and earrings, and he buried them under
the great tree near Shechem. 5 As they set
out, a terror from God spread over the
people in all the towns of that area, so no
one attacked Jacob's family.

6 Eventually, Jacob and his household
arrived at Luz (also called Bethel) in

Canaan. 7 Jacob built an altar there and
named the place El-bethel (which means
"God of Bethel"), because God had appeared to him there when he was fleeing
from his brother, Esau.

8 Soon after this, Rebekah's old nurse,
Deborah, died. She was buried beneath
the oak tree in the valley below Bethel.
Ever since, the tree has been called Allon-
bacuth (which means "oak of weeping").

9 Now that Jacob had returned from
Paddan-aram, God appeared to him again
at Bethel. God blessed him, 10 saying,
"Your name is Jacob, but you will not be
called Jacob any longer. From now on your
name will be Israel."* So God renamed
him Israel.

11 Then God said, "I am El-Shaddai—
'God Almighty.' Be fruitful and multiply.
You will become a great nation, even many
nations. Kings will be among your descendants! 12 And I will give you the land I once
gave to Abraham and Isaac. Yes, I will give
it to you and your descendants after you."
13 Then God went up from the place where
he had spoken to Jacob.

¹⁴Jacob set up a stone pillar to mark the place where God had spoken to him. Then he poured wine over it as an offering to God and anointed the pillar with olive oil. ¹⁵And Jacob named the place Bethel (which means "house of God"), because God had spoken to him there.

¹⁶Leaving Bethel, Jacob and his clan moved on toward Ephrath. But Rachel went into labor while they were still some distance away. Her labor pains were intense. ¹⁷After a very hard delivery, the midwife finally exclaimed, "Don't be afraid—you have another son!" ¹⁸Rachel was about to die, but with her last breath she named the baby Ben-oni (which means "son of my sorrow"). The baby's father, however, called him Benjamin (which means "son of my right hand"). ¹⁹So Rachel died and was buried on the way to Ephrath (that is, Bethlehem). ²⁰Jacob set up a stone monument over Rachel's grave, and it can be seen there to this day.

²¹Then Jacob* traveled on and camped beyond Migdal-eder. ²²While he was living there, Reuben had intercourse with Bilhah, his father's concubine, and Jacob soon heard about it.

These are the names of the twelve sons of Jacob:

²³The sons of Leah were Reuben (Jacob's oldest son), Simeon, Levi, Judah, Issachar, and Zebulun.

²⁴The sons of Rachel were Joseph and Benjamin.

²⁵The sons of Bilhah, Rachel's servant, were Dan and Naphtali.

²⁶The sons of Zilpah, Leah's servant, were Gad and Asher.

These are the names of the sons who were born to Jacob at Paddan-aram.

²⁷So Jacob returned to his father, Isaac, in Mamre, which is near Kiriath-arba (now called Hebron), where Abraham and Isaac had both lived as foreigners. ²⁸Isaac lived for 180 years. ²⁹Then he breathed his last and died at a ripe old age, joining his ancestors in death. And his sons, Esau and Jacob, buried him.

36:1THIS is the account of the descendants of Esau (also known as Edom). ²Esau married two young women from Canaan: Adah, the daughter of Elon the Hittite; and Oholibamah, the daughter of Anah and granddaughter of Zibeon the Hivite. ³He also married his cousin Basemath, who was the daughter of Ishmael and the sister of Nebaioth. ⁴Adah gave birth to a son named Eliphaz for Esau. Basemath gave birth to a son named Reuel. ⁵Oholibamah gave birth to sons named Jeush, Jalam, and Korah. All these sons were born to Esau in the land of Canaan.

⁶Esau took his wives, his children, and his entire household, along with his livestock and cattle—all the wealth he had acquired in the land of Canaan—and moved away from his brother, Jacob. ⁷There was not enough land to support them both because of all the livestock and possessions they had acquired. ⁸So Esau (also known as Edom) settled in the hill country of Seir.

⁹This is the account of Esau's descendants, the Edomites, who lived in the hill country of Seir.

¹⁰These are the names of Esau's sons:
Eliphaz, the son of Esau's wife Adah; and Reuel, the son of Esau's wife Basemath.

¹¹The descendants of Eliphaz were Teman, Omar, Zepho, Gatam, and Kenaz. ¹²Timna, the concubine of Esau's son Eliphaz, gave birth to a son named Amalek. These are the descendants of Esau's wife Adah.

¹³The descendants of Reuel were Nahath, Zerah, Shammah, and Mizzah. These are the descendants of Esau's wife Basemath.

¹⁴Esau also had sons through Oholibamah, the daughter of Anah and granddaughter of Zibeon. Their names were Jeush, Jalam, and Korah.

¹⁵These are the descendants of Esau who became the leaders of various clans:

The descendants of Esau's oldest son, Eliphaz, became the leaders of the clans of Teman, Omar, Zepho, Kenaz, ¹⁶Korah, Gatam, and Amalek. These are the clan leaders in the land of Edom who descended from Eliphaz. All these were descendants of Esau's wife Adah.

17 The descendants of Esau's son Reuel became the leaders of the clans of Nahath, Zerah, Shammah, and Mizzah. These are the clan leaders in the land of Edom who descended from Reuel. All these were descendants of Esau's wife Basemath.

18 The descendants of Esau and his wife Oholibamah became the leaders of the clans of Jeush, Jalam, and Korah. These are the clan leaders who descended from Esau's wife Oholibamah, the daughter of Anah.

19 These are the clans descended from Esau (also known as Edom), identified by their clan leaders.

20 These are the names of the tribes that descended from Seir the Horite. They lived in the land of Edom: Lotan, Shobal, Zibeon, Anah, 21 Dishon, Ezer, and Dishan. These were the Horite clan leaders, the descendants of Seir, who lived in the land of Edom.

22 The descendants of Lotan were Hori and Heman. Lotan also had a sister named Timna.

23 The descendants of Shobal were Alvan, Manahath, Ebal, Shepho, and Onam.

24 The descendants of Zibeon were Aiah and Anah. (This is the Anah who discovered the hot springs in the wilderness while he was grazing his father's donkeys.)

25 The descendants of Anah were his son, Dishon, and his daughter, Oholibamah.

26 The descendants of Dishon* were Hemdan, Eshban, Ithran, and Keran.

27 The descendants of Ezer were Bilhan, Zaavan, and Akan.

28 The descendants of Dishan were Uz and Aran.

29 So these were the leaders of the Horite clans: Lotan, Shobal, Zibeon, Anah, 30 Dishon, Ezer, and Dishan. The Horite clans are named after their clan leaders, who lived in the land of Seir.

31 These are the kings who ruled in the land of Edom before any king ruled over the Israelites*:

32 Bela son of Beor, who ruled in Edom from the city of Dinhabah.

33 After Bela died, Jobab son of Zerah from Bozrah became king in his place.

34 After Jobab died, Husham from the land of the Temanites became king in his place.

35 After Husham died, Hadad son of Bedad became king in his place and ruled from the city of Avith. He was the one who defeated the Midianites in the land of Moab.

36 After Hadad died, Samlah from the city of Masrekah became king in his place.

37 After Samlah died, Shaul from the city of Rehoboth-on-the-River became king in his place.

38 After Shaul died, Baal-hanan son of Acbor became king in his place.

39 After Baal-hanan son of Acbor died, Hadad* became king in his place and ruled from the city of Pau. Hadad's wife was Mehetabel, the daughter of Matred and granddaughter of Mezahab.

40 These are the names of the leaders of the clans descended from Esau, who lived in the places named for them: Timna, Alvah, Jetheth, 41 Oholibamah, Elah, Pinon, 42 Kenaz, Teman, Mibzar, 43 Magdiel, and Iram. These are the leaders of the clans of Edom, listed according to their settlements in the land they occupied. They all descended from Esau, the ancestor of the Edomites.

35:10 *Jacob* sounds like the Hebrew words for "heel" and "deceiver." *Israel* means "God fights."   35:21 Hebrew *Israel;* also in 35:22a. The names "Jacob" and "Israel" are often interchanged throughout the Old Testament, referring sometimes to the individual patriarch and sometimes to the nation.   36:26 Hebrew *Dishan*, a variant spelling of Dishon; compare 36:21, 28.   36:31 Or *before an Israelite king ruled over them.*   36:39 As in some Hebrew manuscripts, Samaritan Pentateuch, and Syriac version (see also 1 Chr 1:50); most Hebrew manuscripts read *Hadar.*

MATTHEW 12:1-21

Jesus showed that the Kingdom of God was bigger than human traditions. He stood so strongly against empty rituals that the religious leadership sought to kill him.

At about that time Jesus was walking through some grainfields on the Sabbath. His disciples were hungry, so they began breaking off some heads of grain and eating them. 2 But some Pharisees saw them do it and protested, "Look, your disciples are breaking the law by harvesting grain on the Sabbath."

³Jesus said to them, "Haven't you read in the Scriptures what David did when he and his companions were hungry? ⁴He went into the house of God, and he and his companions broke the law by eating the sacred loaves of bread that only the priests are allowed to eat. ⁵And haven't you read in the law of Moses that the priests on duty in the Temple may work on the Sabbath? ⁶I tell you, there is one here who is even greater than the Temple! ⁷But you would not have condemned my innocent disciples if you knew the meaning of this Scripture: 'I want you to show mercy, not offer sacrifices.'* ⁸For the Son of Man* is Lord, even over the Sabbath!"

⁹Then Jesus went over to their synagogue, ¹⁰where he noticed a man with a deformed hand. The Pharisees asked Jesus, "Does the law permit a person to work by healing on the Sabbath?" (They were hoping he would say yes, so they could bring charges against him.)

¹¹And he answered, "If you had a sheep that fell into a well on the Sabbath, wouldn't you work to pull it out? Of course you would. ¹²And how much more valuable is a person than a sheep! Yes, the law permits a person to do good on the Sabbath."

¹³Then he said to the man, "Hold out your hand." So the man held out his hand, and it was restored, just like the other one! ¹⁴Then the Pharisees called a meeting to plot how to kill Jesus.

¹⁵But Jesus knew what they were planning. So he left that area, and many people followed him. He healed all the sick among them, ¹⁶but he warned them not to reveal who he was. ¹⁷This fulfilled the prophecy of Isaiah concerning him:

¹⁸ "Look at my Servant, whom I have
    chosen.
    He is my Beloved, who pleases me.
    I will put my Spirit upon him,
    and he will proclaim justice to the
        nations.
¹⁹ He will not fight or shout
    or raise his voice in public.
²⁰ He will not crush the weakest reed
    or put out a flickering candle.
    Finally he will cause justice to be
        victorious.
²¹ And his name will be the hope
    of all the world."*

12:7 Hos 6:6 (Greek version).　12:8 "Son of Man" is a title Jesus used for himself.　12:18-21 Isa 42:1-4 (Greek version for 42:4).

WHO GOD IS
Jesus is Lord

MATTHEW 12:6-8 In the Gospels, Jesus frequently is called *Lord*. Here Jesus speaks of himself as "Lord, even over the Sabbath" (Matthew 12:8). Jesus also said, "You call me 'Teacher' and 'Lord,' and you are right, because that's what I am" (John 13:13, May 23). Jesus is indeed Lord, because he is God who came in the flesh. He is Lord because he is worthy of all honor. Yet even as our Lord, he himself "took the humble position of a slave and was born as a human being. When he appeared in human form, he humbled himself in obedience to God and died a criminal's death on a cross" (Philippians 2:7-8, September 30).　•Paul wrote, "If you confess with your mouth that Jesus is Lord and believe in your heart that God raised him from the dead, you will be saved" (Romans 10:9, July 26). When you call Jesus your Lord, you accept his lordship in all areas of your life. You give him full authority, knowing that he loves you, knows you, and promises to give you his very best. He is Lord, but he gave his life for you. You need not fear giving your life to a Lord who loves you that much.

PSALM 15:1-5
A psalm of David.

¹ **W**ho may worship in your sanctuary,
  LORD?
  Who may enter your presence on
    your holy hill?
² Those who lead blameless lives and
    do what is right,
  speaking the truth from sincere
    hearts.
³ Those who refuse to gossip
  or harm their neighbors
  or speak evil of their friends.
⁴ Those who despise flagrant sinners,
  and honor the faithful followers of
    the LORD,
  and keep their promises even when
    it hurts.

⁵ Those who lend money without
    charging interest,
  and who cannot be bribed to lie
    about the innocent.
  Such people will stand firm forever.

PROVERBS 3:21-26
My child, don't lose sight of common sense and discernment. Hang on to them, for they will refresh your soul. They are like jewels on a necklace. They keep you safe on your way, and your feet will not stumble. You can go to bed without fear; you will lie down and sleep soundly. You need not be afraid of sudden disaster or the destruction that comes upon the wicked, for the LORD is your security. He will keep your foot from being caught in a trap.

JANUARY**18**

GENESIS 37:1-38:30
Today's reading is filled with turmoil and tragedy. The events surrounding Judah and Joseph again show God's grace in continuing to be faithful to his promises to the chosen nation despite the failures of key individuals.

So Jacob settled again in the land of Canaan, where his father had lived as a foreigner.

²This is the account of Jacob and his family. When Joseph was seventeen years old, he often tended his father's flocks. He worked for his half brothers, the sons of his father's wives Bilhah and Zilpah. But Joseph reported to his father some of the bad things his brothers were doing.

³Jacob* loved Joseph more than any of his other children because Joseph had been born to him in his old age. So one day Jacob had a special gift made for Joseph—a beautiful robe.* ⁴But his brothers hated Joseph because their father loved him more than the rest of them. They couldn't say a kind word to him.

⁵One night Joseph had a dream, and when he told his brothers about it, they hated him more than ever. ⁶"Listen to this dream," he said. ⁷"We were out in the field, tying up bundles of grain. Suddenly my bundle stood up, and your bundles all gathered around and bowed low before mine!"

⁸His brothers responded, "So you think you will be our king, do you? Do you actually think you will reign over us?" And they hated him all the more because of his dreams and the way he talked about them.

⁹Soon Joseph had another dream, and again he told his brothers about it. "Listen, I have had another dream," he said. "The sun, moon, and eleven stars bowed low before me!"

¹⁰This time he told the dream to his father as well as to his brothers, but his father scolded him. "What kind of dream is that?" he asked. "Will your mother and I and your brothers actually come and bow to the ground before you?" ¹¹But while his brothers were jealous of Joseph, his father wondered what the dreams meant.

¹²Soon after this, Joseph's brothers went to pasture their father's flocks at Shechem. ¹³When they had been gone for some time, Jacob said to Joseph, "Your

brothers are pasturing the sheep at Shechem. Get ready, and I will send you to them."

"I'm ready to go," Joseph replied.

14"Go and see how your brothers and the flocks are getting along," Jacob said. "Then come back and bring me a report." So Jacob sent him on his way, and Joseph traveled to Shechem from their home in the valley of Hebron.

15When he arrived there, a man from the area noticed him wandering around the countryside. "What are you looking for?" he asked.

16"I'm looking for my brothers," Joseph replied. "Do you know where they are pasturing their sheep?"

17"Yes," the man told him. "They have moved on from here, but I heard them say, 'Let's go on to Dothan.' " So Joseph followed his brothers to Dothan and found them there.

18When Joseph's brothers saw him coming, they recognized him in the distance. As he approached, they made plans to kill him. 19"Here comes the dreamer!" they said. 20"Come on, let's kill him and throw him into one of these cisterns. We can tell our father, 'A wild animal has eaten him.' Then we'll see what becomes of his dreams!"

21But when Reuben heard of their scheme, he came to Joseph's rescue. "Let's not kill him," he said. 22"Why should we shed any blood? Let's just throw him into this empty cistern here in the wilderness. Then he'll die without our laying a hand on him." Reuben was secretly planning to rescue Joseph and return him to his father.

23So when Joseph arrived, his brothers ripped off the beautiful robe he was wearing. 24Then they grabbed him and threw him into the cistern. Now the cistern was empty; there was no water in it. 25Then, just as they were sitting down to eat, they looked up and saw a caravan of camels in the distance coming toward them. It was a group of Ishmaelite traders taking a load of gum, balm, and aromatic resin from Gilead down to Egypt.

26Judah said to his brothers, "What will we gain by killing our brother? His blood would just give us a guilty conscience.

27Instead of hurting him, let's sell him to those Ishmaelite traders. After all, he is our brother—our own flesh and blood!" And his brothers agreed. 28So when the Ishmaelites, who were Midianite traders, came by, Joseph's brothers pulled him out of the cistern and sold him to them for twenty pieces* of silver. And the traders took him to Egypt.

29Some time later, Reuben returned to get Joseph out of the cistern. When he discovered that Joseph was missing, he tore his clothes in grief. 30Then he went back to his brothers and lamented, "The boy is gone! What will I do now?"

31Then the brothers killed a young goat and dipped Joseph's robe in its blood. 32They sent the beautiful robe to their father with this message: "Look at what we found. Doesn't this robe belong to your son?"

33Their father recognized it immediately. "Yes," he said, "it is my son's robe. A wild animal must have eaten him. Joseph has clearly been torn to pieces!" 34Then Jacob tore his clothes and dressed himself in burlap. He mourned deeply for his son for a long time. 35His family all tried to comfort him, but he refused to be comforted. "I will go to my grave* mourning for my son," he would say, and then he would weep.

36Meanwhile, the Midianite traders* arrived in Egypt, where they sold Joseph to Potiphar, an officer of Pharaoh, the king of Egypt. Potiphar was captain of the palace guard.

38:1ABOUT this time, Judah left home and moved to Adullam, where he stayed with a man named Hirah. 2There he saw a Canaanite woman, the daughter of Shua, and he married her. When he slept with her, 3she became pregnant and gave birth to a son, and he named the boy Er. 4Then she became pregnant again and gave birth to another son, and she named him Onan. 5And when she gave birth to a third son, she named him Shelah. At the time of Shelah's birth, they were living at Kezib.

6In the course of time, Judah arranged for his firstborn son, Er, to marry a young woman named Tamar. 7But Er was a wicked man in the LORD's sight, so the

LORD took his life. [8]Then Judah said to Er's brother Onan, "Go and marry Tamar, as our law requires of the brother of a man who has died. You must produce an heir for your brother."

[9]But Onan was not willing to have a child who would not be his own heir. So whenever he had intercourse with his brother's wife, he spilled the semen on the ground. This prevented her from having a child who would belong to his brother. [10]But the LORD considered it evil for Onan to deny a child to his dead brother. So the LORD took Onan's life, too.

[11]Then Judah said to Tamar, his daughter-in-law, "Go back to your parents' home and remain a widow until my son Shelah is old enough to marry you." (But Judah didn't really intend to do this because he was afraid Shelah would also die, like his two brothers.) So Tamar went back to live in her father's home.

[12]Some years later Judah's wife died. After the time of mourning was over, Judah and his friend Hirah the Adullamite went up to Timnah to supervise the shearing of his sheep. [13]Someone told Tamar, "Look, your father-in-law is going up to Timnah to shear his sheep."

[14]Tamar was aware that Shelah had grown up, but no arrangements had been made for her to come and marry him. So she changed out of her widow's clothing and covered herself with a veil to disguise herself. Then she sat beside the road at the entrance to the village of Enaim, which is on the road to Timnah. [15]Judah noticed her and thought she was a prostitute, since she had covered her face. [16]So he stopped and propositioned her. "Let me have sex with you," he said, not realizing that she was his own daughter-in-law.

"How much will you pay to have sex with me?" Tamar asked.

[17]"I'll send you a young goat from my flock," Judah promised.

"But what will you give me to guarantee that you will send the goat?" she asked.

[18]"What kind of guarantee do you want?" he replied.

She answered, "Leave me your identification seal and its cord and the walking stick you are carrying." So Judah gave them to her. Then he had intercourse with her, and she became pregnant. [19]Afterward she went back home, took off her veil, and put on her widow's clothing as usual.

[20]Later Judah asked his friend Hirah the Adullamite to take the young goat to the woman and to pick up the things he had given her as his guarantee. But Hirah couldn't find her. [21]So he asked the men who lived there, "Where can I find the shrine prostitute who was sitting beside the road at the entrance to Enaim?"

"We've never had a shrine prostitute here," they replied.

[22]So Hirah returned to Judah and told him, "I couldn't find her anywhere, and the men of the village claim they've never had a shrine prostitute there."

[23]"Then let her keep the things I gave her," Judah said. "I sent the young goat as we agreed, but you couldn't find her. We'd be the laughingstock of the village if we went back again to look for her."

[24]About three months later, Judah was told, "Tamar, your daughter-in-law, has acted like a prostitute. And now, because of this, she's pregnant."

"Bring her out, and let her be burned!" Judah demanded.

[25]But as they were taking her out to kill her, she sent this message to her father-in-law: "The man who owns these things made me pregnant. Look closely. Whose seal and cord and walking stick are these?"

[26]Judah recognized them immediately and said, "She is more righteous than I am, because I didn't arrange for her to marry my son Shelah." And Judah never slept with Tamar again.

[27]When the time came for Tamar to give birth, it was discovered that she was carrying twins. [28]While she was in labor, one of the babies reached out his hand. The midwife grabbed it and tied a scarlet string around the child's wrist, announcing, "This one came out first." [29]But then he pulled back his hand, and out came his brother! "What!" the midwife exclaimed. "How did you break out first?" So he was named Perez.* [30]Then the baby with the scarlet string on his wrist was born, and he was named Zerah.*

37:3a Hebrew *Israel*; also in 37:13. See note on 35:21.
37:3b Traditionally rendered *a coat of many colors*. The exact meaning of the Hebrew is uncertain. 37:28 Hebrew *20 shekels*, about 8 ounces or 228 grams in weight.

37:35 Hebrew *go down to Sheol.* **37:36** Hebrew *the Medanites.* The relationship between the Midianites and Medanites is unclear; compare 37:28. See also 25:2. **38:29** *Perez* means "breaking out." **38:30** *Zerah* means "scarlet" or "brightness."

MATTHEW 12:22-45

The crowd was beginning to understand. "Could this be the Messiah?" they asked. The religious leaders should have been the first to recognize Jesus as the Messiah; instead, they wanted nothing to do with him.

Then a demon-possessed man, who was blind and couldn't speak, was brought to Jesus. He healed the man so that he could both speak and see. ²³The crowd was amazed and asked, "Could it be that Jesus is the Son of David, the Messiah?"

²⁴But when the Pharisees heard about the miracle, they said, "No wonder he can cast out demons. He gets his power from Satan,* the prince of demons."

²⁵Jesus knew their thoughts and replied, "Any kingdom divided by civil war is doomed. A town or family splintered by feuding will fall apart. ²⁶And if Satan is casting out Satan, he is divided and fighting against himself. His own kingdom will not survive. ²⁷And if I am empowered by Satan, what about your own exorcists? They cast out demons, too, so they will condemn you for what you have said. ²⁸But if I am casting out demons by the Spirit of God, then the Kingdom of God has arrived among you. ²⁹For who is powerful enough to enter the house of a strong man like Satan and plunder his goods? Only someone even stronger—someone who could tie him up and then plunder his house.

³⁰"Anyone who isn't with me opposes me, and anyone who isn't working with me is actually working against me.

³¹"So I tell you, every sin and blasphemy can be forgiven—except blasphemy against the Holy Spirit, which will never be forgiven. ³²Anyone who speaks against the Son of Man can be forgiven, but anyone who speaks against the Holy Spirit will never be forgiven, either in this world or in the world to come.

³³"A tree is identified by its fruit. If a tree is good, its fruit will be good. If a tree is bad, its fruit will be bad. ³⁴You brood of snakes! How could evil men like you speak what is good and right? For whatever is in your heart determines what you say. ³⁵A good person produces good things from the treasury of a good heart, and an evil person produces evil things from the treasury of an evil heart. ³⁶And I tell you this, you must give an account on judgment day for every idle word you speak. ³⁷The words you say will either acquit you or condemn you."

The reality of heaven

WHAT THE BIBLE SAYS

PSALM 16:11 Jesus explained that the only ones who will enter heaven will be those who have accepted him as the way, the truth, and the life—not those who have the best arguments or who have performed the greatest number of good deeds. Plenty of skeptics will try to say that believing in heaven is absurd; but as Christians, we choose to take God at his word. Jesus promised to prepare a place for us (John 14:2-4, May 24), and that place will be beautiful beyond our imagination (Revelation 21–22, December 30, 31). • More important than its beauty, however, is what King David understood: Heaven will be a place of joy in God's presence, a place filled with the pleasures of living with God forever. Lest you think that you're in for eternal choir and harp rehearsals, think again. Joy in God's presence; eternal pleasure. Once again, we are beyond the bounds of our imaginations. • Although heaven is hard to imagine, you can know that in heaven you will be united with the Creator of your soul. Your place in heaven was made the moment you received Christ. Your future is secure and will be filled with joy for eternity.

³⁸One day some teachers of religious law and Pharisees came to Jesus and said, "Teacher, we want you to show us a miraculous sign to prove your authority."

³⁹But Jesus replied, "Only an evil, adulterous generation would demand a miraculous sign; but the only sign I will give them is the sign of the prophet Jonah. ⁴⁰For as Jonah was in the belly of the great fish for three days and three nights, so will the Son of Man be in the heart of the earth for three days and three nights.

⁴¹"The people of Nineveh will stand up against this generation on judgment day and condemn it, for they repented of their sins at the preaching of Jonah. Now someone greater than Jonah is here—but you refuse to repent. ⁴²The queen of Sheba* will also stand up against this generation on judgment day and condemn it, for she came from a distant land to hear the wisdom of Solomon. Now someone greater than Solomon is here—but you refuse to listen.

⁴³"When an evil* spirit leaves a person, it goes into the desert, seeking rest but finding none. ⁴⁴Then it says, 'I will return to the person I came from.' So it returns and finds its former home empty, swept, and in order. ⁴⁵Then the spirit finds seven other spirits more evil than itself, and they all enter the person and live there. And so that person is worse off than before. That will be the experience of this evil generation."

12:24 Greek *Beelzeboul;* also in 12:27. Other manuscripts read *Beezeboul;* Latin version reads *Beelzebub.*   **12:42** Greek *The queen of the south.*   **12:43** Greek *unclean.*

PSALM 16:1-11
A psalm of David.

¹ Keep me safe, O God,
    for I have come to you for refuge.

² I said to the LORD, "You are my
        Master!
    Every good thing I have comes
        from you."
³ The godly people in the land
    are my true heroes!

I take pleasure in them!
⁴ Troubles multiply for those who chase
        after other gods.
    I will not take part in their sacrifices
        of blood
    or even speak the names of their
        gods.

⁵ LORD, you alone are my inheritance,
        my cup of blessing.
    You guard all that is mine.
⁶ The land you have given me is a
        pleasant land.
    What a wonderful inheritance!

⁷ I will bless the LORD who guides me;
    even at night my heart instructs me.
⁸ I know the LORD is always with me.
    I will not be shaken, for he is right
        beside me.

⁹ No wonder my heart is glad, and
        I rejoice.*
    My body rests in safety.
¹⁰ For you will not leave my soul among
        the dead*
    or allow your holy one* to rot in
        the grave.
¹¹ You will show me the way of life,
    granting me the joy of your
        presence
    and the pleasures of living with
        you forever.*

16:9 Greek version reads *and my tongue shouts his praises.* Compare Acts 2:26.   **16:10a** Hebrew *in Sheol.*   **16:10b** Or *your Holy One.*   **16:11** Greek version reads *You have shown me the way of life, / and you will fill me with the joy of your presence.* Compare Acts 2:28.

PROVERBS 3:27-32

Do not withhold good from those who deserve it when it's in your power to help them. If you can help your neighbor now, don't say, "Come back tomorrow, and then I'll help you."   □Don't plot harm against your neighbor, for those who live nearby trust you. Don't pick a fight without reason, when no one has done you harm.   □Don't envy violent people or copy their ways. Such wicked people are detestable to the LORD, but he offers his friendship to the godly.

GENESIS 39:1–41:16

As a young man, eleventh in a line of twelve brothers, Joseph had dreams (literally!) of rising to unlikely leadership over his own family. First came a series of hardships that would position and prepare him for that role.

When Joseph was taken to Egypt by the Ishmaelite traders, he was purchased by Potiphar, an Egyptian officer. Potiphar was captain of the guard for Pharaoh, the king of Egypt.

²The LORD was with Joseph, so he succeeded in everything he did as he served in the home of his Egyptian master. ³Potiphar noticed this and realized that the LORD was with Joseph, giving him success in everything he did. ⁴This pleased Potiphar, so he soon made Joseph his personal attendant. He put him in charge of his entire household and everything he owned. ⁵From the day Joseph was put in charge of his master's household and property, the LORD began to bless Potiphar's household for Joseph's sake. All his household affairs ran smoothly, and his crops and livestock flourished. ⁶So Potiphar gave Joseph complete administrative responsibility over everything he owned. With Joseph there, he didn't worry about a thing—except what kind of food to eat!

Joseph was a very handsome and well-built young man, ⁷and Potiphar's wife soon began to look at him lustfully. "Come and sleep with me," she demanded.

⁸But Joseph refused. "Look," he told her, "my master trusts me with everything in his entire household. ⁹No one here has more authority than I do. He has held back nothing from me except you, because you are his wife. How could I do such a wicked thing? It would be a great sin against God."

¹⁰She kept putting pressure on Joseph day after day, but he refused to sleep with her, and he kept out of her way as much as possible. ¹¹One day, however, no one else was around when he went in to do his work. ¹²She came and grabbed him by his cloak, demanding, "Come on, sleep with me!" Joseph tore himself away, but he left his cloak in her hand as he ran from the house.

¹³When she saw that she was holding his cloak and he had fled, ¹⁴she called out to her servants. Soon all the men came running. "Look!" she said. "My husband has brought this Hebrew slave here to make fools of us! He came into my room to rape me, but I screamed. ¹⁵When he heard me scream, he ran outside and got away, but he left his cloak behind with me."

¹⁶She kept the cloak with her until her husband came home. ¹⁷Then she told him her story. "That Hebrew slave you've brought into our house tried to come in and fool around with me," she said. ¹⁸"But when I screamed, he ran outside, leaving his cloak with me!"

¹⁹Potiphar was furious when he heard his wife's story about how Joseph had treated her. ²⁰So he took Joseph and threw him into the prison where the king's prisoners were held, and there he remained. ²¹But the LORD was with Joseph in the prison and showed him his faithful love. And the LORD made Joseph a favorite with the prison warden. ²²Before long, the warden put Joseph in charge of all the other prisoners and over everything that happened in the prison. ²³The warden had no more worries, because Joseph took care of everything. The LORD was with him and caused everything he did to succeed.

40:1SOME time later, Pharaoh's chief cup-bearer and chief baker offended their royal master. ²Pharaoh became angry with these two officials, ³and he put them in the prison where Joseph was, in the palace of the captain of the guard. ⁴They remained in prison for quite some time, and the captain of the guard assigned them to Joseph, who looked after them.

⁵While they were in prison, Pharaoh's cup-bearer and baker each had a dream one night, and each dream had its own meaning. ⁶When Joseph saw them the next morning, he noticed that they both looked upset. ⁷"Why do you look so worried today?" he asked them.

8 And they replied, "We both had dreams last night, but no one can tell us what they mean."

"Interpreting dreams is God's business," Joseph replied. "Go ahead and tell me your dreams."

9 So the chief cup-bearer told Joseph his dream first. "In my dream," he said, "I saw a grapevine in front of me. 10 The vine had three branches that began to bud and blossom, and soon it produced clusters of ripe grapes. 11 I was holding Pharaoh's wine cup in my hand, so I took a cluster of grapes and squeezed the juice into the cup. Then I placed the cup in Pharaoh's hand."

12 "This is what the dream means," Joseph said. "The three branches represent three days. 13 Within three days Pharaoh will lift you up and restore you to your position as his chief cup-bearer. 14 And please remember me and do me a favor when things go well for you. Mention me to Pharaoh, so he might let me out of this place. 15 For I was kidnapped from my homeland, the land of the Hebrews, and now I'm here in prison, but I did nothing to deserve it."

16 When the chief baker saw that Joseph had given the first dream such a positive interpretation, he said to Joseph, "I had a dream, too. In my dream there were three baskets of white pastries stacked on my head. 17 The top basket contained all kinds of pastries for Pharaoh, but the birds came and ate them from the basket on my head."

18 "This is what the dream means," Joseph told him. "The three baskets also represent three days. 19 Three days from now Pharaoh will lift you up and impale your body on a pole. Then birds will come and peck away at your flesh."

20 Pharaoh's birthday came three days later, and he prepared a banquet for all his officials and staff. He summoned* his chief cup-bearer and chief baker to join the other officials. 21 He then restored the chief cup-bearer to his former position, so he could again hand Pharaoh his cup. 22 But Pharaoh impaled the chief baker, just as Joseph had predicted when he interpreted his dream. 23 Pharaoh's chief cup-bearer, however, forgot all about Joseph, never giving him another thought.

41:1 Two full years later, Pharaoh dreamed that he was standing on the bank of the Nile River. 2 In his dream he saw seven fat, healthy cows come up out of the river and begin grazing in the marsh grass. 3 Then he saw seven more cows come up behind them from the Nile, but these were scrawny and thin. These cows stood beside the fat cows on the riverbank. 4 Then the scrawny, thin cows ate the seven healthy, fat cows! At this point in the dream, Pharaoh woke up.

5 But he fell asleep again and had a second dream. This time he saw seven heads of grain, plump and beautiful, growing on a single stalk. 6 Then seven more heads of grain appeared, but these were shriveled and withered by the east wind. 7 And these thin heads swallowed up the seven plump, well-formed heads! Then Pharaoh woke up again and realized it was a dream.

8 The next morning Pharaoh was very disturbed by the dreams. So he called for all the magicians and wise men of Egypt. When Pharaoh told them his dreams, not one of them could tell him what they meant.

9 Finally, the king's chief cup-bearer spoke up. "Today I have been reminded of my failure," he told Pharaoh. 10 "Some time ago, you were angry with the chief baker and me, and you imprisoned us in the palace of the captain of the guard. 11 One night the chief baker and I each had a dream, and each dream had its own meaning. 12 There was a young Hebrew man with us in the prison who was a slave of the captain of the guard. We told him our dreams, and he told us what each of our dreams meant. 13 And everything happened just as he had predicted. I was restored to my position as cup-bearer, and the chief baker was executed and impaled on a pole."

14 Pharaoh sent for Joseph at once, and he was quickly brought from the prison. After he shaved and changed his clothes, he went in and stood before Pharaoh. 15 Then Pharaoh said to Joseph, "I had a dream last night, and no one here can tell me what it means. But I have heard that when you hear about a dream you can interpret it."

¹⁶"It is beyond my power to do this," Joseph replied. "But God can tell you what it means and set you at ease."

40:20 Hebrew *He lifted up the head of.*

MATTHEW 12:46–13:23
Jesus drew a lot of "lines in the sand"—with his family, with his listeners, with his disciples. He asked the question, "I'm planting the truth. What kind of soil will you be?"

As Jesus was speaking to the crowd, his mother and brothers stood outside, asking to speak to him. ⁴⁷Someone told Jesus, "Your mother and your brothers are outside, and they want to speak to you."*

⁴⁸Jesus asked, "Who is my mother? Who are my brothers?" ⁴⁹Then he pointed to his disciples and said, "Look, these are my mother and brothers. ⁵⁰Anyone who does the will of my Father in heaven is my brother and sister and mother!"

¹³:¹LATER that same day Jesus left the house and sat beside the lake. ²A large crowd soon gathered around him, so he got into a boat. Then he sat there and taught as the people stood on the shore. ³He told many stories in the form of parables, such as this one:

"Listen! A farmer went out to plant some seeds. ⁴As he scattered them across his field, some seeds fell on a footpath, and the birds came and ate them. ⁵Other seeds fell on shallow soil with underlying rock. The seeds sprouted quickly because the soil was shallow. ⁶But the plants soon wilted under the hot sun, and since they didn't have deep roots, they died. ⁷Other seeds fell among thorns that grew up and choked out the tender plants. ⁸Still other seeds fell on fertile soil, and they produced a crop that was thirty, sixty, and even a hundred times as much as had been planted! ⁹Anyone with ears to hear should listen and understand."

¹⁰His disciples came and asked him, "Why do you use parables when you talk to the people?"

¹¹He replied, "You are permitted to understand the secrets* of the Kingdom of Heaven, but others are not. ¹²To those who listen to my teaching, more understanding will be given, and they will have an abundance of knowledge. But for those who are not listening, even what little understanding they have will be taken away from them. ¹³That is why I use these parables,

For they look, but they don't really see.
 They hear, but they don't really
  listen or understand.

¹⁴This fulfills the prophecy of Isaiah that says,

'When you hear what I say,
 you will not understand.

Resisting temptation

GENESIS 39:7-8 Joseph had experienced his share of difficulties—the poor guy deserved a break. But along came this lustful, bored, rich woman with a little too much time on her hands. Joseph, the handsome young man hired by her husband to handle the household, could have taken advantage of the situation. Whether Joseph was tempted by her or not is unknown. But we do know that he had to do something, because "she kept putting pressure on Joseph day after day" (Genesis 39:10). •Joseph tried—he really did. He told her no. He explained in no uncertain terms why he would not sleep with her. It all had to do with integrity, trust, and his faith in God—character traits about which this woman didn't seem to have a clue. In the end, when she actually grabbed him, he had only one choice; he simply got out of the situation. •Temptation is going to hit you at some time or another. You may not be able to anticipate where or when it will strike, but it helps to know your weaknesses, to steer clear when possible, and to run when you need to.

When you see what I do,
you will not comprehend.'
15 For the hearts of these people are
hardened,
and their ears cannot hear,
and they have closed their eyes—
so their eyes cannot see,
and their ears cannot hear,
and their hearts cannot understand,
and they cannot turn to me
and let me heal them.'*

16"But blessed are your eyes, because they see; and your ears, because they hear. 17 I tell you the truth, many prophets and righteous people longed to see what you see, but they didn't see it. And they longed to hear what you hear, but they didn't hear it.

18"Now listen to the explanation of the parable about the farmer planting seeds: 19 The seed that fell on the footpath represents those who hear the message about the Kingdom and don't understand it. Then the evil one comes and snatches away the seed that was planted in their hearts. 20 The seed on the rocky soil represents those who hear the message and immediately receive it with joy. 21 But since they don't have deep roots, they don't last long. They fall away as soon as they have problems or are persecuted for believing God's word. 22 The seed that fell among the thorns represents those who hear God's word, but all too quickly the message is crowded out by the worries of this life and the lure of wealth, so no fruit is produced. 23 The seed that fell on good soil represents those who truly hear and understand God's word and produce a harvest of thirty, sixty, or even a hundred times as much as had been planted!"

12:47 Some manuscripts do not include verse 47. Compare Mark 3:32 and Luke 8:20.   13:11 Greek *the mysteries.*
13:14-15 Isa 6:9-10 (Greek version).

PSALM 17:1-15
A prayer of David.

1 O LORD, hear my plea for justice.
Listen to my cry for help.
Pay attention to my prayer,
for it comes from honest lips.
2 Declare me innocent,
for you see those who do right.

3 You have tested my thoughts and
examined my heart in the night.
You have scrutinized me and found
nothing wrong.
I am determined not to sin in what
I say.
4 I have followed your commands,
which keep me from following
cruel and evil people.
5 My steps have stayed on your path;
I have not wavered from following
you.

6 I am praying to you because I know
you will answer, O God.
Bend down and listen as I pray.
7 Show me your unfailing love in
wonderful ways.
By your mighty power you rescue
those who seek refuge from their
enemies.
8 Guard me as you would guard your
own eyes.*
Hide me in the shadow of your
wings.
9 Protect me from wicked people who
attack me,
from murderous enemies who
surround me.
10 They are without pity.
Listen to their boasting!
11 They track me down and surround me,
watching for the chance to throw
me to the ground.
12 They are like hungry lions, eager to
tear me apart—
like young lions hiding in ambush.

13 Arise, O LORD!
Stand against them, and bring them
to their knees!
Rescue me from the wicked with
your sword!
14 By the power of your hand, O LORD,
destroy those who look to this
world for their reward.
But satisfy the hunger of your
treasured ones.
May their children have plenty,
leaving an inheritance for their
descendants.
15 Because I am righteous, I will see you.
When I awake, I will see you face
to face and be satisfied.

17:8 Hebrew *as the pupil of your eye.*

PROVERBS 3:33-35

The LORD curses the house of the wicked, but he blesses the home of the upright. ☐The LORD mocks the mockers but is gracious to the humble.* ☐The wise inherit honor, but fools are put to shame!

3:34 Greek version reads *The LORD opposes the proud / but favors the humble.* Compare Jas 4:6; 1 Pet 5:5.

JANUARY**20**

GENESIS 41:17–42:17

Years earlier, Joseph's brothers had sold him into slavery, letting their father believe he had been killed. Little did they know that, as they lived their lie, Joseph was rising to power in Egypt, the very place they would go searching for food.

So Pharaoh told Joseph his dream. "In my dream," he said, "I was standing on the bank of the Nile River, 18and I saw seven fat, healthy cows come up out of the river and begin grazing in the marsh grass. 19But then I saw seven sick-looking cows, scrawny and thin, come up after them. I've never seen such sorry-looking animals in all the land of Egypt. 20These thin, scrawny cows ate the seven fat cows. 21But afterward you wouldn't have known it, for they were still as thin and scrawny as before! Then I woke up.

22"Then I fell asleep again, and I had another dream. This time I saw seven heads of grain, full and beautiful, growing on a single stalk. 23Then seven more heads of grain appeared, but these were blighted, shriveled, and withered by the east wind. 24And the shriveled heads swallowed the seven healthy heads. I told these dreams to the magicians, but no one could tell me what they mean."

25Joseph responded, "Both of Pharaoh's dreams mean the same thing. God is telling Pharaoh in advance what he is about to do. 26The seven healthy cows and the seven healthy heads of grain both represent seven years of prosperity. 27The seven thin, scrawny cows that came up later and the seven thin heads of grain, withered by the east wind, represent seven years of famine.

28"This will happen just as I have described it, for God has revealed to Pharaoh in advance what he is about to do. 29The next seven years will be a period of great prosperity throughout the land of Egypt. 30But afterward there will be seven years of famine so great that all the prosperity will be forgotten in Egypt. Famine will destroy the land. 31This famine will be so severe that even the memory of the good years will be erased. 32As for having two similar dreams, it means that these events have been decreed by God, and he will soon make them happen.

33"Therefore, Pharaoh should find an intelligent and wise man and put him in charge of the entire land of Egypt. 34Then Pharaoh should appoint supervisors over the land and let them collect one-fifth of all the crops during the seven good years. 35Have them gather all the food produced in the good years that are just ahead and bring it to Pharaoh's storehouses. Store it away, and guard it so there will be food in the cities. 36That way there will be enough to eat when the seven years of famine come to the land of Egypt. Otherwise this famine will destroy the land."

37Joseph's suggestions were well received by Pharaoh and his officials. 38So Pharaoh asked his officials, "Can we find anyone else like this man so obviously filled with the spirit of God?" 39Then Pharaoh said to Joseph, "Since God has revealed the meaning of the dreams to you, clearly no one else is as intelligent or wise as you are. 40You will be in charge of my court, and all my people will take orders from you. Only I, sitting on my throne, will have a rank higher than yours."

41Pharaoh said to Joseph, "I hereby put you in charge of the entire land of Egypt." 42Then Pharaoh removed his signet ring from his hand and placed it on Joseph's finger. He dressed him in fine linen clothing and hung a gold chain around his neck. ⁴³Then he had Joseph ride in the chariot reserved for his second-in-command. And wherever Joseph went, the command was shouted, "Kneel down!" So Pharaoh put Joseph in charge of all Egypt. ⁴⁴And Pharaoh said to him, "I am Pharaoh, but no one will lift a hand or foot in the entire land of Egypt without your approval."

⁴⁵Then Pharaoh gave Joseph a new Egyptian name, Zaphenath-paneah.* He also gave him a wife, whose name was Asenath. She was the daughter of Potiphera, the priest of On.* So Joseph took charge of the entire land of Egypt. ⁴⁶He was thirty years old when he began serving in the court of Pharaoh, the king of Egypt. And when Joseph left Pharaoh's presence, he inspected the entire land of Egypt.

⁴⁷As predicted, for seven years the land produced bumper crops. ⁴⁸During those years, Joseph gathered all the crops grown in Egypt and stored the grain from the surrounding fields in the cities. ⁴⁹He piled up huge amounts of grain like sand on the seashore. Finally, he stopped keeping records because there was too much to measure.

⁵⁰During this time, before the first of the famine years, two sons were born to Joseph and his wife, Asenath, the daughter of Potiphera, the priest of On. ⁵¹Joseph named his older son Manasseh,* for he said, "God has made me forget all my troubles and everyone in my father's family." ⁵²Joseph named his second son Ephraim,* for he said, "God has made me fruitful in this land of my grief."

⁵³At last the seven years of bumper crops throughout the land of Egypt came to an end. ⁵⁴Then the seven years of famine began, just as Joseph had predicted. The famine also struck all the surrounding countries, but throughout Egypt there was plenty of food. ⁵⁵Eventually, however, the famine spread throughout the land of Egypt as well. And when the people cried out to Pharaoh for food, he told them, "Go to Joseph, and do whatever he tells you." ⁵⁶So with severe famine everywhere, Joseph opened up the storehouses and distributed grain to the Egyptians, for the famine was severe throughout the land of Egypt. ⁵⁷And people from all around came to Egypt to buy grain from Joseph because the famine was severe throughout the world.

⁴²:¹WHEN Jacob heard that grain was available in Egypt, he said to his sons, "Why are you standing around looking at one another? ²I have heard there is grain in Egypt. Go down there, and buy enough grain to keep us alive. Otherwise we'll die."

³So Joseph's ten older brothers went down to Egypt to buy grain. ⁴But Jacob wouldn't let Joseph's younger brother, Benjamin, go with them, for fear some harm might come to him. ⁵So Jacob's* sons arrived in Egypt along with others to buy food, for the famine was in Canaan as well.

⁶Since Joseph was governor of all Egypt and in charge of selling grain to all the people, it was to him that his brothers came. When they arrived, they bowed before him with their faces to the ground. ⁷Joseph recognized his brothers instantly, but he pretended to be a stranger and spoke harshly to them. "Where are you from?" he demanded.

"From the land of Canaan," they replied. "We have come to buy food."

⁸Although Joseph recognized his brothers, they didn't recognize him. ⁹And he remembered the dreams he'd had about them many years before. He said to them, "You are spies! You have come to see how vulnerable our land has become."

¹⁰"No, my lord!" they exclaimed. "Your servants have simply come to buy food. ¹¹We are all brothers—members of the same family. We are honest men, sir! We are not spies!"

¹²"Yes, you are!" Joseph insisted. "You have come to see how vulnerable our land has become."

¹³"Sir," they said, "there are actually twelve of us. We, your servants, are all brothers, sons of a man living in the land of Canaan. Our youngest brother is back there with our father right now, and one of our brothers is no longer with us."

¹⁴But Joseph insisted, "As I said, you are spies! ¹⁵This is how I will test your story.

I swear by the life of Pharaoh that you will never leave Egypt unless your youngest brother comes here! [16] One of you must go and get your brother. I'll keep the rest of you here in prison. Then we'll find out whether or not your story is true. By the life of Pharaoh, if it turns out that you don't have a younger brother, then I'll know you are spies."

[17] So Joseph put them all in prison for three days.

41:45a *Zaphenath-paneah* probably means "God speaks and lives." 41:45b Greek version reads *of Heliopolis;* also in 41:50. 41:51 *Manasseh* sounds like a Hebrew term that means "causing to forget." 41:52 *Ephraim* sounds like a Hebrew term that means "fruitful." 42:5 Hebrew *Israel's.* See note on 35:21.

MATTHEW 13:24-46

Like wheat among weeds, the Kingdom of God grows in preparation for a future harvest. Like a mustard seed and like yeast in dough, it is small but gives amazing results. Like a buried treasure or the perfect pearl, it is worth giving up everything you have to obtain it.

Here is another story Jesus told: "The Kingdom of Heaven is like a farmer who planted good seed in his field. [25] But that night as the workers slept, his enemy came and planted weeds among the wheat, then slipped away. [26] When the crop began to grow and produce grain, the weeds also grew.

[27] "The farmer's workers went to him and said, 'Sir, the field where you planted that good seed is full of weeds! Where did they come from?'

[28] "'An enemy has done this!' the farmer exclaimed.

"'Should we pull out the weeds?' they asked.

[29] "'No,' he replied, 'you'll uproot the wheat if you do. [30] Let both grow together until the harvest. Then I will tell the harvesters to sort out the weeds, tie them into bundles, and burn them, and to put the wheat in the barn.'"

[31] Here is another illustration Jesus used: "The Kingdom of Heaven is like a mustard seed planted in a field. [32] It is the smallest of all seeds, but it becomes the largest of garden plants; it grows into a tree, and birds come and make nests in its branches."

[33] Jesus also used this illustration: "The Kingdom of Heaven is like the yeast a woman used in making bread. Even though she put only a little yeast in three measures of flour, it permeated every part of the dough."

[34] Jesus always used stories and illustrations like these when speaking to the crowds. In fact, he never spoke to them without using such parables. [35] This fulfilled what God had spoken through the prophet:

How to discern truth

WHAT THE BIBLE SAYS

MATTHEW 13:27-30 In its early growth stages, the type of weed (called a tare) Jesus describes in this parable looks exactly like wheat. Jesus used the parable of the wheat and weeds to help his followers realize that Satan's deceptions would produce false believers among the true believers. We need to be able to discern the truth of God's teachings from Satan's distortion of truth. Satan plants half-truths and deception as he tries to lead people astray. Jesus lovingly warned his followers to be vigilant against distortions that may imitate the effects of a life redeemed by Jesus but have nothing to do with the real principles or love present in his teachings. • How can you be a discerning believer? The best way to spot a lie is to know the truth. As you become knowledgeable about God's Word, you will be able to detect teachings and concepts that are contrary to Scripture. The lies are out there. Make sure you know the truth!

"I will speak to you in parables.
I will explain things hidden since
the creation of the world.*"

³⁶Then, leaving the crowds outside, Jesus went into the house. His disciples said, "Please explain to us the story of the weeds in the field."

³⁷Jesus replied, "The Son of Man* is the farmer who plants the good seed. ³⁸The field is the world, and the good seed represents the people of the Kingdom. The weeds are the people who belong to the evil one. ³⁹The enemy who planted the weeds among the wheat is the devil. The harvest is the end of the world,* and the harvesters are the angels.

⁴⁰"Just as the weeds are sorted out and burned in the fire, so it will be at the end of the world. ⁴¹The Son of Man will send his angels, and they will remove from his Kingdom everything that causes sin and all who do evil. ⁴²And the angels will throw them into the fiery furnace, where there will be weeping and gnashing of teeth. ⁴³Then the righteous will shine like the sun in their Father's Kingdom. Anyone with ears to hear should listen and understand!

⁴⁴"The Kingdom of Heaven is like a treasure that a man discovered hidden in a field. In his excitement, he hid it again and sold everything he owned to get enough money to buy the field.

⁴⁵"Again, the Kingdom of Heaven is like a merchant on the lookout for choice pearls. ⁴⁶When he discovered a pearl of great value, he sold everything he owned and bought it!"

13:35 Some manuscripts do not include *of the world.* Ps 78:2. **13:37** "Son of Man" is a title Jesus used for himself. 13:39 Or *the age;* also in 13:40, 49.

PSALM 18:1-15

For the choir director: A psalm of David, the servant of the LORD. He sang this song to the LORD on the day the LORD rescued him from all his enemies and from Saul. He sang:

¹ I love you, LORD;
you are my strength.
² The LORD is my rock, my fortress, and
my savior;
my God is my rock, in whom I find
protection.

He is my shield, the power that saves
me,
and my place of safety.
³ I called on the LORD, who is worthy
of praise,
and he saved me from my
enemies.

⁴ The ropes of death entangled me;
floods of destruction swept
over me.
⁵ The grave* wrapped its ropes
around me;
death laid a trap in my path.
⁶ But in my distress I cried out to the
LORD;
yes, I prayed to my God for help.
He heard me from his sanctuary;
my cry to him reached his ears.

⁷ Then the earth quaked and
trembled.
The foundations of the mountains
shook;
they quaked because of his anger.
⁸ Smoke poured from his nostrils;
fierce flames leaped from his
mouth.
Glowing coals blazed forth from
him.
⁹ He opened the heavens and came
down;
dark storm clouds were beneath
his feet.
¹⁰ Mounted on a mighty angelic being,*
he flew,
soaring on the wings of the wind.
¹¹ He shrouded himself in darkness,
veiling his approach with dark rain
clouds.
¹² Thick clouds shielded the brightness
around him
and rained down hail and burning
coals.*
¹³ The LORD thundered from heaven;
the voice of the Most High
resounded
amid the hail and burning coals.
¹⁴ He shot his arrows and scattered his
enemies;
his lightning flashed, and they were
greatly confused.
¹⁵ Then at your command, O LORD,
at the blast of your breath,
the bottom of the sea could be seen,

and the foundations of the earth
were laid bare.

18:5 Hebrew *Sheol*.   **18:10** Hebrew *a cherub*.   **18:12** Or
and lightning bolts; also in 18:13.

PROVERBS 4:1-6

My children,* listen when your father
corrects you. Pay attention and learn good
judgment, for I am giving you good guidance. Don't turn away from my instructions. For I, too, was once my father's son,
tenderly loved as my mother's only child.
□ My father taught me, "Take my words to
heart. Follow my commands, and you will
live. Get wisdom; develop good judgment.
Don't forget my words or turn away from
them. Don't turn your back on wisdom,
for she will protect you. Love her, and she
will guard you."

4:1 Hebrew *My sons*.

JANUARY**21**

GENESIS 42:18–43:34

Joseph, an official in Egypt, held the well-being of
his brothers within his power. These same brothers
had sold him into slavery years before. They now
bowed before a seeming stranger with no idea that
the man was their long-lost brother.

On the third day Joseph said to them, "I
am a God-fearing man. If you do as I say,
you will live. ¹⁹If you really are honest
men, choose one of your brothers to remain in prison. The rest of you may go
home with grain for your starving families. ²⁰But you must bring your youngest
brother back to me. This will prove that
you are telling the truth, and you will not
die." To this they agreed.

²¹Speaking among themselves, they
said, "Clearly we are being punished because of what we did to Joseph long ago.
We saw his anguish when he pleaded for
his life, but we wouldn't listen. That's why
we're in this trouble."

²²"Didn't I tell you not to sin against the
boy?" Reuben asked. "But you wouldn't
listen. And now we have to answer for his
blood!"

²³Of course, they didn't know that Joseph understood them, for he had been
speaking to them through an interpreter.
²⁴Now he turned away from them and began to weep. When he regained his com-
posure, he spoke to them again. Then he
chose Simeon from among them and had
him tied up right before their eyes.

²⁵Joseph then ordered his servants to fill
the men's sacks with grain, but he also
gave secret instructions to return each
brother's payment at the top of his sack. He
also gave them supplies for their journey
home. ²⁶So the brothers loaded their donkeys with the grain and headed for home.

²⁷But when they stopped for the night
and one of them opened his sack to get
grain for his donkey, he found his money
in the top of his sack. ²⁸"Look!" he exclaimed to his brothers. "My money has
been returned; it's here in my sack!" Then
their hearts sank. Trembling, they said to
each other, "What has God done to us?"

²⁹When the brothers came to their father, Jacob, in the land of Canaan, they told
him everything that had happened to
them. ³⁰"The man who is governor of the
land spoke very harshly to us," they told
him. "He accused us of being spies scouting the land. ³¹But we said, 'We are honest
men, not spies. ³²We are twelve brothers,
sons of one father. One brother is no longer with us, and the youngest is at home
with our father in the land of Canaan.'

³³"Then the man who is governor of the
land told us, 'This is how I will find out if
you are honest men. Leave one of your
brothers here with me, and take grain for
your starving families and go on home.
³⁴But you must bring your youngest
brother back to me. Then I will know you
are honest men and not spies. Then I will
give you back your brother, and you may
trade freely in the land.'"

35As they emptied out their sacks, there in each man's sack was the bag of money he had paid for the grain! The brothers and their father were terrified when they saw the bags of money. 36Jacob exclaimed, "You are robbing me of my children! Joseph is gone! Simeon is gone! And now you want to take Benjamin, too. Everything is going against me!"

37Then Reuben said to his father, "You may kill my two sons if I don't bring Benjamin back to you. I'll be responsible for him, and I promise to bring him back."

38But Jacob replied, "My son will not go down with you. His brother Joseph is dead, and he is all I have left. If anything should happen to him on your journey, you would send this grieving, white-haired man to his grave.*"

43:1But the famine continued to ravage the land of Canaan. 2When the grain they had brought from Egypt was almost gone, Jacob said to his sons, "Go back and buy us a little more food."

3But Judah said, "The man was serious when he warned us, 'You won't see my face again unless your brother is with you.' 4If you send Benjamin with us, we will go down and buy more food. 5But if you don't let Benjamin go, we won't go either. Remember, the man said, 'You won't see my face again unless your brother is with you.'"

6"Why were you so cruel to me?" Jacob* moaned. "Why did you tell him you had another brother?"

7"The man kept asking us questions about our family," they replied. "He asked, 'Is your father still alive? Do you have another brother?' So we answered his questions. How could we know he would say, 'Bring your brother down here'?"

8Judah said to his father, "Send the boy with me, and we will be on our way. Otherwise we will all die of starvation—and not only we, but you and our little ones. 9I personally guarantee his safety. You may hold me responsible if I don't bring him back to you. Then let me bear the blame forever. 10If we hadn't wasted all this time, we could have gone and returned twice by now."

11So their father, Jacob, finally said to them, "If it can't be avoided, then at least do this. Pack your bags with the best products of this land. Take them down to the man as gifts—balm, honey, gum, aromatic resin, pistachio nuts, and almonds. 12Also take double the money that was put back in your sacks, as it was probably someone's mistake. 13Then take your brother, and go back to the man. 14May God Almighty* give you mercy as you go before the man, so that he will release Simeon and let Benjamin return. But if I must lose my children, so be it."

15So the men packed Jacob's gifts and double the money and headed off with Benjamin. They finally arrived in Egypt and presented themselves to Joseph. 16When Joseph saw Benjamin with them, he said to the manager of his household, "These men will eat with me this noon. Take them inside the palace. Then go slaughter an animal, and prepare a big feast." 17So the man did as Joseph told him and took them into Joseph's palace.

18The brothers were terrified when they saw that they were being taken into Joseph's house. "It's because of the money someone put in our sacks last time we were here," they said. "He plans to pretend that we stole it. Then he will seize us, make us slaves, and take our donkeys."

19The brothers approached the manager of Joseph's household and spoke to him at the entrance to the palace. 20"Sir," they said, "we came to Egypt once before to buy food. 21But as we were returning home, we stopped for the night and opened our sacks. Then we discovered that each man's money—the exact amount paid—was in the top of his sack! Here it is; we have brought it back with us. 22We also have additional money to buy more food. We have no idea who put our money in our sacks."

23"Relax. Don't be afraid," the household manager told them. "Your God, the God of your father, must have put this treasure into your sacks. I know I received your payment." Then he released Simeon and brought him out to them.

24The manager then led the men into Joseph's palace. He gave them water to wash their feet and provided food for their donkeys. 25They were told they would be eating there, so they prepared their gifts for Joseph's arrival at noon.

²⁶When Joseph came home, they gave him the gifts they had brought him, then bowed low to the ground before him. ²⁷After greeting them, he asked, "How is your father, the old man you spoke about? Is he still alive?"

²⁸"Yes," they replied. "Our father, your servant, is alive and well." And they bowed low again.

²⁹Then Joseph looked at his brother Benjamin, the son of his own mother. "Is this your youngest brother, the one you told me about?" Joseph asked. "May God be gracious to you, my son." ³⁰Then Joseph hurried from the room because he was overcome with emotion for his brother. He went into his private room, where he broke down and wept. ³¹After washing his face, he came back out, keeping himself under control. Then he ordered, "Bring out the food!"

³²The waiters served Joseph at his own table, and his brothers were served at a separate table. The Egyptians who ate with Joseph sat at their own table, because Egyptians despise Hebrews and refuse to eat with them. ³³Joseph told each of his brothers where to sit, and to their amazement, he seated them according to age,

from oldest to youngest. ³⁴And Joseph filled their plates with food from his own table, giving Benjamin five times as much as he gave the others. So they feasted and drank freely with him.

42:38 Hebrew *to Sheol.* **43:6** Hebrew *Israel;* also in 43:11. See note on 35:21. **43:14** Hebrew *El-Shaddai.*

MATTHEW 13:47–14:12

Not everyone will believe God's truth. Jesus was rejected in his own hometown. John the Baptist was killed. As Jesus explained in his parable, a time will come when believers and unbelievers will be sorted into two separate places—heaven and hell.

"**A**gain, the Kingdom of Heaven is like a fishing net that was thrown into the water and caught fish of every kind. ⁴⁸When the net was full, they dragged it up onto the shore, sat down, and sorted the good fish into crates, but threw the bad ones away. ⁴⁹That is the way it will be at the end of the world. The angels will come and separate the wicked people from the righteous, ⁵⁰throwing the wicked into the fiery furnace, where there will be weeping and gnashing of teeth. ⁵¹Do you understand all these things?"

"Yes," they said, "we do."

⁵²Then he added, "Every teacher of religious law who becomes a disciple in the

HOW WE LIVE | Our relationships

GENESIS 43:29-30 The people we associate with on a regular basis—family, friends, coworkers—have a significant effect on us as we grow in our spiritual and emotional maturity. Rarely are relationships all good or all bad. Family relationships especially exemplify a fascinating mix of devotion and discord. • Like many people, Joseph had a complicated relationship with his family. Even though Joseph's brothers had thrown him in a pit and then sold him into slavery, Joseph's heart welled up with longing and love when he saw his brothers after years of separation. Paul wrote in one of his letters to the Corinthian Christians that love "keeps no record of being wronged" and "rejoices whenever the truth wins out. Love never gives up, never loses faith, is always hopeful, and endures through every circumstance" (1 Corinthians 13:5-7, August 20). Joseph had suffered enough through his own trials to understand that by extending this kind of love toward his brothers, the family could be restored. •Joseph's life teaches us that God's particular kind of love is the only hope of building intimate and influential relationships with one another— even when it seems complicated.

Kingdom of Heaven is like a homeowner who brings from his storeroom new gems of truth as well as old."

⁵³When Jesus had finished telling these stories and illustrations, he left that part of the country. ⁵⁴He returned to Nazareth, his hometown. When he taught there in the synagogue, everyone was amazed and said, "Where does he get this wisdom and the power to do miracles?" ⁵⁵Then they scoffed, "He's just the carpenter's son, and we know Mary, his mother, and his brothers—James, Joseph,* Simon, and Judas. ⁵⁶All his sisters live right here among us. Where did he learn all these things?" ⁵⁷And they were deeply offended and refused to believe in him.

Then Jesus told them, "A prophet is honored everywhere except in his own hometown and among his own family." ⁵⁸And so he did only a few miracles there because of their unbelief.

14:¹WHEN Herod Antipas, the ruler of Galilee,* heard about Jesus, ²he said to his advisers, "This must be John the Baptist raised from the dead! That is why he can do such miracles."

³For Herod had arrested and imprisoned John as a favor to his wife Herodias (the former wife of Herod's brother Philip). ⁴John had been telling Herod, "It is against God's law for you to marry her." ⁵Herod wanted to kill John, but he was afraid of a riot, because all the people believed John was a prophet.

⁶But at a birthday party for Herod, Herodias's daughter performed a dance that greatly pleased him, ⁷so he promised with a vow to give her anything she wanted. ⁸At her mother's urging, the girl said, "I want the head of John the Baptist on a tray!" ⁹Then the king regretted what he had said; but because of the vow he had made in front of his guests, he issued the necessary orders. ¹⁰So John was beheaded in the prison, ¹¹and his head was brought on a tray and given to the girl, who took it to her mother. ¹²Later, John's disciples came for his body and buried it. Then they went and told Jesus what had happened.

13:55 Other manuscripts read *Joses;* still others read *John.*
14:1 Greek *Herod the tetrarch.* Herod Antipas was a son of King Herod and was ruler over Galilee.

PSALM 18:16-36

He reached down from heaven and rescued me;
 he drew me out of deep waters.
¹⁷ He rescued me from my powerful enemies,
 from those who hated me and were too strong for me.
¹⁸ They attacked me at a moment when I was in distress,
 but the LORD supported me.
¹⁹ He led me to a place of safety;
 he rescued me because he delights in me.
²⁰ The LORD rewarded me for doing right;
 he restored me because of my innocence.
²¹ For I have kept the ways of the LORD;
 I have not turned from my God to follow evil.
²² I have followed all his regulations;
 I have never abandoned his decrees.
²³ I am blameless before God;
 I have kept myself from sin.
²⁴ The LORD rewarded me for doing right.
 He has seen my innocence.

²⁵ To the faithful you show yourself faithful;
 to those with integrity you show integrity.
²⁶ To the pure you show yourself pure,
 but to the wicked you show yourself hostile.
²⁷ You rescue the humble,
 but you humiliate the proud.
²⁸ You light a lamp for me.
 The LORD, my God, lights up my darkness.
²⁹ In your strength I can crush an army;
 with my God I can scale any wall.

³⁰ God's way is perfect.
 All the LORD's promises prove true.
 He is a shield for all who look to him for protection.
³¹ For who is God except the LORD?
 Who but our God is a solid rock?
³² God arms me with strength,
 and he makes my way perfect.
³³ He makes me as surefooted as a deer,
 enabling me to stand on mountain heights.

³⁴ He trains my hands for battle;
  he strengthens my arm to draw
    a bronze bow.
³⁵ You have given me your shield
    of victory.
  Your right hand supports me;
  your help has made me
    great.
³⁶ You have made a wide path for
    my feet
  to keep them from slipping.

PROVERBS 4:7-10

"**G**etting wisdom is the wisest thing you can do! And whatever else you do, develop good judgment. If you prize wisdom, she will make you great. Embrace her, and she will honor you. She will place a lovely wreath on your head; she will present you with a beautiful crown." □My child,* listen to me and do as I say, and you will have a long, good life.

4:10 Hebrew *My son;* also in 4:20.

JANUARY**22**

GENESIS 44:1–45:28

From his powerful position as second-in-command in Egypt, Joseph (still unrecognized) interacted with his brothers who, years before, had sold him into slavery. Joseph was finally prepared to reveal his identity, offer forgiveness, and lift a weight of guilt that the brothers had borne for years.

When his brothers were ready to leave, Joseph gave these instructions to his palace manager: "Fill each of their sacks with as much grain as they can carry, and put each man's money back into his sack. ²Then put my personal silver cup at the top of the youngest brother's sack, along with the money for his grain." So the manager did as Joseph instructed him.

³The brothers were up at dawn and were sent on their journey with their loaded donkeys. ⁴But when they had gone only a short distance and were barely out of the city, Joseph said to his palace manager, "Chase after them and stop them. When you catch up with them, ask them, 'Why have you repaid my kindness with such evil? ⁵Why have you stolen my master's silver cup,* which he uses to predict the future? What a wicked thing you have done!'"

⁶When the palace manager caught up with the men, he spoke to them as he had been instructed.

⁷"What are you talking about?" the brothers responded. "We are your servants and would never do such a thing! ⁸Didn't we return the money we found in our sacks? We brought it back all the way from the land of Canaan. Why would we steal silver or gold from your master's house? ⁹If you find his cup with any one of us, let that man die. And all the rest of us, my lord, will be your slaves."

¹⁰"That's fair," the man replied. "But only the one who stole the cup will be my slave. The rest of you may go free."

¹¹They all quickly took their sacks from the backs of their donkeys and opened them. ¹²The palace manager searched the brothers' sacks, from the oldest to the youngest. And the cup was found in Benjamin's sack! ¹³When the brothers saw this, they tore their clothing in despair. Then they loaded their donkeys again and returned to the city.

¹⁴Joseph was still in his palace when Judah and his brothers arrived, and they fell to the ground before him. ¹⁵"What have you done?" Joseph demanded. "Don't you know that a man like me can predict the future?"

¹⁶Judah answered, "Oh, my lord, what can we say to you? How can we explain this? How can we prove our innocence? God is punishing us for our sins. My lord, we have all returned to be your slaves—all of us, not just our brother who had your cup in his sack."

¹⁷"No," Joseph said. "I would never do such a thing! Only the man who stole the cup will be my slave. The rest of you may go back to your father in peace."

¹⁸Then Judah stepped forward and said, "Please, my lord, let your servant say just

one word to you. Please, do not be angry with me, even though you are as powerful as Pharaoh himself.

[19]"My lord, previously you asked us, your servants, 'Do you have a father or a brother?' [20]And we responded, 'Yes, my lord, we have a father who is an old man, and his youngest son is a child of his old age. His full brother is dead, and he alone is left of his mother's children, and his father loves him very much.'

[21]"And you said to us, 'Bring him here so I can see him with my own eyes.' [22]But we said to you, 'My lord, the boy cannot leave his father, for his father would die.' [23]But you told us, 'Unless your youngest brother comes with you, you will never see my face again.'

[24]"So we returned to your servant, our father, and told him what you had said. [25]Later, when he said, 'Go back again and buy us more food,' [26]we replied, 'We can't go unless you let our youngest brother go with us. We'll never get to see the man's face unless our youngest brother is with us.'

[27]"Then my father said to us, 'As you know, my wife had two sons, [28]and one of them went away and never returned. Doubtless he was torn to pieces by some wild animal. I have never seen him since. [29]Now if you take his brother away from me, and any harm comes to him, you will send this grieving, white-haired man to his grave.*'

[30]"And now, my lord, I cannot go back to my father without the boy. Our father's life is bound up in the boy's life. [31]If he sees that the boy is not with us, our father will die. We, your servants, will indeed be responsible for sending that grieving, white-haired man to his grave. [32]My lord, I guaranteed to my father that I would take care of the boy. I told him, 'If I don't bring him back to you, I will bear the blame forever.'

[33]"So please, my lord, let me stay here as a slave instead of the boy, and let the boy return with his brothers. [34]For how can I return to my father if the boy is not with me? I couldn't bear to see the anguish this would cause my father!"

[45:1]JOSEPH could stand it no longer. There were many people in the room, and he said to his attendants, "Out, all of you!" So he was alone with his brothers when he told them who he was. [2]Then he broke down and wept. He wept so loudly the Egyptians could hear him, and word of it quickly carried to Pharaoh's palace.

[3]"I am Joseph!" he said to his brothers. "Is my father still alive?" But his brothers were speechless! They were stunned to realize that Joseph was standing there in front of them. [4]"Please, come closer," he said to them. So they came closer. And he said again, "I am Joseph, your brother, whom you sold into slavery in Egypt. [5]But don't be upset, and don't be angry with yourselves for selling me to this place. It was God who sent me here ahead of you to preserve your lives. [6]This famine that has ravaged the land for two years will last five more years, and there will be neither plowing nor harvesting. [7]God has sent me ahead of you to keep you and your families alive and to preserve many survivors.* [8]So it was God who sent me here, not you! And he is the one who made me an adviser* to Pharaoh—the manager of his entire palace and the governor of all Egypt.

[9]"Now hurry back to my father and tell him, 'This is what your son Joseph says: God has made me master over all the land of Egypt. So come down to me immediately! [10]You can live in the region of Goshen, where you can be near me with all your children and grandchildren, your flocks and herds, and everything you own. [11]I will take care of you there, for there are still five years of famine ahead of us. Otherwise you, your household, and all your animals will starve.'"

[12]Then Joseph added, "Look! You can see for yourselves, and so can my brother Benjamin, that I really am Joseph! [13]Go tell my father of my honored position here in Egypt. Describe for him everything you have seen, and then bring my father here quickly." [14]Weeping with joy, he embraced Benjamin, and Benjamin did the same. [15]Then Joseph kissed each of his brothers and wept over them, and after that they began talking freely with him.

[16]The news soon reached Pharaoh's palace: "Joseph's brothers have arrived!" Pharaoh and his officials were all delighted to hear this.

[17]Pharaoh said to Joseph, "Tell your brothers, 'This is what you must do: Load your pack animals, and hurry back to the land of Canaan. [18]Then get your father and all of your families, and return here to me. I will give you the very best land in Egypt, and you will eat from the best that the land produces.'"

[19]Then Pharaoh said to Joseph, "Tell your brothers, 'Take wagons from the land of Egypt to carry your little children and your wives, and bring your father here. [20]Don't worry about your personal belongings, for the best of all the land of Egypt is yours.'"

[21]So the sons of Jacob* did as they were told. Joseph provided them with wagons, as Pharaoh had commanded, and he gave them supplies for the journey. [22]And he gave each of them new clothes—but to Benjamin he gave five changes of clothes and 300 pieces* of silver. [23]He also sent his father ten male donkeys loaded with the finest products of Egypt, and ten female donkeys loaded with grain and bread and other supplies he would need on his journey.

[24]So Joseph sent his brothers off, and as they left, he called after them, "Don't quarrel about all this along the way!" [25]And they left Egypt and returned to their father, Jacob, in the land of Canaan.

[26]"Joseph is still alive!" they told him. "And he is governor of all the land of Egypt!" Jacob was stunned at the news— he couldn't believe it. [27]But when they repeated to Jacob everything Joseph had told them, and when he saw the wagons Joseph had sent to carry him, their father's spirits revived.

[28]Then Jacob exclaimed, "It must be true! My son Joseph is alive! I must go and see him before I die."

44:5 As in Greek version; Hebrew lacks this phrase.
44:29 Hebrew *to Sheol;* also in 44:31.   45:7 Or *and to save you with an extraordinary rescue.* The meaning of the Hebrew is uncertain.   45:8 Hebrew *a father.*   45:21 Hebrew *Israel;* also in 45:28. See note on 35:21.   45:22 Hebrew *300 shekels,* about 7.5 pounds or 3.4 kilograms in weight.

MATTHEW 14:13-36

Through two amazing miracles—the feeding of five thousand and walking on water—Jesus continued to reveal who he was. His disciples, however, were only beginning to understand.

As soon as Jesus heard the news, he left in a boat to a remote area to be alone. But the crowds heard where he was headed and followed on foot from many towns. [14]Jesus saw the huge crowd as he stepped from the boat, and he had compassion on them and healed their sick.

[15]That evening the disciples came to him and said, "This is a remote place, and it's already getting late. Send the crowds

WHAT THE BIBLE SAYS

Salvation and forgiveness

GENESIS 45:3-5 It couldn't have been easy for Joseph. There stood his malicious brothers who had sold him—*sold* him—into slavery many years earlier. Joseph could have used his position for revenge, but he refused. Instead he looked upon his band of brothers with amazing forgiveness, saying, "Don't be upset, and don't be angry with yourselves for selling me to this place. It was God who sent me here ahead of you to preserve your lives" (Genesis 45:5). Later he added, "You intended to harm me, but God intended it all for good" (Genesis 50:20, January 25). Clearly, Joseph knew that someone much bigger than he was had control of his destiny.   • Are you holding on to hurts from the past? Are you bitter and unforgiving? Chances are, whoever hurt you has gone on with life, hardly thinking (or in some cases without even knowing) the pain he or she has caused. You see, unforgiveness really only hurts one person—you. If you will let it go and trust God to work all things together for good in your life, you will be able to graciously move on with the life he has planned for you.

away so they can go to the villages and buy food for themselves."

¹⁶But Jesus said, "That isn't necessary—you feed them."

¹⁷"But we have only five loaves of bread and two fish!" they answered.

¹⁸"Bring them here," he said. ¹⁹Then he told the people to sit down on the grass. Jesus took the five loaves and two fish, looked up toward heaven, and blessed them. Then, breaking the loaves into pieces, he gave the bread to the disciples, who distributed it to the people. ²⁰They all ate as much as they wanted, and afterward, the disciples picked up twelve baskets of leftovers. ²¹About 5,000 men were fed that day, in addition to all the women and children!

²²Immediately after this, Jesus insisted that his disciples get back into the boat and cross to the other side of the lake, while he sent the people home. ²³After sending them home, he went up into the hills by himself to pray. Night fell while he was there alone.

²⁴Meanwhile, the disciples were in trouble far away from land, for a strong wind had risen, and they were fighting heavy waves. ²⁵About three o'clock in the morning* Jesus came toward them, walking on the water. ²⁶When the disciples saw him walking on the water, they were terrified. In their fear, they cried out, "It's a ghost!"

²⁷But Jesus spoke to them at once. "Don't be afraid," he said. "Take courage. I am here!*"

²⁸Then Peter called to him, "Lord, if it's really you, tell me to come to you, walking on the water."

²⁹"Yes, come," Jesus said.

So Peter went over the side of the boat and walked on the water toward Jesus. ³⁰But when he saw the strong* wind and the waves, he was terrified and began to sink. "Save me, Lord!" he shouted.

³¹Jesus immediately reached out and grabbed him. "You have so little faith," Jesus said. "Why did you doubt me?"

³²When they climbed back into the boat, the wind stopped. ³³Then the disciples worshiped him. "You really are the Son of God!" they exclaimed.

³⁴After they had crossed the lake, they landed at Gennesaret. ³⁵When the people recognized Jesus, the news of his arrival spread quickly throughout the whole area, and soon people were bringing all their sick to be healed. ³⁶They begged him to let the sick touch at least the fringe of his robe, and all who touched him were healed.

14:25 Greek *In the fourth watch of the night.* **14:27** Or *The 'I AM' is here;* Greek reads *I am.* See Exod 3:14. **14:30** Some manuscripts do not include *strong.*

PSALM 18:37-50

I chased my enemies and caught them;
 I did not stop until they were conquered.
³⁸ I struck them down so they could not get up;
 they fell beneath my feet.
³⁹ You have armed me with strength for the battle;
 you have subdued my enemies under my feet.
⁴⁰ You placed my foot on their necks.
 I have destroyed all who hated me.
⁴¹ They called for help, but no one came to their rescue.
 They even cried to the LORD, but he refused to answer.
⁴² I ground them as fine as dust in the wind.
 I swept them into the gutter like dirt.
⁴³ You gave me victory over my accusers.
 You appointed me ruler over nations;
 people I don't even know now serve me.
⁴⁴ As soon as they hear of me, they submit;
 foreign nations cringe before me.
⁴⁵ They all lose their courage
 and come trembling from their strongholds.

⁴⁶ The LORD lives! Praise to my Rock!
 May the God of my salvation be exalted!
⁴⁷ He is the God who pays back those who harm me;
 he subdues the nations under me
⁴⁸ and rescues me from my enemies.
 You hold me safe beyond the reach of my enemies;
 you save me from violent opponents.
⁴⁹ For this, O LORD, I will praise you among the nations;

I will sing praises to your name.
50 You give great victories to your
king;
you show unfailing love to your
anointed,
to David and all his descendants
forever.

GENESIS 46:1–47:31

Joseph's father, Jacob, could hardly believe his ears. He learned that his son Joseph was alive and well, a ruler in Egypt! Joseph settled his family in a land called Goshen. Hundreds of years later their descendants would return to Canaan in the event known as the Exodus.

So Jacob* set out for Egypt with all his possessions. And when he came to Beersheba, he offered sacrifices to the God of his father, Isaac. 2During the night God spoke to him in a vision. "Jacob! Jacob!" he called.

"Here I am," Jacob replied.

3"I am God,* the God of your father," the voice said. "Do not be afraid to go down to Egypt, for there I will make your family into a great nation. 4I will go with you down to Egypt, and I will bring you back again. But you will die in Egypt with Joseph attending to you."

5So Jacob left Beersheba, and his sons took him to Egypt. They carried him and their little ones and their wives in the wagons Pharaoh had provided for them. 6They also took all their livestock and all the personal belongings they had acquired in the land of Canaan. So Jacob and his entire family went to Egypt—7sons and grandsons, daughters and granddaughters—all his descendants.

8These are the names of the descendants of Israel—the sons of Jacob—who went to Egypt:

Reuben was Jacob's oldest son. 9The sons of Reuben were Hanoch, Pallu, Hezron, and Carmi.
10The sons of Simeon were Jemuel, Jamin, Ohad, Jakin, Zohar, and Shaul. (Shaul's mother was a Canaanite woman.)

PROVERBS 4:11-13

I will teach you wisdom's ways and lead you in straight paths. When you walk, you won't be held back; when you run, you won't stumble. Take hold of my instructions; don't let them go. Guard them, for they are the key to life.

JANUARY**23**

11The sons of Levi were Gershon, Kohath, and Merari.
12The sons of Judah were Er, Onan, Shelah, Perez, and Zerah (though Er and Onan had died in the land of Canaan). The sons of Perez were Hezron and Hamul.
13The sons of Issachar were Tola, Puah,* Jashub,* and Shimron.
14The sons of Zebulun were Sered, Elon, and Jahleel.
15These were the sons of Leah and Jacob who were born in Paddan-aram, in addition to their daughter, Dinah. The number of Jacob's descendants (male and female) through Leah was thirty-three.

16The sons of Gad were Zephon,* Haggi, Shuni, Ezbon, Eri, Arodi, and Areli.
17The sons of Asher were Imnah, Ishvah, Ishvi, and Beriah. Their sister was Serah. Beriah's sons were Heber and Malkiel.
18These were the sons of Zilpah, the servant given to Leah by her father, Laban. The number of Jacob's descendants through Zilpah was sixteen.

19The sons of Jacob's wife Rachel were Joseph and Benjamin.
20Joseph's sons, born in the land of Egypt, were Manasseh and Ephraim. Their mother was Asenath, daughter of Potiphera, the priest of On.*
21Benjamin's sons were Bela, Beker, Ashbel, Gera, Naaman, Ehi, Rosh, Muppim, Huppim, and Ard.
22These were the sons of Rachel and Jacob. The number of Jacob's descendants through Rachel was fourteen.

23 The son of Dan was Hushim.

24 The sons of Naphtali were Jahzeel, Guni, Jezer, and Shillem.

25 These were the sons of Bilhah, the servant given to Rachel by her father, Laban. The number of Jacob's descendants through Bilhah was seven.

26 The total number of Jacob's direct descendants who went with him to Egypt, not counting his sons' wives, was sixty-six. 27 In addition, Joseph had two sons* who were born in Egypt. So altogether, there were seventy* members of Jacob's family in the land of Egypt.

28 As they neared their destination, Jacob sent Judah ahead to meet Joseph and get directions to the region of Goshen. And when they finally arrived there, 29 Joseph prepared his chariot and traveled to Goshen to meet his father, Jacob. When Joseph arrived, he embraced his father and wept, holding him for a long time. 30 Finally, Jacob said to Joseph, "Now I am ready to die, since I have seen your face again and know you are still alive."

31 And Joseph said to his brothers and to his father's entire family, "I will go to Pharaoh and tell him, 'My brothers and my father's entire family have come to me from the land of Canaan. 32 These men are shepherds, and they raise livestock. They have brought with them their flocks and herds and everything they own.'"

33 Then he said, "When Pharaoh calls for you and asks you about your occupation, 34 you must tell him, 'We, your servants, have raised livestock all our lives, as our ancestors have always done.' When you tell him this, he will let you live here in the region of Goshen, for the Egyptians despise shepherds."

47:1 THEN Joseph went to see Pharaoh and told him, "My father and my brothers have arrived from the land of Canaan. They have come with all their flocks and herds and possessions, and they are now in the region of Goshen."

2 Joseph took five of his brothers with him and presented them to Pharaoh. 3 And Pharaoh asked the brothers, "What is your occupation?"

They replied, "We, your servants, are shepherds, just like our ancestors. 4 We have come to live here in Egypt for a while, for there is no pasture for our flocks in Canaan. The famine is very severe there. So please, we request permission to live in the region of Goshen."

5 Then Pharaoh said to Joseph, "Now that your father and brothers have joined you here, 6 choose any place in the entire land of Egypt for them to live. Give them the best land of Egypt. Let them live in the region of Goshen. And if any of them have special skills, put them in charge of my livestock, too."

7 Then Joseph brought in his father, Jacob, and presented him to Pharaoh. And Jacob blessed Pharaoh.

8 "How old are you?" Pharaoh asked him.

9 Jacob replied, "I have traveled this earth for 130 hard years. But my life has been short compared to the lives of my ancestors." 10 Then Jacob blessed Pharaoh again before leaving his court.

11 So Joseph assigned the best land of Egypt—the region of Rameses—to his father and his brothers, and he settled them there, just as Pharaoh had commanded. 12 And Joseph provided food for his father and his brothers in amounts appropriate to the number of their dependents, including the smallest children.

13 Meanwhile, the famine became so severe that all the food was used up, and people were starving throughout the lands of Egypt and Canaan. 14 By selling grain to the people, Joseph eventually collected all the money in Egypt and Canaan, and he put the money in Pharaoh's treasury. 15 When the people of Egypt and Canaan ran out of money, all the Egyptians came to Joseph. "Our money is gone!" they cried. "But please give us food, or we will die before your very eyes!"

16 Joseph replied, "Since your money is gone, bring me your livestock. I will give you food in exchange for your livestock." 17 So they brought their livestock to Joseph in exchange for food. In exchange for their horses, flocks of sheep and goats, herds of cattle, and donkeys, Joseph provided them with food for another year.

18 But that year ended, and the next year they came again and said, "We cannot

hide the truth from you, my lord. Our money is gone, and all our livestock and cattle are yours. We have nothing left to give but our bodies and our land. ¹⁹Why should we die before your very eyes? Buy us and our land in exchange for food; we offer our land and ourselves as slaves for Pharaoh. Just give us grain so we may live and not die, and so the land does not become empty and desolate."

²⁰So Joseph bought all the land of Egypt for Pharaoh. All the Egyptians sold him their fields because the famine was so severe, and soon all the land belonged to Pharaoh. ²¹As for the people, he made them all slaves,* from one end of Egypt to the other. ²²The only land he did not buy was the land belonging to the priests. They received an allotment of food directly from Pharaoh, so they didn't need to sell their land.

²³Then Joseph said to the people, "Look, today I have bought you and your land for Pharaoh. I will provide you with seed so you can plant the fields. ²⁴Then when you harvest it, one-fifth of your crop will belong to Pharaoh. You may keep the remaining four-fifths as seed for your fields and as food for you, your households, and your little ones."

²⁵"You have saved our lives!" they exclaimed. "May it please you, my lord, to let us be Pharaoh's servants." ²⁶Joseph

then issued a decree still in effect in the land of Egypt, that Pharaoh should receive one-fifth of all the crops grown on his land. Only the land belonging to the priests was not given to Pharaoh.

²⁷Meanwhile, the people of Israel settled in the region of Goshen in Egypt. There they acquired property, and they were fruitful, and their population grew rapidly. ²⁸Jacob lived for seventeen years after his arrival in Egypt, so he lived 147 years in all.

²⁹As the time of his death drew near, Jacob* called for his son Joseph and said to him, "Please do me this favor. Put your hand under my thigh and swear that you will treat me with unfailing love by honoring this last request: Do not bury me in Egypt. ³⁰When I die, please take my body out of Egypt and bury me with my ancestors."

So Joseph promised, "I will do as you ask."

³¹"Swear that you will do it," Jacob insisted. So Joseph gave his oath, and Jacob bowed humbly at the head of his bed.*

46:1 Hebrew *Israel;* also in 46:29, 30. See note on 35:21. 46:3 Hebrew *I am El.* 46:13a As in Syriac version and Samaritan Pentateuch (see also 1 Chr 7:1); Hebrew reads *Puvah.* 46:13b As in some Greek manuscripts and Samaritan Pentateuch (see also Num 26:24; 1 Chr 7:1); Hebrew reads *Iob.* 46:16 As in Greek version and Samaritan Pentateuch (see also Num 26:15); Hebrew reads *Ziphion.* 46:20 Greek version reads *of Heliopolis.* 46:27a Greek version reads *nine sons,* probably including Joseph's grandsons through Ephraim and Manasseh (see 1 Chr 7:14-20).

HOW WE LIVE — Growing in wisdom

PSALM 19:7-8 Children don't rejoice when they are sent to their rooms for disobeying their parents. Usually they don't thank their parents for their wise advice when told to "stay away from the hot stove" or "look both ways before crossing the street." Common wisdom shows that touching a hot stove causes a burn and crossing the street without looking can land you in the hospital. Yet children ignore these wise words all the time and often end up in their rooms because of it.   • How frequently are we just like stubborn children? How often do we ignore or refuse to listen to God's wisdom in our lives? His love for us causes him to issue warnings and commands—for our own good—yet we regularly ignore this wisdom that would improve our lives.   • The author of this psalm passionately describes God's laws as perfect, trustworthy, making wise the simple. They are right, clear, and give insight for living. To those who long to be wise, God's commands are more desirable than the finest gold. To grow in wisdom in your spiritual life, begin here, with God's Word. See his commands as loving words of wisdom from a loving Father.

46:27b Greek version reads *seventy-five;* see note on Exod 1:5.
47:21 As in Greek version and Samaritan Pentateuch;
Hebrew reads *he moved them all into the towns.*
47:29 Hebrew *Israel;* also in 47:31b. See note on 35:21.
47:31 Greek version reads *and Israel bowed in worship as he leaned on his staff.* Compare Heb 11:21.

MATTHEW 15:1-28

Do you want to be righteous only on the outside where people can see, or on the inside where it matters to God? Jesus wants his people to have their hearts touched and their lives genuinely changed by him. Inner reality is more important than outer performance.

Some Pharisees and teachers of religious law now arrived from Jerusalem to see Jesus. They asked him, ²"Why do your disciples disobey our age-old tradition? For they ignore our tradition of ceremonial hand washing before they eat."

³Jesus replied, "And why do you, by your traditions, violate the direct commandments of God? ⁴For instance, God says, 'Honor your father and mother,'* and 'Anyone who speaks disrespectfully of father or mother must be put to death.'* ⁵But you say it is all right for people to say to their parents, 'Sorry, I can't help you. For I have vowed to give to God what I would have given to you.' ⁶In this way, you say they don't need to honor their parents.* And so you cancel the word of God for the sake of your own tradition. ⁷You hypocrites! Isaiah was right when he prophesied about you, for he wrote,

⁸ 'These people honor me with their lips,
   but their hearts are far from me.
⁹ Their worship is a farce,
   for they teach man-made ideas as
      commands from God.'*"

¹⁰Then Jesus called to the crowd to come and hear. "Listen," he said, "and try to understand. ¹¹It's not what goes into your mouth that defiles you; you are defiled by the words that come out of your mouth."

¹²Then the disciples came to him and asked, "Do you realize you offended the Pharisees by what you just said?"

¹³Jesus replied, "Every plant not planted by my heavenly Father will be uprooted, ¹⁴so ignore them. They are blind guides leading the blind, and if one blind person guides another, they will both fall into a ditch."

¹⁵Then Peter said to Jesus, "Explain to us the parable that says people aren't defiled by what they eat."

¹⁶"Don't you understand yet?" Jesus asked. ¹⁷"Anything you eat passes through the stomach and then goes into the sewer. ¹⁸But the words you speak come from the heart—that's what defiles you. ¹⁹For from the heart come evil thoughts, murder, adultery, all sexual immorality, theft, lying, and slander. ²⁰These are what defile you. Eating with unwashed hands will never defile you."

²¹Then Jesus left Galilee and went north to the region of Tyre and Sidon. ²²A Gentile* woman who lived there came to him, pleading, "Have mercy on me, O Lord, Son of David! For my daughter is possessed by a demon that torments her severely."

²³But Jesus gave her no reply, not even a word. Then his disciples urged him to send her away. "Tell her to go away," they said. "She is bothering us with all her begging."

²⁴Then Jesus said to the woman, "I was sent only to help God's lost sheep—the people of Israel."

²⁵But she came and worshiped him, pleading again, "Lord, help me!"

²⁶Jesus responded, "It isn't right to take food from the children and throw it to the dogs."

²⁷She replied, "That's true, Lord, but even dogs are allowed to eat the scraps that fall beneath their masters' table."

²⁸"Dear woman," Jesus said to her, "your faith is great. Your request is granted." And her daughter was instantly healed.

15:4a Exod 20:12; Deut 5:16.   **15:4b** Exod 21:17 (Greek version); Lev 20:9 (Greek version).   **15:6** Greek *their father;* other manuscripts read *their father or their mother.*   **15:8-9** Isa 29:13 (Greek version).   **15:22** Greek *Canaanite.*

PSALM 19:1-14

For the choir director: A psalm of David.

¹ **T**he heavens proclaim the glory
      of God.
   The skies display his craftsmanship.
² Day after day they continue to
      speak;
   night after night they make him
      known.
³ They speak without a sound or word;
   their voice is never heard.*

[4] Yet their message has gone
      throughout the earth,
   and their words to all the world.

God has made a home in the heavens
   for the sun.
[5] It bursts forth like a radiant
      bridegroom after his wedding.
   It rejoices like a great athlete eager
      to run the race.
[6] The sun rises at one end of the
      heavens
   and follows its course to the
      other end.
   Nothing can hide from its heat.

[7] The instructions of the LORD are
      perfect,
   reviving the soul.
   The decrees of the LORD are
      trustworthy,
   making wise the simple.
[8] The commandments of the LORD
      are right,
   bringing joy to the heart.
   The commands of the LORD
      are clear,
   giving insight for living.
[9] Reverence for the LORD is pure,
      lasting forever.
   The laws of the LORD are true;
      each one is fair.
[10] They are more desirable than gold,
      even the finest gold.
   They are sweeter than honey,
      even honey dripping from
         the comb.

[11] They are a warning to your servant,
      a great reward for those who obey
         them.

[12] How can I know all the sins lurking
      in my heart?
   Cleanse me from these hidden
      faults.
[13] Keep your servant from deliberate
      sins!
   Don't let them control me.
   Then I will be free of guilt
      and innocent of great sin.

[14] May the words of my mouth
      and the meditation of
         my heart
   be pleasing to you,
      O LORD, my rock and my
         redeemer.

19:3 Or *There is no speech or language where their voice is not heard.*

PROVERBS 4:14-19

Don't do as the wicked do, and don't follow the path of evildoers. Don't even think about it; don't go that way. Turn away and keep moving. For evil people can't sleep until they've done their evil deed for the day. They can't rest until they've caused someone to stumble. They eat the food of wickedness and drink the wine of violence! □ The way of the righteous is like the first gleam of dawn, which shines ever brighter until the full light of day. But the way of the wicked is like total darkness. They have no idea what they are stumbling over.

GENESIS 48:1–49:33

Before dying, Jacob blessed Joseph's sons, Manasseh and Ephraim, adopting them as his own. He then prophesied over his other eleven sons as his final good-bye. From these family lines would come the twelve tribes of Israel.

One day not long after this, word came to Joseph, "Your father is failing rapidly." So Joseph went to visit his father, and he took with him his two sons, Manasseh and Ephraim.

[2] When Joseph arrived, Jacob was told, "Your son Joseph has come to see you." So Jacob* gathered his strength and sat up in his bed.

[3] Jacob said to Joseph, "God Almighty* appeared to me at Luz in the land of Canaan and blessed me. [4] He said to me, 'I

JANUARY**24**

will make you fruitful, and I will multiply your descendants. I will make you a multitude of nations. And I will give this land of Canaan to your descendants* after you as an everlasting possession.'

5"Now I am claiming as my own sons these two boys of yours, Ephraim and Manasseh, who were born here in the land of Egypt before I arrived. They will be my sons, just as Reuben and Simeon are. 6But any children born to you in the future will be your own, and they will inherit land within the territories of their brothers Ephraim and Manasseh.

7"Long ago, as I was returning from Paddan-aram, Rachel died in the land of Canaan. We were still on the way, some distance from Ephrath (that is, Bethlehem). So with great sorrow I buried her there beside the road to Ephrath."

8Then Jacob looked over at the two boys. "Are these your sons?" he asked.

9"Yes," Joseph told him, "these are the sons God has given me here in Egypt." And Jacob said, "Bring them closer to me, so I can bless them."

10Jacob was half blind because of his age and could hardly see. So Joseph brought the boys close to him, and Jacob kissed and embraced them. 11Then Jacob said to Joseph, "I never thought I would see your face again, but now God has let me see your children, too!"

12Joseph moved the boys, who were at their grandfather's knees, and he bowed with his face to the ground. 13Then he positioned the boys in front of Jacob. With his right hand he directed Ephraim toward Jacob's left hand, and with his left hand he put Manasseh at Jacob's right hand. 14But Jacob crossed his arms as he reached out to lay his hands on the boys' heads. He put his right hand on the head of Ephraim, though he was the younger boy, and his left hand on the head of Manasseh, though he was the firstborn. 15Then he blessed Joseph and said,

"May the God before whom my
    grandfather Abraham
  and my father, Isaac, walked—
  the God who has been my shepherd
    all my life, to this very day,

16 the Angel who has redeemed me
    from all harm—
  may he bless these boys.
May they preserve my name
    and the names of Abraham and
    Isaac.
And may their descendants multiply
    greatly
  throughout the earth."

17But Joseph was upset when he saw that his father placed his right hand on Ephraim's head. So Joseph lifted it to move it from Ephraim's head to Manasseh's head. 18"No, my father," he said. "This one is the firstborn. Put your right hand on his head."

19But his father refused. "I know, my son; I know," he replied. "Manasseh will also become a great people, but his younger brother will become even greater. And his descendants will become a multitude of nations."

20So Jacob blessed the boys that day with this blessing: "The people of Israel will use your names when they give a blessing. They will say, 'May God make you as prosperous as Ephraim and Manasseh.' " In this way, Jacob put Ephraim ahead of Manasseh.

21Then Jacob said to Joseph, "Look, I am about to die, but God will be with you and will take you back to Canaan, the land of your ancestors. 22And beyond what I have given your brothers, I am giving you an extra portion of the land* that I took from the Amorites with my sword and bow."

49:1THEN Jacob called together all his sons and said, "Gather around me, and I will tell you what will happen to each of you in the days to come.

2 "Come and listen, you sons of Jacob;
    listen to Israel, your father.

3 "Reuben, you are my firstborn, my
    strength,
  the child of my vigorous youth.
  You are first in rank and first in
    power.

4 But you are as unruly as a flood,
    and you will be first no longer.
  For you went to bed with my wife;
    you defiled my marriage couch.

5 "Simeon and Levi are two of a kind;
　　their weapons are instruments
　　　of violence.
6 May I never join in their meetings;
　　may I never be a party to their
　　　plans.
For in their anger they murdered men,
　　and they crippled oxen just for
　　　sport.
7 A curse on their anger, for it is fierce;
　　a curse on their wrath, for it is cruel.
I will scatter them among the
　　descendants of Jacob;
I will disperse them throughout
　　Israel.

8 "Judah, your brothers will praise you.
　　You will grasp your enemies by the
　　　neck.
All your relatives will bow before
　　you.
9 Judah, my son, is a young lion
　　that has finished eating its prey.
Like a lion he crouches and lies down;
　　like a lioness—who dares to rouse
　　　him?
10 The scepter will not depart from
　　Judah,
　　nor the ruler's staff from his
　　　descendants,*
　　until the coming of the one to whom
　　　it belongs,*

the one whom all nations will honor.
11 He ties his foal to a grapevine,
　　the colt of his donkey to a choice
　　　vine.
He washes his clothes in wine,
　　his robes in the blood of grapes.
12 His eyes are darker than wine,
　　and his teeth are whiter than milk.

13 "Zebulun will settle by the seashore
　　and will be a harbor for ships;
　　his borders will extend to Sidon.

14 "Issachar is a sturdy donkey,
　　resting between two saddlepacks.*
15 When he sees how good the
　　countryside is
　　and how pleasant the land,
he will bend his shoulder to the load
　　and submit himself to hard labor.

16 "Dan will govern his people,
　　like any other tribe in Israel.
17 Dan will be a snake beside the road,
　　a poisonous viper along the path
that bites the horse's hooves
　　so its rider is thrown off.
18 I trust in you for salvation, O LORD!

19 "Gad will be attacked by marauding
　　bands,
　　but he will attack them when they
　　　retreat.

WHAT THE BIBLE SAYS

How to discern truth

MATTHEW 16:12 Jesus warned his disciples about the "deceptive teaching of the Pharisees and Sadducees" (the Jewish religious leaders of the day). We too must be able to discern truth and falsehood when dealing with leaders and authority figures within the church. Be alert to some of the more common distortions of the truth. Some people want to add to or subtract from the message of the Bible so that it matches their own strange ideas; others promise salvation apart from Christ and his sacrifice on the cross; others make false promises of wealth and security in order to increase their own wealth; others set aside the clear teaching in Scripture that those who are saved must follow Christ as Lord on a daily basis. In every case, false teachers distort or ignore the Word of God. The best defense against such things is to know the Word yourself.
• You rely on Christian authority figures to feed you spiritually, but a position of authority does not guarantee the soundness of a preacher's doctrine. Be sure that those to whom you listen are teaching God's Word alone.

^{20} "Asher will dine on rich foods
    and produce food fit for kings.

^{21} "Naphtali is a doe set free
    that bears beautiful fawns.

^{22} "Joseph is the foal of a wild donkey,
    the foal of a wild donkey at a
        spring—
    one of the wild donkeys on the
        ridge.*

^{23} Archers attacked him savagely;
    they shot at him and harassed him.

^{24} But his bow remained taut,
    and his arms were strengthened
    by the hands of the Mighty One of
        Jacob,
    by the Shepherd, the Rock of Israel.

^{25} May the God of your father help you;
    May the Almighty bless you
    with the blessings of the heavens
        above,
    and blessings of the watery depths
        below,
    and blessings of the breasts and
        womb.

^{26} May the blessings of your father
    surpass the blessings of the ancient
        mountains,*
    reaching to the heights of the
        eternal hills.
    May these blessings rest on the head
        of Joseph,
    who is a prince among his brothers.

^{27} "Benjamin is a ravenous wolf,
    devouring his enemies in the
        morning
    and dividing his plunder in the
        evening."

^{28}These are the twelve tribes of Israel, and this is what their father said as he told his sons good-bye. He blessed each one with an appropriate message.

^{29}Then Jacob instructed them, "Soon I will die and join my ancestors. Bury me with my father and grandfather in the cave in the field of Ephron the Hittite. ^{30}This is the cave in the field of Machpelah, near Mamre in Canaan, that Abraham bought from Ephron the Hittite as a permanent burial site. ^{31}There Abraham and his wife Sarah are buried. There Isaac and his wife, Rebekah, are buried. And there I buried Leah. ^{32}It is the plot of land

and the cave that my grandfather Abraham bought from the Hittites."

^{33}When Jacob had finished this charge to his sons, he drew his feet into the bed, breathed his last, and joined his ancestors in death.

48:2 Hebrew *Israel;* also in 48:8, 10, 11, 13, 14, 21. See note on 35:21.   **48:3** Hebrew *El-Shaddai.*   **48:4** Hebrew *seed;* also in 48:19.   **48:22** Or *an extra ridge of land.* The meaning of the Hebrew is uncertain.   **49:10a** Hebrew *from between his feet.*   **49:10b** Or *until tribute is brought to him and the peoples obey;* traditionally rendered *until Shiloh comes.*   **49:14** Or *sheepfolds,* or *hearths.*   **49:22** Or *Joseph is a fruitful tree, / a fruitful tree beside a spring. / His branches reach over the wall.* The meaning of the Hebrew is uncertain.   **49:26** Or *of my ancestors.*

MATTHEW 15:29–16:12
Sick people became well. Lame people walked. A few loaves and fish fed a huge crowd. Still, the religious leaders asked for a sign from Jesus that he was really from God. Their questions only revealed their own lack of faith.

Jesus returned to the Sea of Galilee and climbed a hill and sat down. ^{30}A vast crowd brought to him people who were lame, blind, crippled, those who couldn't speak, and many others. They laid them before Jesus, and he healed them all. ^{31}The crowd was amazed! Those who hadn't been able to speak were talking, the crippled were made well, the lame were walking, and the blind could see again! And they praised the God of Israel.

^{32}Then Jesus called his disciples and told them, "I feel sorry for these people. They have been here with me for three days, and they have nothing left to eat. I don't want to send them away hungry, or they will faint along the way."

^{33}The disciples replied, "Where would we get enough food here in the wilderness for such a huge crowd?"

^{34}Jesus asked, "How much bread do you have?"

They replied, "Seven loaves, and a few small fish."

^{35}So Jesus told all the people to sit down on the ground. ^{36}Then he took the seven loaves and the fish, thanked God for them, and broke them into pieces. He gave them to the disciples, who distributed the food to the crowd.

^{37}They all ate as much as they wanted. Afterward, the disciples picked up seven large baskets of leftover food. [38]There were 4,000 men who were fed that day, in addition to all the women and children. [39]Then Jesus sent the people home, and he got into a boat and crossed over to the region of Magadan.

[16:1]ONE day the Pharisees and Sadducees came to test Jesus, demanding that he show them a miraculous sign from heaven to prove his authority.

[2]He replied, "You know the saying, 'Red sky at night means fair weather tomorrow; [3]red sky in the morning means foul weather all day.' You know how to interpret the weather signs in the sky, but you don't know how to interpret the signs of the times!* [4]Only an evil, adulterous generation would demand a miraculous sign, but the only sign I will give them is the sign of the prophet Jonah.*" Then Jesus left them and went away.

[5]Later, after they crossed to the other side of the lake, the disciples discovered they had forgotten to bring any bread. [6]"Watch out!" Jesus warned them. "Beware of the yeast of the Pharisees and Sadducees."

[7]At this they began to argue with each other because they hadn't brought any bread. [8]Jesus knew what they were saying, so he said, "You have so little faith! Why are you arguing with each other about having no bread? [9]Don't you understand even yet? Don't you remember the 5,000 I fed with five loaves, and the baskets of leftovers you picked up? [10]Or the 4,000 I fed with seven loaves, and the large baskets of leftovers you picked up? [11]Why can't you understand that I'm not talking about bread? So again I say, 'Beware of the yeast of the Pharisees and Sadducees.'"

[12]Then at last they understood that he wasn't speaking about the yeast in bread, but about the deceptive teaching of the Pharisees and Sadducees.

16:2-3 Several manuscripts do not include any of the words in 16:2-3 after *He replied.*   16:4 Greek *the sign of Jonah.*

PSALM 20:1-9
For the choir director: A psalm of David.

[1] In times of trouble, may the LORD
answer your cry.

May the name of the God
of Jacob keep you safe from
all harm.
[2] May he send you help from his
sanctuary
and strengthen you from
Jerusalem.*
[3] May he remember all your gifts
and look favorably on your burnt
offerings.   *Interlude*

[4] May he grant your heart's desires
and make all your plans succeed.
[5] May we shout for joy when we hear
of your victory
and raise a victory banner in the
name of our God.
May the LORD answer all your
prayers.

[6] Now I know that the LORD rescues
his anointed king.
He will answer him from his holy
heaven
and rescue him by his great
power.
[7] Some nations boast of their chariots
and horses,
but we boast in the name of the
LORD our God.
[8] Those nations will fall down and
collapse,
but we will rise up and stand firm.

[9] Give victory to our king,
O LORD!
Answer our cry for help.

20:2 Hebrew *Zion.*

PROVERBS 4:20-27
My child, pay attention to what I say. Listen carefully to my words. Don't lose sight of them. Let them penetrate deep into your heart, for they bring life to those who find them, and healing to their whole body. □ Guard your heart above all else, for it determines the course of your life. □ Avoid all perverse talk; stay away from corrupt speech. □ Look straight ahead, and fix your eyes on what lies before you. Mark out a straight path for your feet; stay on the safe path. Don't get sidetracked; keep your feet from following evil.

JANUARY 25

GENESIS 50:1–EXODUS 2:10

During the hundreds of years between the end of Genesis and the beginning of Exodus, Jacob's family grew from an extended family of seventy-plus members living as honored guests in Egypt to an entire nation living as slaves. God knew this would happen, and he would soon intervene in a mighty way.

Joseph threw himself on his father and wept over him and kissed him. ²Then Joseph told the physicians who served him to embalm his father's body; so Jacob* was embalmed. ³The embalming process took the usual forty days. And the Egyptians mourned his death for seventy days.

⁴When the period of mourning was over, Joseph approached Pharaoh's advisers and said, "Please do me this favor and speak to Pharaoh on my behalf. ⁵Tell him that my father made me swear an oath. He said to me, 'Listen, I am about to die. Take my body back to the land of Canaan, and bury me in the tomb I prepared for myself.' So please allow me to go and bury my father. After his burial, I will return without delay."

⁶Pharaoh agreed to Joseph's request. "Go and bury your father, as he made you promise," he said. ⁷So Joseph went up to bury his father. He was accompanied by all of Pharaoh's officials, all the senior members of Pharaoh's household, and all the senior officers of Egypt. ⁸Joseph also took his entire household and his brothers and their households. But they left their little children and flocks and herds in the land of Goshen. ⁹A great number of chariots and charioteers accompanied Joseph.

¹⁰When they arrived at the threshing floor of Atad, near the Jordan River, they held a very great and solemn memorial service, with a seven-day period of mourning for Joseph's father. ¹¹The local residents, the Canaanites, watched them mourning at the threshing floor of Atad. Then they renamed that place (which is near the Jordan) Abel-mizraim,* for they said, "This is a place of deep mourning for these Egyptians."

¹²So Jacob's sons did as he had commanded them. ¹³They carried his body to the land of Canaan and buried him in the cave in the field of Machpelah, near Mamre. This is the cave that Abraham had bought as a permanent burial site from Ephron the Hittite.

¹⁴After burying Jacob, Joseph returned to Egypt with his brothers and all who had accompanied him to his father's burial. ¹⁵But now that their father was dead, Joseph's brothers became fearful. "Now Joseph will show his anger and pay us back for all the wrong we did to him," they said.

¹⁶So they sent this message to Joseph: "Before your father died, he instructed us ¹⁷to say to you: 'Please forgive your brothers for the great wrong they did to you—for their sin in treating you so cruelly.' So we, the servants of the God of your father, beg you to forgive our sin." When Joseph received the message, he broke down and wept. ¹⁸Then his brothers came and threw themselves down before Joseph. "Look, we are your slaves!" they said.

¹⁹But Joseph replied, "Don't be afraid of me. Am I God, that I can punish you? ²⁰You intended to harm me, but God intended it all for good. He brought me to this position so I could save the lives of many people. ²¹No, don't be afraid. I will continue to take care of you and your children." So he reassured them by speaking kindly to them.

²²So Joseph and his brothers and their families continued to live in Egypt. Joseph lived to the age of 110. ²³He lived to see three generations of descendants of his son Ephraim, and he lived to see the birth of the children of Manasseh's son Makir, whom he claimed as his own.*

²⁴"Soon I will die," Joseph told his brothers, "but God will surely come to help you and lead you out of this land of Egypt. He will bring you back to the land he solemnly promised to give to Abraham, to Isaac, and to Jacob." ²⁵Then Joseph made the sons of Israel swear an oath, and he said, "When God

comes to help you and lead you back, you must take my bones with you." ²⁶So Joseph died at the age of 110. The Egyptians embalmed him, and his body was placed in a coffin in Egypt.

1:1THESE are the names of the sons of Israel (that is, Jacob) who moved to Egypt with their father, each with his family: ²Reuben, Simeon, Levi, Judah, ³Issachar, Zebulun, Benjamin, ⁴Dan, Naphtali, Gad, and Asher. ⁵In all, Jacob had seventy* descendants in Egypt, including Joseph, who was already there.

⁶In time, Joseph and all of his brothers died, ending that entire generation. ⁷But their descendants, the Israelites, had many children and grandchildren. In fact, they multiplied so greatly that they became extremely powerful and filled the land.

⁸Eventually, a new king came to power in Egypt who knew nothing about Joseph or what he had done. ⁹He said to his people, "Look, the people of Israel now outnumber us and are stronger than we are. ¹⁰We must make a plan to keep them from growing even more. If we don't, and if war breaks out, they will join our enemies and fight against us. Then they will escape from the country.*"

¹¹So the Egyptians made the Israelites their slaves. They appointed brutal slave drivers over them, hoping to wear them down with crushing labor. They forced them to build the cities of Pithom and Rameses as supply centers for the king. ¹²But the more the Egyptians oppressed them, the more the Israelites multiplied and spread, and the more alarmed the Egyptians became. ¹³So the Egyptians worked the people of Israel without mercy. ¹⁴They made their lives bitter, forcing them to mix mortar and make bricks and do all the work in the fields. They were ruthless in all their demands.

¹⁵Then Pharaoh, the king of Egypt, gave this order to the Hebrew midwives, Shiphrah and Puah: ¹⁶"When you help the Hebrew women as they give birth, watch as they deliver.* If the baby is a boy, kill him; if it is a girl, let her live." ¹⁷But because the midwives feared God, they refused to obey the king's orders. They allowed the boys to live, too.

¹⁸So the king of Egypt called for the midwives. "Why have you done this?" he demanded. "Why have you allowed the boys to live?"

¹⁹"The Hebrew women are not like the Egyptian women," the midwives replied. "They are more vigorous and have their babies so quickly that we cannot get there in time."

²⁰So God was good to the midwives, and the Israelites continued to multiply, growing more and more powerful. ²¹And because the midwives feared God, he gave them families of their own.

²²Then Pharaoh gave this order to all his people: "Throw every newborn Hebrew boy into the Nile River. But you may let the girls live."

2:1ABOUT this time, a man and woman from the tribe of Levi got married. ²The woman became pregnant and gave birth to a son. She saw that he was a special baby and kept him hidden for three months. ³But when she could no longer hide him, she got a basket made of papyrus reeds and waterproofed it with tar and pitch. She put the baby in the basket and laid it among the reeds along the bank of the Nile River. ⁴The baby's sister then stood at a distance, watching to see what would happen to him.

⁵Soon Pharaoh's daughter came down to bathe in the river, and her attendants walked along the riverbank. When the princess saw the basket among the reeds, she sent her maid to get it for her. ⁶When the princess opened it, she saw the baby. The little boy was crying, and she felt sorry for him. "This must be one of the Hebrew children," she said.

⁷Then the baby's sister approached the princess. "Should I go and find one of the Hebrew women to nurse the baby for you?" she asked.

⁸"Yes, do!" the princess replied. So the girl went and called the baby's mother.

⁹"Take this baby and nurse him for me," the princess told the baby's mother. "I will pay you for your help." So the woman took her baby home and nursed him.

¹⁰Later, when the boy was older, his

mother brought him back to Pharaoh's daughter, who adopted him as her own son. The princess named him Moses,* for she explained, "I lifted him out of the water."

50:2 Hebrew *Israel.* See note on 35:21.   **50:11** *Abel-mizraim* means "mourning of the Egyptians."   **50:23** Hebrew *who were born on Joseph's knees.*   **1:5** Dead Sea Scrolls and Greek version read *seventy-five*; see notes on Gen 46:27.   **1:10** Or *will take the country.*   **1:16** Hebrew *look upon the two stones*; perhaps the reference is to a birthstool.   **2:10** *Moses* sounds like a Hebrew term that means "to lift out."

MATTHEW 16:13–17:9

Sometimes we think we understand the truth, only to discover that it goes deeper than we can fathom. Look for Jesus' words to his disciples that seem to shake the very core of their thinking. Jesus was not the earthly king they had anticipated; he was so much more!

When Jesus came to the region of Caesarea Philippi, he asked his disciples, "Who do people say that the Son of Man is?"*

14"Well," they replied, "some say John the Baptist, some say Elijah, and others say Jeremiah or one of the other prophets."

15 Then he asked them, "But who do you say I am?"

16 Simon Peter answered, "You are the Messiah,* the Son of the living God."

17 Jesus replied, "You are blessed, Simon son of John,* because my Father in heaven has revealed this to you. You did not learn this from any human being. 18 Now I say to you that you are Peter (which means 'rock'),* and upon this rock I will build my church, and all the powers of hell* will not conquer it. 19 And I will give you the keys of the Kingdom of Heaven. Whatever you forbid* on earth will be forbidden in heaven, and whatever you permit* on earth will be permitted in heaven."

20 Then he sternly warned the disciples not to tell anyone that he was the Messiah.

21 From then on Jesus* began to tell his disciples plainly that it was necessary for him to go to Jerusalem, and that he would suffer many terrible things at the hands of the elders, the leading priests, and the teachers of religious law. He would be killed, but on the third day he would be raised from the dead.

22 But Peter took him aside and began to reprimand him* for saying such things.

"Heaven forbid, Lord," he said. "This will never happen to you!"

23 Jesus turned to Peter and said, "Get away from me, Satan! You are a dangerous trap to me. You are seeing things merely from a human point of view, not from God's."

24 Then Jesus said to his disciples, "If any of you wants to be my follower, you must turn from your selfish ways, take up your cross, and follow me. 25 If you try to hang on to your life, you will lose it. But if you give up your life for my sake, you will save it. 26 And what do you benefit if you gain the whole world but lose your own soul?* Is anything worth more than your soul? 27 For the Son of Man will come with his angels in the glory of his Father and will judge all people according to their deeds. 28 And I tell you the truth, some standing here right now will not die before they see the Son of Man coming in his Kingdom."

17:1 Six days later Jesus took Peter and the two brothers, James and John, and led them up a high mountain to be alone. 2 As the men watched, Jesus' appearance was transformed so that his face shone like the sun, and his clothes became as white as light. 3 Suddenly, Moses and Elijah appeared and began talking with Jesus.

4 Peter exclaimed, "Lord, it's wonderful for us to be here! If you want, I'll make three shelters as memorials*—one for you, one for Moses, and one for Elijah."

5 But even as he spoke, a bright cloud overshadowed them, and a voice from the cloud said, "This is my dearly loved Son, who brings me great joy. Listen to him." 6 The disciples were terrified and fell face down on the ground.

7 Then Jesus came over and touched them. "Get up," he said. "Don't be afraid." 8 And when they looked up, Moses and Elijah were gone, and they saw only Jesus.

9 As they went back down the mountain, Jesus commanded them, "Don't tell anyone what you have seen until the Son of Man* has been raised from the dead."

16:13 "Son of Man" is a title Jesus used for himself.
16:16 Or *the Christ. Messiah* (a Hebrew term) and *Christ* (a Greek term) both mean "the anointed one."   **16:17** Greek

Simon bar-Jonah; see John 1:42; 21:15-17.   **16:18a** Greek
that you are Peter.   **16:18b** Greek *and the gates of Hades.*
16:19a Or *bind,* or *lock.*   **16:19b** Or *loose,* or *open.*
16:21 Some manuscripts read *Jesus the Messiah.*   **16:22** Or
began to correct him.   **16:26** Or *your self?* also in 16:26b.
17:4 Greek *three tabernacles.*   **17:9** "Son of Man" is a title
Jesus used for himself.

PSALM 21:1-13
For the choir director: A psalm of David.

¹ **H**ow the king rejoices in your strength,
O Lord!
He shouts with joy because you give
him victory.
² For you have given him his heart's
desire;
you have withheld nothing he
requested.   *Interlude*

³ You welcomed him back with success
and prosperity.
You placed a crown of finest gold
on his head.
⁴ He asked you to preserve his life,
and you granted his request.
The days of his life stretch on
forever.
⁵ Your victory brings him great honor,
and you have clothed him with
splendor and majesty.
⁶ You have endowed him with eternal
blessings
and given him the joy of your
presence.

⁷ For the king trusts in the Lord.
The unfailing love of the Most
High will keep him from
stumbling.

⁸ You will capture all your enemies.
Your strong right hand will seize
all who hate you.
⁹ You will throw them in a flaming
furnace
when you appear.
The Lord will consume them in
his anger;
fire will devour them.
¹⁰ You will wipe their children from
the face of the earth;
they will never have descendants.
¹¹ Although they plot against you,
their evil schemes will never
succeed.
¹² For they will turn and run
when they see your arrows aimed
at them.
¹³ Rise up, O Lord, in all your power.
With music and singing we
celebrate your mighty acts.

PROVERBS 5:1-6

My son, pay attention to my wisdom; listen carefully to my wise counsel. Then you will show discernment, and your lips will express what you've learned. For the

Following Jesus

HOW WE LIVE

MATTHEW 16:24-26 Many are on a quest to find personal happiness. The world sets up for us models of wealthy, famous, well-dressed people and says that if we can just become like them, we'll be happy. The Bible has a different message. It says that we find happiness by following Christ into the life he has planned for us.   •The way to be a happy, fulfilled person is found in today's reading in Matthew 16. Jesus gets right to the point by saying to the believer, "If you give up your life for my sake, you will save it." He wasn't talking only about physical death (although in some parts of the world, that is a reality for believers); he was saying that you must submit to him your will, your plans, and your future. The all-knowing, all-powerful God has a plan especially for you. When you gratefully walk in the direction he has planned for you, you will find fulfillment and true happiness.   •That doesn't mean that you can't set goals and work toward attaining them. Instead, you make your plans and set your goals always seeking God's guidance and walking obediently as each step becomes clear.

lips of an immoral woman are as sweet as honey, and her mouth is smoother than oil. But in the end she is as bitter as poison, as dangerous as a double-edged sword. Her feet go down to death; her steps lead straight to the grave.* For she cares nothing about the path to life. She staggers down a crooked trail and doesn't realize it.

5:5 Hebrew *to Sheol.*

JANUARY**26**

EXODUS 2:11–3:22

Moses was born a Hebrew but was adopted into Egyptian royalty. Torn between those worlds, his crime set him upon a path that would lead him to a greater destiny than he could have imagined on his own.

Many years later, when Moses had grown up, he went out to visit his own people, the Hebrews, and he saw how hard they were forced to work. During his visit, he saw an Egyptian beating one of his fellow Hebrews. [12]After looking in all directions to make sure no one was watching, Moses killed the Egyptian and hid the body in the sand.

[13]The next day, when Moses went out to visit his people again, he saw two Hebrew men fighting. "Why are you beating up your friend?" Moses said to the one who had started the fight.

[14]The man replied, "Who appointed you to be our prince and judge? Are you going to kill me as you killed that Egyptian yesterday?"

Then Moses was afraid, thinking, "Everyone knows what I did." [15]And sure enough, Pharaoh heard what had happened, and he tried to kill Moses. But Moses fled from Pharaoh and went to live in the land of Midian.

When Moses arrived in Midian, he sat down beside a well. [16]Now the priest of Midian had seven daughters who came as usual to draw water and fill the water troughs for their father's flocks. [17]But some other shepherds came and chased them away. So Moses jumped up and rescued the girls from the shepherds. Then he drew water for their flocks.

[18]When the girls returned to Reuel, their father, he asked, "Why are you back so soon today?"

[19]"An Egyptian rescued us from the shepherds," they answered. "And then he drew water for us and watered our flocks."

[20]"Then where is he?" their father asked. "Why did you leave him there? Invite him to come and eat with us."

[21]Moses accepted the invitation, and he settled there with him. In time, Reuel gave Moses his daughter Zipporah to be his wife. [22]Later she gave birth to a son, and Moses named him Gershom,* for he explained, "I have been a foreigner in a foreign land."

[23]Years passed, and the king of Egypt died. But the Israelites continued to groan under their burden of slavery. They cried out for help, and their cry rose up to God. [24]God heard their groaning, and he remembered his covenant promise to Abraham, Isaac, and Jacob. [25]He looked down on the people of Israel and knew it was time to act.*

[3:1]ONE day Moses was tending the flock of his father-in-law, Jethro,* the priest of Midian. He led the flock far into the wilderness and came to Sinai,* the mountain of God. [2]There the angel of the LORD appeared to him in a blazing fire from the middle of a bush. Moses stared in amazement. Though the bush was engulfed in flames, it didn't burn up. [3]"This is amazing," Moses said to himself. "Why isn't that bush burning up? I must go see it."

[4]When the LORD saw Moses coming to take a closer look, God called to him from the middle of the bush, "Moses! Moses!"

"Here I am!" Moses replied.

⁵"Do not come any closer," the LORD warned. "Take off your sandals, for you are standing on holy ground. ⁶I am the God of your father*—the God of Abraham, the God of Isaac, and the God of Jacob." When Moses heard this, he covered his face because he was afraid to look at God.

⁷Then the LORD told him, "I have certainly seen the oppression of my people in Egypt. I have heard their cries of distress because of their harsh slave drivers. Yes, I am aware of their suffering. ⁸So I have come down to rescue them from the power of the Egyptians and lead them out of Egypt into their own fertile and spacious land. It is a land flowing with milk and honey—the land where the Canaanites, Hittites, Amorites, Perizzites, Hivites, and Jebusites now live. ⁹Look! The cry of the people of Israel has reached me, and I have seen how harshly the Egyptians abuse them. ¹⁰Now go, for I am sending you to Pharaoh. You must lead my people Israel out of Egypt."

¹¹But Moses protested to God, "Who am I to appear before Pharaoh? Who am I to lead the people of Israel out of Egypt?"

¹²God answered, "I will be with you. And this is your sign that I am the one who has sent you: When you have brought the people out of Egypt, you will worship God at this very mountain."

¹³But Moses protested, "If I go to the people of Israel and tell them, 'The God of your ancestors has sent me to you,' they will ask me, 'What is his name?' Then what should I tell them?"

¹⁴God replied to Moses, "I AM WHO I AM.* Say this to the people of Israel: I AM has sent me to you." ¹⁵God also said to Moses, "Say this to the people of Israel: Yahweh,* the God of your ancestors—the God of Abraham, the God of Isaac, and the God of Jacob—has sent me to you.

This is my eternal name,
my name to remember for all
generations.

¹⁶"Now go and call together all the elders of Israel. Tell them, 'The LORD, the God of your ancestors—the God of Abraham, Isaac, and Jacob—has appeared to me. He told me, "I have been watching closely, and I see how the Egyptians are treating you. ¹⁷I have promised to rescue you from your oppression in Egypt. I will lead you to a land flowing with milk and honey—the land where the Canaanites, Hittites, Amorites, Perizzites, Hivites, and Jebusites now live."'

¹⁸"The elders of Israel will accept your message. Then you and the elders must go to the king of Egypt and tell him, 'The LORD, the God of the Hebrews, has met with us. So please let us take a three-day journey into the wilderness to offer sacrifices to the LORD, our God.'

¹⁹"But I know that the king of Egypt will

HOW WE LIVE

Relying on God's power

EXODUS 3:10-12 God was asking a lot of Moses—and Moses responded with reticence. "Go to Pharaoh? Lead the people out of Egypt? Who am I? How can you expect me . . .?" God's answer? "I will be with you." • Some people look at the Christian life and say, "I can't live that way." Perhaps you've felt that way. Old habits die hard; some relationships become more difficult now that you're a believer; patterns of thinking and living are difficult to change. God's answer to you? "I am with you." •When you asked Jesus into your heart, he gave you the gift of the Holy Spirit. With the helping presence of the Holy Spirit, God empowers his followers to live a Christian life. In Exodus, Moses feared having to confront Pharaoh on his own, believing that he would not be worthy enough to carry God's message. God's reassurance to Moses was, "I will be with you." In that simple statement, you too can be assured of God's presence to guide you in the times of deepest doubt and despair.

not let you go unless a mighty hand forces him.* [20]So I will raise my hand and strike the Egyptians, performing all kinds of miracles among them. Then at last he will let you go. [21]And I will cause the Egyptians to look favorably on you. They will give you gifts when you go so you will not leave empty-handed. [22]Every Israelite woman will ask for articles of silver and gold and fine clothing from her Egyptian neighbors and from the foreign women in their houses. You will dress your sons and daughters with these, stripping the Egyptians of their wealth."

2:22 *Gershom* sounds like a Hebrew term that means "a foreigner there."   **2:25** Or *and acknowledged his obligation to help them.*   **3:1a** Moses' father-in-law went by two names, Jethro and Reuel.   **3:1b** Hebrew *Horeb,* another name for Sinai.   **3:6** Greek version reads *your fathers.*   **3:14** Or *I WILL BE WHAT I WILL BE.*   **3:15** *Yahweh* is a transliteration of the proper name *YHWH* that is sometimes rendered "Jehovah"; in this translation it is usually rendered "the LORD" (note the use of small capitals).   **3:19** As in Greek and Latin versions; Hebrew reads *will not let you go, not by a mighty hand.*

MATTHEW 17:10-27
Jesus described the kind of faith that would enable disciples to do God's work. He spoke of the path his own life must take to offer life by way of death, and of how to get along in this world when you belong in another.

Then his disciples asked him, "Why do the teachers of religious law insist that Elijah must return before the Messiah comes?*"

[11]Jesus replied, "Elijah is indeed coming first to get everything ready. [12]But I tell you, Elijah has already come, but he wasn't recognized, and they chose to abuse him. And in the same way they will also make the Son of Man suffer." [13]Then the disciples realized he was talking about John the Baptist.

[14]At the foot of the mountain, a large crowd was waiting for them. A man came and knelt before Jesus and said, [15]"Lord, have mercy on my son. He has seizures and suffers terribly. He often falls into the fire or into the water. [16]So I brought him to your disciples, but they couldn't heal him."

[17]Jesus said, "You faithless and corrupt people! How long must I be with you? How long must I put up with you? Bring the boy here to me." [18]Then Jesus re-buked the demon in the boy, and it left him. From that moment the boy was well.

[19]Afterward the disciples asked Jesus privately, "Why couldn't we cast out that demon?"

[20]"You don't have enough faith," Jesus told them. "I tell you the truth, if you had faith even as small as a mustard seed, you could say to this mountain, 'Move from here to there,' and it would move. Nothing would be impossible.*"

[22]After they gathered again in Galilee, Jesus told them, "The Son of Man is going to be betrayed into the hands of his enemies. [23]He will be killed, but on the third day he will be raised from the dead." And the disciples were filled with grief.

[24]On their arrival in Capernaum, the collectors of the Temple tax* came to Peter and asked him, "Doesn't your teacher pay the Temple tax?"

[25]"Yes, he does," Peter replied. Then he went into the house.

But before he had a chance to speak, Jesus asked him, "What do you think, Peter?* Do kings tax their own people or the people they have conquered?*"

[26]"They tax the people they have conquered," Peter replied.

"Well, then," Jesus said, "the citizens are free! [27]However, we don't want to offend them, so go down to the lake and throw in a line. Open the mouth of the first fish you catch, and you will find a large silver coin.* Take it and pay the tax for both of us."

17:10 Greek *that Elijah must come first?*   **17:20** Some manuscripts add verse 21, *But this kind of demon won't leave except by prayer and fasting.* Compare Mark 9:29.   **17:24** Greek *the two-drachma [tax];* also in 17:24b. See Exod 30:13-16; Neh 10:32-33.   **17:25a** Greek *Simon?*   **17:25b** Greek *their sons or others?*   **17:27** Greek *a stater* [a Greek coin equivalent to four drachmas].

PSALM 22:1-18
For the choir director: A psalm of David, to be sung to the tune "Doe of the Dawn."

[1]   **M**y God, my God, why have you
          abandoned me?
       Why are you so far away when
          I groan for help?
[2]   Every day I call to you, my God, but
          you do not answer.
       Every night you hear my voice,
          but I find no relief.

3 Yet you are holy,
　enthroned on the praises of Israel.
4 Our ancestors trusted in you,
　and you rescued them.
5 They cried out to you and were saved.
　They trusted in you and were never
　　disgraced.

6 But I am a worm and not a man.
　I am scorned and despised by all!
7 Everyone who sees me mocks me.
　They sneer and shake their heads,
　　saying,
8 "Is this the one who relies on the LORD?
　Then let the LORD save him!
　If the LORD loves him so much,
　　let the LORD rescue him!"

9 Yet you brought me safely from
　　my mother's womb
　and led me to trust you at my
　　mother's breast.
10 I was thrust into your arms at my
　　birth.
　You have been my God from the
　　moment I was born.

11 Do not stay so far from me,
　for trouble is near,
　and no one else can help me.
12 My enemies surround me like a herd
　　of bulls;
　fierce bulls of Bashan have hemmed
　　me in!
13 Like lions they open their jaws
　　against me,
　roaring and tearing into their prey.
14 My life is poured out like water,
　and all my bones are out of joint.

My heart is like wax,
　melting within me.
15 My strength has dried up like
　　sunbaked clay.
　My tongue sticks to the roof
　　of my mouth.
　You have laid me in the dust and
　　left me for dead.
16 My enemies surround me like a pack
　　of dogs;
　an evil gang closes in on me.
　They have pierced my hands and
　　feet.
17 I can count all my bones.
　My enemies stare at me and gloat.
18 They divide my garments among
　　themselves
　and throw dice* for my clothing.

22:18 Hebrew *cast lots.*

PROVERBS 5:7-14

So now, my sons, listen to me. Never stray from what I am about to say: Stay away from her! Don't go near the door of her house! If you do, you will lose your honor and will lose to merciless people all you have achieved. Strangers will consume your wealth, and someone else will enjoy the fruit of your labor. In the end you will groan in anguish when disease consumes your body. You will say, "How I hated discipline! If only I had not ignored all the warnings! Oh, why didn't I listen to my teachers? Why didn't I pay attention to my instructors? I have come to the brink of utter ruin, and now I must face public disgrace."

JANUARY**27**

EXODUS 4:1-5:21

After a few final and unsuccessful protests, Moses obeyed God and returned to Egypt in order to confront Pharaoh and free the Hebrews from bondage.

But Moses protested again, "What if they won't believe me or listen to me? What if

they say, 'The LORD never appeared to you'?"

2 Then the LORD asked him, "What is that in your hand?"

"A shepherd's staff," Moses replied.

3 "Throw it down on the ground," the

LORD told him. So Moses threw down the staff, and it turned into a snake! Moses jumped back.

⁴Then the LORD told him, "Reach out and grab its tail." So Moses reached out and grabbed it, and it turned back into a shepherd's staff in his hand.

⁵"Perform this sign," the LORD told him. "Then they will believe that the LORD, the God of their ancestors—the God of Abraham, the God of Isaac, and the God of Jacob—really has appeared to you."

⁶Then the LORD said to Moses, "Now put your hand inside your cloak." So Moses put his hand inside his cloak, and when he took it out again, his hand was white as snow with a severe skin disease.* ⁷"Now put your hand back into your cloak," the LORD said. So Moses put his hand back in, and when he took it out again, it was as healthy as the rest of his body.

⁸The LORD said to Moses, "If they do not believe you and are not convinced by the first miraculous sign, they will be convinced by the second sign. ⁹And if they don't believe you or listen to you even after these two signs, then take some water from the Nile River and pour it out on the dry ground. When you do, the water from the Nile will turn to blood on the ground."

¹⁰But Moses pleaded with the LORD, "O Lord, I'm not very good with words. I never have been, and I'm not now, even though you have spoken to me. I get tongue-tied, and my words get tangled."

¹¹Then the LORD asked Moses, "Who makes a person's mouth? Who decides whether people speak or do not speak, hear or do not hear, see or do not see? Is it not I, the LORD? ¹²Now go! I will be with you as you speak, and I will instruct you in what to say."

¹³But Moses again pleaded, "Lord, please! Send anyone else."

¹⁴Then the LORD became angry with Moses. "All right," he said. "What about your brother, Aaron the Levite? I know he speaks well. And look! He is on his way to meet you now. He will be delighted to see you. ¹⁵Talk to him, and put the words in his mouth. I will be with both of you as you speak, and I will instruct you both in what to do. ¹⁶Aaron will be your spokes-

man to the people. He will be your mouthpiece, and you will stand in the place of God for him, telling him what to say. ¹⁷And take your shepherd's staff with you, and use it to perform the miraclous signs I have shown you."

¹⁸So Moses went back home to Jethro, his father-in-law. "Please let me return to my relatives in Egypt," Moses said. "I don't even know if they are still alive."

"Go in peace," Jethro replied.

¹⁹Before Moses left Midian, the LORD said to him, "Return to Egypt, for all those who wanted to kill you have died."

²⁰So Moses took his wife and sons, put them on a donkey, and headed back to the land of Egypt. In his hand he carried the staff of God.

²¹And the LORD told Moses, "When you arrive back in Egypt, go to Pharaoh and perform all the miracles I have empowered you to do. But I will harden his heart so he will refuse to let the people go. ²²Then you will tell him, 'This is what the LORD says: Israel is my firstborn son. ²³I commanded you, "Let my son go, so he can worship me." But since you have refused, I will now kill your firstborn son!'"

²⁴On the way to Egypt, at a place where Moses and his family had stopped for the night, the LORD confronted him and was about to kill him. ²⁵But Moses' wife, Zipporah, took a flint knife and circumcised her son. She touched his feet* with the foreskin and said, "Now you are a bridegroom of blood to me." ²⁶(When she said "a bridegroom of blood," she was referring to the circumcision.) After that, the LORD left him alone.

²⁷Now the LORD had said to Aaron, "Go out into the wilderness to meet Moses." So Aaron went and met Moses at the mountain of God, and he embraced him. ²⁸Moses then told Aaron everything the LORD had commanded him to say. And he told him about the miraculous signs the LORD had commanded him to perform.

²⁹Then Moses and Aaron returned to Egypt and called all the elders of Israel together. ³⁰Aaron told them everything the LORD had told Moses, and Moses performed the miraculous signs as they watched. ³¹Then the people of Israel were convinced that the LORD had sent Moses

and Aaron. When they heard that the LORD was concerned about them and had seen their misery, they bowed down and worshiped.

5:1AFTER this presentation to Israel's leaders, Moses and Aaron went and spoke to Pharaoh. They told him, "This is what the LORD, the God of Israel, says: Let my people go so they may hold a festival in my honor in the wilderness."

2"Is that so?" retorted Pharaoh. "And who is the LORD? Why should I listen to him and let Israel go? I don't know the LORD, and I will not let Israel go."

3But Aaron and Moses persisted. "The God of the Hebrews has met with us," they declared. "So let us take a three-day journey into the wilderness so we can offer sacrifices to the LORD our God. If we don't, he will kill us with a plague or with the sword."

4Pharaoh replied, "Moses and Aaron, why are you distracting the people from their tasks? Get back to work! 5Look, there are many of your people in the land, and you are stopping them from their work."

6That same day Pharaoh sent this order to the Egyptian slave drivers and the Israelite foremen: 7"Do not supply any more straw for making bricks. Make the people get it themselves! 8But still require them to make the same number of bricks as before. Don't reduce the quota. They are lazy. That's why they are crying out, 'Let us go and offer sacrifices to our God.' 9Load them down with more work. Make them sweat! That will teach them to listen to lies!"

10So the slave drivers and foremen went out and told the people: "This is what Pharaoh says: I will not provide any more straw for you. 11Go and get it yourselves. Find it wherever you can. But you must produce just as many bricks as before!" 12So the people scattered throughout the land of Egypt in search of stubble to use as straw.

13Meanwhile, the Egyptian slave drivers continued to push hard. "Meet your daily quota of bricks, just as you did when we provided you with straw!" they demanded. 14Then they whipped the Israelite foremen they had put in charge of the work crews. "Why haven't you met your quotas either yesterday or today?" they demanded.

15So the Israelite foremen went to Pharaoh and pleaded with him. "Please don't treat your servants like this," they begged. 16"We are given no straw, but the slave drivers still demand, 'Make bricks!' We are being beaten, but it isn't our fault! Your own people are to blame!"

HOW WE LIVE

Our marriages

PROVERBS 5:15-18 In contrast to what we see in the world, this passage in Proverbs urges married couples to look only to each other for companionship and sexual satisfaction. Adultery, sexually explicit magazines, pornographic videos and images on the Internet are all false ways to satisfy needs. • Temptations assault us from every side. Don't allow yourself to be fooled—giving in to the temptation of the explicit magazine will eventually lead to worse behavior, endangering the health and security of your family. A trusting relationship built upon the vows of marriage can be wiped away the very instant those vows are violated. The unique marriage bond between a man and a woman must be preserved at all costs. • So just how can you safeguard the sanctity of your marriage? (1) Make God the center of your marriage bond. God designed marriage as a place for love and fulfillment, both emotional and physical. (2) Avoid tempting places and situations. (3) Don't allow your marriage to become boring. God created sex for the enjoyment of a husband and wife, as well as for procreation. (4) Keep the lines of communication open with your spouse, and be sure to listen as much as you talk.

[17]But Pharaoh shouted, "You're just lazy! Lazy! That's why you're saying, 'Let us go and offer sacrifices to the LORD.' [18]Now get back to work! No straw will be given to you, but you must still produce the full quota of bricks."

[19]The Israelite foremen could see that they were in serious trouble when they were told, "You must not reduce the number of bricks you make each day." [20]As they left Pharaoh's court, they confronted Moses and Aaron, who were waiting outside for them. [21]The foremen said to them, "May the LORD judge and punish you for making us stink before Pharaoh and his officials. You have put a sword into their hands, an excuse to kill us!"

4:6 Or *with leprosy.* The Hebrew word used here can describe various skin diseases. 4:25 The Hebrew word for "feet" may refer here to the male sex organ.

MATTHEW 18:1-20

The Kingdom of God requires the faith of a child. It demands punishment for those who hurt the innocent. It reveals a God who goes the distance for one wandering soul. It envisions a community in which we deal authentically with conflict and the reality of God's presence.

About that time the disciples came to Jesus and asked, "Who is greatest in the Kingdom of Heaven?"

[2]Jesus called a little child to him and put the child among them. [3]Then he said, "I tell you the truth, unless you turn from your sins and become like little children, you will never get into the Kingdom of Heaven. [4]So anyone who becomes as humble as this little child is the greatest in the Kingdom of Heaven.

[5]"And anyone who welcomes a little child like this on my behalf* is welcoming me. [6]But if you cause one of these little ones who trusts in me to fall into sin, it would be better for you to have a large millstone tied around your neck and be drowned in the depths of the sea.

[7]"What sorrow awaits the world, because it tempts people to sin. Temptations are inevitable, but what sorrow awaits the person who does the tempting. [8]So if your hand or foot causes you to sin, cut it off and throw it away. It's better to enter eternal life with only one hand or one foot than to be thrown into eternal fire with both of your hands and feet. [9]And if your eye causes you to sin, gouge it out and throw it away. It's better to enter eternal life with only one eye than to have two eyes and be thrown into the fire of hell.*

[10]"Beware that you don't look down on any of these little ones. For I tell you that in heaven their angels are always in the presence of my heavenly Father.*

[12]"If a man has a hundred sheep and one of them wanders away, what will he do? Won't he leave the ninety-nine others on the hills and go out to search for the one that is lost? [13]And if he finds it, I tell you the truth, he will rejoice over it more than over the ninety-nine that didn't wander away! [14]In the same way, it is not my heavenly Father's will that even one of these little ones should perish.

[15]"If another believer* sins against you,* go privately and point out the offense. If the other person listens and confesses it, you have won that person back. [16]But if you are unsuccessful, take one or two others with you and go back again, so that everything you say may be confirmed by two or three witnesses. [17]If the person still refuses to listen, take your case to the church. Then if he or she won't accept the church's decision, treat that person as a pagan or a corrupt tax collector.

[18]"I tell you the truth, whatever you forbid* on earth will be forbidden in heaven, and whatever you permit* on earth will be permitted in heaven.

[19]"I also tell you this: If two of you agree here on earth concerning anything you ask, my Father in heaven will do it for you. [20]For where two or three gather together as my followers,* I am there among them."

18:5 Greek *in my name.* 18:9 Greek *the Gehenna of fire.* 18:10 Some manuscripts add verse 11, *And the Son of Man came to save those who are lost.* Compare Luke 19:10. 18:15a Greek *If your brother.* 18:15b Some manuscripts do not include *against you.* 18:18a Or *bind,* or *lock.* 18:18b Or *loose,* or *open.* 18:20 Greek *gather together in my name.*

PSALM 22:19-31

O LORD, do not stay far away!
   You are my strength; come quickly
      to my aid!

²⁰ Save me from the sword;
    spare my precious life from these
    dogs.
²¹ Snatch me from the lion's jaws
    and from the horns of these wild
    oxen.
²² I will proclaim your name to my
    brothers and sisters.*
    I will praise you among your
    assembled people.
²³ Praise the LORD, all you who fear him!
    Honor him, all you descendants
    of Jacob!
    Show him reverence, all you
    descendants of Israel!
²⁴ For he has not ignored or belittled
    the suffering of the needy.
    He has not turned his back on
    them,
    but has listened to their cries for
    help.
²⁵ I will praise you in the great assembly.
    I will fulfill my vows in the
    presence of those who
    worship you.
²⁶ The poor will eat and be satisfied.
    All who seek the LORD will praise
    him.
    Their hearts will rejoice with
    everlasting joy.
²⁷ The whole earth will acknowledge the
    LORD and return to him.
    All the families of the nations will
    bow down before him.

²⁸ For royal power belongs to the LORD.
    He rules all the nations.
²⁹ Let the rich of the earth feast and
    worship.
    Bow before him, all who are
    mortal,
    all whose lives will end as dust.
³⁰ Our children will also serve him.
    Future generations will hear about
    the wonders of the Lord.
³¹ His righteous acts will be told to those
    not yet born.
    They will hear about everything
    he has done.

22:22 Hebrew *my brothers.*

PROVERBS 5:15-21

Drink water from your own well—share your love only with your wife.* Why spill the water of your springs in the streets, having sex with just anyone?* You should reserve it for yourselves. Never share it with strangers. ▫ Let your wife be a fountain of blessing for you. Rejoice in the wife of your youth. She is a loving deer, a graceful doe. Let her breasts satisfy you always. May you always be captivated by her love. Why be captivated, my son, by an immoral woman, or fondle the breasts of a promiscuous woman? ▫ For the LORD sees clearly what a man does, examining every path he takes.

5:15 Hebrew *Drink water from your own cistern, / flowing water from your own well.*   5:16 Hebrew *Why spill your springs in the streets, / your streams in the city squares?*

JANUARY**28**

EXODUS 5:22-7:25

Moses and his brother, Aaron, made initial contact with Pharaoh. Still, his people seemed the worse for his efforts. Moses returned to Pharaoh's courts to begin the process that would result in the Exodus from Egypt.

Then Moses went back to the LORD and protested, "Why have you brought all this trouble on your own people, Lord? Why did you send me? ²³Ever since I came to

Pharaoh as your spokesman, he has been even more brutal to your people. And you have done nothing to rescue them!"

⁶:¹THEN the LORD told Moses, "Now you will see what I will do to Pharaoh. When he feels the force of my strong hand, he will let the people go. In fact, he will force them to leave his land!"

²And God said to Moses, "I am Yahweh—

'the LORD.'* ³I appeared to Abraham, to Isaac, and to Jacob as El-Shaddai—'God Almighty'*—but I did not reveal my name, Yahweh, to them. ⁴And I reaffirmed my covenant with them. Under its terms, I promised to give them the land of Canaan, where they were living as foreigners. ⁵You can be sure that I have heard the groans of the people of Israel, who are now slaves to the Egyptians. And I am well aware of my covenant with them.

⁶"Therefore, say to the people of Israel: 'I am the LORD. I will free you from your oppression and will rescue you from your slavery in Egypt. I will redeem you with a powerful arm and great acts of judgment. ⁷I will claim you as my own people, and I will be your God. Then you will know that I am the LORD your God who has freed you from your oppression in Egypt. ⁸I will bring you into the land I swore to give to Abraham, Isaac, and Jacob. I will give it to you as your very own possession. I am the LORD!'"

⁹So Moses told the people of Israel what the LORD had said, but they refused to listen anymore. They had become too discouraged by the brutality of their slavery.

¹⁰Then the LORD said to Moses, ¹¹"Go back to Pharaoh, the king of Egypt, and tell him to let the people of Israel leave his country."

¹²"But LORD!" Moses objected. "My own people won't listen to me anymore. How can I expect Pharaoh to listen? I'm such a clumsy speaker!*"

¹³But the LORD spoke to Moses and Aaron and gave them orders for the Israelites and for Pharaoh, the king of Egypt. The LORD commanded Moses and Aaron to lead the people of Israel out of Egypt.

¹⁴These are the ancestors of some of the clans of Israel:

The sons of Reuben, Israel's oldest son, were Hanoch, Pallu, Hezron, and Carmi. Their descendants became the clans of Reuben.
¹⁵The sons of Simeon were Jemuel, Jamin, Ohad, Jakin, Zohar, and Shaul. (Shaul's mother was a Canaanite woman.) Their descendants became the clans of Simeon.
¹⁶These are the descendants of Levi, as listed in their family records:

The sons of Levi were Gershon, Kohath, and Merari. (Levi lived to be 137 years old.)
¹⁷The descendants of Gershon included Libni and Shimei, each of whom became the ancestor of a clan.
¹⁸The descendants of Kohath included Amram, Izhar, Hebron, and Uzziel. (Kohath lived to be 133 years old.)
¹⁹The descendants of Merari included Mahli and Mushi.

These are the clans of the Levites, as listed in their family records.

²⁰Amram married his father's sister Jochebed, and she gave birth to his sons, Aaron and Moses. (Amram lived to be 137 years old.)
²¹The sons of Izhar were Korah, Nepheg, and Zicri.
²²The sons of Uzziel were Mishael, Elzaphan, and Sithri.
²³Aaron married Elisheba, the daughter of Amminadab and sister of Nahshon, and she gave birth to his sons, Nadab, Abihu, Eleazar, and Ithamar.
²⁴The sons of Korah were Assir, Elkanah, and Abiasaph. Their descendants became the clans of Korah.
²⁵Eleazar son of Aaron married one of the daughters of Putiel, and she gave birth to his son, Phinehas.

These are the ancestors of the Levite families, listed according to their clans.

²⁶The Aaron and Moses named in this list are the same ones to whom the LORD said, "Lead the people of Israel out of the land of Egypt like an army." ²⁷It was Moses and Aaron who spoke to Pharaoh, the king of Egypt, about leading the people of Israel out of Egypt.

²⁸When the LORD spoke to Moses in the land of Egypt, ²⁹he said to him, "I am the LORD! Tell Pharaoh, the king of Egypt, everything I am telling you." ³⁰But Moses argued with the LORD, saying, "I can't do it! I'm such a clumsy speaker! Why should Pharaoh listen to me?"

7:1THEN the LORD said to Moses, "Pay close attention to this. I will make you seem like God to Pharaoh, and your brother, Aaron, will be your prophet. [2]Tell Aaron everything I command you, and Aaron must command Pharaoh to let the people of Israel leave his country. [3]But I will make Pharaoh's heart stubborn so I can multiply my miraculous signs and wonders in the land of Egypt. [4]Even then Pharaoh will refuse to listen to you. So I will bring down my fist on Egypt. Then I will rescue my forces—my people, the Israelites—from the land of Egypt with great acts of judgment. [5]When I raise my powerful hand and bring out the Israelites, the Egyptians will know that I am the LORD."

[6]So Moses and Aaron did just as the LORD had commanded them. [7]Moses was eighty years old, and Aaron was eighty-three when they made their demands to Pharaoh.

[8]Then the LORD said to Moses and Aaron, [9]"Pharaoh will demand, 'Show me a miracle.' When he does this, say to Aaron, 'Take your staff and throw it down in front of Pharaoh, and it will become a serpent.*'"

[10]So Moses and Aaron went to Pharaoh and did what the LORD had commanded them. Aaron threw down his staff before Pharaoh and his officials, and it became a serpent! [11]Then Pharaoh called in his own wise men and sorcerers, and these Egyptian magicians did the same thing with their magic. [12]They threw down their staffs, which also became serpents! But then Aaron's staff swallowed up their staffs. [13]Pharaoh's heart, however, remained hard. He still refused to listen, just as the LORD had predicted.

[14]Then the LORD said to Moses, "Pharaoh's heart is stubborn,* and he still refuses to let the people go. [15]So go to Pharaoh in the morning as he goes down to the river. Stand on the bank of the Nile and meet him there. Be sure to take along the staff that turned into a snake. [16]Then announce to him, 'The LORD, the God of the Hebrews, has sent me to tell you, "Let my people go, so they can worship me in the wilderness." Until now, you have refused to listen to him. [17]So this is what the LORD says: "I will show you that I am the LORD." Look! I will strike the water of the Nile with this staff in my hand, and the river will turn to blood. [18]The fish in it will die, and the river will stink. The Egyptians will not be able to drink any water from the Nile.'"

WHAT THE BIBLE SAYS

Salvation and forgiveness

MATTHEW 18:21-22 Religious leaders of Jesus' day—the Pharisees and Sadducees—taught that forgiveness was an exhaustible resource. Peter probably thought he was being very generous in offering to forgive someone seven times. How like us! We often think that forgiveness should have an end—that there comes a time when we just shouldn't forgive anymore. Jesus' answer, however, represented a revolutionary change in the way people thought about forgiveness.   • Jesus told Peter to forgive someone not just seven times, but "seventy times seven," or 490 times! In other words, don't even keep count—just keep on forgiving. Jesus was trying to help Peter understand that we should extend unlimited forgiveness to one another, because that's the kind of forgiveness God extends to us. God isn't keeping count of the number of times you must come to him for forgiveness. He continues to forgive. He doesn't erase the consequences that your sins may have set into motion, but he does promise to forgive.   •Jesus commands us to forgive those who have hurt us. When we realize the forgiveness we must constantly ask from God, and how freely he gives it, we can much more easily forgive those who sin against us.

¹⁹Then the LORD said to Moses: "Tell Aaron, 'Take your staff and raise your hand over the waters of Egypt—all its rivers, canals, ponds, and all the reservoirs. Turn all the water to blood. Everywhere in Egypt the water will turn to blood, even the water stored in wooden bowls and stone pots.'"

²⁰So Moses and Aaron did just as the LORD commanded them. As Pharaoh and all of his officials watched, Aaron raised his staff and struck the water of the Nile. Suddenly, the whole river turned to blood! ²¹The fish in the river died, and the water became so foul that the Egyptians couldn't drink it. There was blood everywhere throughout the land of Egypt. ²²But again the magicians of Egypt used their magic, and they, too, turned water into blood. So Pharaoh's heart remained hard. He refused to listen to Moses and Aaron, just as the LORD had predicted. ²³Pharaoh returned to his palace and put the whole thing out of his mind. ²⁴Then all the Egyptians dug along the riverbank to find drinking water, for they couldn't drink the water from the Nile.

²⁵Seven days passed from the time the LORD struck the Nile.

6:2 *Yahweh* is a transliteration of the proper name *YHWH* that is sometimes rendered "Jehovah"; in this translation it is usually rendered "the LORD" (note the use of small capitals).
6:3 *El-Shaddai*, which means "God Almighty," is the name for God used in Gen 17:1; 28:3; 35:11; 43:14; 48:3.
6:12 Hebrew *I have uncircumcised lips;* also in 6:30.
7:9 Hebrew *tannin,* which elsewhere refers to a sea monster. Greek version translates it "dragon." 7:14 Hebrew *heavy.*

MATTHEW 18:21–19:12

In today's reading, Jesus gives a Kingdom perspective on forgiveness and mercy, as well as marriage and divorce.

Then Peter came to him and asked, "Lord, how often should I forgive someone* who sins against me? Seven times?"

²²"No, not seven times," Jesus replied, "but seventy times seven!*

²³"Therefore, the Kingdom of Heaven can be compared to a king who decided to bring his accounts up to date with servants who had borrowed money from him. ²⁴In the process, one of his debtors was brought in who owed him millions of dollars.* ²⁵He couldn't pay, so his master ordered that he be sold—along with his wife, his children, and everything he owned—to pay the debt.

²⁶"But the man fell down before his master and begged him, 'Please, be patient with me, and I will pay it all.' ²⁷Then his master was filled with pity for him, and he released him and forgave his debt.

²⁸"But when the man left the king, he went to a fellow servant who owed him a few thousand dollars.* He grabbed him by the throat and demanded instant payment.

²⁹"His fellow servant fell down before him and begged for a little more time. 'Be patient with me, and I will pay it,' he pleaded. ³⁰But his creditor wouldn't wait. He had the man arrested and put in prison until the debt could be paid in full.

³¹"When some of the other servants saw this, they were very upset. They went to the king and told him everything that had happened. ³²Then the king called in the man he had forgiven and said, 'You evil servant! I forgave you that tremendous debt because you pleaded with me. ³³Shouldn't you have mercy on your fellow servant, just as I had mercy on you?' ³⁴Then the angry king sent the man to prison to be tortured until he had paid his entire debt.

³⁵"That's what my heavenly Father will do to you if you refuse to forgive your brothers and sisters* from your heart."

19:1WHEN Jesus had finished saying these things, he left Galilee and went down to the region of Judea east of the Jordan River. ²Large crowds followed him there, and he healed their sick.

³Some Pharisees came and tried to trap him with this question: "Should a man be allowed to divorce his wife for just any reason?"

⁴"Haven't you read the Scriptures?" Jesus replied. "They record that from the beginning 'God made them male and female.'* ⁵And he said, 'This explains why a man leaves his father and mother and is joined to his wife, and the two are united into one.'* ⁶Since they are no longer two but one, let no one split apart what God has joined together."

⁷"Then why did Moses say in the law that a man could give his wife a written

notice of divorce and send her away?"* they asked.

⁸Jesus replied, "Moses permitted divorce only as a concession to your hard hearts, but it was not what God had originally intended. ⁹And I tell you this, whoever divorces his wife and marries someone else commits adultery—unless his wife has been unfaithful.*"

¹⁰Jesus' disciples then said to him, "If this is the case, it is better not to marry!"

¹¹"Not everyone can accept this statement," Jesus said. "Only those whom God helps. ¹²Some are born as eunuchs, some have been made eunuchs by others, and some choose not to marry* for the sake of the Kingdom of Heaven. Let anyone accept this who can."

18:21 Greek *my brother.*   18:22 Or *seventy-seven times.*   18:24 Greek *10,000 talents* [375 tons or 340 metric tons of silver].   18:28 Greek *100 denarii.* A denarius was equivalent to a laborer's full day's wage.   18:35 Greek *your brother.*   19:4 Gen 1:27; 5:2.   19:5 Gen 2:24.   19:7 See Deut 24:1.   19:9 Some manuscripts add *And anyone who marries a divorced woman commits adultery.* Compare Matt 5:32.   19:12 Greek *and some make themselves eunuchs.*

PSALM 23:1-6
A psalm of David.

¹ **T**he LORD is my shepherd;
    I have all that I need.
² He lets me rest in green meadows;
    he leads me beside peaceful
        streams.
³   He renews my strength.
He guides me along right paths,
    bringing honor to his name.
⁴ Even when I walk
    through the darkest valley,*
I will not be afraid,
    for you are close beside me.
Your rod and your staff
    protect and comfort me.
⁵ You prepare a feast for me
    in the presence of my enemies.
You honor me by anointing my head
    with oil.
    My cup overflows with blessings.
⁶ Surely your goodness and unfailing
        love will pursue me
    all the days of my life,
and I will live in the house of the LORD
    forever.

23:4 Or *the dark valley of death.*

PROVERBS 5:22-23
An evil man is held captive by his own sins; they are ropes that catch and hold him. He will die for lack of self-control; he will be lost because of his great foolishness.

EXODUS 8:1-9:35
Frogs, gnats, flies, dead cows, boil-covered citizens, hail . . . at the height of each plague, Pharaoh pretended that he would allow the Hebrews to leave Egypt. Yet, as each plague passed, he returned to his original refusal. Pharaoh thought he had all the power; he was about to learn otherwise.

¹***T**hen the LORD said to Moses, "Go back to Pharaoh and announce to him, 'This is what the LORD says: Let my people go, so they can worship me. ²If you refuse to let them go, I will send a plague of frogs across your entire land. ³The Nile River will swarm with frogs. They will come up out of the river and into your palace, even into your bedroom and onto your bed!

JANUARY**29**

They will enter the houses of your officials and your people. They will even jump into your ovens and your kneading bowls. ⁴Frogs will jump on you, your people, and all your officials.'"

⁵*Then the LORD said to Moses, "Tell Aaron, 'Raise the staff in your hand over all the rivers, canals, and ponds of Egypt, and bring up frogs over all the land.'" ⁶So Aaron raised his hand over the waters of Egypt, and frogs came up and covered the whole land! ⁷But the magicians were able to do the same thing with their magic. They, too, caused frogs to come up on the land of Egypt.

⁸Then Pharaoh summoned Moses and

Aaron and begged, "Plead with the LORD to take the frogs away from me and my people. I will let your people go, so they can offer sacrifices to the LORD."

9"You set the time!" Moses replied. "Tell me when you want me to pray for you, your officials, and your people. Then you and your houses will be rid of the frogs. They will remain only in the Nile River."

10"Do it tomorrow," Pharaoh said.

"All right," Moses replied, "it will be as you have said. Then you will know that there is no one like the LORD our God. 11The frogs will leave you and your houses, your officials, and your people. They will remain only in the Nile River."

12So Moses and Aaron left Pharaoh's palace, and Moses cried out to the LORD about the frogs he had inflicted on Pharaoh. 13And the LORD did just what Moses had predicted. The frogs in the houses, the courtyards, and the fields all died. 14The Egyptians piled them into great heaps, and a terrible stench filled the land. 15But when Pharaoh saw that relief had come, he became stubborn.* He refused to listen to Moses and Aaron, just as the LORD had predicted.

16So the LORD said to Moses, "Tell Aaron, 'Raise your staff and strike the ground. The dust will turn into swarms of gnats throughout the land of Egypt.' " 17So Moses and Aaron did just as the LORD had commanded them. When Aaron raised his hand and struck the ground with his staff, gnats infested the entire land, covering the Egyptians and their animals. All the dust in the land of Egypt turned into gnats. 18Pharaoh's magicians tried to do the same thing with their secret arts, but this time they failed. And the gnats covered everyone, people and animals alike.

19"This is the finger of God!" the magicians exclaimed to Pharaoh. But Pharaoh's heart remained hard. He wouldn't listen to them, just as the LORD had predicted.

20Then the LORD told Moses, "Get up early in the morning and stand in Pharaoh's way as he goes down to the river. Say to him, 'This is what the LORD says: Let my people go, so they can worship me. 21If you refuse, then I will send swarms of flies on you, your officials, your people, and all the houses. The Egyptian homes will be filled with flies, and the ground will be covered with them. 22But this time I will spare the region of Goshen, where my people live. No flies will be found there. Then you will know that I am the LORD and that I am present even in the heart of your land. 23I will make a clear distinction between* my people and your people. This miraculous sign will happen tomorrow.' "

24And the LORD did just as he had said. A thick swarm of flies filled Pharaoh's palace and the houses of his officials. The whole land of Egypt was thrown into chaos by the flies.

25Pharaoh called for Moses and Aaron. "All right! Go ahead and offer sacrifices to your God," he said. "But do it here in this land."

26But Moses replied, "That wouldn't be right. The Egyptians detest the sacrifices that we offer to the LORD our God. Look, if we offer our sacrifices here where the Egyptians can see us, they will stone us. 27We must take a three-day trip into the wilderness to offer sacrifices to the LORD our God, just as he has commanded us."

28"All right, go ahead," Pharaoh replied. "I will let you go into the wilderness to offer sacrifices to the LORD your God. But don't go too far away. Now hurry and pray for me."

29Moses answered, "As soon as I leave you, I will pray to the LORD, and tomorrow the swarms of flies will disappear from you and your officials and all your people. But I am warning you, Pharaoh, don't lie to us again and refuse to let the people go to sacrifice to the LORD."

30So Moses left Pharaoh's palace and pleaded with the LORD to remove all the flies. 31And the LORD did as Moses asked and caused the swarms of flies to disappear from Pharaoh, his officials, and his people. Not a single fly remained. 32But Pharaoh again became stubborn and refused to let the people go.

9:1"Go back to Pharaoh," the LORD commanded Moses. "Tell him, 'This is what the LORD, the God of the Hebrews, says: Let my people go, so they can worship me. 2If you continue to hold them and refuse to let them go, ³the hand of the LORD will strike all your livestock—your horses, donkeys, camels, cattle, sheep, and goats—with a deadly plague. ⁴But the LORD will again make a distinction between the livestock of the Israelites and that of the Egyptians. Not a single one of Israel's animals will die! ⁵The LORD has already set the time for the plague to begin. He has declared that he will strike the land tomorrow.'"

⁶And the LORD did just as he had said. The next morning all the livestock of the Egyptians died, but the Israelites didn't lose a single animal. ⁷Pharaoh sent his officials to investigate, and they discovered that the Israelites had not lost a single animal! But even so, Pharaoh's heart remained stubborn,* and he still refused to let the people go.

⁸Then the LORD said to Moses and Aaron, "Take handfuls of soot from a brick kiln, and have Moses toss it into the air while Pharaoh watches. ⁹The ashes will spread like fine dust over the whole land of Egypt, causing festering boils to break out on people and animals throughout the land."

¹⁰So they took soot from a brick kiln and went and stood before Pharaoh. As Pharaoh watched, Moses threw the soot

into the air, and boils broke out on people and animals alike. ¹¹Even the magicians were unable to stand before Moses, because the boils had broken out on them and all the Egyptians. ¹²But the LORD hardened Pharaoh's heart, and just as the LORD had predicted to Moses, Pharaoh refused to listen.

¹³Then the LORD said to Moses, "Get up early in the morning and stand before Pharaoh. Tell him, 'This is what the LORD, the God of the Hebrews, says: Let my people go, so they can worship me. ¹⁴If you don't, I will send more plagues on you* and your officials and your people. Then you will know that there is no one like me in all the earth. ¹⁵By now I could have lifted my hand and struck you and your people with a plague to wipe you off the face of the earth. ¹⁶But I have spared you for a purpose—to show you my power* and to spread my fame throughout the earth. ¹⁷But you still lord it over my people and refuse to let them go. ¹⁸So tomorrow at this time I will send a hailstorm more devastating than any in all the history of Egypt. ¹⁹Quick! Order your livestock and servants to come in from the fields to find shelter. Any person or animal left outside will die when the hail falls.'"

²⁰Some of Pharaoh's officials were

WHO GOD IS

God is all-powerful

EXODUS 8:18-19 No question about it: Pharaoh considered himself to be all-powerful and worthy of worship. He was unmoved by the words of Moses and Aaron. After all, the God of a nation of slaves obviously could not be very powerful. To Moses' words, Pharaoh retorted, "Who is the LORD? Why should I listen to him?" (Exodus 5:2, January 27). • God had anticipated the question and had already revealed his plan to Moses. God would take on the self-described "all-powerful" Pharaoh by proving that Pharaoh was not as powerful as he thought. "I know that the king of Egypt will not let you go unless a mighty hand forces him. So I will raise my hand and strike the Egyptians, performing all kinds of miracles among them. Then at last he will let you go" (Exodus 3:19-20, January 26).

•The miracles unleashed on Egypt were not arbitrary—each targeted one of Egypt's many gods and showed its powerlessness. The god of the Nile River couldn't stop the river from being turned to blood; the cow goddess couldn't keep cattle from dying; the sun god couldn't keep darkness from descending on the land. In no uncertain terms, God showed that he is the one, all-powerful God.

afraid because of what the LORD had said. They quickly brought their servants and livestock in from the fields. ²¹But those who paid no attention to the word of the LORD left theirs out in the open.

²²Then the LORD said to Moses, "Lift your hand toward the sky so hail may fall on the people, the livestock, and all the plants throughout the land of Egypt."

²³So Moses lifted his staff toward the sky, and the LORD sent thunder and hail, and lightning flashed toward the earth. The LORD sent a tremendous hailstorm against all the land of Egypt. ²⁴Never in all the history of Egypt had there been a storm like that, with such devastating hail and continuous lightning. ²⁵It left all of Egypt in ruins. The hail struck down everything in the open field—people, animals, and plants alike. Even the trees were destroyed. ²⁶The only place without hail was the region of Goshen, where the people of Israel lived.

²⁷Then Pharaoh quickly summoned Moses and Aaron. "This time I have sinned," he confessed. "The LORD is the righteous one, and my people and I are wrong. ²⁸Please beg the LORD to end this terrifying thunder and hail. We've had enough. I will let you go; you don't need to stay any longer."

²⁹"All right," Moses replied. "As soon as I leave the city, I will lift my hands and pray to the LORD. Then the thunder and hail will stop, and you will know that the earth belongs to the LORD. ³⁰But I know that you and your officials still do not fear the LORD God."

³¹(All the flax and barley were ruined by the hail, because the barley had formed heads and the flax was budding. ³²But the wheat and the emmer wheat were spared, because they had not yet sprouted from the ground.)

³³So Moses left Pharaoh's court and went out of the city. When he lifted his hands to the LORD, the thunder and hail stopped, and the downpour ceased. ³⁴But when Pharaoh saw that the rain, hail, and thunder had stopped, he and his officials sinned again, and Pharaoh again became stubborn.* ³⁵Because his heart was hard, Pharaoh refused to let the people leave, just as the LORD had predicted through Moses.

8:1 Verses 8:1-4 are numbered 7:26-29 in Hebrew text. **8:5** Verses 8:5-32 are numbered 8:1-28 in Hebrew text. **8:15** Hebrew *made his heart heavy*; also in 8:32. **8:23** As in Greek and Latin versions; Hebrew reads *I will set redemption between.* **9:7** Hebrew *heavy.* **9:14** Hebrew *on your heart.* **9:16** Greek version reads *to display my power in you;* compare Rom 9:17. **9:34** Hebrew *made his heart heavy.*

MATTHEW 19:13-30

Jesus called his disciples to give up what they thought was important for all that really matters. If you invest in God's Kingdom, whatever it might cost now, you will come out way ahead in the future.

One day some parents brought their children to Jesus so he could lay his hands on them and pray for them. But the disciples scolded the parents for bothering him.

¹⁴But Jesus said, "Let the children come to me. Don't stop them! For the Kingdom of Heaven belongs to those who are like these children." ¹⁵And he placed his hands on their heads and blessed them before he left.

¹⁶Someone came to Jesus with this question: "Teacher,* what good deed must I do to have eternal life?"

¹⁷"Why ask me about what is good?" Jesus replied. "There is only One who is good. But to answer your question—if you want to receive eternal life, keep* the commandments."

¹⁸"Which ones?" the man asked.

And Jesus replied: "'You must not murder. You must not commit adultery. You must not steal. You must not testify falsely. ¹⁹Honor your father and mother. Love your neighbor as yourself.'*"

²⁰"I've obeyed all these commandments," the young man replied. "What else must I do?"

²¹Jesus told him, "If you want to be perfect, go and sell all your possessions and give the money to the poor, and you will have treasure in heaven. Then come, follow me."

²²But when the young man heard this, he went away sad, for he had many possessions.

²³Then Jesus said to his disciples, "I tell you the truth, it is very hard for a rich person to enter the Kingdom of Heaven. ²⁴I'll say it again—it is easier for a camel to go

through the eye of a needle than for a rich person to enter the Kingdom of God!"

²⁵The disciples were astounded. "Then who in the world can be saved?" they asked.

²⁶Jesus looked at them intently and said, "Humanly speaking, it is impossible. But with God everything is possible."

²⁷Then Peter said to him, "We've given up everything to follow you. What will we get?"

²⁸Jesus replied, "I assure you that when the world is made new* and the Son of Man* sits upon his glorious throne, you who have been my followers will also sit on twelve thrones, judging the twelve tribes of Israel. ²⁹And everyone who has given up houses or brothers or sisters or father or mother or children or property, for my sake, will receive a hundred times as much in return and will inherit eternal life. ³⁰But many who are the greatest now will be least important then, and those who seem least important now will be the greatest then.*"

19:16 Some manuscripts read *Good Teacher.*   19:17 Some manuscripts read *continue to keep.*   19:18-19 Exod 20:12-16; Deut 5:16-20; Lev 19:18.   19:28a Or *in the regeneration.*   19:28b "Son of Man" is a title Jesus used for himself.   19:30 Greek *But many who are first will be last; and the last, first.*

PSALM 24:1-10
A psalm of David.

¹ The earth is the LORD's, and everything
      in it.
   The world and all its people belong
      to him.
² For he laid the earth's foundation on
      the seas
   and built it on the ocean depths.

³ Who may climb the mountain of the
      LORD?
   Who may stand in his holy place?
⁴ Only those whose hands and hearts
      are pure,
   who do not worship idols
   and never tell lies.
⁵ They will receive the LORD's blessing
   and have a right relationship with
      God their savior.
⁶ Such people may seek you
   and worship in your presence,
      O God of Jacob.   *Interlude*

⁷ Open up, ancient gates!
   Open up, ancient doors,
   and let the King of glory enter.
⁸ Who is the King of glory?
   The LORD, strong and mighty;
   the LORD, invincible in battle.
⁹ Open up, ancient gates!
   Open up, ancient doors,
   and let the King of glory enter.
¹⁰ Who is the King of glory?
   The LORD of Heaven's Armies—
   he is the King of glory.   *Interlude*

PROVERBS 6:1-5
My child,* if you have put up security for a friend's debt or agreed to guarantee the debt of a stranger—if you have trapped yourself by your agreement and are caught by what you said—follow my advice and save yourself, for you have placed yourself at your friend's mercy. Now swallow your pride; go and beg to have your name erased. Don't put it off; do it now! Don't rest until you do. Save yourself like a gazelle escaping from a hunter, like a bird fleeing from a net.

6:1 Hebrew *My son.*

EXODUS 10:1-12:13
The plagues culminate in a final plague of death. The Passover paints a picture of Jesus, the Lamb of God, who would one day come to shed his blood and save us from sin and death.

JANUARY**30**

Then the LORD said to Moses, "Return to Pharaoh and make your demands again. I have made him and his officials stubborn* so I can display my miraculous signs among them. [2]I've also done it so you can tell your children and grandchildren about how I made a mockery of the Egyptians and about the signs I displayed among them—and so you will know that I am the LORD."

[3]So Moses and Aaron went to Pharaoh and said, "This is what the LORD, the God of the Hebrews, says: How long will you refuse to submit to me? Let my people go, so they can worship me. [4]If you refuse, watch out! For tomorrow I will bring a swarm of locusts on your country. [5]They will cover the land so that you won't be able to see the ground. They will devour what little is left of your crops after the hailstorm, including all the trees growing in the fields. [6]They will overrun your palaces and the homes of your officials and all the houses in Egypt. Never in the history of Egypt have your ancestors seen a plague like this one!" And with that, Moses turned and left Pharaoh.

[7]Pharaoh's officials now came to Pharaoh and appealed to him. "How long will you let this man hold us hostage? Let the men go to worship the LORD their God! Don't you realize that Egypt lies in ruins?"

[8]So Moses and Aaron were brought back to Pharaoh. "All right," he told them, "go and worship the LORD your God. But who exactly will be going with you?"

[9]Moses replied, "We will all go—young and old, our sons and daughters, and our flocks and herds. We must all join together in celebrating a festival to the LORD."

[10]Pharaoh retorted, "The LORD will certainly need to be with you if I let you take your little ones! I can see through your evil plan. [11]Never! Only the men may go and worship the LORD, since that is what you requested." And Pharaoh threw them out of the palace.

[12]Then the LORD said to Moses, "Raise your hand over the land of Egypt to bring on the locusts. Let them cover the land and devour every plant that survived the hailstorm."

[13]So Moses raised his staff over Egypt, and the LORD caused an east wind to blow over the land all that day and through the night. When morning arrived, the east wind had brought the locusts. [14]And the locusts swarmed over the whole land of Egypt, settling in dense swarms from one end of the country to the other. It was the worst locust plague in Egyptian history, and there has never been another one like it. [15]For the locusts covered the whole country and darkened the land. They devoured every plant in the fields and all the fruit on the trees that had survived the hailstorm. Not a single leaf was left on the trees and plants throughout the land of Egypt.

[16]Pharaoh quickly summoned Moses and Aaron. "I have sinned against the LORD your God and against you," he confessed. [17]"Forgive my sin, just this once, and plead with the LORD your God to take away this death from me."

[18]So Moses left Pharaoh's court and pleaded with the LORD. [19]The LORD responded by shifting the wind, and the strong west wind blew the locusts into the Red Sea.* Not a single locust remained in all the land of Egypt. [20]But the LORD hardened Pharaoh's heart again, so he refused to let the people go.

[21]Then the LORD said to Moses, "Lift your hand toward heaven, and the land of Egypt will be covered with a darkness so thick you can feel it." [22]So Moses lifted his hand to the sky, and a deep darkness covered the entire land of Egypt for three days. [23]During all that time the people could not see each other, and no one moved. But there was light as usual where the people of Israel lived.

[24]Finally, Pharaoh called for Moses. "Go and worship the LORD," he said. "But leave your flocks and herds here. You may even take your little ones with you."

[25]"No," Moses said, "you must provide us with animals for sacrifices and burnt offerings to the LORD our God. [26]All our livestock must go with us, too; not a hoof can be left behind. We must choose our sacrifices for the LORD our God from among these animals. And we won't know how we are to worship the LORD until we get there."

[27]But the LORD hardened Pharaoh's heart once more, and he would not let them go. [28]"Get out of here!" Pharaoh shouted at Moses. "I'm warning you. Never come back to see me again! The day you see my face, you will die!"

²⁹"Very well," Moses replied. "I will never see your face again."

11:1THEN the LORD said to Moses, "I will strike Pharaoh and the land of Egypt with one more blow. After that, Pharaoh will let you leave this country. In fact, he will be so eager to get rid of you that he will force you all to leave. ²Tell all the Israelite men and women to ask their Egyptian neighbors for articles of silver and gold." ³(Now the LORD had caused the Egyptians to look favorably on the people of Israel. And Moses was considered a very great man in the land of Egypt, respected by Pharaoh's officials and the Egyptian people alike.)

⁴Moses had announced to Pharaoh, "This is what the LORD says: At midnight tonight I will pass through the heart of Egypt. ⁵All the firstborn sons will die in every family in Egypt, from the oldest son of Pharaoh, who sits on his throne, to the oldest son of his lowliest servant girl who grinds the flour. Even the firstborn of all the livestock will die. ⁶Then a loud wail will rise throughout the land of Egypt, a wail like no one has heard before or will ever hear again. ⁷But among the Israelites it will be so peaceful that not even a dog will bark. Then you will know that the LORD makes a distinction between the Egyptians and the Israelites. ⁸All the officials of Egypt will run to me and fall to the ground before me. 'Please leave!' they will beg. 'Hurry! And take all your followers with you.' Only then will I go!" Then, burning with anger, Moses left Pharaoh.

⁹Now the LORD had told Moses earlier, "Pharaoh will not listen to you, but then I will do even more mighty miracles in the land of Egypt." ¹⁰Moses and Aaron performed these miracles in Pharaoh's presence, but the LORD hardened Pharaoh's heart, and he wouldn't let the Israelites leave the country.

12:1WHILE the Israelites were still in the land of Egypt, the LORD gave the following instructions to Moses and Aaron: ²"From now on, this month will be the first month of the year for you. ³Announce to the whole community of Israel that on the tenth day of this month each family must choose a lamb or a young goat for a sacrifice, one animal for each household. ⁴If a family is too small to eat a whole animal, let them share with another family in the neighborhood. Divide the animal according to the size of each family and how much they can eat. ⁵The animal you select must be a one-year-old male, either a sheep or a goat, with no defects.

WHAT THE BIBLE SAYS

Old Testament sacrifices

EXODUS 12:13   As you continue to read in the Old Testament, you will find lots of blood. Why? Because for a time God required his people to offer animal sacrifices. These sacrifices served a variety of purposes, but the most important was what they taught about forgiveness of sin.   • When God gave his laws to his people, he said, "It is the blood, given in exchange for a life, that makes purification possible" (Leviticus 17:11, February 25). Why? Because "the wages of sin is death" (Romans 6:23, July 20). Sin requires death; proof of death is in shed blood. In the Old Testament, the people brought their animals as blood sacrifices, for that alone could take away their penalty for sin. All the while, this foreshadowed the coming of Jesus, "the Lamb of God who takes away the sin of the world" (John 1:29, May 1).   • Jesus Christ was the perfect and final sacrifice; he shed his blood for us (your New Testament reading speaks of this; see Matthew 20:17-19). On the cross, Jesus stepped into the line of fire in front of us and absorbed the wrath we deserved. Because of what Jesus did on the cross, God's justice was satisfied and now he can accept those who put their trust in him. Christ took your place by shedding his blood. That blood has given you new life.

⁶"Take special care of this chosen animal until the evening of the fourteenth day of this first month. Then the whole assembly of the community of Israel must slaughter their lamb or young goat at twilight. ⁷They are to take some of the blood and smear it on the sides and top of the doorframes of the houses where they eat the animal. ⁸That same night they must roast the meat over a fire and eat it along with bitter salad greens and bread made without yeast. ⁹Do not eat any of the meat raw or boiled in water. The whole animal—including the head, legs, and internal organs—must be roasted over a fire. ¹⁰Do not leave any of it until the next morning. Burn whatever is not eaten before morning.

¹¹"These are your instructions for eating this meal: Be fully dressed,* wear your sandals, and carry your walking stick in your hand. Eat the meal with urgency, for this is the LORD's Passover. ¹²On that night I will pass through the land of Egypt and strike down every firstborn son and firstborn male animal in the land of Egypt. I will execute judgment against all the gods of Egypt, for I am the LORD! ¹³But the blood on your doorposts will serve as a sign, marking the houses where you are staying. When I see the blood, I will pass over you. This plague of death will not touch you when I strike the land of Egypt."

10:1 Hebrew *have made his heart and his officials' hearts heavy.* 10:19 Hebrew *sea of reeds.* 12:11 Hebrew *Bind up your loins.*

MATTHEW 20:1-28

In God's Kingdom, no one can say, "Give me the blessings I've earned!" All is a gift of God's grace. Similarly, status in the Kingdom is not reckoned as it is in the world. The key to greatness is servanthood. Jesus, who gave his life for us, is our Servant King.

"**F**or the Kingdom of Heaven is like the landowner who went out early one morning to hire workers for his vineyard. ²He agreed to pay the normal daily wage* and sent them out to work.

³"At nine o'clock in the morning he was passing through the marketplace and saw some people standing around doing nothing. ⁴So he hired them, telling them he would pay them whatever was right at the end of the day. ⁵So they went to work

in the vineyard. At noon and again at three o'clock he did the same thing.

⁶"At five o'clock that afternoon he was in town again and saw some more people standing around. He asked them, 'Why haven't you been working today?'

⁷"They replied, 'Because no one hired us.'

"The landowner told them, 'Then go out and join the others in my vineyard.'

⁸"That evening he told the foreman to call the workers in and pay them, beginning with the last workers first. ⁹When those hired at five o'clock were paid, each received a full day's wage. ¹⁰When those hired first came to get their pay, they assumed they would receive more. But they, too, were paid a day's wage. ¹¹When they received their pay, they protested to the owner, ¹²'Those people worked only one hour, and yet you've paid them just as much as you paid us who worked all day in the scorching heat.'

¹³"He answered one of them, 'Friend, I haven't been unfair! Didn't you agree to work all day for the usual wage? ¹⁴Take your money and go. I wanted to pay this last worker the same as you. ¹⁵Is it against the law for me to do what I want with my money? Should you be jealous because I am kind to others?'

¹⁶"So those who are last now will be first then, and those who are first will be last."

¹⁷As Jesus was going up to Jerusalem, he took the twelve disciples aside privately and told them what was going to happen to him. ¹⁸"Listen," he said, "we're going up to Jerusalem, where the Son of Man* will be betrayed to the leading priests and the teachers of religious law. They will sentence him to die. ¹⁹Then they will hand him over to the Romans* to be mocked, flogged with a whip, and crucified. But on the third day he will be raised from the dead."

²⁰Then the mother of James and John, the sons of Zebedee, came to Jesus with her sons. She knelt respectfully to ask a favor. ²¹"What is your request?" he asked.

She replied, "In your Kingdom, please let my two sons sit in places of honor next to you, one on your right and the other on your left."

²²But Jesus answered by saying to them, "You don't know what you are asking! Are you able to drink from the bitter cup of suffering I am about to drink?"

"Oh yes," they replied, "we are able!"

²³Jesus told them, "You will indeed drink from my bitter cup. But I have no right to say who will sit on my right or my left. My Father has prepared those places for the ones he has chosen."

²⁴When the ten other disciples heard what James and John had asked, they were indignant. ²⁵But Jesus called them together and said, "You know that the rulers in this world lord it over their people, and officials flaunt their authority over those under them. ²⁶But among you it will be different. Whoever wants to be a leader among you must be your servant, ²⁷and whoever wants to be first among you must become your slave. ²⁸For even the Son of Man came not to be served but to serve others and to give his life as a ransom for many."

20:2 Greek *a denarius,* the payment for a full day's labor; similarly in 20:9, 10, 13. 20:18 "Son of Man" is a title Jesus used for himself. 20:19 Greek *the Gentiles.*

PSALM 25:1-15*
A psalm of David.

¹ **O** LORD, I give my life to you.
² I trust in you, my God!
Do not let me be disgraced,
    or let my enemies rejoice in my
    defeat.
³ No one who trusts in you will ever
    be disgraced,
    but disgrace comes to those
    who try to deceive others.

⁴ Show me the right path, O LORD;
    point out the road for me
    to follow.
⁵ Lead me by your truth and
    teach me,
    for you are the God who saves me.
    All day long I put my hope in you.
⁶ Remember, O LORD, your compassion
    and unfailing love,

which you have shown from long
    ages past.
⁷ Do not remember the rebellious sins
    of my youth.
Remember me in the light of your
    unfailing love,
    for you are merciful, O LORD.

⁸ The LORD is good and does what
    is right;
    he shows the proper path to those
    who go astray.
⁹ He leads the humble in doing right,
    teaching them his way.
¹⁰ The LORD leads with unfailing love
    and faithfulness
    all who keep his covenant and obey
    his demands.

¹¹ For the honor of your name,
    O LORD,
    forgive my many, many sins.
¹² Who are those who fear the LORD?
    He will show them the path they
    should choose.
¹³ They will live in prosperity,
    and their children will inherit
    the land.
¹⁴ The LORD is a friend to those who
    fear him.
    He teaches them his covenant.
¹⁵ My eyes are always on the LORD,
    for he rescues me from the traps
    of my enemies.

25 This psalm is a Hebrew acrostic poem; each verse begins with a successive letter of the Hebrew alphabet.

PROVERBS 6:6-11
Take a lesson from the ants, you lazybones. Learn from their ways and become wise! Though they have no prince or governor or ruler to make them work, they labor hard all summer, gathering food for the winter. But you, lazybones, how long will you sleep? When will you wake up? A little extra sleep, a little more slumber, a little folding of the hands to rest—then poverty will pounce on you like a bandit; scarcity will attack you like an armed robber.

EXODUS 12:14–13:16

The Passover and Exodus from Egypt would become an often-remembered testimony of God's deliverance for the Hebrew nation. These events remain significant for Christians, who have been delivered from bondage to sin by means of Christ's sacrifice.

"**T**his is a day to remember. Each year, from generation to generation, you must celebrate it as a special festival to the LORD. This is a law for all time. ¹⁵For seven days the bread you eat must be made without yeast. On the first day of the festival, remove every trace of yeast from your homes. Anyone who eats bread made with yeast during the seven days of the festival will be cut off from the community of Israel. ¹⁶On the first day of the festival and again on the seventh day, all the people must observe an official day for holy assembly. No work of any kind may be done on these days except in the preparation of food.

¹⁷"Celebrate this Festival of Unleavened Bread, for it will remind you that I brought your forces out of the land of Egypt on this very day. This festival will be a permanent law for you; celebrate this day from generation to generation. ¹⁸The bread you eat must be made without yeast from the evening of the fourteenth day of the first month until the evening of the twenty-first day of that month. ¹⁹During those seven days, there must be no trace of yeast in your homes. Anyone who eats anything made with yeast during this week will be cut off from the community of Israel. These regulations apply both to the foreigners living among you and to the native-born Israelites. ²⁰During those days you must not eat anything made with yeast. Wherever you live, eat only bread made without yeast."

²¹Then Moses called all the elders of Israel together and said to them, "Go, pick out a lamb or young goat for each of your families, and slaughter the Passover animal. ²²Drain the blood into a basin. Then take a bundle of hyssop branches and dip it into the blood. Brush the hyssop across the top and sides of the doorframes of your houses. And no one may go out through the door until morning. ²³For the LORD will pass through the land to strike down the Egyptians. But when he sees the blood on the top and sides of the doorframe, the LORD will pass over your home. He will not permit his death angel to enter your house and strike you down.

²⁴"Remember, these instructions are a permanent law that you and your descendants must observe forever. ²⁵When you enter the land the LORD has promised to give you, you will continue to observe this ceremony. ²⁶Then your children will ask, 'What does this ceremony mean?' ²⁷And you will reply, 'It is the Passover sacrifice to the LORD, for he passed over the houses of the Israelites in Egypt. And though he struck the Egyptians, he spared our families.'" When Moses had finished speaking, all the people bowed down to the ground and worshiped.

²⁸So the people of Israel did just as the LORD had commanded through Moses and Aaron. ²⁹And that night at midnight, the LORD struck down all the firstborn sons in the land of Egypt, from the firstborn son of Pharaoh, who sat on his throne, to the firstborn son of the prisoner in the dungeon. Even the firstborn of their livestock were killed. ³⁰Pharaoh and all his officials and all the people of Egypt woke up during the night, and loud wailing was heard throughout the land of Egypt. There was not a single house where someone had not died.

³¹Pharaoh sent for Moses and Aaron during the night. "Get out!" he ordered. "Leave my people—and take the rest of the Israelites with you! Go and worship the LORD as you have requested. ³²Take your flocks and herds, as you said, and be gone. Go, but bless me as you leave." ³³All the Egyptians urged the people of Israel to get out of the land as quickly as possible, for they thought, "We will all die!"

³⁴The Israelites took their bread dough before yeast was added. They wrapped their kneading boards in their cloaks and carried them on their shoulders. ³⁵And the people of Israel did as Moses had

instructed; they asked the Egyptians for clothing and articles of silver and gold. ³⁶The LORD caused the Egyptians to look favorably on the Israelites, and they gave the Israelites whatever they asked for. So they stripped the Egyptians of their wealth!

³⁷That night the people of Israel left Rameses and started for Succoth. There were about 600,000 men,* plus all the women and children. ³⁸A rabble of non-Israelites went with them, along with great flocks and herds of livestock. ³⁹For bread they baked flat cakes from the dough without yeast they had brought from Egypt. It was made without yeast because the people were driven out of Egypt in such a hurry that they had no time to prepare the bread or other food.

⁴⁰The people of Israel had lived in Egypt* for 430 years. ⁴¹In fact, it was on the last day of the 430th year that all the LORD's forces left the land. ⁴²On this night the LORD kept his promise to bring his people out of the land of Egypt. So this night belongs to him, and it must be commemorated every year by all the Israelites, from generation to generation.

⁴³Then the LORD said to Moses and Aaron, "These are the instructions for the festival of Passover. No outsiders are allowed to eat the Passover meal. ⁴⁴But any slave who has been purchased may eat it if he has been circumcised. ⁴⁵Temporary residents and hired servants may not eat it. ⁴⁶Each Passover lamb must be eaten in one house. Do not carry any of its meat outside, and do not break any of its bones. ⁴⁷The whole community of Israel must celebrate this Passover festival.

⁴⁸"If there are foreigners living among you who want to celebrate the LORD's Passover, let all their males be circumcised. Only then may they celebrate the Passover with you like any native-born Israelite. But no uncircumcised male may ever eat the Passover meal. ⁴⁹This instruction applies to everyone, whether a native-born Israelite or a foreigner living among you."

⁵⁰So all the people of Israel followed all the LORD's commands to Moses and Aaron. ⁵¹On that very day the LORD brought the people of Israel out of the land of Egypt like an army.

¹³:¹THEN the LORD said to Moses, ²"Dedicate to me every firstborn among the Israelites. The first offspring to be born, of both humans and animals, belongs to me."

³So Moses said to the people, "This is a day to remember forever—the day you left Egypt, the place of your slavery. Today the LORD has brought you out by the power of his mighty hand. (Remember, eat no food containing yeast.) ⁴On this day in early spring, in the month of Abib,* you have been set free. ⁵You must celebrate this event in this month each year after the LORD brings you into the land of the Canaanites, Hittites, Amorites, Hivites, and Jebusites. (He swore to your ancestors that he would give you this land—a land flowing with milk and honey.) ⁶For seven days the bread you eat must be made without yeast. Then on the seventh day, celebrate a feast to the LORD. ⁷Eat bread without yeast during those seven days. In fact, there must be no yeast bread or any yeast at all found within the borders of your land during this time.

⁸"On the seventh day you must explain to your children, 'I am celebrating what the LORD did for me when I left Egypt.' ⁹This annual festival will be a visible sign to you, like a mark branded on your hand or your forehead. Let it remind you always to recite this teaching of the LORD: 'With a strong hand, the LORD rescued you from Egypt.'* ¹⁰So observe the decree of this festival at the appointed time each year.

¹¹"This is what you must do when the LORD fulfills the promise he swore to you and to your ancestors. When he gives you the land where the Canaanites now live, ¹²you must present all firstborn sons and firstborn male animals to the LORD, for they belong to him. ¹³A firstborn donkey may be bought back from the LORD by presenting a lamb or young goat in its place. But if you do not buy it back, you must break its neck. However, you must buy back every firstborn son.

¹⁴"And in the future, your children will ask you, 'What does all this mean?' Then you will tell them, 'With the power of his mighty hand, the LORD brought us out of Egypt, the place of our slavery. ¹⁵Pharaoh stubbornly refused to let us go, so the LORD killed all the firstborn males

throughout the land of Egypt, both people and animals. That is why I now sacrifice all the firstborn males to the LORD—except that the firstborn sons are always bought back.' ¹⁶This ceremony will be like a mark branded on your hand or your forehead. It is a reminder that the power of the LORD's mighty hand brought us out of Egypt."

12:37 Or *fighting men;* Hebrew reads *men on foot.*
12:40 Samaritan Pentateuch reads *in Canaan and Egypt;* Greek version reads *in Egypt and Canaan.*   **13:4** Hebrew *On this day in the month of Abib.* This first month of the ancient Hebrew lunar calendar usually occurs within the months of March and April.   **13:9** Or *Let it remind you always to keep the instructions of the LORD on the tip of your tongue, because with a strong hand, the LORD rescued you from Egypt.*

MATTHEW 20:29-21:22

Jesus entered Jerusalem for what would be the final scene of the drama that would change the world forever.

As Jesus and the disciples left the town of Jericho, a large crowd followed behind. ³⁰Two blind men were sitting beside the road. When they heard that Jesus was coming that way, they began shouting, "Lord, Son of David, have mercy on us!"

³¹"Be quiet!" the crowd yelled at them. But they only shouted louder, "Lord, Son of David, have mercy on us!"

³²When Jesus heard them, he stopped and called, "What do you want me to do for you?"

³³"Lord," they said, "we want to see!"

³⁴Jesus felt sorry for them and touched their eyes. Instantly they could see! Then they followed him.

²¹:¹As Jesus and the disciples approached Jerusalem, they came to the town of Bethphage on the Mount of Olives. Jesus sent two of them on ahead. ²"Go into the village over there," he said. "As soon as you enter it, you will see a donkey tied there, with its colt beside it. Untie them and bring them to me. ³If anyone asks what you are doing, just say, 'The Lord needs them,' and he will immediately let you take them."

⁴This took place to fulfill the prophecy that said,

⁵ "Tell the people of Israel,*
  'Look, your King is coming to you.
He is humble, riding on a donkey—
  riding on a donkey's colt.'"*

⁶The two disciples did as Jesus commanded. ⁷They brought the donkey and the colt to him and threw their garments over the colt, and he sat on it.*

⁸Most of the crowd spread their garments on the road ahead of him, and others cut branches from the trees and spread them on the road. ⁹Jesus was in the center of the procession, and the people all around him were shouting,

"Praise God* for the Son of David!
Blessings on the one who comes in
  the name of the LORD!
Praise God in highest heaven!"*

¹⁰The entire city of Jerusalem was in an uproar as he entered. "Who is this?" they asked.

¹¹And the crowds replied, "It's Jesus, the prophet from Nazareth in Galilee."

¹²Jesus entered the Temple and began to drive out all the people buying and selling animals for sacrifice. He knocked over the tables of the money changers and the chairs of those selling doves. ¹³He said to them, "The Scriptures declare, 'My Temple will be called a house of prayer,' but you have turned it into a den of thieves!"*

¹⁴The blind and the lame came to him in the Temple, and he healed them. ¹⁵The leading priests and the teachers of religious law saw these wonderful miracles and heard even the children in the Temple shouting, "Praise God for the Son of David."

But the leaders were indignant. ¹⁶They asked Jesus, "Do you hear what these children are saying?"

"Yes," Jesus replied. "Haven't you ever read the Scriptures? For they say, 'You have taught children and infants to give you praise.'* " ¹⁷Then he returned to Bethany, where he stayed overnight.

¹⁸In the morning, as Jesus was returning to Jerusalem, he was hungry, ¹⁹and he noticed a fig tree beside the road. He went over to see if there were any figs, but there were only leaves. Then he said to it, "May you never bear fruit again!" And immediately the fig tree withered up.

²⁰The disciples were amazed when they saw this and asked, "How did the fig tree wither so quickly?"

²¹Then Jesus told them, "I tell you the truth, if you have faith and don't doubt, you can do things like this and much more. You can even say to this mountain, 'May you be lifted up and thrown into the sea,' and it will happen. ²²You can pray for anything, and if you have faith, you will receive it."

21:5a Greek *Tell the daughter of Zion.* Isa 62:11.
21:5b Zech 9:9.   **21:7** Greek *over them, and he sat on them.*
21:9a Greek *Hosanna,* an exclamation of praise that literally means "save now"; also in 21:9b, 15.   **21:9b** Pss 118:25-26; 148:1.   **21:13** Isa 56:7; Jer 7:11.   **21:16** Ps 8:2.

PSALM 25:16-22

Turn to me and have mercy,
    for I am alone and in deep distress.
¹⁷ My problems go from bad to worse.
    Oh, save me from them all!
¹⁸ Feel my pain and see my trouble.
    Forgive all my sins.

¹⁹ See how many enemies I have
    and how viciously they hate me!
²⁰ Protect me! Rescue my life from them!
    Do not let me be disgraced, for in
        you I take refuge.
²¹ May integrity and honesty protect me,
    for I put my hope in you.

²² O God, ransom Israel
    from all its troubles.

PROVERBS 6:12-15

What are worthless and wicked people like? They are constant liars, signaling their deceit with a wink of the eye, a nudge of the foot, or the wiggle of fingers. Their perverted hearts plot evil, and they constantly stir up trouble. But they will be destroyed suddenly, broken in an instant beyond all hope of healing.

Jesus is King

WHO GOD IS

MATTHEW 21:5 By entering Jerusalem on a donkey's colt, Jesus was intentionally fulfilling the prophecy recorded in the Old Testament book of Zechariah—and the people knew it. When they spread their cloaks and cut down palm branches, they thought they were honoring a new king. They were right, partially. Jesus was indeed their new King, but he was not the kind of king for which they were hoping. These people thought Jesus would take the throne of Jerusalem and set them free from the rule of Rome.   • Jesus did not come to set up an earthly kingdom, however. As he told Pilate during his trial, "My Kingdom is not an earthly kingdom" (John 18:36, May 30). He is a King, yes, but far greater than any earthly king could ever claim to be. He is King over all creation, and one day he will banish all evil and reign over the earth. Those on Satan's side will "go to war against the Lamb [Jesus], but the Lamb will defeat them because he is Lord of all lords and King of all kings" (Revelation 17:14, see December 26).   •However, Jesus' Kingdom *does* currently exist on this earth, for it is alive in the hearts of his followers. If Jesus rules in your heart and life, then the Kingdom of God is already with you. As your King, Jesus will one day welcome you into his eternal Kingdom to be with him forever.

²⁶Then Jesus told them, "I tell you the truth, if you have faith and don't doubt, you can do things like this and much more. You can even say to this mountain, 'May you be lifted up and thrown into the sea,' and it will happen. ²²You can pray for anything, and if you have faith, you will receive it."

²¹:5 Greek *colt, the daughter of Zion* (Isa 62:11). 21:5b Zech 9:9. 21:12 Greek *overturned the seats of those who*
21:12b Greek *doves*; or *doves, an exclamation of praise that literally means 'save now,' also in 21:9b, 15.* 21:9b Ps 118:25-26.
118:1. 21:13 Isa 56:7. 21:13b Jer 7:11. 21:16 Ps 8:2.

PSALM 25:16-22
turn to me and have mercy,
for I am alone and in deep distress.
¹⁷My problems go from bad to worse.
Oh, save me from them all.
¹⁸Feel my pain and see my trouble.
Forgive all my sins.

¹⁹See how many enemies I have
and how viciously they hate me!
²⁰Protect me! Rescue my life from them!
Do not let me be disgraced, for in
you I take refuge.
²¹May integrity and honesty protect me,
for I put my hope in you.
²²O God, ransom Israel
from all its troubles.

PROVERBS 6:12-15
What are worthless and wicked people like? They are constant liars, signaling their deceit with a wink of the eye, a nudge of the foot, or the wiggle of fingers. Their perverted hearts plot evil, and they constantly stir up trouble. But they will be destroyed suddenly, broken in an instant beyond all hope of healing.

WHO GOD IS

Jesus is King

MATTHEW 21:5 By entering Jerusalem on a donkey's colt, Jesus was intentionally fulfilling the prophecy recorded in the Old Testament book of Zechariah—and the people knew it. When they spread their cloaks and cut down palm branches, they thought they were honoring a new king. They were right, partially. Jesus was indeed their new King, but he was not the kind of king for which they were hoping. These people thought Jesus would take the throne of Jerusalem and set them free from the rule of Rome. ² Jesus did not come to set up an earthly kingdom, however. As he told Pilate during his trial, "My Kingdom is not an earthly kingdom" (John 18:36, May 30). He is a King, yes, but far greater than any earthly king could ever claim to be. He is King over all creation, and one day he will defeat all evil and reign over the earth. Those on Satan's side will "go to war against the Lamb (Jesus), but the Lamb will defeat them because he is Lord of all lords and King of all kings" (Revelation 17:14, see December 26). ³ However, Jesus' Kingdom does currently exist on this earth, for it is alive in the hearts of his followers. If Jesus rules in your heart and life, then the Kingdom of God is already with you. As your King, Jesus will one day welcome you into his eternal Kingdom to be with him forever.

EXODUS 13:17–15:18

The Israelites' journey from slavery to freedom had a few bumps in the road, not the least of which was an angry Egyptian army bearing down on them while they were trapped on the edge of the Red Sea! Watch how God worked to save his people.

When Pharaoh finally let the people go, God did not lead them along the main road that runs through Philistine territory, even though that was the shortest route to the Promised Land. God said, "If the people are faced with a battle, they might change their minds and return to Egypt." ¹⁸So God led them in a roundabout way through the wilderness toward the Red Sea.* Thus the Israelites left Egypt like an army ready for battle.*

¹⁹Moses took the bones of Joseph with him, for Joseph had made the sons of Israel swear to do this. He said, "God will certainly come to help you. When he does, you must take my bones with you from this place."

²⁰The Israelites left Succoth and camped at Etham on the edge of the wilderness. ²¹The LORD went ahead of them. He guided them during the day with a pillar of cloud, and he provided light at night with a pillar of fire. This allowed them to travel by day or by night. ²²And the LORD did not remove the pillar of cloud or pillar of fire from its place in front of the people.

14:1THEN the LORD gave these instructions to Moses: ²"Order the Israelites to turn back and camp by Pi-hahiroth between Migdol and the sea. Camp there along the shore, across from Baal-zephon. ³Then Pharaoh will think, 'The Israelites are confused. They are trapped in the wilderness!' ⁴And once again I will harden Pharaoh's heart, and he will chase after you.* I have planned this in order to display my glory through Pharaoh and his whole army. After this the Egyptians will

know that I am the LORD!" So the Israelites camped there as they were told.

⁵When word reached the king of Egypt that the Israelites had fled, Pharaoh and his officials changed their minds. "What have we done, letting all those Israelite slaves get away?" they asked. ⁶So Pharaoh harnessed his chariot and called up his troops. ⁷He took with him 600 of Egypt's best chariots, along with the rest of the chariots of Egypt, each with its commander. ⁸The LORD hardened the heart of Pharaoh, the king of Egypt, so he chased after the people of Israel, who had left with fists raised in defiance. ⁹The Egyptians chased after them with all the forces in Pharaoh's army—all his horses and chariots, his charioteers, and his troops. The Egyptians caught up with the people of Israel as they were camped beside the shore near Pi-hahiroth, across from Baal-zephon.

¹⁰As Pharaoh approached, the people of Israel looked up and panicked when they saw the Egyptians overtaking them. They cried out to the LORD, ¹¹and they said to Moses, "Why did you bring us out here to die in the wilderness? Weren't there enough graves for us in Egypt? What have you done to us? Why did you make us leave Egypt? ¹²Didn't we tell you this would happen while we were still in Egypt? We said, 'Leave us alone! Let us be slaves to the Egyptians. It's better to be a slave in Egypt than a corpse in the wilderness!'"

¹³But Moses told the people, "Don't be afraid. Just stand still and watch the LORD rescue you today. The Egyptians you see today will never be seen again. ¹⁴The LORD himself will fight for you. Just stay calm."

¹⁵Then the LORD said to Moses, "Why are you crying out to me? Tell the people to get moving! ¹⁶Pick up your staff and

raise your hand over the sea. Divide the water so the Israelites can walk through the middle of the sea on dry ground. ¹⁷And I will harden the hearts of the Egyptians, and they will charge in after the Israelites. My great glory will be displayed through Pharaoh and his troops, his chariots, and his charioteers. ¹⁸When my glory is displayed through them, all Egypt will see my glory and know that I am the LORD!"

¹⁹Then the angel of God, who had been leading the people of Israel, moved to the rear of the camp. The pillar of cloud also moved from the front and stood behind them. ²⁰The cloud settled between the Egyptian and Israelite camps. As darkness fell, the cloud turned to fire, lighting up the night. But the Egyptians and Israelites did not approach each other all night.

²¹Then Moses raised his hand over the sea, and the LORD opened up a path through the water with a strong east wind. The wind blew all that night, turning the seabed into dry land. ²²So the people of Israel walked through the middle of the sea on dry ground, with walls of water on each side!

²³Then the Egyptians—all of Pharaoh's horses, chariots, and charioteers—chased them into the middle of the sea. ²⁴But just before dawn the LORD looked down on the Egyptian army from the pillar of fire and cloud, and he threw their forces into total confusion. ²⁵He twisted* their chariot wheels, making their chariots difficult to drive. "Let's get out of here—away from these Israelites!" the Egyptians shouted. "The LORD is fighting for them against Egypt!"

²⁶When all the Israelites had reached the other side, the LORD said to Moses, "Raise your hand over the sea again. Then the waters will rush back and cover the Egyptians and their chariots and charioteers." ²⁷So as the sun began to rise, Moses raised his hand over the sea, and the water rushed back into its usual place. The Egyptians tried to escape, but the LORD swept them into the sea. ²⁸Then the waters returned and covered all the chariots and charioteers—the entire army of Pharaoh. Of all the Egyptians who had

chased the Israelites into the sea, not a single one survived.

²⁹But the people of Israel had walked through the middle of the sea on dry ground, as the water stood up like a wall on both sides. ³⁰That is how the LORD rescued Israel from the hand of the Egyptians that day. And the Israelites saw the bodies of the Egyptians washed up on the seashore. ³¹When the people of Israel saw the mighty power that the LORD had unleashed against the Egyptians, they were filled with awe before him. They put their faith in the LORD and in his servant Moses.

¹⁵:¹THEN Moses and the people of Israel sang this song to the LORD:

"I will sing to the LORD,
    for he has triumphed gloriously;
he has hurled both horse and rider
    into the sea.
² The LORD is my strength and my song;
    he has given me victory.
This is my God, and I will praise him—
    my father's God, and I will
        exalt him!
³ The LORD is a warrior;
    Yahweh* is his name!
⁴ Pharaoh's chariots and army
    he has hurled into the sea.
The finest of Pharaoh's officers
    are drowned in the Red Sea.*
⁵ The deep waters gushed over them;
    they sank to the bottom like a stone.

⁶ "Your right hand, O LORD,
    is glorious in power.
Your right hand, O LORD,
    smashes the enemy.
⁷ In the greatness of your majesty,
    you overthrow those who rise
        against you.
You unleash your blazing fury;
    it consumes them like straw.
⁸ At the blast of your breath,
    the waters piled up!
The surging waters stood straight
    like a wall;
in the heart of the sea the deep
    waters became hard.

⁹ "The enemy boasted, 'I will chase
    them and catch up with them.
I will plunder them
    and consume them.

I will flash my sword;
my powerful hand will destroy
them.'
[10] But you blew with your breath,
and the sea covered them.
They sank like lead
in the mighty waters.

[11] "Who is like you among the gods,
O Lord—
glorious in holiness,
awesome in splendor,
performing great wonders?
[12] You raised your right hand,
and the earth swallowed our
enemies.

[13] "With your unfailing love you lead
the people you have redeemed.
In your might, you guide them
to your sacred home.
[14] The peoples hear and tremble;
anguish grips those who live
in Philistia.
[15] The leaders of Edom are terrified;
the nobles of Moab tremble.
All who live in Canaan melt away;
[16]   terror and dread fall upon them.
The power of your arm
makes them lifeless as stone
until your people pass by, O Lord,
until the people you purchased
pass by.
[17] You will bring them in and plant
them on your own mountain—

the place, O Lord, reserved for your
own dwelling,
the sanctuary, O Lord, that your
hands have established.
[18] The Lord will reign forever and ever!"

13:18a Hebrew *sea of reeds*.   **13:18b** Greek version reads
left Egypt in the fifth generation.   **14:4** Hebrew *after them*.
14:25 As in Greek version, Samaritan Pentateuch, and Syriac
version; Hebrew reads *He removed*.   **15:3** *Yahweh* is a
transliteration of the proper name *YHWH* that is sometimes
rendered "Jehovah"; in this translation it is usually rendered
"the Lord" (note the use of small capitals).   **15:4** Hebrew *sea
of reeds;* also in 15:22.

MATTHEW 21:23-46
The hypocritical religious establishment demanded
answers; Jesus gave them questions and parables
in order to reveal their hypocritical motives. They
responded with anger and a desire to put him away.

When Jesus returned to the Temple and
began teaching, the leading priests and
elders came up to him. They demanded,
"By what authority are you doing all these
things? Who gave you the right?"

[24]"I'll tell you by what authority I do
these things if you answer one question,"
Jesus replied. [25]"Did John's authority to
baptize come from heaven, or was it
merely human?"

They talked it over among themselves.
"If we say it was from heaven, he will ask
us why we didn't believe John. [26]But if we
say it was merely human, we'll be mobbed
because the people believe John was a
prophet." [27]So they finally replied, "We
don't know."

HOW WE LIVE

Courageous in trials

EXODUS 14:13-14 The Israelites had just been freed from slavery by a
series of miracles. They had left their land of sorrow and were headed
into a bright new future—only now they found themselves trapped at the
edge of the Red Sea with Pharaoh's army in pursuit. You might think their
faith would be strong after all they had seen God do to the Egyptians.
Sadly, the people forgot about God's power and responded in panic as
the dust of the advancing army rose into the sky behind them. • Their
lack of faith is startling, yet how often do we find ourselves losing courage, losing hope, and complaining in the midst of difficulties? God does
not let us experience trials because he wants to see us suffer; he allows
these difficulties to help us live by faith and find courage in the strength
of our Lord. • Don't be like the Israelites, responding with panic when
trouble comes your way. Instead, do as Moses suggested, "Don't be
afraid. Just stand still and watch the Lord rescue you today."

And Jesus responded, "Then I won't tell you by what authority I do these things.

28"But what do you think about this? A man with two sons told the older boy, 'Son, go out and work in the vineyard today.' 29The son answered, 'No, I won't go,' but later he changed his mind and went anyway. 30Then the father told the other son, 'You go,' and he said, 'Yes, sir, I will.' But he didn't go.

31"Which of the two obeyed his father?"

They replied, "The first."*

Then Jesus explained his meaning: "I tell you the truth, corrupt tax collectors and prostitutes will get into the Kingdom of God before you do. 32For John the Baptist came and showed you the right way to live, but you didn't believe him, while tax collectors and prostitutes did. And even when you saw this happening, you refused to believe him and repent of your sins.

33"Now listen to another story. A certain landowner planted a vineyard, built a wall around it, dug a pit for pressing out the grape juice, and built a lookout tower. Then he leased the vineyard to tenant farmers and moved to another country. 34At the time of the grape harvest, he sent his servants to collect his share of the crop. 35But the farmers grabbed his servants, beat one, killed one, and stoned another. 36So the landowner sent a larger group of his servants to collect for him, but the results were the same.

37"Finally, the owner sent his son, thinking, 'Surely they will respect my son.'

38"But when the tenant farmers saw his son coming, they said to one another, 'Here comes the heir to this estate. Come on, let's kill him and get the estate for ourselves!' 39So they grabbed him, dragged him out of the vineyard, and murdered him.

40"When the owner of the vineyard returns," Jesus asked, "what do you think he will do to those farmers?"

41The religious leaders replied, "He will put the wicked men to a horrible death and lease the vineyard to others who will give him his share of the crop after each harvest."

42Then Jesus asked them, "Didn't you ever read this in the Scriptures?

'The stone that the builders rejected
    has now become the cornerstone.
This is the LORD's doing,
    and it is wonderful to see.'*

43I tell you, the Kingdom of God will be taken away from you and given to a nation that will produce the proper fruit. 44Anyone who stumbles over that stone will be broken to pieces, and it will crush anyone it falls on.*"

45When the leading priests and Pharisees heard this parable, they realized he was telling the story against them—they were the wicked farmers. 46They wanted to arrest him, but they were afraid of the crowds, who considered Jesus to be a prophet.

21:29-31 Other manuscripts read *"The second."* In still other manuscripts the first son says "Yes" but does nothing, the second son says "No" but then repents and goes, and the answer to Jesus' question is that the second son obeyed his father.   21:42 Ps 118:22-23.   21:44 This verse is omitted in some early manuscripts. Compare Luke 20:18.

PSALM 26:1-12
A psalm of David.

1 **D**eclare me innocent, O LORD,
    for I have acted with integrity;
    I have trusted in the LORD without
        wavering.
2 Put me on trial, LORD, and cross-
        examine me.
    Test my motives and my heart.
3 For I am always aware of your
        unfailing love,
    and I have lived according to
        your truth.
4 I do not spend time with liars
    or go along with hypocrites.
5 I hate the gatherings of those who
        do evil,
    and I refuse to join in with the wicked.
6 I wash my hands to declare my
        innocence.
    I come to your altar, O LORD,
7 singing a song of thanksgiving
    and telling of all your wonders.
8 I love your sanctuary, LORD,
    the place where your glorious
        presence dwells.
9 Don't let me suffer the fate of sinners.
    Don't condemn me along with
        murderers.

¹⁰ Their hands are dirty with evil schemes,
and they constantly take bribes.
¹¹ But I am not like that; I live with
integrity.
So redeem me and show
me mercy.
¹² Now I stand on solid ground,
and I will publicly praise the LORD.

EXODUS 15:19–17:7

After the miraculous crossing of the Red Sea, the people faced the problem of day-to-day logistics during their journey. God miraculously and lovingly provided food and water for his people, yet it seems that they never quite learned to be thankful.

When Pharaoh's horses, chariots, and charioteers rushed into the sea, the LORD brought the water crashing down on them. But the people of Israel had walked through the middle of the sea on dry ground!

²⁰Then Miriam the prophet, Aaron's sister, took a tambourine and led all the women as they played their tambourines and danced. ²¹And Miriam sang this song:

"Sing to the LORD,
for he has triumphed gloriously;
he has hurled both horse and rider
into the sea."

²²Then Moses led the people of Israel away from the Red Sea, and they moved out into the desert of Shur. They traveled in this desert for three days without finding any water. ²³When they came to the oasis of Marah, the water was too bitter to drink. So they called the place Marah (which means "bitter").

²⁴Then the people complained and turned against Moses. "What are we going to drink?" they demanded. ²⁵So Moses cried out to the LORD for help, and the LORD showed him a piece of wood. Moses threw it into the water, and this made the water good to drink.

It was there at Marah that the LORD set before them the following decree as a

PROVERBS 6:16-19

There are six things the LORD hates—no, seven things he detests: haughty eyes, a lying tongue, hands that kill the innocent, a heart that plots evil, feet that race to do wrong, a false witness who pours out lies, a person who sows discord in a family.

FEBRUARY**2**

standard to test their faithfulness to him. ²⁶He said, "If you will listen carefully to the voice of the LORD your God and do what is right in his sight, obeying his commands and keeping all his decrees, then I will not make you suffer any of the diseases I sent on the Egyptians; for I am the LORD who heals you."

²⁷After leaving Marah, the Israelites traveled on to the oasis of Elim, where they found twelve springs and seventy palm trees. They camped there beside the water.

^{16:1}THEN the whole community of Israel set out from Elim and journeyed into the wilderness of Sin,* between Elim and Mount Sinai. They arrived there on the fifteenth day of the second month, one month after leaving the land of Egypt.* ²There, too, the whole community of Israel complained about Moses and Aaron.

³"If only the LORD had killed us back in Egypt," they moaned. "There we sat around pots filled with meat and ate all the bread we wanted. But now you have brought us into this wilderness to starve us all to death."

⁴Then the LORD said to Moses, "Look, I'm going to rain down food from heaven for you. Each day the people can go out and pick up as much food as they need for that day. I will test them in this to see whether or not they will follow my instructions. ⁵On the sixth day they will gather food, and when they prepare it, there will be twice as much as usual."

⁶So Moses and Aaron said to all the people of Israel, "By evening you will realize it was the LORD who brought you out of the

land of Egypt. ⁷In the morning you will see the glory of the LORD, because he has heard your complaints, which are against him, not against us. What have we done that you should complain about us?" ⁸Then Moses added, "The LORD will give you meat to eat in the evening and bread to satisfy you in the morning, for he has heard all your complaints against him. What have we done? Yes, your complaints are against the LORD, not against us."

⁹Then Moses said to Aaron, "Announce this to the entire community of Israel: 'Present yourselves before the LORD, for he has heard your complaining.'" ¹⁰And as Aaron spoke to the whole community of Israel, they looked out toward the wilderness. There they could see the awesome glory of the LORD in the cloud.

¹¹Then the LORD said to Moses, ¹²"I have heard the Israelites' complaints. Now tell them, 'In the evening you will have meat to eat, and in the morning you will have all the bread you want. Then you will know that I am the LORD your God.'"

¹³That evening vast numbers of quail flew in and covered the camp. And the next morning the area around the camp was wet with dew. ¹⁴When the dew evaporated, a flaky substance as fine as frost blanketed the ground. ¹⁵The Israelites were puzzled when they saw it. "What is it?" they asked each other. They had no idea what it was.

And Moses told them, "It is the food the LORD has given you to eat. ¹⁶These are the LORD's instructions: Each household should gather as much as it needs. Pick up two quarts* for each person in your tent."

¹⁷So the people of Israel did as they were told. Some gathered a lot, some only a little. ¹⁸But when they measured it out,* everyone had just enough. Those who gathered a lot had nothing left over, and those who gathered only a little had enough. Each family had just what it needed.

¹⁹Then Moses told them, "Do not keep any of it until morning." ²⁰But some of them didn't listen and kept some of it until morning. But by then it was full of maggots and had a terrible smell. Moses was very angry with them.

²¹After this the people gathered the food morning by morning, each family according to its need. And as the sun became hot, the flakes they had not picked up melted and disappeared. ²²On the sixth day, they gathered twice as much as usual—four quarts* for each person instead of two. Then all the leaders of the community came and asked Moses for an explanation. ²³He told them, "This is what the LORD commanded: Tomorrow will be a day of complete rest, a holy Sabbath day set apart for the LORD. So bake or boil as much as you want today, and set aside what is left for tomorrow."

²⁴So they put some aside until morning, just as Moses had commanded. And in the morning the leftover food was wholesome and good, without maggots or odor. ²⁵Moses said, "Eat this food today, for today is a Sabbath day dedicated to the LORD. There will be no food on the ground today. ²⁶You may gather the food for six days, but the seventh day is the Sabbath. There will be no food on the ground that day."

²⁷Some of the people went out anyway on the seventh day, but they found no food. ²⁸The LORD asked Moses, "How long will these people refuse to obey my commands and instructions? ²⁹They must realize that the Sabbath is the LORD's gift to you. That is why he gives you a two-day supply on the sixth day, so there will be enough for two days. On the Sabbath day you must each stay in your place. Do not go out to pick up food on the seventh day." ³⁰So the people did not gather any food on the seventh day.

³¹The Israelites called the food manna.* It was white like coriander seed, and it tasted like honey wafers.

³²Then Moses said, "This is what the LORD has commanded: Fill a two-quart container with manna to preserve it for your descendants. Then later generations will be able to see the food I gave you in the wilderness when I set you free from Egypt."

³³Moses said to Aaron, "Get a jar and fill it with two quarts of manna. Then put it in a sacred place before the LORD to preserve it for all future generations." ³⁴Aaron did just as the LORD had commanded Moses. He eventually placed it in the Ark of the

Covenant—in front of the stone tablets inscribed with the terms of the covenant.*

³⁵So the people of Israel ate manna for forty years until they arrived at the land where they would settle. They ate manna until they came to the border of the land of Canaan.

³⁶The container used to measure the manna was an omer, which was one tenth of an ephah; it held about two quarts.*

17:1 At the LORD's command, the whole community of Israel left the wilderness of Sin* and moved from place to place. Eventually they camped at Rephidim, but there was no water there for the people to drink. ²So once more the people complained against Moses. "Give us water to drink!" they demanded.

"Quiet!" Moses replied. "Why are you complaining against me? And why are you testing the LORD?"

³But tormented by thirst, they continued to argue with Moses. "Why did you bring us out of Egypt? Are you trying to kill us, our children, and our livestock with thirst?"

⁴Then Moses cried out to the LORD, "What should I do with these people? They are ready to stone me!"

⁵The LORD said to Moses, "Walk out in front of the people. Take your staff, the one you used when you struck the water of the Nile, and call some of the elders of Israel to join you. ⁶I will stand before you on the rock at Mount Sinai.* Strike the rock, and water will come gushing out. Then the people will be able to drink." So Moses struck the rock as he was told, and water gushed out as the elders looked on.

⁷Moses named the place Massah (which means "test") and Meribah (which means "arguing") because the people of Israel argued with Moses and tested the LORD by saying, "Is the LORD here with us or not?"

16:1a The geographical name *Sin* is related to *Sinai* and should not be confused with the English word *sin*. **16:1b** The Exodus had occurred on the fifteenth day of the first month (see Num 33:3). **16:16** Hebrew *1 omer* (2 liters); also in 16:32, 33. **16:18** Hebrew *measured it with an omer*. **16:22** Hebrew *2 omers* (4 liters). **16:31** *Manna* means "What is it?" See 16:15. **16:34** Hebrew *He placed it in front of the Testimony;* see note on 25:16. **16:36** Hebrew *An omer is one tenth of an ephah*. **17:1** The geographical name *Sin* is related to *Sinai* and should not be confused with the English word *sin*. **17:6** Hebrew *Horeb*, another name for Sinai.

MATTHEW 22:1-33

In his various responses to the Pharisees and Sadducees, the most prominent religious leaders of the day, Jesus revealed truths about the Kingdom of God, the tension of being a citizen of both heaven and earth, and the reality of the afterlife.

Jesus also told them other parables. He said, ²"The Kingdom of Heaven can be illustrated by the story of a king who prepared a great wedding feast for his son. ³When the banquet was ready, he sent

WHAT THE BIBLE SAYS

The reality of heaven

MATTHEW 22:29-32 The Sadducees were an upper-crust religious group who did not believe in life after death. Each time they tried to confound Jesus, he gave answers from which we gain valuable insights. In this case, those insights are about heaven: (1) *Heaven is an absolute certainty— and so is a believer's future presence there.* God's Law—which the Sadducees supposedly knew so well—reveals the truth of life after death in heaven with God. (2) *Life in heaven will not be an extension of this life; it will be new and different.* The ways in which we relate to one another on earth—friend, mother, father, sibling, teacher, student—will be completely redefined in heaven. We will join together on equal footing, worshiping and exploring the glory and mystery of God. (3) *In heaven, we will have a presence in new bodies.* We will not be ghostly spirits, but will have resurrected bodies. To live forever in these present bodies would be a curse, but to live forever in new bodies in God's presence—free of sickness and pain—will be a blessing!

his servants to notify those who were invited. But they all refused to come!

⁴"So he sent other servants to tell them, 'The feast has been prepared. The bulls and fattened cattle have been killed, and everything is ready. Come to the banquet!' ⁵But the guests he had invited ignored them and went their own way, one to his farm, another to his business. ⁶Others seized his messengers and insulted them and killed them.

⁷"The king was furious, and he sent out his army to destroy the murderers and burn their town. ⁸And he said to his servants, 'The wedding feast is ready, and the guests I invited aren't worthy of the honor. ⁹Now go out to the street corners and invite everyone you see.' ¹⁰So the servants brought in everyone they could find, good and bad alike, and the banquet hall was filled with guests.

¹¹"But when the king came in to meet the guests, he noticed a man who wasn't wearing the proper clothes for a wedding. ¹²'Friend,' he asked, 'how is it that you are here without wedding clothes?' But the man had no reply. ¹³Then the king said to his aides, 'Bind his hands and feet and throw him into the outer darkness, where there will be weeping and gnashing of teeth.'

¹⁴"For many are called, but few are chosen."

¹⁵Then the Pharisees met together to plot how to trap Jesus into saying something for which he could be arrested. ¹⁶They sent some of their disciples, along with the supporters of Herod, to meet with him. "Teacher," they said, "we know how honest you are. You teach the way of God truthfully. You are impartial and don't play favorites. ¹⁷Now tell us what you think about this: Is it right to pay taxes to Caesar or not?"

¹⁸But Jesus knew their evil motives. "You hypocrites!" he said. "Why are you trying to trap me? ¹⁹Here, show me the coin used for the tax." When they handed him a Roman coin,* ²⁰he asked, "Whose picture and title are stamped on it?"

²¹"Caesar's," they replied.

"Well, then," he said, "give to Caesar what belongs to Caesar, and give to God what belongs to God."

²²His reply amazed them, and they went away.

²³That same day Jesus was approached by some Sadducees—religious leaders who say there is no resurrection from the dead. They posed this question: ²⁴"Teacher, Moses said, 'If a man dies without children, his brother should marry the widow and have a child who will carry on the brother's name.'* ²⁵Well, suppose there were seven brothers. The oldest one married and then died without children, so his brother married the widow. ²⁶But the second brother also died, and the third brother married her. This continued with all seven of them. ²⁷Last of all, the woman also died. ²⁸So tell us, whose wife will she be in the resurrection? For all seven were married to her."

²⁹Jesus replied, "Your mistake is that you don't know the Scriptures, and you don't know the power of God. ³⁰For when the dead rise, they will neither marry nor be given in marriage. In this respect they will be like the angels in heaven.

³¹"But now, as to whether there will be a resurrection of the dead—haven't you ever read about this in the Scriptures? Long after Abraham, Isaac, and Jacob had died, God said,* ³²'I am the God of Abraham, the God of Isaac, and the God of Jacob.'* So he is the God of the living, not the dead."

³³When the crowds heard him, they were astounded at his teaching.

22:19 Greek *a denarius.*   22:24 Deut 25:5-6.
22:31 Greek *read about this? God said.*   22:32 Exod 3:6.

PSALM 27:1-6
A psalm of David.

¹ The LORD is my light and my
   salvation—
   so why should I be afraid?
The LORD is my fortress, protecting
   me from danger,
   so why should I tremble?
² When evil people come to devour me,
   when my enemies and foes
      attack me,
   they will stumble and fall.
³ Though a mighty army surrounds me,
   my heart will not be afraid.
Even if I am attacked,
   I will remain confident.

⁴ The one thing I ask of the LORD—
   the thing I seek most—
is to live in the house of the LORD all
   the days of my life,
   delighting in the LORD's
      perfections
   and meditating in his Temple.
⁵ For he will conceal me there when
   troubles come;
   he will hide me in his sanctuary.
   He will place me out of reach on
      a high rock.
⁶ Then I will hold my head high
   above my enemies who surround me.
   At his sanctuary I will offer sacrifices
      with shouts of joy,
   singing and praising the LORD
      with music.

EXODUS 17:8–19:15

Today's reading concludes with one of the most significant events in Israel's history—the inauguration of the Sinai Covenant. God formally made the people his covenant nation, and they swore allegiance to him and to the stipulations of the covenant.

While the people of Israel were still at Rephidim, the warriors of Amalek attacked them. ⁹Moses commanded Joshua, "Choose some men to go out and fight the army of Amalek for us. Tomorrow, I will stand at the top of the hill, holding the staff of God in my hand."

¹⁰So Joshua did what Moses had commanded and fought the army of Amalek. Meanwhile, Moses, Aaron, and Hur climbed to the top of a nearby hill. ¹¹As long as Moses held up the staff in his hand, the Israelites had the advantage. But whenever he dropped his hand, the Amalekites gained the advantage. ¹²Moses' arms soon became so tired he could no longer hold them up. So Aaron and Hur found a stone for him to sit on. Then they stood on each side of Moses, holding up his hands. So his hands held steady until sunset. ¹³As a result, Joshua overwhelmed the army of Amalek in battle.

PROVERBS 6:20-26

My son, obey your father's commands, and don't neglect your mother's instruction. Keep their words always in your heart. Tie them around your neck. When you walk, their counsel will lead you. When you sleep, they will protect you. When you wake up, they will advise you. For their command is a lamp and their instruction a light; their corrective discipline is the way to life. It will keep you from the immoral woman, from the smooth tongue of a promiscuous woman. Don't lust for her beauty. Don't let her coy glances seduce you. For a prostitute will bring you to poverty,* but sleeping with another man's wife will cost you your life.

6:26 Hebrew *to a loaf of bread.*

FEBRUARY **3**

¹⁴After the victory, the LORD instructed Moses, "Write this down on a scroll as a permanent reminder, and read it aloud to Joshua: I will erase the memory of Amalek from under heaven." ¹⁵Moses built an altar there and named it Yahweh-nissi (which means "the LORD is my banner"). ¹⁶He said, "They have raised their fist against the LORD's throne, so now* the LORD will be at war with Amalek generation after generation."

¹⁸:¹MOSES' father-in-law, Jethro, the priest of Midian, heard about everything God had done for Moses and his people, the Israelites. He heard especially about how the LORD had rescued them from Egypt.

²Earlier, Moses had sent his wife, Zipporah, and his two sons back to Jethro, who had taken them in. ³(Moses' first son was named Gershom,* for Moses had said when the boy was born, "I have been a foreigner in a foreign land." ⁴His second son was named Eliezer,* for Moses had said, "The God of my ancestors was my helper; he rescued me from the sword of Pharaoh.") ⁵Jethro, Moses' father-in-law, now came to visit Moses in the wilderness. He brought Moses' wife and two sons with

him, and they arrived while Moses and the people were camped near the mountain of God. [6]Jethro had sent a message to Moses, saying, "I, Jethro, your father-in-law, am coming to see you with your wife and your two sons."

[7]So Moses went out to meet his father-in-law. He bowed low and kissed him. They asked about each other's welfare and then went into Moses' tent. [8]Moses told his father-in-law everything the LORD had done to Pharaoh and Egypt on behalf of Israel. He also told about all the hardships they had experienced along the way and how the LORD had rescued his people from all their troubles. [9]Jethro was delighted when he heard about all the good things the LORD had done for Israel as he rescued them from the hand of the Egyptians.

[10]"Praise the LORD," Jethro said, "for he has rescued you from the Egyptians and from Pharaoh. Yes, he has rescued Israel from the powerful hand of Egypt! [11]I know now that the LORD is greater than all other gods, because he rescued his people from the oppression of the proud Egyptians."

[12]Then Jethro, Moses' father-in-law, brought a burnt offering and sacrifices to God. Aaron and all the elders of Israel came out and joined him in a sacrificial meal in God's presence.

[13]The next day, Moses took his seat to hear the people's disputes against each other. They waited before him from morning till evening.

[14]When Moses' father-in-law saw all that Moses was doing for the people, he asked, "What are you really accomplishing here? Why are you trying to do all this alone while everyone stands around you from morning till evening?"

[15]Moses replied, "Because the people come to me to get a ruling from God. [16]When a dispute arises, they come to me, and I am the one who settles the case between the quarreling parties. I inform the people of God's decrees and give them his instructions."

[17]"This is not good!" Moses' father-in-law exclaimed. [18]"You're going to wear yourself out—and the people, too. This job is too heavy a burden for you to handle all by yourself. [19]Now listen to me, and let me give you a word of advice, and may God be with you. You should continue to be the people's representative before God, bringing their disputes to him. [20]Teach them God's decrees, and give them his instructions. Show them how to conduct their lives. [21]But select from all the people some capable, honest men who fear God and hate bribes. Appoint them as leaders over groups of one thousand, one hundred, fifty, and ten. [22]They should always be available to solve the people's common disputes, but have them bring the major cases to you. Let the leaders decide the smaller matters themselves. They will help you carry the load, making the task easier for you. [23]If you follow this advice, and if God commands you to do so, then you will be able to endure the pressures, and all these people will go home in peace."

[24]Moses listened to his father-in-law's advice and followed his suggestions. [25]He chose capable men from all over Israel and appointed them as leaders over the people. He put them in charge of groups of one thousand, one hundred, fifty, and ten. [26]These men were always available to solve the people's common disputes. They brought the major cases to Moses, but they took care of the smaller matters themselves.

[27]Soon after this, Moses said good-bye to his father-in-law, who returned to his own land.

19:1EXACTLY two months after the Israelites left Egypt,* they arrived in the wilderness of Sinai. [2]After breaking camp at Rephidim, they came to the wilderness of Sinai and set up camp there at the base of Mount Sinai.

[3]Then Moses climbed the mountain to appear before God. The LORD called to him from the mountain and said, "Give these instructions to the family of Jacob; announce it to the descendants of Israel: [4]'You have seen what I did to the Egyptians. You know how I carried you on eagles' wings and brought you to myself. [5]Now if you will obey me and keep my covenant, you will be my own special treasure from among all the peoples on earth; for all the earth belongs to me. [6]And you

will be my kingdom of priests, my holy nation.' This is the message you must give to the people of Israel."

[7]So Moses returned from the mountain and called together the elders of the people and told them everything the LORD had commanded him. [8]And all the people responded together, "We will do everything the LORD has commanded." So Moses brought the people's answer back to the LORD.

[9]Then the LORD said to Moses, "I will come to you in a thick cloud, Moses, so the people themselves can hear me when I speak with you. Then they will always trust you."

Moses told the LORD what the people had said. [10]Then the LORD told Moses, "Go down and prepare the people for my arrival. Consecrate them today and tomorrow, and have them wash their clothing. [11]Be sure they are ready on the third day, for on that day the LORD will come down on Mount Sinai as all the people watch. [12]Mark off a boundary all around the mountain. Warn the people, 'Be careful! Do not go up on the mountain or even touch its boundaries. Anyone who touches the mountain will certainly be put to death. [13]No hand may touch the person or animal that crosses the boundary; instead, stone them or shoot them with arrows. They must be put to death.' However, when the ram's horn sounds a long blast, then the people may go up on the mountain.*"

[14]So Moses went down to the people. He consecrated them for worship, and they washed their clothes. [15]He told them, "Get ready for the third day, and until then abstain from having sexual intercourse."

17:16 Or *Hands have been lifted up to the LORD's throne, and now.* 18:3 *Gershom* sounds like a Hebrew term that means "a foreigner there." 18:4 *Eliezer* means "God is my helper." 19:1 Hebrew *In the third month after the Israelites left Egypt, on the very day,* i.e., two lunar months to the day after leaving Egypt. Compare Num 33:3. 19:13 Or *up to the mountain.*

MATTHEW 22:34–23:12

The religious leaders wanted to trick Jesus—or at least cause enough controversy to make people think he was an imposter. Jesus answered their questions well and warned others of their deception.

But when the Pharisees heard that he [Jesus] had silenced the Sadducees with his reply, they met together to question him again. [35]One of them, an expert in religious law, tried to trap him with this question: [36]"Teacher, which is the most important commandment in the law of Moses?"

[37]Jesus replied, "'You must love the LORD your God with all your heart, all your soul, and all your mind.'*[38]This is the first and greatest commandment. [39]A second is equally important: 'Love your neighbor as yourself.'* [40]The entire law and all the demands of the prophets are based on these two commandments."

[41]Then, surrounded by the Pharisees, Jesus asked them a question: [42]"What do

HOW WE LIVE

Loving God and others

MATTHEW 22:37-40 The Pharisees labored to distinguish important laws from the less important ones. Jesus blew their artificial system away when he pointed to the simple way one could fulfill the entire Law—by loving God and loving our neighbor as ourselves. • God made us for relationships. He created us in his image so that we could have a relationship with him. Although human sin fractured that relationship, God made a way through Jesus Christ for that relationship to be restored. Love for God is our highest calling and the path to true fulfillment as a human being. • Love for God always leads to love for one's neighbors. Although the world says, "Look out for number one," true happiness is found when we put the needs of our family, friends, neighbors, and even total strangers before our own. • Learn to love. Love God. Love others. When you do that, you'll find fulfillment that worldly ways of living for oneself simply can't provide.

you think about the Messiah? Whose son is he?"

They replied, "He is the son of David."

[43]Jesus responded, "Then why does David, speaking under the inspiration of the Spirit, call the Messiah 'my Lord'? For David said,

[44] 'The LORD said to my Lord,
   Sit in the place of honor at my right
      hand
   until I humble your enemies
      beneath your feet.'*

[45]Since David called the Messiah 'my Lord,' how can the Messiah be his son?"

[46]No one could answer him. And after that, no one dared to ask him any more questions.

[23:1]THEN Jesus said to the crowds and to his disciples, [2]"The teachers of religious law and the Pharisees are the official interpreters of the law of Moses.* [3]So practice and obey whatever they tell you, but don't follow their example. For they don't practice what they teach. [4]They crush people with unbearable religious demands and never lift a finger to ease the burden.

[5]"Everything they do is for show. On their arms they wear extra wide prayer boxes with Scripture verses inside, and they wear robes with extra long tassels.* [6]And they love to sit at the head table at banquets and in the seats of honor in the synagogues. [7]They love to receive respectful greetings as they walk in the marketplaces, and to be called 'Rabbi.'*

[8]"Don't let anyone call you 'Rabbi,' for you have only one teacher, and all of you are equal as brothers and sisters.* [9]And don't address anyone here on earth as 'Father,' for only God in heaven is your spiritual Father. [10]And don't let anyone call you 'Teacher,' for you have only one teacher, the Messiah. [11]The greatest among you must be a servant. [12]But those who exalt themselves will be humbled, and those who humble themselves will be exalted."

22:37 Deut 6:5.   22:39 Lev 19:18.   22:44 Ps 110:1.
23:2 Greek *and the Pharisees sit in the seat of Moses.*
23:5 Greek *They enlarge their phylacteries and lengthen their tassels.*   23:7 *Rabbi,* from Aramaic, means "master" or "teacher."   23:8 Greek *brothers.*

PSALM 27:7-14

Hear me as I pray, O LORD.
   Be merciful and answer me!
[8] My heart has heard you say,
      "Come and talk with me."
   And my heart responds, "LORD,
      I am coming."
[9] Do not turn your back on me.
   Do not reject your servant
      in anger.
   You have always been my helper.
   Don't leave me now; don't
      abandon me,
   O God of my salvation!
[10] Even if my father and mother
      abandon me,
   the LORD will hold me close.
[11] Teach me how to live, O LORD.
   Lead me along the right path,
      for my enemies are waiting for me.
[12] Do not let me fall into their hands.
   For they accuse me of things I've
      never done;
   with every breath they threaten me
      with violence.
[13] Yet I am confident I will see the LORD's
      goodness
   while I am here in the land of
      the living.
[14] Wait patiently for the LORD.
   Be brave and courageous.
   Yes, wait patiently for the LORD.

PROVERBS 6:27-35

Can a man scoop a flame into his lap and not have his clothes catch on fire? Can he walk on hot coals and not blister his feet? So it is with the man who sleeps with another man's wife. He who embraces her will not go unpunished. □Excuses might be found for a thief who steals because he is starving. But if he is caught, he must pay back seven times what he stole, even if he has to sell everything in his house. But the man who commits adultery is an utter fool, for he destroys himself. He will be wounded and disgraced. His shame will never be erased. For the woman's jealous husband will be furious, and he will show no mercy when he takes revenge. He will accept no compensation, nor be satisfied with a payoff of any size.

EXODUS 19:16–21:21

As God's covenant nation, Israel needed laws to help them function as a just, God-honoring society. Along with many civil and ceremonial laws, God gave the Ten Commandments, a brief but sweeping summary of moral obligations.

On the morning of the third day, thunder roared and lightning flashed, and a dense cloud came down on the mountain. There was a long, loud blast from a ram's horn, and all the people trembled. ¹⁷Moses led them out from the camp to meet with God, and they stood at the foot of the mountain. ¹⁸All of Mount Sinai was covered with smoke because the LORD had descended on it in the form of fire. The smoke billowed into the sky like smoke from a brick kiln, and the whole mountain shook violently. ¹⁹As the blast of the ram's horn grew louder and louder, Moses spoke, and God thundered his reply. ²⁰The LORD came down on the top of Mount Sinai and called Moses to the top of the mountain. So Moses climbed the mountain.

²¹Then the LORD told Moses, "Go back down and warn the people not to break through the boundaries to see the LORD, or they will die. ²²Even the priests who regularly come near to the LORD must purify themselves so that the LORD does not break out and destroy them."

²³"But LORD," Moses protested, "the people cannot come up to Mount Sinai. You already warned us. You told me, 'Mark off a boundary all around the mountain to set it apart as holy.'"

²⁴But the LORD said, "Go down and bring Aaron back up with you. In the meantime, do not let the priests or the people break through to approach the LORD, or he will break out and destroy them."

²⁵So Moses went down to the people and told them what the LORD had said.

²⁰:¹THEN God gave the people all these instructions*:

²"I am the LORD your God, who rescued you from the land of Egypt, the place of your slavery.

³"You must not have any other god but me.

⁴"You must not make for yourself an idol of any kind or an image of anything in the heavens or on the earth or in the sea. ⁵You must not bow down to them or worship them, for I, the LORD your God, am a jealous God who will not tolerate your affection for any other gods. I lay the sins of the parents upon their children; the entire family is affected—even children in the third and fourth generations of those who reject me. ⁶But I lavish unfailing love for a thousand generations on those* who love me and obey my commands.

⁷"You must not misuse the name of the LORD your God. The LORD will not let you go unpunished if you misuse his name.

⁸"Remember to observe the Sabbath day by keeping it holy. ⁹You have six days each week for your ordinary work, ¹⁰but the seventh day is a Sabbath day of rest dedicated to the LORD your God. On that day no one in your household may do any work. This includes you, your sons and daughters, your male and female servants, your livestock, and any foreigners living among you. ¹¹For in six days the LORD made the heavens, the earth, the sea, and everything in them; but on the seventh day he rested. That is why the LORD blessed the Sabbath day and set it apart as holy.

¹²"Honor your father and mother. Then you will live a long, full life in the land the LORD your God is giving you.

¹³"You must not murder.

¹⁴"You must not commit adultery.

¹⁵"You must not steal.

¹⁶"You must not testify falsely against your neighbor.

¹⁷"You must not covet your neighbor's house. You must not covet your neighbor's wife, male or female servant, ox or donkey, or anything else that belongs to your neighbor."

[18]When the people heard the thunder and the loud blast of the ram's horn, and when they saw the flashes of lightning and the smoke billowing from the mountain, they stood at a distance, trembling with fear.

[19]And they said to Moses, "You speak to us, and we will listen. But don't let God speak directly to us, or we will die!"

[20]"Don't be afraid," Moses answered them, "for God has come in this way to test you, and so that your fear of him will keep you from sinning!"

[21]As the people stood in the distance, Moses approached the dark cloud where God was.

[22]And the LORD said to Moses, "Say this to the people of Israel: You saw for yourselves that I spoke to you from heaven. [23]Remember, you must not make any idols of silver or gold to rival me.

[24]"Build for me an altar made of earth, and offer your sacrifices to me—your burnt offerings and peace offerings, your sheep and goats, and your cattle. Build my altar wherever I cause my name to be remembered, and I will come to you and bless you. [25]If you use stones to build my altar, use only natural, uncut stones. Do not shape the stones with a tool, for that would make the altar unfit for holy use. [26]And do not approach my altar by going up steps. If you do, someone might look up under your clothing and see your nakedness.

[21:1]"THESE are the regulations you must present to Israel.

[2]"If you buy a Hebrew slave, he may serve for no more than six years. Set him free in the seventh year, and he will owe you nothing for his freedom. [3]If he was single when he became your slave, he shall leave single. But if he was married before he became a slave, then his wife must be freed with him.

[4]"If his master gave him a wife while he was a slave and they had sons or daughters, then only the man will be free in the seventh year, but his wife and children will still belong to his master. [5]But the slave may declare, 'I love my master, my wife, and my children. I don't want to go free.' [6]If he does this, his master must present him before God.* Then his master must take him to the door or doorpost and publicly pierce his ear with an awl. After that, the slave will serve his master for life.

[7]"When a man sells his daughter as a slave, she will not be freed at the end of six years as the men are. [8]If she does not satisfy her owner, he must allow her to be bought back again. But he is not allowed to sell her to foreigners, since he is the one who broke the contract with her. [9]But if the slave's owner arranges for her to marry his son, he may no longer treat her as a slave but as a daughter.

[10]"If a man who has married a slave wife takes another wife for himself, he must not neglect the rights of the first wife to food, clothing, and sexual intimacy. [11]If he fails in any of these three obligations, she may leave as a free woman without making any payment.

[12]"Anyone who assaults and kills another person must be put to death. [13]But if it was simply an accident permitted by God, I will appoint a place of refuge where the slayer can run for safety. [14]However, if someone deliberately kills another person, then the slayer must be dragged even from my altar and be put to death.

[15]"Anyone who strikes father or mother must be put to death.

[16]"Kidnappers must be put to death, whether they are caught in possession of their victims or have already sold them as slaves.

[17]"Anyone who dishonors* father or mother must be put to death.

[18]"Now suppose two men quarrel, and one hits the other with a stone or fist, and the injured person does not die but is confined to bed. [19]If he is later able to walk outside again, even with a crutch, the assailant will not be punished but must compensate his victim for lost wages and provide for his full recovery.

[20]"If a man beats his male or female slave with a club and the slave dies as a result, the owner must be punished. [21]But if the slave recovers within a day or two, then the owner shall not be punished, since the slave is his property."

20:1 Hebrew *all these words.*   20:6 Hebrew *for thousands of those.*   21:6 Or *before the judges.*   21:17 Greek version reads *Anyone who speaks disrespectfully of.* Compare Matt 15:4; Mark 7:10.

MATTHEW 23:13-39
Jesus stood for the truth no matter how unpopular it made him. He had harsh words for the religious elite who led people astray from the truth by their false holiness.

"**W**hat sorrow awaits you teachers of religious law and you Pharisees. Hypocrites! For you shut the door of the Kingdom of Heaven in people's faces. You won't go in yourselves, and you don't let others enter either.*

15"What sorrow awaits you teachers of religious law and you Pharisees. Hypocrites! For you cross land and sea to make one convert, and then you turn that person into twice the child of hell* you yourselves are!

16"Blind guides! What sorrow awaits you! For you say that it means nothing to swear 'by God's Temple,' but that it is binding to swear 'by the gold in the Temple.' 17Blind fools! Which is more important—the gold or the Temple that makes the gold sacred? 18And you say that to swear 'by the altar' is not binding, but to swear 'by the gifts on the altar' is binding. 19How blind! For which is more important—the gift on the altar or the altar that makes the gift sacred? 20When you swear 'by the altar,' you are swearing by it and by everything on it. 21And when you swear 'by the Temple,' you are swearing by it and by God, who lives in it. 22And when you swear 'by heaven,' you are swearing by the throne of God and by God, who sits on the throne.

23"What sorrow awaits you teachers of religious law and you Pharisees. Hypocrites! For you are careful to tithe even the tiniest income from your herb gardens,* but you ignore the more important aspects of the law—justice, mercy, and faith. You should tithe, yes, but do not neglect the more important things. 24Blind guides! You strain your water so you won't accidentally swallow a gnat, but you swallow a camel!*

25"What sorrow awaits you teachers of religious law and you Pharisees. Hypocrites! For you are so careful to clean the outside of the cup and the dish, but inside you are filthy—full of greed and self-indulgence! 26You blind Pharisee! First wash the inside of the cup and the dish,* and then the outside will become clean, too.

27"What sorrow awaits you teachers of religious law and you Pharisees. Hypocrites! For you are like whitewashed tombs—beautiful on the outside but filled on the inside with dead people's bones and all sorts of impurity. 28Outwardly you look like righteous people, but inwardly your hearts are filled with hypocrisy and lawlessness.

WHAT THE BIBLE SAYS

Right and wrong

EXODUS 20:2-17 The list recorded in Exodus 20:2-17 is known as the Ten Commandments and is the clearest explanation in the Bible of God's moral law. From it, we can understand the difference between right and wrong in almost all areas of life. While this is a list of "do not's," God's law goes much deeper than that. His desire is not just for us to have pure actions, but pure hearts that are focused on him. While some would have us believe that these commandments are no more than archaic laws for another age, their usefulness in society and in people's lives is unsurpassed. • Jesus summed up these commandments by saying, "You must love the LORD your God with all your heart, all your soul, and all your mind" and "Love your neighbor as yourself" (Matthew 22:37, 39, February 3). When your heart and mind are focused on loving God, you will not only know what is right and wrong, but you will be empowered to choose right.

²⁹"What sorrow awaits you teachers of religious law and you Pharisees. Hypocrites! For you build tombs for the prophets your ancestors killed, and you decorate the monuments of the godly people your ancestors destroyed. ³⁰Then you say, 'If we had lived in the days of our ancestors, we would never have joined them in killing the prophets.'

³¹"But in saying that, you testify against yourselves that you are indeed the descendants of those who murdered the prophets. ³²Go ahead and finish what your ancestors started. ³³Snakes! Sons of vipers! How will you escape the judgment of hell?

³⁴"Therefore, I am sending you prophets and wise men and teachers of religious law. But you will kill some by crucifixion, and you will flog others with whips in your synagogues, chasing them from city to city. ³⁵As a result, you will be held responsible for the murder of all godly people of all time—from the murder of righteous Abel to the murder of Zechariah son of Barachiah, whom you killed in the Temple between the sanctuary and the altar. ³⁶I tell you the truth, this judgment will fall on this very generation.

³⁷"O Jerusalem, Jerusalem, the city that kills the prophets and stones God's messengers! How often I have wanted to gather your children together as a hen protects her chicks beneath her wings, but you wouldn't let me. ³⁸And now, look, your house is abandoned and desolate.* ³⁹For I tell you this, you will never see me again until you say, 'Blessings on the one who comes in the name of the LORD!'*"

23:13 Some manuscripts add verse 14, *What sorrow awaits you teachers of religious law and you Pharisees. Hypocrites! You shamelessly cheat widows out of their property and then pretend to be pious by making long prayers in public. Because of this, you will be severely punished.* Compare Mark 12:40 and Luke 20:47. **23:15** Greek *of Gehenna;* also in 23:33. **23:23** Greek *tithe the mint, the dill, and the cumin.* **23:24** See Lev 11:4, 23, where gnats and camels are both forbidden as food. **23:26** Some manuscripts do not include *and the dish.* **23:38** Some manuscripts do not include *and desolate.* **23:39** Ps 118:26.

PSALM 28:1-9
A psalm of David.

¹ I pray to you, O LORD, my rock.
  Do not turn a deaf ear to me.
For if you are silent,
  I might as well give up and die.

² Listen to my prayer for mercy
  as I cry out to you for help,
  as I lift my hands toward your
    holy sanctuary.

³ Do not drag me away with the
    wicked—
  with those who do evil—
those who speak friendly words to
    their neighbors
  while planning evil in their hearts.
⁴ Give them the punishment they so
    richly deserve!
  Measure it out in proportion to
    their wickedness.
Pay them back for all their evil deeds!
  Give them a taste of what they have
    done to others.

⁵ They care nothing for what the LORD
    has done
  or for what his hands have made.
So he will tear them down,
  and they will never be rebuilt!

⁶ Praise the LORD!
  For he has heard my cry for mercy.
⁷ The LORD is my strength and shield.
  I trust him with all my heart.
He helps me, and my heart is filled
    with joy.
  I burst out in songs of thanksgiving.

⁸ The LORD gives his people strength.
  He is a safe fortress for his anointed
    king.
⁹ Save your people!
  Bless Israel, your special
    possession.*
Lead them like a shepherd,
  and carry them in your arms forever.
28:9 Hebrew *Bless your inheritance.*

PROVERBS 7:1-5
Follow my advice, my son; always treasure my commands. Obey my commands and live! Guard my instructions as you guard your own eyes.* Tie them on your fingers as a reminder. Write them deep within your heart. □ Love wisdom like a sister; make insight a beloved member of your family. Let them protect you from an affair with an immoral woman, from listening to the flattery of a promiscuous woman.
7:2 Hebrew *as the pupil of your eye.*

EXODUS 21:22–23:13

The laws God gave his people were guidelines on how they should live together and function as a God-fearing nation.

"**N**ow suppose two men are fighting, and in the process they accidentally strike a pregnant woman so she gives birth prematurely.* If no further injury results, the man who struck the woman must pay the amount of compensation the woman's husband demands and the judges approve. 23But if there is further injury, the punishment must match the injury: a life for a life, 24an eye for an eye, a tooth for a tooth, a hand for a hand, a foot for a foot, 25a burn for a burn, a wound for a wound, a bruise for a bruise.

26"If a man hits his male or female slave in the eye and the eye is blinded, he must let the slave go free to compensate for the eye. 27And if a man knocks out the tooth of his male or female slave, he must let the slave go free to compensate for the tooth.

28"If an ox* gores a man or woman to death, the ox must be stoned, and its flesh may not be eaten. In such a case, however, the owner will not be held liable. 29But suppose the ox had a reputation for goring, and the owner had been informed but failed to keep it under control. If the ox then kills someone, it must be stoned, and the owner must also be put to death. 30However, the dead person's relatives may accept payment to compensate for the loss of life. The owner of the ox may redeem his life by paying whatever is demanded.

31"The same regulation applies if the ox gores a boy or a girl. 32But if the ox gores a slave, either male or female, the animal's owner must pay the slave's owner thirty silver coins,* and the ox must be stoned.

33"Suppose someone digs or uncovers a pit and fails to cover it, and then an ox or a donkey falls into it. 34The owner of the pit must pay full compensation to the owner of the animal, but then he gets to keep the dead animal.

35"If someone's ox injures a neighbor's ox and the injured ox dies, then the two owners must sell the live ox and divide the price equally between them. They must also divide the dead animal. 36But if the ox had a reputation for goring, yet its owner failed to keep it under control, he must pay full compensation—a live ox for the dead one—but he may keep the dead ox.

22:1*"IF someone steals an ox* or sheep and then kills or sells it, the thief must pay back five oxen for each ox stolen, and four sheep for each sheep stolen.

2*"If a thief is caught in the act of breaking into a house and is struck and killed in the process, the person who killed the thief is not guilty of murder. 3But if it happens in daylight, the one who killed the thief is guilty of murder.

"A thief who is caught must pay in full for everything he stole. If he cannot pay, he must be sold as a slave to pay for his theft. 4If someone steals an ox or a donkey or a sheep and it is found in the thief's possession, then the thief must pay double the value of the stolen animal.

5"If an animal is grazing in a field or vineyard and the owner lets it stray into someone else's field to graze, then the animal's owner must pay compensation from the best of his own grain or grapes.

6"If you are burning thornbushes and the fire gets out of control and spreads into another person's field, destroying the sheaves or the uncut grain or the whole crop, the one who started the fire must pay for the lost crop.

7"Suppose someone leaves money or goods with a neighbor for safekeeping, and they are stolen from the neighbor's house. If the thief is caught, the compensation is double the value of what was stolen. 8But if the thief is not caught, the neighbor must appear before God,* who will determine if he stole the property.

9"Suppose there is a dispute between two people who both claim to own a particular ox, donkey, sheep, article of clothing, or any lost property. Both parties must come before God, and the person whom God declares* guilty must pay double compensation to the other.

¹⁰"Now suppose someone leaves a donkey, ox, sheep, or any other animal with a neighbor for safekeeping, but it dies or is injured or gets away, and no one sees what happened. ¹¹The neighbor must then take an oath in the presence of the LORD. If the LORD confirms that the neighbor did not steal the property, the owner must accept the verdict, and no payment will be required. ¹²But if the animal was indeed stolen, the guilty person must pay compensation to the owner. ¹³If it was torn to pieces by a wild animal, the remains of the carcass must be shown as evidence, and no compensation will be required.

¹⁴"If someone borrows an animal from a neighbor and it is injured or dies when the owner is absent, the person who borrowed it must pay full compensation. ¹⁵But if the owner was present, no compensation is required. And no compensation is required if the animal was rented, for this loss is covered by the rental fee.

¹⁶"If a man seduces a virgin who is not engaged to anyone and has sex with her, he must pay the customary bride price and marry her. ¹⁷But if her father refuses to let him marry her, the man must still pay him an amount equal to the bride price of a virgin.

¹⁸"You must not allow a sorceress to live.

¹⁹"Anyone who has sexual relations with an animal must certainly be put to death.

²⁰"Anyone who sacrifices to any god other than the LORD must be destroyed.*

²¹"You must not mistreat or oppress foreigners in any way. Remember, you yourselves were once foreigners in the land of Egypt.

²²"You must not exploit a widow or an orphan. ²³If you exploit them in any way and they cry out to me, then I will certainly hear their cry. ²⁴My anger will blaze against you, and I will kill you with the sword. Then your wives will be widows and your children fatherless.

²⁵"If you lend money to any of my people who are in need, do not charge interest as a money lender would. ²⁶If you take your neighbor's cloak as security for a loan, you must return it before sunset. ²⁷This coat may be the only blanket your neighbor has. How can a person sleep without it? If you do not return it and your neighbor cries out to me for help, then I will hear, for I am merciful.

²⁸"You must not dishonor God or curse any of your rulers.

²⁹"You must not hold anything back when you give me offerings from your crops and your wine.

"You must give me your firstborn sons.

³⁰"You must also give me the firstborn of your cattle, sheep, and goats. But leave the newborn animal with its mother for seven days; then give it to me on the eighth day.

³¹"You must be my holy people. Therefore, do not eat any animal that has been torn up and killed by wild animals. Throw it to the dogs.

²³:¹"You must not pass along false rumors. You must not cooperate with evil people by lying on the witness stand.

²"You must not follow the crowd in doing wrong. When you are called to testify in a dispute, do not be swayed by the crowd to twist justice. ³And do not slant your testimony in favor of a person just because that person is poor.

⁴"If you come upon your enemy's ox or donkey that has strayed away, take it back to its owner. ⁵If you see that the donkey of someone who hates you has collapsed under its load, do not walk by. Instead, stop and help.

⁶"In a lawsuit, you must not deny justice to the poor.

⁷"Be sure never to charge anyone falsely with evil. Never sentence an innocent or blameless person to death, for I never declare a guilty person to be innocent.

⁸"Take no bribes, for a bribe makes you ignore something that you clearly see. A bribe makes even a righteous person twist the truth.

⁹"You must not oppress foreigners. You know what it's like to be a foreigner, for you yourselves were once foreigners in the land of Egypt.

¹⁰"Plant and harvest your crops for six

years, [11]but let the land be renewed and lie uncultivated during the seventh year. Then let the poor among you harvest whatever grows on its own. Leave the rest for wild animals to eat. The same applies to your vineyards and olive groves.

[12]"You have six days each week for your ordinary work, but on the seventh day you must stop working. This gives your ox and your donkey a chance to rest. It also allows your slaves and the foreigners living among you to be refreshed.

[13]"Pay close attention to all my instructions. You must not call on the name of any other gods. Do not even speak their names."

21:22 Or *so she has a miscarriage;* Hebrew reads *so her children come out.* 21:28 Or *bull,* or *cow;* also in 21:29-36. 21:32 Hebrew *30 shekels of silver,* about 12 ounces or 342 grams in weight. 22:1a Verse 22:1 is numbered 21:37 in Hebrew text. 22:1b Or *bull,* or *cow;* also in 22:4, 9, 10. 22:2 Verses 22:2-31 are numbered 22:1-30 in Hebrew text. 22:8 Or *before the judges.* 22:9 Or *before the judges, and the person whom the judges declare.* 22:20 The Hebrew term used here refers to the complete consecration of things or people to the LORD, either by destroying them or by giving them as an offering.

MATTHEW 24:1-28

With his closest companions beside him, Jesus addressed both the immediate future and the distant future. His news was daunting on both counts.

As Jesus was leaving the Temple grounds, his disciples pointed out to him the various Temple buildings. [2]But he responded, "Do you see all these buildings? I tell you the truth, they will be completely demolished. Not one stone will be left on top of another!"

[3]Later, Jesus sat on the Mount of Olives. His disciples came to him privately and said, "Tell us, when will all this happen? What sign will signal your return and the end of the world?*"

[4]Jesus told them, "Don't let anyone mislead you, [5]for many will come in my name, claiming, 'I am the Messiah.' They will deceive many. [6]And you will hear of wars and threats of wars, but don't panic. Yes, these things must take place, but the end won't follow immediately. [7]Nation will go to war against nation, and kingdom against kingdom. There will be famines and earthquakes in many parts of the world. [8]But all this is only the first of the birth pains, with more to come.

[9]"Then you will be arrested, persecuted, and killed. You will be hated all over the world because you are my followers.* [10]And many will turn away from me and betray and hate each other. [11]And many false prophets will appear and will deceive many people. [12]Sin will be rampant everywhere, and the love of many will grow cold. [13]But the one who endures to the end will be saved. [14]And

The laws of the Old Testament

WHAT THE BIBLE SAYS

EXODUS 22:22-24   The Old Testament laws may be divided into three categories. (1) *Moral laws* (such as the command not to steal) include the rules that transcend time. (2) *Ceremonial laws* (such as those about sacrifices that you'll read in Leviticus) focused on Israel's worship. (3) *Civil laws,* such as what you're reading here, gave practical advice about how to keep such a large group of people in order.   • Do we need to follow these laws today? The moral law is still to be followed, for it reveals God's character, and God is unchanging. The ceremonial laws no longer need to be followed because the final sacrifice for sin has been made by Jesus. The civil law should be followed in spirit, for while the cultural details will differ, the point is that God wanted to instill in his people a sense of personal responsibility and justice. Look past the detail of the situations to the overarching truth. While you may not have an ox that gores someone's slave, you may have a child who breaks a neighbor's window with a baseball. The principles of honesty, responsibility, and restitution found in God's Word are what we should follow today.

the Good News about the Kingdom will be preached throughout the whole world, so that all nations* will hear it; and then the end will come.

15"The day is coming when you will see what Daniel the prophet spoke about—the sacrilegious object that causes desecration* standing in the Holy Place." (Reader, pay attention!) 16"Then those in Judea must flee to the hills. 17A person out on the deck of a roof must not go down into the house to pack. 18A person out in the field must not return even to get a coat. 19How terrible it will be for pregnant women and for nursing mothers in those days. 20And pray that your flight will not be in winter or on the Sabbath. 21For there will be greater anguish than at any time since the world began. And it will never be so great again. 22In fact, unless that time of calamity is shortened, not a single person will survive. But it will be shortened for the sake of God's chosen ones.

23"Then if anyone tells you, 'Look, here is the Messiah,' or 'There he is,' don't believe it. 24For false messiahs and false prophets will rise up and perform great signs and wonders so as to deceive, if possible, even God's chosen ones. 25See, I have warned you about this ahead of time.

26"So if someone tells you, 'Look, the Messiah is out in the desert,' don't bother to go and look. Or, 'Look, he is hiding here,' don't believe it! 27For as the lightning flashes in the east and shines to the west, so it will be when the Son of Man* comes. 28Just as the gathering of vultures shows there is a carcass nearby, so these signs indicate that the end is near.*"

24:3 Or *the age?*   **24:9** Greek *on account of my name.*
24:14 Or *all peoples.*   **24:15** Greek *the abomination of desolation.* See Dan 9:27; 11:31; 12:11.   **24:27** "Son of Man" is a title Jesus used for himself.   **24:28** Greek *Wherever the carcass is, the vultures gather.*

PSALM 29:1-11
A psalm of David.

1 Honor the LORD, you heavenly
        beings*;
    honor the LORD for his glory and
        strength.
2 Honor the LORD for the glory of
        his name.

Worship the LORD in the splendor
    of his holiness.
3 The voice of the LORD echoes above
        the sea.
    The God of glory thunders.
    The LORD thunders over the
        mighty sea.
4 The voice of the LORD is powerful;
    the voice of the LORD is majestic.
5 The voice of the LORD splits the
        mighty cedars;
    the LORD shatters the cedars of
        Lebanon.
6 He makes Lebanon's mountains skip
        like a calf;
    he makes Mount Hermon* leap
        like a young wild ox.
7 The voice of the LORD strikes
    with bolts of lightning.
8 The voice of the LORD makes the
        barren wilderness quake;
    the LORD shakes the wilderness
        of Kadesh.
9 The voice of the LORD twists mighty
        oaks*
    and strips the forests bare.
    In his Temple everyone shouts, "Glory!"

10 The LORD rules over the floodwaters.
    The LORD reigns as king forever.
11 The LORD gives his people strength.
    The LORD blesses them with peace.

29:1 Hebrew *you sons of God.*   **29:6** Hebrew *Sirion,* another name for Mount Hermon.   **29:9** Or *causes the deer to writhe in labor.*

PROVERBS 7:6-23
While I was at the window of my house, looking through the curtain, I saw some naive young men, and one in particular who lacked common sense. He was crossing the street near the house of an immoral woman, strolling down the path by her house. It was at twilight, in the evening, as deep darkness fell. The woman approached him, seductively dressed and sly of heart. She was the brash, rebellious type, never content to stay at home. She is often in the streets and markets, soliciting at every corner. She threw her arms around him and kissed him, and with a brazen look she said, "I've just made my peace offerings and fulfilled my vows. You're the one I was looking for! I came

out to find you, and here you are! My bed is spread with beautiful blankets, with colored sheets of Egyptian linen. I've perfumed my bed with myrrh, aloes, and cinnamon. Come, let's drink our fill of love until morning. Let's enjoy each other's caresses, for my husband is not home. He's away on a long trip. He has taken a wallet full of money with him and won't return until later this month.*" □ So she seduced him with her pretty speech and enticed him with her flattery. He followed her at once, like an ox going to the slaughter. He was like a stag caught in a trap, awaiting the arrow that would pierce its heart. He was like a bird flying into a snare, little knowing it would cost him his life.

7:20 Hebrew *until the moon is full.*

FEBRUARY**6**

EXODUS 23:14–25:40

God gave the Israelites festivals to celebrate in order to help them remember his gracious acts on their behalf. He also gave Moses detailed instructions for the Tabernacle, a portable worship center that would be a part of Israelite culture for hundreds of years.

"**E**ach year you must celebrate three festivals in my honor. ¹⁵First, celebrate the Festival of Unleavened Bread. For seven days the bread you eat must be made without yeast, just as I commanded you. Celebrate this festival annually at the appointed time in early spring, in the month of Abib,* for that is the anniversary of your departure from Egypt. No one may appear before me without an offering.

¹⁶"Second, celebrate the Festival of Harvest,* when you bring me the first crops of your harvest.

"Finally, celebrate the Festival of the Final Harvest* at the end of the harvest season, when you have harvested all the crops from your fields. ¹⁷At these three times each year, every man in Israel must appear before the Sovereign, the LORD.

¹⁸"You must not offer the blood of my sacrificial offerings together with any baked goods containing yeast. And do not leave the fat from the festival offerings until the next morning.

¹⁹"As you harvest your crops, bring the very best of the first harvest to the house of the LORD your God.

"You must not cook a young goat in its mother's milk.

²⁰"See, I am sending an angel before you to protect you on your journey and lead you safely to the place I have prepared for you. ²¹Pay close attention to him, and obey his instructions. Do not rebel against him, for he is my representative, and he will not forgive your rebellion. ²²But if you are careful to obey him, following all my instructions, then I will be an enemy to your enemies, and I will oppose those who oppose you. ²³For my angel will go before you and bring you into the land of the Amorites, Hittites, Perizzites, Canaanites, Hivites, and Jebusites, so you may live there. And I will destroy them completely. ²⁴You must not worship the gods of these nations or serve them in any way or imitate their evil practices. Instead, you must utterly destroy them and smash their sacred pillars.

²⁵"You must serve only the LORD your God. If you do, I* will bless you with food and water, and I will protect you from illness. ²⁶There will be no miscarriages or infertility in your land, and I will give you long, full lives.

²⁷"I will send my terror ahead of you and create panic among all the people whose lands you invade. I will make all your enemies turn and run. ²⁸I will send terror* ahead of you to drive out the Hivites, Canaanites, and Hittites. ²⁹But I will not drive them out in a single year, because the land would become desolate and the wild animals would multiply and threaten you. ³⁰I will drive them out a little

at a time until your population has increased enough to take possession of the land. ³¹And I will fix your boundaries from the Red Sea to the Mediterranean Sea,* and from the eastern wilderness to the Euphrates River.* I will hand over to you the people now living in the land, and you will drive them out ahead of you.

³²"Make no treaties with them or their gods. ³³They must not live in your land, or they will cause you to sin against me. If you serve their gods, you will be caught in the trap of idolatry."

²⁴:¹THEN the LORD instructed Moses: "Come up here to me, and bring along Aaron, Nadab, Abihu, and seventy of Israel's elders. All of you must worship from a distance. ²Only Moses is allowed to come near to the LORD. The others must not come near, and none of the other people are allowed to climb up the mountain with him."

³Then Moses went down to the people and repeated all the instructions and regulations the LORD had given him. All the people answered with one voice, "We will do everything the LORD has commanded."

⁴Then Moses carefully wrote down all the LORD's instructions. Early the next morning Moses got up and built an altar at the foot of the mountain. He also set up twelve pillars, one for each of the twelve tribes of Israel. ⁵Then he sent some of the young Israelite men to present burnt offerings and to sacrifice bulls as peace offerings to the LORD. ⁶Moses drained half the blood from these animals into basins. The other half he splattered against the altar.

⁷Then he took the Book of the Covenant and read it aloud to the people. Again they all responded, "We will do everything the LORD has commanded. We will obey."

⁸Then Moses took the blood from the basins and splattered it over the people, declaring, "Look, this blood confirms the covenant the LORD has made with you in giving you these instructions."

⁹Then Moses, Aaron, Nadab, Abihu, and the seventy elders of Israel climbed up the mountain. ¹⁰There they saw the God of Israel. Under his feet there

seemed to be a surface of brilliant blue lapis lazuli, as clear as the sky itself. ¹¹And though these nobles of Israel gazed upon God, he did not destroy them. In fact, they ate a covenant meal, eating and drinking in his presence!

¹²Then the LORD said to Moses, "Come up to me on the mountain. Stay there, and I will give you the tablets of stone on which I have inscribed the instructions and commands so you can teach the people." ¹³So Moses and his assistant Joshua set out, and Moses climbed up the mountain of God.

¹⁴Moses told the elders, "Stay here and wait for us until we come back. Aaron and Hur are here with you. If anyone has a dispute while I am gone, consult with them."

¹⁵Then Moses climbed up the mountain, and the cloud covered it. ¹⁶And the glory of the LORD settled down on Mount Sinai, and the cloud covered it for six days. On the seventh day the LORD called to Moses from inside the cloud. ¹⁷To the Israelites at the foot of the mountain, the glory of the LORD appeared at the summit like a consuming fire. ¹⁸Then Moses disappeared into the cloud as he climbed higher up the mountain. He remained on the mountain forty days and forty nights.

²⁵:¹THE LORD said to Moses, ²"Tell the people of Israel to bring me their sacred offerings. Accept the contributions from all whose hearts are moved to offer them. ³Here is a list of sacred offerings you may accept from them:

gold, silver, and bronze;
⁴ blue, purple, and scarlet thread;
fine linen and goat hair for cloth;
⁵ tanned ram skins and fine goatskin leather;
acacia wood;
⁶ olive oil for the lamps;
spices for the anointing oil and the fragrant incense;
⁷ onyx stones, and other gemstones to be set in the ephod and the priest's chestpiece.

⁸"Have the people of Israel build me a holy sanctuary so I can live among them. ⁹You must build this Tabernacle and its

furnishings exactly according to the pattern I will show you.

¹⁰"Have the people make an Ark of acacia wood—a sacred chest 45 inches long, 27 inches wide, and 27 inches high.* ¹¹Overlay it inside and outside with pure gold, and run a molding of gold all around it. ¹²Cast four gold rings and attach them to its four feet, two rings on each side. ¹³Make poles from acacia wood, and overlay them with gold. ¹⁴Insert the poles into the rings at the sides of the Ark to carry it. ¹⁵These carrying poles must stay inside the rings; never remove them. ¹⁶When the Ark is finished, place inside it the stone tablets inscribed with the terms of the covenant,* which I will give to you.

¹⁷"Then make the Ark's cover—the place of atonement—from pure gold. It must be 45 inches long and 27 inches wide.* ¹⁸Then make two cherubim from hammered gold, and place them on the two ends of the atonement cover. ¹⁹Mold the cherubim on each end of the atonement cover, making it all of one piece of gold. ²⁰The cherubim will face each other and look down on the atonement cover. With their wings spread above it, they will protect it. ²¹Place inside the Ark the stone tablets inscribed with the terms of the covenant, which I will give to you. Then put the atonement cover on top of the Ark. ²²I will meet with you there and talk to you from above the atonement cover between the gold cherubim that hover over the Ark of the Covenant.* From there I will give you my commands for the people of Israel.

²³"Then make a table of acacia wood, 36 inches long, 18 inches wide, and 27 inches high.* ²⁴Overlay it with pure gold and run a gold molding around the edge. ²⁵Decorate it with a 3-inch border* all around, and run a gold molding along the border. ²⁶Make four gold rings for the table and attach them at the four corners next to the four legs. ²⁷Attach the rings near the border to hold the poles that are used to carry the table. ²⁸Make these poles from acacia wood, and overlay them with gold. ²⁹Make special containers of pure gold for the table—bowls, pans, pitchers, and jars—to be used in pouring out liquid offerings. ³⁰Place the Bread of the Presence on the table to remain before me at all times.

³¹"Make a lampstand of pure, hammered gold. Make the entire lampstand and its decorations of one piece—the base, center stem, lamp cups, buds, and petals. ³²Make it with six branches going out from the center stem, three on each side. ³³Each of the six branches will have three lamp cups shaped like almond blossoms, complete with buds and petals.

WHAT THE BIBLE SAYS

Angels

MATTHEW 24:30-31 Popular culture has a certain fascination with angels—whether as the subject of television dramas or atop the Christmas tree. What does the Bible teach us about their true nature and purpose?
• In every Scripture in which they are mentioned, angels are serving God, doing whatever he asks. Aside from their appearance to the shepherds announcing the birth of Jesus, and the angel in the garden announcing Jesus' resurrection, angels are rarely seen in the New Testament. • Why do they remain invisible to the human race? There is little doubt that if God allowed us to see angels on a regular basis, we might be so awed at their beauty that we would begin to worship them instead of their Creator. God created angels as unique spiritual beings who worship Christ and bring messages to his followers. God also at times orders his angels to protect us. And, as mentioned in today's reading, angels will be there to escort you and every other believer on earth to heaven when the final trumpet calls all Christians to our eternal home.

³⁴Craft the center stem of the lampstand with four lamp cups shaped like almond blossoms, complete with buds and petals. ³⁵There will also be an almond bud beneath each pair of branches where the six branches extend from the center stem. ³⁶The almond buds and branches must all be of one piece with the center stem, and they must be hammered from pure gold. ³⁷Then make the seven lamps for the lampstand, and set them so they reflect their light forward. ³⁸The lamp snuffers and trays must also be made of pure gold. ³⁹You will need seventy-five pounds* of pure gold for the lampstand and its accessories.

⁴⁰"Be sure that you make everything according to the pattern I have shown you here on the mountain."

23:15 Hebrew *appointed time in the month of Abib.* This first month of the ancient Hebrew lunar calendar usually occurs within the months of March and April.   23:16a Or *Festival of Weeks.* This was later called the Festival of Pentecost (see Acts 2:1). It is celebrated today as Shavuat (or Shabuoth).   23:16b Or *Festival of Ingathering.* This was later called the Festival of Shelters or Festival of Tabernacles (see Lev 23:33-36). It is celebrated today as Sukkot (or Succoth).   23:25 As in Greek and Latin versions; Hebrew reads *he.*   23:28 Often rendered *the hornet.* The meaning of the Hebrew is uncertain.   23:31a Hebrew *from the sea of reeds to the sea of the Philistines.*   23:31b Hebrew *from the wilderness to the river.*   25:10 Hebrew *2.5 cubits* [115 centimeters] *long, 1.5 cubits* [69 centimeters] *wide, and 1.5 cubits high.*   25:16 Hebrew *Place inside the Ark the Testimony;* similarly in 25:21. The Hebrew word for "testimony" refers to the terms of the LORD's covenant with Israel as written on stone tablets, and also to the covenant itself.   25:17 Hebrew *2.5 cubits* [115 centimeters] *long and 1.5 cubits* [69 centimeters] *wide.*   25:22 Or *Ark of the Testimony.*   25:23 Hebrew *2 cubits* [92 centimeters] *long, 1 cubit* [46 centimeters] *wide, and 1.5 cubits* [69 centimeters] *high.*   25:25 Hebrew *a border of a handbreadth* [8 centimeters].   25:39 Hebrew *1 talent* [34 kilograms].

MATTHEW 24:29-51

One day, the world as we know it will come to an end. Then those who have followed Jesus will enjoy their rewards forever with him. Those who haven't— those who have put it off or who have refused his offer—will find themselves left out of God's presence.

"Immediately after the anguish of those days,

the sun will be darkened,
    the moon will give no light,
    the stars will fall from the sky,
    and the powers in the heavens will
        be shaken.*

³⁰And then at last, the sign that the Son of Man is coming will appear in the heavens, and there will be deep mourning among all the peoples of the earth. And they will see the Son of Man coming on the clouds of heaven with power and great glory.* ³¹And he will send out his angels with the mighty blast of a trumpet, and they will gather his chosen ones from all over the world*—from the farthest ends of the earth and heaven.

³²"Now learn a lesson from the fig tree. When its branches bud and its leaves begin to sprout, you know that summer is near. ³³In the same way, when you see all these things, you can know his return is very near, right at the door. ³⁴I tell you the truth, this generation* will not pass from the scene until all these things take place. ³⁵Heaven and earth will disappear, but my words will never disappear.

³⁶"However, no one knows the day or hour when these things will happen, not even the angels in heaven or the Son himself.* Only the Father knows.

³⁷"When the Son of Man returns, it will be like it was in Noah's day. ³⁸In those days before the flood, the people were enjoying banquets and parties and weddings right up to the time Noah entered his boat. ³⁹People didn't realize what was going to happen until the flood came and swept them all away. That is the way it will be when the Son of Man comes.

⁴⁰"Two men will be working together in the field; one will be taken, the other left. ⁴¹Two women will be grinding flour at the mill; one will be taken, the other left.

⁴²"So you, too, must keep watch! For you don't know what day your Lord is coming. ⁴³Understand this: If a homeowner knew exactly when a burglar was coming, he would keep watch and not permit his house to be broken into. ⁴⁴You also must be ready all the time, for the Son of Man will come when least expected.

⁴⁵"A faithful, sensible servant is one to whom the master can give the responsibility of managing his other household servants and feeding them. ⁴⁶If the master returns and finds that the servant has done a good job, there will be a reward. ⁴⁷I tell you the truth, the master will put that servant in charge of all he owns. ⁴⁸But what if the servant is evil and thinks, 'My master won't be back for a while,' ⁴⁹and he begins

beating the other servants, partying, and getting drunk? ⁵⁰The master will return unannounced and unexpected, ⁵¹and he will cut the servant to pieces and assign him a place with the hypocrites. In that place there will be weeping and gnashing of teeth."

24:29 See Isa 13:10; 34:4; Joel 2:10.   **24:30** See Dan 7:13. **24:31** Greek *from the four winds.*   **24:34** Or *this age,* or *this nation.*   **24:36** Some manuscripts do not include *or the Son himself.*

PSALM 30:1-12
A psalm of David. A song for the dedication of the Temple.

¹ **I** will exalt you, LORD, for you rescued me.
  You refused to let my enemies triumph over me.
² O LORD my God, I cried to you for help, and you restored my health.
³ You brought me up from the grave,*
  O LORD.
  You kept me from falling into the pit of death.

⁴ Sing to the LORD, all you godly ones!
  Praise his holy name.
⁵ For his anger lasts only a moment, but his favor lasts a lifetime!
  Weeping may last through the night, but joy comes with the morning.

⁶ When I was prosperous, I said,
  "Nothing can stop me now!"

⁷ Your favor, O LORD, made me as secure as a mountain.
  Then you turned away from me, and I was shattered.

⁸ I cried out to you, O LORD.
  I begged the Lord for mercy, saying,
⁹ "What will you gain if I die, if I sink into the grave?
  Can my dust praise you?
  Can it tell of your faithfulness?
¹⁰ Hear me, LORD, and have mercy on me.
  Help me, O LORD."

¹¹ You have turned my mourning into joyful dancing.
  You have taken away my clothes of mourning and clothed me with joy,
¹² that I might sing praises to you and not be silent.
  O LORD my God, I will give you thanks forever!

30:3 Hebrew *from Sheol.*

PROVERBS 7:24-27
So listen to me, my sons, and pay attention to my words. Don't let your hearts stray away toward her. Don't wander down her wayward path. For she has been the ruin of many; many men have been her victims. Her house is the road to the grave.* Her bedroom is the den of death.

7:27 Hebrew *to Sheol.*

FEBRUARY**7**

EXODUS 26:1–27:21
Further details for the construction of the Tabernacle, the sanctuary structure that would serve as God's dwelling place among the people. The very act of building this structure was an act of worship.

"**M**ake the Tabernacle from ten curtains of finely woven linen. Decorate the curtains with blue, purple, and scarlet thread and with skillfully embroidered cherubim. ²These ten curtains must all be ex-

actly the same size—42 feet long and 6 feet wide.* ³Join five of these curtains together to make one long curtain, then join the other five into a second long curtain. ⁴Put loops of blue yarn along the edge of the last curtain in each set. ⁵The fifty loops along the edge of one curtain are to match the fifty loops along the edge of the other curtain. ⁶Then make fifty gold clasps and fasten the long curtains together with the clasps. In this way, the Tabernacle will be made of one continuous piece.

[7]"Make eleven curtains of goat-hair cloth to serve as a tent covering for the Tabernacle. [8]These eleven curtains must all be exactly the same size—45 feet long and 6 feet wide.* [9]Join five of these curtains together to make one long curtain, and join the other six into a second long curtain. Allow 3 feet of material from the second set of curtains to hang over the front* of the sacred tent. [10]Make fifty loops for one edge of each large curtain. [11]Then make fifty bronze clasps, and fasten the loops of the long curtains with the clasps. In this way, the tent covering will be made of one continuous piece. [12]The remaining 3 feet* of this tent covering will be left to hang over the back of the Tabernacle. [13]Allow 18 inches* of remaining material to hang down over each side, so the Tabernacle is completely covered. [14]Complete the tent covering with a protective layer of tanned ram skins and a layer of fine goatskin leather.

[15]"For the framework of the Tabernacle, construct frames of acacia wood. [16]Each frame must be 15 feet high and 27 inches wide,* [17]with two pegs under each frame. Make all the frames identical. [18]Make twenty of these frames to support the curtains on the south side of the Tabernacle. [19]Also make forty silver bases—two bases under each frame, with the pegs fitting securely into the bases. [20]For the north side of the Tabernacle, make another twenty frames, [21]with their forty silver bases, two bases under each frame. [22]Make six frames for the rear—the west side of the Tabernacle—[23]along with two additional frames to reinforce the rear corners of the Tabernacle. [24]These corner frames will be matched at the bottom and firmly attached at the top with a single ring, forming a single corner unit. Make both of these corner units the same way. [25]So there will be eight frames at the rear of the Tabernacle, set in sixteen silver bases—two bases under each frame.

[26]"Make crossbars of acacia wood to link the frames, five crossbars for the north side of the Tabernacle [27]and five for the south side. Also make five crossbars for the rear of the Tabernacle, which will face west. [28]The middle crossbar, attached halfway up the frames, will run all the way from one end of the Tabernacle to the other. [29]Overlay the frames with gold, and make gold rings to hold the crossbars. Overlay the crossbars with gold as well.

[30]"Set up this Tabernacle according to the pattern you were shown on the mountain.

[31]"For the inside of the Tabernacle, make a special curtain of finely woven linen. Decorate it with blue, purple, and scarlet thread and with skillfully embroidered cherubim. [32]Hang this curtain on gold hooks attached to four posts of acacia wood. Overlay the posts with gold, and set them in four silver bases. [33]Hang the inner curtain from clasps, and put the Ark of the Covenant* in the room behind it. This curtain will separate the Holy Place from the Most Holy Place.

[34]"Then put the Ark's cover—the place of atonement—on top of the Ark of the Covenant inside the Most Holy Place. [35]Place the table outside the inner curtain on the north side of the Tabernacle, and place the lampstand across the room on the south side.

[36]"Make another curtain for the entrance to the sacred tent. Make it of finely woven linen and embroider it with exquisite designs, using blue, purple, and scarlet thread. [37]Craft five posts from acacia wood. Overlay them with gold, and hang the curtain from them with gold hooks. Cast five bronze bases for the posts.

[27:1]"USING acacia wood, construct a square altar 7½ feet wide, 7½ feet long, and 4½ feet high.* [2]Make horns for each of its four corners so that the horns and altar are all one piece. Overlay the altar with bronze. [3]Make ash buckets, shovels, basins, meat forks, and firepans, all of bronze. [4]Make a bronze grating for it, and attach four bronze rings at its four corners. [5]Install the grating halfway down the side of the altar, under the ledge. [6]For carrying the altar, make poles from acacia wood, and overlay them with bronze. [7]Insert the poles through the rings on the two sides of the altar. [8]The altar must be hollow, made from planks. Build it just as you were shown on the mountain.

9"Then make the courtyard for the Tabernacle, enclosed with curtains made of finely woven linen. On the south side, make the curtains 150 feet long.* 10They will be held up by twenty posts set securely in twenty bronze bases. Hang the curtains with silver hooks and rings. 11Make the curtains the same on the north side—150 feet of curtains held up by twenty posts set securely in bronze bases. Hang the curtains with silver hooks and rings. 12The curtains on the west end of the courtyard will be 75 feet long,* supported by ten posts set into ten bases. 13The east end of the courtyard, the front, will also be 75 feet long. 14The courtyard entrance will be on the east end, flanked by two curtains. The curtain on the right side will be 22½ feet long,* supported by three posts set into three bases. 15The curtain on the left side will also be 22½ feet long, supported by three posts set into three bases.

16"For the entrance to the courtyard, make a curtain that is 30 feet long.* Make it from finely woven linen, and decorate it with beautiful embroidery in blue, purple, and scarlet thread. Support it with four posts, each securely set in its own base. 17All the posts around the courtyard must have silver rings and hooks and bronze bases. 18So the entire courtyard will be 150 feet long and 75 feet wide, with curtain walls 7½ feet high,* made from finely woven linen. The bases for the posts will be made of bronze.

19"All the articles used in the rituals of the Tabernacle, including all the tent pegs used to support the Tabernacle and the courtyard curtains, must be made of bronze.

20"Command the people of Israel to bring you pure oil of pressed olives for the light, to keep the lamps burning continually. 21The lampstand will stand in the Tabernacle, in front of the inner curtain that shields the Ark of the Covenant.* Aaron and his sons must keep the lamps burning in the LORD's presence all night. This is a permanent law for the people of Israel, and it must be observed from generation to generation."

26:2 Hebrew *28 cubits* [12.9 meters] *long and 4 cubits* [1.8 meters] *wide.*   26:8 Hebrew *30 cubits* [13.8 meters] *long and 4 cubits* [1.8 meters] *wide.*   26:9 Hebrew *Double over the sixth sheet at the front.*   26:12 Hebrew *The half sheet that is left over.*   26:13 Hebrew *1 cubit* [46 centimeters].   26:16 Hebrew *10 cubits* [4.6 meters] *high and 1.5 cubits* [69 centimeters] *wide.*   26:33 Or *Ark of the Testimony;* also in 26:34.   27:1 Hebrew *5 cubits* [2.3 meters] *wide, 5 cubits long, a square, and 3 cubits* [1.4 meters] *high.*   27:9 Hebrew *100 cubits* [46 meters]; also in 27:11.   27:12 Hebrew *50 cubits* [23 meters]; also in 27:13.   27:14 Hebrew *15 cubits* [6.9 meters]; also in 27:15.   27:16 Hebrew *20 cubits* [9.2 meters].   27:18 Hebrew *100 cubits* [46 meters] *long and 50 cubits* [23 meters] *wide and 5 cubits* [2.3 meters] *high.*   27:21 Hebrew *in the Tent of Meeting, outside the inner curtain that is in front of the Testimony.* See note on 25:16.

HOW WE LIVE

Following Jesus

MATTHEW 25:13 In today's reading, Jesus used two parables to describe the Kingdom of Heaven and how his followers must be prepared for his return. •The parable of the bridesmaids pictures how every person is responsible for his or her own spiritual condition. Preparation cannot be bought or borrowed at the last minute. The five foolish bridesmaids refused to look after their own oil supply; they hoped that others would pick up the slack for them. As a result, the five foolish bridesmaids missed the opportunity to enjoy the marriage feast. •The parable of the servants entrusted with money points out that God gives each of us time, gifts, and resources according to our abilities, and he expects us to invest them wisely (use them to build his Kingdom) until he returns. •Jesus gave these parables to show that to live as a disciple, you must be willing to grow in your faith, and you must be careful to use the time, treasure, and talents God has given you wisely.

MATTHEW 25:1-30

What will you do with this life you've been given? Jesus told two parables that challenged his listeners to think about that question. The key to living this life well is being prepared for the next one—the one that will last for eternity.

"Then the Kingdom of Heaven will be like ten bridesmaids* who took their lamps and went to meet the bridegroom. ²Five of them were foolish, and five were wise. ³The five who were foolish didn't take enough olive oil for their lamps, ⁴but the other five were wise enough to take along extra oil. ⁵When the bridegroom was delayed, they all became drowsy and fell asleep.

⁶"At midnight they were roused by the shout, 'Look, the bridegroom is coming! Come out and meet him!'

⁷"All the bridesmaids got up and prepared their lamps. ⁸Then the five foolish ones asked the others, 'Please give us some of your oil because our lamps are going out.'

⁹"But the others replied, 'We don't have enough for all of us. Go to a shop and buy some for yourselves.'

¹⁰"But while they were gone to buy oil, the bridegroom came. Then those who were ready went in with him to the marriage feast, and the door was locked. ¹¹Later, when the other five bridesmaids returned, they stood outside, calling, 'Lord! Lord! Open the door for us!'

¹²"But he called back, 'Believe me, I don't know you!'

¹³"So you, too, must keep watch! For you do not know the day or hour of my return.

¹⁴"Again, the Kingdom of Heaven can be illustrated by the story of a man going on a long trip. He called together his servants and entrusted his money to them while he was gone. ¹⁵He gave five bags of silver* to one, two bags of silver to another, and one bag of silver to the last—dividing it in proportion to their abilities. He then left on his trip.

¹⁶"The servant who received the five bags of silver began to invest the money and earned five more. ¹⁷The servant with two bags of silver also went to work and earned two more. ¹⁸But the servant who received the one bag of silver dug a hole in the ground and hid the master's money.

¹⁹"After a long time their master returned from his trip and called them to give an account of how they had used his money. ²⁰The servant to whom he had entrusted the five bags of silver came forward with five more and said, 'Master, you gave me five bags of silver to invest, and I have earned five more.'

²¹"The master was full of praise. 'Well done, my good and faithful servant. You have been faithful in handling this small amount, so now I will give you many more responsibilities. Let's celebrate together!*'

²²"The servant who had received the two bags of silver came forward and said, 'Master, you gave me two bags of silver to invest, and I have earned two more.'

²³"The master said, 'Well done, my good and faithful servant. You have been faithful in handling this small amount, so now I will give you many more responsibilities. Let's celebrate together!'

²⁴"Then the servant with the one bag of silver came and said, 'Master, I knew you were a harsh man, harvesting crops you didn't plant and gathering crops you didn't cultivate. ²⁵I was afraid I would lose your money, so I hid it in the earth. Look, here is your money back.'

²⁶"But the master replied, 'You wicked and lazy servant! If you knew I harvested crops I didn't plant and gathered crops I didn't cultivate, ²⁷why didn't you deposit my money in the bank? At least I could have gotten some interest on it.'

²⁸"Then he ordered, 'Take the money from this servant, and give it to the one with the ten bags of silver. ²⁹To those who use well what they are given, even more will be given, and they will have an abundance. But from those who do nothing, even what little they have will be taken away. ³⁰Now throw this useless servant into outer darkness, where there will be weeping and gnashing of teeth.'"

25:1 Or *virgins;* also in 25:7, 11.   25:15 Greek *talents;* also throughout the story. A talent is equal to 75 pounds or 34 kilograms.   25:21 Greek *Enter into the joy of your master* [or *your Lord*]; also in 25:23.

PSALM 31:1-8
For the choir director: A psalm of David.

¹ **O** LORD, I have come to you for
    protection;
    don't let me be disgraced.
Save me, for you do what is right.
² Turn your ear to listen to me;
    rescue me quickly.
Be my rock of protection,
    a fortress where I will be safe.
³ You are my rock and my fortress.
    For the honor of your name, lead
    me out of this danger.
⁴ Pull me from the trap my enemies
    set for me,
    for I find protection in you
    alone.
⁵ I entrust my spirit into your hand.
    Rescue me, LORD, for you are a
    faithful God.
⁶ I hate those who worship worthless
    idols.
    I trust in the LORD.
⁷ I will be glad and rejoice in your
    unfailing love,
    for you have seen my troubles,

and you care about the anguish
    of my soul.
⁸ You have not handed me over to
    my enemies
    but have set me in a safe place.

PROVERBS 8:1-11
Listen as Wisdom calls out! Hear as understanding raises her voice! On the hilltop along the road, she takes her stand at the crossroads. By the gates at the entrance to the town, on the road leading in, she cries aloud, "I call to you, to all of you! I raise my voice to all people. You simple people, use good judgment. You foolish people, show some understanding. Listen to me! For I have important things to tell you. Everything I say is right, for I speak the truth and detest every kind of deception. My advice is wholesome. There is nothing devious or crooked in it. My words are plain to anyone with understanding, clear to those with knowledge. Choose my instruction rather than silver, and knowledge rather than pure gold. For wisdom is far more valuable than rubies. Nothing you desire can compare with it."

FEBRUARY**8**

EXODUS 28:1-43
Israel's worship at the Tabernacle was to be facilitated by priests who would represent the people before God. Aaron, Moses' brother, was Israel's first high priest.

"**C**all for your [Moses'] brother, Aaron, and his sons, Nadab, Abihu, Eleazar, and Ithamar. Set them apart from the rest of the people of Israel so they may minister to me and be my priests. ²Make sacred garments for Aaron that are glorious and beautiful. ³Instruct all the skilled craftsmen whom I have filled with the spirit of wisdom. Have them make garments for Aaron that will distinguish him as a priest set apart for my service. ⁴These are the garments they are to make: a chestpiece, an ephod, a robe, a patterned tunic,

a turban, and a sash. TOhey are to make these sacred garments for your brother, Aaron, and his sons to wear when they serve me as priests. ⁵So give them fine linen cloth, gold thread, and blue, purple, and scarlet thread.

⁶"The craftsmen must make the ephod of finely woven linen and skillfully embroider it with gold and with blue, purple, and scarlet thread. ⁷It will consist of two pieces, front and back, joined at the shoulders with two shoulder-pieces. ⁸The decorative sash will be made of the same materials: finely woven linen embroidered with gold and with blue, purple, and scarlet thread.

⁹"Take two onyx stones, and engrave on them the names of the tribes of Israel.

¹⁰Six names will be on each stone, arranged in the order of the births of the original sons of Israel. ¹¹Engrave these names on the two stones in the same way a jeweler engraves a seal. Then mount the stones in settings of gold filigree. ¹²Fasten the two stones on the shoulderpieces of the ephod as a reminder that Aaron represents the people of Israel. Aaron will carry these names on his shoulders as a constant reminder whenever he goes before the LORD. ¹³Make the settings of gold filigree, ¹⁴then braid two cords of pure gold and attach them to the filigree settings on the shoulders of the ephod.

¹⁵"Then, with great skill and care, make a chestpiece to be worn for seeking a decision from God.* Make it to match the ephod, using finely woven linen embroidered with gold and with blue, purple, and scarlet thread. ¹⁶Make the chestpiece of a single piece of cloth folded to form a pouch nine inches* square. ¹⁷Mount four rows of gemstones* on it. The first row will contain a red carnelian, a pale-green peridot, and an emerald. ¹⁸The second row will contain a turquoise, a blue lapis lazuli, and a white moonstone. ¹⁹The third row will contain an orange jacinth, an agate, and a purple amethyst. ²⁰The fourth row will contain a blue-green beryl, an onyx, and a green jasper. All these stones will be set in gold filigree. ²¹Each stone will represent one of the twelve sons of Israel, and the name of that tribe will be engraved on it like a seal.

²²"To attach the chestpiece to the ephod, make braided cords of pure gold thread. ²³Then make two gold rings and attach them to the top corners of the chestpiece. ²⁴Tie the two gold cords to the two rings on the chestpiece. ²⁵Tie the other ends of the cords to the gold settings on the shoulder-pieces of the ephod. ²⁶Then make two more gold rings and attach them to the inside edges of the chestpiece next to the ephod. ²⁷And make two more gold rings and attach them to the front of the ephod, below the shoulderpieces, just above the knot where the decorative sash is fastened to the ephod. ²⁸Then attach the bottom rings of the chestpiece to the rings on the ephod with blue cords. This will hold the chestpiece securely to the ephod above the decorative sash.

²⁹"In this way, Aaron will carry the names of the tribes of Israel on the sacred chestpiece* over his heart when he goes into the Holy Place. This will be a continual reminder that he represents the people when he comes before the LORD. ³⁰Insert the Urim and Thummim into the sacred chestpiece so they will be carried over Aaron's heart when he goes into the LORD's presence. In this way, Aaron will always carry over his heart the objects used to determine the LORD's will for his people whenever he goes in before the LORD.

³¹"Make the robe that is worn with the ephod from a single piece of blue cloth, ³²with an opening for Aaron's head in the middle of it. Reinforce the opening with a woven collar* so it will not tear. ³³Make pomegranates out of blue, purple, and scarlet yarn, and attach them to the hem of the robe, with gold bells between them. ³⁴The gold bells and pomegranates are to alternate all around the hem. ³⁵Aaron will wear this robe whenever he ministers before the LORD, and the bells will tinkle as he goes in and out of the LORD's presence in the Holy Place. If he wears it, he will not die.

³⁶"Next make a medallion of pure gold, and engrave it like a seal with these words: HOLY TO THE LORD. ³⁷Attach the medallion with a blue cord to the front of Aaron's turban, where it must remain. ³⁸Aaron must wear it on his forehead so he may take on himself any guilt of the people of Israel when they consecrate their sacred offerings. He must always wear it on his forehead so the LORD will accept the people.

³⁹"Weave Aaron's patterned tunic from fine linen cloth. Fashion the turban from this linen as well. Also make a sash, and decorate it with colorful embroidery.

⁴⁰"For Aaron's sons, make tunics, sashes, and special head coverings that are glorious and beautiful. ⁴¹Clothe your brother, Aaron, and his sons with these garments, and then anoint and ordain them. Consecrate them so they can serve as my priests. ⁴²Also make linen undergarments for them, to be worn next to their bodies,

reaching from their hips to their thighs. [43]These must be worn whenever Aaron and his sons enter the Tabernacle* or approach the altar in the Holy Place to perform their priestly duties. Then they will not incur guilt and die. This is a permanent law for Aaron and all his descendants after him."

28:15 Hebrew *a chestpiece for decision.* 28:16 Hebrew *1 span* [23 centimeters]. 28:17 The identification of some of these gemstones is uncertain. 28:29 Hebrew *the chestpiece for decision;* also in 28:30. See 28:15. 28:32 The meaning of the Hebrew is uncertain. 28:43 Hebrew *Tent of Meeting.*

MATTHEW 25:31–26:13

After teaching his disciples about the coming final judgment of humanity, Jesus again foretold his coming death on the cross. His sacrificial death would make it possible for his disciples to pass through the final judgment unscathed.

"**B**ut when the Son of Man* comes in his glory, and all the angels with him, then he will sit upon his glorious throne. [32]All the nations* will be gathered in his presence, and he will separate the people as a shepherd separates the sheep from the goats. [33]He will place the sheep at his right hand and the goats at his left.

[34]"Then the King will say to those on his right, 'Come, you who are blessed by my Father, inherit the Kingdom prepared for you from the creation of the world. [35]For I was hungry, and you fed me. I was thirsty, and you gave me a drink. I was a stranger, and you invited me into your home. [36]I was naked, and you gave me clothing. I was sick, and you cared for me. I was in prison, and you visited me.'

[37]"Then these righteous ones will reply, 'Lord, when did we ever see you hungry and feed you? Or thirsty and give you something to drink? [38]Or a stranger and show you hospitality? Or naked and give you clothing? [39]When did we ever see you sick or in prison and visit you?'

[40]"And the King will say, 'I tell you the truth, when you did it to one of the least of these my brothers and sisters,* you were doing it to me!'

[41]"Then the King will turn to those on the left and say, 'Away with you, you cursed ones, into the eternal fire prepared for the devil and his demons.* [42]For I was hungry, and you didn't feed me. I was thirsty, and you didn't give me a drink. [43]I was a stranger, and you didn't invite me into your home. I was naked, and you didn't give me clothing. I was sick and in prison, and you didn't visit me.'

[44]"Then they will reply, 'Lord, when did we ever see you hungry or thirsty or a stranger or naked or sick or in prison, and not help you?'

[45]"And he will answer, 'I tell you the

HOW WE LIVE: Serving others

MATTHEW 25:37-40 Just two days before the Passover celebration that preceded his betrayal and crucifixion, Jesus was preparing his disciples for his departure. The key to this preparation was his command that they care for the needs of others, whom he called "the least of these." Jesus went so far as to state that if his followers refused to help the needy members of the human family, they were actually refusing to help him.
• These are radical words. Our natural inclination is to care for those within our own family or circle of acquaintances. We don't necessarily need a command to make us care about those closest to us. Jesus, however, urges us to look beyond serving only those we already love and care about, or those who might meet our needs in return. Instead, he said to reach out beyond our familiar circles to feed the hungry, demonstrate hospitality to the stranger, give our own clothing to those who have none, care for the sick, and visit prisoners. As we serve others in Jesus' name, we are actually serving the Lord himself.

truth, when you refused to help the least of these my brothers and sisters, you were refusing to help me.'

⁴⁶"And they will go away into eternal punishment, but the righteous will go into eternal life."

²⁶:¹WHEN Jesus had finished saying all these things, he said to his disciples, ²"As you know, Passover begins in two days, and the Son of Man* will be handed over to be crucified."

³At that same time the leading priests and elders were meeting at the residence of Caiaphas, the high priest, ⁴plotting how to capture Jesus secretly and kill him. ⁵"But not during the Passover celebration," they agreed, "or the people may riot."

⁶Meanwhile, Jesus was in Bethany at the home of Simon, a man who had previously had leprosy. ⁷While he was eating,* a woman came in with a beautiful alabaster jar of expensive perfume and poured it over his head.

⁸The disciples were indignant when they saw this. "What a waste!" they said. ⁹"It could have been sold for a high price and the money given to the poor."

¹⁰But Jesus, aware of this, replied, "Why criticize this woman for doing such a good thing to me? ¹¹You will always have the poor among you, but you will not always have me. ¹²She has poured this perfume on me to prepare my body for burial. ¹³I tell you the truth, wherever the Good News is preached throughout the world, this woman's deed will be remembered and discussed."

25:31 "Son of Man" is a title Jesus used for himself.   25:32 Or *peoples.*   25:40 Greek *my brothers.*   25:41 Greek *his angels.*   26:2 "Son of Man" is a title Jesus used for himself.   26:7 Or *reclining.*

PSALM 31:9-18

Have mercy on me, LORD, for I am
  in distress.
  Tears blur my eyes.
  My body and soul are withering away.
¹⁰ I am dying from grief;
  my years are shortened by sadness.
  Sin has drained my strength;
  I am wasting away from within.
¹¹ I am scorned by all my enemies
  and despised by my neighbors—
  even my friends are afraid to
    come near me.
  When they see me on the street,
    they run the other way.
¹² I am ignored as if I were dead,
  as if I were a broken pot.
¹³ I have heard the many rumors
    about me,
  and I am surrounded by terror.
  My enemies conspire against me,
    plotting to take my life.
¹⁴ But I am trusting you, O LORD,
  saying, "You are my God!"
¹⁵ My future is in your hands.
  Rescue me from those who hunt
    me down relentlessly.
¹⁶ Let your favor shine on your
    servant.
  In your unfailing love,
    rescue me.
¹⁷ Don't let me be disgraced, O LORD,
  for I call out to you for help.
  Let the wicked be disgraced;
    let them lie silent in the grave.*
¹⁸ Silence their lying lips—
    those proud and arrogant lips
    that accuse the godly.

31:17 Hebrew *in Sheol.*

PROVERBS 8:12-13

"I, Wisdom, live together with good judgment. I know where to discover knowledge and discernment. All who fear the LORD will hate evil. Therefore, I hate pride and arrogance, corruption and perverse speech."

EXODUS 29:1–30:10

God instructed that a special ceremony be conducted to inaugurate the priesthood. The solemnity of the ceremony fit the importance of the priests' role in Israelite worship.

"**T**his is the ceremony you must follow when you consecrate Aaron and his sons to serve me as priests: Take a young bull and two rams with no defects. ²Then, using choice wheat flour and no yeast, make loaves of bread, thin cakes mixed with olive oil, and wafers spread with oil. ³Place them all in a single basket, and present them at the entrance of the Tabernacle, along with the young bull and the two rams.

⁴"Present Aaron and his sons at the entrance of the Tabernacle,* and wash them with water. ⁵Dress Aaron in his priestly garments—the tunic, the robe worn with the ephod, the ephod itself, and the chestpiece. Then wrap the decorative sash of the ephod around him. ⁶Place the turban on his head, and fasten the sacred medallion to the turban. ⁷Then anoint him by pouring the anointing oil over his head. ⁸Next present his sons, and dress them in their tunics. ⁹Wrap the sashes around the waists of Aaron and his sons, and put their special head coverings on them. Then the right to the priesthood will be theirs by law forever. In this way, you will ordain Aaron and his sons.

¹⁰"Bring the young bull to the entrance of the Tabernacle, where Aaron and his sons will lay their hands on its head. ¹¹Then slaughter the bull in the Lord's presence at the entrance of the Tabernacle. ¹²Put some of its blood on the horns of the altar with your finger, and pour out the rest at the base of the altar. ¹³Take all the fat around the internal organs, the long lobe of the liver, and the two kidneys and the fat around them, and burn it all on the altar. ¹⁴Then take the rest of the bull, including its hide, meat, and dung, and burn it outside the camp as a sin offering.

¹⁵"Next Aaron and his sons must lay their hands on the head of one of the rams. ¹⁶Then slaughter the ram, and splatter its blood against all sides of the altar. ¹⁷Cut the ram into pieces, and wash off the internal organs and the legs. Set them alongside the head and the other pieces of the body, ¹⁸then burn the entire animal on the altar. This is a burnt offering to the Lord; it is a pleasing aroma, a special gift presented to the Lord.

¹⁹"Now take the other ram, and have Aaron and his sons lay their hands on its head. ²⁰Then slaughter it, and apply some of its blood to the right earlobes of Aaron and his sons. Also put it on the thumbs of their right hands and the big toes of their right feet. Splatter the rest of the blood against all sides of the altar. ²¹Then take some of the blood from the altar and some of the anointing oil, and sprinkle it on Aaron and his sons and on their garments. In this way, they and their garments will be set apart as holy.

²²"Since this is the ram for the ordination of Aaron and his sons, take the fat of the ram, including the fat of the broad tail, the fat around the internal organs, the long lobe of the liver, and the two kidneys and the fat around them, along with the right thigh. ²³Then take one round loaf of bread, one thin cake mixed with olive oil, and one wafer from the basket of bread without yeast that was placed in the Lord's presence. ²⁴Put all these in the hands of Aaron and his sons to be lifted up as a special offering to the Lord. ²⁵Afterward take the various breads from their hands, and burn them on the altar along with the burnt offering. It is a pleasing aroma to the Lord, a special gift for him. ²⁶Then take the breast of Aaron's ordination ram, and lift it up in the Lord's presence as a special offering to him. Then keep it as your own portion.

²⁷"Set aside the portions of the ordination ram that belong to Aaron and his sons. This includes the breast and the thigh that were lifted up before the Lord as a special offering. ²⁸In the future,

whenever the people of Israel lift up a peace offering, a portion of it must be set aside for Aaron and his descendants. This is their permanent right, and it is a sacred offering from the Israelites to the LORD.

²⁹"Aaron's sacred garments must be preserved for his descendants who succeed him, and they will wear them when they are anointed and ordained. ³⁰The descendant who succeeds him as high priest will wear these clothes for seven days as he ministers in the Tabernacle and the Holy Place.

³¹"Take the ram used in the ordination ceremony, and boil its meat in a sacred place. ³²Then Aaron and his sons will eat this meat, along with the bread in the basket, at the Tabernacle entrance. ³³They alone may eat the meat and bread used for their purification* in the ordination ceremony. No one else may eat them, for these things are set apart and holy. ³⁴If any of the ordination meat or bread remains until the morning, it must be burned. It may not be eaten, for it is holy.

³⁵"This is how you will ordain Aaron and his sons to their offices, just as I have commanded you. The ordination ceremony will go on for seven days. ³⁶Each day you must sacrifice a young bull as a sin offering to purify them, making them right with the LORD.* Afterward, cleanse the altar by purifying it*; make it holy by anointing it with oil. ³⁷Purify the altar, and consecrate it every day for seven days. After that, the altar will be absolutely holy, and whatever touches it will become holy.

³⁸"These are the sacrifices you are to offer regularly on the altar. Each day, offer two lambs that are a year old, ³⁹one in the morning and the other in the evening. ⁴⁰With one of them, offer two quarts of choice flour mixed with one quart of pure oil of pressed olives; also, offer one quart of wine* as a liquid offering. ⁴¹Offer the other lamb in the evening, along with the same offerings of flour and wine as in the morning. It will be a pleasing aroma, a special gift presented to the LORD.

⁴²"These burnt offerings are to be made each day from generation to generation. Offer them in the LORD's presence at the Tabernacle entrance; there I will meet with you and speak with you. ⁴³I will

meet the people of Israel there, in the place made holy by my glorious presence. ⁴⁴Yes, I will consecrate the Tabernacle and the altar, and I will consecrate Aaron and his sons to serve me as priests. ⁴⁵Then I will live among the people of Israel and be their God, ⁴⁶and they will know that I am the LORD their God. I am the one who brought them out of the land of Egypt so that I could live among them. I am the LORD their God.

30:1"THEN make another altar of acacia wood for burning incense. ²Make it 18 inches square and 36 inches high,* with horns at the corners carved from the same piece of wood as the altar itself. ³Overlay the top, sides, and horns of the altar with pure gold, and run a gold molding around the entire altar. ⁴Make two gold rings, and attach them on opposite sides of the altar below the gold molding to hold the carrying poles. ⁵Make the poles of acacia wood and overlay them with gold. ⁶Place the incense altar just outside the inner curtain that shields the Ark of the Covenant,* in front of the Ark's cover—the place of atonement—that covers the tablets inscribed with the terms of the covenant.* I will meet with you there.

⁷"Every morning when Aaron maintains the lamps, he must burn fragrant incense on the altar. ⁸And each evening when he lights the lamps, he must again burn incense in the LORD's presence. This must be done from generation to generation. ⁹Do not offer any unholy incense on this altar, or any burnt offerings, grain offerings, or liquid offerings.

¹⁰"Once a year Aaron must purify* the altar by smearing its horns with blood from the offering made to purify the people from their sin. This will be a regular, annual event from generation to generation, for this is the LORD's most holy altar."

29:4 Hebrew *Tent of Meeting;* also in 29:10, 11, 30, 32, 42, 44.   29:33 Or *their atonement.*   29:36a Or *to make atonement.*   29:36b Or *by making atonement for it;* similarly in 29:37.   29:40 Hebrew ¹⁄₁₀ *of an ephah* [2.2 liters] *of choice flour . . . ¼ of a hin* [1 liter] *of pure oil . . . ¼ of a hin of wine.*   30:2 Hebrew *1 cubit* [46 centimeters] *long and 1 cubit wide, a square, and 2 cubits* [92 centimeters] *high.*   30:6a Or *Ark of the Testimony;* also in 30:26.   30:6b Hebrew *that covers the Testimony;* see note on 25:16.   30:10 Or *make atonement for;* also in 30:10b.

MATTHEW 26:14-46
Jesus sat with his disciples for a final meal, which we now refer to as the Last Supper. It is the basis for the observance of "communion" in churches today. Jesus knew that difficulties were ahead. So after supper, he went to a secluded place to pray.

Then Judas Iscariot, one of the twelve disciples, went to the leading priests [15] and asked, "How much will you pay me to betray Jesus to you?" And they gave him thirty pieces of silver. [16] From that time on, Judas began looking for an opportunity to betray Jesus.

[17] On the first day of the Festival of Unleavened Bread, the disciples came to Jesus and asked, "Where do you want us to prepare the Passover meal for you?"

[18] "As you go into the city," he told them, "you will see a certain man. Tell him, 'The Teacher says: My time has come, and I will eat the Passover meal with my disciples at your house.'" [19] So the disciples did as Jesus told them and prepared the Passover meal there.

[20] When it was evening, Jesus sat down at the table* with the twelve disciples.* [21] While they were eating, he said, "I tell you the truth, one of you will betray me."

[22] Greatly distressed, each one asked in turn, "Am I the one, Lord?"

[23] He replied, "One of you who has just eaten from this bowl with me will betray me. [24] For the Son of Man must die, as the Scriptures declared long ago. But how terrible it will be for the one who betrays him. It would be far better for that man if he had never been born!"

[25] Judas, the one who would betray him, also asked, "Rabbi, am I the one?"

And Jesus told him, "You have said it."

[26] As they were eating, Jesus took some bread and blessed it. Then he broke it in pieces and gave it to the disciples, saying, "Take this and eat it, for this is my body."

[27] And he took a cup of wine and gave thanks to God for it. He gave it to them and said, "Each of you drink from it, [28] for this is my blood, which confirms the covenant* between God and his people. It is poured out as a sacrifice to forgive the sins of many. [29] Mark my words—I will not drink wine again until the day I drink it new with you in my Father's Kingdom."

[30] Then they sang a hymn and went out to the Mount of Olives.

[31] On the way, Jesus told them, "Tonight all of you will desert me. For the Scriptures say,

'God will strike* the Shepherd,
    and the sheep of the flock will
    be scattered.'

[32] But after I have been raised from the dead, I will go ahead of you to Galilee and meet you there."

WHAT THE BIBLE SAYS

Old Testament worship

EXODUS 29:15-18 Approaching God is a serious affair not to be taken lightly. This is precisely why God gave the people so many detailed instructions—even how to cut up and burn the sacrifices. He was teaching the Israelites how to worship, honor, and respect him properly. • Because the sins of the people prevented them from entering into God's holy presence, God gave these guidelines for sacrifices to remind the Israelites that they are can only approach him through the means he graciously provided. • Today, because of Jesus' sacrifice on the cross, we can approach God freely and without fear at any time. We don't need to sacrifice animals because the blood of Jesus "cleanses us from all sin" (1 John 1:7, November 30).

³³Peter declared, "Even if everyone else deserts you, I will never desert you."

³⁴Jesus replied, "I tell you the truth, Peter—this very night, before the rooster crows, you will deny three times that you even know me."

³⁵"No!" Peter insisted. "Even if I have to die with you, I will never deny you!" And all the other disciples vowed the same.

³⁶Then Jesus went with them to the olive grove called Gethsemane, and he said, "Sit here while I go over there to pray." ³⁷He took Peter and Zebedee's two sons, James and John, and he became anguished and distressed. ³⁸He told them, "My soul is crushed with grief to the point of death. Stay here and keep watch with me."

³⁹He went on a little farther and bowed with his face to the ground, praying, "My Father! If it is possible, let this cup of suffering be taken away from me. Yet I want your will to be done, not mine."

⁴⁰Then he returned to the disciples and found them asleep. He said to Peter, "Couldn't you watch with me even one hour? ⁴¹Keep watch and pray, so that you will not give in to temptation. For the spirit is willing, but the body is weak!"

⁴²Then Jesus left them a second time and prayed, "My Father! If this cup cannot be taken away* unless I drink it, your will be done." ⁴³When he returned to them again, he found them sleeping, for they couldn't keep their eyes open.

⁴⁴So he went to pray a third time, saying the same things again. ⁴⁵Then he came to the disciples and said, "Go ahead and sleep. Have your rest. But look—the time has come. The Son of Man is betrayed into the hands of sinners. ⁴⁶Up, let's be going. Look, my betrayer is here!"

26:20a Or *Jesus reclined.*   26:20b Some manuscripts read *the Twelve.*   26:28 Some manuscripts read *the new covenant.*   26:31 Greek *I will strike.* Zech 13:7.   26:42 Greek *If this cannot pass.*

PSALM 31:19-24

How great is the goodness
      you have stored up for those
         who fear you.
You lavish it on those who come
      to you for protection,

blessing them before the watching
         world.
²⁰ You hide them in the shelter of your
         presence,
      safe from those who conspire
         against them.
You shelter them in your presence,
      far from accusing tongues.

²¹ Praise the LORD,
      for he has shown me the wonders
         of his unfailing love.
He kept me safe when my city
      was under attack.
²² In panic I cried out,
      "I am cut off from the LORD!"
But you heard my cry for mercy
      and answered my call for help.

²³ Love the LORD, all you godly ones!
      For the LORD protects those who are
         loyal to him,
      but he harshly punishes the
         arrogant.
²⁴ So be strong and courageous,
      all you who put your hope
         in the LORD!

PROVERBS 8:14-26

"**C**ommon sense and success belong to me. Insight and strength are mine. Because of me, kings reign, and rulers make just decrees. Rulers lead with my help, and nobles make righteous judgments. □"I love all who love me. Those who search will surely find me. I have riches and honor, as well as enduring wealth and justice. My gifts are better than gold, even the purest gold, my wages better than sterling silver! I walk in righteousness, in paths of justice. Those who love me inherit wealth. I will fill their treasuries. □"The LORD formed me from the beginning, before he created anything else. I was appointed in ages past, at the very first, before the earth began. I was born before the oceans were created, before the springs bubbled forth their waters. Before the mountains were formed, before the hills, I was born—before he had made the earth and fields and the first handfuls of soil."

EXODUS 30:11–31:18

Today's reading contains further instructions on the contents and the function of the Tabernacle, as well as instructions concerning keeping the Sabbath. With these topics, this first part of Moses' conversation with God on Mount Sinai came to a close.

Then the LORD said to Moses, [12]"Whenever you take a census of the people of Israel, each man who is counted must pay a ransom for himself to the LORD. Then no plague will strike the people as you count them. [13]Each person who is counted must give a small piece of silver as a sacred offering to the LORD. (This payment is half a shekel,* based on the sanctuary shekel, which equals twenty gerahs.) [14]All who have reached their twentieth birthday must give this sacred offering to the LORD. [15]When this offering is given to the LORD to purify your lives, making you right with him,* the rich must not give more than the specified amount, and the poor must not give less. [16]Receive this ransom money from the Israelites, and use it for the care of the Tabernacle.* It will bring the Israelites to the LORD's attention, and it will purify your lives."

[17]Then the LORD said to Moses, [18]"Make a bronze washbasin with a bronze stand. Place it between the Tabernacle and the altar, and fill it with water. [19]Aaron and his sons will wash their hands and feet there. [20]They must wash with water whenever they go into the Tabernacle to appear before the LORD and when they approach the altar to burn up their special gifts to the LORD—or they will die! [21]They must always wash their hands and feet, or they will die. This is a permanent law for Aaron and his descendants, to be observed from generation to generation."

[22]Then the LORD said to Moses, [23]"Collect choice spices—12½ pounds of pure myrrh, 6¼ pounds of fragrant cinnamon, 6¼ pounds of fragrant calamus* [24]and 12½ pounds of cassia*—as measured by the weight of the sanctuary shekel. Also get one gallon of olive oil.* [25]Like a skilled incense maker, blend these ingredients to make a holy anointing oil. [26]Use this sacred oil to anoint the Tabernacle, the Ark of the Covenant, [27]the table and all its utensils, the lampstand and all its accessories, the incense altar, [28]the altar of burnt offering and all its utensils, and the washbasin with its stand. [29]Consecrate them to make them absolutely holy. After this, whatever touches them will also become holy.

[30]"Anoint Aaron and his sons also, consecrating them to serve me as priests. [31]And say to the people of Israel, 'This holy anointing oil is reserved for me from generation to generation. [32]It must never be used to anoint anyone else, and you must never make any blend like it for yourselves. It is holy, and you must treat it as holy. [33]Anyone who makes a blend like it or anoints someone other than a priest will be cut off from the community.'"

[34]Then the LORD said to Moses, "Gather fragrant spices—resin droplets, mollusk shell, and galbanum—and mix these fragrant spices with pure frankincense, weighed out in equal amounts. [35]Using the usual techniques of the incense maker, blend the spices together and sprinkle them with salt to produce a pure and holy incense. [36]Grind some of the mixture into a very fine powder and put it in front of the Ark of the Covenant,* where I will meet with you in the Tabernacle. You must treat this incense as most holy. [37]Never use this formula to make this incense for yourselves. It is reserved for the LORD, and you must treat it as holy. [38]Anyone who makes incense like this for personal use will be cut off from the community."

[31:1]THEN the LORD said to Moses, [2]"Look, I have specifically chosen Bezalel son of Uri, grandson of Hur, of the tribe of Judah. [3]I have filled him with the Spirit of God, giving him great wisdom, ability, and expertise in all kinds of crafts. [4]He is a master craftsman, expert in working with gold, silver, and bronze. [5]He is skilled in engraving and mounting gemstones and in carving wood. He is a master at every craft!

6"And I have personally appointed Oholiab son of Ahisamach, of the tribe of Dan, to be his assistant. Moreover, I have given special skill to all the gifted craftsmen so they can make all the things I have commanded you to make:

7 the Tabernacle;*

the Ark of the Covenant;*

the Ark's cover—the place of atonement;

all the furnishings of the Tabernacle;

8 the table and its utensils;

the pure gold lampstand with all its accessories;

the incense altar;

9 the altar of burnt offering with all its utensils;

the washbasin with its stand;

10 the beautifully stitched garments—

the sacred garments for Aaron the priest, and the garments for his sons to wear as they minister as priests;

11 the anointing oil;

the fragrant incense for the Holy Place.

The craftsmen must make everything as I have commanded you."

12 The LORD then gave these instructions to Moses: 13"Tell the people of Israel: 'Be careful to keep my Sabbath day, for the Sabbath is a sign of the covenant between me and you from generation to generation. It is given so you may know that I am the LORD, who makes you holy. 14You must keep the Sabbath day, for it is a holy day for you. Anyone who desecrates it must be put to death; anyone who works on that day will be cut off from the community. 15You have six days each week for your ordinary work, but the seventh day must be a Sabbath day of complete rest, a holy day dedicated to the LORD. Anyone who works on the Sabbath must be put to death. 16The people of Israel must keep the Sabbath day by observing it from generation to generation. This is a covenant obligation for all time. 17It is a permanent sign of my covenant with the people of Israel. For in six days the LORD made heaven and earth, but on the seventh day he stopped working and was refreshed.'"

18When the LORD finished speaking with Moses on Mount Sinai, he gave him the two stone tablets inscribed with the terms of the covenant,* written by the finger of God.

30:13 Or *0.2 ounces,* or *6 grams.* 30:15 Or *to make atonement for your lives;* similarly in 30:16. 30:16 Hebrew *Tent of Meeting;* also in 30:18, 20, 26, 36. 30:23 Hebrew *500 shekels* [5.7 kilograms] *of pure myrrh, 250 shekels* [2.9 kilograms] *of fragrant cinnamon, 250 shekels of fragrant calamus.* 30:24a Hebrew *500 shekels* [5.7 kilograms] *of cassia.* 30:24b Hebrew *1 hin* [3.8 liters] *of olive oil.* 30:36 Hebrew *in front of the Testimony;* see note on 25:16. 31:7a Hebrew *the Tent of Meeting.* 31:7b Hebrew *the Ark of the Testimony.* 31:18 Hebrew *the two tablets of the Testimony;* see note on 25:16.

MATTHEW 26:47-68

During Jesus' trial before the Jewish ruling council (called the Sanhedrin), false witnesses came forward in an effort to bring Jesus down. In the end, Jesus admitted to claiming to be the Son of God, which the ruling council considered blasphemy, an offense punishable by death.

And even as Jesus said this, Judas, one of the twelve disciples, arrived with a crowd of men armed with swords and clubs. They had been sent by the leading priests and elders of the people. 48The traitor, Judas, had given them a prearranged signal: "You will know which one to arrest when I greet him with a kiss." 49So Judas came straight to Jesus. "Greetings, Rabbi!" he exclaimed and gave him the kiss.

50Jesus said, "My friend, go ahead and do what you have come for."

Then the others grabbed Jesus and arrested him. 51But one of the men with Jesus pulled out his sword and struck the high priest's slave, slashing off his ear.

52"Put away your sword," Jesus told him. "Those who use the sword will die by the sword. 53Don't you realize that I could ask my Father for thousands* of angels to protect us, and he would send them instantly? 54But if I did, how would the Scriptures be fulfilled that describe what must happen now?"

55Then Jesus said to the crowd, "Am I some dangerous revolutionary, that you come with swords and clubs to arrest me? Why didn't you arrest me in the Temple? I was there teaching every day. 56But this is all happening to fulfill the words of the prophets as recorded in the Scriptures." At that point, all the disciples deserted him and fled.

57Then the people who had arrested

Jesus led him to the home of Caiaphas, the high priest, where the teachers of religious law and the elders had gathered. [58]Meanwhile, Peter followed him at a distance and came to the high priest's courtyard. He went in and sat with the guards and waited to see how it would all end.

[59]Inside, the leading priests and the entire high council* were trying to find witnesses who would lie about Jesus, so they could put him to death. [60]But even though they found many who agreed to give false witness, they could not use anyone's testimony. Finally, two men came forward [61]who declared, "This man said, 'I am able to destroy the Temple of God and rebuild it in three days.'"

[62]Then the high priest stood up and said to Jesus, "Well, aren't you going to answer these charges? What do you have to say for yourself?" [63]But Jesus remained silent. Then the high priest said to him, "I demand in the name of the living God—tell us if you are the Messiah, the Son of God."

[64]Jesus replied, "You have said it. And in the future you will see the Son of Man seated in the place of power at God's right hand* and coming on the clouds of heaven."*

[65]Then the high priest tore his clothing to show his horror and said, "Blasphemy! Why do we need other witnesses? You have all heard his blasphemy. [66]What is your verdict?"

"Guilty!" they shouted. "He deserves to die!"

[67]Then they began to spit in Jesus' face and beat him with their fists. And some slapped him, [68]jeering, "Prophesy to us, you Messiah! Who hit you that time?"

26:53 Greek *twelve legions.* 26:59 Greek *the Sanhedrin.* 26:64a Greek *seated at the right hand of the power.* See Ps 110:1. 26:64b See Dan 7:13.

PSALM 32:1-11
A psalm of David.*

[1] **O**h, what joy for those
        whose disobedience is forgiven,
        whose sin is put out of sight!
[2] Yes, what joy for those
        whose record the LORD has cleared of guilt,*
        whose lives are lived in complete honesty!
[3] When I refused to confess my sin,
        my body wasted away,
        and I groaned all day long.
[4] Day and night your hand of discipline
            was heavy on me.
        My strength evaporated like water
            in the summer heat.   *Interlude*

[5] Finally, I confessed all my sins to you
        and stopped trying to hide my guilt.
    I said to myself, "I will confess my rebellion to the LORD."
        And you forgave me! All my guilt is gone.   *Interlude*

Confessing our sins

HOW WE LIVE

PSALM 32:5 When you became a believer, you confessed your sins to God and accepted his forgiveness and salvation. However, it probably didn't take long for you to realize that you still sin—perhaps *daily*! What then? Go to God *daily* and confess your sins. • The psalmist shared the depth of his sorrow over his sin as well as his joy at being forgiven. As you read this psalm, think upon your own life. Do you recognize certain behaviors, attitudes, or thought patterns that are displeasing to God? Then bring them before God, express your sorrow over them, and ask God to forgive you. Recognizing sin is the first step in repentance. God indeed knows your sins anyway, but you need to admit them and take responsibility for them. Then you can ask for help to keep from committing the same sins again. In addition, if what you did hurt another person, you will need to make things right with him or her. • No matter what the sin, trust in God's willingness to forgive you and then accept his forgiveness. God wants to forgive you. It's part of his nature. All you have to do is ask.

6 Therefore, let all the godly pray to
you while there is still time,
that they may not drown in the
floodwaters of judgment.
7 For you are my hiding place;
you protect me from trouble.
You surround me with songs
of victory.   *Interlude*

8 The LORD says, "I will guide you along
the best pathway for your life.
I will advise you and watch over you.
9 Do not be like a senseless horse
or mule
that needs a bit and bridle to keep
it under control."

10 Many sorrows come to the wicked,
but unfailing love surrounds those
who trust the LORD.
11 So rejoice in the LORD and be glad,
all you who obey him!
Shout for joy, all you whose hearts
are pure!

FEBRUARY**11**

EXODUS 32:1–33:23
As Moses was taking down the laws about not
making idols, Aaron was in the camp doing just
that. Here is a prime example of how quickly we
fall back into old, familiar ways. Aaron should have
known better, but he let the crowd manipulate him.

When the people saw how long it was taking Moses to come back down the mountain, they gathered around Aaron. "Come
on," they said, "make us some gods who
can lead us. We don't know what happened to this fellow Moses, who brought
us here from the land of Egypt."
2 So Aaron said, "Take the gold rings
from the ears of your wives and sons and
daughters, and bring them to me."
3 All the people took the gold rings from
their ears and brought them to Aaron.
4 Then Aaron took the gold, melted it
down, and molded it into the shape of a
calf. When the people saw it, they exclaimed, "O Israel, these are the gods who
brought you out of the land of Egypt!"

32:TITLE Hebrew *maskil*. This may be a literary or musical
term.   32:2 Greek version reads *of sin*. Compare Rom 4:7.

PROVERBS 8:27-32
"**I** [Wisdom] was there when he established the heavens, when he drew the horizon on the oceans. I was there when he
set the clouds above, when he established
springs deep in the earth. I was there
when he set the limits of the seas, so they
would not spread beyond their boundaries. And when he marked off the earth's
foundations, I was the architect at his
side. I was his constant delight, rejoicing
always in his presence. And how happy I
was with the world he created; how I rejoiced with the human family! □ "And so,
my children,* listen to me, for all who follow my ways are joyful."

8:32 Hebrew *my sons*.

5 Aaron saw how excited the people
were, so he built an altar in front of the
calf. Then he announced, "Tomorrow will
be a festival to the LORD!"
6 The people got up early the next
morning to sacrifice burnt offerings and
peace offerings. After this, they celebrated with feasting and drinking, and
they indulged in pagan revelry.
7 The LORD told Moses, "Quick! Go
down the mountain! Your people whom
you brought from the land of Egypt have
corrupted themselves. 8 How quickly
they have turned away from the way I
commanded them to live! They have
melted down gold and made a calf, and
they have bowed down and sacrificed to
it. They are saying, 'These are your gods,
O Israel, who brought you out of the land
of Egypt.'"
9 Then the LORD said, "I have seen how
stubborn and rebellious these people are.

[10]Now leave me alone so my fierce anger can blaze against them, and I will destroy them. Then I will make you, Moses, into a great nation."

[11]But Moses tried to pacify the LORD his God. "O LORD!" he said. "Why are you so angry with your own people whom you brought from the land of Egypt with such great power and such a strong hand? [12]Why let the Egyptians say, 'Their God rescued them with the evil intention of slaughtering them in the mountains and wiping them from the face of the earth'? Turn away from your fierce anger. Change your mind about this terrible disaster you have threatened against your people! [13]Remember your servants Abraham, Isaac, and Jacob.* You bound yourself with an oath to them, saying, 'I will make your descendants as numerous as the stars of heaven. And I will give them all of this land that I have promised to your descendants, and they will possess it forever.'"

[14]So the LORD changed his mind about the terrible disaster he had threatened to bring on his people.

[15]Then Moses turned and went down the mountain. He held in his hands the two stone tablets inscribed with the terms of the covenant.* They were inscribed on both sides, front and back. [16]These tablets were God's work; the words on them were written by God himself.

[17]When Joshua heard the boisterous noise of the people shouting below them, he exclaimed to Moses, "It sounds like war in the camp!"

[18]But Moses replied, "No, it's not a shout of victory nor the wailing of defeat. I hear the sound of a celebration."

[19]When they came near the camp, Moses saw the calf and the dancing, and he burned with anger. He threw the stone tablets to the ground, smashing them at the foot of the mountain. [20]He took the calf they had made and burned it. Then he ground it into powder, threw it into the water, and forced the people to drink it.

[21]Finally, he turned to Aaron and demanded, "What did these people do to you to make you bring such terrible sin upon them?"

[22]"Don't get so upset, my lord," Aaron replied. "You yourself know how evil these people are. [23]They said to me, 'Make us gods who will lead us. We don't know what happened to this fellow Moses, who brought us here from the land of Egypt.' [24]So I told them, 'Whoever has gold jewelry, take it off.' When they brought it to me, I simply threw it into the fire—and out came this calf!"

[25]Moses saw that Aaron had let the people get completely out of control, much to the amusement of their enemies.* [26]So he stood at the entrance to the camp and shouted, "All of you who are on the LORD's side, come here and join me." And all the Levites gathered around him.

[27]Moses told them, "This is what the LORD, the God of Israel, says: Each of you, take your swords and go back and forth from one end of the camp to the other. Kill everyone—even your brothers, friends, and neighbors." [28]The Levites obeyed Moses' command, and about 3,000 people died that day.

[29]Then Moses told the Levites, "Today you have ordained yourselves* for the service of the LORD, for you obeyed him even though it meant killing your own sons and brothers. Today you have earned a blessing."

[30]The next day Moses said to the people, "You have committed a terrible sin, but I will go back up to the LORD on the mountain. Perhaps I will be able to obtain forgiveness* for your sin."

[31]So Moses returned to the LORD and said, "Oh, what a terrible sin these people have committed. They have made gods of gold for themselves. [32]But now, if you will only forgive their sin—but if not, erase my name from the record you have written!"

[33]But the LORD replied to Moses, "No, I will erase the name of everyone who has sinned against me. [34]Now go, lead the people to the place I told you about. Look! My angel will lead the way before you. And when I come to call the people to account, I will certainly hold them responsible for their sins."

[35]Then the LORD sent a great plague upon the people because they had worshiped the calf Aaron had made.

33:1THE LORD said to Moses, "Get going, you and the people you brought up from the land of Egypt. Go up to the land I swore to give to Abraham, Isaac, and Jacob. I told them, 'I will give this land to your descendants.' [2]And I will send an angel before you to drive out the Canaanites, Amorites, Hittites, Perizzites, Hivites, and Jebusites. [3]Go up to this land that flows with milk and honey. But I will not travel among you, for you are a stubborn and rebellious people. If I did, I would surely destroy you along the way."

[4]When the people heard these stern words, they went into mourning and stopped wearing their jewelry and fine clothes. [5]For the LORD had told Moses to tell them, "You are a stubborn and rebellious people. If I were to travel with you for even a moment, I would destroy you. Remove your jewelry and fine clothes while I decide what to do with you." [6]So from the time they left Mount Sinai,* the Israelites wore no more jewelry or fine clothes.

[7]It was Moses' practice to take the Tent of Meeting* and set it up some distance from the camp. Everyone who wanted to make a request of the LORD would go to the Tent of Meeting outside the camp.

[8]Whenever Moses went out to the Tent of Meeting, all the people would get up and stand in the entrances of their own tents. They would all watch Moses until he disappeared inside. [9]As he went into the tent, the pillar of cloud would come down and hover at its entrance while the LORD spoke with Moses. [10]When the people saw the cloud standing at the entrance of the tent, they would stand and bow down in front of their own tents. [11]Inside the Tent of Meeting, the LORD would speak to Moses face to face, as one speaks to a friend. Afterward Moses would return to the camp, but the young man who assisted him, Joshua son of Nun, would remain behind in the Tent of Meeting.

[12]One day Moses said to the LORD, "You have been telling me, 'Take these people up to the Promised Land.' But you haven't told me whom you will send with me. You have told me, 'I know you by name, and I look favorably on you.' [13]If it is true that you look favorably on me, let me know your ways so I may understand you more

fully and continue to enjoy your favor. And remember that this nation is your very own people."

[14]The LORD replied, "I will personally go with you, Moses, and I will give you rest—everything will be fine for you."

[15]Then Moses said, "If you don't personally go with us, don't make us leave this place. [16]How will anyone know that you look favorably on me—on me and on your people—if you don't go with us? For your presence among us sets your people and me apart from all other people on the earth."

[17]The LORD replied to Moses, "I will indeed do what you have asked, for I look favorably on you, and I know you by name."

[18]Moses responded, "Then show me your glorious presence."

[19]The LORD replied, "I will make all my goodness pass before you, and I will call out my name, Yahweh,* before you. For I will show mercy to anyone I choose, and I will show compassion to anyone I choose. [20]But you may not look directly at my face, for no one may see me and live." [21]The LORD continued, "Look, stand near me on this rock. [22]As my glorious presence passes by, I will hide you in the crevice of the rock and cover you with my hand until I have passed by. [23]Then I will remove my hand and let you see me from behind. But my face will not be seen."

32:13 Hebrew *Israel.* The names "Jacob" and "Israel" are often interchanged throughout the Old Testament, referring sometimes to the individual patriarch and sometimes to the nation.   **32:15** Hebrew *the two tablets of the Testimony;* see note on 25:16.   **32:25** Or *out of control, and they mocked anyone who opposed them.* The meaning of the Hebrew is unclear.   **32:29** As in Greek and Latin versions; Hebrew reads *Today ordain yourselves.*   **32:30** Or *to make atonement.*   **33:6** Hebrew *Horeb,* another name for Sinai.   **33:7** This "Tent of Meeting" is different from the Tabernacle described in chapters 26 and 36.   **33:19** *Yahweh* is a transliteration of the proper name *YHWH* that is sometimes rendered "Jehovah"; in this translation it is usually rendered "the LORD" (note the use of small capitals).

MATTHEW 26:69–27:14

Jesus had earlier predicted both Judas's betrayal and Peter's disowning of him. Nothing took Jesus by surprise during this long painful evening.

Meanwhile, Peter was sitting outside in the courtyard. A servant girl came over and said to him, "You were one of those with Jesus the Galilean."

[70]But Peter denied it in front of everyone. "I don't know what you're talking about," he said.

[71]Later, out by the gate, another servant girl noticed him and said to those standing around, "This man was with Jesus of Nazareth.*"

[72]Again Peter denied it, this time with an oath. "I don't even know the man," he said.

[73]A little later some of the other bystanders came over to Peter and said, "You must be one of them; we can tell by your Galilean accent."

[74]Peter swore, "A curse on me if I'm lying—I don't know the man!" And immediately the rooster crowed.

[75]Suddenly, Jesus' words flashed through Peter's mind: "Before the rooster crows, you will deny three times that you even know me." And he went away, weeping bitterly.

27:1VERY early in the morning the leading priests and the elders met again to lay plans for putting Jesus to death. [2]Then they bound him, led him away, and took him to Pilate, the Roman governor.

[3]When Judas, who had betrayed him, realized that Jesus had been condemned to die, he was filled with remorse. So he took the thirty pieces of silver back to the leading priests and the elders. [4]"I have sinned," he declared, "for I have betrayed an innocent man."

"What do we care?" they retorted. "That's your problem."

[5]Then Judas threw the silver coins down in the Temple and went out and hanged himself.

[6]The leading priests picked up the coins. "It wouldn't be right to put this money in the Temple treasury," they said, "since it was payment for murder."* [7]After some discussion they finally decided to buy the potter's field, and they made it into a cemetery for foreigners. [8]That is why the field is still called the Field of Blood. [9]This fulfilled the prophecy of Jeremiah that says,

"They took* the thirty pieces of
    silver—
    the price at which he was valued
        by the people of Israel,
[10] and purchased the potter's field,
        as the LORD directed.*"

[11]Now Jesus was standing before Pilate, the Roman governor. "Are you the king of the Jews?" the governor asked him.

Jesus replied, "You have said it."

[12]But when the leading priests and the elders made their accusations against him, Jesus remained silent. [13]"Don't you hear all these charges they are bringing

---

WHAT THE BIBLE SAYS

Salvation and forgiveness

MATTHEW 27:11-13 As God living in fragile flesh as a human being, Jesus fully experienced the pain of the rejection and the beatings recorded in Scripture. However, his divine insight into God's plan allowed him to forgive the people who caused him pain during the very moment that he was persecuted and rejected by them. Despite the many ways in which his accusers abused him, Jesus never once lashed out or cursed anyone in response. • When we find ourselves suffering or struggling to forgive those who have done us wrong, it helps to remember God's eternal plan. When you seek to forgive as Christ forgave, you acknowledge that God knows and understands how your suffering will work for you in the long run. Forgiveness is not only an act of faith, but a willingness to let go of grudges and hurt and let God set you free.

against you?" Pilate demanded. [14]But Jesus made no response to any of the charges, much to the governor's surprise.

26:71 Or *Jesus the Nazarene.* 27:6 Greek *since it is the price for blood.* 27:9 Or *I took.* 27:9-10 Greek as the LORD *directed me.* Zech 11:12-13; Jer 32:6-9.

PSALM 33:1-11

Let the godly sing for joy to the LORD;
it is fitting for the pure to praise
him.
[2] Praise the LORD with melodies on
the lyre;
make music for him on the ten-
stringed harp.
[3] Sing a new song of praise to him;
play skillfully on the harp, and sing
with joy.
[4] For the word of the LORD holds true,
and we can trust everything he
does.
[5] He loves whatever is just and good;
the unfailing love of the LORD fills
the earth.

[6] The LORD merely spoke,
and the heavens were created.

He breathed the word,
and all the stars were born.
[7] He assigned the sea its boundaries
and locked the oceans in vast
reservoirs.
[8] Let the whole world fear the LORD,
and let everyone stand in awe of
him.
[9] For when he spoke, the world began!
It appeared at his command.

[10] The LORD frustrates the plans of
the nations
and thwarts all their schemes.
[11] But the LORD's plans stand firm
forever;
his intentions can never be shaken.

PROVERBS 8:33-36

"Listen to my [Wisdom's] instruction and be wise. Don't ignore it. Joyful are those who listen to me, watching for me daily at my gates, waiting for me outside my home! For whoever finds me finds life and receives favor from the LORD. But those who miss me injure themselves. All who hate me love death."

FEBRUARY**12**

EXODUS 34:1-35:9

After the Gold Calf incident, God gave Moses another copy of the words of the covenant on two stone tablets along with further instructions.

Then the LORD told Moses, "Chisel out two stone tablets like the first ones. I will write on them the same words that were on the tablets you smashed. [2]Be ready in the morning to climb up Mount Sinai and present yourself to me on the top of the mountain. [3]No one else may come with you. In fact, no one is to appear anywhere on the mountain. Do not even let the flocks or herds graze near the mountain."

[4]So Moses chiseled out two tablets of stone like the first ones. Early in the morning he climbed Mount Sinai as the LORD had commanded him, and he carried the two stone tablets in his hands.

[5]Then the LORD came down in a cloud and stood there with him; and he called out his own name, Yahweh.* [6]The LORD passed in front of Moses, calling out,

"Yahweh!* The LORD!
The God of compassion and mercy!
I am slow to anger
and filled with unfailing love and
faithfulness.
[7] I lavish unfailing love to a thousand
generations.*
I forgive iniquity, rebellion, and sin.
But I do not excuse the guilty.
I lay the sins of the parents upon
their children and grandchildren;
the entire family is affected—
even children in the third and
fourth generations."

[8]Moses immediately threw himself to the ground and worshiped. [9]And he said, "O Lord, if it is true that I have found favor with you, then please travel with us. Yes, this is a stubborn and rebellious people, but please forgive our iniquity and our sins. Claim us as your own special possession."

[10]The LORD replied, "Listen, I am making a covenant with you in the presence of all your people. I will perform miracles that have never been performed anywhere in all the earth or in any nation. And all the people around you will see the power of the LORD—the awesome power I will display for you. [11]But listen carefully to everything I command you today. Then I will go ahead of you and drive out the Amorites, Canaanites, Hittites, Perizzites, Hivites, and Jebusites.

[12]"Be very careful never to make a treaty with the people who live in the land where you are going. If you do, you will follow their evil ways and be trapped. [13]Instead, you must break down their pagan altars, smash their sacred pillars, and cut down their Asherah poles. [14]You must worship no other gods, for the LORD, whose very name is Jealous, is a God who is jealous about his relationship with you.

[15]"You must not make a treaty of any kind with the people living in the land. They lust after their gods, offering sacrifices to them. They will invite you to join them in their sacrificial meals, and you will go with them. [16]Then you will accept their daughters, who sacrifice to other gods, as wives for your sons. And they will seduce your sons to commit adultery against me by worshiping other gods. [17]You must not make any gods of molten metal for yourselves.

[18]"You must celebrate the Festival of Unleavened Bread. For seven days the bread you eat must be made without yeast, just as I commanded you. Celebrate this festival annually at the appointed time in early spring, in the month of Abib,* for that is the anniversary of your departure from Egypt.

[19]"The firstborn of every animal belongs to me, including the firstborn males from your herds of cattle and your flocks of sheep and goats. [20]A firstborn donkey may be bought back from the LORD by presenting a lamb or young goat in its place. But if you do not buy it back, you must break its neck. However, you must buy back every firstborn son.

"No one may appear before me without an offering.

[21]"You have six days each week for your ordinary work, but on the seventh day you must stop working, even during the seasons of plowing and harvest.

[22]"You must celebrate the Festival of Harvest* with the first crop of the wheat harvest, and celebrate the Festival of the Final Harvest* at the end of the harvest season. [23]Three times each year every man in Israel must appear before the Sovereign, the LORD, the God of Israel. [24]I will drive out the other nations ahead of you and expand your territory, so no one will covet and conquer your land while you appear before the LORD your God three times each year.

[25]"You must not offer the blood of my sacrificial offerings together with any baked goods containing yeast. And none of the meat of the Passover sacrifice may be kept over until the next morning.

[26]"As you harvest your crops, bring the very best of the first harvest to the house of the LORD your God.

"You must not cook a young goat in its mother's milk."

[27]Then the LORD said to Moses, "Write down all these instructions, for they represent the terms of the covenant I am making with you and with Israel."

[28]Moses remained there on the mountain with the LORD forty days and forty nights. In all that time he ate no bread and drank no water. And the LORD* wrote the terms of the covenant—the Ten Commandments*—on the stone tablets.

[29]When Moses came down Mount Sinai carrying the two stone tablets inscribed with the terms of the covenant,* he wasn't aware that his face had become radiant because he had spoken to the LORD. [30]So when Aaron and the people of Israel saw the radiance of Moses' face, they were afraid to come near him. [31]But Moses called out to them and asked Aaron and all the leaders of the community to come over, and he talked

with them. ³²Then all the people of Israel approached him, and Moses gave them all the instructions the LORD had given him on Mount Sinai. ³³When Moses finished speaking with them, he covered his face with a veil. ³⁴But whenever he went into the Tent of Meeting to speak with the LORD, he would remove the veil until he came out again. Then he would give the people whatever instructions the LORD had given him, ³⁵and the people of Israel would see the radiant glow of his face. So he would put the veil over his face until he returned to speak with the LORD.

³⁵:¹THEN Moses called together the whole community of Israel and told them, "These are the instructions the LORD has commanded you to follow. ²You have six days each week for your ordinary work, but the seventh day must be a Sabbath day of complete rest, a holy day dedicated to the LORD. Anyone who works on that day must be put to death. ³You must not even light a fire in any of your homes on the Sabbath."

⁴Then Moses said to the whole community of Israel, "This is what the LORD has commanded: ⁵Take a sacred offering for the LORD. Let those with generous hearts present the following gifts to the LORD:

gold, silver, and bronze;
⁶ blue, purple, and scarlet thread;
fine linen and goat hair for cloth;
⁷ tanned ram skins and fine goatskin leather;
acacia wood;
⁸ olive oil for the lamps;
spices for the anointing oil and the fragrant incense;
⁹ onyx stones, and other gemstones to be set in the ephod and the priest's chestpiece."

34:5 *Yahweh* is a transliteration of the proper name *YHWH* that is sometimes rendered "Jehovah"; in this translation it is usually rendered "the LORD" (note the use of small capitals). **34:6** See note on 34:5.   **34:7** Hebrew *for thousands.* **34:18** Hebrew *appointed time in the month of Abib.* This first month of the ancient Hebrew lunar calendar usually occurs within the months of March and April.   **34:22a** Hebrew *Festival of Weeks;* compare 23:16. This was later called the Festival of Pentecost. It is celebrated today as Shavuat (or Shabuoth).   **34:22b** Or *Festival of Ingathering.* This was later called the Festival of Shelters or Festival of Tabernacles (see Lev 23:33-36). It is celebrated today as Sukkot (or Succoth).   **34:28a** Hebrew *he.*   **34:28b** Hebrew *the ten words.*   **34:29** Hebrew *the two tablets of the Testimony;* see note on 25:16.

MATTHEW 27:15-31
The Jews were under Roman occupation and were not allowed to mete out capital punishment. So, after the Jewish high council condemned Jesus, they went to Pilate and urged him to have Jesus crucified.

Now it was the governor's custom each year during the Passover celebration to release one prisoner to the crowd—anyone they wanted. ¹⁶This year there was a notorious prisoner, a man named Barabbas.* ¹⁷As the crowds gathered before Pilate's house that morning, he asked them, "Which one do you want me to release to you—Barabbas, or Jesus who is called the Messiah?" ¹⁸(He knew very well that the religious leaders had arrested Jesus out of envy.)

¹⁹Just then, as Pilate was sitting on the judgment seat, his wife sent him this message: "Leave that innocent man alone. I suffered through a terrible nightmare about him last night."

²⁰Meanwhile, the leading priests and the elders persuaded the crowd to ask for Barabbas to be released and for Jesus to be put to death. ²¹So the governor asked again, "Which of these two do you want me to release to you?"

The crowd shouted back, "Barabbas!"

²²Pilate responded, "Then what should I do with Jesus who is called the Messiah?"

They shouted back, "Crucify him!"

²³"Why?" Pilate demanded. "What crime has he committed?"

But the mob roared even louder, "Crucify him!"

²⁴Pilate saw that he wasn't getting anywhere and that a riot was developing. So he sent for a bowl of water and washed his hands before the crowd, saying, "I am innocent of this man's blood. The responsibility is yours!"

²⁵And all the people yelled back, "We will take responsibility for his death—we and our children!"*

²⁶So Pilate released Barabbas to them. He ordered Jesus flogged with a lead-tipped whip, then turned him over to the Roman soldiers to be crucified.

²⁷Some of the governor's soldiers took Jesus into their headquarters* and called out the entire regiment. ²⁸They stripped

him and put a scarlet robe on him. ²⁹They wove thorn branches into a crown and put it on his head, and they placed a reed stick in his right hand as a scepter. Then they knelt before him in mockery and taunted, "Hail! King of the Jews!" ³⁰And they spit on him and grabbed the stick and struck him on the head with it. ³¹When they were finally tired of mocking him, they took off the robe and put his own clothes on him again. Then they led him away to be crucified.

27:16 Some manuscripts read *Jesus Barabbas;* also in 27:17.
27:25 Greek "His blood be on us and on our children."
27:27 Or *into the Praetorium.*

PSALM 33:12-22

What joy for the nation whose God
    is the LORD,
  whose people he has chosen as
    his inheritance.

¹³ The LORD looks down from heaven
    and sees the whole human race.
¹⁴ From his throne he observes
    all who live on the earth.
¹⁵ He made their hearts,
  so he understands everything
    they do.
¹⁶ The best-equipped army cannot save
    a king,
  nor is great strength enough to save
    a warrior.

¹⁷ Don't count on your warhorse to give
    you victory—
  for all its strength, it cannot save you.

¹⁸ But the LORD watches over those
    who fear him,
  those who rely on his unfailing love.
¹⁹ He rescues them from death
  and keeps them alive in times
    of famine.

²⁰ We put our hope in the LORD.
  He is our help and our shield.
²¹ In him our hearts rejoice,
  for we trust in his holy name.
²² Let your unfailing love surround
    us, LORD,
  for our hope is in you alone.

PROVERBS 9:1-6

Wisdom has built her house; she has carved its seven columns. She has prepared a great banquet, mixed the wines, and set the table. She has sent her servants to invite everyone to come. She calls out from the heights overlooking the city. "Come in with me," she urges the simple. To those who lack good judgment, she says, "Come, eat my food, and drink the wine I have mixed. Leave your simple ways behind, and begin to live; learn to use good judgment."

Why Jesus had to die

WHAT THE BIBLE SAYS

MATTHEW 27:22-23 When Adam and Eve disobeyed God's explicit instructions, sin entered the human race, and a wall went up separating us from God. There was nothing humanity could do to breach that wall and enter the presence of God, who is absolutely holy. Fortunately, God loved us so much that he himself made a way for us to have communion with him again. •The Old Testament animal sacrifices were a temporary way of dealing with sin. God saw the animal blood and provided forgiveness, knowing that he would one day settle the debt once and for all with Jesus' one perfect sacrifice for all sin. Jesus' sacrifice breaks down that wall between us and God and allows us to fellowship with God. It was only by becoming human and actually dying that Jesus could "break the power of the devil, who had the power of death" (Hebrews 2:14, October 31). Jesus healed many broken bodies with just a touch or a word; to heal our sin and to conquer death, however, he had to die and rise again.

EXODUS 35:10–36:38

Moses began to carry out the instructions for the Tabernacle that he had been given on the mountain. God provided a gifted man named Bezalel to oversee the details of the project.

"**C**ome, all of you who are gifted craftsmen. Construct everything that the LORD has commanded:

¹¹ the Tabernacle and its sacred tent, its covering, clasps, frames, crossbars, posts, and bases;

¹² the Ark and its carrying poles;
the Ark's cover—the place of atonement;
the inner curtain to shield the Ark;

¹³ the table, its carrying poles, and all its utensils;
the Bread of the Presence;

¹⁴ for light, the lampstand, its accessories, the lamp cups, and the olive oil for lighting;

¹⁵ the incense altar and its carrying poles;
the anointing oil and fragrant incense;
the curtain for the entrance of the Tabernacle;

¹⁶ the altar of burnt offering;
the bronze grating of the altar and its carrying poles and utensils;
the washbasin with its stand;

¹⁷ the curtains for the walls of the courtyard;
the posts and their bases;
the curtain for the entrance to the courtyard;

¹⁸ the tent pegs of the Tabernacle and courtyard and their ropes;

¹⁹ the beautifully stitched garments for the priests to wear while ministering in the Holy Place—the sacred garments for Aaron the priest, and the garments for his sons to wear as they minister as priests."

²⁰So the whole community of Israel left Moses and returned to their tents. ²¹All whose hearts were stirred and whose spirits were moved came and brought their sacred offerings to the LORD. They brought all the materials needed for the Tabernacle,* for the performance of its rituals, and for the sacred garments. ²²Both men and women came, all whose hearts were willing. They brought to the LORD their offerings of gold—brooches, earrings, rings from their fingers, and necklaces. They presented gold objects of every kind as a special offering to the LORD. ²³All those who owned the following items willingly brought them: blue, purple, and scarlet thread; fine linen and goat hair for cloth; and tanned ram skins and fine goatskin leather. ²⁴And all who had silver and bronze objects gave them as a sacred offering to the LORD. And those who had acacia wood brought it for use in the project.

²⁵All the women who were skilled in sewing and spinning prepared blue, purple, and scarlet thread, and fine linen cloth. ²⁶All the women who were willing used their skills to spin the goat hair into yarn. ²⁷The leaders brought onyx stones and the special gemstones to be set in the ephod and the priest's chestpiece. ²⁸They also brought spices and olive oil for the light, the anointing oil, and the fragrant incense. ²⁹So the people of Israel—every man and woman who was eager to help in the work the LORD had given them through Moses—brought their gifts and gave them freely to the LORD.

³⁰Then Moses told the people of Israel, "The LORD has specifically chosen Bezalel son of Uri, grandson of Hur, of the tribe of Judah. ³¹The LORD has filled Bezalel with the Spirit of God, giving him great wisdom, ability, and expertise in all kinds of crafts. ³²He is a master craftsman, expert in working with gold, silver, and bronze. ³³He is skilled in engraving and mounting gemstones and in carving wood. He is a master at every craft. ³⁴And the LORD has given both him and Oholiab son of Ahisamach, of the tribe of Dan, the ability to teach their skills to others. ³⁵The LORD has given them special skills as engravers, designers, embroiderers in blue, purple, and scarlet thread on fine

linen cloth, and weavers. They excel as craftsmen and as designers.

36:1"THE LORD has gifted Bezalel, Oholiab, and the other skilled craftsmen with wisdom and ability to perform any task involved in building the sanctuary. Let them construct and furnish the Tabernacle, just as the LORD has commanded."

2 So Moses summoned Bezalel and Oholiab and all the others who were specially gifted by the LORD and were eager to get to work. 3 Moses gave them the materials donated by the people of Israel as sacred offerings for the completion of the sanctuary. But the people continued to bring additional gifts each morning. 4 Finally the craftsmen who were working on the sanctuary left their work. 5 They went to Moses and reported, "The people have given more than enough materials to complete the job the LORD has commanded us to do!"

6 So Moses gave the command, and this message was sent throughout the camp: "Men and women, don't prepare any more gifts for the sanctuary. We have enough!" So the people stopped bringing their sacred offerings. 7 Their contributions were more than enough to complete the whole project.

8 The skilled craftsmen made ten curtains of finely woven linen for the Tabernacle. Then Bezalel* decorated the curtains with blue, purple, and scarlet thread and with skillfully embroidered cherubim. 9 All ten curtains were exactly the same size—42 feet long and 6 feet wide.* 10 Five of these curtains were joined together to make one long curtain, and the other five were joined to make a second long curtain. 11 He made fifty loops of blue yarn and put them along the edge of the last curtain in each set. 12 The fifty loops along the edge of one curtain matched the fifty loops along the edge of the other curtain. 13 Then he made fifty gold clasps and fastened the long curtains together with the clasps. In this way, the Tabernacle was made of one continuous piece.

14 He made eleven curtains of goat-hair cloth to serve as a tent covering for the Tabernacle. 15 These eleven curtains were all exactly the same size—45 feet long and 6 feet wide.* 16 Bezalel joined five of these curtains together to make one long curtain, and the other six were joined to make a second long curtain. 17 He made fifty loops for the edge of each large curtain. 18 He also made fifty bronze clasps to fasten the long curtains together. In this way, the tent covering was made of one continuous piece. 19 He completed the tent covering with a layer of tanned ram skins and a layer of fine goatskin leather.

20 For the framework of the Tabernacle, Bezalel constructed frames of acacia wood. 21 Each frame was 15 feet high and 27 inches wide,* 22 with two pegs under each frame. All the frames were identical. 23 He made twenty of these frames to support the curtains on the south side of the Tabernacle. 24 He also made forty silver bases—two bases under each frame, with the pegs fitting securely into the bases. 25 For the north side of the Tabernacle, he made another twenty frames, 26 with their forty silver bases, two bases under each frame. 27 He made six frames for the rear—the west side of the Tabernacle— 28 along with two additional frames to reinforce the rear corners of the Tabernacle. 29 These corner frames were matched at the bottom and firmly attached at the top with a single ring, forming a single corner unit. Both of these corner units were made the same way. 30 So there were eight frames at the rear of the Tabernacle, set in sixteen silver bases—two bases under each frame.

31 Then he made crossbars of acacia wood to link the frames, five crossbars for the north side of the Tabernacle 32 and five for the south side. He also made five crossbars for the rear of the Tabernacle, which faced west. 33 He made the middle crossbar to attach halfway up the frames; it ran all the way from one end of the Tabernacle to the other. 34 He overlaid the frames with gold and made gold rings to hold the crossbars. Then he overlaid the crossbars with gold as well.

35 For the inside of the Tabernacle, Bezalel made a special curtain of finely woven linen. He decorated it with blue, purple, and scarlet thread and with skillfully embroidered cherubim. 36 For the

curtain, he made four posts of acacia wood and four gold hooks. He overlaid the posts with gold and set them in four silver bases.

37Then he made another curtain for the entrance to the sacred tent. He made it of finely woven linen and embroidered it with exquisite designs using blue, purple, and scarlet thread. 38This curtain was hung on gold hooks attached to five posts. The posts with their decorated tops and hooks were overlaid with gold, and the five bases were cast from bronze.

35:21 Hebrew *Tent of Meeting.* 36:8 Hebrew *he;* also in 36:16, 20, 35. See 37:1. 36:9 Hebrew *28 cubits* [12.9 meters] *long and 4 cubits* [1.8 meters] *wide.* 36:15 Hebrew *30 cubits* [13.8 meters] *long and 4 cubits* [1.8 meters] *wide.* 36:21 Hebrew *10 cubits* [4.6 meters] *high and 1.5 cubits* [69 centimeters] *wide.*

MATTHEW 27:32-66

Jesus' death on the cross was an event of great cosmic proportions. The blood sacrifice of a spotless Lamb—Jesus, the Son of God—would take away the sins of the world and mark the sure defeat of Satan.

Along the way, they came across a man named Simon, who was from Cyrene,* and the soldiers forced him to carry Jesus' cross. 33And they went out to a place called Golgotha (which means "Place of the Skull"). 34The soldiers gave him wine mixed with bitter gall, but when he had tasted it, he refused to drink it.

35After they had nailed him to the cross, the soldiers gambled for his clothes by throwing dice.* 36Then they sat around and kept guard as he hung there. 37A sign was fastened to the cross above Jesus' head, announcing the charge against him. It read: "This is Jesus, the King of the Jews." 38Two revolutionaries* were crucified with him, one on his right and one on his left.

39The people passing by shouted abuse, shaking their heads in mockery. 40"Look at you now!" they yelled at him. "You said you were going to destroy the Temple and rebuild it in three days. Well then, if you are the Son of God, save yourself and come down from the cross!"

41The leading priests, the teachers of religious law, and the elders also mocked Jesus. 42"He saved others," they scoffed, "but he can't save himself! So he is the King of Israel, is he? Let him come down from the cross right now, and we will be-

lieve in him! 43He trusted God, so let God rescue him now if he wants him! For he said, 'I am the Son of God.'" 44Even the revolutionaries who were crucified with him ridiculed him in the same way.

45At noon, darkness fell across the whole land until three o'clock. 46At about three o'clock, Jesus called out with a loud voice, *"Eli, Eli,* * *lema sabachthani?"* which means "My God, my God, why have you abandoned me?"*

47Some of the bystanders misunderstood and thought he was calling for the prophet Elijah. 48One of them ran and filled a sponge with sour wine, holding it up to him on a reed stick so he could drink. 49But the rest said, "Wait! Let's see whether Elijah comes to save him."*

50Then Jesus shouted out again, and he released his spirit. 51At that moment the curtain in the sanctuary of the Temple was torn in two, from top to bottom. The earth shook, rocks split apart, 52and tombs opened. The bodies of many godly men and women who had died were raised from the dead. 53They left the cemetery after Jesus' resurrection, went into the holy city of Jerusalem, and appeared to many people.

54The Roman officer* and the other soldiers at the crucifixion were terrified by the earthquake and all that had happened. They said, "This man truly was the Son of God!"

55And many women who had come from Galilee with Jesus to care for him were watching from a distance. 56Among them were Mary Magdalene, Mary (the mother of James and Joseph), and the mother of James and John, the sons of Zebedee.

57As evening approached, Joseph, a rich man from Arimathea who had become a follower of Jesus, 58went to Pilate and asked for Jesus' body. And Pilate issued an order to release it to him. 59Joseph took the body and wrapped it in a long sheet of clean linen cloth. 60He placed it in his own new tomb, which had been carved out of the rock. Then he rolled a great stone across the entrance and left. 61Both Mary Magdalene and the other Mary were sitting across from the tomb and watching.

⁶²The next day, on the Sabbath,* the leading priests and Pharisees went to see Pilate. ⁶³They told him, "Sir, we remember what that deceiver once said while he was still alive: 'After three days I will rise from the dead.' ⁶⁴So we request that you seal the tomb until the third day. This will prevent his disciples from coming and stealing his body and then telling everyone he was raised from the dead! If that happens, we'll be worse off than we were at first."

⁶⁵Pilate replied, "Take guards and secure it the best you can." ⁶⁶So they sealed the tomb and posted guards to protect it.

27:32 *Cyrene* was a city in northern Africa.   27:35 Greek *by casting lots.* A few late manuscripts add *This fulfilled the word of the prophet: "They divided my garments among themselves and cast lots for my robe."* See Ps 22:18.   27:38 Or *criminals;* also in 27:44.   27:46a Some manuscripts read *Eloi, Eloi.* 27:46b Ps 22:1.   27:49 Some manuscripts add *And another took a spear and pierced his side, and out flowed water and blood.* Compare John 19:34.   27:54 Greek *The centurion.* 27:62 Or *On the next day, which is after the Preparation.*

PSALM 34:1-10*

A psalm of David, regarding the time he pretended to be insane in front of Abimelech, who sent him away.

¹ I will praise the LORD at all times.
    I will constantly speak his praises.
² I will boast only in the LORD;
    let all who are helpless take heart.
³ Come, let us tell of the LORD's
        greatness;
    let us exalt his name together.

⁴ I prayed to the LORD, and he
        answered me.
    He freed me from all my fears.
⁵ Those who look to him for help will
        be radiant with joy;
    no shadow of shame will darken
        their faces.
⁶ In my desperation I prayed, and the
        LORD listened;
    he saved me from all my troubles.
⁷ For the angel of the LORD is a guard;
    he surrounds and defends all who
        fear him.

⁸ Taste and see that the LORD is good.
    Oh, the joys of those who take
        refuge in him!
⁹ Fear the LORD, you his godly people,
    for those who fear him will have
        all they need.
¹⁰ Even strong young lions sometimes
        go hungry,
    but those who trust in the LORD
        will lack no good thing.

34 This psalm is a Hebrew acrostic poem; each verse begins with a successive letter of the Hebrew alphabet.

PROVERBS 9:7-8

Anyone who rebukes a mocker will get an insult in return. Anyone who corrects the wicked will get hurt. So don't bother correcting mockers; they will only hate you. But correct the wise, and they will love you.

WHAT THE BIBLE SAYS

Spiritual gifts

EXODUS 35:30-31 The Bible says that God's children have "different gifts for doing certain things well" (Romans 12:6, July 29). You may think to yourself, "I can't stand up and preach to thousands," or "I'm never going to write a book that will change lives." That's okay—God doesn't expect every Christian to preach sermons or to write a best seller! God will use who you are and the experiences you've had in order to help you make full use of whatever spiritual gift he has given you. • The Bible describes some of these gifts, such as teaching, showing mercy, hospitality, and helping others. In this passage in Exodus, you read that Bezalel was blessed by the Spirit of God with "wisdom, ability, and expertise in all kinds of crafts." He and Oholiab, who was also blessed, used these skills not for their own glory or personal satisfaction, but to beautify the Tabernacle of God. Similarly, it is important that we keep the focus of our abilities on glorifying God.

EXODUS 37:1–38:31

The Tabernacle consisted of three main areas: the outermost courtyard, the Holy Place, and the Most Holy Place where the Ark of the Covenant sat. Rules governing these three areas became more stringent the closer one came to God's central dwelling place.

Next Bezalel made the Ark of acacia wood—a sacred chest 45 inches long, 27 inches wide, and 27 inches high.* ²He overlaid it inside and outside with pure gold, and he ran a molding of gold all around it. ³He cast four gold rings and attached them to its four feet, two rings on each side. ⁴Then he made poles from acacia wood and overlaid them with gold. ⁵He inserted the poles into the rings at the sides of the Ark to carry it.

⁶Then he made the Ark's cover—the place of atonement—from pure gold. It was 45 inches long and 27 inches wide.* ⁷He made two cherubim from hammered gold and placed them on the two ends of the atonement cover. ⁸He molded the cherubim on each end of the atonement cover, making it all of one piece of gold. ⁹The cherubim faced each other and looked down on the atonement cover. With their wings spread above it, they protected it.

¹⁰Then Bezalel* made the table of acacia wood, 36 inches long, 18 inches wide, and 27 inches high.* ¹¹He overlaid it with pure gold and ran a gold molding around the edge. ¹²He decorated it with a 3-inch border* all around, and he ran a gold molding along the border. ¹³Then he cast four gold rings for the table and attached them at the four corners next to the four legs. ¹⁴The rings were attached near the border to hold the poles that were used to carry the table. ¹⁵He made these poles from acacia wood and overlaid them with gold. ¹⁶Then he made special containers of pure gold for the table—bowls, pans, jars, and pitchers—to be used in pouring out liquid offerings.

¹⁷Then Bezalel made the lampstand of pure, hammered gold. He made the entire lampstand and its decorations of one piece—the base, center stem, lamp cups, buds, and petals. ¹⁸The lampstand had six branches going out from the center stem, three on each side. ¹⁹Each of the six branches had three lamp cups shaped like almond blossoms, complete with buds and petals. ²⁰The center stem of the lampstand was crafted with four lamp cups shaped like almond blossoms, complete with buds and petals. ²¹There was an almond bud beneath each pair of branches where the six branches extended from the center stem, all made of one piece. ²²The almond buds and branches were all of one piece with the center stem, and they were hammered from pure gold.

²³He also made seven lamps for the lampstand, lamp snuffers, and trays, all of pure gold. ²⁴The entire lampstand, along with its accessories, was made from seventy-five pounds* of pure gold.

²⁵Then Bezalel made the incense altar of acacia wood. It was 18 inches square and 36 inches high,* with horns at the corners carved from the same piece of wood as the altar itself. ²⁶He overlaid the top, sides, and horns of the altar with pure gold, and he ran a gold molding around the entire altar. ²⁷He made two gold rings and attached them on opposite sides of the altar below the gold molding to hold the carrying poles. ²⁸He made the poles of acacia wood and overlaid them with gold.

²⁹Then he made the sacred anointing oil and the fragrant incense, using the techniques of a skilled incense maker.

38:1 Next Bezalel* used acacia wood to construct the square altar of burnt offering. It was 7½ feet wide, 7½ feet long, and 4½ feet high.* ²He made horns for each of its four corners so that the horns and altar were all one piece. He overlaid the altar with bronze. ³Then he made all the altar utensils of bronze—the ash buckets, shovels, basins, meat forks, and firepans. [4]Next he made a bronze grating and installed it halfway down the side of the altar, under the ledge. [5]He cast four rings and attached them to the corners of the bronze grating to hold the carrying poles. [6]He made the poles from acacia wood and overlaid them with bronze. [7]He inserted the poles through the rings on the sides of the altar. The altar was hollow and was made from planks.

[8]Bezalel made the bronze washbasin and its bronze stand from bronze mirrors donated by the women who served at the entrance of the Tabernacle.*

[9]Then Bezalel made the courtyard, which was enclosed with curtains made of finely woven linen. On the south side the curtains were 150 feet long.* [10]They were held up by twenty posts set securely in twenty bronze bases. He hung the curtains with silver hooks and rings. [11]He made a similar set of curtains for the north side—150 feet of curtains held up by twenty posts set securely in bronze bases. He hung the curtains with silver hooks and rings. [12]The curtains on the west end of the courtyard were 75 feet long,* hung with silver hooks and rings and supported by ten posts set into ten bases. [13]The east end, the front, was also 75 feet long.

[14]The courtyard entrance was on the east end, flanked by two curtains. The curtain on the right side was 22½ feet long* and was supported by three posts set into three bases. [15]The curtain on the left side was also 22½ feet long and was supported by three posts set into three bases. [16]All the curtains used in the courtyard were made of finely woven linen. [17]Each post had a bronze base, and all the hooks and rings were silver. The tops of the posts of the courtyard were overlaid with silver, and the rings to hold up the curtains were made of silver.

[18]He made the curtain for the entrance to the courtyard of finely woven linen, and he decorated it with beautiful embroidery in blue, purple, and scarlet thread. It was 30 feet long, and its height was 7½ feet,* just like the curtains of the courtyard walls. [19]It was supported by four posts, each set securely in its own bronze base. The tops of the posts were overlaid with silver, and the hooks and rings were also made of silver.

[20]All the tent pegs used in the Tabernacle and courtyard were made of bronze.

[21]This is an inventory of the materials used in building the Tabernacle of the Covenant.* The Levites compiled the figures, as Moses directed, and Ithamar son of Aaron the priest served as recorder. [22]Bezalel son of Uri, grandson of Hur, of the tribe of Judah, made everything just as the LORD had commanded Moses. [23]He was assisted by Oholiab son of Ahisamach, of the tribe of Dan, a craftsman expert at engraving, designing, and embroidering

HOW WE LIVE

Sharing our faith

MATTHEW 28:19-20 Jesus commands that we go, make disciples, baptize, and teach, so that others may do the same. It doesn't matter whether you share your faith with your next-door neighbor or travel to the far corners of the earth—you are to "go." This was not a suggestion; it was a command to all who call him "Lord." • How do you do this? First Peter 3:15 says, "If someone asks about your Christian hope, always be ready to explain it." Just be willing to share your own story. Think about why you made a decision to put your faith in Jesus. Think about the differences in your life since you became a Christian. Never underestimate the strength of your personal testimony. Those who listen to what you say may be greatly affected, and you may have the joy of welcoming a new member into the family of God!

with blue, purple, and scarlet thread on fine linen cloth.

[24] The people brought special offerings of gold totaling 2,193 pounds,* as measured by the weight of the sanctuary shekel. This gold was used throughout the Tabernacle.

[25] The whole community of Israel gave 7,545 pounds* of silver, as measured by the weight of the sanctuary shekel. [26] This silver came from the tax collected from each man registered in the census. (The tax is one beka, which is half a shekel,* based on the sanctuary shekel.) The tax was collected from 603,550 men who had reached their twentieth birthday. [27] The hundred bases for the frames of the sanctuary walls and for the posts supporting the inner curtain required 7,500 pounds of silver, about 75 pounds for each base.* [28] The remaining 45 pounds* of silver was used to make the hooks and rings and to overlay the tops of the posts.

[29] The people also brought as special offerings 5,310 pounds* of bronze, [30] which was used for casting the bases for the posts at the entrance to the Tabernacle, and for the bronze altar with its bronze grating and all the altar utensils. [31] Bronze was also used to make the bases for the posts that supported the curtains around the courtyard, the bases for the curtain at the entrance of the courtyard, and all the tent pegs for the Tabernacle and the courtyard.

37:1 Hebrew *2.5 cubits* [115 centimeters] *long, 1.5 cubits* [69 centimeters] *wide, and 1.5 cubits high.*   37:6 Hebrew *2.5 cubits* [115 centimeters] *long and 1.5 cubits* [69 centimeters] *wide.*   37:10a Hebrew *he;* also in 37:17, 25.   37:10b Hebrew *2 cubits* [92 centimeters] *long, 1 cubit* [46 centimeters] *wide, and 1.5 cubits* [69 centimeters] *high.* 37:12 Hebrew *a border of a handbreadth* [8 centimeters]. 37:24 Hebrew *1 talent* [34 kilograms].   37:25 Hebrew *1 cubit* [46 centimeters] *long and 1 cubit wide, a square, and 2 cubits* [92 centimeters] *high.*   38:1a Hebrew *he;* also in 38:8, 9.   38:1b Hebrew *5 cubits* [2.3 meters] *wide, 5 cubits long, a square, and 3 cubits* [1.4 meters] *high.*   38:8 Hebrew *Tent of Meeting;* also in 38:30. 38:9 Hebrew *100 cubits* [46 meters]; also in 38:11. 38:12 Hebrew *50 cubits* [23 meters]; also in 38:13. 38:14 Hebrew *15 cubits* [6.9 meters]; also in 38:15. 38:18 Hebrew *20 cubits* [9.2 meters] *long and 5 cubits* [2.3 meters] *high.*   38:21 Hebrew *the Tabernacle, the Tabernacle of the Testimony.*   38:24 Hebrew *29 talents and 730 shekels* [994 kilograms]. Each shekel weighed about 0.4 ounces.   38:25 Hebrew *100 talents and 1,775 shekels* [3,420 kilograms].   38:26 Or *0.2 ounces,* or *6 grams.* 38:27 Hebrew *100 talents* [3,400 kilograms] *of silver, 1 talent* [34 kilograms] *for each base.*   38:28 Hebrew *1,775 shekels* [20.2 kilograms].   38:29 Hebrew *70 talents and 2,400 shekels* [2,407 kilograms].

MATTHEW 28:1-20
The book of Matthew closes with an unforgettable Sunday morning. Jesus, who was dead, came back to life. Jesus' resurrection proved the truth of all he had taught and promised. The weary and worried disciples found new strength and a new commission.

Early on Sunday morning,* as the new day was dawning, Mary Magdalene and the other Mary went out to visit the tomb.

[2] Suddenly there was a great earthquake! For an angel of the Lord came down from heaven, rolled aside the stone, and sat on it. [3] His face shone like lightning, and his clothing was as white as snow. [4] The guards shook with fear when they saw him, and they fell into a dead faint.

[5] Then the angel spoke to the women. "Don't be afraid!" he said. "I know you are looking for Jesus, who was crucified. [6] He isn't here! He is risen from the dead, just as he said would happen. Come, see where his body was lying. [7] And now, go quickly and tell his disciples that he has risen from the dead, and he is going ahead of you to Galilee. You will see him there. Remember what I have told you."

[8] The women ran quickly from the tomb. They were very frightened but also filled with great joy, and they rushed to give the disciples the angel's message. [9] And as they went, Jesus met them and greeted them. And they ran to him, grasped his feet, and worshiped him. [10] Then Jesus said to them, "Don't be afraid! Go tell my brothers to leave for Galilee, and they will see me there."

[11] As the women were on their way, some of the guards went into the city and told the leading priests what had happened. [12] A meeting with the elders was called, and they decided to give the soldiers a large bribe. [13] They told the soldiers, "You must say, 'Jesus' disciples came during the night while we were sleeping, and they stole his body.' [14] If the governor hears about it, we'll stand up for you so you won't get in trouble." [15] So the guards accepted the bribe and said what they were told to say. Their story spread widely among the Jews, and they still tell it today.

¹⁶Then the eleven disciples left for Galilee, going to the mountain where Jesus had told them to go. ¹⁷When they saw him, they worshiped him—but some of them doubted!

¹⁸Jesus came and told his disciples, "I have been given all authority in heaven and on earth. ¹⁹Therefore, go and make disciples of all the nations,* baptizing them in the name of the Father and the Son and the Holy Spirit. ²⁰Teach these new disciples to obey all the commands I have given you. And be sure of this: I am with you always, even to the end of the age."

28:1 Greek *After the Sabbath, on the first day of the week.*
28:19 Or *all peoples.*

PSALM 34:11-22

Come, my children, and listen to me,
    and I will teach you to fear
    the LORD.
¹² Does anyone want to live a life
    that is long and prosperous?
¹³ Then keep your tongue from
    speaking evil
    and your lips from telling lies!
¹⁴ Turn away from evil and do good.
    Search for peace, and work
    to maintain it.
¹⁵ The eyes of the LORD watch over
    those who do right;
    his ears are open to their cries
    for help.

¹⁶ But the LORD turns his face against
    those who do evil;
    he will erase their memory from
    the earth.
¹⁷ The LORD hears his people when
    they call to him for help.
    He rescues them from all their
    troubles.
¹⁸ The LORD is close to the
    brokenhearted;
    he rescues those whose spirits
    are crushed.
¹⁹ The righteous person faces many
    troubles,
    but the LORD comes to the rescue
    each time.
²⁰ For the LORD protects the bones
    of the righteous;
    not one of them is broken!
²¹ Calamity will surely overtake
    the wicked,
    and those who hate the righteous
    will be punished.
²² But the LORD will redeem those who
    serve him.
    No one who takes refuge in him
    will be condemned.

PROVERBS 9:9-10

Instruct the wise, and they will be even wiser. Teach the righteous, and they will learn even more. □ Fear of the LORD is the foundation of wisdom. Knowledge of the Holy One results in good judgment.

FEBRUARY**15**

EXODUS 39:1-40:38

With the Tabernacle completed and in place, the glory of God filled it. God would now be present with them in this special sanctuary every day.

The craftsmen made beautiful sacred garments of blue, purple, and scarlet cloth—clothing for Aaron to wear while ministering in the Holy Place, just as the LORD had commanded Moses.

²Bezalel* made the ephod of finely woven linen and embroidered it with gold and with blue, purple, and scarlet thread. ³He made gold thread by hammering out thin sheets of gold and cutting it into fine strands. With great skill and care, he worked it into the fine linen with the blue, purple, and scarlet thread.

⁴The ephod consisted of two pieces, front and back, joined at the shoulders with two shoulder-pieces. ⁵The decorative sash was made of the same materials: finely woven linen embroidered with gold and with blue, purple, and scarlet thread, just as the LORD had commanded Moses. ⁶They mounted the two onyx stones in settings of gold filigree. The stones were engraved with the names of the tribes of Israel, just as a seal is engraved. ⁷He fastened these stones on the shoulder-pieces of the ephod as a reminder that the priest represents the people of Israel. All this was done just as the LORD had commanded Moses.

⁸Bezalel made the chestpiece with great skill and care. He made it to match the ephod, using finely woven linen embroidered with gold and with blue, purple, and scarlet thread. ⁹He made the chestpiece of a single piece of cloth folded to form a pouch nine inches* square. ¹⁰They mounted four rows of gemstones* on it. The first row contained a red carnelian, a pale-green peridot, and an emerald. ¹¹The second row contained a turquoise, a blue lapis lazuli, and a white moonstone. ¹²The third row contained an orange jacinth, an agate, and a purple amethyst. ¹³The fourth row contained a blue-green beryl, an onyx, and a green jasper. All these stones were set in gold filigree. ¹⁴Each stone represented one of the twelve sons of Israel, and the name of that tribe was engraved on it like a seal.

¹⁵To attach the chestpiece to the ephod, they made braided cords of pure gold thread. ¹⁶They also made two settings of gold filigree and two gold rings and attached them to the top corners of the chestpiece. ¹⁷They tied the two gold cords to the rings on the chestpiece. ¹⁸They tied the other ends of the cords to the gold settings on the shoulder-pieces of the ephod. ¹⁹Then they made two more gold rings and attached them to the inside edges of the chestpiece next to the ephod. ²⁰Then they made two more gold rings and attached them to the front of the ephod, below the shoulder-pieces, just above the knot where the decorative sash was fastened to the ephod. ²¹They attached the bottom rings of the chestpiece to the rings on the ephod with blue cords. In this way, the chestpiece was held securely to the ephod above the decorative sash. All this was done just as the LORD had commanded Moses.

²²Bezalel made the robe that is worn with the ephod from a single piece of blue woven cloth, ²³with an opening for Aaron's head in the middle of it. The opening was reinforced with a woven collar* so it would not tear. ²⁴They made pomegranates of blue, purple, and scarlet yarn, and attached them to the hem of the robe. ²⁵They also made bells of pure gold and placed them between the pomegranates along the hem of the robe, ²⁶with bells and pomegranates alternating all around the hem. This robe was to be worn whenever the priest ministered before the LORD, just as the LORD had commanded Moses.

²⁷They made tunics for Aaron and his sons from fine linen cloth. ²⁸The turban and the special head coverings were made of fine linen, and the undergarments were also made of finely woven linen. ²⁹The sashes were made of finely woven linen and embroidered with blue, purple, and scarlet thread, just as the LORD had commanded Moses.

³⁰Finally, they made the sacred medallion—the badge of holiness—of pure gold. They engraved it like a seal with these words: HOLY TO THE LORD. ³¹They attached the medallion with a blue cord to Aaron's turban, just as the LORD had commanded Moses.

³²And so at last the Tabernacle* was finished. The Israelites had done everything just as the LORD had commanded Moses. ³³And they brought the entire Tabernacle to Moses:

the sacred tent with all its furnishings, clasps, frames, crossbars, posts, and bases;
³⁴ the tent coverings of tanned ram skins and fine goatskin leather;
the inner curtain to shield the Ark;
³⁵ the Ark of the Covenant* and its carrying poles;
the Ark's cover—the place of atonement;
³⁶ the table and all its utensils;
the Bread of the Presence;

[37] the pure gold lampstand with its
symmetrical lamp cups, all its
accessories, and the olive oil for
lighting;
[38] the gold altar;
the anointing oil and fragrant
incense;
the curtain for the entrance of
the sacred tent;
[39] the bronze altar;
the bronze grating and its carrying
poles and utensils;
the washbasin with its stand;
[40] the curtains for the walls of the
courtyard;
the posts and their bases;
the curtain for the entrance to
the courtyard;
the ropes and tent pegs;
all the furnishings to be used in
worship at the Tabernacle;
[41] the beautifully stitched garments
for the priests to wear while
ministering in the Holy Place—
the sacred garments for Aaron
the priest, and the garments for
his sons to wear as they minister
as priests.

[42]So the people of Israel followed all of
the LORD's instructions to Moses. [43]Then
Moses inspected all their work. When he
found it had been done just as the LORD
had commanded him, he blessed them.

40:1THEN the LORD said to Moses, [2]"Set up
the Tabernacle* on the first day of the
new year.* [3]Place the Ark of the Covenant* inside, and install the inner curtain to enclose the Ark within the Most
Holy Place. [4]Then bring in the table, and
arrange the utensils on it. And bring in the
lampstand, and set up the lamps.
[5]"Place the gold incense altar in front of
the Ark of the Covenant. Then hang the
curtain at the entrance of the Tabernacle.
[6]Place the altar of burnt offering in front
of the Tabernacle entrance. [7]Set the washbasin between the Tabernacle* and the
altar, and fill it with water. [8]Then set up
the courtyard around the outside of the
tent, and hang the curtain for the courtyard entrance.
[9]"Take the anointing oil and anoint the

Tabernacle and all its furnishings to consecrate them and make them holy. [10]Anoint
the altar of burnt offering and its utensils
to consecrate them. Then the altar will become absolutely holy. [11]Next anoint the
washbasin and its stand to consecrate
them.
[12]"Present Aaron and his sons at the entrance of the Tabernacle, and wash them
with water. [13]Dress Aaron with the sacred
garments and anoint him, consecrating
him to serve me as a priest. [14]Then present his sons and dress them in their
tunics. [15]Anoint them as you did their father, so they may also serve me as priests.
With their anointing, Aaron's descendants are set apart for the priesthood forever, from generation to generation."
[16]Moses proceeded to do everything
just as the LORD had commanded him.
[17]So the Tabernacle was set up on the first
day of the first month of the second year.
[18]Moses erected the Tabernacle by setting
down its bases, inserting the frames, at-
taching the crossbars, and setting up the
posts. [19]Then he spread the coverings
over the Tabernacle framework and put
on the protective layers, just as the LORD
had commanded him.
[20]He took the stone tablets inscribed
with the terms of the covenant and
placed them* inside the Ark. Then he attached the carrying poles to the Ark, and
he set the Ark's cover—the place of atonement—on top of it. [21]Then he brought the
Ark of the Covenant into the Tabernacle
and hung the inner curtain to shield it
from view, just as the LORD had commanded him.
[22]Next Moses placed the table in the
Tabernacle, along the north side of the
Holy Place, just outside the inner curtain.
[23]And he arranged the Bread of the Presence on the table before the LORD, just as
the LORD had commanded him.
[24]He set the lampstand in the Tabernacle across from the table on the south
side of the Holy Place. [25]Then he lit the
lamps in the LORD's presence, just as the
LORD had commanded him. [26]He also
placed the gold incense altar in the Tabernacle, in the Holy Place in front of the
inner curtain. [27]On it he burned the fra-

grant incense, just as the LORD had commanded him.

[28]He hung the curtain at the entrance of the Tabernacle, [29]and he placed the altar of burnt offering near the Tabernacle entrance. On it he offered a burnt offering and a grain offering, just as the LORD had commanded him.

[30]Next Moses placed the washbasin between the Tabernacle and the altar. He filled it with water so the priests could wash themselves. [31]Moses and Aaron and Aaron's sons used water from it to wash their hands and feet. [32]Whenever they approached the altar and entered the Tabernacle, they washed themselves, just as the LORD had commanded Moses.

[33]Then he hung the curtains forming the courtyard around the Tabernacle and the altar. And he set up the curtain at the entrance of the courtyard. So at last Moses finished the work.

[34]Then the cloud covered the Tabernacle, and the glory of the LORD filled the Tabernacle. [35]Moses could no longer enter the Tabernacle because the cloud had settled down over it, and the glory of the LORD filled the Tabernacle.

[36]Now whenever the cloud lifted from the Tabernacle, the people of Israel would set out on their journey, following it. [37]But if the cloud did not rise, they remained where they were until it lifted. [38]The cloud of the LORD hovered over the Tabernacle during the day, and at night fire glowed inside the cloud so the whole family of Israel could see it. This continued throughout all their journeys.

39:2 Hebrew *He;* also in 39:8, 22.   39:9 Hebrew *1 span* [23 centimeters].   39:10 The identification of some of these gemstones is uncertain.   39:23 The meaning of the Hebrew is uncertain.   39:32 Hebrew *the Tabernacle, the Tent of Meeting;* also in 39:40.   39:35 Or *Ark of the Testimony.* 40:2a Hebrew *the Tabernacle, the Tent of Meeting;* also in 40:6, 29.   40:2b Hebrew *the first day of the first month.* This day of the ancient Hebrew lunar calendar occurred in March or April.   40:3 Or *Ark of the Testimony;* also in 40:5, 21.   40:7 Hebrew *Tent of Meeting;* also in 40:12, 22, 24, 26, 30, 32, 34, 35.   40:20 Hebrew *He placed the Testimony;* see note on 25:16.

MARK 1:1-28

You are starting to read the second Gospel today. Mark's story of Jesus' life jumps right into his ministry in Galilee. John the Baptist was the "front man," preparing the way.

This is the Good News about Jesus the Messiah, the Son of God.* It began [2]just as the prophet Isaiah had written:

"Look, I am sending my messenger
    ahead of you,
and he will prepare your
    way.*
[3] He is a voice shouting in the
    wilderness,
'Prepare the way for the LORD's
    coming!
Clear the road for him!'*"

[4]This messenger was John the Baptist. He was in the wilderness and preached that people should be baptized to show that they had repented of their sins and turned to God to be forgiven. [5]All of Judea, including all the people of Jerusalem, went out to see and hear John. And when they confessed their sins, he baptized them in the Jordan River. [6]His clothes were woven from coarse camel hair, and he wore a leather belt around his waist. For food he ate locusts and wild honey.

[7]John announced: "Someone is coming soon who is greater than I am—so much greater that I'm not even worthy to stoop down like a slave and untie the straps of his sandals. [8]I baptize you with* water, but he will baptize you with the Holy Spirit!"

[9]One day Jesus came from Nazareth in Galilee, and John baptized him in the Jordan River. [10]As Jesus came up out of the water, he saw the heavens splitting apart and the Holy Spirit descending on him* like a dove. [11]And a voice from heaven said, "You are my dearly loved Son, and you bring me great joy."

[12]The Spirit then compelled Jesus to go into the wilderness, [13]where he was tempted by Satan for forty days. He was out among the wild animals, and angels took care of him.

[14]Later on, after John was arrested, Jesus went into Galilee, where he preached God's Good News.* [15]"The time promised by God has come at last!" he announced. "The Kingdom of God is near! Repent of your sins and believe the Good News!"

[16]One day as Jesus was walking along the shore of the Sea of Galilee, he saw Simon* and his brother Andrew throw-

ing a net into the water, for they fished for a living. [17]Jesus called out to them, "Come, follow me, and I will show you how to fish for people!" [18]And they left their nets at once and followed him.

[19]A little farther up the shore Jesus saw Zebedee's sons, James and John, in a boat repairing their nets. [20]He called them at once, and they also followed him, leaving their father, Zebedee, in the boat with the hired men.

[21]Jesus and his companions went to the town of Capernaum. When the Sabbath day came, he went into the synagogue and began to teach. [22]The people were amazed at his teaching, for he taught with real authority—quite unlike the teachers of religious law.

[23]Suddenly, a man in the synagogue who was possessed by an evil* spirit began shouting, [24]"Why are you interfering with us, Jesus of Nazareth? Have you come to destroy us? I know who you are—the Holy One sent from God!"

[25]Jesus cut him short. "Be quiet! Come out of the man," he ordered. [26]At that, the evil spirit screamed, threw the man into a convulsion, and then came out of him.

[27]Amazement gripped the audience, and they began to discuss what had happened. "What sort of new teaching is this?" they asked excitedly. "It has such authority! Even evil spirits obey his orders!" [28]The news about Jesus spread quickly throughout the entire region of Galilee.

1:1 Some manuscripts do not include *the Son of God.*
1:2 Mal 3:1.   1:3 Isa 40:3 (Greek version).   1:8 Or *in;* also in 1:8b.   1:10 Or *toward him,* or *into him.*   1:14 Some manuscripts read *the Good News of the Kingdom of God.*
1:16 *Simon* is called "Peter" in 3:16 and thereafter.
1:23 Greek *unclean;* also in 1:26, 27.

PSALM 35:1-16
A psalm of David.

[1] **O** LORD, oppose those who
oppose me.
Fight those who fight
against me.
[2] Put on your armor, and take up
your shield.
Prepare for battle, and come to
my aid.
[3] Lift up your spear and javelin
against those who pursue me.
Let me hear you say,
"I will give you victory!"
[4] Bring shame and disgrace on those
trying to kill me;
turn them back and humiliate
those who want to harm me.
[5] Blow them away like chaff in the
wind—
a wind sent by the angel of the
LORD.
[6] Make their path dark and slippery,
with the angel of the LORD pursuing
them.
[7] I did them no wrong, but they laid
a trap for me.
I did them no wrong, but they dug
a pit to catch me.

HOW WE LIVE

Responding to God

MARK 1:15 Jesus began his ministry with this proclamation: "The time promised by God has come at last! . . . The Kingdom of God is near! Repent of your sins and believe the Good News!" • These first words spoken by Jesus in the Gospel of Mark reveal the essence of Jesus' ministry on earth—the long-awaited Messiah had arrived to inaugurate the Kingdom of God. This Kingdom would not be what many had expected, however. The Jewish people wanted a king who would set them free from the Romans; Jesus came instead to set them free from sin and bring the Good News of salvation. • People responded differently to Jesus' announcement. Some accepted him, some rejected him. The same is true today. You accepted Jesus when you believed the Good News. As a believer, you are likewise called each day to follow Jesus in a life of obedient discipleship.

8 So let sudden ruin come upon them!
    Let them be caught in the trap they
        set for me!
    Let them be destroyed in the pit
        they dug for me.

9 Then I will rejoice in the LORD.
    I will be glad because he
        rescues me.

10 With every bone in my body I will
        praise him:
    "LORD, who can compare
        with you?
    Who else rescues the helpless
        from the strong?
    Who else protects the helpless
        and poor from those who
        rob them?"

11 Malicious witnesses testify
        against me.
    They accuse me of crimes I know
        nothing about.

12 They repay me evil for good.
    I am sick with despair.

13 Yet when they were ill, I grieved
        for them.
    I denied myself by fasting for them,
        but my prayers returned
        unanswered.

14 I was sad, as though they were
        my friends or family,
    as if I were grieving for my
        own mother.

15 But they are glad now that I am
        in trouble;
    they gleefully join together
        against me.
    I am attacked by people I don't
        even know;
    they slander me constantly.

16 They mock me and call me names;
    they snarl at me.

PROVERBS 9:11-12

Wisdom will multiply your days and add years to your life. If you become wise, you will be the one to benefit. If you scorn wisdom, you will be the one to suffer.

FEBRUARY**16**

LEVITICUS 1:1–3:17

Leviticus was the manual for Old Testament Israelite priests. It included instructions for sacrifices as well as health and sanitation issues. Each regulation taught something about the holiness of God.

The LORD called to Moses from the Tabernacle* and said to him, 2"Give the following instructions to the people of Israel. When you present an animal as an offering to the LORD, you may take it from your herd of cattle or your flock of sheep and goats.

3"If the animal you present as a burnt offering is from the herd, it must be a male with no defects. Bring it to the entrance of the Tabernacle so you* may be accepted by the LORD. 4Lay your hand on the animal's head, and the LORD will accept its death in your place to purify you, making you right with him.* 5Then slaughter the young bull in the LORD's presence, and Aaron's sons, the priests, will present the animal's blood by splattering it against all sides of the altar that stands at the entrance to the Tabernacle. 6Then skin the animal and cut it into pieces. 7The sons of Aaron the priest will build a wood fire on the altar. 8They will arrange the pieces of the offering, including the head and fat, on the wood burning on the altar. 9But the internal organs and the legs must first be washed with water. Then the priest will burn the entire sacrifice on the altar as a burnt offering. It is a special gift, a pleasing aroma to the LORD.

10"If the animal you present as a burnt offering is from the flock, it may be either a sheep or a goat, but it must be a male with no defects. 11Slaughter the animal on the north side of the altar in the LORD's presence, and Aaron's sons, the priests, will splatter its blood against all sides of the altar. [12] Then cut the animal in pieces, and the priests will arrange the pieces of the offering, including the head and fat, on the wood burning on the altar. [13] But the internal organs and the legs must first be washed with water. Then the priest will burn the entire sacrifice on the altar as a burnt offering. It is a special gift, a pleasing aroma to the LORD.

[14] "If you present a bird as a burnt offering to the LORD, choose either a turtledove or a young pigeon. [15] The priest will take the bird to the altar, wring off its head, and burn it on the altar. But first he must drain its blood against the side of the altar. [16] The priest must also remove the crop and the feathers* and throw them in the ashes on the east side of the altar. [17] Then, grasping the bird by its wings, the priest will tear the bird open, but without tearing it apart. Then he will burn it as a burnt offering on the wood burning on the altar. It is a special gift, a pleasing aroma to the LORD.

2:1 "WHEN you present grain as an offering to the LORD, the offering must consist of choice flour. You are to pour olive oil on it, sprinkle it with frankincense, [2] and bring it to Aaron's sons, the priests. The priest will scoop out a handful of the flour moistened with oil, together with all the frankincense, and burn this representative portion on the altar. It is a special gift, a pleasing aroma to the LORD. [3] The rest of the grain offering will then be given to Aaron and his sons. This offering will be considered a most holy part of the special gifts presented to the LORD.

[4] "If your offering is a grain offering baked in an oven, it must be made of choice flour, but without any yeast. It may be presented in the form of thin cakes mixed with olive oil or wafers spread with olive oil. [5] If your grain offering is cooked on a griddle, it must be made of choice flour mixed with olive oil but without any yeast. [6] Break it in pieces and pour olive oil on it; it is a grain offering. [7] If your grain offering is prepared in a pan, it must be made of choice flour and olive oil.

[8] "No matter how a grain offering for the LORD has been prepared, bring it to the priest, who will present it at the altar. [9] The priest will take a representative portion of the grain offering and burn it on the altar. It is a special gift, a pleasing aroma to the LORD. [10] The rest of the grain offering will then be given to Aaron and his sons as their food. This offering will be considered a most holy part of the special gifts presented to the LORD.

[11] "Do not use yeast in preparing any of the grain offerings you present to the LORD, because no yeast or honey may be burned as a special gift presented to the LORD. [12] You may add yeast and honey to an offering of the first crops of your harvest, but these must never be offered on the altar as a pleasing aroma to the LORD. [13] Season all your grain offerings with salt to remind you of God's eternal covenant. Never forget to add salt to your grain offerings.

[14] "If you present a grain offering to the LORD from the first portion of your harvest, bring fresh grain that is coarsely ground and roasted on a fire. [15] Put olive oil on this grain offering, and sprinkle it with frankincense. [16] The priest will take a representative portion of the grain moistened with oil, together with all the frankincense, and burn it as a special gift presented to the LORD.

3:1 "IF you present an animal from the herd as a peace offering to the LORD, it may be a male or a female, but it must have no defects. [2] Lay your hand on the animal's head, and slaughter it at the entrance of the Tabernacle.* Then Aaron's sons, the priests, will splatter its blood against all sides of the altar. [3] The priest must present part of this peace offering as a special gift to the LORD. This includes all the fat around the internal organs, [4] the two kidneys and the fat around them near the loins, and the long lobe of the liver. These must be removed with the kidneys, [5] and Aaron's sons will burn them on top of the burnt offering on the wood burning on the altar. It is a special gift, a pleasing aroma to the LORD.

[6] "If you present an animal from the flock as a peace offering to the LORD, it may be a male or a female, but it must

have no defects. [7]If you present a sheep as your offering, bring it to the LORD, [8]lay your hand on its head, and slaughter it in front of the Tabernacle. Aaron's sons will then splatter the sheep's blood against all sides of the altar. [9]The priest must present the fat of this peace offering as a special gift to the LORD. This includes the fat of the broad tail cut off near the backbone, all the fat around the internal organs, [10]the two kidneys and the fat around them near the loins, and the long lobe of the liver. These must be removed with the kidneys, [11]and the priest will burn them on the altar. It is a special gift of food presented to the LORD.

[12]"If you present a goat as your offering, bring it to the LORD, [13]lay your hand on its head, and slaughter it in front of the Tabernacle. Aaron's sons will then splatter the goat's blood against all sides of the altar. [14]The priest must present part of this offering as a special gift to the LORD. This includes all the fat around the internal organs, [15]the two kidneys and the fat around them near the loins, and the long lobe of the liver. These must be removed with the kidneys, [16]and the priest will burn them on the altar. It is a special gift of food, a pleasing aroma to the LORD. All the fat belongs to the LORD.

[17]"You must never eat any fat or blood. This is a permanent law for you, and it must be observed from generation to generation, wherever you live."

1:1 Hebrew *Tent of Meeting;* also in 1:3, 5.   1:3 Or *it.*
1:4 Or *to make atonement for you.*   1:16 Or *the crop and its contents.* The meaning of the Hebrew is uncertain.
3:2 Hebrew *Tent of Meeting;* also in 3:8, 13.

MARK 1:29–2:12

People came from everywhere to see this man who taught with authority and performed miracles. But when he started forgiving sin, the clash with the religious leaders began. "Who but God can forgive sins?" they asked. Exactly.

After Jesus left the synagogue with James and John, they went to Simon and Andrew's home. [30]Now Simon's mother-in-law was sick in bed with a high fever. They told Jesus about her right away. [31]So he went to her bedside, took her by the hand, and helped her sit up. Then the fever left her, and she prepared a meal for them.

[32]That evening after sunset, many sick and demon-possessed people were brought to Jesus. [33]The whole town gathered at the door to watch. [34]So Jesus healed many people who were sick with various diseases, and he cast out many demons. But because the demons knew who he was, he did not allow them to speak.

[35]Before daybreak the next morning, Jesus got up and went out to an isolated place to pray. [36]Later Simon and the others went out to find him. [37]When they found him, they said, "Everyone is looking for you."

[38]But Jesus replied, "We must go on to other towns as well, and I will preach to them, too. That is why I came." [39]So he traveled throughout the region of Galilee, preaching in the synagogues and casting out demons.

[40]A man with leprosy came and knelt in front of Jesus, begging to be healed. "If you are willing, you can heal me and make me clean," he said.

[41]Moved with compassion,* Jesus reached out and touched him. "I am willing," he said. "Be healed!" [42]Instantly the leprosy disappeared, and the man was healed. [43]Then Jesus sent him on his way with a stern warning: [44]"Don't tell anyone about this. Instead, go to the priest and let him examine you. Take along the offering required in the law of Moses for those who have been healed of leprosy.* This will be a public testimony that you have been cleansed."

[45]But the man went and spread the word, proclaiming to everyone what had happened. As a result, large crowds soon surrounded Jesus, and he couldn't publicly enter a town anywhere. He had to stay out in the secluded places, but people from everywhere kept coming to him.

[2:1]WHEN Jesus returned to Capernaum several days later, the news spread quickly that he was back home. [2]Soon the house where he was staying was so packed with visitors that there was no more room, even outside the door. While he was preaching God's word to them, [3]four men arrived carrying a paralyzed man on a mat. [4]They couldn't bring him to Jesus because of the crowd, so they dug a hole through the roof above his head. Then they lowered the man on his mat, right down in front of Jesus. [5]Seeing their faith, Jesus said to the paralyzed man, "My child, your sins are forgiven."

[6]But some of the teachers of religious law who were sitting there thought to themselves, [7]"What is he saying? This is blasphemy! Only God can forgive sins!"

[8]Jesus knew immediately what they were thinking, so he asked them, "Why do you question this in your hearts? [9]Is it easier to say to the paralyzed man 'Your sins are forgiven,' or 'Stand up, pick up your mat, and walk'? [10]So I will prove to you that the Son of Man* has the authority on earth to forgive sins." Then Jesus turned to the paralyzed man and said, [11]"Stand up, pick up your mat, and go home!"

[12]And the man jumped up, grabbed his mat, and walked out through the stunned onlookers. They were all amazed and praised God, exclaiming, "We've never seen anything like this before!"

1:41 Some manuscripts read *Moved with anger.*
1:44 See Lev 14:2-32.   2:10 "Son of Man" is a title Jesus used for himself.

PSALM 35:17-28

How long, O Lord, will you look on
    and do nothing?
    Rescue me from their fierce attacks.
    Protect my life from these lions!
[18] Then I will thank you in front of the
    great assembly.
    I will praise you before all the
    people.

[19] Don't let my treacherous enemies
    rejoice over my defeat.
    Don't let those who hate me without
    cause gloat over my sorrow.
[20] They don't talk of peace;
    they plot against innocent people
    who mind their own business.
[21] They shout, "Aha! Aha!
    With our own eyes we saw him
    do it!"

[22] O LORD, you know all about this.
    Do not stay silent.
    Do not abandon me now, O Lord.
[23] Wake up! Rise to my defense!
    Take up my case, my God and
    my Lord.
[24] Declare me not guilty, O LORD my God,
    for you give justice.
    Don't let my enemies laugh about
    me in my troubles.
[25] Don't let them say, "Look, we got what
    we wanted!
    Now we will eat him alive!"

[26] May those who rejoice at my troubles
    be humiliated and disgraced.
    May those who triumph over me
    be covered with shame and
    dishonor.
[27] But give great joy to those who came
    to my defense.
    Let them continually say, "Great
    is the LORD,
    who delights in blessing his servant
    with peace!"
[28] Then I will proclaim your justice,
    and I will praise you all day long.

HOW WE LIVE   Prayer

MARK 1:35 Jesus got up while it was still dark and went off alone into the wilderness to pray. He knew the importance of having "quiet time" with God. You also should have a time and a place that is quiet enough for you to pour your heart out to God and also to hear his response to you. Prayer is your vital link to God, like a long-distance phone line to a loved one. Outside distractions make it difficult to clearly communicate. It's difficult to focus your attention on God when the kids are yelling, the oven timer is beeping, and your cat is nimbly walking across the piano keyboard. Like the example set by Jesus, you must break away from the noise and distractions in order to talk with God. Make a point of doing this, even if it means you have to get up early in the morning.

PROVERBS 9:13-18

The woman named Folly is brash. She is ignorant and doesn't know it. She sits in her doorway on the heights overlooking the city. She calls out to men going by who are minding their own business. "Come in with me," she urges the simple.

To those who lack good judgment, she says, "Stolen water is refreshing; food eaten in secret tastes the best!" But little do they know that the dead are there. Her guests are in the depths of the grave.*

9:18 Hebrew *in Sheol.*

FEBRUARY**17**

LEVITICUS 4:1-5:19

Sin offerings made atonement for specific unintentional sins. Guilt offerings included some sort of restitution for the wrong committed. What did all this mean? Holiness was no small matter before God.

Then the LORD said to Moses, ²"Give the following instructions to the people of Israel. This is how you are to deal with those who sin unintentionally by doing anything that violates one of the LORD's commands.

³"If the high priest* sins, bringing guilt upon the entire community, he must give a sin offering for the sin he has committed. He must present to the LORD a young bull with no defects. ⁴He must bring the bull to the LORD at the entrance of the Tabernacle,* lay his hand on the bull's head, and slaughter it before the LORD. ⁵The high priest will then take some of the bull's blood into the Tabernacle, ⁶dip his finger in the blood, and sprinkle it seven times before the LORD in front of the inner curtain of the sanctuary. ⁷The priest will then put some of the blood on the horns of the altar for fragrant incense that stands in the LORD's presence inside the Tabernacle. He will pour out the rest of the bull's blood at the base of the altar for burnt offerings at the entrance of the Tabernacle. ⁸Then the priest must remove all the fat of the bull to be offered as a sin offering. This includes all the fat around the internal organs, ⁹the two kidneys and the fat around them near the loins, and the long lobe of the liver. He must remove these along with the kidneys, ¹⁰just as he does with cattle offered as a peace offering, and burn them on the

altar of burnt offerings. ¹¹But he must take whatever is left of the bull—its hide, meat, head, legs, internal organs, and dung—¹²and carry it away to a place outside the camp that is ceremonially clean, the place where the ashes are dumped. There, on the ash heap, he will burn it on a wood fire.

¹³"If the entire Israelite community sins by violating one of the LORD's commands, but the people don't realize it, they are still guilty. ¹⁴When they become aware of their sin, the people must bring a young bull as an offering for their sin and present it before the Tabernacle. ¹⁵The elders of the community must then lay their hands on the bull's head and slaughter it before the LORD. ¹⁶The high priest will then take some of the bull's blood into the Tabernacle, ¹⁷dip his finger in the blood, and sprinkle it seven times before the LORD in front of the inner curtain. ¹⁸He will then put some of the blood on the horns of the altar for fragrant incense that stands in the LORD's presence inside the Tabernacle. He will pour out the rest of the blood at the base of the altar for burnt offerings at the entrance of the Tabernacle. ¹⁹Then the priest must remove all the animal's fat and burn it on the altar, ²⁰just as he does with the bull offered as a sin offering for the high priest. Through this process, the priest will purify the people, making them right with the LORD,* and they will be forgiven. ²¹Then the priest must take what is left of the bull and carry it outside the camp and burn it there, just as is done with the sin offering for the

high priest. This offering is for the sin of the entire congregation of Israel.

²²"If one of Israel's leaders sins by violating one of the commands of the LORD his God but doesn't realize it, he is still guilty. ²³When he becomes aware of his sin, he must bring as his offering a male goat with no defects. ²⁴He must lay his hand on the goat's head and slaughter it at the place where burnt offerings are slaughtered before the LORD. This is an offering for his sin. ²⁵Then the priest will dip his finger in the blood of the sin offering and put it on the horns of the altar for burnt offerings. He will pour out the rest of the blood at the base of the altar. ²⁶Then he must burn all the goat's fat on the altar, just as he does with the peace offering. Through this process, the priest will purify the leader from his sin, making him right with the LORD, and he will be forgiven.

²⁷"If any of the common people sin by violating one of the LORD's commands, but they don't realize it, they are still guilty. ²⁸When they become aware of their sin, they must bring as an offering for their sin a female goat with no defects. ²⁹They must lay a hand on the head of the sin offering and slaughter it at the place where burnt offerings are slaughtered. ³⁰Then the priest will dip his finger in the blood and put it on the horns of the altar for burnt offerings. He will pour out the rest of the blood at the base of the altar. ³¹Then he must remove all the goat's fat, just as he does with the fat of the peace offering. He will burn the fat on the altar, and it will be a pleasing aroma to the LORD. Through this process, the priest will purify the people, making them right with the LORD, and they will be forgiven.

³²"If the people bring a sheep as their sin offering, it must be a female with no defects. ³³They must lay a hand on the head of the sin offering and slaughter it at the place where burnt offerings are slaughtered. ³⁴Then the priest will dip his finger in the blood of the sin offering and put it on the horns of the altar for burnt offerings. He will pour out the rest of the blood at the base of the altar. ³⁵Then he must remove all the sheep's fat, just as he does with the fat of a sheep presented as a peace offering. He will burn the fat on the

altar on top of the special gifts presented to the LORD. Through this process, the priest will purify the people from their sin, making them right with the LORD, and they will be forgiven.

5:1"IF you are called to testify about something you have seen or that you know about, it is sinful to refuse to testify, and you will be punished for your sin.

²"Or suppose you unknowingly touch something that is ceremonially unclean, such as the carcass of an unclean animal. When you realize what you have done, you must admit your defilement and your guilt. This is true whether it is a wild animal, a domestic animal, or an animal that scurries along the ground.

³"Or suppose you unknowingly touch something that makes a person unclean. When you realize what you have done, you must admit your guilt.

⁴"Or suppose you make a foolish vow of any kind, whether its purpose is for good or for bad. When you realize its foolishness, you must admit your guilt.

⁵"When you become aware of your guilt in any of these ways, you must confess your sin. ⁶Then you must bring to the LORD as the penalty for your sin a female from the flock, either a sheep or a goat. This is a sin offering with which the priest will purify you from your sin, making you right with the LORD.*

⁷"But if you cannot afford to bring a sheep, you may bring to the LORD two turtledoves or two young pigeons as the penalty for your sin. One of the birds will be for a sin offering, and the other for a burnt offering. ⁸You must bring them to the priest, who will present the first bird as the sin offering. He will wring its neck but without severing its head from the body. ⁹Then he will sprinkle some of the blood of the sin offering against the sides of the altar, and the rest of the blood will be drained out at the base of the altar. This is an offering for sin. ¹⁰The priest will then prepare the second bird as a burnt offering, following all the procedures that have been prescribed. Through this process the priest will purify you from your sin, making you right with the LORD, and you will be forgiven.

¹¹"If you cannot afford to bring two turtledoves or two young pigeons, you may bring two quarts* of choice flour for your sin offering. Since it is an offering for sin, you must not moisten it with olive oil or put any frankincense on it. ¹²Take the flour to the priest, who will scoop out a handful as a representative portion. He will burn it on the altar on top of the special gifts presented to the LORD. It is an offering for sin. ¹³Through this process, the priest will purify those who are guilty of any of these sins, making them right with the LORD, and they will be forgiven. The rest of the flour will belong to the priest, just as with the grain offering."

¹⁴Then the LORD said to Moses, ¹⁵"If one of you commits a sin by unintentionally defiling the LORD's sacred property, you must bring a guilt offering to the LORD. The offering must be your own ram with no defects, or you may buy one of equal value with silver, as measured by the weight of the sanctuary shekel.* ¹⁶You must make restitution for the sacred property you have harmed by paying for the loss, plus an additional 20 percent. When you give the payment to the priest, he will purify you with the ram sacrificed as a guilt offering, making you right with the LORD, and you will be forgiven.

¹⁷"Suppose you sin by violating one of the LORD's commands. Even if you are unaware of what you have done, you are guilty and will be punished for your sin. ¹⁸For a guilt offering, you must bring to the priest your own ram with no defects, or you may buy one of equal value. Through this process the priest will purify you from your unintentional sin, making you right with the LORD, and you will be forgiven. ¹⁹This is a guilt offering, for you have been guilty of an offense against the LORD."

4:3 Hebrew *the anointed priest;* also in 4:5, 16. 4:4 Hebrew *Tent of Meeting;* also in 4:5, 7, 14, 16, 18. 4:20 Or *will make atonement for the people;* similarly in 4:26, 31, 35. 5:6 Or *will make atonement for you;* similarly in 5:10, 13, 16, 18. 5:11 Hebrew ¹⁄₁₀ *of an ephah* [2.2 liters]. 5:15 Each shekel was about 0.4 ounces or 11 grams in weight.

MARK 2:13–3:6
From the beginning, Jesus was unconventional. He hung out with the riffraff. He even chose a disciple from among the true sell-outs, the tax collectors. These and other unconventional actions soon had the religious leaders plotting to kill him.

Then Jesus went out to the lakeshore again and taught the crowds that were coming to him. ¹⁴As he walked along, he saw Levi son of Alphaeus sitting at his tax collector's booth. "Follow me and be my disciple," Jesus said to him. So Levi got up and followed him.

¹⁵Later, Levi invited Jesus and his disciples to his home as dinner guests, along with many tax collectors and other disreputable sinners. (There were many people of this kind among Jesus' followers.) ¹⁶But when the teachers of religious law who were Pharisees* saw him eating with tax collectors and other sinners, they asked his disciples, "Why does he eat with such scum?*"

¹⁷When Jesus heard this, he told them, "Healthy people don't need a doctor—sick people do. I have come to call not those who think they are righteous, but those who know they are sinners."

¹⁸Once when John's disciples and the Pharisees were fasting, some people came to Jesus and asked, "Why don't your disciples fast like John's disciples and the Pharisees do?"

¹⁹Jesus replied, "Do wedding guests fast while celebrating with the groom? Of course not. They can't fast while the groom is with them. ²⁰But someday the groom will be taken away from them, and then they will fast.

²¹"Besides, who would patch old clothing with new cloth? For the new patch would shrink and rip away from the old cloth, leaving an even bigger tear than before.

²²"And no one puts new wine into old wineskins. For the wine would burst the wineskins, and the wine and the skins would both be lost. New wine calls for new wineskins."

²³One Sabbath day as Jesus was walking through some grainfields, his disciples began breaking off heads of grain to eat. ²⁴But the Pharisees said to Jesus, "Look, why are they breaking the law by harvesting grain on the Sabbath?"

²⁵Jesus said to them, "Haven't you ever

read in the Scriptures what David did when he and his companions were hungry? [26]He went into the house of God (during the days when Abiathar was high priest) and broke the law by eating the sacred loaves of bread that only the priests are allowed to eat. He also gave some to his companions."

[27]Then Jesus said to them, "The Sabbath was made to meet the needs of people, and not people to meet the requirements of the Sabbath. [28]So the Son of Man is Lord, even over the Sabbath!"

[3:1]JESUS went into the synagogue again and noticed a man with a deformed hand. [2]Since it was the Sabbath, Jesus' enemies watched him closely. If he healed the man's hand, they planned to accuse him of working on the Sabbath.

[3]Jesus said to the man with the deformed hand, "Come and stand in front of everyone." [4]Then he turned to his critics and asked, "Does the law permit good deeds on the Sabbath, or is it a day for doing evil? Is this a day to save life or to destroy it?" But they wouldn't answer him.

[5]He looked around at them angrily and was deeply saddened by their hard hearts. Then he said to the man, "Hold out your hand." So the man held out his hand, and it was restored! [6]At once the Pharisees went away and met with the supporters of Herod to plot how to kill Jesus.

2:16a Greek *the scribes of the Pharisees.*   **2:16b** Greek *with tax collectors and sinners?*

PSALM 36:1-12
For the choir director: A psalm of David, the servant of the LORD.

[1] **S**in whispers to the wicked, deep
    within their hearts.
   They have no fear of God at all.
[2] In their blind conceit,
    they cannot see how wicked they
    really are.
[3] Everything they say is crooked and
    deceitful.
   They refuse to act wisely or do
    good.
[4] They lie awake at night, hatching
    sinful plots.
   Their actions are never good.
   They make no attempt to turn
    from evil.

[5] Your unfailing love, O LORD, is as vast
    as the heavens;
   your faithfulness reaches beyond
    the clouds.
[6] Your righteousness is like the mighty
    mountains,
   your justice like the ocean depths.
  You care for people and animals alike,
    O LORD.

Old Testament sacrifices

WHAT THE BIBLE SAYS

LEVITICUS 4:24 The offerings God prescribed for Israel taught them how to honor him, how to submit to him, how to worship him. Most of the offerings were to make atonement for sin. Sin is a debt that requires payment. Sin ruins any possibility of a relationship with God because God is holy. God wanted that relationship with us, but sin had to be dealt with first. The penalty of sin is death, but God provided that an animal's blood would suffice as an act of obedience until Jesus came. That's why the people brought animals as offerings to God. That was only temporary; Jesus' sacrifice on the cross is what made true forgiveness possible.
• While it's difficult to read the bloody details of the slaughter of animals, it is important to remember that God wanted the people to understand the awful consequences of sin. Having to lay their hands on the head of the animal as it was slain was a strong reminder of God's grace in offering a way to be forgiven.

7   How precious is your unfailing love,
      O God!
All humanity finds shelter
      in the shadow of your wings.
8   You feed them from the abundance
      of your own house,
      letting them drink from your river
      of delights.
9   For you are the fountain of life,
      the light by which we see.

10 Pour out your unfailing love on
      those who love you;
      give justice to those with
      honest hearts.

11 Don't let the proud trample me
      or the wicked push me
      around.
12 Look! Those who do evil have
      fallen!
      They are thrown down, never
      to rise again.

PROVERBS 10:1-2
The proverbs of Solomon: □ A wise child*
brings joy to a father; a foolish child
brings grief to a mother. □ Tainted wealth
has no lasting value, but right living can
save your life.
10:1 Hebrew *son;* also in 10:1b.

FEBRUARY**18**

LEVITICUS 6:1–7:27
There were many different kinds of offerings
designed to fit the occasion—offerings for sin, guilt,
peace, and free will. Some were burnt offerings and
some were not; some were offerings of grain or food
and others of animals. Moses' written instructions
covered all of these.

1***T**hen the LORD said to Moses, 2"Suppose one of you sins against your associate and is unfaithful to the LORD. Suppose
you cheat in a deal involving a security deposit, or you steal or commit fraud, 3 or
you find lost property and lie about it, or
you lie while swearing to tell the truth,
or you commit any other such sin. 4 If you
have sinned in any of these ways, you are
guilty. You must give back whatever you
stole, or the money you took by extortion,
or the security deposit, or the lost property you found, 5 or anything obtained by
swearing falsely. You must make restitution by paying the full price plus an additional 20 percent to the person you have
harmed. On the same day you must present a guilt offering. 6 As a guilt offering to
the LORD, you must bring to the priest
your own ram with no defects, or you may
buy one of equal value. 7 Through this process, the priest will purify you before the

LORD, making you right with him,* and
you will be forgiven for any of these sins
you have committed."

8*Then the LORD said to Moses, 9"Give
Aaron and his sons the following instructions regarding the burnt offering. The
burnt offering must be left on top of the
altar until the next morning, and the fire
on the altar must be kept burning all
night. 10 In the morning, after the priest
on duty has put on his official linen clothing and linen undergarments, he must
clean out the ashes of the burnt offering
and put them beside the altar. 11 Then he
must take off these garments, change
back into his regular clothes, and carry
the ashes outside the camp to a place that
is ceremonially clean. 12 Meanwhile, the
fire on the altar must be kept burning;
it must never go out. Each morning the
priest will add fresh wood to the fire
and arrange the burnt offering on it. He
will then burn the fat of the peace offerings on it. 13 Remember, the fire must
be kept burning on the altar at all times.
It must never go out.

14"These are the instructions regarding the grain offering. Aaron's sons must
present this offering to the LORD in front

of the altar. [15]The priest on duty will take from the grain offering a handful of the choice flour moistened with olive oil, together with all the frankincense. He will burn this representative portion on the altar as a pleasing aroma to the LORD. [16]Aaron and his sons may eat the rest of the flour, but it must be baked without yeast and eaten in a sacred place within the courtyard of the Tabernacle.* [17]Remember, it must never be prepared with yeast. I have given it to the priests as their share of the special gifts presented to me. Like the sin offering and the guilt offering, it is most holy. [18]Any of Aaron's male descendants may eat from the special gifts presented to the LORD. This is their permanent right from generation to generation. Anyone or anything that touches these offerings will become holy."

[19]Then the LORD said to Moses, [20]"On the day Aaron and his sons are anointed, they must present to the LORD a grain offering of two quarts* of choice flour, half to be offered in the morning and half to be offered in the evening. [21]It must be carefully mixed with olive oil and cooked on a griddle. Then slice* this grain offering and present it as a pleasing aroma to the LORD. [22]In each generation, the high priest* who succeeds Aaron must prepare this same offering. It belongs to the LORD and must be burned up completely. This is a permanent law. [23]All such grain offerings of a priest must be burned up entirely. None of it may be eaten."

[24]Then the LORD said to Moses, [25]"Give Aaron and his sons the following instructions regarding the sin offering. The animal given as an offering for sin is a most holy offering, and it must be slaughtered in the LORD's presence at the place where the burnt offerings are slaughtered. [26]The priest who offers the sacrifice as a sin offering must eat his portion in a sacred place within the courtyard of the Tabernacle. [27]Anyone or anything that touches the sacrificial meat will become holy. If any of the sacrificial blood spatters on a person's clothing, the soiled garment must be washed in a sacred place. [28]If a clay pot is used to boil the sacrificial meat, it must then be broken. If a bronze pot is used, it must be scoured and thoroughly

rinsed with water. [29]Any male from a priest's family may eat from this offering; it is most holy. [30]But the offering for sin may not be eaten if its blood was brought into the Tabernacle as an offering for purification* in the Holy Place. It must be completely burned with fire.

[7:1]"THESE are the instructions for the guilt offering. It is most holy. [2]The animal sacrificed as a guilt offering must be slaughtered at the place where the burnt offerings are slaughtered, and its blood must be splattered against all sides of the altar. [3]The priest will then offer all its fat on the altar, including the fat of the broad tail, the fat around the internal organs, [4]the two kidneys and the fat around them near the loins, and the long lobe of the liver. These are to be removed with the kidneys, [5]and the priests will burn them on the altar as a special gift presented to the LORD. This is the guilt offering. [6]Any males from a priest's family may eat the meat. It must be eaten in a sacred place, for it is most holy.

[7]"The same instructions apply to both the guilt offering and the sin offering. Both belong to the priest who uses them to purify someone, making that person right with the LORD.* [8]In the case of the burnt offering, the priest may keep the hide of the sacrificed animal. [9]Any grain offering that has been baked in an oven, prepared in a pan, or cooked on a griddle belongs to the priest who presents it. [10]All other grain offerings, whether made of dry flour or flour moistened with olive oil, are to be shared equally among all the priests, the descendants of Aaron.

[11]"These are the instructions regarding the different kinds of peace offerings that may be presented to the LORD. [12]If you present your peace offering as an expression of thanksgiving, the usual animal sacrifice must be accompanied by various kinds of bread made without yeast—thin cakes mixed with olive oil, wafers spread with oil, and cakes made of choice flour mixed with olive oil. [13]This peace offering of thanksgiving must also be accompanied by loaves of bread made with yeast. [14]One of each kind of bread must be presented as a gift to the LORD. It

will then belong to the priest who splatters the blood of the peace offering against the altar. [15]The meat of the peace offering of thanksgiving must be eaten on the same day it is offered. None of it may be saved for the next morning.

[16]"If you bring an offering to fulfill a vow or as a voluntary offering, the meat must be eaten on the same day the sacrifice is offered, but whatever is left over may be eaten on the second day. [17]Any meat left over until the third day must be completely burned up. [18]If any of the meat from the peace offering is eaten on the third day, the person who presented it will not be accepted by the LORD. You will receive no credit for offering it. By then the meat will be contaminated; if you eat it, you will be punished for your sin.

[19]"Meat that touches anything ceremonially unclean may not be eaten; it must be completely burned up. The rest of the meat may be eaten, but only by people who are ceremonially clean. [20]If you are ceremonially unclean and you eat meat from a peace offering that was presented to the LORD, you will be cut off from the community. [21]If you touch anything that is unclean (whether it is human defilement or an unclean animal or any other unclean, detestable thing) and then eat meat from a peace offering presented to the LORD, you will be cut off from the community."

[22]Then the LORD said to Moses, [23]"Give the following instructions to the people of Israel. You must never eat fat, whether from cattle, sheep, or goats. [24]The fat of an animal found dead or torn to pieces by wild animals must never be eaten, though it may be used for any other purpose. [25]Anyone who eats fat from an animal presented as a special gift to the LORD will be cut off from the community. [26]No matter where you live, you must never consume the blood of any bird or animal. [27]Anyone who consumes blood will be cut off from the community."

6:1 Verses 6:1-7 are numbered 5:20-26 in Hebrew text.
6:7 Or *will make atonement for you before the LORD.*
6:8 Verses 6:8-30 are numbered 6:1-23 in Hebrew text.
6:16 Hebrew *Tent of Meeting;* also in 6:26, 30.   6:20 Hebrew 1⁄10 *of an ephah* [2.2 liters].   6:21 The meaning of this Hebrew term is uncertain.   6:22 Hebrew *the anointed priest.*
6:30 Or *an offering to make atonement.*   7:7 Or *to make atonement.*

MARK 3:7-30
The spirit world, including evil spirits, recognized Jesus as the Son of God even before his closest friends did. The religious leaders claimed that Jesus' authority over evil spirits was evidence that he operated by their power. Read how Jesus showed them their error.

Jesus went out to the lake with his disciples, and a large crowd followed him. They came from all over Galilee, Judea, [8]Jerusalem, Idumea, from east of the Jordan River, and even from as far north as Tyre and Sidon. The news about his miracles had spread far and wide, and vast numbers of people came to see him.

[9]Jesus instructed his disciples to have a boat ready so the crowd would not crush him. [10]He had healed many people that day, so all the sick people eagerly pushed forward to touch him. [11]And whenever those possessed by evil* spirits caught sight of him, the spirits would throw them to the ground in front of him shrieking, "You are the Son of God!" [12]But Jesus sternly commanded the spirits not to reveal who he was.

[13]Afterward Jesus went up on a mountain and called out the ones he wanted to go with him. And they came to him. [14]Then he appointed twelve of them and called them his apostles.* They were to accompany him, and he would send them out to preach, [15]giving them authority to cast out demons. [16]These are the twelve he chose:

Simon (whom he named Peter),
[17] James and John (the sons of Zebedee, but Jesus nicknamed them "Sons of Thunder"*),
[18] Andrew,
Philip,
Bartholomew,
Matthew,
Thomas,
James (son of Alphaeus),
Thaddaeus,
Simon (the zealot*),
[19] Judas Iscariot (who later betrayed him).

[20]One time Jesus entered a house, and the crowds began to gather again. Soon he and his disciples couldn't even find time

to eat. ²¹When his family heard what was happening, they tried to take him away. "He's out of his mind," they said.

²²But the teachers of religious law who had arrived from Jerusalem said, "He's possessed by Satan,* the prince of demons. That's where he gets the power to cast out demons."

²³Jesus called them over and responded with an illustration. "How can Satan cast out Satan?" he asked. ²⁴"A kingdom divided by civil war will collapse. ²⁵Similarly, a family splintered by feuding will fall apart. ²⁶And if Satan is divided and fights against himself, how can he stand? He would never survive. ²⁷Let me illustrate this further. Who is powerful enough to enter the house of a strong man like Satan and plunder his goods? Only someone even stronger—someone who could tie him up and then plunder his house.

²⁸"I tell you the truth, all sin and blasphemy can be forgiven, ²⁹but anyone who blasphemes the Holy Spirit will never be forgiven. This is a sin with eternal consequences." ³⁰He told them this because they were saying, "He's possessed by an evil spirit."

3:11 Greek *unclean;* also in 3:30.   3:14 Some manuscripts do not include *and called them his apostles.*   3:17 Greek *whom he named Boanerges, which means Sons of Thunder.* 3:18 Greek *the Cananean,* an Aramaic term for Jewish nationalists.   3:22 Greek *Beelzeboul;* other manuscripts read *Beezeboul;* Latin version reads *Beelzebub.*

PSALM 37:1-11*
A psalm of David.

¹ **D**on't worry about the wicked
   or envy those who do wrong.
² For like grass, they soon fade away.
   Like spring flowers, they soon
      wither.
³ Trust in the LORD and do good.
   Then you will live safely in the land
      and prosper.
⁴ Take delight in the LORD,
   and he will give you your heart's
      desires.
⁵ Commit everything you do to the
      LORD.
   Trust him, and he will help you.
⁶ He will make your innocence radiate
      like the dawn,
   and the justice of your cause
      will shine like the noonday sun.

⁷ Be still in the presence of the LORD,
   and wait patiently for him to act.
   Don't worry about evil people who
      prosper
   or fret about their wicked
      schemes.
⁸ Stop being angry!
   Turn from your rage!
   Do not lose your temper—
      it only leads to harm.

WHO GOD IS The Holy Spirit is God

MARK 3:29 There is only one true God, but he eternally exists in a triunity of persons: the Father, Son, and Holy Spirit. In the Great Commission recorded in Matthew 28:19-20, Jesus tells his disciples to baptize new believers in the "name" of the Father, the Son and the Holy Spirit, not the "names." The singular "name" pictures the three-in-one nature of God. • It is important to understand that the Holy Spirit is indeed God. Jesus made it clear in his words to the religious leaders that to commit a sin against the Holy Spirit is to commit a sin against God. Resisting and insulting the Holy Spirit will lead to what today's reading calls "a sin with eternal consequences." To blaspheme the Holy Spirit is to have an unbelieving and unrepentant heart attitude, a refusal to admit any need of forgiveness. Since the Bible tells us that Christ is the only way of salvation, deliberate and ongoing rejection of the Holy Spirit is rejection of God himself. And that has eternal consequences.

⁹ For the wicked will be destroyed,
   but those who trust in the LORD
   will possess the land.
¹⁰ Soon the wicked will disappear.
    Though you look for them, they
    will be gone.
¹¹ The lowly will possess the land
    and will live in peace and prosperity.

FEBRUARY**19**

LEVITICUS 7:28–9:6

It was finally time. The instructions for the offerings had been given. Now the priests were anointed for their duties. For seven days Aaron and his sons obeyed specific instructions to inaugurate a lifetime of service for them and their descendants.

Then the LORD said to Moses, ²⁹"Give the following instructions to the people of Israel. When you present a peace offering to the LORD, bring part of it as a gift to the LORD. ³⁰Present it to the LORD with your own hands as a special gift to the LORD. Bring the fat of the animal, together with the breast, and lift up the breast as a special offering to the LORD. ³¹Then the priest will burn the fat on the altar, but the breast will belong to Aaron and his descendants. ³²Give the right thigh of your peace offering to the priest as a gift. ³³The right thigh must always be given to the priest who offers the blood and the fat of the peace offering. ³⁴For I have reserved the breast of the special offering and the right thigh of the sacred offering for the priests. It is the permanent right of Aaron and his descendants to share in the peace offerings brought by the people of Israel. ³⁵This is their rightful share. The special gifts presented to the LORD have been reserved for Aaron and his descendants from the time they were set apart to serve the LORD as priests. ³⁶On the day they were anointed, the LORD commanded the Israelites to give these portions to the priests as their permanent share from generation to generation."

³⁷These are the instructions for the burnt offering, the grain offering, the sin offering, and the guilt offering, as well as the ordination offering and the peace offering. ³⁸The LORD gave these instructions to Moses on Mount Sinai when he commanded the Israelites to present their offerings to the LORD in the wilderness of Sinai.

⁸:¹THEN the LORD said to Moses, ²"Bring Aaron and his sons, along with their sacred garments, the anointing oil, the bull for the sin offering, the two rams, and the basket of bread made without yeast, ³and call the entire community of Israel together at the entrance of the Tabernacle.*"

⁴So Moses followed the LORD's instructions, and the whole community assembled at the Tabernacle entrance. ⁵Moses announced to them, "This is what the LORD has commanded us to do!" ⁶Then he presented Aaron and his sons and washed them with water. ⁷He put the official tunic on Aaron and tied the sash around his waist. He dressed him in the robe, placed the ephod on him, and attached the ephod securely with its decorative sash. ⁸Then Moses placed the chestpiece on Aaron and put the Urim and the Thummim inside it. ⁹He placed the turban on Aaron's head and attached the gold medallion—the badge of holiness—to the front of the turban, just as the LORD had commanded him.

¹⁰Then Moses took the anointing oil and anointed the Tabernacle and everything in it, making them holy. ¹¹He sprinkled the

---

37 This psalm is a Hebrew acrostic poem; each stanza begins with a successive letter of the Hebrew alphabet.

PROVERBS 10:3-4

The LORD will not let the godly go hungry, but he refuses to satisfy the craving of the wicked. □ Lazy people are soon poor; hard workers get rich.

oil on the altar seven times, anointing it and all its utensils, as well as the wash-basin and its stand, making them holy. [12]Then he poured some of the anointing oil on Aaron's head, anointing him and making him holy for his work. [13]Next Moses presented Aaron's sons. He clothed them in their tunics, tied their sashes around them, and put their special head coverings on them, just as the LORD had commanded him.

[14]Then Moses presented the bull for the sin offering. Aaron and his sons laid their hands on the bull's head, [15]and Moses slaughtered it. Moses took some of the blood, and with his finger he put it on the four horns of the altar to purify it. He poured out the rest of the blood at the base of the altar. Through this process, he made the altar holy by purifying it.* [16]Then Moses took all the fat around the internal organs, the long lobe of the liver, and the two kidneys and the fat around them, and he burned it all on the altar. [17]He took the rest of the bull, including its hide, meat, and dung, and burned it on a fire outside the camp, just as the LORD had commanded him.

[18]Then Moses presented the ram for the burnt offering. Aaron and his sons laid their hands on the ram's head, [19]and Moses slaughtered it. Then Moses took the ram's blood and splattered it against all sides of the altar. [20]Then he cut the ram into pieces, and he burned the head, some of its pieces, and the fat on the altar. [21]After washing the internal organs and the legs with water, Moses burned the entire ram on the altar as a burnt offering. It was a pleasing aroma, a special gift presented to the LORD, just as the LORD had commanded him.

[22]Then Moses presented the other ram, which was the ram of ordination. Aaron and his sons laid their hands on the ram's head, [23]and Moses slaughtered it. Then Moses took some of its blood and applied it to the lobe of Aaron's right ear, the thumb of his right hand, and the big toe of his right foot. [24]Next Moses presented Aaron's sons and applied some of the blood to the lobes of their right ears, the thumbs of their right hands, and the big toes of their right feet. He then splattered the rest of the blood against all sides of the altar.

[25]Next Moses took the fat, including the fat of the broad tail, the fat around the internal organs, the long lobe of the liver, and the two kidneys and the fat around them, along with the right thigh. [26]On top of these he placed a thin cake of bread made without yeast, a cake of bread mixed with olive oil, and a wafer spread with olive oil. All these were taken from the basket of bread made without yeast that was placed in the LORD's presence. [27]He put all these in the hands of Aaron and his sons, and he lifted them up as a special offering to the LORD. [28]Moses then took all the offerings back from them and burned them on the altar on top of the burnt offering. This was the ordination offering. It was a pleasing aroma, a special gift presented to the LORD. [29]Then Moses took the breast and lifted it up as a special offering to the LORD. This was Moses' portion of the ram of ordination, just as the LORD had commanded him.

[30]Next Moses took some of the anointing oil and some of the blood that was on the altar, and he sprinkled them on Aaron and his garments and on his sons and their garments. In this way, he made Aaron and his sons and their garments holy.

[31]Then Moses said to Aaron and his sons, "Boil the remaining meat of the offerings at the Tabernacle entrance, and eat it there, along with the bread that is in the basket of offerings for the ordination, just as I commanded when I said, 'Aaron and his sons will eat it.' [32]Any meat or bread that is left over must then be burned up. [33]You must not leave the Tabernacle entrance for seven days, for that is when the ordination ceremony will be completed. [34]Everything we have done today was commanded by the LORD in order to purify you, making you right with him.* [35]Now stay at the entrance of the Tabernacle day and night for seven days, and do everything the LORD requires. If you fail to do this, you will die, for this is what the LORD has commanded." [36]So Aaron and his sons did everything the LORD had commanded through Moses.

9:1AFTER the ordination ceremony, on the

eighth day, Moses called together Aaron and his sons and the elders of Israel. [2]He said to Aaron, "Take a young bull for a sin offering and a ram for a burnt offering, both without defects, and present them to the LORD. [3]Then tell the Israelites, 'Take a male goat for a sin offering, and take a calf and a lamb, both a year old and without defects, for a burnt offering. [4]Also take a bull* and a ram for a peace offering and flour moistened with olive oil for a grain offering. Present all these offerings to the LORD because the LORD will appear to you today.'"

[5]So the people presented all these things at the entrance of the Tabernacle,* just as Moses had commanded. Then the whole community came forward and stood before the LORD. [6]And Moses said, "This is what the LORD has commanded you to do so that the glory of the LORD may appear to you."

8:3 Hebrew *Tent of Meeting;* also in 8:4, 31, 33, 35.
8:15 Or *by making atonement for it;* or *that offerings for purification might be made on it.*   8:34 Or *to make atonement for you.*   9:4 Or *cow;* also in 9:18, 19.
9:5 Hebrew *Tent of Meeting;* also in 9:23.

MARK 3:31–4:25
Jesus taught through stories. He *showed* the truth as well as *told* the truth. Sometimes this left people out in the cold—because of the hardness of their hearts, they just didn't get it.

Then Jesus' mother and brothers came to see him. They stood outside and sent word for him to come out and talk with them. [32]There was a crowd sitting around Jesus, and someone said, "Your mother and your brothers* are outside asking for you."

[33]Jesus replied, "Who is my mother? Who are my brothers?" [34]Then he looked at those around him and said, "Look, these are my mother and brothers. [35]Anyone who does God's will is my brother and sister and mother."

[4:1]ONCE again Jesus began teaching by the lakeshore. A very large crowd soon gathered around him, so he got into a boat. Then he sat in the boat while all the people remained on the shore. [2]He taught them by telling many stories in the form of parables, such as this one:

[3]"Listen! A farmer went out to plant some seed. [4]As he scattered it across his field, some of the seed fell on a footpath, and the birds came and ate it. [5]Other seed fell on shallow soil with underlying rock. The seed sprouted quickly because the soil was shallow. [6]But the plant soon wilted under the hot sun, and since it didn't have deep roots, it died. [7]Other seed fell among thorns that grew up and choked out the tender plants so they produced no grain. [8]Still other seeds fell on fertile soil, and they sprouted, grew, and produced a crop that was thirty, sixty, and even a hundred times as much as had been planted!" [9]Then he said, "Anyone with ears to hear should listen and understand."

[10]Later, when Jesus was alone with the twelve disciples and with the others who were gathered around, they asked him what the parables meant.

[11]He replied, "You are permitted to understand the secret* of the Kingdom of God. But I use parables for everything I say to outsiders, [12]so that the Scriptures might be fulfilled:

'When they see what I do,
     they will learn nothing.
When they hear what I say,
     they will not understand.
Otherwise, they will turn to me
     and be forgiven.'*"

[13]Then Jesus said to them, "If you can't understand the meaning of this parable, how will you understand all the other parables? [14]The farmer plants seed by taking God's word to others. [15]The seed that fell on the footpath represents those who hear the message, only to have Satan come at once and take it away. [16]The seed on the rocky soil represents those who hear the message and immediately receive it with joy. [17]But since they don't have deep roots, they don't last long. They fall away as soon as they have problems or are persecuted for believing God's word. [18]The seed that fell among the thorns represents others who hear God's word, [19]but all too quickly the message is crowded out by the worries of this life, the lure of wealth, and the desire for other things, so no fruit is produced. [20]And the seed that fell on good soil represents those who hear and accept God's word and produce a harvest of thirty,

sixty, or even a hundred times as much as had been planted!"

²¹Then Jesus asked them, "Would anyone light a lamp and then put it under a basket or under a bed? Of course not! A lamp is placed on a stand, where its light will shine. ²²For everything that is hidden will eventually be brought into the open, and every secret will be brought to light. ²³Anyone with ears to hear should listen and understand."

²⁴Then he added, "Pay close attention to what you hear. The closer you listen, the more understanding you will be given*— and you will receive even more. ²⁵To those who listen to my teaching, more understanding will be given. But for those who are not listening, even what little understanding they have will be taken away from them."

3:32 Some manuscripts add *and sisters.*   4:11 Greek *mystery.*   4:12 Isa 6:9-10 (Greek version).   4:24 Or *The measure you give will be the measure you get back.*

PSALM 37:12-29

The wicked plot against the godly;
　　they snarl at them in defiance.
¹³ But the Lord just laughs,
　　for he sees their day of judgment
　　　coming.
¹⁴ The wicked draw their swords
　　and string their bows
to kill the poor and the oppressed,
　　to slaughter those who do right.

¹⁵ But their swords will stab their
　　own hearts,
　　and their bows will be broken.

¹⁶ It is better to be godly and have little
　　than to be evil and rich.
¹⁷ For the strength of the wicked will
　　be shattered,
　　but the Lord takes care of
　　　the godly.

¹⁸ Day by day the Lord takes care
　　of the innocent,
　　and they will receive an inheritance
　　　that lasts forever.
¹⁹ They will not be disgraced in hard times;
　　even in famine they will have more
　　　than enough.

²⁰ But the wicked will die.
　　The Lord's enemies are like flowers
　　　in a field—
　　they will disappear like smoke.

²¹ The wicked borrow and never repay,
　　but the godly are generous givers.
²² Those the Lord blesses will possess
　　the land,
　　but those he curses will die.

²³ The Lord directs the steps
　　of the godly.
　　He delights in every detail
　　　of their lives.
²⁴ Though they stumble, they will
　　never fall,

HOW WE LIVE

Responding to God

MARK 4:16-20 In the parable of the seeds, the four soils represent four different ways that people will respond to Jesus' message. Some are like the hard path, others are like rocky soil, and still others are like thorny ground. The best, of course, are those who receive the seed of Jesus' message in good soil. • Is your enthusiasm for Christ being discouraged by struggles? Be careful not to be like the seed on rocky soil that heard the message, received it with joy, but then wilted. Are you finding that the cares of this life are overshadowing your commitment to Christ? Be careful not to be like the seed on thorny ground with your joy in Christ being crowded out. • Pray that God will help you to be like the good soil so that the faith that's been planted in you can persevere, grow, and produce a harvest. That is, pray that you'll continue to grow in the knowledge of Jesus so that you can share his good news with others.

for the LORD holds them by
the hand.

25 Once I was young, and now I am old.
Yet I have never seen the godly
abandoned
or their children begging for bread.
26 The godly always give generous loans
to others,
and their children are a blessing.

27 Turn from evil and do good,
and you will live in the land
forever.

28 For the LORD loves justice,
and he will never abandon
the godly.

He will keep them safe forever,
but the children of the wicked
will die.
29 The godly will possess the land
and will live there forever.

PROVERBS 10:5
A wise youth harvests in the summer,
but one who sleeps during harvest is a
disgrace.

FEBRUARY**20**

LEVITICUS 9:7–10:20

Aaron began his role as high priest by officiating
the first of many sacrifices he would oversee in his
lifetime. His sons, in their foolishness, didn't take
God seriously. They paid for their irreverence with
their lives.

Then Moses said to Aaron, "Come to the
altar and sacrifice your sin offering and
your burnt offering to purify yourself
and the people. Then present the offerings of the people to purify them, making
them right with the LORD,* just as he
has commanded."

8So Aaron went to the altar and slaughtered the calf as a sin offering for himself. 9His sons brought him the blood,
and he dipped his finger in it and put it
on the horns of the altar. He poured out
the rest of the blood at the base of the altar. 10Then he burned on the altar the fat,
the kidneys, and the long lobe of the liver
from the sin offering, just as the LORD
had commanded Moses. 11The meat and
the hide, however, he burned outside
the camp.

12Next Aaron slaughtered the animal
for the burnt offering. His sons brought
him the blood, and he splattered it
against all sides of the altar. 13Then they
handed him each piece of the burnt
offering, including the head, and he
burned them on the altar. 14Then he
washed the internal organs and the legs
and burned them on the altar along with
the rest of the burnt offering.

15Next Aaron presented the offerings
of the people. He slaughtered the people's
goat and presented it as an offering for
their sin, just as he had first done with the
offering for his own sin. 16Then he presented the burnt offering and sacrificed
it in the prescribed way. 17He also presented the grain offering, burning a handful of the flour mixture on the altar, in
addition to the regular burnt offering for
the morning.

18Then Aaron slaughtered the bull and
the ram for the people's peace offering.
His sons brought him the blood, and he
splattered it against all sides of the altar.
19Then he took the fat of the bull and the
ram—the fat of the broad tail and from
around the internal organs—along with
the kidneys and the long lobes of the
livers. 20He placed these fat portions on
top of the breasts of these animals and
burned them on the altar. 21Aaron then
lifted up the breasts and right thighs as
a special offering to the LORD, just as
Moses had commanded.

22After that, Aaron raised his hands

toward the people and blessed them. Then, after presenting the sin offering, the burnt offering, and the peace offering, he stepped down from the altar. ²³Then Moses and Aaron went into the Tabernacle, and when they came back out, they blessed the people again, and the glory of the LORD appeared to the whole community. ²⁴Fire blazed forth from the LORD's presence and consumed the burnt offering and the fat on the altar. When the people saw this, they shouted with joy and fell face down on the ground.

¹⁰:¹AARON's sons Nadab and Abihu put coals of fire in their incense burners and sprinkled incense over them. In this way, they disobeyed the LORD by burning before him the wrong kind of fire, different than he had commanded. ²So fire blazed forth from the LORD's presence and burned them up, and they died there before the LORD.

³Then Moses said to Aaron, "This is what the LORD meant when he said,

'I will display my holiness
    through those who come near me.
I will display my glory
    before all the people.'"

And Aaron was silent.

⁴Then Moses called for Mishael and Elzaphan, Aaron's cousins, the sons of Aaron's uncle Uzziel. He said to them, "Come forward and carry away the bodies of your relatives from in front of the sanctuary to a place outside the camp." ⁵So they came forward and picked them up by their garments and carried them out of the camp, just as Moses had commanded.

⁶Then Moses said to Aaron and his sons Eleazar and Ithamar, "Do not show grief by leaving your hair uncombed* or by tearing your clothes. If you do, you will die, and the LORD's anger will strike the whole community of Israel. However, the rest of the Israelites, your relatives, may mourn because of the LORD's fiery destruction of Nadab and Abihu. ⁷But you must not leave the entrance of the Tabernacle* or you will die, for you have been anointed with the LORD's anointing oil." So they did as Moses commanded.

⁸Then the LORD said to Aaron, ⁹"You and your descendants must never drink wine or any other alcoholic drink before going into the Tabernacle. If you do, you will die. This is a permanent law for you, and it must be observed from generation to generation. ¹⁰You must distinguish between what is sacred and what is common, between what is ceremonially unclean and what is clean. ¹¹And you must teach the Israelites all the decrees that the LORD has given them through Moses."

¹²Then Moses said to Aaron and his remaining sons, Eleazar and Ithamar, "Take what is left of the grain offering after a portion has been presented as a special gift to the LORD, and eat it beside the altar. Make sure it contains no yeast, for it is most holy. ¹³You must eat it in a sacred place, for it has been given to you and your descendants as your portion of the special gifts presented to the LORD. These are the commands I have been given. ¹⁴But the breast and thigh that were lifted up as a special offering may be eaten in any place that is ceremonially clean. These parts have been given to you and your descendants as your portion of the peace offerings presented by the people of Israel. ¹⁵You must lift up the thigh and breast as a special offering to the LORD, along with the fat of the special gifts. These parts will belong to you and your descendants as your permanent right, just as the LORD has commanded."

¹⁶Moses then asked them what had happened to the goat of the sin offering. When he discovered it had been burned up, he became very angry with Eleazar and Ithamar, Aaron's remaining sons. ¹⁷"Why didn't you eat the sin offering in the sacred area?" he demanded. "It is a holy offering! The LORD has given it to you to remove the guilt of the community and to purify the people, making them right with the LORD.* ¹⁸Since the animal's blood was not brought into the Holy Place, you should have eaten the meat in the sacred area as I ordered you."

¹⁹Then Aaron answered Moses, "Today my sons presented both their sin offering and their burnt offering to the LORD. And yet this tragedy has happened to me. If I had eaten the people's sin offering on

such a tragic day as this, would the LORD have been pleased?" ²⁰And when Moses heard this, he was satisfied.

9:7 Or *to make atonement for them.*   10:6 Or *by uncovering your heads.*   10:7 Hebrew *Tent of Meeting;* also in 10:9.
10:17 Or *to make atonement for the people before the LORD.*

MARK 4:26–5:20
Whether through parables or demonstrations of miraculous power, Jesus often mystified the people who encountered him. He was not out for attention; rather he was confronting people with the most profound truth in the world—the reality of who he is.

Jesus also said, "The Kingdom of God is like a farmer who scatters seed on the ground. ²⁷Night and day, while he's asleep or awake, the seed sprouts and grows, but he does not understand how it happens. ²⁸The earth produces the crops on its own. First a leaf blade pushes through, then the heads of wheat are formed, and finally the grain ripens. ²⁹And as soon as the grain is ready, the farmer comes and harvests it with a sickle, for the harvest time has come."

³⁰Jesus said, "How can I describe the Kingdom of God? What story should I use to illustrate it? ³¹It is like a mustard seed planted in the ground. It is the smallest of all seeds, ³²but it becomes the largest of all garden plants; it grows long branches, and birds can make nests in its shade."

³³Jesus used many similar stories and illustrations to teach the people as much as they could understand. ³⁴In fact, in his public ministry he never taught without using parables, but afterward, when he was alone with his disciples, he explained everything to them.

³⁵As evening came, Jesus said to his disciples, "Let's cross to the other side of the lake." ³⁶So they took Jesus in the boat and started out, leaving the crowds behind (although other boats followed). ³⁷But soon a fierce storm came up. High waves were breaking into the boat, and it began to fill with water.

³⁸Jesus was sleeping at the back of the boat with his head on a cushion. The disciples woke him up, shouting, "Teacher, don't you care that we're going to drown?" ³⁹When Jesus woke up, he rebuked the wind and said to the waves, "Silence! Be still!" Suddenly the wind stopped, and there was a great calm. ⁴⁰Then he asked them, "Why are you afraid? Do you still have no faith?"

⁴¹The disciples were absolutely terrified. "Who is this man?" they asked each other. "Even the wind and waves obey him!"

⁵:¹So they arrived at the other side of the lake, in the region of the Gerasenes.* ²When Jesus climbed out of the boat, a man possessed by an evil* spirit came out from a cemetery to meet him. ³This man lived among the burial caves and could no longer be restrained, even with a chain. ⁴Whenever he was put into chains and shackles—as he often was—he snapped the chains from his wrists and smashed the shackles. No one was strong enough to subdue him. ⁵Day and night he wandered among the burial caves and in the hills, howling and cutting himself with sharp stones.

⁶When Jesus was still some distance away, the man saw him, ran to meet him, and bowed low before him. ⁷With a shriek, he screamed, "Why are you interfering with me, Jesus, Son of the Most High God? In the name of God, I beg you, don't torture me!" ⁸For Jesus had already said to the spirit, "Come out of the man, you evil spirit."

⁹Then Jesus demanded, "What is your name?"

And he replied, "My name is Legion, because there are many of us inside this man." ¹⁰Then the evil spirits begged him again and again not to send them to some distant place.

¹¹There happened to be a large herd of pigs feeding on the hillside nearby. ¹²"Send us into those pigs," the spirits begged. "Let us enter them."

¹³So Jesus gave them permission. The evil spirits came out of the man and entered the pigs, and the entire herd of 2,000 pigs plunged down the steep hillside into the lake and drowned in the water.

¹⁴The herdsmen fled to the nearby town and the surrounding countryside, spreading the news as they ran. People

rushed out to see what had happened. [15]A crowd soon gathered around Jesus, and they saw the man who had been possessed by the legion of demons. He was sitting there fully clothed and perfectly sane, and they were all afraid. [16]Then those who had seen what happened told the others about the demon-possessed man and the pigs. [17]And the crowd began pleading with Jesus to go away and leave them alone.

[18]As Jesus was getting into the boat, the man who had been demon possessed begged to go with him. [19]But Jesus said, "No, go home to your family, and tell them everything the Lord has done for you and how merciful he has been." [20]So the man started off to visit the Ten Towns* of that region and began to proclaim the great things Jesus had done for him; and everyone was amazed at what he told them.

5:1 Other manuscripts read *Gadarenes;* still others read *Gergesenes.* See Matt 8:28; Luke 8:26.   5:2 Greek *unclean;* also in 5:8, 13.   5:20 Greek *Decapolis.*

PSALM 37:30-40

The godly offer good counsel;
    they teach right from wrong.
[31] They have made God's law
    their own,
    so they will never slip from
    his path.

[32] The wicked wait in ambush for
    the godly,
    looking for an excuse to kill them.
[33] But the LORD will not let the wicked
    succeed
    or let the godly be condemned
    when they are put on trial.

[34] Put your hope in the LORD.
    Travel steadily along his path.
    He will honor you by giving you
    the land.
    You will see the wicked
    destroyed.

[35] I have seen wicked and ruthless
    people
    flourishing like a tree in its native
    soil.
[36] But when I looked again, they
    were gone!
    Though I searched for them,
    I could not find them!

[37] Look at those who are honest
    and good,
    for a wonderful future awaits
    those who love peace.
[38] But the rebellious will be destroyed;
    they have no future.

[39] The LORD rescues the godly;
    he is their fortress in times
    of trouble.

HOW WE LIVE

Revering God

LEVITICUS 10:1-3 Because God is holy, he deserves our respect and proper fear. We must never forget that our salvation comes only because God was willing to reach out to us, unworthy as we are, and graciously invite us to be his children.   • In your reading today, two brothers died because they disobeyed God and dared to take his holiness lightly. What was their sin? Indifference, carelessness, and disrespect. God had just reviewed with them the precise manner in which they, as priests, were to conduct worship. They chose to treat those instructions with indifference. The consequence of their sin was immediate and lethal.   • Doing what God asks in the way he asks shows a proper respect for him. God is not looking to blast you if you sin; but you should never think that you can carelessly ignore God's commands without consequence. As you think about God, dwell on his power and his holiness. Be humble in his presence and obey his commands. Never take for granted his gift of salvation given to you.

40 The LORD helps them,
   rescuing them from
      the wicked.
He saves them,
   and they find shelter
      in him.

FEBRUARY**21**

LEVITICUS 11:1–12:8
Israel's laws concerning clean and unclean helped set them apart from the idolatrous cultures of neighboring nations. It further instructed them regarding purity and filth, holiness and sin.

Then the LORD said to Moses and Aaron, 2"Give the following instructions to the people of Israel.

"Of all the land animals, these are the ones you may use for food. 3You may eat any animal that has completely split hooves and chews the cud. 4You may not, however, eat the following animals* that have split hooves or that chew the cud, but not both. The camel chews the cud but does not have split hooves, so it is ceremonially unclean for you. 5The hyrax* chews the cud but does not have split hooves, so it is unclean. 6The hare chews the cud but does not have split hooves, so it is unclean. 7The pig has evenly split hooves but does not chew the cud, so it is unclean. 8You may not eat the meat of these animals or even touch their carcasses. They are ceremonially unclean for you.

9"Of all the marine animals, these are the ones you may use for food. You may eat anything from the water if it has both fins and scales, whether taken from salt water or from streams. 10But you must never eat animals from the sea or from rivers that do not have both fins and scales. They are detestable to you. This applies both to little creatures that live in shallow water and to all creatures that live in deep water. 11They will always be detestable to you. You must never eat their meat or even

PROVERBS 10:6-7
The godly are showered with blessings; the words of the wicked conceal violent intentions. ☐ We have happy memories of the godly, but the name of a wicked person rots away.

touch their dead bodies. 12Any marine animal that does not have both fins and scales is detestable to you.

13"These are the birds that are detestable to you. You must never eat them: the griffon vulture, the bearded vulture, the black vulture, 14the kite, falcons of all kinds, 15ravens of all kinds, 16the eagle owl, the short-eared owl, the seagull, hawks of all kinds, 17the little owl, the cormorant, the great owl, 18the barn owl, the desert owl, the Egyptian vulture, 19the stork, herons of all kinds, the hoopoe, and the bat.

20"You must not eat winged insects that walk along the ground; they are detestable to you. 21You may, however, eat winged insects that walk along the ground and have jointed legs so they can jump. 22The insects you are permitted to eat include all kinds of locusts, bald locusts, crickets, and grasshoppers. 23All other winged insects that walk along the ground are detestable to you.

24"The following creatures will make you ceremonially unclean. If any of you touch their carcasses, you will be defiled until evening. 25If you pick up their carcasses, you must wash your clothes, and you will remain defiled until evening.

26"Any animal that has split hooves that are not evenly divided or that does not chew the cud is unclean for you. If you touch the carcass of such an animal, you will be defiled. 27Of the animals that walk on all fours, those that have paws are unclean. If you touch the carcass of such an animal, you will be defiled until evening. [28]If you pick up its carcass, you must wash your clothes, and you will remain defiled until evening. These animals are unclean for you.

[29]"Of the small animals that scurry along the ground, these are unclean for you: the mole rat, the rat, large lizards of all kinds, [30]the gecko, the monitor lizard, the common lizard, the sand lizard, and the chameleon. [31]All these small animals are unclean for you. If any of you touch the dead body of such an animal, you will be defiled until evening. [32]If such an animal dies and falls on something, that object will be unclean. This is true whether the object is made of wood, cloth, leather, or burlap. Whatever its use, you must dip it in water, and it will remain defiled until evening. After that, it will be ceremonially clean and may be used again.

[33]"If such an animal falls into a clay pot, everything in the pot will be defiled, and the pot must be smashed. [34]If the water from such a container spills on any food, the food will be defiled. And any beverage in such a container will be defiled. [35]Any object on which the carcass of such an animal falls will be defiled. If it is an oven or hearth, it must be destroyed, for it is defiled, and you must treat it accordingly.

[36]"However, if the carcass of such an animal falls into a spring or a cistern, the water will still be clean. But anyone who touches the carcass will be defiled. [37]If the carcass falls on seed grain to be planted in the field, the seed will still be considered clean. [38]But if the seed is wet when the carcass falls on it, the seed will be defiled.

[39]"If an animal you are permitted to eat dies and you touch its carcass, you will be defiled until evening. [40]If you eat any of its meat or carry away its carcass, you must wash your clothes, and you will remain defiled until evening.

[41]"All small animals that scurry along the ground are detestable, and you must never eat them. [42]This includes all animals that slither along on their bellies, as well as those with four legs and those with many feet. All such animals that scurry along the ground are detestable, and you must never eat them. [43]Do not defile yourselves by touching them. You must not make yourselves ceremonially unclean because of them. [44]For I am the LORD your God. You must consecrate yourselves and be holy, because I am holy. So do not defile yourselves with any of these small animals that scurry along the ground. [45]For I, the LORD, am the one who brought you up from the

HOW WE LIVE

Dealing with problems

MARK 5:36 Two people in desperate straits came to Jesus. First, a father came on behalf of his dying daughter. "Please come and lay your hands on her; heal her," he said desperately. Next came the woman who had been hemorrhaging for twelve years. Imagine her weakness, her fear, and especially her feelings of uncleanness. Crawling through the mob, she had only one goal in mind—touch Jesus' robe. She needed his healing power, and she knew she could get it just from a touch to his garment. She was right. Then Christ spoke to her, "Daughter, your faith has made you well. Go in peace. Your suffering is over." The man with the dying daughter? His daughter died before Jesus arrived. The desperate situation turned for the worse. But that was no problem for Jesus—he simply brought the child back to life. • Christ wants you to acknowledge his power to heal and repair what is broken in your life. Whatever the size of your crisis, bring it to Jesus. Nothing is too difficult for him; no situation is too desperate. Reach out your hand. He's there.

land of Egypt, that I might be your God. Therefore, you must be holy because I am holy.

⁴⁶"These are the instructions regarding land animals, birds, marine creatures, and animals that scurry along the ground. ⁴⁷By these instructions you will know what is unclean and clean, and which animals may be eaten and which may not be eaten."

12:1THE LORD said to Moses, "Give the following instructions to the people of Israel. ²If a woman becomes pregnant and gives birth to a son, she will be ceremonially unclean for seven days, just as she is unclean during her menstrual period. ³On the eighth day the boy's foreskin must be circumcised. ⁴After waiting thirty-three days, she will be purified from the bleeding of childbirth. During this time of purification, she must not touch anything that is set apart as holy. And she must not enter the sanctuary until her time of purification is over. ⁵If a woman gives birth to a daughter, she will be ceremonially unclean for two weeks, just as she is unclean during her menstrual period. After waiting sixty-six days, she will be purified from the bleeding of childbirth.

⁶"When the time of purification is completed for either a son or a daughter, the woman must bring a one-year-old lamb for a burnt offering and a young pigeon or turtledove for a purification offering. She must bring her offerings to the priest at the entrance of the Tabernacle.* ⁷The priest will then present them to the LORD to purify her.* Then she will be ceremonially clean again after her bleeding at childbirth. These are the instructions for a woman after the birth of a son or a daughter.

⁸"If a woman cannot afford to bring a lamb, she must bring two turtledoves or two young pigeons. One will be for the burnt offering and the other for the purification offering. The priest will sacrifice them to purify her, and she will be ceremonially clean."

11:4 The identification of some of the animals, birds, and insects in this chapter is uncertain.   11:5 Or *coney,* or *rock badger.*   12:6 Hebrew *Tent of Meeting.*   12:7 Or *to make atonement for her;* also in 12:8.

MARK 5:21-43
Of all the responses Jesus invoked in people, there was one in particular that brought joy to his heart—faith. The same is still true today.

Jesus got into the boat again and went back to the other side of the lake, where a large crowd gathered around him on the shore. ²²Then a leader of the local synagogue, whose name was Jairus, arrived. When he saw Jesus, he fell at his feet, ²³pleading fervently with him. "My little daughter is dying," he said. "Please come and lay your hands on her; heal her so she can live."

²⁴Jesus went with him, and all the people followed, crowding around him. ²⁵A woman in the crowd had suffered for twelve years with constant bleeding. ²⁶She had suffered a great deal from many doctors, and over the years she had spent everything she had to pay them, but she had gotten no better. In fact, she had gotten worse. ²⁷She had heard about Jesus, so she came up behind him through the crowd and touched his robe. ²⁸For she thought to herself, "If I can just touch his robe, I will be healed." ²⁹Immediately the bleeding stopped, and she could feel in her body that she had been healed of her terrible condition.

³⁰Jesus realized at once that healing power had gone out from him, so he turned around in the crowd and asked, "Who touched my robe?"

³¹His disciples said to him, "Look at this crowd pressing around you. How can you ask, 'Who touched me?'"

³²But he kept on looking around to see who had done it. ³³Then the frightened woman, trembling at the realization of what had happened to her, came and fell to her knees in front of him and told him what she had done. ³⁴And he said to her, "Daughter, your faith has made you well. Go in peace. Your suffering is over."

³⁵While he was still speaking to her, messengers arrived from the home of Jairus, the leader of the synagogue. They told him, "Your daughter is dead. There's no use troubling the Teacher now."

³⁶But Jesus overheard* them and said to Jairus, "Don't be afraid. Just have faith."

³⁷Then Jesus stopped the crowd and

wouldn't let anyone go with him except Peter, James, and John (the brother of James). [38]When they came to the home of the synagogue leader, Jesus saw much commotion and weeping and wailing. [39]He went inside and asked, "Why all this commotion and weeping? The child isn't dead; she's only asleep."

[40]The crowd laughed at him. But he made them all leave, and he took the girl's father and mother and his three disciples into the room where the girl was lying. [41]Holding her hand, he said to her, *"Talitha koum,"* which means "Little girl, get up!" [42]And the girl, who was twelve years old, immediately stood up and walked around! They were overwhelmed and totally amazed. [43]Jesus gave them strict orders not to tell anyone what had happened, and then he told them to give her something to eat.

5:36 Or *ignored.*

PSALM 38:1-22

A psalm of David, asking God to remember him.

[1] **O** LORD, don't rebuke me in your
     anger
       or discipline me in your rage!
[2] Your arrows have struck deep,
       and your blows are crushing me.
[3] Because of your anger, my whole body
     is sick;
       my health is broken because of
       my sins.
[4] My guilt overwhelms me—
       it is a burden too heavy to bear.
[5] My wounds fester and stink
       because of my foolish sins.
[6] I am bent over and racked with pain.
     All day long I walk around filled
       with grief.
[7] A raging fever burns within me,
       and my health is broken.
[8] I am exhausted and completely
     crushed.
       My groans come from an anguished
       heart.

[9] You know what I long for, Lord;
       you hear my every sigh.
[10] My heart beats wildly, my strength
     fails,
       and I am going blind.
[11] My loved ones and friends stay away,
       fearing my disease.
     Even my own family stands at
       a distance.
[12] Meanwhile, my enemies lay traps
     to kill me.
     Those who wish me harm make
       plans to ruin me.
     All day long they plan their
       treachery.
[13] But I am deaf to all their threats.
     I am silent before them as one
       who cannot speak.
[14] I choose to hear nothing,
       and I make no reply.
[15] For I am waiting for you, O LORD.
     You must answer for me, O Lord
       my God.
[16] I prayed, "Don't let my enemies gloat
     over me
       or rejoice at my downfall."
[17] I am on the verge of collapse,
       facing constant pain.
[18] But I confess my sins;
     I am deeply sorry for what I have
     done.
[19] I have many aggressive enemies;
       they hate me without reason.
[20] They repay me evil for good
       and oppose me for pursuing good.
[21] Do not abandon me, O LORD.
     Do not stand at a distance,
       my God.
[22] Come quickly to help me,
       O Lord my savior.

PROVERBS 10:8-9

The wise are glad to be instructed, but babbling fools fall flat on their faces. □People with integrity walk safely, but those who follow crooked paths will slip and fall.

FEBRUARY**22**

The laws concerning skin diseases and other infectious conditions combined good hygienic principles with spiritual symbolism.

The LORD said to Moses and Aaron, ²"If anyone has a swelling or a rash or discolored skin that might develop into a serious skin disease,* that person must be brought to Aaron the priest or to one of his sons.* ³The priest will examine the affected area of the skin. If the hair in the affected area has turned white and the problem appears to be more than skin-deep, it is a serious skin disease, and the priest who examines it must pronounce the person ceremonially unclean.

⁴"But if the affected area of the skin is only a white discoloration and does not appear to be more than skin-deep, and if the hair on the spot has not turned white, the priest will quarantine the person for seven days. ⁵On the seventh day the priest will make another examination. If he finds the affected area has not changed and the problem has not spread on the skin, the priest will quarantine the person for seven more days. ⁶On the seventh day the priest will make another examination. If he finds the affected area has faded and has not spread, the priest will pronounce the person ceremonially clean. It was only a rash. The person's clothing must be washed, and the person will be ceremonially clean. ⁷But if the rash continues to spread after the person has been examined by the priest and has been pronounced clean, the infected person must return to be examined again. ⁸If the priest finds that the rash has spread, he must pronounce the person ceremonially unclean, for it is indeed a skin disease.

⁹"Anyone who develops a serious skin disease must go to the priest for an examination. ¹⁰If the priest finds a white swelling on the skin, and some hair on the spot has turned white, and there is an open sore in the affected area, ¹¹it is a chronic skin disease, and the priest must pronounce the person ceremonially unclean. In such cases the person need not be quarantined, for it is obvious that the skin is defiled by the disease.

¹²"Now suppose the disease has spread all over the person's skin, covering the body from head to foot. ¹³When the priest examines the infected person and finds that the disease covers the entire body, he will pronounce the person ceremonially clean. Since the skin has turned completely white, the person is clean. ¹⁴But if any open sores appear, the infected person will be pronounced ceremonially unclean. ¹⁵The priest must make this pronouncement as soon as he sees an open sore, since open sores indicate the presence of a skin disease. ¹⁶However, if the open sores heal and turn white like the rest of the skin, the person must return to the priest ¹⁷for another examination. If the affected areas have indeed turned white, the priest will then pronounce the person ceremonially clean by declaring, 'You are clean!'

¹⁸"If anyone has a boil on the skin that has started to heal, ¹⁹but a white swelling or a reddish white spot develops in its place, that person must go to the priest to be examined. ²⁰If the priest examines it and finds it to be more than skin-deep, and if the hair in the affected area has turned white, the priest must pronounce the person ceremonially unclean. The boil has become a serious skin disease. ²¹But if the priest finds no white hair on the affected area and the problem appears to be no more than skin-deep and has faded, the priest must quarantine the person for seven days. ²²If during that time the affected area spreads on the skin, the priest must pronounce the person ceremonially unclean, because it is a serious disease. ²³But if the area grows no larger and does not spread, it is merely the scar from the boil, and the priest will pronounce the person ceremonially clean.

²⁴"If anyone has suffered a burn on the skin and the burned area changes color, becoming either reddish white or shiny white, ²⁵the priest must examine it. If he finds that the hair in the affected area has

turned white and the problem appears to be more than skin-deep, a skin disease has broken out in the burn. The priest must then pronounce the person ceremonially unclean, for it is clearly a serious skin disease. [26] But if the priest finds no white hair on the affected area and the problem appears to be no more than skin-deep and has faded, the priest must quarantine the infected person for seven days. [27] On the seventh day the priest must examine the person again. If the affected area has spread on the skin, the priest must pronounce that person ceremonially unclean, for it is clearly a serious skin disease. [28] But if the affected area has not changed or spread on the skin and has faded, it is simply a swelling from the burn. The priest will then pronounce the person ceremonially clean, for it is only the scar from the burn.

[29] "If anyone, either a man or woman, has a sore on the head or chin, [30] the priest must examine it. If he finds it is more than skin-deep and has fine yellow hair on it, the priest must pronounce the person ceremonially unclean. It is a scabby sore of the head or chin. [31] If the priest examines the scabby sore and finds that it is only skin-deep but there is no black hair on it, he must quarantine the person for seven days. [32] On the seventh day the priest must examine the sore again. If he finds that the scabby sore has not spread, and there is no yellow hair on it, and it appears to be only skin-deep, [33] the person must shave off all hair except the hair on the affected area. Then the priest must quarantine the person for another seven days. [34] On the seventh day he will examine the sore again. If it has not spread and appears to be no more than skin-deep, the priest will pronounce the person ceremonially clean. The person's clothing must be washed, and the person will be ceremonially clean. [35] But if the scabby sore begins to spread after the person is pronounced clean, [36] the priest must do another examination. If he finds that the sore has spread, the priest does not need to look for yellow hair. The infected person is ceremonially unclean. [37] But if the color of the scabby sore does not change and black hair has grown on it, it has

healed. The priest will then pronounce the person ceremonially clean.

[38] "If anyone, either a man or woman, has shiny white patches on the skin, [39] the priest must examine the affected area. If he finds that the shiny patches are only pale white, this is a harmless skin rash, and the person is ceremonially clean.

[40] "If a man loses his hair and his head becomes bald, he is still ceremonially clean. [41] And if he loses hair on his forehead, he simply has a bald forehead; he is still clean. [42] However, if a reddish white sore appears on the bald area at the top or back of his head, this is a skin disease. [43] The priest must examine him, and if he finds swelling around the reddish white sore anywhere on the man's head and it looks like a skin disease, [44] the man is indeed infected with a skin disease and is unclean. The priest must pronounce him ceremonially unclean because of the sore on his head.

[45] "Those who suffer from a serious skin disease must tear their clothing and leave their hair uncombed.* They must cover their mouth and call out, 'Unclean! Unclean!' [46] As long as the serious disease lasts, they will be ceremonially unclean. They must live in isolation in their place outside the camp.

[47] "Now suppose mildew* contaminates some woolen or linen clothing, [48] woolen or linen fabric, the hide of an animal, or anything made of leather. [49] If the contaminated area in the clothing, the animal hide, the fabric, or the leather article has turned greenish or reddish, it is contaminated with mildew and must be shown to the priest. [50] After examining the affected spot, the priest will put the article in quarantine for seven days. [51] On the seventh day the priest must inspect it again. If the contaminated area has spread, the clothing or fabric or leather is clearly contaminated by a serious mildew and is ceremonially unclean. [52] The priest must burn the item—the clothing, the woolen or linen fabric, or piece of leather—for it has been contaminated by a serious mildew. It must be completely destroyed by fire.

[53] "But if the priest examines it and finds that the contaminated area has not

spread in the clothing, the fabric, or the leather, [54] the priest will order the object to be washed and then quarantined for seven more days. [55] Then the priest must examine the object again. If he finds that the contaminated area has not changed color after being washed, even if it did not spread, the object is defiled. It must be completely burned up, whether the contaminated spot* is on the inside or outside. [56] But if the priest examines it and finds that the contaminated area has faded after being washed, he must cut the spot from the clothing, the fabric, or the leather. [57] If the spot later reappears on the clothing, the fabric, or the leather article, the mildew is clearly spreading, and the contaminated object must be burned up. [58] But if the spot disappears from the clothing, the fabric, or the leather article after it has been washed, it must be washed again; then it will be ceremonially clean.

[59] "These are the instructions for dealing with mildew that contaminates woolen or linen clothing or fabric or anything made of leather. This is how the priest will determine whether these items are ceremonially clean or unclean."

13:2a Traditionally rendered *leprosy*. The Hebrew word used throughout this passage is used to describe various skin diseases.   13:2b Or *one of his descendants*.   13:45 Or *and uncover their heads*.   13:47 Traditionally rendered *leprosy*. The Hebrew term used throughout this passage is the same term used for the various skin diseases described in 13:1-46.   13:55 The meaning of the Hebrew is uncertain.

MARK 6:1-29

Jesus and John the Baptist both faced opposition for preaching truth. In today's reading, Jesus faces opposition from people in his hometown.

Jesus left that part of the country and returned with his disciples to Nazareth, his hometown. [2] The next Sabbath he began teaching in the synagogue, and many who heard him were amazed. They asked, "Where did he get all this wisdom and the power to perform such miracles?" [3] Then they scoffed, "He's just a carpenter, the son of Mary* and the brother of James, Joseph,* Judas, and Simon. And his sisters live right here among us." They were deeply offended and refused to believe in him.

[4] Then Jesus told them, "A prophet is honored everywhere except in his own hometown and among his relatives and his own family." [5] And because of their unbelief, he couldn't do any miracles among them except to place his hands on a few sick people and heal them. [6] And he was amazed at their unbelief.

Then Jesus went from village to village, teaching the people. [7] And he called his twelve disciples together and began sending them out two by two, giving them authority to cast out evil* spirits. [8] He told them to take nothing for their journey except a walking stick—no food, no traveler's bag, no money.* [9] He allowed them to wear sandals but not to take a change of clothes.

[10] "Wherever you go," he said, "stay in the same house until you leave town. [11] But if any place refuses to welcome you or listen to you, shake its dust from your feet as you leave to show that you have abandoned those people to their fate."

[12] So the disciples went out, telling everyone they met to repent of their sins and turn to God. [13] And they cast out many demons and healed many sick people, anointing them with olive oil.

[14] Herod Antipas, the king, soon heard about Jesus, because everyone was talking about him. Some were saying,* "This must be John the Baptist raised from the dead. That is why he can do such miracles." [15] Others said, "He's the prophet Elijah." Still others said, "He's a prophet like the other great prophets of the past."

[16] When Herod heard about Jesus, he said, "John, the man I beheaded, has come back from the dead."

[17] For Herod had sent soldiers to arrest and imprison John as a favor to Herodias. She had been his brother Philip's wife, but Herod had married her. [18] John had been telling Herod, "It is against God's law for you to marry your brother's wife." [19] So Herodias bore a grudge against John and wanted to kill him. But without Herod's approval she was powerless, [20] for Herod respected John; and knowing that he was a good and holy man, he protected him. Herod was greatly disturbed whenever he talked with John, but even so, he liked to listen to him.

[21] Herodias's chance finally came on

Herod's birthday. He gave a party for his high government officials, army officers, and the leading citizens of Galilee. ²²Then his daughter, also named Herodias,* came in and performed a dance that greatly pleased Herod and his guests. "Ask me for anything you like," the king said to the girl, "and I will give it to you." ²³He even vowed, "I will give you whatever you ask, up to half my kingdom!"

²⁴She went out and asked her mother, "What should I ask for?"

Her mother told her, "Ask for the head of John the Baptist!"

²⁵So the girl hurried back to the king and told him, "I want the head of John the Baptist, right now, on a tray!"

²⁶Then the king deeply regretted what he had said; but because of the vows he had made in front of his guests, he couldn't refuse her. ²⁷So he immediately sent an executioner to the prison to cut off John's head and bring it to him. The soldier beheaded John in the prison, ²⁸brought his head on a tray, and gave it to the girl, who took it to her mother. ²⁹When John's disciples heard what had happened, they came to get his body and buried it in a tomb.

6:3a Some manuscripts read *He's just the son of the carpenter and of Mary.*   **6:3b** Most manuscripts read *Joses;* see Matt 13:55.   **6:7** Greek *unclean.*   **6:8** Greek *no copper coins in their money belts.*   **6:14** Some manuscripts read *He was saying.*   **6:22** Some manuscripts read *the daughter of Herodias herself.*

PSALM 39:1-13
For Jeduthun, the choir director: A psalm of David.

¹ I said to myself, "I will watch what I do
    and not sin in what I say.
  I will hold my tongue
    when the ungodly are around me."
² But as I stood there in silence—
    not even speaking of good things—
    the turmoil within me grew worse.
³ The more I thought about it,
    the hotter I got,
    igniting a fire of words:
⁴ "LORD, remind me how brief my time
    on earth will be.
  Remind me that my days are
    numbered—
    how fleeting my life is.
⁵ You have made my life no longer than
    the width of my hand.
  My entire lifetime is just a moment
    to you;
  at best, each of us is but a breath."
                                        Interlude

⁶ We are merely moving shadows,
    and all our busy rushing ends in
    nothing.
  We heap up wealth,
    not knowing who will spend it.
⁷ And so, Lord, where do I put my hope?
    My only hope is in you.
⁸ Rescue me from my rebellion.
    Do not let fools mock me.

Setting priorities

HOW WE LIVE

PSALM 39:5-6 The psalmist David recognized how short life is and how futile it is to make the accumulation of riches one's priority in life. No matter how long your life may be, your years are still only a "breath" when compared to your life in heaven, so you need to set priorities in light of what really matters. If there is something you want or need to do, don't put it off for another day. Make each moment count. Don't neglect what is most important: your relationship with God. • As you look at life from this perspective, remember the words of Jesus: "Don't store up treasures here on earth. . . . Store your treasures in heaven, where moths and rust cannot destroy, and thieves do not break in and steal. Wherever your treasure is, there the desires of your heart will also be" (Matthew 6:19-21, January 7). Your time on earth is short. Ask God to help you spend it on things that count.

9 I am silent before you; I won't say
a word,
for my punishment is from you.
10 But please stop striking me!
I am exhausted by the blows from
your hand.
11 When you discipline us for our sins,
you consume like a moth what is
precious to us.
Each of us is but a breath. *Interlude*

12 Hear my prayer, O LORD!
Listen to my cries for help!
Don't ignore my tears.

For I am your guest—
a traveler passing through,
as my ancestors were
before me.
13 Leave me alone so I can smile again
before I am gone and exist
no more.

PROVERBS 10:10
People who wink at wrong cause trouble,
but a bold reproof promotes peace.*

10:10 As in Greek version; Hebrew reads *but babbling fools
fall flat on their faces.*

FEBRUARY**23**

LEVITICUS 14:1-57
The priest was responsible not just to recognize
impurity—physical or spiritual—but also to
cleanse it.

And the LORD said to Moses, 2"The following instructions are for those seeking
ceremonial purification from a skin disease.* Those who have been healed must
be brought to the priest, 3 who will examine them at a place outside the camp. If
the priest finds that someone has been
healed of a serious skin disease, 4 he will
perform a purification ceremony, using
two live birds that are ceremonially clean,
a stick of cedar,* some scarlet yarn, and a
hyssop branch. 5 The priest will order that
one bird be slaughtered over a clay pot
filled with fresh water. 6 He will take the
live bird, the cedar stick, the scarlet yarn,
and the hyssop branch, and dip them into
the blood of the bird that was slaughtered
over the fresh water. 7 The priest will then
sprinkle the blood of the dead bird seven
times on the person being purified of the
skin disease. When the priest has purified the person, he will release the live
bird in the open field to fly away.

8 "The persons being purified must
then wash their clothes, shave off all their
hair, and bathe themselves in water. Then

they will be ceremonially clean and may
return to the camp. However, they must
remain outside their tents for seven days.
9 On the seventh day they must again
shave all the hair from their heads, including the hair of the beard and eyebrows.
They must also wash their clothes and
bathe themselves in water. Then they will
be ceremonially clean.

10 "On the eighth day each person being
purified must bring two male lambs and a
one-year-old female lamb, all with no defects, along with a grain offering of six
quarts* of choice flour moistened with
olive oil, and a cup* of olive oil. 11 Then the
officiating priest will present that person
for purification, along with the offerings,
before the LORD at the entrance of the
Tabernacle.* 12 The priest will take one of
the male lambs and the olive oil and present them as a guilt offering, lifting them
up as a special offering before the LORD.
13 He will then slaughter the male lamb in
the sacred area where sin offerings and
burnt offerings are slaughtered. As with
the sin offering, the guilt offering belongs
to the priest. It is a most holy offering.
14 The priest will then take some of the
blood of the guilt offering and apply it to
the lobe of the right ear, the thumb of the

right hand, and the big toe of the right foot of the person being purified.

¹⁵"Then the priest will pour some of the olive oil into the palm of his own left hand. ¹⁶He will dip his right finger into the oil in his palm and sprinkle some of it with his finger seven times before the Lord. ¹⁷The priest will then apply some of the oil in his palm over the blood from the guilt offering that is on the lobe of the right ear, the thumb of the right hand, and the big toe of the right foot of the person being purified. ¹⁸The priest will apply the oil remaining in his hand to the head of the person being purified. Through this process, the priest will purify* the person before the Lord.

¹⁹"Then the priest must present the sin offering to purify the person who was cured of the skin disease. After that, the priest will slaughter the burnt offering ²⁰and offer it on the altar along with the grain offering. Through this process, the priest will purify the person who was healed, and the person will be ceremonially clean.

²¹"But anyone who is too poor and cannot afford these offerings may bring one male lamb for a guilt offering, to be lifted up as a special offering for purification. The person must also bring two quarts* of choice flour moistened with olive oil for the grain offering and a cup of olive oil. ²²The offering must also include two turtledoves or two young pigeons, whichever the person can afford. One of the pair must be used for the sin offering and the other for a burnt offering. ²³On the eighth day of the purification ceremony, the person being purified must bring the offerings to the priest in the Lord's presence at the entrance of the Tabernacle. ²⁴The priest will take the lamb for the guilt offering, along with the olive oil, and lift them up as a special offering to the Lord. ²⁵Then the priest will slaughter the lamb for the guilt offering. He will take some of its blood and apply it to the lobe of the right ear, the thumb of the right hand, and the big toe of the right foot of the person being purified.

²⁶"The priest will also pour some of the olive oil into the palm of his own left hand. ²⁷He will dip his right finger into the oil in his palm and sprinkle some of it seven times before the Lord. ²⁸The priest will then apply some of the oil in his palm over the blood from the guilt offering that is on the lobe of the right ear, the thumb of the right hand, and the big toe of the right foot of the person being purified. ²⁹The priest will apply the oil remaining in his hand to the head of the person being purified. Through this process, the priest will purify the person before the Lord.

³⁰"Then the priest will offer the two turtledoves or the two young pigeons, whichever the person can afford. ³¹One of them is for a sin offering and the other for a burnt offering, to be presented along with the grain offering. Through this process, the priest will purify the person before the Lord. ³²These are the instructions for purification for those who have recovered from a serious skin disease but who cannot afford to bring the offerings normally required for the ceremony of purification."

³³Then the Lord said to Moses and Aaron, ³⁴"When you arrive in Canaan, the land I am giving you as your own possession, I may contaminate some of the houses in your land with mildew.* ³⁵The owner of such a house must then go to the priest and say, 'It appears that my house has some kind of mildew.' ³⁶Before the priest goes in to inspect the house, he must have the house emptied so nothing inside will be pronounced ceremonially unclean. ³⁷Then the priest will go in and examine the mildew on the walls. If he finds greenish or reddish streaks and the contamination appears to go deeper than the wall's surface, ³⁸the priest will step outside the door and put the house in quarantine for seven days. ³⁹On the seventh day the priest must return for another inspection. If he finds that the mildew on the walls of the house has spread, ⁴⁰the priest must order that the stones from those areas be removed. The contaminated material will then be taken outside the town to an area designated as ceremonially unclean. ⁴¹Next the inside walls of the entire house must be scraped thoroughly and the scrapings dumped in the unclean place outside the town. ⁴²Other stones will be brought in to

replace the ones that were removed, and the walls will be replastered.

⁴³"But if the mildew reappears after all the stones have been replaced and the house has been scraped and replastered, ⁴⁴the priest must return and inspect the house again. If he finds that the mildew has spread, the walls are clearly contaminated with a serious mildew, and the house is defiled. ⁴⁵It must be torn down, and all its stones, timbers, and plaster must be carried out of town to the place designated as ceremonially unclean. ⁴⁶Those who enter the house during the period of quarantine will be ceremonially unclean until evening, ⁴⁷and all who sleep or eat in the house must wash their clothing.

⁴⁸"But if the priest returns for his inspection and finds that the mildew has not reappeared in the house after the fresh plastering, he will pronounce it clean because the mildew is clearly gone. ⁴⁹To purify the house the priest must take two birds, a stick of cedar, some scarlet yarn, and a hyssop branch. ⁵⁰He will slaughter one of the birds over a clay pot filled with fresh water. ⁵¹He will take the cedar stick, the hyssop branch, the scarlet yarn, and the live bird, and dip them into the blood of the slaughtered bird and into the fresh water. Then he will sprinkle the house seven times. ⁵²When the priest has purified the house in exactly this way, ⁵³he will release the live bird in the open fields outside the town. Through this process, the priest will purify the house, and it will be ceremonially clean.

⁵⁴"These are the instructions for dealing with serious skin diseases,* including scabby sores; ⁵⁵and mildew,* whether on clothing or in a house; ⁵⁶and a swelling on the skin, a rash, or discolored skin. ⁵⁷This procedure will determine whether a person or object is ceremonially clean or unclean.

"These are the instructions regarding skin diseases and mildew."

14:2 Traditionally rendered *leprosy;* see note on 13:2a.
14:4 Or *juniper;* also in 14:6, 49, 51.   14:10a Hebrew ³⁄₁₀ *of an ephah* [6.6 liters].   14:10b Hebrew *1 log* [0.3 liters]; also in 14:21.   14:11 Hebrew *Tent of Meeting;* also in 14:23.
14:18 Or *will make atonement for;* similarly in 14:19, 20, 21, 29, 31, 53.   14:21 Hebrew ¹⁄₁₀ *of an ephah* [2.2 liters].
14:34 Traditionally rendered *leprosy;* see note on 13:47.
14:54 Traditionally rendered *leprosy;* see note on 13:2a.
14:55 Traditionally rendered *leprosy;* see note on 13:47.

MARK 6:30-56
This passage gives lessons on Jesus' divine power and what faith in him can accomplish.

The apostles returned to Jesus from their ministry tour and told him all they had done and taught. ³¹Then Jesus said, "Let's go off by ourselves to a quiet place and rest awhile." He said this because there were so many people coming and going that Jesus and his apostles didn't even have time to eat.

³²So they left by boat for a quiet place, where they could be alone. ³³But many people recognized them and saw them leaving, and people from many towns ran ahead along the shore and got there ahead of them. ³⁴Jesus saw the huge crowd as he stepped from the boat, and he had compassion on them because they were like sheep without a shepherd. So he began teaching them many things.

³⁵Late in the afternoon his disciples came to him and said, "This is a remote place, and it's already getting late. ³⁶Send the crowds away so they can go to the nearby farms and villages and buy something to eat."

³⁷But Jesus said, "You feed them."

"With what?" they asked. "We'd have to work for months to earn enough money* to buy food for all these people!"

³⁸"How much bread do you have?" he asked. "Go and find out."

They came back and reported, "We have five loaves of bread and two fish."

³⁹Then Jesus told the disciples to have the people sit down in groups on the green grass. ⁴⁰So they sat down in groups of fifty or a hundred.

⁴¹Jesus took the five loaves and two fish, looked up toward heaven, and blessed them. Then, breaking the loaves into pieces, he kept giving the bread to the disciples so they could distribute it to the people. He also divided the fish for everyone to share. ⁴²They all ate as much as they wanted, ⁴³and afterward, the disciples picked up twelve baskets of leftover bread and fish. ⁴⁴A total of 5,000 men and their families were fed from those loaves!

⁴⁵Immediately after this, Jesus insisted that his disciples get back into the boat and head across the lake to Bethsaida,

while he sent the people home. ⁴⁶After telling everyone good-bye, he went up into the hills by himself to pray.

⁴⁷Late that night, the disciples were in their boat in the middle of the lake, and Jesus was alone on land. ⁴⁸He saw that they were in serious trouble, rowing hard and struggling against the wind and waves. About three o'clock in the morning* Jesus came toward them, walking on the water. He intended to go past them, ⁴⁹but when they saw him walking on the water, they cried out in terror, thinking he was a ghost. ⁵⁰They were all terrified when they saw him.

But Jesus spoke to them at once. "Don't be afraid," he said. "Take courage! I am here!*" ⁵¹Then he climbed into the boat, and the wind stopped. They were totally amazed, ⁵²for they still didn't understand the significance of the miracle of the loaves. Their hearts were too hard to take it in.

⁵³After they had crossed the lake, they landed at Gennesaret. They brought the boat to shore ⁵⁴and climbed out. The people recognized Jesus at once, ⁵⁵and they ran throughout the whole area, carrying sick people on mats to wherever they heard he was. ⁵⁶Wherever he went—in villages, cities, or the countryside—they brought the sick out to the marketplaces. They begged him to let the sick touch at least the fringe of his robe, and all who touched him were healed.

6:37 Greek *It would take 200 denarii.* A denarius was equivalent to a laborer's full day's wage.   6:48 Greek *About the fourth watch of the night.*   6:50 Or *The 'I AM' is here;* Greek reads *I am.* See Exod 3:14.

PSALM 40:1-10
For the choir director: A psalm of David.

¹ I waited patiently for the LORD to help me,
    and he turned to me and heard my cry.
² He lifted me out of the pit of despair,
    out of the mud and the mire.
He set my feet on solid ground
    and steadied me as I walked along.
³ He has given me a new song to sing,
    a hymn of praise to our God.
Many will see what he has done and be amazed.
    They will put their trust in the LORD.

⁴ Oh, the joys of those who trust the LORD,
    who have no confidence in the proud
    or in those who worship idols.
⁵ O LORD my God, you have performed many wonders for us.
    Your plans for us are too numerous to list.
    You have no equal.
If I tried to recite all your wonderful deeds,
    I would never come to the end of them.

⁶ You take no delight in sacrifice or offerings.
    Now that you have made me listen,
    I finally understand*—

WHO GOD IS
Jesus is God

MARK 6:48-51 Jesus' miracles were powerful evidence that Jesus was more than just a carpenter from Nazareth. His miracles on the Sea of Galilee showed that he was more than just a miracle worker. In the Old Testament, the one who is powerful enough to calm the roaring sea is God himself. "You rule the oceans. You subdue their storm-tossed waves," wrote the psalmist (Psalm 89:9). The disciples' first reaction was fear and astonishment. They did not fully believe for "their hearts were too hard to take it in." Jesus revealed who he was in slow, subtle ways to the disciples, but the cumulative witness of Scripture is clear: Jesus is God.

you don't require burnt offerings
or sin offerings.
⁷ Then I said, "Look, I have come.
As is written about me in
the Scriptures:
⁸ I take joy in doing your will, my God,
for your instructions are written
on my heart."

⁹ I have told all your people about
your justice.
I have not been afraid to speak out,
as you, O LORD, well know.
¹⁰ I have not kept the good news of your
justice hidden in my heart;

I have talked about your
faithfulness and saving power.
I have told everyone in the great
assembly
of your unfailing love and
faithfulness.

40:6 Greek text reads *You have given me a body.* Compare Heb 10:5.

PROVERBS 10:11-12

The words of the godly are a life-giving fountain; the words of the wicked conceal violent intentions. □ Hatred stirs up quarrels, but love makes up for all offenses.

FEBRUARY**24**

LEVITICUS 15:1-16:28
The Day of Atonement became a grand reminder of humanity's need for God's forgiveness and holiness in a dirty, sinful world. Jesus' sacrifice was the ultimate atoning sacrifice.

The LORD said to Moses and Aaron, ²"Give the following instructions to the people of Israel.

"Any man who has a bodily discharge is ceremonially unclean. ³This defilement is caused by his discharge, whether the discharge continues or stops. In either case the man is unclean. ⁴Any bed on which the man with the discharge lies and anything on which he sits will be ceremonially unclean. ⁵So if you touch the man's bed, you must wash your clothes and bathe yourself in water, and you will remain unclean until evening. ⁶If you sit where the man with the discharge has sat, you must wash your clothes and bathe yourself in water, and you will remain unclean until evening. ⁷If you touch the man with the discharge, you must wash your clothes and bathe yourself in water, and you will remain unclean until evening. ⁸If the man spits on you, you must wash your clothes and bathe yourself in water, and you will remain unclean until evening. ⁹Any saddle blanket on which the man

rides will be ceremonially unclean. ¹⁰If you touch anything that was under the man, you will be unclean until evening. You must wash your clothes and bathe yourself in water, and you will remain unclean until evening. ¹¹If the man touches you without first rinsing his hands, you must wash your clothes and bathe yourself in water, and you will remain unclean until evening. ¹²Any clay pot the man touches must be broken, and any wooden utensil he touches must be rinsed with water.

¹³"When the man with the discharge is healed, he must count off seven days for the period of purification. Then he must wash his clothes and bathe himself in fresh water, and he will be ceremonially clean. ¹⁴On the eighth day he must get two turtledoves or two young pigeons and come before the LORD at the entrance of the Tabernacle* and give his offerings to the priest. ¹⁵The priest will offer one bird for a sin offering and the other for a burnt offering. Through this process, the priest will purify* the man before the LORD for his discharge.

¹⁶"Whenever a man has an emission of semen, he must bathe his entire body in

water, and he will remain ceremonially unclean until the next evening.* ¹⁷Any clothing or leather with semen on it must be washed in water, and it will remain unclean until evening. ¹⁸After a man and a woman have sexual intercourse, they must each bathe in water, and they will remain unclean until the next evening.

¹⁹"Whenever a woman has her menstrual period, she will be ceremonially unclean for seven days. Anyone who touches her during that time will be unclean until evening. ²⁰Anything on which the woman lies or sits during the time of her period will be unclean. ²¹If any of you touch her bed, you must wash your clothes and bathe yourself in water, and you will remain unclean until evening. ²²If you touch any object she has sat on, you must wash your clothes and bathe yourself in water, and you will remain unclean until evening. ²³This includes her bed or any other object she has sat on; you will be unclean until evening if you touch it. ²⁴If a man has sexual intercourse with her and her blood touches him, her menstrual impurity will be transmitted to him. He will remain unclean for seven days, and any bed on which he lies will be unclean.

²⁵"If a woman has a flow of blood for many days that is unrelated to her menstrual period, or if the blood continues beyond the normal period, she is ceremonially unclean. As during her menstrual period, the woman will be unclean as long as the discharge continues. ²⁶Any bed she lies on and any object she sits on during that time will be unclean, just as during her normal menstrual period. ²⁷If any of you touch these things, you will be ceremonially unclean. You must wash your clothes and bathe yourself in water, and you will remain unclean until evening.

²⁸"When the woman's bleeding stops, she must count off seven days. Then she will be ceremonially clean. ²⁹On the eighth day she must bring two turtledoves or two young pigeons and present them to the priest at the entrance of the Tabernacle. ³⁰The priest will offer one for a sin offering and the other for a burnt offering. Through this process, the priest will purify her before the LORD for the ceremonial impurity caused by her bleeding.

³¹"This is how you will guard the people of Israel from ceremonial uncleanness. Otherwise they would die, for their impurity would defile my Tabernacle that stands among them. ³²These are the instructions for dealing with anyone who has a bodily discharge—a man who is unclean because of an emission of semen ³³or a woman during her menstrual period. It applies to any man or woman who has a bodily discharge, and to a man who has sexual intercourse with a woman who is ceremonially unclean."

¹⁶:¹THE LORD spoke to Moses after the death of Aaron's two sons, who died after they entered the LORD's presence and burned the wrong kind of fire before him. ²The LORD said to Moses, "Warn your brother, Aaron, not to enter the Most Holy Place behind the inner curtain whenever he chooses; if he does, he will die. For the Ark's cover—the place of atonement—is there, and I myself am present in the cloud above the atonement cover.

³"When Aaron enters the sanctuary area, he must follow these instructions fully. He must bring a young bull for a sin offering and a ram for a burnt offering. ⁴He must put on his linen tunic and the linen undergarments worn next to his body. He must tie the linen sash around his waist and put the linen turban on his head. These are sacred garments, so he must bathe himself in water before he puts them on. ⁵Aaron must take from the community of Israel two male goats for a sin offering and a ram for a burnt offering.

⁶"Aaron will present his own bull as a sin offering to purify himself and his family, making them right with the LORD.* ⁷Then he must take the two male goats and present them to the LORD at the entrance of the Tabernacle.* ⁸He is to cast sacred lots to determine which goat will be reserved as an offering to the LORD and which will carry the sins of the people to the wilderness of Azazel. ⁹Aaron will then present as a sin offering the goat chosen by lot for the LORD. ¹⁰The other goat, the scapegoat chosen by lot to be sent away, will be kept alive, standing before the LORD. When it is sent away to Azazel in

the wilderness, the people will be purified and made right with the LORD.*

11"Aaron will present his own bull as a sin offering to purify himself and his family, making them right with the LORD. After he has slaughtered the bull as a sin offering, 12 he will fill an incense burner with burning coals from the altar that stands before the LORD. Then he will take two handfuls of fragrant powdered incense and will carry the burner and the incense behind the inner curtain. 13 There in the LORD's presence he will put the incense on the burning coals so that a cloud of incense will rise over the Ark's cover— the place of atonement—that rests on the Ark of the Covenant.* If he follows these instructions, he will not die. 14 Then he must take some of the blood of the bull, dip his finger in it, and sprinkle it on the east side of the atonement cover. He must sprinkle blood seven times with his finger in front of the atonement cover.

15"Then Aaron must slaughter the first goat as a sin offering for the people and carry its blood behind the inner curtain. There he will sprinkle the goat's blood over the atonement cover and in front of it, just as he did with the bull's blood. 16 Through this process, he will purify* the Most Holy Place, and he will do the same for the entire Tabernacle, because of the defiling sin and rebellion of the Israelites. 17 No one else is allowed inside the Tabernacle when Aaron enters it for the purification ceremony in the Most Holy Place. No one may enter until he comes out again after purifying himself, his family, and all the congregation of Israel, making them right with the LORD.

18"Then Aaron will come out to purify the altar that stands before the LORD. He will do this by taking some of the blood from the bull and the goat and putting it on each of the horns of the altar. 19 Then he must sprinkle the blood with his finger seven times over the altar. In this way, he will cleanse it from Israel's defilement and make it holy.

20"When Aaron has finished purifying the Most Holy Place and the Tabernacle and the altar, he must present the live goat. 21 He will lay both of his hands on the goat's head and confess over it all the wickedness, rebellion, and sins of the people of Israel. In this way, he will transfer the people's sins to the head of the goat. Then a man specially chosen for the task will drive the goat into the wilderness. 22 As the goat goes into the wilderness, it will carry all the people's sins upon itself into a desolate land.

23"When Aaron goes back into the Tabernacle, he must take off the linen garments he was wearing when he entered the Most Holy Place, and he must leave the garments there. 24 Then he must bathe himself with water in a sacred place, put on his regular garments, and go out to sacrifice a burnt offering for himself and a burnt offering for the people. Through this process, he will purify himself and the people, making them right with the LORD. 25 He must then burn all the fat of the sin offering on the altar.

26"The man chosen to drive the scapegoat into the wilderness of Azazel must wash his clothes and bathe himself in water. Then he may return to the camp.

27"The bull and the goat presented as sin offerings, whose blood Aaron takes into the Most Holy Place for the purification ceremony, will be carried outside the camp. The animals' hides, internal organs, and dung are all to be burned. 28 The man who burns them must wash his clothes and bathe himself in water before returning to the camp."

16:14 Hebrew *Tent of Meeting;* also in 15:29. 15:15 Or *will make atonement for;* also in 15:30. 15:16 Hebrew *until evening;* also in 15:18. 16:6 Or *to make atonement for himself and his family;* similarly in 16:11, 17b, 24, 34. 16:7 Hebrew *Tent of Meeting;* also in 16:16, 17, 20, 23, 33. 16:10 Or *wilderness, it will make atonement for the people.* 16:13 Hebrew *that is above the Testimony.* The Hebrew word for "testimony" refers to the terms of the LORD's covenant with Israel as written on stone tablets, which were kept in the Ark, and also to the covenant itself. 16:16 Or *make atonement for;* similarly in 16:17a, 18, 20, 27, 33.

MARK 7:1-23

Inside versus outside: that was the main issue Jesus tried to make the Pharisees understand. Just because a hand is clean doesn't mean a heart is. Righteousness was meant to be an inside job.

One day some Pharisees and teachers of religious law arrived from Jerusalem to see Jesus. 2 They noticed that some of his disciples failed to follow the Jewish ritual of hand washing before eating. 3(The

Jews, especially the Pharisees, do not eat until they have poured water over their cupped hands,* as required by their ancient traditions. [4]Similarly, they don't eat anything from the market until they immerse their hands* in water. This is but one of many traditions they have clung to—such as their ceremonial washing of cups, pitchers, and kettles.*)

[5]So the Pharisees and teachers of religious law asked him, "Why don't your disciples follow our age-old tradition? They eat without first performing the hand-washing ceremony."

[6]Jesus replied, "You hypocrites! Isaiah was right when he prophesied about you, for he wrote,

'These people honor me with
    their lips,
but their hearts are far from me.
[7] Their worship is a farce,
    for they teach man-made ideas
    as commands from God.'*

[8]For you ignore God's law and substitute your own tradition."

[9]Then he said, "You skillfully sidestep God's law in order to hold on to your own tradition. [10]For instance, Moses gave you this law from God: 'Honor your father and mother,'* and 'Anyone who speaks disrespectfully of father or mother must be put to death.'* [11]But you say it is all right for people to say to their parents, 'Sorry, I can't help you. For I have vowed to give to God what I would have given to you.'* [12]In this way, you let them disregard their needy parents. [13]And so you cancel the word of God in order to hand down your own tradition. And this is only one example among many others."

[14]Then Jesus called to the crowd to come and hear. "All of you listen," he said, "and try to understand. [15]It's not what goes into your body that defiles you; you are defiled by what comes from your heart.*"

[17]Then Jesus went into a house to get away from the crowd, and his disciples asked him what he meant by the parable he had just used. [18]"Don't you understand either?" he asked. "Can't you see that the food you put into your body cannot defile you? [19]Food doesn't go into your heart, but only passes through the stomach and then goes into the sewer." (By saying this, he declared that every kind of food is acceptable in God's eyes.)

[20]And then he added, "It is what comes from inside that defiles you. [21]For from within, out of a person's heart, come evil thoughts, sexual immorality, theft, murder, [22]adultery, greed, wickedness, deceit, lustful desires, envy, slander, pride, and

HOW WE LIVE

Remaining pure

MARK 7:5-7 Both of today's readings focus on purity. In Leviticus, you read about the continual concern for purity in the Israelites' wilderness camp. In Mark 7, you read that the Pharisees were concerned about outward purity—the cleansing of one's hands prior to a meal—and adherence to the age-old cleansing rituals Leviticus describes. • Jesus told these religious leaders that they were wrong to think that they would be acceptable to God just because they were clean on the outside. In fact, Jesus called them hypocrites because they kept the Old Testament laws for the wrong reasons. They were motivated not by love or a genuine desire to help people, but by status. Hypocrisy is pretending you are something you are not and have no intention of ever being. • How can you remain pure and not become a hypocrite? Pay more attention to your character than your reputation. Don't compare yourself to others by extolling your own virtues and emphasizing others' sins. Don't allow your heart to become distant from God while thinking that carefully following religious practices is all that is necessary. Let your desire to honor God guide your daily life.

foolishness. ²³All these vile things come from within; they are what defile you."

7:3 Greek *have washed with the fist.* 7:4a Some manuscripts read *sprinkle themselves.* 7:4b Some manuscripts add *and dining couches.* 7:7 Isa 29:13 (Greek version). 7:10a Exod 20:12; Deut 5:16. 7:10b Exod 21:17 (Greek version); Lev 20:9 (Greek version). 7:11 Greek *'What I would have given to you is Corban' (that is, a gift).* 7:15 Some manuscripts add verse 16, *Anyone with ears to hear should listen and understand.* Compare 4:9, 23.

PSALM 40:11-17

Lord, don't hold back your tender
mercies from me.
Let your unfailing love and
faithfulness always protect me.
¹² For troubles surround me—
too many to count!
My sins pile up so high
I can't see my way out.
They outnumber the hairs on
my head.
I have lost all courage.

¹³ Please, Lord, rescue me!
Come quickly, Lord, and help me.
¹⁴ May those who try to destroy me
be humiliated and put to shame.

May those who take delight in
my trouble
be turned back in disgrace.
¹⁵ Let them be horrified by their shame,
for they said, "Aha! We've got
him now!"

¹⁶ But may all who search for you
be filled with joy and gladness
in you.
May those who love your salvation
repeatedly shout, "The Lord is
great!"
¹⁷ As for me, since I am poor and
needy,
let the Lord keep me in his
thoughts.
You are my helper and my savior.
O my God, do not delay.

PROVERBS 10:13-14

Wise words come from the lips of people with understanding, but those lacking sense will be beaten with a rod. □ Wise people treasure knowledge, but the babbling of a fool invites disaster.

FEBRUARY**25**

LEVITICUS 16:29–18:30

Moses continued his instructions on the yearly Day of Atonement. He also drew lines of decency, propriety, and community.

"On the tenth day of the appointed month in early autumn,* you must deny yourselves.* Neither native-born Israelites nor foreigners living among you may do any kind of work. This is a permanent law for you. ³⁰On that day offerings of purification will be made for you,* and you will be purified in the Lord's presence from all your sins. ³¹It will be a Sabbath day of complete rest for you, and you must deny yourselves. This is a permanent law for you. ³²In future generations, the purification* ceremony will be performed by the priest who has been anointed and ordained to serve as high priest in place of his ancestor Aaron. He will put on the

holy linen garments ³³and purify the Most Holy Place, the Tabernacle, the altar, the priests, and the entire congregation. ³⁴This is a permanent law for you, to purify the people of Israel from their sins, making them right with the Lord once each year."

Moses followed all these instructions exactly as the Lord had commanded him.

¹⁷:¹THEN the Lord said to Moses, ²"Give the following instructions to Aaron and his sons and all the people of Israel. This is what the Lord has commanded.

³"If any native Israelite sacrifices a bull* or a lamb or a goat anywhere inside or outside the camp ⁴instead of bringing it to the entrance of the Tabernacle* to present it as an offering to the Lord, that person will be as guilty as a murderer.* Such a person

has shed blood and will be cut off from the community. ⁵The purpose of this rule is to stop the Israelites from sacrificing animals in the open fields. It will ensure that they bring their sacrifices to the priest at the entrance of the Tabernacle, so he can present them to the LORD as peace offerings. ⁶Then the priest will be able to splatter the blood against the LORD's altar at the entrance of the Tabernacle, and he will burn the fat as a pleasing aroma to the LORD. ⁷The people must no longer be unfaithful to the LORD by offering sacrifices to the goat idols.* This is a permanent law for them, to be observed from generation to generation.

⁸"Give them this command as well. If any native Israelite or foreigner living among you offers a burnt offering or a sacrifice ⁹but does not bring it to the entrance of the Tabernacle to offer it to the LORD, that person will be cut off from the community.

¹⁰"And if any native Israelite or foreigner living among you eats or drinks blood in any form, I will turn against that person and cut him off from the community of your people, ¹¹for the life of the body is in its blood. I have given you the blood on the altar to purify you, making you right with the LORD.* It is the blood, given in exchange for a life, that makes purification possible. ¹²That is why I have said to the people of Israel, 'You must never eat or drink blood—neither you nor the foreigners living among you.'

¹³"And if any native Israelite or foreigner living among you goes hunting and kills an animal or bird that is approved for eating, he must drain its blood and cover it with earth. ¹⁴The life of every creature is in its blood. That is why I have said to the people of Israel, 'You must never eat or drink blood, for the life of any creature is in its blood.' So whoever consumes blood will be cut off from the community.

¹⁵"And if any native-born Israelites or foreigners eat the meat of an animal that died naturally or was torn up by wild animals, they must wash their clothes and bathe themselves in water. They will remain ceremonially unclean until evening, but then they will be clean. ¹⁶But if they do not wash their clothes and bathe

themselves, they will be punished for their sin."

¹⁸:¹THEN the LORD said to Moses, ²"Give the following instructions to the people of Israel. I am the LORD your God. ³So do not act like the people in Egypt, where you used to live, or like the people of Canaan, where I am taking you. You must not imitate their way of life. ⁴You must obey all my regulations and be careful to obey my decrees, for I am the LORD your God. ⁵If you obey my decrees and my regulations, you will find life through them. I am the LORD.

⁶"You must never have sexual relations with a close relative, for I am the LORD.

⁷"Do not violate your father by having sexual relations with your mother. She is your mother; you must not have sexual relations with her.

⁸"Do not have sexual relations with any of your father's wives, for this would violate your father.

⁹"Do not have sexual relations with your sister or half sister, whether she is your father's daughter or your mother's daughter, whether she was born into your household or someone else's.

¹⁰"Do not have sexual relations with your granddaughter, whether she is your son's daughter or your daughter's daughter, for this would violate yourself.

¹¹"Do not have sexual relations with your stepsister, the daughter of any of your father's wives, for she is your sister.

¹²"Do not have sexual relations with your father's sister, for she is your father's close relative.

¹³"Do not have sexual relations with your mother's sister, for she is your mother's close relative.

¹⁴"Do not violate your uncle, your father's brother, by having sexual relations with his wife, for she is your aunt.

¹⁵"Do not have sexual relations with your daughter-in-law; she is your son's wife, so you must not have sexual relations with her.

¹⁶"Do not have sexual relations with your brother's wife, for this would violate your brother.

¹⁷"Do not have sexual relations with both a woman and her daughter. And do not take* her granddaughter, whether her

son's daughter or her daughter's daughter, and have sexual relations with her. They are close relatives, and this would be a wicked act.

¹⁸"While your wife is living, do not marry her sister and have sexual relations with her, for they would be rivals.

¹⁹"Do not have sexual relations with a woman during her period of menstrual impurity.

²⁰"Do not defile yourself by having sexual intercourse with your neighbor's wife.

²¹"Do not permit any of your children to be offered as a sacrifice to Molech, for you must not bring shame on the name of your God. I am the LORD.

²²"Do not practice homosexuality, having sex with another man as with a woman. It is a detestable sin.

²³"A man must not defile himself by having sex with an animal. And a woman must not offer herself to a male animal to have intercourse with it. This is a perverse act.

²⁴"Do not defile yourselves in any of these ways, for the people I am driving out before you have defiled themselves in all these ways. ²⁵Because the entire land has become defiled, I am punishing the people who live there. I will cause the land to vomit them out. ²⁶You must obey all my decrees and regulations. You must not commit any of these detestable sins. This applies both to native-born Israelites and to the foreigners living among you.

²⁷"All these detestable activities are practiced by the people of the land where I am taking you, and this is how the land has become defiled. ²⁸So do not defile the land and give it a reason to vomit you out, as it will vomit out the people who live there now. ²⁹Whoever commits any of these detestable sins will be cut off from the community of Israel. ³⁰So obey my instructions, and do not defile yourselves by committing any of these detestable practices that were committed by the people who lived in the land before you. I am the LORD your God."

16:29a Hebrew *On the tenth day of the seventh month.* This day in the ancient Hebrew lunar calendar occurred in September or October.   16:29b Or *must fast;* also in 16:31.   16:30 Or *atonement will be made for you, to purify you.*   16:32 Or *atonement.*   17:3 Or *cow.*   17:4a Hebrew *Tent of Meeting;* also in 17:5, 6, 9.   17:4b Hebrew *will be guilty of blood.*   17:7 Or *goat demons.*   17:11 Or *to make atonement for you.*   18:17 Or *do not marry.*

MARK 7:24–8:10

Although Israel has served a special place in God's plan, salvation is for the entire world. Jesus' miracles on behalf of non-Jews in today's reading hint at that.

Then Jesus left Galilee and went north to the region of Tyre.* He didn't want anyone to know which house he was staying in, but he couldn't keep it a secret. ²⁵Right away a woman who had heard about him came and fell at his feet. Her little girl was possessed by an evil* spirit, ²⁶and she begged him to cast out the demon from her daughter.

Since she was a Gentile, born in Syrian Phoenicia, ²⁷Jesus told her, "First I should feed the children—my own family, the Jews.* It isn't right to take food from the children and throw it to the dogs."

²⁸She replied, "That's true, Lord, but even the dogs under the table are allowed to eat the scraps from the children's plates."

²⁹"Good answer!" he said. "Now go home, for the demon has left your daughter." ³⁰And when she arrived home, she found her little girl lying quietly in bed, and the demon was gone.

³¹Jesus left Tyre and went up to Sidon before going back to the Sea of Galilee and the region of the Ten Towns.* ³²A deaf man with a speech impediment was brought to him, and the people begged Jesus to lay his hands on the man to heal him.

³³Jesus led him away from the crowd so they could be alone. He put his fingers into the man's ears. Then, spitting on his own fingers, he touched the man's tongue. ³⁴Looking up to heaven, he sighed and said, *"Ephphatha,"* which means, "Be opened!" ³⁵Instantly the man could hear perfectly, and his tongue was freed so he could speak plainly!

³⁶Jesus told the crowd not to tell anyone, but the more he told them not to, the more they spread the news. ³⁷They were completely amazed and said again and again, "Everything he does is wonderful. He even makes the deaf to hear and gives speech to those who cannot speak."

8:1ABOUT this time another large crowd had gathered, and the people ran out of food again. Jesus called his disciples and told them, [2]"I feel sorry for these people. They have been here with me for three days, and they have nothing left to eat. [3]If I send them home hungry, they will faint along the way. For some of them have come a long distance."

[4]His disciples replied, "How are we supposed to find enough food to feed them out here in the wilderness?"

[5]Jesus asked, "How much bread do you have?"

"Seven loaves," they replied.

[6]So Jesus told all the people to sit down on the ground. Then he took the seven loaves, thanked God for them, and broke them into pieces. He gave them to his disciples, who distributed the bread to the crowd. [7]A few small fish were found, too, so Jesus also blessed these and told the disciples to distribute them.

[8]They ate as much as they wanted. Afterward, the disciples picked up seven large baskets of leftover food. [9]There were about 4,000 people in the crowd that day, and Jesus sent them home after they had eaten. [10]Immediately after this, he got into a boat with his disciples and crossed over to the region of Dalmanutha.

7:24 Some manuscripts add *and Sidon.*   7:25 Greek *unclean.*
7:27 Greek *Let the children eat first.*   7:31 Greek *Decapolis.*

PSALM 41:1-13
For the choir director: A psalm of David.

[1] **O**h, the joys of those who are kind
    to the poor!
    The LORD rescues them when they
    are in trouble.
[2] The LORD protects them
    and keeps them alive.
    He gives them prosperity in the
    land
    and rescues them from their
    enemies.
[3] The LORD nurses them when they
    are sick
    and restores them to health.

[4] "O LORD," I prayed, "have mercy on me.
    Heal me, for I have sinned against
    you."
[5] But my enemies say nothing but evil
    about me.
    "How soon will he die and be
    forgotten?" they ask.
[6] They visit me as if they were my
    friends,
    but all the while they gather gossip,
    and when they leave, they spread
    it everywhere.
[7] All who hate me whisper about me,
    imagining the worst.

HOW WE LIVE | Remaining pure

LEVITICUS 18:3-5 This passage contains a long list of rules regarding sexual purity. God had many reasons for listing these sexual aberrations and forbidding his people from practicing them. He wanted to protect his people and their children from physical and mental deformity, disease, and even death. Tolerance of these types of sexual sins disrupts family life and society as a whole, revealing a dismal disregard for the value of oneself and others. • Pay close attention to Leviticus 18:3. God was leading his people from Egypt to Canaan, the Promised Land, and he reminded them to remain pure in the midst of the rampant sexual sins that had been practiced in Egypt and that they would find in their new home. Just as God did not want his people to be absorbed into the culture then, he does not want his people today to conform to popular culture. • Our society flaunts sex in any form with anyone, and society pressures us to be "tolerant" of acts that God has said are wrong. Just as you strive to keep your heart pure, however, make sure to put effort into keeping your body pure as well.

8 "He has some fatal disease," they say.
  "He will never get out of that bed!"
9 Even my best friend, the one I trusted
  completely,
  the one who shared my food,
  has turned against me.

10 LORD, have mercy on me.
  Make me well again, so I can pay
  them back!
11 I know you are pleased with me,
  for you have not let my enemies
  triumph over me.
12 You have preserved my life because
  I am innocent;

you have brought me into your
  presence forever.

13 Praise the LORD, the God of Israel,
  who lives from everlasting
  to everlasting.
  Amen and amen!

PROVERBS 10:15-16
The wealth of the rich is their fortress; the poverty of the poor is their destruction. ☐ The earnings of the godly enhance their lives, but evil people squander their money on sin.

FEBRUARY**26**

LEVITICUS 19:1–20:21
Holiness is not just an individual thing; it affects the entire community. This passage includes many instructions that would help the Israelites establish a just society.

The LORD also said to Moses, 2"Give the following instructions to the entire community of Israel. You must be holy because I, the LORD your God, am holy.

3"Each of you must show great respect for your mother and father, and you must always observe my Sabbath days of rest. I am the LORD your God.

4"Do not put your trust in idols or make metal images of gods for yourselves. I am the LORD your God.

5"When you sacrifice a peace offering to the LORD, offer it properly so you* will be accepted by God. 6The sacrifice must be eaten on the same day you offer it or on the next day. Whatever is left over until the third day must be completely burned up. 7If any of the sacrifice is eaten on the third day, it will be contaminated, and I will not accept it. 8Anyone who eats it on the third day will be punished for defiling what is holy to the LORD and will be cut off from the community.

9"When you harvest the crops of your land, do not harvest the grain along the edges of your fields, and do not pick up

what the harvesters drop. 10It is the same with your grape crop—do not strip every last bunch of grapes from the vines, and do not pick up the grapes that fall to the ground. Leave them for the poor and the foreigners living among you. I am the LORD your God.

11"Do not steal.

"Do not deceive or cheat one another.

12"Do not bring shame on the name of your God by using it to swear falsely. I am the LORD.

13"Do not defraud or rob your neighbor.

"Do not make your hired workers wait until the next day to receive their pay.

14"Do not insult the deaf or cause the blind to stumble. You must fear your God; I am the LORD.

15"Do not twist justice in legal matters by favoring the poor or being partial to the rich and powerful. Always judge people fairly.

16"Do not spread slanderous gossip among your people.*

"Do not stand idly by when your neighbor's life is threatened. I am the LORD.

17"Do not nurse hatred in your heart for any of your relatives.* Confront people directly so you will not be held guilty for their sin.

[18]"Do not seek revenge or bear a grudge against a fellow Israelite, but love your neighbor as yourself. I am the LORD.

[19]"You must obey all my decrees.

"Do not mate two different kinds of animals. Do not plant your field with two different kinds of seed. Do not wear clothing woven from two different kinds of thread.

[20]"If a man has sex with a slave girl whose freedom has never been purchased but who is committed to become another man's wife, he must pay full compensation to her master. But since she is not a free woman, neither the man nor the woman will be put to death. [21]The man, however, must bring a ram as a guilt offering and present it to the LORD at the entrance of the Tabernacle.* [22]The priest will then purify him* before the LORD with the ram of the guilt offering, and the man's sin will be forgiven.

[23]"When you enter the land and plant fruit trees, leave the fruit unharvested for the first three years and consider it forbidden.* Do not eat it. [24]In the fourth year the entire crop must be consecrated to the LORD as a celebration of praise. [25]Finally, in the fifth year you may eat the fruit. If you follow this pattern, your harvest will increase. I am the LORD your God.

[26]"Do not eat meat that has not been drained of its blood.

"Do not practice fortune-telling or witchcraft.

[27]"Do not trim off the hair on your temples or trim your beards.

[28]"Do not cut your bodies for the dead, and do not mark your skin with tattoos. I am the LORD.

[29]"Do not defile your daughter by making her a prostitute, or the land will be filled with prostitution and wickedness.

[30]"Keep my Sabbath days of rest, and show reverence toward my sanctuary. I am the LORD.

[31]"Do not defile yourselves by turning to mediums or to those who consult the spirits of the dead. I am the LORD your God.

[32]"Stand up in the presence of the elderly, and show respect for the aged. Fear your God. I am the LORD.

[33]"Do not take advantage of foreigners who live among you in your land. [34]Treat them like native-born Israelites, and love them as you love yourself. Remember that you were once foreigners living in the land of Egypt. I am the LORD your God.

[35]"Do not use dishonest standards when measuring length, weight, or volume. [36]Your scales and weights must be accurate. Your containers for measuring dry materials or liquids must be accurate.* I am the LORD your God who brought you out of the land of Egypt.

[37]"You must be careful to keep all of my decrees and regulations by putting them into practice. I am the LORD."

20:1THE LORD said to Moses, [2]"Give the people of Israel these instructions, which apply both to native Israelites and to the foreigners living in Israel.

"If any of them offer their children as a sacrifice to Molech, they must be put to death. The people of the community must stone them to death. [3]I myself will turn against them and cut them off from the community, because they have defiled my sanctuary and brought shame on my holy name by offering their children to Molech. [4]And if the people of the community ignore those who offer their children to Molech and refuse to execute them, [5]I myself will turn against them and their families and will cut them off from the community. This will happen to all who commit spiritual prostitution by worshiping Molech.

[6]"I will also turn against those who commit spiritual prostitution by putting their trust in mediums or in those who consult the spirits of the dead. I will cut them off from the community. [7]So set yourselves apart to be holy, for I am the LORD your God. [8]Keep all my decrees by putting them into practice, for I am the LORD who makes you holy.

[9]"Anyone who dishonors* father or mother must be put to death. Such a person is guilty of a capital offense.

[10]"If a man commits adultery with his neighbor's wife, both the man and the woman who have committed adultery must be put to death.

[11]"If a man violates his father by having sex with one of his father's wives, both the

man and the woman must be put to death, for they are guilty of a capital offense.

¹²"If a man has sex with his daughter-in-law, both must be put to death. They have committed a perverse act and are guilty of a capital offense.

¹³"If a man practices homosexuality, having sex with another man as with a woman, both men have committed a detestable act. They must both be put to death, for they are guilty of a capital offense.

¹⁴"If a man marries both a woman and her mother, he has committed a wicked act. The man and both women must be burned to death to wipe out such wickedness from among you.

¹⁵"If a man has sex with an animal, he must be put to death, and the animal must be killed.

¹⁶"If a woman presents herself to a male animal to have intercourse with it, she and the animal must both be put to death. You must kill both, for they are guilty of a capital offense.

¹⁷"If a man marries his sister, the daughter of either his father or his mother, and they have sexual relations, it is a shameful disgrace. They must be publicly cut off from the community. Since the man has violated his sister, he will be punished for his sin.

¹⁸"If a man has sexual relations with a woman during her menstrual period, both of them must be cut off from the community, for together they have exposed the source of her blood flow.

¹⁹"Do not have sexual relations with your aunt, whether your mother's sister or your father's sister. This would dishonor a close relative. Both parties are guilty and will be punished for their sin.

²⁰"If a man has sex with his uncle's wife, he has violated his uncle. Both the man and woman will be punished for their sin, and they will die childless.

²¹"If a man marries his brother's wife, it is an act of impurity. He has violated his brother, and the guilty couple will remain childless."

19:5 Or *it.*   **19:16** Hebrew *Do not act as a merchant toward your own people.*   **19:17** Hebrew *for your brother.*
19:21 Hebrew *Tent of Meeting.*   **19:22** Or *make atonement for him.*   **19:23** Hebrew *consider it uncircumcised.*

19:36 Hebrew *Use an honest ephah* [a dry measure] *and an honest hin* [a liquid measure].   **20:9** Greek version reads *Anyone who speaks disrespectfully of.* Compare Matt 15:4; Mark 7:10.

MARK 8:11-38

Inquiring people wanted to know. The Pharisees demanded a sign to determine who Jesus was. Jesus himself asked his disciples, after all they'd seen, "Who do you say I am?" Read Peter's profound response.

When the Pharisees heard that Jesus had arrived, they came and started to argue with him. Testing him, they demanded that he show them a miraculous sign from heaven to prove his authority.

¹²When he heard this, he sighed deeply in his spirit and said, "Why do these people keep demanding a miraculous sign? I tell you the truth, I will not give this generation any such sign." ¹³So he got back into the boat and left them, and he crossed to the other side of the lake.

¹⁴But the disciples had forgotten to bring any food. They had only one loaf of bread with them in the boat. ¹⁵As they were crossing the lake, Jesus warned them, "Watch out! Beware of the yeast of the Pharisees and of Herod."

¹⁶At this they began to argue with each other because they hadn't brought any bread. ¹⁷Jesus knew what they were saying, so he said, "Why are you arguing about having no bread? Don't you know or understand even yet? Are your hearts too hard to take it in? ¹⁸You have eyes—can't you see? You have ears—can't you hear?'* Don't you remember anything at all? ¹⁹When I fed the 5,000 with five loaves of bread, how many baskets of leftovers did you pick up afterward?"

"Twelve," they said.

²⁰"And when I fed the 4,000 with seven loaves, how many large baskets of leftovers did you pick up?"

"Seven," they said.

²¹"Don't you understand yet?" he asked them.

²²When they arrived at Bethsaida, some people brought a blind man to Jesus, and they begged him to touch the man and heal him. ²³Jesus took the blind man by the hand and led him out of the village. Then, spitting on the man's eyes,

he laid his hands on him and asked, "Can you see anything now?"

²⁴The man looked around. "Yes," he said, "I see people, but I can't see them very clearly. They look like trees walking around."

²⁵Then Jesus placed his hands on the man's eyes again, and his eyes were opened. His sight was completely restored, and he could see everything clearly. ²⁶Jesus sent him away, saying, "Don't go back into the village on your way home."

²⁷Jesus and his disciples left Galilee and went up to the villages near Caesarea Philippi. As they were walking along, he asked them, "Who do people say I am?"

²⁸"Well," they replied, "some say John the Baptist, some say Elijah, and others say you are one of the other prophets."

²⁹Then he asked them, "But who do you say I am?"

Peter replied, "You are the Messiah.*"

³⁰But Jesus warned them not to tell anyone about him.

³¹Then Jesus began to tell them that the Son of Man* must suffer many terrible things and be rejected by the elders, the leading priests, and the teachers of religious law. He would be killed, but three days later he would rise from the dead. ³²As he talked about this openly with his disciples, Peter took him aside and began to reprimand him for saying such things.*

³³Jesus turned around and looked at his disciples, then reprimanded Peter. "Get away from me, Satan!" he said. "You are seeing things merely from a human point of view, not from God's."

³⁴Then, calling the crowd to join his disciples, he said, "If any of you wants to be my follower, you must turn from your selfish ways, take up your cross, and follow me. ³⁵If you try to hang on to your life, you will lose it. But if you give up your life for my sake and for the sake of the Good News, you will save it. ³⁶And what do you benefit if you gain the whole world but lose your own soul?* ³⁷Is anything worth more than your soul? ³⁸If anyone is ashamed of me and my message in these adulterous and sinful days, the Son of Man will be ashamed of that person when he returns in the glory of his Father with the holy angels."

8:18 Jer 5:21.   **8:29** Or *the Christ. Messiah* (a Hebrew term) and *Christ* (a Greek term) both mean "the anointed one."
8:31 "Son of Man" is a title Jesus used for himself.   **8:32** Or *began to correct him.*   **8:36** Or *your self?* also in 8:37.

PSALM 42:1-11
For the choir director: A psalm of the descendants of Korah.*

¹ **A**s the deer longs for streams of water,
  so I long for you, O God.
² I thirst for God, the living God.
   When can I go and stand before him?
³ Day and night I have only tears for food,
   while my enemies continually taunt me, saying,
   "Where is this God of yours?"

⁴ My heart is breaking
   as I remember how it used to be:
  I walked among the crowds of worshipers,

Trusting God

HOW WE LIVE

LEVITICUS 19:4 While you might never bow down and worship a statue, you might begin to allow things or people to take your trust away from God. When that happens, those things become idols in your life. Don't trust in job security; you may be laid off. Don't trust in money; a sudden catastrophe could empty your bank account. The only true constant in life is God. You can know that, no matter what you have done or said, God will always be there waiting for you to place all of your trust in him.

leading a great procession to the
house of God,
singing for joy and giving thanks
amid the sound of a great
celebration!

⁵ Why am I discouraged?
Why is my heart so sad?
I will put my hope in God!
I will praise him again—
my Savior and ⁶my God!

Now I am deeply discouraged,
but I will remember you—
even from distant Mount
Hermon, the source of
the Jordan,
from the land of Mount Mizar.
⁷ I hear the tumult of the raging
seas
as your waves and surging tides
sweep over me.
⁸ But each day the LORD pours his
unfailing love upon me,

and through each night I sing
his songs,
praying to God who gives me life.

⁹ "O God my rock," I cry,
"Why have you forgotten me?
Why must I wander around in grief,
oppressed by my enemies?"
¹⁰ Their taunts break my bones.
They scoff, "Where is this God
of yours?"

¹¹ Why am I discouraged?
Why is my heart so sad?
I will put my hope in God!
I will praise him again—
my Savior and my God!

42:TITLE Hebrew *maskil*. This may be a literary or musical term.

PROVERBS 10:17
People who accept discipline are on the pathway to life, but those who ignore correction will go astray.

FEBRUARY**27**

LEVITICUS 20:22–22:16
Here we read about the special rules the priests had to follow. The importance of their job required strict guidelines.

"**Y**ou must keep all my decrees and regulations by putting them into practice; otherwise the land to which I am bringing you as your new home will vomit you out. ²³Do not live according to the customs of the people I am driving out before you. It is because they do these shameful things that I detest them. ²⁴But I have promised you, 'You will possess their land because I will give it to you as your possession—a land flowing with milk and honey.' I am the LORD your God, who has set you apart from all other people.

²⁵"You must therefore make a distinction between ceremonially clean and unclean animals, and between clean and unclean birds. You must not defile yourselves by eating any unclean animal or

bird or creature that scurries along the ground. I have identified them as being unclean for you. ²⁶You must be holy because I, the LORD, am holy. I have set you apart from all other people to be my very own.

²⁷"Men and women among you who act as mediums or who consult the spirits of the dead must be put to death by stoning. They are guilty of a capital offense."

²¹:¹THE LORD said to Moses, "Give the following instructions to the priests, the descendants of Aaron.

"A priest must not make himself ceremonially unclean by touching the dead body of a relative. ²The only exceptions are his closest relatives—his mother or father, son or daughter, brother, ³or his virgin sister who depends on him because she has no husband. ⁴But a priest must not defile himself and make himself unclean for someone who is related to him only by marriage.

⁵"The priests must not shave their heads or trim their beards or cut their bodies. ⁶They must be set apart as holy to their God and must never bring shame on the name of God. They must be holy, for they are the ones who present the special gifts to the LORD, gifts of food for their God.

⁷"Priests may not marry a woman defiled by prostitution, and they may not marry a woman who is divorced from her husband, for the priests are set apart as holy to their God. ⁸You must treat them as holy because they offer up food to your God. You must consider them holy because I, the LORD, am holy, and I make you holy.

⁹"If a priest's daughter defiles herself by becoming a prostitute, she also defiles her father's holiness, and she must be burned to death.

¹⁰"The high priest has the highest rank of all the priests. The anointing oil has been poured on his head, and he has been ordained to wear the priestly garments. He must never leave his hair uncombed* or tear his clothing. ¹¹He must not defile himself by going near a dead body. He may not make himself ceremonially unclean even for his father or mother. ¹²He must not defile the sanctuary of his God by leaving it to attend to a dead person, for he has been made holy by the anointing oil of his God. I am the LORD.

¹³"The high priest may marry only a virgin. ¹⁴He may not marry a widow, a woman who is divorced, or a woman who has defiled herself by prostitution. She must be a virgin from his own clan, ¹⁵so that he will not dishonor his descendants among his clan, for I am the LORD who makes him holy."

¹⁶Then the LORD said to Moses, ¹⁷"Give the following instructions to Aaron: In all future generations, none of your descendants who has any defect will qualify to offer food to his God. ¹⁸No one who has a defect qualifies, whether he is blind, lame, disfigured, deformed, ¹⁹or has a broken foot or arm, ²⁰or is hunchbacked or dwarfed, or has a defective eye, or skin sores or scabs, or damaged testicles. ²¹No descendant of Aaron who has a defect may approach the altar to present special gifts to the LORD. Since he has a defect, he may not approach the altar to offer food to his God. ²²However, he may eat from the food offered to God, including the holy offerings and the most holy offerings. ²³Yet because of his physical defect, he may not enter the room behind the inner curtain or approach the altar, for this would defile my holy places. I am the LORD who makes them holy."

²⁴So Moses gave these instructions to Aaron and his sons and to all the Israelites.

22:1THE LORD said to Moses, ²"Tell Aaron and his sons to be very careful with the sacred gifts that the Israelites set apart for me, so they do not bring shame on my holy name. I am the LORD. ³Give them the following instructions.

"In all future generations, if any of your descendants is ceremonially unclean when he approaches the sacred offerings that the people of Israel consecrate to the LORD, he must be cut off from my presence. I am the LORD.

⁴"If any of Aaron's descendants has a skin disease* or any kind of discharge that makes him ceremonially unclean, he may not eat from the sacred offerings until he has been pronounced clean. He also becomes unclean by touching a corpse, or by having an emission of semen, ⁵or by touching a small animal that is unclean, or by touching someone who is ceremonially unclean for any reason. ⁶The man who is defiled in any of these ways will remain unclean until evening. He may not eat from the sacred offerings until he has bathed himself in water. ⁷When the sun goes down, he will be ceremonially clean again and may eat from the sacred offerings, for this is his food. ⁸He may not eat an animal that has died a natural death or has been torn apart by wild animals, for this would defile him. I am the LORD.

⁹"The priests must follow my instructions carefully. Otherwise they will be punished for their sin and will die for violating my instructions. I am the LORD who makes them holy.

¹⁰"No one outside a priest's family may eat the sacred offerings. Even guests and

hired workers in a priest's home are not allowed to eat them. [11]However, if the priest buys a slave for himself, the slave may eat from the sacred offerings. And if his slaves have children, they also may share his food. [12]If a priest's daughter marries someone outside the priestly family, she may no longer eat the sacred offerings. [13]But if she becomes a widow or is divorced and has no children to support her, and she returns to live in her father's home as in her youth, she may eat her father's food again. Otherwise, no one outside a priest's family may eat the sacred offerings.

[14]"Any such person who eats the sacred offerings without realizing it must pay the priest for the amount eaten, plus an additional 20 percent. [15]The priests must not let the Israelites defile the sacred offerings brought to the LORD [16]by allowing unauthorized people to eat them. This would bring guilt upon them and require them to pay compensation. I am the LORD who makes them holy."

21:10 Or *never uncover his head.*   **22:4** Traditionally rendered *leprosy;* see note on 13:2a.

MARK 9:1-29
This episode is commonly referred to as the Transfiguration. Peter, James, and John witnessed Jesus revealed ("transfigured") in his glory and conversing with Moses and Elijah.

Jesus went on to say, "I tell you the truth, some standing here right now will not die before they see the Kingdom of God arrive in great power!"

[2]Six days later Jesus took Peter, James, and John, and led them up a high mountain to be alone. As the men watched, Jesus' appearance was transformed, [3]and his clothes became dazzling white, far whiter than any earthly bleach could ever make them. [4]Then Elijah and Moses appeared and began talking with Jesus.

[5]Peter exclaimed, "Rabbi, it's wonderful for us to be here! Let's make three shelters as memorials*—one for you, one for Moses, and one for Elijah." [6]He said this because he didn't really know what else to say, for they were all terrified.

[7]Then a cloud overshadowed them, and a voice from the cloud said, "This is my dearly loved Son. Listen to him." [8]Suddenly, when they looked around, Moses and Elijah were gone, and they saw only Jesus with them.

[9]As they went back down the mountain, he told them not to tell anyone what they had seen until the Son of Man* had risen from the dead. [10]So they kept it to themselves, but they often asked each other what he meant by "rising from the dead."

[11]Then they asked him, "Why do the teachers of religious law insist that Elijah must return before the Messiah comes?*"

[12]Jesus responded, "Elijah is indeed coming first to get everything ready. Yet why do the Scriptures say that the Son of Man must suffer greatly and be treated with utter contempt? [13]But I tell you, Elijah has already come, and they chose to abuse him, just as the Scriptures predicted."

[14]When they returned to the other disciples, they saw a large crowd surrounding them, and some teachers of religious law were arguing with them. [15]When the crowd saw Jesus, they were overwhelmed with awe, and they ran to greet him.

[16]"What is all this arguing about?" Jesus asked.

[17]One of the men in the crowd spoke up and said, "Teacher, I brought my son so you could heal him. He is possessed by an evil spirit that won't let him talk. [18]And whenever this spirit seizes him, it throws him violently to the ground. Then he foams at the mouth and grinds his teeth and becomes rigid.* So I asked your disciples to cast out the evil spirit, but they couldn't do it."

[19]Jesus said to them,* "You faithless people! How long must I be with you? How long must I put up with you? Bring the boy to me."

[20]So they brought the boy. But when the evil spirit saw Jesus, it threw the child into a violent convulsion, and he fell to the ground, writhing and foaming at the mouth.

[21]"How long has this been happening?" Jesus asked the boy's father.

He replied, "Since he was a little boy. [22]The spirit often throws him into the fire or into water, trying to kill him. Have mercy on us and help us, if you can."

²³"What do you mean, 'If I can'?" Jesus asked. "Anything is possible if a person believes."

²⁴The father instantly cried out, "I do believe, but help me overcome my unbelief!"

²⁵When Jesus saw that the crowd of onlookers was growing, he rebuked the evil* spirit. "Listen, you spirit that makes this boy unable to hear and speak," he said. "I command you to come out of this child and never enter him again!"

²⁶Then the spirit screamed and threw the boy into another violent convulsion and left him. The boy appeared to be dead. A murmur ran through the crowd as people said, "He's dead." ²⁷But Jesus took him by the hand and helped him to his feet, and he stood up.

²⁸Afterward, when Jesus was alone in the house with his disciples, they asked him, "Why couldn't we cast out that evil spirit?"

²⁹Jesus replied, "This kind can be cast out only by prayer.*"

9:5 Greek *three tabernacles.*   9:9 "Son of Man" is a title Jesus used for himself.   9:11 Greek *that Elijah must come first?*   9:18 Or *becomes weak.*   9:19 Or *said to his disciples.*   9:25 Greek *unclean.*   9:29 Some manuscripts read *by prayer and fasting.*

PSALM 43:1-5

Declare me innocent, O God!
  Defend me against these ungodly
    people.
  Rescue me from these unjust
    liars.
² For you are God, my only safe haven.
  Why have you tossed me aside?
Why must I wander around in grief,
  oppressed by my enemies?
³ Send out your light and your truth;
    let them guide me.
Let them lead me to your holy
    mountain,
  to the place where you live.
⁴ There I will go to the altar of God,
  to God—the source of all my joy.
I will praise you with my harp,
  O God, my God!

⁵ Why am I discouraged?
  Why is my heart so sad?
I will put my hope in God!
  I will praise him again—
  my Savior and my God!

PROVERBS 10:18

Hiding hatred makes you a liar; slandering others makes you a fool.

WHO GOD IS

Jesus has power to transform

MARK 9:23-24   Everyone who met Jesus was transformed in some way. Sinful people were changed into forgiven people. Blind people were changed into seeing people. Sick people were turned into healthy people. Jesus turned the world around him upside down. Wine became water, water became solid enough to walk on, one loaf became many loaves, a raging storm became calm. He transformed fishermen into disciples; later he changed disciples into leaders. He took tax collectors and made them teachers. He took weak people and made them strong. Like a potter who takes dull clay and turns it into a beautiful pot, Jesus was continuously taking the ugly and making it into something special.   • Jesus wasn't content to merely take a young boy and free him from an evil spirit. His deep desire was to transform the heart of the boy and his father so that they could believe and be saved. He would transform their lives on earth, as he did with so many people he healed, but his greatest desire was to transform their lives for eternity.

FEBRUARY **28**

LEVITICUS 22:17–23:44
The holidays described in today's reading were
object lessons to remind the Israelites of God's
provision for them in the past.

And the LORD said to Moses, [18]"Give Aaron and his sons and all the Israelites these instructions, which apply both to native Israelites and to the foreigners living among you.

"If you present a gift as a burnt offering to the LORD, whether it is to fulfill a vow or is a voluntary offering, [19]you* will be accepted only if your offering is a male animal with no defects. It may be a bull, a ram, or a male goat. [20]Do not present an animal with defects, because the LORD will not accept it on your behalf.

[21]"If you present a peace offering to the LORD from the herd or the flock, whether it is to fulfill a vow or is a voluntary offering, you must offer a perfect animal. It may have no defect of any kind. [22]You must not offer an animal that is blind, crippled, or injured, or that has a wart, a skin sore, or scabs. Such animals must never be offered on the altar as special gifts to the LORD. [23]If a bull* or lamb has a leg that is too long or too short, it may be offered as a voluntary offering, but it may not be offered to fulfill a vow. [24]If an animal has damaged testicles or is castrated, you may not offer it to the LORD. You must never do this in your own land, [25]and you must not accept such an animal from foreigners and then offer it as a sacrifice to your God. Such animals will not be accepted on your behalf, for they are mutilated or defective."

[26]And the LORD said to Moses, [27]"When a calf or lamb or goat is born, it must be left with its mother for seven days. From the eighth day on, it will be acceptable as a special gift to the LORD. [28]But you must not slaughter a mother animal and her offspring on the same day, whether from the herd or the flock. [29]When you bring a thanksgiving offering to the LORD, sacrifice it properly so you will be accepted. [30]Eat the entire sacrificial animal on the day it is presented. Do not leave any of it until the next morning. I am the LORD.

[31]"You must faithfully keep all my commands by putting them into practice, for I am the LORD. [32]Do not bring shame on my holy name, for I will display my holiness among the people of Israel. I am the LORD who makes you holy. [33]It was I who rescued you from the land of Egypt, that I might be your God. I am the LORD."

[23:1]THE LORD said to Moses, [2]"Give the following instructions to the people of Israel. These are the LORD's appointed festivals, which you are to proclaim as official days for holy assembly.

[3]"You have six days each week for your ordinary work, but the seventh day is a Sabbath day of complete rest, an official day for holy assembly. It is the LORD's Sabbath day, and it must be observed wherever you live.

[4]"In addition to the Sabbath, these are the LORD's appointed festivals, the official days for holy assembly that are to be celebrated at their proper times each year.

[5]"The LORD's Passover begins at sundown on the fourteenth day of the first month.* [6]On the next day, the fifteenth day of the month, you must begin celebrating the Festival of Unleavened Bread. This festival to the LORD continues for seven days, and during that time the bread you eat must be made without yeast. [7]On the first day of the festival, all the people must stop their ordinary work and observe an official day for holy assembly. [8]For seven days you must present special gifts to the LORD. On the seventh day the people must again stop all their ordinary work to observe an official day for holy assembly."

[9]Then the LORD said to Moses, [10]"Give the following instructions to the people of Israel. When you enter the land I am giving you and you harvest its first crops, bring the priest a bundle of grain from the first cutting of your grain harvest. [11]On the day after the Sabbath, the priest will lift it up before the LORD so it may be accepted on your behalf. [12]On that same day you

must sacrifice a one-year-old male lamb with no defects as a burnt offering to the LORD. [13] With it you must present a grain offering consisting of four quarts* of choice flour moistened with olive oil. It will be a special gift, a pleasing aroma to the LORD. You must also offer one quart* of wine as a liquid offering. [14] Do not eat any bread or roasted grain or fresh kernels on that day until you bring this offering to your God. This is a permanent law for you, and it must be observed from generation to generation wherever you live.

[15] "From the day after the Sabbath—the day you bring the bundle of grain to be lifted up as a special offering—count off seven full weeks. [16] Keep counting until the day after the seventh Sabbath, fifty days later. Then present an offering of new grain to the LORD. [17] From wherever you live, bring two loaves of bread to be lifted up before the LORD as a special offering. Make these loaves from four quarts of choice flour, and bake them with yeast. They will be an offering to the LORD from the first of your crops. [18] Along with the bread, present seven one-year-old male lambs with no defects, one young bull, and two rams as burnt offerings to the LORD. These burnt offerings, together with the grain offerings and liquid offerings, will be a special gift, a pleasing aroma to the LORD. [19] Then you must offer one male goat as a sin offering and two one-year-old male lambs as a peace offering.

[20] "The priest will lift up the two lambs as a special offering to the LORD, together with the loaves representing the first of your crops. These offerings, which are holy to the LORD, belong to the priests. [21] That same day will be proclaimed an official day for holy assembly, a day on which you do no ordinary work. This is a permanent law for you, and it must be observed from generation to generation wherever you live.*

[22] "When you harvest the crops of your land, do not harvest the grain along the edges of your fields, and do not pick up what the harvesters drop. Leave it for the poor and the foreigners living among you. I am the LORD your God."

[23] The LORD said to Moses, [24] "Give the following instructions to the people of Is-rael. On the first day of the appointed month in early autumn,* you are to observe a day of complete rest. It will be an official day for holy assembly, a day commemorated with loud blasts of a trumpet. [25] You must do no ordinary work on that day. Instead, you are to present special gifts to the LORD."

[26] Then the LORD said to Moses, [27] "Be careful to celebrate the Day of Atonement on the tenth day of that same month—nine days after the Festival of Trumpets.* You must observe it as an official day for holy assembly, a day to deny yourselves* and present special gifts to the LORD. [28] Do no work during that entire day because it is the Day of Atonement, when offerings of purification are made for you, making you right with* the LORD your God. [29] All who do not deny themselves that day will be cut off from God's people. [30] And I will destroy anyone among you who does any work on that day. [31] You must not do any work at all! This is a permanent law for you, and it must be observed from generation to generation wherever you live. [32] This will be a Sabbath day of complete rest for you, and on that day you must deny yourselves. This day of rest will begin at sundown on the ninth day of the month and extend until sundown on the tenth day."

[33] And the LORD said to Moses, [34] "Give the following instructions to the people of Israel. Begin celebrating the Festival of Shelters* on the fifteenth day of the appointed month—five days after the Day of Atonement.* This festival to the LORD will last for seven days. [35] On the first day of the festival you must proclaim an official day for holy assembly, when you do no ordinary work. [36] For seven days you must present special gifts to the LORD. The eighth day is another holy day on which you present your special gifts to the LORD. This will be a solemn occasion, and no ordinary work may be done that day.

[37] ("These are the LORD's appointed festivals. Celebrate them each year as official days for holy assembly by presenting special gifts to the LORD—burnt offerings, grain offerings, sacrifices, and liquid offerings—each on its proper day. [38] These festivals must be observed in addition to the LORD's regular Sabbath days,

and the offerings are in addition to your personal gifts, the offerings you give to fulfill your vows, and the voluntary offerings you present to the LORD.)

³⁹"Remember that this seven-day festival to the LORD—the Festival of Shelters—begins on the fifteenth day of the appointed month,* after you have harvested all the produce of the land. The first day and the eighth day of the festival will be days of complete rest. ⁴⁰On the first day gather branches from magnificent trees*—palm fronds, boughs from leafy trees, and willows that grow by the streams. Then celebrate with joy before the LORD your God for seven days. ⁴¹You must observe this festival to the LORD for seven days every year. This is a permanent law for you, and it must be observed in the appointed month* from generation to generation. ⁴²For seven days you must live outside in little shelters. All native-born Israelites must live in shelters. ⁴³This will remind each new generation of Israelites that I made them live in shelters when I rescued them from the land of Egypt. I am the LORD your God."

⁴⁴So Moses gave the Israelites these instructions regarding the annual festivals of the LORD.

22:19 Or *it.* 22:23 Or *cow.* 23:5 This day in the ancient Hebrew lunar calendar occurred in late March, April, or early May. 23:13a Hebrew ²⁄₁₀ *of an ephah* [4.4 liters]; also in 23:17. 23:13b Hebrew ¼ *of a hin* [1 liter]. 23:21 This celebration, called the Festival of Harvest or the Festival of Weeks, was later called the Festival of Pentecost (see Acts 2:1). It is celebrated today as Shavuat (or Shabuoth). 23:24 Hebrew *On the first day of the seventh month.* This day in the ancient Hebrew lunar calendar occurred in September or October. This festival is celebrated today as Rosh Hashanah, the Jewish new year. 23:27a Hebrew *on the tenth day of the seventh month;* see 23:24 and the note there. This day in the ancient Hebrew lunar calendar occurred in September or October. It is celebrated today as Yom Kippur. 23:27b Or *to fast;* similarly in 23:29, 32. 23:28 Or *when atonement is made for you before.* 23:34a Or *Festival of Booths,* or *Festival of Tabernacles.* This was earlier called the Festival of the Final Harvest or Festival of Ingathering (see Exod 23:16b). It is celebrated today as Sukkot (or Succoth). 23:34b Hebrew *on the fifteenth day of the seventh month;* see 23:27a and the note there. 23:39 Hebrew *on the fifteenth day of the seventh month.* 23:40 Or *gather fruit from majestic trees.* 23:41 Hebrew *the seventh month.*

MARK 9:30–10:12
Jesus has completely different standards than the world. The least is the greatest. The greatest is the least. What is good is useless if it keeps you from the Kingdom. What seems useless is good if it is used by God.

Leaving that region, they traveled through Galilee. Jesus didn't want anyone to know he was there, ³¹for he wanted to spend more time with his disciples and teach them. He said to them, "The Son of Man is going to be betrayed into the hands of his enemies. He will be killed, but three days later he will rise from the dead." ³²They didn't understand what he was saying, however, and they were afraid to ask him what he meant.

³³After they arrived at Capernaum and settled in a house, Jesus asked his disciples, "What were you discussing out on the road?" ³⁴But they didn't answer, because they had been arguing about which of them was the greatest. ³⁵He sat down, called the twelve disciples over to him, and said, "Whoever wants to be first must take last place and be the servant of everyone else."

³⁶Then he put a little child among them. Taking the child in his arms, he said to them, ³⁷"Anyone who welcomes a little child like this on my behalf* welcomes me, and anyone who welcomes me welcomes not only me but also my Father who sent me."

³⁸John said to Jesus, "Teacher, we saw someone using your name to cast out demons, but we told him to stop because he wasn't in our group."

³⁹"Don't stop him!" Jesus said. "No one who performs a miracle in my name will soon be able to speak evil of me. ⁴⁰Anyone who is not against us is for us. ⁴¹If anyone gives you even a cup of water because you belong to the Messiah, I tell you the truth, that person will surely be rewarded.

⁴²"But if you cause one of these little ones who trusts in me to fall into sin, it would be better for you to be thrown into the sea with a large millstone hung around your neck. ⁴³If your hand causes you to sin, cut it off. It's better to enter eternal life with only one hand than to go into the unquenchable fires of hell* with two hands.* ⁴⁵If your foot causes you to sin, cut it off. It's better to enter eternal life with only one foot than to be thrown into hell with two feet.* ⁴⁷And if your eye

causes you to sin, gouge it out. It's better to enter the Kingdom of God with only one eye than to have two eyes and be thrown into hell, [48]'where the maggots never die and the fire never goes out.'*

[49]"For everyone will be tested with fire.* [50]Salt is good for seasoning. But if it loses its flavor, how do you make it salty again? You must have the qualities of salt among yourselves and live in peace with each other."

[10:1]THEN Jesus left Capernaum and went down to the region of Judea and into the area east of the Jordan River. Once again crowds gathered around him, and as usual he was teaching them.

[2]Some Pharisees came and tried to trap him with this question: "Should a man be allowed to divorce his wife?"

[3]Jesus answered them with a question: "What did Moses say in the law about divorce?"

[4]"Well, he permitted it," they replied. "He said a man can give his wife a written notice of divorce and send her away."*

[5]But Jesus responded, "He wrote this commandment only as a concession to your hard hearts. [6]But 'God made them male and female'* from the beginning of creation. [7]This explains why a man leaves his father and mother and is joined to his wife,* [8]and the two are united into one.'* Since they are no longer two but one, [9]let no one split apart what God has joined together."

[10]Later, when he was alone with his disciples in the house, they brought up the subject again. [11]He told them, "Whoever divorces his wife and marries someone else commits adultery against her. [12]And if a woman divorces her husband and marries someone else, she commits adultery."

9:37 Greek *in my name.*   9:43a Greek *Gehenna;* also in 9:45, 47.   9:43b Some manuscripts add verse 44, *'where the maggots never die and the fire never goes out.'* See 9:48. 9:45 Some manuscripts add verse 46, *'where the maggots never die and the fire never goes out.'* See 9:48.   9:48 Isa 66:24.   9:49 Greek *salted with fire;* other manuscripts add *and every sacrifice will be salted with salt.*   10:4 See Deut 24:1.   10:6 Gen 1:27; 5:2.   10:7 Some manuscripts do not include *and is joined to his wife.*   10:7-8 Gen 2:24.

PSALM 44:1-8
For the choir director: A psalm of the descendants of Korah.*

[1] **O** God, we have heard it with our
            own ears—
    our ancestors have told us
of all you did in their day,
    in days long ago:
[2] You drove out the pagan nations
        by your power

HOW WE LIVE | Our marriages

MARK 10:2-9 The Pharisees were trying to trap Jesus when they asked the question, "Should a man be allowed to divorce his wife?" If Jesus answered yes, then he would support the view of the Pharisees. If he answered no, then not only would the people be upset, but he might anger King Herod, who had already beheaded John the Baptist for speaking against divorce. • Jesus, however, saw through their motives and used the question to review God's intended purpose for marriage. As experts in the law, the Pharisees knew what Moses had said about divorce; Jesus went on to explain that it was God's intention that a man and a woman make a commitment to permanence in marriage. In Deuteronomy, divorce was instituted only for the purpose of protecting an injured party within the marriage, and it required the approval of a judge. Yet over time, divorce had become easy and convenient. • Jesus quoted Genesis 2:24, reminding the Pharisees—and us—that when two become one, no one should separate them. We should never enter marriage with the idea that, if it isn't going as we had hoped, we can just end it. Entering marriage with the idea of commitment and permanence no matter what storms assail you will make your marriage work.

and gave all the land to our
ancestors.
You crushed their enemies
and set our ancestors free.
³ They did not conquer the land with
their swords;
it was not their own strong arm that
gave them victory.
It was your right hand and strong arm
and the blinding light from your
face that helped them,
for you loved them.

⁴ You are my King and my God.
You command victories for Israel.*
⁵ Only by your power can we push back
our enemies;
only in your name can we trample
our foes.

⁶ I do not trust in my bow;
I do not count on my sword
to save me.
⁷ You are the one who gives us victory
over our enemies;
you disgrace those who hate us.
⁸ O God, we give glory to you all
day long
and constantly praise your name.
Interlude

44:TITLE Hebrew *maskil*. This may be a literary or musical
term.   44:4 Hebrew *for Jacob*. The names "Jacob" and
"Israel" are often interchanged throughout the Old
Testament, referring sometimes to the individual patriarch
and sometimes to the nation.

PROVERBS 10:19
Too much talk leads to sin. Be sensible
and keep your mouth shut.

LEVITICUS 24:1–25:46

Justice and mercy are prominent themes in Old Testament law. Today's passage provided guidelines for both.

The LORD said to Moses, [2]"Command the people of Israel to bring you pure oil of pressed olives for the light, to keep the lamps burning continually. [3]This is the lampstand that stands in the Tabernacle, in front of the inner curtain that shields the Ark of the Covenant.* Aaron must keep the lamps burning in the LORD's presence all night. This is a permanent law for you, and it must be observed from generation to generation. [4]Aaron and the priests must tend the lamps on the pure gold lampstand continually in the LORD's presence.

[5]"You must bake twelve loaves of bread from choice flour, using four quarts* of flour for each loaf. [6]Place the bread before the LORD on the pure gold table, and arrange the loaves in two rows, with six loaves in each row. [7]Put some pure frankincense near each row to serve as a representative offering, a special gift presented to the LORD. [8]Every Sabbath day this bread must be laid out before the LORD. The bread is to be received from the people of Israel as a requirement of the eternal covenant. [9]The loaves of bread will belong to Aaron and his descendants, who must eat them in a sacred place, for they are most holy. It is the permanent right of the priests to claim this portion of the special gifts presented to the LORD."

[10]One day a man who had an Israelite mother and an Egyptian father came out of his tent and got into a fight with one of the Israelite men. [11]During the fight, this son of an Israelite woman blasphemed the Name of the LORD* with a curse. So the man was brought to Moses for judgment. His mother was Shelomith, the daughter of Dibri of the tribe of Dan. [12]They kept the man in custody until the LORD's will in the matter should become clear to them.

[13]Then the LORD said to Moses, [14]"Take the blasphemer outside the camp, and tell all those who heard the curse to lay their hands on his head. Then let the entire community stone him to death. [15]Say to the people of Israel: Those who curse their God will be punished for their sin. [16]Anyone who blasphemes the Name of the LORD must be stoned to death by the whole community of Israel. Any native-born Israelite or foreigner among you who blasphemes the Name of the LORD must be put to death.

[17]"Anyone who takes another person's life must be put to death.

[18]"Anyone who kills another person's animal must pay for it in full—a live animal for the animal that was killed.

[19]"Anyone who injures another person must be dealt with according to the injury inflicted—[20]a fracture for a fracture, an eye for an eye, a tooth for a tooth. Whatever anyone does to injure another person must be paid back in kind.

[21]"Whoever kills an animal must pay for it in full, but whoever kills another person must be put to death.

[22]"This same standard applies both to native-born Israelites and to the foreigners living among you. I am the LORD your God."

[23]After Moses gave all these instructions to the Israelites, they took the blasphemer outside the camp and stoned him to death. The Israelites did just as the LORD had commanded Moses.

[25:1]WHILE Moses was on Mount Sinai, the LORD said to him, [2]"Give the following instructions to the people of Israel. When you have entered the land I am giving you, the land itself must observe a Sabbath rest before the LORD every seventh year. ³For six years you may plant your fields and prune your vineyards and harvest your crops, ⁴but during the seventh year the land must have a Sabbath year of complete rest. It is the LORD's Sabbath. Do not plant your fields or prune your vineyards during that year. ⁵And don't store away the crops that grow on their own or gather the grapes from your unpruned vines. The land must have a year of complete rest. ⁶But you may eat whatever the land produces on its own during its Sabbath. This applies to you, your male and female servants, your hired workers, and the temporary residents who live with you. ⁷Your livestock and the wild animals in your land will also be allowed to eat what the land produces.

⁸"In addition, you must count off seven Sabbath years, seven sets of seven years, adding up to forty-nine years in all. ⁹Then on the Day of Atonement in the fiftieth year,* blow the ram's horn loud and long throughout the land. ¹⁰Set this year apart as holy, a time to proclaim freedom throughout the land for all who live there. It will be a jubilee year for you, when each of you may return to the land that belonged to your ancestors and return to your own clan. ¹¹This fiftieth year will be a jubilee for you. During that year you must not plant your fields or store away any of the crops that grow on their own, and don't gather the grapes from your unpruned vines. ¹²It will be a jubilee year for you, and you must keep it holy. But you may eat whatever the land produces on its own. ¹³In the Year of Jubilee each of you may return to the land that belonged to your ancestors.

¹⁴"When you make an agreement with your neighbor to buy or sell property, you must not take advantage of each other. ¹⁵When you buy land from your neighbor, the price you pay must be based on the number of years since the last jubilee. The seller must set the price by taking into account the number of years remaining until the next Year of Jubilee. ¹⁶The more years until the next jubilee, the higher the price; the fewer years, the lower the price.

After all, the person selling the land is actually selling you a certain number of harvests. ¹⁷Show your fear of God by not taking advantage of each other. I am the LORD your God.

¹⁸"If you want to live securely in the land, follow my decrees and obey my regulations. ¹⁹Then the land will yield large crops, and you will eat your fill and live securely in it. ²⁰But you might ask, 'What will we eat during the seventh year, since we are not allowed to plant or harvest crops that year?' ²¹Be assured that I will send my blessing for you in the sixth year, so the land will produce a crop large enough for three years. ²²When you plant your fields in the eighth year, you will still be eating from the large crop of the sixth year. In fact, you will still be eating from that large crop when the new crop is harvested in the ninth year.

²³"The land must never be sold on a permanent basis, for the land belongs to me. You are only foreigners and tenant farmers working for me.

²⁴"With every purchase of land you must grant the seller the right to buy it back. ²⁵If one of your fellow Israelites falls into poverty and is forced to sell some family land, then a close relative should buy it back for him. ²⁶If there is no close relative to buy the land, but the person who sold it gets enough money to buy it back, ²⁷he then has the right to redeem it from the one who bought it. The price of the land will be discounted according to the number of years until the next Year of Jubilee. In this way the original owner can then return to the land. ²⁸But if the original owner cannot afford to buy back the land, it will remain with the new owner until the next Year of Jubilee. In the jubilee year, the land must be returned to the original owners so they can return to their family land.

²⁹"Anyone who sells a house inside a walled town has the right to buy it back for a full year after its sale. During that year, the seller retains the right to buy it back. ³⁰But if it is not bought back within a year, the sale of the house within the walled town cannot be reversed. It will become the permanent property of the buyer. It will not be returned to the origi-

nal owner in the Year of Jubilee. ³¹But a house in a village—a settlement without fortified walls—will be treated like property in the countryside. Such a house may be bought back at any time, and it must be returned to the original owner in the Year of Jubilee.

³²"The Levites always have the right to buy back a house they have sold within the towns allotted to them. ³³And any property that is sold by the Levites—all houses within the Levitical towns—must be returned in the Year of Jubilee. After all, the houses in the towns reserved for the Levites are the only property they own in all Israel. ³⁴The open pastureland around the Levitical towns may never be sold. It is their permanent possession.

³⁵"If one of your fellow Israelites falls into poverty and cannot support himself, support him as you would a foreigner or a temporary resident and allow him to live with you. ³⁶Do not charge interest or make a profit at his expense. Instead, show your fear of God by letting him live with you as your relative. ³⁷Remember, do not charge interest on money you lend him or make a profit on food you sell him. ³⁸I am the LORD your God, who brought you out of the land of Egypt to give you the land of Canaan and to be your God.

³⁹"If one of your fellow Israelites falls into poverty and is forced to sell himself to you, do not treat him as a slave. ⁴⁰Treat him instead as a hired worker or as a temporary resident who lives with you, and he will serve you only until the Year of Jubilee. ⁴¹At that time he and his children will no longer be obligated to you, and they will return to their clans and go back to the land originally allotted to their ancestors. ⁴²The people of Israel are my servants, whom I brought out of the land of Egypt, so they must never be sold as slaves. ⁴³Show your fear of God by not treating them harshly.

⁴⁴"However, you may purchase male and female slaves from among the nations around you. ⁴⁵You may also purchase the children of temporary residents who live among you, including those who have been born in your land. You may treat them as your property, ⁴⁶passing them on to your children as a permanent inheritance. You may treat them as slaves, but you must never treat your fellow Israelites this way."

24:3 Hebrew *in the Tent of Meeting, outside the inner curtain of the Testimony;* see note on 16:13.   24:5 Hebrew ²⁄₁₀ *of an ephah* [4.4 liters].   24:11 Hebrew *the Name;* also in 24:16b.   25:9 Hebrew *on the tenth day of the seventh month, on the Day of Atonement;* see 23:27a and the note there.

HOW WE LIVE

Our money

MARK 10:21-22 The young man who came running after Jesus wanted what most people want—eternal life in heaven. Such was his commitment to his goal that he had worked to keep all of the commandments since childhood! • Jesus told the man to "go and sell" all he had and give the money to the poor. Jesus' response exposed a barrier that could keep the young man out of the Kingdom of Heaven—his love of money. Ironically, this attitude toward money and possessions made the young man unable to keep the first commandment, to let nothing be more important than God (Exodus 20:3, February 4). • That is precisely why Jesus pointed out that it is difficult for the rich to enter heaven. Wealth tends to make people self-reliant. Money represents effort, accomplishment, and self-sufficiency. Does this mean that all believers should sell all their possessions? No. What this story shows is that we must not let anything we have (or desire) keep us from serving Jesus. We must be willing to remove all barriers so that we may serve him fully.

MARK 10:13-31

What Jesus valued surprised others. He took time for the people others would have ignored, and he urged the wealthy to seek riches greater than money.

One day some parents brought their children to Jesus so he could touch and bless them. But the disciples scolded the parents for bothering him.

[14]When Jesus saw what was happening, he was angry with his disciples. He said to them, "Let the children come to me. Don't stop them! For the Kingdom of God belongs to those who are like these children. [15]I tell you the truth, anyone who doesn't receive the Kingdom of God like a child will never enter it." [16]Then he took the children in his arms and placed his hands on their heads and blessed them.

[17]As Jesus was starting out on his way to Jerusalem, a man came running up to him, knelt down, and asked, "Good Teacher, what must I do to inherit eternal life?"

[18]"Why do you call me good?" Jesus asked. "Only God is truly good. [19]But to answer your question, you know the commandments: 'You must not murder. You must not commit adultery. You must not steal. You must not testify falsely. You must not cheat anyone. Honor your father and mother.'*"

[20]"Teacher," the man replied, "I've obeyed all these commandments since I was young."

[21]Looking at the man, Jesus felt genuine love for him. "There is still one thing you haven't done," he told him. "Go and sell all your possessions and give the money to the poor, and you will have treasure in heaven. Then come, follow me."

[22]At this the man's face fell, and he went away sad, for he had many possessions.

[23]Jesus looked around and said to his disciples, "How hard it is for the rich to enter the Kingdom of God!" [24]This amazed them. But Jesus said again, "Dear children, it is very hard* to enter the Kingdom of God. [25]In fact, it is easier for a camel to go through the eye of a needle than for a rich person to enter the Kingdom of God!"

[26]The disciples were astounded. "Then who in the world can be saved?" they asked.

[27]Jesus looked at them intently and said, "Humanly speaking, it is impossible. But not with God. Everything is possible with God."

[28]Then Peter began to speak up. "We've given up everything to follow you," he said.

[29]"Yes," Jesus replied, "and I assure you that everyone who has given up house or brothers or sisters or mother or father or children or property, for my sake and for the Good News, [30]will receive now in return a hundred times as many houses, brothers, sisters, mothers, children, and property—along with persecution. And in the world to come that person will have eternal life. [31]But many who are the greatest now will be least important then, and those who seem least important now will be the greatest then.*

10:19 Exod 20:12-16; Deut 5:16-20.   **10:24** Some manuscripts read *very hard for those who trust in riches.* **10:31** Greek *But many who are first will be last; and the last, first.*

PSALM 44:9-26

But now you have tossed us aside
  in dishonor.
    You no longer lead our armies
      to battle.
[10] You make us retreat from our enemies
    and allow those who hate us
      to plunder our land.
[11] You have butchered us like sheep
    and scattered us among the nations.
[12] You sold your precious people for
    a pittance,
    making nothing on the sale.
[13] You let our neighbors mock us.
    We are an object of scorn and
      derision to those around us.
[14] You have made us the butt of their
      jokes;
    they shake their heads at us
      in scorn.
[15] We can't escape the constant
      humiliation;
    shame is written across our faces.
[16] All we hear are the taunts of our
      mockers.
    All we see are our vengeful enemies.

[17] All this has happened though we have
not forgotten you.
  We have not violated your covenant.
[18] Our hearts have not deserted you.
  We have not strayed from your path.
[19] Yet you have crushed us in the jackal's
desert home.
  You have covered us with darkness
and death.
[20] If we had forgotten the name of our God
or spread our hands in prayer
to foreign gods,
[21] God would surely have known it,
  for he knows the secrets of every
heart.
[22] But for your sake we are killed every
day;
  we are being slaughtered like sheep.

[23] Wake up, O Lord! Why do you
sleep?
  Get up! Do not reject us forever.
[24] Why do you look the other way?
  Why do you ignore our suffering
and oppression?
[25] We collapse in the dust,
  lying face down in the dirt.
[26] Rise up! Help us!
  Ransom us because of your
unfailing love.

PROVERBS 10:20-21

The words of the godly are like sterling
silver; the heart of a fool is worthless.
□ The words of the godly encourage
many, but fools are destroyed by their
lack of common sense.

MARCH**2**

LEVITICUS 25:47–27:13

Defeat and exile would surely come if Israel ignored
God's laws and worshiped idols. It's a simple principle: obedience brings blessing; disobedience brings
a curse.

"**S**uppose a foreigner or temporary resident becomes rich while living among
you. If any of your fellow Israelites fall into
poverty and are forced to sell themselves
to such a foreigner or to a member of his
family, [48] they still retain the right to be
bought back, even after they have been
purchased. They may be bought back by
a brother, [49] an uncle, or a cousin. In fact,
anyone from the extended family may buy
them back. They may also redeem themselves if they have prospered. [50] They will
negotiate the price of their freedom with
the person who bought them. The price
will be based on the number of years from
the time they were sold until the next Year
of Jubilee—whatever it would cost to hire a
worker for that period of time. [51] If many
years still remain until the jubilee, they
will repay the proper proportion of what
they received when they sold themselves.
[52] If only a few years remain until the Year

of Jubilee, they will repay a small amount
for their redemption. [53] The foreigner
must treat them as workers hired on a
yearly basis. You must not allow a foreigner to treat any of your fellow Israelites
harshly. [54] If any Israelites have not been
bought back by the time the Year of Jubilee arrives, they and their children must be
set free at that time. [55] For the people of Israel belong to me. They are my servants,
whom I brought out of the land of Egypt. I
am the Lord your God.

[26:1] "Do not make idols or set up carved
images, or sacred pillars, or sculptured
stones in your land so you may worship
them. I am the Lord your God. [2] You must
keep my Sabbath days of rest and show
reverence for my sanctuary. I am the
Lord.

[3] "If you follow my decrees and are careful to obey my commands, [4] I will send you
the seasonal rains. The land will then yield
its crops, and the trees of the field will produce their fruit. [5] Your threshing season
will overlap with the grape harvest, and
your grape harvest will overlap with the

season of planting grain. You will eat your fill and live securely in your own land.

⁶"I will give you peace in the land, and you will be able to sleep with no cause for fear. I will rid the land of wild animals and keep your enemies out of your land. ⁷In fact, you will chase down your enemies and slaughter them with your swords. ⁸Five of you will chase a hundred, and a hundred of you will chase ten thousand! All your enemies will fall beneath your sword.

⁹"I will look favorably upon you, making you fertile and multiplying your people. And I will fulfill my covenant with you. ¹⁰You will have such a surplus of crops that you will need to clear out the old grain to make room for the new harvest! ¹¹I will live among you, and I will not despise you. ¹²I will walk among you; I will be your God, and you will be my people. ¹³I am the LORD your God, who brought you out of the land of Egypt so you would no longer be their slaves. I broke the yoke of slavery from your neck so you can walk with your heads held high.

¹⁴"However, if you do not listen to me or obey all these commands, ¹⁵and if you break my covenant by rejecting my decrees, treating my regulations with contempt, and refusing to obey my commands, ¹⁶I will punish you. I will bring sudden terrors upon you—wasting diseases and burning fevers that will cause your eyes to fail and your life to ebb away. You will plant your crops in vain because your enemies will eat them. ¹⁷I will turn against you, and you will be defeated by your enemies. Those who hate you will rule over you, and you will run even when no one is chasing you!

¹⁸"And if, in spite of all this, you still disobey me, I will punish you seven times over for your sins. ¹⁹I will break your proud spirit by making the skies as unyielding as iron and the earth as hard as bronze. ²⁰All your work will be for nothing, for your land will yield no crops, and your trees will bear no fruit.

²¹"If even then you remain hostile toward me and refuse to obey me, I will inflict disaster on you seven times over for your sins. ²²I will send wild animals that will rob you of your children and

destroy your livestock. Your numbers will dwindle, and your roads will be deserted.

²³"And if you fail to learn the lesson and continue your hostility toward me, ²⁴then I myself will be hostile toward you. I will personally strike you with calamity seven times over for your sins. ²⁵I will send armies against you to carry out the curse of the covenant you have broken. When you run to your towns for safety, I will send a plague to destroy you there, and you will be handed over to your enemies. ²⁶I will destroy your food supply, so that ten women will need only one oven to bake bread for their families. They will ration your food by weight, and though you have food to eat, you will not be satisfied.

²⁷"If in spite of all this you still refuse to listen and still remain hostile toward me, ²⁸then I will give full vent to my hostility. I myself will punish you seven times over for your sins. ²⁹Then you will eat the flesh of your own sons and daughters. ³⁰I will destroy your pagan shrines and knock down your places of worship. I will leave your lifeless corpses piled on top of your lifeless idols,* and I will despise you. ³¹I will make your cities desolate and destroy your places of pagan worship. I will take no pleasure in your offerings that should be a pleasing aroma to me. ³²Yes, I myself will devastate your land, and your enemies who come to occupy it will be appalled at what they see. ³³I will scatter you among the nations and bring out my sword against you. Your land will become desolate, and your cities will lie in ruins. ³⁴Then at last the land will enjoy its neglected Sabbath years as it lies desolate while you are in exile in the land of your enemies. Then the land will finally rest and enjoy the Sabbaths it missed. ³⁵As long as the land lies in ruins, it will enjoy the rest you never allowed it to take every seventh year while you lived in it.

³⁶"And for those of you who survive, I will demoralize you in the land of your enemies. You will live in such fear that the sound of a leaf driven by the wind will send you fleeing. You will run as though fleeing from a sword, and you will fall even when no one pursues you. ³⁷Though no one is chasing you, you will stumble over each other as though fleeing from a

sword. You will have no power to stand up against your enemies. [38]You will die among the foreign nations and be devoured in the land of your enemies. [39]Those of you who survive will waste away in your enemies' lands because of their sins and the sins of their ancestors.

[40]"But at last my people will confess their sins and the sins of their ancestors for betraying me and being hostile toward me. [41]When I have turned their hostility back on them and brought them to the land of their enemies, then at last their stubborn hearts will be humbled, and they will pay for their sins. [42]Then I will remember my covenant with Jacob and my covenant with Isaac and my covenant with Abraham, and I will remember the land. [43]For the land must be abandoned to enjoy its years of Sabbath rest as it lies deserted. At last the people will pay for their sins, for they have continually rejected my regulations and despised my decrees.

[44]"But despite all this, I will not utterly reject or despise them while they are in exile in the land of their enemies. I will not cancel my covenant with them by wiping them out, for I am the LORD their God. [45]For their sakes I will remember my ancient covenant with their ancestors, whom I brought out of the land of Egypt in the sight of all the nations, that I might be their God. I am the LORD."

[46]These are the decrees, regulations, and instructions that the LORD gave through Moses on Mount Sinai as evidence of the relationship between himself and the Israelites.

[27:1]THE LORD said to Moses, [2]"Give the following instructions to the people of Israel. If anyone makes a special vow to dedicate someone to the LORD by paying the value of that person, [3]here is the scale of values to be used. A man between the ages of twenty and sixty is valued at fifty shekels* of silver, as measured by the sanctuary shekel. [4]A woman of that age is valued at thirty shekels* of silver. [5]A boy between the ages of five and twenty is valued at twenty shekels of silver; a girl of that age is valued at ten shekels* of silver. [6]A boy between the ages of one month and five years is valued at five shekels of silver; a girl of that age is valued at three shekels* of silver. [7]A man older than sixty is valued at fifteen shekels of silver; a woman of that age is valued at ten shekels* of silver. [8]If you desire to make such a vow but cannot afford to pay the required amount, take the person to the priest. He will determine the amount for you to pay based on what you can afford.

Serving others

HOW WE LIVE

MARK 10:35-38 The disciples were ordinary men. They loved Christ and wanted to serve him, yet they were also eager to know how they might benefit from their relationship with him. James and John asked Jesus to do them a favor—to guarantee special places of honor for them in his coming Kingdom. • When the other disciples discovered what these two had done, they were indignant. Perhaps they were annoyed that two among them would be requesting preferential treatment, or perhaps they were hoping for such an honor themselves. Jesus used the discussion to teach them all an important lesson: Kingdom values run counter to human values. • As human beings, it is natural for us to enjoy titles, honors, and privileges. Christ teaches us, however, that he views the perks of leadership very differently. "Whoever wants to be a leader among you must be your servant," he said (10:43). Only the man or woman who is willing to serve others is truly worthy of leading them. • Don't be seeking greatness for yourself, Jesus says. Instead, seek to serve others. When you do that, you will be great in the Kingdom of God.

⁹"If your vow involves giving an animal that is acceptable as an offering to the LORD, any gift to the LORD will be considered holy. ¹⁰You may not exchange or substitute it for another animal—neither a good animal for a bad one nor a bad animal for a good one. But if you do exchange one animal for another, then both the original animal and its substitute will be considered holy. ¹¹If your vow involves an unclean animal—one that is not acceptable as an offering to the LORD—then you must bring the animal to the priest. ¹²He will assess its value, and his assessment will be final, whether high or low. ¹³If you want to buy back the animal, you must pay the value set by the priest, plus 20 percent."

26:30 The Hebrew term (literally *round things*) probably alludes to dung. **27:3** Or *20 ounces* [570 grams]. **27:4** Or *12 ounces* [342 grams]. **27:5** Or *A boy . . . 8 ounces* [228 grams] *of silver; a girl . . . 4 ounces* [114 grams]. **27:6** Or *A boy . . . 2 ounces* [57 grams] *of silver; a girl . . . 1.2 ounces* [34 grams]. **27:7** Or *A man . . . 6 ounces* [171 grams] *of silver; a woman . . . 4 ounces* [114 grams].

MARK 10:32-52

Just after Jesus revealed to his disciples that he was going to be betrayed and killed, James and John started begging for places of honor in his Kingdom. They didn't yet understand that Jesus came to suffer in our place.

They [the disciples] were now on the way up to Jerusalem, and Jesus was walking ahead of them. The disciples were filled with awe, and the people following behind were overwhelmed with fear. Taking the twelve disciples aside, Jesus once more began to describe everything that was about to happen to him. ³³"Listen," he said, "we're going up to Jerusalem, where the Son of Man* will be betrayed to the leading priests and the teachers of religious law. They will sentence him to die and hand him over to the Romans.* ³⁴They will mock him, spit on him, flog him with a whip, and kill him, but after three days he will rise again."

³⁵Then James and John, the sons of Zebedee, came over and spoke to him. "Teacher," they said, "we want you to do us a favor."

³⁶"What is your request?" he asked.

³⁷They replied, "When you sit on your glorious throne, we want to sit in places of honor next to you, one on your right and the other on your left."

³⁸But Jesus said to them, "You don't know what you are asking! Are you able to drink from the bitter cup of suffering I am about to drink? Are you able to be baptized with the baptism of suffering I must be baptized with?"

³⁹"Oh yes," they replied, "we are able!"

Then Jesus told them, "You will indeed drink from my bitter cup and be baptized with my baptism of suffering. ⁴⁰But I have no right to say who will sit on my right or my left. God has prepared those places for the ones he has chosen."

⁴¹When the ten other disciples heard what James and John had asked, they were indignant. ⁴²So Jesus called them together and said, "You know that the rulers in this world lord it over their people, and officials flaunt their authority over those under them. ⁴³But among you it will be different. Whoever wants to be a leader among you must be your servant, ⁴⁴and whoever wants to be first among you must be the slave of everyone else. ⁴⁵For even the Son of Man came not to be served but to serve others and to give his life as a ransom for many."

⁴⁶Then they reached Jericho, and as Jesus and his disciples left town, a large crowd followed him. A blind beggar named Bartimaeus (son of Timaeus) was sitting beside the road. ⁴⁷When Bartimaeus heard that Jesus of Nazareth was nearby, he began to shout, "Jesus, Son of David, have mercy on me!"

⁴⁸"Be quiet!" many of the people yelled at him.

But he only shouted louder, "Son of David, have mercy on me!"

⁴⁹When Jesus heard him, he stopped and said, "Tell him to come here."

So they called the blind man. "Cheer up," they said. "Come on, he's calling you!" ⁵⁰Bartimaeus threw aside his coat, jumped up, and came to Jesus.

⁵¹"What do you want me to do for you?" Jesus asked.

"My rabbi,*" the blind man said, "I want to see!"

⁵²And Jesus said to him, "Go, for your faith has healed you." Instantly the man

could see, and he followed Jesus down the road.*

10:33a "Son of Man" is a title Jesus used for himself. **10:33b** Greek *the Gentiles*. **10:51** Greek uses the Hebrew term *Rabboni*. **10:52** Or *on the way*.

PSALM 45:1-17
For the choir director: A love song to be sung to the tune "Lilies." A psalm* of the descendants of Korah.

¹ **B**eautiful words stir my heart.
  I will recite a lovely poem about the king,
  for my tongue is like the pen
  of a skillful poet.

² You are the most handsome of all.
  Gracious words stream from your lips.
  God himself has blessed you forever.

³ Put on your sword, O mighty warrior!
  You are so glorious, so majestic!

⁴ In your majesty, ride out to victory,
  defending truth, humility, and justice.
  Go forth to perform awe-inspiring deeds!

⁵ Your arrows are sharp, piercing your enemies' hearts.
  The nations fall beneath your feet.

⁶ Your throne, O God,* endures forever and ever.
  You rule with a scepter of justice.

⁷ You love justice and hate evil.
  Therefore God, your God, has anointed you,
  pouring out the oil of joy on you
  more than on anyone else.

⁸ Myrrh, aloes, and cassia perfume your robes.

In ivory palaces the music of strings entertains you.

⁹ Kings' daughters are among your noble women.
  At your right side stands the queen,
  wearing jewelry of finest gold from Ophir!

¹⁰ Listen to me, O royal daughter; take to heart what I say.
  Forget your people and your family far away.

¹¹ For your royal husband delights in your beauty;
  honor him, for he is your lord.

¹² The princess of Tyre* will shower you with gifts.
  The wealthy will beg your favor.

¹³ The bride, a princess, looks glorious in her golden gown.

¹⁴ In her beautiful robes, she is led to the king,
  accompanied by her bridesmaids.

¹⁵ What a joyful and enthusiastic procession
  as they enter the king's palace!

¹⁶ Your sons will become kings like their father.
  You will make them rulers over many lands.

¹⁷ I will bring honor to your name in every generation.
  Therefore, the nations will praise you forever and ever.

45:TITLE Hebrew *maskil*. This may be a literary or musical term. **45:6** Or *Your divine throne*. **45:12** Hebrew *The daughter of Tyre*.

PROVERBS 10:22
The blessing of the LORD makes a person rich, and he adds no sorrow with it.

LEVITICUS 27:14–NUMBERS 1:54
Leviticus closes with a discussion of dedicating possessions to God. When the Israelites dedicated their possessions to God, those dedicated items became constant reminders that they themselves belong to God.

"**I**f someone dedicates a house to the LORD, the priest will come to assess its value. The priest's assessment will be final, whether high or low. ¹⁵ If the person who dedicated the house wants to buy it back, he must pay the value set by the priest, plus 20 percent. Then the house will again be his.

¹⁶"If someone dedicates to the LORD a piece of his family property, its value will be assessed according to the amount of seed required to plant it—fifty shekels of silver for a field planted with five bushels of barley seed.* ¹⁷If the field is dedicated to the LORD in the Year of Jubilee, then the entire assessment will apply. ¹⁸But if the field is dedicated after the Year of Jubilee, the priest will assess the land's value in proportion to the number of years left until the next Year of Jubilee. Its assessed value is reduced each year. ¹⁹If the person who dedicated the field wants to buy it back, he must pay the value set by the priest, plus 20 percent. Then the field will again be legally his. ²⁰But if he does not want to buy it back, and it is sold to someone else, the field can no longer be bought back. ²¹When the field is released in the Year of Jubilee, it will be holy, a field specially set apart* for the LORD. It will become the property of the priests.

²²"If someone dedicates to the LORD a field he has purchased but which is not part of his family property, ²³the priest will assess its value based on the number of years left until the next Year of Jubilee. On that day he must give the assessed value of the land as a sacred donation to the LORD. ²⁴In the Year of Jubilee the field must be returned to the person from whom he purchased it, the one who inherited it as family property. ²⁵(All the payments must be measured by the weight of the sanctuary shekel,* which equals twenty gerahs.)

²⁶"You may not dedicate a firstborn animal to the LORD, for the firstborn of your cattle, sheep, and goats already belong to him. ²⁷However, you may buy back the firstborn of a ceremonially unclean animal by paying the priest's assessment of its worth, plus 20 percent. If you do not buy it back, the priest will sell it at its assessed value.

²⁸"However, anything specially set apart for the LORD—whether a person, an animal, or family property—must never be sold or bought back. Anything devoted in this way has been set apart as holy, and it belongs to the LORD. ²⁹No person specially set apart for destruction may be bought back. Such a person must be put to death.

³⁰"One tenth of the produce of the land, whether grain from the fields or fruit from the trees, belongs to the LORD and must be set apart to him as holy. ³¹If you want to buy back the LORD's tenth of the grain or fruit, you must pay its value, plus 20 percent. ³²Count off every tenth animal from your herds and flocks and set them apart for the LORD as holy. ³³You may not pick and choose between good and bad animals, and you may not substitute one for another. But if you do exchange one animal for another, then both the original animal and its substitute will be considered holy and cannot be bought back."

³⁴These are the commands that the LORD gave through Moses on Mount Sinai for the Israelites.

1:1A YEAR after Israel's departure from Egypt, the LORD spoke to Moses in the Tabernacle* in the wilderness of Sinai. On the first day of the second month* of that year he said, ²"From the whole community of Israel, record the names of all the warriors by their clans and families. List all the men ³twenty years old or older who are able to go to war. You and Aaron must register the troops, ⁴and you will be assisted by one family leader from each tribe.

⁵"These are the tribes and the names of the leaders who will assist you:

Tribe	Leader
Reuben	Elizur son of Shedeur
6 Simeon	Shelumiel son of Zurishaddai
7 Judah	Nahshon son of Amminadab
8 Issachar	Nethanel son of Zuar
9 Zebulun	Eliab son of Helon
10 Ephraim son of Joseph	Elishama son of Ammihud
Manasseh son of Joseph	Gamaliel son of Pedahzur
11 Benjamin	Abidan son of Gideoni
12 Dan	Ahiezer son of Ammishaddai
13 Asher	Pagiel son of Ocran
14 Gad	Eliasaph son of Deuel
15 Naphtali	Ahira son of Enan

¹⁶These are the chosen leaders of the

community, the leaders of their ancestral tribes, the heads of the clans of Israel."

¹⁷So Moses and Aaron called together these chosen leaders, ¹⁸and they assembled the whole community of Israel on that very day.* All the people were registered according to their ancestry by their clans and families. The men of Israel who were twenty years old or older were listed one by one, ¹⁹just as the LORD had commanded Moses. So Moses recorded their names in the wilderness of Sinai.

²⁰⁻²¹This is the number of men twenty years old or older who were able to go to war, as their names were listed in the records of their clans and families*:

Tribe	Number
Reuben (Jacob's* oldest son)	46,500
²²⁻²³ Simeon	59,300
²⁴⁻²⁵ Gad	45,650
²⁶⁻²⁷ Judah	74,600
²⁸⁻²⁹ Issachar	54,400
³⁰⁻³¹ Zebulun	57,400
³²⁻³³ Ephraim son of Joseph	40,500
³⁴⁻³⁵ Manasseh son of Joseph	32,200
³⁶⁻³⁷ Benjamin	35,400
³⁸⁻³⁹ Dan	62,700
⁴⁰⁻⁴¹ Asher	41,500
⁴²⁻⁴³ Naphtali	53,400

⁴⁴These were the men registered by Moses and Aaron and the twelve leaders of Israel, all listed according to their ancestral descent. ⁴⁵They were registered by families—all the men of Israel who were twenty years old or older and able to go to war. ⁴⁶The total number was 603,550.

⁴⁷But this total did not include the Levites. ⁴⁸For the LORD had said to Moses, ⁴⁹"Do not include the tribe of Levi in the registration; do not count them with the rest of the Israelites. ⁵⁰Put the Levites in charge of the Tabernacle of the Covenant,* along with all its furnishings and equipment. They must carry the Tabernacle and all its furnishings as you travel, and they must take care of it and camp around it. ⁵¹Whenever it is time for the Tabernacle to move, the Levites will take it down. And when it is time to stop, they will set it up again. But any unauthorized person who goes too near the Tabernacle must be put to death. ⁵²Each tribe of Israel will camp in a designated area with its own family banner. ⁵³But the Levites will camp around the Tabernacle of the Covenant to protect the community of Israel from the LORD's anger. The Levites are responsible to stand guard around the Tabernacle."

⁵⁴So the Israelites did everything just as the LORD had commanded Moses.

2:16 Hebrew *50 shekels* [20 ounces, or 570 grams] *of silver for a homer* [182 liters] *of barley seed.*   2:21 The Hebrew term used here refers to the complete consecration of things

WHAT THE BIBLE SAYS

Salvation and forgiveness

MARK 11:22-25 In Mark 11:22-25, Jesus discusses the power of prayer. If we believe, he says, amazing things can happen. But Jesus adds a crucial qualifier in verse 25: we must be forgiving people.   • So how can we keep from having an unforgiving attitude? Start with remembering God's forgiveness. He established a relationship with us even though he knew we would fail time and again. We surely know that other people are going to fail us as well. It's no surprise. That's why God has a mechanism in place for us to deal with those difficulties—forgiveness.   • To refuse to forgive others means to deny the power of Christ's sacrifice on the cross. Christ died on the cross for all people for all time. Jesus' words here about the power of prayer and the importance of not holding grudges emphasize that if you have confessed your own sin and weakness and have asked him to forgive you, then you must forgive others as well.

or people to the LORD, either by destroying them or by giving them as an offering; also in 27:28, 29. **27:25** Each shekel was about 0.4 ounces [11 grams] in weight. **1:1a** Hebrew *the Tent of Meeting.* **1:1b** This day in the ancient Hebrew lunar calendar occurred in April or May. **1:18** Hebrew *on the first day of the second month;* see 1:1. **1:20-21a** In the Hebrew text, this phrase (*This is the number of men twenty years old or older who were able to go to war, as their names were listed in the records of their clans and families*) is repeated in 1:22, 24, 26, 28, 30, 32, 34, 36, 38, 40, 42. **1:20-21b** Hebrew *Israel's.* The names "Jacob" and "Israel" are often interchanged throughout the Old Testament, referring sometimes to the individual patriarch and sometimes to the nation. **1:50** Or *Tabernacle of the Testimony;* also in 1:53.

MARK 11:1-26

Jesus headed into the hardest week of his life with passion and fervor. He revealed his anger at sin. He ignited faith. No one could just ignore Jesus; it was either follow him or reject him.

As Jesus and his disciples approached Jerusalem, they came to the towns of Bethphage and Bethany on the Mount of Olives. Jesus sent two of them on ahead. ²"Go into that village over there," he told them. "As soon as you enter it, you will see a young donkey tied there that no one has ever ridden. Untie it and bring it here. ³If anyone asks, 'What are you doing?' just say, 'The Lord needs it and will return it soon.'"

⁴The two disciples left and found the colt standing in the street, tied outside the front door. ⁵As they were untying it, some bystanders demanded, "What are you doing, untying that colt?" ⁶They said what Jesus had told them to say, and they were permitted to take it. ⁷Then they brought the colt to Jesus and threw their garments over it, and he sat on it.

⁸Many in the crowd spread their garments on the road ahead of him, and others spread leafy branches they had cut in the fields. ⁹Jesus was in the center of the procession, and the people all around him were shouting,

"Praise God!*
Blessings on the one who comes in
the name of the LORD!
¹⁰ Blessings on the coming Kingdom of
our ancestor David!
Praise God in highest heaven!"*

¹¹So Jesus came to Jerusalem and went into the Temple. After looking around carefully at everything, he left because it was late in the afternoon. Then he returned to Bethany with the twelve disciples.

¹²The next morning as they were leaving Bethany, Jesus was hungry. ¹³He noticed a fig tree in full leaf a little way off, so he went over to see if he could find any figs. But there were only leaves because it was too early in the season for fruit. ¹⁴Then Jesus said to the tree, "May no one ever eat your fruit again!" And the disciples heard him say it.

¹⁵When they arrived back in Jerusalem, Jesus entered the Temple and began to drive out the people buying and selling animals for sacrifices. He knocked over the tables of the money changers and the chairs of those selling doves, ¹⁶and he stopped everyone from using the Temple as a marketplace.* ¹⁷He said to them, "The Scriptures declare, 'My Temple will be called a house of prayer for all nations,' but you have turned it into a den of thieves."*

¹⁸When the leading priests and teachers of religious law heard what Jesus had done, they began planning how to kill him. But they were afraid of him because the people were so amazed at his teaching.

¹⁹That evening Jesus and the disciples left* the city.

²⁰The next morning as they passed by the fig tree he had cursed, the disciples noticed it had withered from the roots up. ²¹Peter remembered what Jesus had said to the tree on the previous day and exclaimed, "Look, Rabbi! The fig tree you cursed has withered and died!"

²²Then Jesus said to the disciples, "Have faith in God. ²³I tell you the truth, you can say to this mountain, 'May you be lifted up and thrown into the sea,' and it will happen. But you must really believe it will happen and have no doubt in your heart. ²⁴I tell you, you can pray for anything, and if you believe that you've received it, it will be yours. ²⁵But when you are praying, first forgive anyone you are holding a grudge against, so that your Father in heaven will forgive your sins, too.*"

11:9 Greek *Hosanna,* an exclamation of praise that literally means "save now"; also in 11:10. **11:9-10** Pss 118:25-26; 148:1. **11:16** Or *from carrying merchandise through the Temple.* **11:17** Isa 56:7; Jer 7:11. **11:19** Greek *they left;* other manuscripts read *he left.* **11:25** Some manuscripts add verse 26, *But if you refuse to forgive, your Father in heaven will not forgive your sins.* Compare Matt 6:15.

PSALM 46:1-11

For the choir director: A song of the descendants of Korah, to be sung by soprano voices.*

¹ God is our refuge and strength,
      always ready to help in times
         of trouble.
² So we will not fear when earthquakes
      come
      and the mountains crumble into
         the sea.
³ Let the oceans roar and foam.
      Let the mountains tremble
         as the waters surge!   *Interlude*

⁴ A river brings joy to the city of our
      God,
      the sacred home of the Most High.
⁵ God dwells in that city; it cannot be
      destroyed.
      From the very break of day, God will
         protect it.
⁶ The nations are in chaos,
      and their kingdoms crumble!
      God's voice thunders,
         and the earth melts!

⁷ The LORD of Heaven's Armies is here
      among us;

the God of Israel* is our
      fortress.   *Interlude*

⁸ Come, see the glorious works of
      the LORD:
      See how he brings destruction upon
         the world.
⁹ He causes wars to end throughout
      the earth.
      He breaks the bow and snaps
         the spear;
      he burns the shields with fire.

¹⁰ "Be still, and know that I am God!
      I will be honored by every
         nation.
      I will be honored throughout
         the world."

¹¹ The LORD of Heaven's Armies is here
      among us;
      the God of Israel is our fortress.
                                   Interlude

46:TITLE Hebrew *according to alamoth.*   **46:7** Hebrew *of Jacob;* also in 46:11. See note on 44:4.

PROVERBS 10:23

Doing wrong is fun for a fool, but living wisely brings pleasure to the sensible.

MARCH**4**

NUMBERS 2:1–3:51

The book of Numbers opens with the first census of the people. The camp was then organized by tribes, according to the descendants of the sons of Jacob. From this point on, each Israelite was to be identified by membership in a tribe.

Then the LORD gave these instructions to Moses and Aaron: ²"When the Israelites set up camp, each tribe will be assigned its own area. The tribal divisions will camp beneath their family banners on all four sides of the Tabernacle,* but at some distance from it.

³⁻⁴"The divisions of Judah, Issachar, and Zebulun are to camp toward the sunrise on the east side of the Tabernacle, beneath their family banners. These are the

names of the tribes, their leaders, and the numbers of their registered troops:

Tribe	Leader	Number
Judah	Nahshon son of Amminadab	74,600
5-6 Issachar	Nethanel son of Zuar	54,400
7-8 Zebulun	Eliab son of Helon	57,400

⁹So the total of all the troops on Judah's side of the camp is 186,400. These three tribes are to lead the way whenever the Israelites travel to a new campsite.

¹⁰⁻¹¹"The divisions of Reuben, Simeon, and Gad are to camp on the south side of the Tabernacle, beneath their family banners. These are the names of the tribes,

their leaders, and the numbers of their registered troops:

Tribe	Leader	Number
Reuben	Elizur son of Shedeur	46,500
12-13 Simeon	Shelumiel son of Zurishaddai	59,300
14-15 Gad	Eliasaph son of Deuel*	45,650

¹⁶So the total of all the troops on Reuben's side of the camp is 151,450. These three tribes will be second in line whenever the Israelites travel.

¹⁷"Then the Tabernacle, carried by the Levites, will set out from the middle of the camp. All the tribes are to travel in the same order that they camp, each in position under the appropriate family banner.

¹⁸⁻¹⁹"The divisions of Ephraim, Manasseh, and Benjamin are to camp on the west side of the Tabernacle, beneath their family banners. These are the names of the tribes, their leaders, and the numbers of their registered troops:

Tribe	Leader	Number
Ephraim	Elishama son of Ammihud	40,500
20-21 Manasseh	Gamaliel son of Pedahzur	32,200
22-23 Benjamin	Abidan son of Gideoni	35,400

²⁴So the total of all the troops on Ephraim's side of the camp is 108,100. These three tribes will be third in line whenever the Israelites travel.

²⁵⁻²⁶"The divisions of Dan, Asher, and Naphtali are to camp on the north side of the Tabernacle, beneath their family banners. These are the names of the tribes, their leaders, and the numbers of their registered troops:

Tribe	Leader	Number
Dan	Ahiezer son of Ammishaddai	62,700
27-28 Asher	Pagiel son of Ocran	41,500
29-30 Naphtali	Ahira son of Enan	53,400

³¹So the total of all the troops on Dan's side of the camp is 157,600. These three tribes will be last, marching under their banners whenever the Israelites travel."

³²In summary, the troops of Israel listed by their families totaled 603,550. ³³But as the LORD had commanded, the Levites were not included in this registration. ³⁴So the people of Israel did everything as the LORD had commanded Moses. Each clan and family set up camp and marched under their banners exactly as the LORD had instructed them.

³:¹THIS is the family line of Aaron and Moses as it was recorded when the LORD spoke to Moses on Mount Sinai: ²The names of Aaron's sons were Nadab (the oldest), Abihu, Eleazar, and Ithamar. ³These sons of Aaron were anointed and ordained to minister as priests. ⁴But Nadab and Abihu died in the LORD's presence in the wilderness of Sinai when they burned before the LORD the wrong kind of fire, different than he had commanded. Since they had no sons, this left only Eleazar and Ithamar to serve as priests with their father, Aaron.

⁵Then the LORD said to Moses, ⁶"Call forward the tribe of Levi, and present them to Aaron the priest to serve as his assistants. ⁷They will serve Aaron and the whole community, performing their sacred duties in and around the Tabernacle.* ⁸They will also maintain all the furnishings of the sacred tent,* serving in the Tabernacle on behalf of all the Israelites. ⁹Assign the Levites to Aaron and his sons. They have been given from among all the people of Israel to serve as their assistants. ¹⁰Appoint Aaron and his sons to carry out the duties of the priesthood. But any unauthorized person who goes too near the sanctuary must be put to death."

¹¹And the LORD said to Moses, ¹²"Look, I have chosen the Levites from among the Israelites to serve as substitutes for all the firstborn sons of the people of Israel. The Levites belong to me, ¹³for all the firstborn males are mine. On the day I struck down all the firstborn sons of the Egyptians, I set apart for myself all the firstborn in Israel, both of people and of animals. They are mine; I am the LORD."

¹⁴The LORD spoke again to Moses in the wilderness of Sinai. He said, ¹⁵"Record the names of the members of the tribe of Levi by their families and clans. List every

male who is one month old or older." [16]So Moses listed them, just as the Lord had commanded.

[17]Levi had three sons, whose names were Gershon, Kohath, and Merari. [18]The clans descended from Gershon were named after two of his descendants, Libni and Shimei. [19]The clans descended from Kohath were named after four of his descendants, Amram, Izhar, Hebron, and Uzziel. [20]The clans descended from Merari were named after two of his descendants, Mahli and Mushi. These were the Levite clans, listed according to their family groups.

[21]The descendants of Gershon were composed of the clans descended from Libni and Shimei. [22]There were 7,500 males one month old or older among these Gershonite clans. [23]They were assigned the area to the west of the Tabernacle for their camp. [24]The leader of the Gershonite clans was Eliasaph son of Lael. [25]These two clans were responsible to care for the Tabernacle, including the sacred tent with its layers of coverings, the curtain at its entrance, [26]the curtains of the courtyard that surrounded the Tabernacle and altar, the curtain at the courtyard entrance, the ropes, and all the equipment related to their use.

[27]The descendants of Kohath were composed of the clans descended from Amram, Izhar, Hebron, and Uzziel. [28]There were 8,600* males one month old or older among these Kohathite clans. They were responsible for the care of the sanctuary, [29]and they were assigned the area south of the Tabernacle for their camp. [30]The leader of the Kohathite clans was Elizaphan son of Uzziel. [31]These four clans were responsible for the care of the Ark, the table, the lampstand, the altars, the various articles used in the sanctuary, the inner curtain, and all the equipment related to their use. [32]Eleazar, son of Aaron the priest, was the chief administrator over all the Levites, with special responsibility for the oversight of the sanctuary.

[33]The descendants of Merari were composed of the clans descended from Mahli and Mushi. [34]There were 6,200 males one month old or older among these Merarite clans. [35]They were assigned the area north of the Tabernacle for their camp. The leader of the Merarite clans was Zuriel son of Abihail. [36]These two clans were responsible for the care of the frames supporting the Tabernacle, the crossbars, the pillars, the bases, and all the equipment related to their use. [37]They were also responsible for the posts of the courtyard and all their bases, pegs, and ropes.

[38]The area in front of the Tabernacle, in

WHO GOD IS
The one true God

PSALM 47:2 Some people claim Christians are too narrow. "Don't all roads lead to God?" they say. God's Word makes it clear that "the great King of all the earth" is the one true God. From the book of Isaiah come these words, "I am the Lord; there is no other God. I have equipped you for battle, though you don't even know me, so all the world from east to west will know there is no other God. I am the Lord, and there is no other" (Isaiah 45:5-6, September 24). He is the one true God and he is sovereign over all things, including the nations. •While other religions may have their gods, prophets, and saviors, no other religion has one who died to save his followers and then rose again from the dead. There is only one God, and Jesus is the only way to him. Jesus said, "I am the way, the truth, and the life. No one can come to the Father except through me" (John 14:6, May 24). Give thanks today that the one true God loves you.

the east toward the sunrise,* was reserved for the tents of Moses and of Aaron and his sons, who had the final responsibility for the sanctuary on behalf of the people of Israel. Anyone other than a priest or Levite who went too near the sanctuary was to be put to death.

³⁹ When Moses and Aaron counted the Levite clans at the LORD's command, the total number was 22,000 males one month old or older.

⁴⁰ Then the LORD said to Moses, "Now count all the firstborn sons in Israel who are one month old or older, and make a list of their names. ⁴¹ The Levites must be reserved for me as substitutes for the firstborn sons of Israel; I am the LORD. And the Levites' livestock must be reserved for me as substitutes for the firstborn livestock of the whole nation of Israel."

⁴² So Moses counted the firstborn sons of the people of Israel, just as the LORD had commanded. ⁴³ The number of firstborn sons who were one month old or older was 22,273.

⁴⁴ Then the LORD said to Moses, ⁴⁵ "Take the Levites as substitutes for the firstborn sons of the people of Israel. And take the livestock of the Levites as substitutes for the firstborn livestock of the people of Israel. The Levites belong to me; I am the LORD. ⁴⁶ There are 273 more firstborn sons of Israel than there are Levites. To redeem these extra firstborn sons, ⁴⁷ collect five pieces of silver* for each of them (each piece weighing the same as the sanctuary shekel, which equals twenty gerahs). ⁴⁸ Give the silver to Aaron and his sons as the redemption price for the extra firstborn sons."

⁴⁹ So Moses collected the silver for redeeming the firstborn sons of Israel who exceeded the number of Levites. ⁵⁰ He collected 1,365 pieces of silver* on behalf of these firstborn sons of Israel (each piece weighing the same as the sanctuary shekel). ⁵¹ And Moses gave the silver for the redemption to Aaron and his sons, just as the LORD had commanded.

2:2 Hebrew *the Tent of Meeting;* also in 2:17.   **2:14-15** As in many Hebrew manuscripts, Samaritan Pentateuch, and Latin Vulgate (see also 1:14); most Hebrew manuscripts read *son of Reuel.*   **3:7** Hebrew *around the Tent of Meeting, doing service at the Tabernacle.*   **3:8** Hebrew *the Tent of Meeting;* also in 3:25.   **3:28** Some Greek manuscripts read *8,300;*

see total in 3:39.   **3:38** Hebrew *toward the sunrise, in front of the Tent of Meeting.*   **3:47** Hebrew *5 shekels* [2 ounces or 57 grams].   **3:50** Hebrew *1,365 shekels* [34 pounds or 15.5 kilograms].

MARK 11:27–12:17

Jesus' very life, not to mention the truths he spoke, confounded the religious leaders of his day. They couldn't see past their own expectations of the Messiah they had been waiting for.

Again they entered Jerusalem. As Jesus was walking through the Temple area, the leading priests, the teachers of religious law, and the elders came up to him. ²⁸ They demanded, "By what authority are you doing all these things? Who gave you the right to do them?"

²⁹ "I'll tell you by what authority I do these things if you answer one question," Jesus replied. ³⁰ "Did John's authority to baptize come from heaven, or was it merely human? Answer me!"

³¹ They talked it over among themselves. "If we say it was from heaven, he will ask why we didn't believe John. ³² But do we dare say it was merely human?" For they were afraid of what the people would do, because everyone believed that John was a prophet. ³³ So they finally replied, "We don't know."

And Jesus responded, "Then I won't tell you by what authority I do these things."

¹²:¹ THEN Jesus began teaching them with stories: "A man planted a vineyard. He built a wall around it, dug a pit for pressing out the grape juice, and built a lookout tower. Then he leased the vineyard to tenant farmers and moved to another country. ²At the time of the grape harvest, he sent one of his servants to collect his share of the crop. ³But the farmers grabbed the servant, beat him up, and sent him back empty-handed. ⁴The owner then sent another servant, but they insulted him and beat him over the head. ⁵The next servant he sent was killed. Others he sent were either beaten or killed, ⁶until there was only one left—his son whom he loved dearly. The owner finally sent him, thinking, 'Surely they will respect my son.'

⁷"But the tenant farmers said to one another, 'Here comes the heir to this estate. Let's kill him and get the estate for ourselves!' ⁸So they grabbed him and mur-

dered him and threw his body out of the vineyard.

⁹"What do you suppose the owner of the vineyard will do?" Jesus asked. "I'll tell you—he will come and kill those farmers and lease the vineyard to others. ¹⁰Didn't you ever read this in the Scriptures?

'The stone that the builders rejected
 has now become the cornerstone.
¹¹ This is the LORD's doing,
 and it is wonderful to see.'*"

¹²The religious leaders* wanted to arrest Jesus because they realized he was telling the story against them—they were the wicked farmers. But they were afraid of the crowd, so they left him and went away.

¹³Later the leaders sent some Pharisees and supporters of Herod to trap Jesus into saying something for which he could be arrested. ¹⁴"Teacher," they said, "we know how honest you are. You are impartial and don't play favorites. You teach the way of God truthfully. Now tell us—is it right to pay taxes to Caesar or not? ¹⁵Should we pay them, or shouldn't we?"

Jesus saw through their hypocrisy and said, "Why are you trying to trap me? Show me a Roman coin,* and I'll tell you." ¹⁶When they handed it to him, he asked, "Whose picture and title are stamped on it?"

"Caesar's," they replied.

¹⁷"Well, then," Jesus said, "give to Caesar what belongs to Caesar, and give to God what belongs to God."

His reply completely amazed them.

12:10-11 Ps 118:22-23. **12:12** Greek *They.* **12:15** Greek *a denarius.*

NUMBERS 4:1–5:31
The family of Levi was not included in the census of chapter one. Their responsibilities with the Tabernacle exempted them from fighting in battle.

PSALM 47:1-9
For the choir director: A psalm of the descendants of Korah.

¹ **C**ome, everyone! Clap your hands!
 Shout to God with joyful praise!
² For the LORD Most High is awesome.
 He is the great King of all the earth.
³ He subdues the nations before us,
 putting our enemies beneath our feet.
⁴ He chose the Promised Land as our inheritance,
 the proud possession of Jacob's descendants, whom he loves.
     Interlude

⁵ God has ascended with a mighty shout.
 The LORD has ascended with trumpets blaring.
⁶ Sing praises to God, sing praises;
 sing praises to our King, sing praises!
⁷ For God is the King over all the earth.
 Praise him with a psalm!
⁸ God reigns above the nations,
 sitting on his holy throne.
⁹ The rulers of the world have gathered together
 with the people of the God of Abraham.
For all the kings of the earth belong to God.
 He is highly honored everywhere.

PROVERBS 10:24-25
The fears of the wicked will be fulfilled; the hopes of the godly will be granted. □When the storms of life come, the wicked are whirled away, but the godly have a lasting foundation.

MARCH**5**

Then the LORD said to Moses and Aaron, ²"Record the names of the members of the clans and families of the Kohathite division of the tribe of Levi. [3]List all the men between the ages of thirty and fifty who are eligible to serve in the Tabernacle.*

[4]"The duties of the Kohathites at the Tabernacle relate to the most sacred objects. [5]When the camp moves, Aaron and his sons must enter the Tabernacle first to take down the inner curtain and cover the Ark of the Covenant* with it. [6]Then they must cover the inner curtain with fine goatskin leather and spread over that a single piece of blue cloth. Finally, they must put the carrying poles of the Ark in place.

[7]"Next they must spread a blue cloth over the table where the Bread of the Presence is displayed, and on the cloth they will place the bowls, pans, jars, pitchers, and the special bread. [8]They must spread a scarlet cloth over all of this, and finally a covering of fine goatskin leather on top of the scarlet cloth. Then they must insert the carrying poles into the table.

[9]"Next they must cover the lampstand with a blue cloth, along with its lamps, lamp snuffers, trays, and special jars of olive oil. [10]Then they must cover the lampstand and its accessories with fine goatskin leather and place the bundle on a carrying frame.

[11]"Next they must spread a blue cloth over the gold incense altar and cover this cloth with fine goatskin leather. Then they must attach the carrying poles to the altar. [12]They must take all the remaining furnishings of the sanctuary and wrap them in a blue cloth, cover them with fine goatskin leather, and place them on the carrying frame.

[13]"They must remove the ashes from the altar for sacrifices and cover the altar with a purple cloth. [14]All the altar utensils—the firepans, meat forks, shovels, basins, and all the containers—must be placed on the cloth, and a covering of fine goatskin leather must be spread over them. Finally, they must put the carrying poles in place. [15]The camp will be ready to move when Aaron and his sons have finished covering the sanctuary and all the sacred articles. The Kohathites will come and carry these things to the next destination. But they must not touch the sacred objects, or they will die. So these are the

things from the Tabernacle that the Kohathites must carry.

[16]"Eleazar son of Aaron the priest will be responsible for the oil of the lampstand, the fragrant incense, the daily grain offering, and the anointing oil. In fact, Eleazar will be responsible for the entire Tabernacle and everything in it, including the sanctuary and its furnishings."

[17]Then the LORD said to Moses and Aaron, [18]"Do not let the Kohathite clans be destroyed from among the Levites! [19]This is what you must do so they will live and not die when they approach the most sacred objects. Aaron and his sons must always go in with them and assign a specific duty or load to each person. [20]The Kohathites must never enter the sanctuary to look at the sacred objects for even a moment, or they will die."

[21]And the LORD said to Moses, [22]"Record the names of the members of the clans and families of the Gershonite division of the tribe of Levi. [23]List all the men between the ages of thirty and fifty who are eligible to serve in the Tabernacle.

[24]"These Gershonite clans will be responsible for general service and carrying loads. [25]They must carry the curtains of the Tabernacle, the Tabernacle itself with its coverings, the outer covering of fine goatskin leather, and the curtain for the Tabernacle entrance. [26]They are also to carry the curtains for the courtyard walls that surround the Tabernacle and altar, the curtain across the courtyard entrance, the ropes, and all the equipment related to their use. The Gershonites are responsible for all these items. [27]Aaron and his sons will direct the Gershonites regarding all their duties, whether it involves moving the equipment or doing other work. They must assign the Gershonites responsibility for the loads they are to carry. [28]So these are the duties assigned to the Gershonite clans at the Tabernacle. They will be directly responsible to Ithamar son of Aaron the priest.

[29]"Now record the names of the members of the clans and families of the Merarite division of the tribe of Levi. [30]List all the men between the ages of thirty and fifty who are eligible to serve in the Tabernacle.

[31]"Their only duty at the Tabernacle will be to carry loads. They will carry the frames of the Tabernacle, the crossbars, the posts, and the bases; [32] also the posts for the courtyard walls with their bases, pegs, and ropes; and all the accessories and everything else related to their use. Assign the various loads to each man by name. [33] So these are the duties of the Merarite clans at the Tabernacle. They are directly responsible to Ithamar son of Aaron the priest."

[34] So Moses, Aaron, and the other leaders of the community listed the members of the Kohathite division by their clans and families. [35] The list included all the men between thirty and fifty years of age who were eligible for service in the Tabernacle, [36] and the total number came to 2,750. [37] So this was the total of all those from the Kohathite clans who were eligible to serve at the Tabernacle. Moses and Aaron listed them, just as the LORD had commanded through Moses.

[38] The Gershonite division was also listed by its clans and families. [39] The list included all the men between thirty and fifty years of age who were eligible for service in the Tabernacle, [40] and the total number came to 2,630. [41] So this was the total of all those from the Gershonite clans who were eligible to serve at the Tabernacle. Moses and Aaron listed them, just as the LORD had commanded.

[42] The Merarite division was also listed by its clans and families. [43] The list included all the men between thirty and fifty years of age who were eligible for service in the Tabernacle, [44] and the total number came to 3,200. [45] So this was the total of all those from the Merarite clans who were eligible for service. Moses and Aaron listed them, just as the LORD had commanded through Moses.

[46] So Moses, Aaron, and the leaders of Israel listed all the Levites by their clans and families. [47] All the men between thirty and fifty years of age who were eligible for service in the Tabernacle and for its transportation [48] numbered 8,580. [49] When their names were recorded, as the LORD had commanded through Moses, each man was assigned his task and told what to carry.

And so the registration was completed, just as the LORD had commanded Moses.

5:1 THE LORD gave these instructions to Moses: [2] "Command the people of Israel to remove from the camp anyone who has a skin disease* or a discharge, or who has become ceremonially unclean by touching a dead person. [3] This command applies to men and women alike. Remove them so they will not defile the camp in which I live among them." [4] So the Israelites did as the LORD had commanded Moses and removed such people from the camp.

[5] Then the LORD said to Moses, [6] "Give the

HOW WE LIVE

Loving God and others

MARK 12:29-31 Jesus' answer to this religious teacher's question showed that all of the laws of the Old Testament could be summed up in two commands: love God and love others. • Loving others is difficult. People can be mean, unfaithful, and downright annoying. Yet Christ calls you to love others as much as you love yourself—to treat others the way you would like to be treated. It's much easier to hold a grudge or to try to hurt in retaliation for hurts you've received. Jesus offers a better way. He knows that those attitudes only end up hurting you, so he commands you to love as you would want to be loved. • Take a look at your relationships with others and hold them up to the standard of loving your neighbor as you love yourself. Are there some changes you need to make? Ask God to help you love as much as Jesus loves you. Fortunately, you don't have to do this on your own: the Holy Spirit will help produce the fruit of love in your life (Galatians 5:22, September 20).

following instructions to the people of Israel: If any of the people—men or women—betray the LORD by doing wrong to another person, they are guilty. [7]They must confess their sin and make full restitution for what they have done, adding an additional 20 percent and returning it to the person who was wronged. [8]But if the person who was wronged is dead, and there are no near relatives to whom restitution can be made, the payment belongs to the LORD and must be given to the priest. Those who are guilty must also bring a ram as a sacrifice, and they will be purified and made right with the LORD.* [9]All the sacred offerings that the Israelites bring to a priest will belong to him. [10]Each priest may keep all the sacred donations that he receives."

[11]And the LORD said to Moses, [12]"Give the following instructions to the people of Israel.

"Suppose a man's wife goes astray, and she is unfaithful to her husband [13]and has sex with another man, but neither her husband nor anyone else knows about it. She has defiled herself, even though there was no witness and she was not caught in the act. [14]If her husband becomes jealous and is suspicious of his wife and needs to know whether or not she has defiled herself, [15]the husband must bring his wife to the priest. He must also bring an offering of two quarts* of barley flour to be presented on her behalf. Do not mix it with olive oil or frankincense, for it is a jealousy offering—an offering to prove whether or not she is guilty.

[16]"The priest will then present her to stand trial before the LORD. [17]He must take some holy water in a clay jar and pour into it dust he has taken from the Tabernacle floor. [18]When the priest has presented the woman before the LORD, he must unbind her hair and place in her hands the offering of proof—the jealousy offering to determine whether her husband's suspicions are justified. The priest will stand before her, holding the jar of bitter water that brings a curse to those who are guilty. [19]The priest will then put the woman under oath and say to her, 'If no other man has had sex with you, and you have not gone astray and defiled yourself while under your husband's authority, may you be immune from the effects of this bitter water that brings on the curse. [20]But if you have gone astray by being unfaithful to your husband, and have defiled yourself by having sex with another man—'

[21]"At this point the priest must put the woman under oath by saying, 'May the people know that the LORD's curse is upon you when he makes you infertile, causing your womb to shrivel* and your abdomen to swell. [22]Now may this water that brings the curse enter your body and cause your abdomen to swell and your womb to shrivel.*' And the woman will be required to say, 'Yes, let it be so.' [23]And the priest will write these curses on a piece of leather and wash them off into the bitter water. [24]He will make the woman drink the bitter water that brings on the curse. When the water enters her body, it will cause bitter suffering if she is guilty.

[25]"The priest will take the jealousy offering from the woman's hand, lift it up before the LORD, and carry it to the altar. [26]He will take a handful of the flour as a token portion and burn it on the altar, and he will require the woman to drink the water. [27]If she has defiled herself by being unfaithful to her husband, the water that brings on the curse will cause bitter suffering. Her abdomen will swell and her womb will shrink,* and her name will become a curse among her people. [28]But if she has not defiled herself and is pure, then she will be unharmed and will still be able to have children.

[29]"This is the ritual law for dealing with suspicion. If a woman goes astray and defiles herself while under her husband's authority, [30]or if a man becomes jealous and is suspicious that his wife has been unfaithful, the husband must present his wife before the LORD, and the priest will apply this entire ritual law to her. [31]The husband will be innocent of any guilt in this matter, but his wife will be held accountable for her sin."

4:3 Hebrew *the Tent of Meeting;* also in 4:4, 15, 23, 25, 28, 30, 31, 33, 35, 37, 39, 41, 43, 47.   **4:5** Or *Ark of the Testimony.*   **5:2** Traditionally rendered *leprosy.* The Hebrew word used here describes various skin diseases.   **5:8** Or *bring a ram for atonement, which will make atonement for them.*   **5:15** Hebrew ¹⁄₁₀ *of an ephah* [2.2 liters].   **5:21** Hebrew *when he causes your thigh to waste away.*   **5:22** Hebrew *and your thigh to waste away.*   **5:27** Hebrew *and her thigh will waste away.*

MARK 12:18-37

Here, as in many other places in the Gospels, there was a lethal game of Q&A going on. Religious leaders like the Sadducees set out to trick Jesus, but he proved to be un-trickable.

Then Jesus was approached by some Sadducees—religious leaders who say there is no resurrection from the dead. They posed this question: [19]"Teacher, Moses gave us a law that if a man dies, leaving a wife without children, his brother should marry the widow and have a child who will carry on the brother's name.* [20]Well, suppose there were seven brothers. The oldest one married and then died without children. [21]So the second brother married the widow, but he also died without children. Then the third brother married her. [22]This continued with all seven of them, and still there were no children. Last of all, the woman also died. [23]So tell us, whose wife will she be in the resurrection? For all seven were married to her."

[24]Jesus replied, "Your mistake is that you don't know the Scriptures, and you don't know the power of God. [25]For when the dead rise, they will neither marry nor be given in marriage. In this respect they will be like the angels in heaven.

[26]"But now, as to whether the dead will be raised—haven't you ever read about this in the writings of Moses, in the story of the burning bush? Long after Abraham, Isaac, and Jacob had died, God said to Moses,* 'I am the God of Abraham, the God of Isaac, and the God of Jacob.'* [27]So he is the God of the living, not the dead. You have made a serious error."

[28]One of the teachers of religious law was standing there listening to the debate. He realized that Jesus had answered well, so he asked, "Of all the commandments, which is the most important?"

[29]Jesus replied, "The most important commandment is this: 'Listen, O Israel! The LORD our God is the one and only LORD. [30]And you must love the LORD your God with all your heart, all your soul, all your mind, and all your strength.'* [31]The second is equally important: 'Love your neighbor as yourself.'* No other commandment is greater than these."

[32]The teacher of religious law replied, "Well said, Teacher. You have spoken the truth by saying that there is only one God and no other. [33]And I know it is important to love him with all my heart and all my understanding and all my strength, and to love my neighbor as myself. This is more important than to offer all of the burnt offerings and sacrifices required in the law."

[34]Realizing how much the man understood, Jesus said to him, "You are not far from the Kingdom of God." And after that, no one dared to ask him any more questions.

[35]Later, as Jesus was teaching the people in the Temple, he asked, "Why do the teachers of religious law claim that the Messiah is the son of David? [36]For David himself, speaking under the inspiration of the Holy Spirit, said,

'The LORD said to my Lord,
   Sit in the place of honor at my right
      hand
      until I humble your enemies
         beneath your feet.'*

[37]Since David himself called the Messiah 'my Lord,' how can the Messiah be his son?" The large crowd listened to him with great delight.

12:19 See Deut 25:5-6. **12:26a** Greek *in the story of the bush? God said to him.* **12:26b** Exod 3:6. **12:29-30** Deut 6:4-5. **12:31** Lev 19:18. **12:36** Ps 110:1.

PSALM 48:1-14

A song. A psalm of the descendants of Korah.

1 **H**ow great is the LORD,
      how deserving of praise,
   in the city of our God,
      which sits on his holy mountain!
2 It is high and magnificent;
      the whole earth rejoices to see it!
   Mount Zion, the holy mountain,*
      is the city of the great King!
3 God himself is in Jerusalem's
      towers,
      revealing himself as its defender.

4 The kings of the earth joined forces
      and advanced against the city.
5 But when they saw it, they were
      stunned;
      they were terrified and ran away.

⁶ They were gripped with terror
    and writhed in pain like a woman
    in labor.
⁷ You destroyed them like the mighty
    ships of Tarshish
    shattered by a powerful east wind.

⁸ We had heard of the city's glory,
    but now we have seen it ourselves—
    the city of the LORD of Heaven's
    Armies.
It is the city of our God;
    he will make it safe forever.
                                    Interlude

⁹ O God, we meditate on your unfailing
    love
    as we worship in your Temple.
¹⁰ As your name deserves, O God,
    you will be praised to the ends
    of the earth.
    Your strong right hand is filled
    with victory.

¹¹ Let the people on Mount Zion
    rejoice.
    Let all the towns of Judah be
    glad
    because of your justice.

¹² Go, inspect the city of Jerusalem.*
    Walk around and count the many
    towers.
¹³ Take note of the fortified walls,
    and tour all the citadels,
    that you may describe them
    to future generations.
¹⁴ For that is what God is like.
    He is our God forever and ever,
    and he will guide us until we die.

48:2 Or *Mount Zion, in the far north;* Hebrew reads *Mount Zion, the heights of Zaphon.*   48:12 Hebrew *Zion.*

PROVERBS 10:26
Lazy people irritate their employers, like vinegar to the teeth or smoke in the eyes.

MARCH6

NUMBERS 6:1–7:89
Nazirites were Israelite men and women who took very specific vows, setting themselves apart in a special way for God. For the consecration of the Tabernacle, every Israelite family was required to set apart a special offering.

Then the LORD said to Moses, "Give the following instructions to the people of Israel.

²"If any of the people, either men or women, take the special vow of a Nazirite, setting themselves apart to the LORD in a special way, ³ they must give up wine and other alcoholic drinks. They must not use vinegar made from wine or from other alcoholic drinks, they must not drink fresh grape juice, and they must not eat grapes or raisins. ⁴As long as they are bound by their Nazirite vow, they are not allowed to eat or drink anything that comes from a grapevine—not even the grape seeds or skins.

⁵"They must never cut their hair throughout the time of their vow, for they are holy and set apart to the LORD. Until the time of their vow has been fulfilled, they must let their hair grow long. ⁶And they must not go near a dead body during the entire period of their vow to the LORD. ⁷Even if the dead person is their own father, mother, brother, or sister, they must not defile themselves, for the hair on their head is the symbol of their separation to God. ⁸This requirement applies as long as they are set apart to the LORD.

⁹"If someone falls dead beside them, the hair they have dedicated will be defiled. They must wait for seven days and then shave their heads. Then they will be cleansed from their defilement. ¹⁰On the eighth day they must bring two turtledoves or two young pigeons to the priest at the entrance of the Tabernacle.* ¹¹The priest will offer one of the birds for a sin offering and the other for a burnt offering. In this way, he will purify them* from

the guilt they incurred through contact with the dead body. Then they must reaffirm their commitment and let their hair begin to grow again. ¹²The days of their vow that were completed before their defilement no longer count. They must rededicate themselves to the LORD as a Nazirite for the full term of their vow, and each must bring a one-year-old male lamb for a guilt offering.

¹³"This is the ritual law for Nazirites. At the conclusion of their time of separation as Nazirites, they must each go to the entrance of the Tabernacle ¹⁴and offer their sacrifices to the LORD: a one-year-old male lamb without defect for a burnt offering, a one-year-old female lamb without defect for a sin offering, a ram without defect for a peace offering, ¹⁵a basket of bread made without yeast—cakes of choice flour mixed with olive oil and wafers spread with olive oil—along with their prescribed grain offerings and liquid offerings. ¹⁶The priest will present these offerings before the LORD: first the sin offering and the burnt offering; ¹⁷then the ram for a peace offering, along with the basket of bread made without yeast. The priest must also present the prescribed grain offering and liquid offering to the LORD.

¹⁸"Then the Nazirites will shave their heads at the entrance of the Tabernacle. They will take the hair that had been dedicated and place it on the fire beneath the peace-offering sacrifice. ¹⁹After the Nazirite's head has been shaved, the priest will take for each of them the boiled shoulder of the ram, and he will take from the basket a cake and a wafer made without yeast. He will put them all into the Nazirite's hands. ²⁰Then the priest will lift them up as a special offering before the LORD. These are holy portions for the priest, along with the breast of the special offering and the thigh of the sacred offering that are lifted up before the LORD. After this ceremony the Nazirites may again drink wine.

²¹"This is the ritual law of the Nazirites, who vow to bring these offerings to the LORD. They may also bring additional offerings if they can afford it. And they must be careful to do whatever they vowed when they set themselves apart as Nazirites."

²²Then the LORD said to Moses, ²³"Tell Aaron and his sons to bless the people of Israel with this special blessing:

²⁴ 'May the LORD bless you
         and protect you.
²⁵ May the LORD smile on you
         and be gracious to you.
²⁶ May the LORD show you his favor
         and give you his peace.'

²⁷Whenever Aaron and his sons bless the people of Israel in my name, I myself will bless them."

⁷:¹ON the day Moses set up the Tabernacle, he anointed it and set it apart as holy. He also anointed and set apart all its furnishings and the altar with its utensils. ²Then the leaders of Israel—the tribal leaders who had registered the troops—came and brought their offerings. ³Together they brought six large wagons and twelve oxen. There was a wagon for every two leaders and an ox for each leader. They presented these to the LORD in front of the Tabernacle.

⁴Then the LORD said to Moses, ⁵"Receive their gifts, and use these oxen and wagons for transporting the Tabernacle.* Distribute them among the Levites according to the work they have to do." ⁶So Moses took the wagons and oxen and presented them to the Levites. ⁷He gave two wagons and four oxen to the Gershonite division for their work, ⁸and he gave four wagons and eight oxen to the Merarite division for their work. All their work was done under the leadership of Ithamar son of Aaron the priest. ⁹But he gave none of the wagons or oxen to the Kohathite division, since they were required to carry the sacred objects of the Tabernacle on their shoulders.

¹⁰The leaders also presented dedication gifts for the altar at the time it was anointed. They each placed their gifts before the altar. ¹¹The LORD said to Moses, "Let one leader bring his gift each day for the dedication of the altar."

¹²On the first day Nahshon son of Aminadab, leader of the tribe of Judah, presented his offering.

[13]His offering consisted of a silver platter weighing 3¼ pounds and a silver basin weighing 1¾ pounds* (as measured by the weight of the sanctuary shekel). These were both filled with grain offerings of choice flour moistened with olive oil. [14]He also brought a gold container weighing four ounces,* which was filled with incense. [15]He brought a young bull, a ram, and a one-year-old male lamb for a burnt offering, [16]and a male goat for a sin offering. [17]For a peace offering he brought two bulls, five rams, five male goats, and five one-year-old male lambs. This was the offering brought by Nahshon son of Amminadab.

[18]On the second day Nethanel son of Zuar, leader of the tribe of Issachar, presented his offering. [19]His offering consisted of a silver platter weighing 3¼ pounds and a silver basin weighing 1¾ pounds (as measured by the weight of the sanctuary shekel). These were both filled with grain offerings of choice flour moistened with olive oil. [20]He also brought a gold container weighing four ounces, which was filled with incense. [21]He brought a young bull, a ram, and a one-year-old male lamb for a burnt offering, [22]and a male goat for a sin offering. [23]For a peace offering he brought two bulls, five rams, five male goats, and five one-year-old male lambs. This was the offering brought by Nethanel son of Zuar.

[24]On the third day Eliab son of Helon, leader of the tribe of Zebulun, presented his offering. [25]His offering consisted of a silver platter weighing 3¼ pounds and a silver basin weighing 1¾ pounds (as measured by the weight of the sanctuary shekel). These were both filled with grain offerings of choice flour moistened with olive oil. [26]He also brought a gold container weighing four ounces, which was filled with incense. [27]He brought a young bull, a ram, and a one-year-old

male lamb for a burnt offering, [28]and a male goat for a sin offering. [29]For a peace offering he brought two bulls, five rams, five male goats, and five one-year-old male lambs. This was the offering brought by Eliab son of Helon.

[30]On the fourth day Elizur son of Shedeur, leader of the tribe of Reuben, presented his offering. [31]His offering consisted of a silver platter weighing 3¼ pounds and a silver basin weighing 1¾ pounds (as measured by the weight of the sanctuary shekel). These were both filled with grain offerings of choice flour moistened with olive oil. [32]He also brought a gold container weighing four ounces, which was filled with incense. [33]He brought a young bull, a ram, and a one-year-old male lamb for a burnt offering, [34]and a male goat for a sin offering. [35]For a peace offering he brought two bulls, five rams, five male goats, and five one-year-old male lambs. This was the offering brought by Elizur son of Shedeur.

[36]On the fifth day Shelumiel son of Zuri-shaddai, leader of the tribe of Simeon, presented his offering. [37]His offering consisted of a silver platter weighing 3¼ pounds and a silver basin weighing 1¾ pounds (as measured by the weight of the sanctuary shekel). These were both filled with grain offerings of choice flour moistened with olive oil. [38]He also brought a gold container weighing four ounces, which was filled with incense. [39]He brought a young bull, a ram, and a one-year-old male lamb for a burnt offering, [40]and a male goat for a sin offering. [41]For a peace offering he brought two bulls, five rams, five male goats, and five one-year-old male lambs. This was the offering brought by Shelumiel son of Zurishaddai.

[42]On the sixth day Eliasaph son of Deuel, leader of the tribe of Gad, presented his offering.

⁴³His offering consisted of a silver platter weighing 3¼ pounds and a silver basin weighing 1¾ pounds (as measured by the weight of the sanctuary shekel). These were both filled with grain offerings of choice flour moistened with olive oil. ⁴⁴He also brought a gold container weighing four ounces, which was filled with incense. ⁴⁵He brought a young bull, a ram, and a one-year-old male lamb for a burnt offering, ⁴⁶and a male goat for a sin offering. ⁴⁷For a peace offering he brought two bulls, five rams, five male goats, and five one-year-old male lambs. This was the offering brought by Eliasaph son of Deuel.

⁴⁸On the seventh day Elishama son of Ammihud, leader of the tribe of Ephraim, presented his offering.

⁴⁹His offering consisted of a silver platter weighing 3¼ pounds and a silver basin weighing 1¾ pounds (as measured by the weight of the sanctuary shekel). These were both filled with grain offerings of choice flour moistened with olive oil. ⁵⁰He also brought a gold container weighing four ounces, which was filled with incense. ⁵¹He brought a young bull, a ram, and a one-year-old male lamb for a burnt offering, ⁵²and a male goat for a sin offering. ⁵³For a peace offering he brought two bulls, five rams, five male goats, and five one-year-old male lambs. This was the offering brought by Elishama son of Ammihud.

⁵⁴On the eighth day Gamaliel son of Pedahzur, leader of the tribe of Manasseh, presented his offering.

⁵⁵His offering consisted of a silver platter weighing 3¼ pounds and a silver basin weighing 1¾ pounds (as measured by the weight of the sanctuary shekel). These were both filled with grain offerings of choice flour moistened with olive oil. ⁵⁶He also brought a gold container weighing four ounces, which was filled with incense. ⁵⁷He brought a young bull, a ram, and a one-year-old male lamb for a burnt offering, ⁵⁸and a male goat for a sin offering. ⁵⁹For a peace offering he brought two bulls, five rams, five male goats, and five one-year-old male lambs. This was the offering brought by Gamaliel son of Pedahzur.

⁶⁰On the ninth day Abidan son of Gideoni, leader of the tribe of Benjamin, presented his offering.

HOW WE LIVE

Our giving

MARK 12:41-44 Why give to God? It's not that God *needs* your money. God commands his people to give (1) so that their faith will grow as they trust him to meet their needs, (2) so that they will remember that everything they have comes from his generous hand, and (3) to give them the privilege of taking part in God's work in the world. • Jesus commended this widow for giving all she had. This is not to say that you must give all that you have; instead, Jesus was teaching that the value of the gift is not determined by its amount, but by the spirit in which it is given. You give not to be noticed or thanked or honored, but because you want to obey God and do what you can with the financial resources he has given you. • So how much should you give? This is a matter for you to work out personally with the Lord. In Scripture, we see the principle of a "tithe"—that is, a tenth of one's income (Deuteronomy 14:22, March 30). However, God may want you to give less or more than a tenth. Bring your financial situation before the Lord in prayer and ask him to guide you.

61His offering consisted of a silver platter weighing 3¼ pounds and a silver basin weighing 1¾ pounds (as measured by the weight of the sanctuary shekel). These were both filled with grain offerings of choice flour moistened with olive oil. 62He also brought a gold container weighing four ounces, which was filled with incense. 63He brought a young bull, a ram, and a one-year-old male lamb for a burnt offering, 64and a male goat for a sin offering. 65For a peace offering he brought two bulls, five rams, five male goats, and five one-year-old male lambs. This was the offering brought by Abidan son of Gideoni.

66On the tenth day Ahiezer son of Ammishaddai, leader of the tribe of Dan, presented his offering.

67His offering consisted of a silver platter weighing 3¼ pounds and a silver basin weighing 1¾ pounds (as measured by the weight of the sanctuary shekel). These were both filled with grain offerings of choice flour moistened with olive oil. 68He also brought a gold container weighing four ounces, which was filled with incense. 69He brought a young bull, a ram, and a one-year-old male lamb for a burnt offering, 70and a male goat for a sin offering. 71For a peace offering he brought two bulls, five rams, five male goats, and five one-year-old male lambs. This was the offering brought by Ahiezer son of Ammishaddai.

72On the eleventh day Pagiel son of Ocran, leader of the tribe of Asher, presented his offering.

73His offering consisted of a silver platter weighing 3¼ pounds and a silver basin weighing 1¾ pounds (as measured by the weight of the sanctuary shekel). These were both filled with grain offerings of choice flour moistened with olive oil. 74He also brought a gold container weighing four ounces, which was filled with incense. 75He brought a young bull, a ram, and a one-year-old

male lamb for a burnt offering, 76and a male goat for a sin offering. 77For a peace offering he brought two bulls, five rams, five male goats, and five one-year-old male lambs. This was the offering brought by Pagiel son of Ocran.

78On the twelfth day Ahira son of Enan, leader of the tribe of Naphtali, presented his offering.

79His offering consisted of a silver platter weighing 3¼ pounds and a silver basin weighing 1¾ pounds (as measured by the weight of the sanctuary shekel). These were both filled with grain offerings of choice flour moistened with olive oil. 80He also brought a gold container weighing four ounces, which was filled with incense. 81He brought a young bull, a ram, and a one-year-old male lamb for a burnt offering, 82and a male goat for a sin offering. 83For a peace offering he brought two bulls, five rams, five male goats, and five one-year-old male lambs. This was the offering brought by Ahira son of Enan.

84So this was the dedication offering brought by the leaders of Israel at the time the altar was anointed: twelve silver platters, twelve silver basins, and twelve gold incense containers. 85Each silver platter weighed 3¼ pounds, and each silver basin weighed 1¾ pounds. The total weight of the silver was 60 pounds* (as measured by the weight of the sanctuary shekel). 86Each of the twelve gold containers that was filled with incense weighed four ounces (as measured by the weight of the sanctuary shekel). The total weight of the gold was three pounds.* 87Twelve young bulls, twelve rams, and twelve one-year-old male lambs were donated for the burnt offerings, along with their prescribed grain offerings. Twelve male goats were brought for the sin offerings. 88Twenty-four bulls, sixty rams, sixty male goats, and sixty one-year-old male lambs were donated for the peace offerings. This was the dedication offering for the altar after it was anointed.

89Whenever Moses went into the Tabernacle to speak with the LORD, he heard the voice speaking to him from between the two cherubim above the Ark's cover—the place of atonement—that rests on the Ark of the Covenant.* The LORD spoke to him from there.

6:10 Hebrew *the Tent of Meeting;* also in 6:13, 18.   6:11 Or *make atonement for them.*   7:5 Hebrew *the Tent of Meeting;* also in 7:89.   7:13 Hebrew *silver platter weighing 130 shekels* [1.5 kilograms] *and a silver basin weighing 70 shekels* [800 grams]; also in 7:19, 25, 31, 37, 43, 49, 55, 61, 67, 73, 79, 85.   7:14 Hebrew *10 shekels* [114 grams]; also in 7:20, 26, 32, 38, 44, 50, 56, 62, 68, 74, 80, 86.   7:85 Hebrew *2,400 shekels* [27.6 kilograms].   7:86 Hebrew *120 shekels* [1.4 kilograms].   7:89 Or *Ark of the Testimony.*

MARK 12:38–13:13

Jesus had no use for pretension. He told the truth—the hard truth, the mysterious truth, even the truth we don't always understand and are not sure we want to hear. He warned his disciples of difficult days to come.

Jesus also taught: "Beware of these teachers of religious law! For they like to parade around in flowing robes and receive respectful greetings as they walk in the marketplaces. [39]And how they love the seats of honor in the synagogues and the head table at banquets. [40]Yet they shamelessly cheat widows out of their property and then pretend to be pious by making long prayers in public. Because of this, they will be more severely punished."

[41]Jesus sat down near the collection box in the Temple and watched as the crowds dropped in their money. Many rich people put in large amounts. [42]Then a poor widow came and dropped in two small coins.*

[43]Jesus called his disciples to him and said, "I tell you the truth, this poor widow has given more than all the others who are making contributions. [44]For they gave a tiny part of their surplus, but she, poor as she is, has given everything she had to live on."

[13:1]As Jesus was leaving the Temple that day, one of his disciples said, "Teacher, look at these magnificent buildings! Look at the impressive stones in the walls."

[2]Jesus replied, "Yes, look at these great buildings. But they will be completely demolished. Not one stone will be left on top of another!"

[3]Later, Jesus sat on the Mount of Olives across the valley from the Temple. Peter, James, John, and Andrew came to him privately and asked him, [4]"Tell us, when will all this happen? What sign will show us that these things are about to be fulfilled?"

[5]Jesus replied, "Don't let anyone mislead you, [6]for many will come in my name, claiming, 'I am the Messiah.'* They will deceive many. [7]And you will hear of wars and threats of wars, but don't panic. Yes, these things must take place, but the end won't follow immediately. [8]Nation will go to war against nation, and kingdom against kingdom. There will be earthquakes in many parts of the world, as well as famines. But this is only the first of the birth pains, with more to come.

[9]"When these things begin to happen, watch out! You will be handed over to the local councils and beaten in the synagogues. You will stand trial before governors and kings because you are my followers. But this will be your opportunity to tell them about me.* [10]For the Good News must first be preached to all nations.* [11]But when you are arrested and stand trial, don't worry in advance about what to say. Just say what God tells you at that time, for it is not you who will be speaking, but the Holy Spirit.

[12]"A brother will betray his brother to death, a father will betray his own child, and children will rebel against their parents and cause them to be killed. [13]And everyone will hate you because you are my followers.* But the one who endures to the end will be saved."

12:42 Greek *two lepta, which is a kodrantes* [i.e., a quadrans]. 13:6 Greek *claiming, 'I am.'*   13:9 Or *But this will be your testimony against them.*   13:10 Or *all peoples.* 13:13 Greek *on account of my name.*

PSALM 49:1-20

For the choir director: A psalm of the descendants of Korah.

[1] Listen to this, all you people!
   Pay attention, everyone in the world!
[2] High and low,
   rich and poor—listen!
[3] For my words are wise,
   and my thoughts are filled within sight.
[4] I listen carefully to many proverbs

and solve riddles with inspiration
from a harp.

5 Why should I fear when trouble
comes,
when enemies surround me?
6 They trust in their wealth
and boast of great riches.
7 Yet they cannot redeem themselves
from death*
by paying a ransom to God.
8 Redemption does not come so easily,
for no one can ever pay enough
9 to live forever
and never see the grave.

10 Those who are wise must finally die,
just like the foolish and senseless,
leaving all their wealth behind.
11 The grave is their eternal home,
where they will stay forever.
They may name their estates after
themselves,
12 but their fame will not last.
They will die, just like animals.
13 This is the fate of fools,
though they are remembered
as being wise.*   *Interlude*

14 Like sheep, they are led to the grave,*
where death will be their shepherd.
In the morning the godly will rule over
them.

Their bodies will rot in the grave,
far from their grand estates.
15 But as for me, God will redeem my life.
He will snatch me from the power
of the grave.   *Interlude*

16 So don't be dismayed when the wicked
grow rich
and their homes become ever more
splendid.
17 For when they die, they take nothing
with them.
Their wealth will not follow them
into the grave.
18 In this life they consider themselves
fortunate
and are applauded for their success.
19 But they will die like all before them
and never again see the light of day.
20 People who boast of their wealth don't
understand;
they will die, just like animals.

49:7 Or *no one can redeem the life of another.*   **49:13** The
meaning of the Hebrew is uncertain.   **49:14** Hebrew *Sheol;*
also in 49:14b, 15.

PROVERBS 10:27-28

Fear of the LORD lengthens one's life,
but the years of the wicked are cut short.
□ The hopes of the godly result in happiness, but the expectations of the wicked
come to nothing.

MARCH**7**

NUMBERS 8:1–9:23
The people remembered God's deliverance and
provision by celebrating the Passover feast and
dedicating their tribe of priests. God's presence
was with them, guiding them hour by hour.

The LORD said to Moses, 2"Give Aaron the
following instructions: When you set up
the seven lamps in the lampstand, place
them so their light shines forward in front
of the lampstand." 3So Aaron did this. He
set up the seven lamps so they reflected
their light forward, just as the LORD had
commanded Moses. 4The entire lampstand, from its base to its decorative blos-

soms, was made of beaten gold. It was
built according to the exact design the
LORD had shown Moses.
5Then the LORD said to Moses, 6"Now
set the Levites apart from the rest of the
people of Israel and make them ceremonially clean. 7Do this by sprinkling them
with the water of purification, and have
them shave their entire body and wash
their clothing. Then they will be ceremonially clean. 8Have them bring a young
bull and a grain offering of choice flour
moistened with olive oil, along with a second young bull for a sin offering. 9Then

assemble the whole community of Israel, and present the Levites at the Tabernacle.* ¹⁰When you present the Levites before the LORD, the people of Israel must lay their hands on them. ¹¹Raising his hands, Aaron must then present the Levites to the LORD as a special offering from the people of Israel, thus dedicating them to the LORD's service.

¹²"Next the Levites will lay their hands on the heads of the young bulls. Present one as a sin offering and the other as a burnt offering to the LORD, to purify the Levites and make them right with the LORD.* ¹³Then have the Levites stand in front of Aaron and his sons, and raise your hands and present them as a special offering to the LORD. ¹⁴In this way, you will set the Levites apart from the rest of the people of Israel, and the Levites will belong to me. ¹⁵After this, they may go into the Tabernacle to do their work, because you have purified them and presented them as a special offering.

¹⁶"Of all the people of Israel, the Levites are reserved for me. I have claimed them for myself in place of all the firstborn sons of the Israelites; I have taken the Levites as their substitutes. ¹⁷For all the firstborn males among the people of Israel are mine, both of people and of animals. I set them apart for myself on the day I struck down all the firstborn sons of the Egyptians. ¹⁸Yes, I have claimed the Levites in place of all the firstborn sons of Israel. ¹⁹And of all the Israelites, I have assigned the Levites to Aaron and his sons. They will serve in the Tabernacle on behalf of the Israelites and make sacrifices to purify* the people so no plague will strike them when they approach the sanctuary."

²⁰So Moses, Aaron, and the whole community of Israel dedicated the Levites, carefully following all the LORD's instructions to Moses. ²¹The Levites purified themselves from sin and washed their clothes, and Aaron lifted them up and presented them to the LORD as a special offering. He then offered a sacrifice to purify them and make them right with the LORD.* ²²After that the Levites went into the Tabernacle to perform their duties, assisting Aaron and his sons. So they

carried out all the commands that the LORD gave Moses concerning the Levites.

²³The LORD also instructed Moses, ²⁴"This is the rule the Levites must follow: They must begin serving in the Tabernacle at the age of twenty-five, ²⁵and they must retire at the age of fifty. ²⁶After retirement they may assist their fellow Levites by serving as guards at the Tabernacle, but they may not officiate in the service. This is how you must assign duties to the Levites."

9:1A YEAR after Israel's departure from Egypt, the LORD spoke to Moses in the wilderness of Sinai. In the first month* of that year he said, ²"Tell the Israelites to celebrate the Passover at the prescribed time, ³at twilight on the fourteenth day of the first month.* Be sure to follow all my decrees and regulations concerning this celebration."

⁴So Moses told the people to celebrate the Passover ⁵in the wilderness of Sinai as twilight fell on the fourteenth day of the month. And they celebrated the festival there, just as the LORD had commanded Moses. ⁶But some of the men had been ceremonially defiled by touching a dead body, so they could not celebrate the Passover that day. They came to Moses and Aaron that day ⁷and said, "We have become ceremonially unclean by touching a dead body. But why should we be prevented from presenting the LORD's offering at the proper time with the rest of the Israelites?"

⁸Moses answered, "Wait here until I have received instructions for you from the LORD."

⁹This was the LORD's reply to Moses. ¹⁰"Give the following instructions to the people of Israel: If any of the people now or in future generations are ceremonially unclean at Passover time because of touching a dead body, or if they are on a journey and cannot be present at the ceremony, they may still celebrate the LORD's Passover. ¹¹They must offer the Passover sacrifice one month later, at twilight on the fourteenth day of the second month.* They must eat the Passover lamb at that time with bitter salad greens and bread made without yeast. ¹²They must not leave any of the lamb until the next morning,

and they must not break any of its bones. They must follow all the normal regulations concerning the Passover.

¹³"But those who neglect to celebrate the Passover at the regular time, even though they are ceremonially clean and not away on a trip, will be cut off from the community of Israel. If they fail to present the LORD's offering at the proper time, they will suffer the consequences of their guilt. ¹⁴And if foreigners living among you want to celebrate the Passover to the LORD, they must follow these same decrees and regulations. The same laws apply both to native-born Israelites and to the foreigners living among you."

¹⁵On the day the Tabernacle was set up, the cloud covered it.* But from evening until morning the cloud over the Tabernacle looked like a pillar of fire. ¹⁶This was the regular pattern—at night the cloud that covered the Tabernacle had the appearance of fire. ¹⁷Whenever the cloud lifted from over the sacred tent, the people of Israel would break camp and follow it. And wherever the cloud settled, the people of Israel would set up camp. ¹⁸In this way, they traveled and camped at the LORD's command wherever he told them to go. Then they remained in their camp as long as the cloud stayed over the Tabernacle. ¹⁹If the cloud remained over the Tabernacle for a long time, the Israelites stayed and performed their duty to the LORD. ²⁰Sometimes the cloud would stay over the Tabernacle for only a few days, so the people would stay for only a few days, as the LORD commanded. Then at the LORD's command they would break camp and move on. ²¹Sometimes the cloud stayed only overnight and lifted the next morning. But day or night, when the cloud lifted, the people broke camp and moved on. ²²Whether the cloud stayed above the Tabernacle for two days, a month, or a year, the people of Israel stayed in camp and did not move on. But as soon as it lifted, they broke camp and moved on. ²³So they camped or traveled at the LORD's command, and they did whatever the LORD told them through Moses.

8:9 Hebrew *the Tent of Meeting;* also in 8:15, 19, 22, 24, 26.
8:12 Or *to make atonement for the Levites.* 8:19 Or *make*

atonement for. 8:21 Or *then made atonement for them to purify them.* 9:1 The first month of the ancient Hebrew lunar calendar usually occurs within the months of March and April. 9:3 This day in the ancient Hebrew lunar calendar occurred in late March, April, or early May. 9:11 This day in the ancient Hebrew lunar calendar occurred in late April, May, or early June. 9:15 Hebrew *covered the Tabernacle, the Tent of the Testimony.*

MARK 13:14-37

No one knows when, but just as summer follows spring, all of what Jesus described here will come to pass.

"The day is coming when you will see the sacrilegious object that causes desecration* standing where he* should not be." (Reader, pay attention!) "Then those in Judea must flee to the hills. ¹⁵A person out on the deck of a roof must not go down into the house to pack. ¹⁶A person out in the field must not return even to get a coat. ¹⁷How terrible it will be for pregnant women and for nursing mothers in those days. ¹⁸And pray that your flight will not be in winter. ¹⁹For there will be greater anguish in those days than at any time since God created the world. And it will never be so great again. ²⁰In fact, unless the Lord shortens that time of calamity, not a single person will survive. But for the sake of his chosen ones he has shortened those days.

²¹"Then if anyone tells you, 'Look, here is the Messiah,' or 'There he is,' don't believe it. ²²For false messiahs and false prophets will rise up and perform signs and wonders so as to deceive, if possible, even God's chosen ones. ²³Watch out! I have warned you about this ahead of time!

²⁴"At that time, after the anguish of those days,

the sun will be darkened,
    the moon will give no light,
²⁵ the stars will fall from the sky,
    and the powers in the heavens will
        be shaken.*

²⁶Then everyone will see the Son of Man* coming on the clouds with great power and glory.* ²⁷And he will send out his angels to gather his chosen ones from all over the world*—from the farthest ends of the earth and heaven.

²⁸"Now learn a lesson from the fig tree.

When its branches bud and its leaves begin to sprout, you know that summer is near. [29]In the same way, when you see all these things taking place, you can know that his return is very near, right at the door. [30]I tell you the truth, this generation* will not pass from the scene before all these things take place. [31]Heaven and earth will disappear, but my words will never disappear.

[32]"However, no one knows the day or hour when these things will happen, not even the angels in heaven or the Son himself. Only the Father knows. [33]And since you don't know when that time will come, be on guard! Stay alert*!

[34]"The coming of the Son of Man can be illustrated by the story of a man going on a long trip. When he left home, he gave each of his slaves instructions about the work they were to do, and he told the gatekeeper to watch for his return. [35]You, too, must keep watch! For you don't know when the master of the household will return—in the evening, at midnight, before dawn, or at daybreak. [36]Don't let him find you sleeping when he arrives without warning. [37]I say to you what I say to everyone: Watch for him!"

13:14a Greek *the abomination of desolation*. See Dan 9:27; 11:31; 12:11. **13:14b** Or *it*. **13:24-25** See Isa 13:10; 34:4; Joel 2:10. **13:26a** "Son of Man" is a title Jesus used for himself. **13:26b** See Dan 7:13. **13:27** Greek *from the four winds*. **13:30** Or *this age*, or *this nation*. **13:33** Some manuscripts add *and pray*.

PSALM 50:1-23
A psalm of Asaph.

[1] **T**he LORD, the Mighty One, is God,
    and he has spoken;
he has summoned all humanity
    from where the sun rises to where
        it sets.
[2] From Mount Zion, the perfection
        of beauty,
    God shines in glorious radiance.
[3] Our God approaches,
    and he is not silent.
Fire devours everything in his way,
    and a great storm rages around him.
[4] He calls on the heavens above and
        earth below
    to witness the judgment of his
        people.
[5] "Bring my faithful people to me—
    those who made a covenant with
        me by giving sacrifices."
[6] Then let the heavens proclaim his
        justice,
    for God himself will be the judge.
                              Interlude

[7] "O my people, listen as I speak.
    Here are my charges against you,
        O Israel:
    I am God, your God!
[8] I have no complaint about your
        sacrifices
    or the burnt offerings you
        constantly offer.

Seeking God's will

NUMBERS 9:15-17 The uncertainties of a journey through the wilderness to Canaan were placated by the divine leadership of God. Whatever the situation, the nation of Israel moved in the direction of God's visible leadership. This manifestation of God was miraculous, but his guidance is not limited to the Old Testament. Thanks to the sacrifice and resurrection of Jesus, God now provides a form of leadership to all believers through the Holy Spirit. On the day of Pentecost, God sent his Holy Spirit to live within every believer. • As a Christian, you have the Holy Spirit inside you. When you seek the guidance of God, you may not receive a visible answer, like a moving pillar of cloud or fire. But he still promises to guide you. That guidance may come through reading his Word, a sermon, or the wise words of a Christian friend. God has made you a promise: "The Lord says, 'I will guide you along the best pathway for your life. I will advise you and watch over you'" (Psalm 32:8, February 10).

⁹ But I do not need the bulls from your
   barns
   or the goats from your pens.
¹⁰ For all the animals of the forest are
   mine,
   and I own the cattle on a thousand
   hills.
¹¹ I know every bird on the mountains,
   and all the animals of the field are
   mine.
¹² If I were hungry, I would not tell you,
   for all the world is mine and
   everything in it.
¹³ Do I eat the meat of bulls?
   Do I drink the blood of goats?
¹⁴ Make thankfulness your sacrifice
   to God,
   and keep the vows you made
   to the Most High.
¹⁵ Then call on me when you are
   in trouble,
   and I will rescue you,
   and you will give me glory."

¹⁶ But God says to the wicked:
   "Why bother reciting my decrees
   and pretending to obey my
   covenant?
¹⁷ For you refuse my discipline
   and treat my words like trash.

¹⁸ When you see thieves, you approve
   of them,
   and you spend your time with
   adulterers.
¹⁹ Your mouth is filled with wickedness,
   and your tongue is full of lies.
²⁰ You sit around and slander your
   brother—
   your own mother's son.
²¹ While you did all this, I remained
   silent,
   and you thought I didn't care.
   But now I will rebuke you,
   listing all my charges against you.
²² Repent, all of you who forget me,
   or I will tear you apart,
   and no one will help you.
²³ But giving thanks is a sacrifice that
   truly honors me.
   If you keep to my path,
   I will reveal to you the salvation
   of God."

PROVERBS 10:29-30

The way of the LORD is a stronghold to
those with integrity, but it destroys the
wicked. □ The godly will never be disturbed, but the wicked will be removed
from the land.

MARCH**8**

NUMBERS 10:1-11:23

God led the people through the desert and
provided for their needs. Yet, what happened?
They grumbled and complained. "The miracle
food you've sent isn't good enough; we want meat."

Now the LORD said to Moses, ²"Make two
trumpets of hammered silver for calling
the community to assemble and for signaling the breaking of camp. ³ When both
trumpets are blown, everyone must
gather before you at the entrance of the
Tabernacle.* ⁴ But if only one trumpet is
blown, then only the leaders—the heads
of the clans of Israel—must present themselves to you.

⁵ "When you sound the signal to move

on, the tribes camped on the east side of
the Tabernacle must break camp and
move forward. ⁶ When you sound the signal a second time, the tribes camped on
the south will follow. You must sound
short blasts as the signal for moving on.
⁷ But when you call the people to an assembly, blow the trumpets with a different signal. ⁸ Only the priests, Aaron's
descendants, are allowed to blow the
trumpets. This is a permanent law for
you, to be observed from generation to
generation.

⁹ "When you arrive in your own land
and go to war against your enemies who
attack you, sound the alarm with the

trumpets. Then the LORD your God will remember you and rescue you from your enemies. [10]Blow the trumpets in times of gladness, too, sounding them at your annual festivals and at the beginning of each month. And blow the trumpets over your burnt offerings and peace offerings. The trumpets will remind the LORD your God of his covenant with you. I am the LORD your God."

[11]In the second year after Israel's departure from Egypt—on the twentieth day of the second month*—the cloud lifted from the Tabernacle of the Covenant.* [12]So the Israelites set out from the wilderness of Sinai and traveled on from place to place until the cloud stopped in the wilderness of Paran.

[13]When the people set out for the first time, following the instructions the LORD had given through Moses, [14]Judah's troops led the way. They marched behind their banner, and their leader was Nahshon son of Amminadab. [15]They were joined by the troops of the tribe of Issachar, led by Nethanel son of Zuar, [16]and the troops of the tribe of Zebulun, led by Eliab son of Helon.

[17]Then the Tabernacle was taken down, and the Gershonite and Merarite divisions of the Levites were next in the line of march, carrying the Tabernacle with them. [18]Reuben's troops went next, marching behind their banner. Their leader was Elizur son of Shedeur. [19]They were joined by the troops of the tribe of Simeon, led by Shelumiel son of Zurishaddai, [20]and the troops of the tribe of Gad, led by Eliasaph son of Deuel.

[21]Next came the Kohathite division of the Levites, carrying the sacred objects from the Tabernacle. Before they arrived at the next camp, the Tabernacle would already be set up at its new location. [22]Ephraim's troops went next, marching behind their banner. Their leader was Elishama son of Ammihud. [23]They were joined by the troops of the tribe of Manasseh, led by Gamaliel son of Pedahzur, [24]and the troops of the tribe of Benjamin, led by Abidan son of Gideoni.

[25]Dan's troops went last, marching behind their banner and serving as the rear guard for all the tribal camps. Their leader was Ahiezer son of Ammishaddai. [26]They were joined by the troops of the tribe of Asher, led by Pagiel son of Ocran, [27]and the troops of the tribe of Naphtali, led by Ahira son of Enan.

[28]This was the order in which the Israelites marched, division by division.

[29]One day Moses said to his brother-in-law, Hobab son of Reuel the Midianite, "We are on our way to the place the LORD promised us, for he said, 'I will give it to you.' Come with us and we will treat you well, for the LORD has promised wonderful blessings for Israel!"

[30]But Hobab replied, "No, I will not go. I must return to my own land and family."

[31]"Please don't leave us," Moses pleaded. "You know the places in the wilderness where we should camp. Come, be our guide. [32]If you do, we'll share with you all the blessings the LORD gives us."

[33]They marched for three days after leaving the mountain of the LORD, with the Ark of the LORD's Covenant moving ahead of them to show them where to stop and rest. [34]As they moved on each day, the cloud of the LORD hovered over them. [35]And whenever the Ark set out, Moses would shout, "Arise, O LORD, and let your enemies be scattered! Let them flee before you!" [36]And when the Ark was set down, he would say, "Return, O LORD, to the countless thousands of Israel!"

[11:1]SOON the people began to complain about their hardship, and the LORD heard everything they said. Then the LORD's anger blazed against them, and he sent a fire to rage among them, and he destroyed some of the people in the outskirts of the camp. [2]Then the people screamed to Moses for help, and when he prayed to the LORD, the fire stopped. [3]After that, the area was known as Taberah (which means "the place of burning"), because fire from the LORD had burned among them there.

[4]Then the foreign rabble who were traveling with the Israelites began to crave the good things of Egypt. And the people of Israel also began to complain. "Oh, for some meat!" they exclaimed. [5]"We remember the fish we used to eat for free in Egypt. And we had all the cucumbers, melons, leeks, onions, and garlic we

wanted. ⁶But now our appetites are gone. All we ever see is this manna!"

⁷The manna looked like small coriander seeds, and it was pale yellow like gum resin. ⁸The people would go out and gather it from the ground. They made flour by grinding it with hand mills or pounding it in mortars. Then they boiled it in a pot and made it into flat cakes. These cakes tasted like pastries baked with olive oil. ⁹The manna came down on the camp with the dew during the night.

¹⁰Moses heard all the families standing in the doorways of their tents whining, and the LORD became extremely angry. Moses was also very aggravated. ¹¹And Moses said to the LORD, "Why are you treating me, your servant, so harshly? Have mercy on me! What did I do to deserve the burden of all these people? ¹²Did I give birth to them? Did I bring them into the world? Why did you tell me to carry them in my arms like a mother carries a nursing baby? How can I carry them to the land you swore to give their ancestors? ¹³Where am I supposed to get meat for all these people? They keep whining to me, saying, 'Give us meat to eat!' ¹⁴I can't carry all these people by myself! The load is far too heavy! ¹⁵If this is how you intend to treat me, just go ahead and kill me. Do me a favor and spare me this misery!"

¹⁶Then the LORD said to Moses, "Gather before me seventy men who are recognized as elders and leaders of Israel. Bring them to the Tabernacle* to stand there with you. ¹⁷I will come down and talk to you there. I will take some of the Spirit that is upon you, and I will put the Spirit upon them also. They will bear the burden of the people along with you, so you will not have to carry it alone.

¹⁸"And say to the people, 'Purify yourselves, for tomorrow you will have meat to eat. You were whining, and the LORD heard you when you cried, "Oh, for some meat! We were better off in Egypt!" Now the LORD will give you meat, and you will have to eat it. ¹⁹And it won't be for just a day or two, or for five or ten or even twenty. ²⁰You will eat it for a whole month until you gag and are sick of it. For you have rejected the LORD, who is here

among you, and you have whined to him, saying, "Why did we ever leave Egypt?"'"

²¹But Moses responded to the LORD, "There are 600,000 foot soldiers here with me, and yet you say, 'I will give them meat for a whole month!' ²²Even if we butchered all our flocks and herds, would that satisfy them? Even if we caught all the fish in the sea, would that be enough?"

²³Then the LORD said to Moses, "Has my arm lost its power? Now you will see whether or not my word comes true!"

10:3 Hebrew *Tent of Meeting*.   **10:11a** This day in the ancient Hebrew lunar calendar occurred in late April, May, or early June.   **10:11b** Or *Tabernacle of the Testimony*.   **11:16** Hebrew *the Tent of Meeting*.

MARK 14:1-21

Was this woman's anointing of Jesus the most practical use for the expensive perfume? The most cost effective? Worship isn't about those things. It's about pleasing the heart of God by giving our best.

It was now two days before Passover and the Festival of Unleavened Bread. The leading priests and the teachers of religious law were still looking for an opportunity to capture Jesus secretly and kill him. ²"But not during the Passover celebration," they agreed, "or the people may riot."

³Meanwhile, Jesus was in Bethany at the home of Simon, a man who had previously had leprosy. While he was eating,* a woman came in with a beautiful alabaster jar of expensive perfume made from essence of nard. She broke open the jar and poured the perfume over his head.

⁴Some of those at the table were indignant. "Why waste such expensive perfume?" they asked. ⁵"It could have been sold for a year's wages* and the money given to the poor!" So they scolded her harshly.

⁶But Jesus replied, "Leave her alone. Why criticize her for doing such a good thing to me? ⁷You will always have the poor among you, and you can help them whenever you want to. But you will not always have me. ⁸She has done what she could and has anointed my body for burial ahead of time. ⁹I tell you the truth, wherever the Good News is preached throughout the world, this woman's deed will be remembered and discussed."

¹⁰Then Judas Iscariot, one of the twelve disciples, went to the leading priests to arrange to betray Jesus to them. ¹¹They were delighted when they heard why he had come, and they promised to give him money. So he began looking for an opportunity to betray Jesus.

¹²On the first day of the Festival of Unleavened Bread, when the Passover lamb is sacrificed, Jesus' disciples asked him, "Where do you want us to go to prepare the Passover meal for you?"

¹³So Jesus sent two of them into Jerusalem with these instructions: "As you go into the city, a man carrying a pitcher of water will meet you. Follow him. ¹⁴At the house he enters, say to the owner, 'The Teacher asks: Where is the guest room where I can eat the Passover meal with my disciples?' ¹⁵He will take you upstairs to a large room that is already set up. That is where you should prepare our meal." ¹⁶So the two disciples went into the city and found everything just as Jesus had said, and they prepared the Passover meal there.

¹⁷In the evening Jesus arrived with the twelve disciples.* ¹⁸As they were at the table* eating, Jesus said, "I tell you the truth, one of you eating with me here will betray me."

¹⁹Greatly distressed, each one asked in turn, "Am I the one?"

²⁰He replied, "It is one of you twelve who is eating from this bowl with me. ²¹For the Son of Man* must die, as the Scriptures declared long ago. But how terrible it will be for the one who betrays him. It would be far better for that man if he had never been born!"

14:3 Or *reclining.* 14:5 Greek *for 300 denarii.* A denarius was equivalent to a laborer's full day's wage. 14:17 Greek *the Twelve.* 14:18 Or *As they reclined.* 14:21 "Son of Man" is a title Jesus used for himself.

PSALM 51:1-19

For the choir director: A psalm of David, regarding the time Nathan the prophet came to him after David had committed adultery with Bathsheba.

¹ **H**ave mercy on me, O God,
  because of your unfailing love.
Because of your great compassion,
  blot out the stain of my sins.
² Wash me clean from my guilt.
  Purify me from my sin.
³ For I recognize my rebellion;
  it haunts me day and night.
⁴ Against you, and you alone, have
    I sinned;
  I have done what is evil in your
    sight.

WHAT THE BIBLE SAYS

Sin and its consequences

PSALM 51:9-12   King David wrote this psalm after Nathan the prophet had come to inform him of God's judgment. David had committed adultery with Bathsheba. Upon discovering that Bathsheba was pregnant, David took measures to cover it up. One thing led to another, and eventually David had Bathsheba's husband murdered (2 Samuel 11–12, May 26–27). • That's the problem with sin. It's a downward spiral that, once begun, is difficult to stop. So often we can justify our actions to ourselves, or we think that we can do what we want as long as it doesn't seem to hurt anyone else. Even more, we may think that no one will ever know what we've done. However, God knocks all of those excuses out of the way. We cannot justify sin. Sin always hurts someone, and God always knows what we've done, even if no one else does. • You are a believer, but you are still going to sin every day. That's part of the battle you'll face until you get to heaven. That's why you need to stay close to God. He can make you aware of the sin so that you can repent and be forgiven.

You will be proved right in what
you say,
and your judgment against me
is just.*
5 For I was born a sinner—
yes, from the moment my mother
conceived me.
6 But you desire honesty from the
womb,*
teaching me wisdom even there.

7 Purify me from my sins,* and I will
be clean;
wash me, and I will be whiter than
snow.
8 Oh, give me back my joy again;
you have broken me—
now let me rejoice.
9 Don't keep looking at my sins.
Remove the stain of my guilt.
10 Create in me a clean heart, O God.
Renew a loyal spirit within me.
11 Do not banish me from your
presence,
and don't take your Holy Spirit*
from me.

12 Restore to me the joy of your salvation,
and make me willing to
obey you.
13 Then I will teach your ways to rebels,
and they will return to you.
14 Forgive me for shedding blood,
O God who saves;

then I will joyfully sing of your
forgiveness.
15 Unseal my lips, O Lord,
that my mouth may praise you.

16 You do not desire a sacrifice, or
I would offer one.
You do not want a burnt
offering.
17 The sacrifice you desire is a broken
spirit.
You will not reject a broken and
repentant heart, O God.
18 Look with favor on Zion and
help her;
rebuild the walls of Jerusalem.
19 Then you will be pleased with
sacrifices offered in the right
spirit—
with burnt offerings and whole
burnt offerings.
Then bulls will again be sacrificed
on your altar.

51:4 Greek version reads *and you will win your case in
court.* Compare Rom 3:4. 51:6 Or *from the heart;* Hebrew
reads *in the inward parts.* 51:7 Hebrew *Purify me with the
hyssop branch.* 51:11 Or *your spirit of holiness.*

PROVERBS 10:31-32
The mouth of the godly person gives
wise advice, but the tongue that deceives
will be cut off. □ The lips of the godly
speak helpful words, but the mouth of the
wicked speaks perverse words.

MARCH9

NUMBERS 11:24-13:33
Here the humility of Moses is in contrast to the pride
of his brother and sister and the stubbornness of the
people, as they refuse to believe that God will ensure
their success in conquering the Promised Land.

So Moses went out and reported the
LORD's words to the people. He gathered
the seventy elders and stationed them
around the Tabernacle.* 25And the LORD
came down in the cloud and spoke to
Moses. Then he gave the seventy elders
the same Spirit that was upon Moses.
And when the Spirit rested upon them,

they prophesied. But this never happened
again.
26Two men, Eldad and Medad, had
stayed behind in the camp. They were
listed among the elders, but they had not
gone out to the Tabernacle. Yet the Spirit
rested upon them as well, so they prophesied there in the camp. 27A young man ran
and reported to Moses, "Eldad and Medad
are prophesying in the camp!"
28Joshua son of Nun, who had been
Moses' assistant since his youth, protested,
"Moses, my master, make them stop!"

[29]But Moses replied, "Are you jealous for my sake? I wish that all the LORD's people were prophets and that the LORD would put his Spirit upon them all!" [30]Then Moses returned to the camp with the elders of Israel.

[31]Now the LORD sent a wind that brought quail from the sea and let them fall all around the camp. For miles in every direction there were quail flying about three feet above the ground.* [32]So the people went out and caught quail all that day and throughout the night and all the next day, too. No one gathered less than fifty bushels*! They spread the quail all around the camp to dry. [33]But while they were gorging themselves on the meat—while it was still in their mouths—the anger of the LORD blazed against the people, and he struck them with a severe plague. [34]So that place was called Kibroth-hattaavah (which means "graves of gluttony") because there they buried the people who had craved meat from Egypt. [35]From Kibroth-hattaavah the Israelites traveled to Hazeroth, where they stayed for some time.

[12:1]WHILE they were at Hazeroth, Miriam and Aaron criticized Moses because he had married a Cushite woman. [2]They said, "Has the LORD spoken only through Moses? Hasn't he spoken through us, too?" But the LORD heard them. [3](Now Moses was very humble—more humble than any other person on earth.)

[4]So immediately the LORD called to Moses, Aaron, and Miriam and said, "Go out to the Tabernacle,* all three of you!" So the three of them went to the Tabernacle. [5]Then the LORD descended in the pillar of cloud and stood at the entrance of the Tabernacle.* "Aaron and Miriam!" he called, and they stepped forward. [6]And the LORD said to them, "Now listen to what I say:

"If there were prophets among you,
I, the LORD, would reveal myself
in visions.
I would speak to them in dreams.
[7] But not with my servant Moses.
Of all my house, he is the one
I trust.
[8] I speak to him face to face,
clearly, and not in riddles!
He sees the LORD as he is.

So why were you not afraid
to criticize my servant Moses?"

[9]The LORD was very angry with them, and he departed. [10]As the cloud moved from above the Tabernacle, there stood Miriam, her skin as white as snow from leprosy.* When Aaron saw what had happened to her, [11]he cried out to Moses, "Oh, my master! Please don't punish us for this sin we have so foolishly committed. [12]Don't let her be like a stillborn baby, already decayed at birth."

[13]So Moses cried out to the LORD, "O God, I beg you, please heal her!"

[14]But the LORD said to Moses, "If her father had done nothing more than spit in her face, wouldn't she be defiled for seven days? So keep her outside the camp for seven days, and after that she may be accepted back."

[15]So Miriam was kept outside the camp for seven days, and the people waited until she was brought back before they traveled again. [16]Then they left Hazeroth and camped in the wilderness of Paran.

[13:1]THE LORD now said to Moses, [2]"Send out men to explore the land of Canaan, the land I am giving to the Israelites. Send one leader from each of the twelve ancestral tribes." [3]So Moses did as the LORD commanded him. He sent out twelve men, all tribal leaders of Israel, from their camp in the wilderness of Paran. [4]These were the tribes and the names of their leaders:

Tribe	Leader
Reuben	Shammua son of Zaccur
[5] Simeon	Shaphat son of Hori
[6] Judah	Caleb son of Jephunneh
[7] Issachar	Igal son of Joseph
[8] Ephraim	Hoshea son of Nun
[9] Benjamin	Palti son of Raphu
[10] Zebulun	Gaddiel son of Sodi
[11] Manasseh son of Joseph	Gaddi son of Susi
[12] Dan	Ammiel son of Gemalli
[13] Asher	Sethur son of Michael
[14] Naphtali	Nahbi son of Vophsi
[15] Gad	Geuel son of Maki

[16]These are the names of the men Moses sent out to explore the land. (Moses called Hoshea son of Nun by the name Joshua.)

¹⁷Moses gave the men these instructions as he sent them out to explore the land: "Go north through the Negev into the hill country. ¹⁸See what the land is like, and find out whether the people living there are strong or weak, few or many. ¹⁹See what kind of land they live in. Is it good or bad? Do their towns have walls, or are they unprotected like open camps? ²⁰Is the soil fertile or poor? Are there many trees? Do your best to bring back samples of the crops you see." (It happened to be the season for harvesting the first ripe grapes.)

²¹So they went up and explored the land from the wilderness of Zin as far as Rehob, near Lebo-hamath. ²²Going north, they passed through the Negev and arrived at Hebron, where Ahiman, Sheshai, and Talmai—all descendants of Anak—lived. (The ancient town of Hebron was founded seven years before the Egyptian city of Zoan.) ²³When they came to the valley of Eshcol, they cut down a branch with a single cluster of grapes so large that it took two of them to carry it on a pole between them! They also brought back samples of the pomegranates and figs. ²⁴That place was called the valley of Eshcol (which means "cluster"), because of the cluster of grapes the Israelite men cut there.

²⁵After exploring the land for forty days, the men returned ²⁶to Moses, Aaron, and the whole community of Israel at Kadesh in the wilderness of Paran. They reported to the whole community what they had seen and showed them the fruit they had taken from the land. ²⁷This was their report to Moses: "We entered the land you sent us to explore, and it is indeed a bountiful country—a land flowing with milk and honey. Here is the kind of fruit it produces. ²⁸But the people living there are powerful, and their towns are large and fortified. We even saw giants there, the descendants of Anak! ²⁹The Amalekites live in the Negev, and the Hittites, Jebusites, and Amorites live in the hill country. The Canaanites live along the coast of the Mediterranean Sea* and along the Jordan Valley."

³⁰But Caleb tried to quiet the people as they stood before Moses. "Let's go at once to take the land," he said. "We can certainly conquer it!"

³¹But the other men who had explored the land with him disagreed. "We can't go up against them! They are stronger than we are!" ³²So they spread this bad report about the land among the Israelites: "The land we traveled through and explored will devour anyone who goes to live there. All the people we saw were huge. ³³We even saw giants* there, the descendants of Anak. Next to them we felt like grasshoppers, and that's what they thought, too!"

11:24 Hebrew *the tent;* also in 11:26.   11:31 Or *there were quail 3 feet* [2 cubits or 92 centimeters] *deep on the ground.*   11:32 Hebrew *10 homers* [1.8 kiloliters].   12:4 Hebrew *the Tent of Meeting.*   12:5 Hebrew *the tent;* also in 12:10.   12:10 Or *with a skin disease.* The Hebrew word used here can describe various skin diseases.   13:29 Hebrew *the sea.*   13:33 Hebrew *nephilim.*

MARK 14:22-52
The theme of spiritual pride also appears in this New Testament passage. Peter was sure that he would not desert Jesus, even if everyone else did. What a contrast his bragging was to Jesus' humble acceptance of God's will for his life—and death.

As they were eating, Jesus took some bread and blessed it. Then he broke it in pieces and gave it to the disciples, saying, "Take it, for this is my body."

²³And he took a cup of wine and gave thanks to God for it. He gave it to them, and they all drank from it. ²⁴And he said to them, "This is my blood, which confirms the covenant* between God and his people. It is poured out as a sacrifice for many. ²⁵I tell you the truth, I will not drink wine again until the day I drink it new in the Kingdom of God."

²⁶Then they sang a hymn and went out to the Mount of Olives.

²⁷On the way, Jesus told them, "All of you will desert me. For the Scriptures say,

'God will strike* the Shepherd,
    and the sheep will be scattered.'

²⁸But after I am raised from the dead, I will go ahead of you to Galilee and meet you there."

²⁹Peter said to him, "Even if everyone else deserts you, I never will."

³⁰Jesus replied, "I tell you the truth, Peter—this very night, before the rooster

crows twice, you will deny three times that you even know me."

[31]"No!" Peter declared emphatically. "Even if I have to die with you, I will never deny you!" And all the others vowed the same.

[32]They went to the olive grove called Gethsemane, and Jesus said, "Sit here while I go and pray." [33]He took Peter, James, and John with him, and he became deeply troubled and distressed. [34]He told them, "My soul is crushed with grief to the point of death. Stay here and keep watch with me."

[35]He went on a little farther and fell to the ground. He prayed that, if it were possible, the awful hour awaiting him might pass him by. [36]"Abba, Father,"* he cried out, "everything is possible for you. Please take this cup of suffering away from me. Yet I want your will to be done, not mine."

[37]Then he returned and found the disciples asleep. He said to Peter, "Simon, are you asleep? Couldn't you watch with me even one hour? [38]Keep watch and pray, so that you will not give in to temptation. For the spirit is willing, but the body is weak."

[39]Then Jesus left them again and prayed the same prayer as before. [40]When he returned to them again, he found them sleeping, for they couldn't keep their eyes open. And they didn't know what to say.

[41]When he returned to them the third time, he said, "Go ahead and sleep. Have your rest. But no—the time has come. The Son of Man is betrayed into the hands of sinners. [42]Up, let's be going. Look, my betrayer is here!"

[43]And immediately, even as Jesus said this, Judas, one of the twelve disciples, arrived with a crowd of men armed with swords and clubs. They had been sent by the leading priests, the teachers of religious law, and the elders. [44]The traitor, Judas, had given them a prearranged signal: "You will know which one to arrest when I greet him with a kiss. Then you can take him away under guard." [45]As soon as they arrived, Judas walked up to Jesus. "Rabbi!" he exclaimed, and gave him the kiss.

[46]Then the others grabbed Jesus and arrested him. [47]But one of the men with Jesus pulled out his sword and struck the high priest's slave, slashing off his ear.

[48]Jesus asked them, "Am I some dangerous revolutionary, that you come with swords and clubs to arrest me? [49]Why didn't you arrest me in the Temple? I was there among you teaching every day. But these things are happening to fulfill what the Scriptures say about me."

[50]Then all his disciples deserted him and ran away. [51]One young man following behind was clothed only in a long linen shirt. When the mob tried to grab

Seeking God's will

HOW WE LIVE

MARK 14:35-36 Was Jesus trying to get out of what lay before him when he prayed, "Please take this cup of suffering away from me"? No, but he was expressing his human emotions—his aversion to the pain, torture, and suffering that would be the end result of his obedience to God's will. In his prayer, Jesus was aware of what doing the Father's will would cost him, but he also saw beyond the horrible experience of crucifixion and recognized that this was part of the plan from the beginning of time. He would take on the sins of the entire world in order to bring us salvation. His death would give us life. • Anything worth having costs something, but sometimes that cost is difficult for us to handle. What should you do when you seek God's will and don't like what you hear? Jesus gave us an example in this passage. First, pray. Second, seek support from other believers. They may have a more objective viewpoint and can offer good advice. Third, focus on the purpose God has given to you. You have to be willing to not only seek his will but to follow it as well.

him, [52]he slipped out of his shirt and ran away naked.

14:24 Some manuscripts read *the new covenant.* **14:27** Greek *I will strike.* Zech 13:7. **14:36** *Abba* is an Aramaic term for "father."

PSALM 52:1-9

For the choir director: A psalm* of David, regarding the time Doeg the Edomite said to Saul, "David has gone to see Ahimelech."

[1] **W**hy do you boast about your crimes, great warrior?
Don't you realize God's justice continues forever?

[2] All day long you plot destruction.
Your tongue cuts like a sharp razor;
you're an expert at telling lies.

[3] You love evil more than good
and lies more than truth.   *Interlude*

[4] You love to destroy others with your words,
you liar!

[5] But God will strike you down once and for all.
He will pull you from your home
and uproot you from the land of the living.   *Interlude*

[6] The righteous will see it and be amazed.
They will laugh and say,

[7] "Look what happens to mighty warriors
who do not trust in God.
They trust their wealth instead
and grow more and more bold
in their wickedness."

[8] But I am like an olive tree, thriving
in the house of God.
I will always trust in God's unfailing love.

[9] I will praise you forever, O God,
for what you have done.
I will trust in your good name
in the presence of your faithful people.

52:TITLE Hebrew *maskil.* This may be a literary or musical term.

PROVERBS 11:1-3

[1] **T**he LORD detests the use of dishonest scales, but he delights in accurate weights. □ Pride leads to disgrace, but with humility comes wisdom. □ Honesty guides good people; dishonesty destroys treacherous people.

MARCH**10**

NUMBERS 14:1-15:16

Taking the Promised Land would not be for the faint-hearted, and faint-hearted is what the people were. They would get their wish: only two from this generation would be allowed to enter the land.

[1] **T**hen the whole community began weeping aloud, and they cried all night. [2] Their voices rose in a great chorus of protest against Moses and Aaron. "If only we had died in Egypt, or even here in the wilderness!" they complained. [3]"Why is the LORD taking us to this country only to have us die in battle? Our wives and our little ones will be carried off as plunder! Wouldn't it be better for us to return to Egypt?" [4]Then they plotted among themselves, "Let's choose a new leader and go back to Egypt!"

[5] Then Moses and Aaron fell face down on the ground before the whole community of Israel. [6]Two of the men who had explored the land, Joshua son of Nun and Caleb son of Jephunneh, tore their clothing. [7] They said to all the people of Israel, "The land we traveled through and explored is a wonderful land! [8]And if the LORD is pleased with us, he will bring us safely into that land and give it to us. It is a rich land flowing with milk and honey. [9]Do not rebel against the LORD, and don't be afraid of the people of the land. They are only helpless prey to us! They have no protection, but the LORD is with us! Don't be afraid of them!"

[10]But the whole community began to talk about stoning Joshua and Caleb. Then

the glorious presence of the LORD appeared to all the Israelites at the Tabernacle.* [11]And the LORD said to Moses, "How long will these people treat me with contempt? Will they never believe me, even after all the miraculous signs I have done among them? [12]I will disown them and destroy them with a plague. Then I will make you into a nation greater and mightier than they are!"

[13]But Moses objected. "What will the Egyptians think when they hear about it?" he asked the LORD. "They know full well the power you displayed in rescuing your people from Egypt. [14]Now if you destroy them, the Egyptians will send a report to the inhabitants of this land, who have already heard that you live among your people. They know, LORD, that you have appeared to your people face to face and that your pillar of cloud hovers over them. They know that you go before them in the pillar of cloud by day and the pillar of fire by night. [15]Now if you slaughter all these people with a single blow, the nations that have heard of your fame will say, [16]'The LORD was not able to bring them into the land he swore to give them, so he killed them in the wilderness.'

[17]"Please, Lord, prove that your power is as great as you have claimed. For you said, [18]'The LORD is slow to anger and filled with unfailing love, forgiving every kind of sin and rebellion. But he does not excuse the guilty. He lays the sins of the parents upon their children; the entire family is affected—even children in the third and fourth generations.' [19]In keeping with your magnificent, unfailing love, please pardon the sins of this people, just as you have forgiven them ever since they left Egypt."

[20]Then the LORD said, "I will pardon them as you have requested. [21]But as surely as I live, and as surely as the earth is filled with the LORD's glory, [22]not one of these people will ever enter that land. They have all seen my glorious presence and the miraculous signs I performed both in Egypt and in the wilderness, but again and again they have tested me by refusing to listen to my voice. [23]They will never even see the land I swore to give their ancestors. None of those who have treated me with contempt will ever see it.

[24]But my servant Caleb has a different attitude than the others have. He has remained loyal to me, so I will bring him into the land he explored. His descendants will possess their full share of that land. [25]Now turn around, and don't go on toward the land where the Amalekites and Canaanites live. Tomorrow you must set out for the wilderness in the direction of the Red Sea.*"

[26]Then the LORD said to Moses and Aaron, [27]"How long must I put up with this wicked community and its complaints about me? Yes, I have heard the complaints the Israelites are making against me. [28]Now tell them this: 'As surely as I live, declares the LORD, I will do to you the very things I heard you say. [29]You will all drop dead in this wilderness! Because you complained against me, every one of you who is twenty years old or older and was included in the registration will die. [30]You will not enter and occupy the land I swore to give you. The only exceptions will be Caleb son of Jephunneh and Joshua son of Nun.

[31]" 'You said your children would be carried off as plunder. Well, I will bring them safely into the land, and they will enjoy what you have despised. [32]But as for you, you will drop dead in this wilderness. [33]And your children will be like shepherds, wandering in the wilderness for forty years. In this way, they will pay for your faithlessness, until the last of you lies dead in the wilderness.

[34]" 'Because your men explored the land for forty days, you must wander in the wilderness for forty years—a year for each day, suffering the consequences of your sins. Then you will discover what it is like to have me for an enemy.' [35]I, the LORD, have spoken! I will certainly do these things to every member of the community who has conspired against me. They will be destroyed here in this wilderness, and here they will die!"

[36]The ten men Moses had sent to explore the land—the ones who incited rebellion against the LORD with their bad report—[37]were struck dead with a plague before the LORD. [38]Of the twelve who had explored the land, only Joshua and Caleb remained alive.

³⁹When Moses reported the LORD's words to all the Israelites, the people were filled with grief. ⁴⁰Then they got up early the next morning and went to the top of the range of hills. "Let's go," they said. "We realize that we have sinned, but now we are ready to enter the land the LORD has promised us."

⁴¹But Moses said, "Why are you now disobeying the LORD's orders to return to the wilderness? It won't work. ⁴²Do not go up into the land now. You will only be crushed by your enemies because the LORD is not with you. ⁴³When you face the Amalekites and Canaanites in battle, you will be slaughtered. The LORD will abandon you because you have abandoned the LORD."

⁴⁴But the people defiantly pushed ahead toward the hill country, even though neither Moses nor the Ark of the LORD's Covenant left the camp. ⁴⁵Then the Amalekites and the Canaanites who lived in those hills came down and attacked them and chased them back as far as Hormah.

15:¹THEN the LORD told Moses, ²"Give the following instructions to the people of Israel.

"When you finally settle in the land I am giving you, ³you will offer special gifts as a pleasing aroma to the LORD. These gifts may take the form of a burnt offering, a sacrifice to fulfill a vow, a voluntary offering, or an offering at any of your annual festivals, and they may be taken from your herds of cattle or your flocks of sheep and goats. ⁴When you present these offerings, you must also give the LORD a grain offering of two quarts* of choice flour mixed with one quart* of olive oil. ⁵For each lamb offered as a burnt offering or a special sacrifice, you must also present one quart of wine as a liquid offering.

⁶"If the sacrifice is a ram, give a grain offering of four quarts* of choice flour mixed with a third of a gallon* of olive oil, ⁷and give a third of a gallon of wine as a liquid offering. This will be a pleasing aroma to the LORD.

⁸"When you present a young bull as a burnt offering or as a sacrifice to fulfill a

vow or as a peace offering to the LORD, ⁹you must also give a grain offering of six quarts* of choice flour mixed with two quarts* of olive oil, ¹⁰and give two quarts of wine as a liquid offering. This will be a special gift, a pleasing aroma to the LORD.

¹¹"Each sacrifice of a bull, ram, lamb, or young goat should be prepared in this way. ¹²Follow these instructions with each offering you present. ¹³All of you native-born Israelites must follow these instructions when you offer a special gift as a pleasing aroma to the LORD. ¹⁴And if any foreigners visit you or live among you and want to present a special gift as a pleasing aroma to the LORD, they must follow these same procedures. ¹⁵Native-born Israelites and foreigners are equal before the LORD and are subject to the same decrees. This is a permanent law for you, to be observed from generation to generation. ¹⁶The same instructions and regulations will apply both to you and to the foreigners living among you."

14:10 Hebrew *the Tent of Meeting.*   **14:25** Hebrew *sea of reeds.*   **15:4a** Hebrew *¹⁄₁₀ of an ephah* [2.2 liters].
15:4b Hebrew *¼ of a hin* [1 liter]; also in 15:5.
15:6a Hebrew *³⁄₁₀ of an ephah* [4.4 liters].   **15:6b** Hebrew *⅓ of a hin* [1.3 liters]; also in 15:7.   **15:9a** Hebrew *³⁄₁₀ of an ephah* [6.6 liters].   **15:9b** Hebrew *½ of a hin* [2 liters]; also in 15:10.

MARK 14:53-72

For a Jewish court, there was no higher crime than blasphemy, which included claiming equality with God. Jesus' claim was clear: he was the Son of God. Blasphemy to the hard-hearted religious hypocrites; good news to the world.

They took Jesus to the high priest's home where the leading priests, the elders, and the teachers of religious law had gathered. ⁵⁴Meanwhile, Peter followed him at a distance and went right into the high priest's courtyard. There he sat with the guards, warming himself by the fire.

⁵⁵Inside, the leading priests and the entire high council* were trying to find evidence against Jesus, so they could put him to death. But they couldn't find any. ⁵⁶Many false witnesses spoke against him, but they contradicted each other. ⁵⁷Finally, some men stood up and gave this false testimony: ⁵⁸"We heard him say, 'I will destroy this Temple made with human hands, and in three days I will build

another, made without human hands.' " ⁵⁹But even then they didn't get their stories straight!

⁶⁰Then the high priest stood up before the others and asked Jesus, "Well, aren't you going to answer these charges? What do you have to say for yourself?" ⁶¹But Jesus was silent and made no reply. Then the high priest asked him, "Are you the Messiah, the Son of the Blessed One?"

⁶²Jesus said, "I AM.* And you will see the Son of Man seated in the place of power at God's right hand* and coming on the clouds of heaven.*"

⁶³Then the high priest tore his clothing to show his horror and said, "Why do we need other witnesses? ⁶⁴You have all heard his blasphemy. What is your verdict?"

"Guilty!" they all cried. "He deserves to die!"

⁶⁵Then some of them began to spit at him, and they blindfolded him and beat him with their fists. "Prophesy to us," they jeered. And the guards slapped him as they took him away.

⁶⁶Meanwhile, Peter was in the courtyard below. One of the servant girls who worked for the high priest came by ⁶⁷and noticed Peter warming himself at the fire. She looked at him closely and said, "You were one of those with Jesus of Nazareth.*"

⁶⁸But Peter denied it. "I don't know what you're talking about," he said, and he went out into the entryway. Just then, a rooster crowed.*

⁶⁹When the servant girl saw him standing there, she began telling the others, "This man is definitely one of them!" ⁷⁰But Peter denied it again.

A little later some of the other bystanders confronted Peter and said, "You must be one of them, because you are a Galilean."

⁷¹Peter swore, "A curse on me if I'm lying—I don't know this man you're talking about!" ⁷²And immediately the rooster crowed the second time.

Suddenly, Jesus' words flashed through Peter's mind: "Before the rooster crows twice, you will deny three times that you even know me." And he broke down and wept.

14:55 Greek *the Sanhedrin.* **14:62a** Or *The 'I AM' is here;* or *I am the LORD.* See Exod 3:14. **14:62b** Greek *at the right hand of the power.* See Ps 110:1. **14:62c** See Dan 7:13. **14:67** Or *Jesus the Nazarene.* **14:68** Some manuscripts do not include *Just then, a rooster crowed.*

PSALM 53:1-6
For the choir director: A meditation; a psalm* of David.

¹ **O**nly fools say in their hearts,
    "There is no God."

HOW WE LIVE | Trusting God

NUMBERS 14:2-4 Days prior, spies saw the Promised Land and came back with a report of giants and walled cities. Two of the spies, Joshua and Caleb, trusted God and told the people, "The LORD is with us! Don't be afraid of them!" (14:9). The other spies were so afraid that they gave a pessimistic report to the people. As a result, the Israelites decided that they would have been better off in Egypt! • It may seem strange that the Israelites refused to believe that God would give them the land he promised them after seeing God send plagues on Egypt, part the Red Sea, and send manna from heaven. Yet how often do we tend to lose perspective in the same way? We trust God to handle certain issues, but then one comes along that seems insurmountable, and we get paralyzed by fear and anxiety. We allow our emotions to take control, and we forget to trust the One who has led us, protected us, and kept his promises. • When you face a seemingly insurmountable situation, don't stop trusting in God. He brought you this far, and he's not about to let you down.

They are corrupt, and their actions are
evil;
not one of them does good!

2 God looks down from heaven
on the entire human race;
he looks to see if anyone is truly wise,
if anyone seeks God.
3 But no, all have turned away;
all have become corrupt.*
No one does good,
not a single one!

4 Will those who do evil never learn?
They eat up my people like bread
and wouldn't think of praying to God.
5 Terror will grip them,
terror like they have never known
before.

God will scatter the bones of your
enemies.
You will put them to shame, for God
has rejected them.

6 Who will come from Mount Zion to
rescue Israel?
When God restores his people,
Jacob will shout with joy, and Israel
will rejoice.

53:TITLE Hebrew *maskil*. This may be a literary or musical
term.   **53:3** Greek version reads *have become useless*.
Compare Rom 3:12.

PROVERBS 11:4
Riches won't help on the day of judgment, but right living can save you from
death.

MARCH**11**

NUMBERS 15:17–16:40
God's commands were reasonable, yet individuals
and groups continued to flaunt them, revealing
deep-seated selfishness and arrogance. Moses left
their fate to God, and all the people witnessed the
results.

Then the LORD said to Moses, [18]"Give the
following instructions to the people of
Israel.

"When you arrive in the land where I
am taking you, [19]and you eat the crops
that grow there, you must set some aside
as a sacred offering to the LORD. [20]Pre-
sent a cake from the first of the flour you
grind, and set it aside as a sacred offering,
as you do with the first grain from the
threshing floor. [21]Throughout the generations to come, you are to present a sacred
offering to the LORD each year from the
first of your ground flour.

[22]"But suppose you unintentionally fail
to carry out all these commands that the
LORD has given you through Moses. [23]And
suppose your descendants in the future
fail to do everything the LORD has commanded through Moses. [24]If the mistake
was made unintentionally, and the community was unaware of it, the whole com-

munity must present a young bull for a
burnt offering as a pleasing aroma to the
LORD. It must be offered along with its
prescribed grain offering and liquid offering and with one male goat for a sin offering. [25]With it the priest will purify the
whole community of Israel, making them
right with the LORD,* and they will be forgiven. For it was an unintentional sin, and
they have corrected it with their offerings
to the LORD—the special gift and the sin
offering. [26]The whole community of Israel will be forgiven, including the foreigners living among you, for all the people
were involved in the sin.

[27]"If one individual commits an unintentional sin, the guilty person must bring
a one-year-old female goat for a sin offering. [28]The priest will sacrifice it to purify*
the guilty person before the LORD, and
that person will be forgiven. [29]These
same instructions apply both to native-
born Israelites and to the foreigners living
among you.

[30]"But those who brazenly violate the
LORD's will, whether native-born Israelites or foreigners, have blasphemed the

LORD, and they must be cut off from the community. ³¹Since they have treated the LORD's word with contempt and deliberately disobeyed his command, they must be completely cut off and suffer the punishment for their guilt."

³²One day while the people of Israel were in the wilderness, they discovered a man gathering wood on the Sabbath day. ³³The people who found him doing this took him before Moses, Aaron, and the rest of the community. ³⁴They held him in custody because they did not know what to do with him. ³⁵Then the LORD said to Moses, "The man must be put to death! The whole community must stone him outside the camp." ³⁶So the whole community took the man outside the camp and stoned him to death, just as the LORD had commanded Moses.

³⁷Then the LORD said to Moses, ³⁸"Give the following instructions to the people of Israel: Throughout the generations to come you must make tassels for the hems of your clothing and attach them with a blue cord. ³⁹When you see the tassels, you will remember and obey all the commands of the LORD instead of following your own desires and defiling yourselves, as you are prone to do. ⁴⁰The tassels will help you remember that you must obey all my commands and be holy to your God. ⁴¹I am the LORD your God who brought you out of the land of Egypt that I might be your God. I am the LORD your God!"

¹⁶:¹ONE day Korah son of Izhar, a descendant of Kohath son of Levi, conspired with Dathan and Abiram, the sons of Eliab, and On son of Peleth, from the tribe of Reuben. ²They incited a rebellion against Moses, along with 250 other leaders of the community, all prominent members of the assembly. ³They united against Moses and Aaron and said, "You have gone too far! The whole community of Israel has been set apart by the LORD, and he is with all of us. What right do you have to act as though you are greater than the rest of the LORD's people?"

⁴When Moses heard what they were saying, he fell face down on the ground. ⁵Then he said to Korah and his followers, "Tomorrow morning the LORD will show

us who belongs to him* and who is holy. The LORD will allow only those whom he selects to enter his own presence. ⁶Korah, you and all your followers must prepare your incense burners. ⁷Light fires in them tomorrow, and burn incense before the LORD. Then we will see whom the LORD chooses as his holy one. You Levites are the ones who have gone too far!"

⁸Then Moses spoke again to Korah: "Now listen, you Levites! ⁹Does it seem insignificant to you that the God of Israel has chosen you from among all the community of Israel to be near him so you can serve in the LORD's Tabernacle and stand before the people to minister to them? ¹⁰Korah, he has already given this special ministry to you and your fellow Levites. Are you now demanding the priesthood as well? ¹¹The LORD is the one you and your followers are really revolting against! For who is Aaron that you are complaining about him?"

¹²Then Moses summoned Dathan and Abiram, the sons of Eliab, but they replied, "We refuse to come before you! ¹³Isn't it enough that you brought us out of Egypt, a land flowing with milk and honey, to kill us here in this wilderness, and that you now treat us like your subjects? ¹⁴What's more, you haven't brought us into another land flowing with milk and honey. You haven't given us a new homeland with fields and vineyards. Are you trying to fool these men?* We will not come."

¹⁵Then Moses became very angry and said to the LORD, "Do not accept their grain offerings! I have not taken so much as a donkey from them, and I have never hurt a single one of them." ¹⁶And Moses said to Korah, "You and all your followers must come here tomorrow and present yourselves before the LORD. Aaron will also be here. ¹⁷You and each of your 250 followers must prepare an incense burner and put incense on it, so you can all present them before the LORD. Aaron will also bring his incense burner."

¹⁸So each of these men prepared an incense burner, lit the fire, and placed incense on it. Then they all stood at the entrance of the Tabernacle* with Moses and Aaron. ¹⁹Meanwhile, Korah had stirred up

the entire community against Moses and Aaron, and they all gathered at the Tabernacle entrance. Then the glorious presence of the LORD appeared to the whole community, [20]and the LORD said to Moses and Aaron, [21]"Get away from all these people so that I may instantly destroy them!"

[22]But Moses and Aaron fell face down on the ground. "O God," they pleaded, "you are the God who gives breath to all creatures. Must you be angry with all the people when only one man sins?"

[23]And the LORD said to Moses, [24]"Then tell all the people to get away from the tents of Korah, Dathan, and Abiram."

[25]So Moses got up and rushed over to the tents of Dathan and Abiram, followed by the elders of Israel. [26]"Quick!" he told the people. "Get away from the tents of these wicked men, and don't touch anything that belongs to them. If you do, you will be destroyed for their sins." [27]So all the people stood back from the tents of Korah, Dathan, and Abiram. Then Dathan and Abiram came out and stood at the entrances of their tents, together with their wives and children and little ones.

[28]And Moses said, "This is how you will know that the LORD has sent me to do all these things that I have done—for I have not done them on my own. [29]If these men die a natural death, or if nothing unusual happens, then the LORD has not sent me. [30]But if the LORD does something entirely new and the ground opens its mouth and swallows them and all their belongings, and they go down alive into the grave,* then you will know that these men have shown contempt for the LORD."

[31]He had hardly finished speaking the words when the ground suddenly split open beneath them. [32]The earth opened its mouth and swallowed the men, along with their households and all their followers who were standing with them, and everything they owned. [33]So they went down alive into the grave, along with all their belongings. The earth closed over them, and they all vanished from among the people of Israel. [34]All the people around them fled when they heard their screams. "The earth will swallow us, too!" they cried. [35]Then fire blazed forth from

the LORD and burned up the 250 men who were offering incense.

[36]*And the LORD said to Moses, [37]"Tell Eleazar son of Aaron the priest to pull all the incense burners from the fire, for they are holy. Also tell him to scatter the burning coals. [38]Take the incense burners of these men who have sinned at the cost of their lives, and hammer the metal into a thin sheet to overlay the altar. Since these burners were used in the LORD's presence, they have become holy. Let them serve as a warning to the people of Israel."

[39]So Eleazar the priest collected the 250 bronze incense burners that had been used by the men who died in the fire, and he hammered them into a thin sheet to overlay the altar. [40]This would warn the Israelites that no unauthorized person—no one who was not a descendant of Aaron—should ever enter the LORD's presence to burn incense. If anyone did, the same thing would happen to him as happened to Korah and his followers. So the LORD's instructions to Moses were carried out.

15:25 Or *will make atonement for the whole community of Israel.* 15:28 Or *to make atonement for.* 16:5 Greek version reads *God has visited and knows those who are his.* Compare 2 Tim 2:19. 16:14 Hebrew *Are you trying to put out the eyes of these men?* 16:18 Hebrew *the Tent of Meeting;* also in 16:19, 42, 43, 50. 16:30 Hebrew *into Sheol;* also in 16:33. 16:36 Verses 16:36-50 are numbered 17:1-15 in Hebrew text.

MARK 15:1-47

From a religious court under a high priest, Jesus was taken to a civil court under a governor named Pilate. From this court, a death sentence could be passed down, which was what the accusers had in mind all along.

Very early in the morning the leading priests, the elders, and the teachers of religious law—the entire high council*—met to discuss their next step. They bound Jesus, led him away, and took him to Pilate, the Roman governor.

[2]Pilate asked Jesus, "Are you the king of the Jews?"

Jesus replied, "You have said it."

[3]Then the leading priests kept accusing him of many crimes, [4]and Pilate asked him, "Aren't you going to answer them? What about all these charges they are

bringing against you?" [5]But Jesus said nothing, much to Pilate's surprise.

[6]Now it was the governor's custom each year during the Passover celebration to release one prisoner—anyone the people requested. [7]One of the prisoners at that time was Barabbas, a revolutionary who had committed murder in an uprising. [8]The crowd went to Pilate and asked him to release a prisoner as usual.

[9]"Would you like me to release to you this 'King of the Jews'?" Pilate asked. [10](For he realized by now that the leading priests had arrested Jesus out of envy.) [11]But at this point the leading priests stirred up the crowd to demand the release of Barabbas instead of Jesus. [12]Pilate asked them, "Then what should I do with this man you call the king of the Jews?"

[13]They shouted back, "Crucify him!"

[14]"Why?" Pilate demanded. "What crime has he committed?"

But the mob roared even louder, "Crucify him!"

[15]So to pacify the crowd, Pilate released Barabbas to them. He ordered Jesus flogged with a lead-tipped whip, then turned him over to the Roman soldiers to be crucified.

[16]The soldiers took Jesus into the courtyard of the governor's headquarters (called the Praetorium) and called out the entire regiment. [17]They dressed him in a purple robe, and they wove thorn branches into a crown and put it on his head. [18]Then they saluted him and taunted, "Hail! King of the Jews!" [19]And they struck him on the head with a reed stick, spit on him, and dropped to their knees in mock worship. [20]When they were finally tired of mocking him, they took off the purple robe and put his own clothes on him again. Then they led him away to be crucified.

[21]A passerby named Simon, who was from Cyrene,* was coming in from the countryside just then, and the soldiers forced him to carry Jesus' cross. (Simon was the father of Alexander and Rufus.) [22]And they brought Jesus to a place called Golgotha (which means "Place of the Skull"). [23]They offered him wine drugged with myrrh, but he refused it.

[24]Then the soldiers nailed him to the cross. They divided his clothes and threw dice* to decide who would get each piece. [25]It was nine o'clock in the morning when they crucified him. [26]A sign was fastened to the cross, announcing the charge against him. It read, "The King of the Jews." [27]Two revolutionaries* were crucified with him, one on his right and one on his left.*

[29]The people passing by shouted abuse, shaking their heads in mockery. "Ha! Look at you now!" they yelled at him. "You said

WHAT THE BIBLE SAYS

Jesus on the cross

MARK 15:34 The Bible teaches that Jesus was both fully human and fully God. As a human, Jesus let himself be subject to the suffering and temptations of this world, yet he remained perfectly sinless through it all.
• Only as a human could Jesus truly experience death. God temporarily removed his power from Jesus and allowed him to die. At that moment Jesus cried out, "My God, my God, why have you abandoned me?" The spiritual burden of carrying the sins of the whole world coupled with the physical burden of extreme pain caused him to cry out to God for help, quoting Psalm 22:1 (see January 26). On the brink of death, tortured physically and spiritually, Jesus was focused on God, calling out for deliverance. And in that moment, God turned away, allowing Jesus to bear the punishment for sin that we deserved. • Three days later, however, Jesus rose from the dead, defeating sin and death forever. Jesus was abandoned, but only for a moment. He is now in heaven at the right hand of God. One day he will bring us to be with him forever.

you were going to destroy the Temple and rebuild it in three days. [30]Well then, save yourself and come down from the cross!"

[31]The leading priests and teachers of religious law also mocked Jesus. "He saved others," they scoffed, "but he can't save himself! [32]Let this Messiah, this King of Israel, come down from the cross so we can see it and believe him!" Even the men who were crucified with Jesus ridiculed him.

[33]At noon, darkness fell across the whole land until three o'clock. [34]Then at three o'clock Jesus called out with a loud voice, *"Eloi, Eloi, lema sabachthani?"* which means "My God, my God, why have you abandoned me?"*

[35]Some of the bystanders misunderstood and thought he was calling for the prophet Elijah. [36]One of them ran and filled a sponge with sour wine, holding it up to him on a reed stick so he could drink. "Wait!" he said. "Let's see whether Elijah comes to take him down!"

[37]Then Jesus uttered another loud cry and breathed his last. [38]And the curtain in the sanctuary of the Temple was torn in two, from top to bottom.

[39]When the Roman officer* who stood facing him* saw how he had died, he exclaimed, "This man truly was the Son of God!"

[40]Some women were there, watching from a distance, including Mary Magdalene, Mary (the mother of James the younger and of Joseph*), and Salome. [41]They had been followers of Jesus and had cared for him while he was in Galilee. Many other women who had come with him to Jerusalem were also there.

[42]This all happened on Friday, the day of preparation,* the day before the Sabbath. As evening approached, [43]Joseph of Arimathea took a risk and went to Pilate and asked for Jesus' body. (Joseph was an honored member of the high council, and he was waiting for the Kingdom of God to come.) [44]Pilate couldn't believe that Jesus was already dead, so he called for the Roman officer and asked if he had died yet. [45]The officer confirmed that Jesus was dead, so Pilate told Joseph he could have the body. [46]Joseph bought a long sheet of linen cloth. Then he took Jesus' body

down from the cross, wrapped it in the cloth, and laid it in a tomb that had been carved out of the rock. Then he rolled a stone in front of the entrance. [47]Mary Magdalene and Mary the mother of Joseph saw where Jesus' body was laid.

15:1 Greek *the Sanhedrin;* also in 15:43.   **15:21** *Cyrene* was a city in northern Africa.   **15:24** Greek *cast lots.* See Ps 22:18.   **15:27a** Or *Two criminals.*   **15:27b** Some manuscripts add verse 28, *And the Scripture was fulfilled that said, "He was counted among those who were rebels."* See Isa 53:12; also compare Luke 22:37.   **15:34** Ps 22:1.   **15:39a** Greek *the centurion;* similarly in 15:44, 45.   **15:39b** Some manuscripts add *heard his cry and.*   **15:40** Greek *Joses;* also in 15:47. See Matt 27:56.   **15:42** Greek *It was the day of preparation.*

PSALM 54:1-7

For the choir director: A psalm of David, regarding the time the Ziphites came and said to Saul, "We know where David is hiding." To be accompanied by stringed instruments.*

[1] **C**ome with great power, O God,
      and rescue me!
   Defend me with your might.
[2] Listen to my prayer, O God.
   Pay attention to my plea.
[3] For strangers are attacking me;
      violent people are trying to kill me.
   They care nothing for God.

Interlude

[4] But God is my helper.
   The Lord keeps me alive!
[5] May the evil plans of my enemies be
      turned against them.
   Do as you promised and put an end
      to them.

[6] I will sacrifice a voluntary offering
      to you;
   I will praise your name, O LORD,
      for it is good.
[7] For you have rescued me from my
      troubles
   and helped me to triumph over
      my enemies.

54:TITLE Hebrew *maskil.* This may be a literary or musical term.

PROVERBS 11:5-6

The godly are directed by honesty; the wicked fall beneath their load of sin.
□ The godliness of good people rescues them; the ambition of treacherous people traps them.

NUMBERS 16:41–18:32

The people continued to grumble. God showed them beyond a shadow of a doubt that Moses and Aaron were his choice to lead the people.

But the very next morning the whole community of Israel began muttering again against Moses and Aaron, saying, "You have killed the LORD's people!" 42As the community gathered to protest against Moses and Aaron, they turned toward the Tabernacle and saw that the cloud had covered it, and the glorious presence of the LORD appeared.

43Moses and Aaron came and stood in front of the Tabernacle, 44and the LORD said to Moses, 45"Get away from all these people so that I can instantly destroy them!" But Moses and Aaron fell face down on the ground.

46And Moses said to Aaron, "Quick, take an incense burner and place burning coals on it from the altar. Lay incense on it, and carry it out among the people to purify them and make them right with the LORD.* The LORD's anger is blazing against them—the plague has already begun."

47Aaron did as Moses told him and ran out among the people. The plague had already begun to strike down the people, but Aaron burned the incense and purified* the people. 48He stood between the dead and the living, and the plague stopped. 49But 14,700 people died in that plague, in addition to those who had died in the affair involving Korah. 50Then because the plague had stopped, Aaron returned to Moses at the entrance of the Tabernacle.

17:1*THEN the LORD said to Moses, 2"Tell the people of Israel to bring you twelve wooden staffs, one from each leader of Israel's ancestral tribes, and inscribe each leader's name on his staff. 3Inscribe Aaron's name on the staff of the tribe of Levi, for there must be one staff for the leader of each ancestral tribe. 4Place these staffs in the Tabernacle in front of the Ark containing the tablets of the Covenant,* where I meet with you. 5Buds will sprout on the staff belonging to the man I choose. Then I will finally put an end to the people's murmuring and complaining against you."

6So Moses gave the instructions to the people of Israel, and each of the twelve tribal leaders, including Aaron, brought Moses a staff. 7Moses placed the staffs in the LORD's presence in the Tabernacle of the Covenant.* 8When he went into the Tabernacle of the Covenant the next day, he found that Aaron's staff, representing the tribe of Levi, had sprouted, budded, blossomed, and produced ripe almonds!

9When Moses brought all the staffs out from the LORD's presence, he showed them to the people. Each man claimed his own staff. 10And the LORD said to Moses: "Place Aaron's staff permanently before the Ark of the Covenant* to serve as a warning to rebels. This should put an end to their complaints against me and prevent any further deaths." 11So Moses did as the LORD commanded him.

12Then the people of Israel said to Moses, "Look, we are doomed! We are dead! We are ruined! 13Everyone who even comes close to the Tabernacle of the LORD dies. Are we all doomed to die?"

18:1THEN the LORD said to Aaron: "You, your sons, and your relatives from the tribe of Levi will be held responsible for any offenses related to the sanctuary. But you and your sons alone will be held responsible for violations connected with the priesthood.

2"Bring your relatives of the tribe of Levi—your ancestral tribe—to assist you and your sons as you perform the sacred duties in front of the Tabernacle of the Covenant.* 3But as the Levites go about all their assigned duties at the Tabernacle, they must be careful not to go near any of the sacred objects or the altar. If they do, both you and they will die. 4The Levites must join you in fulfilling their responsibilities for the care and maintenance of the Tabernacle,* but no unauthorized person may assist you.

5"You yourselves must perform the

sacred duties inside the sanctuary and at the altar. If you follow these instructions, the LORD's anger will never again blaze against the people of Israel. ⁶I myself have chosen your fellow Levites from among the Israelites to be your special assistants. They are a gift to you, dedicated to the LORD for service in the Tabernacle. ⁷But you and your sons, the priests, must personally handle all the priestly rituals associated with the altar and with everything behind the inner curtain. I am giving you the priesthood as your special privilege of service. Any unauthorized person who comes too near the sanctuary will be put to death."

⁸The LORD gave these further instructions to Aaron: "I myself have put you in charge of all the holy offerings that are brought to me by the people of Israel. I have given all these consecrated offerings to you and your sons as your permanent share. ⁹You are allotted the portion of the most holy offerings that is not burned on the fire. This portion of all the most holy offerings—including the grain offerings, sin offerings, and guilt offerings—will be most holy, and it belongs to you and your sons. ¹⁰You must eat it as a most holy offering. All the males may eat of it, and you must treat it as most holy.

¹¹"All the sacred offerings and special offerings presented to me when the Israelites lift them up before the altar also belong to you. I have given them to you and to your sons and daughters as your permanent share. Any member of your family who is ceremonially clean may eat of these offerings.

¹²"I also give you the harvest gifts brought by the people as offerings to the LORD—the best of the olive oil, new wine, and grain. ¹³All the first crops of their land that the people present to the LORD belong to you. Any member of your family who is ceremonially clean may eat this food.

¹⁴"Everything in Israel that is specially set apart for the LORD* also belongs to you.

¹⁵"The firstborn of every mother, whether human or animal, that is offered to the LORD will be yours. But you must always redeem your firstborn sons and the firstborn of ceremonially un-

clean animals. ¹⁶Redeem them when they are one month old. The redemption price is five pieces of silver* (as measured by the weight of the sanctuary shekel, which equals twenty gerahs).

¹⁷"However, you may not redeem the firstborn of cattle, sheep, or goats. They are holy and have been set apart for the LORD. Sprinkle their blood on the altar, and burn their fat as a special gift, a pleasing aroma to the LORD. ¹⁸The meat of these animals will be yours, just like the breast and right thigh that are presented by lifting them up as a special offering before the altar. ¹⁹Yes, I am giving you all these holy offerings that the people of Israel bring to the LORD. They are for you and your sons and daughters, to be eaten as your permanent share. This is an eternal and unbreakable covenant* between the LORD and you, and it also applies to your descendants."

²⁰And the LORD said to Aaron, "You priests will receive no allotment of land or share of property among the people of Israel. I am your share and your allotment. ²¹As for the tribe of Levi, your relatives, I will compensate them for their service in the Tabernacle. Instead of an allotment of land, I will give them the tithes from the entire land of Israel.

²²"From now on, no Israelites except priests or Levites may approach the Tabernacle. If they come too near, they will be judged guilty and will die. ²³Only the Levites may serve at the Tabernacle, and they will be held responsible for any offenses against it. This is a permanent law for you, to be observed from generation to generation. The Levites will receive no allotment of land among the Israelites, ²⁴because I have given them the Israelites' tithes, which have been presented as sacred offerings to the LORD. This will be the Levites' share. That is why I said they would receive no allotment of land among the Israelites."

²⁵The LORD also told Moses, ²⁶"Give these instructions to the Levites: When you receive from the people of Israel the tithes I have assigned as your allotment, give a tenth of the tithes you receive—a tithe of the tithe—to the LORD as a sacred offering. ²⁷The LORD will consider this offering to be your harvest offering, as

though it were the first grain from your own threshing floor or wine from your own winepress. ²⁸You must present one-tenth of the tithe received from the Israelites as a sacred offering to the LORD. This is the LORD's sacred portion, and you must present it to Aaron the priest. ²⁹Be sure to give to the LORD the best portions of the gifts given to you.

³⁰"Also, give these instructions to the Levites: When you present the best part as your offering, it will be considered as though it came from your own threshing floor or winepress. ³¹You Levites and your families may eat this food anywhere you wish, for it is your compensation for serving in the Tabernacle. ³²You will not be considered guilty for accepting the LORD's tithes if you give the best portion to the priests. But be careful not to treat the holy gifts of the people of Israel as though they were common. If you do, you will die."

16:46 Or *to make atonement for them.*   16:47 Or *and made atonement for.*   17:1 Verses 17:1-13 are numbered 17:16-28 in Hebrew text.   17:4 Hebrew *in the Tent of Meeting before the Testimony.* The Hebrew word for "testimony" refers to the terms of the LORD's covenant with Israel as written on stone tablets, which were kept in the Ark, and also to the covenant itself.   17:7 Or *Tabernacle of the Testimony;* also in 17:8.   17:10 Hebrew *before the Testimony;* see note on 17:4.   18:2 Or *Tabernacle of the Testimony.*   18:4 Hebrew *the Tent of Meeting;* also in 18:6, 21, 22, 23, 31.   18:14 The Hebrew term used here refers to the complete consecration of things or people to the LORD, either by destroying them or by giving them as an offering.   18:16 Hebrew *5 shekels* [2 ounces or 57 grams] *of silver.*   18:19 Hebrew *a covenant of salt.*

MARK 16:1-20
Where there should have been a body, there was an angel. Where there should have been death, there was life. Where there should have been the end of a first-century religious movement, there was a beginning.

Saturday evening, when the Sabbath ended, Mary Magdalene, Mary the mother of James, and Salome went out and purchased burial spices so they could anoint Jesus' body. ²Very early on Sunday morning,* just at sunrise, they went to the tomb. ³On the way they were asking each other, "Who will roll away the stone for us from the entrance to the tomb?" ⁴But as they arrived, they looked up and saw that the stone, which was very large, had already been rolled aside.

⁵When they entered the tomb, they saw a young man clothed in a white robe sitting on the right side. The women were shocked, ⁶but the angel said, "Don't be alarmed. You are looking for Jesus of Nazareth,* who was crucified. He isn't here! He is risen from the dead! Look, this is where they laid his body. ⁷Now go and tell his disciples, including Peter, that Jesus is going ahead of you to Galilee. You will see him there, just as he told you before he died."

⁸The women fled from the tomb, trembling and bewildered, and they said

WHAT THE BIBLE SAYS

Jesus' resurrection

MARK 16:5-7   Jesus rose to defeat death once and for all. If he had just died on the cross and stayed buried in the tomb, then nothing would have been accomplished. His claims to be the Son of God would have been false; his promise to rise again would have been a lie.   • Without the resurrection, our "faith is useless," and we are "still guilty" of our sins (1 Corinthians 15:17, August 23). But Jesus did, in fact, rise again from the dead. In doing so, he proved himself to be the Son of God, and he fulfilled not only the promises he made to the disciples, but the Old Testament prophecies about the Messiah as well. The resurrection proves that Jesus is not just another good man or great teacher; he is the Son of God.   • Although death is a fact of life, when we believe in Christ we can be assured that we will ultimately share in his resurrection and be given eternal life. Whatever persecutions or trials you face, you can be confident of the hope you have in Jesus Christ. You will rise again to eternal life—and that's a promise!

nothing to anyone because they were too frightened.*

[Shorter Ending of Mark]

Then they briefly reported all this to Peter and his companions. Afterward Jesus himself sent them out from east to west with the sacred and unfailing message of salvation that gives eternal life. Amen.

[Longer Ending of Mark]

⁹After Jesus rose from the dead early on Sunday morning, the first person who saw him was Mary Magdalene, the woman from whom he had cast out seven demons. ¹⁰She went to the disciples, who were grieving and weeping, and told them what had happened. ¹¹But when she told them that Jesus was alive and she had seen him, they didn't believe her.

¹²Afterward he appeared in a different form to two of his followers who were walking from Jerusalem into the country. ¹³They rushed back to tell the others, but no one believed them.

¹⁴Still later he appeared to the eleven disciples as they were eating together. He rebuked them for their stubborn unbelief because they refused to believe those who had seen him after he had been raised from the dead.*

¹⁵And then he told them, "Go into all the world and preach the Good News to everyone. ¹⁶Anyone who believes and is baptized will be saved. But anyone who refuses to believe will be condemned. ¹⁷These miraculous signs will accompany those who believe: They will cast out demons in my name, and they will speak in new languages.* ¹⁸They will be able to handle snakes with safety, and if they drink anything poisonous, it won't hurt them. They will be able to place their hands on the sick, and they will be healed."

¹⁹When the Lord Jesus had finished talking with them, he was taken up into heaven and sat down in the place of honor at God's right hand. ²⁰And the disciples went everywhere and preached, and the Lord worked through them, confirming what they said by many miraculous signs.

16:2 Greek *on the first day of the week;* also in 16:9.
16:6 Or *Jesus the Nazarene.* 16:8 The most reliable early manuscripts of the Gospel of Mark end at verse 8. Other manuscripts include various endings to the Gospel. A few include both the "shorter ending" and the "longer ending." The majority of manuscripts include the "longer ending" immediately after verse 8. 16:14 Some early manuscripts add: *And they excused themselves, saying, "This age of lawlessness and unbelief is under Satan, who does not permit God's truth and power to conquer the evil [unclean] spirits. Therefore, reveal your justice now." This is what they said to Christ. And Christ replied to them, "The period of years of Satan's power has been fulfilled, but other dreadful things will happen soon. And I was handed over to death for those who have sinned, so that they may return to the truth and sin no more, and so they may inherit the spiritual, incorruptible, and righteous glory in heaven."* 16:17 Or *new tongues;* some manuscripts omit *new.*

PSALM 55:1-23
For the choir director: A psalm of David, to be accompanied by stringed instruments.*

¹ Listen to my prayer, O God.
　　Do not ignore my cry for help!
² Please listen and answer me,
　　for I am overwhelmed by my
　　　troubles.
³ My enemies shout at me,
　　making loud and wicked threats.
　They bring trouble on me
　　and angrily hunt me down.

⁴ My heart pounds in my chest.
　　The terror of death assaults me.
⁵ Fear and trembling overwhelm me,
　　and I can't stop shaking.
⁶ Oh, that I had wings like a dove;
　　then I would fly away and rest!
⁷ I would fly far away
　　to the quiet of the wilderness.
Interlude

⁸ How quickly I would escape—
　　far from this wild storm of hatred.

⁹ Confuse them, Lord, and frustrate
　　their plans,
　for I see violence and conflict
　　in the city.
¹⁰ Its walls are patrolled day and night
　　against invaders,
　but the real danger is wickedness
　　within the city.
¹¹ Everything is falling apart;
　　threats and cheating are rampant
　　in the streets.
¹² It is not an enemy who taunts me—
　　I could bear that.
　It is not my foes who so arrogantly
　　insult me—
　　I could have hidden from them.
¹³ Instead, it is you—my equal,
　　my companion and close friend.

14 What good fellowship we once
enjoyed
as we walked together to the house
of God.

15 Let death stalk my enemies;
let the grave* swallow them alive,
for evil makes its home within
them.

16 But I will call on God,
and the LORD will rescue me.
17 Morning, noon, and night
I cry out in my distress,
and the LORD hears my voice.
18 He ransoms me and keeps me safe
from the battle waged against me,
though many still oppose me.
19 God, who has ruled forever,
will hear me and humble them.
Interlude
For my enemies refuse to change their
ways;
they do not fear God.

20 As for my companion, he betrayed
his friends;
he broke his promises.
21 His words are as smooth as butter,
but in his heart is war.
His words are as soothing as lotion,
but underneath are daggers!

22 Give your burdens to the LORD,
and he will take care of you.
He will not permit the godly to
slip and fall.

23 But you, O God, will send the wicked
down to the pit of destruction.
Murderers and liars will die young,
but I am trusting you to save me.

55:TITLE Hebrew *maskil*. This may be a literary or musical
term.   55:15 Hebrew *let Sheol.*

PROVERBS 11:7
When the wicked die, their hopes die with
them, for they rely on their own feeble
strength.

MARCH**13**

NUMBERS 19:1–20:29
Sometimes it seems that the history of Israel
consists of one stubborn act after another. Indeed,
even Moses and Aaron made a mistake that they
lived to regret.

The LORD said to Moses and Aaron, 2"Here
is another legal requirement commanded
by the LORD: Tell the people of Israel to
bring you a red heifer, a perfect animal
that has no defects and has never been
yoked to a plow. 3Give it to Eleazar the
priest, and it will be taken outside the
camp and slaughtered in his presence.
4Eleazar will take some of its blood on his
finger and sprinkle it seven times toward
the front of the Tabernacle.* 5As Eleazar
watches, the heifer must be burned—its
hide, meat, blood, and dung. 6Eleazar the
priest must then take a stick of cedar,* a
hyssop branch, and some scarlet yarn and
throw them into the fire where the heifer
is burning.

7"Then the priest must wash his clothes
and bathe himself in water. Afterward he
may return to the camp, though he will remain ceremonially unclean until evening.
8The man who burns the animal must also
wash his clothes and bathe himself in water, and he, too, will remain unclean until
evening. 9Then someone who is ceremonially clean will gather up the ashes of the
heifer and deposit them in a purified
place outside the camp. They will be kept
there for the community of Israel to use in
the water for the purification ceremony.
This ceremony is performed for the re-
moval of sin. 10The man who gathers up
the ashes of the heifer must also wash his
clothes, and he will remain ceremonially
unclean until evening. This is a permanent law for the people of Israel and any
foreigners who live among them.

11"All those who touch a dead human
body will be ceremonially unclean for

seven days. ¹²They must purify themselves on the third and seventh days with the water of purification; then they will be purified. But if they do not do this on the third and seventh days, they will continue to be unclean even after the seventh day. ¹³All those who touch a dead body and do not purify themselves in the proper way defile the LORD's Tabernacle, and they will be cut off from the community of Israel. Since the water of purification was not sprinkled on them, their defilement continues.

¹⁴"This is the ritual law that applies when someone dies inside a tent: All those who enter that tent and those who were inside when the death occurred will be ceremonially unclean for seven days. ¹⁵Any open container in the tent that was not covered with a lid is also defiled. ¹⁶And if someone in an open field touches the corpse of someone who was killed with a sword or who died a natural death, or if someone touches a human bone or a grave, that person will be defiled for seven days.

¹⁷"To remove the defilement, put some of the ashes from the burnt purification offering in a jar, and pour fresh water over them. ¹⁸Then someone who is ceremonially clean must take a hyssop branch and dip it into the water. That person must sprinkle the water on the tent, on all the furnishings in the tent, and on the people who were in the tent; also on the person who touched a human bone, or touched someone who was killed or who died naturally, or touched a grave. ¹⁹On the third and seventh days the person who is ceremonially clean must sprinkle the water on those who are defiled. Then on the seventh day the people being cleansed must wash their clothes and bathe themselves, and that evening they will be cleansed of their defilement.

²⁰"But those who become defiled and do not purify themselves will be cut off from the community, for they have defiled the sanctuary of the LORD. Since the water of purification has not been sprinkled on them, they remain defiled. ²¹This is a permanent law for the people. Those who sprinkle the water of purification must afterward wash their clothes, and anyone who then touches the water used for purification will remain defiled until

evening. ²²Anything and anyone that a defiled person touches will be ceremonially unclean until evening."

20:1IN the first month of the year,* the whole community of Israel arrived in the wilderness of Zin and camped at Kadesh. While they were there, Miriam died and was buried.

²There was no water for the people to drink at that place, so they rebelled against Moses and Aaron. ³The people blamed Moses and said, "If only we had died in the LORD's presence with our brothers! ⁴Why have you brought the congregation of the LORD's people into this wilderness to die, along with all our livestock? ⁵Why did you make us leave Egypt and bring us here to this terrible place? This land has no grain, no figs, no grapes, no pomegranates, and no water to drink!"

⁶Moses and Aaron turned away from the people and went to the entrance of the Tabernacle,* where they fell face down on the ground. Then the glorious presence of the LORD appeared to them, ⁷and the LORD said to Moses, ⁸"You and Aaron must take the staff and assemble the entire community. As the people watch, speak to the rock over there, and it will pour out its water. You will provide enough water from the rock to satisfy the whole community and their livestock."

⁹So Moses did as he was told. He took the staff from the place where it was kept before the LORD. ¹⁰Then he and Aaron summoned the people to come and gather at the rock. "Listen, you rebels!" he shouted. "Must we bring you water from this rock?" ¹¹Then Moses raised his hand and struck the rock twice with the staff, and water gushed out. So the entire community and their livestock drank their fill.

¹²But the LORD said to Moses and Aaron, "Because you did not trust me enough to demonstrate my holiness to the people of Israel, you will not lead them into the land I am giving them!" ¹³This place was known as the waters of Meribah (which means "arguing") because there the people of Israel argued with the LORD, and there he demonstrated his holiness among them.

¹⁴While Moses was at Kadesh, he sent

ambassadors to the king of Edom with this message:

"This is what your relatives, the people of Israel, say: You know all the hardships we have been through. [15]Our ancestors went down to Egypt, and we lived there a long time, and we and our ancestors were brutally mistreated by the Egyptians. [16]But when we cried out to the LORD, he heard us and sent an angel who brought us out of Egypt. Now we are camped at Kadesh, a town on the border of your land. [17]Please let us travel through your land. We will be careful not to go through your fields and vineyards. We won't even drink water from your wells. We will stay on the king's road and never leave it until we have passed through your territory."

[18]But the king of Edom said, "Stay out of my land, or I will meet you with an army!"

[19]The Israelites answered, "We will stay on the main road. If our livestock drink your water, we will pay for it. Just let us pass through your country. That's all we ask."

[20]But the king of Edom replied, "Stay out! You may not pass through our land." With that he mobilized his army and marched out against them with an imposing force. [21]Because Edom refused to allow Israel to pass through their country, Israel was forced to turn around.

[22]The whole community of Israel left Kadesh and arrived at Mount Hor. [23]There, on the border of the land of Edom, the LORD said to Moses and Aaron, [24]"The time has come for Aaron to join his ancestors in death. He will not enter the land I am giving the people of Israel, because the two of you rebelled against my instructions concerning the water at Meribah. [25]Now take Aaron and his son Eleazar up Mount Hor. [26]There you will remove Aaron's priestly garments and put them on Eleazar, his son. Aaron will die there and join his ancestors."

[27]So Moses did as the LORD commanded. The three of them went up Mount Hor together as the whole community watched. [28]At the summit, Moses removed the priestly garments from Aaron and put them on Eleazar, Aaron's son. Then Aaron died there on top of the mountain, and Moses and Eleazar went back down. [29]When the people realized that Aaron had died, all Israel mourned for him thirty days.

19:4 Hebrew *the Tent of Meeting.* **19:6** Or *juniper.*
20:1 The first month of the ancient Hebrew lunar calendar usually occurs within the months of March and April. The number of years since leaving Egypt is not specified.
20:6 Hebrew *the Tent of Meeting.*

HOW WE LIVE

Obeying God

NUMBERS 20:11-13 After all Moses had done in leading the people, he still had a will of his own. On this occasion, God told Moses to "speak to the rock over there, and it will pour out its water" (20:8). Moses, in his frustration with God's people, chose instead to strike the rock with his staff, saying, "Must we bring you water from this rock?" When Moses did that, he acted like *he* was the one working the miracle. His punishment was that he would not enter the Promised Land. • Does this punishment seem harsh? Keep in mind that Moses was the leader of an entire nation—one that had been constantly rebelling, complaining, and disobeying God. Moses needed to be a prime example of obedience. His failure, therefore, carried a severe penalty. That penalty itself served as a reminder to the rest of the nation—and to us—that obedience to God is not to be taken lightly. • Because you are a Christian, others will constantly watch what you do. When you faithfully obey God, your actions and words show that your life has been changed, and they glorify the God who has changed you.

LUKE 1:1-25

Luke's Gospel begins with the preparations for the birth of one of Jesus' cousins, John. Later we will know this cousin as John the Baptist, the first-century prophet who prepared the way for the Messiah.

Many people have set out to write accounts about the events that have been fulfilled among us. ²They used the eyewitness reports circulating among us from the early disciples.* ³Having carefully investigated everything from the beginning, I also have decided to write a careful account for you, most honorable Theophilus, ⁴so you can be certain of the truth of everything you were taught.

⁵When Herod was king of Judea, there was a Jewish priest named Zechariah. He was a member of the priestly order of Abijah, and his wife, Elizabeth, was also from the priestly line of Aaron. ⁶Zechariah and Elizabeth were righteous in God's eyes, careful to obey all of the Lord's commandments and regulations. ⁷They had no children because Elizabeth was unable to conceive, and they were both very old.

⁸One day Zechariah was serving God in the Temple, for his order was on duty that week. ⁹As was the custom of the priests, he was chosen by lot to enter the sanctuary of the Lord and burn incense. ¹⁰While the incense was being burned, a great crowd stood outside, praying.

¹¹While Zechariah was in the sanctuary, an angel of the Lord appeared to him, standing to the right of the incense altar. ¹²Zechariah was shaken and overwhelmed with fear when he saw him. ¹³But the angel said, "Don't be afraid, Zechariah! God has heard your prayer. Your wife, Elizabeth, will give you a son, and you are to name him John. ¹⁴You will have great joy and gladness, and many will rejoice at his birth, ¹⁵for he will be great in the eyes of the Lord. He must never touch wine or other alcoholic drinks. He will be filled with the Holy Spirit, even before his birth.* ¹⁶And he will turn many Israelites to the Lord their God. ¹⁷He will be a man with the spirit and power of Elijah. He will prepare the people for the coming of the Lord. He will turn the hearts of the fathers

to their children,* and he will cause those who are rebellious to accept the wisdom of the godly."

¹⁸Zechariah said to the angel, "How can I be sure this will happen? I'm an old man now, and my wife is also well along in years."

¹⁹Then the angel said, "I am Gabriel! I stand in the very presence of God. It was he who sent me to bring you this good news! ²⁰But now, since you didn't believe what I said, you will be silent and unable to speak until the child is born. For my words will certainly be fulfilled at the proper time."

²¹Meanwhile, the people were waiting for Zechariah to come out of the sanctuary, wondering why he was taking so long. ²²When he finally did come out, he couldn't speak to them. Then they realized from his gestures and his silence that he must have seen a vision in the sanctuary.

²³When Zechariah's week of service in the Temple was over, he returned home. ²⁴Soon afterward his wife, Elizabeth, became pregnant and went into seclusion for five months. ²⁵"How kind the Lord is!" she exclaimed. "He has taken away my disgrace of having no children."

1:2 Greek *from those who from the beginning were servants of the word.* 1:15 Or *even from birth.* 1:17 See Mal 4:5-6.

PSALM 56:1-13

For the choir director: A psalm of David, regarding the time the Philistines seized him in Gath. To be sung to the tune "Dove on Distant Oaks."

¹ **O** God, have mercy on me,
    for people are hounding me.
    My foes attack me all day long.
² I am constantly hounded by those who
        slander me,
    and many are boldly attacking me.
³ But when I am afraid,
    I will put my trust in you.
⁴ I praise God for what he has promised.
    I trust in God, so why should I be
        afraid?
    What can mere mortals do to me?

⁵ They are always twisting what I say;
    they spend their days plotting to
        harm me.

⁶ They come together to spy on me—
   watching my every step, eager to
   kill me.
⁷ Don't let them get away with their
   wickedness;
   in your anger, O God, bring them
   down.

⁸ You keep track of all my sorrows.*
   You have collected all my tears
   in your bottle.
   You have recorded each one in
   your book.

⁹ My enemies will retreat when I call
   to you for help.
   This I know: God is on my side!
¹⁰ I praise God for what he has promised;
   Yes, I praise the LORD for what he
   has promised.

¹¹ I trust in God, so why should I be
   afraid?
   What can mere mortals do to me?

¹² I will fulfill my vows to you, O God,
   and will offer a sacrifice of thanks
   for your help.
¹³ For you have rescued me from
   death;
   you have kept my feet from
   slipping.
   So now I can walk in your presence,
   O God,
   in your life-giving light.

56:8 Or *my wanderings.*

PROVERBS 11:8

The godly are rescued from trouble, and it
falls on the wicked instead.

MARCH**14**

NUMBERS 21:1–22:20

For the Israelites, success was a slow, and sometimes bloody, process. Still, they watched their enemies fall before God's power.

The Canaanite king of Arad, who lived in the Negev, heard that the Israelites were approaching on the road through Atharim. So he attacked the Israelites and took some of them as prisoners. ²Then the people of Israel made this vow to the LORD: "If you will hand these people over to us, we will completely destroy* all their towns." ³The LORD heard the Israelites' request and gave them victory over the Canaanites. The Israelites completely destroyed them and their towns, and the place has been called Hormah* ever since.

⁴Then the people of Israel set out from Mount Hor, taking the road to the Red Sea* to go around the land of Edom. But the people grew impatient with the long journey, ⁵and they began to speak against God and Moses. "Why have you brought us out of Egypt to die here in the wilderness?" they complained. "There is nothing to eat here and nothing to drink. And we hate this horrible manna!"

⁶So the LORD sent poisonous snakes among the people, and many were bitten and died. ⁷Then the people came to Moses and cried out, "We have sinned by speaking against the LORD and against you. Pray that the LORD will take away the snakes." So Moses prayed for the people.

⁸Then the LORD told him, "Make a replica of a poisonous snake and attach it to a pole. All who are bitten will live if they simply look at it!" ⁹So Moses made a snake out of bronze and attached it to a pole. Then anyone who was bitten by a snake could look at the bronze snake and be healed!

¹⁰The Israelites traveled next to Oboth and camped there. ¹¹Then they went on to Iye-abarim, in the wilderness on the eastern border of Moab. ¹²From there they traveled to the valley of Zered Brook and set up camp. ¹³Then they moved out and camped on the far side of the Arnon River, in the wilderness adjacent to the territory of the Amorites. The Arnon is the boundary line between the Moabites and the Amorites. ¹⁴For this reason *The*

Book of the Wars of the LORD speaks of "the town of Waheb in the area of Suphah, and the ravines of the Arnon River, [15] and the ravines that extend as far as the settlement of Ar on the border of Moab."

[16] From there the Israelites traveled to Beer,* which is the well where the LORD said to Moses, "Assemble the people, and I will give them water." [17] There the Israelites sang this song:

> "Spring up, O well!
>   Yes, sing its praises!
> [18] Sing of this well,
>   which princes dug,
>   which great leaders hollowed out
>   with their scepters and staffs."

Then the Israelites left the wilderness and proceeded on through Mattanah, [19] Nahaliel, and Bamoth. [20] After that they went to the valley in Moab where Pisgah Peak overlooks the wasteland.*

[21] The Israelites sent ambassadors to King Sihon of the Amorites with this message:

[22] "Let us travel through your land. We will be careful not to go through your fields and vineyards. We won't even drink water from your wells. We will stay on the king's road until we have passed through your territory."

[23] But King Sihon refused to let them cross his territory. Instead, he mobilized his entire army and attacked Israel in the wilderness, engaging them in battle at Jahaz. [24] But the Israelites slaughtered them with their swords and occupied their land from the Arnon River to the Jabbok River. They went only as far as the Ammonite border because the boundary of the Ammonites was fortified.*

[25] So Israel captured all the towns of the Amorites and settled in them, including the city of Heshbon and its surrounding villages. [26] Heshbon had been the capital of King Sihon of the Amorites. He had defeated a former Moabite king and seized all his land as far as the Arnon River. [27] Therefore, the ancient poets wrote this about him:

> "Come to Heshbon and let it be rebuilt!
>   Let the city of Sihon be restored.

> [28] A fire flamed forth from Heshbon,
>   a blaze from the city of Sihon.
> It burned the city of Ar in Moab;
>   it destroyed the rulers of the Arnon
>   heights.
> [29] What sorrow awaits you, O people
>   of Moab!
> You are finished, O worshipers
>   of Chemosh!
> Chemosh has left his sons as refugees,
>   his daughters as captives of Sihon,
>   the Amorite king.
> [30] We have utterly destroyed them,
>   from Heshbon to Dibon.
> We have completely wiped them out
>   as far away as Nophah and
>   Medeba.*"

[31] So the people of Israel occupied the territory of the Amorites. [32] After Moses sent men to explore the Jazer area, they captured all the towns in the region and drove out the Amorites who lived there. [33] Then they turned and marched up the road to Bashan, but King Og of Bashan and all his people attacked them at Edrei. [34] The LORD said to Moses, "Do not be afraid of him, for I have handed him over to you, along with all his people and his land. Do the same to him as you did to King Sihon of the Amorites, who ruled in Heshbon." [35] And Israel killed King Og, his sons, and all his subjects; not a single survivor remained. Then Israel occupied their land.

22:1 THEN the people of Israel traveled to the plains of Moab and camped east of the Jordan River, across from Jericho. [2] Balak son of Zippor, the Moabite king, had seen everything the Israelites did to the Amorites. [3] And when the people of Moab saw how many Israelites there were, they were terrified. [4] The king of Moab said to the elders of Midian, "This mob will devour everything in sight, like an ox devours grass in the field!"

So Balak, king of Moab, [5] sent messengers to call Balaam son of Beor, who was living in his native land of Pethor* near the Euphrates River.* His message said:

"Look, a vast horde of people has arrived from Egypt. They cover the face of the earth and are threatening me.

[6]Please come and curse these people for me because they are too powerful for me. Then perhaps I will be able to conquer them and drive them from the land. I know that blessings fall on any people you bless, and curses fall on people you curse."

[7]Balak's messengers, who were elders of Moab and Midian, set out with money to pay Balaam to place a curse upon Israel.* They went to Balaam and delivered Balak's message to him. [8]"Stay here overnight," Balaam said. "In the morning I will tell you whatever the LORD directs me to say." So the officials from Moab stayed there with Balaam.

[9]That night God came to Balaam and asked him, "Who are these men visiting you?"

[10]Balaam said to God, "Balak son of Zippor, king of Moab, has sent me this message: [11]Look, a vast horde of people has arrived from Egypt, and they cover the face of the earth. Come and curse these people for me. Then perhaps I will be able to stand up to them and drive them from the land.'"

[12]But God told Balaam, "Do not go with them. You are not to curse these people, for they have been blessed!"

[13]The next morning Balaam got up and told Balak's officials, "Go on home! The LORD will not let me go with you."

[14]So the Moabite officials returned to King Balak and reported, "Balaam refused to come with us." [15]Then Balak tried again. This time he sent a larger number of even more distinguished officials than those he had sent the first time. [16]They went to Balaam and delivered this message to him:

"This is what Balak son of Zippor says: Please don't let anything stop you from coming to help me. [17]I will pay you very well and do whatever you tell me. Just come and curse these people for me!"

[18]But Balaam responded to Balak's messengers, "Even if Balak were to give me his palace filled with silver and gold, I would be powerless to do anything against the will of the LORD my God. [19]But stay here one more night, and I will see if the LORD has anything else to say to me."

[20]That night God came to Balaam and told him, "Since these men have come for you, get up and go with them. But do only what I tell you to do."

21:2 The Hebrew term used here refers to the complete consecration of things or people to the LORD, either by destroying them or by giving them as an offering; also in 21:3. **21:3** *Hormah* means "destruction." **21:4** Hebrew *sea of reeds.* **21:16** *Beer* means "well." **21:20** Or *overlooks Jeshimon.* **21:24** Or *because the terrain of the Ammonite frontier was rugged;* Hebrew reads *because the boundary of the Ammonites was strong.* **21:30** Or *until fire spread to Medeba.* The meaning of the Hebrew is uncertain. **22:5a** Or *who was at Pethor in the land of the Amavites.* **22:5b** Hebrew *the river.* **22:7** Hebrew *set out with the money of divination in their hand.*

HOW WE LIVE: Trusting God

LUKE 1:38 Trust is not always easy to obtain, and it is sometimes difficult to give. When you gain the trust of another, you must remain trustworthy in order to keep it. Likewise, when you put your trust in someone, you do so because you believe that person won't let you down. • Imagine how much Mary trusted God when she willingly took on the task of being the mother of God's Son! Sure, she had her questions, but when God answered, she believed without fear. God chose Mary for one of the most important acts of obedience he has ever demanded. Without questioning God's choice, Mary answered by saying, "I am the Lord's servant. May everything you have said about me come true." Because Mary trusted God with her whole heart, he was able to use her for an extraordinary purpose. • If you are unsure about how God can use you, think again. God's plan for you doesn't rest solely on education, ability, or experience. He is looking for people who are willing to wholeheartedly trust him.

LUKE 1:26-56

Elizabeth and Mary shared precious secrets. They were two women with an inside view of how God would change the world forever. Through these two powerless women, the whole world would be turned upside down.

In the sixth month of Elizabeth's pregnancy, God sent the angel Gabriel to Nazareth, a village in Galilee, ²⁷to a virgin named Mary. She was engaged to be married to a man named Joseph, a descendant of King David. ²⁸Gabriel appeared to her and said, "Greetings, favored woman! The Lord is with you!*"

²⁹Confused and disturbed, Mary tried to think what the angel could mean. ³⁰"Don't be afraid, Mary," the angel told her, "for you have found favor with God! ³¹You will conceive and give birth to a son, and you will name him Jesus. ³²He will be very great and will be called the Son of the Most High. The Lord God will give him the throne of his ancestor David. ³³And he will reign over Israel* forever; his Kingdom will never end!"

³⁴Mary asked the angel, "But how can this happen? I am a virgin."

³⁵The angel replied, "The Holy Spirit will come upon you, and the power of the Most High will overshadow you. So the baby to be born will be holy, and he will be called the Son of God. ³⁶What's more, your relative Elizabeth has become pregnant in her old age! People used to say she was barren, but she's now in her sixth month. ³⁷For nothing is impossible with God.*"

³⁸Mary responded, "I am the Lord's servant. May everything you have said about me come true." And then the angel left her.

³⁹A few days later Mary hurried to the hill country of Judea, to the town ⁴⁰where Zechariah lived. She entered the house and greeted Elizabeth. ⁴¹At the sound of Mary's greeting, Elizabeth's child leaped within her, and Elizabeth was filled with the Holy Spirit.

⁴²Elizabeth gave a glad cry and exclaimed to Mary, "God has blessed you above all women, and your child is blessed. ⁴³Why am I so honored, that the mother of my Lord should visit me?

⁴⁴When I heard your greeting, the baby in my womb jumped for joy. ⁴⁵You are blessed because you believed that the Lord would do what he said."

⁴⁶Mary responded,

"Oh, how my soul praises the Lord.
⁴⁷   How my spirit rejoices in God
        my Savior!
⁴⁸ For he took notice of his lowly servant
        girl,
        and from now on all generations
        will call me blessed.
⁴⁹ For the Mighty One is holy,
        and he has done great things
        for me.
⁵⁰ He shows mercy from generation
        to generation
        to all who fear him.
⁵¹ His mighty arm has done tremendous
        things!
        He has scattered the proud and
        haughty ones.
⁵² He has brought down princes from
        their thrones
        and exalted the humble.
⁵³ He has filled the hungry with good
        things
        and sent the rich away with empty
        hands.
⁵⁴ He has helped his servant Israel
        and remembered to be merciful.
⁵⁵ For he made this promise to our
        ancestors,
        to Abraham and his children
        forever."

⁵⁶Mary stayed with Elizabeth about three months and then went back to her own home.

1:28 Some manuscripts add *Blessed are you among women.* 1:33 Greek *over the house of Jacob.* 1:37 Some manuscripts read *For the word of God will never fail.*

PSALM 57:1-11
For the choir director: A psalm of David, regarding the time he fled from Saul and went into the cave. To be sung to the tune "Do Not Destroy!"

¹ **H**ave mercy on me, O God, have mercy!
    I look to you for protection.
    I will hide beneath the shadow
        of your wings
    until the danger passes by.
² I cry out to God Most High,*

to God who will fulfill his purpose
　　for me.
³ He will send help from heaven
　　to rescue me,
　　disgracing those who hound me.
　　　　　　　　　　　　　　Interlude
My God will send forth his unfailing
　　love and faithfulness.

⁴ I am surrounded by fierce lions
　　who greedily devour human prey—
　whose teeth pierce like spears and
　　　arrows,
　　and whose tongues cut like swords.

⁵ Be exalted, O God, above the highest
　　heavens!
　　May your glory shine over all the
　　earth.

⁶ My enemies have set a trap for me.
　　I am weary from distress.
　They have dug a deep pit in my path,
　　but they themselves have fallen
　　　into it.　　　　　　　*Interlude*

⁷ My heart is confident in you, O God;
　　my heart is confident.
　　No wonder I can sing your praises!
⁸ Wake up, my heart!

Wake up, O lyre and harp!
　I will wake the dawn with my
　　song.
⁹ I will thank you, Lord, among
　　all the people.
　I will sing your praises among
　　the nations.
¹⁰ For your unfailing love is as high
　　as the heavens.
　Your faithfulness reaches
　　to the clouds.

¹¹ Be exalted, O God, above the highest
　　heavens.
　May your glory shine over all
　　the earth.

57:2 Hebrew *El-Elyon.*

PROVERBS 11:9-11
With their words, the godless destroy
their friends, but knowledge will rescue
the righteous. □ The whole city celebrates
when the godly succeed; they shout for
joy when the wicked die. □ Upright citizens are good for a city and make it prosper, but the talk of the wicked tears it
apart.

MARCH15

NUMBERS 22:21-23:30
God used a donkey to rebuke a greedy prophet.
He then used that prophet to rebuke an enemy
of Israel.

So the next morning Balaam got up, saddled his donkey, and started off with the
Moabite officials. ²²But God was angry
that Balaam was going, so he sent the angel of the Lord to stand in the road to
block his way. As Balaam and two servants
were riding along, ²³Balaam's donkey saw
the angel of the Lord standing in the road
with a drawn sword in his hand. The donkey bolted off the road into a field, but Balaam beat it and turned it back onto the
road. ²⁴Then the angel of the Lord stood
at a place where the road narrowed between two vineyard walls. ²⁵When the

donkey saw the angel of the Lord, it tried
to squeeze by and crushed Balaam's foot
against the wall. So Balaam beat the donkey again. ²⁶Then the angel of the Lord
moved farther down the road and stood in
a place too narrow for the donkey to get by
at all. ²⁷This time when the donkey saw
the angel, it lay down under Balaam. In a
fit of rage Balaam beat the animal again
with his staff.

²⁸Then the Lord gave the donkey the
ability to speak. "What have I done to you
that deserves your beating me three
times?" it asked Balaam.

²⁹"You have made me look like a fool!"
Balaam shouted. "If I had a sword with me,
I would kill you!"

³⁰"But I am the same donkey you have ridden all your life," the donkey answered. "Have I ever done anything like this before?"

"No," Balaam admitted.

³¹Then the LORD opened Balaam's eyes, and he saw the angel of the LORD standing in the roadway with a drawn sword in his hand. Balaam bowed his head and fell face down on the ground before him.

³²"Why did you beat your donkey those three times?" the angel of the LORD demanded. "Look, I have come to block your way because you are stubbornly resisting me. ³³Three times the donkey saw me and shied away; otherwise, I would certainly have killed you by now and spared the donkey."

³⁴Then Balaam confessed to the angel of the LORD, "I have sinned. I didn't realize you were standing in the road to block my way. I will return home if you are against my going."

³⁵But the angel of the LORD told Balaam, "Go with these men, but say only what I tell you to say." So Balaam went on with Balak's officials. ³⁶When King Balak heard that Balaam was on the way, he went out to meet him at a Moabite town on the Arnon River at the farthest border of his land.

³⁷"Didn't I send you an urgent invitation? Why didn't you come right away?" Balak asked Balaam. "Didn't you believe me when I said I would reward you richly?"

³⁸Balaam replied, "Look, now I have come, but I have no power to say whatever I want. I will speak only the message that God puts in my mouth." ³⁹Then Balaam accompanied Balak to Kiriath-huzoth, ⁴⁰where the king sacrificed cattle and sheep. He sent portions of the meat to Balaam and the officials who were with him. ⁴¹The next morning Balak took Balaam up to Bamoth-baal. From there he could see some of the people of Israel spread out below him.

23:1THEN Balaam said to King Balak, "Build me seven altars here, and prepare seven young bulls and seven rams for me to sacrifice." ²Balak followed his instructions, and the two of them sacrificed a young bull and a ram on each altar.

³Then Balaam said to Balak, "Stand here by your burnt offerings, and I will go to see if the LORD will respond to me. Then I will tell you whatever he reveals to me." So Balaam went alone to the top of a bare hill, ⁴and God met him there. Balaam said to him, "I have prepared seven altars and have sacrificed a young bull and a ram on each altar."

⁵The LORD gave Balaam a message for King Balak. Then he said, "Go back to Balak and give him my message."

⁶So Balaam returned and found the king standing beside his burnt offerings with all the officials of Moab. ⁷This was the message Balaam delivered:

"Balak summoned me to come from Aram;
    the king of Moab brought me from the eastern hills.
'Come,' he said, 'curse Jacob for me!
    Come and announce Israel's doom.'
⁸ But how can I curse those
    whom God has not cursed?
How can I condemn those
    whom the LORD has not condemned?
⁹ I see them from the cliff tops;
    I watch them from the hills.
I see a people who live by themselves,
    set apart from other nations.
¹⁰ Who can count Jacob's descendants,
    as numerous as dust?
Who can count even a fourth
    of Israel's people?
Let me die like the righteous;
    let my life end like theirs."

¹¹Then King Balak demanded of Balaam, "What have you done to me? I brought you to curse my enemies. Instead, you have blessed them!"

¹²But Balaam replied, "I will speak only the message that the LORD puts in my mouth."

¹³Then King Balak told him, "Come with me to another place. There you will see another part of the nation of Israel, but not all of them. Curse at least that many!" ¹⁴So Balak took Balaam to the plateau of Zophim on Pisgah Peak. He built seven altars there and offered a young bull and a ram on each altar.

¹⁵Then Balaam said to the king, "Stand

here by your burnt offerings while I go over there to meet the LORD."

¹⁶And the LORD met Balaam and gave him a message. Then he said, "Go back to Balak and give him my message."

¹⁷So Balaam returned and found the king standing beside his burnt offerings with all the officials of Moab. "What did the LORD say?" Balak asked eagerly.

¹⁸This was the message Balaam delivered:

"Rise up, Balak, and listen!
   Hear me, son of Zippor.
¹⁹ God is not a man, so he does not lie.
   He is not human, so he does not
      change his mind.
Has he ever spoken and failed to act?
   Has he ever promised and not
      carried it through?
²⁰ Listen, I received a command to bless;
   God has blessed, and I cannot
      reverse it!
²¹ No misfortune is in his plan for Jacob;
   no trouble is in store for Israel.
For the LORD their God is with them;
   he has been proclaimed their king.
²² God brought them out of Egypt;
   for them he is as strong as a wild ox.
²³ No curse can touch Jacob;
   no magic has any power against
      Israel.
For now it will be said of Jacob,
   'What wonders God has done
      for Israel!'

²⁴ These people rise up like a lioness,
   like a majestic lion rousing itself.
They refuse to rest
   until they have feasted on prey,
      drinking the blood of the
         slaughtered!"

²⁵ Then Balak said to Balaam, "Fine, but if you won't curse them, at least don't bless them!"

²⁶ But Balaam replied to Balak, "Didn't I tell you that I can do only what the LORD tells me?"

²⁷ Then King Balak said to Balaam, "Come, I will take you to one more place. Perhaps it will please God to let you curse them from there."

²⁸So Balak took Balaam to the top of Mount Peor, overlooking the wasteland.* ²⁹Balaam again told Balak, "Build me seven altars, and prepare seven young bulls and seven rams for me to sacrifice." ³⁰So Balak did as Balaam ordered and offered a young bull and a ram on each altar.

23:28 Or *overlooking Jeshimon.*

LUKE 1:57-80

Zechariah and Elizabeth certainly made a stir. First, Zechariah saw a vision and was struck dumb (Luke 1:8-22, March 13), and then Elizabeth gave their new baby a name out of line with the family heritage. Everyone knew that John would be special.

When it was time for Elizabeth's baby to be born, she gave birth to a son. ⁵⁸And

---

Our money

HOW WE LIVE

NUMBERS 22:37 Balaam was one of those interesting Old Testament people who, although not of the nation of Israel, acknowledged the power of God. His motives, however, were not pure. Balaam loved money. He was ready to do God's bidding as long as he could profit from the experience. King Balak, who was willing to pay any amount in order to bring a curse upon Israel, had his ear too. • Money is a powerful temptation. As Christians, we must have a different attitude toward it. God wants us to use it to further his Kingdom. We can avoid Balaam's mistake by looking past the allure of amassing great wealth to the long-range benefits of tithing, supporting missions, donating to charities, or just buying a needy family a bag of groceries. Be wise with your money and plan for the future, but don't be stingy when the church has a need. The benefits of following God and honoring him with the resources he gives you are great—you can bank on that!

when her neighbors and relatives heard that the Lord had been very merciful to her, everyone rejoiced with her.

⁵⁹When the baby was eight days old, they all came for the circumcision ceremony. They wanted to name him Zechariah, after his father. ⁶⁰But Elizabeth said, "No! His name is John!"

⁶¹"What?" they exclaimed. "There is no one in all your family by that name." ⁶²So they used gestures to ask the baby's father what he wanted to name him. ⁶³He motioned for a writing tablet, and to everyone's surprise he wrote, "His name is John." ⁶⁴Instantly Zechariah could speak again, and he began praising God.

⁶⁵Awe fell upon the whole neighborhood, and the news of what had happened spread throughout the Judean hills. ⁶⁶Everyone who heard about it reflected on these events and asked, "What will this child turn out to be?" For the hand of the Lord was surely upon him in a special way.

⁶⁷Then his father, Zechariah, was filled with the Holy Spirit and gave this prophecy:

⁶⁸ "Praise the Lord, the God of Israel,
      because he has visited and
         redeemed his people.
⁶⁹ He has sent us a mighty Savior*
      from the royal line of his servant
         David,
⁷⁰ just as he promised
      through his holy prophets long ago.
⁷¹ Now we will be saved from our
         enemies
      and from all who hate us.
⁷² He has been merciful to our ancestors
      by remembering his sacred
         covenant—
⁷³ the covenant he swore with an oath
      to our ancestor Abraham.
⁷⁴ We have been rescued from our
         enemies
      so we can serve God without fear,
⁷⁵ in holiness and righteousness
      for as long as we live.
⁷⁶ "And you, my little son,
      will be called the prophet of the
         Most High,
      because you will prepare the way
         for the Lord.

⁷⁷ You will tell his people how to find
         salvation
      through forgiveness of their sins.
⁷⁸ Because of God's tender mercy,
      the morning light from heaven
         is about to break upon us,*
⁷⁹ to give light to those who sit in
         darkness and in the shadow
            of death,
      and to guide us to the path
         of peace."

⁸⁰John grew up and became strong in spirit. And he lived in the wilderness until he began his public ministry to Israel.

1:69 Greek *has raised up a horn of salvation for us.* **1:78** Or *the Morning Light from heaven is about to visit us.*

PSALM 58:1-11
For the choir director: A psalm of David, to be sung to the tune "Do Not Destroy!"

¹ Justice—do you rulers* know the
      meaning of the word?
      Do you judge the people fairly?
² No! You plot injustice in your hearts.
      You spread violence throughout the
         land.
³ These wicked people are born sinners;
      even from birth they have lied and
         gone their own way.
⁴ They spit venom like deadly snakes;
      they are like cobras that refuse to
         listen,
⁵ ignoring the tunes of the snake
         charmers,
      no matter how skillfully they play.

⁶ Break off their fangs, O God!
      Smash the jaws of these lions,
         O LORD!
⁷ May they disappear like water into
         thirsty ground.
      Make their weapons useless in their
         hands.*
⁸ May they be like snails that dissolve
         into slime,
      like a stillborn child who will never
         see the sun.
⁹ God will sweep them away, both young
         and old,
      faster than a pot heats over burning
         thorns.
¹⁰ The godly will rejoice when they see
         injustice avenged.

They will wash their feet in the
blood of the wicked.
[11] Then at last everyone will say,
"There truly is a reward for those
who live for God;
surely there is a God who judges
justly here on earth."

58:1 Or *you gods.*   **58:7** Or *Let them be trodden down and
wither like grass.* The meaning of the Hebrew is uncertain.

NUMBERS 24:1–25:18

How could a mercenary prophet and a foreign king
expect to do damage to people under God's protection? They couldn't, but given the right circumstances, the people could surely do damage to
themselves. This they did when they started sacrificing to other gods.

By now Balaam realized that the LORD
was determined to bless Israel, so he did
not resort to divination as before. Instead,
he turned and looked out toward the wilderness, [2] where he saw the people of Israel camped, tribe by tribe. Then the Spirit
of God came upon him, [3] and this is the
message he delivered:

"This is the message of Balaam son of
Beor,
the message of the man whose eyes
see clearly,
[4] the message of one who hears the
words of God,
who sees a vision from the Almighty,
who bows down with eyes wide
open:
[5] How beautiful are your tents, O Jacob;
how lovely are your homes, O Israel!
[6] They spread before me like palm
groves,*
like gardens by the riverside.
They are like tall trees planted by the
LORD,
like cedars beside the waters.
[7] Water will flow from their buckets;
their offspring have all they need.
Their king will be greater than Agag;
their kingdom will be exalted.

PROVERBS 11:12-13

It is foolish to belittle one's neighbor;
a sensible person keeps quiet. ☐ A gossip
goes around telling secrets, but those who
are trustworthy can keep a confidence.

MARCH**16**

[8] God brought them out of Egypt;
for them he is as strong as a wild ox.
He devours all the nations that oppose
him,
breaking their bones in pieces,
shooting them with arrows.
[9] Like a lion, Israel crouches and lies
down;
like a lioness, who dares to arouse
her?
Blessed is everyone who blesses you,
O Israel,
and cursed is everyone who curses
you."

[10]King Balak flew into a rage against
Balaam. He angrily clapped his hands and
shouted, "I called you to curse my enemies! Instead, you have blessed them
three times. [11]Now get out of here! Go
back home! I promised to reward you
richly, but the LORD has kept you from
your reward."

[12]Balaam told Balak, "Don't you remember what I told your messengers? I said,
[13]'Even if Balak were to give me his palace
filled with silver and gold, I would be powerless to do anything against the will of
the LORD.' I told you that I could say only
what the LORD says! [14]Now I am returning
to my own people. But first let me tell you
what the Israelites will do to your people
in the future."

[15]This is the message Balaam delivered:

"This is the message of Balaam son of
Beor,

the message of the man whose eyes
see clearly,
16 the message of one who hears the
words of God,
who has knowledge from the Most
High,
who sees a vision from the Almighty,
who bows down with eyes wide
open:
17 I see him, but not here and now.
I perceive him, but far in the distant
future.
A star will rise from Jacob;
a scepter will emerge from Israel.
It will crush the foreheads of Moab's
people,
cracking the skulls of the people of
Sheth.
18 Edom will be taken over,
and Seir, its enemy, will be
conquered,
while Israel marches on in triumph.
19 A ruler will rise in Jacob
who will destroy the survivors of Ir."

20Then Balaam looked over toward the
people of Amalek and delivered this message:

"Amalek was the greatest of nations,
but its destiny is destruction!"

21Then he looked over toward the Kenites
and delivered this message:

"Your home is secure;
your nest is set in the rocks.
22 But the Kenites will be destroyed
when Assyria* takes you captive."

23Balaam concluded his messages by
saying:

"Alas, who can survive
unless God has willed it?
24 Ships will come from the coasts of
Cyprus*;
they will oppress Assyria and afflict
Eber,
but they, too, will be utterly
destroyed."

25Then Balaam and Balak returned to
their homes.

25:1WHILE the Israelites were camped
at Acacia Grove,* some of the men defiled
themselves by having* sexual relations
with local Moabite women. 2These women
invited them to attend sacrifices to their
gods, so the Israelites feasted with them
and worshiped the gods of Moab. 3In this
way, Israel joined in the worship of Baal of
Peor, causing the LORD's anger to blaze
against his people.

4The LORD issued the following command to Moses: "Seize all the ringleaders
and execute them before the LORD in
broad daylight, so his fierce anger will turn
away from the people of Israel."

5So Moses ordered Israel's judges,
"Each of you must put to death the men
under your authority who have joined in
worshiping Baal of Peor."

6Just then one of the Israelite men
brought a Midianite woman into his tent,
right before the eyes of Moses and all the
people, as everyone was weeping at the
entrance of the Tabernacle.* 7When Phinehas son of Eleazar and grandson of Aaron
the priest saw this, he jumped up and left
the assembly. He took a spear 8and rushed
after the man into his tent. Phinehas
thrust the spear all the way through the
man's body and into the woman's stomach. So the plague against the Israelites
was stopped, 9but not before 24,000 people had died.

10Then the LORD said to Moses, 11"Phinehas son of Eleazar and grandson of Aaron
the priest has turned my anger away from
the Israelites by being as zealous among
them as I was. So I stopped destroying all
Israel as I had intended to do in my zealous anger. 12Now tell him that I am making
my special covenant of peace with him.
13In this covenant, I give him and his descendants a permanent right to the priesthood, for in his zeal for me, his God, he
purified the people of Israel, making them
right with me.*"

14The Israelite man killed with the
Midianite woman was named Zimri son
of Salu, the leader of a family from the
tribe of Simeon. 15The woman's name was
Cozbi; she was the daughter of Zur, the
leader of a Midianite clan.

16Then the LORD said to Moses, 17"Attack the Midianites and destroy them,
18because they assaulted you with deceit
and tricked you into worshiping Baal of

Peor, and because of Cozbi, the daughter of a Midianite leader, who was killed at the time of the plague because of what happened at Peor."

24:6 Or *like a majestic valley.*   **24:22** Hebrew *Asshur;* also in 24:24.   **24:24** Hebrew *Kittim.*   **25:1a** Hebrew *Shittim.* **25:1b** As in Greek version; Hebrew reads *some of the men began having.*   **25:6** Hebrew *the Tent of Meeting.* **25:13** Or *he made atonement for the people of Israel.*

LUKE 2:1-35
Here is the most familiar of the Christmas narratives, Luke's remarkably detailed account of the events surrounding Jesus' birth. As with John's birth and circumcision, Jesus' birth and circumcision were surrounded by remarkable events.

At that time the Roman emperor, Augustus, decreed that a census should be taken throughout the Roman Empire. ²(This was the first census taken when Quirinius was governor of Syria.) ³All returned to their own ancestral towns to register for this census. ⁴And because Joseph was a descendant of King David, he had to go to Bethlehem in Judea, David's ancient home. He traveled there from the village of Nazareth in Galilee. ⁵He took with him Mary, his fiancée, who was now obviously pregnant.

⁶And while they were there, the time came for her baby to be born. ⁷She gave birth to her first child, a son. She wrapped him snugly in strips of cloth and laid him in a manger, because there was no lodging available for them.

⁸That night there were shepherds staying in the fields nearby, guarding their flocks of sheep. ⁹Suddenly, an angel of the Lord appeared among them, and the radiance of the Lord's glory surrounded them. They were terrified, ¹⁰but the angel reassured them. "Don't be afraid!" he said. "I bring you good news that will bring great joy to all people. ¹¹The Savior—yes, the Messiah, the Lord—has been born today in Bethlehem, the city of David! ¹²And you will recognize him by this sign: You will find a baby wrapped snugly in strips of cloth, lying in a manger."

¹³Suddenly, the angel was joined by a vast host of others—the armies of heaven—praising God and saying,

¹⁴ "Glory to God in highest heaven,
    and peace on earth to those with
        whom God is pleased."

¹⁵When the angels had returned to heaven, the shepherds said to each other, "Let's go to Bethlehem! Let's see this thing that has happened, which the Lord has told us about."

¹⁶They hurried to the village and found Mary and Joseph. And there was the baby, lying in the manger. ¹⁷After seeing him, the shepherds told everyone what had happened and what the angel had said to them about this child. ¹⁸All who heard the shepherds' story were astonished, ¹⁹but Mary kept all these things in her heart and thought about them often. ²⁰The shepherds went back to their flocks, glorifying and praising God for all they had heard and seen. It was just as the angel had told them.

²¹Eight days later, when the baby was

HOW WE LIVE

Praise and thanksgiving

LUKE 2:9-12 It is beyond our understanding how God the Father would let his only Son leave his throne in heaven and take on the garb of humanity. Think about it—the Father sent his Son, himself God Eternal, knowing that he would be rejected and crucified. Death is one thing, but death on a cross was the ultimate symbol of pain and humiliation. He did this in order to give the human race a path to eternal life. Such a sacrifice! Such a gift! Have you stopped to ponder that gift lately?
• God has given us a gift we don't deserve and must never take for granted. Don't let a day go by without thanking God for what he has done. Thank him today for the tiny baby in a manger who came to die for you.

circumcised, he was named Jesus, the name given him by the angel even before he was conceived.

²²Then it was time for their purification offering, as required by the law of Moses after the birth of a child; so his parents took him to Jerusalem to present him to the Lord. ²³The law of the Lord says, "If a woman's first child is a boy, he must be dedicated to the Lord."* ²⁴So they offered the sacrifice required in the law of the Lord—"either a pair of turtledoves or two young pigeons."*

²⁵At that time there was a man in Jerusalem named Simeon. He was righteous and devout and was eagerly waiting for the Messiah to come and rescue Israel. The Holy Spirit was upon him ²⁶and had revealed to him that he would not die until he had seen the Lord's Messiah. ²⁷That day the Spirit led him to the Temple. So when Mary and Joseph came to present the baby Jesus to the Lord as the law required, ²⁸Simeon was there. He took the child in his arms and praised God, saying,

²⁹ "Sovereign Lord, now let your servant
        die in peace,
     as you have promised.
³⁰ I have seen your salvation,
³¹   which you have prepared for all
        people.
³² He is a light to reveal God to the
        nations,
      and he is the glory of your people
        Israel!"

³³Jesus' parents were amazed at what was being said about him. ³⁴Then Simeon blessed them, and he said to Mary, the baby's mother, "This child is destined to cause many in Israel to fall, but he will be a joy to many others. He has been sent as a sign from God, but many will oppose him. ³⁵As a result, the deepest thoughts of many hearts will be revealed. And a sword will pierce your very soul."

2:23 Exod 13:2.   2:24 Lev 12:8.

PSALM 59:1-17
*For the choir director: A psalm of David,
regarding the time Saul sent soldiers to
watch David's house in order to kill him.
To be sung to the tune "Do Not Destroy!"*

¹ **R**escue me from my enemies, O God.
     Protect me from those who have
        come to destroy me.
² Rescue me from these criminals;
     save me from these murderers.
³ They have set an ambush for me.
     Fierce enemies are out there
        waiting, Lord,
     though I have not sinned or
        offended them.
⁴ I have done nothing wrong,
     yet they prepare to attack me.
     Wake up! See what is happening
        and help me!
⁵ O Lord God of Heaven's Armies, the
        God of Israel,
     wake up and punish those hostile
        nations.
     Show no mercy to wicked traitors.
                                              Interlude

⁶ They come out at night,
     snarling like vicious dogs
        as they prowl the streets.
⁷ Listen to the filth that comes from
        their mouths;
     their words cut like swords.
     "After all, who can hear us?" they
        sneer.
⁸ But Lord, you laugh at them.
     You scoff at all the hostile nations.
⁹ You are my strength; I wait for you to
        rescue me,
     for you, O God, are my fortress.
¹⁰ In his unfailing love, my God will stand
        with me.
      He will let me look down in
        triumph on all my enemies.

¹¹ Don't kill them, for my people soon
        forget such lessons;
      stagger them with your power, and
        bring them to their knees,
      O Lord our shield.
¹² Because of the sinful things they say,
      because of the evil that is on their lips,
      let them be captured by their pride,
        their curses, and their lies.
¹³ Destroy them in your anger!
      Wipe them out completely!
      Then the whole world will know
        that God reigns in Israel.* *Interlude*

¹⁴ My enemies come out at night,
      snarling like vicious dogs

as they prowl the streets.
¹⁵ They scavenge for food
    but go to sleep unsatisfied.*
¹⁶ But as for me, I will sing about your
    power.
    Each morning I will sing with joy
       about your unfailing love.
For you have been my refuge,
    a place of safety when I am
    in distress.

¹⁷ O my Strength, to you I sing praises,
    for you, O God, are my refuge,
    the God who shows me unfailing
    love.

59:13 Hebrew *in Jacob*. See note on 44:4.   **59:15** Or *and growl if they don't get enough.*

PROVERBS 11:14

Without wise leadership, a nation falls; there is safety in having many advisers.

MARCH**17**

NUMBERS 26:1-51

It was time to count the people again. Remember that this inhabitation of the land would require battles. Part of the census was knowing what kind of army Israel could muster.

After the plague had ended, the LORD said to Moses and to Eleazar son of Aaron the priest, ²"From the whole community of Israel, record the names of all the warriors by their families. List all the men twenty years old or older who are able to go to war."

³ So there on the plains of Moab beside the Jordan River, across from Jericho, Moses and Eleazar the priest issued these instructions to the leaders of Israel: ⁴"List all the men of Israel twenty years old and older, just as the LORD commanded Moses."

This is the record of all the descendants of Israel who came out of Egypt.

⁵ These were the clans descended from the sons of Reuben, Jacob's* oldest son:
    The Hanochite clan, named after their
      ancestor Hanoch.
    The Palluite clan, named after their
      ancestor Pallu.
⁶ The Hezronite clan, named after their
      ancestor Hezron.
    The Carmite clan, named after their
      ancestor Carmi.
⁷ These were the clans of Reuben. Their registered troops numbered 43,730.

⁸Pallu was the ancestor of Eliab, ⁹and

Eliab was the father of Nemuel, Dathan, and Abiram. This Dathan and Abiram are the same community leaders who conspired with Korah against Moses and Aaron, rebelling against the LORD. ¹⁰But the earth opened up its mouth and swallowed them with Korah, and fire devoured 250 of their followers. This served as a warning to the entire nation of Israel. ¹¹However, the sons of Korah did not die that day.

¹² These were the clans descended from the sons of Simeon:
    The Jemuelite clan, named after their
      ancestor Jemuel.*
    The Jaminite clan, named after their
      ancestor Jamin.
    The Jakinite clan, named after their
      ancestor Jakin.
¹³ The Zoharite clan, named after their
      ancestor Zohar.*
    The Shaulite clan, named after their
      ancestor Shaul.

¹⁴ These were the clans of Simeon. Their registered troops numbered 22,200.

¹⁵ These were the clans descended from the sons of Gad:
    The Zephonite clan, named after their
      ancestor Zephon.
    The Haggite clan, named after their
      ancestor Haggi.
    The Shunite clan, named after their
      ancestor Shuni.

16 The Oznite clan, named after their
   ancestor Ozni.
   The Erite clan, named after their
   ancestor Eri.
17 The Arodite clan, named after their
   ancestor Arodi.*
   The Arelite clan, named after their
   ancestor Areli.

18These were the clans of Gad. Their registered troops numbered 40,500.

19Judah had two sons, Er and Onan, who had died in the land of Canaan. 20These were the clans descended from Judah's surviving sons:
   The Shelanite clan, named after their
   ancestor Shelah.
   The Perezite clan, named after their
   ancestor Perez.
   The Zerahite clan, named after their
   ancestor Zerah.

21These were the subclans descended from the Perezites:
   The Hezronites, named after their
   ancestor Hezron.
   The Hamulites, named after their
   ancestor Hamul.

22These were the clans of Judah. Their registered troops numbered 76,500.

23These were the clans descended from the sons of Issachar:
   The Tolaite clan, named after their
   ancestor Tola.
   The Puite clan, named after their
   ancestor Puah.*
24 The Jashubite clan, named after their
   ancestor Jashub.
   The Shimronite clan, named after
   their ancestor Shimron.

25These were the clans of Issachar. Their registered troops numbered 64,300.

26These were the clans descended from the sons of Zebulun:
   The Seredite clan, named after their
   ancestor Sered.
   The Elonite clan, named after their
   ancestor Elon.
   The Jahleelite clan, named after their
   ancestor Jahleel.

27These were the clans of Zebulun. Their registered troops numbered 60,500.

28Two clans were descended from Joseph through Manasseh and Ephraim.

29These were the clans descended from Manasseh:
   The Makirite clan, named after their
   ancestor Makir.
   The Gileadite clan, named after their
   ancestor Gilead, Makir's son.

30These were the subclans descended from the Gileadites:
   The Iezerites, named after their
   ancestor Iezer.
   The Helekites, named after their
   ancestor Helek.
31 The Asrielites, named after their
   ancestor Asriel.
   The Shechemites, named after their
   ancestor Shechem.
32 The Shemidaites, named after their
   ancestor Shemida.
   The Hepherites, named after their
   ancestor Hepher.
33 (One of Hepher's descendants,
   Zelophehad, had no sons, but his
   daughters' names were Mahlah,
   Noah, Hoglah, Milcah, and Tirzah.)

34These were the clans of Manasseh. Their registered troops numbered 52,700.

35These were the clans descended from the sons of Ephraim:
   The Shuthelahite clan, named after
   their ancestor Shuthelah.
   The Bekerite clan, named after their
   ancestor Beker.
   The Tahanite clan, named after their
   ancestor Tahan.

36This was the subclan descended from the Shuthelahites:
   The Eranites, named after their
   ancestor Eran.

37These were the clans of Ephraim. Their registered troops numbered 32,500.

These clans of Manasseh and Ephraim were all descendants of Joseph.

38These were the clans descended from the sons of Benjamin:
   The Belaite clan, named after their
   ancestor Bela.

The Ashbelite clan, named after their ancestor Ashbel.

The Ahiramite clan, named after their ancestor Ahiram.

[39] The Shuphamite clan, named after their ancestor Shupham.*

The Huphamite clan, named after their ancestor Hupham.

[40] These were the subclans descended from the Belaites:

The Ardites, named after their ancestor Ard.*

The Naamites, named after their ancestor Naaman.

[41] These were the clans of Benjamin. Their registered troops numbered 45,600.

[42] These were the clans descended from the sons of Dan:

The Shuhamite clan, named after their ancestor Shuham.

[43] These were the Shuhamite clans of Dan. Their registered troops numbered 64,400.

[44] These were the clans descended from the sons of Asher:

The Imnite clan, named after their ancestor Imnah.

The Ishvite clan, named after their ancestor Ishvi.

The Beriite clan, named after their ancestor Beriah.

[45] These were the subclans descended from the Beriites:

The Heberites, named after their ancestor Heber.

The Malkielites, named after their ancestor Malkiel.

[46] Asher also had a daughter named Serah.

[47] These were the clans of Asher. Their registered troops numbered 53,400.

[48] These were the clans descended from the sons of Naphtali:

The Jahzeelite clan, named after their ancestor Jahzeel.

The Gunite clan, named after their ancestor Guni.

[49] The Jezerite clan, named after their ancestor Jezer.

The Shillemite clan, named after their ancestor Shillem.

[50] These were the clans of Naphtali. Their registered troops numbered 45,400.

[51] In summary, the registered troops of all Israel numbered 601,730.

26:5 Hebrew *Israel's;* see note on 1:20-21b. 26:12 As in Syriac version (see also Gen 46:10; Exod 6:15); Hebrew reads *Nemuelite . . . Nemuel.* 26:13 As in parallel texts at Gen 46:10 and Exod 6:15; Hebrew reads *Zerahite . . . Zerah.* 26:17 As in Samaritan Pentateuch and Greek and Syriac versions (see also Gen 46:16); Hebrew reads *Arod.* 26:23 As in Samaritan Pentateuch, Greek and Syriac versions, and Latin Vulgate (see also 1 Chr 7:1); Hebrew reads *The Punite clan, named after its ancestor Puvah.* 26:39 As in some Hebrew manuscripts, Samaritan Pentateuch, Greek and Syriac

HOW WE LIVE: Aging

LUKE 2:25-35 (MARCH 16), 36-38 This chapter in Luke contains the account of two individuals of advanced age who played key roles in the first weeks of Jesus' life. Simeon was a righteous, devout man, filled with the Holy Spirit, who had been waiting with eager anticipation for the coming of the promised Messiah. When Mary and Joseph presented their infant son at the Temple, Simeon prophesied over Jesus with great joy. • The widow Anna was a prophet who stayed in the Temple around the clock, fasting and praying. She, too, praised God when her eyes fell upon the Christ child. At age 84, Anna became one of the very first witnesses to tell others about Jesus. • No matter how old you are, God has plans for you! Psalm 92:14 was written with you in mind: "Even in old age they will still produce fruit; they will remain vital and green." Perhaps you are still of younger age. While old age may seem a long way off, seek today—and every day—to please God. Aging will be a joy when you let God walk with you.

versions, and Latin Vulgate; most Hebrew manuscripts read *Shephupham.* **26:40** As in Samaritan Pentateuch, some Greek manuscripts, and Latin Vulgate; Hebrew lacks *named after their ancestor Ard.*

LUKE 2:36-52

Like Simeon from yesterday's reading, Anna was very old. She was a prophet, and she devoted each day to serving in the Temple. So, it was not surprising that she recognized the Son of God when he arrived.

Anna, a prophet, was also there in the Temple. She was the daughter of Phanuel from the tribe of Asher, and she was very old. Her husband died when they had been married only seven years. ³⁷Then she lived as a widow to the age of eighty-four.* She never left the Temple but stayed there day and night, worshiping God with fasting and prayer. ³⁸She came along just as Simeon was talking with Mary and Joseph, and she began praising God. She talked about the child to everyone who had been waiting expectantly for God to rescue Jerusalem.

³⁹When Jesus' parents had fulfilled all the requirements of the law of the Lord, they returned home to Nazareth in Galilee. ⁴⁰There the child grew up healthy and strong. He was filled with wisdom, and God's favor was on him.

⁴¹Every year Jesus' parents went to Jerusalem for the Passover festival. ⁴²When Jesus was twelve years old, they attended the festival as usual. ⁴³After the celebration was over, they started home to Nazareth, but Jesus stayed behind in Jerusalem. His parents didn't miss him at first, ⁴⁴because they assumed he was among the other travelers. But when he didn't show up that evening, they started looking for him among their relatives and friends.

⁴⁵When they couldn't find him, they went back to Jerusalem to search for him there. ⁴⁶Three days later they finally discovered him in the Temple, sitting among the religious teachers, listening to them and asking questions. ⁴⁷All who heard him were amazed at his understanding and his answers.

⁴⁸His parents didn't know what to think. "Son," his mother said to him, "why have you done this to us? Your father and I have been frantic, searching for you everywhere."

⁴⁹"But why did you need to search?" he asked. "Didn't you know that I must be in my Father's house?"* ⁵⁰But they didn't understand what he meant.

⁵¹Then he returned to Nazareth with them and was obedient to them. And his mother stored all these things in her heart.

⁵²Jesus grew in wisdom and in stature and in favor with God and all the people.

2:37 Or *She had been a widow for eighty-four years.*
2:49 Or *"Didn't you realize that I should be involved with my Father's affairs?"*

PSALM 60:1-12

For the choir director: A psalm of David useful for teaching, regarding the time David fought Aram-naharaim and Aram-zobah, and Joab returned and killed 12,000 Edomites in the Valley of Salt. To be sung to the tune "Lily of the Testimony."

¹ **Y**ou have rejected us, O God, and
     broken our defenses.
  You have been angry with us; now
     restore us to your favor.
² You have shaken our land and split it
     open.
  Seal the cracks, for the land trembles.
³ You have been very hard on us,
     making us drink wine that sent us
     reeling.
⁴ But you have raised a banner for those
     who fear you—
  a rallying point in the face of attack.
                                        Interlude

⁵ Now rescue your beloved people.
  Answer and save us by your power.
⁶ God has promised this by his
     holiness*:
  "I will divide up Shechem with joy.
  I will measure out the valley of
     Succoth.
⁷ Gilead is mine,
     and Manasseh, too.
  Ephraim, my helmet, will produce my
     warriors,
  and Judah, my scepter, will produce
     my kings.
⁸ But Moab, my washbasin, will become
     my servant,
  and I will wipe my feet on Edom
     and shout in triumph over Philistia."

⁹ Who will bring me into the fortified
city?
Who will bring me victory over
Edom?
¹⁰ Have you rejected us, O God?
Will you no longer march with
our armies?
¹¹ Oh, please help us against our enemies,
for all human help is useless.

¹² With God's help we will do mighty
things,
for he will trample down our foes.

60:6 Or *in his sanctuary.*

PROVERBS 11:15

There's danger in putting up security for a
stranger's debt; it's safer not to guarantee
another person's debt.

NUMBERS 26:52–28:15

*In the justice of God's law, the Promised Land was
divided fairly among the tribes, and women inherited land to preserve the family property. Moses'
successor was commissioned. It was a new time.*

Then the LORD said to Moses, ⁵³"Divide
the land among the tribes, and distribute
the grants of land in proportion to the
tribes' populations, as indicated by the
number of names on the list. ⁵⁴Give the larger tribes more land and the smaller
tribes less land, each group receiving a
grant in proportion to the size of its population. ⁵⁵But you must assign the land by
lot, and give land to each ancestral tribe
according to the number of names on the
list. ⁵⁶Each grant of land must be assigned
by lot among the larger and smaller tribal
groups."

⁵⁷This is the record of the Levites who
were counted according to their clans:
The Gershonite clan, named after
their ancestor Gershon.
The Kohathite clan, named after their
ancestor Kohath.
The Merarite clan, named after their
ancestor Merari.

⁵⁸The Libnites, the Hebronites, the Mah-
lites, the Mushites, and the Korahites were
all subclans of the Levites.

Now Kohath was the ancestor of Am-
ram, ⁵⁹and Amram's wife was named
Jochebed. She also was a descendant of
Levi, born among the Levites in the land of
Egypt. Amram and Jochebed became the
parents of Aaron, Moses, and their sister,
Miriam. ⁶⁰To Aaron were born Nadab, Abi-
hu, Eleazar, and Ithamar. ⁶¹But Nadab and
Abihu died when they burned before the
LORD the wrong kind of fire, different
than he had commanded.

⁶²The men from the Levite clans who
were one month old or older numbered
23,000. But the Levites were not included
in the registration of the rest of the people
of Israel because they were not given an
allotment of land when it was divided
among the Israelites.

⁶³So these are the results of the registration of the people of Israel as conducted by Moses and Eleazar the priest on
the plains of Moab beside the Jordan
River, across from Jericho. ⁶⁴Not one person on this list had been among those
listed in the previous registration taken
by Moses and Aaron in the wilderness of
Sinai. ⁶⁵For the LORD had said of them,
"They will all die in the wilderness." Not
one of them survived except Caleb son of
Jephunneh and Joshua son of Nun.

²⁷:¹ONE day a petition was presented by
the daughters of Zelophehad—Mahlah,
Noah, Hoglah, Milcah, and Tirzah. Their
father, Zelophehad, was a descendant of
Hepher son of Gilead, son of Makir, son of
Manasseh, son of Joseph. ²These women
stood before Moses, Eleazar the priest, the
tribal leaders, and the entire community

at the entrance of the Tabernacle.* ³"Our father died in the wilderness," they said. "He was not among Korah's followers, who rebelled against the LORD; he died because of his own sin. But he had no sons. ⁴Why should the name of our father disappear from his clan just because he had no sons? Give us property along with the rest of our relatives."

⁵So Moses brought their case before the LORD. ⁶And the LORD replied to Moses, ⁷"The claim of the daughters of Zelophehad is legitimate. You must give them a grant of land along with their father's relatives. Assign them the property that would have been given to their father.

⁸"And give the following instructions to the people of Israel: If a man dies and has no son, then give his inheritance to his daughters. ⁹And if he has no daughter either, transfer his inheritance to his brothers. ¹⁰If he has no brothers, give his inheritance to his father's brothers. ¹¹But if his father has no brothers, give his inheritance to the nearest relative in his clan. This is a legal requirement for the people of Israel, just as the LORD commanded Moses."

¹²One day the LORD said to Moses, "Climb one of the mountains east of the river,* and look out over the land I have given the people of Israel. ¹³After you have seen it, you will die like your brother, Aaron, ¹⁴for you both rebelled against my instructions in the wilderness of Zin. When the people of Israel rebelled, you failed to demonstrate my holiness to them at the waters." (These are the waters of Meribah at Kadesh* in the wilderness of Zin.)

¹⁵Then Moses said to the LORD, ¹⁶"O LORD, you are the God who gives breath to all creatures. Please appoint a new man as leader for the community. ¹⁷Give them someone who will guide them wherever they go and will lead them into battle, so the community of the LORD will not be like sheep without a shepherd."

¹⁸The LORD replied, "Take Joshua son of Nun, who has the Spirit in him, and lay your hands on him. ¹⁹Present him to Eleazar the priest before the whole community, and publicly commission him to lead the people. ²⁰Transfer some of your au-

thority to him so the whole community of Israel will obey him. ²¹When direction from the LORD is needed, Joshua will stand before Eleazar the priest, who will use the Urim—one of the sacred lots cast before the LORD—to determine his will. This is how Joshua and the rest of the community of Israel will determine everything they should do."

²²So Moses did as the LORD commanded. He presented Joshua to Eleazar the priest and the whole community. ²³Moses laid his hands on him and commissioned him to lead the people, just as the LORD had commanded through Moses.

28:1THE LORD said to Moses, ²"Give these instructions to the people of Israel: The offerings you present as special gifts are a pleasing aroma to me; they are my food. See to it that they are brought at the appointed times and offered according to my instructions.

³"Say to the people: This is the special gift you must present to the LORD as your daily burnt offering. You must offer two one-year-old male lambs with no defects. ⁴Sacrifice one lamb in the morning and the other in the evening. ⁵With each lamb you must offer a grain offering of two quarts* of choice flour mixed with one quart* of pure oil of pressed olives. ⁶This is the regular burnt offering instituted at Mount Sinai as a special gift, a pleasing aroma to the LORD. ⁷Along with it you must present the proper liquid offering of one quart of alcoholic drink with each lamb, poured out in the Holy Place as an offering to the LORD. ⁸Offer the second lamb in the evening with the same grain offering and liquid offering. It, too, is a special gift, a pleasing aroma to the LORD.

⁹"On the Sabbath day, sacrifice two one-year-old male lambs with no defects. They must be accompanied by a grain offering of four quarts* of choice flour moistened with olive oil, and a liquid offering. ¹⁰This is the burnt offering to be presented each Sabbath day, in addition to the regular burnt offering and its accompanying liquid offering.

¹¹"On the first day of each month, present an extra burnt offering to the LORD

of two young bulls, one ram, and seven one-year-old male lambs, all with no defects. ¹²These must be accompanied by grain offerings of choice flour moistened with olive oil—six quarts* with each bull, four quarts with the ram, ¹³and two quarts with each lamb. This burnt offering will be a special gift, a pleasing aroma to the LORD. ¹⁴You must also present a liquid offering with each sacrifice: two quarts* of wine for each bull, a third of a gallon* for the ram, and one quart* for each lamb. Present this monthly burnt offering on the first day of each month throughout the year.

¹⁵"On the first day of each month, you must also offer one male goat for a sin offering to the LORD. This is in addition to the regular burnt offering and its accompanying liquid offering."

27:2 Hebrew *the Tent of Meeting.* 27:12 Or *the mountains of Abarim.* 27:14 Hebrew *waters of Meribath-kadesh.*
28:5a Hebrew *1/10 of an ephah* [2.2 liters]; also in 28:13, 21, 29. 28:5b Hebrew *1/4 of a hin* [1 liter]; also in 28:7.
28:9 Hebrew *2/10 of an ephah* [4.4 liters]; also in 28:12, 20, 28.
28:12 Hebrew *3/10 of an ephah* [6.6 liters]; also in 28:20, 28.
28:14a Hebrew *1/2 of a hin* [2 liters]. 28:14b Hebrew *1/3 of a hin* [1.3 liters]. 28:14c Hebrew *1/4 of a hin* [1 liter].

LUKE 3:1-22
John's parents had known since before his birth that his destiny was wrapped up with the destiny of the Messiah. John gave his life to that destiny and drew the attention of his people to a man named Jesus.

It was now the fifteenth year of the reign of Tiberius, the Roman emperor. Pontius Pilate was governor over Judea; Herod Antipas was ruler* over Galilee; his brother Philip was ruler* over Iturea and Traconitis; Lysanias was ruler over Abilene. ²Annas and Caiaphas were the high priests. At this time a message from God came to John son of Zechariah, who was living in the wilderness. ³Then John went from place to place on both sides of the Jordan River, preaching that people should be baptized to show that they had repented of their sins and turned to God to be forgiven. ⁴Isaiah had spoken of John when he said,

"He is a voice shouting in the
     wilderness,
 'Prepare the way for the LORD's
     coming!
  Clear the road for him!
⁵ The valleys will be filled,
  and the mountains and hills made
     level.
  The curves will be straightened,
     and the rough places made
     smooth.
⁶ And then all people will see
     the salvation sent from God.'"*

⁷When the crowds came to John for baptism, he said, "You brood of snakes! Who warned you to flee God's coming wrath? ⁸Prove by the way you live that you

WHO GOD IS

God is just

NUMBERS 26:64-65 You may wonder about the justice of letting an entire generation die in the wilderness. Sure, the people had made some poor choices, but wasn't this punishment a bit harsh? Keep in mind that the people had sinned repeatedly in the wilderness, and God had given them numerous opportunities to change their ways. But they continued to disobey, complain, whine, and rebel. They learned the hard way that one cannot treat God's mercy with contempt. • God must punish sin—and often we face the reality of the consequences of our own sinfulness. However, if God were only just, then none of us could survive, for we deserve punishment every day. Fortunately for us, God is also merciful. He took the punishment for sin upon himself in order to save us. He could not just wink at sin or pretend it isn't so bad; it had to be dealt with and punished as it required—by death. So Jesus died to take our punishment and satisfy God's justice, and then he rose again to promise us eternity with him.

have repented of your sins and turned to God. Don't just say to each other, 'We're safe, for we are descendants of Abraham.' That means nothing, for I tell you, God can create children of Abraham from these very stones. [9]Even now the ax of God's judgment is poised, ready to sever the roots of the trees. Yes, every tree that does not produce good fruit will be chopped down and thrown into the fire."

[10]The crowds asked, "What should we do?"

[11]John replied, "If you have two shirts, give one to the poor. If you have food, share it with those who are hungry."

[12]Even corrupt tax collectors came to be baptized and asked, "Teacher, what should we do?"

[13]He replied, "Collect no more taxes than the government requires."

[14]"What should we do?" asked some soldiers.

John replied, "Don't extort money or make false accusations. And be content with your pay."

[15]Everyone was expecting the Messiah to come soon, and they were eager to know whether John might be the Messiah. [16]John answered their questions by saying, "I baptize you with* water; but someone is coming soon who is greater than I am—so much greater that I'm not even worthy to be his slave and untie the straps of his sandals. He will baptize you with the Holy Spirit and with fire.* [17]He is ready to separate the chaff from the wheat with his winnowing fork. Then he will clean up the threshing area, gathering the wheat into his barn but burning the chaff with never-ending fire." [18]John used many such warnings as he announced the Good News to the people.

[19]John also publicly criticized Herod Antipas, the ruler of Galilee,* for marrying Herodias, his brother's wife, and for many other wrongs he had done. [20]So Herod put John in prison, adding this sin to his many others.

[21]One day when the crowds were being baptized, Jesus himself was baptized. As he was praying, the heavens opened, [22]and the Holy Spirit, in bodily form, descended on him like a dove. And a voice from heaven said, "You are my dearly loved Son, and you bring me great joy.*"

3:1a Greek *Herod was tetrarch.* Herod Antipas was a son of King Herod.   3:1b Greek *tetrarch;* also in 3:1c.   3:4-6 Isa 40:3-5 (Greek version).   3:16a Or *in.*   3:16b Or *in the Holy Spirit and in fire.*   3:19 Greek *Herod the tetrarch.* 3:22 Some manuscripts read *my Son, and today I have become your Father.*

PSALM 61:1-8

For the choir director: A psalm of David, to be accompanied by stringed instruments.

[1] **O** God, listen to my cry!
    Hear my prayer!
[2] From the ends of the earth,
    I cry to you for help
    when my heart is overwhelmed.
    Lead me to the towering rock of safety,
[3]   for you are my safe refuge,
    a fortress where my enemies cannot
        reach me.
[4] Let me live forever in your sanctuary,
    safe beneath the shelter of your
        wings!   *Interlude*

[5] For you have heard my vows, O God.
    You have given me an inheritance
        reserved for those who fear your
        name.
[6] Add many years to the life of the king!
    May his years span the generations!
[7] May he reign under God's protection
        forever.
    May your unfailing love and
        faithfulness watch over him.
[8] Then I will sing praises to your name
        forever
    as I fulfill my vows each day.

PROVERBS 11:16-17

A gracious woman gains respect, but ruthless men gain only wealth. □ Your kindness will reward you, but your cruelty will destroy you.

NUMBERS 28:16–29:40

Festivals were the serious business of ancient Israelite religion. These festivals marked the year and focused the people on God's goodness to them. Each one played a special role in the worship and remembrance of the nation.

"**O**n the fourteenth day of the first month,* you must celebrate the LORD's Passover. ¹⁷On the following day—the fifteenth day of the month—a joyous, seven-day festival will begin, but no bread made with yeast may be eaten. ¹⁸The first day of the festival will be an official day for holy assembly, and no ordinary work may be done on that day. ¹⁹As a special gift you must present a burnt offering to the LORD—two young bulls, one ram, and seven one-year-old male lambs, all with no defects. ²⁰These will be accompanied by grain offerings of choice flour moistened with olive oil—six quarts with each bull, four quarts with the ram, ²¹and two quarts with each of the seven lambs. ²²You must also offer a male goat as a sin offering to purify yourselves and make yourselves right with the LORD.* ²³Present these offerings in addition to your regular morning burnt offering. ²⁴On each of the seven days of the festival, this is how you must prepare the food offering that is presented as a special gift, a pleasing aroma to the LORD. These will be offered in addition to the regular burnt offerings and liquid offerings. ²⁵The seventh day of the festival will be another official day for holy assembly, and no ordinary work may be done on that day.

²⁶"At the Festival of Harvest,* when you present the first of your new grain to the LORD, you must call an official day for holy assembly, and you may do no ordinary work on that day. ²⁷Present a special burnt offering on that day as a pleasing aroma to the LORD. It will consist of two young bulls, one ram, and seven one-year-old male lambs. ²⁸These will be accompanied by grain offerings of choice flour moistened with olive oil—six quarts with each bull, four quarts with the ram, ²⁹and two quarts with each of the seven lambs.

³⁰Also, offer one male goat to purify yourselves and make yourselves right with the LORD. ³¹Prepare these special burnt offerings, along with their liquid offerings, in addition to the regular burnt offering and its accompanying grain offering. Be sure that all the animals you sacrifice have no defects.

²⁹:¹"CELEBRATE the Festival of Trumpets each year on the first day of the appointed month in early autumn.* You must call an official day for holy assembly, and you may do no ordinary work. ²On that day you must present a burnt offering as a pleasing aroma to the LORD. It will consist of one young bull, one ram, and seven one-year-old male lambs, all with no defects. ³These must be accompanied by grain offerings of choice flour moistened with olive oil—six quarts* with the bull, four quarts* with the ram, ⁴and two quarts* with each of the seven lambs. ⁵In addition, you must sacrifice a male goat as a sin offering to purify yourselves and make yourselves right with the LORD.* ⁶These special sacrifices are in addition to your regular monthly and daily burnt offerings, and they must be given with their prescribed grain offerings and liquid offerings. These offerings are given as a special gift to the LORD, a pleasing aroma to him.

⁷"Ten days later, on the tenth day of the same month,* you must call another holy assembly. On that day, the Day of Atonement, the people must go without food and must do no ordinary work. ⁸You must present a burnt offering as a pleasing aroma to the LORD. It will consist of one young bull, one ram, and seven one-year-old male lambs, all with no defects. ⁹These offerings must be accompanied by the prescribed grain offerings of choice flour moistened with olive oil—six quarts of choice flour with the bull, four quarts of choice flour with the ram, ¹⁰and two quarts of choice flour with each of the seven lambs. ¹¹You must also sacrifice one male goat for a sin offering.

This is in addition to the sin offering of atonement and the regular daily burnt offering with its grain offering, and their accompanying liquid offerings.

¹²"Five days later, on the fifteenth day of the same month,* you must call another holy assembly of all the people, and you may do no ordinary work on that day. It is the beginning of the Festival of Shelters,* a seven-day festival to the LORD. ¹³On the first day of the festival, you must present a burnt offering as a special gift, a pleasing aroma to the LORD. It will consist of thirteen young bulls, two rams, and fourteen one-year-old male lambs, all with no defects. ¹⁴Each of these offerings must be accompanied by a grain offering of choice flour moistened with olive oil—six quarts for each of the thirteen bulls, four quarts for each of the two rams, ¹⁵and two quarts for each of the fourteen lambs. ¹⁶You must also sacrifice a male goat as a sin offering, in addition to the regular burnt offering with its accompanying grain offering and liquid offering.

¹⁷"On the second day of this seven-day festival, sacrifice twelve young bulls, two rams, and fourteen one-year-old male lambs, all with no defects. ¹⁸Each of these offerings of bulls, rams, and lambs must be accompanied by its prescribed grain offering and liquid offering. ¹⁹You must also sacrifice a male goat as a sin offering, in addition to the regular burnt offering with its accompanying grain offering and liquid offering.

²⁰"On the third day of the festival, sacrifice eleven young bulls, two rams, and fourteen one-year-old male lambs, all with no defects. ²¹Each of these offerings of bulls, rams, and lambs must be accompanied by its prescribed grain offering and liquid offering. ²²You must also sacrifice a male goat as a sin offering, in addition to the regular burnt offering with its accompanying grain offering and liquid offering.

²³"On the fourth day of the festival, sacrifice ten young bulls, two rams, and fourteen one-year-old male lambs, all with no defects. ²⁴Each of these offerings of bulls, rams, and lambs must be accompanied by its prescribed grain offering and liquid offering. ²⁵You must also sacrifice a male goat as a sin offering, in addition to the regular burnt offering with its accompanying grain offering and liquid offering.

²⁶"On the fifth day of the festival, sacrifice nine young bulls, two rams, and fourteen one-year-old male lambs, all with no defects. ²⁷Each of these offerings of bulls, rams, and lambs must be accompanied by its prescribed grain offering and liquid offering. ²⁸You must also sacrifice a male goat as a sin offering, in addition to the regular burnt offering with its accompanying grain offering and liquid offering.

²⁹"On the sixth day of the festival, sacrifice eight young bulls, two rams, and fourteen one-year-old male lambs, all with no defects. ³⁰Each of these offerings of bulls, rams, and lambs must be accompanied by its prescribed grain offering and liquid offering. ³¹You must also sacrifice a male goat as a sin offering, in addition to the regular burnt offering with its accompanying grain offering and liquid offering.

³²"On the seventh day of the festival, sacrifice seven young bulls, two rams, and fourteen one-year-old male lambs, all with no defects. ³³Each of these offerings of bulls, rams, and lambs must be accompanied by its prescribed grain offering and liquid offering. ³⁴You must also sacrifice one male goat as a sin offering, in addition to the regular burnt offering with its accompanying grain offering and liquid offering.

³⁵"On the eighth day of the festival, proclaim another holy day. You must do no ordinary work on that day. ³⁶You must present a burnt offering as a special gift, a pleasing aroma to the LORD. It will consist of one young bull, one ram, and seven one-year-old male lambs, all with no defects. ³⁷Each of these offerings must be accompanied by its prescribed grain offering and liquid offering. ³⁸You must also sacrifice one male goat as a sin offering, in addition to the regular burnt offering with its accompanying grain offering and liquid offering.

³⁹"You must present these offerings to the LORD at your annual festivals. These are in addition to the sacrifices and offerings you present in connection with vows, or as voluntary offerings, burnt offerings, grain offerings, liquid offerings, or peace offerings."

40*So Moses gave all of these instructions to the people of Israel as the LORD had commanded him.

28:16 This day in the ancient Hebrew lunar calendar occurred in late March, April, or early May.   **28:22** Or *to make atonement for yourselves;* also in 28:30.
28:26 Hebrew *Festival of Weeks.* This was later called the Festival of Pentecost (see Acts 2:1). It is celebrated today as Shavuot (or Shabuoth).   **29:1** Hebrew *the first day of the seventh month.* This day in the ancient Hebrew lunar calendar occurred in September or October. This festival is celebrated today as Rosh Hashanah, the Jewish new year.
29:3a Hebrew ³⁄₁₀ *of an ephah* [6.6 liters]; also in 29:9, 14.
29:3b Hebrew ²⁄₁₀ *of an ephah* [4.4 liters]; also in 29:9, 14.
29:4 Hebrew ¹⁄₁₀ *of an ephah* [2.2 liters]; also in 29:10, 15.
29:5 Or *to make atonement for yourselves.*   **29:7** Hebrew *On the tenth day of the seventh month;* see 29:1 and the note there. This day in the ancient Hebrew lunar calendar occurred in September or October. It is celebrated today as Yom Kippur.   **29:12a** Hebrew *On the fifteenth day of the seventh month;* see 29:1, 7 and the notes there. This day in the ancient Hebrew lunar calendar occurred in late September, October, or early November.   **29:12b** Or *Festival of Booths,* or *Festival of Tabernacles.* This was earlier called the Festival of the Final Harvest or Festival of Ingathering (see Exod 23:16b). It is celebrated today as Sukkot (or Succoth).
29:40 Verse 29:40 is numbered 30:1 in Hebrew text.

LUKE 3:23-38

Going back all the way through Isaac and Abraham, ancestors of the Jewish faith, then through Noah and all the way to Adam, this genealogy demonstrates Jesus' rich heritage and his humanity.

Jesus was about thirty years old when he began his public ministry.

Jesus was known as the son of Joseph.
Joseph was the son of Heli.
24 Heli was the son of Matthat.
Matthat was the son of Levi.
Levi was the son of Melki.

Melki was the son of Jannai.
Jannai was the son of Joseph.
25 Joseph was the son of Mattathias.
Mattathias was the son of Amos.
Amos was the son of Nahum.
Nahum was the son of Esli.
Esli was the son of Naggai.
26 Naggai was the son of Maath.
Maath was the son of Mattathias.
Mattathias was the son of Semein.
Semein was the son of Josech.
Josech was the son of Joda.
27 Joda was the son of Joanan.
Joanan was the son of Rhesa.
Rhesa was the son of Zerubbabel.
Zerubbabel was the son of Shealtiel.
Shealtiel was the son of Neri.
28 Neri was the son of Melki.
Melki was the son of Addi.
Addi was the son of Cosam.
Cosam was the son of Elmadam.
Elmadam was the son of Er.
29 Er was the son of Joshua.
Joshua was the son of Eliezer.
Eliezer was the son of Jorim.
Jorim was the son of Matthat.
Matthat was the son of Levi.
30 Levi was the son of Simeon.
Simeon was the son of Judah.
Judah was the son of Joseph.
Joseph was the son of Jonam.
Jonam was the son of Eliakim.
31 Eliakim was the son of Melea.
Melea was the son of Menna.

HOW WE LIVE — Trusting God

PSALM 62 King David, who wrote this particular psalm, knew a thing or two about enemies rising up against him and trying to destroy him. In the books of 1 and 2 Samuel, you will read about the many ups and downs of King David's life. But David also knew a thing or two about trust. David understood the simple truth that God is trustworthy in everything.   • Have you ever felt like David? Surrounded on every side by troubles, feeling like you need a refuge in the middle of an angry storm? Then do what David did: "I wait quietly before God" (62:1). Place all your hope in God; he is in control no matter how out of control you may feel. When you recognize that, then you can wait patiently as he works through the situation.   • No matter what comes your way, God is your rock, your salvation, your fortress where you will not be shaken. Run to his fortress and wait there. You can trust him to care for you, no matter how fierce the storm may be.

Menna was the son of Mattatha.
Mattatha was the son of Nathan.
Nathan was the son of David.
32 David was the son of Jesse.
Jesse was the son of Obed.
Obed was the son of Boaz.
Boaz was the son of Salmon.*
Salmon was the son of Nahshon.
33 Nahshon was the son of Amminadab.
Amminadab was the son of Admin.
Admin was the son of Arni.*
Arni was the son of Hezron.
Hezron was the son of Perez.
Perez was the son of Judah.
34 Judah was the son of Jacob.
Jacob was the son of Isaac.
Isaac was the son of Abraham.
Abraham was the son of Terah.
Terah was the son of Nahor.
35 Nahor was the son of Serug.
Serug was the son of Reu.
Reu was the son of Peleg.
Peleg was the son of Eber.
Eber was the son of Shelah.
36 Shelah was the son of Cainan.
Cainan was the son of Arphaxad.
Arphaxad was the son of Shem.
Shem was the son of Noah.
Noah was the son of Lamech.
37 Lamech was the son of Methuselah.
Methuselah was the son of Enoch.
Enoch was the son of Jared.
Jared was the son of Mahalalel.
Mahalalel was the son of Kenan.
38 Kenan was the son of Enosh.*
Enosh was the son of Seth.
Seth was the son of Adam.
Adam was the son of God.

3:32 Greek *Sala*, a variant spelling of Salmon; also in 3:32b.
See Ruth 4:22.   3:33 Some manuscripts read *Amminadab
was the son of Aram. Arni* and *Aram* are alternate spellings of
Ram. See 1 Chr 2:9-10.   3:38 Greek *Enos*, a variant spelling
of Enosh; also in 3:38b. See Gen 5:6.

PSALM 62:1-12
*For Jeduthun, the choir director: A psalm
of David.*

1 **I** wait quietly before God,
   for my victory comes from him.
2 He alone is my rock and my salvation,
   my fortress where I will never be
      shaken.

3 So many enemies against one
      man—
   all of them trying to kill me.
   To them I'm just a broken-down wall
      or a tottering fence.
4 They plan to topple me from my high
      position.
   They delight in telling lies about
      me.
   They praise me to my face
      but curse me in their hearts.
                                    Interlude

5 Let all that I am wait quietly before
      God,
   for my hope is in him.
6 He alone is my rock and my
      salvation,
   my fortress where I will not be
      shaken.
7 My victory and honor come from God
      alone.
   He is my refuge, a rock where no
      enemy can reach me.
8 O my people, trust in him at all
      times.
   Pour out your heart to him,
      for God is our refuge.   *Interlude*

9 Common people are as worthless
      as a puff of wind,
   and the powerful are not what they
      appear to be.
   If you weigh them on the scales,
      together they are lighter than
         a breath of air.

10 Don't make your living by extortion
      or put your hope in stealing.
   And if your wealth increases,
      don't make it the center of your life.
11 God has spoken plainly,
      and I have heard it many times:
   Power, O God, belongs to you;
12 unfailing love, O Lord, is yours.
   Surely you repay all people
      according to what they have done.

PROVERBS 11:18-19
Evil people get rich for the moment, but
the reward of the godly will last. □ Godly
people find life; evil people find death.

NUMBERS 30:1–31:54

When the Israelites followed God's command to conquer other peoples, they were fighting the Lord's war, not just ordinary fights between peoples. When they obeyed God's instructions, they were victorious.

¹*Then Moses summoned the leaders of the tribes of Israel and told them, "This is what the LORD has commanded: ²A man who makes a vow to the LORD or makes a pledge under oath must never break it. He must do exactly what he said he would do.

³"If a young woman makes a vow to the LORD or a pledge under oath while she is still living at her father's home, ⁴and her father hears of the vow or pledge and does not object to it, then all her vows and pledges will stand. ⁵But if her father refuses to let her fulfill the vow or pledge on the day he hears of it, then all her vows and pledges will become invalid. The LORD will forgive her because her father would not let her fulfill them.

⁶"Now suppose a young woman makes a vow or binds herself with an impulsive pledge and later marries. ⁷If her husband learns of her vow or pledge and does not object on the day he hears of it, her vows and pledges will stand. ⁸But if her husband refuses to accept her vow or impulsive pledge on the day he hears of it, he nullifies her commitments, and the LORD will forgive her. ⁹If, however, a woman is a widow or is divorced, she must fulfill all her vows and pledges.

¹⁰"But suppose a woman is married and living in her husband's home when she makes a vow or binds herself with a pledge. ¹¹If her husband hears of it and does not object to it, her vow or pledge will stand. ¹²But if her husband refuses to accept it on the day he hears of it, her vow or pledge will be nullified, and the LORD will forgive her. ¹³So her husband may either confirm or nullify any vows or pledges she makes to deny herself. ¹⁴But if he does not object on the day he hears of it, then he is agreeing to all her vows and pledges. ¹⁵If he waits more than a day and then tries to nullify a vow or pledge, he will be punished for her guilt."

¹⁶These are the regulations the LORD gave Moses concerning relationships between a man and his wife, and between a father and a young daughter who still lives at home.

³¹:¹THEN the LORD said to Moses, ²"On behalf of the people of Israel, take revenge on the Midianites for leading them into idolatry. After that, you will die and join your ancestors."

³So Moses said to the people, "Choose some men, and arm them to fight the LORD's war of revenge against Midian. ⁴From each tribe of Israel, send 1,000 men into battle." ⁵So they chose 1,000 men from each tribe of Israel, a total of 12,000 men armed for battle. ⁶Then Moses sent them out, 1,000 men from each tribe, and Phinehas son of Eleazar the priest led them into battle. They carried along the holy objects of the sanctuary and the trumpets for sounding the charge. ⁷They attacked Midian as the LORD had commanded Moses, and they killed all the men. ⁸All five of the Midianite kings—Evi, Rekem, Zur, Hur, and Reba—died in the battle. They also killed Balaam son of Beor with the sword.

⁹Then the Israelite army captured the Midianite women and children and seized their cattle and flocks and all their wealth as plunder. ¹⁰They burned all the towns and villages where the Midianites had lived. ¹¹After they had gathered the plunder and captives, both people and animals, ¹²they brought them all to Moses and Eleazar the priest, and to the whole community of Israel, which was camped on the plains of Moab beside the Jordan River, across from Jericho. ¹³Moses, Eleazar the priest, and all the leaders of the community went to meet them outside the camp. ¹⁴But Moses was furious with all the generals and captains* who had returned from the battle.

¹⁵"Why have you let all the women live?" he demanded. ¹⁶"These are the very ones who followed Balaam's advice and caused the people of Israel to rebel against

the LORD at Mount Peor. They are the ones who caused the plague to strike the LORD's people. ¹⁷So kill all the boys and all the women who have had intercourse with a man. ¹⁸Only the young girls who are virgins may live; you may keep them for yourselves. ¹⁹And all of you who have killed anyone or touched a dead body must stay outside the camp for seven days. You must purify yourselves and your captives on the third and seventh days. ²⁰Purify all your clothing, too, and everything made of leather, goat hair, or wood."

²¹Then Eleazar the priest said to the men who were in the battle, "The LORD has given Moses this legal requirement: ²²Anything made of gold, silver, bronze, iron, tin, or lead—²³that is, all metals that do not burn—must be passed through fire in order to be made ceremonially pure. These metal objects must then be further purified with the water of purification. But everything that burns must be purified by the water alone. ²⁴On the seventh day you must wash your clothes and be purified. Then you may return to the camp."

²⁵And the LORD said to Moses, ²⁶"You and Eleazar the priest and the family leaders of each tribe are to make a list of all the plunder taken in the battle, including the people and animals. ²⁷Then divide the plunder into two parts, and give half to the men who fought the battle and half to the rest of the people. ²⁸From the army's portion, first give the LORD his share of the plunder—one of every 500 of the prisoners and of the cattle, donkeys, sheep, and goats. ²⁹Give this share of the army's half to Eleazar the priest as an offering to the LORD. ³⁰From the half that belongs to the people of Israel, take one of every fifty of the prisoners and of the cattle, donkeys, sheep, goats, and other animals. Give this share to the Levites, who are in charge of maintaining the LORD's Tabernacle." ³¹So Moses and Eleazar the priest did as the LORD commanded Moses.

³²The plunder remaining from everything the fighting men had taken totaled 675,000 sheep and goats, ³³72,000 cattle, ³⁴61,000 donkeys, ³⁵and 32,000 virgin girls. ³⁶Half of the plunder was given to the fighting men. It totaled 337,500 sheep and goats, ³⁷of which 675 were the LORD's share; ³⁸36,000 cattle, of which 72 were the LORD's share; ³⁹30,500 donkeys, of which 61 were the LORD's share; ⁴⁰and 16,000 virgin girls, of whom 32 were the LORD's share. ⁴¹Moses gave all the LORD's share to Eleazar the priest, just as the LORD had directed him.

⁴²Half of the plunder belonged to the people of Israel, and Moses separated it from the half belonging to the fighting men. ⁴³It totaled 337,500 sheep and goats, ⁴⁴36,000 cattle, ⁴⁵30,500 donkeys, ⁴⁶and 16,000 virgin girls. ⁴⁷From the half-share given to the people, Moses took one of every fifty prisoners and animals and gave them to the Levites, who maintained the LORD's Tabernacle. All this was done as the LORD had commanded Moses.

⁴⁸Then all the generals and captains came to Moses ⁴⁹and said, "We, your servants, have accounted for all the men who went out to battle under our command; not one of us is missing! ⁵⁰So we are presenting the items of gold we captured as an offering to the LORD from our share of the plunder—armbands, bracelets, rings, earrings, and necklaces. This will purify our lives before the LORD and make us right with him.*"

⁵¹So Moses and Eleazar the priest received the gold from all the military commanders—all kinds of jewelry and crafted objects. ⁵²In all, the gold that the generals and captains presented as a gift to the LORD weighed about 420 pounds.* ⁵³All the fighting men had taken some of the plunder for themselves. ⁵⁴So Moses and Eleazar the priest accepted the gifts from the generals and captains and brought the gold to the Tabernacle* as a reminder to the LORD that the people of Israel belong to him.

30:1 Verses 30:1-16 are numbered 30:2-17 in Hebrew text.
31:14 Hebrew *the commanders of thousands, and the commanders of hundreds;* also in 31:48, 52, 54.   **31:50** Or *will make atonement for our lives before the LORD.*
31:52 Hebrew *16,750 shekels* [191 kilograms].
31:54 Hebrew *the Tent of Meeting.*

LUKE 4:1-30

In a culture that had looked for the Messiah for centuries, Jesus stood as a seemingly common man from Nazareth claiming to be that long-awaited savior. Many were impressed, but only a few were able to make the leap of faith.

Then Jesus, full of the Holy Spirit, returned from the Jordan River. He was led by the Spirit in the wilderness,* ²where he was tempted by the devil for forty days. Jesus ate nothing all that time and became very hungry.

³Then the devil said to him, "If you are the Son of God, tell this stone to become a loaf of bread."

⁴But Jesus told him, "No! The Scriptures say, 'People do not live by bread alone.'*"

⁵Then the devil took him up and revealed to him all the kingdoms of the world in a moment of time. ⁶"I will give you the glory of these kingdoms and authority over them," the devil said, "because they are mine to give to anyone I please. ⁷I will give it all to you if you will worship me."

⁸Jesus replied, "The Scriptures say,

'You must worship the LORD your God
   and serve only him.'*"

⁹Then the devil took him to Jerusalem, to the highest point of the Temple, and said, "If you are the Son of God, jump off! ¹⁰For the Scriptures say,

'He will order his angels to protect and
   guard you.

¹¹ And they will hold you up with their
   hands
   so you won't even hurt your foot on
   a stone.'*"

¹²Jesus responded, "The Scriptures also say, 'You must not test the LORD your God.'*"

¹³When the devil had finished tempting Jesus, he left him until the next opportunity came.

¹⁴Then Jesus returned to Galilee, filled with the Holy Spirit's power. Reports about him spread quickly through the whole region. ¹⁵He taught regularly in their synagogues and was praised by everyone.

¹⁶When he came to the village of Nazareth, his boyhood home, he went as usual to the synagogue on the Sabbath and stood up to read the Scriptures. ¹⁷The scroll of Isaiah the prophet was handed to him. He unrolled the scroll and found the place where this was written:

¹⁸ "The Spirit of the LORD is upon
   me,
   for he has anointed me to bring
   Good News to the poor.

WHO GOD IS

Jesus fulfilled prophecy

LUKE 4:16-21 The people in the synagogue that day had heard the passage Jesus read many times over the course of their lives. They had wondered at its meaning and looked forward to its fulfillment, for it described the Messiah for whom they were looking. • Jesus read those powerful words of promise, rolled up the scroll, and calmly told the people that the words were being fulfilled that very day! *He* was the one on whom the Spirit of the Lord rested, who had been anointed to bring Good News. Surely this was a very different kind of sermon! • When Jesus came to earth, he came with a clear mission—to fulfill the prophecies of the Old Testament regarding the Messiah, and by doing so to demonstrate God's faithfulness to his promises. From the moment Adam and Eve sinned in the Garden, God promised to deal with sin and Satan in no uncertain terms (Genesis 3:15, January 2). Jesus was appointed by God to come to earth at that specific time to die for sin. His mission was accomplished, and he returned to heaven. One day, he'll come back again with yet another mission—to take us to be with him forever!

He has sent me to proclaim that
captives will be released,
that the blind will see,
that the oppressed will be set free,
19 and that the time of the LORD's
favor has come.*"

20He rolled up the scroll, handed it back to the attendant, and sat down. All eyes in the synagogue looked at him intently. 21Then he began to speak to them. "The Scripture you've just heard has been fulfilled this very day!"

22Everyone spoke well of him and was amazed by the gracious words that came from his lips. "How can this be?" they asked. "Isn't this Joseph's son?"

23Then he said, "You will undoubtedly quote me this proverb: 'Physician, heal yourself'—meaning, 'Do miracles here in your hometown like those you did in Capernaum.' 24But I tell you the truth, no prophet is accepted in his own hometown.

25"Certainly there were many needy widows in Israel in Elijah's time, when the heavens were closed for three and a half years, and a severe famine devastated the land. 26Yet Elijah was not sent to any of them. He was sent instead to a foreigner—a widow of Zarephath in the land of Sidon. 27And there were many lepers in Israel in the time of the prophet Elisha, but the only one healed was Naaman, a Syrian."

28When they heard this, the people in the synagogue were furious. 29Jumping up, they mobbed him and forced him to the edge of the hill on which the town was built. They intended to push him over the cliff, 30but he passed right through the crowd and went on his way.

4:1 Some manuscripts read *into the wilderness.*   4:4 Deut 8:3.   4:8 Deut 6:13.   4:10-11 Ps 91:11-12.   4:12 Deut 6:16.   4:18-19 Or *and to proclaim the acceptable year of the LORD.* Isa 61:1-2 (Greek version); 58:6.

PSALM 63:1-11
A psalm of David, regarding a time when David was in the wilderness of Judah.

1 **O** God, you are my God;
I earnestly search for you.
My soul thirsts for you;
my whole body longs for you
in this parched and weary land
where there is no water.

2 I have seen you in your sanctuary
and gazed upon your power and
glory.

3 Your unfailing love is better than life
itself;
how I praise you!

4 I will praise you as long as I live,
lifting up my hands to you in prayer.

5 You satisfy me more than the richest
feast.
I will praise you with songs of joy.

6 I lie awake thinking of you,
meditating on you through the
night.

7 Because you are my helper,
I sing for joy in the shadow of your
wings.

8 I cling to you;
your strong right hand holds
me securely.

9 But those plotting to destroy me will
come to ruin.
They will go down into the depths
of the earth.

10 They will die by the sword
and become the food of jackals.

11 But the king will rejoice in God.
All who trust in him will praise him,
while liars will be silenced.

PROVERBS 11:20-21
The LORD detests people with crooked hearts, but he delights in those with integrity. □ Evil people will surely be punished, but the children of the godly will go free.

NUMBERS 32:1–33:39

When two of the tribes asked to have land *east* of the Jordan River, Moses launched into a history lesson to better understand their motives. It was important that nothing endanger their taking of the land this time.

The tribes of Reuben and Gad owned vast numbers of livestock. So when they saw that the lands of Jazer and Gilead were ideally suited for their flocks and herds, ²they came to Moses, Eleazar the priest, and the other leaders of the community. They said, ³"Notice the towns of Ataroth, Dibon, Jazer, Nimrah, Heshbon, Elealeh, Sibmah,* Nebo, and Beon. ⁴The LORD has conquered this whole area for the community of Israel, and it is ideally suited for all our livestock. ⁵If we have found favor with you, please let us have this land as our property instead of giving us land across the Jordan River."

⁶"Do you intend to stay here while your brothers go across and do all the fighting?" Moses asked the men of Gad and Reuben. ⁷"Why do you want to discourage the rest of the people of Israel from going across to the land the LORD has given them? ⁸Your ancestors did the same thing when I sent them from Kadesh-barnea to explore the land. ⁹After they went up to the valley of Eshcol and explored the land, they discouraged the people of Israel from entering the land the LORD was giving them. ¹⁰Then the LORD was very angry with them, and he vowed, ¹¹'Of all those I rescued from Egypt, no one who is twenty years old or older will ever see the land I swore to give to Abraham, Isaac, and Jacob, for they have not obeyed me wholeheartedly. ¹²The only exceptions are Caleb son of Jephunneh the Kenizzite and Joshua son of Nun, for they have wholeheartedly followed the LORD.'

¹³"The LORD was angry with Israel and made them wander in the wilderness for forty years until the entire generation that sinned in the LORD's sight had died. ¹⁴But here you are, a brood of sinners, doing exactly the same thing! You are making the LORD even angrier with Israel. ¹⁵If you

turn away from him like this and he abandons them again in the wilderness, you will be responsible for destroying this entire nation!"

¹⁶But they approached Moses and said, "We simply want to build pens for our livestock and fortified towns for our wives and children. ¹⁷Then we will arm ourselves and lead our fellow Israelites into battle until we have brought them safely to their land. Meanwhile, our families will stay in the fortified towns we build here, so they will be safe from any attacks by the local people. ¹⁸We will not return to our homes until all the people of Israel have received their portions of land. ¹⁹But we do not claim any of the land on the other side of the Jordan. We would rather live here on the east side and accept this as our grant of land."

²⁰Then Moses said, "If you keep your word and arm yourselves for the LORD's battles, ²¹and if your troops cross the Jordan and keep fighting until the LORD has driven out his enemies, ²²then you may return when the LORD has conquered the land. You will have fulfilled your duty to the LORD and to the rest of the people of Israel. And the land on the east side of the Jordan will be your property from the LORD. ²³But if you fail to keep your word, then you will have sinned against the LORD, and you may be sure that your sin will find you out. ²⁴Go ahead and build towns for your families and pens for your flocks, but do everything you have promised."

²⁵Then the men of Gad and Reuben replied, "We, your servants, will follow your instructions exactly. ²⁶Our children, wives, flocks, and cattle will stay here in the towns of Gilead. ²⁷But all who are able to bear arms will cross over to fight for the LORD, just as you have said."

²⁸So Moses gave orders to Eleazar the priest, Joshua son of Nun, and the leaders of the clans of Israel. ²⁹He said, "The men of Gad and Reuben who are armed for battle must cross the Jordan with you to fight for the LORD. If they do, give them the land of Gilead as their property when

the land is conquered. ³⁰But if they refuse to arm themselves and cross over with you, then they must accept land with the rest of you in the land of Canaan."

³¹The tribes of Gad and Reuben said again, "We are your servants, and we will do as the LORD has commanded! ³²We will cross the Jordan into Canaan fully armed to fight for the LORD, but our property will be here on this side of the Jordan."

³³So Moses assigned land to the tribes of Gad, Reuben, and half the tribe of Manasseh son of Joseph. He gave them the territory of King Sihon of the Amorites and the land of King Og of Bashan—the whole land with its cities and surrounding lands.

³⁴The descendants of Gad built the towns of Dibon, Ataroth, Aroer, ³⁵Atroth-shophan, Jazer, Jogbehah, ³⁶Beth-nimrah, and Beth-haran. These were all fortified towns with pens for their flocks.

³⁷The descendants of Reuben built the towns of Heshbon, Elealeh, Kiriathaim, ³⁸Nebo, Baal-meon, and Sibmah. They changed the names of some of the towns they conquered and rebuilt.

³⁹Then the descendants of Makir of the tribe of Manasseh went to Gilead and conquered it, and they drove out the Amorites living there. ⁴⁰So Moses gave Gilead to the Makirites, descendants of Manasseh, and they settled there. ⁴¹The people of Jair, another clan of the tribe of Manasseh, captured many of the towns in Gilead and changed the name of that region to the Towns of Jair.* ⁴²Meanwhile, a man named Nobah captured the town of Kenath and its surrounding villages, and he renamed that area Nobah after himself.

33:1THIS is the route the Israelites followed as they marched out of Egypt under the leadership of Moses and Aaron. ²At the LORD's direction, Moses kept a written record of their progress. These are the stages of their march, identified by the different places where they stopped along the way.

³They set out from the city of Rameses in early spring—on the fifteenth day of the first month*—on the morning after the first Passover celebration. The people of Israel left defiantly, in full view of all the Egyptians. ⁴Meanwhile, the Egyptians were burying all their firstborn sons, whom the LORD had killed the night before. The LORD had defeated the gods of Egypt that night with great acts of judgment!

⁵After leaving Rameses, the Israelites set up camp at Succoth.

⁶Then they left Succoth and camped at Etham on the edge of the wilderness.

⁷They left Etham and turned back toward Pi-hahiroth, opposite Baal-zephon, and camped near Migdol.

⁸They left Pi-hahiroth and crossed the Red Sea* into the wilderness beyond. Then they traveled for three days into the Etham wilderness and camped at Marah.

⁹They left Marah and camped at Elim, where there were twelve springs of water and seventy palm trees.

¹⁰They left Elim and camped beside the Red Sea.*

¹¹They left the Red Sea and camped in the wilderness of Sin.*

¹²They left the wilderness of Sin and camped at Dophkah.

¹³They left Dophkah and camped at Alush.

¹⁴They left Alush and camped at Rephidim, where there was no water for the people to drink.

¹⁵They left Rephidim and camped in the wilderness of Sinai.

¹⁶They left the wilderness of Sinai and camped at Kibroth-hattaavah.

¹⁷They left Kibroth-hattaavah and camped at Hazeroth.

¹⁸They left Hazeroth and camped at Rithmah.

¹⁹They left Rithmah and camped at Rimmon-perez.

²⁰They left Rimmon-perez and camped at Libnah.

²¹They left Libnah and camped at Rissah.

²²They left Rissah and camped at Kehelathah.

²³They left Kehelathah and camped at Mount Shepher.

²⁴They left Mount Shepher and camped at Haradah.

²⁵They left Haradah and camped at Makheloth.

²⁶They left Makheloth and camped at Tahath.

²⁷They left Tahath and camped at Terah.
²⁸They left Terah and camped
    at Mithcah.
²⁹They left Mithcah and camped
    at Hashmonah.
³⁰They left Hashmonah and camped
    at Moseroth.
³¹They left Moseroth and camped
    at Bene-jaakan.
³²They left Bene-jaakan and camped
    at Hor-haggidgad.
³³They left Hor-haggidgad and camped
    at Jotbathah.
³⁴They left Jotbathah and camped
    at Abronah.
³⁵They left Abronah and camped
    at Ezion-geber.
³⁶They left Ezion-geber and camped
    at Kadesh in the wilderness of Zin.
³⁷They left Kadesh and camped at
    Mount Hor, at the border of Edom.
³⁸While they were at the foot of Mount
Hor, Aaron the priest was directed by
the Lᴏʀᴅ to go up the mountain, and
there he died. This happened in
midsummer, on the first day of the
fifth month* of the fortieth year after
Israel's departure from Egypt. ³⁹Aaron
was 123 years old when he died there
on Mount Hor.

32:3 As in Samaritan Pentateuch and Greek version (see also
32:38); Hebrew reads *Sebam.*   32:41 Hebrew *Havvoth-jair.*

33:3 This day in the ancient Hebrew lunar calendar occurred
in late March, April, or early May.   33:8 Hebrew *the sea.*
33:10 Hebrew *sea of reeds;* also in 33:11.   33:11 The
geographical name *Sin* is related to *Sinai* and should not be
confused with the English word *sin.*   33:38 This day in the
ancient Hebrew lunar calendar occurred in July or August.

LUKE 4:31-5:11
As Jesus began to reveal his authority over demons
and disease, the people began to ponder where
that authority came from. Jesus was becoming a
mysterious and powerful public figure, adding
followers every day.

Then Jesus went to Capernaum, a town in
Galilee, and taught there in the synagogue
every Sabbath day. ³²There, too, the people were amazed at his teaching, for he
spoke with authority.
    ³³Once when he was in the synagogue,
a man possessed by a demon—an evil*
spirit—began shouting at Jesus, ³⁴"Go
away! Why are you interfering with us,
Jesus of Nazareth? Have you come to destroy us? I know who you are—the Holy
One sent from God!"
    ³⁵Jesus cut him short. "Be quiet! Come
out of the man," he ordered. At that, the
demon threw the man to the floor as the
crowd watched; then it came out of him
without hurting him further.
    ³⁶Amazed, the people exclaimed, "What
authority and power this man's words possess! Even evil spirits obey him, and they

WHAT THE BIBLE SAYS

Jesus' miracles

LUKE 4-5 Jesus' miracles demonstrated his identity and authority. They
gave credibility to his message. When the Pharisees wondered if he
would heal the paralyzed man, Jesus presented this challenge, "Is it
easier to say 'Your sins are forgiven,' or 'Stand up and walk'? So I will
prove to you that the Son of Man has the authority on earth to forgive
sins," and he proved it by healing the man (5:17-26, March 22). When
John the Baptist sent messengers to Jesus to find out whether he was
the Messiah, Jesus pointed to his miracles as the affirmative answer
(Matthew 11:1-6, January 15). • Jesus also did miracles, such as healing, out of compassion—to help alleviate the suffering that sin and Satan
have brought on the world. • Miracles still happen today—yet, as in
Jesus' day, not every bad situation is miraculously made better, not every
sick person is healed, and not every storm is calmed. But the point is
that you know the One who has the power to do great things, and you
know he will keep his promise to one day create a world where sin and
suffering will not exist.

flee at his command!" ³⁷The news about Jesus spread through every village in the entire region.

³⁸After leaving the synagogue that day, Jesus went to Simon's home, where he found Simon's mother-in-law very sick with a high fever. "Please heal her," everyone begged. ³⁹Standing at her bedside, he rebuked the fever, and it left her. And she got up at once and prepared a meal for them.

⁴⁰As the sun went down that evening, people throughout the village brought sick family members to Jesus. No matter what their diseases were, the touch of his hand healed every one. ⁴¹Many were possessed by demons; and the demons came out at his command, shouting, "You are the Son of God!" But because they knew he was the Messiah, he rebuked them and refused to let them speak.

⁴²Early the next morning Jesus went out to an isolated place. The crowds searched everywhere for him, and when they finally found him, they begged him not to leave them. ⁴³But he replied, "I must preach the Good News of the Kingdom of God in other towns, too, because that is why I was sent." ⁴⁴So he continued to travel around, preaching in synagogues throughout Judea.*

⁵:¹ONE day as Jesus was preaching on the shore of the Sea of Galilee,* great crowds pressed in on him to listen to the word of God. ²He noticed two empty boats at the water's edge, for the fishermen had left them and were washing their nets. ³Stepping into one of the boats, Jesus asked Simon,* its owner, to push it out into the water. So he sat in the boat and taught the crowds from there.

⁴When he had finished speaking, he said to Simon, "Now go out where it is deeper, and let down your nets to catch some fish."

⁵"Master," Simon replied, "we worked hard all last night and didn't catch a thing. But if you say so, I'll let the nets down again." ⁶And this time their nets were so full of fish they began to tear! ⁷A shout for help brought their partners in the other boat, and soon both boats were filled with fish and on the verge of sinking.

⁸When Simon Peter realized what had happened, he fell to his knees before Jesus and said, "Oh, Lord, please leave me—I'm too much of a sinner to be around you." ⁹For he was awestruck by the number of fish they had caught, as were the others with him. ¹⁰His partners, James and John, the sons of Zebedee, were also amazed.

Jesus replied to Simon, "Don't be afraid! From now on you'll be fishing for people!" ¹¹And as soon as they landed, they left everything and followed Jesus.

4:33 Greek *unclean;* also in 4:36.   4:44 Some manuscripts read *Galilee.*   5:1 Greek *Lake Gennesaret,* another name for the Sea of Galilee.   5:3 *Simon* is called "Peter" in 6:14 and thereafter.

PSALM 64:1-10
For the choir director: A psalm of David.

¹ **O** God, listen to my complaint.
    Protect my life from my enemies'
      threats.
² Hide me from the plots of this evil
      mob,
    from this gang of wrongdoers.
³ They sharpen their tongues like
      swords
    and aim their bitter words like
      arrows.
⁴ They shoot from ambush at the
      innocent,
    attacking suddenly and fearlessly.
⁵ They encourage each other to do evil
    and plan how to set their traps in
      secret.
    "Who will ever notice?" they ask.
⁶ As they plot their crimes, they say,
    "We have devised the perfect plan!"
    Yes, the human heart and mind are
      cunning.
⁷ But God himself will shoot them with
      his arrows,
    suddenly striking them down.
⁸ Their own tongues will ruin them,
    and all who see them will shake
      their heads in scorn.
⁹ Then everyone will be afraid;
    they will proclaim the mighty acts
      of God
    and realize all the amazing things
      he does.
¹⁰ The godly will rejoice in the LORD
    and find shelter in him.

And those who do what is right
will praise him.

PROVERBS 11:22
A beautiful woman who lacks discretion
is like a gold ring in a pig's snout.

NUMBERS 33:40–35:34

Moses continued his review of the journey of the
Israelites. The people considered this land their
inheritance from God—their financial portfolio and
their net worth. Dividing it and allocating it were of
the utmost interest to everyone involved.

At that time the Canaanite king of Arad,
who lived in the Negev in the land of
Canaan, heard that the people of Israel
were approaching his land.
⁴¹Meanwhile, the Israelites left Mount
Hor and camped at Zalmonah.
⁴²Then they left Zalmonah and camped
at Punon.
⁴³They left Punon and camped at Oboth.
⁴⁴They left Oboth and camped at Iye-
abarim on the border of Moab.
⁴⁵They left Iye-abarim* and camped
at Dibon-gad.
⁴⁶They left Dibon-gad and camped at
Almon-diblathaim.
⁴⁷They left Almon-diblathaim and
camped in the mountains east of the
river,* near Mount Nebo.
⁴⁸They left the mountains east of the
river and camped on the plains of
Moab beside the Jordan River, across
from Jericho. ⁴⁹Along the Jordan River
they camped from Beth-jeshimoth as
far as the meadows of Acacia* on the
plains of Moab.

⁵⁰While they were camped near the
Jordan River on the plains of Moab opposite Jericho, the LORD said to Moses,
⁵¹"Give the following instructions to the
people of Israel: When you cross the Jordan River into the land of Canaan, ⁵²you
must drive out all the people living there.
You must destroy all their carved and molten images and demolish all their pagan
shrines. ⁵³Take possession of the land and
settle in it, because I have given it to you to

occupy. ⁵⁴You must distribute the land
among the clans by sacred lot and in proportion to their size. A larger portion of
land will be allotted to each of the larger
clans, and a smaller portion will be allotted to each of the smaller clans. The decision of the sacred lot is final. In this way,
the portions of land will be divided
among your ancestral tribes. ⁵⁵But if you
fail to drive out the people who live in the
land, those who remain will be like splinters in your eyes and thorns in your sides.
They will harass you in the land where
you live. ⁵⁶And I will do to you what I had
planned to do to them."

³⁴:¹THEN the LORD said to Moses, ²"Give
these instructions to the Israelites: When
you come into the land of Canaan, which I
am giving you as your special possession,
these will be the boundaries. ³The southern portion of your country will extend
from the wilderness of Zin, along the edge
of Edom. The southern boundary will begin on the east at the Dead Sea.* ⁴It will
then run south past Scorpion Pass* in the
direction of Zin. Its southernmost point
will be Kadesh-barnea, from which it will
go to Hazar-addar, and on to Azmon.
⁵From Azmon the boundary will turn toward the Brook of Egypt and end at the
Mediterranean Sea.*

⁶"Your western boundary will be the
coastline of the Mediterranean Sea.

⁷"Your northern boundary will begin at
the Mediterranean Sea and run east to
Mount Hor, ⁸then to Lebo-hamath, and on
through Zedad ⁹and Ziphron to Hazar-
enan. This will be your northern boundary.

¹⁰"The eastern boundary will start at
Hazar-enan and run south to Shepham,
¹¹then down to Riblah on the east side of

Ain. From there the boundary will run down along the eastern edge of the Sea of Galilee,* ¹²and then along the Jordan River to the Dead Sea. These are the boundaries of your land."

¹³Then Moses told the Israelites, "This territory is the homeland you are to divide among yourselves by sacred lot. The LORD has commanded that the land be divided among the nine and a half remaining tribes. ¹⁴The families of the tribes of Reuben, Gad, and half the tribe of Manasseh have already received their grants of land ¹⁵on the east side of the Jordan River, across from Jericho toward the sunrise."

¹⁶And the LORD said to Moses, ¹⁷"Eleazar the priest and Joshua son of Nun are the men designated to divide the grants of land among the people. ¹⁸Enlist one leader from each tribe to help them with the task. ¹⁹These are the tribes and the names of the leaders:

Tribe	Leader
Judah	Caleb son of Jephunneh
²⁰ Simeon	Shemuel son of Ammihud
²¹ Benjamin	Elidad son of Kislon
²² Dan	Bukki son of Jogli
²³ Manasseh son of Joseph	Hanniel son of Ephod
²⁴ Ephraim son of Joseph	Kemuel son of Shiphtan
²⁵ Zebulun	Elizaphan son of Parnach
²⁶ Issachar	Paltiel son of Azzan
²⁷ Asher	Ahihud son of Shelomi
²⁸ Naphtali	Pedahel son of Ammihud

²⁹These are the men the LORD has appointed to divide the grants of land in Canaan among the Israelites."

³⁵:¹WHILE Israel was camped beside the Jordan on the plains of Moab across from Jericho, the LORD said to Moses, ²"Command the people of Israel to give to the Levites from their property certain towns to live in, along with the surrounding pasturelands. ³These towns will be for the Levites to live in, and the surrounding lands will provide pasture for their cattle, flocks, and other livestock. ⁴The pastureland assigned to the Levites around these towns will extend 1,500 feet* from the town walls in every direction. ⁵Measure off 3,000 feet* outside the town walls in every direction—east, south, west, north—with the town at the center. This area will serve as the larger pastureland for the towns.

⁶"Six of the towns you give the Levites will be cities of refuge, where a person who has accidentally killed someone can flee for safety. In addition, give them forty-two other towns. ⁷In all, forty-eight towns with the surrounding pastureland will be given to the Levites. ⁸These towns will come from the property of the people of Israel. The larger tribes will give more towns to the Levites, while the smaller tribes will give fewer. Each tribe will give property in proportion to the size of its land."

⁹The LORD said to Moses, ¹⁰"Give the following instructions to the people of Israel.

"When you cross the Jordan into the land of Canaan, ¹¹designate cities of refuge to which people can flee if they have killed someone accidentally. ¹²These cities will be places of protection from a dead person's relatives who want to avenge the death. The slayer must not be put to death before being tried by the community. ¹³Designate six cities of refuge for yourselves, ¹⁴three on the east side of the Jordan River and three on the west in the land of Canaan. ¹⁵These cities are for the protection of Israelites, foreigners living among you, and traveling merchants. Anyone who accidentally kills someone may flee there for safety.

¹⁶"But if someone strikes and kills another person with a piece of iron, it is murder, and the murderer must be executed. ¹⁷Or if someone with a stone in his hand strikes and kills another person, it is murder, and the murderer must be put to death. ¹⁸Or if someone strikes and kills another person with a wooden object, it is murder, and the murderer must be put to death. ¹⁹The victim's nearest relative is responsible for putting the murderer to death. When they meet, the avenger must put the murderer to death. ²⁰So if someone hates another person and pushes him or throws a dangerous object at him and he dies, it is murder. ²¹Or if someone hates another person and hits him with a fist and he dies, it is murder. In such cases, the avenger must put the murderer to death when they meet.

²²"But suppose someone pushes another person without having shown previous hostility, or throws something that unintentionally hits another person, ²³or accidentally drops a huge stone on someone, though they were not enemies, and the person dies. ²⁴If this should happen, the community must follow these regulations in making a judgment between the slayer and the avenger, the victim's nearest relative: ²⁵The community must protect the slayer from the avenger and must escort the slayer back to live in the city of refuge to which he fled. There he must remain until the death of the high priest, who was anointed with the sacred oil.

²⁶"But if the slayer ever leaves the limits of the city of refuge, ²⁷and the avenger finds him outside the city and kills him, it will not be considered murder. ²⁸The slayer should have stayed inside the city of refuge until the death of the high priest. But after the death of the high priest, the slayer may return to his own property. ²⁹These are legal requirements for you to observe from generation to generation, wherever you may live.

³⁰"All murderers must be put to death, but only if evidence is presented by more than one witness. No one may be put to death on the testimony of only one witness. ³¹Also, you must never accept a ransom payment for the life of someone judged guilty of murder and subject to execution; murderers must always be put to death. ³²And never accept a ransom payment from someone who has fled to a city of refuge, allowing a slayer to return to his property before the death of the high priest. ³³This will ensure that the land where you live will not be polluted, for murder pollutes the land. And no sacrifice except the execution of the murderer can purify the land from murder.* ³⁴You must not defile the land where you live, for I live there myself. I am the LORD, who lives among the people of Israel."

33:45 As in 33:44; Hebrew reads *Iyim,* another name for Iye-abarim.   33:47 Or *the mountains of Abarim;* also in 33:48.   33:49 Hebrew *as far as Abel-shittim.* 34:3 Hebrew *Salt Sea;* also in 34:12.   34:4 Or *the ascent of Akrabbim.*   34:5 Hebrew *the sea;* also in 34:6, 7. 34:11 Hebrew *Sea of Kinnereth.*   35:4 Hebrew *1,000 cubits* [460 meters].   35:5 Hebrew *2,000 cubits* [920 meters]. 35:33 Or *can make atonement for murder.*

LUKE 5:12-28
Lowering a friend through a tile roof was a small price to pay to experience Jesus' power. Meanwhile, the religious leaders listened in confusion as Jesus claimed to forgive sin as only God can do.

In one of the villages, Jesus met a man with an advanced case of leprosy. When the man saw Jesus, he bowed with his face to the ground, begging to be healed. "Lord,"

HOW WE LIVE

Setting priorities

LUKE 5:28 When you became a Christian, many things in your life changed. The way you speak and act as a Christian is (or should be) different now that you've been born again. One significant change will be the way you plan your own future. You must now ask, "How do my ambitions measure up to God's plan?" • In today's reading, Levi (Matthew) made an immediate and life-changing decision. When Jesus asked Levi to join him and be a disciple, "Levi got up, left everything, and followed him." Levi's response is the way God wants all of us to respond. Levi followed the Lord without looking back, and later he gathered his friends to meet Jesus. Levi left his material fortune, a lucrative tax-collecting business, to gain a spiritual fortune. Jesus became his everything, and he wanted to share his Lord with everyone he knew. • It's easy to be drawn into the snares of this life. Wealth, power, position, and fame can seduce us away from our true purpose. When you place God first in your life, you'll want your hopes, dreams, and goals to fall into line with his will. And when your desires match God's, he delights in granting them.

he said, "if you are willing, you can heal me and make me clean."

¹³Jesus reached out and touched him. "I am willing," he said. "Be healed!" And instantly the leprosy disappeared. ¹⁴Then Jesus instructed him not to tell anyone what had happened. He said, "Go to the priest and let him examine you. Take along the offering required in the law of Moses for those who have been healed of leprosy.* This will be a public testimony that you have been cleansed."

¹⁵But despite Jesus' instructions, the report of his power spread even faster, and vast crowds came to hear him preach and to be healed of their diseases. ¹⁶But Jesus often withdrew to the wilderness for prayer.

¹⁷One day while Jesus was teaching, some Pharisees and teachers of religious law were sitting nearby. (It seemed that these men showed up from every village in all Galilee and Judea, as well as from Jerusalem.) And the Lord's healing power was strongly with Jesus.

¹⁸Some men came carrying a paralyzed man on a sleeping mat. They tried to take him inside to Jesus, ¹⁹but they couldn't reach him because of the crowd. So they went up to the roof and took off some tiles. Then they lowered the sick man on his mat down into the crowd, right in front of Jesus. ²⁰Seeing their faith, Jesus said to the man, "Young man, your sins are forgiven."

²¹But the Pharisees and teachers of religious law said to themselves, "Who does he think he is? That's blasphemy! Only God can forgive sins!"

²²Jesus knew what they were thinking, so he asked them, "Why do you question this in your hearts? ²³Is it easier to say 'Your sins are forgiven,' or 'Stand up and walk'? ²⁴So I will prove to you that the Son of Man* has the authority on earth to forgive sins." Then Jesus turned to the paralyzed man and said, "Stand up, pick up your mat, and go home!"

²⁵And immediately, as everyone watched, the man jumped up, picked up his mat, and went home praising God. ²⁶Everyone was gripped with great wonder and awe, and they praised God, exclaiming, "We have seen amazing things today!"

²⁷Later, as Jesus left the town, he saw a tax collector named Levi sitting at his tax collector's booth. "Follow me and be my disciple," Jesus said to him. ²⁸So Levi got up, left everything, and followed him.

5:14 See Lev 14:2-32.   **5:24** "Son of Man" is a title Jesus used for himself.

PSALM 65:1-13
For the choir director: A song. A psalm of David.

¹ **W**hat mighty praise, O God,
   belongs to you in Zion.
We will fulfill our vows to you,
² for you answer our prayers.
   All of us must come to you.
³ Though we are overwhelmed by our sins,
   you forgive them all.
⁴ What joy for those you choose to bring near,
   those who live in your holy courts.
What festivities await us
   inside your holy Temple.

⁵ You faithfully answer our prayers with awesome deeds,
   O God our savior.
You are the hope of everyone on earth,
   even those who sail on distant seas.
⁶ You formed the mountains by your power
   and armed yourself with mighty strength.
⁷ You quieted the raging oceans with their pounding waves
   and silenced the shouting of the nations.
⁸ Those who live at the ends of the earth stand in awe of your wonders.
From where the sun rises to where it sets,
   you inspire shouts of joy.

⁹ You take care of the earth and water it,
   making it rich and fertile.
The river of God has plenty of water;
   it provides a bountiful harvest of grain,
   for you have ordered it so.
¹⁰ You drench the plowed ground with rain,
   melting the clods and leveling the ridges.

You soften the earth with showers
and bless its abundant crops.
[11] You crown the year with a bountiful
harvest;
even the hard pathways overflow
with abundance.
[12] The grasslands of the wilderness
become a lush pasture,
and the hillsides blossom
with joy.

NUMBERS 36:1–DEUTERONOMY 1:46
The book of Numbers gives the account of the long
journey of the Israelites and their preparations to
enter the land. The book of Deuteronomy records
Moses' final words to the people before they
crossed into the Promised Land.

Then the heads of the clans of Gilead—
descendants of Makir, son of Manasseh,
son of Joseph—came to Moses and the
family leaders of Israel with a petition.
[2] They said, "Sir, the LORD instructed you
to divide the land by sacred lot among
the people of Israel. You were told by the
LORD to give the grant of land owned by
our brother Zelophehad to his daughters. [3] But if they marry men from another tribe, their grants of land will go
with them to the tribe into which they
marry. In this way, the total area of our
tribal land will be reduced. [4] Then when
the Year of Jubilee comes, their portion
of land will be added to that of the new
tribe, causing it to be lost forever to our
ancestral tribe."

[5] So Moses gave the Israelites this command from the LORD: "The claim of the
men of the tribe of Joseph is legitimate.
[6] This is what the LORD commands concerning the daughters of Zelophehad: Let
them marry anyone they like, as long as it
is within their own ancestral tribe. [7] None
of the territorial land may pass from tribe
to tribe, for all the land given to each tribe
must remain within the tribe to which
it was first allotted. [8] The daughters
throughout the tribes of Israel who are in

[13] The meadows are clothed with flocks
of sheep,
and the valleys are carpeted with
grain.
They all shout and sing for joy!

PROVERBS 11:23
The godly can look forward to a reward,
while the wicked can expect only judgment.

MARCH**23**

line to inherit property must marry within
their tribe, so that all the Israelites will
keep their ancestral property. [9] No grant of
land may pass from one tribe to another;
each tribe of Israel must keep its allotted
portion of land."

[10] The daughters of Zelophehad did as
the LORD commanded Moses. [11] Mahlah,
Tirzah, Hoglah, Milcah, and Noah all married cousins on their father's side. [12] They
married into the clans of Manasseh son of
Joseph. Thus, their inheritance of land remained within their ancestral tribe.

[13] These are the commands and regulations that the LORD gave to the people of
Israel through Moses while they were
camped on the plains of Moab beside the
Jordan River across from Jericho.

[1:1] THESE are the words that Moses spoke
to all the people of Israel while they were
in the wilderness east of the Jordan River.
They were camped in the Jordan Valley*
near Suph, between Paran on one side and
Tophel, Laban, Hazeroth, and Di-zahab on
the other. [2] Normally it takes only eleven days to
travel from Mount Sinai* to Kadesh-
barnea, going by way of Mount Seir. [3] But
forty years after the Israelites left Egypt,
on the first day of the eleventh month,*
Moses addressed the people of Israel,
telling them everything the LORD had
commanded him to say. [4] This took place
after he had defeated King Sihon of the
Amorites, who had ruled in Heshbon, and

King Og of Bashan, who had ruled in Ashtaroth and Edrei.

⁵While the Israelites were in the land of Moab east of the Jordan River, Moses carefully explained the LORD's instructions as follows.

⁶"When we were at Mount Sinai, the LORD our God said to us, 'You have stayed at this mountain long enough. ⁷It is time to break camp and move on. Go to the hill country of the Amorites and to all the neighboring regions—the Jordan Valley, the hill country, the western foothills,* the Negev, and the coastal plain. Go to the land of the Canaanites and to Lebanon, and all the way to the great Euphrates River. ⁸Look, I am giving all this land to you! Go in and occupy it, for it is the land the LORD swore to give to your ancestors Abraham, Isaac, and Jacob, and to all their descendants.'"

⁹Moses continued, "At that time I told you, 'You are too great a burden for me to carry all by myself. ¹⁰The LORD your God has increased your population, making you as numerous as the stars! ¹¹And may the LORD, the God of your ancestors, multiply you a thousand times more and bless you as he promised! ¹²But you are such a heavy load to carry! How can I deal with all your problems and bickering? ¹³Choose some well-respected men from each tribe who are known for their wisdom and understanding, and I will appoint them as your leaders.'

¹⁴"Then you responded, 'Your plan is a good one.' ¹⁵So I took the wise and respected men you had selected from your tribes and appointed them to serve as judges and officials over you. Some were responsible for a thousand people, some for a hundred, some for fifty, and some for ten.

¹⁶"At that time I instructed the judges, 'You must hear the cases of your fellow Israelites and the foreigners living among you. Be perfectly fair in your decisions ¹⁷and impartial in your judgments. Hear the cases of those who are poor as well as those who are rich. Don't be afraid of anyone's anger, for the decision you make is God's decision. Bring me any cases that are too difficult for you, and I will handle them.'

¹⁸"At that time I gave you instructions about everything you were to do.

¹⁹"Then, just as the LORD our God commanded us, we left Mount Sinai and traveled through the great and terrifying wilderness, as you yourselves remember, and headed toward the hill country of the Amorites. When we arrived at Kadesh-barnea, ²⁰I said to you, 'You have now reached the hill country of the Amorites that the LORD our God is giving us. ²¹Look! He has placed the land in front of you. Go and occupy it as the LORD, the God of your ancestors, has promised you. Don't be afraid! Don't be discouraged!'

²²"But you all came to me and said, 'First, let's send out scouts to explore the land for us. They will advise us on the best route to take and which towns we should enter.'

²³"This seemed like a good idea to me, so I chose twelve scouts, one from each of your tribes. ²⁴They headed for the hill country and came to the valley of Eshcol and explored it. ²⁵They picked some of its fruit and brought it back to us. And they reported, 'The land the LORD our God has given us is indeed a good land.'

²⁶"But you rebelled against the command of the LORD your God and refused to go in. ²⁷You complained in your tents and said, 'The LORD must hate us. That's why he has brought us here from Egypt—to hand us over to the Amorites to be slaughtered. ²⁸Where can we go? Our brothers have demoralized us with their report. They tell us, "The people of the land are taller and more powerful than we are, and their towns are large, with walls rising high into the sky! We even saw giants there—the descendants of Anak!"'

²⁹"But I said to you, 'Don't be shocked or afraid of them! ³⁰The LORD your God is going ahead of you. He will fight for you, just as you saw him do in Egypt. ³¹And you saw how the LORD your God cared for you all along the way as you traveled through the wilderness, just as a father cares for his child. Now he has brought you to this place.'

³²"But even after all he did, you refused to trust the LORD your God, ³³who goes before you looking for the best places to camp, guiding you with a pillar of fire by night and a pillar of cloud by day.

[34]"When the LORD heard your complaining, he became very angry. So he solemnly swore, [35]'Not one of you from this wicked generation will live to see the good land I swore to give your ancestors, [36]except Caleb son of Jephunneh. He will see this land because he has followed the LORD completely. I will give to him and his descendants some of the very land he explored during his scouting mission.'

[37]"And the LORD was also angry with me because of you. He said to me, 'Moses, not even you will enter the Promised Land! [38]Instead, your assistant, Joshua son of Nun, will lead the people into the land. Encourage him, for he will lead Israel as they take possession of it. [39]I will give the land to your little ones—your innocent children. You were afraid they would be captured, but they will be the ones who occupy it. [40]As for you, turn around now and go on back through the wilderness toward the Red Sea.*'

[41]"Then you confessed, 'We have sinned against the LORD! We will go into the land and fight for it, as the LORD our God has commanded us.' So your men strapped on their weapons, thinking it would be easy to attack the hill country.

[42]"But the LORD told me to tell you, 'Do not attack, for I am not with you. If you go ahead on your own, you will be crushed by your enemies.'

[43]"This is what I told you, but you would not listen. Instead, you again rebelled against the LORD's command and arrogantly went into the hill country to fight. [44]But the Amorites who lived there came out against you like a swarm of bees. They chased and battered you all the way from Seir to Hormah. [45]Then you returned and wept before the LORD, but he refused to listen. [46]So you stayed there at Kadesh for a long time."

1:1 Hebrew *the Arabah;* also in 1:7.   1:2 Hebrew *Horeb,* another name for Sinai; also in 1:6, 19.   1:3 Hebrew *In the fortieth year, on the first day of the eleventh month.* This day in the ancient Hebrew lunar calendar occurred in January or February.   1:7 Hebrew *the Shephelah.*   1:40 Hebrew *sea of reeds.*

LUKE 5:29–6:11

The more well-known Jesus became, the less traditional his ways appeared, particularly to the religious select who defined spirituality by conformity.

Later, Levi held a banquet in his home with Jesus as the guest of honor. Many of Levi's fellow tax collectors and other guests also ate with them. [30]But the Pharisees and their teachers of religious law complained bitterly to Jesus' disciples, "Why do you eat and drink with such scum?*"

HOW WE LIVE

Responding to God

DEUTERONOMY 1 Forty years of wandering through the wilderness—that was Israel's punishment for failing to obey God and take Canaan when he originally commanded. Because of their disobedience, an entire generation never enjoyed the bounty of the land God promised to them. Their children learned an important lesson from the whole experience. It taught them the importance of trusting and obeying God when he calls his people to do something.   • As Christians, our spiritual journey will not be easy. The road ahead may be long and painful at times during which our faith is tested. The difficulties you will face might be discouraging, but take heart! God has a purpose as he leads you. Had the Israelites responded positively to God's command to enter the Promised Land, they wouldn't have spent forty years wandering aimlessly. Actively seek God's purpose for you through prayer and the study of his Word. When discouraging times come, keep trusting and responding to what God has revealed to you. Don't make the journey longer or more difficult than it needs to be.

³¹Jesus answered them, "Healthy people don't need a doctor—sick people do. ³²I have come to call not those who think they are righteous, but those who know they are sinners and need to repent."

³³One day some people said to Jesus, "John the Baptist's disciples fast and pray regularly, and so do the disciples of the Pharisees. Why are your disciples always eating and drinking?"

³⁴Jesus responded, "Do wedding guests fast while celebrating with the groom? Of course not. ³⁵But someday the groom will be taken away from them, and then they will fast."

³⁶Then Jesus gave them this illustration: "No one tears a piece of cloth from a new garment and uses it to patch an old garment. For then the new garment would be ruined, and the new patch wouldn't even match the old garment.

³⁷"And no one puts new wine into old wineskins. For the new wine would burst the wineskins, spilling the wine and ruining the skins. ³⁸New wine must be stored in new wineskins. ³⁹But no one who drinks the old wine seems to want the new wine. 'The old is just fine,' they say."

⁶:¹ONE Sabbath day as Jesus was walking through some grainfields, his disciples broke off heads of grain, rubbed off the husks in their hands, and ate the grain. ²But some Pharisees said, "Why are you breaking the law by harvesting grain on the Sabbath?"

³Jesus replied, "Haven't you read in the Scriptures what David did when he and his companions were hungry? ⁴He went into the house of God and broke the law by eating the sacred loaves of bread that only the priests can eat. He also gave some to his companions." ⁵And Jesus added, "The Son of Man* is Lord, even over the Sabbath."

⁶On another Sabbath day, a man with a deformed right hand was in the synagogue while Jesus was teaching. ⁷The teachers of religious law and the Pharisees watched Jesus closely. If he healed the man's hand, they planned to accuse him of working on the Sabbath.

⁸But Jesus knew their thoughts. He said to the man with the deformed hand,

"Come and stand in front of everyone." So the man came forward. ⁹Then Jesus said to his critics, "I have a question for you. Does the law permit good deeds on the Sabbath, or is it a day for doing evil? Is this a day to save life or to destroy it?"

¹⁰He looked around at them one by one and then said to the man, "Hold out your hand." So the man held out his hand, and it was restored! ¹¹At this, the enemies of Jesus were wild with rage and began to discuss what to do with him.

5:30 Greek *with tax collectors and sinners?*   **6:5** "Son of Man" is a title Jesus used for himself.

PSALM 66:1-20
For the choir director: A song. A psalm.

1   **S**hout joyful praises to God, all the earth!
2   Sing about the glory of his name!
      Tell the world how glorious he is.
3   Say to God, "How awesome are your deeds!
      Your enemies cringe before your mighty power.
4   Everything on earth will worship you;
      they will sing your praises,
      shouting your name in glorious songs."   *Interlude*

5   Come and see what our God has done,
      what awesome miracles he performs for people!
6   He made a dry path through the Red Sea,*
      and his people went across on foot.
      There we rejoiced in him.
7   For by his great power he rules forever.
      He watches every movement of the nations;
      let no rebel rise in defiance.   *Interlude*

8   Let the whole world bless our God
      and loudly sing his praises.
9   Our lives are in his hands,
      and he keeps our feet from stumbling.
10   You have tested us, O God;
      you have purified us like silver.
11   You captured us in your net
      and laid the burden of slavery on our backs.
12   Then you put a leader over us.*

We went through fire and flood,
   but you brought us to a place of
   great abundance.

13 Now I come to your Temple with
       burnt offerings
   to fulfill the vows I made to you—
14 yes, the sacred vows that I made
   when I was in deep trouble.
15 That is why I am sacrificing burnt
       offerings to you—
   the best of my rams as a pleasing
       aroma,
   and a sacrifice of bulls and male
       goats.   *Interlude*

16 Come and listen, all you who fear God,
   and I will tell you what he did for me.
17 For I cried out to him for help,
   praising him as I spoke.

18 If I had not confessed the sin in my
       heart,
   the Lord would not have listened.
19 But God did listen!
   He paid attention to my prayer.
20 Praise God, who did not ignore my
       prayer
   or withdraw his unfailing love
       from me.

66:6 Hebrew *the sea.*   **66:12** Or *You made people ride over our heads.*

PROVERBS 11:24-26

Give freely and become more wealthy; be stingy and lose everything. □The generous will prosper; those who refresh others will themselves be refreshed. □People curse those who hoard their grain, but they bless the one who sells in time of need.

MARCH**24**

DEUTERONOMY 2:1–3:29

Moses knew how important it was to always remember what God had done in the lives of his people. Review your own journey, as Moses reviews the journey of his people.

"**T**hen we turned around and headed back across the wilderness toward the Red Sea,* just as the Lord had instructed me, and we wandered around in the region of Mount Seir for a long time.

2"Then at last the Lord said to me, 3'You have been wandering around in this hill country long enough; turn to the north. 4Give these orders to the people: "You will pass through the country belonging to your relatives the Edomites, the descendants of Esau, who live in Seir. The Edomites will feel threatened, so be careful. 5Do not bother them, for I have given them all the hill country around Mount Seir as their property, and I will not give you even one square foot of their land. 6If you need food to eat or water to drink, pay them for it. 7For the Lord your God has blessed you in everything you have done. He has watched your every step through this great wilderness. During these forty years, the Lord your God has been with you, and you have lacked nothing."'

8"So we bypassed the territory of our relatives, the descendants of Esau, who live in Seir. We avoided the road through the Arabah Valley that comes up from Elath and Ezion-geber.

"Then as we turned north along the desert route through Moab, 9the Lord warned us, 'Do not bother the Moabites, the descendants of Lot, or start a war with them. I have given them Ar as their property, and I will not give you any of their land.'"

10(A race of giants called the Emites had once lived in the area of Ar. They were as strong and numerous and tall as the Anakites, another race of giants. 11Both the Emites and the Anakites are also known as the Rephaites, though the Moabites call them Emites. 12In earlier times the Horites had lived in Seir, but they were driven out and displaced by the descendants of Esau, just as Israel drove out the people of Canaan when the Lord gave Israel their land.)

¹³Moses continued, "Then the LORD said to us, 'Get moving. Cross the Zered Brook.' So we crossed the brook.

¹⁴"Thirty-eight years passed from the time we first left Kadesh-barnea until we finally crossed the Zered Brook! By then, all the men old enough to fight in battle had died in the wilderness, as the LORD had vowed would happen. ¹⁵The LORD struck them down until they had all been eliminated from the community.

¹⁶"When all the men of fighting age had died, ¹⁷the LORD said to me, ¹⁸'Today you will cross the border of Moab at Ar ¹⁹and enter the land of the Ammonites, the descendants of Lot. But do not bother them or start a war with them. I have given the land of Ammon to them as their property, and I will not give you any of their land.'"

²⁰(That area was once considered the land of the Rephaites, who had lived there, though the Ammonites call them Zamzummites. ²¹They were also as strong and numerous and tall as the Anakites. But the LORD destroyed them so the Ammonites could occupy their land. ²²He had done the same for the descendants of Esau who lived in Seir, for he destroyed the Horites so they could settle there in their place. The descendants of Esau live there to this day. ²³A similar thing happened when the Caphtorites from Crete* invaded and destroyed the Avvites, who had lived in villages in the area of Gaza.)

²⁴Moses continued, "Then the LORD said, 'Now get moving! Cross the Arnon Gorge. Look, I will hand over to you Sihon the Amorite, king of Heshbon, and I will give you his land. Attack him and begin to occupy the land. ²⁵Beginning today I will make people throughout the earth terrified because of you. When they hear reports about you, they will tremble with dread and fear.'"

²⁶Moses continued, "From the wilderness of Kedemoth I sent ambassadors to King Sihon of Heshbon with this proposal of peace:

²⁷'Let us travel through your land. We will stay on the main road and won't turn off into the fields on either side. ²⁸Sell us food to eat and water to drink, and we will pay for it. All we want is permission to pass through your land. ²⁹The descendants of Esau who live in Seir allowed us to go through their country, and so did the Moabites, who live in Ar. Let us pass through until we cross the Jordan into the land the LORD our God is giving us.'

³⁰"But King Sihon of Heshbon refused to allow us to pass through, because the LORD your God made Sihon stubborn and defiant so he could help you defeat him, as he has now done.

³¹"Then the LORD said to me, 'Look, I have begun to hand King Sihon and his land over to you. Begin now to conquer and occupy his land.'

³²"Then King Sihon declared war on us and mobilized his forces at Jahaz. ³³But the LORD our God handed him over to us, and we crushed him, his sons, and all his people. ³⁴We conquered all his towns and completely destroyed* everyone—men, women, and children. Not a single person was spared. ³⁵We took all the livestock as plunder for ourselves, along with anything of value from the towns we ransacked.

³⁶"The LORD our God also helped us conquer Aroer on the edge of the Arnon Gorge, and the town in the gorge, and the whole area as far as Gilead. No town had walls too strong for us. ³⁷However, we avoided the land of the Ammonites all along the Jabbok River and the towns in the hill country—all the places the LORD our God had commanded us to leave alone.

3:1"NEXT we turned and headed for the land of Bashan, where King Og and his entire army attacked us at Edrei. ²But the LORD told me, 'Do not be afraid of him, for I have given you victory over Og and his entire army, and I will give you all his land. Treat him just as you treated King Sihon of the Amorites, who ruled in Heshbon.'

³"So the LORD our God handed King Og and all his people over to us, and we killed them all. Not a single person survived. ⁴We conquered all sixty of his towns—the entire Argob region in his kingdom of Bashan. Not a single town escaped our conquest. ⁵These towns were all fortified with

high walls and barred gates. We also took many unwalled villages at the same time. [6]We completely destroyed* the kingdom of Bashan, just as we had destroyed King Sihon of Heshbon. We destroyed all the people in every town we conquered—men, women, and children alike. [7]But we kept all the livestock for ourselves and took plunder from all the towns.

[8]"So we took the land of the two Amorite kings east of the Jordan River—all the way from the Arnon Gorge to Mount Hermon. [9](Mount Hermon is called Sirion by the Sidonians, and the Amorites call it Senir.) [10]We had now conquered all the cities on the plateau and all Gilead and Bashan, as far as the towns of Salecah and Edrei, which were part of Og's kingdom in Bashan. [11](King Og of Bashan was the last survivor of the giant Rephaites. His bed was made of iron and was more than thirteen feet long and six feet wide.* It can still be seen in the Ammonite city of Rabbah.)

[12]"When we took possession of this land, I gave to the tribes of Reuben and Gad the territory beyond Aroer along the Arnon Gorge, plus half of the hill country of Gilead with its towns. [13]Then I gave the rest of Gilead and all of Bashan—Og's former kingdom—to the half-tribe of Manasseh. (This entire Argob region of Bashan used to be known as the land of the Rephaites. [14]Jair, a leader from the tribe of Manasseh, conquered the whole Argob region in Bashan, all the way to the border of the Geshurites and Maacathites. Jair renamed this region after himself, calling it the Towns of Jair,* as it is still known today.) [15]I gave Gilead to the clan of Makir. [16]But I also gave part of Gilead to the tribes of Reuben and Gad. The area I gave them extended from the middle of the Arnon Gorge in the south to the Jabbok River on the Ammonite frontier. [17]They also received the Jordan Valley, all the way from the Sea of Galilee down to the Dead Sea,* with the Jordan River serving as the western boundary. To the east were the slopes of Pisgah.

[18]"At that time I gave this command to the tribes that would live east of the Jordan: 'Although the LORD your God has given you this land as your property, all your fighting men must cross the Jordan ahead of your Israelite relatives, armed and ready to assist them. [19]Your wives, children, and numerous livestock, however, may stay behind in the towns I have given you. [20]When the LORD has given security to the rest of the Israelites, as he has

WHAT THE BIBLE SAYS

Conquering the Promised Land

DEUTERONOMY 2:34 When reading these Old Testament passages, many ask, "Wasn't God's instruction to destroy the Canaanites cruel and extreme?" Remember, however, what God said to Abraham hundreds of years earlier: "After four generations your descendants will return here to this land, for the sins of the Amorites do not yet warrant their destruction" (Genesis 15:16, January 6). • The fact that God sent his people into the Promised Land to destroy everything came only after God in his grace had waited until those people's stubbornness and sin was complete and their hearts beyond softening. God did not just kill off everyone so he could put his people in place. The nations in Canaan were a stronghold of rebellion against God, so God commanded his people to take over the land and destroy the wicked people who practiced their idolatry there. God knew that the evil practices and idolatry in the land, were they not eradicated, would prove to be a snare to his people. In fact, Israel's failure to eradicate certain idolatrous peoples in the land later led to their own entanglement in idolatry.

to you, and when they occupy the land the LORD your God is giving them across the Jordan River, then you may all return here to the land I have given you.'

²¹"At that time I gave Joshua this charge: 'You have seen for yourself everything the LORD your God has done to these two kings. He will do the same to all the kingdoms on the west side of the Jordan. ²²Do not be afraid of the nations there, for the LORD your God will fight for you.'

²³"At that time I pleaded with the LORD and said, ²⁴'O Sovereign LORD, you have only begun to show your greatness and the strength of your hand to me, your servant. Is there any god in heaven or on earth who can perform such great and mighty deeds as you do? ²⁵Please let me cross the Jordan to see the wonderful land on the other side, the beautiful hill country and the Lebanon mountains.'

²⁶"But the LORD was angry with me because of you, and he would not listen to me. 'That's enough!' he declared. 'Speak of it no more. ²⁷But go up to Pisgah Peak, and look over the land in every direction. Take a good look, but you may not cross the Jordan River. ²⁸Instead, commission Joshua and encourage and strengthen him, for he will lead the people across the Jordan. He will give them all the land you now see before you as their possession.' ²⁹So we stayed in the valley near Beth-peor."

2:1 Hebrew *sea of reeds.* 2:23 Hebrew *from Caphtor.*
2:34 The Hebrew term used here refers to the complete consecration of things or people to the LORD, either by destroying them or by giving them as an offering. 3:6 The Hebrew term used here refers to the complete consecration of things or people to the LORD, either by destroying them or by giving them as an offering; also in 3:6b. 3:11 Hebrew *9 cubits* [4.1 meters] *long and 4 cubits* [1.8 meters] *wide.* 3:14 Hebrew *Havvoth-jair.* 3:17 Hebrew *from Kinnereth to the Sea of the Arabah, the Salt Sea.*

LUKE 6:12-38

Jesus' message was as unconventional as his leadership style. He called his listeners to lives of love beyond the minimum daily requirement. He offered life and wholeness, a new way of thinking about what it meant to obey God and to be a light in the world.

One day soon afterward Jesus went up on a mountain to pray, and he prayed to God all night. ¹³At daybreak he called together all of his disciples and chose twelve of them to be apostles. Here are their names:

¹⁴ Simon (whom he named Peter),
   Andrew (Peter's brother),
   James,
   John,
   Philip,
   Bartholomew,
¹⁵ Matthew,
   Thomas,
   James (son of Alphaeus),
   Simon (who was called the zealot),
¹⁶ Judas (son of James),
   Judas Iscariot (who later betrayed him).

¹⁷When they came down from the mountain, the disciples stood with Jesus on a large, level area, surrounded by many of his followers and by the crowds. There were people from all over Judea and from Jerusalem and from as far north as the seacoasts of Tyre and Sidon. ¹⁸They had come to hear him and to be healed of their diseases; and those troubled by evil* spirits were healed. ¹⁹Everyone tried to touch him, because healing power went out from him, and he healed everyone.

²⁰Then Jesus turned to his disciples and said,

"God blesses you who are poor,
   for the Kingdom of God is yours.
²¹ God blesses you who are hungry now,
   for you will be satisfied.
God blesses you who weep now,
   for in due time you will laugh.

²²What blessings await you when people hate you and exclude you and mock you and curse you as evil because you follow the Son of Man. ²³When that happens, be happy! Yes, leap for joy! For a great reward awaits you in heaven. And remember, their ancestors treated the ancient prophets that same way.

²⁴ "What sorrow awaits you who are rich,
   for you have your only happiness now.
²⁵ What sorrow awaits you who are fat and prosperous now,
   for a time of awful hunger awaits you.
What sorrow awaits you who laugh now,
   for your laughing will turn to mourning and sorrow.

²⁶ What sorrow awaits you who are
        praised by the crowds,
    for their ancestors also praised false
        prophets.

²⁷"But to you who are willing to listen, I say, love your enemies! Do good to those who hate you. ²⁸Bless those who curse you. Pray for those who hurt you. ²⁹If someone slaps you on one cheek, offer the other cheek also. If someone demands your coat, offer your shirt also. ³⁰Give to anyone who asks; and when things are taken away from you, don't try to get them back. ³¹Do to others as you would like them to do to you.

³²"If you love only those who love you, why should you get credit for that? Even sinners love those who love them! ³³And if you do good only to those who do good to you, why should you get credit? Even sinners do that much! ³⁴And if you lend money only to those who can repay you, why should you get credit? Even sinners will lend to other sinners for a full return.

³⁵"Love your enemies! Do good to them. Lend to them without expecting to be repaid. Then your reward from heaven will be very great, and you will truly be acting as children of the Most High, for he is kind to those who are unthankful and wicked. ³⁶You must be compassionate, just as your Father is compassionate.

³⁷"Do not judge others, and you will not be judged. Do not condemn others, or it will all come back against you. Forgive others, and you will be forgiven. ³⁸Give, and you will receive. Your gift will return to you

in full—pressed down, shaken together to make room for more, running over, and poured into your lap. The amount you give will determine the amount you get back.*"

6:18 Greek *unclean.*   **6:38** Or *The measure you give will be the measure you get back.*

PSALM 67:1-7
For the choir director: A song. A psalm, to be accompanied by stringed instruments.

¹ **M**ay God be merciful and bless us.
    May his face smile with favor on us.
                                        Interlude

² May your ways be known throughout
        the earth,
    your saving power among people
        everywhere.
³ May the nations praise you, O God.
    Yes, may all the nations praise you.
⁴ Let the whole world sing for joy,
    because you govern the nations
        with justice
    and guide the people of the whole
        world.   *Interlude*

⁵ May the nations praise you, O God.
    Yes, may all the nations praise you.
⁶ Then the earth will yield its harvests,
    and God, our God, will richly bless
        us.
⁷ Yes, God will bless us,
    and people all over the world will
        fear him.

PROVERBS 11:27
If you search for good, you will find favor; but if you search for evil, it will find you!

MARCH**25**

DEUTERONOMY 4:1-49
In this, the last section of Moses' first address, he reminded them that what God had wanted all along was purity and devotion.

"**A**nd now, Israel, listen carefully to these decrees and regulations that I am about to teach you. Obey them so that you may live, so you may enter and occupy the land that

the LORD, the God of your ancestors, is giving you. ²Do not add to or subtract from these commands I am giving you. Just obey the commands of the LORD your God that I am giving you.

³"You saw for yourself what the LORD did to you at Baal-peor. There the LORD your God destroyed everyone who had

worshiped Baal, the god of Peor. [4]But all of you who were faithful to the LORD your God are still alive today—every one of you.

[5]"Look, I now teach you these decrees and regulations just as the LORD my God commanded me, so that you may obey them in the land you are about to enter and occupy. [6]Obey them completely, and you will display your wisdom and intelligence among the surrounding nations. When they hear all these decrees, they will exclaim, 'How wise and prudent are the people of this great nation!' [7]For what great nation has a god as near to them as the LORD our God is near to us whenever we call on him? [8]And what great nation has decrees and regulations as righteous and fair as this body of instructions that I am giving you today?

[9]"But watch out! Be careful never to forget what you yourself have seen. Do not let these memories escape from your mind as long as you live! And be sure to pass them on to your children and grandchildren. [10]Never forget the day when you stood before the LORD your God at Mount Sinai,* where he told me, 'Summon the people before me, and I will personally instruct them. Then they will learn to fear me as long as they live, and they will teach their children to fear me also.'

[11]"You came near and stood at the foot of the mountain, while flames from the mountain shot into the sky. The mountain was shrouded in black clouds and deep darkness. [12]And the LORD spoke to you from the heart of the fire. You heard the sound of his words but didn't see his form; there was only a voice. [13]He proclaimed his covenant—the Ten Commandments*— which he commanded you to keep, and which he wrote on two stone tablets. [14]It was at that time that the LORD commanded me to teach you his decrees and regulations so you would obey them in the land you are about to enter and occupy.

[15]"But be very careful! You did not see the LORD's form on the day he spoke to you from the heart of the fire at Mount Sinai. [16]So do not corrupt yourselves by making an idol in any form—whether of a man or a woman, [17]an animal on the ground, a bird in the sky, [18]a small animal that scurries along the ground, or a fish in the deepest

sea. [19]And when you look up into the sky and see the sun, moon, and stars—all the forces of heaven—don't be seduced into worshiping them. The LORD your God gave them to all the peoples of the earth. [20]Remember that the LORD rescued you from the iron-smelting furnace of Egypt in order to make you his very own people and his special possession, which is what you are today.

[21]"But the LORD was angry with me because of you. He vowed that I would not cross the Jordan River into the good land the LORD your God is giving you as your special possession. [22]You will cross the Jordan to occupy the land, but I will not. Instead, I will die here on the east side of the river. [23]So be careful not to break the covenant the LORD your God has made with you. Do not make idols of any shape or form, for the LORD your God has forbidden this. [24]The LORD your God is a devouring fire; he is a jealous God.

[25]"In the future, when you have children and grandchildren and have lived in the land a long time, do not corrupt yourselves by making idols of any kind. This is evil in the sight of the LORD your God and will arouse his anger.

[26]"Today I call on heaven and earth as witnesses against you. If you break my covenant, you will quickly disappear from the land you are crossing the Jordan to occupy. You will live there only a short time; then you will be utterly destroyed. [27]For the LORD will scatter you among the nations, where only a few of you will survive. [28]There, in a foreign land, you will worship idols made from wood and stone—gods that neither see nor hear nor eat nor smell. [29]But from there you will search again for the LORD your God. And if you search for him with all your heart and soul, you will find him.

[30]"In the distant future, when you are suffering all these things, you will finally return to the LORD your God and listen to what he tells you. [31]For the LORD your God is a merciful God; he will not abandon you or destroy you or forget the solemn covenant he made with your ancestors.

[32]"Now search all of history, from the time God created people on the earth until now, and search from one end of the

heavens to the other. Has anything as great as this ever been seen or heard before? [33]Has any nation ever heard the voice of God* speaking from fire—as you did—and survived? [34]Has any other god dared to take a nation for himself out of another nation by means of trials, miraculous signs, wonders, war, a strong hand, a powerful arm, and terrifying acts? Yet that is what the LORD your God did for you in Egypt, right before your eyes.

[35]"He showed you these things so you would know that the LORD is God and there is no other. [36]He let you hear his voice from heaven so he could instruct you. He let you see his great fire here on earth so he could speak to you from it. [37]Because he loved your ancestors, he chose to bless their descendants, and he personally brought you out of Egypt with a great display of power. [38]He drove out nations far greater than you, so he could bring you in and give you their land as your special possession, as it is today.

[39]"So remember this and keep it firmly in mind: The LORD is God both in heaven and on earth, and there is no other. [40]If you obey all the decrees and commands I am giving you today, all will be well with you and your children. I am giving you these instructions so you will enjoy a long life in the land the LORD your God is giving you for all time."

[41]Then Moses set apart three cities of refuge east of the Jordan River. [42]Anyone who killed another person unintentionally, without previous hostility, could flee there to live in safety. [43]These were the cities: Bezer on the wilderness plateau for the tribe of Reuben; Ramoth in Gilead for the tribe of Gad; Golan in Bashan for the tribe of Manasseh.

[44]This is the body of instruction that Moses presented to the Israelites. [45]These are the laws, decrees, and regulations that Moses gave to the people of Israel when they left Egypt, [46]and as they camped in the valley near Beth-peor east of the Jordan River. (This land was formerly occupied by the Amorites under King Sihon, who ruled from Heshbon. But Moses and the Israelites destroyed him and his people when they came up from Egypt. [47]Israel took possession of his land and that of King Og of Bashan—the two Amorite kings east of the Jordan. [48]So Israel conquered the entire area from Aroer at the edge of the Arnon Gorge all the way to Mount Sirion,* also called Mount Hermon. [49]And they conquered the eastern bank of the Jordan River as far south as the Dead Sea,* below the slopes of Pisgah.)

4:10 Hebrew *Horeb*, another name for Sinai; also in 4:15.
4:13 Hebrew *the ten words.*   4:33 Or *voice of a god.*
4:48 As in Syriac version (see also 3:9); Hebrew reads *Mount Sion.*   4:49 Hebrew *took the Arabah on the east side of the Jordan as far as the sea of the Arabah.*

HOW WE LIVE

Courageous in trials

LUKE 6:47-49 Why would someone want to build a house on such unstable ground as sand? This builder might have chosen to ignore the storm warnings, thinking that disaster would not strike him. Whatever his reason, the man who built his house on sand paid a solemn price— he lost everything. Jesus compared this man to those who listen, but do not obey. The sand-builder hears the words of Jesus, but doesn't apply them to his life. Thus, when the storms of life assail him, his faith is weak and he crumbles.   • However, the man who builds on a firm foundation is not swayed, even when the floodwaters break against his house. This is a person of faith and action. In his daily life, he is putting into action the principles he learned from the Bible. He doesn't just listen; he obeys. Such a believer can weather any storm, because his foundation—Jesus Christ—is immovable.   • When you build a strong foundation—by reading God's Word and deepening your understanding of your faith—you can stand strong in any trial. No matter what storms rage around you, your foundation will stand strong.

LUKE 6:39-7:10

Jesus drew believers not only from his own people, the Jews, but also the Romans who occupied his country and other foreigners.

Then Jesus gave the following illustration: "Can one blind person lead another? Won't they both fall into a ditch? ⁴⁰Students* are not greater than their teacher. But the student who is fully trained will become like the teacher.

⁴¹"And why worry about a speck in your friend's eye* when you have a log in your own? ⁴²How can you think of saying, 'Friend,* let me help you get rid of that speck in your eye,' when you can't see past the log in your own eye? Hypocrite! First get rid of the log in your own eye; then you will see well enough to deal with the speck in your friend's eye.

⁴³"A good tree can't produce bad fruit, and a bad tree can't produce good fruit. ⁴⁴A tree is identified by its fruit. Figs are never gathered from thornbushes, and grapes are not picked from bramble bushes. ⁴⁵A good person produces good things from the treasury of a good heart, and an evil person produces evil things from the treasury of an evil heart. What you say flows from what is in your heart.

⁴⁶"So why do you keep calling me 'Lord, Lord!' when you don't do what I say? ⁴⁷I will show you what it's like when someone comes to me, listens to my teaching, and then follows it. ⁴⁸It is like a person building a house who digs deep and lays the foundation on solid rock. When the floodwaters rise and break against that house, it stands firm because it is well built. ⁴⁹But anyone who hears and doesn't obey is like a person who builds a house without a foundation. When the floods sweep down against that house, it will collapse into a heap of ruins."

⁷:¹WHEN Jesus had finished saying all this to the people, he returned to Capernaum. ²At that time the highly valued slave of a Roman officer* was sick and near death. ³When the officer heard about Jesus, he sent some respected Jewish elders to ask him to come and heal his slave. ⁴So they earnestly begged Jesus to help the man. "If anyone deserves your help, he does," they said, ⁵"for he loves the Jewish people and even built a synagogue for us."

⁶So Jesus went with them. But just before they arrived at the house, the officer sent some friends to say, "Lord, don't trouble yourself by coming to my home, for I am not worthy of such an honor. ⁷I am not even worthy to come and meet you. Just say the word from where you are, and my servant will be healed. ⁸I know this because I am under the authority of my superior officers, and I have authority over my soldiers. I only need to say, 'Go,' and they go, or 'Come,' and they come. And if I say to my slaves, 'Do this,' they do it."

⁹When Jesus heard this, he was amazed. Turning to the crowd that was following him, he said, "I tell you, I haven't seen faith like this in all Israel!" ¹⁰And when the officer's friends returned to his house, they found the slave completely healed.

6:40 Or *Disciples.* 6:41 Greek *your brother's eye;* also in 6:42. 6:42 Greek *Brother.* 7:2 Greek *a centurion;* similarly in 7:6.

PSALM 68:1-18
For the choir director: A song. A psalm of David.

¹ **R**ise up, O God, and scatter your
    enemies.
  Let those who hate God run for
    their lives.
² Blow them away like smoke.
  Melt them like wax in a fire.
  Let the wicked perish in the
    presence of God.
³ But let the godly rejoice.
  Let them be glad in God's
    presence.
  Let them be filled with joy.
⁴ Sing praises to God and to his name!
  Sing loud praises to him who rides
    the clouds.
  His name is the LORD—
    rejoice in his presence!

⁵ Father to the fatherless, defender
    of widows—
  this is God, whose dwelling is holy.
⁶ God places the lonely in families;
  he sets the prisoners free and gives
    them joy.
  But he makes the rebellious live
    in a sun-scorched land.

7 O God, when you led your people out
  from Egypt,
    when you marched through the
      dry wasteland,   *Interlude*
8 the earth trembled, and the heavens
    poured down rain
      before you, the God of Sinai,
      before God, the God of Israel.
9 You sent abundant rain, O God,
    to refresh the weary land.
10 There your people finally settled,
    and with a bountiful harvest, O God,
    you provided for your needy people.

11 The Lord gives the word,
    and a great army* brings the good
      news.
12 Enemy kings and their armies flee,
    while the women of Israel divide
      the plunder.
13 Even those who lived among the
      sheepfolds found treasures—
    doves with wings of silver
    and feathers of gold.
14 The Almighty scattered the enemy
      kings
    like a blowing snowstorm on Mount
      Zalmon.

15 The mountains of Bashan are majestic,
    with many peaks stretching high
      into the sky.
16 Why do you look with envy, O rugged
      mountains,
    at Mount Zion, where God has
      chosen to live,
    where the LORD himself will live
      forever?

17 Surrounded by unnumbered
      thousands of chariots,
    the Lord came from Mount Sinai
      into his sanctuary.
18 When you ascended to the heights,
    you led a crowd of captives.
  You received gifts from the people,
    even from those who rebelled
      against you.
    Now the LORD God will live among
      us there.

68:11 Or *a host of women.*

PROVERBS 11:28

Trust in your money and down you go!
But the godly flourish like leaves in
spring.

DEUTERONOMY 5:1–6:25

Moses' reviewed the heart of God's law. He reminded the people of the Ten Commandments,
and he recapped what is known as the great
Shema: the command to love God with all your
heart, soul, and strength.

Moses called all the people of Israel together and said, "Listen carefully, Israel.
Hear the decrees and regulations I am giving you today, so you may learn them and
obey them!

2"The LORD our God made a covenant
with us at Mount Sinai.* 3The LORD did
not make this covenant with our ancestors, but with all of us who are alive today.
4At the mountain the LORD spoke to you
face to face from the heart of the fire. 5I
stood as an intermediary between you

MARCH**26**

and the LORD, for you were afraid of the
fire and did not want to approach the
mountain. He spoke to me, and I passed
his words on to you. This is what he said:

6"I am the LORD your God, who rescued
you from the land of Egypt, the place
of your slavery.
7"You must not have any other god but
me.
8"You must not make for yourself an
idol of any kind, or an image of
anything in the heavens or on the
earth or in the sea. 9You must not
bow down to them or worship them,
for I, the LORD your God, am a
jealous God who will not tolerate
your affection for any other gods.

I lay the sins of the parents upon their children; the entire family is affected—even children in the third and fourth generations of those who reject me. [10]But I lavish unfailing love for a thousand generations on those* who love me and obey my commands.

[11]"You must not misuse the name of the LORD your God. The LORD will not let you go unpunished if you misuse his name.

[12]"Observe the Sabbath day by keeping it holy, as the LORD your God has commanded you. [13]You have six days each week for your ordinary work, [14]but the seventh day is a Sabbath day of rest dedicated to the LORD your God. On that day no one in your household may do any work. This includes you, your sons and daughters, your male and female servants, your oxen and donkeys and other livestock, and any foreigners living among you. All your male and female servants must rest as you do. [15]Remember that you were once slaves in Egypt, but the LORD your God brought you out with his strong hand and powerful arm. That is why the LORD your God has commanded you to rest on the Sabbath day.

[16]"Honor your father and mother, as the LORD your God commanded you. Then you will live a long, full life in the land the LORD your God is giving you.

[17]"You must not murder.

[18]"You must not commit adultery.

[19]"You must not steal.

[20]"You must not testify falsely against your neighbor.

[21]"You must not covet your neighbor's wife. You must not covet your neighbor's house or land, male or female servant, ox or donkey, or anything else that belongs to your neighbor.

[22]"The LORD spoke these words to all of you assembled there at the foot of the mountain. He spoke with a loud voice from the heart of the fire, surrounded by clouds and deep darkness. This was all he said at that time, and he wrote his words on two stone tablets and gave them to me.

[23]"But when you heard the voice from the heart of the darkness, while the mountain was blazing with fire, all your tribal leaders and elders came to me. [24]They said, 'Look, the LORD our God has shown us his glory and greatness, and we have heard his voice from the heart of the fire. Today we have seen that God can speak to us humans, and yet we live! [25]But now, why should we risk death again? If the LORD our God speaks to us again, we will certainly die and be consumed by this awesome fire. [26]Can any living thing hear the voice of the living God from the heart of the fire as we did and yet survive? [27]Go yourself and listen to what the LORD our God says. Then come and tell us everything he tells you, and we will listen and obey.'

[28]"The LORD heard the request you made to me. And he said, 'I have heard what the people said to you, and they are right. [29]Oh, that they would always have hearts like this, that they might fear me and obey all my commands! If they did, they and their descendants would prosper forever. [30]Go and tell them, "Return to your tents." [31]But you stand here with me so I can give you all my commands, decrees, and regulations. You must teach them to the people so they can obey them in the land I am giving them as their possession.'"

[32]So Moses told the people, "You must be careful to obey all the commands of the LORD your God, following his instructions in every detail. [33]Stay on the path that the LORD your God has commanded you to follow. Then you will live long and prosperous lives in the land you are about to enter and occupy.

6:1"THESE are the commands, decrees, and regulations that the LORD your God commanded me to teach you. You must obey them in the land you are about to enter and occupy, [2]and you and your children and grandchildren must fear the LORD your God as long as you live. If you obey all his decrees and commands, you will enjoy a long life. [3]Listen closely, Israel, and be careful to obey. Then all will go well with you, and you will have many children in the land flowing with milk and honey, just as the LORD, the God of your ancestors, promised you.

[4]"Listen, O Israel! The LORD is our God, the LORD alone.* [5]And you must love the LORD your God with all your heart, all your soul, and all your strength. [6]And you must commit yourselves wholeheartedly to these commands that I am giving you today. [7]Repeat them again and again to your children. Talk about them when you are at home and when you are on the road, when you are going to bed and when you are getting up. [8]Tie them to your hands and wear them on your forehead as reminders. [9]Write them on the doorposts of your house and on your gates.

[10]"The LORD your God will soon bring you into the land he swore to give you when he made a vow to your ancestors Abraham, Isaac, and Jacob. It is a land with large, prosperous cities that you did not build. [11]The houses will be richly stocked with goods you did not produce. You will draw water from cisterns you did not dig, and you will eat from vineyards and olive trees you did not plant. When you have eaten your fill in this land, [12]be careful not to forget the LORD, who rescued you from slavery in the land of Egypt. [13]You must

fear the LORD your God and serve him. When you take an oath, you must use only his name.

[14]"You must not worship any of the gods of neighboring nations, [15]for the LORD your God, who lives among you, is a jealous God. His anger will flare up against you, and he will wipe you from the face of the earth. [16]You must not test the LORD your God as you did when you complained at Massah. [17]You must diligently obey the commands of the LORD your God—all the laws and decrees he has given you. [18]Do what is right and good in the LORD's sight, so all will go well with you. Then you will enter and occupy the good land that the LORD swore to give your ancestors. [19]You will drive out all the enemies living in the land, just as the LORD said you would.

[20]"In the future your children will ask you, 'What is the meaning of these laws, decrees, and regulations that the LORD our God has commanded us to obey?'

[21]"Then you must tell them, 'We were Pharaoh's slaves in Egypt, but the LORD brought us out of Egypt with his strong hand. [22]The LORD did miraculous signs and wonders before our eyes, dealing terrifying blows against Egypt and Pharaoh and all his people. [23]He brought us out of Egypt so he could give us this land he had sworn to give our ancestors. [24]And the

HOW WE LIVE

Loving God and others

DEUTERONOMY 6:4-5 In the New Testament, when Jesus was asked what commandment is the greatest (Matthew 22:37-38, February 3), he replied by quoting today's reading. Why is the commandment to love God so important that it is to be held above all others? God is the one true God. Loving him with all of your heart, soul, and strength sets a pattern for everything else in your life. • Loving God is a prerequisite for loving others. Recognizing that God loves your coworkers, neighbors, friends, and family as much as he loves you should make you think twice before being rude, disrespectful, or dismissive. Loving God is the key to obeying him. What God would have you do is most important; bringing glory to him is your soul's desire. The apostle John wrote: "Loving God means keeping his commandments, and his commandments are not burdensome" (1 John 5:3, December 5). • How can we grow in our love for God? Get to know him better. Meditate on his Word and pray to him. The more you get to know him, the more your love for him will grow.

LORD our God commanded us to obey all these decrees and to fear him so he can continue to bless us and preserve our lives, as he has done to this day. ²⁵For we will be counted as righteous when we obey all the commands the LORD our God has given us.'"

5:2 Hebrew *Horeb,* another name for Sinai.   5:10 Hebrew *for thousands of those.*   6:4 Or *The LORD our God is one LORD;* or *The LORD our God, the LORD is one;* or *The LORD is our God, the LORD is one.*

LUKE 7:11-35

Both Jesus and John the Baptist faced difficulty and rejection for speaking the truth. After his arrest, John sent a messenger to Jesus to verify that he was the Messiah. Jesus responded in the affirmative.

Soon afterward Jesus went with his disciples to the village of Nain, and a large crowd followed him. ¹²A funeral procession was coming out as he approached the village gate. The young man who had died was a widow's only son, and a large crowd from the village was with her. ¹³When the Lord saw her, his heart overflowed with compassion. "Don't cry!" he said. ¹⁴Then he walked over to the coffin and touched it, and the bearers stopped. "Young man," he said, "I tell you, get up." ¹⁵Then the dead boy sat up and began to talk! And Jesus gave him back to his mother.

¹⁶Great fear swept the crowd, and they praised God, saying, "A mighty prophet has risen among us," and "God has visited his people today." ¹⁷And the news about Jesus spread throughout Judea and the surrounding countryside.

¹⁸The disciples of John the Baptist told John about everything Jesus was doing. So John called for two of his disciples, ¹⁹and he sent them to the Lord to ask him, "Are you the Messiah we've been expecting,* or should we keep looking for someone else?"

²⁰John's two disciples found Jesus and said to him, "John the Baptist sent us to ask, 'Are you the Messiah we've been expecting, or should we keep looking for someone else?'"

²¹At that very time, Jesus cured many people of their diseases, illnesses, and evil spirits, and he restored sight to many who were blind. ²²Then he told John's disciples, "Go back to John and tell him what you have seen and heard—the blind see, the lame walk, the lepers are cured, the deaf hear, the dead are raised to life, and the Good News is being preached to the poor. ²³And tell him, 'God blesses those who do not turn away because of me.*'"

²⁴After John's disciples left, Jesus began talking about him to the crowds. "What kind of man did you go into the wilderness to see? Was he a weak reed, swayed by every breath of wind? ²⁵Or were you expecting to see a man dressed in expensive clothes? No, people who wear beautiful clothes and live in luxury are found in palaces. ²⁶Were you looking for a prophet? Yes, and he is more than a prophet. ²⁷John is the man to whom the Scriptures refer when they say,

'Look, I am sending my messenger
    ahead of you,
    and he will prepare your way before
        you.'*

²⁸I tell you, of all who have ever lived, none is greater than John. Yet even the least person in the Kingdom of God is greater than he is!"

²⁹When they heard this, all the people—even the tax collectors—agreed that God's way was right,* for they had been baptized by John. ³⁰But the Pharisees and experts in religious law rejected God's plan for them, for they had refused John's baptism.

³¹"To what can I compare the people of this generation?" Jesus asked. "How can I describe them? ³²They are like children playing a game in the public square. They complain to their friends,

'We played wedding songs,
    and you didn't dance,
so we played funeral songs,
    and you didn't weep.'

³³For John the Baptist didn't spend his time eating bread or drinking wine, and you say, 'He's possessed by a demon.' ³⁴The Son of Man,* on the other hand, feasts and drinks, and you say, 'He's a glutton and a drunkard, and a friend of tax collectors and other sinners!' ³⁵But wisdom is shown to be right by the lives of those who follow it.*"

PSALM 68:19-35

Praise the Lord; praise God our savior!
  For each day he carries us in his
    arms.   *Interlude*
20 Our God is a God who saves!
  The Sovereign LORD rescues us
    from death.

21 But God will smash the heads of
    his enemies,
  crushing the skulls of those who
    love their guilty ways.
22 The Lord says, "I will bring my
    enemies down from Bashan;
  I will bring them up from the
    depths of the sea.
23 You, my people, will wash your feet
    in their blood,
  and even your dogs will get their
    share!"

24 Your procession has come into view,
    O God—
  the procession of my God and King
    as he goes into the sanctuary.
25 Singers are in front, musicians behind;
  between them are young women
    playing tambourines.
26 Praise God, all you people of Israel;
  praise the LORD, the source of
    Israel's life.
27 Look, the little tribe of Benjamin leads
    the way.
  Then comes a great throng of rulers
    from Judah
  and all the rulers of Zebulun and
    Naphtali.

28 Summon your might, O God.
  Display your power, O God, as you
    have in the past.
29 The kings of the earth are bringing
    tribute

  to your Temple in Jerusalem.
30 Rebuke these enemy nations—
  these wild animals lurking in
    the reeds,
  this herd of bulls among the
    weaker calves.
  Make them bring bars of silver in
    humble tribute.
  Scatter the nations that delight
    in war.
31 Let Egypt come with gifts of precious
    metals*;
  let Ethiopia* bow in submission
    to God.
32 Sing to God, you kingdoms of
    the earth.
  Sing praises to the Lord.   *Interlude*
33 Sing to the one who rides across the
    ancient heavens,
  his mighty voice thundering from
    the sky.
34 Tell everyone about God's power.
  His majesty shines down on
    Israel;
  his strength is mighty in the
    heavens.
35 God is awesome in his sanctuary.
  The God of Israel gives power and
    strength to his people.

  Praise be to God!

PROVERBS 11:29-31

Those who bring trouble on their families
inherit the wind. The fool will be a servant
to the wise. □ The seeds of good deeds become a tree of life; a wise person wins
friends.* □ If the righteous are rewarded
here on earth, what will happen to wicked
sinners?*

DEUTERONOMY 7:1–8:20

Moses reminded his people that their relationship with God was based on a covenant. God would bless them while they lived within his guidelines.

"**W**hen the LORD your God brings you into the land you are about to enter and occupy, he will clear away many nations ahead of you: the Hittites, Girgashites, Amorites, Canaanites, Perizzites, Hivites, and Jebusites. These seven nations are greater and more numerous than you. ²When the LORD your God hands these nations over to you and you conquer them, you must completely destroy* them. Make no treaties with them and show them no mercy. ³You must not intermarry with them. Do not let your daughters and sons marry their sons and daughters, ⁴for they will lead your children away from me to worship other gods. Then the anger of the LORD will burn against you, and he will quickly destroy you. ⁵This is what you must do. You must break down their pagan altars and shatter their sacred pillars. Cut down their Asherah poles and burn their idols. ⁶For you are a holy people, who belong to the LORD your God. Of all the people on earth, the LORD your God has chosen you to be his own special treasure.

⁷"The LORD did not set his heart on you and choose you because you were more numerous than other nations, for you were the smallest of all nations! ⁸Rather, it was simply that the LORD loves you, and he was keeping the oath he had sworn to your ancestors. That is why the LORD rescued you with such a strong hand from your slavery and from the oppressive hand of Pharaoh, king of Egypt. ⁹Understand, therefore, that the LORD your God is indeed God. He is the faithful God who keeps his covenant for a thousand generations and lavishes his unfailing love on those who love him and obey his commands. ¹⁰But he does not hesitate to punish and destroy those who reject him. ¹¹Therefore, you must obey all these commands, decrees, and regulations I am giving you today.

¹²"If you listen to these regulations and faithfully obey them, the LORD your God will keep his covenant of unfailing love with you, as he promised with an oath to your ancestors. ¹³He will love you and bless you, and he will give you many children. He will give fertility to your land and your animals. When you arrive in the land he swore to give your ancestors, you will have large harvests of grain, new wine, and olive oil, and great herds of cattle, sheep, and goats. ¹⁴You will be blessed above all the nations of the earth. None of your men or women will be childless, and all your livestock will bear young. ¹⁵And the LORD will protect you from all sickness. He will not let you suffer from the terrible diseases you knew in Egypt, but he will inflict them on all your enemies!

¹⁶"You must destroy all the nations the LORD your God hands over to you. Show them no mercy, and do not worship their gods, or they will trap you. ¹⁷Perhaps you will think to yourselves, 'How can we ever conquer these nations that are so much more powerful than we are?' ¹⁸But don't be afraid of them! Just remember what the LORD your God did to Pharaoh and to all the land of Egypt. ¹⁹Remember the great terrors the LORD your God sent against them. You saw it all with your own eyes! And remember the miraculous signs and wonders, and the strong hand and powerful arm with which he brought you out of Egypt. The LORD your God will use this same power against all the people you fear. ²⁰And then the LORD your God will send terror* to drive out the few survivors still hiding from you!

²¹"No, do not be afraid of those nations, for the LORD your God is among you, and he is a great and awesome God. ²²The LORD your God will drive those nations out ahead of you little by little. You will not clear them away all at once, otherwise the wild animals would multiply too quickly for you. ²³But the LORD your God will hand them over to you. He will throw them into complete confusion until they are destroyed. ²⁴He will put their kings in your power, and you will erase their

names from the face of the earth. No one will be able to stand against you, and you will destroy them all.

²⁵"You must burn their idols in fire, and you must not covet the silver or gold that covers them. You must not take it or it will become a trap to you, for it is detestable to the LORD your God. ²⁶Do not bring any detestable objects into your home, for then you will be destroyed, just like them. You must utterly detest such things, for they are set apart for destruction.

8:1"BE careful to obey all the commands I am giving you today. Then you will live and multiply, and you will enter and occupy the land the LORD swore to give your ancestors. ²Remember how the LORD your God led you through the wilderness for these forty years, humbling you and testing you to prove your character, and to find out whether or not you would obey his commands. ³Yes, he humbled you by letting you go hungry and then feeding you with manna, a food previously unknown to you and your ancestors. He did it to teach you that people do not live by bread alone; rather, we live by every word that comes from the mouth of the LORD. ⁴For all these forty years your clothes didn't wear out, and your feet didn't blis-

ter or swell. ⁵Think about it: Just as a parent disciplines a child, the LORD your God disciplines you for your own good.

⁶"So obey the commands of the LORD your God by walking in his ways and fearing him. ⁷For the LORD your God is bringing you into a good land of flowing streams and pools of water, with fountains and springs that gush out in the valleys and hills. ⁸It is a land of wheat and barley; of grapevines, fig trees, and pomegranates; of olive oil and honey. ⁹It is a land where food is plentiful and nothing is lacking. It is a land where iron is as common as stone, and copper is abundant in the hills. ¹⁰When you have eaten your fill, be sure to praise the LORD your God for the good land he has given you.

¹¹"But that is the time to be careful! Beware that in your plenty you do not forget the LORD your God and disobey his commands, regulations, and decrees that I am giving you today. ¹²For when you have become full and prosperous and have built fine homes to live in, ¹³and when your flocks and herds have become very large and your silver and gold have multiplied along with everything else, be careful! ¹⁴Do not become proud at that time and forget the LORD your God, who rescued you from slavery in the land of Egypt. ¹⁵Do

WHO GOD IS

God is faithful

DEUTERONOMY 7:9 Commitment is not very common today. Married couples, for example, promise to stay committed to each other, but the large number of divorces every year indicates that many spouses are not being faithful to their vows. God, on the other hand, always stays true to his word and has been faithful for all eternity. Faithfulness is not something God aspires to; it is an essential part of his character. When God makes a promise, he always keeps it. • In his speech to the Israelites, Moses hammered home this point. The previous generation had refused to believe that God would faithfully keep his promise to give them the land. As punishment, God had sent them to wander until that entire unfaithful generation had died. As the new generation stood ready to enter the land, Moses told them, "Understand, therefore, that the LORD your God is indeed God. He is the faithful God who keeps his covenant for a thousand generations." • Learn this lesson: God's faithfulness doesn't waver. He will keep every promise until the end of time. As David said, "Give thanks to the LORD, for he is good! His faithful love endures forever" (1 Chronicles 16:34, July 13).

not forget that he led you through the great and terrifying wilderness with its poisonous snakes and scorpions, where it was so hot and dry. He gave you water from the rock! [16]He fed you with manna in the wilderness, a food unknown to your ancestors. He did this to humble you and test you for your own good. [17]He did all this so you would never say to yourself, 'I have achieved this wealth with my own strength and energy.' [18]Remember the LORD your God. He is the one who gives you power to be successful, in order to fulfill the covenant he confirmed to your ancestors with an oath.

[19]"But I assure you of this: If you ever forget the LORD your God and follow other gods, worshiping and bowing down to them, you will certainly be destroyed. [20]Just as the LORD has destroyed other nations in your path, you also will be destroyed if you refuse to obey the LORD your God."

7:2 The Hebrew term used here refers to the complete consecration of things or people to the LORD, either by destroying them or by giving them as an offering; also in 7:26. 7:20 Often rendered *the hornet*. The meaning of the Hebrew is uncertain.

LUKE 7:36–8:3

Various women were involved in Jesus' ministry. Some had been healed by him. Some were friends of the family. Some were mothers of the disciples. In a time when women had little voice, Jesus included them in his mission.

One of the Pharisees asked Jesus to have dinner with him, so Jesus went to his home and sat down to eat.* [37]When a certain immoral woman from that city heard he was eating there, she brought a beautiful alabaster jar filled with expensive perfume. [38]Then she knelt behind him at his feet, weeping. Her tears fell on his feet, and she wiped them off with her hair. Then she kept kissing his feet and putting perfume on them.

[39]When the Pharisee who had invited him saw this, he said to himself, "If this man were a prophet, he would know what kind of woman is touching him. She's a sinner!"

[40]Then Jesus answered his thoughts. "Simon," he said to the Pharisee, "I have something to say to you."

"Go ahead, Teacher," Simon replied.

[41]Then Jesus told him this story: "A man loaned money to two people—500 pieces of silver* to one and 50 pieces to the other. [42]But neither of them could repay him, so he kindly forgave them both, canceling their debts. Who do you suppose loved him more after that?"

[43]Simon answered, "I suppose the one for whom he canceled the larger debt."

"That's right," Jesus said. [44]Then he turned to the woman and said to Simon, "Look at this woman kneeling here. When I entered your home, you didn't offer me water to wash the dust from my feet, but she has washed them with her tears and wiped them with her hair. [45]You didn't greet me with a kiss, but from the time I first came in, she has not stopped kissing my feet. [46]You neglected the courtesy of olive oil to anoint my head, but she has anointed my feet with rare perfume.

[47]"I tell you, her sins—and they are many—have been forgiven, so she has shown me much love. But a person who is forgiven little shows only little love." [48]Then Jesus said to the woman, "Your sins are forgiven."

[49]The men at the table said among themselves, "Who is this man, that he goes around forgiving sins?"

[50]And Jesus said to the woman, "Your faith has saved you; go in peace."

[8:1]SOON afterward Jesus began a tour of the nearby towns and villages, preaching and announcing the Good News about the Kingdom of God. He took his twelve disciples with him, [2]along with some women who had been cured of evil spirits and diseases. Among them were Mary Magdalene, from whom he had cast out seven demons; [3]Joanna, the wife of Chuza, Herod's business manager; Susanna; and many others who were contributing their own resources to support Jesus and his disciples.

7:36 Or *and reclined.* 7:41 Greek *500 denarii.* A denarius was equivalent to a laborer's full day's wage.

PSALM 69:1-18

For the choir director: A psalm of David, to be sung to the tune "Lilies."

[1] **S**ave me, O God,

for the floodwaters are up to
my neck.
2 Deeper and deeper I sink into the
mire;
I can't find a foothold.
I am in deep water,
and the floods overwhelm me.
3 I am exhausted from crying
for help;
my throat is parched.
My eyes are swollen with weeping,
waiting for my God to help me.
4 Those who hate me without cause
outnumber the hairs on my head.
Many enemies try to destroy me
with lies,
demanding that I give back what
I didn't steal.
5 O God, you know how foolish I am;
my sins cannot be hidden from you.
6 Don't let those who trust in you be
ashamed because of me,
O Sovereign Lord of Heaven's
Armies.
Don't let me cause them to be
humiliated,
O God of Israel.
7 For I endure insults for your sake;
humiliation is written all over
my face.
8 Even my own brothers pretend they
don't know me;
they treat me like a stranger.
9 Passion for your house has
consumed me,
and the insults of those who insult
you have fallen on me.

10 When I weep and fast,
they scoff at me.
11 When I dress in burlap to show
sorrow,
they make fun of me.
12 I am the favorite topic of town
gossip,
and all the drunks sing
about me.

13 But I keep praying to you, Lord,
hoping this time you will show
me favor.
In your unfailing love, O God,
answer my prayer with your sure
salvation.
14 Rescue me from the mud;
don't let me sink any deeper!
Save me from those who
hate me,
and pull me from these deep
waters.
15 Don't let the floods overwhelm me,
or the deep waters swallow me,
or the pit of death devour me.

16 Answer my prayers, O Lord,
for your unfailing love is wonderful.
Take care of me,
for your mercy is so plentiful.
17 Don't hide from your servant;
answer me quickly, for I am in deep
trouble!
18 Come and redeem me;
free me from my enemies.

PROVERBS 12:1
To learn, you must love discipline; it is stupid to hate correction.

MARCH**28**

DEUTERONOMY 9:1–10:22
You can almost feel the intensity rise as Moses continued to speak: This is what God has done for you! Is there anything to do but follow him with all your heart?

"Listen, O Israel! Today you are about to cross the Jordan River to take over the land belonging to nations much greater and more powerful than you. They live in cities with walls that reach to the sky! 2 The people are strong and tall—descendants of the famous Anakite giants. You've heard the saying, 'Who can stand up to the Anakites?' 3 But recognize today that the Lord your God is the one who will cross over ahead of you like a devouring fire to destroy them. He will subdue them so that you will quickly conquer them and drive them out, just as the LORD has promised.

4"After the LORD your God has done this for you, don't say in your hearts, 'The LORD has given us this land because we are such good people!' No, it is because of the wickedness of the other nations that he is pushing them out of your way. 5It is not because you are so good or have such integrity that you are about to occupy their land. The LORD your God will drive these nations out ahead of you only because of their wickedness, and to fulfill the oath he swore to your ancestors Abraham, Isaac, and Jacob. 6You must recognize that the LORD your God is not giving you this good land because you are good, for you are not—you are a stubborn people.

7"Remember and never forget how angry you made the LORD your God out in the wilderness. From the day you left Egypt until now, you have been constantly rebelling against him. 8Even at Mount Sinai* you made the LORD so angry he was ready to destroy you. 9This happened when I was on the mountain receiving the tablets of stone inscribed with the words of the covenant that the LORD had made with you. I was there for forty days and forty nights, and all that time I ate no food and drank no water. 10The LORD gave me the two tablets on which God had written with his own finger all the words he had spoken to you from the heart of the fire when you were assembled at the mountain.

11"At the end of the forty days and nights, the LORD handed me the two stone tablets inscribed with the words of the covenant. 12Then the LORD said to me, 'Get up! Go down immediately, for the people you brought out of Egypt have corrupted themselves. How quickly they have turned away from the way I commanded them to live! They have melted gold and made an idol for themselves!'

13"The LORD also said to me, 'I have seen how stubborn and rebellious these people are. 14Leave me alone so I may destroy them and erase their name from under heaven. Then I will make a mighty nation of your descendants, a nation larger and more powerful than they are.'

15"So while the mountain was blazing with fire I turned and came down, holding in my hands the two stone tablets inscribed with the terms of the covenant. 16There below me I could see that you had sinned against the LORD your God. You had melted gold and made a calf idol for yourselves. How quickly you had turned away from the path the LORD had commanded you to follow! 17So I took the stone tablets and threw them to the ground, smashing them before your eyes.

18"Then, as before, I threw myself down before the LORD for forty days and nights. I ate no bread and drank no water because of the great sin you had committed by doing what the LORD hated, provoking him to anger. 19I feared that the furious anger of the LORD, which turned him against you, would drive him to destroy you. But again he listened to me. 20The LORD was so angry with Aaron that he wanted to destroy him, too. But I prayed for Aaron, and the LORD spared him. 21I took your sin—the calf you had made—and I melted it down in the fire and ground it into fine dust. Then I threw the dust into the stream that flows down the mountain.

22"You also made the LORD angry at Taberah,* Massah,* and Kibroth-hattaavah.* 23And at Kadesh-barnea the LORD sent you out with this command: 'Go up and take over the land I have given you.' But you rebelled against the command of the LORD your God and refused to put your trust in him or obey him. 24Yes, you have been rebelling against the LORD as long as I have known you.

25"That is why I threw myself down before the LORD for forty days and nights—for the LORD said he would destroy you. 26I prayed to the LORD and said, 'O Sovereign LORD, do not destroy them. They are your own people. They are your special possession, whom you redeemed from Egypt by your mighty power and your strong hand. 27Please overlook the stubbornness and the awful sin of these people, and remember instead your servants Abraham, Isaac, and Jacob. 28If you destroy these people, the Egyptians will say, "The Israelites died because the LORD wasn't able to bring them to the land he had promised to give them." Or they might say,

"He destroyed them because he hated them; he deliberately took them into the wilderness to slaughter them." ²⁹But they are your people and your special possession, whom you brought out of Egypt by your great strength and powerful arm.'

10:1"At that time the LORD said to me, 'Chisel out two stone tablets like the first ones. Also make a wooden Ark—a sacred chest to store them in. Come up to me on the mountain, ²and I will write on the tablets the same words that were on the ones you smashed. Then place the tablets in the Ark.'

³"So I made an Ark of acacia wood and cut two stone tablets like the first two. Then I went up the mountain with the tablets in my hand. ⁴Once again the LORD wrote the Ten Commandments* on the tablets and gave them to me. They were the same words the LORD had spoken to you from the heart of the fire on the day you were assembled at the foot of the mountain. ⁵Then I turned and came down the mountain and placed the tablets in the Ark of the Covenant, which I had made, just as the LORD commanded me. And the tablets are still there in the Ark."

⁶(The people of Israel set out from the wells of the people of Jaakan* and traveled to Moserah, where Aaron died and was buried. His son Eleazar ministered as high priest in his place. ⁷Then they journeyed to Gudgodah, and from there to Jotbathah, a land with many brooks and streams. ⁸At that time the LORD set apart the tribe of Levi to carry the Ark of the LORD's Covenant, and to stand before the LORD as his ministers, and to pronounce blessings in his name. These are their duties to this day. ⁹That is why the Levites have no share of property or possession of land among the other Israelite tribes. The LORD himself is their special possession, as the LORD your God told them.)

¹⁰"As for me, I stayed on the mountain in the LORD's presence for forty days and nights, as I had done the first time. And once again the LORD listened to my pleas and agreed not to destroy you. ¹¹Then the LORD said to me, 'Get up and resume the journey, and lead the people to the land I swore to give to their ancestors, so they may take possession of it.'

¹²"And now, Israel, what does the LORD your God require of you? He requires only that you fear the LORD your God, and live in a way that pleases him, and love him and serve him with all your heart and soul. ¹³And you must always obey the LORD's commands and decrees that I am giving you today for your own good.

HOW WE LIVE

Persevering in faith

LUKE 8:11-15   If you haven't discovered it already, the Christian life can be tough. Perhaps some of your friends don't like it that you've changed. Maybe God is talking to you about some areas of your life that need to change and you're finding that it's hard, even though you want to do it. Or maybe you thought becoming a Christian would solve all those other problems in your life—marriage issues, children problems, job frustrations—and you're discovering that those things are still the same. • When Jesus gave this parable of the seed, he was talking about how sometimes new believers accept the message but then wither because of life's difficulties or fail to grow to maturity because of life's temptations. Jesus wants you to be like the good soil so that the seed of his Word can take root and grow. • So what do you do when the going gets tough? Stay close to God. Read the Bible every day. Pray about the situations that arise. Seek to do what you know is right. As you "hang in there," you'll find that God's Word is taking root. As the roots go down deep, your faith will grow strong.

[14]"Look, the highest heavens and the earth and everything in it all belong to the LORD your God. [15]Yet the LORD chose your ancestors as the objects of his love. And he chose you, their descendants, above all other nations, as is evident today. [16]Therefore, change your hearts* and stop being stubborn.

[17]"For the LORD your God is the God of gods and Lord of lords. He is the great God, the mighty and awesome God, who shows no partiality and cannot be bribed. [18]He ensures that orphans and widows receive justice. He shows love to the foreigners living among you and gives them food and clothing. [19]So you, too, must show love to foreigners, for you yourselves were once foreigners in the land of Egypt. [20]You must fear the LORD your God and worship him and cling to him. Your oaths must be in his name alone. [21]He alone is your God, the only one who is worthy of your praise, the one who has done these mighty miracles that you have seen with your own eyes. [22]When your ancestors went down into Egypt, there were only seventy of them. But now the LORD your God has made you as numerous as the stars in the sky!"

9:8 Hebrew *Horeb,* another name for Sinai. **9:22a** *Taberah* means "place of burning." See Num 11:1-3. **9:22b** *Massah* means "place of testing." See Exod 17:1-7. **9:22c** *Kibroth-hattaavah* means "graves of craving." See Num 11:31-34. **10:4** Hebrew *the ten words.* **10:6** Or *set out from Beeroth of Bene-jaakan.* **10:16** Hebrew *circumcise the foreskin of your hearts.*

LUKE 8:4-21

Seeds that fall and grow or die, lamps that shine or are dimmed, the definition of family—Jesus taught by telling and doing.

One day Jesus told a story in the form of a parable to a large crowd that had gathered from many towns to hear him: [5]"A farmer went out to plant his seed. As he scattered it across his field, some seed fell on a footpath, where it was stepped on, and the birds ate it. [6]Other seed fell among rocks. It began to grow, but the plant soon wilted and died for lack of moisture. [7]Other seed fell among thorns that grew up with it and choked out the tender plants. [8]Still other seed fell on fertile soil. This seed grew and produced a crop that was a hundred times as much as had been planted!" When he

had said this, he called out, "Anyone with ears to hear should listen and understand."

[9]His disciples asked him what this parable meant. [10]He replied, "You are permitted to understand the secrets* of the Kingdom of God. But I use parables to teach the others so that the Scriptures might be fulfilled:

'When they look, they won't really
    see.
When they hear, they won't
    understand.'*

[11]"This is the meaning of the parable: The seed is God's word. [12]The seeds that fell on the footpath represent those who hear the message, only to have the devil come and take it away from their hearts and prevent them from believing and being saved. [13]The seeds on the rocky soil represent those who hear the message and receive it with joy. But since they don't have deep roots, they believe for a while, then they fall away when they face temptation. [14]The seeds that fell among the thorns represent those who hear the message, but all too quickly the message is crowded out by the cares and riches and pleasures of this life. And so they never grow into maturity. [15]And the seeds that fell on the good soil represent honest, good-hearted people who hear God's word, cling to it, and patiently produce a huge harvest.

[16]"No one lights a lamp and then covers it with a bowl or hides it under a bed. A lamp is placed on a stand, where its light can be seen by all who enter the house. [17]For all that is secret will eventually be brought into the open, and everything that is concealed will be brought to light and made known to all.

[18]"So pay attention to how you hear. To those who listen to my teaching, more understanding will be given. But for those who are not listening, even what they think they understand will be taken away from them."

[19]Then Jesus' mother and brothers came to see him, but they couldn't get to him because of the crowd. [20]Someone told Jesus, "Your mother and your brothers are outside, and they want to see you."

[21]Jesus replied, "My mother and my

brothers are all those who hear God's word and obey it."

8:10a Greek *mysteries*.   **8:10b** Isa 6:9 (Greek version).

PSALM 69:19-36

You know of my shame, scorn,
     and disgrace.
   You see all that my enemies are
     doing.
20 Their insults have broken my heart,
     and I am in despair.
   If only one person would show
     some pity;
     if only one would turn and
     comfort me.
21 But instead, they give me poison*
     for food;
     they offer me sour wine for my
     thirst.

22 Let the bountiful table set before
     them become a snare
   and their prosperity become a trap.*
23 Let their eyes go blind so they
     cannot see,
   and make their bodies shake
     continually.*
24 Pour out your fury on them;
   consume them with your burning
     anger.
25 Let their homes become desolate
     and their tents be deserted.
26 To the one you have punished, they
     add insult to injury;
   they add to the pain of those you
     have hurt.
27 Pile their sins up high,
     and don't let them go free.
28 Erase their names from the Book
     of Life;
   don't let them be counted among
     the righteous.

29 I am suffering and in pain.
   Rescue me, O God, by your saving
     power.

30 Then I will praise God's name with
     singing,
   and I will honor him with
     thanksgiving.
31 For this will please the LORD more
     than sacrificing cattle,
   more than presenting a bull with
     its horns and hooves.
32 The humble will see their God at work
     and be glad.
   Let all who seek God's help
     be encouraged.
33 For the LORD hears the cries of the
     needy;
   he does not despise his imprisoned
     people.

34 Praise him, O heaven and earth,
   the seas and all that move in them.
35 For God will save Jerusalem*
     and rebuild the towns of Judah.
   His people will live there
     and settle in their own land.
36 The descendants of those who obey
     him will inherit the land,
   and those who love him will live
     there in safety.

69:21 Or *gall*.   **69:22** Greek version reads *Let their bountiful table set before them become a snare, / a trap that makes them think all is well. / Let their blessings cause them to stumble, / and let them get what they deserve.* Compare Rom 11:9.   **69:23** Greek version reads *and let their backs be bent forever.* Compare Rom 11:10.   **69:35** Hebrew *Zion*.

PROVERBS 12:2-3

The LORD approves of those who are good, but he condemns those who plan wickedness. □ Wickedness never brings stability, but the godly have deep roots.

MARCH**29**

DEUTERONOMY 11:1-12:32

Moses reminded the people of the who, what, when, and where of the offerings and sacrifices, the rituals for worship. These were important reminders in light of the idolatry of the surrounding cultures.

"**Y**ou must love the LORD your God and obey all his requirements, decrees, regulations, and commands. 2Keep in mind that I am not talking now to your children, who have never experienced the discipline of the LORD your God or seen his greatness and his strong hand and powerful arm. ³They didn't see the miraculous signs and wonders he performed in Egypt against Pharaoh and all his land. ⁴They didn't see what the LORD did to the armies of Egypt and to their horses and chariots—how he drowned them in the Red Sea* as they were chasing you. He destroyed them, and they have not recovered to this very day!

⁵"Your children didn't see how the LORD cared for you in the wilderness until you arrived here. ⁶They didn't see what he did to Dathan and Abiram (the sons of Eliab, a descendant of Reuben) when the earth opened its mouth in the Israelite camp and swallowed them, along with their households and tents and every living thing that belonged to them. ⁷But you have seen the LORD perform all these mighty deeds with your own eyes!

⁸"Therefore, be careful to obey every command I am giving you today, so you may have strength to go in and take over the land you are about to enter. ⁹If you obey, you will enjoy a long life in the land the LORD swore to give to your ancestors and to you, their descendants—a land flowing with milk and honey! ¹⁰For the land you are about to enter and take over is not like the land of Egypt from which you came, where you planted your seed and made irrigation ditches with your foot as in a vegetable garden. ¹¹Rather, the land you will soon take over is a land of hills and valleys with plenty of rain—¹²a land that the LORD your God cares for. He watches over it through each season of the year!

¹³"If you carefully obey all the commands I am giving you today, and if you love the LORD your God and serve him with all your heart and soul, ¹⁴then he will send the rains in their proper seasons—the early and late rains—so you can bring in your harvests of grain, new wine, and olive oil. ¹⁵He will give you lush pastureland for your livestock, and you yourselves will have all you want to eat.

¹⁶"But be careful. Don't let your heart be deceived so that you turn away from the LORD and serve and worship other gods. ¹⁷If you do, the LORD's anger will burn against you. He will shut up the sky and hold back the rain, and the ground will fail to produce its harvests. Then you will quickly die in that good land the LORD is giving you.

¹⁸"So commit yourselves wholeheartedly to these words of mine. Tie them to your hands and wear them on your forehead as reminders. ¹⁹Teach them to your children. Talk about them when you are at home and when you are on the road, when you are going to bed and when you are getting up. ²⁰Write them on the doorposts of your house and on your gates, ²¹so that as long as the sky remains above the earth, you and your children may flourish in the land the LORD swore to give your ancestors.

²²"Be careful to obey all these commands I am giving you. Show love to the LORD your God by walking in his ways and holding tightly to him. ²³Then the LORD will drive out all the nations ahead of you, though they are much greater and stronger than you, and you will take over their land. ²⁴Wherever you set foot, that land will be yours. Your frontiers will stretch from the wilderness in the south to Lebanon in the north, and from the Euphrates River in the east to the Mediterranean Sea in the west.* ²⁵No one will be able to stand against you, for the LORD your God will cause the people to fear and dread you, as he promised, wherever you go in the whole land.

²⁶"Look, today I am giving you the choice between a blessing and a curse! ²⁷You will be blessed if you obey the commands of the LORD your God that I am giving you today. ²⁸But you will be cursed if you reject the commands of the LORD your God and turn away from him and worship gods you have not known before.

²⁹"When the LORD your God brings you into the land and helps you take possession of it, you must pronounce the blessing at Mount Gerizim and the curse at Mount Ebal. ³⁰(These two mountains are west of the Jordan River in the land of the Canaanites who live in the Jordan Valley,* near the town of Gilgal, not far from the oaks of Moreh.) ³¹For you are about to cross the Jordan River to take over the land the LORD your God is giving you. When

you take that land and are living in it, ³²you must be careful to obey all the decrees and regulations I am giving you today.

¹²:¹"THESE are the decrees and regulations you must be careful to obey when you live in the land that the LORD, the God of your ancestors, is giving you. You must obey them as long as you live.

²"When you drive out the nations that live there, you must destroy all the places where they worship their gods—high on the mountains, up on the hills, and under every green tree. ³Break down their altars and smash their sacred pillars. Burn their Asherah poles and cut down their carved idols. Completely erase the names of their gods!

⁴"Do not worship the LORD your God in the way these pagan peoples worship their gods. ⁵Rather, you must seek the LORD your God at the place of worship he himself will choose from among all the tribes—the place where his name will be honored. ⁶There you will bring your burnt offerings, your sacrifices, your tithes, your sacred offerings, your offerings to fulfill a vow, your voluntary offerings, and your offerings of the firstborn animals of your herds and flocks. ⁷There you and your families will feast in the presence of the LORD your God, and you will rejoice in all you have accomplished because the LORD your God has blessed you.

⁸"Your pattern of worship will change. Today all of you are doing as you please, ⁹because you have not yet arrived at the place of rest, the land the LORD your God is giving you as your special possession. ¹⁰But you will soon cross the Jordan River and live in the land the LORD your God is giving you. When he gives you rest from all your enemies and you're living safely in the land, ¹¹you must bring everything I command you—your burnt offerings, your sacrifices, your tithes, your sacred offerings, and your offerings to fulfill a vow—to the designated place of worship, the place the LORD your God chooses for his name to be honored.

¹²"You must celebrate there in the presence of the LORD your God with your sons and daughters and all your servants. And remember to include the Levites who live in your towns, for they will receive no allotment of land among you. ¹³Be careful not to sacrifice your burnt offerings just anywhere you like. ¹⁴You may do so only at the place the LORD will choose within one of your tribal territories. There you must offer your burnt offerings and do everything I command you.

¹⁵"But you may butcher your animals and eat their meat in any town whenever you want. You may freely eat the animals with which the LORD your God blesses you. All of you, whether ceremonially

HOW WE LIVE

Studying God's Word

DEUTERONOMY 11:18-20 The Bible is God's book for his followers, the book he left us, the book through which he speaks. While there are many Christian books that you can read, the Bible alone is the book for the ages, the book that you'll want to read every day in order to learn more about your new life in Christ, to understand God's will, to learn how he wants you to live. You see, the Bible is not a book you read from start to finish and then you're "done." God's Word is "alive and powerful. . . . It exposes our innermost thoughts and desires" (Hebrews 4:12, November 2). You can never "finish" reading the Bible. The Bible will speak in different ways at different times and give you guidance when you need it. That's why you need to get into it every day. The more you study, the more you will understand about God's plan for you. • The Bible is not just a book—it is a living testament by which you can pattern your life. Take it off the shelf and keep it near you so that reading it becomes a part of your daily routine.

clean or unclean, may eat that meat, just as you now eat gazelle and deer. ¹⁶But you must not eat the blood. You must pour it out on the ground like water.

¹⁷"But you may not eat your offerings in your hometown—neither the tithe of your grain and new wine and olive oil, nor the firstborn of your flocks and herds, nor any offering to fulfill a vow, nor your voluntary offerings, nor your sacred offerings. ¹⁸You must eat these in the presence of the LORD your God at the place he will choose. Eat them there with your children, your servants, and the Levites who live in your towns, celebrating in the presence of the LORD your God in all you do. ¹⁹And be very careful never to neglect the Levites as long as you live in your land.

²⁰"When the LORD your God expands your territory as he has promised, and you have the urge to eat meat, you may freely eat meat whenever you want. ²¹It might happen that the designated place of worship—the place the LORD your God chooses for his name to be honored—is a long way from your home. If so, you may butcher any of the cattle, sheep, or goats the LORD has given you, and you may freely eat the meat in your hometown, as I have commanded you. ²²Anyone, whether ceremonially clean or unclean, may eat that meat, just as you do now with gazelle and deer. ²³But never eat the blood, for the blood is the life, and you must not eat the lifeblood with the meat. ²⁴Instead, pour out the blood on the ground like water. ²⁵Do not eat the blood, so that all may go well with you and your children after you, because you will be doing what pleases the LORD.

²⁶"Take your sacred gifts and your offerings given to fulfill a vow to the place the LORD chooses. ²⁷You must offer the meat and blood of your burnt offerings on the altar of the LORD your God. The blood of your other sacrifices must be poured out on the altar of the LORD your God, but you may eat the meat. ²⁸Be careful to obey all my commands, so that all will go well with you and your children after you, because you will be doing what is good and pleasing to the LORD your God.

²⁹"When the LORD your God goes ahead of you and destroys the nations and you drive them out and live in their land, ³⁰do not fall into the trap of following their customs and worshiping their gods. Do not inquire about their gods, saying, 'How do these nations worship their gods? I want to follow their example.' ³¹You must not worship the LORD your God the way the other nations worship their gods, for they perform for their gods every detestable act that the LORD hates. They even burn their sons and daughters as sacrifices to their gods.

³²*"So be careful to obey all the commands I give you. You must not add anything to them or subtract anything from them."

11:4 Hebrew *sea of reeds.*   **11:24** Hebrew *to the western sea.*   **11:30** Hebrew *the Arabah.*   **12:32** Verse 12:32 is numbered 13:1 in Hebrew text.

LUKE 8:22-39

Jesus' authority must have been mind-boggling. He spoke to storms and demons. Even more telling, the storms and the demons responded!

One day Jesus said to his disciples, "Let's cross to the other side of the lake." So they got into a boat and started out. ²³As they sailed across, Jesus settled down for a nap. But soon a fierce storm came down on the lake. The boat was filling with water, and they were in real danger.

²⁴The disciples went and woke him up, shouting, "Master, Master, we're going to drown!"

When Jesus woke up, he rebuked the wind and the raging waves. Suddenly the storm stopped and all was calm. ²⁵Then he asked them, "Where is your faith?"

The disciples were terrified and amazed. "Who is this man?" they asked each other. "When he gives a command, even the wind and waves obey him!"

²⁶So they arrived in the region of the Gerasenes,* across the lake from Galilee. ²⁷As Jesus was climbing out of the boat, a man who was possessed by demons came out to meet him. For a long time he had been homeless and naked, living in a cemetery outside the town.

²⁸As soon as he saw Jesus, he shrieked and fell down in front of him. Then he screamed, "Why are you interfering with me, Jesus, Son of the Most High God? Please, I beg you, don't torture me!" ²⁹For

Jesus had already commanded the evil* spirit to come out of him. This spirit had often taken control of the man. Even when he was placed under guard and put in chains and shackles, he simply broke them and rushed out into the wilderness, completely under the demon's power. ³⁰Jesus demanded, "What is your name?"

"Legion," he replied, for he was filled with many demons. ³¹The demons kept begging Jesus not to send them into the bottomless pit.*

³²There happened to be a large herd of pigs feeding on the hillside nearby, and the demons begged him to let them enter into the pigs.

So Jesus gave them permission. ³³Then the demons came out of the man and entered the pigs, and the entire herd plunged down the steep hillside into the lake and drowned.

³⁴When the herdsmen saw it, they fled to the nearby town and the surrounding countryside, spreading the news as they ran. ³⁵People rushed out to see what had happened. A crowd soon gathered around Jesus, and they saw the man who had been freed from the demons. He was sitting at Jesus' feet, fully clothed and perfectly sane, and they were all afraid. ³⁶Then those who had seen what happened told the others how the demon-possessed man had been healed. ³⁷And all the people in the region of the Gerasenes begged Jesus to go away and leave them alone, for a great wave of fear swept over them.

So Jesus returned to the boat and left, crossing back to the other side of the lake.

DEUTERONOMY 13:1-15:23

As Moses finished up his last instructions, he touched on a variety of things—what to eat, practical worship, how to show God's mercy in the world. Never far from his words was the concept of giving God the worship he deserves.

³⁸The man who had been freed from the demons begged to go with him. But Jesus sent him home, saying, ³⁹"No, go back to your family, and tell them everything God has done for you." So he went all through the town proclaiming the great things Jesus had done for him.

8:26 Other manuscripts read *Gadarenes;* still others read *Gergesenes;* also in 8:37. See Matt 8:28; Mark 5:1. **8:29** Greek *unclean.* **8:31** Or *the abyss,* or *the underworld.*

PSALM 70:1-5

For the choir director: A psalm of David, asking God to remember him.

¹ Please, God, rescue me!
    Come quickly, LORD, and
       help me.
² May those who try to kill me
       be humiliated and put to shame.
  May those who take delight in my
       trouble
       be turned back in disgrace.
³ Let them be horrified by their shame,
       for they said, "Aha! We've got him
       now!"
⁴ But may all who search for you
       be filled with joy and gladness
       in you.
  May those who love your salvation
       repeatedly shout, "God is great!"
⁵ But as for me, I am poor and needy;
       please hurry to my aid, O God.
  You are my helper and my savior;
       O LORD, do not delay.

PROVERBS 12:4

A worthy wife is a crown for her husband, but a disgraceful woman is like cancer in his bones.

MARCH**30**

¹*"**S**uppose there are prophets among you or those who dream dreams about the future, and they promise you signs or miracles, ² and the predicted signs or miracles occur. If they then say, 'Come, let us worship other gods'—gods you have not

known before—³do not listen to them. The LORD your God is testing you to see if you truly love him with all your heart and soul. ⁴Serve only the LORD your God and fear him alone. Obey his commands, listen to his voice, and cling to him. ⁵The false prophets or visionaries who try to lead you astray must be put to death, for they encourage rebellion against the LORD your God, who redeemed you from slavery and brought you out of the land of Egypt. Since they try to lead you astray from the way the LORD your God commanded you to live, you must put them to death. In this way you will purge the evil from among you.

⁶"Suppose someone secretly entices you—even your brother, your son or daughter, your beloved wife, or your closest friend—and says, 'Let us go worship other gods'—gods that neither you nor your ancestors have known. ⁷They might suggest that you worship the gods of peoples who live nearby or who come from the ends of the earth. ⁸But do not give in or listen. Have no pity, and do not spare or protect them. ⁹You must put them to death! Strike the first blow yourself, and then all the people must join in. ¹⁰Stone the guilty ones to death because they have tried to draw you away from the LORD your God, who rescued you from the land of Egypt, the place of slavery. ¹¹Then all Israel will hear about it and be afraid, and no one will act so wickedly again.

¹²"When you begin living in the towns the LORD your God is giving you, you may hear ¹³that scoundrels among you are leading their fellow citizens astray by saying, 'Let us go worship other gods'—gods you have not known before. ¹⁴In such cases, you must examine the facts carefully. If you find that the report is true and such a detestable act has been committed among you, ¹⁵you must attack that town and completely destroy* all its inhabitants, as well as all the livestock. ¹⁶Then you must pile all the plunder in the middle of the open square and burn it. Burn the entire town as a burnt offering to the LORD your God. That town must remain a ruin forever; it may never be rebuilt. ¹⁷Keep none of the plunder that has been set apart for destruction. Then the LORD

will turn from his fierce anger and be merciful to you. He will have compassion on you and make you a large nation, just as he swore to your ancestors.

¹⁸"The LORD your God will be merciful only if you listen to his voice and keep all his commands that I am giving you today, doing what pleases him.

¹⁴:¹"SINCE you are the people of the LORD your God, never cut yourselves or shave the hair above your foreheads in mourning for the dead. ²You have been set apart as holy to the LORD your God, and he has chosen you from all the nations of the earth to be his own special treasure.

³"You must not eat any detestable animals that are ceremonially unclean. ⁴These are the animals* you may eat: the ox, the sheep, the goat, ⁵the deer, the gazelle, the roe deer, the wild goat, the addax, the antelope, and the mountain sheep.

⁶"You may eat any animal that has completely split hooves and chews the cud, ⁷but if the animal doesn't have both, it may not be eaten. So you may not eat the camel, the hare, or the hyrax.* They chew the cud but do not have split hooves, so they are ceremonially unclean for you. ⁸And you may not eat the pig. It has split hooves but does not chew the cud, so it is ceremonially unclean for you. You may not eat the meat of these animals or even touch their carcasses.

⁹"Of all the marine animals, you may eat whatever has both fins and scales. ¹⁰You may not, however, eat marine animals that do not have both fins and scales. They are ceremonially unclean for you.

¹¹"You may eat any bird that is ceremonially clean. ¹²These are the birds you may not eat: the griffon vulture, the bearded vulture, the black vulture, ¹³the kite, the falcon, buzzards of all kinds, ¹⁴ravens of all kinds, ¹⁵the eagle owl, the short-eared owl, the seagull, hawks of all kinds, ¹⁶the little owl, the great owl, the barn owl, ¹⁷the desert owl, the Egyptian vulture, the cormorant, ¹⁸the stork, herons of all kinds, the hoopoe, and the bat.

¹⁹"All winged insects that walk along the ground are ceremonially unclean for you and may not be eaten. ²⁰But you may

when you release your servants. Remember that for six years they have given you services worth double the wages of hired workers, and the LORD your God will bless you in all you do.

19"You must set aside for the LORD your God all the firstborn males from your flocks and herds. Do not use the firstborn of your herds to work your fields, and do not shear the firstborn of your flocks. 20Instead, you and your family must eat these animals in the presence of the LORD your God each year at the place he chooses. 21But if this firstborn animal has any defect, such as lameness or blindness, or if anything else is wrong with it, you must not sacrifice it to the LORD your God. 22Instead, use it for food for your family in your hometown. Anyone, whether ceremonially clean or unclean, may eat it, just as anyone may eat a gazelle or deer. 23But you must not eat the blood. You must pour it out on the ground like water."

13:1 Verses 13:1-18 are numbered 13:2-19 in Hebrew text.
13:15 The Hebrew term used here refers to the complete consecration of things or people to the LORD, either by destroying them or by giving them as an offering; similarly in 13:17. 14:4 The identification of some of the animals and birds listed in this chapter is uncertain. 14:7 Or coney, or rock badger. 15:12 Or If a Hebrew man or woman is sold to you.

LUKE 8:40–9:6
An anonymous woman in a crowd, obvious to no one else, drew Jesus' attention by her faith in his power and presence. Jesus sent his disciples out armed with the reality that faith in him would change the world.

On the other side of the lake the crowds welcomed Jesus, because they had been waiting for him. 41Then a man named Jairus, a leader of the local synagogue, came and fell at Jesus' feet, pleading with him to come home with him. 42His only daughter,* who was about twelve years old, was dying.

As Jesus went with him, he was surrounded by the crowds. 43A woman in the crowd had suffered for twelve years with constant bleeding,* and she could find no cure. 44Coming up behind Jesus, she touched the fringe of his robe. Immediately, the bleeding stopped.

45"Who touched me?" Jesus asked.
Everyone denied it, and Peter said,

"Master, this whole crowd is pressing against you."

46But Jesus said, "Someone deliberately touched me, for I felt healing power go out from me." 47When the woman realized that she could not stay hidden, she began to tremble and fell to her knees in front of him. The whole crowd heard her explain why she had touched him and that she had been immediately healed. 48"Daughter," he said to her, "your faith has made you well. Go in peace."

49While he was still speaking to her a messenger arrived from the home of Jairus, the leader of the synagogue. He told him, "Your daughter is dead. There's no use troubling the Teacher now."

50But when Jesus heard what had happened, he said to Jairus, "Don't be afraid. Just have faith, and she will be healed."

51When they arrived at the house, Jesus wouldn't let anyone go in with him except Peter, John, James, and the little girl's father and mother. 52The house was filled with people weeping and wailing, but he said, "Stop the weeping! She isn't dead; she's only asleep."

53But the crowd laughed at him because they all knew she had died. 54Then Jesus took her by the hand and said in a loud voice, "My child, get up!" 55And at that moment her life* returned, and she immediately stood up! Then Jesus told them to give her something to eat. 56Her parents were overwhelmed, but Jesus insisted that they not tell anyone what had happened.

9:1ONE day Jesus called together his twelve disciples* and gave them power and authority to cast out all demons and to heal all diseases. 2Then he sent them out to tell everyone about the Kingdom of God and to heal the sick. 3"Take nothing for your journey," he instructed them. "Don't take a walking stick, a traveler's bag, food, money,* or even a change of clothes. 4Wherever you go, stay in the same house until you leave town. 5And if a town refuses to welcome you, shake its dust from your feet as you leave to show that you have abandoned those people to their fate."

6So they began their circuit of the vil-eat any winged bird or insect that is ceremonially clean.

21"You must not eat anything that has died a natural death. You may give it to a foreigner living in your town, or you may sell it to a stranger. But do not eat it yourselves, for you are set apart as holy to the LORD your God.

"You must not cook a young goat in its mother's milk.

22"You must set aside a tithe of your crops—one-tenth of all the crops you harvest each year. 23Bring this tithe to the designated place of worship—the place the LORD your God chooses for his name to be honored—and eat it there in his presence. This applies to your tithes of grain, new wine, olive oil, and the firstborn males of your flocks and herds. Doing this will teach you always to fear the LORD your God.

24"Now when the LORD your God blesses you with a good harvest, the place of worship he chooses for his name to be honored might be too far for you to bring the tithe. 25If so, you may sell the tithe portion of your crops and herds, put the money in a pouch, and go to the place the LORD your God has chosen. 26When you arrive, you may use the money to buy any kind of food you want—cattle, sheep, goats, wine, or other alcoholic drink. Then feast there in the presence of the LORD your God and celebrate with your household. 27And do not neglect the Levites in your town, for they will receive no allotment of land among you.

28"At the end of every third year, bring the entire tithe of that year's harvest and store it in the nearest town. 29Give it to the Levites, who will receive no allotment of land among you, as well as to the foreigners living among you, the orphans, and the widows in your towns, so they can eat and be satisfied. Then the LORD your God will bless you in all your work.

15:1"At the end of every seventh year you must cancel the debts of everyone who owes you money. 2This is how it must be done. Everyone must cancel the loans they have made to their fellow Israelites. They must not demand payment from their neighbors or relatives, for the LORD's

time of release has arrived. 3This release from debt, however, applies only to your fellow Israelites—not to the foreigners living among you.

4"There should be no poor among you, for the LORD your God will greatly bless you in the land he is giving you as a special possession. 5You will receive this blessing if you are careful to obey all the commands of the LORD your God that I am giving you today. 6The LORD your God will bless you as he has promised. You will lend money to many nations but will never need to borrow. You will rule many nations, but they will not rule over you.

7"But if there are any poor Israelites in your towns when you arrive in the land the LORD your God is giving you, do not be hard-hearted or tightfisted toward them. 8Instead, be generous and lend them whatever they need. 9Do not be mean-spirited and refuse someone a loan because the year for canceling debts is close at hand. If you refuse to make the loan and the needy person cries out to the LORD, you will be considered guilty of sin. 10Give generously to the poor, not grudgingly, for the LORD your God will bless you in everything you do. 11There will always be some in the land who are poor. That is why I am commanding you to share freely with the poor and with other Israelites in need.

12"If a fellow Hebrew sells himself or herself to be your servant* and serves you for six years, in the seventh year you must set that servant free.

13"When you release a male servant, do not send him away empty-handed. 14Give him a generous farewell gift from your flock, your threshing floor, and your winepress. Share with him some of the bounty with which the LORD your God has blessed you. 15Remember that you were once slaves in the land of Egypt and the LORD your God redeemed you! That is why I am giving you this command.

16"But suppose your servant says, 'I will not leave you,' because he loves you and your family, and he has done well with you. 17In that case, take an awl and push it through his earlobe into the door. After that, he will be your servant for life. And do the same for your female servants.

18"You must not consider it a hardship

lages, preaching the Good News and healing the sick.

8:42 Or *His only child, a daughter.* 8:43 Some manuscripts add *having spent everything she had on doctors.* 8:55 Or *her spirit.* 9:1 Greek *the Twelve;* other manuscripts read *the twelve apostles.* 9:3 Or *silver coins.*

PSALM 71:1-24

O LORD, I have come to you
for protection;
don't let me be disgraced.
2 Save me and rescue me,
for you do what is right.
Turn your ear to listen to me,
and set me free.
3 Be my rock of safety
where I can always hide.
Give the order to save me,
for you are my rock and
my fortress.
4 My God, rescue me from the power
of the wicked,
from the clutches of cruel
oppressors.
5 O Lord, you alone are my hope.
I've trusted you, O LORD, from
childhood.
6 Yes, you have been with me from
birth;
from my mother's womb you have
cared for me.
No wonder I am always praising
you!

7 My life is an example to many,
because you have been my strength
and protection.
8 That is why I can never stop praising
you;
I declare your glory all day long.
9 And now, in my old age, don't set me
aside.
Don't abandon me when my
strength is failing.
10 For my enemies are whispering
against me.
They are plotting together to kill
me.
11 They say, "God has abandoned him.
Let's go and get him,
for no one will help him now."
12 O God, don't stay away.
My God, please hurry to help me.
13 Bring disgrace and destruction on
my accusers.
Humiliate and shame those who
want to harm me.
14 But I will keep on hoping for your
help;
I will praise you more and more.
15 I will tell everyone about your
righteousness.
All day long I will proclaim your
saving power,
though I am not skilled with
words.*

How to discern truth

WHAT THE BIBLE SAYS

DEUTERONOMY 13:14 A cornerstone of discernment is the ability to carefully evaluate all aspects of a situation before taking action in that situation. Today, just as in Moses' time, rumor and thoughtless assumption run rampant in families and communities. Rumors often carry portions of the truth but rarely give an accurate and complete depiction of what is really happening. • In Deuteronomy 13:14, Moses implored the nation of Israel to verify and investigate rumors that people were worshiping other gods. Moses knew that if Israel were to rebuke or punish others according to rumor without carefully verifying the facts—without discernment—they could destroy lives and do irreparable harm. • We have the potential to do irreparable harm to our families, friends, and communities if we make assumptions and take action based on nothing but rumors. Discernment is the ability to hold back, consult Scripture, ask for counsel from a trusted friend, and speak to those involved before making a decision. By doing so, we extend the same kind of grace that God extends to us.

¹⁶ I will praise your mighty deeds,
O Sovereign LORD.
I will tell everyone that you alone
are just.

¹⁷ O God, you have taught me from my
earliest childhood,
and I constantly tell others about
the wonderful things you do.
¹⁸ Now that I am old and gray,
do not abandon me, O God.
Let me proclaim your power to this
new generation,
your mighty miracles to all who
come after me.

¹⁹ Your righteousness, O God, reaches to
the highest heavens.
You have done such wonderful
things.
Who can compare with you,
O God?
²⁰ You have allowed me to suffer much
hardship,
but you will restore me to life
again
and lift me up from the depths of
the earth.

²¹ You will restore me to even greater
honor
and comfort me once again.

²² Then I will praise you with music on
the harp,
because you are faithful to your
promises, O my God.
I will sing praises to you with a lyre,
O Holy One of Israel.
²³ I will shout for joy and sing your
praises,
for you have ransomed me.
²⁴ I will tell about your righteous deeds
all day long,
for everyone who tried to hurt me
has been shamed and humiliated.

71:15 Or *though I cannot count it.*

PROVERBS 12:5-7
The plans of the godly are just; the advice of the wicked is treacherous. □ The words of the wicked are like a murderous ambush, but the words of the godly save lives. □ The wicked die and disappear, but the family of the godly stands firm.

MARCH**31**

DEUTERONOMY 16:1–17:20
The Passover reminded Israel of God's provision and protection, but it also pointed ahead to the sacrifice Christ would make. It was years before Israel actually accepted a king, yet here Moses gave the guidelines for how a king might govern justly.

"In honor of the LORD your God, celebrate the Passover each year in the early spring, in the month of Abib,* for that was the month in which the LORD your God brought you out of Egypt by night. ²Your Passover sacrifice may be from either the flock or the herd, and it must be sacrificed to the LORD your God at the designated place of worship—the place he chooses for his name to be honored. ³Eat it with bread made without yeast. For seven days the bread you eat must be made without yeast, as when you escaped from Egypt in such a hurry. Eat this bread—the bread of suffering—so that as long as you live you will remember the day you departed from Egypt. ⁴Let no yeast be found in any house throughout your land for those seven days. And when you sacrifice the Passover lamb on the evening of the first day, do not let any of the meat remain until the next morning.

⁵"You may not sacrifice the Passover in just any of the towns that the LORD your God is giving you. ⁶You must offer it only at the designated place of worship—the place the LORD your God chooses for his name to be honored. Sacrifice it there in the evening as the sun goes down on the anniversary of your exodus from Egypt.

[7]Roast the lamb and eat it in the place the LORD your God chooses. Then you may go back to your tents the next morning. [8]For the next six days you may not eat any bread made with yeast. On the seventh day proclaim another holy day in honor of the LORD your God, and no work may be done on that day.

[9]"Count off seven weeks from when you first begin to cut the grain at the time of harvest. [10]Then celebrate the Festival of Harvest* to honor the LORD your God. Bring him a voluntary offering in proportion to the blessings you have received from him. [11]This is a time to celebrate before the LORD your God at the designated place of worship he will choose for his name to be honored. Celebrate with your sons and daughters, your male and female servants, the Levites from your towns, and the foreigners, orphans, and widows who live among you. [12]Remember that you were once slaves in Egypt, so be careful to obey all these decrees.

[13]"You must observe the Festival of Shelters* for seven days at the end of the harvest season, after the grain has been threshed and the grapes have been pressed. [14]This festival will be a happy time of celebrating with your sons and daughters, your male and female servants, and the Levites, foreigners, orphans, and widows from your towns. [15]For seven days you must celebrate this festival to honor the LORD your God at the place he chooses, for it is he who blesses you with bountiful harvests and gives you success in all your work. This festival will be a time of great joy for all.

[16]"Each year every man in Israel must celebrate these three festivals: the Festival of Unleavened Bread, the Festival of Harvest, and the Festival of Shelters. On each of these occasions, all men must appear before the LORD your God at the place he chooses, but they must not appear before the LORD without a gift for him. [17]All must give as they are able, according to the blessings given to them by the LORD your God.

[18]"Appoint judges and officials for yourselves from each of your tribes in all the towns the LORD your God is giving you. They must judge the people fairly.

[19]You must never twist justice or show partiality. Never accept a bribe, for bribes blind the eyes of the wise and corrupt the decisions of the godly. [20]Let true justice prevail, so you may live and occupy the land that the LORD your God is giving you.

[21]"You must never set up a wooden Asherah pole beside the altar you build for the LORD your God. [22]And never set up sacred pillars for worship, for the LORD your God hates them.

[17:1]"NEVER sacrifice sick or defective cattle, sheep, or goats to the LORD your God, for he detests such gifts.

[2]"When you begin living in the towns the LORD your God is giving you, a man or woman among you might do evil in the sight of the LORD your God and violate the covenant. [3]For instance, they might serve other gods or worship the sun, the moon, or any of the stars—the forces of heaven—which I have strictly forbidden. [4]When you hear about it, investigate the matter thoroughly. If it is true that this detestable thing has been done in Israel, [5]then the man or woman who has committed such an evil act must be taken to the gates of the town and stoned to death. [6]But never put a person to death on the testimony of only one witness. There must always be two or three witnesses. [7]The witnesses must throw the first stones, and then all the people may join in. In this way, you will purge the evil from among you.

[8]"Suppose a case arises in a local court that is too hard for you to decide—for instance, whether someone is guilty of murder or only of manslaughter, or a difficult lawsuit, or a case involving different kinds of assault. Take such legal cases to the place the LORD your God will choose, [9]and present them to the Levitical priests or the judge on duty at that time. They will hear the case and declare the verdict. [10]You must carry out the verdict they announce and the sentence they prescribe at the place the LORD chooses. You must do exactly what they say. [11]After they have interpreted the law and declared their verdict, the sentence they impose must be fully executed; do not modify it in any way. [12]Anyone arrogant enough to reject the verdict of the judge or of the priest who

represents the LORD your God must die. In this way you will purge the evil from Israel. [13] Then everyone else will hear about it and be afraid to act so arrogantly.

[14] "You are about to enter the land the LORD your God is giving you. When you take it over and settle there, you may think, 'We should select a king to rule over us like the other nations around us.' [15] If this happens, be sure to select as king the man the LORD your God chooses. You must appoint a fellow Israelite; he may not be a foreigner.

[16] "The king must not build up a large stable of horses for himself or send his people to Egypt to buy horses, for the LORD has told you, 'You must never return to Egypt.' [17] The king must not take many wives for himself, because they will turn his heart away from the LORD. And he must not accumulate large amounts of wealth in silver and gold for himself.

[18] "When he sits on the throne as king, he must copy for himself this body of instruction on a scroll in the presence of the Levitical priests. [19] He must always keep that copy with him and read it daily as long as he lives. That way he will learn to fear the LORD his God by obeying all the terms of these instructions and decrees. [20] This regular reading will prevent him from becoming proud and acting as if he is above his fellow citizens. It will also prevent him from turning away from these commands in the smallest way. And it will ensure that he and his descendants will reign for many generations in Israel."

16:1 Hebrew *Observe the month of Abib, and keep the Passover unto the LORD your God.* Abib, the first month of the ancient Hebrew lunar calendar, usually occurs within the months of March and April.   **16:10** Hebrew *Festival of Weeks;* also in 16:16. This was later called the Festival of Pentecost (see Acts 2:1). It is celebrated today as Shavuot (or Shabuoth).   **16:13** Or *Festival of Booths,* or *Festival of Tabernacles;* also in 16:16. This was earlier called the Festival of the Final Harvest or Festival of Ingathering (see Exod 23:16b). It is celebrated today as Sukkot (or Succoth).

LUKE 9:7-27

For a time, Jesus let people come to their own conclusions about who he was. Herod did. Peter did. As the end of his ministry neared, though, Jesus began to reveal the truth of who he was and what he had come to do.

When Herod Antipas, the ruler of Galilee,* heard about everything Jesus was doing, he was puzzled. Some were saying that John the Baptist had been raised from the dead. [8] Others thought Jesus was Elijah or one of the other prophets risen from the dead.

[9] "I beheaded John," Herod said, "so who is this man about whom I hear such stories?" And he kept trying to see him.

[10] When the apostles returned, they told Jesus everything they had done. Then he slipped quietly away with them toward the town of Bethsaida. [11] But the crowds found out where he was going, and they followed him. He welcomed them and taught them about the Kingdom of God, and he healed those who were sick.

[12] Late in the afternoon the twelve disciples came to him and said, "Send the crowds away to the nearby villages and farms, so they can find food and lodging for the night. There is nothing to eat here in this remote place."

[13] But Jesus said, "You feed them."

"But we have only five loaves of bread and two fish," they answered. "Or are you expecting us to go and buy enough food for this whole crowd?" [14] For there were about 5,000 men there.

Jesus replied, "Tell them to sit down in groups of about fifty each." [15] So the people all sat down. [16] Jesus took the five loaves and two fish, looked up toward heaven, and blessed them. Then, breaking the loaves into pieces, he kept giving the bread and fish to the disciples so they could distribute it to the people. [17] They all ate as much as they wanted, and afterward, the disciples picked up twelve baskets of leftovers!

[18] One day Jesus left the crowds to pray alone. Only his disciples were with him, and he asked them, "Who do people say I am?"

[19] "Well," they replied, "some say John the Baptist, some say Elijah, and others say you are one of the other ancient prophets risen from the dead."

[20] Then he asked them, "But who do you say I am?"

Peter replied, "You are the Messiah* sent from God!"

[21] Jesus warned his disciples not to tell anyone who he was. [22] "The Son of Man* must suffer many terrible things," he said.

"He will be rejected by the elders, the leading priests, and the teachers of religious law. He will be killed, but on the third day he will be raised from the dead."

²³Then he said to the crowd, "If any of you wants to be my follower, you must turn from your selfish ways, take up your cross daily, and follow me. ²⁴If you try to hang on to your life, you will lose it. But if you give up your life for my sake, you will save it. ²⁵And what do you benefit if you gain the whole world but are yourself lost or destroyed? ²⁶If anyone is ashamed of me and my message, the Son of Man will be ashamed of that person when he returns in his glory and in the glory of the Father and the holy angels. ²⁷I tell you the truth, some standing here right now will not die before they see the Kingdom of God."

9:7 Greek *Herod the tetrarch.* Herod Antipas was a son of King Herod and was ruler over Galilee. **9:20** Or *the Christ. Messiah* (a Hebrew term) and *Christ* (a Greek term) both mean "the anointed one." **9:22** "Son of Man" is a title Jesus used for himself.

PSALM 72:1-20
A psalm of Solomon.

¹ **G**ive your love of justice to the king,
   O God,
   and righteousness to the king's son.
² Help him judge your people in the
   right way;
   let the poor always be treated fairly.

³ May the mountains yield prosperity
   for all,
   and may the hills be fruitful.
⁴ Help him to defend the poor,
   to rescue the children of the needy,
   and to crush their oppressors.
⁵ May they fear you as long as the sun
   shines,
   as long as the moon remains in the
   sky.
   Yes, forever!

⁶ May the king's rule be refreshing like
   spring rain on freshly cut grass,
   like the showers that water the
   earth.
⁷ May all the godly flourish during his
   reign.
   May there be abundant prosperity
   until the moon is no more.
⁸ May he reign from sea to sea,
   and from the Euphrates River*
   to the ends of the earth.
⁹ Desert nomads will bow before him;
   his enemies will fall before him in
   the dust.
¹⁰ The western kings of Tarshish and
   other distant lands
   will bring him tribute.
   The eastern kings of Sheba and Seba
   will bring him gifts.
¹¹ All kings will bow before him,
   and all nations will serve him.

HOW WE LIVE

Following Jesus

LUKE 9:23-25 How can you be a faithful follower of Jesus? Jesus here explained what that entails: (1) *Put your ambition aside.* This is often a question of motivation. Why do you do what you do? When you are surrounded by Christians, are you a little too aware of how you "come off" to those around you? It's tempting to want to look good as well as be good. Your discipleship is then self-serving instead of Christ-serving. (2) *Shoulder your cross.* What is your cross? What sacrifices has God asked you to make? What responsibility and accountability do you take on as a disciple of Christ? How consistent are you with that responsibility? (3) *Follow Jesus.* Discipleship is a daily activity. It means walking as he walked, doing as he would do, grappling with how the teachings in God's Word apply to this day, this week, that conflict, that interaction. To follow is to keep your eyes on one thing and adjust the momentum of your life to keep that one thing in sight. • Discipleship is not effortless, but Christ promises great joy and purpose as a result of living out these precepts.

[12] He will rescue the poor when they cry
to him;
he will help the oppressed, who
have no one to defend them.
[13] He feels pity for the weak and the
needy,
and he will rescue them.
[14] He will redeem them from oppression
and violence,
for their lives are precious to him.

[15] Long live the king!
May the gold of Sheba be given
to him.
May the people always pray for him
and bless him all day long.
[16] May there be abundant grain
throughout the land,
flourishing even on the hilltops.
May the fruit trees flourish like the
trees of Lebanon,
and may the people thrive like grass
in a field.

[17] May the king's name endure forever;
may it continue as long as the sun
shines.
May all nations be blessed through
him
and bring him praise.

[18] Praise the LORD God, the God of Israel,
who alone does such wonderful
things.
[19] Praise his glorious name forever!
Let the whole earth be filled with
his glory.
Amen and amen!

[20] (This ends the prayers of David son
of Jesse.)

72:8 Hebrew *the river.*

PROVERBS 12:8-9

A sensible person wins admiration, but a
warped mind is despised. □ Better to be
an ordinary person with a servant than to
be self-important but have no food.

APRIL 1

DEUTERONOMY 18:1–20:20

Important to this passage is Moses' prophecy about One who would come—the prophet who would arise and speak God's words. The apostle Peter quoted Deuteronomy 18:15 in a sermon in the Temple, saying that Jesus was that prophet (see Acts 3:22, June 5).

"**R**emember that the Levitical priests— that is, the whole of the tribe of Levi—will receive no allotment of land among the other tribes in Israel. Instead, the priests and Levites will eat from the special gifts given to the LORD, for that is their share. ²They will have no land of their own among the Israelites. The LORD himself is their special possession, just as he promised them.

³"These are the parts the priests may claim as their share from the cattle, sheep, and goats that the people bring as offerings: the shoulder, the cheeks, and the stomach. ⁴You must also give to the priests the first share of the grain, the new wine, the olive oil, and the wool at shearing time. ⁵For the LORD your God chose the tribe of Levi out of all your tribes to minister in the LORD's name forever.

⁶"Suppose a Levite chooses to move from his town in Israel, wherever he is living, to the place the LORD chooses for worship. ⁷He may minister there in the name of the LORD his God, just like all his fellow Levites who are serving the LORD there. ⁸He may eat his share of the sacrifices and offerings, even if he also receives support from his family.

⁹"When you enter the land the LORD your God is giving you, be very careful not to imitate the detestable customs of the nations living there. ¹⁰For example, never sacrifice your son or daughter as a burnt offering.* And do not let your people practice fortune-telling, or use sorcery, or interpret omens, or engage in witchcraft, ¹¹or cast spells, or function as mediums

or psychics, or call forth the spirits of the dead. ¹²Anyone who does these things is detestable to the LORD. It is because the other nations have done these detestable things that the LORD your God will drive them out ahead of you. ¹³But you must be blameless before the LORD your God. ¹⁴The nations you are about to displace consult sorcerers and fortune-tellers, but the LORD your God forbids you to do such things."

¹⁵Moses continued, "The LORD your God will raise up for you a prophet like me from among your fellow Israelites. You must listen to him. ¹⁶For this is what you yourselves requested of the LORD your God when you were assembled at Mount Sinai.* You said, 'Don't let us hear the voice of the LORD our God anymore or see this blazing fire, for we will die.'

¹⁷"Then the LORD said to me, 'What they have said is right. ¹⁸I will raise up a prophet like you from among their fellow Israelites. I will put my words in his mouth, and he will tell the people everything I command him. ¹⁹I will personally deal with anyone who will not listen to the messages the prophet proclaims on my behalf. ²⁰But any prophet who falsely claims to speak in my name or who speaks in the name of another god must die.'

²¹"But you may wonder, 'How will we know whether or not a prophecy is from the LORD?' ²²If the prophet speaks in the LORD's name but his prediction does not happen or come true, you will know that the LORD did not give that message. That prophet has spoken without my authority and need not be feared.

¹⁹:¹"WHEN the LORD your God destroys the nations whose land he is giving you, you will take over their land and settle in their towns and homes. ²Then you must set apart three cities of refuge in the land

the Lord your God is giving you. ³Survey the territory,* and divide the land the Lord your God is giving you into three districts, with one of these cities in each district. Then anyone who has killed someone can flee to one of the cities of refuge for safety.

⁴"If someone kills another person unintentionally, without previous hostility, the slayer may flee to any of these cities to live in safety. ⁵For example, suppose someone goes into the forest with a neighbor to cut wood. And suppose one of them swings an ax to chop down a tree, and the ax head flies off the handle, killing the other person. In such cases, the slayer may flee to one of the cities of refuge to live in safety.

⁶"If the distance to the nearest city of refuge is too far, an enraged avenger might be able to chase down and kill the person who caused the death. Then the slayer would die unfairly, since he had never shown hostility toward the person who died. ⁷That is why I am commanding you to set aside three cities of refuge.

⁸"And if the Lord your God enlarges your territory, as he swore to your ancestors, and gives you all the land he promised them, ⁹you must designate three additional cities of refuge. (He will give you this land if you are careful to obey all the commands I have given you—if you always love the Lord your God and walk in his ways.) ¹⁰That way you will prevent the death of innocent people in the land the Lord your God is giving you as your special possession. You will not be held responsible for the death of innocent people.

¹¹"But suppose someone is hostile toward a neighbor and deliberately ambushes and murders him and then flees to one of the cities of refuge. ¹²In that case, the elders of the murderer's hometown must send agents to the city of refuge to bring him back and hand him over to the dead person's avenger to be put to death. ¹³Do not feel sorry for that murderer! Purge from Israel the guilt of murdering innocent people; then all will go well with you.

¹⁴"When you arrive in the land the Lord your God is giving you as your spe-

cial possession, you must never steal anyone's land by moving the boundary markers your ancestors set up to mark their property.

¹⁵"You must not convict anyone of a crime on the testimony of only one witness. The facts of the case must be established by the testimony of two or three witnesses.

¹⁶"If a malicious witness comes forward and accuses someone of a crime, ¹⁷then both the accuser and accused must appear before the Lord by coming to the priests and judges in office at that time. ¹⁸The judges must investigate the case thoroughly. If the accuser has brought false charges against his fellow Israelite, ¹⁹you must impose on the accuser the sentence he intended for the other person. In this way, you will purge such evil from among you. ²⁰Then the rest of the people will hear about it and be afraid to do such an evil thing. ²¹You must show no pity for the guilty! Your rule should be life for life, eye for eye, tooth for tooth, hand for hand, foot for foot.

20:1"When you go out to fight your enemies and you face horses and chariots and an army greater than your own, do not be afraid. The Lord your God, who brought you out of the land of Egypt, is with you! ²When you prepare for battle, the priest must come forward to speak to the troops. ³He will say to them, 'Listen to me, all you men of Israel! Do not be afraid as you go out to fight your enemies today! Do not lose heart or panic or tremble before them. ⁴For the Lord your God is going with you! He will fight for you against your enemies, and he will give you victory!'

⁵"Then the officers of the army must address the troops and say, 'Has anyone here just built a new house but not yet dedicated it? If so, you may go home! You might be killed in the battle, and someone else would dedicate your house. ⁶Has anyone here just planted a vineyard but not yet eaten any of its fruit? If so, you may go home! You might die in battle, and someone else would eat the first fruit. ⁷Has anyone here just become engaged to a woman but not yet married her? Well, you

may go home and get married! You might die in the battle, and someone else would marry her.'

8"Then the officers will also say, 'Is anyone here afraid or worried? If you are, you may go home before you frighten anyone else.' 9When the officers have finished speaking to their troops, they will appoint the unit commanders.

10"As you approach a town to attack it, you must first offer its people terms for peace. 11If they accept your terms and open the gates to you, then all the people inside will serve you in forced labor. 12But if they refuse to make peace and prepare to fight, you must attack the town. 13When the LORD your God hands the town over to you, use your swords to kill every man in the town. 14But you may keep for yourselves all the women, children, livestock, and other plunder. You may enjoy the plunder from your enemies that the LORD your God has given you.

15"But these instructions apply only to distant towns, not to the towns of the nations in the land you will enter. 16In those towns that the LORD your God is giving you as a special possession, destroy every living thing. 17You must completely destroy* the Hittites, Amorites, Canaanites, Perizzites, Hivites, and Jebusites, just as the LORD your God has commanded you.

18This will prevent the people of the land from teaching you to imitate their detestable customs in the worship of their gods, which would cause you to sin deeply against the LORD your God.

19"When you are attacking a town and the war drags on, you must not cut down the trees with your axes. You may eat the fruit, but do not cut down the trees. Are the trees your enemies, that you should attack them? 20You may only cut down trees that you know are not valuable for food. Use them to make the equipment you need to attack the enemy town until it falls."

18:10 Or *never make your son or daughter pass through the fire.* 18:16 Hebrew *Horeb,* another name for Sinai. 19:3 Or *Keep the roads in good repair.* 20:17 The Hebrew term used here refers to the complete consecration of things or people to the LORD, either by destroying them or by giving them as an offering.

LUKE 9:28-50

The disciples didn't always understand Jesus' truth. Even after seeing his glory, his closest followers were only concerned about their status in the earthly kingdom that they thought Jesus would inaugurate.

About eight days later Jesus took Peter, John, and James up on a mountain to pray. 29And as he was praying, the appearance of his face was transformed, and his clothes became dazzling white. 30Suddenly, two men, Moses and Elijah, appeared and be-

HOW WE LIVE

Life's ups and downs

LUKE 9:34-43 Peter, James, and John experienced a wonderful event (often referred to as the Transfiguration) on the mountaintop with Jesus. They were caught up in the supernatural realm of glory when the cloud descended and God spoke directly to them. Imagine how it must have felt to be in God's presence! • Your new faith may have begun as a spiritual "high"—a "mountaintop" experience. Perhaps you're now surprised to discover that life still has its difficulties. We'd prefer to be on the mountaintop, free from life's cares and trials, all the time. That's not realistic, though. Besides, God calls us to help those who are struggling down in the valley. As the disciples came down the mountain, they were confronted by a dark evil, as Jesus saved a young boy from a demon. • Don't be surprised at life's ups and downs. Seek to serve God wherever you are. Even those days that are filled with struggles are opportunities for you to trust God and grow in your faith. Your faith *off* the mountain must be just as strong and courageous as your faith *on* the mountain.

gan talking with Jesus. [31]They were glorious to see. And they were speaking about his exodus from this world, which was about to be fulfilled in Jerusalem.

[32]Peter and the others had fallen asleep. When they woke up, they saw Jesus' glory and the two men standing with him. [33]As Moses and Elijah were starting to leave, Peter, not even knowing what he was saying, blurted out, "Master, it's wonderful for us to be here! Let's make three shelters as memorials*—one for you, one for Moses, and one for Elijah." [34]But even as he was saying this, a cloud overshadowed them, and terror gripped them as the cloud covered them.

[35]Then a voice from the cloud said, "This is my Son, my Chosen One.* Listen to him." [36]When the voice finished, Jesus was there alone. They didn't tell anyone at that time what they had seen.

[37]The next day, after they had come down the mountain, a large crowd met Jesus. [38]A man in the crowd called out to him, "Teacher, I beg you to look at my son, my only child. [39]An evil spirit keeps seizing him, making him scream. It throws him into convulsions so that he foams at the mouth. It batters him and hardly ever leaves him alone. [40]I begged your disciples to cast out the spirit, but they couldn't do it."

[41]Jesus said, "You faithless and corrupt people! How long must I be with you and put up with you?" Then he said to the man, "Bring your son here."

[42]As the boy came forward, the demon knocked him to the ground and threw him into a violent convulsion. But Jesus rebuked the evil* spirit and healed the boy. Then he gave him back to his father. [43]Awe gripped the people as they saw this majestic display of God's power.

While everyone was marveling at everything he was doing, Jesus said to his disciples, [44]"Listen to me and remember what I say. The Son of Man is going to be betrayed into the hands of his enemies." [45]But they didn't know what he meant. Its significance was hidden from them, so they couldn't understand it, and they were afraid to ask him about it.

[46]Then his disciples began arguing about which of them was the greatest.

[47]But Jesus knew their thoughts, so he brought a little child to his side. [48]Then he said to them, "Anyone who welcomes a little child like this on my behalf* welcomes me, and anyone who welcomes me also welcomes my Father who sent me. Whoever is the least among you is the greatest."

[49]John said to Jesus, "Master, we saw someone using your name to cast out demons, but we told him to stop because he isn't in our group."

[50]But Jesus said, "Don't stop him! Anyone who is not against you is for you."

9:33 Greek *three tabernacles.*   9:35 Some manuscripts read *This is my dearly loved Son.*   9:42 Greek *unclean.*
9:48 Greek *in my name.*

PSALM 73:1-28
A psalm of Asaph.

1 **T**ruly God is good to Israel,
      to those whose hearts are pure.
2 But as for me, I almost lost my footing.
      My feet were slipping, and I was
      almost gone.
3 For I envied the proud
      when I saw them prosper despite
      their wickedness.
4 They seem to live such painless lives;
      their bodies are so healthy and
      strong.
5 They don't have troubles like other
      people;
      they're not plagued with problems
      like everyone else.
6 They wear pride like a jeweled
      necklace
      and clothe themselves with cruelty.
7 These fat cats have everything
      their hearts could ever wish for!
8 They scoff and speak only evil;
      in their pride they seek to crush
      others.
9 They boast against the very heavens,
      and their words strut throughout
      the earth.
10 And so the people are dismayed and
      confused,
      drinking in all their words.
11 "What does God know?" they ask.
      "Does the Most High even know
      what's happening?"
12 Look at these wicked people—
      enjoying a life of ease while their
      riches multiply.

¹³ Did I keep my heart pure for nothing?
  Did I keep myself innocent for no
  reason?
¹⁴ I get nothing but trouble all day long;
  every morning brings me pain.

¹⁵ If I had really spoken this way to
  others,
  I would have been a traitor to
  your people.
¹⁶ So I tried to understand why the
  wicked prosper.
  But what a difficult task it is!
¹⁷ Then I went into your sanctuary,
  O God,
  and I finally understood the destiny
  of the wicked.
¹⁸ Truly, you put them on a slippery path
  and send them sliding over the cliff
  to destruction.
¹⁹ In an instant they are destroyed,
  completely swept away by terrors.
²⁰ When you arise, O Lord,
  you will laugh at their silly ideas
  as a person laughs at dreams in the
  morning.

²¹ Then I realized that my heart was
  bitter,
  and I was all torn up inside.

²² I was so foolish and ignorant—
  I must have seemed like a senseless
  animal to you.
²³ Yet I still belong to you;
  you hold my right hand.
²⁴ You guide me with your counsel,
  leading me to a glorious destiny.
²⁵ Whom have I in heaven but you?
  I desire you more than anything
  on earth.
²⁶ My health may fail, and my spirit may
  grow weak,
  but God remains the strength of
  my heart;
  he is mine forever.

²⁷ Those who desert him will perish,
  for you destroy those who abandon
  you.
²⁸ But as for me, how good it is to be near
  God!
  I have made the Sovereign LORD
  my shelter,
  and I will tell everyone about the
  wonderful things you do.

PROVERBS 12:10
The godly care for their animals, but the
wicked are always cruel.

DEUTERONOMY 21:1–22:30
Moses continued to review the various laws
God had given the people to govern all aspects
of society.

"**W**hen you are in the land the LORD your
God is giving you, someone may be found
murdered in a field, and you don't know
who committed the murder. ²In such a
case, your elders and judges must measure the distance from the site of the
crime to the nearby towns. ³When the
nearest town has been determined, that
town's elders must select from the herd a
young cow that has never been trained or
yoked to a plow. ⁴They must lead it down
to a valley that has not been plowed or

planted and that has a stream running
through it. There in the valley they must
break the young cow's neck. ⁵Then the
Levitical priests must step forward, for
the LORD your God has chosen them to
minister before him and to pronounce
blessings in the LORD's name. They are to
decide all legal and criminal cases.

⁶"The elders of the town must wash
their hands over the young cow whose
neck was broken. ⁷Then they must say,
'Our hands did not shed this person's
blood, nor did we see it happen. ⁸O LORD,
forgive your people Israel whom you have
redeemed. Do not charge your people
with the guilt of murdering an innocent

person.' Then they will be absolved of the guilt of this person's blood. [9]By following these instructions, you will do what is right in the LORD's sight and will cleanse the guilt of murder from your community.

[10]"Suppose you go out to war against your enemies and the LORD your God hands them over to you, and you take some of them as captives. [11]And suppose you see among the captives a beautiful woman, and you are attracted to her and want to marry her. [12]If this happens, you may take her to your home, where she must shave her head, cut her nails, [13]and change the clothes she was wearing when she was captured. She will stay in your home, but let her mourn for her father and mother for a full month. Then you may marry her, and you will be her husband and she will be your wife. [14]But if you marry her and she does not please you, you must let her go free. You may not sell her or treat her as a slave, for you have humiliated her.

[15]"Suppose a man has two wives, but he loves one and not the other, and both have given him sons. And suppose the firstborn son is the son of the wife he does not love. [16]When the man divides his inheritance, he may not give the larger inheritance to his younger son, the son of the wife he loves, as if he were the firstborn son. [17]He must recognize the rights of his oldest son, the son of the wife he does not love, by giving him a double portion. He is the first son of his father's virility, and the rights of the firstborn belong to him.

[18]"Suppose a man has a stubborn and rebellious son who will not obey his father or mother, even though they discipline him. [19]In such a case, the father and mother must take the son to the elders as they hold court at the town gate. [20]The parents must say to the elders, 'This son of ours is stubborn and rebellious and refuses to obey. He is a glutton and a drunkard.' [21]Then all the men of his town must stone him to death. In this way, you will purge this evil from among you, and all Israel will hear about it and be afraid.

[22]"If someone has committed a crime worthy of death and is executed and hung on a tree,* [23]the body must not remain hanging from the tree overnight. You must bury the body that same day, for anyone who is hung* is cursed in the sight of God. In this way, you will prevent the defilement of the land the LORD your God is giving you as your special possession.

[22:1]"If you see your neighbor's ox or sheep or goat wandering away, don't ignore your responsibility.* Take it back to its owner. [2]If its owner does not live nearby or you don't know who the owner is, take it to your place and keep it until the owner comes looking for it. Then you must return it. [3]Do the same if you find your neighbor's donkey, clothing, or anything else your neighbor loses. Don't ignore your responsibility.

[4]"If you see that your neighbor's donkey or ox has collapsed on the road, do not look the other way. Go and help your neighbor get it back on its feet!

[5]"A woman must not put on men's clothing, and a man must not wear women's clothing. Anyone who does this is detestable in the sight of the LORD your God.

[6]"If you happen to find a bird's nest in a tree or on the ground, and there are young ones or eggs in it with the mother sitting in the nest, do not take the mother with the young. [7]You may take the young, but let the mother go, so that you may prosper and enjoy a long life.

[8]"When you build a new house, you must build a railing around the edge of its flat roof. That way you will not be considered guilty of murder if someone falls from the roof.

[9]"You must not plant any other crop between the rows of your vineyard. If you do, you are forbidden to use either the grapes from the vineyard or the other crop.

[10]"You must not plow with an ox and a donkey harnessed together.

[11]"You must not wear clothing made of wool and linen woven together.

[12]"You must put four tassels on the hem of the cloak with which you cover yourself—on the front, back, and sides.

[13]"Suppose a man marries a woman, but after sleeping with her, he turns against her [14]and publicly accuses her of shameful conduct, saying, 'When I married this woman, I discovered she was not a virgin.' [15]Then the woman's father and

mother must bring the proof of her virginity to the elders as they hold court at the town gate. [16]Her father must say to them, 'I gave my daughter to this man to be his wife, and now he has turned against her. [17]He has accused her of shameful conduct, saying, "I discovered that your daughter was not a virgin." But here is the proof of my daughter's virginity.' Then they must spread her bed sheet before the elders. [18]The elders must then take the man and punish him. [19]They must also fine him 100 pieces of silver,* which he must pay to the woman's father because he publicly accused a virgin of Israel of shameful conduct. The woman will then remain the man's wife, and he may never divorce her.

[20]"But suppose the man's accusations are true, and he can show that she was not a virgin. [21]The woman must be taken to the door of her father's home, and there the men of the town must stone her to death, for she has committed a disgraceful crime in Israel by being promiscuous while living in her parents' home. In this way, you will purge this evil from among you.

[22]"If a man is discovered committing adultery, both he and the woman must die. In this way, you will purge Israel of such evil.

[23]"Suppose a man meets a young woman, a virgin who is engaged to be married, and he has sexual intercourse with her. If this happens within a town, [24]you must take both of them to the gates of that town and stone them to death. The woman is guilty because she did not scream for help. The man must die because he violated another man's wife. In this way, you will purge this evil from among you.

[25]"But if the man meets the engaged woman out in the country, and he rapes her, then only the man must die. [26]Do nothing to the young woman; she has committed no crime worthy of death. She is as innocent as a murder victim. [27]Since the man raped her out in the country, it must be assumed that she screamed, but there was no one to rescue her.

[28]"Suppose a man has intercourse with a young woman who is a virgin but is not engaged to be married. If they are discovered, [29]he must pay her father fifty pieces of silver.* Then he must marry the young woman because he violated her, and he may never divorce her as long as he lives.

[30]*"A man must not marry his father's former wife, for this would violate his father."

21:22 Or *impaled o a pole;* similarly in 21:23.   **21:23** Greek version reads *for everyone who is hung on a tree.* Compare Gal 3:13.   **22:1** Hebrew *don't hide yourself;* similarly in 22:3.   **22:19** Hebrew *100 shekels onf silver,* about 2.5 pounds or 1.1 kilograms in weight.   **22:29** Hebrew

Demons

LUKE 10:3 Jesus warned his followers that he was sending them out "as lambs among wolves." Forces would indeed be arrayed against them. The spiritual battle is very real, and Christians are Satan's main targets. He wants to ruin your faith, or, failing at that, to at least make you ineffective and fearful. • Make no mistake, Satan has real power. He will seek to tempt you, motivate wicked people to oppose you, cause you to doubt or be afraid, or just make you forget to take time with God and thus hurt your relationship with him. He knows the weak spots humans have and will seek to exploit them. That may sound really creepy, but you need not be afraid. While spiritual warfare is a reality, remember that Satan and demons are not more powerful than God. Scripture promises, "The Spirit who lives in you is greater than the spirit who lives in the world" (1 John 4:4, December 4). • You're already on the winning side. Recognize temptation, doubts, fears, and even too much busyness for what they are. Determine to stay close to God.

50 shekels of silver, about 1.25 pounds or 570 grams in weight.   **22:30** Verse 22:30 is numbered 23:1 in Hebrew text.

LUKE 9:51–10:12

Jesus confronts would-be disciples with the cost of following him. Being a Christian is not a half-hearted, part-time position. It takes your whole heart, your whole being, your whole life.

As the time drew near for him to ascend to heaven, Jesus resolutely set out for Jerusalem. [52]He sent messengers ahead to a Samaritan village to prepare for his arrival. [53]But the people of the village did not welcome Jesus because he was on his way to Jerusalem. [54]When James and John saw this, they said to Jesus, "Lord, should we call down fire from heaven to burn them up*?" [55]But Jesus turned and rebuked them.* [56]So they went on to another village.

[57]As they were walking along, someone said to Jesus, "I will follow you wherever you go."

[58]But Jesus replied, "Foxes have dens to live in, and birds have nests, but the Son of Man has no place even to lay his head."

[59]He said to another person, "Come, follow me."

The man agreed, but he said, "Lord, first let me return home and bury my father."

[60]But Jesus told him, "Let the spiritually dead bury their own dead!* Your duty is to go and preach about the Kingdom of God."

[61]Another said, "Yes, Lord, I will follow you, but first let me say good-bye to my family."

[62]But Jesus told him, "Anyone who puts a hand to the plow and then looks back is not fit for the Kingdom of God."

[10:1]THE Lord now chose seventy-two* other disciples and sent them ahead in pairs to all the towns and places he planned to visit. [2]These were his instructions to them: "The harvest is great, but the workers are few. So pray to the Lord who is in charge of the harvest; ask him to send more workers into his fields. [3]Now go, and remember that I am sending you out as lambs among wolves. [4]Don't take any money with you, nor a traveler's bag, nor an extra pair of sandals. And don't stop to greet anyone on the road.

[5]"Whenever you enter someone's home, first say, 'May God's peace be on this house.' [6]If those who live there are peaceful, the blessing will stand; if they are not, the blessing will return to you. [7]Don't move around from home to home. Stay in one place, eating and drinking what they provide. Don't hesitate to accept hospitality, because those who work deserve their pay.

[8]"If you enter a town and it welcomes you, eat whatever is set before you. [9]Heal the sick, and tell them, 'The Kingdom of God is near you now.' [10]But if a town refuses to welcome you, go out into its streets and say, [11]'We wipe even the dust of your town from our feet to show that we have abandoned you to your fate. And know this—the Kingdom of God is near!' [12]I assure you, even wicked Sodom will be better off than such a town on judgment day."

9:54 Some manuscripts add *as Elijah did.*   **9:55** Some manuscripts add an expanded conclusion to verse 55 and an additional sentence in verse 56: *And he said, "You don't realize what your hearts are like.* [56]*For the Son of Man has not come to destroy people's lives, but to save them."*   **9:60** Greek *Let the dead bury their own dead.*   **10:1** Some manuscripts read *seventy;* also in 10:17.

PSALM 74:1-23
A psalm of Asaph.

[1] **O** God, why have you rejected us so
    long?
  Why is your anger so intense
    against the sheep of your own
    pasture?
[2] Remember that we are the people you
    chose long ago,
  the tribe you redeemed as your own
    special possession!
  And remember Jerusalem,* your
    home here on earth.
[3] Walk through the awful ruins of the
    city;
  see how the enemy has destroyed
    your sanctuary.
[4] There your enemies shouted their
    victorious battle cries;
  there they set up their battle
    standards.
[5] They swung their axes
    like woodcutters in a forest.
[6] With axes and picks,
    they smashed the carved paneling.

7 They burned your sanctuary to the
  ground.
    They defiled the place that bears
    your name.
8 Then they thought, "Let's destroy
  everything!"
    So they burned down all the places
    where God was worshiped.

9 We no longer see your miraculous
  signs.
    All the prophets are gone,
    and no one can tell us when it will
    end.
10 How long, O God, will you allow our
   enemies to insult you?
    Will you let them dishonor your
    name forever?
11 Why do you hold back your strong
   right hand?
    Unleash your powerful fist and
    destroy them.

12 You, O God, are my king from ages
   past,
    bringing salvation to the earth.
13 You split the sea by your strength
    and smashed the heads of the sea
    monsters.
14 You crushed the heads of Leviathan*
    and let the desert animals eat him.
15 You caused the springs and streams
   to gush forth,
    and you dried up rivers that never
    run dry.
16 Both day and night belong to you;

you made the starlight* and the
    sun.
17 You set the boundaries of the earth,
    and you made both summer and
    winter.

18 See how these enemies insult you,
   LORD.
    A foolish nation has dishonored
    your name.
19 Don't let these wild beasts destroy
   your turtledoves.
    Don't forget your suffering people
    forever.

20 Remember your covenant promises,
    for the land is full of darkness and
    violence!
21 Don't let the downtrodden be
   humiliated again.
    Instead, let the poor and needy
    praise your name.

22 Arise, O God, and defend your cause.
    Remember how these fools insult
    you all day long.
23 Don't overlook what your enemies
   have said
    or their growing uproar.

74:TITLE Hebrew *maskil*. This may be a literary or musical
term.   74:2 Hebrew *Mount Zion*.   74:14 The identification
of Leviathan is disputed, ranging from an earthly creature to a
mythical sea monster in ancient literature.   74:16 Or *moon;*
Hebrew reads *light.*

PROVERBS 12:11

A hard worker has plenty of food, but a
person who chases fantasies has no sense.

APRIL**3**

DEUTERONOMY 23:1–25:19

The laws God gave were not merely a list of dos and
don'ts. They were opportunities to honor God in life
and as a society. Obedience was (and still is) the
most meaningful way to express faith.

1*"If a man's testicles are crushed or his
penis is cut off, he may not be admitted to
the assembly of the LORD.

2"If a person is illegitimate by birth,
neither he nor his descendants for ten
generations may be admitted to the assembly of the LORD.

3"No Ammonite or Moabite or any of
their descendants for ten generations
may be admitted to the assembly of the
LORD. 4These nations did not welcome

you with food and water when you came out of Egypt. Instead, they hired Balaam son of Beor from Pethor in distant Aram-naharaim to curse you. ⁵But the LORD your God refused to listen to Balaam. He turned the intended curse into a blessing because the LORD your God loves you. ⁶As long as you live, you must never promote the welfare and prosperity of the Ammonites or Moabites.

⁷"Do not detest the Edomites or the Egyptians, because the Edomites are your relatives and you lived as foreigners among the Egyptians. ⁸The third generation of Edomites and Egyptians may enter the assembly of the LORD.

⁹"When you go to war against your enemies, be sure to stay away from anything that is impure.

¹⁰"Any man who becomes ceremonially defiled because of a nocturnal emission must leave the camp and stay away all day. ¹¹Toward evening he must bathe himself, and at sunset he may return to the camp.

¹²"You must have a designated area outside the camp where you can go to relieve yourself. ¹³Each of you must have a spade as part of your equipment. Whenever you relieve yourself, dig a hole with the spade and cover the excrement. ¹⁴The camp must be holy, for the LORD your God moves around in your camp to protect you and to defeat your enemies. He must not see any shameful thing among you, or he will turn away from you.

¹⁵"If slaves should escape from their masters and take refuge with you, you must not hand them over to their masters. ¹⁶Let them live among you in any town they choose, and do not oppress them.

¹⁷"No Israelite, whether man or woman, may become a temple prostitute. ¹⁸When you are bringing an offering to fulfill a vow, you must not bring to the house of the LORD your God any offering from the earnings of a prostitute, whether a man* or a woman, for both are detestable to the LORD your God.

¹⁹"Do not charge interest on the loans you make to a fellow Israelite, whether you loan money, or food, or anything else. ²⁰You may charge interest to foreigners, but you may not charge interest to Israelites, so that the LORD your God may bless

you in everything you do in the land you are about to enter and occupy.

²¹"When you make a vow to the LORD your God, be prompt in fulfilling whatever you promised him. For the LORD your God demands that you promptly fulfill all your vows, or you will be guilty of sin. ²²However, it is not a sin to refrain from making a vow. ²³But once you have voluntarily made a vow, be careful to fulfill your promise to the LORD your God.

²⁴"When you enter your neighbor's vineyard, you may eat your fill of grapes, but you must not carry any away in a basket. ²⁵And when you enter your neighbor's field of grain, you may pluck the heads of grain with your hand, but you must not harvest it with a sickle.

24:1"SUPPOSE a man marries a woman but she does not please him. Having discovered something wrong with her, he writes her a letter of divorce, hands it to her, and sends her away from his house. ²When she leaves his house, she is free to marry another man. ³But if the second husband also turns against her and divorces her, or if he dies, ⁴the first husband may not marry her again, for she has been defiled. That would be detestable to the LORD. You must not bring guilt upon the land the LORD your God is giving you as a special possession.

⁵"A newly married man must not be drafted into the army or be given any other official responsibilities. He must be free to spend one year at home, bringing happiness to the wife he has married.

⁶"It is wrong to take a set of millstones, or even just the upper millstone, as security for a loan, for the owner uses it to make a living.

⁷"If anyone kidnaps a fellow Israelite and treats him as a slave or sells him, the kidnapper must die. In this way, you will purge the evil from among you.

⁸"In all cases involving serious skin diseases,* be careful to follow the instructions of the Levitical priests; obey all the commands I have given them. ⁹Remember what the LORD your God did to Miriam as you were coming from Egypt.

¹⁰"If you lend anything to your neighbor, do not enter his house to pick up the

item he is giving as security. [11]You must wait outside while he goes in and brings it out to you. [12]If your neighbor is poor and gives you his cloak as security for a loan, do not keep the cloak overnight. [13]Return the cloak to its owner by sunset so he can stay warm through the night and bless you, and the LORD your God will count you as righteous.

[14]"Never take advantage of poor and destitute laborers, whether they are fellow Israelites or foreigners living in your towns. [15]You must pay them their wages each day before sunset because they are poor and are counting on it. If you don't, they might cry out to the LORD against you, and it would be counted against you as sin.

[16]"Parents must not be put to death for the sins of their children, nor children for the sins of their parents. Those deserving to die must be put to death for their own crimes.

[17]"True justice must be given to foreigners living among you and to orphans, and you must never accept a widow's garment as security for her debt. [18]Always remember that you were slaves in Egypt and that the LORD your God redeemed you from your slavery. That is why I have given you this command.

[19]"When you are harvesting your crops and forget to bring in a bundle of grain from your field, don't go back to get it. Leave it for the foreigners, orphans, and widows. Then the LORD your God will bless you in all you do. [20]When you beat the olives from your olive trees, don't go over the boughs twice. Leave the remaining olives for the foreigners, orphans, and widows. [21]When you gather the grapes in your vineyard, don't glean the vines after they are picked. Leave the remaining grapes for the foreigners, orphans, and widows. [22]Remember that you were slaves in the land of Egypt. That is why I am giving you this command.

25:1"SUPPOSE two people take a dispute to court, and the judges declare that one is right and the other is wrong. [2]If the person in the wrong is sentenced to be flogged, the judge must command him to lie down and be beaten in his presence with the number of lashes appropriate to the crime. [3]But never give more than forty lashes; more than forty lashes would publicly humiliate your neighbor.

[4]"You must not muzzle an ox to keep it from eating as it treads out the grain.

[5]"If two brothers are living together on the same property and one of them dies without a son, his widow may not be married to anyone from outside the family. Instead, her husband's brother should marry her and have intercourse with her to fulfill the duties of a brother-in-law. [6]The first

HOW WE LIVE

Having integrity

DEUTERONOMY 25:14-15 When you go to the grocery store, you buy your fruits and vegetables by the pound, trusting that the scales at the checkout are accurate and will charge you the right amount. In Moses' day, much of commerce was governed by weights and measures. It would have been an easy temptation to tamper with scales to get a bigger profit. The Lord commanded that all the people use scales that weighed purchases accurately. Honesty on the part of the merchant would be a reflection of that person's relationship with God. • Would you be characterized as an honest person? Perhaps before you became a believer, your reputation was less than sterling. You can change that, because Jesus can change you! Let your spiritual life affect and permeate everything you do. After all, living a life that is above reproach is one of the greatest testimonies you can give for the Lord. Show that you are dependable, trustworthy, and honest. As you do, you will bring glory and honor to God.

son she bears to him will be considered the son of the dead brother, so that his name will not be forgotten in Israel.

⁷"But if the man refuses to marry his brother's widow, she must go to the town gate and say to the elders assembled there, 'My husband's brother refuses to preserve his brother's name in Israel—he refuses to fulfill the duties of a brother-in-law by marrying me.' ⁸The elders of the town will then summon him and talk with him. If he still refuses and says, 'I don't want to marry her,' ⁹the widow must walk over to him in the presence of the elders, pull his sandal from his foot, and spit in his face. Then she must declare, 'This is what happens to a man who refuses to provide his brother with children.' ¹⁰Ever afterward in Israel his family will be referred to as 'the family of the man whose sandal was pulled off'!

¹¹"If two Israelite men get into a fight and the wife of one tries to rescue her husband by grabbing the testicles of the other man, ¹²you must cut off her hand. Show her no pity.

¹³"You must use accurate scales when you weigh out merchandise, ¹⁴and you must use full and honest measures. ¹⁵Yes, always use honest weights and measures, so that you may enjoy a long life in the land the LORD your God is giving you. ¹⁶All who cheat with dishonest weights and measures are detestable to the LORD your God.

¹⁷"Never forget what the Amalekites did to you as you came from Egypt. ¹⁸They attacked you when you were exhausted and weary, and they struck down those who were straggling behind. They had no fear of God. ¹⁹Therefore, when the LORD your God has given you rest from all your enemies in the land he is giving you as a special possession, you must destroy the Amalekites and erase their memory from under heaven. Never forget this!"

23:1 Verses 23:1-25 are numbered 23:2-26 in Hebrew text. 23:18 Hebrew *a dog*. 24:8 Traditionally rendered *leprosy*. The Hebrew word used here can describe various skin diseases.

LUKE 10:13-37

Obedience matters. Jesus warned entire cities of the judgment their disobedience would bring. When Jesus' followers obey, he is able to work through them to change the world.

"**W**hat sorrow awaits you, Korazin and Bethsaida! For if the miracles I did in you had been done in wicked Tyre and Sidon, their people would have repented of their sins long ago, clothing themselves in burlap and throwing ashes on their heads to show their remorse. ¹⁴Yes, Tyre and Sidon will be better off on judgment day than you. ¹⁵And you people of Capernaum, will you be honored in heaven? No, you will go down to the place of the dead.*"

¹⁶Then he said to the disciples, "Anyone who accepts your message is also accepting me. And anyone who rejects you is rejecting me. And anyone who rejects me is rejecting God, who sent me."

¹⁷When the seventy-two disciples returned, they joyfully reported to him, "Lord, even the demons obey us when we use your name!"

¹⁸"Yes," he told them, "I saw Satan fall from heaven like lightning! ¹⁹Look, I have given you authority over all the power of the enemy, and you can walk among snakes and scorpions and crush them. Nothing will injure you. ²⁰But don't rejoice because evil spirits obey you; rejoice because your names are registered in heaven."

²¹At that same time Jesus was filled with the joy of the Holy Spirit, and he said, "O Father, Lord of heaven and earth, thank you for hiding these things from those who think themselves wise and clever, and for revealing them to the childlike. Yes, Father, it pleased you to do it this way.

²²"My Father has entrusted everything to me. No one truly knows the Son except the Father, and no one truly knows the Father except the Son and those to whom the Son chooses to reveal him."

²³Then when they were alone, he turned to the disciples and said, "Blessed are the eyes that see what you have seen. ²⁴I tell you, many prophets and kings longed to see what you see, but they didn't see it. And they longed to hear what you hear, but they didn't hear it."

²⁵One day an expert in religious law stood up to test Jesus by asking him this question: "Teacher, what should I do to inherit eternal life?"

²⁶Jesus replied, "What does the law of Moses say? How do you read it?"

²⁷The man answered, " 'You must love the LORD your God with all your heart, all your soul, all your strength, and all your mind.' And, 'Love your neighbor as yourself.' "*

²⁸"Right!" Jesus told him. "Do this and you will live!"

²⁹The man wanted to justify his actions, so he asked Jesus, "And who is my neighbor?"

³⁰Jesus replied with a story: "A Jewish man was traveling on a trip from Jerusalem to Jericho, and he was attacked by bandits. They stripped him of his clothes, beat him up, and left him half dead beside the road.

³¹"By chance a priest came along. But when he saw the man lying there, he crossed to the other side of the road and passed him by. ³²A Temple assistant* walked over and looked at him lying there, but he also passed by on the other side.

³³"Then a despised Samaritan came along, and when he saw the man, he felt compassion for him. ³⁴Going over to him, the Samaritan soothed his wounds with olive oil and wine and bandaged them. Then he put the man on his own donkey and took him to an inn, where he took care of him. ³⁵The next day he handed the innkeeper two silver coins,* telling him, 'Take care of this man. If his bill runs higher than this, I'll pay you the next time I'm here.'

³⁶"Now which of these three would you say was a neighbor to the man who was attacked by bandits?" Jesus asked.

³⁷The man replied, "The one who showed him mercy."

Then Jesus said, "Yes, now go and do the same."

10:15 Greek *to Hades.*   10:27 Deut 6:5; Lev 19:18.
10:32 Greek *A Levite.*   10:35 Greek *two denarii.* A denarius was equivalent to a laborer's full day's wage.

PSALM 75:1-10
For the choir director: A psalm of Asaph.
A song to be sung to the tune "Do Not
Destroy!"

¹ **We** thank you, O God!
    We give thanks because you are near.
    People everywhere tell of your
        wonderful deeds.

² God says, "At the time I have planned,
    I will bring justice against the
        wicked.
³ When the earth quakes and its people
        live in turmoil,
    I am the one who keeps its
        foundations firm.   *Interlude*

⁴ "I warned the proud, 'Stop your
        boasting!'
    I told the wicked, 'Don't raise
        your fists!
⁵ Don't raise your fists in defiance
        at the heavens
    or speak with such arrogance.' "
⁶ For no one on earth—from east or
        west,
    or even from the wilderness—
        should raise a defiant fist.*
⁷ It is God alone who judges;
    he decides who will rise and who
        will fall.
⁸ For the LORD holds a cup in his hand
    that is full of foaming wine mixed
        with spices.
He pours out the wine in judgment,
    and all the wicked must drink it,
        draining it to the dregs.

⁹ But as for me, I will always proclaim
        what God has done;
    I will sing praises to the God of
        Jacob.
¹⁰ For God says, "I will break the strength
        of the wicked,
    but I will increase the power
        of the godly."

75:6 Hebrew *should lift.*

PROVERBS 12:12-14
Thieves are jealous of each other's loot, but the godly are well rooted and bear their own fruit. □ The wicked are trapped by their own words, but the godly escape such trouble. □ Wise words bring many benefits, and hard work brings rewards.

APRIL 4

DEUTERONOMY 26:1–27:26

The Israelites were to honor God by giving back to him the first part of their harvest. Believers today do the same by giving a portion of their income back to God. When you do this, you remember that God gives you all you have.

"When you enter the land the LORD your God is giving you as a special possession and you have conquered it and settled there, ²put some of the first produce from each crop you harvest into a basket and bring it to the designated place of worship—the place the LORD your God chooses for his name to be honored. ³Go to the priest in charge at that time and say to him, 'With this gift I acknowledge to the LORD your God that I have entered the land he swore to our ancestors he would give us.' ⁴The priest will then take the basket from your hand and set it before the altar of the LORD your God.

⁵"You must then say in the presence of the LORD your God, 'My ancestor Jacob was a wandering Aramean who went to live as a foreigner in Egypt. His family arrived few in number, but in Egypt they became a large and mighty nation. ⁶When the Egyptians oppressed and humiliated us by making us their slaves, ⁷we cried out to the LORD, the God of our ancestors. He heard our cries and saw our hardship, toil, and oppression. ⁸So the LORD brought us out of Egypt with a strong hand and powerful arm, with overwhelming terror, and with miraculous signs and wonders. ⁹He brought us to this place and gave us this land flowing with milk and honey! ¹⁰And now, O LORD, I have brought you the first portion of the harvest you have given me from the ground.' Then place the produce before the LORD your God, and bow to the ground in worship before him. ¹¹Afterward you may go and celebrate because of all the good things the LORD your God has given to you and your household. Remember to include the Levites and the foreigners living among you in the celebration.

¹²"Every third year you must offer a special tithe of your crops. In this year of the special tithe you must give your tithes to the Levites, foreigners, orphans, and widows, so that they will have enough to eat in your towns. ¹³Then you must declare in the presence of the LORD your God, 'I have taken the sacred gift from my house and have given it to the Levites, foreigners, orphans, and widows, just as you commanded me. I have not violated or forgotten any of your commands. ¹⁴I have not eaten any of it while in mourning; I have not handled it while I was ceremonially unclean; and I have not offered any of it to the dead. I have obeyed the LORD my God and have done everything you commanded me. ¹⁵Now look down from your holy dwelling place in heaven and bless your people Israel and the land you swore to our ancestors to give us—a land flowing with milk and honey.'

¹⁶"Today the LORD your God has commanded you to obey all these decrees and regulations. So be careful to obey them wholeheartedly. ¹⁷You have declared today that the LORD is your God. And you have promised to walk in his ways, and to obey his decrees, commands, and regulations, and to do everything he tells you. ¹⁸The LORD has declared today that you are his people, his own special treasure, just as he promised, and that you must obey all his commands. ¹⁹And if you do, he will set you high above all the other nations he has made. Then you will receive praise, honor, and renown. You will be a nation that is holy to the LORD your God, just as he promised."

²⁷:¹THEN Moses and the leaders of Israel gave this charge to the people: "Obey all these commands that I am giving you today. ²When you cross the Jordan River and enter the land the LORD your God is giving you, set up some large stones and coat them with plaster. ³Write this whole body of instruction on them when you cross the river to enter the land the LORD your God is giving you—a land flowing with milk and honey, just as the LORD, the God of your ancestors, prom-

ised you. ⁴When you cross the Jordan, set up these stones at Mount Ebal and coat them with plaster, as I am commanding you today.

⁵"Then build an altar there to the LORD your God, using natural, uncut stones. You must not shape the stones with an iron tool. ⁶Build the altar of uncut stones, and use it to offer burnt offerings to the LORD your God. ⁷Also sacrifice peace offerings on it, and celebrate by feasting there before the LORD your God. ⁸You must clearly write all these instructions on the stones coated with plaster."

⁹Then Moses and the Levitical priests addressed all Israel as follows: "O Israel, be quiet and listen! Today you have become the people of the LORD your God. ¹⁰So you must obey the LORD your God by keeping all these commands and decrees that I am giving you today."

¹¹That same day Moses also gave this charge to the people: ¹²"When you cross the Jordan River, the tribes of Simeon, Levi, Judah, Issachar, Joseph, and Benjamin must stand on Mount Gerizim to proclaim a blessing over the people. ¹³And the tribes of Reuben, Gad, Asher, Zebulun, Dan, and Naphtali must stand on Mount Ebal to proclaim a curse.

¹⁴"Then the Levites will shout to all the people of Israel:

¹⁵'Cursed is anyone who carves or casts an idol and secretly sets it up. These idols, the work of craftsmen, are detestable to the LORD.'
And all the people will reply, 'Amen.'"

¹⁶'Cursed is anyone who dishonors father or mother.'
And all the people will reply, 'Amen.'

¹⁷'Cursed is anyone who steals property from a neighbor by moving a boundary marker.'
And all the people will reply, 'Amen.'

¹⁸'Cursed is anyone who leads a blind person astray on the road.'
And all the people will reply, 'Amen.'

¹⁹'Cursed is anyone who denies justice to foreigners, orphans, or widows.'
And all the people will reply, 'Amen.'

²⁰'Cursed is anyone who has sexual intercourse with one of his father's wives, for he has violated his father.'
And all the people will reply, 'Amen.'

²¹'Cursed is anyone who has sexual intercourse with an animal.'
And all the people will reply, 'Amen.'

²²'Cursed is anyone who has sexual intercourse with his sister, whether

HOW WE LIVE

Setting priorities

LUKE 10:38-42 It can be easy to lose sight of Jesus in the midst of activity for him. So many Christians are running around doing so much that they forget about worship. The story of Martha and her sister Mary shows the necessity of balancing work and worship. • Martha was so busy getting the big meal ready that she spent all her time fussing in the kitchen. It didn't help that Mary left Martha to get the dinner ready, preferring to sit at Jesus' feet and listen to him. This is what caused Martha such consternation. Mary and Martha both loved Jesus, and on this occasion, both were serving him. But Martha felt that Mary's service was inferior to her own. Jesus didn't tell Martha she was right or wrong—he simply asked her to check her priorities. She was so busy working on the meal and being upset with her sister that she was actually neglecting Jesus. • As you begin to find ways to serve Jesus, don't get so busy that you forget to have a daily quiet time with him. When you strike the right balance between work and worship, you will be more pleasing and effective in your service of him.

she is the daughter of his father or his mother.'

And all the people will reply, 'Amen.'

23'Cursed is anyone who has sexual intercourse with his mother-in-law.'

And all the people will reply, 'Amen.'

24'Cursed is anyone who attacks a neighbor in secret.'

And all the people will reply, 'Amen.'

25'Cursed is anyone who accepts payment to kill an innocent person.'

And all the people will reply, 'Amen.'

26'Cursed is anyone who does not affirm and obey the terms of these instructions.'

And all the people will reply, 'Amen.'"

LUKE 10:38-11:13

Martha needed to learn that spending time with Jesus should always be a priority. For us today, spending time with Jesus happens through Bible reading and prayer. Jesus gave us an example of how to pray.

As Jesus and the disciples continued on their way to Jerusalem, they came to a certain village where a woman named Martha welcomed him into her home. 39Her sister, Mary, sat at the Lord's feet, listening to what he taught. 40But Martha was distracted by the big dinner she was preparing. She came to Jesus and said, "Lord, doesn't it seem unfair to you that my sister just sits here while I do all the work? Tell her to come and help me."

41But the Lord said to her, "My dear Martha, you are worried and upset over all these details! 42There is only one thing worth being concerned about. Mary has discovered it, and it will not be taken away from her."

11:1ONCE Jesus was in a certain place praying. As he finished, one of his disciples came to him and said, "Lord, teach us to pray, just as John taught his disciples."

2Jesus said, "This is how you should pray:*

"Father, may your name be kept holy.
May your Kingdom come soon.
3 Give us each day the food we need,*

4 and forgive us our sins,
as we forgive those who sin against us.
And don't let us yield to temptation.*"

5Then, teaching them more about prayer, he used this story: "Suppose you went to a friend's house at midnight, wanting to borrow three loaves of bread. You say to him, 6'A friend of mine has just arrived for a visit, and I have nothing for him to eat.' 7And suppose he calls out from his bedroom, 'Don't bother me. The door is locked for the night, and my family and I are all in bed. I can't help you.' 8But I tell you this—though he won't do it for friendship's sake, if you keep knocking long enough, he will get up and give you whatever you need because of your shameless persistence.*

9"And so I tell you, keep on asking, and you will receive what you ask for. Keep on seeking, and you will find. Keep on knocking, and the door will be opened to you. 10For everyone who asks, receives. Everyone who seeks, finds. And to everyone who knocks, the door will be opened.

11"You fathers—if your children ask* for a fish, do you give them a snake instead? 12Or if they ask for an egg, do you give them a scorpion? Of course not! 13So if you sinful people know how to give good gifts to your children, how much more will your heavenly Father give the Holy Spirit to those who ask him."

11:2 Some manuscripts add additional phrases from the Lord's Prayer as it reads in Matt 6:9-13. 11:3 Or Give us each day our food for the day; or Give us each day our food for tomorrow. 11:4 Or And keep us from being tested. 11:8 Or in order to avoid shame, or so his reputation won't be damaged. 11:11 Some manuscripts add for bread, do you give them a stone? Or (if they ask).

PSALM 76:1-12

For the choir director: A psalm of Asaph. A song to be accompanied by stringed instruments.

1 **G**od is honored in Judah;
his name is great in Israel.
2 Jerusalem* is where he lives;
Mount Zion is his home.
3 There he has broken the fiery arrows of the enemy,
the shields and swords and weapons of war. *Interlude*

⁴ You are glorious and more majestic
  than the everlasting mountains.*
⁵ Our boldest enemies have been
  plundered.
  They lie before us in the sleep
  of death.
  No warrior could lift a hand
  against us.
⁶ At the blast of your breath, O God
  of Jacob,
  their horses and chariots lay still.

⁷ No wonder you are greatly feared!
  Who can stand before you when
  your anger explodes?
⁸ From heaven you sentenced your
  enemies;
  the earth trembled and stood silent
  before you.
⁹ You stand up to judge those who
  do evil, O God,
  and to rescue the oppressed
  of the earth.   *Interlude*

¹⁰ Human defiance only enhances your
  glory,
  for you use it as a weapon.*
¹¹ Make vows to the LORD your God,
  and keep them.
  Let everyone bring tribute to the
  Awesome One.
¹² For he breaks the pride of
  princes,
  and the kings of the earth fear
  him.

76:2 Hebrew *Salem,* another name for Jerusalem.   76:4 As
in Greek version; Hebrew reads *than mountains filled with
beasts of prey.*   76:10 The meaning of the Hebrew is
uncertain.

PROVERBS 12:15-17

Fools think their own way is right, but the
wise listen to others. ☐ A fool is quick-
tempered, but a wise person stays calm
when insulted. ☐ An honest witness tells
the truth; a false witness tells lies.

DEUTERONOMY 28:1-68

Yesterday you read of a series of curses the Israelites could expect for disobedience; today you read
a series of blessings they could expect for being
obedient.

"**If** you fully obey the LORD your God and
carefully keep all his commands that I am
giving you today, the LORD your God will
set you high above all the nations of the
world. ² You will experience all these
blessings if you obey the LORD your God:

³ Your towns and your fields
  will be blessed.
⁴ Your children and your crops
  will be blessed.
  The offspring of your herds and flocks
  will be blessed.
⁵ Your fruit baskets and breadboards
  will be blessed.
⁶ Wherever you go and whatever you do,
  you will be blessed.

⁷"The LORD will conquer your enemies
when they attack you. They will attack you
from one direction, but they will scatter
from you in seven!

⁸"The LORD will guarantee a blessing
on everything you do and will fill your
storehouses with grain. The LORD your
God will bless you in the land he is giving you.

⁹"If you obey the commands of the
LORD your God and walk in his ways, the
LORD will establish you as his holy people
as he swore he would do. ¹⁰ Then all the
nations of the world will see that you are a
people claimed by the LORD, and they will
stand in awe of you.

¹¹"The LORD will give you prosperity in
the land he swore to your ancestors to give
you, blessing you with many children,
numerous livestock, and abundant crops.
¹²The LORD will send rain at the proper

time from his rich treasury in the heavens and will bless all the work you do. You will lend to many nations, but you will never need to borrow from them. ¹³If you listen to these commands of the LORD your God that I am giving you today, and if you carefully obey them, the LORD will make you the head and not the tail, and you will always be on top and never at the bottom. ¹⁴You must not turn away from any of the commands I am giving you today, nor follow after other gods and worship them.

¹⁵"But if you refuse to listen to the LORD your God and do not obey all the commands and decrees I am giving you today, all these curses will come and overwhelm you:

¹⁶ Your towns and your fields
   will be cursed.
¹⁷ Your fruit baskets and breadboards
   will be cursed.
¹⁸ Your children and your crops
   will be cursed.
   The offspring of your herds and flocks
   will be cursed.
¹⁹ Wherever you go and whatever you do,
   you will be cursed.

²⁰"The LORD himself will send on you curses, confusion, and frustration in everything you do, until at last you are completely destroyed for doing evil and abandoning me. ²¹The LORD will afflict you with diseases until none of you are left in the land you are about to enter and occupy. ²²The LORD will strike you with wasting diseases, fever, and inflammation, with scorching heat and drought, and with blight and mildew. These disasters will pursue you until you die. ²³The skies above will be as unyielding as bronze, and the earth beneath will be as hard as iron. ²⁴The LORD will change the rain that falls on your land into powder, and dust will pour down from the sky until you are destroyed.

²⁵"The LORD will cause you to be defeated by your enemies. You will attack your enemies from one direction, but you will scatter from them in seven! You will be an object of horror to all the kingdoms of the earth. ²⁶Your corpses will be food for all the scavenging birds and wild ani-

mals, and no one will be there to chase them away.

²⁷"The LORD will afflict you with the boils of Egypt and with tumors, scurvy, and the itch, from which you cannot be cured. ²⁸The LORD will strike you with madness, blindness, and panic. ²⁹You will grope around in broad daylight like a blind person groping in the darkness, but you will not find your way. You will be oppressed and robbed continually, and no one will come to save you.

³⁰"You will be engaged to a woman, but another man will sleep with her. You will build a house, but someone else will live in it. You will plant a vineyard, but you will never enjoy its fruit. ³¹Your ox will be butchered before your eyes, but you will not eat a single bite of the meat. Your donkey will be taken from you, never to be returned. Your sheep and goats will be given to your enemies, and no one will be there to help you. ³²You will watch as your sons and daughters are taken away as slaves. Your heart will break for them, but you won't be able to help them. ³³A foreign nation you have never heard about will eat the crops you worked so hard to grow. You will suffer under constant oppression and harsh treatment. ³⁴You will go mad because of all the tragedy you see around you. ³⁵The LORD will cover your knees and legs with incurable boils. In fact, you will be covered from head to foot.

³⁶"The LORD will exile you and your king to a nation unknown to you and your ancestors. There in exile you will worship gods of wood and stone! ³⁷You will become an object of horror, ridicule, and mockery among all the nations to which the LORD sends you.

³⁸"You will plant much but harvest little, for locusts will eat your crops. ³⁹You will plant vineyards and care for them, but you will not drink the wine or eat the grapes, for worms will destroy the vines. ⁴⁰You will grow olive trees throughout your land, but you will never use the olive oil, for the fruit will drop before it ripens. ⁴¹You will have sons and daughters, but you will lose them, for they will be led away into captivity. ⁴²Swarms of insects will destroy your trees and crops.

⁴³"The foreigners living among you will

become stronger and stronger, while you become weaker and weaker. ⁴⁴They will lend money to you, but you will not lend to them. They will be the head, and you will be the tail!

⁴⁵"If you refuse to listen to the LORD your God and to obey the commands and decrees he has given you, all these curses will pursue and overtake you until you are destroyed. ⁴⁶These horrors will serve as a sign and warning among you and your descendants forever. ⁴⁷If you do not serve the LORD your God with joy and enthusiasm for the abundant benefits you have received, ⁴⁸you will serve your enemies whom the LORD will send against you. You will be left hungry, thirsty, naked, and lacking in everything. The LORD will put an iron yoke on your neck, oppressing you harshly until he has destroyed you.

⁴⁹"The LORD will bring a distant nation against you from the end of the earth, and it will swoop down on you like a vulture. It is a nation whose language you do not understand, ⁵⁰a fierce and heartless nation that shows no respect for the old and no pity for the young. ⁵¹Its armies will devour your livestock and crops, and you will be destroyed. They will leave you no grain, new wine, olive oil, calves, or lambs, and you will starve to death. ⁵²They will attack your cities until all the fortified walls in your land—the walls you trusted to protect you—are knocked down. They will attack all the towns in the land the LORD your God has given you.

⁵³"The siege and terrible distress of the enemy's attack will be so severe that you will eat the flesh of your own sons and daughters, whom the LORD your God has given you. ⁵⁴The most tenderhearted man among you will have no compassion for his own brother, his beloved wife, and his surviving children. ⁵⁵He will refuse to share with them the flesh he is devouring—the flesh of one of his own children—because he has nothing else to eat during the siege and terrible distress that your enemy will inflict on all your towns. ⁵⁶The most tender and delicate woman among you—so delicate she would not so much as touch the ground with her foot— will be selfish toward the husband she loves and toward her own son or daughter. ⁵⁷She will hide from them the afterbirth and the new baby she has borne, so that she herself can secretly eat them. She will have nothing else to eat during the siege and terrible distress that your enemy will inflict on all your towns.

⁵⁸"If you refuse to obey all the words of instruction that are written in this book, and if you do not fear the glorious and awesome name of the LORD your God, ⁵⁹then the LORD will overwhelm you and your children with indescribable plagues.

Demons

WHAT THE BIBLE SAYS

LUKE 11:24-26 You may be surprised to read so many accounts of Jesus casting out demons from people. Chances are you've never met a single demon-possessed person, so why did Jesus run into so many? It is possible that God permitted demons to be more active during Jesus' day so that Jesus could demonstrate his power and victory over them. • Satan is still actively working in this world to destroy human souls. Satan will do anything he can to keep people from finding salvation and experiencing the life-saving power of Jesus Christ. Sometimes this involves demon possession. It would not be wise to obsess over demons or to try to figure out who might be possessed and who might not be. Instead, your awareness of the great spiritual battle going on in the world will help you to stay strong and vigilant and will give you all the more reason to share your faith. Jesus is on your side in this fight, and he has the power to defeat any foe, physical or spiritual.

These plagues will be intense and without relief, making you miserable and unbearably sick. 60He will afflict you with all the diseases of Egypt that you feared so much, and you will have no relief. 61The LORD will afflict you with every sickness and plague there is, even those not mentioned in this Book of Instruction, until you are destroyed. 62Though you become as numerous as the stars in the sky, few of you will be left because you would not listen to the LORD your God.

63"Just as the LORD has found great pleasure in causing you to prosper and multiply, the LORD will find pleasure in destroying you. You will be torn from the land you are about to enter and occupy. 64For the LORD will scatter you among all the nations from one end of the earth to the other. There you will worship foreign gods that neither you nor your ancestors have known, gods made of wood and stone! 65There among those nations you will find no peace or place to rest. And the LORD will cause your heart to tremble, your eyesight to fail, and your soul to despair. 66Your life will constantly hang in the balance. You will live night and day in fear, unsure if you will survive. 67In the morning you will say, 'If only it were night!' And in the evening you will say, 'If only it were morning!' For you will be terrified by the awful horrors you see around you. 68Then the LORD will send you back to Egypt in ships, to a destination I promised you would never see again. There you will offer to sell yourselves to your enemies as slaves, but no one will buy you."

LUKE 11:14-36

Where did Jesus get his power? Some attributed his power to Satan, thus making him very dangerous. Jesus described the ludicrousness of such a statement—if his power came from Satan, why would he be casting out demons?

One day Jesus cast out a demon from a man who couldn't speak, and when the demon was gone, the man began to speak. The crowds were amazed, 15but some of them said, "No wonder he can cast out demons. He gets his power from Satan,* the prince of demons." 16Others, trying to test Jesus, demanded that he show them a mi-

raculous sign from heaven to prove his authority.

17He knew their thoughts, so he said, "Any kingdom divided by civil war is doomed. A family splintered by feuding will fall apart. 18You say I am empowered by Satan. But if Satan is divided and fighting against himself, how can his kingdom survive? 19And if I am empowered by Satan, what about your own exorcists? They cast out demons, too, so they will condemn you for what you have said. 20But if I am casting out demons by the power of God,* then the Kingdom of God has arrived among you. 21For when a strong man like Satan is fully armed and guards his palace, his possessions are safe—22until someone even stronger attacks and overpowers him, strips him of his weapons, and carries off his belongings.

23"Anyone who isn't with me opposes me, and anyone who isn't working with me is actually working against me.

24"When an evil* spirit leaves a person, it goes into the desert, searching for rest. But when it finds none, it says, 'I will return to the person I came from.' 25So it returns and finds that its former home is all swept and in order. 26Then the spirit finds seven other spirits more evil than itself, and they all enter the person and live there. And so that person is worse off than before."

27As he was speaking, a woman in the crowd called out, "God bless your mother—the womb from which you came, and the breasts that nursed you!"

28Jesus replied, "But even more blessed are all who hear the word of God and put it into practice."

29As the crowd pressed in on Jesus, he said, "This evil generation keeps asking me to show them a miraculous sign. But the only sign I will give them is the sign of Jonah. 30What happened to him was a sign to the people of Nineveh that God had sent him. What happens to the Son of Man* will be a sign to these people that he was sent by God.

31"The queen of Sheba* will stand up against this generation on judgment day and condemn it, for she came from a distant land to hear the wisdom of Solomon. Now someone greater than Solomon is here—but you refuse to listen. ³²The people of Nineveh will also stand up against this generation on judgment day and condemn it, for they repented of their sins at the preaching of Jonah. Now someone greater than Jonah is here—but you refuse to repent.

³³"No one lights a lamp and then hides it or puts it under a basket.* Instead, a lamp is placed on a stand, where its light can be seen by all who enter the house.

³⁴"Your eye is a lamp that provides light for your body. When your eye is good, your whole body is filled with light. But when it is bad, your body is filled with darkness. ³⁵Make sure that the light you think you have is not actually darkness. ³⁶If you are filled with light, with no dark corners, then your whole life will be radiant, as though a floodlight were filling you with light."

11:15 Greek *Beelzeboul*; also in 11:18, 19. Other manuscripts read *Beezeboul*; Latin version reads *Beelzebub*. 11:20 Greek *by the finger of God.* 11:24 Greek *unclean.* 11:30 "Son of Man" is a title Jesus used for himself. 11:31 Greek *The queen of the south.* 11:33 Some manuscripts omit *or puts it under a basket.*

PSALM 77:1-20
For Jeduthun, the choir director: A psalm of Asaph.

¹ I cry out to God; yes, I shout.
    Oh, that God would listen to me!
² When I was in deep trouble,
    I searched for the Lord.
  All night long I prayed, with hands
    lifted toward heaven,
    but my soul was not comforted.
³ I think of God, and I moan,
    overwhelmed with longing for
    his help.   *Interlude*

⁴ You don't let me sleep.
    I am too distressed even to pray!
⁵ I think of the good old days,
    long since ended,
⁶ when my nights were filled with joyful
    songs.
  I search my soul and ponder the
    difference now.
⁷ Has the Lord rejected me forever?
    Will he never again be kind to me?

⁸ Is his unfailing love gone forever?
    Have his promises permanently
    failed?
⁹ Has God forgotten to be gracious?
    Has he slammed the door on his
    compassion?   *Interlude*

¹⁰ And I said, "This is my fate;
    the Most High has turned his hand
    against me."
¹¹ But then I recall all you have done,
    O LORD;
  I remember your wonderful deeds
    of long ago.
¹² They are constantly in my thoughts.
    I cannot stop thinking about your
    mighty works.

¹³ O God, your ways are holy.
    Is there any god as mighty as you?
¹⁴ You are the God of great wonders!
    You demonstrate your awesome
    power among the nations.
¹⁵ By your strong arm, you redeemed
    your people,
  the descendants of Jacob and
    Joseph.   *Interlude*

¹⁶ When the Red Sea* saw you, O God,
    its waters looked and trembled!
    The sea quaked to its very depths.
¹⁷ The clouds poured down rain;
    the thunder rumbled in the sky.
    Your arrows of lightning flashed.
¹⁸ Your thunder roared from the
    whirlwind;
  the lightning lit up the world!
    The earth trembled and shook.
¹⁹ Your road led through the sea,
    your pathway through the mighty
    waters—
  a pathway no one knew was there!
²⁰ You led your people along that road
    like a flock of sheep,
  with Moses and Aaron as their
    shepherds.

77:16 Hebrew *the waters.*

PROVERBS 12:18
Some people make cutting remarks, but the words of the wise bring healing.

DEUTERONOMY 29:1–30:20

George Santayana, a twentieth-century author, said, "Those who do not remember the past are condemned to repeat it." Moses seemed to have had that thought many centuries ago. He recounted for his people *again* the covenant of obedience they had made with God at Mount Sinai and at Moab.

¹*These are the terms of the covenant the LORD commanded Moses to make with the Israelites while they were in the land of Moab, in addition to the covenant he had made with them at Mount Sinai.*

²*Moses summoned all the Israelites and said to them, "You have seen with your own eyes everything the LORD did in the land of Egypt to Pharaoh and to all his servants and to his whole country—³all the great tests of strength, the miraculous signs, and the amazing wonders. ⁴But to this day the LORD has not given you minds that understand, nor eyes that see, nor ears that hear! ⁵For forty years I led you through the wilderness, yet your clothes and sandals did not wear out. ⁶You ate no bread and drank no wine or other alcoholic drink, but he gave you food so you would know that he is the LORD your God.

⁷"When we came here, King Sihon of Heshbon and King Og of Bashan came out to fight against us, but we defeated them. ⁸We took their land and gave it to the tribes of Reuben and Gad and to the half-tribe of Manasseh as their grant of land.

⁹"Therefore, obey the terms of this covenant so that you will prosper in everything you do. ¹⁰All of you—tribal leaders, elders, officers, all the men of Israel—are standing today in the presence of the LORD your God. ¹¹Your little ones and your wives are with you, as well as the foreigners living among you who chop your wood and carry your water. ¹²You are standing here today to enter into the covenant of the LORD your God. The LORD is making this covenant, including the curses. ¹³By entering into the covenant today, he will establish you as his people and confirm that he is your God, just as he promised you and as he swore to your ancestors Abraham, Isaac, and Jacob.

¹⁴"But you are not the only ones with whom I am making this covenant with its curses. ¹⁵I am making this covenant both with you who stand here today in the presence of the LORD our God, and also with the future generations who are not standing here today.

¹⁶"You remember how we lived in the land of Egypt and how we traveled through the lands of enemy nations as we left. ¹⁷You have seen their detestable practices and their idols* made of wood, stone, silver, and gold. ¹⁸I am making this covenant with you so that no one among you—no man, woman, clan, or tribe—will turn away from the LORD our God to worship these gods of other nations, and so that no root among you bears bitter and poisonous fruit.

¹⁹"Those who hear the warnings of this curse should not congratulate themselves, thinking, 'I am safe, even though I am following the desires of my own stubborn heart.' This would lead to utter ruin! ²⁰The LORD will never pardon such people. Instead his anger and jealousy will burn against them. All the curses written in this book will come down on them, and the LORD will erase their names from under heaven. ²¹The LORD will separate them from all the tribes of Israel, to pour out on them all the curses of the covenant recorded in this Book of Instruction.

²²"Then the generations to come, both your own descendants and the foreigners who come from distant lands, will see the devastation of the land and the diseases the LORD inflicts on it. ²³They will exclaim, 'The whole land is devastated by sulfur and salt. It is a wasteland with nothing planted and nothing growing, not even a blade of grass. It is like the cities of Sodom and Gomorrah, Admah and Zeboiim, which the LORD destroyed in his intense anger.'

²⁴"And all the surrounding nations will ask, 'Why has the LORD done this to this land? Why was he so angry?'

²⁵"And the answer will be, 'This happened because the people of the land

abandoned the covenant that the LORD, the God of their ancestors, made with them when he brought them out of the land of Egypt. [26]Instead, they turned away to serve and worship gods they had not known before, gods that were not from the LORD. [27]That is why the LORD's anger has burned against this land, bringing down on it every curse recorded in this book. [28]In great anger and fury the LORD uprooted his people from their land and banished them to another land, where they still live today!'

[29]"The LORD our God has secrets known to no one. We are not accountable for them, but we and our children are accountable forever for all that he has revealed to us, so that we may obey all the terms of these instructions.

[30:1]"IN the future, when you experience all these blessings and curses I have listed for you, and when you are living among the nations to which the LORD your God has exiled you, take to heart all these instructions. [2]If at that time you and your children return to the LORD your God, and if you obey with all your heart and all your soul all the commands I have given you today, [3]then the LORD your God will restore your fortunes. He will have mercy on you and gather you back from all the nations where he has scattered you. [4]Even though you are banished to the ends of the earth, the LORD your God will gather you from there and bring you back again. [5]The LORD your God will return you to the land that belonged to your ancestors, and you will possess that land again. Then he will make you even more prosperous and numerous than your ancestors!

[6]"The LORD your God will change your heart* and the hearts of all your descendants, so that you will love him with all your heart and soul and so you may live! [7]The LORD your God will inflict all these curses on your enemies and on those who hate and persecute you. [8]Then you will again obey the LORD and keep all his commands that I am giving you today.

[9]"The LORD your God will then make you successful in everything you do. He will give you many children and numerous livestock, and he will cause your fields

to produce abundant harvests, for the LORD will again delight in being good to you as he was to your ancestors. [10]The LORD your God will delight in you if you obey his voice and keep the commands and decrees written in this Book of Instruction, and if you turn to the LORD your God with all your heart and soul.

[11]"This command I am giving you today is not too difficult for you to understand, and it is not beyond your reach. [12]It is not kept in heaven, so distant that you must ask, 'Who will go up to heaven and bring it down so we can hear it and obey?' [13]It is not kept beyond the sea, so far away that you must ask, 'Who will cross the sea to bring it to us so we can hear it and obey?' [14]No, the message is very close at hand; it is on your lips and in your heart so that you can obey it.

[15]"Now listen! Today I am giving you a choice between life and death, between prosperity and disaster. [16]For I command you this day to love the LORD your God and to keep his commands, decrees, and regulations by walking in his ways. If you do this, you will live and multiply, and the LORD your God will bless you and the land you are about to enter and occupy.

[17]"But if your heart turns away and you refuse to listen, and if you are drawn away to serve and worship other gods, [18]then I warn you now that you will certainly be destroyed. You will not live a long, good life in the land you are crossing the Jordan to occupy.

[19]"Today I have given you the choice between life and death, between blessings and curses. Now I call on heaven and earth to witness the choice you make. Oh, that you would choose life, so that you and your descendants might live! [20]You can make this choice by loving the LORD your God, obeying him, and committing yourself firmly to him. This* is the key to your life. And if you love and obey the LORD, you will live long in the land the LORD swore to give your ancestors Abraham, Isaac, and Jacob."

29:1a Verse 29:1 is numbered 28:69 in Hebrew text.
29:1b Hebrew *Horeb,* another name for Sinai.   29:2 Verses 29:2-29 are numbered 29:1-28 in Hebrew text.   29:17 The Hebrew term (literally *round things*) probably alludes to dung.   30:6 Hebrew *circumcise your heart.*   30:20 Or *He.*

LUKE 11:37–12:7

Jesus confronted the pride and pretension of the Pharisees. He warned his followers not to fall into the Pharisees' hypocritical ways.

As Jesus was speaking, one of the Pharisees invited him home for a meal. So he went in and took his place at the table.* ³⁸His host was amazed to see that he sat down to eat without first performing the hand-washing ceremony required by Jewish custom. ³⁹Then the Lord said to him, "You Pharisees are so careful to clean the outside of the cup and the dish, but inside you are filthy—full of greed and wickedness! ⁴⁰Fools! Didn't God make the inside as well as the outside? ⁴¹So clean the inside by giving gifts to the poor, and you will be clean all over.

⁴²"What sorrow awaits you Pharisees! For you are careful to tithe even the tiniest income from your herb gardens,* but you ignore justice and the love of God. You should tithe, yes, but do not neglect the more important things.

⁴³"What sorrow awaits you Pharisees! For you love to sit in the seats of honor in the synagogues and receive respectful greetings as you walk in the marketplaces. ⁴⁴Yes, what sorrow awaits you! For you are like hidden graves in a field. People walk over them without knowing the corruption they are stepping on."

⁴⁵"Teacher," said an expert in religious law, "you have insulted us, too, in what you just said."

⁴⁶"Yes," said Jesus, "what sorrow also awaits you experts in religious law! For you crush people with unbearable religious demands, and you never lift a finger to ease the burden. ⁴⁷What sorrow awaits you! For you build monuments for the prophets your own ancestors killed long ago. ⁴⁸But in fact, you stand as witnesses who agree with what your ancestors did. They killed the prophets, and you join in their crime by building the monuments! ⁴⁹This is what God in his wisdom said about you:* 'I will send prophets and apostles to them, but they will kill some and persecute the others.'

⁵⁰"As a result, this generation will be held responsible for the murder of all God's prophets from the creation of the world—⁵¹from the murder of Abel to the murder of Zechariah, who was killed between the altar and the sanctuary. Yes, it will certainly be charged against this generation.

⁵²"What sorrow awaits you experts in religious law! For you remove the key to knowledge from the people. You don't enter the Kingdom yourselves, and you prevent others from entering."

⁵³As Jesus was leaving, the teachers of religious law and the Pharisees became hostile and tried to provoke him with many questions. ⁵⁴They wanted to trap him into saying something they could use against him.

¹²:¹MEANWHILE, the crowds grew until thousands were milling about and stepping on each other. Jesus turned first to his disciples and warned them, "Beware of the yeast of the Pharisees—their hypocrisy. ²The time is coming when everything that is covered up will be revealed, and all that is secret will be made known to all. ³Whatever you have said in the dark will be heard in the light, and what you have whispered behind closed doors will be shouted from the housetops for all to hear!

⁴"Dear friends, don't be afraid of those who want to kill your body; they cannot do any more to you after that. ⁵But I'll tell you whom to fear. Fear God, who has the power to kill you and then throw you into hell.* Yes, he's the one to fear.

⁶"What is the price of five sparrows—two copper coins*? Yet God does not forget a single one of them. ⁷And the very hairs on your head are all numbered. So don't be afraid; you are more valuable to God than a whole flock of sparrows."

11:37 Or *and reclined.* 11:42 Greek *tithe the mint, the rue, and every herb.* 11:49 Greek *Therefore, the wisdom of God said.* 12:5 Greek *Gehenna.* 12:6 Greek *two assaria* [Roman coins equal to ¹⁄₁₆ of a denarius].

PSALM 78:1-31
A psalm of Asaph.*

¹ **O** my people, listen to my instructions.
  Open your ears to what I am saying,
² for I will speak to you in a parable.
  I will teach you hidden lessons from
    our past—

³ stories we have heard and known,
   stories our ancestors handed down
      to us.
⁴ We will not hide these truths from our
      children;
   we will tell the next generation
about the glorious deeds of the LORD,
   about his power and his mighty
      wonders.
⁵ For he issued his laws to Jacob;
   he gave his instructions to Israel.
He commanded our ancestors
   to teach them to their children,
⁶ so the next generation might know
      them—
   even the children not yet born—
and they in turn will teach their
   own children.
⁷ So each generation should set its hope
      anew on God,
   not forgetting his glorious miracles
and obeying his commands.
⁸ Then they will not be like their
      ancestors—
   stubborn, rebellious, and
      unfaithful,
refusing to give their hearts
   to God.

⁹ The warriors of Ephraim, though
      armed with bows,
   turned their backs and fled on the
      day of battle.

¹⁰ They did not keep God's covenant
    and refused to live by his
       instructions.
¹¹ They forgot what he had done—
    the great wonders he had shown
       them,
¹² the miracles he did for their ancestors
    on the plain of Zoan in the land of
       Egypt.
¹³ For he divided the sea and led them
       through,
    making the water stand up like
       walls!
¹⁴ In the daytime he led them by a cloud,
    and all night by a pillar of fire.
¹⁵ He split open the rocks in the
       wilderness
    to give them water, as from a
       gushing spring.
¹⁶ He made streams pour from the rock,
    making the waters flow down like
       a river!

¹⁷ Yet they kept on sinning against him,
    rebelling against the Most High in
       the desert.
¹⁸ They stubbornly tested God in their
       hearts,
    demanding the foods they craved.
¹⁹ They even spoke against God himself,
       saying,
    "God can't give us food in the
       wilderness."

WHAT THE BIBLE SAYS

Sin and its consequences

DEUTERONOMY 30:19 Christians have been saved from the ultimate effect of sin—eternal separation from God. However, sin still presents problems that must be addressed. It can separate you from the blessings God has for you, and, worse, it can disrupt your fellowship with God himself. Moses here reminded this new generation of Israelites that, even though their parents had turned their backs on God, they could have a fresh start. God would bless them if they would turn from sin and choose to obey him.   • Just as he did for the Hebrew nation, God sets before you the choices each day of obedience or disobedience. And he challenges you to turn away from sin and to obey.   • Your obedience will be imperfect. You will make wrong choices. You will sin. But God is merciful. He wants to forgive you and bring you back into fellowship with himself. Always come to God and ask for his forgiveness. He promises to give it. Then seek to learn a lesson from your sin and move on. Determine that next time you will choose to obey instead.

20 Yes, he can strike a rock so water
        gushes out,
    but he can't give his people bread
        and meat."
21 When the LORD heard them, he was
        furious.
    The fire of his wrath burned
        against Jacob.
    Yes, his anger rose against
        Israel,
22 for they did not believe God
    or trust him to care for them.
23 But he commanded the skies
        to open;
    he opened the doors of heaven.
24 He rained down manna for them
        to eat;
    he gave them bread from heaven.
25 They ate the food of angels!
    God gave them all they could hold.
26 He released the east wind in the
        heavens
    and guided the south wind by his
        mighty power.

27 He rained down meat as thick
        as dust—
    birds as plentiful as the sand on the
        seashore!
28 He caused the birds to fall within their
        camp
    and all around their tents.
29 The people ate their fill.
    He gave them what they craved.
30 But before they satisfied their craving,
    while the meat was yet in their
        mouths,
31 the anger of God rose against them,
    and he killed their strongest men.
    He struck down the finest of Israel's
        young men.

78:TITLE Hebrew *maskil*. This may be a literary or musical term.

PROVERBS 12:19-20

Truthful words stand the test of time, but lies are soon exposed. □ Deceit fills hearts that are plotting evil; joy fills hearts that are planning peace!

APRIL**7**

DEUTERONOMY 31:1-32:27

Moses gave his people a new leader, and with that leader came hope of a new day. Sin, however, could still frustrate God's desire to bless them.

When Moses had finished giving these instructions* to all the people of Israel, ²he said, "I am now 120 years old, and I am no longer able to lead you. The LORD has told me, 'You will not cross the Jordan River.' ³But the LORD your God himself will cross over ahead of you. He will destroy the nations living there, and you will take possession of their land. Joshua will lead you across the river, just as the LORD promised.

⁴"The LORD will destroy the nations living in the land, just as he destroyed Sihon and Og, the kings of the Amorites. ⁵The LORD will hand over to you the people who live there, and you must deal with them as I have commanded you. ⁶So be strong and courageous! Do not be afraid and do not panic before them. For the LORD your God will personally go ahead of you. He will neither fail you nor abandon you."

⁷Then Moses called for Joshua, and as all Israel watched, he said to him, "Be strong and courageous! For you will lead these people into the land that the LORD swore to their ancestors he would give them. You are the one who will divide it among them as their grants of land. ⁸Do not be afraid or discouraged, for the LORD will personally go ahead of you. He will be with you; he will neither fail you nor abandon you."

⁹So Moses wrote this entire body of instruction in a book and gave it to the priests, who carried the Ark of the LORD's Covenant, and to the elders of Israel. ¹⁰Then Moses gave them this command:

"At the end of every seventh year, the Year of Release, during the Festival of Shelters, [11] you must read this Book of Instruction to all the people of Israel when they assemble before the LORD your God at the place he chooses. [12] Call them all together—men, women, children, and the foreigners living in your towns—so they may hear this Book of Instruction and learn to fear the LORD your God and carefully obey all the terms of these instructions. [13] Do this so that your children who have not known these instructions will hear them and will learn to fear the LORD your God. Do this as long as you live in the land you are crossing the Jordan to occupy."

[14] Then the LORD said to Moses, "The time has come for you to die. Call Joshua and present yourselves at the Tabernacle,* so that I may commission him there." So Moses and Joshua went and presented themselves at the Tabernacle. [15] And the LORD appeared to them in a pillar of cloud that stood at the entrance to the sacred tent.

[16] The LORD said to Moses, "You are about to die and join your ancestors. After you are gone, these people will begin to worship foreign gods, the gods of the land where they are going. They will abandon me and break my covenant that I have made with them. [17] Then my anger will blaze forth against them. I will abandon them, hiding my face from them, and they will be devoured. Terrible trouble will come down on them, and on that day they will say, 'These disasters have come down on us because God is no longer among us!' [18] At that time I will hide my face from them on account of all the evil they commit by worshiping other gods.

[19] "So write down the words of this song, and teach it to the people of Israel. Help them learn it, so it may serve as a witness for me against them. [20] For I will bring them into the land I swore to give their ancestors—a land flowing with milk and honey. There they will become prosperous, eat all the food they want, and become fat. But they will begin to worship other gods; they will despise me and break my covenant. [21] And when great disasters come down on them, this song will stand as evidence against them, for it will never be forgotten by their descendants. I know the intentions of these people, even now before they have entered the land I swore to give them."

[22] So that very day Moses wrote down the words of the song and taught it to the Israelites.

[23] Then the LORD commissioned Joshua son of Nun with these words: "Be strong and courageous, for you must bring the people of Israel into the land I swore to give them. I will be with you."

[24] When Moses had finished writing this entire body of instruction in a book, [25] he gave this command to the Levites who carried the Ark of the LORD's Covenant: [26] "Take this Book of Instruction and place it beside the Ark of the Covenant of the LORD your God, so it may remain there as a witness against the people of Israel. [27] For I know how rebellious and stubborn you are. Even now, while I am still alive and am here with you, you have rebelled against the LORD. How much more rebellious will you be after my death!

[28] "Now summon all the elders and officials of your tribes, so that I can speak to them directly and call heaven and earth to witness against them. [29] I know that after my death you will become utterly corrupt and will turn from the way I have commanded you to follow. In the days to come, disaster will come down on you, for you will do what is evil in the LORD's sight, making him very angry with your actions."

[30] So Moses recited this entire song publicly to the assembly of Israel:

32:1 "LISTEN, O heavens, and I will speak!
 Hear, O earth, the words that I say!
[2] Let my teaching fall on you like rain;
 let my speech settle like dew.
Let my words fall like rain on tender
  grass,
 like gentle showers on young
  plants.
[3] I will proclaim the name of the LORD;
 how glorious is our God!
[4] He is the Rock; his deeds are perfect.
 Everything he does is just and fair.
He is a faithful God who does no
  wrong;
 how just and upright he is!

5 "But they have acted corruptly toward
him;
  when they act so perversely,
are they really his children?*
  They are a deceitful and twisted
  generation.

6 Is this the way you repay the LORD,
  you foolish and senseless people?
Isn't he your Father who created you?
  Has he not made you and
  established you?

7 Remember the days of long ago;
  think about the generations past.
Ask your father, and he will inform
  you.
  Inquire of your elders, and they will
  tell you.

8 When the Most High assigned lands
  to the nations,
  when he divided up the human race,
he established the boundaries of the
  peoples
  according to the number in his
  heavenly court.*

9 "For the people of Israel belong to
  the LORD;
  Jacob is his special possession.

10 He found them in a desert land,
  in an empty, howling wasteland.
He surrounded them and watched
  over them;
  he guarded them as he would guard
  his own eyes.*

11 Like an eagle that rouses her chicks
  and hovers over her young,
so he spread his wings to take them up
  and carried them safely on his
  pinions.

12 The LORD alone guided them;
  they followed no foreign gods.

13 He let them ride over the highlands
  and feast on the crops of the fields.
He nourished them with honey from
  the rock
  and olive oil from the stony ground.

14 He fed them yogurt from the herd
  and milk from the flock,
  together with the fat of lambs.
He gave them choice rams from
  Bashan, and goats,
  together with the choicest wheat.
You drank the finest wine,
  made from the juice of grapes.

15 "But Israel* soon became fat and
  unruly;
  the people grew heavy, plump, and
  stuffed!
Then they abandoned the God who
  had made them;
  they made light of the Rock of their
  salvation.

16 They stirred up his jealousy by
  worshiping foreign gods;
  they provoked his fury with
  detestable deeds.

17 They offered sacrifices to demons,
  which are not God,
  to gods they had not known before,
to new gods only recently arrived,
  to gods their ancestors had never
  feared.

18 You neglected the Rock who had
  fathered you;
  you forgot the God who had given
  you birth.

19 "The LORD saw this and drew back,
  provoked to anger by his own sons
  and daughters.

20 He said, 'I will abandon them;
  then see what becomes of them.
For they are a twisted generation,
  children without integrity.

21 They have roused my jealousy by
  worshiping things that are not
  God;
  they have provoked my anger with
  their useless idols.
Now I will rouse their jealousy
  through people who are not even
  a people;
  I will provoke their anger through
  the foolish Gentiles.

22 For my anger blazes forth like fire
  and burns to the depths of the
  grave.*
It devours the earth and all its crops
  and ignites the foundations of the
  mountains.

23 I will heap disasters upon them
  and shoot them down with my
  arrows.

24 I will weaken them with famine,
  burning fever, and deadly disease.
I will send the fangs of wild beasts
  and poisonous snakes that glide
  in the dust.

²⁵ Outside, the sword will bring death,
and inside, terror will strike
both young men and young women,
both infants and the aged.
²⁶ I would have annihilated them,
wiping out even the memory
of them.
²⁷ But I feared the taunt of Israel's enemy,
who might misunderstand and say,
"Our own power has triumphed!
The LORD had nothing to do with
this!"'"

31:1 As in Dead Sea Scrolls and Greek version; Masoretic Text reads *Moses went and spoke.* **31:14** Hebrew *Tent of Meeting;* also in 31:14b. **32:5** The meaning of the Hebrew is uncertain. **32:8** As in Dead Sea Scrolls, which read *the number of the sons of God,* and Greek version, which reads *the number of the angels of God;* Masoretic Text reads *the number of the sons of Israel.* **32:10** Hebrew *as the pupil of his eye.* **32:15** Hebrew *Jeshurun,* a term of endearment for Israel. **32:22** Hebrew *of Sheol.*

LUKE 12:8-34

Things. Money. Stuff. Wealth. So much of our time is spent getting and managing these elements of our lives. Jesus showed his disciples what makes for true wealth.

"I tell you the truth, everyone who acknowledges me publicly here on earth, the Son of Man* will also acknowledge in the presence of God's angels. ⁹But anyone who denies me here on earth will be denied before God's angels. ¹⁰Anyone who speaks against the Son of Man can be for-

given, but anyone who blasphemes the Holy Spirit will not be forgiven.

¹¹"And when you are brought to trial in the synagogues and before rulers and authorities, don't worry about how to defend yourself or what to say, ¹²for the Holy Spirit will teach you at that time what needs to be said."

¹³Then someone called from the crowd, "Teacher, please tell my brother to divide our father's estate with me."

¹⁴Jesus replied, "Friend, who made me a judge over you to decide such things as that?" ¹⁵Then he said, "Beware! Guard against every kind of greed. Life is not measured by how much you own."

¹⁶Then he told them a story: "A rich man had a fertile farm that produced fine crops. ¹⁷He said to himself, 'What should I do? I don't have room for all my crops.' ¹⁸Then he said, 'I know! I'll tear down my barns and build bigger ones. Then I'll have room enough to store all my wheat and other goods. ¹⁹And I'll sit back and say to myself, "My friend, you have enough stored away for years to come. Now take it easy! Eat, drink, and be merry!"'

²⁰"But God said to him, 'You fool! You will die this very night. Then who will get everything you worked for?'

²¹"Yes, a person is a fool to store up earthly wealth but not have a rich relationship with God."

HOW WE LIVE

Our work

LUKE 12:15-21 Jesus' words in this story are a direct contradiction to what the world says. The world tells you to work hard so that you can accumulate lots of money so that you can one day retire and finally enjoy yourself. However, like the man in the story, you don't know when you will die and stand before God. At that moment, whatever wealth you have accumulated on earth will have no bearing on eternity. • Working hard and being responsible at your job are honoring to God. Knowing when and how you can retire can bring a certain peace of mind, but working hard only to accumulate money so that you can hoard it for yourself is disastrous. Are you working only to enlarge your bank account, or are you working so that you can share what God provides through your job in order to further his Kingdom? • Don't be like the rich man in the story. Plan for the future, but also show your gratefulness to God by sharing your income to build God's eternal Kingdom. When you do that, you will have "a rich relationship with God" (12:21). And that lasts forever.

²²Then, turning to his disciples, Jesus said, "That is why I tell you not to worry about everyday life—whether you have enough food to eat or enough clothes to wear. ²³For life is more than food, and your body more than clothing. ²⁴Look at the ravens. They don't plant or harvest or store food in barns, for God feeds them. And you are far more valuable to him than any birds! ²⁵Can all your worries add a single moment to your life? ²⁶And if worry can't accomplish a little thing like that, what's the use of worrying over bigger things?

²⁷"Look at the lilies and how they grow. They don't work or make their clothing, yet Solomon in all his glory was not dressed as beautifully as they are. ²⁸And if God cares so wonderfully for flowers that are here today and thrown into the fire tomorrow, he will certainly care for you. Why do you have so little faith?

²⁹"And don't be concerned about what to eat and what to drink. Don't worry about such things. ³⁰These things dominate the thoughts of unbelievers all over the world, but your Father already knows your needs. ³¹Seek the Kingdom of God above all else, and he will give you everything you need.

³²"So don't be afraid, little flock. For it gives your Father great happiness to give you the Kingdom.

³³"Sell your possessions and give to those in need. This will store up treasure for you in heaven! And the purses of heaven never get old or develop holes. Your treasure will be safe; no thief can steal it and no moth can destroy it. ³⁴Wherever your treasure is, there the desires of your heart will also be."

12:8 "Son of Man" is a title Jesus used for himself.

PSALM 78:32-55

But in spite of this, the people kept sinning.
Despite his wonders, they refused to trust him.
³³ So he ended their lives in failure, their years in terror.
³⁴ When God began killing them, they finally sought him.
They repented and took God seriously.

³⁵ Then they remembered that God was their rock,
that God Most High* was their redeemer.
³⁶ But all they gave him was lip service; they lied to him with their tongues.
³⁷ Their hearts were not loyal to him. They did not keep his covenant.
³⁸ Yet he was merciful and forgave their sins
and did not destroy them all.
Many times he held back his anger and did not unleash his fury!
³⁹ For he remembered that they were merely mortal,
gone like a breath of wind that never returns.

⁴⁰ Oh, how often they rebelled against him in the wilderness
and grieved his heart in that dry wasteland.
⁴¹ Again and again they tested God's patience
and provoked the Holy One of Israel.
⁴² They did not remember his power and how he rescued them from their enemies.
⁴³ They did not remember his miraculous signs in Egypt,
his wonders on the plain of Zoan.
⁴⁴ For he turned their rivers into blood, so no one could drink from the streams.
⁴⁵ He sent vast swarms of flies to consume them
and hordes of frogs to ruin them.
⁴⁶ He gave their crops to caterpillars; their harvest was consumed by locusts.
⁴⁷ He destroyed their grapevines with hail
and shattered their sycamore-figs with sleet.
⁴⁸ He abandoned their cattle to the hail, their livestock to bolts of lightning.
⁴⁹ He loosed on them his fierce anger— all his fury, rage, and hostility.
He dispatched against them a band of destroying angels.
⁵⁰ He turned his anger against them; he did not spare the Egyptians' lives
but ravaged them with the plague.

51 He killed the oldest son in each
        Egyptian family,
    the flower of youth throughout the
        land of Egypt.*
52 But he led his own people like a flock
        of sheep,
    guiding them safely through the
        wilderness.
53 He kept them safe so they were not
        afraid;
    but the sea covered their enemies.
54 He brought them to the border of his
        holy land,
    to this land of hills he had won for
        them.

55 He drove out the nations before them;
    he gave them their inheritance by
        lot.
    He settled the tribes of Israel into
        their homes.

78:35 Hebrew *El-Elyon.*   **78:51** Hebrew *in the tents of Ham.*

PROVERBS 12:21-23
No harm comes to the godly, but the
wicked have their fill of trouble. □ The
LORD detests lying lips, but he delights in
those who tell the truth. □ The wise don't
make a show of their knowledge, but fools
broadcast their foolishness.

APRIL8

DEUTERONOMY 32:28-52
Moses continued his song of faith by reminding the
people of God's place in their history as well as in
their future. Then he faced some difficult realities
of his own. He had served God well, but because of
one important failure, he himself could not enter
the land.

   "**B**ut Israel is a senseless nation;
        the people are foolish, without
        understanding.
29 Oh, that they were wise and could
        understand this!
    Oh, that they might know their
        fate!
30 How could one person chase a
        thousand of them,
    and two people put ten thousand to
        flight,
    unless their Rock had sold them,
    unless the LORD had given them up?
31 But the rock of our enemies is not like
        our Rock,
    as even they recognize.*
32 Their vine grows from the vine of
        Sodom,
    from the vineyards of Gomorrah.
    Their grapes are poison,
    and their clusters are bitter.
33 Their wine is the venom of serpents,
    the deadly poison of cobras.

34 "The LORD says, 'Am I not storing up
        these things,
    sealing them away in my
        treasury?
35 I will take revenge; I will pay them
        back.
    In due time their feet will slip.
    Their day of disaster will arrive,
    and their destiny will overtake
        them.'

36 "Indeed, the LORD will give justice to
        his people,
    and he will change his mind about*
        his servants,
    when he sees their strength is gone
    and no one is left, slave or free.
37 Then he will ask, 'Where are their
        gods,
    the rocks they fled to for refuge?
38 Where now are those gods,
    who ate the fat of their sacrifices
    and drank the wine of their
        offerings?
    Let those gods arise and help you!
    Let them provide you with shelter!
39 Look now; I myself am he!
    There is no other god but me!
    I am the one who kills and gives life;
    I am the one who wounds and heals;

no one can be rescued from my
powerful hand!
⁴⁰ Now I raise my hand to heaven
and declare, "As surely as I live,
⁴¹ when I sharpen my flashing sword
and begin to carry out justice,
I will take revenge on my enemies
and repay those who reject me.
⁴² I will make my arrows drunk with
blood,
and my sword will devour flesh—
the blood of the slaughtered and the
captives,
and the heads of the enemy
leaders.'"

⁴³ "Rejoice with him, you heavens,
and let all of God's angels worship
him.*
Rejoice with his people, you nations,
and let all the angels be
strengthened in him.*
For he will avenge the blood of his
servants;
he will take revenge against his
enemies.
He will repay those who hate him*
and cleanse the land for his
people."

⁴⁴So Moses came with Joshua* son of
Nun and recited all the words of this song
to the people.

⁴⁵When Moses had finished reciting
all these words to the people of Israel,
⁴⁶he added: "Take to heart all the words of
warning I have given you today. Pass them
on as a command to your children so they
will obey every word of these instructions. ⁴⁷These instructions are not empty
words—they are your life! By obeying
them you will enjoy a long life in the land
you will occupy when you cross the Jordan River."

⁴⁸That same day the LORD said to
Moses, ⁴⁹"Go to Moab, to the mountains
east of the river,* and climb Mount Nebo,
which is across from Jericho. Look out
across the land of Canaan, the land I am
giving to the people of Israel as their own
special possession. ⁵⁰Then you will die
there on the mountain. You will join your
ancestors, just as Aaron, your brother,
died on Mount Hor and joined his ancestors. ⁵¹For both of you betrayed me with

the Israelites at the waters of Meribah at
Kadesh* in the wilderness of Zin. You
failed to demonstrate my holiness to the
people of Israel there. ⁵²So you will see
the land from a distance, but you may not
enter the land I am giving to the people of
Israel."

32:31 The meaning of the Hebrew is uncertain. Greek
version reads *our enemies are fools.* 32:36 Or *will take
revenge for.* 32:43a As in Dead Sea Scrolls and Greek
version; Masoretic Text lacks the first two lines. Compare
Heb 1:6. 32:43b As in Greek version; Hebrew text lacks
this line. 32:43c As in Dead Sea Scrolls and Greek version;
Masoretic Text lacks this line. 32:44 Hebrew *Hoshea,* a
variant name for Joshua. 32:49 Hebrew *the mountains
of Abarim.* 32:51 Hebrew *waters of Meribath-kadesh.*

LUKE 12:35-59
Jesus' message constantly caused conflict. He
came to make peace between God and us, but
when his truth was inserted into a less-than-truthful
culture, the results were less than peaceful.

"**B**e dressed for service and keep your
lamps burning, ³⁶as though you were
waiting for your master to return from the
wedding feast. Then you will be ready to
open the door and let him in the moment
he arrives and knocks. ³⁷The servants
who are ready and waiting for his return
will be rewarded. I tell you the truth, he
himself will seat them, put on an apron,
and serve them as they sit and eat! ³⁸He
may come in the middle of the night or
just before dawn.* But whenever he
comes, he will reward the servants who
are ready.

³⁹"Understand this: If a homeowner
knew exactly when a burglar was coming,
he would not permit his house to be broken into. ⁴⁰You also must be ready all the
time, for the Son of Man will come when
least expected."

⁴¹Peter asked, "Lord, is that illustration
just for us or for everyone?"

⁴²And the Lord replied, "A faithful, sensible servant is one to whom the master
can give the responsibility of managing
his other household servants and feeding
them. ⁴³If the master returns and finds
that the servant has done a good job, there
will be a reward. ⁴⁴I tell you the truth, the
master will put that servant in charge of
all he owns. ⁴⁵But what if the servant
thinks, 'My master won't be back for a
while,' and he begins beating the other
servants, partying, and getting drunk?

[46]The master will return unannounced and unexpected, and he will cut the servant in pieces and banish him with the unfaithful.

[47]"And a servant who knows what the master wants, but isn't prepared and doesn't carry out those instructions, will be severely punished. [48]But someone who does not know, and then does something wrong, will be punished only lightly. When someone has been given much, much will be required in return; and when someone has been entrusted with much, even more will be required.

[49]"I have come to set the world on fire, and I wish it were already burning! [50]I have a terrible baptism of suffering ahead of me, and I am under a heavy burden until it is accomplished. [51]Do you think I have come to bring peace to the earth? No, I have come to divide people against each other! [52]From now on families will be split apart, three in favor of me, and two against—or two in favor and three against.

[53] 'Father will be divided against son
    and son against father;
mother against daughter
    and daughter against mother;
and mother-in-law against daughter-
    in-law
and daughter-in-law against
    mother-in-law.'*"

[54]Then Jesus turned to the crowd and said, "When you see clouds beginning to form in the west, you say, 'Here comes a shower.' And you are right. [55]When the south wind blows, you say, 'Today will be a scorcher.' And it is. [56]You fools! You know how to interpret the weather signs of the earth and sky, but you don't know how to interpret the present times.

[57]"Why can't you decide for yourselves what is right? [58]When you are on the way to court with your accuser, try to settle the matter before you get there. Otherwise, your accuser may drag you before the judge, who will hand you over to an officer, who will throw you into prison. [59]And if that happens, you won't be free again until you have paid the very last penny.*"

12:38 Greek *in the second or third watch.*   12:53 Mic 7:6.
12:59 Greek *last lepton* [the smallest Jewish coin].

PSALM 78:56-64
But they kept testing and rebelling
    against God Most High.
They did not obey his laws.
[57] They turned back and were as
    faithless as their parents.

HOW WE LIVE: Accountability to others**LUKE 12:48** When you became a Christian, not only did you obtain the gift of eternal life, but you were given a great responsibility. You have been entrusted with the message of the gospel and are responsible for what you do with it in your life. • According to 12:48, you will be held accountable for what you know. As a new believer, you will constantly be learning new things. You will learn more about God as you read his Word, attend church, and talk with other believers. The more you learn and the more mature you become, the more God will grant you responsibilities in his Kingdom. And he expects you to use your responsibilities wisely. • In the end, all that you have done on this earth will be examined before God. Ultimately, you will be accountable to God for what you did with the responsibilities he gave you. This need not make you fearful; instead, be excited about what God wants to do through you. Your attitude should be like Paul's, who wrote, "For we speak as messengers approved by God to be entrusted with the Good News. Our purpose is to please God, not people. He alone examines the motives of our hearts" (1 Thessalonians 2:4, October 9).

They were as undependable as a
crooked bow.

⁵⁸ They angered God by building shrines
to other gods;
they made him jealous with their
idols.
⁵⁹ When God heard them, he was very
angry,
and he completely rejected Israel.
⁶⁰ Then he abandoned his dwelling at
Shiloh,
the Tabernacle where he had lived
among the people.
⁶¹ He allowed the Ark of his might to be
captured;
he surrendered his glory into
enemy hands.

APRIL**9**

DEUTERONOMY 33:1-29

The people were about to conquer the Promised
Land, and Moses was about to die. Moses
gave each tribe a blessing as his final words.
These blessings serve both as prophecies and
warnings.

This is the blessing that Moses, the man of
God, gave to the people of Israel before his
death:

² "The LORD came from Mount Sinai
and dawned upon us* from Mount
Seir;
he shone forth from Mount Paran
and came from Meribah-kadesh
with flaming fire at his right
hand.*
³ Indeed, he loves his people;*
all his holy ones are in his
hands.
They follow in his steps
and accept his teaching.
⁴ Moses gave us the LORD's instruction,
the special possession of the people
of Israel.*
⁵ The LORD became king in Israel*—
when the leaders of the people
assembled,
when the tribes of Israel gathered
as one."

⁶² He gave his people over to be
butchered by the sword,
because he was so angry with his
own people—his special
possession.
⁶³ Their young men were killed by
fire;
their young women died
before singing their wedding
songs.
⁶⁴ Their priests were slaughtered,
and their widows could not mourn
their deaths.

PROVERBS 12:24

Work hard and become a leader; be lazy
and become a slave.

⁶Moses said this about the tribe of Reuben:*

"Let the tribe of Reuben live and not
die out,
though they are few in number."

⁷ Moses said this about the tribe of
Judah:

"O LORD, hear the cry of Judah
and bring them together as a
people.
Give them strength to defend their
cause;
help them against their enemies!"

⁸Moses said this about the tribe of Levi:

"O LORD, you have given your
Thummim and Urim—the sacred
lots—
to your faithful servants the
Levites.*
You put them to the test at Massah
and struggled with them at the
waters of Meribah.
⁹ The Levites obeyed your word
and guarded your covenant.
They were more loyal to you
than to their own parents.
They ignored their relatives

and did not acknowledge their
own children.
¹⁰ They teach your regulations to
Jacob;
they give your instructions to
Israel.
They present incense before you
and offer whole burnt offerings on
the altar.
¹¹ Bless the ministry of the Levites,
O LORD,
and accept all the work of their
hands.
Hit their enemies where it hurts the
most;
strike down their foes so they never
rise again."

¹²Moses said this about the tribe of Benjamin:

"The people of Benjamin are loved by
the LORD
and live in safety beside him.
He surrounds them continuously
and preserves them from every
harm."

¹³Moses said this about the tribes of Joseph:

"May their land be blessed by the
LORD
with the precious gift of dew from
the heavens

and water from beneath the earth;
¹⁴ with the rich fruit that grows in the
sun,
and the rich harvest produced each
month;
¹⁵ with the finest crops of the ancient
mountains,
and the abundance from the
everlasting hills;
¹⁶ with the best gifts of the earth and its
bounty,
and the favor of the one who
appeared in the burning bush.
May these blessings rest on Joseph's
head,
crowning the brow of the prince
among his brothers.
¹⁷ Joseph has the majesty of a young
bull;
he has the horns of a wild ox.
He will gore distant nations,
driving them to the ends of the
earth.
This is my blessing for the multitudes
of Ephraim
and the thousands of Manasseh."

¹⁸Moses said this about the tribes of Zebulun and Issachar*:

"May the people of Zebulun prosper in
their travels.
May the people of Issachar prosper
at home in their tents.

The Kingdom of God

WHAT THE BIBLE SAYS

LUKE 13:18-21 At his trial, Jesus told Pilate, "My Kingdom is not an earthly
kingdom" (John 18:36, May 30). When Jesus talked about the Kingdom
of God, he was describing a spiritual Kingdom that would begin in the
hearts of his followers and continue for all eternity in heaven. Before he
returned to heaven, Jesus left the Holy Spirit to live in the hearts of his
followers and give us a glimpse of God's Kingdom here and now. •In
these verses, Jesus compared his Kingdom to a small mustard seed that
grows into a large plant. His Kingdom starts out small (just a few followers), but will continue to grow until it covers the world and provides shelter and peace for many. Jesus also compared the Kingdom to yeast.
Although the amount of yeast is small in proportion to the flour, the
yeast permeates every part of the dough. Likewise, the Kingdom of
God will affect everything it touches.

¹⁹ They summon the people to the
mountain
to offer proper sacrifices there.
They benefit from the riches of the sea
and the hidden treasures in the
sand."

²⁰Moses said this about the tribe of Gad:

"Blessed is the one who enlarges Gad's
territory!
Gad is poised there like a lion
to tear off an arm or a head.
²¹ The people of Gad took the best land
for themselves;
a leader's share was assigned to
them.
When the leaders of the people were
assembled,
they carried out the LORD's justice
and obeyed his regulations for
Israel."

²²Moses said this about the tribe of Dan:

"Dan is a lion's cub,
leaping out from Bashan."

²³Moses said this about the tribe of Naphtali:

"O Naphtali, you are rich in favor
and full of the LORD's blessings;
may you possess the west and the
south."

²⁴Moses said this about the tribe of Asher:

"May Asher be blessed above other
sons;
may he be esteemed by his brothers;
may he bathe his feet in olive oil.
²⁵ May the bolts of your gates be of iron
and bronze;
may you be secure all your days."

²⁶ "There is no one like the God of
Israel.*
He rides across the heavens to help
you,
across the skies in majestic
splendor.
²⁷ The eternal God is your refuge,
and his everlasting arms are under
you.
He drives out the enemy before you;
he cries out, 'Destroy them!'
²⁸ So Israel will live in safety,

prosperous Jacob in security,
in a land of grain and new wine,
while the heavens drop down dew.
²⁹ How blessed you are, O Israel!
Who else is like you, a people saved
by the LORD?
He is your protecting shield
and your triumphant sword!
Your enemies will cringe before you,
and you will stomp on their backs!"

33:2a As in Greek and Syriac versions; Hebrew reads *upon
them.* 33:2b Or *came from myriads of holy ones, from the
south, from his mountain slopes.* The meaning of the Hebrew
is uncertain. 33:3 As in Greek version; Hebrew reads
Indeed, lover of the peoples. 33:4 Hebrew *of Jacob.* The
names "Jacob" and "Israel" are often interchanged throughout
the Old Testament, referring sometimes to the individual
patriarch and sometimes to the nation. 33:5 Hebrew *in
Jeshurun,* a term of endearment for Israel. 33:6 Hebrew
lacks *Moses said this about the tribe of Reuben.* 33:8 As in
Greek version; Hebrew lacks *the Levites.* 33:18 Hebrew
lacks *and Issachar.* 33:26 Hebrew *of Jeshurun,* a term of
endearment for Israel.

LUKE 13:1-21
Jesus was all about life—abundant life, fulfilling life,
eternal life. He knew God's true intent behind laws
like the Sabbath regulations. Healing wasn't the
kind of "work" from which people had to refrain.

About this time Jesus was informed that
Pilate had murdered some people from
Galilee as they were offering sacrifices at
the Temple. ²"Do you think those Galileans were worse sinners than all the other
people from Galilee?" Jesus asked. "Is that
why they suffered? ³Not at all! And you
will perish, too, unless you repent of your
sins and turn to God. ⁴And what about the
eighteen people who died when the tower
in Siloam fell on them? Were they the
worst sinners in Jerusalem? ⁵No, and I tell
you again that unless you repent, you will
perish, too."

⁶Then Jesus told this story: "A man
planted a fig tree in his garden and came
again and again to see if there was any fruit
on it, but he was always disappointed. ⁷Finally, he said to his gardener, 'I've waited
three years, and there hasn't been a single
fig! Cut it down. It's just taking up space in
the garden.'

⁸"The gardener answered, 'Sir, give it
one more chance. Leave it another year,
and I'll give it special attention and plenty
of fertilizer. ⁹If we get figs next year, fine.
If not, then you can cut it down.'"

¹⁰One Sabbath day as Jesus was teach-

ing in a synagogue, [11]he saw a woman who had been crippled by an evil spirit. She had been bent double for eighteen years and was unable to stand up straight. [12]When Jesus saw her, he called her over and said, "Dear woman, you are healed of your sickness!" [13]Then he touched her, and instantly she could stand straight. How she praised God!

[14]But the leader in charge of the synagogue was indignant that Jesus had healed her on the Sabbath day. "There are six days of the week for working," he said to the crowd. "Come on those days to be healed, not on the Sabbath."

[15]But the Lord replied, "You hypocrites! Each of you works on the Sabbath day! Don't you untie your ox or your donkey from its stall on the Sabbath and lead it out for water? [16]This dear woman, a daughter of Abraham, has been held in bondage by Satan for eighteen years. Isn't it right that she be released, even on the Sabbath?"

[17]This shamed his enemies, but all the people rejoiced at the wonderful things he did.

[18]Then Jesus said, "What is the Kingdom of God like? How can I illustrate it? [19]It is like a tiny mustard seed that a man planted in a garden; it grows and becomes a tree, and the birds make nests in its branches."

[20]He also asked, "What else is the Kingdom of God like? [21]It is like the yeast a woman used in making bread. Even though she put only a little yeast in three measures of flour, it permeated every part of the dough."

PSALM 78:65-72

Then the Lord rose up as though
    waking from sleep,
    like a warrior aroused from a
        drunken stupor.
[66] He routed his enemies
    and sent them to eternal shame.
[67] But he rejected Joseph's descendants;
    he did not choose the tribe of
        Ephraim.
[68] He chose instead the tribe of Judah,
    and Mount Zion, which he loved.
[69] There he built his sanctuary as high as
        the heavens,
    as solid and enduring as the earth.
[70] He chose his servant David,
    calling him from the sheep pens.
[71] He took David from tending the ewes
        and lambs
    and made him the shepherd of
        Jacob's descendants—
    God's own people, Israel.
[72] He cared for them with a true heart
    and led them with skillful hands.

PROVERBS 12:25

Worry weighs a person down; an encouraging word cheers a person up.

DEUTERONOMY 34:1–JOSHUA 2:24

The passing of an age. The book of Deuteronomy ends with Moses' death. The book of Joshua picks up as the man Joshua prepares to lead the people into the land God had promised to them through their ancestor Abraham.

Then Moses went up to Mount Nebo from the plains of Moab and climbed Pisgah Peak, which is across from Jericho. And the Lord showed him the whole land, from Gilead as far as Dan; [2]all the land of Naphtali; the land of Ephraim and Manasseh; all the land of Judah, extending to the Mediterranean Sea*; [3]the Negev; the Jordan Valley with Jericho—the city of palms—as far as Zoar. [4]Then the Lord said to Moses, "This is the land I promised on oath to Abraham, Isaac, and Jacob when I said, 'I will give it to your descendants.' I have now allowed you to see it with your own eyes, but you will not enter the land."

⁵So Moses, the servant of the LORD, died there in the land of Moab, just as the LORD had said. ⁶The LORD buried him* in a valley near Beth-peor in Moab, but to this day no one knows the exact place. ⁷Moses was 120 years old when he died, yet his eyesight was clear, and he was as strong as ever. ⁸The people of Israel mourned for Moses on the plains of Moab for thirty days, until the customary period of mourning was over.

⁹Now Joshua son of Nun was full of the spirit of wisdom, for Moses had laid his hands on him. So the people of Israel obeyed him, doing just as the LORD had commanded Moses.

¹⁰There has never been another prophet in Israel like Moses, whom the LORD knew face to face. ¹¹The LORD sent him to perform all the miraculous signs and wonders in the land of Egypt against Pharaoh, and all his servants, and his entire land. ¹²With mighty power, Moses performed terrifying acts in the sight of all Israel.

¹:¹AFTER the death of Moses the LORD's servant, the LORD spoke to Joshua son of Nun, Moses' assistant. He said, ²"Moses my servant is dead. Therefore, the time has come for you to lead these people, the Israelites, across the Jordan River into the land I am giving them. ³I promise you what I promised Moses: 'Wherever you set foot, you will be on land I have given you— ⁴from the Negev wilderness in the south to the Lebanon mountains in the north, from the Euphrates River in the east to the Mediterranean Sea* in the west, including all the land of the Hittites.' ⁵No one will be able to stand against you as long as you live. For I will be with you as I was with Moses. I will not fail you or abandon you.

⁶"Be strong and courageous, for you are the one who will lead these people to possess all the land I swore to their ancestors I would give them. ⁷Be strong and very courageous. Be careful to obey all the instructions Moses gave you. Do not deviate from them, turning either to the right or to the left. Then you will be successful in everything you do. ⁸Study this Book of Instruction continually. Meditate on it day and night so you will be sure to obey everything written in it. Only then will you prosper and succeed in all you do. ⁹This is my command—be strong and courageous! Do not be afraid or discouraged. For the LORD your God is with you wherever you go."

¹⁰Joshua then commanded the officers of Israel, ¹¹"Go through the camp and tell the people to get their provisions ready. In three days you will cross the Jordan River and take possession of the land the LORD your God is giving you."

¹²Then Joshua called together the tribes of Reuben, Gad, and the half-tribe of Manasseh. He told them, ¹³"Remember what Moses, the servant of the LORD, commanded you: 'The LORD your God is giving you a place of rest. He has given you this land.' ¹⁴Your wives, children, and livestock may remain here in the land Moses assigned to you on the east side of the Jordan River. But your strong warriors, fully armed, must lead the other tribes across the Jordan to help them conquer their territory. Stay with them ¹⁵until the LORD gives them rest, as he has given you rest, and until they, too, possess the land the LORD your God is giving them. Only then may you return and settle here on the east side of the Jordan River in the land that Moses, the servant of the LORD, assigned to you."

¹⁶They answered Joshua, "We will do whatever you command us, and we will go wherever you send us. ¹⁷We will obey you just as we obeyed Moses. And may the LORD your God be with you as he was with Moses. ¹⁸Anyone who rebels against your orders and does not obey your words and everything you command will be put to death. So be strong and courageous!"

²:¹THEN Joshua secretly sent out two spies from the Israelite camp at Acacia Grove.* He instructed them, "Scout out the land on the other side of the Jordan River, especially around Jericho." So the two men set out and came to the house of a prostitute named Rahab and stayed there that night.

²But someone told the king of Jericho, "Some Israelites have come here tonight to spy out the land." ³So the king of Jericho sent orders to Rahab: "Bring out the men

who have come into your house, for they have come here to spy out the whole land."

[4]Rahab had hidden the two men, but she replied, "Yes, the men were here earlier, but I didn't know where they were from. [5]They left the town at dusk, as the gates were about to close. I don't know where they went. If you hurry, you can probably catch up with them." [6](Actually, she had taken them up to the roof and hidden them beneath bundles of flax she had laid out.) [7]So the king's men went looking for the spies along the road leading to the shallow crossings of the Jordan River. And as soon as the king's men had left, the gate of Jericho was shut.

[8]Before the spies went to sleep that night, Rahab went up on the roof to talk with them. [9]"I know the LORD has given you this land," she told them. "We are all afraid of you. Everyone in the land is living in terror. [10]For we have heard how the LORD made a dry path for you through the Red Sea* when you left Egypt. And we know what you did to Sihon and Og, the two Amorite kings east of the Jordan River, whose people you completely destroyed.* [11]No wonder our hearts have melted in fear! No one has the courage to fight after hearing such things. For the LORD your God is the supreme God of the heavens above and the earth below.

[12]"Now swear to me by the LORD that you will be kind to me and my family since I have helped you. Give me some guarantee that [13]when Jericho is conquered, you will let me live, along with my father and mother, my brothers and sisters, and all their families."

[14]"We offer our own lives as a guarantee for your safety," the men agreed. "If you don't betray us, we will keep our promise and be kind to you when the LORD gives us the land."

[15]Then, since Rahab's house was built into the town wall, she let them down by a rope through the window. [16]"Escape to the hill country," she told them. "Hide there for three days from the men searching for you. Then, when they have returned, you can go on your way."

[17]Before they left, the men told her, "We will be bound by the oath we have taken only if you follow these instructions. [18]When we come into the land, you must leave this scarlet rope hanging from the window through which you let us down. And all your family members— your father, mother, brothers, and all your relatives—must be here inside the house. [19]If they go out into the street and are killed, it will not be our fault. But if anyone lays a hand on people inside this house, we will accept the responsibility for their death. [20]If you betray us, however, we are not bound by this oath in any way."

HOW WE LIVE

Responding to God

JOSHUA 2:8-11 God can work through anyone who is willing to trust in him. In this instance, God worked through a prostitute named Rahab. God looked beyond her profession and saw her faith and her willingness to turn her life over to him. Rahab responded to God's touch on her heart, and God responded in mighty ways. • The whole city of Jericho was buzzing with the news that the Israelites were on their way. Even though she knew she would forfeit her life if she was caught hiding the Israelite spies, Rahab took that risk. She willingly put everything on the line for a God she barely knew. God rewarded her faith by saving her and her family when the city fell. God rewarded Rahab further by placing her in the line of Christ (Matthew 1:5, January 1). • Maybe you still think your past hinders you from being useful to God. Know that God looks past all that you've done and all that has happened to you; he looks into your heart. When you respond to him, he will respond to you in ways beyond your imagining.

²¹"I accept your terms," she replied. And she sent them on their way, leaving the scarlet rope hanging from the window.

²²The spies went up into the hill country and stayed there three days. The men who were chasing them searched everywhere along the road, but they finally returned without success.

²³Then the two spies came down from the hill country, crossed the Jordan River, and reported to Joshua all that had happened to them. ²⁴"The LORD has given us the whole land," they said, "for all the people in the land are terrified of us."

34:2 Hebrew *the western sea.*   34:6 Hebrew *He buried him;* Samaritan Pentateuch and some Greek manuscripts read *They buried him.*   1:4 Hebrew *the Great Sea.*   2:1 Hebrew *Shittim.*   2:10a Hebrew *sea of reeds.*   2:10b The Hebrew term used here refers to the complete consecration of things or people to the LORD, either by destroying them or by giving them as an offering.

LUKE 13:22–14:6

Jesus' life was spent building a bridge between God and humanity. Unfortunately, many of his own people would refuse to see him for who he was.

Jesus went through the towns and villages, teaching as he went, always pressing on toward Jerusalem. ²³Someone asked him, "Lord, will only a few be saved?"

He replied, ²⁴"Work hard to enter the narrow door to God's Kingdom, for many will try to enter but will fail. ²⁵When the master of the house has locked the door, it will be too late. You will stand outside knocking and pleading, 'Lord, open the door for us!' But he will reply, 'I don't know you or where you come from.' ²⁶Then you will say, 'But we ate and drank with you, and you taught in our streets.' ²⁷And he will reply, 'I tell you, I don't know you or where you come from. Get away from me, all you who do evil.'

²⁸"There will be weeping and gnashing of teeth, for you will see Abraham, Isaac, Jacob, and all the prophets in the Kingdom of God, but you will be thrown out. ²⁹And people will come from all over the world—from east and west, north and south—to take their places in the Kingdom of God. ³⁰And note this: Some who seem least important now will be the greatest then, and some who are the greatest now will be least important then.*"

³¹At that time some Pharisees said to him, "Get away from here if you want to live! Herod Antipas wants to kill you!"

³²Jesus replied, "Go tell that fox that I will keep on casting out demons and healing people today and tomorrow; and the third day I will accomplish my purpose. ³³Yes, today, tomorrow, and the next day I must proceed on my way. For it wouldn't do for a prophet of God to be killed except in Jerusalem!

³⁴"O Jerusalem, Jerusalem, the city that kills the prophets and stones God's messengers! How often I have wanted to gather your children together as a hen protects her chicks beneath her wings, but you wouldn't let me. ³⁵And now, look, your house is abandoned. And you will never see me again until you say, 'Blessings on the one who comes in the name of the LORD!'*"

¹⁴:¹ONE Sabbath day Jesus went to eat dinner in the home of a leader of the Pharisees, and the people were watching him closely. ²There was a man there whose arms and legs were swollen.* ³Jesus asked the Pharisees and experts in religious law, "Is it permitted in the law to heal people on the Sabbath day, or not?" ⁴When they refused to answer, Jesus touched the sick man and healed him and sent him away. ⁵Then he turned to them and said, "Which of you doesn't work on the Sabbath? If your son* or your cow falls into a pit, don't you rush to get him out?" ⁶Again they could not answer.

13:30 Greek *Some are last who will be first, and some are first who will be last.*   13:35 Ps 118:26.   14:2 Or *who had dropsy.*   14:5 Some manuscripts read *donkey.*

PSALM 79:1-13

A psalm of Asaph.

¹ **O** God, pagan nations have conquered your land,
　　your special possession.
They have defiled your holy Temple
　　and made Jerusalem a heap of ruins.
² They have left the bodies of your servants
　　as food for the birds of heaven.
The flesh of your godly ones
　　has become food for the wild animals.

³ Blood has flowed like water all around
  Jerusalem;
    no one is left to bury the dead.
⁴ We are mocked by our neighbors,
    an object of scorn and derision
      to those around us.

⁵ O Lᴏʀᴅ, how long will you be angry
    with us? Forever?
      How long will your jealousy burn
        like fire?
⁶ Pour out your wrath on the nations
    that refuse to acknowledge you—
      on kingdoms that do not call upon
        your name.
⁷ For they have devoured your people
    Israel,*
      making the land a desolate
        wilderness.
⁸ Do not hold us guilty for the sins of
    our ancestors!
      Let your compassion quickly meet
        our needs,
          for we are on the brink of despair.

⁹ Help us, O God of our salvation!
    Help us for the glory of your name.
      Save us and forgive our sins
        for the honor of your name.

¹⁰ Why should pagan nations be allowed
    to scoff,
      asking, "Where is their God?"
        Show us your vengeance against
          the nations,
            for they have spilled the blood
              of your servants.
¹¹ Listen to the moaning of the
    prisoners.
      Demonstrate your great power by
        saving those condemned to die.

¹² O Lord, pay back our neighbors seven
    times
      for the scorn they have hurled at
        you.
¹³ Then we your people, the sheep of
    your pasture,
      will thank you forever and ever,
        praising your greatness from
          generation to generation.

79:7 Hebrew *devoured Jacob.* See note on 44:4.

PROVERBS 12:26
The godly give good advice to their
friends;* the wicked lead them astray.

12:26 Or *The godly are cautious in friendship;* or *The godly
are freed from evil.* The meaning of the Hebrew is uncertain.

APRIL**11**

JOSHUA 3:1–4:24
Finally, the nation of Israel crossed the Jordan River
into the Promised Land, leaving a memorial of
twelve stones to mark their journey.

Early the next morning Joshua and all the
Israelites left Acacia Grove* and arrived at
the banks of the Jordan River, where they
camped before crossing. ²Three days
later the Israelite officers went through
the camp, ³giving these instructions to
the people: "When you see the Levitical
priests carrying the Ark of the Covenant
of the Lᴏʀᴅ your God, move out from your
positions and follow them. ⁴Since you
have never traveled this way before, they
will guide you. Stay about a half mile* behind them, keeping a clear distance be-

tween you and the Ark. Make sure you
don't come any closer."

⁵Then Joshua told the people, "Purify
yourselves, for tomorrow the Lᴏʀᴅ will do
great wonders among you."

⁶In the morning Joshua said to the
priests, "Lift up the Ark of the Covenant
and lead the people across the river." And
so they started out and went ahead of the
people.

⁷The Lᴏʀᴅ told Joshua, "Today I will
begin to make you a great leader in
the eyes of all the Israelites. They will
know that I am with you, just as I was
with Moses. ⁸Give this command to the
priests who carry the Ark of the Covenant: 'When you reach the banks of

the Jordan River, take a few steps into the river and stop there.'"

⁹So Joshua told the Israelites, "Come and listen to what the LORD your God says. ¹⁰Today you will know that the living God is among you. He will surely drive out the Canaanites, Hittites, Hivites, Perizzites, Girgashites, Amorites, and Jebusites ahead of you. ¹¹Look, the Ark of the Covenant, which belongs to the Lord of the whole earth, will lead you across the Jordan River! ¹²Now choose twelve men from the tribes of Israel, one from each tribe. ¹³The priests will carry the Ark of the LORD, the Lord of all the earth. As soon as their feet touch the water, the flow of water will be cut off upstream, and the river will stand up like a wall."

¹⁴So the people left their camp to cross the Jordan, and the priests who were carrying the Ark of the Covenant went ahead of them. ¹⁵It was the harvest season, and the Jordan was overflowing its banks. But as soon as the feet of the priests who were carrying the Ark touched the water at the river's edge, ¹⁶the water above that point began backing up a great distance away at a town called Adam, which is near Zarethan. And the water below that point flowed on to the Dead Sea* until the riverbed was dry. Then all the people crossed over near the town of Jericho.

¹⁷Meanwhile, the priests who were carrying the Ark of the LORD's Covenant stood on dry ground in the middle of the riverbed as the people passed by. They waited there until the whole nation of Israel had crossed the Jordan on dry ground.

4:1WHEN all the people had crossed the Jordan, the LORD said to Joshua, ²"Now choose twelve men, one from each tribe. ³Tell them, 'Take twelve stones from the very place where the priests are standing in the middle of the Jordan. Carry them out and pile them up at the place where you will camp tonight.'"

⁴So Joshua called together the twelve men he had chosen—one from each of the tribes of Israel. ⁵He told them, "Go into the middle of the Jordan, in front of the Ark of the LORD your God. Each of you must pick up one stone and carry it out on your shoulder—twelve stones in all, one for each of the twelve tribes of Israel. ⁶We will use these stones to build a memorial. In the future your children will ask you, 'What do these stones mean?' ⁷Then you can tell them, 'They remind us that the Jordan River stopped flowing when the Ark of the LORD's Covenant went across.' These stones will stand as a memorial among the people of Israel forever."

⁸So the men did as Joshua had commanded them. They took twelve stones from the middle of the Jordan River, one for each tribe, just as the LORD had told Joshua. They carried them to the place where they camped for the night and constructed the memorial there.

⁹Joshua also set up another pile of twelve stones in the middle of the Jordan, at the place where the priests who carried the Ark of the Covenant were standing. And they are there to this day.

¹⁰The priests who were carrying the Ark stood in the middle of the river until all of the LORD's commands that Moses had given to Joshua were carried out. Meanwhile, the people hurried across the riverbed. ¹¹And when everyone was safely on the other side, the priests crossed over with the Ark of the LORD as the people watched.

¹²The armed warriors from the tribes of Reuben, Gad, and the half-tribe of Manasseh led the Israelites across the Jordan, just as Moses had directed. ¹³These armed men—about 40,000 strong—were ready for battle, and the LORD was with them as they crossed over to the plains of Jericho.

¹⁴That day the LORD made Joshua a great leader in the eyes of all the Israelites, and for the rest of his life they revered him as much as they had revered Moses.

¹⁵The LORD had said to Joshua, ¹⁶"Command the priests carrying the Ark of the Covenant* to come up out of the riverbed." ¹⁷So Joshua gave the command. ¹⁸As soon as the priests carrying the Ark of the LORD's Covenant came up out of the riverbed and their feet were on high ground, the water of the Jordan returned and overflowed its banks as before.

¹⁹The people crossed the Jordan on the

tenth day of the first month.* Then they camped at Gilgal, just east of Jericho. ²⁰It was there at Gilgal that Joshua piled up the twelve stones taken from the Jordan River.

²¹Then Joshua said to the Israelites, "In the future your children will ask, 'What do these stones mean?' ²²Then you can tell them, 'This is where the Israelites crossed the Jordan on dry ground.' ²³For the LORD your God dried up the river right before your eyes, and he kept it dry until you were all across, just as he did at the Red Sea* when he dried it up until we had all crossed over. ²⁴He did this so all the nations of the earth might know that the LORD's hand is powerful, and so you might fear the LORD your God forever."

3:1 Hebrew *Shittim.* 3:4 Hebrew *about 2,000 cubits* [920 meters]. 3:16 Hebrew *the sea of the Arabah, the Salt Sea.* 4:16 Hebrew *Ark of the Testimony.* 4:19 This day in the ancient Hebrew lunar calendar occurred in late March, April, or early May. 4:23 Hebrew *sea of reeds.*

LUKE 14:7-35

There was (and is) a price to be paid in order to live a life of faith. Jesus never denied it. In fact, he warned people to understand the cost before they make a commitment.

When Jesus noticed that all who had come to the dinner were trying to sit in the seats of honor near the head of the table, he gave them this advice: ⁸"When you are invited to a wedding feast, don't sit in the seat of honor. What if someone who is more distinguished than you has also been invited? ⁹The host will come and say, 'Give this person your seat.' Then you will be embarrassed, and you will have to take whatever seat is left at the foot of the table!

¹⁰"Instead, take the lowest place at the foot of the table. Then when your host sees you, he will come and say, 'Friend, we have a better place for you!' Then you will be honored in front of all the other guests. ¹¹For those who exalt themselves will be humbled, and those who humble themselves will be exalted."

¹²Then he turned to his host. "When you put on a luncheon or a banquet," he said, "don't invite your friends, brothers, relatives, and rich neighbors. For they will invite you back, and that will be your only reward. ¹³Instead, invite the poor, the crippled, the lame, and the blind. ¹⁴Then at the resurrection of the righteous, God will reward you for inviting those who could not repay you."

¹⁵Hearing this, a man sitting at the table with Jesus exclaimed, "What a blessing it will be to attend a banquet* in the Kingdom of God!"

¹⁶Jesus replied with this story: "A man prepared a great feast and sent out many

---

HOW WE LIVE

Following Jesus

LUKE 14:33 Jesus was up front with his followers. He set the bar high. He told potential followers that being a Christian would have a cost. What does that mean? • Perhaps you're experiencing that already. Perhaps your new faith has been ridiculed at home, at school, or at work. Maybe your old friends are wondering what happened to you—and they're backing off a bit, afraid that you've become a fanatic. It could be that your faith is wreaking havoc with some of your old habits. Perhaps you're being convicted to make a greater sacrifice of time or money for God's Kingdom. That's all part of the cost of becoming a believer, so don't think it's unusual. • But it's not all one-sided. The cost you pay is nothing compared to what you have gained. You have been given a new life with the promise of joy and fulfillment. You have been given a worldwide family of believers. You have a true purpose and can experience the joy and fulfillment of living it out. • So what do you do when you face those costly times? Keep the right perspective, pray, and persevere. Greater joy awaits!

invitations. ¹⁷When the banquet was ready, he sent his servant to tell the guests, 'Come, the banquet is ready.' ¹⁸But they all began making excuses. One said, 'I have just bought a field and must inspect it. Please excuse me.' ¹⁹Another said, 'I have just bought five pairs of oxen, and I want to try them out. Please excuse me.' ²⁰Another said, 'I now have a wife, so I can't come.'

²¹"The servant returned and told his master what they had said. His master was furious and said, 'Go quickly into the streets and alleys of the town and invite the poor, the crippled, the blind, and the lame.' ²²After the servant had done this, he reported, 'There is still room for more.' ²³So his master said, 'Go out into the country lanes and behind the hedges and urge anyone you find to come, so that the house will be full. ²⁴For none of those I first invited will get even the smallest taste of my banquet.'"

²⁵A large crowd was following Jesus. He turned around and said to them, ²⁶"If you want to be my disciple, you must hate everyone else by comparison—your father and mother, wife and children, brothers and sisters—yes, even your own life. Otherwise, you cannot be my disciple. ²⁷And if you do not carry your own cross and follow me, you cannot be my disciple.

²⁸"But don't begin until you count the cost. For who would begin construction of a building without first calculating the cost to see if there is enough money to finish it? ²⁹Otherwise, you might complete only the foundation before running out of money, and then everyone would laugh at you. ³⁰They would say, 'There's the person who started that building and couldn't afford to finish it!'

³¹"Or what king would go to war against another king without first sitting down with his counselors to discuss whether his army of 10,000 could defeat the 20,000 soldiers marching against him? ³²And if he can't, he will send a delegation to discuss terms of peace while the enemy is still far away. ³³So you cannot become my disciple without giving up everything you own.

³⁴"Salt is good for seasoning. But if it loses its flavor, how do you make it salty again? ³⁵Flavorless salt is good neither for the soil nor for the manure pile. It is thrown away. Anyone with ears to hear should listen and understand!"

14:15 Greek *to eat bread.*

PSALM 80:1-19

For the choir director: A psalm of Asaph, to be sung to the tune "Lilies of the Covenant."

¹ Please listen, O Shepherd of Israel,
   you who lead Joseph's descendants
      like a flock.
O God, enthroned above the
      cherubim,
   display your radiant glory
² to Ephraim, Benjamin, and
      Manasseh.
Show us your mighty power.
   Come to rescue us!

³ Turn us again to yourself, O God.
   Make your face shine down upon
      us.
   Only then will we be saved.

⁴ O LORD God of Heaven's Armies,
   how long will you be angry with
      our prayers?
⁵ You have fed us with sorrow
   and made us drink tears by the
      bucketful.
⁶ You have made us the scorn* of
      neighboring nations.
   Our enemies treat us as a joke.

⁷ Turn us again to yourself, O God
      of Heaven's Armies.
   Make your face shine down upon
      us.
   Only then will we be saved.

⁸ You brought us from Egypt like
      a grapevine;
   you drove away the pagan nations
      and transplanted us into your
      land.
⁹ You cleared the ground for us,
   and we took root and filled the
      land.
¹⁰ Our shade covered the mountains;
   our branches covered the mighty
      cedars.
¹¹ We spread our branches west to the
      Mediterranean Sea;
   our shoots spread east to the
      Euphrates River.*

[12] But now, why have you broken down
    our walls
  so that all who pass by may steal
    our fruit?
[13] The wild boar from the forest
    devours it,
  and the wild animals feed on it.

[14] Come back, we beg you, O God of
    Heaven's Armies.
  Look down from heaven and see
    our plight.
  Take care of this grapevine
[15]   that you yourself have planted,
  this son you have raised for
    yourself.
[16] For we are chopped up and burned by
    our enemies.
  May they perish at the sight of your
    frown.

[17] Strengthen the man you love,
    the son of your choice.
[18] Then we will never abandon you
    again.
  Revive us so we can call on your
    name once more.

[19] Turn us again to yourself, O LORD God
    of Heaven's Armies.
  Make your face shine down upon us.
  Only then will we be saved.

80:6 As in Syriac version; Hebrew reads *the strife.*
80:11 Hebrew *west to the sea, . . . east to the river.*

PROVERBS 12:27-28

Lazy people don't even cook the game they catch, but the diligent make use of everything they find. □ The way of the godly leads to life; that path does not lead to death.

JOSHUA 5:1–7:15

Circumcision had been the mark of the Israelites since Abraham's original connection with God; nevertheless, a generation had been born on the journey and remained uncircumcised. Only after reconnecting with this part of their covenant heritage could they begin their attacks on the land.

When all the Amorite kings west of the Jordan and all the Canaanite kings who lived along the Mediterranean coast* heard how the LORD had dried up the Jordan River so the people of Israel could cross, they lost heart and were paralyzed with fear because of them.

[2] At that time the LORD told Joshua, "Make flint knives and circumcise this second generation of Israelites.*" [3] So Joshua made flint knives and circumcised the entire male population of Israel at Gibeath-haaraloth.*

[4] Joshua had to circumcise them because all the men who were old enough to fight in battle when they left Egypt had died in the wilderness. [5] Those who left Egypt had all been circumcised, but none of those born after the Exodus, during the

years in the wilderness, had been circumcised. [6] The Israelites had traveled in the wilderness for forty years until all the men who were old enough to fight in battle when they left Egypt had died. For they had disobeyed the LORD, and the LORD vowed he would not let them enter the land he had sworn to give us—a land flowing with milk and honey. [7] So Joshua circumcised their sons—those who had grown up to take their fathers' places—for they had not been circumcised on the way to the Promised Land. [8] After all the males had been circumcised, they rested in the camp until they were healed.

[9] Then the LORD said to Joshua, "Today I have rolled away the shame of your slavery in Egypt." So that place has been called Gilgal* to this day.

[10] While the Israelites were camped at Gilgal on the plains of Jericho, they celebrated Passover on the evening of the fourteenth day of the first month.* [11] The very next day they began to eat unleavened bread and roasted grain harvested from the

land. ¹²No manna appeared on the day they first ate from the crops of the land, and it was never seen again. So from that time on the Israelites ate from the crops of Canaan.

¹³When Joshua was near the town of Jericho, he looked up and saw a man standing in front of him with sword in hand. Joshua went up to him and demanded, "Are you friend or foe?"

¹⁴"Neither one," he replied. "I am the commander of the LORD's army."

At this, Joshua fell with his face to the ground in reverence. "I am at your command," Joshua said. "What do you want your servant to do?"

¹⁵The commander of the LORD's army replied, "Take off your sandals, for the place where you are standing is holy." And Joshua did as he was told.

⁶:¹Now the gates of Jericho were tightly shut because the people were afraid of the Israelites. No one was allowed to go out or in. ²But the LORD said to Joshua, "I have given you Jericho, its king, and all its strong warriors. ³You and your fighting men should march around the town once a day for six days. ⁴Seven priests will walk ahead of the Ark, each carrying a ram's horn. On the seventh day you are to march around the town seven times, with the priests blowing the horns. ⁵When you hear the priests give one long blast on the rams' horns, have all the people shout as loud as they can. Then the walls of the town will collapse, and the people can charge straight into the town."

⁶So Joshua called together the priests and said, "Take up the Ark of the LORD's Covenant, and assign seven priests to walk in front of it, each carrying a ram's horn." ⁷Then he gave orders to the people: "March around the town, and the armed men will lead the way in front of the Ark of the LORD."

⁸After Joshua spoke to the people, the seven priests with the rams' horns started marching in the presence of the LORD, blowing the horns as they marched. And the Ark of the LORD's Covenant followed behind them. ⁹Some of the armed men marched in front of the priests with the horns and some behind the Ark, with the priests continually blowing the horns.

¹⁰"Do not shout; do not even talk," Joshua commanded. "Not a single word from any of you until I tell you to shout. Then shout!" ¹¹So the Ark of the LORD was carried around the town once that day, and then everyone returned to spend the night in the camp.

¹²Joshua got up early the next morning, and the priests again carried the Ark of the LORD. ¹³The seven priests with the rams' horns marched in front of the Ark of the LORD, blowing their horns. Again the armed men marched both in front of the priests with the horns and behind the Ark of the LORD. All this time the priests were blowing their horns. ¹⁴On the second day they again marched around the town once and returned to the camp. They followed this pattern for six days.

¹⁵On the seventh day the Israelites got up at dawn and marched around the town as they had done before. But this time they went around the town seven times. ¹⁶The seventh time around, as the priests sounded the long blast on their horns, Joshua commanded the people, "Shout! For the LORD has given you the town! ¹⁷Jericho and everything in it must be completely destroyed* as an offering to the LORD. Only Rahab the prostitute and the others in her house will be spared, for she protected our spies.

¹⁸"Do not take any of the things set apart for destruction, or you yourselves will be completely destroyed, and you will bring trouble on the camp of Israel. ¹⁹Everything made from silver, gold, bronze, or iron is sacred to the LORD and must be brought into his treasury."

²⁰When the people heard the sound of the rams' horns, they shouted as loud as they could. Suddenly, the walls of Jericho collapsed, and the Israelites charged straight into the town and captured it. ²¹They completely destroyed everything in it with their swords—men and women, young and old, cattle, sheep, goats, and donkeys.

²²Meanwhile, Joshua said to the two spies, "Keep your promise. Go to the prostitute's house and bring her out, along with all her family."

²³The men who had been spies went in and brought out Rahab, her father, mother,

brothers, and all the other relatives who were with her. They moved her whole family to a safe place near the camp of Israel.

²⁴Then the Israelites burned the town and everything in it. Only the things made from silver, gold, bronze, or iron were kept for the treasury of the LORD's house. ²⁵So Joshua spared Rahab the prostitute and her relatives who were with her in the house, because she had hidden the spies Joshua sent to Jericho. And she lives among the Israelites to this day.

²⁶At that time Joshua invoked this curse:

"May the curse of the LORD fall on anyone
   who tries to rebuild the town of Jericho.
At the cost of his firstborn son,
   he will lay its foundation.
At the cost of his youngest son,
   he will set up its gates."

²⁷So the LORD was with Joshua, and his reputation spread throughout the land.

7:1BUT Israel violated the instructions about the things set apart for the LORD.* A man named Achan had stolen some of these dedicated things, so the LORD was very angry with the Israelites. Achan was the son of Carmi, a descendant of Zimri* son of Zerah, of the tribe of Judah.

²Joshua sent some of his men from Jeri-cho to spy out the town of Ai, east of Bethel, near Beth-aven. ³When they returned, they told Joshua, "There's no need for all of us to go up there; it won't take more than two or three thousand men to attack Ai. Since there are so few of them, don't make all our people struggle to go up there."

⁴So approximately 3,000 warriors were sent, but they were soundly defeated. The men of Ai ⁵chased the Israelites from the town gate as far as the quarries,* and they killed about thirty-six who were retreating down the slope. The Israelites were paralyzed with fear at this turn of events, and their courage melted away.

⁶Joshua and the elders of Israel tore their clothing in dismay, threw dust on their heads, and bowed face down to the ground before the Ark of the LORD until evening. ⁷Then Joshua cried out, "Oh, Sovereign LORD, why did you bring us across the Jordan River if you are going to let the Amorites kill us? If only we had been content to stay on the other side! ⁸Lord, what can I say now that Israel has fled from its enemies? ⁹For when the Canaanites and all the other people living in the land hear about it, they will surround us and wipe our name off the face of the earth. And then what will happen to the honor of your great name?"

¹⁰But the LORD said to Joshua, "Get up! Why are you lying on your face like this?

WHAT THE BIBLE SAYS

Salvation and forgiveness

LUKE 15:1-32 Jesus told his followers, "The Son of Man came to seek and save those who are lost" (Luke 19:10, April 18). These parables illustrate this. • In the first two parables, Jesus pictures a God who searches for lost souls until they are found. Not only that, but he's so happy when he finds them that he throws a party and rejoices. Did you know that all heaven rejoiced when you became a believer? • In the third parable, Jesus confronted an ugly attitude he encountered among the religious elite of his day. They were indignant when they saw the large crowds of people coming to Jesus to be saved. Like the older brother in the parable, rather than rejoicing, they began to resent what God was doing. How counter to God's heart. • Believers should be filled with joy whenever someone becomes a believer. It should be our passion to see that happen. We serve a God who is still seeking to save the lost. Let him use you to bring the message, and rejoice when he does.

[11]Israel has sinned and broken my covenant! They have stolen some of the things that I commanded must be set apart for me. And they have not only stolen them but have lied about it and hidden the things among their own belongings. [12]That is why the Israelites are running from their enemies in defeat. For now Israel itself has been set apart for destruction. I will not remain with you any longer unless you destroy the things among you that were set apart for destruction.

[13]"Get up! Command the people to purify themselves in preparation for tomorrow. For this is what the LORD, the God of Israel, says: Hidden among you, O Israel, are things set apart for the LORD. You will never defeat your enemies until you remove these things from among you.

[14]"In the morning you must present yourselves by tribes, and the LORD will point out the tribe to which the guilty man belongs. That tribe must come forward with its clans, and the LORD will point out the guilty clan. That clan will then come forward, and the LORD will point out the guilty family. Finally, each member of the guilty family must come forward one by one. [15]The one who has stolen what was set apart for destruction will himself be burned with fire, along with everything he has, for he has broken the covenant of the LORD and has done a horrible thing in Israel."

5:1 Hebrew *along the sea.*   5:2 Or *circumcise the Israelites a second time.*   5:3 *Gibeath-haaraloth* means "hill of foreskins."   5:9 *Gilgal* sounds like the Hebrew word *galal,* meaning "to roll."   5:10 This day in the ancient Hebrew lunar calendar occurred in late March, April, or early May.   6:17 The Hebrew term used here refers to the complete consecration of things or people to the LORD, either by destroying them or by giving them as an offering; similarly in 6:18, 21.   7:1a The Hebrew term used here refers to the complete consecration of things or people to the LORD, either by destroying them or by giving them as an offering; similarly in 7:11, 12, 13, 15.   7:1b As in Greek version (see also 1 Chr 2:6); Hebrew reads *Zabdi.* Also in 7:17, 18.   7:5 Or *as far as Shebarim.*

LUKE 15:1-32
Sheep, coins, and even children can be lost and then found. In the eyes of God, people can be spiritually lost and found as well. In fact, his Kingdom is all about finding what was lost. That's what he did with you.

Tax collectors and other notorious sinners often came to listen to Jesus teach. [2]This made the Pharisees and teachers of religious law complain that he was associating with such sinful people—even eating with them!

[3]So Jesus told them this story: [4]"If a man has a hundred sheep and one of them gets lost, what will he do? Won't he leave the ninety-nine others in the wilderness and go to search for the one that is lost until he finds it? [5]And when he has found it, he will joyfully carry it home on his shoulders. [6]When he arrives, he will call together his friends and neighbors, saying, 'Rejoice with me because I have found my lost sheep.' [7]In the same way, there is more joy in heaven over one lost sinner who repents and returns to God than over ninety-nine others who are righteous and haven't strayed away!

[8]"Or suppose a woman has ten silver coins* and loses one. Won't she light a lamp and sweep the entire house and search carefully until she finds it? [9]And when she finds it, she will call in her friends and neighbors and say, 'Rejoice with me because I have found my lost coin.' [10]In the same way, there is joy in the presence of God's angels when even one sinner repents."

[11]To illustrate the point further, Jesus told them this story: "A man had two sons. [12]The younger son told his father, 'I want my share of your estate now before you die.' So his father agreed to divide his wealth between his sons.

[13]"A few days later this younger son packed all his belongings and moved to a distant land, and there he wasted all his money in wild living. [14]About the time his money ran out, a great famine swept over the land, and he began to starve. [15]He persuaded a local farmer to hire him, and the man sent him into his fields to feed the pigs. [16]The young man became so hungry that even the pods he was feeding the pigs looked good to him. But no one gave him anything.

[17]"When he finally came to his senses, he said to himself, 'At home even the hired servants have food enough to spare, and here I am dying of hunger! [18]I will go

home to my father and say, "Father, I have sinned against both heaven and you, [19]and I am no longer worthy of being called your son. Please take me on as a hired servant.'"

[20]"So he returned home to his father. And while he was still a long way off, his father saw him coming. Filled with love and compassion, he ran to his son, embraced him, and kissed him. [21]His son said to him, 'Father, I have sinned against both heaven and you, and I am no longer worthy of being called your son.*'

[22]"But his father said to the servants, 'Quick! Bring the finest robe in the house and put it on him. Get a ring for his finger and sandals for his feet. [23]And kill the calf we have been fattening. We must celebrate with a feast, [24]for this son of mine was dead and has now returned to life. He was lost, but now he is found.' So the party began.

[25]"Meanwhile, the older son was in the fields working. When he returned home, he heard music and dancing in the house, [26]and he asked one of the servants what was going on. [27]'Your brother is back,' he was told, 'and your father has killed the fattened calf. We are celebrating because of his safe return.'

[28]"The older brother was angry and wouldn't go in. His father came out and begged him, [29]but he replied, 'All these years I've slaved for you and never once refused to do a single thing you told me to. And in all that time you never gave me even one young goat for a feast with my friends. [30]Yet when this son of yours comes back after squandering your money on prostitutes, you celebrate by killing the fattened calf!'

[31]"His father said to him, 'Look, dear son, you have always stayed by me, and everything I have is yours. [32]We had to celebrate this happy day. For your brother was dead and has come back to life! He was lost, but now he is found!'"

15:8 Greek *ten drachmas.* A drachma was the equivalent of a full day's wage.   15:21 Some manuscripts add *Please take me on as a hired servant.*

PSALM 81:1-16

*For the choir director: A psalm of Asaph, to be accompanied by a stringed instrument.**

[1] **S**ing praises to God, our strength.
   Sing to the God of Jacob.
[2] Sing! Beat the tambourine.
   Play the sweet lyre and the harp.
[3] Blow the ram's horn at new moon,
   and again at full moon to call a festival!
[4] For this is required by the decrees of Israel;
   it is a regulation of the God of Jacob.
[5] He made it a law for Israel*
   when he attacked Egypt to set us free.

I heard an unknown voice say,
[6] "Now I will take the load from your shoulders;
   I will free your hands from their heavy tasks.
[7] You cried to me in trouble, and I saved you;
   I answered out of the thundercloud
   and tested your faith when there was no water at Meribah.

Interlude

[8] "Listen to me, O my people, while I give you stern warnings.
   O Israel, if you would only listen to me!
[9] You must never have a foreign god;
   you must not bow down before a false god.
[10] For it was I, the LORD your God,
   who rescued you from the land of Egypt.
   Open your mouth wide, and I will fill it with good things.

[11] "But no, my people wouldn't listen.
   Israel did not want me around.
[12] So I let them follow their own stubborn desires,
   living according to their own ideas.
[13] Oh, that my people would listen to me!
   Oh, that Israel would follow me, walking in my paths!
[14] How quickly I would then subdue their enemies!
   How soon my hands would be upon their foes!
[15] Those who hate the LORD would cringe before him;
   they would be doomed forever.

¹⁶ But I would feed you with the finest
wheat.
I would satisfy you with wild honey
from the rock."

81:TITLE Hebrew *according to the gittith.*   **81:5** Hebrew *for
Joseph.*

APRIL **13**

JOSHUA 7:16–9:2

Entering the land was serious business, and the
people needed to obey God at every step. Unfortunately, one man allowed greed to get in the way of
his obedience. The consequences were swift and
deadly.

Early the next morning Joshua brought
the tribes of Israel before the LORD, and
the tribe of Judah was singled out.
¹⁷ Then the clans of Judah came forward,
and the clan of Zerah was singled out.
Then the families of Zerah came forward, and the family of Zimri was singled
out. ¹⁸ Every member of Zimri's family
was brought forward person by person,
and Achan was singled out.

¹⁹ Then Joshua said to Achan, "My son,
give glory to the LORD, the God of Israel,
by telling the truth. Make your confession
and tell me what you have done. Don't
hide it from me."

²⁰ Achan replied, "It is true! I have
sinned against the LORD, the God of Israel.
²¹ Among the plunder I saw a beautiful
robe from Babylon,* 200 silver coins,*
and a bar of gold weighing more than a
pound.* I wanted them so much that I
took them. They are hidden in the ground
beneath my tent, with the silver buried
deeper than the rest."

²² So Joshua sent some men to make a
search. They ran to the tent and found the
stolen goods hidden there, just as Achan
had said, with the silver buried beneath
the rest. ²³ They took the things from the
tent and brought them to Joshua and all
the Israelites. Then they laid them on the
ground in the presence of the LORD.

²⁴ Then Joshua and all the Israelites
took Achan, the silver, the robe, the bar of
gold, his sons, daughters, cattle, donkeys,
sheep, goats, tent, and everything he had,

PROVERBS 13:1

A wise child accepts a parent's discipline;* a mocker refuses to listen to correction.

13:1 Hebrew *A wise son accepts his father's discipline.*

and they brought them to the valley of
Achor. ²⁵ Then Joshua said to Achan, "Why
have you brought trouble on us? The
LORD will now bring trouble on you." And
all the Israelites stoned Achan and his
family and burned their bodies. ²⁶ They
piled a great heap of stones over Achan,
which remains to this day. That is why
the place has been called the Valley of
Trouble* ever since. So the LORD was no
longer angry.

⁸:¹ THEN the LORD said to Joshua, "Do not
be afraid or discouraged. Take all your
fighting men and attack Ai, for I have
given you the king of Ai, his people, his
town, and his land. ² You will destroy them
as you destroyed Jericho and its king. But
this time you may keep the plunder and
the livestock for yourselves. Set an ambush behind the town."

³ So Joshua and all the fighting men set
out to attack Ai. Joshua chose 30,000 of
his best warriors and sent them out at
night ⁴ with these orders: "Hide in ambush close behind the town and be ready
for action. ⁵ When our main army attacks,
the men of Ai will come out to fight as
they did before, and we will run away from
them. ⁶ We will let them chase us until we
have drawn them away from the town. For
they will say, 'The Israelites are running
away from us as they did before.' Then,
while we are running from them, ⁷ you will
jump up from your ambush and take possession of the town, for the LORD your
God will give it to you. ⁸ Set the town on
fire, as the LORD has commanded. You
have your orders."

⁹ So they left and went to the place of
ambush between Bethel and the west side
of Ai. But Joshua remained among the

people in the camp that night. ¹⁰Early the next morning Joshua roused his men and started toward Ai, accompanied by the elders of Israel. ¹¹All the fighting men who were with Joshua marched in front of the town and camped on the north side of Ai, with a valley between them and the town. ¹²That night Joshua sent 5,000 men to lie in ambush between Bethel and Ai, on the west side of the town. ¹³So they stationed the main army north of the town and the ambush west of the town. Joshua himself spent that night in the valley.

¹⁴When the king of Ai saw the Israelites across the valley, he and all his army hurried out early in the morning and attacked the Israelites at a place overlooking the Jordan Valley.* But he didn't realize there was an ambush behind the town. ¹⁵Joshua and the Israelite army fled toward the wilderness as though they were badly beaten. ¹⁶Then all the men in the town were called out to chase after them. In this way, they were lured away from the town. ¹⁷There was not a man left in Ai or Bethel* who did not chase after the Israelites, and the town was left wide open.

¹⁸Then the LORD said to Joshua, "Point the spear in your hand toward Ai, for I will hand the town over to you." Joshua did as he was commanded. ¹⁹As soon as Joshua gave this signal, all the men in ambush jumped up from their position and poured into the town. They quickly captured it and set it on fire.

²⁰When the men of Ai looked behind them, smoke from the town was filling the sky, and they had nowhere to go. For the Israelites who had fled in the direction of the wilderness now turned on their pursuers. ²¹When Joshua and all the other Israelites saw that the ambush had succeeded and that smoke was rising from the town, they turned and attacked the men of Ai. ²²Meanwhile, the Israelites who were inside the town came out and attacked the enemy from the rear. So the men of Ai were caught in the middle, with Israelite fighters on both sides. Israel attacked them, and not a single person survived or escaped. ²³Only the king of Ai was taken alive and brought to Joshua.

²⁴When the Israelite army finished chasing and killing all the men of Ai in the open fields, they went back and finished off everyone inside. ²⁵So the entire population of Ai, including men and women, was wiped out that day—12,000 in all. ²⁶For Joshua kept holding out his spear until everyone who had lived in Ai was completely destroyed.* ²⁷Only the livestock and the treasures of the town were not destroyed, for the Israelites kept these as plunder for themselves, as the LORD

WHAT THE BIBLE SAYS

The evil of idolatry

JOSHUA 8:1 You may cringe a bit as you read these passages. Jericho is taken and every person killed (6:21). Achan commits what might seem to be a minor sin, and he and his whole family are stoned to death (7:25). The city of Ai is attacked and destroyed (8:22). Why all this violence? • Lest you think God is arbitrary, understand that God knew this all along and timed the Israelites' invasion for when the destruction was needed. Indeed, hundreds of years earlier, God had told Abraham that his descendants would be enslaved for four hundred years (in Egypt) and only then would return to the land of promise, "for the sins of the Amorites do not yet warrant their destruction" (see Genesis 15:12-16, January 6). The people of the Promised Land were not destroyed until God knew that they were hardened beyond redemption. • Idolatry is a hideous evil. It warrants severe punishment and has no place in the people of God. Today we might not be tempted to worship physical forms, but remember that anything you put before God becomes an idol. Be committed to keeping God first always.

had commanded Joshua. ²⁸So Joshua burned the town of Ai,* and it became a permanent mound of ruins, desolate to this very day.

²⁹Joshua impaled the king of Ai on a sharpened pole and left him there until evening. At sunset the Israelites took down the body, as Joshua commanded, and threw it in front of the town gate. They piled a great heap of stones over him that can still be seen today.

³⁰Then Joshua built an altar to the LORD, the God of Israel, on Mount Ebal. ³¹He followed the commands that Moses the LORD's servant had written in the Book of Instruction: "Make me an altar from stones that are uncut and have not been shaped with iron tools."* Then on the altar they presented burnt offerings and peace offerings to the LORD. ³²And as the Israelites watched, Joshua copied onto the stones of the altar* the instructions Moses had given them.

³³Then all the Israelites—foreigners and native-born alike—along with the elders, officers, and judges, were divided into two groups. One group stood in front of Mount Gerizim, the other in front of Mount Ebal. Each group faced the other, and between them stood the Levitical priests carrying the Ark of the LORD's Covenant. This was all done according to the commands that Moses, the servant of the LORD, had previously given for blessing the people of Israel.

³⁴Joshua then read to them all the blessings and curses Moses had written in the Book of Instruction. ³⁵Every word of every command that Moses had ever given was read to the entire assembly of Israel, including the women and children and the foreigners who lived among them.

⁹:¹Now all the kings west of the Jordan River heard about what had happened. These were the kings of the Hittites, Amorites, Canaanites, Perizzites, Hivites, and Jebusites, who lived in the hill country, in the western foothills,* and along the coast of the Mediterranean Sea* as far north as the Lebanon mountains. ²These kings combined their armies to fight as one against Joshua and the Israelites.

7:21a Hebrew *Shinar.*   **7:21b** Hebrew *200 shekels of silver,* about 5 pounds or 2.3 kilograms in weight.   **7:21c** Hebrew *50 shekels,* about 20 ounces or 570 grams in weight.
7:26 Hebrew *valley of Achor.*   **8:14** Hebrew *the Arabah.*
8:17 Some manuscripts lack *or Bethel.*   **8:26** The Hebrew term used here refers to the complete consecration of things or people to the LORD, either by destroying them or by giving them as an offering.   **8:28** *Ai* means "ruin."   **8:31** Exod 20:25; Deut 27:5-6.   **8:32** Or *onto stones.*   **9:1a** Hebrew *the Shephelah.*   **9:1b** Hebrew *the Great Sea.*

LUKE 16:1-18

Jesus showed respect for the Jewish law that governed his people, but he called those people to an even higher standard. If they would just listen . . .

Jesus told this story to his disciples: "There was a certain rich man who had a manager handling his affairs. One day a report came that the manager was wasting his employer's money. ²So the employer called him in and said, 'What's this I hear about you? Get your report in order, because you are going to be fired.'

³"The manager thought to himself, 'Now what? My boss has fired me. I don't have the strength to dig ditches, and I'm too proud to beg. ⁴Ah, I know how to ensure that I'll have plenty of friends who will give me a home when I am fired.'

⁵"So he invited each person who owed money to his employer to come and discuss the situation. He asked the first one, 'How much do you owe him?' ⁶The man replied, 'I owe him 800 gallons of olive oil.' So the manager told him, 'Take the bill and quickly change it to 400 gallons.*'

⁷"'And how much do you owe my employer?' he asked the next man. 'I owe him 1,000 bushels of wheat,' was the reply. 'Here,' the manager said, 'take the bill and change it to 800 bushels.*'

⁸"The rich man had to admire the dishonest rascal for being so shrewd. And it is true that the children of this world are more shrewd in dealing with the world around them than are the children of the light. ⁹Here's the lesson: Use your worldly resources to benefit others and make friends. Then, when your earthly possessions are gone, they will welcome you to an eternal home.*

¹⁰"If you are faithful in little things, you will be faithful in large ones. But if you are dishonest in little things, you won't be honest with greater responsibilities.

¹¹And if you are untrustworthy about worldly wealth, who will trust you with the true riches of heaven? ¹²And if you are not faithful with other people's things, why should you be trusted with things of your own?

¹³"No one can serve two masters. For you will hate one and love the other; you will be devoted to one and despise the other. You cannot serve both God and money."

¹⁴The Pharisees, who dearly loved their money, heard all this and scoffed at him. ¹⁵Then he said to them, "You like to appear righteous in public, but God knows your hearts. What this world honors is detestable in the sight of God.

¹⁶"Until John the Baptist, the law of Moses and the messages of the prophets were your guides. But now the Good News of the Kingdom of God is preached, and everyone is eager to get in.* ¹⁷But that doesn't mean that the law has lost its force. It is easier for heaven and earth to disappear than for the smallest point of God's law to be overturned.

¹⁸"For example, a man who divorces his wife and marries someone else commits adultery. And anyone who marries a woman divorced from her husband commits adultery."

16:6 Greek *100 baths . . . 50 [baths].* **16:7** Greek *100 korous . . . 80 [korous].* **16:9** Or *you will be welcomed into eternal homes.* **16:16** Or *everyone is urged to enter in.*

JOSHUA 9:3–10:43
The Israelites were to *take over* the land, not *share* it. That's why, from the beginning, Moses had warned them not to make treaties. That's why each battle was an all-or-nothing event. That's why, in this passage, the Gibeonites (Hivites) performed their elaborate masquerade.

But when the people of Gibeon heard what Joshua had done to Jericho and Ai, ⁴they resorted to deception to save themselves. They sent ambassadors to Joshua, loading their donkeys with weathered saddlebags and old, patched wineskins. ⁵They put on worn-out, patched sandals and ragged clothes. And the bread they took with them was dry and moldy. ⁶When they arrived at the camp of Israel at Gilgal, they told Joshua and the men of Israel, "We have come from a distant land to ask you to make a peace treaty with us."

PSALM 82:1-8
A psalm of Asaph.

¹ **G**od presides over heaven's court;
   he pronounces judgment on the heavenly beings:
² "How long will you hand down unjust decisions
   by favoring the wicked?   *Interlude*

³ "Give justice to the poor and the orphan;
   uphold the rights of the oppressed and the destitute.
⁴ Rescue the poor and helpless;
   deliver them from the grasp of evil people.
⁵ But these oppressors know nothing;
   they are so ignorant!
   They wander about in darkness,
   while the whole world is shaken to the core.
⁶ I say, 'You are gods;
   you are all children of the Most High.
⁷ But you will die like mere mortals
   and fall like every other ruler.'"

⁸ Rise up, O God, and judge the earth,
   for all the nations belong to you.

PROVERBS 13:2-3
Wise words will win you a good meal, but treacherous people have an appetite for violence. □Those who control their tongue will have a long life; opening your mouth can ruin everything.

[7] The Israelites replied to these Hivites, "How do we know you don't live nearby? For if you do, we cannot make a treaty with you."

[8] They replied, "We are your servants."

"But who are you?" Joshua demanded. "Where do you come from?"

[9] They answered, "Your servants have come from a very distant country. We have heard of the might of the LORD your God and of all he did in Egypt. [10] We have also heard what he did to the two Amorite kings east of the Jordan River—King Sihon of Heshbon and King Og of Bashan (who lived in Ashtaroth). [11] So our elders and all our people instructed us, 'Take supplies for a long journey. Go meet with the people of Israel and tell them, "We are your servants; please make a treaty with us."'

[12] "This bread was hot from the ovens when we left our homes. But now, as you can see, it is dry and moldy. [13] These wineskins were new when we filled them, but now they are old and split open. And our clothing and sandals are worn out from our very long journey."

[14] So the Israelites examined their food, but they did not consult the LORD. [15] Then Joshua made a peace treaty with them and guaranteed their safety, and the leaders of the community ratified their agreement with a binding oath.

[16] Three days after making the treaty, they learned that these people actually lived nearby! [17] The Israelites set out at once to investigate and reached their towns in three days. The names of these towns were Gibeon, Kephirah, Beeroth, and Kiriath-jearim. [18] But the Israelites did not attack the towns, for the Israelite leaders had made a vow to them in the name of the LORD, the God of Israel.

The people of Israel grumbled against their leaders because of the treaty. [19] But the leaders replied, "Since we have sworn an oath in the presence of the LORD, the God of Israel, we cannot touch them. [20] This is what we must do. We must let them live, for divine anger would come upon us if we broke our oath. [21] Let them live." So they made them woodcutters and water carriers for the entire community, as the Israelite leaders directed.

[22] Joshua called together the Gibeonites and said, "Why did you lie to us? Why did you say that you live in a distant land when you live right here among us? [23] May you be cursed! From now on you will always be servants who cut wood and carry water for the house of my God."

[24] They replied, "We did it because we—your servants—were clearly told that the LORD your God commanded his servant Moses to give you this entire land and to destroy all the people living in it. So we feared greatly for our lives because of you. That is why we have done this. [25] Now we are at your mercy—do to us whatever you think is right."

[26] So Joshua did not allow the people of Israel to kill them. [27] But that day he made the Gibeonites the woodcutters and water carriers for the community of Israel and for the altar of the LORD—wherever the LORD would choose to build it. And that is what they do to this day.

[10:1] ADONI-ZEDEK, king of Jerusalem, heard that Joshua had captured and completely destroyed* Ai and killed its king, just as he had destroyed the town of Jericho and killed its king. He also learned that the Gibeonites had made peace with Israel and were now their allies. [2] He and his people became very afraid when they heard all this because Gibeon was a large town—as large as the royal cities and larger than Ai. And the Gibeonite men were strong warriors.

[3] So King Adoni-zedek of Jerusalem sent messengers to several other kings: Hoham of Hebron, Piram of Jarmuth, Japhia of Lachish, and Debir of Eglon. [4] "Come and help me destroy Gibeon," he urged them, "for they have made peace with Joshua and the people of Israel." [5] So these five Amorite kings combined their armies for a united attack. They moved all their troops into place and attacked Gibeon.

[6] The men of Gibeon quickly sent messengers to Joshua at his camp in Gilgal. "Don't abandon your servants now!" they pleaded. "Come at once! Save us! Help us! For all the Amorite kings who live in the hill country have joined forces to attack us."

[7]So Joshua and his entire army, including his best warriors, left Gilgal and set out for Gibeon. [8]"Do not be afraid of them," the LORD said to Joshua, "for I have given you victory over them. Not a single one of them will be able to stand up to you."

[9]Joshua traveled all night from Gilgal and took the Amorite armies by surprise. [10]The LORD threw them into a panic, and the Israelites slaughtered great numbers of them at Gibeon. Then the Israelites chased the enemy along the road to Beth-horon, killing them all along the way to Azekah and Makkedah. [11]As the Amorites retreated down the road from Beth-horon, the LORD destroyed them with a terrible hailstorm from heaven that continued until they reached Azekah. The hail killed more of the enemy than the Israelites killed with the sword.

[12]On the day the LORD gave the Israelites victory over the Amorites, Joshua prayed to the LORD in front of all the people of Israel. He said,

"Let the sun stand still over Gibeon,
and the moon over the valley of Aijalon."

[13]So the sun stood still and the moon stayed in place until the nation of Israel had defeated its enemies.

Is this event not recorded in *The Book of Jashar**? The sun stayed in the middle of the sky, and it did not set as on a normal day.* [14]There has never been a day like this one before or since, when the LORD answered such a prayer. Surely the LORD fought for Israel that day!

[15]Then Joshua and the Israelite army returned to their camp at Gilgal.

[16]During the battle the five kings escaped and hid in a cave at Makkedah. [17]When Joshua heard that they had been found, [18]he issued this command: "Cover the opening of the cave with large rocks, and place guards at the entrance to keep the kings inside. [19]The rest of you continue chasing the enemy and cut them down from the rear. Don't give them a chance to get back to their towns, for the LORD your God has given you victory over them."

[20]So Joshua and the Israelite army continued the slaughter and completely crushed the enemy. They totally wiped out the five armies except for a tiny remnant that managed to reach their fortified towns. [21]Then the Israelites returned

WHAT THE BIBLE SAYS

The reality of hell

LUKE 16:19-31 This parable isn't meant to give a full theology about hell, but it does give some insights. (1) *The reality of an afterlife*. Some contend that there is no life beyond this earthly one, that the soul is not eternal. If that were true, it would seem strange for Jesus to invent an afterlife just to tell a story of accountability. (2) *There are only two destinies in the afterlife*. Lazarus and the rich man landed in different destinations, aware of each other but unable to reach each other. Each destination reflected choices they had made in their earthly lives. (3) *We have the information we need in this life to make the choice of how we'll spend the next*. The rich man wanted Abraham to send Lazarus back from the dead to warn his brothers, but Abraham told him that the brothers had the information they needed to make the right choice. • We can be certain that beyond this life there is a heaven and hell. In one place, people are eternally connected to God. In the other, people are eternally separated from him. How people choose to connect with God in this life determines how they will spend eternity. Since you have put your faith in Christ, your destination is determined. Share the faith, so that others will be there, too.

safely to Joshua in the camp at Makkedah. After that, no one dared to speak even a word against Israel.

[22] Then Joshua said, "Remove the rocks covering the opening of the cave, and bring the five kings to me." [23] So they brought the five kings out of the cave—the kings of Jerusalem, Hebron, Jarmuth, Lachish, and Eglon. [24] When they brought them out, Joshua told the commanders of his army, "Come and put your feet on the kings' necks." And they did as they were told.

[25] "Don't ever be afraid or discouraged," Joshua told his men. "Be strong and courageous, for the LORD is going to do this to all of your enemies." [26] Then Joshua killed each of the five kings and impaled them on five sharpened poles, where they hung until evening.

[27] As the sun was going down, Joshua gave instructions for the bodies of the kings to be taken down from the poles and thrown into the cave where they had been hiding. Then they covered the opening of the cave with a pile of large rocks, which remains to this very day.

[28] That same day Joshua captured and destroyed the town of Makkedah. He killed everyone in it, including the king, leaving no survivors. He destroyed them all, and he killed the king of Makkedah as he had killed the king of Jericho. [29] Then Joshua and the Israelites went to Libnah and attacked it. [30] There, too, the LORD gave them the town and its king. He killed everyone in it, leaving no survivors. Then Joshua killed the king of Libnah as he had killed the king of Jericho.

[31] From Libnah, Joshua and the Israelites went to Lachish and attacked it. [32] Here again, the LORD gave them Lachish. Joshua took it on the second day and killed everyone in it, just as he had done at Libnah. [33] During the attack on Lachish, King Horam of Gezer arrived with his army to help defend the town. But Joshua's men killed him and his army, leaving no survivors.

[34] Then Joshua and the Israelite army went on to Eglon and attacked it. [35] They captured it that day and killed everyone in it. He completely destroyed everyone, just as he had done at Lachish. [36] From Eglon, Joshua and the Israelite army went up to Hebron and attacked it. [37] They captured the town and killed everyone in it, including its king, leaving no survivors. They did the same thing to all of its surrounding villages. And just as he had done at Eglon, he completely destroyed the entire population.

[38] Then Joshua and the Israelites turned back and attacked Debir. [39] He captured the town, its king, and all of its surrounding villages. He completely destroyed everyone in it, leaving no survivors. He did to Debir and its king just what he had done to Hebron and to Libnah and its king.

[40] So Joshua conquered the whole region—the kings and people of the hill country, the Negev, the western foothills,* and the mountain slopes. He completely destroyed everyone in the land, leaving no survivors, just as the LORD, the God of Israel, had commanded. [41] Joshua slaughtered them from Kadesh-barnea to Gaza and from the region around the town of Goshen up to Gibeon. [42] Joshua conquered all these kings and their land in a single campaign, for the LORD, the God of Israel, was fighting for his people.

[43] Then Joshua and the Israelite army returned to their camp at Gilgal.

10:1 The Hebrew term used here refers to the complete consecration of things or people to the LORD, either by destroying them or by giving them as an offering; also in 10:28, 35, 37, 39, 40.   **10:13a** Or *The Book of the Upright.*   **10:13b** Or *did not set for about a whole day.*   **10:40** Hebrew *the Shephelah.*

LUKE 16:19–17:10

The story of Lazarus and the rich man reveals some hard realities. If people are going to believe, they'll believe. If they don't want to, they won't. The point is not to wait for miracles but to have an open heart.

Jesus said, "There was a certain rich man who was splendidly clothed in purple and fine linen and who lived each day in luxury. [20] At his gate lay a poor man named Lazarus who was covered with sores. [21] As Lazarus lay there longing for scraps from the rich man's table, the dogs would come and lick his open sores.

[22] "Finally, the poor man died and was carried by the angels to be with Abraham.*

The rich man also died and was buried, [23] and his soul went to the place of the dead.* There, in torment, he saw Abraham in the far distance with Lazarus at his side.

[24]"The rich man shouted, 'Father Abraham, have some pity! Send Lazarus over here to dip the tip of his finger in water and cool my tongue. I am in anguish in these flames.'

[25]"But Abraham said to him, 'Son, remember that during your lifetime you had everything you wanted, and Lazarus had nothing. So now he is here being comforted, and you are in anguish. [26]And besides, there is a great chasm separating us. No one can cross over to you from here, and no one can cross over to us from there.'

[27]"Then the rich man said, 'Please, Father Abraham, at least send him to my father's home. [28]For I have five brothers, and I want him to warn them so they don't end up in this place of torment.'

[29]"But Abraham said, 'Moses and the prophets have warned them. Your brothers can read what they wrote.'

[30]"The rich man replied, 'No, Father Abraham! But if someone is sent to them from the dead, then they will repent of their sins and turn to God.'

[31]"But Abraham said, 'If they won't listen to Moses and the prophets, they won't listen even if someone rises from the dead.'"

[17:1]ONE day Jesus said to his disciples, "There will always be temptations to sin, but what sorrow awaits the person who does the tempting! [2]It would be better to be thrown into the sea with a millstone hung around your neck than to cause one of these little ones to fall into sin. [3]So watch yourselves!

"If another believer* sins, rebuke that person; then if there is repentance, forgive. [4]Even if that person wrongs you seven times a day and each time turns again and asks forgiveness, you must forgive."

[5]The apostles said to the Lord, "Show us how to increase our faith."

[6]The Lord answered, "If you had faith even as small as a mustard seed, you could say to this mulberry tree, 'May you be up-

rooted and thrown into the sea,' and it would obey you!

[7]"When a servant comes in from plowing or taking care of sheep, does his master say, 'Come in and eat with me'? [8]No, he says, 'Prepare my meal, put on your apron, and serve me while I eat. Then you can eat later.' [9]And does the master thank the servant for doing what he was told to do? Of course not. [10]In the same way, when you obey me you should say, 'We are unworthy servants who have simply done our duty.'"

16:22 Greek *into Abraham's bosom.*   16:23 Greek *to Hades.*
17:3 Greek *If your brother.*

PSALM 83:1-18
A song. A psalm of Asaph.

[1] **O** God, do not be silent!
    Do not be deaf.
    Do not be quiet, O God.
[2] Don't you hear the uproar of your
      enemies?
    Don't you see that your arrogant
      enemies are rising up?
[3] They devise crafty schemes against
      your people;
    they conspire against your precious
      ones.
[4] "Come," they say, "let us wipe out Israel
      as a nation.
    We will destroy the very memory
      of its existence."
[5] Yes, this was their unanimous
      decision.
    They signed a treaty as allies against
      you—
[6] these Edomites and Ishmaelites;
      Moabites and Hagrites;
[7] Gebalites, Ammonites, and
      Amalekites;
    and people from Philistia and Tyre.
[8] Assyria has joined them, too,
    and is allied with the descendants
      of Lot.   *Interlude*

[9] Do to them as you did to the
      Midianites
    and as you did to Sisera and Jabin
      at the Kishon River.
[10] They were destroyed at Endor,
    and their decaying corpses
      fertilized the soil.
[11] Let their mighty nobles die as Oreb
      and Zeeb did.

Let all their princes die like Zebah
and Zalmunna,
[12] for they said, "Let us seize for our
own use
these pasturelands of God!"
[13] O my God, scatter them like
tumbleweed,
like chaff before the wind!
[14] As a fire burns a forest
and as a flame sets mountains
ablaze,
[15] chase them with your fierce storm;
terrify them with your tempest.

[16] Utterly disgrace them
until they submit to your name,
O LORD.
[17] Let them be ashamed and terrified
forever.
Let them die in disgrace.
[18] Then they will learn that you alone
are called the LORD,
that you alone are the Most High,
supreme over all the earth.

PROVERBS 13:4
Lazy people want much but get little, but
those who work hard will prosper.

APRIL**15**

JOSHUA 11:1–12:24
In today's passage, Joshua defeats the northern
kings of Canaan. The plan was to take out several
of the key cities, and then leave the tribes to do
the cleanup work in their own territories.

When King Jabin of Hazor heard what
had happened, he sent messages to the
following kings: King Jobab of Madon; the
king of Shimron; the king of Acshaph; [2] all
the kings of the northern hill country; the
kings in the Jordan Valley south of Galilee*; the kings in the Galilean foothills*;
the kings of Naphoth-dor on the west;
[3] the kings of Canaan, both east and west;
the kings of the Amorites, the Hittites, the
Perizzites, the Jebusites in the hill country, and the Hivites in the towns on the
slopes of Mount Hermon in the land of
Mizpah.

[4] All these kings came out to fight.
Their combined armies formed a vast
horde. And with all their horses and chariots, they covered the landscape like the
sand on the seashore. [5] The kings joined
forces and established their camp around
the water near Merom to fight against
Israel.

[6] Then the LORD said to Joshua, "Do not
be afraid of them. By this time tomorrow I
will hand all of them over to Israel as dead
men. Then you must cripple their horses
and burn their chariots."

[7] So Joshua and all his fighting men
traveled to the water near Merom and
attacked suddenly. [8] And the LORD gave
them victory over their enemies. The Israelites chased them as far as Greater Sidon
and Misrephoth-maim, and eastward into
the valley of Mizpah, until not one enemy
warrior was left alive. [9] Then Joshua crippled the horses and burned all the chariots, as the LORD had instructed.

[10] Joshua then turned back and captured Hazor and killed its king. (Hazor
had at one time been the capital of all
these kingdoms.) [11] The Israelites completely destroyed* every living thing in
the city, leaving no survivors. Not a single
person was spared. And then Joshua
burned the city.

[12] Joshua slaughtered all the other
kings and their people, completely destroying them, just as Moses, the servant
of the LORD, had commanded. [13] But the
Israelites did not burn any of the towns
built on mounds except Hazor, which
Joshua burned. [14] And the Israelites took
all the plunder and livestock of the ravaged towns for themselves. But they killed
all the people, leaving no survivors. [15] As
the LORD had commanded his servant
Moses, so Moses commanded Joshua.
And Joshua did as he was told, carefully

obeying all the commands that the LORD had given to Moses.

¹⁶So Joshua conquered the entire region—the hill country, the entire Negev, the whole area around the town of Goshen, the western foothills, the Jordan Valley,* the mountains of Israel, and the Galilean foothills. ¹⁷The Israelite territory now extended all the way from Mount Halak, which leads up to Seir in the south, as far north as Baal-gad at the foot of Mount Hermon in the valley of Lebanon. Joshua killed all the kings of those territories, ¹⁸waging war for a long time to accomplish this. ¹⁹No one in this region made peace with the Israelites except the Hivites of Gibeon. All the others were defeated. ²⁰For the LORD hardened their hearts and caused them to fight the Israelites. So they were completely destroyed without mercy, as the LORD had commanded Moses.

²¹During this period Joshua destroyed all the descendants of Anak, who lived in the hill country of Hebron, Debir, Anab, and the entire hill country of Judah and Israel. He killed them all and completely destroyed their towns. ²²None of the descendants of Anak were left in all the land of Israel, though some still remained in Gaza, Gath, and Ashdod.

²³So Joshua took control of the entire land, just as the LORD had instructed Moses. He gave it to the people of Israel as their special possession, dividing the land among the tribes. So the land finally had rest from war.

12:1THESE are the kings east of the Jordan River who had been killed by the Israelites and whose land was taken. Their territory extended from the Arnon Gorge to Mount Hermon and included all the land east of the Jordan Valley.*

²King Sihon of the Amorites, who lived in Heshbon, was defeated. His kingdom included Aroer, on the edge of the Arnon Gorge, and extended from the middle of the Arnon Gorge to the Jabbok River, which serves as a border for the Ammonites. This territory included the southern half of the territory of Gilead. ³Sihon also controlled the Jordan Valley and regions to the east—from as far north as the Sea of Galilee to as far south as the Dead Sea,* in-

cluding the road to Beth-jeshimoth and southward to the slopes of Pisgah.

⁴King Og of Bashan, the last of the Rephaites, lived at Ashtaroth and Edrei. ⁵He ruled a territory stretching from Mount Hermon to Salecah in the north and to all of Bashan in the east, and westward to the borders of the kingdoms of Geshur and Maacah. This territory included the northern half of Gilead, as far as the boundary of King Sihon of Heshbon.

⁶Moses, the servant of the LORD, and the Israelites had destroyed the people of King Sihon and King Og. And Moses gave their land as a possession to the tribes of Reuben, Gad, and the half-tribe of Manasseh.

⁷The following is a list of the kings that Joshua and the Israelite armies defeated on the west side of the Jordan, from Baal-gad in the valley of Lebanon to Mount Halak, which leads up to Seir. (Joshua gave this land to the tribes of Israel as their possession, ⁸including the hill country, the western foothills,* the Jordan Valley, the mountain slopes, the Judean wilderness, and the Negev. The people who lived in this region were the Hittites, the Amorites, the Canaanites, the Perizzites, the Hivites, and the Jebusites.) These are the kings Israel defeated:

⁹ The king of Jericho
  The king of Ai, near Bethel
¹⁰ The king of Jerusalem
  The king of Hebron
¹¹ The king of Jarmuth
  The king of Lachish
¹² The king of Eglon
  The king of Gezer
¹³ The king of Debir
  The king of Geder
¹⁴ The king of Hormah
  The king of Arad
¹⁵ The king of Libnah
  The king of Adullam
¹⁶ The king of Makkedah
  The king of Bethel
¹⁷ The king of Tappuah
  The king of Hepher
¹⁸ The king of Aphek
  The king of Lasharon
¹⁹ The king of Madon
  The king of Hazor

20 The king of Shimron-meron
 The king of Acshaph
21 The king of Taanach
 The king of Megiddo
22 The king of Kedesh
 The king of Jokneam in Carmel
23 The king of Dor in the town of
    Naphoth-dor*
 The king of Goyim in Gilgal*
24 The king of Tirzah.

In all, thirty-one kings were defeated.

11:2a Hebrew *in the Arabah south of Kinnereth.*
11:2b Hebrew *the Shephelah;* also in 11:16. 11:11 The
Hebrew term used here refers to the complete consecration
of things or people to the LORD, either by destroying them or
by giving them as an offering; also in 11:12, 20, 21.
11:16 Hebrew *the Shephelah, the Arabah.* 12:1 Hebrew
the Arabah; also in 12:3, 8. 12:3 Hebrew *from the Sea of
Kinnereth to the Sea of the Arabah, which is the Salt Sea.*
12:8 Hebrew *the Shephelah.* 12:23a Hebrew *Naphath-dor,*
a variant spelling of Naphoth-dor. 12:23b Greek version
reads *Goyim in Galilee.*

LUKE 17:11-37
After Jesus healed ten men of leprosy (with only one
returning to express thanks), he revealed that the
Kingdom of God is not like an earthly kingdom with
geographical boundaries. Instead, it begins in
people's hearts.

As Jesus continued on toward Jerusalem,
he reached the border between Galilee
and Samaria. 12As he entered a village
there, ten lepers stood at a distance, 13cry-
ing out, "Jesus, Master, have mercy on us!"

14He looked at them and said, "Go show
yourselves to the priests."* And as they
went, they were cleansed of their leprosy.

15One of them, when he saw that he was
healed, came back to Jesus, shouting,
"Praise God!" 16He fell to the ground at
Jesus' feet, thanking him for what he had
done. This man was a Samaritan.

17Jesus asked, "Didn't I heal ten men?
Where are the other nine? 18Has no one
returned to give glory to God except this
foreigner?" 19And Jesus said to the man,
"Stand up and go. Your faith has healed
you.*"

20One day the Pharisees asked Jesus,
"When will the Kingdom of God come?"

Jesus replied, "The Kingdom of God
can't be detected by visible signs.* 21You
won't be able to say, 'Here it is!' or 'It's over
there!' For the Kingdom of God is already
among you.*"

22Then he said to his disciples, "The
time is coming when you will long to see
the day when the Son of Man returns,* but
you won't see it. 23People will tell you,
'Look, there is the Son of Man,' or 'Here he
is,' but don't go out and follow them. 24For
as the lightning flashes and lights up the
sky from one end to the other, so it will be
on the day when the Son of Man comes.
25But first the Son of Man must suffer terribly* and be rejected by this generation.

26"When the Son of Man returns, it will
be like it was in Noah's day. 27In those
days, the people enjoyed banquets and
parties and weddings right up to the time
Noah entered his boat and the flood came
and destroyed them all.

28"And the world will be as it was in the
days of Lot. People went about their daily
business—eating and drinking, buying
and selling, farming and building—29un-
til the morning Lot left Sodom. Then fire
and burning sulfur rained down from
heaven and destroyed them all. 30Yes, it
will be 'business as usual' right up to the
day when the Son of Man is revealed. 31On
that day a person out on the deck of a roof
must not go down into the house to pack.
A person out in the field must not return
home. 32Remember what happened to
Lot's wife! 33If you cling to your life, you
will lose it, and if you let your life go, you
will save it. 34That night two people will be
asleep in one bed; one will be taken, the
other left. 35Two women will be grinding
flour together at the mill; one will be
taken, the other left.*"

37"Where will this happen, Lord?"* the
disciples asked.

Jesus replied, "Just as the gathering of
vultures shows there is a carcass nearby, so
these signs indicate that the end is near."*

17:14 See Lev 14:2-32. 17:19 Or *Your faith has saved you.*
17:20 Or *by your speculations.* 17:21 Or *is within you,* or
is in your grasp. 17:22 Or *long for even one day with the
Son of Man.* "Son of Man" is a title Jesus used for himself.
17:25 Or *suffer many things.* 17:35 Some manuscripts
add verse 36, *Two men will be working in the field; one will
be taken, the other left.* Compare Matt 24:40. 17:37a Greek
"*Where, Lord?*" 17:37b Greek "*Wherever the carcass is, the
vultures gather.*"

PSALM 84:1-12
*For the choir director: A psalm of the
descendants of Korah, to be accompanied
by a stringed instrument.*

¹ **H**ow lovely is your dwelling place,
   O LORD of Heaven's Armies.
² I long, yes, I faint with longing
     to enter the courts of the LORD.
   With my whole being, body and soul,
     I will shout joyfully to the living God.
³ Even the sparrow finds a home,
     and the swallow builds her nest and
       raises her young
   at a place near your altar,
     O LORD of Heaven's Armies, my
       King and my God!
⁴ What joy for those who can live in
     your house,
   always singing your praises.
                                    Interlude

⁵ What joy for those whose strength
     comes from the LORD,
   who have set their minds on a
     pilgrimage to Jerusalem.
⁶ When they walk through the Valley of
     Weeping,*
   it will become a place of refreshing
     springs.
   The autumn rains will clothe it with
     blessings.
⁷ They will continue to grow stronger,
     and each of them will appear before
       God in Jerusalem.*

⁸ O LORD God of Heaven's Armies, hear
     my prayer.
   Listen, O God of Jacob.   *Interlude*

⁹ O God, look with favor upon the king,
     our shield!
   Show favor to the one you have
     anointed.
¹⁰ A single day in your courts
     is better than a thousand anywhere
       else!
   I would rather be a gatekeeper in the
     house of my God
   than live the good life in the homes
     of the wicked.
¹¹ For the LORD God is our sun and our
     shield.
   He gives us grace and glory.
   The LORD will withhold no good thing
     from those who do what is right.
¹² O LORD of Heaven's Armies,
     what joy for those who trust in you.

84:TITLE Hebrew *according to the gittith.*   **84:6** Or *Valley of Poplars;* Hebrew reads *valley of Baca.*   **84:7** Hebrew *Zion.*

PROVERBS 13:5-6
The godly hate lies; the wicked cause shame and disgrace. ☐ Godliness guards the path of the blameless, but the evil are misled by sin.

HOW WE LIVE

Praise and thanksgiving

LUKE 17:11-19 Ten individuals afflicted with leprosy, a dreaded skin disease, witnessed Jesus' entrance into a nearby village and cried out for mercy. Christ looked at them with compassion and commanded them "Go show yourselves to the priests." As they obeyed, their healing became apparent. Yet only one man, a Samaritan, returned to express his gratitude. • Jesus used this occasion of healing to teach an important lesson about thankfulness. "Didn't I heal ten men?" he asked. "Where are the other nine?" Jesus recognized our human propensity to ask for miracles from God and yet fail to give him the glory. • Why is expressing thanks so important? It's really a question of need: God doesn't need your thanks, but thankfulness acknowledges your dependence upon him. When you acknowledge what he has done for you, you are completing the cycle that God begins when he promises to meet all of your needs. God gives to you out of his great love and compassion, and you "return thanks" to him. Developing a heart of praise and thanksgiving gives you a proper perspective of your place in God's plan. Being thankful is not so much about what it does for God as what it does for you.

APRIL 16

Key cities in various territories had been conquered; now it would be up to the tribes to clear the remaining enemies from their allotted areas. Caleb, Joshua's faithful friend, received the land God had promised him over 45 years before.

When Joshua was an old man, the LORD said to him, "You are growing old, and much land remains to be conquered. ²This is the territory that remains: all the regions of the Philistines and the Geshurites, ³and the larger territory of the Canaanites, extending from the stream of Shihor on the border of Egypt, northward to the boundary of Ekron. It includes the territory of the five Philistine rulers of Gaza, Ashdod, Ashkelon, Gath, and Ekron. The land of the Avvites ⁴in the south also remains to be conquered. In the north, the following area has not yet been conquered: all the land of the Canaanites, including Mearah (which belongs to the Sidonians), stretching northward to Aphek on the border of the Amorites; ⁵the land of the Gebalites and all of the Lebanon mountain area to the east, from Baal-gad below Mount Hermon to Lebo-hamath; ⁶and all the hill country from Lebanon to Misrephoth-maim, including all the land of the Sidonians.

"I myself will drive these people out of the land ahead of the Israelites. So be sure to give this land to Israel as a special possession, just as I have commanded you. ⁷Include all this territory as Israel's possession when you divide this land among the nine tribes and the half-tribe of Manasseh."

⁸Half the tribe of Manasseh and the tribes of Reuben and Gad had already received their grants of land on the east side of the Jordan, for Moses, the servant of the LORD, had previously assigned this land to them.

⁹Their territory extended from Aroer on the edge of the Arnon Gorge (including the town in the middle of the gorge) to the plain beyond Medeba, as far as Dibon. ¹⁰It also included all the towns of King Sihon of the Amorites, who had reigned in Heshbon, and extended as far as the borders of Ammon. ¹¹It included Gilead, the territory of the kingdoms of Geshur and Maacah, all of Mount Hermon, all of Bashan as far as Salecah, ¹²and all the territory of King Og of Bashan, who had reigned in Ashtaroth and Edrei. King Og was the last of the Rephaites, for Moses had attacked them and driven them out. ¹³But the Israelites failed to drive out the people of Geshur and Maacah, so they continue to live among the Israelites to this day.

¹⁴Moses did not assign any allotment of land to the tribe of Levi. Instead, as the LORD had promised them, their allotment came from the offerings burned on the altar to the LORD, the God of Israel.

¹⁵Moses had assigned the following area to the clans of the tribe of Reuben.

¹⁶Their territory extended from Aroer on the edge of the Arnon Gorge (including the town in the middle of the gorge) to the plain beyond Medeba. ¹⁷It included Heshbon and the other towns on the plain—Dibon, Bamoth-baal, Beth-baal-meon, ¹⁸Jahaz, Kedemoth, Mephaath, ¹⁹Kiriathaim, Sibmah, Zereth-shahar on the hill above the valley, ²⁰Beth-peor, the slopes of Pisgah, and Beth-jeshimoth.

²¹The land of Reuben also included all the towns of the plain and the entire kingdom of Sihon. Sihon was the Amorite king who had reigned in Heshbon and was killed by Moses along with the leaders of Midian—Evi, Rekem, Zur, Hur, and Reba—princes living in the region who were allied with Sihon. ²²The Israelites had also killed Balaam son of Beor, who used magic to tell the future. ²³The Jordan River marked the western boundary for the tribe of Reuben. The towns and their surrounding villages in this area

were given as a homeland to the clans of the tribe of Reuben.

²⁴Moses had assigned the following area to the clans of the tribe of Gad.

²⁵Their territory included Jazer, all the towns of Gilead, and half of the land of Ammon, as far as the town of Aroer just west of* Rabbah. ²⁶It extended from Heshbon to Ramath-mizpeh and Betonim, and from Mahanaim to Lo-debar.* ²⁷In the valley were Beth-haram, Beth-nimrah, Succoth, Zaphon, and the rest of the kingdom of King Sihon of Heshbon. The western boundary ran along the Jordan River, extended as far north as the tip of the Sea of Galilee,* and then turned eastward. ²⁸The towns and their surrounding villages in this area were given as a homeland to the clans of the tribe of Gad.

²⁹Moses had assigned the following area to the clans of the half-tribe of Manasseh.

³⁰Their territory extended from Mahanaim, including all of Bashan, all the former kingdom of King Og, and the sixty towns of Jair in Bashan. ³¹It also included half of Gilead and King Og's royal cities of Ashtaroth and Edrei. All this was given to the clans of the descendants of Makir, who was Manasseh's son.

³²These are the allotments Moses had made while he was on the plains of Moab, across the Jordan River, east of Jericho. ³³But Moses gave no allotment of land to the tribe of Levi, for the LORD, the God of Israel, had promised that he himself would be their allotment.

¹⁴:¹THE remaining tribes of Israel received land in Canaan as allotted by Eleazar the priest, Joshua son of Nun, and the tribal leaders. ²These nine and a half tribes received their grants of land by means of sacred lots, in accordance with the LORD's command through Moses. ³Moses had already given a grant of land to the two and a half tribes on the east side of the Jordan River, but he had given the Levites no such allotment. ⁴The descendants of Joseph had become two separate tribes—Manasseh and Ephraim. And the Levites were given no land at all, only towns to live in with surrounding pasturelands for their livestock and all their possessions. ⁵So the land was distributed in strict accordance with the LORD's commands to Moses.

⁶A delegation from the tribe of Judah, led

HOW WE LIVE

Persevering in faith

JOSHUA 14:6-14 Caleb was one of the spies whom Moses sent to explore the Promised Land. Upon returning, only he and Joshua reported that the Israelites should obey God and enter the land. The other spies insisted that such a mission would be too dangerous, and the people sided with them. That entire generation died in the wilderness (see Numbers 13–14, March 9–10). Only Caleb and Joshua were allowed to live and eventually enter the land. • What was the secret to Caleb's faith? He persevered. Caleb refused to go with the majority opinion when it contradicted what he knew to be God's will. Because of his faithfulness to the will and purposes of God, Caleb never lost his spiritual edge. He had to endure forty years of desert wandering before he could enter the Promised Land, yet he never doubted God's ability to carry through on his promise. • You've begun a spiritual walk with the Lord that will last the rest of your life. You will face "desert" times that might cause you to doubt God's promises. Like Caleb, stand for God's truth, no matter what the rest of the crowd says. Like Caleb, trust God to carry through on his promises.

by Caleb son of Jephunneh the Kenizzite, came to Joshua at Gilgal. Caleb said to Joshua, "Remember what the LORD said to Moses, the man of God, about you and me when we were at Kadesh-barnea. ⁷I was forty years old when Moses, the servant of the LORD, sent me from Kadesh-barnea to explore the land of Canaan. I returned and gave an honest report, ⁸but my brothers who went with me frightened the people from entering the Promised Land. For my part, I wholeheartedly followed the LORD my God. ⁹So that day Moses solemnly promised me, 'The land of Canaan on which you were just walking will be your grant of land and that of your descendants forever, because you wholeheartedly followed the LORD my God.'

¹⁰"Now, as you can see, the LORD has kept me alive and well as he promised for all these forty-five years since Moses made this promise—even while Israel wandered in the wilderness. Today I am eighty-five years old. ¹¹I am as strong now as I was when Moses sent me on that journey, and I can still travel and fight as well as I could then. ¹²So give me the hill country that the LORD promised me. You will remember that as scouts we found the descendants of Anak living there in great, walled towns. But if the LORD is with me, I will drive them out of the land, just as the LORD said."

¹³So Joshua blessed Caleb son of Jephunneh and gave Hebron to him as his portion of land. ¹⁴Hebron still belongs to the descendants of Caleb son of Jephunneh the Kenizzite because he wholeheartedly followed the LORD, the God of Israel. ¹⁵(Previously Hebron had been called Kiriath-arba. It had been named after Arba, a great hero of the descendants of Anak.)

And the land had rest from war.

13:25 Hebrew *in front of.* 13:26 Or *to the territory of Debir.* 13:27 Hebrew *Sea of Kinnereth.*

LUKE 18:1-17

Jesus talked a lot about prayer; he knew that once he was gone, prayer would be his people's primary method of communication with him. He taught that we should always pray and never give up, and that we should come with an attitude of humility, like little children.

One day Jesus told his disciples a story to show that they should always pray and never give up. ²"There was a judge in a certain city," he said, "who neither feared God nor cared about people. ³A widow of that city came to him repeatedly, saying, 'Give me justice in this dispute with my enemy.' ⁴The judge ignored her for a while, but finally he said to himself, 'I don't fear God or care about people, ⁵but this woman is driving me crazy. I'm going to see that she gets justice, because she is wearing me out with her constant requests!'"

⁶Then the Lord said, "Learn a lesson from this unjust judge. ⁷Even he rendered a just decision in the end. So don't you think God will surely give justice to his chosen people who cry out to him day and night? Will he keep putting them off? ⁸I tell you, he will grant justice to them quickly! But when the Son of Man* returns, how many will he find on the earth who have faith?"

⁹Then Jesus told this story to some who had great confidence in their own righteousness and scorned everyone else: ¹⁰"Two men went to the Temple to pray. One was a Pharisee, and the other was a despised tax collector. ¹¹The Pharisee stood by himself and prayed this prayer*: 'I thank you, God, that I am not a sinner like everyone else. For I don't cheat, I don't sin, and I don't commit adultery. I'm certainly not like that tax collector! ¹²I fast twice a week, and I give you a tenth of my income.'

¹³"But the tax collector stood at a distance and dared not even lift his eyes to heaven as he prayed. Instead, he beat his chest in sorrow, saying, 'O God, be merciful to me, for I am a sinner.' ¹⁴I tell you, this sinner, not the Pharisee, returned home justified before God. For those who exalt themselves will be humbled, and those who humble themselves will be exalted."

¹⁵One day some parents brought their little children to Jesus so he could touch and bless them. But when the disciples saw this, they scolded the parents for bothering him.

¹⁶Then Jesus called for the children and said to the disciples, "Let the children come to me. Don't stop them! For the Kingdom of God belongs to those who are like these children. ¹⁷I tell you the truth,

anyone who doesn't receive the Kingdom of God like a child will never enter it."

18:8 "Son of Man" is a title Jesus used for himself. 18:11 Some manuscripts read *stood and prayed this prayer to himself.*

PSALM 85:1-13
For the choir director: A psalm of the descendants of Korah.

[1] LORD, you poured out blessings on
   your land!
   You restored the fortunes of
   Israel.*

[2] You forgave the guilt of your people—
   yes, you covered all their sins.
                    Interlude

[3] You held back your fury.
   You kept back your blazing anger.

[4] Now restore us again, O God of our
   salvation.
   Put aside your anger against us once
   more.

[5] Will you be angry with us always?
   Will you prolong your wrath to all
   generations?

[6] Won't you revive us again,
   so your people can rejoice in you?

[7] Show us your unfailing love, O LORD,
   and grant us your salvation.

[8] I listen carefully to what God the LORD
   is saying,

for he speaks peace to his faithful
   people.
   But let them not return to their
   foolish ways.

[9] Surely his salvation is near to those
   who fear him,
   so our land will be filled with his
   glory.

[10] Unfailing love and truth have met
    together.
    Righteousness and peace have
    kissed!

[11] Truth springs up from the earth,
    and righteousness smiles down
    from heaven.

[12] Yes, the LORD pours down his
    blessings.
    Our land will yield its bountiful
    harvest.

[13] Righteousness goes as a herald before
    him,
    preparing the way for his steps.

85:1 Hebrew *of Jacob.* See note on 44:4.

PROVERBS 13:7-8
Some who are poor pretend to be rich; others who are rich pretend to be poor. □The rich can pay a ransom for their lives, but the poor won't even get threatened.

JOSHUA 15:1-63
The tribe of Judah played a huge role in the history of the Jewish nation. King David came from this tribe, as did Jesus himself.

The allotment for the clans of the tribe of Judah reached southward to the border of Edom, as far south as the wilderness of Zin.

[2] The southern boundary began at the south bay of the Dead Sea,* [3] ran south of Scorpion Pass* into the wilderness of Zin, and then went south of Kadesh-barnea to Hezron. Then it went up to Addar, where it turned toward Karka. [4] From there it passed

to Azmon until it finally reached the Brook of Egypt, which it followed to the Mediterranean Sea.* This was their* southern boundary.

[5] The eastern boundary extended along the Dead Sea to the mouth of the Jordan River.

The northern boundary began at the bay where the Jordan River empties into the Dead Sea, [6] went up from there to Beth-hoglah, then proceeded north of Beth-arabah to the Stone of Bohan. (Bohan was Reuben's son.) [7] From that point it went through the valley of Achor to Debir, turning north toward

APRIL**17**

Gilgal, which is across from the slopes of Adummim on the south side of the valley. From there the boundary extended to the springs at En-shemesh and on to En-rogel. ⁸The boundary then passed through the valley of Ben-Hinnom, along the southern slopes of the Jebusites, where the city of Jerusalem is located. Then it went west to the top of the mountain above the valley of Hinnom, and on up to the northern end of the valley of Rephaim. ⁹From there the boundary extended from the top of the mountain to the spring at the waters of Nephtoah,* and from there to the towns on Mount Ephron. Then it turned toward Baalah (that is, Kiriath-jearim). ¹⁰The boundary circled west of Baalah to Mount Seir, passed along to the town of Kesalon on the northern slope of Mount Jearim, and went down to Beth-shemesh and on to Timnah. ¹¹The boundary then proceeded to the slope of the hill north of Ekron, where it turned toward Shikkeron and Mount Baalah. It passed Jabneel and ended at the Mediterranean Sea.

¹²The western boundary was the shoreline of the Mediterranean Sea.*

These are the boundaries for the clans of the tribe of Judah.

¹³The LORD commanded Joshua to assign some of Judah's territory to Caleb son of Jephunneh. So Caleb was given the town of Kiriath-arba (that is, Hebron), which had been named after Anak's ancestor. ¹⁴Caleb drove out the three groups of Anakites—the descendants of Sheshai, Ahiman, and Talmai, the sons of Anak.

¹⁵From there he went to fight against the people living in the town of Debir (formerly called Kiriath-sepher). ¹⁶Caleb said, "I will give my daughter Acsah in marriage to the one who attacks and captures Kiriath-sepher." ¹⁷Othniel, the son of Caleb's brother Kenaz, was the one who conquered it, so Acsah became Othniel's wife.

¹⁸When Acsah married Othniel, she urged him* to ask her father for a field. As she got down off her donkey, Caleb asked her, "What's the matter?"

¹⁹She said, "Give me another gift. You have already given me land in the Negev; now please give me springs of water, too." So Caleb gave her the upper and lower springs.

²⁰This was the homeland allocated to the clans of the tribe of Judah.

²¹The towns of Judah situated along the borders of Edom in the extreme south were Kabzeel, Eder, Jagur, ²²Kinah, Dimonah, Adadah, ²³Kedesh, Hazor, Ithnan, ²⁴Ziph, Telem, Bealoth, ²⁵Hazor-hadattah, Kerioth-hezron (that is, Hazor), ²⁶Amam, Shema, Moladah, ²⁷Hazar-gaddah, Heshmon, Beth-pelet, ²⁸Hazar-shual, Beersheba, Biziothiah, ²⁹Baalah, Iim, Ezem, ³⁰Eltolad, Kesil, Hormah, ³¹Ziklag, Madmannah, Sansannah, ³²Lebaoth, Shilhim, Ain, and Rimmon—twenty-nine towns with their surrounding villages.

³³The following towns situated in the western foothills* were also given to Judah: Eshtaol, Zorah, Ashnah, ³⁴Zanoah, En-gannim, Tappuah, Enam, ³⁵Jarmuth, Adullam, Socoh, Azekah, ³⁶Shaaraim, Adithaim, Gederah, and Gederothaim—fourteen towns with their surrounding villages.

³⁷Also included were Zenan, Hadashah, Migdal-gad, ³⁸Dilean, Mizpeh, Joktheel, ³⁹Lachish, Bozkath, Eglon, ⁴⁰Cabbon, Lahmam, Kitlish, ⁴¹Gederoth, Beth-dagon, Naamah, and Makkedah—sixteen towns with their surrounding villages.

⁴²Besides these, there were Libnah, Ether, Ashan, ⁴³Iphtah, Ashnah, Nezib, ⁴⁴Keilah, Aczib, and Mareshah—nine towns with their surrounding villages.

⁴⁵The territory of the tribe of Judah also included Ekron and its surrounding settlements and villages. ⁴⁶From Ekron the boundary extended west and included the towns near Ashdod with their surrounding villages. ⁴⁷It also included Ashdod with its surrounding settlements and villages and Gaza with its settlements and villages, as far as the Brook of Egypt and along the coast of the Mediterranean Sea.

⁴⁸Judah also received the following towns in the hill country: Shamir,

Jattir, Socoh, [49]Dannah, Kiriath-sannah (that is, Debir), [50]Anab, Eshtemoh, Anim, [51]Goshen, Holon, and Giloh—eleven towns with their surrounding villages.

[52]Also included were the towns of Arab, Dumah, Eshan, [53]Janim, Beth-tappuah, Aphekah, [54]Humtah, Kiriath-arba (that is, Hebron), and Zior—nine towns with their surrounding villages.

[55]Besides these, there were Maon, Carmel, Ziph, Juttah, [56]Jezreel, Jokdeam, Zanoah, [57]Kain, Gibeah, and Timnah—ten towns with their surrounding villages.

[58]In addition, there were Halhul, Beth-zur, Gedor, [59]Maarath, Beth-anoth, and Eltekon—six towns with their surrounding villages.

[60]There were also Kiriath-baal (that is, Kiriath-jearim) and Rabbah—two towns with their surrounding villages.

[61]In the wilderness there were the towns of Beth-arabah, Middin, Secacah, [62]Nibshan, the City of Salt, and En-gedi—six towns with their surrounding villages.

[63]But the tribe of Judah could not drive out the Jebusites, who lived in the city of Jerusalem, so the Jebusites live there among the people of Judah to this day.

15:2 Hebrew *the Salt Sea;* also in 15:5.   15:3 Hebrew *Akrabbim.*   15:4a Hebrew *the sea;* also in 15:11.   15:4b Hebrew *your.*   15:9 Or *the spring at Me-nephtoah.*

15:12 Hebrew *the Great Sea;* also in 15:47.   15:18 Some Greek manuscripts read *he urged her.*   15:33 Hebrew *the Shephelah.*

LUKE 18:18-43

If not handled with care, Jesus taught that wealth can work against faith. Why? Money has a way of making people feel self-sufficient, thinking they have no need for God.

Once a religious leader asked Jesus this question: "Good Teacher, what should I do to inherit eternal life?"

[19]"Why do you call me good?" Jesus asked him. "Only God is truly good. [20]But to answer your question, you know the commandments: 'You must not commit adultery. You must not murder. You must not steal. You must not testify falsely. Honor your father and mother.'*"

[21]The man replied, "I've obeyed all these commandments since I was young."

[22]When Jesus heard his answer, he said, "There is still one thing you haven't done. Sell all your possessions and give the money to the poor, and you will have treasure in heaven. Then come, follow me."

[23]But when the man heard this he became very sad, for he was very rich.

[24]When Jesus saw this,* he said, "How hard it is for the rich to enter the Kingdom of God! [25]In fact, it is easier for a camel to go through the eye of a needle than for a rich person to enter the Kingdom of God!"

Setting priorities

HOW WE LIVE

LUKE 18:18-25 A wealthy man came to Jesus, concerned about whether he was on the right path. He was wealthy, and, according to him anyway, he had managed to keep every law required of him. So Jesus got right to the heart of the matter by telling him to get rid of his wealth. This zeroed in on a fact that the man couldn't see for himself—that his unwillingness to give up his wealth showed that he wasn't even keeping the first of the Ten Commandments, to not let anything be more important than his relationship with God (see Exodus 20:2-3, February 4). • Jesus doesn't ask you to sell everything you own, but he does ask you to get rid of anything in your life that adversely affects your relationship with God. Consider where you focus your time and energy. The focus of your life establishes your priorities. Jesus says to make *him* your priority. When you do, you won't need to fret about whether you're *doing* enough. Instead, you'll be doing just what he calls you to do.

²⁶Those who heard this said, "Then who in the world can be saved?"

²⁷He replied, "What is impossible for people is possible with God."

²⁸Peter said, "We've left our homes to follow you."

²⁹"Yes," Jesus replied, "and I assure you that everyone who has given up house or wife or brothers or parents or children, for the sake of the Kingdom of God, ³⁰will be repaid many times over in this life, and will have eternal life in the world to come."

³¹Taking the twelve disciples aside, Jesus said, "Listen, we're going up to Jerusalem, where all the predictions of the prophets concerning the Son of Man will come true. ³²He will be handed over to the Romans,* and he will be mocked, treated shamefully, and spit upon. ³³They will flog him with a whip and kill him, but on the third day he will rise again."

³⁴But they didn't understand any of this. The significance of his words was hidden from them, and they failed to grasp what he was talking about.

³⁵As Jesus approached Jericho, a blind beggar was sitting beside the road. ³⁶When he heard the noise of a crowd going past, he asked what was happening. ³⁷They told him that Jesus the Nazarene* was going by. ³⁸So he began shouting, "Jesus, Son of David, have mercy on me!"

³⁹"Be quiet!" the people in front yelled at him.

But he only shouted louder, "Son of David, have mercy on me!"

⁴⁰When Jesus heard him, he stopped and ordered that the man be brought to him. As the man came near, Jesus asked him, ⁴¹"What do you want me to do for you?"

"Lord," he said, "I want to see!"

⁴²And Jesus said, "All right, receive your sight! Your faith has healed you." ⁴³Instantly the man could see, and he followed Jesus, praising God. And all who saw it praised God, too.

18:20 Exod 20:12-16; Deut 5:16-20.   18:24 Some manuscripts read *When Jesus saw how sad the man was.*   18:32 Greek *the Gentiles.*   18:37 Or *Jesus of Nazareth.*

PSALM 86:1-17
A prayer of David.

¹ **B**end down, O L ORD, and hear my prayer;

answer me, for I need your help.
² Protect me, for I am devoted to you.
Save me, for I serve you and
trust you.
You are my God.
³ Be merciful to me, O Lord,
for I am calling on you constantly.
⁴ Give me happiness, O Lord,
for I give myself to you.
⁵ O Lord, you are so good, so ready to
forgive,
so full of unfailing love for all who
ask for your help.
⁶ Listen closely to my prayer, O L ORD;
hear my urgent cry.
⁷ I will call to you whenever I'm in
trouble,
and you will answer me.

⁸ No pagan god is like you, O Lord.
None can do what you do!
⁹ All the nations you made
will come and bow before you,
Lord;
they will praise your holy name.
¹⁰ For you are great and perform
wonderful deeds.
You alone are God.

¹¹ Teach me your ways, O L ORD,
that I may live according to your
truth!
Grant me purity of heart,
so that I may honor you.
¹² With all my heart I will praise you,
O Lord my God.
I will give glory to your name
forever,
¹³ for your love for me is very great.
You have rescued me from the
depths of death.*

¹⁴ O God, insolent people rise up
against me;
a violent gang is trying to kill me.
You mean nothing to them.
¹⁵ But you, O Lord,
are a God of compassion and
mercy,
slow to get angry
and filled with unfailing love and
faithfulness.
¹⁶ Look down and have mercy on me.
Give your strength to your servant;
save me, the son of your servant.

¹⁷ Send me a sign of your favor.
Then those who hate me will be put
to shame,
for you, O LORD, help and comfort
me.

86:13 Hebrew *of Sheol.*

JOSHUA 16:1–18:28
Joshua continued allotting the land to the tribes.
While no region was assigned to Joseph (one of the
original twelve sons of Jacob), his sons, Ephraim
and Manasseh, each received an allotment of land.

The allotment for the descendants of
Joseph extended from the Jordan
River near Jericho, east of the springs
of Jericho, through the wilderness and
into the hill country of Bethel. ²From
Bethel (that is, Luz)* it ran over to
Ataroth in the territory of the Arkites.
³Then it descended westward to the
territory of the Japhletites as far as
Lower Beth-horon, then to Gezer and
over to the Mediterranean Sea.*

⁴This was the homeland allocated to the
families of Joseph's sons, Manasseh and
Ephraim.

⁵The following territory was given to
the clans of the tribe of Ephraim.

The boundary of their homeland
began at Ataroth-addar in the east.
From there it ran to Upper Beth-
horon, ⁶then on to the Mediterranean
Sea. From Micmethath on the north,
the boundary curved eastward past
Taanath-shiloh to the east of Janoah.
⁷From Janoah it turned southward to
Ataroth and Naarah, touched Jericho,
and ended at the Jordan River. ⁸From
Tappuah the boundary extended
westward, following the Kanah Ravine
to the Mediterranean Sea. This is the
homeland allocated to the clans of the
tribe of Ephraim.

⁹In addition, some towns with their
surrounding villages in the territory
allocated to the half-tribe of Manasseh
were set aside for the tribe of Ephraim.

PROVERBS 13:9-10
The life of the godly is full of light and joy,
but the light of the wicked will be snuffed
out. □ Pride leads to conflict; those who
take advice are wise.

APRIL**18**

¹⁰They did not drive the Canaanites
out of Gezer, however, so the people of
Gezer live as slaves among the people
of Ephraim to this day.

^{17:1}THE next allotment of land was given
to the half-tribe of Manasseh, the descendants of Joseph's older son. Makir, the
firstborn son of Manasseh, was the father
of Gilead. Because his descendants were
experienced soldiers, the regions of Gilead and Bashan on the east side of the Jordan had already been given to them. ²So
the allotment on the west side of the Jordan was for the remaining families within
the clans of the tribe of Manasseh: Abiezer, Helek, Asriel, Shechem, Hepher, and
Shemida. These clans represent the male
descendants of Manasseh son of Joseph.

³However, Zelophehad, a descendant
of Hepher son of Gilead, son of Makir, son
of Manasseh, had no sons. He had only
daughters, whose names were Mahlah,
Noah, Hoglah, Milcah, and Tirzah. ⁴These
women came to Eleazar the priest, Joshua
son of Nun, and the Israelite leaders and
said, "The LORD commanded Moses to
give us a grant of land along with the men
of our tribe."

So Joshua gave them a grant of land
along with their uncles, as the LORD had
commanded. ⁵As a result, Manasseh's total allocation came to ten parcels of land,
in addition to the land of Gilead and
Bashan across the Jordan River, ⁶because
the female descendants of Manasseh received a grant of land along with the male
descendants. (The land of Gilead was
given to the rest of the male descendants
of Manasseh.)

⁷The boundary of the tribe of
Manasseh extended from the border

of Asher to Micmethath, near Shechem. Then the boundary went south from Micmethath to the settlement near the spring of Tappuah. ⁸The land surrounding Tappuah belonged to Manasseh, but the town of Tappuah itself, on the border of Manasseh's territory, belonged to the tribe of Ephraim. ⁹From the spring of Tappuah, the boundary of Manasseh followed the Kanah Ravine to the Mediterranean Sea.* Several towns south of the ravine were inside Manasseh's territory, but they actually belonged to the tribe of Ephraim. ¹⁰In general, however, the land south of the ravine belonged to Ephraim, and the land north of the ravine belonged to Manasseh. Manasseh's boundary ran along the northern side of the ravine and ended at the Mediterranean Sea. North of Manasseh was the territory of Asher, and to the east was the territory of Issachar.

¹¹The following towns within the territory of Issachar and Asher, however, were given to Manasseh: Beth-shan,* Ibleam, Dor (that is, Naphoth-dor),* Endor, Taanach, and Megiddo, each with their surrounding settlements.

¹²But the descendants of Manasseh were unable to occupy these towns. They could not drive out the Canaanites who continued to live there. ¹³Later, however, when the Israelites became strong enough, they forced the Canaanites to work as slaves. But they did not drive them out of the land.

¹⁴The descendants of Joseph came to Joshua and asked, "Why have you given us only one portion of land as our homeland when the LORD has blessed us with so many people?"

¹⁵Joshua replied, "If there are so many of you, and if the hill country of Ephraim is not large enough for you, clear out land for yourselves in the forest where the Perizzites and Rephaites live."

¹⁶The descendants of Joseph responded, "It's true that the hill country is not large enough for us. But all the Canaanites in the lowlands have iron chariots, both those in Beth-shan and its surrounding settlements and those in the valley of Jezreel. They are too strong for us."

¹⁷Then Joshua said to the tribes of Ephraim and Manasseh, the descendants of Joseph, "Since you are so large and strong, you will be given more than one portion. ¹⁸The forests of the hill country will be yours as well. Clear as much of the land as you wish, and take possession of its farthest corners. And you will drive out the Canaanites from the valleys, too, even though they are strong and have iron chariots."

18:1 Now that the land was under Israelite control, the entire community of Israel gathered at Shiloh and set up the Tabernacle.* ²But there remained seven tribes who had not yet been allotted their grants of land.

³Then Joshua asked them, "How long are you going to wait before taking possession of the remaining land the LORD, the God of your ancestors, has given to you? ⁴Select three men from each tribe, and I will send them out to explore the land and map it out. They will then return to me with a written report of their proposed divisions of their new homeland. ⁵Let them divide the land into seven sections, excluding Judah's territory in the south and Joseph's territory in the north. ⁶And when you record the seven divisions of the land and bring them to me, I will cast sacred lots in the presence of the LORD our God to assign land to each tribe.

⁷"The Levites, however, will not receive any allotment of land. Their role as priests of the LORD is their allotment. And the tribes of Gad, Reuben, and the half-tribe of Manasseh won't receive any more land, for they have already received their grant of land, which Moses, the servant of the LORD, gave them on the east side of the Jordan River."

⁸As the men started on their way to map out the land, Joshua commanded them, "Go and explore the land and write a description of it. Then return to me, and I will assign the land to the tribes by casting sacred lots here in the presence of the LORD at Shiloh." ⁹The men did as they

were told and mapped the entire territory into seven sections, listing the towns in each section. They made a written record and then returned to Joshua in the camp at Shiloh. ¹⁰And there at Shiloh, Joshua cast sacred lots in the presence of the LORD to determine which tribe should have each section.

¹¹The first allotment of land went to the clans of the tribe of Benjamin. It lay between the territory assigned to the tribes of Judah and Joseph.

¹²The northern boundary of Benjamin's land began at the Jordan River, went north of the slope of Jericho, then west through the hill country and the wilderness of Beth-aven. ¹³From there the boundary went south to Luz (that is, Bethel) and proceeded down to Ataroth-addar on the hill that lies south of Lower Beth-horon.

¹⁴The boundary then made a turn and swung south along the western edge of the hill facing Beth-horon, ending at the village of Kiriath-baal (that is, Kiriath-jearim), a town belonging to the tribe of Judah. This was the western boundary.

¹⁵The southern boundary began at the outskirts of Kiriath-jearim. From that western point it ran* to the spring at the waters of Neph-toah,* ¹⁶and down to the base of the mountain beside the valley of Ben-Hinnom, at the northern end of the valley of Rephaim. From there it went down the valley of Hinnom, crossing south of the slope where the Jebusites lived, and continued down to En-rogel. ¹⁷From En-rogel the boundary proceeded in a northerly direction and came to En-shemesh and on to Geliloth (which is across from the slopes of Adummim). Then it went down to the Stone of Bohan. (Bohan was Reuben's son.) ¹⁸From there it passed along the north side of the slope overlooking the Jordan Valley.* The border then went down into the valley, ¹⁹ran past the north slope of Beth-hoglah, and ended at the north bay of the Dead Sea,* which is the southern end of the Jordan River. This was the southern boundary.

²⁰The eastern boundary was the Jordan River.

These were the boundaries of the homeland allocated to the clans of the tribe of Benjamin.

²¹These were the towns given to the clans of the tribe of Benjamin.

Jericho, Beth-hoglah, Emek-keziz, ²²Beth-arabah, Zemaraim, Bethel, ²³Avvim, Parah, Ophrah, ²⁴Kephar-ammoni, Ophni, and Geba—twelve

HOW WE LIVE

Accountability to others

LUKE 19:11-26 Although Jesus could have worked it out that the moment we were saved we could go straight to heaven, he chose instead to leave us here on earth. Why? He has jobs for us to do. • The Bible makes it clear that each believer is given "gifts"—a unique mix of abilities. Jesus fashioned you for a particular purpose and wastes nothing of your life in the plan he has for your future. Like the nobleman in this story who divided up the silver among his servants, Jesus gives his people gifts and expects us to "invest" them while he is gone to heaven. Some of us will have huge amounts of return, some not so much. But in both of those cases, Jesus' response will be, "Well done!" However, if you, like the third servant, bury your gift out of selfishness or fear, you will be held accountable and judged. • You see, you have been given gifts for the purpose of serving God while you remain on this earth. You have a job to do. Whatever you do, do it well, and do it for God's glory. Then God will say to you, "Well done."

towns with their surrounding villages. [25]Also Gibeon, Ramah, Beeroth, [26]Mizpeh, Kephirah, Mozah, [27]Rekem, Irpeel, Taralah, [28]Zela, Haeleph, Jebus (that is, Jerusalem), Gibeah, and Kiriath-jearim*—fourteen towns with their surrounding villages.

This was the homeland allocated to the clans of the tribe of Benjamin.

16:2 As in Greek version (also see 18:13); Hebrew reads *From Bethel to Luz.* **16:3** Hebrew *the sea;* also in 16:6, 8. **17:9** Hebrew *the sea;* also in 17:10. **17:11a** Hebrew *Beth-shean,* a variant spelling of Beth-shan; also in 17:16. **17:11b** The meaning of the Hebrew here is uncertain. **18:1** Hebrew *Tent of Meeting.* **18:15a** Or *From there it went to Mozah.* The meaning of the Hebrew is uncertain. **18:15b** Or *the spring at Me-nephtoah.* **18:18** Hebrew *overlooking the Arabah,* or *overlooking Beth-arabah.* **18:19** Hebrew *Salt Sea.* **18:28** As in Greek version; Hebrew reads *Kiriath.*

LUKE 19:1-27

Jesus accepts all who are willing to turn from sin and follow him. Zacchaeus, a despised tax collector, was willing. Jesus accepted him and told a parable about how his followers have a new opportunity to make the most of what God has given them.

Jesus entered Jericho and made his way through the town. [2]There was a man there named Zacchaeus. He was the chief tax collector in the region, and he had become very rich. [3]He tried to get a look at Jesus, but he was too short to see over the crowd. [4]So he ran ahead and climbed a sycamore-fig tree beside the road, for Jesus was going to pass that way.

[5]When Jesus came by, he looked up at Zacchaeus and called him by name. "Zacchaeus!" he said. "Quick, come down! I must be a guest in your home today."

[6]Zacchaeus quickly climbed down and took Jesus to his house in great excitement and joy. [7]But the people were displeased. "He has gone to be the guest of a notorious sinner," they grumbled.

[8]Meanwhile, Zacchaeus stood before the Lord and said, "I will give half my wealth to the poor, Lord, and if I have cheated people on their taxes, I will give them back four times as much!"

[9]Jesus responded, "Salvation has come to this home today, for this man has shown himself to be a true son of Abraham. [10]For the Son of Man* came to seek and save those who are lost."

[11]The crowd was listening to everything Jesus said. And because he was nearing Jerusalem, he told them a story to correct the impression that the Kingdom of God would begin right away. [12]He said, "A nobleman was called away to a distant empire to be crowned king and then return. [13]Before he left, he called together ten of his servants and divided among them ten pounds of silver,* saying, 'Invest this for me while I am gone.' [14]But his people hated him and sent a delegation after him to say, 'We do not want him to be our king.'

[15]"After he was crowned king, he returned and called in the servants to whom he had given the money. He wanted to find out what their profits were. [16]The first servant reported, 'Master, I invested your money and made ten times the original amount!'

[17]"'Well done!' the king exclaimed. 'You are a good servant. You have been faithful with the little I entrusted to you, so you will be governor of ten cities as your reward.'

[18]"The next servant reported, 'Master, I invested your money and made five times the original amount.'

[19]"'Well done!' the king said. 'You will be governor over five cities.'

[20]"But the third servant brought back only the original amount of money and said, 'Master, I hid your money and kept it safe. [21]I was afraid because you are a hard man to deal with, taking what isn't yours and harvesting crops you didn't plant.'

[22]"'You wicked servant!' the king roared. 'Your own words condemn you. If you knew that I'm a hard man who takes what isn't mine and harvests crops I didn't plant, [23]why didn't you deposit my money in the bank? At least I could have gotten some interest on it.'

[24]"Then, turning to the others standing nearby, the king ordered, 'Take the money from this servant, and give it to the one who has ten pounds.'

[25]"'But, master,' they said, 'he already has ten pounds!'

[26]"'Yes,' the king replied, 'and to those who use well what they are given, even more will be given. But from those who do nothing, even what little they have will be taken away. [27]And as for these enemies of mine who didn't want me to be their

king—bring them in and execute them right here in front of me.'"

19:10 "Son of Man" is a title Jesus used for himself.
19:13 Greek *ten minas;* one mina was worth about three months' wages.

PSALM 87:1-7
A song. A psalm of the descendants of Korah.

¹ **O**n the holy mountain
    stands the city founded by the LORD.
² He loves the city of Jerusalem
    more than any other city in Israel.*
³ O city of God,
    what glorious things are said of you!
                                    Interlude

⁴ I will count Egypt* and Babylon
    among those who know me—
    also Philistia and Tyre, and even
    distant Ethiopia.*
    They have all become citizens of
    Jerusalem!

⁵ Regarding Jerusalem* it will be said,
    "Everyone enjoys the rights of
    citizenship there."
    And the Most High will personally
    bless this city.
⁶ When the LORD registers the nations,
    he will say,
    "They have all become citizens of
    Jerusalem."   *Interlude*

⁷ The people will play flutes* and sing,
    "The source of my life springs from
    Jerusalem!"

87:2 Hebrew *He loves the gates of Zion more than all the dwellings of Jacob.* See note on 44:4.   87:4a Hebrew *Rahab,* the name of a mythical sea monster that represents chaos in ancient literature. The name is used here as a poetic name for Egypt.   87:4b Hebrew *Cush.*   87:5 Hebrew *Zion.*   87:7 Or *will dance.*

PROVERBS 13:11
Wealth from get-rich-quick schemes quickly disappears; wealth from hard work grows over time.

APRIL**19**

JOSHUA 19:1-20:9
One by one, the tribes each received a portion of land to claim as their own. To help with administering justice in capital cases, God told Joshua to set aside cities of refuge where people could go in the case of unintentional murder.

The second allotment of land went to the clans of the tribe of Simeon. Their homeland was surrounded by Judah's territory.

²Simeon's homeland included Beersheba, Sheba, Moladah, ³Hazar-shual, Balah, Ezem, ⁴Eltolad, Bethul, Hormah, ⁵Ziklag, Beth-marcaboth, Hazar-susah, ⁶Beth-lebaoth, and Sharuhen—thirteen towns with their surrounding villages. ⁷It also included Ain, Rimmon, Ether, and Ashan—four towns with their villages, ⁸including all the surrounding villages as far south as Baalath-beer (also known as Ramah of the Negev).

This was the homeland allocated to the clans of the tribe of Simeon. ⁹Their allo-

cation of land came from part of what had been given to Judah because Judah's territory was too large for them. So the tribe of Simeon received an allocation within the territory of Judah.

¹⁰The third allotment of land went to the clans of the tribe of Zebulun.

The boundary of Zebulun's homeland started at Sarid. ¹¹From there it went west, going past Maralah, touching Dabbesheth, and proceeding to the brook east of Jokneam. ¹²In the other direction, the boundary went east from Sarid to the border of Kisloth-tabor, and from there to Daberath and up to Japhia. ¹³Then it continued east to Gath-hepher, Eth-kazin, and Rimmon and turned toward Neah. ¹⁴The northern boundary of Zebulun passed Hannathon and ended at the valley of Iphtah-el. ¹⁵The towns in these areas included Kattath, Nahalal, Shimron,

Idalah, and Bethlehem—twelve towns with their surrounding villages.

[16]The homeland allocated to the clans of the tribe of Zebulun included these towns and their surrounding villages.

[17]The fourth allotment of land went to the clans of the tribe of Issachar.

[18]Its boundaries included the following towns: Jezreel, Kesulloth, Shunem, [19]Hapharaim, Shion, Anaharath, [20]Rabbith, Kishion, Ebez, [21]Remeth, En-gannim, En-haddah, and Beth-pazzez. [22]The boundary also touched Tabor, Shahazumah, and Beth-shemesh, ending at the Jordan River—sixteen towns with their surrounding villages.

[23]The homeland allocated to the clans of the tribe of Issachar included these towns and their surrounding villages.

[24]The fifth allotment of land went to the clans of the tribe of Asher.

[25]Its boundaries included these towns: Helkath, Hali, Beten, Acshaph, [26]Allammelech, Amad, and Mishal. The boundary on the west touched Carmel and Shihor-libnath, [27]then it turned east toward Beth-dagon, and ran as far as Zebulun in the valley of Iphtah-el, going north to Beth-emek and Neiel. It then continued north to Cabul, [28]Abdon,* Rehob, Hammon, Kanah, and as far as Greater Sidon. [29]Then the boundary turned toward Ramah and the fortress of Tyre, where it turned toward Hosah and came to the Mediterranean Sea.* The territory also included Mehebel, Aczib, [30]Ummah, Aphek, and Rehob—twenty-two towns with their surrounding villages.

[31]The homeland allocated to the clans of the tribe of Asher included these towns and their surrounding villages.

[32]The sixth allotment of land went to the clans of the tribe of Naphtali.

[33]Its boundary ran from Heleph, from the oak at Zaanannim, and extended across to Adami-nekeb, Jabneel, and as

far as Lakkum, ending at the Jordan River. [34]The western boundary ran past Aznoth-tabor, then to Hukkok, and touched the border of Zebulun in the south, the border of Asher on the west, and the Jordan River* on the east. [35]The fortified towns included in this territory were Ziddim, Zer, Hammath, Rakkath, Kinnereth, [36]Adamah, Ramah, Hazor, [37]Kedesh, Edrei, En-hazor, [38]Yiron, Migdal-el, Horem, Beth-anath, and Beth-shemesh—nineteen towns with their surrounding villages.

[39]The homeland allocated to the clans of the tribe of Naphtali included these towns and their surrounding villages.

[40]The seventh allotment of land went to the clans of the tribe of Dan.

[41]The land allocated as their homeland included the following towns: Zorah, Eshtaol, Ir-shemesh, [42]Shaalabbin, Aijalon, Ithlah, [43]Elon, Timnah, Ekron, [44]Eltekeh, Gibbethon, Baalath, [45]Jehud, Bene-berak, Gath-rimmon, [46]Me-jarkon, Rakkon, and the territory across from Joppa.

[47]But the tribe of Dan had trouble taking possession of their land,* so they attacked the town of Laish.* They captured it, slaughtered its people, and settled there. They renamed the town Dan after their ancestor.

[48]The homeland allocated to the clans of the tribe of Dan included these towns and their surrounding villages.

[49]After all the land was divided among the tribes, the Israelites gave a piece of land to Joshua as his allocation. [50]For the LORD had said he could have any town he wanted. He chose Timnath-serah in the hill country of Ephraim. He rebuilt the town and lived there.

[51]These are the territories that Eleazar the priest, Joshua son of Nun, and the tribal leaders allocated as grants of land to the tribes of Israel by casting sacred lots in the presence of the LORD at the entrance of the Tabernacle* at Shiloh. So the division of the land was completed.

20:1THE LORD said to Joshua, 2"Now tell the Israelites to designate the cities of refuge, as I instructed Moses. 3Anyone who kills another person accidentally and unintentionally can run to one of these cities; they will be places of refuge from relatives seeking revenge for the person who was killed.

4"Upon reaching one of these cities, the one who caused the death will appear before the elders at the city gate and present his case. They must allow him to enter the city and give him a place to live among them. 5If the relatives of the victim come to avenge the killing, the leaders must not release the slayer to them, for he killed the other person unintentionally and without previous hostility. 6But the slayer must stay in that city and be tried by the local assembly, which will render a judgment. And he must continue to live in that city until the death of the high priest who was in office at the time of the accident. After that, he is free to return to his own home in the town from which he fled."

7The following cities were designated as cities of refuge: Kedesh of Galilee, in the hill country of Naphtali; Shechem, in the hill country of Ephraim; and Kiriatharba (that is, Hebron), in the hill country of Judah. 8On the east side of the Jordan River, across from Jericho, the following cities were designated: Bezer, in the wilderness plain of the tribe of Reuben; Ramoth in Gilead, in the territory of the tribe of Gad; and Golan in Bashan, in the land of the tribe of Manasseh. 9These cities were set apart for all the Israelites as well as the foreigners living among them. Anyone who accidentally killed another person could take refuge in one of these cities. In this way, they could escape being killed in revenge prior to standing trial before the local assembly.

19:28 As in some Hebrew manuscripts (see also 21:30); most Hebrew manuscripts read *Ebron.* 19:29 Hebrew *the sea.* 19:34 Hebrew *and Judah at the Jordan River.* 19:47a Or *had trouble holding onto their land.* 19:47b Hebrew *Leshem,* a variant spelling of Laish. 19:51 Hebrew *Tent of Meeting.*

LUKE 19:28-48
The people thought that their king had come, and they went wild! Unfortunately, they didn't understand the kind of Kingdom he came to bring. He would not overthrow Rome; he would overthrow sin and death.

After telling this story, Jesus went on toward Jerusalem, walking ahead of his disciples. 29As he came to the towns of Bethphage and Bethany on the Mount of Olives, he sent two disciples ahead. 30"Go into that village over there," he told them. "As you enter it, you will see a young donkey tied there that no one has ever ridden. Untie it and bring it here. 31If anyone asks, 'Why are you untying that colt?' just say, 'The Lord needs it.'"

HOW WE LIVE: Revering God

LUKE 19:45-46 Upon entering the Temple, Jesus found merchants selling items for sacrifice and money changers charging exorbitant exchange rates. Jesus became justifiably angry that a house of worship had become a place of extortion and a barrier to those who wanted to focus on God. • As a new believer, you've gone from taking Sunday as just another weekend day to setting it aside to go to church for teaching, fellowship, and worship. Or maybe you've gone to church all your life but only out of habit or coercion; now church has taken on new meaning. • Depending on the type of church you attend, you will find many different styles of worship. No particular style is by necessity right or wrong. What matters is whether what is done is done to God's glory. The focus of worship must be God himself, and there must be no genuine barrier to your focusing on him. • As you enter the doors of your church, think about why you're there. As you take your seat, say a quick prayer, asking God to draw close and teach you something new. Ask him to help church be a time of confession, reflection, instruction, and inspiration.

³²So they went and found the colt, just as Jesus had said. ³³And sure enough, as they were untying it, the owners asked them, "Why are you untying that colt?" ³⁴And the disciples simply replied, "The Lord needs it." ³⁵So they brought the colt to Jesus and threw their garments over it for him to ride on.

³⁶As he rode along, the crowds spread out their garments on the road ahead of him. ³⁷When he reached the place where the road started down the Mount of Olives, all of his followers began to shout and sing as they walked along, praising God for all the wonderful miracles they had seen.

³⁸ "Blessings on the King who comes in
the name of the LORD!
Peace in heaven, and glory in
highest heaven!"*

³⁹But some of the Pharisees among the crowd said, "Teacher, rebuke your followers for saying things like that!"

⁴⁰He replied, "If they kept quiet, the stones along the road would burst into cheers!"

⁴¹But as he came closer to Jerusalem and saw the city ahead, he began to weep. ⁴²"How I wish today that you of all people would understand the way to peace. But now it is too late, and peace is hidden from your eyes. ⁴³Before long your enemies will build ramparts against your walls and encircle you and close in on you from every side. ⁴⁴They will crush you into the ground, and your children with you. Your enemies will not leave a single stone in place, because you did not accept your opportunity for salvation."

⁴⁵Then Jesus entered the Temple and began to drive out the people selling animals for sacrifices. ⁴⁶He said to them, "The Scriptures declare, 'My Temple will be a house of prayer,' but you have turned it into a den of thieves."*

⁴⁷After that, he taught daily in the Temple, but the leading priests, the teachers of religious law, and the other leaders of the people began planning how to kill him. ⁴⁸But they could think of nothing, because all the people hung on every word he said.

19:38 Pss 118:26; 148:1.   19:46 Isa 56:7; Jer 7:11.

PSALM 88:1-18
For the choir director: A psalm of the descendants of Korah. A song to be sung to the tune "The Suffering of Affliction." A psalm* of Heman the Ezrahite.

¹ **O** LORD, God of my salvation,
I cry out to you by day.
I come to you at night.
² Now hear my prayer;
listen to my cry.
³ For my life is full of troubles,
and death* draws near.
⁴ I am as good as dead,
like a strong man with no strength
left.
⁵ They have left me among
the dead,
and I lie like a corpse in
a grave.
I am forgotten,
cut off from your care.
⁶ You have thrown me into the lowest
pit,
into the darkest depths.
⁷ Your anger weighs me down;
with wave after wave you have
engulfed me.   *Interlude*
⁸ You have driven my friends away
by making me repulsive to them.
I am in a trap with no way of escape.
⁹   My eyes are blinded by my tears.
Each day I beg for your help, O LORD;
I lift my hands to you for mercy.
¹⁰ Are your wonderful deeds of any use
to the dead?
Do the dead rise up and praise you?
Interlude
¹¹ Can those in the grave declare your
unfailing love?
Can they proclaim your
faithfulness in the place
of destruction?*
¹² Can the darkness speak of your
wonderful deeds?
Can anyone in the land of
forgetfulness talk about your
righteousness?
¹³ O LORD, I cry out to you.
I will keep on pleading day
by day.
¹⁴ O LORD, why do you reject me?

Why do you turn your face
   from me?
¹⁵ I have been sick and close to death
   since my youth.
   I stand helpless and desperate
   before your terrors.
¹⁶ Your fierce anger has overwhelmed
   me.
   Your terrors have paralyzed me.
¹⁷ They swirl around me like floodwaters
   all day long.
   They have engulfed me
   completely.

¹⁸ You have taken away my companions
   and loved ones.
   Darkness is my closest friend.

88:TITLE Hebrew *maskil*. This may be a literary or musical
term.   **88:3** Hebrew *Sheol*.   **88:11** Hebrew *in Abaddon?*

PROVERBS 13:12-14

Hope deferred makes the heart sick, but a
dream fulfilled is a tree of life. □ People
who despise advice are asking for trouble;
those who respect a command will succeed. □ The instruction of the wise is like
a life-giving fountain; those who accept it
avoid the snares of death.

APRIL**20**

JOSHUA 21:1-22:20
The Levites were granted certain towns instead of
an entire region.

Then the leaders of the tribe of Levi came
to consult with Eleazar the priest, Joshua
son of Nun, and the leaders of the other
tribes of Israel. ²They came to them at
Shiloh in the land of Canaan and said,
"The LORD commanded Moses to give us
towns to live in and pasturelands for our
livestock." ³So by the command of the
LORD the people of Israel gave the Levites
the following towns and pasturelands out
of their own grants of land.

⁴The descendants of Aaron, who were
members of the Kohathite clan within
the tribe of Levi, were allotted thirteen
towns that were originally assigned to
the tribes of Judah, Simeon, and Benja-
min. ⁵The other families of the Kohathite
clan were allotted ten towns from the
tribes of Ephraim, Dan, and the half-tribe
of Manasseh.

⁶The clan of Gershon was allotted thir-
teen towns from the tribes of Issachar,
Asher, Naphtali, and the half-tribe of Manasseh in Bashan.

⁷The clan of Merari was allotted twelve
towns from the tribes of Reuben, Gad, and
Zebulun.

⁸So the Israelites obeyed the LORD's

command to Moses and assigned these
towns and pasturelands to the Levites by
casting sacred lots.

⁹The Israelites gave the following
towns from the tribes of Judah and Simeon ¹⁰to the descendants of Aaron, who
were members of the Kohathite clan
within the tribe of Levi, since the sacred
lot fell to them first: ¹¹Kiriath-arba (that is,
Hebron), in the hill country of Judah,
along with its surrounding pasturelands.
(Arba was an ancestor of Anak.) ¹²But the
open fields beyond the town and the surrounding villages were given to Caleb son
of Jephunneh as his possession.

¹³The following towns with their pas-
turelands were given to the descendants of
Aaron the priest: Hebron (a city of refuge
for those who accidentally killed some-
one), Libnah, ¹⁴Jattir, Eshtemoa, ¹⁵Holon,
Debir, ¹⁶Ain, Juttah, and Beth-shemesh—
nine towns from these two tribes.

¹⁷From the tribe of Benjamin the priests
were given the following towns with their
pasturelands: Gibeon, Geba, ¹⁸Anathoth,
and Almon—four towns. ¹⁹So in all, thirteen towns with their pasturelands were
given to the priests, the descendants of
Aaron.

²⁰The rest of the Kohathite clan from
the tribe of Levi was allotted the following

towns and pasturelands from the tribe of Ephraim: ²¹Shechem in the hill country of Ephraim (a city of refuge for those who accidentally killed someone), Gezer, ²²Kibzaim, and Beth-horon—four towns.

²³The following towns and pasturelands were allotted to the priests from the tribe of Dan: Eltekeh, Gibbethon, ²⁴Aijalon, and Gath-rimmon—four towns.

²⁵The half-tribe of Manasseh allotted the following towns with their pasturelands to the priests: Taanach and Gath-rimmon—two towns. ²⁶So in all, ten towns with their pasturelands were given to the rest of the Kohathite clan.

²⁷The descendants of Gershon, another clan within the tribe of Levi, received the following towns with their pasturelands from the half-tribe of Manasseh: Golan in Bashan (a city of refuge for those who accidentally killed someone) and Be-eshterah—two towns.

²⁸From the tribe of Issachar they received the following towns with their pasturelands: Kishion, Daberath, ²⁹Jarmuth, and En-gannim—four towns.

³⁰From the tribe of Asher they received the following towns with their pasturelands: Mishal, Abdon, ³¹Helkath, and Rehob—four towns.

³²From the tribe of Naphtali they received the following towns with their pasturelands: Kedesh in Galilee (a city of refuge for those who accidentally killed someone), Hammoth-dor, and Kartan—three towns. ³³So in all, thirteen towns with their pasturelands were allotted to the clan of Gershon.

³⁴The rest of the Levites—the Merari clan—were given the following towns with their pasturelands from the tribe of Zebulun: Jokneam, Kartah, ³⁵Dimnah, and Nahalal—four towns.

³⁶From the tribe of Reuben they received the following towns with their pasturelands: Bezer, Jahaz,* ³⁷Kedemoth, and Mephaath—four towns.

³⁸From the tribe of Gad they received the following towns with their pasturelands: Ramoth in Gilead (a city of refuge for those who accidentally killed someone), Mahanaim, ³⁹Heshbon, and Jazer—four towns. ⁴⁰So in all, twelve towns were allotted to the clan of Merari.

⁴¹The total number of towns and pasturelands within Israelite territory given to the Levites came to forty-eight. ⁴²Every one of these towns had pasturelands surrounding it.

⁴³So the LORD gave to Israel all the land he had sworn to give their ancestors, and they took possession of it and settled there. ⁴⁴And the LORD gave them rest on every side, just as he had solemnly promised their ancestors. None of their enemies could stand against them, for the LORD helped them conquer all their enemies. ⁴⁵Not a single one of all the good promises the LORD had given to the family of Israel was left unfulfilled; everything he had spoken came true.

^{22:1}THEN Joshua called together the tribes of Reuben, Gad, and the half-tribe of Manasseh. ²He told them, "You have done as Moses, the servant of the LORD, commanded you, and you have obeyed every order I have given you. ³During all this time you have not deserted the other tribes. You have been careful to obey the commands of the LORD your God right up to the present day. ⁴And now the LORD your God has given the other tribes rest, as he promised them. So go back home to the land that Moses, the servant of the LORD, gave you as your possession on the east side of the Jordan River. ⁵But be very careful to obey all the commands and the instructions that Moses gave to you. Love the LORD your God, walk in all his ways, obey his commands, hold firmly to him, and serve him with all your heart and all your soul." ⁶So Joshua blessed them and sent them away, and they went home.

⁷Moses had given the land of Bashan, east of the Jordan River, to the half-tribe of Manasseh. (The other half of the tribe was given land west of the Jordan.) As Joshua sent them away and blessed them, ⁸he said to them, "Go back to your homes with the great wealth you have taken from your enemies—the vast herds of livestock, the silver, gold, bronze, and iron, and the large supply of clothing. Share the plunder with your relatives."

⁹So the men of Reuben, Gad, and the half-tribe of Manasseh left the rest of Isra-

el at Shiloh in the land of Canaan. They started the journey back to their own land of Gilead, the territory that belonged to them according to the LORD's command through Moses.

¹⁰But while they were still in Canaan, and when they came to a place called Geliloth* near the Jordan River, the men of Reuben, Gad, and the half-tribe of Manasseh stopped to build a large and imposing altar.

¹¹The rest of Israel heard that the people of Reuben, Gad, and the half-tribe of Manasseh had built an altar at Geliloth at the edge of the land of Canaan, on the west side of the Jordan River. ¹²So the whole community of Israel gathered at Shiloh and prepared to go to war against them. ¹³First, however, they sent a delegation led by Phinehas son of Eleazar, the priest, to talk with the tribes of Reuben, Gad, and the half-tribe of Manasseh. ¹⁴In this delegation were ten leaders of Israel, one from each of the ten tribes, and each the head of his family within the clans of Israel.

¹⁵When they arrived in the land of Gilead, they said to the tribes of Reuben, Gad, and the half-tribe of Manasseh, ¹⁶"The whole community of the LORD demands to know why you are betraying the God of Israel. How could you turn away from the LORD and build an altar for yourselves in rebellion against him? ¹⁷Was our sin at Peor not enough? To this day we are not fully cleansed of it, even after the plague that struck the entire community of the LORD. ¹⁸And yet today you are turning away from following the LORD. If you rebel against the LORD today, he will be angry with all of us tomorrow.

¹⁹"If you need the altar because the land you possess is defiled, then join us in the LORD's land, where the Tabernacle of the LORD is situated, and share our land with us. But do not rebel against the LORD or against us by building an altar other than the one true altar of the LORD our God. ²⁰Didn't divine anger fall on the entire community of Israel when Achan, a member of the clan of Zerah, sinned by stealing the things set apart for the LORD*? He was not the only one who died because of his sin."

21:36 Hebrew *Jahzah,* a variant spelling of Jahaz.   **22:10** Or *to the circle of stones;* similarly in 22:11.   **22:20** The Hebrew term used here refers to the complete consecration of things or people to the LORD, either by destroying them or by giving them as an offering.

LUKE 20:1-26

The religious leaders tried to undermine Jesus' authority with traps veiled as questions. Jesus' response was often veiled as well, as in the parable of the wicked tenant farmers, where he left it to the listener to decide the implications.

One day as Jesus was teaching the people and preaching the Good News in the

HOW WE LIVE

Living responsibly

JOSHUA 22:1-5 The tribes of Reuben, Gad, and Manasseh had done exactly what they said they would do, completing the job Moses had asked of them (see Numbers 32, March 21). Now that key cities had been taken and the rest of the tribes allotted their land, Joshua sent these three tribes home with the admonition to continue to do the right thing, not forgetting that although they lived across the river, they were still part of God's people. • Joshua especially reminded these men to "be very careful to obey all the commands and the instructions that Moses gave to you. Love the LORD your God, walk in all his ways, obey his commands, hold firmly to him, and serve him with all your heart and all your soul" (22:5). It doesn't get much clearer than that. The key to living responsibly on the other side of the river is to keep God and his Word at the center of life. Similarly, wherever you are in life, it is your responsibility to keep God first in your life through things like praying, studying his Word, and serving others.

Temple, the leading priests, the teachers of religious law, and the elders came up to him. ²They demanded, "By what authority are you doing all these things? Who gave you the right?"

³"Let me ask you a question first," he replied. ⁴"Did John's authority to baptize come from heaven, or was it merely human?"

⁵They talked it over among themselves. "If we say it was from heaven, he will ask why we didn't believe John. ⁶But if we say it was merely human, the people will stone us because they are convinced John was a prophet." ⁷So they finally replied that they didn't know.

⁸And Jesus responded, "Then I won't tell you by what authority I do these things."

⁹Now Jesus turned to the people again and told them this story: "A man planted a vineyard, leased it to tenant farmers, and moved to another country to live for several years. ¹⁰At the time of the grape harvest, he sent one of his servants to collect his share of the crop. But the farmers attacked the servant, beat him up, and sent him back empty-handed. ¹¹So the owner sent another servant, but they also insulted him, beat him up, and sent him away empty-handed. ¹²A third man was sent, and they wounded him and chased him away.

¹³" 'What will I do?' the owner asked himself. 'I know! I'll send my cherished son. Surely they will respect him.'

¹⁴"But when the tenant farmers saw his son, they said to each other, 'Here comes the heir to this estate. Let's kill him and get the estate for ourselves!' ¹⁵So they dragged him out of the vineyard and murdered him.

"What do you suppose the owner of the vineyard will do to them?" Jesus asked. ¹⁶"I'll tell you—he will come and kill those farmers and lease the vineyard to others."

"How terrible that such a thing should ever happen," his listeners protested.

¹⁷Jesus looked at them and said, "Then what does this Scripture mean?

'The stone that the builders rejected
    has now become the
    cornerstone.'*

¹⁸Everyone who stumbles over that stone will be broken to pieces, and it will crush anyone it falls on."

¹⁹The teachers of religious law and the leading priests wanted to arrest Jesus immediately because they realized he was telling the story against them—they were the wicked farmers. But they were afraid of the people's reaction.

²⁰Watching for their opportunity, the leaders sent spies pretending to be honest men. They tried to get Jesus to say something that could be reported to the Roman governor so he would arrest Jesus. ²¹"Teacher," they said, "we know that you speak and teach what is right and are not influenced by what others think. You teach the way of God truthfully. ²²Now tell us—is it right for us to pay taxes to Caesar or not?"

²³He saw through their trickery and said, ²⁴"Show me a Roman coin.* Whose picture and title are stamped on it?"

"Caesar's," they replied.

²⁵"Well then," he said, "give to Caesar what belongs to Caesar, and give to God what belongs to God."

²⁶So they failed to trap him by what he said in front of the people. Instead, they were amazed by his answer, and they became silent.

20:17 Ps 118:22. 20:24 Greek *a denarius.*

PSALM 89:1-13

A psalm* of Ethan the Ezrahite.

¹ **I** will sing of the Lord's unfailing love
        forever!
    Young and old will hear of your
        faithfulness.
² Your unfailing love will last forever.
    Your faithfulness is as enduring
        as the heavens.

³ The Lord said, "I have made a
        covenant with David, my chosen
        servant.
    I have sworn this oath to him:
⁴ 'I will establish your descendants as
        kings forever;
    they will sit on your throne from
        now until eternity.'"   *Interlude*

⁵ All heaven will praise your great
        wonders, Lord;

myriads of angels will praise you for
your faithfulness.

6 For who in all of heaven can compare
with the LORD?
What mightiest angel is anything
like the LORD?

7 The highest angelic powers stand
in awe of God.
He is far more awesome than all
who surround his throne.

8 O LORD God of Heaven's Armies!
Where is there anyone as mighty
as you, O LORD?
You are entirely faithful.

9 You rule the oceans.
You subdue their storm-tossed
waves.

10 You crushed the great sea
monster.*
You scattered your enemies with
your mighty arm.

11 The heavens are yours, and the earth
is yours;
everything in the world is yours—
you created it all.

12 You created north and south.
Mount Tabor and Mount Hermon
praise your name.

13 Powerful is your arm!
Strong is your hand!
Your right hand is lifted high in
glorious strength.

89:TITLE Hebrew *maskil*. This may be a literary or musical
term.   **89:10** Hebrew *Rahab*, the name of a mythical sea
monster that represents chaos in ancient literature.

PROVERBS 13:15-16

A person with good sense is respected;
a treacherous person is headed for destruction.* ▢ Wise people think before
they act; fools don't—and even brag about
their foolishness.

13:15 As in Greek version; Hebrew reads *the way of the
treacherous is lasting.*

APRIL**21**

JOSHUA 22:21–23:16

Since Moses' death, Joshua had led the people
through victories, defeats, internal negotiations,
and logistical nightmares. Just as Moses had done
before him, he offered wisdom to his people as his
last act of leadership.

Then the people of Reuben, Gad, and the
half-tribe of Manasseh answered the
heads of the clans of Israel: 22"The LORD,
the Mighty One, is God! The LORD, the
Mighty One, is God! He knows the truth,
and may Israel know it, too! We have not
built the altar in treacherous rebellion
against the LORD. If we have done so, do
not spare our lives this day. 23If we have
built an altar for ourselves to turn away
from the LORD or to offer burnt offerings
or grain offerings or peace offerings, may
the LORD himself punish us.

24"The truth is, we have built this altar
because we fear that in the future your descendants will say to ours, 'What right do
you have to worship the LORD, the God of

Israel? 25 The LORD has placed the Jordan
River as a barrier between our people and
you people of Reuben and Gad. You have
no claim to the LORD.' So your descendants may prevent our descendants from
worshiping the LORD.

26"So we decided to build the altar, not
for burnt offerings or sacrifices, 27 but as a
memorial. It will remind our descendants
and your descendants that we, too, have
the right to worship the LORD at his sanctuary with our burnt offerings, sacrifices,
and peace offerings. Then your descendants will not be able to say to ours, 'You
have no claim to the LORD.'

28"If they say this, our descendants
can reply, 'Look at this copy of the LORD's
altar that our ancestors made. It is not
for burnt offerings or sacrifices; it is a reminder of the relationship both of us
have with the LORD.' 29Far be it from us to
rebel against the LORD or turn away from
him by building our own altar for burnt

offerings, grain offerings, or sacrifices. Only the altar of the LORD our God that stands in front of the Tabernacle may be used for that purpose."

³⁰When Phinehas the priest and the leaders of the community—the heads of the clans of Israel—heard this from the tribes of Reuben, Gad, and the half-tribe of Manasseh, they were satisfied. ³¹Phinehas son of Eleazar, the priest, replied to them, "Today we know the LORD is among us because you have not committed this treachery against the LORD as we thought. Instead, you have rescued Israel from being destroyed by the hand of the LORD."

³²Then Phinehas son of Eleazar, the priest, and the other leaders left the tribes of Reuben and Gad in Gilead and returned to the land of Canaan to tell the Israelites what had happened. ³³And all the Israelites were satisfied and praised God and spoke no more of war against Reuben and Gad.

³⁴The people of Reuben and Gad named the altar "Witness,"* for they said, "It is a witness between us and them that the LORD is our God, too."

²³:¹THE years passed, and the LORD had given the people of Israel rest from all their enemies. Joshua, who was now very old, ²called together all the elders, leaders, judges, and officers of Israel. He said to them, "I am now a very old man. ³You have seen everything the LORD your God has done for you during my lifetime. The LORD your God has fought for you against your enemies. ⁴I have allotted to you as your homeland all the land of the nations yet unconquered, as well as the land of those we have already conquered—from the Jordan River to the Mediterranean Sea* in the west. ⁵This land will be yours, for the LORD your God will himself drive out all the people living there now. You will take possession of their land, just as the LORD your God promised you.

⁶"So be very careful to follow everything Moses wrote in the Book of Instruction. Do not deviate from it, turning either to the right or to the left. ⁷Make sure you do not associate with the other people still remaining in the land. Do not even mention the names of their gods, much less swear

by them or serve them or worship them. ⁸Rather, cling tightly to the LORD your God as you have done until now.

⁹"For the LORD has driven out great and powerful nations for you, and no one has yet been able to defeat you. ¹⁰Each one of you will put to flight a thousand of the enemy, for the LORD your God fights for you, just as he has promised. ¹¹So be very careful to love the LORD your God.

¹²"But if you turn away from him and cling to the customs of the survivors of these nations remaining among you, and if you intermarry with them, ¹³then know for certain that the LORD your God will no longer drive them out of your land. Instead, they will be a snare and a trap to you, a whip for your backs and thorny brambles in your eyes, and you will vanish from this good land the LORD your God has given you.

¹⁴"Soon I will die, going the way of everything on earth. Deep in your hearts you know that every promise of the LORD your God has come true. Not a single one has failed! ¹⁵But as surely as the LORD your God has given you the good things he promised, he will also bring disaster on you if you disobey him. He will completely destroy you from this good land he has given you. ¹⁶If you break the covenant of the LORD your God by worshiping and serving other gods, his anger will burn against you, and you will quickly vanish from the good land he has given you."

22:34 Some manuscripts lack this word. 23:4 Hebrew *the Great Sea.*

LUKE 20:27-47

The Sadducees were another group of Jewish religious leaders. They did not believe in the resurrection from the dead, and according to some early church fathers, they accepted only the books of Genesis to Deuteronomy as Scripture. They came to Jesus hoping to stump him with a trick question, but Jesus turned the tables.

Then Jesus was approached by some Sadducees—religious leaders who say there is no resurrection from the dead. ²⁸They posed this question: "Teacher, Moses gave us a law that if a man dies, leaving a wife but no children, his brother should marry the widow and have a child who will carry on the brother's name.* ²⁹Well, suppose there were seven brothers. The oldest one married and then died without children. ³⁰So the second brother married the widow, but he also died. ³¹Then the third brother married her. This continued with all seven of them, who died without children. ³²Finally, the woman also died. ³³So tell us, whose wife will she be in the resurrection? For all seven were married to her!"

³⁴Jesus replied, "Marriage is for people here on earth. ³⁵But in the age to come, those worthy of being raised from the dead will neither marry nor be given in marriage. ³⁶And they will never die again. In this respect they will be like angels. They are children of God and children of the resurrection.

³⁷"But now, as to whether the dead will be raised—even Moses proved this when he wrote about the burning bush. Long after Abraham, Isaac, and Jacob had died, he referred to the Lord* as 'the God of Abraham, the God of Isaac, and the God of Jacob.'* ³⁸So he is the God of the living, not the dead, for they are all alive to him."

³⁹"Well said, Teacher!" remarked some of the teachers of religious law who were standing there. ⁴⁰And then no one dared to ask him any more questions.

⁴¹Then Jesus presented them with a question. "Why is it," he asked, "that the Messiah is said to be the son of David? ⁴²For David himself wrote in the book of Psalms:

'The LORD said to my Lord,
   Sit in the place of honor at my right
      hand
⁴³ until I humble your enemies,
      making them a footstool under your
         feet.'*

⁴⁴Since David called the Messiah 'Lord,' how can the Messiah be his son?"

⁴⁵Then, with the crowds listening, he turned to his disciples and said, ⁴⁶"Beware of these teachers of religious law! For they like to parade around in flowing robes and love to receive respectful greetings as they walk in the marketplaces. And how they love the seats of honor in the synagogues and the head table at banquets. ⁴⁷Yet they shamelessly cheat widows out of their property and then pretend to be pious by making long prayers in public. Because of this, they will be severely punished."

20:28 See Deut 25:5-6.   20:37a Greek *when he wrote about the bush. He referred to the Lord.*   20:37b Exod 3:6.
20:42-43 Ps 110:1.

PSALM 89:14-37

Righteousness and justice are the
   foundation of your throne.
Unfailing love and truth walk
   before you as attendants.

Growing in wisdom

HOW WE LIVE

JOSHUA 23 Wisdom can be defined as the ability to make edifying decisions about the future by evaluating the consequences of actions taken in the past. History is full of leaders who watched their kingdoms crumble because they believed they were immune to the consequences their forebears had suffered when making the same ignorant or foolish decisions.   • Joshua 23 records the final words of wisdom from a leader who loved his nation like children. This short chapter is filled with advice for living wisely. Joshua stresses the wisdom of following a few basic rules of faith by reminding Israel of its past—the mistakes as well as the victories.   • When you are called upon to make a wise decision for yourself, your family, or your community, remember the ways in which God taught you a principle of life through mistakes you've made, or times when you were blessed because you held fast to God's teachings. If you're still new to this and don't have a lot of faithful past to build on, you can learn from past mistakes; and you can get advice from mature, godly leaders who can draw upon their own experiences with the Lord.

¹⁵ Happy are those who hear the joyful
          call to worship,
  for they will walk in the light of
          your presence, LORD.
¹⁶ They rejoice all day long in your
          wonderful reputation.
  They exult in your righteousness.
¹⁷ You are their glorious strength.
  It pleases you to make us strong.
¹⁸ Yes, our protection comes from the
          LORD,
  and he, the Holy One of Israel, has
          given us our king.

¹⁹ Long ago you spoke in a vision to your
          faithful people.
  You said, "I have raised up a warrior.
  I have selected him from the
          common people to be king.
²⁰ I have found my servant David.
  I have anointed him with my holy oil.
²¹ I will steady him with my hand;
  with my powerful arm I will make
          him strong.
²² His enemies will not defeat him,
  nor will the wicked overpower him.
²³ I will beat down his adversaries before
          him
  and destroy those who hate him.
²⁴ My faithfulness and unfailing love will
          be with him,
  and by my authority he will grow
          in power.
²⁵ I will extend his rule over the sea,
  his dominion over the rivers.
²⁶ And he will call out to me, 'You are
          my Father,
  my God, and the Rock of my
          salvation.'
²⁷ I will make him my firstborn son,
  the mightiest king on earth.

²⁸ I will love him and be kind to him
          forever;
  my covenant with him will never
          end.
²⁹ I will preserve an heir for him;
  his throne will be as endless as
          the days of heaven.
³⁰ But if his descendants forsake my
          instructions
  and fail to obey my regulations,
³¹ if they do not obey my decrees
  and fail to keep my commands,
³² then I will punish their sin with
          the rod,
  and their disobedience with
          beating.
³³ But I will never stop loving him
  nor fail to keep my promise to
          him.
³⁴ No, I will not break my covenant;
  I will not take back a single word
          I said.
³⁵ I have sworn an oath to David,
  and in my holiness I cannot lie:
³⁶ His dynasty will go on forever;
  his kingdom will endure as
          the sun.
³⁷ It will be as eternal as the moon,
  my faithful witness in the sky!"
                     Interlude

PROVERBS 13:17-19

An unreliable messenger stumbles into trouble, but a reliable messenger brings healing. □If you ignore criticism, you will end in poverty and disgrace; if you accept correction, you will be honored. □It is pleasant to see dreams come true, but fools refuse to turn from evil to attain them.

APRIL **22**

JOSHUA 24:1-33

As Joshua prepared to die, he reminded the people of the journey that was described in Exodus, Numbers, and then Deuteronomy. He reminded them of the promises they had made to God along the way. Would they keep these promises?

Then Joshua summoned all the tribes of Israel to Shechem, including their elders, leaders, judges, and officers. So they came and presented themselves to God.

²Joshua said to the people, "This is

what the LORD, the God of Israel, says: Long ago your ancestors, including Terah, the father of Abraham and Nahor, lived beyond the Euphrates River,* and they worshiped other gods. ³But I took your ancestor Abraham from the land beyond the Euphrates and led him into the land of Canaan. I gave him many descendants through his son Isaac. ⁴To Isaac I gave Jacob and Esau. To Esau I gave the mountains of Seir, while Jacob and his children went down into Egypt.

⁵"Then I sent Moses and Aaron, and I brought terrible plagues on Egypt; and afterward I brought you out as a free people. ⁶But when your ancestors arrived at the Red Sea,* the Egyptians chased after you with chariots and charioteers. ⁷When your ancestors cried out to the LORD, I put darkness between you and the Egyptians. I brought the sea crashing down on the Egyptians, drowning them. With your very own eyes you saw what I did. Then you lived in the wilderness for many years.

⁸"Finally, I brought you into the land of the Amorites on the east side of the Jordan. They fought against you, but I destroyed them before you. I gave you victory over them, and you took possession of their land. ⁹Then Balak son of Zippor, king of Moab, started a war against Israel. He summoned Balaam son of Beor to curse you, ¹⁰but I would not listen to him. Instead, I made Balaam bless you, and so I rescued you from Balak.

¹¹"When you crossed the Jordan River and came to Jericho, the men of Jericho fought against you, as did the Amorites, the Perizzites, the Canaanites, the Hittites, the Girgashites, the Hivites, and the Jebusites. But I gave you victory over them. ¹²And I sent terror* ahead of you to drive out the two kings of the Amorites. It was not your swords or bows that brought you victory. ¹³I gave you land you had not worked on, and I gave you towns you did not build—the towns where you are now living. I gave you vineyards and olive groves for food, though you did not plant them.

¹⁴"So fear the LORD and serve him wholeheartedly. Put away forever the idols your ancestors worshiped when they lived beyond the Euphrates River and in Egypt. Serve the LORD alone. ¹⁵But if you refuse to serve the LORD, then choose today whom you will serve. Would you prefer the gods your ancestors served beyond the Euphrates? Or will it be the gods of the Amorites in whose land you now live? But as for me and my family, we will serve the LORD."

¹⁶The people replied, "We would never abandon the LORD and serve other gods. ¹⁷For the LORD our God is the one who rescued us and our ancestors from slavery in the land of Egypt. He performed mighty miracles before our very eyes. As we traveled through the wilderness among our enemies, he preserved us. ¹⁸It was the LORD who drove out the Amorites and the other nations living here in the land. So we, too, will serve the LORD, for he alone is our God."

¹⁹Then Joshua warned the people, "You are not able to serve the LORD, for he is a holy and jealous God. He will not forgive your rebellion and your sins. ²⁰If you abandon the LORD and serve other gods, he will turn against you and destroy you, even though he has been so good to you."

²¹But the people answered Joshua, "No, we will serve the LORD!"

²²"You are a witness to your own decision," Joshua said. "You have chosen to serve the LORD."

"Yes," they replied, "we are witnesses to what we have said."

²³"All right then," Joshua said, "destroy the idols among you, and turn your hearts to the LORD, the God of Israel."

²⁴The people said to Joshua, "We will serve the LORD our God. We will obey him alone."

²⁵So Joshua made a covenant with the people that day at Shechem, committing them to follow the decrees and regulations of the LORD. ²⁶Joshua recorded these things in the Book of God's Instructions. As a reminder of their agreement, he took a huge stone and rolled it beneath the terebinth tree beside the Tabernacle of the LORD.

²⁷Joshua said to all the people, "This stone has heard everything the LORD said to us. It will be a witness to testify against you if you go back on your word to God."

²⁸Then Joshua sent all the people away to their own homelands.

²⁹After this, Joshua son of Nun, the servant of the LORD, died at the age of 110. ³⁰They buried him in the land he had been allocated, at Timnath-serah in the hill country of Ephraim, north of Mount Gaash.

³¹The people of Israel served the LORD throughout the lifetime of Joshua and of the elders who outlived him—those who had personally experienced all that the LORD had done for Israel.

³²The bones of Joseph, which the Israelites had brought along with them when they left Egypt, were buried at Shechem, in the parcel of ground Jacob had bought from the sons of Hamor for 100 pieces of silver.* This land was located in the territory allotted to the descendants of Joseph.

³³Eleazar son of Aaron also died. He was buried in the hill country of Ephraim, in the town of Gibeah, which had been given to his son Phinehas.

24:2 Hebrew *the river;* also in 24:3, 14, 15. **24:6** Hebrew *sea of reeds.* **24:12** Often rendered *the hornet.* The meaning of the Hebrew is uncertain. **24:32** Hebrew *100 kesitahs;* the value or weight of the kesitah is no longer known.

LUKE 21:1-28

For centuries, the Jews had hoped for a Messiah who would lead them into victory as a nation. When you read Jesus' teachings in this passage, you can understand why those Jews were disappointed. Jesus didn't come to bring the kind of victory they were expecting—at least, not immediately.

While Jesus was in the Temple, he watched the rich people dropping their gifts in the collection box. ²Then a poor widow came by and dropped in two small coins.*

³"I tell you the truth," Jesus said, "this poor widow has given more than all the rest of them. ⁴For they have given a tiny part of their surplus, but she, poor as she is, has given everything she has."

⁵Some of his disciples began talking about the majestic stonework of the Temple and the memorial decorations on the walls. But Jesus said, ⁶"The time is coming when all these things will be completely demolished. Not one stone will be left on top of another!"

⁷"Teacher," they asked, "when will all this happen? What sign will show us that these things are about to take place?"

⁸He replied, "Don't let anyone mislead you, for many will come in my name, claiming, 'I am the Messiah,'* and saying, 'The time has come!' But don't believe them. ⁹And when you hear of wars and insurrections, don't panic. Yes, these things must take place first, but the end won't follow immediately." ¹⁰Then he added, "Nation will go to war against nation, and kingdom against kingdom. ¹¹There will be great earthquakes, and there will be famines and plagues in many lands, and there will be terrifying things and great miraculous signs from heaven.

¹²"But before all this occurs, there will be a time of great persecution. You will be dragged into synagogues and prisons, and you will stand trial before kings and governors because you are my followers. ¹³But this will be your opportunity to tell them about me.* ¹⁴So don't worry in advance about how to answer the charges against you, ¹⁵for I will give you the right words and such wisdom that none of your opponents will be able to reply or refute you! ¹⁶Even those closest to you—your parents, brothers, relatives, and friends—will betray you. They will even kill some of you. ¹⁷And everyone will hate you because you are my followers.* ¹⁸But not a hair of your head will perish! ¹⁹By standing firm, you will win your souls.

²⁰"And when you see Jerusalem surrounded by armies, then you will know that the time of its destruction has arrived. ²¹Then those in Judea must flee to the hills. Those in Jerusalem must get out, and those out in the country should not return to the city. ²²For those will be days of God's vengeance, and the prophetic words of the Scriptures will be fulfilled. ²³How terrible it will be for pregnant women and for nursing mothers in those days. For there will be disaster in the land and great anger against this people. ²⁴They will be killed by the sword or sent away as captives to all the nations of the world. And Jerusalem will be trampled

down by the Gentiles until the period of the Gentiles comes to an end.

²⁵"And there will be strange signs in the sun, moon, and stars. And here on earth the nations will be in turmoil, perplexed by the roaring seas and strange tides. ²⁶People will be terrified at what they see coming upon the earth, for the powers in the heavens will be shaken. ²⁷Then everyone will see the Son of Man* coming on a cloud with power and great glory.* ²⁸So when all these things begin to happen, stand and look up, for your salvation is near!"

21:2 Greek *two lepta* [the smallest of Jewish coins]. **21:8** Greek *claiming, 'I am.'* **21:13** Or *This will be your testimony against them.* **21:17** Greek *on account of my name.* **21:27a** "Son of Man" is a title Jesus used for himself. **21:27b** See Dan 7:13.

PSALM 89:38-52

But now you have rejected him and cast him off.
    You are angry with your anointed king.
³⁹ You have renounced your covenant with him;
    you have thrown his crown in the dust.
⁴⁰ You have broken down the walls protecting him
    and ruined every fort defending him.
⁴¹ Everyone who comes along has robbed him,

and he has become a joke to his neighbors.
⁴² You have strengthened his enemies
    and made them all rejoice.
⁴³ You have made his sword useless
    and refused to help him in battle.
⁴⁴ You have ended his splendor
    and overturned his throne.
⁴⁵ You have made him old before his time
    and publicly disgraced him.
                                    Interlude

⁴⁶ O LORD, how long will this go on?
    Will you hide yourself forever?
    How long will your anger burn like fire?
⁴⁷ Remember how short my life is,
    how empty and futile this human existence!
⁴⁸ No one can live forever; all will die.
    No one can escape the power of the grave.*   *Interlude*
⁴⁹ Lord, where is your unfailing love?
    You promised it to David with a faithful pledge.
⁵⁰ Consider, Lord, how your servants are disgraced!
    I carry in my heart the insults of so many people.

WHAT THE BIBLE SAYS

The future

LUKE 21:5-28 The picture painted in this passage is rather gloomy. Why? Because the world is winding toward a certain predetermined end time when Jesus will return from heaven and set up his eternal kingdom. Until that time, however, a spiritual battle wages in the realm beyond our senses—we can't see it or hear it, but it's there. Satan and his demons are fighting what will ultimately be a losing battle. The part of the battle that we do see, the evil that continues to escalate—culminating in persecution, wars, natural disaster, betrayal, and widespread destruction—will keep occurring until Jesus returns and "everyone will see the Son of Man coming on a cloud with power and great glory" (21:27).   • Jesus gave these warnings to keep us from being disheartened. While God's plans for us are always good, we must be prepared that the world will not always be an easy place. No matter what happens here, however, the promises to you will be kept in eternity.

51 Your enemies have mocked me,
O LORD;
they mock your anointed king
wherever he goes.

52 Praise the LORD forever!
Amen and amen!

89:48 Hebrew *of Sheol.*

APRIL**23**

JUDGES 1:1-2:9

After the strong leadership of Moses and then Joshua, the book of Judges opens with no one in charge over all the tribes. Spiritual complacency soon followed, with unfortunate consequences.

After the death of Joshua, the Israelites asked the LORD, "Which tribe should go first to attack the Canaanites?"

2 The LORD answered, "Judah, for I have given them victory over the land."

3 The men of Judah said to their relatives from the tribe of Simeon, "Join with us to fight against the Canaanites living in the territory allotted to us. Then we will help you conquer your territory." So the men of Simeon went with Judah.

4 When the men of Judah attacked, the LORD gave them victory over the Canaanites and Perizzites, and they killed 10,000 enemy warriors at the town of Bezek. 5 While at Bezek they encountered King Adoni-bezek and fought against him, and the Canaanites and Perizzites were defeated. 6 Adoni-bezek escaped, but the Israelites soon captured him and cut off his thumbs and big toes.

7 Adoni-bezek said, "I once had seventy kings with their thumbs and big toes cut off, eating scraps from under my table. Now God has paid me back for what I did to them." They took him to Jerusalem, and he died there.

8 The men of Judah attacked Jerusalem and captured it, killing all its people and setting the city on fire. 9 Then they went down to fight the Canaanites living in the hill country, the Negev, and the western

PROVERBS 13:20-23

Walk with the wise and become wise; associate with fools and get in trouble. □ Trouble chases sinners, while blessings reward the righteous. □ Good people leave an inheritance to their grandchildren, but the sinner's wealth passes to the godly. □ A poor person's farm may produce much food, but injustice sweeps it all away.

foothills.* 10 Judah marched against the Canaanites in Hebron (formerly called Kiriath-arba), defeating the forces of Sheshai, Ahiman, and Talmai.

11 From there they went to fight against the people living in the town of Debir (formerly called Kiriath-sepher). 12 Caleb said, "I will give my daughter Acsah in marriage to the one who attacks and captures Kiriath-sepher." 13 Othniel, the son of Caleb's younger brother, Kenaz, was the one who conquered it, so Acsah became Othniel's wife.

14 When Acsah married Othniel, she urged him* to ask her father for a field. As she got down off her donkey, Caleb asked her, "What's the matter?"

15 She said, "Let me have another gift. You have already given me land in the Negev; now please give me springs of water, too." So Caleb gave her the upper and lower springs.

16 When the tribe of Judah left Jericho—the city of palms—the Kenites, who were descendants of Moses' father-in-law, traveled with them into the wilderness of Judah. They settled among the people there, near the town of Arad in the Negev.

17 Then Judah joined with Simeon to fight against the Canaanites living in Zephath, and they completely destroyed* the town. So the town was named Hormah.* 18 In addition, Judah captured the towns of Gaza, Ashkelon, and Ekron, along with their surrounding territories.

19 The LORD was with the people of Ju-

dah, and they took possession of the hill country. But they failed to drive out the people living in the plains, who had iron chariots. [20]The town of Hebron was given to Caleb as Moses had promised. And Caleb drove out the people living there, who were descendants of the three sons of Anak.

[21]The tribe of Benjamin, however, failed to drive out the Jebusites, who were living in Jerusalem. So to this day the Jebusites live in Jerusalem among the people of Benjamin.

[22]The descendants of Joseph attacked the town of Bethel, and the LORD was with them. [23]They sent men to scout out Bethel (formerly known as Luz). [24]They confronted a man coming out of the town and said to him, "Show us a way into the town, and we will have mercy on you." [25]So he showed them a way in, and they killed everyone in the town except that man and his family. [26]Later the man moved to the land of the Hittites, where he built a town. He named it Luz, which is its name to this day.

[27]The tribe of Manasseh failed to drive out the people living in Beth-shan,* Taanach, Dor, Ibleam, Megiddo, and all their surrounding settlements, because the Canaanites were determined to stay in that region. [28]When the Israelites grew stronger, they forced the Canaanites to work as slaves, but they never did drive them completely out of the land.

[29]The tribe of Ephraim failed to drive out the Canaanites living in Gezer, so the Canaanites continued to live there among them.

[30]The tribe of Zebulun failed to drive out the residents of Kitron and Nahalol, so the Canaanites continued to live among them. But the Canaanites were forced to work as slaves for the people of Zebulun.

[31]The tribe of Asher failed to drive out the residents of Acco, Sidon, Ahlab, Aczib, Helbah, Aphik, and Rehob. [32]Instead, the people of Asher moved in among the Canaanites, who controlled the land, for they failed to drive them out.

[33]Likewise, the tribe of Naphtali failed to drive out the residents of Beth-shemesh and Beth-anath. Instead, they moved in among the Canaanites, who controlled the land. Nevertheless, the people of Beth-shemesh and Beth-anath were forced to work as slaves for the people of Naphtali.

[34]As for the tribe of Dan, the Amorites forced them back into the hill country and would not let them come down into the plains. [35]The Amorites were determined to stay in Mount Heres, Aijalon, and Shaalbim, but when the descendants of Joseph became stronger, they forced the Amorites to work as slaves. [36]The boundary of the Amorites ran from Scorpion Pass* to Sela and continued upward from there.

[2:1]THE angel of the LORD went up from Gilgal to Bokim and said to the Israelites, "I brought you out of Egypt into this land that I swore to give your ancestors, and I said I would never break my covenant with you. [2]For your part, you were not to make any covenants with the people living in this land; instead, you were to destroy their altars. But you disobeyed my command. Why did you do this? [3]So now I declare that I will no longer drive out the people living in your land. They will be thorns in your sides,* and their gods will be a constant temptation to you."

[4]When the angel of the LORD finished speaking to all the Israelites, the people wept loudly. [5]So they called the place Bokim (which means "weeping"), and they offered sacrifices there to the LORD.

[6]After Joshua sent the people away, each of the tribes left to take possession of the land allotted to them. [7]And the Israelites served the LORD throughout the lifetime of Joshua and the leaders who outlived him—those who had seen all the great things the LORD had done for Israel.

[8]Joshua son of Nun, the servant of the LORD, died at the age of 110. [9]They buried him in the land he had been allocated, at Timnath-serah* in the hill country of Ephraim, north of Mount Gaash.

1:9 Hebrew *the Shephelah.*   1:14 Greek version and Latin Vulgate read *he urged her.*   1:17a The Hebrew term used here refers to the complete consecration of things or people to the LORD, either by destroying them or by giving them as an offering.   1:17b *Hormah* means "destruction."   1:27 Hebrew *Beth-shean,* a variant spelling of Beth-shan.   1:36 Hebrew *Akrabbim.*   2:3 Hebrew *They will be in your sides;* compare Num 33:55.   2:9 As in parallel text at Josh 24:30; Hebrew reads *Timnath-heres,* a variant spelling of Timnath-serah.

LUKE 21:29-22:13
Jesus continued his teachings every day in the Temple during the week before his death. He taught about his return and about being watchful. Then it was time for preparations—Judas and Jesus both had arrangements to make.

Then he gave them this illustration: "Notice the fig tree, or any other tree. ³⁰When the leaves come out, you know without being told that summer is near. ³¹In the same way, when you see all these things taking place, you can know that the Kingdom of God is near. ³²I tell you the truth, this generation will not pass from the scene until all these things have taken place. ³³Heaven and earth will disappear, but my words will never disappear.

³⁴"Watch out! Don't let your hearts be dulled by carousing and drunkenness, and by the worries of this life. Don't let that day catch you unaware, ³⁵like a trap. For that day will come upon everyone living on the earth. ³⁶Keep alert at all times. And pray that you might be strong enough to escape these coming horrors and stand before the Son of Man."

³⁷Every day Jesus went to the Temple to teach, and each evening he returned to spend the night on the Mount of Olives. ³⁸The crowds gathered at the Temple early each morning to hear him.

22:1THE Festival of Unleavened Bread, which is also called Passover, was approaching. ²The leading priests and teachers of religious law were plotting how to kill Jesus, but they were afraid of the people's reaction.

³Then Satan entered into Judas Iscariot, who was one of the twelve disciples, ⁴and he went to the leading priests and captains of the Temple guard to discuss the best way to betray Jesus to them. ⁵They were delighted, and they promised to give him money. ⁶So he agreed and began looking for an opportunity to betray Jesus so they could arrest him when the crowds weren't around.

⁷Now the Festival of Unleavened Bread arrived, when the Passover lamb is sacrificed. ⁸Jesus sent Peter and John ahead and said, "Go and prepare the Passover meal, so we can eat it together."

⁹"Where do you want us to prepare it?" they asked him.

¹⁰He replied, "As soon as you enter Jerusalem, a man carrying a pitcher of water will meet you. Follow him. At the house he enters, ¹¹say to the owner, 'The Teacher asks: Where is the guest room where I can eat the Passover meal with my disciples?' ¹²He will take you upstairs to a large room that is already set up. That is where you should prepare our meal." ¹³They went off to the city and found everything just as Jesus had said, and they prepared the Passover meal there.

PSALM 90:1-91:16
A prayer of Moses, the man of God.

¹ Lord, through all the generations
  you have been our home!
² Before the mountains were born,
  before you gave birth to the earth
    and the world,
  from beginning to end, you
    are God.

³ You turn people back to dust, saying,
  "Return to dust, you mortals!"
⁴ For you, a thousand years are as
    a passing day,
  as brief as a few night hours.
⁵ You sweep people away like dreams
    that disappear.
  They are like grass that springs up
    in the morning.
⁶ In the morning it blooms and
    flourishes,
  but by evening it is dry and
    withered.
⁷ We wither beneath your anger;
  we are overwhelmed by your fury.
⁸ You spread out our sins before you—
  our secret sins—and you see them
    all.
⁹ We live our lives beneath your wrath,
  ending our years with a groan.
¹⁰ Seventy years are given to us!
  Some even live to eighty.
  But even the best years are filled with
    pain and trouble;
  soon they disappear, and we fly
    away.
¹¹ Who can comprehend the power of
  your anger?

Your wrath is as awesome as the
fear you deserve.
12 Teach us to realize the brevity of life,
so that we may grow in wisdom.

13 O LORD, come back to us!
How long will you delay?
Take pity on your servants!
14 Satisfy us each morning with your
unfailing love,
so we may sing for joy to the end
of our lives.
15 Give us gladness in proportion to our
former misery!
Replace the evil years with good.
16 Let us, your servants, see you work
again;
let our children see your glory.
17 And may the Lord our God show us
his approval
and make our efforts successful.
Yes, make our efforts successful!

91:1 THOSE who live in the shelter of
the Most High
will find rest in the shadow of
the Almighty.
2 This I declare about the LORD:
He alone is my refuge, my place of
safety;
he is my God, and I trust him.
3 For he will rescue you from every trap
and protect you from deadly disease.

4 He will cover you with his feathers.
He will shelter you with his wings.
His faithful promises are your
armor and protection.
5 Do not be afraid of the terrors of the
night,
nor the arrow that flies in the day.
6 Do not dread the disease that stalks in
darkness,
nor the disaster that strikes at
midday.
7 Though a thousand fall at your side,
though ten thousand are dying
around you,
these evils will not touch you.
8 Just open your eyes,
and see how the wicked are
punished.
9 If you make the LORD your refuge,
if you make the Most High your
shelter,
10 no evil will conquer you;
no plague will come near
your home.
11 For he will order his angels
to protect you wherever you go.
12 They will hold you up with their
hands
so you won't even hurt your foot
on a stone.
13 You will trample upon lions and
cobras;

Living responsibly

HOW WE LIVE

JUDGES 2:1-5 God gave the Israelites the responsibility of conquering and settling the land of Canaan. The opening of the book of Judges gives a good picture of how the Israelites had failed in that responsibility. It reads like a sad litany, "The tribe of Manasseh failed to drive out the people" (1:27); "as for the tribe of Dan, the Amorites forced them back into the hill country and would not let them come down into the plains" (1:34). And so on. As God had warned, the Israelites found it impossible to maintain pure worship with other religions all around them. The weaker they became spiritually, the weaker they became politically. Imagine how different their history might have been had they taken care of the responsibilities God had given them. • God has given you responsibilities as well. Like the ancient Israelites, when given a job by God, you should complete it without fear or doubt. You should not be lazy, thinking that you know better than God and so choosing to only meet him halfway. You should not live carelessly, unintentionally, or irresponsibly. Otherwise, you will repeat an ancient mistake and will be weaker for it.

you will crush fierce lions and
serpents under your feet!

14 The LORD says, "I will rescue those
who love me.
I will protect those who trust
in my name.
15 When they call on me, I will answer;
I will be with them in trouble.
I will rescue and honor them.

16 I will reward them with a long life
and give them my salvation."

PROVERBS 13:24-25
Those who spare the rod of discipline
hate their children. Those who love their
children care enough to discipline them.
□ The godly eat to their hearts' content,
but the belly of the wicked goes hungry.

APRIL **24**

JUDGES 2:10–3:31
The book of Judges describes a series of cycles.
Each time the people grew weak spiritually, they
were oppressed by foreigners. The judges were
national champions God raised up from within the
Israelite ranks to rescue the people from their own
wickedness.

After that generation died, another generation grew up who did not acknowledge
the LORD or remember the mighty things
he had done for Israel.

11The Israelites did evil in the LORD's
sight and served the images of Baal.
12They abandoned the LORD, the God of
their ancestors, who had brought them
out of Egypt. They went after other gods,
worshiping the gods of the people around
them. And they angered the LORD. 13They
abandoned the LORD to serve Baal and the
images of Ashtoreth. 14This made the
LORD burn with anger against Israel, so
he handed them over to raiders who stole
their possessions. He turned them over to
their enemies all around, and they were
no longer able to resist them. 15Every time
Israel went out to battle, the LORD fought
against them, causing them to be defeated, just as he had warned. And the
people were in great distress.

16Then the LORD raised up judges to
rescue the Israelites from their attackers.
17Yet Israel did not listen to the judges but
prostituted themselves by worshiping
other gods. How quickly they turned away
from the path of their ancestors, who had

walked in obedience to the LORD's commands.

18Whenever the LORD raised up a judge
over Israel, he was with that judge and
rescued the people from their enemies
throughout the judge's lifetime. For the
LORD took pity on his people, who were
burdened by oppression and suffering.
19But when the judge died, the people
returned to their corrupt ways, behaving
worse than those who had lived before
them. They went after other gods, serving
and worshiping them. And they refused
to give up their evil practices and stubborn ways.

20So the LORD burned with anger
against Israel. He said, "Because these
people have violated my covenant, which
I made with their ancestors, and have ignored my commands, 21I will no longer
drive out the nations that Joshua left unconquered when he died. 22I did this to
test Israel—to see whether or not they
would follow the ways of the LORD as their
ancestors did." 23That is why the LORD
left those nations in place. He did not
quickly drive them out or allow Joshua to
conquer them all.

3:1THESE are the nations that the LORD left
in the land to test those Israelites who had
not experienced the wars of Canaan. 2He
did this to teach warfare to generations of
Israelites who had no experience in battle. 3These are the nations: the Philistines
(those living under the five Philistine rul-

ers), all the Canaanites, the Sidonians, and the Hivites living in the mountains of Lebanon from Mount Baal-hermon to Lebo-hamath. ⁴These people were left to test the Israelites—to see whether they would obey the commands the LORD had given to their ancestors through Moses.

⁵So the people of Israel lived among the Canaanites, Hittites, Amorites, Perizzites, Hivites, and Jebusites, ⁶and they intermarried with them. Israelite sons married their daughters, and Israelite daughters were given in marriage to their sons. And the Israelites served their gods.

⁷The Israelites did evil in the LORD's sight. They forgot about the LORD their God, and they served the images of Baal and the Asherah poles. ⁸Then the LORD burned with anger against Israel, and he turned them over to King Cushan-rishathaim of Aram-naharaim.* And the Israelites served Cushan-rishathaim for eight years.

⁹But when the people of Israel cried out to the LORD for help, the LORD raised up a rescuer to save them. His name was Othniel, the son of Caleb's younger brother, Kenaz. ¹⁰The Spirit of the LORD came upon him, and he became Israel's judge. He went to war against King Cushan-rishathaim of Aram, and the LORD gave Othniel victory over him. ¹¹So there was peace in the land for forty years. Then Othniel son of Kenaz died.

¹²Once again the Israelites did evil in the LORD's sight, and the LORD gave King Eglon of Moab control over Israel because of their evil. ¹³Eglon enlisted the Ammonites and Amalekites as allies, and then he went out and defeated Israel, taking possession of Jericho, the city of palms. ¹⁴And the Israelites served Eglon of Moab for eighteen years.

¹⁵But when the people of Israel cried out to the LORD for help, the LORD again raised up a rescuer to save them. His name was Ehud son of Gera, a left-handed man of the tribe of Benjamin. The Israelites sent Ehud to deliver their tribute money to King Eglon of Moab. ¹⁶So Ehud made a double-edged dagger that was about a foot* long, and he strapped it to his right thigh, keeping it hidden under his clothing. ¹⁷He brought the tribute money to Eglon, who was very fat.

¹⁸After delivering the payment, Ehud started home with those who had helped carry the tribute. ¹⁹But when Ehud reached the stone idols near Gilgal, he turned back. He came to Eglon and said, "I have a secret message for you."

So the king commanded his servants, "Be quiet!" and he sent them all out of the room.

²⁰Ehud walked over to Eglon, who was sitting alone in a cool upstairs room. And Ehud said, "I have a message from God for you!" As King Eglon rose from his seat, ²¹Ehud reached with his left hand, pulled out the dagger strapped to his right thigh, and plunged it into the king's belly. ²²The dagger went so deep that the handle disappeared beneath the king's fat. So Ehud did not pull out the dagger, and the king's bowels emptied.* ²³Then Ehud closed and locked the doors of the room and escaped down the latrine.*

²⁴After Ehud was gone, the king's servants returned and found the doors to the upstairs room locked. They thought he might be using the latrine in the room, ²⁵so they waited. But when the king didn't come out after a long delay, they became concerned and got a key. And when they opened the doors, they found their master dead on the floor.

²⁶While the servants were waiting, Ehud escaped, passing the stone idols on his way to Seirah. ²⁷When he arrived in the hill country of Ephraim, Ehud sounded a call to arms. Then he led a band of Israelites down from the hills.

²⁸"Follow me," he said, "for the LORD has given you victory over Moab your enemy." So they followed him. And the Israelites took control of the shallow crossings of the Jordan River across from Moab, preventing anyone from crossing.

²⁹They attacked the Moabites and killed about 10,000 of their strongest and most able-bodied warriors. Not one of them escaped. ³⁰So Moab was conquered by Israel that day, and there was peace in the land for eighty years.

³¹After Ehud, Shamgar son of Anath rescued Israel. He once killed 600 Philistines with an ox goad.

3:8 *Aram-naharaim* means "Aram of the two rivers," thought to have been located between the Euphrates and Balih Rivers in northwestern Mesopotamia.   3:16 Hebrew *gomed*, the length of which is uncertain.   3:22 Or *and it came out behind.*   3:23 Or *and went out through the porch*; the meaning of the Hebrew is uncertain.

LUKE 22:14-34

Jesus gathered his closest and most beloved companions together to share a meal of great significance. He spoke the truth, even when it was difficult for them to hear.

When the time came, Jesus and the apostles sat down together at the table.* [15] Jesus said, "I have been very eager to eat this Passover meal with you before my suffering begins. [16] For I tell you now that I won't eat this meal again until its meaning is fulfilled in the Kingdom of God."

[17] Then he took a cup of wine, and gave thanks to God for it. Then he said, "Take this and share it among yourselves. [18] For I will not drink wine again until the Kingdom of God has come."

[19] He took some bread and gave thanks to God for it. Then he broke it in pieces and gave it to the disciples, saying, "This is my body, which is given for you. Do this to remember me."

[20] After supper he took another cup of wine and said, "This cup is the new covenant between God and his people— an agreement confirmed with my blood, which is poured out as a sacrifice for you.*

[21] "But here at this table, sitting among us as a friend, is the man who will betray me. [22] For it has been determined that the Son of Man* must die. But what sorrow awaits the one who betrays him." [23] The disciples began to ask each other which of them would ever do such a thing.

[24] Then they began to argue among themselves about who would be the greatest among them. [25] Jesus told them, "In this world the kings and great men lord it over their people, yet they are called 'friends of the people.' [26] But among you it will be different. Those who are the greatest among you should take the lowest rank, and the leader should be like a servant. [27] Who is more important, the one who sits at the table or the one who serves? The one who sits at the table, of course. But not here! For I am among you as one who serves.

[28] "You have stayed with me in my time of trial. [29] And just as my Father has granted me a Kingdom, I now grant you the right [30] to eat and drink at my table in my Kingdom. And you will sit on thrones, judging the twelve tribes of Israel.

[31] "Simon, Simon, Satan has asked to sift each of you like wheat. [32] But I have pleaded in prayer for you, Simon, that your faith should not fail. So when you have repented and turned to me again, strengthen your brothers."

[33] Peter said, "Lord, I am ready to go to prison with you, and even to die with you."

[34] But Jesus said, "Peter, let me tell you something. Before the rooster crows tomorrow morning, you will deny three times that you even know me."

22:14 Or *reclined together.*   22:19-20 Some manuscripts omit 22:19b-20, *which is given for you . . . which is poured out as a sacrifice for you.*   22:22 "Son of Man" is a title Jesus used for himself.

PSALM 92:1-93:5

A psalm. A song to be sung on the Sabbath Day.

1 It is good to give thanks to the LORD,
    to sing praises to the Most High.
2 It is good to proclaim your unfailing
        love in the morning,
    your faithfulness in the evening,
3 accompanied by the ten-stringed harp
    and the melody of the lyre.

4 You thrill me, LORD, with all you have
        done for me!
    I sing for joy because of what you
        have done.
5 O LORD, what great works you do!
    And how deep are your thoughts.
6 Only a simpleton would not know,
    and only a fool would not
        understand this:
7 Though the wicked sprout like
        weeds
    and evildoers flourish,
    they will be destroyed forever.

8 But you, O LORD, will be exalted
        forever.
9 Your enemies, LORD, will surely
        perish;
    all evildoers will be scattered.
10 But you have made me as strong
    as a wild ox.

You have anointed me with the
finest oil.
11 My eyes have seen the downfall of
my enemies;
my ears have heard the defeat of
my wicked opponents.
12 But the godly will flourish like palm
trees
and grow strong like the cedars
of Lebanon.
13 For they are transplanted to the LORD's
own house.
They flourish in the courts of our
God.
14 Even in old age they will still produce
fruit;
they will remain vital and green.
15 They will declare, "The LORD
is just!
He is my rock!
There is no evil in him!"

93:1 THE LORD is king! He is robed
in majesty.
Indeed, the LORD is robed in
majesty and armed with
strength.

The world stands firm
and cannot be shaken.
2 Your throne, O LORD, has stood from
time immemorial.
You yourself are from the
everlasting past.
3 The floods have risen up, O LORD.
The floods have roared like
thunder;
the floods have lifted their
pounding waves.
4 But mightier than the violent raging
of the seas,
mightier than the breakers on the
shore—
the LORD above is mightier than
these!
5 Your royal laws cannot be changed.
Your reign, O LORD, is holy forever
and ever.

PROVERBS 14:1-2

A wise woman builds her home, but a
foolish woman tears it down with her own
hands. □ Those who follow the right path
fear the LORD; those who take the wrong
path despise him.

WHAT THE BIBLE SAYS

The Lord's Supper

LUKE 22:14-20 The Lord's Supper (also called "Communion" in many
churches) is a very special moment for a believer, a time of deep intimacy
with God. Believers join together to partake of the bread and wine, and
by doing so they draw close to God on many different levels. It is a time
to remember and reflect on the amazing sacrifice that Jesus made for
us. A deep bond is formed when believers celebrate the Lord's Supper
together; it unites all believers in the one sacrifice of Jesus Christ. On a
personal level, it is also a very private moment of reflection, where you
can look inside your own heart, repent of your sins, and ask God to make
you clean. When you partake of communion with the family of believers,
you show your deep gratitude for Christ's work on your behalf, and you
are expressing your faith that he will come again.   • The next time you are
about to participate in the Lord's Supper, be sure to pause for a moment
to prepare your heart. Don't let it be an activity you engage in mindlessly.
Take the opportunity to draw close to God in a special way.

JUDGES 4:1–5:31

Deborah was faithful and available to God, so God used her, even though the cultural norms of the day made female leadership rare, if not impossible. She not only led her people into battle; she led them to victory.

After Ehud's death, the Israelites again did evil in the LORD's sight. ²So the LORD turned them over to King Jabin of Hazor, a Canaanite king. The commander of his army was Sisera, who lived in Harosheth-haggoyim. ³Sisera, who had 900 iron chariots, ruthlessly oppressed the Israelites for twenty years. Then the people of Israel cried out to the LORD for help.

⁴Deborah, the wife of Lappidoth, was a prophet who was judging Israel at that time. ⁵She would sit under the Palm of Deborah, between Ramah and Bethel in the hill country of Ephraim, and the Israelites would go to her for judgment. ⁶One day she sent for Barak son of Abinoam, who lived in Kedesh in the land of Naphtali. She said to him, "This is what the LORD, the God of Israel, commands you: Call out 10,000 warriors from the tribes of Naphtali and Zebulun at Mount Tabor. ⁷And I will call out Sisera, commander of Jabin's army, along with his chariots and warriors, to the Kishon River. There I will give you victory over him."

⁸Barak told her, "I will go, but only if you go with me."

⁹"Very well," she replied, "I will go with you. But you will receive no honor in this venture, for the LORD's victory over Sisera will be at the hands of a woman." So Deborah went with Barak to Kedesh. ¹⁰At Kedesh, Barak called together the tribes of Zebulun and Naphtali, and 10,000 warriors went up with him. Deborah also went with him.

¹¹Now Heber the Kenite, a descendant of Moses' brother-in-law* Hobab, had moved away from the other members of his tribe and pitched his tent by the oak of Zaanannim near Kedesh.

¹²When Sisera was told that Barak son of Abinoam had gone up to Mount Tabor, ¹³he called for all 900 of his iron chariots and all of his warriors, and they marched from Harosheth-haggoyim to the Kishon River.

¹⁴Then Deborah said to Barak, "Get ready! This is the day the LORD will give you victory over Sisera, for the LORD is marching ahead of you." So Barak led his 10,000 warriors down the slopes of Mount Tabor into battle. ¹⁵When Barak attacked, the LORD threw Sisera and all his chariots and warriors into a panic. Sisera leaped down from his chariot and escaped on foot. ¹⁶Then Barak chased the chariots and the enemy army all the way to Harosheth-haggoyim, killing all of Sisera's warriors. Not a single one was left alive.

¹⁷Meanwhile, Sisera ran to the tent of Jael, the wife of Heber the Kenite, because Heber's family was on friendly terms with King Jabin of Hazor. ¹⁸Jael went out to meet Sisera and said to him, "Come into my tent, sir. Come in. Don't be afraid." So he went into her tent, and she covered him with a blanket.

¹⁹"Please give me some water," he said. "I'm thirsty." So she gave him some milk from a leather bag and covered him again.

²⁰"Stand at the door of the tent," he told her. "If anybody comes and asks you if there is anyone here, say no."

²¹But when Sisera fell asleep from exhaustion, Jael quietly crept up to him with a hammer and tent peg in her hand. Then she drove the tent peg through his temple and into the ground, and so he died.

²²When Barak came looking for Sisera, Jael went out to meet him. She said, "Come, and I will show you the man you are looking for." So he followed her into the tent and found Sisera lying there dead, with the tent peg through his temple.

²³So on that day Israel saw God defeat Jabin, the Canaanite king. ²⁴And from that time on Israel became stronger and stronger against King Jabin until they finally destroyed him.

⁵:¹On that day Deborah and Barak son of Abinoam sang this song:

² "Israel's leaders took charge,
    and the people gladly followed.
  Praise the LORD!

³ "Listen, you kings!
    Pay attention, you mighty rulers!
  For I will sing to the LORD.
  I will make music to the LORD,
    the God of Israel.

⁴ "LORD, when you set out from Seir
    and marched across the fields
        of Edom,
  the earth trembled,
    and the cloudy skies poured down
        rain.

⁵ The mountains quaked in the
        presence of the LORD,
    the God of Mount Sinai—
  in the presence of the LORD,
    the God of Israel.

⁶ "In the days of Shamgar son of Anath,
    and in the days of Jael,
  people avoided the main roads,
    and travelers stayed on winding
        pathways.

⁷ There were few people left in the
        villages of Israel*—
    until Deborah arose as a mother
        for Israel.

⁸ When Israel chose new gods,
    war erupted at the city gates.
  Yet not a shield or spear could be seen
    among forty thousand warriors in
        Israel!

⁹ My heart is with the commanders
        of Israel,
    with those who volunteered
        for war.
  Praise the LORD!

¹⁰ "Consider this, you who ride on fine
        donkeys,
    you who sit on fancy saddle
        blankets,
  and you who walk along the road.

¹¹ Listen to the village musicians*
    gathered at the watering holes.
  They recount the righteous victories
        of the LORD
    and the victories of his villagers
        in Israel.
  Then the people of the LORD
    marched down to the city gates.

¹² "Wake up, Deborah, wake up!
    Wake up, wake up, and sing a song!
  Arise, Barak!
    Lead your captives away, son of
        Abinoam!

¹³ "Down from Tabor marched the few
        against the nobles.
    The people of the LORD marched
        down against mighty warriors.

¹⁴ They came down from Ephraim—
    a land that once belonged to the
        Amalekites;
  they followed you, Benjamin, with
        your troops.
  From Makir the commanders
        marched down;
    from Zebulun came those who
        carry a commander's staff.

¹⁵ The princes of Issachar were with
        Deborah and Barak.
    They followed Barak, rushing into
        the valley.
  But in the tribe of Reuben
    there was great indecision.

¹⁶ Why did you sit at home among the
        sheepfolds—
    to hear the shepherds whistle for
        their flocks?
  Yes, in the tribe of Reuben
    there was great indecision.

¹⁷ Gilead remained east of the Jordan.
    And why did Dan stay home?
  Asher sat unmoved at the seashore,
    remaining in his harbors.

¹⁸ But Zebulun risked his life,
    as did Naphtali, on the heights
        of the battlefield.

¹⁹ "The kings of Canaan came and
        fought,
    at Taanach near Megiddo's springs,
  but they carried off no silver
        treasures.

²⁰ The stars fought from heaven.
    The stars in their orbits fought
        against Sisera.

²¹ The Kishon River swept them away—
    that ancient torrent, the Kishon.
  March on with courage, my soul!

²² Then the horses' hooves hammered
        the ground,
    the galloping, galloping of Sisera's
        mighty steeds.

²³ 'Let the people of Meroz be cursed,'
      said the angel of the LORD.
   'Let them be utterly cursed,
   because they did not come to help
      the LORD—
         to help the LORD against the mighty
            warriors.'

²⁴ "Most blessed among women is Jael,
      the wife of Heber the Kenite.
   May she be blessed above all
      women who live in tents.
²⁵ Sisera asked for water,
      and she gave him milk.
   In a bowl fit for nobles,
      she brought him yogurt.
²⁶ Then with her left hand she reached
      for a tent peg,
   and with her right hand for the
      workman's hammer.
   She struck Sisera with the hammer,
      crushing his head.
   With a shattering blow, she pierced
      his temples.
²⁷ He sank, he fell,
      he lay still at her feet.
   And where he sank,
      there he died.

²⁸ "From the window Sisera's mother
      looked out.
   Through the window she watched
      for his return, saying,
   'Why is his chariot so long in coming?
      Why don't we hear the sound of
         chariot wheels?'

²⁹ "Her wise women answer,
      and she repeats these words to
         herself:
³⁰ 'They must be dividing the captured
      plunder—
   with a woman or two for every man.
   There will be colorful robes for Sisera,
      and colorful, embroidered robes
         for me.
   Yes, the plunder will include
      colorful robes embroidered on both
         sides.'

³¹ "LORD, may all your enemies die like
      Sisera!
   But may those who love you rise like
      the sun in all its power!"

Then there was peace in the land for forty years.

4:11 Or *father-in-law.*   5:7 The meaning of the Hebrew is uncertain.   5:11 The meaning of the Hebrew is uncertain.

LUKE 22:35-53

Knowing his suffering was about to begin, Jesus warned Peter of his impending failure, gave the disciples instructions for the battle that would be theirs for the remainder of their lives, and agonized in prayer in the Garden of Gethsemane.

Then Jesus asked them, "When I sent you out to preach the Good News and you did not have money, a traveler's bag, or extra clothing, did you need anything?"

"No," they replied.

³⁶"But now," he said, "take your money and a traveler's bag. And if you don't have a sword, sell your cloak and buy one! ³⁷For the time has come for this prophecy about me to be fulfilled: 'He was counted among the rebels.'* Yes, everything written about me by the prophets will come true."

³⁸"Look, Lord," they replied, "we have two swords among us."

"That's enough," he said.

³⁹Then, accompanied by the disciples, Jesus left the upstairs room and went as usual to the Mount of Olives. ⁴⁰There he told them, "Pray that you will not give in to temptation."

⁴¹He walked away, about a stone's throw, and knelt down and prayed, ⁴²"Father, if you are willing, please take this cup of suffering away from me. Yet I want your will to be done, not mine." ⁴³Then an angel from heaven appeared and strengthened him. ⁴⁴He prayed more fervently, and he was in such agony of spirit that his sweat fell to the ground like great drops of blood.*

⁴⁵At last he stood up again and returned to the disciples, only to find them asleep, exhausted from grief. ⁴⁶"Why are you sleeping?" he asked them. "Get up and pray, so that you will not give in to temptation."

⁴⁷But even as Jesus said this, a crowd approached, led by Judas, one of the twelve disciples. Judas walked over to Jesus to greet him with a kiss. ⁴⁸But Jesus said, "Judas, would you betray the Son of Man with a kiss?"

⁴⁹When the other disciples saw what was about to happen, they exclaimed, "Lord, should we fight? We brought the swords!" ⁵⁰And one of them struck at the high priest's slave, slashing off his right ear.

⁵¹But Jesus said, "No more of this." And he touched the man's ear and healed him.

⁵²Then Jesus spoke to the leading priests, the captains of the Temple guard, and the elders who had come for him. "Am I some dangerous revolutionary," he asked, "that you come with swords and clubs to arrest me? ⁵³Why didn't you arrest me in the Temple? I was there every day. But this is your moment, the time when the power of darkness reigns."

22:37 Isa 53:12. 22:43-44 Verses 43 and 44 are not included in many ancient manuscripts.

PSALM 94:1-23

O LORD, the God of vengeance,
  O God of vengeance, let your
    glorious justice shine forth!
² Arise, O judge of the earth.
  Give the proud what they deserve.
³ How long, O LORD?
  How long will the wicked be
    allowed to gloat?
⁴ How long will they speak with
    arrogance?
  How long will these evil people
    boast?

⁵ They crush your people, LORD,
    hurting those you claim as your
    own.
⁶ They kill widows and foreigners
    and murder orphans.
⁷ "The LORD isn't looking," they say,
    "and besides, the God of Israel*
    doesn't care."

⁸ Think again, you fools!
    When will you finally catch on?
⁹ Is he deaf—the one who made your
    ears?
  Is he blind—the one who formed
    your eyes?
¹⁰ He punishes the nations—won't he
    also punish you?
  He knows everything—doesn't he
    also know what you are doing?
¹¹ The LORD knows people's thoughts;
    he knows they are worthless!

¹² Joyful are those you discipline, LORD,
    those you teach with your
    instructions.
¹³ You give them relief from troubled
    times
    until a pit is dug to capture the
    wicked.
¹⁴ The LORD will not reject his
    people;
    he will not abandon his special
    possession.

WHO GOD IS

Jesus suffered for us

LUKE 22:44 In a mystery that we will never fully understand, Jesus, the eternal Son of God, became fully human without losing any of his divinity. He had to be fully human *and* fully divine in order to pay the penalty for our sins (Hebrews 2:14, October 31). • As a human being, Jesus went through pain beyond our imagining when he willingly went to the cross on our behalf. Even before his arrest, his pain was intense: "He was in such agony of spirit that his sweat fell to the ground like great drops of blood" (Luke 22:44). His trial and death would fulfill what the prophet had written, "He was pierced for our rebellion, crushed for our sins. He was beaten so we could be whole. He was whipped so we could be healed. . . . The LORD laid on him the sins of us all" (Isaiah 53:5-6, September 27). Without his death, there would be no salvation for any of us. • Jesus' suffering also makes him able to understand the pain you will experience in life. When you cry out to God, when you yearn for relief, you can be assured that Jesus doesn't just hear you, he understands.

¹⁵ Judgment will again be founded
    on justice,
    and those with virtuous hearts
    will pursue it.

¹⁶ Who will protect me from the wicked?
    Who will stand up for me against
    evildoers?
¹⁷ Unless the LORD had helped me,
    I would soon have settled in the
    silence of the grave.
¹⁸ I cried out, "I am slipping!"
    but your unfailing love, O LORD,
    supported me.
¹⁹ When doubts filled my mind,
    your comfort gave me renewed
    hope and cheer.

²⁰ Can unjust leaders claim that God
    is on their side—
    leaders whose decrees permit
    injustice?

²¹ They gang up against the
    righteous
    and condemn the innocent
    to death.
²² But the LORD is my fortress;
    my God is the mighty rock where
    I hide.
²³ God will turn the sins of evil people
    back on them.
    He will destroy them for their sins.
    The LORD our God will destroy
    them.

94:7 Hebrew *of Jacob.* See note on 44:4.

PROVERBS 14:3-4

A fool's proud talk becomes a rod that
beats him, but the words of the wise keep
them safe. □ Without oxen a stable stays
clean, but you need a strong ox for a large
harvest.

APRIL**26**

JUDGES 6:1-40

Gideon was a hesitant champion. He needed
a lot of reassurance. His story reminds us that
God sometimes uses the unlikely and even the
unwilling.

The Israelites did evil in the LORD's sight.
So the LORD handed them over to the
Midianites for seven years. ²The Midianites were so cruel that the Israelites made
hiding places for themselves in the mountains, caves, and strongholds. ³Whenever
the Israelites planted their crops, ma-
rauders from Midian, Amalek, and the
people of the east would attack Israel,
⁴camping in the land and destroying
crops as far away as Gaza. They left the Israelites with nothing to eat, taking all the
sheep, goats, cattle, and donkeys. ⁵These
enemy hordes, coming with their livestock and tents, were as thick as locusts;
they arrived on droves of camels too numerous to count. And they stayed until
the land was stripped bare. ⁶So Israel was
reduced to starvation by the Midianites.

Then the Israelites cried out to the LORD
for help.

⁷When they cried out to the LORD because of Midian, ⁸the LORD sent a prophet
to the Israelites. He said, "This is what the
LORD, the God of Israel, says: I brought you
up out of slavery in Egypt. ⁹I rescued you
from the Egyptians and from all who oppressed you. I drove out your enemies
and gave you their land. ¹⁰I told you, 'I am
the LORD your God. You must not worship
the gods of the Amorites, in whose land
you now live.' But you have not listened
to me."

¹¹Then the angel of the LORD came and
sat beneath the great tree at Ophrah,
which belonged to Joash of the clan of
Abiezer. Gideon son of Joash was threshing wheat at the bottom of a winepress to
hide the grain from the Midianites. ¹²The
angel of the LORD appeared to him and
said, "Mighty hero, the LORD is with you!"
¹³"Sir," Gideon replied, "if the LORD is
with us, why has all this happened to us?

And where are all the miracles our ancestors told us about? Didn't they say, 'The LORD brought us up out of Egypt'? But now the LORD has abandoned us and handed us over to the Midianites."

¹⁴Then the LORD turned to him and said, "Go with the strength you have, and rescue Israel from the Midianites. I am sending you!"

¹⁵"But Lord," Gideon replied, "how can I rescue Israel? My clan is the weakest in the whole tribe of Manasseh, and I am the least in my entire family!"

¹⁶The LORD said to him, "I will be with you. And you will destroy the Midianites as if you were fighting against one man."

¹⁷Gideon replied, "If you are truly going to help me, show me a sign to prove that it is really the LORD speaking to me. ¹⁸Don't go away until I come back and bring my offering to you."

He answered, "I will stay here until you return."

¹⁹Gideon hurried home. He cooked a young goat, and with a basket* of flour he baked some bread without yeast. Then, carrying the meat in a basket and the broth in a pot, he brought them out and presented them to the angel, who was under the great tree.

²⁰The angel of God said to him, "Place the meat and the unleavened bread on this rock, and pour the broth over it." And Gideon did as he was told. ²¹Then the angel of the LORD touched the meat and bread with the tip of the staff in his hand, and fire flamed up from the rock and consumed all he had brought. And the angel of the LORD disappeared.

²²When Gideon realized that it was the angel of the LORD, he cried out, "Oh, Sovereign LORD, I'm doomed! I have seen the angel of the LORD face to face!"

²³"It is all right," the LORD replied. "Do not be afraid. You will not die." ²⁴And Gideon built an altar to the LORD there and named it Yahweh-Shalom (which means "the LORD is peace"). The altar remains in Ophrah in the land of the clan of Abiezer to this day.

²⁵That night the LORD said to Gideon, "Take the second bull from your father's herd, the one that is seven years old. Pull down your father's altar to Baal, and cut down the Asherah pole standing beside it. ²⁶Then build an altar to the LORD your God here on this hilltop sanctuary, laying the stones carefully. Sacrifice the bull as a burnt offering on the altar, using as fuel the wood of the Asherah pole you cut down."

²⁷So Gideon took ten of his servants and did as the LORD had commanded. But he did it at night because he was afraid of the other members of his father's household and the people of the town.

²⁸Early the next morning, as the people of the town began to stir, someone discovered that the altar of Baal had been broken down and that the Asherah pole beside it had been cut down. In their place a new altar had been built, and on it were the remains of the bull that had been sacrificed. ²⁹The people said to each other, "Who did this?" And after asking around and making a careful search, they learned that it was Gideon, the son of Joash.

³⁰"Bring out your son," the men of the town demanded of Joash. "He must die for destroying the altar of Baal and for cutting down the Asherah pole."

³¹But Joash shouted to the mob that confronted him, "Why are you defending Baal? Will you argue his case? Whoever pleads his case will be put to death by morning! If Baal truly is a god, let him defend himself and destroy the one who broke down his altar!" ³²From then on Gideon was called Jerub-baal, which means "Let Baal defend himself," because he broke down Baal's altar.

³³Soon afterward the armies of Midian, Amalek, and the people of the east formed an alliance against Israel and crossed the Jordan, camping in the valley of Jezreel. ³⁴Then the Spirit of the LORD took possession of Gideon. He blew a ram's horn as a call to arms, and the men of the clan of Abiezer came to him. ³⁵He also sent messengers throughout Manasseh, Asher, Zebulun, and Naphtali, summoning their warriors, and all of them responded.

³⁶Then Gideon said to God, "If you are truly going to use me to rescue Israel as you promised, ³⁷prove it to me in this way. I will put a wool fleece on the threshing floor tonight. If the fleece is wet with dew

in the morning but the ground is dry, then I will know that you are going to help me rescue Israel as you promised." [38]And that is just what happened. When Gideon got up early the next morning, he squeezed the fleece and wrung out a whole bowlful of water.

[39]Then Gideon said to God, "Please don't be angry with me, but let me make one more request. Let me use the fleece for one more test. This time let the fleece remain dry while the ground around it is wet with dew." [40]So that night God did as Gideon asked. The fleece was dry in the morning, but the ground was covered with dew.

6:19 Hebrew *an ephah* [20 quarts or 22 liters].

LUKE 22:54–23:12

Jesus' followers deserted him; one denied him. Jesus' various trials were a mockery, and Jesus knew the outcome. But he also knew that this was part of the plan and why he had come.

So they arrested him and led him to the high priest's home. And Peter followed at a distance. [55]The guards lit a fire in the middle of the courtyard and sat around it, and Peter joined them there. [56]A servant girl noticed him in the firelight and began staring at him. Finally she said, "This man was one of Jesus' followers!"

[57]But Peter denied it. "Woman," he said, "I don't even know him!"

[58]After a while someone else looked at him and said, "You must be one of them!"

"No, man, I'm not!" Peter retorted.

[59]About an hour later someone else insisted, "This must be one of them, because he is a Galilean, too."

[60]But Peter said, "Man, I don't know what you are talking about." And immediately, while he was still speaking, the rooster crowed.

[61]At that moment the Lord turned and looked at Peter. Suddenly, the Lord's words flashed through Peter's mind: "Before the rooster crows tomorrow morning, you will deny three times that you even know me." [62]And Peter left the courtyard, weeping bitterly.

[63]The guards in charge of Jesus began mocking and beating him. [64]They blindfolded him and said, "Prophesy to us! Who hit you that time?" [65]And they hurled all sorts of terrible insults at him.

[66]At daybreak all the elders of the people assembled, including the leading priests and the teachers of religious law. Jesus was led before this high council,* [67]and they said, "Tell us, are you the Messiah?"

But he replied, "If I tell you, you won't believe me. [68]And if I ask you a question, you won't answer. [69]But from now on the Son of Man will be seated in the place of power at God's right hand.*"

[70]They all shouted, "So, are you claiming to be the Son of God?"

And he replied, "You say that I am."

[71]"Why do we need other witnesses?" they said. "We ourselves heard him say it."

23:1 THEN the entire council took Jesus to Pilate, the Roman governor. [2]They began to state their case: "This man has been leading our people astray by telling them not to pay their taxes to the Roman government and by claiming he is the Messiah, a king."

[3]So Pilate asked him, "Are you the king of the Jews?"

Jesus replied, "You have said it."

[4]Pilate turned to the leading priests and to the crowd and said, "I find nothing wrong with this man!"

[5]Then they became insistent. "But he is causing riots by his teaching wherever he goes—all over Judea, from Galilee to Jerusalem!"

[6]"Oh, is he a Galilean?" Pilate asked. [7]When they said that he was, Pilate sent him to Herod Antipas, because Galilee was under Herod's jurisdiction, and Herod happened to be in Jerusalem at the time.

[8]Herod was delighted at the opportunity to see Jesus, because he had heard about him and had been hoping for a long time to see him perform a miracle. [9]He asked Jesus question after question, but Jesus refused to answer. [10]Meanwhile, the leading priests and the teachers of religious law stood there shouting their accusations. [11]Then Herod and his soldiers began mocking and ridiculing Jesus. Finally, they put a royal robe on him and sent him back to Pilate. [12](Herod and Pi-

late, who had been enemies before, became friends that day.)

22:66 Greek *before their Sanhedrin.*   **22:69** See Ps 110:1.

PSALM 95:1–96:13

Come, let us sing to the LORD!
Let us shout joyfully to the Rock
of our salvation.
² Let us come to him with
thanksgiving.
Let us sing psalms of praise
to him.
³ For the LORD is a great God,
a great King above all gods.
⁴ He holds in his hands the depths
of the earth
and the mightiest mountains.
⁵ The sea belongs to him, for he
made it.
His hands formed the dry
land, too.

⁶ Come, let us worship and
bow down.
Let us kneel before the LORD
our maker,
⁷ for he is our God.
We are the people he watches over,
the flock under his care.

If only you would listen to his voice
today!
⁸ The LORD says, "Don't harden your
hearts as Israel did at Meribah,
as they did at Massah in the
wilderness.

⁹ For there your ancestors tested and
tried my patience,
even though they saw everything
I did.
¹⁰ For forty years I was angry with them,
and I said,
'They are a people whose hearts turn
away from me.
They refuse to do what I tell them.'
¹¹ So in my anger I took an oath:
'They will never enter my place
of rest.'"

⁹⁶:¹ SING a new song to the LORD!
Let the whole earth sing to the
LORD!
² Sing to the LORD; praise his name.
Each day proclaim the good news
that he saves.
³ Publish his glorious deeds among
the nations.
Tell everyone about the amazing
things he does.
⁴ Great is the LORD! He is most worthy
of praise!
He is to be feared above all gods.
⁵ The gods of other nations are mere
idols,
but the LORD made the heavens!
⁶ Honor and majesty surround him;
strength and beauty fill his sanctuary.

⁷ O nations of the world, recognize
the LORD;
recognize that the LORD is glorious
and strong.

HOW WE LIVE

Seeking God's will

JUDGES 6:36-40 Gideon's motive was good (to obey God and defeat the enemy), but his method was less than commendable. God had already communicated his will to him, yet he sought multiple confirmations. Deep down he just didn't believe, yet God mercifully granted Gideon's requests because Gideon had a job to do. • When you truly believe God has a plan for your life, God will make clear the path you are to take. Once the direction is obvious, you should not fearfully sit back and ask for more and more confirmation; you should take action! Waiting for more signs to confirm what you already know is a waste of your time and God's—and it shows doubt, fear, and laziness. Study God's Word, pray, and consult with wise Christians—these will serve as the best references for learning God's will in the decisions you must make.

8 Give to the LORD the glory he deserves!
Bring your offering and come into
his courts.
9 Worship the LORD in all his holy
splendor.
Let all the earth tremble before
him.
10 Tell all the nations, "The LORD reigns!"
The world stands firm and cannot
be shaken.
He will judge all peoples fairly.

11 Let the heavens be glad, and the earth
rejoice!
Let the sea and everything in it
shout his praise!

12 Let the fields and their crops burst out
with joy!
Let the trees of the forest rustle
with praise
13 before the LORD, for he is coming!
He is coming to judge the earth.
He will judge the world with justice,
and the nations with his truth.

PROVERBS 14:5-6

An honest witness does not lie; a false witness breathes lies. □ A mocker seeks wisdom and never finds it, but knowledge comes easily to those with understanding.

APRIL**27**

JUDGES 7:1–8:17

Gideon commanded his army in some unexpected ways: Winning with fewer men, deriving hope and strength from a dream about a runaway loaf of bread, a surprise attack where men seemed to appear out of nowhere. Success came because God was the real commander.

So Jerub-baal (that is, Gideon) and his army got up early and went as far as the spring of Harod. The armies of Midian were camped north of them in the valley near the hill of Moreh. 2 The LORD said to Gideon, "You have too many warriors with you. If I let all of you fight the Midianites, the Israelites will boast to me that they saved themselves by their own strength. 3 Therefore, tell the people, 'Whoever is timid or afraid may leave this mountain* and go home.'" So 22,000 of them went home, leaving only 10,000 who were willing to fight.

4 But the LORD told Gideon, "There are still too many! Bring them down to the spring, and I will test them to determine who will go with you and who will not." 5 When Gideon took his warriors down to the water, the LORD told him, "Divide the men into two groups. In one group put all those who cup water in their hands and lap it up with their tongues like dogs. In the other group put all those who kneel down and drink with their mouths in the stream." 6 Only 300 of the men drank from their hands. All the others got down on their knees and drank with their mouths in the stream.

7 The LORD told Gideon, "With these 300 men I will rescue you and give you victory over the Midianites. Send all the others home." 8 So Gideon collected the provisions and rams' horns of the other warriors and sent them home. But he kept the 300 men with him.

The Midianite camp was in the valley just below Gideon. 9 That night the LORD said, "Get up! Go down into the Midianite camp, for I have given you victory over them! 10 But if you are afraid to attack, go down to the camp with your servant Purah. 11 Listen to what the Midianites are saying, and you will be greatly encouraged. Then you will be eager to attack."

So Gideon took Purah and went down to the edge of the enemy camp. 12 The armies of Midian, Amalek, and the people of the east had settled in the valley like a swarm of locusts. Their camels were like grains of sand on the seashore—too many to count! 13 Gideon crept up just as a man was telling his companion about a dream.

The man said, "I had this dream, and in my dream a loaf of barley bread came tumbling down into the Midianite camp. It hit a tent, turned it over, and knocked it flat!"

¹⁴His companion answered, "Your dream can mean only one thing—God has given Gideon son of Joash, the Israelite, victory over Midian and all its allies!"

¹⁵When Gideon heard the dream and its interpretation, he bowed in worship before the LORD.* Then he returned to the Israelite camp and shouted, "Get up! For the LORD has given you victory over the Midianite hordes!" ¹⁶He divided the 300 men into three groups and gave each man a ram's horn and a clay jar with a torch in it.

¹⁷Then he said to them, "Keep your eyes on me. When I come to the edge of the camp, do just as I do. ¹⁸As soon as I and those with me blow the rams' horns, blow your horns, too, all around the entire camp, and shout, 'For the LORD and for Gideon!'"

¹⁹It was just after midnight,* after the changing of the guard, when Gideon and the 100 men with him reached the edge of the Midianite camp. Suddenly, they blew the rams' horns and broke their clay jars. ²⁰Then all three groups blew their horns and broke their jars. They held the blazing torches in their left hands and the horns in their right hands, and they all shouted, "A sword for the LORD and for Gideon!"

²¹Each man stood at his position around the camp and watched as all the Midianites rushed around in a panic, shouting as they ran to escape. ²²When the 300 Israelites blew their rams' horns, the LORD caused the warriors in the camp to fight against each other with their swords. Those who were not killed fled to places as far away as Beth-shittah near Zererah and to the border of Abel-meholah near Tabbath.

²³Then Gideon sent for the warriors of Naphtali, Asher, and Manasseh, who joined in chasing the army of Midian. ²⁴Gideon also sent messengers throughout the hill country of Ephraim, saying, "Come down to attack the Midianites. Cut them off at the shallow crossings of the Jordan River at Beth-barah."

So all the men of Ephraim did as they were told. ²⁵They captured Oreb and Zeeb, the two Midianite commanders, killing Oreb at the rock of Oreb, and Zeeb at the winepress of Zeeb. And they continued to chase the Midianites. Afterward the Israelites brought the heads of Oreb and Zeeb to Gideon, who was by the Jordan River.

8:1THEN the people of Ephraim asked Gideon, "Why have you treated us this way? Why didn't you send for us when you first went out to fight the Midianites?" And they argued heatedly with Gideon.

²But Gideon replied, "What have I accomplished compared to you? Aren't even the leftover grapes of Ephraim's harvest better than the entire crop of my little clan of Abiezer? ³God gave you victory over Oreb and Zeeb, the commanders of the Midianite army. What have I accomplished compared to that?" When the men of Ephraim heard Gideon's answer, their anger subsided.

⁴Gideon then crossed the Jordan River with his 300 men, and though exhausted, they continued to chase the enemy. ⁵When they reached Succoth, Gideon asked the leaders of the town, "Please give my warriors some food. They are very tired. I am chasing Zebah and Zalmunna, the kings of Midian."

⁶But the officials of Succoth replied, "Catch Zebah and Zalmunna first, and then we will feed your army."

⁷So Gideon said, "After the LORD gives me victory over Zebah and Zalmunna, I will return and tear your flesh with the thorns and briers from the wilderness."

⁸From there Gideon went up to Peniel* and again asked for food, but he got the same answer. ⁹So he said to the people of Peniel, "After I return in victory, I will tear down this tower."

¹⁰By this time Zebah and Zalmunna were in Karkor with 15,000 warriors—all that remained of the allied armies of the east, for 120,000 had already been killed. ¹¹Gideon circled around by the caravan route east of Nobah and Jogbehah, taking the Midianite army by surprise. ¹²Zebah and Zalmunna, the two Midianite kings,

fled, but Gideon chased them down and captured all their warriors.

13After this, Gideon returned from the battle by way of Heres Pass. 14There he captured a young man from Succoth and demanded that he write down the names of all the seventy-seven officials and elders in the town. 15Gideon then returned to Succoth and said to the leaders, "Here are Zebah and Zalmunna. When we were here before, you taunted me, saying, 'Catch Zebah and Zalmunna first, and then we will feed your exhausted army.'" 16Then Gideon took the elders of the town and taught them a lesson, punishing them with thorns and briers from the wilderness. 17He also tore down the tower of Peniel and killed all the men in the town.

7:3 Hebrew *may leave Mount Gilead.* The identity of Mount Gilead is uncertain in this context. It is perhaps used here as another name for Mount Gilboa.   7:15 As in Greek version; Hebrew reads *he bowed.*   7:19 Hebrew *at the beginning of the second watch.*   8:8 Hebrew *Penuel,* a variant spelling of Peniel; also in 8:9, 17.

LUKE 23:13-43

The Old Testament describes the Messiah as an innocent lamb led to the slaughter. On this night, Jesus was led to the slaughter to save us from our sins.

Then Pilate called together the leading priests and other religious leaders, along with the people, 14and he announced his verdict. "You brought this man to me, accusing him of leading a revolt. I have examined him thoroughly on this point in your presence and find him innocent. 15Herod came to the same conclusion and sent him back to us. Nothing this man has done calls for the death penalty. 16So I will have him flogged, and then I will release him."*

18Then a mighty roar rose from the crowd, and with one voice they shouted, "Kill him, and release Barabbas to us!" 19(Barabbas was in prison for taking part in an insurrection in Jerusalem against the government, and for murder.) 20Pilate argued with them, because he wanted to release Jesus. 21But they kept shouting, "Crucify him! Crucify him!"

22For the third time he demanded, "Why? What crime has he committed? I have found no reason to sentence him to death. So I will have him flogged, and then I will release him."

23But the mob shouted louder and louder, demanding that Jesus be crucified, and their voices prevailed. 24So Pilate sentenced Jesus to die as they demanded. 25As they had requested, he released Barabbas, the man in prison for insurrection and murder. But he turned Jesus over to them to do as they wished.

26As they led Jesus away, a man named Simon, who was from Cyrene,* happened to be coming in from the countryside. The soldiers seized him and put the cross on him and made him carry it behind Jesus. 27A large crowd trailed behind, including many grief-stricken women. 28But Jesus turned and said to them, "Daughters of Jerusalem, don't weep for me, but weep for yourselves and for your children. 29For the days are coming when they will say, 'Fortunate indeed are the women who are childless, the wombs that have not borne a child and the breasts that have never nursed.' 30People will beg the mountains, 'Fall on us,' and plead with the hills, 'Bury us.'* 31For if these things are done when the tree is green, what will happen when it is dry?*"

32Two others, both criminals, were led out to be executed with him. 33When they came to a place called The Skull,* they nailed him to the cross. And the criminals were also crucified—one on his right and one on his left.

34Jesus said, "Father, forgive them, for they don't know what they are doing."* And the soldiers gambled for his clothes by throwing dice.*

35The crowd watched and the leaders scoffed. "He saved others," they said, "let him save himself if he is really God's Messiah, the Chosen One." 36The soldiers mocked him, too, by offering him a drink of sour wine. 37They called out to him, "If you are the King of the Jews, save yourself!" 38A sign was fastened to the cross above him with these words: "This is the King of the Jews."

39One of the criminals hanging beside him scoffed, "So you're the Messiah, are you? Prove it by saving yourself—and us, too, while you're at it!"

⁴⁰But the other criminal protested, "Don't you fear God even when you have been sentenced to die? ⁴¹We deserve to die for our crimes, but this man hasn't done anything wrong." ⁴²Then he said, "Jesus, remember me when you come into your Kingdom."

⁴³And Jesus replied, "I assure you, today you will be with me in paradise."

23:16 Some manuscripts add verse 17, *Now it was necessary for him to release one prisoner to them during the Passover celebration.* Compare Matt 27:15; Mark 15:6; John 18:39. 23:26 *Cyrene* was a city in northern Africa. 23:30 Hos 10:8. 23:31 Or *If these things are done to me, the living tree, what will happen to you, the dry tree?* 23:33 Sometimes rendered *Calvary,* which comes from the Latin word for "skull." 23:34a This sentence is not included in many ancient manuscripts. 23:34b Greek *by casting lots.* See Ps 22:18.

PSALM 97:1-98:9

The LORD is king!
  Let the earth rejoice!
  Let the farthest coastlands be glad.
² Dark clouds surround him.
  Righteousness and justice are
    the foundation of his throne.
³ Fire spreads ahead of him
  and burns up all his foes.
⁴ His lightning flashes out across
    the world.
  The earth sees and trembles.
⁵ The mountains melt like wax before
    the LORD,

before the Lord of all the earth.
⁶ The heavens proclaim his
    righteousness;
  every nation sees his glory.
⁷ Those who worship idols are
    disgraced—
  all who brag about their worthless
    gods—
  for every god must bow to him.
⁸ Jerusalem* has heard and rejoiced,
  and all the towns of Judah are
    glad
  because of your justice, O LORD!
⁹ For you, O LORD, are supreme over all
    the earth;
  you are exalted far above all gods.

¹⁰ You who love the LORD, hate evil!
  He protects the lives of his godly
    people
  and rescues them from the power
    of the wicked.
¹¹ Light shines on the godly,
  and joy on those whose hearts are
    right.
¹² May all who are godly rejoice in
    the LORD
  and praise his holy name!

⁹⁸:¹ SING a new song to the LORD,
  for he has done wonderful
    deeds.

WHAT THE BIBLE SAYS

Salvation and forgiveness

LUKE 23:32-43 Even on the verge of death, Jesus asked God to forgive those who were responsible for killing him. He also promised a dying thief a place in paradise. From Jesus' example of forgiveness we learn some important things: (1) *Jesus recognized the brokenness that causes sin.* Jesus said that his assailants didn't really understand their actions. He knew their wickedness revealed brokenness and spiritual blindness. He didn't turn a blind eye to their sin, but he did keep their humanity in clear sight. (2) *Jesus forgave freely.* The thief on the cross had nothing to give in exchange for the gift of paradise. (3) *Jesus left judgment to God.* It wasn't that Jesus was unaware of the wrongs being done. He could see people jeering at his suffering. Jesus' role at that point was to sacrifice himself. He left the judgment up to God. • You have been saved from eternal death because God chose to save you. You have been forgiven for your sins because God chose to forgive you. Jesus then calls you to live a life of forgiveness by passing on that gift by forgiving as freely as you have been forgiven.

His right hand has won a mighty
victory;
his holy arm has shown his saving
power!
2 The LORD has announced his victory
and has revealed his righteousness
to every nation!
3 He has remembered his promise to
love and be faithful to Israel.
The ends of the earth have seen the
victory of our God.

4 Shout to the LORD, all the earth;
break out in praise and sing
for joy!
5 Sing your praise to the LORD with
the harp,
with the harp and melodious song,
6 with trumpets and the sound of
the ram's horn.
Make a joyful symphony before
the LORD, the King!

7 Let the sea and everything in it shout
his praise!
Let the earth and all living things
join in.
8 Let the rivers clap their hands in
glee!
Let the hills sing out their songs
of joy
9 before the LORD.
For the LORD is coming to judge
the earth.
He will judge the world with justice,
and the nations with fairness.

97:8 Hebrew *Zion*.

PROVERBS 14:7-8

Stay away from fools, for you won't find
knowledge on their lips. □ The prudent
understand where they are going, but
fools deceive themselves.

APRIL **28**

JUDGES 8:18–9:21

Gideon had certainly made some mistakes, but
he brought peace to Israel for about forty years.
As soon as he was gone, however, trouble was
on the horizon.

Then Gideon asked Zebah and Zalmunna,
"The men you killed at Tabor—what were
they like?"

"Like you," they replied. "They all had
the look of a king's son."

19"They were my brothers, the sons of
my own mother!" Gideon exclaimed. "As
surely as the LORD lives, I wouldn't kill
you if you hadn't killed them."

20Turning to Jether, his oldest son, he
said, "Kill them!" But Jether did not draw
his sword, for he was only a boy and was
afraid.

21Then Zebah and Zalmunna said to
Gideon, "Be a man! Kill us yourself!" So
Gideon killed them both and took the
royal ornaments from the necks of their
camels.

22Then the Israelites said to Gideon,
"Be our ruler! You and your son and your
grandson will be our rulers, for you have
rescued us from Midian."

23But Gideon replied, "I will not rule
over you, nor will my son. The LORD will
rule over you! 24However, I do have one
request—that each of you give me an earring from the plunder you collected from
your fallen enemies." (The enemies, being
Ishmaelites, all wore gold earrings.)

25"Gladly!" they replied. They spread
out a cloak, and each one threw in a gold
earring he had gathered from the plunder. 26The weight of the gold earrings
was forty-three pounds,* not including
the royal ornaments and pendants, the
purple clothing worn by the kings of
Midian, or the chains around the necks
of their camels.

27Gideon made a sacred ephod from
the gold and put it in Ophrah, his hometown. But soon all the Israelites prosti-

tuted themselves by worshiping it, and it became a trap for Gideon and his family.

²⁸That is the story of how the people of Israel defeated Midian, which never recovered. Throughout the rest of Gideon's lifetime—about forty years—there was peace in the land.

²⁹Then Gideon* son of Joash returned home. ³⁰He had seventy sons born to him, for he had many wives. ³¹He also had a concubine in Shechem, who gave birth to a son, whom he named Abimelech. ³²Gideon died when he was very old, and he was buried in the grave of his father, Joash, at Ophrah in the land of the clan of Abiezer.

³³As soon as Gideon died, the Israelites prostituted themselves by worshiping the images of Baal, making Baal-berith their god. ³⁴They forgot the LORD their God, who had rescued them from all their enemies surrounding them. ³⁵Nor did they show any loyalty to the family of Jerubbaal (that is, Gideon), despite all the good he had done for Israel.

⁹:¹ONE day Gideon's* son Abimelech went to Shechem to visit his uncles—his mother's brothers. He said to them and to the rest of his mother's family, ²"Ask the leading citizens of Shechem whether they want to be ruled by all seventy of Gideon's sons or by one man. And remember that I am your own flesh and blood!"

³So Abimelech's uncles gave his message to all the citizens of Shechem on his behalf. And after listening to this proposal, the people of Shechem decided in favor of Abimelech because he was their relative. ⁴They gave him seventy silver coins from the temple of Baal-berith, which he used to hire some reckless troublemakers who agreed to follow him. ⁵He went to his father's home at Ophrah, and there, on one stone, they killed all seventy of his half brothers, the sons of Gideon.* But the youngest brother, Jotham, escaped and hid.

⁶Then all the leading citizens of Shechem and Beth-millo called a meeting under the oak beside the pillar* at Shechem and made Abimelech their king.

⁷When Jotham heard about this, he climbed to the top of Mount Gerizim and shouted,

"Listen to me, citizens of Shechem!
    Listen to me if you want God to
        listen to you!
⁸ Once upon a time the trees decided
        to elect a king.
    First they said to the olive tree,
        'Be our king!'
⁹ But the olive tree refused, saying,
    'Should I quit producing the olive
        oil
        that blesses both God and people,

just to wave back and forth over
the trees?'

¹⁰ "Then they said to the fig tree,
'You be our king!'
¹¹ But the fig tree also refused, saying,
'Should I quit producing my sweet
fruit
just to wave back and forth over
the trees?'
¹² "Then they said to the grapevine,
'You be our king!'
¹³ But the grapevine also refused, saying,
'Should I quit producing the wine
that cheers both God and people,
just to wave back and forth over
the trees?'
¹⁴ "Then all the trees finally turned
to the thornbush and said,
'Come, you be our king!'
¹⁵ And the thornbush replied to the
trees,
'If you truly want to make me your
king,
come and take shelter in my shade.
If not, let fire come out from me
and devour the cedars of Lebanon.'"

¹⁶Jotham continued, "Now make sure
you have acted honorably and in good
faith by making Abimelech your king, and
that you have done right by Gideon and all
of his descendants. Have you treated him
with the honor he deserves for all he accomplished? ¹⁷For he fought for you and
risked his life when he rescued you from
the Midianites. ¹⁸But today you have revolted against my father and his descendants, killing his seventy sons on one
stone. And you have chosen his slave
woman's son, Abimelech, to be your king
just because he is your relative.

¹⁹"If you have acted honorably and in
good faith toward Gideon and his descendants today, then may you find joy in
Abimelech, and may he find joy in you.
²⁰But if you have not acted in good faith,
then may fire come out from Abimelech
and devour the leading citizens of Shechem and Beth-millo; and may fire come
out from the citizens of Shechem and
Beth-millo and devour Abimelech!"

²¹Then Jotham escaped and lived in

Beer because he was afraid of his brother
Abimelech.

8:26 Hebrew *1,700 shekels* [19.4 kilograms].   **8:29** Hebrew
Jerub-baal; see 6:32.   **9:1** Hebrew *Jerub-baal's* (see 6:32);
also in 9:2, 24.   **9:5** Hebrew *Jerub-baal* (see 6:32); also
in 9:16, 19, 28, 57.   **9:6** The meaning of the Hebrew is
uncertain.

LUKE 23:44–24:12
The heart of Christ's work can be found in his sacrifice—his suffering and death—and the power of his
resurrection. It was through this very sacrifice that
salvation was brought to sinners. Only by death
could there be life.

By this time it was noon, and darkness fell
across the whole land until three o'clock.
⁴⁵The light from the sun was gone. And
suddenly, the curtain in the sanctuary of
the Temple was torn down the middle.
⁴⁶Then Jesus shouted, "Father, I entrust
my spirit into your hands!"* And with
those words he breathed his last.

⁴⁷When the Roman officer* oversee-
ing the execution saw what had happened, he worshiped God and said,
"Surely this man was innocent.*" ⁴⁸And
when all the crowd that came to see the
crucifixion saw what had happened, they
went home in deep sorrow.* ⁴⁹But Jesus'
friends, including the women who had
followed him from Galilee, stood at a distance watching.

⁵⁰Now there was a good and righteous
man named Joseph. He was a member of
the Jewish high council, ⁵¹but he had not
agreed with the decision and actions of
the other religious leaders. He was from
the town of Arimathea in Judea, and he
was waiting for the Kingdom of God to
come. ⁵²He went to Pilate and asked for
Jesus' body. ⁵³Then he took the body
down from the cross and wrapped it in a
long sheet of linen cloth and laid it in a
new tomb that had been carved out of
rock. ⁵⁴This was done late on Friday
afternoon, the day of preparation,* as the
Sabbath was about to begin.

⁵⁵As his body was taken away, the wom-
en from Galilee followed and saw the
tomb where his body was placed. ⁵⁶Then
they went home and prepared spices and
ointments to anoint his body. But by the
time they were finished the Sabbath had

begun, so they rested as required by the law.

24:1BUT very early on Sunday morning* the women went to the tomb, taking the spices they had prepared. 2They found that the stone had been rolled away from the entrance. 3So they went in, but they didn't find the body of the Lord Jesus. 4As they stood there puzzled, two men suddenly appeared to them, clothed in dazzling robes.

5The women were terrified and bowed with their faces to the ground. Then the men asked, "Why are you looking among the dead for someone who is alive? 6He isn't here! He is risen from the dead! Remember what he told you back in Galilee, 7that the Son of Man* must be betrayed into the hands of sinful men and be crucified, and that he would rise again on the third day."

8Then they remembered that he had said this. 9So they rushed back from the tomb to tell his eleven disciples—and everyone else—what had happened. 10It was Mary Magdalene, Joanna, Mary the mother of James, and several other women who told the apostles what had happened. 11But the story sounded like nonsense to the men, so they didn't believe it. 12However, Peter jumped up and ran to the tomb to look. Stooping, he peered in and saw the empty linen wrappings; then he went home again, wondering what had happened.

23:46 Ps 31:5.   23:47a Greek *the centurion.*   23:47b Or *righteous.*   23:48 Greek *went home beating their breasts.* 23:54 Greek *It was the day of preparation.*   24:1 Greek *But on the first day of the week, very early in the morning.* 24:7 "Son of Man" is a title Jesus used for himself.

PSALM 99:1-9

The LORD is king!
  Let the nations tremble!
He sits on his throne between the
    cherubim.
  Let the whole earth quake!
2 The LORD sits in majesty in
    Jerusalem,*
  exalted above all the nations.
3 Let them praise your great and
    awesome name.
  Your name is holy!
4 Mighty King, lover of justice,
  you have established fairness.
You have acted with justice
  and righteousness throughout
    Israel.*
5 Exalt the LORD our God!
  Bow low before his feet, for he
    is holy!

6 Moses and Aaron were among his
    priests;
  Samuel also called on his name.
They cried to the LORD for help,
  and he answered them.
7 He spoke to Israel from the pillar
    of cloud,
  and they followed the laws and
    decrees he gave them.
8 O LORD our God, you answered
    them.
  You were a forgiving God to them,
  but you punished them when they
    went wrong.

9 Exalt the LORD our God,
  and worship at his holy mountain
    in Jerusalem,
  for the LORD our God is holy!

99:2 Hebrew *Zion.*   99:4 Hebrew *Jacob.* See note on 44:4.

PROVERBS 14:9-10

Fools make fun of guilt, but the godly acknowledge it and seek reconciliation. □Each heart knows its own bitterness, and no one else can fully share its joy.

APRIL**29**

JUDGES 9:22–10:18

Abimelech desired power but didn't know how to use it wisely. He seized power after his father, Gideon, died and became a ruthless leader.

After Abimelech had ruled over Israel for three years, 23God sent a spirit that stirred up trouble between Abimelech and the leading citizens of Shechem, and they revolted. [24]God was punishing Abimelech for murdering Gideon's seventy sons, and the citizens of Shechem for supporting him in this treachery of murdering his brothers. [25]The citizens of Shechem set an ambush for Abimelech on the hilltops and robbed everyone who passed that way. But someone warned Abimelech about their plot.

[26]One day Gaal son of Ebed moved to Shechem with his brothers and gained the confidence of the leading citizens of Shechem. [27]During the annual harvest festival at Shechem, held in the temple of the local god, the wine flowed freely, and everyone began cursing Abimelech. [28]"Who is Abimelech?" Gaal shouted. "He's not a true son of Shechem,* so why should we be his servants? He's merely the son of Gideon, and this Zebul is merely his deputy. Serve the true sons of Hamor, the founder of Shechem. Why should we serve Abimelech? [29]If I were in charge here, I would get rid of Abimelech. I would say* to him, 'Get some soldiers, and come out and fight!'"

[30]But when Zebul, the leader of the city, heard what Gaal was saying, he was furious. [31]He sent messengers to Abimelech in Arumah,* telling him, "Gaal son of Ebed and his brothers have come to live in Shechem, and now they are inciting the city to rebel against you. [32]Come by night with an army and hide out in the fields. [33]In the morning, as soon as it is daylight, attack the city. When Gaal and those who are with him come out against you, you can do with them as you wish."

[34]So Abimelech and all his men went by night and split into four groups, stationing themselves around Shechem. [35]Gaal was standing at the city gates when Abimelech and his army came out of hiding. [36]When Gaal saw them, he said to Zebul, "Look, there are people coming down from the hilltops!"

Zebul replied, "It's just the shadows on the hills that look like men."

[37]But again Gaal said, "No, people are coming down from the hills.* And another group is coming down the road past the Diviners' Oak.*"

[38]Then Zebul turned on him and asked,

"Now where is that big mouth of yours? Wasn't it you that said, 'Who is Abimelech, and why should we be his servants?' The men you mocked are right outside the city! Go out and fight them!"

[39]So Gaal led the leading citizens of Shechem into battle against Abimelech. [40]But Abimelech chased him, and many of Shechem's men were wounded and fell along the road as they retreated to the city gate. [41]Abimelech returned to Arumah, and Zebul drove Gaal and his brothers out of Shechem.

[42]The next day the people of Shechem went out into the fields to battle. When Abimelech heard about it, [43]he divided his men into three groups and set an ambush in the fields. When Abimelech saw the people coming out of the city, he and his men jumped up from their hiding places and attacked them. [44]Abimelech and his group stormed the city gate to keep the men of Shechem from getting back in, while Abimelech's other two groups cut them down in the fields. [45]The battle went on all day before Abimelech finally captured the city. He killed the people, leveled the city, and scattered salt all over the ground.

[46]When the leading citizens who lived in the tower of Shechem heard what had happened, they ran and hid in the temple of Baal-berith.* [47]Someone reported to Abimelech that the citizens had gathered in the temple, [48]so he led his forces to Mount Zalmon. He took an ax and chopped some branches from a tree, then put them on his shoulder. "Quick, do as I have done!" he told his men. [49]So each of them cut down some branches, following Abimelech's example. They piled the branches against the walls of the temple and set them on fire. So all the people who had lived in the tower of Shechem died—about 1,000 men and women.

[50]Then Abimelech attacked the town of Thebez and captured it. [51]But there was a strong tower inside the town, and all the men and women—the entire population—fled to it. They barricaded themselves in and climbed up to the roof of the tower. [52]Abimelech followed them to attack the tower. But as he prepared to set fire to the entrance, [53]a woman on the

roof dropped a millstone that landed on Abimelech's head and crushed his skull.

⁵⁴He quickly said to his young armor bearer, "Draw your sword and kill me! Don't let it be said that a woman killed Abimelech!" So the young man ran him through with his sword, and he died. ⁵⁵When Abimelech's men saw that he was dead, they disbanded and returned to their homes.

⁵⁶In this way, God punished Abimelech for the evil he had done against his father by murdering his seventy brothers. ⁵⁷God also punished the men of Shechem for all their evil. So the curse of Jotham son of Gideon was fulfilled.

10:1AFTER Abimelech died, Tola son of Puah, son of Dodo, was the next person to rescue Israel. He was from the tribe of Issachar but lived in the town of Shamir in the hill country of Ephraim. ²He judged Israel for twenty-three years. When he died, he was buried in Shamir.

³After Tola died, Jair from Gilead judged Israel for twenty-two years. ⁴His thirty sons rode around on thirty donkeys, and they owned thirty towns in the land of Gilead, which are still called the Towns of Jair.* ⁵When Jair died, he was buried in Kamon.

⁶Again the Israelites did evil in the LORD's sight. They served the images of Baal and Ashtoreth, and the gods of Aram, Sidon, Moab, Ammon, and Philistia. They abandoned the LORD and no longer served him at all. ⁷So the LORD burned with anger against Israel, and he turned them over to the Philistines and the Ammonites, ⁸who began to oppress them that year. For eighteen years they oppressed all the Israelites east of the Jordan River in the land of the Amorites (that is, in Gilead). ⁹The Ammonites also crossed to the west side of the Jordan and attacked Judah, Benjamin, and Ephraim.

The Israelites were in great distress. ¹⁰Finally, they cried out to the LORD for help, saying, "We have sinned against you because we have abandoned you as our God and have served the images of Baal."

¹¹The LORD replied, "Did I not rescue you from the Egyptians, the Amorites, the Ammonites, the Philistines, ¹²the Sidonians, the Amalekites, and the Maonites? When they oppressed you, you cried out to me for help, and I rescued you. ¹³Yet you have abandoned me and served other gods. So I will not rescue you anymore. ¹⁴Go and cry out to the gods you have chosen! Let them rescue you in your hour of distress!"

¹⁵But the Israelites pleaded with the LORD and said, "We have sinned. Punish us as you see fit, only rescue us today from our enemies." ¹⁶Then the Israelites put

HOW WE LIVE | Studying God's Word

LUKE 24 Even though the men Jesus encountered on the road to Emmaus had been with Jesus before his death, they hadn't grasped the fact that his death had been prophesied by the Old Testament and by Jesus himself. So Jesus connected the dots for them. He started from the writings of Moses and then walked them through all of the prophets, "explaining from all the Scriptures the things concerning himself" (24:27). Now that would have been quite a Bible study! Jesus opened their minds to the meaning of all of the prophecies regarding him. And finally, Jesus opened their eyes, and they got it! • God's Word needs to be understood and applied to life. You won't understand everything you read, but the more you read, the more you'll learn and the more you'll understand. From beginning to end, the Bible is about Jesus. It tells what happened to humanity, why we needed a Savior, and what God did about it. It tells of God's great love for us. It assures us of eternity. Ask God to help you "get it" when you read his Word.

aside their foreign gods and served the LORD. And he was grieved by their misery.

[17]At that time the armies of Ammon had gathered for war and were camped in Gilead, and the people of Israel assembled and camped at Mizpah. [18]The leaders of Gilead said to each other, "Whoever attacks the Ammonites first will become ruler over all the people of Gilead."

9:28 Hebrew *Who is Shechem?*   **9:29** As in Greek version; Hebrew reads *And he said.*   **9:31** Or *in secret;* Hebrew reads *in Tormah;* compare 9:41.   **9:37a** Or *the center of the land.*   **9:37b** Hebrew *Elon-meonenim.*   **9:46** Hebrew *El-berith,* another name for Baal-berith; compare 9:4.   **10:4** Hebrew *Havvoth-jair.*

LUKE 24:13-53

After his resurrection, Jesus continued to reveal to his disciples the truth of who he was. He opened their eyes to understand how the Old Testament had pointed to his life, death, and resurrection.

That same day two of Jesus' followers were walking to the village of Emmaus, seven miles* from Jerusalem. [14]As they walked along they were talking about everything that had happened. [15]As they talked and discussed these things, Jesus himself suddenly came and began walking with them. [16]But God kept them from recognizing him.

[17]He asked them, "What are you discussing so intently as you walk along?"

They stopped short, sadness written across their faces. [18]Then one of them, Cleopas, replied, "You must be the only person in Jerusalem who hasn't heard about all the things that have happened there the last few days."

[19]"What things?" Jesus asked.

"The things that happened to Jesus, the man from Nazareth," they said. "He was a prophet who did powerful miracles, and he was a mighty teacher in the eyes of God and all the people. [20]But our leading priests and other religious leaders handed him over to be condemned to death, and they crucified him. [21]We had hoped he was the Messiah who had come to rescue Israel. This all happened three days ago. [22]"Then some women from our group of his followers were at his tomb early this morning, and they came back with an amazing report. [23]They said his body was missing, and they had seen angels who told them Jesus is alive! [24]Some of our men ran out to see, and sure enough, his body was gone, just as the women had said."

[25]Then Jesus said to them, "You foolish people! You find it so hard to believe all that the prophets wrote in the Scriptures. [26]Wasn't it clearly predicted that the Messiah would have to suffer all these things before entering his glory?" [27]Then Jesus took them through the writings of Moses and all the prophets, explaining from all the Scriptures the things concerning himself.

[28]By this time they were nearing Emmaus and the end of their journey. Jesus acted as if he were going on, [29]but they begged him, "Stay the night with us, since it is getting late." So he went home with them. [30]As they sat down to eat,* he took the bread and blessed it. Then he broke it and gave it to them. [31]Suddenly, their eyes were opened, and they recognized him. And at that moment he disappeared!

[32]They said to each other, "Didn't our hearts burn within us as he talked with us on the road and explained the Scriptures to us?" [33]And within the hour they were on their way back to Jerusalem. There they found the eleven disciples and the others who had gathered with them, [34]who said, "The Lord has really risen! He appeared to Peter.*"

[35]Then the two from Emmaus told their story of how Jesus had appeared to them as they were walking along the road, and how they had recognized him as he was breaking the bread. [36]And just as they were telling about it, Jesus himself was suddenly standing there among them. "Peace be with you," he said. [37]But the whole group was startled and frightened, thinking they were seeing a ghost!

[38]"Why are you frightened?" he asked. "Why are your hearts filled with doubt? [39]Look at my hands. Look at my feet. You can see that it's really me. Touch me and make sure that I am not a ghost, because ghosts don't have bodies, as you see that I do." [40]As he spoke, he showed them his hands and his feet.

[41]Still they stood there in disbelief, filled with joy and wonder. Then he asked

them, "Do you have anything here to eat?" [42] They gave him a piece of broiled fish, [43] and he ate it as they watched.

[44] Then he said, "When I was with you before, I told you that everything written about me in the law of Moses and the prophets and in the Psalms must be fulfilled." [45] Then he opened their minds to understand the Scriptures. [46] And he said, "Yes, it was written long ago that the Messiah would suffer and die and rise from the dead on the third day. [47] It was also written that this message would be proclaimed in the authority of his name to all the nations,* beginning in Jerusalem: 'There is forgiveness of sins for all who repent.' [48] You are witnesses of all these things.

[49] "And now I will send the Holy Spirit, just as my Father promised. But stay here in the city until the Holy Spirit comes and fills you with power from heaven."

[50] Then Jesus led them to Bethany, and lifting his hands to heaven, he blessed them. [51] While he was blessing them, he left them and was taken up to heaven.* [52] So they worshiped him and then returned to Jerusalem filled with great joy. [53] And they spent all of their time in the Temple, praising God.

24:13 Greek *60 stadia* [11.1 kilometers]. 24:30 Or *As they reclined.* 24:34 Greek *Simon.* 24:47 Or *all peoples.* 24:51 Some manuscripts do not include *and was taken up to heaven.*

PSALM 100:1-5
A psalm of thanksgiving.

[1] **S**hout with joy to the LORD, all
　　the earth!
[2] 　Worship the LORD with gladness.
　　Come before him, singing with joy.
[3] Acknowledge that the LORD is God!
　　He made us, and we are his.
　　We are his people, the sheep of
　　　his pasture.
[4] Enter his gates with thanksgiving;
　　go into his courts with praise.
　　Give thanks to him and praise
　　　his name.
[5] For the LORD is good.
　　His unfailing love continues
　　　forever,
　　and his faithfulness continues
　　　to each generation.

PROVERBS 14:11-12

The house of the wicked will be destroyed, but the tent of the godly will flourish. □ There is a path before each person that seems right, but it ends in death.

APRIL**30**

JUDGES 11:1–12:15

In spite of his heritage and rejection, God used Jephthah. Even unjust circumstances can be turned around for good if a person is available to God. Unfortunately, Jephthah is most well known for making a rash promise that caused much pain to his own family.

Now Jephthah of Gilead was a great warrior. He was the son of Gilead, but his mother was a prostitute. [2] Gilead's wife also had several sons, and when these half brothers grew up, they chased Jephthah off the land. "You will not get any of our father's inheritance," they said, "for you are the son of a prostitute." [3] So Jephthah

fled from his brothers and lived in the land of Tob. Soon he had a band of worthless rebels following him.

[4] At about this time, the Ammonites began their war against Israel. [5] When the Ammonites attacked, the elders of Gilead sent for Jephthah in the land of Tob. The elders said, [6] "Come and be our commander! Help us fight the Ammonites!"

[7] But Jephthah said to them, "Aren't you the ones who hated me and drove me from my father's house? Why do you come to me now when you're in trouble?"

[8] "Because we need you," the elders replied. "If you lead us in battle against the

Ammonites, we will make you ruler over all the people of Gilead."

⁹Jephthah said to the elders, "Let me get this straight. If I come with you and if the LORD gives you victory over the Ammonites, will you really make me ruler over all the people?"

¹⁰"The LORD is our witness," the elders replied. "We promise to do whatever you say."

¹¹So Jephthah went with the elders of Gilead, and the people made him their ruler and commander of the army. At Mizpah, in the presence of the LORD, Jephthah repeated what he had said to the elders.

¹²Then Jephthah sent messengers to the king of Ammon, asking, "Why have you come out to fight against my land?"

¹³The king of Ammon answered Jephthah's messengers, "When the Israelites came out of Egypt, they stole my land from the Arnon River to the Jabbok River and all the way to the Jordan. Now then, give back the land peaceably."

¹⁴Jephthah sent this message back to the Ammonite king:

¹⁵"This is what Jephthah says: Israel did not steal any land from Moab or Ammon. ¹⁶When the people of Israel arrived at Kadesh on their journey from Egypt after crossing the Red Sea,* ¹⁷they sent messengers to the king of Edom asking for permission to pass through his land. But their request was denied. Then they asked the king of Moab for similar permission, but he wouldn't let them pass through either. So the people of Israel stayed in Kadesh.

¹⁸"Finally, they went around Edom and Moab through the wilderness. They traveled along Moab's eastern border and camped on the other side of the Arnon River. But they never once crossed the Arnon River into Moab, for the Arnon was the border of Moab.

¹⁹"Then Israel sent messengers to King Sihon of the Amorites, who ruled from Heshbon, asking for permission to cross through his land to get to their destination. ²⁰But King Sihon didn't trust Israel to pass through his land. Instead, he mobilized his army at Jahaz and attacked them. ²¹But the LORD, the God of Israel, gave his people victory over King Sihon. So Israel took control of all the land of the Amorites, who lived in that region, ²²from the Arnon River to the Jabbok River, and from the eastern wilderness to the Jordan.

²³"So you see, it was the LORD, the God of Israel, who took away the land from the Amorites and gave it to Israel. Why, then, should we give it back to you? ²⁴You keep whatever your god Chemosh gives you, and we will keep whatever the LORD our God gives us. ²⁵Are you any better than Balak son of Zippor, king of Moab? Did he try to make a case against Israel for disputed land? Did he go to war against them?

²⁶"Israel has been living here for 300 years, inhabiting Heshbon and its surrounding settlements, all the way to Aroer and its settlements, and in all the towns along the Arnon River. Why have you made no effort to recover it before now? ²⁷Therefore, I have not sinned against you. Rather, you have wronged me by attacking me. Let the LORD, who is judge, decide today which of us is right—Israel or Ammon."

²⁸But the king of Ammon paid no attention to Jephthah's message.

²⁹At that time the Spirit of the LORD came upon Jephthah, and he went throughout the land of Gilead and Manasseh, including Mizpah in Gilead, and from there he led an army against the Ammonites. ³⁰And Jephthah made a vow to the LORD. He said, "If you give me victory over the Ammonites, ³¹I will give to the LORD whatever comes out of my house to meet me when I return in triumph. I will sacrifice it as a burnt offering."

³²So Jephthah led his army against the Ammonites, and the LORD gave him victory. ³³He crushed the Ammonites, devastating about twenty towns from Aroer to an area near Minnith and as far away as Abel-keramim. In this way Israel defeated the Ammonites.

³⁴When Jephthah returned home to Mizpah, his daughter came out to meet him, playing on a tambourine and dancing for joy. She was his one and only child; he had no other sons or daughters. ³⁵When he saw her, he tore his clothes in anguish. "Oh, my daughter!" he cried out. "You have completely destroyed me! You've brought disaster on me! For I have made a vow to the LORD, and I cannot take it back."

³⁶And she said, "Father, if you have made a vow to the LORD, you must do to me what you have vowed, for the LORD has given you a great victory over your enemies, the Ammonites. ³⁷But first let me do this one thing: Let me go up and roam in the hills and weep with my friends for two months, because I will die a virgin."

³⁸"You may go," Jephthah said. And he sent her away for two months. She and her friends went into the hills and wept because she would never have children. ³⁹When she returned home, her father kept the vow he had made, and she died a virgin.

So it has become a custom in Israel ⁴⁰for young Israelite women to go away for four days each year to lament the fate of Jephthah's daughter.

¹²:¹THEN the people of Ephraim mobilized an army and crossed over the Jordan River to Zaphon. They sent this message to Jephthah: "Why didn't you call for us to help you fight against the Ammonites? We are going to burn down your house with you in it!"

²Jephthah replied, "I summoned you at the beginning of the dispute, but you refused to come! You failed to help us in our struggle against Ammon. ³So when I realized you weren't coming, I risked my life and went to battle without you, and the LORD gave me victory over the Ammonites. So why have you now come to fight me?"

⁴The people of Ephraim responded, "You men of Gilead are nothing more than fugitives from Ephraim and Manasseh." So Jephthah gathered all the men of Gilead and attacked the men of Ephraim and defeated them.

⁵Jephthah captured the shallow crossings of the Jordan River, and whenever a fugitive from Ephraim tried to go back across, the men of Gilead would challenge him. "Are you a member of the tribe of Ephraim?" they would ask. If the man said, "No, I'm not," ⁶they would tell him to say "Shibboleth." If he was from Ephraim, he would say "Sibboleth," because people from Ephraim cannot pronounce the word correctly. Then they would take him and kill him at the shallow crossings of

WHO GOD IS — Jesus is the Son of God

JOHN 1 The Gospel of John opens by reminding us that Jesus is eternal. He existed from before time began, before he became human and made his home among us. Jesus is eternal because he is God. This fact relates to one of Christianity's key doctrines—the doctrine of the Trinity. • The term *Trinity* is not found in the Bible; however, the idea is there. The Bible speaks of God being eternally existent as the Father, the Son, and the Holy Spirit. Not three gods, but one God eternally existent in three distinct persons. Not one God who can switch back and forth from different modes, but one God ever present as three distinct persons. Admittedly, this is a great mystery, but it is central to our faith. • John wrote in one of his letters, "We know that the Son of God has come, and he has given us understanding so that we can know the true God. And now we live in fellowship with the true God because we live in fellowship with his Son, Jesus Christ" (1 John 5:20, December 5). The Son became human not only in order to die for our sins but also so that we might know God better.

the Jordan. In all, 42,000 Ephraimites were killed at that time.

⁷Jephthah judged Israel for six years. When he died, he was buried in one of the towns of Gilead.

⁸After Jephthah died, Ibzan from Bethlehem judged Israel. ⁹He had thirty sons and thirty daughters. He sent his daughters to marry men outside his clan, and he brought in thirty young women from outside his clan to marry his sons. Ibzan judged Israel for seven years. ¹⁰When he died, he was buried at Bethlehem.

¹¹After Ibzan died, Elon from the tribe of Zebulun judged Israel for ten years. ¹²When he died, he was buried at Aijalon in Zebulun.

¹³After Elon died, Abdon son of Hillel, from Pirathon, judged Israel. ¹⁴He had forty sons and thirty grandsons, who rode on seventy donkeys. He judged Israel for eight years. ¹⁵When he died, he was buried at Pirathon in Ephraim, in the hill country of the Amalekites.

11:16 Hebrew *sea of reeds.*

JOHN 1:1-28
The Gospel of John opens with a beautiful description of Jesus' presence in the world.

In the beginning the Word already
        existed.
    The Word was with God,
        and the Word was God.
² He existed in the beginning with God.
³ God created everything through him,
        and nothing was created except
        through him.
⁴ The Word gave life to everything that
        was created,*
    and his life brought light to
        everyone.
⁵ The light shines in the darkness,
        and the darkness can never
        extinguish it.*

⁶God sent a man, John the Baptist,* ⁷to tell about the light so that everyone might believe because of his testimony. ⁸John himself was not the light; he was simply a witness to tell about the light. ⁹The one who is the true light, who gives light to everyone, was coming into the world.

¹⁰He came into the very world he created, but the world didn't recognize him.

¹¹He came to his own people, and even they rejected him. ¹²But to all who believed him and accepted him, he gave the right to become children of God. ¹³They are reborn—not with a physical birth resulting from human passion or plan, but a birth that comes from God.

¹⁴So the Word became human* and made his home among us. He was full of unfailing love and faithfulness.* And we have seen his glory, the glory of the Father's one and only Son.

¹⁵John testified about him when he shouted to the crowds, "This is the one I was talking about when I said, 'Someone is coming after me who is far greater than I am, for he existed long before me.'"

¹⁶From his abundance we have all received one gracious blessing after another.* ¹⁷For the law was given through Moses, but God's unfailing love and faithfulness came through Jesus Christ. ¹⁸No one has ever seen God. But the unique One, who is himself God,* is near to the Father's heart. He has revealed God to us.

¹⁹This was John's testimony when the Jewish leaders sent priests and Temple assistants* from Jerusalem to ask John, "Who are you?" ²⁰He came right out and said, "I am not the Messiah."

²¹"Well then, who are you?" they asked. "Are you Elijah?"

"No," he replied.

"Are you the Prophet we are expecting?"*

"No."

²²"Then who are you? We need an answer for those who sent us. What do you have to say about yourself?"

²³John replied in the words of the prophet Isaiah:

"I am a voice shouting in the
        wilderness,
    'Clear the way for the LORD's
        coming!'"*

²⁴Then the Pharisees who had been sent ²⁵asked him, "If you aren't the Messiah or Elijah or the Prophet, what right do you have to baptize?"

²⁶John told them, "I baptize with* water, but right here in the crowd is someone you do not recognize. ²⁷Though his ministry follows mine, I'm not even worthy

to be his slave and untie the straps of his sandal."

28This encounter took place in Bethany, an area east of the Jordan River, where John was baptizing.

1:3-4 Or *and nothing that was created was created except through him. The Word gave life to everything.*   1:5 Or *and the darkness has not understood it.*   1:6 Greek *a man named John.*   1:14a Greek *became flesh.*   1:14b Or *grace and truth;* also in 1:17.   1:16 Or *received the grace of Christ rather than the grace of the law;* Greek reads *received grace upon grace.*   1:18 Some manuscripts read *But the one and only Son.*   1:19 Greek *and Levites.*   1:21 Greek *Are you the Prophet?* See Deut 18:15, 18; Mal 4:5-6.   1:23 Isa 40:3.   1:26 Or *in;* also in 1:31, 33.

PSALM 101:1-8
A psalm of David.

1 I will sing of your love and justice,
        LORD.
    I will praise you with songs.
2 I will be careful to live a blameless
        life—
    when will you come to help me?
    I will lead a life of integrity
        in my own home.
3 I will refuse to look at
        anything vile and vulgar.
    I hate all who deal crookedly;

I will have nothing to do with
        them.
4 I will reject perverse ideas
    and stay away from every evil.
5 I will not tolerate people who
        slander their neighbors.
    I will not endure conceit and
        pride.

6 I will search for faithful people
        to be my companions.
    Only those who are above
        reproach
        will be allowed to serve me.
7 I will not allow deceivers to serve
        in my house,
    and liars will not stay in my
        presence.
8 My daily task will be to ferret out
        the wicked
    and free the city of the LORD from
        their grip.

PROVERBS 14:13-14
Laughter can conceal a heavy heart, but when the laughter ends, the grief remains. □ Backsliders get what they deserve; good people receive their reward.

to be his slave and untie the straps of his sandal."

This encounter took place in Bethany, an area east of the Jordan River, where John was baptizing.

PSALM 101:1-8
A psalm of David.

1 I will sing of your love and justice, LORD.
I will praise you with songs.
2 I will be careful to live a blameless life—
when will you come to help me?
I will lead a life of integrity
in my own home.
3 I will refuse to look at
anything vile and vulgar.
I hate all who deal crookedly;

I will have nothing to do with them.
4 I will reject perverse ideas
and stay away from every evil.
5 I will not tolerate people who
slander their neighbors.
I will not endure conceit and pride.
6 I will search for faithful people
to be my companions.
Only those who are above reproach
will be allowed to serve me.
7 I will not allow deceivers to serve in my house,
and liars will not stay in my presence.
8 My daily task will be to ferret out the wicked
and free the city of the LORD from their grip.

PROVERBS 14:13-14
Laughter can conceal a heavy heart, but when the laughter ends, the grief remains. 14 Backsliders get what they deserve; good people receive their reward.

JUDGES 13:1–14:20

Samson was a powerful deliverer of Israel. However, he was a bit of a loose cannon, and his antics got him into numerous unfortunate predicaments.

Again the Israelites did evil in the LORD's sight, so the LORD handed them over to the Philistines, who oppressed them for forty years.

²In those days a man named Manoah from the tribe of Dan lived in the town of Zorah. His wife was unable to become pregnant, and they had no children. ³The angel of the LORD appeared to Manoah's wife and said, "Even though you have been unable to have children, you will soon become pregnant and give birth to a son. ⁴So be careful; you must not drink wine or any other alcoholic drink nor eat any forbidden food.* ⁵You will become pregnant and give birth to a son, and his hair must never be cut. For he will be dedicated to God as a Nazirite from birth. He will begin to rescue Israel from the Philistines."

⁶The woman ran and told her husband, "A man of God appeared to me! He looked like one of God's angels, terrifying to see. I didn't ask where he was from, and he didn't tell me his name. ⁷But he told me, 'You will become pregnant and give birth to a son. You must not drink wine or any other alcoholic drink nor eat any forbidden food. For your son will be dedicated to God as a Nazirite from the moment of his birth until the day of his death.'"

⁸Then Manoah prayed to the LORD, saying, "Lord, please let the man of God come back to us again and give us more instructions about this son who is to be born."

⁹God answered Manoah's prayer, and the angel of God appeared once again to his wife as she was sitting in the field. But her husband, Manoah, was not with her. ¹⁰So she quickly ran and told her husband, "The man who appeared to me the other day is here again!"

¹¹Manoah ran back with his wife and asked, "Are you the man who spoke to my wife the other day?"

"Yes," he replied, "I am."

¹²So Manoah asked him, "When your words come true, what kind of rules should govern the boy's life and work?"

¹³The angel of the LORD replied, "Be sure your wife follows the instructions I gave her. ¹⁴She must not eat grapes or raisins, drink wine or any other alcoholic drink, or eat any forbidden food."

¹⁵Then Manoah said to the angel of the LORD, "Please stay here until we can prepare a young goat for you to eat."

¹⁶"I will stay," the angel of the LORD replied, "but I will not eat anything. However, you may prepare a burnt offering as a sacrifice to the LORD." (Manoah didn't realize it was the angel of the LORD.)

¹⁷Then Manoah asked the angel of the LORD, "What is your name? For when all this comes true, we want to honor you."

¹⁸"Why do you ask my name?" the angel of the LORD replied. "It is too wonderful for you to understand."

¹⁹Then Manoah took a young goat and a grain offering and offered it on a rock as a sacrifice to the LORD. And as Manoah and his wife watched, the LORD did an amazing thing. ²⁰As the flames from the altar shot up toward the sky, the angel of the LORD ascended in the fire. When Manoah and his wife saw this, they fell with their faces to the ground.

²¹The angel did not appear again to Manoah and his wife. Manoah finally realized it was the angel of the LORD, ²²and he said to his wife, "We will certainly die, for we have seen God!"

²³But his wife said, "If the LORD were going to kill us, he wouldn't have accepted our burnt offering and grain offering. He wouldn't have appeared to us and told us this wonderful thing and done these miracles."

²⁴When her son was born, she named him Samson. And the LORD blessed him as he grew up. ²⁵And the Spirit of the LORD began to stir him while he lived in Mahaneh-dan, which is located between the towns of Zorah and Eshtaol.

¹⁴:¹ONE day when Samson was in Timnah, one of the Philistine women caught his eye. ²When he returned home, he told his father and mother, "A young Philistine woman in Timnah caught my eye. I want to marry her. Get her for me."

³His father and mother objected. "Isn't there even one woman in our tribe or among all the Israelites you could marry?" they asked. "Why must you go to the pagan Philistines to find a wife?"

But Samson told his father, "Get her for me! She looks good to me." ⁴His father and mother didn't realize the LORD was at work in this, creating an opportunity to work against the Philistines, who ruled over Israel at that time.

⁵As Samson and his parents were going down to Timnah, a young lion suddenly attacked Samson near the vineyards of Timnah. ⁶At that moment the Spirit of the LORD came powerfully upon him, and he ripped the lion's jaws apart with his bare hands. He did it as easily as if it were a young goat. But he didn't tell his father or mother about it. ⁷When Samson arrived in Timnah, he talked with the woman and was very pleased with her.

⁸Later, when he returned to Timnah for the wedding, he turned off the path to look at the carcass of the lion. And he found that a swarm of bees had made some honey in the carcass. ⁹He scooped some of the honey into his hands and ate it along the way. He also gave some to his father and mother, and they ate it. But he didn't tell them he had taken the honey from the carcass of the lion.

¹⁰As his father was making final arrangements for the marriage, Samson threw a party at Timnah, as was the custom for elite young men. ¹¹When the bride's parents* saw him, they selected thirty young men from the town to be his companions.

¹²Samson said to them, "Let me tell you a riddle. If you solve my riddle during these seven days of the celebration, I will give you thirty fine linen robes and thirty sets of festive clothing. ¹³But if you can't solve it, then you must give me thirty fine linen robes and thirty sets of festive clothing."

"All right," they agreed, "let's hear your riddle."

¹⁴So he said:

"Out of the one who eats came
     something to eat;
  out of the strong came something
     sweet."

Three days later they were still trying to figure it out. ¹⁵On the fourth* day they said to Samson's wife, "Entice your husband to explain the riddle for us, or we will burn down your father's house with you in it. Did you invite us to this party just to make us poor?"

¹⁶So Samson's wife came to him in tears and said, "You don't love me; you hate me! You have given my people a riddle, but you haven't told me the answer."

"I haven't even given the answer to my father or mother," he replied. "Why should I tell you?" ¹⁷So she cried whenever she was with him and kept it up for the rest of the celebration. At last, on the seventh day he told her the answer because she was tormenting him with her nagging. Then she explained the riddle to the young men.

¹⁸So before sunset of the seventh day, the men of the town came to Samson with their answer:

"What is sweeter than honey?
  What is stronger than a lion?"

Samson replied, "If you hadn't plowed with my heifer, you wouldn't have solved my riddle!"

¹⁹Then the Spirit of the LORD came powerfully upon him. He went down to the town of Ashkelon, killed thirty men, took their belongings, and gave their clothing to the men who had solved his riddle. But Samson was furious about what had happened, and he went back home to live with his father and mother. ²⁰So his wife was given in marriage to the man who had been Samson's best man at the wedding.

13:4 Hebrew *any unclean thing;* also in 13:7, 14.
14:11 Hebrew *they.*   **14:15** As in Greek version; Hebrew reads *seventh.*

JOHN 1:29-51
John the Baptist, whose role was to herald the Messiah, did so by identifying Jesus as the Lamb of God—the sacrifice to save us from sin and death.

The next day John saw Jesus coming toward him and said, "Look! The Lamb of God who takes away the sin of the world! ³⁰He is the one I was talking about when I said, 'A man is coming after me who is far greater than I am, for he existed long before me.' ³¹I did not recognize him as the Messiah, but I have been baptizing with water so that he might be revealed to Israel."

³²Then John testified, "I saw the Holy Spirit descending like a dove from heaven and resting upon him. ³³I didn't know he was the one, but when God sent me to baptize with water, he told me, 'The one on whom you see the Spirit descend and rest is the one who will baptize with the Holy Spirit.' ³⁴I saw this happen to Jesus, so I testify that he is the Chosen One of God.*"

³⁵The following day John was again standing with two of his disciples. ³⁶As Jesus walked by, John looked at him and declared, "Look! There is the Lamb of God!" ³⁷When John's two disciples heard this, they followed Jesus.

³⁸Jesus looked around and saw them following. "What do you want?" he asked them.

They replied, "Rabbi" (which means "Teacher"), "where are you staying?"

³⁹"Come and see," he said. It was about four o'clock in the afternoon when they went with him to the place where he was staying, and they remained with him the rest of the day.

⁴⁰Andrew, Simon Peter's brother, was one of these men who heard what John said and then followed Jesus. ⁴¹Andrew went to find his brother, Simon, and told him, "We have found the Messiah" (which means "Christ"*).

⁴²Then Andrew brought Simon to meet Jesus. Looking intently at Simon, Jesus said, "Your name is Simon, son of John—but you will be called Cephas" (which means "Peter"*).

⁴³The next day Jesus decided to go to Galilee. He found Philip and said to him, "Come, follow me." ⁴⁴Philip was from Bethsaida, Andrew and Peter's hometown.

⁴⁵Philip went to look for Nathanael and told him, "We have found the very person Moses* and the prophets wrote about! His name is Jesus, the son of Joseph from Nazareth."

⁴⁶"Nazareth!" exclaimed Nathanael. "Can anything good come from Nazareth?"

HOW WE LIVE | Sharing our faith

JOHN 1:46 Andrew was so excited about finding the long-awaited Messiah that the first thing he did was to bring his brother Simon to meet Jesus. The result: Simon Peter followed Jesus too. Not long after that, Jesus called Philip to be his disciple. Philip then went and told Nathanael, who had some doubts. When Philip brought Nathanael to meet Jesus for himself, Nathanael was hooked! • The disciples didn't have all the answers. In fact, some of their original ideas about the Messiah were simply wrong. But when they encountered Jesus, something deep inside of them stirred. They not only believed in him, but they were eager to tell their friends and relatives about Jesus. • You don't need to have all the answers about Jesus before you follow him. You don't even need to know all the questions. In order to share your faith, all you need is a willingness to tell other people about what you've found. Then invite them to "come and see" for themselves.

"Come and see for yourself," Philip replied.

⁴⁷As they approached, Jesus said, "Now here is a genuine son of Israel—a man of complete integrity."

⁴⁸"How do you know about me?" Nathanael asked.

Jesus replied, "I could see you under the fig tree before Philip found you."

⁴⁹Then Nathanael exclaimed, "Rabbi, you are the Son of God—the King of Israel!"

⁵⁰Jesus asked him, "Do you believe this just because I told you I had seen you under the fig tree? You will see greater things than this." ⁵¹Then he said, "I tell you the truth, you will all see heaven open and the angels of God going up and down on the Son of Man, the one who is the stairway between heaven and earth.*"

1:34 Some manuscripts read *the Son of God*.   1:41 *Messiah* (a Hebrew term) and *Christ* (a Greek term) both mean "the anointed one."   1:42 The names *Cephas* (from Aramaic) and *Peter* (from Greek) both mean "rock."   1:45 Greek *Moses in the law*.   1:51 Greek *going up and down on the Son of Man;* see Gen 28:10-17. "Son of Man" is a title Jesus used for himself.

PSALM 102:1-28
A prayer of one overwhelmed with trouble, pouring out problems before the LORD.

¹ LORD, hear my prayer!
    Listen to my plea!
² Don't turn away from me
    in my time of distress.
  Bend down to listen,
    and answer me quickly when
        I call to you.
³ For my days disappear like smoke,
    and my bones burn like red-hot
        coals.
⁴ My heart is sick, withered like grass,
    and I have lost my appetite.
⁵ Because of my groaning,
    I am reduced to skin and bones.
⁶ I am like an owl in the desert,
    like a little owl in a far-off
        wilderness.
⁷ I lie awake,
    lonely as a solitary bird on
        the roof.
⁸ My enemies taunt me day after day.
    They mock and curse me.
⁹ I eat ashes for food.
    My tears run down into
        my drink

¹⁰ because of your anger and wrath.
    For you have picked me up and
        thrown me out.
¹¹ My life passes as swiftly as the evening
        shadows.
    I am withering away like grass.

¹² But you, O LORD, will sit on your
        throne forever.
    Your fame will endure to every
        generation.
¹³ You will arise and have mercy
        on Jerusalem*—
    and now is the time to pity her,
        now is the time you promised to help.
¹⁴ For your people love every stone
        in her walls
    and cherish even the dust in
        her streets.
¹⁵ Then the nations will tremble before
        the LORD.
    The kings of the earth will tremble
        before his glory.
¹⁶ For the LORD will rebuild Jerusalem.
    He will appear in his glory.
¹⁷ He will listen to the prayers of
        the destitute.
    He will not reject their pleas.

¹⁸ Let this be recorded for future
        generations,
    so that a people not yet born will
        praise the LORD.
¹⁹ Tell them the LORD looked down
        from his heavenly sanctuary.
    He looked down to earth from heaven
²⁰   to hear the groans of the prisoners,
        to release those condemned to die.
²¹ And so the LORD's fame will
        be celebrated in Zion,
    his praises in Jerusalem,
²² when multitudes gather together
    and kingdoms come to worship
        the LORD.

²³ He broke my strength in midlife,
    cutting short my days.
²⁴ But I cried to him, "O my God,
        who lives forever,
    don't take my life while I am
        so young!
²⁵ Long ago you laid the foundation
        of the earth
    and made the heavens with your
        hands.

²⁶ They will perish, but you remain
    forever;
  they will wear out like old
    clothing.
You will change them like
    a garment
    and discard them.
²⁷ But you are always the same;
    you will live forever.
²⁸ The children of your people
    will live in security.

Their children's children
    will thrive in your presence."

102:13 Hebrew *Zion*; also in 102:16.

PROVERBS 14:15-16

Only simpletons believe everything
they're told! The prudent carefully consider their steps. □ The wise are cautious*
and avoid danger; fools plunge ahead
with reckless confidence.

14:16 Hebrew *The wise fear.*

JUDGES 15:1–16:31

The Philistines were one of Israel's most troublesome neighbors. Samson, who had significant
victories against them, ultimately died in their
hands, but not without taking many Philistines
with him.

Later on, during the wheat harvest, Samson took a young goat as a present to his
wife. He said, "I'm going into my wife's
room to sleep with her," but her father
wouldn't let him in.

²"I truly thought you must hate her,"
her father explained, "so I gave her in
marriage to your best man. But look, her
younger sister is even more beautiful
than she is. Marry her instead."

³Samson said, "This time I cannot be
blamed for everything I am going to do to
you Philistines." ⁴Then he went out and
caught 300 foxes. He tied their tails together in pairs, and he fastened a torch to
each pair of tails. ⁵Then he lit the torches
and let the foxes run through the grain
fields of the Philistines. He burned all
their grain to the ground, including the
sheaves and the uncut grain. He also destroyed their vineyards and olive groves.

⁶"Who did this?" the Philistines demanded.

"Samson," was the reply, "because his
father-in-law from Timnah gave Samson's
wife to be married to his best man." So the
Philistines went and got the woman and
her father and burned them to death.

⁷"Because you did this," Samson vowed,
"I won't rest until I take my revenge on
you!" ⁸So he attacked the Philistines with
great fury and killed many of them. Then
he went to live in a cave in the rock of
Etam.

⁹The Philistines retaliated by setting
up camp in Judah and spreading out near
the town of Lehi. ¹⁰The men of Judah
asked the Philistines, "Why are you attacking us?"

The Philistines replied, "We've come to
capture Samson. We've come to pay him
back for what he did to us."

¹¹So 3,000 men of Judah went down to
get Samson at the cave in the rock of
Etam. They said to Samson, "Don't you realize the Philistines rule over us? What
are you doing to us?"

But Samson replied, "I only did to them
what they did to me."

¹²But the men of Judah told him, "We
have come to tie you up and hand you
over to the Philistines."

"All right," Samson said. "But promise
that you won't kill me yourselves."

¹³"We will only tie you up and hand you
over to the Philistines," they replied. "We
won't kill you." So they tied him up with
two new ropes and brought him up from
the rock.

¹⁴As Samson arrived at Lehi, the Philistines came shouting in triumph. But the
Spirit of the LORD came powerfully upon

Samson, and he snapped the ropes on his arms as if they were burnt strands of flax, and they fell from his wrists. ¹⁵Then he found the jawbone of a recently killed donkey. He picked it up and killed 1,000 Philistines with it. ¹⁶Then Samson said,

"With the jawbone of a donkey,
    I've piled them in heaps!
With the jawbone of a donkey,
    I've killed a thousand men!"

¹⁷When he finished his boasting, he threw away the jawbone; and the place was named Jawbone Hill.*

¹⁸Samson was now very thirsty, and he cried out to the LORD, "You have accomplished this great victory by the strength of your servant. Must I now die of thirst and fall into the hands of these pagans?" ¹⁹So God caused water to gush out of a hollow in the ground at Lehi, and Samson was revived as he drank. Then he named that place "The Spring of the One Who Cried Out,"* and it is still in Lehi to this day.

²⁰Samson judged Israel for twenty years during the period when the Philistines dominated the land.

¹⁶:¹ONE day Samson went to the Philistine town of Gaza and spent the night with a prostitute. ²Word soon spread* that Samson was there, so the men of Gaza gathered together and waited all night at the town gates. They kept quiet during the night, saying to themselves, "When the light of morning comes, we will kill him."

³But Samson stayed in bed only until midnight. Then he got up, took hold of the doors of the town gate, including the two posts, and lifted them up, bar and all. He put them on his shoulders and carried them all the way to the top of the hill across from Hebron.

⁴Some time later Samson fell in love with a woman named Delilah, who lived in the valley of Sorek. ⁵The rulers of the Philistines went to her and said, "Entice Samson to tell you what makes him so strong and how he can be overpowered and tied up securely. Then each of us will give you 1,100 pieces* of silver."

⁶So Delilah said to Samson, "Please tell me what makes you so strong and what it would take to tie you up securely."

⁷Samson replied, "If I were tied up with seven new bowstrings that have not yet been dried, I would become as weak as anyone else."

⁸So the Philistine rulers brought Delilah seven new bowstrings, and she tied Samson up with them. ⁹She had hidden some men in one of the inner rooms of her house, and she cried out, "Samson! The Philistines have come to capture you!" But Samson snapped the bowstrings as a piece of string snaps when it is burned by a fire. So the secret of his strength was not discovered.

¹⁰Afterward Delilah said to him, "You've been making fun of me and telling me lies! Now please tell me how you can be tied up securely."

¹¹Samson replied, "If I were tied up with brand-new ropes that had never been used, I would become as weak as anyone else."

¹²So Delilah took new ropes and tied him up with them. The men were hiding in the inner room as before, and again Delilah cried out, "Samson! The Philistines have come to capture you!" But again Samson snapped the ropes from his arms as if they were thread.

¹³Then Delilah said, "You've been making fun of me and telling me lies! Now tell me how you can be tied up securely."

Samson replied, "If you were to weave the seven braids of my hair into the fabric on your loom and tighten it with the loom shuttle, I would become as weak as anyone else."

So while he slept, Delilah wove the seven braids of his hair into the fabric. ¹⁴Then she tightened it with the loom shuttle.* Again she cried out, "Samson! The Philistines have come to capture you!" But Samson woke up, pulled back the loom shuttle, and yanked his hair away from the loom and the fabric.

¹⁵Then Delilah pouted, "How can you tell me, 'I love you,' when you don't share your secrets with me? You've made fun of me three times now, and you still haven't told me what makes you so strong!" ¹⁶She tormented him with her nagging day after day until he was sick to death of it.

¹⁷Finally, Samson shared his secret with her. "My hair has never been cut," he

confessed, "for I was dedicated to God as a Nazirite from birth. If my head were shaved, my strength would leave me, and I would become as weak as anyone else."

[18]Delilah realized he had finally told her the truth, so she sent for the Philistine rulers. "Come back one more time," she said, "for he has finally told me his secret." So the Philistine rulers returned with the money in their hands. [19]Delilah lulled Samson to sleep with his head in her lap, and then she called in a man to shave off the seven locks of his hair. In this way she began to bring him down,* and his strength left him.

[20]Then she cried out, "Samson! The Philistines have come to capture you!"

When he woke up, he thought, "I will do as before and shake myself free." But he didn't realize the LORD had left him.

[21]So the Philistines captured him and gouged out his eyes. They took him to Gaza, where he was bound with bronze chains and forced to grind grain in the prison.

[22]But before long, his hair began to grow back.

[23]The Philistine rulers held a great festival, offering sacrifices and praising their god, Dagon. They said, "Our god has given us victory over our enemy Samson!"

[24]When the people saw him, they praised their god, saying, "Our god has delivered our enemy to us! The one who killed so many of us is now in our power!"

[25]Half drunk by now, the people demanded, "Bring out Samson so he can amuse us!" So he was brought from the prison to amuse them, and they had him stand between the pillars supporting the roof.

[26]Samson said to the young servant who was leading him by the hand, "Place my hands against the pillars that hold up the temple. I want to rest against them." [27]Now the temple was completely filled with people. All the Philistine rulers were there, and there were about 3,000 men and women on the roof who were watching as Samson amused them.

[28]Then Samson prayed to the LORD, "Sovereign LORD, remember me again. O God, please strengthen me just one more time. With one blow let me pay back the Philistines for the loss of my two eyes." [29]Then Samson put his hands on the two center pillars that held up the temple. Pushing against them with both hands, [30]he prayed, "Let me die with the Philistines." And the temple crashed down on the Philistine rulers and all the people. So he killed more people when he died than he had during his entire lifetime.

[31]Later his brothers and other relatives went down to get his body. They took him

Our relationships

JUDGES 16:4 Samson's life shows us how being unwise in our relationships can lead to negative consequences. Samson seems to have just blundered through life, forging his way with his strength more than his wits. He fluctuated between conflict and compromise with Israel's ongoing enemy, the Philistines. His unwise association with Delilah eventually led to his downfall. • Samson's sad story causes us to wonder what was going on in his head and in his heart. Why wasn't he intentional about pleasing God in his relationships? Why was he so stubborn in constantly choosing to associate with people who hurt him? With all of his leadership potential, why wasn't he wiser in choosing the sort of relationships to have? Samson's life reminds us that we need to seek God's discernment and help in our relationships. • How can you do that? Choose your relationships wisely, and when you can't choose (you're stuck with your relatives!), be intentional in treating them in ways that please God.

back home and buried him between Zorah and Eshtaol, where his father, Manoah, was buried. Samson had judged Israel for twenty years.

15:17 Hebrew *Ramath-lehi*.   15:19 Hebrew *En-hakkore*.
16:2 As in Greek and Syriac versions and Latin Vulgate; Hebrew lacks *Word soon spread*.   16:5 Hebrew *1,100 shekels*, about 28 pounds or 12.5 kilograms in weight.
16:13-14 As in Greek version and Latin Vulgate; Hebrew lacks *I would become as weak as anyone else. / So while he slept, Delilah wove the seven braids of his hair into the fabric.* *¹⁴Then she tightened it with the loom shuttle.*   16:19 Or *she began to torment him.* Greek version reads *He began to grow weak.*

JOHN 2:1-25

Water to wine at a wedding to an angry outburst at the Temple—onlookers found Jesus' ministry to be unexpected, sometimes perplexing, and always astonishing.

The next day* there was a wedding celebration in the village of Cana in Galilee. Jesus' mother was there, ²and Jesus and his disciples were also invited to the celebration. ³The wine supply ran out during the festivities, so Jesus' mother told him, "They have no more wine."

⁴"Dear woman, that's not our problem," Jesus replied. "My time has not yet come."

⁵But his mother told the servants, "Do whatever he tells you."

⁶Standing nearby were six stone water jars, used for Jewish ceremonial washing. Each could hold twenty to thirty gallons.* ⁷Jesus told the servants, "Fill the jars with water." When the jars had been filled, ⁸he said, "Now dip some out, and take it to the master of ceremonies." So the servants followed his instructions.

⁹When the master of ceremonies tasted the water that was now wine, not knowing where it had come from (though, of course, the servants knew), he called the bridegroom over. ¹⁰"A host always serves the best wine first," he said. "Then, when everyone has had a lot to drink, he brings out the less expensive wine. But you have kept the best until now!"

¹¹This miraculous sign at Cana in Galilee was the first time Jesus revealed his glory. And his disciples believed in him.

¹²After the wedding he went to Capernaum for a few days with his mother, his brothers, and his disciples.

¹³It was nearly time for the Jewish Passover celebration, so Jesus went to Jerusa-lem. ¹⁴In the Temple area he saw merchants selling cattle, sheep, and doves for sacrifices; he also saw dealers at tables exchanging foreign money. ¹⁵Jesus made a whip from some ropes and chased them all out of the Temple. He drove out the sheep and cattle, scattered the money changers' coins over the floor, and turned over their tables. ¹⁶Then, going over to the people who sold doves, he told them, "Get these things out of here. Stop turning my Father's house into a marketplace!"

¹⁷Then his disciples remembered this prophecy from the Scriptures: "Passion for God's house will consume me."*

¹⁸But the Jewish leaders demanded, "What are you doing? If God gave you authority to do this, show us a miraculous sign to prove it."

¹⁹"All right," Jesus replied. "Destroy this temple, and in three days I will raise it up."

²⁰"What!" they exclaimed. "It has taken forty-six years to build this Temple, and you can rebuild it in three days?" ²¹But when Jesus said "this temple," he meant his own body. ²²After he was raised from the dead, his disciples remembered he had said this, and they believed both the Scriptures and what Jesus had said.

²³Because of the miraculous signs Jesus did in Jerusalem at the Passover celebration, many began to trust in him. ²⁴But Jesus didn't trust them, because he knew human nature. ²⁵No one needed to tell him what mankind is really like.

2:1 Greek *On the third day*; see 1:35, 43.   2:6 Greek *2 or 3 measures* [75 to 113 liters].   2:17 Or *"Concern for God's house will be my undoing."* Ps 69:9.

PSALM 103:1-22
A psalm of David.

¹ **L**et all that I am praise the LORD;
      with my whole heart, I will praise
      his holy name.
² Let all that I am praise the LORD;
      may I never forget the good things
      he does for me.
³ He forgives all my sins
      and heals all my diseases.
⁴ He redeems me from death
      and crowns me with love and
      tender mercies.
⁵ He fills my life with good things.
      My youth is renewed like the eagle's!

⁶ The LORD gives righteousness
    and justice to all who are treated
    unfairly.

⁷ He revealed his character to Moses
    and his deeds to the people of Israel.
⁸ The LORD is compassionate and
    merciful,
    slow to get angry and filled with
    unfailing love.
⁹ He will not constantly accuse us,
    nor remain angry forever.
¹⁰ He does not punish us for all our sins;
    he does not deal harshly with us,
    as we deserve.
¹¹ For his unfailing love toward those
    who fear him
    is as great as the height of the
    heavens above the earth.
¹² He has removed our sins as far from us
    as the east is from the west.
¹³ The LORD is like a father to his
    children,
    tender and compassionate to those
    who fear him.
¹⁴ For he knows how weak we are;
    he remembers we are only dust.
¹⁵ Our days on earth are like grass;
    like wildflowers, we bloom and die.
¹⁶ The wind blows, and we are gone—
    as though we had never been here.
¹⁷ But the love of the LORD remains
    forever
    with those who fear him.

His salvation extends to the children's
    children
¹⁸ of those who are faithful to his
    covenant,
    of those who obey his
    commandments!

¹⁹ The LORD has made the heavens
    his throne;
    from there he rules over
    everything.
²⁰ Praise the LORD, you angels,
    you mighty ones who carry out
    his plans,
    listening for each of his
    commands.
²¹ Yes, praise the LORD, you armies
    of angels
    who serve him and do his will!
²² Praise the LORD, everything he has
    created,
    everything in all his kingdom.

Let all that I am praise the LORD.

PROVERBS 14:17-19

Short-tempered people do foolish things,
and schemers are hated. □ Simpletons
are clothed with foolishness,* but the
prudent are crowned with knowledge.
□ Evil people will bow before good people; the wicked will bow at the gates of
the godly.

14:18 Or *inherit foolishness.*

JUDGES 17:1–18:31

From the earliest Israelite history, the people struggled with the one thing God asked of them—purity
of faith. The story of Micah shows what happens
when believers let themselves get confused about
what it means to worship God alone.

There was a man named Micah, who lived
in the hill country of Ephraim. ²One day
he said to his mother, "I heard you place a
curse on the person who stole 1,100
pieces* of silver from you. Well, I have the
money. I was the one who took it."

"The LORD bless you for admitting it,"
his mother replied. ³He returned the
money to her, and she said, "I now dedicate these silver coins to the LORD. In
honor of my son, I will have an image
carved and an idol cast."

⁴So when he returned the money to his
mother, she took 200 silver coins and gave
them to a silversmith, who made them
into an image and an idol. And these were
placed in Micah's house. ⁵Micah set up a
shrine for the idol, and he made a sacred

ephod and some household idols. Then he installed one of his sons as his personal priest.

⁶In those days Israel had no king; all the people did whatever seemed right in their own eyes.

⁷One day a young Levite, who had been living in Bethlehem in Judah, arrived in that area. ⁸He had left Bethlehem in search of another place to live, and as he traveled, he came to the hill country of Ephraim. He happened to stop at Micah's house as he was traveling through. ⁹"Where are you from?" Micah asked him.

He replied, "I am a Levite from Bethlehem in Judah, and I am looking for a place to live."

¹⁰"Stay here with me," Micah said, "and you can be a father and priest to me. I will give you ten pieces* of silver a year, plus a change of clothes and your food." ¹¹The Levite agreed to this, and the young man became like one of Micah's sons.

¹²So Micah installed the Levite as his personal priest, and he lived in Micah's house. ¹³"I know the LORD will bless me now," Micah said, "because I have a Levite serving as my priest."

18:1 Now in those days Israel had no king. And the tribe of Dan was trying to find a place where they could settle, for they had not yet moved into the land assigned to them when the land was divided among the tribes of Israel. ²So the men of Dan chose from their clans five capable warriors from the towns of Zorah and Eshtaol to scout out a land for them to settle in.

When these warriors arrived in the hill country of Ephraim, they came to Micah's house and spent the night there. ³While at Micah's house, they recognized the young Levite's accent, so they went over and asked him, "Who brought you here, and what are you doing in this place? Why are you here?" ⁴He told them about his agreement with Micah and that he had been hired as Micah's personal priest.

⁵Then they said, "Ask God whether or not our journey will be successful."

⁶"Go in peace," the priest replied. "For the LORD is watching over your journey."

⁷So the five men went on to the town of Laish, where they noticed the people living carefree lives, like the Sidonians; they were peaceful and secure.* The people were also wealthy because their land was very fertile. And they lived a great distance from Sidon and had no allies nearby.

⁸When the men returned to Zorah and Eshtaol, their relatives asked them, "What did you find?"

⁹The men replied, "Come on, let's attack them! We have seen the land, and it is very good. What are you waiting for? Don't hesitate to go and take possession of it. ¹⁰When you get there, you will find the people living carefree lives. God has given us a spacious and fertile land, lacking in nothing!"

¹¹So 600 men from the tribe of Dan, armed with weapons of war, set out from Zorah and Eshtaol. ¹²They camped at a place west of Kiriath-jearim in Judah, which is called Mahaneh-dan* to this day. ¹³Then they went on from there into the hill country of Ephraim and came to the house of Micah.

¹⁴The five men who had scouted out the land around Laish explained to the others, "These buildings contain a sacred ephod, as well as some household idols, a carved image, and a cast idol. What do you think you should do?" ¹⁵Then the five men turned off the road and went over to Micah's house, where the young Levite lived, and greeted him kindly. ¹⁶As the 600 armed warriors from the tribe of Dan stood at the entrance of the gate, ¹⁷the five scouts entered the shrine and removed the carved image, the sacred ephod, the household idols, and the cast idol. Meanwhile, the priest was standing at the gate with the 600 armed warriors.

¹⁸When the priest saw the men carrying all the sacred objects out of Micah's shrine, he said, "What are you doing?"

¹⁹"Be quiet and come with us," they said. "Be a father and priest to all of us. Isn't it better to be a priest for an entire tribe and clan of Israel than for the household of just one man?"

²⁰The young priest was quite happy to go with them, so he took along the sacred ephod, the household idols, and the carved image. ²¹They turned and started on their way again, placing their children, livestock, and possessions in front of them.

²²When the people from the tribe of Dan were quite a distance from Micah's house, the people who lived near Micah came chasing after them. ²³They were shouting as they caught up with them. The men of Dan turned around and said to Micah, "What's the matter? Why have you called these men together and chased after us like this?"

²⁴"What do you mean, 'What's the matter?'" Micah replied. "You've taken away all the gods I have made, and my priest, and I have nothing left!"

²⁵The men of Dan said, "Watch what you say! There are some short-tempered men around here who might get angry and kill you and your family." ²⁶So the men of Dan continued on their way. When Micah saw that there were too many of them for him to attack, he turned around and went home.

²⁷Then, with Micah's idols and his priest, the men of Dan came to the town of Laish, whose people were peaceful and secure. They attacked with swords and burned the town to the ground. ²⁸There was no one to rescue the people, for they lived a great distance from Sidon and had no allies nearby. This happened in the valley near Beth-rehob.

Then the people of the tribe of Dan rebuilt the town and lived there. ²⁹They renamed the town Dan after their ancestor, Israel's son, but it had originally been called Laish.

³⁰Then they set up the carved image, and they appointed Jonathan son of Gershom, son of Moses,* as their priest. This family continued as priests for the tribe of Dan until the Exile. ³¹So Micah's carved image was worshiped by the tribe of Dan as long as the Tabernacle of God remained at Shiloh.

17:2 Hebrew *1,100 shekels*, about 28 pounds or 12.5 kilograms in weight.   17:10 Hebrew *10 shekels*, about 4 ounces or 114 grams in weight.   18:7 The meaning of the Hebrew is uncertain.   18:12 *Mahaneh-dan* means "the camp of Dan."   18:30 As in an ancient Hebrew tradition, some Greek manuscripts, and Latin Vulgate; Masoretic Text reads *son of Manasseh.*

JOHN 3:1-21

Nicodemus, a Pharisee, came secretly one evening to ask Jesus some honest questions. In this frank conversation some of Christianity's most basic truths are recorded.

There was a man named Nicodemus, a Jewish religious leader who was a Pharisee. ²After dark one evening, he came to speak with Jesus. "Rabbi," he said, "we all know that God has sent you to teach us. Your miraculous signs are evidence that God is with you."

³Jesus replied, "I tell you the truth, unless you are born again,* you cannot see the Kingdom of God."

⁴"What do you mean?" exclaimed Nicodemus. "How can an old man go back into his mother's womb and be born again?"

WHO GOD IS

God is loving

JOHN 3:16 The entire message of Scripture comes into focus with this one verse. Here Jesus explained to Nicodemus the depth of God's love for the people he created—God so loved that he *gave*. What he gave is beyond our imagination: He gave his Son to die. Why would he do such a thing? So that "everyone who believes in him will not perish but have eternal life." • How painful it must have been for the all-powerful God to witness the brutal torture and murder of his child when, with a breath, he could have stopped it! Yet he knew that the death and subsequent resurrection of Jesus would clear a path to heaven for all who would believe in him. • Some try to question God's love by asking how a loving God could allow evil and suffering. No matter what God's purpose is in allowing these things, it is important to remember that God, in his love, promises that for those who believe in Jesus, all evil and suffering will one day be banished forever. This is how much God loves you.

⁵Jesus replied, "I assure you, no one can enter the Kingdom of God without being born of water and the Spirit.* ⁶Humans can reproduce only human life, but the Holy Spirit gives birth to spiritual life.* ⁷So don't be surprised when I say, 'You* must be born again.' ⁸The wind blows wherever it wants. Just as you can hear the wind but can't tell where it comes from or where it is going, so you can't explain how people are born of the Spirit."

⁹"How are these things possible?" Nicodemus asked.

¹⁰Jesus replied, "You are a respected Jewish teacher, and yet you don't understand these things? ¹¹I assure you, we tell you what we know and have seen, and yet you won't believe our testimony. ¹²But if you don't believe me when I tell you about earthly things, how can you possibly believe if I tell you about heavenly things? ¹³No one has ever gone to heaven and returned. But the Son of Man* has come down from heaven. ¹⁴And as Moses lifted up the bronze snake on a pole in the wilderness, so the Son of Man must be lifted up, ¹⁵so that everyone who believes in him will have eternal life.*

¹⁶"For God loved the world so much that he gave his one and only Son, so that everyone who believes in him will not perish but have eternal life. ¹⁷God sent his Son into the world not to judge the world, but to save the world through him.

¹⁸"There is no judgment against anyone who believes in him. But anyone who does not believe in him has already been judged for not believing in God's one and only Son. ¹⁹And the judgment is based on this fact: God's light came into the world, but people loved the darkness more than the light, for their actions were evil. ²⁰All who do evil hate the light and refuse to go near it for fear their sins will be exposed. ²¹But those who do what is right come to the light so others can see that they are doing what God wants.*"

3:3 Or *born from above;* also in 3:7. 3:5 Or *and spirit.* The Greek word for *Spirit* can also be translated *wind;* see 3:8. 3:6 Greek *what is born of the Spirit is spirit.* 3:7 The Greek word for *you* is plural; also in 3:12. 3:13 Some manuscripts add *who lives in heaven.* "Son of Man" is a title Jesus used for himself. 3:15 Or *everyone who believes will have eternal life in him.* 3:21 Or *can see God at work in what he is doing.*

PSALM 104:1-23

Let all that I am praise the LORD.

O LORD my God, how great you are!
　You are robed with honor and
　　majesty.
² 　You are dressed in a robe of light.
You stretch out the starry curtain
　of the heavens;
³ 　you lay out the rafters of your home
　in the rain clouds.
You make the clouds your chariot;
　you ride upon the wings of the wind.
⁴ The winds are your messengers;
　flames of fire are your servants.*

⁵ You placed the world on its
　foundation
　so it would never be moved.
⁶ You clothed the earth with floods
　of water,
　water that covered even the
　mountains.
⁷ At your command, the water fled;
　at the sound of your thunder,
　it hurried away.
⁸ Mountains rose and valleys sank
　to the levels you decreed.
⁹ Then you set a firm boundary
　for the seas,
　so they would never again cover
　the earth.

¹⁰ You make springs pour water into
　the ravines,
　so streams gush down from
　the mountains.
¹¹ They provide water for all the animals,
　and the wild donkeys quench their
　thirst.
¹² The birds nest beside the streams
　and sing among the branches
　of the trees.
¹³ You send rain on the mountains from
　your heavenly home,
　and you fill the earth with the fruit
　of your labor.
¹⁴ You cause grass to grow for the
　livestock
　and plants for people to use.
You allow them to produce food from
　the earth—
¹⁵ 　wine to make them glad,
　olive oil to soothe their skin,
　and bread to give them strength.

16 The trees of the LORD are well cared
for—
  the cedars of Lebanon that
  he planted.
17 There the birds make their nests,
  and the storks make their homes
  in the cypresses.
18 High in the mountains live the wild
goats,
  and the rocks form a refuge
  for the hyraxes.*
19 You made the moon to mark
the seasons,
  and the sun knows when to set.
20 You send the darkness, and it
becomes night,
  when all the forest animals prowl
  about.

21 Then the young lions roar for their
prey,
  stalking the food provided
  by God.
22 At dawn they slink back
  into their dens to rest.
23 Then people go off to their work,
  where they labor until evening.

104:4 Greek version reads *He sends his angels like the
winds, / his servants like flames of fire.* Compare Heb 1:7.
104:18 Or *coneys,* or *rock badgers.*

PROVERBS 14:20-21

The poor are despised even by their
neighbors, while the rich have many
"friends." □It is a sin to belittle one's
neighbor; blessed are those who help
the poor.

JUDGES 19:1-20:48

Prepare yourself. There is probably no more graphic
or violent account in all of Scripture than the one
you're about to read. It reveals much about the
horrible effects of sin on the culture of the day.

Now in those days Israel had no king.
There was a man from the tribe of Levi living in a remote area of the hill country of
Ephraim. One day he brought home a
woman from Bethlehem in Judah to be
his concubine. 2But she became angry
with him* and returned to her father's
home in Bethlehem.

After about four months, 3 her husband
set out for Bethlehem to speak personally
to her and persuade her to come back. He
took with him a servant and a pair of donkeys. When he arrived at* her father's
house, her father saw him and welcomed
him. 4Her father urged him to stay awhile,
so he stayed three days, eating, drinking,
and sleeping there.

5On the fourth day the man was up
early, ready to leave, but the woman's father said to his son-in-law, "Have something to eat before you go." 6So the two
men sat down together and had some-

MAY**4**

thing to eat and drink. Then the woman's
father said, "Please stay another night and
enjoy yourself." 7 The man got up to leave,
but his father-in-law kept urging him to
stay, so he finally gave in and stayed the
night.

8On the morning of the fifth day he was
up early again, ready to leave, and again
the woman's father said, "Have something
to eat; then you can leave later this afternoon." So they had another day of feasting. 9Later, as the man and his concubine
and servant were preparing to leave, his
father-in-law said, "Look, it's almost evening. Stay the night and enjoy yourself.
Tomorrow you can get up early and be on
your way."

10But this time the man was determined to leave. So he took his two saddled donkeys and his concubine and
headed in the direction of Jebus (that is,
Jerusalem). 11It was late in the day when
they neared Jebus, and the man's servant
said to him, "Let's stop at this Jebusite
town and spend the night there."

12"No," his master said, "we can't stay in

this foreign town where there are no Israelites. Instead, we will go on to Gibeah. ¹³Come on, let's try to get as far as Gibeah or Ramah, and we'll spend the night in one of those towns." ¹⁴So they went on. The sun was setting as they came to Gibeah, a town in the land of Benjamin, ¹⁵so they stopped there to spend the night. They rested in the town square, but no one took them in for the night.

¹⁶That evening an old man came home from his work in the fields. He was from the hill country of Ephraim, but he was living in Gibeah, where the people were from the tribe of Benjamin. ¹⁷When he saw the travelers sitting in the town square, he asked them where they were from and where they were going.

¹⁸"We have been in Bethlehem in Judah," the man replied. "We are on our way to a remote area in the hill country of Ephraim, which is my home. I traveled to Bethlehem, and now I'm returning home.* But no one has taken us in for the night, ¹⁹even though we have everything we need. We have straw and feed for our donkeys and plenty of bread and wine for ourselves."

²⁰"You are welcome to stay with me," the old man said. "I will give you anything you might need. But whatever you do, don't spend the night in the square." ²¹So he took them home with him and fed the donkeys. After they washed their feet, they ate and drank together.

²²While they were enjoying themselves, a crowd of troublemakers from the town surrounded the house. They began beating at the door and shouting to the old man, "Bring out the man who is staying with you so we can have sex with him."

²³The old man stepped outside to talk to them. "No, my brothers, don't do such an evil thing. For this man is a guest in my house, and such a thing would be shameful. ²⁴Here, take my virgin daughter and this man's concubine. I will bring them out to you, and you can abuse them and do whatever you like. But don't do such a shameful thing to this man."

²⁵But they wouldn't listen to him. So the Levite took hold of his concubine and pushed her out the door. The men of the town abused her all night, taking turns

raping her until morning. Finally, at dawn they let her go. ²⁶At daybreak the woman returned to the house where her husband was staying. She collapsed at the door of the house and lay there until it was light.

²⁷When her husband opened the door to leave, there lay his concubine with her hands on the threshold. ²⁸He said, "Get up! Let's go!" But there was no answer.* So he put her body on his donkey and took her home.

²⁹When he got home, he took a knife and cut his concubine's body into twelve pieces. Then he sent one piece to each tribe throughout all the territory of Israel.

³⁰Everyone who saw it said, "Such a horrible crime has not been committed in all the time since Israel left Egypt. Think about it! What are we going to do? Who's going to speak up?"

²⁰:¹THEN all the Israelites were united as one man, from Dan in the north to Beersheba in the south, including those from across the Jordan in the land of Gilead. The entire community assembled in the presence of the LORD at Mizpah. ²The leaders of all the people and all the tribes of Israel—400,000 warriors armed with swords—took their positions in the assembly of the people of God. ³(Word soon reached the land of Benjamin that the other tribes had gone up to Mizpah.) The Israelites then asked how this terrible crime had happened.

⁴The Levite, the husband of the woman who had been murdered, said, "My concubine and I came to spend the night in Gibeah, a town that belongs to the people of Benjamin. ⁵That night some of the leading citizens of Gibeah surrounded the house, planning to kill me, and they raped my concubine until she was dead. ⁶So I cut her body into twelve pieces and sent the pieces throughout the territory assigned to Israel, for these men have committed a terrible and shameful crime. ⁷Now then, all of you—the entire community of Israel—must decide here and now what should be done about this!"

⁸And all the people rose to their feet in unison and declared, "None of us will return home! No, not even one of us! ⁹Instead, this is what we will do to Gibeah;

we will draw lots to decide who will attack it. ¹⁰One tenth of the men* from each tribe will be chosen to supply the warriors with food, and the rest of us will take revenge on Gibeah* of Benjamin for this shameful thing they have done in Israel." ¹¹So all the Israelites were completely united, and they gathered together to attack the town.

¹²The Israelites sent messengers to the tribe of Benjamin, saying, "What a terrible thing has been done among you! ¹³Give up those evil men, those troublemakers from Gibeah, so we can execute them and purge Israel of this evil."

But the people of Benjamin would not listen. ¹⁴Instead, they came from their towns and gathered at Gibeah to fight the Israelites. ¹⁵In all, 26,000 of their warriors armed with swords arrived in Gibeah to join the 700 elite troops who lived there. ¹⁶Among Benjamin's elite troops, 700 were left-handed, and each of them could sling a rock and hit a target within a hairsbreadth without missing. ¹⁷Israel had 400,000 experienced soldiers armed with swords, not counting Benjamin's warriors.

¹⁸Before the battle the Israelites went to Bethel and asked God, "Which tribe should go first to attack the people of Benjamin?"

The LORD answered, "Judah is to go first."

¹⁹So the Israelites left early the next morning and camped near Gibeah. ²⁰Then they advanced toward Gibeah to attack the men of Benjamin. ²¹But Benjamin's warriors, who were defending the town, came out and killed 22,000 Israelites on the battlefield that day.

²²But the Israelites encouraged each other and took their positions again at the same place they had fought the previous day. ²³For they had gone up to Bethel and wept in the presence of the LORD until evening. They had asked the LORD, "Should we fight against our relatives from Benjamin again?"

And the LORD had said, "Go out and fight against them."

²⁴So the next day they went out again to fight against the men of Benjamin, ²⁵but the men of Benjamin killed another 18,000 Israelites, all of whom were experienced with the sword.

²⁶Then all the Israelites went up to Bethel and wept in the presence of the LORD and fasted until evening. They also brought burnt offerings and peace offerings to the LORD. ²⁷The Israelites went up seeking direction from the LORD. (In those days the Ark of the Covenant of God was in Bethel, ²⁸and Phinehas son of

Being humble

HOW WE LIVE

JOHN 3:30 An Old Testament prophecy foretold that there would be a voice in the wilderness announcing the Messiah's coming (see Isaiah 40:3). Like a messenger who arrived at a city ahead of an ancient king in order to announce the king's imminent arrival, John the Baptist was the messenger preparing people's hearts for the coming of Jesus. That's pretty heady stuff for a young guy. But instead of busting his buttons in pride, John showed remarkable humility. • John knew his purpose in life was to point others to Christ, so he didn't get wrapped up in his own popularity. Even when John's own disciples began to follow Jesus, John took it all in stride. "He [Jesus] must become greater and greater, and I must become less and less." • John had everything in perspective, and so he was able to humbly submit his abilities to God. He was content to do what he had been called to do. How about you? Are you thankful for who God has made you to be? Take your eyes off yourself and focus your energies on making Jesus known. He must become greater and greater.

Eleazar and grandson of Aaron was the priest.) The Israelites asked the LORD, "Should we fight against our relatives from Benjamin again, or should we stop?"

The LORD said, "Go! Tomorrow I will hand them over to you."

²⁹So the Israelites set an ambush all around Gibeah. ³⁰They went out on the third day and took their positions at the same place as before. ³¹When the men of Benjamin came out to attack, they were drawn away from the town. And as they had done before, they began to kill the Israelites. About thirty Israelites died in the open fields and along the roads, one leading to Bethel and the other leading back to Gibeah.

³²Then the warriors of Benjamin shouted, "We're defeating them as we did before!" But the Israelites had planned in advance to run away so that the men of Benjamin would chase them along the roads and be drawn away from the town.

³³When the main group of Israelite warriors reached Baal-tamar, they turned and took up their positions. Meanwhile, the Israelites hiding in ambush to the west* of Gibeah jumped up to fight. ³⁴There were 10,000 elite Israelite troops who advanced against Gibeah. The fighting was so heavy that Benjamin didn't realize the impending disaster. ³⁵So the LORD helped Israel defeat Benjamin, and that day the Israelites killed 25,100 of Benjamin's warriors, all of whom were experienced swordsmen. ³⁶Then the men of Benjamin saw that they were beaten.

The Israelites had retreated from Benjamin's warriors in order to give those hiding in ambush more room to maneuver against Gibeah. ³⁷Then those who were hiding rushed in from all sides and killed everyone in the town. ³⁸They had arranged to send up a large cloud of smoke from the town as a signal. ³⁹When the Israelites saw the smoke, they turned and attacked Benjamin's warriors.

By that time Benjamin's warriors had killed about thirty Israelites, and they shouted, "We're defeating them as we did in the first battle!" ⁴⁰But when the warriors of Benjamin looked behind them and saw the smoke rising into the sky from every part of the town, ⁴¹the men of

Israel turned and attacked. At this point the men of Benjamin became terrified, because they realized disaster was close at hand. ⁴²So they turned around and fled before the Israelites toward the wilderness. But they couldn't escape the battle, and the people who came out of the nearby towns were also killed.* ⁴³The Israelites surrounded the men of Benjamin and chased them relentlessly, finally overtaking them east of Gibeah.* ⁴⁴That day 18,000 of Benjamin's strongest warriors died in battle. ⁴⁵The survivors fled into the wilderness toward the rock of Rimmon, but Israel killed 5,000 of them along the road. They continued the chase until they had killed another 2,000 near Gidom.

⁴⁶So that day the tribe of Benjamin lost 25,000 strong warriors armed with swords, ⁴⁷leaving only 600 men who escaped to the rock of Rimmon, where they lived for four months. ⁴⁸And the Israelites returned and slaughtered every living thing in all the towns—the people, the livestock, and everything they found. They also burned down all the towns they came to.

19:2 Or *she was unfaithful to him.*   19:3 As in Greek version; Hebrew reads *When she brought him to.*   19:18 As in Greek version (see also 19:29); Hebrew reads *now I'm going to the Tabernacle of the LORD.*   19:28 Greek version adds *for she was dead.*   20:10a Hebrew *10 men from every hundred, 100 men from every thousand, and 1,000 men from every 10,000.*   20:10b Hebrew *Geba,* in this case a variant spelling of Gibeah; also in 20:33.   20:33 As in Greek and Syriac versions and Latin Vulgate; Hebrew reads *hiding in the open space.*   20:42 Or *battle, for the people from the nearby towns also came out and killed them.*   20:43 The meaning of the Hebrew is uncertain.

JOHN 3:22–4:3

John the Baptist knew his place and his purpose. He was not worried when he heard that his followers were now following Jesus; he was overjoyed.

Then Jesus and his disciples left Jerusalem and went into the Judean countryside. Jesus spent some time with them there, baptizing people.

²³At this time John the Baptist was baptizing at Aenon, near Salim, because there was plenty of water there; and people kept coming to him for baptism. ²⁴(This was before John was thrown into prison.) ²⁵A debate broke out between John's disciples and a certain Jew* over ceremonial cleansing. ²⁶So John's disciples came to him and

said, "Rabbi, the man you met on the other side of the Jordan River, the one you identified as the Messiah, is also baptizing people. And everybody is going to him instead of coming to us."

27 John replied, "No one can receive anything unless God gives it from heaven. 28 You yourselves know how plainly I told you, 'I am not the Messiah. I am only here to prepare the way for him.' 29 It is the bridegroom who marries the bride, and the best man is simply glad to stand with him and hear his vows. Therefore, I am filled with joy at his success. 30 He must become greater and greater, and I must become less and less.

31 "He has come from above and is greater than anyone else. We are of the earth, and we speak of earthly things, but he has come from heaven and is greater than anyone else.* 32 He testifies about what he has seen and heard, but how few believe what he tells them! 33 Anyone who accepts his testimony can affirm that God is true. 34 For he is sent by God. He speaks God's words, for God gives him the Spirit without limit. 35 The Father loves his Son and has put everything into his hands. 36 And anyone who believes in God's Son has eternal life. Anyone who doesn't obey the Son will never experience eternal life but remains under God's angry judgment."

4:1 JESUS* knew the Pharisees had heard that he was baptizing and making more disciples than John 2(though Jesus himself didn't baptize them—his disciples did). 3 So he left Judea and returned to Galilee.

3:25 Some manuscripts read *some Jews.*   3:31 Some manuscripts omit *and is greater than anyone else.*
4:1 Some manuscripts read *The Lord.*

PSALM 104:24-35

O LORD, what a variety of things you
    have made!
In wisdom you have made them all.
    The earth is full of your creatures.

25 Here is the ocean, vast and wide,
    teeming with life of every kind,
    both large and small.
26 See the ships sailing along,
    and Leviathan,* which you made to
    play in the sea.

27 They all depend on you
    to give them food as they need it.
28 When you supply it, they gather it.
    You open your hand to feed them,
    and they are richly satisfied.
29 But if you turn away from them, they
    panic.
    When you take away their breath,
    they die and turn again to dust.
30 When you give them your breath,*
    life is created,
    and you renew the face of the earth.

31 May the glory of the LORD continue
    forever!
    The LORD takes pleasure in all he
    has made!
32 The earth trembles at his glance;
    the mountains smoke at his touch.

33 I will sing to the LORD as long as I live.
    I will praise my God to my last
    breath!
34 May all my thoughts be pleasing to
    him,
    for I rejoice in the LORD.
35 Let all sinners vanish from the face
    of the earth;
    let the wicked disappear forever.

Let all that I am praise the LORD.

Praise the LORD!

104:26 The identification of Leviathan is disputed, ranging from an earthly creature to a mythical sea monster in ancient literature.   104:30 Or *When you send your Spirit.*

PROVERBS 14:22-24

If you plan to do evil, you will be lost; if you plan to do good, you will receive unfailing love and faithfulness. □ Work brings profit, but mere talk leads to poverty! □ Wealth is a crown for the wise; the effort of fools yields only foolishness.

JUDGES 21:1–RUTH 1:22
The book of Judges closes with Israel's struggle to decide whether to allow one of its twelve tribes to die out. Their odd solution preserved the twelfth tribe but showed yet again that during this period people did "whatever seemed right in their own eyes" rather than honor God.

The Israelites had vowed at Mizpah, "We will never give our daughters in marriage to a man from the tribe of Benjamin." ²Now the people went to Bethel and sat in the presence of God until evening, weeping loudly and bitterly. ³"O Lord, God of Israel," they cried out, "why has this happened in Israel? Now one of our tribes is missing from Israel!"

⁴Early the next morning the people built an altar and presented their burnt offerings and peace offerings on it. ⁵Then they said, "Who among the tribes of Israel did not join us at Mizpah when we held our assembly in the presence of the Lord?" At that time they had taken a solemn oath in the Lord's presence, vowing that anyone who refused to come would be put to death.

⁶The Israelites felt sorry for their brother Benjamin and said, "Today one of the tribes of Israel has been cut off. ⁷How can we find wives for the few who remain, since we have sworn by the Lord not to give them our daughters in marriage?"

⁸So they asked, "Who among the tribes of Israel did not join us at Mizpah when we assembled in the presence of the Lord?" And they discovered that no one from Jabesh-gilead had attended the assembly. ⁹For after they counted all the people, no one from Jabesh-gilead was present.

¹⁰So the assembly sent 12,000 of their best warriors to Jabesh-gilead with orders to kill everyone there, including women and children. ¹¹"This is what you are to do," they said. "Completely destroy* all the males and every woman who is not a virgin." ¹²Among the residents of Jabesh-gilead they found 400 young virgins who had never slept with a man, and they brought them to the camp at Shiloh in the land of Canaan.

¹³The Israelite assembly sent a peace delegation to the remaining people of Benjamin who were living at the rock of Rimmon. ¹⁴Then the men of Benjamin returned to their homes, and the 400 women of Jabesh-gilead who had been spared were given to them as wives. But there were not enough women for all of them.

¹⁵The people felt sorry for Benjamin because the Lord had made this gap among the tribes of Israel. ¹⁶So the elders of the assembly asked, "How can we find wives for the few who remain, since the women of the tribe of Benjamin are dead? ¹⁷There must be heirs for the survivors so that an entire tribe of Israel is not wiped out. ¹⁸But we cannot give them our own daughters in marriage because we have sworn with a solemn oath that anyone who does this will fall under God's curse."

¹⁹Then they thought of the annual festival of the Lord held in Shiloh, south of Lebonah and north of Bethel, along the east side of the road that goes from Bethel to Shechem. ²⁰They told the men of Benjamin who still needed wives, "Go and hide in the vineyards. ²¹When you see the young women of Shiloh come out for their dances, rush out from the vineyards, and each of you can take one of them home to the land of Benjamin to be your wife! ²²And when their fathers and brothers come to us in protest, we will tell them, 'Please be sympathetic. Let them have your daughters, for we didn't find wives for all of them when we destroyed Jabesh-gilead. And you are not guilty of breaking the vow since you did not actually give your daughters to them in marriage.'"

²³So the men of Benjamin did as they were told. Each man caught one of the women as she danced in the celebration and carried her off to be his wife. They returned to their own land, and they rebuilt their towns and lived in them.

²⁴Then the people of Israel departed by

tribes and families, and they returned to their own homes.

[25] In those days Israel had no king; all the people did whatever seemed right in their own eyes.

[1:1] In the days when the judges ruled in Israel, a severe famine came upon the land. So a man from Bethlehem in Judah left his home and went to live in the country of Moab, taking his wife and two sons with him. [2] The man's name was Elimelech, and his wife was Naomi. Their two sons were Mahlon and Kilion. They were Ephrathites from Bethlehem in the land of Judah. And when they reached Moab, they settled there.

[3] Then Elimelech died, and Naomi was left with her two sons. [4] The two sons married Moabite women. One married a woman named Orpah, and the other a woman named Ruth. But about ten years later, [5] both Mahlon and Kilion died. This left Naomi alone, without her two sons or her husband.

[6] Then Naomi heard in Moab that the LORD had blessed his people in Judah by giving them good crops again. So Naomi and her daughters-in-law got ready to leave Moab to return to her homeland. [7] With her two daughters-in-law she set out from the place where she had been living, and they took the road that would lead them back to Judah.

[8] But on the way, Naomi said to her two daughters-in-law, "Go back to your mothers' homes. And may the LORD reward you for your kindness to your husbands and to me. [9] May the LORD bless you with the security of another marriage." Then she kissed them good-bye, and they all broke down and wept.

[10] "No," they said. "We want to go with you to your people."

[11] But Naomi replied, "Why should you go on with me? Can I still give birth to other sons who could grow up to be your husbands? [12] No, my daughters, return to your parents' homes, for I am too old to marry again. And even if it were possible, and I were to get married tonight and bear sons, then what? [13] Would you wait for them to grow up and refuse to marry someone else? No, of course not, my daughters! Things are far more bitter for me than for you, because the LORD himself has raised his fist against me."

[14] And again they wept together, and Orpah kissed her mother-in-law good-bye. But Ruth clung tightly to Naomi. [15] "Look," Naomi said to her, "your sister-in-law has gone back to her people and to her gods. You should do the same."

[16] But Ruth replied, "Don't ask me to leave you and turn back. Wherever you go, I will go; wherever you live, I will live. Your people will be my people, and your God will be my God. [17] Wherever you die, I will die, and there I will be buried. May the LORD punish me severely if I allow anything but death to separate us!" [18] When Naomi saw that Ruth was determined to go with her, she said nothing more.

[19] So the two of them continued on their journey. When they came to Bethlehem, the entire town was excited by their arrival. "Is it really Naomi?" the women asked.

[20] "Don't call me Naomi," she responded. "Instead, call me Mara,* for the Almighty has made life very bitter for me. [21] I went away full, but the LORD has brought me home empty. Why call me Naomi when the LORD has caused me to suffer* and the Almighty has sent such tragedy upon me?"

[22] So Naomi returned from Moab, accompanied by her daughter-in-law Ruth, the young Moabite woman. They arrived in Bethlehem in late spring, at the beginning of the barley harvest.

21:11 The Hebrew term used here refers to the complete consecration of things or people to the LORD, either by destroying them or by giving them as an offering. **1:20** *Naomi* means "pleasant"; *Mara* means "bitter." **1:21** Or *has testified against me.*

JOHN 4:4-42

The Jews and the Samaritans didn't mix. The Jews considered Samaritans half-breeds, and the hostility between them was the same sort of hateful bigotry that has plagued humanity through the centuries. That's part of what makes Jesus' conversation with this woman so amazing.

He [Jesus] had to go through Samaria on the way. [5] Eventually he came to the Samaritan village of Sychar, near the field that Jacob gave to his son Joseph. [6] Jacob's well was there; and Jesus, tired from the long walk, sat wearily beside the well about noontime. [7]Soon a Samaritan woman came to draw water, and Jesus said to her, "Please give me a drink." [8]He was alone at the time because his disciples had gone into the village to buy some food.

[9]The woman was surprised, for Jews refuse to have anything to do with Samaritans.* She said to Jesus, "You are a Jew, and I am a Samaritan woman. Why are you asking me for a drink?"

[10]Jesus replied, "If you only knew the gift God has for you and who you are speaking to, you would ask me, and I would give you living water."

[11]"But sir, you don't have a rope or a bucket," she said, "and this well is very deep. Where would you get this living water? [12]And besides, do you think you're greater than our ancestor Jacob, who gave us this well? How can you offer better water than he and his sons and his animals enjoyed?"

[13]Jesus replied, "Anyone who drinks this water will soon become thirsty again. [14]But those who drink the water I give will never be thirsty again. It becomes a fresh, bubbling spring within them, giving them eternal life."

[15]"Please, sir," the woman said, "give me this water! Then I'll never be thirsty again, and I won't have to come here to get water."

[16]"Go and get your husband," Jesus told her.

[17]"I don't have a husband," the woman replied.

Jesus said, "You're right! You don't have a husband—[18]for you have had five husbands, and you aren't even married to the man you're living with now. You certainly spoke the truth!"

[19]"Sir," the woman said, "you must be a prophet. [20]So tell me, why is it that you Jews insist that Jerusalem is the only place of worship, while we Samaritans claim it is here at Mount Gerizim,* where our ancestors worshiped?"

[21]Jesus replied, "Believe me, dear woman, the time is coming when it will no longer matter whether you worship the Father on this mountain or in Jerusalem. [22]You Samaritans know very little about the one you worship, while we Jews know all about him, for salvation comes through the Jews. [23]But the time is coming—indeed it's here now—when true worshipers will worship the Father in spirit and in truth. The Father is looking for those who will worship him that way. [24]For God is Spirit, so those who worship him must worship in spirit and in truth."

[25]The woman said, "I know the Messiah is coming—the one who is called Christ. When he comes, he will explain everything to us."

[26]Then Jesus told her, "I AM the Messiah!"*

[27]Just then his disciples came back. They were shocked to find him talking to a woman, but none of them had the nerve to ask, "What do you want with her?" or "Why are you talking to her?" [28]The woman left her water jar beside the well and ran back to the village, telling everyone, [29]"Come and see a man who told me everything I ever did! Could he possibly be the Messiah?" [30]So the people came streaming from the village to see him.

[31]Meanwhile, the disciples were urging Jesus, "Rabbi, eat something."

[32]But Jesus replied, "I have a kind of food you know nothing about."

[33]"Did someone bring him food while we were gone?" the disciples asked each other.

[34]Then Jesus explained: "My nourishment comes from doing the will of God, who sent me, and from finishing his work. [35]You know the saying, 'Four months between planting and harvest.' But I say, wake up and look around. The fields are already ripe* for harvest. [36]The harvesters are paid good wages, and the fruit they harvest is people brought to eternal life. What joy awaits both the planter and the harvester alike! [37]You know the saying, 'One plants and another harvests.' And it's true. [38]I sent you to harvest where you didn't plant; others had already done the work, and now you will get to gather the harvest."

[39]Many Samaritans from the village believed in Jesus because the woman had said, "He told me everything I ever did!" [40]When they came out to see him, they begged him to stay in their village. So he

stayed for two days, ⁴¹long enough for many more to hear his message and believe. ⁴²Then they said to the woman, "Now we believe, not just because of what you told us, but because we have heard him ourselves. Now we know that he is indeed the Savior of the world."

4:9 Some manuscripts omit this sentence.   **4:20** Greek *on this mountain.*   **4:26** Or "*The 'I AM' is here*"; or "*I am the LORD*"; Greek reads *I am, the one speaking to you.*" See Exod 3:14.   **4:35** Greek *white.*

PSALM 105:1-15

Give thanks to the LORD and proclaim his greatness.
Let the whole world know what he has done.
² Sing to him; yes, sing his praises.
Tell everyone about his wonderful deeds.
³ Exult in his holy name;
rejoice, you who worship the LORD.
⁴ Search for the LORD and for his strength;
continually seek him.
⁵ Remember the wonders he has performed,
his miracles, and the rulings he has given,
⁶ you children of his servant Abraham,
you descendants of Jacob, his chosen ones.

⁷ He is the LORD our God.
His justice is seen throughout the land.
⁸ He always stands by his covenant—
the commitment he made to a thousand generations.
⁹ This is the covenant he made with Abraham
and the oath he swore to Isaac.
¹⁰ He confirmed it to Jacob as a decree,
and to the people of Israel as a never-ending covenant:
¹¹ "I will give you the land of Canaan as your special possession."
¹² He said this when they were few in number,
a tiny group of strangers in Canaan.
¹³ They wandered from nation to nation,
from one kingdom to another.
¹⁴ Yet he did not let anyone oppress them.
He warned kings on their behalf:
¹⁵ "Do not touch my chosen people,
and do not hurt my prophets."

PROVERBS 14:25

A truthful witness saves lives, but a false witness is a traitor.

HOW WE LIVE

Accepting others

JOHN 4:9-10 The story of Jesus' encounter with the woman at the well is interesting for several reasons: (1) She was a Samaritan, a group composed of Jews that had intermarried with non-Jews. Many Jews looked down on this "impure" group of people. (2) She had a bad reputation. As Jesus said, she had already gone through five husbands and was currently living with a man to whom she was not married. Most religious teachers in Jesus' day would not associate with such a person. (3) She was in a public place. No self-respecting Jewish man would speak to a mixed-race woman in public for fear of tarnishing his own reputation. •But Jesus *did* speak to this Samaritan woman. Jesus came for both the poor and destitute and for those of power and means. He came for people of every race. He came for all who will believe in him, regardless of their past sins. • Examine your own prejudices. Are you accepting and serving people who are different from you? Where do you need to change? Ask God to help you follow Jesus' example.

MAY 6

RUTH 2:1–4:22

The love story of Ruth and Boaz gives us a peek into ancient social customs such as courtship and marriage and shows us the importance of maintaining the family inheritance in that culture.

Now there was a wealthy and influential man in Bethlehem named Boaz, who was a relative of Naomi's husband, Elimelech.

²One day Ruth the Moabite said to Naomi, "Let me go out into the harvest fields to pick up the stalks of grain left behind by anyone who is kind enough to let me do it."

Naomi replied, "All right, my daughter, go ahead." ³So Ruth went out to gather grain behind the harvesters. And as it happened, she found herself working in a field that belonged to Boaz, the relative of her father-in-law, Elimelech.

⁴While she was there, Boaz arrived from Bethlehem and greeted the harvesters. "The LORD be with you!" he said.

"The LORD bless you!" the harvesters replied.

⁵Then Boaz asked his foreman, "Who is that young woman over there? Who does she belong to?"

⁶And the foreman replied, "She is the young woman from Moab who came back with Naomi. ⁷She asked me this morning if she could gather grain behind the harvesters. She has been hard at work ever since, except for a few minutes' rest in the shelter."

⁸Boaz went over and said to Ruth, "Listen, my daughter. Stay right here with us when you gather grain; don't go to any other fields. Stay right behind the young women working in my field. ⁹See which part of the field they are harvesting, and then follow them. I have warned the young men not to treat you roughly. And when you are thirsty, help yourself to the water they have drawn from the well."

¹⁰Ruth fell at his feet and thanked him warmly. "What have I done to deserve such kindness?" she asked. "I am only a foreigner."

¹¹"Yes, I know," Boaz replied. "But I also know about everything you have done for your mother-in-law since the death of your husband. I have heard how you left your father and mother and your own land to live here among complete strangers. ¹²May the LORD, the God of Israel, under whose wings you have come to take refuge, reward you fully for what you have done."

¹³"I hope I continue to please you, sir," she replied. "You have comforted me by speaking so kindly to me, even though I am not one of your workers."

¹⁴At mealtime Boaz called to her, "Come over here, and help yourself to some food. You can dip your bread in the sour wine." So she sat with his harvesters, and Boaz gave her some roasted grain to eat. She ate all she wanted and still had some left over.

¹⁵When Ruth went back to work again, Boaz ordered his young men, "Let her gather grain right among the sheaves without stopping her. ¹⁶And pull out some heads of barley from the bundles and drop them on purpose for her. Let her pick them up, and don't give her a hard time!"

¹⁷So Ruth gathered barley there all day, and when she beat out the grain that evening, it filled an entire basket.* ¹⁸She carried it back into town and showed it to her mother-in-law. Ruth also gave her the roasted grain that was left over from her meal.

¹⁹"Where did you gather all this grain today?" Naomi asked. "Where did you work? May the LORD bless the one who helped you!"

So Ruth told her mother-in-law about the man in whose field she had worked. She said, "The man I worked with today is named Boaz."

²⁰"May the LORD bless him!" Naomi told her daughter-in-law. "He is showing his kindness to us as well as to your dead husband.* That man is one of our closest relatives, one of our family redeemers."

²¹Then Ruth* said, "What's more, Boaz even told me to come back and stay with

his harvesters until the entire harvest is completed."

²²"Good!" Naomi exclaimed. "Do as he said, my daughter. Stay with his young women right through the whole harvest. You might be harassed in other fields, but you'll be safe with him."

²³So Ruth worked alongside the women in Boaz's fields and gathered grain with them until the end of the barley harvest. Then she continued working with them through the wheat harvest in early summer. And all the while she lived with her mother-in-law.

3:1ONE day Naomi said to Ruth, "My daughter, it's time that I found a permanent home for you, so that you will be provided for. ²Boaz is a close relative of ours, and he's been very kind by letting you gather grain with his young women. Tonight he will be winnowing barley at the threshing floor. ³Now do as I tell you—take a bath and put on perfume and dress in your nicest clothes. Then go to the threshing floor, but don't let Boaz see you until he has finished eating and drinking. ⁴Be sure to notice where he lies down; then go and uncover his feet and lie down there. He will tell you what to do."

⁵"I will do everything you say," Ruth replied. ⁶So she went down to the threshing floor that night and followed the instructions of her mother-in-law.

⁷After Boaz had finished eating and drinking and was in good spirits, he lay down at the far end of the pile of grain and went to sleep. Then Ruth came quietly, uncovered his feet, and lay down. ⁸Around midnight Boaz suddenly woke up and turned over. He was surprised to find a woman lying at his feet! ⁹"Who are you?" he asked.

"I am your servant Ruth," she replied. "Spread the corner of your covering over me, for you are my family redeemer."

¹⁰"The LORD bless you, my daughter!" Boaz exclaimed. "You are showing even more family loyalty now than you did before, for you have not gone after a younger man, whether rich or poor. ¹¹Now don't worry about a thing, my daughter. I will do what is necessary, for everyone in town knows you are a virtuous woman. ¹²But

while it's true that I am one of your family redeemers, there is another man who is more closely related to you than I am. ¹³Stay here tonight, and in the morning I will talk to him. If he is willing to redeem you, very well. Let him marry you. But if he is not willing, then as surely as the LORD lives, I will redeem you myself! Now lie down here until morning."

¹⁴So Ruth lay at Boaz's feet until the morning, but she got up before it was light enough for people to recognize each other. For Boaz had said, "No one must know that a woman was here at the threshing floor." ¹⁵Then Boaz said to her, "Bring your cloak and spread it out." He measured six scoops* of barley into the cloak and placed it on her back. Then he* returned to the town.

¹⁶When Ruth went back to her mother-in-law, Naomi asked, "What happened, my daughter?"

Ruth told Naomi everything Boaz had done for her, ¹⁷and she added, "He gave me these six scoops of barley and said, 'Don't go back to your mother-in-law empty-handed.'"

¹⁸Then Naomi said to her, "Just be patient, my daughter, until we hear what happens. The man won't rest until he has settled things today."

4:1BOAZ went to the town gate and took a seat there. Just then the family redeemer he had mentioned came by, so Boaz called out to him, "Come over here and sit down, friend. I want to talk to you." So they sat down together. ²Then Boaz called ten leaders from the town and asked them to sit as witnesses. ³And Boaz said to the family redeemer, "You know Naomi, who came back from Moab. She is selling the land that belonged to our relative Elimelech. ⁴I thought I should speak to you about it so that you can redeem it if you wish. If you want the land, then buy it here in the presence of these witnesses. But if you don't want it, let me know right away, because I am next in line to redeem it after you."

The man replied, "All right, I'll redeem it."

⁵Then Boaz told him, "Of course, your purchase of the land from Naomi also

requires that you marry Ruth, the Moabite widow. That way she can have children who will carry on her husband's name and keep the land in the family."

⁶"Then I can't redeem it," the family redeemer replied, "because this might endanger my own estate. You redeem the land; I cannot do it."

⁷Now in those days it was the custom in Israel for anyone transferring a right of purchase to remove his sandal and hand it to the other party. This publicly validated the transaction. ⁸So the other family redeemer drew off his sandal as he said to Boaz, "You buy the land."

⁹Then Boaz said to the elders and to the crowd standing around, "You are witnesses that today I have bought from Naomi all the property of Elimelech, Kilion, and Mahlon. ¹⁰And with the land I have acquired Ruth, the Moabite widow of Mahlon, to be my wife. This way she can have a son to carry on the family name of her dead husband and to inherit the family property here in his hometown. You are all witnesses today."

¹¹Then the elders and all the people standing in the gate replied, "We are witnesses! May the LORD make this woman who is coming into your home like Rachel and Leah, from whom all the nation of Israel descended! May you prosper in Ephrathah and be famous in Bethlehem. ¹²And may the LORD give you descendants by this young woman who will be like those of our ancestor Perez, the son of Tamar and Judah."

¹³So Boaz took Ruth into his home, and she became his wife. When he slept with her, the LORD enabled her to become pregnant, and she gave birth to a son. ¹⁴Then the women of the town said to Naomi, "Praise the LORD, who has now provided a redeemer for your family! May this child be famous in Israel. ¹⁵May he restore your youth and care for you in your old age. For he is the son of your daughter-in-law who loves you and has been better to you than seven sons!"

¹⁶Naomi took the baby and cuddled him to her breast. And she cared for him as if he were her own. ¹⁷The neighbor women said, "Now at last Naomi has a son again!" And they named him Obed. He became

the father of Jesse and the grandfather of David.

¹⁸This is the genealogical record of their ancestor Perez:

Perez was the father of Hezron.
¹⁹ Hezron was the father of Ram.
Ram was the father of Amminadab.
²⁰ Amminadab was the father of Nahshon.
Nahshon was the father of Salmon.*
²¹ Salmon was the father of Boaz.
Boaz was the father of Obed.
²² Obed was the father of Jesse.
Jesse was the father of David.

2:17 Hebrew *it was about an ephah* [20 quarts or 22 liters]. 2:20 Hebrew *to the living and to the dead.* 2:21 Hebrew *Ruth the Moabite.* 3:15a Hebrew *six measures,* an unknown quantity. 3:15b Most Hebrew manuscripts read *he;* many Hebrew manuscripts, Syriac version, and Latin Vulgate read *she.* 4:20 As in some Greek manuscripts (see also 4:21); Hebrew reads *Salma.*

JOHN 4:43-54
Sometimes the greatest act of faith can seem very small in human terms. Watch this father simply take Jesus at his word, and see the amazing result.

At the end of the two days, Jesus went on to Galilee. ⁴⁴He himself had said that a prophet is not honored in his own hometown. ⁴⁵Yet the Galileans welcomed him, for they had been in Jerusalem at the Passover celebration and had seen everything he did there.

⁴⁶As he traveled through Galilee, he came to Cana, where he had turned the water into wine. There was a government official in nearby Capernaum whose son was very sick. ⁴⁷When he heard that Jesus had come from Judea to Galilee, he went and begged Jesus to come to Capernaum to heal his son, who was about to die.

⁴⁸Jesus asked, "Will you never believe in me unless you see miraculous signs and wonders?"

⁴⁹The official pleaded, "Lord, please come now before my little boy dies."

⁵⁰Then Jesus told him, "Go back home. Your son will live!" And the man believed what Jesus said and started home.

⁵¹While the man was on his way, some of his servants met him with the news that his son was alive and well. ⁵²He asked them when the boy had begun to

get better, and they replied, "Yesterday afternoon at one o'clock his fever suddenly disappeared!" [53] Then the father realized that that was the very time Jesus had told him, "Your son will live." And he and his entire household believed in Jesus. [54]This was the second miraculous sign Jesus did in Galilee after coming from Judea.

PSALM 105:16-36

He [the LORD] called for a famine on
    the land of Canaan,
    cutting off its food supply.
[17] Then he sent someone to Egypt ahead
        of them—
    Joseph, who was sold as a slave.
[18] They bruised his feet with fetters
    and placed his neck in an iron collar.
[19] Until the time came to fulfill his
        dreams,*
    the LORD tested Joseph's character.
[20] Then Pharaoh sent for him and set
        him free;
    the ruler of the nation opened
        his prison door.
[21] Joseph was put in charge of all the
        king's household;
    he became ruler over all the king's
        possessions.
[22] He could instruct the king's aides
        as he pleased
    and teach the king's advisers.

[23] Then Israel arrived in Egypt;
    Jacob lived as a foreigner in the land
        of Ham.
[24] And the LORD multiplied the people
        of Israel
    until they became too mighty
        for their enemies.
[25] Then he turned the Egyptians against
        the Israelites,
    and they plotted against the LORD's
        servants.
[26] But the LORD sent his servant Moses,
    along with Aaron, whom he had
        chosen.
[27] They performed miraculous signs
        among the Egyptians,
    and wonders in the land of Ham.
[28] The LORD blanketed Egypt
        in darkness,
    for they had defied his commands
        to let his people go.
[29] He turned their water into blood,
    poisoning all the fish.
[30] Then frogs overran the land
    and even invaded the king's
        bedrooms.
[31] When the LORD spoke, flies
        descended on the Egyptians,
    and gnats swarmed across Egypt.
[32] He sent them hail instead of rain,
    and lightning flashed over
        the land.

HOW WE LIVE

Life's ups and downs

RUTH 4:13-22 Ruth had plenty of ups and downs in her life. Here she was in a foreign land having to glean leftover grain from a stranger's field. She could have wallowed in self-pity as she went about the degrading task of collecting cast-off food for herself and Naomi. But Ruth's character and faith in Naomi's God kept her from despair.
• As Ruth faithfully went about her task, the field workers noticed her work ethic and determination. God knew his plans for Ruth. She just *happened* to glean in the field of a man who also just *happened* to be a descendent of a common ancestor. Everything worked together for good (Romans 8:28, July 24); Ruth became the great-grandmother of King David, and thus she was an ancestor of Jesus Christ. • Often we look at the circumstances of our present life and hopelessness threatens to overwhelm us. Although it may be difficult, sometimes the best thing to do is go on about our daily tasks to the best of our ability, trusting that God will make a way. Just as God had plans for Ruth, he has plans for you.

³³ He ruined their grapevines and
  fig trees
  and shattered all the trees.
³⁴ He spoke, and hordes of locusts
  came—
  young locusts beyond number.
³⁵ They ate up everything green in the
  land,
  destroying all the crops in their
  fields.

³⁶ Then he killed the oldest son in each
  Egyptian home,
  the pride and joy of each family.

105:19 Hebrew *his word.*

PROVERBS 14:26-27

Those who fear the LORD are secure; he
will be a refuge for their children. □ Fear
of the LORD is a life-giving fountain; it
offers escape from the snares of death.

MAY**7**

1 SAMUEL 1:1-2:21
The first book of Samuel opens with the story of
Samuel's birth. Samuel was considered the last
judge of Israel, and he anointed both the first and
second kings of Israel, Saul and David.

There was a man named Elkanah who
lived in Ramah in the region of Zuph* in
the hill country of Ephraim. He was the
son of Jeroham, son of Elihu, son of Tohu,
son of Zuph, of Ephraim. ²Elkanah had
two wives, Hannah and Peninnah. Peninnah had children, but Hannah did not.

³Each year Elkanah would travel to Shiloh to worship and sacrifice to the LORD
of Heaven's Armies at the Tabernacle. The
priests of the LORD at that time were the
two sons of Eli—Hophni and Phinehas.
⁴On the days Elkanah presented his sacrifice, he would give portions of the meat to
Peninnah and each of her children. ⁵And
though he loved Hannah, he would give
her only one choice portion* because the
LORD had given her no children. ⁶So Peninnah would taunt Hannah and make
fun of her because the LORD had kept her
from having children. ⁷Year after year it
was the same—Peninnah would taunt
Hannah as they went to the Tabernacle.*
Each time, Hannah would be reduced to
tears and would not even eat.

⁸"Why are you crying, Hannah?" Elkanah would ask. "Why aren't you eating?
Why be downhearted just because you
have no children? You have me—isn't that
better than having ten sons?"

⁹Once after a sacrificial meal at Shiloh,

Hannah got up and went to pray. Eli the
priest was sitting at his customary place
beside the entrance of the Tabernacle.*
¹⁰Hannah was in deep anguish, crying bitterly as she prayed to the LORD. ¹¹And she
made this vow: "O LORD of Heaven's Armies, if you will look upon my sorrow and
answer my prayer and give me a son, then
I will give him back to you. He will be
yours for his entire lifetime, and as a sign
that he has been dedicated to the LORD,
his hair will never be cut.*"

¹²As she was praying to the LORD, Eli
watched her. ¹³Seeing her lips moving but
hearing no sound, he thought she had
been drinking. ¹⁴"Must you come here
drunk?" he demanded. "Throw away your
wine!"

¹⁵"Oh no, sir!" she replied. "I haven't
been drinking wine or anything stronger.
But I am very discouraged, and I was
pouring out my heart to the LORD. ¹⁶Don't
think I am a wicked woman! For I have
been praying out of great anguish and
sorrow."

¹⁷"In that case," Eli said, "go in peace!
May the God of Israel grant the request
you have asked of him."

¹⁸"Oh, thank you, sir!" she exclaimed.
Then she went back and began to eat
again, and she was no longer sad.

¹⁹The entire family got up early the
next morning and went to worship the
LORD once more. Then they returned
home to Ramah. When Elkanah slept
with Hannah, the LORD remembered her

plea, [20]and in due time she gave birth to a son. She named him Samuel,* for she said, "I asked the LORD for him."

[21]The next year Elkanah and his family went on their annual trip to offer a sacrifice to the LORD. [22]But Hannah did not go. She told her husband, "Wait until the boy is weaned. Then I will take him to the Tabernacle and leave him there with the LORD permanently.*"

[23]"Whatever you think is best," Elkanah agreed. "Stay here for now, and may the LORD help you keep your promise." So she stayed home and nursed the boy until he was weaned.

[24]When the child was weaned, Hannah took him to the Tabernacle in Shiloh. They brought along a three-year-old bull* for the sacrifice and a basket* of flour and some wine. [25]After sacrificing the bull, they brought the boy to Eli. [26]"Sir, do you remember me?" Hannah asked. "I am the woman who stood here several years ago praying to the LORD. [27]I asked the LORD to give me this boy, and he has granted my request. [28]Now I am giving him to the LORD, and he will belong to the LORD his whole life." And they* worshiped the LORD there.

2:1THEN Hannah prayed:

"My heart rejoices in the LORD!
  The LORD has made me strong.*

Now I have an answer for my enemies;
  I rejoice because you rescued me.
[2] No one is holy like the LORD!
    There is no one besides you;
    there is no Rock like our God.

[3] "Stop acting so proud and haughty!
    Don't speak with such arrogance!
  For the LORD is a God who knows what you have done;
    he will judge your actions.
[4] The bow of the mighty is now broken,
    and those who stumbled are now strong.
[5] Those who were well fed are now starving,
    and those who were starving are now full.
  The childless woman now has seven children,
    and the woman with many children wastes away.
[6] The LORD gives both death and life;
    he brings some down to the grave*
    but raises others up.
[7] The LORD makes some poor and others rich;
    he brings some down and lifts others up.
[8] He lifts the poor from the dust
    and the needy from the garbage dump.
  He sets them among princes,
    placing them in seats of honor.

HOW WE LIVE

Trusting God

1 SAMUEL 1:1-18 Hannah was barren. In the ancient Near East, the inability to bear children was considered a grave misfortune. A husband would almost certainly take another wife in order to produce heirs. For many women, barrenness meant ostracism and shame. Hannah was tormented by Peninnah but fortunately had the constant love and devotion of her husband. • Hannah had something else as well—faith in God and complete trust in him. She brought her sorrow and pain before God with complete honesty. She poured out her anguish in such a way that Eli, the priest at the Tabernacle, accused her of being drunk! She prayed, trusted that her request would be granted, went back to her life, and waited for God's answer. • If you are having a tough time trusting God, remember Hannah. Pour out your heart to God, knowing that he hears you. Then get on with the tasks at hand. You can certainly continue to pray for that same request—God loves persistent prayer—but don't *worry* about it anymore. Put the situation in God's hands and leave it there.

For all the earth is the LORD's,
and he has set the world in order.

⁹ "He will protect his faithful ones,
but the wicked will disappear
in darkness.
No one will succeed by strength alone.
¹⁰ Those who fight against the LORD
will be shattered.
He thunders against them from
heaven;
the LORD judges throughout the
earth.
He gives power to his king;
he increases the strength* of his
anointed one."

¹¹Then Elkanah returned home to Ramah without Samuel. And the boy served the LORD by assisting Eli the priest.

¹²Now the sons of Eli were scoundrels who had no respect for the LORD ¹³or for their duties as priests. Whenever anyone offered a sacrifice, Eli's sons would send over a servant with a three-pronged fork. While the meat of the sacrificed animal was still boiling, ¹⁴the servant would stick the fork into the pot and demand that whatever it brought up be given to Eli's sons. All the Israelites who came to worship at Shiloh were treated this way. ¹⁵Sometimes the servant would come even before the animal's fat had been burned on the altar. He would demand raw meat before it had been boiled so that it could be used for roasting.

¹⁶The man offering the sacrifice might reply, "Take as much as you want, but the fat must be burned first." Then the servant would demand, "No, give it to me now, or I'll take it by force." ¹⁷So the sin of these young men was very serious in the LORD's sight, for they treated the LORD's offerings with contempt.

¹⁸But Samuel, though he was only a boy, served the LORD. He wore a linen garment like that of a priest.* ¹⁹Each year his mother made a small coat for him and brought it to him when she came with her husband for the sacrifice. ²⁰Before they returned home, Eli would bless Elkanah and his wife and say, "May the LORD give you other children to take the place of this one she gave to the LORD.*" ²¹And the LORD gave Hannah three sons and two daughters. Meanwhile, Samuel grew up in the presence of the LORD.

1:1 As in Greek version; Hebrew reads *in Ramathaim-zophim;* compare 1:19. 1:5 Or *And because he loved Hannah, he would give her a choice portion.* The meaning of the Hebrew is uncertain. 1:7 Hebrew *the house of the LORD;* also in 1:24. 1:9 Hebrew *the Temple of the LORD.* 1:11 Some manuscripts add *He will drink neither wine nor intoxicants.* 1:20 *Samuel* sounds like the Hebrew term for "asked of God" or "heard by God." 1:22 Some manuscripts add *I will offer him as a Nazirite for all time.* 1:24a As in Dead Sea Scrolls, Greek and Syriac versions; Masoretic Text reads *three bulls.* 1:24b Hebrew *and an ephah* [20 quarts or 22 liters]. 1:28 Hebrew *he.* 2:1 Hebrew *has exalted my horn.* 2:6 Hebrew *to Sheol.* 2:10 Hebrew *he exalts the horn.* 2:18 Hebrew *He wore a linen ephod.* 2:20 As in Dead Sea Scrolls and Greek version; Masoretic Text reads *this one she requested of the LORD in prayer.*

JOHN 5:1-23

Jesus did not disregard the Sabbath, or any other Old Testament institution. As the Son of God, he was Lord over them and fulfilled their true meaning and purpose.

Afterward Jesus returned to Jerusalem for one of the Jewish holy days. ²Inside the city, near the Sheep Gate, was the pool of Bethesda,* with five covered porches. ³Crowds of sick people—blind, lame, or paralyzed—lay on the porches.* ⁵One of the men lying there had been sick for thirty-eight years. ⁶When Jesus saw him and knew he had been ill for a long time, he asked him, "Would you like to get well?"

⁷"I can't, sir," the sick man said, "for I have no one to put me into the pool when the water bubbles up. Someone else always gets there ahead of me."

⁸Jesus told him, "Stand up, pick up your mat, and walk!"

⁹Instantly, the man was healed! He rolled up his sleeping mat and began walking! But this miracle happened on the Sabbath, ¹⁰so the Jewish leaders objected. They said to the man who was cured, "You can't work on the Sabbath! The law doesn't allow you to carry that sleeping mat!"

¹¹But he replied, "The man who healed me told me, 'Pick up your mat and walk.'"

¹²"Who said such a thing as that?" they demanded.

¹³The man didn't know, for Jesus had disappeared into the crowd. ¹⁴But afterward Jesus found him in the Temple and told him, "Now you are well; so stop sinning, or something even worse

may happen to you." [15]Then the man went and told the Jewish leaders that it was Jesus who had healed him.

[16]So the Jewish leaders began harassing* Jesus for breaking the Sabbath rules. [17]But Jesus replied, "My Father is always working, and so am I." [18]So the Jewish leaders tried all the harder to find a way to kill him. For he not only broke the Sabbath, he called God his Father, thereby making himself equal with God.

[19]So Jesus explained, "I tell you the truth, the Son can do nothing by himself. He does only what he sees the Father doing. Whatever the Father does, the Son also does. [20]For the Father loves the Son and shows him everything he is doing. In fact, the Father will show him how to do even greater works than healing this man. Then you will truly be astonished. [21]For just as the Father gives life to those he raises from the dead, so the Son gives life to anyone he wants. [22]In addition, the Father judges no one. Instead, he has given the Son absolute authority to judge, [23]so that everyone will honor the Son, just as they honor the Father. Anyone who does not honor the Son is certainly not honoring the Father who sent him."

5:2 Other manuscripts read *Beth-zatha;* still others read *Bethsaida.* 5:3 Some manuscripts add an expanded conclusion to verse 3 and all of verse 4: *waiting for a certain movement of the water, [4]for an angel of the Lord came from time to time and stirred up the water. And the first person to step in after the water was stirred was healed of whatever disease he had.* 5:16 Or *persecuting.*

PSALM 105:37-45

The LORD brought his people out
    of Egypt, loaded with silver
    and gold;

1 SAMUEL 2:22–4:22

From the earliest days of the Israelites' journey, the Ark of the Covenant represented God's presence among the people. How crushing to have an enemy capture it!

Now Eli was very old, but he was aware of what his sons were doing to the people of

and not one among the tribes
    of Israel even stumbled.
[38] Egypt was glad when they were
    gone,
    for they feared them greatly.
[39] The LORD spread a cloud above
    them as a covering
    and gave them a great fire to light
    the darkness.
[40] They asked for meat, and he sent
    them quail;
    he satisfied their hunger
    with manna—bread from
    heaven.
[41] He split open a rock, and water
    gushed out
    to form a river through the dry
    wasteland.
[42] For he remembered his sacred
    promise
    to his servant Abraham.
[43] So he brought his people out of Egypt
    with joy,
    his chosen ones with rejoicing.
[44] He gave his people the lands of pagan
    nations,
    and they harvested crops that
    others had planted.
[45] All this happened so they would follow
    his decrees
    and obey his instructions.

Praise the LORD!

PROVERBS 14:28-29

A growing population is a king's glory; a prince without subjects has nothing. □ People with understanding control their anger; a hot temper shows great foolishness.

Israel. He knew, for instance, that his sons were seducing the young women who assisted at the entrance of the Tabernacle.* [23]Eli said to them, "I have been hearing reports from all the people about the wicked things you are doing. Why do you keep sinning? [24]You must stop, my sons!

The reports I hear among the LORD's people are not good. ²⁵If someone sins against another person, God* can mediate for the guilty party. But if someone sins against the LORD, who can intercede?" But Eli's sons wouldn't listen to their father, for the LORD was already planning to put them to death.

²⁶Meanwhile, the boy Samuel grew taller and grew in favor with the LORD and with the people.

²⁷One day a man of God came to Eli and gave him this message from the LORD: "I revealed myself* to your ancestors when the people of Israel were slaves in Egypt. ²⁸I chose your ancestor Aaron* from among all the tribes of Israel to be my priest, to offer sacrifices on my altar, to burn incense, and to wear the priestly vest* as he served me. And I assigned the sacrificial offerings to you priests. ²⁹So why do you scorn my sacrifices and offerings? Why do you give your sons more honor than you give me—for you and they have become fat from the best offerings of my people Israel!

³⁰"Therefore, the LORD, the God of Israel, says: I promised that your branch of the tribe of Levi* would always be my priests. But I will honor those who honor me, and I will despise those who think lightly of me. ³¹The time is coming when I will put an end to your family, so it will no longer serve as my priests. All the members of your family will die before their time. None will reach old age. ³²You will watch with envy as I pour out prosperity on the people of Israel. But no members of your family will ever live out their days. ³³Those who survive will live in sadness and grief, and their children will die a violent death.* ³⁴And to prove that what I have said will come true, I will cause your two sons, Hophni and Phinehas, to die on the same day!

³⁵"Then I will raise up a faithful priest who will serve me and do what I desire. I will establish his family, and they will be priests to my anointed kings forever. ³⁶Then all of your surviving family will bow before him, begging for money and food. 'Please,' they will say, 'give us jobs among the priests so we will have enough to eat.'"

³:¹MEANWHILE, the boy Samuel served the LORD by assisting Eli. Now in those days messages from the LORD were very rare, and visions were quite uncommon.

²One night Eli, who was almost blind by now, had gone to bed. ³The lamp of God had not yet gone out, and Samuel was sleeping in the Tabernacle* near the Ark of God. ⁴Suddenly the LORD called out, "Samuel!"

"Yes?" Samuel replied. "What is it?" ⁵He got up and ran to Eli. "Here I am. Did you call me?"

"I didn't call you," Eli replied. "Go back to bed." So he did.

⁶Then the LORD called out again, "Samuel!"

Again Samuel got up and went to Eli. "Here I am. Did you call me?"

"I didn't call you, my son," Eli said. "Go back to bed."

⁷Samuel did not yet know the LORD because he had never had a message from the LORD before. ⁸So the LORD called a third time, and once more Samuel got up and went to Eli. "Here I am. Did you call me?"

Then Eli realized it was the LORD who was calling the boy. ⁹So he said to Samuel, "Go and lie down again, and if someone calls again, say, 'Speak, LORD, your servant is listening.'" So Samuel went back to bed.

¹⁰And the LORD came and called as before, "Samuel! Samuel!"

And Samuel replied, "Speak, your servant is listening."

¹¹Then the LORD said to Samuel, "I am about to do a shocking thing in Israel. ¹²I am going to carry out all my threats against Eli and his family, from beginning to end. ¹³I have warned him that judgment is coming upon his family forever, because his sons are blaspheming God* and he hasn't disciplined them. ¹⁴So I have vowed that the sins of Eli and his sons will never be forgiven by sacrifices or offerings."

¹⁵Samuel stayed in bed until morning, then got up and opened the doors of the Tabernacle* as usual. He was afraid to tell Eli what the LORD had said to him. ¹⁶But Eli called out to him, "Samuel, my son."

"Here I am," Samuel replied.

¹⁷"What did the LORD say to you? Tell

me everything. And may God strike you and even kill you if you hide anything from me!" ¹⁸So Samuel told Eli everything; he didn't hold anything back. "It is the LORD's will," Eli replied. "Let him do what he thinks best."

¹⁹As Samuel grew up, the LORD was with him, and everything Samuel said proved to be reliable. ²⁰And all Israel, from Dan in the north to Beersheba in the south, knew that Samuel was confirmed as a prophet of the LORD. ²¹The LORD continued to appear at Shiloh and gave messages to Samuel there at the Tabernacle. ⁴:¹And Samuel's words went out to all the people of Israel.

⁴:¹AT that time Israel was at war with the Philistines. The Israelite army was camped near Ebenezer, and the Philistines were at Aphek. ²The Philistines attacked and defeated the army of Israel, killing 4,000 men. ³After the battle was over, the troops retreated to their camp, and the elders of Israel asked, "Why did the LORD allow us to be defeated by the Philistines?" Then they said, "Let's bring the Ark of the Covenant of the LORD from Shiloh. If we carry it into battle with us, it* will save us from our enemies."

⁴So they sent men to Shiloh to bring the Ark of the Covenant of the LORD of Heaven's Armies, who is enthroned between the cherubim. Hophni and Phinehas, the sons of Eli, were also there with the Ark of the Covenant of God. ⁵When all the Israelites saw the Ark of the Covenant of the LORD coming into the camp, their shout of joy was so loud it made the ground shake!

⁶"What's going on?" the Philistines asked. "What's all the shouting about in the Hebrew camp?" When they were told it was because the Ark of the LORD had arrived, ⁷they panicked. "The gods have* come into their camp!" they cried. "This is a disaster! We have never had to face anything like this before! ⁸Help! Who can save us from these mighty gods of Israel? They are the same gods who destroyed the Egyptians with plagues when Israel was in the wilderness. ⁹Fight as never before, Philistines! If you don't, we will become the Hebrews' slaves just as they have been ours! Stand up like men and fight!"

¹⁰So the Philistines fought desperately, and Israel was defeated again. The slaughter was great; 30,000 Israelite soldiers died that day. The survivors turned and fled to their tents. ¹¹The Ark of God was captured, and Hophni and Phinehas, the two sons of Eli, were killed.

¹²A man from the tribe of Benjamin ran from the battlefield and arrived at Shiloh later that same day. He had torn his clothes and put dust on his head to show

WHO GOD IS

Jesus is our Savior

JOHN 5:24 Jesus came to do many things. He was a teacher, a carpenter, and a friend. He was a worker of miracles and a spokesman for God. But his greatest purpose was to "save his people from their sins" (Matthew 1:21, January 1). The name *Jesus* means "the Lord saves." God in his great love has provided a way to have a right relationship with him for anyone who believes in his Son, Jesus. • When you trust and believe in Jesus as your Savior, many things happen. You accept that he died for your sins on the cross. You are forgiven and given a clean slate. You walk out of darkness and into light. You have power to live differently here on earth. And Jesus says here that when you believe in him, you have eternal life! As hard as it is to understand, our eternal life—living with God forever—begins here and now. "All this and heaven too!" as the saying goes. • It's an uneven exchange, that's for sure. There's nothing we've done to deserve what we gain in Christ. Take time to thank Jesus, your Savior, for all he has provided for your life now and into eternity.

his grief. [13]Eli was waiting beside the road to hear the news of the battle, for his heart trembled for the safety of the Ark of God. When the messenger arrived and told what had happened, an outcry resounded throughout the town.

[14]"What is all the noise about?" Eli asked.

The messenger rushed over to Eli, [15]who was ninety-eight years old and blind. [16]He said to Eli, "I have just come from the battlefield—I was there this very day."

"What happened, my son?" Eli demanded.

[17]"Israel has been defeated by the Philistines," the messenger replied. "The people have been slaughtered, and your two sons, Hophni and Phinehas, were also killed. And the Ark of God has been captured."

[18]When the messenger mentioned what had happened to the Ark of God, Eli fell backward from his seat beside the gate. He broke his neck and died, for he was old and overweight. He had been Israel's judge for forty years.

[19]Eli's daughter-in-law, the wife of Phinehas, was pregnant and near her time of delivery. When she heard that the Ark of God had been captured and that her father-in-law and husband were dead, she went into labor and gave birth. [20]She died in childbirth, but before she passed away the midwives tried to encourage her. "Don't be afraid," they said. "You have a baby boy!" But she did not answer or pay attention to them.

[21]She named the child Ichabod (which means "Where is the glory?"), for she said, "Israel's glory is gone." She named him this because the Ark of God had been captured and because her father-in-law and husband were dead. [22]Then she said, "The glory has departed from Israel, for the Ark of God has been captured."

2:22 Hebrew *Tent of Meeting.* Some manuscripts lack this entire sentence.   2:25 Or *the judges.*   2:27 As in Greek and Syriac versions; Hebrew reads *Did I reveal myself.*   2:28a Hebrew *your father.*   2:28b Hebrew *an ephod.*   2:30 Hebrew *that your house and your father's house.*   2:33 As in Dead Sea Scrolls, which read *die by the sword;* Masoretic Text reads *die like mortals.*   3:3 Hebrew *the Temple of the LORD.*   3:13 As in Greek version; Hebrew reads *his sons have made themselves contemptible.*   3:15 Hebrew *the house of the LORD.*   4:3 Or *he.*   4:7 Or *A god has.*

JOHN 5:24-47
Jesus' miracles and teachings gave witness to who he was. But it was still hard for many to accept him. The Jews had been looking for the Messiah for centuries; when he arrived many could not believe it.

"I [Jesus] tell you the truth, those who listen to my message and believe in God who sent me have eternal life. They will never be condemned for their sins, but they have already passed from death into life.

[25]"And I assure you that the time is coming, indeed it's here now, when the dead will hear my voice—the voice of the Son of God. And those who listen will live. [26]The Father has life in himself, and he has granted that same life-giving power to his Son. [27]And he has given him authority to judge everyone because he is the Son of Man.* [28]Don't be so surprised! Indeed, the time is coming when all the dead in their graves will hear the voice of God's Son, [29]and they will rise again. Those who have done good will rise to experience eternal life, and those who have continued in evil will rise to experience judgment. [30]I can do nothing on my own. I judge as God tells me. Therefore, my judgment is just, because I carry out the will of the one who sent me, not my own will.

[31]"If I were to testify on my own behalf, my testimony would not be valid. [32]But someone else is also testifying about me, and I assure you that everything he says about me is true. [33]In fact, you sent investigators to listen to John the Baptist, and his testimony about me was true. [34]Of course, I have no need of human witnesses, but I say these things so you might be saved. [35]John was like a burning and shining lamp, and you were excited for a while about his message. [36]But I have a greater witness than John—my teachings and my miracles. The Father gave me these works to accomplish, and they prove that he sent me. [37]And the Father who sent me has testified about me himself. You have never heard his voice or seen him face to face, [38]and you do not have his message in your hearts, because you do not believe me—the one he sent to you.

[39]"You search the Scriptures because you think they give you eternal life. But the Scriptures point to me! [40]Yet you refuse to come to me to receive this life.

[41]"Your approval means nothing to me, [42]because I know you don't have God's love within you. [43]For I have come to you in my Father's name, and you have rejected me. Yet if others come in their own name, you gladly welcome them. [44]No wonder you can't believe! For you gladly honor each other, but you don't care about the honor that comes from the one who alone is God.*

[45]"Yet it isn't I who will accuse you before the Father. Moses will accuse you! Yes, Moses, in whom you put your hopes. [46]If you really believed Moses, you would believe me, because he wrote about me. [47]But since you don't believe what he wrote, how will you believe what I say?"

5:27 "Son of Man" is a title Jesus used for himself.
5:44 Some manuscripts read *from the only One.*

PSALM 106:1-12

Praise the LORD!

Give thanks to the LORD,
    for he is good!
His faithful love endures forever.
[2] Who can list the glorious miracles
    of the LORD?
Who can ever praise him enough?
[3] There is joy for those who deal justly
    with others
and always do what is right.

[4] Remember me, LORD, when you show
    favor to your people;
come near and rescue me.
[5] Let me share in the prosperity of your
    chosen ones.

Let me rejoice in the joy of your
    people;
let me praise you with those who
    are your heritage.

[6] Like our ancestors, we have sinned.
    We have done wrong! We have
    acted wickedly!
[7] Our ancestors in Egypt
    were not impressed by the LORD's
    miraculous deeds.
They soon forgot his many acts
    of kindness to them.
Instead, they rebelled against him
    at the Red Sea.*
[8] Even so, he saved them—
    to defend the honor of his name
    and to demonstrate his mighty
    power.
[9] He commanded the Red Sea*
    to dry up.
He led Israel across the sea
    as if it were a desert.
[10] So he rescued them from their
    enemies
and redeemed them from their
    foes.
[11] Then the water returned and covered
    their enemies;
not one of them survived.
[12] Then his people believed his
    promises.
Then they sang his praise.

106:7 Hebrew *at the sea, the sea of reeds.*   106:9 Hebrew *sea of reeds;* also in 106:22.

PROVERBS 14:30-31

A peaceful heart leads to a healthy body; jealousy is like cancer in the bones.
□Those who oppress the poor insult their Maker, but helping the poor honors him.

1 SAMUEL 5:1-7:17
The Philistines soon became sorry they had stolen the Ark! God punished them wherever they took the Ark, and Samuel stepped to the forefront to lead the Israelites in victory against them.

MAY**9**

After the Philistines captured the Ark of God, they took it from the battleground at Ebenezer to the town of Ashdod. [2]They carried the Ark of God into the temple of

Dagon and placed it beside an idol of Dagon. ³But when the citizens of Ashdod went to see it the next morning, Dagon had fallen with his face to the ground in front of the Ark of the LORD! So they took Dagon and put him in his place again. ⁴But the next morning the same thing happened—Dagon had fallen face down before the Ark of the LORD again. This time his head and hands had broken off and were lying in the doorway. Only the trunk of his body was left intact. ⁵That is why to this day neither the priests of Dagon nor anyone who enters the temple of Dagon in Ashdod will step on its threshold.

⁶Then the LORD's heavy hand struck the people of Ashdod and the nearby villages with a plague of tumors.* ⁷When the people realized what was happening, they cried out, "We can't keep the Ark of the God of Israel here any longer! He is against us! We will all be destroyed along with Dagon, our god." ⁸So they called together the rulers of the Philistine towns and asked, "What should we do with the Ark of the God of Israel?"

The rulers discussed it and replied, "Move it to the town of Gath." So they moved the Ark of the God of Israel to Gath. ⁹But when the Ark arrived at Gath, the LORD's heavy hand fell on its men, young and old; he struck them with a plague of tumors, and there was a great panic.

¹⁰So they sent the Ark of God to the town of Ekron, but when the people of Ekron saw it coming they cried out, "They are bringing the Ark of the God of Israel here to kill us, too!" ¹¹The people summoned the Philistine rulers again and begged them, "Please send the Ark of the God of Israel back to its own country, or it* will kill us all." For the deadly plague from God had already begun, and great fear was sweeping across the town. ¹²Those who didn't die were afflicted with tumors; and the cry from the town rose to heaven.

6:1THE Ark of the LORD remained in Philistine territory seven months in all. ²Then the Philistines called in their priests and diviners and asked them, "What should we do about the Ark of the LORD? Tell us how to return it to its own country."

³"Send the Ark of the God of Israel back with a gift," they were told. "Send a guilt offering so the plague will stop. Then, if you are healed, you will know it was his hand that caused the plague."

⁴"What sort of guilt offering should we send?" they asked.

And they were told, "Since the plague has struck both you and your five rulers, make five gold tumors and five gold rats, just like those that have ravaged your land. ⁵Make these things to show honor to the God of Israel. Perhaps then he will stop afflicting you, your gods, and your land. ⁶Don't be stubborn and rebellious as Pharaoh and the Egyptians were. By the time God was finished with them, they were eager to let Israel go.

⁷"Now build a new cart, and find two cows that have just given birth to calves. Make sure the cows have never been yoked to a cart. Hitch the cows to the cart, but shut their calves away from them in a pen. ⁸Put the Ark of the LORD on the cart, and beside it place a chest containing the gold rats and gold tumors you are sending as a guilt offering. Then let the cows go wherever they want. ⁹If they cross the border of our land and go to Beth-shemesh, we will know it was the LORD who brought this great disaster upon us. If they don't, we will know it was not his hand that caused the plague. It came simply by chance."

¹⁰So these instructions were carried out. Two cows were hitched to the cart, and their newborn calves were shut up in a pen. ¹¹Then the Ark of the LORD and the chest containing the gold rats and gold tumors were placed on the cart. ¹²And sure enough, without veering off in other directions, the cows went straight along the road toward Beth-shemesh, lowing as they went. The Philistine rulers followed them as far as the border of Beth-shemesh.

¹³The people of Beth-shemesh were harvesting wheat in the valley, and when they saw the Ark, they were overjoyed! ¹⁴The cart came into the field of a man named Joshua and stopped beside a large rock. So the people broke up the wood of the cart for a fire and killed the cows and sacrificed them to the LORD as a burnt of-

fering. [15]Several men of the tribe of Levi lifted the Ark of the LORD and the chest containing the gold rats and gold tumors from the cart and placed them on the large rock. Many sacrifices and burnt offerings were offered to the LORD that day by the people of Beth-shemesh. [16]The five Philistine rulers watched all this and then returned to Ekron that same day.

[17]The five gold tumors sent by the Philistines as a guilt offering to the LORD were gifts from the rulers of Ashdod, Gaza, Ashkelon, Gath, and Ekron. [18]The five gold rats represented the five Philistine towns and their surrounding villages, which were controlled by the five rulers. The large rock at Beth-shemesh, where they set the Ark of the LORD, still stands in the field of Joshua as a witness to what happened there.

[19]But the LORD killed seventy men* from Beth-shemesh because they looked into the Ark of the LORD. And the people mourned greatly because of what the LORD had done. [20]"Who is able to stand in the presence of the LORD, this holy God?" they cried out. "Where can we send the Ark from here?"

[21]So they sent messengers to the people at Kiriath-jearim and told them, "The Philistines have returned the Ark of the LORD. Come here and get it!"

[7:1]So the men of Kiriath-jearim came to get the Ark of the LORD. They took it to the hillside home of Abinadab and ordained Eleazar, his son, to be in charge of it. [2]The Ark remained in Kiriath-jearim for a long time—twenty years in all. During that time all Israel mourned because it seemed the LORD had abandoned them.

[3]Then Samuel said to all the people of Israel, "If you are really serious about wanting to return to the LORD, get rid of your foreign gods and your images of Ashtoreth. Determine to obey only the LORD; then he will rescue you from the Philistines." [4]So the Israelites got rid of their images of Baal and Ashtoreth and worshiped only the LORD.

[5]Then Samuel told them, "Gather all of Israel to Mizpah, and I will pray to the LORD for you." [6]So they gathered at Mizpah and, in a great ceremony, drew water from a well and poured it out before the LORD. They also went without food all day and confessed that they had sinned against the LORD. (It was at Mizpah that Samuel became Israel's judge.)

[7]When the Philistine rulers heard that Israel had gathered at Mizpah, they mobilized their army and advanced. The Israelites were badly frightened when they learned that the Philistines were approaching. [8]"Don't stop pleading with

HOW WE LIVE

Our giving

JOHN 6:8-9 When Jesus asked Philip where they could buy food for the multitude that had followed them into the hill country, he was testing Philip's faith. Philip had a rational answer: Even if they had the time to walk to the nearest city, they didn't have the funds to purchase the vast quantity of food necessary. Remember, there were five thousand men; the number of women and children is not recorded. • But there was one child who offered what he had to Jesus. He may have been carrying the meal for his family—someone, at least, had thought ahead. But though he and his family might go hungry, he offered the small lunch anyway. Andrew still insisted, "What good is that with this huge crowd?" Jesus answered by performing one of the most spectacular miracles recorded in the Gospels. The boy gave the little he had, and Jesus multiplied it beyond human comprehension. • Even today, there are no barriers to what Jesus can do. Neither age nor financial resources can keep God from doing what seems impossible. If you give joyfully of your time, talents, and resources—no matter how meager—the possibilities are endless. Little is much with God.

the LORD our God to save us from the Philistines!" they begged Samuel. ⁹So Samuel took a young lamb and offered it to the LORD as a whole burnt offering. He pleaded with the LORD to help Israel, and the LORD answered him.

¹⁰Just as Samuel was sacrificing the burnt offering, the Philistines arrived to attack Israel. But the LORD spoke with a mighty voice of thunder from heaven that day, and the Philistines were thrown into such confusion that the Israelites defeated them. ¹¹The men of Israel chased them from Mizpah to a place below Bethcar, slaughtering them all along the way.

¹²Samuel then took a large stone and placed it between the towns of Mizpah and Jeshanah.* He named it Ebenezer (which means "the stone of help"), for he said, "Up to this point the LORD has helped us!"

¹³So the Philistines were subdued and didn't invade Israel again for some time. And throughout Samuel's lifetime, the LORD's powerful hand was raised against the Philistines. ¹⁴The Israelite villages near Ekron and Gath that the Philistines had captured were restored to Israel, along with the rest of the territory that the Philistines had taken. And there was peace between Israel and the Amorites in those days.

¹⁵Samuel continued as Israel's judge for the rest of his life. ¹⁶Each year he traveled around, setting up his court first at Bethel, then at Gilgal, and then at Mizpah. He judged the people of Israel at each of these places. ¹⁷Then he would return to his home at Ramah, and he would hear cases there, too. And Samuel built an altar to the LORD at Ramah.

5:6 Greek version and Latin Vulgate read *tumors; and rats appeared in their land, and death and destruction were throughout the city.* 5:11 Or *he.* 6:19 As in a few Hebrew manuscripts; most Hebrew manuscripts read *70 men, 50,000 men.* Perhaps the text should be understood to read *the LORD killed 70 men and 50 oxen.* 7:12 As in Greek and Syriac versions; Hebrew reads *Shen.*

JOHN 6:1-21

Jesus often withdrew from the crowds who witnessed his miracle-working power. He had a mission to complete and did not want people trying to make him king before his time.

After this, Jesus crossed over to the far side of the Sea of Galilee, also known as the Sea of Tiberias. ²A huge crowd kept following him wherever he went, because they saw his miraculous signs as he healed the sick. ³Then Jesus climbed a hill and sat down with his disciples around him. ⁴(It was nearly time for the Jewish Passover celebration.) ⁵Jesus soon saw a huge crowd of people coming to look for him. Turning to Philip, he asked, "Where can we buy bread to feed all these people?" ⁶He was testing Philip, for he already knew what he was going to do.

⁷Philip replied, "Even if we worked for months, we wouldn't have enough money* to feed them!"

⁸Then Andrew, Simon Peter's brother, spoke up. ⁹"There's a young boy here with five barley loaves and two fish. But what good is that with this huge crowd?"

¹⁰"Tell everyone to sit down," Jesus said. So they all sat down on the grassy slopes. (The men alone numbered about 5,000.) ¹¹Then Jesus took the loaves, gave thanks to God, and distributed them to the people. Afterward he did the same with the fish. And they all ate as much as they wanted. ¹²After everyone was full, Jesus told his disciples, "Now gather the leftovers, so that nothing is wasted." ¹³So they picked up the pieces and filled twelve baskets with scraps left by the people who had eaten from the five barley loaves.

¹⁴When the people saw him* do this miraculous sign, they exclaimed, "Surely, he is the Prophet we have been expecting!"* ¹⁵When Jesus saw that they were ready to force him to be their king, he slipped away into the hills by himself.

¹⁶That evening Jesus' disciples went down to the shore to wait for him. ¹⁷But as darkness fell and Jesus still hadn't come back, they got into the boat and headed across the lake toward Capernaum. ¹⁸Soon a gale swept down upon them, and the sea grew very rough. ¹⁹They had rowed three or four miles* when suddenly they saw Jesus walking on the water toward the boat. They were terrified, ²⁰but he called out to them, "Don't be afraid. I am here!*" ²¹Then they were eager to let him in the boat, and immediately they arrived at their destination!

6:7 Greek *Two hundred denarii would not be enough.* A denarius was equivalent to a laborer's full day's wage. 6:14a Some manuscripts read *Jesus.* 6:14b See Deut 18:15,

18; Mal 4:5-6.   **6:19** Greek *25 or 30 stadia* [4.6 or 5.5 kilometers].   **6:20** Or *The 'I AM' is here;* Greek reads *I am.* See Exod 3:14.

PSALM 106:13-31

Yet how quickly they forgot what he
    had done!
    They wouldn't wait for his counsel!
[14] In the wilderness their desires ran
    wild,
    testing God's patience in that dry
        wasteland.
[15] So he gave them what they asked for,
    but he sent a plague along with it.
[16] The people in the camp were jealous
        of Moses
    and envious of Aaron, the LORD's
        holy priest.
[17] Because of this, the earth opened up;
    it swallowed Dathan
    and buried Abiram and the other
        rebels.
[18] Fire fell upon their followers;
    a flame consumed the wicked.

[19] The people made a calf at Mount
        Sinai*;
    they bowed before an image made
        of gold.
[20] They traded their glorious God
    for a statue of a grass-eating bull.
[21] They forgot God, their savior,
    who had done such great things
        in Egypt—
[22] such wonderful things in the land
        of Ham,
    such awesome deeds at the Red Sea.
[23] So he declared he would destroy them.
    But Moses, his chosen one, stepped
        between the LORD and the people.

He begged him to turn from his
    anger and not destroy them.
[24] The people refused to enter the
    pleasant land,
    for they wouldn't believe his
        promise to care for them.
[25] Instead, they grumbled in their tents
    and refused to obey the LORD.
[26] Therefore, he solemnly swore
    that he would kill them in
        the wilderness,
[27] that he would scatter their
        descendants among the
        nations,
    exiling them to distant lands.
[28] Then our ancestors joined in the
        worship of Baal at Peor;
    they even ate sacrifices offered
        to the dead!
[29] They angered the LORD with all
        these things,
    so a plague broke out among them.
[30] But Phinehas had the courage
        to intervene,
    and the plague was stopped.
[31] So he has been regarded as a
        righteous man
    ever since that time.

106:19 Hebrew *at Horeb*, another name for Sinai.

PROVERBS 14:32-33

The wicked are crushed by disaster, but the godly have a refuge when they die. □ Wisdom is enshrined in an understanding heart; wisdom is not* found among fools.

14:33 As in Greek and Syriac versions; Hebrew lacks *not.*

1 SAMUEL 8:1-9:27

Although Israel had had leaders such as Moses, Joshua, and the judges, these were spiritual rather than political leaders. Now the people demanded a king, which was a rejection of God's leadership.

As Samuel grew old, he appointed his sons to be judges over Israel. [2] Joel and

MAY**10**

Abijah, his oldest sons, held court in Beersheba. [3] But they were not like their father, for they were greedy for money. They accepted bribes and perverted justice.

[4] Finally, all the elders of Israel met at Ramah to discuss the matter with Samuel. [5] "Look," they told him, "you are now old,

and your sons are not like you. Give us a king to judge us like all the other nations have."

⁶Samuel was displeased with their request and went to the LORD for guidance. ⁷"Do everything they say to you," the LORD replied, "for it is me they are rejecting, not you. They don't want me to be their king any longer. ⁸Ever since I brought them from Egypt they have continually abandoned me and followed other gods. And now they are giving you the same treatment. ⁹Do as they ask, but solemnly warn them about the way a king will reign over them."

¹⁰So Samuel passed on the LORD's warning to the people who were asking him for a king. ¹¹"This is how a king will reign over you," Samuel said. "The king will draft your sons and assign them to his chariots and his charioteers, making them run before his chariots. ¹²Some will be generals and captains in his army,* some will be forced to plow in his fields and harvest his crops, and some will make his weapons and chariot equipment. ¹³The king will take your daughters from you and force them to cook and bake and make perfumes for him. ¹⁴He will take away the best of your fields and vineyards and olive groves and give them to his own officials. ¹⁵He will take a tenth of your grain and your grape harvest and distribute it among his officers and attendants. ¹⁶He will take your male and female slaves and demand the finest of your cattle* and donkeys for his own use. ¹⁷He will demand a tenth of your flocks, and you will be his slaves. ¹⁸When that day comes, you will beg for relief from this king you are demanding, but then the LORD will not help you."

¹⁹But the people refused to listen to Samuel's warning. "Even so, we still want a king," they said. ²⁰"We want to be like the nations around us. Our king will judge us and lead us into battle."

²¹So Samuel repeated to the LORD what the people had said, ²²and the LORD replied, "Do as they say, and give them a king." Then Samuel agreed and sent the people home.

⁹:¹THERE was a wealthy, influential man named Kish from the tribe of Benjamin.

He was the son of Abiel, son of Zeror, son of Becorath, son of Aphiah, of the tribe of Benjamin. ²His son Saul was the most handsome man in Israel—head and shoulders taller than anyone else in the land.

³One day Kish's donkeys strayed away, and he told Saul, "Take a servant with you, and go look for the donkeys." ⁴So Saul took one of the servants and traveled through the hill country of Ephraim, the land of Shalishah, the Shaalim area, and the entire land of Benjamin, but they couldn't find the donkeys anywhere.

⁵Finally, they entered the region of Zuph, and Saul said to his servant, "Let's go home. By now my father will be more worried about us than about the donkeys!"

⁶But the servant said, "I've just thought of something! There is a man of God who lives here in this town. He is held in high honor by all the people because everything he says comes true. Let's go find him. Perhaps he can tell us which way to go."

⁷"But we don't have anything to offer him," Saul replied. "Even our food is gone, and we don't have a thing to give him."

⁸"Well," the servant said, "I have one small silver piece.* We can at least offer it to the man of God and see what happens!" ⁹(In those days if people wanted a message from God, they would say, "Let's go and ask the seer," for prophets used to be called seers.)

¹⁰"All right," Saul agreed, "let's try it!" So they started into the town where the man of God lived.

¹¹As they were climbing the hill to the town, they met some young women coming out to draw water. So Saul and his servant asked, "Is the seer here today?"

¹²"Yes," they replied. "Stay right on this road. He is at the town gates. He has just arrived to take part in a public sacrifice up at the place of worship. ¹³Hurry and catch him before he goes up there to eat. The guests won't begin eating until he arrives to bless the food."

¹⁴So they entered the town, and as they passed through the gates, Samuel was coming out toward them to go up to the place of worship.

¹⁵Now the LORD had told Samuel the previous day, ¹⁶"About this time tomorrow I will send you a man from the land of

Benjamin. Anoint him to be the leader of my people, Israel. He will rescue them from the Philistines, for I have looked down on my people in mercy and have heard their cry."

[17] When Samuel saw Saul, the LORD said, "That's the man I told you about! He will rule my people."

[18] Just then Saul approached Samuel at the gateway and asked, "Can you please tell me where the seer's house is?"

[19] "I am the seer!" Samuel replied. "Go up to the place of worship ahead of me. We will eat there together, and in the morning I'll tell you what you want to know and send you on your way. [20] And don't worry about those donkeys that were lost three days ago, for they have been found. And I am here to tell you that you and your family are the focus of all Israel's hopes."

[21] Saul replied, "But I'm only from the tribe of Benjamin, the smallest tribe in Israel, and my family is the least important of all the families of that tribe! Why are you talking like this to me?"

[22] Then Samuel brought Saul and his servant into the hall and placed them at the head of the table, honoring them above the thirty special guests. [23] Samuel then instructed the cook to bring Saul the finest cut of meat, the piece that had been set aside for the guest of honor. [24] So the cook brought in the meat and placed it

before Saul. "Go ahead and eat it," Samuel said. "I was saving it for you even before I invited these others!" So Saul ate with Samuel that day.

[25] When they came down from the place of worship and returned to town, Samuel took Saul up to the roof of the house and prepared a bed for him there.* [26] At daybreak the next morning, Samuel called to Saul, "Get up! It's time you were on your way." So Saul got ready, and he and Samuel left the house together. [27] When they reached the edge of town, Samuel told Saul to send his servant on ahead. After the servant was gone, Samuel said, "Stay here, for I have received a special message for you from God."

8:12 Hebrew *commanders of thousands and commanders of fifties.*   8:16 As in Greek version; Hebrew reads *young men.*   9:8 Hebrew *¼ shekel of silver,* about 0.1 ounces or 3 grams in weight.   9:25 As in Greek version; Hebrew reads *and talked with him there.*

JOHN 6:22-42

Having heard of Jesus' power, people came to be fed on miracle bread. Jesus instead informed them of the true bread of life.

The next day the crowd that had stayed on the far shore saw that the disciples had taken the only boat, and they realized Jesus had not gone with them. [23] Several boats from Tiberias landed near the place where the Lord had blessed the bread and the people had eaten. [24] So when the

HOW WE LIVE

Obeying God

1 SAMUEL 8:1-21   Samuel knew the consequences of the nation's choice to move from a theocracy (God in charge) to a monarchy (a king in charge). He warned the people about the many changes that would occur with a king in control of their lives: He will draft your sons, he will make some of you slaves, he will take the best crops. But the people persisted. They thought a king would bring much needed change and prestige to their nation. They would "fit in" with the other nations who had kings and would have a strong leader in battle. They didn't think about any long-term consequences.   • When we begin to follow Jesus, we are asking him to be our Lord and King. We cannot continue to live by the standards and values of those around us. We cannot give in to the peer pressure of popular media or compromise our moral standards in order to "fit in." Everything we do, right or wrong, has a consequence. Make the choice to reap the benefits and blessings of obeying your loving King.

crowd saw that neither Jesus nor his disciples were there, they got into the boats and went across to Capernaum to look for him. 25 They found him on the other side of the lake and asked, "Rabbi, when did you get here?"

26 Jesus replied, "I tell you the truth, you want to be with me because I fed you, not because you understood the miraculous signs. 27 But don't be so concerned about perishable things like food. Spend your energy seeking the eternal life that the Son of Man* can give you. For God the Father has given me the seal of his approval."

28 They replied, "We want to perform God's works, too. What should we do?"

29 Jesus told them, "This is the only work God wants from you: Believe in the one he has sent."

30 They answered, "Show us a miraculous sign if you want us to believe in you. What can you do? 31 After all, our ancestors ate manna while they journeyed through the wilderness! The Scriptures say, 'Moses gave them bread from heaven to eat.'*"

32 Jesus said, "I tell you the truth, Moses didn't give you bread from heaven. My Father did. And now he offers you the true bread from heaven. 33 The true bread of God is the one who comes down from heaven and gives life to the world."

34 "Sir," they said, "give us that bread every day."

35 Jesus replied, "I am the bread of life. Whoever comes to me will never be hungry again. Whoever believes in me will never be thirsty. 36 But you haven't believed in me even though you have seen me. 37 However, those the Father has given me will come to me, and I will never reject them. 38 For I have come down from heaven to do the will of God who sent me, not to do my own will. 39 And this is the will of God, that I should not lose even one of all those he has given me, but that I should raise them up at the last day. 40 For it is my Father's will that all who see his Son and believe in him should have eternal life. I will raise them up at the last day."

41 Then the people* began to murmur in disagreement because he had said, "I am the bread that came down from heaven." 42 They said, "Isn't this Jesus, the son of Joseph? We know his father and mother. How can he say, 'I came down from heaven'?"

6:27 "Son of Man" is a title Jesus used for himself.
6:31 Exod 16:4; Ps 78:24. 6:41 Greek *Jewish people;* also in 6:52.

PSALM 106:32-48

At Meribah, too, they angered the LORD,
    causing Moses serious trouble.
33 They made Moses angry,*
    and he spoke foolishly.
34 Israel failed to destroy the nations
    in the land,
    as the LORD had commanded them.
35 Instead, they mingled among the
    pagans
    and adopted their evil customs.
36 They worshiped their idols,
    which led to their downfall.
37 They even sacrificed their sons
    and their daughters to the
    demons.
38 They shed innocent blood,
    the blood of their sons and
    daughters.
By sacrificing them to the idols
    of Canaan,
    they polluted the land with murder.
39 They defiled themselves by their evil
    deeds,
    and their love of idols was adultery
    in the LORD's sight.

40 That is why the LORD's anger burned
    against his people,
    and he abhorred his own special
    possession.
41 He handed them over to pagan
    nations,
    and they were ruled by those who
    hated them.
42 Their enemies crushed them
    and brought them under their
    cruel power.
43 Again and again he rescued them,
    but they chose to rebel against him,
    and they were finally destroyed
    by their sin.
44 Even so, he pitied them in their
    distress
    and listened to their cries.

⁴⁵ He remembered his covenant
    with them
    and relented because of his
        unfailing love.
⁴⁶ He even caused their captors
    to treat them with kindness.

⁴⁷ Save us, O LORD our God!
    Gather us back from among
        the nations,
    so we can thank your holy
        name
    and rejoice and praise you.

⁴⁸ Praise the LORD, the God of Israel,
    who lives from everlasting to
        everlasting!
    Let all the people say, "Amen!"

Praise the LORD!

106:33 Hebrew *They embittered his spirit.*

PROVERBS 14:34-35

Godliness makes a nation great, but sin is a disgrace to any people. ◻ A king rejoices in wise servants but is angry with those who disgrace him.

MAY**11**

1 SAMUEL 10:1–11:15

Saul went looking for runaway donkeys and found himself appointed as the first king of Israel. He tried to hide from that fate, but he could not.

Then Samuel took a flask of olive oil and poured it over Saul's head. He kissed Saul and said, "I am doing this because the LORD has appointed you to be the ruler over Israel, his special possession.* ² When you leave me today, you will see two men beside Rachel's tomb at Zelzah, on the border of Benjamin. They will tell you that the donkeys have been found and that your father has stopped worrying about them and is now worried about you. He is asking, 'Have you seen my son?'

³ "When you get to the oak of Tabor, you will see three men coming toward you who are on their way to worship God at Bethel. One will be bringing three young goats, another will have three loaves of bread, and the third will be carrying a wineskin full of wine. ⁴ They will greet you and offer you two of the loaves, which you are to accept.

⁵ "When you arrive at Gibeah of God,* where the garrison of the Philistines is located, you will meet a band of prophets coming down from the place of worship. They will be playing a harp, a tambourine, a flute, and a lyre, and they will be prophesying. ⁶ At that time the Spirit of the LORD will come powerfully upon you, and you will prophesy with them. You will be changed into a different person. ⁷ After these signs take place, do what must be done, for God is with you. ⁸ Then go down to Gilgal ahead of me. I will join you there to sacrifice burnt offerings and peace offerings. You must wait for seven days until I arrive and give you further instructions."

⁹ As Saul turned and started to leave, God gave him a new heart, and all Samuel's signs were fulfilled that day. ¹⁰ When Saul and his servant arrived at Gibeah, they saw a group of prophets coming toward them. Then the Spirit of God came powerfully upon Saul, and he, too, began to prophesy. ¹¹ When those who knew Saul heard about it, they exclaimed, "What? Is even Saul a prophet? How did the son of Kish become a prophet?"

¹² And one of those standing there said, "Can anyone become a prophet, no matter who his father is?"* So that is the origin of the saying "Is even Saul a prophet?"

¹³ When Saul had finished prophesying, he went up to the place of worship. ¹⁴ "Where have you been?" Saul's uncle asked him and his servant.

"We were looking for the donkeys," Saul replied, "but we couldn't find them. So we went to Samuel to ask him where they were."

¹⁵ "Oh? And what did he say?" his uncle asked.

¹⁶"He told us that the donkeys had already been found," Saul replied. But Saul didn't tell his uncle what Samuel said about the kingdom.

¹⁷Later Samuel called all the people of Israel to meet before the LORD at Mizpah. ¹⁸And he said, "This is what the LORD, the God of Israel, has declared: I brought you from Egypt and rescued you from the Egyptians and from all of the nations that were oppressing you. ¹⁹But though I have rescued you from your misery and distress, you have rejected your God today and have said, 'No, we want a king instead!' Now, therefore, present yourselves before the LORD by tribes and clans."

²⁰So Samuel brought all the tribes of Israel before the LORD, and the tribe of Benjamin was chosen by lot. ²¹Then he brought each family of the tribe of Benjamin before the LORD, and the family of the Matrites was chosen. And finally Saul son of Kish was chosen from among them. But when they looked for him, he had disappeared! ²²So they asked the LORD, "Where is he?"

And the LORD replied, "He is hiding among the baggage." ²³So they found him and brought him out, and he stood head and shoulders above anyone else.

²⁴Then Samuel said to all the people, "This is the man the LORD has chosen as your king. No one in all Israel is like him!"

And all the people shouted, "Long live the king!"

²⁵Then Samuel told the people what the rights and duties of a king were. He wrote them down on a scroll and placed it before the LORD. Then Samuel sent the people home again.

²⁶When Saul returned to his home at Gibeah, a group of men whose hearts God had touched went with him. ²⁷But there were some scoundrels who complained, "How can this man save us?" And they scorned him and refused to bring him gifts. But Saul ignored them.

[Nahash, king of the Ammonites, had been grievously oppressing the people of Gad and Reuben who lived east of the Jordan River. He gouged out the right eye of each of the Israelites living there, and he didn't allow anyone to come and rescue them. In fact, of all the Israelites east of the Jordan, there wasn't a single one whose right eye Nahash had not gouged out. But there were 7,000 men who had escaped from the Ammonites, and they had settled in Jabesh-gilead.]*

11:1ABOUT a month later,* King Nahash of Ammon led his army against the Israelite town of Jabesh-gilead. But all the citizens of Jabesh asked for peace. "Make a treaty with us, and we will be your servants," they pleaded.

²"All right," Nahash said, "but only on one condition. I will gouge out the right eye of every one of you as a disgrace to all Israel!"

³"Give us seven days to send messengers throughout Israel!" replied the elders of Jabesh. "If no one comes to save us, we will agree to your terms."

⁴When the messengers came to Gibeah of Saul and told the people about their plight, everyone broke into tears. ⁵Saul had been plowing a field with his oxen, and when he returned to town, he asked, "What's the matter? Why is everyone crying?" So they told him about the message from Jabesh.

⁶Then the Spirit of God came powerfully upon Saul, and he became very angry. ⁷He took two oxen and cut them into pieces and sent the messengers to carry them throughout Israel with this message: "This is what will happen to the oxen of anyone who refuses to follow Saul and Samuel into battle!" And the LORD made the people afraid of Saul's anger, and all of them came out together as one. ⁸When Saul mobilized them at Bezek, he found that there were 300,000 men from Israel and 30,000* men from Judah.

⁹So Saul sent the messengers back to Jabesh-gilead to say, "We will rescue you by noontime tomorrow!" There was great joy throughout the town when that message arrived!

¹⁰The men of Jabesh then told their enemies, "Tomorrow we will come out to you, and you can do to us whatever you wish." ¹¹But before dawn the next morning, Saul arrived, having divided his army into three detachments. He launched a surprise attack against the Ammonites and slaughtered them the whole morn-

ing. The remnant of their army was so badly scattered that no two of them were left together.

¹²Then the people exclaimed to Samuel, "Now where are those men who said, 'Why should Saul rule over us?' Bring them here, and we will kill them!"

¹³But Saul replied, "No one will be executed today, for today the LORD has rescued Israel!"

¹⁴Then Samuel said to the people, "Come, let us all go to Gilgal to renew the kingdom." ¹⁵So they all went to Gilgal, and in a solemn ceremony before the LORD they made Saul king. Then they offered peace offerings to the LORD, and Saul and all the Israelites were filled with joy.

10:1 Greek version reads *over Israel. And you will rule over the LORD's people and save them from their enemies around them. This will be the sign to you that the LORD has appointed you to be leader over his special possession.* **10:5** Hebrew *Gibeath-elohim.* **10:12** Hebrew *said, "Who is their father?"* **10:27** This paragraph, which is not included in the Masoretic Text, is found in Dead Sea Scroll 4QSamª. **11:1** As in Greek version; Hebrew lacks *About a month later.* **11:8** Dead Sea Scrolls and Greek version read *70,000.*

JOHN 6:43-71
Jesus challenged complacency with outrageous words about eating his flesh. His words seemed offensive on the surface, and those who could not look deeper deserted him.

But Jesus replied, "Stop complaining about what I said. ⁴⁴For no one can come to me unless the Father who sent me draws them to me, and at the last day I will raise them up. ⁴⁵As it is written in the Scriptures,* 'They will all be taught by God.' Everyone who listens to the Father and learns from him comes to me. ⁴⁶(Not that anyone has ever seen the Father; only I, who was sent from God, have seen him.)

⁴⁷"I tell you the truth, anyone who believes has eternal life. ⁴⁸Yes, I am the bread of life! ⁴⁹Your ancestors ate manna in the wilderness, but they all died. ⁵⁰Anyone who eats the bread from heaven, however, will never die. ⁵¹I am the living bread that came down from heaven. Anyone who eats this bread will live forever; and this bread, which I will offer so the world may live, is my flesh."

⁵²Then the people began arguing with each other about what he meant. "How can this man give us his flesh to eat?" they asked.

⁵³So Jesus said again, "I tell you the truth, unless you eat the flesh of the Son of Man and drink his blood, you cannot have eternal life within you. ⁵⁴But anyone who eats my flesh and drinks my blood has eternal life, and I will raise that person at the last day. ⁵⁵For my flesh is true food, and my blood is true drink. ⁵⁶Anyone who eats my flesh and drinks my blood remains in me, and I in him. ⁵⁷I live because of the living Father who sent me; in the same way, anyone who feeds on me will live because of me. ⁵⁸I am the true bread that came down from heaven. Anyone who eats this

HOW WE LIVE

Growing in faith

JOHN 6:51-66 The idea of drinking blood is as repugnant to us as it was to Jesus' followers. Jesus was not talking about literal blood; he was saying that they had to radically internalize him by faith. His life had to become their own. Still, "many of his disciples turned away and deserted him" (6:66). Jesus' radical language had put them to the test. Many, who followed him merely to benefit from his miracle-working power, deserted him. The more the people heard Jesus' real message, the more they divided into two camps—the honest seekers who wanted to understand more, and those who didn't want to accept Jesus on his terms.   • As you gain maturity in your faith, you may become frustrated at some of what you read in the Bible. You may not understand or you may think something is just too difficult to actually live out. When this happens, ask God to show you what the teachings mean and how they apply to your life. Then have the courage to cling to and act on God's truth.

bread will not die as your ancestors did (even though they ate the manna) but will live forever."

⁵⁹He said these things while he was teaching in the synagogue in Capernaum.

⁶⁰Many of his disciples said, "This is very hard to understand. How can anyone accept it?"

⁶¹Jesus was aware that his disciples were complaining, so he said to them, "Does this offend you? ⁶²Then what will you think if you see the Son of Man ascend to heaven again? ⁶³The Spirit alone gives eternal life. Human effort accomplishes nothing. And the very words I have spoken to you are spirit and life. ⁶⁴But some of you do not believe me." (For Jesus knew from the beginning which ones didn't believe, and he knew who would betray him.) ⁶⁵Then he said, "That is why I said that people can't come to me unless the Father gives them to me."

⁶⁶At this point many of his disciples turned away and deserted him. ⁶⁷Then Jesus turned to the Twelve and asked, "Are you also going to leave?"

⁶⁸Simon Peter replied, "Lord, to whom would we go? You have the words that give eternal life. ⁶⁹We believe, and we know you are the Holy One of God.*"

⁷⁰Then Jesus said, "I chose the twelve of you, but one is a devil." ⁷¹He was speaking of Judas, son of Simon Iscariot, one of the Twelve, who would later betray him.

6:45 Greek *in the prophets.* Isa 54:13.   6:69 Other manuscripts read *you are the Christ, the Holy One of God;* still others read *you are the Christ, the Son of God;* and still others read *you are the Christ, the Son of the living God.*

PSALM 107:1-43

Give thanks to the Lord, for he is good!
  His faithful love endures forever.
² Has the Lord redeemed you? Then
      speak out!
  Tell others he has redeemed you
      from your enemies.
³ For he has gathered the exiles from
      many lands,
  from east and west,
  from north and south.

⁴ Some wandered in the wilderness,
  lost and homeless.
⁵ Hungry and thirsty,
  they nearly died.

⁶ "Lord, help!" they cried in their
      trouble,
  and he rescued them from their
      distress.
⁷ He led them straight to safety,
  to a city where they could live.
⁸ Let them praise the Lord for his great
      love
  and for the wonderful things he has
      done for them.
⁹ For he satisfies the thirsty
  and fills the hungry with good things.

¹⁰ Some sat in darkness and deepest
      gloom,
  imprisoned in iron chains of misery.
¹¹ They rebelled against the words of
      God,
  scorning the counsel of the Most
      High.
¹² That is why he broke them with hard
      labor;
  they fell, and no one was there
      to help them.
¹³ "Lord, help!" they cried in their
      trouble,
  and he saved them from their
      distress.
¹⁴ He led them from the darkness and
      deepest gloom;
  he snapped their chains.
¹⁵ Let them praise the Lord for his great
      love
  and for the wonderful things
      he has done for them.
¹⁶ For he broke down their prison gates
      of bronze;
  he cut apart their bars of iron.

¹⁷ Some were fools; they rebelled
  and suffered for their sins.
¹⁸ They couldn't stand the thought
      of food,
  and they were knocking on death's
      door.
¹⁹ "Lord, help!" they cried in their trouble,
  and he saved them from their
      distress.
²⁰ He sent out his word and healed them,
  snatching them from the door
      of death.
²¹ Let them praise the Lord for his great
      love
  and for the wonderful things
      he has done for them.

22 Let them offer sacrifices of
    thanksgiving
    and sing joyfully about his glorious
    acts.

23 Some went off to sea in ships,
    plying the trade routes of the world.
24 They, too, observed the LORD's power
    in action,
    his impressive works on the deepest
    seas.
25 He spoke, and the winds rose,
    stirring up the waves.
26 Their ships were tossed to the heavens
    and plunged again to the depths;
    the sailors cringed in terror.
27 They reeled and staggered like
    drunkards
    and were at their wits' end.
28 "LORD, help!" they cried in their
    trouble,
    and he saved them from their
    distress.
29 He calmed the storm to a whisper
    and stilled the waves.
30 What a blessing was that stillness
    as he brought them safely into
    harbor!
31 Let them praise the LORD for his great
    love
    and for the wonderful things he has
    done for them.
32 Let them exalt him publicly before
    the congregation
    and before the leaders of the
    nation.

33 He changes rivers into deserts,
    and springs of water into dry,
    thirsty land.
34 He turns the fruitful land into salty
    wastelands,

because of the wickedness of those
    who live there.
35 But he also turns deserts into pools
    of water,
    the dry land into springs of water.
36 He brings the hungry to settle there
    and to build their cities.
37 They sow their fields, plant their
    vineyards,
    and harvest their bumper crops.
38 How he blesses them!
    They raise large families there,
    and their herds of livestock
    increase.

39 When they decrease in number and
    become impoverished
    through oppression, trouble,
    and sorrow,
40 the LORD pours contempt on their
    princes,
    causing them to wander in trackless
    wastelands.
41 But he rescues the poor from trouble
    and increases their families like
    flocks of sheep.
42 The godly will see these things and
    be glad,
    while the wicked are struck silent.
43 Those who are wise will take all this
    to heart;
    they will see in our history the
    faithful love of the LORD.

PROVERBS 15:1-3
A gentle answer deflects anger, but harsh
words make tempers flare. □ The tongue
of the wise makes knowledge appealing,
but the mouth of a fool belches out foolishness. □ The LORD is watching everywhere, keeping his eye on both the evil
and the good.

1 SAMUEL 12:1–13:23
Saul quickly took the reins of leadership and just
as quickly made a bad decision. Samuel was there
to inform Saul that as a result of Saul's poor decision, his leadership would end.

MAY**12**

Then Samuel addressed all Israel: "I have
done as you asked and given you a king.
2 Your king is now your leader. I stand here
before you—an old, gray-haired man—

and my sons serve you. I have served as your leader from the time I was a boy to this very day. ³Now testify against me in the presence of the LORD and before his anointed one. Whose ox or donkey have I stolen? Have I ever cheated any of you? Have I ever oppressed you? Have I ever taken a bribe and perverted justice? Tell me and I will make right whatever I have done wrong."

⁴"No," they replied, "you have never cheated or oppressed us, and you have never taken even a single bribe."

⁵"The LORD and his anointed one are my witnesses today," Samuel declared, "that my hands are clean."

"Yes, he is a witness," they replied.

⁶"It was the LORD who appointed Moses and Aaron," Samuel continued. "He brought your ancestors out of the land of Egypt. ⁷Now stand here quietly before the LORD as I remind you of all the great things the LORD has done for you and your ancestors.

⁸"When the Israelites were* in Egypt and cried out to the LORD, he sent Moses and Aaron to rescue them from Egypt and to bring them into this land. ⁹But the people soon forgot about the LORD their God, so he handed them over to Sisera, the commander of Hazor's army, and also to the Philistines and to the king of Moab, who fought against them.

¹⁰"Then they cried to the LORD again and confessed, 'We have sinned by turning away from the LORD and worshiping the images of Baal and Ashtoreth. But we will worship you and you alone if you will rescue us from our enemies.' ¹¹Then the LORD sent Gideon,* Bedan,* Jephthah, and Samuel* to save you, and you lived in safety.

¹²"But when you were afraid of Nahash, the king of Ammon, you came to me and said that you wanted a king to reign over you, even though the LORD your God was already your king. ¹³All right, here is the king you have chosen. You asked for him, and the LORD has granted your request.

¹⁴"Now if you fear and worship the LORD and listen to his voice, and if you do not rebel against the LORD's commands, then both you and your king will show

that you recognize the LORD as your God. ¹⁵But if you rebel against the LORD's commands and refuse to listen to him, then his hand will be as heavy upon you as it was upon your ancestors.

¹⁶"Now stand here and see the great thing the LORD is about to do. ¹⁷You know that it does not rain at this time of the year during the wheat harvest. I will ask the LORD to send thunder and rain today. Then you will realize how wicked you have been in asking the LORD for a king!"

¹⁸So Samuel called to the LORD, and the LORD sent thunder and rain that day. And all the people were terrified of the LORD and of Samuel. ¹⁹"Pray to the LORD your God for us, or we will die!" they all said to Samuel. "For now we have added to our sins by asking for a king."

²⁰"Don't be afraid," Samuel reassured them. "You have certainly done wrong, but make sure now that you worship the LORD with all your heart, and don't turn your back on him. ²¹Don't go back to worshiping worthless idols that cannot help or rescue you—they are totally useless! ²²The LORD will not abandon his people, because that would dishonor his great name. For it has pleased the LORD to make you his very own people.

²³"As for me, I will certainly not sin against the LORD by ending my prayers for you. And I will continue to teach you what is good and right. ²⁴But be sure to fear the LORD and faithfully serve him. Think of all the wonderful things he has done for you. ²⁵But if you continue to sin, you and your king will be swept away."

13:1SAUL was thirty* years old when he became king, and he reigned for forty-two years.*

²Saul selected 3,000 special troops from the army of Israel and sent the rest of the men home. He took 2,000 of the chosen men with him to Micmash and the hill country of Bethel. The other 1,000 went with Saul's son Jonathan to Gibeah in the land of Benjamin.

³Soon after this, Jonathan attacked and defeated the garrison of Philistines at Geba. The news spread quickly among the Philistines. So Saul blew the ram's horn throughout the land, saying, "Hebrews,

hear this! Rise up in revolt!" ⁴All Israel heard the news that Saul had destroyed the Philistine garrison at Geba and that the Philistines now hated the Israelites more than ever. So the entire Israelite army was summoned to join Saul at Gilgal.

⁵The Philistines mustered a mighty army of 3,000* chariots, 6,000 charioteers, and as many warriors as the grains of sand on the seashore! They camped at Micmash east of Beth-aven. ⁶The men of Israel saw what a tight spot they were in; and because they were hard pressed by the enemy, they tried to hide in caves, thickets, rocks, holes, and cisterns. ⁷Some of them crossed the Jordan River and escaped into the land of Gad and Gilead.

Meanwhile, Saul stayed at Gilgal, and his men were trembling with fear. ⁸Saul waited there seven days for Samuel, as Samuel had instructed him earlier, but Samuel still didn't come. Saul realized that his troops were rapidly slipping away. ⁹So he demanded, "Bring me the burnt offering and the peace offerings!" And Saul sacrificed the burnt offering himself.

¹⁰Just as Saul was finishing with the burnt offering, Samuel arrived. Saul went out to meet and welcome him, ¹¹but Samuel said, "What is this you have done?"

Saul replied, "I saw my men scattering from me, and you didn't arrive when you said you would, and the Philistines are at Micmash ready for battle. ¹²So I said, 'The Philistines are ready to march against us at Gilgal, and I haven't even asked for the LORD's help!' So I felt compelled to offer the burnt offering myself before you came."

¹³"How foolish!" Samuel exclaimed. "You have not kept the command the LORD your God gave you. Had you kept it, the LORD would have established your kingdom over Israel forever. ¹⁴But now your kingdom must end, for the LORD has sought out a man after his own heart. The LORD has already appointed him to be the leader of his people, because you have not kept the LORD's command."

¹⁵Samuel then left Gilgal and went on his way, but the rest of the troops went with Saul to meet the army. They went up from Gilgal to Gibeah in the land of Benjamin.* When Saul counted the men who were still with him, he found only 600 were left! ¹⁶Saul and Jonathan and the troops with them were staying at Geba in the land of Benjamin. The Philistines set up their camp at Micmash. ¹⁷Three raiding parties soon left the camp of the Philistines. One went north toward Ophrah in the land of Shual, ¹⁸another went west to Beth-horon, and the third moved toward the border above the valley of Zeboim near the wilderness.

¹⁹There were no blacksmiths in the land of Israel in those days. The Philistines wouldn't allow them for fear they would

---

HOW WE LIVE

Obeying God

1 SAMUEL 13:13-14 Saul experienced his greatest successes as a king when he obeyed God's commands. His greatest failures were the direct results of acting on his own. In this passage we see that his disobedience and attempts to rationalize his sin cost him his kingship. Samuel later reminded him that "obedience is better than sacrifice" (1 Samuel 15:22, May 14). • One of the most difficult aspects of discipleship is simply obeying what God says. Why does God require obedience? Because he's an ogre who wants his way? Because he rules his people with an iron fist? Just the opposite: it is because he loves us. Obedience shows our true love for him, and love is what God is all about. He always has our greater good in mind. • Obedience is the mark of a Christian. In the New Testament, Jesus said, "When you obey my commandments, you remain in my love. . . . You are my friends if you do what I command" (John 15:10, 14, May 26).

make swords and spears for the Hebrews. [20]So whenever the Israelites needed to sharpen their plowshares, picks, axes, or sickles,* they had to take them to a Philistine blacksmith. [21](The charges were as follows: a quarter of an ounce of silver* for sharpening a plowshare or a pick, and an eighth of an ounce* for sharpening an ax, a sickle, or an ox goad.) [22]So on the day of the battle none of the people of Israel had a sword or spear, except for Saul and Jonathan.

[23]The pass at Micmash had meanwhile been secured by a contingent of the Philistine army.

12:8 Hebrew *When Jacob was.* The names "Jacob" and "Israel" are often interchanged throughout the Old Testament, referring sometimes to the individual patriarch and sometimes to the nation. **12:11a** Hebrew *Jerub-baal,* another name for Gideon; see Judg 6:32. **12:11b** Greek and Syriac versions read *Barak.* **12:11c** Greek and Syriac versions read *Samson.* **13:1a** As in a few Greek manuscripts; the number is missing in the Hebrew. **13:1b** Hebrew *reigned . . . and two;* the number is incomplete in the Hebrew. Compare Acts 13:21. **13:5** As in Greek and Syriac versions; Hebrew reads *30,000.* **13:15** As in Greek version; Hebrew reads *Samuel then left Gilgal and went to Gibeah in the land of Benjamin.* **13:20** As in Greek version; Hebrew reads *or plowshares.* **13:21a** Hebrew *1 pim* [8 grams]. **13:21b** Hebrew ⅓ *of a shekel* [4 grams].

JOHN 7:1-30

The Festival of Shelters commemorated their journey from Egypt, living in tents as they went. At the Festival, Jesus was steeped in controversy.

After this, Jesus traveled around Galilee. He wanted to stay out of Judea, where the Jewish leaders were plotting his death. [2]But soon it was time for the Jewish Festival of Shelters, [3]and Jesus' brothers said to him, "Leave here and go to Judea, where your followers can see your miracles! [4]You can't become famous if you hide like this! If you can do such wonderful things, show yourself to the world!" [5]For even his brothers didn't believe in him.

[6]Jesus replied, "Now is not the right time for me to go, but you can go anytime. [7]The world can't hate you, but it does hate me because I accuse it of doing evil. [8]You go on. I'm not going* to this festival, because my time has not yet come." [9]After saying these things, Jesus remained in Galilee.

[10]But after his brothers left for the festival, Jesus also went, though secretly, staying out of public view. [11]The Jewish leaders tried to find him at the festival and kept asking if anyone had seen him. [12]There was a lot of grumbling about him among the crowds. Some argued, "He's a good man," but others said, "He's nothing but a fraud who deceives the people." [13]But no one had the courage to speak favorably about him in public, for they were afraid of getting in trouble with the Jewish leaders.

[14]Then, midway through the festival, Jesus went up to the Temple and began to teach. [15]The people* were surprised when they heard him. "How does he know so much when he hasn't been trained?" they asked.

[16]So Jesus told them, "My message is not my own; it comes from God who sent me. [17]Anyone who wants to do the will of God will know whether my teaching is from God or is merely my own. [18]Those who speak for themselves want glory only for themselves, but a person who seeks to honor the one who sent him speaks truth, not lies. [19]Moses gave you the law, but none of you obeys it! In fact, you are trying to kill me."

[20]The crowd replied, "You're demon possessed! Who's trying to kill you?"

[21]Jesus replied, "I did one miracle on the Sabbath, and you were amazed. [22]But you work on the Sabbath, too, when you obey Moses' law of circumcision. (Actually, this tradition of circumcision began with the patriarchs, long before the law of Moses.) [23]For if the correct time for circumcising your son falls on the Sabbath, you go ahead and do it so as not to break the law of Moses. So why should you be angry with me for healing a man on the Sabbath? [24]Look beneath the surface so you can judge correctly."

[25]Some of the people who lived in Jerusalem started to ask each other, "Isn't this the man they are trying to kill? [26]But here he is, speaking in public, and they say nothing to him. Could our leaders possibly believe that he is the Messiah? [27]But how could he be? For we know where this man comes from. When the Messiah comes, he will simply appear; no one will know where he comes from."

[28]While Jesus was teaching in the Temple, he called out, "Yes, you know me, and

you know where I come from. But I'm not here on my own. The one who sent me is true, and you don't know him. 29But I know him because I come from him, and he sent me to you." 30Then the leaders tried to arrest him; but no one laid a hand on him, because his time* had not yet come.

7:8 Some manuscripts read *not yet going.* 7:15 Greek *Jewish people.* 7:30 Greek *his hour.*

PSALM 108:1-13
A song. A psalm of David.

1 **M**y heart is confident in you, O God;
    no wonder I can sing your praises
        with all my heart!
2 Wake up, lyre and harp!
    I will wake the dawn with
        my song.
3 I will thank you, LORD, among all
        the people.
    I will sing your praises among
        the nations.
4 For your unfailing love is higher
        than the heavens.
    Your faithfulness reaches to
        the clouds.
5 Be exalted, O God, above the highest
        heavens.
    May your glory shine over all
        the earth.
6 Now rescue your beloved people.
    Answer and save us by your power.

7 God has promised this by his
        holiness*:
"I will divide up Shechem with joy.
    I will measure out the valley
        of Succoth.
8 Gilead is mine,
    and Manasseh, too.
Ephraim, my helmet, will produce
        my warriors,
    and Judah, my scepter, will produce
        my kings.
9 But Moab, my washbasin, will become
        my servant,
    and I will wipe my feet on Edom
    and shout in triumph over Philistia."

10 Who will bring me into the fortified
        city?
    Who will bring me victory over
        Edom?
11 Have you rejected us, O God?
    Will you no longer march with
        our armies?
12 Oh, please help us against our enemies,
    for all human help is useless.
13 With God's help we will do mighty
        things,
    for he will trample down our foes.

108:7 Or *in his sanctuary.*

PROVERBS 15:4
Gentle words are a tree of life; a deceitful tongue crushes the spirit.

MAY**13**

1 SAMUEL 14:1-52
Saul's son Jonathan came to the forefront as a man trusting in God. Jonathan was Saul's oldest son, thus the heir to the throne. Yet he recognized and accepted that God had chosen David, his best friend, to be the next king.

One day Jonathan said to his armor bearer, "Come on, let's go over to where the Philistines have their outpost." But Jonathan did not tell his father what he was doing.

2Meanwhile, Saul and his 600 men were camped on the outskirts of Gibeah, around the pomegranate tree* at Migron. 3Among Saul's men was Ahijah the priest, who was wearing the ephod, the priestly vest. Ahijah was the son of Ichabod's brother Ahitub, son of Phinehas, son of Eli, the priest of the LORD who had served at Shiloh.

No one realized that Jonathan had left the Israelite camp. 4To reach the Philistine outpost, Jonathan had to go down between two rocky cliffs that were called

Bozez and Seneh. ⁵The cliff on the north was in front of Micmash, and the one on the south was in front of Geba. ⁶"Let's go across to the outpost of those pagans," Jonathan said to his armor bearer. "Perhaps the LORD will help us, for nothing can hinder the LORD. He can win a battle whether he has many warriors or only a few!"

⁷"Do what you think is best," the armor bearer replied. "I'm with you completely, whatever you decide."

⁸"All right then," Jonathan told him. "We will cross over and let them see us. ⁹If they say to us, 'Stay where you are or we'll kill you,' then we will stop and not go up to them. ¹⁰But if they say, 'Come on up and fight,' then we will go up. That will be the LORD's sign that he will help us defeat them."

¹¹When the Philistines saw them coming, they shouted, "Look! The Hebrews are crawling out of their holes!" ¹²Then the men from the outpost shouted to Jonathan, "Come on up here, and we'll teach you a lesson!"

"Come on, climb right behind me," Jonathan said to his armor bearer, "for the LORD will help us defeat them!"

¹³So they climbed up using both hands and feet, and the Philistines fell before Jonathan, and his armor bearer killed those who came behind them. ¹⁴They killed some twenty men in all, and their bodies were scattered over about half an acre.*

¹⁵Suddenly, panic broke out in the Philistine army, both in the camp and in the field, including even the outposts and raiding parties. And just then an earthquake struck, and everyone was terrified.

¹⁶Saul's lookouts in Gibeah of Benjamin saw a strange sight—the vast army of Philistines began to melt away in every direction. ¹⁷"Call the roll and find out who's missing," Saul ordered. And when they checked, they found that Jonathan and his armor bearer were gone.

¹⁸Then Saul shouted to Ahijah, "Bring the ephod here!" For at that time Ahijah was wearing the ephod in front of the Israelites.* ¹⁹But while Saul was talking to the priest, the confusion in the Philistine camp grew louder and louder. So Saul said to the priest, "Never mind; let's get going!"*

²⁰Then Saul and all his men rushed out to the battle and found the Philistines killing each other. There was terrible confusion everywhere. ²¹Even the Hebrews who had previously gone over to the Philistine army revolted and joined in with Saul, Jonathan, and the rest of the Israelites. ²²Likewise, the men of Israel who were hiding in the hill country of Ephraim joined the chase when they saw the Philistines running away. ²³So the LORD saved Israel that day, and the battle continued to rage even beyond Beth-aven.

²⁴Now the men of Israel were pressed to exhaustion that day, because Saul had placed them under an oath, saying, "Let a curse fall on anyone who eats before evening—before I have full revenge on my enemies." So no one ate anything all day, ²⁵even though they had all found honeycomb on the ground in the forest. ²⁶They didn't dare touch the honey because they all feared the oath they had taken.

²⁷But Jonathan had not heard his father's command, and he dipped the end of his stick into a piece of honeycomb and ate the honey. After he had eaten it, he felt refreshed.* ²⁸But one of the men saw him and said, "Your father made the army take a strict oath that anyone who eats food today will be cursed. That is why everyone is weary and faint."

²⁹"My father has made trouble for us all!" Jonathan exclaimed. "A command like that only hurts us. See how refreshed I am now that I have eaten this little bit of honey. ³⁰If the men had been allowed to eat freely from the food they found among our enemies, think how many more Philistines we could have killed!"

³¹They chased and killed the Philistines all day from Micmash to Aijalon, growing more and more faint. ³²That evening they rushed for the battle plunder and butchered the sheep, goats, cattle, and calves, but they ate them without draining the blood. ³³Someone reported to Saul, "Look, the men are sinning against the LORD by eating meat that still has blood in it."

"That is very wrong," Saul said. "Find a large stone and roll it over here. ³⁴Then go out among the troops and tell them,

'Bring the cattle, sheep, and goats here to me. Kill them here, and drain the blood before you eat them. Do not sin against the Lord by eating meat with the blood still in it.'"

So that night all the troops brought their animals and slaughtered them there. ³⁵Then Saul built an altar to the Lord; it was the first of the altars he built to the Lord.

³⁶Then Saul said, "Let's chase the Philistines all night and plunder them until sunrise. Let's destroy every last one of them."

His men replied, "We'll do whatever you think is best."

But the priest said, "Let's ask God first."

³⁷So Saul asked God, "Should we go after the Philistines? Will you help us defeat them?" But God made no reply that day.

³⁸Then Saul said to the leaders, "Something's wrong! I want all my army commanders to come here. We must find out what sin was committed today. ³⁹I vow by the name of the Lord who rescued Israel that the sinner will surely die, even if it is my own son Jonathan!" But no one would tell him what the trouble was.

⁴⁰Then Saul said, "Jonathan and I will stand over here, and all of you stand over there."

And the people responded to Saul, "Whatever you think is best."

⁴¹Then Saul prayed, "O Lord, God of Israel, please show us who is guilty and who is innocent.*" Then they cast sacred lots, and Jonathan and Saul were chosen as the guilty ones, and the people were declared innocent.

⁴²Then Saul said, "Now cast lots again and choose between me and Jonathan." And Jonathan was shown to be the guilty one.

⁴³"Tell me what you have done," Saul demanded of Jonathan.

"I tasted a little honey," Jonathan admitted. "It was only a little bit on the end of my stick. Does that deserve death?"

⁴⁴"Yes, Jonathan," Saul said, "you must die! May God strike me and even kill me if you do not die for this."

⁴⁵But the people broke in and said to Saul, "Jonathan has won this great victory for Israel. Should he die? Far from it! As surely as the Lord lives, not one hair on his head will be touched, for God helped him do a great deed today." So the people rescued Jonathan, and he was not put to death.

⁴⁶Then Saul called back the army from chasing the Philistines, and the Philistines returned home.

⁴⁷Now when Saul had secured his grasp on Israel's throne, he fought against his enemies in every direction—against Moab, Ammon, Edom, the kings of Zobah, and

Relying on God's power

HOW WE LIVE

1 SAMUEL 14:6-10 Most of what we read about Jonathan is in the context of his role as David's trusted friend and ally. This story in 1 Samuel 14 reveals that Jonathan was a great man of faith in his own right. He believed that whatever God called him to do was possible. Who would have thought that two soldiers could set in motion the defeat of a whole army? But Jonathan followed God step by step. First he decided to go. Then he recruited the logical assistant, his armor-bearer who had accompanied him in the heat of battle before. Then he watched for the Lord's guidance: "That will be the Lord's sign that he will help us defeat them" (14:9-10). Jonathan was right. With each step he followed what he believed was God's guidance, and he found the strength to do what was required. • Jonathan took action and relied on God for guidance and power. It is not the strength that you find in yourself that carries you through the challenges. Instead, it is the strength of God's presence that enables you to face life, as precarious as it can be, and accomplish great things.

the Philistines. And wherever he turned, he was victorious. [48]He performed great deeds and conquered the Amalekites, saving Israel from all those who had plundered them.

[49]Saul's sons included Jonathan, Ishbosheth,* and Malkishua. He also had two daughters: Merab, who was older, and Michal. [50]Saul's wife was Ahinoam, the daughter of Ahimaaz. The commander of Saul's army was Abner, the son of Saul's uncle Ner. [51]Saul's father, Kish, and Abner's father, Ner, were both sons of Abiel.

[52]The Israelites fought constantly with the Philistines throughout Saul's lifetime. So whenever Saul observed a young man who was brave and strong, he drafted him into his army.

14:2 Or *around the rock of Rimmon;* compare Judg 20:45, 47; 21:13.   14:14 Hebrew *half a yoke;* a "yoke" was the amount of land plowed by a pair of yoked oxen in one day.   14:18 As in some Greek manuscripts; Hebrew reads *"Bring the Ark of God." For at that time the Ark of God was with the Israelites.*   14:19 Hebrew *Withdraw your hand.*   14:27 Or *his eyes brightened;* similarly in 14:29.   14:41 Greek version adds *If the fault is with me or my son Jonathan, respond with Urim; but if the men of Israel are at fault, respond with Thummim.*   14:49 Hebrew *Ishvi,* a variant name for Ishbosheth; also known as Esh-baal.

JOHN 7:31-53

Jesus' controversial teaching and miracles led to much speculation and disagreement over who he was. Those with open hearts eventually got it right, but his hardhearted enemies plotted against him.

Many among the crowds at the Temple believed in him [Jesus]. "After all," they said, "would you expect the Messiah to do more miraculous signs than this man has done?"

[32]When the Pharisees heard that the crowds were whispering such things, they and the leading priests sent Temple guards to arrest Jesus. [33]But Jesus told them, "I will be with you only a little longer. Then I will return to the one who sent me. [34]You will search for me but not find me. And you cannot go where I am going."

[35]The Jewish leaders were puzzled by this statement. "Where is he planning to go?" they asked. "Is he thinking of leaving the country and going to the Jews in other lands?* Maybe he will even teach the Greeks! [36]What does he mean when

he says, 'You will search for me but not find me,' and 'You cannot go where I am going'?"

[37]On the last day, the climax of the festival, Jesus stood and shouted to the crowds, "Anyone who is thirsty may come to me! [38]Anyone who believes in me may come and drink! For the Scriptures declare, 'Rivers of living water will flow from his heart.' "* [39](When he said "living water," he was speaking of the Spirit, who would be given to everyone believing in him. But the Spirit had not yet been given,* because Jesus had not yet entered into his glory.)

[40]When the crowds heard him say this, some of them declared, "Surely this man is the Prophet we've been expecting."* [41]Others said, "He is the Messiah." Still others said, "But he can't be! Will the Messiah come from Galilee? [42]For the Scriptures clearly state that the Messiah will be born of the royal line of David, in Bethlehem, the village where King David was born."* [43]So the crowd was divided about him. [44]Some even wanted him arrested, but no one laid a hand on him.

[45]When the Temple guards returned without having arrested Jesus, the leading priests and Pharisees demanded, "Why didn't you bring him in?"

[46]"We have never heard anyone speak like this!" the guards responded.

[47]"Have you been led astray, too?" the Pharisees mocked. [48]"Is there a single one of us rulers or Pharisees who believes in him? [49]This foolish crowd follows him, but they are ignorant of the law. God's curse is on them!"

[50]Then Nicodemus, the leader who had met with Jesus earlier, spoke up. [51]"Is it legal to convict a man before he is given a hearing?" he asked.

[52]They replied, "Are you from Galilee, too? Search the Scriptures and see for yourself—no prophet ever comes* from Galilee!"

[The most ancient Greek manuscripts do not include John 7:53–8:11.]

[53]Then the meeting broke up, and everybody went home.

7:35 Or *the Jews who live among the Greeks?*   7:37-38 Or *"Let anyone who is thirsty come to me and drink. [38]For the*

Scriptures declare, 'Rivers of living water will flow from the heart of anyone who believes in me.'" **7:39** Some manuscripts read *But as yet there was no Spirit.* Still others read *But as yet there was no Holy Spirit.* **7:40** See Deut 18:15, 18; Mal 4:5-6. **7:42** See Mic 5:2. **7:52** Some manuscripts read *the prophet does not come.*

PSALM 109:1-31
For the choir director: A psalm of David.

¹ **O** God, whom I praise,
    don't stand silent and aloof
² while the wicked slander me
    and tell lies about me.
³ They surround me with hateful
        words
    and fight against me for no reason.
⁴ I love them, but they try to destroy me
        with accusations
    even as I am praying for them!
⁵ They repay evil for good,
    and hatred for my love.

⁶ They say,* "Get an evil person to turn
        against him.
    Send an accuser to bring him to trial.
⁷ When his case comes up for
        judgment,
    let him be pronounced guilty.
    Count his prayers as sins.
⁸ Let his years be few;
    let someone else take his position.
⁹ May his children become fatherless,
    and his wife a widow.
¹⁰ May his children wander as beggars
    and be driven from their ruined
        homes.
¹¹ May creditors seize his entire estate,
    and strangers take all he has earned.
¹² Let no one be kind to him;
    let no one pity his fatherless
        children.
¹³ May all his offspring die.
    May his family name be blotted
        out in a single generation.
¹⁴ May the LORD never forget the sins
        of his fathers;
    may his mother's sins never
        be erased from the record.
¹⁵ May the LORD always remember
        these sins,
    and may his name disappear from
        human memory.
¹⁶ For he refused all kindness to others;
    he persecuted the poor and needy,
    and he hounded the brokenhearted
        to death.

¹⁷ He loved to curse others;
    now you curse him.
    He never blessed others;
    now don't you bless him.
¹⁸ Cursing is as natural to him
        as his clothing,
    or the water he drinks,
    or the rich food he eats.
¹⁹ Now may his curses return and cling
        to him like clothing;
    may they be tied around him like
        a belt."

²⁰ May those curses become the LORD's
        punishment
    for my accusers who speak evil
        of me.
²¹ But deal well with me, O Sovereign
        LORD,
    for the sake of your own reputation!
    Rescue me
    because you are so faithful and good.
²² For I am poor and needy,
    and my heart is full of pain.
²³ I am fading like a shadow at dusk;
    I am brushed off like a locust.
²⁴ My knees are weak from fasting,
    and I am skin and bones.
²⁵ I am a joke to people everywhere;
    when they see me, they shake their
        heads in scorn.

²⁶ Help me, O LORD my God!
    Save me because of your unfailing
        love.
²⁷ Let them see that this is your doing,
    that you yourself have done it,
        LORD.
²⁸ Then let them curse me if they like,
    but you will bless me!
    When they attack me, they will
        be disgraced!
    But I, your servant, will go right
        on rejoicing!
²⁹ May my accusers be clothed with
        disgrace;
    may their humiliation cover them
        like a cloak.
³⁰ But I will give repeated thanks
        to the LORD,
    praising him to everyone.
³¹ For he stands beside the needy,
    ready to save them from those
        who condemn them.

109:6 Hebrew lacks *They say.*

PROVERBS 15:5-7

Only a fool despises a parent's* discipline; whoever learns from correction is wise. □There is treasure in the house of the godly, but the earnings of the wicked bring trouble. □The lips of the wise give good advice; the heart of a fool has none to give.

15:5 Hebrew *father's.*

MAY**14**

1 SAMUEL 15:1–16:23

Because of Saul's refusal to be a holy king, God rejected him and put a young man named David in place to become Israel's next king—although many years would pass before David would reign.

One day Samuel said to Saul, "It was the LORD who told me to anoint you as king of his people, Israel. Now listen to this message from the LORD! ²This is what the LORD of Heaven's Armies has declared: I have decided to settle accounts with the nation of Amalek for opposing Israel when they came from Egypt. ³Now go and completely destroy* the entire Amalekite nation—men, women, children, babies, cattle, sheep, goats, camels, and donkeys."

⁴So Saul mobilized his army at Telaim. There were 200,000 soldiers from Israel and 10,000 men from Judah. ⁵Then Saul and his army went to a town of the Amalekites and lay in wait in the valley. ⁶Saul sent this warning to the Kenites: "Move away from where the Amalekites live, or you will die with them. For you showed kindness to all the people of Israel when they came up from Egypt." So the Kenites packed up and left.

⁷Then Saul slaughtered the Amalekites from Havilah all the way to Shur, east of Egypt. ⁸He captured Agag, the Amalekite king, but completely destroyed everyone else. ⁹Saul and his men spared Agag's life and kept the best of the sheep and goats, the cattle, the fat calves, and the lambs—everything, in fact, that appealed to them. They destroyed only what was worthless or of poor quality.

¹⁰Then the LORD said to Samuel, ¹¹"I am sorry that I ever made Saul king, for he has not been loyal to me and has refused to obey my command." Samuel was so deeply moved when he heard this that he cried out to the LORD all night.

¹²Early the next morning Samuel went to find Saul. Someone told him, "Saul went to the town of Carmel to set up a monument to himself; then he went on to Gilgal."

¹³When Samuel finally found him, Saul greeted him cheerfully. "May the LORD bless you," he said. "I have carried out the LORD's command!"

¹⁴"Then what is all the bleating of sheep and goats and the lowing of cattle I hear?" Samuel demanded.

¹⁵"It's true that the army spared the best of the sheep, goats, and cattle," Saul admitted. "But they are going to sacrifice them to the LORD your God. We have destroyed everything else."

¹⁶Then Samuel said to Saul, "Stop! Listen to what the LORD told me last night!"

"What did he tell you?" Saul asked.

¹⁷And Samuel told him, "Although you may think little of yourself, are you not the leader of the tribes of Israel? The LORD has anointed you king of Israel. ¹⁸And the LORD sent you on a mission and told you, 'Go and completely destroy the sinners, the Amalekites, until they are all dead.' ¹⁹Why haven't you obeyed the LORD? Why did you rush for the plunder and do what was evil in the LORD's sight?"

²⁰"But I did obey the LORD," Saul insisted. "I carried out the mission he gave me. I brought back King Agag, but I destroyed everyone else. ²¹Then my troops brought in the best of the sheep, goats, cattle, and plunder to sacrifice to the LORD your God in Gilgal."

²²But Samuel replied,

"What is more pleasing
  to the LORD:
  your burnt offerings and
    sacrifices
  or your obedience to his voice?
Listen! Obedience is better than
    sacrifice,
  and submission is better than
    offering the fat of rams.
²³ Rebellion is as sinful as witchcraft,
  and stubbornness as bad as
    worshiping idols.
So because you have rejected
    the command of the LORD,
  he has rejected you as king."

²⁴Then Saul admitted to Samuel, "Yes, I have sinned. I have disobeyed your instructions and the LORD's command, for I was afraid of the people and did what they demanded. ²⁵But now, please forgive my sin and come back with me so that I may worship the LORD."

²⁶But Samuel replied, "I will not go back with you! Since you have rejected the LORD's command, he has rejected you as king of Israel."

²⁷As Samuel turned to go, Saul tried to hold him back and tore the hem of his robe. ²⁸And Samuel said to him, "The LORD has torn the kingdom of Israel from you today and has given it to someone else—one who is better than you. ²⁹And he who is the Glory of Israel will not lie, nor will he change his mind, for he is not human that he should change his mind!"

³⁰Then Saul pleaded again, "I know I have sinned. But please, at least honor me before the elders of my people and before Israel by coming back with me so that I may worship the LORD your God." ³¹So Samuel finally agreed and went back with him, and Saul worshiped the LORD.

³²Then Samuel said, "Bring King Agag to me." Agag arrived full of hope, for he thought, "Surely the worst is over, and I have been spared!"* ³³But Samuel said, "As your sword has killed the sons of many mothers, now your mother will be childless." And Samuel cut Agag to pieces before the LORD at Gilgal.

³⁴Then Samuel went home to Ramah, and Saul returned to his house at Gibeah of Saul. ³⁵Samuel never went to meet with Saul again, but he mourned constantly for him. And the LORD was sorry he had ever made Saul king of Israel.

16:1Now the LORD said to Samuel, "You have mourned long enough for Saul. I have rejected him as king of Israel, so fill your flask with olive oil and go to Bethlehem. Find a man named Jesse who lives there, for I have selected one of his sons to be my king."

²But Samuel asked, "How can I do that? If Saul hears about it, he will kill me."

"Take a heifer with you," the LORD replied, "and say that you have come to make a sacrifice to the LORD. ³Invite Jesse to the sacrifice, and I will show you which of his sons to anoint for me."

⁴So Samuel did as the LORD instructed. When he arrived at Bethlehem, the elders of the town came trembling to meet him. "What's wrong?" they asked. "Do you come in peace?"

⁵"Yes," Samuel replied. "I have come to sacrifice to the LORD. Purify yourselves and come with me to the sacrifice." Then Samuel performed the purification rite for Jesse and his sons and invited them to the sacrifice, too.

⁶When they arrived, Samuel took one look at Eliab and thought, "Surely this is the LORD's anointed!"

⁷But the LORD said to Samuel, "Don't judge by his appearance or height, for I have rejected him. The LORD doesn't see things the way you see them. People judge by outward appearance, but the LORD looks at the heart."

⁸Then Jesse told his son Abinadab to step forward and walk in front of Samuel. But Samuel said, "This is not the one the LORD has chosen." ⁹Next Jesse summoned Shimea,* but Samuel said, "Neither is this the one the LORD has chosen." ¹⁰In the same way all seven of Jesse's sons were presented to Samuel. But Samuel said to Jesse, "The LORD has not chosen any of these." ¹¹Then Samuel asked, "Are these all the sons you have?"

"There is still the youngest," Jesse

replied. "But he's out in the fields watching the sheep and goats."

"Send for him at once," Samuel said. "We will not sit down to eat until he arrives."

[12] So Jesse sent for him. He was dark and handsome, with beautiful eyes.

And the LORD said, "This is the one; anoint him."

[13] So as David stood there among his brothers, Samuel took the flask of olive oil he had brought and anointed David with the oil. And the Spirit of the LORD came powerfully upon David from that day on. Then Samuel returned to Ramah.

[14] Now the Spirit of the LORD had left Saul, and the LORD sent a tormenting spirit* that filled him with depression and fear.

[15] Some of Saul's servants said to him, "A tormenting spirit from God is troubling you. [16] Let us find a good musician to play the harp whenever the tormenting spirit troubles you. He will play soothing music, and you will soon be well again."

[17] "All right," Saul said. "Find me someone who plays well, and bring him here."

[18] One of the servants said to Saul, "One of Jesse's sons from Bethlehem is a talented harp player. Not only that—he is a brave warrior, a man of war, and has good judgment. He is also a fine-looking young man, and the LORD is with him."

[19] So Saul sent messengers to Jesse to say, "Send me your son David, the shepherd." [20] Jesse responded by sending David to Saul, along with a young goat, a donkey loaded with bread, and a wineskin full of wine.

[21] So David went to Saul and began serving him. Saul loved David very much, and David became his armor bearer.

[22] Then Saul sent word to Jesse asking, "Please let David remain in my service, for I am very pleased with him."

[23] And whenever the tormenting spirit from God troubled Saul, David would play the harp. Then Saul would feel better, and the tormenting spirit would go away.

15:3 The Hebrew term used here refers to the complete consecration of things or people to the LORD, either by destroying them or by giving them as an offering; also in 15:8, 9, 15, 18, 20, 21. 15:32 Dead Sea Scrolls and Greek version read *Agag arrived hesitantly, for he thought, "Surely this is the bitterness of death."* 16:9 Hebrew *Shammah,* a variant spelling of Shimea; compare 1 Chr 2:13; 20:7. 16:14 Or *an evil spirit;* also in 16:15, 16, 23.

JOHN 8:1-20

In the following story, Jesus refused to condemn a woman who had done condemnable acts. He knew he was being set up, so he turned people's expectations inside out for the sake of love, forgiveness, and truth.

Jesus returned to the Mount of Olives, [2] but early the next morning he was back again at the Temple. A crowd soon gathered, and he sat down and taught them. [3] As he was speaking, the teachers of religious law and the Pharisees brought a woman who had been caught in the act of adultery. They put her in front of the crowd.

[4] "Teacher," they said to Jesus, "this woman was caught in the act of adultery. [5] The law of Moses says to stone her. What do you say?"

[6] They were trying to trap him into saying something they could use against him, but Jesus stooped down and wrote in the dust with his finger. [7] They kept demanding an answer, so he stood up again and said, "All right, but let the one who has never sinned throw the first stone!" [8] Then he stooped down again and wrote in the dust.

[9] When the accusers heard this, they slipped away one by one, beginning with the oldest, until only Jesus was left in the middle of the crowd with the woman. [10] Then Jesus stood up again and said to the woman, "Where are your accusers? Didn't even one of them condemn you?"

[11] "No, Lord," she said.

And Jesus said, "Neither do I. Go and sin no more."

---

[12] Jesus spoke to the people once more and said, "I am the light of the world. If you follow me, you won't have to walk in darkness, because you will have the light that leads to life."

[13] The Pharisees replied, "You are making those claims about yourself! Such testimony is not valid."

[14] Jesus told them, "These claims are valid even though I make them about myself. For I know where I came from and where I am going, but you don't know this about me. [15] You judge me by human standards, but I do not judge anyone.

[16]And if I did, my judgment would be correct in every respect because I am not alone. The Father* who sent me is with me. [17]Your own law says that if two people agree about something, their witness is accepted as fact.* [18]I am one witness, and my Father who sent me is the other."

[19]"Where is your father?" they asked.

Jesus answered, "Since you don't know who I am, you don't know who my Father is. If you knew me, you would also know my Father." [20]Jesus made these statements while he was teaching in the section of the Temple known as the Treasury. But he was not arrested, because his time* had not yet come.

8:16 Some manuscripts read *The One.*   **8:17** See Deut 19:15.   **8:20** Greek *his hour.*

PSALM 110:1-7
A psalm of David.

[1] The LORD said to my Lord,
    "Sit in the place of honor at my
        right hand
until I humble your enemies,
    making them a footstool under
        your feet."

[2] The LORD will extend your powerful
        kingdom from Jerusalem*;
    you will rule over your enemies.

[3] When you go to war,
    your people will serve you willingly.
You are arrayed in holy garments,
    and your strength will be renewed
        each day like the morning dew.

[4] The LORD has taken an oath and will
        not break his vow:
    "You are a priest forever in the
        order of Melchizedek."

[5] The Lord stands at your right hand
        to protect you.
He will strike down many kings
    when his anger erupts.
[6] He will punish the nations
    and fill their lands with corpses;
he will shatter heads over the whole
        earth.
[7] But he himself will be refreshed from
        brooks along the way.
He will be victorious.

110:2 Hebrew *Zion.*

PROVERBS 15:8-10
The LORD detests the sacrifice of the wicked, but he delights in the prayers of the upright. ▫ The LORD detests the way of the wicked, but he loves those who pursue godliness. ▫ Whoever abandons the right path will be severely disciplined; whoever hates correction will die.

HOW WE LIVE

Standing firm in our beliefs

1 SAMUEL 15:22 Saul tried to obey partially, but he discovered that compromising on obedience is no better than disobedience. Samuel made that abundantly clear. • Saul thought God would be pleased with compromised obedience. Even though God had said to destroy everything, Saul and the army kept the animals alive "to sacrifice them to the Lord" (15:15). Samuel countered with, "Obedience is better than sacrifice, and submission is better than offering the fat of rams" (15:22). Of course sacrifice was important—it was a central part of the Jewish faith at this time. But God put a higher premium on full obedience to his commands. • Sacrifice without obedience or repentance is a hollow ritual, just as the acts of going to church, tithing, or volunteering on a committee aren't enough to save us. God is far more pleased by complete obedience and refusal to compromise than by whatever things you think you are sacrificing in order to follow him.

MAY 15

David's victory over Goliath garnered him attention as a national champion. Saul's first impression of David as a warrior eventually led to Saul's jealousy of him as a potential rival.

The Philistines now mustered their army for battle and camped between Socoh in Judah and Azekah at Ephes-dammim. ²Saul countered by gathering his Israelite troops near the valley of Elah. ³So the Philistines and Israelites faced each other on opposite hills, with the valley between them.

⁴Then Goliath, a Philistine champion from Gath, came out of the Philistine ranks to face the forces of Israel. He was over nine feet* tall! ⁵He wore a bronze helmet, and his bronze coat of mail weighed 125 pounds.* ⁶He also wore bronze leg armor, and he carried a bronze javelin on his shoulder. ⁷The shaft of his spear was as heavy and thick as a weaver's beam, tipped with an iron spearhead that weighed 15 pounds.* His armor bearer walked ahead of him carrying a shield.

⁸Goliath stood and shouted a taunt across to the Israelites. "Why are you all coming out to fight?" he called. "I am the Philistine champion, but you are only the servants of Saul. Choose one man to come down here and fight me! ⁹If he kills me, then we will be your slaves. But if I kill him, you will be our slaves! ¹⁰I defy the armies of Israel today! Send me a man who will fight me!" ¹¹When Saul and the Israelites heard this, they were terrified and deeply shaken.

¹²Now David was the son of a man named Jesse, an Ephrathite from Bethlehem in the land of Judah. Jesse was an old man at that time, and he had eight sons. ¹³Jesse's three oldest sons—Eliab, Abinadab, and Shimea*—had already joined Saul's army to fight the Philistines. ¹⁴David was the youngest son. David's three oldest brothers stayed with Saul's army, ¹⁵but David went back and forth so he could help his father with the sheep in Bethlehem.

¹⁶For forty days, every morning and evening, the Philistine champion strutted in front of the Israelite army.

¹⁷One day Jesse said to David, "Take this basket* of roasted grain and these ten loaves of bread, and carry them quickly to your brothers. ¹⁸And give these ten cuts of cheese to their captain. See how your brothers are getting along, and bring back a report on how they are doing.*" ¹⁹David's brothers were with Saul and the Israelite army at the valley of Elah, fighting against the Philistines.

²⁰So David left the sheep with another shepherd and set out early the next morning with the gifts, as Jesse had directed him. He arrived at the camp just as the Israelite army was leaving for the battlefield with shouts and battle cries. ²¹Soon the Israelite and Philistine forces stood facing each other, army against army. ²²David left his things with the keeper of supplies and hurried out to the ranks to greet his brothers. ²³As he was talking with them, Goliath, the Philistine champion from Gath, came out from the Philistine ranks. Then David heard him shout his usual taunt to the army of Israel.

²⁴As soon as the Israelite army saw him, they began to run away in fright. ²⁵"Have you seen the giant?" the men asked. "He comes out each day to defy Israel. The king has offered a huge reward to anyone who kills him. He will give that man one of his daughters for a wife, and the man's entire family will be exempted from paying taxes!"

²⁶David asked the soldiers standing nearby, "What will a man get for killing this Philistine and ending his defiance of Israel? Who is this pagan Philistine anyway, that he is allowed to defy the armies of the living God?"

²⁷And these men gave David the same reply. They said, "Yes, that is the reward for killing him."

²⁸But when David's oldest brother, Eliab, heard David talking to the men, he was angry. "What are you doing around here anyway?" he demanded. "What about those few sheep you're supposed

to be taking care of? I know about your pride and deceit. You just want to see the battle!"

²⁹"What have I done now?" David replied. "I was only asking a question!" ³⁰He walked over to some others and asked them the same thing and received the same answer. ³¹Then David's question was reported to King Saul, and the king sent for him.

³²"Don't worry about this Philistine," David told Saul. "I'll go fight him!"

³³"Don't be ridiculous!" Saul replied. "There's no way you can fight this Philistine and possibly win! You're only a boy, and he's been a man of war since his youth."

³⁴But David persisted. "I have been taking care of my father's sheep and goats," he said. "When a lion or a bear comes to steal a lamb from the flock, ³⁵I go after it with a club and rescue the lamb from its mouth. If the animal turns on me, I catch it by the jaw and club it to death. ³⁶I have done this to both lions and bears, and I'll do it to this pagan Philistine, too, for he has defied the armies of the living God! ³⁷The LORD who rescued me from the claws of the lion and the bear will rescue me from this Philistine!"

Saul finally consented. "All right, go ahead," he said. "And may the LORD be with you!"

³⁸Then Saul gave David his own armor—a bronze helmet and a coat of mail.

³⁹David put it on, strapped the sword over it, and took a step or two to see what it was like, for he had never worn such things before.

"I can't go in these," he protested to Saul. "I'm not used to them." So David took them off again. ⁴⁰He picked up five smooth stones from a stream and put them into his shepherd's bag. Then, armed only with his shepherd's staff and sling, he started across the valley to fight the Philistine.

⁴¹Goliath walked out toward David with his shield bearer ahead of him, ⁴²sneering in contempt at this ruddy-faced boy. ⁴³"Am I a dog," he roared at David, "that you come at me with a stick?" And he cursed David by the names of his gods. ⁴⁴"Come over here, and I'll give your flesh to the birds and wild animals!" Goliath yelled.

⁴⁵David replied to the Philistine, "You come to me with sword, spear, and javelin, but I come to you in the name of the LORD of Heaven's Armies—the God of the armies of Israel, whom you have defied. ⁴⁶Today the LORD will conquer you, and I will kill you and cut off your head. And then I will give the dead bodies of your men to the birds and wild animals, and the whole world will know that there is a God in Israel! ⁴⁷And everyone assembled here will know that the LORD rescues his people, but not with sword and spear. This is the LORD's battle, and he will give you to us!"

Relying on God's power

HOW WE LIVE

1 SAMUEL 17 Most of us know the story of David and Goliath. It is referred to in every arena from sports to business. The little guy beats the big guy, and everyone cheers! • The truth is that the people around David thought he was a little crazy. In their minds, he didn't have a chance. But David saw it differently. The giant across the valley wasn't just a bully; he was disrespecting David's God. This placed the fight on a whole different level—it was not a fight about weapons, it was a fight about faith. David so believed that God was his strength that he set about to do what appeared to be impossible—and he didn't seem to think twice. • That's what happens to us, too, when we are living in God's strength. When we are connected with God and familiar with his presence, we can face down giant problems. Your strength is no longer the determining factor. God's strength in you is what matters.

⁴⁸As Goliath moved closer to attack, David quickly ran out to meet him. ⁴⁹Reaching into his shepherd's bag and taking out a stone, he hurled it with his sling and hit the Philistine in the forehead. The stone sank in, and Goliath stumbled and fell face down on the ground.

⁵⁰So David triumphed over the Philistine with only a sling and a stone, for he had no sword. ⁵¹Then David ran over and pulled Goliath's sword from its sheath. David used it to kill him and cut off his head.

When the Philistines saw that their champion was dead, they turned and ran. ⁵²Then the men of Israel and Judah gave a great shout of triumph and rushed after the Philistines, chasing them as far as Gath* and the gates of Ekron. The bodies of the dead and wounded Philistines were strewn all along the road from Shaaraim, as far as Gath and Ekron. ⁵³Then the Israelite army returned and plundered the deserted Philistine camp. ⁵⁴(David took the Philistine's head to Jerusalem, but he stored the man's armor in his own tent.)

⁵⁵As Saul watched David go out to fight the Philistine, he asked Abner, the commander of his army, "Abner, whose son is this young man?"

"I really don't know," Abner declared.

⁵⁶"Well, find out who he is!" the king told him.

⁵⁷As soon as David returned from killing Goliath, Abner brought him to Saul with the Philistine's head still in his hand. ⁵⁸"Tell me about your father, young man," Saul said.

And David replied, "His name is Jesse, and we live in Bethlehem."

¹⁸:¹AFTER David had finished talking with Saul, he met Jonathan, the king's son. There was an immediate bond between them, for Jonathan loved David. ²From that day on Saul kept David with him and wouldn't let him return home. ³And Jonathan made a solemn pact with David, because he loved him as he loved himself. ⁴Jonathan sealed the pact by taking off his robe and giving it to David, together with his tunic, sword, bow, and belt.

17:4 Hebrew *6 cubits and 1 span* [which totals about 9.75 feet or 3 meters]; Dead Sea Scrolls and Greek version read *4 cubits and 1 span* [which totals about 6.75 feet or 2 meters].   17:5 Hebrew *5,000 shekels* [57 kilograms]. 17:7 Hebrew *600 shekels* [6.8 kilograms].   17:13 Hebrew *Shammah*, a variant spelling of Shimea; compare 1 Chr 2:13; 20:7.   17:17 Hebrew *ephah* [20 quarts or 22 liters]. 17:18 Hebrew *and take their pledge*.   17:52 As in some Greek manuscripts; Hebrew reads *a valley*.

JOHN 8:21-30

At times people had difficulty understanding Jesus' message. Even though they didn't understand him fully, many believed in him.

Later Jesus said to them again, "I am going away. You will search for me but will die in your sin. You cannot come where I am going."

²²The people* asked, "Is he planning to commit suicide? What does he mean, 'You cannot come where I am going'?"

²³Jesus continued, "You are from below; I am from above. You belong to this world; I do not. ²⁴That is why I said that you will die in your sins; for unless you believe that I AM who I claim to be,* you will die in your sins."

²⁵"Who are you?" they demanded.

Jesus replied, "The one I have always claimed to be.* ²⁶I have much to say about you and much to condemn, but I won't. For I say only what I have heard from the one who sent me, and he is completely truthful." ²⁷But they still didn't understand that he was talking about his Father.

²⁸So Jesus said, "When you have lifted up the Son of Man on the cross, then you will understand that I AM he.* I do nothing on my own but say only what the Father taught me. ²⁹And the one who sent me is with me—he has not deserted me. For I always do what pleases him." ³⁰Then many who heard him say these things believed in him.

8:22 Greek *Jewish people*; also in 8:31, 48, 52, 57.
8:24 Greek *unless you believe that I am*. See Exod 3:14.
8:25 Or *Why do I speak to you at all?*   8:28 Greek *When you have lifted up the Son of Man, then you will know that I am*. "Son of Man" is a title Jesus used for himself.

PSALM 111:1-10*

Praise the LORD!

I will thank the LORD with all my heart
    as I meet with his godly people.
² How amazing are the deeds of the
    LORD!

All who delight in him should
    ponder them.
3 Everything he does reveals his glory
        and majesty.
    His righteousness never fails.
4 He causes us to remember his
        wonderful works.
    How gracious and merciful
        is our LORD!
5 He gives food to those who fear him;
    he always remembers his covenant.
6 He has shown his great power to his
        people
    by giving them the lands of other
        nations.
7 All he does is just and good,
    and all his commandments are
        trustworthy.
8 They are forever true,
    to be obeyed faithfully and with
        integrity.

9 He has paid a full ransom for his
        people.
    He has guaranteed his covenant
        with them forever.
    What a holy, awe-inspiring name
        he has!
10 Fear of the LORD is the foundation
        of true wisdom.
    All who obey his commandments
        will grow in wisdom.

Praise him forever!

111 This psalm is a Hebrew acrostic poem; after the
introductory note of praise, each line begins with a
successive letter of the Hebrew alphabet.

PROVERBS 15:11

Even Death and Destruction* hold no secrets from the LORD. How much more
does he know the human heart!

15:11 Hebrew *Sheol and Abaddon.*

MAY**16**

1 SAMUEL 18:5–19:24

Saul's jealousy of David elevated to the point of
repeated assassination attempts. This part of the
story reads like an action/adventure sequence as
David tries to escape Saul's aggression.

Whatever Saul asked David to do, David
did it successfully. So Saul made him a
commander over the men of war, an appointment that was welcomed by the people and Saul's officers alike.

6 When the victorious Israelite army
was returning home after David had
killed the Philistine, women from all the
towns of Israel came out to meet King
Saul. They sang and danced for joy with
tambourines and cymbals.* 7 This was
their song:

"Saul has killed his thousands,
    and David his ten thousands!"

8 This made Saul very angry. "What's
this?" he said. "They credit David with ten
thousands and me with only thousands.
Next they'll be making him their king!"

9 So from that time on Saul kept a jealous
eye on David.

10 The very next day a tormenting spirit*
from God overwhelmed Saul, and he began to rave in his house like a madman.
David was playing the harp, as he did each
day. But Saul had a spear in his hand, 11 and
he suddenly hurled it at David, intending
to pin him to the wall. But David escaped
him twice.

12 Saul was then afraid of David, for the
LORD was with David and had turned
away from Saul. 13 Finally, Saul sent him
away and appointed him commander
over 1,000 men, and David faithfully led
his troops into battle.

14 David continued to succeed in everything he did, for the LORD was with him.
15 When Saul recognized this, he became
even more afraid of him. 16 But all Israel
and Judah loved David because he was
so successful at leading his troops into
battle.

17 One day Saul said to David, "I am

ready to give you my older daughter, Merab, as your wife. But first you must prove yourself to be a real warrior by fighting the LORD's battles." For Saul thought, "I'll send him out against the Philistines and let them kill him rather than doing it myself."

¹⁸"Who am I, and what is my family in Israel that I should be the king's son-in-law?" David exclaimed. "My father's family is nothing!" ¹⁹So* when the time came for Saul to give his daughter Merab in marriage to David, he gave her instead to Adriel, a man from Meholah.

²⁰In the meantime, Saul's daughter Michal had fallen in love with David, and Saul was delighted when he heard about it. ²¹"Here's another chance to see him killed by the Philistines!" Saul said to himself. But to David he said, "Today you have a second chance to become my son-in-law!"

²²Then Saul told his men to say to David, "The king really likes you, and so do we. Why don't you accept the king's offer and become his son-in-law?"

²³When Saul's men said these things to David, he replied, "How can a poor man from a humble family afford the bride price for the daughter of a king?"

²⁴When Saul's men reported this back to the king, ²⁵he told them, "Tell David that all I want for the bride price is 100 Philistine foreskins! Vengeance on my enemies is all I really want." But what Saul had in mind was that David would be killed in the fight.

²⁶David was delighted to accept the offer. Before the time limit expired, ²⁷he and his men went out and killed 200 Phiistines. Then David fulfilled the king's requirement by presenting all their foreskins to him. So Saul gave his daughter Michal to David to be his wife.

²⁸When Saul realized that the LORD was with David and how much his daughter Michal loved him, ²⁹Saul became even more afraid of him, and he remained David's enemy for the rest of his life.

³⁰Every time the commanders of the Philistines attacked, David was more successful against them than all the rest of Saul's officers. So David's name became very famous.

¹⁹:¹SAUL now urged his servants and his son Jonathan to assassinate David. But Jonathan, because of his strong affection for David, ²told him what his father was planning. "Tomorrow morning," he warned him, "you must find a hiding place out in the fields. ³I'll ask my father to go out there with me, and I'll talk to him about you. Then I'll tell you everything I can find out."

⁴The next morning Jonathan spoke with his father about David, saying many good things about him. "The king must not sin against his servant David," Jonathan said. "He's never done anything to harm you. He has always helped you in any way he could. ⁵Have you forgotten about the time he risked his life to kill the Philistine giant and how the LORD brought a great victory to all Israel as a result? You were certainly happy about it then. Why should you murder an innocent man like David? There is no reason for it at all!"

⁶So Saul listened to Jonathan and vowed, "As surely as the LORD lives, David will not be killed."

⁷Afterward Jonathan called David and told him what had happened. Then he brought David to Saul, and David served in the court as before.

⁸War broke out again after that, and David led his troops against the Philistines. He attacked them with such fury that they all ran away.

⁹But one day when Saul was sitting at home, with spear in hand, the tormenting spirit* from the LORD suddenly came upon him again. As David played his harp, ¹⁰Saul hurled his spear at David. But David dodged out of the way, and leaving the spear stuck in the wall, he fled and escaped into the night.

¹¹Then Saul sent troops to watch David's house. They were told to kill David when he came out the next morning. But Michal, David's wife, warned him, "If you don't escape tonight, you will be dead by morning." ¹²So she helped him climb out through a window, and he fled and escaped. ¹³Then she took an idol* and put it in his bed, covered it with blankets, and put a cushion of goat's hair at its head. ¹⁴When the troops came to arrest

David, she told them he was sick and couldn't get out of bed.

¹⁵But Saul sent the troops back to get David. He ordered, "Bring him to me in his bed so I can kill him!" ¹⁶But when they came to carry David out, they discovered that it was only an idol in the bed with a cushion of goat's hair at its head.

¹⁷"Why have you betrayed me like this and let my enemy escape?" Saul demanded of Michal.

"I had to," Michal replied. "He threatened to kill me if I didn't help him."

¹⁸So David escaped and went to Ramah to see Samuel, and he told him all that Saul had done to him. Then Samuel took David with him to live at Naioth. ¹⁹When the report reached Saul that David was at Naioth in Ramah, ²⁰he sent troops to capture him. But when they arrived and saw Samuel leading a group of prophets who were prophesying, the Spirit of God came upon Saul's men, and they also began to prophesy. ²¹When Saul heard what had happened, he sent other troops, but they, too, prophesied! The same thing happened a third time. ²²Finally, Saul himself went to Ramah and arrived at the great well in Secu. "Where are Samuel and David?" he demanded.

"They are at Naioth in Ramah," someone told him.

²³But on the way to Naioth in Ramah the Spirit of God came even upon Saul, and he, too, began to prophesy all the way to Naioth! ²⁴He tore off his clothes and lay naked on the ground all day and all night, prophesying in the presence of Samuel. The people who were watching exclaimed, "What? Is even Saul a prophet?"

18:6 The type of instrument represented by the word *cymbals* is uncertain.   18:10 Or *an evil spirit*.   18:19 Or *But*.   19:9 Or *evil spirit*.   19:13 Hebrew *teraphim;* also in 19:16.

JOHN 8:31-59

According to the Old Testament, Abraham, the chief patriarch of the Jews, was righteous before God because of his faith. It would make sense, then, that Jesus would hearken back to Abraham to teach his contemporaries about faith.

Jesus said to the people who believed in him, "You are truly my disciples if you remain faithful to my teachings. ³²And you will know the truth, and the truth will set you free."

³³"But we are descendants of Abraham," they said. "We have never been slaves to anyone. What do you mean, 'You will be set free'?"

³⁴Jesus replied, "I tell you the truth, everyone who sins is a slave of sin. ³⁵A slave is not a permanent member of the family, but a son is part of the family

HOW WE LIVE

Our relationships

1 SAMUEL 19:1-6 Saul, the first king of Israel, had a good relationship with David at first, but as David grew more popular, Saul grew more bitter and insecure. Saul was not pleased with the jingle that was going around the kingdom: "Saul has killed his thousands, and David his ten thousands!" (1 Samuel 18:7). So much for job security. • Enter Jonathan, Saul's son. When Jonathan met David, they became friends and their loyalty to each other extended through long and difficult days to come. Jonathan was technically in line for the throne, and he might easily have turned traitor against David in order to have the throne for himself, but he knew better than to try to thwart God's plan. So deep was their friendship that David later made a pact to take care of Jonathan's family. David kept that promise, taking Jonathan's crippled son under his own roof (2 Samuel 9, May 26). • Friends are blessings from the Lord. True friendships are invaluable, and true friends are sometimes too hard to find. Be a good friend—loyal, caring, honest, understanding, and willing to go out of your way when needed.

forever. ³⁶So if the Son sets you free, you are truly free. ³⁷Yes, I realize that you are descendants of Abraham. And yet some of you are trying to kill me because there's no room in your hearts for my message. ³⁸I am telling you what I saw when I was with my Father. But you are following the advice of your father."

³⁹"Our father is Abraham!" they declared.

"No," Jesus replied, "for if you were really the children of Abraham, you would follow his example.* ⁴⁰Instead, you are trying to kill me because I told you the truth, which I heard from God. Abraham never did such a thing. ⁴¹No, you are imitating your real father."

They replied, "We aren't illegitimate children! God himself is our true Father."

⁴²Jesus told them, "If God were your Father, you would love me, because I have come to you from God. I am not here on my own, but he sent me. ⁴³Why can't you understand what I am saying? It's because you can't even hear me! ⁴⁴For you are the children of your father the devil, and you love to do the evil things he does. He was a murderer from the beginning. He has always hated the truth, because there is no truth in him. When he lies, it is consistent with his character; for he is a liar and the father of lies. ⁴⁵So when I tell the truth, you just naturally don't believe me! ⁴⁶Which of you can truthfully accuse me of sin? And since I am telling you the truth, why don't you believe me? ⁴⁷Anyone who belongs to God listens gladly to the words of God. But you don't listen because you don't belong to God."

⁴⁸The people retorted, "You Samaritan devil! Didn't we say all along that you were possessed by a demon?"

⁴⁹"No," Jesus said, "I have no demon in me. For I honor my Father—and you dishonor me. ⁵⁰And though I have no wish to glorify myself, God is going to glorify me. He is the true judge. ⁵¹I tell you the truth, anyone who obeys my teaching will never die!"

⁵²The people said, "Now we know you are possessed by a demon. Even Abraham and the prophets died, but you say, 'Anyone who obeys my teaching will never die!' ⁵³Are you greater than our father Abraham? He died, and so did the prophets. Who do you think you are?"

⁵⁴Jesus answered, "If I want glory for myself, it doesn't count. But it is my Father who will glorify me. You say, 'He is our God,*' ⁵⁵but you don't even know him. I know him. If I said otherwise, I would be as great a liar as you! But I do know him and obey him. ⁵⁶Your father Abraham rejoiced as he looked forward to my coming. He saw it and was glad."

⁵⁷The people said, "You aren't even fifty years old. How can you say you have seen Abraham?*"

⁵⁸Jesus answered, "I tell you the truth, before Abraham was even born, I AM!*" ⁵⁹At that point they picked up stones to throw at him. But Jesus was hidden from them and left the Temple.

8:39 Some manuscripts read *if you are really the children of Abraham, follow his example.* **8:54** Some manuscripts read *your God.* **8:57** Some manuscripts read *How can you say Abraham has seen you?* **8:58** Or *before Abraham was even born, I have always been alive;* Greek reads *before Abraham was, I am.* See Exod 3:14.

PSALM 112:1-10*

Praise the LORD!

How joyful are those who fear the LORD
  and delight in obeying his
    commands.
² Their children will be successful
  everywhere;
  an entire generation of godly people
    will be blessed.
³ They themselves will be wealthy,
  and their good deeds will last forever.
⁴ Light shines in the darkness for the
  godly.
  They are generous, compassionate,
    and righteous.
⁵ Good comes to those who lend money
  generously
  and conduct their business
    fairly.
⁶ Such people will not be overcome
  by evil.
  Those who are righteous will be
    long remembered.
⁷ They do not fear bad news;
  they confidently trust the LORD
    to care for them.
⁸ They are confident and fearless
  and can face their foes
    triumphantly.

⁹ They share freely and give generously
to those in need.
Their good deeds will be
remembered forever.
They will have influence and honor.
¹⁰ The wicked will see this and be
infuriated.
They will grind their teeth in anger;
they will slink away, their hopes
thwarted.

112 This psalm is a Hebrew acrostic poem; after the
introductory note of praise, each line begins with a
successive letter of the Hebrew alphabet.

PROVERBS 15:12-14

Mockers hate to be corrected, so they stay
away from the wise. ▢A glad heart makes
a happy face; a broken heart crushes the
spirit. ▢A wise person is hungry for
knowledge, while the fool feeds on trash.

MAY**17**

1 SAMUEL 20:1-21:15

In his flight from Saul's maniacal jealousy, David
was blessed to have such a faithful ally in Jonathan.
Ahimelech the priest risked his life to help David
and his men. Tomorrow's reading tells of Ahimelech's sad fate in Saul's hands.

David now fled from Naioth in Ramah
and found Jonathan. "What have I done?"
he exclaimed. "What is my crime? How
have I offended your father that he is so
determined to kill me?"

²"That's not true!" Jonathan protested.
"You're not going to die. He always tells
me everything he's going to do, even the
little things. I know my father wouldn't
hide something like this from me. It just
isn't so!"

³Then David took an oath before Jonathan and said, "Your father knows perfectly well about our friendship, so he has
said to himself, 'I won't tell Jonathan—
why should I hurt him?' But I swear to you
that I am only a step away from death!
I swear it by the LORD and by your own
soul!"

⁴"Tell me what I can do to help you,"
Jonathan exclaimed.

⁵David replied, "Tomorrow we celebrate the new moon festival. I've always
eaten with the king on this occasion, but
tomorrow I'll hide in the field and stay
there until the evening of the third day. ⁶If
your father asks where I am, tell him I
asked permission to go home to Bethlehem for an annual family sacrifice. ⁷If he

says, 'Fine!' you will know all is well. But if
he is angry and loses his temper, you will
know he is determined to kill me. ⁸Show
me this loyalty as my sworn friend—for
we made a solemn pact before the LORD—
or kill me yourself if I have sinned against
your father. But please don't betray me to
him!"

⁹"Never!" Jonathan exclaimed. "You
know that if I had the slightest notion my
father was planning to kill you, I would
tell you at once."

¹⁰Then David asked, "How will I know
whether or not your father is angry?"

¹¹"Come out to the field with me," Jonathan replied. And they went out there together. ¹²Then Jonathan told David, "I
promise by the LORD, the God of Israel,
that by this time tomorrow, or the next
day at the latest, I will talk to my father
and let you know at once how he feels
about you. If he speaks favorably about
you, I will let you know. ¹³But if he is angry
and wants you killed, may the LORD strike
me and even kill me if I don't warn you so
you can escape and live. May the LORD be
with you as he used to be with my father.
¹⁴And may you treat me with the faithful
love of the LORD as long as I live. But if I
die, ¹⁵treat my family with this faithful
love, even when the LORD destroys all
your enemies from the face of the earth."

¹⁶So Jonathan made a solemn pact with
David,* saying, "May the LORD destroy all

your enemies!" ¹⁷And Jonathan made David reaffirm his vow of friendship again, for Jonathan loved David as he loved himself.

¹⁸Then Jonathan said, "Tomorrow we celebrate the new moon festival. You will be missed when your place at the table is empty. ¹⁹The day after tomorrow, toward evening, go to the place where you hid before, and wait there by the stone pile.* ²⁰I will come out and shoot three arrows to the side of the stone pile as though I were shooting at a target. ²¹Then I will send a boy to bring the arrows back. If you hear me tell him, 'They're on this side,' then you will know, as surely as the LORD lives, that all is well, and there is no trouble. ²²But if I tell him, 'Go farther—the arrows are still ahead of you,' then it will mean that you must leave immediately, for the LORD is sending you away. ²³And may the LORD make us keep our promises to each other, for he has witnessed them."

²⁴So David hid himself in the field, and when the new moon festival began, the king sat down to eat. ²⁵He sat at his usual place against the wall, with Jonathan sitting opposite him* and Abner beside him. But David's place was empty. ²⁶Saul didn't say anything about it that day, for he said to himself, "Something must have made David ceremonially unclean." ²⁷But when David's place was empty again the next day, Saul asked Jonathan, "Why hasn't the son of Jesse been here for the meal either yesterday or today?"

²⁸Jonathan replied, "David earnestly asked me if he could go to Bethlehem. ²⁹He said, 'Please let me go, for we are having a family sacrifice. My brother demanded that I be there. So please let me get away to see my brothers.' That's why he isn't here at the king's table."

³⁰Saul boiled with rage at Jonathan. "You stupid son of a whore!"* he swore at him. "Do you think I don't know that you want him to be king in your place, shaming yourself and your mother? ³¹As long as that son of Jesse is alive, you'll never be king. Now go and get him so I can kill him!"

³²"But why should he be put to death?" Jonathan asked his father. "What has he done?" ³³Then Saul hurled his spear at

Jonathan, intending to kill him. So at last Jonathan realized that his father was really determined to kill David.

³⁴Jonathan left the table in fierce anger and refused to eat on that second day of the festival, for he was crushed by his father's shameful behavior toward David.

³⁵The next morning, as agreed, Jonathan went out into the field and took a young boy with him to gather his arrows. ³⁶"Start running," he told the boy, "so you can find the arrows as I shoot them." So the boy ran, and Jonathan shot an arrow beyond him. ³⁷When the boy had almost reached the arrow, Jonathan shouted, "The arrow is still ahead of you. ³⁸Hurry, hurry, don't wait." So the boy quickly gathered up the arrows and ran back to his master. ³⁹He, of course, suspected nothing; only Jonathan and David understood the signal. ⁴⁰Then Jonathan gave his bow and arrows to the boy and told him to take them back to town.

⁴¹As soon as the boy was gone, David came out from where he had been hiding near the stone pile.* Then David bowed three times to Jonathan with his face to the ground. Both of them were in tears as they embraced each other and said goodbye, especially David.

⁴²At last Jonathan said to David, "Go in peace, for we have sworn loyalty to each other in the LORD's name. The LORD is the witness of a bond between us and our children forever." Then David left, and Jonathan returned to the town.*

²¹:¹*DAVID went to the town of Nob to see Ahimelech the priest. Ahimelech trembled when he saw him. "Why are you alone?" he asked. "Why is no one with you?"

²"The king has sent me on a private matter," David said. "He told me not to tell anyone why I am here. I have told my men where to meet me later. ³Now, what is there to eat? Give me five loaves of bread or anything else you have."

⁴"We don't have any regular bread," the priest replied. "But there is the holy bread, which you can have if your young men have not slept with any women recently."

⁵"Don't worry," David replied. "I never allow my men to be with women when

they are on a campaign. And since they stay clean even on ordinary trips, how much more on this one!"

⁶Since there was no other food available, the priest gave him the holy bread—the Bread of the Presence that was placed before the LORD in the Tabernacle. It had just been replaced that day with fresh bread.

⁷Now Doeg the Edomite, Saul's chief herdsman, was there that day, having been detained before the LORD.*

⁸David asked Ahimelech, "Do you have a spear or sword? The king's business was so urgent that I didn't even have time to grab a weapon!"

⁹"I only have the sword of Goliath the Philistine, whom you killed in the valley of Elah," the priest replied. "It is wrapped in a cloth behind the ephod. Take that if you want it, for there is nothing else here."

"There is nothing like it!" David replied. "Give it to me!"

¹⁰So David escaped from Saul and went to King Achish of Gath. ¹¹But the officers of Achish were unhappy about his being there. "Isn't this David, the king of the land?" they asked. "Isn't he the one the people honor with dances, singing,

'Saul has killed his thousands,
     and David his ten thousands'?"

¹²David heard these comments and was very afraid of what King Achish of Gath might do to him. ¹³So he pretended

to be insane, scratching on doors and drooling down his beard.

¹⁴Finally, King Achish said to his men, "Must you bring me a madman? ¹⁵We already have enough of them around here! Why should I let someone like this be my guest?"

20:16 Hebrew *with the house of David.* 20:19 Hebrew *the stone Ezel.* The meaning of the Hebrew is uncertain. 20:25 As in Greek version; Hebrew reads *with Jonathan standing.* 20:30 Hebrew *You son of a perverse and rebellious woman.* 20:41 As in Greek version; Hebrew reads *near the south edge.* 20:42 This sentence is numbered 21:1 in Hebrew text. 21:1 Verses 21:1-15 are numbered 21:2-16 in Hebrew text. 21:7 The meaning of the Hebrew is uncertain.

JOHN 9:1-41
Physical blindness is a handicap. Spiritual blindness is a sickness of the soul. Jesus healed both.

As Jesus was walking along, he saw a man who had been blind from birth. ²"Rabbi," his disciples asked him, "why was this man born blind? Was it because of his own sins or his parents' sins?"

³"It was not because of his sins or his parents' sins," Jesus answered. "This happened so the power of God could be seen in him. ⁴We must quickly carry out the tasks assigned us by the one who sent us.* The night is coming, and then no one can work. ⁵But while I am here in the world, I am the light of the world."

⁶Then he spit on the ground, made mud with the saliva, and spread the mud over the blind man's eyes. ⁷He told him, "Go wash yourself in the pool of Siloam"

(Siloam means "sent"). So the man went and washed and came back seeing!

[8]His neighbors and others who knew him as a blind beggar asked each other, "Isn't this the man who used to sit and beg?" [9]Some said he was, and others said, "No, he just looks like him!"

But the beggar kept saying, "Yes, I am the same one!"

[10]They asked, "Who healed you? What happened?"

[11]He told them, "The man they call Jesus made mud and spread it over my eyes and told me, 'Go to the pool of Siloam and wash yourself.' So I went and washed, and now I can see!"

[12]"Where is he now?" they asked.

"I don't know," he replied.

[13]Then they took the man who had been blind to the Pharisees, [14]because it was on the Sabbath that Jesus had made the mud and healed him. [15]The Pharisees asked the man all about it. So he told them, "He put the mud over my eyes, and when I washed it away, I could see!"

[16]Some of the Pharisees said, "This man Jesus is not from God, for he is working on the Sabbath." Others said, "But how could an ordinary sinner do such miraculous signs?" So there was a deep division of opinion among them.

[17]Then the Pharisees again questioned the man who had been blind and demanded, "What's your opinion about this man who healed you?"

The man replied, "I think he must be a prophet."

[18]The Jewish leaders still refused to believe the man had been blind and could now see, so they called in his parents. [19]They asked them, "Is this your son? Was he born blind? If so, how can he now see?"

[20]His parents replied, "We know this is our son and that he was born blind, [21]but we don't know how he can see or who healed him. Ask him. He is old enough to speak for himself." [22]His parents said this because they were afraid of the Jewish leaders, who had announced that anyone saying Jesus was the Messiah would be expelled from the synagogue. [23]That's why they said, "He is old enough. Ask him."

[24]So for the second time they called in the man who had been blind and told

him, "God should get the glory for this,* because we know this man Jesus is a sinner."

[25]"I don't know whether he is a sinner," the man replied. "But I know this: I was blind, and now I can see!"

[26]"But what did he do?" they asked. "How did he heal you?"

[27]"Look!" the man exclaimed. "I told you once. Didn't you listen? Why do you want to hear it again? Do you want to become his disciples, too?"

[28]Then they cursed him and said, "You are his disciple, but we are disciples of Moses! [29]We know God spoke to Moses, but we don't even know where this man comes from."

[30]"Why, that's very strange!" the man replied. "He healed my eyes, and yet you don't know where he comes from? [31]We know that God doesn't listen to sinners, but he is ready to hear those who worship him and do his will. [32]Ever since the world began, no one has been able to open the eyes of someone born blind. [33]If this man were not from God, he couldn't have done it."

[34]"You were born a total sinner!" they answered. "Are you trying to teach us?" And they threw him out of the synagogue.

[35]When Jesus heard what had happened, he found the man and asked, "Do you believe in the Son of Man?*"

[36]The man answered, "Who is he, sir? I want to believe in him."

[37]"You have seen him," Jesus said, "and he is speaking to you!"

[38]"Yes, Lord, I believe!" the man said. And he worshiped Jesus.

[39]Then Jesus told him,* "I entered this world to render judgment—to give sight to the blind and to show those who think they see* that they are blind."

[40]Some Pharisees who were standing nearby heard him and asked, "Are you saying we're blind?"

[41]"If you were blind, you wouldn't be guilty," Jesus replied. "But you remain guilty because you claim you can see."

9:4 Other manuscripts read *I must quickly carry out the tasks assigned me by the one who sent me;* still others read *We must quickly carry out the tasks assigned us by the one who sent me.* **9:24** Or *Give glory to God, not to Jesus;* Greek reads *Give glory to God.* **9:35** Some manuscripts read *the Son of God?* "Son of Man" is a title Jesus used for himself. **9:38-39a** Some manuscripts do not include *"Yes, Lord,*

I believe!" the man said. And he worshiped Jesus. Then Jesus told him. **9:39b** Greek *those who see.*

PSALM 113:1–114:8

Praise the LORD!

Yes, give praise, O servants of the
LORD.
Praise the name of the LORD!
2 Blessed be the name of the LORD
now and forever.
3 Everywhere—from east to west—
praise the name of the LORD.
4 For the LORD is high above the
nations;
his glory is higher than the heavens.
5 Who can be compared with the LORD
our God,
who is enthroned on high?
6 He stoops to look down
on heaven and on earth.
7 He lifts the poor from the dust
and the needy from the garbage
dump.
8 He sets them among princes,
even the princes of his own people!
9 He gives the childless woman a family,
making her a happy mother.

Praise the LORD!

114:1 WHEN the Israelites escaped from
Egypt—
when the family of Jacob left that
foreign land—

2 the land of Judah became God's
sanctuary,
and Israel became his kingdom.
3 The Red Sea* saw them coming and
hurried out of their way!
The water of the Jordan River
turned away.
4 The mountains skipped like rams,
the hills like lambs!
5 What's wrong, Red Sea, that made you
hurry out of their way?
What happened, Jordan River, that
you turned away?
6 Why, mountains, did you skip like
rams?
Why, hills, like lambs?
7 Tremble, O earth, at the presence of
the Lord,
at the presence of the God of Jacob.
8 He turned the rock into a pool of
water;
yes, a spring of water flowed from
solid rock.

114:3 Hebrew *the sea;* also in 114:5.

PROVERBS 15:15-17

For the despondent, every day brings
trouble; for the happy heart, life is a continual feast. □ Better to have little, with
fear for the LORD, than to have great treasure and inner turmoil. □ A bowl of vegetables with someone you love is better
than steak with someone you hate.

MAY**18**

1 SAMUEL 22:1-23:29

Because of Saul's obsession, David had to hide in
caves and wilderness areas with his army of disen-
franchised but loyal soldiers. He had already been
anointed king by Samuel, yet he waited on God to
put him in power.

So David left Gath and escaped to the
cave of Adullam. Soon his brothers and
all his other relatives joined him there.
2 Then others began coming—men who
were in trouble or in debt or who were just

discontented—until David was the captain of about 400 men.

3 Later David went to Mizpeh in Moab,
where he asked the king, "Please allow my
father and mother to live here with you
until I know what God is going to do for
me." 4 So David's parents stayed in Moab
with the king during the entire time David
was living in his stronghold.

5 One day the prophet Gad told David,
"Leave the stronghold and return to the

land of Judah." So David went to the forest of Hereth.

⁶The news of his arrival in Judah soon reached Saul. At the time, the king was sitting beneath the tamarisk tree on the hill at Gibeah, holding his spear and surrounded by his officers.

⁷"Listen here, you men of Benjamin!" Saul shouted to his officers when he heard the news. "Has that son of Jesse promised every one of you fields and vineyards? Has he promised to make you all generals and captains in his army?* ⁸Is that why you have conspired against me? For not one of you told me when my own son made a solemn pact with the son of Jesse. You're not even sorry for me. Think of it! My own son—encouraging him to kill me, as he is trying to do this very day!"

⁹Then Doeg the Edomite, who was standing there with Saul's men, spoke up. "When I was at Nob," he said, "I saw the son of Jesse talking to the priest, Ahimelech son of Ahitub. ¹⁰Ahimelech consulted the LORD for him. Then he gave him food and the sword of Goliath the Philistine."

¹¹King Saul immediately sent for Ahimelech and all his family, who served as priests at Nob. ¹²When they arrived, Saul shouted at him, "Listen to me, you son of Ahitub!"

"What is it, my king?" Ahimelech asked.

¹³"Why have you and the son of Jesse conspired against me?" Saul demanded. "Why did you give him food and a sword? Why have you consulted God for him? Why have you encouraged him to kill me, as he is trying to do this very day?"

¹⁴"But sir," Ahimelech replied, "is anyone among all your servants as faithful as David, your son-in-law? Why, he is the captain of your bodyguard and a highly honored member of your household! ¹⁵This was certainly not the first time I had consulted God for him! May the king not accuse me and my family in this matter, for I knew nothing at all of any plot against you."

¹⁶"You will surely die, Ahimelech, along with your entire family!" the king shouted. ¹⁷And he ordered his bodyguards, "Kill these priests of the LORD, for they are allies

and conspirators with David! They knew he was running away from me, but they didn't tell me!" But Saul's men refused to kill the LORD's priests.

¹⁸Then the king said to Doeg, "You do it." So Doeg the Edomite turned on them and killed them that day, eighty-five priests in all, still wearing their priestly garments. ¹⁹Then he went to Nob, the town of the priests, and killed the priests' families—men and women, children and babies—and all the cattle, donkeys, sheep, and goats.

²⁰Only Abiathar, one of the sons of Ahimelech, escaped and fled to David. ²¹When he told David that Saul had killed the priests of the LORD, ²²David exclaimed, "I knew it! When I saw Doeg the Edomite there that day, I knew he was sure to tell Saul. Now I have caused the death of all your father's family. ²³Stay here with me, and don't be afraid. I will protect you with my own life, for the same person wants to kill us both."

²³:¹ONE day news came to David that the Philistines were at Keilah stealing grain from the threshing floors. ²David asked the LORD, "Should I go and attack them?"

"Yes, go and save Keilah," the LORD told him.

³But David's men said, "We're afraid even here in Judah. We certainly don't want to go to Keilah to fight the whole Philistine army!"

⁴So David asked the LORD again, and again the LORD replied, "Go down to Keilah, for I will help you conquer the Philistines."

⁵So David and his men went to Keilah. They slaughtered the Philistines and took all their livestock and rescued the people of Keilah. ⁶Now when Abiathar son of Ahimelech fled to David at Keilah, he brought the ephod with him.

⁷Saul soon learned that David was at Keilah. "Good!" he exclaimed. "We've got him now! God has handed him over to me, for he has trapped himself in a walled town!" ⁸So Saul mobilized his entire army to march to Keilah and besiege David and his men.

⁹But David learned of Saul's plan and told Abiathar the priest to bring the

ephod and ask the LORD what he should do. [10]Then David prayed, "O LORD, God of Israel, I have heard that Saul is planning to come and destroy Keilah because I am here. [11]Will the leaders of Keilah betray me to him?* And will Saul actually come as I have heard? O LORD, God of Israel, please tell me."

And the LORD said, "He will come."

[12]Again David asked, "Will the leaders of Keilah betray me and my men to Saul?"

And the LORD replied, "Yes, they will betray you."

[13]So David and his men—about 600 of them now—left Keilah and began roaming the countryside. Word soon reached Saul that David had escaped, so he didn't go to Keilah after all. [14]David now stayed in the strongholds of the wilderness and in the hill country of Ziph. Saul hunted him day after day, but God didn't let Saul find him.

[15]One day near Horesh, David received the news that Saul was on the way to Ziph to search for him and kill him. [16]Jonathan went to find David and encouraged him to stay strong in his faith in God. [17]"Don't be afraid," Jonathan reassured him. "My father will never find you! You are going to be the king of Israel, and I will be next to you, as my father, Saul, is well aware." [18]So the two of them renewed their solemn pact before the LORD. Then Jonathan returned home, while David stayed at Horesh.

[19]But now the men of Ziph went to Saul in Gibeah and betrayed David to him. "We know where David is hiding," they said. "He is in the strongholds of Horesh on the hill of Hakilah, which is in the southern part of Jeshimon. [20]Come down whenever you're ready, O king, and we will catch him and hand him over to you!"

[21]"The LORD bless you," Saul said. "At last someone is concerned about me! [22]Go and check again to be sure of where he is staying and who has seen him there, for I know that he is very crafty. [23]Discover his hiding places, and come back when you are sure. Then I'll go with you. And if he is in the area at all, I'll track him down, even if I have to search every hiding place in Judah!" [24]So the men of Ziph returned home ahead of Saul.

Meanwhile, David and his men had moved into the wilderness of Maon in the Arabah Valley south of Jeshimon. [25]When David heard that Saul and his men were searching for him, he went even farther into the wilderness to the great rock, and he remained there in the wilderness of Maon. But Saul kept after him in the wilderness.

[26]Saul and David were now on opposite sides of a mountain. Just as Saul and his men began to close in on David and his men, [27]an urgent message reached Saul that the Philistines were raiding Israel again. [28]So Saul quit chasing David and

WHO GOD IS

Jesus is the Good Shepherd

JOHN 10:1-16 A shepherd's job is difficult. He is constantly on guard, watching over his flock of sheep day and night. He protects them when predators try to attack or thieves try to steal them away. The shepherd is at times tender and loving, and at other times he is strong and forceful. But at all times he is focused on the best interests of the sheep. • We, of course, are like sheep. Sheep are vulnerable, rather dumb, and tend to wander away. They can be hardheaded and stubborn. Sound familiar? We often think we know what is best for us, but invariably we end up in trouble. Jesus, the good shepherd, watches out for us. He speaks our name as he calls us back to safety. And he willingly gave up his life for us in order to give us "a rich and satisfying life" (10:10). If you find yourself off the path or in a fix, just call out to Jesus. Then stay close—follow where he leads, stay where he rests, and respond to his voice. There you will find safety.

returned to fight the Philistines. Ever since that time, the place where David was camped has been called the Rock of Escape.* [29]*David then went to live in the strongholds of En-gedi.

22:7 Hebrew *commanders of thousands and commanders of hundreds?* 23:11 Some manuscripts lack the first sentence of 23:11. 23:28 Hebrew *Sela-hammahlekoth.* 23:29 Verse 23:29 is numbered 24:1 in Hebrew text.

JOHN 10:1-21

Jesus taught in pictures. He wove illustrations from people, objects, and events that were familiar to his listeners. A good shepherd was something that these agrarian people understood.

"**I** [Jesus] tell you the truth, anyone who sneaks over the wall of a sheepfold, rather than going through the gate, must surely be a thief and a robber! [2]But the one who enters through the gate is the shepherd of the sheep. [3]The gatekeeper opens the gate for him, and the sheep recognize his voice and come to him. He calls his own sheep by name and leads them out. [4]After he has gathered his own flock, he walks ahead of them, and they follow him because they know his voice. [5]They won't follow a stranger; they will run from him because they don't know his voice."

[6]Those who heard Jesus use this illustration didn't understand what he meant, [7]so he explained it to them: "I tell you the truth, I am the gate for the sheep. [8]All who came before me* were thieves and robbers. But the true sheep did not listen to them. [9]Yes, I am the gate. Those who come in through me will be saved.* They will come and go freely and will find good pastures. [10]The thief's purpose is to steal and kill and destroy. My purpose is to give them a rich and satisfying life.

[11]"I am the good shepherd. The good shepherd sacrifices his life for the sheep. [12]A hired hand will run when he sees a wolf coming. He will abandon the sheep because they don't belong to him and he isn't their shepherd. And so the wolf attacks them and scatters the flock. [13]The hired hand runs away because he's working only for the money and doesn't really care about the sheep.

[14]"I am the good shepherd; I know my own sheep, and they know me, [15]just as my Father knows me and I know the Fa-

ther. So I sacrifice my life for the sheep. [16]I have other sheep, too, that are not in this sheepfold. I must bring them also. They will listen to my voice, and there will be one flock with one shepherd.

[17]"The Father loves me because I sacrifice my life so I may take it back again. [18]No one can take my life from me. I sacrifice it voluntarily. For I have the authority to lay it down when I want to and also to take it up again. For this is what my Father has commanded."

[19]When he said these things, the people* were again divided in their opinions about him. [20]Some said, "He's demon possessed and out of his mind. Why listen to a man like that?" [21]Others said, "This doesn't sound like a man possessed by a demon! Can a demon open the eyes of the blind?"

10:8 Some manuscripts do not include *before me.* 10:9 Or *will find safety.* 10:19 Greek *Jewish people;* also in 10:24, 31.

PSALM 115:1-18

Not to us, O LORD, not to us,
   but to your name goes all the glory
   for your unfailing love and
      faithfulness.
[2] Why let the nations say,
   "Where is their God?"
[3] Our God is in the heavens,
   and he does as he wishes.
[4] Their idols are merely things of silver
      and gold,
   shaped by human hands.
[5] They have mouths but cannot speak,
   and eyes but cannot see.
[6] They have ears but cannot hear,
   and noses but cannot smell.
[7] They have hands but cannot feel,
   and feet but cannot walk,
   and throats but cannot make
      a sound.
[8] And those who make idols are just
      like them,
   as are all who trust in them.
[9] O Israel, trust the LORD!
   He is your helper and your shield.
[10] O priests, descendants of Aaron, trust
      the LORD!
   He is your helper and your shield.
[11] All you who fear the LORD, trust
      the LORD!
   He is your helper and your shield.

¹² The LORD remembers us and will
　　bless us.
　He will bless the people of Israel
　　and bless the priests, the
　　descendants of Aaron.
¹³ He will bless those who fear the LORD,
　　both great and lowly.

¹⁴ May the LORD richly bless
　　both you and your children.
¹⁵ May you be blessed by the LORD,
　　who made heaven and earth.
¹⁶ The heavens belong to the LORD,
　　but he has given the earth to all
　　humanity.

¹⁷ The dead cannot sing praises
　　to the LORD,
　for they have gone into the silence
　　of the grave.
¹⁸ But we can praise the LORD
　　both now and forever!

Praise the LORD!

PROVERBS 15:18-19

A hot-tempered person starts fights; a
cool-tempered person stops them. □ A
lazy person's way is blocked with briers,
but the path of the upright is an open
highway.

MAY**19**

1 SAMUEL 24:1-25:44

*The striking difference between David and Saul was
that David surrendered to God's will, whereas Saul
insisted on taking matters into his own hands.*

¹*After Saul returned from fighting the
Philistines, he was told that David had
gone into the wilderness of En-gedi. ²So
Saul chose 3,000 elite troops from all Israel and went to search for David and his
men near the rocks of the wild goats.

³At the place where the road passes
some sheepfolds, Saul went into a cave to
relieve himself. But as it happened, David
and his men were hiding farther back in
that very cave!

⁴"Now's your opportunity!" David's
men whispered to him. "Today the LORD
is telling you, 'I will certainly put your enemy into your power, to do with as you
wish.'" So David crept forward and cut off
a piece of the hem of Saul's robe.

⁵But then David's conscience began
bothering him because he had cut Saul's
robe. ⁶"The LORD knows I shouldn't have
done that to my lord the king," he said to
his men. "The LORD forbid that I should
do this to my lord the king and attack the
LORD's anointed one, for the LORD himself has chosen him." ⁷So David re-

strained his men and did not let them kill
Saul.

After Saul had left the cave and gone on
his way, ⁸David came out and shouted after him, "My lord the king!" And when
Saul looked around, David bowed low before him.

⁹Then he shouted to Saul, "Why do you
listen to the people who say I am trying to
harm you? ¹⁰This very day you can see
with your own eyes it isn't true. For the
LORD placed you at my mercy back there
in the cave. Some of my men told me to
kill you, but I spared you. For I said, 'I will
never harm the king—he is the LORD's
anointed one.' ¹¹Look, my father, at what I
have in my hand. It is a piece of the hem of
your robe! I cut it off, but I didn't kill you.
This proves that I am not trying to harm
you and that I have not sinned against you,
even though you have been hunting for
me to kill me.

¹²"May the LORD judge between us.
Perhaps the LORD will punish you for
what you are trying to do to me, but I will
never harm you. ¹³As that old proverb
says, 'From evil people come evil deeds.'
So you can be sure I will never harm you.
¹⁴Who is the king of Israel trying to catch

anyway? Should he spend his time chasing one who is as worthless as a dead dog or a single flea? [15]May the LORD therefore judge which of us is right and punish the guilty one. He is my advocate, and he will rescue me from your power!"

[16]When David had finished speaking, Saul called back, "Is that really you, my son David?" Then he began to cry. [17]And he said to David, "You are a better man than I am, for you have repaid me good for evil. [18]Yes, you have been amazingly kind to me today, for when the LORD put me in a place where you could have killed me, you didn't do it. [19]Who else would let his enemy get away when he had him in his power? May the LORD reward you well for the kindness you have shown me today. [20]And now I realize that you are surely going to be king, and that the kingdom of Israel will flourish under your rule. [21]Now swear to me by the LORD that when that happens you will not kill my family and destroy my line of descendants!"

[22]So David promised this to Saul with an oath. Then Saul went home, but David and his men went back to their stronghold.

[25:1]Now Samuel died, and all Israel gathered for his funeral. They buried him at his house in Ramah.

Then David moved down to the wilderness of Maon.* [2]There was a wealthy man from Maon who owned property near the town of Carmel. He had 3,000 sheep and 1,000 goats, and it was sheep-shearing time. [3]This man's name was Nabal, and his wife, Abigail, was a sensible and beautiful woman. But Nabal, a descendant of Caleb, was crude and mean in all his dealings.

[4]When David heard that Nabal was shearing his sheep, [5]he sent ten of his young men to Carmel with this message for Nabal: [6]"Peace and prosperity to you, your family, and everything you own! [7]I am told that it is sheep-shearing time. While your shepherds stayed among us near Carmel, we never harmed them, and nothing was ever stolen from them. [8]Ask your own men, and they will tell you this is true. So would you be kind to us, since we have come at a time of celebration? Please share any provisions you might have on hand with us and with your friend David."

[9]David's young men gave this message to Nabal in David's name, and they waited for a reply.

[10]"Who is this fellow David?" Nabal sneered to the young men. "Who does this son of Jesse think he is? There are lots of servants these days who run away from their masters. [11]Should I take my bread and my water and my meat that I've slaughtered for my shearers and give it to a band of outlaws who come from who knows where?"

[12]So David's young men returned and told him what Nabal had said. [13]"Get your swords!" was David's reply as he strapped on his own. Then 400 men started off with David, and 200 remained behind to guard their equipment.

[14]Meanwhile, one of Nabal's servants went to Abigail and told her, "David sent messengers from the wilderness to greet our master, but he screamed insults at them. [15]These men have been very good to us, and we never suffered any harm from them. Nothing was stolen from us the whole time they were with us. [16]In fact, day and night they were like a wall of protection to us and the sheep. [17]You need to know this and figure out what to do, for there is going to be trouble for our master and his whole family. He's so ill-tempered that no one can even talk to him!"

[18]Abigail wasted no time. She quickly gathered 200 loaves of bread, two wineskins full of wine, five sheep that had been slaughtered, nearly a bushel* of roasted grain, 100 clusters of raisins, and 200 fig cakes. She packed them on donkeys [19]and said to her servants, "Go on ahead. I will follow you shortly." But she didn't tell her husband Nabal what she was doing.

[20]As she was riding her donkey into a mountain ravine, she saw David and his men coming toward her. [21]David had just been saying, "A lot of good it did to help this fellow. We protected his flocks in the wilderness, and nothing he owned was lost or stolen. But he has repaid me evil for good. [22]May God strike me and kill me* if even one man of his household is still alive tomorrow morning!"

²³When Abigail saw David, she quickly got off her donkey and bowed low before him. ²⁴She fell at his feet and said, "I accept all blame in this matter, my lord. Please listen to what I have to say. ²⁵I know Nabal is a wicked and ill-tempered man; please don't pay any attention to him. He is a fool, just as his name suggests.* But I never even saw the young men you sent.

²⁶"Now, my lord, as surely as the LORD lives and you yourself live, since the LORD has kept you from murdering and taking vengeance into your own hands, let all your enemies and those who try to harm you be as cursed as Nabal is. ²⁷And here is a present that I, your servant, have brought to you and your young men. ²⁸Please forgive me if I have offended you in any way. The LORD will surely reward you with a lasting dynasty, for you are fighting the LORD's battles. And you have not done wrong throughout your entire life.

²⁹"Even when you are chased by those who seek to kill you, your life is safe in the care of the LORD your God, secure in his treasure pouch! But the lives of your enemies will disappear like stones shot from a sling! ³⁰When the LORD has done all he promised and has made you leader of Israel, ³¹don't let this be a blemish on your record. Then your conscience won't have to bear the staggering burden of needless bloodshed and vengeance. And when the LORD has done these great things for you, please remember me, your servant!"

³²David replied to Abigail, "Praise the LORD, the God of Israel, who has sent you to meet me today! ³³Thank God for your good sense! Bless you for keeping me from murder and from carrying out vengeance with my own hands. ³⁴For I swear by the LORD, the God of Israel, who has kept me from hurting you, that if you had not hurried out to meet me, not one of Nabal's men would still be alive tomorrow morning." ³⁵Then David accepted her present and told her, "Return home in peace. I have heard what you said. We will not kill your husband."

³⁶When Abigail arrived home, she found that Nabal was throwing a big party and was celebrating like a king. He was very drunk, so she didn't tell him anything about her meeting with David until dawn the next day. ³⁷In the morning when Nabal was sober, his wife told him what had happened. As a result he had a stroke,* and he lay paralyzed on his bed like a stone. ³⁸About ten days later, the LORD struck him, and he died.

³⁹When David heard that Nabal was dead, he said, "Praise the LORD, who has

HOW WE LIVE

Obeying God

1 SAMUEL 24:1-22 When David's men saw Saul enter their cave, they wrongly assumed that God was delivering Saul into their hands. David might have assumed that as well. After all, David knew he would be king . . . someday. Yet he also knew that to strike down the man God had placed on the throne would be worse than murder. In addition, if he assassinated Saul, what kind of example would that set for the men who were following him? It would indeed set a dangerous precedent with unforeseen consequences. So even though it meant continued running and living in caves, David chose to honor God and display loyalty to his king. His men probably thought he was crazy. • When you're in a tough situation where revenge may feel justified, do what David did. Think about what God would have you do. God never contradicts himself, so consider if your actions are against God's revealed will in his Word. Always obey that which God has revealed clearly even though circumstances might be confusing.

avenged the insult I received from Nabal and has kept me from doing it myself. Nabal has received the punishment for his sin." Then David sent messengers to Abigail to ask her to become his wife.

⁴⁰When the messengers arrived at Carmel, they told Abigail, "David has sent us to take you back to marry him."

⁴¹She bowed low to the ground and responded, "I, your servant, would be happy to marry David. I would even be willing to become a slave, washing the feet of his servants!" ⁴²Quickly getting ready, she took along five of her servant girls as attendants, mounted her donkey, and went with David's messengers. And so she became his wife. ⁴³David also married Ahinoam from Jezreel, making both of them his wives. ⁴⁴Saul, meanwhile, had given his daughter Michal, David's wife, to a man from Gallim named Palti son of Laish.

24:1 Verses 24:1-22 are numbered 24:2-23 in Hebrew text. 25:1 As in Greek version (see also 25:2); Hebrew reads *Paran*. 25:18 Hebrew 5 *seahs* [30 liters]. 25:22 As in Greek version; Hebrew reads *May God strike and kill the enemies of David*. 25:25 The name *Nabal* means "fool." 25:37 Hebrew *his heart failed him*.

JOHN 10:22-42

Jesus made it clear that those who didn't recognize his deity were making more of a statement about themselves than about him.

It was now winter, and Jesus was in Jerusalem at the time of Hanukkah, the Festival of Dedication. ²³He was in the Temple, walking through the section known as Solomon's Colonnade. ²⁴The people surrounded him and asked, "How long are you going to keep us in suspense? If you are the Messiah, tell us plainly."

²⁵Jesus replied, "I have already told you, and you don't believe me. The proof is the work I do in my Father's name. ²⁶But you don't believe me because you are not my sheep. ²⁷My sheep listen to my voice; I know them, and they follow me. ²⁸I give them eternal life, and they will never perish. No one can snatch them away from me, ²⁹for my Father has given them to me, and he is more powerful than anyone else.* No one can snatch them from the Father's hand. ³⁰The Father and I are one."

³¹Once again the people picked up stones to kill him. ³²Jesus said, "At my Father's direction I have done many good

works. For which one are you going to stone me?"

³³They replied, "We're stoning you not for any good work, but for blasphemy! You, a mere man, claim to be God."

³⁴Jesus replied, "It is written in your own Scriptures* that God said to certain leaders of the people, 'I say, you are gods!'* ³⁵And you know that the Scriptures cannot be altered. So if those people who received God's message were called 'gods,' ³⁶why do you call it blasphemy when I say, 'I am the Son of God'? After all, the Father set me apart and sent me into the world. ³⁷Don't believe me unless I carry out my Father's work. ³⁸But if I do his work, believe in the evidence of the miraculous works I have done, even if you don't believe me. Then you will know and understand that the Father is in me, and I am in the Father."

³⁹Once again they tried to arrest him, but he got away and left them. ⁴⁰He went beyond the Jordan River near the place where John was first baptizing and stayed there awhile. ⁴¹And many followed him. "John didn't perform miraculous signs," they remarked to one another, "but everything he said about this man has come true." ⁴²And many who were there believed in Jesus.

10:29 Other manuscripts read *for what my Father has given me is more powerful than anything*; still others read *regarding that which my Father has given me, he is greater than all*. 10:34a Greek *your own law*. 10:34b Ps 82:6.

PSALM 116:1-19

I love the LORD because he hears
    my voice
    and my prayer for mercy.
² Because he bends down to listen,
    I will pray as long as I have breath!
³ Death wrapped its ropes around me;
    the terrors of the grave* overtook
    me.
    I saw only trouble and sorrow.
⁴ Then I called on the name of the
    LORD:
    "Please, LORD, save me!"
⁵ How kind the LORD is! How good he is!
    So merciful, this God of ours!
⁶ The LORD protects those of childlike
    faith;
    I was facing death, and he
    saved me.

7 Let my soul be at rest again,
    for the LORD has been good to me.
8 He has saved me from death,
    my eyes from tears,
    my feet from stumbling.
9 And so I walk in the LORD's presence
    as I live here on earth!
10 I believed in you, so I said,
    "I am deeply troubled, LORD."
11 In my anxiety I cried out to you,
    "These people are all liars!"
12 What can I offer the LORD
    for all he has done for me?
13 I will lift up the cup of salvation
    and praise the LORD's name for
        saving me.
14 I will keep my promises to the LORD
    in the presence of all his people.

15 The LORD cares deeply
    when his loved ones die.

16 O LORD, I am your servant;
    yes, I am your servant, born into
        your household;
    you have freed me from my chains.
17 I will offer you a sacrifice of
        thanksgiving
    and call on the name of the LORD.
18 I will fulfill my vows to the LORD
    in the presence of all his people—
19 in the house of the LORD
    in the heart of Jerusalem.

Praise the LORD!

116:3 Hebrew *of Sheol.*

PROVERBS 15:20-21

Sensible children bring joy to their father;
foolish children despise their mother.
□Foolishness brings joy to those with no
sense; a sensible person stays on the right
path.

MAY**20**

1 SAMUEL 26:1–28:25

As Saul and David sorted through their options,
they both came to surprising conclusions. David
found refuge with Israel's enemies. Saul sought
guidance from the very person he had outlawed.

Now some men from Ziph came to Saul at
Gibeah to tell him, "David is hiding on
the hill of Hakilah, which overlooks Jeshimon."

2 So Saul took 3,000 of Israel's elite
troops and went to hunt him down in the
wilderness of Ziph. 3 Saul camped along
the road beside the hill of Hakilah, near
Jeshimon, where David was hiding. When
David learned that Saul had come after
him into the wilderness, 4 he sent out
spies to verify the report of Saul's arrival.

5 David slipped over to Saul's camp one
night to look around. Saul and Abner son
of Ner, the commander of his army, were
sleeping inside a ring formed by the
slumbering warriors. 6 "Who will volunteer to go in there with me?" David asked
Ahimelech the Hittite and Abishai son of
Zeruiah, Joab's brother.

"I'll go with you," Abishai replied. 7 So
David and Abishai went right into Saul's
camp and found him asleep, with his
spear stuck in the ground beside his head.
Abner and the soldiers were lying asleep
around him.

8 "God has surely handed your enemy
over to you this time!" Abishai whispered
to David. "Let me pin him to the ground
with one thrust of the spear; I won't need
to strike twice!"

9 "No!" David said. "Don't kill him. For
who can remain innocent after attacking
the LORD's anointed one? 10 Surely the
LORD will strike Saul down someday, or he
will die of old age or in battle. 11 The LORD
forbid that I should kill the one he has
anointed! But take his spear and that jug
of water beside his head, and then let's get
out of here!"

12 So David took the spear and jug of
water that were near Saul's head. Then he
and Abishai got away without anyone seeing them or even waking up, because the

LORD had put Saul's men into a deep sleep.

¹³David climbed the hill opposite the camp until he was at a safe distance. ¹⁴Then he shouted down to the soldiers and to Abner son of Ner, "Wake up, Abner!"

"Who is it?" Abner demanded.

¹⁵"Well, Abner, you're a great man, aren't you?" David taunted. "Where in all Israel is there anyone as mighty? So why haven't you guarded your master the king when someone came to kill him? ¹⁶This isn't good at all! I swear by the LORD that you and your men deserve to die, because you failed to protect your master, the LORD's anointed! Look around! Where are the king's spear and the jug of water that were beside his head?"

¹⁷Saul recognized David's voice and called out, "Is that you, my son David?"

And David replied, "Yes, my lord the king. ¹⁸Why are you chasing me? What have I done? What is my crime? ¹⁹But now let my lord the king listen to his servant. If the LORD has stirred you up against me, then let him accept my offering. But if this is simply a human scheme, then may those involved be cursed by the LORD. For they have driven me from my home, so I can no longer live among the LORD's people, and they have said, 'Go, worship pagan gods.' ²⁰Must I die on foreign soil, far from the presence of the LORD? Why has the king of Israel come out to search for a single flea? Why does he hunt me down like a partridge on the mountains?"

²¹Then Saul confessed, "I have sinned. Come back home, my son, and I will no longer try to harm you, for you valued my life today. I have been a fool and very, very wrong."

²²"Here is your spear, O king," David replied. "Let one of your young men come over and get it. ²³The LORD gives his own reward for doing good and for being loyal, and I refused to kill you even when the LORD placed you in my power, for you are the LORD's anointed one. ²⁴Now may the LORD value my life, even as I have valued yours today. May he rescue me from all my troubles."

²⁵And Saul said to David, "Blessings on you, my son David. You will do many he-roic deeds, and you will surely succeed." Then David went away, and Saul returned home.

27:1BUT David kept thinking to himself, "Someday Saul is going to get me. The best thing I can do is escape to the Philistines. Then Saul will stop hunting for me in Israelite territory, and I will finally be safe."

²So David took his 600 men and went over and joined Achish son of Maoch, the king of Gath. ³David and his men and their families settled there with Achish at Gath. David brought his two wives along with him—Ahinoam from Jezreel and Abigail, Nabal's widow from Carmel. ⁴Word soon reached Saul that David had fled to Gath, so he stopped hunting for him.

⁵One day David said to Achish, "If it is all right with you, we would rather live in one of the country towns instead of here in the royal city."

⁶So Achish gave him the town of Ziklag (which still belongs to the kings of Judah to this day), ⁷and they lived there among the Philistines for a year and four months.

⁸David and his men spent their time raiding the Geshurites, the Girzites, and the Amalekites—people who had lived near Shur, toward the land of Egypt, since ancient times. ⁹David did not leave one person alive in the villages he attacked. He took the sheep, goats, cattle, donkeys, camels, and clothing before returning home to see King Achish.

¹⁰"Where did you make your raid today?" Achish would ask.

And David would reply, "Against the south of Judah, the Jerahmeelites, and the Kenites."

¹¹No one was left alive to come to Gath and tell where he had really been. This happened again and again while he was living among the Philistines. ¹²Achish believed David and thought to himself, "By now the people of Israel must hate him bitterly. Now he will have to stay here and serve me forever!"

28:1ABOUT that time the Philistines mustered their armies for another war with Israel. King Achish told David, "You and your men will be expected to join me in battle."

[2]"Very well!" David agreed. "Now you will see for yourself what we can do."

Then Achish told David, "I will make you my personal bodyguard for life."

[3]Meanwhile, Samuel had died, and all Israel had mourned for him. He was buried in Ramah, his hometown. And Saul had banned from the land of Israel all mediums and those who consult the spirits of the dead.

[4]The Philistines set up their camp at Shunem, and Saul gathered all the army of Israel and camped at Gilboa. [5]When Saul saw the vast Philistine army, he became frantic with fear. [6]He asked the LORD what he should do, but the LORD refused to answer him, either by dreams or by sacred lots* or by the prophets. [7]Saul then said to his advisers, "Find a woman who is a medium, so I can go and ask her what to do."

His advisers replied, "There is a medium at Endor."

[8]So Saul disguised himself by wearing ordinary clothing instead of his royal robes. Then he went to the woman's home at night, accompanied by two of his men. "I have to talk to a man who has died," he said. "Will you call up his spirit for me?"

[9]"Are you trying to get me killed?" the woman demanded. "You know that Saul has outlawed all the mediums and all who consult the spirits of the dead. Why are you setting a trap for me?"

[10]But Saul took an oath in the name of the LORD and promised, "As surely as the LORD lives, nothing bad will happen to you for doing this."

[11]Finally, the woman said, "Well, whose spirit do you want me to call up?"

"Call up Samuel," Saul replied.

[12]When the woman saw Samuel, she screamed, "You've deceived me! You are Saul!"

[13]"Don't be afraid!" the king told her. "What do you see?"

"I see a god* coming up out of the earth," she said.

[14]"What does he look like?" Saul asked.

"He is an old man wrapped in a robe," she replied. Saul realized it was Samuel, and he fell to the ground before him.

[15]"Why have you disturbed me by calling me back?" Samuel asked Saul.

"Because I am in deep trouble," Saul replied. "The Philistines are at war with me, and God has left me and won't reply by prophets or dreams. So I have called for you to tell me what to do."

[16]But Samuel replied, "Why ask me, since the LORD has left you and has become your enemy? [17]The LORD has done just as he said he would. He has torn the

---

WHAT THE BIBLE SAYS

Warning against divination

1 SAMUEL 28:1-3 For many people today, reading your horoscope while standing in line at the supermarket may not seem like a big deal. Television shows have mediums who consult with the dead and psychics who solve crimes. All this has the appearance of harmless fun and games. However, God takes these things very seriously indeed and he does not want us to play around with them. He says very clearly that his people must have nothing to do with anything from the occult (Deuteronomy 18:10-12, April 1). • It comes down to a matter of trust. God has told us to trust in him and him alone. Consulting a medium, using a palmreader, or even just looking at a horoscope implies that our trust is actually not in God. When we lose our focus on God, we end up like Saul. Fear and doubt creep into our hearts and we have a tendency to want to take matters into our own hands. • Don't let desire to know the future or the belief that superstition is harmless lead you into condoning occult practices. They are counterfeits of God's power and have at their root a system of beliefs totally opposed to God.

kingdom from you and given it to your rival, David. ¹⁸The LORD has done this to you today because you refused to carry out his fierce anger against the Amalekites. ¹⁹What's more, the LORD will hand you and the army of Israel over to the Philistines tomorrow, and you and your sons will be here with me. The LORD will bring down the entire army of Israel in defeat."

²⁰Saul fell full length on the ground, paralyzed with fright because of Samuel's words. He was also faint with hunger, for he had eaten nothing all day and all night.

²¹When the woman saw how distraught he was, she said, "Sir, I obeyed your command at the risk of my life. ²²Now do what I say, and let me give you a little something to eat so you can regain your strength for the trip back."

²³But Saul refused. The men who were with him also urged him to eat, so he finally yielded and got up from the ground and sat on the couch.

²⁴The woman had been fattening a calf, so she hurried out and killed it. She took some flour, kneaded it into dough and baked unleavened bread. ²⁵She brought the meal to Saul and his men, and they ate it. Then they went out into the night.

28:6 Hebrew *by Urim.* **28:13** Or *gods.*

JOHN 11:1-54

Imagine seeing someone raised from the dead. When Jesus raised the dead, some of the observers believed that Jesus was God himself. Others believed that Jesus should die, and very soon.

A man named Lazarus was sick. He lived in Bethany with his sisters, Mary and Martha. ²This is the Mary who later poured the expensive perfume on the Lord's feet and wiped them with her hair.* Her brother, Lazarus, was sick. ³So the two sisters sent a message to Jesus telling him, "Lord, your dear friend is very sick."

⁴But when Jesus heard about it he said, "Lazarus's sickness will not end in death. No, it happened for the glory of God so that the Son of God will receive glory from this." ⁵So although Jesus loved Martha, Mary, and Lazarus, ⁶he stayed where he was for the next two days. ⁷Finally, he said to his disciples, "Let's go back to Judea."

⁸But his disciples objected. "Rabbi,"

they said, "only a few days ago the people* in Judea were trying to stone you. Are you going there again?"

⁹Jesus replied, "There are twelve hours of daylight every day. During the day people can walk safely. They can see because they have the light of this world. ¹⁰But at night there is danger of stumbling because they have no light." ¹¹Then he said, "Our friend Lazarus has fallen asleep, but now I will go and wake him up."

¹²The disciples said, "Lord, if he is sleeping, he will soon get better!" ¹³They thought Jesus meant Lazarus was simply sleeping, but Jesus meant Lazarus had died.

¹⁴So he told them plainly, "Lazarus is dead. ¹⁵And for your sakes, I'm glad I wasn't there, for now you will really believe. Come, let's go see him."

¹⁶Thomas, nicknamed the Twin,* said to his fellow disciples, "Let's go, too—and die with Jesus."

¹⁷When Jesus arrived at Bethany, he was told that Lazarus had already been in his grave for four days. ¹⁸Bethany was only a few miles* down the road from Jerusalem, ¹⁹and many of the people had come to console Martha and Mary in their loss. ²⁰When Martha got word that Jesus was coming, she went to meet him. But Mary stayed in the house. ²¹Martha said to Jesus, "Lord, if only you had been here, my brother would not have died. ²²But even now I know that God will give you whatever you ask."

²³Jesus told her, "Your brother will rise again."

²⁴"Yes," Martha said, "he will rise when everyone else rises, at the last day."

²⁵Jesus told her, "I am the resurrection and the life.* Anyone who believes in me will live, even after dying. ²⁶Everyone who lives in me and believes in me will never ever die. Do you believe this, Martha?"

²⁷"Yes, Lord," she told him. "I have always believed you are the Messiah, the Son of God, the one who has come into the world from God." ²⁸Then she returned to Mary. She called Mary aside from the mourners and told her, "The Teacher is here and wants to see you." ²⁹So Mary immediately went to him.

³⁰Jesus had stayed outside the village,

at the place where Martha met him. [31]When the people who were at the house consoling Mary saw her leave so hastily, they assumed she was going to Lazarus's grave to weep. So they followed her there. [32]When Mary arrived and saw Jesus, she fell at his feet and said, "Lord, if only you had been here, my brother would not have died."

[33]When Jesus saw her weeping and saw the other people wailing with her, a deep anger welled up within him,* and he was deeply troubled. [34]"Where have you put him?" he asked them.

They told him, "Lord, come and see."

[35]Then Jesus wept. [36]The people who were standing nearby said, "See how much he loved him!" [37]But some said, "This man healed a blind man. Couldn't he have kept Lazarus from dying?"

[38]Jesus was still angry as he arrived at the tomb, a cave with a stone rolled across its entrance. [39]"Roll the stone aside," Jesus told them.

But Martha, the dead man's sister, protested, "Lord, he has been dead for four days. The smell will be terrible."

[40]Jesus responded, "Didn't I tell you that you would see God's glory if you believe?" [41]So they rolled the stone aside. Then Jesus looked up to heaven and said, "Father, thank you for hearing me. [42]You always hear me, but I said it out loud for the sake of all these people standing here, so that they will believe you sent me." [43]Then Jesus shouted, "Lazarus, come out!" [44]And the dead man came out, his hands and feet bound in graveclothes, his face wrapped in a headcloth. Jesus told them, "Unwrap him and let him go!"

[45]Many of the people who were with Mary believed in Jesus when they saw this happen. [46]But some went to the Pharisees and told them what Jesus had done. [47]Then the leading priests and Pharisees called the high council* together. "What are we going to do?" they asked

each other. "This man certainly performs many miraculous signs. [48]If we allow him to go on like this, soon everyone will believe in him. Then the Roman army will come and destroy both our Temple* and our nation."

[49]Caiaphas, who was high priest at that time,* said, "You don't know what you're talking about! [50]You don't realize that it's better for you that one man should die for the people than for the whole nation to be destroyed."

[51]He did not say this on his own; as high priest at that time he was led to prophesy that Jesus would die for the entire nation. [52]And not only for that nation, but to bring together and unite all the children of God scattered around the world.

[53]So from that time on, the Jewish leaders began to plot Jesus' death. [54]As a result, Jesus stopped his public ministry among the people and left Jerusalem. He went to a place near the wilderness, to the village of Ephraim, and stayed there with his disciples.

11:2 This incident is recorded in chapter 12.   **11:8** Greek *Jewish people;* also in 11:19, 31, 33, 36, 45, 54.   **11:16** Greek *Thomas, who was called Didymus.*   **11:18** Greek *was about 15 stadia* [about 2.8 kilometers].   **11:25** Some manuscripts do not include *and the life.*   **11:33** Or *he was angry in his spirit.*   **11:47** Greek *the Sanhedrin.*   **11:48** Or *our position;* Greek reads *our place.*   **11:49** Greek *that year;* also in 11:51.

PSALM 117:1-2

Praise the LORD, all you nations.
  Praise him, all you people of the
    earth.
2 For he loves us with unfailing love;
  the LORD's faithfulness endures
    forever.

Praise the LORD!

PROVERBS 15:22-23

Plans go wrong for lack of advice; many advisers bring success. □ Everyone enjoys a fitting reply; it is wonderful to say the right thing at the right time!

1 SAMUEL 29:1–31:13
The first book of Samuel ends with the death of Saul and his sons. God already had a plan and would bring the young King David into his rightful place.

The entire Philistine army now mobilized at Aphek, and the Israelites camped at the spring in Jezreel. ²As the Philistine rulers were leading out their troops in groups of hundreds and thousands, David and his men marched at the rear with King Achish. ³But the Philistine commanders demanded, "What are these Hebrews doing here?"

And Achish told them, "This is David, the servant of King Saul of Israel. He's been with me for years, and I've never found a single fault in him from the day he arrived until today."

⁴But the Philistine commanders were angry. "Send him back to the town you've given him!" they demanded. "He can't go into the battle with us. What if he turns against us in battle and becomes our adversary? Is there any better way for him to reconcile himself with his master than by handing our heads over to him? ⁵Isn't this the same David about whom the women of Israel sing in their dances,

'Saul has killed his thousands,
 and David his ten thousands'?"

⁶So Achish finally summoned David and said to him, "I swear by the LORD that you have been a trustworthy ally. I think you should go with me into battle, for I've never found a single flaw in you from the day you arrived until today. But the other Philistine rulers won't hear of it. ⁷Please don't upset them, but go back quietly."

⁸"What have I done to deserve this treatment?" David demanded. "What have you ever found in your servant, that I can't go and fight the enemies of my lord the king?"

⁹But Achish insisted, "As far as I'm concerned, you're as perfect as an angel of God. But the Philistine commanders are afraid to have you with them in the battle. ¹⁰Now get up early in the morning, and leave with your men as soon as it gets light."

¹¹So David and his men headed back into the land of the Philistines, while the Philistine army went on to Jezreel.

30:1THREE days later, when David and his men arrived home at their town of Ziklag, they found that the Amalekites had made a raid into the Negev and Ziklag; they had crushed Ziklag and burned it to the ground. ²They had carried off the women and children and everyone else but without killing anyone.

³When David and his men saw the ruins and realized what had happened to their families, ⁴they wept until they could weep no more. ⁵David's two wives, Ahinoam from Jezreel and Abigail, the widow of Nabal from Carmel, were among those captured. ⁶David was now in great danger because all his men were very bitter about losing their sons and daughters, and they began to talk of stoning him. But David found strength in the LORD his God.

⁷Then he said to Abiathar the priest, "Bring me the ephod!" So Abiathar brought it. ⁸Then David asked the LORD, "Should I chase after this band of raiders? Will I catch them?"

And the LORD told him, "Yes, go after them. You will surely recover everything that was taken from you!"

⁹So David and his 600 men set out, and they came to the brook Besor. ¹⁰But 200 of the men were too exhausted to cross the brook, so David continued the pursuit with 400 men.

¹¹Along the way they found an Egyptian man in a field and brought him to David. They gave him some bread to eat and water to drink. ¹²They also gave him part of a fig cake and two clusters of raisins, for he hadn't had anything to eat or drink for three days and nights. Before long his strength returned.

¹³"To whom do you belong, and where do you come from?" David asked him.

"I am an Egyptian—the slave of an Amalekite," he replied. "My master abandoned me three days ago because I was sick. ¹⁴We were on our way back from raiding the Kerethites in the Negev, the territory of Judah, and the land of Caleb, and we had just burned Ziklag."

¹⁵"Will you lead me to this band of raiders?" David asked.

The young man replied, "If you take an oath in God's name that you will not kill me or give me back to my master, then I will guide you to them."

¹⁶So he led David to them, and they found the Amalekites spread out across the fields, eating and drinking and dancing with joy because of the vast amount of plunder they had taken from the Philistines and the land of Judah. ¹⁷David and his men rushed in among them and slaughtered them throughout that night and the entire next day until evening. None of the Amalekites escaped except 400 young men who fled on camels. ¹⁸David got back everything the Amalekites had taken, and he rescued his two wives. ¹⁹Nothing was missing: small or great, son or daughter, nor anything else that had been taken. David brought everything back. ²⁰He also recovered all the flocks and herds, and his men drove them ahead of the other livestock. "This plunder belongs to David!" they said.

²¹Then David returned to the brook Besor and met up with the 200 men who had been left behind because they were too exhausted to go with him. They went out to meet David and his men, and David greeted them joyfully. ²²But some evil troublemakers among David's men said, "They didn't go with us, so they can't have any of the plunder we recovered. Give them their wives and children, and tell them to be gone."

²³But David said, "No, my brothers! Don't be selfish with what the LORD has given us. He has kept us safe and helped us defeat the band of raiders that attacked us. ²⁴Who will listen when you talk like this? We share and share alike—those who go to battle and those who guard the equipment." ²⁵From then on David made this a decree and regulation for Israel, and it is still followed today.

²⁶When he arrived at Ziklag, David sent part of the plunder to the elders of Judah, who were his friends. "Here is a present for you, taken from the LORD's enemies," he said.

²⁷The gifts were sent to the people of the following towns David had visited: Bethel, Ramoth-negev, Jattir, ²⁸Aroer, Siphmoth, Eshtemoa, ²⁹Racal,* the towns of the Jerahmeelites, the towns of the Kenites, ³⁰Hormah, Bor-ashan, Athach, ³¹Hebron, and all the other places David and his men had visited.

³¹:¹Now the Philistines attacked Israel, and the men of Israel fled before them. Many were slaughtered on the slopes of Mount Gilboa. ²The Philistines closed in on Saul and his sons, and they killed three of his sons—Jonathan, Abinadab, and Malkishua. ³The fighting grew very fierce around Saul, and the Philistine archers caught up with him and wounded him severely.

⁴Saul groaned to his armor bearer, "Take your sword and kill me before these pagan Philistines come to run me through and taunt and torture me."

But his armor bearer was afraid and would not do it. So Saul took his own sword and fell on it. ⁵When his armor bearer realized that Saul was dead, he fell on his own sword and died beside the king. ⁶So Saul, his three sons, his armor bearer, and his troops all died together that same day.

⁷When the Israelites on the other side of the Jezreel Valley and beyond the Jordan saw that the Israelite army had fled and that Saul and his sons were dead, they abandoned their towns and fled. So the Philistines moved in and occupied their towns.

⁸The next day, when the Philistines went out to strip the dead, they found the bodies of Saul and his three sons on Mount Gilboa. ⁹So they cut off Saul's head and stripped off his armor. Then they proclaimed the good news of Saul's death in their pagan temple and to the people throughout the land of Philistia. ¹⁰They placed his armor in the temple of the Ashtoreths, and they fastened his body to the wall of the city of Beth-shan.

¹¹But when the people of Jabesh-gilead heard what the Philistines had done to

Saul, [12]all their mighty warriors traveled through the night to Beth-shan and took the bodies of Saul and his sons down from the wall. They brought them to Jabesh, where they burned the bodies. [13]Then they took their bones and buried them beneath the tamarisk tree at Jabesh, and they fasted for seven days.

30:29 Greek version reads *Carmel*.

JOHN 11:55–12:19

Having heard of Jesus raising Lazarus from the dead, those attending the Passover in Jerusalem were excited, to say the least. They thought their king had come at last to free them from Rome and usher in a Golden Age for their nation.

It was now almost time for the Jewish Passover celebration, and many people from all over the country arrived in Jerusalem several days early so they could go through the purification ceremony before Passover began. [56]They kept looking for Jesus, but as they stood around in the Temple, they said to each other, "What do you think? He won't come for Passover, will he?" [57]Meanwhile, the leading priests and Pharisees had publicly ordered that anyone seeing Jesus must report it immediately so they could arrest him.

[12:1]Six days before the Passover celebration began, Jesus arrived in Bethany, the home of Lazarus—the man he had raised from the dead. [2]A dinner was prepared in Jesus' honor. Martha served, and Lazarus was among those who ate* with him. [3]Then Mary took a twelve-ounce jar* of expensive perfume made from essence of nard, and she anointed Jesus' feet with it, wiping his feet with her hair. The house was filled with the fragrance.

[4]But Judas Iscariot, the disciple who would soon betray him, said, [5]"That perfume was worth a year's wages.* It should have been sold and the money given to the poor." [6]Not that he cared for the poor—he was a thief, and since he was in charge of the disciples' money, he often stole some for himself.

[7]Jesus replied, "Leave her alone. She did this in preparation for my burial. [8]You will always have the poor among you, but you will not always have me."

[9]When all the people* heard of Jesus' arrival, they flocked to see him and also to see Lazarus, the man Jesus had raised from the dead. [10]Then the leading priests decided to kill Lazarus, too, [11]for it was because of him that many of the people had deserted them* and believed in Jesus.

[12]The next day, the news that Jesus was on the way to Jerusalem swept through the city. A large crowd of Passover visitors [13]took palm branches and went down the road to meet him. They shouted,

"Praise God!*
Blessings on the one who comes
in the name of the LORD!
Hail to the King of Israel!"*

[14]Jesus found a young donkey and rode on it, fulfilling the prophecy that said:

[15] "Don't be afraid, people of Jerusalem.*
Look, your King is coming,
riding on a donkey's colt."*

[16]His disciples didn't understand at the time that this was a fulfillment of prophecy. But after Jesus entered into his glory, they remembered what had happened and realized that these things had been written about him.

[17]Many in the crowd had seen Jesus call Lazarus from the tomb, raising him from the dead, and they were telling others* about it. [18]That was the reason so many went out to meet him—because they had heard about this miraculous sign. [19]Then the Pharisees said to each other, "There's nothing we can do. Look, everyone* has gone after him!"

12:2 Or *who reclined.*   12:3 Greek *took 1 litra* [327 grams].   12:5 Greek *worth 300 denarii.* A denarius was equivalent to a laborer's full day's wage.   12:9 Greek *Jewish people;* also in 12:11.   12:11 Or *had deserted their traditions;* Greek reads *had deserted.*   12:13a Greek *Hosanna,* an exclamation of praise adapted from a Hebrew expression that means "save now."   12:13b Ps 118:25-26; Zeph 3:15.   12:15a Greek *daughter of Zion.*   12:15b Zech 9:9.   12:17 Greek *were testifying.*   12:19 Greek *the world.*

PSALM 118:1-18

Give thanks to the LORD,
for he is good!
His faithful love endures
forever.

[2] Let all Israel repeat:
"His faithful love endures
forever."

3 Let Aaron's descendants, the priests,
    repeat:
    "His faithful love endures forever."
4 Let all who fear the LORD repeat:
    "His faithful love endures forever."

5 In my distress I prayed to the LORD,
    and the LORD answered me and set
    me free.
6 The LORD is for me, so I will have
    no fear.
    What can mere people do to me?
7 Yes, the LORD is for me; he will
    help me.
    I will look in triumph at those
    who hate me.
8 It is better to take refuge in the LORD
    than to trust in people.
9 It is better to take refuge in the LORD
    than to trust in princes.

10 Though hostile nations surrounded
    me,
    I destroyed them all with the
    authority of the LORD.
11 Yes, they surrounded and attacked me,
    but I destroyed them all with the
    authority of the LORD.
12 They swarmed around me like bees;
    they blazed against me like
    a crackling fire.

But I destroyed them all with the
    authority of the LORD.
13 My enemies did their best to kill me,
    but the LORD rescued me.
14 The LORD is my strength and
    my song;
    he has given me victory.
15 Songs of joy and victory are sung
    in the camp of the godly.
    The strong right arm of the LORD
    has done glorious things!
16 The strong right arm of the LORD
    is raised in triumph.
    The strong right arm of the LORD
    has done glorious things!
17 I will not die; instead, I will live
    to tell what the LORD has done.
18 The LORD has punished me
    severely,
    but he did not let me die.

PROVERBS 15:24-26
The path of life leads upward for the wise;
they leave the grave* behind. □ The LORD
tears down the house of the proud, but he
protects the property of widows. □ The
LORD detests evil plans, but he delights in
pure words.

15:24 Hebrew *Sheol.*

WHO GOD IS — Jesus fulfilled prophecy

JOHN 12:12-16 A great throng ran in front of Jesus, waving palm branches
and shouting, "Hail to the King of Israel!" And what did this king do?
He rode on a donkey for a humble entry into the city. • Then verse 14
comments that this was "fulfilling the prophecy." Centuries earlier the
prophet Zechariah had written: "Rejoice, O people of Zion! . . . Look, your
king is coming to you. He is righteous and victorious, yet he is humble,
riding on a donkey—riding on a donkey's colt" (Zechariah 9:9, December
26). Now it was happening. Their king had arrived just as the prophet had
foretold. • Jesus fulfilled all the Old Testament prophecies. His birth-
place in Bethlehem was foretold by the prophet Micah (Micah 5:2 and
Matthew 2:5-6, December 16 and January 1). His death for us was prophesied by Isaiah (Isaiah 53, September 27). The point? The crowds were
right—this was their king. But they were wrong about what kind of king
he would be. Like the men on the road to Emmaus, they didn't understand how all of the Scriptures pointed to Jesus (Luke 24, April 29).

2 SAMUEL 1:1–2:11

The second book of Samuel opens with the news of Saul's death and the death of his sons. For David, who had long known that in God's time he was to be the next king of Israel, this news prompted mixed emotions.

After the death of Saul, David returned from his victory over the Amalekites and spent two days in Ziklag. ²On the third day a man arrived from Saul's army camp. He had torn his clothes and put dirt on his head to show that he was in mourning. He fell to the ground before David in deep respect.

³"Where have you come from?" David asked.

"I escaped from the Israelite camp," the man replied.

⁴"What happened?" David demanded. "Tell me how the battle went."

The man replied, "Our entire army fled from the battle. Many of the men are dead, and Saul and his son Jonathan are also dead."

⁵"How do you know Saul and Jonathan are dead?" David demanded of the young man.

⁶The man answered, "I happened to be on Mount Gilboa, and there was Saul leaning on his spear with the enemy chariots and charioteers closing in on him. ⁷When he turned and saw me, he cried out for me to come to him. 'How can I help?' I asked him.

⁸"He responded, 'Who are you?'

"'I am an Amalekite,' I told him.

⁹"Then he begged me, 'Come over here and put me out of my misery, for I am in terrible pain and want to die.'

¹⁰"So I killed him," the Amalekite told David, "for I knew he couldn't live. Then I took his crown and his armband, and I have brought them here to you, my lord."

¹¹David and his men tore their clothes in sorrow when they heard the news. ¹²They mourned and wept and fasted all day for Saul and his son Jonathan, and for the LORD's army and the nation of Israel, because they had died by the sword that day.

¹³Then David said to the young man who had brought the news, "Where are you from?"

And he replied, "I am a foreigner, an Amalekite, who lives in your land."

¹⁴"Why were you not afraid to kill the LORD's anointed one?" David asked.

¹⁵Then David said to one of his men, "Kill him!" So the man thrust his sword into the Amalekite and killed him. ¹⁶"You have condemned yourself," David said, "for you yourself confessed that you killed the LORD's anointed one."

¹⁷Then David composed a funeral song for Saul and Jonathan, ¹⁸and he commanded that it be taught to the people of Judah. It is known as the Song of the Bow, and it is recorded in *The Book of Jashar*.*

¹⁹ Your pride and joy, O Israel, lies dead
       on the hills!
    Oh, how the mighty heroes have
       fallen!
²⁰ Don't announce the news in Gath,
       don't proclaim it in the streets
          of Ashkelon,
    or the daughters of the Philistines
       will rejoice
    and the pagans will laugh in triumph.

²¹ O mountains of Gilboa,
       let there be no dew or rain upon you,
    nor fruitful fields producing
          offerings of grain.*
    For there the shield of the mighty
       heroes was defiled;
    the shield of Saul will no longer
       be anointed with oil.
²² The bow of Jonathan was powerful,
       and the sword of Saul did its mighty
          work.
    They shed the blood of their enemies
       and pierced the bodies of mighty
          heroes.

²³ How beloved and gracious were Saul
       and Jonathan!
    They were together in life and
       in death.
    They were swifter than eagles,
       stronger than lions.

²⁴ O women of Israel, weep for Saul,
for he dressed you in luxurious
scarlet clothing,
in garments decorated with gold.

²⁵ Oh, how the mighty heroes have fallen
in battle!
Jonathan lies dead on the hills.
²⁶ How I weep for you, my brother
Jonathan!
Oh, how much I loved you!
And your love for me was deep,
deeper than the love of women!

²⁷ Oh, how the mighty heroes have
fallen!
Stripped of their weapons,
they lie dead.

2:1AFTER this, David asked the LORD, "Should I move back to one of the towns of Judah?"

"Yes," the LORD replied.

Then David asked, "Which town should I go to?"

"To Hebron," the LORD answered.

²David's two wives were Ahinoam from Jezreel and Abigail, the widow of Nabal from Carmel. So David and his wives ³ and his men and their families all moved to Judah, and they settled in the villages near Hebron. ⁴Then the men of Judah came to David and crowned him king over the people of Judah.

When David heard that the men of Jabesh-gilead had buried Saul, ⁵he sent them this message: "May the LORD bless you for being so loyal to your master Saul and giving him a decent burial. ⁶May the LORD be loyal to you in return and reward you with his unfailing love! And I, too, will reward you for what you have done. ⁷Now that Saul is dead, I ask you to be my strong and loyal subjects like the people of Judah, who have anointed me as their new king."

⁸But Abner son of Ner, the commander of Saul's army, had already gone to Mahanaim with Saul's son Ishbosheth.* ⁹There he proclaimed Ishbosheth king over Gilead, Jezreel, Ephraim, Benjamin, the land of the Ashurites, and all the rest of Israel.

¹⁰Ishbosheth, Saul's son, was forty years old when he became king, and he ruled from Mahanaim for two years. Meanwhile, the people of Judah remained loyal to David. ¹¹David made Hebron his capital, and he ruled as king of Judah for seven and a half years.

1:18 Or *The Book of the Upright.*   1:21 The meaning of the Hebrew is uncertain.   2:8 *Ishbosheth* is another name for Esh-baal.

JOHN 12:20-50

For the entire history of the Israelite nation, there had been a promise of one who would come to make things right. He would triumph over all evil. Jesus claimed to be that one, yet he talked more and more about dying. His death would bring life—eternal life.

Following Jesus

HOW WE LIVE

JOHN 12:26 One aspect of following Jesus means spending time with him. That seems obvious. But think about it. When Jesus was here on earth, people who believed in Jesus' teachings literally *followed* him. They walked with him. They traveled together, ate together, prayed together, saw awesome things together, and suffered together. • So how do we follow Jesus today? How do we spend time with him? One way to spend time with Jesus is through prayer and reading the Bible. We need to take quiet times to sense his presence and to welcome him into our lives. We need to read and study God's Word so we can do what he wants us to do. Though we cannot see or touch Jesus today (he is risen and in heaven!), he has given every new believer his Holy Spirit. Through the Spirit, we can live in the awareness of God's presence as we go through our daily lives. We are never out of his sight. We are never separated from his love.

Some Greeks who had come to Jerusalem for the Passover celebration [21] paid a visit to Philip, who was from Bethsaida in Galilee. They said, "Sir, we want to meet Jesus." [22] Philip told Andrew about it, and they went together to ask Jesus.

[23] Jesus replied, "Now the time has come for the Son of Man* to enter into his glory. [24] I tell you the truth, unless a kernel of wheat is planted in the soil and dies, it remains alone. But its death will produce many new kernels—a plentiful harvest of new lives. [25] Those who love their life in this world will lose it. Those who care nothing for their life in this world will keep it for eternity. [26] Anyone who wants to be my disciple must follow me, because my servants must be where I am. And the Father will honor anyone who serves me.

[27] "Now my soul is deeply troubled. Should I pray, 'Father, save me from this hour'? But this is the very reason I came! [28] Father, bring glory to your name."

Then a voice spoke from heaven, saying, "I have already brought glory to my name, and I will do so again." [29] When the crowd heard the voice, some thought it was thunder, while others declared an angel had spoken to him.

[30] Then Jesus told them, "The voice was for your benefit, not mine. [31] The time for judging this world has come, when Satan, the ruler of this world, will be cast out. [32] And when I am lifted up from the earth, I will draw everyone to myself." [33] He said this to indicate how he was going to die.

[34] The crowd responded, "We understood from Scripture* that the Messiah would live forever. How can you say the Son of Man will die? Just who is this Son of Man, anyway?"

[35] Jesus replied, "My light will shine for you just a little longer. Walk in the light while you can, so the darkness will not overtake you. Those who walk in the darkness cannot see where they are going. [36] Put your trust in the light while there is still time; then you will become children of the light."

After saying these things, Jesus went away and was hidden from them.

[37] But despite all the miraculous signs Jesus had done, most of the people still did not believe in him. [38] This is exactly what Isaiah the prophet had predicted:

"Lord, who has believed our message?
To whom has the Lord revealed his
powerful arm?"*

[39] But the people couldn't believe, for as Isaiah also said,

[40] "The Lord has blinded their eyes
and hardened their hearts—
so that their eyes cannot see,
and their hearts cannot understand,
and they cannot turn to me
and have me heal them."*

[41] Isaiah was referring to Jesus when he said this, because he saw the future and spoke of the Messiah's glory. [42] Many people did believe in him, however, including some of the Jewish leaders. But they wouldn't admit it for fear that the Pharisees would expel them from the synagogue. [43] For they loved human praise more than the praise of God.

[44] Jesus shouted to the crowds, "If you trust me, you are trusting not only me, but also God who sent me. [45] For when you see me, you are seeing the one who sent me. [46] I have come as a light to shine in this dark world, so that all who put their trust in me will no longer remain in the dark. [47] I will not judge those who hear me but don't obey me, for I have come to save the world and not to judge it. [48] But all who reject me and my message will be judged on the day of judgment by the truth I have spoken. [49] I don't speak on my own authority. The Father who sent me has commanded me what to say and how to say it. [50] And I know his commands lead to eternal life; so I say whatever the Father tells me to say."

12:23 "Son of Man" is a title Jesus used for himself. 12:34 Greek *from the law.* 12:38 Isa 53:1. 12:40 Isa 6:10.

PSALM 118:19-29

Open for me the gates where the
righteous enter,
and I will go in and thank
the Lord.
[20] These gates lead to the presence
of the Lord,
and the godly enter there.

²¹ I thank you for answering my prayer
and giving me victory!

²² The stone that the builders rejected
has now become the cornerstone.
²³ This is the LORD's doing,
and it is wonderful to see.
²⁴ This is the day the LORD has made.
We will rejoice and be glad in it.
²⁵ Please, LORD, please save us.
Please, LORD, please give
us success.
²⁶ Bless the one who comes in the name
of the LORD.
We bless you from the house
of the LORD.

²⁷ The LORD is God, shining upon us.
Take the sacrifice and bind it with
cords on the altar.
²⁸ You are my God, and I will praise you!
You are my God, and I will exalt you!

²⁹ Give thanks to the LORD, for he is
good!
His faithful love endures forever.

PROVERBS 15:27-28
Greed brings grief to the whole family,
but those who hate bribes will live. □ The
heart of the godly thinks carefully before
speaking; the mouth of the wicked overflows with evil words.

MAY**23**

2 SAMUEL 2:12–3:39
Israel was experiencing growing pains; two
separate claims to the throne emerged. One was
official (Saul's family line) and one was more
grassroots (David). Each camp had a strong-willed
military commander. However, only one had God's
anointing.

One day Abner led Ishbosheth's troops
from Mahanaim to Gibeon. ¹³About the
same time, Joab son of Zeruiah led David's
troops out and met them at the pool of
Gibeon. The two groups sat down there,
facing each other from opposite sides of
the pool.
¹⁴Then Abner suggested to Joab, "Let's
have a few of our warriors fight hand to
hand here in front of us."
"All right," Joab agreed. ¹⁵So twelve
men were chosen to fight from each
side—twelve men of Benjamin representing Ishbosheth son of Saul, and twelve
representing David. ¹⁶Each one grabbed
his opponent by the hair and thrust his
sword into the other's side so that all of
them died. So this place at Gibeon has
been known ever since as the Field of
Swords.*
¹⁷A fierce battle followed that day, and
Abner and the men of Israel were defeated by the forces of David.

¹⁸Joab, Abishai, and Asahel—the three
sons of Zeruiah—were among David's
forces that day. Asahel could run like a gazelle, ¹⁹and he began chasing Abner. He
pursued him relentlessly, not stopping for
anything. ²⁰When Abner looked back and
saw him coming, he called out, "Is that
you, Asahel?"
"Yes, it is," he replied.
²¹"Go fight someone else!" Abner
warned. "Take on one of the younger men,
and strip him of his weapons." But Asahel
kept right on chasing Abner.
²²Again Abner shouted to him, "Get
away from here! I don't want to kill you.
How could I ever face your brother Joab
again?"
²³But Asahel refused to turn back, so
Abner thrust the butt end of his spear
through Asahel's stomach, and the spear
came out through his back. He stumbled
to the ground and died there. And everyone who came by that spot stopped and
stood still when they saw Asahel lying
there.
²⁴When Joab and Abishai found out
what had happened, they set out after Abner. The sun was just going down as they
arrived at the hill of Ammah near Giah,

along the road to the wilderness of Gibeon. ²⁵Abner's troops from the tribe of Benjamin regrouped there at the top of the hill to take a stand.

²⁶Abner shouted down to Joab, "Must we always be killing each other? Don't you realize that bitterness is the only result? When will you call off your men from chasing their Israelite brothers?"

²⁷Then Joab said, "God only knows what would have happened if you hadn't spoken, for we would have chased you all night if necessary." ²⁸So Joab blew the ram's horn, and his men stopped chasing the troops of Israel.

²⁹All that night Abner and his men retreated through the Jordan Valley.* They crossed the Jordan River, traveling all through the morning,* and didn't stop until they arrived at Mahanaim.

³⁰Meanwhile, Joab and his men also returned home. When Joab counted his casualties, he discovered that only 19 men were missing in addition to Asahel. ³¹But 360 of Abner's men had been killed, all from the tribe of Benjamin. ³²Joab and his men took Asahel's body to Bethlehem and buried him there in his father's tomb. Then they traveled all night and reached Hebron at daybreak.

³:¹THAT was the beginning of a long war between those who were loyal to Saul and those loyal to David. As time passed David became stronger and stronger, while Saul's dynasty became weaker and weaker.

²These are the sons who were born to David in Hebron:

The oldest was Amnon, whose mother was Ahinoam from Jezreel.
³ The second was Daniel,* whose mother was Abigail, the widow of Nabal from Carmel.
The third was Absalom, whose mother was Maacah, the daughter of Talmai, king of Geshur.
⁴ The fourth was Adonijah, whose mother was Haggith.
The fifth was Shephatiah, whose mother was Abital.
⁵ The sixth was Ithream, whose mother was Eglah, David's wife.

These sons were all born to David in Hebron.

⁶As the war between the house of Saul and the house of David went on, Abner became a powerful leader among those loyal to Saul. ⁷One day Ishbosheth,* Saul's son, accused Abner of sleeping with one of his father's concubines, a woman named Rizpah, daughter of Aiah.

⁸Abner was furious. "Am I some Judean dog to be kicked around like this?" he shouted. "After all I have done for your father, Saul, and his family and friends by not handing you over to David, is this my reward—that you find fault with me about this woman? ⁹May God strike me and even kill me if I don't do everything I can to help David get what the LORD has promised him! ¹⁰I'm going to take Saul's kingdom and give it to David. I will establish the throne of David over Israel as well as Judah, all the way from Dan in the north to Beersheba in the south." ¹¹Ishbosheth didn't dare say another word because he was afraid of what Abner might do.

¹²Then Abner sent messengers to David, saying, "Doesn't the entire land belong to you? Make a solemn pact with me, and I will help turn over all of Israel to you."

¹³"All right," David replied, "but I will not negotiate with you unless you bring back my wife Michal, Saul's daughter, when you come."

¹⁴David then sent this message to Ishbosheth, Saul's son: "Give me back my wife Michal, for I bought her with the lives* of 100 Philistines."

¹⁵So Ishbosheth took Michal away from her husband, Palti* son of Laish. ¹⁶Palti followed along behind her as far as Bahurim, weeping as he went. Then Abner told him, "Go back home!" So Palti returned.

¹⁷Meanwhile, Abner had consulted with the elders of Israel. "For some time now," he told them, "you have wanted to make David your king. ¹⁸Now is the time! For the LORD has said, 'I have chosen David to save my people Israel from the hands of the Philistines and from all their other enemies.'" ¹⁹Abner also spoke with the men of Benjamin. Then he went to

Hebron to tell David that all the people of Israel and Benjamin had agreed to support him.

[20]When Abner and twenty of his men came to Hebron, David entertained them with a great feast. [21]Then Abner said to David, "Let me go and call an assembly of all Israel to support my lord the king. They will make a covenant with you to make you their king, and you will rule over everything your heart desires." So David sent Abner safely on his way.

[22]But just after David had sent Abner away in safety, Joab and some of David's troops returned from a raid, bringing much plunder with them. [23]When Joab arrived, he was told that Abner had just been there visiting the king and had been sent away in safety.

[24]Joab rushed to the king and demanded, "What have you done? What do you mean by letting Abner get away? [25]You know perfectly well that he came to spy on you and find out everything you're doing!"

[26]Joab then left David and sent messengers to catch up with Abner, asking him to return. They found him at the well of Sirah and brought him back, though David knew nothing about it. [27]When Abner arrived back at Hebron, Joab took him aside at the gateway as if to speak with him privately. But then he stabbed Abner in the stomach and killed him in revenge for killing his brother Asahel.

[28]When David heard about it, he declared, "I vow by the LORD that I and my kingdom are forever innocent of this crime against Abner son of Ner. [29]Joab and his family are the guilty ones. May the family of Joab be cursed in every generation with a man who has open sores or leprosy* or who walks on crutches* or dies by the sword or begs for food!"

[30]So Joab and his brother Abishai killed Abner because Abner had killed their brother Asahel at the battle of Gibeon.

[31]Then David said to Joab and all those who were with him, "Tear your clothes and put on burlap. Mourn for Abner." And King David himself walked behind the procession to the grave. [32]They buried Abner in Hebron, and the king and all the people wept at his graveside. [33]Then the king sang this funeral song for Abner:

"Should Abner have died as
        fools die?
[34] Your hands were not bound;
        your feet were not chained.
No, you were murdered—
        the victim of a wicked plot."

All the people wept again for Abner. [35]David had refused to eat anything on the day of the funeral, and now everyone begged him to eat. But David had made a vow, saying, "May God strike me and even kill me if I eat anything before sundown." [36]This pleased the people very much. In fact, everything the king did pleased

---

WHO GOD IS | Jesus is the perfect servant

JOHN 13:1-17 In Bible times people walked on dusty roads. Washing the feet of guests was an ancient custom of hospitality that was performed by the household servants. It was a lowly job. So what was Jesus doing washing his disciples' feet? • Jesus came to demonstrate God's love, and one way he showed that love was by serving people. Washing the feet of the disciples was a loving act of humility. This was a reflection of who Jesus was. It was his whole purpose: "The Son of Man came not to be served but to serve others and to give his life as a ransom for many" (Matthew 20:28, January 30). • This act set a precedent for how Jesus wanted his followers to act after he left them: "I have given you an example to follow. Do as I have done to you" (13:15). If the Son of God is willing to serve, then we his followers must also be willing to serve. Are you ready to follow Jesus' example?

them! [37]So everyone in Judah and all Israel understood that David was not responsible for Abner's murder.

[38]Then King David said to his officials, "Don't you realize that a great commander has fallen today in Israel? [39]And even though I am the anointed king, these two sons of Zeruiah—Joab and Abishai—are too strong for me to control. So may the LORD repay these evil men for their evil deeds."

2:16 Hebrew *Helkath-hazzurim*.   2:29a Hebrew *the Arabah*.   2:29b Or *continued on through the Bithron*. The meaning of the Hebrew is uncertain.   3:3 As in parallel text at 1 Chr 3:1 (see also Greek version, which reads *Daluia*, and Dead Sea Scrolls, which read *Dan[iel]*); Hebrew reads *Kileab*.   3:7 *Ishbosheth* is another name for Esh-baal.   3:14 Hebrew *the foreskins*.   3:15 As in 1 Sam 25:44; Hebrew reads *Paltiel*, a variant spelling of Palti.   3:29a Or *a contagious skin disease*. The Hebrew word used here can describe various skin diseases.   3:29b Or *who is effeminate*; Hebrew reads *who handles a spindle*.

JOHN 13:1-30

On the evening he was betrayed and arrested, Jesus demonstrated his love for his disciples by washing their feet after supper. Foot-washing was a servant's task, but Jesus had come to serve. His ultimate act of service—dying for our sins—was looming on the horizon.

Before the Passover celebration, Jesus knew that his hour had come to leave this world and return to his Father. He had loved his disciples during his ministry on earth, and now he loved them to the very end.* [2]It was time for supper, and the devil had already prompted Judas,* son of Simon Iscariot, to betray Jesus. [3]Jesus knew that the Father had given him authority over everything and that he had come from God and would return to God. [4]So he got up from the table, took off his robe, wrapped a towel around his waist, [5]and poured water into a basin. Then he began to wash the disciples' feet, drying them with the towel he had around him.

[6]When Jesus came to Simon Peter, Peter said to him, "Lord, are you going to wash my feet?"

[7]Jesus replied, "You don't understand now what I am doing, but someday you will."

[8]"No," Peter protested, "you will never ever wash my feet!"

Jesus replied, "Unless I wash you, you won't belong to me."

[9]Simon Peter exclaimed, "Then wash my hands and head as well, Lord, not just my feet!"

[10]Jesus replied, "A person who has bathed all over does not need to wash, except for the feet,* to be entirely clean. And you disciples are clean, but not all of you." [11]For Jesus knew who would betray him. That is what he meant when he said, "Not all of you are clean."

[12]After washing their feet, he put on his robe again and sat down and asked, "Do you understand what I was doing? [13]You call me 'Teacher' and 'Lord,' and you are right, because that's what I am. [14]And since I, your Lord and Teacher, have washed your feet, you ought to wash each other's feet. [15]I have given you an example to follow. Do as I have done to you. [16]I tell you the truth, slaves are not greater than their master. Nor is the messenger more important than the one who sends the message. [17]Now that you know these things, God will bless you for doing them.

[18]"I am not saying these things to all of you; I know the ones I have chosen. But this fulfills the Scripture that says, 'The one who eats my food has turned against me.'* [19]I tell you this beforehand, so that when it happens you will believe that I AM the Messiah.* [20]I tell you the truth, anyone who welcomes my messenger is welcoming me, and anyone who welcomes me is welcoming the Father who sent me."

[21]Now Jesus was deeply troubled,* and he exclaimed, "I tell you the truth, one of you will betray me!"

[22]The disciples looked at each other, wondering whom he could mean. [23]The disciple Jesus loved was sitting next to Jesus at the table.* [24]Simon Peter motioned to him to ask, "Who's he talking about?" [25]So that disciple leaned over to Jesus and asked, "Lord, who is it?"

[26]Jesus responded, "It is the one to whom I give the bread I dip in the bowl." And when he had dipped it, he gave it to Judas, son of Simon Iscariot. [27]When Judas had eaten the bread, Satan entered into him. Then Jesus told him, "Hurry and do what you're going to do." [28]None of the others at the table knew what Jesus meant. [29]Since Judas was their treasurer,

some thought Jesus was telling him to go and pay for the food or to give some money to the poor. ³⁰So Judas left at once, going out into the night.

13:1 Or *he showed them the full extent of his love.*
13:2 Or *the devil had already intended for Judas.*
13:10 Some manuscripts do not include *except for the feet.*
13:18 Ps 41:9.　13:19 Or *that the 'I AM' has come;* or *that I am the LORD;* Greek reads *that I am.* See Exod 3:14.
13:21 Greek *was troubled in his spirit.*　13:23 Greek *was reclining on Jesus' bosom.* The "disciple Jesus loved" was probably John.

PSALM 119:1-16

Aleph*

¹ Joyful are people of integrity,
　　who follow the instructions
　　　of the LORD.
² Joyful are those who obey his laws
　　and search for him with all their
　　　hearts.
³ They do not compromise with evil,
　　and they walk only in his paths.
⁴ You have charged us
　　to keep your commandments
　　　carefully.
⁵ Oh, that my actions would consistently
　　reflect your decrees!
⁶ Then I will not be ashamed
　　when I compare my life with your
　　　commands.
⁷ As I learn your righteous regulations,
　　I will thank you by living as I should!

⁸ I will obey your decrees.
　　Please don't give up on me!

Beth

⁹ How can a young person stay pure?
　　By obeying your word.
¹⁰ I have tried hard to find you—
　　don't let me wander from your
　　　commands.
¹¹ I have hidden your word in my heart,
　　that I might not sin against you.
¹² I praise you, O LORD;
　　teach me your decrees.
¹³ I have recited aloud
　　all the regulations you have
　　　given us.
¹⁴ I have rejoiced in your laws
　　as much as in riches.
¹⁵ I will study your commandments
　　and reflect on your ways.
¹⁶ I will delight in your decrees
　　and not forget your word.

119 This psalm is a Hebrew acrostic poem; there are twenty-two stanzas, one for each successive letter of the Hebrew alphabet. Each of the eight verses within each stanza begins with the Hebrew letter named in its heading.

PROVERBS 15:29-30

The LORD is far from the wicked, but he hears the prayers of the righteous. □A cheerful look brings joy to the heart; good news makes for good health.

2 SAMUEL 4:1–6:23

Today's reading is like looking into David's trophy case—the memories of his biggest moments. For him, ascending to the throne was gradual—reigning first over Judah, then all of Israel.

When Ishbosheth,* Saul's son, heard about Abner's death at Hebron, he lost all courage, and all Israel became paralyzed with fear. ²Now there were two brothers, Baanah and Recab, who were captains of Ishbosheth's raiding parties. They were sons of Rimmon, a member of the tribe of Benjamin who lived in Beeroth. The town of Beeroth is now part of Benjamin's territory ³because the original people of Bee-

roth fled to Gittaim, where they still live as foreigners.

⁴(Saul's son Jonathan had a son named Mephibosheth,* who was crippled as a child. He was five years old when the report came from Jezreel that Saul and Jonathan had been killed in battle. When the child's nurse heard the news, she picked him up and fled. But as she hurried away, she dropped him, and he became crippled.)

⁵One day Recab and Baanah, the sons of Rimmon from Beeroth, went to Ishbosheth's house around noon as he was taking his midday rest. ⁶The doorkeeper, who

had been sifting wheat, became drowsy and fell asleep. So Recab and Baanah slipped past her.* [7]They went into the house and found Ishbosheth sleeping on his bed. They struck and killed him and cut off his head. Then, taking his head with them, they fled across the Jordan Valley* through the night. [8]When they arrived at Hebron, they presented Ishbosheth's head to David. "Look!" they exclaimed to the king. "Here is the head of Ishbosheth, the son of your enemy Saul who tried to kill you. Today the LORD has given my lord the king revenge on Saul and his entire family!"

[9]But David said to Recab and Baanah, "The LORD, who saves me from all my enemies, is my witness. [10]Someone once told me, 'Saul is dead,' thinking he was bringing me good news. But I seized him and killed him at Ziklag. That's the reward I gave him for his news! [11]How much more should I reward evil men who have killed an innocent man in his own house and on his own bed? Shouldn't I hold you responsible for his blood and rid the earth of you?"

[12]So David ordered his young men to kill them, and they did. They cut off their hands and feet and hung their bodies beside the pool in Hebron. Then they took Ishbosheth's head and buried it in Abner's tomb in Hebron.

5:1THEN all the tribes of Israel went to David at Hebron and told him, "We are your own flesh and blood. [2]In the past,* when Saul was our king, you were the one who really led the forces of Israel. And the LORD told you, 'You will be the shepherd of my people Israel. You will be Israel's leader.'"

[3]So there at Hebron, King David made a covenant before the LORD with all the elders of Israel. And they anointed him king of Israel.

[4]David was thirty years old when he began to reign, and he reigned forty years in all. [5]He had reigned over Judah from Hebron for seven years and six months, and from Jerusalem he reigned over all Israel and Judah for thirty-three years.

[6]David then led his men to Jerusalem to fight against the Jebusites, the original inhabitants of the land who were living there. The Jebusites taunted David, saying, "You'll never get in here! Even the blind and lame could keep you out!" For the Jebusites thought they were safe. [7]But David captured the fortress of Zion, which is now called the City of David.

[8]On the day of the attack, David said to his troops, "I hate those 'lame' and 'blind' Jebusites.* Whoever attacks them should strike by going into the city through the water tunnel.*" That is the origin of the saying, "The blind and the lame may not enter the house."*

[9]So David made the fortress his home, and he called it the City of David. He extended the city, starting at the supporting terraces* and working inward. [10]And David became more and more powerful, because the LORD God of Heaven's Armies was with him.

[11]Then King Hiram of Tyre sent messengers to David, along with cedar timber and carpenters and stonemasons, and they built David a palace. [12]And David realized that the LORD had confirmed him as king over Israel and had blessed his kingdom for the sake of his people Israel.

[13]After moving from Hebron to Jerusalem, David married more concubines and wives, and they had more sons and daughters. [14]These are the names of David's sons who were born in Jerusalem: Shammua, Shobab, Nathan, Solomon, [15]Ibhar, Elishua, Nepheg, Japhia, [16]Elishama, Eliada, and Eliphelet.

[17]When the Philistines heard that David had been anointed king of Israel, they mobilized all their forces to capture him. But David was told they were coming, so he went into the stronghold. [18]The Philistines arrived and spread out across the valley of Rephaim. [19]So David asked the LORD, "Should I go out to fight the Philistines? Will you hand them over to me?"

The LORD replied to David, "Yes, go ahead. I will certainly hand them over to you."

[20]So David went to Baal-perazim and defeated the Philistines there. "The LORD did it!" David exclaimed. "He burst through my enemies like a raging flood!" So he named that place Baal-perazim (which means "the Lord who bursts

through"). ²¹The Philistines had abandoned their idols there, so David and his men confiscated them.

²²But after a while the Philistines returned and again spread out across the valley of Rephaim. ²³And again David asked the LORD what to do. "Do not attack them straight on," the LORD replied. "Instead, circle around behind and attack them near the poplar* trees. ²⁴When you hear a sound like marching feet in the tops of the poplar trees, be on the alert! That will be the signal that the LORD is moving ahead of you to strike down the Philistine army." ²⁵So David did what the LORD commanded, and he struck down the Philistines all the way from Gibeon* to Gezer.

6:1THEN David again gathered all the elite troops in Israel, 30,000 in all. ²He led them to Baalah of Judah* to bring back the Ark of God, which bears the name of the LORD of Heaven's Armies,* who is enthroned between the cherubim. ³They placed the Ark of God on a new cart and brought it from Abinadab's house, which was on a hill. Uzzah and Ahio, Abinadab's sons, were guiding the cart as it left the house, ⁴carrying the Ark of God. Ahio walked in front of the Ark. ⁵David and all the people of Israel were celebrating before the LORD, singing songs* and playing all kinds of musical instruments—lyres, harps, tambourines, castanets, and cymbals.

⁶But when they arrived at the threshing floor of Nacon, the oxen stumbled, and Uzzah reached out his hand and steadied the Ark of God. ⁷Then the LORD's anger was aroused against Uzzah, and God struck him dead because of this.* So Uzzah died right there beside the Ark of God.

⁸David was angry because the LORD's anger had burst out against Uzzah. He named that place Perez-uzzah (which means "to burst out against Uzzah"), as it is still called today.

⁹David was now afraid of the LORD, and he asked, "How can I ever bring the Ark of the LORD back into my care?" ¹⁰So David decided not to move the Ark of the LORD into the City of David. Instead, he took it to the house of Obed-edom of Gath. ¹¹The Ark of the LORD remained there in Obed-edom's house for three months, and the LORD blessed Obed-edom and his entire household.

¹²Then King David was told, "The LORD has blessed Obed-edom's household and everything he has because of the Ark of God." So David went there and brought the Ark of God from the house of Obed-edom to the City of David with a great celebration. ¹³After the men who were carrying the Ark of the LORD had gone six steps, David sacrificed a bull and a fattened calf. ¹⁴And David danced before the LORD with all his might, wearing a priestly garment.* ¹⁵So David and all the people

WHO GOD IS   The Way, the Truth, the Life

JOHN 14:6 If you're lost, you need a map. And that's what Jesus offers to everyone—a roadmap for navigating life. More than that, he says he *is* the road. Jesus says that nothing you find in this world will provide lasting meaning and direction; only he can do that for you. Jesus is the pathway that leads to real purpose. Jesus doesn't point you in the right direction; he *is* the right direction. Jesus doesn't provide us with different options to try; he says, "I *am* the way you should go. I *am* the only meaningful pursuit." He is the route to the ultimate destination—eternal life with God in heaven.   • So what does this mean for us? Take him at his word and see if what he says is true. Believe in him, follow in his way by doing what he commands, and you'll have abundant life that will never end. Jesus isn't a twelve-step plan of self-improvement; he is a one-step plan to eternal life.

of Israel brought up the Ark of the LORD with shouts of joy and the blowing of rams' horns.

[16]But as the Ark of the LORD entered the City of David, Michal, the daughter of Saul, looked down from her window. When she saw King David leaping and dancing before the LORD, she was filled with contempt for him.

[17]They brought the Ark of the LORD and set it in its place inside the special tent David had prepared for it. And David sacrificed burnt offerings and peace offerings to the LORD. [18]When he had finished his sacrifices, David blessed the people in the name of the LORD of Heaven's Armies. [19]Then he gave to every Israelite man and woman in the crowd a loaf of bread, a cake of dates,* and a cake of raisins. Then all the people returned to their homes.

[20]When David returned home to bless his own family, Michal, the daughter of Saul, came out to meet him. She said in disgust, "How distinguished the king of Israel looked today, shamelessly exposing himself to the servant girls like any vulgar person might do!"

[21]David retorted to Michal, "I was dancing before the LORD, who chose me above your father and all his family! He appointed me as the leader of Israel, the people of the LORD, so I celebrate before the LORD. [22]Yes, and I am willing to look even more foolish than this, even to be humiliated in my own eyes! But those servant girls you mentioned will indeed think I am distinguished!" [23]So Michal, the daughter of Saul, remained childless throughout her entire life.

4:1 *Ishbosheth* is another name for Esh-baal.
4:4 *Mephibosheth* is another name for Merib-baal.
4:6 As in Greek version; Hebrew reads *So they went into the house pretending to fetch wheat, but they stabbed him in the stomach. Then Recab and Baanah escaped.* 4:7 Hebrew *the Arabah.* 5:2 Or *For some time.* 5:8a Or *Those 'lame' and 'blind' Jebusites hate me.* 5:8b Or *with scaling hooks.* The meaning of the Hebrew is uncertain. 5:9 Hebrew *the millo.* The meaning of the Hebrew is uncertain. 5:23 Or *aspen,* or *balsam;* also in 5:24. The exact identification of this tree is uncertain. 5:25 As in Greek version (see also 1 Chr 14:16); Hebrew reads *Geba.* 6:2a *Baalah of Judah* is another name for Kiriath-jearim; compare 1 Chr 13:6. 6:2b Or *the Ark of God where the Name is proclaimed—the name of the LORD of Heaven's Armies.* 6:5 As in Greek version (see also 1 Chr 13:8); Hebrew reads *before the LORD with all manner of cypress trees.* 6:7 As in Dead Sea Scrolls; Masoretic Text reads *because of his irreverence.* 6:14 Hebrew *a linen ephod.* 6:19 Or *a portion of meat.* The meaning of the Hebrew is uncertain.

JOHN 13:31–14:14
Jesus' announcement of his imminent departure was disquieting to the disciples. He comforted them with the promise to return for them and bring them with him to heaven.

As soon as Judas left the room, Jesus said, "The time has come for the Son of Man* to enter into his glory, and God will be glorified because of him. [32]And since God receives glory because of the Son,* he will soon give glory to the Son. [33]Dear children, I will be with you only a little longer. And as I told the Jewish leaders, you will search for me, but you can't come where I am going. [34]So now I am giving you a new commandment: Love each other. Just as I have loved you, you should love each other. [35]Your love for one another will prove to the world that you are my disciples."

[36]Simon Peter asked, "Lord, where are you going?"

And Jesus replied, "You can't go with me now, but you will follow me later."

[37]"But why can't I come now, Lord?" he asked. "I'm ready to die for you."

[38]Jesus answered, "Die for me? I tell you the truth, Peter—before the rooster crows tomorrow morning, you will deny three times that you even know me.

14:1"DON'T let your hearts be troubled. Trust in God, and trust also in me. [2]There is more than enough room in my Father's home.* If this were not so, would I have told you that I am going to prepare a place for you?* [3]When everything is ready, I will come and get you, so that you will always be with me where I am. [4]And you know the way to where I am going."

[5]"No, we don't know, Lord," Thomas said. "We have no idea where you are going, so how can we know the way?"

[6]Jesus told him, "I am the way, the truth, and the life. No one can come to the Father except through me. [7]If you had really known me, you would know who my Father is.* From now on, you do know him and have seen him!"

[8]Philip said, "Lord, show us the Father, and we will be satisfied."

[9]Jesus replied, "Have I been with you all this time, Philip, and yet you still don't know who I am? Anyone who has seen me has seen the Father! So why are you asking

me to show him to you? ¹⁰Don't you believe that I am in the Father and the Father is in me? The words I speak are not my own, but my Father who lives in me does his work through me. ¹¹Just believe that I am in the Father and the Father is in me. Or at least believe because of the work you have seen me do.

¹²"I tell you the truth, anyone who believes in me will do the same works I have done, and even greater works, because I am going to be with the Father. ¹³You can ask for anything in my name, and I will do it, so that the Son can bring glory to the Father. ¹⁴Yes, ask me for anything in my name, and I will do it!"

13:31 "Son of Man" is a title Jesus used for himself. 13:32 Some manuscripts omit *And since God receives glory because of the Son.* 14:2a Or *There are many rooms in my Father's house.* 14:2b Or *If this were not so, I would have told you that I am going to prepare a place for you.* Some manuscripts read *If this were not so, I would have told you. I am going to prepare a place for you.* 14:7 Some manuscripts read *If you have really known me, you will know who my Father is.*

PSALM 119:17-32

Gimel

¹⁷ **B**e good to your servant,
that I may live and obey your
word.
¹⁸ Open my eyes to see
the wonderful truths in your
instructions.
¹⁹ I am only a foreigner in the land.
Don't hide your commands
from me!
²⁰ I am always overwhelmed
with a desire for your regulations.

²¹ You rebuke the arrogant;
those who wander from your
commands are cursed.
²² Don't let them scorn and insult me,
for I have obeyed your laws.
²³ Even princes sit and speak against me,
but I will meditate on your decrees.
²⁴ Your laws please me;
they give me wise advice.

Daleth

²⁵ I lie in the dust;
revive me by your word.
²⁶ I told you my plans, and you answered.
Now teach me your decrees.
²⁷ Help me understand the meaning
of your commandments,
and I will meditate on your
wonderful deeds.
²⁸ I weep with sorrow;
encourage me by your word.
²⁹ Keep me from lying to myself;
give me the privilege of knowing
your instructions.
³⁰ I have chosen to be faithful;
I have determined to live by your
regulations.
³¹ I cling to your laws.
LORD, don't let me be put to shame!
³² I will pursue your commands,
for you expand my understanding.

PROVERBS 15:31-32

If you listen to constructive criticism, you will be at home among the wise. □ If you reject discipline, you only harm yourself; but if you listen to correction, you grow in understanding.

MAY**25**

2 SAMUEL 7:1-8:18

God promised David an eternal kingdom—his dynasty would not end. Through Jesus Christ, that promise was fulfilled. He was of David's family line, and his Kingdom will never end.

When King David was settled in his palace and the LORD had given him rest from all the surrounding enemies, ²the king summoned Nathan the prophet. "Look," David said, "I am living in a beautiful ce-

dar palace,* but the Ark of God is out there in a tent!"

³Nathan replied to the king, "Go ahead and do whatever you have in mind, for the LORD is with you."

⁴But that same night the LORD said to Nathan,

⁵"Go and tell my servant David, 'This is what the LORD has declared: Are you

the one to build a house for me to live in? ⁶I have never lived in a house, from the day I brought the Israelites out of Egypt until this very day. I have always moved from one place to another with a tent and a Tabernacle as my dwelling. ⁷Yet no matter where I have gone with the Israelites, I have never once complained to Israel's tribal leaders, the shepherds of my people Israel. I have never asked them, "Why haven't you built me a beautiful cedar house?"'

⁸"Now go and say to my servant David, 'This is what the LORD of Heaven's Armies has declared: I took you from tending sheep in the pasture and selected you to be the leader of my people Israel. ⁹I have been with you wherever you have gone, and I have destroyed all your enemies before your eyes. Now I will make your name as famous as anyone who has ever lived on the earth! ¹⁰And I will provide a homeland for my people Israel, planting them in a secure place where they will never be disturbed. Evil nations won't oppress them as they've done in the past, ¹¹starting from the time I appointed judges to rule my people Israel. And I will give you rest from all your enemies.

"'Furthermore, the LORD declares that he will make a house for you—a dynasty of kings! ¹²For when you die and are buried with your ancestors, I will raise up one of your descendants, your own offspring, and I will make his kingdom strong. ¹³He is the one who will build a house—a temple—for my name. And I will secure his royal throne forever. ¹⁴I will be his father, and he will be my son. If he sins, I will correct and discipline him with the rod, like any father would do. ¹⁵But my favor will not be taken from him as I took it from Saul, whom I removed from your sight. ¹⁶Your house and your kingdom will continue before me* for all time, and your throne will be secure forever.'"

¹⁷So Nathan went back to David and told him everything the LORD had said in this vision.

¹⁸Then King David went in and sat before the LORD and prayed,

"Who am I, O Sovereign LORD, and what is my family, that you have brought me this far? ¹⁹And now, Sovereign LORD, in addition to everything else, you speak of giving your servant a lasting dynasty! Do you deal with everyone this way, O Sovereign LORD?*

²⁰"What more can I say to you? You know what your servant is really like, Sovereign LORD. ²¹Because of your promise and according to your will, you have done all these great things and have made them known to your servant.

²²"How great you are, O Sovereign LORD! There is no one like you. We have never even heard of another God like you! ²³What other nation on earth is like your people Israel? What other nation, O God, have you redeemed from slavery to be your own people? You made a great name for yourself when you redeemed your people from Egypt. You performed awesome miracles and drove out the nations and gods that stood in their way.* ²⁴You made Israel your very own people forever, and you, O LORD, became their God.

²⁵"And now, O LORD God, I am your servant; do as you have promised concerning me and my family. Confirm it as a promise that will last forever. ²⁶And may your name be honored forever so that everyone will say, 'The LORD of Heaven's Armies is God over Israel!' And may the house of your servant David continue before you forever.

²⁷"O LORD of Heaven's Armies, God of Israel, I have been bold enough to pray this prayer to you because you have revealed all this to your servant, saying, 'I will build a house for you—a dynasty of kings!' ²⁸For you are God, O Sovereign LORD. Your words are truth, and you have promised these good things to your servant. ²⁹And now, may it please you to bless the house of your servant, so that it may continue forever before you. For you

have spoken, and when you grant a blessing to your servant, O Sovereign LORD, it is an eternal blessing!"

8:1AFTER this, David defeated and subdued the Philistines by conquering Gath, their largest town.* 2David also conquered the land of Moab. He made the people lie down on the ground in a row, and he measured them off in groups with a length of rope. He measured off two groups to be executed for every one group to be spared. The Moabites who were spared became David's subjects and paid him tribute money.

3David also destroyed the forces of Hadadezer son of Rehob, king of Zobah, when Hadadezer marched out to strengthen his control along the Euphrates River. 4David captured 1,700 charioteers* and 20,000 foot soldiers. He crippled all the chariot horses except enough for 100 chariots.

5When Arameans from Damascus arrived to help King Hadadezer, David killed 22,000 of them. 6Then he placed several army garrisons in Damascus, the Aramean capital, and the Arameans became David's subjects and paid him tribute money. So the LORD made David victorious wherever he went.

7David brought the gold shields of Hadadezer's officers to Jerusalem, 8along with a large amount of bronze from Hadadezer's towns of Tebah* and Berothai.

9When King Toi of Hamath heard that David had destroyed the entire army of Hadadezer, 10he sent his son Joram to congratulate King David for his successful campaign. Hadadezer and Toi had been enemies and were often at war. Joram presented David with many gifts of silver, gold, and bronze.

11King David dedicated all these gifts to the LORD, as he did with the silver and gold from the other nations he had defeated—12from Edom,* Moab, Ammon, Philistia, and Amalek—and from Hadadezer son of Rehob, king of Zobah.

13So David became very famous. After his return he destroyed 18,000 Edomites* in the Valley of Salt. 14He placed army garrisons throughout Edom, and all the Edomites became David's subjects. In fact, the LORD made David victorious wherever he went.

15So David reigned over all Israel and did what was just and right for all his people. 16Joab son of Zeruiah was commander of the army. Jehoshaphat son of Ahilud was the royal historian. 17Zadok son of Ahitub and Ahimelech son of Abiathar were the priests. Seraiah was the court secretary. 18Benaiah son of Jehoiada was captain of the king's bodyguard.* And David's sons served as priestly leaders.*

7:2 Hebrew *a house of cedar.*   7:16 As in Greek version and some Hebrew manuscripts; Masoretic text reads *before you.*
7:19 Or *This is your instruction for all humanity, O Sovereign LORD.*   7:23 As in Greek version (see also 1 Chr

WHO GOD IS
The Holy Spirit is our helper

JOHN 14:15-17 In this reading, Jesus mentions his imminent departure to his disciples; he was going to leave them and yet *not* leave them. How could this possibly be? Jesus promised that the Holy Spirit—the Spirit of God himself—would come to comfort and guide the disciples, and all believers. • So who is the Holy Spirit? Chapters 14 and 16 of the Gospel of John give some insight into the nature of the Holy Spirit. He is a Counselor (14:16), someone who comforts and advises. He will never leave us (14:16)—no matter what the circumstance, we have the powerful Holy Spirit on our side. The Holy Spirit helps us recognize sin and our need for salvation through Jesus. When we believe in Jesus, the Holy Spirit lives with us and in us (14:17), helping us live as God wants us to live. He teaches us and reminds us of Jesus' words (14:26). The Holy Spirit guides us in truth, gives us insight for the future, and brings glory to Jesus Christ (16:13-14, May 27).

17:21); Hebrew reads *You made a great name for yourself and performed awesome miracles for your land. You did this in the sight of your people, whom you redeemed from Egypt, from nations and their gods.*   **8:1** Hebrew *by conquering Metheg-ammah,* a name that means "the bridle," possibly referring to the size of the town or the tribute money taken from it. Compare 1 Chr 18:1.   **8:4** Greek version reads *1,000 chariots and 7,000 charioteers;* compare 1 Chr 18:4.   **8:8** As in some Greek manuscripts (see also 1 Chr 18:8); Hebrew reads *Betah.*   **8:12** As in a few Hebrew manuscripts and Greek and Syriac versions (see also 8:14; 1 Chr 18:11); most Hebrew manuscripts read *Aram.*   **8:13** As in a few Hebrew manuscripts and Greek and Syriac versions (see also 8:14; 1 Chr 18:12); most Hebrew manuscripts read *Arameans.*   **8:18a** Hebrew *of the Kerethites and Pelethites.*   **8:18b** Hebrew *David's sons were priests;* compare parallel text at 1 Chr 18:17.

JOHN 14:15-31

Jesus further comforted his disciples that fateful evening with the promise that God's Spirit would be present with them. The book of Acts revealed the coming of that Spirit and the work that began the church.

"**If** you love me [Jesus], obey* my commandments. ¹⁶And I will ask the Father, and he will give you another Advocate,* who will never leave you. ¹⁷He is the Holy Spirit, who leads into all truth. The world cannot receive him, because it isn't looking for him and doesn't recognize him. But you know him, because he lives with you now and later will be in you.* ¹⁸No, I will not abandon you as orphans—I will come to you. ¹⁹Soon the world will no longer see me, but you will see me. Since I live, you also will live. ²⁰When I am raised to life again, you will know that I am in my Father, and you are in me, and I am in you. ²¹Those who accept my commandments and obey them are the ones who love me. And because they love me, my Father will love them. And I will love them and reveal myself to each of them."

²²Judas (not Judas Iscariot, but the other disciple with that name) said to him, "Lord, why are you going to reveal yourself only to us and not to the world at large?"

²³Jesus replied, "All who love me will do what I say. My Father will love them, and we will come and make our home with each of them. ²⁴Anyone who doesn't love me will not obey me. And remember, my words are not my own. What I am telling you is from the Father who sent me. ²⁵I am telling you these things now while I am still with you. ²⁶But when the Father sends the Advocate as my representative—that is, the Holy Spirit—he will teach you everything and will remind you of everything I have told you.

²⁷"I am leaving you with a gift—peace of mind and heart. And the peace I give is a gift the world cannot give. So don't be troubled or afraid. ²⁸Remember what I told you: I am going away, but I will come back to you again. If you really loved me, you would be happy that I am going to the Father, who is greater than I am. ²⁹I have told you these things before they happen so that when they do happen, you will believe.

³⁰"I don't have much more time to talk to you, because the ruler of this world approaches. He has no power over me, ³¹but I will do what the Father requires of me, so that the world will know that I love the Father. Come, let's be going."

14:15 Other manuscripts read *you will obey;* still others read *you should obey.*   **14:16** Or *Comforter,* or *Encourager,* or *Counselor.* Greek reads *Paraclete;* also in 14:26.   **14:17** Some manuscripts read *and is in you.*

PSALM 119:33-48

He

³³ **T**each me your decrees, O LORD;
>   I will keep them to the end.
³⁴ Give me understanding and I will obey
>   your instructions;
>   I will put them into practice with
>   all my heart.
³⁵ Make me walk along the path of your
>   commands,
>   for that is where my happiness
>   is found.
³⁶ Give me an eagerness for your laws
>   rather than a love for money!
³⁷ Turn my eyes from worthless things,
>   and give me life through your
>   word.*
³⁸ Reassure me of your promise,
>   made to those who fear you.
³⁹ Help me abandon my shameful ways;
>   for your regulations are good.
⁴⁰ I long to obey your commandments!
>   Renew my life with your goodness.

Waw

⁴¹ LORD, give me your unfailing love,
>   the salvation that you promised me.
⁴² Then I can answer those who taunt me,
>   for I trust in your word.

⁴³ Do not snatch your word of truth
        from me,
    for your regulations are my only hope.
⁴⁴ I will keep on obeying your
        instructions
    forever and ever.
⁴⁵ I will walk in freedom,
    for I have devoted myself to your
        commandments.
⁴⁶ I will speak to kings about your laws,
    and I will not be ashamed.

⁴⁷ How I delight in your commands!
    How I love them!
⁴⁸ I honor and love your commands.
    I meditate on your decrees.

119:37 Some manuscripts read *in your ways.*

PROVERBS 15:33
Fear of the LORD teaches wisdom; humility precedes honor.

MAY**26**

2 SAMUEL 9:1–11:27
King David was a mix of whole-hearted spirituality and big mistakes. Today's reading gives a good dose of both.

One day David asked, "Is anyone in Saul's family still alive—anyone to whom I can show kindness for Jonathan's sake?" ²He summoned a man named Ziba, who had been one of Saul's servants. "Are you Ziba?" the king asked.

"Yes sir, I am," Ziba replied.

³The king then asked him, "Is anyone still alive from Saul's family? If so, I want to show God's kindness to them."

Ziba replied, "Yes, one of Jonathan's sons is still alive. He is crippled in both feet."

⁴"Where is he?" the king asked.

"In Lo-debar," Ziba told him, "at the home of Makir son of Ammiel."

⁵So David sent for him and brought him from Makir's home. ⁶His name was Mephibosheth*; he was Jonathan's son and Saul's grandson. When he came to David, he bowed low to the ground in deep respect. David said, "Greetings, Mephibosheth."

Mephibosheth replied, "I am your servant."

⁷"Don't be afraid!" David said. "I intend to show kindness to you because of my promise to your father, Jonathan. I will give you all the property that once belonged to your grandfather Saul, and you will eat here with me at the king's table!"

⁸Mephibosheth bowed respectfully and exclaimed, "Who is your servant, that you should show such kindness to a dead dog like me?"

⁹Then the king summoned Saul's servant Ziba and said, "I have given your master's grandson everything that belonged to Saul and his family. ¹⁰You and your sons and servants are to farm the land for him to produce food for your master's household.* But Mephibosheth, your master's grandson, will eat here at my table." (Ziba had fifteen sons and twenty servants.)

Ziba replied, ¹¹"Yes, my lord the king; I am your servant, and I will do all that you have commanded." And from that time on, Mephibosheth ate regularly at David's table,* like one of the king's own sons.

¹²Mephibosheth had a young son named Mica. From then on, all the members of Ziba's household were Mephibosheth's servants. ¹³And Mephibosheth, who was crippled in both feet, lived in Jerusalem and ate regularly at the king's table.

¹⁰:¹SOME time after this, King Nahash* of the Ammonites died, and his son Hanun became king. ²David said, "I am going to show loyalty to Hanun just as his father, Nahash, was always loyal to me." So David sent ambassadors to express sympathy to Hanun about his father's death.

But when David's ambassadors arrived in the land of Ammon, ³the Ammonite commanders said to Hanun, their master, "Do you really think these men are coming here to honor your father? No! David has sent them to spy out the city so they can come in and conquer it!" 4So Hanun seized David's ambassadors and shaved off half of each man's beard, cut off their robes at the buttocks, and sent them back to David in shame.

5When David heard what had happened, he sent messengers to tell the men, "Stay at Jericho until your beards grow out, and then come back." For they felt deep shame because of their appearance.

6When the people of Ammon realized how seriously they had angered David, they sent and hired 20,000 Aramean foot soldiers from the lands of Beth-rehob and Zobah, 1,000 from the king of Maacah, and 12,000 from the land of Tob. 7When David heard about this, he sent Joab and all his warriors to fight them. 8The Ammonite troops came out and drew up their battle lines at the entrance of the city gate, while the Arameans from Zobah and Rehob and the men from Tob and Maacah positioned themselves to fight in the open fields.

9When Joab saw that he would have to fight on both the front and the rear, he chose some of Israel's elite troops and placed them under his personal command to fight the Arameans in the fields. 10He left the rest of the army under the command of his brother Abishai, who was to attack the Ammonites. 11"If the Arameans are too strong for me, then come over and help me," Joab told his brother. "And if the Ammonites are too strong for you, I will come and help you. 12Be courageous! Let us fight bravely for our people and the cities of our God. May the LORD's will be done."

13When Joab and his troops attacked, the Arameans began to run away. 14And when the Ammonites saw the Arameans running, they ran from Abishai and retreated into the city. After the battle was over, Joab returned to Jerusalem.

15The Arameans now realized that they were no match for Israel. So when they regrouped, 16they were joined by additional Aramean troops summoned by Hadadezer from the other side of the Euphrates River.* These troops arrived at Helam under the command of Shobach, the commander of Hadadezer's forces.

17When David heard what was happening, he mobilized all Israel, crossed the Jordan River, and led the army to Helam. The Arameans positioned themselves in battle formation and fought against David. 18But again the Arameans fled from the Israelites. This time David's forces killed 700 charioteers and 40,000 foot soldiers,* including Shobach, the commander of their army. 19When all the kings allied with Hadadezer saw that they had been defeated by Israel, they surrendered to Israel and became their subjects. After that, the Arameans were afraid to help the Ammonites.

11:1In the spring of the year,* when kings normally go out to war, David sent Joab and the Israelite army to fight the Ammonites. They destroyed the Ammonite army and laid siege to the city of Rabbah. However, David stayed behind in Jerusalem.

2Late one afternoon, after his midday rest, David got out of bed and was walking on the roof of the palace. As he looked out over the city, he noticed a woman of unusual beauty taking a bath. 3He sent someone to find out who she was, and he was told, "She is Bathsheba, the daughter of Eliam and the wife of Uriah the Hittite." 4Then David sent messengers to get her; and when she came to the palace, he slept with her. She had just completed the purification rites after having her menstrual period. Then she returned home. 5Later, when Bathsheba discovered that she was pregnant, she sent a message, saying, "I'm pregnant."

6Then David sent word to Joab: "Send me Uriah the Hittite." So Joab sent him to David. 7When Uriah arrived, David asked him how Joab and the army were getting along and how the war was progressing. 8Then he told Uriah, "Go on home and relax.*" David even sent a gift to Uriah after he had left the palace. 9But Uriah didn't go home. He slept that night at the palace entrance with the king's palace guard.

10When David heard that Uriah had not gone home, he summoned him and asked, "What's the matter? Why didn't you go home last night after being away for so long?"

[11]Uriah replied, "The Ark and the armies of Israel and Judah are living in tents,* and Joab and my master's men are camping in the open fields. How could I go home to wine and dine and sleep with my wife? I swear that I would never do such a thing."

[12]"Well, stay here today," David told him, "and tomorrow you may return to the army." So Uriah stayed in Jerusalem that day and the next. [13]Then David invited him to dinner and got him drunk. But even then he couldn't get Uriah to go home to his wife. Again he slept at the palace entrance with the king's palace guard.

[14]So the next morning David wrote a letter to Joab and gave it to Uriah to deliver. [15]The letter instructed Joab, "Station Uriah on the front lines where the battle is fiercest. Then pull back so that he will be killed." [16]So Joab assigned Uriah to a spot close to the city wall where he knew the enemy's strongest men were fighting. [17]And when the enemy soldiers came out of the city to fight, Uriah the Hittite was killed along with several other Israelite soldiers.

[18]Then Joab sent a battle report to David. [19]He told his messenger, "Report all the news of the battle to the king. [20]But he might get angry and ask, 'Why did the troops go so close to the city? Didn't they know there would be shooting from the walls? [21]Wasn't Abimelech son of Gideon* killed at Thebez by a woman who threw a millstone down on him from the wall? Why would you get so close to the wall?' Then tell him, 'Uriah the Hittite was killed, too.'"

[22]So the messenger went to Jerusalem and gave a complete report to David. [23]"The enemy came out against us in the open fields," he said. "And as we chased them back to the city gate, [24]the archers on the wall shot arrows at us. Some of the king's men were killed, including Uriah the Hittite."

[25]"Well, tell Joab not to be discouraged," David said. "The sword devours this one today and that one tomorrow! Fight harder next time, and conquer the city!"

[26]When Uriah's wife heard that her husband was dead, she mourned for him. [27]When the period of mourning was over, David sent for her and brought her to the palace, and she became one of his wives.

HOW WE LIVE

Remaining pure

2 SAMUEL 11:1-27 David, once called "a man after [God's] own heart" (1 Samuel 13:14, May 12), allowed himself to fall to the temptation of lust. And the first submission to temptation led him deeper and deeper into sin. • This was the time of year when kings went off to war (11:1). Yet David remained at home, shirking his duty. This led to an even greater battle within himself, and he made three life-altering mistakes: (1) David could have turned his back and walked away, but he chose to stay and watch Bathsheba. (2) Even after he found out that she was married, he summoned Bathsheba, knowing that she would come (to refuse a king could mean punishment or even death). When she arrived, he slept with her. The consequence? The same as it often is: pregnancy. (3) He orchestrated the murder of Bathsheba's husband, Uriah. • There would have been no temptation, no pregnancy, and no murder had David been doing his duty as king in the first place. You can remain pure by staying away from places, people, and situations that can lead you into temptation. When tempted, you can remain pure by considering the consequences and choosing to do the right thing. When you fail, you can avoid falling deeper and deeper into sin by owning up to the consequences of your bad choices instead of trying to cover them up.

Then she gave birth to a son. But the LORD was displeased with what David had done.

9:6 *Mephibosheth* is another name for Merib-baal. 9:10 As in Greek version; Hebrew reads *your master's grandson.* 9:11 As in Greek version; Hebrew reads *my table.* 10:1 As in parallel text at 1 Chr 19:1; Hebrew reads *the king.* 10:16 Hebrew *the river.* 10:18 As in some Greek manuscripts (see also 1 Chr 19:18); Hebrew reads *charioteers.* 11:1 Hebrew *At the turn of the year.* The first day of the year in the ancient Hebrew lunar calendar occurred in March or April. 11:8 Hebrew *and wash your feet,* an expression that may also have a connotation of ritualistic washing. 11:11 Or *at Succoth.* 11:21 Hebrew *son of Jerub-besheth.* Jerub-besheth is a variation on the name Jerub-baal, which is another name for Gideon; see Judg 6:32.

JOHN 15:1-27

Jesus' life and ministry were about connecting us to God. Here, he elaborates on that connection. We are connected in the same way that branches are connected to the vine. We are only alive when we are drawing nourishment from the vine.

"**I** [Jesus] am the true grapevine, and my Father is the gardener. ²He cuts off every branch of mine that doesn't produce fruit, and he prunes the branches that do bear fruit so they will produce even more. ³You have already been pruned and purified by the message I have given you. ⁴Remain in me, and I will remain in you. For a branch cannot produce fruit if it is severed from the vine, and you cannot be fruitful unless you remain in me.

⁵"Yes, I am the vine; you are the branches. Those who remain in me, and I in them, will produce much fruit. For apart from me you can do nothing. ⁶Anyone who does not remain in me is thrown away like a useless branch and withers. Such branches are gathered into a pile to be burned. ⁷But if you remain in me and my words remain in you, you may ask for anything you want, and it will be granted! ⁸When you produce much fruit, you are my true disciples. This brings great glory to my Father.

⁹"I have loved you even as the Father has loved me. Remain in my love. ¹⁰When you obey my commandments, you remain in my love, just as I obey my Father's commandments and remain in his love. ¹¹I have told you these things so that you will be filled with my joy. Yes, your joy will overflow! ¹²This is my commandment: Love each other in the same way I have loved you. ¹³There is no greater love than

to lay down one's life for one's friends. ¹⁴You are my friends if you do what I command. ¹⁵I no longer call you slaves, because a master doesn't confide in his slaves. Now you are my friends, since I have told you everything the Father told me. ¹⁶You didn't choose me. I chose you. I appointed you to go and produce lasting fruit, so that the Father will give you whatever you ask for, using my name. ¹⁷This is my command: Love each other.

¹⁸"If the world hates you, remember that it hated me first. ¹⁹The world would love you as one of its own if you belonged to it, but you are no longer part of the world. I chose you to come out of the world, so it hates you. ²⁰Do you remember what I told you? 'A slave is not greater than the master.' Since they persecuted me, naturally they will persecute you. And if they had listened to me, they would listen to you. ²¹They will do all this to you because of me, for they have rejected the One who sent me. ²²They would not be guilty if I had not come and spoken to them. But now they have no excuse for their sin. ²³Anyone who hates me also hates my Father. ²⁴If I hadn't done such miraculous signs among them that no one else could do, they would not be guilty. But as it is, they have seen everything I did, yet they still hate me and my Father. ²⁵This fulfills what is written in their Scriptures*: 'They hated me without cause.'

²⁶"But I will send you the Advocate*— the Spirit of truth. He will come to you from the Father and will testify all about me. ²⁷And you must also testify about me because you have been with me from the beginning of my ministry."

15:25 Greek *in their law.* Pss 35:19; 69:4.   15:26 Or *Comforter,* or *Encourager,* or *Counselor.* Greek reads *Paraclete.*

PSALM 119:49-64

Zayin

⁴⁹ **R**emember your promise to me;
    it is my only hope.
⁵⁰ Your promise revives me;
    it comforts me in all my troubles.
⁵¹ The proud hold me in utter contempt,
    but I do not turn away from your
    instructions.
⁵² I meditate on your age-old regulations;
    O LORD, they comfort me.

53 I become furious with the wicked,
  because they reject your
  instructions.
54 Your decrees have been the theme
  of my songs
  wherever I have lived.
55 I reflect at night on who you are,
  O LORD;
  therefore, I obey your instructions.
56 This is how I spend my life:
  obeying our commandments.

Heth

57 LORD, you are mine!
  I promise to obey your words!
58 With all my heart I want your blessings.
  Be merciful as you promised.
59 I pondered the direction of my life,
  and I turned to follow your laws.
60 I will hurry, without delay,
  to obey your commands.

61 Evil people try to drag me into sin,
  but I am firmly anchored to your
  instructions.
62 I rise at midnight to thank you
  for your just regulations.
63 I am a friend to anyone who fears
  you—
  anyone who obeys your
  commandments.
64 O LORD, your unfailing love fills the
  earth;
  teach me your decrees.

PROVERBS 16:1-3

We can make our own plans, but the LORD
gives the right answer. □ People may be
pure in their own eyes, but the LORD examines their motives. □ Commit your actions to the LORD, and your plans will
succeed.

MAY**27**

2 SAMUEL 12:1-31

David was the king of the land, but he was also a
man who desired to please God. Therefore, when
faced with his own wickedness, he didn't shoot the
messenger. Instead, he got really honest and faced
some severe consequences.

So the LORD sent Nathan the prophet to
tell David this story: "There were two men
in a certain town. One was rich, and one
was poor. ²The rich man owned a great
many sheep and cattle. ³The poor man
owned nothing but one little lamb he had
bought. He raised that little lamb, and it
grew up with his children. It ate from the
man's own plate and drank from his cup.
He cuddled it in his arms like a baby
daughter. ⁴One day a guest arrived at the
home of the rich man. But instead of killing an animal from his own flock or herd,
he took the poor man's lamb and killed it
and prepared it for his guest."

⁵David was furious. "As surely as the
LORD lives," he vowed, "any man who
would do such a thing deserves to die! ⁶He
must repay four lambs to the poor man

for the one he stole and for having no
pity."

⁷Then Nathan said to David, "You are
that man! The LORD, the God of Israel,
says: I anointed you king of Israel and
saved you from the power of Saul. ⁸I gave
you your master's house and his wives
and the kingdoms of Israel and Judah.
And if that had not been enough, I would
have given you much, much more. ⁹Why,
then, have you despised the word of the
LORD and done this horrible deed? For
you have murdered Uriah the Hittite with
the sword of the Ammonites and stolen
his wife. ¹⁰From this time on, your family
will live by the sword because you have
despised me by taking Uriah's wife to be
your own.

¹¹"This is what the LORD says: Because
of what you have done, I will cause your
own household to rebel against you. I will
give your wives to another man before
your very eyes, and he will go to bed with
them in public view. ¹²You did it secretly,

but I will make this happen to you openly in the sight of all Israel."

¹³Then David confessed to Nathan, "I have sinned against the LORD."

Nathan replied, "Yes, but the LORD has forgiven you, and you won't die for this sin. ¹⁴Nevertheless, because you have shown utter contempt for the LORD* by doing this, your child will die."

¹⁵After Nathan returned to his home, the LORD sent a deadly illness to the child of David and Uriah's wife. ¹⁶David begged God to spare the child. He went without food and lay all night on the bare ground. ¹⁷The elders of his household pleaded with him to get up and eat with them, but he refused.

¹⁸Then on the seventh day the child died. David's advisers were afraid to tell him. "He wouldn't listen to reason while the child was ill," they said. "What drastic thing will he do when we tell him the child is dead?"

¹⁹When David saw them whispering, he realized what had happened. "Is the child dead?" he asked.

"Yes," they replied, "he is dead."

²⁰Then David got up from the ground, washed himself, put on lotions,* and changed his clothes. He went to the Tabernacle and worshiped the LORD. After that, he returned to the palace and was served food and ate.

²¹His advisers were amazed. "We don't understand you," they told him. "While the child was still living, you wept and refused to eat. But now that the child is dead, you have stopped your mourning and are eating again."

²²David replied, "I fasted and wept while the child was alive, for I said, 'Perhaps the LORD will be gracious to me and let the child live.' ²³But why should I fast when he is dead? Can I bring him back again? I will go to him one day, but he cannot return to me."

²⁴Then David comforted Bathsheba, his wife, and slept with her. She became pregnant and gave birth to a son, and they named him Solomon. The LORD loved the child ²⁵and sent word through Nathan the prophet that they should name him Jedidiah (which means "beloved of the LORD"), as the LORD had commanded.*

²⁶Meanwhile, Joab was fighting against Rabbah, the capital of Ammon, and he captured the royal fortifications.* ²⁷Joab sent messengers to tell David, "I have fought against Rabbah and captured its water supply.* ²⁸Now bring the rest of the army and capture the city. Otherwise, I will capture it and get credit for the victory."

²⁹So David gathered the rest of the army and went to Rabbah, and he fought against it and captured it. ³⁰David removed the crown from the king's head,* and it was placed on his own head. The crown was made of gold and set with gems, and it weighed seventy-five pounds.* David took a vast amount of plunder from the city. ³¹He also made slaves of the people of Rabbah and forced them to labor with* saws, iron picks, and iron axes, and to work in the brick kilns.* That is how he dealt with the people of all the Ammonite towns. Then David and all the army returned to Jerusalem.

12:14 As in Dead Sea Scrolls; Masoretic Text reads *the LORD's enemies.* 12:20 Hebrew *anointed himself.* 12:25 As in Greek version; Hebrew reads *because of the LORD.* 12:26 Or *the royal city.* 12:27 Or *captured the city of water.* 12:30a Or *from the head of Milcom* (as in Greek version). Milcom, also called Molech, was the god of the Ammonites. 12:30b Hebrew *1 talent* [34 kilograms]. 12:31a Or *He also brought out the people of Rabbah and put them under.* 12:31b Or *and he made them pass through the brick kilns.*

JOHN 16:1-33

After Jesus' death, the disciples would face trouble and persecution themselves. However, Jesus' death and resurrection would secure the ultimate victory.

"**I** [Jesus] have told you these things so that you won't abandon your faith. ²For you will be expelled from the synagogues, and the time is coming when those who kill you will think they are doing a holy service for God. ³This is because they have never known the Father or me. ⁴Yes, I'm telling you these things now, so that when they happen, you will remember my warning. I didn't tell you earlier because I was going to be with you for a while longer.

⁵"But now I am going away to the One who sent me, and not one of you is asking where I am going. ⁶Instead, you grieve because of what I've told you. ⁷But in fact, it is best for you that I go away, because if I don't, the Advocate* won't come. If I do go away, then I will send him to you. ⁸And

when he comes, he will convict the world of its sin, and of God's righteousness, and of the coming judgment. [9]The world's sin is that it refuses to believe in me. [10]Righteousness is available because I go to the Father, and you will see me no more. [11]Judgment will come because the ruler of this world has already been judged.

[12]"There is so much more I want to tell you, but you can't bear it now. [13]When the Spirit of truth comes, he will guide you into all truth. He will not speak on his own but will tell you what he has heard. He will tell you about the future. [14]He will bring me glory by telling you whatever he receives from me. [15]All that belongs to the Father is mine; this is why I said, 'The Spirit will tell you whatever he receives from me.'

[16]"In a little while you won't see me anymore. But a little while after that, you will see me again."

[17]Some of the disciples asked each other, "What does he mean when he says, 'In a little while you won't see me, but then you will see me,' and 'I am going to the Father'? [18]And what does he mean by 'a little while'? We don't understand."

[19]Jesus realized they wanted to ask him about it, so he said, "Are you asking yourselves what I meant? I said in a little while you won't see me, but a little while after that you will see me again. [20]I tell you the truth, you will weep and mourn over what is going to happen to me, but the world will rejoice. You will grieve, but your grief will suddenly turn to wonderful joy. [21]It will be like a woman suffering the pains of labor. When her child is born, her anguish gives way to joy because she has brought a new baby into the world. [22]So you have sorrow now, but I will see you again; then you will rejoice, and no one can rob you of that joy. [23]At that time you won't need to ask me for anything. I tell you the truth, you will ask the Father directly, and he will grant your request because you use my name. [24]You haven't done this before. Ask, using my name, and you will receive, and you will have abundant joy.

[25]"I have spoken of these matters in figures of speech, but soon I will stop speaking figuratively and will tell you plainly all about the Father. [26]Then you will ask in my name. I'm not saying I will ask the Father on your behalf, [27]for the Father himself loves you dearly because you love me and believe that I came from God.* [28]Yes, I came from the Father into the world, and now I will leave the world and return to the Father."

[29]Then his disciples said, "At last you are speaking plainly and not figuratively. [30]Now we understand that you know

---

HOW WE LIVE | Prayer

JOHN 16:23-24 Prayer is an amazing mystery. How can we connect with a God who is above and beyond anything we can imagine? The Bible tells us over and over again that our great God and Creator wants us to praise him, call on him, talk to him, and ask for help—that's prayer. Here, Jesus tells his followers that they can ask anything in his name. Through Christ, we are able to commune directly with God. • The apostle Paul says in 1 Timothy 2:5 that Jesus is the "Mediator" between God and humanity (see October 17). By using Christ's name in prayer, we acknowledge that Jesus is our go-between, our Mediator, and that we accept his death on the cross for our sins. It reminds us of the cost he paid to make a relationship with God possible. • This passage does not advocate that you demand things from God as though he were some cosmic butler prepared to answer your every beck and call. God wants to bless you because you are his child. You can bring any need or request to him. Because of Jesus, you can come into God's presence with confidence and assurance that he hears and will answer.

everything, and there's no need to question you. From this we believe that you came from God."

³¹Jesus asked, "Do you finally believe? ³²But the time is coming—indeed it's here now—when you will be scattered, each one going his own way, leaving me alone. Yet I am not alone because the Father is with me. ³³I have told you all this so that you may have peace in me. Here on earth you will have many trials and sorrows. But take heart, because I have overcome the world."

16:7 Or *Comforter*, or *Encourager*, or *Counselor*. Greek reads *Paraclete.* **16:27** Some manuscripts read *from the Father.*

PSALM 119:65-80

Teth

⁶⁵ **Y**ou have done many good things
for me, LORD,
just as you promised.
⁶⁶ I believe in your commands;
now teach me good judgment
and knowledge.
⁶⁷ I used to wander off until you
disciplined me;
but now I closely follow your word.
⁶⁸ You are good and do only good;
teach me your decrees.
⁶⁹ Arrogant people smear me with lies,
but in truth I obey your
commandments with all
my heart.
⁷⁰ Their hearts are dull and stupid,
but I delight in your instructions.
⁷¹ My suffering was good for me,
for it taught me to pay attention
to your decrees.

⁷² Your instructions are more valuable
to me
than millions in gold and silver.

Yodh

⁷³ You made me; you created me.
Now give me the sense to follow
your commands.
⁷⁴ May all who fear you find in me
a cause for joy,
for I have put my hope in your
word.
⁷⁵ I know, O LORD, that your regulations
are fair;
you disciplined me because
I needed it.
⁷⁶ Now let your unfailing love comfort
me,
just as you promised me, your
servant.
⁷⁷ Surround me with your tender
mercies so I may live,
for your instructions are my delight.
⁷⁸ Bring disgrace upon the arrogant
people who lied about me;
meanwhile, I will concentrate on
your commandments.
⁷⁹ Let me be united with all who fear you,
with those who know your laws.
⁸⁰ May I be blameless in keeping your
decrees;
then I will never be ashamed.

PROVERBS 16:4-5

The LORD has made everything for his own purposes, even the wicked for a day of disaster. ☐ The LORD detests the proud; they will surely be punished.

MAY**28**

2 SAMUEL 13:1-39
David's family wasn't immune from strife. Unfortunately, the conflicts at times became bloody and violent. Today's reading is a good example of such a conflict.

Now David's son Absalom had a beautiful sister named Tamar. And Amnon, her half brother, fell desperately in love with her. ²Amnon became so obsessed with Tamar that he became ill. She was a virgin, and Amnon thought he could never have her.

³But Amnon had a very crafty friend—his cousin Jonadab. He was the son of David's brother Shimea.* ⁴One day Jonadab said to Amnon, "What's the trouble? Why

should the son of a king look so dejected morning after morning?"

So Amnon told him, "I am in love with Tamar, my brother Absalom's sister."

⁵"Well," Jonadab said, "I'll tell you what to do. Go back to bed and pretend you are ill. When your father comes to see you, ask him to let Tamar come and prepare some food for you. Tell him you'll feel better if she prepares it as you watch and feeds you with her own hands."

⁶So Amnon lay down and pretended to be sick. And when the king came to see him, Amnon asked him, "Please let my sister Tamar come and cook my favorite dish* as I watch. Then I can eat it from her own hands." ⁷So David agreed and sent Tamar to Amnon's house to prepare some food for him.

⁸When Tamar arrived at Amnon's house, she went to the place where he was lying down so he could watch her mix some dough. Then she baked his favorite dish for him. ⁹But when she set the serving tray before him, he refused to eat. "Everyone get out of here," Amnon told his servants. So they all left.

¹⁰Then he said to Tamar, "Now bring the food into my bedroom and feed it to me here." So Tamar took his favorite dish to him. ¹¹But as she was feeding him, he grabbed her and demanded, "Come to bed with me, my darling sister."

¹²"No, my brother!" she cried. "Don't be foolish! Don't do this to me! Such wicked things aren't done in Israel. ¹³Where could I go in my shame? And you would be called one of the greatest fools in Israel. Please, just speak to the king about it, and he will let you marry me."

¹⁴But Amnon wouldn't listen to her, and since he was stronger than she was, he raped her. ¹⁵Then suddenly Amnon's love turned to hate, and he hated her even more than he had loved her. "Get out of here!" he snarled at her.

¹⁶"No, no!" Tamar cried. "Sending me away now is worse than what you've already done to me."

But Amnon wouldn't listen to her. ¹⁷He shouted for his servant and demanded, "Throw this woman out, and lock the door behind her!"

¹⁸So the servant put her out and locked the door behind her. She was wearing a long, beautiful robe,* as was the custom in those days for the king's virgin daughters. ¹⁹But now Tamar tore her robe and put ashes on her head. And then, with her face in her hands, she went away crying.

²⁰Her brother Absalom saw her and asked, "Is it true that Amnon has been with you? Well, my sister, keep quiet for now, since he's your brother. Don't you worry about it." So Tamar lived as a desolate woman in her brother Absalom's house.

²¹When King David heard what had happened, he was very angry.* ²²And though Absalom never spoke to Amnon about this, he hated Amnon deeply because of what he had done to his sister.

²³Two years later, when Absalom's sheep were being sheared at Baal-hazor near Ephraim, Absalom invited all the king's sons to come to a feast. ²⁴He went to the king and said, "My sheep-shearers are now at work. Would the king and his servants please come to celebrate the occasion with me?"

²⁵The king replied, "No, my son. If we all came, we would be too much of a burden on you." Absalom pressed him, but the king would not come, though he gave Absalom his blessing.

²⁶"Well, then," Absalom said, "if you can't come, how about sending my brother Amnon with us?"

"Why Amnon?" the king asked. ²⁷But Absalom kept on pressing the king until he finally agreed to let all his sons attend, including Amnon. So Absalom prepared a feast fit for a king.*

²⁸Absalom told his men, "Wait until Amnon gets drunk; then at my signal, kill him! Don't be afraid. I'm the one who has given the command. Take courage and do it!" ²⁹So at Absalom's signal they murdered Amnon. Then the other sons of the king jumped on their mules and fled.

³⁰As they were on the way back to Jerusalem, this report reached David: "Absalom has killed all the king's sons; not one is left alive!" ³¹The king got up, tore his robe, and threw himself on the ground. His advisers also tore their clothes in horror and sorrow.

³²But just then Jonadab, the son of

David's brother Shimea, arrived and said, "No, don't believe that all the king's sons have been killed! It was only Amnon! Absalom has been plotting this ever since Amnon raped his sister Tamar. [33]No, my lord the king, your sons aren't all dead! It was only Amnon." [34]Meanwhile Absalom escaped.

Then the watchman on the Jerusalem wall saw a great crowd coming toward the city from the west. He ran to tell the king, "I see a crowd of people coming from the Horonaim road* along the side of the hill."

[35]"Look!" Jonadab told the king. "There they are now! The king's sons are coming, just as I said."

[36]They soon arrived, weeping and sobbing, and the king and all his servants wept bitterly with them. [37]And David mourned many days for his son Amnon.

Absalom fled to his grandfather, Talmai son of Ammihud, the king of Geshur. [38]He stayed in Geshur for three years. [39]And King David, now reconciled to Amnon's death, longed to be reunited with his son Absalom.*

13:3 Hebrew *Shimeah* (also in 13:32), a variant spelling of Shimea; compare 1 Chr 2:13.   13:6 Or *a couple of cakes;* also in 13:8, 10.   13:18 Or *a robe with sleeves,* or *an ornamented robe.* The meaning of the Hebrew is uncertain. 13:21 Dead Sea Scrolls and Greek version add *But he did not punish his son Amnon, because he loved him, for he was his firstborn.*   13:27 As in Greek and Latin versions (compare also Dead Sea Scrolls); the Hebrew text omits this sentence. 13:34 As in Greek version; Hebrew reads *from the road behind him.*   13:39 Or *no longer felt a need to go out after Absalom.*

JOHN 17:1-26

This chapter records an especially intimate moment between Jesus and his heavenly Father. In it we see Jesus' love for his Father, for the world, and especially for those who follow him.

After saying all these things, Jesus looked up to heaven and said, "Father, the hour has come. Glorify your Son so he can give glory back to you. [2]For you have given him authority over everyone. He gives eternal life to each one you have given him. [3]And this is the way to have eternal life—to know you, the only true God, and Jesus Christ, the one you sent to earth. [4]I brought glory to you here on earth by completing the work you gave me to do. [5]Now, Father, bring me into the glory we shared before the world began.

[6]"I have revealed you* to the ones you gave me from this world. They were always yours. You gave them to me, and they have kept your word. [7]Now they know that everything I have is a gift from you, [8]for I have passed on to them the message you gave me. They accepted it and know that I came from you, and they believe you sent me.

[9]"My prayer is not for the world, but for those you have given me, because they belong to you. [10]All who are mine belong to you, and you have given them to me, so they bring me glory. [11]Now I am departing from the world; they are staying in this world, but I am coming to you. Holy Father, you have given me your name;* now protect them by the power of your name so that they will be united just as we are. [12]During my time here, I protected them by the power of the name you gave me.* I guarded them so that not one was lost, except the one headed for destruction, as the Scriptures foretold.

[13]"Now I am coming to you. I told them many things while I was with them in this world so they would be filled with my joy. [14]I have given them your word. And the world hates them because they do not belong to the world, just as I do not belong to the world. [15]I'm not asking you to take them out of the world, but to keep them safe from the evil one. [16]They do not belong to this world any more than I do. [17]Make them holy by your truth; teach them your word, which is truth. [18]Just as you sent me into the world, I am sending them into the world. [19]And I give myself as a holy sacrifice for them so they can be made holy by your truth.

[20]"I am praying not only for these disciples but also for all who will ever believe in me through their message. [21]I pray that they will all be one, just as you and I are one—as you are in me, Father, and I am in you. And may they be in us so that the world will believe you sent me.

[22]"I have given them the glory you gave me, so they may be one as we are one. [23]I am in them and you are in me. May they experience such perfect unity that the world will know that you sent me and that you love them as much as you love me. [24]Father, I want these whom you have

given me to be with me where I am. Then they can see all the glory you gave me because you loved me even before the world began!

²⁵"O righteous Father, the world doesn't know you, but I do; and these disciples know you sent me. ²⁶I have revealed you to them, and I will continue to do so. Then your love for me will be in them, and I will be in them."

17:6 Greek *have revealed your name;* also in 17:26.
17:11 Some manuscripts read *you have given me these [disciples].*   17:12 Some manuscripts read *I protected those you gave me, by the power of your name.*

PSALM 119:81-96

Kaph

⁸¹ I am worn out waiting for your
      rescue,
   but I have put my hope in your
      word.
⁸² My eyes are straining to see your
      promises come true.
   When will you comfort me?
⁸³ I am shriveled like a wineskin in
      the smoke,
   but I have not forgotten to obey
      your decrees.
⁸⁴ How long must I wait?
   When will you punish those who
      persecute me?
⁸⁵ These arrogant people who hate your
      instructions
   have dug deep pits to trap me.

⁸⁶ All your commands are trustworthy.
   Protect me from those who
      hunt me down without
      cause.
⁸⁷ They almost finished me off,
   but I refused to abandon your
      commandments.
⁸⁸ In your unfailing love, spare
      my life;
   then I can continue to obey
      your laws.

Lamedh

⁸⁹ Your eternal word, O LORD,
   stands firm in heaven.
⁹⁰ Your faithfulness extends to every
      generation,
   as enduring as the earth you
      created.
⁹¹ Your regulations remain true to
      this day,
   for everything serves your
      plans.
⁹² If your instructions hadn't sustained
      me with joy,
   I would have died in my misery.
⁹³ I will never forget your
      commandments,
   for by them you give me life.
⁹⁴ I am yours; rescue me!
   For I have worked hard at obeying
      your commandments.
⁹⁵ Though the wicked hide along the
      way to kill me,

HOW WE LIVE

In the world, not of it

JOHN 17:15 It would be nice to just go straight to heaven, wouldn't it? Become a believer and—poof—you're on streets of gold. No more worries, no more tears, no more bills, no more illness. • God could have done it that way, but he didn't. He chose instead to leave us in the world with all of our foibles and propensities to sin. He chose to have us continue to face hardship, pain, persecution, and yes, even physical death. • Why? Well, because we have a job to do: to share the gospel message with those who haven't heard. We are in the world, yet we're awaiting the next world. We know that heaven is our true home, and we eagerly anticipate that eternal abode. So we live differently while here. We are in the world, but we are not of it. • Because Jesus sends you into the world, you should not try to escape from the world, nor should you avoid all relationships with non-Christians. You are called to be salt and light (Matthew 5:13-16, January 5).

I will quietly keep my mind
     on your laws.
⁹⁶ Even perfection has its limits,
     but your commands have
     no limit.

MAY**29**

2 SAMUEL 14:1–15:22
The king's eldest son is usually the next in line to rule the kingdom. Trouble arises, however, when that son decides he's ready to be king while Dad is still on the throne. Absalom had such aspirations.

Joab realized how much the king longed to see Absalom. ²So he sent for a woman from Tekoa who had a reputation for great wisdom. He said to her, "Pretend you are in mourning; wear mourning clothes and don't put on lotions.* Act like a woman who has been mourning for the dead for a long time. ³Then go to the king and tell him the story I am about to tell you." Then Joab told her what to say.

⁴When the woman from Tekoa approached the king, she bowed with her face to the ground in deep respect and cried out, "O king! Help me!"

⁵"What's the trouble?" the king asked.

"Alas, I am a widow!" she replied. "My husband is dead. ⁶My two sons had a fight out in the field. And since no one was there to stop it, one of them was killed. ⁷Now the rest of the family is demanding, 'Let us have your son. We will execute him for murdering his brother. He doesn't deserve to inherit his family's property.' They want to extinguish the only coal I have left, and my husband's name and family will disappear from the face of the earth."

⁸"Leave it to me," the king told her. "Go home, and I'll see to it that no one touches him."

⁹"Oh, thank you, my lord the king," the woman from Tekoa replied. "If you are criticized for helping me, let the blame fall on me and on my father's house, and let the king and his throne be innocent."

¹⁰"If anyone objects," the king said,

PROVERBS 16:6-7
Unfailing love and faithfulness make atonement for sin. By fearing the LORD, people avoid evil. ☐ When people's lives please the LORD, even their enemies are at peace with them.

"bring him to me. I can assure you he will never complain again!"

¹¹Then she said, "Please swear to me by the LORD your God that you won't let anyone take vengeance against my son. I want no more bloodshed."

"As surely as the LORD lives," he replied, "not a hair on your son's head will be disturbed!"

¹²"Please allow me to ask one more thing of my lord the king," she said.

"Go ahead and speak," he responded.

¹³She replied, "Why don't you do as much for the people of God as you have promised to do for me? You have convicted yourself in making this decision, because you have refused to bring home your own banished son. ¹⁴All of us must die eventually. Our lives are like water spilled out on the ground, which cannot be gathered up again. But God does not just sweep life away; instead, he devises ways to bring us back when we have been separated from him.

¹⁵"I have come to plead with my lord the king because people have threatened me. I said to myself, 'Perhaps the king will listen to me ¹⁶and rescue us from those who would cut us off from the inheritance* God has given us. ¹⁷Yes, my lord the king will give us peace of mind again.' I know that you are like an angel of God in discerning good from evil. May the LORD your God be with you."

¹⁸"I must know one thing," the king replied, "and tell me the truth."

"Yes, my lord the king," she responded.

¹⁹"Did Joab put you up to this?"

And the woman replied, "My lord the king, how can I deny it? Nobody can hide anything from you. Yes, Joab sent me and told me what to say. 20He did it to place the matter before you in a different light. But you are as wise as an angel of God, and you understand everything that happens among us!"

21So the king sent for Joab and told him, "All right, go and bring back the young man Absalom."

22Joab bowed with his face to the ground in deep respect and said, "At last I know that I have gained your approval, my lord the king, for you have granted me this request!"

23Then Joab went to Geshur and brought Absalom back to Jerusalem. 24But the king gave this order: "Absalom may go to his own house, but he must never come into my presence." So Absalom did not see the king.

25Now Absalom was praised as the most handsome man in all Israel. He was flawless from head to foot. 26He cut his hair only once a year, and then only because it was so heavy. When he weighed it out, it came to five pounds!* 27He had three sons and one daughter. His daughter's name was Tamar, and she was very beautiful.

28Absalom lived in Jerusalem for two years, but he never got to see the king. 29Then Absalom sent for Joab to ask him to intercede for him, but Joab refused to come. Absalom sent for him a second time, but again Joab refused to come. 30So Absalom said to his servants, "Go and set fire to Joab's barley field, the field next to mine." So they set his field on fire, as Absalom had commanded.

31Then Joab came to Absalom at his house and demanded, "Why did your servants set my field on fire?"

32And Absalom replied, "Because I wanted you to ask the king why he brought me back from Geshur if he didn't intend to see me. I might as well have stayed there. Let me see the king; if he finds me guilty of anything, then let him kill me."

33So Joab told the king what Absalom had said. Then at last David summoned Absalom, who came and bowed low before the king, and the king kissed him.

15:1AFTER this, Absalom bought a chariot and horses, and he hired fifty bodyguards to run ahead of him. 2He got up early every morning and went out to the gate of the city. When people brought a case to the king for judgment, Absalom would ask where in Israel they were from, and they would tell him their tribe. 3Then Absalom would say, "You've really got a strong case here! It's too bad the king doesn't have anyone to hear it. 4I wish I were the judge. Then everyone could bring their cases to me for judgment, and I would give them justice!"

5When people tried to bow before him, Absalom wouldn't let them. Instead, he took them by the hand and kissed them. 6Absalom did this with everyone who came to the king for judgment, and so he stole the hearts of all the people of Israel.

7After four years,* Absalom said to the king, "Let me go to Hebron to offer a sacrifice to the LORD and fulfill a vow I made to him. 8For while your servant was at Geshur in Aram, I promised to sacrifice to the LORD in Hebron* if he would bring me back to Jerusalem."

9"All right," the king told him. "Go and fulfill your vow."

So Absalom went to Hebron. 10But while he was there, he sent secret messengers to all the tribes of Israel to stir up a rebellion against the king. "As soon as you hear the ram's horn," his message read, "you are to say, 'Absalom has been crowned king in Hebron.'" 11He took 200 men from Jerusalem with him as guests, but they knew nothing of his intentions. 12While Absalom was offering the sacrifices, he sent for Ahithophel, one of David's counselors who lived in Giloh. Soon many others also joined Absalom, and the conspiracy gained momentum.

13A messenger soon arrived in Jerusalem to tell David, "All Israel has joined Absalom in a conspiracy against you!"

14"Then we must flee at once, or it will be too late!" David urged his men. "Hurry! If we get out of the city before Absalom arrives, both we and the city of Jerusalem will be spared from disaster."

15"We are with you," his advisers replied. "Do what you think is best."

16So the king and all his household set out at once. He left no one behind except ten of his concubines to look after the palace. 17The king and all his people set out on foot, pausing at the last house 18to let all the king's men move past to lead the way. There were 600 men from Gath who had come with David, along with the king's bodyguard.*

19Then the king turned and said to Ittai, a leader of the men from Gath, "Why are you coming with us? Go on back to King Absalom, for you are a guest in Israel, a foreigner in exile. 20You arrived only recently, and should I force you today to wander with us? I don't even know where we will go. Go on back and take your kinsmen with you, and may the LORD show you his unfailing love and faithfulness.*"

21But Ittai said to the king, "I vow by the LORD and by your own life that I will go wherever my lord the king goes, no matter what happens—whether it means life or death."

22David replied, "All right, come with us." So Ittai and all his men and their families went along.

14:2 Hebrew *don't anoint yourself with oil.* **14:16** Or *the property;* or *the people.* **14:26** Hebrew *200 shekels* [2.3 kilograms] *by the royal standard.* **15:7** As in Greek and Syriac versions; Hebrew reads *forty years.* **15:8** As in some Greek manuscripts; Hebrew lacks *in Hebron.* **15:18** Hebrew *the Kerethites and Pelethites.* **15:20** As in Greek version; Hebrew reads *and may unfailing love and faithfulness go with you.*

JOHN 18:1-24
Jesus walked into the suffering that awaited him with his eyes wide open. This was why he had come to Earth.

After saying these things, Jesus crossed the Kidron Valley with his disciples and entered a grove of olive trees. 2Judas, the betrayer, knew this place, because Jesus had often gone there with his disciples. 3The leading priests and Pharisees had given Judas a contingent of Roman soldiers and Temple guards to accompany him. Now with blazing torches, lanterns, and weapons, they arrived at the olive grove.

4Jesus fully realized all that was going to happen to him, so he stepped forward to meet them. "Who are you looking for?" he asked.

5"Jesus the Nazarene,"* they replied.

"I AM he,"* Jesus said. (Judas, who betrayed him, was standing with them.) 6As Jesus said "I AM he," they all drew back and fell to the ground! 7Once more he asked them, "Who are you looking for?"

And again they replied, "Jesus the Nazarene."

8"I told you that I AM he," Jesus said. "And since I am the one you want, let these others go." 9He did this to fulfill his own statement: "I did not lose a single one of those you have given me."*

10Then Simon Peter drew a sword and slashed off the right ear of Malchus, the high priest's slave. 11But Jesus said to Peter, "Put your sword back into its sheath. Shall I not drink from the cup of suffering the Father has given me?"

12So the soldiers, their commanding officer, and the Temple guards arrested Jesus and tied him up. 13First they took him to Annas, the father-in-law of Caiaphas, the high priest at that time.* 14Caiaphas was the one who had told the other Jewish leaders, "It's better that one man should die for the people."

15Simon Peter followed Jesus, as did another of the disciples. That other disciple was acquainted with the high priest, so he was allowed to enter the high priest's courtyard with Jesus. 16Peter had to stay outside the gate. Then the disciple who knew the high priest spoke to the woman watching at the gate, and she let Peter in. 17The woman asked Peter, "You're not one of that man's disciples, are you?"

"No," he said, "I am not."

18Because it was cold, the household servants and the guards had made a charcoal fire. They stood around it, warming themselves, and Peter stood with them, warming himself.

19Inside, the high priest began asking Jesus about his followers and what he had been teaching them. 20Jesus replied, "Everyone knows what I teach. I have preached regularly in the synagogues and the Temple, where the people* gather. I have not spoken in secret. 21Why are you asking me this question? Ask those who heard me. They know what I said."

22Then one of the Temple guards standing nearby slapped Jesus across the face.

"Is that the way to answer the high priest?" he demanded.

²³ Jesus replied, "If I said anything wrong, you must prove it. But if I'm speaking the truth, why are you beating me?"

²⁴ Then Annas bound Jesus and sent him to Caiaphas, the high priest.

18:5a Or *Jesus of Nazareth;* also in 18:7. **18:5b** Or *"The 'I AM' is here";* or *"I am the LORD";* Greek reads *I am;* also in 18:6, 8. See Exod 3:14. **18:9** See John 6:39 and 17:12. **18:13** Greek *that year.* **18:20** Greek *Jewish people;* also in 18:38.

PSALM 119:97-112

Mem

⁹⁷ **O**h, how I love your instructions!
　　I think about them all day long.
⁹⁸ Your commands make me wiser than
　　　my enemies,
　　for they are my constant guide.
⁹⁹ Yes, I have more insight than my
　　　teachers,
　　for I am always thinking of your laws.
¹⁰⁰ I am even wiser than my elders,
　　for I have kept your commandments.
¹⁰¹ I have refused to walk on any evil
　　　path,
　　so that I may remain obedient to
　　　your word.
¹⁰² I haven't turned away from your
　　　regulations,
　　for you have taught me well.
¹⁰³ How sweet your words taste to me;
　　they are sweeter than honey.

¹⁰⁴ Your commandments give me
　　　understanding;
　　no wonder I hate every false way
　　　of life.

Nun

¹⁰⁵ Your word is a lamp to guide my feet
　　and a light for my path.
¹⁰⁶ I've promised it once, and I'll promise
　　　it again:
　　I will obey your righteous
　　　regulations.
¹⁰⁷ I have suffered much, O LORD;
　　restore my life again as you
　　　promised.
¹⁰⁸ LORD, accept my offering of praise,
　　and teach me your regulations.
¹⁰⁹ My life constantly hangs in the
　　　balance,
　　but I will not stop obeying your
　　　instructions.
¹¹⁰ The wicked have set their traps for me,
　　but I will not turn from your
　　　commandments.
¹¹¹ Your laws are my treasure;
　　they are my heart's delight.
¹¹² I am determined to keep your decrees
　　to the very end.

PROVERBS 16:8-9

Better to have little, with godliness, than to be rich and dishonest. □ We can make our plans, but the LORD determines our steps.

Raising our children

HOW WE LIVE

2 SAMUEL 14–15 God warned that David's family would suffer because of his sin against Bathsheba and Uriah (2 Samuel 12:7-12, May 27). Even though God forgave David, the resulting family discord was inevitable. David must have been horrified as he witnessed his own son running wild, refusing good advice, and plotting his father's destruction. • When David did not discipline his son Amnon for his sin of rape or Absalom for his sin of murder, he failed to hold them accountable and give them the opportunity to change. Sometimes when the kids are causing a ruckus and parents are at their wit's end, it's tempting to take the easy road and just ignore the problem for a while. Don't give in to this temptation! Children's lives are shaped by their parents. Children need guidance and support. They need to be held accountable for their actions. If you are a parent, ask God for wisdom in raising your children. Give them the chance to become people of good character.

MAY**30**

2 SAMUEL 15:23–16:23

The only thing worse than a spoiled, angry prince rebelling against his father is such a prince getting the upper hand. King David had to flee Jerusalem, running for his life from his own son.

Everyone cried loudly as the king and his followers passed by. They crossed the Kidron Valley and then went out toward the wilderness.

²⁴Zadok and all the Levites also came along, carrying the Ark of the Covenant of God. They set down the Ark of God, and Abiathar offered sacrifices* until everyone had passed out of the city.

²⁵Then the king instructed Zadok to take the Ark of God back into the city. "If the Lord sees fit," David said, "he will bring me back to see the Ark and the Tabernacle* again. ²⁶But if he is through with me, then let him do what seems best to him."

²⁷The king also told Zadok the priest, "Look,* here is my plan. You and Abiathar* should return quietly to the city with your son Ahimaaz and Abiathar's son Jonathan. ²⁸I will stop at the shallows of the Jordan River* and wait there for a report from you." ²⁹So Zadok and Abiathar took the Ark of God back to the city and stayed there.

³⁰David walked up the road to the Mount of Olives, weeping as he went. His head was covered and his feet were bare as a sign of mourning. And the people who were with him covered their heads and wept as they climbed the hill. ³¹When someone told David that his adviser Ahithophel was now backing Absalom, David prayed, "O Lord, let Ahithophel give Absalom foolish advice!"

³²When David reached the summit of the Mount of Olives where people worshiped God, Hushai the Arkite was waiting there for him. Hushai had torn his clothing and put dirt on his head as a sign of mourning. ³³But David told him, "If you go with me, you will only be a burden. ³⁴Return to Jerusalem and tell Absalom, 'I will now be your adviser, O king, just as I was your father's adviser in the past.'

Then you can frustrate and counter Ahithophel's advice. ³⁵Zadok and Abiathar, the priests, will be there. Tell them about the plans being made in the king's palace, ³⁶and they will send their sons Ahimaaz and Jonathan to tell me what is going on."

³⁷So David's friend Hushai returned to Jerusalem, getting there just as Absalom arrived.

¹⁶:¹When David had gone a little beyond the summit of the Mount of Olives, Ziba, the servant of Mephibosheth,* was waiting there for him. He had two donkeys loaded with 200 loaves of bread, 100 clusters of raisins, 100 bunches of summer fruit, and a wineskin full of wine.

²"What are these for?" the king asked Ziba.

Ziba replied, "The donkeys are for the king's people to ride on, and the bread and summer fruit are for the young men to eat. The wine is for those who become exhausted in the wilderness."

³"And where is Mephibosheth, Saul's grandson?" the king asked him.

"He stayed in Jerusalem," Ziba replied. "He said, 'Today I will get back the kingdom of my grandfather Saul.'"

⁴"In that case," the king told Ziba, "I give you everything Mephibosheth owns."

"I bow before you," Ziba replied. "May I always be pleasing to you, my lord the king."

⁵As King David came to Bahurim, a man came out of the village cursing them. It was Shimei son of Gera, from the same clan as Saul's family. ⁶He threw stones at the king and the king's officers and all the mighty warriors who surrounded him. ⁷"Get out of here, you murderer, you scoundrel!" he shouted at David. ⁸"The Lord is paying you back for all the bloodshed in Saul's clan. You stole his throne, and now the Lord has given it to your son Absalom. At last you will taste some of your own medicine, for you are a murderer!"

⁹"Why should this dead dog curse my

lord the king?" Abishai son of Zeruiah demanded. "Let me go over and cut off his head!"

¹⁰"No!" the king said. "Who asked your opinion, you sons of Zeruiah! If the LORD has told him to curse me, who are you to stop him?"

¹¹Then David said to Abishai and to all his servants, "My own son is trying to kill me. Doesn't this relative of Saul* have even more reason to do so? Leave him alone and let him curse, for the LORD has told him to do it. ¹²And perhaps the LORD will see that I am being wronged and will bless me because of these curses today."

¹³So David and his men continued down the road, and Shimei kept pace with them on a nearby hillside, cursing as he went and throwing stones at David and tossing dust into the air.

¹⁴The king and all who were with him grew weary along the way, so they rested when they reached the Jordan River.*

¹⁵Meanwhile, Absalom and all the army of Israel arrived at Jerusalem, accompanied by Ahithophel. ¹⁶When David's friend Hushai the Arkite arrived, he went immediately to see Absalom. "Long live the king!" he exclaimed. "Long live the king!"

¹⁷"Is this the way you treat your friend David?" Absalom asked him. "Why aren't you with him?"

¹⁸"I'm here because I belong to the man who is chosen by the LORD and by all the men of Israel," Hushai replied. ¹⁹"And anyway, why shouldn't I serve you? Just as I was your father's adviser, now I will be your adviser!"

²⁰Then Absalom turned to Ahithophel and asked him, "What should I do next?"

²¹Ahithophel told him, "Go and sleep with your father's concubines, for he has left them here to look after the palace. Then all Israel will know that you have insulted your father beyond hope of reconciliation, and they will throw their support to you." ²²So they set up a tent on the palace roof where everyone could see it, and Absalom went in and had sex with his father's concubines.

²³Absalom followed Ahithophel's advice, just as David had done. For every word Ahithophel spoke seemed as wise as though it had come directly from the mouth of God.

15:24 Or *Abiathar went up.*   15:25 Hebrew *and his dwelling place.*   15:27a As in Greek version; Hebrew reads *Are you a seer?* or *Do you see?*   15:27b Hebrew lacks *and Abiathar;* compare 15:29.   15:28 Hebrew *at the crossing points of the wilderness.*   16:1 Mephibosheth is another name for Merib-baal.   16:11 Hebrew *this Benjaminite.*   16:14 As in Greek version (see also 17:16); Hebrew reads *when they reached their destination.*

JOHN 18:25–19:22

The hostility of the religious leaders rose against Jesus in a constant crescendo. They wanted him out of the picture, no matter what it took. They had to convince the Roman government that he was a criminal worthy of death.

Meanwhile, as Simon Peter was standing by the fire warming himself, they asked him again, "You're not one of his disciples, are you?"

He denied it, saying, "No, I am not."

Our work

HOW WE LIVE

PROVERBS 16:11 Many workplaces are run on an unspoken rule: the end justifies any means. And the "end" usually involves making more money than the other guy. So to get your share, it's okay to cut corners on a little quality here or shave off workers' wages there. It's acceptable to pad your expense account every once in a while; everybody does it. Why not take credit for something a coworker did? You're all on the same team, after all. It's alright to "enhance" profit reports to your shareholders. It's just the way you have to do business these days, right? • Wrong. Proverbs 16:11 reminds us how much the Lord values—even demands—honesty and integrity. When we follow Jesus, we are called to walk to the beat of a different drummer. The "end" for us is much more than making money or coming out on top; our chief end is to please God.

26But one of the household slaves of the high priest, a relative of the man whose ear Peter had cut off, asked, "Didn't I see you out there in the olive grove with Jesus?" 27Again Peter denied it. And immediately a rooster crowed.

28Jesus' trial before Caiaphas ended in the early hours of the morning. Then he was taken to the headquarters of the Roman governor.* His accusers didn't go inside because it would defile them, and they wouldn't be allowed to celebrate the Passover. 29So Pilate, the governor, went out to them and asked, "What is your charge against this man?"

30"We wouldn't have handed him over to you if he weren't a criminal!" they retorted.

31"Then take him away and judge him by your own law," Pilate told them.

"Only the Romans are permitted to execute someone," the Jewish leaders replied. 32(This fulfilled Jesus' prediction about the way he would die.*)

33Then Pilate went back into his headquarters and called for Jesus to be brought to him. "Are you the king of the Jews?" he asked him.

34Jesus replied, "Is this your own question, or did others tell you about me?"

35"Am I a Jew?" Pilate retorted. "Your own people and their leading priests brought you to me for trial. Why? What have you done?"

36Jesus answered, "My Kingdom is not an earthly kingdom. If it were, my followers would fight to keep me from being handed over to the Jewish leaders. But my Kingdom is not of this world."

37Pilate said, "So you are a king?"

Jesus responded, "You say I am a king. Actually, I was born and came into the world to testify to the truth. All who love the truth recognize that what I say is true."

38"What is truth?" Pilate asked. Then he went out again to the people and told them, "He is not guilty of any crime. 39But you have a custom of asking me to release one prisoner each year at Passover. Would you like me to release this 'King of the Jews'?"

40But they shouted back, "No! Not this man. We want Barabbas!" (Barabbas was a revolutionary.)

19:1Then Pilate had Jesus flogged with a lead-tipped whip. 2The soldiers wove a crown of thorns and put it on his head, and they put a purple robe on him. 3"Hail! King of the Jews!" they mocked, as they slapped him across the face.

4Pilate went outside again and said to the people, "I am going to bring him out to you now, but understand clearly that I find him not guilty." 5Then Jesus came out wearing the crown of thorns and the purple robe. And Pilate said, "Look, here is the man!"

6When they saw him, the leading priests and Temple guards began shouting, "Crucify him! Crucify him!"

"Take him yourselves and crucify him," Pilate said. "I find him not guilty."

7The Jewish leaders replied, "By our law he ought to die because he called himself the Son of God."

8When Pilate heard this, he was more frightened than ever. 9He took Jesus back into the headquarters* again and asked him, "Where are you from?" But Jesus gave no answer. 10"Why don't you talk to me?" Pilate demanded. "Don't you realize that I have the power to release you or crucify you?"

11Then Jesus said, "You would have no power over me at all unless it were given to you from above. So the one who handed me over to you has the greater sin."

12Then Pilate tried to release him, but the Jewish leaders shouted, "If you release this man, you are no 'friend of Caesar.'* Anyone who declares himself a king is a rebel against Caesar."

13When they said this, Pilate brought Jesus out to them again. Then Pilate sat down on the judgment seat on the platform that is called the Stone Pavement (in Hebrew, *Gabbatha*). 14It was now about noon on the day of preparation for the Passover. And Pilate said to the people,* "Look, here is your king!"

15"Away with him," they yelled. "Away with him! Crucify him!"

"What? Crucify your king?" Pilate asked.

"We have no king but Caesar," the leading priests shouted back.

¹⁶Then Pilate turned Jesus over to them to be crucified.

So they took Jesus away. ¹⁷Carrying the cross by himself, he went to the place called Place of the Skull (in Hebrew, *Golgotha*). ¹⁸There they nailed him to the cross. Two others were crucified with him, one on either side, with Jesus between them. ¹⁹And Pilate posted a sign over him that read, "Jesus of Nazareth,* the King of the Jews." ²⁰The place where Jesus was crucified was near the city, and the sign was written in Hebrew, Latin, and Greek, so that many people could read it.

²¹Then the leading priests objected and said to Pilate, "Change it from 'The King of the Jews' to 'He said, I am King of the Jews.'"

²²Pilate replied, "No, what I have written, I have written."

18:28 Greek *to the Praetorium;* also in 18:33.
18:32 See John 12:32-33.   **19:9** Greek *the Praetorium.*
19:12 "Friend of Caesar" is a technical term that refers to an ally of the emperor.   **19:14** Greek *Jewish people;* also in 19:20.   **19:19** Or *Jesus the Nazarene.*

PSALM 119:113-128

Samekh

¹¹³I hate those with divided loyalties,
    but I love your instructions.
¹¹⁴You are my refuge and my shield;
    your word is my source of hope.
¹¹⁵Get out of my life, you evil-minded people,
    for I intend to obey the commands of my God.
¹¹⁶LORD, sustain me as you promised, that I may live!
    Do not let my hope be crushed.

¹¹⁷Sustain me, and I will be rescued;
    then I will meditate continually on your decrees.
¹¹⁸But you have rejected all who stray from your decrees.
    They are only fooling themselves.
¹¹⁹You skim off the wicked of the earth like scum;
    no wonder I love to obey your laws!
¹²⁰I tremble in fear of you;
    I stand in awe of your regulations.

Ayin

¹²¹Don't leave me to the mercy of my enemies,
    for I have done what is just and right.
¹²²Please guarantee a blessing for me.
    Don't let the arrogant oppress me!
¹²³My eyes strain to see your rescue,
    to see the truth of your promise fulfilled.
¹²⁴I am your servant; deal with me in unfailing love,
    and teach me your decrees.
¹²⁵Give discernment to me, your servant;
    then I will understand your laws.
¹²⁶LORD, it is time for you to act,
    for these evil people have violated your instructions.
¹²⁷Truly, I love your commands
    more than gold, even the finest gold.
¹²⁸Each of your commandments is right.
    That is why I hate every false way.

PROVERBS 16:10-11

The king speaks with divine wisdom; he must never judge unfairly. □ The LORD demands accurate scales and balances; he sets the standards for fairness.

2 SAMUEL 17:1-29

How do you know who to listen to? That was a question on the mind of Absalom, the prince-run-wild. Fortunately for David, a king defending his throne, Absalom chose poorly.

Now Ahithophel urged Absalom, "Let me choose 12,000 men to start out after David tonight. ²I will catch up with him while he is weary and discouraged. He and his troops will panic, and everyone will run away. Then I will kill only the king, ³and I will bring all the people back to you as a bride returns to her husband. After all, it is only one man's life that you seek.* Then you will be at peace with all the people." ⁴This plan seemed good to Absalom and to all the elders of Israel.

⁵But then Absalom said, "Bring in Hushai the Arkite. Let's see what he thinks about this." ⁶When Hushai arrived, Absalom told him what Ahithophel had said. Then he asked, "What is your opinion? Should we follow Ahithophel's advice? If not, what do you suggest?"

⁷"Well," Hushai replied to Absalom, "this time Ahithophel has made a mistake. ⁸You know your father and his men; they are mighty warriors. Right now they are as enraged as a mother bear who has been robbed of her cubs. And remember that your father is an experienced man of war. He won't be spending the night among the troops. ⁹He has probably already hidden in some pit or cave. And when he comes out and attacks and a few of your men fall, there will be panic among your troops, and the word will spread that Absalom's men are being slaughtered. ¹⁰Then even the bravest soldiers, though they have the heart of a lion, will be paralyzed with fear. For all Israel knows what a mighty warrior your father is and how courageous his men are.

¹¹"I recommend that you mobilize the entire army of Israel, bringing them from as far away as Dan in the north and Beersheba in the south. That way you will have an army as numerous as the sand on the seashore. And I advise that you personally lead the troops. ¹²When we find David, we'll fall on him like dew that falls on the ground. Then neither he nor any of his men will be left alive. ¹³And if David were to escape into some town, you will have all Israel there at your command. Then we can take ropes and drag the walls of the town into the nearest valley until every stone is torn down."

¹⁴Then Absalom and all the men of Israel said, "Hushai's advice is better than Ahithophel's." For the LORD had determined to defeat the counsel of Ahithophel, which really was the better plan, so that he could bring disaster on Absalom!

¹⁵Hushai told Zadok and Abiathar, the priests, what Ahithophel had said to Absalom and the elders of Israel and what he himself had advised instead. ¹⁶"Quick!" he told them. "Find David and urge him not to stay at the shallows of the Jordan River* tonight. He must go across at once into the wilderness beyond. Otherwise he will die and his entire army with him."

¹⁷Jonathan and Ahimaaz had been staying at En-rogel so as not to be seen entering and leaving the city. Arrangements had been made for a servant girl to bring them the message they were to take to King David. ¹⁸But a boy spotted them at En-rogel, and he told Absalom about it. So they quickly escaped to Bahurim, where a man hid them down inside a well in his courtyard. ¹⁹The man's wife put a cloth over the top of the well and scattered grain on it to dry in the sun; so no one suspected they were there.

²⁰When Absalom's men arrived, they asked her, "Have you seen Ahimaaz and Jonathan?"

The woman replied, "They were here, but they crossed over the brook." Absalom's men looked for them without success and returned to Jerusalem.

²¹Then the two men crawled out of the well and hurried on to King David. "Quick!" they told him, "cross the Jordan tonight!" And they told him how Ahithophel had advised that he be captured and killed. ²²So David and all the people with him went across the Jordan River during the night, and they were all on the other bank before dawn.

²³When Ahithophel realized that his advice had not been followed, he saddled his donkey, went to his hometown, set his affairs in order, and hanged himself. He died there and was buried in the family tomb.

²⁴David soon arrived at Mahanaim. By now, Absalom had mobilized the entire army of Israel and was leading his troops across the Jordan River. ²⁵Absalom had appointed Amasa as commander of his army, replacing Joab, who had been commander under David. (Amasa was Joab's cousin. His father was Jether,* an Ishma-

elite.* His mother, Abigail daughter of Nahash, was the sister of Joab's mother, Zeruiah.) 26Absalom and the Israelite army set up camp in the land of Gilead.

27When David arrived at Mahanaim, he was warmly greeted by Shobi son of Nahash, who came from Rabbah of the Ammonites, and by Makir son of Ammiel from Lo-debar, and by Barzillai of Gilead from Rogelim. 28They brought sleeping mats, cooking pots, serving bowls, wheat and barley, flour and roasted grain, beans, lentils, 29honey, butter, sheep, goats, and cheese for David and those who were with him. For they said, "You must all be very hungry and tired and thirsty after your long march through the wilderness."

17:3 As in Greek version; Hebrew reads *like the return of all is the man whom you seek.*   17:16 Hebrew *at the crossing points of the wilderness.*   17:25a Hebrew *Ithra,* a variant spelling of Jether.   17:25b As in some Greek manuscripts (see also 1 Chr 2:17); Hebrew reads *an Israelite.*

JOHN 19:23-42
Jesus did what he came to do. He was offered up as the sacrificial Lamb of God. Those who hatefully prompted his death only served to facilitate his mission. With that last breath some may have seen defeat, but it was victory in the making.

When the soldiers had crucified Jesus, they divided his clothes among the four of them. They also took his robe, but it was seamless, woven in one piece from top to bottom. 24So they said, "Rather than tearing it apart, let's throw dice* for it." This fulfilled the Scripture that says, "They divided my garments among themselves and threw dice for my clothing."* So that is what they did.

25Standing near the cross were Jesus' mother, and his mother's sister, Mary (the wife of Clopas), and Mary Magdalene. 26When Jesus saw his mother standing there beside the disciple he loved, he said to her, "Dear woman, here is your son." 27And he said to this disciple, "Here is your mother." And from then on this disciple took her into his home.

28Jesus knew that his mission was now finished, and to fulfill Scripture he said, "I am thirsty."* 29A jar of sour wine was sitting there, so they soaked a sponge in it, put it on a hyssop branch, and held it up to his lips. 30When Jesus had tasted it, he said, "It is finished!" Then he bowed his head and released his spirit.

31It was the day of preparation, and the Jewish leaders didn't want the bodies hanging there the next day, which was the Sabbath (and a very special Sabbath, because it was the Passover). So they asked Pilate to hasten their deaths by ordering that their legs be broken. Then their bodies could be taken down. 32So the soldiers came and broke the legs of the two men

HOW WE LIVE

Studying God's Word

PSALM 119:129-152 How many books do you own? Hundreds? Many people view their books as beloved friends and take joy in rereading them or quoting favorite passages. Of all of the books you own, the Bible is the most important. How much of the Bible can you quote? Do you know how to find your favorite passages? In today's reading, the psalmist talks about the joy that comes when he follows the principles set forth in God's Word. How can we know those principles unless we read and study them? • The most amazing thing about studying the Bible is that we have the direct assistance of its Author. God has not only provided guidelines for life, he is also accessible to us through prayer. "Help me understand the meaning of your commandments" (119:27) is the prayer of the psalmist. And he continues, "Teach me your decrees, O Lord" (119:33); "Give me understanding" (119:34); "Give me an eagerness for your laws" (119:36). It's a mystery, but somehow, when we read the Bible with open hearts, asking God to speak, it comes alive and changes us. Always keep the daily reading of his Word a top priority in your life.

crucified with Jesus. ³³But when they came to Jesus, they saw that he was already dead, so they didn't break his legs. ³⁴One of the soldiers, however, pierced his side with a spear, and immediately blood and water flowed out. ³⁵(This report is from an eyewitness giving an accurate account. He speaks the truth so that you also can believe.*) ³⁶These things happened in fulfillment of the Scriptures that say, "Not one of his bones will be broken,"* ³⁷and "They will look on the one they pierced."*

³⁸Afterward Joseph of Arimathea, who had been a secret disciple of Jesus (because he feared the Jewish leaders), asked Pilate for permission to take down Jesus' body. When Pilate gave permission, Joseph came and took the body away. ³⁹With him came Nicodemus, the man who had come to Jesus at night. He brought seventy-five pounds* of perfumed ointment made from myrrh and aloes. ⁴⁰Following Jewish burial custom, they wrapped Jesus' body with the spices in long sheets of linen cloth. ⁴¹The place of crucifixion was near a garden, where there was a new tomb, never used before. ⁴²And so, because it was the day of preparation for the Jewish Passover* and since the tomb was close at hand, they laid Jesus there.

19:24a Greek *cast lots.* **19:24b** Ps 22:18. **19:28** See Pss 22:15; 69:21. **19:35** Some manuscripts read *can continue to believe.* **19:36** Exod 12:46; Num 9:12; Ps 34:20. **19:37** Zech 12:10. **19:39** Greek *100 litras* [32.7 kilograms]. **19:42** Greek *because of the Jewish day of preparation.*

PSALM 119:129-152

Pe

129 **Y**our laws are wonderful.
No wonder I obey them!
130 The teaching of your word gives light,
so even the simple can understand.
131 I pant with expectation,
longing for your commands.
132 Come and show me your mercy,
as you do for all who love your name.
133 Guide my steps by your word,
so I will not be overcome by evil.
134 Ransom me from the oppression
of evil people;
then I can obey your
commandments.
135 Look upon me with love;
teach me your decrees.

136 Rivers of tears gush from my eyes
because people disobey your
instructions.

Tsadhe

137 O LORD, you are righteous,
and your regulations are fair.
138 Your laws are perfect
and completely trustworthy.
139 I am overwhelmed with indignation,
for my enemies have disregarded
your words.
140 Your promises have been thoroughly
tested;
that is why I love them so much.
141 I am insignificant and despised,
but I don't forget your
commandments.
142 Your justice is eternal,
and your instructions are perfectly
true.
143 As pressure and stress bear down on me,
I find joy in your commands.
144 Your laws are always right;
help me to understand them
so I may live.

Qoph

145 I pray with all my heart; answer me,
LORD!
I will obey your decrees.
146 I cry out to you; rescue me,
that I may obey your laws.
147 I rise early, before the sun is up;
I cry out for help and put my hope
in your words.
148 I stay awake through the night,
thinking about your promise.
149 In your faithful love, O LORD, hear
my cry;
let me be revived by following your
regulations.
150 Lawless people are coming to attack
me;
they live far from your instructions.
151 But you are near, O LORD,
and all your commands are true.
152 I have known from my earliest days
that your laws will last forever.

PROVERBS 16:12-13

A king detests wrongdoing, for his rule is built on justice. □ The king is pleased with words from righteous lips; he loves those who speak honestly.

2 SAMUEL 18:1–19:10

David had the ability to love people despite their failures and shortcomings. Although Saul had tried to kill him, David mourned when Saul himself was killed in battle. Here David showed the same compassion for Absalom, his son-turned-traitor.

David now mustered the men who were with him and appointed generals and captains* to lead them. ²He sent the troops out in three groups, placing one group under Joab, one under Joab's brother Abishai son of Zeruiah, and one under Ittai, the man from Gath. The king told his troops, "I am going out with you."

³But his men objected strongly. "You must not go," they urged. "If we have to turn and run—and even if half of us die— it will make no difference to Absalom's troops; they will be looking only for you. You are worth 10,000 of us,* and it is better that you stay here in the town and send help if we need it."

⁴"If you think that's the best plan, I'll do it," the king answered. So he stood alongside the gate of the town as all the troops marched out in groups of hundreds and of thousands.

⁵And the king gave this command to Joab, Abishai, and Ittai: "For my sake, deal gently with young Absalom." And all the troops heard the king give this order to his commanders.

⁶So the battle began in the forest of Ephraim, ⁷and the Israelite troops were beaten back by David's men. There was a great slaughter that day, and 20,000 men laid down their lives. ⁸The battle raged all across the countryside, and more men died because of the forest than were killed by the sword.

⁹During the battle, Absalom happened to come upon some of David's men. He tried to escape on his mule, but as he rode beneath the thick branches of a great tree, his hair* got caught in the tree. His mule kept going and left him dangling in the

air. ¹⁰One of David's men saw what had happened and told Joab, "I saw Absalom dangling from a great tree."

¹¹"What?" Joab demanded. "You saw him there and didn't kill him? I would have rewarded you with ten pieces of silver* and a hero's belt!"

¹²"I would not kill the king's son for even a thousand pieces of silver,*" the man replied to Joab. "We all heard the king say to you and Abishai and Ittai, 'For my sake, please spare young Absalom.' ¹³And if I had betrayed the king by killing his son—and the king would certainly find out who did it—you yourself would be the first to abandon me."

¹⁴"Enough of this nonsense," Joab said. Then he took three daggers and plunged them into Absalom's heart as he dangled, still alive, in the great tree. ¹⁵Ten of Joab's young armor bearers then surrounded Absalom and killed him.

¹⁶Then Joab blew the ram's horn, and his men returned from chasing the army of Israel. ¹⁷They threw Absalom's body into a deep pit in the forest and piled a great heap of stones over it. And all Israel fled to their homes.

¹⁸During his lifetime, Absalom had built a monument to himself in the King's Valley, for he said, "I have no son to carry on my name." He named the monument after himself, and it is known as Absalom's Monument to this day.

¹⁹Then Zadok's son Ahimaaz said, "Let me run to the king with the good news that the LORD has rescued him from his enemies."

²⁰"No," Joab told him, "it wouldn't be good news to the king that his son is dead. You can be my messenger another time, but not today."

²¹Then Joab said to a man from Ethiopia,* "Go tell the king what you have seen." The man bowed and ran off.

²²But Ahimaaz continued to plead with Joab, "Whatever happens, please let me go, too."

"Why should you go, my son?" Joab replied. "There will be no reward for your news."

²³"Yes, but let me go anyway," he begged.

Joab finally said, "All right, go ahead." So Ahimaaz took the less demanding route by way of the plain and ran to Mahanaim ahead of the Ethiopian.

²⁴While David was sitting between the inner and outer gates of the town, the watchman climbed to the roof of the gateway by the wall. As he looked, he saw a lone man running toward them. ²⁵He shouted the news down to David, and the king replied, "If he is alone, he has news."

As the messenger came closer, ²⁶the watchman saw another man running toward them. He shouted down, "Here comes another one!"

The king replied, "He also will have news."

²⁷"The first man runs like Ahimaaz son of Zadok," the watchman said.

"He is a good man and comes with good news," the king replied.

²⁸Then Ahimaaz cried out to the king, "Everything is all right!" He bowed before the king with his face to the ground and said, "Praise to the LORD your God, who has handed over the rebels who dared to stand against my lord the king."

²⁹"What about young Absalom?" the king demanded. "Is he all right?"

Ahimaaz replied, "When Joab told me to come, there was a lot of commotion. But I didn't know what was happening."

³⁰"Wait here," the king told him. So Ahimaaz stepped aside.

³¹Then the man from Ethiopia arrived and said, "I have good news for my lord the king. Today the LORD has rescued you from all those who rebelled against you."

³²"What about young Absalom?" the king demanded. "Is he all right?"

And the Ethiopian replied, "May all of your enemies, my lord the king, both now and in the future, share the fate of that young man!"

³³*The king was overcome with emotion. He went up to the room over the gateway and burst into tears. And as he went, he cried, "O my son Absalom! My son, my son Absalom! If only I had died instead of you! O Absalom, my son, my son."

19:1*WORD soon reached Joab that the king was weeping and mourning for Absalom. ²As all the people heard of the king's deep grief for his son, the joy of that day's victory was turned into deep sadness. ³They crept back into the town that day as though they were ashamed and had deserted in battle. ⁴The king covered his face with his hands and kept on crying, "O my son Absalom! O Absalom, my son, my son!"

⁵Then Joab went to the king's room and said to him, "We saved your life today and the lives of your sons, your daughters, and your wives and concubines. Yet you act like this, making us feel ashamed of ourselves. ⁶You seem to love those who hate you and hate those who love you. You have made it clear today that your commanders and troops mean nothing to you. It seems that if Absalom had lived and all of us had died, you would be pleased. ⁷Now go out there and congratulate your troops, for I swear by the LORD that if you don't go out, not a single one of them will remain here tonight. Then you will be worse off than ever before."

⁸So the king went out and took his seat at the town gate, and as the news spread throughout the town that he was there, everyone went to him.

Meanwhile, the Israelites who had supported Absalom fled to their homes. ⁹And throughout all the tribes of Israel there was much discussion and argument going on. The people were saying, "The king rescued us from our enemies and saved us from the Philistines, but Absalom chased him out of the country. ¹⁰Now Absalom, whom we anointed to rule over us, is dead. Why not ask David to come back and be our king again?"

18:1 Hebrew *appointed commanders of thousands and commanders of hundreds.* **18:3** As in two Hebrew manuscripts and some Greek and Latin manuscripts; most Hebrew manuscripts read *Now there are 10,000 like us.* **18:9** Hebrew *his head.* **18:11** Hebrew *10 shekels of silver,* about 4 ounces or 114 grams in weight. **18:12** Hebrew *1,000 shekels,* about 25 pounds or 11.4 kilograms in weight. **18:21** Hebrew *from Cush;* similarly in 18:23, 31, 32. **18:33** Verse 18:33 is numbered 19:1 in Hebrew text. **19:1** Verses 19:1-43 are numbered 19:2-44 in Hebrew text.

JOHN 20:1-31

Jesus had been tortured and executed. Those closest to him were trying to accept the reality of Jesus' death and understand why it had occurred. Then, the unexpected happened. . . .

Early on Sunday morning,* while it was still dark, Mary Magdalene came to the tomb and found that the stone had been rolled away from the entrance. ²She ran and found Simon Peter and the other disciple, the one whom Jesus loved. She said, "They have taken the Lord's body out of the tomb, and we don't know where they have put him!"

³Peter and the other disciple started out for the tomb. ⁴They were both running, but the other disciple outran Peter and reached the tomb first. ⁵He stooped and looked in and saw the linen wrappings lying there, but he didn't go in. ⁶Then Simon Peter arrived and went inside. He also noticed the linen wrappings lying there, ⁷while the cloth that had covered Jesus' head was folded up and lying apart from the other wrappings. ⁸Then the disciple who had reached the tomb first also went in, and he saw and believed—⁹for until then they still hadn't understood the Scriptures that said Jesus must rise from the dead. ¹⁰Then they went home.

¹¹Mary was standing outside the tomb crying, and as she wept, she stooped and looked in. ¹²She saw two white-robed angels, one sitting at the head and the other at the foot of the place where the body of Jesus had been lying. ¹³"Dear woman, why are you crying?" the angels asked her.

"Because they have taken away my Lord," she replied, "and I don't know where they have put him."

¹⁴She turned to leave and saw someone standing there. It was Jesus, but she didn't recognize him. ¹⁵"Dear woman, why are you crying?" Jesus asked her. "Who are you looking for?"

She thought he was the gardener. "Sir," she said, "if you have taken him away, tell me where you have put him, and I will go and get him."

¹⁶"Mary!" Jesus said.

She turned to him and cried out, "Rabboni!" (which is Hebrew for "Teacher").

¹⁷"Don't cling to me," Jesus said, "for I haven't yet ascended to the Father. But go find my brothers and tell them, 'I am ascending to my Father and your Father, to my God and your God.'"

¹⁸Mary Magdalene found the disciples and told them, "I have seen the Lord!" Then she gave them his message.

¹⁹That Sunday evening* the disciples

The danger of doubt

WHAT THE BIBLE SAYS

JOHN 20:24-25 It is easy to doubt what we cannot see. That was Thomas's problem—he needed evidence to reassure him that Jesus had truly come back to life. Often referred to as "Doubting Thomas," this disciple did not cling to his disbelief; rather, he was eager to discover the truth for himself. • It is normal to experience doubt from time to time. However, if doubt becomes a way of life and doubters choose to remain stubborn in their questions without attempting to find answers, then doubt is harmful to faith. But doubt can be productive if handled correctly. Questioning leads to a search for answers, and finding the answers strengthens one's beliefs. • Don't let doubt stop you from moving forward in your walk with God. Search out answers—from the Bible, your pastor, Christian authors, and through prayer. God is not afraid of your doubts and your questions. Questioning and finding answers will allow you to make your faith your own. Then, when you are challenged to answer why you believe the way you do, you can respond with the assurance of one who has a personal understanding of faith in Jesus Christ.

were meeting behind locked doors because they were afraid of the Jewish leaders. Suddenly, Jesus was standing there among them! "Peace be with you," he said. [20]As he spoke, he showed them the wounds in his hands and his side. They were filled with joy when they saw the Lord! [21]Again he said, "Peace be with you. As the Father has sent me, so I am sending you." [22]Then he breathed on them and said, "Receive the Holy Spirit. [23]If you forgive anyone's sins, they are forgiven. If you do not forgive them, they are not forgiven."

[24]One of the twelve disciples, Thomas (nicknamed the Twin),* was not with the others when Jesus came. [25]They told him, "We have seen the Lord!"

But he replied, "I won't believe it unless I see the nail wounds in his hands, put my fingers into them, and place my hand into the wound in his side."

[26]Eight days later the disciples were together again, and this time Thomas was with them. The doors were locked; but suddenly, as before, Jesus was standing among them. "Peace be with you," he said. [27]Then he said to Thomas, "Put your finger here, and look at my hands. Put your hand into the wound in my side. Don't be faithless any longer. Believe!"

[28]"My Lord and my God!" Thomas exclaimed.

[29]Then Jesus told him, "You believe because you have seen me. Blessed are those who believe without seeing me."

[30]The disciples saw Jesus do many other miraculous signs in addition to the ones recorded in this book. [31]But these are written so that you may continue to believe* that Jesus is the Messiah, the Son of God, and that by believing in him you will have life by the power of his name.

20:1 Greek *On the first day of the week.*   **20:19** Greek *In the evening of that day, the first day of the week.*
20:24 Greek *Thomas, who was called Didymus.*
20:31 Some manuscripts read *that you may believe.*

PSALM 119:153-176

Resh

[153]**L**ook upon my suffering and rescue me,
for I have not forgotten your instructions.

[154]Argue my case; take my side!
Protect my life as you promised.
[155]The wicked are far from rescue,
for they do not bother with your decrees.
[156]LORD, how great is your mercy;
let me be revived by following your regulations.
[157]Many persecute and trouble me,
yet I have not swerved from your laws.
[158]Seeing these traitors makes me sick at heart,
because they care nothing for your word.
[159]See how I love your commandments, LORD.
Give back my life because of your unfailing love.
[160]The very essence of your words is truth;
all your just regulations will stand forever.

Shin

[161]Powerful people harass me without cause,
but my heart trembles only at your word.
[162]I rejoice in your word
like one who discovers a great treasure.
[163]I hate and abhor all falsehood,
but I love your instructions.
[164]I will praise you seven times a day
because all your regulations are just.
[165]Those who love your instructions
have great peace
and do not stumble.
[166]I long for your rescue, LORD,
so I have obeyed your commands.
[167]I have obeyed your laws,
for I love them very much.
[168]Yes, I obey your commandments and laws
because you know everything I do.

Taw

[169]O LORD, listen to my cry;
give me the discerning mind you promised.
[170]Listen to my prayer;
rescue me as you promised.
[171]Let praise flow from my lips,
for you have taught me your decrees.

172 Let my tongue sing about your word,
　　for all your commands are right.
173 Give me a helping hand,
　　for I have chosen to follow your
　　　commandments.
174 O LORD, I have longed for your rescue,
　　and your instructions are my
　　　delight.
175 Let me live so I can praise you,
　　and may your regulations help me.

176 I have wandered away like a lost sheep;
　　come and find me,
　　for I have not forgotten your
　　　commands.

PROVERBS 16:14-15

The anger of the king is a deadly threat; the wise will try to appease it. □ When the king smiles, there is life; his favor refreshes like a spring rain.

2 SAMUEL 19:11–20:13

David returned to Jerusalem to once again take up his throne. The atmosphere was still mixed. In these days, power was always up for grabs. Watch as David's friends and enemies negotiate their place in his kingdom.

Then King David sent Zadok and Abiathar, the priests, to say to the elders of Judah, "Why are you the last ones to welcome back the king into his palace? For I have heard that all Israel is ready. 12 You are my relatives, my own tribe, my own flesh and blood! So why are you the last ones to welcome back the king?" 13 And David told them to tell Amasa, "Since you are my own flesh and blood, like Joab, may God strike me and even kill me if I do not appoint you as commander of my army in his place."

14 Then Amasa* convinced all the men of Judah, and they responded unanimously. They sent word to the king, "Return to us, and bring back all who are with you."

15 So the king started back to Jerusalem. And when he arrived at the Jordan River, the people of Judah came to Gilgal to meet him and escort him across the river. 16 Shimei son of Gera, the man from Bahurim in Benjamin, hurried across with the men of Judah to welcome King David. 17 A thousand other men from the tribe of Benjamin were with him, including Ziba, the chief servant of the house of Saul, and Ziba's fifteen sons and twenty servants. They rushed down to the Jordan to meet

the king. 18 They crossed the shallows of the Jordan to bring the king's household across the river, helping him in every way they could.

As the king was about to cross the river, Shimei fell down before him. 19 "My lord the king, please forgive me," he pleaded. "Forget the terrible thing your servant did when you left Jerusalem. May the king put it out of his mind. 20 I know how much I sinned. That is why I have come here today, the very first person in all Israel* to greet my lord the king."

21 Then Abishai son of Zeruiah said, "Shimei should die, for he cursed the LORD's anointed king!"

22 "Who asked your opinion, you sons of Zeruiah!" David exclaimed. "Why have you become my adversary* today? This is not a day for execution but for celebration! Today I am once again the king of Israel!" 23 Then, turning to Shimei, David vowed, "Your life will be spared."

24 Now Mephibosheth,* Saul's grandson, came down from Jerusalem to meet the king. He had not cared for his feet, trimmed his beard, or washed his clothes since the day the king left Jerusalem. 25 "Why didn't you come with me, Mephibosheth?" the king asked him.

26 Mephibosheth replied, "My lord the king, my servant Ziba deceived me. I told him, 'Saddle my donkey* so I can go with the king.' For as you know I am crippled. 27 Ziba has slandered me by saying that I

refused to come. But I know that my lord the king is like an angel of God, so do what you think is best. ²⁸All my relatives and I could expect only death from you, my lord, but instead you have honored me by allowing me to eat at your own table! What more can I ask?"

²⁹"You've said enough," David replied. "I've decided that you and Ziba will divide your land equally between you."

³⁰"Give him all of it," Mephibosheth said. "I am content just to have you safely back again, my lord the king!"

³¹Barzillai of Gilead had come down from Rogelim to escort the king across the Jordan. ³²He was very old, about eighty, and very wealthy. He was the one who had provided food for the king during his stay in Mahanaim. ³³"Come across with me and live in Jerusalem," the king said to Barzillai. "I will take care of you there."

³⁴"No," he replied, "I am far too old to go with the king to Jerusalem. ³⁵I am eighty years old today, and I can no longer enjoy anything. Food and wine are no longer tasty, and I cannot hear the singers as they sing. I would only be a burden to my lord the king. ³⁶Just to go across the Jordan River with the king is all the honor I need! ³⁷Then let me return again to die in my own town, where my father and mother are buried. But here is your servant, my son Kimham. Let him go with my lord the king and receive whatever you want to give him."

³⁸"Good," the king agreed. "Kimham will go with me, and I will help him in any way you would like. And I will do for you anything you want." ³⁹So all the people crossed the Jordan with the king. After David had blessed Barzillai and kissed him, Barzillai returned to his own home.

⁴⁰The king then crossed over to Gilgal, taking Kimham with him. All the troops of Judah and half the troops of Israel escorted the king on his way.

⁴¹But all the men of Israel complained to the king, "The men of Judah stole the king and didn't give us the honor of helping take you, your household, and all your men across the Jordan."

⁴²The men of Judah replied, "The king is one of our own kinsmen. Why should this make you angry? We haven't eaten any of the king's food or received any special favors!"

⁴³"But there are ten tribes in Israel," the others replied. "So we have ten times as much right to the king as you do. What right do you have to treat us with such contempt? Weren't we the first to speak of bringing him back to be our king again?" The argument continued back and forth, and the men of Judah spoke even more harshly than the men of Israel.

20:1THERE happened to be a troublemaker there named Sheba son of Bicri, a man from the tribe of Benjamin. Sheba blew a ram's horn and began to chant:

"Down with the dynasty of David!
    We have no interest in the son
        of Jesse.
Come on, you men of Israel,
    back to your homes!"

²So all the men of Israel deserted David and followed Sheba son of Bicri. But the men of Judah stayed with their king and escorted him from the Jordan River to Jerusalem.

³When David came to his palace in Jerusalem, he took the ten concubines he had left to look after the palace and placed them in seclusion. Their needs were provided for, but he no longer slept with them. So each of them lived like a widow until she died.

⁴Then the king told Amasa, "Mobilize the army of Judah within three days, and report back at that time." ⁵So Amasa went out to notify Judah, but it took him longer than the time he had been given.

⁶Then David said to Abishai, "Sheba son of Bicri is going to hurt us more than Absalom did. Quick, take my troops and chase after him before he gets into a fortified town where we can't reach him."

⁷So Abishai and Joab,* together with the king's bodyguard* and all the mighty warriors, set out from Jerusalem to go after Sheba. ⁸As they arrived at the great stone in Gibeon, Amasa met them. Joab was wearing his military tunic with a dagger strapped to his belt. As he stepped forward to greet Amasa, he slipped the dagger from its sheath.*

⁹"How are you, my cousin?" Joab said and took him by the beard with his right

hand as though to kiss him. [10]Amasa didn't notice the dagger in his left hand, and Joab stabbed him in the stomach with it so that his insides gushed out onto the ground. Joab did not need to strike again, and Amasa soon died. Joab and his brother Abishai left him lying there and continued after Sheba.

[11]One of Joab's young men shouted to Amasa's troops, "If you are for Joab and David, come and follow Joab." [12]But Amasa lay in his blood in the middle of the road, and Joab's man saw that everyone was stopping to stare at him. So he pulled him off the road into a field and threw a cloak over him. [13]With Amasa's body out of the way, everyone went on with Joab to capture Sheba son of Bicri.

19:14 As in Greek version; Hebrew reads *he.*   19:20 Hebrew *in the house of Joseph.*   19:22 Or *my prosecutor.* 19:24 *Mephibosheth* is another name for Merib-baal. 19:26 As in Greek, Syriac, and Latin versions; Hebrew reads *I will saddle a donkey for myself.*   20:7a Hebrew *So Joab's men.*   20:7b Hebrew *the Kerethites and Pelethites;* also in 20:23.   20:8 Hebrew *As he stepped forward, it fell out.*

JOHN 21:1-25
What would you ask Jesus if you had the opportunity to have breakfast with him on the beach? What would you expect him to say to you? What advice do you think he'd give? Today, sit in with the disciples and listen.

Later, Jesus appeared again to the disciples beside the Sea of Galilee.* This is

how it happened. [2]Several of the disciples were there—Simon Peter, Thomas (nicknamed the Twin),* Nathanael from Cana in Galilee, the sons of Zebedee, and two other disciples.

[3]Simon Peter said, "I'm going fishing."

"We'll come, too," they all said. So they went out in the boat, but they caught nothing all night.

[4]At dawn Jesus was standing on the beach, but the disciples couldn't see who he was. [5]He called out, "Fellows,* have you caught any fish?"

"No," they replied.

[6]Then he said, "Throw out your net on the right-hand side of the boat, and you'll get some!" So they did, and they couldn't haul in the net because there were so many fish in it.

[7]Then the disciple Jesus loved said to Peter, "It's the Lord!" When Simon Peter heard that it was the Lord, he put on his tunic (for he had stripped for work), jumped into the water, and headed to shore. [8]The others stayed with the boat and pulled the loaded net to the shore, for they were only about a hundred yards* from shore. [9]When they got there, they found breakfast waiting for them—fish cooking over a charcoal fire, and some bread.

[10]"Bring some of the fish you've just caught," Jesus said. [11]So Simon Peter went aboard and dragged the net to the shore.

HOW WE LIVE

Loving God and others

JOHN 21:15-17 This was a tough time for Peter—and it was made even tougher as he was singled out for this conversation. Three times during Jesus' trial, Peter had denied even knowing him (Luke 22:54-62, April 26). Peter probably felt like he was sidelined, out of the game for good, a total loser. • Jesus wasn't finished with Peter, but he needed to make sure Peter was well prepared for the tasks ahead of him. Earlier in his ministry, Jesus had said to Peter, "You are Peter (which means 'rock'), and upon this rock I will build my church" (Matthew 16:18, January 25). But Peter had failed miserably—hardly a "rock," he seemed more like a jellyfish. • Then came Jesus' resurrection and this breakfast on the beach. Three times Jesus asked Peter to reaffirm his love—once for each denial. In essence, Jesus was saying to Peter, "I can use you Peter. You already know how much I love you. I need your wholehearted love in return." • You can serve God best when your love for him is genuine. Jesus knows your heart. He whether your love is superficial or reaches into the depths of your soul.

There were 153 large fish, and yet the net hadn't torn.

[12]"Now come and have some breakfast!" Jesus said. None of the disciples dared to ask him, "Who are you?" They knew it was the Lord. [13]Then Jesus served them the bread and the fish. [14]This was the third time Jesus had appeared to his disciples since he had been raised from the dead.

[15]After breakfast Jesus asked Simon Peter, "Simon son of John, do you love me more than these?*"

"Yes, Lord," Peter replied, "you know I love you."

"Then feed my lambs," Jesus told him.

[16]Jesus repeated the question: "Simon son of John, do you love me?"

"Yes, Lord," Peter said, "you know I love you."

"Then take care of my sheep," Jesus said.

[17]A third time he asked him, "Simon son of John, do you love me?"

Peter was hurt that Jesus asked the question a third time. He said, "Lord, you know everything. You know that I love you."

Jesus said, "Then feed my sheep.

[18]"I tell you the truth, when you were young, you were able to do as you liked; you dressed yourself and went wherever you wanted to go. But when you are old, you will stretch out your hands, and others* will dress you and take you where you don't want to go." [19]Jesus said this to let him know by what kind of death he would glorify God. Then Jesus told him, "Follow me."

[20]Peter turned around and saw behind them the disciple Jesus loved—the one who had leaned over to Jesus during supper and asked, "Lord, who will betray you?" [21]Peter asked Jesus, "What about him, Lord?"

[22]Jesus replied, "If I want him to remain alive until I return, what is that to you? As for you, follow me." [23]So the rumor spread among the community of believers* that this disciple wouldn't die. But that isn't what Jesus said at all. He only said, "If I want him to remain alive until I return, what is that to you?"

[24]This disciple is the one who testifies to these events and has recorded them here. And we know that his account of these things is accurate.

[25]Jesus also did many other things. If they were all written down, I suppose the whole world could not contain the books that would be written.

21:1 Greek *Sea of Tiberias,* another name for the Sea of Galilee. 21:2 Greek *Thomas, who was called Didymus.* 21:5 Greek *Children.* 21:8 Greek *200 cubits* [90 meters]. 21:15 Or *more than these others do?* 21:18 Some manuscripts read *and another one.* 21:23 Greek *the brothers.*

PSALM 120:1-7
A song for pilgrims ascending to Jerusalem.

[1] I took my troubles to the LORD;
    I cried out to him, and he answered
        my prayer.
[2] Rescue me, O LORD, from liars
    and from all deceitful people.
[3] O deceptive tongue, what will God
        do to you?
    How will he increase your
        punishment?
[4] You will be pierced with sharp arrows
    and burned with glowing coals.

[5] How I suffer in far-off Meshech.
    It pains me to live in distant Kedar.
[6] I am tired of living
    among people who hate peace.
[7] I search for peace;
    but when I speak of peace, they
        want war!

PROVERBS 16:16-17
How much better to get wisdom than gold, and good judgment than silver! □ The path of the virtuous leads away from evil; whoever follows that path is safe.

2 SAMUEL 20:14–21:22

The Gibeonites and the Philistines both had a long history of interaction with David's people. In today's reading, David makes peace with one and war with the other.

Meanwhile, Sheba traveled through all the tribes of Israel and eventually came to the town of Abel-beth-maacah. All the members of his own clan, the Bicrites,* assembled for battle and followed him into the town. ¹⁵When Joab's forces arrived, they attacked Abel-beth-maacah. They built a siege ramp against the town's fortifications and began battering down the wall. ¹⁶But a wise woman in the town called out to Joab, "Listen to me, Joab. Come over here so I can talk to you." ¹⁷As he approached, the woman asked, "Are you Joab?"

"I am," he replied.

So she said, "Listen carefully to your servant."

"I'm listening," he said.

¹⁸Then she continued, "There used to be a saying, 'If you want to settle an argument, ask advice at the town of Abel.' ¹⁹I am one who is peace loving and faithful in Israel. But you are destroying an important town in Israel.* Why do you want to devour what belongs to the LORD?"

²⁰And Joab replied, "Believe me, I don't want to devour or destroy your town! ²¹That's not my purpose. All I want is a man named Sheba son of Bicri from the hill country of Ephraim, who has revolted against King David. If you hand over this one man to me, I will leave the town in peace."

"All right," the woman replied, "we will throw his head over the wall to you." ²²Then the woman went to all the people with her wise advice, and they cut off Sheba's head and threw it out to Joab. So he blew the ram's horn and called his troops back from the attack. They all returned to their homes, and Joab returned to the king at Jerusalem.

²³Now Joab was the commander of the army of Israel. Benaiah son of Jehoiada was captain of the king's bodyguard. ²⁴Ad-

oniram* was in charge of the labor force. Jehoshaphat son of Ahilud was the royal historian. ²⁵Sheva was the court secretary. Zadok and Abiathar were the priests. ²⁶And Ira, a descendant of Jair, was David's personal priest.

²¹:¹THERE was a famine during David's reign that lasted for three years, so David asked the LORD about it. And the LORD said, "The famine has come because Saul and his family are guilty of murdering the Gibeonites."

²So the king summoned the Gibeonites. They were not part of Israel but were all that was left of the nation of the Amorites. The people of Israel had sworn not to kill them, but Saul, in his zeal for Israel and Judah, had tried to wipe them out. ³David asked them, "What can I do for you? How can I make amends so that you will bless the LORD's people again?"

⁴"Well, money can't settle this matter between us and the family of Saul," the Gibeonites replied. "Neither can we demand the life of anyone in Israel."

"What can I do then?" David asked. "Just tell me and I will do it for you."

⁵Then they replied, "It was Saul who planned to destroy us, to keep us from having any place at all in the territory of Israel. ⁶So let seven of Saul's sons be handed over to us, and we will execute them before the LORD at Gibeon, on the mountain of the LORD.*"

"All right," the king said, "I will do it." ⁷The king spared Jonathan's son Mephibosheth,* who was Saul's grandson, because of the oath David and Jonathan had sworn before the LORD. ⁸But he gave them Saul's two sons Armoni and Mephibosheth, whose mother was Rizpah daughter of Aiah. He also gave them the five sons of Saul's daughter Merab,* the wife of Adriel son of Barzillai from Meholah. ⁹The men of Gibeon executed them on the mountain before the LORD. So all seven of them died together at the beginning of the barley harvest.

¹⁰Then Rizpah daughter of Aiah, the

mother of two of the men, spread burlap on a rock and stayed there the entire harvest season. She prevented the scavenger birds from tearing at their bodies during the day and stopped wild animals from eating them at night. [11]When David learned what Rizpah, Saul's concubine, had done, [12]he went to the people of Jabesh-gilead and retrieved the bones of Saul and his son Jonathan. (When the Philistines had killed Saul and Jonathan on Mount Gilboa, the people of Jabesh-gilead stole their bodies from the public square of Beth-shan, where the Philistines had hung them.) [13]So David obtained the bones of Saul and Jonathan, as well as the bones of the men the Gibeonites had executed.

[14]Then the king ordered that they bury the bones in the tomb of Kish, Saul's father, at the town of Zela in the land of Benjamin. After that, God ended the famine in the land.

[15]Once again the Philistines were at war with Israel. And when David and his men were in the thick of battle, David became weak and exhausted. [16]Ishbi-benob was a descendant of the giants*; his bronze spearhead weighed more than seven pounds,* and he was armed with a new sword. He had cornered David and was about to kill him. [17]But Abishai son of Zeruiah came to David's rescue and killed the Philistine. Then David's men declared, "You are not going out to battle with us again! Why risk snuffing out the light of Israel?"

[18]After this, there was another battle against the Philistines at Gob. As they fought, Sibbecai from Hushah killed Saph, another descendant of the giants.

[19]During another battle at Gob, Elhanan son of Jair* from Bethlehem killed the brother of Goliath of Gath.* The handle of his spear was as thick as a weaver's beam!

[20]In another battle with the Philistines at Gath, they encountered a huge man with six fingers on each hand and six toes on each foot, twenty-four in all, who was also a descendant of the giants. [21]But when he defied and taunted Israel, he was killed by Jonathan, the son of David's brother Shimea.*

[22]These four Philistines were descendants of the giants of Gath, but David and his warriors killed them.

20:14 As in Greek and Latin versions; Hebrew reads *All the Berites.*   **20:19** Hebrew *a town that is a mother in Israel.*   **20:24** As in Greek version (see also 1 Kgs 4:6; 5:14); Hebrew reads *Adoram.*   **21:6** As in Greek version (see also 21:9); Hebrew reads *at Gibeah of Saul, the chosen of the LORD.*   **21:7** *Mephibosheth* is another name for Merib-baal.   **21:8** As in a few Hebrew and Greek manuscripts and Syriac version (see also 1 Sam 18:19); most Hebrew manuscripts read *Michal.*   **21:16a** As in Greek version; Hebrew reads *a descendant of the Rephaites;* also in 21:18, 20, 22.   **21:16b** Hebrew *300 shekels* [3.4 kilograms].   **21:19a** As in parallel text at 1 Chr 20:5; Hebrew reads *son of Jaare-oregim.*   **21:19b** As in parallel text at 1 Chr 20:5; Hebrew reads *killed Goliath of Gath.*   **21:21** As in parallel text at 1 Chr 20:7; Hebrew reads *Shimei,* a variant spelling of Shimea.

ACTS 1:1-26

The book of Acts opens with Jesus' last days before he ascended back into heaven. After his departure, the disciples asked the question, "Where do we go from here?" The answers became the foundation of the New Testament church.

In my first book* I told you, Theophilus, about everything Jesus began to do and teach [2]until the day he was taken up to heaven after giving his chosen apostles further instructions through the Holy Spirit. [3]During the forty days after his crucifixion, he appeared to the apostles from time to time, and he proved to them in many ways that he was actually alive. And he talked to them about the Kingdom of God.

[4]Once when he was eating with them, he commanded them, "Do not leave Jerusalem until the Father sends you the gift he promised, as I told you before. [5]John baptized with* water, but in just a few days you will be baptized with the Holy Spirit."

[6]So when the apostles were with Jesus, they kept asking him, "Lord, has the time come for you to free Israel and restore our kingdom?"

[7]He replied, "The Father alone has the authority to set those dates and times, and they are not for you to know. [8]But you will receive power when the Holy Spirit comes upon you. And you will be my witnesses, telling people about me everywhere—in Jerusalem, throughout Judea, in Samaria, and to the ends of the earth."

[9]After saying this, he was taken up into a cloud while they were watching, and they could no longer see him. [10]As they strained

to see him rising into heaven, two white-robed men suddenly stood among them. [11]"Men of Galilee," they said, "why are you standing here staring into heaven? Jesus has been taken from you into heaven, but someday he will return from heaven in the same way you saw him go!"

[12]Then the apostles returned to Jerusalem from the Mount of Olives, a distance of half a mile.* [13]When they arrived, they went to the upstairs room of the house where they were staying.

Here are the names of those who were present: Peter, John, James, Andrew, Philip, Thomas, Bartholomew, Matthew, James (son of Alphaeus), Simon (the Zealot), and Judas (son of James). [14]They all met together and were constantly united in prayer, along with Mary the mother of Jesus, several other women, and the brothers of Jesus.

[15]During this time, when about 120 believers* were together in one place, Peter stood up and addressed them. [16]"Brothers," he said, "the Scriptures had to be fulfilled concerning Judas, who guided those who arrested Jesus. This was predicted long ago by the Holy Spirit, speaking through King David. [17]Judas was one of us and shared in the ministry with us."

[18](Judas had bought a field with the money he received for his treachery. Falling headfirst there, his body split open, spilling out all his intestines. [19]The news of his death spread to all the people of Jerusalem, and they gave the place the Aramaic name *Akeldama,* which means "Field of Blood.")

[20]Peter continued, "This was written in the book of Psalms, where it says, 'Let his home become desolate, with no one living in it.' It also says, 'Let someone else take his position.'*

[21]"So now we must choose a replacement for Judas from among the men who were with us the entire time we were traveling with the Lord Jesus—[22]from the time he was baptized by John until the day he was taken from us. Whoever is chosen will join us as a witness of Jesus' resurrection."

[23]So they nominated two men: Joseph called Barsabbas (also known as Justus) and Matthias. [24]Then they all prayed, "O Lord, you know every heart. Show us which of these men you have chosen [25]as an apostle to replace Judas in this ministry, for he has deserted us and gone where he belongs." [26]Then they cast lots, and Matthias was selected to become an apostle with the other eleven.

1:1 The reference is to the Gospel of Luke.   1:5 Or *in;* also in 1:5b.   1:12 Greek *a Sabbath day's journey.*   1:15 Greek *brothers.*   1:20 Pss 69:25; 109:8.

PSALM 121:1-8
A song for pilgrims ascending to Jerusalem.

[1] I look up to the mountains—
        does my help come from there?

HOW WE LIVE

Relying on God's power

ACTS 1:8 Just prior to Jesus' ascension, his disciples still had questions about the fate of the nation of Israel. The Messiah had long been expected to lead Israel to a great political victory. The mission Jesus came to accomplish was different, however, and now with him ascended to heaven, the disciples had an important and difficult mission themselves. How would this humble and somewhat confused group take the gospel to the nations of the world? How would they meet the challenges that come from bearing witness to Jesus? • It was not by their skills or intelligence. Rather, God's Spirit himself empowered them for their mission. Through the Spirit, they had the power to do things they would never have tried before. • Jesus' followers today still have the same mandate to bear witness of Jesus. The same Holy Spirit who indwelt those early believers and changed the world is in the heart of every believer. He empowers you to make Jesus known in this dark world.

2 My help comes from the LORD,
who made heaven and earth!

3 He will not let you stumble;
the one who watches over you will
not slumber.

4 Indeed, he who watches over Israel
never slumbers or sleeps.

5 The LORD himself watches over you!
The LORD stands beside you as your
protective shade.

6 The sun will not harm you by day,
nor the moon at night.

7 The LORD keeps you from all harm
and watches over your life.

8 The LORD keeps watch over you as you
come and go,
both now and forever.

PROVERBS 16:18

Pride goes before destruction, and haughtiness before a fall.

JUNE**4**

2 SAMUEL 22:1–23:23

After reading so much about David's role as a king
and warrior, it's easy to forget that he was also
an artist. In today's reading he expresses himself
through that artistry as he also did in many of
the psalms.

David sang this song to the LORD on the
day the LORD rescued him from all his enemies and from Saul. 2He sang:

"The LORD is my rock, my fortress,
and my savior;
3   my God is my rock, in whom I find
protection.
He is my shield, the power that saves
me,
and my place of safety.
He is my refuge, my savior,
the one who saves me from
violence.

4 I called on the LORD, who is worthy
of praise,
and he saved me from my enemies.

5 "The waves of death overwhelmed me;
floods of destruction swept over
me.

6 The grave* wrapped its ropes around
me;
death laid a trap in my path.

7 But in my distress I cried out to
the LORD;
yes, I cried to my God for help.
He heard me from his sanctuary;
my cry reached his ears.

8 "Then the earth quaked and trembled.
The foundations of the heavens
shook;
they quaked because of his anger.

9 Smoke poured from his nostrils;
fierce flames leaped from his
mouth.
Glowing coals blazed forth from
him.

10 He opened the heavens and came
down;
dark storm clouds were beneath
his feet.

11 Mounted on a mighty angelic being,*
he flew,
soaring* on the wings of the wind.

12 He shrouded himself in darkness,
veiling his approach with dense
rain clouds.

13 A great brightness shone around him,
and burning coals* blazed forth.

14 The LORD thundered from heaven;
the voice of the Most High
resounded.

15 He shot arrows and scattered his
enemies;
his lightning flashed, and they
were confused.

16 Then at the command of the LORD,
at the blast of his breath,
the bottom of the sea could be seen,
and the foundations of the earth
were laid bare.

¹⁷ "He reached down from heaven and
rescued me;
    he drew me out of deep waters.
¹⁸ He rescued me from my powerful
enemies,
    from those who hated me and were
too strong for me.
¹⁹ They attacked me at a moment when
I was in distress,
    but the LORD supported me.
²⁰ He led me to a place of safety;
    he rescued me because he delights
in me.
²¹ The LORD rewarded me for doing right;
    he restored me because of
my innocence.
²² For I have kept the ways of the LORD;
    I have not turned from my God
to follow evil.
²³ I have followed all his regulations;
    I have never abandoned his decrees.
²⁴ I am blameless before God;
    I have kept myself from sin.
²⁵ The LORD rewarded me for doing right.
    He has seen my innocence.

²⁶ "To the faithful you show yourself
faithful;
    to those with integrity you show
integrity.
²⁷ To the pure you show yourself pure,
    but to the wicked you show yourself
hostile.
²⁸ You rescue the humble,
    but your eyes watch the proud and
humiliate them.
²⁹ O LORD, you are my lamp.
    The LORD lights up my darkness.
³⁰ In your strength I can crush an army;
    with my God I can scale any wall.

³¹ "God's way is perfect.
    All the LORD's promises prove true.
    He is a shield for all who look to
him for protection.
³² For who is God except the LORD?
    Who but our God is a solid rock?
³³ God is my strong fortress,
    and he makes my way perfect.
³⁴ He makes me as surefooted as a deer,
    enabling me to stand on mountain
heights.
³⁵ He trains my hands for battle;
    he strengthens my arm to draw
a bronze bow.

³⁶ You have given me your shield
of victory;
    your help* has made me great.
³⁷ You have made a wide path for my feet
    to keep them from slipping.

³⁸ "I chased my enemies and destroyed
them;
    I did not stop until they were
conquered.
³⁹ I consumed them;
    I struck them down so they did
not get up;
    they fell beneath my feet.
⁴⁰ You have armed me with strength
for the battle;
    you have subdued my enemies
under my feet.
⁴¹ You placed my foot on their necks.
    I have destroyed all who hated me.
⁴² They looked for help, but no one came
to their rescue.
    They even cried to the LORD,
    but he refused to answer.
⁴³ I ground them as fine as the dust
of the earth;
    I trampled them* in the gutter
like dirt.

⁴⁴ "You gave me victory over my accusers.
    You preserved me as the ruler over
nations;
    people I don't even know now serve
me.
⁴⁵ Foreign nations cringe before me;
    as soon as they hear of me, they
submit.
⁴⁶ They all lose their courage
    and come trembling* from their
strongholds.

⁴⁷ "The LORD lives! Praise to my Rock!
    May God, the Rock of my salvation,
be exalted!
⁴⁸ He is the God who pays back those
who harm me;
    he brings down the nations under me
⁴⁹ and delivers me from my enemies.
    You hold me safe beyond the reach
of my enemies;
    you save me from violent
opponents.
⁵⁰ For this, O LORD, I will praise you
among the nations;
    I will sing praises to your name.

⁵¹ You give great victories to your king;
   you show unfailing love to your
      anointed,
   to David and all his descendants
      forever."

23:1THESE are the last words of David:

"David, the son of Jesse, speaks—
   David, the man who was raised up
      so high,
David, the man anointed by the God
      of Jacob,
   David, the sweet psalmist of Israel.*

² "The Spirit of the LORD speaks
      through me;
   his words are upon my tongue.
³ The God of Israel spoke.
   The Rock of Israel said to me:
   'The one who rules righteously,
   who rules in the fear of God,
⁴ is like the light of morning at sunrise,
   like a morning without clouds,
   like the gleaming of the sun
      on new grass after rain.'

⁵ "Is it not my family God has chosen?
   Yes, he has made an everlasting
      covenant with me.
His agreement is arranged and
      guaranteed in every detail.
   He will ensure my safety and
      success.
⁶ But the godless are like thorns
   to be thrown away,
   for they tear the hand that touches
      them.
⁷ One must use iron tools to chop
      them down;
   they will be totally consumed
      by fire."

⁸These are the names of David's might-
iest warriors. The first was Jashobeam
the Hacmonite,* who was leader of the
Three*—the three mightiest warriors
among David's men. He once used his
spear to kill 800 enemy warriors in a sin-
gle battle.* ⁹Next in rank among the Three was Eleazar son of Dodai, a descendant of Ahoah.
Once Eleazar and David stood together
against the Philistines when the entire Israelite army had fled. ¹⁰He killed Philistines until his hand was too tired to lift his
sword, and the LORD gave him a great victory that day. The rest of the army did not
return until it was time to collect the
plunder!

¹¹Next in rank was Shammah son of
Agee from Harar. One time the Philistines
gathered at Lehi and attacked the Israelites in a field full of lentils. The Israelite
army fled, ¹²but Shammah* held his
ground in the middle of the field and beat
back the Philistines. So the LORD brought
about a great victory.

¹³Once during the harvest, when David
was at the cave of Adullam, the Philistine
army was camped in the valley of Rephaim.
The Three (who were among the Thirty—
an elite group among David's fighting men)
went down to meet him there. ¹⁴David was
staying in the stronghold at the time, and a
Philistine detachment had occupied the
town of Bethlehem.

¹⁵David remarked longingly to his men,
"Oh, how I would love some of that good
water from the well by the gate in Bethlehem." ¹⁶So the Three broke through the
Philistine lines, drew some water from the
well by the gate in Bethlehem, and brought
it back to David. But he refused to drink it.
Instead, he poured it out as an offering to
the LORD. ¹⁷"The LORD forbid that I should
drink this!" he exclaimed. "This water is as
precious as the blood of these men* who
risked their lives to bring it to me." So David did not drink it. These are examples of
the exploits of the Three.

¹⁸Abishai son of Zeruiah, the brother of
Joab, was the leader of the Thirty.* He
once used his spear to kill 300 enemy
warriors in a single battle. It was by such
feats that he became as famous as the
Three. ¹⁹Abishai was the most famous of
the Thirty* and was their commander,
though he was not one of the Three.

²⁰There was also Benaiah son of Jehoia-
da, a valiant warrior* from Kabzeel. He
did many heroic deeds, which included
killing two champions* of Moab. Another
time, on a snowy day, he chased a lion
down into a pit and killed it. ²¹Once,
armed only with a club, he killed a great
Egyptian warrior who was armed with a
spear. Benaiah wrenched the spear from
the Egyptian's hand and killed him with it.
²²Deeds like these made Benaiah as fa-

mous as the Three mightiest warriors.
²³He was more honored than the other
members of the Thirty, though he was not
one of the Three. And David made him
captain of his bodyguard.

22:6 Hebrew *Sheol.*   22:11a Hebrew *a cherub.*   22:11b As in
some Hebrew manuscripts (see also Ps 18:10); other Hebrew
manuscripts read *appearing.*   22:13 Or *and lightning bolts.*
22:36 As in Dead Sea Scrolls (see also Ps 18:35); Masoretic Text
reads *your answering.*   22:43 As in Dead Sea Scrolls (see also
Ps 18:42); Masoretic Text reads *I crushed and trampled them.*
22:46 As in parallel text at Ps 18:45; Hebrew reads *come girding
themselves.*   23:1 Or *the favorite subject of the songs of Israel;*
or *the favorite of the Strong One of Israel.*   23:8a As in parallel
text at 1 Chr 11:11; Hebrew reads *Josheb-basshebeth the
Tahkemonite.*   23:8b As in Greek and Latin versions (see
also 1 Chr 11:11); the meaning of the Hebrew is uncertain.
23:8c As in some Greek manuscripts (see also 1 Chr 11:11);
the meaning of the Hebrew is uncertain, though it might be
rendered *the Three. It was Adino the Eznite who killed
800 men at one time.*   23:12 Hebrew *he.*   23:17 Hebrew
Shall I drink the blood of these men?   23:18 As in a few
Hebrew manuscripts and Syriac version; most Hebrew
manuscripts read *the Three.*   23:19 As in Syriac version;
Hebrew reads *the Three.*   23:20a Or *son of Jehoiada, son
of Ish-hai.*   23:20b Or *two sons of Ariel.*

ACTS 2:1-47

Today's reading describes the coming of God's Holy
Spirit, just as Jesus had promised. The Holy Spirit
provided the power necessary to establish the
church.

On the day of Pentecost* all the believers
were meeting together in one place. ²Suddenly, there was a sound from heaven like
the roaring of a mighty windstorm, and it
filled the house where they were sitting.
³Then, what looked like flames or tongues
of fire appeared and settled on each of
them. ⁴And everyone present was filled
with the Holy Spirit and began speaking
in other languages,* as the Holy Spirit
gave them this ability.

⁵At that time there were devout Jews
from every nation living in Jerusalem.
⁶When they heard the loud noise, everyone came running, and they were bewildered to hear their own languages being
spoken by the believers.

⁷They were completely amazed. "How
can this be?" they exclaimed. "These people are all from Galilee, ⁸and yet we hear
them speaking in our own native languages! ⁹Here we are—Parthians, Medes,
Elamites, people from Mesopotamia,
Judea, Cappadocia, Pontus, the province of
Asia, ¹⁰Phrygia, Pamphylia, Egypt, and the
areas of Libya around Cyrene, visitors from
Rome ¹¹(both Jews and converts to Judaism), Cretans, and Arabs. And we all hear
these people speaking in our own languages about the wonderful things God
has done!" ¹²They stood there amazed and
perplexed. "What can this mean?" they
asked each other.

¹³But others in the crowd ridiculed
them, saying, "They're just drunk, that's
all!"

The Holy Spirit empowers us

WHO GOD IS

ACTS 2:1-4 The arrival of the Holy Spirit fulfilled the prophecies of John
the Baptist (Luke 3:16, March 18), the Old Testament prophet Joel
(Joel 2:28-29, December 9), and Jesus himself (John 14:15-18, May 25).
•The Holy Spirit spoke through these believers in the languages of the
many different peoples so that they all heard the Good News spoken in
their own language! Three thousand people believed that day alone
(Acts 2:41), many of them returning to their homelands with the gospel
message fresh in their hearts! •The power of the Holy Spirit within you
is meant to guide you, help you, and comfort you. His primary goal,
however, is to draw attention to Jesus. Jesus' physical presence is
absent from the earth, but he is still here through every believer—meaning he's all over the world talking, preaching, singing, healing, caring,
loving, understanding, and comforting. Without the Holy Spirit's help, you
might not have the courage to tell someone about Jesus or the ability to
live as a good example of Christianity. With his help, you can represent
Christ to others by the things you do and say. Allow him to work through
you and bring glory to God.

¹⁴Then Peter stepped forward with the eleven other apostles and shouted to the crowd, "Listen carefully, all of you, fellow Jews and residents of Jerusalem! Make no mistake about this. ¹⁵These people are not drunk, as some of you are assuming. Nine o'clock in the morning is much too early for that. ¹⁶No, what you see was predicted long ago by the prophet Joel:

¹⁷ 'In the last days,' God says,
  'I will pour out my Spirit upon
    all people.
  Your sons and daughters will
    prophesy.
  Your young men will see visions,
    and your old men will dream
    dreams.
¹⁸ In those days I will pour out my Spirit
    even on my servants—men and
    women alike—
  and they will prophesy.
¹⁹ And I will cause wonders in the
    heavens above
  and signs on the earth below—
  blood and fire and clouds of smoke.
²⁰ The sun will become dark,
  and the moon will turn blood red
  before that great and glorious day
    of the LORD arrives.
²¹ But everyone who calls on the name
    of the LORD
  will be saved.'*

²²"People of Israel, listen! God publicly endorsed Jesus the Nazarene* by doing powerful miracles, wonders, and signs through him, as you well know. ²³But God knew what would happen, and his prearranged plan was carried out when Jesus was betrayed. With the help of lawless Gentiles, you nailed him to a cross and killed him. ²⁴But God released him from the horrors of death and raised him back to life, for death could not keep him in its grip. ²⁵King David said this about him:

  'I see that the LORD is always with me.
  I will not be shaken, for he is right
    beside me.
²⁶ No wonder my heart is glad,
  and my tongue shouts his praises!
  My body rests in hope.
²⁷ For you will not leave my soul among
    the dead*

  or allow your Holy One to rot
    in the grave.
²⁸ You have shown me the way
    of life,
  and you will fill me with
    the joy of your presence.'*

²⁹"Dear brothers, think about this! You can be sure that the patriarch David wasn't referring to himself, for he died and was buried, and his tomb is still here among us. ³⁰But he was a prophet, and he knew God had promised with an oath that one of David's own descendants would sit on his throne. ³¹David was looking into the future and speaking of the Messiah's resurrection. He was saying that God would not leave him among the dead or allow his body to rot in the grave.

³²"God raised Jesus from the dead, and we are all witnesses of this. ³³Now he is exalted to the place of highest honor in heaven, at God's right hand. And the Father, as he had promised, gave him the Holy Spirit to pour out upon us, just as you see and hear today. ³⁴For David himself never ascended into heaven, yet he said,

  'The LORD said to my Lord,
    "Sit in the place of honor
      at my right hand
³⁵ until I humble your enemies,
    making them a footstool under
      your feet."'*

³⁶"So let everyone in Israel know for certain that God has made this Jesus, whom you crucified, to be both Lord and Messiah!"

³⁷Peter's words pierced their hearts, and they said to him and to the other apostles, "Brothers, what should we do?"

³⁸Peter replied, "Each of you must repent of your sins and turn to God, and be baptized in the name of Jesus Christ for the forgiveness of your sins. Then you will receive the gift of the Holy Spirit. ³⁹This promise is to you, and to your children, and even to the Gentiles*—all who have been called by the Lord our God." ⁴⁰Then Peter continued preaching for a long time, strongly urging all his listeners, "Save yourselves from this crooked generation!"

⁴¹Those who believed what Peter said

were baptized and added to the church that day—about 3,000 in all.

[42] All the believers devoted themselves to the apostles' teaching, and to fellowship, and to sharing in meals (including the Lord's Supper*), and to prayer.

[43] A deep sense of awe came over them all, and the apostles performed many miraculous signs and wonders. [44] And all the believers met together in one place and shared everything they had. [45] They sold their property and possessions and shared the money with those in need. [46] They worshiped together at the Temple each day, met in homes for the Lord's Supper, and shared their meals with great joy and generosity*—[47] all the while praising God and enjoying the goodwill of all the people. And each day the Lord added to their fellowship those who were being saved.

2:1 The Festival of Pentecost came 50 days after Passover (when Jesus was crucified).   2:4 Or *in other tongues.*
2:17-21 Joel 2:28-32.   2:22 Or *Jesus of Nazareth.*
2:27 Greek *in Hades;* also in 2:31.   2:25-28 Ps 16:8-11 (Greek version).   2:34-35 Ps 110:1.   2:39 Or *and to people far in the future;* Greek reads *and to those far away.*
2:42 Greek *the breaking of bread;* also in 2:46.   2:46 Or *and sincere hearts.*

PSALM 122:1-9
A song for pilgrims ascending to Jerusalem. A psalm of David.

[1] **I** was glad when they said to me,
    "Let us go to the house of the
       LORD."

[2] And now here we are,
       standing inside your gates,
         O Jerusalem.
[3] Jerusalem is a well-built city;
       its seamless walls cannot be
         breached.
[4] All the tribes of Israel—the LORD's
         people—
       make their pilgrimage here.
    They come to give thanks to the name
         of the LORD,
       as the law requires of Israel.
[5] Here stand the thrones where
         judgment is given,
       the thrones of the dynasty of David.

[6] Pray for peace in Jerusalem.
       May all who love this city prosper.
[7] O Jerusalem, may there be peace
         within your walls
       and prosperity in your palaces.
[8] For the sake of my family and friends,
         I will say,
       "May you have peace."
[9] For the sake of the house of the LORD
         our God,
       I will seek what is best for you,
         O Jerusalem.

PROVERBS 16:19-20
Better to live humbly with the poor than to share plunder with the proud. □ Those who listen to instruction will prosper; those who trust the LORD will be joyful.

2 SAMUEL 23:24–24:25
While running from King Saul's rage, David had gathered a ragamuffin band of warriors. Some of them became known as his mighty men. Second Samuel closes with the recognition of these men and the description of one final mistake on the part of David.

Other members of the Thirty included:

    Asahel, Joab's brother;
    Elhanan son of Dodo from
       Bethlehem;

[25] Shammah from Harod;
       Elika from Harod;
[26] Helez from Pelon*;
       Ira son of Ikkesh from Tekoa;
[27] Abiezer from Anathoth;
       Sibbecai* from Hushah;
[28] Zalmon from Ahoah;
       Maharai from Netophah;
[29] Heled* son of Baanah from Netophah;
       Ithai* son of Ribai from Gibeah
          (in the land of Benjamin);

30 Benaiah from Pirathon;
   Hurai* from Nahale-gaash*;
31 Abi-albon from Arabah;
   Azmaveth from Bahurim;
32 Eliahba from Shaalbon;
   the sons of Jashen;
33 Jonathan son of Shagee* from Harar;
   Ahiam son of Sharar from Harar;
34 Eliphelet son of Ahasbai from Maacah;
   Eliam son of Ahithophel from Giloh;
35 Hezro from Carmel;
   Paarai from Arba;
36 Igal son of Nathan from Zobah;
   Bani from Gad;
37 Zelek from Ammon;
   Naharai from Beeroth, Joab's armor
   bearer;
38 Ira from Jattir;
   Gareb from Jattir;
39 Uriah the Hittite.

There were thirty-seven in all.

24:1 ONCE again the anger of the LORD burned against Israel, and he caused David to harm them by taking a census. "Go and count the people of Israel and Judah," the LORD told him.

² So the king said to Joab and the commanders* of the army, "Take a census of all the tribes of Israel—from Dan in the north to Beersheba in the south—so I may know how many people there are."

³ But Joab replied to the king, "May the LORD your God let you live to see a hundred times as many people as there are now! But why, my lord the king, do you want to do this?"

⁴ But the king insisted that they take the census, so Joab and the commanders of the army went out to count the people of Israel. ⁵ First they crossed the Jordan and camped at Aroer, south of the town in the valley, in the direction of Gad. Then they went on to Jazer, ⁶ then to Gilead in the land of Tahtim-hodshi* and to Dan-jaan and around to Sidon. ⁷ Then they came to the fortress of Tyre, and all the towns of the Hivites and Canaanites. Finally, they went south to Judah* as far as Beersheba.

⁸ Having gone through the entire land for nine months and twenty days, they returned to Jerusalem. ⁹ Joab reported the number of people to the king. There were 800,000 capable warriors in Israel who

could handle a sword, and 500,000 in Judah.

¹⁰ But after he had taken the census, David's conscience began to bother him. And he said to the LORD, "I have sinned greatly by taking this census. Please forgive my guilt, LORD, for doing this foolish thing."

¹¹ The next morning the word of the LORD came to the prophet Gad, who was David's seer. This was the message: ¹²"Go and say to David, 'This is what the LORD says: I will give you three choices. Choose one of these punishments, and I will inflict it on you.'"

¹³ So Gad came to David and asked him, "Will you choose three* years of famine throughout your land, three months of fleeing from your enemies, or three days of severe plague throughout your land? Think this over and decide what answer I should give the LORD who sent me."

¹⁴"I'm in a desperate situation!" David replied to Gad. "But let us fall into the hands of the LORD, for his mercy is great. Do not let me fall into human hands."

¹⁵ So the LORD sent a plague upon Israel that morning, and it lasted for three days.* A total of 70,000 people died throughout the nation, from Dan in the north to Beersheba in the south. ¹⁶ But as the angel was preparing to destroy Jerusalem, the LORD relented and said to the death angel, "Stop! That is enough!" At that moment the angel of the LORD was by the threshing floor of Araunah the Jebusite.

¹⁷ When David saw the angel, he said to the LORD, "I am the one who has sinned and done wrong! But these people are as innocent as sheep—what have they done? Let your anger fall against me and my family."

¹⁸ That day Gad came to David and said to him, "Go up and build an altar to the LORD on the threshing floor of Araunah the Jebusite."

¹⁹ So David went up to do what the LORD had commanded him. ²⁰ When Araunah saw the king and his men coming toward him, he came and bowed before the king with his face to the ground. ²¹"Why have you come, my lord the king?" Araunah asked.

David replied, "I have come to buy

your threshing floor and to build an altar to the LORD there, so that he will stop the plague."

22"Take it, my lord the king, and use it as you wish," Araunah said to David. "Here are oxen for the burnt offering, and you can use the threshing boards and ox yokes for wood to build a fire on the altar. 23I will give it all to you, Your Majesty, and may the LORD your God accept your sacrifice."

24But the king replied to Araunah, "No, I insist on buying it, for I will not present burnt offerings to the LORD my God that have cost me nothing." So David paid him fifty pieces of silver* for the threshing floor and the oxen.

25David built an altar there to the LORD and sacrificed burnt offerings and peace offerings. And the LORD answered his prayer for the land, and the plague on Israel was stopped.

23:26 As in parallel text at 1 Chr 11:27 (see also 1 Chr 27:10); Hebrew reads *from Palti.*   23:27 As in some Greek manuscripts (see also 1 Chr 11:29); Hebrew reads *Mebunnai.* 23:29a As in some Hebrew manuscripts (see also 1 Chr 11:30); most Hebrew manuscripts read *Heleb.*   23:29b As in parallel text at 1 Chr 11:31; Hebrew reads *Ittai.*   23:30a As in some Greek manuscripts (see also 1 Chr 11:32); Hebrew reads *Hiddai.*   23:30b Or *from the ravines of Gaash.* 23:33 As in parallel text at 1 Chr 11:34; Hebrew reads *Jonathan, Shammah;* some Greek manuscripts read *Jonathan son of Shammah.* 24:2 As in Greek version (see also 24:4 and 1 Chr 21:2); Hebrew reads *Joab the commander.*   24:6 Greek version reads *to Gilead and to Kadesh in the land of the Hittites.*   24:7 Or *they went to the Negev of Judah.*   24:13 As in Greek version (see also 1 Chr 21:12); Hebrew reads *seven.*   24:15 Hebrew *for the designated time.*   24:24 Hebrew *50 shekels of silver,* about 20 ounces or 570 grams in weight.

ACTS 3:1-26
Peter and John, two key apostles, performed miracles and proclaimed the message of Jesus. Peter gave his hearers a lesson in the real meaning behind recent events.

Peter and John went to the Temple one afternoon to take part in the three o'clock prayer service. 2As they approached the Temple, a man lame from birth was being carried in. Each day he was put beside the Temple gate, the one called the Beautiful Gate, so he could beg from the people going into the Temple. 3When he saw Peter and John about to enter, he asked them for some money.

4Peter and John looked at him intently, and Peter said, "Look at us!" 5The lame man looked at them eagerly, expecting some money. 6But Peter said, "I don't have any silver or gold for you. But I'll give you what I have. In the name of Jesus Christ the Nazarene,* get up and* walk!"

7Then Peter took the lame man by the right hand and helped him up. And as he did, the man's feet and ankles were instantly healed and strengthened. 8He jumped up, stood on his feet, and began to walk! Then, walking, leaping, and praising God, he went into the Temple with them.

9All the people saw him walking and heard him praising God. 10When they realized he was the lame beggar they had seen so often at the Beautiful Gate, they

HOW WE LIVE | Our speech

PROVERBS 16:23 Jesus said, "Whatever is in your heart determines what you say" (Matthew 12:34, January 18). Now that your heart has been cleansed and changed because of your new relationship with Jesus, the words you say are going to change as well. • What does wise speech look like? Wise speech is made up of words that are encouraging, uplifting, kind, and caring. Wise speech gives good and helpful advice. Words are wise when they are well considered before they are spoken, or are silent when silence is required. Words are wise when they are filled with good motives and speak only the truth. • As you seek to please God with your words, trust his Spirit to help you. It may take time, so don't get discouraged. Perhaps you've been used to gossiping, using coarse language, or speaking harshly to others. Those habits will die hard, but the Spirit will go to work on your words, helping you take control of what you say and how you say it. He will help you to use the "wise speech" that this proverb describes.

were absolutely astounded! [11]They all rushed out in amazement to Solomon's Colonnade, where the man was holding tightly to Peter and John.

[12]Peter saw his opportunity and addressed the crowd. "People of Israel," he said, "what is so surprising about this? And why stare at us as though we had made this man walk by our own power or godliness? [13]For it is the God of Abraham, Isaac, and Jacob—the God of all our ancestors—who has brought glory to his servant Jesus by doing this. This is the same Jesus whom you handed over and rejected before Pilate, despite Pilate's decision to release him. [14]You rejected this holy, righteous one and instead demanded the release of a murderer. [15]You killed the author of life, but God raised him from the dead. And we are witnesses of this fact!

[16]"Through faith in the name of Jesus, this man was healed—and you know how crippled he was before. Faith in Jesus' name has healed him before your very eyes.

[17]"Friends,* I realize that what you and your leaders did to Jesus was done in ignorance. [18]But God was fulfilling what all the prophets had foretold about the Messiah—that he must suffer these things. [19]Now repent of your sins and turn to God, so that your sins may be wiped away. [20]Then times of refreshment will come from the presence of the Lord, and he will again send you Jesus, your appointed Messiah. [21]For he must remain in heaven until the time for the final restoration of all things, as God promised long ago through his holy prophets. [22]Moses said, 'The LORD your God will raise up for you a Prophet like me from among your own people. Listen carefully to everything he tells you.'* [23]Then Moses said, 'Anyone who will not listen to that Prophet will be completely cut off from God's people.'*

[24]"Starting with Samuel, every prophet spoke about what is happening today. [25]You are the children of those prophets, and you are included in the covenant God promised to your ancestors. For God said to Abraham, 'Through your descendants* all the families on earth will be blessed.' [26]When God raised up his servant, Jesus, he sent him first to you people of Israel, to bless you by turning each of you back from your sinful ways."

3:6a Or *Jesus Christ of Nazareth.* **3:6b** Some manuscripts omit *get up and.* **3:17** Greek *Brothers.* **3:22** Deut 18:15. **3:23** Deut 18:19; Lev 23:29. **3:25** Greek *your seed;* see Gen 12:3; 22:18.

PSALM 123:1-4
A song for pilgrims ascending to Jerusalem.

[1] I lift my eyes to you,
    O God, enthroned in heaven.
[2] We keep looking to the LORD our God
      for his mercy,
    just as servants keep their eyes
      on their master,
    as a slave girl watches her mistress
      for the slightest signal.
[3] Have mercy on us, LORD, have mercy,
    for we have had our fill of
      contempt.
[4] We have had more than our fill of the
      scoffing of the proud
    and the contempt of the arrogant.

PROVERBS 16:21-23
The wise are known for their understanding, and pleasant words are persuasive. □ Discretion is a life-giving fountain to those who possess it, but discipline is wasted on fools. □ From a wise mind comes wise speech; the words of the wise are persuasive.

JUNE**6**

1 KINGS 1:1-53
The first book of Kings picks up where Samuel left off. King David's reign was essentially over, but which of his sons would ascend his throne? Watch as one son tries a power grab.

King David was now very old, and no matter how many blankets covered him, he could not keep warm. [2]So his advisers told him, "Let us find a young virgin to wait on you and look after you, my lord. She will lie in your arms and keep you warm."

[3]So they searched throughout the land of Israel for a beautiful girl, and they found Abishag from Shunem and brought her to the king. [4]The girl was very beautiful, and she looked after the king and took care of him. But the king had no sexual relations with her.

[5]About that time David's son Adonijah, whose mother was Haggith, began boasting, "I will make myself king." So he provided himself with chariots and charioteers and recruited fifty men to run in front of him. [6]Now his father, King David, had never disciplined him at any time, even by asking, "Why are you doing that?" Adonijah had been born next after Absalom, and he was very handsome.

[7]Adonijah took Joab son of Zeruiah and Abiathar the priest into his confidence, and they agreed to help him become king. [8]But Zadok the priest, Benaiah son of Jehoiada, Nathan the prophet, Shimei, Rei, and David's personal bodyguard refused to support Adonijah.

[9]Adonijah went to the Stone of Zoheleth* near the spring of En-rogel, where he sacrificed sheep, cattle, and fattened calves. He invited all his brothers—the other sons of King David—and all the royal officials of Judah. [10]But he did not invite Nathan the prophet or Benaiah or the king's bodyguard or his brother Solomon.

[11]Then Nathan went to Bathsheba, Solomon's mother, and asked her, "Haven't you heard that Haggith's son, Adonijah, has made himself king, and our lord David doesn't even know about it? [12]If you want to save your own life and the life of your son Solomon, follow my advice. [13]Go at once to King David and say to him, 'My lord the king, didn't you make a vow and say to me, "Your son Solomon will surely be the next king and will sit on my throne"? Why then has Adonijah become king?' [14]And while you are still talking with him, I will come and confirm everything you have said."

[15]So Bathsheba went into the king's bedroom. (He was very old now, and Abishag was taking care of him.) [16]Bathsheba bowed down before the king.

"What can I do for you?" he asked her.

[17]She replied, "My lord, you made a vow before the LORD your God when you said to me, 'Your son Solomon will surely be the next king and will sit on my throne.' [18]But instead, Adonijah has made himself king, and my lord the king does not even know about it. [19]He has sacrificed many cattle, fattened calves, and sheep, and he has invited all the king's sons to attend the celebration. He also invited Abiathar the priest and Joab, the commander of the army. But he did not invite your servant Solomon. [20]And now, my lord the king, all Israel is waiting for you to announce who will become king after you. [21]If you do not act, my son Solomon and I will be treated as criminals as soon as my lord the king has died."

[22]While she was still speaking with the king, Nathan the prophet arrived. [23]The king's officials told him, "Nathan the prophet is here to see you."

Nathan went in and bowed before the king with his face to the ground. [24]Nathan asked, "My lord the king, have you decided that Adonijah will be the next king and that he will sit on your throne? [25]Today he has sacrificed many cattle, fattened calves, and sheep, and he has invited all the king's sons to attend the celebration. He also invited the commanders of the army and Abiathar the priest. They are feasting and drinking with him and shouting, 'Long live King Adonijah!' [26]But he did not invite me or Zadok the priest or Benaiah or your servant Solomon. [27]Has my lord the king really done this without letting any of his officials know who should be the next king?"

[28]King David responded, "Call Bathsheba!" So she came back in and stood before the king. [29]And the king repeated his vow: "As surely as the LORD lives, who has rescued me from every danger, [30]your son Solomon will be the next king and will sit on my throne this very day, just as I vowed to you before the LORD, the God of Israel."

[31]Then Bathsheba bowed down with her face to the ground before the king and exclaimed, "May my lord King David live forever!"

[32]Then King David ordered, "Call Zadok the priest, Nathan the prophet, and Benaiah son of Jehoiada." When they

came into the king's presence, ³³the king said to them, "Take Solomon and my officials down to Gihon Spring. Solomon is to ride on my own mule. ³⁴There Zadok the priest and Nathan the prophet are to anoint him king over Israel. Blow the ram's horn and shout, 'Long live King Solomon!' ³⁵Then escort him back here, and he will sit on my throne. He will succeed me as king, for I have appointed him to be ruler over Israel and Judah."

³⁶"Amen!" Benaiah son of Jehoiada replied. "May the LORD, the God of my lord the king, decree that it happen. ³⁷And may the LORD be with Solomon as he has been with you, my lord the king, and may he make Solomon's reign even greater than yours!"

³⁸So Zadok the priest, Nathan the prophet, Benaiah son of Jehoiada, and the king's bodyguard* took Solomon down to Gihon Spring, with Solomon riding on King David's own mule. ³⁹There Zadok the priest took the flask of olive oil from the sacred tent and anointed Solomon with the oil. Then they sounded the ram's horn and all the people shouted, "Long live King Solomon!" ⁴⁰And all the people followed Solomon into Jerusalem, playing flutes and shouting for joy. The celebration was so joyous and noisy that the earth shook with the sound.

⁴¹Adonijah and his guests heard the celebrating and shouting just as they were finishing their banquet. When Joab heard the sound of the ram's horn, he asked, "What's going on? Why is the city in such an uproar?"

⁴²And while he was still speaking, Jonathan son of Abiathar the priest arrived. "Come in," Adonijah said to him, "for you are a good man. You must have good news."

⁴³"Not at all!" Jonathan replied. "Our lord King David has just declared Solomon king! ⁴⁴The king sent him down to Gihon Spring with Zadok the priest, Nathan the prophet, and Benaiah son of Jehoiada, protected by the king's bodyguard. They had him ride on the king's own mule, ⁴⁵and Zadok and Nathan have anointed him at Gihon Spring as the new king. They have just returned, and the whole city is celebrating and rejoicing. That's what all the

noise is about. ⁴⁶What's more, Solomon is now sitting on the royal throne as king. ⁴⁷And all the royal officials have gone to King David and congratulated him, saying, 'May your God make Solomon's fame even greater than your own, and may Solomon's reign be even greater than yours!' Then the king bowed his head in worship as he lay in his bed, ⁴⁸and he said, 'Praise the LORD, the God of Israel, who today has chosen a successor to sit on my throne while I am still alive to see it.'"

⁴⁹Then all of Adonijah's guests jumped up in panic from the banquet table and quickly scattered. ⁵⁰Adonijah was afraid of Solomon, so he rushed to the sacred tent and grabbed onto the horns of the altar. ⁵¹Word soon reached Solomon that Adonijah had seized the horns of the altar in fear, and that he was pleading, "Let King Solomon swear today that he will not kill me!"

⁵²Solomon replied, "If he proves himself to be loyal, not a hair on his head will be touched. But if he makes trouble, he will die." ⁵³So King Solomon summoned Adonijah, and they brought him down from the altar. He came and bowed respectfully before King Solomon, who dismissed him, saying, "Go on home."

1:9 Or *to the Serpent's Stone;* Greek version supports reading *Zoheleth* as a proper name.   1:38 Hebrew the *Kerethites and Pelethites;* also in 1:44.

ACTS 4:1-37

The Jewish religious leaders were incensed that Jesus claimed to be God. Now, even after Jesus had been put to death, a crowd of his disciples continued to claim that Jesus was God, the Messiah for whom the Jews had waited for centuries.

While Peter and John were speaking to the people, they were confronted by the priests, the captain of the Temple guard, and some of the Sadducees. ²These leaders were very disturbed that Peter and John were teaching the people that through Jesus there is a resurrection of the dead. ³They arrested them and, since it was already evening, put them in jail until morning. ⁴But many of the people who heard their message believed it, so the number of believers now totaled about 5,000 men, not counting women and children.*

⁵The next day the council of all the rul-

ers and elders and teachers of religious law met in Jerusalem. [6]Annas the high priest was there, along with Caiaphas, John, Alexander, and other relatives of the high priest. [7]They brought in the two disciples and demanded, "By what power, or in whose name, have you done this?"

[8]Then Peter, filled with the Holy Spirit, said to them, "Rulers and elders of our people, [9]are we being questioned today because we've done a good deed for a crippled man? Do you want to know how he was healed? [10]Let me clearly state to all of you and to all the people of Israel that he was healed by the powerful name of Jesus Christ the Nazarene,* the man you crucified but whom God raised from the dead. [11]For Jesus is the one referred to in the Scriptures, where it says,

'The stone that you builders rejected has now become the cornerstone.'*

[12]There is salvation in no one else! God has given no other name under heaven by which we must be saved."

[13]The members of the council were amazed when they saw the boldness of Peter and John, for they could see that they were ordinary men with no special training in the Scriptures. They also recognized them as men who had been with Jesus. [14]But since they could see the man who had been healed standing right there among them, there was nothing the council could say. [15]So they ordered Peter and John out of the council chamber* and conferred among themselves.

[16]"What should we do with these men?" they asked each other. "We can't deny that they have performed a miraculous sign, and everybody in Jerusalem knows about it. [17]But to keep them from spreading their propaganda any further, we must warn them not to speak to anyone in Jesus' name again." [18]So they called the apostles back in and commanded them never again to speak or teach in the name of Jesus.

[19]But Peter and John replied, "Do you think God wants us to obey you rather than him? [20]We cannot stop telling about everything we have seen and heard."

[21]The council then threatened them further, but they finally let them go because they didn't know how to punish them without starting a riot. For everyone was praising God [22]for this miraculous sign—the healing of a man who had been lame for more than forty years.

[23]As soon as they were freed, Peter and John returned to the other believers and told them what the leading priests and elders had said. [24]When they heard the report, all the believers lifted their voices together in prayer to God: "O Sovereign

Is Jesus the only way to God?

ACTS 4:12 Inevitably there will be people who will challenge your new faith by saying, "How can Jesus be the *only* way to God? I believe that all religions lead to God. We all get to God by different roads." • Nothing could be further from the truth. The fact that "there is salvation in no one else" is not something Peter made up; it was a teaching of Jesus himself. Jesus said, "I am the way. . . . No one can come to the Father except through me" (John 14:6, May 24). This was not arrogance; it was a truthful statement that only Jesus could fulfill the Father's required punishment for sin—and hence, conquer sin itself. • Jesus came as the only perfect, sinless human to ever live, and he took the punishment for sin. No other religious teacher could die for our sins; no other religious teacher came to earth as God's only Son; no other religious teacher rose from the dead. Only one road takes you to God; only one road guarantees forgiveness of sin and everlasting life—that road is Jesus himself.

WHAT THE BIBLE SAYS

Lord, Creator of heaven and earth, the sea, and everything in them—[25]you spoke long ago by the Holy Spirit through our ancestor David, your servant, saying,

'Why were the nations so angry?
Why did they waste their time
with futile plans?
[26] The kings of the earth prepared
for battle;
the rulers gathered together
against the LORD
and against his Messiah.'*

[27]"In fact, this has happened here in this very city! For Herod Antipas, Pontius Pilate the governor, the Gentiles, and the people of Israel were all united against Jesus, your holy servant, whom you anointed. [28]But everything they did was determined beforehand according to your will. [29]And now, O Lord, hear their threats, and give us, your servants, great boldness in preaching your word. [30]Stretch out your hand with healing power; may miraculous signs and wonders be done through the name of your holy servant Jesus."

[31]After this prayer, the meeting place shook, and they were all filled with the Holy Spirit. Then they preached the word of God with boldness.

[32]All the believers were united in heart and mind. And they felt that what they owned was not their own, so they shared everything they had. [33]The apostles testified powerfully to the resurrection of the Lord Jesus, and God's great blessing was upon them all. [34]There were no needy people among them, because those who owned land or houses would sell them [35]and bring the money to the apostles to give to those in need.

[36]For instance, there was Joseph, the one the apostles nicknamed Barnabas (which means "Son of Encouragement"). He was from the tribe of Levi and came from the island of Cyprus. [37]He sold a field he owned and brought the money to the apostles.

4:4 Greek 5,000 adult males.   4:10 Or Jesus Christ of Nazareth.   4:11 Ps 118:22.   4:15 Greek the Sanhedrin. 4:25-26 Or his anointed one; or his Christ. Ps 2:1-2.

PSALM 124:1-8
*A song for pilgrims ascending to Jerusalem.
A psalm of David.*

[1] **W**hat if the LORD had not been
on our side?
Let all Israel repeat:
[2] What if the LORD had not been
on our side
when people attacked us?
[3] They would have swallowed us alive
in their burning anger.
[4] The waters would have engulfed us;
a torrent would have overwhelmed
us.
[5] Yes, the raging waters of their fury
would have overwhelmed our
very lives.

[6] Praise the LORD,
who did not let their teeth tear us
apart!
[7] We escaped like a bird from a hunter's
trap.
The trap is broken, and we are free!
[8] Our help is from the LORD,
who made heaven and earth.

PROVERBS 16:24
Kind words are like honey—sweet to the soul and healthy for the body.

JUNE**7**

1 KINGS 2:1-3:2
Often when modern executives come into a new position, they fire the current employees and bring in their own. They "clean house." According to today's reading, Solomon also had some house-cleaning to do.

As the time of King David's death approached, he gave this charge to his son Solomon:

[2]"I am going where everyone on earth must someday go. Take courage and be a

man. ³Observe the requirements of the LORD your God, and follow all his ways. Keep the decrees, commands, regulations, and laws written in the Law of Moses so that you will be successful in all you do and wherever you go. ⁴If you do this, then the LORD will keep the promise he made to me. He told me, 'If your descendants live as they should and follow me faithfully with all their heart and soul, one of them will always sit on the throne of Israel.'

⁵"And there is something else. You know what Joab son of Zeruiah did to me when he murdered my two army commanders, Abner son of Ner and Amasa son of Jether. He pretended that it was an act of war, but it was done in a time of peace,* staining his belt and sandals with innocent blood.* ⁶Do with him what you think best, but don't let him grow old and go to his grave in peace.*

⁷"Be kind to the sons of Barzillai of Gilead. Make them permanent guests at your table, for they took care of me when I fled from your brother Absalom.

⁸"And remember Shimei son of Gera, the man from Bahurim in Benjamin. He cursed me with a terrible curse as I was fleeing to Mahanaim. When he came down to meet me at the Jordan River, I swore by the LORD that I would not kill him. ⁹But that oath does not make him innocent. You are a wise man, and you will know how to arrange a bloody death for him.*"

¹⁰Then David died and was buried with his ancestors in the City of David. ¹¹David had reigned over Israel for forty years, seven of them in Hebron and thirty-three in Jerusalem. ¹²Solomon became king and sat on the throne of David his father, and his kingdom was firmly established.

¹³One day Adonijah, whose mother was Haggith, came to see Bathsheba, Solomon's mother. "Have you come with peaceful intentions?" she asked him.

"Yes," he said, "I come in peace. ¹⁴In fact, I have a favor to ask of you."

"What is it?" she asked.

¹⁵He replied, "As you know, the kingdom was rightfully mine; all Israel wanted me to be the next king. But the tables were turned, and the kingdom went to my brother instead; for that is the way the LORD wanted it. ¹⁶So now I have just one favor to ask of you. Please don't turn me down."

"What is it?" she asked.

¹⁷He replied, "Speak to King Solomon on my behalf, for I know he will do anything you request. Ask him to let me marry Abishag, the girl from Shunem."

¹⁸"All right," Bathsheba replied. "I will speak to the king for you."

¹⁹So Bathsheba went to King Solomon to speak on Adonijah's behalf. The king rose from his throne to meet her, and he bowed down before her. When he sat down on his throne again, the king ordered that a throne be brought for his mother, and she sat at his right hand.

²⁰"I have one small request to make of you," she said. "I hope you won't turn me down."

"What is it, my mother?" he asked. "You know I won't refuse you."

²¹"Then let your brother Adonijah marry Abishag, the girl from Shunem," she replied.

²²"How can you possibly ask me to give Abishag to Adonijah?" King Solomon demanded. "You might as well ask me to give him the kingdom! You know that he is my older brother, and that he has Abiathar the priest and Joab son of Zeruiah on his side."

²³Then King Solomon made a vow before the LORD: "May God strike me and even kill me if Adonijah has not sealed his fate with this request. ²⁴The LORD has confirmed me and placed me on the throne of my father, David; he has established my dynasty as he promised. So as surely as the LORD lives, Adonijah will die this very day!" ²⁵So King Solomon ordered Benaiah son of Jehoiada to execute him, and Adonijah was put to death.

²⁶Then the king said to Abiathar the priest, "Go back to your home in Anathoth. You deserve to die, but I will not kill you now, because you carried the Ark of the Sovereign LORD for David my father and you shared all his hardships." ²⁷So Solomon deposed Abiathar from his position as priest of the LORD, thereby fulfilling the prophecy the LORD had given at Shiloh concerning the descendants of Eli.

28Joab had not joined Absalom's earlier rebellion, but he had joined Adonijah's rebellion. So when Joab heard about Adonijah's death, he ran to the sacred tent of the LORD and grabbed onto the horns of the altar. 29When this was reported to King Solomon, he sent Benaiah son of Jehoiada to execute him.

30Benaiah went to the sacred tent of the LORD and said to Joab, "The king orders you to come out!"

But Joab answered, "No, I will die here."

So Benaiah returned to the king and told him what Joab had said.

31"Do as he said," the king replied. "Kill him there beside the altar and bury him. This will remove the guilt of Joab's senseless murders from me and from my father's family. 32The LORD will repay him* for the murders of two men who were more righteous and better than he. For my father knew nothing about the deaths of Abner son of Ner, commander of the army of Israel, and of Amasa son of Jether, commander of the army of Judah. 33May their blood be on Joab and his descendants forever, and may the LORD grant peace forever to David, his descendants, his dynasty, and his throne."

34So Benaiah son of Jehoiada returned to the sacred tent and killed Joab, and he was buried at his home in the wilderness. 35Then the king appointed Benaiah to command the army in place of Joab, and he installed Zadok the priest to take the place of Abiathar.

36The king then sent for Shimei and told him, "Build a house here in Jerusalem and live there. But don't step outside the city to go anywhere else. 37On the day you so much as cross the Kidron Valley, you will surely die; and your blood will be on your own head."

38Shimei replied, "Your sentence is fair; I will do whatever my lord the king commands." So Shimei lived in Jerusalem for a long time.

39But three years later two of Shimei's slaves ran away to King Achish son of Maacah of Gath. When Shimei learned where they were, 40he saddled his donkey and went to Gath to search for them. When he found them, he brought them back to Jerusalem.

41Solomon heard that Shimei had left Jerusalem and had gone to Gath and returned. 42So the king sent for Shimei and demanded, "Didn't I make you swear by the LORD and warn you not to go anywhere else or you would surely die? And you replied, 'The sentence is fair; I will do as you say.' 43Then why haven't you kept your oath to the LORD and obeyed my command?"

44The king also said to Shimei, "You certainly remember all the wicked things you did to my father, David. May the LORD now bring that evil on your own head. 45But may I, King Solomon, receive the LORD's blessings, and may one of David's descendants always sit on this throne in the presence of the LORD." 46Then, at the king's command, Benaiah son of Jehoiada took Shimei outside and killed him.

So the kingdom was now firmly in Solomon's grip.

3:1SOLOMON made an alliance with Pharaoh, the king of Egypt, and married one of his daughters. He brought her to live in the City of David until he could finish building his palace and the Temple of the LORD and the wall around the city. 2At that time the people of Israel sacrificed their offerings at local places of worship, for a temple honoring the name of the LORD had not yet been built.

2:5a Or *He murdered them during a time of peace as revenge for deaths they had caused in time of war.* 2:5b As in some Greek and Old Latin manuscripts; Hebrew reads *with the blood of war.* 2:6 Hebrew *don't let his white head go down to Sheol in peace.* 2:9 Hebrew *how to bring his white head down to Sheol in blood.* 2:32 Hebrew *will return his blood on his own head.*

ACTS 5:1-42

The first-century believers did their best to walk in Jesus' footsteps and live as he did. They shared everything. They traded personal ambitions for a mission and a calling. At least, most of them did. God punished harshly those who took God's requirements lightly.

But there was a certain man named Ananias who, with his wife, Sapphira, sold some property. 2He brought part of the money to the apostles, claiming it was the full amount. With his wife's consent, he kept the rest.

3Then Peter said, "Ananias, why have

you let Satan fill your heart? You lied to the Holy Spirit, and you kept some of the money for yourself. [4]The property was yours to sell or not sell, as you wished. And after selling it, the money was also yours to give away. How could you do a thing like this? You weren't lying to us but to God!"

[5]As soon as Ananias heard these words, he fell to the floor and died. Everyone who heard about it was terrified. [6]Then some young men got up, wrapped him in a sheet, and took him out and buried him.

[7]About three hours later his wife came in, not knowing what had happened. [8]Peter asked her, "Was this the price you and your husband received for your land?"

"Yes," she replied, "that was the price."

[9]And Peter said, "How could the two of you even think of conspiring to test the Spirit of the Lord like this? The young men who buried your husband are just outside the door, and they will carry you out, too."

[10]Instantly, she fell to the floor and died. When the young men came in and saw that she was dead, they carried her out and buried her beside her husband. [11]Great fear gripped the entire church and everyone else who heard what had happened.

[12]The apostles were performing many miraculous signs and wonders among the people. And all the believers were meeting regularly at the Temple in the area known as Solomon's Colonnade. [13]But no one else dared to join them, even though all the people had high regard for them. [14]Yet more and more people believed and were brought to the Lord—crowds of both men and women. [15]As a result of the apostles' work, sick people were brought out into the streets on beds and mats so that Peter's shadow might fall across some of them as he went by. [16]Crowds came from the villages around Jerusalem, bringing their sick and those possessed by evil* spirits, and they were all healed.

[17]The high priest and his officials, who were Sadducees, were filled with jealousy. [18]They arrested the apostles and put them in the public jail. [19]But an angel of the Lord came at night, opened the gates of the jail, and brought them out. Then he told them, [20]"Go to the Temple and give the people this message of life!"

[21]So at daybreak the apostles entered the Temple, as they were told, and immediately began teaching.

When the high priest and his officials arrived, they convened the high council*—the full assembly of the elders of Israel. Then they sent for the apostles to be brought from the jail for trial. [22]But when the Temple guards went to the jail, the men were gone. So they returned to the council and reported, [23]"The jail was securely locked, with the guards standing

---

HOW WE LIVE

Standing firm in our beliefs

ACTS 5:1-10 On a first reading, one might wonder why God handed down such a harsh and immediate punishment. A clue to this story lies in the last verses of the previous reading (Acts 4:36-37, June 6). Apparently a man named Barnabas had sold a field and brought the money to the apostles. It appears that Ananias and Sapphira wanted to look as generous as Barnabas, so they, too, sold some property and brought money to the apostles, lying about the real amount of the sale. This sin was judged harshly to set an example in the early church, making the believers realize how seriously God regards sin. • Dishonesty, greed, and covetousness are destructive in the church. When Christians compromise, we destroy our testimony about Christ and our fellowship with him is eroded. Bottom line: Don't compromise on what you know to be true. Live in honesty and integrity, in awe of the God who calls you to honor him in all you do and say.

outside, but when we opened the gates, no one was there!"

²⁴When the captain of the Temple guard and the leading priests heard this, they were perplexed, wondering where it would all end. ²⁵Then someone arrived with startling news: "The men you put in jail are standing in the Temple, teaching the people!"

²⁶The captain went with his Temple guards and arrested the apostles, but without violence, for they were afraid the people would stone them. ²⁷Then they brought the apostles before the high council, where the high priest confronted them. ²⁸"Didn't we tell you never again to teach in this man's name?" he demanded. "Instead, you have filled all Jerusalem with your teaching about him, and you want to make us responsible for his death!"

²⁹But Peter and the apostles replied, "We must obey God rather than any human authority. ³⁰The God of our ancestors raised Jesus from the dead after you killed him by hanging him on a cross.* ³¹Then God put him in the place of honor at his right hand as Prince and Savior. He did this so the people of Israel would repent of their sins and be forgiven. ³²We are witnesses of these things and so is the Holy Spirit, who is given by God to those who obey him."

³³When they heard this, the high council was furious and decided to kill them. ³⁴But one member, a Pharisee named Gamaliel, who was an expert in religious law and respected by all the people, stood up and ordered that the men be sent outside the council chamber for a while. ³⁵Then he said to his colleagues, "Men of Israel, take care what you are planning to do to these men! ³⁶Some time ago there was that fellow Theudas, who pretended to be someone great. About 400 others joined him, but he was killed, and all his followers went their various ways. The whole movement came to nothing. ³⁷After him, at the time of the census, there was Judas of Galilee. He got people to follow him, but he was killed, too, and all his followers were scattered.

³⁸"So my advice is, leave these men alone. Let them go. If they are planning and doing these things merely on their own, it will soon be overthrown. ³⁹But if it is from God, you will not be able to overthrow them. You may even find yourselves fighting against God!"

⁴⁰The others accepted his advice. They called in the apostles and had them flogged. Then they ordered them never again to speak in the name of Jesus, and they let them go.

⁴¹The apostles left the high council rejoicing that God had counted them worthy to suffer disgrace for the name of Jesus.* ⁴²And every day, in the Temple and from house to house, they continued to teach and preach this message: "Jesus is the Messiah."

5:16 Greek *unclean.* 5:21 Greek *Sanhedrin;* also in 5:27, 41. 5:30 Greek *on a tree.* 5:41 Greek *for the name.*

PSALM 125:1-5
A song for pilgrims ascending to Jerusalem.

¹ Those who trust in the LORD are
  as secure as Mount Zion;
  they will not be defeated but will
   endure forever.
² Just as the mountains surround
   Jerusalem,
  so the LORD surrounds his people,
   both now and forever.
³ The wicked will not rule the land
   of the godly,
  for then the godly might be
   tempted to do wrong.
⁴ O LORD, do good to those who
   are good,
  whose hearts are in tune
   with you.
⁵ But banish those who turn to crooked
   ways, O LORD.
  Take them away with those who
   do evil.

  May Israel have peace!

PROVERBS 16:25
There is a path before each person that seems right, but it ends in death.

1 KINGS 3:3–4:34

One of the most famous stories about King Solomon appears in today's reading: When offered to have anything he wanted, he asked for an understanding heart in order to rule God's people wisely. God was very pleased with this request.

Solomon loved the LORD and followed all the decrees of his father, David, except that Solomon, too, offered sacrifices and burned incense at the local places of worship. ⁴The most important of these places of worship was at Gibeon, so the king went there and sacrificed 1,000 burnt offerings. ⁵That night the LORD appeared to Solomon in a dream, and God said, "What do you want? Ask, and I will give it to you!"

⁶Solomon replied, "You showed faithful love to your servant my father, David, because he was honest and true and faithful to you. And you have continued your faithful love to him today by giving him a son to sit on his throne.

⁷"Now, O LORD my God, you have made me king instead of my father, David, but I am like a little child who doesn't know his way around. ⁸And here I am in the midst of your own chosen people, a nation so great and numerous they cannot be counted! ⁹Give me an understanding heart so that I can govern your people well and know the difference between right and wrong. For who by himself is able to govern this great people of yours?"

¹⁰The Lord was pleased that Solomon had asked for wisdom. ¹¹So God replied, "Because you have asked for wisdom in governing my people with justice and have not asked for a long life or wealth or the death of your enemies—¹²I will give you what you asked for! I will give you a wise and understanding heart such as no one else has had or ever will have! ¹³And I will also give you what you did not ask for—riches and fame! No other king in all the world will be compared to you for the rest of your life! ¹⁴And if you follow me and obey my decrees and my commands as your father, David, did, I will give you a long life."

¹⁵Then Solomon woke up and realized it had been a dream. He returned to Jerusalem and stood before the Ark of the LORD's Covenant, where he sacrificed burnt offerings and peace offerings. Then he invited all his officials to a great banquet.

¹⁶Some time later two prostitutes came to the king to have an argument settled. ¹⁷"Please, my lord," one of them began, "this woman and I live in the same house. I gave birth to a baby while she was with me in the house. ¹⁸Three days later this woman also had a baby. We were alone; there were only two of us in the house.

¹⁹"But her baby died during the night when she rolled over on it. ²⁰Then she got up in the night and took my son from beside me while I was asleep. She laid her dead child in my arms and took mine to sleep beside her. ²¹And in the morning when I tried to nurse my son, he was dead! But when I looked more closely in the morning light, I saw that it wasn't my son at all."

²²Then the other woman interrupted, "It certainly was your son, and the living child is mine."

"No," the first woman said, "the living child is mine, and the dead one is yours." And so they argued back and forth before the king.

²³Then the king said, "Let's get the facts straight. Both of you claim the living child is yours, and each says that the dead one belongs to the other. ²⁴All right, bring me a sword." So a sword was brought to the king.

²⁵Then he said, "Cut the living child in two, and give half to one woman and half to the other!"

²⁶Then the woman who was the real mother of the living child, and who loved him very much, cried out, "Oh no, my lord! Give her the child—please do not kill him!"

But the other woman said, "All right, he will be neither yours nor mine; divide him between us!"

²⁷Then the king said, "Do not kill the child, but give him to the woman who wants him to live, for she is his mother!"

²⁸When all Israel heard the king's decision, the people were in awe of the king, for they saw the wisdom God had given him for rendering justice.

4:1KING Solomon now ruled over all Israel, ²and these were his high officials:

Azariah son of Zadok was the priest.
³ Elihoreph and Ahijah, the sons of Shisha, were court secretaries.
Jehoshaphat son of Ahilud was the royal historian.
⁴ Benaiah son of Jehoiada was commander of the army.
Zadok and Abiathar were priests.
⁵ Azariah son of Nathan was in charge of the district governors.
Zabud son of Nathan, a priest, was a trusted adviser to the king.
⁶ Ahishar was manager of the palace property.
Adoniram son of Abda was in charge of the labor force.

⁷ Solomon also had twelve district governors who were over all Israel. They were responsible for providing food for the king's household. Each of them arranged provisions for one month of the year. ⁸These are the names of the twelve governors:

Ben-hur, in the hill country of Ephraim.
⁹ Ben-deker, in Makaz, Shaalbim, Beth-shemesh, and Elon-bethhanan.
¹⁰ Ben-hesed, in Arubboth, including Socoh and all the land of Hepher.
¹¹ Ben-abinadab, in all of Naphoth-dor.* (He was married to Taphath, one of Solomon's daughters.)
¹² Baana son of Ahilud, in Taanach and Megiddo, all of Beth-shan* near Zarethan below Jezreel, and all the territory from Beth-shan to Abel-meholah and over to Jokmeam.
¹³ Ben-geber, in Ramoth-gilead, including the Towns of Jair (named for Jair of the tribe of Manasseh*) in Gilead, and in the Argob region of Bashan, including sixty large fortified towns with bronze bars on their gates.
¹⁴ Ahinadab son of Iddo, in Mahanaim.
¹⁵ Ahimaaz, in Naphtali. (He was married to Basemath, another of Solomon's daughters.)

¹⁶ Baana son of Hushai, in Asher and in Aloth.
¹⁷ Jehoshaphat son of Paruah, in Issachar.
¹⁸ Shimei son of Ela, in Benjamin.
¹⁹ Geber son of Uri, in the land of Gilead,* including the territories of King Sihon of the Amorites and King Og of Bashan.
There was also one governor over the land of Judah.*

²⁰The people of Judah and Israel were as numerous as the sand on the seashore. They were very contented, with plenty to eat and drink. ²¹*Solomon ruled over all the kingdoms from the Euphrates River* in the north to the land of the Philistines and the border of Egypt in the south. The conquered peoples of those lands sent tribute money to Solomon and continued to serve him throughout his lifetime.

²²The daily food requirements for Solomon's palace were 150 bushels of choice flour and 300 bushels of meal*; ²³also 10 oxen from the fattening pens, 20 pasture-fed cattle, 100 sheep or goats, as well as deer, gazelles, roe deer, and choice poultry.*

²⁴Solomon's dominion extended over all the kingdoms west of the Euphrates River, from Tiphsah to Gaza. And there was peace on all his borders. ²⁵During the lifetime of Solomon, all of Judah and Israel lived in peace and safety. And from Dan in the north to Beersheba in the south, each family had its own home and garden.*

²⁶Solomon had 4,000* stalls for his chariot horses, and he had 12,000 horses.*

²⁷The district governors faithfully provided food for King Solomon and his court; each made sure nothing was lacking during the month assigned to him. ²⁸They also brought the necessary barley and straw for the royal horses in the stables.

²⁹God gave Solomon very great wisdom and understanding, and knowledge as vast as the sands of the seashore. ³⁰In fact, his wisdom exceeded that of all the wise men of the East and the wise men of Egypt. ³¹He was wiser than anyone else, including Ethan the Ezrahite and the sons of Mahol—Heman, Calcol, and Darda. His

fame spread throughout all the surrounding nations. [32]He composed some 3,000 proverbs and wrote 1,005 songs. [33]He could speak with authority about all kinds of plants, from the great cedar of Lebanon to the tiny hyssop that grows from cracks in a wall. He could also speak about animals, birds, small creatures, and fish. [34]And kings from every nation sent their ambassadors to listen to the wisdom of Solomon.

4:11 Hebrew *Naphath-dor,* a variant spelling of Naphoth-dor. 4:12 Hebrew *Beth-shean,* a variant spelling of Beth-shan; also in 4:12b.   4:13 Hebrew *Jair son of Manasseh;* compare 1 Chr 2:22.   4:19a Greek version reads *of Gad;* compare 4:13.   4:19b As in some Greek manuscripts; Hebrew lacks *of Judah.* The meaning of the Hebrew is uncertain. 4:21a Verses 4:21-34 are numbered 5:1-14 in Hebrew text. 4:21b Hebrew *the river;* also in 4:24.   4:22 Hebrew *30 cors* [5.5 kiloliters] *of choice flour and 60 cors* [11 kiloliters] *of meal.*   4:23 Or *and fattened geese.*   4:25 Hebrew *each family lived under its own grapevine and under its own fig tree.*   4:26a As in some Greek manuscripts (see also 2 Chr 9:25); Hebrew reads *40,000.*   4:26b Or *12,000 charioteers.*

ACTS 6:1-15
The fledgling church had to organize on the most practical of issues. Watch God's wisdom go to work in the decision-making process of these church leaders.

But as the believers* rapidly multiplied, there were rumblings of discontent. The Greek-speaking believers complained about the Hebrew-speaking believers, saying that their widows were being discriminated against in the daily distribution of food.

[2]So the Twelve called a meeting of all the believers. They said, "We apostles should spend our time teaching the word of God, not running a food program. [3]And so, brothers, select seven men who are well respected and are full of the Spirit and wisdom. We will give them this responsibility. [4]Then we apostles can spend our time in prayer and teaching the word."

[5]Everyone liked this idea, and they chose the following: Stephen (a man full of faith and the Holy Spirit), Philip, Procorus, Nicanor, Timon, Parmenas, and Nicolas of Antioch (an earlier convert to the Jewish faith). [6]These seven were presented to the apostles, who prayed for them as they laid their hands on them.

[7]So God's message continued to spread. The number of believers greatly increased in Jerusalem, and many of the Jewish priests were converted, too.

[8]Stephen, a man full of God's grace and power, performed amazing miracles and signs among the people. [9]But one day some men from the Synagogue of Freed Slaves, as it was called, started to debate with him. They were Jews from Cyrene, Alexandria, Cilicia, and the province of Asia. [10]None of them could stand against the wisdom and the Spirit with which Stephen spoke.

[11]So they persuaded some men to lie about Stephen, saying, "We heard him

Growing in wisdom

1 KINGS 3:9 King Solomon knew something important: All the power and wealth in the world were worth nothing if he didn't have the wisdom to use them well. He also knew that the responsibility he had been given to rule the nation of Israel was beyond his ability. So, when given the opportunity, Solomon asked God for "an understanding heart"—wisdom—so that he could rule the nation well. God was pleased with Solomon's request and responded by making his wisdom legendary. • It may surprise you to learn that you've been given a similar offer from God. James wrote, "If you need wisdom, ask our generous God, and he will give it to you" (James 1:5, November 17). God wants to give you wisdom, so he generously offers to give it if you ask. Of course, you won't wake up tomorrow and be completely wise. Instead, wisdom is a process. But when you ask God to work this way in your life, he helps you to grow wise through the many situations you face.

blaspheme Moses, and even God." [12]This roused the people, the elders, and the teachers of religious law. So they arrested Stephen and brought him before the high council.*

[13]The lying witnesses said, "This man is always speaking against the holy Temple and against the law of Moses. [14]We have heard him say that this Jesus of Nazareth* will destroy the Temple and change the customs Moses handed down to us."

[15]At this point everyone in the high council stared at Stephen, because his face became as bright as an angel's.

6:1 Greek *disciples;* also in 6:2, 7. 6:12 Greek *Sanhedrin;* also in 6:15. 6:14 Or *Jesus the Nazarene.*

PSALM 126:1-6
A song for pilgrims ascending to Jerusalem.

[1] **W**hen the LORD brought back
his exiles to Jerusalem,*
it was like a dream!
[2] We were filled with laughter,
and we sang for joy.

And the other nations said,
"What amazing things the LORD
has done for them."
[3] Yes, the LORD has done amazing
things for us!
What joy!

[4] Restore our fortunes, LORD,
as streams renew the desert.
[5] Those who plant in tears
will harvest with shouts
of joy.
[6] They weep as they go to plant
their seed,
but they sing as they return
with the harvest.

126:1 Hebrew *Zion.*

PROVERBS 16:26-27
It is good for workers to have an appetite; an empty stomach drives them on. □Scoundrels create trouble; their words are a destructive blaze.

JUNE**9**

1 KINGS 5:1-6:38
King David was the first to envision a permanent Temple that would replace the moveable Tabernacle; it was to be built in Jerusalem. His son Solomon made that vision a reality.

[1]***K**ing Hiram of Tyre had always been a loyal friend of David. When Hiram learned that David's son Solomon was the new king of Israel, he sent ambassadors to congratulate him.

[2]Then Solomon sent this message back to Hiram:

[3]"You know that my father, David, was not able to build a Temple to honor the name of the LORD his God because of the many wars waged against him by surrounding nations. He could not build until the LORD gave him victory over all his enemies. [4]But now the LORD my God has given me peace on every side; I have no enemies, and all is well.

[5]So I am planning to build a Temple to honor the name of the LORD my God, just as he had instructed my father, David. For the LORD told him, 'Your son, whom I will place on your throne, will build the Temple to honor my name.'

[6]"Therefore, please command that cedars from Lebanon be cut for me. Let my men work alongside yours, and I will pay your men whatever wages you ask. As you know, there is no one among us who can cut timber like you Sidonians!"

[7]When Hiram received Solomon's message, he was very pleased and said, "Praise the LORD today for giving David a wise son to be king of the great nation of Israel." [8]Then he sent this reply to Solomon:

"I have received your message, and I will supply all the cedar and cypress timber you need. ⁹My servants will bring the logs from the Lebanon mountains to the Mediterranean Sea* and make them into rafts and float them along the coast to whatever place you choose. Then we will break the rafts apart so you can carry the logs away. You can pay me by supplying me with food for my household."

¹⁰So Hiram supplied as much cedar and cypress timber as Solomon desired. ¹¹In return, Solomon sent him an annual payment of 100,000 bushels* of wheat for his household and 110,000 gallons* of pure olive oil. ¹²So the LORD gave wisdom to Solomon, just as he had promised. And Hiram and Solomon made a formal alliance of peace.

¹³Then King Solomon conscripted a labor force of 30,000 men from all Israel. ¹⁴He sent them to Lebanon in shifts, 10,000 every month, so that each man would be one month in Lebanon and two months at home. Adoniram was in charge of this labor force. ¹⁵Solomon also had 70,000 common laborers, 80,000 quarry workers in the hill country, ¹⁶and 3,600* foremen to supervise the work. ¹⁷At the king's command, they quarried large blocks of high-quality stone and shaped them to make the foundation of the Temple. ¹⁸Men from the city of Gebal helped Solomon's and Hiram's builders prepare the timber and stone for the Temple.

6:1IT was in midspring, in the month of Ziv,* during the fourth year of Solomon's reign, that he began to construct the Temple of the LORD. This was 480 years after the people of Israel were rescued from their slavery in the land of Egypt.

²The Temple that King Solomon built for the LORD was 90 feet long, 30 feet wide, and 45 feet high.* ³The entry room at the front of the Temple was 30 feet* wide, running across the entire width of the Temple. It projected outward 15 feet* from the front of the Temple. ⁴Solomon also made narrow recessed windows throughout the Temple.

⁵He built a complex of rooms against the outer walls of the Temple, all the way around the sides and rear of the building.

⁶The complex was three stories high, the bottom floor being 7½ feet wide, the second floor 9 feet wide, and the top floor 10½ feet wide.* The rooms were connected to the walls of the Temple by beams resting on ledges built out from the wall. So the beams were not inserted into the walls themselves.

⁷The stones used in the construction of the Temple were finished at the quarry, so there was no sound of hammer, ax, or any other iron tool at the building site.

⁸The entrance to the bottom floor* was on the south side of the Temple. There were winding stairs going up to the second floor, and another flight of stairs between the second and third floors. ⁹After completing the Temple structure, Solomon put in a ceiling made of cedar beams and planks. ¹⁰As already stated, he built a complex of rooms on three sides of the building, attached to the Temple walls by cedar timbers. Each story of the complex was 7½ feet* high.

¹¹Then the LORD gave this message to Solomon: ¹²"Concerning this Temple you are building, if you keep all my decrees and regulations and obey all my commands, I will fulfill through you the promise I made to your father, David. ¹³I will live among the Israelites and will never abandon my people Israel."

¹⁴So Solomon finished building the Temple. ¹⁵The entire inside, from floor to ceiling, was paneled with wood. He paneled the walls and ceilings with cedar, and he used planks of cypress for the floors. ¹⁶He partitioned off an inner sanctuary— the Most Holy Place—at the far end of the Temple. It was 30 feet deep and was paneled with cedar from floor to ceiling. ¹⁷The main room of the Temple, outside the Most Holy Place, was 60 feet* long. ¹⁸Cedar paneling completely covered the stone walls throughout the Temple, and the paneling was decorated with carvings of gourds and open flowers.

¹⁹He prepared the inner sanctuary at the far end of the Temple, where the Ark of the LORD's Covenant would be placed. ²⁰This inner sanctuary was 30 feet long, 30 feet wide, and 30 feet high. He overlaid the inside with solid gold. He also overlaid the altar made of cedar.* ²¹Then

Solomon overlaid the rest of the Temple's interior with solid gold, and he made gold chains to protect the entrance* to the Most Holy Place. [22] So he finished overlaying the entire Temple with gold, including the altar that belonged to the Most Holy Place.

[23] He made two cherubim of wild olive* wood, each 15 feet* tall, and placed them in the inner sanctuary. [24] The wingspan of each of the cherubim was 15 feet, each wing being 7½ feet* long. [25] The two cherubim were identical in shape and size; [26] each was 15 feet tall. [27] He placed them side by side in the inner sanctuary of the Temple. Their outspread wings reached from wall to wall, while their inner wings touched at the center of the room. [28] He overlaid the two cherubim with gold.

[29] He decorated all the walls of the inner sanctuary and the main room with carvings of cherubim, palm trees, and open flowers. [30] He overlaid the floor in both rooms with gold.

[31] For the entrance to the inner sanctuary, he made double doors of wild olive wood with five-sided doorposts.* [32] These double doors were decorated with carvings of cherubim, palm trees, and open flowers. The doors, including the decorations of cherubim and palm trees, were overlaid with gold.

[33] Then he made four-sided doorposts of wild olive wood for the entrance to the Temple. [34] There were two folding doors of cypress wood, and each door was hinged to fold back upon itself. [35] These doors were decorated with carvings of cherubim, palm trees, and open flowers— all overlaid evenly with gold.

[36] The walls of the inner courtyard were built so that there was one layer of cedar beams between every three layers of finished stone.

[37] The foundation of the LORD's Temple was laid in midspring, in the month of Ziv,* during the fourth year of Solomon's reign. [38] The entire building was completed in every detail by midautumn, in the month of Bul,* during the eleventh year of his reign. So it took seven years to build the Temple.

5:1 Verses 5:1-18 are numbered 5:15-32 in Hebrew text. 5:9 Hebrew *the sea.* 5:11a Hebrew *20,000 cors* [3,640

kiloliters]. **5:11b** As in Greek version, which reads *20,000 baths* [420 kiloliters] (see also 2 Chr 2:10); Hebrew reads *20 cors,* about 800 gallons or 3.6 kiloliters in volume. **5:16** As in some Greek manuscripts (see also 2 Chr 2:2, 18); Hebrew reads *3,300.* **6:1** Hebrew *It was in the month of Ziv, which is the second month.* This month of the ancient Hebrew lunar calendar usually occurs within the months of April and May. **6:2** Hebrew *60 cubits* [27.6 meters] *long, 20 cubits* [9.2 meters] *wide, and 30 cubits* [13.8 meters] *high.* **6:3a** Hebrew *20 cubits* [9.2 meters]; also in 6:16, 20. **6:3b** Hebrew *10 cubits* [4.6 meters]. **6:6** Hebrew *the bottom floor being 5 cubits* [2.3 meters] *wide, the second floor 6 cubits* [2.8 meters] *wide, and the top floor 7 cubits* [3.2 meters] *wide.* **6:8** As in Greek version; Hebrew reads *middle floor.* **6:10** Hebrew *5 cubits* [2.3 meters]. **6:17** Hebrew *40 cubits* [18.4 meters]. **6:20** Or *overlaid the altar with cedar.* The meaning of the Hebrew is uncertain. **6:21** Or *to draw curtains across.* The meaning of the Hebrew is uncertain. **6:23a** Or *pine;* Hebrew reads *oil tree;* also in 6:31, 33. **6:23b** Hebrew *10 cubits* [4.6 meters]; also in 6:24, 25. **6:24** Hebrew *5 cubits* [2.3 meters]. **6:31** The meaning of the Hebrew is uncertain. **6:37** Hebrew *was laid in the month of Ziv.* This month of the ancient Hebrew lunar calendar usually occurs within the months of April and May. **6:38** Hebrew *by the month of Bul, which is the eighth month.* This month of the ancient Hebrew lunar calendar usually occurs within the months of October and November.

ACTS 7:1-29

Just as they persecuted Jesus for his message, the Jewish leaders persecuted his followers for spreading that message. Early church leaders were imprisoned, interrogated, and even killed for the faith they professed. Watch Stephen's trial unfold.

Then the high priest asked Stephen, "Are these accusations true?"

[2] This was Stephen's reply: "Brothers and fathers, listen to me. Our glorious God appeared to our ancestor Abraham in Mesopotamia before he settled in Haran.* [3] God told him, 'Leave your native land and your relatives, and come into the land that I will show you.'* [4] So Abraham left the land of the Chaldeans and lived in Haran until his father died. Then God brought him here to the land where you now live.

[5] "But God gave him no inheritance here, not even one square foot of land. God did promise, however, that eventually the whole land would belong to Abraham and his descendants—even though he had no children yet. [6] God also told him that his descendants would live in a foreign land, where they would be oppressed as slaves for 400 years. [7] 'But I will punish the nation that enslaves them,' God said, 'and in the end they will come out and worship me here in this place.'*

[8] "God also gave Abraham the covenant of circumcision at that time. So when Abraham became the father of Isaac, he

circumcised him on the eighth day. And the practice was continued when Isaac became the father of Jacob, and when Jacob became the father of the twelve patriarchs of the Israelite nation.

9"These patriarchs were jealous of their brother Joseph, and they sold him to be a slave in Egypt. But God was with him 10and rescued him from all his troubles. And God gave him favor before Pharaoh, king of Egypt. God also gave Joseph unusual wisdom, so that Pharaoh appointed him governor over all of Egypt and put him in charge of the palace.

11"But a famine came upon Egypt and Canaan. There was great misery, and our ancestors ran out of food. 12Jacob heard that there was still grain in Egypt, so he sent his sons—our ancestors—to buy some. 13The second time they went, Joseph revealed his identity to his brothers,* and they were introduced to Pharaoh. 14Then Joseph sent for his father, Jacob, and all his relatives to come to Egypt, seventy-five persons in all. 15So Jacob went to Egypt. He died there, as did our ancestors. 16Their bodies were taken to Shechem and buried in the tomb Abraham had bought for a certain price from Hamor's sons in Shechem.

17"As the time drew near when God would fulfill his promise to Abraham, the number of our people in Egypt greatly increased. 18But then a new king came to the throne of Egypt who knew nothing about Joseph. 19This king exploited our people and oppressed them, forcing parents to abandon their newborn babies so they would die.

20"At that time Moses was born—a beautiful child in God's eyes. His parents cared for him at home for three months. 21When they had to abandon him, Pharaoh's daughter adopted him and raised him as her own son. 22Moses was taught all the wisdom of the Egyptians, and he was powerful in both speech and action.

23"One day when Moses was forty years old, he decided to visit his relatives, the people of Israel. 24He saw an Egyptian mistreating an Israelite. So Moses came to the man's defense and avenged him, killing the Egyptian. 25Moses assumed his fellow Israelites would realize that God had sent him to rescue them, but they didn't.

26"The next day he visited them again and saw two men of Israel fighting. He tried to be a peacemaker. 'Men,' he said, 'you are brothers. Why are you fighting each other?'

27"But the man in the wrong pushed Moses aside. 'Who made you a ruler and judge over us?' he asked. 28'Are you going to kill me as you killed that Egyptian yesterday?' ²⁹When Moses heard that, he fled the country and lived as a foreigner in the land of Midian. There his two sons were born."

7:2 *Mesopotamia* was the region now called Iraq. *Haran* was a city in what is now called Syria.   7:3 Gen 12:1.   7:5-7 Gen 12:7; 15:13-14; Exod 3:12.   7:13 Other manuscripts read *Joseph was recognized by his brothers.*

PSALM 127:1-5
A song for pilgrims ascending to Jerusalem. A psalm of Solomon.

¹ Unless the LORD builds a house,
   the work of the builders is wasted.
Unless the LORD protects a city,
   guarding it with sentries will do no good.
² It is useless for you to work so hard
   from early morning until late at night,

anxiously working for food to eat;
   for God gives rest to his loved ones.

³ Children are a gift from the LORD;
   they are a reward from him.
⁴ Children born to a young man
   are like arrows in a warrior's hands.
⁵ How joyful is the man whose quiver
   is full of them!
He will not be put to shame when
   he confronts his accusers at the city gates.

PROVERBS 16:28-30
A troublemaker plants seeds of strife; gossip separates the best of friends. □ Violent people mislead their companions, leading them down a harmful path. □ With narrowed eyes, people plot evil; with a smirk, they plan their mischief.

JUNE**10**

1 KINGS 7:1-51
Solomon built the Temple first and then began work on his own palace. Watch the details unfold in today's reading. The grandeur of Solomon's palace mirrored the grandeur of his whole reign, the Golden Age of Israel's history.

Solomon also built a palace for himself, and it took him thirteen years to complete the construction.

²One of Solomon's buildings was called the Palace of the Forest of Lebanon. It was 150 feet long, 75 feet wide, and 45 feet high.* There were four rows of cedar pillars, and great cedar beams rested on the pillars. ³The hall had a cedar roof. Above the beams on the pillars were forty-five side rooms,* arranged in three tiers of fifteen each. ⁴On each end of the long hall were three rows of windows facing each other. ⁵All the doorways and doorposts* had rectangular frames and were arranged in sets of three, facing each other.

⁶Solomon also built the Hall of Pillars, which was 75 feet long and 45 feet wide.* There was a porch in front, along with a canopy supported by pillars.

⁷Solomon also built the throne room, known as the Hall of Justice, where he sat to hear legal matters. It was paneled with cedar from floor to ceiling.* ⁸Solomon's living quarters surrounded a courtyard behind this hall, and they were constructed the same way. He also built similar living quarters for Pharaoh's daughter, whom he had married.

⁹From foundation to eaves, all these buildings were built from huge blocks of high-quality stone, cut with saws and trimmed to exact measure on all sides. ¹⁰Some of the huge foundation stones were 15 feet long, and some were 12 feet* long. ¹¹The blocks of high-quality stone used in the walls were also cut to measure, and cedar beams were also used. ¹²The walls of the great courtyard were built so that there was one layer of cedar beams between every three layers of finished stone, just like the walls of the inner courtyard of the LORD's Temple with its entry room.

¹³King Solomon then asked for a man

named Huram* to come from Tyre. [14]He was half Israelite, since his mother was a widow from the tribe of Naphtali, and his father had been a craftsman in bronze from Tyre. Huram was extremely skillful and talented in any work in bronze, and he came to do all the metal work for King Solomon.

[15]Huram cast two bronze pillars, each 27 feet tall and 18 feet in circumference.* [16]For the tops of the pillars he cast bronze capitals, each 7½ feet* tall. [17]Each capital was decorated with seven sets of latticework and interwoven chains. [18]He also encircled the latticework with two rows of pomegranates to decorate the capitals over the pillars. [19]The capitals on the columns inside the entry room were shaped like water lilies, and they were six feet* tall. [20]The capitals on the two pillars had 200 pomegranates in two rows around them, beside the rounded surface next to the latticework. [21]Huram set the pillars at the entrance of the Temple, one toward the south and one toward the north. He named the one on the south Jakin, and the one on the north Boaz.* [22]The capitals on the pillars were shaped like water lilies. And so the work on the pillars was finished.

[23]Then Huram cast a great round basin, 15 feet across from rim to rim, called the Sea. It was 7½ feet deep and about 45 feet in circumference.* [24]It was encircled just below its rim by two rows of decorative gourds. There were about six gourds per foot* all the way around, and they were cast as part of the basin.

[25]The Sea was placed on a base of twelve bronze oxen,* all facing outward. Three faced north, three faced west, three faced south, and three faced east, and the Sea rested on them. [26]The walls of the Sea were about three inches* thick, and its rim flared out like a cup and resembled a water lily blossom. It could hold about 11,000 gallons* of water.

[27]Huram also made ten bronze water carts, each 6 feet long, 6 feet wide, and 4½ feet tall.* [28]They were constructed with side panels braced with crossbars. [29]Both the panels and the crossbars were decorated with carved lions, oxen, and cherubim. Above and below the lions and

oxen were wreath decorations. [30]Each of these carts had four bronze wheels and bronze axles. There were supporting posts for the bronze basins at the corners of the carts; these supports were decorated on each side with carvings of wreaths. [31]The top of each cart had a rounded frame for the basin. It projected 1½ feet* above the cart's top like a round pedestal, and its opening was 2¼ feet* across; it was decorated on the outside with carvings of wreaths. The panels of the carts were square, not round. [32]Under the panels were four wheels that were connected to axles that had been cast as one unit with the cart. The wheels were 2¼ feet in diameter [33]and were similar to chariot wheels. The axles, spokes, rims, and hubs were all cast from molten bronze.

[34]There were handles at each of the four corners of the carts, and these, too, were cast as one unit with the cart. [35]Around the top of each cart was a rim nine inches wide.* The corner supports and side panels were cast as one unit with the cart. [36]Carvings of cherubim, lions, and palm trees decorated the panels and corner supports wherever there was room, and there were wreaths all around. [37]All ten water carts were the same size and were made alike, for each was cast from the same mold.

[38]Huram also made ten smaller bronze basins, one for each cart. Each basin was six feet across and could hold 220 gallons* of water. [39]He set five water carts on the south side of the Temple and five on the north side. The great bronze basin called the Sea was placed near the southeast corner of the Temple. [40]He also made the necessary washbasins, shovels, and bowls.

So at last Huram completed everything King Solomon had assigned him to make for the Temple of the LORD:

[41] the two pillars;
the two bowl-shaped capitals on top of the pillars;
the two networks of interwoven chains that decorated the capitals;
[42] the 400 pomegranates that hung from the chains on the capitals (two rows of pomegranates for each of the

chain networks that decorated the capitals on top of the pillars); 43 the ten water carts holding the ten basins; 44 the Sea and the twelve oxen under it; 45 the ash buckets, the shovels, and the bowls.

Huram made all these things of burnished bronze for the Temple of the LORD, just as King Solomon had directed. 46The king had them cast in clay molds in the Jordan Valley between Succoth and Zarethan. 47 Solomon did not weigh all these things because there were so many; the weight of the bronze could not be measured.

48Solomon also made all the furnishings of the Temple of the LORD:

the gold altar;
the gold table for the Bread of the Presence;
49 the lampstands of solid gold, five on the south and five on the north, in front of the Most Holy Place;
the flower decorations, lamps, and tongs—all of gold;
50 the small bowls, lamp snuffers, bowls, dishes, and incense burners—all of solid gold;
the doors for the entrances to the Most Holy Place and the main room of the Temple, with their fronts overlaid with gold.

51So King Solomon finished all his work on the Temple of the LORD. Then he brought all the gifts his father, David, had dedicated—the silver, the gold, and the various articles—and he stored them in the treasuries of the LORD's Temple.

7:2 Hebrew *100 cubits* [46 meters] *long, 50 cubits* [23 meters] *wide, and 30 cubits* [13.5 meters] *high.*   7:3 Or *45 rafters,* or *45 beams,* or *45 pillars.* The architectural details in 7:2-6 can be interpreted in many different ways.   7:5 Greek version reads *windows.*   7:6 Hebrew *50 cubits* [23 meters] *long and 30 cubits* [13.8 meters] *wide.*   7:7 As in Syriac version and Latin Vulgate; Hebrew reads *from floor to floor.*   7:10 Hebrew *10 cubits* [4.6 meters] . . . *8 cubits* [3.7 meters].   7:13 Hebrew *Hiram* (also in 7:40, 45); compare 2 Chr 2:13. This is not the same person mentioned in 5:1.   7:15 Hebrew *18 cubits* [8.3 meters] *tall and 12 cubits* [5.5 meters] *in circumference.*   7:16 Hebrew *5 cubits* [2.3 meters].   7:19 Hebrew *4 cubits* [1.8 meters]; also in 7:38.   7:21 *Jakin* probably means "he establishes"; *Boaz* probably means "in him is strength."   7:23 Hebrew *10 cubits* [4.6 meters] *across.* . . . *5 cubits* [2.3 meters] *deep and 30 cubits* [13.8 meters] *in circumference.*   7:24 Or *20 gourds per meter;* Hebrew reads *10 per cubit.*   7:25 Hebrew *12 oxen;* compare 2 Kgs 16:17, which specifies *bronze oxen.*   7:26a Hebrew *a handbreadth* [8 centimeters].

7:26b Hebrew *2,000 baths* [42 kiloliters].   7:27 Hebrew *4 cubits* [1.8 meters] *long, 4 cubits wide, and 3 cubits* [1.4 meters] *high.*   7:31a Hebrew *a cubit* [46 centimeters].   7:31b Hebrew *1½ cubits* [69 centimeters]; also in 7:32.   7:35 Hebrew *half a cubit wide* [23 centimeters].   7:38 Hebrew *40 baths* [840 liters].

ACTS 7:30-50
Stephen connected the dots from Jewish history to the coming of Jesus, the promised Messiah.

"Forty years later, in the desert near Mount Sinai, an angel appeared to Moses in the flame of a burning bush. 31When Moses saw it, he was amazed at the sight. As he went to take a closer look, the voice of the LORD called out to him, 32'I am the God of your ancestors—the God of Abraham, Isaac, and Jacob.' Moses shook with terror and did not dare to look.

33"Then the LORD said to him, 'Take off your sandals, for you are standing on holy ground. 34I have certainly seen the oppression of my people in Egypt. I have heard their groans and have come down to rescue them. Now go, for I am sending you back to Egypt.'*

35"So God sent back the same man his people had previously rejected when they demanded, 'Who made you a ruler and judge over us?' Through the angel who appeared to him in the burning bush, God sent Moses to be their ruler and savior. 36And by means of many wonders and miraculous signs, he led them out of Egypt, through the Red Sea, and through the wilderness for forty years.

37"Moses himself told the people of Israel, 'God will raise up for you a Prophet like me from among your own people.'* 38Moses was with our ancestors, the assembly of God's people in the wilderness, when the angel spoke to him at Mount Sinai. And there Moses received life-giving words to pass on to us.*

39"But our ancestors refused to listen to Moses. They rejected him and wanted to return to Egypt. 40They told Aaron, 'Make us some gods who can lead us, for we don't know what has become of this Moses, who brought us out of Egypt.' 41So they made an idol shaped like a calf, and they sacrificed to it and celebrated over this thing they had made. 42Then God turned away from them and abandoned them to serve the stars of heaven as their gods! In the book of the prophets it is written,

'Was it to me you were bringing
sacrifices and offerings
during those forty years in the
wilderness, Israel?
[43] No, you carried your pagan gods—
the shrine of Molech,
the star of your god Rephan,
and the images you made
to worship them.
So I will send you into exile
as far away as Babylon.'*

[44]"Our ancestors carried the Tabernacle* with them through the wilderness. It was constructed according to the plan God had shown to Moses. [45]Years later, when Joshua led our ancestors in battle against the nations that God drove out of this land, the Tabernacle was taken with them into their new territory. And it stayed there until the time of King David.
[46]"David found favor with God and asked for the privilege of building a permanent Temple for the God of Jacob.* [47]But it was Solomon who actually built it. [48]However, the Most High doesn't live in temples made by human hands. As the prophet says,

[49] 'Heaven is my throne,
and the earth is my footstool.
Could you build me a temple as good
as that?'
asks the LORD.

'Could you build me such a resting
place?
[50] Didn't my hands make both heaven
and earth?'*"

7:31-34 Exod 3:5-10.   **7:37** Deut 18:15.   **7:38** Some manuscripts read *to you.*   **7:42-43** Amos 5:25-27 (Greek version).   **7:44** Greek *the tent of witness.*   **7:46** Some manuscripts read *the house of Jacob.*   **7:49-50** Isa 66:1-2.

PSALM 128:1-6
*A song for pilgrims ascending
to Jerusalem.*

[1] **H**ow joyful are those who fear the
LORD—
all who follow his ways!
[2] You will enjoy the fruit of
your labor.
How joyful and prosperous
you will be!
[3] Your wife will be like a fruitful
grapevine,
flourishing within your home.
Your children will be like vigorous
young olive trees
as they sit around your table.
[4] That is the LORD's blessing
for those who fear him.

[5] May the LORD continually bless you
from Zion.
May you see Jerusalem prosper
as long as you live.
[6] May you live to enjoy your
grandchildren.
May Israel have peace!

HOW WE LIVE | Aging

PROVERBS 16:31 As followers of Christ, we do not need to fear old age. We have assurance from the Scriptures that we will never outlive our value to God. Proverbs teaches us that the gray hair we try so hard to hide is actually "a crown of glory." • Do you fear the physical effects of aging? Are you concerned that your later decades of life might bring serious health problems or a loss of independence? Perhaps you are worried about living on a reduced income: Will your financial needs be met after you retire? • Scripture contains reassurance from our heavenly Father that he will not abandon us in our later years. Consider this wonderful promise from Isaiah 46:4: "I will be your God throughout your lifetime—until your hair is white with age. I made you, and I will care for you. I will carry you along and save you" (see September 25). • You're never too old for God. He continues to walk with you every day of your life—and then from there into eternity.

PROVERBS 16:31-33

Gray hair is a crown of glory; it is gained by living a godly life. □ Better to be patient than powerful; better to have self-control than to conquer a city. □ We may throw the dice,* but the LORD determines how they fall.

16:33 Hebrew *We may cast lots.*

JUNE**11**

1 KINGS 8:1-66

The Ark of the Lord's Covenant was the most sacred religious item of the Israelite nation. It was kept in the innermost chamber of the Tabernacle and Temple, for it was the place where God had his throne on earth.

Solomon then summoned to Jerusalem the elders of Israel and all the heads of the tribes—the leaders of the ancestral families of the Israelites. They were to bring the Ark of the LORD's Covenant to the Temple from its location in the City of David, also known as Zion. ²So all the men of Israel assembled before King Solomon at the annual Festival of Shelters, which is held in early autumn in the month of Ethanim.*

³When all the elders of Israel arrived, the priests picked up the Ark. ⁴The priests and Levites brought up the Ark of the LORD along with the special tent* and all the sacred items that had been in it. ⁵There, before the Ark, King Solomon and the entire community of Israel sacrificed so many sheep, goats, and cattle that no one could keep count!

⁶Then the priests carried the Ark of the LORD's Covenant into the inner sanctuary of the Temple—the Most Holy Place—and placed it beneath the wings of the cherubim. ⁷The cherubim spread their wings over the Ark, forming a canopy over the Ark and its carrying poles. ⁸These poles were so long that their ends could be seen from the Temple's main room—the Holy Place—but not from the outside. They are still there to this day. ⁹Nothing was in the Ark except the two stone tablets that Moses had placed in it at Mount Sinai,* where the LORD made a covenant with the people of Israel when they left the land of Egypt.

¹⁰When the priests came out of the Holy Place, a thick cloud filled the Temple of the LORD. ¹¹The priests could not continue their service because of the cloud, for the glorious presence of the LORD filled the Temple.

¹²Then Solomon prayed, "O LORD, you have said that you would live in a thick cloud of darkness. ¹³Now I have built a glorious Temple for you, a place where you can live forever!*"

¹⁴Then the king turned around to the entire community of Israel standing before him and gave this blessing: ¹⁵"Praise the LORD, the God of Israel, who has kept the promise he made to my father, David. For he told my father, ¹⁶'From the day I brought my people Israel out of Egypt, I have never chosen a city among any of the tribes of Israel as the place where a Temple should be built to honor my name. But I have chosen David to be king over my people Israel.'"

¹⁷Then Solomon said, "My father, David, wanted to build this Temple to honor the name of the LORD, the God of Israel. ¹⁸But the LORD told him, 'You wanted to build the Temple to honor my name. Your intention is good, ¹⁹but you are not the one to do it. One of your own sons will build the Temple to honor me.'

²⁰"And now the LORD has fulfilled the promise he made, for I have become king in my father's place, and I now sit on the throne of Israel, just as the LORD promised. I have built this Temple to honor the name of the LORD, the God of Israel. ²¹And I have prepared a place there for the Ark, which contains the covenant that the LORD made with our ancestors when he brought them out of Egypt."

²²Then Solomon stood before the altar of the LORD in front of the entire community of Israel. He lifted his hands toward heaven, ²³and he prayed,

"O LORD, God of Israel, there is no God like you in all of heaven above or on the earth below. You keep your covenant and show unfailing love to all who walk before you in wholehearted devotion. ²⁴You have kept your promise to your servant David, my father. You made that promise with your own mouth, and with your own hands you have fulfilled it today.

²⁵"And now, O LORD, God of Israel, carry out the additional promise you made to your servant David, my father. For you said to him, 'If your descendants guard their behavior and faithfully follow me as you have done, one of them will always sit on the throne of Israel.' ²⁶Now, O God of Israel, fulfill this promise to your servant David, my father.

²⁷"But will God really live on earth? Why, even the highest heavens cannot contain you. How much less this Temple I have built! ²⁸Nevertheless, listen to my prayer and my plea, O LORD my God. Hear the cry and the prayer that your servant is making to you today. ²⁹May you watch over this Temple night and day, this place where you have said, 'My name will be there.' May you always hear the prayers I make toward this place. ³⁰May you hear the humble and earnest requests from me and your people Israel when we pray toward this place. Yes, hear us from heaven where you live, and when you hear, forgive.

³¹"If someone wrongs another person and is required to take an oath of innocence in front of your altar in this Temple, ³²then hear from heaven and judge between your servants—the accuser and the accused. Punish the guilty as they deserve. Acquit the innocent because of their innocence.

³³"If your people Israel are defeated by their enemies because they have sinned against you, and if they turn to you and acknowledge your name and pray to you here in this Temple, ³⁴then hear from heaven and forgive the sin of your people Israel and return them to this land you gave their ancestors.

³⁵"If the skies are shut up and there is no rain because your people have sinned against you, and if they pray toward this Temple and acknowledge your name and turn from their sins because you have punished them, ³⁶then hear from heaven and forgive the sins of your servants, your people Israel. Teach them to follow the right path, and send rain on your land that you have given to your people as their special possession.

³⁷"If there is a famine in the land or a plague or crop disease or attacks of locusts or caterpillars, or if your people's enemies are in the land besieging their towns—whatever disaster or disease there is—³⁸and if your people Israel pray about their troubles, raising their hands toward this Temple, ³⁹then hear from heaven where you live, and forgive. Give your people what their actions deserve, for you alone know each human heart. ⁴⁰Then they will fear you as long as they live in the land you gave to our ancestors.

⁴¹"In the future, foreigners who do not belong to your people Israel will hear of you. They will come from distant lands because of your name, ⁴²for they will hear of your great name and your strong hand and your powerful arm. And when they pray toward this Temple, ⁴³then hear from heaven where you live, and grant what they ask of you. In this way, all the people of the earth will come to know and fear you, just as your own people Israel do. They, too, will know that this Temple I have built honors your name.

⁴⁴"If your people go out where you send them to fight their enemies, and if they pray to the LORD by turning toward this city you have chosen and toward this Temple I have built to honor your name, ⁴⁵then hear their prayers from heaven and uphold their cause.

⁴⁶"If they sin against you—and who has never sinned?—you might become angry with them and let their enemies conquer them and take them captive to their land far away or near. ⁴⁷But in that land of exile, they might turn to you in repentance and pray, 'We have sinned, done evil, and acted wickedly.' ⁴⁸If they turn to you with their whole heart and soul in the land of their enemies and pray toward the land you gave to their ancestors—toward this city you have chosen, and toward this Temple I have built to honor your name—⁴⁹then hear their prayers and their petition from heaven where you live, and uphold their cause. ⁵⁰Forgive your people who have sinned against you. Forgive all the offenses they have committed against you. Make their captors merciful to them, ⁵¹for they are your people—your special possession—whom you brought out of the iron-smelting furnace of Egypt.

⁵²"May your eyes be open to my requests and to the requests of your people Israel. May you hear and answer them whenever they cry out to you. ⁵³For when you brought our ancestors out of Egypt, O Sovereign LORD, you told your servant Moses that you had set Israel apart from all the nations of the earth to be your own special possession."

⁵⁴When Solomon finished making these prayers and petitions to the LORD, he stood up in front of the altar of the LORD, where he had been kneeling with his hands raised toward heaven. ⁵⁵He stood and in a loud voice blessed the entire congregation of Israel:

⁵⁶"Praise the LORD who has given rest to his people Israel, just as he promised. Not one word has failed of all the wonderful promises he gave through his servant Moses. ⁵⁷May the LORD our God be with us as he was with our ancestors; may he never leave us or abandon us. ⁵⁸May he give us the desire to do his will in everything and to obey all the commands, decrees, and regulations that he gave our ancestors. ⁵⁹And may these words that I have prayed in the presence of the LORD

be before him constantly, day and night, so that the LORD our God may give justice to me and to his people Israel, according to each day's needs. ⁶⁰Then people all over the earth will know that the LORD alone is God and there is no other. ⁶¹And may you be completely faithful to the LORD our God. May you always obey his decrees and commands, just as you are doing today."

⁶²Then the king and all Israel with him offered sacrifices to the LORD. ⁶³Solomon offered to the LORD a peace offering of 22,000 cattle and 120,000 sheep and goats. And so the king and all the people of Israel dedicated the Temple of the LORD.

⁶⁴That same day the king consecrated the central area of the courtyard in front of the LORD's Temple. He offered burnt offerings, grain offerings, and the fat of peace offerings there, because the bronze altar in the LORD's presence was too small to hold all the burnt offerings, grain offerings, and the fat of the peace offerings.

⁶⁵Then Solomon and all Israel celebrated the Festival of Shelters* in the presence of the LORD our God. A large congregation had gathered from as far away as Lebo-hamath in the north and the Brook of Egypt in the south. The celebration went on for fourteen days in all—seven days for the dedication of the altar and seven days for the Festival of Shelters.* ⁶⁶After the festival was over,* Solomon sent the people home. They blessed the king and went to their homes joyful and glad because the LORD had been good to his servant David and to his people Israel.

8:2 Hebrew *at the festival in the month Ethanim, which is the seventh month.* The Festival of Shelters began on the fifteenth day of the seventh month of the ancient Hebrew lunar calendar. This day occurred in late September, October, or early November. 8:4 Hebrew *the Tent of Meeting;* i.e., the tent mentioned in 2 Sam 6:17 and 1 Chr 16:1. 8:9 Hebrew *at Horeb,* another name for Sinai. 8:13 Some Greek texts add the line *Is this not written in the Book of Jashar?* 8:65a Hebrew *the festival;* see note on 8:2. 8:65b Hebrew *seven days and seven days, fourteen days;* compare parallel text at 2 Chr 7:8-10. 8:66 Hebrew *On the eighth day,* probably referring to the day following the seven-day Festival of Shelters; compare parallel text at 2 Chr 7:9-10.

ACTS 7:51–8:13

It's easy to remember the mob rule that surrounded Jesus' death as you witness Stephen's martyrdom. Stephen's death sent a distinct message: Faith in

Jesus is something not only worth living for but also worth dying for.

"You stubborn people! You are heathen* at heart and deaf to the truth. Must you forever resist the Holy Spirit? That's what your ancestors did, and so do you! 52Name one prophet your ancestors didn't persecute! They even killed the ones who predicted the coming of the Righteous One— the Messiah whom you betrayed and murdered. 53You deliberately disobeyed God's law, even though you received it from the hands of angels."

54The Jewish leaders were infuriated by Stephen's accusation, and they shook their fists at him in rage.* 55But Stephen, full of the Holy Spirit, gazed steadily into heaven and saw the glory of God, and he saw Jesus standing in the place of honor at God's right hand. 56And he told them, "Look, I see the heavens opened and the Son of Man standing in the place of honor at God's right hand!"

57Then they put their hands over their ears and began shouting. They rushed at him 58and dragged him out of the city and began to stone him. His accusers took off their coats and laid them at the feet of a young man named Saul.*

59As they stoned him, Stephen prayed, "Lord Jesus, receive my spirit." 60He fell to his knees, shouting, "Lord, don't charge them with this sin!" And with that, he died.

8:1SAUL was one of the witnesses, and he agreed completely with the killing of Stephen.

A great wave of persecution began that day, sweeping over the church in Jerusalem; and all the believers except the apostles were scattered through the regions of Judea and Samaria. 2(Some devout men came and buried Stephen with great mourning.) 3But Saul was going everywhere to destroy the church. He went from house to house, dragging out both men and women to throw them into prison.

4But the believers who were scattered preached the Good News about Jesus wherever they went. 5Philip, for example, went to the city of Samaria and told the people there about the Messiah. 6Crowds listened intently to Philip because they were eager to hear his message and see the miraculous signs he did. 7Many evil* spirits were cast out, screaming as they left their victims. And many who had been paralyzed or lame were healed. 8So there was great joy in that city.

9A man named Simon had been a sorcerer there for many years, amazing the people of Samaria and claiming to be someone great. 10Everyone, from the least to the greatest, often spoke of him as "the Great One—the Power of God." 11They listened closely to him because for a long time he had astounded them with his magic. 12But now the people believed Philip's

---

HOW WE LIVE

Sharing our faith

ACTS 8:4-8 The Philip in this passage was not the apostle Philip; this is one of the seven men who had been chosen to help with the food distribution program in the church (see Acts 6:3-5, June 9). Along with that important duty, Philip was led by the Holy Spirit to preach, convert, and heal in a city in Samaria. • God uses all kinds of people to spread his Good News. From this story, you learn that you don't need to be a preacher or evangelist to share your faith. You just need to follow the Holy Spirit as he leads you to someone who needs to hear the Good News of salvation. You may not always feel comfortable—Philip may not have been comfortable venturing into Samaritan territory—but he went anyway. You may not feel knowledgeable enough, but Philip didn't decide that only the apostles could share the Good News. Instead, he followed the Spirit and went with the knowledge he had. God did the rest.

message of Good News concerning the Kingdom of God and the name of Jesus Christ. As a result, many men and women were baptized. ¹³Then Simon himself believed and was baptized. He began following Philip wherever he went, and he was amazed by the signs and great miracles Philip performed.

7:51 Greek *uncircumcised.* **7:54** Greek *they were grinding their teeth against him.* **7:58** Saul is later called Paul; see 13:9. **8:7** Greek *unclean.*

PSALM 129:1-8
A song for pilgrims ascending to Jerusalem.

¹ From my earliest youth my enemies
  have persecuted me.
  Let all Israel repeat this:
² From my earliest youth my enemies
  have persecuted me,
  but they have never defeated me.
³ My back is covered with cuts,
  as if a farmer had plowed long
  furrows.

⁴ But the LORD is good;
  he has cut me free from the ropes
  of the ungodly.

⁵ May all who hate Jerusalem*
  be turned back in shameful
  defeat.
⁶ May they be as useless as grass
  on a rooftop,
  turning yellow when only
  half grown,
⁷ ignored by the harvester,
  despised by the binder.
⁸ And may those who pass by
  refuse to give them this
  blessing:
"The LORD bless you;
  we bless you in the LORD's name."

129:5 Hebrew *Zion.*

PROVERBS 17:1
Better a dry crust eaten in peace than a house filled with feasting—and conflict.

JUNE**12**

1 KINGS 9:1-10:29
Solomon ushered in a golden age in Israel's history. He spent twenty years constructing extravagant buildings, brought Israel to political prominence, and built a reputation as a wise king.

So Solomon finished building the Temple of the LORD, as well as the royal palace. He completed everything he had planned to do. ²Then the LORD appeared to Solomon a second time, as he had done before at Gibeon. ³The LORD said to him,

"I have heard your prayer and your petition. I have set this Temple apart to be holy—this place you have built where my name will be honored forever. I will always watch over it, for it is dear to my heart. ⁴"As for you, if you will follow me with integrity and godliness, as David your father did, obeying all my commands, decrees, and regulations, ⁵then I will establish the throne of

your dynasty over Israel forever. For I made this promise to your father, David: 'One of your descendants will always sit on the throne of Israel.'

⁶"But if you or your descendants abandon me and disobey the commands and decrees I have given you, and if you serve and worship other gods, ⁷then I will uproot Israel from this land that I have given them. I will reject this Temple that I have made holy to honor my name. I will make Israel an object of mockery and ridicule among the nations. ⁸And though this Temple is impressive now, all who pass by will be appalled and will shake their heads in amazement. They will ask, 'Why did the LORD do such terrible things to this land and to this Temple?'

⁹"And the answer will be, 'Because his people abandoned the LORD their

God, who brought their ancestors out of Egypt, and they worshiped other gods instead and bowed down to them. That is why the LORD has brought all these disasters on them.'"

¹⁰It took Solomon twenty years to build the LORD's Temple and his own royal palace. At the end of that time, ¹¹he gave twenty towns in the land of Galilee to King Hiram of Tyre. (Hiram had previously provided all the cedar and cypress timber and gold that Solomon had requested.) ¹²But when Hiram came from Tyre to see the towns Solomon had given him, he was not at all pleased with them. ¹³"What kind of towns are these, my brother?" he asked. So Hiram called that area Cabul (which means "worthless"), as it is still known today. ¹⁴Nevertheless, Hiram paid* Solomon 9,000 pounds* of gold.

¹⁵This is the account of the forced labor that King Solomon conscripted to build the LORD's Temple, the royal palace, the supporting terraces,* the wall of Jerusalem, and the cities of Hazor, Megiddo, and Gezer. ¹⁶(Pharaoh, the king of Egypt, had attacked and captured Gezer, killing the Canaanite population and burning it down. He gave the city to his daughter as a wedding gift when she married Solomon. ¹⁷So Solomon rebuilt the city of Gezer.) He also built up the towns of Lower Beth-horon, ¹⁸Baalath, and Tamar* in the wilderness within his land. ¹⁹He built towns as supply centers and constructed towns where his chariots and horses* could be stationed. He built everything he desired in Jerusalem and Lebanon and throughout his entire realm.

²⁰There were still some people living in the land who were not Israelites, including Amorites, Hittites, Perizzites, Hivites, and Jebusites. ²¹These were descendants of the nations whom the people of Israel had not completely destroyed.* So Solomon conscripted them for his labor force, and they serve in the labor force to this day. ²²But Solomon did not conscript any of the Israelites for forced labor. Instead, he assigned them to serve as fighting men, government officials, officers and captains in his army, commanders of his chariots, and charioteers. ²³Solomon ap-

pointed 550 of them to supervise the people working on his various projects.

²⁴Solomon moved his wife, Pharaoh's daughter, from the City of David to the new palace he had built for her. Then he constructed the supporting terraces.

²⁵Three times each year Solomon presented burnt offerings and peace offerings on the altar he had built for the LORD. He also burned incense to the LORD. And so he finished the work of building the Temple.

²⁶King Solomon also built a fleet of ships at Ezion-geber, a port near Elath* in the land of Edom, along the shore of the Red Sea.* ²⁷Hiram sent experienced crews of sailors to sail the ships with Solomon's men. ²⁸They sailed to Ophir and brought back to Solomon some sixteen tons* of gold.

¹⁰:¹WHEN the queen of Sheba heard of Solomon's fame, which brought honor to the name of the LORD,* she came to test him with hard questions. ²She arrived in Jerusalem with a large group of attendants and a great caravan of camels loaded with spices, large quantities of gold, and precious jewels. When she met with Solomon, she talked with him about everything she had on her mind. ³Solomon had answers for all her questions; nothing was too hard for the king to explain to her. ⁴When the queen of Sheba realized how very wise Solomon was, and when she saw the palace he had built, ⁵she was overwhelmed. She was also amazed at the food on his tables, the organization of his officials and their splendid clothing, the cup-bearers, and the burnt offerings Solomon made at the Temple of the LORD.

⁶She exclaimed to the king, "Everything I heard in my country about your achievements* and wisdom is true! ⁷I didn't believe what was said until I arrived here and saw it with my own eyes. In fact, I had not heard the half of it! Your wisdom and prosperity are far beyond what I was told. ⁸How happy your people* must be! What a privilege for your officials to stand here day after day, listening to your wisdom! ⁹Praise the LORD your God, who delights in you and has placed you on the throne of Israel. Because of the LORD's

eternal love for Israel, he has made you king so you can rule with justice and righteousness."

10Then she gave the king a gift of 9,000 pounds* of gold, great quantities of spices, and precious jewels. Never again were so many spices brought in as those the queen of Sheba gave to King Solomon.

11(In addition, Hiram's ships brought gold from Ophir, and they also brought rich cargoes of red sandalwood* and precious jewels. 12The king used the sandalwood to make railings for the Temple of the LORD and the royal palace, and to construct lyres and harps for the musicians. Never before or since has there been such a supply of sandalwood.)

13King Solomon gave the queen of Sheba whatever she asked for, besides all the customary gifts he had so generously given. Then she and all her attendants returned to their own land.

14Each year Solomon received about 25 tons* of gold. 15This did not include the additional revenue he received from merchants and traders, all the kings of Arabia, and the governors of the land.

16King Solomon made 200 large shields of hammered gold, each weighing more than fifteen pounds.* 17He also made 300 smaller shields of hammered gold, each weighing nearly four pounds.* The king placed these shields in the Palace of the Forest of Lebanon.

18Then the king made a huge throne, decorated with ivory and overlaid with fine gold. 19The throne had six steps and a rounded back. There were armrests on both sides of the seat, and the figure of a lion stood on each side of the throne. 20There were also twelve other lions, one standing on each end of the six steps. No other throne in all the world could be compared with it!

21All of King Solomon's drinking cups were solid gold, as were all the utensils in the Palace of the Forest of Lebanon. They were not made of silver, for silver was considered worthless in Solomon's day!

22The king had a fleet of trading ships* that sailed with Hiram's fleet. Once every three years the ships returned, loaded with gold, silver, ivory, apes, and peacocks.*

23So King Solomon became richer and wiser than any other king on earth. 24People from every nation came to consult him and to hear the wisdom God had given him. 25Year after year everyone who visited brought him gifts of silver and gold, clothing, weapons, spices, horses, and mules.

26Solomon built up a huge force of chariots and horses.* He had 1,400 chariots and 12,000 horses. He stationed some of them in the chariot cities and some near him in Jerusalem. 27The king made silver as plentiful in Jerusalem as stone. And valuable cedar timber was as common as the sycamore-fig trees that grow in the foothills of Judah.* 28Solomon's horses were imported from Egypt* and from Cilicia*; the king's traders acquired them from Cilicia at the standard price. 29At that time chariots from Egypt could be purchased for 600 pieces of silver,* and horses for 150 pieces of silver.* They were then exported to the kings of the Hittites and the kings of Aram.

9:14a Or *For Hiram had paid.* 9:14b Hebrew *120 talents* [4,000 kilograms]. 9:15 Hebrew *the millo;* also in 9:24. The meaning of the Hebrew is uncertain. 9:18 An alternate reading in the Masoretic Text reads *Tadmor.* 9:19 Or *and charioteers.* 9:21 The Hebrew term used here refers to the complete consecration of things or people to the LORD, either by destroying them or by giving them as an offering. 9:26a As in Greek version (see also 2 Kgs 14:22; 16:6); Hebrew reads *Eloth,* a variant spelling of Elath. 9:26b Hebrew *sea of reeds.* 9:28 Hebrew *420 talents* [14 metric tons]. 10:1 Or *which was due to the name of the LORD.* The meaning of the Hebrew is uncertain. 10:6 Hebrew *your words.* 10:8 Greek and Syriac versions and Latin Vulgate read *your wives.* 10:10 Hebrew *120 talents* [4,000 kilograms]. 10:11 Hebrew *almug wood;* also in 10:12. 10:14 Hebrew *666 talents* [23 metric tons]. 10:16 Hebrew *600 shekels* [6.8 kilograms]. 10:17 Hebrew *3 minas* [1.8 kilograms]. 10:22a Hebrew *fleet of ships of Tarshish.* 10:22b Or *and baboons.* 10:26 Or *charioteers;* also in 10:26b. 10:27 Hebrew *the Shephelah.* 10:28a Possibly *Muzur,* a district near Cilicia; also in 10:29. 10:28b Hebrew *Kue,* probably another name for Cilicia. 10:29a Hebrew *600 shekels of silver,* about 15 pounds or 6.8 kilograms in weight. 10:29b Hebrew *150* [shekels], about 3.8 pounds or 1.7 kilograms in weight.

ACTS 8:14-40

Jesus had told his disciples that the Holy Spirit would give them power to take the message everywhere—"in Jerusalem, throughout Judea, in Samaria, and to the ends of the earth" (Acts 1:8, June 3). Watch the message spread from Jerusalem outward like ripples in a pond.

When the apostles in Jerusalem heard that the people of Samaria had accepted God's message, they sent Peter and John there.

[15]As soon as they arrived, they prayed for these new believers to receive the Holy Spirit. [16]The Holy Spirit had not yet come upon any of them, for they had only been baptized in the name of the Lord Jesus. [17]Then Peter and John laid their hands upon these believers, and they received the Holy Spirit.

[18]When Simon saw that the Spirit was given when the apostles laid their hands on people, he offered them money to buy this power. [19]"Let me have this power, too," he exclaimed, "so that when I lay my hands on people, they will receive the Holy Spirit!"

[20]But Peter replied, "May your money be destroyed with you for thinking God's gift can be bought! [21]You can have no part in this, for your heart is not right with God. [22]Repent of your wickedness and pray to the Lord. Perhaps he will forgive your evil thoughts, [23]for I can see that you are full of bitter jealousy and are held captive by sin."

[24]"Pray to the Lord for me," Simon exclaimed, "that these terrible things you've said won't happen to me!"

[25]After testifying and preaching the word of the Lord in Samaria, Peter and John returned to Jerusalem. And they stopped in many Samaritan villages along the way to preach the Good News.

[26]As for Philip, an angel of the Lord said to him, "Go south* down the desert road that runs from Jerusalem to Gaza." [27]So he started out, and he met the treasurer of Ethiopia, a eunuch of great authority under the Kandake, the queen of Ethiopia. The eunuch had gone to Jerusalem to worship, [28]and he was now returning. Seated in his carriage, he was reading aloud from the book of the prophet Isaiah.

[29]The Holy Spirit said to Philip, "Go over and walk along beside the carriage."

[30]Philip ran over and heard the man reading from the prophet Isaiah. Philip asked, "Do you understand what you are reading?"

[31]The man replied, "How can I, unless someone instructs me?" And he urged Philip to come up into the carriage and sit with him.

[32]The passage of Scripture he had been reading was this:

"He was led like a sheep to the
    slaughter.
And as a lamb is silent before
    the shearers,
he did not open his mouth.
[33] He was humiliated and received
    no justice.
Who can speak of his descendants?
For his life was taken from
    the earth."*

[34]The eunuch asked Philip, "Tell me, was the prophet talking about himself or someone else?" [35]So beginning with this

HOW WE LIVE

Accepting others

ACTS 8:26-39 Having followed God's leading to head toward Gaza, Philip encountered an Ethiopian government official who had great faith. This man was devout in his belief in God, so much so that he traveled a great distance to worship in Jerusalem. • Philip could have allowed his human nature to take over. He could have chosen to ignore this Ethiopian foreigner. But Philip was obedient to the Holy Spirit's direction to speak to the man. Because Philip obeyed God, this man from Ethiopia was baptized. As a result, the nation of Ethiopia was opened to the gospel of Jesus Christ. The conversion of one man brought Christianity to the power structure of another nation's government. • Sometimes God may send you to places that don't make sense. He may send you to the "desert" when you were having such a good ministry where you were. Take a lesson from Philip and follow. Someone out in that desert is thirsty and needs the water of life!

same Scripture, Philip told him the Good News about Jesus.

³⁶As they rode along, they came to some water, and the eunuch said, "Look! There's some water! Why can't I be baptized?"* ³⁸He ordered the carriage to stop, and they went down into the water, and Philip baptized him.

³⁹When they came up out of the water, the Spirit of the Lord snatched Philip away. The eunuch never saw him again but went on his way rejoicing. ⁴⁰Meanwhile, Philip found himself farther north at the town of Azotus. He preached the Good News there and in every town along the way until he came to Caesarea.

8:26 Or *Go at noon.*   **8:32-33** Isa 53:7-8 (Greek version).
8:36 Some manuscripts add verse 37, *"You can," Philip answered, "if you believe with all your heart." And the eunuch replied, "I believe that Jesus Christ is the Son of God."*

PSALM 130:1-8
A song for pilgrims ascending to Jerusalem.

¹ **F**rom the depths of despair, O Lord,
    I call for your help.
² Hear my cry, O Lord.
    Pay attention to my prayer.

JUNE**13**

1 KINGS 11:1-12:19
Solomon may have led his nation to greatness, but he wearied his people in the process. The grand construction projects he took on and the taxes to support the efforts left a bitter taste. Worse, he allowed his desire for women to overrule the wisdom that had characterized his reign.

Now King Solomon loved many foreign women. Besides Pharaoh's daughter, he married women from Moab, Ammon, Edom, Sidon, and from among the Hittites. ²The Lord had clearly instructed the people of Israel, 'You must not marry them, because they will turn your hearts to their gods.' Yet Solomon insisted on loving them anyway. ³He had 700 wives of royal birth and 300 concubines. And in fact, they did turn his heart away from the Lord.

³ Lord, if you kept a record of our sins,
    who, O Lord, could ever survive?
⁴ But you offer forgiveness,
    that we might learn to fear you.

⁵ I am counting on the Lord;
    yes, I am counting on him.
    I have put my hope in his word.
⁶ I long for the Lord
    more than sentries long
        for the dawn,
    yes, more than sentries long
        for the dawn.

⁷ O Israel, hope in the Lord;
    for with the Lord there is unfailing
        love.
    His redemption overflows.
⁸ He himself will redeem Israel
    from every kind of sin.

PROVERBS 17:2-3
A wise servant will rule over the master's disgraceful son and will share the inheritance of the master's children. □ Fire tests the purity of silver and gold, but the Lord tests the heart.

⁴In Solomon's old age, they turned his heart to worship other gods instead of being completely faithful to the Lord his God, as his father, David, had been. ⁵Solomon worshiped Ashtoreth, the goddess of the Sidonians, and Molech,* the detestable god of the Ammonites. ⁶In this way, Solomon did what was evil in the Lord's sight; he refused to follow the Lord completely, as his father, David, had done.

⁷On the Mount of Olives, east of Jerusalem,* he even built a pagan shrine for Chemosh, the detestable god of Moab, and another for Molech, the detestable god of the Ammonites. ⁸Solomon built such shrines for all his foreign wives to use for burning incense and sacrificing to their gods.

⁹The Lord was very angry with Solo-

mon, for his heart had turned away from the LORD, the God of Israel, who had appeared to him twice. [10]He had warned Solomon specifically about worshiping other gods, but Solomon did not listen to the LORD's command. [11]So now the LORD said to him, "Since you have not kept my covenant and have disobeyed my decrees, I will surely tear the kingdom away from you and give it to one of your servants. [12]But for the sake of your father, David, I will not do this while you are still alive. I will take the kingdom away from your son. [13]And even so, I will not take away the entire kingdom; I will let him be king of one tribe, for the sake of my servant David and for the sake of Jerusalem, my chosen city."

[14]Then the LORD raised up Hadad the Edomite, a member of Edom's royal family, to be Solomon's adversary. [15]Years before, David had defeated Edom. Joab, his army commander, had stayed to bury some of the Israelite soldiers who had died in battle. While there, they killed every male in Edom. [16]Joab and the army of Israel had stayed there for six months, killing them.

[17]But Hadad and a few of his father's royal officials escaped and headed for Egypt. (Hadad was just a boy at the time.) [18]They set out from Midian and went to Paran, where others joined them. Then they traveled to Egypt and went to Pharaoh, who gave them a home, food, and some land. [19]Pharaoh grew very fond of Hadad, and he gave him his wife's sister in marriage—the sister of Queen Tahpenes. [20]She bore him a son named Genubath. Tahpenes raised him* in Pharaoh's palace among Pharaoh's own sons.

[21]When the news reached Hadad in Egypt that David and his commander Joab were both dead, he said to Pharaoh, "Let me return to my own country."

[22]"Why?" Pharaoh asked him. "What do you lack here that makes you want to go home?"

"Nothing," he replied. "But even so, please let me return home."

[23]God also raised up Rezon son of Eliada as Solomon's adversary. Rezon had fled from his master, King Hadadezer of Zobah, [24]and had become the leader of a gang of rebels. After David conquered Hadadezer, Rezon and his men fled to Damascus, where he became king. [25]Rezon was Israel's bitter adversary for the rest of Solomon's reign, and he made trouble, just as Hadad did. Rezon hated Israel intensely and continued to reign in Aram.

[26]Another rebel leader was Jeroboam son of Nebat, one of Solomon's own officials. He came from the town of Zeredah in Ephraim, and his mother was Zeruah, a widow.

[27]This is the story behind his rebellion. Solomon was rebuilding the supporting terraces* and repairing the walls of the city of his father, David. [28]Jeroboam was a very capable young man, and when Solomon saw how industrious he was, he put him in charge of the labor force from the tribes of Ephraim and Manasseh, the descendants of Joseph.

[29]One day as Jeroboam was leaving Jerusalem, the prophet Ahijah from Shiloh met him along the way. Ahijah was wearing a new cloak. The two of them were alone in a field, [30]and Ahijah took hold of the new cloak he was wearing and tore it into twelve pieces. [31]Then he said to Jeroboam, "Take ten of these pieces, for this is what the LORD, the God of Israel, says: 'I am about to tear the kingdom from the hand of Solomon, and I will give ten of the tribes to you! [32]But I will leave him one tribe for the sake of my servant David and for the sake of Jerusalem, which I have chosen out of all the tribes of Israel. [33]For Solomon has* abandoned me and worshiped Ashtoreth, the goddess of the Sidonians; Chemosh, the god of Moab; and Molech, the god of the Ammonites. He has not followed my ways and done what is pleasing in my sight. He has not obeyed my decrees and regulations as David his father did.

[34]" 'But I will not take the entire kingdom from Solomon at this time. For the sake of my servant David, the one whom I chose and who obeyed my commands and decrees, I will keep Solomon as leader for the rest of his life. [35]But I will take the kingdom away from his son and give ten of the tribes to you. [36]His son will have one tribe so that the descendants of David my servant will continue to reign, shining like

a lamp in Jerusalem, the city I have chosen to be the place for my name. ³⁷And I will place you on the throne of Israel, and you will rule over all that your heart desires. ³⁸If you listen to what I tell you and follow my ways and do whatever I consider to be right, and if you obey my decrees and commands, as my servant David did, then I will always be with you. I will establish an enduring dynasty for you as I did for David, and I will give Israel to you. ³⁹Because of Solomon's sin I will punish the descendants of David—though not forever.'"

⁴⁰Solomon tried to kill Jeroboam, but he fled to King Shishak of Egypt and stayed there until Solomon died.

⁴¹The rest of the events in Solomon's reign, including all his deeds and his wisdom, are recorded in *The Book of the Acts of Solomon*. ⁴²Solomon ruled in Jerusalem over all Israel for forty years. ⁴³When he died, he was buried in the City of David, named for his father. Then his son Rehoboam became the next king.

12:1REHOBOAM went to Shechem, where all Israel had gathered to make him king. ²When Jeroboam son of Nebat heard of this, he returned from Egypt,* for he had fled to Egypt to escape from King Solomon. ³The leaders of Israel summoned him, and Jeroboam and the whole assembly of Israel went to speak with Rehoboam. ⁴"Your father was a hard master," they said. "Lighten the harsh labor demands and heavy taxes that your father imposed on us. Then we will be your loyal subjects."

⁵Rehoboam replied, "Give me three days to think this over. Then come back for my answer." So the people went away.

⁶Then King Rehoboam discussed the matter with the older men who had counseled his father, Solomon. "What is your advice?" he asked. "How should I answer these people?"

⁷The older counselors replied, "If you are willing to be a servant to these people today and give them a favorable answer, they will always be your loyal subjects."

⁸But Rehoboam rejected the advice of the older men and instead asked the opinion of the young men who had grown up with him and were now his advisers.

⁹"What is your advice?" he asked them. "How should I answer these people who want me to lighten the burdens imposed by my father?"

¹⁰The young men replied, "This is what you should tell those complainers who want a lighter burden: 'My little finger is thicker than my father's waist! ¹¹Yes, my father laid heavy burdens on you, but I'm going to make them even heavier! My father beat you with whips, but I will beat you with scorpions!'"

¹²Three days later Jeroboam and all the people returned to hear Rehoboam's decision, just as the king had ordered. ¹³But Rehoboam spoke harshly to the people, for he rejected the advice of the older counselors ¹⁴and followed the counsel of his younger advisers. He told the people, "My father laid heavy burdens on you, but I'm going to make them even heavier! My father beat you with whips, but I will beat you with scorpions!"

¹⁵So the king paid no attention to the people. This turn of events was the will of the LORD, for it fulfilled the LORD's message to Jeroboam son of Nebat through the prophet Ahijah from Shiloh.

¹⁶When all Israel realized that the king had refused to listen to them, they responded,

"Down with the dynasty of David!
We have no interest in the son of Jesse.
Back to your homes, O Israel!
Look out for your own house,
O David!"

So the people of Israel returned home. ¹⁷But Rehoboam continued to rule over the Israelites who lived in the towns of Judah.

¹⁸King Rehoboam sent Adoniram,* who was in charge of the labor force, to restore order, but the people of Israel stoned him to death. When this news reached King Rehoboam, he quickly jumped into his chariot and fled to Jerusalem. ¹⁹And to this day the northern tribes of Israel have refused to be ruled by a descendant of David.

11:5 Hebrew *Milcom*, a variant spelling of Molech; also in 11:33. **11:7** Hebrew *On the mountain east of Jerusalem.* **11:20** As in Greek version; Hebrew reads *weaned him.*

11:27 Hebrew *the millo.* The meaning of the Hebrew is uncertain.   11:33 As in Greek, Syriac, and Latin Vulgate; Hebrew reads *For they have.*   12:2 As in Greek version and Latin Vulgate (see also 2 Chr 10:2); Hebrew reads *he lived in Egypt.*   12:18 As in some Greek manuscripts and Syriac version (see also 4:6; 5:14); Hebrew reads *Adoram.*

ACTS 9:1-25

As the message of salvation spread like wildfire, the persecution of those who believed followed right behind. Saul was on a mission to find and arrest Christians. But God would literally stop him in his tracks and send him on an entirely new mission.

Meanwhile, Saul was uttering threats with every breath and was eager to kill the Lord's followers.* So he went to the high priest. ²He requested letters addressed to the synagogues in Damascus, asking for their cooperation in the arrest of any followers of the Way he found there. He wanted to bring them—both men and women—back to Jerusalem in chains.

³As he was approaching Damascus on this mission, a light from heaven suddenly shone down around him. ⁴He fell to the ground and heard a voice saying to him, "Saul! Saul! Why are you persecuting me?"

⁵"Who are you, lord?" Saul asked.

And the voice replied, "I am Jesus, the one you are persecuting! ⁶Now get up and go into the city, and you will be told what you must do."

⁷The men with Saul stood speechless, for they heard the sound of someone's voice but saw no one! ⁸Saul picked himself up off the ground, but when he opened his eyes he was blind. So his companions led him by the hand to Damascus. ⁹He remained there blind for three days and did not eat or drink.

¹⁰Now there was a believer* in Damascus named Ananias. The Lord spoke to him in a vision, calling, "Ananias!"

"Yes, Lord!" he replied.

¹¹The Lord said, "Go over to Straight Street, to the house of Judas. When you get there, ask for a man from Tarsus named Saul. He is praying to me right now. ¹²I have shown him a vision of a man named Ananias coming in and laying hands on him so he can see again."

¹³"But Lord," exclaimed Ananias, "I've heard many people talk about the terrible things this man has done to the believers* in Jerusalem! ¹⁴And he is authorized by the leading priests to arrest everyone who calls upon your name."

¹⁵But the Lord said, "Go, for Saul is my chosen instrument to take my message to the Gentiles and to kings, as well as to the people of Israel. ¹⁶And I will show him how much he must suffer for my name's sake."

¹⁷So Ananias went and found Saul. He laid his hands on him and said, "Brother Saul, the Lord Jesus, who appeared to you on the road, has sent me so that you might regain your sight and be filled with the

---

HOW WE LIVE — Standing firm in our beliefs

1 KINGS 11:1-13 Solomon's actions remind us how easy it is to know what is right but do what is wrong. Solomon didn't revolt against God all at once. Rather, his turning away from God began with a tiny departure from God's laws—he married Pharaoh's daughter (1 Kings 3:1, June 7). The Israelites had been told by God not to intermarry with foreigners because he did not want his people influenced in idol worship. At that point, Solomon still loved the Lord, but that first marriage, justified as a political alliance, led Solomon into a downward spiral. More and more political marriages ensued and these new wives brought the worship of their gods into the nation. Solomon's compromise resulted in the division of his kingdom for many centuries to follow. • While you will make mistakes in your Christian life, be sure to stay close to God and be sensitive. That first little compromise need not lead to a downward spiral if you become aware of it and turn away from that pattern.

Holy Spirit." [18]Instantly something like scales fell from Saul's eyes, and he regained his sight. Then he got up and was baptized. [19]Afterward he ate some food and regained his strength.

Saul stayed with the believers* in Damascus for a few days. [20]And immediately he began preaching about Jesus in the synagogues, saying, "He is indeed the Son of God!"

[21]All who heard him were amazed. "Isn't this the same man who caused such devastation among Jesus' followers in Jerusalem?" they asked. "And didn't he come here to arrest them and take them in chains to the leading priests?"

[22]Saul's preaching became more and more powerful, and the Jews in Damascus couldn't refute his proofs that Jesus was indeed the Messiah. [23]After a while some of the Jews plotted together to kill him. [24]They were watching for him day and night at the city gate so they could murder him, but Saul was told about their plot. [25]So during the night, some of the other believers* lowered him in a large basket through an opening in the city wall.

9:1 Greek *disciples.*   9:10 Greek *disciple;* also in 9:26, 36. 9:13 Greek *God's holy people;* also in 9:32, 41.   9:19 Greek *disciples;* also in 9:26, 38.   9:25 Greek *his disciples.*

PSALM 131:1-3
A song for pilgrims ascending to Jerusalem. A psalm of David.

[1] Lord, my heart is not proud;
    my eyes are not haughty.
I don't concern myself with matters
        too great
    or too awesome for me to grasp.
[2] Instead, I have calmed and quieted
        myself,
    like a weaned child who no longer
        cries for its mother's milk.
    Yes, like a weaned child is my soul
        within me.

[3] O Israel, put your hope in the Lord—
    now and always.

PROVERBS 17:4-5
Wrongdoers eagerly listen to gossip; liars pay close attention to slander. □ Those who mock the poor insult their Maker; those who rejoice at the misfortune of others will be punished.

JUNE**14**

1 KINGS 12:20–13:34
After Solomon's reign, the united kingdom of Israel began to fall apart. The nation eventually divided, with ten tribes forming the northern kingdom called Israel, and two tribes forming the southern kingdom called Judah.

When the people of Israel learned of Jeroboam's return from Egypt, they called an assembly and made him king over all Israel. So only the tribe of Judah remained loyal to the family of David.

[21]When Rehoboam arrived at Jerusalem, he mobilized the men of Judah and the tribe of Benjamin—180,000 select troops—to fight against the men of Israel and to restore the kingdom to himself.

[22]But God said to Shemaiah, the man of God, [23]"Say to Rehoboam son of Solomon, king of Judah, and to all the people of Judah and Benjamin, and to the rest of the people, [24]'This is what the Lord says: Do not fight against your relatives, the Israelites. Go back home, for what has happened is my doing!'" So they obeyed the message of the Lord and went home, as the Lord had commanded.

[25]Jeroboam then built up the city of Shechem in the hill country of Ephraim, and it became his capital. Later he went and built up the town of Peniel.*

[26]Jeroboam thought to himself, "Unless I am careful, the kingdom will return to the dynasty of David. [27]When these people go to Jerusalem to offer sacrifices at the Temple of the Lord, they will again

give their allegiance to King Rehoboam of Judah. They will kill me and make him their king instead."

²⁸So on the advice of his counselors, the king made two gold calves. He said to the people,* "It is too much trouble for you to worship in Jerusalem. Look, Israel, these are the gods who brought you out of Egypt!"

²⁹He placed these calf idols in Bethel and in Dan—at either end of his kingdom. ³⁰But this became a great sin, for the people worshiped the idols, traveling as far north as Dan to worship the one there.

³¹Jeroboam also erected buildings at the pagan shrines and ordained priests from the common people—those who were not from the priestly tribe of Levi. ³²And Jeroboam instituted a religious festival in Bethel, held on the fifteenth day of the eighth month,* in imitation of the annual Festival of Shelters in Judah. There at Bethel he himself offered sacrifices to the calves he had made, and he appointed priests for the pagan shrines he had made. ³³So on the fifteenth day of the eighth month, a day that he himself had designated, Jeroboam offered sacrifices on the altar at Bethel. He instituted a religious festival for Israel, and he went up to the altar to burn incense.

¹³:¹At the LORD's command, a man of God from Judah went to Bethel, arriving there just as Jeroboam was approaching the altar to burn incense. ²Then at the LORD's command, he shouted, "O altar, altar! This is what the LORD says: A child named Josiah will be born into the dynasty of David. On you he will sacrifice the priests from the pagan shrines who come here to burn incense, and human bones will be burned on you." ³That same day the man of God gave a sign to prove his message. He said, "The LORD has promised to give this sign: This altar will split apart, and its ashes will be poured out on the ground."

⁴When King Jeroboam heard the man of God speaking against the altar at Bethel, he pointed at him and shouted, "Seize that man!" But instantly the king's hand became paralyzed in that position, and he couldn't pull it back. ⁵At the same time a wide crack appeared in the altar, and the ashes poured out, just as the man of God

had predicted in his message from the LORD.

⁶The king cried out to the man of God, "Please ask the LORD your God to restore my hand again!" So the man of God prayed to the LORD, and the king's hand was restored and he could move it again.

⁷Then the king said to the man of God, "Come to the palace with me and have something to eat, and I will give you a gift."

⁸But the man of God said to the king, "Even if you gave me half of everything you own, I would not go with you. I would not eat or drink anything in this place. ⁹For the LORD gave me this command: 'You must not eat or drink anything while you are there, and do not return to Judah by the same way you came.'" ¹⁰So he left Bethel and went home another way.

¹¹As it happened, there was an old prophet living in Bethel, and his sons* came home and told him what the man of God had done in Bethel that day. They also told their father what the man had said to the king. ¹²The old prophet asked them, "Which way did he go?" So they showed their father* which road the man of God had taken. ¹³"Quick, saddle the donkey," the old man said. So they saddled the donkey for him, and he mounted it.

¹⁴Then he rode after the man of God and found him sitting under a great tree. The old prophet asked him, "Are you the man of God who came from Judah?"

"Yes, I am," he replied.

¹⁵Then he said to the man of God, "Come home with me and eat some food."

¹⁶"No, I cannot," he replied. "I am not allowed to eat or drink anything here in this place. ¹⁷For the LORD gave me this command: 'You must not eat or drink anything while you are there, and do not return to Judah by the same way you came.'"

¹⁸But the old prophet answered, "I am a prophet, too, just as you are. And an angel gave me this command from the LORD: 'Bring him home with you so he can have something to eat and drink.'" But the old man was lying to him. ¹⁹So they went back together, and the man of God ate and drank at the prophet's home.

²⁰Then while they were sitting at the table, a command from the LORD came to the old prophet. ²¹He cried out to the man

of God from Judah, "This is what the LORD says: You have defied the word of the LORD and have disobeyed the command the LORD your God gave you. [22]You came back to this place and ate and drank where he told you not to eat or drink. Because of this, your body will not be buried in the grave of your ancestors."

[23]After the man of God had finished eating and drinking, the old prophet saddled his own donkey for him, [24]and the man of God started off again. But as he was traveling along, a lion came out and killed him. His body lay there on the road, with the donkey and the lion standing beside it. [25]People who passed by saw the body lying in the road and the lion standing beside it, and they went and reported it in Bethel, where the old prophet lived.

[26]When the prophet heard the report, he said, "It is the man of God who disobeyed the LORD's command. The LORD has fulfilled his word by causing the lion to attack and kill him."

[27]Then the prophet said to his sons, "Saddle a donkey for me." So they saddled a donkey, [28]and he went out and found the body lying in the road. The donkey and lion were still standing there beside it, for the lion had not eaten the body nor attacked the donkey. [29]So the prophet laid the body of the man of God on the donkey and took it back to the town to mourn over him and bury him. [30]He laid the body in his own grave, crying out in grief, "Oh, my brother!"

[31]Afterward the prophet said to his sons, "When I die, bury me in the grave where the man of God is buried. Lay my bones beside his bones. [32]For the message the LORD told him to proclaim against the altar in Bethel and against the pagan shrines in the towns of Samaria will certainly come true."

[33]But even after this, Jeroboam did not turn from his evil ways. He continued to choose priests from the common people. He appointed anyone who wanted to become a priest for the pagan shrines. [34]This became a great sin and resulted in the utter destruction of Jeroboam's dynasty from the face of the earth.

12:25 Hebrew *Penuel*, a variant spelling of Peniel.
12:28 Hebrew *to them.* 12:32 This day of the ancient

Hebrew lunar calendar occurred in late October or early November, exactly one month after the annual Festival of Shelters in Judah (see Lev 23:34). 13:11 As in Greek version; Hebrew reads *son.* 13:12 As in Greek version; Hebrew reads *They had seen.*

ACTS 9:26-43

After having distinguished himself as a zealous persecutor of the church, Saul began claiming to be a convert to Christianity. To say the people hesitated to trust him at first would be an understatement.

When Saul arrived in Jerusalem, he tried to meet with the believers, but they were all afraid of him. They did not believe he had truly become a believer! [27]Then Barnabas brought him to the apostles and told them how Saul had seen the Lord on the way to Damascus and how the Lord had spoken to Saul. He also told them that Saul had preached boldly in the name of Jesus in Damascus.

[28]So Saul stayed with the apostles and went all around Jerusalem with them, preaching boldly in the name of the Lord. [29]He debated with some Greek-speaking Jews, but they tried to murder him. [30]When the believers* heard about this, they took him down to Caesarea and sent him away to Tarsus, his hometown.

[31]The church then had peace throughout Judea, Galilee, and Samaria, and it became stronger as the believers lived in the fear of the Lord. And with the encouragement of the Holy Spirit, it also grew in numbers.

[32]Meanwhile, Peter traveled from place to place, and he came down to visit the believers in the town of Lydda. [33]There he met a man named Aeneas, who had been paralyzed and bedridden for eight years. [34]Peter said to him, "Aeneas, Jesus Christ heals you! Get up, and roll up your sleeping mat!" And he was healed instantly. [35]Then the whole population of Lydda and Sharon saw Aeneas walking around, and they turned to the Lord.

[36]There was a believer in Joppa named Tabitha (which in Greek is Dorcas*). She was always doing kind things for others and helping the poor. [37]About this time she became ill and died. Her body was washed for burial and laid in an upstairs room. [38]But the believers had heard that Peter was nearby at Lydda, so they sent two men to beg him, "Please come as soon as possible!"

[39]So Peter returned with them; and as soon as he arrived, they took him to the upstairs room. The room was filled with widows who were weeping and showing him the coats and other clothes Dorcas had made for them. [40]But Peter asked them all to leave the room; then he knelt and prayed. Turning to the body he said, "Get up, Tabitha." And she opened her eyes! When she saw Peter, she sat up! [41]He gave her his hand and helped her up. Then he called in the widows and all the believers, and he presented her to them alive.

[42]The news spread through the whole town, and many believed in the Lord. [43]And Peter stayed a long time in Joppa, living with Simon, a tanner of hides.

9:30 Greek *brothers*.   9:36 The names *Tabitha* in Aramaic and *Dorcas* in Greek both mean "gazelle."

PSALM 132:1-18
A song for pilgrims ascending to Jerusalem.

[1] LORD, remember David
   and all that he suffered.
[2] He made a solemn promise
   to the LORD.
   He vowed to the Mighty One
   of Israel,*
[3] "I will not go home;
   I will not let myself rest.
[4] I will not let my eyes sleep
   nor close my eyelids in slumber

[5] until I find a place to build a house
   for the LORD,
   a sanctuary for the Mighty One
   of Israel."

[6] We heard that the Ark was
   in Ephrathah;
   then we found it in the distant
   countryside of Jaar.
[7] Let us go to the sanctuary
   of the LORD;
   let us worship at the footstool
   of his throne.
[8] Arise, O LORD, and enter your resting
   place,
   along with the Ark, the symbol
   of your power.
[9] May your priests be clothed
   in godliness;
   may your loyal servants sing for joy.
[10] For the sake of your servant David,
   do not reject the king you have
   anointed.
[11] The LORD swore an oath to David
   with a promise he will never take
   back:
   "I will place one of your descendants
   on your throne.
[12] If your descendants obey the terms
   of my covenant
   and the laws that I teach them,
   then your royal line
   will continue forever and ever."

HOW WE LIVE

Standing firm in our beliefs

1 KINGS 12:25-33 God planned to give Jeroboam part of Solomon's son's kingdom as punishment for Solomon's sins. God made it quite clear that if Jeroboam followed his commands, God would be with him and make his kingdom a great dynasty (11:38). Unfortunately, Jeroboam decided that God's word to him wasn't good enough. Rather than follow God's instructions and see his promise fulfilled, Jeroboam decided to do whatever was necessary to secure his position as king. In doing so, he led his people away from the God who allowed him to reign. As a result, his family line was eventually wiped out, along with his kingdom.   • Compromise with sin is not justifiable; its consequences are guaranteed. Sometimes the consequences are immediate, but often they are not, causing us to believe that we got away with our disobedience. We cannot predict the timing, or the intensity, of the result of a sin. Don't think that you know better than God or you'll learn your lesson the hard way and perhaps hurt many others along with you.

13 For the LORD has chosen Jerusalem*;
   he has desired it for his home.
14 "This is my resting place forever,"
   he said.
   "I will live here, for this is the home
   I desired.
15 I will bless this city and make
   it prosperous;
   I will satisfy its poor with food.
16 I will clothe its priests with godliness;
   its faithful servants will sing for joy.
17 Here I will increase the power
   of David;

my anointed one will be a light for
   my people.
18 I will clothe his enemies with
   shame,
   but he will be a glorious king."

132:2 Hebrew *of Jacob;* also in 132:5. See note on 44:4.
132:13 Hebrew *Zion.*

PROVERBS 17:6

Grandchildren are the crowning glory of
the aged; parents* are the pride of their
children.

17:6 Hebrew *fathers.*

JUNE**15**

1 KINGS 14:1–15:24

The remainder of the books of Kings and Chronicles
traces the dual kingdoms of Judah and Israel. The
kings who chose to follow God saw revival and
prosperity. The kings who allowed idolatry into the
kingdom saw spiritual and political decay.

At that time Jeroboam's son Abijah became very sick. ²So Jeroboam told his
wife, "Disguise yourself so that no one will
recognize you as my wife. Then go to the
prophet Ahijah at Shiloh—the man who
told me I would become king. ³Take him a
gift of ten loaves of bread, some cakes,
and a jar of honey, and ask him what will
happen to the boy."

⁴So Jeroboam's wife went to Ahijah's
home at Shiloh. He was an old man now
and could no longer see. ⁵But the LORD
had told Ahijah, "Jeroboam's wife will
come here, pretending to be someone
else. She will ask you about her son, for he
is very sick. Give her the answer I give
you."

⁶So when Ahijah heard her footsteps at
the door, he called out, "Come in, wife of
Jeroboam! Why are you pretending to be
someone else?" Then he told her, "I have
bad news for you. ⁷Give your husband,
Jeroboam, this message from the LORD,
the God of Israel: 'I promoted you from
the ranks of the common people and
made you ruler over my people Israel. ⁸I
ripped the kingdom away from the family

of David and gave it to you. But you have
not been like my servant David, who
obeyed my commands and followed me
with all his heart and always did whatever
I wanted. ⁹You have done more evil than
all who lived before you. You have made
other gods for yourself and have made me
furious with your gold calves. And since
you have turned your back on me, ¹⁰I will
bring disaster on your dynasty and will
destroy every one of your male descendants, slave and free alike, anywhere in Israel. I will burn up your royal dynasty as
one burns up trash until it is all gone.
¹¹The members of Jeroboam's family who
die in the city will be eaten by dogs, and
those who die in the field will be eaten by
vultures. I, the LORD, have spoken.'"

¹²Then Ahijah said to Jeroboam's wife,
"Go on home, and when you enter the city,
the child will die. ¹³All Israel will mourn
for him and bury him. He is the only member of your family who will have a proper
burial, for this child is the only good thing
that the LORD, the God of Israel, sees in the
entire family of Jeroboam.

¹⁴"In addition, the LORD will raise up a
king over Israel who will destroy the family of Jeroboam. This will happen today,
even now! ¹⁵Then the LORD will shake Israel like a reed whipped about in a stream.
He will uproot the people of Israel from

this good land that he gave their ancestors and will scatter them beyond the Euphrates River,* for they have angered the LORD with the Asherah poles they have set up for worship. [16]He will abandon Israel because Jeroboam sinned and made Israel sin along with him."

[17]So Jeroboam's wife returned to Tirzah, and the child died just as she walked through the door of her home. [18]And all Israel buried him and mourned for him, as the LORD had promised through the prophet Ahijah.

[19]The rest of the events in Jeroboam's reign, including all his wars and how he ruled, are recorded in *The Book of the History of the Kings of Israel.* [20]Jeroboam reigned in Israel twenty-two years. When Jeroboam died, his son Nadab became the next king.

[21]Meanwhile, Rehoboam son of Solomon was king in Judah. He was forty-one years old when he became king, and he reigned seventeen years in Jerusalem, the city the LORD had chosen from among all the tribes of Israel as the place to honor his name. Rehoboam's mother was Naamah, an Ammonite woman.

[22]During Rehoboam's reign, the people of Judah did what was evil in the LORD's sight, provoking his anger with their sin, for it was even worse than that of their ancestors. [23]For they also built for themselves pagan shrines and set up sacred pillars and Asherah poles on every high hill and under every green tree. [24]There were even male and female shrine prostitutes throughout the land. The people imitated the detestable practices of the pagan nations the LORD had driven from the land ahead of the Israelites.

[25]In the fifth year of King Rehoboam's reign, King Shishak of Egypt came up and attacked Jerusalem. [26]He ransacked the treasuries of the LORD's Temple and the royal palace; he stole everything, including all the gold shields Solomon had made. [27]King Rehoboam later replaced them with bronze shields as substitutes, and he entrusted them to the care of the commanders of the guard who protected the entrance to the royal palace. [28]Whenever the king went to the Temple of the LORD, the guards would also take the shields and then return them to the guardroom.

[29]The rest of the events in Rehoboam's reign and everything he did are recorded in *The Book of the History of the Kings of Judah.* [30]There was constant war between Rehoboam and Jeroboam. [31]When Rehoboam died, he was buried among his ancestors in the City of David. His mother was Naamah, an Ammonite woman. Then his son Abijam* became the next king.

15:1ABIJAM* began to rule over Judah in the eighteenth year of Jeroboam's reign in Israel. [2]He reigned in Jerusalem three

---

HOW WE LIVE

Responding to God

ACTS 10:5-7 Cornelius was a Roman, a Gentile, yet a man of great faith. He prayed regularly and gave generously to those in need, but he didn't have the whole story of salvation in Jesus. So God told him to send for Peter because Peter would be able to give Cornelius more knowledge and answers about the God whom he was already seeking. • Many Christians ask the question, "What will happen to those who never hear about Christ?" In this passage we find that although Cornelius wasn't a believer in Christ, he was actively seeking to please God and was reverent in his attitude toward God in prayer. Cornelius is an example of Hebrews 11:6, "Anyone who wants to come to him must believe that God exists and that he rewards those who sincerely seek him" (see November 12). God knew Cornelius was seeking, so he sent Peter to tell Cornelius about Christ. God sees sincerity of faith and will reward those who respond to his calling.

years. His mother was Maacah, the daughter of Absalom.*

³He committed the same sins as his father before him, and he was not faithful to the LORD his God, as his ancestor David had been. ⁴But for David's sake, the LORD his God allowed his descendants to continue ruling, shining like a lamp, and he gave Abijam a son to rule after him in Jerusalem. ⁵For David had done what was pleasing in the LORD's sight and had obeyed the LORD's commands throughout his life, except in the affair concerning Uriah the Hittite.

⁶There was war between Abijam and Jeroboam* throughout Abijam's reign. ⁷The rest of the events in Abijam's reign and everything he did are recorded in *The Book of the History of the Kings of Judah.* There was constant war between Abijam and Jeroboam. ⁸When Abijam died, he was buried in the City of David. Then his son Asa became the next king.

⁹Asa began to rule over Judah in the twentieth year of Jeroboam's reign in Israel. ¹⁰He reigned in Jerusalem forty-one years. His grandmother* was Maacah, the daughter of Absalom.

¹¹Asa did what was pleasing in the LORD's sight, as his ancestor David had done. ¹²He banished the male and female shrine prostitutes from the land and got rid of all the idols* his ancestors had made. ¹³He even deposed his grandmother Maacah from her position as queen mother because she had made an obscene Asherah pole. He cut down her obscene pole and burned it in the Kidron Valley. ¹⁴Although the pagan shrines were not removed, Asa's heart remained completely faithful to the LORD throughout his life. ¹⁵He brought into the Temple of the LORD the silver and gold and the various items that he and his father had dedicated.

¹⁶There was constant war between King Asa of Judah and King Baasha of Israel. ¹⁷King Baasha of Israel invaded Judah and fortified Ramah in order to prevent anyone from entering or leaving King Asa's territory in Judah.

¹⁸Asa responded by removing all the silver and gold that was left in the treasuries of the Temple of the LORD and the royal palace. He sent it with some of his officials to Ben-hadad son of Tabrimmon, son of Hezion, the king of Aram, who was ruling in Damascus, along with this message:

> ¹⁹"Let there be a treaty* between you and me like the one between your father and my father. See, I am sending you a gift of silver and gold. Break your treaty with King Baasha of Israel so that he will leave me alone."

²⁰Ben-hadad agreed to King Asa's request and sent the commanders of his army to attack the towns of Israel. They conquered the towns of Ijon, Dan, Abel-beth-maacah, and all Kinnereth, and all the land of Naphtali. ²¹As soon as Baasha of Israel heard what was happening, he abandoned his project of fortifying Ramah and withdrew to Tirzah. ²²Then King Asa sent an order throughout Judah, requiring that everyone, without exception, help to carry away the building stones and timbers that Baasha had been using to fortify Ramah. Asa used these materials to fortify the town of Geba in Benjamin and the town of Mizpah.

²³The rest of the events in Asa's reign—the extent of his power, everything he did, and the names of the cities he built—are recorded in *The Book of the History of the Kings of Judah.* In his old age his feet became diseased. ²⁴When Asa died, he was buried with his ancestors in the City of David.

Then Jehoshaphat, Asa's son, became the next king.

14:15 Hebrew *the river.* 14:31 Also known as *Abijah.* 15:1 Also known as *Abijah.* 15:2 Hebrew *Abishalom* (also in 15:10), a variant spelling of Absalom; compare 2 Chr 11:20. 15:6 As in a few Hebrew and Greek manuscripts; most Hebrew manuscripts read *between Rehoboam and Jeroboam.* 15:10 Or *The queen mother;* Hebrew reads *His mother* (also in 15:13); compare 15:2. 15:12 The Hebrew term (literally *round things*) probably alludes to dung. 15:19 As in Greek version; Hebrew reads *There is a treaty.*

ACTS 10:1-23

God used a dream about eating "unclean" animals to help Peter make a mental shift—namely, that the gospel message was meant to go not just to the Jews, but also to Gentiles.

In Caesarea there lived a Roman army officer* named Cornelius, who was a captain of the Italian Regiment. ²He was a devout, God-fearing man, as was everyone in his household. He gave generously to the poor and prayed regularly to God. [3]One afternoon about three o'clock, he had a vision in which he saw an angel of God coming toward him. "Cornelius!" the angel said.

[4]Cornelius stared at him in terror. "What is it, sir?" he asked the angel.

And the angel replied, "Your prayers and gifts to the poor have been received by God as an offering! [5]Now send some men to Joppa, and summon a man named Simon Peter. [6]He is staying with Simon, a tanner who lives near the seashore."

[7]As soon as the angel was gone, Cornelius called two of his household servants and a devout soldier, one of his personal attendants. [8]He told them what had happened and sent them off to Joppa.

[9]The next day as Cornelius's messengers were nearing the town, Peter went up on the flat roof to pray. It was about noon, [10]and he was hungry. But while a meal was being prepared, he fell into a trance. [11]He saw the sky open, and something like a large sheet was let down by its four corners. [12]In the sheet were all sorts of animals, reptiles, and birds. [13]Then a voice said to him, "Get up, Peter; kill and eat them."

[14]"No, Lord," Peter declared. "I have never eaten anything that our Jewish laws have declared impure and unclean.*"

[15]But the voice spoke again: "Do not call something unclean if God has made it clean." [16]The same vision was repeated three times. Then the sheet was suddenly pulled up to heaven.

[17]Peter was very perplexed. What could the vision mean? Just then the men sent by Cornelius found Simon's house. Standing outside the gate, [18]they asked if a man named Simon Peter was staying there.

[19]Meanwhile, as Peter was puzzling over the vision, the Holy Spirit said to him, "Three men have come looking for you. [20]Get up, go downstairs, and go with them without hesitation. Don't worry, for I have sent them."

[21]So Peter went down and said, "I'm the man you are looking for. Why have you come?"

[22]They said, "We were sent by Cornelius, a Roman officer. He is a devout and God-fearing man, well respected by all the Jews. A holy angel instructed him to summon you to his house so that he can hear your message." [23]So Peter invited the men to stay for the night. The next day he went with them, accompanied by some of the brothers from Joppa.

10:1 Greek *a centurion;* similarly in 10:22.   10:14 Greek *anything common and unclean.*

PSALM 133:1-3
A song for pilgrims ascending to Jerusalem. A psalm of David.

[1] **H**ow wonderful and pleasant it is
     when brothers live together in
     harmony!
[2] For harmony is as precious as the
     anointing oil
     that was poured over Aaron's head,
     that ran down his beard
     and onto the border of his robe.
[3] Harmony is as refreshing as the dew
     from Mount Hermon
     that falls on the mountains of Zion.
   And there the LORD has pronounced
     his blessing,
     even life everlasting.

PROVERBS 17:7-8
Eloquent words are not fitting for a fool; even less are lies fitting for a ruler. □A bribe is like a lucky charm; whoever gives one will prosper!

1 KINGS 15:25–17:24
During this up-and-down time of Israel's history, God's prophets spoke out in an effort to guide the people. Elijah was one of the most famous Israelite prophets of this era.

JUNE**16**

Nadab son of Jeroboam began to rule over Israel in the second year of King Asa's reign in Judah. He reigned in Israel two years. [26]But he did what was evil in the

LORD's sight and followed the example of his father, continuing the sins that Jeroboam had led Israel to commit.

²⁷ Then Baasha son of Ahijah, from the tribe of Issachar, plotted against Nadab and assassinated him while he and the Israelite army were laying siege to the Philistine town of Gibbethon. ²⁸Baasha killed Nadab in the third year of King Asa's reign in Judah, and he became the next king of Israel.

²⁹He immediately slaughtered all the descendants of King Jeroboam, so that not one of the royal family was left, just as the LORD had promised concerning Jeroboam by the prophet Ahijah from Shiloh. ³⁰This was done because Jeroboam had provoked the anger of the LORD, the God of Israel, by the sins he had committed and the sins he had led Israel to commit.

³¹The rest of the events in Nadab's reign and everything he did are recorded in *The Book of the History of the Kings of Israel.*

³² There was constant war between King Asa of Judah and King Baasha of Israel. ³³Baasha son of Ahijah began to rule over all Israel in the third year of King Asa's reign in Judah. Baasha reigned in Tirzah twenty-four years. ³⁴But he did what was evil in the LORD's sight and followed the example of Jeroboam, continuing the sins that Jeroboam had led Israel to commit.

16:1THIS message from the LORD was delivered to King Baasha by the prophet Jehu son of Hanani: ²"I lifted you out of the dust to make you ruler of my people Israel, but you have followed the evil example of Jeroboam. You have provoked my anger by causing my people Israel to sin. ³So now I will destroy you and your family, just as I destroyed the descendants of Jeroboam son of Nebat. ⁴The members of Baasha's family who die in the city will be eaten by dogs, and those who die in the field will be eaten by vultures."

⁵The rest of the events in Baasha's reign and the extent of his power are recorded in *The Book of the History of the Kings of Israel.* ⁶When Baasha died, he was buried in Tirzah. Then his son Elah became the next king.

⁷The message from the LORD against Baasha and his family came through the prophet Jehu son of Hanani. It was delivered because Baasha had done what was evil in the LORD's sight (just as the family of Jeroboam had done), and also because Baasha had destroyed the family of Jeroboam. The LORD's anger was provoked by Baasha's sins.

⁸Elah son of Baasha began to rule over Israel in the twenty-sixth year of King Asa's reign in Judah. He reigned in the city of Tirzah for two years.

⁹Then Zimri, who commanded half of the royal chariots, made plans to kill him. One day in Tirzah, Elah was getting drunk at the home of Arza, the supervisor of the palace. ¹⁰Zimri walked in and struck him down and killed him. This happened in the twenty-seventh year of King Asa's reign in Judah. Then Zimri became the next king.

¹¹Zimri immediately killed the entire royal family of Baasha, leaving him not even a single male child. He even destroyed distant relatives and friends. ¹²So Zimri destroyed the dynasty of Baasha as the LORD had promised through the prophet Jehu. ¹³This happened because of all the sins Baasha and his son Elah had committed, and because of the sins they led Israel to commit. They provoked the anger of the LORD, the God of Israel, with their worthless idols.

¹⁴The rest of the events in Elah's reign and everything he did are recorded in *The Book of the History of the Kings of Israel.*

¹⁵Zimri began to rule over Israel in the twenty-seventh year of King Asa's reign in Judah, but his reign in Tirzah lasted only seven days. The army of Israel was then attacking the Philistine town of Gibbethon. ¹⁶When they heard that Zimri had committed treason and had assassinated the king, that very day they chose Omri, commander of the army, as the new king of Israel. ¹⁷So Omri led the entire army of Israel up from Gibbethon to attack Tirzah, Israel's capital. ¹⁸When Zimri saw that the city had been taken, he went into the citadel of the palace and burned it down over himself and died in the flames. ¹⁹For he, too, had done what was evil in the LORD's sight. He followed the example of Jeroboam in all the sins he had committed and led Israel to commit.

²⁰The rest of the events in Zimri's reign and his conspiracy are recorded in *The Book of the History of the Kings of Israel.*

²¹But now the people of Israel were split into two factions. Half the people tried to make Tibni son of Ginath their king, while the other half supported Omri. ²²But Omri's supporters defeated the supporters of Tibni. So Tibni was killed, and Omri became the next king.

²³Omri began to rule over Israel in the thirty-first year of King Asa's reign in Judah. He reigned twelve years in all, six of them in Tirzah. ²⁴Then Omri bought the hill now known as Samaria from its owner, Shemer, for 150 pounds of silver.* He built a city on it and called the city Samaria in honor of Shemer.

²⁵But Omri did what was evil in the LORD's sight, even more than any of the kings before him. ²⁶He followed the example of Jeroboam son of Nebat in all the sins he had committed and led Israel to commit. The people provoked the anger of the LORD, the God of Israel, with their worthless idols.

²⁷The rest of the events in Omri's reign, the extent of his power, and everything he did are recorded in *The Book of the History of the Kings of Israel.* ²⁸When Omri died, he was buried in Samaria. Then his son Ahab became the next king.

²⁹Ahab son of Omri began to rule over Israel in the thirty-eighth year of King Asa's reign in Judah. He reigned in Samaria twenty-two years. ³⁰But Ahab son of Omri did what was evil in the LORD's sight, even more than any of the kings before him. ³¹And as though it were not enough to follow the example of Jeroboam, he married Jezebel, the daughter of King Ethbaal of the Sidonians, and he began to bow down in worship of Baal. ³²First Ahab built a temple and an altar for Baal in Samaria. ³³Then he set up an Asherah pole. He did more to provoke the anger of the LORD, the God of Israel, than any of the other kings of Israel before him.

³⁴It was during his reign that Hiel, a man from Bethel, rebuilt Jericho. When he laid its foundations, it cost him the life of his oldest son, Abiram. And when he completed it and set up its gates, it cost him the life of his youngest son, Segub.* This all happened according to the message from the LORD concerning Jericho spoken by Joshua son of Nun.

¹⁷:¹Now Elijah, who was from Tishbe in Gilead, told King Ahab, "As surely as the LORD, the God of Israel, lives—the God I serve—there will be no dew or rain during the next few years until I give the word!"

²Then the LORD said to Elijah, ³"Go to

HOW WE LIVE

Accepting others

ACTS 10:34-35 Peter had to overcome Jewish prejudice against non-Jews when he set foot in Cornelius's house. Yet Peter obeyed God in spite of his background and personal feelings. He shared the gospel message with a Gentile man, along with his family and friends. Peter's message was clear and concise, and it had a profound effect on those present. God made it clear to Peter that salvation was for both the Jews and Gentiles by blessing the new believers with an outpouring of the Holy Spirit. Peter then baptized them and remained with Cornelius for a few days, probably instructing him further about Jesus. •Cornelius needed Peter's presentation of the gospel in order to find salvation. Peter needed to witness Cornelius's conversion in order to understand that salvation is for everyone who believes. The conversion of this Roman army officer was a major stepping-stone for spreading the gospel to the Gentiles. •When you share the gospel message, you're helping someone. But don't allow your willingness to serve become arrogance. Realize that the people you serve have much to offer you in return.

the east and hide by Kerith Brook, near where it enters the Jordan River. ⁴Drink from the brook and eat what the ravens bring you, for I have commanded them to bring you food."

⁵So Elijah did as the LORD told him and camped beside Kerith Brook, east of the Jordan. ⁶The ravens brought him bread and meat each morning and evening, and he drank from the brook. ⁷But after a while the brook dried up, for there was no rainfall anywhere in the land.

⁸Then the LORD said to Elijah, ⁹"Go and live in the village of Zarephath, near the city of Sidon. I have instructed a widow there to feed you."

¹⁰So he went to Zarephath. As he arrived at the gates of the village, he saw a widow gathering sticks, and he asked her, "Would you please bring me a little water in a cup?" ¹¹As she was going to get it, he called to her, "Bring me a bite of bread, too."

¹²But she said, "I swear by the LORD your God that I don't have a single piece of bread in the house. And I have only a handful of flour left in the jar and a little cooking oil in the bottom of the jug. I was just gathering a few sticks to cook this last meal, and then my son and I will die."

¹³But Elijah said to her, "Don't be afraid! Go ahead and do just what you've said, but make a little bread for me first. Then use what's left to prepare a meal for yourself and your son. ¹⁴For this is what the LORD, the God of Israel, says: There will always be flour and olive oil left in your containers until the time when the LORD sends rain and the crops grow again!"

¹⁵So she did as Elijah said, and she and Elijah and her son continued to eat for many days. ¹⁶There was always enough flour and olive oil left in the containers, just as the LORD had promised through Elijah.

¹⁷Some time later the woman's son became sick. He grew worse and worse, and finally he died. ¹⁸Then she said to Elijah, "O man of God, what have you done to me? Have you come here to point out my sins and kill my son?"

¹⁹But Elijah replied, "Give me your son." And he took the child's body from her arms, carried him up the stairs to the room where he was staying, and laid the body on his bed. ²⁰Then Elijah cried out to the LORD, "O LORD my God, why have you brought tragedy to this widow who has opened her home to me, causing her son to die?"

²¹And he stretched himself out over the child three times and cried out to the LORD, "O LORD my God, please let this child's life return to him." ²²The LORD heard Elijah's prayer, and the life of the child returned, and he revived! ²³Then Elijah brought him down from the upper room and gave him to his mother. "Look!" he said. "Your son is alive!"

²⁴Then the woman told Elijah, "Now I know for sure that you are a man of God, and that the LORD truly speaks through you."

16:24 Hebrew *for 2 talents* [68 kilograms] *of silver.*
16:34 An ancient Hebrew scribal tradition reads *He killed his oldest son when he laid its foundations, and he killed his youngest son when he set up its gates.*

ACTS 10:24-48

God had led Peter to a new understanding of God's plan to save people from every nation. The cultural doors were now thrown open and the church leaders began to see that their mission field was the whole world, not just Israel.

They [Peter and the other believers] arrived in Caesarea the following day. Cornelius was waiting for them and had called together his relatives and close friends. ²⁵As Peter entered his home, Cornelius fell at his feet and worshiped him. ²⁶But Peter pulled him up and said, "Stand up! I'm a human being just like you!" ²⁷So they talked together and went inside, where many others were assembled.

²⁸Peter told them, "You know it is against our laws for a Jewish man to enter a Gentile home like this or to associate with you. But God has shown me that I should no longer think of anyone as impure or unclean. ²⁹So I came without objection as soon as I was sent for. Now tell me why you sent for me."

³⁰Cornelius replied, "Four days ago I was praying in my house about this same time, three o'clock in the afternoon. Suddenly, a man in dazzling clothes was standing in front of me. ³¹He told me, '-Cornelius, your prayer has been heard,

and your gifts to the poor have been noticed by God! [32]Now send messengers to Joppa, and summon a man named Simon Peter. He is staying in the home of Simon, a tanner who lives near the seashore.' [33]So I sent for you at once, and it was good of you to come. Now we are all here, waiting before God to hear the message the Lord has given you."

[34]Then Peter replied, "I see very clearly that God shows no favoritism. [35]In every nation he accepts those who fear him and do what is right. [36]This is the message of Good News for the people of Israel—that there is peace with God through Jesus Christ, who is Lord of all. [37]You know what happened throughout Judea, beginning in Galilee, after John began preaching his message of baptism. [38]And you know that God anointed Jesus of Nazareth with the Holy Spirit and with power. Then Jesus went around doing good and healing all who were oppressed by the devil, for God was with him.

[39]"And we apostles are witnesses of all he did throughout Judea and in Jerusalem. They put him to death by hanging him on a cross,* [40]but God raised him to life on the third day. Then God allowed him to appear, [41]not to the general public,* but to us whom God had chosen in advance to be his witnesses. We were those who ate and drank with him after he rose from the dead. [42]And he ordered us to preach everywhere and to testify that Jesus is the one appointed by God to be the judge of all—the living and the dead. [43]He is the one all the prophets testified about, saying that everyone who believes in him will have their sins forgiven through his name."

[44]Even as Peter was saying these things, the Holy Spirit fell upon all who were listening to the message. [45]The Jewish believers* who came with Peter were amazed that the gift of the Holy Spirit had been poured out on the Gentiles, too. [46]For they heard them speaking in tongues and praising God.

Then Peter asked, [47]"Can anyone object to their being baptized, now that they have received the Holy Spirit just as we did?" [48]So he gave orders for them to be baptized in the name of Jesus Christ. Afterward Cornelius asked him to stay with them for several days.

10:39 Greek *on a tree.*   **10:41** Greek *the people.*
10:45 Greek *The faithful ones of the circumcision.*

PSALM 134:1-3
A song for pilgrims ascending to Jerusalem.

[1] **Oh**, praise the LORD, all you servants
          of the LORD,
     you who serve at night in the house
          of the LORD.
[2] Lift up holy hands in prayer,
     and praise the LORD.
[3] May the LORD, who made heaven and
          earth,
     bless you from Jerusalem.*

134:3 Hebrew *Zion.*

PROVERBS 17:9-11
Love prospers when a fault is forgiven, but dwelling on it separates close friends. □ A single rebuke does more for a person of understanding than a hundred lashes on the back of a fool. □ Evil people are eager for rebellion, but they will be severely punished.

1 KINGS 18:1-46
Elijah put his faith on the line when he challenged the prophets of Baal. His faith, in turn, challenges us. How many of us would believe in a miracle at the risk of national humiliation? Elijah did. Watch the miracle happen.

JUNE**17**

Later on, in the third year of the drought, the LORD said to Elijah, "Go and present yourself to King Ahab. Tell him that I will soon send rain!" [2]So Elijah went to appear before Ahab.

Meanwhile, the famine had become very severe in Samaria. ³So Ahab summoned Obadiah, who was in charge of the palace. (Obadiah was a devoted follower of the LORD. ⁴Once when Jezebel had tried to kill all the LORD's prophets, Obadiah had hidden 100 of them in two caves. He put fifty prophets in each cave and supplied them with food and water.) ⁵Ahab said to Obadiah, "We must check every spring and valley in the land to see if we can find enough grass to save at least some of my horses and mules." ⁶So they divided the land between them. Ahab went one way by himself, and Obadiah went another way by himself.

⁷As Obadiah was walking along, he suddenly saw Elijah coming toward him. Obadiah recognized him at once and bowed low to the ground before him. "Is it really you, my lord Elijah?" he asked.

⁸"Yes, it is," Elijah replied. "Now go and tell your master, 'Elijah is here.'"

⁹"Oh, sir," Obadiah protested, "what harm have I done to you that you are sending me to my death at the hands of Ahab? ¹⁰For I swear by the LORD your God that the king has searched every nation and kingdom on earth from end to end to find you. And each time he was told, 'Elijah isn't here,' King Ahab forced the king of that nation to swear to the truth of his claim. ¹¹And now you say, 'Go and tell your master, "Elijah is here."' ¹²But as soon as I leave you, the Spirit of the LORD will carry you away to who knows where. When Ahab comes and cannot find you, he will kill me. Yet I have been a true servant of the LORD all my life. ¹³Has no one told you, my lord, about the time when Jezebel was trying to kill the LORD's prophets? I hid 100 of them in two caves and supplied them with food and water. ¹⁴And now you say, 'Go and tell your master, "Elijah is here."' Sir, if I do that, Ahab will certainly kill me."

¹⁵But Elijah said, "I swear by the LORD Almighty, in whose presence I stand, that I will present myself to Ahab this very day."

¹⁶So Obadiah went to tell Ahab that Elijah had come, and Ahab went out to meet Elijah. ¹⁷When Ahab saw him, he exclaimed, "So, is it really you, you troublemaker of Israel?"

¹⁸"I have made no trouble for Israel," Elijah replied. "You and your family are the troublemakers, for you have refused to obey the commands of the LORD and have worshiped the images of Baal instead. ¹⁹Now summon all Israel to join me at Mount Carmel, along with the 450 prophets of Baal and the 400 prophets of Asherah who are supported by Jezebel.*"

²⁰So Ahab summoned all the people of Israel and the prophets to Mount Carmel. ²¹Then Elijah stood in front of them and said, "How much longer will you waver, hobbling between two opinions? If the LORD is God, follow him! But if Baal is God, then follow him!" But the people were completely silent.

²²Then Elijah said to them, "I am the only prophet of the LORD who is left, but Baal has 450 prophets. ²³Now bring two bulls. The prophets of Baal may choose whichever one they wish and cut it into pieces and lay it on the wood of their altar, but without setting fire to it. I will prepare the other bull and lay it on the wood on the altar, but not set fire to it. ²⁴Then call on the name of your god, and I will call on the name of the LORD. The god who answers by setting fire to the wood is the true God!" And all the people agreed.

²⁵Then Elijah said to the prophets of Baal, "You go first, for there are many of you. Choose one of the bulls, and prepare it and call on the name of your god. But do not set fire to the wood."

²⁶So they prepared one of the bulls and placed it on the altar. Then they called on the name of Baal from morning until noontime, shouting, "O Baal, answer us!" But there was no reply of any kind. Then they danced, hobbling around the altar they had made.

²⁷About noontime Elijah began mocking them. "You'll have to shout louder," he scoffed, "for surely he is a god! Perhaps he is daydreaming, or is relieving himself.* Or maybe he is away on a trip, or is asleep and needs to be wakened!"

²⁸So they shouted louder, and following their normal custom, they cut themselves with knives and swords until the blood gushed out. ²⁹They raved all afternoon

until the time of the evening sacrifice, but still there was no sound, no reply, no response.

³⁰Then Elijah called to the people, "Come over here!" They all crowded around him as he repaired the altar of the LORD that had been torn down. ³¹He took twelve stones, one to represent each of the tribes of Israel,* ³²and he used the stones to rebuild the altar in the name of the LORD. Then he dug a trench around the altar large enough to hold about three gallons.* ³³He piled wood on the altar, cut the bull into pieces, and laid the pieces on the wood.

Then he said, "Fill four large jars with water, and pour the water over the offering and the wood."

³⁴After they had done this, he said, "Do the same thing again!" And when they were finished, he said, "Now do it a third time!" So they did as he said, ³⁵and the water ran around the altar and even filled the trench.

³⁶At the usual time for offering the evening sacrifice, Elijah the prophet walked up to the altar and prayed, "O LORD, God of Abraham, Isaac, and Jacob,* prove today that you are God in Israel and that I am your servant. Prove that I have done all this at your command. ³⁷O LORD, answer me! Answer me so these people will know

that you, O LORD, are God and that you have brought them back to yourself."

³⁸Immediately the fire of the LORD flashed down from heaven and burned up the young bull, the wood, the stones, and the dust. It even licked up all the water in the trench! ³⁹And when all the people saw it, they fell face down on the ground and cried out, "The LORD—he is God! Yes, the LORD is God!"

⁴⁰Then Elijah commanded, "Seize all the prophets of Baal. Don't let a single one escape!" So the people seized them all, and Elijah took them down to the Kishon Valley and killed them there.

⁴¹Then Elijah said to Ahab, "Go get something to eat and drink, for I hear a mighty rainstorm coming!"

⁴²So Ahab went to eat and drink. But Elijah climbed to the top of Mount Carmel and bowed low to the ground and prayed with his face between his knees.

⁴³Then he said to his servant, "Go and look out toward the sea."

The servant went and looked, then returned to Elijah and said, "I didn't see anything."

Seven times Elijah told him to go and look. ⁴⁴Finally the seventh time, his servant told him, "I saw a little cloud about the size of a man's hand rising from the sea."

Then Elijah shouted, "Hurry to Ahab

HOW WE LIVE

Relying on God's power

1 KINGS 18:18-40 Elijah challenged the people of his nation to take a stand against evil. King Ahab and Queen Jezebel—two of the most ominous characters in all of Scripture—had led the northern kingdom of Israel into the worst sort of idolatry. So Elijah took a stand, calling for a sort of "prophet duel"—him against 450 prophets of Baal. Were the odds stacked against Elijah? Not with God on his side. Elijah had faith, but people can have loads of faith and still be weak because their faith is in the wrong place. The 450 prophets of Baal had plenty of faith, but it was in a god that did not exist and had no power. • Where is your faith— ultimately? Put faith in friends or family, and you'll find that they let you down. Put faith in government, and you'll be disappointed by corruption. Put faith in money, and you'll see that it doesn't buy happiness. Put faith in fame, and you'll find it fleeting. Put your faith in the God of the universe, however, and you will find strength beyond what you can imagine. You will be able to face down evil fearlessly if your faith is in the right place.

and tell him, 'Climb into your chariot and go back home. If you don't hurry, the rain will stop you!'"

45And soon the sky was black with clouds. A heavy wind brought a terrific rainstorm, and Ahab left quickly for Jezreel. 46Then the LORD gave special strength to Elijah. He tucked his cloak into his belt* and ran ahead of Ahab's chariot all the way to the entrance of Jezreel.

18:19 Hebrew *who eat at Jezebel's table.* 18:27 Or *is busy somewhere else,* or *is engaged in business.* 18:31 Hebrew *each of the tribes of the sons of Jacob to whom the LORD had said "Your name will be Israel."* 18:32 Hebrew *2 seahs* [12 liters] *of seed.* 18:36 Hebrew *and Israel.* The names "Jacob" and "Israel" are often interchanged throughout the Old Testament, referring sometimes to the individual patriarch and sometimes to the nation. 18:46 Hebrew *He bound up his loins.*

ACTS 11:1-30

As the fledgling church began to come to terms with the inclusion of Gentiles in God's plan, God was raising up Paul and Barnabas as leaders in the church. They would soon begin a major push into Gentile lands to spread the Good News.

Soon the news reached the apostles and other believers* in Judea that the Gentiles had received the word of God. 2But when Peter arrived back in Jerusalem, the Jewish believers* criticized him. 3"You entered the home of Gentiles* and even ate with them!" they said.

4Then Peter told them exactly what had happened. 5"I was in the town of Joppa," he said, "and while I was praying, I went into a trance and saw a vision. Something like a large sheet was let down by its four corners from the sky. And it came right down to me. 6When I looked inside the sheet, I saw all sorts of small animals, wild animals, reptiles, and birds. 7And I heard a voice say, 'Get up, Peter; kill and eat them.'

8" 'No, Lord,' I replied. 'I have never eaten anything that our Jewish laws have declared impure or unclean.*'

9"But the voice from heaven spoke again: 'Do not call something unclean if God has made it clean.' 10This happened three times before the sheet and all it contained was pulled back up to heaven.

11"Just then three men who had been sent from Caesarea arrived at the house where we were staying. 12The Holy Spirit told me to go with them and not to worry that they were Gentiles. These six broth-

ers here accompanied me, and we soon entered the home of the man who had sent for us. 13He told us how an angel had appeared to him in his home and had told him, 'Send messengers to Joppa, and summon a man named Simon Peter. 14He will tell you how you and everyone in your household can be saved!'

15"As I began to speak," Peter continued, "the Holy Spirit fell on them, just as he fell on us at the beginning. 16Then I thought of the Lord's words when he said, 'John baptized with* water, but you will be baptized with the Holy Spirit.' 17And since God gave these Gentiles the same gift he gave us when we believed in the Lord Jesus Christ, who was I to stand in God's way?"

18When the others heard this, they stopped objecting and began praising God. They said, "We can see that God has also given the Gentiles the privilege of repenting of their sins and receiving eternal life."

19Meanwhile, the believers who had been scattered during the persecution after Stephen's death traveled as far as Phoenicia, Cyprus, and Antioch of Syria. They preached the word of God, but only to Jews. 20However, some of the believers who went to Antioch from Cyprus and Cyrene began preaching to the Gentiles* about the Lord Jesus. 21The power of the Lord was with them, and a large number of these Gentiles believed and turned to the Lord.

22When the church at Jerusalem heard what had happened, they sent Barnabas to Antioch. 23When he arrived and saw this evidence of God's blessing, he was filled with joy, and he encouraged the believers to stay true to the Lord. 24Barnabas was a good man, full of the Holy Spirit and strong in faith. And many people were brought to the Lord.

25Then Barnabas went on to Tarsus to look for Saul. 26When he found him, he brought him back to Antioch. Both of them stayed there with the church for a full year, teaching large crowds of people. (It was at Antioch that the believers* were first called Christians.)

27During this time some prophets traveled from Jerusalem to Antioch. 28One of them named Agabus stood up in one of the meetings and predicted by the Spirit that a great famine was coming upon the entire Roman world. (This was fulfilled during the reign of Claudius.) [29]So the believers in Antioch decided to send relief to the brothers and sisters* in Judea, everyone giving as much as they could. [30]This they did, entrusting their gifts to Barnabas and Saul to take to the elders of the church in Jerusalem.

11:1 Greek *brothers.* 11:2 Greek *those of the circumcision.* 11:3 Greek *of uncircumcised men.* 11:8 Greek *anything common or unclean.* 11:16 Or *in;* also in 11:16b. 11:20 Greek *the Hellenists* (i.e., those who speak Greek); other manuscripts read *the Greeks.* 11:26 Greek *disciples;* also in 11:29. 11:29 Greek *the brothers.*

PSALM 135:1-21

Praise the LORD!

Praise the name of the LORD!
  Praise him, you who serve
    the LORD,
[2] you who serve in the house of
    the LORD,
  in the courts of the house of our God.

[3] Praise the LORD, for the LORD is good;
  celebrate his lovely name with
    music.
[4] For the LORD has chosen Jacob for
    himself,
  Israel for his own special treasure.

[5] I know the greatness of the LORD—
  that our Lord is greater than any
    other god.
[6] The LORD does whatever pleases him
  throughout all heaven and earth,
  and on the seas and in their depths.
[7] He causes the clouds to rise over
    the whole earth.
  He sends the lightning with the rain
  and releases the wind from his
    storehouses.

[8] He destroyed the firstborn in each
    Egyptian home,
  both people and animals.

[9] He performed miraculous signs
    and wonders in Egypt
  against Pharaoh and all his people.
[10] He struck down great nations
  and slaughtered mighty kings—
[11] Sihon king of the Amorites,
  Og king of Bashan,
  and all the kings of Canaan.
[12] He gave their land as an inheritance,
  a special possession to his people
    Israel.

[13] Your name, O LORD, endures forever;
  your fame, O LORD, is known
    to every generation.
[14] For the LORD will give justice
    to his people
  and have compassion on
    his servants.

[15] The idols of the nations are merely
    things of silver and gold,
  shaped by human hands.
[16] They have mouths but cannot speak,
  and eyes but cannot see.
[17] They have ears but cannot hear,
  and noses but cannot smell.
[18] And those who make idols are just
    like them,
  as are all who trust in them.

[19] O Israel, praise the LORD!
  O priests—descendants of Aaron—
    praise the LORD!
[20] O Levites, praise the LORD!
  All you who fear the LORD, praise
    the LORD!
[21] The LORD be praised from Zion,
  for he lives here in Jerusalem.

Praise the LORD!

PROVERBS 17:12-13

It is safer to meet a bear robbed of her cubs than to confront a fool caught in foolishness. ❑ If you repay good with evil, evil will never leave your house.

JUNE18

Elijah had just had a tremendous victory for God on Mount Carmel, but an outraged queen sent him fleeing into the desert, begging God to let him die. God understood his prophet's low moment, ministered to him, and then sent him right back into the fray.

When Ahab got home, he told Jezebel everything Elijah had done, including the way he had killed all the prophets of Baal. ²So Jezebel sent this message to Elijah: "May the gods strike me and even kill me if by this time tomorrow I have not killed you just as you killed them."

³Elijah was afraid and fled for his life. He went to Beersheba, a town in Judah, and he left his servant there. ⁴Then he went on alone into the wilderness, traveling all day. He sat down under a solitary broom tree and prayed that he might die. "I have had enough, LORD," he said. "Take my life, for I am no better than my ancestors who have already died."

⁵Then he lay down and slept under the broom tree. But as he was sleeping, an angel touched him and told him, "Get up and eat!" ⁶He looked around and there beside his head was some bread baked on hot stones and a jar of water! So he ate and drank and lay down again.

⁷Then the angel of the LORD came again and touched him and said, "Get up and eat some more, or the journey ahead will be too much for you."

⁸So he got up and ate and drank, and the food gave him enough strength to travel forty days and forty nights to Mount Sinai,* the mountain of God. ⁹There he came to a cave, where he spent the night.

But the LORD said to him, "What are you doing here, Elijah?"

¹⁰Elijah replied, "I have zealously served the LORD God Almighty. But the people of Israel have broken their covenant with you, torn down your altars, and killed every one of your prophets. I am the only one left, and now they are trying to kill me, too."

¹¹"Go out and stand before me on the mountain," the LORD told him. And as Elijah stood there, the LORD passed by, and a mighty windstorm hit the mountain. It was such a terrible blast that the rocks were torn loose, but the LORD was not in the wind. After the wind there was an earthquake, but the LORD was not in the earthquake. ¹²And after the earthquake there was a fire, but the LORD was not in the fire. And after the fire there was the sound of a gentle whisper. ¹³When Elijah heard it, he wrapped his face in his cloak and went out and stood at the entrance of the cave.

And a voice said, "What are you doing here, Elijah?"

¹⁴He replied again, "I have zealously served the LORD God Almighty. But the people of Israel have broken their covenant with you, torn down your altars, and killed every one of your prophets. I am the only one left, and now they are trying to kill me, too."

¹⁵Then the LORD told him, "Go back the same way you came, and travel to the wilderness of Damascus. When you arrive there, anoint Hazael to be king of Aram. ¹⁶Then anoint Jehu son of Nimshi to be king of Israel, and anoint Elisha son of Shaphat from the town of Abel-meholah to replace you as my prophet. ¹⁷Anyone who escapes from Hazael will be killed by Jehu, and those who escape Jehu will be killed by Elisha! ¹⁸Yet I will preserve 7,000 others in Israel who have never bowed down to Baal or kissed him!"

¹⁹So Elijah went and found Elisha son of Shaphat plowing a field. There were twelve teams of oxen in the field, and Elisha was plowing with the twelfth team. Elijah went over to him and threw his cloak across his shoulders and then walked away. ²⁰Elisha left the oxen standing there, ran after Elijah, and said to him, "First let me go and kiss my father and mother good-bye, and then I will go with you!"

Elijah replied, "Go on back, but think about what I have done to you."

²¹So Elisha returned to his oxen and slaughtered them. He used the wood from the plow to build a fire to roast their flesh. He passed around the meat to the

townspeople, and they all ate. Then he went with Elijah as his assistant.

19:8 Hebrew *to Horeb,* another name for Sinai.

ACTS 12:1-23

Martyrdom was a harsh reality for the first-century Christians. Herod Agrippa I, grandson of Herod the Great, who had tried to have the baby Jesus killed (Matthew 2:16-18, January 2), saw an opportunity for political gain by killing James and arresting Peter.

About that time King Herod Agrippa* began to persecute some believers in the church. ²He had the apostle James (John's brother) killed with a sword. ³When Herod saw how much this pleased the Jewish people, he also arrested Peter. (This took place during the Passover celebration.*) ⁴Then he imprisoned him, placing him under the guard of four squads of four soldiers each. Herod intended to bring Peter out for public trial after the Passover. ⁵But while Peter was in prison, the church prayed very earnestly for him.

⁶The night before Peter was to be placed on trial, he was asleep, fastened with two chains between two soldiers. Others stood guard at the prison gate. ⁷Suddenly, there was a bright light in the cell, and an angel of the Lord stood before Peter. The angel struck him on the side to awaken him and said, "Quick! Get up!" And the chains fell off his wrists. ⁸Then the angel told him,

"Get dressed and put on your sandals." And he did. "Now put on your coat and follow me," the angel ordered.

⁹So Peter left the cell, following the angel. But all the time he thought it was a vision. He didn't realize it was actually happening. ¹⁰They passed the first and second guard posts and came to the iron gate leading to the city, and this opened for them all by itself. So they passed through and started walking down the street, and then the angel suddenly left him.

¹¹Peter finally came to his senses. "It's really true!" he said. "The Lord has sent his angel and saved me from Herod and from what the Jewish leaders* had planned to do to me!"

¹²When he realized this, he went to the home of Mary, the mother of John Mark, where many were gathered for prayer. ¹³He knocked at the door in the gate, and a servant girl named Rhoda came to open it. ¹⁴When she recognized Peter's voice, she was so overjoyed that, instead of opening the door, she ran back inside and told everyone, "Peter is standing at the door!"

¹⁵"You're out of your mind!" they said. When she insisted, they decided, "It must be his angel."

¹⁶Meanwhile, Peter continued knocking. When they finally opened the door and saw him, they were amazed. ¹⁷He motioned for them to quiet down and told

HOW WE LIVE

Seeking God's will

1 KINGS 19:11-13 Elijah had fled to the mountain, fearful for his life. God knew his prophet was feeling alone and overwhelmed, but God still had work for Elijah to do. So he called him to come out of the cave and provided a spectacular show of power—a mighty windstorm, an earthquake, and a fire—but did not speak to Elijah in these. Instead, he asked in a gentle whisper, "What are you doing here, Elijah?" • Where are you looking for God's guidance? He may indeed speak to you in an unmistakable audiovisual display. More likely, however, he will speak in a gentle whisper as you read his Word or sit quietly before him. When you need direction, answer God's first question to Elijah, "What are you doing here?" God has you right where you are for a reason, and he may have a job for you to do—a job you're missing because you're too worried about "what next" instead of "what now." • As you pray for God's direction, listen. Turn down the noise of a busy life so you can hear God's gentle whisper. It may come when you least expect it.

them how the Lord had led him out of prison. "Tell James and the other brothers what happened," he said. And then he went to another place.

[18]At dawn there was a great commotion among the soldiers about what had happened to Peter. [19]Herod Agrippa ordered a thorough search for him. When he couldn't be found, Herod interrogated the guards and sentenced them to death. Afterward Herod left Judea to stay in Caesarea for a while.

[20]Now Herod was very angry with the people of Tyre and Sidon. So they sent a delegation to make peace with him because their cities were dependent upon Herod's country for food. The delegates won the support of Blastus, Herod's personal assistant, [21]and an appointment with Herod was granted. When the day arrived, Herod put on his royal robes, sat on his throne, and made a speech to them. [22]The people gave him a great ovation, shouting, "It's the voice of a god, not of a man!"

[23]Instantly, an angel of the Lord struck Herod with a sickness, because he accepted the people's worship instead of giving the glory to God. So he was consumed with worms and died.

12:1 Greek *Herod the king.* He was the nephew of Herod Antipas and a grandson of Herod the Great.   12:3 Greek *the days of unleavened bread.*   12:11 Or *the Jewish people.*

PSALM 136:1-26

Give thanks to the LORD, for he is good!
His faithful love endures forever.
[2] Give thanks to the God of gods.
His faithful love endures forever.
[3] Give thanks to the Lord of lords.
His faithful love endures forever.
[4] Give thanks to him who alone does mighty miracles.
His faithful love endures forever.
[5] Give thanks to him who made the heavens so skillfully.
His faithful love endures forever.
[6] Give thanks to him who placed the earth among the waters.
His faithful love endures forever.
[7] Give thanks to him who made the heavenly lights—
His faithful love endures forever.
[8] the sun to rule the day,
His faithful love endures forever.

[9] and the moon and stars to rule the night.
His faithful love endures forever.
[10] Give thanks to him who killed the firstborn of Egypt.
His faithful love endures forever.
[11] He brought Israel out of Egypt.
His faithful love endures forever.
[12] He acted with a strong hand and powerful arm.
His faithful love endures forever.
[13] Give thanks to him who parted the Red Sea.*
His faithful love endures forever.
[14] He led Israel safely through,
His faithful love endures forever.
[15] but he hurled Pharaoh and his army into the Red Sea.
His faithful love endures forever.
[16] Give thanks to him who led his people through the wilderness.
His faithful love endures forever.
[17] Give thanks to him who struck down mighty kings.
His faithful love endures forever.
[18] He killed powerful kings—
His faithful love endures forever.
[19] Sihon king of the Amorites,
His faithful love endures forever.
[20] and Og king of Bashan.
His faithful love endures forever.
[21] God gave the land of these kings as an inheritance—
His faithful love endures forever.
[22] a special possession to his servant Israel.
His faithful love endures forever.
[23] He remembered us in our weakness.
His faithful love endures forever.
[24] He saved us from our enemies.
His faithful love endures forever.
[25] He gives food to every living thing.
His faithful love endures forever.
[26] Give thanks to the God of heaven.
His faithful love endures forever.

136:13 Hebrew *sea of reeds;* also in 136:15.

PROVERBS 17:14-15

Starting a quarrel is like opening a floodgate, so stop before a dispute breaks out. ☐ Acquitting the guilty and condemning the innocent—both are detestable to the LORD.

1 KINGS 20:1–21:29

Jezebel and Ahab were just about as corrupt as any pair in leadership could be. They took what they wanted, manipulated as they pleased, and murdered if necessary. These stories reveal their ugly character.

About that time King Ben-hadad of Aram mobilized his army, supported by the chariots and horses of thirty-two allied kings. They went to besiege Samaria, the capital of Israel, and launched attacks against it. ²Ben-hadad sent messengers into the city to relay this message to King Ahab of Israel: "This is what Ben-hadad says: ³'Your silver and gold are mine, and so are your wives and the best of your children!'"

⁴"All right, my lord the king," Israel's king replied. "All that I have is yours!"

⁵Soon Ben-hadad's messengers returned again and said, "This is what Ben-hadad says: 'I have already demanded that you give me your silver, gold, wives, and children. ⁶But about this time tomorrow I will send my officials to search your palace and the homes of your people. They will take away everything you consider valuable!'"

⁷Then Ahab summoned all the elders of the land and said to them, "Look how this man is stirring up trouble! I already agreed with his demand that I give him my wives and children and silver and gold."

⁸"Don't give in to any more demands," all the elders and the people advised.

⁹So Ahab told the messengers from Ben-hadad, "Say this to my lord the king: 'I will give you everything you asked for the first time, but I cannot accept this last demand of yours.'" So the messengers returned to Ben-hadad with that response.

¹⁰Then Ben-hadad sent this message to Ahab: "May the gods strike me and even kill me if there remains enough dust from Samaria to provide even a handful for each of my soldiers."

¹¹The king of Israel sent back this answer: "A warrior putting on his sword for battle should not boast like a warrior who has already won."

¹²Ahab's reply reached Ben-hadad and the other kings as they were drinking in their tents.* "Prepare to attack!" Ben-hadad commanded his officers. So they prepared to attack the city.

¹³Then a certain prophet came to see King Ahab of Israel and told him, "This is what the LORD says: Do you see all these enemy forces? Today I will hand them all over to you. Then you will know that I am the LORD."

¹⁴Ahab asked, "How will he do it?"

And the prophet replied, "This is what the LORD says: The troops of the provincial commanders will do it."

"Should we attack first?" Ahab asked.

"Yes," the prophet answered.

¹⁵So Ahab mustered the troops of the 232 provincial commanders. Then he called out the rest of the army of Israel, some 7,000 men. ¹⁶About noontime, as Ben-hadad and the thirty-two allied kings were still in their tents drinking themselves into a stupor, ¹⁷the troops of the provincial commanders marched out of the city as the first contingent.

As they approached, Ben-hadad's scouts reported to him, "Some troops are coming from Samaria."

¹⁸"Take them alive," Ben-hadad commanded, "whether they have come for peace or for war."

¹⁹But Ahab's provincial commanders and the entire army had now come out to fight. ²⁰Each Israelite soldier killed his Aramean opponent, and suddenly the entire Aramean army panicked and fled. The Israelites chased them, but King Ben-hadad and a few of his charioteers escaped on horses. ²¹However, the king of Israel destroyed the other horses and chariots and slaughtered the Arameans.

²²Afterward the prophet said to King Ahab, "Get ready for another attack. Begin making plans now, for the king of Aram will come back next spring.*"

²³After their defeat, Ben-hadad's officers said to him, "The Israelite gods are gods of the hills; that is why they won. But we can beat them easily on the plains. ²⁴Only this time replace the kings with

field commanders! ²⁵Recruit another army like the one you lost. Give us the same number of horses, chariots, and men, and we will fight against them on the plains. There's no doubt that we will beat them." So King Ben-hadad did as they suggested.

²⁶The following spring he called up the Aramean army and marched out against Israel, this time at Aphek. ²⁷Israel then mustered its army, set up supply lines, and marched out for battle. But the Israelite army looked like two little flocks of goats in comparison to the vast Aramean forces that filled the countryside!

²⁸Then the man of God went to the king of Israel and said, "This is what the LORD says: The Arameans have said, 'The LORD is a god of the hills and not of the plains.' So I will defeat this vast army for you. Then you will know that I am the LORD."

²⁹The two armies camped opposite each other for seven days, and on the seventh day the battle began. The Israelites killed 100,000 Aramean foot soldiers in one day. ³⁰The rest fled into the town of Aphek, but the wall fell on them and killed another 27,000. Ben-hadad fled into the town and hid in a secret room.

³¹Ben-hadad's officers said to him, "Sir, we have heard that the kings of Israel are merciful. So let's humble ourselves by wearing burlap around our waists and putting ropes on our heads, and surrender to the king of Israel. Then perhaps he will let you live."

³²So they put on burlap and ropes, and they went to the king of Israel and begged, "Your servant Ben-hadad says, 'Please let me live!'"

The king of Israel responded, "Is he still alive? He is my brother!"

³³The men took this as a good sign and quickly picked up on his words. "Yes," they said, "your brother Ben-hadad!"

"Go and get him," the king of Israel told them. And when Ben-hadad arrived, Ahab invited him up into his chariot.

³⁴Ben-hadad told him, "I will give back the towns my father took from your father, and you may establish places of trade in Damascus, as my father did in Samaria."

Then Ahab said, "I will release you under these conditions." So they made a new treaty, and Ben-hadad was set free.

³⁵Meanwhile, the LORD instructed one of the group of prophets to say to another man, "Hit me!" But the man refused to hit the prophet. ³⁶Then the prophet told him, "Because you have not obeyed the voice of the LORD, a lion will kill you as soon as you leave me." And when he had gone, a lion did attack and kill him.

³⁷Then the prophet turned to another man and said, "Hit me!" So he struck the prophet and wounded him.

³⁸The prophet placed a bandage over his eyes to disguise himself and then waited beside the road for the king. ³⁹As the king passed by, the prophet called out to him, "Sir, I was in the thick of battle, and suddenly a man brought me a prisoner. He said, 'Guard this man; if for any reason he gets away, you will either die or pay a fine of seventy-five pounds* of silver!' ⁴⁰But while I was busy doing something else, the prisoner disappeared!"

"Well, it's your own fault," the king replied. "You have brought the judgment on yourself."

⁴¹Then the prophet quickly pulled the bandage from his eyes, and the king of Israel recognized him as one of the prophets. ⁴²The prophet said to him, "This is what the LORD says: Because you have spared the man I said must be destroyed,* now you must die in his place, and your people will die instead of his people." ⁴³So the king of Israel went home to Samaria angry and sullen.

²¹:¹Now there was a man named Naboth, from Jezreel, who owned a vineyard in Jezreel beside the palace of King Ahab of Samaria. ²One day Ahab said to Naboth, "Since your vineyard is so convenient to my palace, I would like to buy it to use as a vegetable garden. I will give you a better vineyard in exchange, or if you prefer, I will pay you for it."

³But Naboth replied, "The LORD forbid that I should give you the inheritance that was passed down by my ancestors."

⁴So Ahab went home angry and sullen because of Naboth's answer. The king went to bed with his face to the wall and refused to eat!

⁵"What's the matter?" his wife Jezebel

asked him. "What's made you so upset that you're not eating?"

⁶"I asked Naboth to sell me his vineyard or trade it, but he refused!" Ahab told her.

⁷"Are you the king of Israel or not?" Jezebel demanded. "Get up and eat something, and don't worry about it. I'll get you Naboth's vineyard!"

⁸So she wrote letters in Ahab's name, sealed them with his seal, and sent them to the elders and other leaders of the town where Naboth lived. ⁹In her letters she commanded: "Call the citizens together for fasting and prayer, and give Naboth a place of honor. ¹⁰And then seat two scoundrels across from him who will accuse him of cursing God and the king. Then take him out and stone him to death."

¹¹So the elders and other town leaders followed the instructions Jezebel had written in the letters. ¹²They called for a fast and put Naboth at a prominent place before the people. ¹³Then the two scoundrels came and sat down across from him. And they accused Naboth before all the people, saying, "He cursed God and the king." So he was dragged outside the town and stoned to death. ¹⁴The town leaders then sent word to Jezebel, "Naboth has been stoned to death."

¹⁵When Jezebel heard the news, she said to Ahab, "You know the vineyard Naboth wouldn't sell you? Well, you can have it now! He's dead!" ¹⁶So Ahab immediately went down to the vineyard of Naboth to claim it.

¹⁷But the LORD said to Elijah,* ¹⁸"Go down to meet King Ahab of Israel, who rules in Samaria. He will be at Naboth's vineyard in Jezreel, claiming it for himself. ¹⁹Give him this message: 'This is what the LORD says: Wasn't it enough that you killed Naboth? Must you rob him, too? Because you have done this, dogs will lick your blood at the very place where they licked the blood of Naboth!'"

²⁰"So, my enemy, you have found me!" Ahab exclaimed to Elijah.

"Yes," Elijah answered, "I have come because you have sold yourself to what is evil in the LORD's sight. ²¹So now the LORD says, 'I will bring disaster on you and consume you. I will destroy every one of your male descendants, slave and free alike, anywhere in Israel! ²²I am going to destroy your family as I did the family of Jeroboam son of Nebat and the family of Baasha son of Ahijah, for you have made me very angry and have led Israel into sin.'

²³"And regarding Jezebel, the LORD says, 'Dogs will eat Jezebel's body at the plot of land in Jezreel.*'

WHAT THE BIBLE SAYS

The apostle Paul

ACTS 13:2-3 God chooses the most unlikely people to do his greatest works. For the very important mission to the Gentiles, he called upon a zealous Jewish Pharisee. The man most zealous to put Christians in prison became the leading spokesman for the Christian faith. • Paul (his Jewish name was Saul) took the final step in Jesus' call to his followers to take the Good News to the ends of the earth. Paul tirelessly traveled much of the Roman Empire with the gospel message. The remainder of the book of Acts follows Paul all the way to Rome, the capital of the empire. Much of the rest of the New Testament is made up of Paul's letters to the churches in cities he had visited, and even some he had not. • Paul had been chosen for this by God himself: "Saul is my chosen instrument to take my message to the Gentiles and to kings, as well as to the people of Israel. And I will show him how much he must suffer for my name's sake" (Acts 9:15-16, June 13). Eventually, Paul would die for his faith. • Paul was chosen, he followed Jesus, was beaten, was martyred, and was key to the spread of the gospel across the world and to the writing of the New Testament you hold in your hands.

²⁴"The members of Ahab's family who die in the city will be eaten by dogs, and those who die in the field will be eaten by vultures."

²⁵(No one else so completely sold himself to what was evil in the LORD's sight as Ahab did under the influence of his wife Jezebel. ²⁶His worst outrage was worshiping idols* just as the Amorites had done—the people whom the LORD had driven out from the land ahead of the Israelites.)

²⁷But when Ahab heard this message, he tore his clothing, dressed in burlap, and fasted. He even slept in burlap and went about in deep mourning.

²⁸Then another message from the LORD came to Elijah: ²⁹"Do you see how Ahab has humbled himself before me? Because he has done this, I will not do what I promised during his lifetime. It will happen to his sons; I will destroy his dynasty."

20:12 Or *in Succoth;* also in 20:16. **20:22** Hebrew *at the turn of the year;* similarly in 20:26. The first day of the year in the ancient Hebrew lunar calendar occurred in March or April. **20:39** Hebrew *1 talent* [34 kilograms]. **20:42** The Hebrew term used here refers to the complete consecration of things or people to the LORD, either by destroying them or by giving them as an offering. **21:17** Hebrew *Elijah the Tishbite;* also in 21:28. **21:23** As in several Hebrew manuscripts, Syriac, and Latin Vulgate (see also 2 Kgs 9:26, 36); most Hebrew manuscripts read *at the city wall.* **21:26** The Hebrew term (literally *round things*) probably alludes to dung.

ACTS 12:24–13:15

From the growing church in Antioch, Paul and Barnabas were sent out on what would be known as the first of Paul's three (possibly four) missionary journeys.

Meanwhile, the word of God continued to spread, and there were many new believers.

²⁵When Barnabas and Saul had finished their mission to Jerusalem, they returned,* taking John Mark with them.

¹³:¹AMONG the prophets and teachers of the church at Antioch of Syria were Barnabas, Simeon (called "the black man"*), Lucius (from Cyrene), Manaen (the childhood companion of King Herod Antipas*), and Saul. ²One day as these men were worshiping the Lord and fasting, the Holy Spirit said, "Dedicate Barnabas and Saul for the special work to which I have called them." ³So after more fasting and prayer, the men laid their hands on them and sent them on their way.

⁴So Barnabas and Saul were sent out by the Holy Spirit. They went down to the seaport of Seleucia and then sailed for the island of Cyprus. ⁵There, in the town of Salamis, they went to the Jewish synagogues and preached the word of God. John Mark went with them as their assistant.

⁶Afterward they traveled from town to town across the entire island until finally they reached Paphos, where they met a Jewish sorcerer, a false prophet named Bar-Jesus. ⁷He had attached himself to the governor, Sergius Paulus, who was an intelligent man. The governor invited Barnabas and Saul to visit him, for he wanted to hear the word of God. ⁸But Elymas, the sorcerer (as his name means in Greek), interfered and urged the governor to pay no attention to what Barnabas and Saul said. He was trying to keep the governor from believing.

⁹Saul, also known as Paul, was filled with the Holy Spirit, and he looked the sorcerer in the eye. ¹⁰Then he said, "You son of the devil, full of every sort of deceit and fraud, and enemy of all that is good! Will you never stop perverting the true ways of the Lord? ¹¹Watch now, for the Lord has laid his hand of punishment upon you, and you will be struck blind. You will not see the sunlight for some time." Instantly mist and darkness came over the man's eyes, and he began groping around begging for someone to take his hand and lead him.

¹²When the governor saw what had happened, he became a believer, for he was astonished at the teaching about the Lord.

¹³Paul and his companions then left Paphos by ship for Pamphylia, landing at the port town of Perga. There John Mark left them and returned to Jerusalem. ¹⁴But Paul and Barnabas traveled inland to Antioch of Pisidia.*

On the Sabbath they went to the synagogue for the services. ¹⁵After the usual readings from the books of Moses* and the prophets, those in charge of the service sent them this message: "Brothers, if you have any word of encouragement for the people, come and give it."

12:25 Or *mission, they returned to Jerusalem.* Other manuscripts read *mission, they returned from Jerusalem;* still others read *mission, they returned from Jerusalem to Antioch.* 13:1a Greek *who was called Niger.* 13:1b Greek *Herod the tetrarch.* 13:13-14 *Pamphylia* and *Pisidia* were districts in what is now Turkey. 13:15 Greek *from the law.*

PSALM 137:1-9

Beside the rivers of Babylon, we sat
    and wept
    as we thought of Jerusalem.*
² We put away our harps,
    hanging them on the branches
    of poplar trees.
³ For our captors demanded a song
    from us.
    Our tormentors insisted on a joyful
    hymn:
    "Sing us one of those songs
    of Jerusalem!"
⁴ But how can we sing the songs
    of the LORD
    while in a pagan land?

⁵ If I forget you, O Jerusalem,
    let my right hand forget how to play
    the harp.

⁶ May my tongue stick to the roof
    of my mouth
    if I fail to remember you,
    if I don't make Jerusalem my
    greatest joy.

⁷ O LORD, remember what the
    Edomites did
    on the day the armies of Babylon
    captured Jerusalem.
    "Destroy it!" they yelled.
    "Level it to the ground!"
⁸ O Babylon, you will be destroyed.
    Happy is the one who pays
    you back
    for what you have done to us.
⁹ Happy is the one who takes your
    babies
    and smashes them against the
    rocks!

137:1 Hebrew *Zion;* also in 137:3.

PROVERBS 17:16

It is senseless to pay tuition to educate a fool, since he has no heart for learning.

JUNE**20**

1 KINGS 22:1-53

After the kingdom of Israel split, relations between the northern kingdom (Israel, at times called Samaria for its capital) and the southern kingdom (Judah) were not always friendly. Here the two kingdoms joined their efforts against a common enemy. Unfortunately, God was not pleased.

For three years there was no war between Aram and Israel. ²Then during the third year, King Jehoshaphat of Judah went to visit King Ahab of Israel. ³During the visit, the king of Israel said to his officials, "Do you realize that the town of Ramoth-gilead belongs to us? And yet we've done nothing to recapture it from the king of Aram!"

⁴Then he turned to Jehoshaphat and asked, "Will you join me in battle to recover Ramoth-gilead?"

Jehoshaphat replied to the king of Israel, "Why, of course! You and I are as one. My troops are your troops, and my horses are your horses." ⁵Then Jehoshaphat added, "But first let's find out what the LORD says."

⁶So the king of Israel summoned the prophets, about 400 of them, and asked them, "Should I go to war against Ramoth-gilead, or should I hold back?"

They all replied, "Yes, go right ahead! The Lord will give the king victory."

⁷But Jehoshaphat asked, "Is there not also a prophet of the LORD here? We should ask him the same question."

⁸The king of Israel replied to Jehoshaphat, "There is one more man who could consult the LORD for us, but I hate him. He never prophesies anything but trouble for me! His name is Micaiah son of Imlah."

Jehoshaphat replied, "That's not the way a king should talk! Let's hear what he has to say."

⁹So the king of Israel called one of his officials and said, "Quick! Bring Micaiah son of Imlah."

¹⁰King Ahab of Israel and King Jehoshaphat of Judah, dressed in their royal robes, were sitting on thrones at the threshing floor near the gate of Samaria. All of Ahab's prophets were prophesying there in front of them. ¹¹One of them, Zedekiah son of Kenaanah, made some iron horns and proclaimed, "This is what the LORD says: With these horns you will gore the Arameans to death!"

¹²All the other prophets agreed. "Yes," they said, "go up to Ramoth-gilead and be victorious, for the LORD will give the king victory!"

¹³Meanwhile, the messenger who went to get Micaiah said to him, "Look, all the prophets are promising victory for the king. Be sure that you agree with them and promise success."

¹⁴But Micaiah replied, "As surely as the LORD lives, I will say only what the LORD tells me to say."

¹⁵When Micaiah arrived before the king, Ahab asked him, "Micaiah, should we go to war against Ramoth-gilead, or should we hold back?"

Micaiah replied sarcastically, "Yes, go up and be victorious, for the LORD will give the king victory!"

¹⁶But the king replied sharply, "How many times must I demand that you speak only the truth to me when you speak for the LORD?"

¹⁷Then Micaiah told him, "In a vision I saw all Israel scattered on the mountains, like sheep without a shepherd. And the LORD said, 'Their master has been killed.* Send them home in peace.'"

¹⁸"Didn't I tell you?" the king of Israel exclaimed to Jehoshaphat. "He never prophesies anything but trouble for me."

¹⁹Then Micaiah continued, "Listen to what the LORD says! I saw the LORD sitting on his throne with all the armies of heaven around him, on his right and on his left. ²⁰And the LORD said, 'Who can entice Ahab to go into battle against Ramoth-gilead so he can be killed?'

"There were many suggestions, ²¹and finally a spirit approached the LORD and said, 'I can do it!'

²²" 'How will you do this?' the LORD asked.

"And the spirit replied, 'I will go out and inspire all of Ahab's prophets to speak lies.'

" 'You will succeed,' said the LORD. 'Go ahead and do it.'

²³"So you see, the LORD has put a lying spirit in the mouths of all your prophets. For the LORD has pronounced your doom."

²⁴Then Zedekiah son of Kenaanah walked up to Micaiah and slapped him across the face. "Since when did the Spirit of the LORD leave me to speak to you?" he demanded.

²⁵And Micaiah replied, "You will find out soon enough when you are trying to hide in some secret room!"

²⁶"Arrest him!" the king of Israel ordered. "Take him back to Amon, the governor of the city, and to my son Joash. ²⁷Give them this order from the king: 'Put this man in prison, and feed him nothing but bread and water until I return safely from the battle!'"

²⁸But Micaiah replied, "If you return safely, it will mean that the LORD has not spoken through me!" Then he added to those standing around, "Everyone mark my words!"

²⁹So King Ahab of Israel and King Jehoshaphat of Judah led their armies against Ramoth-gilead. ³⁰The king of Israel said to Jehoshaphat, "As we go into battle, I will disguise myself so no one will recognize me, but you wear your royal robes." So the king of Israel disguised himself, and they went into battle.

³¹Meanwhile, the king of Aram had issued these orders to his thirty-two chariot commanders: "Attack only the king of Israel. Don't bother with anyone else!" ³²So when the Aramean chariot commanders saw Jehoshaphat in his royal robes, they went after him. "There is the king of Israel!" they shouted. But when Jehoshaphat called out, ³³the chariot commanders realized he was not the king of Israel, and they stopped chasing him.

³⁴An Aramean soldier, however, randomly shot an arrow at the Israelite troops and hit the king of Israel between the joints of his armor. "Turn the horses* and get me out of here!" Ahab groaned

to the driver of his chariot. "I'm badly wounded!"

³⁵The battle raged all that day, and the king remained propped up in his chariot facing the Arameans. The blood from his wound ran down to the floor of his chariot, and as evening arrived he died. ³⁶Just as the sun was setting, the cry ran through his troops: "We're done for! Run for your lives!"

³⁷So the king died, and his body was taken to Samaria and buried there. ³⁸Then his chariot was washed beside the pool of Samaria, and dogs came and licked his blood at the place where the prostitutes bathed,* just as the LORD had promised.

³⁹The rest of the events in Ahab's reign and everything he did, including the story of the ivory palace and the towns he built, are recorded in *The Book of the History of the Kings of Israel.* ⁴⁰So Ahab died, and his son Ahaziah became the next king.

⁴¹Jehoshaphat son of Asa began to rule over Judah in the fourth year of King Ahab's reign in Israel. ⁴²Jehoshaphat was thirty-five years old when he became king, and he reigned in Jerusalem twenty-five years. His mother was Azubah, the daughter of Shilhi.

⁴³Jehoshaphat was a good king, following the example of his father, Asa. He did what was pleasing in the LORD's sight.

*During his reign, however, he failed to remove all the pagan shrines, and the people still offered sacrifices and burned incense there. ⁴⁴Jehoshaphat also made peace with the king of Israel.

⁴⁵The rest of the events in Jehoshaphat's reign, the extent of his power, and the wars he waged are recorded in *The Book of the History of the Kings of Judah.* ⁴⁶He banished from the land the rest of the male and female shrine prostitutes, who still continued their practices from the days of his father, Asa.

⁴⁷(There was no king in Edom at that time, only a deputy.)

⁴⁸Jehoshaphat also built a fleet of trading ships* to sail to Ophir for gold. But the ships never set sail, for they met with disaster in their home port of Ezion-geber. ⁴⁹At one time Ahaziah son of Ahab had proposed to Jehoshaphat, "Let my men sail with your men in the ships." But Jehoshaphat refused the request.

⁵⁰When Jehoshaphat died, he was buried with his ancestors in the City of David. Then his son Jehoram became the next king.

⁵¹Ahaziah son of Ahab began to rule over Israel in the seventeenth year of King Jehoshaphat's reign in Judah. He reigned in Samaria two years. ⁵²But he did what was evil in the LORD's sight, following the example of his father and mother and the

WHAT THE BIBLE SAYS

Salvation and forgiveness

ACTS 13:38-39 Christ's death on the cross made forgiveness of sin possible. We could not be forgiven without Jesus' sacrifice. Because God is holy, he could not accept us by simply disregarding or ignoring our sins, nor could he negate the required punishment for sin. Sinful human nature had to be dealt with. God did this through the sacrificial death of his Son—born as a human, so he could die; born God in the flesh, so he could be the perfect sacrifice. • You could never have been acceptable to God by working hard to obey. Your only hope was in accepting Jesus' sacrifice on your behalf. On the basis of what Christ did, God gave an acquittal that sets free all those who are otherwise hopeless prisoners of sin. Because of Christ's shed blood on the cross, people no longer have to bear the penalty for their sin. Jesus paid it all. Through Jesus, you have been made right with God.

example of Jeroboam son of Nebat, who had led Israel to sin. [53]He served Baal and worshiped him, provoking the anger of the LORD, the God of Israel, just as his father had done.

22:17 Hebrew *These people have no master.*   **22:34** Hebrew *Turn your hand.*   **22:38** Or *his blood, and the prostitutes bathed [in it]; or his blood, and they washed his armor.* **22:43** Verses 22:43b-53 are numbered 22:44-54 in Hebrew text.   **22:48** Hebrew *fleet of ships of Tarshish.*

ACTS 13:16-41

For the rest of the book of Acts, Paul stepped to the forefront as the main spokesperson for faith in Christ. Paul's message was this: "Jesus was who he said he was. You can be right with God by believing in him."

So Paul stood, lifted his hand to quiet them [those in the synagogue], and started speaking. "Men of Israel," he said, "and you God-fearing Gentiles, listen to me. [17]"The God of this nation of Israel chose our ancestors and made them multiply and grow strong during their stay in Egypt. Then with a powerful arm he led them out of their slavery. [18]He put up with them* through forty years of wandering in the wilderness. [19]Then he destroyed seven nations in Canaan and gave their land to Israel as an inheritance. [20]All this took about 450 years.

"After that, God gave them judges to rule until the time of Samuel the prophet. [21]Then the people begged for a king, and God gave them Saul son of Kish, a man of the tribe of Benjamin, who reigned for forty years. [22]But God removed Saul and replaced him with David, a man about whom God said, 'I have found David son of Jesse, a man after my own heart. He will do everything I want him to do.'*

[23]"And it is one of King David's descendants, Jesus, who is God's promised Savior of Israel! [24]Before he came, John the Baptist preached that all the people of Israel needed to repent of their sins and turn to God and be baptized. [25]As John was finishing his ministry he asked, 'Do you think I am the Messiah? No, I am not! But he is coming soon—and I'm not even worthy to be his slave and untie the sandals on his feet.'

[26]"Brothers—you sons of Abraham, and also you God-fearing Gentiles—this mes-

sage of salvation has been sent to us! [27]The people in Jerusalem and their leaders did not recognize Jesus as the one the prophets had spoken about. Instead, they condemned him, and in doing this they fulfilled the prophets' words that are read every Sabbath. [28]They found no legal reason to execute him, but they asked Pilate to have him killed anyway.

[29]"When they had done all that the prophecies said about him, they took him down from the cross* and placed him in a tomb. [30]But God raised him from the dead! [31]And over a period of many days he appeared to those who had gone with him from Galilee to Jerusalem. They are now his witnesses to the people of Israel.

[32]"And now we are here to bring you this Good News. The promise was made to our ancestors, [33]and God has now fulfilled it for us, their descendants, by raising Jesus. This is what the second psalm says about Jesus:

'You are my Son.
    Today I have become your Father.*'

[34]For God had promised to raise him from the dead, not leaving him to rot in the grave. He said, 'I will give you the sacred blessings I promised to David.'* [35]Another psalm explains it more fully: 'You will not allow your Holy One to rot in the grave.'* [36]This is not a reference to David, for after David had done the will of God in his own generation, he died and was buried with his ancestors, and his body decayed. [37]No, it was a reference to someone else—someone whom God raised and whose body did not decay.

[38]*"Brothers, listen! We are here to proclaim that through this man Jesus there is forgiveness for your sins. [39]Everyone who believes in him is declared right with God—something the law of Moses could never do. [40]Be careful! Don't let the prophets' words apply to you. For they said,

[41] 'Look, you mockers,
        be amazed and die!
    For I am doing something in your
        own day,
    something you wouldn't believe
        even if someone told you about it.'*"

13:18 Some manuscripts read *He cared for them;* compare Deut 1:31. **13:22** 1 Sam 13:14. **13:29** Greek *from the tree.* **13:33** Or *Today I reveal you as my Son.* Ps 2:7. **13:34** Isa 55:3. **13:35** Ps 16:10. **13:38** English translations divide verses 38 and 39 in various ways. **13:41** Hab 1:5 (Greek version).

PSALM 138:1-8
A psalm of David.

¹ I give you thanks, O LORD, with all
my heart;
I will sing your praises before
the gods.
² I bow before your holy Temple
as I worship.
I praise your name for your
unfailing love and faithfulness;
for your promises are backed
by all the honor of your name.
³ As soon as I pray, you answer me;
you encourage me by giving me
strength.

⁴ Every king in all the earth will thank
you, LORD,
for all of them will hear your
words.

⁵ Yes, they will sing about the LORD's
ways,
for the glory of the LORD is very
great.
⁶ Though the LORD is great, he cares
for the humble,
but he keeps his distance from
the proud.

⁷ Though I am surrounded by troubles,
you will protect me from the anger
of my enemies.
You reach out your hand,
and the power of your right hand
saves me.
⁸ The LORD will work out his plans
for my life—
for your faithful love, O LORD,
endures forever.
Don't abandon me, for you made me.

PROVERBS 17:17-18

A friend is always loyal, and a brother is born to help in time of need. □It's poor judgment to guarantee another person's debt or put up security for a friend.

JUNE**21**

2 KINGS 1:1-2:25
The two books of Kings in the Bible were originally one book, so 2 Kings picks up right where 1 Kings left off. Elijah was a prophet in the northern kingdom of Israel. He ministered alongside other prophets of Israel, including his protégé, Elisha.

After King Ahab's death, the land of Moab rebelled against Israel.

²One day Israel's new king, Ahaziah, fell through the latticework of an upper room at his palace in Samaria and was seriously injured. So he sent messengers to the temple of Baal-zebub, the god of Ekron, to ask whether he would recover.

³But the angel of the LORD told Elijah, who was from Tishbe, "Go and confront the messengers of the king of Samaria and ask them, 'Is there no God in Israel? Why are you going to Baal-zebub, the god of Ekron, to ask whether the king will recover? ⁴Now, therefore, this is what the LORD says: You will never leave the bed you are lying on; you will surely die.'" So Elijah went to deliver the message.

⁵When the messengers returned to the king, he asked them, "Why have you returned so soon?"

⁶They replied, "A man came up to us and told us to go back to the king and give him this message. 'This is what the LORD says: Is there no God in Israel? Why are you sending men to Baal-zebub, the god of Ekron, to ask whether you will recover? Therefore, because you have done this, you will never leave the bed you are lying on; you will surely die.'"

[7]"What sort of man was he?" the king demanded. "What did he look like?"

[8]They replied, "He was a hairy man,* and he wore a leather belt around his waist."

"Elijah from Tishbe!" the king exclaimed.

[9]Then he sent an army captain with fifty soldiers to arrest him. They found him sitting on top of a hill. The captain said to him, "Man of God, the king has commanded you to come down with us."

[10]But Elijah replied to the captain, "If I am a man of God, let fire come down from heaven and destroy you and your fifty men!" Then fire fell from heaven and killed them all.

[11]So the king sent another captain with fifty men. The captain said to him, "Man of God, the king demands that you come down at once."

[12]Elijah replied, "If I am a man of God, let fire come down from heaven and destroy you and your fifty men!" And again the fire of God fell from heaven and killed them all.

[13]Once more the king sent a third captain with fifty men. But this time the captain went up the hill and fell to his knees before Elijah. He pleaded with him, "O man of God, please spare my life and the lives of these, your fifty servants. [14]See how the fire from heaven came down and destroyed the first two groups. But now please spare my life!"

[15]Then the angel of the LORD said to Elijah, "Go down with him, and don't be afraid of him." So Elijah got up and went with him to the king.

[16]And Elijah said to the king, "This is what the LORD says: Why did you send messengers to Baal-zebub, the god of Ekron, to ask whether you will recover? Is there no God in Israel to answer your question? Therefore, because you have done this, you will never leave the bed you are lying on; you will surely die."

[17]So Ahaziah died, just as the LORD had promised through Elijah. Since Ahaziah did not have a son to succeed him, his brother Joram* became the next king. This took place in the second year of the reign of Jehoram son of Jehoshaphat, king of Judah.

[18]The rest of the events in Ahaziah's reign are recorded in *The Book of the History of the Kings of Israel.*

2:1WHEN the LORD was about to take Elijah up to heaven in a whirlwind, Elijah and Elisha were traveling from Gilgal. [2]And Elijah said to Elisha, "Stay here, for the LORD has told me to go to Bethel."

But Elisha replied, "As surely as the LORD lives and you yourself live, I will never leave you!" So they went down together to Bethel.

[3]The group of prophets from Bethel came to Elisha and asked him, "Did you know that the LORD is going to take your master away from you today?"

"Of course I know," Elisha answered. "But be quiet about it."

[4]Then Elijah said to Elisha, "Stay here, for the LORD has told me to go to Jericho."

But Elisha replied again, "As surely as the LORD lives and you yourself live, I will never leave you." So they went on together to Jericho.

[5]Then the group of prophets from Jericho came to Elisha and asked him, "Did you know that the LORD is going to take your master away from you today?"

"Of course I know," Elisha answered. "But be quiet about it."

[6]Then Elijah said to Elisha, "Stay here, for the LORD has told me to go to the Jordan River."

But again Elisha replied, "As surely as the LORD lives and you yourself live, I will never leave you." So they went on together.

[7]Fifty men from the group of prophets also went and watched from a distance as Elijah and Elisha stopped beside the Jordan River. [8]Then Elijah folded his cloak together and struck the water with it. The river divided, and the two of them went across on dry ground!

[9]When they came to the other side, Elijah said to Elisha, "Tell me what I can do for you before I am taken away."

And Elisha replied, "Please let me inherit a double share of your spirit and become your successor."

[10]"You have asked a difficult thing," Elijah replied. "If you see me when I am taken from you, then you will get your request. But if not, then you won't."

[11]As they were walking along and talking, suddenly a chariot of fire appeared, drawn by horses of fire. It drove between the two men, separating them, and Elijah was carried by a whirlwind into heaven. [12]Elisha saw it and cried out, "My father! My father! I see the chariots and charioteers of Israel!" And as they disappeared from sight, Elisha tore his clothes in distress.

[13]Elisha picked up Elijah's cloak, which had fallen when he was taken up. Then Elisha returned to the bank of the Jordan River. [14]He struck the water with Elijah's cloak and cried out, "Where is the LORD, the God of Elijah?" Then the river divided, and Elisha went across.

[15]When the group of prophets from Jericho saw from a distance what happened, they exclaimed, "Elijah's spirit rests upon Elisha!" And they went to meet him and bowed to the ground before him. [16]"Sir," they said, "just say the word and fifty of our strongest men will search the wilderness for your master. Perhaps the Spirit of the LORD has left him on some mountain or in some valley."

"No," Elisha said, "don't send them." [17]But they kept urging him until they shamed him into agreeing, and he finally said, "All right, send them." So fifty men searched for three days but did not find Elijah. [18]Elisha was still at Jericho when they returned. "Didn't I tell you not to go?" he asked.

[19]One day the leaders of the town of Jericho visited Elisha. "We have a problem, my lord," they told him. "This town is located in pleasant surroundings, as you can see. But the water is bad, and the land is unproductive."

[20]Elisha said, "Bring me a new bowl with salt in it." So they brought it to him. [21]Then he went out to the spring that supplied the town with water and threw the salt into it. And he said, "This is what the LORD says: I have purified this water. It will no longer cause death or infertility.*" [22]And the water has remained pure ever since, just as Elisha said.

[23]Elisha left Jericho and went up to Bethel. As he was walking along the road, a group of boys from the town began mocking and making fun of him. "Go away, baldy!" they chanted. "Go away, baldy!" [24]Elisha turned around and looked at them, and he cursed them in the name of the LORD. Then two bears came out of the woods and mauled forty-two of them. [25]From there Elisha went to Mount Carmel and finally returned to Samaria.

1:8 Or *He was wearing clothing made of hair.*   **1:17** Hebrew *Jehoram,* a variant spelling of Joram.   **2:21** Or *or make the land unproductive;* Hebrew reads *or barrenness.*

WHAT THE BIBLE SAYS

The reality of heaven

2 KINGS 2:11-12 Elijah was taken to heaven without dying. God came one day with a chariot of fire and "Elijah was carried by a whirlwind into heaven." The only other person we know of to have been taken to heaven without actually dying was Enoch, who walked "in close fellowship with God. Then one day he disappeared, because God took him" (Genesis 5:24, January 3). • Why God did this for only these two men in all of Scripture is unknown. Other men who walked closely with God— such as Isaiah, Peter, and Paul—faced martyrdom. Still others who played significant roles in Scripture—like Abraham, Moses, and David— simply died naturally. • From the events of Elijah and Enoch simply being taken to heaven without dying, we learn that God has control of the passage from earth to heaven, and one need not necessarily die in order to get there. Most people do die, but the point is that God decides when and how that passage will be made. Our job on this side is to be prepared to make that passage when the time comes.

ACTS 13:42-14:7

Change never happens effortlessly, so conflicts are unavoidable. As wonderful as this news of Jesus was to some, it was a whole new way of thinking. Some people would rather have destroyed a new way of thinking than have to deal with it.

As Paul and Barnabas left the synagogue that day, the people begged them to speak about these things again the next week. 43Many Jews and devout converts to Judaism followed Paul and Barnabas, and the two men urged them to continue to rely on the grace of God.

44The following week almost the entire city turned out to hear them preach the word of the Lord. 45But when some of the Jews saw the crowds, they were jealous; so they slandered Paul and argued against whatever he said.

46Then Paul and Barnabas spoke out boldly and declared, "It was necessary that we first preach the word of God to you Jews. But since you have rejected it and judged yourselves unworthy of eternal life, we will offer it to the Gentiles. 47For the Lord gave us this command when he said,

'I have made you a light to the
    Gentiles,
to bring salvation to the farthest
    corners of the earth.'*"

48When the Gentiles heard this, they were very glad and thanked the Lord for his message; and all who were chosen for eternal life became believers. 49So the Lord's message spread throughout that region.

50Then the Jews stirred up the influential religious women and the leaders of the city, and they incited a mob against Paul and Barnabas and ran them out of town. 51So they shook the dust from their feet as a sign of rejection and went to the town of Iconium. 52And the believers* were filled with joy and with the Holy Spirit.

14:1THE same thing happened in Iconium.* Paul and Barnabas went to the Jewish synagogue and preached with such power that a great number of both Jews and Greeks became believers. 2Some of the Jews, however, spurned God's message and poisoned the minds of the Gentiles

against Paul and Barnabas. 3But the apostles stayed there a long time, preaching boldly about the grace of the Lord. And the Lord proved their message was true by giving them power to do miraculous signs and wonders. 4But the people of the town were divided in their opinion about them. Some sided with the Jews, and some with the apostles.

5Then a mob of Gentiles and Jews, along with their leaders, decided to attack and stone them. 6When the apostles learned of it, they fled to the region of Lycaonia—to the towns of Lystra and Derbe and the surrounding area. 7And there they preached the Good News.

13:47 Isa 49:6. 13:52 Greek *the disciples.* 14:1 *Iconium,* as well as *Lystra* and *Derbe* (14:6), were towns in what is now Turkey.

PSALM 139:1-24
For the choir director: A psalm of David.

1 **O** LORD, you have examined my heart
    and know everything about me.
2 You know when I sit down or stand up.
    You know my thoughts even when
        I'm far away.
3 You see me when I travel
    and when I rest at home.
    You know everything I do.
4 You know what I am going to say
    even before I say it, LORD.
5 You go before me and follow me.
    You place your hand of blessing on
        my head.
6 Such knowledge is too wonderful
        for me,
    too great for me to understand!

7 I can never escape from your Spirit!
    I can never get away from your
        presence!
8 If I go up to heaven, you are there;
    if I go down to the grave,* you are
        there.
9 If I ride the wings of the morning,
    if I dwell by the farthest oceans,
10 even there your hand will guide me,
    and your strength will support me.
11 I could ask the darkness to hide me
    and the light around me to become
        night—
12   but even in darkness I cannot hide
        from you.

To you the night shines as bright as day.
Darkness and light are the same
to you.

¹³ You made all the delicate, inner parts
of my body
and knit me together in my
mother's womb.
¹⁴ Thank you for making me so
wonderfully complex!
Your workmanship is marvelous—
how well I know it.
¹⁵ You watched me as I was being
formed in utter seclusion,
as I was woven together in the dark
of the womb.
¹⁶ You saw me before I was born.
Every day of my life was recorded
in your book.
Every moment was laid out
before a single day had passed.

¹⁷ How precious are your thoughts about
me,* O God.
They cannot be numbered!
¹⁸ I can't even count them;
they outnumber the grains of sand!
And when I wake up,
you are still with me!

¹⁹ O God, if only you would destroy
the wicked!
Get out of my life, you murderers!
²⁰ They blaspheme you;
your enemies misuse your name.
²¹ O LORD, shouldn't I hate those who
hate you?
Shouldn't I despise those who
oppose you?
²² Yes, I hate them with total hatred,
for your enemies are my enemies.

²³ Search me, O God, and know my heart;
test me and know my anxious
thoughts.
²⁴ Point out anything in me that offends
you,
and lead me along the path
of everlasting life.

139:8 Hebrew *to Sheol.*   **139:17** Or *How precious to me are your thoughts.*

PROVERBS 17:19-21

Anyone who loves to quarrel loves sin; anyone who trusts in high walls invites disaster. ☐ The crooked heart will not prosper; the lying tongue tumbles into trouble. ☐ It is painful to be the parent of a fool; there is no joy for the father of a rebel.

JUNE**22**

2 KINGS 3:1–4:17

When the Israelites traveled back to the land God had promised to Abraham centuries before, they inhabited the land, but they did not fully conquer it. Because of that, they constantly struggled to maintain a pure worship of the one true God.

Ahab's son Joram* began to rule over Israel in the eighteenth year of King Jehoshaphat's reign in Judah. He reigned in Samaria twelve years. ²He did what was evil in the LORD's sight, but not to the same extent as his father and mother. He at least tore down the sacred pillar of Baal that his father had set up. ³Nevertheless, he continued in the sins that Jeroboam son of Nebat had committed and led the people of Israel to commit.

⁴King Mesha of Moab was a sheep breeder. He used to pay the king of Israel an annual tribute of 100,000 lambs and the wool of 100,000 rams. ⁵But after Ahab's death, the king of Moab rebelled against the king of Israel. ⁶So King Joram promptly mustered the army of Israel and marched from Samaria. ⁷On the way, he sent this message to King Jehoshaphat of Judah: "The king of Moab has rebelled against me. Will you join me in battle against him?"

And Jehoshaphat replied, "Why, of course! You and I are as one. My troops are your troops, and my horses are your horses." ⁸Then Jehoshaphat asked, "What route will we take?"

"We will attack from the wilderness of Edom," Joram replied.

⁹The king of Edom and his troops joined them, and all three armies traveled along a roundabout route through the wilderness for seven days. But there was no water for the men or their animals.

¹⁰"What should we do?" the king of Israel cried out. "The LORD has brought the three of us here to let the king of Moab defeat us."

¹¹But King Jehoshaphat of Judah asked, "Is there no prophet of the LORD with us? If there is, we can ask the LORD what to do through him."

One of King Joram's officers replied, "Elisha son of Shaphat is here. He used to be Elijah's personal assistant.*"

¹²Jehoshaphat said, "Yes, the LORD speaks through him." So the kings of Israel, Judah, and Edom went to consult with Elisha.

¹³"Why are you coming to me?"* Elisha asked the king of Israel. "Go to the pagan prophets of your father and mother!"

But King Joram of Israel said, "No! For it was the LORD who called us three kings here—only to be defeated by the king of Moab!"

¹⁴Elisha replied, "As surely as the LORD Almighty lives, whom I serve, I wouldn't even bother with you except for my respect for King Jehoshaphat of Judah. ¹⁵Now bring me someone who can play the harp."

While the harp was being played, the power* of the LORD came upon Elisha, ¹⁶and he said, "This is what the LORD says: This dry valley will be filled with pools of water! ¹⁷You will see neither wind nor rain, says the LORD, but this valley will be filled with water. You will have plenty for yourselves and your cattle and other animals. ¹⁸But this is only a simple thing for the LORD, for he will make you victorious over the army of Moab! ¹⁹You will conquer the best of their towns, even the fortified ones. You will cut down all their good trees, stop up all their springs, and ruin all their good land with stones."

²⁰The next day at about the time when the morning sacrifice was offered, water suddenly appeared! It was flowing from the direction of Edom, and soon there was water everywhere.

²¹Meanwhile, when the people of Moab heard about the three armies marching against them, they mobilized every man who was old enough to strap on a sword, and they stationed themselves along their border. ²²But when they got up the next morning, the sun was shining across the water, making it appear red to the Moabites—like blood. ²³"It's blood!" the Moabites exclaimed. "The three armies must have attacked and killed each other! Let's go, men of Moab, and collect the plunder!"

²⁴But when the Moabites arrived at the Israelite camp, the army of Israel rushed out and attacked them until they turned and ran. The army of Israel chased them into the land of Moab, destroying everything as they went.* ²⁵They destroyed the towns, covered their good land with stones, stopped up all the springs, and cut down all the good trees. Finally, only Kir-hareseth and its stone walls were left, but men with slings surrounded and attacked it.

²⁶When the king of Moab saw that he was losing the battle, he led 700 of his swordsmen in a desperate attempt to break through the enemy lines near the king of Edom, but they failed. ²⁷Then the king of Moab took his oldest son, who would have been the next king, and sacrificed him as a burnt offering on the wall. So there was great anger against Israel,* and the Israelites withdrew and returned to their own land.

4:1ONE day the widow of a member of the group of prophets came to Elisha and cried out, "My husband who served you is dead, and you know how he feared the LORD. But now a creditor has come, threatening to take my two sons as slaves."

²"What can I do to help you?" Elisha asked. "Tell me, what do you have in the house?"

"Nothing at all, except a flask of olive oil," she replied.

³And Elisha said, "Borrow as many empty jars as you can from your friends and neighbors. ⁴Then go into your house with your sons and shut the door behind you. Pour olive oil from your flask into

the jars, setting each one aside when it is filled."

⁵So she did as she was told. Her sons kept bringing jars to her, and she filled one after another. ⁶Soon every container was full to the brim!

"Bring me another jar," she said to one of her sons.

"There aren't any more!" he told her. And then the olive oil stopped flowing.

⁷When she told the man of God what had happened, he said to her, "Now sell the olive oil and pay your debts, and you and your sons can live on what is left over."

⁸One day Elisha went to the town of Shunem. A wealthy woman lived there, and she urged him to come to her home for a meal. After that, whenever he passed that way, he would stop there for something to eat.

⁹She said to her husband, "I am sure this man who stops in from time to time is a holy man of God. ¹⁰Let's build a small room for him on the roof and furnish it with a bed, a table, a chair, and a lamp. Then he will have a place to stay whenever he comes by."

¹¹One day Elisha returned to Shunem, and he went up to this upper room to rest. ¹²He said to his servant Gehazi, "Tell the woman from Shunem I want to speak to her." When she appeared, ¹³Elisha said to Gehazi, "Tell her, 'We appreciate the kind concern you have shown us. What can we do for you? Can we put in a good word for you to the king or to the commander of the army?'"

"No," she replied, "my family takes good care of me."

¹⁴Later Elisha asked Gehazi, "What can we do for her?"

Gehazi replied, "She doesn't have a son, and her husband is an old man."

¹⁵"Call her back again," Elisha told him. When the woman returned, Elisha said to her as she stood in the doorway, ¹⁶"Next year at this time you will be holding a son in your arms!"

"No, my lord!" she cried. "O man of God, don't deceive me and get my hopes up like that."

¹⁷But sure enough, the woman soon became pregnant. And at that time the following year she had a son, just as Elisha had said.

3:1 Hebrew *Jehoram,* a variant spelling of Joram; also in 3:6. 3:11 Hebrew *He used to pour water on the hands of Elijah.* 3:13 Hebrew *What is there in common between you and me?* 3:15 Hebrew *the hand.* 3:24 The meaning of the Hebrew is uncertain. 3:27 Or *So Israel's anger was great.* The meaning of the Hebrew is uncertain.

ACTS 14:8-28
Paul and Barnabas continued on their missionary journeys. They went from town to town with a powerful message. It was so disturbing to some people that they were willing to kill Paul and Barnabas over it. For others, it was truly Good News.

WHAT THE BIBLE SAYS
Old Testament prophets

2 KINGS 3:11 2 Kings concludes the story of Elijah and continues with the story of Elisha, his protégé (although neither have books with their name in the prophetic books of the Old Testament—not all the prophets wrote down their prophecies). Elijah was the first in a long line of important prophets God sent to Israel and Judah. Israel had no faithful kings throughout its history; the southern kingdom of Judah had a few good kings. The prophets brought God's messages to the good kings and warnings to the bad kings. These men and women played vital roles in both nations, encouraging the people and leaders to turn back to God.

• Muddying up the waters, however, were false prophets who pretended to have messages from God, saying not God's words but what the king and people wanted to hear. They were often popular, whereas God's prophets were often sorely mistreated. The test to know if a prophet was from God? "Only when his predictions come true can we know that he is really from the Lord" (Jeremiah 28:9, October 16).

While they were at Lystra, Paul and Barnabas came upon a man with crippled feet. He had been that way from birth, so he had never walked. He was sitting ⁹and listening as Paul preached. Looking straight at him, Paul realized he had faith to be healed. ¹⁰So Paul called to him in a loud voice, "Stand up!" And the man jumped to his feet and started walking.

¹¹When the crowd saw what Paul had done, they shouted in their local dialect, "These men are gods in human form!" ¹²They decided that Barnabas was the Greek god Zeus and that Paul was Hermes, since he was the chief speaker. ¹³Now the temple of Zeus was located just outside the town. So the priest of the temple and the crowd brought bulls and wreaths of flowers to the town gates, and they prepared to offer sacrifices to the apostles.

¹⁴But when the apostles Barnabas and Paul heard what was happening, they tore their clothing in dismay and ran out among the people, shouting, ¹⁵"Friends,* why are you doing this? We are merely human beings—just like you! We have come to bring you the Good News that you should turn from these worthless things and turn to the living God, who made heaven and earth, the sea, and everything in them. ¹⁶In the past he permitted all the nations to go their own ways, ¹⁷but he never left them without evidence of himself and his goodness. For instance, he sends you rain and good crops and gives you food and joyful hearts." ¹⁸But even with these words, Paul and Barnabas could scarcely restrain the people from sacrificing to them.

¹⁹Then some Jews arrived from Antioch and Iconium and won the crowds to their side. They stoned Paul and dragged him out of town, thinking he was dead. ²⁰But as the believers* gathered around him, he got up and went back into the town. The next day he left with Barnabas for Derbe.

²¹After preaching the Good News in Derbe and making many disciples, Paul and Barnabas returned to Lystra, Iconium, and Antioch of Pisidia, ²²where they strengthened the believers. They encouraged them to continue in the faith, reminding them that we must suffer many hardships to enter the Kingdom of God.

²³Paul and Barnabas also appointed elders in every church. With prayer and fasting, they turned the elders over to the care of the Lord, in whom they had put their trust. ²⁴Then they traveled back through Pisidia to Pamphylia. ²⁵They preached the word in Perga, then went down to Attalia.

²⁶Finally, they returned by ship to Antioch of Syria, where their journey had begun. The believers there had entrusted them to the grace of God to do the work they had now completed. ²⁷Upon arriving in Antioch, they called the church together and reported everything God had done through them and how he had opened the door of faith to the Gentiles, too. ²⁸And they stayed there with the believers for a long time.

14:15 Greek *Men.*   14:20 Greek *disciples;* also in 14:22, 28.

PSALM 140:1-13
For the choir director: A psalm of David.

¹ **O** LORD, rescue me from evil people.
  Protect me from those who are
    violent,
² those who plot evil in their hearts
    and stir up trouble all day long.
³ Their tongues sting like a snake;
    the venom of a viper drips from
      their lips.   *Interlude*

⁴ O LORD, keep me out of the hands
    of the wicked.
  Protect me from those who are
    violent,
  for they are plotting against me.
⁵ The proud have set a trap to catch me;
    they have stretched out a net;
    they have placed traps all along
      the way.   *Interlude*

⁶ I said to the LORD, "You are my God!"
  Listen, O LORD, to my cries for
    mercy!
⁷ O Sovereign LORD, the strong one who
    rescued me,
  you protected me on the day
    of battle.
⁸ LORD, do not let evil people have
    their way.
  Do not let their evil schemes
    succeed,
  or they will become proud.
                         Interlude

⁹ Let my enemies be destroyed
   by the very evil they have planned
   for me.
¹⁰ Let burning coals fall down on their
   heads.
   Let them be thrown into the fire
   or into watery pits from which they
   can't escape.
¹¹ Don't let liars prosper here in our land.
   Cause great disasters to fall on the
   violent.

¹² But I know the LORD will help those
   they persecute;
   he will give justice to the poor.
¹³ Surely righteous people are praising
   your name;
   the godly will live in your
   presence.

PROVERBS 17:22
A cheerful heart is good medicine, but a
broken spirit saps a person's strength.

JUNE**23**

2 KINGS 4:18–5:27
Just as Jesus performed miracles to show that God's
power was at work through him, so the prophets of
the Old Testament performed miracles for the same
reason. Always, the goal was to honor God.

One day when her child was older, he
went out to help his father, who was working with the harvesters. ¹⁹Suddenly he
cried out, "My head hurts! My head hurts!"

His father said to one of the servants,
"Carry him home to his mother."
²⁰So the servant took him home, and
his mother held him on her lap. But
around noontime he died. ²¹She carried
him up and laid him on the bed of the
man of God, then shut the door and left
him there. ²²She sent a message to her
husband: "Send one of the servants and a
donkey so that I can hurry to the man of
God and come right back."

²³"Why go today?" he asked. "It is neither a new moon festival nor a Sabbath."

But she said, "It will be all right."
²⁴So she saddled the donkey and said to
the servant, "Hurry! Don't slow down unless I tell you to."

²⁵As she approached the man of God at
Mount Carmel, Elisha saw her in the distance. He said to Gehazi, "Look, the
woman from Shunem is coming. ²⁶Run
out to meet her and ask her, 'Is everything
all right with you, your husband, and your
child?'"

"Yes," the woman told Gehazi, "everything is fine."

²⁷But when she came to the man of God
at the mountain, she fell to the ground
before him and caught hold of his feet.
Gehazi began to push her away, but the
man of God said, "Leave her alone. She is
deeply troubled, but the LORD has not
told me what it is."

²⁸Then she said, "Did I ask you for a son,
my lord? And didn't I say, 'Don't deceive
me and get my hopes up'?"

²⁹Then Elisha said to Gehazi, "Get ready
to travel*; take my staff and go! Don't talk
to anyone along the way. Go quickly and
lay the staff on the child's face."

³⁰But the boy's mother said, "As surely
as the LORD lives and you yourself live, I
won't go home unless you go with me." So
Elisha returned with her.

³¹Gehazi hurried on ahead and laid the
staff on the child's face, but nothing happened. There was no sign of life. He returned to meet Elisha and told him, "The
child is still dead."

³²When Elisha arrived, the child was
indeed dead, lying there on the prophet's
bed. ³³He went in alone and shut the door
behind him and prayed to the LORD.
³⁴Then he lay down on the child's body,
placing his mouth on the child's mouth,
his eyes on the child's eyes, and his hands
on the child's hands. And as he stretched
out on him, the child's body began to grow
warm again! ³⁵Elisha got up, walked back
and forth across the room once, and then

stretched himself out again on the child. This time the boy sneezed seven times and opened his eyes!

³⁶Then Elisha summoned Gehazi. "Call the child's mother!" he said. And when she came in, Elisha said, "Here, take your son!" ³⁷She fell at his feet and bowed before him, overwhelmed with gratitude. Then she took her son in her arms and carried him downstairs.

³⁸Elisha now returned to Gilgal, and there was a famine in the land. One day as the group of prophets was seated before him, he said to his servant, "Put a large pot on the fire, and make some stew for the rest of the group."

³⁹One of the young men went out into the field to gather herbs and came back with a pocketful of wild gourds. He shredded them and put them into the pot without realizing they were poisonous. ⁴⁰Some of the stew was served to the men. But after they had eaten a bite or two they cried out, "Man of God, there's poison in this stew!" So they would not eat it.

⁴¹Elisha said, "Bring me some flour." Then he threw it into the pot and said, "Now it's all right; go ahead and eat." And then it did not harm them.

⁴²One day a man from Baal-shalishah brought the man of God a sack of fresh grain and twenty loaves of barley bread made from the first grain of his harvest. Elisha said, "Give it to the people so they can eat."

⁴³"What?" his servant exclaimed. "Feed a hundred people with only this?"

But Elisha repeated, "Give it to the people so they can eat, for this is what the LORD says: Everyone will eat, and there will even be some left over!" ⁴⁴And when they gave it to the people, there was plenty for all and some left over, just as the LORD had promised.

5:1THE king of Aram had great admiration for Naaman, the commander of his army, because through him the LORD had given Aram great victories. But though Naaman was a mighty warrior, he suffered from leprosy.*

²At this time Aramean raiders had invaded the land of Israel, and among their captives was a young girl who had been given to Naaman's wife as a maid. ³One day the girl said to her mistress, "I wish my master would go to see the prophet in Samaria. He would heal him of his leprosy."

⁴So Naaman told the king what the young girl from Israel had said. ⁵"Go and visit the prophet," the king of Aram told him. "I will send a letter of introduction for you to take to the king of Israel." So Naaman started out, carrying as gifts 750 pounds of silver, 150 pounds of gold,* and ten sets of clothing. ⁶The letter to the king of Israel said: "With this letter I present my servant Naaman. I want you to heal him of his leprosy."

⁷When the king of Israel read the letter, he tore his clothes in dismay and said, "This man sends me a leper to heal! Am I God, that I can give life and take it away? I can see that he's just trying to pick a fight with me."

⁸But when Elisha, the man of God, heard that the king of Israel had torn his clothes in dismay, he sent this message to him: "Why are you so upset? Send Naaman to me, and he will learn that there is a true prophet here in Israel."

⁹So Naaman went with his horses and chariots and waited at the door of Elisha's house. ¹⁰But Elisha sent a messenger out to him with this message: "Go and wash yourself seven times in the Jordan River. Then your skin will be restored, and you will be healed of your leprosy."

¹¹But Naaman became angry and stalked away. "I thought he would certainly come out to meet me!" he said. "I expected him to wave his hand over the leprosy and call on the name of the LORD his God and heal me! ¹²Aren't the rivers of Damascus, the Abana and the Pharpar, better than any of the rivers of Israel? Why shouldn't I wash in them and be healed?" So Naaman turned and went away in a rage.

¹³But his officers tried to reason with him and said, "Sir,* if the prophet had told you to do something very difficult, wouldn't you have done it? So you should certainly obey him when he says simply, 'Go and wash and be cured!'" ¹⁴So Naaman went down to the Jordan River and dipped himself seven times, as the man of God had instructed him. And his skin be-

came as healthy as the skin of a young child's, and he was healed!

¹⁵Then Naaman and his entire party went back to find the man of God. They stood before him, and Naaman said, "Now I know that there is no God in all the world except in Israel. So please accept a gift from your servant."

¹⁶But Elisha replied, "As surely as the LORD lives, whom I serve, I will not accept any gifts." And though Naaman urged him to take the gift, Elisha refused.

¹⁷Then Naaman said, "All right, but please allow me to load two of my mules with earth from this place, and I will take it back home with me. From now on I will never again offer burnt offerings or sacrifices to any other god except the LORD. ¹⁸However, may the LORD pardon me in this one thing: When my master the king goes into the temple of the god Rimmon to worship there and leans on my arm, may the LORD pardon me when I bow, too."

¹⁹"Go in peace," Elisha said. So Naaman started home again.

²⁰But Gehazi, the servant of Elisha, the man of God, said to himself, "My master should not have let this Aramean get away without accepting any of his gifts. As surely as the LORD lives, I will chase after him and get something from him." ²¹So Gehazi set off after Naaman.

When Naaman saw Gehazi running after him, he climbed down from his chariot and went to meet him. "Is everything all right?" Naaman asked.

²²"Yes," Gehazi said, "but my master has sent me to tell you that two young prophets from the hill country of Ephraim have just arrived. He would like 75 pounds* of silver and two sets of clothing to give to them."

²³"By all means, take twice as much* silver," Naaman insisted. He gave him two sets of clothing, tied up the money in two bags, and sent two of his servants to carry the gifts for Gehazi. ²⁴But when they arrived at the citadel,* Gehazi took the gifts from the servants and sent the men back. Then he went and hid the gifts inside the house.

²⁵When he went in to his master, Elisha asked him, "Where have you been, Gehazi?"

"I haven't been anywhere," he replied.

²⁶But Elisha asked him, "Don't you realize that I was there in spirit when Naaman stepped down from his chariot to

WHAT THE BIBLE SAYS

The Jerusalem Council

ACTS 15:1-31 This council at Jerusalem was a watershed moment in the life of the early church. The question of whether Gentile believers should obey the Law of Moses in order to be saved was extremely critical at this point in Christianity's history and could have potentially split the early church if not handled carefully. • The question: Do the Gentiles have to adhere to the laws of Moses and other Jewish traditions to be saved? One group of Jewish Christians insisted that following the law, including circumcision, was necessary for salvation. The council rightly decided that the Jewish laws, including circumcision, were not essential for salvation. • A letter was drafted and sent to the Gentile believers in Antioch. The council made a compromise agreement: Legalistic Jews no longer insisted that the Gentiles had to be circumcised to be saved, and Gentiles accepted a change in their eating habits. These decisions should not be regarded as divine ordinances but rather as stipulations for fellowship between the two disparate parties. Because a wise and careful approach to conflict resolution had been followed, and because the Jewish and Gentile Christians were willing to abide by the compromise, church unity was saved, laying the groundwork for the church to explode among the Gentiles.

meet you? Is this the time to receive money and clothing, olive groves and vineyards, sheep and cattle, and male and female servants? ²⁷Because you have done this, you and your descendants will suffer from Naaman's leprosy forever." When Gehazi left the room, he was covered with leprosy; his skin was white as snow.

4:29 Hebrew *Bind up your loins.* **5:1** Or *from a contagious skin disease.* The Hebrew word used here and throughout this passage can describe various skin diseases. **5:5** Hebrew *10 talents [340 kilograms] of silver, 6,000 shekels* [68 kilograms] *of gold.* **5:13** Hebrew *My father.* **5:22** Hebrew *1 talent* [34 kilograms]. **5:23** Hebrew *take 2 talents* [68 kilograms]. **5:24** Hebrew *the Ophel.*

ACTS 15:1-35

As Christianity spread beyond the Jewish community, a new question arose: Did a person first have to convert to Judaism in order to become a Christian? This was a crisis point in the church—and the decision would affect the future of the Christian faith.

While Paul and Barnabas were at Antioch of Syria, some men from Judea arrived and began to teach the believers*: "Unless you are circumcised as required by the law of Moses, you cannot be saved." ²Paul and Barnabas disagreed with them, arguing vehemently. Finally, the church decided to send Paul and Barnabas to Jerusalem, accompanied by some local believers, to talk to the apostles and elders about this question. ³The church sent the delegates to Jerusalem, and they stopped along the way in Phoenicia and Samaria to visit the believers. They told them—much to everyone's joy—that the Gentiles, too, were being converted.

⁴When they arrived in Jerusalem, Barnabas and Paul were welcomed by the whole church, including the apostles and elders. They reported everything God had done through them. ⁵But then some of the believers who belonged to the sect of the Pharisees stood up and insisted, "The Gentile converts must be circumcised and required to follow the law of Moses."

⁶So the apostles and elders met together to resolve this issue. ⁷At the meeting, after a long discussion, Peter stood and addressed them as follows: "Brothers, you all know that God chose me from among you some time ago to preach to the

Gentiles so that they could hear the Good News and believe. ⁸God knows people's hearts, and he confirmed that he accepts Gentiles by giving them the Holy Spirit, just as he did to us. ⁹He made no distinction between us and them, for he cleansed their hearts through faith. ¹⁰So why are you now challenging God by burdening the Gentile believers* with a yoke that neither we nor our ancestors were able to bear? ¹¹We believe that we are all saved the same way, by the undeserved grace of the Lord Jesus."

¹²Everyone listened quietly as Barnabas and Paul told about the miraculous signs and wonders God had done through them among the Gentiles.

¹³When they had finished, James stood and said, "Brothers, listen to me. ¹⁴Peter* has told you about the time God first visited the Gentiles to take from them a people for himself. ¹⁵And this conversion of Gentiles is exactly what the prophets predicted. As it is written:

¹⁶ 'Afterward I will return
    and restore the fallen house*
      of David.
   I will rebuild its ruins
      and restore it,
¹⁷ so that the rest of humanity might
      seek the LORD,
   including the Gentiles—
      all those I have called to be mine.
   The LORD has spoken—
¹⁸   he who made these things known
      so long ago.'*

¹⁹"And so my judgment is that we should not make it difficult for the Gentiles who are turning to God. ²⁰Instead, we should write and tell them to abstain from eating food offered to idols, from sexual immorality, from eating the meat of strangled animals, and from consuming blood. ²¹For these laws of Moses have been preached in Jewish synagogues in every city on every Sabbath for many generations."

²²Then the apostles and elders together with the whole church in Jerusalem chose delegates, and they sent them to Antioch of Syria with Paul and Barnabas to report on this decision. The men chosen were two of the church leaders*—

Judas (also called Barsabbas) and Silas. ²³This is the letter they took with them:

"This letter is from the apostles and elders, your brothers in Jerusalem. It is written to the Gentile believers in Antioch, Syria, and Cilicia. Greetings!

²⁴"We understand that some men from here have troubled you and upset you with their teaching, but we did not send them! ²⁵So we decided, having come to complete agreement, to send you official representatives, along with our beloved Barnabas and Paul, ²⁶who have risked their lives for the name of our Lord Jesus Christ. ²⁷We are sending Judas and Silas to confirm what we have decided concerning your question.

²⁸"For it seemed good to the Holy Spirit and to us to lay no greater burden on you than these few requirements: ²⁹You must abstain from eating food offered to idols, from consuming blood or the meat of strangled animals, and from sexual immorality. If you do this, you will do well. Farewell."

³⁰The messengers went at once to Antioch, where they called a general meeting of the believers and delivered the letter. ³¹And there was great joy throughout the church that day as they read this encouraging message.

³²Then Judas and Silas, both being prophets, spoke at length to the believers, encouraging and strengthening their faith. ³³They stayed for a while, and then the believers sent them back to the church in Jerusalem with a blessing of peace.* ³⁵Paul and Barnabas stayed in Antioch. They and many others taught and preached the word of the Lord there.

15:1 Greek *brothers;* also in 15:3, 23, 32, 33, 36, 40. 15:10 Greek *disciples.*   15:14 Greek *Symeon.*   15:16 Or *kingdom;* Greek reads *tent.*   15:16-18 Amos 9:11-12 (Greek version); Isa 45:21.   15:22 Greek *were leaders among the brothers.*   15:33 Some manuscripts add verse 34, *But Silas decided to stay there.*

PSALM 141:1-10
A psalm of David.

¹ **O** LORD, I am calling to you. Please hurry!
   Listen when I cry to you for help!
² Accept my prayer as incense offered to you,
   and my upraised hands as an evening offering.

³ Take control of what I say, O LORD,
   and guard my lips.
⁴ Don't let me drift toward evil
   or take part in acts of wickedness.
   Don't let me share in the delicacies of those who do wrong.

⁵ Let the godly strike me!
   It will be a kindness!
   If they correct me, it is soothing medicine.
   Don't let me refuse it.

   But I pray constantly
   against the wicked and their deeds.
⁶ When their leaders are thrown down from a cliff,
   the wicked will listen to my words and find them true.
⁷ Like rocks brought up by a plow,
   the bones of the wicked will lie scattered without burial.*

⁸ I look to you for help, O Sovereign LORD.
   You are my refuge; don't let them kill me.
⁹ Keep me from the traps they have set for me,
   from the snares of those who do wrong.
¹⁰ Let the wicked fall into their own nets,
   but let me escape.

141:7 Hebrew *scattered at the mouth of Sheol.*

PROVERBS 17:23
The wicked take secret bribes to pervert the course of justice.

2 KINGS 6:1–7:20

In the ancient Near East, boundaries were only as strong as the army that defended them. Some of Israel's victories were hard-won. Some, on the other hand, were quite miraculous. In today's reading, a victory came without a battle.

One day the group of prophets came to Elisha and told him, "As you can see, this place where we meet with you is too small. ²Let's go down to the Jordan River, where there are plenty of logs. There we can build a new place for us to meet."

"All right," he told them, "go ahead."

³"Please come with us," someone suggested.

"I will," he said. ⁴So he went with them.

When they arrived at the Jordan, they began cutting down trees. ⁵But as one of them was cutting a tree, his ax head fell into the river. "Oh, sir!" he cried. "It was a borrowed ax!"

⁶"Where did it fall?" the man of God asked. When he showed him the place, Elisha cut a stick and threw it into the water at that spot. Then the ax head floated to the surface. ⁷"Grab it," Elisha said. And the man reached out and grabbed it.

⁸When the king of Aram was at war with Israel, he would confer with his officers and say, "We will mobilize our forces at such and such a place."

⁹But immediately Elisha, the man of God, would warn the king of Israel, "Do not go near that place, for the Arameans are planning to mobilize their troops there." ¹⁰So the king of Israel would send word to the place indicated by the man of God. Time and again Elisha warned the king, so that he would be on the alert there.

¹¹The king of Aram became very upset over this. He called his officers together and demanded, "Which of you is the traitor? Who has been informing the king of Israel of my plans?"

¹²"It's not us, my lord the king," one of the officers replied. "Elisha, the prophet in Israel, tells the king of Israel even the words you speak in the privacy of your bedroom!"

¹³"Go and find out where he is," the king commanded, "so I can send troops to seize him."

And the report came back: "Elisha is at Dothan." ¹⁴So one night the king of Aram sent a great army with many chariots and horses to surround the city.

¹⁵When the servant of the man of God got up early the next morning and went outside, there were troops, horses, and chariots everywhere. "Oh, sir, what will we do now?" the young man cried to Elisha.

¹⁶"Don't be afraid!" Elisha told him. "For there are more on our side than on theirs!" ¹⁷Then Elisha prayed, "O LORD, open his eyes and let him see!" The LORD opened the young man's eyes, and when he looked up, he saw that the hillside around Elisha was filled with horses and chariots of fire.

¹⁸As the Aramean army advanced toward him, Elisha prayed, "O LORD, please make them blind." So the LORD struck them with blindness as Elisha had asked.

¹⁹Then Elisha went out and told them, "You have come the wrong way! This isn't the right city! Follow me, and I will take you to the man you are looking for." And he led them to the city of Samaria.

²⁰As soon as they had entered Samaria, Elisha prayed, "O LORD, now open their eyes and let them see." So the LORD opened their eyes, and they discovered that they were in the middle of Samaria.

²¹When the king of Israel saw them, he shouted to Elisha, "My father, should I kill them? Should I kill them?"

²²"Of course not!" Elisha replied. "Do we kill prisoners of war? Give them food and drink and send them home again to their master."

²³So the king made a great feast for them and then sent them home to their master. After that, the Aramean raiders stayed away from the land of Israel.

²⁴Some time later, however, King Benhadad of Aram mustered his entire army and besieged Samaria. ²⁵As a result, there was a great famine in the city. The siege lasted so long that a donkey's head sold

for eighty pieces of silver, and a cup of dove's dung sold for five pieces* of silver.

²⁶One day as the king of Israel was walking along the wall of the city, a woman called to him, "Please help me, my lord the king!"

²⁷He answered, "If the LORD doesn't help you, what can I do? I have neither food from the threshing floor nor wine from the press to give you." ²⁸But then the king asked, "What is the matter?"

She replied, "This woman said to me: 'Come on, let's eat your son today, then we will eat my son tomorrow.' ²⁹So we cooked my son and ate him. Then the next day I said to her, 'Kill your son so we can eat him,' but she has hidden her son."

³⁰When the king heard this, he tore his clothes in despair. And as the king walked along the wall, the people could see that he was wearing burlap under his robe next to his skin.* ³¹"May God strike me and even kill me if I don't separate Elisha's head from his shoulders this very day," the king vowed.

³²Elisha was sitting in his house with the elders of Israel when the king sent a messenger to summon him. But before the messenger arrived, Elisha said to the elders, "A murderer has sent a man to cut off my head. When he arrives, shut the door and keep him out. We will soon hear his master's steps following him."

³³While Elisha was still saying this, the messenger arrived. And the king* said, "All this misery is from the LORD! Why should I wait for the LORD any longer?"

⁷:¹ELISHA replied, "Listen to this message from the LORD! This is what the LORD says: By this time tomorrow in the markets of Samaria, five quarts of choice flour will cost only one piece of silver,* and ten quarts of barley grain will cost only one piece of silver.*"

²The officer assisting the king said to the man of God, "That couldn't happen even if the LORD opened the windows of heaven!"

But Elisha replied, "You will see it happen with your own eyes, but you won't be able to eat any of it!"

³Now there were four men with leprosy* sitting at the entrance of the city gates. "Why should we sit here waiting to die?" they asked each other. ⁴"We will starve if we stay here, but with the famine in the city, we will starve if we go back there. So we might as well go out and surrender to the Aramean army. If they let us live, so much the better. But if they kill us, we would have died anyway."

⁵So at twilight they set out for the camp of the Arameans. But when they came to the edge of the camp, no one was there! ⁶For the Lord had caused the Aramean army to hear the clatter of speeding chariots and the galloping of horses and the sounds of a great army approaching. "The king of Israel has hired the Hittites and Egyptians* to attack us!" they cried to one another. ⁷So they panicked and ran into the night, abandoning their tents, horses, donkeys, and everything else, as they fled for their lives.

⁸When the lepers arrived at the edge of the camp, they went into one tent after another, eating and drinking wine; and they carried off silver and gold and clothing and hid it. ⁹Finally, they said to each other, "This is not right. This is a day of good news, and we aren't sharing it with anyone! If we wait until morning, some calamity will certainly fall upon us. Come on, let's go back and tell the people at the palace."

¹⁰So they went back to the city and told the gatekeepers what had happened. "We went out to the Aramean camp," they said, "and no one was there! The horses and donkeys were tethered and the tents were all in order, but there wasn't a single person around!" ¹¹Then the gatekeepers shouted the news to the people in the palace.

¹²The king got out of bed in the middle of the night and told his officers, "I know what has happened. The Arameans know we are starving, so they have left their camp and have hidden in the fields. They are expecting us to leave the city, and then they will take us alive and capture the city."

¹³One of his officers replied, "We had better send out scouts to check into this. Let them take five of the remaining horses. If something happens to them, it

will be no worse than if they stay here and die with the rest of us."

¹⁴So two chariots with horses were prepared, and the king sent scouts to see what had happened to the Aramean army. ¹⁵They went all the way to the Jordan River, following a trail of clothing and equipment that the Arameans had thrown away in their mad rush to escape. The scouts returned and told the king about it. ¹⁶Then the people of Samaria rushed out and plundered the Aramean camp. So it was true that five quarts of choice flour were sold that day for one piece of silver, and ten quarts of barley grain were sold for one piece of silver, just as the LORD had promised. ¹⁷The king appointed his officer to control the traffic at the gate, but he was knocked down and trampled to death as the people rushed out.

So everything happened exactly as the man of God had predicted when the king came to his house. ¹⁸The man of God had said to the king, "By this time tomorrow in the markets of Samaria, five quarts of choice flour will cost one piece of silver, and ten quarts of barley grain will cost one piece of silver."

¹⁹The king's officer had replied, "That couldn't happen even if the LORD opened the windows of heaven!" And the man of God had said, "You will see it happen with your own eyes, but you won't be able to eat any of it!" ²⁰And so it was, for the people trampled him to death at the gate!

6:25 Hebrew *sold for 80 shekels* [2 pounds, or 0.9 kilograms] *of silver, and ¼ of a cab* [0.3 liters] *of dove's dung sold for 5 shekels* [2 ounces, or 57 grams]. *Dove's dung* may be a variety of wild vegetable.   6:30 As in Greek version; Hebrew reads *wearing burlap next to his skin from the house.* 6:33 Hebrew *he.*   7:1a Hebrew *1 seah* [6 liters] *of choice flour will cost 1 shekel* [0.4 ounces, or 11 grams]; also in 7:16, 18.   7:1b Hebrew *2 seahs* [12 liters] *of barley grain will cost 1 shekel* [0.4 ounces, or 11 grams]; also in 7:16, 18. 7:3 Or *with a contagious skin disease.* The Hebrew word used here and throughout this passage can describe various skin diseases.   7:6 Possibly *and the people of Muzur,* a district near Cilicia.

ACTS 15:36–16:15

Paul and Barnabas prepared for a second journey to return to those churches they had established on their first journey. Conflict threw a wrench in the cogs. God worked through the conflict, however, and used the conflict to double the missionary effort.

After some time Paul said to Barnabas, "Let's go back and visit each city where we previously preached the word of the Lord, to see how the new believers are doing." ³⁷Barnabas agreed and wanted to take along John Mark. ³⁸But Paul disagreed strongly, since John Mark had deserted them in Pamphylia and had not continued with them in their work. ³⁹Their disagreement was so sharp that they separated. Barnabas took John Mark with him and sailed for Cyprus. ⁴⁰Paul chose Silas, and as he left, the believers entrusted him to the Lord's gracious care. ⁴¹Then he traveled throughout Syria and Cilicia, strengthening the churches there.

¹⁶:¹PAUL went first to Derbe and then to Lystra, where there was a young disciple named Timothy. His mother was a Jewish believer, but his father was a Greek. ²Timothy was well thought of by the believers* in Lystra and Iconium, ³so Paul wanted him to join them on their journey. In deference to the Jews of the area, he arranged for Timothy to be circumcised before they left, for everyone knew that his father was a Greek. ⁴Then they went from town to town, instructing the believers to follow the decisions made by the apostles and elders in Jerusalem. ⁵So the churches were strengthened in their faith and grew larger every day.

⁶Next Paul and Silas traveled through the area of Phrygia and Galatia, because the Holy Spirit had prevented them from preaching the word in the province of Asia at that time. ⁷Then coming to the borders of Mysia, they headed north for the province of Bithynia,* but again the Spirit of Jesus did not allow them to go there. ⁸So instead, they went on through Mysia to the seaport of Troas.

⁹That night Paul had a vision: A man from Macedonia in northern Greece was standing there, pleading with him, "Come over to Macedonia and help us!" ¹⁰So we* decided to leave for Macedonia at once, having concluded that God was calling us to preach the Good News there.

¹¹We boarded a boat at Troas and sailed straight across to the island of Samothrace, and the next day we landed at Neapolis. ¹²From there we reached Philippi,

a major city of that district of Macedonia and a Roman colony. And we stayed there several days.

[13]On the Sabbath we went a little way outside the city to a riverbank, where we thought people would be meeting for prayer, and we sat down to speak with some women who had gathered there. [14]One of them was Lydia from Thyatira, a merchant of expensive purple cloth, who worshiped God. As she listened to us, the Lord opened her heart, and she accepted what Paul was saying. [15]She was baptized along with other members of her household, and she asked us to be her guests. "If you agree that I am a true believer in the Lord," she said, "come and stay at my home." And she urged us until we agreed.

16:2 Greek *brothers;* also in 16:40.   **16:6-7** *Phrygia, Galatia, Asia, Mysia,* and *Bithynia* were all districts in what is now Turkey.   **16:10** Luke, the writer of this book, here joined Paul and accompanied him on his journey.

PSALM 142:1-7
A psalm* of David, regarding his experience in the cave. A prayer.

[1] I cry out to the LORD;
      I plead for the LORD's mercy.
[2] I pour out my complaints before him
      and tell him all my troubles.
[3] When I am overwhelmed,

you alone know the way I should turn.
Wherever I go,
      my enemies have set traps for me.
[4] I look for someone to come and help me,
      but no one gives me a passing thought!
No one will help me;
      no one cares a bit what happens to me.
[5] Then I pray to you, O LORD.
      I say, "You are my place of refuge.
      You are all I really want in life.
[6] Hear my cry,
      for I am very low.
Rescue me from my persecutors,
      for they are too strong for me.
[7] Bring me out of prison
      so I can thank you.
The godly will crowd around me,
      for you are good to me."

142:TITLE Hebrew *maskil.* This may be a literary or musical term.

PROVERBS 17:24-25
Sensible people keep their eyes glued on wisdom, but a fool's eyes wander to the ends of the earth. □ Foolish children* bring grief to their father and bitterness to the one who gave them birth.

17:25 Hebrew *A foolish son.*

HOW WE LIVE — Seeking God's will

ACTS 16:6-10 Paul and Silas wanted to preach, to spread the gospel to anyone whom they could reach. They headed in one direction, then in another, but the Holy Spirit blocked them both times. Why would the Holy Spirit prevent these two eager preachers from heading in a certain direction?   • While the question is a good one, it is probably unanswerable. Only God knows why he chose to send this missionary team in the direction he did. This must have been disconcerting to Paul and Timothy. Although we don't know exactly how the Holy Spirit prevented them from going in the planned directions—perhaps it was the words of a prophet, an inner conviction, or even weather that made the trek impossible—we do know that a vision led them in the direction God wanted them to go. And they obediently followed.   • When God says no to you, it doesn't necessarily mean your plan was a bad one. Instead, he simply has another place he needs you for the time being. So when a door closes, don't attempt to barge through it. Trust that God has a reason and will guide you in another direction.

2 KINGS 8:1–9:13

The influence of the surrounding pagan cultures affected the kings and, in turn, the people of both Israel and Judah. Prophets like Elisha continued to call people to faith in the one true God in the midst of such decline.

Elisha had told the woman whose son he had brought back to life, "Take your family and move to some other place, for the LORD has called for a famine on Israel that will last for seven years." ²So the woman did as the man of God instructed. She took her family and settled in the land of the Philistines for seven years.

³After the famine ended she returned from the land of the Philistines, and she went to see the king about getting back her house and land. ⁴As she came in, the king was talking with Gehazi, the servant of the man of God. The king had just said, "Tell me some stories about the great things Elisha has done." ⁵And Gehazi was telling the king about the time Elisha had brought a boy back to life. At that very moment, the mother of the boy walked in to make her appeal to the king about her house and land.

"Look, my lord the king!" Gehazi exclaimed. "Here is the woman now, and this is her son—the very one Elisha brought back to life!"

⁶"Is this true?" the king asked her. And she told him the story. So he directed one of his officials to see that everything she had lost was restored to her, including the value of any crops that had been harvested during her absence.

⁷Elisha went to Damascus, the capital of Aram, where King Ben-hadad lay sick. When someone told the king that the man of God had come, ⁸the king said to Hazael, "Take a gift to the man of God. Then tell him to ask the LORD, 'Will I recover from this illness?'"

⁹So Hazael loaded down forty camels with the finest products of Damascus as a gift for Elisha. He went to him and said, "Your servant Ben-hadad, the king of Aram, has sent me to ask, 'Will I recover from this illness?'"

¹⁰And Elisha replied, "Go and tell him, 'You will surely recover.' But actually the LORD has shown me that he will surely die!" ¹¹Elisha stared at Hazael* with a fixed gaze until Hazael became uneasy.* Then the man of God started weeping.

¹²"What's the matter, my lord?" Hazael asked him.

Elisha replied, "I know the terrible things you will do to the people of Israel. You will burn their fortified cities, kill their young men with the sword, dash their little children to the ground, and rip open their pregnant women!"

¹³Hazael responded, "How could a nobody like me* ever accomplish such great things?"

Elisha answered, "The LORD has shown me that you are going to be the king of Aram."

¹⁴When Hazael left Elisha and went back, the king asked him, "What did Elisha tell you?"

And Hazael replied, "He told me that you will surely recover."

¹⁵But the next day Hazael took a blanket, soaked it in water, and held it over the king's face until he died. Then Hazael became the next king of Aram.

¹⁶Jehoram son of King Jehoshaphat of Judah began to rule over Judah in the fifth year of the reign of Joram son of Ahab, king of Israel. ¹⁷Jehoram was thirty-two years old when he became king, and he reigned in Jerusalem eight years. ¹⁸But Jehoram followed the example of the kings of Israel and was as wicked as King Ahab, for he had married one of Ahab's daughters. So Jehoram did what was evil in the LORD's sight. ¹⁹But the LORD did not want to destroy Judah, for he had made a covenant with David and promised that his descendants would continue to rule, shining like a lamp forever.

²⁰During Jehoram's reign, the Edomites revolted against Judah and crowned their own king. ²¹So Jehoram* went with all his chariots to attack the town of Zair.* The Edomites surrounded him and his chariot commanders, but he went out at night

and attacked them* under cover of darkness. But Jehoram's army deserted him and fled to their homes. ²²So Edom has been independent from Judah to this day. The town of Libnah also revolted about that same time.

²³The rest of the events in Jehoram's reign and everything he did are recorded in *The Book of the History of the Kings of Judah*. ²⁴When Jehoram died, he was buried with his ancestors in the City of David. Then his son Ahaziah became the next king.

²⁵Ahaziah son of Jehoram began to rule over Judah in the twelfth year of the reign of Joram son of Ahab, king of Israel.

²⁶Ahaziah was twenty-two years old when he became king, and he reigned in Jerusalem one year. His mother was Athaliah, a granddaughter of King Omri of Israel. ²⁷Ahaziah followed the evil example of King Ahab's family. He did what was evil in the LORD's sight, just as Ahab's family had done, for he was related by marriage to the family of Ahab.

²⁸Ahaziah joined Joram son of Ahab, the king of Israel, in his war against King Hazael of Aram at Ramoth-gilead. When the Arameans wounded King Joram in the battle, ²⁹he returned to Jezreel to recover from the wounds he had received at Ramoth.* Because Joram was wounded, King Ahaziah of Judah went to Jezreel to visit him.

⁹:¹MEANWHILE, Elisha the prophet had summoned a member of the group of prophets. "Get ready to travel,"* he told him, "and take this flask of olive oil with you. Go to Ramoth-gilead, ²and find Jehu son of Jehoshaphat, son of Nimshi. Call him into a private room away from his friends, ³and pour the oil over his head. Say to him, 'This is what the LORD says: I anoint you to be the king over Israel.' Then open the door and run for your life!"

⁴So the young prophet did as he was told and went to Ramoth-gilead. ⁵When he arrived there, he found Jehu sitting around with the other army officers. "I have a message for you, Commander," he said.

"For which one of us?" Jehu asked.

"For you, Commander," he replied.

⁶So Jehu left the others and went into the house. Then the young prophet poured the oil over Jehu's head and said, "This is what the LORD, the God of Israel, says: I anoint you king over the LORD's people, Israel. ⁷You are to destroy the family of Ahab, your master. In this way, I will avenge the murder of my prophets and all the LORD's servants who were killed by Jezebel. ⁸The entire family of Ahab must be wiped out.

Experiencing joy

HOW WE LIVE

ACTS 16:25 Stripped, beaten, placed in stocks, and locked in an inner cell in a prison—Paul and Silas had every reason to moan about their unfortunate situation. Amazingly, they did not. Why? Because of the joy that Jesus had given them. • Joy is not the same as happiness. You will feel happy when everything is going well in life; but not so happy when the car needs repairs, the bank account is overdrawn, or the medical report is not good. You may not be happy, but you can still be joyful. Joy comes from deep within, from the knowledge that ultimately God is in control of all that occurs in your life and he will help you through it. • Jesus promised his followers: "I have told you these things so that you will be filled with my joy. Yes, your joy will overflow!" (John 15:11, May 26). When you are saved, you are given a well of joy deep within that can never run dry. Even more, that joy bubbles up like a fountain and overflows to everyone around you. Just as Paul and Silas's joyful response in prison impacted the other prisoners and the jailer, so you can impact others.

I will destroy every one of his male descendants, slave and free alike, anywhere in Israel. [9]I will destroy the family of Ahab as I destroyed the families of Jeroboam son of Nebat and of Baasha son of Ahijah. [10]Dogs will eat Ahab's wife Jezebel at the plot of land in Jezreel, and no one will bury her." Then the young prophet opened the door and ran.

[11]Jehu went back to his fellow officers, and one of them asked him, "What did that madman want? Is everything all right?"

"You know how a man like that babbles on," Jehu replied.

[12]"You're hiding something," they said. "Tell us."

So Jehu told them, "He said to me, 'This is what the LORD says: I have anointed you to be king over Israel.'"

[13]Then they quickly spread out their cloaks on the bare steps and blew the ram's horn, shouting, "Jehu is king!"

8:11a Hebrew *He stared at him.*   8:11b The meaning of the Hebrew is uncertain.   8:13 Hebrew *a dog.*   8:21a Hebrew *Joram,* a variant spelling of Jehoram; also in 8:23, 24.   8:21b Greek version reads *Seir.*   8:21c Or *he went out and escaped.* The meaning of the Hebrew is uncertain.   8:29 Hebrew *Ramah,* a variant spelling of Ramoth.   9:1 Hebrew *Bind up your loins.*

ACTS 16:16-40

When Paul set a young child free from a demon, he angered her masters who made money on her fortune-telling. Paul and Silas ended up in prison—but nothing could stop their joy. Besides, God had an appointment set up between his missionaries and a certain jailer.

One day as we [Luke, Paul, and their companions] were going down to the place of prayer, we met a demon-possessed slave girl. She was a fortune-teller who earned a lot of money for her masters. [17]She followed Paul and the rest of us, shouting, "These men are servants of the Most High God, and they have come to tell you how to be saved."

[18]This went on day after day until Paul got so exasperated that he turned and said to the demon within her, "I command you in the name of Jesus Christ to come out of her." And instantly it left her.

[19]Her masters' hopes of wealth were now shattered, so they grabbed Paul and Silas and dragged them before the authorities at the marketplace. [20]"The whole city is in an uproar because of these Jews!" they shouted to the city officials. [21]"They are teaching customs that are illegal for us Romans to practice."

[22]A mob quickly formed against Paul and Silas, and the city officials ordered them stripped and beaten with wooden rods. [23]They were severely beaten, and then they were thrown into prison. The jailer was ordered to make sure they didn't escape. [24]So the jailer put them into the inner dungeon and clamped their feet in the stocks.

[25]Around midnight Paul and Silas were praying and singing hymns to God, and the other prisoners were listening. [26]Suddenly, there was a massive earthquake, and the prison was shaken to its foundations. All the doors immediately flew open, and the chains of every prisoner fell off! [27]The jailer woke up to see the prison doors wide open. He assumed the prisoners had escaped, so he drew his sword to kill himself. [28]But Paul shouted to him, "Stop! Don't kill yourself! We are all here!"

[29]The jailer called for lights and ran to the dungeon and fell down trembling before Paul and Silas. [30]Then he brought them out and asked, "Sirs, what must I do to be saved?"

[31]They replied, "Believe in the Lord Jesus and you will be saved, along with everyone in your household." [32]And they shared the word of the Lord with him and with all who lived in his household. [33]Even at that hour of the night, the jailer cared for them and washed their wounds. Then he and everyone in his household were immediately baptized. [34]He brought them into his house and set a meal before them, and he and his entire household rejoiced because they all believed in God.

[35]The next morning the city officials sent the police to tell the jailer, "Let those men go!" [36]So the jailer told Paul, "The city officials have said you and Silas are free to leave. Go in peace."

[37]But Paul replied, "They have publicly beaten us without a trial and put us in prison—and we are Roman citizens. So now they want us to leave secretly? Cer-

tainly not! Let them come themselves to release us!"

[38]When the police reported this, the city officials were alarmed to learn that Paul and Silas were Roman citizens. [39]So they came to the jail and apologized to them. Then they brought them out and begged them to leave the city. [40]When Paul and Silas left the prison, they returned to the home of Lydia. There they met with the believers and encouraged them once more. Then they left town.

PSALM 143:1-12
A psalm of David.

[1] **H**ear my prayer, O LORD;
      listen to my plea!
   Answer me because you are faithful
      and righteous.
[2] Don't put your servant on trial,
      for no one is innocent before you.
[3] My enemy has chased me.
   He has knocked me to the ground
      and forces me to live in darkness
         like those in the grave.
[4] I am losing all hope;
      I am paralyzed with fear.
[5] I remember the days of old.
   I ponder all your great works
      and think about what you have done.
[6] I lift my hands to you in prayer.

I thirst for you as parched land
      thirsts for rain.   *Interlude*

[7] Come quickly, LORD, and answer
      me,
      for my depression deepens.
   Don't turn away from me,
      or I will die.
[8] Let me hear of your unfailing love
      each morning,
      for I am trusting you.
   Show me where to walk,
      for I give myself to you.
[9] Rescue me from my enemies, LORD;
      I run to you to hide me.
[10] Teach me to do your will,
      for you are my God.
   May your gracious Spirit lead
      me forward
      on a firm footing.
[11] For the glory of your name, O LORD,
      preserve my life.
   Because of your faithfulness,
      bring me out of this distress.
[12] In your unfailing love, silence all
      my enemies
   and destroy all my foes,
      for I am your servant.

PROVERBS 17:26
It is wrong to punish the godly for being good or to flog leaders for being honest.

JUNE**26**

2 KINGS 9:14-10:31
The same old problems followed the people of Israel and Judah when they turned away from God's law. The same old violence took place as one family dynasty defeated another. Sometimes it makes you wonder if people ever learn.

So Jehu son of Jehoshaphat, son of Nimshi, led a conspiracy against King Joram. (Now Joram had been with the army at Ramoth-gilead, defending Israel against the forces of King Hazael of Aram. [15]But King Joram* was wounded in the fighting and returned to Jezreel to recover from his wounds.) So Jehu told the men with him, "If you want me to be king, don't let

anyone leave town and go to Jezreel to report what we have done."

[16]Then Jehu got into a chariot and rode to Jezreel to find King Joram, who was lying there wounded. King Ahaziah of Judah was there, too, for he had gone to visit him. [17]The watchman on the tower of Jezreel saw Jehu and his company approaching, so he shouted to Joram, "I see a company of troops coming!"

"Send out a rider to ask if they are coming in peace," King Joram ordered.

[18]So a horseman went out to meet Jehu and said, "The king wants to know if you are coming in peace."

Jehu replied, "What do you know about peace? Fall in behind me!"

The watchman called out to the king, "The messenger has met them, but he's not returning."

¹⁹So the king sent out a second horseman. He rode up to them and said, "The king wants to know if you come in peace."

Again Jehu answered, "What do you know about peace? Fall in behind me!"

²⁰The watchman exclaimed, "The messenger has met them, but he isn't returning either! It must be Jehu son of Nimshi, for he's driving like a madman."

²¹"Quick! Get my chariot ready!" King Joram commanded.

Then King Joram of Israel and King Ahaziah of Judah rode out in their chariots to meet Jehu. They met him at the plot of land that had belonged to Naboth of Jezreel. ²²King Joram demanded, "Do you come in peace, Jehu?"

Jehu replied, "How can there be peace as long as the idolatry and witchcraft of your mother, Jezebel, are all around us?"

²³Then King Joram turned the horses around* and fled, shouting to King Ahaziah, "Treason, Ahaziah!" ²⁴But Jehu drew his bow and shot Joram between the shoulders. The arrow pierced his heart, and he sank down dead in his chariot.

²⁵Jehu said to Bidkar, his officer, "Throw him into the plot of land that belonged to Naboth of Jezreel. Do you remember when you and I were riding along behind his father, Ahab? The LORD pronounced this message against him: ²⁶'I solemnly swear that I will repay him here on this plot of land, says the LORD, for the murder of Naboth and his sons that I saw yesterday.' So throw him out on Naboth's property, just as the LORD said."

²⁷When King Ahaziah of Judah saw what was happening, he fled along the road to Beth-haggan. Jehu rode after him, shouting, "Shoot him, too!" So they shot Ahaziah in his chariot at the Ascent of Gur, near Ibleam. He was able to go on as far as Megiddo, but he died there. ²⁸His servants took him by chariot to Jerusalem, where they buried him with his ancestors in the City of David. ²⁹Ahaziah had become king over Judah in the eleventh year of the reign of Joram son of Ahab.

³⁰When Jezebel, the queen mother, heard that Jehu had come to Jezreel, she painted her eyelids and fixed her hair and sat at a window. ³¹When Jehu entered the gate of the palace, she shouted at him, "Have you come in peace, you murderer? You're just like Zimri, who murdered his master!"*

³²Jehu looked up and saw her at the window and shouted, "Who is on my side?" And two or three eunuchs looked out at him. ³³"Throw her down!" Jehu yelled. So they threw her out the window, and her blood spattered against the wall and on the horses. And Jehu trampled her body under his horses' hooves.

³⁴Then Jehu went into the palace and ate and drank. Afterward he said, "Someone go and bury this cursed woman, for she is the daughter of a king." ³⁵But when they went out to bury her, they found only her skull, her feet, and her hands.

³⁶When they returned and told Jehu, he stated, "This fulfills the message from the LORD, which he spoke through his servant Elijah from Tishbe: 'At the plot of land in Jezreel, dogs will eat Jezebel's body. ³⁷Her remains will be scattered like dung on the plot of land in Jezreel, so that no one will be able to recognize her.'"

10:¹AHAB had seventy sons living in the city of Samaria. So Jehu wrote letters and sent them to Samaria, to the elders and officials of the city,* and to the guardians of King Ahab's sons. He said, ²"The king's sons are with you, and you have at your disposal chariots, horses, a fortified city, and weapons. As soon as you receive this letter, ³select the best qualified of your master's sons to be your king, and prepare to fight for Ahab's dynasty."

⁴But they were paralyzed with fear and said, "We've seen that two kings couldn't stand against this man! What can we do?"

⁵So the palace and city administrators, together with the elders and the guardians of the king's sons, sent this message to Jehu: "We are your servants and will do anything you tell us. We will not make anyone king; do whatever you think is best."

⁶Jehu responded with a second letter: "If you are on my side and are going to

obey me, bring the heads of your master's sons to me at Jezreel by this time tomorrow." Now the seventy sons of the king were being cared for by the leaders of Samaria, where they had been raised since childhood. ⁷When the letter arrived, the leaders killed all seventy of the king's sons. They placed their heads in baskets and presented them to Jehu at Jezreel.

⁸A messenger went to Jehu and said, "They have brought the heads of the king's sons."

So Jehu ordered, "Pile them in two heaps at the entrance of the city gate, and leave them there until morning."

⁹In the morning he went out and spoke to the crowd that had gathered around them. "You are not to blame," he told them. "I am the one who conspired against my master and killed him. But who killed all these? ¹⁰You can be sure that the message of the LORD that was spoken concerning Ahab's family will not fail. The LORD declared through his servant Elijah that this would happen." ¹¹Then Jehu killed all who were left of Ahab's relatives living in Jezreel and all his important officials, his personal friends, and his priests. So Ahab was left without a single survivor.

¹²Then Jehu set out for Samaria. Along the way, while he was at Beth-eked of the Shepherds, ¹³he met some relatives of King Ahaziah of Judah. "Who are you?" he asked them.

And they replied, "We are relatives of King Ahaziah. We are going to visit the sons of King Ahab and the sons of the queen mother."

¹⁴"Take them alive!" Jehu shouted to his men. And they captured all forty-two of them and killed them at the well of Beth-eked. None of them escaped.

¹⁵When Jehu left there, he met Jehonadab son of Recab, who was coming to meet him. After they had greeted each other, Jehu said to him, "Are you as loyal to me as I am to you?"

"Yes, I am," Jehonadab replied.

"If you are," Jehu said, "then give me your hand." So Jehonadab put out his hand, and Jehu helped him into the chariot. ¹⁶Then Jehu said, "Now come with me, and see how devoted I am to the LORD." So Jehonadab rode along with him.

¹⁷When Jehu arrived in Samaria, he killed everyone who was left there from Ahab's family, just as the LORD had promised through Elijah.

¹⁸Then Jehu called a meeting of all the people of the city and said to them, "Ahab's worship of Baal was nothing compared to the way I will worship him! ¹⁹Therefore, summon all the prophets and worshipers of Baal, and call together all his priests. See to it that every one of them comes, for I am going to offer a great sacrifice to Baal. Anyone who fails to come will be put to death." But Jehu's cunning plan was to destroy all the worshipers of Baal.

²⁰Then Jehu ordered, "Prepare a solemn assembly to worship Baal!" So they did. ²¹He sent messengers throughout all Israel summoning those who worshiped Baal. They all came—not a single one remained behind—and they filled the temple of Baal from one end to the other. ²²And Jehu instructed the keeper of the wardrobe, "Be sure that every worshiper of Baal wears one of these robes." So robes were given to them.

²³Then Jehu went into the temple of Baal with Jehonadab son of Recab. Jehu said to the worshipers of Baal, "Make sure no one who worships the LORD is here—only those who worship Baal." ²⁴So they were all inside the temple to offer sacrifices and burnt offerings. Now Jehu had stationed eighty of his men outside the building and had warned them, "If you let anyone escape, you will pay for it with your own life."

²⁵As soon as Jehu had finished sacrificing the burnt offering, he commanded his guards and officers, "Go in and kill all of them. Don't let a single one escape!" So they killed them all with their swords, and the guards and officers dragged their bodies outside.* Then Jehu's men went into the innermost fortress* of the temple of Baal. ²⁶They dragged out the sacred pillar* used in the worship of Baal and burned it. ²⁷They smashed the sacred pillar and wrecked the temple of Baal, converting it into a public toilet, as it remains to this day.

²⁸In this way, Jehu destroyed every trace of Baal worship from Israel. ²⁹He did

not, however, destroy the gold calves at Bethel and Dan, with which Jeroboam son of Nebat had caused Israel to sin.

30Nonetheless the LORD said to Jehu, "You have done well in following my instructions to destroy the family of Ahab. Therefore, your descendants will be kings of Israel down to the fourth generation." 31But Jehu did not obey the Law of the LORD, the God of Israel, with all his heart. He refused to turn from the sins that Jeroboam had led Israel to commit.

9:15 Hebrew *Jehoram,* a variant spelling of Joram; also in 9:17, 21, 22, 23, 24.   **9:23** Hebrew *turned his hands.*
9:31 See 1 Kgs 16:9-10, where Zimri killed his master, King Elah.   **10:1** As in some Greek manuscripts and Latin Vulgate (see also 10:6); Hebrew reads *of Jezreel.*   **10:25a** Or *they left their bodies lying there;* or *they threw them out into the outermost court.*   **10:25b** Hebrew *city.*   **10:26** As in Greek and Syriac versions and Latin Vulgate; Hebrew reads *sacred pillars.*

ACTS 17:1-34

Paul returned to visit the churches he had started on his first missionary journey and made some new stops as well. When he preached, he began where the culture was, and then from that point led the people to a new way of thinking.

Paul and Silas then traveled through the towns of Amphipolis and Apollonia and came to Thessalonica, where there was a Jewish synagogue. 2As was Paul's custom, he went to the synagogue service, and for three Sabbaths in a row he used the Scriptures to reason with the people. 3He explained the prophecies and proved that the Messiah must suffer and rise from the dead. He said, "This Jesus I'm telling you about is the Messiah." 4Some of the Jews who listened were persuaded and joined Paul and Silas, along with many God-fearing Greek men and quite a few prominent women.*

5But some of the Jews were jealous, so they gathered some troublemakers from the marketplace to form a mob and start a riot. They attacked the home of Jason, searching for Paul and Silas so they could drag them out to the crowd.* 6Not finding them there, they dragged out Jason and some of the other believers* instead and took them before the city council. "Paul and Silas have caused trouble all over the world," they shouted, "and now they are here disturbing our city, too. 7And Jason has welcomed them into his home. They are all guilty of treason against Caesar, for they profess allegiance to another king, named Jesus."

8The people of the city, as well as the city council, were thrown into turmoil by these reports. 9So the officials forced Jason and the other believers to post bond, and then they released them.

10That very night the believers sent Paul and Silas to Berea. When they arrived there, they went to the Jewish synagogue. 11And the people of Berea were more open-minded than those in Thessalonica, and they listened eagerly to Paul's message. They searched the Scriptures day after day to see if Paul and Silas were teaching the truth. 12As a result, many Jews believed, as did many of the prominent Greek women and men.

13But when some Jews in Thessalonica learned that Paul was preaching the word of God in Berea, they went there and stirred up trouble. 14The believers acted at once, sending Paul on to the coast, while Silas and Timothy remained behind. 15Those escorting Paul went with him all the way to Athens; then they returned to Berea with instructions for Silas and Timothy to hurry and join him.

16While Paul was waiting for them in Athens, he was deeply troubled by all the idols he saw everywhere in the city. 17He went to the synagogue to reason with the Jews and the God-fearing Gentiles, and he spoke daily in the public square to all who happened to be there. 18He also had a debate with some of the Epicurean and Stoic philosophers. When he told them about Jesus and his resurrection, they said, "What's this babbler trying to say with these strange ideas he's picked up?" Others said, "He seems to be preaching about some foreign gods."

19Then they took him to the high council of the city.* "Come and tell us about this new teaching," they said. 20"You are saying some rather strange things, and we want to know what it's all about." 21(It should be explained that all the Athenians as well as the foreigners in Athens seemed to spend all their time discussing the latest ideas.)

22So Paul, standing before the council,* addressed them as follows: "Men of Athens, I notice that you are very religious in every way, ²³for as I was walking along I saw your many shrines. And one of your altars had this inscription on it: 'To an Unknown God.' This God, whom you worship without knowing, is the one I'm telling you about.

²⁴"He is the God who made the world and everything in it. Since he is Lord of heaven and earth, he doesn't live in man-made temples, ²⁵and human hands can't serve his needs—for he has no needs. He himself gives life and breath to everything, and he satisfies every need. ²⁶From one man* he created all the nations throughout the whole earth. He decided beforehand when they should rise and fall, and he determined their boundaries.

²⁷"His purpose was for the nations to seek after God and perhaps feel their way toward him and find him—though he is not far from any one of us. ²⁸For in him we live and move and exist. As some of your* own poets have said, 'We are his offspring.' ²⁹And since this is true, we shouldn't think of God as an idol designed by craftsmen from gold or silver or stone.

³⁰"God overlooked people's ignorance about these things in earlier times, but now he commands everyone everywhere to repent of their sins and turn to him. ³¹For he has set a day for judging the world with justice by the man he has ap-pointed, and he proved to everyone who this is by raising him from the dead."

³²When they heard Paul speak about the resurrection of the dead, some laughed in contempt, but others said, "We want to hear more about this later." ³³That ended Paul's discussion with them, ³⁴but some joined him and became believers. Among them were Dionysius, a member of the council,* a woman named Damaris, and others with them.

17:4 Some manuscripts read *quite a few of the wives of the leading men.*   17:5 Or *the city council.*   17:6 Greek *brothers;* also in 17:10, 14.   17:19 Or *the most learned society of philosophers in the city.* Greek reads *the Areopagus.*   17:22 Traditionally rendered *standing in the middle of Mars Hill;* Greek reads *standing in the middle of the Areopagus.*   17:26 Greek *From one;* other manuscripts read *From one blood.*   17:28 Some manuscripts read *our.* 17:34 Greek *an Areopagite.*

PSALM 144:1-15
A psalm of David.

¹ **P**raise the LORD, who is my rock.
  He trains my hands for war
   and gives my fingers skill for battle.
² He is my loving ally and my fortress,
   my tower of safety, my rescuer.
 He is my shield, and I take refuge in him.
   He makes the nations* submit to me.

³ O LORD, what are human beings that
   you should notice them,
  mere mortals that you should think
   about them?

WHAT THE BIBLE SAYS
How to discern truth

ACTS 17:11 We hear phrases like "blind faith" and get the impression that faith can require us to hang our brains at the door. That's not the case, however. It certainly wasn't with the Bereans as they are described in Acts: "They listened eagerly to Paul's message. They searched the Scriptures day after day to see if Paul and Silas were teaching the truth." The Bereans listened to Paul, then they studied for themselves to see if what Paul taught agreed with what the Scriptures said. • Discernment requires your brain and heart to be in full cooperation. It means receiving wisdom from God, remaining aware of logic and good reason, and keeping your undying faith in plain view. It means deciding for yourself what God wants of you, even when it might be easier to let someone else decide for you. Life is a process with as many exceptions as there are rules. Believing is a lifelong journey. Discernment is the ability to keep the train on the tracks through all the twists and turns of life.

4 For they are like a breath of air;
  their days are like a passing shadow.

5 Open the heavens, LORD, and come
    down.
  Touch the mountains so they billow
    smoke.

6 Hurl your lightning bolts and scatter
    your enemies!
  Shoot your arrows and confuse
    them!

7 Reach down from heaven and rescue
    me;
  rescue me from deep waters,
  from the power of my enemies.

8 Their mouths are full of lies;
  they swear to tell the truth,
    but they lie instead.

9 I will sing a new song to you, O God!
  I will sing your praises with a ten-
    stringed harp.

10 For you grant victory to kings!
   You rescued your servant David
     from the fatal sword.

11 Save me!
   Rescue me from the power of
     my enemies.
   Their mouths are full of lies;
   they swear to tell the truth,
     but they lie instead.

12 May our sons flourish in their youth
   like well-nurtured plants.
   May our daughters be like graceful
     pillars,
   carved to beautify a palace.

13 May our barns be filled
   with crops of every kind.
   May the flocks in our fields multiply
     by the thousands,
   even tens of thousands,

14 and may our oxen be loaded down
   with produce.
   May there be no enemy breaking
     through our walls,
   no going into captivity,
   no cries of alarm in our town
     squares.

15 Yes, joyful are those who live like this!
   Joyful indeed are those whose God
     is the LORD.

144:2 Some manuscripts read *my people.*

PROVERBS 17:27-28

A truly wise person uses few words; a person with understanding is even-tempered. ☐ Even fools are thought wise when they keep silent; with their mouths shut, they seem intelligent.

JUNE**27**

2 KINGS 10:32–12:21
While Joash chose to follow God's law and care for the Temple, he unfortunately didn't choose to exert that influence over the whole nation. Altars and idols still stood throughout Judah. Joash took a "live and let live" stance. Watch what happened as a result.

At about that time the LORD began to cut down the size of Israel's territory. King Hazael conquered several sections of the country 33 east of the Jordan River, including all of Gilead, Gad, Reuben, and Manasseh. He conquered the area from the town of Aroer by the Arnon Gorge to as far north as Gilead and Bashan.

34 The rest of the events in Jehu's reign—everything he did and all his achievements—are recorded in *The Book of the History of the Kings of Israel.*

35 When Jehu died, he was buried in Samaria. Then his son Jehoahaz became the next king. 36 In all, Jehu reigned over Israel from Samaria for twenty-eight years.

11:1 WHEN Athaliah, the mother of King Ahaziah of Judah, learned that her son was dead, she began to destroy the rest of the royal family. 2 But Ahaziah's sister Jehosheba, the daughter of King Jehoram,* took Ahaziah's infant son, Joash, and stole him away from among the rest of the king's children, who were about to be killed. She put Joash and his nurse in a bedroom to hide him from Athaliah, so the child was not murdered. ³Joash remained hidden in the Temple of the LORD for six years while Athaliah ruled over the land.

⁴In the seventh year of Athaliah's reign, Jehoiada the priest summoned the commanders, the Carite mercenaries, and the palace guards to come to the Temple of the LORD. He made a solemn pact with them and made them swear an oath of loyalty there in the LORD's Temple; then he showed them the king's son.

⁵Jehoiada told them, "This is what you must do. A third of you who are on duty on the Sabbath are to guard the royal palace itself. ⁶Another third of you are to stand guard at the Sur Gate. And the final third must stand guard behind the palace guard. These three groups will all guard the palace. ⁷The other two units who are off duty on the Sabbath must stand guard for the king at the LORD's Temple. ⁸Form a bodyguard around the king and keep your weapons in hand. Kill anyone who tries to break through. Stay with the king wherever he goes."

⁹So the commanders did everything as Jehoiada the priest ordered. The commanders took charge of the men reporting for duty that Sabbath, as well as those who were going off duty. They brought them all to Jehoiada the priest, ¹⁰and he supplied them with the spears and small shields that had once belonged to King David and were stored in the Temple of the LORD. ¹¹The palace guards stationed themselves around the king, with their weapons ready. They formed a line from the south side of the Temple around to the north side and all around the altar.

¹²Then Jehoiada brought out Joash, the king's son, placed the crown on his head, and presented him with a copy of God's laws.* They anointed him and proclaimed him king, and everyone clapped their hands and shouted, "Long live the king!"

¹³When Athaliah heard all the noise made by the palace guards and the people, she hurried to the LORD's Temple to see what was happening. ¹⁴When she ar-

rived, she saw the newly crowned king standing in his place of authority by the pillar, as was the custom at times of coronation. The commanders and trumpeters were surrounding him, and people from all over the land were rejoicing and blowing trumpets. When Athaliah saw all this, she tore her clothes in despair and shouted, "Treason! Treason!"

¹⁵Then Jehoiada the priest ordered the commanders who were in charge of the troops, "Take her to the soldiers in front of the Temple,* and kill anyone who tries to rescue her." For the priest had said, "She must not be killed in the Temple of the LORD." ¹⁶So they seized her and led her out to the gate where horses enter the palace grounds, and she was killed there.

¹⁷Then Jehoiada made a covenant between the LORD and the king and the people that they would be the LORD's people. He also made a covenant between the king and the people. ¹⁸And all the people of the land went over to the temple of Baal and tore it down. They demolished the altars and smashed the idols to pieces, and they killed Mattan the priest of Baal in front of the altars.

Jehoiada the priest stationed guards at the Temple of the LORD. ¹⁹Then the commanders, the Carite mercenaries, the palace guards, and all the people of the land escorted the king from the Temple of the LORD. They went through the gate of the guards and into the palace, and the king took his seat on the royal throne. ²⁰So all the people of the land rejoiced, and the city was peaceful because Athaliah had been killed at the king's palace.

²¹*Joash* was seven years old when he became king.

12:1*JOASH* began to rule over Judah in the seventh year of King Jehu's reign in Israel. He reigned in Jerusalem forty years. His mother was Zibiah from Beersheba. ²All his life Joash did what was pleasing in the LORD's sight because Jehoiada the priest instructed him. ³Yet even so, he did not destroy the pagan shrines, and the people still offered sacrifices and burned incense there.

⁴One day King Joash said to the priests, "Collect all the money brought as a sacred

offering to the LORD's Temple, whether it is a regular assessment, a payment of vows, or a voluntary gift. ⁵Let the priests take some of that money to pay for whatever repairs are needed at the Temple."

⁶But by the twenty-third year of Joash's reign, the priests still had not repaired the Temple. ⁷So King Joash called for Jehoiada and the other priests and asked them, "Why haven't you repaired the Temple? Don't use any more money for your own needs. From now on, it must all be spent on Temple repairs." ⁸So the priests agreed not to accept any more money from the people, and they also agreed to let others take responsibility for repairing the Temple.

⁹Then Jehoiada the priest bored a hole in the lid of a large chest and set it on the right-hand side of the altar at the entrance of the Temple of the LORD. The priests guarding the entrance put all of the people's contributions into the chest. ¹⁰Whenever the chest became full, the court secretary and the high priest counted the money that had been brought to the LORD's Temple and put it into bags. ¹¹Then they gave the money to the construction supervisors, who used it to pay the people working on the LORD's Temple—the carpenters, the builders, ¹²the masons, and the stonecutters. They also used the money to buy the timber and the finished stone needed for repairing the LORD's Temple, and they paid any other expenses related to the Temple's restoration.

¹³The money brought to the Temple was not used for making silver bowls, lamp snuffers, basins, trumpets, or other articles of gold or silver for the Temple of the LORD. ¹⁴It was paid to the workmen, who used it for the Temple repairs. ¹⁵No accounting of this money was required from the construction supervisors, because they were honest and trustworthy men. ¹⁶However, the money that was contributed for guilt offerings and sin offerings was not brought into the LORD's Temple. It was given to the priests for their own use.

¹⁷About this time King Hazael of Aram went to war against Gath and captured it. Then he turned to attack Jerusalem. ¹⁸King Joash collected all the sacred objects that Jehoshaphat, Jehoram, and Ahaziah, the previous kings of Judah, had dedicated, along with what he himself had dedicated. He sent them all to Hazael, along with all the gold in the treasuries of the LORD's Temple and the royal palace. So Hazael called off his attack on Jerusalem.

¹⁹The rest of the events in Joash's reign and everything he did are recorded in *The Book of the History of the Kings of Judah*.

²⁰Joash's officers plotted against him and assassinated him at Beth-millo on the road to Silla. ²¹The assassins were Jozacar* son of Shimeath and Jehozabad son of Shomer—both trusted advisers. Joash was buried with his ancestors in the City of David. Then his son Amaziah became the next king.

11:2 Hebrew *Joram*, a variant spelling of Jehoram.
11:12 Or *a copy of the covenant*.   11:15 Or *Bring her out from between the ranks;* or *Take her out of the Temple precincts*. The meaning of the Hebrew is uncertain.
11:21a Verse 11:21 is numbered 12:1 in Hebrew text.
11:21b Hebrew *Jehoash*, a variant spelling of Joash.
12:1a Verses 12:1-21 are numbered 12:2-22 in Hebrew text.
12:1b Hebrew *Jehoash*, a variant spelling of Joash; also in 12:2, 4, 6, 7, 18.   12:21 As in Greek and Syriac versions; Hebrew reads *Jozabad*.

ACTS 18:1-22

With all the trouble that followed him as he spread the news about Jesus, it would have been easy for Paul to get discouraged or fearful. While facing the wrath of the Jewish leaders at Corinth, Paul received from the Lord a special message of encouragement.

Then Paul left Athens and went to Corinth.* ²There he became acquainted with a Jew named Aquila, born in Pontus, who had recently arrived from Italy with his wife, Priscilla. They had left Italy when Claudius Caesar deported all Jews from Rome. ³Paul lived and worked with them, for they were tentmakers* just as he was.

⁴Each Sabbath found Paul at the synagogue, trying to convince the Jews and Greeks alike. ⁵And after Silas and Timothy came down from Macedonia, Paul spent all his time preaching the word. He testified to the Jews that Jesus was the Messiah. ⁶But when they opposed and insulted him, Paul shook the dust from his clothes and said, "Your blood is upon your own heads—I am innocent. From now on I will go preach to the Gentiles."

⁷Then he left and went to the home of Titus Justus, a Gentile who worshiped God and lived next door to the synagogue. ⁸Crispus, the leader of the synagogue, and everyone in his household believed in the Lord. Many others in Corinth also heard Paul, became believers, and were baptized.

⁹One night the Lord spoke to Paul in a vision and told him, "Don't be afraid! Speak out! Don't be silent! ¹⁰For I am with you, and no one will attack and harm you, for many people in this city belong to me." ¹¹So Paul stayed there for the next year and a half, teaching the word of God.

¹²But when Gallio became governor of Achaia, some Jews rose up together against Paul and brought him before the governor for judgment. ¹³They accused Paul of "persuading people to worship God in ways that are contrary to our law."

¹⁴But just as Paul started to make his defense, Gallio turned to Paul's accusers and said, "Listen, you Jews, if this were a case involving some wrongdoing or a serious crime, I would have a reason to accept your case. ¹⁵But since it is merely a question of words and names and your Jewish law, take care of it yourselves. I refuse to judge such matters." ¹⁶And he threw them out of the courtroom.

¹⁷The crowd* then grabbed Sosthenes, the leader of the synagogue, and beat him right there in the courtroom. But Gallio paid no attention.

¹⁸Paul stayed in Corinth for some time after that, then said good-bye to the brothers and sisters* and went to nearby Cenchrea. There he shaved his head according to Jewish custom, marking the end of a vow. Then he set sail for Syria, taking Priscilla and Aquila with him.

¹⁹They stopped first at the port of Ephesus, where Paul left the others behind. While he was there, he went to the synagogue to reason with the Jews. ²⁰They asked him to stay longer, but he declined. ²¹As he left, however, he said, "I will come back later,* God willing." Then he set sail from Ephesus. ²²The next stop was at the port of Caesarea. From there he went up and visited the church at Jerusalem* and then went back to Antioch.

18:1 *Athens* and *Corinth* were major cities in Achaia, the region in the southern portion of the Greek peninsula. 18:3 Or *leatherworkers.* 18:17 Greek *Everyone;* other manuscripts read *All the Greeks.* 18:18 Greek *brothers;* also in 18:27. 18:21 Some manuscripts read "I must by all means be at Jerusalem for the upcoming festival, but I will come back later." 18:22 Greek *the church.*

PSALM 145:1-21*
A psalm of praise of David.

¹ I will exalt you, my God and King,
    and praise your name forever and
    ever.
² I will praise you every day;
    yes, I will praise you forever.
³ Great is the LORD! He is most worthy
    of praise!

Having integrity

HOW WE LIVE

2 KINGS 12:15 The construction supervisors in the Temple were completely honest, so honest in fact that no accounting of the money was required. What a contrast between them and the priests who couldn't be trusted to set some of their funds aside for the Temple (12:7-8). What an example these construction supervisors were to the men who should have been the spiritual guides for the nation! • Honesty should come naturally, but it doesn't always come easily. Honesty is vital, for a dishonest act can ruin your witness for Christ. How honest are you? Are your words honest, or are you guilty of passing along gossip? Are you completely trustworthy at work—not stealing time from your employer, but putting in a day's work for a day's wage? If you are an employer, do you run your business honestly—without cooking the books? • Take a lesson from these Old Testament men. Be so honest that others will always know that you tell the truth and can be trusted.

No one can measure his
greatness.

4 Let each generation tell its children
of your mighty acts;
let them proclaim your power.
5 I will meditate* on your majestic,
glorious splendor
and your wonderful miracles.
6 Your awe-inspiring deeds will be
on every tongue;
I will proclaim your greatness.
7 Everyone will share the story of your
wonderful goodness;
they will sing with joy about your
righteousness.

8 The LORD is merciful and
compassionate,
slow to get angry and filled with
unfailing love.
9 The LORD is good to everyone.
He showers compassion on all
his creation.
10 All of your works will thank you, LORD,
and your faithful followers will
praise you.
11 They will speak of the glory of your
kingdom;
they will give examples of your
power.
12 They will tell about your mighty deeds
and about the majesty and glory
of your reign.
13 For your kingdom is an everlasting
kingdom.
You rule throughout all generations.

The LORD always keeps his promises;
he is gracious in all he does.*
14 The LORD helps the fallen
and lifts those bent beneath
their loads.
15 The eyes of all look to you in hope;
you give them their food as they
need it.
16 When you open your hand,
you satisfy the hunger and thirst
of every living thing.
17 The LORD is righteous in everything
he does;
he is filled with kindness.
18 The LORD is close to all who call
on him,
yes, to all who call on him in truth.
19 He grants the desires of those who
fear him;
he hears their cries for help and
rescues them.
20 The LORD protects all those who love
him,
but he destroys the wicked.

21 I will praise the LORD,
and may everyone on earth bless
his holy name
forever and ever.

145 This psalm is a Hebrew acrostic poem; each verse
(including 13b) begins with a successive letter of the Hebrew
alphabet. **145:5** Some manuscripts read *They will speak.*
145:13 The last two lines of 145:13 are not found in many
of the ancient manuscripts.

PROVERBS 18:1
Unfriendly people care only about themselves; they lash out at common sense.

JUNE **28**

2 KINGS 13:1–14:29
Jehoahaz is described as doing evil, yet when his
nation was in trouble, he prayed to God. God was
merciful to him and to his people. Don't let past
failures keep you from turning back to God.

Jehoahaz son of Jehu began to rule over
Israel in the twenty-third year of King Joash's reign in Judah. He reigned in Samar-

ia seventeen years. 2But he did what was
evil in the LORD's sight. He followed the
example of Jeroboam son of Nebat, continuing the sins that Jeroboam had led Israel to commit. 3So the LORD was very
angry with Israel, and he allowed King
Hazael of Aram and his son Ben-hadad to
defeat them repeatedly.

⁴Then Jehoahaz prayed for the LORD's help, and the LORD heard his prayer, for he could see how severely the king of Aram was oppressing Israel. ⁵So the LORD provided someone to rescue the Israelites from the tyranny of the Arameans. Then Israel lived in safety again as they had in former days.

⁶But they continued to sin, following the evil example of Jeroboam. They also allowed the Asherah pole in Samaria to remain standing. ⁷Finally, Jehoahaz's army was reduced to 50 charioteers, 10 chariots, and 10,000 foot soldiers. The king of Aram had killed the others, trampling them like dust under his feet.

⁸The rest of the events in Jehoahaz's reign—everything he did and the extent of his power—are recorded in *The Book of the History of the Kings of Israel.* ⁹When Jehoahaz died, he was buried in Samaria. Then his son Jehoash* became the next king.

¹⁰Jehoash son of Jehoahaz began to rule over Israel in the thirty-seventh year of King Joash's reign in Judah. He reigned in Samaria sixteen years. ¹¹But he did what was evil in the LORD's sight. He refused to turn from the sins that Jeroboam son of Nebat had led Israel to commit.

¹²The rest of the events in Jehoash's reign and everything he did, including the extent of his power and his war with King Amaziah of Judah, are recorded in *The Book of the History of the Kings of Israel.* ¹³When Jehoash died, he was buried in Samaria with the kings of Israel. Then his son Jeroboam II became the next king.

¹⁴When Elisha was in his last illness, King Jehoash of Israel visited him and wept over him. "My father! My father! I see the chariots and charioteers of Israel!" he cried.

¹⁵Elisha told him, "Get a bow and some arrows." And the king did as he was told. ¹⁶Elisha told him, "Put your hand on the bow," and Elisha laid his own hands on the king's hands.

¹⁷Then he commanded, "Open that eastern window," and he opened it. Then he said, "Shoot!" So he shot an arrow. Elisha proclaimed, "This is the LORD's arrow, an arrow of victory over Aram, for you will completely conquer the Arameans at Aphek."

¹⁸Then he said, "Now pick up the other arrows and strike them against the ground." So the king picked them up and struck the ground three times. ¹⁹But the man of God was angry with him. "You should have struck the ground five or six times!" he exclaimed. "Then you would have beaten Aram until it was entirely destroyed. Now you will be victorious only three times."

²⁰Then Elisha died and was buried.

Groups of Moabite raiders used to invade the land each spring. ²¹Once when some Israelites were burying a man, they spied a band of these raiders. So they hastily threw the corpse into the tomb of Elisha and fled. But as soon as the body touched Elisha's bones, the dead man revived and jumped to his feet!

²²King Hazael of Aram had oppressed Israel during the entire reign of King Jehoahaz. ²³But the LORD was gracious and merciful to the people of Israel, and they were not totally destroyed. He pitied them because of his covenant with Abraham, Isaac, and Jacob. And to this day he still has not completely destroyed them or banished them from his presence.

²⁴King Hazael of Aram died, and his son Ben-hadad became the next king. ²⁵Then Jehoash son of Jehoahaz recaptured from Ben-hadad son of Hazael the towns that had been taken from Jehoash's father, Jehoahaz. Jehoash defeated Ben-hadad on three occasions, and he recovered the Israelite towns.

14:1AMAZIAH son of Joash began to rule over Judah in the second year of the reign of King Jehoash* of Israel. ²Amaziah was twenty-five years old when he became king, and he reigned in Jerusalem twenty-nine years. His mother was Jehoaddin from Jerusalem. ³Amaziah did what was pleasing in the LORD's sight, but not like his ancestor David. Instead, he followed the example of his father, Joash. ⁴Amaziah did not destroy the pagan shrines, and the people still offered sacrifices and burned incense there.

⁵When Amaziah was well established as king, he executed the officials who had assassinated his father. ⁶However, he did not kill the children of the assassins, for he

obeyed the command of the LORD as written by Moses in the Book of the Law: "Parents must not be put to death for the sins of their children, nor children for the sins of their parents. Those deserving to die must be put to death for their own crimes."*

⁷Amaziah also killed 10,000 Edomites in the Valley of Salt. He also conquered Sela and changed its name to Joktheel, as it is called to this day.

⁸One day Amaziah sent messengers with this challenge to Israel's king Jehoash, the son of Jehoahaz and grandson of Jehu: "Come and meet me in battle!"*

⁹But King Jehoash of Israel replied to King Amaziah of Judah with this story: "Out in the Lebanon mountains, a thistle sent a message to a mighty cedar tree: 'Give your daughter in marriage to my son.' But just then a wild animal of Lebanon came by and stepped on the thistle, crushing it!

¹⁰"You have indeed defeated Edom, and you are very proud of it. But be content with your victory and stay at home! Why stir up trouble that will only bring disaster on you and the people of Judah?"

¹¹But Amaziah refused to listen, so King Jehoash of Israel mobilized his army against King Amaziah of Judah. The two armies drew up their battle lines at Bethshemesh in Judah. ¹²Judah was routed by the army of Israel, and its army scattered and fled for home. ¹³King Jehoash of Israel captured Judah's king, Amaziah son of Joash and grandson of Ahaziah, at Bethshemesh. Then he marched to Jerusalem, where he demolished 600 feet* of Jerusalem's wall, from the Ephraim Gate to the Corner Gate. ¹⁴He carried off all the gold and silver and all the articles from the Temple of the LORD. He also seized the treasures from the royal palace, along with hostages, and then returned to Samaria.

¹⁵The rest of the events in Jehoash's reign and everything he did, including the extent of his power and his war with King Amaziah of Judah, are recorded in *The Book of the History of the Kings of Israel.* ¹⁶When Jehoash died, he was buried in Samaria with the kings of Israel. And his son Jeroboam II became the next king.

¹⁷King Amaziah of Judah lived for fifteen years after the death of King Jehoash

of Israel. ¹⁸The rest of the events in Amaziah's reign are recorded in *The Book of the History of the Kings of Judah.*

¹⁹There was a conspiracy against Amaziah's life in Jerusalem, and he fled to Lachish. But his enemies sent assassins after him, and they killed him there. ²⁰They brought his body back to Jerusalem on a horse, and he was buried with his ancestors in the City of David.

²¹All the people of Judah had crowned Amaziah's sixteen-year-old son, Uzziah,* as king in place of his father, Amaziah. ²²After his father's death, Uzziah rebuilt the town of Elath and restored it to Judah.

²³Jeroboam II, the son of Jehoash, began to rule over Israel in the fifteenth year of King Amaziah's reign in Judah. Jeroboam reigned in Samaria forty-one years. ²⁴He did what was evil in the LORD's sight. He refused to turn from the sins that Jeroboam son of Nebat had led Israel to commit. ²⁵Jeroboam II recovered the territories of Israel between Lebo-hamath and the Dead Sea,* just as the LORD, the God of Israel, had promised through Jonah son of Amittai, the prophet from Gath-hepher.

²⁶For the LORD saw the bitter suffering of everyone in Israel, and that there was no one in Israel, slave or free, to help them. ²⁷And because the LORD had not said he would blot out the name of Israel completely, he used Jeroboam II, the son of Jehoash, to save them.

²⁸The rest of the events in the reign of Jeroboam II and everything he did—including the extent of his power, his wars, and how he recovered for Israel both Damascus and Hamath, which had belonged to Judah*—are recorded in *The Book of the History of the Kings of Israel.* ²⁹When Jeroboam II died, he was buried in Samaria* with the kings of Israel. Then his son Zechariah became the next king.

13:9 Hebrew *Joash,* a variant spelling of Jehoash; also in 13:10, 12, 13, 14, 25.   **14:1** Hebrew *Joash,* a variant spelling of Jehoash; also in 14:13, 23, 27.   **14:6** Deut 24:16.   **14:8** Hebrew *Come, let us look one another in the face.*   **14:13** Hebrew *400 cubits* [180 meters].   **14:21** Hebrew *Azariah,* a variant spelling of Uzziah.   **14:25** Hebrew *the sea of the Arabah.*   **14:28** Or *to Yaudi.* The meaning of the Hebrew is uncertain.   **14:29** As in some Greek manuscripts; Hebrew omits *in Samaria.*

ACTS 18:23–19:12

So much had changed from Jesus' resurrection to the coming of the Holy Spirit (described at the beginning of Acts). Paul met people all along the spectrum of that knowledge. They knew bits and pieces, but not the whole picture.

After spending some time in Antioch, Paul went back through Galatia and Phrygia, visiting and strengthening all the believers.*

24Meanwhile, a Jew named Apollos, an eloquent speaker who knew the Scriptures well, had arrived in Ephesus from Alexandria in Egypt. 25He had been taught the way of the Lord, and he taught others about Jesus with an enthusiastic spirit* and with accuracy. However, he knew only about John's baptism. 26When Priscilla and Aquila heard him preaching boldly in the synagogue, they took him aside and explained the way of God even more accurately.

27Apollos had been thinking about going to Achaia, and the brothers and sisters in Ephesus encouraged him to go. They wrote to the believers in Achaia, asking them to welcome him. When he arrived there, he proved to be of great benefit to those who, by God's grace, had believed. 28He refuted the Jews with powerful arguments in public debate. Using the Scriptures, he explained to them that Jesus was the Messiah.

19:1WHILE Apollos was in Corinth, Paul traveled through the interior regions until he reached Ephesus, on the coast, where he found several believers.* 2"Did you receive the Holy Spirit when you believed?" he asked them.

"No," they replied, "we haven't even heard that there is a Holy Spirit."

3"Then what baptism did you experience?" he asked.

And they replied, "The baptism of John."

4Paul said, "John's baptism called for repentance from sin. But John himself told the people to believe in the one who would come later, meaning Jesus."

5As soon as they heard this, they were baptized in the name of the Lord Jesus. 6Then when Paul laid his hands on them, the Holy Spirit came on them, and they spoke in other tongues and prophesied. 7There were about twelve men in all.

8Then Paul went to the synagogue and preached boldly for the next three months, arguing persuasively about the Kingdom of God. 9But some became stubborn, rejecting his message and publicly speaking against the Way. So Paul left the synagogue and took the believers with him. Then he held daily discussions at the lecture hall of Tyrannus. 10This went on for the next two years, so that people throughout the province of Asia—both Jews and Greeks—heard the word of the Lord.

11God gave Paul the power to perform unusual miracles. 12When handkerchiefs

WHAT THE BIBLE SAYS The kings of Israel and Judah

2 KINGS 13-14 Reading about all these kings can get long and tedious, but some important lessons can be learned as you read about them. Hundreds of years previously, the Israelites clamored for a king so that they could be "like all the other nations" (1 Samuel 8:5, May 10). That should be a clue right there that by asking for a king, the people were headed for trouble. • God knew this would happen way back in the days of Moses (Deuteronomy 17:14-20, March 31). At that time, he gave guidelines for the kings the people would someday have. A king was to (1) have a copy of the Law made for his personal use, (2) keep it with him, (3) read from it daily, and (4) obey it completely. Through this process he would learn respect for God, keep himself from feeling more important than others, and avoid neglecting God in times of prosperity. • These kings teach us the consequences of failing to take God into account when in a leadership position. No matter where God has placed you—whether you run a company or family—your focus should always be on God.

or aprons that had merely touched his skin were placed on sick people, they were healed of their diseases, and evil spirits were expelled.

18:23 Greek *disciples;* also in 18:27. 18:25 Or *with enthusiasm in the Spirit.* 19:1 Greek *disciples;* also in 19:9, 30.

PSALM 146:1-10
Praise the LORD!

Let all that I am praise the LORD.
2 I will praise the LORD as long as
    I live.
  I will sing praises to my God with
    my dying breath.
3 Don't put your confidence in powerful
    people;
  there is no help for you there.
4 When they breathe their last, they
    return to the earth,
  and all their plans die with them.
5 But joyful are those who have the God
    of Israel* as their helper,
  whose hope is in the LORD their God.
6 He made heaven and earth,
    the sea, and everything in them.
  He keeps every promise forever.

7 He gives justice to the oppressed
    and food to the hungry.
  The LORD frees the prisoners.
8   The LORD opens the eyes of the
       blind.
  The LORD lifts up those who are
    weighed down.
  The LORD loves the godly.
9 The LORD protects the foreigners
    among us.
  He cares for the orphans and
    widows,
  but he frustrates the plans
    of the wicked.
10 The LORD will reign forever.
  He will be your God, O Jerusalem,*
    throughout the generations.

  Praise the LORD!

146:5 Hebrew *of Jacob.* See note on 44:4.   146:10 Hebrew *Zion.*

PROVERBS 18:2-3
Fools have no interest in understanding; they only want to air their own opinions. ◻ Doing wrong leads to disgrace, and scandalous behavior brings contempt.

JUNE**29**

2 KINGS 15:1-16:20
The assassination of King Zechariah brought an end to the dynasty of Jehu, just as the Lord had promised. In both Judah and Israel, persistent wickedness brought each kingdom closer and closer to the judgments the Lord had warned about.

Uzziah* son of Amaziah began to rule over Judah in the twenty-seventh year of the reign of King Jeroboam II of Israel. 2He was sixteen years old when he became king, and he reigned in Jerusalem fifty-two years. His mother was Jecoliah from Jerusalem.

3He did what was pleasing in the LORD's sight, just as his father, Amaziah, had done. 4But he did not destroy the pagan shrines, and the people still offered sacrifices and burned incense there. 5The

LORD struck the king with leprosy,* which lasted until the day he died. He lived in isolation in a separate house. The king's son Jotham was put in charge of the royal palace, and he governed the people of the land.

6The rest of the events in Uzziah's reign and everything he did are recorded in *The Book of the History of the Kings of Judah.* 7When Uzziah died, he was buried with his ancestors in the City of David. And his son Jotham became the next king.

8Zechariah son of Jeroboam II began to rule over Israel in the thirty-eighth year of King Uzziah's reign in Judah. He reigned in Samaria six months. 9Zechariah did what was evil in the LORD's sight, as his ancestors had done. He refused to turn from the sins that Jeroboam son of Nebat had led Israel to commit. [10]Then Shallum son of Jabesh conspired against Zechariah, assassinated him in public,* and became the next king.

[11]The rest of the events in Zechariah's reign are recorded in *The Book of the History of the Kings of Israel.* [12]So the LORD's message to Jehu came true: "Your descendants will be kings of Israel down to the fourth generation."

[13]Shallum son of Jabesh began to rule over Israel in the thirty-ninth year of King Uzziah's reign in Judah. Shallum reigned in Samaria only one month. [14]Then Menahem son of Gadi went to Samaria from Tirzah and assassinated him, and he became the next king.

[15]The rest of the events in Shallum's reign, including his conspiracy, are recorded in *The Book of the History of the Kings of Israel.*

[16]At that time Menahem destroyed the town of Tappuah* and all the surrounding countryside as far as Tirzah, because its citizens refused to surrender the town. He killed the entire population and ripped open the pregnant women.

[17]Menahem son of Gadi began to rule over Israel in the thirty-ninth year of King Uzziah's reign in Judah. He reigned in Samaria ten years. [18]But Menahem did what was evil in the LORD's sight. During his entire reign, he refused to turn from the sins that Jeroboam son of Nebat had led Israel to commit.

[19]Then King Tiglath-pileser* of Assyria invaded the land. But Menahem paid him thirty-seven tons* of silver to gain his support in tightening his grip on royal power. [20]Menahem extorted the money from the rich of Israel, demanding that each of them pay fifty pieces* of silver to the king of Assyria. So the king of Assyria turned from attacking Israel and did not stay in the land.

[21]The rest of the events in Menahem's reign and everything he did are recorded in *The Book of the History of the Kings of Israel.* [22]When Menahem died, his son Pekahiah became the next king.

[23]Pekahiah son of Menahem began to rule over Israel in the fiftieth year of King Uzziah's reign in Judah. He reigned in Samaria two years. [24]But Pekahiah did what was evil in the LORD's sight. He refused to turn from the sins that Jeroboam son of Nebat had led Israel to commit.

[25]Then Pekah son of Remaliah, the commander of Pekahiah's army, conspired against him. With fifty men from Gilead, Pekah assassinated the king, along with Argob and Arieh, in the citadel of the palace at Samaria. And Pekah reigned in his place.

[26]The rest of the events in Pekahiah's reign and everything he did are recorded in *The Book of the History of the Kings of Israel.*

[27]Pekah son of Remaliah began to rule over Israel in the fifty-second year of King Uzziah's reign in Judah. He reigned in Samaria twenty years. [28]But Pekah did what was evil in the LORD's sight. He refused to turn from the sins that Jeroboam son of Nebat had led Israel to commit.

[29]During Pekah's reign, King Tiglath-pileser of Assyria attacked Israel again, and he captured the towns of Ijon, Abel-beth-maacah, Janoah, Kedesh, and Hazor. He also conquered the regions of Gilead, Galilee, and all of Naphtali, and he took the people to Assyria as captives. [30]Then Hoshea son of Elah conspired against Pekah and assassinated him. He began to rule over Israel in the twentieth year of Jotham son of Uzziah.

[31]The rest of the events in Pekah's reign and everything he did are recorded in *The Book of the History of the Kings of Israel.*

[32]Jotham son of Uzziah began to rule over Judah in the second year of King Pekah's reign in Israel. [33]He was twenty-five years old when he became king, and he reigned in Jerusalem sixteen years. His mother was Jerusha, the daughter of Zadok.

[34]Jotham did what was pleasing in the LORD's sight. He did everything his father, Uzziah, had done. [35]But he did not destroy the pagan shrines, and the people still offered sacrifices and burned incense there. He rebuilt the upper gate of the Temple of the LORD.

[36]The rest of the events in Jotham's reign and everything he did are recorded in *The Book of the History of the Kings of*

Judah. [37] In those days the LORD began to send King Rezin of Aram and King Pekah of Israel to attack Judah. [38] When Jotham died, he was buried with his ancestors in the City of David. And his son Ahaz became the next king.

[16:1] AHAZ son of Jotham began to rule over Judah in the seventeenth year of King Pekah's reign in Israel. [2] Ahaz was twenty years old when he became king, and he reigned in Jerusalem sixteen years. He did not do what was pleasing in the sight of the LORD his God, as his ancestor David had done. [3] Instead, he followed the example of the kings of Israel, even sacrificing his own son in the fire.* In this way, he followed the detestable practices of the pagan nations the LORD had driven from the land ahead of the Israelites. [4] He offered sacrifices and burned incense at the pagan shrines and on the hills and under every green tree.

[5] Then King Rezin of Aram and King Pekah of Israel came up to attack Jerusalem. They besieged Ahaz but could not conquer him. [6] At that time the king of Edom* recovered the town of Elath for Edom.* He drove out the people of Judah and sent Edomites* to live there, as they do to this day.

[7] King Ahaz sent messengers to King Tiglath-pileser of Assyria with this message: "I am your servant and your vassal.* Come up and rescue me from the attacking armies of Aram and Israel." [8] Then Ahaz took the silver and gold from the Temple of the LORD and the palace treasury and sent it as a payment to the Assyrian king. [9] So the king of Assyria attacked the Aramean capital of Damascus and led its population away as captives, resettling them in Kir. He also killed King Rezin.

[10] King Ahaz then went to Damascus to meet with King Tiglath-pileser of Assyria. While he was there, he took special note of the altar. Then he sent a model of the altar to Uriah the priest, along with its design in full detail. [11] Uriah followed the king's instructions and built an altar just like it, and it was ready before the king returned from Damascus. [12] When the king returned, he inspected the altar and made offerings on it. [13] He presented a burnt of-

fering and a grain offering, he poured out a liquid offering, and he sprinkled the blood of peace offerings on the altar.

[14] Then King Ahaz removed the old bronze altar from its place in front of the LORD's Temple, between the entrance and the new altar, and placed it on the north side of the new altar. [15] He told Uriah the priest, "Use the new altar* for the morning sacrifices of burnt offering, the evening grain offering, the king's burnt offering and grain offering, and the burnt offerings of all the people, as well as their grain offerings and liquid offerings. Sprinkle the blood from all the burnt offerings and sacrifices on the new altar. The bronze altar will be for my personal use only." [16] Uriah the priest did just as King Ahaz commanded him.

[17] Then the king removed the side panels and basins from the portable water carts. He also removed the great bronze basin called the Sea from the backs of the bronze oxen and placed it on the stone pavement. [18] In deference to the king of Assyria, he also removed the canopy that had been constructed inside the palace for use on the Sabbath day,* as well as the king's outer entrance to the Temple of the LORD.

[19] The rest of the events in Ahaz's reign and everything he did are recorded in *The Book of the History of the Kings of Judah.* [20] When Ahaz died, he was buried with his ancestors in the City of David. Then his son Hezekiah became the next king.

15:1 Hebrew *Azariah,* a variant spelling of Uzziah; also in 15:6, 7, 8, 17, 23, 27.   15:5 Or *with a contagious skin disease.* The Hebrew word used here and throughout this passage can describe various skin diseases.   15:10 Or *at Ibleam.*   15:16 As in some Greek manuscripts; other Greek manuscripts read *at Ibleam.* Hebrew reads *Tiphsah.*
15:19a Hebrew *Pul,* another name for Tiglath-pileser.
15:19b Hebrew *1,000 talents* [34 metric tons].
15:20 Hebrew *50 shekels* [20 ounces, or 570 grams].
16:3 Or *even making his son pass through the fire.*
16:6a As in Latin Vulgate; Hebrew reads *Rezin king of Aram.*
16:6b As in Latin Vulgate; Hebrew reads *Aram.*   16:6c As in Greek version, Latin Vulgate, and an alternate reading of the Masoretic Text; the other alternate reads *Arameans.*
16:7 Hebrew *your son.*   16:15 Hebrew *the great altar.*
16:18 The meaning of the Hebrew is uncertain.

ACTS 19:13-41
During the first century, most of Paul's world was under the rule of Rome. This included Ephesus, a significant stop on Paul's journey. The people's desire to avoid drawing the attention of the Roman

authorities at times worked to Paul's benefit, as in today's reading.

A group of Jews was traveling from town to town casting out evil spirits. They tried to use the name of the Lord Jesus in their incantation, saying, "I command you in the name of Jesus, whom Paul preaches, to come out!" [14]Seven sons of Sceva, a leading priest, were doing this. [15]But one time when they tried it, the evil spirit replied, "I know Jesus, and I know Paul, but who are you?" [16]Then the man with the evil spirit leaped on them, overpowered them, and attacked them with such violence that they fled from the house, naked and battered.

[17]The story of what happened spread quickly all through Ephesus, to Jews and Greeks alike. A solemn fear descended on the city, and the name of the Lord Jesus was greatly honored. [18]Many who became believers confessed their sinful practices. [19]A number of them who had been practicing sorcery brought their incantation books and burned them at a public bonfire. The value of the books was several million dollars.* [20]So the message about the Lord spread widely and had a powerful effect.

[21]Afterward Paul felt compelled by the Spirit* to go over to Macedonia and Acha-ia before going to Jerusalem. "And after that," he said, "I must go on to Rome!" [22]He sent his two assistants, Timothy and Erastus, ahead to Macedonia while he stayed awhile longer in the province of Asia.

[23]About that time, serious trouble developed in Ephesus concerning the Way. [24]It began with Demetrius, a silversmith who had a large business manufacturing silver shrines of the Greek goddess Artemis.* He kept many craftsmen busy. [25]He called them together, along with others employed in similar trades, and addressed them as follows:

"Gentlemen, you know that our wealth comes from this business. [26]But as you have seen and heard, this man Paul has persuaded many people that handmade gods aren't really gods at all. And he's done this not only here in Ephesus but throughout the entire province! [27]Of course, I'm not just talking about the loss of public respect for our business. I'm also concerned that the temple of the great goddess Artemis will lose its influence and that Artemis—this magnificent goddess worshiped throughout the province of Asia and all around the world—will be robbed of her great prestige!"

[28]At this their anger boiled, and they began shouting, "Great is Artemis of the

WHAT THE BIBLE SAYS

Demons

ACTS 19:13-20 Ephesus was a center for black magic and other occult practices. The people cooked up magical formulas in search of wealth, happiness, and fertility. Superstition and sorcery were commonplace. Many Ephesians engaged in exorcism and occult practices for profit. The sons of Sceva were impressed by Paul's work, whose power to drive out demons came from God's Holy Spirit, not from witchcraft, and was obviously more powerful than theirs. They discovered, however, that no one can control or duplicate God's power. • One of Satan's schemes is to make demonically influenced activities seem normal, commonplace, or even "good." Even today, demonic activities are masked as harmless fun, and too many people are falling for it. Christians have no business going to fortune-tellers, putting trust in horoscopes, channeling people who lived long ago, or getting involved in Wicca activities and casting spells. God clearly forbids such practices (Deuteronomy 18:9-13, April 1). Moreover, they are harmful to the soul. There's no fooling around when it comes to Satan.

Ephesians!" ²⁹Soon the whole city was filled with confusion. Everyone rushed to the amphitheater, dragging along Gaius and Aristarchus, who were Paul's traveling companions from Macedonia. ³⁰Paul wanted to go in, too, but the believers wouldn't let him. ³¹Some of the officials of the province, friends of Paul, also sent a message to him, begging him not to risk his life by entering the amphitheater.

³²Inside, the people were all shouting, some one thing and some another. Everything was in confusion. In fact, most of them didn't even know why they were there. ³³The Jews in the crowd pushed Alexander forward and told him to explain the situation. He motioned for silence and tried to speak. ³⁴But when the crowd realized he was a Jew, they started shouting again and kept it up for two hours: "Great is Artemis of the Ephesians! Great is Artemis of the Ephesians!"

³⁵At last the mayor was able to quiet them down enough to speak. "Citizens of Ephesus," he said. "Everyone knows that Ephesus is the official guardian of the temple of the great Artemis, whose image fell down to us from heaven. ³⁶Since this is an undeniable fact, you should stay calm and not do anything rash. ³⁷You have brought these men here, but they have stolen nothing from the temple and have not spoken against our goddess.

³⁸"If Demetrius and the craftsmen have a case against them, the courts are in session and the officials can hear the case at once. Let them make formal charges. ³⁹And if there are complaints about other matters, they can be settled in a legal assembly. ⁴⁰I am afraid we are in danger of being charged with rioting by the Roman government, since there is no cause for all this commotion. And if Rome demands an explanation, we won't know what to say." ⁴¹*Then he dismissed them, and they dispersed.

19:19 Greek *50,000 pieces of silver,* each of which was the equivalent of a day's wage.   19:21 Or *decided in his spirit.*   19:24 *Artemis* is otherwise known as Diana.   19:41 Some translations include verse 41 as part of verse 40.

PSALM 147:1-20

Praise the LORD!

How good to sing praises to our God!
    How delightful and how fitting!

² The LORD is rebuilding Jerusalem
    and bringing the exiles back to
        Israel.
³ He heals the brokenhearted
    and bandages their wounds.
⁴ He counts the stars
    and calls them all by name.
⁵ How great is our Lord! His power
        is absolute!
    His understanding is beyond
        comprehension!
⁶ The LORD supports the humble,
    but he brings the wicked down into
        the dust.

⁷ Sing out your thanks to the LORD;
    sing praises to our God with a harp.
⁸ He covers the heavens with clouds,
    provides rain for the earth,
    and makes the grass grow in
        mountain pastures.
⁹ He gives food to the wild animals
    and feeds the young ravens when
        they cry.
¹⁰ He takes no pleasure in the strength
        of a horse
    or in human might.
¹¹ No, the LORD's delight is in those
        who fear him,
    those who put their hope in his
        unfailing love.

¹² Glorify the LORD, O Jerusalem!
    Praise your God, O Zion!
¹³ For he has strengthened the bars
        of your gates
    and blessed your children within
        your walls.
¹⁴ He sends peace across your nation
    and satisfies your hunger with the
        finest wheat.
¹⁵ He sends his orders to the world—
    how swiftly his word flies!
¹⁶ He sends the snow like white wool;
    he scatters frost upon the ground
        like ashes.
¹⁷ He hurls the hail like stones.*
    Who can stand against his freezing
        cold?
¹⁸ Then, at his command, it all melts.
    He sends his winds, and the ice
        thaws.
¹⁹ He has revealed his words to Jacob,
    his decrees and regulations
        to Israel.

²⁰ He has not done this for any other nation;
   they do not know his regulations.

   Praise the LORD!

147:17 Hebrew *like bread crumbs.*

PROVERBS 18:4-5
Wise words are like deep waters; wisdom flows from the wise like a bubbling brook. □ It is not right to acquit the guilty or deny justice to the innocent.

JUNE**30**

2 KINGS 17:1–18:12
As judgment on Israel's persistent sin, God allowed the Assyrian empire to conquer the northern kingdom and the capital city Samaria, taking its people into captivity. Only a few survivors remained in the land. They would intermarry and become known as the Samaritans.

Hoshea son of Elah began to rule over Israel in the twelfth year of King Ahaz's reign in Judah. He reigned in Samaria nine years. ²He did what was evil in the LORD's sight, but not to the same extent as the kings of Israel who ruled before him.

³King Shalmaneser of Assyria attacked King Hoshea, so Hoshea was forced to pay heavy tribute to Assyria. ⁴But Hoshea stopped paying the annual tribute and conspired against the king of Assyria by asking King So of Egypt* to help him shake free of Assyria's power. When the king of Assyria discovered this treachery, he seized Hoshea and put him in prison.

⁵Then the king of Assyria invaded the entire land, and for three years he besieged the city of Samaria. ⁶Finally, in the ninth year of King Hoshea's reign, Samaria fell, and the people of Israel were exiled to Assyria. They were settled in colonies in Halah, along the banks of the Habor River in Gozan, and in the cities of the Medes.

⁷This disaster came upon the people of Israel because they worshiped other gods. They sinned against the LORD their God, who had brought them safely out of Egypt and had rescued them from the power of Pharaoh, the king of Egypt. ⁸They had followed the practices of the pagan nations the LORD had driven from the land ahead of them, as well as the practices the kings of Israel had introduced. ⁹The people of Israel had also secretly done many things that were not pleasing to the LORD their God. They built pagan shrines for themselves in all their towns, from the smallest outpost to the largest walled city. ¹⁰They set up sacred pillars and Asherah poles at the top of every hill and under every green tree. ¹¹They offered sacrifices on all the hilltops, just like the nations the LORD had driven from the land ahead of them. So the people of Israel had done many evil things, arousing the LORD's anger. ¹²Yes, they worshiped idols,* despite the LORD's specific and repeated warnings.

¹³Again and again the LORD had sent his prophets and seers to warn both Israel and Judah: "Turn from all your evil ways. Obey my commands and decrees—the entire law that I commanded your ancestors to obey, and that I gave you through my servants the prophets."

¹⁴But the Israelites would not listen. They were as stubborn as their ancestors who had refused to believe in the LORD their God. ¹⁵They rejected his decrees and the covenant he had made with their ancestors, and they despised all his warnings. They worshiped worthless idols, so they became worthless themselves. They followed the example of the nations around them, disobeying the LORD's command not to imitate them.

¹⁶They rejected all the commands of the LORD their God and made two calves from metal. They set up an Asherah pole and worshiped Baal and all the forces of heaven. ¹⁷They even sacrificed their own sons and daughters in the fire.* They consulted fortune-tellers and practiced sorcery and sold themselves to evil, arousing the LORD's anger.

¹⁸Because the LORD was very angry with Israel, he swept them away from his presence. Only the tribe of Judah remained in the land. ¹⁹But even the people of Judah refused to obey the commands of the LORD their God, for they followed the evil practices that Israel had introduced. ²⁰The LORD rejected all the descendants of Israel. He punished them by handing them over to their attackers until he had banished Israel from his presence.

²¹For when the LORD* tore Israel away from the kingdom of David, they chose Jeroboam son of Nebat as their king. But Jeroboam drew Israel away from following the LORD and made them commit a great sin. ²²And the people of Israel persisted in all the evil ways of Jeroboam. They did not turn from these sins ²³until the LORD finally swept them away from his presence, just as all his prophets had warned. So Israel was exiled from their land to Assyria, where they remain to this day.

²⁴The king of Assyria transported groups of people from Babylon, Cuthah, Avva, Hamath, and Sepharvaim and resettled them in the towns of Samaria, replacing the people of Israel. They took possession of Samaria and lived in its towns. ²⁵But since these foreign settlers did not worship the LORD when they first arrived, the LORD sent lions among them, which killed some of them.

²⁶So a message was sent to the king of Assyria: "The people you have sent to live in the towns of Samaria do not know the religious customs of the God of the land. He has sent lions among them to destroy them because they have not worshiped him correctly."

²⁷The king of Assyria then commanded, "Send one of the exiled priests back to Samaria. Let him live there and teach the new residents the religious customs of the God of the land." ²⁸So one of the priests who had been exiled from Samaria returned to Bethel and taught the new residents how to worship the LORD.

²⁹But these various groups of foreigners also continued to worship their own gods. In town after town where they lived, they placed their idols at the pagan shrines that the people of Samaria had built. ³⁰Those from Babylon worshiped idols of their god Succoth-benoth. Those from Cuthah worshiped their god Nergal. And those from Hamath worshiped Ashima. ³¹The Avvites worshiped their gods Nibhaz and Tartak. And the people from Sepharvaim even burned their own children as sacrifices to their gods Adrammelech and Anammelech.

³²These new residents worshiped the LORD, but they also appointed from among themselves all sorts of people as priests to offer sacrifices at their places of worship. ³³And though they worshiped the LORD, they continued to follow their own gods according to the religious customs of the nations from which they came. ³⁴And this is still going on today. They continue to follow their former practices instead of truly worshiping the LORD and obeying the decrees, regulations, instructions, and commands he gave the descendants of Jacob, whose name he changed to Israel.

³⁵For the LORD had made a covenant with the descendants of Jacob and commanded them: "Do not worship any other gods or bow before them or serve them or offer sacrifices to them. ³⁶But worship only the LORD, who brought you out of Egypt with great strength and a powerful arm. Bow down to him alone, and offer sacrifices only to him. ³⁷Be careful at all times to obey the decrees, regulations, instructions, and commands that he wrote for you. You must not worship other gods. ³⁸Do not forget the covenant I made with you, and do not worship other gods. ³⁹You must worship only the LORD your God. He is the one who will rescue you from all your enemies."

⁴⁰But the people would not listen and continued to follow their former practices. ⁴¹So while these new residents worshiped the LORD, they also worshiped their idols. And to this day their descendants do the same.

18:1HEZEKIAH son of Ahaz began to rule over Judah in the third year of King Hoshea's reign in Israel. ²He was twenty-five years old when he became king, and he reigned in Jerusalem twenty-nine years. His mother was Abijah,* the daughter of Zechariah. ³He did what was pleasing in the LORD's sight, just as his ancestor David had done. ⁴He removed the pagan shrines, smashed the sacred pillars, and cut down the Asherah poles. He broke up the bronze serpent that Moses had made, because the people of Israel had been offering sacrifices to it. The bronze serpent was called Nehushtan.*

⁵Hezekiah trusted in the LORD, the God of Israel. There was no one like him among all the kings of Judah, either before or after his time. ⁶He remained faithful to the LORD in everything, and he carefully obeyed all the commands LORD had given Moses. ⁷So the LORD was with him, and Hezekiah was successful in everything he did. He revolted against the king of Assyria and refused to pay him tribute. ⁸He also conquered the Philistines as far distant as Gaza and its territory, from their smallest outpost to their largest walled city.

⁹During the fourth year of Hezekiah's reign, which was the seventh year of King Hoshea's reign in Israel, King Shalmaneser of Assyria attacked the city of Samaria and began a siege against it. ¹⁰Three years later, during the sixth year of King Hezekiah's reign and the ninth year of King Hoshea's reign in Israel, Samaria fell. ¹¹At that time the king of Assyria exiled the Israelites to Assyria and placed them in colonies in Halah, along the banks of the Habor River in Gozan, and in the cities of the Medes. ¹²For they refused to listen to the LORD their God and obey him. Instead, they violated his covenant—all the laws that Moses the LORD's servant had commanded them to obey.

17:4 Or *by asking the king of Egypt at Sais.*   17:12 The Hebrew term (literally *round things*) probably alludes to dung.   17:17 Or *They even made their sons and daughters pass through the fire.*   17:21 Hebrew *he;* compare 1 Kgs 11:31-32.   18:2 As in parallel text at 2 Chr 29:1; Hebrew reads *Abi,* a variant spelling of Abijah.   18:4 *Nehushtan* sounds like the Hebrew terms that mean "snake," "bronze," and "unclean thing."

ACTS 20:1-38

On his return to Jerusalem, Paul was leaving behind people in whom he had invested greatly, both spiritually and personally. Believing that he would not see the Ephesian elders again, he charged them to shepherd the church as he had and then prayed for them before an emotional departure.

When the uproar was over, Paul sent for the believers* and encouraged them. Then he said good-bye and left for Macedonia. ²While there, he encouraged the believers in all the towns he passed through. Then he traveled down to Greece, ³where he stayed for three months. He was preparing to sail back to Syria when he discovered a plot by some Jews against his life, so he decided to return through Macedonia.

⁴Several men were traveling with him. They were Sopater son of Pyrrhus from Berea; Aristarchus and Secundus from Thessalonica; Gaius from Derbe; Timothy; and Tychicus and Trophimus from the province of Asia. ⁵They went on ahead and waited for us at Troas. ⁶After the Passover* ended, we boarded a ship at Philippi in Macedonia and five days later joined them in Troas, where we stayed a week.

⁷On the first day of the week, we gathered with the local believers to share in the Lord's Supper.* Paul was preaching to them, and since he was leaving the next day, he kept talking until midnight. ⁸The upstairs room where we met was lighted with many flickering lamps. ⁹As Paul spoke on and on, a young man named Eutychus, sitting on the windowsill, became very drowsy. Finally, he fell sound asleep and dropped three stories to his death below. ¹⁰Paul went down, bent over him, and took him into his arms. "Don't worry," he said, "he's alive!" ¹¹Then they all went back upstairs, shared in the Lord's Supper,* and ate together. Paul continued talking to them until dawn, and then he left. ¹²Meanwhile, the young man was taken home unhurt, and everyone was greatly relieved.

¹³Paul went by land to Assos, where he had arranged for us to join him, while we traveled by ship. ¹⁴He joined us there, and we sailed together to Mitylene. ¹⁵The next day we sailed past the island of Kios. The following day we crossed to the island of Samos, and* a day later we arrived at Miletus.

¹⁶Paul had decided to sail on past Ephesus, for he didn't want to spend any more time in the province of Asia. He was hurrying to get to Jerusalem, if possible, in time for the Festival of Pentecost. ¹⁷But

when we landed at Miletus, he sent a message to the elders of the church at Ephesus, asking them to come and meet him.

¹⁸When they arrived he declared, "You know that from the day I set foot in the province of Asia until now ¹⁹I have done the Lord's work humbly and with many tears. I have endured the trials that came to me from the plots of the Jews. ²⁰I never shrank back from telling you what you needed to hear, either publicly or in your homes. ²¹I have had one message for Jews and Greeks alike—the necessity of repenting from sin and turning to God, and of having faith in our Lord Jesus.

²²"And now I am bound by the Spirit* to go to Jerusalem. I don't know what awaits me, ²³except that the Holy Spirit tells me in city after city that jail and suffering lie ahead. ²⁴But my life is worth nothing to me unless I use it for finishing the work assigned me by the Lord Jesus—the work of telling others the Good News about the wonderful grace of God.

²⁵"And now I know that none of you to whom I have preached the Kingdom will ever see me again. ²⁶I declare today that I have been faithful. If anyone suffers eternal death, it's not my fault,* ²⁷for I didn't shrink from declaring all that God wants you to know.

²⁸"So guard yourselves and God's people. Feed and shepherd God's flock—his church, purchased with his own blood*—over which the Holy Spirit has appointed you as elders.* ²⁹I know that false teachers, like vicious wolves, will come in among you after I leave, not sparing the flock. ³⁰Even some men from your own group will rise up and distort the truth in order to draw a following. ³¹Watch out! Remember the three years I was with you—my constant watch and care over you night and day, and my many tears for you.

³²"And now I entrust you to God and the message of his grace that is able to build you up and give you an inheritance with all those he has set apart for himself.

³³"I have never coveted anyone's silver or gold or fine clothes. ³⁴You know that these hands of mine have worked to supply my own needs and even the needs of those who were with me. ³⁵And I have

been a constant example of how you can help those in need by working hard. You should remember the words of the Lord Jesus: 'It is more blessed to give than to receive.'"

³⁶When he had finished speaking, he knelt and prayed with them. ³⁷They all cried as they embraced and kissed him good-bye. ³⁸They were sad most of all because he had said that they would never see him again. Then they escorted him down to the ship.

20:1 Greek *disciples.*   20:6 Greek *the days of unleavened bread.*   20:7 Greek *to break bread.*   20:11 Greek *broke the bread.*   20:15 Some manuscripts read *and having stayed at Trogyllium.*   20:22 Or *by my spirit,* or *by an inner compulsion;* Greek reads *by the spirit.*   20:26 Greek *I am innocent of the blood of all.*   20:28a Or *with the blood of his own [Son].*   20:28b Greek *overseers.*

PSALM 148:1-14

Praise the LORD!

Praise the LORD from the heavens!
　Praise him from the skies!
² Praise him, all his angels!
　Praise him, all the armies of heaven!
³ Praise him, sun and moon!
　Praise him, all you twinkling stars!
⁴ Praise him, skies above!
　Praise him, vapors high above the
　　clouds!
⁵ Let every created thing give praise
　　to the LORD,
　for he issued his command, and
　　they came into being.
⁶ He set them in place forever and ever.
　His decree will never be revoked.

⁷ Praise the LORD from the earth,
　you creatures of the ocean depths,
⁸ fire and hail, snow and clouds,*
　wind and weather that obey him,
⁹ mountains and all hills,
　fruit trees and all cedars,
¹⁰ wild animals and all livestock,
　small scurrying animals and birds,
¹¹ kings of the earth and all people,
　rulers and judges of the earth,
¹² young men and young women,
　old men and children.

¹³ Let them all praise the name of the
　　LORD.
　For his name is very great;
　his glory towers over the earth
　　and heaven!

14 He has made his people strong,
  honoring his faithful ones—
    the people of Israel who are close
    to him.

Praise the LORD!

148:8 Or *mist*, or *smoke*.

PROVERBS 18:6-7
Fools' words get them into constant quarrels; they are asking for a beating. □ The mouths of fools are their ruin; they trap themselves with their lips.

HOW WE LIVE

Obeying God

2 KINGS 17:7-23   God had had enough. "Again and again" he had warned his people that their sins would be punished (17:13), but they wouldn't listen. They forgot the importance and the blessings of honoring God's commandments and his Word. While God's patience and mercy are beyond human comprehension, after hundreds of years of sending prophets to warn his wayward people of the error of their ways, God made good on his promise. He allowed Assyria to invade, defeat, and disperse the nation.   • As he pursued the Israelites, so God pursues mankind with his love and warns of the consequences of choosing a path other than salvation. People either respond to his call or become hardhearted and unreachable. Even those of us who are believers must take care not to let the fallen morals of the world intertwine with the truth of God's Word. Sin always brings consequences, and sometimes the consequences are irreversible. Obeying God is always the better option.

He has made his people strong,
honoring his faithful ones—
the people of Israel who are close
to him.

Praise the Lord!

PROVERBS 18:6-7
Fools' words get them into constant quarrels; they are asking for a beating. The
mouths of fools are their ruin; they trap
themselves with their lips.

Obeying God

HOW WE LIVE

1 KINGS 17:1-23 God had had enough. "Again and again" he had warned
his people that their sins would be punished (17:13), but they wouldn't
listen. They forgot the importance and the blessings of honoring God's
commandments and his Word. While God's patience and mercy are
beyond human comprehension, after hundreds of years of sending prophets to warn his wayward people of the error of their ways, God made good
on his promise. He allowed Assyria to invade, defeat, and disperse the
nation. As he pursued the Israelites, so God pursues mankind with his
love and warns of the consequences of choosing a path other than salvation. People either respond to his call or become hardhearted and
unreachable. Even those of us who are believers must take care not to
let the fallen morals of the world intertwine with the truth of God's Word.
Sin always brings consequences, and sometimes the consequences are
irreversible. Obeying God is always the better option.

2 KINGS 18:13–19:37

Assyria was a huge empire, growing as it conquered nations in its path. However, King Sennacherib and his army got more than they bargained for when they came up against the tiny kingdom of Judah.

In the fourteenth year of King Hezekiah's reign,* King Sennacherib of Assyria came to attack the fortified towns of Judah and conquered them. ¹⁴King Hezekiah sent this message to the king of Assyria at Lachish: "I have done wrong. I will pay whatever tribute money you demand if you will only withdraw." The king of Assyria then demanded a settlement of more than eleven tons of silver and one ton of gold.* ¹⁵To gather this amount, King Hezekiah used all the silver stored in the Temple of the LORD and in the palace treasury. ¹⁶Hezekiah even stripped the gold from the doors of the LORD's Temple and from the doorposts he had overlaid with gold, and he gave it all to the Assyrian king.

¹⁷Nevertheless, the king of Assyria sent his commander in chief, his field commander, and his chief of staff* from Lachish with a huge army to confront King Hezekiah in Jerusalem. The Assyrians took up a position beside the aqueduct that feeds water into the upper pool, near the road leading to the field where cloth is washed.* ¹⁸They summoned King Hezekiah, but the king sent these officials to meet with them: Eliakim son of Hilkiah, the palace administrator; Shebna the court secretary; and Joah son of Asaph, the royal historian.

¹⁹Then the Assyrian king's chief of staff told them to give this message to Hezekiah:

"This is what the great king of Assyria says: What are you trusting in that makes you so confident? ²⁰Do you think that mere words can substitute for military skill and strength? Who are you counting on, that you have rebelled against me? ²¹On Egypt? If you lean on Egypt, it will be like a reed that splinters beneath your weight and pierces your hand. Pharaoh, the king of Egypt, is completely unreliable!

²²"But perhaps you will say to me, 'We are trusting in the LORD our God!' But isn't he the one who was insulted by Hezekiah? Didn't Hezekiah tear down his shrines and altars and make everyone in Judah and Jerusalem worship only at the altar here in Jerusalem?

²³"I'll tell you what! Strike a bargain with my master, the king of Assyria. I will give you 2,000 horses if you can find that many men to ride on them! ²⁴With your tiny army, how can you think of challenging even the weakest contingent of my master's troops, even with the help of Egypt's chariots and charioteers? ²⁵What's more, do you think we have invaded your land without the LORD's direction? The LORD himself told us, 'Attack this land and destroy it!'"

²⁶Then Eliakim son of Hilkiah, Shebna, and Joah said to the Assyrian chief of staff, "Please speak to us in Aramaic, for we understand it well. Don't speak in Hebrew,* for the people on the wall will hear."

²⁷But Sennacherib's chief of staff replied, "Do you think my master sent this message only to you and your master? He wants all the people to hear it, for when we put this city under siege, they will suffer along with you. They will be so hungry and thirsty that they will eat their own dung and drink their own urine."

²⁸Then the chief of staff stood and shouted in Hebrew to the people on the wall, "Listen to this message from the great king of Assyria! ²⁹This is what the king says: Don't let Hezekiah deceive you. He

will never be able to rescue you from my power. ³⁰Don't let him fool you into trusting in the LORD by saying, 'The LORD will surely rescue us. This city will never fall into the hands of the Assyrian king!'

³¹"Don't listen to Hezekiah! These are the terms the king of Assyria is offering: Make peace with me—open the gates and come out. Then each of you can continue eating from your own grapevine and fig tree and drinking from your own well. ³²Then I will arrange to take you to another land like this one—a land of grain and new wine, bread and vineyards, olive groves and honey. Choose life instead of death!

"Don't listen to Hezekiah when he tries to mislead you by saying, 'The LORD will rescue us!' ³³Have the gods of any other nations ever saved their people from the king of Assyria? ³⁴What happened to the gods of Hamath and Arpad? And what about the gods of Sepharvaim, Hena, and Ivvah? Did any god rescue Samaria from my power? ³⁵What god of any nation has ever been able to save its people from my power? So what makes you think that the LORD can rescue Jerusalem from me?"

³⁶But the people were silent and did not utter a word because Hezekiah had commanded them, "Do not answer him."

³⁷Then Eliakim son of Hilkiah, the palace administrator; Shebna the court secretary; and Joah son of Asaph, the royal historian, went back to Hezekiah. They tore their clothes in despair, and they went in to see the king and told him what the Assyrian chief of staff had said.

19:1WHEN King Hezekiah heard their report, he tore his clothes and put on burlap and went into the Temple of the LORD. ²And he sent Eliakim the palace administrator, Shebna the court secretary, and the leading priests, all dressed in burlap, to the prophet Isaiah son of Amoz. ³They told him, "This is what King Hezekiah says: Today is a day of trouble, insults, and disgrace. It is like when a child is ready to be born, but the mother has no strength to deliver the baby. ⁴But perhaps the LORD your God has heard the Assyrian chief of staff,* sent by the king to defy the living God, and will punish him for his words. Oh, pray for those of us who are left!"

⁵After King Hezekiah's officials delivered the king's message to Isaiah, ⁶the prophet replied, "Say to your master, 'This is what the LORD says: Do not be disturbed by this blasphemous speech against me from the Assyrian king's messengers. ⁷Listen! I myself will move against him,* and the king will receive a message that he is needed at home. So he will return to his land, where I will have him killed with a sword.'"

⁸Meanwhile, the Assyrian chief of staff left Jerusalem and went to consult the king of Assyria, who had left Lachish and was attacking Libnah.

⁹Soon afterward King Sennacherib received word that King Tirhakah of Ethiopia* was leading an army to fight against him. Before leaving to meet the attack, he sent messengers back to Hezekiah in Jerusalem with this message:

¹⁰"This message is for King Hezekiah of Judah. Don't let your God, in whom you trust, deceive you with promises that Jerusalem will not be captured by the king of Assyria. ¹¹You know perfectly well what the kings of Assyria have done wherever they have gone. They have completely destroyed everyone who stood in their way! Why should you be any different? ¹²Have the gods of other nations rescued them—such nations as Gozan, Haran, Rezeph, and the people of Eden who were in Tel-assar? My predecessors destroyed them all! ¹³What happened to the king of Hamath and the king of Arpad? What happened to the kings of Sepharvaim, Hena, and Ivvah?"

¹⁴After Hezekiah received the letter from the messengers and read it, he went up to the LORD's Temple and spread it out before the LORD. ¹⁵And Hezekiah prayed this prayer before the LORD: "O LORD, God of Israel, you are enthroned between the mighty cherubim! You alone are God of all the kingdoms of the earth. You alone created the heavens and the earth. ¹⁶Bend down, O LORD, and listen! Open your eyes, O LORD, and see! Listen to Sennacherib's words of defiance against the living God.

[17]"It is true, LORD, that the kings of Assyria have destroyed all these nations. [18]And they have thrown the gods of these nations into the fire and burned them. But of course the Assyrians could destroy them! They were not gods at all—only idols of wood and stone shaped by human hands. [19]Now, O LORD our God, rescue us from his power; then all the kingdoms of the earth will know that you alone, O LORD, are God."

[20]Then Isaiah son of Amoz sent this message to Hezekiah: "This is what the LORD, the God of Israel, says: I have heard your prayer about King Sennacherib of Assyria. [21]And the LORD has spoken this word against him:

"The virgin daughter of Zion
despises you and laughs at you.
The daughter of Jerusalem
shakes her head in derision
as you flee.

[22] "Whom have you been defying and
ridiculing?
Against whom did you raise your
voice?
At whom did you look with such
haughty eyes?
It was the Holy One of Israel!

[23] By your messengers you have defied
the Lord.
You have said, 'With my many
chariots
I have conquered the highest
mountains—
yes, the remotest peaks of Lebanon.
I have cut down its tallest cedars
and its finest cypress trees.
I have reached its farthest corners
and explored its deepest forests.

[24] I have dug wells in many foreign
lands
and refreshed myself with their
water.
With the sole of my foot
I stopped up all the rivers of Egypt!'

[25] "But have you not heard?
I decided this long ago.
Long ago I planned it,
and now I am making it happen.
I planned for you to crush fortified
cities
into heaps of rubble.

[26] That is why their people have so little
power
and are so frightened and
confused.
They are as weak as grass,
as easily trampled as tender green
shoots.
They are like grass sprouting on
a housetop,
scorched before it can grow lush
and tall.

[27] "But I know you well—
where you stay

HOW WE LIVE

Dealing with problems

2 KINGS 19:14 What is your first reaction when a seemingly impossible situation rears its ugly head? When you are befuddled, caught off guard, gut punched, or waylaid, how do you respond? • Christians are not above being stymied by life's difficulties. As we grow in our faith, however, we should find that our knee-jerk reactions change. Hezekiah's did. When the conquering, evil king sent a horrifying message, Hezekiah didn't panic. He went straight to God instead. Instead of simply reacting, Hezekiah created a space where God could breathe his power into the situation. • That's a good example to follow. Becoming a believer does not remove life's problems. When the problem arrives—by mail, from the doctor's office, in a phone call—"spread it out before the Lord." Invite God into the problem. Instead of bustling around in your own strength or giving up because you know you're not strong enough, lay it before God and see what *he* says.

and when you come and go.
     I know the way you have raged
          against me.
²⁸ And because of your raging against me
     and your arrogance, which I have
          heard for myself,
     I will put my hook in your nose
          and my bit in your mouth.
     I will make you return
          by the same road on which you
               came."

²⁹ Then Isaiah said to Hezekiah, "Here is
the proof that what I say is true:

     "This year you will eat only what grows
          up by itself,
     and next year you will eat what
          springs up from that.
     But in the third year you will plant
          crops and harvest them;
     you will tend vineyards and eat
          their fruit.
³⁰ And you who are left in Judah,
     who have escaped the ravages of
          the siege,
     will put roots down in your own soil
          and will grow up and flourish.
³¹ For a remnant of my people will
          spread out from Jerusalem,
     a group of survivors from Mount
          Zion.
     The passionate commitment of the
          LORD of Heaven's Armies*
     will make this happen!

³²"And this is what the LORD says about
the king of Assyria:

     "His armies will not enter Jerusalem.
     They will not even shoot an arrow
          at it.
     They will not march outside its gates
          with their shields
     nor build banks of earth against its
          walls.
³³ The king will return to his own
          country
     by the same road on which he came.
     He will not enter this city,
          says the LORD.
³⁴ For my own honor and for the sake
          of my servant David,
     I will defend this city and
          protect it."

³⁵ That night the angel of the LORD
went out to the Assyrian camp and killed
185,000 Assyrian soldiers. When the
surviving Assyrians* woke up the next
morning, they found corpses everywhere.
³⁶ Then King Sennacherib of Assyria
broke camp and returned to his own land.
He went home to his capital of Nineveh
and stayed there.

³⁷ One day while he was worshiping in
the temple of his god Nisroch, his sons*
Adrammelech and Sharezer killed him
with their swords. They then escaped to
the land of Ararat, and another son, Esarhaddon, became the next king of Assyria.

18:13 The fourteenth year of Hezekiah's reign was 701 B.C.
18:14 Hebrew *300 talents* [10 metric tons] *of silver and
30 talents* [1 metric ton] *of gold.* 18:17a Or *the rabshakeh;*
also in 18:19, 26, 27, 28, 37. 18:17b Or *bleached.*
18:26 Hebrew *in the dialect of Judah;* also in 18:28.
19:4 Or *the rabshakeh;* also in 19:8. 19:7 Hebrew *I will
put a spirit in him.* 19:9 Hebrew *of Cush.* 19:31 As in
Greek and Syriac versions, Latin Vulgate, and an alternate
reading of the Masoretic Text (see also Isa 37:32); the other
alternate reads *the LORD.* 19:35 Hebrew *When they.*
19:37 As in Greek version and an alternate reading of the
Masoretic Text (see also Isa 37:38); the other alternate
reading lacks *his sons.*

ACTS 21:1-17
Paul spent a significant amount of time in jails.
Some of the New Testament books authored by
Paul were actually written while he was in jail. Paul
could handle whatever circumstances came his way
because he knew God was in control.

After saying farewell to the Ephesian elders, we [Luke, Paul, and their compan-
ions] sailed straight to the island of Cos.
The next day we reached Rhodes and then
went to Patara. ² There we boarded a ship
sailing for Phoenicia. ³ We sighted the island of Cyprus, passed it on our left, and
landed at the harbor of Tyre, in Syria,
where the ship was to unload its cargo.

⁴ We went ashore, found the local believers,* and stayed with them a week.
These believers prophesied through the
Holy Spirit that Paul should not go on to
Jerusalem. ⁵ When we returned to the
ship at the end of the week, the entire
congregation, including women* and
children, left the city and came down to
the shore with us. There we knelt, prayed,
⁶ and said our farewells. Then we went
aboard, and they returned home.

⁷ The next stop after leaving Tyre was

Ptolemais, where we greeted the brothers and sisters* and stayed for one day. ⁸The next day we went on to Caesarea and stayed at the home of Philip the Evangelist, one of the seven men who had been chosen to distribute food. ⁹He had four unmarried daughters who had the gift of prophecy.

¹⁰Several days later a man named Agabus, who also had the gift of prophecy, arrived from Judea. ¹¹He came over, took Paul's belt, and bound his own feet and hands with it. Then he said, "The Holy Spirit declares, 'So shall the owner of this belt be bound by the Jewish leaders in Jerusalem and turned over to the Gentiles.'" ¹²When we heard this, we and the local believers all begged Paul not to go on to Jerusalem.

¹³But he said, "Why all this weeping? You are breaking my heart! I am ready not only to be jailed at Jerusalem but even to die for the sake of the Lord Jesus." ¹⁴When it was clear that we couldn't persuade him, we gave up and said, "The Lord's will be done."

¹⁵After this we packed our things and left for Jerusalem. ¹⁶Some believers from Caesarea accompanied us, and they took us to the home of Mnason, a man originally from Cyprus and one of the early believers. ¹⁷When we arrived, the brothers and sisters in Jerusalem welcomed us warmly.

21:4 Greek *disciples;* also in 21:16.   21:5 Or *wives.*
21:7 Greek *brothers;* also in 21:17.

---

2 KINGS 20:1–22:2

Healed of a deadly sickness, Hezekiah made an unwise decision. Even worse, his son Manasseh undid the many good things Hezekiah had done for Judah. Manasseh turned to the Lord later in life, but by then the damage he had caused could not be easily reversed.

About that time Hezekiah became deathly ill, and the prophet Isaiah son of Amoz went to visit him. He gave the king this

PSALM 149:1-9

Praise the LORD!

Sing to the LORD a new song.
    Sing his praises in the assembly
        of the faithful.

² O Israel, rejoice in your Maker.
    O people of Jerusalem,* exult in
        your King.
³ Praise his name with dancing,
    accompanied by tambourine
        and harp.
⁴ For the LORD delights in his people;
    he crowns the humble with victory.
⁵ Let the faithful rejoice that he honors
        them.
    Let them sing for joy as they lie on
        their beds.

⁶ Let the praises of God be in their
        mouths,
    and a sharp sword in their hands—
⁷ to execute vengeance on the nations
        and punishment on the peoples,
⁸ to bind their kings with shackles
        and their leaders with iron chains,
⁹ to execute the judgment written
        against them.
    This is the glorious privilege of his
        faithful ones.

Praise the LORD!
149:2 Hebrew *Zion.*

PROVERBS 18:8

Rumors are dainty morsels that sink deep into one's heart.

JULY2

message: "This is what the LORD says: Set your affairs in order, for you are going to die. You will not recover from this illness."

²When Hezekiah heard this, he turned his face to the wall and prayed to the LORD, ³"Remember, O LORD, how I have always been faithful to you and have served you single-mindedly, always doing what pleases you." Then he broke down and wept bitterly.

⁴But before Isaiah had left the middle courtyard, this message came to him from the LORD: ⁵"Go back to Hezekiah, the leader of my people. Tell him, 'This is what the LORD, the God of your ancestor David, says: I have heard your prayer and seen your tears. I will heal you, and three days from now you will get out of bed and go to the Temple of the LORD. ⁶I will add fifteen years to your life, and I will rescue you and this city from the king of Assyria. I will defend this city for my own honor and for the sake of my servant David.'"

⁷Then Isaiah said, "Make an ointment from figs." So Hezekiah's servants spread the ointment over the boil, and Hezekiah recovered!

⁸Meanwhile, Hezekiah had said to Isaiah, "What sign will the LORD give to prove that he will heal me and that I will go to the Temple of the LORD three days from now?"

⁹Isaiah replied, "This is the sign from the LORD to prove that he will do as he promised. Would you like the shadow on the sundial to go forward ten steps or backward ten steps?*"

¹⁰"The shadow always moves forward," Hezekiah replied, "so that would be easy. Make it go ten steps backward instead." ¹¹So Isaiah the prophet asked the LORD to do this, and he caused the shadow to move ten steps backward on the sundial* of Ahaz!

¹²Soon after this, Merodach-baladan son of Baladan, king of Babylon, sent Hezekiah his best wishes and a gift, for he had heard that Hezekiah had been very sick. ¹³Hezekiah received the Babylonian envoys and showed them everything in his treasure-houses—the silver, the gold, the spices, and the aromatic oils. He also took them to see his armory and showed them everything in his royal treasuries! There was nothing in his palace or kingdom that Hezekiah did not show them.

¹⁴Then Isaiah the prophet went to King Hezekiah and asked him, "What did those men want? Where were they from?"

Hezekiah replied, "They came from the distant land of Babylon."

¹⁵"What did they see in your palace?" Isaiah asked.

"They saw everything," Hezekiah replied. "I showed them everything I own—all my royal treasuries."

¹⁶Then Isaiah said to Hezekiah, "Listen to this message from the LORD: ¹⁷The time is coming when everything in your palace—all the treasures stored up by your ancestors until now—will be carried off to Babylon. Nothing will be left, says the LORD. ¹⁸Some of your very own sons will be taken away into exile. They will become eunuchs who will serve in the palace of Babylon's king."

¹⁹Then Hezekiah said to Isaiah, "This message you have given me from the LORD is good." For the king was thinking, "At least there will be peace and security during my lifetime."

²⁰The rest of the events in Hezekiah's reign, including the extent of his power and how he built a pool and dug a tunnel* to bring water into the city, are recorded in *The Book of the History of the Kings of Judah*. ²¹Hezekiah died, and his son Manasseh became the next king.

²¹:¹MANASSEH was twelve years old when he became king, and he reigned in Jerusalem fifty-five years. His mother was Hephzibah. ²He did what was evil in the LORD's sight, following the detestable practices of the pagan nations that the LORD had driven from the land ahead of the Israelites. ³He rebuilt the pagan shrines his father, Hezekiah, had destroyed. He constructed altars for Baal and set up an Asherah pole, just as King Ahab of Israel had done. He also bowed before all the powers of the heavens and worshiped them.

⁴He built pagan altars in the Temple of the LORD, the place where the LORD had said, "My name will remain in Jerusalem forever." ⁵He built these altars for all the powers of the heavens in both courtyards of the LORD's Temple. ⁶Manasseh also sacrificed his own son in the fire.* He practiced sorcery and divination, and he consulted with mediums and psychics. He did much that was evil in the LORD's sight, arousing his anger.

⁷Manasseh even made a carved image of Asherah and set it up in the Temple, the very place where the LORD had told David and his son Solomon: "My name will be

honored forever in this Temple and in Jerusalem—the city I have chosen from among all the tribes of Israel. ⁸If the Israelites will be careful to obey my commands—all the laws my servant Moses gave them—I will not send them into exile from this land that I gave their ancestors." ⁹But the people refused to listen, and Manasseh led them to do even more evil than the pagan nations that the LORD had destroyed when the people of Israel entered the land.

¹⁰Then the LORD said through his servants the prophets: ¹¹"King Manasseh of Judah has done many detestable things. He is even more wicked than the Amorites, who lived in this land before Israel. He has caused the people of Judah to sin with his idols.* ¹²So this is what the LORD, the God of Israel, says: I will bring such disaster on Jerusalem and Judah that the ears of those who hear about it will tingle with horror. ¹³I will judge Jerusalem by the same standard I used for Samaria and the same measure* I used for the family of Ahab. I will wipe away the people of Jerusalem as one wipes a dish and turns it upside down. ¹⁴Then I will reject even the remnant of my own people who are left, and I will hand them over as plunder for their enemies. ¹⁵For they have done great evil in my sight and have angered me ever since their ancestors came out of Egypt."

¹⁶Manasseh also murdered many innocent people until Jerusalem was filled from one end to the other with innocent blood. This was in addition to the sin that he caused the people of Judah to commit, leading them to do evil in the LORD's sight.

¹⁷The rest of the events in Manasseh's reign and everything he did, including the sins he committed, are recorded in *The Book of the History of the Kings of Judah.* ¹⁸When Manasseh died, he was buried in the palace garden, the garden of Uzza. Then his son Amon became the next king.

¹⁹Amon was twenty-two years old when he became king, and he reigned in Jerusalem two years. His mother was Meshullemeth, the daughter of Haruz from Jotbah. ²⁰He did what was evil in the LORD's sight, just as his father, Manasseh, had done. ²¹He followed the example of his father, worshiping the same idols his father had worshiped. ²²He abandoned the LORD, the God of his ancestors, and he refused to follow the LORD's ways.

²³Then Amon's own officials conspired against him and assassinated him in his palace. ²⁴But the people of the land killed all those who had conspired against King Amon, and they made his son Josiah the next king.

²⁵The rest of the events in Amon's reign and what he did are recorded in *The Book of the History of the Kings of Judah.* ²⁶He

---

HOW WE LIVE

Praise and thanksgiving

PSALM 150 Some parents and grandparents can't stop talking about their kids or grandkids. When you love someone, it's easy to brag about him or her. And when you love God, it's easy to praise him! That's what Psalm 150 is all about—pure praise out of pure love. • The author of this psalm apparently was a musician, and the psalms are literally "songs" that the people of God sang as they worshiped the Lord in the Temple. They pulled out all the stops to praise God. Imagine the symphony of sounds at this praise service! Horns blowing, harps plucking, flutes tooting, tambourines banging, and cymbals clanging—everything was used to express love and praise to God. Why? Because God is great, God is unequaled, and God is mighty. They just couldn't stop talking about him. • If you find yourself feeling down, take a minute to remember that God is great and good. Remember all he has done for you. Thank him for his great love and grace. Then love him back by joining in the praise party.

was buried in his tomb in the garden of Uzza. Then his son Josiah became the next king.

22:1JOSIAH was eight years old when he became king, and he reigned in Jerusalem thirty-one years. His mother was Jedidah, the daughter of Adaiah from Bozkath. 2He did what was pleasing in the LORD's sight and followed the example of his ancestor David. He did not turn away from doing what was right.

20:9 Or *The shadow on the sundial has gone forward ten steps; do you want it to go backward ten steps?*   20:11 Hebrew *the steps.*   20:20 Hebrew *watercourse.*   21:6 Or *also made his son pass through the fire.*   21:11 The Hebrew term (literally *round things*) probably alludes to dung; also in 21:21.   21:13 Hebrew *the same plumb line I used for Samaria and the same plumb bob.*

ACTS 21:18-36

Paul's ministry did not go quietly unnoticed by those who opposed the gospel. At Jerusalem, Paul was engulfed by an angry mob much like the mobs that called for Jesus' execution.

The next day Paul went with us [Luke and Paul's other companions] to meet with James, and all the elders of the Jerusalem church were present. 19After greeting them, Paul gave a detailed account of the things God had accomplished among the Gentiles through his ministry.

20After hearing this, they praised God. And then they said, "You know, dear brother, how many thousands of Jews have also believed, and they all follow the law of Moses very seriously. 21But the Jewish believers here in Jerusalem have been told that you are teaching all the Jews who live among the Gentiles to turn their backs on the laws of Moses. They've heard that you teach them not to circumcise their children or follow other Jewish customs. 22What should we do? They will certainly hear that you have come.

23"Here's what we want you to do. We have four men here who have completed their vow. 24Go with them to the Temple and join them in the purification ceremony, paying for them to have their heads ritually shaved. Then everyone will know that the rumors are all false and that you yourself observe the Jewish laws.

25"As for the Gentile believers, they should do what we already told them in a

letter: They should abstain from eating food offered to idols, from consuming blood or the meat of strangled animals, and from sexual immorality."

26So Paul went to the Temple the next day with the other men. They had already started the purification ritual, so he publicly announced the date when their vows would end and sacrifices would be offered for each of them.

27The seven days were almost ended when some Jews from the province of Asia saw Paul in the Temple and roused a mob against him. They grabbed him, 28yelling, "Men of Israel, help us! This is the man who preaches against our people everywhere and tells everybody to disobey the Jewish laws. He speaks against the Temple—and even defiles this holy place by bringing in Gentiles.*" 29(For earlier that day they had seen him in the city with Trophimus, a Gentile from Ephesus,* and they assumed Paul had taken him into the Temple.)

30The whole city was rocked by these accusations, and a great riot followed. Paul was grabbed and dragged out of the Temple, and immediately the gates were closed behind him. 31As they were trying to kill him, word reached the commander of the Roman regiment that all Jerusalem was in an uproar. 32He immediately called out his soldiers and officers* and ran down among the crowd. When the mob saw the commander and the troops coming, they stopped beating Paul.

33Then the commander arrested him and ordered him bound with two chains. He asked the crowd who he was and what he had done. 34Some shouted one thing and some another. Since he couldn't find out the truth in all the uproar and confusion, he ordered that Paul be taken to the fortress. 35As Paul reached the stairs, the mob grew so violent the soldiers had to lift him to their shoulders to protect him. 36And the crowd followed behind, shouting, "Kill him, kill him!"

21:28 Greek *Greeks.*   21:29 Greek *Trophimus, the Ephesian.* 21:32 Greek *centurions.*

PSALM 150:1-6

Praise the LORD!

Praise God in his sanctuary;
    praise him in his mighty heaven!

² Praise him for his mighty works;
    praise his unequaled greatness!
³ Praise him with a blast of the ram's horn;
    praise him with the lyre and harp!
⁴ Praise him with the tambourine and
    dancing;
    praise him with strings and flutes!
⁵ Praise him with a clash of cymbals;
    praise him with loud clanging
    cymbals.

⁶ Let everything that breathes sing
    praises to the LORD!

Praise the LORD!

PROVERBS 18:9-10
A lazy person is as bad as someone who destroys things. ☐ The name of the LORD is a strong fortress; the godly run to him and are safe.

JULY**3**

2 KINGS 22:3–23:30
Fortunately for Judah, after the evil reign of Manasseh, his son Josiah came to the throne. Josiah followed in the faith of his grandfather Hezekiah. After the Book of the Law was discovered deep in the Temple, Josiah read it and instituted much-needed reforms.

In the eighteenth year of his reign, King Josiah sent Shaphan son of Azaliah and grandson of Meshullam, the court secretary, to the Temple of the LORD. He told him, ⁴"Go to Hilkiah the high priest and have him count the money the gatekeepers have collected from the people at the LORD's Temple. ⁵Entrust this money to the men assigned to supervise the Temple's restoration. Then they can use it to pay workers to repair the Temple of the LORD. ⁶They will need to hire carpenters, builders, and masons. Also have them buy the timber and the finished stone needed to repair the Temple. ⁷But don't require the construction supervisors to keep account of the money they receive, for they are honest and trustworthy men."

⁸Hilkiah the high priest said to Shaphan the court secretary, "I have found the Book of the Law in the LORD's Temple!" Then Hilkiah gave the scroll to Shaphan, and he read it.

⁹Shaphan went to the king and reported, "Your officials have turned over the money collected at the Temple of the LORD to the workers and supervisors at the Temple." ¹⁰Shaphan also told the king, "Hilkiah the priest has given me a scroll." So Shaphan read it to the king.

¹¹When the king heard what was written in the Book of the Law, he tore his clothes in despair. ¹²Then he gave these orders to Hilkiah the priest, Ahikam son of Shaphan, Acbor son of Micaiah, Shaphan the court secretary, and Asaiah the king's personal adviser: ¹³"Go to the Temple and speak to the LORD for me and for the people and for all Judah. Inquire about the words written in this scroll that has been found. For the LORD's great anger is burning against us because our ancestors have not obeyed the words in this scroll. We have not been doing everything it says we must do."

¹⁴So Hilkiah the priest, Ahikam, Acbor, Shaphan, and Asaiah went to the New Quarter* of Jerusalem to consult with the prophet Huldah. She was the wife of Shallum son of Tikvah, son of Harhas, the keeper of the Temple wardrobe.

¹⁵She said to them, "The LORD, the God of Israel, has spoken! Go back and tell the man who sent you, ¹⁶'This is what the LORD says: I am going to bring disaster on this city* and its people. All the words written in the scroll that the king of Judah has read will come true. ¹⁷For my people have abandoned me and offered sacrifices to pagan gods, and I am very angry with them for everything they have done. My anger will burn against this place, and it will not be quenched.'

18"But go to the king of Judah who sent you to seek the LORD and tell him: 'This is what the LORD, the God of Israel, says concerning the message you have just heard: 19You were sorry and humbled yourself before the LORD when you heard what I said against this city and its people—that this land would be cursed and become desolate. You tore your clothing in despair and wept before me in repentance. And I have indeed heard you, says the LORD. 20So I will not send the promised disaster until after you have died and been buried in peace. You will not see the disaster I am going to bring on this city.'"

So they took her message back to the king.

23:1THEN the king summoned all the elders of Judah and Jerusalem. 2And the king went up to the Temple of the LORD with all the people of Judah and Jerusalem, along with the priests and the prophets—all the people from the least to the greatest. There the king read to them the entire Book of the Covenant that had been found in the LORD's Temple. 3The king took his place of authority beside the pillar and renewed the covenant in the LORD's presence. He pledged to obey the LORD by keeping all his commands, laws, and decrees with all his heart and soul. In this way, he confirmed all the terms of the covenant that were written in the scroll, and all the people pledged themselves to the covenant.

4Then the king instructed Hilkiah the high priest and the priests of the second rank and the Temple gatekeepers to remove from the LORD's Temple all the articles that were used to worship Baal, Asherah, and all the powers of the heavens. The king had all these things burned outside Jerusalem on the terraces of the Kidron Valley, and he carried the ashes away to Bethel. 5He did away with the idolatrous priests, who had been appointed by the previous kings of Judah, for they had offered sacrifices at the pagan shrines throughout Judah and even in the vicinity of Jerusalem. They had also offered sacrifices to Baal, and to the sun, the moon, the constellations, and to all the powers of the heavens. 6The king re-

moved the Asherah pole from the LORD's Temple and took it outside Jerusalem to the Kidron Valley, where he burned it. Then he ground the ashes of the pole to dust and threw the dust over the graves of the people. 7He also tore down the living quarters of the male and female shrine prostitutes that were inside the Temple of the LORD, where the women wove coverings for the Asherah pole.

8Josiah brought to Jerusalem all the priests who were living in other towns of Judah. He also defiled the pagan shrines, where they had offered sacrifices—all the way from Geba to Beersheba. He destroyed the shrines at the entrance to the gate of Joshua, the governor of Jerusalem. This gate was located to the left of the city gate as one enters the city. 9The priests who had served at the pagan shrines were not allowed* to serve at the LORD's altar in Jerusalem, but they were allowed to eat unleavened bread with the other priests.

10Then the king defiled the altar of Topheth in the valley of Ben-Hinnom, so no one could ever again use it to sacrifice a son or daughter in the fire* as an offering to Molech. 11He removed from the entrance of the LORD's Temple the horse statues that the former kings of Judah had dedicated to the sun. They were near the quarters of Nathan-melech the eunuch, an officer of the court.* The king also burned the chariots dedicated to the sun.

12Josiah tore down the altars that the kings of Judah had built on the palace roof above the upper room of Ahaz. The king destroyed the altars that Manasseh had built in the two courtyards of the LORD's Temple. He smashed them to bits* and scattered the pieces in the Kidron Valley. 13The king also desecrated the pagan shrines east of Jerusalem, to the south of the Mount of Corruption, where King Solomon of Israel had built shrines for Ashtoreth, the detestable goddess of the Sidonians; and for Chemosh, the detestable god of the Moabites; and for Molech,* the vile god of the Ammonites. 14He smashed the sacred pillars and cut down the Asherah poles. Then he desecrated these places by scattering human bones over them.

15The king also tore down the altar at

Bethel—the pagan shrine that Jeroboam son of Nebat had made when he caused Israel to sin. He burned down the shrine and ground it to dust, and he burned the Asherah pole. ¹⁶Then Josiah turned around and noticed several tombs in the side of the hill. He ordered that the bones be brought out, and he burned them on the altar at Bethel to desecrate it. (This happened just as the LORD had promised through the man of God when Jeroboam stood beside the altar at the festival.)

Then Josiah turned and looked up at the tomb of the man of God* who had predicted these things. ¹⁷"What is that monument over there?" Josiah asked.

And the people of the town told him, "It is the tomb of the man of God who came from Judah and predicted the very things that you have just done to the altar at Bethel!"

¹⁸Josiah replied, "Leave it alone. Don't disturb his bones." So they did not burn his bones or those of the old prophet from Samaria.

¹⁹Then Josiah demolished all the buildings at the pagan shrines in the towns of Samaria, just as he had done at Bethel. They had been built by the various kings of Israel and had made the LORD* very angry. ²⁰He executed the priests of the pagan shrines on their own altars, and

he burned human bones on the altars to desecrate them. Finally, he returned to Jerusalem.

²¹King Josiah then issued this order to all the people: "You must celebrate the Passover to the LORD your God, as required in this Book of the Covenant." ²²There had not been a Passover celebration like that since the time when the judges ruled in Israel, nor throughout all the years of the kings of Israel and Judah. ²³This Passover was celebrated to the LORD in Jerusalem in the eighteenth year of King Josiah's reign.

²⁴Josiah also got rid of the mediums and psychics, the household gods, the idols,* and every other kind of detestable practice, both in Jerusalem and throughout the land of Judah. He did this in obedience to the laws written in the scroll that Hilkiah the priest had found in the LORD's Temple. ²⁵Never before had there been a king like Josiah, who turned to the LORD with all his heart and soul and strength, obeying all the laws of Moses. And there has never been a king like him since.

²⁶Even so, the LORD was very angry with Judah because of all the wicked things Manasseh had done to provoke him. ²⁷For the LORD said, "I will also banish Judah from my presence just as I have

HOW WE LIVE

Studying God's Word

2 KINGS 22:8-20 If you wonder about the power of Bible study, consider what happened with Josiah. As the king listened to the reading of the law, he was so convicted that he tore his clothes, showing his remorse. Things had to change, and they had to change right then. Reforms were instituted immediately. Shrines to other gods were destroyed, and all the people pledged to renew their covenant with the Lord. The reading of God's Word produced drastic changes for the better in an entire nation.
• You have right here in your hand the most amazing resource for living—including the words read to Josiah so many centuries ago. Praying is how you communicate with God; studying God's Word is how he communicates with you. It is powerful and sharp as a sword (Hebrews 4:12, November 2), but you need to read with an open heart, ready to do what it says. God had mercy on Josiah because he humbled himself and repented. Whenever a verse of Scripture pierces your soul, don't be afraid to admit where you've been wrong and ask for God's forgiveness. Then do as Josiah did—get moving in the right direction!

banished Israel. And I will reject my chosen city of Jerusalem and the Temple where my name was to be honored."

²⁸The rest of the events in Josiah's reign and all his deeds are recorded in *The Book of the History of the Kings of Judah.*

²⁹While Josiah was king, Pharaoh Neco, king of Egypt, went to the Euphrates River to help the king of Assyria. King Josiah and his army marched out to fight him,* but King Neco* killed him when they met at Megiddo. ³⁰Josiah's officers took his body back in a chariot from Megiddo to Jerusalem and buried him in his own tomb. Then the people of the land anointed Josiah's son Jehoahaz and made him the next king.

22:14 Or *the Second Quarter,* a newer section of Jerusalem. Hebrew reads *the Mishneh.*   22:16 Hebrew *this place;* also in 22:19, 20.   23:9 Hebrew *did not come up.*   23:10 Or *to make a son or daughter pass through the fire.*   23:11 The meaning of the Hebrew is uncertain.   23:12 Or *He quickly removed them.*   23:13 Hebrew *Milcom,* a variant spelling of Molech.   23:16 As in Greek version; Hebrew lacks *when Jeroboam stood beside the altar at the festival. Then Josiah turned and looked up at the tomb of the man of God.* 23:19 As in Greek and Syriac versions and Latin Vulgate; Hebrew lacks *the LORD.*   23:24 The Hebrew term (literally *round things*) probably alludes to dung.   23:29a Or *Josiah went out to meet him.*   23:29b Hebrew *he.*

ACTS 21:37–22:16

Having been taken into custody in the midst of a violent mob, Paul decided to take advantage of the fact that he had the people's attention; he told his story and, in so doing, pointed people to Jesus.

As Paul was about to be taken inside, he said to the commander, "May I have a word with you?"

"Do you know Greek?" the commander asked, surprised. ³⁸"Aren't you the Egyptian who led a rebellion some time ago and took 4,000 members of the Assassins out into the desert?"

³⁹"No," Paul replied, "I am a Jew and a citizen of Tarsus in Cilicia, which is an important city. Please, let me talk to these people." ⁴⁰The commander agreed, so Paul stood on the stairs and motioned to the people to be quiet. Soon a deep silence enveloped the crowd, and he addressed them in their own language, Aramaic.*

22:1"**BROTHERS** and esteemed fathers," Paul said, "listen to me as I offer my defense." ²When they heard him speaking in their own language,* the silence was even greater.

³Then Paul said, "I am a Jew, born in Tarsus, a city in Cilicia, and I was brought up and educated here in Jerusalem under Gamaliel. As his student, I was carefully trained in our Jewish laws and customs. I became very zealous to honor God in everything I did, just like all of you today. ⁴And I persecuted the followers of the Way, hounding some to death, arresting both men and women and throwing them in prison. ⁵The high priest and the whole council of elders can testify that this is so. For I received letters from them to our Jewish brothers in Damascus, authorizing me to bring the Christians from there to Jerusalem, in chains, to be punished.

⁶"As I was on the road, approaching Damascus about noon, a very bright light from heaven suddenly shone down around me. ⁷I fell to the ground and heard a voice saying to me, 'Saul, Saul, why are you persecuting me?'

⁸"'Who are you, lord?' I asked.

"And the voice replied, 'I am Jesus the Nazarene,* the one you are persecuting.' ⁹The people with me saw the light but didn't understand the voice speaking to me.

¹⁰"I asked, 'What should I do, Lord?'

"And the Lord told me, 'Get up and go into Damascus, and there you will be told everything you are to do.'

¹¹"I was blinded by the intense light and had to be led by the hand to Damascus by my companions. ¹²A man named Ananias lived there. He was a godly man, deeply devoted to the law, and well regarded by all the Jews of Damascus. ¹³He came and stood beside me and said, 'Brother Saul, regain your sight.' And that very moment I could see him!

¹⁴"Then he told me, 'The God of our ancestors has chosen you to know his will and to see the Righteous One and hear him speak. ¹⁵For you are to be his witness, telling everyone what you have seen and heard. ¹⁶What are you waiting for? Get up and be baptized. Have your sins washed away by calling on the name of the Lord.'"

21:40 Or *Hebrew.*   22:2 Greek *in Aramaic,* or *in Hebrew.* 22:8 Or *Jesus of Nazareth.*

PSALM 1:1-6

Oh, the joys of those who do not
   follow the advice of the wicked,

or stand around with sinners,
   or join in with mockers.
² But they delight in the law of the
   LORD,
   meditating on it day and night.
³ They are like trees planted along the
   riverbank,
   bearing fruit each season.
   Their leaves never wither,
   and they prosper in all they do.

⁴ But not the wicked!
   They are like worthless chaff,
      scattered by the wind.

---

2 KINGS 23:31–25:30
When Israel and Judah followed God, he blessed
them. When they rebelled, he punished them. After
both kingdoms persistently disobeyed, God allowed
them to be taken into exile. He even allowed his
own Temple to be destroyed.

Jehoahaz was twenty-three years old when
he became king, and he reigned in Jerusalem three months. His mother was Hamutal, the daughter of Jeremiah from Libnah.
³²He did what was evil in the LORD's sight,
just as his ancestors had done.

³³Pharaoh Neco put Jehoahaz in prison
at Riblah in the land of Hamath to prevent
him from ruling* in Jerusalem. He also demanded that Judah pay 7,500 pounds of
silver and 75 pounds of gold* as tribute.

³⁴Pharaoh Neco then installed Eliakim,
another of Josiah's sons, to reign in place
of his father, and he changed Eliakim's
name to Jehoiakim. Jehoahaz was taken to
Egypt as a prisoner, where he died.

³⁵In order to get the silver and gold demanded as tribute by Pharaoh Neco, Jehoiakim collected a tax from the people
of Judah, requiring them to pay in proportion to their wealth.

³⁶Jehoiakim was twenty-five years old
when he became king, and he reigned in
Jerusalem eleven years. His mother was
Zebidah, the daughter of Pedaiah from

⁵ They will be condemned at the time of
   judgment.
   Sinners will have no place among
   the godly.
⁶ For the LORD watches over the path of
   the godly,
   but the path of the wicked leads to
   destruction.

PROVERBS 18:11-12
The rich think of their wealth as a strong
defense; they imagine it to be a high wall
of safety. □ Haughtiness goes before
destruction; humility precedes honor.

Rumah. ³⁷He did what was evil in the
LORD's sight, just as his ancestors had
done.

²⁴:¹DURING Jehoiakim's reign, King Nebuchadnezzar of Babylon invaded the land
of Judah. Jehoiakim surrendered and
paid him tribute for three years but then
rebelled. ²Then the LORD sent bands of
Babylonian,* Aramean, Moabite, and Ammonite raiders against Judah to destroy it,
just as the LORD had promised through
his prophets. ³These disasters happened
to Judah because of the LORD's command.
He had decided to banish Judah from
his presence because of the many sins of
Manasseh, ⁴who had filled Jerusalem
with innocent blood. The LORD would not
forgive this.

⁵The rest of the events in Jehoiakim's
reign and all his deeds are recorded in *The
Book of the History of the Kings of Judah.*
⁶When Jehoiakim died, his son Jehoiachin became the next king.

⁷The king of Egypt did not venture out
of his country after that, for the king of
Babylon captured the entire area formerly
claimed by Egypt—from the Brook of
Egypt to the Euphrates River.

⁸Jehoiachin was eighteen years old
when he became king, and he reigned in

JULY 4

Jerusalem three months. His mother was Nehushta, the daughter of Elnathan from Jerusalem. ⁹Jehoiachin did what was evil in the LORD's sight, just as his father had done.

¹⁰During Jehoiachin's reign, the officers of King Nebuchadnezzar of Babylon came up against Jerusalem and besieged it. ¹¹Nebuchadnezzar himself arrived at the city during the siege. ¹²Then King Jehoiachin, along with the queen mother, his advisers, his commanders, and his officials, surrendered to the Babylonians.

In the eighth year of Nebuchadnezzar's reign, he took Jehoiachin prisoner. ¹³As the LORD had said beforehand, Nebuchadnezzar carried away all the treasures from the LORD's Temple and the royal palace. He stripped away* all the gold objects that King Solomon of Israel had placed in the Temple. ¹⁴King Nebuchadnezzar took all of Jerusalem captive, including all the commanders and the best of the soldiers, craftsmen, and artisans— 10,000 in all. Only the poorest people were left in the land.

¹⁵Nebuchadnezzar led King Jehoiachin away as a captive to Babylon, along with the queen mother, his wives and officials, and all Jerusalem's elite. ¹⁶He also exiled 7,000 of the best troops and 1,000 craftsmen and artisans, all of whom were strong and fit for war. ¹⁷Then the king of Babylon installed Mattaniah, Jehoiachin's* uncle, as the next king, and he changed Mattaniah's name to Zedekiah.

¹⁸Zedekiah was twenty-one years old when he became king, and he reigned in Jerusalem eleven years. His mother was Hamutal, the daughter of Jeremiah from Libnah. ¹⁹But Zedekiah did what was evil in the LORD's sight, just as Jehoiakim had done. ²⁰These things happened because of the LORD's anger against the people of Jerusalem and Judah, until he finally banished them from his presence and sent them into exile.

Zedekiah rebelled against the king of Babylon.

25:1 So on January 15,* during the ninth year of Zedekiah's reign, King Nebuchadnezzar of Babylon led his entire army against Jerusalem. They surrounded the city and built siege ramps against its walls. ²Jerusalem was kept under siege until the eleventh year of King Zedekiah's reign.

³By July 18 in the eleventh year of Zedekiah's reign,* the famine in the city had become very severe, and the last of the food was entirely gone. ⁴Then a section of the city wall was broken down, and all the soldiers fled. Since the city was surrounded by the Babylonians,* they waited for nightfall. Then they slipped through the gate between the two walls behind the king's garden and headed toward the Jordan Valley.*

⁵But the Babylonian* troops chased the king and caught him on the plains of Jericho, for his men had all deserted him and scattered. ⁶They took him to the king of Babylon at Riblah, where they pronounced judgment upon Zedekiah. ⁷They made Zedekiah watch as they slaughtered his sons. Then they gouged out Zedekiah's eyes, bound him in bronze chains, and led him away to Babylon.

⁸On August 14 of that year,* which was the nineteenth year of King Nebuchadnezzar's reign, Nebuzaradan, the captain of the guard and an official of the Babylonian king, arrived in Jerusalem. ⁹He burned down the Temple of the LORD, the royal palace, and all the houses of Jerusalem. He destroyed all the important buildings* in the city. ¹⁰Then he supervised the entire Babylonian army as they tore down the walls of Jerusalem on every side. ¹¹Nebuzaradan, the captain of the guard, then took as exiles the rest of the people who remained in the city, the defectors who had declared their allegiance to the king of Babylon, and the rest of the population. ¹²But the captain of the guard allowed some of the poorest people to stay behind in Judah to care for the vineyards and fields.

¹³The Babylonians broke up the bronze pillars in front of the LORD's Temple, the bronze water carts, and the great bronze basin called the Sea, and they carried all the bronze away to Babylon. ¹⁴They also took all the ash buckets, shovels, lamp snuffers, dishes, and all the other bronze articles used for making sacrifices at the Temple. ¹⁵Nebuzaradan, the captain of

the guard, also took the incense burners and basins, and all the other articles made of pure gold or silver.

¹⁶The weight of the bronze from the two pillars, the Sea, and the water carts was too great to be measured. These things had been made for the LORD's Temple in the days of King Solomon. ¹⁷Each of the pillars was 27 feet* tall. The bronze capital on top of each pillar was 7½ feet* high and was decorated with a network of bronze pomegranates all the way around.

¹⁸Nebuzaradan, the captain of the guard, took with him as prisoners Seraiah the high priest, Zephaniah the priest of the second rank, and the three chief gatekeepers. ¹⁹And from among the people still hiding in the city, he took an officer who had been in charge of the Judean army; five of the king's personal advisers; the army commander's chief secretary, who was in charge of recruitment; and sixty other citizens. ²⁰Nebuzaradan, the captain of the guard, took them all to the king of Babylon at Riblah. ²¹And there at Riblah, in the land of Hamath, the king of Babylon had them all put to death. So the people of Judah were sent into exile from their land.

²²Then King Nebuchadnezzar appointed Gedaliah son of Ahikam and grandson of Shaphan as governor over the people he had left in Judah. ²³When all the army commanders and their men learned that the king of Babylon had appointed Gedaliah as governor, they went to see him at Mizpah. These included Ishmael son of Nethaniah, Johanan son of Kareah, Seraiah son of Tanhumeth the Netophathite, and Jezaniah* son of the Maacathite, and all their men.

²⁴Gedaliah vowed to them that the Babylonian officials meant them no harm. "Don't be afraid of them. Live in the land and serve the king of Babylon, and all will go well for you," he promised.

²⁵But in midautumn of that year,* Ishmael son of Nethaniah and grandson of Elishama, who was of the royal family, went to Mizpah with ten men and killed Gedaliah. He also killed all the Judeans and Babylonians who were with Gedaliah at Mizpah.

²⁶Then all the people of Judah, from the least to the greatest, as well as the army commanders, fled in panic to Egypt, for they were afraid of what the Babylonians would do to them.

²⁷In the thirty-seventh year of the exile of King Jehoiachin of Judah, Evilmerodach ascended to the Babylonian throne. He was kind to* Jehoiachin and released him from prison on April 2 of that year.* ²⁸He spoke kindly to Jehoiachin and gave him a higher place than all the other exiled kings in Babylon. ²⁹He supplied Jehoiachin with new clothes to

HOW WE LIVE

Obeying God

2 KINGS 25:1-21 "You reap what you sow," the old saying goes. And the nation of Judah learned the truth of that statement firsthand. God gave them many opportunities to turn from their sin, but evil permeated the nation. Therefore God allowed the Babylonians to conquer and destroy Jerusalem and pillage the Temple. • As Christians, we have received all the benefits of salvation through Jesus Christ. We can never lose that salvation. Yet, the promise of salvation does not mean there are no longer any consequences to our choices. As human beings, we are still tainted with sin. The pull of wanting to do our own thing, just as the Israelites did, is strong. The destruction of Jerusalem stands as a startling reminder that even as believers we can reap significant negative consequences from sin. • When you fail, don't give up on your faith or on yourself. God's promises will not fail. In his faithfulness, he will forgive you when you repent, and he will help you get back on the right path.

replace his prison garb and allowed him to dine in the king's presence for the rest of his life. [30]So the Babylonian king gave him a regular food allowance as long as he lived.

23:33a The meaning of the Hebrew is uncertain.
23:33b Hebrew *100 talents* [3,400 kilograms] *of silver and 1 talent* [34 kilograms] *of gold.* 24:2 Or *Chaldean.* 24:13 Or *He cut apart.* 24:17 Hebrew *his.* 25:1 Hebrew *on the tenth day of the tenth month,* of the ancient Hebrew lunar calendar. A number of events in 2 Kings can be cross-checked with dates in surviving Babylonian records and related accurately to our modern calendar. This day was January 15, 588 B.C. 25:3 Hebrew *By the ninth day of the (fourth) month* [in the eleventh year of Zedekiah's reign] (compare Jer 52:6 and the note there). This day was July 18, 586 B.C.; also see note on 25:1. 25:4a Or *the Chaldeans;* also in 25:13, 25, 26. 25:4b Hebrew *the Arabah.* 25:5 Or *Chaldean;* also in 25:10, 24. 25:8 Hebrew *On the seventh day of the fifth month,* of the ancient Hebrew lunar calendar. This day was August 14, 586 B.C.; also see note on 25:1. 25:9 Or *destroyed the houses of all the important people.* 25:17a Hebrew *18 cubits* [8.1 meters]. 25:17b As in parallel texts at 1 Kgs 7:16, 2 Chr 3:15, and Jer 52:22, all of which read *5 cubits* [2.3 meters]; Hebrew reads *3 cubits,* which is 4.5 feet or 1.4 meters. 25:23 As in parallel text at Jer 40:8; Hebrew reads *Jaazaniah,* a variant spelling of Jezaniah. 25:25 Hebrew *in the seventh month,* of the ancient Hebrew lunar calendar. This month occurred within the months of October and November 586 B.C.; also see note on 25:1. 25:27a Hebrew *He raised the head of.* 25:27b Hebrew *on the twenty-seventh day of the twelfth month,* of the ancient Hebrew lunar calendar. This day was April 2, 561 B.C.; also see note on 25:1.

ACTS 22:17-23:10

How can freedom exist in the midst of chains and religious oppression? For Paul freedom was a heart issue, a matter of perspective rather than location. Paul's arrest at Jerusalem was a doorway for new ministry—in Rome, the most influential city in the world.

"**A**fter I [Paul] returned to Jerusalem, I was praying in the Temple and fell into a trance. [18]I saw a vision of Jesus* saying to me, 'Hurry! Leave Jerusalem, for the people here won't accept your testimony about me.'

[19] 'But Lord,' I argued, 'they certainly know that in every synagogue I imprisoned and beat those who believed in you. [20]And I was in complete agreement when your witness Stephen was killed. I stood by and kept the coats they took off when they stoned him.'

[21]"But the Lord said to me, 'Go, for I will send you far away to the Gentiles!'"

[22]The crowd listened until Paul said that word. Then they all began to shout, "Away with such a fellow! He isn't fit to live!" [23]They yelled, threw off their coats, and tossed handfuls of dust into the air.

[24]The commander brought Paul inside and ordered him lashed with whips to make him confess his crime. He wanted to find out why the crowd had become so furious. [25]When they tied Paul down to lash him, Paul said to the officer* standing there, "Is it legal for you to whip a Roman citizen who hasn't even been tried?"

[26]When the officer heard this, he went to the commander and asked, "What are you doing? This man is a Roman citizen!"

[27]So the commander went over and asked Paul, "Tell me, are you a Roman citizen?"

"Yes, I certainly am," Paul replied.

[28]"I am, too," the commander muttered, "and it cost me plenty!"

Paul answered, "But I am a citizen by birth!"

[29]The soldiers who were about to interrogate Paul quickly withdrew when they heard he was a Roman citizen, and the commander was frightened because he had ordered him bound and whipped.

[30]The next day the commander ordered the leading priests into session with the Jewish high council.* He wanted to find out what the trouble was all about, so he released Paul to have him stand before them.

23:1GAZING intently at the high council,* Paul began: "Brothers, I have always lived before God with a clear conscience!"

[2]Instantly Ananias the high priest commanded those close to Paul to slap him on the mouth. [3]But Paul said to him, "God will slap you, you corrupt hypocrite!* What kind of judge are you to break the law yourself by ordering me struck like that?"

[4]Those standing near Paul said to him, "Do you dare to insult God's high priest?"

[5]"I'm sorry, brothers. I didn't realize he was the high priest," Paul replied, "for the Scriptures say, 'You must not speak evil of any of your rulers.'*"

[6]Paul realized that some members of the high council were Sadducees and some were Pharisees, so he shouted, "Brothers, I am a Pharisee, as were my ancestors! And I am on trial because my hope is in the resurrection of the dead!"

[7]This divided the council—the Pharisees against the Sadducees—[8]for the Sad-

ducees say there is no resurrection or angels or spirits, but the Pharisees believe in all of these. ⁹So there was a great uproar. Some of the teachers of religious law who were Pharisees jumped up and began to argue forcefully. "We see nothing wrong with him," they shouted. "Perhaps a spirit or an angel spoke to him." ¹⁰As the conflict grew more violent, the commander was afraid they would tear Paul apart. So he ordered his soldiers to go and rescue him by force and take him back to the fortress.

22:18 Greek *him.*   **22:25** Greek *the centurion;* also in 22:26.   **22:30** Greek *Sanhedrin.*   **23:1** Greek *Sanhedrin;* also in 23:6, 15, 20, 28.   **23:3** Greek *you whitewashed wall.* **23:5** Exod 22:28.

PSALM 2:1-12

Why are the nations so angry?
     Why do they waste their time with
          futile plans?
² The kings of the earth prepare for
          battle;
     the rulers plot together
against the LORD
     and against his anointed one.
³ "Let us break their chains," they cry,
     "and free ourselves from slavery to
          God."

⁴ But the one who rules in heaven
          laughs.
     The Lord scoffs at them.
⁵ Then in anger he rebukes them,

1 CHRONICLES 1:1–2:17

First Chronicles opens with a genealogy that begins with Adam and continues through David. For the Jews, a genealogy was an important way to keep track of their history and, in fact, to remember their own identity. You'll see some names you recognize in 1:1-4; 1:34-35; 2:1; and 2:12-15.

The descendants of Adam were Seth, Enosh, ²Kenan, Mahalalel, Jared, ³Enoch, Methuselah, Lamech, ⁴and Noah.
The sons of Noah were* Shem, Ham, and Japheth.

terrifying them with his fierce fury.
⁶ For the Lord declares, "I have placed
     my chosen king on the throne
     in Jerusalem,* on my holy
          mountain."

⁷ The king proclaims the LORD's decree:
     "The LORD said to me, 'You are my
          son.*
     Today I have become your Father.*
⁸ Only ask, and I will give you the
          nations as your inheritance,
     the whole earth as your possession.
⁹ You will break* them with an iron rod
     and smash them like clay pots.'"

¹⁰ Now then, you kings, act wisely!
     Be warned, you rulers of the earth!
¹¹ Serve the LORD with reverent fear,
     and rejoice with trembling.
¹² Submit to God's royal son,* or he will
          become angry,
     and you will be destroyed in the
          midst of all your activities—
     for his anger flares up in an instant.
     But what joy for all who take refuge
          in him!

2:6 Hebrew *on Zion.*   **2:7a** Or *Son;* also in 2:12.   **2:7b** Or *Today I reveal you as my son.*   **2:9** Greek version reads *rule.* Compare Rev 2:27.   **2:12** The meaning of the Hebrew is uncertain.

PROVERBS 18:13

Spouting off before listening to the facts is both shameful and foolish.

JULY**5**

⁵The descendants of Japheth were
     Gomer, Magog, Madai, Javan, Tubal,
     Meshech, and Tiras.
⁶The descendants of Gomer were
     Ashkenaz, Riphath,* and Togarmah.
⁷The descendants of Javan were Elishah,
     Tarshish, Kittim, and Rodanim.

⁸The descendants of Ham were Cush,
     Mizraim,* Put, and Canaan.
⁹The descendants of Cush were Seba,
     Havilah, Sabtah, Raamah, and Sabteca.

The descendants of Raamah were Sheba and Dedan. [10]Cush was also the ancestor of Nimrod, who was the first heroic warrior on earth.

[11]Mizraim was the ancestor of the Ludites, Anamites, Lehabites, Naphtuhites, [12]Pathrusites, Casluhites, and the Caphtorites, from whom the Philistines came.*

[13]Canaan's oldest son was Sidon, the ancestor of the Sidonians. Canaan was also the ancestor of the Hittites, [14]Jebusites, Amorites, Girgashites, [15]Hivites, Arkites, Sinites, [16]Arvadites, Zemarites, and Hamathites.

[17]The descendants of Shem were Elam, Asshur, Arphaxad, Lud, and Aram.

The descendants of Aram were* Uz, Hul, Gether, and Mash.*

[18]Arphaxad was the father of Shelah.

Shelah was the father of Eber.

[19]Eber had two sons. The first was named Peleg (which means "division"), for during his lifetime the people of the world were divided into different language groups. His brother's name was Joktan.

[20]Joktan was the ancestor of Almodad, Sheleph, Hazarmaveth, Jerah, [21]Hadoram, Uzal, Diklah, [22]Obal,* Abimael, Sheba, [23]Ophir, Havilah, and Jobab. All these were descendants of Joktan.

[24]So this is the family line descended from Shem: Arphaxad, Shelah,* [25]Eber, Peleg, Reu, [26]Serug, Nahor, Terah, [27]and Abram, later known as Abraham.

[28]The sons of Abraham were Isaac and Ishmael. [29]These are their genealogical records:

The sons of Ishmael were Nebaioth (the oldest), Kedar, Adbeel, Mibsam, [30]Mishma, Dumah, Massa, Hadad, Tema, [31]Jetur, Naphish, and Kedemah. These were the sons of Ishmael.

[32]The sons of Keturah, Abraham's concubine, were Zimran, Jokshan, Medan, Midian, Ishbak, and Shuah.

The sons of Jokshan were Sheba and Dedan.

[33]The sons of Midian were Ephah, Epher, Hanoch, Abida, and Eldaah.

All these were descendants of Abraham through his concubine Keturah.

[34]Abraham was the father of Isaac. The sons of Isaac were Esau and Israel.*

[35]The sons of Esau were Eliphaz, Reuel, Jeush, Jalam, and Korah.

[36]The sons of Eliphaz were Teman, Omar, Zepho,* Gatam, Kenaz, and Amalek, who was born to Timna.*

[37]The sons of Reuel were Nahath, Zerah, Shammah, and Mizzah.

[38]The sons of Seir were Lotan, Shobal, Zibeon, Anah, Dishon, Ezer, and Dishan.

[39]The sons of Lotan were Hori and Heman.* Lotan's sister was named Timna.

[40]The sons of Shobal were Alvan,* Manahath, Ebal, Shepho,* and Onam.

The sons of Zibeon were Aiah and Anah.

[41]The son of Anah was Dishon.

The sons of Dishon were Hemdan,* Eshban, Ithran, and Keran.

[42]The sons of Ezer were Bilhan, Zaavan, and Akan.*

The sons of Dishan* were Uz and Aran.

[43]These are the kings who ruled in Edom before there were kings in Israel*:

Bela son of Beor, who ruled from his city of Dinhabah.

[44]When Bela died, Jobab son of Zerah from Bozrah became king.

[45]When Jobab died, Husham from the land of the Temanites became king.

[46]When Husham died, Hadad son of Bedad became king and ruled from the city of Avith. He was the one who destroyed the Midianite army in the land of Moab.

[47]When Hadad died, Samlah from the city of Masrekah became king.

[48]When Samlah died, Shaul from the city of Rehoboth on the river became king.

[49]When Shaul died, Baal-hanan son of Acbor became king.

[50]When Baal-hanan died, Hadad became king and ruled from the city of Pau.* His wife was Mehetabel, the daughter of Matred and granddaughter of Mezahab. [51]Then Hadad died.

The clan leaders of Edom were Timna, Alvah,* Jetheth, [52]Oholibamah, Elah,

Pinon, [53]Kenaz, Teman, Mibzar, [54]Magdiel, and Iram. These were the clan leaders of Edom.

2:1THE sons of Israel* were Reuben, Simeon, Levi, Judah, Issachar, Zebulun, [2]Dan, Joseph, Benjamin, Naphtali, Gad, and Asher.

[3]Judah had three sons from Bathshua, a Canaanite woman. Their names were Er, Onan, and Shelah. But the LORD saw that the oldest son, Er, was a wicked man, so he killed him. [4]Later Judah had twin sons from Tamar, his widowed daughter-in-law. Their names were Perez and Zerah. So Judah had five sons in all.

[5]The sons of Perez were Hezron and Hamul.

[6]The sons of Zerah were Zimri, Ethan, Heman, Calcol, and Darda*—five in all.

[7]The son of Carmi (a descendant of Zimri) was Achan,* who brought disaster on Israel by taking plunder that had been set apart for the LORD.*

[8]The son of Ethan was Azariah.

[9]The sons of Hezron were Jerahmeel, Ram, and Caleb.*

[10]Ram was the father of Amminadab. Amminadab was the father of Nahshon, a leader of Judah.

[11]Nahshon was the father of Salmon.* Salmon was the father of Boaz.

[12]Boaz was the father of Obed. Obed was the father of Jesse.

[13]Jesse's first son was Eliab, his second was Abinadab, his third was Shimea, [14]his fourth was Nethanel, his fifth was Raddai, [15]his sixth was Ozem, and his seventh was David.

[16]Their sisters were named Zeruiah and Abigail. Zeruiah had three sons named Abishai, Joab, and Asahel.

[17]Abigail married a man named Jether, an Ishmaelite, and they had a son named Amasa.

1:4 As in Greek version (see also Gen 5:3-32); Hebrew lacks *The sons of Noah were.*   **1:6** As in some Hebrew manuscripts and Greek version (see also Gen 10:3); most Hebrew manuscripts read *Diphath.*   **1:8** Or *Egypt;* also in 1:11.   **1:12** Hebrew *Casluhites, from whom the Philistines came, Caphtorites.* See Jer 47:4; Amos 9:7.   **1:17a** As in one Hebrew manuscript and some Greek manuscripts (see also Gen 10:23); most Hebrew manuscripts lack *The descendants of Aram were.*   **1:17b** As in parallel text at Gen 10:23; Hebrew reads *and Meshech.*   **1:22** As in some Hebrew manuscripts and Syriac version (see also Gen 10:28); most Hebrew manuscripts read *Ebal.*   **1:24** Some Greek manuscripts read *Arphaxad, Cainan, Shelah.* See notes on Gen 10:24; 11:12-13.   **1:34** *Israel* is the name that God gave to Jacob.   **1:36a** As in many Hebrew manuscripts and a few

WHAT THE BIBLE SAYS

The purpose of genealogies

1 CHRONICLES 1–9   The Bible contains several lists of ancestors, called *genealogies.* Why? What is their purpose?   • 1 Chronicles contains the most genealogical information of any book in the Bible. It was compiled after the people of Judah had been taken captive to Babylon. As the exiles looked forward to the day when they would return to their homeland, it was important that their heritage not be lost.   • The Hebrews passed on their beliefs through oral tradition. Stories were told to children who passed them on to their children. Genealogies gave a skeletal outline that helped people remember their place in the grand story of God's dealings with Israel. The genealogies preserved family tradition, but even more importantly, they confirmed the Bible's promise that the coming Messiah, Jesus Christ, would be born into the line of Abraham. The genealogies at the beginning of Matthew (1:1-17, January 1) and Luke (3:23-38, March 19) show this very clearly.   • Genealogies point out an interesting characteristic of God. People are important to him as individuals, not just as races or nations. Therefore God refers to people by name, mentioning their life span and descendants. The next time you feel overwhelmed in a vast crowd, remember that the focus of God's attention and love is on the individual—and on you!

Greek manuscripts (see also Gen 36:11); most Hebrew manuscripts read *Zephi*. **1:36b** As in some Greek manuscripts (see also Gen 36:12); Hebrew reads *Kenaz, Timna, and Amalek*. **1:39** As in parallel text at Gen 36:22; Hebrew reads *and Homam*. **1:40a** As in many Hebrew manuscripts and a few Greek manuscripts (see also Gen 36:23); most Hebrew manuscripts read *Alian*. **1:40b** As in some Hebrew manuscripts (see also Gen 36:23); most Hebrew manuscripts read *Shephi*. **1:41** As in many Hebrew manuscripts and some Greek manuscripts (see also Gen 36:26); most Hebrew manuscripts read *Hamran*. **1:42a** As in many Hebrew and Greek manuscripts (see also Gen 36:27); most Hebrew manuscripts read *Jaakan*. **1:42b** Hebrew *Dishon;* compare 1:38 and parallel text at Gen 36:28. **1:43** Or *before an Israelite king ruled over them*. **1:50** As in many Hebrew manuscripts, some Greek manuscripts, Syriac version, and Latin Vulgate (see also Gen 36:39); most Hebrew manuscripts read *Pai*. **1:51** As in parallel text at Gen 36:40; Hebrew reads *Aliah*. **2:1** *Israel* is the name that God gave to Jacob. **2:6** As in many Hebrew manuscripts, some Greek manuscripts, and Syriac version (see also 1 Kgs 4:31); Hebrew reads *Dara*. **2:7a** Hebrew *Achar;* compare Josh 7:1. *Achar* means "disaster." **2:7b** The Hebrew term used here refers to the complete consecration of things or people to the LORD, either by destroying them or by giving them as an offering. **2:9** Hebrew *Kelubai*, a variant spelling of Caleb; compare 2:18. **2:11** As in Greek version (see also Ruth 4:21); Hebrew reads *Salma*.

ACTS 23:11-35

Being in imperial custody spared Paul from being killed by a Jewish mob. Leave it to God to find a creative way to protect his servant!

That night the Lord appeared to Paul and said, "Be encouraged, Paul. Just as you have been a witness to me here in Jerusalem, you must preach the Good News in Rome as well."

¹²The next morning a group of Jews* got together and bound themselves with an oath not to eat or drink until they had killed Paul. ¹³There were more than forty of them in the conspiracy. ¹⁴They went to the leading priests and elders and told them, "We have bound ourselves with an oath to eat nothing until we have killed Paul. ¹⁵So you and the high council should ask the commander to bring Paul back to the council again. Pretend you want to examine his case more fully. We will kill him on the way."

¹⁶But Paul's nephew—his sister's son—heard of their plan and went to the fortress and told Paul. ¹⁷Paul called for one of the Roman officers* and said, "Take this young man to the commander. He has something important to tell him."

¹⁸So the officer did, explaining, "Paul, the prisoner, called me over and asked me to bring this young man to you because he has something to tell you."

¹⁹The commander took his hand, led him aside, and asked, "What is it you want to tell me?"

²⁰Paul's nephew told him, "Some Jews are going to ask you to bring Paul before the high council tomorrow, pretending they want to get some more information. ²¹But don't do it! There are more than forty men hiding along the way ready to ambush him. They have vowed not to eat or drink anything until they have killed him. They are ready now, just waiting for your consent."

²²"Don't let anyone know you told me this," the commander warned the young man.

²³Then the commander called two of his officers and ordered, "Get 200 soldiers ready to leave for Caesarea at nine o'clock tonight. Also take 200 spearmen and 70 mounted troops. ²⁴Provide horses for Paul to ride, and get him safely to Governor Felix." ²⁵Then he wrote this letter to the governor:

²⁶"From Claudius Lysias, to his Excellency, Governor Felix: Greetings!

²⁷"This man was seized by some Jews, and they were about to kill him when I arrived with the troops. When I learned that he was a Roman citizen, I removed him to safety. ²⁸Then I took him to their high council to try to learn the basis of the accusations against him. ²⁹I soon discovered the charge was something regarding their religious law—certainly nothing worthy of imprisonment or death. ³⁰But when I was informed of a plot to kill him, I immediately sent him on to you. I have told his accusers to bring their charges before you."

³¹So that night, as ordered, the soldiers took Paul as far as Antipatris. ³²They returned to the fortress the next morning, while the mounted troops took him on to Caesarea. ³³When they arrived in Caesarea, they presented Paul and the letter to Governor Felix. ³⁴He read it and then asked Paul what province he was from. "Cilicia," Paul answered.

³⁵"I will hear your case myself when your accusers arrive," the governor told

him. Then the governor ordered him kept in the prison at Herod's headquarters.*

23:12 Greek *the Jews.*   **23:17** Greek *centurions;* also in 23:23.   **23:35** Greek *Herod's Praetorium.*

PSALM 3:1-8

A psalm of David, regarding the time David fled from his son Absalom.

¹ **O** LORD, I have so many enemies;
    so many are against me.
² So many are saying,
    "God will never rescue him!"
                                    *Interlude**

³ But you, O LORD, are a shield around me;
    you are my glory, the one who holds my head high.
⁴ I cried out to the LORD,
    and he answered me from his holy mountain.   *Interlude*

⁵ I lay down and slept,
    yet I woke up in safety,
    for the LORD was watching over me.
⁶ I am not afraid of ten thousand enemies
    who surround me on every side.

⁷ Arise, O LORD!
    Rescue me, my God!
Slap all my enemies in the face!
    Shatter the teeth of the wicked!
⁸ Victory comes from you, O LORD.
    May you bless your people.
                                    Interlude

3:2 Hebrew *Selah.* The meaning of this word is uncertain, though it is probably a musical or literary term. It is rendered *Interlude* throughout the Psalms.

PROVERBS 18:14-15

The human spirit can endure a sick body, but who can bear a crushed spirit? □Intelligent people are always ready to learn. Their ears are open for knowledge.

JULY**6**

1 CHRONICLES 2:18–4:4

This Jewish family history continues through David's family and into the family of his son, Solomon, who led Israel to international greatness. David belonged to the tribe of Judah (the same tribe to which Jesus belonged).

Hezron's son Caleb had sons from his wife Azubah and from Jerioth.* Her sons were named Jesher, Shobab, and Ardon. ¹⁹After Azubah died, Caleb married Ephrathah,* and they had a son named Hur. ²⁰Hur was the father of Uri. Uri was the father of Bezalel.

²¹When Hezron was sixty years old, he married Gilead's sister, the daughter of Makir. They had a son named Segub. ²²Segub was the father of Jair, who ruled twenty-three towns in the land of Gilead. ²³(But Geshur and Aram captured the Towns of Jair* and also took Kenath and its sixty surrounding villages.) All these were descendants of Makir, the father of Gilead.

²⁴Soon after Hezron died in the town of Caleb-ephrathah, his wife Abijah gave birth to a son named Ashhur (the father of* Tekoa).

²⁵The sons of Jerahmeel, the oldest son of Hezron, were Ram (the firstborn), Bunah, Oren, Ozem, and Ahijah. ²⁶Jerahmeel had a second wife named Atarah. She was the mother of Onam. ²⁷The sons of Ram, the oldest son of Jerahmeel, were Maaz, Jamin, and Eker. ²⁸The sons of Onam were Shammai and Jada.

The sons of Shammai were Nadab and Abishur. ²⁹The sons of Abishur and his wife Abihail were Ahban and Molid. ³⁰The sons of Nadab were Seled and Appaim. Seled died without children, ³¹but Appaim had a son named Ishi. The son of Ishi was Sheshan. Sheshan had a descendant named Ahlai.

³²The sons of Jada, Shammai's brother, were Jether and Jonathan. Jether died without children, ³³but Jonathan had two sons named Peleth and Zaza.

These were all descendants of Jerahmeel.

³⁴Sheshan had no sons, though he did have daughters. He also had an Egyptian servant named Jarha. ³⁵Sheshan gave one of his daughters to be the wife of Jarha, and they had a son named Attai.

³⁶ Attai was the father of Nathan. Nathan was the father of Zabad.

³⁷ Zabad was the father of Ephlal. Ephlal was the father of Obed.

³⁸ Obed was the father of Jehu. Jehu was the father of Azariah.

³⁹ Azariah was the father of Helez. Helez was the father of Eleasah.

⁴⁰ Eleasah was the father of Sismai. Sismai was the father of Shallum.

⁴¹ Shallum was the father of Jekamiah. Jekamiah was the father of Elishama.

⁴²The descendants of Caleb, the brother of Jerahmeel, included Mesha (the firstborn), who became the father of Ziph. Caleb's descendants also included the sons of Mareshah, the father of Hebron.*

⁴³The sons of Hebron were Korah, Tappuah, Rekem, and Shema. ⁴⁴Shema was the father of Raham. Raham was the father of Jorkeam. Rekem was the father of Shammai. ⁴⁵The son of Shammai was Maon. Maon was the father of Beth-zur.

⁴⁶Caleb's concubine Ephah gave birth to Haran, Moza, and Gazez. Haran was the father of Gazez.

⁴⁷The sons of Jahdai were Regem, Jotham, Geshan, Pelet, Ephah, and Shaaph.

⁴⁸Another of Caleb's concubines, Maacah, gave birth to Sheber and Tirhanah. ⁴⁹She also gave birth to Shaaph (the father of Madmannah) and Sheva (the father of Macbenah and Gibea). Caleb also had a daughter named Acsah.

⁵⁰These were all descendants of Caleb.

The sons of Hur, the oldest son of Caleb's wife Ephrathah, were Shobal (the founder of Kiriath-jearim), ⁵¹Salma (the founder of Bethlehem), and Hareph (the founder of Beth-gader).

⁵²The descendants of Shobal (the founder of Kiriath-jearim) were Haroeh, half the Manahathites, ⁵³and the families of Kiriath-jearim—the Ithrites, Puthites, Shumathites, and Mishraites, from whom came the people of Zorah and Eshtaol.

⁵⁴The descendants of Salma were the people of Bethlehem, the Netophathites, Atroth-beth-joab, the other half of the Manahathites, the Zorites, ⁵⁵and the families of scribes living at Jabez—the Tirathites, Shimeathites, and Sucathites. All these were Kenites who descended from Hammath, the father of the family of Recab.*

3:1THESE are the sons of David who were born in Hebron:

The oldest was Amnon, whose mother was Ahinoam from Jezreel.
The second was Daniel, whose mother was Abigail from Carmel.
² The third was Absalom, whose mother was Maacah, the daughter of Talmai, king of Geshur.
The fourth was Adonijah, whose mother was Haggith.
³ The fifth was Shephatiah, whose mother was Abital.
The sixth was Ithream, whose mother was Eglah, David's wife.

⁴These six sons were born to David in Hebron, where he reigned seven and a half years.

Then David reigned another thirty-three years in Jerusalem. ⁵The sons born to David in Jerusalem included Shammua,* Shobab, Nathan, and Solomon. Their mother was Bathsheba,* the daughter of Ammiel. ⁶David also had nine other sons: Ibhar, Elishua,* El-pelet,* ⁷Nogah, Nepheg, Japhia, ⁸Elishama, Eliada, and Eliphelet.

⁹These were the sons of David, not including his sons born to his concubines. Their sister was named Tamar.

¹⁰The descendants of Solomon were Rehoboam, Abijah, Asa, Jehoshaphat,

[11]Jehoram,* Ahaziah, Joash, [12]Amaziah, Uzziah,* Jotham, [13]Ahaz, Hezekiah, Manasseh, [14]Amon, and Josiah.

[15]The sons of Josiah were Johanan (the oldest), Jehoiakim (the second), Zedekiah (the third), and Jehoahaz* (the fourth).

[16]The successors of Jehoiakim were his son Jehoiachin and his brother Zedekiah.*

[17]The sons of Jehoiachin,* who was taken prisoner by the Babylonians, were Shealtiel, [18]Malkiram, Pedaiah, Shenazzar, Jekamiah, Hoshama, and Nedabiah.

[19]The sons of Pedaiah were Zerubbabel and Shimei.

The sons of Zerubbabel were Meshullam and Hananiah. (Their sister was Shelomith.) [20]His five other sons were Hashubah, Ohel, Berekiah, Hasadiah, and Jushab-hesed.

[21]The sons of Hananiah were Pelatiah and Jeshaiah. Jeshaiah's son was Rephaiah. Rephaiah's son was Arnan. Arnan's son was Obadiah. Obadiah's son was Shecaniah.

[22]The descendants of Shecaniah were Shemaiah and his sons, Hattush, Igal, Bariah, Neariah, and Shaphat—six in all.

[23]The sons of Neariah were Elioenai, Hizkiah, and Azrikam—three in all.

[24]The sons of Elioenai were Hodaviah, Eliashib, Pelaiah, Akkub, Johanan, Delaiah, and Anani—seven in all.

4:1THE descendants of Judah were Perez, Hezron, Carmi, Hur, and Shobal.
[2]Shobal's son Reaiah was the father of Jahath. Jahath was the father of Ahumai and Lahad. These were the families of the Zorathites.
[3]The descendants of* Etam were Jezreel, Ishma, Idbash, their sister Hazzelelponi, [4]Penuel (the father of* Gedor), and Ezer (the father of Hushah). These were the descendants of Hur (the firstborn of Ephrathah), the ancestor of Bethlehem.

2:18 Or *Caleb had a daughter named Jerioth from his wife, Azubah.* The meaning of the Hebrew is uncertain. **2:19** Hebrew *Ephrath,* a variant spelling of Ephrathah; compare 2:50 and 4:4. **2:23** Or *captured Havvoth-jair.* **2:24** Or *the founder of;* also in 2:42, 45, 49. **2:42** Or *who founded Hebron.* The meaning of the Hebrew is uncertain. **2:55** Or *the founder of Beth-recab.* **3:5a** As in Syriac version (see also 14:4; 2 Sam 5:14); Hebrew reads *Shimea.* **3:5b** Hebrew *Bathshua,* a variant spelling of Bathsheba. **3:6a** As in some Hebrew and Greek manuscripts (see also 14:5-7 and 2 Sam 5:15); most Hebrew manuscripts read *Elishama.* **3:6b** Hebrew *Eliphelet;* compare parallel text at 14:5-7. **3:11** Hebrew *Joram,* a variant spelling of Jehoram. **3:12** Hebrew *Azariah,* a variant spelling of Uzziah. **3:15** Hebrew *Shallum,* another name for Jehoahaz. **3:16** Hebrew *The sons of Jehoiakim were his son Jeconiah* [a variant spelling of Jehoiachin] *and his son Zedekiah.* **3:17** Hebrew *Jeconiah,* a variant spelling of Jehoiachin. **4:3** As in Greek version; Hebrew reads *father of.* The meaning of the Hebrew is uncertain. **4:4** Or *the founder of;* also in 4:5, 12, 14, 17, 18, and perhaps other instances where the text reads *the father of.*

HOW WE LIVE

Knowing God's peace

PSALM 4:8 When we lay our heads on the pillow at night, the only security we have is God's presence. For all of our security systems, yearly physicals, savings accounts, and pension plans, the only real peace we can find comes from knowing that we will never face life alone. God will always be there with us. • The psalmist, David, understood this. As a soldier he carried swords. As a general he had an army. As a king he had guards. But what he knew in his heart was that only God's presence was a true source of peace. • What about you? Have you begun to experience this peace promised by God? Becoming a believer didn't erase all your problems or change the world to a rosy shade of pink, but becoming a believer does put you in the lap of One who will protect you, watch over you, help you through the problems, and make you a better person because of them. You can rest in peace knowing that you will never be alone again. God is watching over you.

ACTS 24:1-27

Tertullus was the prosecuting attorney, Felix was the judge, and Paul was in the hot seat. He was put under house arrest for two years before his trial resumed. During that time he witnessed to Felix on numerous occasions.

Five days later Ananias, the high priest, arrived with some of the Jewish elders and the lawyer* Tertullus, to present their case against Paul to the governor. ²When Paul was called in, Tertullus presented the charges against Paul in the following address to the governor:

"Your Excellency, you have provided a long period of peace for us Jews and with foresight have enacted reforms for us. ³For all of this we are very grateful to you. ⁴But I don't want to bore you, so please give me your attention for only a moment. ⁵We have found this man to be a troublemaker who is constantly stirring up riots among the Jews all over the world. He is a ringleader of the cult known as the Nazarenes. ⁶Furthermore, he was trying to desecrate the Temple when we arrested him.* ⁸You can find out the truth of our accusations by examining him yourself." ⁹Then the other Jews chimed in, declaring that everything Tertullus said was true.

¹⁰The governor then motioned for Paul to speak. Paul said, "I know, sir, that you have been a judge of Jewish affairs for many years, so I gladly present my defense before you. ¹¹You can quickly discover that I arrived in Jerusalem no more than twelve days ago to worship at the Temple. ¹²My accusers never found me arguing with anyone in the Temple, nor stirring up a riot in any synagogue or on the streets of the city. ¹³These men cannot prove the things they accuse me of doing.

¹⁴"But I admit that I follow the Way, which they call a cult. I worship the God of our ancestors, and I firmly believe the Jewish law and everything written in the prophets. ¹⁵I have the same hope in God that these men have, that he will raise both the righteous and the unrighteous. ¹⁶Because of this, I always try to maintain a clear conscience before God and all people.

¹⁷"After several years away, I returned to Jerusalem with money to aid my people and to offer sacrifices to God. ¹⁸My accusers saw me in the Temple as I was completing a purification ceremony. There was no crowd around me and no rioting. ¹⁹But some Jews from the province of Asia were there—and they ought to be here to bring charges if they have anything against me! ²⁰Ask these men here what crime the Jewish high council* found me guilty of, ²¹except for the one time I shouted out, 'I am on trial before you today because I believe in the resurrection of the dead!'"

²²At that point Felix, who was quite familiar with the Way, adjourned the hearing and said, "Wait until Lysias, the garrison commander, arrives. Then I will decide the case." ²³He ordered an officer* to keep Paul in custody but to give him some freedom and allow his friends to visit him and take care of his needs.

²⁴A few days later Felix came back with his wife, Drusilla, who was Jewish. Sending for Paul, they listened as he told them about faith in Christ Jesus. ²⁵As he reasoned with them about righteousness and self-control and the coming day of judgment, Felix became frightened. "Go away for now," he replied. "When it is more convenient, I'll call for you again." ²⁶He also hoped that Paul would bribe him, so he sent for him quite often and talked with him.

²⁷After two years went by in this way, Felix was succeeded by Porcius Festus. And because Felix wanted to gain favor with the Jewish people, he left Paul in prison.

24:1 Greek *some elders and an orator.* **24:6** Some manuscripts add an expanded conclusion to verse 6, all of verse 7, and an additional phrase in verse 8: *We would have judged him by our law,* ⁷*but Lysias, the commander of the garrison, came and violently took him away from us,* ⁸*commanding his accusers to come before you.* **24:20** Greek *Sanhedrin.* **24:23** Greek *a centurion.*

PSALM 4:1-8

For the choir director: A psalm of David, to be accompanied by stringed instruments.

¹ **A**nswer me when I call to you,
    O God who declares me innocent.
  Free me from my troubles.
    Have mercy on me and hear my
      prayer.

² How long will you people ruin my
    reputation?

How long will you make groundless
accusations?
How long will you continue your
lies?   *Interlude*
³ You can be sure of this:
The LORD set apart the godly for
himself.
The LORD will answer when I call to
him.

⁴ Don't sin by letting anger control you.
Think about it overnight and remain
silent.   *Interlude*
⁵ Offer sacrifices in the right spirit,
and trust the LORD.

⁶ Many people say, "Who will show us
better times?"

Let your face smile on us,
LORD.
⁷ You have given me greater joy
than those who have abundant
harvests of grain and new wine.
⁸ In peace I will lie down and sleep,
for you alone, O LORD, will keep
me safe.

PROVERBS 18:16-18
Giving a gift can open doors; it gives access to important people! □ The first to
speak in court sounds right—until the
cross-examination begins. □ Flipping a
coin* can end arguments; it settles disputes between powerful opponents.
18:18 Hebrew *Casting lots.*

JULY**7**

1 CHRONICLES 4:5–5:17
Today's reading wraps up the genealogy of Judah
and moves on to the descendants of some of
Jacob's other sons—Simeon, Reuben, and Gad.

Ashhur (the father of Tekoa) had two wives,
named Helah and Naarah. ⁶ Naarah gave
birth to Ahuzzam, Hepher, Temeni, and
Haahashtari. ⁷ Helah gave birth to Zereth,
Izhar, Ethnan, ⁸ and Koz, who became the
ancestor of Anub, Zobebah, and all the
families of Aharhel son of Harum.
⁹ There was a man named Jabez who was
more honorable than any of his
brothers. His mother named him
Jabez* because his birth had been so
painful. ¹⁰ He was the one who prayed
to the God of Israel, "Oh, that you
would bless me and expand my
territory! Please be with me in all that
I do, and keep me from all trouble and
pain!" And God granted him his
request.
¹¹ Kelub (the brother of Shuhah) was the
father of Mehir. Mehir was the father
of Eshton. ¹² Eshton was the father of
Beth-rapha, Paseah, and Tehinnah.
Tehinnah was the father of Ir-nahash.
These were the descendants of Recah.

¹³ The sons of Kenaz were Othniel and
Seraiah. Othniel's sons were Hathath
and Meonothai.* ¹⁴ Meonothai was the
father of Ophrah. Seraiah was the
father of Joab, the founder of the
Valley of Craftsmen,* so called
because they were craftsmen.
¹⁵ The sons of Caleb son of Jephunneh
were Iru, Elah, and Naam. The son of
Elah was Kenaz.
¹⁶ The sons of Jehallelel were Ziph,
Ziphah, Tiria, and Asarel.
¹⁷ The sons of Ezrah were Jether, Mered,
Epher, and Jalon. One of Mered's wives
became* the mother of Miriam,
Shammai, and Ishbah (the father of
Eshtemoa). ¹⁸ He married a woman
from Judah, who became the mother
of Jered (the father of Gedor), Heber
(the father of Soco), and Jekuthiel (the
father of Zanoah). Mered also married
Bithia, a daughter of Pharaoh, and she
bore him children.
¹⁹ Hodiah's wife was the sister of Naham.
One of her sons was the father of
Keilah the Garmite, and another was
the father of Eshtemoa the
Maacathite.

20The sons of Shimon were Amnon, Rinnah, Ben-hanan, and Tilon.

The descendants of Ishi were Zoheth and Ben-zoheth.

21Shelah was one of Judah's sons. The descendants of Shelah were Er (the father of Lecah); Laadah (the father of Mareshah); the families of linen workers at Beth-ashbea; 22Jokim; the men of Cozeba; and Joash and Saraph, who ruled over Moab and Jashubi-lehem. These names all come from ancient records. 23They were the pottery makers who lived in Netaim and Gederah. They lived there and worked for the king.

24The sons of Simeon were Jemuel,* Jamin, Jarib, Zohar,* and Shaul.

25The descendants of Shaul were Shallum, Mibsam, and Mishma.

26The descendants of Mishma were Hammuel, Zaccur, and Shimei.

27Shimei had sixteen sons and six daughters, but none of his brothers had large families. So Simeon's tribe never grew as large as the tribe of Judah.

28They lived in Beersheba, Moladah, Hazar-shual, 29Bilhah, Ezem, Tolad, 30Bethuel, Hormah, Ziklag, 31Beth-marcaboth, Hazar-susim, Beth-biri, and Shaaraim. These towns were under their control until the time of King David. 32Their descendants also lived in Etam, Ain, Rimmon, Token, and Ashan—five towns 33and their surrounding villages as far away as Baalath.* This was their territory, and these names are listed in their genealogical records.

34Other descendants of Simeon included Meshobab, Jamlech, Joshah son of Amaziah, 35Joel, Jehu son of Joshibiah, son of Seraiah, son of Asiel, 36Elioenai, Jaakobah, Jesho-haiah, Asaiah, Adiel, Jesimiel, Benaiah, 37and Ziza son of Shiphi, son of Allon, son of Jedaiah, son of Shimri, son of Shemaiah.

38These were the names of some of the leaders of Simeon's wealthy clans. Their families grew, 39and they traveled to the region of Gerar,* in the east part of the val-ley, seeking pastureland for their flocks. 40They found lush pastures there, and the land was quiet and peaceful.

Some of Ham's descendants had been living in that region. 41But during the reign of King Hezekiah of Judah, these leaders of Simeon invaded the region and completely destroyed* the homes of the descendants of Ham and of the Meunites. No trace of them remains today. They killed everyone who lived there and took the land for themselves, because they wanted its good pastureland for their flocks. 42Five hundred of these invaders from the tribe of Simeon went to Mount Seir, led by Pelatiah, Neariah, Rephaiah, and Uzziel—all sons of Ishi. 43They destroyed the few Amalekites who had survived, and they have lived there ever since.

5:1THE oldest son of Israel* was Reuben. But since he dishonored his father by sleeping with one of his father's concubines, his birthright was given to the sons of his brother Joseph. For this reason, Reuben is not listed in the genealogical records as the firstborn son. 2The descendants of Judah became the most powerful tribe and provided a ruler for the nation,* but the birthright belonged to Joseph.

3The sons of Reuben, the oldest son of Israel, were Hanoch, Pallu, Hezron, and Carmi.

4The descendants of Joel were Shemaiah, Gog, Shimei, 5Micah, Reaiah, Baal, 6and Beerah. Beerah was the leader of the Reubenites when they were taken into captivity by King Tiglath-pileser* of Assyria.

7Beerah's* relatives are listed in their genealogical records by their clans: Jeiel (the leader), Zechariah, 8and Bela son of Azaz, son of Shema, son of Joel.

The Reubenites lived in the area that stretches from Aroer to Nebo and Baal-meon. 9And since they had so many livestock in the land of Gilead, they spread east toward the edge of the desert that stretches to the Euphrates River.

10During the reign of Saul, the Reubenites defeated the Hagrites in battle. Then they moved into the

Hagrite settlements all along the eastern edge of Gilead.

[11]Next to the Reubenites, the descendants of Gad lived in the land of Bashan as far east as Salecah. [12]Joel was the leader in the land of Bashan, and Shapham was second-in-command, followed by Janai and Shaphat. [13]Their relatives, the leaders of seven other clans, were Michael, Meshullam, Sheba, Jorai, Jacan, Zia, and Eber. [14]These were all descendants of Abihail son of Huri, son of Jaroah, son of Gilead, son of Michael, son of Jeshishai, son of Jahdo, son of Buz. [15]Ahi son of Abdiel, son of Guni, was the leader of their clans.

[16]The Gadites lived in the land of Gilead, in Bashan and its villages, and throughout all the pasturelands of Sharon. [17]All of these were listed in the genealogical records during the days of King Jotham of Judah and King Jeroboam of Israel.

4:9 *Jabez* sounds like a Hebrew word meaning "distress" or "pain."   **4:13** As in some Greek manuscripts and Latin Vulgate; Hebrew lacks *and Meonothai.*   **4:14** Or *Joab, the father of Ge-harashim.*   **4:17** Or *Jether's wife became;* Hebrew reads *She became.*   **4:24a** As in Syriac version (see also Gen 46:10; Exod 6:15); Hebrew reads *Nemuel.*   **4:24b** As in parallel texts at Gen 46:10 and Exod 6:15; Hebrew reads *Zerah.*   **4:33** As in some Greek manuscripts (see also Josh 19:8); Hebrew reads *Baal.*   **4:39** As in Greek version; Hebrew reads *Gedor.*   **4:41** The Hebrew term used here refers to the complete consecration of things or people to the LORD, either by destroying them or by giving them as an offering.   **5:1** *Israel* is the name that God gave to Jacob.   **5:2** Or *and from Judah came a prince.*   **5:6** Hebrew *Tilgath-pilneser,* a variant spelling of Tiglath-pileser; also in 5:26.   **5:7** Hebrew *His.*

ACTS 25:1-27
Paul wanted to go to Rome—the center of the empire, the place where all roads led. He made use of his heritage as a Roman citizen to get his trial brought to the supreme court of the land—that is, to Caesar himself.

Three days after Festus arrived in Caesarea to take over his new responsibilities, he left for Jerusalem, [2]where the leading priests and other Jewish leaders met with him and made their accusations against Paul. [3]They asked Festus as a favor to transfer Paul to Jerusalem (planning to ambush and kill him on the way). [4]But Festus replied that Paul was at Caesarea and he himself would be returning there soon. [5]So he said, "Those of you in authority can return with me. If Paul has done anything wrong, you can make your accusations."

[6]About eight or ten days later Festus returned to Caesarea, and on the following day he took his seat in court and ordered that Paul be brought in. [7]When Paul arrived, the Jewish leaders from Jerusalem gathered around and made many serious accusations they couldn't prove.

Blessed by God

1 CHRONICLES 4:9 Several chapters of the book of 1 Chronicles contain genealogies listing many family ties and relationships. Countless names are spelled out, and it can be a little confusing. Then, in the midst of it all, we read about the personality of one man called Jabez. It says his birth was painful for his mother, and perhaps he, too, suffered pain of some kind. But why is Jabez singled out? Because of his bold request. He asked God to bless him, give him more land, be with him, and keep him from trouble and pain. It is a short, simple prayer, but it reveals something of the character of Jabez. He didn't let his circumstances stop him from earnestly seeking God. He had his priorities straight—God was first in his life. It is for his devotion that he is remembered.   • You, too, have a unique lineage and life circumstances that are all your own. Be thankful for the person God has made you. Ask God to pour out his blessings on you as you follow him. Be a shining example of the love of Jesus Christ that will live on in the hearts of those who come after you.

⁸Paul denied the charges. "I am not guilty of any crime against the Jewish laws or the Temple or the Roman government," he said.

⁹Then Festus, wanting to please the Jews, asked him, "Are you willing to go to Jerusalem and stand trial before me there?"

¹⁰But Paul replied, "No! This is the official Roman court, so I ought to be tried right here. You know very well I am not guilty of harming the Jews. ¹¹If I have done something worthy of death, I don't refuse to die. But if I am innocent, no one has a right to turn me over to these men to kill me. I appeal to Caesar!"

¹²Festus conferred with his advisers and then replied, "Very well! You have appealed to Caesar, and to Caesar you will go!"

¹³A few days later King Agrippa arrived with his sister, Bernice,* to pay their respects to Festus. ¹⁴During their stay of several days, Festus discussed Paul's case with the king. "There is a prisoner here," he told him, "whose case was left for me by Felix. ¹⁵When I was in Jerusalem, the leading priests and Jewish elders pressed charges against him and asked me to condemn him. ¹⁶I pointed out to them that Roman law does not convict people without a trial. They must be given an opportunity to confront their accusers and defend themselves.

¹⁷"When his accusers came here for the trial, I didn't delay. I called the case the very next day and ordered Paul brought in. ¹⁸But the accusations made against him weren't any of the crimes I expected. ¹⁹Instead, it was something about their religion and a dead man named Jesus, who Paul insists is alive. ²⁰I was at a loss to know how to investigate these things, so I asked him whether he would be willing to stand trial on these charges in Jerusalem. ²¹But Paul appealed to have his case decided by the emperor. So I ordered that he be held in custody until I could arrange to send him to Caesar."

²²"I'd like to hear the man myself," Agrippa said.

And Festus replied, "You will—tomorrow!"

²³So the next day Agrippa and Bernice arrived at the auditorium with great pomp, accompanied by military officers and prominent men of the city. Festus ordered that Paul be brought in. ²⁴Then Festus said, "King Agrippa and all who are here, this is the man whose death is demanded by all the Jews, both here and in Jerusalem. ²⁵But in my opinion he has done nothing deserving death. However, since he appealed his case to the emperor, I have decided to send him to Rome.

²⁶"But what shall I write the emperor? For there is no clear charge against him. So I have brought him before all of you, and especially you, King Agrippa, so that after we examine him, I might have something to write. ²⁷For it makes no sense to send a prisoner to the emperor without specifying the charges against him!"

25:13 Greek *Agrippa the king and Bernice arrived.*

PSALM 5:1-12
For the choir director: A psalm of David, to be accompanied by the flute.

¹ O LORD, hear me as I pray;
    pay attention to my groaning.
² Listen to my cry for help, my King and my God,
    for I pray to no one but you.
³ Listen to my voice in the morning, LORD.
    Each morning I bring my requests to you and wait expectantly.

⁴ O God, you take no pleasure in wickedness;
    you cannot tolerate the sins of the wicked.
⁵ Therefore, the proud may not stand in your presence,
    for you hate all who do evil.
⁶ You will destroy those who tell lies.
    The LORD detests murderers and deceivers.

⁷ Because of your unfailing love, I can enter your house;
    I will worship at your Temple with deepest awe.
⁸ Lead me in the right path, O LORD,
    or my enemies will conquer me.
    Make your way plain for me to follow.

⁹ My enemies cannot speak a truthful word.
    Their deepest desire is to destroy others.

Their talk is foul, like the stench from
an open grave.
Their tongues are filled with
flattery.*
[10] O God, declare them guilty.
Let them be caught in their own
traps.
Drive them away because of their
many sins,
for they have rebelled against you.

[11] But let all who take refuge in you
rejoice;
let them sing joyful praises forever.

Spread your protection over
them,
that all who love your name may
be filled with joy.
[12] For you bless the godly, O Lord;
you surround them with your shield
of love.

5:9 Greek version reads *with lies.* Compare Rom 3:12.

PROVERBS 18:19

An offended friend is harder to win back
than a fortified city. Arguments separate
friends like a gate locked with bars.

JULY**8**

1 CHRONICLES 5:18–6:81

All the tribes received allotments of land with the
exception of the tribe of Levi. The Levites, who were
responsible for worship at the Tabernacle and later
the Temple, received cities in the territories belonging to the other tribes and were to be supported by
the tithes from those tribes.

There were 44,760 capable warriors in
the armies of Reuben, Gad, and the half-
tribe of Manasseh. They were all skilled in
combat and armed with shields, swords,
and bows. [19] They waged war against the
Hagrites, the Jeturites, the Naphishites,
and the Nodabites. [20] They cried out to
God during the battle, and he answered
their prayer because they trusted in him.
So the Hagrites and all their allies were
defeated. [21] The plunder taken from the
Hagrites included 50,000 camels,
250,000 sheep and goats, 2,000 donkeys,
and 100,000 captives. [22] Many of the
Hagrites were killed in the battle because
God was fighting against them. The people of Reuben, Gad, and Manasseh lived in
their land until they were taken into exile.

[23] The half-tribe of Manasseh was very
large and spread through the land from
Bashan to Baal-hermon, Senir, and Mount
Hermon. [24] These were the leaders of
their clans: Epher,* Ishi, Eliel, Azriel, Jeremiah, Hodaviah, and Jahdiel. These men

had a great reputation as mighty warriors
and leaders of their clans.

[25] But these tribes were unfaithful to
the God of their ancestors. They worshiped the gods of the nations that God
had destroyed. [26] So the God of Israel
caused King Pul of Assyria (also known as
Tiglath-pileser) to invade the land and
take away the people of Reuben, Gad, and
the half-tribe of Manasseh as captives.
The Assyrians exiled them to Halah,
Habor, Hara, and the Gozan River, where
they remain to this day.

[6:1]*THE sons of Levi were Gershon,
Kohath, and Merari.
[2] The descendants of Kohath included
Amram, Izhar, Hebron, and Uzziel.
[3] The children of Amram were Aaron,
Moses, and Miriam.
The sons of Aaron were Nadab, Abihu,
Eleazar, and Ithamar.
[4] Eleazar was the father of Phinehas.
Phinehas was the father of Abishua.
[5] Abishua was the father of Bukki.
Bukki was the father of Uzzi.
[6] Uzzi was the father of Zerahiah.
Zerahiah was the father of Meraioth.
[7] Meraioth was the father of Amariah.
Amariah was the father of Ahitub.
[8] Ahitub was the father of Zadok.
Zadok was the father of Ahimaaz.

9 Ahimaaz was the father of Azariah. Azariah was the father of Johanan.

10 Johanan was the father of Azariah, the high priest at the Temple* built by Solomon in Jerusalem.

11 Azariah was the father of Amariah. Amariah was the father of Ahitub.

12 Ahitub was the father of Zadok. Zadok was the father of Shallum.

13 Shallum was the father of Hilkiah. Hilkiah was the father of Azariah.

14 Azariah was the father of Seraiah. Seraiah was the father of Jehozadak, 15who went into exile when the LORD sent the people of Judah and Jerusalem into captivity under Nebuchadnezzar.

16*The sons of Levi were Gershon,* Kohath, and Merari.

17 The descendants of Gershon included Libni and Shimei.

18 The descendants of Kohath included Amram, Izhar, Hebron, and Uzziel.

19 The descendants of Merari included Mahli and Mushi.

The following were the Levite clans, listed according to their ancestral descent:

20The descendants of Gershon included Libni, Jahath, Zimmah, 21Joah, Iddo, Zerah, and Jeatherai.

22 The descendants of Kohath included Amminadab, Korah, Assir, 23Elkanah, Abiasaph,* Assir, 24Tahath, Uriel, Uzziah, and Shaul.

25 The descendants of Elkanah included Amasai, Ahimoth, 26Elkanah, Zophai, Nahath, 27Eliab, Jeroham, Elkanah, and Samuel.*

28The sons of Samuel were Joel* (the older) and Abijah (the second).

29 The descendants of Merari included Mahli, Libni, Shimei, Uzzah, 30Shimea, Haggiah, and Asaiah.

31David assigned the following men to lead the music at the house of the LORD after the Ark was placed there. 32They ministered with music at the Tabernacle* until Solomon built the Temple of the LORD in Jerusalem. They carried out their work, following all the regulations handed down to them. 33These are the men who served, along with their sons:

Heman the musician was from the clan of Kohath. His genealogy was traced back through Joel, Samuel, 34Elkanah, Jeroham, Eliel, Toah, 35Zuph, Elkanah, Mahath, Amasai, 36Elkanah, Joel, Azariah, Zephaniah, 37Tahath, Assir, Abiasaph, Korah, 38Izhar, Kohath, Levi, and Israel.*

39Heman's first assistant was Asaph from the clan of Gershon.* Asaph's genealogy was traced back through Berekiah, Shimea, 40Michael, Baaseiah, Malkijah, 41Ethni, Zerah, Adaiah, 42Ethan, Zimmah, Shimei, 43Jahath, Gershon, and Levi.

44Heman's second assistant was Ethan from the clan of Merari. Ethan's genealogy was traced back through Kishi, Abdi, Malluch, 45Hashabiah, Amaziah, Hilkiah, 46Amzi, Bani, Shemer, 47Mahli, Mushi, Merari, and Levi.

48Their fellow Levites were appointed to various other tasks in the Tabernacle, the house of God.

49Only Aaron and his descendants served as priests. They presented the offerings on the altar of burnt offering and the altar of incense, and they performed all the other duties related to the Most Holy Place. They made atonement for Israel by doing everything that Moses, the servant of God, had commanded them.

50The descendants of Aaron were Eleazar, Phinehas, Abishua, 51Bukki, Uzzi, Zerahiah, 52Meraioth, Amariah, Ahitub, 53Zadok, and Ahimaaz.

54This is a record of the towns and territory assigned by means of sacred lots to the descendants of Aaron, who were from the clan of Kohath. 55This territory included Hebron and its surrounding pasturelands in Judah, 56but the fields and outlying areas belonging to the city were given to Caleb son of Jephunneh. 57So the descendants of Aaron were given the following towns, each with its pasturelands: Hebron (a city of refuge),* Libnah, Jattir, Eshtemoa, 58Holon,* Debir, 59Ain,* Juttah,* and Beth-shemesh. 60And from the territory of Benjamin they were given Gibeon,* Geba, Alemeth, and Anathoth, each with its pasturelands. So thirteen towns were given to the descendants of Aaron. ⁶¹The remaining descendants of Kohath received ten towns from the territory of the half-tribe of Manasseh by means of sacred lots.

⁶²The descendants of Gershon received by sacred lots thirteen towns from the territories of Issachar, Asher, Naphtali, and from the Bashan area of Manasseh, east of the Jordan.

⁶³The descendants of Merari received by sacred lots twelve towns from the territories of Reuben, Gad, and Zebulun.

⁶⁴So the people of Israel assigned all these towns and pasturelands to the Levites. ⁶⁵The towns in the territories of Judah, Simeon, and Benjamin, mentioned above, were assigned to them by means of sacred lots.

⁶⁶The descendants of Kohath were given the following towns from the territory of Ephraim, each with its pasturelands: ⁶⁷Shechem (a city of refuge in the hill country of Ephraim),* Gezer, ⁶⁸Jokmeam, Beth-horon, ⁶⁹Aijalon, and Gathrimmon. ⁷⁰The remaining descendants of Kohath were assigned the towns of Aner and Bileam from the territory of the half-tribe of Manasseh, each with its pasturelands.

⁷¹The descendants of Gershon received the towns of Golan (in Bashan) and Ashtaroth from the territory of the half-tribe of Manasseh, each with its pasturelands. ⁷²From the territory of Issachar, they were given Kedesh, Daberath, ⁷³Ramoth, and Anem, each with its pasturelands. ⁷⁴From the territory of Asher, they received Mashal, Abdon, ⁷⁵Hukok, and Rehob, each with its pasturelands. ⁷⁶From the territory of Naphtali, they were given Kedesh in Galilee, Hammon, and Kiriathaim, each with its pasturelands.

⁷⁷The remaining descendants of Merari received the towns of Jokneam, Kartah,* Rimmon,* and Tabor from the territory of Zebulun, each with its pasturelands. ⁷⁸From the territory of Reuben, east of the Jordan River opposite Jericho, they received Bezer (a desert town), Jahaz,* ⁷⁹Kedemoth, and Mephaath, each with its pasturelands. ⁸⁰And from the territory of Gad, they received Ramoth in Gilead, Mahanaim, ⁸¹Heshbon, and Jazer, each with its pasturelands.

5:24 As in Greek version and Latin Vulgate; Hebrew reads *and Epher.*   6:1 Verses 6:1-15 are numbered 5:27-41 in Hebrew text.   6:10 Hebrew *the house.*   6:16a Verses 6:16-81 are numbered 6:1-66 in Hebrew text.   6:16b Hebrew *Gershom,* a variant spelling of Gershon (see 6:1); also in 6:17, 20, 43, 62, 71.   6:23 Hebrew *Ebiasaph,* a variant spelling of Abiasaph (also in 6:37); compare parallel text at Exod 6:24.   6:27 As in some Greek manuscripts (see also 6:33-34); Hebrew lacks *and Samuel.*   6:28 As in some Greek manuscripts and the Syriac version (see also 6:33 and 1 Sam 8:2); Hebrew lacks *Joel.*

HOW WE LIVE

Responding to God

ACTS 26:1-32 In this passage three different kinds of responses to the Good News are illustrated: Paul had believed in Jesus, Festus scoffed, and Agrippa answered in sarcasm. • You may already have experienced the scoffing of a friend or coworker or the sarcasm of a family member regarding your new faith. Why do some people respond to Christ and others don't? While there are many reasons, the root of a refusal to respond to God is a failure to understand or acknowledge one's own sin and God's love in spite of it. When we see ourselves as we really are and truly understand the depths of God's love and mercy toward us, there's no other response but to bow before him. We show our love by responding to his love. "We love . . . because he loved us first" (1 John 4:19, December 4). • Wherever he went, Paul told his story and shared the gospel message. He let God handle each person's response. No matter what your road to faith has been, you can share your story with anyone who will listen. Don't worry if someone responds negatively. Who knows? Perhaps the seed you planted in that person's life will later sprout into faith!

6:32 Hebrew *the Tabernacle, the Tent of Meeting.* 6:38 *Israel* is the name that God gave to Jacob. 6:39 Hebrew lacks *from the clan of Gershon;* see 6:43. 6:57 As in parallel text at Josh 21:13; Hebrew reads *were given the cities of refuge: Hebron, and the following towns, each with its pasturelands.* 6:58 As in parallel text at Josh 21:15; Hebrew reads *Hilen.* 6:59a As in parallel text at Josh 21:16; Hebrew reads *Ashan.* 6:59b As in Syriac version (see also Josh 21:16); Hebrew lacks *Juttah.* 6:60 As in parallel text at Josh 21:17; Hebrew lacks *Gibeon.* 6:66-67 As in parallel text at Josh 21:21. Hebrew text reads *were given the cities of refuge: Shechem in the hill country of Ephraim, and the following towns, each with its pasturelands.* 6:77a As in Greek version (see also Josh 21:34); Hebrew lacks *Jokneam, Kartah.* 6:77b As in Greek version (see also Josh 19:13); Hebrew reads *Rimmono.* 6:78 Hebrew *Jahzah,* a variant spelling of Jahaz.

ACTS 26:1-32

Most of us would consider it a stressful, worst-day-you-could-imagine kind of event if we were put on trial before the highest court in the land. For Paul it was just one more opportunity to tell the story of how his life had been changed by Jesus.

Then Agrippa said to Paul, "You may speak in your defense."

So Paul, gesturing with his hand, started his defense: ²"I am fortunate, King Agrippa, that you are the one hearing my defense today against all these accusations made by the Jewish leaders, ³for I know you are an expert on all Jewish customs and controversies. Now please listen to me patiently!

⁴"As the Jewish leaders are well aware, I was given a thorough Jewish training from my earliest childhood among my own people and in Jerusalem. ⁵If they would admit it, they know that I have been a member of the Pharisees, the strictest sect of our religion. ⁶Now I am on trial because of my hope in the fulfillment of God's promise made to our ancestors. ⁷In fact, that is why the twelve tribes of Israel zealously worship God night and day, and they share the same hope I have. Yet, Your Majesty, they accuse me for having this hope! ⁸Why does it seem incredible to any of you that God can raise the dead?

⁹"I used to believe that I ought to do everything I could to oppose the very name of Jesus the Nazarene.* ¹⁰Indeed, I did just that in Jerusalem. Authorized by the leading priests, I caused many believers* there to be sent to prison. And I cast my vote against them when they were condemned to death. ¹¹Many times I had them punished in the synagogues to get them to curse Jesus.* I was so violently opposed to them that I even chased them down in foreign cities.

¹²"One day I was on such a mission to Damascus, armed with the authority and commission of the leading priests. ¹³About noon, Your Majesty, as I was on the road, a light from heaven brighter than the sun shone down on me and my companions. ¹⁴We all fell down, and I heard a voice saying to me in Aramaic,* 'Saul, Saul, why are you persecuting me? It is useless for you to fight against my will.*'

¹⁵"'Who are you, lord?' I asked.

"And the Lord replied, 'I am Jesus, the one you are persecuting. ¹⁶Now get to your feet! For I have appeared to you to appoint you as my servant and witness. You are to tell the world what you have seen and what I will show you in the future. ¹⁷And I will rescue you from both your own people and the Gentiles. Yes, I am sending you to the Gentiles ¹⁸to open their eyes, so they may turn from darkness to light and from the power of Satan to God. Then they will receive forgiveness for their sins and be given a place among God's people, who are set apart by faith in me.'

¹⁹"And so, King Agrippa, I obeyed that vision from heaven. ²⁰I preached first to those in Damascus, then in Jerusalem and throughout all Judea, and also to the Gentiles, that all must repent of their sins and turn to God—and prove they have changed by the good things they do. ²¹Some Jews arrested me in the Temple for preaching this, and they tried to kill me. ²²But God has protected me right up to this present time so I can testify to everyone, from the least to the greatest. I teach nothing except what the prophets and Moses said would happen—²³that the Messiah would suffer and be the first to rise from the dead, and in this way announce God's light to Jews and Gentiles alike."

²⁴Suddenly, Festus shouted, "Paul, you are insane. Too much study has made you crazy!"

²⁵But Paul replied, "I am not insane, Most Excellent Festus. What I am saying is the sober truth. ²⁶And King Agrippa knows about these things. I speak boldly, for I am sure these events are all familiar

to him, for they were not done in a corner! ²⁷King Agrippa, do you believe the prophets? I know you do—"

²⁸Agrippa interrupted him. "Do you think you can persuade me to become a Christian so quickly?"*

²⁹Paul replied, "Whether quickly or not, I pray to God that both you and everyone here in this audience might become the same as I am, except for these chains."

³⁰Then the king, the governor, Bernice, and all the others stood and left. ³¹As they went out, they talked it over and agreed, "This man hasn't done anything to deserve death or imprisonment."

³²And Agrippa said to Festus, "He could have been set free if he hadn't appealed to Caesar."

26:9 Or *Jesus of Nazareth.* 26:10 Greek *many of God's holy people.* 26:11 Greek *to blaspheme.* 26:14a Or *Hebrew.* 26:14b Greek *It is hard for you to kick against the oxgoads.* 26:28 Or *"A little more, and your arguments would make me a Christian."*

PSALM 6:1-10
*For the choir director: A psalm of David, to be accompanied by an eight-stringed instrument.**

¹ O LORD, don't rebuke me in your anger
    or discipline me in your rage.
² Have compassion on me, LORD, for
        I am weak.
    Heal me, LORD, for my bones are
        in agony.

³ I am sick at heart.
    How long, O LORD, until you restore
        me?

⁴ Return, O LORD, and rescue me.
    Save me because of your unfailing
        love.
⁵ For the dead do not remember you.
    Who can praise you from the
        grave?*

⁶ I am worn out from sobbing.
    All night I flood my bed with
        weeping,
    drenching it with my tears.
⁷ My vision is blurred by grief;
    my eyes are worn out because of all
        my enemies.

⁸ Go away, all you who do evil,
    for the LORD has heard my weeping.
⁹ The LORD has heard my plea;
    the LORD will answer my prayer.
¹⁰ May all my enemies be disgraced and
        terrified.
    May they suddenly turn back in
        shame.

6:TITLE Hebrew *with stringed instruments; according to the sheminith.* 6:5 Hebrew *from Sheol?*

PROVERBS 18:20-21
Wise words satisfy like a good meal; the right words bring satisfaction. □ The tongue can bring death or life; those who love to talk will reap the consequences.

JULY 9

1 CHRONICLES 7:1–8:40
This detailed history of the Jewish nation continues with descendants of more sons of Jacob, including Benjamin. Saul, Israel's first king, came from the tribe of Benjamin.

The four sons of Issachar were Tola, Puah, Jashub, and Shimron.

² The sons of Tola were Uzzi, Rephaiah, Jeriel, Jahmai, Ibsam, and Shemuel. Each of them was the leader of an ancestral clan. At the time of King David, the total number of mighty warriors listed in the records of these clans was 22,600.

³ The son of Uzzi was Izrahiah. The sons of Izrahiah were Michael, Obadiah, Joel, and Isshiah. These five became the leaders of clans. ⁴All of them had many wives and many sons, so the total number of men available for military service among their descendants was 36,000.

⁵ The total number of mighty warriors from all the clans of the tribe of Issachar

was 87,000. All of them were listed in their genealogical records.

⁶Three of Benjamin's sons were Bela, Beker, and Jediael.

⁷The five sons of Bela were Ezbon, Uzzi, Uzziel, Jerimoth, and Iri. Each of them was the leader of an ancestral clan. The total number of mighty warriors from these clans was 22,034, as listed in their genealogical records.

⁸The sons of Beker were Zemirah, Joash, Eliezer, Elioenai, Omri, Jeremoth, Abijah, Anathoth, and Alemeth. ⁹Each of them was the leader of an ancestral clan. The total number of mighty warriors and leaders from these clans was 20,200, as listed in their genealogical records.

¹⁰The son of Jediael was Bilhan. The sons of Bilhan were Jeush, Benjamin, Ehud, Kenaanah, Zethan, Tarshish, and Ahishahar. ¹¹Each of them was the leader of an ancestral clan. From these clans the total number of mighty warriors ready for war was 17,200.

¹²The sons of Ir were Shuppim and Huppim. Hushim was the son of Aher.

¹³The sons of Naphtali were Jahzeel,* Guni, Jezer, and Shillem.* They were all descendants of Jacob's concubine Bilhah.

¹⁴The descendants of Manasseh through his Aramean concubine included Asriel. She also bore Makir, the father of Gilead. ¹⁵Makir found wives for* Huppim and Shuppim. Makir had a sister named Maacah. One of his descendants was Zelophehad, who had only daughters.

¹⁶Makir's wife, Maacah, gave birth to a son whom she named Peresh. His brother's name was Sheresh. The sons of Peresh were Ulam and Rakem. ¹⁷The son of Ulam was Bedan. All these were considered Gileadites, descendants of Makir son of Manasseh.

¹⁸Makir's sister Hammoleketh gave birth to Ishhod, Abiezer, and Mahlah.

¹⁹The sons of Shemida were Ahian, Shechem, Likhi, and Aniam.

²⁰The descendants of Ephraim were Shuthelah, Bered, Tahath, Eleadah, Tahath, ²¹Zabad, Shuthelah, Ezer, and Elead. These two were killed trying to steal livestock from the local farmers near Gath. ²²Their father, Ephraim, mourned for them a long time, and his relatives came to comfort him.

²³Afterward Ephraim slept with his wife, and she became pregnant and gave birth to a son. Ephraim named him Beriah* because of the tragedy his family had suffered. ²⁴He had a daughter named Sheerah. She built the towns of Lower and Upper Beth-horon and Uzzen-sheerah.

²⁵The descendants of Ephraim included Rephah, Resheph, Telah, Tahan, ²⁶Ladan, Ammihud, Elishama, ²⁷Nun, and Joshua.

²⁸The descendants of Ephraim lived in the territory that included Bethel and its surrounding towns to the south, Naaran to the east, Gezer and its villages to the west, and Shechem and its surrounding villages to the north as far as Ayyah and its towns. ²⁹Along the border of Manasseh were the towns of Beth-shan,* Taanach, Megiddo, Dor, and their surrounding villages. The descendants of Joseph son of Israel* lived in these towns.

³⁰The sons of Asher were Imnah, Ishvah, Ishvi, and Beriah. They had a sister named Serah.

³¹The sons of Beriah were Heber and Malkiel (the father of Birzaith).

³²The sons of Heber were Japhlet, Shomer, and Hotham. They had a sister named Shua.

³³The sons of Japhlet were Pasach, Bimhal, and Ashvath.

³⁴The sons of Shomer were Ahi,* Rohgah, Hubbah, and Aram.

³⁵The sons of his brother Helem* were Zophah, Imna, Shelesh, and Amal.

³⁶The sons of Zophah were Suah, Harnepher, Shual, Beri, Imrah, ³⁷Bezer, Hod, Shamma, Shilshah, Ithran,* and Beera.

³⁸The sons of Jether were Jephunneh, Pispah, and Ara.

³⁹The sons of Ulla were Arah, Hanniel, and Rizia.

⁴⁰Each of these descendants of Asher was the head of an ancestral clan. They were

all select men—mighty warriors and out-standing leaders. The total number of men available for military service was 26,000, as listed in their genealogical records.

8:1BENJAMIN's first son was Bela, the second was Ashbel, the third was Aharah, 2the fourth was Nohah, and the fifth was Rapha.

3The sons of Bela were Addar, Gera, Abihud,* 4Abishua, Naaman, Ahoah, 5Gera, Shephuphan, and Huram.

6The sons of Ehud, leaders of the clans living at Geba, were exiled to Manahath. 7Ehud's sons were Naaman, Ahijah, and Gera. Gera, who led them into exile, was the father of Uzza and Ahihud.*

8After Shaharaim divorced his wives Hushim and Baara, he had children in the land of Moab. 9Hodesh, his new wife, gave birth to Jobab, Zibia, Mesha, Malcam, 10Jeuz, Sakia, and Mirmah. These sons all became the leaders of clans.

11Shaharaim's wife Hushim had already given birth to Abitub and Elpaal. 12The sons of Elpaal were Eber, Misham, Shemed (who built the towns of Ono and Lod and their nearby villages), 13Beriah, and Shema. They were the leaders of the clans living in Aijalon, and they drove out the inhabitants of Gath.

14Ahio, Shashak, Jeremoth, 15Zebadiah, Arad, Eder, 16Michael, Ishpah, and Joha were the sons of Beriah.

17Zebadiah, Meshullam, Hizki, Heber, 18Ishmerai, Izliah, and Jobab were the sons of Elpaal.

19Jakim, Zicri, Zabdi, 20Elienai, Zillethai, Eliel, 21Adaiah, Beraiah, and Shimrath were the sons of Shimei.

22Ishpan, Eber, Eliel, 23Abdon, Zicri, Hanan, 24Hananiah, Elam, Anthothijah, 25Iphdeiah, and Penuel were the sons of Shashak.

26Shamsherai, Shehariah, Athaliah, 27Jaareshiah, Elijah, and Zicri were the sons of Jeroham.

28These were the leaders of the ancestral clans; they were listed in their genealogical records, and they all lived in Jerusalem.

29Jeiel* (the father of* Gibeon) lived in the town of Gibeon. His wife's name was Maacah, 30and his oldest son was named Abdon. Jeiel's other sons were Zur, Kish, Baal, Ner,* Nadab, 31Gedor, Ahio, Zechariah,* 32and Mikloth, who was the father of Shimeam.* All these families lived near each other in Jerusalem.

33 Ner was the father of Kish.
Kish was the father of Saul.
Saul was the father of Jonathan, Malkishua, Abinadab, and Esh-baal.

HOW WE LIVE

Our marriages

PROVERBS 18:22 When we think of treasure, we picture buried gold, material wealth, or a priceless object that has great worth. People are not usually put in the treasure category. But Proverbs 18:22 says just that: the one who finds a spouse finds a *treasure,* and receives favor from God. • Husbands and wives are many things: companions, lovers, parents, business partners. But what might happen if you also thought of your spouse as a precious and rare treasure? Honor your husband's great worth as a human being made in God's image. Admire your wife's unique gifts. Brag on each other in public with pride. Treat each other gently, accepting the little chips and cracks, as you would lovingly handle a precious piece of art. • It is crucial that you invite God to reside at the center of your marriage. Pray for your spouse daily. Never take your husband or wife for granted. Share in the sorrows as well as the joys. Pray together. Above all, remember that your spouse is a treasure from God and thank him each day for this gift.

³⁴ Jonathan was the father of Merib-baal.
Merib-baal was the father of Micah.
³⁵ Micah was the father of Pithon,
Melech, Tahrea,* and Ahaz.
³⁶ Ahaz was the father of Jadah.*
Jadah was the father of Alemeth,
Azmaveth, and Zimri.
Zimri was the father of Moza.
³⁷ Moza was the father of Binea.
Binea was the father of Rephaiah.*
Rephaiah was the father of Eleasah.
Eleasah was the father of Azel.
³⁸Azel had six sons: Azrikam, Bokeru,
Ishmael, Sheariah, Obadiah, and
Hanan. These were the sons of Azel.
³⁹Azel's brother Eshek had three sons:
the first was Ulam, the second was
Jeush, and the third was Eliphelet.
⁴⁰Ulam's sons were all mighty warriors
and expert archers. They had many
sons and grandsons—150 in all.

All these were descendants of Benjamin.

7:13a As in parallel text at Gen 46:24; Hebrew reads *Jahziel*,
a variant spelling of Jahzeel.   7:13b As in some Hebrew and
Greek manuscripts (see also Gen 46:24; Num 26:49); most
Hebrew manuscripts read *Shallum*.   7:15 Or *Makir took a
wife from*. The meaning of the Hebrew is uncertain.
7:23 *Beriah* sounds like a Hebrew term meaning "tragedy" or
"misfortune."   7:29a Hebrew *Beth-shean*, a variant spelling
of Beth-shan.   7:29b *Israel* is the name that God gave to
Jacob.   7:34 Or *The sons of Shomer, his brother, were*.
7:35 Possibly another name for *Hotham*; compare 7:32.
7:37 Possibly another name for *Jether*; compare 7:38.
8:3 Possibly *Gera the father of Ehud*; compare 8:6.   8:7 Or
Gera, that is Heglam, was the father of Uzza and Ahihud.
8:29a As in some Greek manuscripts (see also 9:35); Hebrew
lacks *Jeiel*.   8:29b Or *the founder of*.   8:30 As in some
Greek manuscripts (see also 9:36); Hebrew lacks *Ner*.
8:31 As in parallel text at 9:37; Hebrew reads *Zeker*, a variant
spelling of Zechariah.   8:32 As in parallel text at 9:38;
Hebrew reads *Shimeah*, a variant spelling of Shimeam.
8:35 As in parallel text at 9:41; Hebrew reads *Tarea*, a variant
spelling of Tahrea.   8:36 As in parallel text at 9:42; Hebrew
reads *Jehoaddah*, a variant spelling of Jadah.   8:37 As in
parallel text at 9:43; Hebrew reads *Raphah*, a variant spelling
of Rephaiah.

ACTS 27:1-20
Danger at sea! Today's passage reads like an
action-adventure story. It's a good reminder that
following God doesn't necessarily mean the path
will be free of bumps (or waves!).

When the time came, we [Luke, Paul, and
his companions] set sail for Italy. Paul and
several other prisoners were placed in the
custody of a Roman officer* named Julius,
a captain of the Imperial Regiment. ²Aris-
tarchus, a Macedonian from Thessalonica,
was also with us. We left on a ship whose
home port was Adramyttium on the north-

west coast of the province of Asia;* it was
scheduled to make several stops at ports
along the coast of the province.
³The next day when we docked at Sidon, Julius was very kind to Paul and
let him go ashore to visit with friends
so they could provide for his needs. ⁴Put-
ting out to sea from there, we encountered strong headwinds that made it
difficult to keep the ship on course, so we
sailed north of Cyprus between the island
and the mainland. ⁵Keeping to the open
sea, we passed along the coast of Cilicia
and Pamphylia, landing at Myra, in the
province of Lycia. ⁶There the commanding officer found an Egyptian ship from
Alexandria that was bound for Italy, and
he put us on board.
⁷We had several days of slow sailing,
and after great difficulty we finally neared
Cnidus. But the wind was against us, so we
sailed across to Crete and along the sheltered coast of the island, past the cape of
Salmone. ⁸We struggled along the coast
with great difficulty and finally arrived at
Fair Havens, near the town of Lasea. ⁹We
had lost a lot of time. The weather was becoming dangerous for sea travel because
it was so late in the fall,* and Paul spoke to
the ship's officers about it.
¹⁰"Men," he said, "I believe there is
trouble ahead if we go on—shipwreck,
loss of cargo, and danger to our lives as
well." ¹¹But the officer in charge of the
prisoners listened more to the ship's captain and the owner than to Paul. ¹²And
since Fair Havens was an exposed harbor—a poor place to spend the winter—
most of the crew wanted to go on to Phoenix, farther up the coast of Crete, and
spend the winter there. Phoenix was a
good harbor with only a southwest and
northwest exposure.
¹³When a light wind began blowing
from the south, the sailors thought they
could make it. So they pulled up anchor
and sailed close to the shore of Crete.
¹⁴But the weather changed abruptly, and a
wind of typhoon strength (called a "north-
easter") burst across the island and blew
us out to sea. ¹⁵The sailors couldn't turn
the ship into the wind, so they gave up and
let it run before the gale. ¹⁶We sailed along the sheltered side of

a small island named Cauda,* where with great difficulty we hoisted aboard the lifeboat being towed behind us. [17]Then the sailors bound ropes around the hull of the ship to strengthen it. They were afraid of being driven across to the sandbars of Syrtis off the African coast, so they lowered the sea anchor to slow the ship and were driven before the wind.

[18]The next day, as gale-force winds continued to batter the ship, the crew began throwing the cargo overboard. [19]The following day they even took some of the ship's gear and threw it overboard. [20]The terrible storm raged for many days, blotting out the sun and the stars, until at last all hope was gone.

27:1 Greek *centurion;* similarly in 27:6, 11, 31, 43.
27:2 Asia was a Roman province in what is now western Turkey.   27:9 Greek *because the fast was now already gone by.* This fast was associated with the Day of Atonement (*Yom Kippur*), which occurred in late September or early October.
27:16 Some manuscripts read *Clauda.*

PSALM 7:1-17
A psalm of David, which he sang to the LORD concerning Cush of the tribe of Benjamin.

[1] I come to you for protection, O LORD
   my God.
   Save me from my persecutors—
      rescue me!
[2] If you don't, they will maul me like
      a lion,
   tearing me to pieces with no one
      to rescue me.
[3] O LORD my God, if I have done wrong
   or am guilty of injustice,
[4] if I have betrayed a friend
   or plundered my enemy without
      cause,
[5] then let my enemies capture me.
   Let them trample me into the
      ground
   and drag my honor in the dust.
                              Interlude

[6] Arise, O LORD, in anger!
   Stand up against the fury of my
      enemies!
   Wake up, my God, and bring justice!
[7] Gather the nations before you.
   Rule over them from on high.
[8]   The LORD judges the nations.
   Declare me righteous, O LORD,
      for I am innocent, O Most High!
[9] End the evil of those who are wicked,
   and defend the righteous.
   For you look deep within the mind
      and heart,
      O righteous God.

[10] God is my shield,
   saving those whose hearts are true
      and right.
[11] God is an honest judge.
   He is angry with the wicked every
      day.

[12] If a person does not repent,
   God* will sharpen his sword;
   he will bend and string his bow.
[13] He will prepare his deadly weapons
   and shoot his flaming arrows.

[14] The wicked conceive evil;
   they are pregnant with trouble
   and give birth to lies.
[15] They dig a deep pit to trap others,
   then fall into it themselves.
[16] The trouble they make for others
      backfires on them.
   The violence they plan falls on their
      own heads.

[17] I will thank the LORD because he is just;
   I will sing praise to the name of the
      LORD Most High.

7:12 Hebrew *he.*

PROVERBS 18:22
The man who finds a wife finds a treasure, and he receives favor from the LORD.

JULY 10

1 CHRONICLES 9:1–10:14

Today's reading makes reference to the people of Judah returning from exile. Years after David's reign, the kingdom divided. The northern kingdom was later conquered and exiled by Assyria; Babylon did likewise to the southern kingdom over a century later. The Chronicles were written after a remnant of those exiles returned to Jerusalem.

So all Israel was listed in the genealogical records in *The Book of the Kings of Israel*.

The people of Judah were exiled to Babylon because they were unfaithful to the LORD. ²The first of the exiles to return to their property in their former towns were priests, Levites, Temple servants, and other Israelites. ³Some of the people from the tribes of Judah, Benjamin, Ephraim, and Manasseh came and settled in Jerusalem.

⁴One family that returned was that of Uthai son of Ammihud, son of Omri, son of Imri, son of Bani, a descendant of Perez son of Judah.

⁵Others returned from the Shilonite clan, including Asaiah (the oldest) and his sons.

⁶From the Zerahite clan, Jeuel returned with his relatives.

In all, 690 families from the tribe of Judah returned.

⁷From the tribe of Benjamin came Sallu son of Meshullam, son of Hodaviah, son of Hassenuah; ⁸Ibneiah son of Jeroham; Elah son of Uzzi, son of Micri; and Meshullam son of Shephatiah, son of Reuel, son of Ibnijah.

⁹These men were all leaders of clans, and they were listed in their genealogical records. In all, 956 families from the tribe of Benjamin returned.

¹⁰Among the priests who returned were Jedaiah, Jehoiarib, Jakin, ¹¹Azariah son of Hilkiah, son of Meshullam, son of Zadok, son of Meraioth, son of Ahitub. Azariah was the chief officer of the house of God.

¹²Other returning priests were Adaiah son of Jeroham, son of Pashhur, son of Malkijah, and Maasai son of Adiel, son of Jahzerah, son of Meshullam, son of Meshillemith, son of Immer.

¹³In all, 1,760 priests returned. They were heads of clans and very able men. They were responsible for ministering at the house of God.

¹⁴The Levites who returned were Shemaiah son of Hasshub, son of Azrikam, son of Hashabiah, a descendant of Merari; ¹⁵Bakbakkar; Heresh; Galal; Mattaniah son of Mica, son of Zicri, son of Asaph; ¹⁶Obadiah son of Shemaiah, son of Galal, son of Jeduthun; and Berekiah son of Asa, son of Elkanah, who lived in the area of Netophah.

¹⁷The gatekeepers who returned were Shallum, Akkub, Talmon, Ahiman, and their relatives. Shallum was the chief gatekeeper. ¹⁸Prior to this time, they were responsible for the King's Gate on the east side. These men served as gatekeepers for the camps of the Levites. ¹⁹Shallum was the son of Kore, a descendant of Abiasaph,* from the clan of Korah. He and his relatives, the Korahites, were responsible for guarding the entrance to the sanctuary, just as their ancestors had guarded the Tabernacle in the camp of the LORD. ²⁰Phinehas son of Eleazar had been in charge of the gatekeepers in earlier times, and the LORD had been with him. ²¹And later Zechariah son of Meshelemiah was responsible for guarding the entrance to the Tabernacle.*

²²In all, there were 212 gatekeepers in those days, and they were listed according to the genealogies in their villages. David and Samuel the seer had appointed their ancestors because they were reliable men. ²³These gatekeepers and their descendants, by their divisions, were responsible for guarding the entrance to the house of the LORD when that house was a tent. ²⁴The gatekeepers were stationed on all four sides—east, west, north, and south. ²⁵Their relatives in the villages

came regularly to share their duties for seven-day periods.

²⁶The four chief gatekeepers, all Levites, were trusted officials, for they were responsible for the rooms and treasuries at the house of God. ²⁷They would spend the night around the house of God, since it was their duty to guard it and to open the gates every morning.

²⁸Some of the gatekeepers were assigned to care for the various articles used in worship. They checked them in and out to avoid any loss. ²⁹Others were responsible for the furnishings, the items in the sanctuary, and the supplies, such as choice flour, wine, olive oil, frankincense, and spices. ³⁰But it was the priests who blended the spices. ³¹Mattithiah, a Levite and the oldest son of Shallum the Korahite, was entrusted with baking the bread used in the offerings. ³²And some members of the clan of Kohath were in charge of preparing the bread to be set on the table each Sabbath day.

³³The musicians, all prominent Levites, lived at the Temple. They were exempt from other responsibilities since they were on duty at all hours. ³⁴All these men lived in Jerusalem. They were the heads of Levite families and were listed as prominent leaders in their genealogical records.

³⁵Jeiel (the father of* Gibeon) lived in the town of Gibeon. His wife's name was Maacah, ³⁶and his oldest son was named Abdon. Jeiel's other sons were Zur, Kish, Baal, Ner, Nadab, ³⁷Gedor, Ahio, Zechariah, and Mikloth. ³⁸Mikloth was the father of Shimeam. All these families lived near each other in Jerusalem.

³⁹ Ner was the father of Kish.
Kish was the father of Saul.
Saul was the father of Jonathan,
    Malkishua, Abinadab, and Esh-baal.
⁴⁰ Jonathan was the father of Merib-baal.
Merib-baal was the father of Micah.
⁴¹ The sons of Micah were Pithon,
    Melech, Tahrea, and Ahaz.*
⁴² Ahaz was the father of Jadah.*
Jadah was the father of Alemeth,
    Azmaveth, and Zimri.
Zimri was the father of Moza.
⁴³ Moza was the father of Binea.
Binea's son was Rephaiah.
Rephaiah's son was Eleasah.
Eleasah's son was Azel.
⁴⁴Azel had six sons, whose names were Azrikam, Bokeru, Ishmael, Sheariah, Obadiah, and Hanan. These were the sons of Azel.

¹⁰:¹Now the Philistines attacked Israel, and the men of Israel fled before them. Many were slaughtered on the slopes of Mount Gilboa. ²The Philistines closed in on Saul and his sons, and they killed three of his sons—Jonathan, Abinadab,

WHAT THE BIBLE SAYS

Does the Bible repeat material?

1 CHRONICLES 10 It's not so much that the Bible repeats material. Rather, at a couple of places the Bible covers the same period of history from different angles. This is especially true of the four Gospels, which give us a rich combination of perspectives on Jesus' life, death, and resurrection. • Some of the material you read in Chronicles will remind you of what you read in Kings. In a few places, it's almost verbatim. On the whole, however, Chronicles provides a fresh opportunity to understand the history of Israel and Judah. The key difference between the books of Kings and Chronicles is that the books of Kings go back and forth between the kingdoms of Israel and Judah, while the books of Chronicles focus on Judah. • Layering the stories recorded in Kings and Chronicles will give you a better picture of the nation's history—the good, the bad, and the ugly—and give you a glimpse of how God continued to watch over his people through it all.

and Malkishua. [3]The fighting grew very fierce around Saul, and the Philistine archers caught up with him and wounded him.

[4]Saul groaned to his armor bearer, "Take your sword and kill me before these pagan Philistines come to taunt and torture me."

But his armor bearer was afraid and would not do it. So Saul took his own sword and fell on it. [5]When his armor bearer realized that Saul was dead, he fell on his own sword and died. [6]So Saul and his three sons died there together, bringing his dynasty to an end.

[7]When all the Israelites in the Jezreel Valley saw that their army had fled and that Saul and his sons were dead, they abandoned their towns and fled. So the Philistines moved in and occupied their towns.

[8]The next day, when the Philistines went out to strip the dead, they found the bodies of Saul and his sons on Mount Gilboa. [9]So they stripped off Saul's armor and cut off his head. Then they proclaimed the good news of Saul's death before their idols and to the people throughout the land of Philistia. [10]They placed his armor in the temple of their gods, and they fastened his head to the temple of Dagon.

[11]But when everyone in Jabesh-gilead heard about everything the Philistines had done to Saul, [12]all their mighty warriors brought the bodies of Saul and his sons back to Jabesh. Then they buried their bones beneath the great tree at Jabesh, and they fasted for seven days.

[13]So Saul died because he was unfaithful to the LORD. He failed to obey the LORD's command, and he even consulted a medium [14]instead of asking the LORD for guidance. So the LORD killed him and turned the kingdom over to David son of Jesse.

9:19 Hebrew *Ebiasaph*, a variant spelling of Abiasaph; compare Exod 6:24.   **9:21** Hebrew *Tent of Meeting*.
9:35 Or *the founder of.*   **9:41** As in Syriac version and Latin Vulgate (see also 8:35); Hebrew lacks *and Ahaz.*   **9:42** As in some Hebrew manuscripts and Greek version (see also 8:36); Hebrew reads *Jarah.*

ACTS 27:21-44

Paul was traveling by boat—as a prisoner. In light of his status, it is all the more astounding that he took charge of the situation. It was Paul who called the crew together and cared for their well-being. Paul remained a man with a mission defined by God—no matter what situation.

No one had eaten for a long time. Finally, Paul called the crew together and said, "Men, you should have listened to me in the first place and not left Crete. You would have avoided all this damage and loss. [22]But take courage! None of you will lose your lives, even though the ship will go down. [23]For last night an angel of the God to whom I belong and whom I serve stood beside me, [24]and he said, 'Don't be afraid, Paul, for you will surely stand trial before Caesar! What's more, God in his goodness has granted safety to everyone sailing with you.' [25]So take courage! For I believe God. It will be just as he said. [26]But we will be shipwrecked on an island."

[27]About midnight on the fourteenth night of the storm, as we were being driven across the Sea of Adria,* the sailors sensed land was near. [28]They dropped a weighted line and found that the water was 120 feet deep. But a little later they measured again and found it was only 90 feet deep.* [29]At this rate they were afraid we would soon be driven against the rocks along the shore, so they threw out four anchors from the back of the ship and prayed for daylight.

[30]Then the sailors tried to abandon the ship; they lowered the lifeboat as though they were going to put out anchors from the front of the ship. [31]But Paul said to the commanding officer and the soldiers, "You will all die unless the sailors stay aboard." [32]So the soldiers cut the ropes to the lifeboat and let it drift away.

[33]Just as day was dawning, Paul urged everyone to eat. "You have been so worried that you haven't touched food for two weeks," he said. [34]"Please eat something now for your own good. For not a hair of your heads will perish." [35]Then he took some bread, gave thanks to God before them all, and broke off a piece and ate it. [36]Then everyone was encouraged and began to eat—[37]all 276 of us who were on board. [38]After eating, the crew lightened the ship further by throwing the cargo of wheat overboard.

[39]When morning dawned, they didn't recognize the coastline, but they saw a bay with a beach and wondered if they could get to shore by running the ship aground. [40]So they cut off the anchors and left them in the sea. Then they lowered the rudders, raised the foresail, and headed toward shore. [41]But they hit a shoal and ran the ship aground too soon. The bow of the ship stuck fast, while the stern was repeatedly smashed by the force of the waves and began to break apart.

[42]The soldiers wanted to kill the prisoners to make sure they didn't swim ashore and escape. [43]But the commanding officer wanted to spare Paul, so he didn't let them carry out their plan. Then he ordered all who could swim to jump overboard first and make for land. [44]The others held onto planks or debris from the broken ship.* So everyone escaped safely to shore.

27:27 The *Sea of Adria* includes the central portion of the Mediterranean. 27:28 Greek *20 fathoms . . . 15 fathoms* [37 meters . . . 27 meters]. 27:44 Or *or were helped by members of the ship's crew.*

PSALM 8:1-9
*For the choir director: A psalm of David, to be accompanied by a stringed instrument.**

[1] **O** Lord, our Lord, your majestic name
       fills the earth!
   Your glory is higher than the
       heavens.
[2] You have taught children and infants
       to tell of your strength,*
   silencing your enemies
       and all who oppose you.

[3] When I look at the night sky
       and see the work of your
       fingers—
   the moon and the stars you set
       in place—
[4] what are mere mortals that you should
       think about them,
   human beings that you should care
       for them?*
[5] Yet you made them only a little lower
       than God*
   and crowned them* with glory and
       honor.
[6] You gave them charge of everything
       you made,
   putting all things under their
       authority—
[7] the flocks and the herds
       and all the wild animals,
[8] the birds in the sky, the fish
       in the sea,
   and everything that swims
       the ocean currents.

[9] O Lord, our Lord, your majestic name
       fills the earth!

8:title Hebrew *according to the gittith.* 8:2 Greek version reads *to give you praise.* Compare Matt 21:16. 8:4 Hebrew *what is man that you should think of him, / the son of man that you should care for him?* 8:5a Or *Yet you made them only a little lower than the angels;* Hebrew reads *Yet you made him* [i.e., man] *a little lower than Elohim.* 8:5b Hebrew *him* [i.e., man]; similarly in 8:6.

PROVERBS 18:23-24
The poor plead for mercy; the rich answer with insults. □ There are "friends" who destroy each other, but a real friend sticks closer than a brother.

JULY**11**

1 CHRONICLES 11:1–12:18
Saul, David's predecessor, had been the very first king of Israel. With Saul's passing, a power struggle ensued. David first ruled only a small portion of the kingdom—Judah, the territory of David's family.

Then all Israel gathered before David at Hebron and told him, "We are your own flesh and blood. [2]In the past,* even when Saul was king, you were the one who really led the forces of Israel. And the Lord your God told you, 'You will be the shepherd of my people Israel. You will be the leader of my people Israel.'"

[3]So there at Hebron, David made a covenant before the Lord with all the elders of Israel. And they anointed him king of Israel, just as the Lord had promised through Samuel.

[4]Then David and all Israel went to Jerusalem (or Jebus, as it used to be called),

where the Jebusites, the original inhabitants of the land, were living. [5]The people of Jebus taunted David, saying, "You'll never get in here!" But David captured the fortress of Zion, which is now called the City of David.

[6]David had said to his troops, "Whoever is first to attack the Jebusites will become the commander of my armies!" And Joab, the son of David's sister Zeruiah, was first to attack, so he became the commander of David's armies.

[7]David made the fortress his home, and that is why it is called the City of David. [8]He extended the city from the supporting terraces* to the surrounding area, while Joab rebuilt the rest of Jerusalem. [9]And David became more and more powerful, because the LORD of Heaven's Armies was with him.

[10]These are the leaders of David's mighty warriors. Together with all Israel, they decided to make David their king, just as the LORD had promised concerning Israel.

[11]Here is the record of David's mightiest warriors: The first was Jashobeam the Hacmonite, who was leader of the Three— the mightiest warriors among David's men.* He once used his spear to kill 300 enemy warriors in a single battle.

[12]Next in rank among the Three was Eleazar son of Dodai,* a descendant of Ahoah. [13]He was with David in the battle against the Philistines at Pas-dammim. The battle took place in a field full of barley, and the Israelite army fled. [14]But Eleazar and David* held their ground in the middle of the field and beat back the Philistines. So the LORD saved them by giving them a great victory.

[15]Once when David was at the rock near the cave of Adullam, the Philistine army was camped in the valley of Rephaim. The Three (who were among the Thirty—an elite group among David's fighting men) went down to meet him there. [16]David was staying in the stronghold at the time, and a Philistine detachment had occupied the town of Bethlehem. [17]David remarked longingly to his men, "Oh, how I would love some of that good water from the well by the gate in Bethlehem." [18]So the Three broke through the Philistine lines, drew some water from the well by the gate in Bethlehem, and brought it back to David. But David refused to drink it. Instead, he poured it out as an offering to the LORD. [19]"God forbid that I should drink this!" he exclaimed. "This water is as precious as the blood of these men* who risked their lives to bring it to me." So David did not drink it. These are examples of the exploits of the Three.

[20]Abishai, the brother of Joab, was the leader of the Thirty.* He once used his spear to kill 300 enemy warriors in a single battle. It was by such feats that he became as famous as the Three. [21]Abishai was the most famous of the Thirty and was their commander, though he was not one of the Three.

[22]There was also Benaiah son of Jehoiada, a valiant warrior from Kabzeel. He did many heroic deeds, which included killing two champions* of Moab. Another time, on a snowy day, he chased a lion down into a pit and killed it. [23]Once, armed only with a club, he killed an Egyptian warrior who was 7½ feet* tall and whose spear was as thick as a weaver's beam. Benaiah wrenched the spear from the Egyptian's hand and killed him with it. [24]Deeds like these made Benaiah as famous as the three mightiest warriors. [25]He was more honored than the other members of the Thirty, though he was not one of the Three. And David made him captain of his bodyguard.

[26]David's mighty warriors also included:

Asahel, Joab's brother;
Elhanan son of Dodo from Bethlehem;
[27] Shammah from Harod;*
Helez from Pelon;
[28] Ira son of Ikkesh from Tekoa;
Abiezer from Anathoth;
[29] Sibbecai from Hushah;
Zalmon* from Ahoah;
[30] Maharai from Netophah;
Heled son of Baanah from Netophah;
[31] Ithai son of Ribai from Gibeah (in the land of Benjamin);
Benaiah from Pirathon;
[32] Hurai from near Nahale-gaash*;
Abi-albon* from Arabah;
[33] Azmaveth from Bahurim*;
Eliahba from Shaalbon;

³⁴ the sons of Jashen* from Gizon;
Jonathan son of Shagee from Harar;
³⁵ Ahiam son of Sharar* from Harar;
Eliphal son of Ur;
³⁶ Hepher from Mekerah;
Ahijah from Pelon;
³⁷ Hezro from Carmel;
Paarai* son of Ezbai;
³⁸ Joel, the brother of Nathan;
Mibhar son of Hagri;
³⁹ Zelek from Ammon;
Naharai from Beeroth, Joab's armor
bearer;
⁴⁰ Ira from Jattir;
Gareb from Jattir;
⁴¹ Uriah the Hittite;
Zabad son of Ahlai;
⁴² Adina son of Shiza, the Reubenite
leader who had thirty men with him;
⁴³ Hanan son of Maacah;
Joshaphat from Mithna;
⁴⁴ Uzzia from Ashtaroth;
Shama and Jeiel, the sons of Hotham,
from Aroer;
⁴⁵ Jediael son of Shimri;
Joha, his brother, from Tiz;
⁴⁶ Eliel from Mahavah;
Jeribai and Joshaviah, the sons
of Elnaam;
Ithmah from Moab;
⁴⁷ Eliel and Obed;
Jaasiel from Zobah.*

^{12:1}THE following men joined David at
Ziklag while he was hiding from Saul son
of Kish. They were among the warriors
who fought beside David in battle. ²All
of them were expert archers, and they
could shoot arrows or sling stones with
their left hand as well as their right. They
were all relatives of Saul from the tribe of
Benjamin. ³Their leader was Ahiezer son
of Shemaah from Gibeah; his brother Joash was second-in-command. These were
the other warriors:

Jeziel and Pelet, sons of Azmaveth;
Beracah;
Jehu from Anathoth;
⁴ Ishmaiah from Gibeon, a famous
warrior and leader among the
Thirty;
*Jeremiah, Jahaziel, Johanan, and
Jozabad from Gederah;
⁵ Eluzai, Jerimoth, Bealiah, Shemariah,
and Shephatiah from Haruph;
⁶ Elkanah, Isshiah, Azarel, Joezer,
and Jashobeam, who were
Korahites;
⁷ Joelah and Zebadiah, sons of Jeroham
from Gedor.

⁸Some brave and experienced warriors
from the tribe of Gad also defected to David while he was at the stronghold in the

---

HOW WE LIVE

Following Jesus

ACTS 28:1-31 Acts closes with Paul's harrowing journey to Rome where he
would spend two years under house arrest . . . but preaching the Good
News nonetheless. • What made this man so strong, so bold, so fearless—so unstoppable? The answer is easy: Paul followed Jesus. Paul
had faith that bore itself out in actions over and over again. He believed
that God would do what he promised—guide, protect, teach, and heal.
Paul was completely and utterly sold out to God's will. His life was given
for the gospel. As far as we know, he never married, never had kids,
never worried about his retirement plan, and never took a cruise that
wasn't on his missionary itinerary. He was a man for the time, specially
chosen to take the gospel message across the known world. The road
was tough. He was persecuted, hated, maligned, imprisoned, and eventually martyred. • By following Jesus, you are not guaranteed an easy
road; his road does promise, however, to be the most fulfilling place to
be in the entire world. When you follow Jesus, you change the world—
one person, one day, one life at a time.

wilderness. They were expert with both shield and spear, as fierce as lions and as swift as deer on the mountains.

⁹ Ezer was their leader.
  Obadiah was second.
  Eliab was third.
¹⁰ Mishmannah was fourth.
  Jeremiah was fifth.
¹¹ Attai was sixth.
  Eliel was seventh.
¹² Johanan was eighth.
  Elzabad was ninth.
¹³ Jeremiah was tenth.
  Macbannai was eleventh.

¹⁴These warriors from Gad were army commanders. The weakest among them could take on a hundred regular troops, and the strongest could take on a thousand! ¹⁵These were the men who crossed the Jordan River during its seasonal flooding at the beginning of the year and drove out all the people living in the lowlands on both the east and west banks.

¹⁶Others from Benjamin and Judah came to David at the stronghold. ¹⁷David went out to meet them and said, "If you have come in peace to help me, we are friends. But if you have come to betray me to my enemies when I am innocent, then may the God of our ancestors see it and punish you."

¹⁸Then the Spirit came upon Amasai, the leader of the Thirty, and he said,

"We are yours, David!
  We are on your side, son of Jesse.
Peace and prosperity be with you,
  and success to all who help you,
  for your God is the one who helps
    you."

So David let them join him, and he made them officers over his troops.

11:2 Or *For some time.*   11:8 Hebrew *the millo.* The meaning of the Hebrew is uncertain.   11:11 As in some Greek manuscripts (see also 2 Sam 23:8); Hebrew reads *leader of the Thirty,* or *leader of the captains.*   11:12 As in parallel text at 2 Sam 23:9 (see also 1 Chr 27:4); Hebrew reads *Dodo,* a variant spelling of Dodai.   11:14 Hebrew *they.*   11:19 Hebrew *Shall I drink the lifeblood of these men?*   11:20 As in Syriac version; Hebrew reads *the Three;* also in 11:21.   11:22 Or *two sons of Ariel.*   11:23 Hebrew *5 cubits* [2.3 meters].   11:27 As in parallel text at 2 Sam 23:25; Hebrew reads *Shammoth from Haror.*   11:29 As in parallel text at 2 Sam 23:28; Hebrew reads *Ilai.*   11:32a Or *from the ravines of Gaash.*   11:32b As in parallel text at 2 Sam 23:31; Hebrew reads *Abiel.*   11:33 As in parallel text at 2 Sam 23:31; Hebrew reads *Baharum.*   11:34 As in parallel text at

2 Sam 23:32; Hebrew reads *sons of Hashem.*   11:35 As in parallel text at 2 Sam 23:33; Hebrew reads *son of Sacar.*   11:37 As in parallel text at 2 Sam 23:35; Hebrew reads *Naarai.*   11:47 Or *the Mezobaite.*   12:4 Verses 12:4b-40 are numbered 12:5-41 in Hebrew text.

ACTS 28:1-31

The book of Acts closes with Paul in Rome, imprisoned yet still preaching about Jesus. Throughout Paul's life, he took what seemed to be definite negatives and used them as platforms from which to do God's work.

Once we [Luke, Paul, and his companions] were safe on shore, we learned that we were on the island of Malta. ²The people of the island were very kind to us. It was cold and rainy, so they built a fire on the shore to welcome us.

³As Paul gathered an armful of sticks and was laying them on the fire, a poisonous snake, driven out by the heat, bit him on the hand. ⁴The people of the island saw it hanging from his hand and said to each other, "A murderer, no doubt! Though he escaped the sea, justice will not permit him to live." ⁵But Paul shook off the snake into the fire and was unharmed. ⁶The people waited for him to swell up or suddenly drop dead. But when they had waited a long time and saw that he wasn't harmed, they changed their minds and decided he was a god.

⁷Near the shore where we landed was an estate belonging to Publius, the chief official of the island. He welcomed us and treated us kindly for three days. ⁸As it happened, Publius's father was ill with fever and dysentery. Paul went in and prayed for him, and laying his hands on him, he healed him. ⁹Then all the other sick people on the island came and were healed. ¹⁰As a result we were showered with honors, and when the time came to sail, people supplied us with everything we would need for the trip.

¹¹It was three months after the shipwreck that we set sail on another ship that had wintered at the island—an Alexandrian ship with the twin gods* as its figurehead. ¹²Our first stop was Syracuse,* where we stayed three days. ¹³From there we sailed across to Rhegium.* A day later a south wind began blowing, so the following day we sailed up the coast to Puteoli. ¹⁴There we found some believers,* who

invited us to spend a week with them. And so we came to Rome.

¹⁵The brothers and sisters* in Rome had heard we were coming, and they came to meet us at the Forum* on the Appian Way. Others joined us at The Three Taverns.* When Paul saw them, he was encouraged and thanked God.

¹⁶When we arrived in Rome, Paul was permitted to have his own private lodging, though he was guarded by a soldier.

¹⁷Three days after Paul's arrival, he called together the local Jewish leaders. He said to them, "Brothers, I was arrested in Jerusalem and handed over to the Roman government, even though I had done nothing against our people or the customs of our ancestors. ¹⁸The Romans tried me and wanted to release me, because they found no cause for the death sentence. ¹⁹But when the Jewish leaders protested the decision, I felt it necessary to appeal to Caesar, even though I had no desire to press charges against my own people. ²⁰I asked you to come here today so we could get acquainted and so I could explain to you that I am bound with this chain because I believe that the hope of Israel—the Messiah—has already come."

²¹They replied, "We have had no letters from Judea or reports against you from anyone who has come here. ²²But we want to hear what you believe, for the only thing we know about this movement is that it is denounced everywhere."

²³So a time was set, and on that day a large number of people came to Paul's lodging. He explained and testified about the Kingdom of God and tried to persuade them about Jesus from the Scriptures. Using the law of Moses and the books of the prophets, he spoke to them from morning until evening. ²⁴Some were persuaded by the things he said, but others did not believe. ²⁵And after they had argued back and forth among themselves, they left with this final word from Paul: "The Holy Spirit was right when he said to your ancestors through Isaiah the prophet,

²⁶ 'Go and say to this people:
When you hear what I say,
    you will not understand.

When you see what I do,
    you will not comprehend.
²⁷ For the hearts of these people are hardened,
    and their ears cannot hear,
    and they have closed their eyes—
so their eyes cannot see,
    and their ears cannot hear,
    and their hearts cannot understand,
and they cannot turn to me
    and let me heal them.'*

²⁸So I want you to know that this salvation from God has also been offered to the Gentiles, and they will accept it."*

³⁰For the next two years, Paul lived in Rome at his own expense.* He welcomed all who visited him, ³¹boldly proclaiming the Kingdom of God and teaching about the Lord Jesus Christ. And no one tried to stop him.

28:11 The *twin gods* were the Roman gods Castor and Pollux. **28:12** *Syracuse* was on the island of Sicily.   **28:13** *Rhegium* was on the southern tip of Italy.   **28:14** Greek *brothers*. **28:15a** Greek *brothers*.   **28:15b** *The Forum* was about 43 miles (70 kilometers) from Rome.   **28:15c** *The Three Taverns* was about 35 miles (57 kilometers) from Rome. **28:26-27** Isa 6:9-10 (Greek version).   **28:28** Some manuscripts add verse 29, *And when he had said these words, the Jews departed, greatly disagreeing with each other.*   **28:30** Or *in his own rented quarters.*

PSALM 9:1-12

For the choir director: A psalm of David, to be sung to the tune "Death of the Son."

¹ **I** will praise you, LORD, with all
        my heart;
    I will tell of all the marvelous things
        you have done.
² I will be filled with joy because of you.
    I will sing praises to your name,
        O Most High.

³ My enemies retreated;
    they staggered and died when you
        appeared.
⁴ For you have judged in my favor;
    from your throne you have judged
        with fairness.
⁵ You have rebuked the nations and
        destroyed the wicked;
    you have erased their names
        forever.
⁶ The enemy is finished, in endless
        ruins;
    the cities you uprooted are now
        forgotten.

7 But the LORD reigns forever,
    executing judgment from
      his throne.
8 He will judge the world with justice
    and rule the nations with fairness.
9 The LORD is a shelter for the
      oppressed,
    a refuge in times of trouble.
10 Those who know your name trust in
      you,
    for you, O LORD, do not abandon
      those who search for you.

11 Sing praises to the LORD who reigns
    in Jerusalem.*

JULY**12**

1 CHRONICLES 12:19–14:17

David soon amassed a powerful army of warriors.
But it was David's determination to bring the Ark to
the forefront that communicated what sort of king
he was: he was a man of God and his people were
a people of God.

Some men from Manasseh defected
from the Israelite army and joined David
when he set out with the Philistines to
fight against Saul. But as it turned out, the
Philistine rulers refused to let David and
his men go with them. After much discussion, they sent them back, for they said, "It
will cost us our heads if David switches
loyalties to Saul and turns against us."

20Here is a list of the men from Manasseh who defected to David as he was returning to Ziklag: Adnah, Jozabad, Jediael,
Michael, Jozabad, Elihu, and Zillethai.
Each commanded 1,000 troops from the
tribe of Manasseh. 21They helped David
chase down bands of raiders, for they
were all brave and able warriors who became commanders in his army. 22Day after day more men joined David until he
had a great army, like the army of God.

23These are the numbers of armed
warriors who joined David at Hebron.
They were all eager to see David become
king instead of Saul, just as the LORD had
promised.

Tell the world about his
    unforgettable deeds.
12 For he who avenges murder cares
    for the helpless.
  He does not ignore the cries
    of those who suffer.

9:11 Hebrew *Zion;* also in 9:14.

PROVERBS 19:1-3

Better to be poor and honest than to be
dishonest and a fool. □ Enthusiasm without knowledge is no good; haste makes
mistakes. □ People ruin their lives by their
own foolishness and then are angry at the
LORD.

24From the tribe of Judah, there were
    6,800 warriors armed with shields
    and spears.
25From the tribe of Simeon, there were
    7,100 brave warriors.
26From the tribe of Levi, there were
    4,600 warriors. 27This included
    Jehoiada, leader of the family of Aaron,
    who had 3,700 under his command.
    28This also included Zadok, a brave
    young warrior, with 22 members of
    his family who were all officers.
29From the tribe of Benjamin, Saul's
    relatives, there were 3,000 warriors.
    Most of the men from Benjamin had
    remained loyal to Saul until this time.
30From the tribe of Ephraim, there were
    20,800 brave warriors, each highly
    respected in his own clan.
31From the half-tribe of Manasseh west
    of the Jordan, 18,000 men were
    designated by name to help David
    become king.
32From the tribe of Issachar, there were
    200 leaders of the tribe with their
    relatives. All these men understood
    the signs of the times and knew the
    best course for Israel to take.
33From the tribe of Zebulun, there were
    50,000 skilled warriors. They were

fully armed and prepared for battle and completely loyal to David.

[34] From the tribe of Naphtali, there were 1,000 officers and 37,000 warriors armed with shields and spears.

[35] From the tribe of Dan, there were 28,600 warriors, all prepared for battle.

[36] From the tribe of Asher, there were 40,000 trained warriors, all prepared for battle.

[37] From the east side of the Jordan River—where the tribes of Reuben and Gad and the half-tribe of Manasseh lived—there were 120,000 troops armed with every kind of weapon.

[38] All these men came in battle array to Hebron with the single purpose of making David the king over all Israel. In fact, everyone in Israel agreed that David should be their king. [39] They feasted and drank with David for three days, for preparations had been made by their relatives for their arrival. [40] And people from as far away as Issachar, Zebulun, and Naphtali brought food on donkeys, camels, mules, and oxen. Vast supplies of flour, fig cakes, clusters of raisins, wine, olive oil, cattle, sheep, and goats were brought to the celebration. There was great joy throughout the land of Israel.

13:1 DAVID consulted with all his officials, including the generals and captains of his army.* [2] Then he addressed the entire assembly of Israel as follows: "If you approve and if it is the will of the LORD our God, let us send messages to all the Israelites throughout the land, including the priests and Levites in their towns and pasturelands. Let us invite them to come and join us. [3] It is time to bring back the Ark of our God, for we neglected it during the reign of Saul."

[4] The whole assembly agreed to this, for the people could see it was the right thing to do. [5] So David summoned all Israel, from the Shihor Brook of Egypt in the south all the way to the town of Lebo-hamath in the north, to join in bringing the Ark of God from Kiriath-jearim. [6] Then David and all Israel went to Baalah of Judah (also called Kiriath-jearim) to bring back the Ark of God, which bears the name* of the LORD who is enthroned between the cherubim. [7] They placed the Ark of God on a new cart and brought it from Abinadab's house. Uzzah and Ahio were guiding the cart. [8] David and all Israel were celebrating before God with all their might, singing songs and playing all kinds of musical instruments—lyres, harps, tambourines, cymbals, and trumpets.

[9] But when they arrived at the threshing floor of Nacon,* the oxen stumbled, and Uzzah reached out his hand to steady the Ark. [10] Then the LORD's anger was aroused against Uzzah, and he struck him dead

HOW WE LIVE | Sharing our faith

ROMANS 1:16 Good news lifts the spirits, brings a smile, and helps you believe in humanity again. It's powerful stuff. The apostle Paul had some good news he was eager to talk about with anyone who would listen: "I am not ashamed of this Good News about Christ. It is the power of God at work." And what is that Good News? That through Jesus Christ, the crucified Savior and resurrected Lord, we can be righteous in God's sight. • Like Paul, we have good news to share with whoever will listen. But it is not always easy to share our faith. No one likes to feel like he or she is imposing on someone, and no one likes to be rejected. When you feel timid, just remember that you bear genuinely good news. Remember that God sent his only Son to take your place by dying for your sins. Think about how you can go to him in prayer, in sorrow, and in joy. Focus on where you will spend eternity. Wow! That's powerful stuff. Why not tell someone about it today?

because he had laid his hand on the Ark. So Uzzah died there in the presence of God.

[11]David was angry because the LORD's anger had burst out against Uzzah. He named that place Perez-uzzah (which means "to burst out against Uzzah"), as it is still called today.

[12]David was now afraid of God, and he asked, "How can I ever bring the Ark of God back into my care?" [13]So David did not move the Ark into the City of David. Instead, he took it to the house of Obed-edom of Gath. [14]The Ark of God remained there in Obed-edom's house for three months, and the LORD blessed the household of Obed-edom and everything he owned.

[14:1]THEN King Hiram of Tyre sent messengers to David, along with cedar timber, and stonemasons and carpenters to build him a palace. [2]And David realized that the LORD had confirmed him as king over Israel and had greatly blessed his kingdom for the sake of his people Israel.

[3]Then David married more wives in Jerusalem, and they had more sons and daughters. [4]These are the names of David's sons who were born in Jerusalem: Shammua, Shobab, Nathan, Solomon, [5]Ibhar, Elishua, Elpelet, [6]Nogah, Nepheg, Japhia, [7]Elishama, Eliada,* and Eliphelet.

[8]When the Philistines heard that David had been anointed king over all Israel, they mobilized all their forces to capture him. But David was told they were coming, so he marched out to meet them. [9]The Philistines arrived and made a raid in the valley of Rephaim. [10]So David asked God, "Should I go out to fight the Philistines? Will you hand them over to me?"

The LORD replied, "Yes, go ahead. I will hand them over to you."

[11]So David and his troops went up to Baal-perazim and defeated the Philistines there. "God did it!" David exclaimed. "He used me to burst through my enemies like a raging flood!" So they named that place Baal-perazim (which means "the Lord who bursts through"). [12]The Philistines had abandoned their gods there, so David gave orders to burn them.

[13]But after a while the Philistines re-turned and raided the valley again. [14]And once again David asked God what to do. "Do not attack them straight on," God replied. "Instead, circle around behind and attack them near the poplar* trees. [15]When you hear a sound like marching feet in the tops of the poplar trees, go out and attack! That will be the signal that God is moving ahead of you to strike down the Philistine army." [16]So David did what God commanded, and they struck down the Philistine army all the way from Gibeon to Gezer.

[17]So David's fame spread everywhere, and the LORD caused all the nations to fear David.

13:1 Hebrew *the commanders of thousands and of hundreds.* 13:6 Or *the Ark of God, where the Name is proclaimed—the name.* 13:9 As in parallel text at 2 Sam 6:6; Hebrew reads *Kidon.* 14:7 Hebrew *Beeliada,* a variant spelling of Eliada; compare 3:8 and parallel text at 2 Sam 5:16. 14:14 Or *aspen,* or *balsam;* also in 14:15. The exact identification of this tree is uncertain.

ROMANS 1:1-17

Paul wrote the book of Romans from Corinth to the Christians in Rome before he had ever visited them. He wanted to "get on the same page" with the Roman Christians before his visit. The result is one of Christianity's most highly formative and dearly loved books.

This letter is from Paul, a slave of Christ Jesus, chosen by God to be an apostle and sent out to preach his Good News. [2]God promised this Good News long ago through his prophets in the holy Scriptures. [3]The Good News is about his Son. In his earthly life he was born into King David's family line, [4]and he was shown to be* the Son of God when he was raised from the dead by the power of the Holy Spirit.* He is Jesus Christ our Lord. [5]Through Christ, God has given us the privilege* and authority as apostles to tell Gentiles everywhere what God has done for them, so that they will believe and obey him, bringing glory to his name.

[6]And you are included among those Gentiles who have been called to belong to Jesus Christ. [7]I am writing to all of you in Rome who are loved by God and are called to be his own holy people.

May God our Father and the Lord Jesus Christ give you grace and peace.

[8]Let me say first that I thank my God

through Jesus Christ for all of you, because your faith in him is being talked about all over the world. [9]God knows how often I pray for you. Day and night I bring you and your needs in prayer to God, whom I serve with all my heart* by spreading the Good News about his Son.

[10]One of the things I always pray for is the opportunity, God willing, to come at last to see you. [11]For I long to visit you so I can bring you some spiritual gift that will help you grow strong in the faith. [12]When we get together, I want to encourage you in your faith, but I also want to be encouraged by yours.

[13]I want you to know, dear brothers and sisters,* that I planned many times to visit you, but I was prevented until now. I want to work among you and see spiritual fruit, just as I have seen among other Gentiles. [14]For I have a great sense of obligation to people in both the civilized world and the rest of the world,* to the educated and uneducated alike. [15]So I am eager to come to you in Rome, too, to preach the Good News.

[16]For I am not ashamed of this Good News about Christ. It is the power of God at work, saving everyone who believes—the Jew first and also the Gentile.* [17]This Good News tells us how God makes us right in his sight. This is accomplished from start to finish by faith. As the Scriptures say, "It is through faith that a righteous person has life."*

1:4a Or and was designated.   1:4b Or by the Spirit of holiness; or in the new realm of the Spirit.   1:5 Or the grace.   1:9 Or in my spirit.   1:13 Greek brothers.   1:14 Greek to Greeks and barbarians.   1:16 Greek also the Greek.   1:17 Or "The righteous will live by faith." Hab 2:4.

1 CHRONICLES 15:1–16:36

The Ark of God was a wooden chest covered with gold. It represented God's presence among the people. By returning it to the capital city and central place of worship, David showed that God was the real King of Israel.

PSALM 9:13-20

LORD, have mercy on me.
    See how my enemies torment me.
    Snatch me back from the jaws of
        death.
[14] Save me so I can praise you publicly
        at Jerusalem's gates,
    so I can rejoice that you have
        rescued me.

[15] The nations have fallen into the pit
        they dug for others.
    Their own feet have been caught
        in the trap they set.
[16] The LORD is known for his justice.
    The wicked are trapped by their
        own deeds.   Quiet Interlude*

[17] The wicked will go down to the grave.*
    This is the fate of all the nations
        who ignore God.
[18] But the needy will not be ignored
        forever;
    the hopes of the poor will not
        always be crushed.

[19] Arise, O LORD!
    Do not let mere mortals defy you!
    Judge the nations!
[20] Make them tremble in fear, O LORD.
    Let the nations know they are merely
        human.   Interlude

9:16 Hebrew Higgaion Selah. The meaning of this phrase is uncertain.   9:17 Hebrew to Sheol.

PROVERBS 19:4-5

Wealth makes many "friends"; poverty drives them all away. □A false witness will not go unpunished, nor will a liar escape.

JULY 13

David now built several buildings for himself in the City of David. He also prepared a place for the Ark of God and set up a special tent for it. [2]Then he commanded, "No one except the Levites may carry the Ark of God. The LORD has chosen them to carry the Ark of the LORD and to serve him forever."

³Then David summoned all Israel to Jerusalem to bring the Ark of the LORD to the place he had prepared for it. ⁴This is the number of the descendants of Aaron (the priests) and the Levites who were called together:

⁵From the clan of Kohath, 120, with Uriel as their leader.

⁶From the clan of Merari, 220, with Asaiah as their leader.

⁷From the clan of Gershon,* 130, with Joel as their leader.

⁸From the descendants of Elizaphan, 200, with Shemaiah as their leader.

⁹From the descendants of Hebron, 80, with Eliel as their leader.

¹⁰From the descendants of Uzziel, 112, with Amminadab as their leader.

¹¹Then David summoned the priests, Zadok and Abiathar, and these Levite leaders: Uriel, Asaiah, Joel, Shemaiah, Eliel, and Amminadab. ¹²He said to them, "You are the leaders of the Levite families. You must purify yourselves and all your fellow Levites, so you can bring the Ark of the LORD, the God of Israel, to the place I have prepared for it. ¹³Because you Levites did not carry the Ark the first time, the anger of the LORD our God burst out against us. We failed to ask God how to move it properly." ¹⁴So the priests and the Levites purified themselves in order to bring the Ark of the LORD, the God of Israel, to Jerusalem. ¹⁵Then the Levites carried the Ark of God on their shoulders with its carrying poles, just as the LORD had instructed Moses.

¹⁶David also ordered the Levite leaders to appoint a choir of Levites who were singers and musicians to sing joyful songs to the accompaniment of harps, lyres, and cymbals. ¹⁷So the Levites appointed Heman son of Joel along with his fellow Levites: Asaph son of Berekiah, and Ethan son of Kushaiah from the clan of Merari. ¹⁸The following men were chosen as their assistants: Zechariah, Jaaziel,* Shemiramoth, Jehiel, Unni, Eliab, Benaiah, Maaseiah, Mattithiah, Eliphelehu, Mikneiah, and the gatekeepers—Obed-edom and Jeiel.

¹⁹The musicians Heman, Asaph, and Ethan were chosen to sound the bronze cymbals. ²⁰Zechariah, Aziel, Shemiramoth, Jehiel, Unni, Eliab, Maaseiah, and Benaiah were chosen to play the harps.* ²¹Mattithiah, Eliphelehu, Mikneiah, Obed-edom, Jeiel, and Azaziah were chosen to play the lyres.* ²²Kenaniah, the head Levite, was chosen as the choir leader because of his skill.

²³Berekiah and Elkanah were chosen to guard* the Ark. ²⁴Shebaniah, Joshaphat, Nethanel, Amasai, Zechariah, Benaiah, and Eliezer—all of whom were priests—were chosen to blow the trumpets as they marched in front of the Ark of God. Obed-edom and Jehiah were chosen to guard the Ark.

²⁵Then David and the elders of Israel and the generals of the army* went to the house of Obed-edom to bring the Ark of the LORD's Covenant up to Jerusalem with a great celebration. ²⁶And because God was clearly helping the Levites as they carried the Ark of the LORD's Covenant, they sacrificed seven bulls and seven rams.

²⁷David was dressed in a robe of fine linen, as were all the Levites who carried the Ark, and also the singers, and Kenaniah the choir leader. David was also wearing a priestly garment.* ²⁸So all Israel brought up the Ark of the LORD's Covenant with shouts of joy, the blowing of rams' horns and trumpets, the crashing of cymbals, and loud playing on harps and lyres.

²⁹But as the Ark of the LORD's Covenant entered the City of David, Michal, the daughter of Saul, looked down from her window. When she saw King David skipping about and laughing with joy, she was filled with contempt for him.

16:1THEY brought the Ark of God and placed it inside the special tent David had prepared for it. And they presented burnt offerings and peace offerings to God. ²When he had finished his sacrifices, David blessed the people in the name of the LORD. ³Then he gave to every man and woman in all Israel a loaf of bread, a cake of dates,* and a cake of raisins.

⁴David appointed the following Levites to lead the people in worship before the

Ark of the LORD—to invoke his blessings, to give thanks, and to praise the LORD, the God of Israel. ⁵Asaph, the leader of this group, sounded the cymbals. Second to him was Zechariah, followed by Jeiel, Shemiramoth, Jehiel, Mattithiah, Eliab, Benaiah, Obed-edom, and Jeiel. They played the harps and lyres. ⁶The priests, Benaiah and Jahaziel, played the trumpets regularly before the Ark of God's Covenant.

⁷On that day David gave to Asaph and his fellow Levites this song of thanksgiving to the LORD:

⁸ Give thanks to the LORD and proclaim his greatness.
    Let the whole world know what he has done.
⁹ Sing to him; yes, sing his praises.
    Tell everyone about his wonderful deeds.
¹⁰ Exult in his holy name;
    rejoice, you who worship the LORD.
¹¹ Search for the LORD and for his strength;
    continually seek him.
¹² Remember the wonders he has performed,
    his miracles, and the rulings he has given,
¹³ you children of his servant Israel,
    you descendants of Jacob, his chosen ones.

¹⁴ He is the LORD our God.
    His justice is seen throughout the land.
¹⁵ Remember his covenant forever—
    the commitment he made to a thousand generations.
¹⁶ This is the covenant he made with Abraham
    and the oath he swore to Isaac.
¹⁷ He confirmed it to Jacob as a decree,
    and to the people of Israel as a never-ending covenant:
¹⁸ "I will give you the land of Canaan
    as your special possession."

¹⁹ He said this when you were few in number,
    a tiny group of strangers in Canaan.
²⁰ They wandered from nation to nation,
    from one kingdom to another.
²¹ Yet he did not let anyone oppress them.
    He warned kings on their behalf:
²² "Do not touch my chosen people,
    and do not hurt my prophets."

²³ Let the whole earth sing to the LORD!
    Each day proclaim the good news that he saves.
²⁴ Publish his glorious deeds among the nations.
    Tell everyone about the amazing things he does.

WHAT THE BIBLE SAYS

Those who never hear about Jesus

ROMANS 1:18-20 How could a loving God send someone to hell when that person never heard the Good News of Jesus? In fact, says Paul, in creation God has revealed himself plainly to *all* people. Also, everyone has an inner sense of what God requires. All people are wired for a personal relationship with God, and if they seek him they will find him. No one will go to hell simply because he or she missed out. God watches over every individual, knowing the number of hairs on every head. He reveals himself and touches lives, but people must choose to respond appropriately to whatever understanding they have. • God could have kept humans in ignorance about himself, but he chose to reveal himself in nature, through the Scriptures, and in Jesus Christ. Those who've been given greater revelation have a greater responsibility to respond to it, but no one has been left completely in the dark. Because God has made certain facts about himself plain, people will someday have to give an account before God of why they chose to ignore his existence and his character.

²⁵ Great is the LORD! He is most worthy
of praise!

He is to be feared above all gods.

²⁶ The gods of other nations are mere
idols,

but the LORD made the heavens!

²⁷ Honor and majesty surround him;

strength and joy fill his dwelling.

²⁸ O nations of the world, recognize
the LORD,

recognize that the LORD is glorious
and strong.

²⁹ Give to the LORD the glory he deserves!

Bring your offering and come into
his presence.

Worship the LORD in all his holy
splendor.

³⁰   Let all the earth tremble before him.

The world stands firm and cannot
be shaken.

³¹ Let the heavens be glad, and the earth
rejoice!

Tell all the nations, "The LORD
reigns!"

³² Let the sea and everything in it shout
his praise!

Let the fields and their crops burst
out with joy!

³³ Let the trees of the forest rustle
with praise,

for the LORD is coming to judge
the earth.

³⁴ Give thanks to the LORD, for he
is good!

His faithful love endures forever.

³⁵ Cry out, "Save us, O God of our
salvation!

Gather and rescue us from among
the nations,

so we can thank your holy name
and rejoice and praise you."

³⁶ Praise the LORD, the God of Israel,

who lives from everlasting
to everlasting!

And all the people shouted "Amen!" and
praised the LORD.

15:7 Hebrew *Gershom*, a variant spelling of Gershon.
15:18 Or *Zechariah son of Jaaziel;* or *Zechariah, Ben, Jaaziel.*
15:20 Hebrew adds *according to Alamoth*, which is probably
a musical term. The meaning of the Hebrew is uncertain.
15:21 Hebrew adds *according to the Sheminith*, which
is probably a musical term. The meaning of the Hebrew

is uncertain.   15:23 Hebrew *chosen as gatekeepers for;* also
in 15:24.   15:25 Hebrew *the commanders of thousands.*
15:27 Hebrew *a linen ephod.*   16:3 Or *a portion of
meat.* The meaning of the Hebrew is uncertain.

ROMANS 1:18-32

Paul started with the basics: the evidence of God
is all around in creation—who are we to disregard
him? God is a loving Father and a rightful Judge.
How we live matters to him.

But God shows his anger from heaven
against all sinful, wicked people who suppress the truth by their wickedness.*
¹⁹ They know the truth about God because
he has made it obvious to them. ²⁰ For ever
since the world was created, people have
seen the earth and sky. Through everything God made, they can clearly see his
invisible qualities—his eternal power and
divine nature. So they have no excuse for
not knowing God.

²¹ Yes, they knew God, but they wouldn't
worship him as God or even give him
thanks. And they began to think up foolish ideas of what God was like. As a result,
their minds became dark and confused.
²² Claiming to be wise, they instead be-
came utter fools. ²³ And instead of worshiping the glorious, ever-living God,
they worshiped idols made to look like
mere people and birds and animals and
reptiles.

²⁴ So God abandoned them to do
whatever shameful things their hearts
desired. As a result, they did vile and degrading things with each other's bodies.
²⁵ They traded the truth about God for a
lie. So they worshiped and served the
things God created instead of the Creator
himself, who is worthy of eternal praise!
Amen. ²⁶ That is why God abandoned
them to their shameful desires. Even the
women turned against the natural way to
have sex and instead indulged in sex with
each other. ²⁷ And the men, instead of having normal sexual relations with women,
burned with lust for each other. Men did
shameful things with other men, and as a
result of this sin, they suffered within
themselves the penalty they deserved.

²⁸ Since they thought it foolish to ac-
knowledge God, he abandoned them to
their foolish thinking and let them do
things that should never be done. ²⁹ Their

lives became full of every kind of wickedness, sin, greed, hate, envy, murder, quarreling, deception, malicious behavior, and gossip. [30]They are backstabbers, haters of God, insolent, proud, and boastful. They invent new ways of sinning, and they disobey their parents. [31]They refuse to understand, break their promises, are heartless, and have no mercy. [32]They know God's justice requires that those who do these things deserve to die, yet they do them anyway. Worse yet, they encourage others to do them, too.

1:18 Or *who, by their wickedness, prevent the truth from being known.*

PSALM 10:1-15

O LORD, why do you stand so far away?
　　Why do you hide when I am
　　　in trouble?
[2] The wicked arrogantly hunt down
　　　the poor.
　　Let them be caught in the evil they
　　　plan for others.
[3] For they brag about their evil desires;
　　they praise the greedy and curse
　　　the LORD.
[4] The wicked are too proud to seek God.
　　They seem to think that God
　　　is dead.
[5] Yet they succeed in everything
　　they do.
　　They do not see your punishment
　　　awaiting them.
　　They sneer at all their enemies.
[6] They think, "Nothing bad will ever
　　　happen to us!
　　We will be free of trouble forever!"
[7] Their mouths are full of cursing, lies,
　　and threats.*
　　Trouble and evil are on the tips
　　　of their tongues.

[8] They lurk in ambush in the villages,
　　waiting to murder innocent people.
　　They are always searching for
　　　helpless victims.
[9] Like lions crouched in hiding,
　　they wait to pounce on the helpless.
　　Like hunters they capture the helpless
　　and drag them away in nets.
[10] Their helpless victims are crushed;
　　they fall beneath the strength
　　　of the wicked.
[11] The wicked think, "God isn't watching
　　　us!
　　He has closed his eyes and won't
　　　even see what we do!"

[12] Arise, O LORD!
　　Punish the wicked, O God!
　　Do not ignore the helpless!
[13] Why do the wicked get away with
　　　despising God?
　　They think, "God will never call us
　　　to account."
[14] But you see the trouble and grief they
　　　cause.
　　You take note of it and punish
　　　them.
　　The helpless put their trust in you.
　　You defend the orphans.

[15] Break the arms of these wicked,
　　　evil people!
　　Go after them until the last one
　　　is destroyed.

10:7 Greek version reads *cursing and bitterness.* Compare Rom 3:14.

PROVERBS 19:6-7

Many seek favors from a ruler; everyone is the friend of a person who gives gifts! □ The relatives of the poor despise them; how much more will their friends avoid them! Though the poor plead with them, their friends are gone.

1 CHRONICLES 16:37–18:17
Today's reading includes a promise and prophecy from God to David. While this prophecy included David's son, Solomon, who would build the great

JULY**14**

Temple in Jerusalem, it was about much more than that. The promise of an eternal Kingdom actually would be fulfilled in Jesus, a descendant of David.

David arranged for Asaph and his fellow Levites to serve regularly before the Ark of the LORD's Covenant, doing whatever needed to be done each day. ³⁸This group included Obed-edom (son of Jeduthun), Hosah, and sixty-eight other Levites as gatekeepers.

³⁹Meanwhile, David stationed Zadok the priest and his fellow priests at the Tabernacle of the LORD at the place of worship in Gibeon, where they continued to minister before the LORD. ⁴⁰They sacrificed the regular burnt offerings to the LORD each morning and evening on the altar set aside for that purpose, obeying everything written in the Law of the LORD, as he had commanded Israel. ⁴¹David also appointed Heman, Jeduthun, and the others chosen by name to give thanks to the LORD, for "his faithful love endures forever." ⁴²They used their trumpets, cymbals, and other instruments to accompany their songs of praise to God.* And the sons of Jeduthun were appointed as gatekeepers.

⁴³Then all the people returned to their homes, and David turned and went home to bless his own family.

¹⁷:¹WHEN David was settled in his palace, he summoned Nathan the prophet. "Look," David said, "I am living in a beautiful cedar palace,* but the Ark of the LORD's Covenant is out there under a tent!"

²Nathan replied to David, "Do whatever you have in mind, for God is with you."

³But that same night God said to Nathan,

⁴"Go and tell my servant David, 'This is what the LORD has declared: You are not the one to build a house for me to live in. ⁵I have never lived in a house, from the day I brought the Israelites out of Egypt until this very day. My home has always been a tent, moving from one place to another in a Tabernacle. ⁶Yet no matter where I have gone with the Israelites, I have never once complained to Israel's leaders,* the shepherds of my people. I have never asked them, "Why haven't you built me a beautiful cedar house?"'

⁷"Now go and say to my servant David, 'This is what the LORD of Heaven's Armies has declared: I took you from tending sheep in the pasture and selected you to be the leader of my people Israel. ⁸I have been with you wherever you have gone, and I have destroyed all your enemies before your eyes. Now I will make your name as famous as anyone who has ever lived on the earth! ⁹And I will provide a homeland for my people Israel, planting them in a secure place where they will never be disturbed. Evil nations won't oppress them as they've done in the past, ¹⁰starting from the time I appointed judges to rule my people Israel. And I will defeat all your enemies

"'Furthermore, I declare that the LORD will build a house for you— a dynasty of kings! ¹¹For when you die and join your ancestors, I will raise up one of your descendants, one of your sons, and I will make his kingdom strong. ¹²He is the one who will build a house—a temple—for me. And I will secure his throne forever. ¹³I will be his father, and he will be my son. I will never take my favor from him as I took it from the one who ruled before you. ¹⁴I will confirm him as king over my house and my kingdom for all time, and his throne will be secure forever.'"

¹⁵So Nathan went back to David and told him everything the LORD had said in this vision.

¹⁶Then King David went in and sat before the LORD and prayed,

"Who am I, O LORD God, and what is my family, that you have brought me this far? ¹⁷And now, O God, in addition to everything else, you speak of giving your servant a lasting dynasty! You speak as though I were someone very great,* O LORD God!

¹⁸"What more can I say to you about the way you have honored me? You know what your servant is really like. ¹⁹For the sake of your servant, O LORD, and according to your will, you have done all these great things and have made them known.

²⁰"O LORD, there is no one like you. We have never even heard of another

God like you! [21]What other nation on earth is like your people Israel? What other nation, O God, have you redeemed from slavery to be your own people? You made a great name for yourself when you redeemed your people from Egypt. You performed awesome miracles and drove out the nations that stood in their way. [22]You chose Israel to be your very own people forever, and you, O LORD, became their God.

[23]"And now, O LORD, I am your servant; do as you have promised concerning me and my family. May it be a promise that will last forever. [24]And may your name be established and honored forever so that everyone will say, 'The LORD of Heaven's Armies, the God of Israel, is Israel's God!' And may the house of your servant David continue before you forever.

[25]"O my God, I have been bold enough to pray to you because you have revealed to your servant that you will build a house for him—a dynasty of kings! [26]For you are God, O LORD. And you have promised these good things to your servant. [27]And now, it has pleased you to bless the house of your servant, so that it will continue forever before you. For when you grant a blessing, O LORD, it is an eternal blessing!"

[18:1]AFTER this, David defeated and subdued the Philistines by conquering Gath and its surrounding towns. [2]David also conquered the land of Moab, and the Moabites who were spared became David's subjects and paid him tribute money.

[3]David also destroyed the forces of Hadadezer, king of Zobah, as far as Hamath,* when Hadadezer marched out to strengthen his control along the Euphrates River. [4]David captured 1,000 chariots, 7,000 charioteers, and 20,000 foot soldiers. He crippled all the chariot horses except enough for 100 chariots.

[5]When Arameans from Damascus arrived to help King Hadadezer, David killed 22,000 of them. [6]Then he placed several army garrisons* in Damascus, the Aramean capital, and the Arameans became David's subjects and paid him tribute money. So the LORD made David victorious wherever he went.

[7]David brought the gold shields of Hadadezer's officers to Jerusalem, [8]along with a large amount of bronze from Hadadezer's towns of Tebah* and Cun. Later Solomon melted the bronze and molded

WHAT THE BIBLE SAYS

The covenants of the Bible

1 CHRONICLES 17 The first covenant in the Bible was with Noah after the Flood. God gave him a reassuring promise that never again would a flood destroy the earth. The rainbow is a continuing sign of this covenant (Genesis 9:8-17, January 4). • Another covenant was given to Abraham, telling him that he would found a great nation and that the other nations of the earth would be blessed through Abraham's descendants. Through Abraham's family tree, Jesus Christ was born to save humanity (Genesis 12:1-3, January 5). • At Mount Sinai, God made a covenant with the Hebrew people promising to bless and care for them if they obeyed him. The people did not keep their part of the bargain, but God kept his (Exodus 19:5-8, February 3) • In the covenant with David, God promised to carry on David's line and kingdom forever. This was fulfilled in the birth of Jesus, whose reign will go on for eternity (2 Samuel 7:8-16, May 25). • Jesus said that he came to bring a new covenant in his blood (Luke 22:20, April 24). People under the old covenant (those who lived before Jesus) could approach God only through a priest and an animal sacrifice. Now all people can come directly to God through faith because Jesus' death has made those who believe acceptable in God's eyes.

it into the great bronze basin called the Sea, the pillars, and the various bronze articles used at the Temple.

⁹When King Toi* of Hamath heard that David had destroyed the entire army of King Hadadezer of Zobah, ¹⁰he sent his son Joram* to congratulate King David for his successful campaign. Hadadezer and Toi had been enemies and were often at war. Joram presented David with many gifts of gold, silver, and bronze.

¹¹King David dedicated all these gifts to the LORD, along with the silver and gold he had taken from the other nations—from Edom, Moab, Ammon, Philistia, and Amalek.

¹²Abishai son of Zeruiah destroyed 18,000 Edomites in the Valley of Salt. ¹³He placed army garrisons in Edom, and all the Edomites became David's subjects. In fact, the LORD made David victorious wherever he went.

¹⁴So David reigned over all Israel and did what was just and right for all his people. ¹⁵Joab son of Zeruiah was commander of the army. Jehoshaphat son of Ahilud was the royal historian. ¹⁶Zadok son of Ahitub and Ahimelech* son of Abiathar were the priests. Seraiah* was the court secretary. ¹⁷Benaiah son of Jehoiada was captain of the king's bodyguard.* And David's sons served as the king's chief assistants.

16:42 Or *to accompany the sacred music;* or *to accompany singing to God.* **17:1** Hebrew *a house of cedar.* **17:6** As in Greek version (see also 2 Sam 7:7); Hebrew reads *judges.* **17:17** The meaning of the Hebrew is uncertain. **18:3** The meaning of the Hebrew is uncertain. **18:6** As in Greek version and Latin Vulgate (see also 2 Sam 8:6); Hebrew lacks *several army garrisons.* **18:8** Hebrew reads *Tibhath,* a variant spelling of Tebah; compare parallel text at 2 Sam 8:8. **18:9** As in parallel text at 2 Sam 8:9; Hebrew reads *Tou;* also in 18:10. **18:10** As in parallel text at 2 Sam 8:10; Hebrew reads *Hadoram,* a variant spelling of Joram. **18:16a** As in some Hebrew manuscripts, Syriac version, and Latin Vulgate (see also 2 Sam 8:17); most Hebrew manuscripts read *Abimelech.* **18:16b** As in parallel text at 2 Sam 8:17; Hebrew reads *Shavsha.* **18:17** Hebrew *of the Kerethites and Pelethites.*

ROMANS 2:1-24

Do some of us get off the hook because we only dabble in the least destructive of behaviors (at least by our own definitions)? Do our religious traditions protect us from full accountability for our actions? Paul does not hesitate to answer, "No."

You may think you can condemn such people, but you are just as bad, and you have no excuse! When you say they are wicked and should be punished, you are condemning yourself, for you who judge others do these very same things. ²And we know that God, in his justice, will punish anyone who does such things. ³Since you judge others for doing these things, why do you think you can avoid God's judgment when you do the same things? ⁴Don't you see how wonderfully kind, tolerant, and patient God is with you? Does this mean nothing to you? Can't you see that his kindness is intended to turn you from your sin?

⁵But because you are stubborn and refuse to turn from your sin, you are storing up terrible punishment for yourself. For a day of anger is coming, when God's righteous judgment will be revealed. ⁶He will judge everyone according to what they have done. ⁷He will give eternal life to those who keep on doing good, seeking after the glory and honor and immortality that God offers. ⁸But he will pour out his anger and wrath on those who live for themselves, who refuse to obey the truth and instead live lives of wickedness. ⁹There will be trouble and calamity for everyone who keeps on doing what is evil—for the Jew first and also for the Gentile.* ¹⁰But there will be glory and honor and peace from God for all who do good—for the Jew first and also for the Gentile. ¹¹For God does not show favoritism.

¹²When the Gentiles sin, they will be destroyed, even though they never had God's written law. And the Jews, who do have God's law, will be judged by that law when they fail to obey it. ¹³For merely listening to the law doesn't make us right with God. It is obeying the law that makes us right in his sight. ¹⁴Even Gentiles, who do not have God's written law, show that they know his law when they instinctively obey it, even without having heard it. ¹⁵They demonstrate that God's law is written in their hearts, for their own conscience and thoughts either accuse them or tell them they are doing right. ¹⁶And this is the message I proclaim—that the day is coming when God, through Christ Jesus, will judge everyone's secret life.

¹⁷You who call yourselves Jews are relying on God's law, and you boast about your

special relationship with him. [18]You know what he wants; you know what is right because you have been taught his law. [19]You are convinced that you are a guide for the blind and a light for people who are lost in darkness. [20]You think you can instruct the ignorant and teach children the ways of God. For you are certain that God's law gives you complete knowledge and truth.

[21]Well then, if you teach others, why don't you teach yourself? You tell others not to steal, but do you steal? [22]You say it is wrong to commit adultery, but do you commit adultery? You condemn idolatry, but do you use items stolen from pagan temples?* [23]You are so proud of knowing the law, but you dishonor God by breaking it. [24]No wonder the Scriptures say, "The Gentiles blaspheme the name of God because of you."*

2:9 Greek *also for the Greek;* also in 2:10.

2:22 Greek *do you steal from temples?*   2:24 Isa 52:5 (Greek version).

PSALM 10:16-18

[16]The LORD is king forever and ever!
   The godless nations will vanish
      from the land.
[17] LORD, you know the hopes of the
      helpless.
   Surely you will hear their cries and
      comfort them.
[18] You will bring justice to the orphans
      and the oppressed,
   so mere people can no longer
      terrify them.

PROVERBS 19:8-9

[8]To acquire wisdom is to love oneself; people who cherish understanding will prosper. □A false witness will not go unpunished, and a liar will be destroyed.

JULY**15**

1 CHRONICLES 19:1–21:30

In today's reading, David sins by taking a census. Census-taking was not sinful in itself. In this case, however, David's motive was likely pride or a desire to revel in his military strength. For whatever reason, God was not pleased, and the people suffered because of their leader's actions.

[1]Some time after this, King Nahash of the Ammonites died, and his son Hanun* became king. [2]David said, "I am going to show loyalty to Hanun because his father, Nahash, was always loyal to me." So David sent messengers to express sympathy to Hanun about his father's death.

But when David's ambassadors arrived in the land of Ammon, [3]the Ammonite commanders said to Hanun, "Do you really think these men are coming here to honor your father? No! David has sent them to spy out the land so they can come in and conquer it!" [4]So Hanun seized David's ambassadors and shaved them, cut off their robes at the buttocks, and sent them back to David in shame.

[5]When David heard what had happened to the men, he sent messengers to tell them, "Stay at Jericho until your beards grow out, and then come back." For they felt deep shame because of their appearance.

[6]When the people of Ammon realized how seriously they had angered David, Hanun and the Ammonites sent 75,000 pounds* of silver to hire chariots and charioteers from Aram-naharaim, Aram-maacah, and Zobah. [7]They also hired 32,000 chariots and secured the support of the king of Maacah and his army. These forces camped at Medeba, where they were joined by the Ammonite troops that Hanun had recruited from his own towns. [8]When David heard about this, he sent Joab and all his warriors to fight them. [9]The Ammonite troops came out and drew up their battle lines at the entrance of the city, while the other kings positioned themselves to fight in the open fields.

¹⁰When Joab saw that he would have to fight on both the front and the rear, he chose some of Israel's elite troops and placed them under his personal command to fight the Arameans in the fields. ¹¹He left the rest of the army under the command of his brother Abishai, who was to attack the Ammonites. ¹²"If the Arameans are too strong for me, then come over and help me," Joab told his brother. "And if the Ammonites are too strong for you, I will help you. ¹³Be courageous! Let us fight bravely for our people and the cities of our God. May the LORD's will be done."

¹⁴When Joab and his troops attacked, the Arameans began to run away. ¹⁵And when the Ammonites saw the Arameans running, they also ran from Abishai and retreated into the city. Then Joab returned to Jerusalem.

¹⁶The Arameans now realized that they were no match for Israel, so they sent messengers and summoned additional Aramean troops from the other side of the Euphrates River.* These troops were under the command of Shobach,* the commander of Hadadezer's forces.

¹⁷When David heard what was happening, he mobilized all Israel, crossed the Jordan River, and positioned his troops in battle formation. Then David engaged the Arameans in battle, and they fought against him. ¹⁸But again the Arameans fled from the Israelites. This time David's forces killed 7,000 charioteers and 40,000 foot soldiers, including Shobach, the commander of their army. ¹⁹When Hadadezer's allies saw that they had been defeated by Israel, they surrendered to David and became his subjects. After that, the Arameans were no longer willing to help the Ammonites.

²⁰:¹In the spring of the year,* when kings normally go out to war, Joab led the Israelite army in successful attacks against the land of the Ammonites. In the process he laid siege to the city of Rabbah. However, David stayed behind in Jerusalem.

²When David arrived at Rabbah, he removed the crown from the king's head,* and it was placed on his own head. The crown was made of gold and set with gems, and he found that it weighed seventy-five pounds.* David took a vast amount of plunder from the city. ³He also made slaves of the people of Rabbah and forced them to labor with* saws, iron picks, and iron axes.* That is how David dealt with the people of all the Ammonite towns. Then David and all the army returned to Jerusalem.

⁴After this, war broke out with the Philistines at Gezer. As they fought, Sibbecai from Hushah killed Saph,* a descendant of the giants,* and so the Philistines were subdued.

⁵During another battle with the Philistines, Elhanan son of Jair killed Lahmi, the brother of Goliath of Gath. The handle of Lahmi's spear was as thick as a weaver's beam!

⁶In another battle with the Philistines at Gath, they encountered a huge man with six fingers on each hand and six toes on each foot, twenty-four in all, who was also a descendant of the giants. ⁷But when he defied and taunted Israel, he was killed by Jonathan, the son of David's brother Shimea.

⁸These Philistines were descendants of the giants of Gath, but David and his warriors killed them.

²¹:¹Satan rose up against Israel and caused David to take a census of the people of Israel. ²So David said to Joab and the commanders of the army, "Take a census of all the people of Israel—from Beersheba in the south to Dan in the north—and bring me a report so I may know how many there are."

³But Joab replied, "May the LORD increase the number of his people a hundred times over! But why, my lord the king, do you want to do this? Are they not all your servants? Why must you cause Israel to sin?"

⁴But the king insisted that they take the census, so Joab traveled throughout all Israel to count the people. Then he returned to Jerusalem ⁵and reported the number of people to David. There were 1,100,000 warriors in all Israel who could handle a sword, and 470,000 in Judah. ⁶But Joab did not include the tribes of Levi and Benjamin in the census be-

cause he was so distressed at what the king had made him do.

[7] God was very displeased with the census, and he punished Israel for it. [8] Then David said to God, "I have sinned greatly by taking this census. Please forgive my guilt for doing this foolish thing."

[9] Then the LORD spoke to Gad, David's seer. This was the message: [10] "Go and say to David, 'This is what the LORD says: I will give you three choices. Choose one of these punishments, and I will inflict it on you.'"

[11] So Gad came to David and said, "These are the choices the LORD has given you. [12] You may choose three years of famine, three months of destruction by the sword of your enemies, or three days of severe plague as the angel of the LORD brings devastation throughout the land of Israel. Decide what answer I should give the LORD who sent me."

[13] "I'm in a desperate situation!" David replied to Gad. "But let me fall into the hands of the LORD, for his mercy is very great. Do not let me fall into human hands."

[14] So the LORD sent a plague upon Israel, and 70,000 people died as a result. [15] And God sent an angel to destroy Jerusalem. But just as the angel was preparing to destroy it, the LORD relented and said to the death angel, "Stop! That is enough!" At that moment the angel of the LORD was standing by the threshing floor of Araunah* the Jebusite.

[16] David looked up and saw the angel of the LORD standing between heaven and earth with his sword drawn, reaching out over Jerusalem. So David and the leaders of Israel put on burlap to show their deep distress and fell face down on the ground. [17] And David said to God, "I am the one who called for the census! I am the one who has sinned and done wrong! But these people are as innocent as sheep— what have they done? O LORD my God, let your anger fall against me and my family, but do not destroy your people."

[18] Then the angel of the LORD told Gad to instruct David to go up and build an altar to the LORD on the threshing floor of Araunah the Jebusite. [19] So David went up to do what the LORD had commanded him through Gad. [20] Araunah, who was busy threshing wheat at the time, turned and saw the angel there. His four sons, who were with him, ran away and hid. [21] When Araunah saw David approaching, he left his threshing floor and bowed before David with his face to the ground.

[22] David said to Araunah, "Let me buy this threshing floor from you at its full price. Then I will build an altar to the LORD there, so that he will stop the plague."

HOW WE LIVE

Our giving

1 CHRONICLES 21:18-27 When David offered to purchase Araunah's threshing floor to build an altar, Araunah graciously offered it free of charge. But David insisted upon paying for it. David understood that he would not truly be worshiping the Lord if building the altar for sacrifice cost him nothing. So he paid 600 pieces of gold—no small change, even for a king. Because David loved God, he did what God told him to do. His worship was not just show; it was from his heart and from his pocketbook. • What about you? Do you worship God sacrificially from the heart? There are many ways to give of our resources to God, and each of us may "sacrifice" in different ways. We should never judge others because we think they aren't giving enough—they may be giving in ways we can't see. You can give of your time to teach a Sunday school class or volunteer at a homeless shelter. You can give by praying for others' needs. You can give money. Whatever your method of giving may be, it should mean something to you, it should be done joyfully, and it should benefit God's Kingdom.

23"Take it, my lord the king, and use it as you wish," Araunah said to David. "I will give the oxen for the burnt offerings, and the threshing boards for wood to build a fire on the altar, and the wheat for the grain offering. I will give it all to you." 24But King David replied to Araunah, "No, I insist on buying it for the full price. I will not take what is yours and give it to the LORD. I will not present burnt offerings that have cost me nothing!" 25So David gave Araunah 600 pieces of gold* in payment for the threshing floor.

26David built an altar there to the LORD and sacrificed burnt offerings and peace offerings. And when David prayed, the LORD answered him by sending fire from heaven to burn up the offering on the altar. 27Then the LORD spoke to the angel, who put the sword back into its sheath.

28When David saw that the LORD had answered his prayer, he offered sacrifices there at Araunah's threshing floor. 29At that time the Tabernacle of the LORD and the altar of burnt offering that Moses had made in the wilderness were located at the place of worship in Gibeon. 30But David was not able to go there to inquire of God, because he was terrified by the drawn sword of the angel of the LORD.

19:1 As in parallel text at 2 Sam 10:1; Hebrew lacks *Hanun.* 19:6 Hebrew *1,000 talents* [34,000 kilograms]. 19:16a Hebrew *the river.* 19:16b As in parallel text at 2 Sam 10:16; Hebrew reads *Shophach;* also in 19:18. 20:1 Hebrew *At the turn of the year.* The first day of the year in the ancient Hebrew lunar calendar occurred in March or April. 20:2a Or *from the head of Milcom* (as in Greek version and Latin Vulgate). Milcom, also called Molech, was the god of the Ammonites. 20:2b Hebrew *1 talent* [34 kilograms]. 20:3a Or *He also brought out the people of Rabbah and cut them with.* 20:3b As in parallel text at 2 Sam 12:31; Hebrew reads *and saws.* 20:4a As in parallel text at 2 Sam 21:18; Hebrew reads *Sippai.* 20:4b Hebrew *descendant of the Rephaites;* also in 20:6, 8. 21:15 As in parallel text at 2 Sam 24:16; Hebrew reads *Ornan,* another name for Araunah; also in 21:18-28. 21:25 Hebrew *600 shekels of gold,* about 15 pounds or 6.8 kilograms in weight.

ROMANS 2:25–3:8
Christianity began as a primarily Jewish movement. As the Good News spread to the nations, however, conflict grew regarding whether a person needed to become a Jew first in order to become a Christian. Paul was very clear that the answer is no.

The Jewish ceremony of circumcision has value only if you obey God's law. But if you don't obey God's law, you are no better off than an uncircumcised Gentile. 26And if the Gentiles obey God's law, won't God declare them to be his own people? 27In fact, uncircumcised Gentiles who keep God's law will condemn you Jews who are circumcised and possess God's law but don't obey it.

28For you are not a true Jew just because you were born of Jewish parents or because you have gone through the ceremony of circumcision. 29No, a true Jew is one whose heart is right with God. And true circumcision is not merely obeying the letter of the law; rather, it is a change of heart produced by God's Spirit. And a person with a changed heart seeks praise* from God, not from people.

3:1THEN what's the advantage of being a Jew? Is there any value in the ceremony of circumcision? 2Yes, there are great benefits! First of all, the Jews were entrusted with the whole revelation of God.*

3True, some of them were unfaithful; but just because they were unfaithful, does that mean God will be unfaithful? 4Of course not! Even if everyone else is a liar, God is true. As the Scriptures say about him,

"You will be proved right in what you
     say,
     and you will win your case in court."*

5"But," some might say, "our sinfulness serves a good purpose, for it helps people see how righteous God is. Isn't it unfair, then, for him to punish us?" (This is merely a human point of view.) 6Of course not! If God were not entirely fair, how would he be qualified to judge the world? 7"But," someone might still argue, "how can God condemn me as a sinner if my dishonesty highlights his truthfulness and brings him more glory?" 8And some people even slander us by claiming that we say, "The more we sin, the better it is!" Those who say such things deserve to be condemned.

2:29 Or *receives praise.* 3:2 Greek *the oracles of God.* 3:4 Ps 51:4 (Greek version).

PSALM 11:1-7
For the choir director: A psalm of David.

1 **I** trust in the LORD for protection.
     So why do you say to me,

"Fly like a bird to the mountains
for safety!
² The wicked are stringing their bows
and fitting their arrows on the
bowstrings.
They shoot from the shadows
at those whose hearts are right.
³ The foundations of law and order
have collapsed.
What can the righteous do?"

⁴ But the LORD is in his holy Temple;
the LORD still rules from heaven.
He watches everyone closely,
examining every person on earth.
⁵ The LORD examines both the
righteous and the wicked.

He hates those who love
violence.
⁶ He will rain down blazing coals and
burning sulfur on the wicked,
punishing them with scorching
winds.
⁷ For the righteous LORD loves justice.
The virtuous will see his face.

PROVERBS 19:10-12

It isn't right for a fool to live in luxury or
for a slave to rule over princes! ☐ Sensible
people control their temper; they earn respect by overlooking wrongs. ☐ The king's
anger is like a lion's roar, but his favor is
like dew on the grass.

JULY**16**

1 CHRONICLES 22:1–23:32

While David did not build the Temple in Jerusalem,
he did make preparations for it. He collected materials and craftsmen. He even began training the
Levites to run the Temple—a permanent structure
as opposed to the portable Tabernacle the Levites
were accustomed to maintaining.

Then David said, "This will be the location
for the Temple of the LORD God and the
place of the altar for Israel's burnt offerings!"
²So David gave orders to call together
the foreigners living in Israel, and he assigned them the task of preparing finished stone for building the Temple of
God. ³David provided large amounts of
iron for the nails that would be needed for
the doors in the gates and for the clamps,
and he gave more bronze than could be
weighed. ⁴He also provided innumerable
cedar logs, for the men of Tyre and Sidon
had brought vast amounts of cedar to
David.
⁵David said, "My son Solomon is still
young and inexperienced. And since the
Temple to be built for the LORD must be
a magnificent structure, famous and
glorious throughout the world, I will be-

gin making preparations for it now." So
David collected vast amounts of building
materials before his death.
⁶Then David sent for his son Solomon
and instructed him to build a Temple for
the LORD, the God of Israel. ⁷"My son, I
wanted to build a Temple to honor the
name of the LORD my God," David told
him. ⁸"But the LORD said to me, 'You have
killed many men in the battles you have
fought. And since you have shed so much
blood in my sight, you will not be the one
to build a Temple to honor my name. ⁹But
you will have a son who will be a man of
peace. I will give him peace with his enemies in all the surrounding lands. His
name will be Solomon,* and I will give
peace and quiet to Israel during his reign.
¹⁰He is the one who will build a Temple to
honor my name. He will be my son, and I
will be his father. And I will secure the
throne of his kingdom over Israel forever.'
¹¹"Now, my son, may the LORD be with
you and give you success as you follow his
directions in building the Temple of the
LORD your God. ¹²And may the LORD give
you wisdom and understanding, that you
may obey the Law of the LORD your God as

you rule over Israel. [13]For you will be successful if you carefully obey the decrees and regulations that the LORD gave to Israel through Moses. Be strong and courageous; do not be afraid or lose heart!

[14]"I have worked hard to provide materials for building the Temple of the LORD—nearly 4,000 tons of gold, 40,000 tons of silver,* and so much iron and bronze that it cannot be weighed. I have also gathered timber and stone for the walls, though you may need to add more. [15]You have a large number of skilled stonemasons and carpenters and craftsmen of every kind. [16]You have expert goldsmiths and silversmiths and workers of bronze and iron. Now begin the work, and may the LORD be with you!"

[17]Then David ordered all the leaders of Israel to assist Solomon in this project. [18]"The LORD your God is with you," he declared. "He has given you peace with the surrounding nations. He has handed them over to me, and they are now subject to the LORD and his people. [19]Now seek the LORD your God with all your heart and soul. Build the sanctuary of the LORD God so that you can bring the Ark of the LORD's Covenant and the holy vessels of God into the Temple built to honor the LORD's name."

[23:1]WHEN David was an old man, he appointed his son Solomon to be king over Israel. [2]David summoned all the leaders of Israel, together with the priests and Levites. [3]All the Levites who were thirty years old or older were counted, and the total came to 38,000. [4]Then David said, "From all the Levites, 24,000 will supervise the work at the Temple of the LORD. Another 6,000 will serve as officials and judges. [5]Another 4,000 will work as gatekeepers, and 4,000 will praise the LORD with the musical instruments I have made." [6]Then David divided the Levites into divisions named after the clans descended from the three sons of Levi—Gershon, Kohath, and Merari.

[7]The Gershonite family units were defined by their lines of descent from Libni* and Shimei, the sons of Gershon. [8]Three of the descendants of Libni were Jehiel (the family leader), Zetham, and Joel. [9]These were the leaders of the family of Libni.

Three of the descendants of Shimei were Shelomoth, Haziel, and Haran. [10]Four other descendants of Shimei were Jahath, Ziza,* Jeush, and Beriah. [11]Jahath was the family leader, and Ziza was next. Jeush and Beriah were counted as a single family because neither had many sons.

[12]Four of the descendants of Kohath were Amram, Izhar, Hebron, and Uzziel.

[13]The sons of Amram were Aaron and Moses. Aaron and his descendants were set apart to dedicate the most holy things, to offer sacrifices in the LORD's presence, to serve the LORD, and to pronounce blessings in his name forever.

[14]As for Moses, the man of God, his sons were included with the tribe of Levi. [15]The sons of Moses were Gershom and Eliezer. [16]The descendants of Gershom included Shebuel, the family leader. [17]Eliezer had only one son, Rehabiah, the family leader. Rehabiah had numerous descendants.

[18]The descendants of Izhar included Shelomith, the family leader.

[19]The descendants of Hebron included Jeriah (the family leader), Amariah (the second), Jahaziel (the third), and Jekameam (the fourth).

[20]The descendants of Uzziel included Micah (the family leader) and Isshiah (the second).

[21]The descendants of Merari included Mahli and Mushi.

The sons of Mahli were Eleazar and Kish. [22]Eleazar died with no sons, only daughters. His daughters married their cousins, the sons of Kish.

[23]Three of the descendants of Mushi were Mahli, Eder, and Jerimoth.

[24]These were the descendants of Levi by clans, the leaders of their family groups, registered carefully by name. Each had to be twenty years old or older to qualify for service in the house of the LORD. [25]For David said, "The LORD, the God of Is-

rael, has given us peace, and he will always live in Jerusalem. ²⁶Now the Levites will no longer need to carry the Tabernacle and its furnishings from place to place." ²⁷In accordance with David's final instructions, all the Levites twenty years old or older were registered for service.

²⁸The work of the Levites was to assist the priests, the descendants of Aaron, as they served at the house of the LORD. They also took care of the courtyards and side rooms, helped perform the ceremonies of purification, and served in many other ways in the house of God. ²⁹They were in charge of the sacred bread that was set out on the table, the choice flour for the grain offerings, the wafers made without yeast, the cakes cooked in olive oil, and the other mixed breads. They were also responsible to check all the weights and measures. ³⁰And each morning and evening they stood before the LORD to sing songs of thanks and praise to him. ³¹They assisted with the burnt offerings that were presented to the LORD on Sabbath days, at new moon celebrations, and at all the appointed festivals. The required number of Levites served in the LORD's presence at all times, following all the procedures they had been given.

³²And so, under the supervision of the priests, the Levites watched over the Tabernacle and the Temple* and faithfully carried out their duties of service at the house of the LORD.

ROMANS 3:9-31
Although Paul denied that Gentiles needed to become Jews in order to be saved, he did not disregard the continuing value of the Old Testament. In this passage he quotes the Old Testament repeatedly to show humanity's need for salvation and how Christ's atonement meets that need.

Well then, should we conclude that we Jews are better than others? No, not at all, for we have already shown that all people, whether Jews or Gentiles,* are under the power of sin. ¹⁰As the Scriptures say,

"No one is righteous—
    not even one.
¹¹ No one is truly wise;
    no one is seeking God.
¹² All have turned away;
    all have become useless.
No one does good,
    not a single one."*
¹³ "Their talk is foul, like the stench from
    an open grave.
    Their tongues are filled with lies."
"Snake venom drips from their lips."*

WHAT THE BIBLE SAYS
Why we need a Savior

ROMANS 3:10, 20, 23 Paul uses Old Testament references to show that humanity in general, in its present sinful condition, is unacceptable before God. Some people think they're not too bad, that they're pretty good people. Unfortunately, no one is good enough to be saved. In thought, word, and deed, everyone in the world stands guilty before God. •A holy God cannot have anything to do with sin. That means that God couldn't have anything to do with us sinful people; therefore, we were completely alienated from him. You know what the really good news is? God came after us. He put on human form (without sin) and came to earth in order to die for us. Sin required punishment. God couldn't change that fact, but he could take the punishment himself. •We need a Savior because we cannot save ourselves. There is no way to get to heaven without him. Thank God for Jesus, your Savior, who has made you right with God and given you eternity with him. What a blessing that he loves us that much!

14   "Their mouths are full of cursing
       and bitterness."*
15 "They rush to commit murder.
16   Destruction and misery always
       follow them.
17 They don't know where to find
       peace."*
18   "They have no fear of God at all."*

19 Obviously, the law applies to those to
whom it was given, for its purpose is to
keep people from having excuses, and
to show that the entire world is guilty before God. 20 For no one can ever be made
right with God by doing what the law
commands. The law simply shows us how
sinful we are.

21 But now God has shown us a way to
be made right with him without keeping
the requirements of the law, as was promised in the writings of Moses* and the
prophets long ago. 22 We are made right
with God by placing our faith in Jesus
Christ. And this is true for everyone who
believes, no matter who we are.

23 For everyone has sinned; we all fall
short of God's glorious standard. 24 Yet
God, with undeserved kindness, declares
that we are righteous. He did this through
Christ Jesus when he freed us from the
penalty for our sins. 25 For God presented
Jesus as the sacrifice for sin. People are
made right with God when they believe
that Jesus sacrificed his life, shedding his
blood. This sacrifice shows that God was
being fair when he held back and did not
punish those who sinned in times past,
26 for he was looking ahead and including
them in what he would do in this present
time. God did this to demonstrate his
righteousness, for he himself is fair and
just, and he declares sinners to be right in
his sight when they believe in Jesus.

27 Can we boast, then, that we have done
anything to be accepted by God? No, because our acquittal is not based on obeying the law. It is based on faith. 28 So we are
made right with God through faith and
not by obeying the law.

29 After all, is God the God of the Jews
only? Isn't he also the God of the Gentiles?
Of course he is. 30 There is only one God,
and he makes people right with himself
only by faith, whether they are Jews or Gen-

tiles.* 31 Well then, if we emphasize faith,
does this mean that we can forget about
the law? Of course not! In fact, only when
we have faith do we truly fulfill the law.

3:9 Greek *or Greeks.* **3:10-12** Pss 14:1-3; 53:1-3 (Greek
version). **3:13** Pss 5:9 (Greek version); 140:3. **3:14** Ps
10:7 (Greek version). **3:15-17** Isa 59:7-8. **3:18** Ps 36:1.
3:21 Greek *in the law.* **3:30** Greek *whether they are
circumcised or uncircumcised.*

PSALM 12:1-8
*For the choir director: A psalm of David,
to be accompanied by an eight-stringed
instrument.*

1 **H**elp, O Lord, for the godly are fast
       disappearing!
     The faithful have vanished from
       the earth!
2 Neighbors lie to each other,
     speaking with flattering lips and
       deceitful hearts.
3 May the Lord cut off their flattering
       lips
     and silence their boastful tongues.
4 They say, "We will lie to our hearts'
       content.
     Our lips are our own—who can stop
       us?"
5 The Lord replies, "I have seen
       violence done to the helpless,
     and I have heard the groans of the
       poor.
     Now I will rise up to rescue them,
       as they have longed for me to do."
6 The Lord's promises are pure,
     like silver refined in a furnace,
       purified seven times over.
7 Therefore, Lord, we know you will
       protect the oppressed,
     preserving them forever from this
       lying generation,
8 even though the wicked strut about,
     and evil is praised throughout the
       land.

12:TITLE Hebrew *according to the sheminith.*

PROVERBS 19:13-14
A foolish child* is a calamity to a father; a
quarrelsome wife is as annoying as constant dripping. □ Fathers can give their
sons an inheritance of houses and wealth,
but only the Lord can give an understanding wife.

19:13 Hebrew *son;* also in 19:27.

1 CHRONICLES 24:1–26:11

David showed his commitment to the Temple, and thus to God, by the care and attention he gave to preparing those who would serve God in it.

This is how Aaron's descendants, the priests, were divided into groups for service. The sons of Aaron were Nadab, Abihu, Eleazar, and Ithamar. ²But Nadab and Abihu died before their father, and they had no sons. So only Eleazar and Ithamar were left to carry on as priests.

³With the help of Zadok, who was a descendant of Eleazar, and of Ahimelech, who was a descendant of Ithamar, David divided Aaron's descendants into groups according to their various duties. ⁴Eleazar's descendants were divided into sixteen groups and Ithamar's into eight, for there were more family leaders among the descendants of Eleazar.

⁵All tasks were assigned to the various groups by means of sacred lots so that no preference would be shown, for there were many qualified officials serving God in the sanctuary from among the descendants of both Eleazar and Ithamar. ⁶Shemaiah son of Nethanel, a Levite, acted as secretary and wrote down the names and assignments in the presence of the king, the officials, Zadok the priest, Ahimelech son of Abiathar, and the family leaders of the priests and Levites. The descendants of Eleazar and Ithamar took turns casting lots.

⁷ The first lot fell to Jehoiarib.
The second lot fell to Jedaiah.
⁸ The third lot fell to Harim.
The fourth lot fell to Seorim.
⁹ The fifth lot fell to Malkijah.
The sixth lot fell to Mijamin.
¹⁰ The seventh lot fell to Hakkoz.
The eighth lot fell to Abijah.
¹¹ The ninth lot fell to Jeshua.
The tenth lot fell to Shecaniah.
¹² The eleventh lot fell to Eliashib.
The twelfth lot fell to Jakim.
¹³ The thirteenth lot fell to Huppah.
The fourteenth lot fell to Jeshebeab.
¹⁴ The fifteenth lot fell to Bilgah.
The sixteenth lot fell to Immer.

¹⁵ The seventeenth lot fell to Hezir.
The eighteenth lot fell to Happizzez.
¹⁶ The nineteenth lot fell to Pethahiah.
The twentieth lot fell to Jehezkel.
¹⁷ The twenty-first lot fell to Jakin.
The twenty-second lot fell to Gamul.
¹⁸ The twenty-third lot fell to Delaiah.
The twenty-fourth lot fell to Maaziah.

¹⁹Each group carried out its appointed duties in the house of the LORD according to the procedures established by their ancestor Aaron in obedience to the commands of the LORD, the God of Israel.

²⁰These were the other family leaders descended from Levi:

From the descendants of Amram, the leader was Shebuel.*
From the descendants of Shebuel, the leader was Jehdeiah.
²¹ From the descendants of Rehabiah, the leader was Isshiah.
²² From the descendants of Izhar, the leader was Shelomith.*
From the descendants of Shelomith, the leader was Jahath.
²³ From the descendants of Hebron, Jeriah was the leader,* Amariah was second, Jahaziel was third, and Jekameam was fourth.
²⁴ From the descendants of Uzziel, the leader was Micah.
From the descendants of Micah, the leader was Shamir, ²⁵along with Isshiah, the brother of Micah.
From the descendants of Isshiah, the leader was Zechariah.
²⁶ From the descendants of Merari, the leaders were Mahli and Mushi.
From the descendants of Jaaziah, the leader was Beno.
²⁷ From the descendants of Merari through Jaaziah, the leaders were Beno, Shoham, Zaccur, and Ibri.
²⁸ From the descendants of Mahli, the leader was Eleazar, though he had no sons.
²⁹ From the descendants of Kish, the leader was Jerahmeel.

30 From the descendants of Mushi, the leaders were Mahli, Eder, and Jerimoth.

These were the descendants of Levi in their various families. 31Like the descendants of Aaron, they were assigned to their duties by means of sacred lots, without regard to age or rank. Lots were drawn in the presence of King David, Zadok, Ahimelech, and the family leaders of the priests and the Levites.

25:1DAVID and the army commanders then appointed men from the families of Asaph, Heman, and Jeduthun to proclaim God's messages to the accompaniment of lyres, harps, and cymbals. Here is a list of their names and their work:

2From the sons of Asaph, there were Zaccur, Joseph, Nethaniah, and Asarelah. They worked under the direction of their father, Asaph, who proclaimed God's messages by the king's orders.

3From the sons of Jeduthun, there were Gedaliah, Zeri, Jeshaiah, Shimei,* Hashabiah, and Mattithiah, six in all. They worked under the direction of their father, Jeduthun, who proclaimed God's messages to the accompaniment of the lyre, offering thanks and praise to the LORD.

4From the sons of Heman, there were Bukkiah, Mattaniah, Uzziel, Shubael,* Jerimoth, Hananiah, Hanani, Eliathah, Giddalti, Romamti-ezer, Joshbekashah, Mallothi, Hothir, and Mahazioth. 5All these were the sons of Heman, the king's seer, for God had honored him with fourteen sons and three daughters.

6All these men were under the direction of their fathers as they made music at the house of the LORD. Their responsibilities included the playing of cymbals, harps, and lyres at the house of God. Asaph, Jeduthun, and Heman reported directly to the king. 7They and their families were all trained in making music before the LORD, and each of them—288 in all—was an accomplished musician. 8The musicians were appointed to their term of service by means of sacred lots, without regard to

whether they were young or old, teacher or student.

9 The first lot fell to Joseph of the Asaph clan and twelve of his sons and relatives.*

The second lot fell to Gedaliah and twelve of his sons and relatives.

10 The third lot fell to Zaccur and twelve of his sons and relatives.

11 The fourth lot fell to Zeri* and twelve of his sons and relatives.

12 The fifth lot fell to Nethaniah and twelve of his sons and relatives.

13 The sixth lot fell to Bukkiah and twelve of his sons and relatives.

14 The seventh lot fell to Asarelah* and twelve of his sons and relatives.

15 The eighth lot fell to Jeshaiah and twelve of his sons and relatives.

16 The ninth lot fell to Mattaniah and twelve of his sons and relatives.

17 The tenth lot fell to Shimei and twelve of his sons and relatives.

18 The eleventh lot fell to Uzziel* and twelve of his sons and relatives.

19 The twelfth lot fell to Hashabiah and twelve of his sons and relatives.

20 The thirteenth lot fell to Shubael and twelve of his sons and relatives.

21 The fourteenth lot fell to Mattithiah and twelve of his sons and relatives.

22 The fifteenth lot fell to Jerimoth* and twelve of his sons and relatives.

23 The sixteenth lot fell to Hananiah and twelve of his sons and relatives.

24 The seventeenth lot fell to Joshbekashah* and twelve of his sons and relatives.

25 The eighteenth lot fell to Hanani and twelve of his sons and relatives.

26 The nineteenth lot fell to Mallothi and twelve of his sons and relatives.

27 The twentieth lot fell to Eliathah and twelve of his sons and relatives.

28 The twenty-first lot fell to Hothir and twelve of his sons and relatives.

29 The twenty-second lot fell to Giddalti and twelve of his sons and relatives.

30 The twenty-third lot fell to Mahazioth and twelve of his sons and relatives.

31 The twenty-fourth lot fell to Romamti-ezer and twelve of his sons and relatives.

26:1THESE are the divisions of the gatekeepers:

From the Korahites, there was Meshelemiah son of Kore, of the family of Abiasaph.* ²The sons of Meshelemiah were Zechariah (the oldest), Jediael (the second), Zebadiah (the third), Jathniel (the fourth), ³Elam (the fifth), Jehohanan (the sixth), and Eliehoenai (the seventh).

⁴The sons of Obed-edom, also gatekeepers, were Shemaiah (the oldest), Jehozabad (the second), Joah (the third), Sacar (the fourth), Nethanel (the fifth), ⁵Ammiel (the sixth), Issachar (the seventh), and Peullethai (the eighth). God had richly blessed Obed-edom.

⁶Obed-edom's son Shemaiah had sons with great ability who earned positions of great authority in the clan. ⁷Their names were Othni, Rephael, Obed, and Elzabad. Their relatives, Elihu and Semakiah, were also very capable men.

⁸All of these descendants of Obed-edom, including their sons and grandsons—sixty-two of them in all—were very capable men, well qualified for their work.

⁹Meshelemiah's eighteen sons and relatives were also very capable men.

¹⁰Hosah, of the Merari clan, appointed Shimri as the leader among his sons, though he was not the oldest. ¹¹His other sons included Hilkiah (the second), Tebaliah (the third), and Zechariah (the fourth). Hosah's sons and relatives, who served as gatekeepers, numbered thirteen in all.

24:20 Hebrew *Shubael* (also in 24:20b), a variant spelling of Shebuel; compare 23:16 and 26:24. **24:22** Hebrew *Shelomoth* (also in 24:22b), a variant spelling of Shelomith; compare 23:18. **24:23** Hebrew *From the descendants of Jeriah;* compare 23:19. **25:3** As in one Hebrew manuscript and some Greek manuscripts (see also 25:17); most Hebrew manuscripts lack *Shimei.* **25:4** Hebrew *Shebuel,* a variant spelling of Shubael; compare 25:20. **25:9** As in Greek version; Hebrew lacks *and twelve of his sons and relatives.* **25:11** Hebrew *Izri,* a variant spelling of Zeri; compare 25:3. **25:14** Hebrew *Jesarelah, a variant spelling of Asarelah; compare 25:2.* **25:18** Hebrew *Azarel,* a variant spelling of Uzziel; compare 25:4. **25:22** Hebrew *Jeremoth,* a variant spelling of Jerimoth; compare 25:4. **25:24** Hebrew *Joshbekasha,* a variant spelling of Joshbekashah; compare 25:4. **26:1** As in Greek version (see also Exod 6:24); Hebrew reads *Asaph.*

ROMANS 4:1-12

Abraham was the father of the Jewish nation, their ancestor to whom God had promised a nation of descendants with a land of their own. Abraham was righteous because of his faith in God—not because of his heritage or personal holiness.

Abraham was, humanly speaking, the founder of our Jewish nation. What did he discover about being made right with God? ²If his good deeds had made him acceptable to God, he would have had something to boast about. But that was not God's way. ³For the Scriptures tell us, "Abraham believed God, and God counted him as righteous because of his faith."*

⁴When people work, their wages are not a gift, but something they have earned. ⁵But people are counted as righteous, not because of their work, but because of their faith in God who forgives sinners. ⁶David also spoke of this when he described the happiness of those who are declared righteous without working for it:

⁷ "Oh, what joy for those
    whose disobedience is forgiven,
    whose sins are put out of sight.
⁸ Yes, what joy for those
    whose record the LORD has cleared
        of sin."*

⁹Now, is this blessing only for the Jews, or is it also for uncircumcised Gentiles?* Well, we have been saying that Abraham was counted as righteous by God because of his faith. ¹⁰But how did this happen? Was he counted as righteous only after he was circumcised, or was it before he was circumcised? Clearly, God accepted Abraham before he was circumcised!

¹¹Circumcision was a sign that Abraham already had faith and that God had already accepted him and declared him to be righteous—even before he was circumcised. So Abraham is the spiritual father of those who have faith but have not been circumcised. They are counted as righteous because of their faith. ¹²And Abraham is also the spiritual father of those

who have been circumcised, but only if they have the same kind of faith Abraham had before he was circumcised.

4:3 Gen 15:6.   **4:7-8** Ps 32:1-2 (Greek version).   **4:9** Greek *is this blessing only for the circumcised, or is it also for the uncircumcised?*

PSALM 13:1-6
For the choir director: A psalm of David.

¹ **O** LORD, how long will you forget me?
        Forever?
    How long will you look the other
        way?
² How long must I struggle with anguish
        in my soul,
    with sorrow in my heart every day?
    How long will my enemy have the
        upper hand?

³ Turn and answer me, O LORD my God!
    Restore the sparkle to my eyes,
        or I will die.
⁴ Don't let my enemies gloat, saying,
        "We have defeated him!"
    Don't let them rejoice at my
        downfall.

⁵ But I trust in your unfailing love.
    I will rejoice because you have
        rescued me.
⁶ I will sing to the LORD
    because he is good to me.

PROVERBS 19:15-16
Lazy people sleep soundly, but idleness leaves them hungry. □ Keep the commandments and keep your life; despising them leads to death.

JULY**18**

1 CHRONICLES 26:12–27:34
David not only organized and trained men for the Temple construction and use, he also organized civil and military roles.

These divisions of the gatekeepers were named for their family leaders, and like the other Levites, they served at the house of the LORD. ¹³They were assigned by fam-

ilies for guard duty at the various gates, without regard to age or training, for it was all decided by means of sacred lots.

¹⁴The responsibility for the east gate went to Meshelemiah* and his group. The north gate was assigned to his son Zechariah, a man of unusual wisdom. ¹⁵The south gate went to Obed-edom, and his

sons were put in charge of the storehouse. [16]Shuppim and Hosah were assigned the west gate and the gateway leading up to the Temple.* Guard duties were divided evenly. [17]Six Levites were assigned each day to the east gate, four to the north gate, four to the south gate, and two pairs at the storehouse. [18]Six were assigned each day to the west gate, four to the gateway leading up to the Temple, and two to the courtyard.*

[19]These were the divisions of the gatekeepers from the clans of Korah and Merari.

[20]Other Levites, led by Ahijah, were in charge of the treasuries of the house of God and the treasuries of the gifts dedicated to the LORD. [21]From the family of Libni* in the clan of Gershon, Jehiel* was the leader. [22]The sons of Jehiel, Zetham and his brother Joel, were in charge of the treasuries of the house of the LORD.

[23]These are the leaders that descended from Amram, Izhar, Hebron, and Uzziel:

[24]From the clan of Amram, Shebuel was a descendant of Gershom son of Moses. He was the chief officer of the treasuries. [25]His relatives through Eliezer were Rehabiah, Jeshaiah, Joram, Zicri, and Shelomoth.

[26]Shelomoth and his relatives were in charge of the treasuries containing the gifts that King David, the family leaders, and the generals and captains* and other officers of the army had dedicated to the LORD. [27]These men dedicated some of the plunder they had gained in battle to maintain the house of the LORD. [28]Shelomoth* and his relatives also cared for the gifts dedicated to the LORD by Samuel the seer, Saul son of Kish, Abner son of Ner, and Joab son of Zeruiah. All the other dedicated gifts were in their care, too.

[29]From the clan of Izhar came Kenaniah. He and his sons were given administrative responsibilities* over Israel as officials and judges.

[30]From the clan of Hebron came Hashabiah. He and his relatives— 1,700 capable men—were put in charge of the Israelite lands west of the Jordan River. They were responsible for all matters related to the things of the LORD and the service of the king in that area.

[31]Also from the clan of Hebron came Jeriah,* who was the leader of the Hebronites according to the genealogical records. (In the fortieth year of David's reign, a search was made in the records, and capable men from the clan of Hebron were found at Jazer in the land of Gilead.) [32]There were 2,700 capable men among the relatives of Jeriah. King David sent them to the east side of the Jordan River and put them in charge of the tribes of Reuben and Gad and the half-tribe of Manasseh. They were responsible for all matters related to God and to the king.

[27:1]THIS is the list of Israelite generals and captains,* and their officers, who served the king by supervising the army divisions that were on duty each month of the year. Each division served for one month and had 24,000 troops.

[2]Jashobeam son of Zabdiel was commander of the first division of 24,000 troops, which was on duty during the first month. [3]He was a descendant of Perez and was in charge of all the army officers for the first month.

[4]Dodai, a descendant of Ahoah, was commander of the second division of 24,000 troops, which was on duty during the second month. Mikloth was his chief officer.

[5]Benaiah son of Jehoiada the priest was commander of the third division of 24,000 troops, which was on duty during the third month. [6]This was the Benaiah who commanded David's elite military group known as the Thirty. His son Ammizabad was his chief officer.

[7]Asahel, the brother of Joab, was commander of the fourth division of 24,000 troops, which was on duty during the fourth month. Asahel was succeeded by his son Zebadiah.

[8]Shammah* the Izrahite was commander of the fifth division of

24,000 troops, which was on duty during the fifth month.

9 Ira son of Ikkesh from Tekoa was commander of the sixth division of 24,000 troops, which was on duty during the sixth month.

10 Helez, a descendant of Ephraim from Pelon, was commander of the seventh division of 24,000 troops, which was on duty during the seventh month.

11 Sibbecai, a descendant of Zerah from Hushah, was commander of the eighth division of 24,000 troops, which was on duty during the eighth month.

12 Abiezer from Anathoth in the territory of Benjamin was commander of the ninth division of 24,000 troops, which was on duty during the ninth month.

13 Maharai, a descendant of Zerah from Netophah, was commander of the tenth division of 24,000 troops, which was on duty during the tenth month.

14 Benaiah from Pirathon in Ephraim was commander of the eleventh division of 24,000 troops, which was on duty during the eleventh month.

15 Heled,* a descendant of Othniel from Netophah, was commander of the twelfth division of 24,000 troops, which was on duty during the twelfth month.

16 The following were the tribes of Israel and their leaders:

Tribe	Leader
Reuben	Eliezer son of Zicri
Simeon	Shephatiah son of Maacah
17 Levi	Hashabiah son of Kemuel
Aaron (the priests)	Zadok
18 Judah	Elihu (a brother of David)
Issachar	Omri son of Michael
19 Zebulun	Ishmaiah son of Obadiah
Naphtali	Jeremoth son of Azriel
20 Ephraim	Hoshea son of Azaziah
Manasseh (west)	Joel son of Pedaiah
21 Manasseh in Gilead (east)	Iddo son of Zechariah
Benjamin	Jaasiel son of Abner
22 Dan	Azarel son of Jeroham

These were the leaders of the tribes of Israel.

23 When David took his census, he did not count those who were younger than twenty years of age, because the LORD had promised to make the Israelites as numerous as the stars in heaven. 24 Joab son of Zeruiah began the census but never finished it because* the anger of God fell on Israel. The total number was never recorded in King David's official records.

25 Azmaveth son of Adiel was in charge of the palace treasuries.

Jonathan son of Uzziah was in charge of the regional treasuries throughout the towns, villages, and fortresses of Israel.

26 Ezri son of Kelub was in charge of the field workers who farmed the king's lands.

27 Shimei from Ramah was in charge of the king's vineyards.

Zabdi from Shepham was responsible for the grapes and the supplies of wine.

28 Baal-hanan from Geder was in charge of the king's olive groves and sycamore-fig trees in the foothills of Judah.*

Joash was responsible for the supplies of olive oil.

29 Shitrai from Sharon was in charge of the cattle on the Sharon Plain.

Shaphat son of Adlai was responsible for the cattle in the valleys.

30 Obil the Ishmaelite was in charge of the camels.

Jehdeiah from Meronoth was in charge of the donkeys.

31 Jaziz the Hagrite was in charge of the king's flocks of sheep and goats.

All these officials were overseers of King David's property.

32 Jonathan, David's uncle, was a wise counselor to the king, a man of great insight, and a scribe. Jehiel the Hacmonite was responsible for teaching the king's sons. 33 Ahithophel was the royal adviser. Hushai the Arkite was the king's friend. 34 Ahithophel was succeeded by Jehoiada son of Benaiah and by Abiathar. Joab was commander of the king's army.

26:14 Hebrew *Shelemiah*, a variant spelling of Meshelemiah; compare 26:2. 26:16 Or *the gate of Shalleketh on the upper road* (also in 26:18). The meaning of the Hebrew is uncertain. 26:18 Or *the colonnade*. The meaning of the Hebrew is uncertain. 26:21a Hebrew *Ladan*, a variant spelling of Libni; compare 6:17. 26:21b Hebrew *Jehieli* (also in 26:22), a variant spelling of Jehiel; compare 23:8.

26:26 Hebrew *the commanders of thousands and of hundreds.*   26:28 Hebrew *Shelomith,* a variant spelling of Shelomoth.   26:29 Or *were given outside work;* or *were given work away from the Temple area.*   26:31 Hebrew *Jerijah,* a variant spelling of Jeriah; compare 23:19.
27:1 Hebrew *commanders of thousands and of hundreds.*   27:8 Hebrew *Shamhuth,* a variant spelling of Shammah; compare 11:27 and 2 Sam 23:25.   27:15 Hebrew *Heldai,* a variant spelling of Heled; compare 11:30 and 2 Sam 23:29.   27:24 Or *never finished it, and yet.*   27:28 Hebrew *the Shephelah.*

ROMANS 4:13-5:5

Paul continues to show that obedience to the Jewish laws is not what is required to be justified. We have hope because God himself has made a way for us to be justified: It is through the death and resurrection of his Son.

Clearly, God's promise to give the whole earth to Abraham and his descendants was based not on his obedience to God's law, but on a right relationship with God that comes by faith. ¹⁴If God's promise is only for those who obey the law, then faith is not necessary and the promise is pointless. ¹⁵For the law always brings punishment on those who try to obey it. (The only way to avoid breaking the law is to have no law to break!)

¹⁶So the promise is received by faith. It is given as a free gift. And we are all certain to receive it, whether or not we live according to the law of Moses, if we have faith like Abraham's. For Abraham is the father of all who believe. ¹⁷That is what the Scriptures mean when God told him, "I have made you the father of many nations."* This happened because Abraham believed in the God who brings the dead back to life and who creates new things out of nothing.

¹⁸Even when there was no reason for hope, Abraham kept hoping—believing that he would become the father of many nations. For God had said to him, "That's how many descendants you will have!"* ¹⁹And Abraham's faith did not weaken, even though, at about 100 years of age, he figured his body was as good as dead—and so was Sarah's womb.

²⁰Abraham never wavered in believing God's promise. In fact, his faith grew stronger, and in this he brought glory to God. ²¹He was fully convinced that God is able to do whatever he promises. ²²And because of Abraham's faith, God counted him as righteous. ²³And when God counted him as righteous, it wasn't just for Abraham's benefit. It was recorded ²⁴for our benefit, too, assuring us that God will also count us as righteous if we believe in him, the one who raised Jesus our Lord from the dead. ²⁵He was handed over to die because of our sins, and he was raised to life to make us right with God.

⁵:¹THEREFORE, since we have been made right in God's sight by faith, we have peace

WHAT THE BIBLE SAYS

Why does God allow suffering?

ROMANS 5:1-5   After Adam and Eve's sin in the Garden, the world slipped into a pretty sorry state. It will remain that way until Jesus comes again and sets up his Kingdom in the new creation. Sure, we all want a world where nothing bad happens. But we're getting ahead of ourselves. Jesus promises just that—but in eternity, not the present. In this world we have to fight against Satan and bring as many people as we can out from under his grip. And, right now, we face times of suffering. • Some suffering we bring on ourselves—we do dumb things and get hurt. Some suffering is caused by sin. Some suffering—such as natural disasters like floods, fire, or storms—is the result of the curse that came over creation after the Fall in the Garden of Eden. We do not always know why certain bad things happen. • God may not always stop suffering, but that doesn't lessen his power. He does something even better: He uses our suffering to teach us, mature us, and help us to reach out to others who are also suffering. In this way God takes suffering and redeems it.

with God because of what Jesus Christ our Lord has done for us. ²Because of our faith, Christ has brought us into this place of undeserved privilege where we now stand, and we confidently and joyfully look forward to sharing God's glory.

³We can rejoice, too, when we run into problems and trials, for we know that they help us develop endurance. ⁴And endurance develops strength of character, and character strengthens our confident hope of salvation. ⁵And this hope will not lead to disappointment. For we know how dearly God loves us, because he has given us the Holy Spirit to fill our hearts with his love.

4:17 Gen 17:5.　4:18 Gen 15:5.

PSALM 14:1-7
For the choir director: A psalm of David.

¹ **O**nly fools say in their hearts,
　"There is no God."
　They are corrupt, and their actions are
　　evil;
　not one of them does good!

² The LORD looks down from heaven
　on the entire human race;

he looks to see if anyone is truly wise,
　if anyone seeks God.
³ But no, all have turned away;
　all have become corrupt.*
No one does good,
　not a single one!

⁴ Will those who do evil never learn?
　They eat up my people like bread
　and wouldn't think of praying to
　　the LORD.
⁵ Terror will grip them,
　for God is with those who obey him.
⁶ The wicked frustrate the plans of the
　　oppressed,
　but the LORD will protect his
　　people.

⁷ Who will come from Mount Zion to
　　rescue Israel?
　When the LORD restores his people,
　Jacob will shout with joy, and Israel
　　will rejoice.

14:3 Greek version reads *have become useless.* Compare Rom 3:12.

PROVERBS 19:17
If you help the poor, you are lending to the LORD— and he will repay you!

JULY**19**

1 CHRONICLES 28:1–29:30
David's reign was drawing to a close. He had done all he could to prepare for the construction of the Temple; the rest was up to Solomon.

David summoned all the officials of Israel to Jerusalem—the leaders of the tribes, the commanders of the army divisions, the other generals and captains,* the overseers of the royal property and livestock, the palace officials, the mighty men, and all the other brave warriors in the kingdom. ²David rose to his feet and said: "My brothers and my people! It was my desire to build a temple where the Ark of the LORD's Covenant, God's footstool, could rest permanently. I made the necessary preparations for building it, ³but God

said to me, 'You must not build a temple to honor my name, for you are a warrior and have shed much blood.'

⁴"Yet the LORD, the God of Israel, has chosen me from among all my father's family to be king over Israel forever. For he has chosen the tribe of Judah to rule, and from among the families of Judah he chose my father's family. And from among my father's sons the LORD was pleased to make me king over all Israel. ⁵And from among my sons—for the LORD has given me many—he chose Solomon to succeed me on the throne of Israel and to rule over the LORD's kingdom. ⁶He said to me, 'Your son Solomon will build my Temple and its courtyards, for I have chosen him as my

son, and I will be his father. ⁷And if he continues to obey my commands and regulations as he does now, I will make his kingdom last forever.'

⁸"So now, with God as our witness, and in the sight of all Israel—the LORD's assembly—I give you this charge. Be careful to obey all the commands of the LORD your God, so that you may continue to possess this good land and leave it to your children as a permanent inheritance.

⁹"And Solomon, my son, learn to know the God of your ancestors intimately. Worship and serve him with your whole heart and a willing mind. For the LORD sees every heart and knows every plan and thought. If you seek him, you will find him. But if you forsake him, he will reject you forever. ¹⁰So take this seriously. The LORD has chosen you to build a Temple as his sanctuary. Be strong, and do the work."

¹¹Then David gave Solomon the plans for the Temple and its surroundings, including the entry room, the storerooms, the upstairs rooms, the inner rooms, and the inner sanctuary—which was the place of atonement. ¹²David also gave Solomon all the plans he had in mind* for the courtyards of the LORD's Temple, the outside rooms, the treasuries, and the rooms for the gifts dedicated to the LORD. ¹³The king also gave Solomon the instructions concerning the work of the various divisions of priests and Levites in the Temple of the LORD. And he gave specifications for the items in the Temple that were to be used for worship.

¹⁴David gave instructions regarding how much gold and silver should be used to make the items needed for service. ¹⁵He told Solomon the amount of gold needed for the gold lampstands and lamps, and the amount of silver for the silver lampstands and lamps, depending on how each would be used. ¹⁶He designated the amount of gold for the table on which the Bread of the Presence would be placed and the amount of silver for other tables.

¹⁷David also designated the amount of gold for the solid gold meat hooks used to handle the sacrificial meat and for the basins, pitchers, and dishes, as well as the amount of silver for every dish. ¹⁸He des-

ignated the amount of refined gold for the altar of incense. Finally, he gave him a plan for the LORD's "chariot"—the gold cherubim* whose wings were stretched out over the Ark of the LORD's Covenant. ¹⁹"Every part of this plan," David told Solomon, "was given to me in writing from the hand of the LORD.*"

²⁰Then David continued, "Be strong and courageous, and do the work. Don't be afraid or discouraged, for the LORD God, my God, is with you. He will not fail you or forsake you. He will see to it that all the work related to the Temple of the LORD is finished correctly. ²¹The various divisions of priests and Levites will serve in the Temple of God. Others with skills of every kind will volunteer, and the officials and the entire nation are at your command."

²⁹:¹THEN King David turned to the entire assembly and said, "My son Solomon, whom God has clearly chosen as the next king of Israel, is still young and inexperienced. The work ahead of him is enormous, for the Temple he will build is not for mere mortals—it is for the LORD God himself! ²Using every resource at my command, I have gathered as much as I could for building the Temple of my God. Now there is enough gold, silver, bronze, iron, and wood, as well as great quantities of onyx, other precious stones, costly jewels, and all kinds of fine stone and marble.

³"And now, because of my devotion to the Temple of my God, I am giving all of my own private treasures of gold and silver to help in the construction. This is in addition to the building materials I have already collected for his holy Temple. ⁴I am donating more than 112 tons of gold* from Ophir and 262 tons of refined silver* to be used for overlaying the walls of the buildings ⁵and for the other gold and silver work to be done by the craftsmen. Now then, who will follow my example and give offerings to the LORD today?"

⁶Then the family leaders, the leaders of the tribes of Israel, the generals and captains of the army,* and the king's administrative officers all gave willingly. ⁷For the construction of the Temple of God, they gave about 188 tons of gold,* 10,000 gold coins,* 375 tons of silver,*

675 tons of bronze,* and 3,750 tons of iron.* ⁸They also contributed numerous precious stones, which were deposited in the treasury of the house of the LORD under the care of Jehiel, a descendant of Gershon. ⁹The people rejoiced over the offerings, for they had given freely and wholeheartedly to the LORD, and King David was filled with joy.

¹⁰Then David praised the LORD in the presence of the whole assembly:

"O LORD, the God of our ancestor Israel,* may you be praised forever and ever! ¹¹Yours, O LORD, is the greatness, the power, the glory, the victory, and the majesty. Everything in the heavens and on earth is yours, O LORD, and this is your kingdom. We adore you as the one who is over all things. ¹²Wealth and honor come from you alone, for you rule over everything. Power and might are in your hand, and at your discretion people are made great and given strength.

¹³"O our God, we thank you and praise your glorious name! ¹⁴But who am I, and who are my people, that we could give anything to you? Everything we have has come from you, and we give you only what you first gave us! ¹⁵We are here for only a moment, visitors and strangers in the land as our ancestors were before us. Our days on earth are like a passing shadow, gone so soon without a trace.

¹⁶"O LORD our God, even this material we have gathered to build a Temple to honor your holy name comes from you! It all belongs to you! ¹⁷I know, my God, that you examine our hearts and rejoice when you find integrity there. You know I have done all this with good motives, and I have watched your people offer their gifts willingly and joyously.

¹⁸"O LORD, the God of our ancestors Abraham, Isaac, and Israel, make your people always want to obey you. See to it that their love for you never changes. ¹⁹Give my son Solomon the wholehearted desire to obey all your commands, laws, and decrees, and to do everything necessary to build this Temple, for which I have made these preparations."

²⁰Then David said to the whole assembly, "Give praise to the LORD your God!" And the entire assembly praised the LORD, the God of their ancestors, and they bowed low and knelt before the LORD and the king.

²¹The next day they brought 1,000 bulls, 1,000 rams, and 1,000 male lambs as burnt offerings to the LORD. They also brought liquid offerings and many other sacrifices on behalf of all Israel. ²²They feasted and drank in the LORD's presence with great joy that day.

And again they crowned David's son Solomon as their new king. They anointed him before the LORD as their leader, and they anointed Zadok as priest. ²³So Solomon took the throne of the LORD in place of his father, David, and he succeeded in everything, and all Israel obeyed him. ²⁴All the officials, the warriors, and the sons of King David pledged their loyalty to King Solomon. ²⁵And the LORD exalted Solomon in the sight of all Israel, and he gave Solomon greater royal splendor than any king in Israel before him.

²⁶So David son of Jesse reigned over all Israel. ²⁷He reigned over Israel for forty years, seven of them in Hebron and thirty-three in Jerusalem. ²⁸He died at a ripe old age, having enjoyed long life, wealth, and honor. Then his son Solomon ruled in his place.

²⁹All the events of King David's reign, from beginning to end, are written in *The Record of Samuel the Seer, The Record of Nathan the Prophet,* and *The Record of Gad the Seer.* ³⁰These accounts include the mighty deeds of his reign and everything that happened to him and to Israel and to all the surrounding kingdoms.

28:1 Hebrew *the commanders of thousands and commanders of hundreds.* **28:12** Or *the plans of the spirit that was with him.* **28:18** Hebrew *for the gold cherub chariot.* **28:19** Or *was written under the direction of the* LORD. **29:4a** Hebrew *3,000 talents* [102 metric tons] *of gold.* **29:4b** Hebrew *7,000 talents* [238 metric tons] *of silver.* **29:6** Hebrew *the commanders of thousands and commanders of hundreds.* **29:7a** Hebrew *5,000 talents* [170 metric tons] *of gold.* **29:7b** Hebrew *10,000 darics* [a Persian coin] *of gold,* about 185 pounds or 84 kilograms in weight. **29:7c** Hebrew *10,000 talents* [340 metric tons] *of silver.* **29:7d** Hebrew *18,000 talents* [612 metric tons] *of bronze.* **29:7e** Hebrew *100,000 talents* [3,400 metric tons] *of iron.* **29:10** *Israel* is the name that God gave to Jacob.

ROMANS 5:6-21
Paul refers back even earlier than Abraham. He compares the work of Jesus to the work of Adam. Adam introduced sin. Jesus Christ introduced the remedy for sin.

When we were utterly helpless, Christ came at just the right time and died for us sinners. [7]Now, most people would not be willing to die for an upright person, though someone might perhaps be willing to die for a person who is especially good. [8]But God showed his great love for us by sending Christ to die for us while we were still sinners. [9]And since we have been made right in God's sight by the blood of Christ, he will certainly save us from God's condemnation. [10]For since our friendship with God was restored by the death of his Son while we were still his enemies, we will certainly be saved through the life of his Son. [11]So now we can rejoice in our wonderful new relationship with God because our Lord Jesus Christ has made us friends of God.

[12]When Adam sinned, sin entered the world. Adam's sin brought death, so death spread to everyone, for everyone sinned. [13]Yes, people sinned even before the law was given. But it was not counted as sin because there was not yet any law to break. [14]Still, everyone died—from the time of Adam to the time of Moses—even those who did not disobey an explicit commandment of God, as Adam did. Now Adam is a symbol, a representation of Christ, who was yet to come. [15]But there is a great difference between Adam's sin and God's gracious gift. For the sin of this one man, Adam, brought death to many. But even greater is God's wonderful grace and his gift of forgiveness to many through this other man, Jesus Christ. [16]And the result of God's gracious gift is very different from the result of that one man's sin. For Adam's sin led to condemnation, but God's free gift leads to our being made right with God, even though we are guilty of many sins. [17]For the sin of this one man, Adam, caused death to rule over many. But even greater is God's wonderful grace and his gift of righteousness, for all who receive it will live in triumph over sin and death through this one man, Jesus Christ.

[18]Yes, Adam's one sin brings condemnation for everyone, but Christ's one act of righteousness brings a right relationship with God and new life for everyone. [19]Because one person disobeyed God, many became sinners. But because one other person obeyed God, many will be made righteous.

[20]God's law was given so that all people could see how sinful they were. But as people sinned more and more, God's wonderful grace became more abundant.

WHO GOD IS

God is loving

ROMANS 5:8-11 *While we were still sinners*—these are amazing words. God sent Jesus Christ to die for us, not because we were good enough, but because he loved us. • We were sinners, doomed to death, "utterly helpless." Instead of punishing us with the death we deserve, however, Christ took our sins upon himself and took our punishment by dying on the cross. Now we can "rejoice in God." Through faith in *Christ's* work, we have been reconciled to God rather than being enemies and outcasts. We have been saved from God's judgment. We will be delivered from eternal punishment by his life. We can rejoice in our wonderful new relationship with God. We are friends with God. • The love that caused Christ to die is the same love that sends the Holy Spirit to live in you and guide you every day. The power that raised Christ from the dead is the same power that saved you and is available to you in your daily life. You can be assured that, having begun a life with Christ, you have a reserve of power and love to call on each day to help you meet every challenge and trial.

²¹So just as sin ruled over all people and brought them to death, now God's wonderful grace rules instead, giving us right standing with God and resulting in eternal life through Jesus Christ our Lord.

PSALM 15:1-5
A psalm of David.

¹ **W**ho may worship in your sanctuary,
  LORD?
  Who may enter your presence on
  your holy hill?
² Those who lead blameless lives and
  do what is right,
  speaking the truth from sincere
  hearts.
³ Those who refuse to gossip
  or harm their neighbors

or speak evil of their friends.
⁴ Those who despise flagrant
  sinners,
  and honor the faithful followers
  of the LORD,
  and keep their promises even when
  it hurts.
⁵ Those who lend money without
  charging interest,
  and who cannot be bribed to lie
  about the innocent.
Such people will stand firm forever.

PROVERBS 19:18-19
Discipline your children while there is hope. Otherwise you will ruin their lives. □ Hot-tempered people must pay the penalty. If you rescue them once, you will have to do it again.

JULY**20**

2 CHRONICLES 1:1–3:17
David had done a lot to ensure a secure transition from his reign to that of his son Solomon. Solomon would still need God's help to be a good king, so he asked for wisdom—a request God was happy to grant.

Solomon son of David took firm control of his kingdom, for the LORD his God was with him and made him very powerful.

²Solomon called together all the leaders of Israel—the generals and captains of the army,* the judges, and all the political and clan leaders. ³Then he led the entire assembly to the place of worship in Gibeon, for God's Tabernacle* was located there. (This was the Tabernacle that Moses, the LORD's servant, had made in the wilderness.)

⁴David had already moved the Ark of God from Kiriath-jearim to the tent he had prepared for it in Jerusalem. ⁵But the bronze altar made by Bezalel son of Uri and grandson of Hur was there* at Gibeon in front of the Tabernacle of the LORD. So Solomon and the people gathered in front of it to consult the LORD.* ⁶There in front of the Tabernacle, Solomon went

up to the bronze altar in the LORD's presence and sacrificed 1,000 burnt offerings on it.

⁷That night God appeared to Solomon and said, "What do you want? Ask, and I will give it to you!"

⁸Solomon replied to God, "You showed faithful love to David, my father, and now you have made me king in his place. ⁹O LORD God, please continue to keep your promise to David my father, for you have made me king over a people as numerous as the dust of the earth! ¹⁰Give me the wisdom and knowledge to lead them properly,* for who could possibly govern this great people of yours?"

¹¹God said to Solomon, "Because your greatest desire is to help your people, and you did not ask for wealth, riches, fame, or even the death of your enemies or a long life, but rather you asked for wisdom and knowledge to properly govern my people—¹²I will certainly give you the wisdom and knowledge you requested. But I will also give you wealth, riches, and fame such as no other king has had before you or will ever have in the future!"

¹³Then Solomon returned to Jerusalem from the Tabernacle at the place of worship in Gibeon, and he reigned over Israel.

¹⁴Solomon built up a huge force of chariots and horses.* He had 1,400 chariots and 12,000 horses. He stationed some of them in the chariot cities and some near him in Jerusalem. ¹⁵The king made silver and gold as plentiful in Jerusalem as stone. And valuable cedar timber was as common as the sycamore-fig trees that grow in the foothills of Judah.* ¹⁶Solomon's horses were imported from Egypt* and from Cilicia*; the king's traders acquired them from Cilicia at the standard price. ¹⁷At that time chariots from Egypt could be purchased for 600 pieces of silver,* and horses for 150 pieces of silver.* They were then exported to the kings of the Hittites and the kings of Aram.

²:¹*SOLOMON decided to build a Temple to honor the name of the LORD, and also a royal palace for himself. ²*He enlisted a force of 70,000 laborers, 80,000 men to quarry stone in the hill country, and 3,600 foremen.

³Solomon also sent this message to King Hiram* at Tyre:

"Send me cedar logs as you did for my father, David, when he was building his palace. ⁴I am about to build a Temple to honor the name of the LORD my God. It will be a place set apart to burn fragrant incense before him, to display the special sacrificial bread, and to sacrifice burnt offerings each morning and evening, on the Sabbaths, at new moon celebrations, and at the other appointed festivals of the LORD our God. He has commanded Israel to do these things forever.

⁵"This must be a magnificent Temple because our God is greater than all other gods. ⁶But who can really build him a worthy home? Not even the highest heavens can contain him! So who am I to consider building a Temple for him, except as a place to burn sacrifices to him?

⁷"So send me a master craftsman who can work with gold, silver, bronze, and iron, as well as with purple, scarlet, and blue cloth. He must be a skilled engraver who can work with the craftsmen of Judah and Jerusalem who were selected by my father, David.

⁸"Also send me cedar, cypress, and red sandalwood* logs from Lebanon, for I know that your men are without equal at cutting timber in Lebanon. I will send my men to help them. ⁹An immense amount of timber will be needed, for the Temple I am going to build will be very large and magnificent. ¹⁰In payment for your woodcutters, I will send 100,000 bushels of crushed wheat, 100,000 bushels of barley,* 110,000 gallons of wine, and 110,000 gallons of olive oil.*"

¹¹King Hiram sent this letter of reply to Solomon:

"It is because the LORD loves his people that he has made you their king!
¹²Praise the LORD, the God of Israel, who made the heavens and the earth! He has given King David a wise son, gifted with skill and understanding, who will build a Temple for the LORD and a royal palace for himself.

¹³"I am sending you a master craftsman named Huram-abi, who is extremely talented. ¹⁴His mother is from the tribe of Dan in Israel, and his father is from Tyre. He is skillful at making things from gold, silver, bronze, and iron, and he also works with stone and wood. He can work with purple, blue, and scarlet cloth and fine linen. He is also an engraver and can follow any design given to him. He will work with your craftsmen and those appointed by my lord David, your father.

¹⁵"Send along the wheat, barley, olive oil, and wine that my lord has mentioned. ¹⁶We will cut whatever timber you need from the Lebanon mountains and will float the logs in rafts down the coast of the Mediterranean Sea* to Joppa. From there you can transport the logs up to Jerusalem."

¹⁷Solomon took a census of all foreigners in the land of Israel, like the census

his father had taken, and he counted 153,600. [18]He assigned 70,000 of them as common laborers, 80,000 as quarry workers in the hill country, and 3,600 as foremen.

[3:1]So Solomon began to build the Temple of the LORD in Jerusalem on Mount Moriah, where the LORD had appeared to David, his father. The Temple was built on the threshing floor of Araunah* the Jebusite, the site that David had selected. [2]The construction began in midspring,* during the fourth year of Solomon's reign.

[3]These are the dimensions Solomon used for the foundation of the Temple of God (using the old standard of measurement).* It was 90 feet long and 30 feet wide.* [4]The entry room at the front of the Temple was 30 feet* wide, running across the entire width of the Temple, and 30 feet* high. He overlaid the inside with pure gold.

[5]He paneled the main room of the Temple with cypress wood, overlaid it with fine gold, and decorated it with carvings of palm trees and chains. [6]He decorated the walls of the Temple with beautiful jewels and with gold from the land of Parvaim. [7]He overlaid the beams, thresholds, walls, and doors throughout the Temple with gold, and he carved figures of cherubim on the walls.

[8]He made the Most Holy Place 30 feet wide, corresponding to the width of the Temple, and 30 feet deep. He overlaid its interior with 23 tons* of fine gold. [9]The gold nails that were used weighed 20 ounces* each. He also overlaid the walls of the upper rooms with gold.

[10]He made two figures shaped like cherubim, overlaid them with gold, and placed them in the Most Holy Place. [11]The total wingspan of the two cherubim standing side by side was 30 feet. One wing of the first figure was 7½ feet* long, and it touched the Temple wall. The other wing, also 7½ feet long, touched one of the wings of the second figure. [12]In the same way, the second figure had one wing 7½ feet long that touched the opposite wall. The other wing, also 7½ feet long, touched the wing of the first figure. [13]So the wingspan of the two cherubim side by side was 30 feet. They stood on their feet and faced out toward the main room of the Temple.

[14]Across the entrance of the Most Holy Place he hung a curtain made of fine linen, decorated with blue, purple, and scarlet thread and embroidered with figures of cherubim.

[15]For the front of the Temple, he made two pillars that were 27 feet* tall, each topped by a capital extending upward another 7½ feet. [16]He made a network of interwoven chains and used them to decorate the tops of the pillars. He also made 100 decorative pomegranates and attached them to the chains. [17]Then he set up the two pillars at the entrance of the Temple, one to the south of the entrance and the other to the north. He named the one on the south Jakin, and the one on the north Boaz.*

1:2 Hebrew *the commanders of thousands and of hundreds.*
1:3 Hebrew *Tent of Meeting;* also in 1:6, 13.   **1:5a** As in Greek version and Latin Vulgate, and some Hebrew manuscripts. Masoretic Text reads *he placed.*   **1:5b** Hebrew *to consult him.*   **1:10** Hebrew *to go out and come in before this people.*   **1:14** Or *charioteers;* also in 1:14b.
1:15 Hebrew *the Shephelah.*   **1:16a** Possibly *Muzur,* a district near Cilicia; also in 1:17.   **1:16b** Hebrew *Kue,* probably another name for Cilicia.   **1:17a** Hebrew *600 shekels of silver,* about 15 pounds or 6.8 kilograms in weight.   **1:17b** Hebrew *150 shekels,* about 3.8 pounds or 1.7 kilograms in weight.   **2:1** Verse 2:1 is numbered 1:18 in Hebrew text.   **2:2** Verses 2:2-18 are numbered 2:1-17 in Hebrew text.   **2:3** Hebrew *Huram,* a variant spelling of Hiram; also in 2:11.   **2:8** Or *juniper;* Hebrew reads *algum,* perhaps a variant spelling of *almug;* compare 9:10-11 and parallel text at 1 Kgs 10:11-12.   **2:10a** Hebrew *20,000 cors* [3,640 kiloliters] *of crushed wheat, 20,000 cors of barley.*   **2:10b** Hebrew *20,000 baths* [420 kiloliters] *of wine, and 20,000 baths of olive oil.*   **2:16** Hebrew *the sea.*
3:1 Hebrew reads *Ornan,* a variant spelling of Araunah; compare 2 Sam 24:16.   **3:2** Hebrew *on the second day of the second month.* This day of the ancient Hebrew lunar calendar occurred in April or May.   **3:3a** The "old standard of measurement" was a cubit equal to 18 inches [46 centimeters]. The new standard was a cubit of approximately 21 inches [53 centimeters].   **3:3b** Hebrew *60 cubits* [27.6 meters] *long and 20 cubits* [9.2 meters] *wide.*
3:4a Hebrew *20 cubits* [9.2 meters]; also in 3:8, 11, 13.
3:4b As in some Greek and Syriac manuscripts, which read *20 cubits* [9.2 meters]; Hebrew reads *120 cubits,* which is 180 feet or 55 meters.   **3:8** Hebrew *600 talents* [20.4 metric tons].   **3:9** Hebrew *50 shekels* [570 grams].
3:11 Hebrew *5 cubits* [2.3 meters]; also in 3:11b, 12, 15.
3:15 As in Syriac version (see also 1 Kgs 7:15; 2 Kgs 25:17; Jer 52:21), which reads *18 cubits* [8.3 meters]; Hebrew reads *35 cubits,* which is 52.5 feet or 16.5 meters.   **3:17** *Jakin* probably means "he establishes"; *Boaz* probably means "in him is strength."

ROMANS 6:1-23

If through Christ's work we have forgiveness, then does it matter how we live? Paul reveals that even though we've been forgiven once and for all, how we live matters because we are connected to God and should therefore want to please him.

Well then, should we keep on sinning so that God can show us more and more of his wonderful grace? [2]Of course not! Since we have died to sin, how can we continue to live in it? [3]Or have you forgotten that when we were joined with Christ Jesus in baptism, we joined him in his death? [4]For we died and were buried with Christ by baptism. And just as Christ was raised from the dead by the glorious power of the Father, now we also may live new lives.

[5]Since we have been united with him in his death, we will also be raised to life as he was. [6]We know that our old sinful selves were crucified with Christ so that sin might lose its power in our lives. We are no longer slaves to sin. [7]For when we died with Christ we were set free from the power of sin. [8]And since we died with Christ, we know we will also live with him. [9]We are sure of this because Christ was raised from the dead, and he will never die again. Death no longer has any power over him. [10]When he died, he died once to break the power of sin. But now that he lives, he lives for the glory of God. [11]So you also should consider yourselves to be dead to the power of sin and alive to God through Christ Jesus.

[12]Do not let sin control the way you live;* do not give in to sinful desires. [13]Do not let any part of your body become an instrument of evil to serve sin. Instead, give yourselves completely to God, for you were dead, but now you have new life. So use your whole body as an instrument to do what is right for the glory of God. [14]Sin is no longer your master, for you no longer live under the requirements of the law. Instead, you live under the freedom of God's grace.

[15]Well then, since God's grace has set us free from the law, does that mean we can go on sinning? Of course not! [16]Don't you realize that you become the slave of whatever you choose to obey? You can be a slave to sin, which leads to death, or you can choose to obey God, which leads to righteous living. [17]Thank God! Once you were slaves of sin, but now you wholeheartedly obey this teaching we have given you. [18]Now you are free from your slavery to sin, and you have become slaves to righteous living.

[19]Because of the weakness of your human nature, I am using the illustration of slavery to help you understand all this. Previously, you let yourselves be slaves to impurity and lawlessness, which led ever deeper into sin. Now you must give yourselves to be slaves to righteous living so that you will become holy.

[20]When you were slaves to sin, you were free from the obligation to do right. [21]And what was the result? You are now ashamed of the things you used to do, things that

---

HOW WE LIVE

Following Jesus

ROMANS 6:15-18 Following Jesus doesn't mean that you're suddenly perfect. We will still struggle with sin, but we don't have to be slaves to sin. As followers of Christ, we have been set free from the enslaving power of sin. "Well then, since God's grace has set us free from the law, does that mean we can go on sinning?" Paul asked. Short answer: Of course not! • Following Jesus means desiring to be like him. It means knowing him well enough to have an idea of what he would do in the situations we face. Even when we sin, when we fail and flounder, we can choose to repent and obey God and pursue his way. We can become slaves to righteousness instead of slaves to sin. • What is your honest estimation of yourself in this area? Do you want to be like Jesus? Do you deal honestly with sin in your life? Live under God's grace, and keep on following Jesus.

end in eternal doom. [22]But now you are free from the power of sin and have become slaves of God. Now you do those things that lead to holiness and result in eternal life. [23]For the wages of sin is death, but the free gift of God is eternal life through Christ Jesus our Lord.

6:12 Or *Do not let sin reign in your body, which is subject to death.*

PSALM 16:1-11
A psalm of David.

[1] Keep me safe, O God,
  for I have come to you for refuge.

[2] I said to the LORD, "You are my Master!
  Every good thing I have comes from you."
[3] The godly people in the land
  are my true heroes!
  I take pleasure in them!

[4] Troubles multiply for those who chase after other gods.
  I will not take part in their sacrifices of blood
  or even speak the names of their gods.

[5] LORD, you alone are my inheritance,
  my cup of blessing.
  You guard all that is mine.

[6] The land you have given me is a pleasant land.
  What a wonderful inheritance!

[7] I will bless the LORD who guides me;
  even at night my heart instructs me.
[8] I know the LORD is always with me.
  I will not be shaken, for he is right beside me.

[9] No wonder my heart is glad, and I rejoice.*
  My body rests in safety.
[10] For you will not leave my soul among the dead*
  or allow your holy one* to rot in the grave.
[11] You will show me the way of life,
  granting me the joy of your presence
  and the pleasures of living with you forever.*

16:9 Greek version reads *and my tongue shouts his praises.* Compare Acts 2:26.   16:10a Hebrew *in Sheol.*   16:10b Or *your Holy One.*   16:11 Greek version reads *You have shown me the way of life, / and you will fill me with the joy of your presence.* Compare Acts 2:28.

PROVERBS 19:20-21
Get all the advice and instruction you can, so you will be wise the rest of your life. ☐ You can make many plans, but the LORD's purpose will prevail.

JULY**21**

2 CHRONICLES 4:1–6:11
The Ark of the Covenant was the most sacred symbol of God's presence. To bring that Ark to a permanent resting place at the nation's capital had huge significance for Israel.

Solomon* also made a bronze altar 30 feet long, 30 feet wide, and 15 feet high.* [2]Then he cast a great round basin, 15 feet across from rim to rim, called the Sea. It was 7½ feet deep and about 45 feet in circumference.* [3]It was encircled just below its rim by two rows of figures that resembled oxen. There were about six oxen per foot* all the way around, and they were cast as part of the basin.

[4]The Sea was placed on a base of twelve bronze oxen, all facing outward. Three faced north, three faced west, three faced south, and three faced east, and the Sea rested on them. [5]The walls of the Sea were about three inches* thick, and its rim flared out like a cup and resembled a water lily blossom. It could hold about 16,500 gallons* of water.

[6]He also made ten smaller basins for washing the utensils for the burnt offerings. He set five on the south side and five on the north. But the priests washed themselves in the Sea.

[7]He then cast ten gold lampstands ac-

cording to the specifications that had been given, and he put them in the Temple. Five were placed against the south wall, and five were placed against the north wall.

[8]He also built ten tables and placed them in the Temple, five along the south wall and five along the north wall. Then he molded 100 gold basins.

[9]He then built a courtyard for the priests, and also the large outer courtyard. He made doors for the courtyard entrances and overlaid them with bronze. [10]The great bronze basin called the Sea was placed near the southeast corner of the Temple.

[11]Huram-abi also made the necessary washbasins, shovels, and bowls.

So at last Huram-abi completed everything King Solomon had assigned him to make for the Temple of God:

[12] the two pillars;
the two bowl-shaped capitals on top of the pillars;
the two networks of interwoven chains that decorated the capitals;
[13] the 400 pomegranates that hung from the chains on the capitals (two rows of pomegranates for each of the chain networks that decorated the capitals on top of the pillars);
[14] the water carts holding the basins;
[15] the Sea and the twelve oxen under it;
[16] the ash buckets, the shovels, the meat hooks, and all the related articles.

Huram-abi made all these things of burnished bronze for the Temple of the LORD, just as King Solomon had directed. [17]The king had them cast in clay molds in the Jordan Valley between Succoth and Zarethan.* [18]Solomon used such great quantities of bronze that its weight could not be determined.

[19]Solomon also made all the furnishings for the Temple of God:

the gold altar;
the tables for the Bread of the Presence;
[20] the lampstands and their lamps of solid gold, to burn in front of the Most Holy Place as prescribed;
[21] the flower decorations, lamps, and tongs—all of the purest gold;

[22] the lamp snuffers, bowls, dishes, and incense burners—all of solid gold;
the doors for the entrances to the Most Holy Place and the main room of the Temple, overlaid with gold.

5:1 So Solomon finished all his work on the Temple of the LORD. Then he brought all the gifts his father, David, had dedicated—the silver, the gold, and the various articles—and he stored them in the treasuries of the Temple of God.

[2]Solomon then summoned to Jerusalem the elders of Israel and all the heads of tribes—the leaders of the ancestral families of Israel. They were to bring the Ark of the LORD's Covenant to the Temple from its location in the City of David, also known as Zion. [3]So all the men of Israel assembled before the king at the annual Festival of Shelters, which is held in early autumn.*

[4]When all the elders of Israel arrived, the Levites picked up the Ark. [5]The priests and Levites brought up the Ark along with the special tent* and all the sacred items that had been in it. [6]There, before the Ark, King Solomon and the entire community of Israel sacrificed so many sheep, goats, and cattle that no one could keep count!

[7]Then the priests carried the Ark of the LORD's Covenant into the inner sanctuary of the Temple—the Most Holy Place—and placed it beneath the wings of the cherubim. [8]The cherubim spread their wings over the Ark, forming a canopy over the Ark and its carrying poles. [9]These poles were so long that their ends could be seen from the Temple's main room—the Holy Place*—but not from the outside. They are still there to this day. [10]Nothing was in the Ark except the two stone tablets that Moses had placed in it at Mount Sinai,* where the LORD made a covenant with the people of Israel when they left Egypt.

[11]Then the priests left the Holy Place. All the priests who were present had purified themselves, whether or not they were on duty that day. [12]And the Levites who were musicians—Asaph, Heman, Jeduthun, and all their sons and brothers—were dressed in fine linen robes and stood at the east side of the altar playing

cymbals, lyres, and harps. They were joined by 120 priests who were playing trumpets. ¹³The trumpeters and singers performed together in unison to praise and give thanks to the LORD. Accompanied by trumpets, cymbals, and other instruments, they raised their voices and praised the LORD with these words:

"He is good!
His faithful love endures forever!"

At that moment a thick cloud filled the Temple of the LORD. ¹⁴The priests could not continue their service because of the cloud, for the glorious presence of the LORD filled the Temple of God.

⁶:¹THEN Solomon prayed, "O LORD, you have said that you would live in a thick cloud of darkness. ²Now I have built a glorious Temple for you, a place where you can live forever!"

³Then the king turned around to the entire community of Israel standing before him and gave this blessing: ⁴"Praise the LORD, the God of Israel, who has kept the promise he made to my father, David. For he told my father, ⁵'From the day I brought my people out of the land of Egypt, I have never chosen a city among any of the tribes of Israel as the place where a Temple should be built to honor my name. Nor have I chosen a king to lead my people Israel. ⁶But now I have chosen Jerusalem as the place for my name to be honored, and I have chosen David to be king over my people Israel.'"

⁷Then Solomon said, "My father, David, wanted to build this Temple to honor the name of the LORD, the God of Israel. ⁸But the LORD told him, 'You wanted to build the Temple to honor my name. Your intention is good, ⁹but you are not the one to do it. One of your own sons will build the Temple to honor me.'

¹⁰"And now the LORD has fulfilled the promise he made, for I have become king in my father's place, and now I sit on the throne of Israel, just as the LORD promised. I have built this Temple to honor the name of the LORD, the God of Israel. ¹¹There I have placed the Ark, which contains the covenant that the LORD made with the people of Israel."

4:1a Or *Huram-abi;* Hebrew reads *He.*   **4:1b** Hebrew *20 cubits* [9.2 meters] *long, 20 cubits wide, and 10 cubits* [4.6 meters] *high.*   **4:2** Hebrew *10 cubits* [4.6 meters] *across . . . 5 cubits* [2.3 meters] *deep and 30 cubits* [13.8 meters] *in circumference.*   **4:3** Or *20 oxen per meter;* Hebrew reads *10 per cubit.*   **4:5a** Hebrew *a handbreadth* [8 centimeters].   **4:5b** Hebrew *3,000 baths* [63 kiloliters].   **4:17** As in parallel text at 1 Kgs 7:46; Hebrew reads *Zeredah.*   **5:3** Hebrew *at the festival that is in the seventh month.* The Festival of Shelters began on the fifteenth day of the seventh month of the ancient Hebrew lunar calendar. This day occurred in late September, October, or early November.   **5:5** Hebrew *the Tent of Meeting;* i.e., the tent mentioned in 2 Sam 6:17 and 1 Chr 16:1.   **5:9** As in parallel text at 1 Kgs 8:8; Hebrew reads *from the Ark in front of the Most Holy Place.*   **5:10** Hebrew *Horeb,* another name for Sinai.

ROMANS 7:1-13

So what good are all of God's rules and laws anyway? They teach us that we don't have the ability to follow them. They show us that we need redemption, the very thing that God generously provides.

Now, dear brothers and sisters*—you who are familiar with the law—don't you know that the law applies only while a person is living? ²For example, when a woman marries, the law binds her to her husband as long as he is alive. But if he dies, the laws of marriage no longer apply to her. ³So while her husband is alive, she would be committing adultery if she married another man. But if her husband dies, she is free from that law and does not commit adultery when she remarries.

⁴So, my dear brothers and sisters, this is the point: You died to the power of the law when you died with Christ. And now you are united with the one who was raised from the dead. As a result, we can produce a harvest of good deeds for God. ⁵When we were controlled by our old nature,* sinful desires were at work within us, and the law aroused these evil desires that produced a harvest of sinful deeds, resulting in death. ⁶But now we have been released from the law, for we died to it and are no longer captive to its power. Now we can serve God, not in the old way of obeying the letter of the law, but in the new way of living in the Spirit.

⁷Well then, am I suggesting that the law of God is sinful? Of course not! In fact, it was the law that showed me my sin. I would never have known that coveting is wrong if the law had not said, "You must not covet."* ⁸But sin used this command to arouse all kinds of covetous desires

within me! If there were no law, sin would not have that power. [9]At one time I lived without understanding the law. But when I learned the command not to covet, for instance, the power of sin came to life, [10]and I died. So I discovered that the law's commands, which were supposed to bring life, brought spiritual death instead. [11]Sin took advantage of those commands and deceived me; it used the commands to kill me. [12]But still, the law itself is holy, and its commands are holy and right and good.

[13]But how can that be? Did the law, which is good, cause my death? Of course not! Sin used what was good to bring about my condemnation to death. So we can see how terrible sin really is. It uses God's good commands for its own evil purposes.

7:1 Greek *brothers;* also in 7:4.   7:5 Greek *When we were in the flesh.*   7:7 Exod 20:17; Deut 5:21.

PSALM 17:1-15
A prayer of David.

[1] **O** LORD, hear my plea for justice.
　　Listen to my cry for help.
　Pay attention to my prayer,
　　for it comes from honest lips.
[2] Declare me innocent,
　　for you see those who do right.

[3] You have tested my thoughts and
　　examined my heart in the
　　night.
　You have scrutinized me and found
　　nothing wrong.

I am determined not to sin in what
　　I say.
[4] I have followed your commands,
　　which keep me from following
　　cruel and evil people.
[5] My steps have stayed on your path;
　　I have not wavered from following
　　you.

[6] I am praying to you because I know
　　you will answer, O God.
　Bend down and listen as I pray.
[7] Show me your unfailing love in
　　wonderful ways.
　By your mighty power you rescue
　　those who seek refuge from their
　　enemies.
[8] Guard me as you would guard your
　　own eyes.*
　Hide me in the shadow of your
　　wings.
[9] Protect me from wicked people
　　who attack me,
　　from murderous enemies who
　　surround me.
[10] They are without pity.
　　Listen to their boasting!
[11] They track me down and surround me,
　　watching for the chance to throw
　　me to the ground.
[12] They are like hungry lions, eager to
　　tear me apart—
　　like young lions hiding in ambush.
[13] Arise, O LORD!
　　Stand against them, and bring them
　　to their knees!

HOW WE LIVE | Faith and works

ROMANS 7:4 As a new believer, you have put your faith in Jesus Christ as your Savior. The Bible says that true faith is then revealed by "a harvest of good deeds for God." But how is that harvest produced? • Paul says here that we have died with Christ, and now we have access to the power that raised him from the dead. This power helps us yield a rich harvest of good deeds.   • Your faith is not only a list of beliefs or doctrines; real faith is your surrender and connection with God and his subsequent work in and through you. As the apostle Paul said, "What is important is faith expressing itself in love" (Galatians 5:6, September 19). Jesus said, "I am the vine; you are the branches. Those who remain in me, and I in them, will produce much fruit" (John 15:5, May 26). What kind of harvest is your life producing?

Rescue me from the wicked with
your sword!
[14] By the power of your hand, O LORD,
destroy those who look to this
world for their reward.
But satisfy the hunger of your
treasured ones.
May their children have plenty,
leaving an inheritance for their
descendants.

[15] Because I am righteous, I will see you.
When I awake, I will see you face to
face and be satisfied.

17:8 Hebrew *as the pupil of your eye.*

PROVERBS 19:22-23

Loyalty makes a person attractive. It is
better to be poor than dishonest. □ Fear
of the LORD leads to life, bringing security
and protection from harm.

JULY**22**

2 CHRONICLES 6:12–8:10

Throughout the centuries the Temple was the center
of Jewish life. In fact, the welfare of the Temple was
often a good indicator of the spiritual life of the
people. Today's reading reveals a people dedicated
to God with much to celebrate.

Then Solomon stood before the altar of
the LORD in front of the entire community of Israel, and he lifted his hands
in prayer. [13] Now Solomon had made a
bronze platform 7½ feet long, 7½ feet
wide, and 4½ feet high* and had placed it
at the center of the Temple's outer courtyard. He stood on the platform, and then
he knelt in front of the entire community
of Israel and lifted his hands toward
heaven. [14] He prayed,

"O LORD, God of Israel, there is no God
like you in all of heaven and earth. You
keep your covenant and show
unfailing love to all who walk before
you in wholehearted devotion. [15] You
have kept your promise to your
servant David, my father. You made
that promise with your own mouth,
and with your own hands you have
fulfilled it today.
[16] "And now, O LORD, God of Israel,
carry out the additional promise you
made to your servant David, my father.
For you said to him, 'If your
descendants guard their behavior and
faithfully follow my Law as you have
done, one of them will always sit on

the throne of Israel.' [17] Now, O LORD,
God of Israel, fulfill this promise to
your servant David.
[18] "But will God really live on earth
among people? Why, even the highest
heavens cannot contain you. How
much less this Temple I have built!
[19] Nevertheless, listen to my prayer and
my plea, O LORD my God. Hear the cry
and the prayer that your servant is
making to you. [20] May you watch over
this Temple day and night, this place
where you have said you would put
your name. May you always hear the
prayers I make toward this place.
[21] May you hear the humble and
earnest requests from me and your
people Israel when we pray toward
this place. Yes, hear us from heaven
where you live, and when you hear,
forgive.
[22] "If someone wrongs another
person and is required to take an oath
of innocence in front of your altar at
this Temple, [23] then hear from heaven
and judge between your servants—the
accuser and the accused. Pay back the
guilty as they deserve. Acquit the
innocent because of their innocence.
[24] "If your people Israel are defeated
by their enemies because they have
sinned against you, and if they turn
back and acknowledge your name and
pray to you here in this Temple, [25] then
hear from heaven and forgive the sin

of your people Israel and return them to this land you gave to them and to their ancestors.

26"If the skies are shut up and there is no rain because your people have sinned against you, and if they pray toward this Temple and acknowledge your name and turn from their sins because you have punished them, 27then hear from heaven and forgive the sins of your servants, your people Israel. Teach them to follow the right path, and send rain on your land that you have given to your people as their special possession.

28"If there is a famine in the land or a plague or crop disease or attacks of locusts or caterpillars, or if your people's enemies are in the land besieging their towns—whatever disaster or disease there is—29and if your people Israel pray about their troubles or sorrow, raising their hands toward this Temple, 30then hear from heaven where you live, and forgive. Give your people what their actions deserve, for you alone know each human heart. 31Then they will fear you and walk in your ways as long as they live in the land you gave to our ancestors.

32"In the future, foreigners who do not belong to your people Israel will hear of you. They will come from distant lands when they hear of your great name and your strong hand and your powerful arm. And when they pray toward this Temple, 33then hear from heaven where you live, and grant what they ask of you. In this way, all the people of the earth will come to know and fear you, just as your own people Israel do. They, too, will know that this Temple I have built honors your name.

34"If your people go out where you send them to fight their enemies, and if they pray to you by turning toward this city you have chosen and toward this Temple I have built to honor your name, 35then hear their prayers from heaven and uphold their cause.

36"If they sin against you—and who has never sinned?—you might become

angry with them and let their enemies conquer them and take them captive to a foreign land far away or near. 37But in that land of exile, they might turn to you in repentance and pray, 'We have sinned, done evil, and acted wickedly.' 38If they turn to you with their whole heart and soul in the land of their captivity and pray toward the land you gave to their ancestors—toward this city you have chosen, and toward this Temple I have built to honor your name—39then hear their prayers and their petitions from heaven where you live, and uphold their cause. Forgive your people who have sinned against you.

40"O my God, may your eyes be open and your ears attentive to all the prayers made to you in this place.

41 "And now arise, O LORD God, and
    enter your resting place,
    along with the Ark, the symbol of
    your power.
May your priests, O LORD God, be
    clothed with salvation;
    may your loyal servants rejoice in
    your goodness.
42 O LORD God, do not reject the king
    you have anointed.
Remember your unfailing love
    for your servant David."

7:1WHEN Solomon finished praying, fire flashed down from heaven and burned up the burnt offerings and sacrifices, and the glorious presence of the LORD filled the Temple. 2The priests could not enter the Temple of the LORD because the glorious presence of the LORD filled it. 3When all the people of Israel saw the fire coming down and the glorious presence of the LORD filling the Temple, they fell face down on the ground and worshiped and praised the LORD, saying,

"He is good!
    His faithful love endures forever!"

4Then the king and all the people offered sacrifices to the LORD. 5King Solomon offered a sacrifice of 22,000 cattle and 120,000 sheep and goats. And so the king and all the people dedicated the Temple of God. 6The priests took their assigned positions, and so did the Levites who were singing, "His faithful love endures forever!" They accompanied the singing with music from the instruments King David had made for praising the LORD. Across from the Levites, the priests blew the trumpets, while all Israel stood.

⁷Solomon then consecrated the central area of the courtyard in front of the LORD's Temple. He offered burnt offerings and the fat of peace offerings there, because the bronze altar he had built could not hold all the burnt offerings, grain offerings, and sacrificial fat.

⁸For the next seven days Solomon and all Israel celebrated the Festival of Shelters.* A large congregation had gathered from as far away as Lebo-hamath in the north and the Brook of Egypt in the south. ⁹On the eighth day they had a closing ceremony, for they had celebrated the dedication of the altar for seven days and the Festival of Shelters for seven days. ¹⁰Then at the end of the celebration,* Solomon sent the people home. They were all joyful and glad because the LORD had been so good to David and to Solomon and to his people Israel.

¹¹So Solomon finished the Temple of the LORD, as well as the royal palace. He completed everything he had planned to do in the construction of the Temple and the palace. ¹²Then one night the LORD appeared to Solomon and said,

"I have heard your prayer and have chosen this Temple as the place for making sacrifices. ¹³At times I might shut up the heavens so that no rain falls, or command grasshoppers to devour your crops, or send plagues among you. ¹⁴Then if my people who are called by my name will humble themselves and pray and seek my face and turn from their wicked ways, I will hear from heaven and will forgive their sins and restore their land. ¹⁵My eyes will be open and my ears attentive to every prayer made in this place. ¹⁶For I have chosen this Temple and set it apart to be holy—a place where my name will be honored forever. I will always watch over it, for it is dear to my heart.

¹⁷"As for you, if you faithfully follow me as David your father did, obeying all my commands, decrees, and regulations, ¹⁸then I will establish the throne of your dynasty. For I made this covenant with your father, David, when I said, 'One of your descendants will always rule over Israel.'

¹⁹"But if you or your descendants abandon me and disobey the decrees and commands I have given you, and if you serve and worship other gods, ²⁰then I will uproot the people from this land that I have given them. I will reject this Temple that I have made holy to honor my name. I will make it an object of mockery and ridicule among the nations. ²¹And though this Temple is impressive now, all who pass by will be appalled. They will ask, 'Why did the LORD do such terrible things to this land and to this Temple?' ²²"And the answer will be, 'Because his people abandoned the LORD, the God of their ancestors, who brought them out of Egypt, and they worshiped other gods instead and bowed down to them. That is why he has brought all these disasters on them.'"

8:1IT took Solomon twenty years to build the LORD's Temple and his own royal palace. At the end of that time, ²Solomon turned his attention to rebuilding the towns that King Hiram* had given him, and he settled Israelites in them.

³Solomon also fought against the town of Hamath-zobah and conquered it. ⁴He rebuilt Tadmor in the wilderness and built towns in the region of Hamath as supply centers. ⁵He fortified the towns of Upper Beth-horon and Lower Beth-horon, rebuilding their walls and installing barred gates. ⁶He also rebuilt Baalath and other supply centers and constructed towns where his chariots and horses* could be stationed. He built everything he desired in Jerusalem and Lebanon and throughout his entire realm.

⁷There were still some people living in the land who were not Israelites, including the Hittites, Amorites, Perizzites, Hivites, and Jebusites. ⁸These were descendants of the nations whom the people of Israel had

not destroyed. So Solomon conscripted them for his labor force, and they serve in the labor force to this day. 9But Solomon did not conscript any of the Israelites for his labor force. Instead, he assigned them to serve as fighting men, officers in his army, commanders of his chariots, and charioteers. 10King Solomon appointed 250 of them to supervise the people.

6:13 Hebrew *5 cubits* [2.3 meters] *long, 5 cubits wide, and 3 cubits* [1.4 meters] *high.*   7:8 Hebrew *the festival* (also in 7:9); see note on 5:3.   7:10 Hebrew *Then on the twenty-third day of the seventh month.* This day of the ancient Hebrew lunar calendar occurred in October or early November.   8:2 Hebrew *Huram,* a variant spelling of Hiram; also in 8:18.   8:6 Or *and charioteers.*

ROMANS 7:14–8:8
Our struggle with sin is indeed a struggle. Paul didn't hesitate to admit that he struggled—certain things still tripped him up. God offers forgiveness and transformation so that our struggle can be less and less.

So the trouble is not with the law, for it is spiritual and good. The trouble is with me, [Paul] for I am all too human, a slave to sin. 15I don't really understand myself, for I want to do what is right, but I don't do it. Instead, I do what I hate. 16But if I know that what I am doing is wrong, this shows that I agree that the law is good. 17So I am not the one doing wrong; it is sin living in me that does it.

18And I know that nothing good lives in me, that is, in my sinful nature.* I want to do what is right, but I can't. 19I want to do what is good, but I don't. I don't want to do what is wrong, but I do it anyway. 20But if I do what I don't want to do, I am not really the one doing wrong; it is sin living in me that does it.

21I have discovered this principle of life—that when I want to do what is right, I inevitably do what is wrong. 22I love God's law with all my heart. 23But there is another power* within me that is at war with my mind. This power makes me a slave to the sin that is still within me. 24Oh, what a miserable person I am! Who will free me from this life that is dominated by sin and death? 25Thank God! The answer is in Jesus Christ our Lord. So you see how it is: In my mind I really want to obey God's law, but because of my sinful nature I am a slave to sin.

8:1So now there is no condemnation for those who belong to Christ Jesus. 2And because you belong to him, the power* of the life-giving Spirit has freed you* from the power of sin that leads to death. 3The law of Moses was unable to save us because of the weakness of our sinful nature.* So God did what the law could not do. He sent his own Son in a body like the bodies we sinners have. And in that body

---

WHAT THE BIBLE SAYS

The Temple

2 CHRONICLES 7:1-10 For the Israelites, the Temple was central to their religious and national identity. It was a holy and sacred location where God's presence was manifest in a special way. In its beauty and its mystery (no one entered into the Most Holy Place except the high priest, and he could do that only once a year), it represented the holy character of God and taught the people about worship and holiness. In a theocracy, God's presence in the capital city created a sense of national solidarity and strength. Before the Temple there was the Tabernacle—a beautiful, portable, tent-like structure where God himself dwelt among his people as they traveled through the wilderness (Exodus 40:34-38, February 15).
• In the Temple, God was present to his people. No wonder the people rejoiced so much when this awesome structure was completed and God's glorious presence filled it! How horrible it must have been for those who saw it destroyed by the invading Babylonians centuries later.

God declared an end to sin's control over us by giving his Son as a sacrifice for our sins. ⁴He did this so that the just requirement of the law would be fully satisfied for us, who no longer follow our sinful nature but instead follow the Spirit.

⁵Those who are dominated by the sinful nature think about sinful things, but those who are controlled by the Holy Spirit think about things that please the Spirit. ⁶So letting your sinful nature control your mind leads to death. But letting the Spirit control your mind leads to life and peace. ⁷For the sinful nature is always hostile to God. It never did obey God's laws, and it never will. ⁸That's why those who are still under the control of their sinful nature can never please God.

7:18 Greek *my flesh;* also in 7:25. 7:23 Greek *law;* also in 7:23b. 8:2a Greek *the law;* also in 8:2b. 8:2b Some manuscripts read *me.* 8:3 Greek *our flesh;* similarly in 8:4, 5, 6, 7, 8, 9, 12.

PSALM 18:1-15

For the choir director: A psalm of David, the servant of the LORD. He sang this song to the LORD on the day the LORD rescued him from all his enemies and from Saul. He sang:

¹ I love you, LORD;
  you are my strength.
² The LORD is my rock, my fortress, and
  my savior;
  my God is my rock, in whom I find
  protection.
He is my shield, the power that saves
  me,
  and my place of safety.
³ I called on the LORD, who is worthy
  of praise,
  and he saved me from my enemies.

⁴ The ropes of death entangled me;
  floods of destruction swept
  over me.
⁵ The grave* wrapped its ropes
  around me;
  death laid a trap in my path.
⁶ But in my distress I cried out to the
  LORD;

yes, I prayed to my God for
  help.
He heard me from his sanctuary;
  my cry to him reached his ears.

⁷ Then the earth quaked and trembled.
  The foundations of the mountains
  shook;
  they quaked because of his anger.
⁸ Smoke poured from his nostrils;
  fierce flames leaped from his
  mouth.
  Glowing coals blazed forth
  from him.
⁹ He opened the heavens and came
  down;
  dark storm clouds were beneath
  his feet.
¹⁰ Mounted on a mighty angelic being,*
  he flew,
  soaring on the wings of the wind.
¹¹ He shrouded himself in darkness,
  veiling his approach with dark rain
  clouds.
¹² Thick clouds shielded the brightness
  around him
  and rained down hail and burning
  coals.*
¹³ The LORD thundered from heaven;
  the voice of the Most High
  resounded
  amid the hail and burning coals.
¹⁴ He shot his arrows and scattered his
  enemies;
  his lightning flashed, and they were
  greatly confused.
¹⁵ Then at your command, O LORD,
  at the blast of your breath,
  the bottom of the sea could be seen,
  and the foundations of the earth
  were laid bare.

18:5 Hebrew *Sheol.* 18:10 Hebrew *a cherub.* 18:12 Or *and lightning bolts;* also in 18:13.

PROVERBS 19:24-25

Lazy people take food in their hand but don't even lift it to their mouth. □ If you punish a mocker, the simpleminded will learn a lesson; if you correct the wise, they will be all the wiser.

2 CHRONICLES 8:11–10:19

Solomon's indiscretions toward the end of his reign ended up costing the people of Israel greatly. The unified kingdom was to be no more.

Solomon moved his wife, Pharaoh's daughter, from the City of David to the new palace he had built for her. He said, "My wife must not live in King David's palace, for the Ark of the LORD has been there, and it is holy ground."

¹²Then Solomon presented burnt offerings to the LORD on the altar he had built for him in front of the entry room of the Temple. ¹³He offered the sacrifices for the Sabbaths, the new moon festivals, and the three annual festivals—the Passover celebration, the Festival of Harvest,* and the Festival of Shelters—as Moses had commanded.

¹⁴In assigning the priests to their duties, Solomon followed the regulations of his father, David. He also assigned the Levites to lead the people in praise and to assist the priests in their daily duties. And he assigned the gatekeepers to their gates by their divisions, following the commands of David, the man of God. ¹⁵Solomon did not deviate in any way from David's commands concerning the priests and Levites and the treasuries.

¹⁶So Solomon made sure that all the work related to building the Temple of the LORD was carried out, from the day its foundation was laid to the day of its completion.

¹⁷Later Solomon went to Ezion-geber and Elath,* ports along the shore of the Red Sea* in the land of Edom. ¹⁸Hiram sent him ships commanded by his own officers and manned by experienced crews of sailors. These ships sailed to Ophir with Solomon's men and brought back to Solomon almost seventeen tons* of gold.

⁹:¹WHEN the queen of Sheba heard of Solomon's fame, she came to Jerusalem to test him with hard questions. She arrived with a large group of attendants and a great caravan of camels loaded with spices, large quantities of gold, and precious jewels. When she met with Solomon, she talked with him about everything she had on her mind. ²Solomon had answers for all her questions; nothing was too hard for him to explain to her. ³When the queen of Sheba realized how wise Solomon was, and when she saw the palace he had built, ⁴she was overwhelmed. She was also amazed at the food on his tables, the organization of his officials and their splendid clothing, the cup-bearers and their robes, and the burnt offerings Solomon made at the Temple of the LORD.

⁵She exclaimed to the king, "Everything I heard in my country about your achievements* and wisdom is true! ⁶I didn't believe what was said until I arrived here and saw it with my own eyes. In fact, I had not heard the half of your great wisdom! It is far beyond what I was told. ⁷How happy your people must be! What a privilege for your officials to stand here day after day, listening to your wisdom! ⁸Praise the LORD your God, who delights in you and has placed you on the throne as king to rule for him. Because God loves Israel and desires this kingdom to last forever, he has made you king over them so you can rule with justice and righteousness."

⁹Then she gave the king a gift of 9,000 pounds* of gold, great quantities of spices, and precious jewels. Never before had there been spices as fine as those the queen of Sheba gave to King Solomon.

¹⁰(In addition, the crews of Hiram and Solomon brought gold from Ophir, and they also brought red sandalwood* and precious jewels. ¹¹The king used the sandalwood to make steps* for the Temple of the LORD and the royal palace, and to construct lyres and harps for the musicians. Never before had such beautiful things been seen in Judah.)

¹²King Solomon gave the queen of Sheba whatever she asked for—gifts of greater value than the gifts she had given him. Then she and all her attendants returned to their own land.

¹³Each year Solomon received about

25 tons* of gold. ¹⁴This did not include the additional revenue he received from merchants and traders. All the kings of Arabia and the governors of the provinces also brought gold and silver to Solomon.

¹⁵King Solomon made 200 large shields of hammered gold, each weighing more than 15 pounds.* ¹⁶He also made 300 smaller shields of hammered gold, each weighing more than 7½ pounds.* The king placed these shields in the Palace of the Forest of Lebanon.

¹⁷Then the king made a huge throne, decorated with ivory and overlaid with pure gold. ¹⁸The throne had six steps, with a footstool of gold. There were armrests on both sides of the seat, and the figure of a lion stood on each side of the throne. ¹⁹There were also twelve other lions, one standing on each end of the six steps. No other throne in all the world could be compared with it!

²⁰All of King Solomon's drinking cups were solid gold, as were all the utensils in the Palace of the Forest of Lebanon. They were not made of silver, for silver was considered worthless in Solomon's day!

²¹The king had a fleet of trading ships* manned by the sailors sent by Hiram.* Once every three years the ships returned, loaded with gold, silver, ivory, apes, and peacocks.*

²²So King Solomon became richer and wiser than any other king on earth. ²³Kings from every nation came to consult him and to hear the wisdom God had given him. ²⁴Year after year everyone who visited brought him gifts of silver and gold, clothing, weapons, spices, horses, and mules.

²⁵Solomon had 4,000 stalls for his horses and chariots, and he had 12,000 horses.* He stationed some of them in the chariot cities, and some near him in Jerusalem. ²⁶He ruled over all the kings from the Euphrates River* in the north to the land of the Philistines and the border of Egypt in the south. ²⁷The king made silver as plentiful in Jerusalem as stone. And valuable cedar timber was as common as the sycamore-fig trees that grow in the foothills of Judah.* ²⁸Solomon's horses were imported from Egypt* and many other countries.

²⁹The rest of the events of Solomon's reign, from beginning to end, are recorded in *The Record of Nathan the Prophet,* and *The Prophecy of Ahijah from Shiloh,* and also in *The Visions of Iddo the Seer,* concerning Jeroboam son of Nebat. ³⁰Solomon ruled in Jerusalem over all Israel for forty years. ³¹When he died, he was buried in the City of David, named for his father. Then his son Rehoboam became the next king.

10:1 Rehoboam went to Shechem, where all Israel had gathered to make him king. ²When Jeroboam son of Nebat heard of this, he returned from Egypt, for he had fled to Egypt to escape from King Solomon. ³The leaders of Israel summoned him, and Jeroboam and all Israel went to speak with Rehoboam. ⁴"Your father was a hard master," they said. "Lighten the harsh labor demands and heavy taxes that your father imposed on us. Then we will be your loyal subjects."

⁵Rehoboam replied, "Come back in three days for my answer." So the people went away.

⁶Then King Rehoboam discussed the matter with the older men who had counseled his father, Solomon. "What is your advice?" he asked. "How should I answer these people?"

⁷The older counselors replied, "If you are good to these people and do your best to please them and give them a favorable answer, they will always be your loyal subjects."

⁸But Rehoboam rejected the advice of the older men and instead asked the opinion of the young men who had grown up with him and were now his advisers. ⁹"What is your advice?" he asked them. "How should I answer these people who want me to lighten the burdens imposed by my father?"

¹⁰The young men replied, "This is what you should tell those complainers who want a lighter burden: 'My little finger is thicker than my father's waist! ¹¹Yes, my father laid heavy burdens on you, but I'm going to make them even heavier! My father beat you with whips, but I will beat you with scorpions!'"

¹²Three days later Jeroboam and all the

people returned to hear Rehoboam's decision, just as the king had ordered. ¹³But Rehoboam spoke harshly to them, for he rejected the advice of the older counselors ¹⁴and followed the counsel of his younger advisers. He told the people, "My father laid* heavy burdens on you, but I'm going to make them even heavier! My father beat you with whips, but I will beat you with scorpions!"

¹⁵So the king paid no attention to the people. This turn of events was the will of God, for it fulfilled the LORD's message to Jeroboam son of Nebat through the prophet Ahijah from Shiloh.

¹⁶When all Israel realized* that the king had refused to listen to them, they responded,

"Down with the dynasty of David!
We have no interest in the son of Jesse.
Back to your homes, O Israel!
Look out for your own house, O David!"

So all the people of Israel returned home. ¹⁷But Rehoboam continued to rule over the Israelites who lived in the towns of Judah.

¹⁸King Rehoboam sent Adoniram,* who was in charge of the labor force, to restore order, but the people of Israel stoned him to death. When this news reached King Rehoboam, he quickly jumped into his chariot and fled to Jerusalem. ¹⁹And to this day the northern tribes of Israel have refused to be ruled by a descendant of David.

8:13 Or *Festival of Weeks.* **8:17a** As in Greek version (see also 2 Kgs 14:22; 16:6); Hebrew reads *Eloth,* a variant spelling of Elath. **8:17b** As in parallel text at 1 Kgs 9:26; Hebrew reads *the sea.* **8:18** Hebrew *450 talents* [15.3 metric tons]. **9:5** Hebrew *your words.* **9:9** Hebrew *120 talents* [4,000 kilograms]. **9:10** Hebrew *algum wood* (also in 9:11); perhaps a variant spelling of *almug.* Compare parallel text at 1 Kgs 10:11-12. **9:11** Or *gateways.* The meaning of the Hebrew is uncertain. **9:13** Hebrew *666 talents* [23 metric tons]. **9:15** Hebrew *600 shekels* [6.8 kilograms]. **9:16** Hebrew *300 shekels* [3.4 kilograms]. **9:21a** Hebrew *fleet of ships that could sail to Tarshish.* **9:21b** Hebrew *Huram,* a variant spelling of Hiram. **9:21c** Or *and baboons.* **9:25** Or *12,000 charioteers.* **9:26** Hebrew *the river.* **9:27** Hebrew *the Shephelah.* **9:28** Possibly *Muzur,* a district near Cilicia. **10:14** As in Greek version and many Hebrew manuscripts (see also 1 Kgs 12:14); Masoretic Text reads *I will lay.* **10:16** As in Syriac version, Latin Vulgate, and many Hebrew manuscripts (see also 1 Kgs 12:16); Masoretic Text lacks *realized.* **10:18** Hebrew *Hadoram,* a variant spelling of Adoniram; compare 1 Kgs 4:6; 5:14; 12:18.

ROMANS 8:9-25
God provides us with an invaluable resource—his Spirit. The Holy Spirit empowers us to live in such a way that we could not in our own strength. Will we still struggle with sin? Yes. Will we struggle alone with no hope? Never again.

But you are not controlled by your sinful nature. You are controlled by the Spirit if you have the Spirit of God living in you.

HOW WE LIVE: Relying on God's power

ROMANS 8:9-14 Perhaps you've already experienced the yo-yo syndrome in your Christian life—feeling strong in your faith one minute and then giving in to temptation the next minute. Back and forth. Up and down. Sometimes it feels as if the pull of sin is so strong that there is nothing that can overpower it. But there *is* something stronger in us: "the Spirit of God . . . lives in you" (8:11). And "the Spirit who lives in you is greater than the spirit who lives in the world" (1 John 4:4, December 4). ● If God's Spirit is in us, why do we still struggle with sin? One reason is that even though we are God's children, we still have our human nature. We will wrestle with the old nature until we go to heaven. But Paul reminded his Roman readers that they had no obligation to that little voice that says, "Go ahead, you know you want to . . . " Once we become Christians, our only obligation is to the Spirit, who calls us to a better life, a more *alive* life. ● Learning how to live by God's Spirit is the process through which we grow as Christians. Learn to pray for God's Spirit to give you strength to stand—even against your own sinful nature when necessary.

(And remember that those who do not have the Spirit of Christ living in them do not belong to him at all.) [10]And Christ lives within you, so even though your body will die because of sin, the Spirit gives you life* because you have been made right with God. [11]The Spirit of God, who raised Jesus from the dead, lives in you. And just as God raised Christ Jesus from the dead, he will give life to your mortal bodies by this same Spirit living within you.

[12]Therefore, dear brothers and sisters,* you have no obligation to do what your sinful nature urges you to do. [13]For if you live by its dictates, you will die. But if through the power of the Spirit you put to death the deeds of your sinful nature,* you will live. [14]For all who are led by the Spirit of God are children* of God.

[15]So you have not received a spirit that makes you fearful slaves. Instead, you received God's Spirit when he adopted you as his own children.* Now we call him, "Abba, Father."* [16]For his Spirit joins with our spirit to affirm that we are God's children. [17]And since we are his children, we are his heirs. In fact, together with Christ we are heirs of God's glory. But if we are to share his glory, we must also share his suffering.

[18]Yet what we suffer now is nothing compared to the glory he will reveal to us later. [19]For all creation is waiting eagerly for that future day when God will reveal who his children really are. [20]Against its will, all creation was subjected to God's curse. But with eager hope, [21]the creation looks forward to the day when it will join God's children in glorious freedom from death and decay. [22]For we know that all creation has been groaning as in the pains of childbirth right up to the present time. [23]And we believers also groan, even though we have the Holy Spirit within us as a foretaste of future glory, for we long for our bodies to be released from sin and suffering. We, too, wait with eager hope for the day when God will give us our full rights as his adopted children,* including the new bodies he has promised us. [24]We were given this hope when we were saved. (If we already have something, we don't need to hope* for it. [25]But if we look for-

ward to something we don't yet have, we must wait patiently and confidently.)

8:10 Or *your spirit is alive.*   **8:12** Greek *brothers;* also in 8:29.
8:13 Greek *deeds of the body.*   **8:14** Greek *sons;* also in 8:19.
8:15a Greek *you received a spirit of sonship.*   **8:15b** *Abba* is an Aramaic term for "father."   **8:23** Greek *wait anxiously for sonship.*   **8:24** Some manuscripts read *wait.*

PSALM 18:16-36

He [the LORD] reached down from
 heaven and rescued me;
 he drew me out of deep waters.
[17] He rescued me from my powerful
 enemies,
 from those who hated me and were
 too strong for me.
[18] They attacked me at a moment when I
 was in distress,
 but the LORD supported me.
[19] He led me to a place of safety;
 he rescued me because he delights
 in me.
[20] The LORD rewarded me for doing
 right;
 he restored me because of my
 innocence.
[21] For I have kept the ways of the LORD;
 I have not turned from my God to
 follow evil.
[22] I have followed all his regulations;
 I have never abandoned his decrees.
[23] I am blameless before God;
 I have kept myself from sin.
[24] The LORD rewarded me for doing
 right.
 He has seen my innocence.

[25] To the faithful you show yourself
 faithful;
 to those with integrity you show
 integrity.
[26] To the pure you show yourself pure,
 but to the wicked you show yourself
 hostile.
[27] You rescue the humble,
 but you humiliate the proud.
[28] You light a lamp for me.
 The LORD, my God, lights up my
 darkness.
[29] In your strength I can crush an army;
 with my God I can scale any wall.

[30] God's way is perfect.
 All the LORD's promises prove true.
 He is a shield for all who look to
 him for protection.

31 For who is God except the LORD?
   Who but our God is a solid rock?
32 God arms me with strength,
   and he makes my way perfect.
33 He makes me as surefooted
      as a deer,
   enabling me to stand on mountain
      heights.
34 He trains my hands for battle;
   he strengthens my arm to draw
      a bronze bow.

35 You have given me your shield
      of victory.
   Your right hand supports me;
   your help has made me great.
36 You have made a wide path for my feet
   to keep them from slipping.

PROVERBS 19:26

Children who mistreat their father or chase away their mother are an embarrassment and a public disgrace.

JULY**24**

2 CHRONICLES 11:1–13:22

Not long after securing his reign over Judah, Rehoboam abandoned the Lord. He soon learned a lesson that too few subsequent kings of Israel and Judah learned—that if you abandon the Lord you reap the consequences.

When Rehoboam arrived at Jerusalem, he mobilized the men of Judah and Benjamin—180,000 select troops—to fight against Israel and to restore the kingdom to himself.

2 But the LORD said to Shemaiah, the man of God, 3 "Say to Rehoboam son of Solomon, king of Judah, and to all the Israelites in Judah and Benjamin: 4 This is what the LORD says: Do not fight against your relatives. Go back home, for what has happened is my doing!' " So they obeyed the message of the LORD and did not fight against Jeroboam.

5 Rehoboam remained in Jerusalem and fortified various towns for the defense of Judah. 6 He built up Bethlehem, Etam, Tekoa, 7 Beth-zur, Soco, Adullam, 8 Gath, Mareshah, Ziph, 9 Adoraim, Lachish, Azekah, 10 Zorah, Aijalon, and Hebron. These became the fortified towns of Judah and Benjamin. 11 Rehoboam strengthened their defenses and stationed commanders in them, and he stored supplies of food, olive oil, and wine. 12 He also put shields and spears in these towns as a further safety measure.

So only Judah and Benjamin remained under his control.

13 But all the priests and Levites living among the northern tribes of Israel sided with Rehoboam. 14 The Levites even abandoned their pasturelands and property and moved to Judah and Jerusalem, because Jeroboam and his sons would not allow them to serve the LORD as priests. 15 Jeroboam appointed his own priests to serve at the pagan shrines, where they worshiped the goat and calf idols he had made. 16 From all the tribes of Israel, those who sincerely wanted to worship the LORD, the God of Israel, followed the Levites to Jerusalem, where they could offer sacrifices to the LORD, the God of their ancestors. 17 This strengthened the kingdom of Judah, and for three years they supported Rehoboam son of Solomon, for during those years they faithfully followed in the footsteps of David and Solomon.

18 Rehoboam married his cousin Mahalath, the daughter of David's son Jerimoth and of Abihail, the daughter of Eliab son of Jesse. 19 Mahalath had three sons—Jeush, Shemariah, and Zaham.

20 Later Rehoboam married another cousin, Maacah, the daughter of Absalom. Maacah gave birth to Abijah, Attai, Ziza, and Shelomith. 21 Rehoboam loved Maacah more than any of his other wives and concubines. In all, he had eighteen wives

and sixty concubines, and they gave birth to twenty-eight sons and sixty daughters.

²²Rehoboam appointed Maacah's son Abijah as leader among the princes, making it clear that he would be the next king. ²³Rehoboam also wisely gave responsibilities to his other sons and stationed some of them in the fortified towns throughout the land of Judah and Benjamin. He provided them with generous provisions, and he found many wives for them.

12:1BUT when Rehoboam was firmly established and strong, he abandoned the Law of the LORD, and all Israel followed him in this sin. ²Because they were unfaithful to the LORD, King Shishak of Egypt came up and attacked Jerusalem in the fifth year of King Rehoboam's reign. ³He came with 1,200 chariots, 60,000 horses,* and a countless army of foot soldiers, including Libyans, Sukkites, and Ethiopians.* ⁴Shishak conquered Judah's fortified towns and then advanced to attack Jerusalem.

⁵The prophet Shemaiah then met with Rehoboam and Judah's leaders, who had all fled to Jerusalem because of Shishak. Shemaiah told them, "This is what the LORD says: You have abandoned me, so I am abandoning you to Shishak."

⁶Then the leaders of Israel and the king humbled themselves and said, "The LORD is right in doing this to us!"

⁷When the LORD saw their change of heart, he gave this message to Shemaiah: "Since the people have humbled themselves, I will not completely destroy them and will soon give them some relief. I will not use Shishak to pour out my anger on Jerusalem. ⁸But they will become his subjects, so they will know the difference between serving me and serving earthly rulers."

⁹So King Shishak of Egypt came up and attacked Jerusalem. He ransacked the treasuries of the LORD's Temple and the royal palace; he stole everything, including all the gold shields Solomon had made. ¹⁰King Rehoboam later replaced them with bronze shields as substitutes, and he entrusted them to the care of the commanders of the guard who protected the entrance to the royal palace.

¹¹Whenever the king went to the Temple of the LORD, the guards would also take the shields and then return them to the guardroom. ¹²Because Rehoboam humbled himself, the LORD's anger was turned away, and he did not destroy him completely. There were still some good things in the land of Judah.

¹³King Rehoboam firmly established himself in Jerusalem and continued to rule. He was forty-one years old when he became king, and he reigned seventeen years in Jerusalem, the city the LORD had chosen from among all the tribes of Israel as the place to honor his name. Rehoboam's mother was Naamah, a woman from Ammon. ¹⁴But he was an evil king, for he did not seek the LORD with all his heart.

¹⁵The rest of the events of Rehoboam's reign, from beginning to end, are recorded in *The Record of Shemaiah the Prophet* and *The Record of Iddo the Seer*, which are part of the genealogical record. Rehoboam and Jeroboam were continually at war with each other. ¹⁶When Rehoboam died, he was buried in the City of David. Then his son Abijah became the next king.

13:1ABIJAH began to rule over Judah in the eighteenth year of Jeroboam's reign in Israel. ²He reigned in Jerusalem three years. His mother was Maacah,* the daughter of Uriel from Gibeah.

Then war broke out between Abijah and Jeroboam. ³Judah, led by King Abijah, fielded 400,000 select warriors, while Jeroboam mustered 800,000 select troops from Israel.

⁴When the army of Judah arrived in the hill country of Ephraim, Abijah stood on Mount Zemaraim and shouted to Jeroboam and all Israel: "Listen to me! ⁵Don't you realize that the LORD, the God of Israel, made a lasting covenant* with David, giving him and his descendants the throne of Israel forever? ⁶Yet Jeroboam son of Nebat, a mere servant of David's son Solomon, rebelled against his master. ⁷Then a whole gang of scoundrels joined him, defying Solomon's son Rehoboam when he was young and inexperienced and could not stand up to them.

⁸"Do you really think you can stand

against the kingdom of the LORD that is led by the descendants of David? You may have a vast army, and you have those gold calves that Jeroboam made as your gods. ⁹But you have chased away the priests of the LORD (the descendants of Aaron) and the Levites, and you have appointed your own priests, just like the pagan nations. You let anyone become a priest these days! Whoever comes to be dedicated with a young bull and seven rams can become a priest of these so-called gods of yours!

¹⁰"But as for us, the LORD is our God, and we have not abandoned him. Only the descendants of Aaron serve the LORD as priests, and the Levites alone may help them in their work. ¹¹They present burnt offerings and fragrant incense to the LORD every morning and evening. They place the Bread of the Presence on the holy table, and they light the gold lampstand every evening. We are following the instructions of the LORD our God, but you have abandoned him. ¹²So you see, God is with us. He is our leader. His priests blow their trumpets and lead us into battle against you. O people of Israel, do not fight against the LORD, the God of your ancestors, for you will not succeed!"

¹³Meanwhile, Jeroboam had secretly sent part of his army around behind the men of Judah to ambush them. ¹⁴When Judah realized that they were being attacked from the front and the rear, they cried out to the LORD for help. Then the priests blew the trumpets, ¹⁵and the men of Judah began to shout. At the sound of their battle cry, God defeated Jeroboam and all Israel and routed them before Abijah and the army of Judah.

¹⁶The Israelite army fled from Judah, and God handed them over to Judah in defeat. ¹⁷Abijah and his army inflicted heavy losses on them; 500,000 of Israel's select troops were killed that day. ¹⁸So Judah defeated Israel on that occasion because they trusted in the LORD, the God of their ancestors. ¹⁹Abijah and his army pursued Jeroboam's troops and captured some of his towns, including Bethel, Jeshanah, and Ephron, along with their surrounding villages.

²⁰So Jeroboam of Israel never regained his power during Abijah's lifetime, and finally the LORD struck him down and he died. ²¹Meanwhile, Abijah of Judah grew more and more powerful. He married fourteen wives and had twenty-two sons and sixteen daughters.

²²The rest of the events of Abijah's reign, including his words and deeds, are recorded in *The Commentary of Iddo the Prophet.*

HOW WE LIVE

Trusting God

ROMANS 8:28-31, 38-39 If you're alive, you have problems. You will continue to face tough times of one kind or another. Christians are not exempt from hardship. So where is God in the tough times? Can he really be trusted when things turn bad? • In those difficult times, you may feel set aside by God, unloved, forgotten. But that's not possible. You see, the Bible tells us that God is always at work behind the scenes of our lives, fulfilling his purposes and using "all things," even hard times, to mature and shape our faith. This does not mean that all that happens to us is good. Evil is prevalent in our fallen world, but God is able to turn every circumstance around for our long-range good. This promise is not for everybody; it can be claimed only by those who love God and are called according to his purpose. • As a believer, you are one of those "called" people. As such, you can trust that no matter how big your problems are, God will work them together for good. He will redeem trouble. Nothing— *nothing!*—can separate you from God's love. Whether you live or die, you cannot be separated from him.

12:3a Or *charioteers*, or *horsemen*.   12:3b Hebrew *and Cushites*.   13:2 As in most Greek manuscripts and Syriac version (see also 2 Chr 11:20-21; 1 Kgs 15:2); Hebrew reads *Micaiah*, a variant spelling of Maacah.   13:5 Hebrew *a covenant of salt*.

ROMANS 8:26-39

Many of us go through life feeling alone, unnoticed, and even unloved. Yet Paul's words reflect the truth that, in relationship with God through Christ, there is no place we can go, no attitude we can cop, no mistake that we can make that will separate us from God's love.

And the Holy Spirit helps us in our weakness. For example, we don't know what God wants us to pray for. But the Holy Spirit prays for us with groanings that cannot be expressed in words. 27And the Father who knows all hearts knows what the Spirit is saying, for the Spirit pleads for us believers* in harmony with God's own will. 28And we know that God causes everything to work together* for the good of those who love God and are called according to his purpose for them. 29For God knew his people in advance, and he chose them to become like his Son, so that his Son would be the firstborn among many brothers and sisters. 30And having chosen them, he called them to come to him. And having called them, he gave them right standing with himself. And having given them right standing, he gave them his glory.

31What shall we say about such wonderful things as these? If God is for us, who can ever be against us? 32Since he did not spare even his own Son but gave him up for us all, won't he also give us everything else? 33Who dares accuse us whom God has chosen for his own? No one—for God himself has given us right standing with himself. 34Who then will condemn us? No one—for Christ Jesus died for us and was raised to life for us, and he is sitting in the place of honor at God's right hand, pleading for us.

35Can anything ever separate us from Christ's love? Does it mean he no longer loves us if we have trouble or calamity, or are persecuted, or hungry, or destitute, or in danger, or threatened with death? 36(As the Scriptures say, "For your sake we are killed every day; we are being slaughtered like sheep."*) 37No, despite all these things, overwhelming victory is ours through Christ, who loved us.

38And I am convinced that nothing can ever separate us from God's love. Neither death nor life, neither angels nor demons,* neither our fears for today nor our worries about tomorrow—not even the powers of hell can separate us from God's love. 39No power in the sky above or in the earth below—indeed, nothing in all creation will ever be able to separate us from the love of God that is revealed in Christ Jesus our Lord.

8:27 Greek *for God's holy people*.   8:28 Some manuscripts read *And we know that everything works together*.
8:36 Ps 44:22.   8:38 Greek *nor rulers*.

PSALM 18:37-50

I chased my enemies and caught them;
  I did not stop until they were conquered.
38 I struck them down so they could not get up;
  they fell beneath my feet.
39 You have armed me with strength for the battle;
  you have subdued my enemies under my feet.
40 You placed my foot on their necks.
  I have destroyed all who hated me.
41 They called for help, but no one came to their rescue.
  They even cried to the Lord, but he refused to answer.
42 I ground them as fine as dust in the wind.
  I swept them into the gutter like dirt.
43 You gave me victory over my accusers.
  You appointed me ruler over nations;
  people I don't even know now serve me.
44 As soon as they hear of me, they submit;
  foreign nations cringe before me.
45 They all lose their courage
  and come trembling from their strongholds.
46 The Lord lives! Praise to my Rock!
  May the God of my salvation be exalted!

⁴⁷ He is the God who pays back those
   who harm me;
he subdues the nations under me
⁴⁸   and rescues me from my
   enemies.
You hold me safe beyond the reach
   of my enemies;
you save me from violent
   opponents.
⁴⁹ For this, O LORD, I will praise you
   among the nations;
I will sing praises to your name.
⁵⁰ You give great victories to your king;

you show unfailing love to your
   anointed,
to David and all his descendants
   forever.

PROVERBS 19:27-29

If you stop listening to instruction, my
child, you will turn your back on knowledge. ☐ A corrupt witness makes a mockery of justice; the mouth of the wicked
gulps down evil. ☐ Punishment is made
for mockers, and the backs of fools are
made to be beaten.

2 CHRONICLES 14:1–16:14

The rest of 2 Chronicles records the story of the
kings of Judah (while the books of Kings recorded
the stories of both Israel and Judah). Today's reading is about King Asa of Judah who succeeded his
father, Abijah.

¹*When Abijah died, he was buried in the
City of David. Then his son Asa became the
next king. There was peace in the land for
ten years. ²*Asa did what was pleasing and
good in the sight of the LORD his God. ³He
removed the foreign altars and the pagan
shrines. He smashed the sacred pillars and
cut down the Asherah poles. ⁴He commanded the people of Judah to seek the
LORD, the God of their ancestors, and to
obey his law and his commands. ⁵Asa also
removed the pagan shrines, as well as the
incense altars from every one of Judah's
towns. So Asa's kingdom enjoyed a period
of peace. ⁶During those peaceful years, he
was able to build up the fortified towns
throughout Judah. No one tried to make
war against him at this time, for the LORD
was giving him rest from his enemies.
⁷Asa told the people of Judah, "Let us
build towns and fortify them with walls,
towers, gates, and bars. The land is still
ours because we sought the LORD our God,
and he has given us peace on every side."
So they went ahead with these projects
and brought them to completion.

⁸King Asa had an army of 300,000 warriors from the tribe of Judah, armed with
large shields and spears. He also had an
army of 280,000 warriors from the tribe
of Benjamin, armed with small shields
and bows. Both armies were composed of
well-trained fighting men.
⁹Once an Ethiopian* named Zerah attacked Judah with an army of 1,000,000
men* and 300 chariots. They advanced to
the town of Mareshah, ¹⁰so Asa deployed
his armies for battle in the valley north of
Mareshah.* ¹¹Then Asa cried out to the
LORD his God, "O LORD, no one but you
can help the powerless against the
mighty! Help us, O LORD our God, for we
trust in you alone. It is in your name that
we have come against this vast horde.
O LORD, you are our God; do not let mere
men prevail against you!"
¹²So the LORD defeated the Ethiopians* in the presence of Asa and the
army of Judah, and the enemy fled. ¹³Asa
and his army pursued them as far as
Gerar, and so many Ethiopians fell that
they were unable to rally. They were destroyed by the LORD and his army, and the
army of Judah carried off a vast amount of
plunder.
¹⁴While they were at Gerar, they attacked all the towns in that area, and terror

from the LORD came upon the people there. As a result, a vast amount of plunder was taken from these towns, too. [15]They also attacked the camps of herdsmen and captured many sheep, goats, and camels before finally returning to Jerusalem.

[15:1]THEN the Spirit of God came upon Azariah son of Oded, [2]and he went out to meet King Asa as he was returning from the battle. "Listen to me, Asa!" he shouted. "Listen, all you people of Judah and Benjamin! The LORD will stay with you as long as you stay with him! Whenever you seek him, you will find him. But if you abandon him, he will abandon you. [3]For a long time Israel was without the true God, without a priest to teach them, and without the Law to instruct them. [4]But whenever they were in trouble and turned to the LORD, the God of Israel, and sought him out, they found him.

[5]"During those dark times, it was not safe to travel. Problems troubled the people of every land. [6]Nation fought against nation, and city against city, for God was troubling them with every kind of problem. [7]But as for you, be strong and courageous, for your work will be rewarded."

[8]When Asa heard this message from Azariah the prophet,* he took courage and removed all the detestable idols from the land of Judah and Benjamin and in the towns he had captured in the hill country of Ephraim. And he repaired the altar of the LORD, which stood in front of the entry room of the LORD's Temple.

[9]Then Asa called together all the people of Judah and Benjamin, along with the people of Ephraim, Manasseh, and Simeon who had settled among them. For many from Israel had moved to Judah during Asa's reign when they saw that the LORD his God was with him. [10]The people gathered at Jerusalem in late spring,* during the fifteenth year of Asa's reign.

[11]On that day they sacrificed to the LORD 700 cattle and 7,000 sheep and goats from the plunder they had taken in the battle. [12]Then they entered into a covenant to seek the LORD, the God of their ancestors, with all their heart and soul. [13]They agreed that anyone who refused to seek the LORD, the God of Israel, would be

put to death—whether young or old, man or woman. [14]They shouted out their oath of loyalty to the LORD with trumpets blaring and rams' horns sounding. [15]All in Judah were happy about this covenant, for they had entered into it with all their heart. They earnestly sought after God, and they found him. And the LORD gave them rest from their enemies on every side.

[16]King Asa even deposed his grandmother* Maacah from her position as queen mother because she had made an obscene Asherah pole. He cut down her obscene pole, broke it up, and burned it in the Kidron Valley. [17]Although the pagan shrines were not removed from Israel, Asa's heart remained completely faithful throughout his life. [18]He brought into the Temple of God the silver and gold and the various items that he and his father had dedicated.

[19]So there was no more war until the thirty-fifth year of Asa's reign.

[16:1]IN the thirty-sixth year of Asa's reign, King Baasha of Israel invaded Judah and fortified Ramah in order to prevent anyone from entering or leaving King Asa's territory in Judah.

[2]Asa responded by removing the silver and gold from the treasuries of the Temple of the LORD and the royal palace. He sent it to King Ben-hadad of Aram, who was ruling in Damascus, along with this message:

> [3]"Let there be a treaty between you and me like the one between your father and my father. See, I am sending you silver and gold. Break your treaty with King Baasha of Israel so that he will leave me alone."

[4]Ben-hadad agreed to King Asa's request and sent the commanders of his army to attack the towns of Israel. They conquered the towns of Ijon, Dan, Abel-beth-maacah,* and all the store cities in Naphtali. [5]As soon as Baasha of Israel heard what was happening, he abandoned his project of fortifying Ramah and stopped all work on it. [6]Then King Asa called out all the men of Judah to carry away the building stones and timbers that

Baasha had been using to fortify Ramah. Asa used these materials to fortify the towns of Geba and Mizpah.

[7]At that time Hanani the seer came to King Asa and told him, "Because you have put your trust in the king of Aram instead of in the LORD your God, you missed your chance to destroy the army of the king of Aram. [8]Don't you remember what happened to the Ethiopians* and Libyans and their vast army, with all of their chariots and charioteers?* At that time you relied on the LORD, and he handed them over to you. [9]The eyes of the LORD search the whole earth in order to strengthen those whose hearts are fully committed to him. What a fool you have been! From now on you will be at war."

[10]Asa became so angry with Hanani for saying this that he threw him into prison and put him in stocks. At that time Asa also began to oppress some of his people.

[11]The rest of the events of Asa's reign, from beginning to end, are recorded in *The Book of the Kings of Judah and Israel*. [12]In the thirty-ninth year of his reign, Asa developed a serious foot disease. Yet even with the severity of his disease, he did not seek the LORD's help but turned only to his physicians. [13]So he died in the forty-first year of his reign. [14]He was buried in the tomb he had carved out for himself in the City of David. He was laid on a bed perfumed with sweet spices and fragrant ointments, and the people built a huge funeral fire in his honor.

14:1 Verse 14:1 is numbered 13:23 in the Hebrew text.
14:2 Verses 14:2-15 are numbered 14:1-14 in Hebrew text.
14:9a Hebrew *a Cushite*.   **14:9b** Or *an army of thousands and thousands;* Hebrew reads *an army of a thousand thousands*.   **14:10** Or *in the Zephathah Valley near Mareshah*.   **14:12** Hebrew *Cushites;* also in 14:13.
15:8 As in Syriac version and Latin Vulgate (see also 15:1); Hebrew reads *from Oded the prophet*.   **15:10** Hebrew *in the third month*. This month of the ancient Hebrew lunar calendar usually occurs within the months of May and June.
15:16 Hebrew *his mother*.   **16:4** As in parallel text at 1 Kgs 15:20; Hebrew reads *Abel-maim,* a variant spelling of *Abel-beth-maacah*.   **16:8a** Hebrew *Cushites*.   **16:8b** Or *and horsemen?*

ROMANS 9:1-24

God chooses us. He pursues us. Just as he chose Abraham, then Isaac, then Jacob (the Jewish patriarchs), so he chooses us to be his own. We can't manipulate it, earn it or demand it. We can only receive it.

With Christ as my witness, I [Paul] speak with utter truthfulness. My conscience and the Holy Spirit confirm it. [2]My heart is filled with bitter sorrow and unending grief [3]for my people, my Jewish brothers and sisters.* I would be willing to be forever cursed—cut off from Christ!— if that would save them. [4]They are the people of Israel, chosen to be God's adopted children.* God revealed his glory to them. He made covenants with them and gave them his law. He gave them the privilege of worshiping him and receiving his wonderful promises. [5]Abraham, Isaac, and Jacob are their ancestors, and Christ himself was an

---

HOW WE LIVE

Setting priorities

2 CHRONICLES 16:7-9 It wasn't wrong of Asa to make treaties or to seek an alliance. No, the issue was much deeper: "You have put your trust in the king of Aram instead of in the LORD," Hanani the seer said. Asa had his priorities all wrong; he was relying on all the wrong things. • Think about how you make decisions in your life. Reflect on how you deal with difficulties. On what are you relying? The first human response is usually to rely on our own wits. But learn a lesson from King Asa. To please God we must have our priorities in order—relying first on God, trusting in his power, leaning on him. God is looking for people "whose hearts are fully committed to him." You are not left to flounder in your decisions alone; God will advise you through his Word and strengthen you. When you make it your priority to pray for God's guidance, he will help set all of your other priorities in order.

Israelite as far as his human nature is concerned. And he is God, the one who rules over everything and is worthy of eternal praise! Amen.*

⁶Well then, has God failed to fulfill his promise to Israel? No, for not all who are born into the nation of Israel are truly members of God's people! ⁷Being descendants of Abraham doesn't make them truly Abraham's children. For the Scriptures say, "Isaac is the son through whom your descendants will be counted,"* though Abraham had other children, too. ⁸This means that Abraham's physical descendants are not necessarily children of God. Only the children of the promise are considered to be Abraham's children. ⁹For God had promised, "I will return about this time next year, and Sarah will have a son."*

¹⁰This son was our ancestor Isaac. When he married Rebekah, she gave birth to twins.* ¹¹But before they were born, before they had done anything good or bad, she received a message from God. (This message shows that God chooses people according to his own purposes; ¹²he calls people, but not according to their good or bad works.) She was told, "Your older son will serve your younger son."* ¹³In the words of the Scriptures, "I loved Jacob, but I rejected Esau."*

¹⁴Are we saying, then, that God was unfair? Of course not! ¹⁵For God said to Moses,

"I will show mercy to anyone I choose,
and I will show compassion to
anyone I choose."*

¹⁶So it is God who decides to show mercy. We can neither choose it nor work for it.

¹⁷For the Scriptures say that God told Pharaoh, "I have appointed you for the very purpose of displaying my power in you and to spread my fame throughout the earth."* ¹⁸So you see, God chooses to show mercy to some, and he chooses to harden the hearts of others so they refuse to listen.

¹⁹Well then, you might say, "Why does God blame people for not responding? Haven't they simply done what he makes them do?"

²⁰No, don't say that. Who are you, a mere human being, to argue with God? Should the thing that was created say to the one who created it, "Why have you made me like this?" ²¹When a potter makes jars out of clay, doesn't he have a right to use the same lump of clay to make one jar for decoration and another to throw garbage into? ²²In the same way, even though God has the right to show his anger and his power, he is very patient with those on whom his anger falls, who are destined for destruction. ²³He does this to make the riches of his glory shine even brighter on those to whom he shows mercy, who were prepared in advance for glory. ²⁴And we are among those whom he selected, both from the Jews and from the Gentiles.

9:3 Greek *my brothers.*   9:4 Greek *chosen for sonship.*
9:5 Or *May God, the one who rules over everything, be praised forever. Amen.*   9:7 Gen 21:12.   9:9 Gen 18:10, 14.
9:10 Greek *she conceived children through this one man.*
9:12 Gen 25:23.   9:13 Mal 1:2-3.   9:15 Exod 33:19.
9:17 Exod 9:16 (Greek version).

PSALM 19:1-14
For the choir director: A psalm of David.

¹ The heavens proclaim the glory
    of God.
   The skies display his craftsmanship.
² Day after day they continue to speak;
   night after night they make him
    known.
³ They speak without a sound or word;
   their voice is never heard.*
⁴ Yet their message has gone
    throughout the earth,
   and their words to all the world.

God has made a home in the heavens
    for the sun.
⁵ It bursts forth like a radiant
    bridegroom after his wedding.
   It rejoices like a great athlete eager
    to run the race.
⁶ The sun rises at one end of the
    heavens
   and follows its course to the other
    end.
   Nothing can hide from its heat.

⁷ The instructions of the LORD are
    perfect,
   reviving the soul.
   The decrees of the LORD are
    trustworthy,
   making wise the simple.

⁸ The commandments of the LORD are
right,
bringing joy to the heart.
The commands of the LORD are clear,
giving insight for living.
⁹ Reverence for the LORD is pure,
lasting forever.
The laws of the LORD are true;
each one is fair.
¹⁰ They are more desirable than gold,
even the finest gold.
They are sweeter than honey,
even honey dripping from the comb.
¹¹ They are a warning to your servant,
a great reward for those who obey
them.
¹² How can I know all the sins lurking in
my heart?

Cleanse me from these hidden
faults.
¹³ Keep your servant from deliberate
sins!
Don't let them control me.
Then I will be free of guilt
and innocent of great sin.

¹⁴ May the words of my mouth
and the meditation of my heart
be pleasing to you,
O LORD, my rock and my redeemer.

19:3 Or *There is no speech or language where their voice is
not heard.*

PROVERBS 20:1

Wine produces mockers; alcohol leads to
brawls. Those led astray by drink cannot
be wise.

JULY**26**

2 CHRONICLES 17:1–18:34

Jehoshaphat ruled in Judah, succeeding his father,
Asa. Jehoshaphat was a diplomat and a negotiator,
sometimes erring on the side of diplomacy (note
his relationship with the evil King Ahab of Israel).
Nevertheless, he is remembered for his positive
reforms.

Then Jehoshaphat, Asa's son, became the
next king. He strengthened Judah to
stand against any attack from Israel. ²He
stationed troops in all the fortified towns
of Judah, and he assigned additional garrisons to the land of Judah and to the
towns of Ephraim that his father, Asa, had
captured.

³The LORD was with Jehoshaphat because he followed the example of his father's early years* and did not worship
the images of Baal. ⁴He sought his father's
God and obeyed his commands instead of
following the evil practices of the kingdom of Israel. ⁵So the LORD established
Jehoshaphat's control over the kingdom
of Judah. All the people of Judah brought
gifts to Jehoshaphat, so he became very
wealthy and highly esteemed. ⁶He was

deeply committed to* the ways of the
LORD. He removed the pagan shrines and
Asherah poles from Judah.

⁷In the third year of his reign Jehoshaphat sent his officials to teach in all the
towns of Judah. These officials included
Ben-hail, Obadiah, Zechariah, Nethanel,
and Micaiah. ⁸He sent Levites along with
them, including Shemaiah, Nethaniah,
Zebadiah, Asahel, Shemiramoth, Jehonathan, Adonijah, Tobijah, and Tob-
adonijah. He also sent out the priests
Elishama and Jehoram. ⁹They took copies
of the Book of the Law of the LORD and
traveled around through all the towns of
Judah, teaching the people.

¹⁰Then the fear of the LORD fell over all
the surrounding kingdoms so that none
of them wanted to declare war on Jehoshaphat. ¹¹Some of the Philistines brought
him gifts and silver as tribute, and the
Arabs brought 7,700 rams and 7,700 male
goats.

¹²So Jehoshaphat became more and
more powerful and built fortresses and
storage cities throughout Judah. ¹³He

stored numerous supplies in Judah's towns and stationed an army of seasoned troops at Jerusalem. ¹⁴His army was enrolled according to ancestral clans.

From Judah there were 300,000 troops organized in units of 1,000, under the command of Adnah. ¹⁵Next in command was Jehohanan, who commanded 280,000 troops. ¹⁶Next was Amasiah son of Zicri, who volunteered for the LORD's service, with 200,000 troops under his command. ¹⁷From Benjamin there were 200,000 troops equipped with bows and shields. They were under the command of Eliada, a veteran soldier. ¹⁸Next in command was Jehozabad, who commanded 180,000 armed men.

¹⁹These were the troops stationed in Jerusalem to serve the king, besides those Jehoshaphat stationed in the fortified towns throughout Judah.

¹⁸:¹JEHOSHAPHAT enjoyed great riches and high esteem, and he made an alliance with Ahab of Israel by having his son marry Ahab's daughter. ²A few years later he went to Samaria to visit Ahab, who prepared a great banquet for him and his officials. They butchered great numbers of sheep, goats, and cattle for the feast. Then Ahab enticed Jehoshaphat to join forces with him to recover Ramoth-gilead.

³"Will you go with me to Ramoth-gilead?" King Ahab of Israel asked King Jehoshaphat of Judah.

Jehoshaphat replied, "Why, of course! You and I are as one, and my troops are your troops. We will certainly join you in battle." ⁴Then Jehoshaphat added, "But first let's find out what the LORD says."

⁵So the king of Israel summoned the prophets, 400 of them, and asked them, "Should we go to war against Ramoth-gilead, or should I hold back?"

They all replied, "Yes, go right ahead! God will give the king victory."

⁶But Jehoshaphat asked, "Is there not also a prophet of the LORD here? We should ask him the same question."

⁷The king of Israel replied to Jehoshaphat, "There is one more man who could consult the LORD for us, but I hate him. He never prophesies anything but trouble for me! His name is Micaiah son of Imlah."

Jehoshaphat replied, "That's not the way a king should talk! Let's hear what he has to say."

⁸So the king of Israel called one of his officials and said, "Quick! Bring Micaiah son of Imlah."

⁹King Ahab of Israel and King Jehoshaphat of Judah, dressed in their royal robes, were sitting on thrones at the threshing floor near the gate of Samaria. All of Ahab's prophets were prophesying there in front of them. ¹⁰One of them, Zedekiah son of Kenaanah, made some iron horns and proclaimed, "This is what the LORD says: With these horns you will gore the Arameans to death!"

¹¹All the other prophets agreed. "Yes," they said, "go up to Ramoth-gilead and be victorious, for the LORD will give the king victory!"

¹²Meanwhile, the messenger who went to get Micaiah said to him, "Look, all the prophets are promising victory for the king. Be sure that you agree with them and promise success."

¹³But Micaiah replied, "As surely as the LORD lives, I will say only what my God says."

¹⁴When Micaiah arrived before the king, Ahab asked him, "Micaiah, should we go to war against Ramoth-gilead, or should I hold back?"

Micaiah replied sarcastically, "Yes, go up and be victorious, for you will have victory over them!"

¹⁵But the king replied sharply, "How many times must I demand that you speak only the truth to me when you speak for the LORD?"

¹⁶Then Micaiah told him, "In a vision I saw all Israel scattered on the mountains, like sheep without a shepherd. And the LORD said, 'Their master has been killed.* Send them home in peace.'"

¹⁷"Didn't I tell you?" the king of Israel exclaimed to Jehoshaphat. "He never prophesies anything but trouble for me."

¹⁸Then Micaiah continued, "Listen to what the LORD says! I saw the LORD sitting on his throne with all the armies of heaven around him, on his right and on

his left. ¹⁹And the LORD said, 'Who can entice King Ahab of Israel to go into battle against Ramoth-gilead so he can be killed?'

"There were many suggestions, ²⁰and finally a spirit approached the LORD and said, 'I can do it!'

"'How will you do this?' the LORD asked.

²¹"And the spirit replied, 'I will go out and inspire all of Ahab's prophets to speak lies.'

"'You will succeed,' said the LORD. 'Go ahead and do it.'

²²"So you see, the LORD has put a lying spirit in the mouths of your prophets. For the LORD has pronounced your doom."

²³Then Zedekiah son of Kenaanah walked up to Micaiah and slapped him across the face. "Since when did the Spirit of the LORD leave me to speak to you?" he demanded.

²⁴And Micaiah replied, "You will find out soon enough when you are trying to hide in some secret room!"

²⁵"Arrest him!" the king of Israel ordered. "Take him back to Amon, the governor of the city, and to my son Joash. ²⁶Give them this order from the king: 'Put this man in prison, and feed him nothing but bread and water until I return safely from the battle!'"

²⁷But Micaiah replied, "If you return safely, it will mean that the LORD has not spoken through me!" Then he added to those standing around, "Everyone mark my words!"

²⁸So King Ahab of Israel and King Jehoshaphat of Judah led their armies against Ramoth-gilead. ²⁹The king of Israel said to Jehoshaphat, "As we go into battle, I will disguise myself so no one will recognize me, but you wear your royal robes." So the king of Israel disguised himself, and they went into battle.

³⁰Meanwhile, the king of Aram had issued these orders to his chariot commanders: "Attack only the king of Israel! Don't bother with anyone else." ³¹So when the Aramean chariot commanders saw Jehoshaphat in his royal robes, they went after him. "There is the king of Israel!" they shouted. But Jehoshaphat called out and the LORD saved him. God helped him by turning the attackers away from him. ³²As soon as the chariot commanders realized he was not the king of Israel, they stopped chasing him.

³³An Aramean soldier, however, randomly shot an arrow at the Israelite troops and hit the king of Israel between the joints of his armor. "Turn the horses* and get me out of here!" Ahab groaned to the driver of the chariot. "I'm badly wounded!"

³⁴The battle raged all that day, and the

WHAT THE BIBLE SAYS

Jews and Gentiles

ROMANS 9:11-13 Jews are physical descendants of Abraham who were chosen as his special nation to receive God's law and through whom the Messiah, the Savior of the entire world, would come. The term *Gentiles* refers to all non-Jews. • Jesus was Jewish, as were many of the first Christians. However, it wasn't long before the message of salvation spread out to the Gentile nations. God's plan all along had been to bring salvation *through* the Jews, not just *to* the Jews. • Jews took great pride in their ancestry and the fact that they had descended from Abraham. Paul made the case, however, that Abraham became God's child not because of who he was but because of his faith in God. Therefore, true descendants of Abraham are not just those who are in his physical lineage, but instead, it is those who likewise have faith in God and in salvation through his Son, Jesus (Romans 9:6-8, July 25).

king of Israel propped himself up in his chariot facing the Arameans. In the evening, just as the sun was setting, he died.

17:3 Some Hebrew manuscripts read *the example of his father, David.*   17:6 Hebrew *His heart was courageous in.*   18:16 Hebrew *These people have no master.*   18:33 Hebrew *Turn your hand.*

ROMANS 9:25-10:13

No matter what externals we might believe make us right with God—family heritage, traditions, rules we've never broken—they aren't enough. Being a Jew was not enough. It takes faith to connect with God. It takes God's grace to become his child.

Concerning the Gentiles, God says in the prophecy of Hosea,

"Those who were not my people,
    I will now call my people.
And I will love those
    whom I did not love before."*

²⁶And,

"Then, at the place where they were told,
    'You are not my people,'
    there they will be called
    'children of the living God.'"*

²⁷And concerning Israel, Isaiah the prophet cried out,

"Though the people of Israel are as numerous as the sand of the seashore,
    only a remnant will be saved.
²⁸ For the LORD will carry out his sentence upon the earth
    quickly and with finality."*

²⁹And Isaiah said the same thing in another place:

"If the LORD of Heaven's Armies had not spared a few of our children,
we would have been wiped out like Sodom,
    destroyed like Gomorrah."*

³⁰What does all this mean? Even though the Gentiles were not trying to follow God's standards, they were made right with God. And it was by faith that this took place. ³¹But the people of Israel, who tried so hard to get right with God by keeping the law, never succeeded. ³²Why not? Because they were trying to get right with God by keeping the law* instead of by trusting in him. They stumbled over the great rock in their path. ³³God warned them of this in the Scriptures when he said,

"I am placing a stone in Jerusalem*
    that makes people stumble,
    a rock that makes them fall.
But anyone who trusts in him
    will never be disgraced."*

¹⁰:¹DEAR brothers and sisters,* the longing of my heart and my prayer to God is for the people of Israel to be saved. ²I know what enthusiasm they have for God, but it is misdirected zeal. ³For they don't understand God's way of making people right with himself. Refusing to accept God's way, they cling to their own way of getting right with God by trying to keep the law. ⁴For Christ has already accomplished the purpose for which the law was given.* As a result, all who believe in him are made right with God.

⁵For Moses writes that the law's way of making a person right with God requires obedience to all of its commands.* ⁶But faith's way of getting right with God says, "Don't say in your heart, 'Who will go up to heaven' (to bring Christ down to earth). ⁷And don't say, 'Who will go down to the place of the dead' (to bring Christ back to life again)." ⁸In fact, it says,

"The message is very close at hand;
    it is on your lips and in your heart."*

And that message is the very message about faith that we preach: ⁹If you confess with your mouth that Jesus is Lord and believe in your heart that God raised him from the dead, you will be saved. ¹⁰For it is by believing in your heart that you are made right with God, and it is by confessing with your mouth that you are saved. ¹¹As the Scriptures tell us, "Anyone who trusts in him will never be disgraced."* ¹²Jew and Gentile* are the same in this respect. They have the same Lord, who gives generously to all who call on him. ¹³For "Everyone who calls on the name of the LORD will be saved."*

9:25 Hos 2:23.   9:26 Greek *sons of the living God.* Hos 1:10.   9:27-28 Isa 10:22-23 (Greek version).   9:29 Isa 1:9.   9:32 Greek *by works.*   9:33a Greek *in Zion.*   9:33b Isa

8:14; 28:16 (Greek version).   **10:1** Greek *Brothers.*   **10:4** Or
For Christ is the end of the law.   **10:5** See Lev 18:5.
10:6-8 Deut 30:12-14.   **10:11** Isa 28:16 (Greek version).
10:12 Greek *and Greek.*   **10:13** Joel 2:32.

PSALM 20:1-9
For the choir director: A psalm of David.

¹ In times of trouble, may the LORD
  answer your cry.
  May the name of the God of Jacob
  keep you safe from all harm.
² May he send you help from his
  sanctuary
  and strengthen you from
  Jerusalem.*
³ May he remember all your gifts
  and look favorably on your burnt
  offerings.   *Interlude*

⁴ May he grant your heart's desires
  and make all your plans succeed.
⁵ May we shout for joy when we hear of
  your victory
  and raise a victory banner in the
  name of our God.

  May the LORD answer all your prayers.

⁶ Now I know that the LORD rescues his
  anointed king.
  He will answer him from his holy
  heaven
  and rescue him by his great power.
⁷ Some nations boast of their chariots
  and horses,
  but we boast in the name of the
  LORD our God.
⁸ Those nations will fall down and
  collapse,
  but we will rise up and stand firm.

⁹ Give victory to our king, O LORD!
  Answer our cry for help.

20:2 Hebrew *Zion.*

PROVERBS 20:2-3
The king's fury is like a lion's roar; to rouse
his anger is to risk your life. □ Avoiding a
fight is a mark of honor; only fools insist
on quarreling.

JULY**27**

2 CHRONICLES 19:1–20:37
At the end of today's reading, Jehoshaphat's life is
summarized. A paraphrase might be, "He honored
God's ways, but not one hundred percent." It's a
little intimidating to think of a life summarized in
a few sentences. How would your life summary
compare to Jehoshaphat's?

When King Jehoshaphat of Judah arrived
safely home in Jerusalem, ²Jehu son of
Hanani the seer went out to meet him.
"Why should you help the wicked and
love those who hate the LORD?" he asked
the king. "Because of what you have done,
the LORD is very angry with you. ³Even so,
there is some good in you, for you have removed the Asherah poles throughout the
land, and you have committed yourself to
seeking God."

⁴Jehoshaphat lived in Jerusalem, but he
went out among the people, traveling
from Beersheba to the hill country of

Ephraim, encouraging the people to
return to the LORD, the God of their ancestors. ⁵He appointed judges throughout
the nation in all the fortified towns, ⁶and
he said to them, "Always think carefully
before pronouncing judgment. Remember that you do not judge to please people
but to please the LORD. He will be with
you when you render the verdict in each
case. ⁷Fear the LORD and judge with integrity, for the LORD our God does not tolerate perverted justice, partiality, or the
taking of bribes."

⁸In Jerusalem, Jehoshaphat appointed
some of the Levites and priests and clan
leaders in Israel to serve as judges for
cases involving the LORD's regulations and
for civil disputes. ⁹These were his instructions to them: "You must always act in the
fear of the LORD, with faithfulness and an
undivided heart. ¹⁰Whenever a case

comes to you from fellow citizens in an outlying town, whether a murder case or some other violation of God's laws, commands, decrees, or regulations, you must warn them not to sin against the LORD, so that he will not be angry with you and them. Do this and you will not be guilty.

¹¹"Amariah the high priest will have final say in all cases involving the LORD. Zebadiah son of Ishmael, a leader from the tribe of Judah, will have final say in all civil cases. The Levites will assist you in making sure that justice is served. Take courage as you fulfill your duties, and may the LORD be with those who do what is right."

²⁰:¹AFTER this, the armies of the Moabites, Ammonites, and some of the Meunites* declared war on Jehoshaphat. ²Messengers came and told Jehoshaphat, "A vast army from Edom* is marching against you from beyond the Dead Sea.* They are already at Hazazon-tamar." (This was another name for En-gedi.)

³Jehoshaphat was terrified by this news and begged the LORD for guidance. He also ordered everyone in Judah to begin fasting. ⁴So people from all the towns of Judah came to Jerusalem to seek the LORD's help.

⁵Jehoshaphat stood before the community of Judah and Jerusalem in front of the new courtyard at the Temple of the LORD. ⁶He prayed, "O LORD, God of our ancestors, you alone are the God who is in heaven. You are ruler of all the kingdoms of the earth. You are powerful and mighty; no one can stand against you! ⁷O our God, did you not drive out those who lived in this land when your people Israel arrived? And did you not give this land forever to the descendants of your friend Abraham? ⁸Your people settled here and built this Temple to honor your name. ⁹They said, 'Whenever we are faced with any calamity such as war,* plague, or famine, we can come to stand in your presence before this Temple where your name is honored. We can cry out to you to save us, and you will hear us and rescue us.'

¹⁰"And now see what the armies of Ammon, Moab, and Mount Seir are doing. You would not let our ancestors invade those nations when Israel left Egypt, so they went around them and did not destroy them. ¹¹Now see how they reward us! For they have come to throw us out of your land, which you gave us as an inheritance. ¹²O our God, won't you stop them? We are powerless against this mighty army that is about to attack us. We do not know what to do, but we are looking to you for help."

¹³As all the men of Judah stood before the LORD with their little ones, wives, and children, ¹⁴the Spirit of the LORD came upon one of the men standing there. His name was Jahaziel son of Zechariah, son of Benaiah, son of Jeiel, son of Mattaniah, a Levite who was a descendant of Asaph.

¹⁵He said, "Listen, all you people of Judah and Jerusalem! Listen, King Jehoshaphat! This is what the LORD says: Do not be afraid! Don't be discouraged by this mighty army, for the battle is not yours, but God's. ¹⁶Tomorrow, march out against them. You will find them coming up through the ascent of Ziz at the end of the valley that opens into the wilderness of Jeruel. ¹⁷But you will not even need to fight. Take your positions; then stand still and watch the LORD's victory. He is with you, O people of Judah and Jerusalem. Do not be afraid or discouraged. Go out against them tomorrow, for the LORD is with you!"

¹⁸Then King Jehoshaphat bowed low with his face to the ground. And all the people of Judah and Jerusalem did the same, worshiping the LORD. ¹⁹Then the Levites from the clans of Kohath and Korah stood to praise the LORD, the God of Israel, with a very loud shout.

²⁰Early the next morning the army of Judah went out into the wilderness of Tekoa. On the way Jehoshaphat stopped and said, "Listen to me, all you people of Judah and Jerusalem! Believe in the LORD your God, and you will be able to stand firm. Believe in his prophets, and you will succeed."

²¹After consulting the people, the king appointed singers to walk ahead of the army, singing to the LORD and praising him for his holy splendor. This is what they sang:

"Give thanks to the LORD;
   his faithful love endures forever!"

²²At the very moment they began to sing and give praise, the LORD caused the armies of Ammon, Moab, and Mount Seir to start fighting among themselves. ²³The armies of Moab and Ammon turned against their allies from Mount Seir and killed every one of them. After they had destroyed the army of Seir, they began attacking each other. ²⁴So when the army of Judah arrived at the lookout point in the wilderness, all they saw were dead bodies lying on the ground as far as they could see. Not a single one of the enemy had escaped.

²⁵King Jehoshaphat and his men went out to gather the plunder. They found vast amounts of equipment, clothing,* and other valuables—more than they could carry. There was so much plunder that it took them three days just to collect it all! ²⁶On the fourth day they gathered in the Valley of Blessing,* which got its name that day because the people praised and thanked the LORD there. It is still called the Valley of Blessing today.

²⁷Then all the men returned to Jerusalem, with Jehoshaphat leading them, overjoyed that the LORD had given them victory over their enemies. ²⁸They marched into Jerusalem to the music of harps, lyres, and trumpets, and they proceeded to the Temple of the LORD.

²⁹When all the surrounding kingdoms heard that the LORD himself had fought against the enemies of Israel, the fear of God came over them. ³⁰So Jehoshaphat's kingdom was at peace, for his God had given him rest on every side.

³¹So Jehoshaphat ruled over the land of Judah. He was thirty-five years old when he became king, and he reigned in Jerusalem twenty-five years. His mother was Azubah, the daughter of Shilhi.

³²Jehoshaphat was a good king, following the ways of his father, Asa. He did what was pleasing in the LORD's sight. ³³During his reign, however, he failed to remove all the pagan shrines, and the people never fully committed themselves to follow the God of their ancestors.

³⁴The rest of the events of Jehoshaphat's reign, from beginning to end, are recorded in *The Record of Jehu Son of Hanani,* which is included in *The Book of the Kings of Israel.*

³⁵Some time later King Jehoshaphat of Judah made an alliance with King Ahaziah of Israel, who was very wicked.* ³⁶Together they built a fleet of trading ships* at the port of Ezion-geber. ³⁷Then Eliezer son of Dodavahu from Mareshah prophesied against Jehoshaphat. He said, "Because you have allied yourself with King Ahaziah, the LORD will destroy your work." So the ships met with disaster and never put out to sea.*

20:1 As in some Greek manuscripts (see also 26:7); Hebrew repeats *Ammonites.*   20:2a As in one Hebrew manuscript; most Hebrew manuscripts and ancient versions read *Aram.*   20:2b Hebrew *the sea.*   20:9 Or *sword of judgment;* or

HOW WE LIVE

Prayer

2 CHRONICLES 20:5-17   As a believer in Jesus you can come boldly into your heavenly Father's throne room and seek his help and mercy. King Jehoshaphat did just that. His nation was in obvious jeopardy and he immediately sought God's help in a public manner, calling together all of his people to fast and pray.   •His prayer had six essential parts: (1) He acknowledged that God's intervention was the only way their nation would be saved; (2) He acknowledged how God had helped them over and over again; (3) He admitted God's complete sovereignty over the situation; (4) He praised God; (5) He took comfort in God's promises; (6) He placed his dependence on God alone for the deliverance of his people.   •Because of Jehoshaphat's prayer, God spoke through Jahaziel, assuring the people that they should have no fear—the battle would be God's, not theirs. But it all began with a humble prayer. God always listens to his children when they humbly turn to him in prayer.

sword, judgment. **20:25** As in some Hebrew manuscripts and Latin Vulgate; most Hebrew manuscripts read *corpses.* **20:26** Hebrew *valley of Beracah.* **20:35** Or *who made him do what was wicked.* **20:36** Hebrew *fleet of ships that could go to Tarshish.* **20:37** Hebrew *never set sail for Tarshish.*

ROMANS 10:14–11:12

It is a sad fact that not everyone welcomes the Good News. God is patient—both with Israel and the whole world, allowing his messengers to reach more and more people while there is still time.

But how can they call on him to save them unless they believe in him? And how can they believe in him if they have never heard about him? And how can they hear about him unless someone tells them? ¹⁵And how will anyone go and tell them without being sent? That is why the Scriptures say, "How beautiful are the feet of messengers who bring good news!"*

¹⁶But not everyone welcomes the Good News, for Isaiah the prophet said, "LORD, who has believed our message?"* ¹⁷So faith comes from hearing, that is, hearing the Good News about Christ. ¹⁸But I ask, have the people of Israel actually heard the message? Yes, they have:

"The message has gone throughout
     the earth,
   and the words to all the world."*

¹⁹But I ask, did the people of Israel really understand? Yes, they did, for even in the time of Moses, God said,

"I will rouse your jealousy through
     people who are not even a nation.
   I will provoke your anger through
     the foolish Gentiles."*

²⁰And later Isaiah spoke boldly for God, saying,

"I was found by people who were not
     looking for me.
   I showed myself to those who were
     not asking for me."*

²¹But regarding Israel, God said,

"All day long I opened my arms to
     them,
   but they were disobedient and
     rebellious."*

11:¹I ASK, then, has God rejected his own people, the nation of Israel? Of course

not! I myself am an Israelite, a descendant of Abraham and a member of the tribe of Benjamin.

²No, God has not rejected his own people, whom he chose from the very beginning. Do you realize what the Scriptures say about this? Elijah the prophet complained to God about the people of Israel and said, ³"LORD, they have killed your prophets and torn down your altars. I am the only one left, and now they are trying to kill me, too."*

⁴And do you remember God's reply? He said, "No, I have 7,000 others who have never bowed down to Baal!"*

⁵It is the same today, for a few of the people of Israel* have remained faithful because of God's grace—his undeserved kindness in choosing them. ⁶And since it is through God's kindness, then it is not by their good works. For in that case, God's grace would not be what it really is—free and undeserved.

⁷So this is the situation: Most of the people of Israel have not found the favor of God they are looking for so earnestly. A few have—the ones God has chosen—but the hearts of the rest were hardened. ⁸As the Scriptures say,

"God has put them into a deep sleep.
To this day he has shut their eyes
     so they do not see,
   and closed their ears so they
     do not hear."*

⁹Likewise, David said,

"Let their bountiful table become a
     snare,
   a trap that makes them think all
     is well.
Let their blessings cause them
     to stumble,
   and let them get what they deserve.
¹⁰ Let their eyes go blind so they cannot
     see,
   and let their backs be bent forever."*

¹¹Did God's people stumble and fall beyond recovery? Of course not! They were disobedient, so God made salvation available to the Gentiles. But he wanted his own people to become jealous and claim it for themselves. ¹²Now if the Gentiles were enriched because the people of Israel turned

down God's offer of salvation, think how much greater a blessing the world will share when they finally accept it.

10:15 Isa 52:7.   10:16 Isa 53:1.   10:18 Ps 19:4.
10:19 Deut 32:21.   10:20 Isa 65:1 (Greek version).
10:21 Isa 65:2 (Greek version).   11:3 1 Kgs 19:10, 14.
11:4 1 Kgs 19:18.   11:5 Greek *for a remnant*.   11:8 Isa
29:10; Deut 29:4.   11:9-10 Ps 69:22-23 (Greek version).

PSALM 21:1-13
For the choir director: A psalm of David.

¹ How the king rejoices in your strength,
O LORD!
He shouts with joy because you give
him victory.
² For you have given him his heart's
desire;
you have withheld nothing he
requested.   *Interlude*

³ You welcomed him back with success
and prosperity.
You placed a crown of finest gold
on his head.
⁴ He asked you to preserve his life,
and you granted his request.
The days of his life stretch on forever.
⁵ Your victory brings him great honor,
and you have clothed him with
splendor and majesty.
⁶ You have endowed him with eternal
blessings
and given him the joy of your
presence.

⁷ For the king trusts in the LORD.
The unfailing love of the Most High
will keep him from stumbling.

⁸ You will capture all your enemies.
Your strong right hand will seize all
who hate you.
⁹ You will throw them in a flaming
furnace
when you appear.
The LORD will consume them in his
anger;
fire will devour them.
¹⁰ You will wipe their children from the
face of the earth;
they will never have descendants.
¹¹ Although they plot against you,
their evil schemes will never
succeed.
¹² For they will turn and run
when they see your arrows aimed
at them.
¹³ Rise up, O LORD, in all your power.
With music and singing we
celebrate your mighty acts.

PROVERBS 20:4-6
Those too lazy to plow in the right season will have no food at the harvest. □ Though good advice lies deep within the heart, a person with understanding will draw it out. □ Many will say they are loyal friends, but who can find one who is truly reliable?

JULY**28**

2 CHRONICLES 21:1–23:21
A king's oldest son was his natural successor. But as God's people fell further and further away from God's laws, politics became dirtier and dirtier. Evil Jehoram secured his power through cold-blooded murder.

When Jehoshaphat died, he was buried with his ancestors in the City of David. Then his son Jehoram became the next king.

²Jehoram's brothers—the other sons of Jehoshaphat—were Azariah, Jehiel, Zech-ariah, Azariahu, Michael, and Shephatiah; all these were the sons of Jehoshaphat king of Judah.* ³Their father had given each of them valuable gifts of silver, gold, and costly items, and also some of Judah's fortified towns. However, he designated Jehoram as the next king because he was the oldest. ⁴But when Jehoram had become solidly established as king, he killed all his brothers and some of the other leaders of Judah.

⁵Jehoram was thirty-two years old

when he became king, and he reigned in Jerusalem eight years. ⁶But Jehoram followed the example of the kings of Israel and was as wicked as King Ahab, for he had married one of Ahab's daughters. So Jehoram did what was evil in the LORD's sight. ⁷But the LORD did not want to destroy David's dynasty, for he had made a covenant with David and promised that his descendants would continue to rule, shining like a lamp forever.

⁸During Jehoram's reign, the Edomites revolted against Judah and crowned their own king. ⁹So Jehoram went out with his full army and all his chariots. The Edomites surrounded him and his chariot commanders, but he went out at night and attacked them* under cover of darkness. ¹⁰Even so, Edom has been independent from Judah to this day. The town of Libnah also revolted about that same time. All this happened because Jehoram had abandoned the LORD, the God of his ancestors. ¹¹He had built pagan shrines in the hill country of Judah and had led the people of Jerusalem and Judah to give themselves to pagan gods and to go astray.

¹²Then Elijah the prophet wrote Jehoram this letter:

> "This is what the LORD, the God of your ancestor David, says: You have not followed the good example of your father, Jehoshaphat, or your grandfather King Asa of Judah. ¹³Instead, you have been as evil as the kings of Israel. You have led the people of Jerusalem and Judah to worship idols, just as King Ahab did in Israel. And you have even killed your own brothers, men who were better than you. ¹⁴So now the LORD is about to strike you, your people, your children, your wives, and all that is yours with a heavy blow. ¹⁵You yourself will suffer with a severe intestinal disease that will get worse each day until your bowels come out."

¹⁶Then the LORD stirred up the Philistines and the Arabs, who lived near the Ethiopians,* to attack Jehoram. ¹⁷They marched against Judah, broke down its defenses, and carried away everything of value in the royal palace, including the king's sons and his wives. Only his youngest son, Ahaziah,* was spared.

¹⁸After all this, the LORD struck Jehoram with the severe intestinal disease. ¹⁹The disease grew worse and worse, and at the end of two years it caused his bowels to come out, and he died in agony. His people did not build a great funeral fire to honor him as they had done for his ancestors.

²⁰Jehoram was thirty-two years old when he became king, and he reigned in Jerusalem eight years. No one was sorry when he died. They buried him in the City of David, but not in the royal cemetery.

²²:¹THEN the people of Jerusalem made Ahaziah, Jehoram's youngest son, their next king, since the marauding bands who came with the Arabs* had killed all the older sons. So Ahaziah son of Jehoram reigned as king of Judah.

²Ahaziah was twenty-two* years old when he became king, and he reigned in Jerusalem one year. His mother was Athaliah, a granddaughter of King Omri. ³Ahaziah also followed the evil example of King Ahab's family, for his mother encouraged him in doing wrong. ⁴He did what was evil in the LORD's sight, just as Ahab's family had done. They even became his advisers after the death of his father, and they led him to ruin.

⁵Following their evil advice, Ahaziah joined King Joram,* the son of King Ahab of Israel, in his war against King Hazael of Aram at Ramoth-gilead. When the Arameans wounded Joram in the battle, ⁶he returned to Jezreel to recover from the wounds he had received at Ramoth.* Because Joram was wounded, King Ahaziah* of Judah went to Jezreel to visit him.

⁷But God had decided that this visit would be Ahaziah's downfall. While he was there, Ahaziah went out with Joram to meet Jehu son of Nimshi, whom the LORD had appointed to destroy the dynasty of Ahab.

⁸While Jehu was executing judgment against the family of Ahab, he happened to meet some of Judah's officials and Ahaziah's relatives* who were traveling with Ahaziah. So Jehu killed them all. ⁹Then Jehu's men searched for Ahaziah, and they found him hiding in the city of Samaria.

They brought him to Jehu, who killed him. Ahaziah was given a decent burial because the people said, "He was the grandson of Jehoshaphat—a man who sought the LORD with all his heart." But none of the surviving members of Ahaziah's family was capable of ruling the kingdom.

¹⁰When Athaliah, the mother of King Ahaziah of Judah, learned that her son was dead, she began to destroy the rest of Judah's royal family. ¹¹But Ahaziah's sister Jehosheba,* the daughter of King Jehoram, took Ahaziah's infant son, Joash, and stole him away from among the rest of the king's children, who were about to be killed. She put Joash and his nurse in a bedroom. In this way, Jehosheba, wife of Jehoiada the priest and sister of Ahaziah, hid the child so that Athaliah could not murder him. ¹²Joash remained hidden in the Temple of God for six years while Athaliah ruled over the land.

²³:¹In the seventh year of Athaliah's reign, Jehoiada the priest decided to act. He summoned his courage and made a pact with five army commanders: Azariah son of Jeroham, Ishmael son of Jehohanan, Azariah son of Obed, Maaseiah son of Adaiah, and Elishaphat son of Zicri. ²These men traveled secretly throughout Judah and summoned the Levites and clan leaders in all the towns to come to Jerusalem. ³They all gathered at the Temple of God, where they made a solemn pact with Joash, the young king.

Jehoiada said to them, "Here is the king's son! The time has come for him to reign! The LORD has promised that a descendant of David will be our king. ⁴This is what you must do. When you priests and Levites come on duty on the Sabbath, a third of you will serve as gatekeepers. ⁵Another third will go over to the royal palace, and the final third will be at the Foundation Gate. Everyone else should stay in the courtyards of the LORD's Temple. ⁶Remember, only the priests and Levites on duty may enter the Temple of the LORD, for they are set apart as holy. The rest of the people must obey the LORD's instructions and stay outside. ⁷You Levites, form a bodyguard around the king and keep your weapons in hand. Kill anyone who tries to enter the Temple. Stay with the king wherever he goes."

⁸So the Levites and all the people of Judah did everything as Jehoiada the priest ordered. The commanders took charge of the men reporting for duty that Sabbath, as well as those who were going off duty. Jehoiada the priest did not let anyone go home after their shift ended. ⁹Then Jehoiada supplied the commanders with the spears and the large and small shields that had once belonged to King David and were stored in the Temple of God. ¹⁰He stationed all the people around the king, with their weapons ready. They formed a line from the south side of the Temple around to the north side and all around the altar.

HOW WE LIVE

Courageous in trials

PSALM 22 David was no stranger to trials. Rejected by friends, and feeling abandoned by God, he obviously was suffering a great deal when he penned Psalm 22. In spite of this emotional turmoil, he believed God would lead him out of desolation. This psalm goes from the depths of despair to the heights of great joy. Where does that courageous faith come from? How does one believe during tough times? • We will face difficult times and feel that people despise us. At times we may feel just as David described in verse 6—less than human. Like worms, we want to crawl underground and hide from the rejection. But these are the times that we must do what David did: turn toward God, not away from God. God is our only source of ultimate comfort and strength and perspective. We can be strong because we know he will never leave us nor forsake us.

11Then Jehoiada and his sons brought out Joash, the king's son, placed the crown on his head, and presented him with a copy of God's laws.* They anointed him and proclaimed him king, and everyone shouted, "Long live the king!"

12When Athaliah heard the noise of the people running and the shouts of praise to the king, she hurried to the LORD's Temple to see what was happening. 13When she arrived, she saw the newly crowned king standing in his place of authority by the pillar at the Temple entrance. The commanders and trumpeters were surrounding him, and people from all over the land were rejoicing and blowing trumpets. Singers with musical instruments were leading the people in a great celebration. When Athaliah saw all this, she tore her clothes in despair and shouted, "Treason! Treason!"

14Then Jehoiada the priest ordered the commanders who were in charge of the troops, "Take her to the soldiers in front of the Temple,* and kill anyone who tries to rescue her." For the priest had said, "She must not be killed in the Temple of the LORD." 15So they seized her and led her out to the entrance of the Horse Gate on the palace grounds, and they killed her there.

16Then Jehoiada made a covenant between himself and the king and the people that they would be the LORD's people. 17And all the people went over to the temple of Baal and tore it down. They demolished the altars and smashed the idols, and they killed Mattan the priest of Baal in front of the altars.

18Jehoiada now put the priests and Levites in charge of the Temple of the LORD, following all the directions given by David. He also commanded them to present burnt offerings to the LORD, as prescribed by the Law of Moses, and to sing and rejoice as David had instructed. 19He also stationed gatekeepers at the gates of the LORD's Temple to keep out those who for any reason were ceremonially unclean.

20Then the commanders, nobles, rulers, and all the people of the land escorted the king from the Temple of the LORD. They went through the upper gate and into the palace, and they seated the king on the royal throne. 21So all the people of the land rejoiced, and the city was peaceful because Athaliah had been killed.

21:2 Hebrew *of Israel;* also in 21:4. The author of Chronicles sees Judah as representative of the true Israel. See also some Hebrew manuscripts, Greek and Syriac versions, and Latin Vulgate. 21:9 Or *he went out and escaped.* The meaning of the Hebrew is uncertain. 21:16 Hebrew *the Cushites.* 21:17 Hebrew *Jehoahaz,* a variant spelling of Ahaziah; compare 22:1. 22:1 Or *marauding bands of Arabs.* 22:2 As in some Greek manuscripts and Syriac version (see also 2 Kgs 8:26); Hebrew reads *forty-two.* 22:5 Hebrew *Jehoram,* a variant spelling of Joram; also in 22:6, 7. 22:6a Hebrew *Ramah,* a variant spelling of Ramoth. 22:6b As in some Hebrew manuscripts, Greek and Syriac versions, and Latin Vulgate (see also 2 Kgs 8:29); most Hebrew manuscripts read *Azariah.* 22:8 As in Greek version (see also 2 Kgs 10:13); Hebrew reads *and sons of the brothers of Ahaziah.* 22:11 As in parallel text at 2 Kgs 11:2; Hebrew omits *Ahaziah's sister* and reads *Jehoshabeath* (a variant spelling of Jehosheba). 23:11 Or *a copy of the covenant.* 23:14 Or *Bring her out from between the ranks;* or *Take her out of the Temple precincts.* The meaning of the Hebrew is uncertain.

ROMANS 11:13-36

For many first-century Jews, the idea that God's salvation is for both Gentiles and Jews was a startling new way of thinking. Paul had to warn some of the Gentile believers in Rome not to let their acceptance lead to pride.

I [Paul] am saying all this especially for you Gentiles. God has appointed me as the apostle to the Gentiles. I stress this, 14for I want somehow to make the people of Israel jealous of what you Gentiles have, so I might save some of them. 15For since their rejection meant that God offered salvation to the rest of the world, their acceptance will be even more wonderful. It will be life for those who were dead! 16And since Abraham and the other patriarchs were holy, their descendants will also be holy—just as the entire batch of dough is holy because the portion given as an offering is holy. For if the roots of the tree are holy, the branches will be, too.

17But some of these branches from Abraham's tree—some of the people of Israel—have been broken off. And you Gentiles, who were branches from a wild olive tree, have been grafted in. So now you also receive the blessing God has promised Abraham and his children, sharing in the rich nourishment from the root of God's special olive tree. 18But you must not brag about being grafted in to replace the branches that were broken off. You are just a branch, not the root.

¹⁹"Well," you may say, "those branches were broken off to make room for me." ²⁰Yes, but remember—those branches were broken off because they didn't believe in Christ, and you are there because you do believe. So don't think highly of yourself, but fear what could happen. ²¹For if God did not spare the original branches, he won't* spare you either.

²²Notice how God is both kind and severe. He is severe toward those who disobeyed, but kind to you if you continue to trust in his kindness. But if you stop trusting, you also will be cut off. ²³And if the people of Israel turn from their unbelief, they will be grafted in again, for God has the power to graft them back into the tree. ²⁴You, by nature, were a branch cut from a wild olive tree. So if God was willing to do something contrary to nature by grafting you into his cultivated tree, he will be far more eager to graft the original branches back into the tree where they belong.

²⁵I want you to understand this mystery, dear brothers and sisters,* so that you will not feel proud about yourselves. Some of the people of Israel have hard hearts, but this will last only until the full number of Gentiles comes to Christ. ²⁶And so all Israel will be saved. As the Scriptures say,

"The one who rescues will come from Jerusalem,*
and he will turn Israel* away from ungodliness.
²⁷ And this is my covenant with them,
that I will take away their sins."*

²⁸Many of the people of Israel are now enemies of the Good News, and this benefits you Gentiles. Yet they are still the people he loves because he chose their ancestors Abraham, Isaac, and Jacob. ²⁹For God's gifts and his call can never be withdrawn. ³⁰Once, you Gentiles were rebels against God, but when the people of Israel rebelled against him, God was merciful to you instead. ³¹Now they are the rebels, and God's mercy has come to you so that they, too, will share* in God's mercy. ³²For God has imprisoned everyone in disobedience so he could have mercy on everyone.

³³Oh, how great are God's riches and wisdom and knowledge! How impossible it is for us to understand his decisions and his ways!

³⁴ For who can know the LORD's thoughts?
Who knows enough to give him advice?*
³⁵ And who has given him so much that he needs to pay it back?*

³⁶For everything comes from him and exists by his power and is intended for his glory. All glory to him forever! Amen.

11:21 Some manuscripts read *perhaps he won't.*
11:25 Greek *brothers.*   11:26a Greek *from Zion.*
11:26b Greek *Jacob.*   11:26-27 Isa 59:20-21; 27:9 (Greek version).   11:31 Other manuscripts read *will now share;* still others read *will someday share.*   11:34 Isa 40:13 (Greek version).   11:35 See Job 41:11.

PSALM 22:1-18

For the choir director: A psalm of David, to be sung to the tune "Doe of the Dawn."

¹ My God, my God, why have you abandoned me?
Why are you so far away when I groan for help?
² Every day I call to you, my God, but you do not answer.
Every night you hear my voice, but I find no relief.

³ Yet you are holy,
enthroned on the praises of Israel.
⁴ Our ancestors trusted in you,
and you rescued them.
⁵ They cried out to you and were saved.
They trusted in you and were never disgraced.

⁶ But I am a worm and not a man.
I am scorned and despised by all!
⁷ Everyone who sees me mocks me.
They sneer and shake their heads, saying,
⁸ "Is this the one who relies on the LORD?
Then let the LORD save him!
If the LORD loves him so much,
let the LORD rescue him!"

⁹ Yet you brought me safely from my mother's womb
and led me to trust you at my mother's breast.

¹⁰ I was thrust into your arms at my
    birth.
  You have been my God from the
    moment I was born.

¹¹ Do not stay so far from me,
    for trouble is near,
  and no one else can help me.
¹² My enemies surround me like a herd
    of bulls;
  fierce bulls of Bashan have hemmed
    me in!
¹³ Like lions they open their jaws
    against me,
  roaring and tearing into their prey.
¹⁴ My life is poured out like water,
    and all my bones are out of joint.
  My heart is like wax,
    melting within me.
¹⁵ My strength has dried up like
    sunbaked clay.

My tongue sticks to the roof of my
    mouth.
  You have laid me in the dust and
    left me for dead.
¹⁶ My enemies surround me like a pack
    of dogs;
  an evil gang closes in on me.
  They have pierced my hands and
    feet.
¹⁷ I can count all my bones.
  My enemies stare at me and
    gloat.
¹⁸ They divide my garments among
    themselves
  and throw dice* for my clothing.

22:18 Hebrew *cast lots.*

PROVERBS 20:7
The godly walk with integrity; blessed are
their children who follow them.

JULY 29

2 CHRONICLES 24:1–25:28
Joash started out well but then faltered miserably—
even killing the son of the priest who had helped
him so many years. His son Amaziah followed God,
but not wholeheartedly.

Joash was seven years old when he became king, and he reigned in Jerusalem
forty years. His mother was Zibiah from
Beersheba. ²Joash did what was pleasing
in the LORD's sight throughout the lifetime of Jehoiada the priest. ³Jehoiada
chose two wives for Joash, and he had
sons and daughters.

⁴At one point Joash decided to repair
and restore the Temple of the LORD. ⁵He
summoned the priests and Levites and
gave them these instructions: "Go to all the
towns of Judah and collect the required
annual offerings, so that we can repair the
Temple of your God. Do not delay!" But the
Levites did not act immediately.

⁶So the king called for Jehoiada the
high priest and asked him, "Why haven't
you demanded that the Levites go out and
collect the Temple taxes from the towns

of Judah and from Jerusalem? Moses, the
servant of the LORD, levied this tax on the
community of Israel in order to maintain
the Tabernacle of the Covenant.*"

⁷Over the years the followers of wicked
Athaliah had broken into the Temple of
God, and they had used all the dedicated
things from the Temple of the LORD to
worship the images of Baal.

⁸So now the king ordered a chest to be
made and set outside the gate leading to
the Temple of the LORD. ⁹Then a proclamation was sent throughout Judah and Jerusalem, telling the people to bring to the
LORD the tax that Moses, the servant of
God, had required of the Israelites in the
wilderness. ¹⁰This pleased all the leaders
and the people, and they gladly brought
their money and filled the chest with it.

¹¹Whenever the chest became full, the
Levites would carry it to the king's officials. Then the court secretary and an officer of the high priest would come and
empty the chest and take it back to the
Temple again. This went on day after day,

and a large amount of money was collected. [12] The king and Jehoiada gave the money to the construction supervisors, who hired masons and carpenters to restore the Temple of the LORD. They also hired metalworkers, who made articles of iron and bronze for the LORD's Temple.

[13] The men in charge of the renovation worked hard and made steady progress. They restored the Temple of God according to its original design and strengthened it. [14] When all the repairs were finished, they brought the remaining money to the king and Jehoiada. It was used to make various articles for the Temple of the LORD—articles for worship services and for burnt offerings, including ladles and other articles made of gold and silver. And the burnt offerings were sacrificed continually in the Temple of the LORD during the lifetime of Jehoiada the priest.

[15] Jehoiada lived to a very old age, finally dying at 130. [16] He was buried among the kings in the City of David, because he had done so much good in Judah* for God and his Temple.

[17] But after Jehoiada's death, the leaders of Judah came and bowed before King Joash and persuaded him to listen to their advice. [18] They decided to abandon the Temple of the LORD, the God of their ancestors, and they worshiped Asherah poles and idols instead! Because of this sin, divine anger fell on Judah and Jerusalem. [19] Yet the LORD sent prophets to bring them back to him. The prophets warned them, but still the people would not listen.

[20] Then the Spirit of God came upon Zechariah son of Jehoiada the priest. He stood before the people and said, "This is what God says: Why do you disobey the LORD's commands and keep yourselves from prospering? You have abandoned the LORD, and now he has abandoned you!"

[21] Then the leaders plotted to kill Zechariah, and King Joash ordered that they stone him to death in the courtyard of the LORD's Temple. [22] That was how King Joash repaid Jehoiada for his loyalty—by killing his son. Zechariah's last words as he died were, "May the LORD see what they are doing and avenge my death!"

[23] In the spring of the year* the Aramean army marched against Joash. They invaded Judah and Jerusalem and killed all the leaders of the nation. Then they sent all the plunder back to their king in Damascus. [24] Although the Arameans attacked with only a small army, the LORD helped them conquer the much larger army of Judah. The people of Judah had abandoned the LORD, the God of their ancestors, so judgment was carried out against Joash.

[25] The Arameans withdrew, leaving Joash severely wounded. But his own officials plotted to kill him for murdering the son* of Jehoiada the priest. They assassinated him as he lay in bed. Then he was buried in the City of David, but not in the royal cemetery. [26] The assassins were Jozacar,* the son of an Ammonite woman named Shimeath, and Jehozabad, the son of a Moabite woman named Shomer.*

[27] The account of the sons of Joash, the prophecies about him, and the record of his restoration of the Temple of God are written in *The Commentary on the Book of the Kings.* His son Amaziah became the next king.

[25:1] AMAZIAH was twenty-five years old when he became king, and he reigned in Jerusalem twenty-nine years. His mother was Jehoaddin* from Jerusalem. [2] Amaziah did what was pleasing in the LORD's sight, but not wholeheartedly.

[3] When Amaziah was well established as king, he executed the officials who had assassinated his father. [4] However, he did not kill the children of the assassins, for he obeyed the command of the LORD as written by Moses in the Book of the Law: "Parents must not be put to death for the sins of their children, nor children for the sins of their parents. Those deserving to die must be put to death for their own crimes."*

[5] Then Amaziah organized the army, assigning generals and captains* for all Judah and Benjamin. He took a census and found that he had an army of 300,000 select troops, twenty years old and older, all trained in the use of spear and shield. [6] He also paid about 7,500 pounds* of silver to hire 100,000 experienced fighting men from Israel.

[7]But a man of God came to him and said, "Your Majesty, do not hire troops from Israel, for the LORD is not with Israel. He will not help those people of Ephraim! [8]If you let them go with your troops into battle, you will be defeated by the enemy no matter how well you fight. God will overthrow you, for he has the power to help you or to trip you up."

[9]Amaziah asked the man of God, "But what about all that silver I paid to hire the army of Israel?"

The man of God replied, "The LORD is able to give you much more than this!" [10]So Amaziah discharged the hired troops and sent them back to Ephraim. This made them very angry with Judah, and they returned home in a great rage.

[11]Then Amaziah summoned his courage and led his army to the Valley of Salt, where they killed 10,000 Edomite troops from Seir. [12]They captured another 10,000 and took them to the top of a cliff and threw them off, dashing them to pieces on the rocks below.

[13]Meanwhile, the hired troops that Amaziah had sent home raided several of the towns of Judah between Samaria and Beth-horon. They killed 3,000 people and carried off great quantities of plunder.

[14]When King Amaziah returned from slaughtering the Edomites, he brought with him idols taken from the people of Seir. He set them up as his own gods, bowed down in front of them, and offered sacrifices to them! [15]This made the LORD very angry, and he sent a prophet to ask, "Why do you turn to gods who could not even save their own people from you?"

[16]But the king interrupted him and said, "Since when have I made you the king's counselor? Be quiet now before I have you killed!"

So the prophet stopped with this warning: "I know that God has determined to destroy you because you have done this and have refused to accept my counsel."

[17]After consulting with his advisers, King Amaziah of Judah sent this challenge to Israel's king Jehoash,* the son of Jehoahaz and grandson of Jehu: "Come and meet me in battle!"*

[18]But King Jehoash of Israel replied to King Amaziah of Judah with this story: "Out in the Lebanon mountains, a thistle sent a message to a mighty cedar tree: 'Give your daughter in marriage to my son.' But just then a wild animal of Lebanon came by and stepped on the thistle, crushing it!

[19]"You are saying, 'I have defeated Edom,' and you are very proud of it. But my advice is to stay at home. Why stir up trouble that will only bring disaster on you and the people of Judah?"

[20]But Amaziah refused to listen, for God was determined to destroy him for turning to the gods of Edom. [21]So King Jehoash of Israel mobilized his army against King Amaziah of Judah. The two armies drew up their battle lines at Beth-shemesh in Judah. [22]Judah was routed by the army of Israel, and its army scattered and fled for home. [23]King Jehoash of Israel captured Judah's king, Amaziah son of Joash and grandson of Ahaziah, at Beth-shemesh. Then he brought him to Jerusalem, where he demolished 600 feet* of Jerusalem's wall, from the Ephraim Gate to the Corner Gate. [24]He carried off all the gold and silver and all the articles from the Temple of God that had been in the care of Obed-edom. He also seized the treasures of the royal palace, along with hostages, and then returned to Samaria.

[25]King Amaziah of Judah lived on for fifteen years after the death of King Jehoash of Israel. [26]The rest of the events in Amaziah's reign, from beginning to end, are recorded in *The Book of the Kings of Judah and Israel.*

[27]After Amaziah turned away from the LORD, there was a conspiracy against his life in Jerusalem, and he fled to Lachish. But his enemies sent assassins after him, and they killed him there. [28]They brought his body back on a horse, and he was buried with his ancestors in the City of David.*

24:6 Hebrew *Tent of the Testimony.*   24:16 Hebrew *in Israel.* The author of Chronicles sees Judah as representative of the true Israel.   24:23 Hebrew *At the turn of the year.* The first day of the year in the ancient Hebrew lunar calendar occurred in March or April.   24:25 As in Greek version and Latin Vulgate; Hebrew reads *sons.*   24:26a As in parallel text at 2 Kgs 12:21; Hebrew reads *Zabad.*   24:26b As in parallel text at 2 Kgs 12:21; Hebrew reads *Shimrith,* a variant spelling of Shomer.   25:1 As in parallel text at 2 Kgs 14:2; Hebrew reads *Jehoaddan,* a variant spelling of Jehoaddin.   25:4 Deut

ROMANS 12:1-21

Having spent 11 chapters expounding right doctrine, Paul's focus now shifts to right living. The two are related. Right living is the proper manifestation of understanding all that God had done for us in Jesus Christ.

And so, dear brothers and sisters,* I plead with you to give your bodies to God because of all he has done for you. Let them be a living and holy sacrifice—the kind he will find acceptable. This is truly the way to worship him.* ²Don't copy the behavior and customs of this world, but let God transform you into a new person by changing the way you think. Then you will learn to know God's will for you, which is good and pleasing and perfect.

³Because of the privilege and authority* God has given me, I give each of you this warning: Don't think you are better than you really are. Be honest in your evaluation of yourselves, measuring yourselves by the faith God has given us.* ⁴Just as our bodies have many parts and each part has a special function, ⁵so it is with Christ's body. We are many parts of one body, and we all belong to each other.

⁶In his grace, God has given us different gifts for doing certain things well. So if God has given you the ability to prophesy, speak out with as much faith as God has given you. ⁷If your gift is serving others, serve them well. If you are a teacher, teach well. ⁸If your gift is to encourage others, be encouraging. If it is giving, give generously. If God has given you leadership ability, take the responsibility seriously. And if you have a gift for showing kindness to others, do it gladly.

⁹Don't just pretend to love others. Really love them. Hate what is wrong. Hold tightly to what is good. ¹⁰Love each other with genuine affection,* and take delight in honoring each other. ¹¹Never be lazy, but work hard and serve the Lord enthusiastically.* ¹²Rejoice in our confident hope. Be patient in trouble, and keep on praying. ¹³When God's people are in need, be ready to help them. Always be eager to practice hospitality.

¹⁴Bless those who persecute you. Don't curse them; pray that God will bless them. ¹⁵Be happy with those who are happy, and weep with those who weep. ¹⁶Live in harmony with each other. Don't be too proud to enjoy the company of ordinary people. And don't think you know it all!

HOW WE LIVE

Seeking God's will

ROMANS 12:1-2 It's easy just to follow the crowd, to fit in and be like everyone else. But Christians are called to be different from this world. God wants us to offer ourselves as a "living sacrifice." What does this mean?

• First, it means that we are to put aside our personal, selfish desires and follow him. He has good and perfect plans for us. As we study his Word and pray daily, we become more attuned to what his plans are.

• Second, we are to put all our energy and resources at his disposal. Because he wants what is best for us, and because he gave his Son as a sacrifice for our sin, we can joyfully give of our time, talents and finances.

• Third, we are to trust his guidance in our lives. We may question why he is leading us down a certain path, especially when we desire another road. But when we follow his leading, he will use us to bless others and we will be blessed, too.   • Copying the behaviors and customs of the world will only leave us on a dead-end street. Let God transform you. Let his Word change the way you think about things, and then you will be on the road to knowing God's will for you.

[17]Never pay back evil with more evil. Do things in such a way that everyone can see you are honorable. [18]Do all that you can to live in peace with everyone.

[19]Dear friends, never take revenge. Leave that to the righteous anger of God. For the Scriptures say,

"I will take revenge;
I will pay them back,"*
says the LORD.

[20]Instead,

"If your enemies are hungry, feed them.
If they are thirsty, give them something to drink.
In doing this, you will heap burning coals of shame on their heads."*

[21]Don't let evil conquer you, but conquer evil by doing good.

12:1a Greek *brothers.* 12:1b Or *This is your spiritual worship;* or *This is your reasonable service.* 12:3a Or *Because of the grace;* compare 1:5. 12:3b Or *by the faith God has given you;* or *by the standard of our God-given faith.* 12:10 Greek *with brotherly love.* 12:11 Or *but serve the Lord with a zealous spirit;* or *but let the Spirit excite you as you serve the Lord.* 12:19 Deut 32:35. 12:20 Prov 25:21-22.

PSALM 22:19-31

O LORD, do not stay far away!
You are my strength; come quickly to my aid!
[20] Save me from the sword;
spare my precious life from these dogs.
[21] Snatch me from the lion's jaws
and from the horns of these wild oxen.

[22] I will proclaim your name to my brothers and sisters.*
I will praise you among your assembled people.
[23] Praise the LORD, all you who fear him!

Honor him, all you descendants of Jacob!
Show him reverence, all you descendants of Israel!
[24] For he has not ignored or belittled the suffering of the needy.
He has not turned his back on them, but has listened to their cries for help.

[25] I will praise you in the great assembly.
I will fulfill my vows in the presence of those who worship you.
[26] The poor will eat and be satisfied.
All who seek the LORD will praise him.
Their hearts will rejoice with everlasting joy.
[27] The whole earth will acknowledge the LORD and return to him.
All the families of the nations will bow down before him.
[28] For royal power belongs to the LORD.
He rules all the nations.

[29] Let the rich of the earth feast and worship.
Bow before him, all who are mortal, all whose lives will end as dust.
[30] Our children will also serve him.
Future generations will hear about the wonders of the Lord.
[31] His righteous acts will be told to those not yet born.
They will hear about everything he has done.

22:22 Hebrew *my brothers.*

PROVERBS 20:8-10

When a king sits in judgment, he weighs all the evidence, distinguishing the bad from the good. □ Who can say, "I have cleansed my heart; I am pure and free from sin"? □ False weights and unequal measures*—the LORD detests double standards of every kind.

20:10 Hebrew *A stone and a stone, an ephah and an ephah.*

JULY30

2 CHRONICLES 26:1–28:27

The history of Judah seemed a one-step-forward-two-steps-back kind of story at best. From king to king, the spiritual state of the population fluctuated but ultimately declined to the point of ruin. That decline is clearly seen in Ahaz's action of shutting down the Temple.

All the people of Judah had crowned Amaziah's sixteen-year-old son, Uzziah, as king in place of his father. ²After his father's death, Uzziah rebuilt the town of Elath* and restored it to Judah.

³Uzziah was sixteen years old when he became king, and he reigned in Jerusalem fifty-two years. His mother was Jecoliah from Jerusalem. ⁴He did what was pleasing in the LORD's sight, just as his father, Amaziah, had done. ⁵Uzziah sought God during the days of Zechariah, who taught him to fear God.* And as long as the king sought guidance from the LORD, God gave him success.

⁶Uzziah declared war on the Philistines and broke down the walls of Gath, Jabneh, and Ashdod. Then he built new towns in the Ashdod area and in other parts of Philistia. ⁷God helped him in his wars against the Philistines, his battles with the Arabs of Gur,* and his wars with the Meunites. ⁸The Meunites* paid annual tribute to him, and his fame spread even to Egypt, for he had become very powerful.

⁹Uzziah built fortified towers in Jerusalem at the Corner Gate, at the Valley Gate, and at the angle in the wall. ¹⁰He also constructed forts in the wilderness and dug many water cisterns, because he kept great herds of livestock in the foothills of Judah* and on the plains. He was also a man who loved the soil. He had many workers who cared for his farms and vineyards, both on the hillsides and in the fertile valleys.

¹¹Uzziah had an army of well-trained warriors, ready to march into battle, unit by unit. This army had been mustered and organized by Jeiel, the secretary of the army, and his assistant, Maaseiah. They were under the direction of Hananiah, one of the king's officials. ¹²These regiments of mighty warriors were commanded by

2,600 clan leaders. ¹³The army consisted of 307,500 men, all elite troops. They were prepared to assist the king against any enemy.

¹⁴Uzziah provided the entire army with shields, spears, helmets, coats of mail, bows, and sling stones. ¹⁵And he built structures on the walls of Jerusalem, designed by experts to protect those who shot arrows and hurled large stones* from the towers and the corners of the wall. His fame spread far and wide, for the LORD gave him marvelous help, and he became very powerful.

¹⁶But when he had become powerful, he also became proud, which led to his downfall. He sinned against the LORD his God by entering the sanctuary of the LORD's Temple and personally burning incense on the incense altar. ¹⁷Azariah the high priest went in after him with eighty other priests of the LORD, all brave men. ¹⁸They confronted King Uzziah and said, "It is not for you, Uzziah, to burn incense to the LORD. That is the work of the priests alone, the descendants of Aaron who are set apart for this work. Get out of the sanctuary, for you have sinned. The LORD God will not honor you for this!"

¹⁹Uzziah, who was holding an incense burner, became furious. But as he was standing there raging at the priests before the incense altar in the LORD's Temple, leprosy* suddenly broke out on his forehead. ²⁰When Azariah the high priest and all the other priests saw the leprosy, they rushed him out. And the king himself was eager to get out because the LORD had struck him. ²¹So King Uzziah had leprosy until the day he died. He lived in isolation in a separate house, for he was excluded from the Temple of the LORD. His son Jotham was put in charge of the royal palace, and he governed the people of the land.

²²The rest of the events of Uzziah's reign, from beginning to end, are recorded by the prophet Isaiah son of Amoz. ²³When Uzziah died, he was buried with

his ancestors; his grave was in a nearby burial field belonging to the kings, for the people said, "He had leprosy." And his son Jotham became the next king.

27:1 JOTHAM was twenty-five years old when he became king, and he reigned in Jerusalem sixteen years. His mother was Jerusha, the daughter of Zadok.

²Jotham did what was pleasing in the LORD's sight. He did everything his father, Uzziah, had done, except that Jotham did not sin by entering the Temple of the LORD. But the people continued in their corrupt ways.

³Jotham rebuilt the upper gate of the Temple of the LORD. He also did extensive rebuilding on the wall at the hill of Ophel. ⁴He built towns in the hill country of Judah and constructed fortresses and towers in the wooded areas. ⁵Jotham went to war against the Ammonites and conquered them. Over the next three years he received from them an annual tribute of 7,500 pounds* of silver, 50,000 bushels of wheat, and 50,000 bushels of barley.*

⁶King Jotham became powerful because he was careful to live in obedience to the LORD his God.

⁷The rest of the events of Jotham's reign, including all his wars and other activities, are recorded in *The Book of the Kings of Israel and Judah.* ⁸He was twenty-five years old when he became king, and he reigned in Jerusalem sixteen years. ⁹When Jotham died, he was buried in the City of David. And his son Ahaz became the next king.

28:1 AHAZ was twenty years old when he became king, and he reigned in Jerusalem sixteen years. He did not do what was pleasing in the sight of the LORD, as his ancestor David had done. ²Instead, he followed the example of the kings of Israel. He cast metal images for the worship of Baal. ³He offered sacrifices in the valley of Ben-Hinnom, even sacrificing his own sons in the fire.* In this way, he followed the detestable practices of the pagan nations the LORD had driven from the land ahead of the Israelites. ⁴He offered sacrifices and burned incense at the pagan shrines and on the hills and under every green tree.

⁵Because of all this, the LORD his God allowed the king of Aram to defeat Ahaz and to exile large numbers of his people to Damascus. The armies of the king of Israel also defeated Ahaz and inflicted many casualties on his army. ⁶In a single day Pekah son of Remaliah, Israel's king, killed 120,000 of Judah's troops, all of them experienced warriors, because they had abandoned the LORD, the God of their ancestors. ⁷Then Zicri, a warrior from Ephraim, killed Maaseiah, the king's son; Azrikam, the king's palace commander; and Elkanah, the king's second-in-command. ⁸The armies of Israel captured 200,000 women and children from Judah and seized tremendous amounts of plunder, which they took back to Samaria.

⁹But a prophet of the LORD named Oded was there in Samaria when the army of Israel returned home. He went out to meet them and said, "The LORD, the God of your ancestors, was angry with Judah and let you defeat them. But you have gone too far, killing them without mercy, and all heaven is disturbed. ¹⁰And now you are planning to make slaves of these people from Judah and Jerusalem. What about your own sins against the LORD your God? ¹¹Listen to me and return these prisoners you have taken, for they are your own relatives. Watch out, because now the LORD's fierce anger has been turned against you!"

¹²Then some of the leaders of Israel*— Azariah son of Jehohanan, Berekiah son of Meshillemoth, Jehizkiah son of Shallum, and Amasa son of Hadlai—agreed with this and confronted the men returning from battle. ¹³"You must not bring the prisoners here!" they declared. "We cannot afford to add to our sins and guilt. Our guilt is already great, and the LORD's fierce anger is already turned against Israel."

¹⁴So the warriors released the prisoners and handed over the plunder in the sight of the leaders and all the people. ¹⁵Then the four men just mentioned by name came forward and distributed clothes from the plunder to the prisoners who were naked. They provided clothing and sandals to wear, gave them enough food and drink, and dressed their wounds with olive oil. They put those who were weak on

donkeys and took all the prisoners back to their own people in Jericho, the city of palms. Then they returned to Samaria.

16At that time King Ahaz of Judah asked the king of Assyria for help. 17The armies of Edom had again invaded Judah and taken captives. 18And the Philistines had raided towns located in the foothills of Judah* and in the Negev of Judah. They had already captured and occupied Beth-shemesh, Aijalon, Gederoth, Soco with its villages, Timnah with its villages, and Gimzo with its villages. 19The LORD was humbling Judah because of King Ahaz of Judah,* for he had encouraged his people to sin and had been utterly unfaithful to the LORD.

20So when King Tiglath-pileser* of Assyria arrived, he attacked Ahaz instead of helping him. 21Ahaz took valuable items from the LORD's Temple, the royal palace, and from the homes of his officials and gave them to the king of Assyria as tribute. But this did not help him.

22Even during this time of trouble, King Ahaz continued to reject the LORD. 23He offered sacrifices to the gods of Damascus who had defeated him, for he said, "Since these gods helped the kings of Aram, they will help me, too, if I sacrifice to them." But instead, they led to his ruin and the ruin of all Judah.

24The king took the various articles from the Temple of God and broke them into pieces. He shut the doors of the LORD's Temple so that no one could worship there, and he set up altars to pagan gods in every corner of Jerusalem. 25He made pagan shrines in all the towns of Judah for offering sacrifices to other gods. In this way, he aroused the anger of the LORD, the God of his ancestors.

26The rest of the events of Ahaz's reign and everything he did, from beginning to end, are recorded in *The Book of the Kings of Judah and Israel.* 27When Ahaz died, he was buried in Jerusalem but not in the royal cemetery of the kings of Judah. Then his son Hezekiah became the next king.

26:2 As in Greek version (see also 2 Kgs 14:22; 16:6); Hebrew reads *Eloth,* a variant spelling of Elath.   26:5 As in Syriac and Greek versions; Hebrew reads *who instructed him in divine visions.*   26:7 As in Greek version; Hebrew reads *Gurbaal.*   26:8 As in Greek version; Hebrew reads *Ammonites.* Compare 26:7.   26:10 Hebrew *the Shephelah.*   26:15 Or *to shoot arrows and hurl large stones.*   26:19 Or *a contagious skin disease.* The Hebrew word used here and throughout this passage can describe various skin diseases.   27:5a Hebrew *100 talents* [3,400 kilograms].   27:5b Hebrew *10,000 cors* [1,820 kiloliters] *of wheat, and 10,000 cors of barley.*   28:3 Or *even making his sons pass through the fire.*   28:12 Hebrew *Ephraim,* referring to the northern kingdom of Israel.   28:18 Hebrew *the Shephelah.* 28:19 Hebrew *of Israel;* also in 28:23, 27. The author of Chronicles sees Judah as representative of the true Israel. See also some Hebrew manuscripts, Greek and Syriac versions, and Latin Vulgate.   28:20 Hebrew *Tilgath-pileser,* a variant spelling of Tiglath-pileser.

Obeying authority

HOW WE LIVE

ROMANS 13 In today's passage, Paul reminds believers that no longer conforming to this world does not mean we can ignore civil laws or refuse to pay taxes. Christians should be law-abiding citizens. • Are there times when believers should not submit to the government? Paul does not address this question here, but other passages of Scripture give guidelines and examples. The government can demand respect, obedience, taxes, and honor from its citizens inasmuch as God appoints governments to protect people. When a government demands allegiance that conflicts with a believer's loyalty to God, however, Christians must respond in a different way. Believers should never allow the government to force them to disobey God. • Jesus and his apostles never disobeyed the government for personal reasons; when they disobeyed, they were following their higher loyalty to God (Acts 5:29, June 7). Their disobedience was not cheap; they were threatened, beaten, thrown into jail, tortured, and executed for their convictions. If you are compelled to disobey, you must be ready to accept the consequences.

ROMANS 13:1-14

If believers are no longer to allow themselves to be conformed to behaviors and customs of this world (Romans 12:2, July 29), where does that leave us in terms of civil laws and paying taxes? Paul answers these questions here.

Everyone must submit to governing authorities. For all authority comes from God, and those in positions of authority have been placed there by God. ²So anyone who rebels against authority is rebelling against what God has instituted, and they will be punished. ³For the authorities do not strike fear in people who are doing right, but in those who are doing wrong. Would you like to live without fear of the authorities? Do what is right, and they will honor you. ⁴The authorities are God's servants, sent for your good. But if you are doing wrong, of course you should be afraid, for they have the power to punish you. They are God's servants, sent for the very purpose of punishing those who do what is wrong. ⁵So you must submit to them, not only to avoid punishment, but also to keep a clear conscience.

⁶Pay your taxes, too, for these same reasons. For government workers need to be paid. They are serving God in what they do. ⁷Give to everyone what you owe them: Pay your taxes and government fees to those who collect them, and give respect and honor to those who are in authority.

⁸Owe nothing to anyone—except for your obligation to love one another. If you love your neighbor, you will fulfill the requirements of God's law. ⁹For the commandments say, "You must not commit adultery. You must not murder. You must not steal. You must not covet."* These— and other such commandments—are summed up in this one commandment: "Love your neighbor as yourself."* ¹⁰Love does no wrong to others, so love fulfills the requirements of God's law.

¹¹This is all the more urgent, for you know how late it is; time is running out. Wake up, for our salvation is nearer now than when we first believed. ¹²The night is almost gone; the day of salvation will soon be here. So remove your dark deeds like dirty clothes, and put on the shining armor of right living. ¹³Because we belong to the day, we must live decent lives for all to see. Don't participate in the darkness of wild parties and drunkenness, or in sexual promiscuity and immoral living, or in quarreling and jealousy. ¹⁴Instead, clothe yourself with the presence of the Lord Jesus Christ. And don't let yourself think about ways to indulge your evil desires.

13:9a Exod 20:13-15, 17.   13:9b Lev 19:18.

PSALM 23:1-6
A psalm of David.

¹ **T**he LORD is my shepherd;
   I have all that I need.
² He lets me rest in green meadows;
   he leads me beside peaceful
     streams.
³   He renews my strength.
He guides me along right paths,
   bringing honor to his name.
⁴ Even when I walk
   through the darkest valley,*
I will not be afraid,
   for you are close beside me.
Your rod and your staff
   protect and comfort me.
⁵ You prepare a feast for me
   in the presence of my enemies.
You honor me by anointing my
   head with oil.
My cup overflows with
   blessings.
⁶ Surely your goodness and unfailing
   love will pursue me
all the days of my life,
and I will live in the house of the LORD
   forever.

23:4 Or *the dark valley of death.*

PROVERBS 20:11

Even children are known by the way they act, whether their conduct is pure, and whether it is right.

2 CHRONICLES 29:1-36

King Hezekiah was a bright light in an otherwise dark period. As the king breathed life into that national history again, the people received yet another opportunity to become the nation God had intended for them to be.

Hezekiah was twenty-five years old when he became the king of Judah, and he reigned in Jerusalem twenty-nine years. His mother was Abijah, the daughter of Zechariah. ²He did what was pleasing in the LORD's sight, just as his ancestor David had done.

³In the very first month of the first year of his reign, Hezekiah reopened the doors of the Temple of the LORD and repaired them. ⁴He summoned the priests and Levites to meet him at the courtyard east of the Temple. ⁵He said to them, "Listen to me, you Levites! Purify yourselves, and purify the Temple of the LORD, the God of your ancestors. Remove all the defiled things from the sanctuary. ⁶Our ancestors were unfaithful and did what was evil in the sight of the LORD our God. They abandoned the LORD and his dwelling place; they turned their backs on him. ⁷They also shut the doors to the Temple's entry room, and they snuffed out the lamps. They stopped burning incense and presenting burnt offerings at the sanctuary of the God of Israel.

⁸"That is why the LORD's anger has fallen upon Judah and Jerusalem. He has made them an object of dread, horror, and ridicule, as you can see with your own eyes. ⁹Because of this, our fathers have been killed in battle, and our sons and daughters and wives have been captured. ¹⁰But now I will make a covenant with the LORD, the God of Israel, so that his fierce anger will turn away from us. ¹¹My sons, do not neglect your duties any longer! The LORD has chosen you to stand in his presence, to minister to him, and to lead the people in worship and present offerings to him."

¹²Then these Levites got right to work:

From the clan of Kohath: Mahath son of Amasai and Joel son of Azariah.

From the clan of Merari: Kish son of Abdi and Azariah son of Jehallelel.

From the clan of Gershon: Joah son of Zimmah and Eden son of Joah.

¹³ From the family of Elizaphan: Shimri and Jeiel.

From the family of Asaph: Zechariah and Mattaniah.

¹⁴ From the family of Heman: Jehiel and Shimei.

From the family of Jeduthun: Shemaiah and Uzziel.

¹⁵These men called together their fellow Levites, and they all purified themselves. Then they began to cleanse the Temple of the LORD, just as the king had commanded. They were careful to follow all the LORD's instructions in their work. ¹⁶The priests went into the sanctuary of the Temple of the LORD to cleanse it, and they took out to the Temple courtyard all the defiled things they found. From there the Levites carted it all out to the Kidron Valley.

¹⁷They began the work in early spring, on the first day of the new year,* and in eight days they had reached the entry room of the LORD's Temple. Then they purified the Temple of the LORD itself, which took another eight days. So the entire task was completed in sixteen days.

¹⁸Then the Levites went to King Hezekiah and gave him this report: "We have cleansed the entire Temple of the LORD, the altar of burnt offering with all its utensils, and the table of the Bread of the Presence with all its utensils. ¹⁹We have also recovered all the items discarded by King Ahaz when he was unfaithful and closed the Temple. They are now in front of the altar of the LORD, purified and ready for use."

²⁰Early the next morning King Hezekiah gathered the city officials and went to the Temple of the LORD. ²¹They brought seven bulls, seven rams, and seven male lambs as a burnt offering, together with seven male goats as a sin offering for the

kingdom, for the Temple, and for Judah. The king commanded the priests, who were descendants of Aaron, to sacrifice the animals on the altar of the LORD.

²²So they killed the bulls, and the priests took the blood and sprinkled it on the altar. Next they killed the rams and sprinkled their blood on the altar. And finally, they did the same with the male lambs. ²³The male goats for the sin offering were then brought before the king and the assembly of people, who laid their hands on them. ²⁴The priests then killed the goats as a sin offering and sprinkled their blood on the altar to make atonement for the sins of all Israel. The king had specifically commanded that this burnt offering and sin offering should be made for all Israel.

²⁵King Hezekiah then stationed the Levites at the Temple of the LORD with cymbals, lyres, and harps. He obeyed all the commands that the LORD had given to King David through Gad, the king's seer, and the prophet Nathan. ²⁶The Levites then took their positions around the Temple with the instruments of David, and the priests took their positions with the trumpets.

²⁷Then Hezekiah ordered that the burnt offering be placed on the altar. As the burnt offering was presented, songs of praise to the LORD were begun, accompanied by the trumpets and other instruments of David, the former king of Israel. ²⁸The entire assembly worshiped the LORD as the singers sang and the trumpets blew, until all the burnt offerings were finished. ²⁹Then the king and everyone with him bowed down in worship. ³⁰King Hezekiah and the officials ordered the Levites to praise the LORD with the psalms written by David and by Asaph the seer. So they offered joyous praise and bowed down in worship.

³¹Then Hezekiah declared, "Now that you have consecrated yourselves to the LORD, bring your sacrifices and thanksgiving offerings to the Temple of the LORD." So the people brought their sacrifices and thanksgiving offerings, and all whose hearts were willing brought burnt offerings, too. ³²The people brought to the LORD 70 bulls, 100 rams, and 200 male

lambs for burnt offerings. ³³They also brought 600 cattle and 3,000 sheep and goats as sacred offerings.

³⁴But there were too few priests to prepare all the burnt offerings. So their relatives the Levites helped them until the work was finished and more priests had been purified, for the Levites had been more conscientious about purifying themselves than the priests had been. ³⁵There was an abundance of burnt offerings, along with the usual liquid offerings, and a great deal of fat from the many peace offerings.

So the Temple of the LORD was restored to service. ³⁶And Hezekiah and all the people rejoiced because of what God had done for the people, for everything had been accomplished so quickly.

29:17 Hebrew *on the first day of the first month.* This day in the ancient Hebrew lunar calendar occurred in March or early April, 715 B.C.

ROMANS 14:1-23

Opinions. Everybody's got one . . . or two . . . or fifty. Paul instructs believers to be careful not to turn what God considers matters of personal conviction into matters of universal dogma by which we condemn others.

Accept other believers who are weak in faith, and don't argue with them about what they think is right or wrong. ²For instance, one person believes it's all right to eat anything. But another believer with a sensitive conscience will eat only vegetables. ³Those who feel free to eat anything must not look down on those who don't. And those who don't eat certain foods must not condemn those who do, for God has accepted them. ⁴Who are you to condemn someone else's servants? They are responsible to the Lord, so let him judge whether they are right or wrong. And with the Lord's help, they will do what is right and will receive his approval.

⁵In the same way, some think one day is more holy than another day, while others think every day is alike. You should each be fully convinced that whichever day you choose is acceptable. ⁶Those who worship the Lord on a special day do it to honor him. Those who eat any kind of food do so to honor the Lord, since they give thanks to God before eating. And

those who refuse to eat certain foods also want to please the Lord and give thanks to God. [7] For we don't live for ourselves or die for ourselves. [8] If we live, it's to honor the Lord. And if we die, it's to honor the Lord. So whether we live or die, we belong to the Lord. [9] Christ died and rose again for this very purpose—to be Lord both of the living and of the dead.

[10] So why do you condemn another believer*? Why do you look down on another believer? Remember, we will all stand before the judgment seat of God. [11] For the Scriptures say,

"'As surely as I live,' says the
        LORD,
'every knee will bend to me,
    and every tongue will confess
        and give praise to God.*'"

[12] Yes, each of us will give a personal account to God. [13] So let's stop condemning each other. Decide instead to live in such a way that you will not cause another believer to stumble and fall.

[14] I know and am convinced on the authority of the Lord Jesus that no food, in and of itself, is wrong to eat. But if someone believes it is wrong, then for that person it is wrong. [15] And if another believer is distressed by what you eat, you are not acting in love if you eat it. Don't let your eating ruin someone for whom Christ died. [16] Then you will not be criticized for doing something you believe is good. [17] For the Kingdom of God is not a matter of what we eat or drink, but of living a life of goodness and peace and joy in the Holy Spirit. [18] If you serve Christ with this attitude, you will please God, and others will approve of you, too. [19] So then, let us aim for harmony in the church and try to build each other up.

[20] Don't tear apart the work of God over what you eat. Remember, all foods are acceptable, but it is wrong to eat something if it makes another person stumble. [21] It is better not to eat meat or drink wine or do anything else if it might cause another believer to stumble. [22] You may believe there's nothing wrong with what you are doing, but keep it between yourself and God. Blessed are those who don't feel guilty for doing something they have decided is right. [23] But if you have doubts about whether or not you should eat something, you are sinning if you go ahead and do it. For you are not following your convictions. If you do anything you believe is not right, you are sinning.

14:10 Greek *your brother;* also in 14:10b, 13, 15, 21.
14:11 Or *confess allegiance to God.* Isa 49:18; 45:23 (Greek version).

HOW WE LIVE   Dealing with differences

ROMANS 14:4 It's sometimes confusing that even among believers attending the same church there are different takes on how faith should work itself out. Some differences come from different interpretations of Scripture. Others come from the fact that different people have different convictions about gray areas. What is a temptation for one is not for another. What is a weakness for one is not for another. • So how should Christians handle differences in gray areas? (1) Keep a clean conscience before God. Each of us must stand before God as an obedient child. It is him we are trying to please, not other people. It is him we worship, not the approval of other Christians. It's easier to handle different opinions if you honestly know and accept God's requirements on your own life. (2) Give up the right to judge. Paul said it over and over again—it's not your responsibility to condemn anyone else. Don't try to do God's job. (3) Get comfortable talking about differences. Practice it. Work on a vocabulary and a tone of voice that allows you to engage in conversation in which you don't necessarily agree, but you offer respect to everyone involved.

PSALM 24:1-10
A psalm of David.

[1] **T**he earth is the LORD's, and everything
      in it.
   The world and all its people belong
      to him.
[2] For he laid the earth's foundation
      on the seas
   and built it on the ocean depths.

[3] Who may climb the mountain of the
      LORD?
   Who may stand in his holy place?
[4] Only those whose hands and hearts
      are pure,
   who do not worship idols
      and never tell lies.
[5] They will receive the LORD's blessing
   and have a right relationship with
      God their savior.

[6] Such people may seek you
   and worship in your presence, O God
      of Jacob.   *Interlude*

[7] Open up, ancient gates!
   Open up, ancient doors,
      and let the King of glory enter.
[8] Who is the King of glory?
   The LORD, strong and mighty;
      the LORD, invincible in battle.
[9] Open up, ancient gates!
   Open up, ancient doors,
      and let the King of glory enter.
[10] Who is the King of glory?
   The LORD of Heaven's Armies—
      he is the King of glory.   *Interlude*

PROVERBS 20:12
Ears to hear and eyes to see—both are
gifts from the LORD.

2 CHRONICLES 30:1–31:21

The Passover feast was named for the last plague in the story of the Exodus in which the angel of death "passed over" each home marked with lamb's blood. Passover was one of the most important of all the Jewish feasts. To reinstate this feast was to reclaim their national spiritual heritage.

King Hezekiah now sent word to all Israel and Judah, and he wrote letters of invitation to the people of Ephraim and Manasseh. He asked everyone to come to the Temple of the LORD at Jerusalem to celebrate the Passover of the LORD, the God of Israel. ²The king, his officials, and all the community of Jerusalem decided to celebrate Passover a month later than usual.* ³They were unable to celebrate it at the prescribed time because not enough priests could be purified by then, and the people had not yet assembled at Jerusalem.

⁴This plan for keeping the Passover seemed right to the king and all the people. ⁵So they sent a proclamation throughout all Israel, from Beersheba in the south to Dan in the north, inviting everyone to come to Jerusalem to celebrate the Passover of the LORD, the God of Israel. The people had not been celebrating it in great numbers as required in the Law.

⁶At the king's command, runners were sent throughout Israel and Judah. They carried letters that said:

"O people of Israel, return to the LORD, the God of Abraham, Isaac, and Israel,* so that he will return to the few of us who have survived the conquest of the Assyrian kings. ⁷Do not be like your ancestors and relatives who abandoned the LORD, the God of their ancestors, and became an object of derision, as you yourselves can see. ⁸Do not be stubborn, as they were, but submit yourselves to the LORD. Come to his Temple, which he has set apart

as holy forever. Worship the LORD your God so that his fierce anger will turn away from you.

⁹"For if you return to the LORD, your relatives and your children will be treated mercifully by their captors, and they will be able to return to this land. For the LORD your God is gracious and merciful. If you return to him, he will not continue to turn his face from you."

¹⁰The runners went from town to town throughout Ephraim and Manasseh and as far as the territory of Zebulun. But most of the people just laughed at the runners and made fun of them. ¹¹However, some people from Asher, Manasseh, and Zebulun humbled themselves and went to Jerusalem.

¹²At the same time, God's hand was on the people in the land of Judah, giving them all one heart to obey the orders of the king and his officials, who were following the word of the LORD. ¹³So a huge crowd assembled at Jerusalem in midspring* to celebrate the Festival of Unleavened Bread. ¹⁴They set to work and removed the pagan altars from Jerusalem. They took away all the incense altars and threw them into the Kidron Valley.

¹⁵On the fourteenth day of the second month, one month later than usual,* the people slaughtered the Passover lamb. This shamed the priests and Levites, so they purified themselves and brought burnt offerings to the Temple of the LORD. ¹⁶Then they took their places at the Temple as prescribed in the Law of Moses, the man of God. The Levites brought the sacrificial blood to the priests, who then sprinkled it on the altar.

¹⁷Since many of the people had not purified themselves, the Levites had to slaughter their Passover lamb for them, to set them apart for the LORD. ¹⁸Most of

those who came from Ephraim, Manasseh, Issachar, and Zebulun had not purified themselves. But King Hezekiah prayed for them, and they were allowed to eat the Passover meal anyway, even though this was contrary to the requirements of the Law. For Hezekiah said, "May the LORD, who is good, pardon those ¹⁹who decide to follow the LORD, the God of their ancestors, even though they are not properly cleansed for the ceremony." ²⁰And the LORD listened to Hezekiah's prayer and healed the people.

²¹So the people of Israel who were present in Jerusalem joyously celebrated the Festival of Unleavened Bread for seven days. Each day the Levites and priests sang to the LORD, accompanied by loud instruments.* ²²Hezekiah encouraged all the Levites regarding the skill they displayed as they served the LORD. The celebration continued for seven days. Peace offerings were sacrificed, and the people gave thanks to the LORD, the God of their ancestors.

²³The entire assembly then decided to continue the festival another seven days, so they celebrated joyfully for another week. ²⁴King Hezekiah gave the people 1,000 bulls and 7,000 sheep and goats for offerings, and the officials donated 1,000 bulls and 10,000 sheep and goats. Meanwhile, many more priests purified themselves.

²⁵The entire assembly of Judah rejoiced, including the priests, the Levites, all who came from the land of Israel, the foreigners who came to the festival, and all those who lived in Judah. ²⁶There was great joy in the city, for Jerusalem had not seen a celebration like this one since the days of Solomon, King David's son. ²⁷Then the priests and Levites stood and blessed the people, and God heard their prayer from his holy dwelling in heaven.

31:1WHEN the festival ended, the Israelites who attended went to all the towns of Judah, Benjamin, Ephraim, and Manasseh, and they smashed all the sacred pillars, cut down the Asherah poles, and removed the pagan shrines and altars. After this, the Israelites returned to their own towns and homes.

²Hezekiah then organized the priests and Levites into divisions to offer the burnt offerings and peace offerings, and to worship and give thanks and praise to the LORD at the gates of the Temple. ³The king also made a personal contribution of animals for the daily morning and evening burnt offerings, the weekly Sabbath festivals, the monthly new moon festivals, and the annual festivals as prescribed in the Law of the LORD. ⁴In addition, he required the people in Jerusalem to bring a portion of their goods to the priests and Levites, so they could devote themselves fully to the Law of the LORD.

⁵The people of Israel responded immediately and generously by bringing the first of their crops and grain, new wine, olive oil, honey, and all the produce of their fields. They brought a large quantity—a tithe of all they produced. ⁶The people who had moved to Judah from Israel, and the people of Judah themselves, brought in the tithes of their cattle, sheep, and goats and a tithe of the things that had been dedicated to the LORD their God, and they piled them up in great heaps. ⁷They began piling them up in late spring, and the heaps continued to grow until early autumn.* ⁸When Hezekiah and his officials came and saw these huge piles, they thanked the LORD and his people Israel!

⁹"Where did all this come from?" Hezekiah asked the priests and Levites.

¹⁰And Azariah the high priest, from the family of Zadok, replied, "Since the people began bringing their gifts to the LORD's Temple, we have had enough to eat and plenty to spare. The LORD has blessed his people, and all this is left over."

¹¹Hezekiah ordered that storerooms be prepared in the Temple of the LORD. When this was done, ¹²the people faithfully brought all the tithes and gifts to the Temple. Conaniah the Levite was put in charge, assisted by his brother Shimei. ¹³The supervisors under them were Jehiel, Azaziah, Nahath, Asahel, Jerimoth, Jozabad, Eliel, Ismakiah, Mahath, and Benaiah. These appointments were made by King Hezekiah and Azariah, the chief official in the Temple of God.

¹⁴Kore son of Imnah the Levite, who was the gatekeeper at the East Gate, was put in charge of distributing the voluntary offer-

ings given to God, the gifts, and the things that had been dedicated to the LORD. ¹⁵His faithful assistants were Eden, Miniamin, Jeshua, Shemaiah, Amariah, and Shecaniah. They distributed the gifts among the families of priests in their towns by their divisions, dividing the gifts fairly among old and young alike. ¹⁶They distributed the gifts to all males three years old or older, regardless of their place in the genealogical records. The distribution went to all who would come to the LORD's Temple to perform their daily duties according to their divisions. ¹⁷They distributed gifts to the priests who were listed by their families in the genealogical records, and to the Levites twenty years old or older who were listed according to their jobs and their divisions. ¹⁸Food allotments were also given to the families of all those listed in the genealogical records, including their little babies, wives, sons, and daughters. For they had all been faithful in purifying themselves.

¹⁹As for the priests, the descendants of Aaron, who were living in the open villages around the towns, men were appointed by name to distribute portions to every male among the priests and to all the Levites listed in the genealogical records.

²⁰In this way, King Hezekiah handled the distribution throughout all Judah, doing what was pleasing and good in the sight of the LORD his God. ²¹In all that he did in the service of the Temple of God and in his efforts to follow God's laws and commands, Hezekiah sought his God wholeheartedly. As a result, he was very successful.

30:2 Hebrew *in the second month.* Passover was normally observed in the first month (of the ancient Hebrew lunar calendar). 30:6 *Israel* is the name that God gave to Jacob. 30:13 Hebrew *in the second month.* The second month of the ancient Hebrew lunar calendar usually occurs within the months of April and May. 30:15 Hebrew *On the fourteenth day of the second month.* Passover normally began on the fourteenth day of the first month (see Lev 23:5). 30:21 Or *sang to the LORD with all their strength.* 31:7 Hebrew *in the third month . . . until the seventh month.* The third month of the ancient Hebrew lunar calendar usually occurs within the months of May and June; the seventh month usually occurs within September and October.

ROMANS 15:1-22
Christians will disagree about lots of things, but because of our common faith in Jesus Christ as Savior, we all need to learn to live in harmony.

We [Paul and other Christians] who are strong must be considerate of those who are sensitive about things like this. We must not just please ourselves. ²We should help others do what is right and build them up in the Lord. ³For even Christ didn't live to please himself. As the Scriptures say, "The insults of those who insult you, O God, have fallen on me."* ⁴Such things were written in the Scriptures long ago to teach us. And the Scriptures give us hope and encouragement as we wait patiently for God's promises to be fulfilled.

⁵May God, who gives this patience and encouragement, help you live in complete harmony with each other, as is fitting for followers of Christ Jesus. ⁶Then all of you

HOW WE LIVE

Experiencing joy

ROMANS 15:10 Christians of every background have a source of unending joy: their salvation in Jesus Christ. Jesus came to bring his message of salvation to his people, the Jews; but the plan had always been to offer salvation to the Gentiles also. It took awhile for the Jews to catch on to this (Remember the story of Peter visiting the Roman soldier Cornelius in Acts 10–11, June 15–17?). Finally, the Jews began to understand that God was creating something new—a church filled with Christians from every ethnic background united by their faith in Jesus Christ. • Your salvation is not an accident or a fluke—it is part of God's grand plan for the world. Nor is it a tenuous proposal that you hope works out in the end—your salvation is sure. He who sent his Son to die for you will not allow that event to be wasted. You will indeed inherit eternal life. This is reason to rejoice!

can join together with one voice, giving praise and glory to God, the Father of our Lord Jesus Christ.

⁷Therefore, accept each other just as Christ has accepted you so that God will be given glory. ⁸Remember that Christ came as a servant to the Jews* to show that God is true to the promises he made to their ancestors. ⁹He also came so that the Gentiles might give glory to God for his mercies to them. That is what the psalmist meant when he wrote:

"For this, I will praise you among
the Gentiles;
I will sing praises to your name."*

¹⁰And in another place it is written,

"Rejoice with his people,
you Gentiles."*

¹¹And yet again,

"Praise the Lᴏʀᴅ, all you Gentiles.
Praise him, all you people of
the earth."*

¹²And in another place Isaiah said,

"The heir to David's throne* will come,
and he will rule over the Gentiles.
They will place their hope on him."*

¹³I pray that God, the source of hope, will fill you completely with joy and peace because you trust in him. Then you will overflow with confident hope through the power of the Holy Spirit.

¹⁴I am fully convinced, my dear brothers and sisters,* that you are full of goodness. You know these things so well you can teach each other all about them. ¹⁵Even so, I have been bold enough to write about some of these points, knowing that all you need is this reminder. For by God's grace, ¹⁶I am a special messenger from Christ Jesus to you Gentiles. I bring you the Good News so that I might present you as an acceptable offering to God, made holy by the Holy Spirit. ¹⁷So I have reason to be enthusiastic about all Christ Jesus has done through me in my service to God. ¹⁸Yet I dare not boast about anything except what Christ has done through me, bringing the Gentiles to God by my message and by the way I worked among them. ¹⁹They were convinced by the power of miraculous signs and wonders and by the power of God's Spirit.* In this way, I have fully presented the Good News of Christ from Jerusalem all the way to Illyricum.*

²⁰My ambition has always been to preach the Good News where the name of Christ has never been heard, rather than where a church has already been started by someone else. ²¹I have been following the plan spoken of in the Scriptures, where it says,

"Those who have never been told
about him will see,
and those who have never heard
of him will understand."*

²²In fact, my visit to you has been delayed so long because I have been preaching in these places.

15:3 Greek *who insult you have fallen on me.* Ps 69:9.
15:8 Greek *servant of circumcision.* **15:9** Ps 18:49.
15:10 Deut 32:43. **15:11** Ps 117:1. **15:12a** Greek *The root of Jesse.* David was the son of Jesse. **15:12b** Isa 11:10 (Greek version). **15:14** Greek *brothers;* also in 15:30.
15:19a Other manuscripts read *the Spirit;* still others read *the Holy Spirit.* **15:19b** *Illyricum* was a region northeast of Italy. **15:21** Isa 52:15 (Greek version).

*PSALM 25:1-15
A psalm of David.

¹ **O** Lᴏʀᴅ, I give my life to you.
²   I trust in you, my God!
Do not let me be disgraced,
or let my enemies rejoice
in my defeat.
³ No one who trusts in you will ever
be disgraced,
but disgrace comes to those who
try to deceive others.

⁴ Show me the right path, O Lᴏʀᴅ;
point out the road for me to follow.
⁵ Lead me by your truth and teach me,
for you are the God who saves me.
All day long I put my hope in you.
⁶ Remember, O Lᴏʀᴅ, your compassion
and unfailing love,
which you have shown from long
ages past.
⁷ Do not remember the rebellious sins
of my youth.
Remember me in the light of your
unfailing love,
for you are merciful, O Lᴏʀᴅ.

⁸ The Lᴏʀᴅ is good and does what
is right;

he shows the proper path to those
who go astray.
9 He leads the humble in doing right,
teaching them his way.
10 The LORD leads with unfailing love
and faithfulness
all who keep his covenant and obey
his demands.

11 For the honor of your name, O LORD,
forgive my many, many sins.
12 Who are those who fear the LORD?
He will show them the path they
should choose.
13 They will live in prosperity,
and their children will inherit
the land.

14 The LORD is a friend to those who fear
him.
He teaches them his covenant.
15 My eyes are always on the LORD,
for he rescues me from the traps
of my enemies.

25 This psalm is a Hebrew acrostic poem; each verse begins
with a successive letter of the Hebrew alphabet.

PROVERBS 20:13-15

If you love sleep, you will end in poverty.
Keep your eyes open, and there will be
plenty to eat! □ The buyer haggles over
the price, saying, "It's worthless," then
brags about getting a bargain! □ Wise
words are more valuable than much gold
and many rubies.

AUGUST 2

2 CHRONICLES 32:1-33:13

Throughout their history, Israel and Judah faced
threats from surrounding nations. The Assyrians
were an especially dangerous threat. King Hezekiah
witnessed the Lord's protection against the Assyrian
invasion of Judah.

After Hezekiah had faithfully carried out
this work, King Sennacherib of Assyria invaded Judah. He laid siege to the fortified
towns, giving orders for his army to break
through their walls. 2 When Hezekiah realized that Sennacherib also intended to
attack Jerusalem, 3 he consulted with his
officials and military advisers, and they
decided to stop the flow of the springs
outside the city. 4 They organized a huge
work crew to stop the flow of the springs,
cutting off the brook that ran through the
fields. For they said, "Why should the
kings of Assyria come here and find
plenty of water?"

5 Then Hezekiah worked hard at repairing all the broken sections of the wall,
erecting towers, and constructing a second wall outside the first. He also reinforced the supporting terraces* in the
City of David and manufactured large

numbers of weapons and shields. 6 He appointed military officers over the people
and assembled them before him in the
square at the city gate. Then Hezekiah encouraged them by saying: 7 "Be strong and
courageous! Don't be afraid or discouraged because of the king of Assyria or his
mighty army, for there is a power far
greater on our side! 8 He may have a great
army, but they are merely men. We have
the LORD our God to help us and to fight
our battles for us!" Hezekiah's words
greatly encouraged the people.

9 While King Sennacherib of Assyria
was still besieging the town of Lachish, he
sent his officers to Jerusalem with this
message for Hezekiah and all the people
in the city:

10 "This is what King Sennacherib of
Assyria says: What are you trusting in
that makes you think you can survive
my siege of Jerusalem? 11 Hezekiah
has said, 'The LORD our God will
rescue us from the king of Assyria.'
Surely Hezekiah is misleading you,
sentencing you to death by famine

and thirst! ¹²Don't you realize that Hezekiah is the very person who destroyed all the Lord's shrines and altars? He commanded Judah and Jerusalem to worship only at the altar at the Temple and to offer sacrifices on it alone.

¹³"Surely you must realize what I and the other kings of Assyria before me have done to all the people of the earth! Were any of the gods of those nations able to rescue their people from my power? ¹⁴Which of their gods was able to rescue its people from the destructive power of my predecessors? What makes you think your God can rescue you from me? ¹⁵Don't let Hezekiah deceive you! Don't let him fool you like this! I say it again—no god of any nation or kingdom has ever yet been able to rescue his people from me or my ancestors. How much less will your God rescue you from my power!"

¹⁶And Sennacherib's officers further mocked the Lord God and his servant Hezekiah, heaping insult upon insult. ¹⁷The king also sent letters scorning the Lord, the God of Israel. He wrote, "Just as the gods of all the other nations failed to rescue their people from my power, so the God of Hezekiah will also fail." ¹⁸The Assyrian officials who brought the letters shouted this in Hebrew* to the people gathered on the walls of the city, trying to terrify them so it would be easier to capture the city. ¹⁹These officers talked about the God of Jerusalem as though he were one of the pagan gods, made by human hands.

²⁰Then King Hezekiah and the prophet Isaiah son of Amoz cried out in prayer to God in heaven. ²¹And the Lord sent an angel who destroyed the Assyrian army with all its commanders and officers. So Sennacherib was forced to return home in disgrace to his own land. And when he entered the temple of his god, some of his own sons killed him there with a sword.

²²That is how the Lord rescued Hezekiah and the people of Jerusalem from King Sennacherib of Assyria and from all the others who threatened them. So there was peace throughout the land. ²³From then on King Hezekiah became highly respected among all the surrounding nations, and many gifts for the Lord arrived at Jerusalem, with valuable presents for King Hezekiah, too.

²⁴About that time Hezekiah became deathly ill. He prayed to the Lord, who healed him and gave him a miraculous sign. ²⁵But Hezekiah did not respond appropriately to the kindness shown him, and he became proud. So the Lord's anger came against him and against Judah and Jerusalem. ²⁶Then Hezekiah humbled himself and repented of his pride, as did the people of Jerusalem. So the Lord's anger did not fall on them during Hezekiah's lifetime.

²⁷Hezekiah was very wealthy and highly honored. He built special treasury buildings for his silver, gold, precious stones, and spices, and for his shields and other valuable items. ²⁸He also constructed many storehouses for his grain, new wine, and olive oil; and he made many stalls for his cattle and pens for his flocks of sheep and goats. ²⁹He built many towns and acquired vast flocks and herds, for God had given him great wealth. ³⁰He blocked up the upper spring of Gihon and brought the water down through a tunnel to the west side of the City of David. And so he succeeded in everything he did.

³¹However, when ambassadors arrived from Babylon to ask about the remarkable events that had taken place in the land, God withdrew from Hezekiah in order to test him and to see what was really in his heart.

³²The rest of the events in Hezekiah's reign and his acts of devotion are recorded in *The Vision of the Prophet Isaiah Son of Amoz*, which is included in *The Book of the Kings of Judah and Israel*. ³³When Hezekiah died, he was buried in the upper area of the royal cemetery, and all Judah and Jerusalem honored him at his death. And his son Manasseh became the next king.

³³:¹Manasseh was twelve years old when he became king, and he reigned in Jerusalem fifty-five years. ²He did what was evil

in the LORD's sight, following the detestable practices of the pagan nations that the LORD had driven from the land ahead of the Israelites. ³He rebuilt the pagan shrines his father, Hezekiah, had broken down. He constructed altars for the images of Baal and set up Asherah poles. He also bowed before all the powers of the heavens and worshiped them.

⁴He built pagan altars in the Temple of the LORD, the place where the LORD had said, "My name will remain in Jerusalem forever." ⁵He built these altars for all the powers of the heavens in both courtyards of the LORD's Temple. ⁶Manasseh also sacrificed his own sons in the fire* in the valley of Ben-Hinnom. He practiced sorcery, divination, and witchcraft, and he consulted with mediums and psychics. He did much that was evil in the LORD's sight, arousing his anger.

⁷Manasseh even took a carved idol he had made and set it up in God's Temple, the very place where God had told David and his son Solomon: "My name will be honored forever in this Temple and in Jerusalem—the city I have chosen from among all the tribes of Israel. ⁸If the Israelites will be careful to obey my commands—all the laws, decrees, and regulations given through Moses—I will not send them into exile from this land that I set aside for your ancestors." ⁹But Manasseh led the people of Judah and Jerusalem to do even more evil than the pagan nations that the LORD had destroyed when the people of Israel entered the land.

¹⁰The LORD spoke to Manasseh and his people, but they ignored all his warnings. ¹¹So the LORD sent the commanders of the Assyrian armies, and they took Manasseh prisoner. They put a ring through his nose, bound him in bronze chains, and led him away to Babylon. ¹²But while in deep distress, Manasseh sought the LORD his God and sincerely humbled himself before the God of his ancestors. ¹³And when he prayed, the LORD listened to him and was moved by his request. So the LORD brought Manasseh back to Jerusalem and to his kingdom. Then Manasseh finally realized that the LORD alone is God!

32:5 Hebrew *the millo*. The meaning of the Hebrew is uncertain.   32:18 Hebrew *in the dialect of Judah*.   33:6 Or *also made his sons pass through the fire*.

ROMANS 15:23–16:9
Paul closes his letter with his future travel plans and greetings to friends. He invites them to pray for his well-being so that he can continue to spread the message of salvation.

But now I [Paul] have finished my work in these regions, and after all these long

Revering God

HOW WE LIVE

2 CHRONICLES 33:12-13 The list of evils perpetrated by Manasseh might make you queasy. Not only did he worship idols and desecrate the Temple, he sacrificed his own children to pagan gods. He led his whole nation astray and paid no attention when God spoke to him (33:10). Reverence for God? Manasseh was more into proud defiance.   • Yet, when Manasseh hit rock bottom, shackled and led around by a ring in his nose by his captors, he cried out "in deep distress" to God—not to the pagan gods he had worshiped. He humbled himself in reverence of the "God of his ancestors." And God responded with forgiveness and restored him to his throne. Because he finally came to honor the Lord as the only true God, Manasseh's life was changed. God extended his grace to this man whose sins had been sickening. Thanks to this example, we know God will forgive any sin as long as there is heartfelt repentance on the sinner's part.   • Learn from Manasseh's example. Failing to revere God brings disaster; turning back to him when we've sinned brings restoration.

years of waiting, I am eager to visit you. [24]I am planning to go to Spain, and when I do, I will stop off in Rome. And after I have enjoyed your fellowship for a little while, you can provide for my journey.

[25]But before I come, I must go to Jerusalem to take a gift to the believers* there. [26]For you see, the believers in Macedonia and Achaia* have eagerly taken up an offering for the poor among the believers in Jerusalem. [27]They were glad to do this because they feel they owe a real debt to them. Since the Gentiles received the spiritual blessings of the Good News from the believers in Jerusalem, they feel the least they can do in return is to help them financially. [28]As soon as I have delivered this money and completed this good deed of theirs, I will come to see you on my way to Spain. [29]And I am sure that when I come, Christ will richly bless our time together.

[30]Dear brothers and sisters, I urge you in the name of our Lord Jesus Christ to join in my struggle by praying to God for me. Do this because of your love for me, given to you by the Holy Spirit. [31]Pray that I will be rescued from those in Judea who refuse to obey God. Pray also that the believers there will be willing to accept the donation* I am taking to Jerusalem. [32]Then, by the will of God, I will be able to come to you with a joyful heart, and we will be an encouragement to each other.

[33]And now may God, who gives us his peace, be with you all. Amen.*

[16:1]I COMMEND to you our sister Phoebe, who is a deacon in the church in Cenchrea. [2]Welcome her in the Lord as one who is worthy of honor among God's people. Help her in whatever she needs, for she has been helpful to many, and especially to me.

[3]Give my greetings to Priscilla and Aquila, my co-workers in the ministry of Christ Jesus. [4]In fact, they once risked their lives for me. I am thankful to them, and so are all the Gentile churches. [5]Also

give my greetings to the church that meets in their home.

Greet my dear friend Epenetus. He was the first person from the province of Asia to become a follower of Christ. [6]Give my greetings to Mary, who has worked so hard for your benefit. [7]Greet Andronicus and Junia,* my fellow Jews,* who were in prison with me. They are highly respected among the apostles and became followers of Christ before I did. [8]Greet Ampliatus, my dear friend in the Lord. [9]Greet Urbanus, our co-worker in Christ, and my dear friend Stachys.

15:25 Greek *God's holy people;* also in 15:26, 31.
15:26 *Macedonia* and *Achaia* were the northern and southern regions of Greece.   **15:31** Greek *the ministry;* other manuscripts read *the gift.*   **15:33** Some manuscripts omit *Amen.* One very early manuscript places 16:25-27 here.
16:7a *Junia* is a feminine name. Some late manuscripts accent the word so it reads *Junias,* a masculine name; still others read *Julia* (feminine).   **16:7b** Or *compatriots;* also in 16:21.

PSALM 25:16-22

Turn to me and have mercy,
for I am alone and in deep distress.
[17] My problems go from bad to worse.
Oh, save me from them all!
[18] Feel my pain and see my trouble.
Forgive all my sins.
[19] See how many enemies I have
and how viciously they hate me!
[20] Protect me! Rescue my life from them!
Do not let me be disgraced,
for in you I take refuge.
[21] May integrity and honesty protect me,
for I put my hope in you.

[22] O God, ransom Israel
from all its troubles.

PROVERBS 20:16-18

Get security from someone who guarantees a stranger's debt. Get a deposit if he does it for foreigners.* □Stolen bread tastes sweet, but it turns to gravel in the mouth. □Plans succeed through good counsel; don't go to war without wise advice.

20:16 An alternate reading in the Hebrew text is *for a promiscuous woman.*

2 CHRONICLES 33:14–34:33

Every few generations in Judah, a righteous king came to the throne, rose above the cultural decline, and called the nation back to its spiritual roots. Josiah was that kind of king.

After this Manasseh rebuilt the outer wall of the City of David, from west of the Gihon Spring in the Kidron Valley to the Fish Gate, and continuing around the hill of Ophel. He built the wall very high. And he stationed his military officers in all of the fortified towns of Judah. ¹⁵Manasseh also removed the foreign gods and the idol from the LORD's Temple. He tore down all the altars he had built on the hill where the Temple stood and all the altars that were in Jerusalem, and he dumped them outside the city. ¹⁶Then he restored the altar of the LORD and sacrificed peace offerings and thanksgiving offerings on it. He also encouraged the people of Judah to worship the LORD, the God of Israel. ¹⁷However, the people still sacrificed at the pagan shrines, though only to the LORD their God.

¹⁸The rest of the events of Manasseh's reign, his prayer to God, and the words the seers spoke to him in the name of the LORD, the God of Israel, are recorded in *The Book of the Kings of Israel.* ¹⁹Manasseh's prayer, the account of the way God answered him, and an account of all his sins and unfaithfulness are recorded in *The Record of the Seers.** It includes a list of the locations where he built pagan shrines and set up Asherah poles and idols before he humbled himself and repented. ²⁰When Manasseh died, he was buried in his palace. Then his son Amon became the next king.

²¹Amon was twenty-two years old when he became king, and he reigned in Jerusalem two years. ²²He did what was evil in the LORD's sight, just as his father, Manasseh, had done. He worshiped and sacrificed to all the idols his father had made. ²³But unlike his father, he did not humble himself before the LORD. Instead, Amon sinned even more.

²⁴Then Amon's own officials conspired against him and assassinated him in his palace. ²⁵But the people of the land killed all those who had conspired against King Amon, and they made his son Josiah the next king.

34:¹JOSIAH was eight years old when he became king, and he reigned in Jerusalem thirty-one years. ²He did what was pleasing in the LORD's sight and followed the example of his ancestor David. He did not turn away from doing what was right.

³During the eighth year of his reign, while he was still young, Josiah began to seek the God of his ancestor David. Then in the twelfth year he began to purify Judah and Jerusalem, destroying all the pagan shrines, the Asherah poles, and the carved idols and cast images. ⁴He ordered that the altars of Baal be demolished and that the incense altars which stood above them be broken down. He also made sure that the Asherah poles, the carved idols, and the cast images were smashed and scattered over the graves of those who had sacrificed to them. ⁵He burned the bones of the pagan priests on their own altars, and so he purified Judah and Jerusalem.

⁶He did the same thing in the towns of Manasseh, Ephraim, and Simeon, even as far as Naphtali, and in the regions* all around them. ⁷He destroyed the pagan altars and the Asherah poles, and he crushed the idols into dust. He cut down all the incense altars throughout the land of Israel. Finally, he returned to Jerusalem.

⁸In the eighteenth year of his reign, after he had purified the land and the Temple, Josiah appointed Shaphan son of Azaliah, Maaseiah the governor of Jerusalem, and Joah son of Joahaz, the royal historian, to repair the Temple of the LORD his God. ⁹They gave Hilkiah the high priest the money that had been collected by the Levites who served as gatekeepers at the Temple of God. The gifts were brought by people from Manasseh, Ephraim, and from all the remnant of Israel, as

well as from all Judah, Benjamin, and the people of Jerusalem.

[10]He entrusted the money to the men assigned to supervise the restoration of the LORD's Temple. Then they paid the workers who did the repairs and renovation of the Temple. [11]They hired carpenters and builders, who purchased finished stone for the walls and timber for the rafters and beams. They restored what earlier kings of Judah had allowed to fall into ruin.

[12]The workers served faithfully under the leadership of Jahath and Obadiah, Levites of the Merarite clan, and Zechariah and Meshullam, Levites of the Kohathite clan. Other Levites, all of whom were skilled musicians, [13]were put in charge of the laborers of the various trades. Still others assisted as secretaries, officials, and gatekeepers.

[14]While they were bringing out the money collected at the LORD's Temple, Hilkiah the priest found the Book of the Law of the LORD that was written by Moses. [15]Hilkiah said to Shaphan the court secretary, "I have found the Book of the Law in the LORD's Temple!" Then Hilkiah gave the scroll to Shaphan.

[16]Shaphan took the scroll to the king and reported, "Your officials are doing everything they were assigned to do. [17]The money that was collected at the Temple of the LORD has been turned over to the supervisors and workmen." [18]Shaphan also told the king, "Hilkiah the priest has given me a scroll." So Shaphan read it to the king.

[19]When the king heard what was written in the Law, he tore his clothes in despair. [20]Then he gave these orders to Hilkiah, Ahikam son of Shaphan, Acbor son of Micaiah,* Shaphan the court secretary, and Asaiah the king's personal adviser: [21]"Go to the Temple and speak to the LORD for me and for all the remnant of Israel and Judah. Inquire about the words written in the scroll that has been found. For the LORD's great anger has been poured out on us because our ancestors have not obeyed the word of the LORD. We have not been doing everything this scroll says we must do."

[22]So Hilkiah and the other men went to the New Quarter* of Jerusalem to consult with the prophet Huldah. She was the wife of Shallum son of Tikvah, son of Harhas,* the keeper of the Temple wardrobe.

[23]She said to them, "The LORD, the God of Israel, has spoken! Go back and tell the man who sent you, [24]'This is what the LORD says: I am going to bring disaster on this city* and its people. All the curses written in the scroll that was read to the king of Judah will come true. [25]For my people have abandoned me and offered sacrifices to pagan gods, and I am very angry with them for everything they have done. My anger will be poured out on this place, and it will not be quenched.'

[26]"But go to the king of Judah who sent you to seek the LORD and tell him: 'This is what the LORD, the God of Israel, says concerning the message you have just heard: [27]You were sorry and humbled yourself before God when you heard his words against this city and its people. You humbled yourself and tore your clothing in despair and wept before me in repentance. And I have indeed heard you, says the LORD. [28]So I will not send the promised disaster until after you have died and been buried in peace. You yourself will not see the disaster I am going to bring on this city and its people.'"

So they took her message back to the king.

[29]Then the king summoned all the elders of Judah and Jerusalem. [30]And the king went up to the Temple of the LORD with all the people of Judah and Jerusalem, along with the priests and the Levites—all the people from the greatest to the least. There the king read to them the entire Book of the Covenant that had been found in the LORD's Temple. [31]The king took his place of authority beside the pillar and renewed the covenant in the LORD's presence. He pledged to obey the LORD by keeping all his commands, laws, and decrees with all his heart and soul. He promised to obey all the terms of the covenant that were written in the scroll. [32]And he required everyone in Jerusalem and the people of Benjamin to make a similar pledge. The people of Jerusalem did so, renewing their covenant with God, the God of their ancestors.

³³So Josiah removed all detestable idols from the entire land of Israel and required everyone to worship the LORD their God. And throughout the rest of his lifetime, they did not turn away from the LORD, the God of their ancestors.

33:19 Or *The Record of Hozai.*   **34:6** As in Syriac version. Hebrew reads *in their temples,* or *in their ruins.* The meaning of the Hebrew is uncertain.   **34:20** As in parallel text at 2 Kgs 22:12; Hebrew reads *Abdon son of Micah.*   **34:22a** Or *the Second Quarter,* a newer section of Jerusalem. Hebrew reads *the Mishneh.*   **34:22b** As in parallel text at 2 Kgs 22:14; Hebrew reads *son of Tokhath, son of Hasrah.*   **34:24** Hebrew *this place;* also in 34:27, 28.

ROMANS 16:10-27

Final words are often our strongest. After some final greetings and encouragements, Paul returned to the most important topic of all: God's glory as it is revealed in the Good News of Jesus Christ.

Greet Apelles, a good man whom Christ approves. And give my [Paul's] greetings to the believers from the household of Aristobulus. ¹¹Greet Herodion, my fellow Jew.* Greet the Lord's people from the household of Narcissus. ¹²Give my greetings to Tryphena and Tryphosa, the Lord's workers, and to dear Persis, who has worked so hard for the Lord. ¹³Greet Rufus, whom the Lord picked out to be his very own; and also his dear mother, who has been a mother to me.

¹⁴Give my greetings to Asyncritus, Phlegon, Hermes, Patrobas, Hermas, and the brothers and sisters* who meet with them. ¹⁵Give my greetings to Philologus, Julia, Nereus and his sister, and to Olympas and all the believers* who meet with them. ¹⁶Greet each other in Christian love.* All the churches of Christ send you their greetings.

¹⁷And now I make one more appeal, my dear brothers and sisters. Watch out for people who cause divisions and upset people's faith by teaching things contrary to what you have been taught. Stay away from them. ¹⁸Such people are not serving Christ our Lord; they are serving their own personal interests. By smooth talk and glowing words they deceive innocent people. ¹⁹But everyone knows that you are obedient to the Lord. This makes me very happy. I want you to be wise in doing right and to stay innocent of any wrong. ²⁰The God of peace will soon crush Satan under your feet. May the grace of our Lord Jesus* be with you.

²¹Timothy, my fellow worker, sends you his greetings, as do Lucius, Jason, and Sosipater, my fellow Jews.

²²I, Tertius, the one writing this letter for Paul, send my greetings, too, as one of the Lord's followers.

²³Gaius says hello to you. He is my host and also serves as host to the whole

---

HOW WE LIVE

Our speech

PROVERBS 20:19 One of the more visible ways Christians represent Jesus is through their words. It has been said that a person speaks about thirty thousand words in an average day. That is a considerable amount of "representation time"—especially when you consider the power of the spoken word. Your words have the power to build up or to destroy, help or hurt, encourage or discourage. The tongue is small but can do great damage (James 3:6, November 19). • Proverbs 20:19 speaks in particular of gossip, warning us not to keep company with people who talk too much. Gossip takes many forms. We can put someone down in order to feel superior. We can say things behind a person's back in order to cause hurt. We can gossip just to have a good laugh. Unfortunately, gossip "separates the best of friends" (Proverbs 16:28, June 9) and will ruin your good reputation (Proverbs 25:10, October 12). Jesus said that we will be held accountable for every idle word we speak (Matthew 12:36, January 18). Ask God to give you the courage not to participate in gossip. Instead, turn the conversation to more positive and uplifting topics.

church. Erastus, the city treasurer, sends you his greetings, and so does our brother Quartus.*

25Now all glory to God, who is able to make you strong, just as my Good News says. This message about Jesus Christ has revealed his plan for you Gentiles, a plan kept secret from the beginning of time. 26But now as the prophets* foretold and as the eternal God has commanded, this message is made known to all Gentiles everywhere, so that they too might believe and obey him. 27All glory to the only wise God, through Jesus Christ, forever. Amen.

16:11 Or *compatriot.* 16:14 Greek *brothers;* also in 16:17. 16:15 Greek *all of God's holy people.* 16:16 Greek *with a sacred kiss.* 16:20 Some manuscripts read *Lord Jesus Christ.* 16:23 Some manuscripts add verse 24, *May the grace of our Lord Jesus Christ be with you all. Amen.* Still others add this sentence after verse 27. 16:26 Greek *the prophetic writings.*

PSALM 26:1-12
A psalm of David.

1 **D**eclare me innocent, O LORD,
  for I have acted with integrity;
  I have trusted in the LORD without
    wavering.
2 Put me on trial, LORD, and cross-
    examine me.
  Test my motives and my heart.
3 For I am always aware of your
    unfailing love,

and I have lived according to your
    truth.
4 I do not spend time with liars
  or go along with hypocrites.
5 I hate the gatherings of those who
    do evil,
  and I refuse to join in with the
    wicked.
6 I wash my hands to declare my
    innocence.
  I come to your altar, O LORD,
7 singing a song of thanksgiving
  and telling of all your wonders.
8 I love your sanctuary, LORD,
  the place where your glorious
    presence dwells.

9 Don't let me suffer the fate of sinners.
  Don't condemn me along with
    murderers.
10 Their hands are dirty with evil
    schemes,
  and they constantly take bribes.
11 But I am not like that; I live with
    integrity.
  So redeem me and show me mercy.
12 Now I stand on solid ground,
  and I will publicly praise the LORD.

PROVERBS 20:19
A gossip goes around telling secrets, so don't hang around with chatterers.

AUGUST**4**

2 CHRONICLES 35:1–36:23
Josiah had revitalized the nation, but his efforts were short-lived. He was followed by a chain of evil kings that brought the nation to the brink of destruction. In the end, as God had warned, the nation fell and its people were taken into captivity in Babylon.

Then Josiah announced that the Passover of the LORD would be celebrated in Jerusalem, and so the Passover lamb was slaughtered on the fourteenth day of the first month.* 2Josiah also assigned the priests to their duties and encouraged them in

their work at the Temple of the LORD. 3He issued this order to the Levites, who were to teach all Israel and who had been set apart to serve the LORD: "Put the holy Ark in the Temple that was built by Solomon son of David, the king of Israel. You no longer need to carry it back and forth on your shoulders. Now spend your time serving the LORD your God and his people Israel. 4Report for duty according to the family divisions of your ancestors, following the directions of King David of Israel and the directions of his son Solomon.

[5]"Then stand in the sanctuary at the place appointed for your family division and help the families assigned to you as they bring their offerings to the Temple. [6]Slaughter the Passover lambs, purify yourselves, and prepare to help those who come. Follow all the directions that the LORD gave through Moses."

[7]Then Josiah provided 30,000 lambs and young goats for the people's Passover offerings, along with 3,000 cattle, all from the king's own flocks and herds. [8]The king's officials also made willing contributions to the people, priests, and Levites. Hilkiah, Zechariah, and Jehiel, the administrators of God's Temple, gave the priests 2,600 lambs and young goats and 300 cattle as Passover offerings. [9]The Levite leaders—Conaniah and his brothers Shemaiah and Nethanel, as well as Hashabiah, Jeiel, and Jozabad—gave 5,000 lambs and young goats and 500 cattle to the Levites for their Passover offerings.

[10]When everything was ready for the Passover celebration, the priests and the Levites took their places, organized by their divisions, as the king had commanded. [11]The Levites then slaughtered the Passover lambs and presented the blood to the priests, who sprinkled the blood on the altar while the Levites prepared the animals. [12]They divided the burnt offerings among the people by their family groups, so they could offer them to the LORD as prescribed in the Book of Moses. They did the same with the cattle. [13]Then they roasted the Passover lambs as prescribed; and they boiled the holy offerings in pots, kettles, and pans, and brought them out quickly so the people could eat them.

[14]Afterward the Levites prepared Passover offerings for themselves and for the priests—the descendants of Aaron—because the priests had been busy from morning till night offering the burnt offerings and the fat portions. The Levites took responsibility for all these preparations.

[15]The musicians, descendants of Asaph, were in their assigned places, following the commands that had been given by David, Asaph, Heman, and Jeduthun, the king's seer. The gatekeepers guarded the gates and did not need to leave their posts of duty, for their Passover offerings were prepared for them by their fellow Levites.

[16]The entire ceremony for the LORD's Passover was completed that day. All the burnt offerings were sacrificed on the altar of the LORD, as King Josiah had commanded. [17]All the Israelites present in Jerusalem celebrated Passover and the Festival of Unleavened Bread for seven days. [18]Never since the time of the prophet Samuel had there been such a Passover. None of the kings of Israel had ever kept a Passover as Josiah did, involving all the priests and Levites, all the people of Jerusalem, and people from all over Judah and Israel. [19]This Passover celebration took place in the eighteenth year of Josiah's reign.

[20]After Josiah had finished restoring the Temple, King Neco of Egypt led his army up from Egypt to do battle at Carchemish on the Euphrates River, and Josiah and his army marched out to fight him.* [21]But King Neco sent messengers to Josiah with this message:

"What do you want with me, king of Judah? I have no quarrel with you today! I am on my way to fight another nation, and God has told me to hurry! Do not interfere with God, who is with me, or he will destroy you."

[22]But Josiah refused to listen to Neco, to whom God had indeed spoken, and he would not turn back. Instead, he disguised himself and led his army into battle on the plain of Megiddo. [23]But the enemy archers hit King Josiah with their arrows and wounded him. He cried out to his men, "Take me from the battle, for I am badly wounded!"

[24]So they lifted Josiah out of his chariot and placed him in another chariot. Then they brought him back to Jerusalem, where he died. He was buried there in the royal cemetery. And all Judah and Jerusalem mourned for him. [25]The prophet Jeremiah composed funeral songs for Josiah, and to this day choirs still sing these sad songs about his death. These songs of sorrow have become a tradition and are recorded in *The Book of Laments*.

[26]The rest of the events of Josiah's reign

and his acts of devotion (carried out according to what was written in the Law of the LORD), 27 from beginning to end—all are recorded in *The Book of the Kings of Israel and Judah*.

36:1 THEN the people of the land took Josiah's son Jehoahaz and made him the next king in Jerusalem.

2 Jehoahaz* was twenty-three years old when he became king, and he reigned in Jerusalem three months.

3 Then he was deposed by the king of Egypt, who demanded that Judah pay 7,500 pounds of silver and 75 pounds of gold* as tribute.

4 The king of Egypt then installed Eliakim, the brother of Jehoahaz, as the next king of Judah and Jerusalem, and he changed Eliakim's name to Jehoiakim. Then Neco took Jehoahaz to Egypt as a prisoner.

5 Jehoiakim was twenty-five years old when he became king, and he reigned in Jerusalem eleven years. He did what was evil in the sight of the LORD his God.

6 Then King Nebuchadnezzar of Babylon came to Jerusalem and captured it, and he bound Jehoiakim in bronze chains and led him away to Babylon. 7 Nebuchadnezzar also took some of the treasures from the Temple of the LORD, and he placed them in his palace* in Babylon.

8 The rest of the events in Jehoiakim's reign, including all the evil things he did and everything found against him, are recorded in *The Book of the Kings of Israel and Judah*. Then his son Jehoiachin became the next king.

9 Jehoiachin was eighteen* years old when he became king, and he reigned in Jerusalem three months and ten days. Jehoiachin did what was evil in the LORD's sight.

10 In the spring of the year* King Nebuchadnezzar took Jehoiachin to Babylon. Many treasures from the Temple of the LORD were also taken to Babylon at that time. And Nebuchadnezzar installed Jehoiachin's uncle,* Zedekiah, as the next king in Judah and Jerusalem.

11 Zedekiah was twenty-one years old when he became king, and he reigned in Jerusalem eleven years. 12 He did what was evil in the sight of the LORD his God, and he refused to humble himself when the prophet Jeremiah spoke to him directly from the LORD. 13 He also rebelled against King Nebuchadnezzar, even though he had taken an oath of loyalty in God's name. Zedekiah was a hard and stubborn man, refusing to turn to the LORD, the God of Israel.

14 Likewise, all the leaders of the priests and the people became more and more unfaithful. They followed all the pagan practices of the surrounding nations, desecrating the Temple of the LORD that had been consecrated in Jerusalem.

15 The LORD, the God of their ancestors, repeatedly sent his prophets to warn them, for he had compassion on his people and his Temple. 16 But the people mocked these messengers of God and despised their words. They scoffed at the prophets until the LORD's anger could no longer be restrained and nothing could be done.

17 So the LORD brought the king of Babylon against them. The Babylonians* killed Judah's young men, even chasing after them into the Temple. They had no pity on the people, killing both young men and young women, the old and the infirm. God handed all of them over to Nebuchadnezzar. 18 The king took home to Babylon all the articles, large and small, used in the Temple of God, and the treasures from both the LORD's Temple and from the palace of the king and his officials. 19 Then his army burned the Temple of God, tore down the walls of Jerusalem, burned all the palaces, and completely destroyed everything of value.* 20 The few who survived were taken as exiles to Babylon, and they became servants to the king and his sons until the kingdom of Persia came to power.

21 So the message of the LORD spoken through Jeremiah was fulfilled. The land finally enjoyed its Sabbath rest, lying desolate until the seventy years were fulfilled, just as the prophet had said.

22 In the first year of King Cyrus of Persia,* the LORD fulfilled the prophecy he had given through Jeremiah.* He stirred the heart of Cyrus to put this proclama-

tion in writing and to send it throughout his kingdom:

²³"This is what King Cyrus of Persia says:

"The LORD, the God of heaven, has given me all the kingdoms of the earth. He has appointed me to build him a Temple at Jerusalem, which is in Judah. Any of you who are the LORD's people may go there for this task. And may the LORD your God be with you!"

35:1 This day in the ancient Hebrew lunar calendar was April 5, 622 B.C.   35:20 Or *Josiah went out to meet him.* 36:2 Hebrew *Joahaz*, a variant spelling of Jehoahaz; also in 36:4.   36:3 Hebrew *100 talents* [3,400 kilograms] *of silver and 1 talent* [34 kilograms] *of gold.*   36:7 Or *temple.* 36:9 As in one Hebrew manuscript, some Greek manuscripts, and Syriac version (see also 2 Kgs 24:8); most Hebrew manuscripts read *eight.*   36:10a Hebrew *At the turn of the year.* The first day of this year in the ancient Hebrew lunar calendar was April 13, 597 B.C.   36:10b As in parallel text at 2 Kgs 24:17; Hebrew reads *brother,* or *relative.*   36:17 Or *Chaldeans.*   36:19 Or *destroyed all the valuable articles from the Temple.*   36:22a The first year of Cyrus's reign over Babylon was 538 B.C.   36:22b See Jer 25:11-12; 29:10.

1 CORINTHIANS 1:1-17

Corinth was a major metropolitan city in Paul's day. Paul had spent about eighteen months in Corinth, starting the Christian church there (Acts 18:1-18, June 27). Five years later, he heard that the church was struggling, so he wrote this letter to the believers.

This letter is from Paul, chosen by the will of God to be an apostle of Christ Jesus, and from our brother Sosthenes.

²I am writing to God's church in Corinth,* to you who have been called by God to be his own holy people. He made you holy by means of Christ Jesus,* just as he did for all people everywhere who call on the name of our Lord Jesus Christ, their Lord and ours.

³May God our Father and the Lord Jesus Christ give you grace and peace.

⁴I always thank my God for you and for the gracious gifts he has given you, now that you belong to Christ Jesus. ⁵Through him, God has enriched your church in every way—with all of your eloquent words and all of your knowledge. ⁶This confirms that what I told you about Christ is true. ⁷Now you have every spiritual gift you need as you eagerly wait for the return of our Lord Jesus Christ. ⁸He will keep you strong to the end so that you will be free from all blame on the day when our Lord Jesus Christ returns. ⁹God will do this, for he is faithful to do what he says, and he has invited you into partnership with his Son, Jesus Christ our Lord.

¹⁰I appeal to you, dear brothers and sisters,* by the authority of our Lord Jesus Christ, to live in harmony with each other. Let there be no divisions in the church. Rather, be of one mind, united in thought and purpose. ¹¹For some members of Chloe's household have told me about your quarrels, my dear brothers and sisters. ¹²Some of you are saying, "I am a follower

HOW WE LIVE

Growing in wisdom

1 CORINTHIANS 1:10-17 Human beings find countless reasons to disagree and divide. Paul saw it happening in the church in Corinth. Factions were developing around different personalities, and the church was in danger of dissolving into splinter groups. • Paul urged the Corinthian Christians to get some perspective. They had been saved by Christ—not by Paul or Apollos or Peter. Their unity in Christ must trump anything else. They must not allow themselves to get caught up in disagreements that would separate them and render them ineffective in their witness to their fellow Corinthians. God had called them to live in unity and wisdom. • "The LORD grants wisdom! From his mouth come knowledge and understanding" (Proverbs 2:6, January 8). Growing in wisdom means that we live according to the principles in God's Word, not according to the latest political or religious guru with the most hype. Growing in wisdom means not getting sidetracked from where your faith lies—in Jesus Christ.

of Paul." Others are saying, "I follow Apollos," or "I follow Peter,*" or "I follow Christ."

¹³Has Christ been divided into factions? Was I, Paul, crucified for you? Were any of you baptized in the name of Paul? Of course not! ¹⁴I thank God that I did not baptize any of you except Crispus and Gaius, ¹⁵for now no one can say they were baptized in my name. ¹⁶(Oh yes, I also baptized the household of Stephanas, but I don't remember baptizing anyone else.) ¹⁷For Christ didn't send me to baptize, but to preach the Good News—and not with clever speech, for fear that the cross of Christ would lose its power.

1:2a *Corinth* was the capital city of Achaia, the southern region of the Greek peninsula. 1:2b Or *because you belong to Christ Jesus.* 1:10 Greek *brothers;* also in 1:11, 26. 1:12 Greek *Cephas.*

PSALM 27:1-6
A psalm of David.

¹ The LORD is my light and my
    salvation—
    so why should I be afraid?
The LORD is my fortress, protecting
    me from danger,
    so why should I tremble?
² When evil people come to devour me,

when my enemies and foes attack me,
    they will stumble and fall.
³ Though a mighty army surrounds me,
    my heart will not be afraid.
Even if I am attacked,
    I will remain confident.

⁴ The one thing I ask of the LORD—
    the thing I seek most—
is to live in the house of the LORD all
    the days of my life,
    delighting in the LORD's perfections
    and meditating in his Temple.
⁵ For he will conceal me there when
    troubles come;
    he will hide me in his sanctuary.
    He will place me out of reach on
    a high rock.
⁶ Then I will hold my head high
    above my enemies who surround me.
At his sanctuary I will offer sacrifices
    with shouts of joy,
    singing and praising the LORD with
    music.

PROVERBS 20:20-21
If you insult your father or mother, your light will be snuffed out in total darkness.
□ An inheritance obtained too early in life is not a blessing in the end.

AUGUST5

EZRA 1:1–2:70
The Babylonians were eventually defeated by the next world empire—the Medo-Persians. God moved Cyrus, their king, to allow the Jewish exiles to return to their homeland. Ezra tells the story of the Jews who returned from exile many years later in order to begin rebuilding their nation.

In the first year of King Cyrus of Persia,* the LORD fulfilled the prophecy he had given through Jeremiah.* He stirred the heart of Cyrus to put this proclamation in writing and to send it throughout his kingdom:

²"This is what King Cyrus of Persia says: "The LORD, the God of heaven, has

given me all the kingdoms of the earth. He has appointed me to build him a Temple at Jerusalem, which is in Judah. ³Any of you who are his people may go to Jerusalem in Judah to rebuild this Temple of the LORD, the God of Israel, who lives in Jerusalem. And may your God be with you! ⁴Wherever this Jewish remnant is found, let their neighbors contribute toward their expenses by giving them silver and gold, supplies for the journey, and livestock, as well as a voluntary offering for the Temple of God in Jerusalem."

⁵Then God stirred the hearts of the priests and Levites and the leaders of the tribes of Judah and Benjamin to go to Jerusalem to rebuild the Temple of the LORD. ⁶And all their neighbors assisted by giving them articles of silver and gold, supplies for the journey, and livestock. They gave them many valuable gifts in addition to all the voluntary offerings.

⁷King Cyrus himself brought out the articles that King Nebuchadnezzar had taken from the LORD's Temple in Jerusalem and had placed in the temple of his own gods. ⁸Cyrus directed Mithredath, the treasurer of Persia, to count these items and present them to Sheshbazzar, the leader of the exiles returning to Judah.* ⁹This is a list of the items that were returned:

gold basins	30
silver basins	1,000
silver incense burners*	29
¹⁰ gold bowls	30
silver bowls	410
other items	1,000

¹¹In all, there were 5,400 articles of gold and silver. Sheshbazzar brought all of these along when the exiles went from Babylon to Jerusalem.

2:1HERE is the list of the Jewish exiles of the provinces who returned from their captivity. King Nebuchadnezzar had deported them to Babylon, but now they returned to Jerusalem and the other towns in Judah where they originally lived. ²Their leaders were Zerubbabel, Jeshua, Nehemiah, Seraiah, Reelaiah, Mordecai, Bilshan, Mispar, Bigvai, Rehum, and Baanah.

This is the number of the men of Israel who returned from exile:

³	The family of Parosh	2,172
⁴	The family of Shephatiah	372
⁵	The family of Arah	775
⁶	The family of Pahath-moab (descendants of Jeshua and Joab)	2,812
⁷	The family of Elam	1,254
⁸	The family of Zattu	945
⁹	The family of Zaccai	760
¹⁰	The family of Bani	642
¹¹	The family of Bebai	623
¹²	The family of Azgad	1,222
¹³	The family of Adonikam	666
¹⁴	The family of Bigvai	2,056
¹⁵	The family of Adin	454
¹⁶	The family of Ater (descendants of Hezekiah)	98
¹⁷	The family of Bezai	323
¹⁸	The family of Jorah	112
¹⁹	The family of Hashum	223
²⁰	The family of Gibbar	95
²¹	The people of Bethlehem	123
²²	The people of Netophah	56
²³	The people of Anathoth	128
²⁴	The people of Beth-azmaveth*	42
²⁵	The people of Kiriath-jearim,* Kephirah, and Beeroth	743
²⁶	The people of Ramah and Geba	621
²⁷	The people of Micmash	122
²⁸	The people of Bethel and Ai	223
²⁹	The citizens of Nebo	52
³⁰	The citizens of Magbish	156
³¹	The citizens of Elam	1,254
³²	The citizens of Harim	320
³³	The citizens of Lod, Hadid, and Ono	725
³⁴	The citizens of Jericho	345
³⁵	The citizens of Senaah	3,630

³⁶These are the priests who returned from exile:

	The family of Jedaiah (through the line of Jeshua)	973
³⁷	The family of Immer	1,052
³⁸	The family of Pashhur	1,247
³⁹	The family of Harim	1,017

⁴⁰These are the Levites who returned from exile:

	The families of Jeshua and Kadmiel (descendants of Hodaviah)	74
⁴¹	The singers of the family of Asaph	128
⁴²	The gatekeepers of the families of Shallum, Ater, Talmon, Akkub, Hatita, and Shobai	139

⁴³The descendants of the following Temple servants returned from exile:
Ziha, Hasupha, Tabbaoth,
⁴⁴Keros, Siaha, Padon,
⁴⁵Lebanah, Hagabah, Akkub,
⁴⁶Hagab, Shalmai,* Hanan,
⁴⁷Giddel, Gahar, Reaiah,
⁴⁸Rezin, Nekoda, Gazzam,
⁴⁹Uzza, Paseah, Besai,
⁵⁰Asnah, Meunim, Nephusim,

51 Bakbuk, Hakupha, Harhur,
52 Bazluth, Mehida, Harsha,
53 Barkos, Sisera, Temah,
54 Neziah, and Hatipha.

55 The descendants of these servants of King Solomon returned from exile:
Sotai, Hassophereth, Peruda,
56 Jaalah, Darkon, Giddel,
57 Shephatiah, Hattil, Pokereth-hazzebaim, and Ami.

58 In all, the Temple servants and the descendants of Solomon's servants numbered 392.

59 Another group returned at this time from the towns of Tel-melah, Tel-harsha, Kerub, Addan, and Immer. However, they could not prove that they or their families were descendants of Israel. 60 This group included the families of Delaiah, Tobiah, and Nekoda—a total of 652 people.

61 Three families of priests—Hobaiah, Hakkoz, and Barzillai—also returned. (This Barzillai had married a woman who was a descendant of Barzillai of Gilead, and he had taken her family name.) 62 They searched for their names in the genealogical records, but they were not found, so they were disqualified from serving as priests. 63 The governor told them not to eat the priests' share of food from the sacrifices until a priest could consult the LORD about the matter by using the Urim and Thummim—the sacred lots.

64 So a total of 42,360 people returned to Judah, 65 in addition to 7,337 servants and 200 singers, both men and women. 66 They took with them 736 horses, 245 mules, 67 435 camels, and 6,720 donkeys.

68 When they arrived at the Temple of the LORD in Jerusalem, some of the family leaders made voluntary offerings toward the rebuilding of God's Temple on its original site, 69 and each leader gave as much as he could. The total of their gifts came to 61,000 gold coins,* 6,250 pounds* of silver, and 100 robes for the priests.

70 So the priests, the Levites, the singers, the gatekeepers, the Temple servants, and some of the common people settled in villages near Jerusalem. The rest of the people returned to their own towns throughout Israel.

1:1a The first year of Cyrus's reign over Babylon was 538 B.C. **1:1b** See Jer 25:11-12; 29:10. **1:8** Hebrew *Sheshbazzar, the prince of Judah.* **1:9** The meaning of this Hebrew word is uncertain. **2:24** As in parallel text at Neh 7:28; Hebrew reads *Azmaveth.* **2:25** As in some Hebrew manuscripts and Greek version (see also Neh 7:29); Hebrew reads *Kiriatharim.* **2:46** As in an alternate reading of the Masoretic Text (see also Neh 7:48); the other alternate reads *Shamlai.* **2:69a** Hebrew *61,000 darics of gold,* about 1,100 pounds or 500 kilograms in weight. **2:69b** Hebrew *5,000 minas* [3,000 kilograms].

1 CORINTHIANS 1:18–2:5

Sectarian divisions were plaguing the Corinthian church. Paul called the church to focus once again on the Cross—the wisdom and power of God. In light of the Cross, human pride begins to fade.

The message of the cross is foolish to those who are headed for destruction! But we who are being saved know it is the very power of God. 19 As the Scriptures say,

> "I will destroy the wisdom of the wise
>   and discard the intelligence of the
>   intelligent."*

20 So where does this leave the philosophers, the scholars, and the world's brilliant debaters? God has made the wisdom of this world look foolish. 21 Since God in his wisdom saw to it that the world would never know him through human wisdom, he has used our foolish preaching to save those who believe. 22 It is foolish to the Jews, who ask for signs from heaven. And it is foolish to the Greeks, who seek human wisdom. 23 So when we preach that Christ was crucified, the Jews are offended and the Gentiles say it's all nonsense.

24 But to those called by God to salvation, both Jews and Gentiles,* Christ is the power of God and the wisdom of God. 25 This foolish plan of God is wiser than the wisest of human plans, and God's weakness is stronger than the greatest of human strength.

26 Remember, dear brothers and sisters, that few of you were wise in the world's eyes or powerful or wealthy* when God called you. 27 Instead, God chose things the world considers foolish in order to shame those who think they are wise. And he chose things that are powerless to shame those who are powerful. 28 God chose things despised by the world,* things counted as nothing at all, and used them to bring to nothing what the world

considers important. [29]As a result, no one can ever boast in the presence of God.

[30]God has united you with Christ Jesus. For our benefit God made him to be wisdom itself. Christ made us right with God; he made us pure and holy, and he freed us from sin. [31]Therefore, as the Scriptures say, "If you want to boast, boast only about the LORD."*

[2:1]WHEN I [Paul] first came to you, dear brothers and sisters,* I didn't use lofty words and impressive wisdom to tell you God's secret plan.* [2]For I decided that while I was with you I would forget everything except Jesus Christ, the one who was crucified. [3]I came to you in weakness—timid and trembling. [4]And my message and my preaching were very plain. Rather than using clever and persuasive speeches, I relied only on the power of the Holy Spirit. [5]I did this so you would trust not in human wisdom but in the power of God.

1:19 Isa 29:14.   1:24 Greek *and Greeks*.   1:26 Or *high born*.   1:28 Or *God chose those who are low born*.   1:31 Jer 9:24.   2:1a Greek *brothers*.   2:1b Greek *God's mystery; other manuscripts read God's testimony*.

PSALM 27:7-14
Hear me as I pray, O LORD.
    Be merciful and answer me!
[8] My heart has heard you say, "Come and
    talk with me."

And my heart responds, "LORD,
    I am coming."
[9] Do not turn your back on me.
    Do not reject your servant in anger.
    You have always been my helper.
    Don't leave me now; don't abandon me,
    O God of my salvation!
[10] Even if my father and mother
        abandon me,
    the LORD will hold me close.

[11] Teach me how to live, O LORD.
    Lead me along the right path,
    for my enemies are waiting for me.
[12] Do not let me fall into their hands.
    For they accuse me of things I've
        never done;
    with every breath they threaten
        me with violence.
[13] Yet I am confident I will see the LORD's
        goodness
    while I am here in the land of the
        living.

[14] Wait patiently for the LORD.
    Be brave and courageous.
    Yes, wait patiently for the LORD.

PROVERBS 20:22-23
Don't say, "I will get even for this wrong."
Wait for the LORD to handle the matter.
□ The LORD detests double standards; he
is not pleased by dishonest scales.

HOW WE LIVE — Sharing our faith

1 CORINTHIANS 2:1-5 Paul was an intelligent individual. He spoke multiple languages, was highly educated, and was a former Pharisee. His intellect was formidable—he knew both what to say and when and how to say it. But when it came to sharing the message of salvation, he kept it plain and simple, relying upon the power of the Holy Spirit rather than his skill as an orator.   • When you share with others about Jesus, what approach do you take? Paul set a good example for us all. His message was basic and understandable to all who heard him speak. It can be tempting for us to think our skillful or impassioned presentation is the reason someone is attracted to Jesus. Paul warns us against such pride.   • This does not mean we should not be prepared when asked about certain Scriptures; we must take time to read and study the Bible. But when you have the opportunity to share your faith with someone, take a moment to pray and ask for guidance, that your words may be exactly what the unbeliever needs to hear. And then thank God for allowing you to plant a seed in someone's heart.

EZRA 3:1–4:23

The people had spent many years in exile, and now they were returning to their homeland. First order of business: Rebuild the altar and the Temple so they could once again offer sacrifices for sin and worship the Lord as prescribed in God's law.

In early autumn,* when the Israelites had settled in their towns, all the people assembled in Jerusalem with a unified purpose. ²Then Jeshua son of Jehozadak* joined his fellow priests and Zerubbabel son of Shealtiel with his family in rebuilding the altar of the God of Israel. They wanted to sacrifice burnt offerings on it, as instructed in the Law of Moses, the man of God. ³Even though the people were afraid of the local residents, they rebuilt the altar at its old site. Then they began to sacrifice burnt offerings on the altar to the LORD each morning and evening.

⁴They celebrated the Festival of Shelters as prescribed in the Law, sacrificing the number of burnt offerings specified for each day of the festival. ⁵They also offered the regular burnt offerings and the offerings required for the new moon celebrations and the annual festivals as prescribed by the LORD. The people also gave voluntary offerings to the LORD. ⁶Fifteen days before the Festival of Shelters began,* the priests had begun to sacrifice burnt offerings to the LORD. This was even before they had started to lay the foundation of the LORD's Temple.

⁷Then the people hired masons and carpenters and bought cedar logs from the people of Tyre and Sidon, paying them with food, wine, and olive oil. The logs were brought down from the Lebanon mountains and floated along the coast of the Mediterranean Sea* to Joppa, for King Cyrus had given permission for this.

⁸The construction of the Temple of God began in midspring,* during the second year after they arrived in Jerusalem. The work force was made up of everyone who had returned from exile, including Zerubbabel son of Shealtiel, Jeshua son of Jehozadak and his fellow priests, and all the Levites. The Levites who were twenty years old or older were put in charge of rebuilding the LORD's Temple. ⁹The workers at the Temple of God were supervised by Jeshua with his sons and relatives, and Kadmiel and his sons, all descendants of Hodaviah.* They were helped in this task by the Levites of the family of Henadad.

¹⁰When the builders completed the foundation of the LORD's Temple, the priests put on their robes and took their places to blow their trumpets. And the Levites, descendants of Asaph, clashed their cymbals to praise the LORD, just as King David had prescribed. ¹¹With praise and thanks, they sang this song to the LORD:

"He is so good!
His faithful love for Israel endures forever!"

Then all the people gave a great shout, praising the LORD because the foundation of the LORD's Temple had been laid.

¹²But many of the older priests, Levites, and other leaders who had seen the first Temple wept aloud when they saw the new Temple's foundation. The others, however, were shouting for joy. ¹³The joyful shouting and weeping mingled together in a loud noise that could be heard far in the distance.

4:1THE enemies of Judah and Benjamin heard that the exiles were rebuilding a Temple to the LORD, the God of Israel. ²So they approached Zerubbabel and the other leaders and said, "Let us build with you, for we worship your God just as you do. We have sacrificed to him ever since King Esarhaddon of Assyria brought us here."

³But Zerubbabel, Jeshua, and the other leaders of Israel replied, "You may have no part in this work. We alone will build the Temple for the LORD, the God of Israel, just as King Cyrus of Persia commanded us."

⁴Then the local residents tried to discourage and frighten the people of Judah to keep them from their work. ⁵They bribed agents to work against them and to frustrate their plans. This went on during the entire reign of King Cyrus of Persia and lasted until King Darius of Persia took the throne.*

⁶Years later when Xerxes* began his reign, the enemies of Judah wrote a letter of accusation against the people of Judah and Jerusalem.

⁷Even later, during the reign of King Artaxerxes of Persia,* the enemies of Judah, led by Bishlam, Mithredath, and Tabeel, sent a letter to Artaxerxes in the Aramaic language, and it was translated for the king. ⁸*Rehum the governor and Shimshai the court secretary wrote the letter, telling King Artaxerxes about the situation in Jerusalem. ⁹They greeted the king for all their colleagues—the judges and local leaders, the people of Tarpel, the Persians, the Babylonians, and the people of Erech and Susa (that is, Elam). ¹⁰They also sent greetings from the rest of the people whom the great and noble Ashurbanipal* had deported and relocated in Samaria and throughout the neighboring lands of the province west of the Euphrates River.* ¹¹This is a copy of their letter:

"To King Artaxerxes, from your loyal subjects in the province west of the Euphrates River.

¹²"The king should know that the Jews who came here to Jerusalem from Babylon are rebuilding this rebellious and evil city. They have already laid the foundation and will soon finish its walls. ¹³And the king should know that if this city is rebuilt

and its walls are completed, it will be much to your disadvantage, for the Jews will then refuse to pay their tribute, customs, and tolls to you.

¹⁴"Since we are your loyal subjects* and do not want to see the king dishonored in this way, we have sent the king this information. ¹⁵We suggest that a search be made in your ancestors' records, where you will discover what a rebellious city this has been in the past. In fact, it was destroyed because of its long and troublesome history of revolt against the kings and countries who controlled it. ¹⁶We declare to the king that if this city is rebuilt and its walls are completed, the province west of the Euphrates River will be lost to you."

¹⁷Then King Artaxerxes sent this reply:

"To Rehum the governor, Shimshai the court secretary, and their colleagues living in Samaria and throughout the province west of the Euphrates River. Greetings.

¹⁸"The letter you sent has been translated and read to me. ¹⁹I ordered a search of the records and have found that Jerusalem has indeed been a hotbed of insurrection against many kings. In fact, rebellion and revolt are normal there! ²⁰Powerful kings have

HOW WE LIVE

Praise and thanksgiving

EZRA 3:11 Rebuilding the altar was a priority of the highest order for these exiles who had long been denied the ability to worship freely. This altar was used twice daily for burnt offerings that were sacrificed to the Lord. Once the altar was complete, the rebuilding of the Temple itself began. But when the builders had completed the foundation, construction halted for a public service of praise and thanksgiving. The people raised their voices to openly acknowledge God's hand in forgiving their sins and bringing them back home. The words to their song are preserved for us: "He is so good! His faithful love for Israel endures forever!" • As a Christian, "your body is the temple of the Holy Spirit" (1 Corinthians 6:19, August 10). He is always at work in your life—past, present, and future—even when you feel as if you are in "exile" or as if your life is on hold. Can you look back in your life and find evidence of God's faithful love, even before you started following Christ? Stop everything and thank God for all he has done and all he will continue to do for the rest of your life!

ruled over Jerusalem and the entire province west of the Euphrates River, receiving tribute, customs, and tolls. [21]Therefore, issue orders to have these men stop their work. That city must not be rebuilt except at my express command. [22]Be diligent, and don't neglect this matter, for we must not permit the situation to harm the king's interests."

[23]When this letter from King Artaxerxes was read to Rehum, Shimshai, and their colleagues, they hurried to Jerusalem. Then, with a show of strength, they forced the Jews to stop building.

3:1 Hebrew *in the seventh month.* The year is not specified, so it may have been during Cyrus's first year (538 B.C.) or second year (537 B.C.). The seventh month of the ancient Hebrew lunar calendar occurred within the months of September/October 538 B.C. and October/November 537 B.C. 3:2 Hebrew *Jozadak,* a variant spelling of Jehozadak; also in 3:8. 3:6 Hebrew *On the first day of the seventh month.* This day in the ancient Hebrew lunar calendar occurred in September or October. The Festival of Shelters began on the fifteenth day of the seventh month. 3:7 Hebrew *the sea.* 3:8 Hebrew *in the second month.* This month in the ancient Hebrew lunar calendar occurred within the months of April and May 536 B.C. 3:9 Hebrew *sons of Judah* (i.e., *bene Yehudah). Bene* might also be read here as the proper name Binnui; *Yehudah* is probably another name for Hodaviah. Compare 2:40; Neh 7:43; 1 Esdras 5:58. 4:5 Darius reigned 521–486 B.C. 4:6 Hebrew *Ahasuerus,* another name for Xerxes. He reigned 486–465 B.C. 4:7 Artaxerxes reigned 465–424 B.C. 4:8 The original text of 4:8–6:18 is in Aramaic. 4:10a Aramaic *Osnappar,* another name for Ashurbanipal. 4:10b Aramaic *the province beyond the river;* also in 4:11, 16, 17, 20. 4:14 Aramaic *Since we eat the salt of the palace.*

1 CORINTHIANS 2:6–3:4

What does it mean to be mature spiritually? What does it mean to live according to God's wisdom? How do we look as the body of Christ when we really live as God has called us?

Yet when I [Paul] am among mature believers, I do speak with words of wisdom, but not the kind of wisdom that belongs to this world or to the rulers of this world, who are soon forgotten. [7]No, the wisdom we speak of is the mystery of God*—his plan that was previously hidden, even though he made it for our ultimate glory before the world began. [8]But the rulers of this world have not understood it; if they had, they would not have crucified our glorious Lord. [9]That is what the Scriptures mean when they say,

"No eye has seen, no ear has heard,
and no mind has imagined

what God has prepared
for those who love him."*

[10]But* it was to us that God revealed these things by his Spirit. For his Spirit searches out everything and shows us God's deep secrets. [11]No one can know a person's thoughts except that person's own spirit, and no one can know God's thoughts except God's own Spirit. [12]And we have received God's Spirit (not the world's spirit), so we can know the wonderful things God has freely given us.

[13]When we tell you these things, we do not use words that come from human wisdom. Instead, we speak words given to us by the Spirit, using the Spirit's words to explain spiritual truths.* [14]But people who aren't spiritual* can't receive these truths from God's Spirit. It all sounds foolish to them and they can't understand it, for only those who are spiritual can understand what the Spirit means. [15]Those who are spiritual can evaluate all things, but they themselves cannot be evaluated by others. [16]For,

"Who can know the LORD's thoughts?
Who knows enough to teach
him?"*

But we understand these things, for we have the mind of Christ.

3:1 DEAR brothers and sisters,* when I was with you I couldn't talk to you as I would to spiritual people.* I had to talk as though you belonged to this world or as though you were infants in the Christian life.* [2]I had to feed you with milk, not with solid food, because you weren't ready for anything stronger. And you still aren't ready, [3]for you are still controlled by your sinful nature. You are jealous of one another and quarrel with each other. Doesn't that prove you are controlled by your sinful nature? Aren't you living like people of the world? [4]When one of you says, "I am a follower of Paul," and another says, "I follow Apollos," aren't you acting just like people of the world?

2:7 Greek *But we speak God's wisdom in a mystery.* 2:9 Isa 64:4. 2:10 Some manuscripts read *For.* 2:13 Or *explaining spiritual truths in spiritual language,* or *explaining spiritual truths to spiritual people.* 2:14 Or *who don't have the Spirit;* or *who have only physical life.* 2:16 Isa 40:13 (Greek version). 3:1a Greek *Brothers.* 3:1b Or *to people who have the Spirit.* 3:1c Greek *in Christ.*

PSALM 28:1-9
A psalm of David.

¹ **I** pray to you, O LORD, my rock.
    Do not turn a deaf ear to me.
For if you are silent,
    I might as well give up and die.
² Listen to my prayer for mercy
    as I cry out to you for help,
    as I lift my hands toward your holy
        sanctuary.
³ Do not drag me away with the
        wicked—
    with those who do evil—
those who speak friendly words to
        their neighbors
    while planning evil in their hearts.
⁴ Give them the punishment they so
        richly deserve!
    Measure it out in proportion to
        their wickedness.
Pay them back for all their evil deeds!
    Give them a taste of what they have
        done to others.
⁵ They care nothing for what the LORD
        has done
    or for what his hands have made.

So he will tear them down,
    and they will never be rebuilt!
⁶ Praise the LORD!
    For he has heard my cry for mercy.
⁷ The LORD is my strength and shield.
    I trust him with all my heart.
He helps me, and my heart is filled
        with joy.
    I burst out in songs of thanksgiving.
⁸ The LORD gives his people strength.
    He is a safe fortress for his anointed
        king.
⁹ Save your people!
    Bless Israel, your special
        possession.*
Lead them like a shepherd,
    and carry them in your arms
        forever.

28:9 Hebrew *Bless your inheritance.*

PROVERBS 20:24-25
The LORD directs our steps, so why try to understand everything along the way? □Don't trap yourself by making a rash promise to God and only later counting the cost.

EZRA 4:24–6:22
Even in the ancient world, bureaucracy played a role in government. Here, the work of the Jews was almost stalled by those who knew how to work the system.

So the work on the Temple of God in Jerusalem had stopped, and it remained at a standstill until the second year of the reign of King Darius of Persia.*

⁵:¹At that time the prophets Haggai and Zechariah son of Iddo prophesied to the Jews in Judah and Jerusalem. They prophesied in the name of the God of Israel who was over them. ²Zerubbabel son of Shealtiel and Jeshua son of Jehozadak* responded by starting again to rebuild the

Temple of God in Jerusalem. And the prophets of God were with them and helped them.

³But Tattenai, governor of the province west of the Euphrates River,* and Shethar-bozenai and their colleagues soon arrived in Jerusalem and asked, "Who gave you permission to rebuild this Temple and restore this structure?" ⁴They also asked for the names of all the men working on the Temple. ⁵But because their God was watching over them, the leaders of the Jews were not prevented from building until a report was sent to Darius and he returned his decision.

⁶This is a copy of the letter that Tattenai

AUGUST**7**

the governor, Shethar-bozenai, and the other officials of the province west of the Euphrates River sent to King Darius:

7"To King Darius. Greetings.

8"The king should know that we went to the construction site of the Temple of the great God in the province of Judah. It is being rebuilt with specially prepared stones, and timber is being laid in its walls. The work is going forward with great energy and success.

9"We asked the leaders, 'Who gave you permission to rebuild this Temple and restore this structure?' 10And we demanded their names so that we could tell you who the leaders were.

11"This was their answer: 'We are the servants of the God of heaven and earth, and we are rebuilding the Temple that was built here many years ago by a great king of Israel. 12But because our ancestors angered the God of heaven, he abandoned them to King Nebuchadnezzar of Babylon,* who destroyed this Temple and exiled the people to Babylonia. 13However, King Cyrus of Babylon,* during the first year of his reign, issued a decree that the Temple of God should be rebuilt. 14King Cyrus returned the gold and silver cups that Nebuchadnezzar had taken from the Temple of God in Jerusalem and had placed in the temple of Babylon. These cups were taken from that temple and presented to a man named Sheshbazzar, whom King Cyrus appointed as governor of Judah. 15The king instructed him to return the cups to their place in Jerusalem and to rebuild the Temple of God there on its original site. 16So this Sheshbazzar came and laid the foundations of the Temple of God in Jerusalem. The people have been working on it ever since, though it is not yet completed.'

17"Therefore, if it pleases the king, we request that a search be made in the royal archives of Babylon to discover whether King Cyrus ever issued a decree to rebuild God's Temple in Jerusalem. And then let the king send us his decision in this matter."

6:1So King Darius issued orders that a search be made in the Babylonian archives, which were stored in the treasury. 2But it was at the fortress at Ecbatana in the province of Media that a scroll was found. This is what it said:

"Memorandum:

3"In the first year of King Cyrus's reign, a decree was sent out concerning the Temple of God at Jerusalem.

"Let the Temple be rebuilt on the site where Jews used to offer their sacrifices, using the original foundations. Its height will be ninety feet, and its width will be ninety feet.* 4Every three layers of specially prepared stones will be topped by a layer of timber. All expenses will be paid by the royal treasury. 5Furthermore, the gold and silver cups, which were taken to Babylon by Nebuchadnezzar from the Temple of God in Jerusalem, must be returned to Jerusalem and put back where they belong. Let them be taken back to the Temple of God."

6So King Darius sent this message:

"Now therefore, Tattenai, governor of the province west of the Euphrates River,* and Shethar-bozenai, and your colleagues and other officials west of the Euphrates River—stay away from there! 7Do not disturb the construction of the Temple of God. Let it be rebuilt on its original site, and do not hinder the governor of Judah and the elders of the Jews in their work.

8"Moreover, I hereby decree that you are to help these elders of the Jews as they rebuild this Temple of God. You must pay the full construction costs, without delay, from my taxes collected in the province west of the Euphrates River so that the work will not be interrupted.

9"Give the priests in Jerusalem whatever is needed in the way of young bulls, rams, and male lambs for the burnt offerings presented to the

God of heaven. And without fail, provide them with as much wheat, salt, wine, and olive oil as they need each day. [10]Then they will be able to offer acceptable sacrifices to the God of heaven and pray for the welfare of the king and his sons.

[11]"Those who violate this decree in any way will have a beam pulled from their house. Then they will be tied to it and flogged, and their house will be reduced to a pile of rubble.* [12]May the God who has chosen the city of Jerusalem as the place to honor his name destroy any king or nation that violates this command and destroys this Temple.

"I, Darius, have issued this decree. Let it be obeyed with all diligence."

[13]Tattenai, governor of the province west of the Euphrates River, and Shethar-bozenai and their colleagues complied at once with the command of King Darius. [14]So the Jewish elders continued their work, and they were greatly encouraged by the preaching of the prophets Haggai and Zechariah son of Iddo. The Temple was finally finished, as had been commanded by the God of Israel and decreed by Cyrus, Darius, and Artaxerxes, the kings of Persia. [15]The Temple was completed on March 12,* during the sixth year of King Darius's reign.

[16]The Temple of God was then dedicated with great joy by the people of Isra-el, the priests, the Levites, and the rest of the people who had returned from exile. [17]During the dedication ceremony for the Temple of God, 100 young bulls, 200 rams, and 400 male lambs were sacrificed. And 12 male goats were presented as a sin offering for the twelve tribes of Israel. [18]Then the priests and Levites were divided into their various divisions to serve at the Temple of God in Jerusalem, as prescribed in the Book of Moses.

[19]On April 21* the returned exiles celebrated Passover. [20]The priests and Levites had purified themselves and were ceremonially clean. So they slaughtered the Passover lamb for all the returned exiles, for their fellow priests, and for themselves. [21]The Passover meal was eaten by the people of Israel who had returned from exile and by the others in the land who had turned from their immoral customs to worship the LORD, the God of Israel. [22]Then they celebrated the Festival of Unleavened Bread for seven days. There was great joy throughout the land because the LORD had caused the king of Assyria* to be favorable to them, so that he helped them to rebuild the Temple of God, the God of Israel.

4:24 The second year of Darius's reign was 520 B.C. The narrative started in 4:1-5 is resumed at verse 24.
5:2 Aramaic *Jozadak*, a variant spelling of Jehozadak.
5:3 Aramaic *the province beyond the river*; also in 5:6.
5:12 Aramaic *Nebuchadnezzar the Chaldean.*   5:13 King Cyrus of Persia is here identified as the king of Babylon because Persia had conquered the Babylonian Empire.
6:3 Aramaic *Its height will be 60 cubits* [27.6 meters], *and*

Relying on God's power

1 CORINTHIANS 3:7-9 In today's passage, Paul brings a word of warning to Christian servants. It would be foolish for those who had a part in people coming to Christ or growing in their commitment to him to think this was the result of their own skill or talent. God is the one who makes the seed of faith grow into a life that bears fruit for his kingdom. We are tools in his hand. • This is a great encouragement when you think about it. Sharing our faith can be an intimidating thing. We will face rejection and scorn at times. We can try to help others along in their commitment to Christ, but there will be times when it seems people are taking two steps back for every step forward. Were it up to us, we could become discouraged quickly. The great thing is that it's not up to us. We rely on God's power to bring the results. We just need to be obedient when he calls us to a task. He will take care of the rest.

its width will be 60 cubits. It is commonly held that this verse should be emended to read: "Its height will be 30 cubits [45 feet, or 13.8 meters], its length will be 60 cubits [90 feet, or 27.6 meters], and its width will be 20 meters [30 feet, or 9.2 meters]"; compare 1 Kgs 6:2. The emendation regarding the width is supported by the Syriac version. **6:6** Aramaic *the province beyond the river;* also in 6:6b, 8, 13. **6:11** Aramaic *a dunghill.* **6:15** Aramaic *on the third day of the month Adar,* of the ancient Hebrew lunar calendar. A number of events in Ezra can be cross-checked with dates in surviving Persian records and related accurately to our modern calendar. This day was March 12, 515 B.C. **6:19** Hebrew *On the fourteenth day of the first month,* of the ancient Hebrew lunar calendar. This day was April 21, 515 B.C.; also see note on 6:15. **6:22** King Darius of Persia is here identified as the king of Assyria because Persia had conquered the Babylonian Empire, which included the earlier Assyrian Empire.

1 CORINTHIANS 3:5-23

Divisions in the church emerge whenever people assign their loyalties to this leader or that leader rather than join in unified allegiance to the Lord. Paul had to address this problem in first-century Corinth.

After all, who is Apollos? Who is Paul? We are only God's servants through whom you believed the Good News. Each of us did the work the Lord gave us. 6I planted the seed in your hearts, and Apollos watered it, but it was God who made it grow. 7It's not important who does the planting, or who does the watering. What's important is that God makes the seed grow. 8The one who plants and the one who waters work together with the same purpose. And both will be rewarded for their own hard work. 9For we are both God's workers. And you are God's field. You are God's building.

10Because of God's grace to me, I have laid the foundation like an expert builder. Now others are building on it. But whoever is building on this foundation must be very careful. 11For no one can lay any foundation other than the one we already have—Jesus Christ.

12Anyone who builds on that foundation may use a variety of materials—gold, silver, jewels, wood, hay, or straw. 13But on the judgment day, fire will reveal what kind of work each builder has done. The fire will show if a person's work has any value. 14If the work survives, that builder will receive a reward. 15But if the work is burned up, the builder will suffer great loss. The builder will be saved, but like someone barely escaping through a wall of flames.

16Don't you realize that all of you together are the temple of God and that the Spirit of God lives in* you? 17God will destroy anyone who destroys this temple. For God's temple is holy, and you are that temple.

18Stop deceiving yourselves. If you think you are wise by this world's standards, you need to become a fool to be truly wise. 19For the wisdom of this world is foolishness to God. As the Scriptures say,

"He traps the wise
    in the snare of their own
        cleverness."*

20And again,

"The LORD knows the thoughts of the
        wise;
    he knows they are worthless."*

21So don't boast about following a particular human leader. For everything belongs to you—22whether Paul or Apollos or Peter,* or the world, or life and death, or the present and the future. Everything belongs to you, 23and you belong to Christ, and Christ belongs to God.

3:16 Or *among.* **3:19** Job 5:13. **3:20** Ps 94:11. **3:22** Greek *Cephas.*

PSALM 29:1-11
A psalm of David.

1 **H**onor the LORD, you heavenly beings*;
    honor the LORD for his glory and
        strength.
2 Honor the LORD for the glory of his
        name.
    Worship the LORD in the splendor
        of his holiness.

3 The voice of the LORD echoes above
        the sea.
    The God of glory thunders.
    The LORD thunders over the mighty
        sea.
4 The voice of the LORD is powerful;
    the voice of the LORD is majestic.
5 The voice of the LORD splits the
        mighty cedars;
    the LORD shatters the cedars of
        Lebanon.
6 He makes Lebanon's mountains skip
        like a calf;
    he makes Mount Hermon* leap like
        a young wild ox.

⁷ The voice of the LORD strikes
    with bolts of lightning.
⁸ The voice of the LORD makes the
        barren wilderness quake;
    the LORD shakes the wilderness
        of Kadesh.
⁹ The voice of the LORD twists mighty
        oaks*
    and strips the forests bare.
    In his Temple everyone shouts, "Glory!"

¹⁰ The LORD rules over the floodwaters.
    The LORD reigns as king forever.

¹¹ The LORD gives his people strength.
    The LORD blesses them with peace.

29:1 Hebrew *you sons of God.*   29:6 Hebrew *Sirion,* another
name for Mount Hermon.   29:9 Or *causes the deer to
writhe in labor.*

PROVERBS 20:26-27

A wise king scatters the wicked like
wheat, then runs his threshing wheel over
them. □ The LORD's light penetrates the
human spirit,* exposing every hidden
motive.

20:27 Or *The human spirit is the LORD's light.*

AUGUST**8**

EZRA 7:1–8:20

*A second consignment of Jews returned to Jerusa-
lem with Ezra. They returned with a letter that
turned the bureaucratic tide. City hall was finally
listening.*

Many years later, during the reign of King
Artaxerxes of Persia,* there was a man
named Ezra. He was the son* of Seraiah,
son of Azariah, son of Hilkiah, ²son of
Shallum, son of Zadok, son of Ahitub,
³son of Amariah, son of Azariah, son* of
Meraioth, ⁴son of Zerahiah, son of Uzzi,
son of Bukki, ⁵son of Abishua, son of
Phinehas, son of Eleazar, son of Aaron the
high priest.* ⁶This Ezra was a scribe who
was well versed in the Law of Moses,
which the LORD, the God of Israel, had
given to the people of Israel. He came up
to Jerusalem from Babylon, and the king
gave him everything he asked for, because
the gracious hand of the LORD his God
was on him. ⁷Some of the people of Israel,
as well as some of the priests, Levites,
singers, gatekeepers, and Temple servants, traveled up to Jerusalem with him
in the seventh year of King Artaxerxes'
reign.
⁸Ezra arrived in Jerusalem in August* of
that year. ⁹He had arranged to leave Babylon on April 8, the first day of the new
year,* and he arrived at Jerusalem on August 4,* for the gracious hand of his God
was on him. ¹⁰This was because Ezra had

determined to study and obey the Law of
the LORD and to teach those decrees and
regulations to the people of Israel.
¹¹King Artaxerxes had given a copy of
the following letter to Ezra, the priest and
scribe who studied and taught the commands and decrees of the LORD to Israel:

¹²*"From Artaxerxes, the king of kings,
to Ezra the priest, the teacher of the
law of the God of heaven. Greetings.
¹³"I decree that any of the people of
Israel in my kingdom, including the
priests and Levites, may volunteer to
return to Jerusalem with you. ¹⁴I and
my council of seven hereby instruct
you to conduct an inquiry into the
situation in Judah and Jerusalem,
based on your God's law, which is in
your hand. ¹⁵We also commission you
to take with you silver and gold, which
we are freely presenting as an offering
to the God of Israel who lives in
Jerusalem.
¹⁶"Furthermore, you are to take any
silver and gold that you may obtain
from the province of Babylon, as well
as the voluntary offerings of the
people and the priests that are
presented for the Temple of their God
in Jerusalem. ¹⁷These donations are to
be used specifically for the purchase
of bulls, rams, male lambs, and the

appropriate grain offerings and liquid offerings, all of which will be offered on the altar of the Temple of your God in Jerusalem. ¹⁸Any silver and gold that is left over may be used in whatever way you and your colleagues feel is the will of your God.

¹⁹"But as for the cups we are entrusting to you for the service of the Temple of your God, deliver them all to the God of Jerusalem. ²⁰If you need anything else for your God's Temple or for any similar needs, you may take it from the royal treasury.

²¹"I, Artaxerxes the king, hereby send this decree to all the treasurers in the province west of the Euphrates River*: 'You are to give Ezra, the priest and teacher of the law of the God of heaven, whatever he requests of you. ²²You are to give him up to 7,500 pounds* of silver, 500 bushels* of wheat, 550 gallons of wine, 550 gallons of olive oil,* and an unlimited supply of salt. ²³Be careful to provide whatever the God of heaven demands for his Temple, for why should we risk bringing God's anger against the realm of the king and his sons? ²⁴I also decree that no priest, Levite, singer, gate-keeper, Temple servant, or other worker in this Temple of God will be required to pay tribute, customs, or tolls of any kind.'

²⁵"And you, Ezra, are to use the wisdom your God has given you to appoint magistrates and judges who know your God's laws to govern all the people in the province west of the Euphrates River. Teach the law to anyone who does not know it. ²⁶Anyone who refuses to obey the law of your God and the law of the king will be punished immediately, either by death, banishment, confiscation of goods, or imprisonment."

²⁷Praise the LORD, the God of our ancestors, who made the king want to beautify the Temple of the LORD in Jerusalem! ²⁸And praise him for demonstrating such unfailing love to me by honoring me before the king, his council, and all his mighty nobles! I felt encouraged because the gracious hand of the LORD my God was on me. And I gathered some of the leaders of Israel to return with me to Jerusalem.

8:¹HERE is a list of the family leaders and the genealogies of those who came with me from Babylon during the reign of King Artaxerxes:

² From the family of Phinehas: Gershom.
From the family of Ithamar: Daniel.
From the family of David: Hattush, ³a descendant of Shecaniah.
From the family of Parosh: Zechariah and 150 other men were registered.
⁴ From the family of Pahath-moab: Eliehoenai son of Zerahiah and 200 other men.
⁵ From the family of Zattu*: Shecaniah son of Jahaziel and 300 other men.
⁶ From the family of Adin: Ebed son of Jonathan and 50 other men.
⁷ From the family of Elam: Jeshaiah son of Athaliah and 70 other men.
⁸ From the family of Shephatiah: Zebadiah son of Michael and 80 other men.
⁹ From the family of Joab: Obadiah son of Jehiel and 218 other men.
¹⁰ From the family of Bani*: Shelomith son of Josiphiah and 160 other men.
¹¹ From the family of Bebai: Zechariah son of Bebai and 28 other men.
¹² From the family of Azgad: Johanan son of Hakkatan and 110 other men.
¹³ From the family of Adonikam, who came later*: Eliphelet, Jeuel, Shemaiah, and 60 other men.
¹⁴ From the family of Bigvai: Uthai, Zaccur,* and 70 other men.

¹⁵I assembled the exiles at the Ahava Canal, and we camped there for three days while I went over the lists of the people and the priests who had arrived. I found that not one Levite had volunteered to come along. ¹⁶So I sent for Eliezer, Ariel, Shemaiah, Elnathan, Jarib, Elnathan, Nathan, Zechariah, and Meshullam, who were leaders of the people. I also sent for Joiarib and Elnathan, who were men of

discernment. [17] I sent them to Iddo, the leader of the Levites at Casiphia, to ask him and his relatives and the Temple servants to send us ministers for the Temple of God at Jerusalem.

[18] Since the gracious hand of our God was on us, they sent us a man named Sherebiah, along with eighteen of his sons and brothers. He was a very astute man and a descendant of Mahli, who was a descendant of Levi son of Israel.* [19] They also sent Hashabiah, together with Jeshaiah from the descendants of Merari, and twenty of his sons and brothers, [20] and 220 Temple servants. The Temple servants were assistants to the Levites—a group of Temple workers first instituted by King David and his officials. They were all listed by name.

7:1a Artaxerxes reigned 465–424 B.C.   7:1b Or *descendant;* see 1 Chr 6:14.   7:3 Or *descendant;* see 1 Chr 6:6-10.
7:5 Or *the first priest.*   7:8 Hebrew *in the fifth month.* This month in the ancient Hebrew lunar calendar occurred within the months of August and September 458 B.C.   7:9a Hebrew *on the first day of the first month,* of the ancient Hebrew lunar calendar. This day was April 8, 458 B.C.; also see note on 6:15.   7:9b Hebrew *on the first day of the fifth month,* of the ancient Hebrew lunar calendar. This day was August 4, 458 B.C.; also see note on 6:15.   7:12 The original text of 7:12-26 is in Aramaic.   7:21 Aramaic *the province beyond the river;* also in 7:25.   7:22a Aramaic *100 talents* [3,400 kilograms].   7:22b Aramaic *100 cors* [18.2 kiloliters].
7:22c Aramaic *100 baths* [2.1 kiloliters] *of wine, 100 baths of olive oil.*   8:5 As in some Greek manuscripts (see also 1 Esdras 8:32); Hebrew lacks *Zattu.*   8:10 As in some Greek manuscripts (see also 1 Esdras 8:36); Hebrew lacks *Bani.*
8:13 Or *who were the last of his family.*   8:14 As in Greek and Syriac versions and an alternate reading of the Masoretic

Text; the other alternate reads *Zabbud.*   8:18 *Israel* is the name that God gave to Jacob.

1 CORINTHIANS 4:1-21
As an apostle of Christ, Paul asserted his shepherding authority over the Corinthian church. They needed to shape up, and Paul pulled no punches to see that this would happen.

So look at Apollos and me [Paul] as mere servants of Christ who have been put in charge of explaining God's mysteries. [2] Now, a person who is put in charge as a manager must be faithful. [3] As for me, it matters very little how I might be evaluated by you or by any human authority. I don't even trust my own judgment on this point. [4] My conscience is clear, but that doesn't prove I'm right. It is the Lord himself who will examine me and decide.

[5] So don't make judgments about anyone ahead of time—before the Lord returns. For he will bring our darkest secrets to light and will reveal our private motives. Then God will give to each one whatever praise is due.

[6] Dear brothers and sisters,* I have used Apollos and myself to illustrate what I've been saying. If you pay attention to what I have quoted from the Scriptures,* you won't be proud of one of your leaders at the expense of another. [7] For what gives you the right to make such a judgment?

HOW WE LIVE
Following Jesus
EZRA 7:8-10 The Jews had been captives in Babylon (which was now controlled by Persia) for many years. They had settled in. Children had grown up and had children and grandchildren of their own. Some of the captive Jews had never known life back home in Judah, nor were they particularly interested in returning. When given the chance to return home, however, Ezra took it, even though returning home meant difficulty and hardship. Returning to Jerusalem entailed a long journey and strenuous work to rebuild a ruined city, a burnt-out Temple, and a broken-down city wall. But it also led the way for Ezra's nation of Israel to become what it was meant to be in the land that it had been given.   • We experience something similar when we begin following Jesus. God wants to restore us to *his* vision for our lives through faith. That sometimes requires that we do the difficult thing instead of the cushy thing. Be willing to follow where he leads so that you can do the task he wants you to do for his Kingdom.

What do you have that God hasn't given you? And if everything you have is from God, why boast as though it were not a gift?

[8]You think you already have everything you need. You think you are already rich. You have begun to reign in God's kingdom without us! I wish you really were reigning already, for then we would be reigning with you. [9]Instead, I sometimes think God has put us apostles on display, like prisoners of war at the end of a victor's parade, condemned to die. We have become a spectacle to the entire world—to people and angels alike.

[10]Our dedication to Christ makes us look like fools, but you claim to be so wise in Christ! We are weak, but you are so powerful! You are honored, but we are ridiculed. [11]Even now we go hungry and thirsty, and we don't have enough clothes to keep warm. We are often beaten and have no home. [12]We work wearily with our own hands to earn our living. We bless those who curse us. We are patient with those who abuse us. [13]We appeal gently when evil things are said about us. Yet we are treated like the world's garbage, like everybody's trash—right up to the present moment.

[14]I am not writing these things to shame you, but to warn you as my beloved children. [15]For even if you had ten thousand others to teach you about Christ, you have only one spiritual father. For I became your father in Christ Jesus when I preached the Good News to you. [16]So I urge you to imitate me.

[17]That's why I have sent Timothy, my beloved and faithful child in the Lord. He will remind you of how I follow Christ Jesus, just as I teach in all the churches wherever I go.

[18]Some of you have become arrogant, thinking I will not visit you again. [19]But I will come—and soon—if the Lord lets me, and then I'll find out whether these arrogant people just give pretentious speeches or whether they really have God's power. [20]For the Kingdom of God is not just a lot of talk; it is living by God's power. [21]Which do you choose? Should I come with a rod to punish you, or should I come with love and a gentle spirit?

4:6a Greek *Brothers.* **4:6b** Or *If you learn not to go beyond "what is written."*

PSALM 30:1-12

A psalm of David. A song for the dedication of the Temple.

[1] I will exalt you, LORD, for you rescued me.
You refused to let my enemies triumph over me.
[2] O LORD my God, I cried to you for help, and you restored my health.
[3] You brought me up from the grave,*
O LORD.
You kept me from falling into the pit of death.

[4] Sing to the LORD, all you godly ones! Praise his holy name.
[5] For his anger lasts only a moment, but his favor lasts a lifetime!
Weeping may last through the night, but joy comes with the morning.

[6] When I was prosperous, I said, "Nothing can stop me now!"
[7] Your favor, O LORD, made me as secure as a mountain.
Then you turned away from me, and I was shattered.

[8] I cried out to you, O LORD.
I begged the Lord for mercy, saying,
[9] "What will you gain if I die, if I sink into the grave?
Can my dust praise you?
Can it tell of your faithfulness?
[10] Hear me, LORD, and have mercy on me. Help me, O LORD."

[11] You have turned my mourning into joyful dancing.
You have taken away my clothes of mourning and clothed me with joy,
[12] that I might sing praises to you and not be silent.
O LORD my God, I will give you thanks forever!

30:3 Hebrew *from Sheol.*

PROVERBS 20:28-30

Unfailing love and faithfulness protect the king; his throne is made secure through love. □ The glory of the young is their strength; the gray hair of experience is the splendor of the old. □ Physical punishment cleanses away evil;* such discipline purifies the heart.

20:30 The meaning of the Hebrew is uncertain.

EZRA 8:21–9:15

When God brought the Israelites into their land, he gave them a command not to marry into surrounding tribes. Doing so would lead the Israelites into idolatry. Upon returning from the exile, intermarriage with idolatrous people was again a temptation that had to be dealt with.

And there by the Ahava Canal, I [Ezra] gave orders for all of us to fast and humble ourselves before our God. We prayed that he would give us a safe journey and protect us, our children, and our goods as we traveled. ²²For I was ashamed to ask the king for soldiers and horsemen* to accompany us and protect us from enemies along the way. After all, we had told the king, "Our God's hand of protection is on all who worship him, but his fierce anger rages against those who abandon him." ²³So we fasted and earnestly prayed that our God would take care of us, and he heard our prayer.

²⁴I appointed twelve leaders of the priests—Sherebiah, Hashabiah, and ten other priests—²⁵to be in charge of transporting the silver, the gold, the gold bowls, and the other items that the king, his council, his officials, and all the people of Israel had presented for the Temple of God. ²⁶I weighed the treasure as I gave it to them and found the totals to be as follows:

24 tons* of silver,
7,500 pounds* of silver articles,
7,500 pounds of gold,
²⁷ 20 gold bowls, equal in value to 1,000 gold coins,*
2 fine articles of polished bronze, as precious as gold.

²⁸And I said to these priests, "You and these treasures have been set apart as holy to the LORD. This silver and gold is a voluntary offering to the LORD, the God of our ancestors. ²⁹Guard these treasures well until you present them to the leading priests, the Levites, and the leaders of Israel, who will weigh them at the storerooms of the LORD's Temple in Jerusalem." ³⁰So the priests and the Levites accepted the task of transporting these treasures of silver and gold to the Temple of our God in Jerusalem.

³¹We broke camp at the Ahava Canal on April 19* and started off to Jerusalem. And the gracious hand of our God protected us and saved us from enemies and bandits along the way. ³²So we arrived safely in Jerusalem, where we rested for three days.

³³On the fourth day after our arrival, the silver, gold, and other valuables were weighed at the Temple of our God and entrusted to Meremoth son of Uriah the priest and to Eleazar son of Phinehas, along with Jozabad son of Jeshua and Noadiah son of Binnui—both of whom were Levites. ³⁴Everything was accounted for by number and weight, and the total weight was officially recorded.

³⁵Then the exiles who had come out of captivity sacrificed burnt offerings to the God of Israel. They presented twelve bulls for all the people of Israel, as well as ninety-six rams and seventy-seven male lambs. They also offered twelve male goats as a sin offering. All this was given as a burnt offering to the LORD. ³⁶The king's decrees were delivered to his highest officers and the governors of the province west of the Euphrates River,* who then cooperated by supporting the people and the Temple of God.

⁹:¹WHEN these things had been done, the Jewish leaders came to me and said, "Many of the people of Israel, and even some of the priests and Levites, have not kept themselves separate from the other peoples living in the land. They have taken up the detestable practices of the Canaanites, Hittites, Perizzites, Jebusites, Ammonites, Moabites, Egyptians, and Amorites. ²For the men of Israel have married women from these people and have taken them as wives for their sons. So the holy race has become polluted by these mixed marriages. Worse yet, the leaders and officials have led the way in this outrage."

³When I heard this, I tore my cloak and my shirt, pulled hair from my head and

beard, and sat down utterly shocked. [4]Then all who trembled at the words of the God of Israel came and sat with me because of this outrage committed by the returned exiles. And I sat there utterly appalled until the time of the evening sacrifice.

[5]At the time of the sacrifice, I stood up from where I had sat in mourning with my clothes torn. I fell to my knees and lifted my hands to the LORD my God. [6]I prayed,

"O my God, I am utterly ashamed; I blush to lift up my face to you. For our sins are piled higher than our heads, and our guilt has reached to the heavens. [7]From the days of our ancestors until now, we have been steeped in sin. That is why we and our kings and our priests have been at the mercy of the pagan kings of the land. We have been killed, captured, robbed, and disgraced, just as we are today.

[8]"But now we have been given a brief moment of grace, for the LORD our God has allowed a few of us to survive as a remnant. He has given us security in this holy place. Our God has brightened our eyes and granted us some relief from our slavery. [9]For we were slaves, but in his unfailing love our God did not abandon us in our slavery. Instead, he caused the kings of Persia to treat us favorably. He revived us so we could rebuild the Temple of our God and repair its ruins. He has given us a protective wall in Judah and Jerusalem.

[10]"And now, O our God, what can we say after all of this? For once again we have abandoned your commands! [11]Your servants the prophets warned us when they said, 'The land you are entering to possess is totally defiled by the detestable practices of the people living there. From one end to the other, the land is filled with corruption. [12]Don't let your daughters marry their sons! Don't take their daughters as wives for your sons. Don't ever promote the peace and prosperity of those nations. If you follow these instructions, you will be strong and will

enjoy the good things the land produces, and you will leave this prosperity to your children forever.'

[13]"Now we are being punished because of our wickedness and our great guilt. But we have actually been punished far less than we deserve, for you, our God, have allowed some of us to survive as a remnant. [14]But even so, we are again breaking your commands and intermarrying with people who do these detestable things. Won't your anger be enough to destroy us, so that even this little remnant no longer survives? [15]O LORD, God of Israel, you are just. We come before you in our guilt as nothing but an escaped remnant, though in such a condition none of us can stand in your presence."

8:22 Or *charioteers.*   8:26a Hebrew *650 talents* [22 metric tons].   8:26b Hebrew *100 talents* [3,400 kilograms]; also in 8:26c.   8:27 Hebrew *1,000 darics,* about 19 pounds or 8.6 kilograms in weight.   8:31 Hebrew *on the twelfth day of the first month,* of the ancient Hebrew lunar calendar. This day was April 19, 458 B.C.; also see note on 6:15.   8:36 Hebrew *the province beyond the river.*

1 CORINTHIANS 5:1-13

There was an elephant in the room in Corinth—a topic that everyone knew about but no one would actually address. Leave it to Paul to uncover the beast and tell everybody, in no uncertain terms, what to do about it.

1 [Paul] can hardly believe the report about the sexual immorality going on among you—something that even pagans don't do. I am told that a man in your church is living in sin with his step-mother.* [2]You are so proud of yourselves, but you should be mourning in sorrow and shame. And you should remove this man from your fellowship.

[3]Even though I am not with you in person, I am with you in the Spirit.* And as though I were there, I have already passed judgment on this man [4]in the name of the Lord Jesus. You must call a meeting of the church.* I will be present with you in spirit, and so will the power of our Lord Jesus. [5]Then you must throw this man out and hand him over to Satan so that his sinful nature will be destroyed* and he himself* will be saved on the day the Lord* returns.

[6]Your boasting about this is terrible.

Don't you realize that this sin is like a little yeast that spreads through the whole batch of dough? [7] Get rid of the old "yeast" by removing this wicked person from among you. Then you will be like a fresh batch of dough made without yeast, which is what you really are. Christ, our Passover Lamb, has been sacrificed for us.* [8] So let us celebrate the festival, not with the old bread* of wickedness and evil, but with the new bread* of sincerity and truth.

[9] When I wrote to you before, I told you not to associate with people who indulge in sexual sin. [10] But I wasn't talking about unbelievers who indulge in sexual sin, or are greedy, or cheat people, or worship idols. You would have to leave this world to avoid people like that. [11] I meant that you are not to associate with anyone who claims to be a believer* yet indulges in sexual sin, or is greedy, or worships idols, or is abusive, or is a drunkard, or cheats people. Don't even eat with such people.

[12] It isn't my responsibility to judge outsiders, but it certainly is your responsibility to judge those inside the church who are sinning. [13] God will judge those on the outside; but as the Scriptures say, "You must remove the evil person from among you."*

5:1 Greek *his father's wife.* 5:3 Or *in spirit.* 5:4 Or *In the name of the Lord Jesus, you must call a meeting of the church.*

5:5a Or *so that his body will be destroyed;* Greek reads *for the destruction of the flesh.* 5:5b Greek *and the spirit.* 5:5c Other manuscripts read *the Lord Jesus;* still others read *our Lord Jesus Christ.* 5:7 Greek *has been sacrificed.* 5:8a Greek *not with old leaven.* 5:8b Greek *but with unleavened [bread].* 5:11 Greek *a brother.* 5:13 Deut 17:7.

PSALM 31:1-8
For the choir director: A psalm of David.

[1] O LORD, I have come to you for protection;
don't let me be disgraced.
Save me, for you do what
is right.
[2] Turn your ear to listen to me;
rescue me quickly.
Be my rock of protection,
a fortress where I will be safe.
[3] You are my rock and my fortress.
For the honor of your name, lead
me out of this danger.
[4] Pull me from the trap my enemies set
for me,
for I find protection in you alone.
[5] I entrust my spirit into your hand.
Rescue me, LORD, for you are a
faithful God.
[6] I hate those who worship worthless
idols.
I trust in the LORD.
[7] I will be glad and rejoice in your
unfailing love,

In the world, not of it

HOW WE LIVE

1 CORINTHIANS 5:1 It's got to be pretty bad when Christians are doing things even pagans don't do! Sure, the world is pretty loose when it comes to sexual sin, but a man living in sin with his father's wife (most likely a stepmother—maybe a young one at that)? That was sinking pretty low. • Corinth had a reputation for being one of the most decadent cities of the time. The believers in that culture probably were pretty jaded. To them, sex had merely been part of the worship of some of their gods. Temple prostitutes offered their services to men and women as a form of "worship." So when it came to sexual sin, maybe they just didn't see what the big deal was. Paul needed to explain that it didn't matter what the culture thought about sex; the believers were to be different. They were to be pure before God by living according to his Word. • The same is true for us. It doesn't matter what the culture says or how low the standards dip. God's Word defines the boundaries for God's people. Your standards come from his Word, not from the world.

for you have seen my troubles,
and you care about the anguish of
my soul.
[8] You have not handed me over to my
enemies
but have set me in a safe place.

AUGUST**10**

EZRA 10:1-44
Today's reading is a good example of tough choices. Marriages had taken place. Families had been formed, yet the purity of the Jewish faith and the worship of the one true God were at stake. When God's honor is at stake, tough choices have to be made.

While Ezra prayed and made this confession, weeping and lying face down on the ground in front of the Temple of God, a very large crowd of people from Israel—men, women, and children—gathered and wept bitterly with him. [2] Then Shecaniah son of Jehiel, a descendant of Elam, said to Ezra, "We have been unfaithful to our God, for we have married these pagan women of the land. But in spite of this there is hope for Israel. [3] Let us now make a covenant with our God to divorce our pagan wives and to send them away with their children. We will follow the advice given by you and by the others who respect the commands of our God. Let it be done according to the Law of God. [4] Get up, for it is your duty to tell us how to proceed in setting things straight. We are behind you, so be strong and take action."

[5] So Ezra stood up and demanded that the leaders of the priests and the Levites and all the people of Israel swear that they would do as Shecaniah had said. And they all swore a solemn oath. [6] Then Ezra left the front of the Temple of God and went to the room of Jehohanan son of Eliashib. He spent the night* there without eating or drinking anything. He was still in mourning because of the unfaithfulness of the returned exiles.

PROVERBS 21:1-2
The king's heart is like a stream of water directed by the LORD; he guides it wherever he pleases. □ People may be right in their own eyes, but the LORD examines their heart.

[7] Then a proclamation was made throughout Judah and Jerusalem that all the exiles should come to Jerusalem. [8] Those who failed to come within three days would, if the leaders and elders so decided, forfeit all their property and be expelled from the assembly of the exiles.

[9] Within three days, all the people of Judah and Benjamin had gathered in Jerusalem. This took place on December 19,* and all the people were sitting in the square before the Temple of God. They were trembling both because of the seriousness of the matter and because it was raining. [10] Then Ezra the priest stood and said to them: "You have committed a terrible sin. By marrying pagan women, you have increased Israel's guilt. [11] So now confess your sin to the LORD, the God of your ancestors, and do what he demands. Separate yourselves from the people of the land and from these pagan women."

[12] Then the whole assembly raised their voices and answered, "Yes, you are right; we must do as you say!" [13] Then they added, "This isn't something that can be done in a day or two, for many of us are involved in this extremely sinful affair. And this is the rainy season, so we cannot stay out here much longer. [14] Let our leaders act on behalf of us all. Let everyone who has a pagan wife come at a scheduled time, accompanied by the leaders and judges of his city, so that the fierce anger of our God concerning this affair may be turned away from us."

[15] Only Jonathan son of Asahel and Jahzeiah son of Tikvah opposed this course

of action, and they were supported by Meshullam and Shabbethai the Levite.

[16]So this was the plan they followed. Ezra selected leaders to represent their families, designating each of the representatives by name. On December 29,* the leaders sat down to investigate the matter. [17]By March 27, the first day of the new year,* they had finished dealing with all the men who had married pagan wives.

[18]These are the priests who had married pagan wives:

From the family of Jeshua son of Jehozadak* and his brothers: Maaseiah, Eliezer, Jarib, and Gedaliah. [19]They vowed to divorce their wives, and they each acknowledged their guilt by offering a ram as a guilt offering.

[20]From the family of Immer: Hanani and Zebadiah.

[21]From the family of Harim: Maaseiah, Elijah, Shemaiah, Jehiel, and Uzziah.

[22]From the family of Pashhur: Elioenai, Maaseiah, Ishmael, Nethanel, Jozabad, and Elasah.

[23]These are the Levites who were guilty: Jozabad, Shimei, Kelaiah(also called Kelita), Pethahiah, Judah, and Eliezer.

[24]This is the singer who was guilty: Eliashib.

These are the gatekeepers who were guilty: Shallum, Telem, and Uri.

[25]These are the other people of Israel who were guilty:

From the family of Parosh: Ramiah, Izziah, Malkijah, Mijamin, Eleazar, Hashabiah,* and Benaiah.

[26]From the family of Elam: Mattaniah, Zechariah, Jehiel, Abdi, Jeremoth, and Elijah.

[27]From the family of Zattu: Elioenai, Eliashib, Mattaniah, Jeremoth, Zabad, and Aziza.

[28]From the family of Bebai: Jehohanan, Hananiah, Zabbai, and Athlai.

[29]From the family of Bani: Meshullam, Malluch, Adaiah, Jashub, Sheal, and Jeremoth.

[30]From the family of Pahath-moab: Adna, Kelal, Benaiah, Maaseiah, Mattaniah, Bezalel, Binnui, and Manasseh.

[31]From the family of Harim: Eliezer, Ishijah, Malkijah, Shemaiah, Shimeon, [32]Benjamin, Malluch, and Shemariah.

[33]From the family of Hashum: Mattenai, Mattattah, Zabad, Eliphelet, Jeremai, Manasseh, and Shimei.

[34]From the family of Bani: Maadai, Amram, Uel, [35]Benaiah, Bedeiah, Keluhi, [36]Vaniah, Meremoth, Eliashib,

---

Right and wrong

1 CORINTHIANS 6:9-20 It's a common refrain in our day: "Don't impose on me your concept of right and wrong." The problem with that attitude is that it makes each person a god—answerable to no one. Because humanity is inherently sinful and selfish, what one person decides is "right" might be harmful to someone else. One person may feel justified and right in murdering someone. That's why societies have laws; otherwise, anarchy and chaos would result. • People need a standard that exists outside of their sinful selves. God has given standards in his Word. The more you mature in your faith, the more discerning you will become. The Holy Spirit will help you distinguish right from wrong. You'll be more able to incorporate principles of right thinking and right action from the Bible, and they will help you correctly judge moral situations. • God draws a line for right and wrong because he loves us. The guidelines he gives keep us safe and happy. The boundaries he sets protect us. When you begin to see that God's rules protect us, you begin to understand that knowing right and wrong—and choosing right—are always the best way to go.

[37] Mattaniah, Mattenai, and Jaasu.
[38] From the family of Binnui*: Shimei,
[39] Shelemiah, Nathan, Adaiah,
[40] Macnadebai, Shashai, Sharai,
[41] Azarel, Shelemiah, Shemariah,
[42] Shallum, Amariah, and Joseph.
[43] From the family of Nebo: Jeiel,
Mattithiah, Zabad, Zebina, Jaddai, Joel,
and Benaiah.

[44] Each of these men had a pagan wife,
and some even had children by these
wives.*

10:6 As in parallel text at 1 Esdras 9:2; Hebrew reads *He
went.* 10:9 Hebrew *on the twentieth day of the ninth
month,* of the ancient Hebrew lunar calendar. This day was
December 19, 458 B.C.; also see note on 6:15. 10:16 Hebrew
On the first day of the tenth month, of the ancient Hebrew
lunar calendar. This day was December 29, 458 B.C.; also see
note on 6:15. 10:17 Hebrew *By the first day of the first
month,* of the ancient Hebrew lunar calendar. This day was
March 27, 457 B.C.; also see note on 6:15. 10:18 Hebrew
Jozadak, a variant spelling of Jehozadak. 10:25 As in
parallel text at 1 Esdras 9:26; Hebrew reads *Malkijah.*
10:37-38 As in Greek version; Hebrew reads *Jaasu,* [38]*Bani,
Binnui.* 10:44 Or *and they sent them away with their
children.* The meaning of the Hebrew is uncertain.

1 CORINTHIANS 6:1-20
How should we treat each other as a Christian family? How do we deal with conflicts? Lawsuits? Did
you know the Bible addresses such things?

When one of you has a dispute with another believer, how dare you file a lawsuit
and ask a secular court to decide the matter instead of taking it to other believers*!
[2] Don't you realize that someday we believers will judge the world? And since you are
going to judge the world, can't you decide
even these little things among yourselves?
[3] Don't you realize that we will judge angels? So you should surely be able to resolve ordinary disputes in this life. [4] If you
have legal disputes about such matters,
why go to outside judges who are not respected by the church? [5] I am saying this to
shame you. Isn't there anyone in all the
church who is wise enough to decide these
issues? [6] But instead, one believer* sues
another—right in front of unbelievers!
[7] Even to have such lawsuits with one another is a defeat for you. Why not just accept the injustice and leave it at that? Why
not let yourselves be cheated? [8] Instead,
you yourselves are the ones who do wrong
and cheat even your fellow believers.*
[9] Don't you realize that those who do
wrong will not inherit the Kingdom of

God? Don't fool yourselves. Those who indulge in sexual sin, or who worship idols,
or commit adultery, or are male prostitutes, or practice homosexuality, [10] or are
thieves, or greedy people, or drunkards,
or are abusive, or cheat people—none of
these will inherit the Kingdom of God.
[11] Some of you were once like that. But you
were cleansed; you were made holy; you
were made right with God by calling on
the name of the Lord Jesus Christ and by
the Spirit of our God.

[12] You say, "I am allowed to do anything"—but not everything is good for you.
And even though "I am allowed to do anything," I must not become a slave to anything. [13] You say, "Food was made for the
stomach, and the stomach for food." (This
is true, though someday God will do away
with both of them.) But you can't say that
our bodies were made for sexual immorality. They were made for the Lord, and the
Lord cares about our bodies. [14] And God
will raise us from the dead by his power,
just as he raised our Lord from the dead.

[15] Don't you realize that your bodies are
actually parts of Christ? Should a man
take his body, which is part of Christ, and
join it to a prostitute? Never! [16] And don't
you realize that if a man joins himself to a
prostitute, he becomes one body with
her? For the Scriptures say, "The two are
united into one."* [17] But the person who is
joined to the Lord is one spirit with him.

[18] Run from sexual sin! No other sin so
clearly affects the body as this one does.
For sexual immorality is a sin against your
own body. [19] Don't you realize that your
body is the temple of the Holy Spirit, who
lives in you and was given to you by God?
You do not belong to yourself, [20] for God
bought you with a high price. So you must
honor God with your body.

6:1 Greek *God's holy people;* also in 6:2. 6:6 Greek *one
brother.* 6:8 Greek *even the brothers.* 6:16 Gen 2:24.

PSALM 31:9-18
Have mercy on me, LORD, for I am in
distress.
Tears blur my eyes.
My body and soul are withering
away.
[10] I am dying from grief;
my years are shortened by sadness.

Sin has drained my strength;
　　I am wasting away from within.
[11] I am scorned by all my enemies
　　and despised by my neighbors—
　　even my friends are afraid to come
　　　near me.
When they see me on the street,
　　they run the other way.
[12] I am ignored as if I were dead,
　　as if I were a broken pot.
[13] I have heard the many rumors about
　　me,
　　and I am surrounded by terror.
My enemies conspire against me,
　　plotting to take my life.

[14] But I am trusting you, O LORD,
　　saying, "You are my God!"

[15] My future is in your hands.
　　Rescue me from those who hunt me
　　　down relentlessly.
[16] Let your favor shine on your servant.
　　In your unfailing love, rescue me.
[17] Don't let me be disgraced, O LORD,
　　for I call out to you for help.
Let the wicked be disgraced;
　　let them lie silent in the grave.*
[18] Silence their lying lips—
　　those proud and arrogant lips that
　　　accuse the godly.

31:17 Hebrew *in Sheol.*

PROVERBS 21:3

The LORD is more pleased when we do
what is right and just than when we offer
him sacrifices.

AUGUST**11**

NEHEMIAH 1:1–3:14

The books of Ezra and Nehemiah both deal with the
return of exiles to the Holy Land. The book of Ezra
centered on the rebuilding of the Temple; Nehemiah's task, several years later, was to rebuild Jerusalem's city wall.

These are the memoirs of Nehemiah son
of Hacaliah.

In late autumn, in the month of Kislev,
in the twentieth year of King Artaxerxes'
reign,* I was at the fortress of Susa. [2]Ha-
nani, one of my brothers, came to visit me
with some other men who had just arrived from Judah. I asked them about the
Jews who had returned there from captivity and about how things were going in Jerusalem.

[3]They said to me, "Things are not going
well for those who returned to the province of Judah. They are in great trouble
and disgrace. The wall of Jerusalem has
been torn down, and the gates have been
destroyed by fire."

[4]When I heard this, I sat down and
wept. In fact, for days I mourned, fasted,
and prayed to the God of heaven. [5]Then
I said,

"O LORD, God of heaven, the great and
awesome God who keeps his covenant
of unfailing love with those who love
him and obey his commands, [6]listen
to my prayer! Look down and see me
praying night and day for your people
Israel. I confess that we have sinned
against you. Yes, even my own family
and I have sinned! [7]We have sinned
terribly by not obeying the commands,
decrees, and regulations that you gave
us through your servant Moses.

[8]"Please remember what you told
your servant Moses: 'If you are
unfaithful to me, I will scatter you
among the nations. [9]But if you return
to me and obey my commands and
live by them, then even if you are
exiled to the ends of the earth, I will
bring you back to the place I have
chosen for my name to be honored.'

[10]"The people you rescued by your
great power and strong hand are your
servants. [11]O Lord, please hear my
prayer! Listen to the prayers of those
of us who delight in honoring you.
Please grant me success today by

making the king favorable to me.* Put it into his heart to be kind to me."

In those days I was the king's cup-bearer.

2:1EARLY the following spring, in the month of Nisan,* during the twentieth year of King Artaxerxes' reign, I was serving the king his wine. I had never before appeared sad in his presence. 2So the king asked me, "Why are you looking so sad? You don't look sick to me. You must be deeply troubled."

Then I was terrified, 3but I replied, "Long live the king! How can I not be sad? For the city where my ancestors are buried is in ruins, and the gates have been destroyed by fire."

4The king asked, "Well, how can I help you?"

With a prayer to the God of heaven, 5I replied, "If it please the king, and if you are pleased with me, your servant, send me to Judah to rebuild the city where my ancestors are buried."

6The king, with the queen sitting beside him, asked, "How long will you be gone? When will you return?" After I told him how long I would be gone, the king agreed to my request.

7I also said to the king, "If it please the king, let me have letters addressed to the governors of the province west of the Euphrates River,* instructing them to let me travel safely through their territories on my way to Judah. 8And please give me a letter addressed to Asaph, the manager of the king's forest, instructing him to give me timber. I will need it to make beams for the gates of the Temple fortress, for the city walls, and for a house for myself." And the king granted these requests, because the gracious hand of God was on me.

9When I came to the governors of the province west of the Euphrates River, I delivered the king's letters to them. The king, I should add, had sent along army officers and horsemen* to protect me. 10But when Sanballat the Horonite and Tobiah the Ammonite official heard of my arrival, they were very displeased that someone had come to help the people of Israel.

11So I arrived in Jerusalem. Three days later, 12I slipped out during the night, taking only a few others with me. I had not told anyone about the plans God had put in my heart for Jerusalem. We took no pack animals with us except the donkey I was riding. 13After dark I went out through the Valley Gate, past the Jackal's Well,* and over to the Dung Gate to inspect the broken walls and burned gates. 14Then I went to the Fountain Gate and to the King's Pool, but my donkey couldn't get through the rubble. 15So, though it was still dark, I went up the Kidron Valley* instead, inspecting the wall before I turned back and entered again at the Valley Gate.

16The city officials did not know I had been out there or what I was doing, for I had not yet said anything to anyone about my plans. I had not yet spoken to the Jewish leaders—the priests, the nobles, the officials, or anyone else in the administration. 17But now I said to them, "You know very well what trouble we are in. Jerusalem lies in ruins, and its gates have been destroyed by fire. Let us rebuild the wall of Jerusalem and end this disgrace!" 18Then I told them about how the gracious hand of God had been on me, and about my conversation with the king.

They replied at once, "Yes, let's rebuild the wall!" So they began the good work.

19But when Sanballat, Tobiah, and Geshem the Arab heard of our plan, they scoffed contemptuously. "What are you doing? Are you rebelling against the king?" they asked.

20I replied, "The God of heaven will help us succeed. We, his servants, will start rebuilding this wall. But you have no share, legal right, or historic claim in Jerusalem."

3:1THEN Eliashib the high priest and the other priests started to rebuild at the Sheep Gate. They dedicated it and set up its doors, building the wall as far as the Tower of the Hundred, which they dedicated, and the Tower of Hananel. 2People from the town of Jericho worked next to them, and beyond them was Zaccur son of Imri.

3The Fish Gate was built by the sons of Hassenaah. They laid the beams, set up its doors, and installed its bolts and bars. 4Meremoth son of Uriah and grandson of Hakkoz repaired the next section of wall.

Beside him were Meshullam son of Berekiah and grandson of Meshezabel, and then Zadok son of Baana. ⁵Next were the people from Tekoa, though their leaders refused to work with the construction supervisors.

⁶The Old City Gate* was repaired by Joiada son of Paseah and Meshullam son of Besodeiah. They laid the beams, set up its doors, and installed its bolts and bars. ⁷Next to them were Melatiah from Gibeon, Jadon from Meronoth, people from Gibeon, and people from Mizpah, the headquarters of the governor of the province west of the Euphrates River.* ⁸Next was Uzziel son of Harhaiah, a goldsmith by trade, who also worked on the wall. Beyond him was Hananiah, a manufacturer of perfumes. They left out a section of Jerusalem as they built the Broad Wall.*

⁹Rephaiah son of Hur, the leader of half the district of Jerusalem, was next to them on the wall. ¹⁰Next Jedaiah son of Harumaph repaired the wall across from his own house, and next to him was Hattush son of Hashabneiah. ¹¹Then came Malkijah son of Harim and Hasshub son of Pahath-moab, who repaired another section of the wall and the Tower of the Ovens. ¹²Shallum son of Hallohesh and his daughters repaired the next section. He was the leader of the other half of the district of Jerusalem.

¹³The Valley Gate was repaired by the people from Zanoah, led by Hanun. They set up its doors and installed its bolts and bars. They also repaired the 1,500 feet* of wall to the Dung Gate.

¹⁴The Dung Gate was repaired by Malkijah son of Recab, the leader of the Beth-hakkerem district. He rebuilt it, set up its doors, and installed its bolts and bars.

1:1 Hebrew *In the month of Kislev of the twentieth year.* A number of dates in the book of Nehemiah can be cross-checked with dates in surviving Persian records and related accurately to our modern calendar. This month of the ancient Hebrew lunar calendar occurred within the months of November and December 446 B.C. The *twentieth year* probably refers to the reign of King Artaxerxes I; compare 2:1; 5:14.   1:11 Hebrew *today in the sight of this man.*   2:1 Hebrew *In the month of Nisan.* This month of the ancient Hebrew lunar calendar occurred within the months of April and May 445 B.C.   2:7 Hebrew *the province beyond the river;* also in 2:9.   2:9 Or *charioteers.*   2:13 Or *Serpent's Well.*   2:15 Hebrew *the valley.*   3:6 Or *The Mishneh Gate,* or *The Jeshanah Gate.*   3:7 Hebrew *the province beyond the river.*   3:8 Or *They fortified Jerusalem up to the Broad Wall.*   3:13 Hebrew *1,000 cubits* [450 meters].

1 CORINTHIANS 7:1-24

Is it better to be married or not? Can you serve God more effectively one way than the other? The Corinthians asked similar questions. Here's what Paul had to say. . . .

Now regarding the questions you [Corinthians] asked in your letter. Yes, it is good to live a celibate life.* ²But because there is so much sexual immorality, each man should have his own wife, and each woman should have her own husband.

HOW WE LIVE

Prayer

NEHEMIAH 1:4; 2:4 Nehemiah was a Jew who lived in Persia. Still, his heart was with his people in the Promised Land. News from those who had returned indicated that the wall of Jerusalem remained a shambles. A city without a wall was unprotected, vulnerable to attack. Nehemiah fasted and prayed for several days, expressing his sorrow for Israel's sin and his desire that Jerusalem would again come alive with the worship of the one true God. By the end of his prayer time, Nehemiah knew what action he had to take (Nehemiah 1:11). • Eight times in this book we read that Nehemiah also prayed spontaneously when he was put on the spot (Nehemiah 2:4; 4:4-5, 9; 5:19; 6:14; 13:14, 22, 29). Nehemiah prayed at any time, even while talking with others. Nehemiah could confidently send up short prayers when needed because he had established an intimate relationship with God during times of extended prayer (Nehemiah 1:4-7). • Develop a habit of prayer. Whether in times of quiet or in an emergency, make room for God through prayer. Watch how he responds.

³The husband should fulfill his wife's sexual needs, and the wife should fulfill her husband's needs. ⁴The wife gives authority over her body to her husband, and the husband gives authority over his body to his wife.

⁵Do not deprive each other of sexual relations, unless you both agree to refrain from sexual intimacy for a limited time so you can give yourselves more completely to prayer. Afterward, you should come together again so that Satan won't be able to tempt you because of your lack of self-control. ⁶I say this as a concession, not as a command. ⁷But I wish everyone were single, just as I am. But God gives to some the gift of marriage, and to others the gift of singleness.

⁸So I say to those who aren't married and to widows—it's better to stay unmarried, just as I am. ⁹But if they can't control themselves, they should go ahead and marry. It's better to marry than to burn with lust.

¹⁰But for those who are married, I have a command that comes not from me, but from the Lord.* A wife must not leave her husband. ¹¹But if she does leave him, let her remain single or else be reconciled to him. And the husband must not leave his wife.

¹²Now, I will speak to the rest of you, though I do not have a direct command from the Lord. If a Christian man* has a wife who is not a believer and she is willing to continue living with him, he must not leave her. ¹³And if a Christian woman has a husband who is not a believer and he is willing to continue living with her, she must not leave him. ¹⁴For the Christian wife brings holiness to her marriage, and the Christian husband* brings holiness to his marriage. Otherwise, your children would not be holy, but now they are holy. ¹⁵(But if the husband or wife who isn't a believer insists on leaving, let them go. In such cases the Christian husband or wife* is no longer bound to the other, for God has called you* to live in peace.) ¹⁶Don't you wives realize that your husbands might be saved because of you? And don't you husbands realize that your wives might be saved because of you?

¹⁷Each of you should continue to live in whatever situation the Lord has placed you, and remain as you were when God first called you. This is my rule for all the churches. ¹⁸For instance, a man who was circumcised before he became a believer should not try to reverse it. And the man who was uncircumcised when he became a believer should not be circumcised now. ¹⁹For it makes no difference whether or not a man has been circumcised. The important thing is to keep God's commandments.

²⁰Yes, each of you should remain as you were when God called you. ²¹Are you a slave? Don't let that worry you—but if you get a chance to be free, take it. ²²And remember, if you were a slave when the Lord called you, you are now free in the Lord. And if you were free when the Lord called you, you are now a slave of Christ. ²³God paid a high price for you, so don't be enslaved by the world.* ²⁴Each of you, dear brothers and sisters,* should remain as you were when God first called you.

7:1 Greek *It is good for a man not to touch a woman.*
7:10 See Matt 5:32; 19:9; Mark 10:11-12; Luke 16:18.
7:12 Greek *a brother.* **7:14** Greek *the brother.* **7:15a** Greek *the brother or sister.* **7:15b** Some manuscripts read *us.*
7:23 Greek *don't become slaves of people.* **7:24** Greek *brothers;* also in 7:29.

PSALM 31:19-24

How great is the goodness
    you have stored up for those who
        fear you.
You lavish it on those who come to you
        for protection,
    blessing them before the watching
        world.
²⁰ You hide them in the shelter of your
        presence,
    safe from those who conspire
        against them.
You shelter them in your presence,
    far from accusing tongues.

²¹ Praise the LORD,
    for he has shown me the wonders
        of his unfailing love.
    He kept me safe when my city was
        under attack.
²² In panic I cried out,
    "I am cut off from the LORD!"
    But you heard my cry for mercy
        and answered my call for help.

²³ Love the LORD, all you godly ones!
    For the LORD protects those
        who are loyal to him,
    but he harshly punishes the arrogant.

24 So be strong and courageous,
    all you who put your hope in the
    LORD!

NEHEMIAH 3:15–5:13

Nehemiah faced struggles from within and without as he led the people to rebuild. An external fortification was one thing; but did the people have the inner strength to finish the job?

The Fountain Gate was repaired by Shallum* son of Col-hozeh, the leader of the Mizpah district. He rebuilt it, roofed it, set up its doors, and installed its bolts and bars. Then he repaired the wall of the pool of Siloam* near the king's garden, and he rebuilt the wall as far as the stairs that descend from the City of David. 16Next to him was Nehemiah son of Azbuk, the leader of half the district of Bethzur. He rebuilt the wall from a place across from the tombs of David's family as far as the water reservoir and the House of the Warriors.

17Next to him, repairs were made by a group of Levites working under the supervision of Rehum son of Bani. Then came Hashabiah, the leader of half the district of Keilah, who supervised the building of the wall on behalf of his own district. 18Next down the line were his countrymen led by Binnui* son of Henadad, the leader of the other half of the district of Keilah.

19Next to them, Ezer son of Jeshua, the leader of Mizpah, repaired another section of wall across from the ascent to the armory near the angle in the wall. 20Next to him was Baruch son of Zabbai, who zealously repaired an additional section from the angle to the door of the house of Eliashib the high priest. 21Meremoth son of Uriah and grandson of Hakkoz rebuilt another section of the wall extending

PROVERBS 21:4

Haughty eyes, a proud heart, and evil actions are all sin.

AUGUST**12**

from the door of Eliashib's house to the end of the house.

22The next repairs were made by the priests from the surrounding region. 23After them, Benjamin and Hasshub repaired the section across from their house, and Azariah son of Maaseiah and grandson of Ananiah repaired the section across from his house. 24Next was Binnui son of Henadad, who rebuilt another section of the wall from Azariah's house to the angle and the corner. 25Palal son of Uzai carried on the work from a point opposite the angle and the tower that projects up from the king's upper house beside the court of the guard. Next to him were Pedaiah son of Parosh, 26with the Temple servants living on the hill of Ophel, who repaired the wall as far as a point across from the Water Gate to the east and the projecting tower. 27Then came the people of Tekoa, who repaired another section across from the great projecting tower and over to the wall of Ophel.

28Above the Horse Gate, the priests repaired the wall. Each one repaired the section immediately across from his own house. 29Next Zadok son of Immer also rebuilt the wall across from his own house, and beyond him was Shemaiah son of Shecaniah, the gatekeeper of the East Gate. 30Next Hananiah son of Shelemiah and Hanun, the sixth son of Zalaph, repaired another section, while Meshullam son of Berekiah rebuilt the wall across from where he lived. 31Malkijah, one of the goldsmiths, repaired the wall as far as the housing for the Temple servants and merchants, across from the Inspection Gate. Then he continued as far as the upper room at the corner. [32] The other goldsmiths and merchants repaired the wall from that corner to the Sheep Gate.

[4:1] *SANBALLAT was very angry when he learned that we were rebuilding the wall. He flew into a rage and mocked the Jews, [2] saying in front of his friends and the Samarian army officers, "What does this bunch of poor, feeble Jews think they're doing? Do they think they can build the wall in a single day by just offering a few sacrifices?* Do they actually think they can make something of stones from a rubbish heap—and charred ones at that?"

[3] Tobiah the Ammonite, who was standing beside him, remarked, "That stone wall would collapse if even a fox walked along the top of it!"

[4] Then I prayed, "Hear us, our God, for we are being mocked. May their scoffing fall back on their own heads, and may they themselves become captives in a foreign land! [5] Do not ignore their guilt. Do not blot out their sins, for they have provoked you to anger here in front of* the builders."

[6] At last the wall was completed to half its height around the entire city, for the people had worked with enthusiasm.

[7] *But when Sanballat and Tobiah and the Arabs, Ammonites, and Ashdodites heard that the work was going ahead and that the gaps in the wall of Jerusalem were being repaired, they were furious. [8] They all made plans to come and fight against Jerusalem and throw us into confusion. [9] But we prayed to our God and guarded the city day and night to protect ourselves.

[10] Then the people of Judah began to complain, "The workers are getting tired, and there is so much rubble to be moved. We will never be able to build the wall by ourselves."

[11] Meanwhile, our enemies were saying, "Before they know what's happening, we will swoop down on them and kill them and end their work."

[12] The Jews who lived near the enemy came and told us again and again, "They will come from all directions and attack us!"* [13] So I placed armed guards behind the lowest parts of the wall in the exposed areas. I stationed the people to stand guard by families, armed with swords, spears, and bows.

[14] Then as I looked over the situation, I called together the nobles and the rest of the people and said to them, "Don't be afraid of the enemy! Remember the Lord, who is great and glorious, and fight for your brothers, your sons, your daughters, your wives, and your homes!"

[15] When our enemies heard that we knew of their plans and that God had frustrated them, we all returned to our work on the wall. [16] But from then on, only half my men worked while the other half stood guard with spears, shields, bows, and coats of mail. The leaders stationed themselves behind the people of Judah [17] who were building the wall. The laborers carried on their work with one hand supporting their load and one hand holding a weapon. [18] All the builders had a sword belted to their side. The trumpeter stayed with me to sound the alarm.

[19] Then I explained to the nobles and officials and all the people, "The work is very spread out, and we are widely separated from each other along the wall. [20] When you hear the blast of the trumpet, rush to wherever it is sounding. Then our God will fight for us!"

[21] We worked early and late, from sunrise to sunset. And half the men were always on guard. [22] I also told everyone living outside the walls to stay in Jerusalem. That way they and their servants could help with guard duty at night and work during the day. [23] During this time, none of us—not I, nor my relatives, nor my servants, nor the guards who were with me—ever took off our clothes. We carried our weapons with us at all times, even when we went for water.*

[5:1] ABOUT this time some of the men and their wives raised a cry of protest against their fellow Jews. [2] They were saying, "We have such large families. We need more food to survive."

[3] Others said, "We have mortgaged our fields, vineyards, and homes to get food during the famine."

[4] And others said, "We have had to borrow money on our fields and vineyards to pay our taxes. [5] We belong to the same family as those who are wealthy, and our children are just like theirs. Yet we must sell our children into slavery just to get enough

money to live. We have already sold some of our daughters, and we are helpless to do anything about it, for our fields and vineyards are already mortgaged to others."

[6] When I heard their complaints, I was very angry. [7] After thinking it over, I spoke out against these nobles and officials. I told them, "You are hurting your own relatives by charging interest when they borrow money!" Then I called a public meeting to deal with the problem.

[8] At the meeting I said to them, "We are doing all we can to redeem our Jewish relatives who have had to sell themselves to pagan foreigners, but you are selling them back into slavery again. How often must we redeem them?" And they had nothing to say in their defense.

[9] Then I pressed further, "What you are doing is not right! Should you not walk in the fear of our God in order to avoid being mocked by enemy nations? [10] I myself, as well as my brothers and my workers, have been lending the people money and grain, but now let us stop this business of charging interest. [11] You must restore their fields, vineyards, olive groves, and homes to them this very day. And repay the interest you charged when you lent them money, grain, new wine, and olive oil."

[12] They replied, "We will give back everything and demand nothing more from the people. We will do as you say." Then I called the priests and made the nobles and officials swear to do what they had promised. [13] I shook out the folds of my robe and said, "If you fail to keep your promise, may God shake you like this from your homes and from your property!"

The whole assembly responded, "Amen," and they praised the LORD. And the people did as they had promised.

3:15a As in Syriac version; Hebrew reads *Shallun*.
3:15b Hebrew *pool of Shelah*, another name for the pool of Siloam.   3:18 As in a few Hebrew manuscripts, some Greek manuscripts, and Syriac version (see also 3:24; 10:9); most Hebrew manuscripts read *Bavvai*.   4:1 Verses 4:1-6 are numbered 3:33-38 in Hebrew text.   4:2 The meaning of the Hebrew is uncertain.   4:5 Or *for they have thrown insults in the face of.*   4:7 Verses 4:7-23 are numbered 4:1-17 in Hebrew text.   4:12 The meaning of the Hebrew is uncertain.
4:23 Or *Each carried his weapon in his right hand.* Hebrew reads *Each his weapon the water.* The meaning of the Hebrew is uncertain.

1 CORINTHIANS 7:25-40

Paul urged believers not to regard marriage, home, or financial security as the ultimate goals of life. As much as possible, believers should live unhindered by the cares of this world so we can focus on serving Christ.

Now regarding your question about the young women who are not yet married. I [Paul] do not have a command from the

HOW WE LIVE

Our marriages

1 CORINTHIANS 7:39 The Corinthian believers had written to Paul with questions about marriage. The biggest problem may have been concern on the part of those who had unbelieving spouses. Should they leave those spouses and find believers to marry? Should they leave their spouses altogether in order to serve the Lord? • Paul explained that being single definitely had its advantages, for one could serve the Lord completely unhindered by concerns over a spouse and family. However, Paul also explained that the married believers were not to leave their unbelieving spouses, but instead to pray diligently for them and to live in a way that might draw their spouses to the faith. Instead of suddenly marrying or divorcing, the believers were to be content in their current situation—married or single—and seek God's guidance regarding the future. • Both marriage and singleness are gifts from God. If you are a new believer married to an unbeliever, don't seek to get out of your marriage. Instead, patiently serve the Lord and pray for your spouse. If you're single, allow God to work out his plan for your life in his timing. Be content and serve God where he has placed you.

Lord for them. But the Lord in his mercy has given me wisdom that can be trusted, and I will share it with you. [26] Because of the present crisis,* I think it is best to remain as you are. [27] If you have a wife, do not seek to end the marriage. If you do not have a wife, do not seek to get married. [28] But if you do get married, it is not a sin. And if a young woman gets married, it is not a sin. However, those who get married at this time will have troubles, and I am trying to spare you those problems.

[29] But let me say this, dear brothers and sisters: The time that remains is very short. So from now on, those with wives should not focus only on their marriage. [30] Those who weep or who rejoice or who buy things should not be absorbed by their weeping or their joy or their possessions. [31] Those who use the things of the world should not become attached to them. For this world as we know it will soon pass away.

[32] I want you to be free from the concerns of this life. An unmarried man can spend his time doing the Lord's work and thinking how to please him. [33] But a married man has to think about his earthly responsibilities and how to please his wife. [34] His interests are divided. In the same way, a woman who is no longer married or has never been married can be devoted to the Lord and holy in body and in spirit. But a married woman has to think about her earthly responsibilities and how to please her husband. [35] I am saying this for your benefit, not to place restrictions on you. I want you to do whatever will help you serve the Lord best, with as few distractions as possible.

[36] But if a man thinks that he's treating his fiancée improperly and will inevitably give in to his passion, let him marry her as he wishes. It is not a sin. [37] But if he has decided firmly not to marry and there is no urgency and he can control his passion, he does well not to marry. [38] So the person who marries his fiancée does well, and the person who doesn't marry does even better.

[39] A wife is bound to her husband as long as he lives. If her husband dies, she is free to marry anyone she wishes, but only if he loves the Lord.* [40] But in my opinion it would be better for her to stay single, and I think I am giving you counsel from God's Spirit when I say this.

7:26 Or *the pressures of life.*   **7:39** Greek *but only in the Lord.*

PSALM 32:1-11
A psalm* of David.

1 **O**h, what joy for those
　　whose disobedience is forgiven,
　　whose sin is put out of sight!
2 Yes, what joy for those
　　whose record the LORD has cleared
　　　　of guilt,*
　　whose lives are lived in complete
　　　　honesty!
3 When I refused to confess my sin,
　　my body wasted away,
　　and I groaned all day long.
4 Day and night your hand of discipline
　　was heavy on me.
　　My strength evaporated like water
　　　　in the summer heat.   *Interlude*

5 Finally, I confessed all my sins to you
　　and stopped trying to hide my guilt.
　　I said to myself, "I will confess my
　　　　rebellion to the LORD."
　　And you forgave me! All my guilt
　　　　is gone.   *Interlude*

6 Therefore, let all the godly pray to you
　　while there is still time,
　　that they may not drown in the
　　　　floodwaters of judgment.
7 For you are my hiding place;
　　you protect me from trouble.
　　You surround me with songs
　　　　of victory.   *Interlude*

8 The LORD says, "I will guide you along
　　　　the best pathway for your life.
　　I will advise you and watch over
　　　　you.
9 Do not be like a senseless horse or mule
　　that needs a bit and bridle to keep it
　　　　under control."

10 Many sorrows come to the wicked,
　　but unfailing love surrounds those
　　　　who trust the LORD.
11 So rejoice in the LORD and be glad,
　　　　all you who obey him!
　　Shout for joy, all you whose hearts
　　　　are pure!

32:TITLE Hebrew *maskil.* This may be a literary or musical term.   **32:2** Greek version reads *of sin.* Compare Rom 4:7.

PROVERBS 21:5-7

Good planning and hard work lead to prosperity, but hasty shortcuts lead to poverty. □ Wealth created by a lying tongue is a vanishing mist and a deadly trap.* □ The violence of the wicked sweeps them away, because they refuse to do what is just.

21:6 As in Greek version; Hebrew reads *mist for those who seek death.*

AUGUST**13**

NEHEMIAH 5:14–7:73A

There's a particular feeling of satisfaction when a long, difficult task is finished. The people had worked on their portions of the wall, even when their lives were in danger. They kept going—persevering until the wall was finished in record time.

For the entire twelve years that I was governor of Judah—from the twentieth year to the thirty-second year of the reign of King Artaxerxes*—neither I nor my officials drew on our official food allowance. [15] The former governors, in contrast, had laid heavy burdens on the people, demanding a daily ration of food and wine, besides forty pieces* of silver. Even their assistants took advantage of the people. But because I feared God, I did not act that way.

[16] I also devoted myself to working on the wall and refused to acquire any land. And I required all my servants to spend time working on the wall. [17] I asked for nothing, even though I regularly fed 150 Jewish officials at my table, besides all the visitors from other lands! [18] The provisions I paid for each day included one ox, six choice sheep or goats, and a large number of poultry. And every ten days we needed a large supply of all kinds of wine. Yet I refused to claim the governor's food allowance because the people already carried a heavy burden.

[19] Remember, O my God, all that I have done for these people, and bless me for it.

6:1 SANBALLAT, Tobiah, Geshem the Arab, and the rest of our enemies found out that I had finished rebuilding the wall and that no gaps remained—though we had not yet set up the doors in the gates. [2] So Sanbal-lat and Geshem sent a message asking me to meet them at one of the villages* in the plain of Ono.

But I realized they were plotting to harm me, [3] so I replied by sending this message to them: "I am engaged in a great work, so I can't come. Why should I stop working to come and meet with you?"

[4] Four times they sent the same message, and each time I gave the same reply. [5] The fifth time, Sanballat's servant came with an open letter in his hand, [6] and this is what it said:

"There is a rumor among the surrounding nations, and Geshem* tells me it is true, that you and the Jews are planning to rebel and that is why you are building the wall. According to his reports, you plan to be their king. [7] He also reports that you have appointed prophets in Jerusalem to proclaim about you, 'Look! There is a king in Judah!'

"You can be very sure that this report will get back to the king, so I suggest that you come and talk it over with me."

[8] I replied, "There is no truth in any part of your story. You are making up the whole thing."

[9] They were just trying to intimidate us, imagining that they could discourage us and stop the work. So I continued the work with even greater determination.*

[10] Later I went to visit Shemaiah son of Delaiah and grandson of Mehetabel, who was confined to his home. He said, "Let us meet together inside the Temple of God and bolt the doors shut. Your enemies are coming to kill you tonight."

¹¹But I replied, "Should someone in my position run from danger? Should someone in my position enter the Temple to save his life? No, I won't do it!" ¹²I realized that God had not spoken to him, but that he had uttered this prophecy against me because Tobiah and Sanballat had hired him. ¹³They were hoping to intimidate me and make me sin. Then they would be able to accuse and discredit me.

¹⁴Remember, O my God, all the evil things that Tobiah and Sanballat have done. And remember Noadiah the prophet and all the prophets like her who have tried to intimidate me.

¹⁵So on October 2* the wall was finished—just fifty-two days after we had begun. ¹⁶When our enemies and the surrounding nations heard about it, they were frightened and humiliated. They realized this work had been done with the help of our God.

¹⁷During those fifty-two days, many letters went back and forth between Tobiah and the nobles of Judah. ¹⁸For many in Judah had sworn allegiance to him because his father-in-law was Shecaniah son of Arah, and his son Jehohanan was married to the daughter of Meshullam son of Berekiah. ¹⁹They kept telling me about Tobiah's good deeds, and then they told him everything I said. And Tobiah kept sending threatening letters to intimidate me.

⁷:¹After the wall was finished and I had set up the doors in the gates, the gatekeepers, singers, and Levites were appointed. ²I gave the responsibility of governing Jerusalem to my brother Hanani, along with Hananiah, the commander of the fortress, for he was a faithful man who feared God more than most. ³I said to them, "Do not leave the gates open during the hottest part of the day.* And even while the gatekeepers are on duty, have them shut and bar the doors. Appoint the residents of Jerusalem to act as guards, everyone on a regular watch. Some will serve at sentry posts and some in front of their own homes."

⁴At that time the city was large and spacious, but the population was small, and none of the houses had been rebuilt. ⁵So

my God gave me the idea to call together all the nobles and leaders of the city, along with the ordinary citizens, for registration. I had found the genealogical record of those who had first returned to Judah. This is what was written there:

⁶Here is the list of the Jewish exiles of the provinces who returned from their captivity. King Nebuchadnezzar had deported them to Babylon, but now they returned to Jerusalem and the other towns in Judah where they originally lived. ⁷Their leaders were Zerubbabel, Jeshua, Nehemiah, Seraiah,* Reelaiah,* Nahamani, Mordecai, Bilshan, Mispar,* Bigvai, Rehum,* and Baanah.

This is the number of the men of Israel who returned from exile:

⁸ The family of Parosh	2,172
⁹ The family of Shephatiah	372
¹⁰ The family of Arah	652
¹¹ The family of Pahath-moab (descendants of Jeshua and Joab)	2,818
¹² The family of Elam	1,254
¹³ The family of Zattu	845
¹⁴ The family of Zaccai	760
¹⁵ The family of Bani*	648
¹⁶ The family of Bebai	628
¹⁷ The family of Azgad	2,322
¹⁸ The family of Adonikam	667
¹⁹ The family of Bigvai	2,067
²⁰ The family of Adin	655
²¹ The family of Ater (descendants of Hezekiah)	98
²² The family of Hashum	328
²³ The family of Bezai	324
²⁴ The family of Jorah*	112
²⁵ The family of Gibbar*	95
²⁶ The people of Bethlehem and Netophah	188
²⁷ The people of Anathoth	128
²⁸ The people of Beth-azmaveth	42
²⁹ The people of Kiriath-jearim, Kephirah, and Beeroth	743
³⁰ The people of Ramah and Geba	621
³¹ The people of Micmash	122
³² The people of Bethel and Ai	123
³³ The people of Nebo	52
³⁴ The citizens of Elam	1,254
³⁵ The citizens of Harim	320

³⁶ The citizens of Jericho........ 345
³⁷ The citizens of Lod, Hadid,
and Ono.................. 721
³⁸ The citizens of Senaah....... 3,930

³⁹These are the priests who returned
from exile:
The family of Jedaiah
(through the line of Jeshua) .. 973
⁴⁰ The family of Immer........ 1,052
⁴¹ The family of Pashhur 1,247
⁴² The family of Harim......... 1,017

⁴³These are the Levites who returned
from exile:
The families of Jeshua and
Kadmiel (descendants of
Hodaviah*)................. 74
⁴⁴ The singers of the family
of Asaph.................. 148
⁴⁵ The gatekeepers of the families
of Shallum, Ater, Talmon,
Akkub, Hatita, and Shobai ... 138

⁴⁶The descendants of the following
Temple servants returned from exile:
Ziha, Hasupha, Tabbaoth,
⁴⁷ Keros, Siaha,* Padon,
⁴⁸ Lebanah, Hagabah, Shalmai,
⁴⁹ Hanan, Giddel, Gahar,
⁵⁰ Reaiah, Rezin, Nekoda,
⁵¹ Gazzam, Uzza, Paseah,
⁵² Besai, Meunim, Nephusim,*
⁵³ Bakbuk, Hakupha, Harhur,
⁵⁴ Bazluth,* Mehida, Harsha,

⁵⁵ Barkos, Sisera, Temah,
⁵⁶ Neziah, and Hatipha.

⁵⁷The descendants of these servants
of King Solomon returned from exile:
Sotai, Hassophereth, Peruda,*
⁵⁸ Jaalah,* Darkon, Giddel,
⁵⁹ Shephatiah, Hattil,
Pokereth-hazzebaim, and Ami.*

⁶⁰In all, the Temple servants and the
descendants of Solomon's servants
numbered 392.

⁶¹Another group returned at this
time from the towns of Tel-melah, Tel-
harsha, Kerub, Addan,* and Immer.
However, they could not prove that they
or their families were descendants of
Israel. ⁶²This group included the families of Delaiah, Tobiah, and Nekoda—
a total of 642 people.

⁶³Three families of priests—Hobaiah,
Hakkoz, and Barzillai—also returned.
(This Barzillai had married a woman
who was a descendant of Barzillai of
Gilead, and he had taken her family
name.) ⁶⁴They searched for their
names in the genealogical records,
but they were not found, so they were
disqualified from serving as priests.
⁶⁵The governor told them not to eat the
priests' share of food from the sacrifices
until a priest could consult the LORD
about the matter by using the Urim
and Thummim—the sacred lots.

HOW WE LIVE

Dealing with problems

NEHEMIAH 6:15-16 As Nehemiah began the work on the walls, he faced
constant opposition. How did he deal with these problems? He didn't
give up. He inspired his people to keep on until the job was done. He
confronted their fears while enabling their continued work. He reminded
them of the reason that they worked. He trusted God and was able to see
through deception. • You're going to face problems—today, tomorrow,
and in the days to come. No one is immune. However, as a believer, you
have a new way to deal with problems because your faith now plays a
role in helping you find a solution. You no longer have to depend on your
own ingenuity. You no longer have to just hope you're doing the right
thing. You can take every problem to God and ask for his guidance,
protection, and wisdom. With God leading you, you will find strength
to not only tackle problems but to surmount them and then to use
them as a resource of knowledge and understanding in the future.

⁶⁶So a total of 42,360 people returned to Judah, ⁶⁷in addition to 7,337 servants and 245 singers, both men and women. ⁶⁸They took with them 736 horses, 245 mules,* ⁶⁹435 camels, and 6,720 donkeys.

⁷⁰Some of the family leaders gave gifts for the work. The governor gave to the treasury 1,000 gold coins,* 50 gold basins, and 530 robes for the priests. ⁷¹The other leaders gave to the treasury a total of 20,000 gold coins* and some 2,750 pounds* of silver for the work. ⁷²The rest of the people gave 20,000 gold coins, about 2,500 pounds* of silver, and 67 robes for the priests.

⁷³So the priests, the Levites, the gatekeepers, the singers, the Temple servants, and some of the common people settled near Jerusalem. The rest of the people returned to their own towns throughout Israel.

5:14 That is, 445–433 B.C. 5:15 Hebrew 40 shekels [1 pound, or 456 grams]. 6:2 As in Greek version; Hebrew reads at Kephirim. 6:6 Hebrew Gashmu, a variant spelling of Geshem. 6:9 As in Greek version; Hebrew reads But now to strengthen my hands. 6:15 Hebrew on the twenty-fifth day of the month Elul, of the ancient Hebrew lunar calendar. This day was October 2, 445 B.C.; also see note on 1:1. 7:3 Or Keep the gates of Jerusalem closed until the sun is hot. 7:7a As in parallel text at Ezra 2:2; Hebrew reads Azariah. 7:7b As in parallel text at Ezra 2:2; Hebrew reads Raamiah. 7:7c As in parallel text at Ezra 2:2; Hebrew reads Mispereth. 7:7d As in parallel text at Ezra 2:2; Hebrew reads Nehum. 7:15 As in parallel text at Ezra 2:10; Hebrew reads Binnui. 7:24 As in parallel text at Ezra 2:18; Hebrew reads Hariph. 7:25 As in parallel text at Ezra 2:20; Hebrew reads Gibeon. 7:43 As in parallel text at Ezra 2:40; Hebrew reads Hodevah. 7:47 As in parallel text at Ezra 2:44; Hebrew reads Sia. 7:52 As in parallel text at Ezra 2:50; Hebrew reads Nephushesim. 7:54 As in parallel text at Ezra 2:52; Hebrew reads Bazlith. 7:57 As in parallel text at Ezra 2:55; Hebrew reads Sotai, Sophereth, Perida. 7:58 As in parallel text at Ezra 2:56; Hebrew reads Jaala. 7:59 As in parallel text at Ezra 2:57; Hebrew reads Amon. 7:61 As in parallel text at Ezra 2:59; Hebrew reads Addon. 7:68 As in some Hebrew manuscripts (see also Ezra 2:66); most Hebrew manuscripts lack this verse. Verses 7:69-73 are numbered 7:68-72 in Hebrew text. 7:70 Hebrew 1,000 darics of gold, about 19 pounds or 8.6 kilograms in weight. 7:71a Hebrew 20,000 darics of gold, about 375 pounds or 170 kilograms in weight; also in 7:72. 7:71b Hebrew 2,200 minas [1,300 kilograms]. 7:72 Hebrew 2,000 minas [1,200 kilograms].

1 CORINTHIANS 8:1-13

Meat purchased in the marketplaces of Corinth had most likely been offered to an idol in one of the many pagan temples. The believers at Corinth had asked Paul for advice on whether eating such meat was okay.

Now regarding your [Corinthians] question about food that has been offered to idols. Yes, we know that "we all have knowledge" about this issue. But while knowledge makes us feel important, it is love that strengthens the church. ²Anyone who claims to know all the answers doesn't really know very much. ³But the person who loves God is the one whom God recognizes.*

⁴So, what about eating meat that has been offered to idols? Well, we all know that an idol is not really a god and that there is only one God. ⁵There may be so-called gods both in heaven and on earth, and some people actually worship many gods and many lords. ⁶But we know that there is only one God, the Father, who created everything, and we live for him. And there is only one Lord, Jesus Christ, through whom God made everything and through whom we have been given life.

⁷However, not all believers know this. Some are accustomed to thinking of idols as being real, so when they eat food that has been offered to idols, they think of it as the worship of real gods, and their weak consciences are violated. ⁸It's true that we can't win God's approval by what we eat. We don't lose anything if we don't eat it, and we don't gain anything if we do.

⁹But you must be careful so that your freedom does not cause others with a weaker conscience to stumble. ¹⁰For if others see you—with your "superior knowledge"—eating in the temple of an idol, won't they be encouraged to violate their conscience by eating food that has been offered to an idol? ¹¹So because of your superior knowledge, a weak believer* for whom Christ died will be destroyed. ¹²And when you sin against other believers* by encouraging them to do something they believe is wrong, you are sinning against Christ. ¹³So if what I eat causes another believer to sin, I will never eat meat again as long as I live—for I don't want to cause another believer to stumble.

8:3 Some manuscripts read the person who loves has full knowledge. 8:11 Greek brother; also in 8:13. 8:12 Greek brothers.

PSALM 33:1-11

Let the godly sing for joy to the LORD;
it is fitting for the pure to praise
him.

² Praise the LORD with melodies
  on the lyre;
    make music for him on the ten-
      stringed harp.
³ Sing a new song of praise to him;
  play skillfully on the harp, and sing
    with joy.
⁴ For the word of the LORD holds true,
  and we can trust everything he does.
⁵ He loves whatever is just and good;
  the unfailing love of the LORD fills
    the earth.

⁶ The LORD merely spoke,
  and the heavens were created.
He breathed the word,
  and all the stars were born.
⁷ He assigned the sea its boundaries
  and locked the oceans in vast
    reservoirs.

⁸ Let the whole world fear the LORD,
  and let everyone stand in awe
    of him.
⁹ For when he spoke, the world began!
  It appeared at his command.

¹⁰ The LORD frustrates the plans of the
    nations
  and thwarts all their schemes.
¹¹ But the LORD's plans stand firm
    forever;
  his intentions can never be shaken.

PROVERBS 21:8-10

The guilty walk a crooked path; the innocent travel a straight road. □ It's better to
live alone in the corner of an attic than
with a quarrelsome wife in a lovely home.
□ Evil people desire evil; their neighbors
get no mercy from them.

AUGUST**14**

NEHEMIAH 7:73B–9:21

As always with Israel, it wasn't enough for the
people to do the right thing with their hands if they
weren't going to do the right thing with their hearts.
They needed to return to God's law and become the
people he had called them to be.

In October,* when the Israelites had settled in their towns, ⁸:¹ all the people assembled with a unified purpose at the
square just inside the Water Gate. They
asked Ezra the scribe to bring out the
Book of the Law of Moses, which the
LORD had given for Israel to obey.

²So on October 8* Ezra the priest
brought the Book of the Law before the
assembly, which included the men and
women and all the children old enough to
understand. ³He faced the square just inside the Water Gate from early morning
until noon and read aloud to everyone
who could understand. All the people listened closely to the Book of the Law.

⁴Ezra the scribe stood on a high
wooden platform that had been made for
the occasion. To his right stood Mattithiah, Shema, Anaiah, Uriah, Hilkiah, and

Maaseiah. To his left stood Pedaiah, Mishael, Malkijah, Hashum, Hashbaddanah,
Zechariah, and Meshullam. ⁵Ezra stood
on the platform in full view of all the people. When they saw him open the book,
they all rose to their feet.

⁶Then Ezra praised the LORD, the great
God, and all the people chanted, "Amen!
Amen!" as they lifted their hands. Then
they bowed down and worshiped the
LORD with their faces to the ground.

⁷The Levites—Jeshua, Bani, Sherebiah,
Jamin, Akkub, Shabbethai, Hodiah, Maaseiah, Kelita, Azariah, Jozabad, Hanan,
and Pelaiah—then instructed the people
in the Law while everyone remained in
their places. ⁸They read from the Book of
the Law of God and clearly explained the
meaning of what was being read, helping
the people understand each passage.

⁹Then Nehemiah the governor, Ezra
the priest and scribe, and the Levites who
were interpreting for the people said to
them, "Don't mourn or weep on such a
day as this! For today is a sacred day before

the LORD your God." For the people had all been weeping as they listened to the words of the Law.

¹⁰And Nehemiah* continued, "Go and celebrate with a feast of rich foods and sweet drinks, and share gifts of food with people who have nothing prepared. This is a sacred day before our Lord. Don't be dejected and sad, for the joy of the LORD is your strength!"

¹¹And the Levites, too, quieted the people, telling them, "Hush! Don't weep! For this is a sacred day." ¹²So the people went away to eat and drink at a festive meal, to share gifts of food, and to celebrate with great joy because they had heard God's words and understood them.

¹³On October 9* the family leaders of all the people, together with the priests and Levites, met with Ezra the scribe to go over the Law in greater detail. ¹⁴As they studied the Law, they discovered that the LORD had commanded through Moses that the Israelites should live in shelters during the festival to be held that month.* ¹⁵He had said that a proclamation should be made throughout their towns and in Jerusalem, telling the people to go to the hills to get branches from olive, wild olive,* myrtle, palm, and other leafy trees. They were to use these branches to make shelters in which they would live during the festival, as prescribed in the Law.

¹⁶So the people went out and cut branches and used them to build shelters on the roofs of their houses, in their courtyards, in the courtyards of God's Temple, or in the squares just inside the Water Gate and the Ephraim Gate. ¹⁷So everyone who had returned from captivity lived in these shelters during the festival, and they were all filled with great joy! The Israelites had not celebrated like this since the days of Joshua* son of Nun.

¹⁸Ezra read from the Book of the Law of God on each of the seven days of the festival. Then on the eighth day they held a solemn assembly, as was required by law.

⁹:¹ON October 31* the people assembled again, and this time they fasted and dressed in burlap and sprinkled dust on their heads. ²Those of Israelite descent separated themselves from all foreigners as they confessed their own sins and the sins of their ancestors. ³They remained standing in place for three hours* while the Book of the Law of the LORD their God was read aloud to them. Then for three more hours they confessed their sins and worshiped the LORD their God. ⁴The Levites—Jeshua, Bani, Kadmiel, Shebaniah, Bunni, Sherebiah, Bani, and Kenani—stood on the stairway of the Levites and cried out to the LORD their God with loud voices.

⁵Then the leaders of the Levites—Jeshua, Kadmiel, Bani, Hashabneiah, Sherebiah, Hodiah, Shebaniah, and Pethahiah—called out to the people: "Stand up and praise the LORD your God, for he lives from everlasting to everlasting!" Then they prayed:

"May your glorious name be praised! May it be exalted above all blessing and praise!

⁶"You alone are the LORD. You made the skies and the heavens and all the stars. You made the earth and the seas and everything in them. You preserve them all, and the angels of heaven worship you.

⁷"You are the LORD God, who chose Abram and brought him from Ur of the Chaldeans and renamed him Abraham. ⁸When he had proved himself faithful, you made a covenant with him to give him and his descendants the land of the Canaanites, Hittites, Amorites, Perizzites, Jebusites, and Girgashites. And you have done what you promised, for you are always true to your word.

⁹"You saw the misery of our ancestors in Egypt, and you heard their cries from beside the Red Sea.* ¹⁰You displayed miraculous signs and wonders against Pharaoh, his officials, and all his people, for you knew how arrogantly they were treating our ancestors. You have a glorious reputation that has never been forgotten. ¹¹You divided the sea for your people so they could walk through on dry land! And then you hurled their enemies into the depths of the sea. They sank like stones beneath the mighty waters. ¹²You led our ancestors by a pillar of cloud

during the day and a pillar of fire at night so that they could find their way. ¹³"You came down at Mount Sinai and spoke to them from heaven. You gave them regulations and instructions that were just, and decrees and commands that were good. ¹⁴You instructed them concerning your holy Sabbath. And you commanded them, through Moses your servant, to obey all your commands, decrees, and instructions.

¹⁵"You gave them bread from heaven when they were hungry and water from the rock when they were thirsty. You commanded them to go and take possession of the land you had sworn to give them.

¹⁶"But our ancestors were proud and stubborn, and they paid no attention to your commands. ¹⁷They refused to obey and did not remember the miracles you had done for them. Instead, they became stubborn and appointed a leader to take them back to their slavery in Egypt! But you are a God of forgiveness, gracious and merciful, slow to become angry, and rich in unfailing love. You did not abandon them, ¹⁸even when they made an idol shaped like a calf and said, 'This is your god who brought you out of Egypt!' They committed terrible blasphemies.

¹⁹"But in your great mercy you did not abandon them to die in the wilderness. The pillar of cloud still led them forward by day, and the pillar of fire showed them the way through the night. ²⁰You sent your good Spirit to instruct them, and you did not stop giving them manna from heaven or water for their thirst. ²¹For forty years you sustained them in the wilderness, and they lacked nothing. Their clothes did not wear out, and their feet did not swell!"

7:73 Hebrew *in the seventh month.* This month of the ancient Hebrew lunar calendar occurred within the months of October and November 445 B.C.   8:2 Hebrew *on the first day of the seventh month,* of the ancient Hebrew lunar calendar. This day was October 8, 445 B.C.; also see note on 1:1.   8:10 Hebrew *he.*   8:13 Hebrew *On the second day,* of the seventh month of the ancient Hebrew lunar calendar. This day was October 9, 445 B.C.; also see notes on 1:1 and 8:2.   8:14 Hebrew *in the seventh month.* This month of the ancient Hebrew lunar calendar usually occurs within the months of September and October. See Lev 23:39-43.   8:15 Or *pine;* Hebrew reads *oil tree.*   8:17 Hebrew *Jeshua,* a variant spelling of Joshua.   9:1 Hebrew *On the twenty-fourth day of that same month,* the seventh month of the ancient Hebrew lunar calendar. This day was October 31, 445 B.C.; also see notes on 1:1 and 8:2.   9:3 Hebrew *for a quarter of a day.*   9:9 Hebrew *sea of reeds.*

1 CORINTHIANS 9:1-18
In today's reading, Paul defends his authority as an apostle of Jesus Christ. Paul had not been one of the original twelve disciples of Jesus. But he did meet Jesus in a vision after Jesus had been resurrected and ascended back into heaven.

Am I [Paul] not as free as anyone else? Am I not an apostle? Haven't I seen Jesus our

HOW WE LIVE

Experiencing joy

NEHEMIAH 8:9-11 After hearing the Book of the Law, the Israelites wept because they realized how far they had strayed from God. Instead of chastising them further, Nehemiah gave them hope. This was not a sad day; this was a holy day to celebrate. God was working in their hearts. "Don't be dejected and sad, for the joy of the LORD is your strength!" • We can learn a few important lessons from this Old Testament scene: (1) God's Word is powerful and helps us see ourselves as we really are—sinners who need to turn from our sin back to God. (2) Seeing ourselves as we really are is pretty depressing at times. We often can feel like failures. No joy there. (3) God never leaves us in our guilt and shame! Once we have turned back to him, he forgives and restores our relationship with him. • God's love and forgiveness are great cause for joy. At times in your Christian life, you will stray from God. During those times, turn to the Lord and tell him you're sorry. Then wipe your eyes and be joyful. God has work for you to do! The joy of the Lord is your strength!

Lord with my own eyes? Isn't it because of my work that you belong to the Lord? [2]Even if others think I am not an apostle, I certainly am to you. You yourselves are proof that I am the Lord's apostle.

[3]This is my answer to those who question my authority.* [4]Don't we have the right to live in your homes and share your meals? [5]Don't we have the right to bring a Christian wife with us as the other apostles and the Lord's brothers do, and as Peter* does? [6]Or is it only Barnabas and I who have to work to support ourselves?

[7]What soldier has to pay his own expenses? What farmer plants a vineyard and doesn't have the right to eat some of its fruit? What shepherd cares for a flock of sheep and isn't allowed to drink some of the milk? [8]Am I expressing merely a human opinion, or does the law say the same thing? [9]For the law of Moses says, "You must not muzzle an ox to keep it from eating as it treads out the grain."* Was God thinking only about oxen when he said this? [10]Wasn't he actually speaking to us? Yes, it was written for us, so that the one who plows and the one who threshes the grain might both expect a share of the harvest.

[11]Since we have planted spiritual seed among you, aren't we entitled to a harvest of physical food and drink? [12]If you support others who preach to you, shouldn't we have an even greater right to be supported? But we have never used this right. We would rather put up with anything than be an obstacle to the Good News about Christ.

[13]Don't you realize that those who work in the temple get their meals from the offerings brought to the temple? And those who serve at the altar get a share of the sacrificial offerings. [14]In the same way, the Lord ordered that those who preach the Good News should be supported by those who benefit from it. [15]Yet I have never used any of these rights. And I am not writing this to suggest that I want to start now. In fact, I would rather die than lose my right to boast about preaching without charge. [16]Yet preaching the Good News is not something I can boast about. I am compelled by God to do it. How terrible for me if I didn't preach the Good News!

[17]If I were doing this on my own initiative, I would deserve payment. But I have no choice, for God has given me this sacred trust. [18]What then is my pay? It is the opportunity to preach the Good News without charging anyone. That's why I never demand my rights when I preach the Good News.

9:3 Greek *those who examine me.* **9:5** Greek *Cephas.* **9:9** Deut 25:4.

PSALM 33:12-22

What joy for the nation whose God is the LORD,
whose people he has chosen as his inheritance.

[13] The LORD looks down from heaven
and sees the whole human race.
[14] From his throne he observes
all who live on the earth.
[15] He made their hearts,
so he understands everything
they do.
[16] The best-equipped army cannot save
a king,
nor is great strength enough to save
a warrior.
[17] Don't count on your warhorse to give
you victory—
for all its strength, it cannot save
you.
[18] But the LORD watches over those who
fear him,
those who rely on his unfailing love.
[19] He rescues them from death
and keeps them alive in times
of famine.
[20] We put our hope in the LORD.
He is our help and our shield.
[21] In him our hearts rejoice,
for we trust in his holy name.
[22] Let your unfailing love surround us,
LORD,
for our hope is in you alone.

PROVERBS 21:11-12

If you punish a mocker, the simpleminded become wise; if you instruct the wise, they will be all the wiser. ◻ The Righteous One* knows what is going on in the homes of the wicked; he will bring disaster on them.

21:12 Or *The righteous man.*

NEHEMIAH 9:22–10:39
Who hasn't made a recommitment of some kind?
Whether it was a New Year's resolution or a healing
of a relationship, most of us know the feeling of
saying, "I'm going to do better this time." That was
what was required of the Jews here.

"**T**hen you [the Lord] helped our
ancestors conquer kingdoms and
nations, and you placed your people in
every corner of the land.* They took
over the land of King Sihon of
Heshbon and the land of King Og of
Bashan. 23 You made their descendants
as numerous as the stars in the sky
and brought them into the land you
had promised to their ancestors.

24"They went in and took
possession of the land. You subdued
whole nations before them. Even the
Canaanites, who inhabited the land,
were powerless! Your people could
deal with these nations and their
kings as they pleased. 25Our ancestors
captured fortified cities and fertile
land. They took over houses full of
good things, with cisterns already dug
and vineyards and olive groves and
fruit trees in abundance. So they ate
until they were full and grew fat and
enjoyed themselves in all your
blessings.

26"But despite all this, they were
disobedient and rebelled against you.
They turned their backs on your Law,
they killed your prophets who warned
them to return to you, and they
committed terrible blasphemies.
27So you handed them over to their
enemies, who made them suffer. But
in their time of trouble they cried to
you, and you heard them from heaven.
In your great mercy, you sent them
liberators who rescued them from
their enemies.

28"But as soon as they were at peace,
your people again committed evil in
your sight, and once more you let their
enemies conquer them. Yet whenever
your people turned and cried to you
again for help, you listened once more

from heaven. In your wonderful
mercy, you rescued them many times!

29"You warned them to return to
your Law, but they became proud
and obstinate and disobeyed your
commands. They did not follow your
regulations, by which people will find
life if only they obey. They stubbornly
turned their backs on you and refused
to listen. 30In your love, you were
patient with them for many years.
You sent your Spirit, who warned
them through the prophets. But still
they wouldn't listen! So once again
you allowed the peoples of the land
to conquer them. 31But in your great
mercy, you did not destroy them
completely or abandon them forever.
What a gracious and merciful God
you are!

32"And now, our God, the great and
mighty and awesome God, who keeps
his covenant of unfailing love, do not
let all the hardships we have suffered
seem insignificant to you. Great
trouble has come upon us and upon
our kings and leaders and priests and
prophets and ancestors—all of your
people—from the days when the kings
of Assyria first triumphed over us
until now. 33Every time you punished
us you were being just. We have
sinned greatly, and you gave us only
what we deserved. 34Our kings,
leaders, priests, and ancestors did
not obey your Law or listen to the
warnings in your commands and laws.
35Even while they had their own
kingdom, they did not serve you,
though you showered your goodness
on them. You gave them a large, fertile
land, but they refused to turn from
their wickedness.

36"So now today we are slaves in
the land of plenty that you gave our
ancestors for their enjoyment! We are
slaves here in this good land. 37 The
lush produce of this land piles up in
the hands of the kings whom you have
set over us because of our sins. They

have power over us and our livestock. We serve them at their pleasure, and we are in great misery."

38*The people responded, "In view of all this,* we are making a solemn promise and putting it in writing. On this sealed document are the names of our leaders and Levites and priests."

10:1*THE document was ratified and sealed with the following names:

The governor:
Nehemiah son of Hacaliah, and also Zedekiah.
2 The following priests:
Seraiah, Azariah, Jeremiah, 3Pashhur, Amariah, Malkijah, 4Hattush, Shebaniah, Malluch, 5Harim, Meremoth, Obadiah, 6Daniel, Ginnethon, Baruch, 7Meshullam, Abijah, Mijamin, 8Maaziah, Bilgai, and Shemaiah. These were the priests.
9 The following Levites:
Jeshua son of Azaniah, Binnui from the family of Henadad, Kadmiel, 10and their fellow Levites: Shebaniah, Hodiah, Kelita, Pelaiah, Hanan, 11Mica, Rehob, Hashabiah, 12Zaccur, Sherebiah, Shebaniah, 13Hodiah, Bani, and Beninu.
14The following leaders:
Parosh, Pahath-moab, Elam, Zattu, Bani, 15Bunni, Azgad, Bebai, 16Adonijah, Bigvai, Adin, 17Ater, Hezekiah, Azzur, 18Hodiah, Hashum, Bezai, 19Hariph, Anathoth, Nebai, 20Magpiash, Meshullam, Hezir, 21Meshezabel, Zadok, Jaddua, 22Pelatiah, Hanan, Anaiah, 23Hoshea, Hananiah, Hasshub, 24Hallohesh, Pilha, Shobek, 25Rehum, Hashabnah, Maaseiah, 26Ahiah, Hanan, Anan, 27Malluch, Harim, and Baanah.

28Then the rest of the people—the priests, Levites, gatekeepers, singers, Temple servants, and all who had separated themselves from the pagan people of the land in order to obey the Law of God, together with their wives, sons, daughters, and all who were old enough to understand—29joined their leaders and bound themselves with an oath. They swore a curse on themselves if they failed to obey the Law of God as issued by his servant Moses. They solemnly promised to carefully follow all the commands, regulations, and decrees of the LORD our Lord:

30"We promise not to let our daughters marry the pagan people of the land, and not to let our sons marry their daughters.
31"We also promise that if the people of the land should bring any merchandise or grain to be sold on the Sabbath or on any other holy day, we will refuse to buy it. Every seventh year we will let our land rest, and we will cancel all debts owed to us.
32"In addition, we promise to obey the command to pay the annual Temple tax of one-eighth of an ounce of silver* for the care of the Temple of our God. 33This will provide for the Bread of the Presence; for the regular grain offerings and burnt offerings; for the offerings on the Sabbaths, the new moon celebrations, and the annual festivals; for the holy offerings; and for the sin offerings to make atonement for Israel. It will provide for everything necessary for the work of the Temple of our God.
34"We have cast sacred lots to determine when—at regular times each year—the families of the priests, Levites, and the common people should bring wood to God's Temple to be burned on the altar of the LORD our God, as is written in the Law.
35"We promise to bring the first part of every harvest to the LORD's Temple year after year—whether it be a crop from the soil or from our fruit trees. 36We agree to give God our oldest sons and the firstborn of all our herds and flocks, as prescribed in the Law. We will present them to the priests who minister in the Temple of our God. 37We will store the produce in the storerooms of the Temple of our God. We will bring the best of our flour and other grain offerings, the best of our fruit, and the best of our new wine and olive oil. And we promise to bring to the Levites a tenth of everything our land produces, for it is the Levites who collect the tithes in all our rural towns.

³⁸"A priest—a descendant of Aaron—will be with the Levites as they receive these tithes. And a tenth of all that is collected as tithes will be delivered by the Levites to the Temple of our God and placed in the storerooms. ³⁹The people and the Levites must bring these offerings of grain, new wine, and olive oil to the storerooms and place them in the sacred containers near the ministering priests, the gatekeepers, and the singers.

"We promise together not to neglect the Temple of our God."

9:22 The meaning of the Hebrew is uncertain.
9:38a Verse 9:38 is numbered 10:1 in Hebrew text.
9:38b Or *In spite of all this.*   10:1 Verses 10:1-39 are numbered 10:2-40 in Hebrew text.   10:32 Hebrew *tax of ⅓ of a shekel* [4 grams].

1 CORINTHIANS 9:19–10:13
As an apostle, Paul could have demanded certain things from the churches he started and oversaw. He gladly denied these rights so that his ministry would not be hindered in any way.

Even though I [Paul] am a free man with no master, I have become a slave to all people to bring many to Christ. ²⁰When I was with the Jews, I lived like a Jew to bring the Jews to Christ. When I was with those who follow the Jewish law, I too lived under that law. Even though I am not subject to the law, I did this so I could bring to Christ those who are under the law. ²¹When I am with

the Gentiles who do not follow the Jewish law,* I too live apart from that law so I can bring them to Christ. But I do not ignore the law of God; I obey the law of Christ.

²²When I am with those who are weak, I share their weakness, for I want to bring the weak to Christ. Yes, I try to find common ground with everyone, doing everything I can to save some. ²³I do everything to spread the Good News and share in its blessings.

²⁴Don't you realize that in a race everyone runs, but only one person gets the prize? So run to win! ²⁵All athletes are disciplined in their training. They do it to win a prize that will fade away, but we do it for an eternal prize. ²⁶So I run with purpose in every step. I am not just shadowboxing. ²⁷I discipline my body like an athlete, training it to do what it should. Otherwise, I fear that after preaching to others I myself might be disqualified.

10:¹I DON'T want you to forget, dear brothers and sisters,* about our ancestors in the wilderness long ago. All of them were guided by a cloud that moved ahead of them, and all of them walked through the sea on dry ground. ²In the cloud and in the sea, all of them were baptized as followers of Moses. ³All of them ate the same spiritual food, ⁴and all of them drank the same spiritual water. For they drank from the spiritual rock that traveled with them,

Resisting temptation

HOW WE LIVE

1 CORINTHIANS 10:13 You don't have to look far to find temptation. Actually, all you have to do is try to quit a bad habit. Suddenly the reality of temptation is all too clear. The appeal of doing what we shouldn't is a part of our sinful nature. Even as a new believer, old temptations linger. Maybe even some new ones have emerged. You want to please God, but the temptation to sin can be very strong. What can you do? • Paul offers assurance. Not only does God make sure that your temptations are not too strong for you, he also provides you with a way out. In other words, the temptation will loom very large in front of you, but take your focus off of it for a moment and look around. You will see it—the way out. You just have to learn where to look and what to look for. • You can take God at his word. In those white-knuckle moments of temptation when you are simply trying to resist and hold on—hold on to God. Ask him to show you that escape hatch. And then run for all you're worth!

and that rock was Christ. ⁵ Yet God was not pleased with most of them, and their bodies were scattered in the wilderness.

⁶These things happened as a warning to us, so that we would not crave evil things as they did, ⁷or worship idols as some of them did. As the Scriptures say, "The people celebrated with feasting and drinking, and they indulged in pagan revelry."* ⁸And we must not engage in sexual immorality as some of them did, causing 23,000 of them to die in one day.

⁹Nor should we put Christ* to the test, as some of them did and then died from snakebites. ¹⁰And don't grumble as some of them did, and then were destroyed by the angel of death. ¹¹These things happened to them as examples for us. They were written down to warn us who live at the end of the age.

¹²If you think you are standing strong, be careful not to fall. ¹³The temptations in your life are no different from what others experience. And God is faithful. He will not allow the temptation to be more than you can stand. When you are tempted, he will show you a way out so that you can endure.

9:21 Greek *those without the law.*   **10:1** Greek *brothers.*
10:7 Exod 32:6.   **10:9** Some manuscripts read *the Lord.*

*PSALM 34:1-10
A psalm of David, regarding the time he pretended to be insane in front of Abimelech, who sent him away.

¹ **I** will praise the LORD at all times.
    I will constantly speak his praises.

² I will boast only in the LORD;
    let all who are helpless take heart.
³ Come, let us tell of the LORD's
        greatness;
    let us exalt his name together.

⁴ I prayed to the LORD, and he answered
        me.
    He freed me from all my fears.
⁵ Those who look to him for help will
        be radiant with joy;
    no shadow of shame will darken
        their faces.

⁶ In my desperation I prayed, and the
        LORD listened;
    he saved me from all my troubles.
⁷ For the angel of the LORD is a guard;
    he surrounds and defends all who
        fear him.

⁸ Taste and see that the LORD is good.
    Oh, the joys of those who take
        refuge in him!
⁹ Fear the LORD, you his godly people,
    for those who fear him will have all
        they need.
¹⁰ Even strong young lions sometimes
        go hungry,
    but those who trust in the LORD will
        lack no good thing.

34 This psalm is a Hebrew acrostic poem; each verse begins with a successive letter of the Hebrew alphabet.

PROVERBS 21:13
Those who shut their ears to the cries of the poor will be ignored in their own time of need.

AUGUST**16**

NEHEMIAH 11:1–12:26
With the city walls rebuilt, there was a need to repopulate the city. Some were chosen by lot to move back to Jerusalem. Others volunteered.

The leaders of the people were living in Jerusalem, the holy city. A tenth of the people from the other towns of Judah and Benjamin were chosen by sacred lots to live there, too, while the rest stayed where

they were. ²And the people commended everyone who volunteered to resettle in Jerusalem.

³Here is a list of the names of the provincial officials who came to live in Jerusalem. (Most of the people, priests, Levites, Temple servants, and descendants of Solomon's servants continued to live in their own homes in the various towns of Judah,

⁴but some of the people from Judah and Benjamin resettled in Jerusalem.)

From the tribe of Judah:

Athaiah son of Uzziah, son of Zechariah, son of Amariah, son of Shephatiah, son of Mahalalel, of the family of Perez. ⁵Also Maaseiah son of Baruch, son of Col-hozeh, son of Hazaiah, son of Adaiah, son of Joiarib, son of Zechariah, of the family of Shelah.* ⁶There were 468 descendants of Perez who lived in Jerusalem—all outstanding men.

⁷From the tribe of Benjamin:

Sallu son of Meshullam, son of Joed, son of Pedaiah, son of Kolaiah, son of Maaseiah, son of Ithiel, son of Jeshaiah. ⁸After him were Gabbai and Sallai and a total of 928 relatives. ⁹Their chief officer was Joel son of Zicri, who was assisted by Judah son of Hassenuah, second-in-command over the city.

¹⁰From the priests:

Jedaiah son of Joiarib; Jakin; ¹¹and Seraiah son of Hilkiah, son of Meshullam, son of Zadok, son of Meraioth, son of Ahitub, the supervisor of the Temple of God. ¹²Also 822 of their associates, who worked at the Temple. Also Adaiah son of Jeroham, son of Pelaliah, son of Amzi, son of Zechariah, son of Pashhur, son of Malkijah, ¹³along with 242 of his associates, who were heads of their families. Also Amashsai son of Azarel, son of Ahzai, son of Meshillemoth, son of Immer, ¹⁴and 128 of his* outstanding associates. Their chief officer was Zabdiel son of Haggedolim.

¹⁵From the Levites:

Shemaiah son of Hasshub, son of Azrikam, son of Hashabiah, son of Bunni. ¹⁶Also Shabbethai and Jozabad, who were in charge of the work outside the Temple of God. ¹⁷Also Mattaniah son of Mica, son of Zabdi, a descendant of Asaph, who led in thanksgiving and prayer. Also Bakbukiah, who was Mattaniah's assistant, and Abda son of Shammua, son of Galal, son of Jeduthun. ¹⁸In all, there were 284 Levites in the holy city.

¹⁹From the gatekeepers:

Akkub, Talmon, and 172 of their associates, who guarded the gates.

²⁰The other priests, Levites, and the rest of the Israelites lived wherever their family inheritance was located in any of the towns of Judah. ²¹The Temple servants, however, whose leaders were Ziha and Gishpa, all lived on the hill of Ophel.

²²The chief officer of the Levites in Jerusalem was Uzzi son of Bani, son of Hashabiah, son of Mattaniah, son of Mica, a descendant of Asaph, whose family served as singers at God's Temple. ²³Their daily responsibilities were carried out according to the terms of a royal command.

²⁴Pethahiah son of Meshezabel, a descendant of Zerah son of Judah, was the royal adviser in all matters of public administration.

²⁵As for the surrounding villages with their open fields, some of the people of Judah lived in Kiriath-arba with its settlements, Dibon with its settlements, and Jekabzeel with its villages. ²⁶They also lived in Jeshua, Moladah, Beth-pelet, ²⁷Hazar-shual, Beersheba with its settlements, ²⁸Ziklag, and Meconah with its settlements. ²⁹They also lived in En-rimmon, Zorah, Jarmuth, ³⁰Zanoah, and Adullam with their surrounding villages. They also lived in Lachish with its nearby fields and Azekah with its surrounding villages. So the people of Judah were living all the way from Beersheba in the south to the valley of Hinnom.

³¹Some of the people of Benjamin lived at Geba, Micmash, Aija, and Bethel with its settlements. ³²They also lived in Anathoth, Nob, Ananiah, ³³Hazor, Ramah, Gittaim, ³⁴Hadid, Zeboim, Neballat, ³⁵Lod, Ono, and the Valley of Craftsmen.* ³⁶Some of the Levites who lived in Judah were sent to live with the tribe of Benjamin.

12:1HERE is the list of the priests and Levites who returned with Zerubbabel son of Shealtiel and Jeshua the high priest:

Seraiah, Jeremiah, Ezra,
² Amariah, Malluch, Hattush,
³ Shecaniah, Harim,* Meremoth,
⁴ Iddo, Ginnethon,* Abijah,
⁵ Miniamin, Moadiah,* Bilgah,

⁶ Shemaiah, Joiarib, Jedaiah,
⁷ Sallu, Amok, Hilkiah, and Jedaiah.
These were the leaders of the priests and their associates in the days of Jeshua.

⁸The Levites who returned with them were Jeshua, Binnui, Kadmiel, Sherebiah, Judah, and Mattaniah, who with his associates was in charge of the songs of thanksgiving. ⁹Their associates, Bakbukiah and Unni, stood opposite them during the service.

¹⁰ Jeshua the high priest was the father of Joiakim.
Joiakim was the father of Eliashib.
Eliashib was the father of Joiada.
¹¹ Joiada was the father of Johanan.*
Johanan was the father of Jaddua.

¹²Now when Joiakim was high priest, the family leaders of the priests were as follows:

Meraiah was leader of the family of Seraiah.
Hananiah was leader of the family of Jeremiah.
¹³ Meshullam was leader of the family of Ezra.
Jehohanan was leader of the family of Amariah.
¹⁴ Jonathan was leader of the family of Malluch.*
Joseph was leader of the family of Shecaniah.*
¹⁵ Adna was leader of the family of Harim.
Helkai was leader of the family of Meremoth.*
¹⁶ Zechariah was leader of the family of Iddo.
Meshullam was leader of the family of Ginnethon.
¹⁷ Zicri was leader of the family of Abijah.
There was also a* leader of the family of Miniamin.
Piltai was leader of the family of Moadiah.
¹⁸ Shammua was leader of the family of Bilgah.
Jehonathan was leader of the family of Shemaiah.
¹⁹ Mattenai was leader of the family of Joiarib.

Uzzi was leader of the family of Jedaiah.
²⁰ Kallai was leader of the family of Sallu.*
Eber was leader of the family of Amok.
²¹ Hashabiah was leader of the family of Hilkiah.
Nethanel was leader of the family of Jedaiah.

²²A record of the Levite families was kept during the years when Eliashib, Joiada, Johanan, and Jaddua served as high priest. Another record of the priests was kept during the reign of Darius the Persian.* ²³A record of the heads of the Levite families was kept in *The Book of History* down to the days of Johanan, the grandson* of Eliashib.

²⁴These were the family leaders of the Levites: Hashabiah, Sherebiah, Jeshua, Binnui,* Kadmiel, and other associates, who stood opposite them during the ceremonies of praise and thanksgiving, one section responding to the other, as commanded by David, the man of God. ²⁵This included Mattaniah, Bakbukiah, and Obadiah.

Meshullam, Talmon, and Akkub were the gatekeepers in charge of the storerooms at the gates. ²⁶These all served in the days of Joiakim son of Jeshua, son of Jehozadak,* and in the days of Nehemiah the governor and of Ezra the priest and scribe.

11:5 Hebrew *son of the Shilonite.*   11:14 As in Greek version; Hebrew reads *their.*   11:35 Or *and Ge-harashim.*
12:3 Hebrew *Rehum;* compare 7:42; 12:15; Ezra 2:39.
12:4 As in some Hebrew manuscripts and Latin Vulgate (see also 12:16); most Hebrew manuscripts read *Gennethoi.*
12:5 Hebrew *Mijamin, Maadiah;* compare 12:17.
12:11 Hebrew *Jonathan;* compare 12:22.   12:14a As in Greek version (see also 10:4; 12:2); Hebrew reads *Malluchi.*
12:14b As in many Hebrew manuscripts, some Greek manuscripts, and Syriac version (see also 12:3); most Hebrew manuscripts read *Shebaniah.*   12:15 As in some Greek manuscripts (see also 12:3); Hebrew reads *Meraioth.*
12:17 Hebrew lacks the name of this family leader.
12:20 Hebrew *Sallai;* compare 12:7.   12:22 *Darius the Persian* is probably Darius II, who reigned 423–404 B.C., or possibly Darius III, who reigned 336–331 B.C.
12:23 Hebrew *son;* compare 12:10-11.   12:24 Hebrew *son of* (i.e., *ben*), which should probably be read here as the proper name Binnui; compare Ezra 3:9 and the note there.
12:26 Hebrew *Jozadak,* a variant spelling of Jehozadak.

---

1 CORINTHIANS 10:14-33

The Christian life boils down to this: Whatever you do, do it to the glory of God. That statement carries both great freedom and great responsibility.

So, my dear friends, flee from the worship of idols. ¹⁵You are reasonable people. Decide for yourselves if what I am saying is true. [16]When we bless the cup at the Lord's Table, aren't we sharing in the blood of Christ? And when we break the bread, aren't we sharing in the body of Christ? [17]And though we are many, we all eat from one loaf of bread, showing that we are one body. [18]Think about the people of Israel. Weren't they united by eating the sacrifices at the altar?

[19]What am I trying to say? Am I saying that food offered to idols has some significance, or that the idols are real gods? [20]No, not at all. I am saying that these sacrifices are offered to demons, not to God. And I don't want you to participate with demons. [21]You cannot drink from the cup of the Lord and from the cup of demons, too. You cannot eat at the Lord's Table and at the table of demons, too. [22]What? Do we dare to rouse the Lord's jealousy? Do you think we are stronger than he is?

[23]You say, "I am allowed to do anything"*—but not everything is good for you. You say, "I am allowed to do anything"—but not everything is beneficial. [24]Don't be concerned for your own good but for the good of others.

[25]So you may eat any meat that is sold in the marketplace without raising questions of conscience. [26]For "the earth is the LORD's, and everything in it."*

[27]If someone who isn't a believer asks you home for dinner, accept the invitation if you want to. Eat whatever is offered to you without raising questions of conscience. [28](But suppose someone tells you, "This meat was offered to an idol." Don't eat it, out of consideration for the conscience of the one who told you. [29]It might not be a matter of conscience for you, but it is for the other person.) For why should my freedom be limited by what someone else thinks? [30]If I can thank God for the food and enjoy it, why should I be condemned for eating it?

[31]So whether you eat or drink, or whatever you do, do it all for the glory of God. [32]Don't give offense to Jews or Gentiles* or the church of God. [33]I, too, try to please everyone in everything I do. I don't just do what is best for me; I do what is best for others so that many may be saved.

10:23 Greek *All things are lawful;* also in 10:23b.
10:26 Ps 24:1.   **10:32** Greek *or Greeks.*

PSALM 34:11-22

Come, my children, and listen to me,
    and I will teach you to fear the
    LORD.
[12] Does anyone want to live a life
    that is long and prosperous?

HOW WE LIVE

Living responsibly

1 CORINTHIANS 10:23-31   As a Christian, you are now part of the body of Christ and you have a certain responsibility to other Christians. Paul's point in this chapter is that when it comes to gray areas, believers need to be understanding and gracious to one another. There is room for different convictions among believers. For example, in that day, the issue of eating meat offered to idols was a sticking point for the believers. Paul explained that it will be okay for some of them because they know that idols aren't even real anyway. However, others might not be able to eat that same meat with a clear conscience. Since this was not a black and white issue, there was room for differing practices. Paul's only qualification was that those who could eat such meat with a clear conscience needed to take care not to lead a weaker believer to violate his or her conscience by eating it.   • Likewise, we, at times, must be willing to give up certain liberties to avoid causing someone else to sin. There are higher values and higher purposes than your own freedom and wants. Let love and seeking the "glory of God" be your guide in all your actions. Then whatever you do will bring honor to God.

13 Then keep your tongue from speaking
  evil
  and your lips from telling lies!
14 Turn away from evil and do good.
  Search for peace, and work to
  maintain it.

15 The eyes of the LORD watch over those
  who do right;
  his ears are open to their cries for
  help.
16 But the LORD turns his face against
  those who do evil;
  he will erase their memory from
  the earth.
17 The LORD hears his people when they
  call to him for help.
  He rescues them from all their
  troubles.
18 The LORD is close to the
  brokenhearted;
  he rescues those whose spirits are
  crushed.

19 The righteous person faces many
  troubles,
  but the LORD comes to the rescue
  each time.
20 For the LORD protects the bones
  of the righteous;
  not one of them is broken!

21 Calamity will surely overtake the
  wicked,
  and those who hate the righteous
  will be punished.
22 But the LORD will redeem those who
  serve him.
  No one who takes refuge in him will
  be condemned.

PROVERBS 21:14-16
A secret gift calms anger; a bribe under the table pacifies fury. □ Justice is a joy to the godly, but it terrifies evildoers. □ The person who strays from common sense will end up in the company of the dead.

AUGUST**17**

NEHEMIAH 12:27–13:31
When the wall was finally completed, the joy of the people's celebration could be heard for miles. The joy of forgiveness and restoration is difficult to contain.

For the dedication of the new wall of Jerusalem, the Levites throughout the land were asked to come to Jerusalem to assist in the ceremonies. They were to take part in the joyous occasion with their songs of thanksgiving and with the music of cymbals, harps, and lyres. 28The singers were brought together from the region around Jerusalem and from the villages of the Netophathites. 29They also came from Bethgilgal and the rural areas near Geba and Azmaveth, for the singers had built their own settlements around Jerusalem. 30The priests and Levites first purified themselves; then they purified the people, the gates, and the wall.

31I led the leaders of Judah to the top of the wall and organized two large choirs to give thanks. One of the choirs proceeded southward* along the top of the wall to the Dung Gate. 32Hoshaiah and half the leaders of Judah followed them, 33along with Azariah, Ezra, Meshullam, 34Judah, Benjamin, Shemaiah, and Jeremiah. 35Then came some priests who played trumpets, including Zechariah son of Jonathan, son of Shemaiah, son of Mattaniah, son of Micaiah, son of Zaccur, a descendant of Asaph. 36And Zechariah's colleagues were Shemaiah, Azarel, Milalai, Gilalai, Maai, Nethanel, Judah, and Hanani. They used the musical instruments prescribed by David, the man of God. Ezra the scribe led this procession. 37At the Fountain Gate they went straight up the steps on the ascent of the city wall toward the City of David. They passed the house of David and then proceeded to the Water Gate on the east.

38The second choir giving thanks went northward* around the other way to meet them. I followed them, together with the other half of the people, along the top of the wall past the Tower of the Ovens to the Broad Wall, [39] then past the Ephraim Gate to the Old City Gate,* past the Fish Gate and the Tower of Hananel, and on to the Tower of the Hundred. Then we continued on to the Sheep Gate and stopped at the Guard Gate.

[40] The two choirs that were giving thanks then proceeded to the Temple of God, where they took their places. So did I, together with the group of leaders who were with me. [41] We went together with the trumpet-playing priests—Eliakim, Maaseiah, Miniamin, Micaiah, Elioenai, Zechariah, and Hananiah—[42] and the singers—Maaseiah, Shemaiah, Eleazar, Uzzi, Jehohanan, Malkijah, Elam, and Ezer. They played and sang loudly under the direction of Jezrahiah the choir director.

[43] Many sacrifices were offered on that joyous day, for God had given the people cause for great joy. The women and children also participated in the celebration, and the joy of the people of Jerusalem could be heard far away.

[44] On that day men were appointed to be in charge of the storerooms for the offerings, the first part of the harvest, and the tithes. They were responsible to collect from the fields outside the towns the portions required by the Law for the priests and Levites. For all the people of Judah took joy in the priests and Levites and their work. [45] They performed the service of their God and the service of purification, as commanded by David and his son Solomon, and so did the singers and the gatekeepers. [46] The custom of having choir directors to lead the choirs in hymns of praise and thanksgiving to God began long ago in the days of David and Asaph. [47] So now, in the days of Zerubbabel and of Nehemiah, all Israel brought a daily supply of food for the singers, the gatekeepers, and the Levites. The Levites, in turn, gave a portion of what they received to the priests, the descendants of Aaron.

[13:1] ON that same day, as the Book of Moses was being read to the people, the passage was found that said no Ammonite or Mo-

abite should ever be permitted to enter the assembly of God.* [2] For they had not provided the Israelites with food and water in the wilderness. Instead, they hired Balaam to curse them, though our God turned the curse into a blessing. [3] When this passage of the Law was read, all those of foreign descent were immediately excluded from the assembly.

[4] Before this had happened, Eliashib the priest, who had been appointed as supervisor of the storerooms of the Temple of our God and who was also a relative of Tobiah, [5] had converted a large storage room and placed it at Tobiah's disposal. The room had previously been used for storing the grain offerings, the frankincense, various articles for the Temple, and the tithes of grain, new wine, and olive oil (which were prescribed for the Levites, the singers, and the gatekeepers), as well as the offerings for the priests.

[6] I was not in Jerusalem at that time, for I had returned to King Artaxerxes of Babylon in the thirty-second year of his reign,* though I later asked his permission to return. [7] When I arrived back in Jerusalem, I learned about Eliashib's evil deed in providing Tobiah with a room in the courtyards of the Temple of God. [8] I became very upset and threw all of Tobiah's belongings out of the room. [9] Then I demanded that the rooms be purified, and I brought back the articles for God's Temple, the grain offerings, and the frankincense.

[10] I also discovered that the Levites had not been given their prescribed portions of food, so they and the singers who were to conduct the worship services had all returned to work their fields. [11] I immediately confronted the leaders and demanded, "Why has the Temple of God been neglected?" Then I called all the Levites back again and restored them to their proper duties. [12] And once more all the people of Judah began bringing their tithes of grain, new wine, and olive oil to the Temple storerooms.

[13] I assigned supervisors for the storerooms: Shelemiah the priest, Zadok the scribe, and Pedaiah, one of the Levites. And I appointed Hanan son of Zaccur and grandson of Mattaniah as their assistant.

These men had an excellent reputation, and it was their job to make honest distributions to their fellow Levites.

14Remember this good deed, O my God, and do not forget all that I have faithfully done for the Temple of my God and its services.

15In those days I saw men of Judah treading out their winepresses on the Sabbath. They were also bringing in grain, loading it on donkeys, and bringing their wine, grapes, figs, and all sorts of produce to Jerusalem to sell on the Sabbath. So I rebuked them for selling their produce on that day. 16Some men from Tyre, who lived in Jerusalem, were bringing in fish and all kinds of merchandise. They were selling it on the Sabbath to the people of Judah—and in Jerusalem at that!

17So I confronted the nobles of Judah. "Why are you profaning the Sabbath in this evil way?" I asked. 18"Wasn't it just this sort of thing that your ancestors did that caused our God to bring all this trouble upon us and our city? Now you are bringing even more wrath upon Israel by permitting the Sabbath to be desecrated in this way!"

19Then I commanded that the gates of Jerusalem should be shut as darkness fell every Friday evening,* not to be opened until the Sabbath ended. I sent some of my own servants to guard the gates so that no merchandise could be brought in on the Sabbath day. 20The merchants and tradesmen with a variety of wares camped outside Jerusalem once or twice. 21But I spoke sharply to them and said, "What are you doing out here, camping around the wall? If you do this again, I will arrest you!" And that was the last time they came on the Sabbath. 22Then I commanded the Levites to purify themselves and to guard the gates in order to preserve the holiness of the Sabbath.

Remember this good deed also, O my God! Have compassion on me according to your great and unfailing love.

23About the same time I realized that some of the men of Judah had married women from Ashdod, Ammon, and Moab.

24Furthermore, half their children spoke the language of Ashdod or of some other people and could not speak the language of Judah at all. 25So I confronted them and called down curses on them. I beat some of them and pulled out their hair. I made them swear in the name of God that they would not let their children intermarry with the pagan people of the land.

26"Wasn't this exactly what led King Solomon of Israel into sin?" I demanded. "There was no king from any nation who could compare to him, and God loved him and made him king over all Israel. But even he was led into sin by his foreign wives. 27How could you even think of committing this sinful deed and acting unfaithfully toward God by marrying foreign women?"

28One of the sons of Joiada son of Eliashib the high priest had married a daughter of Sanballat the Horonite, so I banished him from my presence.

29Remember them, O my God, for they have defiled the priesthood and the solemn vows of the priests and Levites.

30So I purged out everything foreign and assigned tasks to the priests and Levites, making certain that each knew his work. 31I also made sure that the supply of wood for the altar and the first portions of the harvest were brought at the proper times.

Remember this in my favor, O my God.

12:31 Hebrew *to the right.*   12:38 Hebrew *to the left.*   12:39 Or *the Mishneh Gate,* or *the Jeshanah Gate.*   13:1 See Deut 23:3-6.   13:6 King Artaxerxes of Persia is here identified as the king of Babylon because Persia had conquered the Babylonian Empire. The thirty-second year of Artaxerxes was 433 B.C.   13:19 Hebrew *on the day before the Sabbath.*

1 CORINTHIANS 11:1-16
Even as customs change, the basic truth remains that God is not the author of confusion, but of order. And everything is to be done for his glory and honor.

And you [Corinthians] should imitate me [Paul], just as I imitate Christ.

2I am so glad that you always keep me in your thoughts, and that you are following the teachings I passed on to you. 3But there is one thing I want you to know: The head of every man is Christ, the head of woman is man, and the head of Christ is God.* ⁴A man dishonors his head* if he covers his head while praying or prophesying. ⁵But a woman dishonors her head* if she prays or prophesies without a covering on her head, for this is the same as shaving her head. ⁶Yes, if she refuses to wear a head covering, she should cut off all her hair! But since it is shameful for a woman to have her hair cut or her head shaved, she should wear a covering.*

⁷A man should not wear anything on his head when worshiping, for man is made in God's image and reflects God's glory. And woman reflects man's glory. ⁸For the first man didn't come from woman, but the first woman came from man. ⁹And man was not made for woman, but woman was made for man. ¹⁰For this reason, and because the angels are watching, a woman should wear a covering on her head to show she is under authority.*

¹¹But among the Lord's people, women are not independent of men, and men are not independent of women. ¹²For although the first woman came from man, every other man was born from a woman, and everything comes from God.

¹³Judge for yourselves. Is it right for a woman to pray to God in public without covering her head? ¹⁴Isn't it obvious that it's disgraceful for a man to have long hair? ¹⁵And isn't long hair a woman's pride and joy? For it has been given to her as a covering. ¹⁶But if anyone wants to argue about this, I simply say that we have no other custom than this, and neither do God's other churches.

11:3 Or *to know: The source of every man is Christ, the source of woman is man, and the source of Christ is God.* Or *to know: Every man is responsible to Christ, a woman is responsible to her husband, and Christ is responsible to God.* 11:4 Or *dishonors Christ.* 11:5 Or *dishonors her husband.* 11:6 Or *should have long hair.* 11:10 Greek *should have an authority on her head.*

PSALM 35:1-16
A psalm of David.

¹ O LORD, oppose those who oppose me.
　　Fight those who fight against me.
² Put on your armor, and take up your shield.
　　Prepare for battle, and come to my aid.
³ Lift up your spear and javelin against those who pursue me.
　　Let me hear you say,
　　"I will give you victory!"

Praise and thanksgiving

NEHEMIAH 12:43 Most of us have attended sporting events between two evenly matched teams. Those in attendance who are rooting for their favorite team are avidly interested in the outcome, and they express their excitement in various ways. When their team scores, they erupt in spontaneous exclamations of joy. • Flashback a few centuries to Jerusalem in Nehemiah's day: When the city wall was finally rebuilt despite tremendous opposition, the people of Israel were not content to sit quietly by. When it came time to dedicate the wall, Nehemiah organized two large choirs to give thanks. Nehemiah 12:43 tells us that "God had given the people cause for great joy," and that "the joy of the people of Jerusalem could be heard far away." • How about you? Has God given you cause for great joy? One of the greatest privileges we have as his people is the ability to worship him with passionate, exuberant praise. It's not just about raising your hands or shouting "Amen!" While these elements may or may not be part of your own worship, God is more concerned that you not sit idly by while the "professionals" do your worship for you. Praise is not a spectator sport!

⁴ Bring shame and disgrace on those
trying to kill me;
turn them back and humiliate those
who want to harm me.
⁵ Blow them away like chaff in the wind—
a wind sent by the angel of the LORD.
⁶ Make their path dark and slippery,
with the angel of the LORD pursuing
them.
⁷ I did them no wrong, but they laid
a trap for me.
I did them no wrong, but they dug
a pit to catch me.
⁸ So let sudden ruin come upon them!
Let them be caught in the trap they
set for me!
Let them be destroyed in the pit
they dug for me.

⁹ Then I will rejoice in the LORD.
I will be glad because he rescues me.
¹⁰ With every bone in my body I will
praise him:
"LORD, who can compare with you?
Who else rescues the helpless from
the strong?
Who else protects the helpless and
poor from those who rob them?"

¹¹ Malicious witnesses testify against me.

They accuse me of crimes I know
nothing about.
¹² They repay me evil for good.
I am sick with despair.
¹³ Yet when they were ill, I grieved for
them.
I denied myself by fasting for them,
but my prayers returned
unanswered.
¹⁴ I was sad, as though they were my
friends or family,
as if I were grieving for my own
mother.
¹⁵ But they are glad now that I am in
trouble;
they gleefully join together against
me.
I am attacked by people I don't even
know;
they slander me constantly.
¹⁶ They mock me and call me names;
they snarl at me.

PROVERBS 21:17-18

Those who love pleasure become poor;
those who love wine and luxury will never
be rich. ☐ The wicked are punished in
place of the godly, and traitors in place of
the honest.

AUGUST**18**

ESTHER 1:1–3:15

Esther's story occurred while Judah was in exile in
Persia, prior to the events recorded in Ezra and Nehemiah. The Hebrew people had been exiled because
of their sin, but God did not abandon them. At times
he worked behind the scenes to protect the Jews.

These events happened in the days of King
Xerxes,* who reigned over 127 provinces
stretching from India to Ethiopia.* ²At
that time Xerxes ruled his empire from his
royal throne at the fortress of Susa. ³In the
third year of his reign, he gave a banquet
for all his nobles and officials. He invited
all the military officers of Persia and Me-

dia as well as the princes and nobles of
the provinces. ⁴The celebration lasted
180 days—a tremendous display of the
opulent wealth of his empire and the
pomp and splendor of his majesty.

⁵When it was all over, the king gave a
banquet for all the people, from the greatest to the least, who were in the fortress of
Susa. It lasted for seven days and was held
in the courtyard of the palace garden.
⁶The courtyard was beautifully decorated
with white cotton curtains and blue hang-
ings, which were fastened with white
linen cords and purple ribbons to silver

rings embedded in marble pillars. Gold and silver couches stood on a mosaic pavement of porphyry, marble, mother-of-pearl, and other costly stones.

[7]Drinks were served in gold goblets of many designs, and there was an abundance of royal wine, reflecting the king's generosity. [8]By edict of the king, no limits were placed on the drinking, for the king had instructed all his palace officials to serve each man as much as he wanted.

[9]At the same time, Queen Vashti gave a banquet for the women in the royal palace of King Xerxes.

[10]On the seventh day of the feast, when King Xerxes was in high spirits because of the wine, he told the seven eunuchs who attended him—Mehuman, Biztha, Harbona, Bigtha, Abagtha, Zethar, and Carcas—[11]to bring Queen Vashti to him with the royal crown on her head. He wanted the nobles and all the other men to gaze on her beauty, for she was a very beautiful woman. [12]But when they conveyed the king's order to Queen Vashti, she refused to come. This made the king furious, and he burned with anger.

[13]He immediately consulted with his wise advisers, who knew all the Persian laws and customs, for he always asked their advice. [14]The names of these men were Carshena, Shethar, Admatha, Tarshish, Meres, Marsena, and Memucan—seven nobles of Persia and Media. They met with the king regularly and held the highest positions in the empire.

[15]"What must be done to Queen Vashti?" the king demanded. "What penalty does the law provide for a queen who refuses to obey the king's orders, properly sent through his eunuchs?"

[16]Memucan answered the king and his nobles, "Queen Vashti has wronged not only the king but also every noble and citizen throughout your empire. [17]Women everywhere will begin to despise their husbands when they learn that Queen Vashti has refused to appear before the king. [18]Before this day is out, the wives of all the king's nobles throughout Persia and Media will hear what the queen did and will start treating their husbands the same way. There will be no end to their contempt and anger.

[19]"So if it please the king, we suggest that you issue a written decree, a law of the Persians and Medes that cannot be revoked. It should order that Queen Vashti be forever banished from the presence of King Xerxes, and that the king should choose another queen more worthy than she. [20]When this decree is published throughout the king's vast empire, husbands everywhere, whatever their rank, will receive proper respect from their wives!"

[21]The king and his nobles thought this made good sense, so he followed Memucan's counsel. [22]He sent letters to all parts of the empire, to each province in its own script and language, proclaiming that every man should be the ruler of his own home and should say whatever he pleases.*

[2:1]But after Xerxes' anger had subsided, he began thinking about Vashti and what she had done and the decree he had made. [2]So his personal attendants suggested, "Let us search the empire to find beautiful young virgins for the king. [3]Let the king appoint agents in each province to bring these beautiful young women into the royal harem at the fortress of Susa. Hegai, the king's eunuch in charge of the harem, will see that they are all given beauty treatments. [4]After that, the young woman who most pleases the king will be made queen instead of Vashti." This advice was very appealing to the king, so he put the plan into effect.

[5]At that time there was a Jewish man in the fortress of Susa whose name was Mordecai son of Jair. He was from the tribe of Benjamin and was a descendant of Kish and Shimei. [6]His family* had been among those who, with King Jehoiachin* of Judah, had been exiled from Jerusalem to Babylon by King Nebuchadnezzar. [7]This man had a very beautiful and lovely young cousin, Hadassah, who was also called Esther. When her father and mother died, Mordecai adopted her into his family and raised her as his own daughter.

[8]As a result of the king's decree, Esther, along with many other young women, was brought to the king's harem at the fortress of Susa and placed in Hegai's care. [9]Hegai

was very impressed with Esther and treated her kindly. He quickly ordered a special menu for her and provided her with beauty treatments. He also assigned her seven maids specially chosen from the king's palace, and he moved her and her maids into the best place in the harem.

¹⁰Esther had not told anyone of her nationality and family background, because Mordecai had directed her not to do so. ¹¹Every day Mordecai would take a walk near the courtyard of the harem to find out about Esther and what was happening to her.

¹²Before each young woman was taken to the king's bed, she was given the prescribed twelve months of beauty treatments—six months with oil of myrrh, followed by six months with special perfumes and ointments. ¹³When it was time for her to go to the king's palace, she was given her choice of whatever clothing or jewelry she wanted to take from the harem. ¹⁴That evening she was taken to the king's private rooms, and the next morning she was brought to the second harem,* where the king's wives lived. There she would be under the care of Shaashgaz, the king's eunuch in charge of the concubines. She would never go to the king again unless he had especially enjoyed her and requested her by name.

¹⁵Esther was the daughter of Abihail, who was Mordecai's uncle. (Mordecai had adopted his younger cousin Esther.) When it was Esther's turn to go to the king, she accepted the advice of Hegai, the eunuch in charge of the harem. She asked for nothing except what he suggested, and she was admired by everyone who saw her.

¹⁶Esther was taken to King Xerxes at the royal palace in early winter* of the seventh year of his reign. ¹⁷And the king loved Esther more than any of the other young women. He was so delighted with her that he set the royal crown on her head and declared her queen instead of Vashti. ¹⁸To celebrate the occasion, he gave a great banquet in Esther's honor for all his nobles and officials, declaring a public holiday for the provinces and giving generous gifts to everyone.

¹⁹Even after all the young women had

been transferred to the second harem* and Mordecai had become a palace official,* ²⁰Esther continued to keep her family background and nationality a secret. She was still following Mordecai's directions, just as she did when she lived in his home.

²¹One day as Mordecai was on duty at the king's gate, two of the king's eunuchs, Bigthana* and Teresh—who were guards at the door of the king's private quarters—became angry at King Xerxes and plotted to assassinate him. ²²But Mordecai heard about the plot and gave the information to Queen Esther. She then told the king about it and gave Mordecai credit for the report. ²³When an investigation was made and Mordecai's story was found to be true, the two men were impaled on a sharpened pole. This was all recorded in *The Book of the History of King Xerxes' Reign.*

³:¹Some time later King Xerxes promoted Haman son of Hammedatha the Agagite over all the other nobles, making him the most powerful official in the empire. ²All the king's officials would bow down before Haman to show him respect whenever he passed by, for so the king had commanded. But Mordecai refused to bow down or show him respect.

³Then the palace officials at the king's gate asked Mordecai, "Why are you disobeying the king's command?" ⁴They spoke to him day after day, but still he refused to comply with the order. So they spoke to Haman about this to see if he would tolerate Mordecai's conduct, since Mordecai had told them he was a Jew.

⁵When Haman saw that Mordecai would not bow down or show him respect, he was filled with rage. ⁶He had learned of Mordecai's nationality, so he decided it was not enough to lay hands on Mordecai alone. Instead, he looked for a way to destroy all the Jews throughout the entire empire of Xerxes.

⁷So in the month of April,* during the twelfth year of King Xerxes' reign, lots were cast in Haman's presence (the lots were called *purim*) to determine the best day and month to take action. And the day selected was March 7, nearly a year later.*

⁸Then Haman approached King Xerxes

and said, "There is a certain race of people scattered through all the provinces of your empire who keep themselves separate from everyone else. Their laws are different from those of any other people, and they refuse to obey the laws of the king. So it is not in the king's interest to let them live. ⁹If it please the king, issue a decree that they be destroyed, and I will give 10,000 large sacks* of silver to the government administrators to be deposited in the royal treasury."

¹⁰The king agreed, confirming his decision by removing his signet ring from his finger and giving it to Haman son of Hammedatha the Agagite, the enemy of the Jews. ¹¹The king said, "The money and the people are both yours to do with as you see fit."

¹²So on April 17* the king's secretaries were summoned, and a decree was written exactly as Haman dictated. It was sent to the king's highest officers, the governors of the respective provinces, and the nobles of each province in their own scripts and languages. The decree was written in the name of King Xerxes and sealed with the king's signet ring. ¹³Dispatches were sent by swift messengers into all the provinces of the empire, giving the order that all Jews—young and old, including women and children—must be killed, slaughtered, and annihilated on a single day. This was scheduled to happen on March 7 of the next year.* The property of the Jews would be given to those who killed them.

¹⁴A copy of this decree was to be issued as law in every province and proclaimed to all peoples, so that they would be ready to do their duty on the appointed day. ¹⁵At the king's command, the decree went out by swift messengers, and it was also proclaimed in the fortress of Susa. Then the king and Haman sat down to drink, but the city of Susa fell into confusion.

1:1a Hebrew *Ahasuerus,* another name for Xerxes; also throughout the book of Esther. Xerxes reigned 486–465 B.C. **1:1b** Hebrew *to Cush.* **1:22** Or *and should speak in the language of his own people.* **2:6a** Hebrew *He.* **2:6b** Hebrew *Jeconiah,* a variant spelling of Jehoiachin. **2:14** Or *to another part of the harem.* **2:16** Hebrew *in the tenth month, the month of Tebeth.* A number of dates in the book of Esther can be cross-checked with dates in surviving Persian records and related accurately to our modern calendar. This month of the ancient Hebrew lunar calendar occurred within the months of December 479 B.C. and January 478 B.C. **2:19a** The meaning of the Hebrew is uncertain. **2:19b** Hebrew *and Mordecai was sitting in the gate of the king.* **2:21** Hebrew *Bigthan;* compare 6:2. **3:7a** Hebrew *in the first month, the month of Nisan.* This month of the ancient Hebrew lunar calendar occurred within the months of April and May 474 B.C.; also see note on 2:16. **3:7b** As in Greek version, which reads *the thirteenth day of the twelfth month, the month of Adar* (see also 3:13). Hebrew reads *in the twelfth month,* of the ancient Hebrew lunar calendar. The date selected was March 7, 473 B.C.; also see note on 2:16. **3:9** Hebrew *10,000 talents,* about 375 tons or 340 metric tons in weight. **3:12** Hebrew *On the thirteenth day of the first month,* of the ancient Hebrew lunar calendar. This day was April 17, 474 B.C.; also see note on 2:16. **3:13** Hebrew *on the thirteenth day of the twelfth month, the month of Adar,* of the ancient Hebrew lunar calendar. The date selected was March 7, 473 B.C.; also see note on 2:16.

HOW WE LIVE

Following Jesus

ESTHER 2:18 What happened in Esther's life was beyond anything the young Jewish captive could have ever imagined. Who would have expected that she, a young foreigner, would become queen of an empire? Who could have believed that she would rise to this position at the very time when the existence of her people would be threatened? Who could have known that she would have the opportunity to save her entire nation? God is not mentioned overtly in this story, but his work behind the scenes is unmistakable. • Part of the adventure of following Jesus is allowing God to do the unexpected in our lives, too. We can trace his hand in the most unpredictable places if we look closely. We can follow Jesus in the least likely situations if we will commit our heart to doing so. And we can see God do amazing things if we are willing and open, no matter where we are or what we are doing. • What are you facing right now? Could it be that God brought you to this place at this time for a specific purpose? Stay connected with God and take the next step.

1 CORINTHIANS 11:17-34

The Lord's Supper, instituted by Jesus himself (Matthew 26:26-30, February 9), is a vital part of Christian community. The church in Corinth was not giving it the reverence and respect it deserves.

But in the following instructions, I [Paul] cannot praise you [Corinthians]. For it sounds as if more harm than good is done when you meet together. ¹⁸First, I hear that there are divisions among you when you meet as a church, and to some extent I believe it. ¹⁹But, of course, there must be divisions among you so that you who have God's approval will be recognized!

²⁰When you meet together, you are not really interested in the Lord's Supper. ²¹For some of you hurry to eat your own meal without sharing with others. As a result, some go hungry while others get drunk. ²²What? Don't you have your own homes for eating and drinking? Or do you really want to disgrace God's church and shame the poor? What am I supposed to say? Do you want me to praise you? Well, I certainly will not praise you for this!

²³For I pass on to you what I received from the Lord himself. On the night when he was betrayed, the Lord Jesus took some bread ²⁴and gave thanks to God for it. Then he broke it in pieces and said, "This is my body, which is given for you.* Do this to remember me." ²⁵In the same way, he took the cup of wine after supper, saying, "This cup is the new covenant between God and his people—an agreement confirmed with my blood. Do this to remember me as often as you drink it." ²⁶For every time you eat this bread and drink this cup, you are announcing the Lord's death until he comes again.

²⁷So anyone who eats this bread or drinks this cup of the Lord unworthily is guilty of sinning against* the body and blood of the Lord. ²⁸That is why you should examine yourself before eating the bread and drinking the cup. ²⁹For if you eat the bread or drink the cup without honoring the body of Christ,* you are eating and drinking God's judgment upon yourself. ³⁰That is why many of you are weak and sick and some have even died. ³¹But if we would examine ourselves, we would not be judged by God in this way.

³²Yet when we are judged by the Lord, we are being disciplined so that we will not be condemned along with the world.

³³So, my dear brothers and sisters,* when you gather for the Lord's Supper, wait for each other. ³⁴If you are really hungry, eat at home so you won't bring judgment upon yourselves when you meet together. I'll give you instructions about the other matters after I arrive.

11:24 Greek *which is for you;* other manuscripts read *which is broken for you.* 11:27 Or *is responsible for.* 11:29 Greek *the body;* other manuscripts read *the Lord's body.* 11:33 Greek *brothers.*

PSALM 35:17-28

How long, O Lord, will you look
   on and do nothing?
   Rescue me from their fierce attacks.
   Protect my life from these lions!
¹⁸ Then I will thank you in front of
      the great assembly.
   I will praise you before all the people.
¹⁹ Don't let my treacherous enemies
      rejoice over my defeat.
   Don't let those who hate me without
      cause gloat over my sorrow.
²⁰ They don't talk of peace;
   they plot against innocent people
      who mind their own business.
²¹ They shout, "Aha! Aha!
   With our own eyes we saw him do it!"

²² O LORD, you know all about this.
   Do not stay silent.
   Do not abandon me now, O Lord.
²³ Wake up! Rise to my defense!
   Take up my case, my God and
      my Lord.
²⁴ Declare me not guilty, O LORD my God,
      for you give justice.
   Don't let my enemies laugh about
      me in my troubles.
²⁵ Don't let them say, "Look, we got what
      we wanted!
   Now we will eat him alive!"

²⁶ May those who rejoice at my troubles
      be humiliated and disgraced.
   May those who triumph over me
      be covered with shame and dishonor.
²⁷ But give great joy to those who came
      to my defense.
   Let them continually say, "Great is
      the LORD,

who delights in blessing his servant
with peace!"

28 Then I will proclaim your justice,
and I will praise you all
day long.

ESTHER 4:1–7:10

*Esther was selected as queen because God had a
job for her to do. Because she realized her moment
in history—at "such a time as this"—she saved her
people from genocide.*

When Mordecai learned about all that
had been done, he tore his clothes, put on
burlap and ashes, and went out into the
city, crying with a loud and bitter wail. 2He
went as far as the gate of the palace, for no
one was allowed to enter the palace gate
while wearing clothes of mourning. 3And
as news of the king's decree reached all
the provinces, there was great mourning
among the Jews. They fasted, wept, and
wailed, and many people lay in burlap and
ashes.

4When Queen Esther's maids and eunuchs came and told her about Mordecai,
she was deeply distressed. She sent clothing to him to replace the burlap, but he refused it. 5Then Esther sent for Hathach,
one of the king's eunuchs who had been
appointed as her attendant. She ordered
him to go to Mordecai and find out what
was troubling him and why he was in
mourning. 6So Hathach went out to Mordecai in the square in front of the palace
gate.

7Mordecai told him the whole story,
including the exact amount of money
Haman had promised to pay into the royal
treasury for the destruction of the Jews.
8Mordecai gave Hathach a copy of the decree issued in Susa that called for the
death of all Jews. He asked Hathach to
show it to Esther and explain the situation
to her. He also asked Hathach to direct

PROVERBS 21:19-20

It's better to live alone in the desert than
with a quarrelsome, complaining wife.
□ The wise have wealth and luxury, but
fools spend whatever they get.

AUGUST**19**

her to go to the king to beg for mercy and
plead for her people. 9So Hathach returned to Esther with Mordecai's message.

10Then Esther told Hathach to go back
and relay this message to Mordecai: 11"All
the king's officials and even the people
in the provinces know that anyone who
appears before the king in his inner court
without being invited is doomed to die
unless the king holds out his gold scepter.
And the king has not called for me to
come to him for thirty days." 12So Hathach* gave Esther's message to Mordecai.

13Mordecai sent this reply to Esther:
"Don't think for a moment that because
you're in the palace you will escape when
all other Jews are killed. 14If you keep
quiet at a time like this, deliverance and
relief for the Jews will arise from some
other place, but you and your relatives will
die. Who knows if perhaps you were
made queen for just such a time as this?"

15Then Esther sent this reply to Mordecai: 16"Go and gather together all the Jews
of Susa and fast for me. Do not eat or
drink for three days, night or day. My
maids and I will do the same. And then,
though it is against the law, I will go in to
see the king. If I must die, I must die."
17So Mordecai went away and did everything as Esther had ordered him.

5:1ON the third day of the fast, Esther put
on her royal robes and entered the inner
court of the palace, just across from the
king's hall. The king was sitting on his
royal throne, facing the entrance. 2When
he saw Queen Esther standing there in the

inner court, he welcomed her and held out the gold scepter to her. So Esther approached and touched the end of the scepter.

³Then the king asked her, "What do you want, Queen Esther? What is your request? I will give it to you, even if it is half the kingdom!"

⁴And Esther replied, "If it please the king, let the king and Haman come today to a banquet I have prepared for the king."

⁵The king turned to his attendants and said, "Tell Haman to come quickly to a banquet, as Esther has requested." So the king and Haman went to Esther's banquet.

⁶And while they were drinking wine, the king said to Esther, "Now tell me what you really want. What is your request? I will give it to you, even if it is half the kingdom!"

⁷Esther replied, "This is my request and deepest wish. ⁸If I have found favor with the king, and if it pleases the king to grant my request and do what I ask, please come with Haman tomorrow to the banquet I will prepare for you. Then I will explain what this is all about."

⁹Haman was a happy man as he left the banquet! But when he saw Mordecai sitting at the palace gate, not standing up or trembling nervously before him, Haman became furious. ¹⁰However, he restrained himself and went on home.

Then Haman gathered together his friends and Zeresh, his wife, ¹¹and boasted to them about his great wealth and his many children. He bragged about the honors the king had given him and how he had been promoted over all the other nobles and officials.

¹²Then Haman added, "And that's not all! Queen Esther invited only me and the king himself to the banquet she prepared for us. And she has invited me to dine with her and the king again tomorrow!" ¹³Then he added, "But this is all worth nothing as long as I see Mordecai the Jew just sitting there at the palace gate."

¹⁴So Haman's wife, Zeresh, and all his friends suggested, "Set up a sharpened pole that stands seventy-five feet* tall, and in the morning ask the king to impale Mordecai on it. When this is done, you can go on your merry way to the banquet with the king." This pleased Haman, and he ordered the pole set up.

⁶:¹THAT night the king had trouble sleeping, so he ordered an attendant to bring the book of the history of his reign so it could be read to him. ²In those records he discovered an account of how Mordecai had exposed the plot of Bigthana and Teresh, two of the eunuchs who guarded the door to the king's private quarters. They had plotted to assassinate King Xerxes.

³"What reward or recognition did we ever give Mordecai for this?" the king asked.

His attendants replied, "Nothing has been done for him."

⁴"Who is that in the outer court?" the king inquired. As it happened, Haman had just arrived in the outer court of the palace to ask the king to impale Mordecai on the pole he had prepared.

⁵So the attendants replied to the king, "Haman is out in the court."

"Bring him in," the king ordered. ⁶So Haman came in, and the king said, "What should I do to honor a man who truly pleases me?"

Haman thought to himself, "Whom would the king wish to honor more than me?" ⁷So he replied, "If the king wishes to honor someone, ⁸he should bring out one of the king's own royal robes, as well as a horse that the king himself has ridden— one with a royal emblem on its head. ⁹Let the robes and the horse be handed over to one of the king's most noble officials. And let him see that the man whom the king wishes to honor is dressed in the king's robes and led through the city square on the king's horse. Have the official shout as they go, 'This is what the king does for someone he wishes to honor!'"

¹⁰"Excellent!" the king said to Haman. "Quick! Take the robes and my horse, and do just as you have said for Mordecai the Jew, who sits at the gate of the palace. Leave out nothing you have suggested!"

¹¹So Haman took the robes and put them on Mordecai, placed him on the king's own horse, and led him through the city square, shouting, "This is what the king does for someone he wishes to

honor!" ¹²Afterward Mordecai returned to the palace gate, but Haman hurried home dejected and completely humiliated.

¹³When Haman told his wife, Zeresh, and all his friends what had happened, his wise advisers and his wife said, "Since Mordecai—this man who has humiliated you—is of Jewish birth, you will never succeed in your plans against him. It will be fatal to continue opposing him."

¹⁴While they were still talking, the king's eunuchs arrived and quickly took Haman to the banquet Esther had prepared.

⁷:¹So the king and Haman went to Queen Esther's banquet. ²On this second occasion, while they were drinking wine, the king again said to Esther, "Tell me what you want, Queen Esther. What is your request? I will give it to you, even if it is half the kingdom!"

³Queen Esther replied, "If I have found favor with the king, and if it pleases the king to grant my request, I ask that my life and the lives of my people will be spared. ⁴For my people and I have been sold to those who would kill, slaughter, and annihilate us. If we had merely been sold as slaves, I could remain quiet, for that would be too trivial a matter to warrant disturbing the king."

⁵"Who would do such a thing?" King Xerxes demanded. "Who would be so presumptuous as to touch you?"

⁶Esther replied, "This wicked Haman is our adversary and our enemy." Haman grew pale with fright before the king and queen. ⁷Then the king jumped to his feet in a rage and went out into the palace garden.

Haman, however, stayed behind to plead for his life with Queen Esther, for he knew that the king intended to kill him. ⁸In despair he fell on the couch where Queen Esther was reclining, just as the king was returning from the palace garden.

The king exclaimed, "Will he even assault the queen right here in the palace, before my very eyes?" And as soon as the king spoke, his attendants covered Haman's face, signaling his doom.

⁹Then Harbona, one of the king's eunuchs, said, "Haman has set up a sharpened pole that stands seventy-five feet* tall in his own courtyard. He intended to use it to impale Mordecai, the man who saved the king from assassination."

"Then impale Haman on it!" the king ordered. ¹⁰So they impaled Haman on the pole he had set up for Mordecai, and the king's anger subsided.

4:12 As in Greek version; Hebrew reads *they.*   5:14 Hebrew *50 cubits* [22.5 meters].   7:9 Hebrew *50 cubits* [22.5 meters].

WHAT THE BIBLE SAYS

Spiritual gifts

1 CORINTHIANS 12:4-30 The words "spiritual gifts" refer to special abilities given to believers by the Holy Spirit. These gifts are just that—gifts. Every believer has at least one spiritual gift to help build the church. • The gifts listed here are not the only gifts God gives; instead, this gives an idea of the types of gifts. Some gifts help those in the church to grow closer to Christ; other gifts bring outsiders in; others give encouragement or comfort. • As a new believer, you may wonder what gift God gave you. You can find out by: (1) being available to God and seeking to serve others for Christ's sake, (2) helping out in your church when needs arise, (3) finding out what you're good at and what you enjoy, (4) asking for feedback from fellow believers. As you serve in various capacities, your gift will come to the surface. • The church, like a body, needs all the parts working together to get the job done. So be a willing servant, use your gifts, and help when needed. The ultimate goal is always that more people will come to know Jesus.

1 CORINTHIANS 12:1-26

As a part of the body of Christ, we all have something to offer and something to do. We work together to be the physical manifestation of Christ in the world.

Now, dear brothers and sisters,* regarding your [Corinthians] question about the special abilities the Spirit gives us. I [Paul] don't want you to misunderstand this. ²You know that when you were still pagans, you were led astray and swept along in worshiping speechless idols. ³So I want you to know that no one speaking by the Spirit of God will curse Jesus, and no one can say Jesus is Lord, except by the Holy Spirit.

⁴There are different kinds of spiritual gifts, but the same Spirit is the source of them all. ⁵There are different kinds of service, but we serve the same Lord. ⁶God works in different ways, but it is the same God who does the work in all of us.

⁷A spiritual gift is given to each of us so we can help each other. ⁸To one person the Spirit gives the ability to give wise advice*; to another the same Spirit gives a message of special knowledge.* ⁹The same Spirit gives great faith to another, and to someone else the one Spirit gives the gift of healing. ¹⁰He gives one person the power to perform miracles, and another the ability to prophesy. He gives someone else the ability to discern whether a message is from the Spirit of God or from another spirit. Still another person is given the ability to speak in unknown languages,* while another is given the ability to interpret what is being said. ¹¹It is the one and only Spirit who distributes all these gifts. He alone decides which gift each person should have.

¹²The human body has many parts, but the many parts make up one whole body. So it is with the body of Christ. ¹³Some of us are Jews, some are Gentiles,* some are slaves, and some are free. But we have all been baptized into one body by one Spirit, and we all share the same Spirit.*

¹⁴Yes, the body has many different parts, not just one part. ¹⁵If the foot says, "I am not a part of the body because I am not a hand," that does not make it any less a part of the body. ¹⁶And if the ear says, "I am not part of the body because I am not an eye," would that make it any less a part of the body? ¹⁷If the whole body were an eye, how would you hear? Or if your whole body were an ear, how would you smell anything?

¹⁸But our bodies have many parts, and God has put each part just where he wants it. ¹⁹How strange a body would be if it had only one part! ²⁰Yes, there are many parts, but only one body. ²¹The eye can never say to the hand, "I don't need you." The head can't say to the feet, "I don't need you."

²²In fact, some parts of the body that seem weakest and least important are actually the most necessary. ²³And the parts we regard as less honorable are those we clothe with the greatest care. So we carefully protect those parts that should not be seen, ²⁴while the more honorable parts do not require this special care. So God has put the body together such that extra honor and care are given to those parts that have less dignity. ²⁵This makes for harmony among the members, so that all the members care for each other. ²⁶If one part suffers, all the parts suffer with it, and if one part is honored, all the parts are glad.

12:1 Greek *brothers.*   12:8a Or *gives a word of wisdom.*
12:8b Or *gives a word of knowledge.*   12:10 Or *in various tongues;* also in 12:28, 30.   12:13a Greek *some are Greeks.*
12:13b Greek *we were all given one Spirit to drink.*

PSALM 36:1-12

For the choir director: A psalm of David, the servant of the LORD.

¹ **S**in whispers to the wicked, deep
     within their hearts.
   They have no fear of God at all.
² In their blind conceit,
     they cannot see how wicked they
       really are.
³ Everything they say is crooked and
     deceitful.
   They refuse to act wisely or do
     good.
⁴ They lie awake at night, hatching
     sinful plots.
   Their actions are never good.
   They make no attempt to turn
     from evil.

⁵ Your unfailing love, O LORD, is as vast
     as the heavens;

your faithfulness reaches beyond
the clouds.
⁶ Your righteousness is like the mighty
mountains,
your justice like the ocean depths.
You care for people and animals alike,
O LORD.
⁷ How precious is your unfailing love,
O God!
All humanity finds shelter
in the shadow of your wings.
⁸ You feed them from the abundance
of your own house,
letting them drink from your river
of delights.
⁹ For you are the fountain of life,
the light by which we see.

¹⁰ Pour out your unfailing love on those
who love you;
give justice to those with honest
hearts.
¹¹ Don't let the proud trample me
or the wicked push me around.
¹² Look! Those who do evil have
fallen!
They are thrown down, never to rise
again.

PROVERBS 21:21-22
Whoever pursues righteousness and unfailing love will find life, righteousness,
and honor. □ The wise conquer the city of
the strong and level the fortress in which
they trust.

AUGUST**20**

ESTHER 8:1-10:3
The Jews' victory over Haman became the basis for
the Jewish festival known as Purim.

On that same day King Xerxes gave the
property of Haman, the enemy of the
Jews, to Queen Esther. Then Mordecai
was brought before the king, for Esther
had told the king how they were related.
²The king took off his signet ring—which
he had taken back from Haman—and
gave it to Mordecai. And Esther appointed Mordecai to be in charge of Haman's
property.

³Then Esther went again before the
king, falling down at his feet and begging
him with tears to stop the evil plot de-
vised by Haman the Agagite against the
Jews. ⁴Again the king held out the gold
scepter to Esther. So she rose and stood
before him.

⁵Esther said, "If it please the king, and if
I have found favor with him, and if he
thinks it is right, and if I am pleasing to
him, let there be a decree that reverses the
orders of Haman son of Hammedatha the
Agagite, who ordered that Jews throughout all the king's provinces should be destroyed. ⁶For how can I endure to see my

people and my family slaughtered and
destroyed?"

⁷Then King Xerxes said to Queen Esther and Mordecai the Jew, "I have given
Esther the property of Haman, and he has
been impaled on a pole because he tried
to destroy the Jews. ⁸Now go ahead and
send a message to the Jews in the king's
name, telling them whatever you want,
and seal it with the king's signet ring.
But remember that whatever has already
been written in the king's name and
sealed with his signet ring can never be
revoked."

⁹So on June 25* the king's secretaries
were summoned, and a decree was written exactly as Mordecai dictated. It was
sent to the Jews and to the highest officers, the governors, and the nobles of all
the 127 provinces stretching from India
to Ethiopia.* The decree was written in
the scripts and languages of all the peoples of the empire, including that of the
Jews. ¹⁰The decree was written in the
name of King Xerxes and sealed with
the king's signet ring. Mordecai sent the
dispatches by swift messengers, who

rode fast horses especially bred for the king's service.

[11]The king's decree gave the Jews in every city authority to unite to defend their lives. They were allowed to kill, slaughter, and annihilate anyone of any nationality or province who might attack them or their children and wives, and to take the property of their enemies. [12]The day chosen for this event throughout all the provinces of King Xerxes was March 7 of the next year.*

[13]A copy of this decree was to be issued as law in every province and proclaimed to all peoples, so that the Jews would be ready to take revenge on their enemies on the appointed day. [14]So urged on by the king's command, the messengers rode out swiftly on fast horses bred for the king's service. The same decree was also proclaimed in the fortress of Susa.

[15]Then Mordecai left the king's presence, wearing the royal robe of blue and white, the great crown of gold, and an outer cloak of fine linen and purple. And the people of Susa celebrated the new decree. [16]The Jews were filled with joy and gladness and were honored everywhere. [17]In every province and city, wherever the king's decree arrived, the Jews rejoiced and had a great celebration and declared a public festival and holiday. And many of the people of the land became Jews themselves, for they feared what the Jews might do to them.

9:1 So on March 7* the two decrees of the king were put into effect. On that day, the enemies of the Jews had hoped to overpower them, but quite the opposite happened. It was the Jews who over-powered their enemies. [2]The Jews gathered in their cities throughout all the king's provinces to attack anyone who tried to harm them. But no one could make a stand against them, for everyone was afraid of them. [3]And all the nobles of the provinces, the highest officers, the governors, and the royal officials helped the Jews for fear of Mordecai. [4]For Mordecai had been promoted in the king's palace, and his fame spread throughout all the provinces as he became more and more powerful.

[5]So the Jews went ahead on the ap-

pointed day and struck down their enemies with the sword. They killed and annihilated their enemies and did as they pleased with those who hated them. [6]In the fortress of Susa itself, the Jews killed 500 men. [7]They also killed Parshandatha, Dalphon, Aspatha, [8]Poratha, Adalia, Aridatha, [9]Parmashta, Arisai, Aridai, and Vaizatha—[10]the ten sons of Haman son of Hammedatha, the enemy of the Jews. But they did not take any plunder.

[11]That very day, when the king was informed of the number of people killed in the fortress of Susa, [12]he called for Queen Esther. He said, "The Jews have killed 500 men in the fortress of Susa alone, as well as Haman's ten sons. If they have done that here, what has happened in the rest of the provinces? But now, what more do you want? It will be granted to you; tell me and I will do it."

[13]Esther responded, "If it please the king, give the Jews in Susa permission to do again tomorrow as they have done today, and let the bodies of Haman's ten sons be impaled on a pole."

[14]So the king agreed, and the decree was announced in Susa. And they impaled the bodies of Haman's ten sons. [15]Then the Jews at Susa gathered together on March 8* and killed 300 more men, and again they took no plunder.

[16]Meanwhile, the other Jews throughout the king's provinces had gathered together to defend their lives. They gained relief from all their enemies, killing 75,000 of those who hated them. But they did not take any plunder. [17]This was done throughout the provinces on March 7, and on March 8 they rested,* celebrating their victory with a day of feasting and gladness. [18](The Jews at Susa killed their enemies on March 7 and again on March 8, then rested on March 9,* making that their day of feasting and gladness.) [19]So to this day, rural Jews living in remote villages celebrate an annual festival and holiday on the appointed day in late winter,* when they rejoice and send gifts of food to each other.

[20]Mordecai recorded these events and sent letters to the Jews near and far, throughout all the provinces of King Xerxes, [21]calling on them to celebrate an

annual festival on these two days.* ²²He told them to celebrate these days with feasting and gladness and by giving gifts of food to each other and presents to the poor. This would commemorate a time when the Jews gained relief from their enemies, when their sorrow was turned into gladness and their mourning into joy.

²³So the Jews accepted Mordecai's proposal and adopted this annual custom. ²⁴Haman son of Hammedatha the Agagite, the enemy of the Jews, had plotted to crush and destroy them on the date determined by casting lots (the lots were called *purim*). ²⁵But when Esther came before the king, he issued a decree causing Haman's evil plot to backfire, and Haman and his sons were impaled on a sharpened pole. ²⁶That is why this celebration is called Purim, because it is the ancient word for casting lots.

So because of Mordecai's letter and because of what they had experienced, ²⁷the Jews throughout the realm agreed to inaugurate this tradition and to pass it on to their descendants and to all who became Jews. They declared they would never fail to celebrate these two prescribed days at the appointed time each year. ²⁸These days would be remembered and kept from generation to generation and cele-

brated by every family throughout the provinces and cities of the empire. This Festival of Purim would never cease to be celebrated among the Jews, nor would the memory of what happened ever die out among their descendants.

²⁹Then Queen Esther, the daughter of Abihail, along with Mordecai the Jew, wrote another letter putting the queen's full authority behind Mordecai's letter to establish the Festival of Purim. ³⁰Letters wishing peace and security were sent to the Jews throughout the 127 provinces of the empire of Xerxes. ³¹These letters established the Festival of Purim—an annual celebration of these days at the appointed time, decreed by both Mordecai the Jew and Queen Esther. (The people decided to observe this festival, just as they had decided for themselves and their descendants to establish the times of fasting and mourning.) ³²So the command of Esther confirmed the practices of Purim, and it was all written down in the records.

10:1KING Xerxes imposed a tribute throughout his empire, even to the distant coastlands. ²His great achievements and the full account of the greatness of Mordecai, whom the king had promoted, are recorded in *The Book of the History of*

HOW WE LIVE

Loving God and others

1 CORINTHIANS 13:1-13 It seems that *love* has little meaning any more. In most popular books, television shows, and movies, the term "lust" would be more appropriate than "love." Rarely do we see the kind of love Paul describes here—patient, kind, not jealous, not boastful, not proud, not rude, not demanding its own way, not irritable, not keeping records of wrongs done, always persistent, always hopeful, able to endure any circumstance. Surely such love would revolutionize marriages, families, churches, and neighborhoods. • This kind of love is God's kind of love. This is the kind of love God wants you to show to everyone around you. You see, love has little to do with feelings and more to do with decisions and choices. Think of the people with whom you interact every day— a spouse, children, a boss, employees, friends, neighbors, teachers, students. How can you show love? Can you be less irritable, more hopeful, willing to persist through the difficult times, more patient, less jealous? It doesn't come easy, but true love isn't easy. It is important, however. In fact, of faith, hope and love, "the greatest of these is love."

the Kings of Media and Persia. ³Mordecai the Jew became the prime minister, with authority next to that of King Xerxes himself. He was very great among the Jews, who held him in high esteem, because he continued to work for the good of his people and to speak up for the welfare of all their descendants.

8:9a Hebrew *on the twenty-third day of the third month, the month of Sivan,* of the ancient Hebrew lunar calendar. This day was June 25, 474 B.C.; also see note on 2:16. 8:9b Hebrew *to Cush.*   8:12 Hebrew *the thirteenth day of the twelfth month, the month of Adar,* of the ancient Hebrew lunar calendar. The date selected was March 7, 473 B.C.; also see note on 2:16.   9:1 Hebrew *on the thirteenth day of the twelfth month, the month of Adar,* of the ancient Hebrew lunar calendar. This day was March 7, 473 B.C.; also see note on 2:16.   9:15 Hebrew *the fourteenth day of the month of Adar,* of the Hebrew lunar calendar. This day was March 8, 473 B.C.; also see note on 2:16.   9:17 Hebrew *on the thirteenth day of the month of Adar, and on the fourteenth day they rested.* These days were March 7 and 8, 473 B.C.; also see note on 2:16.   9:18 Hebrew *killed their enemies on the thirteenth day and the fourteenth day, and then rested on the fifteenth day,* of the Hebrew month of Adar. 9:19 Hebrew *on the fourteenth day of the month of Adar.* This day of the Hebrew lunar calendar occurs in February or March.   9:21 Hebrew *on the fourteenth and fifteenth days of Adar,* of the Hebrew lunar calendar.

1 CORINTHIANS 12:27–13:13

Believers have different gifts with which to serve the church. Those very differences can cause conflict, jealousy, and division, or they can lead to strength. The way to have the latter? Do everything with love.

All of you [believers] together are Christ's body, and each of you is a part of it. ²⁸Here are some of the parts God has appointed for the church:

> first are apostles,
> second are prophets,
> third are teachers,
> then those who do miracles,
> those who have the gift of healing,
> those who can help others,
> those who have the gift of leadership,
> those who speak in unknown
>   languages.

²⁹Are we all apostles? Are we all prophets? Are we all teachers? Do we all have the power to do miracles? ³⁰Do we all have the gift of healing? Do we all have the ability to speak in unknown languages? Do we all have the ability to interpret unknown languages? Of course not! ³¹So you should earnestly desire the most helpful gifts.

But now let me show you a way of life that is best of all.

13:1 If I could speak all the languages of earth and of angels, but didn't love others, I would only be a noisy gong or a clanging cymbal. ²If I had the gift of prophecy, and if I understood all of God's secret plans and possessed all knowledge, and if I had such faith that I could move mountains, but didn't love others, I would be nothing. ³If I gave everything I have to the poor and even sacrificed my body, I could boast about it;* but if I didn't love others, I would have gained nothing.

⁴Love is patient and kind. Love is not jealous or boastful or proud ⁵or rude. It does not demand its own way. It is not irritable, and it keeps no record of being wronged. ⁶It does not rejoice about injustice but rejoices whenever the truth wins out. ⁷Love never gives up, never loses faith, is always hopeful, and endures through every circumstance.

⁸Prophecy and speaking in unknown languages* and special knowledge will become useless. But love will last forever! ⁹Now our knowledge is partial and incomplete, and even the gift of prophecy reveals only part of the whole picture! ¹⁰But when full understanding comes, these partial things will become useless.

¹¹When I was a child, I spoke and thought and reasoned as a child. But when I grew up, I put away childish things. ¹²Now we see things imperfectly as in a cloudy mirror, but then we will see everything with perfect clarity.* All that I know now is partial and incomplete, but then I will know everything completely, just as God now knows me completely.

¹³Three things will last forever—faith, hope, and love—and the greatest of these is love.

13:3 Some manuscripts read *sacrificed my body to be burned.*   13:8 Or *in tongues.*   13:12 Greek *see face to face.*

*PSALM 37:1-11
A psalm of David.

¹ **D**on't worry about the wicked
>   or envy those who do wrong.
² For like grass, they soon fade away.
>   Like spring flowers, they soon
>   wither.

³ Trust in the LORD and do good.
Then you will live safely in the land
and prosper.
⁴ Take delight in the LORD,
and he will give you your heart's
desires.

⁵ Commit everything you do to the LORD.
Trust him, and he will help you.
⁶ He will make your innocence radiate
like the dawn,
and the justice of your cause will
shine like the noonday sun.

⁷ Be still in the presence of the LORD,
and wait patiently for him to act.
Don't worry about evil people who
prosper
or fret about their wicked schemes.

⁸ Stop being angry!
Turn from your rage!

Do not lose your temper—
it only leads to harm.
⁹ For the wicked will be
destroyed,
but those who trust in the LORD will
possess the land.

¹⁰ Soon the wicked will disappear.
Though you look for them, they will
be gone.
¹¹ The lowly will possess the land
and will live in peace and
prosperity.

37 This psalm is a Hebrew acrostic poem; each stanza begins
with a successive letter of the Hebrew alphabet.

PROVERBS 21:23-24

Watch your tongue and keep your mouth
shut, and you will stay out of trouble.
☐ Mockers are proud and haughty; they
act with boundless arrogance.

AUGUST**21**

JOB 1:1–3:26
The book of Job tells the story of a man named Job
who has come to symbolize suffering. He lost everything—but held on to God. And God held on to him.

There once was a man named Job who
lived in the land of Uz. He was blameless—a man of complete integrity. He
feared God and stayed away from evil.
²He had seven sons and three daughters.
³He owned 7,000 sheep, 3,000 camels,
500 teams of oxen, and 500 female donkeys. He also had many servants. He was,
in fact, the richest person in that entire
area.

⁴Job's sons would take turns preparing
feasts in their homes, and they would also
invite their three sisters to celebrate with
them. ⁵When these celebrations ended—
sometimes after several days—Job would
purify his children. He would get up early
in the morning and offer a burnt offering
for each of them. For Job said to himself,
"Perhaps my children have sinned and
have cursed God in their hearts." This was
Job's regular practice.

⁶One day the members of the heavenly
court* came to present themselves before
the LORD, and the Accuser, Satan,* came
with them. ⁷"Where have you come
from?" the LORD asked Satan.

Satan answered the LORD, "I have been
patrolling the earth, watching everything
that's going on."

⁸Then the LORD asked Satan, "Have you
noticed my servant Job? He is the finest
man in all the earth. He is blameless—a
man of complete integrity. He fears God
and stays away from evil."

⁹Satan replied to the LORD, "Yes, but
Job has good reason to fear God. ¹⁰You
have always put a wall of protection
around him and his home and his property. You have made him prosper in everything he does. Look how rich he is! ¹¹But
reach out and take away everything he
has, and he will surely curse you to your
face!"

¹²"All right, you may test him," the LORD
said to Satan. "Do whatever you want with

everything he possesses, but don't harm him physically." So Satan left the LORD's presence.

¹³One day when Job's sons and daughters were feasting at the oldest brother's house, ¹⁴a messenger arrived at Job's home with this news: "Your oxen were plowing, with the donkeys feeding beside them, ¹⁵when the Sabeans raided us. They stole all the animals and killed all the farmhands. I am the only one who escaped to tell you."

¹⁶While he was still speaking, another messenger arrived with this news: "The fire of God has fallen from heaven and burned up your sheep and all the shepherds. I am the only one who escaped to tell you."

¹⁷While he was still speaking, a third messenger arrived with this news: "Three bands of Chaldean raiders have stolen your camels and killed your servants. I am the only one who escaped to tell you."

¹⁸While he was still speaking, another messenger arrived with this news: "Your sons and daughters were feasting in their oldest brother's home. ¹⁹Suddenly, a powerful wind swept in from the wilderness and hit the house on all sides. The house collapsed, and all your children are dead. I am the only one who escaped to tell you."

²⁰Job stood up and tore his robe in grief. Then he shaved his head and fell to the ground to worship. ²¹He said,

"I came naked from my mother's womb,
    and I will be naked when I leave.
The LORD gave me what I had,
    and the LORD has taken it away.
Praise the name of the LORD!"

²²In all of this, Job did not sin by blaming God.

2:1ONE day the members of the heavenly court* came again to present themselves before the LORD, and the Accuser, Satan,* came with them. ²"Where have you come from?" the LORD asked Satan.

Satan answered the LORD, "I have been patrolling the earth, watching everything that's going on."

³Then the LORD asked Satan, "Have you noticed my servant Job? He is the finest man in all the earth. He is blameless—a

man of complete integrity. He fears God and stays away from evil. And he has maintained his integrity, even though you urged me to harm him without cause."

⁴Satan replied to the LORD, "Skin for skin! A man will give up everything he has to save his life. ⁵But reach out and take away his health, and he will surely curse you to your face!"

⁶"All right, do with him as you please," the LORD said to Satan. "But spare his life." ⁷So Satan left the LORD's presence, and he struck Job with terrible boils from head to foot.

⁸Job scraped his skin with a piece of broken pottery as he sat among the ashes. ⁹His wife said to him, "Are you still trying to maintain your integrity? Curse God and die."

¹⁰But Job replied, "You talk like a foolish woman. Should we accept only good things from the hand of God and never anything bad?" So in all this, Job said nothing wrong.

¹¹When three of Job's friends heard of the tragedy he had suffered, they got together and traveled from their homes to comfort and console him. Their names were Eliphaz the Temanite, Bildad the Shuhite, and Zophar the Naamathite. ¹²When they saw Job from a distance, they scarcely recognized him. Wailing loudly, they tore their robes and threw dust into the air over their heads to show their grief. ¹³Then they sat on the ground with him for seven days and nights. No one said a word to Job, for they saw that his suffering was too great for words.

3:1AT last Job spoke, and he cursed the day of his birth. ²He said:

³ "Let the day of my birth be erased,
    and the night I was conceived.
⁴ Let that day be turned to darkness.
    Let it be lost even to God on high,
    and let no light shine on it.
⁵ Let the darkness and utter gloom
        claim that day for its own.
    Let a black cloud overshadow it,
    and let the darkness terrify it.
⁶ Let that night be blotted off the
        calendar,
    never again to be counted among
        the days of the year,

never again to appear among
the months.

[7] Let that night be childless.
Let it have no joy.

[8] Let those who are experts at cursing—
whose cursing could rouse
Leviathan*—
curse that day.

[9] Let its morning stars remain dark.
Let it hope for light, but in vain;
may it never see the morning light.

[10] Curse that day for failing to shut my
mother's womb,
for letting me be born to see all this
trouble.

[11] "Why wasn't I born dead?
Why didn't I die as I came from
the womb?

[12] Why was I laid on my mother's lap?
Why did she nurse me at her
breasts?

[13] Had I died at birth, I would now be
at peace.
I would be asleep and at rest.

[14] I would rest with the world's kings and
prime ministers,
whose great buildings now lie
in ruins.

[15] I would rest with princes, rich in gold,
whose palaces were filled with
silver.

[16] Why wasn't I buried like a stillborn
child,
like a baby who never lives to see
the light?

[17] For in death the wicked cause
no trouble,
and the weary are at rest.

[18] Even captives are at ease in death,
with no guards to curse them.

[19] Rich and poor are both there,
and the slave is free from his
master.

[20] "Oh, why give light to those in misery,
and life to those who are bitter?

[21] They long for death, and it won't
come.
They search for death more eagerly
than for hidden treasure.

[22] They're filled with joy when they
finally die,
and rejoice when they find
the grave.

[23] Why is life given to those with
no future,
those God has surrounded with
difficulties?

[24] I cannot eat for sighing;
my groans pour out like water.

[25] What I always feared has happened
to me.
What I dreaded has come true.

WHAT THE BIBLE SAYS

The devil

JOB 1:6 We know little about the details of the spiritual world, but the opening scenario in the book of Job gives us some hints. Describing a confrontation between God and Satan almost like a courtroom scene, we find that God and Satan are very familiar with each other. Satan originally was an angel of God who became corrupt. He rebelled against God and was cast out of heaven. Satan is a hostile adversary, but he is not more powerful than God. In fact, Satan has to ask God's permission to act, is accountable to God, and must live within God's boundaries. He is not able to be present everywhere at all times—as God is—but he has legions of demons that help do his evil work on the earth. • You will find that Satan wants to fight against your faith, make you doubt, or at least make you ineffective. He will use every means at his disposal, but remember that he can bring nothing into your life that God hasn't allowed. Don't be surprised by any spiritual struggles you begin to face. Realize their source, and then go directly to God and trust him to see you through.

²⁶ I have no peace, no quietness.
I have no rest; only trouble comes."

1:6a Hebrew *the sons of God.*　**1:6b** Hebrew *and the satan;* similarly throughout this chapter.　**2:1a** Hebrew *the sons of God.*　**2:1b** Hebrew *and the satan;* similarly throughout this chapter.　**3:8** The identification of Leviathan is disputed, ranging from an earthly creature to a mythical sea monster in ancient literature.

1 CORINTHIANS 14:1-17

The Corinthian Christians were obsessing about certain spiritual gifts. Paul reminded them that spiritual gifts are given in order to build up the church and teach people about God. If they don't do that, then they are being misused.

Let love be your highest goal! But you should also desire the special abilities the Spirit gives—especially the ability to prophesy. ²For if you have the ability to speak in tongues,* you will be talking only to God, since people won't be able to understand you. You will be speaking by the power of the Spirit, but it will all be mysterious. ³But one who prophesies strengthens others, encourages them, and comforts them. ⁴A person who speaks in tongues is strengthened personally, but one who speaks a word of prophecy strengthens the entire church.

⁵I wish you could all speak in tongues, but even more I wish you could all prophesy. For prophecy is greater than speaking in tongues, unless someone interprets what you are saying so that the whole church will be strengthened.

⁶Dear brothers and sisters,* if I should come to you speaking in an unknown language,* how would that help you? But if I bring you a revelation or some special knowledge or prophecy or teaching, that will be helpful. ⁷Even lifeless instruments like the flute or the harp must play the notes clearly, or no one will recognize the melody. ⁸And if the bugler doesn't sound a clear call, how will the soldiers know they are being called to battle?

⁹It's the same for you. If you speak to people in words they don't understand, how will they know what you are saying? You might as well be talking into empty space.

¹⁰There are many different languages in the world, and every language has meaning. ¹¹But if I don't understand a language,

I will be a foreigner to someone who speaks it, and the one who speaks it will be a foreigner to me. ¹²And the same is true for you. Since you are so eager to have the special abilities the Spirit gives, seek those that will strengthen the whole church.

¹³So anyone who speaks in tongues should pray also for the ability to interpret what has been said. ¹⁴For if I pray in tongues, my spirit is praying, but I don't understand what I am saying.

¹⁵Well then, what shall I do? I will pray in the spirit,* and I will also pray in words I understand. I will sing in the spirit, and I will also sing in words I understand. ¹⁶For if you praise God only in the spirit, how can those who don't understand you praise God along with you? How can they join you in giving thanks when they don't understand what you are saying? ¹⁷You will be giving thanks very well, but it won't strengthen the people who hear you.

14:2 Or *in unknown languages;* also in 14:4, 5, 13, 14, 18, 22, 26, 27, 28, 39.　**14:6a** Greek *brothers;* also in 14:20, 26, 39.　**14:6b** Or *in tongues;* also in 14:19, 23.　**14:15** Or *in the spirit;* also in 14:15b, 16.

PSALM 37:12-29

The wicked plot against the godly;
they snarl at them in defiance.
¹³ But the Lord just laughs,
for he sees their day of judgment
coming.

¹⁴ The wicked draw their swords
and string their bows
to kill the poor and the oppressed,
to slaughter those who do right.
¹⁵ But their swords will stab their own
hearts,
and their bows will be broken.

¹⁶ It is better to be godly and have little
than to be evil and rich.
¹⁷ For the strength of the wicked will be
shattered,
but the LORD takes care of the godly.

¹⁸ Day by day the LORD takes care of the
innocent,
and they will receive an inheritance
that lasts forever.
¹⁹ They will not be disgraced in hard
times;
even in famine they will have more
than enough.

20 But the wicked will die.
The LORD's enemies are like flowers
in a field—
they will disappear like smoke.

21 The wicked borrow and never repay,
but the godly are generous givers.
22 Those the LORD blesses will possess
the land,
but those he curses will die.

23 The LORD directs the steps of the godly.
He delights in every detail of their
lives.
24 Though they stumble, they will never
fall,
for the LORD holds them by the hand.

25 Once I was young, and now I am old.
Yet I have never seen the godly
abandoned

or their children begging for bread.
26 The godly always give generous loans
to others,
and their children are a blessing.

27 Turn from evil and do good,
and you will live in the land forever.
28 For the LORD loves justice,
and he will never abandon the godly.

He will keep them safe forever,
but the children of the wicked
will die.
29 The godly will possess the land
and will live there forever.

PROVERBS 21:25-26
Despite their desires, the lazy will come
to ruin, for their hands refuse to work.
□ Some people are always greedy for
more, but the godly love to give!

AUGUST**22**

JOB 4:1–7:21
Eliphaz was from Teman, a place in Edom with
a reputation for wisdom. He took the traditional
approach with Job: "You must have done something
wrong in order to deserve all of the horrible stuff
that's happening to you!"

Then Eliphaz the Temanite replied to Job:

2 "Will you be patient and let me say
a word?
For who could keep from speaking
out?

3 "In the past you have encouraged
many people;
you have strengthened those who
were weak.
4 Your words have supported those who
were falling;
you encouraged those with shaky
knees.
5 But now when trouble strikes, you lose
heart.
You are terrified when it touches
you.
6 Doesn't your reverence for God give
you confidence?

Doesn't your life of integrity give
you hope?

7 "Stop and think! Do the innocent die?
When have the upright been
destroyed?
8 My experience shows that those who
plant trouble
and cultivate evil will harvest
the same.
9 A breath from God destroys them.
They vanish in a blast of his anger.
10 The lion roars and the wildcat snarls,
but the teeth of strong lions will be
broken.
11 The fierce lion will starve for lack
of prey,
and the cubs of the lioness will
be scattered.

12 "This truth was given to me in secret,
as though whispered in my ear.
13 It came to me in a disturbing vision
at night,
when people are in a deep sleep.
14 Fear gripped me,
and my bones trembled.

15 A spirit* swept past my face,
and my hair stood on end.*
16 The spirit stopped, but I couldn't see
its shape.
There was a form before my eyes.
In the silence I heard a voice say,
17 'Can a mortal be innocent before God?
Can anyone be pure before the
Creator?'

18 "If God does not trust his own angels
and has charged his messengers
with foolishness,
19 how much less will he trust people
made of clay!
They are made of dust, crushed as
easily as a moth.
20 They are alive in the morning but dead
by evening,
gone forever without a trace.
21 Their tent-cords are pulled and the
tent collapses,
and they die in ignorance.

5:1 "CRY for help, but will anyone answer
you?
Which of the angels* will help you?
2 Surely resentment destroys the fool,
and jealousy kills the simple.
3 I have seen that fools may be
successful for the moment,
but then comes sudden disaster.
4 Their children are abandoned far
from help;
they are crushed in court with no
one to defend them.
5 The hungry devour their harvest,
even when it is guarded by
brambles.*
The thirsty pant after their wealth.
6 But evil does not spring from the soil,
and trouble does not sprout from
the earth.
7 People are born for trouble
as readily as sparks fly up from a fire.

8 "If I were you, I would go to God
and present my case to him.
9 He does great things too marvelous
to understand.
He performs countless miracles.
10 He gives rain for the earth
and water for the fields.
11 He gives prosperity to the poor
and protects those who suffer.

12 He frustrates the plans of schemers
so the work of their hands will not
succeed.
13 He traps the wise in their own
cleverness
so their cunning schemes are
thwarted.
14 They find it is dark in the daytime,
and they grope at noon as if it were
night.
15 He rescues the poor from the cutting
words of the strong,
and rescues them from the clutches
of the powerful.
16 And so at last the poor have hope,
and the snapping jaws of the
wicked are shut.

17 "But consider the joy of those
corrected by God!
Do not despise the discipline of the
Almighty when you sin.
18 For though he wounds, he also
bandages.
He strikes, but his hands also heal.
19 From six disasters he will rescue you;
even in the seventh, he will keep
you from evil.
20 He will save you from death in time
of famine,
from the power of the sword in
time of war.
21 You will be safe from slander
and have no fear when destruction
comes.
22 You will laugh at destruction and
famine;
wild animals will not terrify you.
23 You will be at peace with the stones
of the field,
and its wild animals will be at peace
with you.
24 You will know that your home is safe.
When you survey your possessions,
nothing will be missing.
25 You will have many children;
your descendants will be as
plentiful as grass!
26 You will go to the grave at a ripe old
age,
like a sheaf of grain harvested at the
proper time!
27 "We have studied life and found all
this to be true.

Listen to my counsel, and apply it to
yourself."

6:1 THEN Job spoke again:

2 "If my misery could be weighed
and my troubles be put on the
scales,
3 they would outweigh all the sands
of the sea.
That is why I spoke impulsively.
4 For the Almighty has struck me down
with his arrows.
Their poison infects my spirit.
God's terrors are lined up against
me.
5 Don't I have a right to complain?
Don't wild donkeys bray when they
find no grass,
and oxen bellow when they have
no food?
6 Don't people complain about unsalted
food?
Does anyone want the tasteless
white of an egg?*
7 My appetite disappears when I look
at it;
I gag at the thought of eating it!

8 "Oh, that I might have my request,
that God would grant my desire.
9 I wish he would crush me.

I wish he would reach out his hand
and kill me.
10 At least I can take comfort in this:
Despite the pain,
I have not denied the words of the
Holy One.
11 But I don't have the strength to
endure.
I have nothing to live for.
12 Do I have the strength of a stone?
Is my body made of bronze?
13 No, I am utterly helpless,
without any chance of success.

14 "One should be kind to a fainting
friend,
but you accuse me without any fear
of the Almighty.*
15 My brothers, you have proved as
unreliable as a seasonal brook
that overflows its banks in the
spring
16 when it is swollen with ice and
melting snow.
17 But when the hot weather arrives,
the water disappears.
The brook vanishes in the heat.
18 The caravans turn aside to be
refreshed,
but there is nothing to drink,
so they die.

HOW WE LIVE

Remaining pure

JOB 4:17 Job was a man who was careful not to worship his possessions,
idols, or anything other than God alone. One might think his heart was as
pure as is humanly possible. But one of his friends, the unhelpful Eliphaz,
told Job that he was suffering because he had sinned. In reality, it was
Job's unwavering purity of heart—his faith that God would help him in
this time of need—that brought about this unprecedented test of faith.
• Although Eliphaz made some worthwhile comments, he made three
wrong assumptions. First, he assumed that an innocent person never
suffers (4:7). Second, he believed that anyone who suffers must be
paying for past sins (4:8-9). Third, he asserted that Job must have sinned
against God, otherwise he would not be suffering so much (5:8-18).
• The perfect example that disproves Eliphaz's claims is Jesus Christ.
Sinless, blameless, and pure, he suffered pain, humiliation, and death in
order to bring us life. "Can a mortal be innocent before God? Can anyone
be pure before the Creator?" The answer is a resounding "Yes!" when
that person has been purified by Jesus Christ's blood which washes away
all sin.

19 The caravans from Tema search for
this water;
the travelers from Sheba hope to
find it.
20 They count on it but are disappointed.
When they arrive, their hopes are
dashed.
21 You, too, have given no help.
You have seen my calamity, and you
are afraid.
22 But why? Have I ever asked you for
a gift?
Have I begged for anything of yours
for myself?
23 Have I asked you to rescue me from
my enemies,
or to save me from ruthless
people?
24 Teach me, and I will keep quiet.
Show me what I have done wrong.
25 Honest words can be painful,
but what do your criticisms amount
to?
26 Do you think your words are
convincing
when you disregard my cry
of desperation?
27 You would even send an orphan into
slavery*
or sell a friend.
28 Look at me!
Would I lie to your face?
29 Stop assuming my guilt,
for I have done no wrong.
30 Do you think I am lying?
Don't I know the difference
between right and wrong?

7:1 "Is not all human life a struggle?
Our lives are like that of a hired hand,
2 like a worker who longs for the shade,
like a servant waiting to be paid.
3 I, too, have been assigned months
of futility,
long and weary nights of misery.
4 Lying in bed, I think, 'When will it be
morning?'
But the night drags on, and I toss till
dawn.
5 My body is covered with maggots and
scabs.
My skin breaks open, oozing with
pus.

6 "My days fly faster than a weaver's
shuttle.
They end without hope.
7 O God, remember that my life is but
a breath,
and I will never again feel happiness.
8 You see me now, but not for long.
You will look for me, but I will
be gone.
9 Just as a cloud dissipates and vanishes,
those who die* will not come back.
10 They are gone forever from their
home—
never to be seen again.

11 "I cannot keep from speaking.
I must express my anguish.
My bitter soul must complain.
12 Am I a sea monster or a dragon
that you must place me under
guard?
13 I think, 'My bed will comfort me,
and sleep will ease my misery,'
14 but then you shatter me with dreams
and terrify me with visions.
15 I would rather be strangled—
rather die than suffer like this.
16 I hate my life and don't want to go
on living.
Oh, leave me alone for my few
remaining days.

17 "What are people, that you should
make so much of us,
that you should think of us so
often?
18 For you examine us every morning
and test us every moment.
19 Why won't you leave me alone,
at least long enough for me to
swallow!
20 If I have sinned, what have I done
to you,
O watcher of all humanity?
Why make me your target?
Am I a burden to you?
21 Why not just forgive my sin
and take away my guilt?
For soon I will lie down in the dust and
die.
When you look for me, I will
be gone."

4:15a Or *wind;* also in 4:16. 4:15b Or *its wind sent shivers*
up my spine. 5:1 Hebrew *the holy ones.* 5:5 The meaning

of the Hebrew for this phrase is uncertain.   **6:6** Or *the tasteless juice of the mallow plant?*   **6:14** Or *friend, / or he might lose his fear of the Almighty.*   **6:27** Hebrew *even gamble over an orphan.*   **7:9** Hebrew *who go down to Sheol.*

1 CORINTHIANS 14:18-40

Paul continued his discussion of speaking in tongues, again bringing the believers back to the basic understanding that everything done in church should be orderly and for the purpose of bringing people to faith and strengthening faith.

I [Paul] thank God that I speak in tongues more than any of you. ¹⁹But in a church meeting I would rather speak five understandable words to help others than ten thousand words in an unknown language.

²⁰Dear brothers and sisters, don't be childish in your understanding of these things. Be innocent as babies when it comes to evil, but be mature in understanding matters of this kind. ²¹It is written in the Scriptures*:

"I will speak to my own people
    through strange languages
    and through the lips of foreigners.
But even then, they will not listen
        to me,"*
    says the LORD.

²²So you see that speaking in tongues is a sign, not for believers, but for unbelievers. Prophecy, however, is for the benefit of believers, not unbelievers. ²³Even so, if unbelievers or people who don't understand these things come into your church meeting and hear everyone speaking in an unknown language, they will think you are crazy. ²⁴But if all of you are prophesying, and unbelievers or people who don't understand these things come into your meeting, they will be convicted of sin and judged by what you say. ²⁵As they listen, their secret thoughts will be exposed, and they will fall to their knees and worship God, declaring, "God is truly here among you."

²⁶Well, my brothers and sisters, let's summarize. When you meet together, one will sing, another will teach, another will tell some special revelation God has given, one will speak in tongues, and another will interpret what is said. But everything that is done must strengthen all of you.

²⁷No more than two or three should speak in tongues. They must speak one at a time, and someone must interpret what they say. ²⁸But if no one is present who can interpret, they must be silent in your church meeting and speak in tongues to God privately.

²⁹Let two or three people prophesy, and let the others evaluate what is said. ³⁰But if someone is prophesying and another person receives a revelation from the Lord, the one who is speaking must stop. ³¹In this way, all who prophesy will have a turn to speak, one after the other, so that everyone will learn and be encouraged. ³²Remember that people who prophesy are in control of their spirit and can take turns. ³³For God is not a God of disorder but of peace, as in all the meetings of God's holy people.*

³⁴Women should be silent during the church meetings. It is not proper for them to speak. They should be submissive, just as the law says. ³⁵If they have any questions, they should ask their husbands at home, for it is improper for women to speak in church meetings.*

³⁶Or do you think God's word originated with you Corinthians? Are you the only ones to whom it was given? ³⁷If you claim to be a prophet or think you are spiritual, you should recognize that what I am saying is a command from the Lord himself. ³⁸But if you do not recognize this, you yourself will not be recognized.*

³⁹So, my dear brothers and sisters, be eager to prophesy, and don't forbid speaking in tongues. ⁴⁰But be sure that everything is done properly and in order.

14:21a Greek *in the law.*   **14:21b** Isa 28:11-12.
14:33 The phrase *as in all the meetings of God's holy people* could instead be joined to the beginning of 14:34.
14:35 Some manuscripts place verses 34-35 after 14:40.
14:38 Some manuscripts read *If you are ignorant of this, stay in your ignorance.*

PSALM 37:30-40

The godly offer good counsel;
    they teach right from wrong.
³¹ They have made God's law their own,
    so they will never slip from his path.

³² The wicked wait in ambush for the godly,
    looking for an excuse to kill them.
³³ But the LORD will not let the wicked succeed

or let the godly be condemned
  when they are put on trial.

34 Put your hope in the LORD.
    Travel steadily along his path.
  He will honor you by giving you
      the land.
    You will see the wicked destroyed.

35 I have seen wicked and ruthless
      people
    flourishing like a tree in its native
      soil.
36 But when I looked again, they were
      gone!
    Though I searched for them, I could
      not find them!

37 Look at those who are honest and good,
for a wonderful future awaits those
  who love peace.
38 But the rebellious will be
    destroyed;
  they have no future.

39 The LORD rescues the godly;
    he is their fortress in times
      of trouble.
40 The LORD helps them,
    rescuing them from the wicked.
  He saves them,
    and they find shelter in him.

PROVERBS 21:27
The sacrifice of an evil person is detestable, especially when it is offered with wrong motives.

AUGUST**23**

JOB 8:1–11:20
Bildad and Zophar were Job's next advisors. Bildad reminded Job that God punishes the wicked. This was a backhanded way of saying that Job wouldn't be suffering if he wasn't wicked.

Then Bildad the Shuhite replied to Job:

2 "How long will you go on like this?
    You sound like a blustering wind.
3 Does God twist justice?
    Does the Almighty twist what is
      right?
4 Your children must have sinned
      against him,
    so their punishment was well
      deserved.
5 But if you pray to God
    and seek the favor of the Almighty,
6 and if you are pure and live with
      integrity,
    he will surely rise up and restore
      your happy home.
7 And though you started with little,
    you will end with much.

8 "Just ask the previous generation.
    Pay attention to the experience of
      our ancestors.
9 For we were born but yesterday and
      know nothing.
    Our days on earth are as fleeting as
      a shadow.
10 But those who came before us will
      teach you.
    They will teach you the wisdom of
      old.
11 "Can papyrus reeds grow tall without a
      marsh?
    Can marsh grass flourish without
      water?
12 While they are still flowering, not
      ready to be cut,
    they begin to wither more quickly
      than grass.
13 The same happens to all who forget
      God.
    The hopes of the godless evaporate.
14 Their confidence hangs by a thread.
    They are leaning on a spider's web.
15 They cling to their home for security,
    but it won't last.
    They try to hold it tight, but it will
      not endure.
16 The godless seem like a lush plant
      growing in the sunshine,

its branches spreading across the garden.

17 Its roots grow down through a pile of stones;
it takes hold on a bed of rocks.

18 But when it is uprooted,
it's as though it never existed!

19 That's the end of its life,
and others spring up from the earth to replace it.

20 "But look, God will not reject a person of integrity,
nor will he lend a hand to the wicked.

21 He will once again fill your mouth with laughter
and your lips with shouts of joy.

22 Those who hate you will be clothed with shame,
and the home of the wicked will be destroyed."

9:1 THEN Job spoke again:

2 "Yes, I know all this is true in principle.
But how can a person be declared innocent in God's sight?

3 If someone wanted to take God to court,*
would it be possible to answer him even once in a thousand times?

4 For God is so wise and so mighty.
Who has ever challenged him successfully?

5 "Without warning, he moves the mountains,
overturning them in his anger.

6 He shakes the earth from its place,
and its foundations tremble.

7 If he commands it, the sun won't rise and the stars won't shine.

8 He alone has spread out the heavens and marches on the waves of the sea.

9 He made all the stars—the Bear and Orion,
the Pleiades and the constellations of the southern sky.

10 He does great things too marvelous to understand.
He performs countless miracles.

11 "Yet when he comes near, I cannot see him.

When he moves by, I do not see him go.

12 If he snatches someone in death, who can stop him?
Who dares to ask, 'What are you doing?'

13 And God does not restrain his anger.
Even the monsters of the sea* are crushed beneath his feet.

14 "So who am I, that I should try to answer God
or even reason with him?

15 Even if I were right, I would have no defense.
I could only plead for mercy.

16 And even if I summoned him and he responded,
I'm not sure he would listen to me.

17 For he attacks me with a storm
and repeatedly wounds me without cause.

18 He will not let me catch my breath,
but fills me instead with bitter sorrows.

19 If it's a question of strength, he's the strong one.
If it's a matter of justice, who dares to summon him to court?

20 Though I am innocent, my own mouth would pronounce me guilty.
Though I am blameless, it* would prove me wicked.

21 "I am innocent,
but it makes no difference to me—
I despise my life.

22 Innocent or wicked, it is all the same to God.
That's why I say, 'He destroys both the blameless and the wicked.'

23 When a plague* sweeps through,
he laughs at the death of the innocent.

24 The whole earth is in the hands of the wicked,
and God blinds the eyes of the judges.
If he's not the one who does it, who is?

25 "My life passes more swiftly than a runner.
It flees away without a glimpse of happiness.

²⁶ It disappears like a swift papyrus boat,
like an eagle swooping down on its
prey.
²⁷ If I decided to forget my complaints,
to put away my sad face and be
cheerful,
²⁸ I would still dread all the pain,
for I know you will not find me
innocent, O God.
²⁹ Whatever happens, I will be found
guilty.
So what's the use of trying?
³⁰ Even if I were to wash myself with soap
and clean my hands with lye,
³¹ you would plunge me into a muddy
ditch,
and my own filthy clothing would
hate me.

³² "God is not a mortal like me,
so I cannot argue with him or take
him to trial.
³³ If only there were a mediator between
us,
someone who could bring us
together.
³⁴ The mediator could make God stop
beating me,
and I would no longer live in terror
of his punishment.
³⁵ Then I could speak to him without
fear,
but I cannot do that in my own
strength.

^{10:1} "I AM disgusted with my life.
Let me complain freely.
My bitter soul must complain.
² I will say to God, 'Don't simply
condemn me—
tell me the charge you are bringing
against me.
³ What do you gain by oppressing me?
Why do you reject me, the work
of your own hands,
while smiling on the schemes of the
wicked?
⁴ Are your eyes like those of a human?
Do you see things only as people see
them?
⁵ Is your lifetime only as long as ours?
Is your life so short
⁶ that you must quickly probe for my
guilt
and search for my sin?

⁷ Although you know I am not guilty,
no one can rescue me from your
hands.

⁸ "'You formed me with your hands; you
made me,
yet now you completely destroy me.
⁹ Remember that you made me from
dust—
will you turn me back to dust so
soon?
¹⁰ You guided my conception
and formed me in the womb.*
¹¹ You clothed me with skin and flesh,
and you knit my bones and sinews
together.
¹² You gave me life and showed me your
unfailing love.
My life was preserved by your care.

¹³ "'Yet your real motive—
your true intent—
¹⁴ was to watch me, and if I sinned,
you would not forgive my guilt.
¹⁵ If I am guilty, too bad for me;
and even if I'm innocent, I can't
hold my head high,
because I am filled with shame and
misery.
¹⁶ And if I hold my head high, you hunt
me like a lion
and display your awesome power
against me.
¹⁷ Again and again you witness against
me.
You pour out your growing anger on
me
and bring fresh armies against me.

¹⁸ "'Why, then, did you deliver me from
my mother's womb?
Why didn't you let me die at birth?
¹⁹ It would be as though I had never
existed,
going directly from the womb to the
grave.
²⁰ I have only a few days left, so leave me
alone,
that I may have a moment of
comfort
²¹ before I leave—never to return—
for the land of darkness and utter
gloom.
²² It is a land as dark as midnight,
a land of gloom and confusion,

where even the light is dark as
midnight.'"

11:1THEN Zophar the Naamathite replied
to Job:

2 "Shouldn't someone answer this
torrent of words?
Is a person proved innocent just by
a lot of talking?
3 Should I remain silent while you
babble on?
When you mock God, shouldn't
someone make you ashamed?
4 You claim, 'My beliefs are pure,'
and 'I am clean in the sight of God.'
5 If only God would speak;
if only he would tell you what he
thinks!
6 If only he would tell you the secrets
of wisdom,
for true wisdom is not a simple
matter.
Listen! God is doubtless punishing you
far less than you deserve!

7 "Can you solve the mysteries of God?
Can you discover everything about
the Almighty?
8 Such knowledge is higher than the
heavens—
and who are you?
It is deeper than the underworld*—
what do you know?

9 It is broader than the earth
and wider than the sea.
10 If God comes and puts a person
in prison
or calls the court to order, who can
stop him?
11 For he knows those who are false,
and he takes note of all their sins.
12 An empty-headed person won't
become wise
any more than a wild donkey can
bear a human child.*

13 "If only you would prepare your heart
and lift up your hands to him
in prayer!
14 Get rid of your sins,
and leave all iniquity behind you.
15 Then your face will brighten with
innocence.
You will be strong and free of fear.
16 You will forget your misery;
it will be like water flowing away.
17 Your life will be brighter than the
noonday.
Even darkness will be as bright
as morning.
18 Having hope will give you courage.
You will be protected and will rest
in safety.
19 You will lie down unafraid,
and many will look to you
for help.

HOW WE LIVE

Overcoming doubt

1 CORINTHIANS 15:3-9 There will always be people who refuse to believe that
Jesus Christ rose from the dead. In fact, most churches have a few unbelievers in their congregations. They believe that Jesus was a good man,
a teacher, or a prophet, but they just can't (or won't) wrap their minds
around the concept of him being the Son of God who rose from the dead.
• Paul was dealing with doubters when he wrote to the church in Corinth.
But he had something at his disposal that we do not have today: living
eyewitnesses. In 1 Corinthians 15:5-7, he reminds the Corinthians of all
the people who saw Jesus after his resurrection. Jesus appeared to
Peter, the Twelve, and 500 others at the same time. Then he appeared
to James, the apostles, and to Paul as he traveled on the road to Damascus. Because so many folks witnessed the resurrection of Jesus, it is
recorded many places in the New Testament. We have this written record;
beyond that, we must have faith. • Don't be discouraged by doubters.
Rather, be filled with hope that one day everyone—doubters and believers alike—will see living proof when Christ returns.

20 But the wicked will be blinded.
    They will have no escape.
    Their only hope is death."

9:3 Or *If God wanted to take someone to court.*
9:13 Hebrew *the helpers of Rahab,* the name of a mythical
sea monster that represents chaos in ancient literature.
9:20 Or *he.* 9:23 Or *disaster.* 10:10 Hebrew *You poured
me out like milk / and curdled me like cheese.* 11:8 Hebrew
than Sheol. 11:12 Or *than a wild male donkey can bear
a tame colt.*

1 CORINTHIANS 15:1-28
Resurrection; life beyond death; life out of death;
life in spite of death: these are all offered to us by
Jesus, who saved us from the power of sin and
death.

Let me [Paul] now remind you, dear brothers and sisters,* of the Good News I
preached to you before. You welcomed it
then, and you still stand firm in it. ²It is
this Good News that saves you if you continue to believe the message I told you—
unless, of course, you believed something
that was never true in the first place.*

³I passed on to you what was most important and what had also been passed on
to me. Christ died for our sins, just as the
Scriptures said. ⁴He was buried, and he
was raised from the dead on the third day,
just as the Scriptures said. ⁵He was seen
by Peter* and then by the Twelve . ⁶After
that, he was seen by more than 500 of his
followers* at one time, most of whom are
still alive, though some have died. ⁷Then
he was seen by James and later by all the
apostles. ⁸Last of all, as though I had been
born at the wrong time, I also saw him.
⁹For I am the least of all the apostles. In
fact, I'm not even worthy to be called an
apostle after the way I persecuted God's
church.

¹⁰But whatever I am now, it is all because God poured out his special favor on
me—and not without results. For I have
worked harder than any of the other apostles; yet it was not I but God who was
working through me by his grace. ¹¹So it
makes no difference whether I preach or
they preach, for we all preach the same
message you have already believed.

¹²But tell me this—since we preach that
Christ rose from the dead, why are some
of you saying there will be no resurrection
of the dead? ¹³For if there is no resurrection of the dead, then Christ has not been

raised either. ¹⁴And if Christ has not been
raised, then all our preaching is useless,
and your faith is useless. ¹⁵And we apostles would all be lying about God—for we
have said that God raised Christ from the
grave. But that can't be true if there is no
resurrection of the dead. ¹⁶And if there is
no resurrection of the dead, then Christ
has not been raised. ¹⁷And if Christ has
not been raised, then your faith is useless
and you are still guilty of your sins. ¹⁸In
that case, all who have died believing in
Christ are lost! ¹⁹And if our hope in Christ
is only for this life, we are more to be pitied than anyone in the world.

²⁰But in fact, Christ has been raised
from the dead. He is the first of a great
harvest of all who have died.

²¹So you see, just as death came into the
world through a man, now the resurrection from the dead has begun through
another man. ²²Just as everyone dies because we all belong to Adam, everyone
who belongs to Christ will be given new
life. ²³But there is an order to this resurrection: Christ was raised as the first of
the harvest; then all who belong to Christ
will be raised when he comes back.

²⁴After that the end will come, when he
will turn the Kingdom over to God the Father, having destroyed every ruler and authority and power. ²⁵For Christ must reign
until he humbles all his enemies beneath
his feet. ²⁶And the last enemy to be destroyed is death. ²⁷For the Scriptures say,
"God has put all things under his authority."* (Of course, when it says "all things
are under his authority," that does not include God himself, who gave Christ his
authority.) ²⁸Then, when all things are
under his authority, the Son will put himself under God's authority, so that God,
who gave his Son authority over all things,
will be utterly supreme over everything
everywhere.

15:1 Greek *brothers;* also in 15:31, 50, 58. 15:2 Or *unless
you never believed it in the first place.* 15:5 Greek *Cephas.*
15:6 Greek *the brothers.* 15:27 Ps 8:6.

PSALM 38:1-22
*A psalm of David, asking God to remember
him.*

¹ **O** Lord, don't rebuke me in your anger
    or discipline me in your rage!

2 Your arrows have struck deep,
   and your blows are crushing me.
3 Because of your anger, my whole body
   is sick;
   my health is broken because of
   my sins.
4 My guilt overwhelms me—
   it is a burden too heavy to bear.
5 My wounds fester and stink
   because of my foolish sins.
6 I am bent over and racked with pain.
   All day long I walk around filled
   with grief.
7 A raging fever burns within me,
   and my health is broken.
8 I am exhausted and completely crushed.
   My groans come from an anguished
   heart.
9 You know what I long for, Lord;
   you hear my every sigh.
10 My heart beats wildly, my strength fails,
   and I am going blind.
11 My loved ones and friends stay away,
   fearing my disease.
   Even my own family stands at
   a distance.
12 Meanwhile, my enemies lay traps
   to kill me.
   Those who wish me harm make
   plans to ruin me.
   All day long they plan their
   treachery.

13 But I am deaf to all their threats.
   I am silent before them as one who
   cannot speak.
14 I choose to hear nothing,
   and I make no reply.
15 For I am waiting for you, O LORD.
   You must answer for me, O Lord
   my God.
16 I prayed, "Don't let my enemies gloat
   over me
   or rejoice at my downfall."
17 I am on the verge of collapse,
   facing constant pain.
18 But I confess my sins;
   I am deeply sorry for what I have
   done.
19 I have many aggressive enemies;
   they hate me without reason.
20 They repay me evil for good
   and oppose me for pursuing
   good.
21 Do not abandon me, O LORD.
   Do not stand at a distance,
   my God.
22 Come quickly to help me,
   O Lord my savior.

PROVERBS 21:28-29
A false witness will be cut off, but a credible witness will be allowed to speak. □ The wicked bluff their way through, but the virtuous think before they act.

AUGUST**24**

JOB 12:1–15:35
Job responded to each of his advisors. He had searched his heart and found no sin for which God would have destroyed his life in this way. He awaited some other explanation.

Then Job spoke again:

2 "You people really know everything,
   don't you?
   And when you die, wisdom will die
   with you!
3 Well, I know a few things myself—
   and you're no better than I am.
   Who doesn't know these things
   you've been saying?

4 Yet my friends laugh at me,
   for I call on God and expect an
   answer.
   I am a just and blameless man,
   yet they laugh at me.
5 People who are at ease mock those
   in trouble.
   They give a push to people who
   are stumbling.
6 But robbers are left in peace,
   and those who provoke God live
   in safety—
   though God keeps them in his
   power.

7 "Just ask the animals, and they will
teach you.
Ask the birds of the sky, and they
will tell you.
8 Speak to the earth, and it will instruct
you.
Let the fish in the sea speak to you.
9 For they all know
that my disaster* has come from
the hand of the LORD.
10 For the life of every living thing is in
his hand,
and the breath of every human
being.
11 The ear tests the words it hears
just as the mouth distinguishes
between foods.
12 Wisdom belongs to the aged,
and understanding to the old.

13 "But true wisdom and power are found
in God;
counsel and understanding are his.
14 What he destroys cannot be rebuilt.
When he puts someone in prison,
there is no escape.
15 If he holds back the rain, the earth
becomes a desert.
If he releases the waters, they flood
the earth.
16 Yes, strength and wisdom are his;
deceivers and deceived are both
in his power.
17 He leads counselors away, stripped
of good judgment;
wise judges become fools.
18 He removes the royal robe of kings.
They are led away with ropes
around their waist.
19 He leads priests away, stripped
of status;
he overthrows those with long years
in power.
20 He silences the trusted adviser
and removes the insight of the
elders.
21 He pours disgrace upon princes
and disarms the strong.

22 "He uncovers mysteries hidden
in darkness;
he brings light to the deepest
gloom.
23 He builds up nations, and he destroys
them.

He expands nations, and he
abandons them.
24 He strips kings of understanding
and leaves them wandering in
a pathless wasteland.
25 They grope in the darkness without
a light.
He makes them stagger like
drunkards.

13:1 "LOOK, I have seen all this with my
own eyes
and heard it with my own ears,
and now I understand.
2 I know as much as you do.
You are no better than I am.
3 As for me, I would speak directly to
the Almighty.
I want to argue my case with God
himself.
4 As for you, you smear me with lies.
As physicians, you are worthless
quacks.
5 If only you could be silent!
That's the wisest thing you could
do.
6 Listen to my charge;
pay attention to my arguments.

7 "Are you defending God with lies?
Do you make your dishonest
arguments for his sake?
8 Will you slant your testimony in his
favor?
Will you argue God's case for him?
9 What will happen when he finds out
what you are doing?
Can you fool him as easily as you
fool people?
10 No, you will be in trouble with him
if you secretly slant your testimony
in his favor.
11 Doesn't his majesty terrify you?
Doesn't your fear of him overwhelm
you?
12 Your platitudes are as valuable
as ashes.
Your defense is as fragile as a clay
pot.

13 "Be silent now and leave me alone.
Let me speak, and I will face the
consequences.
14 Yes, I will take my life in my hands
and say what I really think.

15 God might kill me, but I have no other
   hope.
   I am going to argue my case with
      him.
16 But this is what will save me—I am not
   godless.
   If I were, I could not stand before
      him.
17 "Listen closely to what I am about
   to say.
   Hear me out.
18 I have prepared my case;
   I will be proved innocent.
19 Who can argue with me over this?
   And if you prove me wrong, I will
      remain silent and die.

20 "O God, grant me these two things,
   and then I will be able to face you.
21 Remove your heavy hand from me,
   and don't terrify me with your
      awesome presence.
22 Now summon me, and I will answer!
   Or let me speak to you, and you
      reply.
23 Tell me, what have I done wrong?
   Show me my rebellion and
      my sin.
24 Why do you turn away from me?
   Why do you treat me as your
      enemy?

25 Would you terrify a leaf blown by
   the wind?
   Would you chase dry straw?
26 "You write bitter accusations against
   me
   and bring up all the sins of
      my youth.
27 You put my feet in stocks.
   You examine all my paths.
   You trace all my footprints.
28 I waste away like rotting wood,
   like a moth-eaten coat.

14:1 "How frail is humanity!
   How short is life, how full
      of trouble!
2 We blossom like a flower and then
   wither.
   Like a passing shadow, we quickly
      disappear.
3 Must you keep an eye on such a frail
   creature
   and demand an accounting from
      me?
4 Who can bring purity out of an
   impure person?
   No one!
5 You have decided the length of
   our lives.
   You know how many months
      we will live,

WHAT THE BIBLE SAYS

The future

1 CORINTHIANS 15:50-58 Satan seemed to be victorious in the Garden of
Eden and at the cross of Jesus. But God turned Satan's apparent victory
into defeat when Jesus Christ rose from the dead. Death is no longer a
source of fear for those who believe in Jesus. Death has been defeated,
and we have hope beyond the grave. There is a future beyond death,
beyond the grave. • However, for most of us, the bodies we have now
are going to die. Or, if we happen to be alive at the time of Christ's
return, our bodies will still have to be changed. Our resurrected bodies
have to be different from our present, physical bodies because "physical
bodies cannot inherit the Kingdom of God." Our bodies cannot go into
God's eternal Kingdom because these present bodies were not made
to live forever. So God has prepared new bodies that *will* live forever. The
resurrection is a fact; new bodies ready for life in eternity is also a fact.
• For those who have no hope in Christ, death is something to fear. Christians have been given a different perspective. For believers, death is not
the end; it is a doorway into eternal life.

and we are not given a minute
longer.

⁶ So leave us alone and let us rest!
We are like hired hands, so let us
finish our work in peace.

⁷ "Even a tree has more hope!
If it is cut down, it will sprout again
and grow new branches.
⁸ Though its roots have grown old in
the earth
and its stump decays,
⁹ at the scent of water it will bud
and sprout again like a new
seedling.

¹⁰ "But when people die, their strength
is gone.
They breathe their last, and then
where are they?
¹¹ As water evaporates from a lake
and a river disappears in drought,
¹² people are laid to rest and do not rise
again.
Until the heavens are no more, they
will not wake up
nor be roused from their sleep.

¹³ "I wish you would hide me in the
grave*
and forget me there until your
anger has passed.
But mark your calendar to think
of me again!
¹⁴ Can the dead live again?
If so, this would give me hope
through all my years of struggle,
and I would eagerly await the
release of death.
¹⁵ You would call and I would answer,
and you would yearn for me, your
handiwork.
¹⁶ For then you would guard my steps,
instead of watching for my sins.
¹⁷ My sins would be sealed in a pouch,
and you would cover my guilt.

¹⁸ "But instead, as mountains fall and
crumble
and as rocks fall from a cliff,
¹⁹ as water wears away the stones
and floods wash away the soil,
so you destroy people's hope.
²⁰ You always overpower them, and
they pass from the scene.

You disfigure them in death and
send them away.
²¹ They never know if their children
grow up in honor
or sink to insignificance.
²² They suffer painfully;
their life is full of trouble."

15:1 THEN Eliphaz the Temanite replied:

² "A wise man wouldn't answer with
such empty talk!
You are nothing but a windbag.
³ The wise don't engage in empty
chatter.
What good are such words?
⁴ Have you no fear of God,
no reverence for him?
⁵ Your sins are telling your mouth what
to say.
Your words are based on clever
deception.
⁶ Your own mouth condemns you,
not I.
Your own lips testify against you.

⁷ "Were you the first person ever born?
Were you born before the hills were
made?
⁸ Were you listening at God's secret
council?
Do you have a monopoly on
wisdom?
⁹ What do you know that we don't?
What do you understand that we
do not?
¹⁰ On our side are aged, gray-haired men
much older than your father!

¹¹ "Is God's comfort too little for you?
Is his gentle word not enough?
¹² What has taken away your reason?
What has weakened your vision,*
¹³ that you turn against God
and say all these evil things?
¹⁴ Can any mortal be pure?
Can anyone born of a woman
be just?
¹⁵ Look, God does not even trust the
angels.*
Even the heavens are not absolutely
pure in his sight.
¹⁶ How much less pure is a corrupt and
sinful person
with a thirst for wickedness!

[17] "If you will listen, I will show you.
I will answer you from my own
experience.
[18] And it is confirmed by the reports
of wise men
who have heard the same thing
from their fathers—
[19] from those to whom the land
was given
long before any foreigners arrived.

[20] "The wicked writhe in pain
throughout their lives.
Years of trouble are stored up for
the ruthless.
[21] The sound of terror rings in their ears,
and even on good days they fear the
attack of the destroyer.
[22] They dare not go out into the
darkness
for fear they will be murdered.
[23] They wander around, saying, 'Where
can I find bread?'*
They know their day of destruction
is near.
[24] That dark day terrifies them.
They live in distress and anguish,
like a king preparing for battle.
[25] For they shake their fists at God,
defying the Almighty.
[26] Holding their strong shields,
they defiantly charge against him.

[27] "These wicked people are heavy and
prosperous;
their waists bulge with fat.
[28] But their cities will be ruined.
They will live in abandoned houses
that are ready to tumble down.
[29] Their riches will not last,
and their wealth will not endure.
Their possessions will no longer
spread across the horizon.

[30] "They will not escape the darkness.
The burning sun will wither their
shoots,
and the breath of God will destroy
them.
[31] Let them no longer fool themselves by
trusting in empty riches,
for emptiness will be their only
reward.
[32] Like trees, they will be cut down in the
prime of life;

their branches will never again
be green.
[33] They will be like a vine whose grapes
are harvested too early,
like an olive tree that loses its
blossoms before the fruit can
form.
[34] For the godless are barren.
Their homes, enriched through
bribery, will burn.
[35] They conceive trouble and give birth
to evil.
Their womb produces deceit."

12:9 Hebrew *that this.*   **14:13** Hebrew *in Sheol.*   **15:12** Or
Why do your eyes flash with anger; Hebrew reads *Why
do your eyes blink.*   **15:15** Hebrew *the holy ones.*
15:23 Greek version reads *He is appointed to be food
for a vulture.*

1 CORINTHIANS 15:29-58
What will it be like on the other side of this material
world and these physical bodies? What will it really
mean to be "transformed"?

If the dead will not be raised, what point is
there in people being baptized for those
who are dead? Why do it unless the dead
will someday rise again?

[30]And why should we ourselves risk our
lives hour by hour? [31]For I swear, dear
brothers and sisters, that I face death
daily. This is as certain as my pride in
what Christ Jesus our Lord has done in
you. [32]And what value was there in fighting wild beasts—those people of Ephesus*—if there will be no resurrection
from the dead? And if there is no resurrection, "Let's feast and drink, for tomorrow we die!"* [33]Don't be fooled by those
who say such things, for "bad company
corrupts good character." [34]Think carefully about what is right, and stop sinning.
For to your shame I say that some of you
don't know God at all.

[35]But someone may ask, "How will the
dead be raised? What kind of bodies will
they have?" [36]What a foolish question!
When you put a seed into the ground, it
doesn't grow into a plant unless it dies
first. [37]And what you put in the ground is
not the plant that will grow, but only a
bare seed of wheat or whatever you are
planting. [38]Then God gives it the new
body he wants it to have. A different plant
grows from each kind of seed. [39]Similarly

there are different kinds of flesh—one kind for humans, another for animals, another for birds, and another for fish.

⁴⁰There are also bodies in the heavens and bodies on the earth. The glory of the heavenly bodies is different from the glory of the earthly bodies. ⁴¹The sun has one kind of glory, while the moon and stars each have another kind. And even the stars differ from each other in their glory.

⁴²It is the same way with the resurrection of the dead. Our earthly bodies are planted in the ground when we die, but they will be raised to live forever. ⁴³Our bodies are buried in brokenness, but they will be raised in glory. They are buried in weakness, but they will be raised in strength. ⁴⁴They are buried as natural human bodies, but they will be raised as spiritual bodies. For just as there are natural bodies, there are also spiritual bodies.

⁴⁵The Scriptures tell us, "The first man, Adam, became a living person."* But the last Adam—that is, Christ—is a life-giving Spirit. ⁴⁶What comes first is the natural body, then the spiritual body comes later. ⁴⁷Adam, the first man, was made from the dust of the earth, while Christ, the second man, came from heaven. ⁴⁸Earthly people are like the earthly man, and heavenly people are like the heavenly man. ⁴⁹Just as we are now like the earthly man, we will someday be like* the heavenly man.

⁵⁰What I am saying, dear brothers and sisters, is that our physical bodies cannot inherit the Kingdom of God. These dying bodies cannot inherit what will last forever.

⁵¹But let me reveal to you a wonderful secret. We will not all die, but we will all be transformed! ⁵²It will happen in a moment, in the blink of an eye, when the last trumpet is blown. For when the trumpet sounds, those who have died will be raised to live forever. And we who are living will also be transformed. ⁵³For our dying bodies must be transformed into bodies that will never die; our mortal bodies must be transformed into immortal bodies.

⁵⁴Then, when our dying bodies have been transformed into bodies that will never die,* this Scripture will be fulfilled:

"Death is swallowed up in victory.*
⁵⁵ O death, where is your victory?
    O death, where is your sting?*"

⁵⁶For sin is the sting that results in death, and the law gives sin its power. ⁵⁷But thank God! He gives us victory over sin and death through our Lord Jesus Christ.

⁵⁸So, my dear brothers and sisters, be strong and immovable. Always work enthusiastically for the Lord, for you know that nothing you do for the Lord is ever useless.

15:32a Greek *fighting wild beasts in Ephesus.* **15:32b** Isa 22:13. **15:45** Gen 2:7. **15:49** Some manuscripts read *let us be like.* **15:54a** Some manuscripts add *and our mortal bodies have been transformed into immortal bodies.* **15:54b** Isa 25:8. **15:55** Hos 13:14 (Greek version).

PSALM 39:1-13
For Jeduthun, the choir director: A psalm of David.

¹ I said to myself, "I will watch what I do
    and not sin in what I say.
I will hold my tongue
    when the ungodly are around me."
² But as I stood there in silence—
    not even speaking of good things—
    the turmoil within me grew worse.
³ The more I thought about it,
    the hotter I got,
    igniting a fire of words:
⁴ "LORD, remind me how brief my time
    on earth will be.
Remind me that my days are
    numbered—
    how fleeting my life is.
⁵ You have made my life no longer than
    the width of my hand.
My entire lifetime is just a moment
    to you;
    at best, each of us is but a breath."
                                        Interlude

⁶ We are merely moving shadows,
    and all our busy rushing ends in
    nothing.
We heap up wealth,
    not knowing who will spend it.
⁷ And so, Lord, where do I put my hope?
    My only hope is in you.
⁸ Rescue me from my rebellion.
    Do not let fools mock me.
⁹ I am silent before you; I won't say
    a word,

for my punishment is from you.
¹⁰ But please stop striking me!
I am exhausted by the blows from
your hand.
¹¹ When you discipline us for our sins,
you consume like a moth what
is precious to us.
Each of us is but a breath.

Interlude

¹² Hear my prayer, O LORD!
Listen to my cries for help!
Don't ignore my tears.

PROVERBS 21:30-31

No human wisdom or understanding or plan can stand against the LORD. □ The horse is prepared for the day of battle, but the victory belongs to the LORD.

For I am your guest—
a traveler passing through,
as my ancestors were before me.
¹³ Leave me alone so I can smile again
before I am gone and exist
no more.

AUGUST**25**

JOB 16:1-19:29
Back and forth the men grappled with Job's plight, the same plight that we often struggle with today. Where is God when life goes awry? Where is God when we suffer?

Then Job spoke again:

² "I have heard all this before.
What miserable comforters you are!
³ Won't you ever stop blowing hot air?
What makes you keep on talking?
⁴ I could say the same things if you were
in my place.
I could spout off criticism and
shake my head at you.
⁵ But if it were me, I would encourage
you.
I would try to take away your grief.
⁶ Instead, I suffer if I defend myself,
and I suffer no less if I refuse
to speak.

⁷ "O God, you have ground me down
and devastated my family.
⁸ As if to prove I have sinned, you've
reduced me to skin and bones.
My gaunt flesh testifies against me.
⁹ God hates me and angrily tears
me apart.
He snaps his teeth at me
and pierces me with his eyes.
¹⁰ People jeer and laugh at me.
They slap my cheek in contempt.
A mob gathers against me.

¹¹ God has handed me over to sinners.
He has tossed me into the hands
of the wicked.
¹² "I was living quietly until he shattered
me.
He took me by the neck and broke
me in pieces.
Then he set me up as his target,
¹³ and now his archers surround me.
His arrows pierce me without mercy.
The ground is wet with my blood.*
¹⁴ Again and again he smashes against
me,
charging at me like a warrior.
¹⁵ I wear burlap to show my grief.
My pride lies in the dust.
¹⁶ My eyes are red with weeping;
dark shadows circle my eyes.
¹⁷ Yet I have done no wrong,
and my prayer is pure.

¹⁸ "O earth, do not conceal my blood.
Let it cry out on my behalf.
¹⁹ Even now my witness is in heaven.
My advocate is there on high.
²⁰ My friends scorn me,
but I pour out my tears to God.
²¹ I need someone to mediate between
God and me,
as a person mediates between
friends.
²² For soon I must go down that road
from which I will never return.

17:1"My spirit is crushed,
  and my life is nearly snuffed out.
  The grave is ready to receive me.
2 I am surrounded by mockers.
  I watch how bitterly they taunt me.

3 "You must defend my innocence,
    O God,
  since no one else will stand up
    for me.
4 You have closed their minds
    to understanding,
  but do not let them triumph.
5 They betray their friends for their own
    advantage,
  so let their children faint with
    hunger.

6 "God has made a mockery of me
    among the people;
  they spit in my face.
7 My eyes are swollen with weeping,
  and I am but a shadow of my
    former self.
8 The virtuous are horrified when they
    see me.
  The innocent rise up against the
    ungodly.
9 The righteous keep moving forward,
  and those with clean hands become
    stronger and stronger.

10 "As for all of you, come back with
    a better argument,
  though I still won't find a wise man
    among you.
11 My days are over.
  My hopes have disappeared.
  My heart's desires are broken.
12 These men say that night is day;
  they claim that the darkness is light.
13 What if I go to the grave*
  and make my bed in darkness?
14 What if I call the grave my father,
  and the maggot my mother or my
    sister?
15 Where then is my hope?
  Can anyone find it?
16 No, my hope will go down with me
    to the grave.
  We will rest together in the dust!"

18:1Then Bildad the Shuhite replied:

2 "How long before you stop talking?
  Speak sense if you want us to answer!

3 Do you think we are mere animals?
  Do you think we are stupid?
4 You may tear out your hair in anger,
  but will that destroy the earth?
  Will it make the rocks tremble?

5 "Surely the light of the wicked will be
    snuffed out.
  The sparks of their fire will not
    glow.
6 The light in their tent will grow dark.
  The lamp hanging above them will
    be quenched.
7 The confident stride of the wicked
    will be shortened.
  Their own schemes will be their
    downfall.
8 The wicked walk into a net.
  They fall into a pit.
9 A trap grabs them by the heel.
  A snare holds them tight.
10 A noose lies hidden on the ground.
  A rope is stretched across their
    path.

11 "Terrors surround the wicked
  and trouble them at every step.
12 Hunger depletes their strength,
  and calamity waits for them to
    stumble.
13 Disease eats their skin;
  death devours their limbs.
14 They are torn from the security of
    their homes
  and are brought down to the king of
    terrors.
15 The homes of the wicked will burn
    down;
  burning sulfur rains on their
    houses.
16 Their roots will dry up,
  and their branches will wither.
17 All memory of their existence will
    fade from the earth,
  No one will remember their names.
18 They will be thrust from light into
    darkness,
  driven from the world.
19 They will have neither children nor
    grandchildren,
  nor any survivor in the place where
    they lived.
20 People in the west are appalled at their
    fate;
  people in the east are horrified.

21 They will say, 'This was the home of a
  wicked person,
    the place of one who rejected God.'"

19:1THEN Job spoke again:

2 "How long will you torture me?
  How long will you try to crush me
    with your words?
3 You have already insulted me ten
    times.
  You should be ashamed of treating
    me so badly.
4 Even if I have sinned,
  that is my concern, not yours.
5 You think you're better than I am,
  using my humiliation as evidence
    of my sin.
6 But it is God who has wronged me,
  capturing me in his net.*

7 "I cry out, 'Help!' but no one answers
    me.
  I protest, but there is no justice.
8 God has blocked my way so I cannot
    move.
  He has plunged my path into
    darkness.
9 He has stripped me of my honor
  and removed the crown from my
    head.
10 He has demolished me on every side,
    and I am finished.

He has uprooted my hope like
  a fallen tree.
11 His fury burns against me;
  he counts me as an enemy.
12 His troops advance.
  They build up roads to attack me.
  They camp all around my tent.

13 "My relatives stay far away,
  and my friends have turned against
    me.
14 My family is gone,
  and my close friends have forgotten
    me.
15 My servants and maids consider me
    a stranger.
  I am like a foreigner to them.
16 When I call my servant, he doesn't
    come;
  I have to plead with him!
17 My breath is repulsive to my wife.
  I am rejected by my own family.
18 Even young children despise me.
  When I stand to speak, they turn
    their backs on me.
19 My close friends detest me.
  Those I loved have turned against
    me.
20 I have been reduced to skin and
    bones
  and have escaped death by the skin
    of my teeth.

WHAT THE BIBLE SAYS

Why does God allow suffering?

JOB 17:1 The main question in the book of Job is timely: Why does God allow suffering? Like Job's friends, people today make a mistake when they assume that all misfortune *must be* a sign of unconfessed sin or lack of faith. Though following God normally (but not always) leads to a happier life, and rebelling against God normally (but not always) leads to an unhappy life, in this fallen world, calamity and suffering come to good and bad alike. • This does not mean that God is indifferent, uncaring, unjust, or powerless to protect us. Bad things happen because we live in a fallen world where both believers and unbelievers are hit with the tragic consequences of sin. God will one day eradicate evil and suffering. In the meantime, believers can take courage that God turns suffering around for their good (Romans 8:28, July 24). • Often it is impossible to know why God allows certain tragic events to happen, but we can be sure he is all-powerful and knows what he is doing. The next time you face trials and dilemmas, see them as opportunities to turn to God for strength.

²¹ "Have mercy on me, my friends,
> have mercy,
> for the hand of God has struck me.
²² Must you also persecute me, like God
> does?
> Haven't you chewed me up enough?

²³ "Oh, that my words could be recorded.
> Oh, that they could be inscribed
> on a monument,
²⁴ carved with an iron chisel and filled
> with lead,
> engraved forever in the rock.

²⁵ "But as for me, I know that my
> Redeemer lives,
> and he will stand upon the earth
> at last.
²⁶ And after my body has decayed,
> yet in my body I will see God!*
²⁷ I will see him for myself.
> Yes, I will see him with my own
> eyes.
> I am overwhelmed at the thought!

²⁸ "How dare you go on persecuting me,
> saying, 'It's his own fault'?
²⁹ You should fear punishment
> yourselves,
> for your attitude deserves
> punishment.
> Then you will know that there
> is indeed a judgment."

16:13 Hebrew *my gall.*   17:13 Hebrew *to Sheol;* also in
17:16.   19:6 Or *for I am like a city under siege.*   19:26 Or
without my body I will see God. The meaning of the Hebrew
is uncertain.

1 CORINTHIANS 16:1-24
Paul wanted the Corinthian believers to have a part
in the offering that he was collecting to help the
Christians in Jerusalem. The letter closes with final
greetings and exhortations.

Now regarding your [Corinthians] question about the money being collected for
God's people in Jerusalem. You should
follow the same procedure I gave to the
churches in Galatia. ²On the first day of
each week, you should each put aside a
portion of the money you have earned.
Don't wait until I get there and then try to
collect it all at once. ³When I come, I will
write letters of recommendation for the
messengers you choose to deliver your
gift to Jerusalem. ⁴And if it seems appro-

priate for me to go along, they can travel
with me.

⁵I am coming to visit you after I have
been to Macedonia,* for I am planning to
travel through Macedonia. ⁶Perhaps I will
stay awhile with you, possibly all winter,
and then you can send me on my way to
my next destination. ⁷This time I don't
want to make just a short visit and then go
right on. I want to come and stay awhile, if
the Lord will let me. ⁸In the meantime, I
will be staying here at Ephesus until the
Festival of Pentecost. ⁹There is a wide-
open door for a great work here, although
many oppose me.

¹⁰When Timothy comes, don't intimi-
date him. He is doing the Lord's work, just
as I am. ¹¹Don't let anyone treat him with
contempt. Send him on his way with your
blessing when he returns to me. I expect
him to come with the other believers.*

¹²Now about our brother Apollos—I
urged him to visit you with the other believers, but he was not willing to go right
now. He will see you later when he has the
opportunity.

¹³Be on guard. Stand firm in the faith.
Be courageous.* Be strong. ¹⁴And do everything with love.

¹⁵You know that Stephanas and his
household were the first of the harvest of
believers in Greece,* and they are spending their lives in service to God's people. I
urge you, dear brothers and sisters,* ¹⁶to
submit to them and others like them
who serve with such devotion. ¹⁷I am very
glad that Stephanas, Fortunatus, and
Achaicus have come here. They have been
providing the help you weren't here to
give me. ¹⁸They have been a wonderful
encouragement to me, as they have been
to you. You must show your appreciation
to all who serve so well.

¹⁹The churches here in the province of
Asia* send greetings in the Lord, as do Aquila and Priscilla* and all the others who
gather in their home for church meetings.
²⁰All the brothers and sisters here send
greetings to you. Greet each other with
Christian love.*

²¹HERE IS MY GREETING IN MY OWN
HANDWRITING—PAUL.

²²If anyone does not love the Lord, that
person is cursed. Our Lord, come!*

²³May the grace of the Lord Jesus be with you.

²⁴My love to all of you in Christ Jesus.*

16:5 *Macedonia* was in the northern region of Greece. **16:11** Greek *with the brothers;* also in 16:12. **16:13** Greek *Be men.* **16:15a** Greek *in Achaia,* the southern region of the Greek peninsula. **16:15b** Greek *brothers;* also in 16:20. **16:19a** *Asia* was a Roman province in what is now western Turkey. **16:19b** Greek *Prisca.* **16:20** Greek *with a sacred kiss.* **16:22** From Aramaic, *Marana tha.* Some manuscripts read *Maran atha, "Our Lord has come."* **16:24** Some manuscripts add *Amen.*

PSALM 40:1-10
For the choir director: A psalm of David.

¹ **I** waited patiently for the LORD to help me,
    and he turned to me and heard my cry.
² He lifted me out of the pit of despair,
    out of the mud and the mire.
He set my feet on solid ground
    and steadied me as I walked along.
³ He has given me a new song to sing,
    a hymn of praise to our God.
Many will see what he has done and
    be amazed.
    They will put their trust in the LORD.

⁴ Oh, the joys of those who trust the
    LORD,
    who have no confidence in the
        proud
    or in those who worship idols.
⁵ O LORD my God, you have performed
    many wonders for us.
    Your plans for us are too numerous
        to list.
    You have no equal.

JOB 20:1-22:30
And what about the wicked? The only thing more perplexing than a good person facing horrible adversity is a wicked person who seems to get away with his wickedness and even profit from it.

Then Zophar the Naamathite replied:

² "I must reply
    because I am greatly disturbed.

If I tried to recite all your wonderful
    deeds,
    I would never come to the end
        of them.
⁶ You take no delight in sacrifices or
    offerings.
    Now that you have made me listen,
        I finally understand*—
    you don't require burnt offerings
        or sin offerings.
⁷ Then I said, "Look, I have come.
    As is written about me in the
        Scriptures:
⁸ I take joy in doing your will,
    my God,
    for your instructions are written
        on my heart."

⁹ I have told all your people about your
    justice.
    I have not been afraid to speak out,
        as you, O LORD, well know.
¹⁰ I have not kept the good news of your
    justice hidden in my heart;
    I have talked about your
        faithfulness and saving power.
I have told everyone in the great
    assembly
    of your unfailing love and
        faithfulness.

40:6 Greek text reads *You have given me a body.* Compare Heb 10:5.

PROVERBS 22:1
Choose a good reputation over great riches; being held in high esteem is better than silver or gold.

AUGUST**26**

³ I've had to endure your insults,
    but now my spirit prompts me
        to reply.

⁴ "Don't you realize that from the
    beginning of time,
    ever since people were first placed
        on the earth,
⁵ the triumph of the wicked has been
    short lived

and the joy of the godless has been
only temporary?

6 Though the pride of the godless
reaches to the heavens
and their heads touch the clouds,

7 yet they will vanish forever,
thrown away like their own dung.
Those who knew them will ask,
'Where are they?'

8 They will fade like a dream and not
be found.
They will vanish like a vision in the
night.

9 Those who once saw them will see
them no more.
Their families will never see them
again.

10 Their children will beg from the poor,
for they must give back their stolen
riches.

11 Though they are young,
their bones will lie in the dust.

12 "They enjoyed the sweet taste of
wickedness,
letting it melt under their tongue.

13 They savored it,
holding it long in their mouths.

14 But suddenly the food in their bellies
turns sour,
a poisonous venom in their
stomach.

15 They will vomit the wealth they
swallowed.
God won't let them keep it down.

16 They will suck the poison of cobras.
The viper will kill them.

17 They will never again enjoy streams
of olive oil
or rivers of milk and honey.

18 They will give back everything they
worked for.
Their wealth will bring them no joy.

19 For they oppressed the poor and left
them destitute.
They foreclosed on their homes.

20 They were always greedy and never
satisfied.
Nothing remains of all the things
they dreamed about.

21 Nothing is left after they finish
gorging themselves.
Therefore, their prosperity will not
endure.

22 "In the midst of plenty, they will run
into trouble
and be overcome by misery.

23 May God give them a bellyful of
trouble.
May God rain down his anger upon
them.

24 When they try to escape an iron
weapon,
a bronze-tipped arrow will pierce
them.

25 The arrow is pulled from their back,
and the arrowhead glistens with
blood.*
The terrors of death are upon them.

26   Their treasures will be thrown into
deepest darkness.
A wildfire will devour their goods,
consuming all they have left.

27 The heavens will reveal their guilt,
and the earth will testify against
them.

28 A flood will sweep away their house.
God's anger will descend on them
in torrents.

29 This is the reward that God gives the
wicked.
It is the inheritance decreed by God."

21:1 THEN Job spoke again:

2 "Listen closely to what I am saying.
That's one consolation you can
give me.

3 Bear with me, and let me speak.
After I have spoken, you may
resume mocking me.

4 "My complaint is with God, not with
people.
I have good reason to be so
impatient.

5 Look at me and be stunned.
Put your hand over your mouth
in shock.

6 When I think about what I am saying,
I shudder.
My body trembles.

7 "Why do the wicked prosper,
growing old and powerful?

8 They live to see their children grow up
and settle down,
and they enjoy their grandchildren.

9 Their homes are safe from every fear,
and God does not punish them.

10 Their bulls never fail to breed.
   Their cows bear calves and never
      miscarry.
11 They let their children frisk about like
      lambs.
   Their little ones skip and dance.
12 They sing with tambourine and harp.
   They celebrate to the sound of the
      flute.
13 They spend their days in prosperity,
      then go down to the grave*
      in peace.
14 And yet they say to God, 'Go away.
   We want no part of you and your
      ways.
15 Who is the Almighty, and why should
      we obey him?
   What good will it do us to pray?'
16 (They think their prosperity is of their
      own doing,
   but I will have nothing to do with
      that kind of thinking.)

17 "Yet the light of the wicked never
      seems to be extinguished.
   Do they ever have trouble?
   Does God distribute sorrows
      to them in anger?
18 Are they driven before the wind like
      straw?
   Are they carried away by the storm
      like chaff?
   Not at all!

19 "'Well,' you say, 'at least God will
      punish their children!'
   But I say he should punish the ones
      who sin,
   so that they understand his
      judgment.
20 Let them see their destruction with
      their own eyes.
   Let them drink deeply of the anger
      of the Almighty.
21 For they will not care what happens
      to their family
   after they are dead.

22 "But who can teach a lesson to God,
      since he judges even the most
      powerful?
23 One person dies in prosperity,
   completely comfortable and secure,
24 the picture of good health,
   vigorous and fit.
25 Another person dies in bitter poverty,
   never having tasted the good life.
26 But both are buried in the same dust,
   both eaten by the same maggots.

27 "Look, I know what you're thinking.
   I know the schemes you plot
      against me.
28 You will tell me of rich and wicked
      people
   whose houses have vanished
      because of their sins.

HOW WE LIVE

Courageous in trials

2 CORINTHIANS 1:3-7 Paul had seen many people suffer for their faith in Jesus (some at his own hands). He also had personally endured some unpleasant consequences of following Jesus. In this passage, he reminded the Corinthians that they suffered not only *for* Christ, but also *with* him. And their comfort would come from Christ and from each other. • Many Christians are surprised when they suffer hardship or face tough times. Wasn't believing in Jesus supposed to make things better? Becoming a Christian doesn't make our troubles disappear. If this were the case, people would flock to Jesus out of the selfish desire to make their lives easier. But we can take courage in our trials because God promises to "shower us with his comfort." • Remember, when you are feeling overwhelmed by what you are going through, allow God to comfort you. The more you suffer, the more strength you will be given. And when the clouds part, you will be better able to help and encourage others in their trials.

29 But ask those who have been around,
and they will tell you the truth.
30 Evil people are spared in times of
calamity
and are allowed to escape disaster.
31 No one criticizes them openly
or pays them back for what they
have done.
32 When they are carried to the grave,
an honor guard keeps watch at their
tomb.
33 A great funeral procession goes to the
cemetery.
Many pay their respects as the body
is laid to rest,
and the earth gives sweet repose.

34 "How can your empty clichés comfort
me?
All your explanations are lies!"

22:1 THEN Eliphaz the Temanite replied:

2 "Can a person do anything to help God?
Can even a wise person be helpful
to him?
3 Is it any advantage to the Almighty if
you are righteous?
Would it be any gain to him if you
were perfect?
4 Is it because you're so pious that he
accuses you
and brings judgment against you?
5 No, it's because of your wickedness!
There's no limit to your sins.

6 "For example, you must have lent
money to your friend
and demanded clothing as security.
Yes, you stripped him to the bone.
7 You must have refused water for the
thirsty
and food for the hungry.
8 You probably think the land belongs
to the powerful
and only the privileged have a right
to it!
9 You must have sent widows away
empty-handed
and crushed the hopes of orphans.
10 That is why you are surrounded
by traps
and tremble from sudden fears.
11 That is why you cannot see in the
darkness,
and waves of water cover you.

12 "God is so great—higher than the
heavens,
higher than the farthest stars.
13 But you reply, 'That's why God can't see
what I am doing!
How can he judge through the thick
darkness?
14 For thick clouds swirl about him,
and he cannot see us.
He is way up there, walking on
the vault of heaven.'

15 "Will you continue on the old paths
where evil people have walked?
16 They were snatched away in the prime
of life,
the foundations of their lives
washed away.
17 For they said to God, 'Leave us
alone!
What can the Almighty do to us?'
18 Yet he was the one who filled their
homes with good things,
so I will have nothing to do with
that kind of thinking.

19 "The righteous will be happy to see
the wicked destroyed,
and the innocent will laugh
in contempt.
20 They will say, 'See how our enemies
have been destroyed.
The last of them have been
consumed in the fire.'

21 "Submit to God, and you will have
peace;
then things will go well for you.
22 Listen to his instructions,
and store them in your heart.
23 If you return to the Almighty, you will
be restored—
so clean up your life.
24 If you give up your lust for money
and throw your precious gold into
the river,
25 the Almighty himself will be your
treasure.
He will be your precious silver!

26 "Then you will take delight in the
Almighty
and look up to God.
27 You will pray to him, and he will
hear you,

and you will fulfill your vows
to him.
²⁸ You will succeed in whatever you
choose to do,
and light will shine on the road
ahead of you.
²⁹ If people are in trouble and you say,
'Help them,'
God will save them.
³⁰ Even sinners will be rescued;
they will be rescued because your
hands are pure."

20:25 Hebrew *with gall.*   **21:13** Hebrew *to Sheol.*

2 CORINTHIANS 1:1-11
In this second letter to the church in Corinth, Paul
follows up on some of the questions and details
that had arisen from his previous letter.

This letter is from Paul, chosen by the will
of God to be an apostle of Christ Jesus,
and from our brother Timothy.

I am writing to God's church in Corinth
and to all of his holy people throughout
Greece.*
²May God our Father and the Lord Jesus
Christ give you grace and peace.
³All praise to God, the Father of our
Lord Jesus Christ. God is our merciful Father and the source of all comfort.
⁴He comforts us in all our troubles so
that we can comfort others. When they are
troubled, we will be able to give them the
same comfort God has given us. ⁵For the
more we suffer for Christ, the more God
will shower us with his comfort through
Christ. ⁶Even when we are weighed down
with troubles, it is for your comfort and
salvation! For when we ourselves are comforted, we will certainly comfort you. Then
you can patiently endure the same things
we suffer. ⁷We are confident that as you
share in our sufferings, you will also share
in the comfort God gives us.
⁸We think you ought to know, dear
brothers and sisters,* about the trouble we
went through in the province of Asia. We
were crushed and overwhelmed beyond
our ability to endure, and we thought we
would never live through it. ⁹In fact, we expected to die. But as a result, we stopped
relying on ourselves and learned to rely
only on God, who raises the dead. ¹⁰And he
did rescue us from mortal danger, and he

will rescue us again. We have placed our
confidence in him, and he will continue to
rescue us. ¹¹And you are helping us by
praying for us. Then many people will give
thanks because God has graciously answered so many prayers for our safety.

1:1 Greek *Achaia,* the southern region of the Greek
peninsula.   **1:8** Greek *brothers.*

PSALM 40:11-17
L̲ord, don't hold back your tender
mercies from me.
Let your unfailing love and
faithfulness always protect me.
¹² For troubles surround me—
too many to count!
My sins pile up so high
I can't see my way out.
They outnumber the hairs on
my head.
I have lost all courage.

¹³ Please, L̲ord, rescue me!
Come quickly, L̲ord, and
help me.
¹⁴ May those who try to destroy me
be humiliated and put to shame.
May those who take delight in my
trouble
be turned back in disgrace.
¹⁵ Let them be horrified by their
shame,
for they said, "Aha! We've got
him now!"

¹⁶ But may all who search for you
be filled with joy and gladness
in you.
May those who love your salvation
repeatedly shout, "The L̲ord is
great!"
¹⁷ As for me, since I am poor and needy,
let the Lord keep me in his
thoughts.
You are my helper and my savior.
O my God, do not delay.

PROVERBS 22:2-4
The rich and poor have this in common:
The L̲ord made them both. □ A prudent
person foresees danger and takes precautions. The simpleton goes blindly on and
suffers the consequences. □ True humility and fear of the L̲ord lead to riches,
honor, and long life.

AUGUST27

JOB 23:1–27:23

Job's plight involved bitter suffering. At times he became emotional, yet he didn't curse God. We have to remember that we aren't required to be stoic. We are just required to have a faith that honors God in the midst of life's confusion.

Then Job spoke again:

2 "My complaint today is still a bitter one,
  and I try hard not to groan aloud.
3 If only I knew where to find God,
  I would go to his court.
4 I would lay out my case
  and present my arguments.
5 Then I would listen to his reply
  and understand what he says to me.
6 Would he use his great power to argue with me?
  No, he would give me a fair hearing.
7 Honest people can reason with him,
  so I would be forever acquitted by my judge.
8 I go east, but he is not there.
  I go west, but I cannot find him.
9 I do not see him in the north, for he is hidden.
  I look to the south, but he is concealed.

10 "But he knows where I am going.
  And when he tests me, I will come out as pure as gold.
11 For I have stayed on God's paths;
  I have followed his ways and not turned aside.
12 I have not departed from his commands,
  but have treasured his words more than daily food.
13 But once he has made his decision, who can change his mind?
  Whatever he wants to do, he does.
14 So he will do to me whatever he has planned.
  He controls my destiny.
15 No wonder I am so terrified in his presence.
  When I think of it, terror grips me.
16 God has made me sick at heart;
  the Almighty has terrified me.

17 Darkness is all around me;
  thick, impenetrable darkness is everywhere.

24:1 "WHY doesn't the Almighty bring the wicked to judgment?
  Why must the godly wait for him in vain?
2 Evil people steal land by moving the boundary markers.
  They steal livestock and put them in their own pastures.
3 They take the orphan's donkey
  and demand the widow's ox as security for a loan.
4 The poor are pushed off the path;
  the needy must hide together for safety.
5 Like wild donkeys in the wilderness,
  the poor must spend all their time looking for food,
  searching even in the desert for food for their children.
6 They harvest a field they do not own,
  and they glean in the vineyards of the wicked.
7 All night they lie naked in the cold,
  without clothing or covering.
8 They are soaked by mountain showers,
  and they huddle against the rocks for want of a home.

9 "The wicked snatch a widow's child from her breast,
  taking the baby as security for a loan.
10 The poor must go about naked, without any clothing.
  They harvest food for others while they themselves are starving.
11 They press out olive oil without being allowed to taste it,
  and they tread in the winepress as they suffer from thirst.
12 The groans of the dying rise from the city,
  and the wounded cry for help,
  yet God ignores their moaning.

13 "Wicked people rebel against the light.

They refuse to acknowledge its ways
or stay in its paths.
¹⁴ The murderer rises in the early dawn
to kill the poor and needy;
at night he is a thief.
¹⁵ The adulterer waits for the twilight,
saying, 'No one will see me then.'
He hides his face so no one will
know him.
¹⁶ Thieves break into houses at night
and sleep in the daytime.
They are not acquainted with
the light.
¹⁷ The black night is their morning.
They ally themselves with the
terrors of the darkness.

¹⁸ "But they disappear like foam down
a river.
Everything they own is cursed,
and they are afraid to enter their
own vineyards.
¹⁹ The grave* consumes sinners
just as drought and heat consume
snow.
²⁰ Their own mothers will forget them.
Maggots will find them sweet to eat.
No one will remember them.
Wicked people are broken like
a tree in the storm.
²¹ They cheat the woman who has no son
to help her.
They refuse to help the needy
widow.
²² "God, in his power, drags away the rich.
They may rise high, but they have
no assurance of life.
²³ They may be allowed to live in
security,
but God is always watching them.
²⁴ And though they are great now,
in a moment they will be gone like
all others,
cut off like heads of grain.
²⁵ Can anyone claim otherwise?
Who can prove me wrong?"

^{25:1} THEN Bildad the Shuhite replied:

² "God is powerful and dreadful.
He enforces peace in the heavens.
³ Who is able to count his heavenly
army?
Doesn't his light shine on all
the earth?

⁴ How can a mortal be innocent before
God?
Can anyone born of a woman
be pure?
⁵ God is more glorious than the moon;
he shines brighter than the stars.
⁶ In comparison, people are maggots;
we mortals are mere worms."

^{26:1} THEN Job spoke again:

² "How you have helped the powerless!
How you have saved the weak!
³ How you have enlightened my
stupidity!
What wise advice you have offered!
⁴ Where have you gotten all these wise
sayings?
Whose spirit speaks through you?

⁵ "The dead tremble—
those who live beneath the waters.
⁶ The underworld* is naked in God's
presence.
The place of destruction* is
uncovered.
⁷ God stretches the northern sky over
empty space
and hangs the earth on nothing.
⁸ He wraps the rain in his thick clouds,
and the clouds don't burst with
the weight.
⁹ He covers the face of the moon,*
shrouding it with his clouds.
¹⁰ He created the horizon when he
separated the waters;
he set the boundary between day
and night.
¹¹ The foundations of heaven tremble;
they shudder at his rebuke.
¹² By his power the sea grew calm.
By his skill he crushed the great sea
monster.*
¹³ His Spirit made the heavens beautiful,
and his power pierced the gliding
serpent.
¹⁴ These are just the beginning of all that
he does,
merely a whisper of his power.
Who, then, can comprehend the
thunder of his power?"

^{27:1} JOB continued speaking:

² "I vow by the living God, who has
taken away my rights,

by the Almighty who has
embittered my soul—
³ As long as I live,
while I have breath from God,
⁴ my lips will speak no evil,
and my tongue will speak no lies.
⁵ I will never concede that you are right;
I will defend my integrity until I die.
⁶ I will maintain my innocence without
wavering.
My conscience is clear for as long as
I live.

⁷ "May my enemy be punished like the
wicked,
my adversary like those who do evil.
⁸ For what hope do the godless have
when God cuts them off
and takes away their life?
⁹ Will God listen to their cry
when trouble comes upon them?
¹⁰ Can they take delight in the Almighty?
Can they call to God at any time?
¹¹ I will teach you about God's power.
I will not conceal anything
concerning the Almighty.
¹² But you have seen all this,
yet you say all these useless things
to me.

¹³ "This is what the wicked will receive
from God;
this is their inheritance from the
Almighty.
¹⁴ They may have many children,
but the children will die in war or
starve to death.
¹⁵ Those who survive will die of a plague,
and not even their widows will
mourn them.

¹⁶ "Evil people may have piles of money
and may store away mounds of
clothing.
¹⁷ But the righteous will wear that
clothing,
and the innocent will divide that
money.
¹⁸ The wicked build houses as fragile as
a spider's web,*
as flimsy as a shelter made of
branches.
¹⁹ The wicked go to bed rich
but wake to find that all their
wealth is gone.

²⁰ Terror overwhelms them like a flood,
and they are blown away in the
storms of the night.
²¹ The east wind carries them away, and
they are gone.
It sweeps them away.
²² It whirls down on them without mercy.
They struggle to flee from its power.
²³ But everyone jeers at them
and mocks them."

24:19 Hebrew *Sheol.*   26:6a Hebrew *Sheol.*   26:6b Hebrew
Abaddon.   26:9 Or *covers his throne.*   26:12 Hebrew
Rahab, the name of a mythical sea monster that represents
chaos in ancient literature.   27:18 As in Greek and Syriac
versions (see also 8:14); Hebrew reads *a moth.*

2 CORINTHIANS 1:12–2:11
Paul's plan to visit the Corinthians had to be
altered due to circumstances. Apparently some in
the Corinthian church took Paul's change of plans
the wrong way.

We [Paul and his coworkers] can say with
confidence and a clear conscience that
we have lived with a God-given holiness*
and sincerity in all our dealings. We have
depended on God's grace, not on our own
human wisdom. That is how we have conducted ourselves before the world, and
especially toward you. ¹³Our letters have
been straightforward, and there is nothing written between the lines and nothing
you can't understand. I hope someday
you will fully understand us, ¹⁴even if you
don't understand us now. Then on the day
when the Lord Jesus* returns, you will be
proud of us in the same way we are proud
of you.

¹⁵Since I was so sure of your understanding and trust, I wanted to give you a
double blessing by visiting you twice—
¹⁶first on my way to Macedonia and again
when I returned from Macedonia.* Then
you could send me on my way to Judea.

¹⁷You may be asking why I changed my
plan. Do you think I make my plans carelessly? Do you think I am like people of
the world who say "Yes" when they really
mean "No"? ¹⁸As surely as God is faithful,
my word to you does not waver between
"Yes" and "No." ¹⁹For Jesus Christ, the Son
of God, does not waver between "Yes" and
"No." He is the one whom Silas,* Timothy,
and I preached to you, and as God's ultimate "Yes," he always does what he says.

²⁰For all of God's promises have been fulfilled in Christ with a resounding "Yes!" And through Christ, our "Amen" (which means "Yes") ascends to God for his glory. ²¹It is God who enables us, along with you, to stand firm for Christ. He has commissioned us, ²²and he has identified us as his own by placing the Holy Spirit in our hearts as the first installment that guarantees everything he has promised us.

²³Now I call upon God as my witness that I am telling the truth. The reason I didn't return to Corinth was to spare you from a severe rebuke. ²⁴But that does not mean we want to dominate you by telling you how to put your faith into practice. We want to work together with you so you will be full of joy, for it is by your own faith that you stand firm.

2:1So I decided that I would not bring you grief with another painful visit. ²For if I cause you grief, who will make me glad? Certainly not someone I have grieved. ³That is why I wrote to you as I did, so that when I do come, I won't be grieved by the very ones who ought to give me the greatest joy. Surely you all know that my joy comes from your being joyful. ⁴I wrote that letter in great anguish, with a troubled heart and many tears. I didn't want to grieve you, but I wanted to let you know how much love I have for you.

⁵I am not overstating it when I say that the man who caused all the trouble hurt all of you more than he hurt me. ⁶Most of you opposed him, and that was punishment enough. ⁷Now, however, it is time to forgive and comfort him. Otherwise he may be overcome by discouragement. ⁸So I urge you now to reaffirm your love for him.

⁹I wrote to you as I did to test you and see if you would fully comply with my instructions. ¹⁰When you forgive this man, I forgive him, too. And when I forgive whatever needs to be forgiven, I do so with Christ's authority for your benefit, ¹¹so that Satan will not outsmart us. For we are familiar with his evil schemes.

1:12 Some manuscripts read *honesty.* 1:14 Some manuscripts read *our Lord Jesus.* 1:16 *Macedonia* was in the northern region of Greece. 1:19 Greek *Silvanus.*

PSALM 41:1-13
For the choir director: A psalm of David.

¹ **O**h, the joys of those who are kind
    to the poor!
    The LORD rescues them when they
    are in trouble.
² The LORD protects them
    and keeps them alive.

HOW WE LIVE Raising our children

PROVERBS 22:6 It has often been said that experience is the best teacher. That's only half of the story. Parental guidance and discipline is also crucial. We offer the kind of direction this verse is describing when we model good decision-making to our children, and then provide them security, wisdom, patience, and discipline while they learn to make decisions for themselves.   • Of course, no responsible parent would give their three-year-old complete freedom to decide whether it's okay to play in the street or run with a sharp object in hand. However, it is also irresponsible to overprotect a child, never allowing children to learn how to think and act responsibly on their own. When parents teach their children how to make decisions based upon God's standards, goodness, kindness, responsibility, and love, they equip their children with the sort of character and skills that will keep them on the right track in the long run.   • Raising children can be a difficult, scary job. Take courage that as you seek to be a godly parent, love and nurture your children, and prepare them to be the men and women God wants them to be, God is also there working right alongside you.

He gives them prosperity in the land
and rescues them from their
enemies.
3 The LORD nurses them when they
are sick
and restores them to health.

4 "O LORD," I prayed, "have mercy on
me.
Heal me, for I have sinned against
you."
5 But my enemies say nothing but evil
about me.
"How soon will he die and be
forgotten?" they ask.
6 They visit me as if they were my
friends,
but all the while they gather
gossip,
and when they leave, they spread it
everywhere.
7 All who hate me whisper about me,
imagining the worst.
8 "He has some fatal disease," they say.
"He will never get out of that bed!"

9 Even my best friend, the one I trusted
completely,
the one who shared my food, has
turned against me.
10 LORD, have mercy on me.
Make me well again, so I can pay
them back!
11 I know you are pleased with me,
for you have not let my enemies
triumph over me.
12 You have preserved my life because
I am innocent;
you have brought me into your
presence forever.
13 Praise the LORD, the God of Israel,
who lives from everlasting to
everlasting.
Amen and amen!

PROVERBS 22:5-6

Corrupt people walk a thorny, treacherous road; whoever values life will avoid it. □ Direct your children onto the right path, and when they are older, they will not leave it.

AUGUST**28**

JOB 28:1–30:31
Job's final words encompass anguish, loss, and godly wisdom. Notice his feeling of despair and the frustration of seemingly unanswered prayer.

"**P**eople know where to mine silver
and how to refine gold.
2 They know where to dig iron from
the earth
and how to smelt copper from rock.
3 They know how to shine light in the
darkness
and explore the farthest regions
of the earth
as they search in the dark for ore.
4 They sink a mine shaft into the earth
far from where anyone lives.
They descend on ropes, swinging
back and forth.

5 Food is grown on the earth above,
but down below, the earth is melted
as by fire.
6 Here the rocks contain precious lapis
lazuli,
and the dust contains gold.
7 These are treasures no bird of prey
can see,
no falcon's eye observe.
8 No wild animal has walked upon these
treasures;
no lion has ever set his paw there.
9 People know how to tear apart flinty
rocks
and overturn the roots
of mountains.
10 They cut tunnels in the rocks
and uncover precious stones.

¹¹ They dam up the trickling streams
   and bring to light the hidden
   treasures.

¹² "But do people know where to find
   wisdom?
   Where can they find understanding?
¹³ No one knows where to find it,
   for it is not found among the living.
¹⁴ 'It is not here,' says the ocean.
   'Nor is it here,' says the sea.
¹⁵ It cannot be bought with gold.
   It cannot be purchased with silver.
¹⁶ It's worth more than all the gold of
   Ophir,
   greater than precious onyx or lapis
   lazuli.
¹⁷ Wisdom is more valuable than gold
   and crystal.
   It cannot be purchased with jewels
   mounted in fine gold.
¹⁸ Coral and jasper are worthless in
   trying to get it.
   The price of wisdom is far above
   rubies.
¹⁹ Precious peridot from Ethiopia*
   cannot be exchanged for it.
   It's worth more than the purest
   gold.

²⁰ "But do people know where to find
   wisdom?
   Where can they find
   understanding?
²¹ It is hidden from the eyes of all
   humanity.
   Even the sharp-eyed birds in the sky
   cannot discover it.
²² Destruction* and Death say,
   'We've heard only rumors of where
   wisdom can be found.'

²³ "God alone understands the way
   to wisdom;
   he knows where it can be found,
²⁴ for he looks throughout the whole
   earth
   and sees everything under the
   heavens.
²⁵ He decided how hard the winds
   should blow
   and how much rain should fall.
²⁶ He made the laws for the rain
   and laid out a path for the
   lightning.

²⁷ Then he saw wisdom and evaluated it.
   He set it in place and examined
   it thoroughly.
²⁸ And this is what he says to all humanity:
   'The fear of the Lord is true wisdom;
   to forsake evil is real
   understanding.'"

²⁹:¹ JOB continued speaking:

² "I long for the years gone by
   when God took care of me,
³ when he lit up the way before me
   and I walked safely through the
   darkness.
⁴ When I was in my prime,
   God's friendship was felt in
   my home.
⁵ The Almighty was still with me,
   and my children were around me.
⁶ My cows produced milk in abundance,
   and my groves poured out streams
   of olive oil.

⁷ "Those were the days when I went
   to the city gate
   and took my place among the
   honored leaders.
⁸ The young stepped aside when they
   saw me,
   and even the aged rose in respect
   at my coming.
⁹ The princes stood in silence
   and put their hands over their
   mouths.
¹⁰ The highest officials of the city stood
   quietly,
   holding their tongues in respect.

¹¹ "All who heard me praised me.
   All who saw me spoke well of me.
¹² For I assisted the poor in their need
   and the orphans who required help.
¹³ I helped those without hope, and they
   blessed me.
   And I caused the widows' hearts
   to sing for joy.
¹⁴ Everything I did was honest.
   Righteousness covered me like
   a robe,
   and I wore justice like a turban.
¹⁵ I served as eyes for the blind
   and feet for the lame.
¹⁶ I was a father to the poor
   and assisted strangers who needed
   help.

17 I broke the jaws of godless oppressors
  and plucked their victims from
    their teeth.
18 "I thought, 'Surely I will die
    surrounded by my family
    after a long, good life.*
19 For I am like a tree whose roots reach
    the water,
  whose branches are refreshed with
    the dew.
20 New honors are constantly bestowed
    on me,
  and my strength is continually
    renewed.'

21 "Everyone listened to my advice.
  They were silent as they waited for
    me to speak.
22 And after I spoke, they had nothing to
    add,
  for my counsel satisfied them.
23 They longed for me to speak as people
    long for rain.
  They drank my words like a
    refreshing spring rain.
24 When they were discouraged, I smiled
    at them.
  My look of approval was precious
    to them.
25 Like a chief, I told them what to do.
  I lived like a king among his troops
  and comforted those who mourned.

30:1 "BUT now I am mocked by people
    younger than I,
  by young men whose fathers are not
    worthy to run with my
    sheepdogs.
2 A lot of good they are to me—
  those worn-out wretches!
3 They are gaunt with hunger
  and flee to the deserts,
  to desolate and gloomy wastelands.
4 They pluck wild greens from among
    the bushes
  and eat from the roots of broom
    trees.
5 They are driven from human society,
  and people shout at them as if they
    were thieves.
6 So now they live in frightening ravines,
  in caves and among the rocks.
7 They sound like animals howling
  among the bushes,

  huddled together beneath
    the nettles.
8 They are nameless fools,
  outcasts from society.

9 "And now they mock me with vulgar
    songs!
  They taunt me!
10 They despise me and won't come
    near me,
  except to spit in my face.
11 For God has cut my bowstring.
  He has humbled me,
  so they have thrown off all restraint.
12 These outcasts oppose me to my face.
  They send me sprawling
  and lay traps in my path.
13 They block my road
  and do everything they can to
    destroy me.
  They know I have no one to help me.
14   They come at me from all
    directions.
  They jump on me when I am down.
15   I live in terror now.
  My honor has blown away in the wind,
  and my prosperity has vanished like
    a cloud.

16 "And now my life seeps away.
  Depression haunts my days.
17 At night my bones are filled with pain,
  which gnaws at me relentlessly.
18 With a strong hand, God grabs my
    shirt.
  He grips me by the collar of my coat.
19 He has thrown me into the mud.
  I'm nothing more than dust and
    ashes.

20 "I cry to you, O God, but you don't
    answer.
  I stand before you, but you don't
    even look.
21 You have become cruel toward me.
  You use your power to persecute me.
22 You throw me into the whirlwind
  and destroy me in the storm.
23 And I know you are sending me to
    my death—
  the destination of all who live.

24 "Surely no one would turn against
    the needy
  when they cry for help in their
    trouble.

²⁵ Did I not weep for those in trouble?
   Was I not deeply grieved for the
      needy?
²⁶ So I looked for good, but evil came
      instead.
   I waited for the light, but darkness
      fell.
²⁷ My heart is troubled and restless.
   Days of suffering torment me.
²⁸ I walk in gloom, without sunlight.
   I stand in the public square and cry
      for help.
²⁹ Instead, I am considered a brother
      to jackals
   and a companion to owls.
³⁰ My skin has turned dark,
   and my bones burn with fever.
³¹ My harp plays sad music,
   and my flute accompanies those
      who weep."

28:19 Hebrew *from Cush.*   **28:22** Hebrew *Abaddon.*
29:18 Hebrew *after I have counted my days like sand.*

2 CORINTHIANS 2:12-17
Some at Corinth had begun to view Paul's constant suffering for the gospel negatively. Paul reminded them that such suffering was a pleasing thing in God's eyes.

When I [Paul] came to the city of Troas to preach the Good News of Christ, the Lord opened a door of opportunity for me. ¹³But I had no peace of mind because my dear brother Titus hadn't yet arrived with a report from you. So I said good-bye and went on to Macedonia to find him.

¹⁴But thank God! He has made us his captives and continues to lead us along in Christ's triumphal procession. Now he uses us to spread the knowledge of Christ everywhere, like a sweet perfume. ¹⁵Our lives are a Christ-like fragrance rising up to God. But this fragrance is perceived differently by those who are being saved and by those who are perishing. ¹⁶To those who are perishing, we are a dreadful smell of death and doom. But to those who are being saved, we are a life-giving perfume. And who is adequate for such a task as this?

¹⁷You see, we are not like the many hucksters* who preach for personal profit. We preach the word of God with sincerity and with Christ's authority, knowing that God is watching us.

2:17 Some manuscripts read *the rest of the hucksters.*

PSALM 42:1-11
For the choir director: A psalm* of the descendants of Korah.

¹ **A**s the deer longs for streams of water,
   so I long for you, O God.
² I thirst for God, the living God.
   When can I go and stand before
      him?
³ Day and night I have only tears for food,

HOW WE LIVE
Overcoming doubt

PSALM 42:1-11 The writer of this psalm was feeling low. He wondered, *Where are you, God? Have you forgotten me?* Yet somehow he was able to remember what God had done for him, and somehow he was able to praise God in the dark times.   • We all face times of discouragement, times when we wonder if God is really there. Some of us even face extended periods of depression. When you feel yourself slipping into the zone of doubt, one antidote is praise—remembering God's goodness to you. Read the Bible to recall what God has done for others in the past. If you have kept a journal of your Christian walk, review your own personal record of God's answered prayer in your life.   • Just as a deer depends upon water for life, so we believers depend upon God for spiritual life. When you begin to feel separated from God or wonder if he cares about your situation, take advantage of the psalmist's "antidepressant": praise. Think about how much God blesses you and takes care of you day by day. Dwell upon his goodness and mercy. You'll be amazed by what happens when you start praising instead of doubting.

while my enemies continually taunt
me, saying,
"Where is this God of yours?"

4 My heart is breaking
as I remember how it used to be:
I walked among the crowds of
worshipers,
leading a great procession to the
house of God,
singing for joy and giving thanks
amid the sound of a great
celebration!

5 Why am I discouraged?
Why is my heart so sad?
I will put my hope in God!
I will praise him again—
my Savior and 6 my God!

Now I am deeply discouraged,
but I will remember you—
even from distant Mount
Hermon, the source of the
Jordan,
from the land of Mount Mizar.
7 I hear the tumult of the raging seas

as your waves and surging tides
sweep over me.
8 But each day the LORD pours his
unfailing love upon me,
and through each night I sing
his songs,
praying to God who gives me life.

9 "O God my rock," I cry,
"Why have you forgotten me?
Why must I wander around in grief,
oppressed by my enemies?"
10 Their taunts break my bones.
They scoff, "Where is this God
of yours?"

11 Why am I discouraged?
Why is my heart so sad?
I will put my hope in God!
I will praise him again—
my Savior and my God!

42:TITLE Hebrew *maskil*. This may be a literary or musical
term.

PROVERBS 22:7
Just as the rich rule the poor, so the borrower is servant to the lender.

AUGUST**29**

JOB 31:1–33:33
Job's words end here, and then a fourth friend
appears—Elihu. This is the only time he speaks.
Instead of thinking of suffering as mere punishment, Elihu describes it more as discipline—that
which trains us and makes us strong. Still, his
answer ultimately misses the mark.

"I [Job] made a covenant with my eyes
not to look with lust at a young
woman.
2 For what has God above chosen for us?
What is our inheritance from the
Almighty on high?
3 Isn't it calamity for the wicked
and misfortune for those who
do evil?
4 Doesn't he see everything I do
and every step I take?

5 "Have I lied to anyone
or deceived anyone?
6 Let God weigh me on the scales
of justice,
for he knows my integrity.
7 If I have strayed from his pathway,
or if my heart has lusted for what
my eyes have seen,
or if I am guilty of any other sin,
8 then let someone else eat the crops
I have planted.
Let all that I have planted be
uprooted.
9 "If my heart has been seduced by
a woman,
or if I have lusted for my neighbor's
wife,

10 then let my wife belong to* another
man;
let other men sleep with her.
11 For lust is a shameful sin,
a crime that should be punished.
12 It is a fire that burns all the way
to hell.*
It would wipe out everything I own.

13 "If I have been unfair to my male
or female servants
when they brought their complaints
to me,
14 how could I face God?
What could I say when he
questioned me?
15 For God created both me and my
servants.
He created us both in the womb.

16 "Have I refused to help the poor,
or crushed the hopes of widows?
17 Have I been stingy with my food
and refused to share it with
orphans?
18 No, from childhood I have cared for
orphans like a father,
and all my life I have cared for
widows.
19 Whenever I saw the homeless without
clothes
and the needy with nothing to wear,
20 did they not praise me
for providing wool clothing to keep
them warm?

21 "If I raised my hand against an orphan,
knowing the judges would take my
side,
22 then let my shoulder be wrenched out
of place!
Let my arm be torn from its socket!
23 That would be better than facing
God's judgment.
For if the majesty of God opposes
me, what hope is there?

24 "Have I put my trust in money
or felt secure because of my gold?
25 Have I gloated about my wealth
and all that I own?

26 "Have I looked at the sun shining in
the skies,
or the moon walking down its silver
pathway,

27 and been secretly enticed in my heart
to throw kisses at them in worship?
28 If so, I should be punished by the
judges,
for it would mean I had denied the
God of heaven.

29 "Have I ever rejoiced when disaster
struck my enemies,
or become excited when harm
came their way?
30 No, I have never sinned by cursing
anyone
or by asking for revenge.

31 "My servants have never said,
'He let others go hungry.'
32 I have never turned away a stranger
but have opened my doors to
everyone.

33 "Have I tried to hide my sins like other
people do,
concealing my guilt in my heart?
34 Have I feared the crowd
or the contempt of the masses,
so that I kept quiet and stayed
indoors?

35 "If only someone would listen to me!
Look, I will sign my name to my
defense.
Let the Almighty answer me.
Let my accuser write out the
charges against me.
36 I would face the accusation proudly.
I would wear it like a crown.
37 For I would tell him exactly what
I have done.
I would come before him like a
prince.

38 "If my land accuses me
and all its furrows cry out together,
39 or if I have stolen its crops
or murdered its owners,
40 then let thistles grow on that land
instead of wheat,
and weeds instead of barley."

Job's words are ended.

32:1 JOB's three friends refused to reply
further to him because he kept insisting
on his innocence.
2 Then Elihu son of Barakel the Buzite,
of the clan of Ram, became angry. He was

angry because Job refused to admit that he had sinned and that God was right in punishing him. ³He was also angry with Job's three friends, for they made God* appear to be wrong by their inability to answer Job's arguments. ⁴Elihu had waited for the others to speak to Job because they were older than he. ⁵But when he saw that they had no further reply, he spoke out angrily. ⁶Elihu son of Barakel the Buzite said,

"I am young and you are old,
so I held back from telling you what
I think.
⁷ I thought, 'Those who are older should
speak,
for wisdom comes with age.'
⁸ But there is a spirit* within people,
the breath of the Almighty within
them,
that makes them intelligent.
⁹ Sometimes the elders are not wise.
Sometimes the aged do not
understand justice.
¹⁰ So listen to me,
and let me tell you what I think.

¹¹ "I have waited all this time,
listening very carefully to your
arguments,
listening to you grope for words.
¹² I have listened,
but not one of you has refuted Job
or answered his arguments.
¹³ And don't tell me, 'He is too wise for
us.
Only God can convince him.'
¹⁴ If Job had been arguing with me,
I would not answer with your kind
of logic!
¹⁵ You sit there baffled,
with nothing more to say.
¹⁶ Should I continue to wait, now that
you are silent?
Must I also remain silent?
¹⁷ No, I will say my piece.
I will speak my mind.
¹⁸ For I am full of pent-up words,
and the spirit within me urges me
on.
¹⁹ I am like a cask of wine without a vent,
like a new wineskin ready to burst!
²⁰ I must speak to find relief,
so let me give my answers.

²¹ I won't play favorites
or try to flatter anyone.
²² For if I tried flattery,
my Creator would soon
destroy me.

33:1 "LISTEN to my words, Job;
pay attention to what I have to say.
² Now that I have begun to speak,
let me continue.
³ I speak with all sincerity;
I speak the truth.
⁴ For the Spirit of God has made me,
and the breath of the Almighty
gives me life.
⁵ Answer me, if you can;
make your case and take your stand.
⁶ Look, you and I both belong to God.
I, too, was formed from clay.
⁷ So you don't need to be afraid of me.
I won't come down hard on you.

⁸ "You have spoken in my hearing,
and I have heard your very words.
⁹ You said, 'I am pure; I am without sin;
I am innocent; I have no guilt.
¹⁰ God is picking a quarrel with me,
and he considers me his enemy.
¹¹ He puts my feet in the stocks
and watches my every move.'

¹² "But you are wrong, and I will show
you why.
For God is greater than any human
being.
¹³ So why are you bringing a charge
against him?
Why say he does not respond to
people's complaints?
¹⁴ For God speaks again and again,
though people do not recognize it.
¹⁵ He speaks in dreams, in visions of
the night,
when deep sleep falls on people
as they lie in their beds.
¹⁶ He whispers in their ears
and terrifies them with warnings.
¹⁷ He makes them turn from doing
wrong;
he keeps them from pride.
¹⁸ He protects them from the grave,
from crossing over the river
of death.

¹⁹ "Or God disciplines people with pain
on their sickbeds,

with ceaseless aching in their
   bones.

20 They lose their appetite
   for even the most delicious food.

21 Their flesh wastes away,
   and their bones stick out.

22 They are at death's door;
   the angels of death wait for them.

23 "But if an angel from heaven
      appears—
   a special messenger to intercede for
      a person
   and declare that he is upright—

24 he will be gracious and say,
   'Rescue him from the grave,
   for I have found a ransom for his life.'

25 Then his body will become as healthy
      as a child's,
   firm and youthful again.

26 When he prays to God,
   he will be accepted.
   And God will receive him with joy
   and restore him to good standing.

27 He will declare to his friends,
   'I sinned and twisted the truth,
   but it was not worth it.*

28 God rescued me from the grave,
   and now my life is filled with light.'

29 "Yes, God does these things
   again and again for people.

30 He rescues them from the grave
   so they may enjoy the light of life.

31 Mark this well, Job. Listen to me,
   for I have more to say.

32 But if you have anything to say, go
      ahead.
   Speak, for I am anxious to see you
      justified.

33 But if not, then listen to me.
   Keep silent and I will teach you
      wisdom!"

31:10 Hebrew *grind for.*   **31:12** Hebrew *to Abaddon.*
32:3 As in ancient Hebrew scribal tradition; the Masoretic
Text reads *Job.*   **32:8** Or *Spirit;* also in 32:18.   **33:27** Greek
version reads *but he* [God] *did not punish me as my sin
deserved.*

2 CORINTHIANS 3:1-18

Paul uses powerful imagery from the Old Testament
to describe the new covenant. God has put his Spirit
in our hearts, giving us new power to live for him.

Are we [Paul and his coworkers] beginning to praise ourselves again? Are we like
others, who need to bring you letters of
recommendation, or who ask you to write
such letters on their behalf? Surely not!
²The only letter of recommendation we
need is you yourselves. Your lives are a letter written in our* hearts; everyone can
read it and recognize our good work
among you. ³Clearly, you are a letter from
Christ showing the result of our ministry
among you. This "letter" is written not
with pen and ink, but with the Spirit of
the living God. It is carved not on tablets
of stone, but on human hearts.

⁴We are confident of all this because of
our great trust in God through Christ. ⁵It
is not that we think we are qualified to do

WHO GOD IS
The Holy Spirit helps us grow

2 CORINTHIANS 3:16-18   The Holy Spirit is the identifying mark of a Christian.
When Jesus ascended to heaven after his resurrection, he promised that
he would send the Holy Spirit (Acts 1:8, June 3). We do not live out our
Christian lives alone. We have God's Spirit dwelling in us, helping us live
the Christian life.   • You may feel a bit overwhelmed. As you read God's
Word and all of these devotional thoughts about how to act and live, you
may feel like throwing in the towel and saying, "This is just too hard!"
However, no one is asking you to do all of this on your own. In fact, it
would be too hard if that were the case. Instead, the Holy Spirit has been
sent to empower you to live the Christian life. He will help to bring about
the needed changes in your life. Far more than just a self-help fix, the
Holy Spirit draws you closer to the Lord and is the empowering force
to live a life pleasing to God (John 14:15-21, May 25).

anything on our own. Our qualification comes from God. ⁶He has enabled us to be ministers of his new covenant. This is a covenant not of written laws, but of the Spirit. The old written covenant ends in death; but under the new covenant, the Spirit gives life.

⁷The old way,* with laws etched in stone, led to death, though it began with such glory that the people of Israel could not bear to look at Moses' face. For his face shone with the glory of God, even though the brightness was already fading away. ⁸Shouldn't we expect far greater glory under the new way, now that the Holy Spirit is giving life? ⁹If the old way, which brings condemnation, was glorious, how much more glorious is the new way, which makes us right with God! ¹⁰In fact, that first glory was not glorious at all compared with the overwhelming glory of the new way. ¹¹So if the old way, which has been replaced, was glorious, how much more glorious is the new, which remains forever!

¹²Since this new way gives us such confidence, we can be very bold. ¹³We are not like Moses, who put a veil over his face so the people of Israel would not see the glory, even though it was destined to fade away. ¹⁴But the people's minds were hardened, and to this day whenever the old covenant is being read, the same veil covers their minds so they cannot understand the truth. And this veil can be removed only by believing in Christ. ¹⁵Yes, even today when they read Moses' writings, their hearts are covered with that veil, and they do not understand.

¹⁶But whenever someone turns to the Lord, the veil is taken away. ¹⁷For the Lord is the Spirit, and wherever the Spirit of the Lord is, there is freedom. ¹⁸So all of us who have had that veil removed can see and reflect the glory of the Lord. And the Lord—who is the Spirit—makes us more and more like him as we are changed into his glorious image.

3:2 Some manuscripts read *your.* 3:7 Or *ministry;* also in 3:8, 9, 10, 11, 12.

PSALM 43:1-5

Declare me innocent, O God!
    Defend me against these ungodly
        people.
    Rescue me from these unjust liars.
² For you are God, my only safe haven.
    Why have you tossed me aside?
Why must I wander around in grief,
    oppressed by my enemies?
³ Send out your light and your truth;
    let them guide me.
Let them lead me to your holy
        mountain,
    to the place where you live.
⁴ There I will go to the altar of God,
    to God—the source of all my joy.
I will praise you with my harp,
    O God, my God!

⁵ Why am I discouraged?
    Why is my heart so sad?
I will put my hope in God!
    I will praise him again—
        my Savior and my God!

PROVERBS 22:8-9

Those who plant injustice will harvest disaster, and their reign of terror will come to an end.* □ Blessed are those who are generous, because they feed the poor.

22:8 The Greek version includes an additional proverb: *God blesses a man who gives cheerfully, / but his worthless deeds will come to an end.* Compare 2 Cor 9:7.

AUGUST**30**

JOB 34:1–36:33
Elihu correctly affirms God's justice in the midst of a world that is unjust. In the end, God will execute justice. We can hang on to that truth. Elihu failed, however, to realize that not all suffering is the result of sin.

Then Elihu said:

² "Listen to me, you wise men.
    Pay attention, you who have
        knowledge.

3 Job said, 'The ear tests the words it hears
    just as the mouth distinguishes
    between foods.'
4 So let us discern for ourselves what
    is right;
    let us learn together what is good.
5 For Job also said, 'I am innocent,
    but God has taken away my rights.
6 I am innocent, but they call me a liar.
    My suffering is incurable, though
    I have not sinned.'

7 "Tell me, has there ever been a man
    like Job,
    with his thirst for irreverent talk?
8 He chooses evil people as
    companions.
    He spends his time with wicked
    men.
9 He has even said, 'Why waste time
    trying to please God?'

10 "Listen to me, you who have
    understanding.
    Everyone knows that God doesn't sin!
    The Almighty can do no wrong.
11 He repays people according to their
    deeds.
    He treats people as they deserve.
12 Truly, God will not do wrong.
    The Almighty will not twist justice.
13 Did someone else put the world in
    his care?
    Who set the whole world in place?
14 If God were to take back his spirit
    and withdraw his breath,
15 all life would cease,
    and humanity would turn again
    to dust.

16 "Now listen to me if you are wise.
    Pay attention to what I say.
17 Could God govern if he hated justice?
    Are you going to condemn the
    almighty judge?
18 For he says to kings, 'You are wicked,'
    and to nobles, 'You are unjust.'
19 He doesn't care how great a person
    may be,
    and he pays no more attention to
    the rich than to the poor.
    He made them all.
20 In a moment they die.
    In the middle of the night they pass
    away;

the mighty are removed without
    human hand.

21 "For God watches how people live;
    he sees everything they do.
22 No darkness is thick enough
    to hide the wicked from his eyes.
23 We don't set the time
    when we will come before God
    in judgment.
24 He brings the mighty to ruin without
    asking anyone,
    and he sets up others in their place.
25 He knows what they do,
    and in the night he overturns and
    destroys them.
26 He strikes them down because they
    are wicked,
    doing it openly for all to see.
27 For they turned away from following
    him.
    They have no respect for any
    of his ways.
28 They cause the poor to cry out,
    catching God's attention.
    He hears the cries of the needy.
29 But if he chooses to remain quiet,
    who can criticize him?
    When he hides his face, no one can
    find him,
    whether an individual or a nation.
30 He prevents the godless from ruling
    so they cannot be a snare to the
    people.

31 "Why don't people say to God, 'I have
    sinned,
    but I will sin no more'?
32 Or 'I don't know what evil I have
    done—tell me.
    If I have done wrong, I will stop
    at once'?

33 "Must God tailor his justice to your
    demands?
    But you have rejected him!
    The choice is yours, not mine.
    Go ahead, share your wisdom with
    us.
34 After all, bright people will tell me,
    and wise people will hear me say,
35 'Job speaks out of ignorance;
    his words lack insight.'
36 Job, you deserve the maximum penalty
    for the wicked way you have talked.

³⁷ For you have added rebellion to your
sin;
you show no respect,
and you speak many angry words
against God."

^{35:1} THEN Elihu said:

² "Do you think it is right for you
to claim,
'I am righteous before God'?
³ For you also ask, 'What's in it for me?
What's the use of living a righteous
life?'

⁴ "I will answer you
and all your friends, too.
⁵ Look up into the sky,
and see the clouds high above you.
⁶ If you sin, how does that affect God?
Even if you sin again and again,
what effect will it have on him?
⁷ If you are good, is this some great gift
to him?
What could you possibly give him?
⁸ No, your sins affect only people like
yourself,
and your good deeds also affect
only humans.

⁹ "People cry out when they are
oppressed.
They groan beneath the power
of the mighty.
¹⁰ Yet they don't ask, 'Where is God
my Creator,
the one who gives songs in the
night?
¹¹ Where is the one who makes us
smarter than the animals
and wiser than the birds of the sky?'
¹² And when they cry out, God does not
answer
because of their pride.
¹³ But it is wrong to say God doesn't
listen,
to say the Almighty isn't concerned.
¹⁴ You say you can't see him,
but he will bring justice if you will
only wait.*
¹⁵ You say he does not respond to sinners
with anger
and is not greatly concerned about
wickedness.*
¹⁶ But you are talking nonsense, Job.
You have spoken like a fool."

^{36:1} ELIHU continued speaking:

² "Let me go on, and I will show you
the truth.
For I have not finished defending
God!
³ I will present profound arguments
for the righteousness of my Creator.
⁴ I am telling you nothing but the truth,
for I am a man of great knowledge.

⁵ "God is mighty, but he does not
despise anyone!
He is mighty in both power and
understanding.
⁶ He does not let the wicked live
but gives justice to the afflicted.
⁷ He never takes his eyes off the innocent,
but he sets them on thrones with
kings
and exalts them forever.
⁸ If they are bound in chains
and caught up in a web of trouble,
⁹ he shows them the reason.
He shows them their sins of pride.
¹⁰ He gets their attention
and commands that they turn
from evil.

¹¹ "If they listen and obey God,
they will be blessed with prosperity
throughout their lives.
All their years will be pleasant.
¹² But if they refuse to listen to him,
they will be killed by the sword*
and die from lack of understanding.
¹³ For the godless are full of resentment.
Even when he punishes them,
they refuse to cry out to him for help.
¹⁴ They die when they are young,
after wasting their lives in immoral
living.
¹⁵ But by means of their suffering, he
rescues those who suffer.
For he gets their attention through
adversity.

¹⁶ "God is leading you away from danger,
Job,
to a place free from distress.
He is setting your table with the
best food.
¹⁷ But you are obsessed with whether the
godless will be judged.
Don't worry, judgment and justice
will be upheld.

¹⁸ But watch out, or you may be seduced
    by wealth.*
    Don't let yourself be bribed into sin.
¹⁹ Could all your wealth*
    or all your mighty efforts
    keep you from distress?
²⁰ Do not long for the cover of night,
    for that is when people will be
    destroyed.*
²¹ Be on guard! Turn back from evil,
    for God sent this suffering
    to keep you from a life of evil.

²² "Look, God is all-powerful.
    Who is a teacher like him?
²³ No one can tell him what to do,
    or say to him, 'You have done wrong.'
²⁴ Instead, glorify his mighty works,
    singing songs of praise.
²⁵ Everyone has seen these things,
    though only from a distance.

²⁶ "Look, God is greater than we can
    understand.
    His years cannot be counted.
²⁷ He draws up the water vapor
    and then distills it into rain.
²⁸ The rain pours down from the clouds,
    and everyone benefits.
²⁹ Who can understand the spreading of
    the clouds

    and the thunder that rolls forth
    from heaven?
³⁰ See how he spreads the lightning
    around him
    and how it lights up the depths of
    the sea.
³¹ By these mighty acts he nourishes*
    the people,
    giving them food in abundance.
³² He fills his hands with lightning bolts
    and hurls each at its target.
³³ The thunder announces his presence;
    the storm announces his indignant
    anger.*"

35:13-14 These verses can also be translated as follows: ¹³*Indeed, God doesn't listen to their empty plea; / the Almighty is not concerned. /* ¹⁴*How much less will he listen when you say you don't see him, / and that your case is before him and you're waiting for justice.* **35:15** As in Greek and Latin versions; the meaning of this Hebrew word is uncertain. **36:12** Or *they will cross the river* [of death]. **36:18** Or *But don't let your anger lead you to mockery.* **36:19** Or *Could all your cries for help.* **36:16-20** The meaning of the Hebrew in this passage is uncertain. **36:31** Or *he governs.* **36:33** Or *even the cattle know when a storm is coming.* The meaning of the Hebrew is uncertain.

2 CORINTHIANS 4:1-12
Can something eternal be kept in something disposable? Evidently so, since our eternal souls are in these aging bodies.

Therefore, since God in his mercy has given us [Paul and his coworkers] this

WHAT THE BIBLE SAYS

The devil

2 CORINTHIANS 4:3-4 Paul's description here of the way Satan blinds unbelievers is reminiscent of his conversion experience on the Damascus road. Although Paul could see perfectly well, he had been blinded to spiritual truth. Unknowingly, Paul had been an instrument of Satan. In one magnificent moment, however, Christ had broken through Satan's deception and had revealed the truth to Paul (Acts 9:1-18, June 13). • The "god of this world" is a title for Satan, the great deceiver. This present world is in Satan's grasp. But Jesus' life and death began an all-out war on Satan. The church—the community of believers—is awaiting Jesus' victorious return, when Satan will finally be imprisoned and Jesus will reign forever. In the meantime, however, Satan continues to try to trap believers in sin—or at least make them ineffective in spreading the Good News. • "The Lord is faithful; he will strengthen you and guard you from the evil one" (2 Thessalonians 3:3, October 15). You can be strong against him by wearing the armor that God provides (Ephesians 6:10-17, September 28). You may be no match for someone who can blind you to the truth, but God is.

new way,* we never give up. ²We reject all shameful deeds and underhanded methods. We don't try to trick anyone or distort the word of God. We tell the truth before God, and all who are honest know this.

³If the Good News we preach is hidden behind a veil, it is hidden only from people who are perishing. ⁴Satan, who is the god of this world, has blinded the minds of those who don't believe. They are unable to see the glorious light of the Good News. They don't understand this message about the glory of Christ, who is the exact likeness of God.

⁵You see, we don't go around preaching about ourselves. We preach that Jesus Christ is Lord, and we ourselves are your servants for Jesus' sake. ⁶For God, who said, "Let there be light in the darkness," has made this light shine in our hearts so we could know the glory of God that is seen in the face of Jesus Christ.

⁷We now have this light shining in our hearts, but we ourselves are like fragile clay jars containing this great treasure.* This makes it clear that our great power is from God, not from ourselves.

⁸We are pressed on every side by troubles, but we are not crushed. We are perplexed, but not driven to despair. ⁹We are hunted down, but never abandoned by God. We get knocked down, but we are not destroyed. ¹⁰Through suffering, our bodies continue to share in the death of Jesus so that the life of Jesus may also be seen in our bodies.

¹¹Yes, we live under constant danger of death because we serve Jesus, so that the life of Jesus will be evident in our dying bodies. ¹²So we live in the face of death, but this has resulted in eternal life for you.

4:1 Or *ministry.*   4:7 Greek *We now have this treasure in clay jars.*

PSALM 44:1-8
For the choir director: A psalm* of the descendants of Korah.

¹ **O** God, we have heard it with our own ears—

our ancestors have told us
  of all you did in their day,
  in days long ago:
² You drove out the pagan nations
  by your power
and gave all the land to our
  ancestors.
You crushed their enemies
  and set our ancestors free.
³ They did not conquer the land
  with their swords;
it was not their own strong arm
  that gave them victory.
It was your right hand and strong
  arm
and the blinding light from your
  face that helped them,
  for you loved them.

⁴ You are my King and my God.
You command victories for
  Israel.*
⁵ Only by your power can we push
  back our enemies;
only in your name can we
  trample our foes.
⁶ I do not trust in my bow;
I do not count on my sword to
  save me.
⁷ You are the one who gives us victory
  over our enemies;
you disgrace those who
  hate us.
⁸ O God, we give glory to you all day
  long
and constantly praise your name.
              Interlude

44:TITLE Hebrew *maskil.* This may be a literary or musical term.   44:4 Hebrew *for Jacob.* The names "Jacob" and "Israel" are often interchanged throughout the Old Testament, referring sometimes to the individual patriarch and sometimes to the nation.

PROVERBS 22:10-12
Throw out the mocker, and fighting goes, too. Quarrels and insults will disappear. □ Whoever loves a pure heart and gracious speech will have the king as a friend. □ The Lord preserves those with knowledge, but he ruins the plans of the treacherous.

JOB 37:1–39:30

After Elihu speaks, God himself has a word with Job. No matter how circumstances change, for better or worse, God remains the same. It's one thing to want your circumstances changed; it's another altogether to let God change you in the midst of your circumstances.

"**M**y [Elihu's] heart pounds as I think of this.
  It trembles within me.
² Listen carefully to the thunder of God's voice
  as it rolls from his mouth.
³ It rolls across the heavens,
  and his lightning flashes in every direction.
⁴ Then comes the roaring of the thunder—
  the tremendous voice of his majesty.
  He does not restrain it when he speaks.
⁵ God's voice is glorious in the thunder.
  We can't even imagine the greatness of his power.

⁶ "He directs the snow to fall on the earth
  and tells the rain to pour down.
⁷ Then everyone stops working
  so they can watch his power.
⁸ The wild animals take cover
  and stay inside their dens.
⁹ The stormy wind comes from its chamber,
  and the driving winds bring the cold.
¹⁰ God's breath sends the ice,
  freezing wide expanses of water.
¹¹ He loads the clouds with moisture,
  and they flash with his lightning.
¹² The clouds churn about at his direction.
  They do whatever he commands throughout the earth.
¹³ He makes these things happen either to punish people
  or to show his unfailing love.

¹⁴ "Pay attention to this, Job.
  Stop and consider the wonderful miracles of God!

¹⁵ Do you know how God controls the storm
  and causes the lightning to flash from his clouds?
¹⁶ Do you understand how he moves the clouds
  with wonderful perfection and skill?
¹⁷ When you are sweltering in your clothes
  and the south wind dies down and everything is still,
¹⁸ he makes the skies reflect the heat like a bronze mirror.
  Can you do that?

¹⁹ "So teach the rest of us what to say to God.
  We are too ignorant to make our own arguments.
²⁰ Should God be notified that I want to speak?
  Can people even speak when they are confused?*
²¹ We cannot look at the sun,
  for it shines brightly in the sky when the wind clears away the clouds.
²² So also, golden splendor comes from the mountain of God.*
  He is clothed in dazzling splendor.
²³ We cannot imagine the power of the Almighty;
  but even though he is just and righteous,
  he does not destroy us.
²⁴ No wonder people everywhere fear him.
  All who are wise show him reverence."

38:1THEN the LORD answered Job from the whirlwind:

² "Who is this that questions my wisdom
  with such ignorant words?
³ Brace yourself like a man,
  because I have some questions for you,
  and you must answer them.

⁴ "Where were you when I laid the
foundations of the earth?
Tell me, if you know so much.
⁵ Who determined its dimensions
and stretched out the surveying
line?
⁶ What supports its foundations,
and who laid its cornerstone
⁷ as the morning stars sang together
and all the angels* shouted for joy?

⁸ "Who kept the sea inside its
boundaries
as it burst from the womb,
⁹ and as I clothed it with clouds
and wrapped it in thick darkness?
¹⁰ For I locked it behind barred gates,
limiting its shores.
¹¹ I said, 'This far and no farther will you
come.
Here your proud waves must stop!'

¹² "Have you ever commanded the
morning to appear
and caused the dawn to rise in the
east?
¹³ Have you made daylight spread to the
ends of the earth,
to bring an end to the night's
wickedness?
¹⁴ As the light approaches,
the earth takes shape like clay
pressed beneath a seal;
it is robed in brilliant colors.*
¹⁵ The light disturbs the wicked
and stops the arm that is raised in
violence.

¹⁶ "Have you explored the springs from
which the seas come?
Have you explored their depths?
¹⁷ Do you know where the gates of death
are located?
Have you seen the gates of utter
gloom?
¹⁸ Do you realize the extent of the earth?
Tell me about it if you know!

¹⁹ "Where does light come from,
and where does darkness go?
²⁰ Can you take each to its home?
Do you know how to get there?
²¹ But of course you know all this!
For you were born before it was all
created,
and you are so very experienced!

²² "Have you visited the storehouses of
the snow
or seen the storehouses of hail?
²³ (I have reserved them as weapons for
the time of trouble,
for the day of battle and war.)
²⁴ Where is the path to the source of
light?
Where is the home of the east wind?

²⁵ "Who created a channel for the
torrents of rain?
Who laid out the path for
the lightning?
²⁶ Who makes the rain fall on barren
land,
in a desert where no one lives?
²⁷ Who sends rain to satisfy the parched
ground
and make the tender grass spring up?

²⁸ "Does the rain have a father?
Who gives birth to the dew?
²⁹ Who is the mother of the ice?
Who gives birth to the frost from
the heavens?
³⁰ For the water turns to ice as hard
as rock,
and the surface of the water
freezes.

³¹ "Can you direct the movement of
the stars—
binding the cluster of the Pleiades
or loosening the cords of Orion?
³² Can you direct the sequence of the
seasons
or guide the Bear with her cubs
across the heavens?
³³ Do you know the laws of the universe?
Can you use them to regulate
the earth?

³⁴ "Can you shout to the clouds
and make it rain?
³⁵ Can you make lightning appear
and cause it to strike as you direct?
³⁶ Who gives intuition to the heart
and instinct to the mind?
³⁷ Who is wise enough to count all
the clouds?
Who can tilt the water jars of
heaven
³⁸ when the parched ground is dry
and the soil has hardened into
clods?

³⁹ "Can you stalk prey for a lioness
and satisfy the young lions'
appetites
⁴⁰ as they lie in their dens
or crouch in the thicket?
⁴¹ Who provides food for the ravens
when their young cry out to God
and wander about in hunger?

³⁹:¹ "Do you know when the wild goats
give birth?
Have you watched as deer are born
in the wild?
² Do you know how many months they
carry their young?
Are you aware of the time of their
delivery?
³ They crouch down to give birth to
their young
and deliver their offspring.
⁴ Their young grow up in the open
fields,
then leave home and never return.

⁵ "Who gives the wild donkey its
freedom?
Who untied its ropes?
⁶ I have placed it in the wilderness;
its home is the wasteland.
⁷ It hates the noise of the city
and has no driver to shout at it.
⁸ The mountains are its pastureland,
where it searches for every blade of
grass.

⁹ "Will the wild ox consent to being
tamed?
Will it spend the night in your stall?
¹⁰ Can you hitch a wild ox to a plow?
Will it plow a field for you?
¹¹ Given its strength, can you trust it?
Can you leave and trust the ox to do
your work?
¹² Can you rely on it to bring home your
grain
and deliver it to your threshing
floor?

¹³ "The ostrich flaps her wings grandly,
but they are no match for the
feathers of the stork.
¹⁴ She lays her eggs on top of the earth,
letting them be warmed in the dust.
¹⁵ She doesn't worry that a foot might
crush them
or a wild animal might destroy
them.
¹⁶ She is harsh toward her young,
as if they were not her own.
She doesn't care if they die.
¹⁷ For God has deprived her of wisdom.
He has given her no understanding.
¹⁸ But whenever she jumps up to run,
she passes the swiftest horse with
its rider.

¹⁹ "Have you given the horse its strength
or clothed its neck with a flowing
mane?

WHAT THE BIBLE SAYS

Facing death with hope

2 CORINTHIANS 5:5-8 Death is never an easy topic to discuss. It comes with sorrow, tears, and grief—no matter when or how it happens, those left behind must bear the pain. That's what Satan gave us when sin entered the human race. Everyone must face death. Everyone must die. • For Christians, however, death is not the end of the story. It is merely the close of Act One and the opening of Act Two of a two-act play. Death is the doorway through which we must walk in order to enter eternity. • Paul was not afraid to die, because he was confident of spending eternity with Christ. Like Paul, you can have that same confidence. When believers die, we will be with Jesus. And when Jesus returns in glory, all believers will be given heavenly bodies that will be perfect and will last forever. • The Holy Spirit guarantees that we will be resurrected to eternal glory. "God himself has prepared us for this, and as a guarantee he has given us his Holy Spirit" (5:5). Because you have the Holy Spirit, you are guaranteed eternal life.

20 Did you give it the ability to leap like
   a locust?
     Its majestic snorting is terrifying!
21 It paws the earth and rejoices in its
   strength
     when it charges out to battle.
22 It laughs at fear and is unafraid.
     It does not run from the sword.
23 The arrows rattle against it,
     and the spear and javelin flash.
24 It paws the ground fiercely
     and rushes forward into battle
     when the ram's horn blows.
25 It snorts at the sound of the horn.
     It senses the battle in the distance.
     It quivers at the captain's
     commands and the noise
     of battle.
26 "Is it your wisdom that makes the
   hawk soar
     and spread its wings toward
     the south?
27 Is it at your command that the eagle
   rises
     to the heights to make its nest?
28 It lives on the cliffs,
     making its home on a distant, rocky
     crag.
29 From there it hunts its prey,
     keeping watch with piercing eyes.
30 Its young gulp down blood.
     Where there's a carcass, there you'll
     find it."

37:20 Or *speak without being swallowed up?*   **37:22** Or
from the north; or *from the abode.*   **38:7** Hebrew *the sons of
God.*   **38:14** Or *its features stand out like folds in a robe.*

2 CORINTHIANS 4:13–5:10
Paul had faced sufferings, trials, and distress as he
preached the Good News. But he knew that they
would one day be over and he would obtain God's
rest and rewards. We, too, have the assurance that
one day all suffering will end and all sorrow will be
gone.

But we [Paul and his coworkers] continue
to preach because we have the same kind
of faith the psalmist had when he said, "I
believed in God, so I spoke."* 14We know
that God, who raised the Lord Jesus,* will
also raise us with Jesus and present us
to himself together with you. 15All of this
is for your benefit. And as God's grace
reaches more and more people, there will

be great thanksgiving, and God will receive more and more glory.
   16That is why we never give up. Though
our bodies are dying, our spirits are* being renewed every day. 17For our present
troubles are small and won't last very
long. Yet they produce for us a glory that
vastly outweighs them and will last forever! 18So we don't look at the troubles we
can see now; rather, we fix our gaze on
things that cannot be seen. For the things
we see now will soon be gone, but the
things we cannot see will last forever.

5:1FOR we know that when this earthly
tent we live in is taken down (that is, when
we die and leave this earthly body), we will
have a house in heaven, an eternal body
made for us by God himself and not by human hands. 2We grow weary in our present bodies, and we long to put on our
heavenly bodies like new clothing. 3For
we will put on heavenly bodies; we will not
be spirits without bodies.* 4While we live
in these earthly bodies, we groan and sigh,
but it's not that we want to die and get rid
of these bodies that clothe us. Rather, we
want to put on our new bodies so that
these dying bodies will be swallowed up
by life. 5God himself has prepared us for
this, and as a guarantee he has given us his
Holy Spirit.
   6So we are always confident, even
though we know that as long as we live in
these bodies we are not at home with the
Lord. 7For we live by believing and not by
seeing. 8Yes, we are fully confident, and
we would rather be away from these
earthly bodies, for then we will be at
home with the Lord. 9So whether we are
here in this body or away from this body,
our goal is to please him. 10For we must all
stand before Christ to be judged. We will
each receive whatever we deserve for the
good or evil we have done in this earthly
body.

4:13 Ps 116:10.   **4:14** Some manuscripts read *who raised
Jesus.*   **4:16** Greek *our inner being is.*   **5:3** Greek *we will
not be naked.*

PSALM 44:9-26
But now you [God] have tossed us
   aside in dishonor.
     You no longer lead our armies to
     battle.

10 You make us retreat from our enemies
    and allow those who hate us to
      plunder our land.
11 You have butchered us like sheep
    and scattered us among the nations.
12 You sold your precious people for a
      pittance,
    making nothing on the sale.
13 You let our neighbors mock us.
    We are an object of scorn and
      derision to those around us.
14 You have made us the butt of their
      jokes;
    they shake their heads at us in scorn.
15 We can't escape the constant
      humiliation;
    shame is written across our faces.
16 All we hear are the taunts of our
      mockers.
    All we see are our vengeful enemies.

17 All this has happened though we have
      not forgotten you.
    We have not violated your covenant.
18 Our hearts have not deserted you.
    We have not strayed from your path.
19 Yet you have crushed us in the jackal's
      desert home.

You have covered us with darkness
      and death.
20 If we had forgotten the name of our
      God
    or spread our hands in prayer to
      foreign gods,
21 God would surely have known it,
    for he knows the secrets of every
      heart.
22 But for your sake we are killed every
      day;
    we are being slaughtered like
      sheep.

23 Wake up, O Lord! Why do you sleep?
    Get up! Do not reject us forever.
24 Why do you look the other way?
    Why do you ignore our suffering
      and oppression?
25 We collapse in the dust,
    lying face down in the dirt.
26 Rise up! Help us!
    Ransom us because of your
      unfailing love.

PROVERBS 22:13
The lazy person claims, "There's a lion out
there! If I go outside, I might be killed!"

You make us retreat from our enemies,
and allow those who hate us to
plunder our land.
You have butchered us like sheep
and scattered us among the nations.
You sold your precious people for a
pittance,
making nothing on the sale.
You let our neighbors mock us.
We are an object of scorn and
derision to those around us.
You have made us the butt of their
jokes.
They shake their heads at us in scorn.
We can't escape the constant
humiliation;
shame is written across our faces.
All we hear are the taunts of our
mockers.
All we see are our vengeful enemies.
All this has happened though we have
not forgotten you.
We have not violated your covenant.
Our hearts have not deserted you.
We have not strayed from your path.
Yet you have crushed us in the jackal's
desert home,

You have covered us with darkness
and death.
If we had forgotten the name of our
God
or spread out our hands in prayer to
foreign gods,
God would surely have known it,
for he knows the secrets of every
heart.
But for your sake we are killed every
day;
we are being slaughtered like
sheep.

Wake up, O Lord! Why do you sleep?
Get up! Do not reject us forever.
Why do you look the other way?
Why do you ignore our suffering
and oppression?
We collapse in the dust,
lying face down in the dirt.
Rise up! Help us!
Ransom us because of your
unfailing love.

PROVERBS 22:13
The lazy person claims, "There's a lion out
there! If I go outside, I might be killed!"

JOB 40:1-42:17

We tend to define our lives by what we have. Job lost everything. His trial completely altered his expectations of being able to control his own life, but his view of God remained intact. Read his perspective after the crisis.

Then the LORD said to Job,

2 "Do you still want to argue with
      the Almighty?
    You are God's critic, but do you have
      the answers?"

3 Then Job replied to the LORD,

4 "I am nothing—how could I ever find
      the answers?
    I will cover my mouth with my hand.
5 I have said too much already.
    I have nothing more to say."

6 Then the LORD answered Job from the whirlwind:

7 "Brace yourself like a man,
      because I have some questions
        for you,
    and you must answer them.

8 "Will you discredit my justice
      and condemn me just to prove you
        are right?
9 Are you as strong as God?
    Can you thunder with a voice
      like his?
10 All right, put on your glory and
      splendor,
    your honor and majesty.
11 Give vent to your anger.
    Let it overflow against the proud.
12 Humiliate the proud with a glance;
    walk on the wicked where they stand.
13 Bury them in the dust.
    Imprison them in the world of
      the dead.
14 Then even I would praise you,
    for your own strength would
      save you.

15 "Take a look at Behemoth,*
    which I made, just as I made you.
    It eats grass like an ox.
16 See its powerful loins
    and the muscles of its belly.
17 Its tail is as strong as a cedar.
    The sinews of its thighs are knit
      tightly together.
18 Its bones are tubes of bronze.
    Its limbs are bars of iron.
19 It is a prime example of God's
      handiwork,
    and only its Creator can threaten it.
20 The mountains offer it their best food,
    where all the wild animals play.
21 It lies under the lotus plants,*
    hidden by the reeds in the marsh.
22 The lotus plants give it shade
      among the willows beside
        the stream.
23 It is not disturbed by the raging river,
    not concerned when the swelling
      Jordan rushes around it.
24 No one can catch it off guard
    or put a ring in its nose and lead
      it away.

41:1 *"CAN you catch Leviathan* with
      a hook
    or put a noose around its jaw?
2 Can you tie it with a rope through
      the nose
    or pierce its jaw with a spike?
3 Will it beg you for mercy
    or implore you for pity?
4 Will it agree to work for you,
    to be your slave for life?
5 Can you make it a pet like a bird,
    or give it to your little girls to
      play with?
6 Will merchants try to buy it
    to sell it in their shops?
7 Will its hide be hurt by spears
    or its head by a harpoon?
8 If you lay a hand on it,

you will certainly remember the battle that follows.
You won't try that again!

9*No, it is useless to try to capture it.
The hunter who attempts it will be knocked down.

10 And since no one dares to disturb it, who then can stand up to me?

11 Who has given me anything that I need to pay back?
Everything under heaven is mine.

12 "I want to emphasize Leviathan's limbs
and its enormous strength and graceful form.

13 Who can strip off its hide,
and who can penetrate its double layer of armor?*

14 Who could pry open its jaws?
For its teeth are terrible!

15 Its scales are like rows of shields tightly sealed together.

16 They are so close together that no air can get between them.

17 Each scale sticks tight to the next.
They interlock and cannot be penetrated.

18 "When it sneezes, it flashes light!
Its eyes are like the red of dawn.

19 Lightning leaps from its mouth;
flames of fire flash out.

20 Smoke streams from its nostrils like steam from a pot heated over burning rushes.

21 Its breath would kindle coals,
for flames shoot from its mouth.

22 "The tremendous strength in Leviathan's neck
strikes terror wherever it goes.

23 Its flesh is hard and firm and cannot be penetrated.

24 Its heart is hard as rock,
hard as a millstone.

25 When it rises, the mighty are afraid, gripped by terror.

26 No sword can stop it,
no spear, dart, or javelin.

27 Iron is nothing but straw to that creature,
and bronze is like rotten wood.

28 Arrows cannot make it flee.

Stones shot from a sling are like bits of grass.

29 Clubs are like a blade of grass,
and it laughs at the swish of javelins.

30 Its belly is covered with scales as sharp as glass.
It plows up the ground as it drags through the mud.

31 "Leviathan makes the water boil with its commotion.
It stirs the depths like a pot of ointment.

32 The water glistens in its wake,
making the sea look white.

33 Nothing on earth is its equal,
no other creature so fearless.

34 Of all the creatures, it is the proudest.
It is the king of beasts."

42:1THEN Job replied to the LORD:

2 "I know that you can do anything,
and no one can stop you.

3 You asked, 'Who is this that questions my wisdom with such ignorance?'
It is I—and I was talking about things I knew nothing about,
things far too wonderful for me.

4 You said, 'Listen and I will speak!
I have some questions for you,
and you must answer them.'

5 I had only heard about you before,
but now I have seen you with my own eyes.

6 I take back everything I said,
and I sit in dust and ashes to show my repentance."

7After the LORD had finished speaking to Job, he said to Eliphaz the Temanite: "I am angry with you and your two friends, for you have not spoken accurately about me, as my servant Job has. 8So take seven bulls and seven rams and go to my servant Job and offer a burnt offering for yourselves. My servant Job will pray for you, and I will accept his prayer on your behalf. I will not treat you as you deserve, for you have not spoken accurately about me, as my servant Job has." 9So Eliphaz the Temanite, Bildad the Shuhite, and Zophar the Naamathite did as the LORD commanded them, and the LORD accepted Job's prayer.

¹⁰When Job prayed for his friends, the LORD restored his fortunes. In fact, the LORD gave him twice as much as before! ¹¹Then all his brothers, sisters, and former friends came and feasted with him in his home. And they consoled him and comforted him because of all the trials the LORD had brought against him. And each of them brought him a gift of money* and a gold ring.

¹²So the LORD blessed Job in the second half of his life even more than in the beginning. For now he had 14,000 sheep, 6,000 camels, 1,000 teams of oxen, and 1,000 female donkeys. ¹³He also gave Job seven more sons and three more daughters. ¹⁴He named his first daughter Jemimah, the second Keziah, and the third Keren-happuch. ¹⁵In all the land no women were as lovely as the daughters of Job. And their father put them into his will along with their brothers.

¹⁶Job lived 140 years after that, living to see four generations of his children and grandchildren. ¹⁷Then he died, an old man who had lived a long, full life.

40:15 The identification of Behemoth is disputed, ranging from an earthly creature to a mythical sea monster in ancient literature. 40:21 Or *bramble bushes;* also in 40:22. 41:1a Verses 41:1-8 are numbered 40:25-32 in Hebrew text. 41:1b The identification of Leviathan is disputed, ranging from an earthly creature to a mythical sea monster in ancient literature. 41:9 Verses 41:9-34 are numbered 41:1-26 in Hebrew text. 41:13 As in Greek version; Hebrew reads *its bridle?* 42:11 Hebrew *a kesitah;* the value or weight of the kesitah is no longer known.

2 CORINTHIANS 5:11-21
An *ambassador* is a representative, an official messenger with a specialized mission. We are God's ambassadors. We show the world what life is like in God's Kingdom.

Because we [Paul and his co-workers] understand our fearful responsibility to the Lord, we work hard to persuade others. God knows we are sincere, and I hope you [Corinthians] know this, too. ¹²Are we commending ourselves to you again? No, we are giving you a reason to be proud of us,* so you can answer those who brag about having a spectacular ministry rather than having a sincere heart. ¹³If it seems we are crazy, it is to bring glory to God. And if we are in our right minds, it is for your benefit. ¹⁴Either way, Christ's love controls us.* Since we believe that Christ died for all, we also believe that we have all died to our old life.* ¹⁵He died for everyone so that those who receive his new life will no longer live for themselves. Instead, they will live for Christ, who died and was raised for them.

¹⁶So we have stopped evaluating others from a human point of view. At one time we thought of Christ merely from a human point of view. How differently we know him now! ¹⁷This means that anyone who belongs to Christ has become a new person. The old life is gone; a new life has begun!

HOW WE LIVE Responding to God

2 CORINTHIANS 5:17 When you put your trust in Christ to save you, he made you a new creation. You look the same on the outside, but on the inside—in your heart—you have been transformed. You may say, "I don't feel that much different. In fact, I don't even act that much different." You may wonder if maybe this new faith "didn't take" somehow, or if you missed out on something. • You didn't miss anything. Just as a person grows physically—growth that is imperceptible from day to day—so it is with spiritual growth. You are just now beginning the spiritual growth process. It's going to take some time and you may not see big changes on a daily basis. But over the course of time, you'll begin to see those transformations in your life. Through Bible reading and prayer, you will discover some changes God wants you to make or areas of service to which he is calling you. As you respond to him, you will get to know him better. And you will grow as a result. The desire to respond to God—to sense his leading and obey him—is part of the fruit of salvation.

¹⁸And all of this is a gift from God, who brought us back to himself through Christ. And God has given us this task of reconciling people to him. ¹⁹For God was in Christ, reconciling the world to himself, no longer counting people's sins against them. And he gave us this wonderful message of reconciliation. ²⁰So we are Christ's ambassadors; God is making his appeal through us. We speak for Christ when we plead, "Come back to God!" ²¹For God made Christ, who never sinned, to be the offering for our sin,* so that we could be made right with God through Christ.

5:12 Some manuscripts read *proud of yourselves.*   5:14a Or *urges us on.*   5:14b Greek *Since one died for all, then all died.*   5:21 Or *to become sin itself.*

PSALM 45:1-17

For the choir director: A love song to be sung to the tune "Lilies." A psalm of the descendants of Korah.*

¹ **B**eautiful words stir my heart.
   I will recite a lovely poem about
      the king,
   for my tongue is like the pen of
      a skillful poet.

² You are the most handsome of all.
   Gracious words stream from
      your lips.
   God himself has blessed you
      forever.

³ Put on your sword, O mighty warrior!
   You are so glorious, so majestic!

⁴ In your majesty, ride out to victory,
   defending truth, humility, and
      justice.
   Go forth to perform awe-inspiring
      deeds!

⁵ Your arrows are sharp, piercing your
      enemies' hearts.
   The nations fall beneath your feet.

⁶ Your throne, O God,* endures forever
      and ever.
   You rule with a scepter of justice.

⁷ You love justice and hate evil.

   Therefore God, your God, has
      anointed you,
   pouring out the oil of joy on you
      more than on anyone else.

⁸ Myrrh, aloes, and cassia perfume
      your robes.
   In ivory palaces the music of strings
      entertains you.

⁹ Kings' daughters are among your
      noble women.
   At your right side stands the queen,
      wearing jewelry of finest gold from
      Ophir!

¹⁰ Listen to me, O royal daughter; take
      to heart what I say.
   Forget your people and your family
      far away.

¹¹ For your royal husband delights in
      your beauty;
   honor him, for he is your lord.

¹² The princess of Tyre* will shower you
      with gifts.
   The wealthy will beg your favor.

¹³ The bride, a princess, looks glorious
      in her golden gown.

¹⁴ In her beautiful robes, she is led to the
      king,
   accompanied by her bridesmaids.

¹⁵ What a joyful and enthusiastic
      procession
   as they enter the king's palace!

¹⁶ Your sons will become kings like
      their father.
   You will make them rulers over
      many lands.

¹⁷ I will bring honor to your name in
      every generation.
   Therefore, the nations will praise
      you forever and ever.

45:TITLE Hebrew *maskil.* This may be a literary or musical term.   45:6 Or *Your divine throne.*   45:12 Hebrew *The daughter of Tyre.*

PROVERBS 22:14

The mouth of an immoral woman is a dangerous trap; those who make the LORD angry will fall into it.

ECCLESIASTES 1:1–3:22

While Job is a book about a man who lost everything, Ecclesiastes is a book about a man who had everything. King Solomon could enjoy every pleasure money could buy. This book provides a test case: Can money buy happiness?

These are the words of the Teacher,* King David's son, who ruled in Jerusalem.

²"Everything is meaningless," says the Teacher, "completely meaningless!"

³What do people get for all their hard work under the sun? ⁴Generations come and generations go, but the earth never changes. ⁵The sun rises and the sun sets, then hurries around to rise again. ⁶The wind blows south, and then turns north. Around and around it goes, blowing in circles. ⁷Rivers run into the sea, but the sea is never full. Then the water returns again to the rivers and flows out again to the sea. ⁸Everything is wearisome beyond description. No matter how much we see, we are never satisfied. No matter how much we hear, we are not content.

⁹History merely repeats itself. It has all been done before. Nothing under the sun is truly new. ¹⁰Sometimes people say, "Here is something new!" But actually it is old; nothing is ever truly new. ¹¹We don't remember what happened in the past, and in future generations, no one will remember what we are doing now.

¹²I, the Teacher, was king of Israel, and I lived in Jerusalem. ¹³I devoted myself to search for understanding and to explore by wisdom everything being done under heaven. I soon discovered that God has dealt a tragic existence to the human race. ¹⁴I observed everything going on under the sun, and really, it is all meaningless—like chasing the wind.

15 What is wrong cannot be made right.
　　What is missing cannot be
　　　recovered.

¹⁶I said to myself, "Look, I am wiser than any of the kings who ruled in Jerusalem before me. I have greater wisdom and knowledge than any of them." ¹⁷So I set out to learn everything from wisdom to madness and folly. But I learned firsthand that pursuing all this is like chasing the wind.

18 The greater my wisdom, the greater
　　my grief.
　　To increase knowledge only
　　　increases sorrow.

2:1I SAID to myself, "Come on, let's try pleasure. Let's look for the 'good things' in life." But I found that this, too, was meaningless. ²So I said, "Laughter is silly. What good does it do to seek pleasure?" ³After much thought, I decided to cheer myself with wine. And while still seeking wisdom, I clutched at foolishness. In this way, I tried to experience the only happiness most people find during their brief life in this world.

⁴I also tried to find meaning by building huge homes for myself and by planting beautiful vineyards. ⁵I made gardens and parks, filling them with all kinds of fruit trees. ⁶I built reservoirs to collect the water to irrigate my many flourishing groves. ⁷I bought slaves, both men and women, and others were born into my household. I also owned large herds and flocks, more than any of the kings who had lived in Jerusalem before me. ⁸I collected great sums of silver and gold, the treasure of many kings and provinces. I hired wonderful singers, both men and women, and had many beautiful concubines. I had everything a man could desire!

⁹So I became greater than all who had lived in Jerusalem before me, and my wisdom never failed me. ¹⁰Anything I wanted, I would take. I denied myself no pleasure. I even found great pleasure in hard work, a reward for all my labors. ¹¹But as I looked at everything I had worked so hard to accomplish, it was all so meaningless—like chasing the wind. There was nothing really worthwhile anywhere.

¹²So I decided to compare wisdom with foolishness and madness (for who can do this better than I, the king?*). ¹³I thought, "Wisdom is better than foolishness, just

as light is better than darkness. ¹⁴For the wise can see where they are going, but fools walk in the dark." Yet I saw that the wise and the foolish share the same fate. ¹⁵Both will die. So I said to myself, "Since I will end up the same as the fool, what's the value of all my wisdom? This is all so meaningless!" ¹⁶For the wise and the foolish both die. The wise will not be remembered any longer than the fool. In the days to come, both will be forgotten.

¹⁷So I came to hate life because everything done here under the sun is so troubling. Everything is meaningless—like chasing the wind.

¹⁸I came to hate all my hard work here on earth, for I must leave to others everything I have earned. ¹⁹And who can tell whether my successors will be wise or foolish? Yet they will control everything I have gained by my skill and hard work under the sun. How meaningless! ²⁰So I gave up in despair, questioning the value of all my hard work in this world.

²¹Some people work wisely with knowledge and skill, then must leave the fruit of their efforts to someone who hasn't worked for it. This, too, is meaningless, a great tragedy. ²²So what do people get in this life for all their hard work and anxiety? ²³Their days of labor are filled with pain and grief; even at night their minds cannot rest. It is all meaningless.

²⁴So I decided there is nothing better than to enjoy food and drink and to find satisfaction in work. Then I realized that these pleasures are from the hand of God. ²⁵For who can eat or enjoy anything apart from him?* ²⁶God gives wisdom, knowledge, and joy to those who please him. But if a sinner becomes wealthy, God takes the wealth away and gives it to those who please him. This, too, is meaningless—like chasing the wind.

³:¹ FOR everything there is a season,
    a time for every activity under
        heaven.
² A time to be born and a time to die.
    A time to plant and a time to
        harvest.
³ A time to kill and a time to heal.
    A time to tear down and a time
        to build up.

⁴ A time to cry and a time to laugh.
    A time to grieve and a time to
        dance.
⁵ A time to scatter stones and a time
        to gather stones.
    A time to embrace and a time
        to turn away.
⁶ A time to search and a time to quit
        searching.
    A time to keep and a time to throw
        away.
⁷ A time to tear and a time to mend.
    A time to be quiet and a time
        to speak.
⁸ A time to love and a time to hate.
    A time for war and a time
        for peace.

⁹What do people really get for all their hard work? ¹⁰I have seen the burden God has placed on us all. ¹¹Yet God has made everything beautiful for its own time. He has planted eternity in the human heart, but even so, people cannot see the whole scope of God's work from beginning to end. ¹²So I concluded there is nothing better than to be happy and enjoy ourselves as long as we can. ¹³And people should eat and drink and enjoy the fruits of their labor, for these are gifts from God.

¹⁴And I know that whatever God does is final. Nothing can be added to it or taken from it. God's purpose is that people should fear him. ¹⁵What is happening now has happened before, and what will happen in the future has happened before, because God makes the same things happen over and over again.

¹⁶I also noticed that under the sun there is evil in the courtroom. Yes, even the courts of law are corrupt! ¹⁷I said to myself, "In due season God will judge everyone, both good and bad, for all their deeds."

¹⁸I also thought about the human condition—how God proves to people that they are like animals. ¹⁹For people and animals share the same fate—both breathe* and both must die. So people have no real advantage over the animals. How meaningless! ²⁰Both go to the same place—they came from dust and they return to dust. ²¹For who can prove that the human spirit

goes up and the spirit of animals goes down into the earth? ²²So I saw that there is nothing better for people than to be happy in their work. That is why we are here! No one will bring us back from death to enjoy life after we die.

1:1 Hebrew *Qoheleth;* this term is rendered "the Teacher" throughout this book.   2:12 The meaning of the Hebrew is uncertain.   2:25 As in Greek and Syriac versions; Hebrew reads *apart from me?*   3:19 Or *both have the same spirit.*

2 CORINTHIANS 6:1-13

Paul's suffering gives us a view into the persecution that many Christians of the first century faced. The fact that Paul never lost sight of his mission in the midst of that suffering is an inspiration.

As God's partners,* we [Paul and his co-workers] beg you [Corinthians] not to accept this marvelous gift of God's kindness and then ignore it. ²For God says,

"At just the right time, I heard you.
 On the day of salvation, I helped
  you."*

Indeed, the "right time" is now. Today is the day of salvation.

³We live in such a way that no one will stumble because of us, and no one will find fault with our ministry. ⁴In everything we do, we show that we are true ministers of God. We patiently endure troubles and hardships and calamities of every kind. ⁵We have been beaten, been put in prison, faced angry mobs, worked to exhaustion, endured sleepless nights, and gone without food. ⁶We prove ourselves by our purity, our understanding, our patience, our kindness, by the Holy Spirit within us,* and by our sincere love. ⁷We faithfully preach the truth. God's power is working in us. We use the weapons of righteousness in the right hand for attack and the left hand for defense. ⁸We serve God whether people honor us or despise us, whether they slander us or praise us. We are honest, but they call us impostors. ⁹We are ignored, even though we are well known. We live close to death, but we are still alive. We have been beaten, but we have not been killed. ¹⁰Our hearts ache, but we always have joy. We are poor, but we give spiritual riches to others. We own nothing, and yet we have everything.

¹¹Oh, dear Corinthian friends! We have spoken honestly with you, and our hearts are open to you. ¹²There is no lack of love on our part, but you have withheld your love from us. ¹³I am asking you to respond as if you were my own children. Open your hearts to us!

6:1 Or *As we work together.*   6:2 Isa 49:8 (Greek version).
6:6 Or *by our holiness of spirit.*

PSALM 46:1-11

*For the choir director: A song of the descendants of Korah, to be sung by soprano voices.**

HOW WE LIVE

Worshiping God

ECCLESIASTES 3:11 Look around you. Are people ever completely satisfied? Who has enough money? Who has a perfect marriage or family relationship? Who has perfect health? Who has all of his or her desires fulfilled? We are always searching for more.   •King Solomon had everything under the sun, but nothing truly satisfied him. And like Solomon, even if *we* had it all, we would discover that deep within is a need that nothing can fill. That need is a desire for something eternal, for something more than what we find from day to day. God planted that desire in us, and only he can satisfy it.   •So we search for him. And as his Word promises, when we search with all our hearts, we will find him. And when we find him, we can't help but respond in love and worship. As you respond in worship, thank God for giving you purpose in life and hope for something beyond this life. Worship allows us to experience a glimpse of the glory that awaits us in heaven.

¹ **G**od is our refuge and strength,
   always ready to help in times
   of trouble.
² So we will not fear when earthquakes
   come
   and the mountains crumble into
   the sea.
³ Let the oceans roar and foam.
   Let the mountains tremble as the
   waters surge!   *Interlude*

⁴ A river brings joy to the city of
   our God,
   the sacred home of the Most High.
⁵ God dwells in that city; it cannot be
   destroyed.
   From the very break of day, God
   will protect it.
⁶ The nations are in chaos,
   and their kingdoms crumble!
   God's voice thunders,
   and the earth melts!
⁷ The LORD of Heaven's Armies is here
   among us;
   the God of Israel* is our
   fortress.   *Interlude*

⁸ Come, see the glorious works of
   the LORD:
   See how he brings destruction upon
   the world.
⁹ He causes wars to end throughout
   the earth.
   He breaks the bow and snaps the
   spear;
   he burns the shields with fire.

¹⁰ "Be still, and know that I am God!
   I will be honored by every nation.
   I will be honored throughout the
   world."

¹¹ The LORD of Heaven's Armies is here
   among us;
   the God of Israel is our fortress.
                                        Interlude

46:TITLE Hebrew *according to alamoth.*   **46:7** Hebrew *of
Jacob;* also in 46:11. See note on 44:4.

PROVERBS 22:15
A youngster's heart is filled with foolishness, but physical discipline will drive it
far away.

SEPTEMBER**3**

ECCLESIASTES 4:1–6:12
What are the real tragedies a person faces? Losing
your life? How about not really living the one you're
given?

Again, I [the Teacher] observed all the oppression that takes place under the sun. I
saw the tears of the oppressed, with no
one to comfort them. The oppressors
have great power, and their victims are
helpless. ²So I concluded that the dead
are better off than the living. ³But most
fortunate of all are those who are not yet
born. For they have not seen all the evil
that is done under the sun.

⁴Then I observed that most people are
motivated to success because they envy
their neighbors. But this, too, is meaningless—like chasing the wind.

⁵ "Fools fold their idle hands,
   leading them to ruin."

⁶And yet,

   "Better to have one handful with
   quietness
   than two handfuls with hard work
   and chasing the wind."

⁷I observed yet another example of
something meaningless under the sun.
⁸This is the case of a man who is all alone,
without a child or a brother, yet who
works hard to gain as much wealth as he
can. But then he asks himself, "Who am I
working for? Why am I giving up so much
pleasure now?" It is all so meaningless
and depressing.

⁹Two people are better off than one, for
they can help each other succeed. ¹⁰If one
person falls, the other can reach out and
help. But someone who falls alone is in
real trouble. ¹¹Likewise, two people lying

close together can keep each other warm. But how can one be warm alone? [12] A person standing alone can be attacked and defeated, but two can stand back-to-back and conquer. Three are even better, for a triple-braided cord is not easily broken.

[13] It is better to be a poor but wise youth than an old and foolish king who refuses all advice. [14] Such a youth could rise from poverty and succeed. He might even become king, though he has been in prison. [15] But then everyone rushes to the side of yet another youth* who replaces him. [16] Endless crowds stand around him,* but then another generation grows up and rejects him, too. So it is all meaningless—like chasing the wind.

[5:1]*As you enter the house of God, keep your ears open and your mouth shut. It is evil to make mindless offerings to God. [2]*Don't make rash promises, and don't be hasty in bringing matters before God. After all, God is in heaven, and you are here on earth. So let your words be few.

[3] Too much activity gives you restless dreams; too many words make you a fool.

[4] When you make a promise to God, don't delay in following through, for God takes no pleasure in fools. Keep all the promises you make to him. [5] It is better to say nothing than to make a promise and not keep it. [6] Don't let your mouth make you sin. And don't defend yourself by telling the Temple messenger that the promise you made was a mistake. That would make God angry, and he might wipe out everything you have achieved.

[7] Talk is cheap, like daydreams and other useless activities. Fear God instead.

[8] Don't be surprised if you see a poor person being oppressed by the powerful and if justice is being miscarried throughout the land. For every official is under orders from higher up, and matters of justice get lost in red tape and bureaucracy. [9] Even the king milks the land for his own profit!*

[10] Those who love money will never have enough. How meaningless to think that wealth brings true happiness! [11] The more you have, the more people come to help you spend it. So what good is wealth—except perhaps to watch it slip through your fingers!

[12] People who work hard sleep well, whether they eat little or much. But the rich seldom get a good night's sleep.

[13] There is another serious problem I have seen under the sun. Hoarding riches

HOW WE LIVE

Our relationships

2 CORINTHIANS 6:14–7:1 As a new believer you should be building some new relationships with other Christians. Perhaps, though, some of your closest friends, coworkers, a spouse, or parents are not believers. How do you please God in those relationships? • Paul's words here are not to be interpreted to mean that you must leave an unbelieving spouse or sever your relationship with your family (see 1 Corinthians 7:12-16, August 11). Nor do you have to leave your job in order to work with only Christians. Paul wanted his readers—fairly new believers themselves—to be careful about entering into new binding associations. Would they be free to live according to their core beliefs and values within that relationship? Would their desire to obey God put them between a rock and a hard place?
• Be careful about what kind of partner you team up with, whether in business, marriage, or close friendship. When two people come at life from completely different worldviews and attitudes, there are many places where conflict will arise. If you are already in a marriage or business relationship with an unbeliever, prayerfully seek ways to introduce your partner to Jesus.

harms the saver. [14]Money is put into risky investments that turn sour, and everything is lost. In the end, there is nothing left to pass on to one's children. [15]We all come to the end of our lives as naked and empty-handed as on the day we were born. We can't take our riches with us.

[16]And this, too, is a very serious problem. People leave this world no better off than when they came. All their hard work is for nothing—like working for the wind. [17]Throughout their lives, they live under a cloud—frustrated, discouraged, and angry.

[18]Even so, I have noticed one thing, at least, that is good. It is good for people to eat, drink, and enjoy their work under the sun during the short life God has given them, and to accept their lot in life. [19]And it is a good thing to receive wealth from God and the good health to enjoy it. To enjoy your work and accept your lot in life—this is indeed a gift from God. [20]God keeps such people so busy enjoying life that they take no time to brood over the past.

[6:1]THERE is another serious tragedy I have seen under the sun, and it weighs heavily on humanity. [2]God gives some people great wealth and honor and everything they could ever want, but then he doesn't give them the chance to enjoy these things. They die, and someone else, even a stranger, ends up enjoying their wealth! This is meaningless—a sickening tragedy.

[3]A man might have a hundred children and live to be very old. But if he finds no satisfaction in life and doesn't even get a decent burial, it would have been better for him to be born dead. [4]His birth would have been meaningless, and he would have ended in darkness. He wouldn't even have had a name, [5]and he would never have seen the sun or known of its existence. Yet he would have had more peace than in growing up to be an unhappy man. [6]He might live a thousand years twice over but still not find contentment. And since he must die like everyone else—well, what's the use?

[7]All people spend their lives scratching for food, but they never seem to have enough. [8]So are wise people really better off than fools? Do poor people gain anything by being wise and knowing how to act in front of others?

[9]Enjoy what you have rather than desiring what you don't have. Just dreaming about nice things is meaningless—like chasing the wind.

[10]Everything has already been decided. It was known long ago what each person would be. So there's no use arguing with God about your destiny.

[11]The more words you speak, the less they mean. So what good are they?

[12]In the few days of our meaningless lives, who knows how our days can best be spent? Our lives are like a shadow. Who can tell what will happen on this earth after we are gone?

4:15 Hebrew *the second youth.*   **4:16** Hebrew *There is no end to all the people, to all those who are before them.* **5:1** Verse 5:1 is numbered 4:17 in Hebrew text.   **5:2** Verses 5:2-20 are numbered 5:1-19 in Hebrew text.   **5:9** The meaning of the Hebrew in verses 8 and 9 is uncertain.

2 CORINTHIANS 6:14–7:7

Paul urged the Corinthian believers to be careful not to become entangled with unbelievers in harmful ways. Believers are to be a light in the darkness, not a partner with it.

Don't team up with those who are unbelievers. How can righteousness be a partner with wickedness? How can light live with darkness? [15]What harmony can there be between Christ and the devil*? How can a believer be a partner with an unbeliever? [16]And what union can there be between God's temple and idols? For we are the temple of the living God. As God said:

"I will live in them
    and walk among them.
I will be their God,
    and they will be my people.*
[17] Therefore, come out from among
        unbelievers,
    and separate yourselves from them,
        says the LORD.
Don't touch their filthy things,
    and I will welcome you.*
[18] And I will be your Father,
    and you will be my sons and
        daughters,
        says the LORD Almighty.*"

[7:1]BECAUSE we have these promises, dear friends, let us cleanse ourselves from everything that can defile our body or spirit. And let us work toward complete holiness because we fear God.

²Please open your hearts to us. We have not done wrong to anyone, nor led anyone astray, nor taken advantage of anyone. ³I'm not saying this to condemn you. I said before that you are in our hearts, and we live or die together with you. ⁴I have the highest confidence in you, and I take great pride in you. You have greatly encouraged me and made me happy despite all our troubles.

⁵When we arrived in Macedonia, there was no rest for us. We faced conflict from every direction, with battles on the outside and fear on the inside. ⁶But God, who encourages those who are discouraged, encouraged us by the arrival of Titus. ⁷His presence was a joy, but so was the news he brought of the encouragement he received from you. When he told us how much you long to see me, and how sorry you are for what happened, and how loyal you are to me, I was filled with joy!

6:15 Greek *Beliar;* various other manuscripts render this proper name of the devil as *Belian, Beliab,* or *Belial.* 6:16 Lev 26:12; Ezek 37:27. 6:17 Isa 52:11; Ezek 20:34 (Greek version). 6:18 2 Sam 7:14.

PSALM 47:1-9
For the choir director: A psalm of the descendants of Korah.

¹ **C**ome, everyone! Clap your hands!
    Shout to God with joyful praise!
² For the LORD Most High is
        awesome.

He is the great King of all the earth.
³ He subdues the nations before us,
    putting our enemies beneath our
        feet.
⁴ He chose the Promised Land as our
    inheritance,
    the proud possession of Jacob's
        descendants, whom he loves.
                                    Interlude

⁵ God has ascended with a mighty
    shout.
    The LORD has ascended with
        trumpets blaring.
⁶ Sing praises to God, sing praises;
    sing praises to our King, sing
        praises!
⁷ For God is the King over all
    the earth.
    Praise him with a psalm!
⁸ God reigns above the nations,
    sitting on his holy throne.
⁹ The rulers of the world have gathered
    together
    with the people of the God
        of Abraham.
For all the kings of the earth belong
    to God.
    He is highly honored everywhere.

PROVERBS 22:16
A person who gets ahead by oppressing the poor or by showering gifts on the rich will end in poverty.

ECCLESIASTES 7:1-9:18
Today's reading is reminiscent of the book of Proverbs, a book that Solomon penned a large portion of. Instead of being a linear narrative, it's a collection of nuggets that cover a variety of topics.

A good reputation is more valuable
        than costly perfume.
    And the day you die is better than
        the day you are born.
² Better to spend your time at funerals
        than at parties.

After all, everyone dies—
    so the living should take this to heart.
³ Sorrow is better than laughter,
    for sadness has a refining influence
        on us.
⁴ A wise person thinks a lot about death,
    while a fool thinks only about
        having a good time.
⁵ Better to be criticized by a wise
    person
    than to be praised by a fool.

SEPTEMBER**4**

6 A fool's laughter is quickly gone,
    like thorns crackling in a fire.
    This also is meaningless.

7 Extortion turns wise people into fools,
    and bribes corrupt the heart.

8 Finishing is better than starting.
    Patience is better than pride.

9 Control your temper,
    for anger labels you a fool.

10 Don't long for "the good old days."
    This is not wise.

11 Wisdom is even better when you have
        money.
    Both are a benefit as you go through
        life.

12 Wisdom and money can get you
        almost anything,
    but only wisdom can save your life.

13 Accept the way God does things,
    for who can straighten what he has
        made crooked?

14 Enjoy prosperity while you can,
    but when hard times strike, realize
        that both come from God.
    Remember that nothing is certain
        in this life.

15 I have seen everything in this meaningless life, including the death of good young people and the long life of wicked people. 16 So don't be too good or too wise! Why destroy yourself? 17 On the other hand, don't be too wicked either. Don't be a fool! Why die before your time? 18 Pay attention to these instructions, for anyone who fears God will avoid both extremes.*

19 One wise person is stronger than ten leading citizens of a town!

20 Not a single person on earth is always good and never sins.

21 Don't eavesdrop on others—you may hear your servant curse you. 22 For you know how often you yourself have cursed others.

23 I have always tried my best to let wisdom guide my thoughts and actions. I said to myself, "I am determined to be wise." But it didn't work. 24 Wisdom is always distant and difficult to find. 25 I searched everywhere, determined to find wisdom and to understand the reason for things. I was determined to prove to myself that wickedness is stupid and that foolishness is madness.

26 I discovered that a seductive woman* is a trap more bitter than death. Her passion is a snare, and her soft hands are chains. Those who are pleasing to God will escape her, but sinners will be caught in her snare.

27 "This is my conclusion," says the Teacher. "I discovered this after looking at the matter from every possible angle. 28 Though I have searched repeatedly, I have not found what I was looking for. Only one out of a thousand men is virtuous, but not one woman! 29 But I did find this: God created people to be virtuous, but they have each turned to follow their own downward path."

8:1 How wonderful to be wise,
    to analyze and interpret things.
    Wisdom lights up a person's face,
        softening its harshness.

2 Obey the king since you vowed to God that you would. 3 Don't try to avoid doing your duty, and don't stand with those who plot evil, for the king can do whatever he wants. 4 His command is backed by great power. No one can resist or question it. 5 Those who obey him will not be punished. Those who are wise will find a time and a way to do what is right, 6 for there is a time and a way for everything, even when a person is in trouble.

7 Indeed, how can people avoid what they don't know is going to happen? 8 None of us can hold back our spirit from departing. None of us has the power to prevent the day of our death. There is no escaping that obligation, that dark battle. And in the face of death, wickedness will certainly not rescue the wicked.

9 I have thought deeply about all that goes on here under the sun, where people have the power to hurt each other. 10 I have seen wicked people buried with honor. Yet they were the very ones who frequented the Temple and are now praised* in the same city where they committed their crimes! This, too, is meaningless. 11 When a crime is not punished quickly, people feel it is safe to do wrong. 12 But even though a person sins a hundred

times and still lives a long time, I know that those who fear God will be better off. [13] The wicked will not prosper, for they do not fear God. Their days will never grow long like the evening shadows.

[14] And this is not all that is meaningless in our world. In this life, good people are often treated as though they were wicked, and wicked people are often treated as though they were good. This is so meaningless!

[15] So I recommend having fun, because there is nothing better for people in this world than to eat, drink, and enjoy life. That way they will experience some happiness along with all the hard work God gives them under the sun.

[16] In my search for wisdom and in my observation of people's burdens here on earth, I discovered that there is ceaseless activity, day and night. [17] I realized that no one can discover everything God is doing under the sun. Not even the wisest people discover everything, no matter what they claim.

[9:1] This, too, I carefully explored: Even though the actions of godly and wise people are in God's hands, no one knows whether God will show them favor. [2] The same destiny ultimately awaits everyone, whether righteous or wicked, good or bad,* ceremonially clean or unclean, reli-

gious or irreligious. Good people receive the same treatment as sinners, and people who make promises to God are treated like people who don't.

[3] It seems so tragic that everyone under the sun suffers the same fate. That is why people are not more careful to be good. Instead, they choose their own mad course, for they have no hope. There is nothing ahead but death anyway. [4] There is hope only for the living. As they say, "It's better to be a live dog than a dead lion!"

[5] The living at least know they will die, but the dead know nothing. They have no further reward, nor are they remembered. [6] Whatever they did in their lifetime—loving, hating, envying—is all long gone. They no longer play a part in anything here on earth. [7] So go ahead. Eat your food with joy, and drink your wine with a happy heart, for God approves of this! [8] Wear fine clothes, with a splash of cologne!

[9] Live happily with the woman you love through all the meaningless days of life that God has given you under the sun. The wife God gives you is your reward for all your earthly toil. [10] Whatever you do, do well. For when you go to the grave,* there will be no work or planning or knowledge or wisdom.

[11] I have observed something else under the sun. The fastest runner doesn't always win the race, and the strongest

---

HOW WE LIVE

Responding to God

2 CORINTHIANS 7:10 We see from this passage that sorrow is not always a bad thing. Yet God wants our sorrow to lead us somewhere, to make a difference in our lives. Many people are sorry for their actions when they get caught in the act, but not sorry enough to stop sinning. What is the kind of sorrow God wants us to have? The kind of heartfelt remorse over sin that results in a change of behavior. (By the way, you will often hear this sort of thing referred to as "repentance.") When we make that change, sorrow is soon turned to joy.   • Remember Peter from your readings in the Gospels and Acts? Three times Peter denied even knowing Jesus (Matthew 26:75, February 11). But in his sorrow and remorse afterward, he repented of his sin and went on to become a strong church leader.   • When you are confronted with your wrongdoings, are you defensive or willing to change? Do you try to rationalize your behavior, or do you accept God's correction and make a change for the better? Responding in humble repentance can be difficult, but it will always be life-changing.

warrior doesn't always win the battle. The wise sometimes go hungry, and the skillful are not necessarily wealthy. And those who are educated don't always lead successful lives. It is all decided by chance, by being in the right place at the right time.

¹²People can never predict when hard times might come. Like fish in a net or birds in a trap, people are caught by sudden tragedy.

¹³Here is another bit of wisdom that has impressed me as I have watched the way our world works. ¹⁴There was a small town with only a few people, and a great king came with his army and besieged it. ¹⁵A poor, wise man knew how to save the town, and so it was rescued. But afterward no one thought to thank him. ¹⁶So even though wisdom is better than strength, those who are wise will be despised if they are poor. What they say will not be appreciated for long.

¹⁷ Better to hear the quiet words of a
　　wise person
　　than the shouts of a foolish king.
¹⁸ Better to have wisdom than weapons
　　of war,
　　but one sinner can destroy much
　　that is good.

7:18 Or *will follow them both.*　7:26 Hebrew *a woman.*
8:10 As in some Hebrew manuscripts and Greek version; many Hebrew manuscripts read *and are forgotten.*　9:2 As in Greek and Syriac versions and Latin Vulgate; Hebrew lacks *or bad.*　9:10 Hebrew *to Sheol.*

2 CORINTHIANS 7:8-16

There is a world of difference between guilt and godly sorrow. With guilt comes condemnation. With godly sorrow comes redemption and renewal.

❚ [Paul] am not sorry that I sent that severe letter to you [Corinthians], though I was sorry at first, for I know it was painful to you for a little while. ⁹Now I am glad I sent it, not because it hurt you, but because the pain caused you to repent and change your ways. It was the kind of sorrow God wants his people to have, so you were not harmed by us in any way. ¹⁰For the kind of sorrow God wants us to experience leads us away from sin and results in salvation. There's no regret for that kind of sorrow. But worldly sorrow, which lacks repentance, results in spiritual death.

¹¹Just see what this godly sorrow produced in you! Such earnestness, such concern to clear yourselves, such indignation, such alarm, such longing to see me, such zeal, and such a readiness to punish wrong. You showed that you have done everything necessary to make things right. ¹²My purpose, then, was not to write about who did the wrong or who was wronged. I wrote to you so that in the sight of God you could see for yourselves how loyal you are to us. ¹³We have been greatly encouraged by this.

In addition to our own encouragement, we were especially delighted to see how happy Titus was about the way all of you welcomed him and set his mind* at ease. ¹⁴I had told him how proud I was of you— and you didn't disappoint me. I have always told you the truth, and now my boasting to Titus has also proved true! ¹⁵Now he cares for you more than ever when he remembers the way all of you obeyed him and welcomed him with such fear and deep respect. ¹⁶I am very happy now because I have complete confidence in you.

7:13 Greek *his spirit.*

PSALM 48:1-14
A song. A psalm of the descendants of Korah.

¹ **H**ow great is the LORD,
　　how deserving of praise,
　in the city of our God,
　　which sits on his holy mountain!
² It is high and magnificent;
　　the whole earth rejoices to see it!
　Mount Zion, the holy mountain,*
　　is the city of the great King!
³ God himself is in Jerusalem's towers,
　　revealing himself as its defender.

⁴ The kings of the earth joined forces
　　and advanced against the city.
⁵ But when they saw it, they were
　　stunned;
　　they were terrified and ran away.
⁶ They were gripped with terror
　　and writhed in pain like a woman
　　in labor.
⁷ You destroyed them like the mighty
　　ships of Tarshish
　　shattered by a powerful east wind.

⁸ We had heard of the city's glory,
     but now we have seen it ourselves—
     the city of the LORD of Heaven's
          Armies.
  It is the city of our God;
     he will make it safe forever.

Interlude

⁹ O God, we meditate on your unfailing
          love
     as we worship in your Temple.
¹⁰ As your name deserves, O God,
     you will be praised to the ends
          of the earth.
     Your strong right hand is filled with
          victory.
¹¹ Let the people on Mount Zion rejoice.
     Let all the towns of Judah be glad
     because of your justice.

¹² Go, inspect the city of Jerusalem.*
     Walk around and count the many
          towers.
¹³ Take note of the fortified walls,
     and tour all the citadels,
     that you may describe them
          to future generations.
¹⁴ For that is what God is like.
     He is our God forever and ever,
     and he will guide us until we die.

48:2 Or *Mount Zion, in the far north;* Hebrew reads *Mount Zion, the heights of Zaphon.*   **48:12** Hebrew *Zion.*

PROVERBS 22:17-19

Listen to the words of the wise; apply your heart to my instruction. For it is good to keep these sayings in your heart and always ready on your lips. I am teaching you today—yes, you—so you will trust in the LORD.

SEPTEMBER**5**

ECCLESIASTES 10:1–12:14
Solomon continues on with more wise proverbs. He reminds us that no matter our season of life, connecting with God is really the only thing that satisfies our souls.

As dead flies cause even a bottle of
          perfume to stink,
     so a little foolishness spoils great
          wisdom and honor.

² A wise person chooses the right road;
     a fool takes the wrong one.

³ You can identify fools
     just by the way they walk down
          the street!

⁴ If your boss is angry at you, don't quit!
     A quiet spirit can overcome even
          great mistakes.

⁵ There is another evil I have seen under the sun. Kings and rulers make a grave mistake ⁶when they give great authority to foolish people and low positions to people of proven worth. ⁷I have even seen servants riding horseback like princes—and princes walking like servants!

⁸ When you dig a well,
     you might fall in.
  When you demolish an old wall,
     you could be bitten by a snake.
⁹ When you work in a quarry,
     stones might fall and crush you.
  When you chop wood,
     there is danger with each stroke
          of your ax.

¹⁰ Using a dull ax requires great strength,
     so sharpen the blade.
  That's the value of wisdom;
     it helps you succeed.

¹¹ If a snake bites before you charm it,
     what's the use of being a snake
          charmer?

¹² Wise words bring approval,
     but fools are destroyed by their own
          words.

¹³ Fools base their thoughts on foolish
          assumptions,
     so their conclusions will be wicked
          madness;
¹⁴   they chatter on and on.

No one really knows what is going
to happen;
no one can predict the future.

[15] Fools are so exhausted by a little work
that they can't even find their way
home.

[16] What sorrow for the land ruled by
a servant,*
the land whose leaders feast in
the morning.

[17] Happy is the land whose king is
a noble leader
and whose leaders feast at the
proper time
to gain strength for their work,
not to get drunk.

[18] Laziness leads to a sagging roof;
idleness leads to a leaky house.

[19] A party gives laughter,
wine gives happiness,
and money gives everything!

[20] Never make light of the king, even
in your thoughts.
And don't make fun of the powerful,
even in your own bedroom.
For a little bird might deliver your
message
and tell them what you said.

[11:1] SEND your grain across the seas,
and in time, profits will flow back
to you.*

[2] But divide your investments among
many places,*
for you do not know what risks
might lie ahead.

[3] When clouds are heavy, the rains
come down.
Whether a tree falls north or south,
it stays where it falls.

[4] Farmers who wait for perfect weather
never plant.
If they watch every cloud, they
never harvest.

[5] Just as you cannot understand the path of the wind or the mystery of a tiny baby growing in its mother's womb,* so you cannot understand the activity of God, who does all things.

[6] Plant your seed in the morning and

keep busy all afternoon, for you don't know if profit will come from one activity or another—or maybe both.

[7] Light is sweet; how pleasant to see a new day dawning.

[8] When people live to be very old, let them rejoice in every day of life. But let them also remember there will be many dark days. Everything still to come is meaningless.

[9] Young people,* it's wonderful to be young! Enjoy every minute of it. Do everything you want to do; take it all in. But remember that you must give an account to God for everything you do. [10] So refuse to worry, and keep your body healthy. But remember that youth, with a whole life before you, is meaningless.

[12:1] DON'T let the excitement of youth cause you to forget your Creator. Honor him in your youth before you grow old and say, "Life is not pleasant anymore." [2] Remember him before the light of the sun, moon, and stars is dim to your old eyes, and rain clouds continually darken your sky. [3] Remember him before your legs—the guards of your house—start to tremble; and before your shoulders—the strong men—stoop. Remember him before your teeth—your few remaining servants—stop grinding; and before your eyes—the women looking through the windows—see dimly.

[4] Remember him before the door to life's opportunities is closed and the sound of work fades. Now you rise at the first chirping of the birds, but then all their sounds will grow faint.

[5] Remember him before you become fearful of falling and worry about danger in the streets; before your hair turns white like an almond tree in bloom, and you drag along without energy like a dying grasshopper, and the caperberry no longer inspires sexual desire. Remember him before you near the grave, your everlasting home, when the mourners will weep at your funeral.

[6] Yes, remember your Creator now while you are young, before the silver cord of life snaps and the golden bowl is broken. Don't wait until the water jar is smashed at the spring and the pulley is

broken at the well. ⁷For then the dust will return to the earth, and the spirit will return to God who gave it.

⁸"Everything is meaningless," says the Teacher, "completely meaningless."

⁹Keep this in mind: The Teacher was considered wise, and he taught the people everything he knew. He listened carefully to many proverbs, studying and classifying them. ¹⁰The Teacher sought to find just the right words to express truths clearly.*

¹¹The words of the wise are like cattle prods—painful but helpful. Their collected sayings are like a nail-studded stick with which a shepherd* drives the sheep.

¹²But, my child,* let me give you some further advice: Be careful, for writing books is endless, and much study wears you out.

¹³That's the whole story. Here now is my final conclusion: Fear God and obey his commands, for this is everyone's duty. ¹⁴God will judge us for everything we do, including every secret thing, whether good or bad.

10:16 Or a child.   11:1 Or Give generously, / for your gifts will return to you later. Hebrew reads Throw your bread on the waters, / for after many days you will find it again.   11:2 Hebrew among seven or even eight.   11:5 Some manuscripts read Just as you cannot understand how breath comes to a tiny baby in its mother's womb.   11:9 Hebrew Young man.   12:10 Or sought to write what was upright and true.   12:11 Or one shepherd.   12:12 Hebrew my son.

2 CORINTHIANS 8:1-15
Supporting the church financially has always been an element of the Christian life. Designating part of our money for God's work is part of serving him.

Now I [Paul] want you to know, dear brothers and sisters,* what God in his kindness has done through the churches in Macedonia. ²They are being tested by many troubles, and they are very poor. But they are also filled with abundant joy, which has overflowed in rich generosity.

³For I can testify that they gave not only what they could afford, but far more. And they did it of their own free will. ⁴They begged us again and again for the privilege of sharing in the gift for the believers* in Jerusalem. ⁵They even did more than we had hoped, for their first action was to give themselves to the Lord and to us, just as God wanted them to do.

⁶So we have urged Titus, who encouraged your giving in the first place, to return to you and encourage you to finish this ministry of giving. ⁷Since you excel in so many ways—in your faith, your gifted speakers, your knowledge, your enthusiasm, and your love from us*—I want you to excel also in this gracious act of giving.

⁸I am not commanding you to do this. But I am testing how genuine your love is by comparing it with the eagerness of the other churches.

HOW WE LIVE
Revering God

ECCLESIASTES 12:8-14 Solomon was a man who had it all—power, success, wisdom, and wealth. Yet in the book of Ecclesiastes, Solomon, the "Teacher," candidly revealed how almost everything in his life was completely meaningless to him. How could someone of his immense intellect and good fortune say such a pessimistic thing? Simply because all that the world had to offer came up short. In the end, his relationship with God was the only thing that gave his life meaning.   • He sums up his reasoning in the last two verses of the book: "Fear God and obey his commands." The word *fear* in this sense means to "have a reverential awe of, to respect." If anyone deserves our reverence, it is God. God is awesome and holy. God is righteous and all-powerful. God is our final Judge and Redeemer.   • Your time on earth is short. Solomon has already learned the tough lesson for you. Rather than spending time seeking worldly things that give no meaning, focus your attention on God's Word and learn how to apply it to your life. This is your duty—and joy—as a new Christian.

[9] You know the generous grace of our Lord Jesus Christ. Though he was rich, yet for your sakes he became poor, so that by his poverty he could make you rich.

[10] Here is my advice: It would be good for you to finish what you started a year ago. Last year you were the first who wanted to give, and you were the first to begin doing it. [11] Now you should finish what you started. Let the eagerness you showed in the beginning be matched now by your giving. Give in proportion to what you have. [12] Whatever you give is acceptable if you give it eagerly. And give according to what you have, not what you don't have. [13] Of course, I don't mean your giving should make life easy for others and hard for yourselves. I only mean that there should be some equality. [14] Right now you have plenty and can help those who are in need. Later, they will have plenty and can share with you when you need it. In this way, things will be equal. [15] As the Scriptures say,

> "Those who gathered a lot had
>   nothing left over,
> and those who gathered only a little
>   had enough."*

8:1 Greek *brothers.*   8:4 Greek *for God's holy people.*
8:7 Some manuscripts read *your love for us.*   8:15 Exod 16:18.

PSALM 49:1-20

For the choir director: A psalm of the descendants of Korah.

[1] Listen to this, all you people!
    Pay attention, everyone in the world!
[2] High and low,
    rich and poor—listen!
[3] For my words are wise,
    and my thoughts are filled with
        insight.
[4] I listen carefully to many proverbs
    and solve riddles with inspiration
        from a harp.

[5] Why should I fear when trouble
        comes,
    when enemies surround me?
[6] They trust in their wealth
    and boast of great riches.
[7] Yet they cannot redeem themselves
        from death*
    by paying a ransom to God.

[8] Redemption does not come so easily,
    for no one can ever pay enough
[9] to live forever
    and never see the grave.

[10] Those who are wise must finally die,
    just like the foolish and senseless,
    leaving all their wealth behind.
[11] The grave is their eternal home,
    where they will stay forever.
    They may name their estates after
        themselves,
[12]   but their fame will not last.
    They will die, just like animals.

[13] This is the fate of fools,
    though they are remembered
        as being wise.*   *Interlude*

[14] Like sheep, they are led to the grave,*
    where death will be their shepherd.
    In the morning the godly will rule over
        them.
    Their bodies will rot in the grave,
    far from their grand estates.
[15] But as for me, God will redeem my life.
    He will snatch me from the power
        of the grave.   *Interlude*

[16] So don't be dismayed when the wicked
        grow rich
    and their homes become ever more
        splendid.
[17] For when they die, they take nothing
        with them.
    Their wealth will not follow them
        into the grave.
[18] In this life they consider themselves
        fortunate
    and are applauded for their success.
[19] But they will die like all before them
    and never again see the light of day.
[20] People who boast of their wealth don't
        understand;
    they will die, just like animals.

49:7 Or *no one can redeem the life of another.*   49:13 The meaning of the Hebrew is uncertain.   49:14 Hebrew *Sheol;* also in 49:14b, 15.

PROVERBS 22:20-21

I have written thirty sayings* for you, filled with advice and knowledge. In this way, you may know the truth and take an accurate report to those who sent you.

22:20 Or *excellent sayings;* the meaning of the Hebrew is uncertain.

SONG OF SONGS 1:1–4:16

While intimacy between a man and a woman is God-given, it has been so corrupted in the modern world that we feel almost embarrassed of it rather than able to celebrate it. Song of Songs reclaims the God-given intimacy of marital love.

This is Solomon's song of songs, more wonderful than any other.

Young Woman*
² Kiss me and kiss me again,
    for your love is sweeter than wine.
³ How fragrant your cologne;
    your name is like its spreading
      fragrance.
    No wonder all the young women
      love you!
⁴ Take me with you; come, let's run!
    The king has brought me into
      his bedroom.

Young Women of Jerusalem
How happy we are for you, O king.
    We praise your love even more
      than wine.

Young Woman
How right they are to adore you.

⁵ I am dark but beautiful,
    O women of Jerusalem—
dark as the tents of Kedar,
    dark as the curtains of Solomon's
      tents.
⁶ Don't stare at me because I am dark—
    the sun has darkened my skin.
My brothers were angry with me;
    they forced me to care for their
      vineyards,
so I couldn't care for myself—
    my own vineyard.

⁷ Tell me, my love, where are you leading
    your flock today?
Where will you rest your sheep
    at noon?
For why should I wander like
    a prostitute*
among your friends and their flocks?

Young Man
⁸ If you don't know, O most beautiful
    woman,

follow the trail of my flock,
    and graze your young goats by the
      shepherds' tents.
⁹ You are as exciting, my darling,
    as a mare among Pharaoh's
      stallions.
¹⁰ How lovely are your cheeks;
    your earrings set them afire!
How lovely is your neck,
    enhanced by a string of jewels.
¹¹ We will make for you earrings of gold
    and beads of silver.

Young Woman
¹² The king is lying on his couch,
    enchanted by the fragrance of
      my perfume.
¹³ My lover is like a sachet of myrrh
    lying between my breasts.
¹⁴ He is like a bouquet of sweet henna
      blossoms
    from the vineyards of En-gedi.

Young Man
¹⁵ How beautiful you are, my darling,
    how beautiful!
Your eyes are like doves.

Young Woman
¹⁶ You are so handsome, my love,
    pleasing beyond words!
The soft grass is our bed;
¹⁷   fragrant cedar branches are the
      beams of our house,
    and pleasant smelling firs are
      the rafters.

Young Woman
²:¹ I AM the spring crocus blooming
    on the Sharon Plain,*
    the lily of the valley.

Young Man
² Like a lily among thistles
    is my darling among young women.

Young Woman
³ Like the finest apple tree in
    the orchard
    is my lover among other young men.
I sit in his delightful shade
    and taste his delicious fruit.

4 He escorts me to the banquet hall;
   it's obvious how much he loves me.
5 Strengthen me with raisin cakes,
   refresh me with apples,
   for I am weak with love.
6 His left arm is under my head,
   and his right arm embraces me.

7 Promise me, O women of Jerusalem,
   by the gazelles and wild deer,
   not to awaken love until the time
   is right.*

8 Ah, I hear my lover coming!
   He is leaping over the mountains,
   bounding over the hills.
9 My lover is like a swift gazelle
   or a young stag.
   Look, there he is behind the wall,
   looking through the window,
   peering into the room.

10 My lover said to me,
   "Rise up, my darling!
   Come away with me, my fair one!
11 Look, the winter is past,
   and the rains are over and gone.
12 The flowers are springing up,
   the season of singing birds*
   has come,
   and the cooing of turtledoves fills
   the air.
13 The fig trees are forming young fruit,
   and the fragrant grapevines are
   blossoming.
   Rise up, my darling!
   Come away with me, my fair one!"

Young Man
14 My dove is hiding behind the rocks,
   behind an outcrop on the cliff.
   Let me see your face;
   let me hear your voice.
   For your voice is pleasant,
   and your face is lovely.

Young Women of Jerusalem
15 Catch all the foxes,
   those little foxes,
   before they ruin the vineyard of love,
   for the grapevines are blossoming!

Young Woman
16 My lover is mine, and I am his.
   He browses among the lilies.
17 Before the dawn breezes blow
   and the night shadows flee,

return to me, my love, like a gazelle
   or a young stag on the rugged
   mountains.*

Young Woman
3:1 ONE night as I lay in bed, I yearned
   for my lover.
   I yearned for him, but he did
   not come.
2 So I said to myself, "I will get up and
   roam the city,
   searching in all its streets and
   squares.
   I will search for the one I love."
   So I searched everywhere but did
   not find him.
3 The watchmen stopped me as they
   made their rounds,
   and I asked, "Have you seen the one
   I love?"
4 Then scarcely had I left them
   when I found my love!
   I caught and held him tightly,
   then I brought him to my mother's
   house,
   into my mother's bed, where I had
   been conceived.

5 Promise me, O women of Jerusalem,
   by the gazelles and wild deer,
   not to awaken love until the time
   is right.*

Young Women of Jerusalem
6 Who is this sweeping in from
   the wilderness
   like a cloud of smoke?
   Who is it, fragrant with myrrh and
   frankincense
   and every kind of spice?
7 Look, it is Solomon's carriage,
   surrounded by sixty heroic men,
   the best of Israel's soldiers.
8 They are all skilled swordsmen,
   experienced warriors.
   Each wears a sword on his thigh,
   ready to defend the king against
   an attack in the night.
9 King Solomon's carriage is built
   of wood imported from Lebanon.
10 Its posts are silver,
   its canopy gold;
   its cushions are purple.
   It was decorated with love
   by the young women of Jerusalem.

Young Woman

11 Come out to see King Solomon,
      young women of Jerusalem.*
  He wears the crown his mother gave
      him on his wedding day,
      his most joyous day.

Young Man

4:1 You are beautiful, my darling,
      beautiful beyond words.
  Your eyes are like doves
      behind your veil.
  Your hair falls in waves,
      like a flock of goats winding down
          the slopes of Gilead.
2 Your teeth are as white as sheep,
      recently shorn and freshly washed.
  Your smile is flawless,
      each tooth matched with its twin.*
3 Your lips are like scarlet ribbon;
      your mouth is inviting.
  Your cheeks are like rosy
          pomegranates
      behind your veil.
4 Your neck is as beautiful as the tower
          of David,
      jeweled with the shields of a
          thousand heroes.
5 Your breasts are like two fawns,
      twin fawns of a gazelle grazing
          among the lilies.
6 Before the dawn breezes blow
      and the night shadows flee,

  I will hurry to the mountain of myrrh
      and to the hill of frankincense.
7 You are altogether beautiful,
      my darling,
      beautiful in every way.

8 Come with me from Lebanon,
      my bride,
      come with me from Lebanon.
  Come down* from Mount Amana,
      from the peaks of Senir and
          Hermon,
  where the lions have their dens
      and leopards live among the hills.

9 You have captured my heart,
      my treasure,* my bride.
  You hold it hostage with one glance
          of your eyes,
      with a single jewel of your necklace.
10 Your love delights me,
      my treasure, my bride.
  Your love is better than wine,
      your perfume more fragrant
          than spices.
11 Your lips are as sweet as nectar,
      my bride.
  Honey and milk are under your
          tongue.
  Your clothes are scented
      like the cedars of Lebanon.
12 You are my private garden, my
      treasure, my bride,

HOW WE LIVE

Our marriages

SONG OF SONGS 4:1-16 The entire book of the Song of Songs is a dialogue of love between a man and a woman. As you read you may feel like an awkward bystander as they express their longing to be together. The poetic imagery may seem "over the top" to some readers, but the love and admiration this couple has for each other is unmistakable. • Words and expressions of love can bring a new spark to any marriage. Solomon's bride was like a refreshing fountain to him, and he compares her to a "private garden." Sex was created by God as part of the loving relationship between a man and a woman committed to each other in marriage. Sex outside the boundary of marriage is cheap and self-gratifying. It cannot compare to the joy of giving yourself totally to the one who is committed to you. • Over the years of marriage, many things, including sex, can become routine. The familiarity of marriage can sometimes cause us to forget the feelings of longing and desire that felt so overwhelming in the beginning. Let Song of Songs inspire you to renew the joy and excitement of marriage through words and other creative expressions of love.

a secluded spring, a hidden
   fountain.
13 Your thighs shelter a paradise of
      pomegranates
   with rare spices—
   henna with nard,
14   nard and saffron,
      fragrant calamus and cinnamon,
   with all the trees of frankincense,
      myrrh, and aloes,
   and every other lovely spice.
15 You are a garden fountain,
   a well of fresh water
   streaming down from Lebanon's
      mountains.

Young Woman
16 Awake, north wind!
      Rise up, south wind!
   Blow on my garden
   and spread its fragrance all around.
   Come into your garden, my love;
      taste its finest fruits.

1:1 The headings identifying the speakers are not in the
original text, though the Hebrew usually gives clues by means
of the gender of the person speaking.   1:7 Hebrew *like a
veiled woman.*   2:1 Traditionally rendered *I am the rose
of Sharon.* Sharon Plain is a region in the coastal plain of
Palestine.   2:7 Or *not to awaken love until it is ready.*
2:12 Or *the season of pruning vines.*   2:17 Or *on the hills
of Bether.*   3:5 Or *not to awaken love until it is ready.*
3:11 Hebrew *of Zion.*   4:2 Hebrew *Not one is missing; each
has a twin.*   4:8 Or *Look down.*   4:9 Hebrew *my sister;* also
in 4:10, 12.

2 CORINTHIANS 8:16-24

Titus was one of the first-century Gentile church
leaders whom Paul introduced to the Christian faith
and trained as a leader. Paul sent Titus to Corinth
to help solve some of the problems that plagued
the church there.

But thank God! He has given Titus the same
enthusiasm for you [Corinthians] that I
[Paul] have. 17 Titus welcomed our request
that he visit you again. In fact, he himself
was very eager to go and see you. 18 We are
also sending another brother with Titus.
All the churches praise him as a preacher
of the Good News. 19 He was appointed by
the churches to accompany us as we take
the offering to Jerusalem*—a service that
glorifies the Lord and shows our eagerness
to help.

20 We are traveling together to guard
against any criticism for the way we are
handling this generous gift. 21 We are
careful to be honorable before the Lord,

but we also want everyone else to see that
we are honorable.

22 We are also sending with them another of our brothers who has proven himself many times and has shown on many
occasions how eager he is. He is now even
more enthusiastic because of his great
confidence in you. 23 If anyone asks about
Titus, say that he is my partner who works
with me to help you. And the brothers with
him have been sent by the churches,* and
they bring honor to Christ. 24 So show them
your love, and prove to all the churches
that our boasting about you is justified.

8:19 See 1 Cor 16:3-4.   8:23 Greek *are apostles of the
churches.*

PSALM 50:1-23
A psalm of Asaph.

1 **T**he LORD, the Mighty One, is God,
      and he has spoken;
   he has summoned all humanity
      from where the sun rises to where
         it sets.
2 From Mount Zion, the perfection
      of beauty,
   God shines in glorious radiance.
3 Our God approaches,
      and he is not silent.
   Fire devours everything in his way,
      and a great storm rages around him.
4 He calls on the heavens above and
      earth below
   to witness the judgment of his
      people.
5 "Bring my faithful people to me—
      those who made a covenant with
         me by giving sacrifices."
6 Then let the heavens proclaim his
      justice,
   for God himself will be the judge.
                              Interlude

7 "O my people, listen as I speak.
   Here are my charges against you,
      O Israel:
   I am God, your God!
8 I have no complaint about your
      sacrifices
   or the burnt offerings you
      constantly offer.
9 But I do not need the bulls from
      your barns
   or the goats from your pens.

10 For all the animals of the forest
    are mine,
    and I own the cattle on a thousand
    hills.
11 I know every bird on the mountains,
    and all the animals of the field
    are mine.
12 If I were hungry, I would not
    tell you,
    for all the world is mine and
    everything in it.
13 Do I eat the meat of bulls?
    Do I drink the blood of goats?
14 Make thankfulness your sacrifice
    to God,
    and keep the vows you made to the
    Most High.
15 Then call on me when you are
    in trouble,
    and I will rescue you,
    and you will give me glory."

16 But God says to the wicked:
    "Why bother reciting my decrees
    and pretending to obey my
    covenant?
17 For you refuse my discipline
    and treat my words like trash.

18 When you see thieves, you approve
    of them,
    and you spend your time with
    adulterers.
19 Your mouth is filled with wickedness,
    and your tongue is full of lies.
20 You sit around and slander your
    brother—
    your own mother's son.
21 While you did all this, I remained silent,
    and you thought I didn't care.
    But now I will rebuke you,
    listing all my charges against you.
22 Repent, all of you who forget me,
    or I will tear you apart,
    and no one will help you.
23 But giving thanks is a sacrifice that
    truly honors me.
    If you keep to my path,
    I will reveal to you the salvation
    of God."

PROVERBS 22:22-23

Don't rob the poor just because you can,
or exploit the needy in court. For the
LORD is their defender. He will ruin anyone who ruins them.

SEPTEMBER**7**

SONG OF SONGS 5:1-8:14

The love story continues. Love is "as strong as
death." Love cannot be bought at any price, for it is
freely given. Love is the greatest of all God's gifts.

Young Man
I have entered my garden, my
    treasure,* my bride!
    I gather myrrh with my spices
    and eat honeycomb with my honey.
    I drink wine with my milk.

Young Women of Jerusalem
    Oh, lover and beloved, eat and drink!
    Yes, drink deeply of your love!

Young Woman
2 I slept, but my heart was awake,
    when I heard my lover knocking
    and calling:

"Open to me, my treasure, my darling,
    my dove, my perfect one.
My head is drenched with dew,
    my hair with the dampness of the
    night."

3 But I responded,
"I have taken off my robe.
    Should I get dressed again?
I have washed my feet.
    Should I get them soiled?"

4 My lover tried to unlatch the door,
    and my heart thrilled within me.
5 I jumped up to open the door for
    my love,
    and my hands dripped with perfume.
My fingers dripped with lovely myrrh
    as I pulled back the bolt.

6 I opened to my lover,
  but he was gone!
  My heart sank.
I searched for him
  but could not find him anywhere.
I called to him,
  but there was no reply.
7 The night watchmen found me
  as they made their rounds.
They beat and bruised me
  and stripped off my veil,
  those watchmen on the walls.

8 Make this promise, O women
    of Jerusalem—
  If you find my lover,
  tell him I am weak with love.

Young Women of Jerusalem
9 Why is your lover better than all
    others,
  O woman of rare beauty?
What makes your lover so special
  that we must promise this?

Young Woman
10 My lover is dark and dazzling,
  better than ten thousand others!
11 His head is finest gold,
  his wavy hair is black as a raven.
12 His eyes sparkle like doves
  beside springs of water;
they are set like jewels
  washed in milk.
13 His cheeks are like gardens of spices
  giving off fragrance.
His lips are like lilies,
  perfumed with myrrh.
14 His arms are like rounded bars of gold,
  set with beryl.
His body is like bright ivory,
  glowing with lapis lazuli.
15 His legs are like marble pillars
  set in sockets of finest gold.
His posture is stately,
  like the noble cedars of Lebanon.
16 His mouth is sweetness itself;
  he is desirable in every way.
Such, O women of Jerusalem,
  is my lover, my friend.

Young Women of Jerusalem
6:1 WHERE has your lover gone,
  O woman of rare beauty?
Which way did he turn
  so we can help you find him?

Young Woman
2 My lover has gone down to his garden,
  to his spice beds,
  to browse in the gardens
  and gather the lilies.
3 I am my lover's, and my lover is mine.
  He browses among the lilies.

Young Man
4 You are beautiful, my darling,
  like the lovely city of Tirzah.
Yes, as beautiful as Jerusalem,
  as majestic as an army with
    billowing banners.
5 Turn your eyes away,
  for they overpower me.
Your hair falls in waves,
  like a flock of goats winding down
    the slopes of Gilead.
6 Your teeth are as white as sheep
  that are freshly washed.
Your smile is flawless,
  each tooth matched with its twin.*
7 Your cheeks are like rosy
    pomegranates
  behind your veil.

8 Even among sixty queens
  and eighty concubines
  and countless young women,
9 I would still choose my dove, my
    perfect one—
  the favorite of her mother,
  dearly loved by the one who bore
    her.
The young women see her and praise
    her;
  even queens and royal concubines
    sing her praises:
10 "Who is this, arising like the dawn,
  as fair as the moon,
as bright as the sun,
  as majestic as an army with
    billowing banners?"

11 I went down to the grove of walnut
    trees
  and out to the valley to see the new
    spring growth,
to see whether the grapevines had
    budded
  or the pomegranates were in bloom.
12 Before I realized it,
  I found myself in the royal chariot
    with my beloved.*

Young Women of Jerusalem

13*Return, return to us, O maid
  of Shulam.
  Come back, come back, that we may
  see you again.

Young Man

  Why do you stare at this young woman
  of Shulam,
  as she moves so gracefully between
  two lines of dancers?*

7:1*How beautiful are your sandaled feet,
  O queenly maiden.
  Your rounded thighs are like jewels,
  the work of a skilled craftsman.
2 Your navel is perfectly formed
  like a goblet filled with mixed wine.
  Between your thighs lies a mound
  of wheat
  bordered with lilies.
3 Your breasts are like two fawns,
  twin fawns of a gazelle.
4 Your neck is as beautiful as an ivory
  tower.
  Your eyes are like the sparkling pools
  in Heshbon
  by the gate of Bath-rabbim.
  Your nose is as fine as the tower
  of Lebanon
  overlooking Damascus.

5 Your head is as majestic as Mount
  Carmel,
  and the sheen of your hair radiates
  royalty.
  The king is held captive by
  its tresses.
6 Oh, how beautiful you are!
  How pleasing, my love, how full
  of delights!
7 You are slender like a palm tree,
  and your breasts are like its clusters
  of fruit.
8 I said, "I will climb the palm tree
  and take hold of its fruit."
  May your breasts be like grape
  clusters,
  and the fragrance of your breath
  like apples.
9 May your kisses be as exciting as the
  best wine,
  flowing gently over lips and teeth.*

Young Woman

10 I am my lover's,
  and he claims me as his own.
11 Come, my love, let us go out to
  the fields
  and spend the night among
  the wildflowers.*
12 Let us get up early and go to the
  vineyards

HOW WE LIVE

Our giving

2 CORINTHIANS 9:6-12 Paul commends the Corinthian Christians for the
financial help they sent to the church in Jerusalem. All believers are
called to generous giving. Those who sow few seeds will have a small
harvest, and those who plant generously will reap a large harvest.
• Churches are usually self-supporting; they depend on the gifts of their
members in order to continue to operate. What you give is between you
and God. Paul says each person should decide how much he or she can
give. The important thing is not how much we give, but how we give.
Give cheerfully! Remember that you have nothing except what God has
provided. Be joyful as you give back to him. It is a tangible way to express
your trust in him to continue to provide for your needs. Failure to give
boils down to a failure to trust. • When you invest what God has given
you in the lives and ministries around you, he will use your gifts, no
matter how small, to help meet a need. Your attitude should be generous
and cheerful, not selfish and grudging. Consider it a joy to have a part in
building God's Kingdom!

to see if the grapevines have
budded,
if the blossoms have opened,
and if the pomegranates have
bloomed.
There I will give you my love.
13 There the mandrakes give off their
fragrance,
and the finest fruits are at our door,
new delights as well as old,
which I have saved for you,
my lover.

Young Woman

8:1 OH, I wish you were my brother,
who nursed at my mother's breasts.
Then I could kiss you no matter who
was watching,
and no one would criticize me.
2 I would bring you to my childhood
home,
and there you would teach me.*
I would give you spiced wine to drink,
my sweet pomegranate wine.
3 Your left arm would be under my
head,
and your right arm would embrace
me.

4 Promise me, O women of Jerusalem,
not to awaken love until the time
is right.*

Young Women of Jerusalem
5 Who is this sweeping in from the
desert,
leaning on her lover?

Young Woman

I aroused you under the apple tree,
where your mother gave you birth,
where in great pain she delivered
you.
6 Place me like a seal over your heart,
like a seal on your arm.
For love is as strong as death,
its jealousy* as enduring as the
grave.*
Love flashes like fire,
the brightest kind of flame.
7 Many waters cannot quench love,
nor can rivers drown it.
If a man tried to buy love
with all his wealth,
his offer would be utterly scorned.

The Young Woman's Brothers
8 We have a little sister
too young to have breasts.
What will we do for our sister
if someone asks to marry her?
9 If she is a virgin, like a wall,
we will protect her with a silver
tower.
But if she is promiscuous, like
a swinging door,
we will block her door with
a cedar bar.

Young Woman
10 I was a virgin, like a wall;
now my breasts are like towers.
When my lover looks at me,
he is delighted with what he sees.

11 Solomon has a vineyard at Baal-
hamon,
which he leases out to tenant
farmers.
Each of them pays a thousand pieces
of silver*
for harvesting its fruit.
12 But my vineyard is mine to give,
and Solomon need not pay a
thousand pieces of silver.
But I will give two hundred pieces
to those who care for its vines.

Young Man
13 O my darling, lingering in the gardens,
your companions are fortunate
to hear your voice.
Let me hear it, too!

Young Woman
14 Come away, my love! Be like a gazelle
or a young stag on the mountains
of spices.

5:1 Hebrew *my sister;* also in 5:2. **6:6** Hebrew *Not one is
missing; each has a twin.* **6:12** Or *among the royal
chariots of my people,* or *among the chariots of Amminadab.*
The meaning of the Hebrew is uncertain. **6:13a** Verse 6:13
is numbered 7:1 in Hebrew text. **6:13b** Or *as you would at
the movements of two armies?* or *as you would at the dance
of Mahanaim?* The meaning of the Hebrew is uncertain.
7:1 Verses 7:1-13 are numbered 7:2-14 in Hebrew text.
7:9 As in Greek and Syriac versions and Latin Vulgate;
Hebrew reads *over lips of sleepers.* **7:11** Or *in the villages.*
8:2 Or *there she will teach me;* or *there she bore me.* **8:4** Or
not to awaken love until it is ready. **8:6a** Or *its passion.*
8:6b Hebrew *as Sheol.* **8:11** Hebrew *1,000 shekels of silver.*

2 CORINTHIANS 9:1-15
The offering Paul was collecting for the church in
Jerusalem was important because Christianity

emanated from there. Other churches, especially those composed primarily of Gentiles, needed to show their support for the primarily Jewish church from which the Good News originally went forth.

❙ [Paul] really don't need to write to you about this ministry of giving for the believers in Jerusalem.* ²For I know how eager you are to help, and I have been boasting to the churches in Macedonia that you in Greece* were ready to send an offering a year ago. In fact, it was your enthusiasm that stirred up many of the Macedonian believers to begin giving.

³But I am sending these brothers to be sure you really are ready, as I have been telling them, and that your money is all collected. I don't want to be wrong in my boasting about you. ⁴We would be embarrassed—not to mention your own embarrassment—if some Macedonian believers came with me and found that you weren't ready after all I had told them! ⁵So I thought I should send these brothers ahead of me to make sure the gift you promised is ready. But I want it to be a willing gift, not one given grudgingly.

⁶Remember this—a farmer who plants only a few seeds will get a small crop. But the one who plants generously will get a generous crop. ⁷You must each decide in your heart how much to give. And don't give reluctantly or in response to pressure. "For God loves a person who gives cheerfully."* ⁸And God will generously provide all you need. Then you will always have everything you need and plenty left over to share with others. ⁹As the Scriptures say,

"They share freely and give generously
    to the poor.
Their good deeds will be
    remembered forever."*

¹⁰For God is the one who provides seed for the farmer and then bread to eat. In the same way, he will provide and increase your resources and then produce a great harvest of generosity* in you.

¹¹Yes, you will be enriched in every way so that you can always be generous. And when we take your gifts to those who need them, they will thank God. ¹²So two good things will result from this ministry of giving—the needs of the believers in Jerusa-

lem* will be met, and they will joyfully express their thanks to God.

¹³As a result of your ministry, they will give glory to God. For your generosity to them and to all believers will prove that you are obedient to the Good News of Christ. ¹⁴And they will pray for you with deep affection because of the overflowing grace God has given to you. ¹⁵Thank God for this gift* too wonderful for words!

9:1 Greek *about the offering for God's holy people.*
9:2 Greek *in Achaia,* the southern region of the Greek peninsula. *Macedonia* was in the northern region of Greece.
9:7 See footnote on Prov 22:8.   9:9 Ps 112:9.   9:10 Greek *righteousness.*   9:12 Greek *of God's holy people.*
9:15 Greek *his gift.*

PSALM 51:1-19
For the choir director: A psalm of David, regarding the time Nathan the prophet came to him after David had committed adultery with Bathsheba.

¹ **H**ave mercy on me, O God,
        because of your unfailing love.
Because of your great compassion,
        blot out the stain of my sins.
² Wash me clean from my guilt.
        Purify me from my sin.
³ For I recognize my rebellion;
        it haunts me day and night.
⁴ Against you, and you alone, have
            I sinned;
        I have done what is evil in your sight.
You will be proved right in what
            you say,
        and your judgment against me
            is just.*
⁵ For I was born a sinner—
        yes, from the moment my mother
            conceived me.
⁶ But you desire honesty from the
            womb,*
        teaching me wisdom even there.

⁷ Purify me from my sins,* and I will
            be clean;
        wash me, and I will be whiter than
            snow.
⁸ Oh, give me back my joy again;
        you have broken me—
        now let me rejoice.
⁹ Don't keep looking at my sins.
        Remove the stain of my guilt.
¹⁰ Create in me a clean heart, O God.
        Renew a loyal spirit within me.

11 Do not banish me from your presence,
  and don't take your Holy Spirit*
  from me.
12 Restore to me the joy of your salvation,
  and make me willing to obey you.
13 Then I will teach your ways to rebels,
  and they will return to you.
14 Forgive me for shedding blood, O God
  who saves;
  then I will joyfully sing of your
  forgiveness.
15 Unseal my lips, O Lord,
  that my mouth may praise you.

16 You do not desire a sacrifice, or
  I would offer one.
  You do not want a burnt offering.
17 The sacrifice you desire is a broken
  spirit.

  You will not reject a broken and
  repentant heart, O God.
18 Look with favor on Zion and help her;
  rebuild the walls of Jerusalem.
19 Then you will be pleased with
  sacrifices offered in the right
  spirit—
  with burnt offerings and whole
  burnt offerings.
  Then bulls will again be sacrificed
  on your altar.

51:4 Greek version reads *and you will win your case in court.* Compare Rom 3:4.   **51:6** Or *from the heart;* Hebrew reads *in the inward parts.*   **51:7** Hebrew *Purify me with the hyssop branch.*   **51:11** Or *your spirit of holiness.*

PROVERBS 22:24-25
Don't befriend angry people or associate with hot-tempered people, or you will learn to be like them and endanger your soul.

SEPTEMBER**8**

ISAIAH 1:1–2:22
Isaiah was a Judean prophet of the eighth century BC. While he moved easily among the king's court, the truth that he preached did not always find receptive listeners.

These are the visions that Isaiah son of Amoz saw concerning Judah and Jerusalem. He saw these visions during the years when Uzziah, Jotham, Ahaz, and Hezekiah were kings of Judah.*

2 Listen, O heavens! Pay attention, earth!
  This is what the LORD says:
  "The children I raised and cared for
  have rebelled against me.
3 Even an ox knows its owner,
  and a donkey recognizes its
  master's care—
  but Israel doesn't know its master.
  My people don't recognize my care
  for them."
4 Oh, what a sinful nation they are—
  loaded down with a burden of guilt.
  They are evil people,
  corrupt children who have rejected
  the LORD.

  They have despised the Holy One
  of Israel
  and turned their backs on him.

5 Why do you continue to invite
  punishment?
  Must you rebel forever?
  Your head is injured,
  and your heart is sick.
6 You are battered from head
  to foot—
  covered with bruises, welts, and
  infected wounds—
  without any soothing ointments
  or bandages.
7 Your country lies in ruins,
  and your towns are burned.
  Foreigners plunder your fields before
  your eyes
  and destroy everything they see.
8 Beautiful Jerusalem* stands abandoned
  like a watchman's shelter in a
  vineyard,
  like a lean-to in a cucumber field after
  the harvest,
  like a helpless city under siege.

⁹ If the Lord of Heaven's Armies
   had not spared a few of us,*
we would have been wiped out like
   Sodom,
destroyed like Gomorrah.

¹⁰ Listen to the Lord, you leaders of
   "Sodom."
   Listen to the law of our God, people
   of "Gomorrah."
¹¹ "What makes you think I want all your
   sacrifices?"
   says the Lord.
   "I am sick of your burnt offerings
   of rams
   and the fat of fattened cattle.
I get no pleasure from the blood
   of bulls and lambs and goats.
¹² When you come to worship me,
   who asked you to parade through
   my courts with all your
   ceremony?
¹³ Stop bringing me your meaningless
   gifts;
   the incense of your offerings
   disgusts me!
As for your celebrations of the new
   moon and the Sabbath
   and your special days for fasting—
they are all sinful and false.
   I want no more of your pious
   meetings.
¹⁴ I hate your new moon celebrations
   and your annual festivals.
   They are a burden to me. I cannot
   stand them!
¹⁵ When you lift up your hands in prayer,
   I will not look.
   Though you offer many prayers,
   I will not listen,
   for your hands are covered with the
   blood of innocent victims.
¹⁶ Wash yourselves and be clean!
   Get your sins out of my sight.
   Give up your evil ways.
¹⁷ Learn to do good.
   Seek justice.
Help the oppressed.
   Defend the cause of orphans.
   Fight for the rights of widows.

¹⁸ "Come now, let's settle this,"
   says the Lord.
   "Though your sins are like scarlet,
   I will make them as white as snow.

Though they are red like crimson,
   I will make them as white as wool.
¹⁹ If you will only obey me,
   you will have plenty to eat.
²⁰ But if you turn away and refuse
   to listen,
   you will be devoured by the sword
   of your enemies.
   I, the Lord, have spoken!"

²¹ See how Jerusalem, once so faithful,
   has become a prostitute.
Once the home of justice and
   righteousness,
   she is now filled with murderers.
²² Once like pure silver,
   you have become like worthless
   slag.
Once so pure,
   you are now like watered-down
   wine.
²³ Your leaders are rebels,
   the companions of thieves.
All of them love bribes
   and demand payoffs,
but they refuse to defend the cause
   of orphans
   or fight for the rights of widows.

²⁴ Therefore, the Lord, the Lord of
   Heaven's Armies,
   the Mighty One of Israel, says,
"I will take revenge on my enemies
   and pay back my foes!
²⁵ I will raise my fist against you.
   I will melt you down and skim off
   your slag.
   I will remove all your impurities.
²⁶ Then I will give you good judges again
   and wise counselors like you used
   to have.
Then Jerusalem will again be called
   the Home of Justice
   and the Faithful City."

²⁷ Zion will be restored by justice;
   those who repent will be revived
   by righteousness.
²⁸ But rebels and sinners will be
   completely destroyed,
   and those who desert the Lord will
   be consumed.

²⁹ You will be ashamed of your idol
   worship
   in groves of sacred oaks.

You will blush because you worshiped
in gardens dedicated to idols.
³⁰ You will be like a great tree with
withered leaves,
like a garden without water.
³¹ The strongest among you will
disappear like straw;
their evil deeds will be the spark
that sets it on fire.
They and their evil works will burn up
together,
and no one will be able to put out
the fire.

2:1THIS is a vision that Isaiah son of Amoz
saw concerning Judah and Jerusalem:

² In the last days, the mountain of the
LORD's house
will be the highest of all—
the most important place on earth.
It will be raised above the other hills,
and people from all over the world
will stream there to worship.
³ People from many nations will come
and say,
"Come, let us go up to the mountain
of the LORD,
to the house of Jacob's God.
There he will teach us his ways,
and we will walk in his paths."
For the LORD's teaching will go out
from Zion;
his word will go out from
Jerusalem.
⁴ The LORD will mediate between
nations
and will settle international
disputes.
They will hammer their swords into
plowshares
and their spears into pruning
hooks.
Nation will no longer fight against
nation,
nor train for war anymore.

⁵ Come, descendants of Jacob,
let us walk in the light of the LORD!
⁶ For the LORD has rejected his people,
the descendants of Jacob,
because they have filled their land
with practices from the East
and with sorcerers, as the
Philistines do.

They have made alliances with
pagans.
⁷ Israel is full of silver and gold;
there is no end to its treasures.
Their land is full of warhorses;
there is no end to its chariots.
⁸ Their land is full of idols;
the people worship things they
have made
with their own hands.
⁹ So now they will be humbled,
and all will be brought low—
do not forgive them.
¹⁰ Crawl into caves in the rocks.
Hide in the dust
from the terror of the LORD
and the glory of his majesty.
¹¹ Human pride will be brought down,
and human arrogance will be
humbled.
Only the LORD will be exalted
on that day of judgment.

¹² For the LORD of Heaven's Armies
has a day of reckoning.
He will punish the proud and mighty
and bring down everything that is
exalted.
¹³ He will cut down the tall cedars of
Lebanon
and all the mighty oaks of Bashan.
¹⁴ He will level all the high mountains
and all the lofty hills.
¹⁵ He will break down every high tower
and every fortified wall.
¹⁶ He will destroy all the great trading
ships*
and every magnificent vessel.
¹⁷ Human pride will be humbled,
and human arrogance will be
brought down.
Only the LORD will be exalted
on that day of judgment.

¹⁸ Idols will completely disappear.
¹⁹ When the LORD rises to shake the
earth,
his enemies will crawl into holes
in the ground.
They will hide in caves in the rocks
from the terror of the LORD
and the glory of his majesty.
²⁰ On that day of judgment they will
abandon the gold and silver idols

they made for themselves to
worship.
They will leave their gods to the
rodents and bats,
21   while they crawl away into
caverns
and hide among the jagged rocks
in the cliffs.
They will try to escape the terror
of the LORD
and the glory of his majesty
as he rises to shake the earth.
22 Don't put your trust in mere humans.
They are as frail as breath.
What good are they?

1:1 These kings reigned from 792 to 686 B.C.   1:8 Hebrew
The daughter of Zion.   1:9 Greek version reads *a few of our
children.* Compare Rom 9:29.   2:16 Hebrew *every ship of
Tarshish.*

2 CORINTHIANS 10:1-18

Paul was a rock of the faith with faults and idiosyn-
crasies of his own. Some people were put off by him
while others welcomed him as a mentor. Here, he
shares personal information to defend his role as
an early church leader.

Now I, Paul, appeal to you [Corinthians]
with the gentleness and kindness of
Christ—though I realize you think I am
timid in person and bold only when I
write from far away. ²Well, I am begging
you now so that when I come I won't have
to be bold with those who think we act
from human motives.

³We are human, but we don't wage war
as humans do. ⁴*We use God's mighty
weapons, not worldly weapons, to knock
down the strongholds of human reasoning and to destroy false arguments. ⁵We
destroy every proud obstacle that keeps
people from knowing God. We capture
their rebellious thoughts and teach them
to obey Christ. ⁶And after you have become fully obedient, we will punish
everyone who remains disobedient.

⁷Look at the obvious facts.* Those who
say they belong to Christ must recognize
that we belong to Christ as much as they
do. ⁸I may seem to be boasting too much
about the authority given to us by the
Lord. But our authority builds you up; it
doesn't tear you down. So I will not be
ashamed of using my authority.

⁹I'm not trying to frighten you by my
letters. ¹⁰For some say, "Paul's letters are
demanding and forceful, but in person he
is weak, and his speeches are worthless!"
¹¹Those people should realize that our actions when we arrive in person will be as
forceful as what we say in our letters from
far away.

¹²Oh, don't worry; we wouldn't dare say
that we are as wonderful as these other
men who tell you how important they are!

WHAT THE BIBLE SAYS

Salvation and forgiveness

ISAIAH 1:18 Salvation involves being delivered from the eternal consequences of sin. But salvation means so much more than that! Imagine
a drowning person who is pulled from the ocean. It's not just about being
saved from drowning; it's also about the new opportunity *to live* that
person has been given. • Isaiah's words create a powerful picture of a
white garment with a scarlet stain. Only the blood of Christ can take that
red, crimson stain and make it white as snow. No sin is so big and no
stain is so deep that it cannot be cleansed by God's saving grace. When
we come to God in true humility and repentance, we are completely
redeemed, washed white as snow. • Salvation is not something that you
do; it's something that God does for you. God does not say, "You can
take care of your sins by doing this. . . ." Instead, he says, "Come to me;
I will make your dirty sins as white as snow." Salvation and forgiveness
are costly gifts offered freely to you. Since you have accepted that salvation, live like someone who has been saved from drowning. Take that
glorious new opportunity at life!

But they are only comparing themselves with each other, using themselves as the standard of measurement. How ignorant! [13] We will not boast about things done outside our area of authority. We will boast only about what has happened within the boundaries of the work God has given us, which includes our working with you. [14] We are not reaching beyond these boundaries when we claim authority over you, as if we had never visited you. For we were the first to travel all the way to Corinth with the Good News of Christ.

[15] Nor do we boast and claim credit for the work someone else has done. Instead, we hope that your faith will grow so that the boundaries of our work among you will be extended. [16] Then we will be able to go and preach the Good News in other places far beyond you, where no one else is working. Then there will be no question of our boasting about work done in someone else's territory. [17] As the Scriptures say, "If you want to boast, boast only about the LORD."*

[18] When people commend themselves, it doesn't count for much. The important thing is for the Lord to commend them.

10:4 English translations divide verses 4 and 5 in various ways.   10:7 Or *You look at things only on the basis of appearance.*   10:17 Jer 9:24.

PSALM 52:1-9

For the choir director: A psalm* of David, regarding the time Doeg the Edomite said to Saul, "David has gone to see Ahimelech."

[1] **W**hy do you boast about your crimes,
    great warrior?
  Don't you realize God's justice
    continues forever?
[2] All day long you plot destruction.

Your tongue cuts like a sharp razor;
    you're an expert at telling lies.
[3] You love evil more than good
    and lies more than truth.
Interlude

[4] You love to destroy others with
    your words,
    you liar!
[5] But God will strike you down once and
    for all.
  He will pull you from your home
    and uproot you from the land
    of the living.   *Interlude*

[6] The righteous will see it and be
    amazed.
  They will laugh and say,
[7] "Look what happens to mighty
    warriors
    who do not trust in God.
  They trust their wealth instead
    and grow more and more bold
    in their wickedness."

[8] But I am like an olive tree, thriving
    in the house of God.
  I will always trust in God's unfailing
    love.
[9] I will praise you forever, O God,
    for what you have done.
  I will trust in your good name
    in the presence of your faithful
    people.

52:TITLE Hebrew *maskil.* This may be a literary or musical term.

PROVERBS 22:26-27

Don't agree to guarantee another person's debt or put up security for someone else. If you can't pay it, even your bed will be snatched from under you.

SEPTEMBER9

ISAIAH 3:1-5:30
The people of Judah had a choice. If the people obeyed God, their path was filled with hope. If the people disobeyed God, destruction was certain. But even in the deepest and darkest of their consequences, God promised eventual restoration for his people.

The Lord, the LORD of Heaven's Armies,
    will take away from Jerusalem and
    Judah
everything they depend on:
    every bit of bread
    and every drop of water,

2 all their heroes and soldiers,
   judges and prophets,
   fortune-tellers and elders,
3 army officers and high officials,
   advisers, skilled craftsmen, and
   astrologers.

4 I will make boys their leaders,
   and toddlers their rulers.
5 People will oppress each other—
   man against man,
   neighbor against neighbor.
Young people will insult their elders,
   and vulgar people will sneer at the
   honorable.

6 In those days a man will say to his
   brother,
   "Since you have a coat, you be our
   leader!
   Take charge of this heap of ruins!"
7 But he will reply,
   "No! I can't help.
I don't have any extra food or clothes.
   Don't put me in charge!"

8 For Jerusalem will stumble,
   and Judah will fall,
because they speak out against the
   LORD and refuse to obey him.
   They provoke him to his face.
9 The very look on their faces gives
   them away.
   They display their sin like the
   people of Sodom
   and don't even try to hide it.
They are doomed!
   They have brought destruction
   upon themselves.

10 Tell the godly that all will be well for
   them.
   They will enjoy the rich reward they
   have earned!
11 But the wicked are doomed,
   for they will get exactly what they
   deserve.

12 Childish leaders oppress my people,
   and women rule over them.
O my people, your leaders mislead you;
   they send you down the wrong road.

13 The LORD takes his place in court
   and presents his case against his
   people!

14 The LORD comes forward to
   pronounce judgment
   on the elders and rulers of his
   people:
"You have ruined Israel, my vineyard.
   Your houses are filled with things
   stolen from the poor.
15 How dare you crush my people,
   grinding the faces of the poor into
   the dust?"
   demands the Lord, the LORD
   of Heaven's Armies.

16 The LORD says, "Beautiful Zion*
   is haughty:
craning her elegant neck,
   flirting with her eyes,
walking with dainty steps,
   tinkling her ankle bracelets.
17 So the Lord will send scabs on her
   head;
   the LORD will make beautiful Zion
   bald."

18 On that day of judgment
   the Lord will strip away everything
   that makes her beautiful:
ornaments, headbands, crescent
   necklaces,
19   earrings, bracelets, and veils;
20 scarves, ankle bracelets, sashes,
   perfumes, and charms;
21 rings, jewels,
22   party clothes, gowns, capes,
   and purses;
23 mirrors, fine linen garments,
   head ornaments, and shawls.

24 Instead of smelling of sweet perfume,
   she will stink.
   She will wear a rope for a sash,
   and her elegant hair will fall out.
She will wear rough burlap instead
   of rich robes.
   Shame will replace her beauty.*
25 The men of the city will be killed with
   the sword,
   and her warriors will die in battle.
26 The gates of Zion will weep and
   mourn.
   The city will be like a ravaged woman,
   huddled on the ground.

4:1IN that day so few men will be left that
seven women will fight for each man, saying, "Let us all marry you! We will provide

our own food and clothing. Only let us take your name so we won't be mocked as old maids."

2 But in that day, the branch* of the
LORD
   will be beautiful and glorious;
the fruit of the land will be the pride
   and glory
   of all who survive in Israel.
3 All who remain in Zion
   will be a holy people—
those who survive the destruction of
   Jerusalem
   and are recorded among the living.
4 The Lord will wash the filth from
   beautiful Zion*
   and cleanse Jerusalem of its
   bloodstains
   with the hot breath of fiery
   judgment.
5 Then the LORD will provide shade for
   Mount Zion
   and all who assemble there.
He will provide a canopy of cloud
   during the day
   and smoke and flaming fire
   at night,
   covering the glorious land.
6 It will be a shelter from daytime heat
   and a hiding place from storms
   and rain.

5:1 Now I will sing for the one I love
   a song about his vineyard:
My beloved had a vineyard
   on a rich and fertile hill.
2 He plowed the land, cleared its stones,
   and planted it with the best vines.
In the middle he built a watchtower
   and carved a winepress in the
   nearby rocks.
Then he waited for a harvest of sweet
   grapes,
   but the grapes that grew were bitter.

3 Now, you people of Jerusalem
   and Judah,
   you judge between me and my
   vineyard.
4 What more could I have done for my
   vineyard
   that I have not already done?
When I expected sweet grapes,

why did my vineyard give me bitter
   grapes?

5 Now let me tell you
   what I will do to my vineyard:
I will tear down its hedges
   and let it be destroyed.
I will break down its walls
   and let animals trample it.
6 I will make it a wild place
   where the vines are not pruned
   and the ground is not hoed,
   a place overgrown with briers
   and thorns.
I will command the clouds
   to drop no rain on it.

7 The nation of Israel is the vineyard of
   the LORD of Heaven's Armies.
The people of Judah are his
   pleasant garden.
He expected a crop of justice,
   but instead he found oppression.
He expected to find righteousness,
   but instead he heard cries of
   violence.

8 What sorrow for you who buy up
   house after house and field after
   field,
   until everyone is evicted and you
   live alone in the land.
9 But I have heard the LORD of Heaven's
   Armies
   swear a solemn oath:
"Many houses will stand deserted;
   even beautiful mansions will be
   empty.
10 Ten acres* of vineyard will not
   produce even six gallons* of
   wine.
   Ten baskets of seed will yield only
   one basket* of grain."

11 What sorrow for those who get up
   early in the morning
   looking for a drink of alcohol
and spend long evenings drinking
   wine
   to make themselves flaming drunk.
12 They furnish wine and lovely music at
   their grand parties—
   lyre and harp, tambourine and
   flute—
but they never think about the LORD
   or notice what he is doing.

¹³ So my people will go into exile far away
    because they do not know me.
Those who are great and honored will
        starve,
    and the common people will die
        of thirst.
¹⁴ The grave* is licking its lips in
        anticipation,
    opening its mouth wide.
The great and the lowly
    and all the drunken mob will be
        swallowed up.
¹⁵ Humanity will be destroyed, and
        people brought down;
    even the arrogant will lower their
        eyes in humiliation.
¹⁶ But the LORD of Heaven's Armies will
        be exalted by his justice.
The holiness of God will be
        displayed by his righteousness.
¹⁷ In that day lambs will find good
        pastures,
    and fattened sheep and young
        goats* will feed among the ruins.

¹⁸ What sorrow for those who drag their
        sins behind them
    with ropes made of lies,
    who drag wickedness behind them
        like a cart!
¹⁹ They even mock God and say,
    "Hurry up and do something!
    We want to see what you can do.

Let the Holy One of Israel carry out
        his plan,
    for we want to know what it is."

²⁰ What sorrow for those who say
        that evil is good and good is evil,
    that dark is light and light is dark,
        that bitter is sweet and sweet
            is bitter.
²¹ What sorrow for those who are wise
        in their own eyes
    and think themselves so clever.
²² What sorrow for those who are heroes
        at drinking wine
    and boast about all the alcohol they
        can hold.
²³ They take bribes to let the wicked
        go free,
    and they punish the innocent.

²⁴ Therefore, just as fire licks up
        stubble
    and dry grass shrivels in the flame,
so their roots will rot
    and their flowers wither.
For they have rejected the law of the
        LORD of Heaven's Armies;
    they have despised the word of the
        Holy One of Israel.
²⁵ That is why the LORD's anger burns
        against his people,
    and why he has raised his fist
        to crush them.

WHAT THE BIBLE SAYS

The devil

2 CORINTHIANS 11:14-15 Satan is a deceiver. In the Garden of Eden he undermined Eve's relationship with God. Jesus said that the devil is the father of lies and that he hates the truth. •Paul warned the Corinthian church that Satan can disguise himself as an angel of light. He made this statement in the context of talking about false apostles and teachers. The tricky thing about those teachers was how close they were to the truth. They were close enough to skirt the edges of Christianity, but far enough away to do some damage. •Paul compares false teachers to Satan: If even Satan can charade as an angel, certainly these false teachers can sneak into the camp of truth. So how can you know? How can you defend yourself against deceivers in disguise? First, always keep God's Word the standard by which all teaching is judged. If a teaching you hear or an action you're called to do would go against the Bible, then steer clear. Second, pray for wisdom to discern the truth. God will not let those who love the truth be deceived by lies.

The mountains tremble,
and the corpses of his people litter
the streets like garbage.
But even then the LORD's anger is
not satisfied.
His fist is still poised to strike!

26 He will send a signal to distant nations
far away
and whistle to those at the ends
of the earth.
They will come racing toward
Jerusalem.
27 They will not get tired or stumble.
They will not stop for rest or sleep.
Not a belt will be loose,
not a sandal strap broken.
28 Their arrows will be sharp
and their bows ready for battle.
Sparks will fly from their horses'
hooves,
and the wheels of their chariots will
spin like a whirlwind.
29 They will roar like lions,
like the strongest of lions.
Growling, they will pounce on their
victims and carry them off,
and no one will be there to rescue
them.
30 They will roar over their victims
on that day of destruction
like the roaring of the sea.
If someone looks across the land,
only darkness and distress will
be seen;
even the light will be darkened
by clouds.

3:16 Or *The women of Zion* (with corresponding changes to plural forms through verse 24); Hebrew reads *The daughters of Zion;* also in 3:17.   **3:24** As in Dead Sea Scrolls; Masoretic Text reads *robes / because instead of beauty.*   **4:2** Or *the Branch.*   **4:4** Or *from the women of Zion;* Hebrew reads *from the daughters of Zion.*   **5:10a** Hebrew *A ten yoke,* that is, the area of land plowed by ten teams of oxen in one day.   **5:10b** Hebrew *a bath* [21 liters].   **5:10c** Hebrew *A homer* [5 bushels or 182 liters] *of seed will yield only an ephah* [20 quarts or 22 liters].   **5:14** Hebrew *Sheol.*   **5:17** As in Greek version; Hebrew reads *and strangers.*

2 CORINTHIANS 11:1-15

Even in the early years of the Christian faith, the church had to deal with false teachers. The basics of the faith are clear from Scripture. Those who deviate from those truths are dangerous false teachers.

I [Paul] hope you [Corinthians] will put up with a little more of my foolishness. Please bear with me. 2For I am jealous for you with the jealousy of God himself. I promised you as a pure bride* to one husband—Christ. 3But I fear that somehow your pure and undivided devotion to Christ will be corrupted, just as Eve was deceived by the cunning ways of the serpent. 4You happily put up with whatever anyone tells you, even if they preach a different Jesus than the one we preach, or a different kind of Spirit than the one you received, or a different kind of gospel than the one you believed.

5But I don't consider myself inferior in any way to these "super apostles" who teach such things. 6I may be unskilled as a speaker, but I'm not lacking in knowledge. We have made this clear to you in every possible way.

7Was I wrong when I humbled myself and honored you by preaching God's Good News to you without expecting anything in return? 8I "robbed" other churches by accepting their contributions so I could serve you at no cost. 9And when I was with you and didn't have enough to live on, I did not become a financial burden to anyone. For the brothers who came from Macedonia brought me all that I needed. I have never been a burden to you, and I never will be. 10As surely as the truth of Christ is in me, no one in all of Greece* will ever stop me from boasting about this. 11Why? Because I don't love you? God knows that I do.

12But I will continue doing what I have always done. This will undercut those who are looking for an opportunity to boast that their work is just like ours. 13These people are false apostles. They are deceitful workers who disguise themselves as apostles of Christ. 14But I am not surprised! Even Satan disguises himself as an angel of light. 15So it is no wonder that his servants also disguise themselves as servants of righteousness. In the end they will get the punishment their wicked deeds deserve.

11:2 Greek *a virgin.*   **11:10** Greek *Achaia,* the southern region of the Greek peninsula.

PSALM 53:1-6
For the choir director: A meditation; a psalm of David.*

1 Only fools say in their hearts,
"There is no God."

They are corrupt, and their actions
  are evil;
    not one of them does good!

2 God looks down from heaven
    on the entire human race;
  he looks to see if anyone is truly wise,
    if anyone seeks God.
3 But no, all have turned away;
    all have become corrupt.*
  No one does good,
    not a single one!

4 Will those who do evil never learn?
    They eat up my people like bread
    and wouldn't think of praying
      to God.
5 Terror will grip them,
    terror like they have never known
      before.

God will scatter the bones of your
  enemies.
    You will put them to shame, for God
      has rejected them.

6 Who will come from Mount Zion
    to rescue Israel?
  When God restores his people,
    Jacob will shout with joy, and Israel
      will rejoice.

53:TITLE Hebrew *maskil*. This may be a literary or musical
term.   53:3 Greek version reads *have become useless.*
Compare Rom 3:12.

PROVERBS 22:28-29

Don't cheat your neighbor by moving the
ancient boundary markers set up by previous generations. □ Do you see any truly
competent workers? They will serve kings
rather than working for ordinary people.

SEPTEMBER**10**

ISAIAH 6:1–7:25

Isaiah shares the events surrounding his call to be a
prophet. All of us face defining moments in our lives,
in which we are called upon to answer, "Send me."

It was in the year King Uzziah died* that I
[Isaiah] saw the Lord. He was sitting on a
lofty throne, and the train of his robe
filled the Temple. 2 Attending him were
mighty seraphim, each having six wings.
With two wings they covered their faces,
with two they covered their feet, and with
two they flew. 3 They were calling out to
each other,

"Holy, holy, holy is the LORD of
  Heaven's Armies!
    The whole earth is filled with
      his glory!"

4 Their voices shook the Temple to its
foundations, and the entire building was
filled with smoke.

5 Then I said, "It's all over! I am doomed,
for I am a sinful man. I have filthy lips, and
I live among a people with filthy lips. Yet
I have seen the King, the LORD of Heaven's
Armies."

6 Then one of the seraphim flew to me
with a burning coal he had taken from the
altar with a pair of tongs. 7 He touched my
lips with it and said, "See, this coal has
touched your lips. Now your guilt is removed, and your sins are forgiven."

8 Then I heard the Lord asking, "Whom
should I send as a messenger to this people? Who will go for us?"

I said, "Here I am. Send me."

9 And he said, "Yes, go, and say to this
people,

'Listen carefully, but do not
    understand.
  Watch closely, but learn nothing.'
10 Harden the hearts of these people.
  Plug their ears and shut their eyes.
  That way, they will not see with their
    eyes,
    nor hear with their ears,
  nor understand with their hearts
    and turn to me for healing."*

11 Then I said, "Lord, how long will this
go on?"

And he replied,

"Until their towns are empty,
their houses are deserted,
and the whole country is
a wasteland;
12 until the LORD has sent everyone
away,
and the entire land of Israel lies
deserted.
13 If even a tenth—a remnant—survive,
it will be invaded again and burned.
But as a terebinth or oak tree leaves
a stump when it is cut down,
so Israel's stump will be a
holy seed."

7:1WHEN Ahaz, son of Jotham and grandson of Uzziah, was king of Judah, King Rezin of Syria* and Pekah son of Remaliah, the king of Israel, set out to attack Jerusalem. However, they were unable to carry out their plan.

2 The news had come to the royal court of Judah: "Syria is allied with Israel* against us!" So the hearts of the king and his people trembled with fear, like trees shaking in a storm.

3 Then the LORD said to Isaiah, "Take your son Shear-jashub* and go out to meet King Ahaz. You will find him at the end of the aqueduct that feeds water into the upper pool, near the road leading to the field where cloth is washed.* 4 Tell him to stop worrying. Tell him he doesn't need to fear the fierce anger of those two burned-out embers, King Rezin of Syria and Pekah son of Remaliah. 5 Yes, the kings of Syria and Israel are plotting against him, saying, 6'We will attack Judah and capture it for ourselves. Then we will install the son of Tabeel as Judah's king.' 7 But this is what the Sovereign LORD says:

"This invasion will never happen;
it will never take place;
8 for Syria is no stronger than its capital,
Damascus,
and Damascus is no stronger than
its king, Rezin.
As for Israel, within sixty-five years
it will be crushed and completely
destroyed.
9 Israel is no stronger than its capital,
Samaria,

and Samaria is no stronger than its
king, Pekah son of Remaliah.
Unless your faith is firm,
I cannot make you stand firm."

10 Later, the LORD sent this message to King Ahaz: 11"Ask the LORD your God for a sign of confirmation, Ahaz. Make it as difficult as you want—as high as heaven or as deep as the place of the dead.*"

12 But the king refused. "No," he said, "I will not test the LORD like that."

13 Then Isaiah said, "Listen well, you royal family of David! Isn't it enough to exhaust human patience? Must you exhaust the patience of my God as well? 14 All right then, the Lord himself will give you the sign. Look! The virgin* will conceive a child! She will give birth to a son and will call him Immanuel (which means 'God is with us'). 15 By the time this child is old enough to choose what is right and reject what is wrong, he will be eating yogurt* and honey. 16 For before the child is that old, the lands of the two kings you fear so much will both be deserted.

17"Then the LORD will bring things on you, your nation, and your family unlike anything since Israel broke away from Judah. He will bring the king of Assyria upon you!"

18 In that day the LORD will whistle for the army of southern Egypt and for the army of Assyria. They will swarm around you like flies and bees. 19 They will come in vast hordes and settle in the fertile areas and also in the desolate valleys, caves, and thorny places. 20 In that day the Lord will hire a "razor" from beyond the Euphrates River*—the king of Assyria— and use it to shave off everything: your land, your crops, and your people.*

21 In that day a farmer will be fortunate to have a cow and two sheep or goats left. 22 Nevertheless, there will be enough milk for everyone because so few people will be left in the land. They will eat their fill of yogurt and honey. 23 In that day the lush vineyards, now worth 1,000 pieces of silver,* will become patches of briers and thorns. 24 The entire land will become a vast expanse of briers and thorns, a hunting ground overrun by wildlife. 25 No one will go to the fertile hillsides where the

gardens once grew, for briers and thorns will cover them. Cattle, sheep, and goats will graze there.

6:1 King Uzziah died in 740 B.C. 6:9-10 Greek version reads *And he said, "Go and say to this people, / 'When you hear what I say, you will not understand. / When you see what I do, you will not comprehend.' / For the hearts of these people are hardened, / and their ears cannot hear, and they have closed their eyes— / so their eyes cannot see, / and their ears cannot hear, / and their hearts cannot understand, / and they cannot turn to me and let me heal them."* Compare Matt 13:14-15; Mark 4:12; Luke 8:10; Acts 28:26-27. 7:1 Hebrew *Aram;* also in 7:2, 4, 5, 8. 7:2 Hebrew *Ephraim,* referring to the northern kingdom of Israel; also in 7:5, 8, 9, 17. 7:3a *Shear-jashub* means "A remnant will return." 7:3b Or *bleached.* 7:11 Hebrew *as deep as Sheol.* 7:14 Or *young woman.* 7:15 Or *curds;* also in 7:22. 7:20a Hebrew *the river.* 7:20b Hebrew *shave off the head, the hair of the legs, and the beard.* 7:23 Hebrew *1,000 shekels of silver,* about 25 pounds or 11.4 kilograms in weight.

2 CORINTHIANS 11:16-33

Some false teachers not only tried to spread damaging doctrine, they also tried to discredit Paul, a true apostle. Paul defended himself primarily by pointing to the suffering he endured while serving Christ.

Again I [Paul] say, don't think that I am a fool to talk like this. But even if you do, listen to me, as you would to a foolish person, while I also boast a little. [17]Such boasting is not from the Lord, but I am acting like a fool. [18]And since others boast about their human achievements, I will, too. [19]After all, you think you are so wise, but you enjoy putting up with fools! [20]You put up with it when someone enslaves you, takes everything you have, takes advantage of you,

takes control of everything, and slaps you in the face. [21]I'm ashamed to say that we've been too "weak" to do that!

But whatever they dare to boast about— I'm talking like a fool again—I dare to boast about it, too. [22]Are they Hebrews? So am I. Are they Israelites? So am I. Are they descendants of Abraham? So am I. [23]Are they servants of Christ? I know I sound like a madman, but I have served him far more! I have worked harder, been put in prison more often, been whipped times without number, and faced death again and again. [24]Five different times the Jewish leaders gave me thirty-nine lashes. [25]Three times I was beaten with rods. Once I was stoned. Three times I was shipwrecked. Once I spent a whole night and a day adrift at sea. [26]I have traveled on many long journeys. I have faced danger from rivers and from robbers. I have faced danger from my own people, the Jews, as well as from the Gentiles. I have faced danger in the cities, in the deserts, and on the seas. And I have faced danger from men who claim to be believers but are not.* [27]I have worked hard and long, enduring many sleepless nights. I have been hungry and thirsty and have often gone without food. I have shivered in the cold, without enough clothing to keep me warm. [28]Then, besides all this, I have the daily burden of my concern for all the churches.

WHO GOD IS

God is holy

ISAIAH 6:1-8 In a time of moral and spiritual decay in the kingdom of Judah, the prophet Isaiah was allowed to witness the glory of God's holiness. *Holy* means morally pure, perfect, and set apart from all sin. When Isaiah saw the seraphim (angels), the throne, and the Lord whose robe filled the Temple, he realized his own unworthiness to be in the Lord's presence. Then one of the seraphim touched his lips with a burning coal and told Isaiah that his sins had been forgiven. It was not the coal that brought forgiveness, but God's willingness to cleanse Isaiah from his unrighteousness. Isaiah responded by giving himself over totally to God's service. • We have no hope of measuring up to God's holiness on our own. But when we confess our sins and submit to God's control, God is faithful to forgive and cleanse us. The process may be as painful as a hot coal, but it is necessary. Isaiah never set out to be a prophet, but his encounter with the holy God changed his life forever. Imagine what God can do through you if you'll let him!

29 Who is weak without my feeling that weakness? Who is led astray, and I do not burn with anger?

30 If I must boast, I would rather boast about the things that show how weak I am. 31 God, the Father of our Lord Jesus, who is worthy of eternal praise, knows I am not lying. 32 When I was in Damascus, the governor under King Aretas kept guards at the city gates to catch me. 33 I had to be lowered in a basket through a window in the city wall to escape from him.

11:26 Greek *from false brothers.*

PSALM 54:1-7

For the choir director: A psalm* of David, regarding the time the Ziphites came and said to Saul, "We know where David is hiding." To be accompanied by stringed instruments.

1 **C**ome with great power, O God,
       and rescue me!
   Defend me with your might.
2 Listen to my prayer, O God.
   Pay attention to my plea.
3 For strangers are attacking me;

violent people are trying to kill me.
   They care nothing for God.

Interlude

4 But God is my helper.
   The Lord keeps me alive!
5 May the evil plans of my enemies be
       turned against them.
   Do as you promised and put an end
       to them.
6 I will sacrifice a voluntary offering
       to you;
   I will praise your name, O LORD,
       for it is good.
7 For you have rescued me from
       my troubles
   and helped me to triumph over
       my enemies.

54:TITLE Hebrew *maskil.* This may be a literary or musical term.

PROVERBS 23:1-3

While dining with a ruler, pay attention to what is put before you. If you are a big eater, put a knife to your throat; don't desire all the delicacies, for he might be trying to trick you.

SEPTEMBER**11**

ISAIAH 8:1–9:21

Isaiah's prophecy includes some of the most poignant prophecies of the Messiah in Scripture. The Messiah would be a savior, one who would defend Israel and make it the nation it was meant to be.

Then the LORD said to me [Isaiah], "Make a large signboard and clearly write this name on it: Maher-shalal-hash-baz.*" 2 I asked Uriah the priest and Zechariah son of Jeberekiah, both known as honest men, to witness my doing this.

3 Then I slept with my wife, and she became pregnant and gave birth to a son. And the LORD said, "Call him Maher-shalal-hash-baz. 4 For before this child is old enough to say 'Papa' or 'Mama,' the king of Assyria will carry away both the abundance of Damascus and the riches of Samaria."

5 Then the LORD spoke to me again and said, 6 "My care for the people of Judah is like the gently flowing waters of Shiloah, but they have rejected it. They are rejoicing over what will happen to* King Rezin and King Pekah.* 7 Therefore, the Lord will overwhelm them with a mighty flood from the Euphrates River*—the king of Assyria and all his glory. This flood will overflow all its channels 8 and sweep into Judah until it is chin deep. It will spread its wings, submerging your land from one end to the other, O Immanuel.

9 "Huddle together, you nations, and be
       terrified.
   Listen, all you distant lands.
   Prepare for battle, but you will be
       crushed!

Yes, prepare for battle, but you will
be crushed!
¹⁰ Call your councils of war, but they will
be worthless.
Develop your strategies, but they
will not succeed.
For God is with us!*"

¹¹The LORD has given me a strong
warning not to think like everyone else
does. He said,

¹² "Don't call everything a conspiracy,
like they do,
and don't live in dread of what
frightens them.
¹³ Make the LORD of Heaven's Armies
holy in your life.
He is the one you should fear.
He is the one who should make you
tremble.
¹⁴ He will keep you safe.
But to Israel and Judah
he will be a stone that makes people
stumble,
a rock that makes them fall.
And for the people of Jerusalem
he will be a trap and a snare.
¹⁵ Many will stumble and fall,
never to rise again.
They will be snared and captured."

¹⁶ Preserve the teaching of God;
entrust his instructions to those
who follow me.
¹⁷ I will wait for the LORD,
who has turned away from the
descendants of Jacob.
I will put my hope in him.

¹⁸I and the children the LORD has given
me serve as signs and warnings to Israel
from the LORD of Heaven's Armies who
dwells in his Temple on Mount Zion.
¹⁹Someone may say to you, "Let's ask
the mediums and those who consult the
spirits of the dead. With their whis-
perings and mutterings, they will tell us
what to do." But shouldn't people ask God
for guidance? Should the living seek guidance from the dead?
²⁰Look to God's instructions and teachings! People who contradict his word are
completely in the dark. ²¹They will go
from one place to another, weary and
hungry. And because they are hungry, they

will rage and curse their king and their
God. They will look up to heaven ²²and
down at the earth, but wherever they look,
there will be trouble and anguish and
dark despair. They will be thrown out into
the darkness.

⁹:¹*NEVERTHELESS, that time of darkness
and despair will not go on forever. The
land of Zebulun and Naphtali will be humbled, but there will be a time in the future
when Galilee of the Gentiles, which lies
along the road that runs between the Jordan and the sea, will be filled with glory.

²*The people who walk in darkness
will see a great light.
For those who live in a land of deep
darkness,*
a light will shine.
³ You will enlarge the nation of Israel,
and its people will rejoice.
They will rejoice before you
as people rejoice at the harvest
and like warriors dividing the
plunder.
⁴ For you will break the yoke of their
slavery
and lift the heavy burden from their
shoulders.
You will break the oppressor's rod,
just as you did when you destroyed
the army of Midian.
⁵ The boots of the warrior
and the uniforms bloodstained by
war
will all be burned.
They will be fuel for the fire.

⁶ For a child is born to us,
a son is given to us.
The government will rest on his
shoulders.
And he will be called:
Wonderful Counselor,* Mighty God,
Everlasting Father, Prince of Peace.
⁷ His government and its peace
will never end.
He will rule with fairness and justice
from the throne of his ancestor
David
for all eternity.
The passionate commitment of the
LORD of Heaven's Armies
will make this happen!

8 The Lord has spoken out against Jacob;
   his judgment has fallen upon Israel.
9 And the people of Israel* and Samaria,
   who spoke with such pride and
   arrogance,
   will soon know it.
10 They said, "We will replace the broken
   bricks of our ruins with finished
   stone,
   and replant the felled sycamore-fig
   trees with cedars."
11 But the Lord will bring Rezin's
   enemies against Israel
   and stir up all their foes.
12 The Syrians* from the east and the
   Philistines from the west
   will bare their fangs and devour
   Israel.
   But even then the Lord's anger will
   not be satisfied.
   His fist is still poised to strike.

13 For after all this punishment, the
   people will still not repent.
   They will not seek the Lord of
   Heaven's Armies.
14 Therefore, in a single day the Lord
   will destroy both the head and
   the tail,
   the noble palm branch and the
   lowly reed.
15 The leaders of Israel are the head,
   and the lying prophets are the tail.
16 For the leaders of the people have
   misled them.
   They have led them down the path
   of destruction.
17 That is why the Lord takes no pleasure
   in the young men
   and shows no mercy even to the
   widows and orphans.
   For they are all wicked hypocrites,
   and they all speak foolishness.
   But even then the Lord's anger will
   not be satisfied.
   His fist is still poised to strike.

18 This wickedness is like a brushfire.
   It burns not only briers and thorns
   but also sets the forests ablaze.
   Its burning sends up clouds
   of smoke.
19 The land will be blackened

by the fury of the Lord of Heaven's
   Armies.
The people will be fuel for the fire,
   and no one will spare even his own
   brother.
20 They will attack their neighbor
   on the right
   but will still be hungry.
They will devour their neighbor
   on the left
   but will not be satisfied.
In the end they will even eat their own
   children.*
21 Manasseh will feed on Ephraim,
   Ephraim will feed on Manasseh,
   and both will devour Judah.
But even then the Lord's anger will
   not be satisfied.
   His fist is still poised to strike.

8:1 *Maher-shalal-hash-baz* means "Swift to plunder and
quick to carry away." **8:6a** Or *They are rejoicing because of.*
8:6b Hebrew *and the son of Remaliah.* **8:7** Hebrew *the
river.* **8:10** Hebrew *Immanuel!* **9:1** Verse 9:1 is numbered
8:23 in Hebrew text. **9:2a** Verses 9:2-21 are numbered 9:1-
20 in Hebrew text. **9:2b** Greek version reads *a land where
death casts its shadow.* Compare Matt 4:16. **9:6** Or
Wonderful, Counselor. **9:9** Hebrew *of Ephraim,* referring to
the northern kingdom of Israel. **9:12** Hebrew *Arameans.*
9:20 Or *eat their own arms.*

2 CORINTHIANS 12:1-10

Is there some problem you've prayed repeatedly
about? Paul could relate. God does not take away
every problem, but he is able to work through any
problem, even your most irksome imperfections, for
your growth and his glory.

This boasting will do no good, but I [Paul]
must go on. I will reluctantly tell about visions and revelations from the Lord. 2 I*
was caught up to the third heaven fourteen years ago. Whether I was in my body
or out of my body, I don't know—only God
knows. 3 Yes, only God knows whether I
was in my body or outside my body. But
I do know 4 that I was caught up* to paradise and heard things so astounding that
they cannot be expressed in words, things
no human is allowed to tell.
   5 That experience is worth boasting
about, but I'm not going to do it. I will
boast only about my weaknesses. 6 If I
wanted to boast, I would be no fool in
doing so, because I would be telling the
truth. But I won't do it, because I don't
want anyone to give me credit beyond
what they can see in my life or hear in my

message, [7]even though I have received such wonderful revelations from God. So to keep me from becoming proud, I was given a thorn in my flesh, a messenger from Satan to torment me and keep me from becoming proud.

[8]Three different times I begged the Lord to take it away. [9]Each time he said, "My grace is all you need. My power works best in weakness." So now I am glad to boast about my weaknesses, so that the power of Christ can work through me. [10]That's why I take pleasure in my weaknesses, and in the insults, hardships, persecutions, and troubles that I suffer for Christ. For when I am weak, then I am strong.

12:2 Greek *I know a man in Christ who*. 12:3-4 Greek *But I know such a man, that he was caught up.*

PSALM 55:1-23

For the choir director: A psalm of David, to be accompanied by stringed instruments.*

[1] Listen to my prayer, O God.
        Do not ignore my cry for help!
[2] Please listen and answer me,
        for I am overwhelmed by my
            troubles.
[3] My enemies shout at me,
        making loud and wicked threats.
    They bring trouble on me
        and angrily hunt me down.
[4] My heart pounds in my chest.
        The terror of death assaults me.

[5] Fear and trembling overwhelm me,
        and I can't stop shaking.
[6] Oh, that I had wings like a dove;
        then I would fly away and rest!
[7] I would fly far away
        to the quiet of the wilderness.
                                    Interlude
[8] How quickly I would escape—
        far from this wild storm
            of hatred.

[9] Confuse them, Lord, and frustrate
            their plans,
        for I see violence and conflict
            in the city.
[10] Its walls are patrolled day and night
            against invaders,
        but the real danger is wickedness
            within the city.
[11] Everything is falling apart;
        threats and cheating are rampant
            in the streets.

[12] It is not an enemy who taunts me—
        I could bear that.
    It is not my foes who so arrogantly
            insult me—
        I could have hidden from them.
[13] Instead, it is you—my equal,
        my companion and close friend.
[14] What good fellowship we once
            enjoyed
        as we walked together to the house
            of God.

HOW WE LIVE

Growing in faith

2 CORINTHIANS 12:7-10 Paul described having a "thorn" in his flesh—apparently some kind of physical debilitation that was a "torment" to him. Whether it was malaria, epilepsy, or a disease of the eyes (Galatians 4:13-15, September 18), it was a chronic and debilitating problem that sometimes affected his ministry. No wonder Paul prayed for it to be removed. Wouldn't you? • Yet God refused. Doesn't make much sense, does it? Here's Paul, a high-energy spokesman for the Good News, yet when he's not sitting in prison, he's sometimes sick with a debilitating ailment. Couldn't he have been so much more effective never in prison and never sick? • Although God did not remove Paul's physical affliction, he promised to demonstrate his power in Paul. The fact that God displays his power through weak people should give us courage. If we could do it all on our own, we would become proud. When we have to rely on God, he works through us and we grow. Commit whatever difficulties you face to God and ask him to help you to grow in faith through them.

15 Let death stalk my enemies;
  let the grave* swallow them alive,
  for evil makes its home within
  them.

16 But I will call on God,
  and the LORD will rescue me.
17 Morning, noon, and night
  I cry out in my distress,
  and the LORD hears my voice.
18 He ransoms me and keeps me safe
  from the battle waged against me,
  though many still oppose me.
19 God, who has ruled forever,
  will hear me and humble them.
      Interlude
  For my enemies refuse to change
  their ways;
  they do not fear God.

20 As for my companion, he betrayed
  his friends;
  he broke his promises.

21 His words are as smooth as butter,
  but in his heart is war.
  His words are as soothing as lotion,
  but underneath are daggers!

22 Give your burdens to the LORD,
  and he will take care of you.
  He will not permit the godly to slip
  and fall.

23 But you, O God, will send the wicked
  down to the pit of destruction.
  Murderers and liars will die young,
  but I am trusting you to save me.

55:TITLE Hebrew *maskil*. This may be a literary or musical
term. 55:15 Hebrew *let Sheol*.

PROVERBS 23:4-5

Don't wear yourself out trying to get rich.
Be wise enough to know when to quit.
In the blink of an eye wealth disappears,
for it will sprout wings and fly away like
an eagle.

SEPTEMBER**12**

ISAIAH 10:1–11:16

The Old Testament contains numerous prophecies
against the enemies of God's people. Today's reading mentions Assyria, the brutal neighbor to the
northeast, who conquered and destroyed the northern kingdom and threatened the southern kingdom
during Isaiah's lifetime.

What sorrow awaits the unjust
  judges
  and those who issue unfair laws.
2 They deprive the poor of justice
  and deny the rights of the needy
  among my people.
  They prey on widows
  and take advantage of orphans.
3 What will you do when I punish you,
  when I send disaster upon you from
  a distant land?
  To whom will you turn for help?
  Where will your treasures
  be safe?
4 You will stumble along as prisoners
  or lie among the dead.

But even then the LORD's anger will
  not be satisfied.
  His fist is still poised to strike.

5 "What sorrow awaits Assyria, the rod
  of my anger.
  I use it as a club to express my
  anger.
6 I am sending Assyria against a godless
  nation,
  against a people with whom
  I am angry.
  Assyria will plunder them,
  trampling them like dirt beneath
  its feet.
7 But the king of Assyria will not
  understand that he is my tool;
  his mind does not work that way.
  His plan is simply to destroy,
  to cut down nation after nation.
8 He will say,
  'Each of my princes will soon
  be a king.

⁹ We destroyed Calno just as we did
   Carchemish.
   Hamath fell before us as Arpad did.
   And we destroyed Samaria just as
      we did Damascus.
¹⁰ Yes, we have finished off many
      a kingdom
   whose gods were greater than those
      in Jerusalem and Samaria.
¹¹ So we will defeat Jerusalem and
      her gods,
   just as we destroyed Samaria
      with hers.'"

¹²After the Lord has used the king of
Assyria to accomplish his purposes on
Mount Zion and in Jerusalem, he will turn
against the king of Assyria and punish
him—for he is proud and arrogant. ¹³He
boasts,

"By my own powerful arm I have done
   this.
With my own shrewd wisdom
   I planned it.
I have broken down the defenses
   of nations
and carried off their treasures.
I have knocked down their kings
   like a bull.
¹⁴ I have robbed their nests of riches
   and gathered up kingdoms as
      a farmer gathers eggs.
No one can even flap a wing
   against me
or utter a peep of protest."

¹⁵ But can the ax boast greater power
      than the person who uses it?
   Is the saw greater than the person
      who saws?
   Can a rod strike unless a hand
      moves it?
   Can a wooden cane walk by itself?
¹⁶ Therefore, the Lord, the LORD of
      Heaven's Armies,
   will send a plague among Assyria's
      proud troops,
   and a flaming fire will consume
      its glory.
¹⁷ The LORD, the Light of Israel, will
      be a fire;
   the Holy One will be a flame.
   He will devour the thorns and briers
      with fire,

burning up the enemy in a single
   night.
¹⁸ The LORD will consume Assyria's glory
   like a fire consumes a forest in
      a fruitful land;
   it will waste away like sick people
      in a plague.
¹⁹ Of all that glorious forest, only a few
      trees will survive—
   so few that a child could count
      them!

²⁰ In that day the remnant left in Israel,
   the survivors in the house
      of Jacob,
will no longer depend on allies
   who seek to destroy them.
But they will faithfully trust the LORD,
   the Holy One of Israel.
²¹ A remnant will return;*
   yes, the remnant of Jacob will return
      to the Mighty God.
²² But though the people of Israel are
      as numerous
   as the sand of the seashore,
only a remnant of them will return.
   The LORD has rightly decided
      to destroy his people.
²³ Yes, the Lord, the LORD of Heaven's
      Armies,
   has already decided to destroy
      the entire land.*

²⁴So this is what the Lord, the LORD of
Heaven's Armies, says: "O my people in
Zion, do not be afraid of the Assyrians
when they oppress you with rod and club
as the Egyptians did long ago. ²⁵In a little
while my anger against you will end, and
then my anger will rise up to destroy
them." ²⁶The LORD of Heaven's Armies
will lash them with his whip, as he did
when Gideon triumphed over the Midianites at the rock of Oreb, or when the
LORD's staff was raised to drown the Egyptian army in the sea.

²⁷ In that day the LORD will end the
      bondage of his people.
   He will break the yoke of slavery
   and lift it from their shoulders.*

²⁸ Look, the Assyrians are now at Aiath.
   They are passing through Migron
   and are storing their equipment
      at Micmash.

²⁹ They are crossing the pass
   and are camping at Geba.
Fear strikes the town of Ramah.
   All the people of Gibeah, the
      hometown of Saul,
   are running for their lives.

³⁰ Scream in terror,
   you people of Gallim!
Shout out a warning to Laishah.
   Oh, poor Anathoth!

³¹ There go the people of Madmenah,
   all fleeing.
   The citizens of Gebim are trying
      to hide.

³² The enemy stops at Nob for the rest
   of that day.
He shakes his fist at beautiful Mount
   Zion, the mountain of Jerusalem.

³³ But look! The Lord, the LORD of
   Heaven's Armies,
   will chop down the mighty tree
      of Assyria with great power!
He will cut down the proud.
   That lofty tree will be brought down.

³⁴ He will cut down the forest trees with
   an ax.
   Lebanon will fall to the Mighty
      One.*

¹¹:¹ OUT of the stump of David's family*
   will grow a shoot—
   yes, a new Branch bearing fruit
      from the old root.

² And the Spirit of the LORD will rest
   on him—
   the Spirit of wisdom and
      understanding,
   the Spirit of counsel and might,
   the Spirit of knowledge and the fear
      of the LORD.

³ He will delight in obeying the LORD.
   He will not judge by appearance
   nor make a decision based
      on hearsay.

⁴ He will give justice to the poor
   and make fair decisions for the
      exploited.
The earth will shake at the force
   of his word,
   and one breath from his mouth will
      destroy the wicked.

⁵ He will wear righteousness like a belt
   and truth like an undergarment.

⁶ In that day the wolf and the lamb will
   live together;
   the leopard will lie down with the
      baby goat.
The calf and the yearling will be safe
   with the lion,
   and a little child will lead them all.

⁷ The cow will graze near the bear.
   The cub and the calf will lie down
      together.
   The lion will eat hay like a cow.

⁸ The baby will play safely near the hole
   of a cobra.
   Yes, a little child will put its hand in
      a nest of deadly snakes without
      harm.

⁹ Nothing will hurt or destroy in all my
   holy mountain,
   for as the waters fill the sea,
   so the earth will be filled with
      people who know the LORD.

¹⁰ In that day the heir to David's throne*
   will be a banner of salvation to all
      the world.
The nations will rally to him,
   and the land where he lives will
      be a glorious place.*

¹¹ In that day the Lord will reach out his
   hand a second time
   to bring back the remnant of
      his people—
those who remain in Assyria and
   northern Egypt;
   in southern Egypt, Ethiopia,*
      and Elam;
   in Babylonia,* Hamath, and all the
      distant coastlands.

¹² He will raise a flag among the nations
   and assemble the exiles of Israel.
He will gather the scattered people
   of Judah
   from the ends of the earth.

¹³ Then at last the jealousy between
   Israel* and Judah will end.
   They will not be rivals anymore.

¹⁴ They will join forces to swoop down
   on Philistia to the west.
   Together they will attack and
      plunder the nations to the east.
They will occupy the lands of Edom
   and Moab,
   and Ammon will obey them.

¹⁵ The LORD will make a dry path
        through the gulf of the Red Sea.*
    He will wave his hand over the
        Euphrates River,*
    sending a mighty wind to divide it into
        seven streams
    so it can easily be crossed on foot.
¹⁶ He will make a highway for the
        remnant of his people,
    the remnant coming from Assyria,
    just as he did for Israel long ago
        when they returned from Egypt.

10:21 Hebrew *Shear-jashub;* see 7:3; 8:18.   10:22-23 Greek version reads *only a remnant of them will be saved. / For he will carry out his sentence quickly and with finality and righteousness; / for God will carry out his sentence upon all the world with finality.* Compare Rom 9:27-28.   10:27 As in Greek version; Hebrew reads *The yoke will be broken, / for you have grown so fat.*   10:34 Or *with an ax / as even the mighty trees of Lebanon fall.*   11:1 Hebrew *the stump of the line of Jesse. Jesse* was King David's father.   11:10a Hebrew *the root of Jesse.*   11:10b Greek version reads *In that day the heir to David's throne* [literally *the root of Jesse*] *will come, / and he will rule over the Gentiles. / They will place their hopes on him.* Compare Rom 15:12.   11:11a Hebrew *in Pathros, Cush.*   11:11b Hebrew *in Shinar.*   11:13 Hebrew *Ephraim,* referring to the northern kingdom of Israel. 11:15a Hebrew *will destroy the tongue of the sea of Egypt.* 11:15b Hebrew *the river.*

2 CORINTHIANS 12:11-21
Paul did not want to speak of his credentials as an apostle, but the Corinthian believers drove him to it. Enough was enough. It was time to let the chips fall where they may and get on with ministering to these people.

You [Corinthians] have made me [Paul] act like a fool—boasting like this.* You ought to be writing commendations for me, for I am not at all inferior to these "super apostles," even though I am nothing at all. ¹²When I was with you, I certainly gave you proof that I am an apostle. For I patiently did many signs and wonders and miracles among you. ¹³The only thing I failed to do, which I do in the other churches, was to become a financial burden to you. Please forgive me for this wrong!

¹⁴Now I am coming to you for the third time, and I will not be a burden to you. I don't want what you have—I want you. After all, children don't provide for their parents. Rather, parents provide for their children. ¹⁵I will gladly spend myself and all I have for you, even though it seems that the more I love you, the less you love me.

¹⁶Some of you admit I was not a burden to you. But others still think I was sneaky and took advantage of you by trickery. ¹⁷But how? Did any of the men I sent to you take advantage of you? ¹⁸When I urged Titus to visit you and sent our other brother with him, did Titus take advantage of you? No! For we have the same spirit and walk in each other's steps, doing things the same way.

¹⁹Perhaps you think we're saying these things just to defend ourselves. No, we tell

WHO GOD IS

Jesus fulfilled prophecy

ISAIAH 11:1-5 In the midst of promises of judgment, God made another promise through the prophet Isaiah: "Out of the stump of David's family will grow . . . a new Branch." • From David's line of descendants would come another leader, an altogether different King. This King would have God's Spirit resting on him with wisdom and knowledge. He would bring justice and renewal. This new Branch would bear new fruit and bring light into darkness. Earlier Isaiah also said, "A child is born to us, a son is given to us," and he will be called the Prince of Peace (Isaiah 9:6, September 11). What hope this must have given the people who were listening to Isaiah's words! • And hundreds of years later, it all happened. Jesus came—the new Branch, the promised Messiah and King. He healed the sick and fed the hungry. He taught truth. He led by being a servant. He revolutionized what it means to love others. Most importantly, he bore the sins of the world so that all who put their trust in him could be forgiven and have eternal life. • Jesus came as the promised One, fulfilling the prophecy from today's reading.

you this as Christ's servants, and with God as our witness. Everything we do, dear friends, is to strengthen you. ²⁰For I am afraid that when I come I won't like what I find, and you won't like my response. I am afraid that I will find quarreling, jealousy, anger, selfishness, slander, gossip, arrogance, and disorderly behavior. ²¹Yes, I am afraid that when I come again, God will humble me in your presence. And I will be grieved because many of you have not given up your old sins. You have not repented of your impurity, sexual immorality, and eagerness for lustful pleasure.

12:11 Some manuscripts omit *boasting like this.*

PSALM 56:1-13
For the choir director: A psalm of David, regarding the time the Philistines seized him in Gath. To be sung to the tune "Dove on Distant Oaks."

¹ **O** God, have mercy on me,
    for people are hounding me.
    My foes attack me all day long.
² I am constantly hounded by those who
        slander me,
    and many are boldly attacking me.
³ But when I am afraid,
    I will put my trust in you.
⁴ I praise God for what he has promised.
    I trust in God, so why should I be
        afraid?
    What can mere mortals do to me?

⁵ They are always twisting what I say;
    they spend their days plotting to
        harm me.
⁶ They come together to spy on me—
    watching my every step, eager to
        kill me.

⁷ Don't let them get away with their
        wickedness;
    in your anger, O God, bring them
        down.

⁸ You keep track of all my sorrows.*
    You have collected all my tears in
        your bottle.
    You have recorded each one in
        your book.

⁹ My enemies will retreat when I call to
        you for help.
    This I know: God is on my side!
¹⁰ I praise God for what he has promised;
    Yes, I praise the LORD for what he
        has promised.
¹¹ I trust in God, so why should I be
        afraid?
    What can mere mortals do to me?

¹² I will fulfill my vows to you, O God,
    and will offer a sacrifice of thanks
        for your help.
¹³ For you have rescued me from death;
    you have kept my feet from
        slipping.
    So now I can walk in your presence,
        O God,
    in your life-giving light.

56:8 Or *my wanderings.*

PROVERBS 23:6-8
Don't eat with people who are stingy; don't desire their delicacies. They are always thinking about how much it costs.* "Eat and drink," they say, but they don't mean it. You will throw up what little you've eaten, and your compliments will be wasted.

23:7 The meaning of the Hebrew is uncertain.

SEPTEMBER**13**

ISAIAH 12:1-14:32
Babylon was another enemy of the Jews. It was Babylon that would eventually conquer and exile the citizens of the southern kingdom of Judah, destroying the city of Jerusalem in the process.

In that day you [Israel] will sing:
"I will praise you, O LORD!
    You were angry with me, but not any
        more.
    Now you comfort me.

2 See, God has come to save me.
  I will trust in him and not be afraid.
The LORD GOD is my strength and
    my song;
  he has given me victory."

3 With joy you will drink deeply
  from the fountain of salvation!
4 In that wonderful day you will sing:
  "Thank the LORD! Praise his name!
Tell the nations what he has done.
  Let them know how mighty he is!
5 Sing to the LORD, for he has done
    wonderful things.
  Make known his praise around
    the world.
6 Let all the people of Jerusalem* shout
    his praise with joy!
  For great is the Holy One of Israel
    who lives among you."

13:1 ISAIAH son of Amoz received this message concerning the destruction of Babylon:

2 "Raise a signal flag on a bare hilltop.
  Call up an army against Babylon.
Wave your hand to encourage them
  as they march into the palaces of
    the high and mighty.
3 I, the LORD, have dedicated these
    soldiers for this task.
  Yes, I have called mighty warriors
    to express my anger,
  and they will rejoice when I am
    exalted."

4 Hear the noise on the mountains!
  Listen, as the vast armies march!
It is the noise and shouting of many
    nations.
  The LORD of Heaven's Armies has
    called this army together.
5 They come from distant countries,
  from beyond the farthest horizons.
They are the LORD's weapons to carry
    out his anger.
  With them he will destroy the
    whole land.

6 Scream in terror, for the day of the
    LORD has arrived—
  the time for the Almighty to destroy.
7 Every arm is paralyzed with fear.
  Every heart melts,
8   and people are terrified.

Pangs of anguish grip them,
  like those of a woman in labor.
They look helplessly at one another,
  their faces aflame with fear.

9 For see, the day of the LORD
    is coming—
  the terrible day of his fury and
    fierce anger.
The land will be made desolate,
  and all the sinners destroyed with it.
10 The heavens will be black above them;
  the stars will give no light.
The sun will be dark when it rises,
  and the moon will provide no light.

11 "I, the LORD, will punish the world for
    its evil
  and the wicked for their sin.
I will crush the arrogance of the proud
  and humble the pride of the mighty.
12 I will make people scarcer than gold—
  more rare than the fine gold
    of Ophir.
13 For I will shake the heavens.
  The earth will move from its place
when the LORD of Heaven's Armies
    displays his wrath
  in the day of his fierce anger."

14 Everyone in Babylon will run about
    like a hunted gazelle,
  like sheep without a shepherd.
They will try to find their own people
  and flee to their own land.
15 Anyone who is captured will be cut
    down—
  run through with a sword.
16 Their little children will be dashed
    to death before their eyes.
  Their homes will be sacked, and
    their wives will be raped.

17 "Look, I will stir up the Medes against
    Babylon.
  They cannot be tempted by silver
    or bribed with gold.
18 The attacking armies will shoot down
    the young men with arrows.
  They will have no mercy on helpless
    babies
  and will show no compassion
    for children."

19 Babylon, the most glorious of kingdoms,
  the flower of Chaldean pride,

will be devastated like Sodom and
   Gomorrah
   when God destroyed them.
20 Babylon will never be inhabited again.
   It will remain empty for generation
      after generation.
Nomads will refuse to camp there,
   and shepherds will not bed down
      their sheep.
21 Desert animals will move into the
      ruined city,
   and the houses will be haunted
      by howling creatures.
Owls will live among the ruins,
   and wild goats will go there to dance.
22 Hyenas will howl in its fortresses,
   and jackals will make dens in its
      luxurious palaces.
Babylon's days are numbered;
   its time of destruction will soon
      arrive.

14:1BUT the LORD will have mercy on the descendants of Jacob. He will choose Israel as his special people once again. He will bring them back to settle once again in their own land. And people from many different nations will come and join them there and unite with the people of Israel.* 2 The nations of the world will help the LORD's people to return, and those who come to live in their land will serve them. Those who captured Israel will themselves be captured, and Israel will rule over its enemies.

3 In that wonderful day when the LORD gives his people rest from sorrow and fear, from slavery and chains, 4 you will taunt the king of Babylon. You will say,

"The mighty man has been destroyed.
   Yes, your insolence* is ended.
5 For the LORD has crushed your wicked
      power
   and broken your evil rule.
6 You struck the people with endless
      blows of rage
   and held the nations in your angry
      grip
   with unrelenting tyranny.
7 But finally the earth is at rest and quiet.
   Now it can sing again!
8 Even the trees of the forest—
   the cypress trees and the cedars
      of Lebanon—
   sing out this joyous song:

'Since you have been cut down,
   no one will come now to cut us
      down!'

9 "In the place of the dead* there is
      excitement
   over your arrival.
The spirits of world leaders and
      mighty kings long dead
   stand up to see you.
10 With one voice they all cry out,
   'Now you are as weak as we are!
11 Your might and power were buried
      with you.*
   The sound of the harp in your
      palace has ceased.
Now maggots are your sheet,
   and worms your blanket.'

12 "How you are fallen from heaven,
   O shining star, son of the morning!
You have been thrown down to the
      earth,
   you who destroyed the nations of
      the world.
13 For you said to yourself,
   'I will ascend to heaven and set my
      throne above God's stars.
I will preside on the mountain of the
      gods
   far away in the north.*
14 I will climb to the highest heavens
   and be like the Most High.'
15 Instead, you will be brought down to
      the place of the dead,
   down to its lowest depths.
16 Everyone there will stare at you and
      ask,
   'Can this be the one who shook the
      earth
   and made the kingdoms of the
      world tremble?
17 Is this the one who destroyed the
      world
   and made it into a wasteland?
Is this the king who demolished the
      world's greatest cities
   and had no mercy on his prisoners?'

18 "The kings of the nations lie in stately
      glory,
   each in his own tomb,
19 but you will be thrown out of your
      grave
   like a worthless branch.

Like a corpse trampled underfoot,
  you will be dumped into a mass
    grave
  with those killed in battle.
You will descend to the pit.
20 You will not be given a proper
      burial,
  for you have destroyed your nation
    and slaughtered your people.
  The descendants of such an evil
    person
  will never again receive honor.
21 Kill this man's children!
  Let them die because of their
    father's sins!
  They must not rise and conquer the
    earth,
  filling the world with their cities."

22 This is what the LORD of Heaven's
    Armies says:
  "I, myself, have risen against
    Babylon!
  I will destroy its children and its
    children's children,"
  says the LORD.
23 "I will make Babylon a desolate place
    of owls,
  filled with swamps and marshes.
  I will sweep the land with the broom
    of destruction.
  I, the LORD of Heaven's Armies, have
    spoken!"

24The LORD of Heaven's Armies has
sworn this oath:

  "It will all happen as I have planned.
    It will be as I have decided.
25 I will break the Assyrians when they
      are in Israel;
  I will trample them on my
    mountains.
  My people will no longer be their slaves
    nor bow down under their heavy
      loads.
26 I have a plan for the whole earth,
    a hand of judgment upon all the
      nations.
27 The LORD of Heaven's Armies has
    spoken—
  who can change his plans?
  When his hand is raised,
    who can stop him?"

28This message came to me the year
King Ahaz died:*

29 Do not rejoice, you Philistines,
    that the rod that struck you is
      broken—
  that the king who attacked you
    is dead.
  For from that snake a more poisonous
    snake will be born,
    a fiery serpent to destroy you!
30 I will feed the poor in my pasture;
    the needy will lie down in peace.

WHAT THE BIBLE SAYS

Old Testament prophets

ISAIAH 13:1 The remainder of the Old Testament consists mostly of prophetic writings. The prophets of the Old Testament were God's mouthpiece not only to Israel and Judah, but to the surrounding nations as well. They warned of the consequences of sin and promised hope for those who turned to the Lord. • At the time of this prophecy recorded in Isaiah 13 against Babylon, the nation was not even a world power—it was still part of the Assyrian Empire. Tomorrow you'll read about Moab—and learn that "the glory of Moab will be ended" (Isaiah 16:14, September 14). You'll also read in Jeremiah 48:35 (October 25) that God will "put an end to Moab." Moab ceased to exist—you'll not find it on any current maps. The point is, what God says comes true. He has complete control over the course of history. • Far more important than political history, God is in control of "salvation history." In the Old Testament prophets we read of God's plan to send the Savior, Jesus Christ, at just the right time. Even before this world fell into sin, God had a plan to redeem it, and he faithfully carried out that plan in Jesus Christ.

But as for you, I will wipe you out with
famine
and destroy the few who remain.
³¹ Wail at the gates! Weep in the cities!
Melt with fear, you Philistines!
A powerful army comes like smoke
from the north.
Each soldier rushes forward eager
to fight.

³²What should we tell the Philistine
messengers? Tell them,

"The LORD has built Jerusalem*;
its walls will give refuge to his
oppressed people."

12:6 Hebrew *Zion.* **14:1** Hebrew *the house of Jacob.* The
names "Jacob" and "Israel" are often interchanged throughout
the Old Testament, referring sometimes to the individual
patriarch and sometimes to the nation. **14:4** As in Dead
Sea Scrolls; the meaning of the Masoretic Text is uncertain.
14:9 Hebrew *Sheol;* also in 14:15. **14:11** Hebrew *were
brought down to Sheol.* **14:13** Or *on the heights of Zaphon.*
14:28 King Ahaz died in 715 B.C. **14:32** Hebrew *Zion.*

2 CORINTHIANS 13:1-13

Paul spent quite a bit of this letter evaluating his
own life and role in the Kingdom of God. Then he
invited the church of Corinth to do the same thing.
He closed his letter by asking them to look at their
own lives and their own relationship with Christ.

This is the third time I am coming to visit
you (and as the Scriptures say, "The facts
of every case must be established by the
testimony of two or three witnesses"*). ²I
have already warned those who had been
sinning when I was there on my second
visit. Now I again warn them and all others, just as I did before, that next time I
will not spare them.

³I will give you all the proof you want
that Christ speaks through me. Christ is
not weak when he deals with you; he is
powerful among you. ⁴Although he was
crucified in weakness, he now lives by the
power of God. We, too, are weak, just as
Christ was, but when we deal with you we
will be alive with him and will have God's
power.

⁵Examine yourselves to see if your faith
is genuine. Test yourselves. Surely you
know that Jesus Christ is among you*; if
not, you have failed the test of genuine
faith. ⁶As you test yourselves, I hope you
will recognize that we have not failed the
test of apostolic authority.

⁷We pray to God that you will not do
what is wrong by refusing our correction.
I hope we won't need to demonstrate our
authority when we arrive. Do the right
thing before we come—even if that makes
it look like we have failed to demonstrate
our authority. ⁸For we cannot oppose the
truth, but must always stand for the truth.
⁹We are glad to seem weak if it helps show
that you are actually strong. We pray that
you will become mature.

¹⁰I am writing this to you before I come,
hoping that I won't need to deal severely
with you when I do come. For I want to
use the authority the Lord has given me to
strengthen you, not to tear you down.

¹¹Dear brothers and sisters,* I close my
letter with these last words: Be joyful.
Grow to maturity. Encourage each other.
Live in harmony and peace. Then the God
of love and peace will be with you.

¹²Greet each other with Christian love.*
¹³All of God's people here send you their
greetings.

¹⁴*May the grace of the Lord Jesus
Christ, the love of God, and the fellowship
of the Holy Spirit be with you all.

13:1 Deut 19:15. **13:5** Or *in you.* **13:11** Greek *Brothers.*
13:12 Greek *with a sacred kiss.* **13:14** Some English
translations include verse 13 as part of verse 12, and then
verse 14 becomes verse 13.

PSALM 57:1-11

*For the choir director: A psalm of David,
regarding the time he fled from Saul and
went into the cave. To be sung to the tune
"Do Not Destroy!"*

¹ **H**ave mercy on me, O God, have mercy!
I look to you for protection.
I will hide beneath the shadow of your
wings
until the danger passes by.
² I cry out to God Most High,*
to God who will fulfill his purpose
for me.
³ He will send help from heaven to
rescue me,
disgracing those who hound me.
Interlude
My God will send forth his unfailing
love and faithfulness.

⁴ I am surrounded by fierce lions
who greedily devour human prey—

whose teeth pierce like spears and
arrows,
and whose tongues cut like swords.

5 Be exalted, O God, above the highest
heavens!
May your glory shine over all the
earth.

6 My enemies have set a trap for me.
I am weary from distress.
They have dug a deep pit in my path,
but they themselves have fallen
into it.   *Interlude*

7 My heart is confident in you, O God;
my heart is confident.
No wonder I can sing your praises!
8 Wake up, my heart!
Wake up, O lyre and harp!
I will wake the dawn with my song.
9 I will thank you, Lord, among all the
people.

I will sing your praises among the
nations.
10 For your unfailing love is as high as
the heavens.
Your faithfulness reaches to the
clouds.

11 Be exalted, O God, above the highest
heavens!
May your glory shine over all the
earth.

57:2 Hebrew *El-Elyon*.

PROVERBS 23:9-11

Don't waste your breath on fools, for they
will despise the wisest advice. ☐ Don't
cheat your neighbor by moving the ancient boundary markers; don't take the
land of defenseless orphans. For their Redeemer* is strong; he himself will bring
their charges against you.

23:11 Or *redeemer*.

ISAIAH 15:1–18:7

The people of Moab were the descendants of Abraham's nephew, Lot. You'd think they would have
cared about their "brothers" in Judah. Instead, they
were glad to hear of their misfortune. This attitude
would not go unpunished.

This message came to me concerning
Moab:

In one night the town of Ar will
be leveled,
and the city of Kir will be destroyed.
2 Your people will go to their temple in
Dibon to mourn.
They will go to their sacred shrines
to weep.
They will wail for the fate of Nebo and
Medeba,
shaving their heads in sorrow and
cutting off their beards.
3 They will wear burlap as they wander
the streets.
From every home and public square
will come the sound of wailing.

SEPTEMBER**14**

4 The people of Heshbon and Elealeh
will cry out;
their voices will be heard as far
away as Jahaz!
The bravest warriors of Moab will cry
out in utter terror.
They will be helpless with fear.

5 My heart weeps for Moab.
Its people flee to Zoar and Eglath-
shelishiyah.
Weeping, they climb the road to
Luhith.
Their cries of distress can be heard
all along the road to Horonaim.
6 Even the waters of Nimrim are
dried up!
The grassy banks are scorched.
The tender plants are gone;
nothing green remains.
7 The people grab their possessions
and carry them across the Ravine
of Willows.

8 A cry of distress echoes through the
land of Moab
  from one end to the other—
  from Eglaim to Beer-elim.
9 The stream near Dibon* runs red with
blood,
  but I am still not finished with Dibon!
Lions will hunt down the survivors—
  both those who try to escape
  and those who remain behind.

16:1 SEND lambs from Sela as tribute
to the ruler of the land.
Send them through the desert
  to the mountain of beautiful Zion.
2 The women of Moab are left like
homeless birds
  at the shallow crossings of the
  Arnon River.
3 "Help us," they cry.
  "Defend us against our enemies.
Protect us from their relentless attack.
Do not betray us now that we have
escaped.
4 Let our refugees stay among you.
  Hide them from our enemies until
  the terror is past."

When oppression and destruction
have ended
  and enemy raiders have disappeared,
5 then God will establish one of David's
descendants as king.
  He will rule with mercy and truth.
  He will always do what is just
  and be eager to do what is right.

6 We have heard about proud Moab—
about its pride and arrogance and
rage.
  But all that boasting has
  disappeared.
7 The entire land of Moab weeps.
  Yes, everyone in Moab mourns
  for the cakes of raisins from Kir-
  hareseth.
  They are all gone now.
8 The farms of Heshbon are abandoned;
the vineyards at Sibmah are
deserted.
The rulers of the nations have broken
down Moab—
  that beautiful grapevine.
Its tendrils spread north as far as the
town of Jazer

and trailed eastward into the
wilderness.
Its shoots reached so far west
  that they crossed over the Dead
  Sea.*

9 So now I weep for Jazer and the
vineyards of Sibmah;
  my tears will flow for Heshbon and
  Elealeh.
There are no more shouts of joy
  over your summer fruits and harvest.
10 Gone now is the gladness,
  gone the joy of harvest.
There will be no singing in the
vineyards,
  no more happy shouts,
  no treading of grapes in the
  winepresses.
  I have ended all their harvest joys.
11 My heart's cry for Moab is like
a lament on a harp.
  I am filled with anguish for
  Kir-hareseth.*
12 The people of Moab will worship
at their pagan shrines,
  but it will do them no good.
They will cry to the gods in their
temples,
  but no one will be able to save them.

13 The LORD has already said these
things about Moab in the past. 14But now
the LORD says, "Within three years, counting each day,* the glory of Moab will be
ended. From its great population, only a
few of its people will be left alive."

17:1 THIS message came to me concerning
Damascus:

  "Look, the city of Damascus will
  disappear!
  It will become a heap of ruins.
2 The towns of Aroer will be deserted.
  Flocks will graze in the streets and
  lie down undisturbed,
  with no one to chase them away.
3 The fortified towns of Israel* will also
be destroyed,
  and the royal power of Damascus
  will end.
All that remains of Syria*
  will share the fate of Israel's
  departed glory,"

declares the LORD of Heaven's Armies.

4 "In that day Israel's* glory will grow dim;
    its robust body will waste away.
5 The whole land will look like a grainfield
    after the harvesters have gathered the grain.
It will be desolate,
    like the fields in the valley of Rephaim after the harvest.
6 Only a few of its people will be left,
    like stray olives left on a tree after the harvest.
Only two or three remain in the highest branches,
    four or five scattered here and there on the limbs,"
declares the LORD, the God of Israel.

7 Then at last the people will look to their Creator
    and turn their eyes to the Holy One of Israel.
8 They will no longer look to their idols for help
    or worship what their own hands have made.
They will never again bow down to their Asherah poles

or worship at the pagan shrines they have built.
9 Their largest cities will be like a deserted forest,
    like the land the Hivites and Amorites abandoned*
when the Israelites came here so long ago.
It will be utterly desolate.
10 Why? Because you have turned from the God who can save you.
    You have forgotten the Rock who can hide you.
So you may plant the finest grapevines and import the most expensive seedlings.
11 They may sprout on the day you set them out;
    yes, they may blossom on the very morning you plant them,
but you will never pick any grapes from them.
    Your only harvest will be a load of grief and unrelieved pain.

12 Listen! The armies of many nations roar like the roaring of the sea.
Hear the thunder of the mighty forces as they rush forward like thundering waves.
13 But though they thunder like breakers on a beach,

HOW WE LIVE

Standing firm in our beliefs

GALATIANS 1:6-7 Some false teachers were wandering around Galatia teaching that salvation required faith *plus* certain Old Testament practices. At issue were the very different backgrounds of the Jewish and Gentile believers. As more and more Gentiles became believers, false teachers arose who said that the Gentiles had to be circumcised and obey Old Testament laws. In other words, they had to become Jews before they could become Christians. This confused the Galatian believers; it was not what Paul had taught them. • There will always be people who twist the truth and pervert the Good News. They may do so out of misunderstanding of the Bible, or they may be uncomfortable with the truth as it stands in Scripture. Make sure the church you attend, Bible study group you belong to, and the books you read are all committed to understanding Scripture rightly and holding firm to its truth. • Paul warned that Satan masquerades as an angel of light (2 Corinthians 11:14-15, September 9). Often lies don't look like lies; they sound good, tolerant, and politically correct—but that doesn't make them true. The only way to beware of compromise is to always use God's Word as your standard.

God will silence them, and they will
run away.
They will flee like chaff scattered by
the wind,
like a tumbleweed whirling before
a storm.

14 In the evening Israel waits in terror,
but by dawn its enemies are dead.
This is the just reward of those who
plunder us,
a fitting end for those who
destroy us.

18:1 LISTEN, Ethiopia*—land of fluttering
sails*
that lies at the headwaters of
the Nile,
2 that sends ambassadors in swift boats
down the river.

Go, swift messengers!
Take a message to a tall, smooth-
skinned people,
who are feared far and wide
for their conquests and destruction,
and whose land is divided by rivers.

3 All you people of the world,
everyone who lives on the earth—
when I raise my battle flag on the
mountain, look!
When I blow the ram's horn, listen!
4 For the LORD has told me this:
"I will watch quietly from my dwelling
place—
as quietly as the heat rises on a
summer day,
or as the morning dew forms
during the harvest."
5 Even before you begin your attack,
while your plans are ripening like
grapes,
the LORD will cut off your new growth
with pruning shears.
He will snip off and discard your
spreading branches.
6 Your mighty army will be left dead
in the fields
for the mountain vultures and wild
animals.
The vultures will tear at the corpses
all summer.
The wild animals will gnaw at the
bones all winter.

7 At that time the LORD of Heaven's
Armies will receive gifts
from this land divided by rivers,
from this tall, smooth-skinned people,
who are feared far and wide for
their conquests and destruction.
They will bring the gifts to Jerusalem,*
where the LORD of Heaven's Armies
dwells.

15:9 As in Dead Sea Scrolls, some Greek manuscripts, and
Latin Vulgate; Masoretic Text reads *Dimon;* also in 15:9b.
16:8 Hebrew *the sea.*   16:11 Hebrew *Kir-heres,* a variant
spelling of Kir-haraseth.   16:14 Hebrew *Within three
years, as a servant bound by contract would count them.*
17:3a Hebrew *of Ephraim,* referring to the northern kingdom
of Israel.   17:3b Hebrew *Aram.*   17:4 Hebrew *Jacob's.* See
note on 14:1.   17:9 As in Greek version; Hebrew reads *like
places of the wood and the highest bough.*   18:1a Hebrew
Cush.   18:1b Or *land of many locusts;* Hebrew reads *land
of whirring wings.*   18:7 Hebrew *to Mount Zion.*

GALATIANS 1:1-24

Galatia was a region northwest of Israel. On Paul's
first missionary journey, he traveled through Galatia
establishing churches there. The book of Galatians
is a letter Paul wrote back to those churches to
strengthen their faith and refute false teachers.

This letter is from Paul, an apostle. I was
not appointed by any group of people or
any human authority, but by Jesus Christ
himself and by God the Father, who raised
Jesus from the dead.
2 All the brothers and sisters* here join
me in sending this letter to the churches
of Galatia.
3 May God our Father and the Lord Jesus
Christ* give you grace and peace. 4 Jesus
gave his life for our sins, just as God our
Father planned, in order to rescue us from
this evil world in which we live. 5 All glory
to God forever and ever! Amen.
6 I am shocked that you are turning
away so soon from God, who called you to
himself through the loving mercy of
Christ.* You are following a different way
that pretends to be the Good News 7 but is
not the Good News at all. You are being
fooled by those who deliberately twist the
truth concerning Christ.
8 Let God's curse fall on anyone, including us or even an angel from heaven, who
preaches a different kind of Good News
than the one we preached to you. 9 I say
again what we have said before: If anyone
preaches any other Good News than the

one you welcomed, let that person be cursed.

[10]Obviously, I'm not trying to win the approval of people, but of God. If pleasing people were my goal, I would not be Christ's servant.

[11]Dear brothers and sisters, I want you to understand that the gospel message I preach is not based on mere human reasoning. [12]I received my message from no human source, and no one taught me. Instead, I received it by direct revelation from Jesus Christ.*

[13]You know what I was like when I followed the Jewish religion—how I violently persecuted God's church. I did my best to destroy it. [14]I was far ahead of my fellow Jews in my zeal for the traditions of my ancestors.

[15]But even before I was born, God chose me and called me by his marvelous grace. Then it pleased him [16]to reveal his Son to me* so that I would proclaim the Good News about Jesus to the Gentiles.

When this happened, I did not rush out to consult with any human being.* [17]Nor did I go up to Jerusalem to consult with those who were apostles before I was. Instead, I went away into Arabia, and later I returned to the city of Damascus.

[18]Then three years later I went to Jerusalem to get to know Peter,* and I stayed with him for fifteen days. [19]The only other apostle I met at that time was James, the Lord's brother. [20]I declare before God that what I am writing to you is not a lie.

[21]After that visit I went north into the provinces of Syria and Cilicia. [22]And still the Christians in the churches in Judea didn't know me personally. [23]All they knew was that people were saying, "The one who used to persecute us is now preaching the very faith he tried to destroy!" [24]And they praised God because of me.

1:2 Greek *brothers;* also in 1:11.　1:3 Some manuscripts read *God the Father and our Lord Jesus Christ.*　1:6 Some manuscripts read *through loving mercy.*　1:12 Or *by the revelation of Jesus Christ.*　1:16a Or *in me.*　1:16b Greek *with flesh and blood.*　1:18 Greek *Cephas.*

PSALM 58:1-11

For the choir director: A psalm of David, to be sung to the tune "Do Not Destroy!"

[1] **J**ustice—do you rulers* know the
　　meaning of the word?
　　Do you judge the people fairly?
[2] No! You plot injustice in your hearts.
　　You spread violence throughout
　　　the land.
[3] These wicked people are born sinners;
　　even from birth they have lied and
　　　gone their own way.
[4] They spit venom like deadly snakes;
　　they are like cobras that refuse to
　　　listen,
[5] ignoring the tunes of the snake
　　　charmers,
　　no matter how skillfully they play.

[6] Break off their fangs, O God!
　　Smash the jaws of these lions,
　　　O Lord!
[7] May they disappear like water into
　　　thirsty ground.
　　Make their weapons useless in their
　　　hands.*
[8] May they be like snails that dissolve
　　　into slime,
　　like a stillborn child who will never
　　　see the sun.
[9] God will sweep them away, both young
　　　and old,
　　faster than a pot heats over burning
　　　thorns.

[10] The godly will rejoice when they see
　　　injustice avenged.
　　They will wash their feet in the
　　　blood of the wicked.
[11] Then at last everyone will say,
　　"There truly is a reward for those
　　　who live for God;
　　surely there is a God who judges
　　　justly here on earth."

58:1 Or *you gods.*　**58:7** Or *Let them be trodden down and wither like grass.* The meaning of the Hebrew is uncertain.

PROVERBS 23:12

Commit yourself to instruction; listen carefully to words of knowledge.

SEPTEMBER 15

ISAIAH 19:1–21:17

The people of Edom were the descendants of Esau. The people of Judah were descendants of Jacob. Jacob had tricked his brother Esau out of birthright and inheritance. The enmity between Esau and Jacob continued in the nations descended from them.

This message came to me [Isaiah] concerning Egypt:

Look! The LORD is advancing against
Egypt,
riding on a swift cloud.
The idols of Egypt tremble.
The hearts of the Egyptians melt
with fear.

2 "I will make Egyptian fight against
Egyptian—
brother against brother,
neighbor against neighbor,
city against city,
province against province.
3 The Egyptians will lose heart,
and I will confuse their plans.
They will plead with their idols
for wisdom
and call on spirits, mediums, and
those who consult the spirits of
the dead.
4 I will hand Egypt over
to a hard, cruel master.
A fierce king will rule them,"
says the Lord, the LORD of Heaven's
Armies.

5 The waters of the Nile will fail to rise
and flood the fields.
The riverbed will be parched
and dry.
6 The canals of the Nile will dry up,
and the streams of Egypt will stink
with rotting reeds and rushes.
7 All the greenery along the riverbank
and all the crops along the river
will dry up and blow away.
8 The fishermen will lament for lack
of work.
Those who cast hooks into the Nile
will groan,
and those who use nets will lose
heart.

9 There will be no flax for the
harvesters,
no thread for the weavers.
10 They will be in despair,
and all the workers will be sick
at heart.

11 What fools are the officials of Zoan!
Their best counsel to the king of
Egypt is stupid and wrong.
Will they still boast to Pharaoh of their
wisdom?
Will they dare brag about all their
wise ancestors?
12 Where are your wise counselors,
Pharaoh?
Let them tell you what God plans,
what the LORD of Heaven's Armies
is going to do to Egypt.
13 The officials of Zoan are fools,
and the officials of Memphis* are
deluded.
The leaders of the people
have led Egypt astray.
14 The LORD has sent a spirit of
foolishness on them,
so all their suggestions are wrong.
They cause Egypt to stagger
like a drunk in his vomit.
15 There is nothing Egypt can do.
All are helpless—
the head and the tail,
the noble palm branch and the
lowly reed.

16 In that day the Egyptians will be as weak as women. They will cower in fear beneath the upraised fist of the LORD of Heaven's Armies. 17 Just to speak the name of Israel will terrorize them, for the LORD of Heaven's Armies has laid out his plans against them.

18 In that day five of Egypt's cities will follow the LORD of Heaven's Armies. They will even begin to speak Hebrew, the language of Canaan. One of these cities will be Heliopolis, the City of the Sun.* 19 In that day there will be an altar to the LORD in the heart of Egypt, and there will be a monument to the LORD at its border. 20 It will be a sign and a witness that the

LORD of Heaven's Armies is worshiped in the land of Egypt. When the people cry to the LORD for help against those who oppress them, he will send them a savior who will rescue them. ²¹The LORD will make himself known to the Egyptians. Yes, they will know the LORD and will give their sacrifices and offerings to him. They will make a vow to the LORD and will keep it. ²²The LORD will strike Egypt, and then he will bring healing. For the Egyptians will turn to the LORD, and he will listen to their pleas and heal them.

²³In that day Egypt and Assyria will be connected by a highway. The Egyptians and Assyrians will move freely between their lands, and they will both worship God. ²⁴And Israel will be their ally. The three will be together, and Israel will be a blessing to them. ²⁵For the LORD of Heaven's Armies will say, "Blessed be Egypt, my people. Blessed be Assyria, the land I have made. Blessed be Israel, my special possession!"

²⁰:¹IN the year when King Sargon of Assyria sent his commander in chief to capture the Philistine city of Ashdod,* ²the LORD told Isaiah son of Amoz, "Take off the burlap you have been wearing, and remove your sandals." Isaiah did as he was told and walked around naked and barefoot.

³Then the LORD said, "My servant Isaiah has been walking around naked and barefoot for the last three years. This is a sign—a symbol of the terrible troubles I will bring upon Egypt and Ethiopia.* ⁴For the king of Assyria will take away the Egyptians and Ethiopians* as prisoners. He will make them walk naked and barefoot, both young and old, their buttocks bared, to the shame of Egypt. ⁵Then the Philistines will be thrown into panic, for they counted on the power of Ethiopia and boasted of their allies in Egypt! ⁶They will say, 'If this can happen to Egypt, what chance do we have? We were counting on Egypt to protect us from the king of Assyria.'"

²¹:¹THIS message came to me concerning Babylon—the desert by the sea*:

Disaster is roaring down on you from the desert,

like a whirlwind sweeping in from the Negev.
² I see a terrifying vision:
    I see the betrayer betraying,
    the destroyer destroying.
Go ahead, you Elamites and Medes,
    attack and lay siege.
I will make an end to all the groaning Babylon caused.
³ My stomach aches and burns with pain.
    Sharp pangs of anguish are upon me,
    like those of a woman in labor.
I grow faint when I hear what God is planning;
    I am too afraid to look.
⁴ My mind reels and my heart races.
    I longed for evening to come,
    but now I am terrified of the dark.

⁵ Look! They are preparing a great feast.
    They are spreading rugs for people to sit on.
Everyone is eating and drinking.
But quick! Grab your shields and prepare for battle.
    You are being attacked!

⁶ Meanwhile, the Lord said to me,
    "Put a watchman on the city wall.
    Let him shout out what he sees.
⁷ He should look for chariots
    drawn by pairs of horses,
and for riders on donkeys and camels.
    Let the watchman be fully alert."

⁸ Then the watchman* called out,
    "Day after day I have stood on the watchtower, my lord.
    Night after night I have remained at my post.
⁹ Now at last—look!
Here comes a man in a chariot
    with a pair of horses!"
Then the watchman said,
    "Babylon is fallen, fallen!
All the idols of Babylon
    lie broken on the ground!"
¹⁰ O my people, threshed and winnowed,
    I have told you everything the LORD of Heaven's Armies has said,
    everything the God of Israel has told me.

¹¹This message came to me concerning Edom*:

Someone from Edom* keeps calling to me,
"Watchman, how much longer until morning?
When will the night be over?"
¹² The watchman replies,
"Morning is coming, but night will soon return.
If you wish to ask again, then come back and ask."

¹³This message came to me concerning Arabia:

O caravans from Dedan,
hide in the deserts of Arabia.
¹⁴ O people of Tema,
bring water to these thirsty people,
food to these weary refugees.
¹⁵ They have fled from the sword,
from the drawn sword,
from the bent bow
and the terrors of battle.

¹⁶The Lord said to me, "Within a year, counting each day,* all the glory of Kedar will come to an end. ¹⁷Only a few of its courageous archers will survive. I, the LORD, the God of Israel, have spoken!"

19:13 Hebrew *Noph.* 19:18 Or *will be the City of Destruction.* 20:1 Ashdod was captured by Assyria in 711 B.C. 20:3 Hebrew *Cush;* also in 20:5. 20:4 Hebrew *Cushites.* 21:1 Hebrew *concerning the desert by the sea.* 21:8 As in Dead Sea Scrolls and Syriac version; Masoretic Text reads a *lion.* 21:11a Hebrew *Dumah,* which means "silence" or "stillness." It is a wordplay on the word *Edom.* 21:11b Hebrew *Seir,* another name for Edom. 21:16 Hebrew *Within a year, as a servant bound by contract would count it.* Some ancient manuscripts read *Within three years,* as in 16:14.

GALATIANS 2:1-16
One of the key issues of the early Christian church was whether a person had to become a Jew first in order to become a Christian. In addressing this issue Paul had to confront Peter, who acted hypocritically under Jewish peer pressure.

Then fourteen years later I [Paul] went back to Jerusalem again, this time with Barnabas; and Titus came along, too. ²I went there because God revealed to me that I should go. While I was there I met privately with those considered to be leaders of the church and shared with them the message I had been preaching

to the Gentiles. I wanted to make sure that we were in agreement, for fear that all my efforts had been wasted and I was running the race for nothing. ³And they supported me and did not even demand that my companion Titus be circumcised, though he was a Gentile.*

⁴Even that question came up only because of some so-called Christians there—false ones, really*—who were secretly brought in. They sneaked in to spy on us and take away the freedom we have in Christ Jesus. They wanted to enslave us and force us to follow their Jewish regulations. ⁵But we refused to give in to them for a single moment. We wanted to preserve the truth of the gospel message for you.

⁶And the leaders of the church had nothing to add to what I was preaching. (By the way, their reputation as great leaders made no difference to me, for God has no favorites.) ⁷Instead, they saw that God had given me the responsibility of preaching the gospel to the Gentiles, just as he had given Peter the responsibility of preaching to the Jews. ⁸For the same God who worked through Peter as the apostle to the Jews also worked through me as the apostle to the Gentiles.

⁹In fact, James, Peter,* and John, who were known as pillars of the church, recognized the gift God had given me, and they accepted Barnabas and me as their co-workers. They encouraged us to keep preaching to the Gentiles, while they continued their work with the Jews. ¹⁰Their only suggestion was that we keep on helping the poor, which I have always been eager to do.

¹¹But when Peter came to Antioch, I had to oppose him to his face, for what he did was very wrong. ¹²When he first arrived, he ate with the Gentile Christians, who were not circumcised. But afterward, when some friends of James came, Peter wouldn't eat with the Gentiles anymore. He was afraid of criticism from these people who insisted on the necessity of circumcision. ¹³As a result, other Jewish Christians followed Peter's hypocrisy, and even Barnabas was led astray by their hypocrisy. ¹⁴When I saw that they were not follow-

ing the truth of the gospel message, I said to Peter in front of all the others, "Since you, a Jew by birth, have discarded the Jewish laws and are living like a Gentile, why are you now trying to make these Gentiles follow the Jewish traditions?

15"You and I are Jews by birth, not 'sinners' like the Gentiles. 16Yet we know that a person is made right with God by faith in Jesus Christ, not by obeying the law. And we have believed in Christ Jesus, so that we might be made right with God because of our faith in Christ, not because we have obeyed the law. For no one will ever be made right with God by obeying the law."*

2:3 Greek *a Greek.* 2:4 Greek *some false brothers.*
2:9 Greek *Cephas;* also in 2:11, 14. 2:16 Some translators hold that the quotation extends through verse 14; others through verse 16; and still others through verse 21.

PSALM 59:1-17
For the choir director: A psalm of David, regarding the time Saul sent soldiers to watch David's house in order to kill him. To be sung to the tune "Do Not Destroy!"

1 **R**escue me from my enemies, O God.
　　Protect me from those who have
　　　come to destroy me.
2 Rescue me from these criminals;
　　save me from these murderers.
3 They have set an ambush for me.

Fierce enemies are out there
　　waiting, LORD,
though I have not sinned or
　　offended them.
4 I have done nothing wrong,
　　yet they prepare to attack me.
Wake up! See what is happening
　　and help me!
5 O LORD God of Heaven's Armies, the
　　God of Israel,
wake up and punish those hostile
　　nations.
Show no mercy to wicked traitors.
　　　　　　　　　　　　Interlude

6 They come out at night,
　　snarling like vicious dogs
　　as they prowl the streets.
7 Listen to the filth that comes from
　　their mouths;
their words cut like swords.
"After all, who can hear us?" they
　　sneer.
8 But LORD, you laugh at them.
　　You scoff at all the hostile nations.
9 You are my strength; I wait for you to
　　rescue me,
for you, O God, are my fortress.
10 In his unfailing love, my God will stand
　　with me.
He will let me look down in
　　triumph on all my enemies.

Standing firm in our beliefs

GALATIANS 2:3-5, 11-14 What does it take to be a Christian? Do you have to dress a certain way or have a particular haircut? Listen to Christian music only? Read only books by Christian authors? • Some churches today have lists of man-made standards like these. Those who insist on such standards may be morally upright people, but if they make these standards requirements for being "saved," then they are twisting the truth. They are trying to take away the freedom believers have in Christ. • The temptation to equate cultural preferences with requirements for salvation can be a big one. Paul had to confront the apostle Peter himself for acting one way with the Gentile believers and another way with the Jewish believers. Paul called that hypocrisy. • Always remember that believing in Jesus Christ, not following man-made regulations, is the only way to be saved. Saving faith will result in a changed life. But those who profess to be believers must show their faith by heart-level obedience to what God truly demands, not by outward conformity to man-made rules.

¹¹ Don't kill them, for my people soon
    forget such lessons;
  stagger them with your power, and
    bring them to their knees,
  O Lord our shield.
¹² Because of the sinful things they say,
    because of the evil that is on
      their lips,
  let them be captured by their pride,
    their curses, and their lies.
¹³ Destroy them in your anger!
    Wipe them out completely!
  Then the whole world will know
    that God reigns in Israel.*

Interlude

¹⁴ My enemies come out at night,
    snarling like vicious dogs
    as they prowl the streets.
¹⁵ They scavenge for food
    but go to sleep unsatisfied.*

¹⁶ But as for me, I will sing about
    your power.
  Each morning I will sing with joy
    about your unfailing love.
  For you have been my refuge,
    a place of safety when I am
      in distress.
¹⁷ O my Strength, to you I sing praises,
    for you, O God, are my refuge,
  the God who shows me unfailing
    love.

59:13 Hebrew *in Jacob*. See note on 44:4.   **59:15** Or *and growl if they don't get enough.*

PROVERBS 23:13-14
Don't fail to discipline your children.
They won't die if you spank them. Physical discipline may well save them from
death.*

23:14 Hebrew *from Sheol.*

SEPTEMBER**16**

ISAIAH 22:1–24:23
Isaiah described a scene that was spiraling downward toward destruction. Jerusalem was the most
sacred place for the Jews. To think of Jerusalem in
a state of devastation was the same as thinking of
the nation in defeat.

This message came to me [Isaiah] concerning Jerusalem—the Valley of Vision*:

  What is happening?
    Why is everyone running to the
      rooftops?
² The whole city is in a terrible uproar.
    What do I see in this reveling city?
  Bodies are lying everywhere,
    killed not in battle but by famine
      and disease.
³ All your leaders have fled.
    They surrendered without
      resistance.
  The people tried to slip away,
    but they were captured, too.
⁴ That's why I said, "Leave me alone
    to weep;
  do not try to comfort me.

  Let me cry for my people
    as I watch them being destroyed."

⁵ Oh, what a day of crushing defeat!
    What a day of confusion and terror
  brought by the Lord, the LORD of
      Heaven's Armies,
    upon the Valley of Vision!
  The walls of Jerusalem have been
      broken,
    and cries of death echo from the
      mountainsides.
⁶ Elamites are the archers,
    with their chariots and charioteers.
  The men of Kir hold up the shields.
⁷ Chariots fill your beautiful valleys,
    and charioteers storm your gates.
⁸ Judah's defenses have been stripped
      away.
  You run to the armory* for your
      weapons.
⁹ You inspect the breaks in the walls
    of Jerusalem.*
  You store up water in the lower
      pool.

¹⁰ You survey the houses and tear
some down
for stone to strengthen the walls.
¹¹ Between the city walls, you build
a reservoir
for water from the old pool.
But you never ask for help from the
One who did all this.
You never considered the One who
planned this long ago.

¹² At that time the Lord, the Lᴏʀᴅ of
Heaven's Armies,
called you to weep and mourn.
He told you to shave your heads in
sorrow for your sins
and to wear clothes of burlap to
show your remorse.
¹³ But instead, you dance and play;
you slaughter cattle and kill sheep.
You feast on meat and drink wine.
You say, "Let's feast and drink,
for tomorrow we die!"

¹⁴The Lᴏʀᴅ of Heaven's Armies has re-
vealed this to me: "Till the day you die, you
will never be forgiven for this sin." That is
the judgment of the Lord, the Lᴏʀᴅ of
Heaven's Armies.

¹⁵This is what the Lord, the Lᴏʀᴅ of
Heaven's Armies, said to me: "Confront
Shebna, the palace administrator, and
give him this message:

¹⁶ "Who do you think you are,
and what are you doing here,
building a beautiful tomb for
yourself—
a monument high up in the rock?
¹⁷ For the Lᴏʀᴅ is about to hurl you away,
mighty man.
He is going to grab you,
¹⁸ crumple you into a ball,
and toss you away into a distant,
barren land.
There you will die,
and your glorious chariots will be
broken and useless.
You are a disgrace to your master!

¹⁹"Yes, I will drive you out of office,"
says the Lᴏʀᴅ. "I will pull you down from
your high position. ²⁰And then I will call
my servant Eliakim son of Hilkiah to replace you. ²¹I will dress him in your royal
robes and will give him your title and your
authority. And he will be a father to the
people of Jerusalem and Judah. ²²I will
give him the key to the house of David—
the highest position in the royal court.
When he opens doors, no one will be able
to close them; when he closes doors, no
one will be able to open them. ²³He will
bring honor to his family name, for I will
drive him firmly in place like a nail in the
wall. ²⁴They will give him great responsibility, and he will bring honor to even the
lowliest members of his family.*"

²⁵But the Lᴏʀᴅ of Heaven's Armies also
says: "The time will come when I will pull
out the nail that seemed so firm. It will
come out and fall to the ground. Everything it supports will fall with it. I, the
Lᴏʀᴅ, have spoken!"

^{23:1}Tʜɪs message came to me concerning
Tyre:

Weep, O ships of Tarshish,
for the harbor and houses of Tyre
are gone!
The rumors you heard in Cyprus*
are all true.
² Mourn in silence, you people of the
coast
and you merchants of Sidon.
Your traders crossed the sea,
³   sailing over deep waters.
They brought you grain from Egypt*
and harvests from along the Nile.
You were the marketplace of the world.

⁴ But now you are put to shame, city
of Sidon,
for Tyre, the fortress of the sea, says,
"Now I am childless;
I have no sons or daughters."
⁵ When Egypt hears the news about
Tyre,
there will be great sorrow.
⁶ Send word now to Tarshish!
Wail, you people who live in distant
lands!
⁷ Is this silent ruin all that is left of your
once joyous city?
What a long history was yours!
Think of all the colonists you sent
to distant places.
⁸ Who has brought this disaster on Tyre,
that great creator of kingdoms?

Her traders were all princes,
her merchants were nobles.

9 The LORD of Heaven's Armies has done it
to destroy your pride
and bring low all earth's nobility.

10 Come, people of Tarshish,
sweep over the land like the flooding Nile,
for Tyre is defenseless.*

11 The LORD held out his hand over the sea
and shook the kingdoms of the earth.
He has spoken out against Phoenicia,*
ordering that her fortresses be destroyed.

12 He says, "Never again will you rejoice,
O daughter of Sidon, for you have been crushed.
Even if you flee to Cyprus,
you will find no rest."

13 Look at the land of Babylonia*—
the people of that land are gone!
The Assyrians have handed Babylon over
to the wild animals of the desert.
They have built siege ramps against its walls,
torn down its palaces,
and turned it to a heap of rubble.

14 Wail, O ships of Tarshish,
for your harbor is destroyed!

15For seventy years, the length of a king's life, Tyre will be forgotten. But then the city will come back to life as in the song about the prostitute:

16 Take a harp and walk the streets,
you forgotten harlot.
Make sweet melody and sing
your songs
so you will be remembered again.

17Yes, after seventy years the LORD will revive Tyre. But she will be no different than she was before. She will again be a prostitute to all kingdoms around the world. 18But in the end her profits will be given to the LORD. Her wealth will not be hoarded but will provide good food and fine clothing for the LORD's priests.

24:1LOOK! The LORD is about to destroy the earth
and make it a vast wasteland.
He devastates the surface of the earth
and scatters the people.

2 Priests and laypeople,
servants and masters,
maids and mistresses,
buyers and sellers,
lenders and borrowers,
bankers and debtors—none will be spared.

3 The earth will be completely emptied and looted.
The LORD has spoken!

4 The earth mourns and dries up,
and the crops waste away and wither.
Even the greatest people on earth waste away.

5 The earth suffers for the sins of its people,
for they have twisted God's instructions,
violated his laws,
and broken his everlasting covenant.

6 Therefore, a curse consumes the earth.
Its people must pay the price for their sin.
They are destroyed by fire,
and only a few are left alive.

7 The grapevines waste away,
and there is no new wine.
All the merrymakers sigh and mourn.

8 The cheerful sound of tambourines is stilled;
the happy cries of celebration are heard no more.
The melodious chords of the harp are silent.

9 Gone are the joys of wine and song;
alcoholic drink turns bitter in the mouth.

10 The city writhes in chaos;
every home is locked to keep out intruders.

11 Mobs gather in the streets, crying out for wine.
Joy has turned to gloom.
Gladness has been banished from the land.

12 The city is left in ruins,
its gates battered down.

13 Throughout the earth the story
    is the same—
    only a remnant is left,
    like the stray olives left on the tree
    or the few grapes left on the vine
    after harvest.

14 But all who are left shout and sing
    for joy.
    Those in the west praise the LORD's
    majesty.
15 In eastern lands, give glory to
    the LORD.
    In the lands beyond the sea, praise
    the name of the LORD, the God
    of Israel.
16 We hear songs of praise from the ends
    of the earth,
    songs that give glory to the
    Righteous One!

But my heart is heavy with grief.
    Weep for me, for I wither away.
Deceit still prevails,
    and treachery is everywhere.
17 Terror and traps and snares will be
    your lot,
    you people of the earth.
18 Those who flee in terror will fall into
    a trap,
    and those who escape the trap will
    be caught in a snare.

Destruction falls like rain from the
    heavens;

the foundations of the earth
    shake.
19 The earth has broken up.
    It has utterly collapsed;
    it is violently shaken.
20 The earth staggers like a drunk.
    It trembles like a tent in a storm.
It falls and will not rise again,
    for the guilt of its rebellion is very
    heavy.

21 In that day the LORD will punish the
    gods in the heavens
    and the proud rulers of the nations
    on earth.
22 They will be rounded up and put
    in prison.
    They will be shut up in prison
    and will finally be punished.
23 Then the glory of the moon will wane,
    and the brightness of the sun will
    fade,
for the LORD of Heaven's Armies will
    rule on Mount Zion.
He will rule in great glory in
    Jerusalem,
    in the sight of all the leaders of his
    people.

22:1 Hebrew *concerning the Valley of Vision.*   **22:8** Hebrew
to the House of the Forest; see 1 Kgs 7:2-5.   **22:9** Hebrew
the city of David.   **22:24** Hebrew *They will hang on him all
the glory of his father's house: its offspring and offshoots, all
its lesser vessels, from the bowls to all the jars.*   **23:1** Hebrew
Kittim; also in 23:12.   **23:3** Hebrew *from Shihor,* a branch
of the Nile River.   **23:10** The meaning of the Hebrew in this
verse is uncertain.   **23:11** Hebrew *Canaan.*   **23:13** Or
Chaldea.

HOW WE LIVE

Relying on God's power

GALATIANS 2:20 Salvation is a life and death event. When you trusted in
Christ, you died. And yet you live—in fact you are more alive now than
you ever were before. How so? Your old self, your old nature, was crucified with Christ when you believed. God looks at you as if you died with
Christ. Because your sins died with him, you are no longer condemned.
Now Christ is living in and through you. You have become one with Christ.
You share the relationship he has with the Father. • These are wonderful
truths. But what about ongoing sin? How is that possible? Your old nature
is dead in the sense that you are no longer a slave to it. It will at times
pull itself out of the grave and try to regain control. You may occasionally
fold under the pressure. But that doesn't change the reality of who you
are in Christ. It doesn't change the truth of your new life that is a result
of him living in you. Each day we must put to death the desires of the old
self and rely on Christ's life to transform us.

GALATIANS 2:17-3:9

The father of all Jews was Abraham, a man who was considered righteous by God based on his belief in God. That was centuries before Moses wrote the Old Testament law, proving that righteousness comes through faith, not the law.

But suppose we [Paul and other believers] seek to be made right with God through faith in Christ and then we are found guilty because we have abandoned the law. Would that mean Christ has led us into sin? Absolutely not! ¹⁸Rather, I am a sinner if I rebuild the old system of law I already tore down. ¹⁹For when I tried to keep the law, it condemned me. So I died to the law—I stopped trying to meet all its requirements—so that I might live for God. ²⁰My old self has been crucified with Christ.* It is no longer I who live, but Christ lives in me. So I live in this earthly body by trusting in the Son of God, who loved me and gave himself for me. ²¹I do not treat the grace of God as meaningless. For if keeping the law could make us right with God, then there was no need for Christ to die.

³:¹OH, foolish Galatians! Who has cast an evil spell on you? For the meaning of Jesus Christ's death was made as clear to you as if you had seen a picture of his death on the cross. ²Let me ask you this one question: Did you receive the Holy Spirit by obeying the law of Moses? Of course not! You received the Spirit because you believed the message you heard about Christ. ³How foolish can you be? After starting your Christian lives in the Spirit, why are you now trying to become perfect by your own human effort? ⁴Have you experienced* so much for nothing? Surely it was not in vain, was it?

⁵I ask you again, does God give you the Holy Spirit and work miracles among you because you obey the law? Of course not! It is because you believe the message you heard about Christ.

⁶In the same way, "Abraham believed God, and God counted him as righteous because of his faith."* ⁷The real children of Abraham, then, are those who put their faith in God.

⁸What's more, the Scriptures looked forward to this time when God would declare the Gentiles to be righteous because of their faith. God proclaimed this good news to Abraham long ago when he said, "All nations will be blessed through you."* ⁹So all who put their faith in Christ share the same blessing Abraham received because of his faith.

2:20 Some English translations put this sentence in verse 19.
3:4 Or *Have you suffered.*   3:6 Gen 15:6.   3:8 Gen 12:3;
18:18; 22:18.

PSALM 60:1-12

For the choir director: A psalm of David useful for teaching, regarding the time David fought Aram-naharaim and Aram-zobah, and Joab returned and killed 12,000 Edomites in the Valley of Salt. To be sung to the tune "Lily of the Testimony."

¹ **Y**ou have rejected us, O God, and
    broken our defenses.
    You have been angry with us; now
    restore us to your favor.
² You have shaken our land and split
    it open.
    Seal the cracks, for the land trembles.
³ You have been very hard on us,
    making us drink wine that sent
    us reeling.
⁴ But you have raised a banner for those
    who fear you—
    a rallying point in the face of attack.
                        Interlude

⁵ Now rescue your beloved people.
    Answer and save us by your power.
⁶ God has promised this by his
    holiness*:
    "I will divide up Shechem with joy.
    I will measure out the valley of
    Succoth.
⁷ Gilead is mine,
    and Manasseh, too.
    Ephraim, my helmet, will produce
    my warriors,
    and Judah, my scepter, will produce
    my kings.
⁸ But Moab, my washbasin, will become
    my servant,
    and I will wipe my feet on Edom
    and shout in triumph over Philistia."
⁹ Who will bring me into the fortified
    city?

Who will bring me victory over
Edom?
¹⁰ Have you rejected us, O God?
Will you no longer march with
our armies?
¹¹ Oh, please help us against our enemies,
for all human help is useless.
¹² With God's help we will do mighty
things,

for he will trample down
our foes.

60:6 Or *in his sanctuary.*

PROVERBS 23:15-16

My child,* if your heart is wise, my own
heart will rejoice! Everything in me will
celebrate when you speak what is right.

23:15 Hebrew *My son;* also in 23:19.

SEPTEMBER**17**

ISAIAH 25:1–28:13

Even in the midst of judgment, there was hope. This
hope was based on God's commitment to restore
his people. That commitment was based on God's
promise made to Abraham centuries before Isaiah
lived.

O LORD, I [Isaiah] will honor and
praise your name,
for you are my God.
You do such wonderful things!
You planned them long ago,
and now you have accomplished
them.
² You turn mighty cities into heaps of
ruins.
Cities with strong walls are turned
to rubble.
Beautiful palaces in distant lands
disappear
and will never be rebuilt.
³ Therefore, strong nations will declare
your glory;
ruthless nations will fear you.
⁴ But you are a tower of refuge to the
poor, O LORD,
a tower of refuge to the needy in
distress.
You are a refuge from the storm
and a shelter from the heat.
For the oppressive acts of ruthless
people
are like a storm beating against a
wall,
⁵ or like the relentless heat of
the desert.

But you silence the roar of foreign
nations.
As the shade of a cloud cools
relentless heat,
so the boastful songs of ruthless
people are stilled.

⁶ In Jerusalem,* the LORD of Heaven's
Armies
will spread a wonderful feast
for all the people of the world.
It will be a delicious banquet
with clear, well-aged wine and
choice meat.
⁷ There he will remove the cloud of
gloom,
the shadow of death that hangs over
the earth.
⁸ He will swallow up death forever!*
The Sovereign LORD will wipe away
all tears.
He will remove forever all insults and
mockery
against his land and people.
The LORD has spoken!

⁹ In that day the people will proclaim,
"This is our God!
We trusted in him, and he saved us!
This is the LORD, in whom we trusted.
Let us rejoice in the salvation he
brings!"
¹⁰ For the LORD's hand of blessing will
rest on Jerusalem.
But Moab will be crushed.

It will be like straw trampled down
and left to rot.

[11] God will push down Moab's people
as a swimmer pushes down water
with his hands.
He will end their pride
and all their evil works.

[12] The high walls of Moab will be
demolished.
They will be brought down to
the ground,
down into the dust.

26:1 IN that day, everyone in the land of Judah will sing this song:

Our city is strong!
We are surrounded by the walls
of God's salvation.

[2] Open the gates to all who are
righteous;
allow the faithful to enter.

[3] You will keep in perfect peace
all who trust in you,
all whose thoughts are fixed on you!

[4] Trust in the LORD always,
for the LORD GOD is the eternal
Rock.

[5] He humbles the proud
and brings down the arrogant city.
He brings it down to the dust.

[6] The poor and oppressed trample it
underfoot,
and the needy walk all over it.

[7] But for those who are righteous,
the way is not steep and rough.
You are a God who does what is right,
and you smooth out the path ahead
of them.

[8] LORD, we show our trust in you by
obeying your laws;
our heart's desire is to glorify your
name.

[9] All night long I search for you;
in the morning I earnestly seek
for God.
For only when you come to judge
the earth
will people learn what is right.

[10] Your kindness to the wicked
does not make them do good.
Although others do right, the wicked
keep doing wrong

and take no notice of the LORD's
majesty.

[11] O LORD, they pay no attention to your
upraised fist.
Show them your eagerness to
defend your people.
Then they will be ashamed.
Let your fire consume your
enemies.

[12] LORD, you will grant us peace;
all we have accomplished is really
from you.

[13] O LORD our God, others have ruled us,
but you alone are the one we
worship.

[14] Those we served before are dead and
gone.
Their departed spirits will never
return!
You attacked them and destroyed
them,
and they are long forgotten.

[15] O LORD, you have made our nation
great;
yes, you have made us great.
You have extended our borders,
and we give you the glory!

[16] LORD, in distress we searched for you.
We prayed beneath the burden of
your discipline.

[17] Just as a pregnant woman
writhes and cries out in pain as she
gives birth,
so were we in your presence, LORD.

[18] We, too, writhe in agony,
but nothing comes of our suffering.
We have not given salvation to
the earth,
nor brought life into the world.

[19] But those who die in the LORD will
live;
their bodies will rise again!
Those who sleep in the earth
will rise up and sing for joy!
For your life-giving light will fall like
dew
on your people in the place of
the dead!

[20] Go home, my people,
and lock your doors!
Hide yourselves for a little while
until the LORD's anger has passed.

21 Look! The LORD is coming from heaven
    to punish the people of the earth
    for their sins.
The earth will no longer hide those
    who have been killed.
    They will be brought out for all
    to see.

27:1 IN that day the LORD will take his terrible, swift sword and punish Leviathan,*
the swiftly moving serpent, the coiling,
writhing serpent. He will kill the dragon
of the sea.

2 "In that day,
    sing about the fruitful vineyard.
3 I, the LORD, will watch over it,
    watering it carefully.
Day and night I will watch so no one
    can harm it.
4   My anger will be gone.
If I find briers and thorns growing,
    I will attack them;
I will burn them up—
5   unless they turn to me for help.
Let them make peace with me;
    yes, let them make peace with me."
6 The time is coming when Jacob's
    descendants will take root.
Israel will bud and blossom
    and fill the whole earth with fruit!

7 Has the LORD struck Israel
    as he struck her enemies?

Has he punished her
    as he punished them?
8 No, but he exiled Israel to call her
    to account.
She was exiled from her land
    as though blown away in a storm
    from the east.
9 The LORD did this to purge Israel's*
    wickedness,
    to take away all her sin.
As a result, all the pagan altars will
    be crushed to dust.
No Asherah pole or pagan shrine
    will be left standing.
10 The fortified towns will be silent
    and empty,
    the houses abandoned, the streets
    overgrown with weeds.
Calves will graze there,
    chewing on twigs and branches.
11 The people are like the dead branches
    of a tree,
    broken off and used for kindling
    beneath the cooking pots.
Israel is a foolish and stupid nation,
    for its people have turned away
    from God.
Therefore, the one who made them
    will show them no pity or mercy.

12 Yet the time will come when the
LORD will gather them together like hand-
picked grain. One by one he will gather

HOW WE LIVE

Knowing God's peace

ISAIAH 26:3-4 It isn't easy finding peace in a violent world. This task
was no less daunting for the people in the Bible who followed God in the
midst of brutal and oppressive times. Isaiah lived in such times. He saw
Israel (the northern kingdom) conquered and destroyed by the Assyrians,
who then turned their sights on Judah (the southern kingdom). Yet he
spoke of knowing peace—not just any peace but *perfect* peace. In fact,
he said that if we trust in God and fix our thoughts on him, he will not
only give us perfect peace, but will *keep us* in perfect peace. • The key
to knowing God's peace in a violent world is to fix our thoughts on him
and trust him. When we fix our thoughts on him, the dizzying tornado
of stress and confusion fades into the distance. Circumstances may
change, but God doesn't change. He is "the eternal Rock" (Isaiah
26:4)—immoveable, unchangeable, firm, and steady. We can entrust
ourselves to him. • No matter what circumstances you face, keep your
thoughts on and your trust in God. He will give you peace.

them—from the Euphrates River* in the east to the Brook of Egypt in the west. [13]In that day the great trumpet will sound. Many who were dying in exile in Assyria and Egypt will return to Jerusalem to worship the LORD on his holy mountain.

28:1WHAT sorrow awaits the proud city
  of Samaria—
    the glorious crown of the drunks
    of Israel.*
  It sits at the head of a fertile valley,
    but its glorious beauty will fade like
    a flower.
  It is the pride of a people
    brought down by wine.
[2] For the Lord will send a mighty army
  against it.
  Like a mighty hailstorm and a
    torrential rain,
  they will burst upon it like a surging
    flood
  and smash it to the ground.
[3] The proud city of Samaria—
  the glorious crown of the drunks of
    Israel*—
  will be trampled beneath its
    enemies' feet.
[4] It sits at the head of a fertile valley,
  but its glorious beauty will fade like
    a flower.
  Whoever sees it will snatch it up,
    as an early fig is quickly picked
    and eaten.
[5] Then at last the LORD of Heaven's
  Armies
  will himself be Israel's glorious
    crown.
  He will be the pride and joy
    of the remnant of his people.
[6] He will give a longing for justice
    to their judges.
  He will give great courage
    to their warriors who stand at the
    gates.
[7] Now, however, Israel is led by drunks
    who reel with wine and stagger with
    alcohol.
  The priests and prophets stagger
    with alcohol
    and lose themselves in wine.
  They reel when they see visions
    and stagger as they render decisions.

[8] Their tables are covered with vomit;
    filth is everywhere.
[9] "Who does the LORD think we are?"
    they ask.
  "Why does he speak to us like this?
  Are we little children,
    just recently weaned?
[10] He tells us everything over and over—
    one line at a time,
      one line at a time,
    a little here,
      and a little there!"

[11] So now God will have to speak to his
    people
    through foreign oppressors who
      speak a strange language!
[12] God has told his people,
  "Here is a place of rest;
    let the weary rest here.
  This is a place of quiet rest."
    But they would not listen.
[13] So the LORD will spell out his message
    for them again,
    one line at a time,
      one line at a time,
    a little here,
      and a little there,
    so that they will stumble and fall.
    They will be injured, trapped,
      and captured.

25:6 Hebrew *On this mountain;* also in 25:10.   25:8 Greek version reads *Death is swallowed up in victory.* Compare 1 Cor 15:54.   27:1 The identification of Leviathan is disputed, ranging from an earthly creature to a mythical sea monster in ancient literature.   27:9 Hebrew *Jacob's.* See note on 14:1.   27:12 Hebrew *the river.*   28:1 Hebrew *What sorrow awaits the crowning glory of the drunks of Ephraim,* referring to Samaria, capital of the northern kingdom of Israel.   28:3 Hebrew *The crowning glory of the drunks of Ephraim;* see note on 28:1.

GALATIANS 3:10-22
In the debate concerning the law of Moses, Paul had to readjust people's focus beyond Moses to Abraham. Jesus fulfilled the promises given to Abraham before the law was ever given. Just as the promise came apart from the law, so did the blessings of the promise's fulfillment.

But those who depend on the law to make them right with God are under his curse, for the Scriptures say, "Cursed is everyone who does not observe and obey all the commands that are written in God's Book of the Law."* [11]So it is clear that no one can be made right with God by trying to keep the law. For the Scriptures say, "It is through faith that a righteous person has life."* [12] This way of faith is very different from the way of law, which says, "It is through obeying the law that a person has life."*

[13] But Christ has rescued us from the curse pronounced by the law. When he was hung on the cross, he took upon himself the curse for our wrongdoing. For it is written in the Scriptures, "Cursed is everyone who is hung on a tree."* [14] Through Christ Jesus, God has blessed the Gentiles with the same blessing he promised to Abraham, so that we who are believers might receive the promised* Holy Spirit through faith.

[15] Dear brothers and sisters,* here's an example from everyday life. Just as no one can set aside or amend an irrevocable agreement, so it is in this case. [16] God gave the promises to Abraham and his child.* And notice that the Scripture doesn't say "to his children,*" as if it meant many descendants. Rather, it says "to his child"—and that, of course, means Christ. [17] This is what I am trying to say: The agreement God made with Abraham could not be canceled 430 years later when God gave the law to Moses. God would be breaking his promise. [18] For if the inheritance could be received by keeping the law, then it would not be the result of accepting God's promise. But God graciously gave it to Abraham as a promise.

[19] Why, then, was the law given? It was given alongside the promise to show people their sins. But the law was designed to last only until the coming of the child who was promised. God gave his law through angels to Moses, who was the mediator between God and the people. [20] Now a mediator is helpful if more than one party must reach an agreement. But God, who is one, did not use a mediator when he gave his promise to Abraham.

[21] Is there a conflict, then, between God's law and God's promises?* Absolutely not! If the law could give us new life, we could be made right with God by obeying it. [22] But the Scriptures declare that we are all prisoners of sin, so we receive God's promise of freedom only by believing in Jesus Christ.

3:10 Deut 27:26.   **3:11** Hab 2:4.   **3:12** Lev 18:5.
3:13 Deut 21:23 (Greek version).   **3:14** Some manuscripts read *the blessing of the.*   **3:15** Greek *Brothers.*   **3:16a** Greek *seed;* also in 3:16c, 19. See Gen 12:7 and 13:15.   **3:16b** Greek *seeds.*   **3:21** Some manuscripts read *and the promises?*

PSALM 61:1-8

For the choir director: A psalm of David, to be accompanied by stringed instruments.

[1] O God, listen to my cry!
  Hear my prayer!
[2] From the ends of the earth,
  I cry to you for help
  when my heart is overwhelmed.
  Lead me to the towering rock of safety,
[3]   for you are my safe refuge,
    a fortress where my enemies cannot reach me.
[4] Let me live forever in your sanctuary,
  safe beneath the shelter of your wings!
                                          Interlude

[5] For you have heard my vows, O God.
  You have given me an inheritance
    reserved for those who fear your name.
[6] Add many years to the life of the king!
  May his years span the generations!
[7] May he reign under God's protection forever.
  May your unfailing love and
    faithfulness watch over him.
[8] Then I will sing praises to your name forever
  as I fulfill my vows each day.

PROVERBS 23:17-18

Don't envy sinners, but always continue to fear the LORD. You will be rewarded for this; your hope will not be disappointed.

ISAIAH 28:14-30:11

It was one thing for the people to have confidence *in* God, but another thing entirely for them to have confidence apart from God. Throughout their history, it had been God that protected them and supplied their every need. To have confidence in anything but God's strength meant certain destruction.

Therefore, listen to this message from the LORD,
  you scoffing rulers in Jerusalem.
15 You boast, "We have struck a bargain
    to cheat death
  and have made a deal to dodge
    the grave.*
The coming destruction can never
    touch us,
  for we have built a strong refuge
    made of lies and deception."

16 Therefore, this is what the Sovereign
    LORD says:
  "Look! I am placing a foundation stone
    in Jerusalem,*
  a firm and tested stone.
It is a precious cornerstone that is safe
    to build on.
  Whoever believes need never
    be shaken.*
17 I will test you with the measuring line
    of justice
  and the plumb line of
    righteousness.
Since your refuge is made of lies,
  a hailstorm will knock it down.
Since it is made of deception,
  a flood will sweep it away.
18 I will cancel the bargain you made
    to cheat death,
  and I will overturn your deal
    to dodge the grave.
When the terrible enemy sweeps
    through,
  you will be trampled into the
    ground.
19 Again and again that flood will come,
    morning after morning,
  day and night,
    until you are carried away."

This message will bring terror to your
    people.

20 The bed you have made is too short
    to lie on.
  The blankets are too narrow
    to cover you.
21 The LORD will come as he did against
    the Philistines at Mount Perazim
  and against the Amorites at Gibeon.
He will come to do a strange thing;
  he will come to do an unusual deed:
22 For the Lord, the LORD of Heaven's
    Armies,
  has plainly said that he is
    determined to crush the
    whole land.
So scoff no more,
  or your punishment will be even
    greater.

23 Listen to me;
  listen, and pay close attention.
24 Does a farmer always plow and
    never sow?
  Is he forever cultivating the soil and
    never planting?
25 Does he not finally plant his seeds—
    black cumin, cumin, wheat, barley,
    and emmer wheat—
  each in its proper way,
    and each in its proper place?
26 The farmer knows just what to do,
  for God has given him
    understanding.
27 A heavy sledge is never used to thresh
    black cumin;
  rather, it is beaten with a light stick.
A threshing wheel is never rolled on
    cumin;
  instead, it is beaten lightly with
    a flail.
28 Grain for bread is easily crushed,
  so he doesn't keep on pounding it.
He threshes it under the wheels of
    a cart,
  but he doesn't pulverize it.
29 The LORD of Heaven's Armies is
    a wonderful teacher,
  and he gives the farmer great
    wisdom.

29:1 "WHAT sorrow awaits Ariel,* the City
    of David.

Year after year you celebrate
your feasts.
2 Yet I will bring disaster upon you,
and there will be much weeping
and sorrow.
For Jerusalem will become what her
name Ariel means—
an altar covered with blood.
3 I will be your enemy,
surrounding Jerusalem and
attacking its walls.
I will build siege towers
and destroy it.
4 Then deep from the earth you will
speak;
from low in the dust your words
will come.
Your voice will whisper from the
ground
like a ghost conjured up from the
grave.

5 "But suddenly, your ruthless enemies
will be crushed
like the finest of dust.
Your many attackers will be driven
away
like chaff before the wind.
Suddenly, in an instant,
6   I, the LORD of Heaven's Armies, will
act for you
with thunder and earthquake and
great noise,
with whirlwind and storm and
consuming fire.
7 All the nations fighting against
Jerusalem*
will vanish like a dream!
Those who are attacking her walls
will vanish like a vision in the night.
8 A hungry person dreams of eating
but wakes up still hungry.
A thirsty person dreams of drinking
but is still faint from thirst when
morning comes.
So it will be with your enemies,
with those who attack Mount Zion."

9 Are you amazed and incredulous?
Don't you believe it?
Then go ahead and be blind.
You are stupid, but not from wine!
You stagger, but not from liquor!
10 For the LORD has poured out on you a
spirit of deep sleep.

He has closed the eyes of your
prophets and visionaries.

11 All the future events in this vision are
like a sealed book to them. When you give
it to those who can read, they will say, "We
can't read it because it is sealed." 12 When
you give it to those who cannot read, they
will say, "We don't know how to read."

13 And so the Lord says,
"These people say they are mine.
They honor me with their lips,
but their hearts are far from me.
And their worship of me
is nothing but man-made rules
learned by rote.*
14 Because of this, I will once again
astound these hypocrites
with amazing wonders.
The wisdom of the wise will pass away,
and the intelligence of the
intelligent will disappear."

15 What sorrow awaits those who try to
hide their plans from the LORD,
who do their evil deeds in the dark!
"The LORD can't see us," they say.
"He doesn't know what's going on!"
16 How foolish can you be?
He is the Potter, and he is certainly
greater than you, the clay!
Should the created thing say to the
one who made it,
"He didn't make me"?
Does a jar ever say,
"The potter who made me is
stupid"?

17 Soon—and it will not be very long—
the forests of Lebanon will become
a fertile field,
and the fertile field will yield
bountiful crops.
18 In that day the deaf will hear words
read from a book,
and the blind will see through the
gloom and darkness.
19 The humble will be filled with fresh
joy from the LORD.
The poor will rejoice in the Holy
One of Israel.
20 The scoffer will be gone,
the arrogant will disappear,
and those who plot evil will
be killed.

21 Those who convict the innocent
     by their false testimony will
         disappear.
   A similar fate awaits those who use
         trickery to pervert justice
     and who tell lies to destroy the
         innocent.

22 That is why the LORD, who redeemed
Abraham, says to the people of Israel,*

   "My people will no longer be ashamed
         or turn pale with fear.
23 For when they see their many children
         and all the blessings I have given
             them,
   they will recognize the holiness of the
         Holy One of Israel.
   They will stand in awe of the God
         of Jacob.
24 Then the wayward will gain
         understanding,
     and complainers will accept
         instruction.

30:1 "WHAT sorrow awaits my rebellious
         children,"
     says the LORD.
   "You make plans that are contrary
         to mine.
     You make alliances not directed by
         my Spirit,
         thus piling up your sins.
2 For without consulting me,
     you have gone down to Egypt for
         help.
   You have put your trust in Pharaoh's
         protection.
     You have tried to hide in his shade.
3 But by trusting Pharaoh, you will be
         humiliated,
     and by depending on him, you will
         be disgraced.
4 For though his power extends to Zoan
         and his officials have arrived in
             Hanes,
5 all who trust in him will be ashamed.
   He will not help you.
     Instead, he will disgrace you."

6 This message came to me concerning
the animals in the Negev:

   The caravan moves slowly
         across the terrible desert to Egypt—
     donkeys weighed down with riches

and camels loaded with treasure—
         all to pay for Egypt's protection.
   They travel through the wilderness,
         a place of lionesses and lions,
         a place where vipers and poisonous
             snakes live.
   All this, and Egypt will give you
         nothing in return.
7   Egypt's promises are worthless!
   Therefore, I call her Rahab—
         the Harmless Dragon.*

8 Now go and write down these words.
     Write them in a book.
   They will stand until the end of time
         as a witness
9 that these people are stubborn rebels
     who refuse to pay attention to the
         LORD's instructions.
10 They tell the seers,
     "Stop seeing visions!"
   They tell the prophets,
     "Don't tell us what is right.
     Tell us nice things.
     Tell us lies.
11 Forget all this gloom.
     Get off your narrow path.
   Stop telling us about your
     'Holy One of Israel.'"

28:15 Hebrew *Sheol;* also in 28:18.   28:16a Hebrew *in
Zion.*   28:16b Greek version reads *Look! I am placing a
stone in the foundation of Jerusalem* (literally *Zion*), */ a
precious cornerstone for its foundation, chosen for great
honor. / Anyone who trusts in him will never be disgraced.*
Compare Rom 9:33; 1 Pet 2:6.   29:1 *Ariel* sounds like a
Hebrew term that means "hearth" or "altar."   29:7 Hebrew
Ariel.   29:13 Greek version reads *Their worship is a farce, /
for they teach man-made ideas as commands from God.*
Compare Mark 7:7.   29:22 Hebrew *of Jacob.* See note on
14:1.   30:7 Hebrew *Rahab who sits still.* Rahab is the name
of a mythical sea monster that represents chaos in ancient
literature. The name is used here as a poetic name for Egypt.

GALATIANS 3:23–4:31
What does it mean to become a child of God?
What is Christ's role in our adoption into God's family? Paul addressed these questions with a concern
to steer the Galatians away from harmful teaching
that had crept into their midst.

Before the way of faith in Christ was available to us, we were placed under guard by
the law. We were kept in protective custody, so to speak, until the way of faith was
revealed. 24 Let me put it another way. The law
was our guardian until Christ came; it
protected us until we could be made right

with God through faith. ²⁵And now that the way of faith has come, we no longer need the law as our guardian.

²⁶For you are all children* of God through faith in Christ Jesus. ²⁷And all who have been united with Christ in baptism have put on Christ, like putting on new clothes.* ²⁸There is no longer Jew or Gentile,* slave or free, male and female. For you are all one in Christ Jesus. ²⁹And now that you belong to Christ, you are the true children* of Abraham. You are his heirs, and God's promise to Abraham belongs to you.

4:¹THINK of it this way. If a father dies and leaves an inheritance for his young children, those children are not much better off than slaves until they grow up, even though they actually own everything their father had. ²They have to obey their guardians until they reach whatever age their father set. ³And that's the way it was with us before Christ came. We were like children; we were slaves to the basic spiritual principles* of this world.

⁴But when the right time came, God sent his Son, born of a woman, subject to the law. ⁵God sent him to buy freedom for us who were slaves to the law, so that he could adopt us as his very own children.* ⁶And because we* are his children, God has sent the Spirit of his Son into our hearts, prompting us to call out, "Abba, Father."* ⁷Now you are no longer a slave but God's own child.* And since you are his child, God has made you his heir.

⁸Before you Gentiles knew God, you were slaves to so-called gods that do not even exist. ⁹So now that you know God (or should I say, now that God knows you), why do you want to go back again and become slaves once more to the weak and useless spiritual principles of this world? ¹⁰You are trying to earn favor with God by observing certain days or months or seasons or years. ¹¹I fear for you. Perhaps all my hard work with you was for nothing. ¹²Dear brothers and sisters,* I plead with you to live as I do in freedom from these things, for I have become like you Gentiles—free from those laws.

You did not mistreat me when I first preached to you. ¹³Surely you remember that I was sick when I first brought you the Good News. ¹⁴But even though my condition tempted you to reject me, you did not despise me or turn me away. No, you took me in and cared for me as though I were an angel from God or even Christ Jesus himself. ¹⁵Where is that joyful and grateful spirit you felt then? I am sure you would have taken out your own eyes and given them to me if it had been possible. ¹⁶Have I now become your enemy because I am telling you the truth?

WHO GOD IS | God is our Father

GALATIANS 4:5-7 The God of the Bible is our Creator, the Lord of the universe. He is all-powerful, all-knowing, holy, and awesome. But the Bible also reveals something astounding: this great God is our Father! • Does that seem irreverent? How can we call the great God of the universe, who is beyond our understanding, our Father? The apostle Paul reminds us that a new relationship was made available when God sent his Son to be the Savior of the world. When we believe in Jesus Christ, we become God's children, with all the rights and privileges that go with it. • God is the ultimate parent. He provides and cares for us. He gives us a spiritual inheritance. He nurtures us and teaches us. We can call God "Abba," an Aramaic term that can be translated as "Daddy." No earthly parent can meet all your needs, and many are much less than perfect. But as a follower of Jesus, you have a heavenly Father who will never leave you nor forsake you. You are adopted as God's own child, in his care forever. There is no safer place to be.

[17] Those false teachers are so eager to win your favor, but their intentions are not good. They are trying to shut you off from me so that you will pay attention only to them. [18] If someone is eager to do good things for you, that's all right; but let them do it all the time, not just when I'm with you.

[19] Oh, my dear children! I feel as if I'm going through labor pains for you again, and they will continue until Christ is fully developed in your lives. [20] I wish I were with you right now so I could change my tone. But at this distance I don't know how else to help you.

[21] Tell me, you who want to live under the law, do you know what the law actually says? [22] The Scriptures say that Abraham had two sons, one from his slave wife and one from his freeborn wife.* [23] The son of the slave wife was born in a human attempt to bring about the fulfillment of God's promise. But the son of the freeborn wife was born as God's own fulfillment of his promise.

[24] These two women serve as an illustration of God's two covenants. The first woman, Hagar, represents Mount Sinai where people received the law that enslaved them. [25] And now Jerusalem is just like Mount Sinai in Arabia,* because she and her children live in slavery to the law. [26] But the other woman, Sarah, represents the heavenly Jerusalem. She is the free woman, and she is our mother. [27] As Isaiah said,

"Rejoice, O childless woman,
　you who have never given birth!
Break into a joyful shout,
　you who have never been in labor!
For the desolate woman now has more
　children
than the woman who lives with her
　husband!"*

[28] And you, dear brothers and sisters, are children of the promise, just like Isaac. [29] But you are now being persecuted by those who want you to keep the law, just as Ishmael, the child born by human effort, persecuted Isaac, the child born by the power of the Spirit. [30] But what do the Scriptures say about that? "Get rid of the slave and her son, for the son of the slave woman will not share the inheritance with the free woman's son."* [31] So, dear brothers and sisters, we are not children of the slave woman; we are children of the free woman.

3:26 Greek *sons.* **3:27** Greek *have put on Christ.*
3:28 Greek *Jew or Greek.* **3:29** Greek *seed.* **4:3** Or *powers;* also in 4:9. **4:5** Greek *sons;* also in 4:6. **4:6a** Greek *you.*
4:6b *Abba* is an Aramaic term for "father." **4:7** Greek *son;* also in 4:7b. **4:12** Greek *brothers;* also in 4:28, 31.
4:22 See Gen 16:15; 21:2-3. **4:25** Greek *And Hagar, which is Mount Sinai in Arabia, is now like Jerusalem;* other manuscripts read *And Mount Sinai in Arabia is now like Jerusalem.* **4:27** Isa 54:1. **4:30** Gen 21:10.

PSALM 62:1-12

For Jeduthun, the choir director: A psalm of David.

[1] I wait quietly before God,
　for my victory comes from him.
[2] He alone is my rock and my salvation,
　my fortress where I will never be
　　shaken.

[3] So many enemies against one man—
　all of them trying to kill me.
To them I'm just a broken-down wall
　or a tottering fence.
[4] They plan to topple me from my high
　position.
They delight in telling lies about
　me.
They praise me to my face
　but curse me in their hearts. *Interlude*

[5] Let all that I am wait quietly before
　God,
　for my hope is in him.
[6] He alone is my rock and my salvation,
　my fortress where I will not be
　　shaken.
[7] My victory and honor come from God
　alone.
He is my refuge, a rock where no
　enemy can reach me.
[8] O my people, trust in him at all times.
Pour out your heart to him,
　for God is our refuge. *Interlude*

[9] Common people are as worthless
　as a puff of wind,
and the powerful are not what they
　appear to be.
If you weigh them on the scales,
　together they are lighter than a
　　breath of air.

¹⁰ Don't make your living by extortion
    or put your hope in stealing.
And if your wealth increases,
    don't make it the center of your life.

¹¹ God has spoken plainly,
    and I have heard it many times:
Power, O God, belongs to you;
¹²   unfailing love, O Lord, is yours.

Surely you repay all people
    according to what they have done.

PROVERBS 23:19-21

My child, listen and be wise: Keep your heart on the right course. Do not carouse with drunkards or feast with gluttons, for they are on their way to poverty, and too much sleep clothes them in rags.

ISAIAH 30:12–33:9

Isaiah prophesied during a time of international turmoil. All of Judah's neighboring nations (especially Assyria and Babylon) were potential threats. To rely on an alliance with any of them was like trusting a snake.

This is the reply of the Holy One of Israel:

"Because you [Israel] despise what
        I tell you
    and trust instead in oppression and
        lies,
¹³ calamity will come upon you
        suddenly—
    like a bulging wall that bursts and
        falls.
In an instant it will collapse
    and come crashing down.
¹⁴ You will be smashed like a piece of
        pottery—
    shattered so completely that
there won't be a piece big enough
    to carry coals from a fireplace
    or a little water from the well."

¹⁵ This is what the Sovereign LORD,
    the Holy One of Israel, says:
"Only in returning to me
    and resting in me will you be saved.
In quietness and confidence is your
        strength.
    But you would have none of it.
¹⁶ You said, 'No, we will get our help from
        Egypt.
    They will give us swift horses for
        riding into battle.'

SEPTEMBER**19**

But the only swiftness you are going
        to see
    is the swiftness of your enemies
        chasing you!
¹⁷ One of them will chase a thousand
        of you.
    Five of them will make all of you
        flee.
You will be left like a lonely flagpole
        on a hill
    or a tattered banner on a distant
        mountaintop."

¹⁸ So the LORD must wait for you to come
        to him
    so he can show you his love and
        compassion.
For the LORD is a faithful God.
    Blessed are those who wait for
        his help.

¹⁹ O people of Zion, who live in
        Jerusalem,
    you will weep no more.
He will be gracious if you ask for help.
    He will surely respond to the sound
        of your cries.
²⁰ Though the Lord gave you adversity
        for food
    and suffering for drink,
he will still be with you to teach you.
    You will see your teacher with your
        own eyes.
²¹ Your own ears will hear him.
    Right behind you a voice will say,
"This is the way you should go,"

whether to the right or to
the left.

²² Then you will destroy all your silver
idols
and your precious gold images.
You will throw them out like filthy rags,
saying to them, "Good riddance!"

²³ Then the LORD will bless you with
rain at planting time. There will be wonderful harvests and plenty of pastureland
for your livestock. ²⁴ The oxen and donkeys that till the ground will eat good
grain, its chaff blown away by the wind.
²⁵ In that day, when your enemies are
slaughtered and the towers fall, there will
be streams of water flowing down every
mountain and hill. ²⁶ The moon will be as
bright as the sun, and the sun will be
seven times brighter—like the light of
seven days in one! So it will be when the
LORD begins to heal his people and cure
the wounds he gave them.

²⁷ Look! The LORD is coming from far
away,
burning with anger,
surrounded by thick, rising smoke.
His lips are filled with fury;
his words consume like fire.

²⁸ His hot breath pours out like a flood
up to the neck of his enemies.
He will sift out the proud nations for
destruction.
He will bridle them and lead them
away to ruin.

²⁹ But the people of God will sing a song
of joy,
like the songs at the holy festivals.
You will be filled with joy,
as when a flutist leads a group of
pilgrims
to Jerusalem, the mountain of the
LORD—
to the Rock of Israel.

³⁰ And the LORD will make his majestic
voice heard.
He will display the strength of his
mighty arm.
It will descend with devouring flames,
with cloudbursts, thunderstorms,
and huge hailstones.

³¹ At the LORD's command, the Assyrians
will be shattered.

He will strike them down with his
royal scepter.

³² And as the LORD strikes them with his
rod of punishment,
his people will celebrate with
tambourines and harps.
Lifting his mighty arm, he will fight
the Assyrians.

³³ Topheth—the place of burning—
has long been ready for the Assyrian
king;
the pyre is piled high with wood.
The breath of the LORD, like fire from
a volcano,
will set it ablaze.

31:1 WHAT sorrow awaits those who look
to Egypt for help,
trusting their horses, chariots, and
charioteers
and depending on the strength of
human armies
instead of looking to the LORD,
the Holy One of Israel.

² In his wisdom, the LORD will send
great disaster;
he will not change his mind.
He will rise against the wicked
and against their helpers.

³ For these Egyptians are mere humans,
not God!
Their horses are puny flesh, not
mighty spirits!
When the LORD raises his fist against
them,
those who help will stumble,
and those being helped will fall.
They will all fall down and die
together.

⁴ But this is what the LORD has told me:

"When a strong young lion
stands growling over a sheep it has
killed,
it is not frightened by the shouts and
noise
of a whole crowd of shepherds.
In the same way, the LORD of Heaven's
Armies
will come down and fight on Mount
Zion.

⁵ The LORD of Heaven's Armies will
hover over Jerusalem

and protect it like a bird protecting
   its nest.
He will defend and save the city;
   he will pass over it and rescue it."

[6]Though you are such wicked rebels,
my people, come and return to the LORD.
[7]I know the glorious day will come when
each of you will throw away the gold idols
and silver images your sinful hands have
made.

[8] "The Assyrians will be destroyed,
   but not by the swords of men.
The sword of God will strike them,
   and they will panic and flee.
The strong young Assyrians
   will be taken away as captives.
[9] Even the strongest will quake with
   terror,
   and princes will flee when they see
     your battle flags,"
says the LORD, whose fire burns in Zion,
   whose flame blazes from Jerusalem.

[32:1]LOOK, a righteous king is coming!
   And honest princes will rule under
     him.
[2] Each one will be like a shelter from
   the wind
   and a refuge from the storm,
like streams of water in the desert

and the shadow of a great rock
   in a parched land.
[3] Then everyone who has eyes will
   be able to see the truth,
   and everyone who has ears will be
     able to hear it.
[4] Even the hotheads will be full of sense
   and understanding.
Those who stammer will speak out
   plainly.
[5] In that day ungodly fools will not be
   heroes.
Scoundrels will not be respected.
[6] For fools speak foolishness
   and make evil plans.
They practice ungodliness
   and spread false teachings about
     the LORD.
They deprive the hungry of food
   and give no water to the thirsty.
[7] The smooth tricks of scoundrels
   are evil.
They plot crooked schemes.
They lie to convict the poor,
   even when the cause of the poor
     is just.
[8] But generous people plan to do what
   is generous,
   and they stand firm in their
     generosity.

HOW WE LIVE | Following Jesus

GALATIANS 5:1, 13-14 One of the great conflicts of the first century was over
the requirements of becoming a Christian. Did it require converting to
Judaism? Jesus was Jewish, after all! As you read through the book of
Acts and this letter to the Galatians, you discover conflicts and councils
about this very thing. •Paul was clear on this issue: Gentiles did not
need to convert to Judaism before they could be saved. Jesus brought
freedom from the ritual aspects of Judaism. Paul was also clear, however,
that Christian freedom is not permission to do anything we want. Rather,
it is the opportunity to do what Christ wants, without fear that our performance will be counted against us. We are free from endless ceremonial
laws, sin, and fear. But we are not free in the sense of totally governing
ourselves or being totally autonomous from Christ. We are under the
restraint of the Holy Spirit and the constraint of the higher law, the law
of love. Freedom must be used to glorify Christ and serve others, not just
to fulfill our personal desires. •Following Jesus does not enslave you—
it sets you free to be all that God created you to be!

⁹ Listen, you women who lie around
in ease.
Listen to me, you who are so smug.
¹⁰ In a short time—just a little more than
a year—
you careless ones will suddenly
begin to care.
For your fruit crops will fail,
and the harvest will never take
place.
¹¹ Tremble, you women of ease;
throw off your complacency.
Strip off your pretty clothes,
and put on burlap to show your
grief.
¹² Beat your breasts in sorrow for your
bountiful farms
and your fruitful grapevines.
¹³ For your land will be overgrown with
thorns and briers.
Your joyful homes and happy towns
will be gone.
¹⁴ The palace and the city will be
deserted,
and busy towns will be empty.
Wild donkeys will frolic and flocks
will graze
in the empty forts* and watchtowers
¹⁵ until at last the Spirit is poured out
on us from heaven.
Then the wilderness will become
a fertile field,
and the fertile field will yield
bountiful crops.

¹⁶ Justice will rule in the wilderness
and righteousness in the fertile
field.
¹⁷ And this righteousness will bring
peace.
Yes, it will bring quietness and
confidence forever.
¹⁸ My people will live in safety, quietly at
home.
They will be at rest.
¹⁹ Even if the forest should be destroyed
and the city torn down,
²⁰ the LORD will greatly bless his people.
Wherever they plant seed, bountiful
crops will spring up.
Their cattle and donkeys will graze
freely.

³³:¹ WHAT sorrow awaits you Assyrians,
who have destroyed others*

but have never been destroyed
yourselves.
You betray others,
but you have never been betrayed.
When you are done destroying,
you will be destroyed.
When you are done betraying,
you will be betrayed.
² But LORD, be merciful to us,
for we have waited for you.
Be our strong arm each day
and our salvation in times of
trouble.
³ The enemy runs at the sound of your
voice.
When you stand up, the nations
flee!
⁴ Just as caterpillars and locusts strip
the fields and vines,
so the fallen army of Assyria will be
stripped!
⁵ Though the LORD is very great and
lives in heaven,
he will make Jerusalem* his home
of justice and righteousness.
⁶ In that day he will be your sure
foundation,
providing a rich store of salvation,
wisdom, and knowledge.
The fear of the LORD will be your
treasure.

⁷ But now your brave warriors weep in
public.
Your ambassadors of peace cry in
bitter disappointment.
⁸ Your roads are deserted;
no one travels them anymore.
The Assyrians have broken their peace
treaty
and care nothing for the promises
they made before witnesses.*
They have no respect for anyone.
⁹ The land of Israel wilts in mourning.
Lebanon withers with shame.
The plain of Sharon is now a
wilderness.
Bashan and Carmel have been
plundered.

32:14 Hebrew *the Ophel.* **33:1** Hebrew *What sorrow
awaits you, O destroyer.* The Hebrew text does not
specifically name Assyria as the object of the prophecy in
this chapter. **33:5** Hebrew *Zion;* also in 33:14. **33:8** As
in Dead Sea Scrolls; Masoretic Text reads *care nothing for
the cities.*

GALATIANS 5:1-12

The Galatians had come to faith in Christ, but then something happened. They got weighed down by unnecessary rules and regulations rather than enjoying the liberty found in "faith expressing itself in love" (Galatians 5:6).

So Christ has truly set us free. Now make sure that you stay free, and don't get tied up again in slavery to the law.

²Listen! I, Paul, tell you this: If you are counting on circumcision to make you right with God, then Christ will be of no benefit to you. ³I'll say it again. If you are trying to find favor with God by being circumcised, you must obey every regulation in the whole law of Moses. ⁴For if you are trying to make yourselves right with God by keeping the law, you have been cut off from Christ! You have fallen away from God's grace.

⁵But we who live by the Spirit eagerly wait to receive by faith the righteousness God has promised to us. ⁶For when we place our faith in Christ Jesus, there is no benefit in being circumcised or being uncircumcised. What is important is faith expressing itself in love.

⁷You were running the race so well. Who has held you back from following the truth? ⁸It certainly isn't God, for he is the one who called you to freedom. ⁹This false teaching is like a little yeast that spreads through the whole batch of dough! ¹⁰I am trusting the Lord to keep you from believing false teachings. God will judge that person, whoever he is, who has been confusing you.

¹¹Dear brothers and sisters,* if I were still preaching that you must be circumcised—as some say I do—why am I still being persecuted? If I were no longer preaching salvation through the cross of Christ, no one would be offended. ¹²I just wish that those troublemakers who want to mutilate you by circumcision would mutilate themselves.*

5:11 Greek *Brothers;* similarly in 5:13.   5:12 Or *castrate themselves, or cut themselves off from you;* Greek reads *cut themselves off.*

PSALM 63:1-11

A psalm of David, regarding a time when David was in the wilderness of Judah.

¹ **O** God, you are my God;
    I earnestly search for you.
My soul thirsts for you;
    my whole body longs for you
in this parched and weary land
    where there is no water.
² I have seen you in your sanctuary
    and gazed upon your power and
        glory.
³ Your unfailing love is better than life
        itself;
    how I praise you!
⁴ I will praise you as long as I live,
    lifting up my hands to you in prayer.
⁵ You satisfy me more than the richest
        feast.
    I will praise you with songs of joy.

⁶ I lie awake thinking of you,
    meditating on you through the night.
⁷ Because you are my helper,
    I sing for joy in the shadow of your
        wings.
⁸ I cling to you;
    your strong right hand holds me
        securely.

⁹ But those plotting to destroy me will
        come to ruin.
    They will go down into the depths
        of the earth.
¹⁰ They will die by the sword
    and become the food of jackals.
¹¹ But the king will rejoice in God.
    All who trust in him will praise him,
    while liars will be silenced.

PROVERBS 23:22

Listen to your father, who gave you life, and don't despise your mother when she is old.

SEPTEMBER**20**

ISAIAH 33:10–36:22

Isaiah's prophecy cuts in and out of historical accounts and then back to prophecy. In today's reading, Isaiah gives God's perspective on the future of Israel, then cuts to the actual events of Assyria invading Judah.

But the LORD says: "Now I will stand up.
 Now I will show my power and might.
11 You Assyrians produce nothing but dry grass and stubble.
 Your own breath will turn to fire and consume you.
12 Your people will be burned up completely,
 like thornbushes cut down and tossed in a fire.
13 Listen to what I have done, you nations far away!
 And you that are near, acknowledge my might!"
14 The sinners in Jerusalem shake with fear.
 Terror seizes the godless.
 "Who can live with this devouring fire?" they cry.
 "Who can survive this all-consuming fire?"
15 Those who are honest and fair,
 who refuse to profit by fraud,
 who stay far away from bribes,
 who refuse to listen to those who plot murder,
 who shut their eyes to all enticement to do wrong—
16 these are the ones who will dwell on high.
 The rocks of the mountains will be their fortress.
 Food will be supplied to them,
 and they will have water in abundance.

17 Your eyes will see the king in all his splendor,
 and you will see a land that stretches into the distance.
18 You will think back to this time of terror, asking,

"Where are the Assyrian officers who counted our towers?
 Where are the bookkeepers who recorded the plunder taken from our fallen city?"
19 You will no longer see these fierce, violent people
 with their strange, unknown language.
20 Instead, you will see Zion as a place of holy festivals.
 You will see Jerusalem, a city quiet and secure.
 It will be like a tent whose ropes are taut
 and whose stakes are firmly fixed.
21 The LORD will be our Mighty One.
 He will be like a wide river of protection
 that no enemy can cross,
 that no enemy ship can sail upon.
22 For the LORD is our judge,
 our lawgiver, and our king.
 He will care for us and save us.
23 The enemies' sails hang loose
 on broken masts with useless tackle.
 Their treasure will be divided by the people of God.
 Even the lame will take their share!
24 The people of Israel will no longer say,
 "We are sick and helpless,"
 for the LORD will forgive their sins.

34:1COME here and listen, O nations of the earth.
 Let the world and everything in it hear my words.
2 For the LORD is enraged against the nations.
 His fury is against all their armies.
 He will completely destroy* them,
 dooming them to slaughter.
3 Their dead will be left unburied,
 and the stench of rotting bodies will fill the land.
 The mountains will flow with their blood.
4 The heavens above will melt away
 and disappear like a rolled-up scroll.
 The stars will fall from the sky

like withered leaves from
    a grapevine,
    or shriveled figs from a fig tree.

5 And when my sword has finished its
    work in the heavens,
    it will fall upon Edom,
    the nation I have marked for
    destruction.
6 The sword of the Lord is drenched
    with blood
    and covered with fat—
with the blood of lambs and goats,
    with the fat of rams prepared for
    sacrifice.
Yes, the Lord will offer a sacrifice in
    the city of Bozrah.
    He will make a mighty slaughter
    in Edom.
7 Even men as strong as wild oxen
    will die—
    the young men alongside the
    veterans.
The land will be soaked with blood
    and the soil enriched with fat.

8 For it is the day of the Lord's revenge,
    the year when Edom will be paid
    back for all it did to Israel.*
9 The streams of Edom will be filled
    with burning pitch,
    and the ground will be covered with
    fire.
10 This judgment on Edom will never
    end;
    the smoke of its burning will rise
    forever.
The land will lie deserted from
    generation to generation.
    No one will live there anymore.
11 It will be haunted by the desert owl
    and the screech owl,
    the great owl and the raven.*
For God will measure that land
    carefully;
    he will measure it for chaos and
    destruction.
12 It will be called the Land of Nothing,
    and all its nobles will soon be gone.*
13 Thorns will overrun its palaces;
    nettles and thistles will grow in its
    forts.
The ruins will become a haunt for
    jackals
    and a home for owls.

14 Desert animals will mingle there
    with hyenas,
    their howls filling the night.
Wild goats will bleat at one another
    among the ruins,
    and night creatures* will come
    there to rest.
15 There the owl will make her nest and
    lay her eggs.
    She will hatch her young and cover
    them with her wings.
And the buzzards will come,
    each one with its mate.

16 Search the book of the Lord,
    and see what he will do.
Not one of these birds and animals
    will be missing,
    and none will lack a mate,
for the Lord has promised this.
    His Spirit will make it all come true.
17 He has surveyed and divided the land
    and deeded it over to those creatures.
They will possess it forever,
    from generation to generation.

35:1 Even the wilderness and desert will
    be glad in those days.
    The wasteland will rejoice and
    blossom with spring crocuses.
2 Yes, there will be an abundance of
    flowers
    and singing and joy!
The deserts will become as green as
    the mountains of Lebanon,
    as lovely as Mount Carmel or the
    plain of Sharon.
There the Lord will display his glory,
    the splendor of our God.
3 With this news, strengthen those who
    have tired hands,
    and encourage those who have
    weak knees.
4 Say to those with fearful hearts,
    "Be strong, and do not fear,
for your God is coming to destroy your
    enemies.
    He is coming to save you."

5 And when he comes, he will open the
    eyes of the blind
    and unplug the ears of the deaf.
6 The lame will leap like a deer,
    and those who cannot speak will
    sing for joy!

Springs will gush forth in the
wilderness,
and streams will water the
wasteland.
7 The parched ground will become
a pool,
and springs of water will satisfy the
thirsty land.
Marsh grass and reeds and rushes will
flourish
where desert jackals once lived.
8 And a great road will go through that
once deserted land.
It will be named the Highway
of Holiness.
Evil-minded people will never travel
on it.
It will only be for those who walk
in God's ways;
fools will never walk there.
9 Lions will not lurk along its course,
nor any other ferocious beasts.
There will be no other dangers.
Only the redeemed will walk on it.
10 Those who have been ransomed by
the LORD will return.
They will enter Jerusalem* singing,
crowned with everlasting joy.
Sorrow and mourning will disappear,
and they will be filled with joy and
gladness.

36:1IN the fourteenth year of King Hezekiah's reign,* King Sennacherib of Assyria
came to attack the fortified towns of Judah and conquered them. ²Then the king
of Assyria sent his chief of staff* from Lachish with a huge army to confront King
Hezekiah in Jerusalem. The Assyrians
took up a position beside the aqueduct
that feeds water into the upper pool, near
the road leading to the field where cloth is
washed.*
³These are the officials who went out
to meet with them: Eliakim son of Hilkiah,
the palace administrator; Shebna the
court secretary; and Joah son of Asaph,
the royal historian.
⁴Then the Assyrian king's chief of staff
told them to give this message to Hezekiah:

"This is what the great king of Assyria
says: What are you trusting in that
makes you so confident? ⁵Do you

think that mere words can substitute
for military skill and strength? Who
are you counting on, that you have
rebelled against me? ⁶On Egypt? If you
lean on Egypt, it will be like a reed that
splinters beneath your weight and
pierces your hand. Pharaoh, the king
of Egypt, is completely unreliable!
⁷"But perhaps you will say to me,
'We are trusting in the LORD our God!'
But isn't he the one who was insulted
by Hezekiah? Didn't Hezekiah tear
down his shrines and altars and make
everyone in Judah and Jerusalem
worship only at the altar here in
Jerusalem?
⁸"I'll tell you what! Strike a bargain
with my master, the king of Assyria.
I will give you 2,000 horses if you can
find that many men to ride on them!
⁹With your tiny army, how can you
think of challenging even the weakest
contingent of my master's troops, even
with the help of Egypt's chariots and
charioteers? ¹⁰What's more, do you
think we have invaded your land
without the LORD's direction? The
LORD himself told us, 'Attack this
land and destroy it!'"

¹¹Then Eliakim, Shebna, and Joah said
to the Assyrian chief of staff, "Please
speak to us in Aramaic, for we understand
it well. Don't speak in Hebrew,* for the
people on the wall will hear."
¹²But Sennacherib's chief of staff replied, "Do you think my master sent this
message only to you and your master? He
wants all the people to hear it, for when
we put this city under siege, they will suffer along with you. They will be so hungry
and thirsty that they will eat their own
dung and drink their own urine."
¹³Then the chief of staff stood and
shouted in Hebrew to the people on the
wall, "Listen to this message from the
great king of Assyria! ¹⁴This is what
the king says: Don't let Hezekiah deceive
you. He will never be able to rescue you.
¹⁵Don't let him fool you into trusting in
the LORD by saying, 'The LORD will surely
rescue us. This city will never fall into the
hands of the Assyrian king!'
¹⁶"Don't listen to Hezekiah! These are

the terms the king of Assyria is offering: Make peace with me—open the gates and come out. Then each of you can continue eating from your own grapevine and fig tree and drinking from your own well. ¹⁷Then I will arrange to take you to another land like this one—a land of grain and new wine, bread and vineyards.

¹⁸"Don't let Hezekiah mislead you by saying, 'The LORD will rescue us!' Have the gods of any other nations ever saved their people from the king of Assyria? ¹⁹What happened to the gods of Hamath and Arpad? And what about the gods of Sepharvaim? Did any god rescue Samaria from my power? ²⁰What god of any nation has ever been able to save its people from my power? So what makes you think that the LORD can rescue Jerusalem from me?"

²¹But the people were silent and did not utter a word because Hezekiah had commanded them, "Do not answer him."

²²Then Eliakim son of Hilkiah, the palace administrator; Shebna the court secretary; and Joah son of Asaph, the royal historian, went back to Hezekiah. They tore their clothes in despair, and they went in to see the king and told him what the Assyrian chief of staff had said.

34:2 The Hebrew term used here refers to the complete consecration of things or people to the LORD, either by destroying them or by giving them as an offering; similarly in 34:5. **34:8** Hebrew *to Zion.* **34:11** The identification of some of these birds is uncertain. **34:12** The meaning of the Hebrew is uncertain. **34:14** Hebrew *Lilith,* possibly a reference to a mythical demon of the night. **35:10** Hebrew *Zion.* **36:1** The fourteenth year of Hezekiah's reign was 701 B.C. **36:2a** Or *the rabshakeh;* also in 36:4, 11, 12, 22. **36:2b** Or *bleached.* **36:11** Hebrew *in the dialect of Judah;* also in 36:13.

GALATIANS 5:13-26

An apple tree bears apples. A pear tree bears pears. Through us, the Holy Spirit bears fruit—the evidence of God's work in our lives.

For you have been called to live in freedom, my brothers and sisters. But don't use your freedom to satisfy your sinful nature. Instead, use your freedom to serve one another in love. ¹⁴For the whole law can be summed up in this one command: "Love your neighbor as yourself."* ¹⁵But if you are always biting and devouring one another, watch out! Beware of destroying one another.

¹⁶So I say, let the Holy Spirit guide your lives. Then you won't be doing what your sinful nature craves. ¹⁷The sinful nature wants to do evil, which is just the opposite of what the Spirit wants. And the Spirit gives us desires that are the opposite of what the sinful nature desires. These two forces are constantly fighting each other, so you are not free to carry out your good intentions. ¹⁸But when you are directed

WHO GOD IS · The Holy Spirit produces fruit in us

GALATIANS 5:16-26 Love, joy, peace, patience. . . . The "fruit" of the Holy Spirit is the visible result of God's Spirit working within us. Yet there is a struggle going on in the heart: human nature versus the Holy Spirit. As a follower of Jesus, you are sealed with his Spirit. You have the Holy Spirit living in you, convicting you of your sin and effecting changes in your life to help you become more like Jesus (2 Corinthians 3:18, August 29). But you have a choice every day. You can choose to follow your own desires or you can choose to follow the Spirit's leading. •Paul says, "Let the Holy Spirit guide your lives." It is important to allow the Holy Spirit to control our lives because he produces character traits that are not natural for us, but which are found abundantly in the nature of Jesus Christ. Jesus is the "true grapevine" (John 15:1-5, May 26). By staying rooted in the vine (through things like Bible study and prayer), we allow the Spirit to produce fruit in us. •Submit every aspect of your life to the Spirit's guidance, keep in step with the Spirit's leading, and then watch for fruit to blossom in your life.

by the Spirit, you are not under obligation to the law of Moses.

[19] When you follow the desires of your sinful nature, the results are very clear: sexual immorality, impurity, lustful pleasures, [20] idolatry, sorcery, hostility, quarreling, jealousy, outbursts of anger, selfish ambition, dissension, division, [21] envy, drunkenness, wild parties, and other sins like these. Let me tell you again, as I have before, that anyone living that sort of life will not inherit the Kingdom of God.

[22] But the Holy Spirit produces this kind of fruit in our lives: love, joy, peace, patience, kindness, goodness, faithfulness, [23] gentleness, and self-control. There is no law against these things!

[24] Those who belong to Christ Jesus have nailed the passions and desires of their sinful nature to his cross and crucified them there. [25] Since we are living by the Spirit, let us follow the Spirit's leading in every part of our lives. [26] Let us not become conceited, or provoke one another, or be jealous of one another.

5:14 Lev 19:18.

PSALM 64:1-10
For the choir director: A psalm of David.

[1] **O** God, listen to my complaint.
     Protect my life from my enemies'
        threats.
[2] Hide me from the plots of this evil mob,
     from this gang of wrongdoers.

[3] They sharpen their tongues like
        swords
     and aim their bitter words like
        arrows.
[4] They shoot from ambush at the
        innocent,
     attacking suddenly and fearlessly.
[5] They encourage each other to do evil
     and plan how to set their traps in
        secret.
     "Who will ever notice?" they ask.
[6] As they plot their crimes, they say,
     "We have devised the perfect plan!"
     Yes, the human heart and mind are
        cunning.

[7] But God himself will shoot them with
        his arrows,
     suddenly striking them down.
[8] Their own tongues will ruin them,
     and all who see them will shake
        their heads in scorn.
[9] Then everyone will be afraid;
     they will proclaim the mighty acts
        of God
     and realize all the amazing things
        he does.
[10] The godly will rejoice in the LORD
     and find shelter in him.
     And those who do what is right
        will praise him.

PROVERBS 23:23
Get the truth and never sell it; also get wisdom, discipline, and good judgment.

SEPTEMBER**21**

ISAIAH 37:1–38:22
Hezekiah was a good king among many kings that were not. "Good" means that a king tried to turn the people back to the worship of God. Hezekiah's heart can be seen in his choice to turn to God when things heated up politically.

When King Hezekiah heard their report, he tore his clothes and put on burlap and went into the Temple of the LORD. [2] And he sent Eliakim the palace administrator, Shebna the court secretary, and the lead-ing priests, all dressed in burlap, to the prophet Isaiah son of Amoz. [3] They told him, "This is what King Hezekiah says: Today is a day of trouble, insults, and disgrace. It is like when a child is ready to be born, but the mother has no strength to deliver the baby. [4] But perhaps the LORD your God has heard the Assyrian chief of staff,* sent by the king to defy the living God, and will punish him for his words. Oh, pray for those of us who are left!"

⁵After King Hezekiah's officials delivered the king's message to Isaiah, ⁶the prophet replied, "Say to your master, 'This is what the Lord says: Do not be disturbed by this blasphemous speech against me from the Assyrian king's messengers. ⁷Listen! I myself will move against him,* and the king will receive a message that he is needed at home. So he will return to his land, where I will have him killed with a sword.'"

⁸Meanwhile, the Assyrian chief of staff left Jerusalem and went to consult the king of Assyria, who had left Lachish and was attacking Libnah.

⁹Soon afterward King Sennacherib received word that King Tirhakah of Ethiopia* was leading an army to fight against him. Before leaving to meet the attack, he sent messengers back to Hezekiah in Jerusalem with this message:

¹⁰"This message is for King Hezekiah of Judah. Don't let your God, in whom you trust, deceive you with promises that Jerusalem will not be captured by the king of Assyria. ¹¹You know perfectly well what the kings of Assyria have done wherever they have gone. They have completely destroyed everyone who stood in their way! Why should you be any different? ¹²Have the gods of other nations rescued them—such nations as Gozan, Haran, Rezeph, and the people of Eden who were in Tel-assar? My predecessors destroyed them all! ¹³What happened to the king of Hamath and the king of Arpad? What happened to the kings of Sepharvaim, Hena, and Ivvah?"

¹⁴After Hezekiah received the letter from the messengers and read it, he went up to the Lord's Temple and spread it out before the Lord. ¹⁵And Hezekiah prayed this prayer before the Lord: ¹⁶"O Lord of Heaven's Armies, God of Israel, you are enthroned between the mighty cherubim! You alone are God of all the kingdoms of the earth. You alone created the heavens and the earth. ¹⁷Bend down, O Lord, and listen! Open your eyes, O Lord, and see! Listen to Sennacherib's words of defiance against the living God.

¹⁸"It is true, Lord, that the kings of As-

syria have destroyed all these nations. ¹⁹And they have thrown the gods of these nations into the fire and burned them. But of course the Assyrians could destroy them! They were not gods at all—only idols of wood and stone shaped by human hands. ²⁰Now, O Lord our God, rescue us from his power; then all the kingdoms of the earth will know that you alone, O Lord, are God.*"

²¹Then Isaiah son of Amoz sent this message to Hezekiah: "This is what the Lord, the God of Israel, says: Because you prayed about King Sennacherib of Assyria, ²²the Lord has spoken this word against him:

"The virgin daughter of Zion
    despises you and laughs at you.
The daughter of Jerusalem
    shakes her head in derision
        as you flee.

²³ "Whom have you been defying and
        ridiculing?
    Against whom did you raise your
        voice?
At whom did you look with such
        haughty eyes?
    It was the Holy One of Israel!
²⁴ By your messengers you have defied
        the Lord.
    You have said, 'With my many
        chariots
I have conquered the highest
        mountains—
    yes, the remotest peaks of Lebanon.
I have cut down its tallest cedars
    and its finest cypress trees.
I have reached its farthest heights
    and explored its deepest forests.
²⁵ I have dug wells in many foreign
        lands*
    and refreshed myself with their
        water.
With the sole of my foot,
    I stopped up all the rivers of Egypt!'

²⁶ "But have you not heard?
    I decided this long ago.
Long ago I planned it,
    and now I am making it happen.
I planned for you to crush fortified
        cities
    into heaps of rubble.

²⁷ That is why their people have so little
power
and are so frightened and confused.
They are as weak as grass,
as easily trampled as tender green
shoots.
They are like grass sprouting on
a housetop,
scorched* before it can grow lush
and tall.

²⁸ "But I know you well—
where you stay
and when you come and go.
I know the way you have raged
against me.

²⁹ And because of your raging against me
and your arrogance, which I have
heard for myself,
I will put my hook in your nose
and my bit in your mouth.
I will make you return
by the same road on which
you came."

³⁰Then Isaiah said to Hezekiah, "Here is
the proof that what I say is true:

"This year you will eat only what grows
up by itself,
and next year you will eat what
springs up from that.
But in the third year you will plant
crops and harvest them;
you will tend vineyards and eat
their fruit.

³¹ And you who are left in Judah,
who have escaped the ravages of
the siege,
will put roots down in your own soil
and grow up and flourish.

³² For a remnant of my people will
spread out from Jerusalem,
a group of survivors from Mount
Zion.
The passionate commitment of the
LORD of Heaven's Armies
will make this happen!

³³"And this is what the LORD says about
the king of Assyria:

"'His armies will not enter Jerusalem.
They will not even shoot an arrow
at it.

They will not march outside its gates
with their shields
nor build banks of earth against
its walls.

³⁴ The king will return to his own
country
by the same road on which
he came.
He will not enter this city,'
says the LORD.

³⁵ 'For my own honor and for the sake of
my servant David,
I will defend this city and
protect it.'"

³⁶That night the angel of the LORD went
out to the Assyrian camp and killed
185,000 Assyrian soldiers. When the
surviving Assyrians* woke up the next
morning, they found corpses everywhere.
³⁷Then King Sennacherib of Assyria
broke camp and returned to his own land.
He went home to his capital of Nineveh
and stayed there.

³⁸One day while he was worshiping in
the temple of his god Nisroch, his sons
Adrammelech and Sharezer killed him
with their swords. They then escaped to
the land of Ararat, and another son, Esarhaddon, became the next king of Assyria.

^{38:1}ABOUT that time Hezekiah became
deathly ill, and the prophet Isaiah son of
Amoz went to visit him. He gave the king
this message: "This is what the LORD says:
'Set your affairs in order, for you are going
to die. You will not recover from this illness.'"

²When Hezekiah heard this, he turned
his face to the wall and prayed to the
LORD, ³"Remember, O LORD, how I have
always been faithful to you and have
served you single-mindedly, always doing
what pleases you." Then he broke down
and wept bitterly.

⁴Then this message came to Isaiah
from the LORD: ⁵"Go back to Hezekiah
and tell him, 'This is what the LORD, the
God of your ancestor David, says: I have
heard your prayer and seen your tears. I
will add fifteen years to your life, ⁶and
I will rescue you and this city from the
king of Assyria. Yes, I will defend this city.

⁷"'And this is the sign from the LORD to
prove that he will do as he promised: ⁸I

will cause the sun's shadow to move ten steps backward on the sundial* of Ahaz!'" So the shadow on the sundial moved backward ten steps.

[9] When King Hezekiah was well again, he wrote this poem:

[10] I said, "In the prime of my life,
must I now enter the place of
the dead?*
Am I to be robbed of the rest of
my years?"
[11] I said, "Never again will I see the LORD
GOD
while still in the land of the living.
Never again will I see my friends
or be with those who live in this
world.
[12] My life has been blown away
like a shepherd's tent in a storm.
It has been cut short,
as when a weaver cuts cloth from
a loom.
Suddenly, my life was over.
[13] I waited patiently all night,
but I was torn apart as though by
lions.
Suddenly, my life was over.
[14] Delirious, I chattered like a swallow
or a crane,
and then I moaned like a mourning
dove.
My eyes grew tired of looking
to heaven for help.
I am in trouble, Lord. Help me!"

[15] But what could I say?
For he himself sent this sickness.
Now I will walk humbly throughout
my years
because of this anguish I have felt.
[16] Lord, your discipline is good,
for it leads to life and health.
You restore my health
and allow me to live!
[17] Yes, this anguish was good for me,
for you have rescued me from death
and forgiven all my sins.
[18] For the dead* cannot praise you;
they cannot raise their voices
in praise.
Those who go down to the grave
can no longer hope in your
faithfulness.
[19] Only the living can praise you as
I do today.
Each generation tells of your
faithfulness to the next.
[20] Think of it—the LORD is ready to
heal me!
I will sing his praises with
instruments
every day of my life
in the Temple of the LORD.

HOW WE LIVE

Our relationships

GALATIANS 6:1-3 According to today's reading in Galatians, we please God in our relationships when we are helpful and giving. Sounds easy—so why do we often fail to do it? (1) *We become focused on ourselves and don't want to be distracted.* Life, by itself, is pretty overwhelming. It's okay to take care of ourselves; we just have to keep a good balance with focusing on others so that we aren't completely self-centered. (2) *We become afraid to get involved with other people's problems.* Certain boundaries are wise and necessary, but we must be willing to get our hands dirty. (3) *We don't want to enable someone's problem.* There's always the danger that the person you're helping won't appreciate it or will only ask for more. However, we are only called to give, not to govern what is done with the gift or judge whether it is adequately appreciated. • From wherever you are, you can take a small step toward how God wants you to live in relationship with others. Maybe it means calling your difficult family member when it's easier to stay away. Maybe it means just being there for a hurting friend. Whatever it is, step out of your comfort zone and be a blessing to others.

²¹Isaiah had said to Hezekiah's servants, "Make an ointment from figs and spread it over the boil, and Hezekiah will recover."

²²And Hezekiah had asked, "What sign will prove that I will go to the Temple of the LORD?"

37:4 Or *the rabshakeh;* also in 37:8.   **37:7** Hebrew *I will put a spirit in him.*   **37:9** Hebrew *of Cush.*   **37:20** As in Dead Sea Scrolls (see also 2 Kgs 19:19); Masoretic Text reads *you alone are the LORD.*   **37:25** As in Dead Sea Scrolls (see also 2 Kgs 19:24); Masoretic Text lacks *in many foreign lands.*   **37:27** As in Dead Sea Scrolls and some Greek manuscripts (see also 2 Kgs 19:26); most Hebrew manuscripts read *like a terraced field.*   **37:36** Hebrew *When they.*   **38:8** Hebrew *the steps.*   **38:10** Hebrew *enter the gates of Sheol?*   **38:18** Hebrew *Sheol.*

GALATIANS 6:1-18

Paul closes his letter to the Galatians with one of the foundational principles of life: We reap what we sow.

Dear brothers and sisters, if another believer* is overcome by some sin, you who are godly* should gently and humbly help that person back onto the right path. And be careful not to fall into the same temptation yourself. ²Share each other's burdens, and in this way obey the law of Christ. ³If you think you are too important to help someone, you are only fooling yourself. You are not that important.

⁴Pay careful attention to your own work, for then you will get the satisfaction of a job well done, and you won't need to compare yourself to anyone else. ⁵For we are each responsible for our own conduct.

⁶Those who are taught the word of God should provide for their teachers, sharing all good things with them.

⁷Don't be misled—you cannot mock the justice of God. You will always harvest what you plant. ⁸Those who live only to satisfy their own sinful nature will harvest decay and death from that sinful nature. But those who live to please the Spirit will harvest everlasting life from the Spirit. ⁹So let's not get tired of doing what is good. At just the right time we will reap a harvest of blessing if we don't give up. ¹⁰Therefore, whenever we have the opportunity, we should do good to everyone—especially to those in the family of faith.

¹¹NOTICE WHAT LARGE LETTERS I USE AS I WRITE THESE CLOSING WORDS IN MY OWN HANDWRITING.

¹²Those who are trying to force you to be circumcised want to look good to others. They don't want to be persecuted for teaching that the cross of Christ alone can save. ¹³And even those who advocate circumcision don't keep the whole law themselves. They only want you to be circumcised so they can boast about it and claim you as their disciples.

¹⁴As for me, may I never boast about anything except the cross of our Lord Jesus Christ. Because of that cross,* my interest in this world has been crucified, and the world's interest in me has also died. ¹⁵It doesn't matter whether we have been circumcised or not. What counts is whether we have been transformed into a new creation. ¹⁶May God's peace and mercy be upon all who live by this principle; they are the new people of God.*

¹⁷From now on, don't let anyone trouble me with these things. For I bear on my body the scars that show I belong to Jesus.

¹⁸Dear brothers and sisters,* may the grace of our Lord Jesus Christ be with your spirit. Amen.

6:1a Greek *Brothers, if a man.*   **6:1b** Greek *spiritual.*   **6:14** Or *Because of him.*   **6:16** Greek *this principle, and upon the Israel of God.*   **6:18** Greek *Brothers.*

PSALM 65:1-13

For the choir director: A song. A psalm of David.

¹ **W**hat mighty praise, O God,
    belongs to you in Zion.
  We will fulfill our vows to you,
²   for you answer our prayers.
    All of us must come to you.
³ Though we are overwhelmed by our sins,
    you forgive them all.
⁴ What joy for those you choose to bring near,
    those who live in your holy courts.
  What festivities await us
    inside your holy Temple.

⁵ You faithfully answer our prayers with awesome deeds,
    O God our savior.
  You are the hope of everyone on earth,
    even those who sail on distant seas.
⁶ You formed the mountains by your power

and armed yourself with mighty
strength.
7 You quieted the raging oceans
with their pounding waves
and silenced the shouting of the
nations.
8 Those who live at the ends of
the earth
stand in awe of your wonders.
From where the sun rises to where
it sets,
you inspire shouts of joy.

9 You take care of the earth and
water it,
making it rich and fertile.
The river of God has plenty of water;
it provides a bountiful harvest
of grain,
for you have ordered it so.
10 You drench the plowed ground
with rain,

melting the clods and leveling
the ridges.
You soften the earth with showers
and bless its abundant crops.
11 You crown the year with a bountiful
harvest;
even the hard pathways overflow
with abundance.
12 The grasslands of the wilderness
become a lush pasture,
and the hillsides blossom with joy.
13 The meadows are clothed with flocks
of sheep,
and the valleys are carpeted with
grain.
They all shout and sing for joy!

PROVERBS 23:24
The father of godly children has cause for
joy. What a pleasure to have children who
are wise.*
23:24 Hebrew *to have a wise son.*

SEPTEMBER**22**

ISAIAH 39:1–41:16
It was a balancing act for an ancient king to show
enough of his riches to garner the respect of
foreigners, but not so much that they were tempted
to conquer him. Hezekiah crossed over that line
with the envoys from Babylon.

Soon after this, Merodach-baladan son of
Baladan, king of Babylon, sent Hezekiah
his best wishes and a gift. He had heard
that Hezekiah had been very sick and that
he had recovered. 2 Hezekiah was delighted with the Babylonian envoys and
showed them everything in his treasure-
houses—the silver, the gold, the spices,
and the aromatic oils. He also took them
to see his armory and showed them everything in his royal treasuries! There was
nothing in his palace or kingdom that
Hezekiah did not show them.

3 Then Isaiah the prophet went to King
Hezekiah and asked him, "What did those
men want? Where were they from?"

Hezekiah replied, "They came from the
distant land of Babylon."

4 "What did they see in your palace?"
asked Isaiah.

"They saw everything," Hezekiah replied. "I showed them everything I own—
all my royal treasuries."

5 Then Isaiah said to Hezekiah, "Listen
to this message from the LORD of Heaven's
Armies: 6 'The time is coming when everything in your palace—all the treasures
stored up by your ancestors until now—
will be carried off to Babylon. Nothing will
be left,' says the LORD. 7 'Some of your very
own sons will be taken away into exile.
They will become eunuchs who will serve
in the palace of Babylon's king.'"

8 Then Hezekiah said to Isaiah, "This
message you have given me from the
LORD is good." For the king was thinking,
"At least there will be peace and security
during my lifetime."

40:1 "COMFORT, comfort my people,"
  says your God.
2 "Speak tenderly to Jerusalem.
  Tell her that her sad days are gone
    and her sins are pardoned.
  Yes, the LORD has punished her
    twice over
    for all her sins."

3 Listen! It's the voice of someone
    shouting,
  "Clear the way through the wilderness
    for the LORD!
  Make a straight highway through
    the wasteland
    for our God!
4 Fill in the valleys,
    and level the mountains and hills.
  Straighten the curves,
    and smooth out the rough places.
5 Then the glory of the LORD will be
    revealed,
  and all people will see it together.
    The LORD has spoken!"*

6 A voice said, "Shout!"
  I asked, "What should I shout?"

  "Shout that people are like the grass.
    Their beauty fades as quickly
    as the flowers in a field.
7 The grass withers and the flowers fade
    beneath the breath of the LORD.
    And so it is with people.
8 The grass withers and the flowers fade,
    but the word of our God stands
    forever."

9 O Zion, messenger of good news,
    shout from the mountaintops!
  Shout it louder, O Jerusalem.*
    Shout, and do not be afraid.
  Tell the towns of Judah,
    "Your God is coming!"
10 Yes, the Sovereign LORD is coming in
    power.
  He will rule with a powerful arm.
    See, he brings his reward with him
    as he comes.
11 He will feed his flock like a shepherd.
    He will carry the lambs in his arms,
  holding them close to his heart.
    He will gently lead the mother
    sheep with their young.

12 Who else has held the oceans in
    his hand?

Who has measured off the heavens
    with his fingers?
Who else knows the weight of the
    earth
  or has weighed the mountains and
    hills on a scale?
13 Who is able to advise the Spirit of
    the LORD?*
  Who knows enough to give him
    advice or teach him?
14 Has the LORD ever needed anyone's
    advice?
  Does he need instruction about
    what is good?
  Did someone teach him what is right
    or show him the path of justice?

15 No, for all the nations of the world
    are but a drop in the bucket.
  They are nothing more
    than dust on the scales.
  He picks up the whole earth
    as though it were a grain of sand.
16 All the wood in Lebanon's forests
    and all Lebanon's animals
  would not be enough
    to make a burnt offering worthy
    of our God.
17 The nations of the world are worth
    nothing to him.
  In his eyes they count for less than
    nothing—
    mere emptiness and froth.

18 To whom can you compare God?
  What image can you find to
    resemble him?
19 Can he be compared to an idol formed
    in a mold,
    overlaid with gold, and decorated
    with silver chains?
20 Or if people are too poor for that,
    they might at least choose wood
    that won't decay
  and a skilled craftsman
    to carve an image that won't fall
    down!

21 Haven't you heard? Don't you
    understand?
  Are you deaf to the words of God—
  the words he gave before the world
    began?
  Are you so ignorant?
22 God sits above the circle of the earth.

The people below seem like
grasshoppers to him!
He spreads out the heavens like
a curtain
and makes his tent from them.
²³ He judges the great people of
the world
and brings them all to nothing.
²⁴ They hardly get started, barely taking
root,
when he blows on them and they
wither.
The wind carries them off like
chaff.

²⁵ "To whom will you compare me?
Who is my equal?" asks the
Holy One.

²⁶ Look up into the heavens.
Who created all the stars?
He brings them out like an army, one
after another,
calling each by its name.
Because of his great power and
incomparable strength,
not a single one is missing.
²⁷ O Jacob, how can you say the LORD
does not see your troubles?
O Israel, how can you say God
ignores your rights?
²⁸ Have you never heard?
Have you never understood?
The LORD is the everlasting God,

the Creator of all the earth.
He never grows weak or weary.
No one can measure the depths of
his understanding.
²⁹ He gives power to the weak
and strength to the powerless.
³⁰ Even youths will become weak and
tired,
and young men will fall in
exhaustion.
³¹ But those who trust in the LORD will
find new strength.
They will soar high on wings like
eagles.
They will run and not grow weary.
They will walk and not faint.

⁴¹:¹"LISTEN in silence before me, you
lands beyond the sea.
Bring your strongest arguments.
Come now and speak.
The court is ready for your case.

² "Who has stirred up this king from
the east,
rightly calling him to God's service?
Who gives this man victory over many
nations
and permits him to trample their
kings underfoot?
With his sword, he reduces armies to
dust.
With his bow, he scatters them like
chaff before the wind.

Relying on God's power

EPHESIANS 1:19-20 What a tremendous truth: God's great power is at work on our behalf—the same power that created the universe and raised Jesus from the dead. Here are some things to remember: (1) God is on your side, ready to help you meet each and every obstacle. (2) God's power is never stagnant or out of commission—it is always actively working on your behalf. (3) God is always fighting against the forces of evil on your behalf—no human strength or spiritual power from the evil world (not even Satan himself) can deter or change God's power at work on your behalf. • When you truly grasp this truth, you begin to understand the strength that you have. The power that set the galaxies spinning, that holds the earth in place, that calmed the seas, that turned water into wine—*that* power is in your life. Why would we go through life trying to do things in our own strength? And yet, so many of us fall into that very temptation. Be different. Thank God for his power at work in your life and on your behalf. Rely on him instead of yourself.

HOW WE LIVE

³ He chases them away and goes
on safely,
though he is walking over
unfamiliar ground.
⁴ Who has done such mighty deeds,
summoning each new generation
from the beginning of time?
It is I, the LORD, the First and the Last.
I alone am he."

⁵ The lands beyond the sea watch
in fear.
Remote lands tremble and mobilize
for war.
⁶ The idol makers encourage one
another,
saying to each other, "Be strong!"
⁷ The carver encourages the goldsmith,
and the molder helps at the anvil.
"Good," they say. "It's coming along
fine."
Carefully they join the parts together,
then fasten the thing in place so it
won't fall over.

⁸ "But as for you, Israel my servant,
Jacob my chosen one,
descended from Abraham
my friend,
⁹ I have called you back from the ends
of the earth,
saying, 'You are my servant.'
For I have chosen you
and will not throw you away.
¹⁰ Don't be afraid, for I am with you.
Don't be discouraged, for I am your
God.
I will strengthen you and help you.
I will hold you up with my
victorious right hand.

¹¹ "See, all your angry enemies lie there,
confused and humiliated.
Anyone who opposes you will die
and come to nothing.
¹² You will look in vain
for those who tried to conquer you.
Those who attack you
will come to nothing.
¹³ For I hold you by your right hand—
I, the LORD your God.
And I say to you,
'Don't be afraid. I am here to
help you.
¹⁴ Though you are a lowly worm, O Jacob,

don't be afraid, people of Israel,
for I will help you.
I am the LORD, your Redeemer.
I am the Holy One of Israel.'
¹⁵ You will be a new threshing
instrument
with many sharp teeth.
You will tear your enemies apart,
making chaff of mountains.
¹⁶ You will toss them into the air,
and the wind will blow them
all away;
a whirlwind will scatter them.
Then you will rejoice in the LORD.
You will glory in the Holy One
of Israel."

40:3-5 Greek version reads *He is a voice shouting in the wilderness, / "Prepare the way for the LORD's coming! / Clear a road for our God! / Fill in the valleys, / and level the mountains and hills. / And then the glory of the LORD will be revealed, / and all people will see the salvation sent from God. / The LORD has spoken!"* Compare Matt 3:3; Mark 1:3; Luke 3:4-6. **40:9** Or *O messenger of good news, shout to Zion from the mountaintops! Shout it louder to Jerusalem.* **40:13** Greek version reads *Who can know the LORD's thoughts?* Compare Rom 11:34; 1 Cor 2:16.

EPHESIANS 1:1-23

Paul wrote this letter to the Ephesian believers from a prison in Rome. Because of his faith, he found a way to talk about freedom and life despite being incarcerated.

This letter is from Paul, chosen by the will of God to be an apostle of Christ Jesus.

I am writing to God's holy people in Ephesus,* who are faithful followers of Christ Jesus.

²May God our Father and the Lord Jesus Christ give you grace and peace.

³All praise to God, the Father of our Lord Jesus Christ, who has blessed us with every spiritual blessing in the heavenly realms because we are united with Christ. ⁴Even before he made the world, God loved us and chose us in Christ to be holy and without fault in his eyes. ⁵God decided in advance to adopt us into his own family by bringing us to himself through Jesus Christ. This is what he wanted to do, and it gave him great pleasure. ⁶So we praise God for the glorious grace he has poured out on us who belong to his dear Son.* ⁷He is so rich in kindness and grace that he purchased our freedom with the blood of his Son and forgave our sins. ⁸He has showered

his kindness on us, along with all wisdom and understanding.

[9] God has now revealed to us his mysterious plan regarding Christ, a plan to fulfill his own good pleasure. [10] And this is the plan: At the right time he will bring everything together under the authority of Christ—everything in heaven and on earth. [11] Furthermore, because we are united with Christ, we have received an inheritance from God,* for he chose us in advance, and he makes everything work out according to his plan.

[12] God's purpose was that we Jews who were the first to trust in Christ would bring praise and glory to God. [13] And now you Gentiles have also heard the truth, the Good News that God saves you. And when you believed in Christ, he identified you as his own* by giving you the Holy Spirit, whom he promised long ago. [14] The Spirit is God's guarantee that he will give us the inheritance he promised and that he has purchased us to be his own people. He did this so we would praise and glorify him.

[15] Ever since I first heard of your strong faith in the Lord Jesus and your love for God's people everywhere,* [16] I have not stopped thanking God for you. I pray for you constantly, [17] asking God, the glorious Father of our Lord Jesus Christ, to give you spiritual wisdom* and insight so that you might grow in your knowledge of God. [18] I pray that your hearts will be flooded with light so that you can understand the confident hope he has given to those he called—his holy people who are his rich and glorious inheritance.*

[19] I also pray that you will understand the incredible greatness of God's power for us who believe him. This is the same mighty power [20] that raised Christ from the dead and seated him in the place of honor at God's right hand in the heavenly realms. [21] Now he is far above any ruler or authority or power or leader or anything else—not only in this world but also in the world to come. [22] God has put all things under the authority of Christ and has made him head over all things for the benefit of the church. [23] And the church is his body; it is made full and complete by Christ, who fills all things everywhere with himself.

1:1 The most ancient manuscripts do not include *in Ephesus.*
1:6 Greek *to us in the beloved.*   **1:11** Or *we have become God's inheritance.*   **1:13** Or *he put his seal on you.*
1:15 Some manuscripts read *your faithfulness to the Lord Jesus and to God's people everywhere.*   **1:17** Or *to give you the Spirit of wisdom.*   **1:18** Or *called, and the rich and glorious inheritance he has given to his holy people.*

PSALM 66:1-20
For the choir director: A song. A psalm.

[1] **S**hout joyful praises to God, all
the earth!
[2] Sing about the glory of his name!
Tell the world how glorious he is.
[3] Say to God, "How awesome are your deeds!
Your enemies cringe before your mighty power.
[4] Everything on earth will worship you;
they will sing your praises,
shouting your name in glorious songs."   *Interlude*

[5] Come and see what our God has done,
what awesome miracles he performs for people!
[6] He made a dry path through the Red Sea,*
and his people went across on foot.
There we rejoiced in him.
[7] For by his great power he rules forever.
He watches every movement of the nations;
let no rebel rise in defiance.   *Interlude*

[8] Let the whole world bless our God
and loudly sing his praises.
[9] Our lives are in his hands,
and he keeps our feet from stumbling.
[10] You have tested us, O God;
you have purified us like silver.
[11] You captured us in your net
and laid the burden of slavery on our backs.
[12] Then you put a leader over us.*
We went through fire and flood,
but you brought us to a place of great abundance.

[13] Now I come to your Temple with burnt offerings
to fulfill the vows I made to you—
[14] yes, the sacred vows that I made
when I was in deep trouble.

¹⁵ That is why I am sacrificing burnt
offerings to you—
the best of my rams as a pleasing
aroma,
and a sacrifice of bulls and
male goats.   *Interlude*

¹⁶ Come and listen, all you who fear God,
and I will tell you what he did for me.
¹⁷ For I cried out to him for help,
praising him as I spoke.
¹⁸ If I had not confessed the sin in my
heart,
the Lord would not have listened.
¹⁹ But God did listen!
He paid attention to my prayer.

SEPTEMBER**23**

ISAIAH 41:17–43:13
The later chapters of Isaiah cycle through similar
themes: God's faithfulness, Israel's unfaithfulness,
Israel's restoration from exile, the coming Messiah.
The Messiah would extend God's blessings on Israel
to the entire world.

"**W**hen the poor and needy search for
water and there is none,
and their tongues are parched
from thirst,
then I, the Lord, will answer them.
I, the God of Israel, will never
abandon them.
¹⁸ I will open up rivers for them on the
high plateaus.
I will give them fountains of water
in the valleys.
I will fill the desert with pools
of water.
Rivers fed by springs will flow
across the parched ground.
¹⁹ I will plant trees in the barren desert—
cedar, acacia, myrtle, olive, cypress,
fir, and pine.
²⁰ I am doing this so all who see this
miracle
will understand what it means—
that it is the Lord who has done this,
the Holy One of Israel who created it.

²⁰ Praise God, who did not ignore
my prayer
or withdraw his unfailing love
from me.

66:6 Hebrew *the sea.* 66:12 Or *You made people ride over
our heads.*

PROVERBS 23:25-28
So give your father and mother joy! May
she who gave you birth be happy. □ O my
son, give me your heart. May your eyes take
delight in following my ways. A prostitute
is a dangerous trap; a promiscuous woman
is as dangerous as falling into a narrow
well. She hides and waits like a robber, eager to make more men unfaithful.

²¹ "Present the case for your idols,"
says the Lord.
"Let them show what they can do,"
says the King of Israel.*
²² "Let them try to tell us what happened
long ago
so that we may consider the
evidence.
Or let them tell us what the future
holds,
so we can know what's going to
happen.
²³ Yes, tell us what will occur in the days
ahead.
Then we will know you are gods.
In fact, do anything—good or bad!
Do something that will amaze and
frighten us.
²⁴ But no! You are less than nothing and
can do nothing at all.
Those who choose you pollute
themselves.
²⁵ "But I have stirred up a leader who will
come from the north.
I have called him by name from
the east.
I will give him victory over kings
and princes.

He will trample them as a potter
   treads on clay.

26 "Who told you from the beginning
      that this would happen?
   Who predicted this,
      making you admit that he was right?
      No one said a word!
27 I was the first to tell Zion,
      'Look! Help is on the way!'*
   I will send Jerusalem a messenger
      with good news.
28 Not one of your idols told you this.
      Not one gave any answer when
      I asked.
29 See, they are all foolish, worthless
      things.
   All your idols are as empty as the
      wind.

42:1 "Look at my servant, whom
      I strengthen.
   He is my chosen one, who pleases
      me.
   I have put my Spirit upon him.
   He will bring justice to the nations.
2 He will not shout
      or raise his voice in public.
3 He will not crush the weakest reed
      or put out a flickering candle.
   He will bring justice to all who have
      been wronged.
4 He will not falter or lose heart
      until justice prevails throughout the
      earth.
   Even distant lands beyond the sea
      will wait for his instruction.*"

5 God, the Lord, created the heavens
      and stretched them out.
   He created the earth and everything
      in it.
   He gives breath to everyone,
      life to everyone who walks the
      earth.
   And it is he who says,
6 "I, the Lord, have called you to
      demonstrate my righteousness.
   I will take you by the hand and
      guard you,
   and I will give you to my people, Israel,
      as a symbol of my covenant with
      them.
   And you will be a light to guide
      the nations.

7   You will open the eyes of the blind.
   You will free the captives from prison,
      releasing those who sit in dark
      dungeons.

8 "I am the Lord; that is my name!
   I will not give my glory to anyone
      else,
   nor share my praise with carved
      idols.
9 Everything I prophesied has come
      true,
   and now I will prophesy again.
   I will tell you the future before it
      happens."

10 Sing a new song to the Lord!
   Sing his praises from the ends of
      the earth!
   Sing, all you who sail the seas,
      all you who live in distant
      coastlands.
11 Join in the chorus, you desert towns;
      let the villages of Kedar rejoice!
   Let the people of Sela sing for joy;
      shout praises from the
      mountaintops!
12 Let the whole world glorify the Lord;
      let it sing his praise.
13 The Lord will march forth like a
      mighty hero;
   he will come out like a warrior, full
      of fury.
   He will shout his battle cry
      and crush all his enemies.

14 He will say, "I have long been silent;
      yes, I have restrained myself.
   But now, like a woman in labor,
      I will cry and groan and pant.
15 I will level the mountains and hills
      and blight all their greenery.
   I will turn the rivers into dry land
      and will dry up all the pools.
16 I will lead blind Israel down a
      new path,
   guiding them along an unfamiliar
      way.
   I will brighten the darkness before
      them
   and smooth out the road ahead
      of them.
   Yes, I will indeed do these things;
      I will not forsake them.
17 But those who trust in idols,

who say, 'You are our gods,'
will be turned away in shame.

18 "Listen, you who are deaf!
Look and see, you blind!
19 Who is as blind as my own people,
my servant?
Who is as deaf as my messenger?
Who is as blind as my chosen people,
the servant of the LORD?
20 You see and recognize what is right
but refuse to act on it.
You hear with your ears,
but you don't really listen."

21 Because he is righteous,
the LORD has exalted his glorious law.
22 But his own people have been robbed
and plundered,
enslaved, imprisoned, and trapped.
They are fair game for anyone
and have no one to protect them,
no one to take them back home.

23 Who will hear these lessons from
the past
and see the ruin that awaits you
in the future?
24 Who allowed Israel to be robbed
and hurt?
It was the LORD, against whom
we sinned,
for the people would not walk in
his path,
nor would they obey his law.
25 Therefore, he poured out his fury
on them
and destroyed them in battle.
They were enveloped in flames,
but they still refused to understand.
They were consumed by fire,
but they did not learn their lesson.

43:1But now, O Jacob, listen to the LORD
who created you.
O Israel, the one who formed
you says,
"Do not be afraid, for I have ransomed
you.
I have called you by name; you are
mine.
2 When you go through deep waters,
I will be with you.
When you go through rivers
of difficulty,
you will not drown.

When you walk through the fire of
oppression,
you will not be burned up;
the flames will not consume you.
3 For I am the LORD, your God,
the Holy One of Israel, your Savior.
I gave Egypt as a ransom for your
freedom;
I gave Ethiopia* and Seba in your
place.
4 Others were given in exchange for
you.
I traded their lives for yours
because you are precious to me.
You are honored, and I love you.

5 "Do not be afraid, for I am with you.
I will gather you and your children
from east and west.
6 I will say to the north and south,
'Bring my sons and daughters back
to Israel
from the distant corners of the
earth.
7 Bring all who claim me as their God,
for I have made them for my glory.
It was I who created them.'"

8 Bring out the people who have eyes
but are blind,
who have ears but are deaf.
9 Gather the nations together!
Assemble the peoples of the world!
Which of their idols has ever foretold
such things?
Which can predict what will
happen tomorrow?
Where are the witnesses of such
predictions?
Who can verify that they spoke the
truth?

10 "But you are my witnesses, O Israel!"
says the LORD.
"You are my servant.
You have been chosen to know me,
believe in me,
and understand that I alone am
God.
There is no other God—
there never has been, and there
never will be.
11 I, yes I, am the LORD,
and there is no other Savior.
12 First I predicted your rescue,

then I saved you and proclaimed
　　it to the world.
No foreign god has ever done this.
You are witnesses that I am the
　　only God,"
　　says the LORD.
13 "From eternity to eternity I am God.
No one can snatch anyone out
　　of my hand.
No one can undo what I have done."

41:21 Hebrew *the King of Jacob.* See note on 14:1.
41:27 Or '*Look! They are coming home.*'   42:4 Greek
version reads *And his name will be the hope of all the world.*
Compare Matt 12:21.   43:3 Hebrew *Cush.*

EPHESIANS 2:1-22
Christ offers life, peace, and unity—not just to his
people, the Jews, but to all people. How does your
life reflect what Christ offers?

Once you [believers] were dead because
of your disobedience and your many sins.
² You used to live in sin, just like the rest of
the world, obeying the devil—the commander of the powers in the unseen
world.* He is the spirit at work in the
hearts of those who refuse to obey God.
³ All of us used to live that way, following
the passionate desires and inclinations of
our sinful nature. By our very nature we
were subject to God's anger, just like
everyone else.

⁴ But God is so rich in mercy, and he
loved us so much, ⁵ that even though we
were dead because of our sins, he gave us

life when he raised Christ from the dead.
(It is only by God's grace that you have been
saved!) ⁶ For he raised us from the dead
along with Christ and seated us with him
in the heavenly realms because we are
united with Christ Jesus. ⁷ So God can point
to us in all future ages as examples of the
incredible wealth of his grace and kindness toward us, as shown in all he has done
for us who are united with Christ Jesus.

⁸ God saved you by his grace when you
believed. And you can't take credit for this;
it is a gift from God. ⁹ Salvation is not a reward for the good things we have done, so
none of us can boast about it. ¹⁰ For we are
God's masterpiece. He has created us
anew in Christ Jesus, so we can do the
good things he planned for us long ago.

¹¹ Don't forget that you Gentiles used
to be outsiders. You were called "uncircumcised heathens" by the Jews, who
were proud of their circumcision, even
though it affected only their bodies and
not their hearts. ¹² In those days you were
living apart from Christ. You were excluded from citizenship among the people of Israel, and you did not know the
covenant promises God had made to
them. You lived in this world without God
and without hope. ¹³ But now you have
been united with Christ Jesus. Once you
were far away from God, but now you have
been brought near to him through the
blood of Christ.

HOW WE LIVE

Dealing with problems

ISAIAH 43:2 One of the things that should be affected by our faith is how
we deal with problems. It's not that we have any *fewer* problems, that's
for sure. In fact, sometimes having faith creates problems because we
are often called to live in a counter-cultural way. But when it comes to
problems, God has promised that we are in some ways untouchable—not
by pain, not by misfortune, but by abandonment and destruction. What
we face in life, we never face alone. God is with us. What we endure
cannot completely destroy us. Our souls are eternally safe. • Granted,
the problems you face on a daily basis are usually not issues of complete
destruction or ultimate abandonment. Nevertheless, you can face even
the smallest tricky details from a position of strength instead of worry
and fear. God has promised that nothing will overwhelm you. You can
face the deep waters, the rivers of difficulty, and the fire of oppression
with the promise from God, "I will be with you."

[14]For Christ himself has brought peace to us. He united Jews and Gentiles into one people when, in his own body on the cross, he broke down the wall of hostility that separated us. [15]He did this by ending the system of law with its commandments and regulations. He made peace between Jews and Gentiles by creating in himself one new people from the two groups. [16]Together as one body, Christ reconciled both groups to God by means of his death on the cross, and our hostility toward each other was put to death.

[17]He brought this Good News of peace to you Gentiles who were far away from him, and peace to the Jews who were near. [18]Now all of us can come to the Father through the same Holy Spirit because of what Christ has done for us.

[19]So now you Gentiles are no longer strangers and foreigners. You are citizens along with all of God's holy people. You are members of God's family. [20]Together, we are his house, built on the foundation of the apostles and the prophets. And the cornerstone is Christ Jesus himself. [21]We are carefully joined together in him, becoming a holy temple for the Lord. [22]Through him you Gentiles are also being made part of this dwelling where God lives by his Spirit.

2:2 Greek *obeying the commander of the power of the air.*

PSALM 67:1-7
For the choir director: A song. A psalm, to be accompanied by stringed instruments.

[1] May God be merciful and bless us.
    May his face smile with favor on us.
               Interlude

[2] May your ways be known throughout the earth,
    your saving power among people everywhere.
[3] May the nations praise you, O God.
    Yes, may all the nations praise you.
[4] Let the whole world sing for joy,
    because you govern the nations with justice
    and guide the people of the whole world.   *Interlude*
[5] May the nations praise you,
    O God.
    Yes, may all the nations praise you.
[6] Then the earth will yield its harvests,
    and God, our God, will richly bless us.
[7] Yes, God will bless us,
    and people all over the world will fear him.

PROVERBS 23:29-35
Who has anguish? Who has sorrow? Who is always fighting? Who is always complaining? Who has unnecessary bruises? Who has bloodshot eyes? It is the one who spends long hours in the taverns, trying out new drinks. Don't gaze at the wine, seeing how red it is, how it sparkles in the cup, how smoothly it goes down. For in the end it bites like a poisonous snake; it stings like a viper. You will see hallucinations, and you will say crazy things. You will stagger like a sailor tossed at sea, clinging to a swaying mast. And you will say, "They hit me, but I didn't feel it. I didn't even know it when they beat me up. When will I wake up so I can look for another drink?"

SEPTEMBER**24**

ISAIAH 43:14–45:10
Isaiah prophesied from about 740–681 BC. In Isaiah 44:28–45:1, he gives the name of the Persian king who would allow the exiles to return to Judah. That man's name was Cyrus—and he didn't come to the throne until about 150 years after this prophecy!

This is what the LORD says—your Redeemer, the Holy One of Israel:

    "For your sakes I will send an army against Babylon,
    forcing the Babylonians* to flee
    in those ships they are so proud of.

15 I am the LORD, your Holy One,
  Israel's Creator and King.
16 I am the LORD, who opened a way
    through the waters,
  making a dry path through the sea.
17 I called forth the mighty army of Egypt
    with all its chariots and horses.
  I drew them beneath the waves, and
    they drowned,
    their lives snuffed out like a
    smoldering candlewick.

18 "But forget all that—
    it is nothing compared to what I am
    going to do.
19 For I am about to do something new.
  See, I have already begun! Do you
    not see it?
  I will make a pathway through the
    wilderness.
  I will create rivers in the dry
    wasteland.
20 The wild animals in the fields will
    thank me,
    the jackals and owls, too,
    for giving them water in the desert.
  Yes, I will make rivers in the dry
    wasteland
    so my chosen people can be
    refreshed.
21 I have made Israel for myself,
    and they will someday honor me
    before the whole world.

22 "But, dear family of Jacob, you refuse
    to ask for my help.
  You have grown tired of me,
    O Israel!
23 You have not brought me sheep or
    goats for burnt offerings.
  You have not honored me with
    sacrifices,
  though I have not burdened and
    wearied you
    with requests for grain offerings
    and frankincense.
24 You have not brought me fragrant
    calamus
    or pleased me with the fat from
    sacrifices.
  Instead, you have burdened me with
    your sins
    and wearied me with your faults.

25 "I—yes, I alone—will blot out your sins
    for my own sake
    and will never think of them again.
26 Let us review the situation together,
    and you can present your case to
    prove your innocence.
27 From the very beginning, your first
    ancestor sinned against me;
    all your leaders broke my laws.
28 That is why I have disgraced your
    priests;
  I have decreed complete
    destruction* for Jacob
    and shame for Israel.

44:1 "BUT now, listen to me, Jacob my
    servant,
    Israel my chosen one.
2 The LORD who made you and helps
    you says:
  Do not be afraid, O Jacob, my servant,
    O dear Israel,* my chosen one.
3 For I will pour out water to quench
    your thirst
    and to irrigate your parched fields.
  And I will pour out my Spirit on your
    descendants,
    and my blessing on your children.
4 They will thrive like watered grass,
    like willows on a riverbank.
5 Some will proudly claim, 'I belong to
    the LORD.'
  Others will say, 'I am a descendant
    of Jacob.'
  Some will write the LORD's name on
    their hands
    and will take the name of Israel as
    their own."

6 This is what the LORD says—Israel's
King and Redeemer, the LORD of Heaven's
Armies:

  "I am the First and the Last;
    there is no other God.
7 Who is like me?
  Let him step forward and prove to
    you his power.
  Let him do as I have done since
    ancient times
    when I established a people and
    explained its future.
8 Do not tremble; do not be afraid.
  Did I not proclaim my purposes for
    you long ago?

You are my witnesses—is there any
other God?
No! There is no other Rock—
not one!"

9 How foolish are those who
manufacture idols.
These prized objects are really
worthless.
The people who worship idols don't
know this,
so they are all put to shame.
10 Who but a fool would make his
own god—
an idol that cannot help him
one bit?
11 All who worship idols will be
disgraced
along with all these craftsmen—
mere humans—
who claim they can make a god.
They may all stand together,
but they will stand in terror and
shame.

12 The blacksmith stands at his forge to
make a sharp tool,
pounding and shaping it with all his
might.
His work makes him hungry and
weak.
It makes him thirsty and faint.
13 Then the wood-carver measures a
block of wood
and draws a pattern on it.
He works with chisel and plane
and carves it into a human figure.
He gives it human beauty
and puts it in a little shrine.
14 He cuts down cedars;
he selects the cypress and the oak;
he plants the pine in the forest
to be nourished by the rain.
15 Then he uses part of the wood to
make a fire.
With it he warms himself and bakes
his bread.
Then—yes, it's true—he takes the rest
of it
and makes himself a god
to worship!
He makes an idol
and bows down in front of it!
16 He burns part of the tree to roast
his meat

and to keep himself warm.
He says, "Ah, that fire feels good."
17 Then he takes what's left
and makes his god: a carved idol!
He falls down in front of it,
worshiping and praying to it.
"Rescue me!" he says.
"You are my god!"

18 Such stupidity and ignorance!
Their eyes are closed, and they
cannot see.
Their minds are shut, and they
cannot think.
19 The person who made the idol never
stops to reflect,
"Why, it's just a block of wood!
I burned half of it for heat
and used it to bake my bread and
roast my meat.
How can the rest of it be a god?
Should I bow down to worship a
piece of wood?"
20 The poor, deluded fool feeds
on ashes.
He trusts something that can't help
him at all.
Yet he cannot bring himself to ask,
"Is this idol that I'm holding in my
hand a lie?"

21 "Pay attention, O Jacob,
for you are my servant, O Israel.
I, the LORD, made you,
and I will not forget you.
22 I have swept away your sins like
a cloud.
I have scattered your offenses like
the morning mist.
Oh, return to me,
for I have paid the price to set
you free."

23 Sing, O heavens, for the LORD has
done this wondrous thing.
Shout for joy, O depths of the earth!
Break into song,
O mountains and forests and every
tree!
For the LORD has redeemed Jacob
and is glorified in Israel.

24 This is what the LORD says—
your Redeemer and Creator:
"I am the LORD, who made all things.
I alone stretched out the heavens.

Who was with me
    when I made the earth?
25 I expose the false prophets as liars
    and make fools of fortune-tellers.
I cause the wise to give bad advice,
    thus proving them to be fools.
26 But I carry out the predictions of
    my prophets!
    By them I say to Jerusalem, 'People
      will live here again,'
and to the towns of Judah, 'You will be
    rebuilt;
    I will restore all your ruins!'
27 When I speak to the rivers and say,
    'Dry up!'
    they will be dry.
28 When I say of Cyrus, 'He is my
    shepherd,'
    he will certainly do as I say.
He will command, 'Rebuild Jerusalem';
    he will say, 'Restore the Temple.'"

45:1 THIS is what the LORD says to Cyrus,
    his anointed one,
    whose right hand he will empower.
Before him, mighty kings will be
    paralyzed with fear.
    Their fortress gates will be opened,
    never to shut again.
2 This is what the LORD says:

"I will go before you, Cyrus,
    and level the mountains.*
I will smash down gates of bronze
    and cut through bars of iron.

3 And I will give you treasures hidden
    in the darkness—
    secret riches.
I will do this so you may know that
    I am the LORD,
    the God of Israel, the one who calls
    you by name.

4 "And why have I called you for
    this work?
    Why did I call you by name when
    you did not know me?
It is for the sake of Jacob my servant,
    Israel my chosen one.
5 I am the LORD;
    there is no other God.
I have equipped you for battle,
    though you don't even know me,
6 so all the world from east to west
    will know there is no other God.
I am the LORD, and there is no other.
7   I create the light and make the
    darkness.
I send good times and bad times.
    I, the LORD, am the one who does
    these things.

8 "Open up, O heavens,
    and pour out your righteousness.
Let the earth open wide
    so salvation and righteousness can
    sprout up together.
    I, the LORD, created them.

9 "What sorrow awaits those who argue
    with their Creator.

WHO GOD IS   God is loving

EPHESIANS 3:18-19   Have you ever seen a toddler answer the question, "How much does daddy love you?" Having been well coached, the child spreads her arms as wide as she can and says with great delight, "THIS much!" • So how much does our Father God love us? Apparently words can barely describe it, for Paul knows that the love of Christ "is too great to understand fully." But Paul attempts a description anyway: God's love is so wide that it reaches around the whole earth, offering salvation to any who are willing to believe; so long that it stretches from the creation of the world to the return of Jesus, surrounding all people across all of time; so high that it stretches from earth right up to heaven; so deep that it reaches into the depths of our struggles, depression, and grief—no darkness is so deep that God's love cannot shine into it. • So how much does God love you? Jesus spread his arms as wide as he could and had them nailed to a cross. *That's* how much you are loved.

Does a clay pot argue with
  its maker?
Does the clay dispute with the one
  who shapes it, saying,
  'Stop, you're doing it wrong!'
Does the pot exclaim,
  'How clumsy can you be?'
10 How terrible it would be if a newborn
  baby said to its father,
  'Why was I born?'
or if it said to its mother,
  'Why did you make me this way?'"

43:14 Or *Chaldeans.* **43:28** The Hebrew term used here
refers to the complete consecration of things or people to
the LORD, either by destroying them or by giving them as an
offering. **44:2** Hebrew *Jeshurun,* a term of endearment for
Israel. **45:2** As in Dead Sea Scrolls and Greek version;
Masoretic Text reads *the swellings.*

EPHESIANS 3:1-21
Paul reminded the predominantly Gentile Christians
in Ephesus of the amazing fact that God had
included them in his plan of salvation. Paul was
specially chosen to bring this Good News to the
Gentiles.

When I think of all this, I, Paul, a prisoner
of Christ Jesus for the benefit of you Gentiles* . . . ²assuming, by the way, that you
know God gave me the special responsibility of extending his grace to you Gentiles. ³As I briefly wrote earlier, God
himself revealed his mysterious plan to
me. ⁴As you read what I have written, you
will understand my insight into this plan
regarding Christ. ⁵God did not reveal it to
previous generations, but now by his
Spirit he has revealed it to his holy
apostles and prophets.

⁶And this is God's plan: Both Gentiles
and Jews who believe the Good News
share equally in the riches inherited by
God's children. Both are part of the same
body, and both enjoy the promise of
blessings because they belong to Christ
Jesus.* ⁷By God's grace and mighty power,
I have been given the privilege of serving
him by spreading this Good News.

⁸Though I am the least deserving of all
God's people, he graciously gave me the
privilege of telling the Gentiles about the
endless treasures available to them in
Christ. ⁹I was chosen to explain to everyone* this mysterious plan that God, the
Creator of all things, had kept secret from
the beginning.

¹⁰God's purpose in all this was to use
the church to display his wisdom in its
rich variety to all the unseen rulers and
authorities in the heavenly places. ¹¹This
was his eternal plan, which he carried out
through Christ Jesus our Lord.

¹²Because of Christ and our faith in
him,* we can now come boldly and confidently into God's presence. ¹³So please
don't lose heart because of my trials here.
I am suffering for you, so you should feel
honored.

¹⁴When I think of all this, I fall to my
knees and pray to the Father,* ¹⁵the Creator of everything in heaven and on
earth.* ¹⁶I pray that from his glorious, unlimited resources he will empower you
with inner strength through his Spirit.
¹⁷Then Christ will make his home in your
hearts as you trust in him. Your roots will
grow down into God's love and keep you
strong. ¹⁸And may you have the power to
understand, as all God's people should,
how wide, how long, how high, and how
deep his love is. ¹⁹May you experience the
love of Christ, though it is too great to
understand fully. Then you will be made
complete with all the fullness of life and
power that comes from God.

²⁰Now all glory to God, who is able,
through his mighty power at work within
us, to accomplish infinitely more than we
might ask or think. ²¹Glory to him in the
church and in Christ Jesus through all
generations forever and ever! Amen.

3:1 Paul resumes this thought in verse 14: "When I think of
all this, I fall to my knees and pray to the Father." **3:6** Or
because they are united with Christ Jesus. **3:9** Some
manuscripts omit *to everyone.* **3:12** Or *Because of Christ's
faithfulness.* **3:14** Some manuscripts read *the Father of our
Lord Jesus Christ.* **3:15** Or *from whom every family in
heaven and on earth takes its name.*

PSALM 68:1-18
*For the choir director: A song. A psalm
of David.*

¹ **R**ise up, O God, and scatter your
  enemies.
  Let those who hate God run for
    their lives.
² Blow them away like smoke.
  Melt them like wax in a fire.
  Let the wicked perish in the
    presence of God.
³ But let the godly rejoice.

Let them be glad in God's presence.
Let them be filled with joy.
⁴ Sing praises to God and to his name!
Sing loud praises to him who rides
the clouds.
His name is the LORD—
rejoice in his presence!

⁵ Father to the fatherless, defender of
widows—
this is God, whose dwelling is holy.
⁶ God places the lonely in families;
he sets the prisoners free and gives
them joy.
But he makes the rebellious live in a
sun-scorched land.

⁷ O God, when you led your people out
from Egypt,
when you marched through the dry
wasteland,   *Interlude*
⁸ the earth trembled, and the heavens
poured down rain
before you, the God of Sinai,
before God, the God of Israel.
⁹ You sent abundant rain, O God,
to refresh the weary land.
¹⁰ There your people finally settled,
and with a bountiful harvest, O God,
you provided for your needy people.

¹¹ The Lord gives the word,
and a great army* brings the good
news.
¹² Enemy kings and their armies flee,
while the women of Israel divide
the plunder.

---

¹³ Even those who lived among the
sheepfolds found treasures—
doves with wings of silver
and feathers of gold.
¹⁴ The Almighty scattered the enemy
kings
like a blowing snowstorm on
Mount Zalmon.

¹⁵ The mountains of Bashan are majestic,
with many peaks stretching high
into the sky.
¹⁶ Why do you look with envy, O rugged
mountains,
at Mount Zion, where God has
chosen to live,
where the LORD himself will live
forever?

¹⁷ Surrounded by unnumbered
thousands of chariots,
the Lord came from Mount Sinai
into his sanctuary.
¹⁸ When you ascended to the heights,
you led a crowd of captives.
You received gifts from the people,
even from those who rebelled
against you.
Now the LORD God will live among
us there.

68:11 Or *a host of women.*

PROVERBS 24:1-2

Don't envy evil people or desire their
company. For their hearts plot violence,
and their words always stir up trouble.

SEPTEMBER**25**

ISAIAH 45:11–48:11

Throughout history God used whomever he chose
to enact his plan. Nebuchadnezzar of Babylon took
the Jews into exile, fulfilling the fall God predicted
if his people didn't follow him. Then it was Cyrus of
Persia who defeated Babylon and eventually began
the return of the exiles.

This is what the LORD says—
the Holy One of Israel and your
Creator:

"Do you question what I do for my
children?
Do you give me orders about the
work of my hands?
¹² I am the one who made
the earth
and created people to live on it.
With my hands I stretched out the
heavens.

All the stars are at my command.
¹³ I will raise up Cyrus to fulfill my
righteous purpose,
and I will guide his actions.
He will restore my city and free my
captive people—
without seeking a reward!
I, the LORD of Heaven's Armies,
have spoken!"

¹⁴This is what the LORD says:

"You will rule the Egyptians,
the Ethiopians,* and the Sabeans.
They will come to you with all their
merchandise,
and it will all be yours.
They will follow you as prisoners
in chains.
They will fall to their knees in front
of you and say,
'God is with you, and he is the only God.
There is no other.'"

¹⁵ Truly, O God of Israel, our Savior,
you work in mysterious ways.
¹⁶ All craftsmen who make idols will be
humiliated.
They will all be disgraced together.
¹⁷ But the LORD will save the people
of Israel
with eternal salvation.
Throughout everlasting ages,
they will never again be humiliated
and disgraced.

¹⁸ For the LORD is God,
and he created the heavens
and earth
and put everything in place.
He made the world to be lived in,
not to be a place of empty chaos.
"I am the LORD," he says,
"and there is no other.
¹⁹ I publicly proclaim bold promises.
I do not whisper obscurities in
some dark corner.
I would not have told the people of
Israel* to seek me
if I could not be found.
I, the LORD, speak only what is true
and declare only what is right.

²⁰ "Gather together and come,
you fugitives from surrounding
nations.

What fools they are who carry around
their wooden idols
and pray to gods that cannot save!
²¹ Consult together, argue your case.
Get together and decide what to say.
Who made these things known so
long ago?
What idol ever told you they would
happen?
Was it not I, the LORD?
For there is no other God but me,
a righteous God and Savior.
There is none but me.
²² Let all the world look to me for
salvation!
For I am God; there is no other.
²³ I have sworn by my own name;
I have spoken the truth,
and I will never go back on my
word:
Every knee will bend to me,
and every tongue will confess
allegiance to me.*"
²⁴ The people will declare,
"The LORD is the source of all my
righteousness and strength."
And all who were angry with him
will come to him and be ashamed.
²⁵ In the LORD all the generations of
Israel will be justified,
and in him they will boast.

^{46:1} BEL and Nebo, the gods of Babylon,
bow as they are lowered to the
ground.
They are being hauled away on
ox carts.
The poor beasts stagger under
the weight.
² Both the idols and their owners are
bowed down.
The gods cannot protect the people,
and the people cannot protect
the gods.
They go off into captivity together.

³ "Listen to me, descendants of Jacob,
all you who remain in Israel.
I have cared for you since you were
born.
Yes, I carried you before you were
born.
⁴ I will be your God throughout your
lifetime—
until your hair is white with age.

I made you, and I will care for you.
I will carry you along and save you.

5 "To whom will you compare me?
Who is my equal?
6 Some people pour out their silver
and gold
and hire a craftsman to make a god
from it.
Then they bow down and
worship it!
7 They carry it around on their
shoulders,
and when they set it down, it
stays there.
It can't even move!
And when someone prays to it, there
is no answer.
It can't rescue anyone from
trouble.

8 "Do not forget this! Keep it in mind!
Remember this, you guilty ones.
9 Remember the things I have done
in the past.
For I alone am God!
I am God, and there is none like me.
10 Only I can tell you the future
before it even happens.
Everything I plan will come to pass,
for I do whatever I wish.
11 I will call a swift bird of prey from
the east—

a leader from a distant land to come
and do my bidding.
I have said what I would do,
and I will do it.

12 "Listen to me, you stubborn people
who are so far from doing right.
13 For I am ready to set things right,
not in the distant future, but right
now!
I am ready to save Jerusalem*
and show my glory to Israel.

47:1 COME down, virgin daughter of
Babylon, and sit in the dust.
For your days of sitting on a throne
have ended.
O daughter of Babylonia,* never again
will you be
the lovely princess, tender and
delicate.
2 Take heavy millstones and grind flour.
Remove your veil, and strip off your
robe.
Expose yourself to public view.
3 You will be naked and burdened
with shame.
I will take vengeance against you
without pity."

4 Our Redeemer, whose name is the
LORD of Heaven's Armies,
is the Holy One of Israel.

HOW WE LIVE Church involvement

EPHESIANS 4:3-6 All believers across the world are "united in the Spirit"
(4:3), part of one body, one Spirit, one glorious hope, one Lord, one faith,
one baptism. Paul's point is difficult to miss. As a believer, you've joined
a worldwide body that is united by faith in Christ. We will have our minor
differences, but the bottom line is the same.   • As great as that worldwide family is, every believer needs to be part of a local family of believers, a local church. Why is that? Because we can't do the Christian life
alone. God has given his church an enormous responsibility—to make
disciples in every nation (Matthew 28:18-20, February 14). This involves
preaching, teaching, healing, nurturing, giving, administering, building,
and many other tasks. If we had to fulfill this command as individuals,
we might as well give up without trying—it would be impossible. But God
calls us as members of his body. Some of us can do one task; some can
do another. Together we can obey God more fully than any of us could
alone. Working together, the church can express the fullness of Christ
to a hungry, thirsty, hurting, dying world.

5 "O beautiful Babylon, sit now in
    darkness and silence.
  Never again will you be known as
    the queen of kingdoms.
6 For I was angry with my chosen people
    and punished them by letting them
    fall into your hands.
  But you, Babylon, showed them no
    mercy.
  You oppressed even the elderly.
7 You said, 'I will reign forever as queen
    of the world!'
  You did not reflect on your actions
    or think about their consequences.

8 "Listen to this, you pleasure-loving
    kingdom,
    living at ease and feeling secure.
  You say, 'I am the only one, and there is
    no other.
  I will never be a widow or lose my
    children.'
9 Well, both these things will come
    upon you in a moment:
    widowhood and the loss of your
    children.
  Yes, these calamities will come upon
    you,
    despite all your witchcraft
    and magic.

10 "You felt secure in your wickedness.
    'No one sees me,' you said.
  But your 'wisdom' and 'knowledge'
    have led you astray,
    and you said, 'I am the only one, and
    there is no other.'
11 So disaster will overtake you,
    and you won't be able to charm
    it away.
  Calamity will fall upon you,
    and you won't be able to buy your
    way out.
  A catastrophe will strike you suddenly,
    one for which you are not prepared.

12 "Now use your magical charms!
    Use the spells you have worked at
    all these years!
  Maybe they will do you some good.
    Maybe they can make someone
    afraid of you.
13 All the advice you receive has made
    you tired.
  Where are all your astrologers,

those stargazers who make
    predictions each month?
  Let them stand up and save you
    from what the future holds.
14 But they are like straw burning in
    a fire;
    they cannot save themselves from
    the flame.
  You will get no help from them at all;
    their hearth is no place to sit for
    warmth.
15 And all your friends,
    those with whom you've done
    business since childhood,
  will go their own ways,
    turning a deaf ear to your cries.

48:1 "LISTEN to me, O family of Jacob,
    you who are called by the name of
    Israel
    and born into the family of Judah.
  Listen, you who take oaths in the name
    of the LORD
    and call on the God of Israel.
  You don't keep your promises,
2   even though you call yourself the
    holy city
    and talk about depending on the God
    of Israel,
    whose name is the LORD of
    Heaven's Armies.
3 Long ago I told you what was going to
    happen.
  Then suddenly I took action,
    and all my predictions came true.
4 For I know how stubborn and
    obstinate you are.
  Your necks are as unbending as
    iron.
  Your heads are as hard as bronze.
5 That is why I told you what would
    happen;
    I told you beforehand what I was
    going to do.
  Then you could never say, 'My idols
    did it.
  My wooden image and metal god
    commanded it to happen!'
6 You have heard my predictions and
    seen them fulfilled,
    but you refuse to admit it.
  Now I will tell you new things,
    secrets you have not yet heard.

[7] They are brand new, not things from
the past.
So you cannot say, 'We knew that all
the time!'

[8] "Yes, I will tell you of things that are
entirely new,
things you never heard of before.
For I know so well what traitors you
are.
You have been rebels from birth.
[9] Yet for my own sake and for the honor
of my name,
I will hold back my anger and not
wipe you out.
[10] I have refined you, but not as silver
is refined.
Rather, I have refined you in the
furnace of suffering.
[11] I will rescue you for my sake—
yes, for my own sake!
I will not let my reputation be
tarnished,
and I will not share my glory with
idols!"

45:14 Hebrew *Cushites.*   **45:19** Hebrew *of Jacob.* See note
on 14:1.   **45:23** Hebrew *will confess;* Greek version reads
will confess and give praise to God. Compare Rom 14:11.
46:13 Hebrew *Zion.*   **47:1** Or *Chaldea;* also in 47:5.

EPHESIANS 4:1-16

Ephesians 1–3 explains the objective reality of our
salvation. Ephesians 4–6 explains how we should
live in light of all that Christ has done.

Therefore I [Paul], a prisoner for serving
the Lord, beg you to lead a life worthy of
your calling, for you have been called by
God. [2]Always be humble and gentle. Be
patient with each other, making allowance
for each other's faults because of your
love. [3]Make every effort to keep yourselves united in the Spirit, binding yourselves together with peace. [4]For there is
one body and one Spirit, just as you have
been called to one glorious hope for the
future. [5]There is one Lord, one faith, one
baptism, [6]and one God and Father, who is
over all and in all and living through all.

[7]However, he has given each one of us a
special gift* through the generosity of
Christ. [8]That is why the Scriptures say,

"When he ascended to the heights,
he led a crowd of captives
and gave gifts to his people."*

[9]Notice that it says "he ascended." This
clearly means that Christ also descended
to our lowly world.* [10]And the same one
who descended is the one who ascended
higher than all the heavens, so that he
might fill the entire universe with himself.

[11]Now these are the gifts Christ gave to
the church: the apostles, the prophets, the
evangelists, and the pastors and teachers.
[12]Their responsibility is to equip God's
people to do his work and build up the
church, the body of Christ. [13]This will
continue until we all come to such unity
in our faith and knowledge of God's Son
that we will be mature in the Lord, measuring up to the full and complete standard of Christ.

[14]Then we will no longer be immature
like children. We won't be tossed and
blown about by every wind of new teaching. We will not be influenced when people try to trick us with lies so clever they
sound like the truth. [15]Instead, we will
speak the truth in love, growing in every
way more and more like Christ, who is the
head of his body, the church. [16]He makes
the whole body fit together perfectly. As
each part does its own special work, it
helps the other parts grow, so that the
whole body is healthy and growing and
full of love.

4:7 Greek *a grace.*   **4:8** Ps 68:18.   **4:9** Or *to the lowest
parts of the earth.*

PSALM 68:19-35

Praise the Lord; praise God our savior!
For each day he carries us in his
arms.   *Interlude*
[20] Our God is a God who saves!
The Sovereign LORD rescues us
from death.

[21] But God will smash the heads of his
enemies,
crushing the skulls of those who
love their guilty ways.
[22] The Lord says, "I will bring my
enemies down from Bashan;
I will bring them up from the
depths of the sea.
[23] You, my people, will wash your feet
in their blood,
and even your dogs will get their
share!"

24 Your procession has come into view,
    O God—
      the procession of my God and King
      as he goes into the sanctuary.
25 Singers are in front, musicians behind;
    between them are young women
    playing tambourines.
26 Praise God, all you people of Israel;
    praise the LORD, the source of
    Israel's life.
27 Look, the little tribe of Benjamin leads
    the way.
    Then comes a great throng of rulers
      from Judah
    and all the rulers of Zebulun and
      Naphtali.

28 Summon your might, O God.
    Display your power, O God, as you
    have in the past.
29 The kings of the earth are bringing
    tribute
    to your Temple in Jerusalem.
30 Rebuke these enemy nations—
    these wild animals lurking in the
      reeds,
    this herd of bulls among the weaker
      calves.
    Make them bring bars of silver in
      humble tribute.

    Scatter the nations that delight in
      war.
31 Let Egypt come with gifts of precious
    metals*;
    let Ethiopia* bow in submission to
      God.
32 Sing to God, you kingdoms of the
    earth.
    Sing praises to the Lord.
               Interlude
33 Sing to the one who rides across the
    ancient heavens,
    his mighty voice thundering from
      the sky.
34 Tell everyone about God's power.
    His majesty shines down on Israel;
    his strength is mighty in the
      heavens.
35 God is awesome in his sanctuary.
    The God of Israel gives power and
      strength to his people.

    Praise be to God!

68:31a Or *of rich cloth.*   **68:31b** Hebrew *Cush.*

PROVERBS 24:3-4
A house is built by wisdom and becomes strong through good sense. Through knowledge its rooms are filled with all sorts of precious riches and valuables.

SEPTEMBER**26**

ISAIAH 48:12–50:11
The Jews returned to their homeland, which was a shadow of its former magnificence. But God promised them that the restoration of their home would exceed what they could imagine.

    "Listen to me, O family of Jacob,
      Israel my chosen one!
    I alone am God,
      the First and the Last.
13 It was my hand that laid the
      foundations of the earth,
    my right hand that spread out the
      heavens above.
    When I call out the stars,
      they all appear in order."

14 Have any of your idols ever told
      you this?
    Come, all of you, and listen:
    The LORD has chosen Cyrus as his ally.
    He will use him to put an end to the
      empire of Babylon
    and to destroy the Babylonian*
      armies.

15 "I have said it: I am calling Cyrus!
    I will send him on this errand and
      will help him succeed.
16 Come closer, and listen to this.
    From the beginning I have told you
      plainly what would happen."

And now the Sovereign Lord and his
  Spirit
    have sent me with this message.

¹⁷ This is what the Lord says—
    your Redeemer, the Holy One of
      Israel:
  "I am the Lord your God,
    who teaches you what is good for
      you
    and leads you along the paths you
      should follow.

¹⁸ Oh, that you had listened to my
    commands!
    Then you would have had peace
      flowing like a gentle river
    and righteousness rolling over you
      like waves in the sea.

¹⁹ Your descendants would have been
    like the sands along the
      seashore—
    too many to count!
  There would have been no need for
    your destruction,
    or for cutting off your family name."

²⁰ Yet even now, be free from your
      captivity!
    Leave Babylon and the
      Babylonians.*
  Sing out this message!
    Shout it to the ends of the earth!
  The Lord has redeemed his servants,
    the people of Israel.*

²¹ They were not thirsty
    when he led them through
      the desert.
  He divided the rock,
    and water gushed out for them
      to drink.

²² "But there is no peace for the wicked,"
    says the Lord.

49:1 Listen to me, all you in distant lands!
    Pay attention, you who are far away!
  The Lord called me before my birth;
    from within the womb he called me
      by name.

² He made my words of judgment as
    sharp as a sword.
  He has hidden me in the shadow
    of his hand.
  I am like a sharp arrow in his quiver.

³ He said to me, "You are my servant,
    Israel,

and you will bring me
    glory."

⁴ I replied, "But my work seems
    so useless!
  I have spent my strength for
    nothing and to no purpose.
  Yet I leave it all in the Lord's hand;
    I will trust God for my reward."

⁵ And now the Lord speaks—
    the one who formed me in my
      mother's womb to be his servant,
    who commissioned me to bring
      Israel back to him.
  The Lord has honored me,
    and my God has given me strength.

⁶ He says, "You will do more than
    restore the people of Israel to me.
  I will make you a light to the
    Gentiles,
    and you will bring my salvation to
      the ends of the earth."

⁷ The Lord, the Redeemer
    and Holy One of Israel,
  says to the one who is despised and
    rejected by the nations,
    to the one who is the servant of rulers:
  "Kings will stand at attention when
    you pass by.
  Princes will also bow low
  because of the Lord, the faithful one,
    the Holy One of Israel, who has
      chosen you."

⁸This is what the Lord says:

"At just the right time, I will respond
    to you.*
  On the day of salvation I will
    help you.
  I will protect you and give you to
    the people
    as my covenant with them.
  Through you I will reestablish the land
    of Israel
    and assign it to its own people
      again.

⁹ I will say to the prisoners, 'Come out in
    freedom,'
    and to those in darkness, 'Come into
      the light.'
  They will be my sheep, grazing in
    green pastures

and on hills that were
previously bare.
10 They will neither hunger nor thirst.
The searing sun will not reach them
anymore.
For the LORD in his mercy will
lead them;
he will lead them beside cool waters.
11 And I will make my mountains into
level paths for them.
The highways will be raised above
the valleys.
12 See, my people will return from
far away,
from lands to the north and west,
and from as far south as Egypt.*"

13 Sing for joy, O heavens!
Rejoice, O earth!
Burst into song, O mountains!
For the LORD has comforted his
people
and will have compassion on them
in their suffering.

14 Yet Jerusalem* says, "The LORD has
deserted us;
the Lord has forgotten us."

15 "Never! Can a mother forget her
nursing child?
Can she feel no love for the child
she has borne?
But even if that were possible,
I would not forget you!
16 See, I have written your name on the
palms of my hands.
Always in my mind is a picture of
Jerusalem's walls in ruins.
17 Soon your descendants will come
back,
and all who are trying to destroy you
will go away.
18 Look around you and see,
for all your children will come back
to you.
As surely as I live," says the LORD,
"they will be like jewels or bridal
ornaments for you to display.

19 "Even the most desolate parts of your
abandoned land
will soon be crowded with your
people.
Your enemies who enslaved you
will be far away.

20 The generations born in exile will
return and say,
'We need more room! It's crowded
here!'
21 Then you will think to yourself,
'Who has given me all these
descendants?
For most of my children were killed,
and the rest were carried away into
exile.
I was left here all alone.
Where did all these people come
from?
Who bore these children?
Who raised them for me?'"

22 This is what the Sovereign LORD says:
"See, I will give a signal to the
godless nations.
They will carry your little sons back to
you in their arms;
they will bring your daughters on
their shoulders.
23 Kings and queens will serve you
and care for all your needs.
They will bow to the earth before you
and lick the dust from your feet.
Then you will know that I am the
LORD.
Those who trust in me will never be
put to shame."

24 Who can snatch the plunder of war
from the hands of a warrior?
Who can demand that a tyrant* let
his captives go?
25 But the LORD says,
"The captives of warriors will be
released,
and the plunder of tyrants will be
retrieved.
For I will fight those who fight you,
and I will save your children.
26 I will feed your enemies with their
own flesh.
They will be drunk with rivers of
their own blood.
All the world will know that I, the
LORD,
am your Savior and your Redeemer,
the Mighty One of Israel.*"

50:1THIS is what the LORD says:

"Was your mother sent away because
I divorced her?

Did I sell you as slaves to my
creditors?
No, you were sold because of
your sins.
And your mother, too, was taken
because of your sins.
² Why was no one there when I came?
Why didn't anyone answer when
I called?
Is it because I have no power to
rescue?
No, that is not the reason!
For I can speak to the sea and make it
dry up!
I can turn rivers into deserts
covered with dying fish.
³ I dress the skies in darkness,
covering them with clothes
of mourning."

⁴ The Sovereign LORD has given me his
words of wisdom,
so that I know how to comfort the
weary.
Morning by morning he wakens me
and opens my understanding to
his will.
⁵ The Sovereign LORD has spoken to me,
and I have listened.
I have not rebelled or turned away.
⁶ I offered my back to those who
beat me

and my cheeks to those who pulled
out my beard.
I did not hide my face
from mockery and spitting.

⁷ Because the Sovereign LORD helps me,
I will not be disgraced.
Therefore, I have set my face like
a stone,
determined to do his will.
And I know that I will not be put
to shame.
⁸ He who gives me justice is near.
Who will dare to bring charges
against me now?
Where are my accusers?
Let them appear!
⁹ See, the Sovereign LORD is on my side!
Who will declare me guilty?
All my enemies will be destroyed
like old clothes that have been
eaten by moths!
¹⁰ Who among you fears the LORD
and obeys his servant?
If you are walking in darkness,
without a ray of light,
trust in the LORD
and rely on your God.
¹¹ But watch out, you who live in your
own light
and warm yourselves by your
own fires.

HOW WE LIVE · Our speech

EPHESIANS 4:29 As part of Christ's body, believers must not use "foul or abusive language." This includes gossip, slander, and coarse language (swearing, telling coarse jokes, or otherwise speaking in an off-color manner). Such speech is worthless, spreads worthlessness, and leads hearers to think about worthless matters. Such speech does not please God. • This can be a tough one, for words slip out quickly—especially if we're frustrated or angry. At other times, we may change our speech slightly in order to fit in with a particular group. Yet to be transformed by Christ means the transforming of your mouth. If you want to please God in your conversations, watch your words. They should be clean and truthful, encouraging those who hear them. • Proverbs 15:28 (May 22) says, "The heart of the godly thinks carefully before speaking; the mouth of the wicked overflows with evil words." Improper language should have no place in your conversation because it does not reflect God's gracious presence in you. How can you praise God and remind others of his goodness when you are speaking coarsely?

This is the reward you will receive
from me:
　　You will soon fall down in great
　　torment.

48:14 Or *Chaldean*.　**48:20a** Or *the Chaldeans*.
48:20b Hebrew *his servant, Jacob*. See note on 14:1.
49:8 Greek version reads *I heard you*. Compare 2 Cor 6:2.
49:12 As in Dead Sea Scrolls, which read *from the region of
Aswan*, which is in southern Egypt. Masoretic Text reads *from
the region of Sinim*.　**49:14** Hebrew *Zion*.　**49:24** As in
Dead Sea Scrolls, Syriac version, and Latin Vulgate (also
see 49:25); Masoretic Text reads *a righteous person*.
49:26 Hebrew *of Jacob*. See note on 14:1.

EPHESIANS 4:17-32

Believers are to live in a way that pleases God, not
out of their own effort but out of the newness of life
that God has created in us. We are transformed by
God into new people.

With the Lord's authority I [Paul] say this:
Live no longer as the Gentiles do, for they
are hopelessly confused. ¹⁸Their minds
are full of darkness; they wander far from
the life God gives because they have
closed their minds and hardened their
hearts against him. ¹⁹They have no sense
of shame. They live for lustful pleasure
and eagerly practice every kind of
impurity.

²⁰But that isn't what you learned about
Christ. ²¹Since you have heard about Jesus
and have learned the truth that comes
from him, ²²throw off your old sinful nature and your former way of life, which is
corrupted by lust and deception. ²³In-
stead, let the Spirit renew your thoughts
and attitudes. ²⁴Put on your new nature,
created to be like God—truly righteous
and holy.

²⁵So stop telling lies. Let us tell our
neighbors the truth, for we are all parts of
the same body. ²⁶And "don't sin by letting
anger control you."* Don't let the sun go
down while you are still angry, ²⁷for anger
gives a foothold to the devil.

²⁸If you are a thief, quit stealing. Instead, use your hands for good hard work,
and then give generously to others in
need. ²⁹Don't use foul or abusive language. Let everything you say be good and
helpful, so that your words will be an encouragement to those who hear them.

³⁰And do not bring sorrow to God's
Holy Spirit by the way you live. Remember, he has identified you as his own,*

guaranteeing that you will be saved on the
day of redemption.

³¹Get rid of all bitterness, rage, anger,
harsh words, and slander, as well as all
types of evil behavior. ³²Instead, be kind
to each other, tenderhearted, forgiving
one another, just as God through Christ
has forgiven you.

4:26 Ps 4:4.　**4:30** Or *has put his seal on you*.

PSALM 69:1-18

*For the choir director: A psalm of David,
to be sung to the tune "Lilies."*

¹ **S**ave me, O God,
　　for the floodwaters are up to
　　　my neck.
² Deeper and deeper I sink into the mire;
　　I can't find a foothold.
　I am in deep water,
　　and the floods overwhelm me.
³ I am exhausted from crying for help;
　　my throat is parched.
　My eyes are swollen with weeping,
　　waiting for my God to help me.
⁴ Those who hate me without cause
　　outnumber the hairs on my head.
　Many enemies try to destroy me
　　with lies,
　　　demanding that I give back what
　　　　I didn't steal.

⁵ O God, you know how foolish I am;
　　my sins cannot be hidden from you.
⁶ Don't let those who trust in you be
　　ashamed because of me,
　O Sovereign LORD of Heaven's
　　Armies.
　Don't let me cause them to be
　　humiliated,
　O God of Israel.
⁷ For I endure insults for your sake;
　　humiliation is written all over
　　　my face.
⁸ Even my own brothers pretend they
　　don't know me;
　　they treat me like a stranger.

⁹ Passion for your house has
　　consumed me,
　　and the insults of those who insult
　　　you have fallen on me.
¹⁰ When I weep and fast,
　　they scoff at me.

11 When I dress in burlap to show
        sorrow,
    they make fun of me.
12 I am the favorite topic of town gossip,
    and all the drunks sing about me.

13 But I keep praying to you, LORD,
    hoping this time you will show me
        favor.
    In your unfailing love, O God,
        answer my prayer with your sure
        salvation.
14 Rescue me from the mud;
    don't let me sink any deeper!
    Save me from those who hate me,
        and pull me from these deep waters.
15 Don't let the floods overwhelm me,
    or the deep waters swallow me,
    or the pit of death devour me.

16 Answer my prayers, O LORD,
    for your unfailing love is
        wonderful.
    Take care of me,
        for your mercy is so plentiful.
17 Don't hide from your servant;
    answer me quickly, for I am in deep
        trouble!
18 Come and redeem me;
    free me from my enemies.

PROVERBS 24:5-6
The wise are mightier than the strong,*
and those with knowledge grow stronger
and stronger. So don't go to war without
wise guidance; victory depends on having
many advisers.

24:5 As in Greek version; Hebrew reads *A wise man is
strength.*

ISAIAH 51:1–53:12
Today's reading includes one of the most quoted
Messianic passages. Isaiah 53 prophesies the
suffering and the sacrifice that the Gospels later
describe in the life and death of Jesus Christ.

    "**L**isten to me, all who hope for
        deliverance—
    all who seek the LORD!
    Consider the rock from which you
        were cut,
        the quarry from which you were
        mined.
2 Yes, think about Abraham, your
        ancestor,
    and Sarah, who gave birth to your
        nation.
    Abraham was only one man when I
        called him.
    But when I blessed him, he became
        a great nation."

3 The LORD will comfort Israel* again
    and have pity on her ruins.
    Her desert will blossom like Eden,
        her barren wilderness like the
        garden of the LORD.

SEPTEMBER**27**

    Joy and gladness will be found there.
        Songs of thanksgiving will fill the air.

4 "Listen to me, my people.
        Hear me, Israel,
    for my law will be proclaimed,
        and my justice will become a light
        to the nations.
5 My mercy and justice are coming
        soon.
    My salvation is on the way.
    My strong arm will bring justice to
        the nations.
    All distant lands will look to me
        and wait in hope for my powerful
        arm.
6 Look up to the skies above,
    and gaze down on the earth below.
    For the skies will disappear like
        smoke,
        and the earth will wear out like a
        piece of clothing.
    The people of the earth will die like
        flies,
    but my salvation lasts forever.
    My righteous rule will never end!

⁷ "Listen to me, you who know right
from wrong
you who cherish my law in your
hearts.
Do not be afraid of people's scorn,
nor fear their insults.
⁸ For the moth will devour them as it
devours clothing.
The worm will eat at them as it eats
wool.
But my righteousness will last forever.
My salvation will continue from
generation to generation."

⁹ Wake up, wake up, O Lᴏʀᴅ! Clothe
yourself with strength!
Flex your mighty right arm!
Rouse yourself as in the days of old
when you slew Egypt, the dragon of
the Nile.*
¹⁰ Are you not the same today,
the one who dried up the sea,
making a path of escape through
the depths
so that your people could cross
over?
¹¹ Those who have been ransomed by
the Lᴏʀᴅ will return.
They will enter Jerusalem* singing,
crowned with everlasting joy.
Sorrow and mourning will disappear,
and they will be filled with joy and
gladness.

¹² "I, yes I, am the one who comforts you.
So why are you afraid of mere
humans,
who wither like the grass and
disappear?
¹³ Yet you have forgotten the Lᴏʀᴅ, your
Creator,
the one who stretched out the sky
like a canopy
and laid the foundations of the
earth.
Will you remain in constant dread of
human oppressors?
Will you continue to fear the anger
of your enemies?
Where is their fury and anger now?
It is gone!
¹⁴ Soon all you captives will be released!
Imprisonment, starvation, and
death will not be your fate!
¹⁵ For I am the Lᴏʀᴅ your God,

who stirs up the sea, causing its
waves to roar.
My name is the Lᴏʀᴅ of Heaven's
Armies.
¹⁶ And I have put my words in your
mouth
and hidden you safely in my hand.
I stretched out* the sky like a canopy
and laid the foundations of the
earth.
I am the one who says to Israel,
'You are my people!'"

¹⁷ Wake up, wake up, O Jerusalem!
You have drunk the cup of the
Lᴏʀᴅ's fury.
You have drunk the cup of terror,
tipping out its last drops.
¹⁸ Not one of your children is left alive
to take your hand and guide you.
¹⁹ These two calamities have fallen on
you:
desolation and destruction, famine
and war.
And who is left to sympathize with
you?
Who is left to comfort you?*
²⁰ For your children have fainted and lie
in the streets,
helpless as antelopes caught in
a net.
The Lᴏʀᴅ has poured out his fury;
God has rebuked them.

²¹ But now listen to this, you afflicted
ones
who sit in a drunken stupor,
though not from drinking wine.
²² This is what the Sovereign Lᴏʀᴅ,
your God and Defender, says:
"See, I have taken the terrible cup
from your hands.
You will drink no more of my fury.
²³ Instead, I will hand that cup to your
tormentors,
those who said, 'We will trample
you into the dust
and walk on your backs.'"

⁵²:¹ Wᴀᴋᴇ up, wake up, O Zion!
Clothe yourself with strength.
Put on your beautiful clothes, O holy
city of Jerusalem,
for unclean and godless people will
enter your gates no longer.

² Rise from the dust, O Jerusalem.
    Sit in a place of honor.
    Remove the chains of slavery from
        your neck,
    O captive daughter of Zion.
³ For this is what the LORD says:
    "When I sold you into exile,
    I received no payment.
    Now I can redeem you
        without having to pay for you."

⁴This is what the Sovereign LORD says: "Long ago my people chose to live in Egypt. Now they are oppressed by Assyria. ⁵What is this?" asks the LORD. "Why are my people enslaved again? Those who rule them shout in exultation. My name is blasphemed all day long.* ⁶But I will reveal my name to my people, and they will come to know its power. Then at last they will recognize that I am the one who speaks to them."

⁷ How beautiful on the mountains
    are the feet of the messenger who
        brings good news,
    the good news of peace and salvation,
    the news that the God of Israel*
        reigns!
⁸ The watchmen shout and sing with joy,
    for before their very eyes
    they see the LORD returning to
        Jerusalem.*

⁹ Let the ruins of Jerusalem break into
        joyful song,
    for the LORD has comforted his
        people.
    He has redeemed Jerusalem.
¹⁰ The LORD has demonstrated his holy
        power
    before the eyes of all the nations.
    All the ends of the earth will see
        the victory of our God.

¹¹ Get out! Get out and leave your
        captivity,
    where everything you touch is
        unclean.
    Get out of there and purify yourselves,
    you who carry home the sacred
        objects of the LORD.
¹² You will not leave in a hurry,
        running for your lives.
    For the LORD will go ahead of you;
    yes, the God of Israel will protect
        you from behind.

¹³ See, my servant will prosper;
    he will be highly exalted.
¹⁴ But many were amazed when they saw
        him.*
    His face was so disfigured he
        seemed hardly human,
    and from his appearance, one
        would scarcely know he was
        a man.

WHO GOD IS Jesus is our sacrifice

ISAIAH 53 Isaiah 53 is an astounding prophecy of the coming Messiah. These words portray a Messiah who would come, not as a conquering king, but as a servant and a sacrifice. Listen to Isaiah's description: He's not attractive or majestic (in other words, he doesn't look like a king); he's despised and rejected; he's a man of sorrows. • So many in Jesus' day wanted a conquering king who would ride into Jerusalem, overthrow Rome, and restore the nation's glory. But Jesus did not come to do that. He came to carry our weaknesses and sorrows, to take our punishment, to be crushed for our sin and rebellion. Who would have imagined that God would choose to save the world through a humble, suffering servant rather than a glorious king? The idea is contrary to human pride and worldly ways. But God often works in ways we don't expect. • The animal sacrifices offered by the Old Testament people were merely a picture of the sacrifice of the One to come. He shed his blood and "the Lord laid on him the sins of us all" (53:6). Jesus is "the Lamb of God who takes away the sin of the world!" (John 1:29, May 1).

15 And he will startle* many nations.
    Kings will stand speechless in
       his presence.
For they will see what they had not
      been told;
    they will understand what they had
      not heard about.*

53:1 Who has believed our message?
    To whom has the Lord revealed his
      powerful arm?
2 My servant grew up in the Lord's
      presence like a tender green
      shoot,
    like a root in dry ground.
There was nothing beautiful or
      majestic about his appearance,
    nothing to attract us to him.
3 He was despised and rejected—
    a man of sorrows, acquainted with
      deepest grief.
We turned our backs on him and
      looked the other way.
He was despised, and we did
      not care.

4 Yet it was our weaknesses he carried;
    it was our sorrows* that weighed
      him down.
And we thought his troubles were a
      punishment from God,
    a punishment for his own sins!
5 But he was pierced for our rebellion,
      crushed for our sins.
He was beaten so we could be whole.
He was whipped so we could be
      healed.
6 All of us, like sheep, have strayed away.
    We have left God's paths to follow
      our own.
Yet the Lord laid on him
    the sins of us all.

7 He was oppressed and treated harshly,
    yet he never said a word.
He was led like a lamb to the
      slaughter.
    And as a sheep is silent before
      the shearers,
    he did not open his mouth.
8 Unjustly condemned,
    he was led away.*
No one cared that he died without
      descendants,

    that his life was cut short
      in midstream.*
But he was struck down
    for the rebellion of my people.
9 He had done no wrong
    and had never deceived anyone.
But he was buried like a criminal;
    he was put in a rich man's grave.

10 But it was the Lord's good plan to
      crush him
    and cause him grief.
Yet when his life is made an offering
      for sin,
    he will have many descendants.
He will enjoy a long life,
    and the Lord's good plan will
      prosper in his hands.
11 When he sees all that is accomplished
      by his anguish,
    he will be satisfied.
And because of his experience,
    my righteous servant will make it
      possible
for many to be counted righteous,
    for he will bear all their sins.
12 I will give him the honors of a
      victorious soldier,
    because he exposed himself to
      death.
He was counted among the rebels.
He bore the sins of many and
      interceded for rebels.

51:3 Hebrew *Zion;* also in 51:16. **51:9** Hebrew *You slew
Rahab; you pierced the dragon.* Rahab is the name of a
mythical sea monster that represents chaos in ancient
literature. The name is used here as a poetic name for Egypt.
51:11 Hebrew *Zion.* **51:16** As in Syriac version (see also
51:13); Hebrew reads *planted.* **51:19** As in Dead Sea Scrolls
and Greek, Latin, and Syriac versions; Masoretic Text reads
How can I comfort you? **52:5** Greek version reads *The
Gentiles continually blaspheme my name because of you.*
Compare Rom 2:24. **52:7** Hebrew *of Zion.* **52:8** Hebrew
to Zion. **52:14** As in Syriac version; Hebrew reads *you.*
52:15a Or *cleanse.* **52:15b** Greek version reads *Those who
have never been told about him will see, / and those who
have never heard of him will understand.* Compare Rom
15:21. **53:4** Or *Yet it was our sicknesses he carried; / it was
our diseases.* **53:8a** Greek version reads *He was humiliated
and received no justice.* Compare Acts 8:33. **53:8b** Or *As
for his contemporaries, / who cared that his life was cut short
in midstream?* Greek version reads *Who can speak of his
descendants? / For his life was taken from the earth.*
Compare Acts 8:33.

EPHESIANS 5:1-33

Paul continued his theme of how to live as a Christian. We live in light and in the power of the Holy
Spirit. This affects every part of our lives—even
behind the closed doors of our own homes.

Imitate God, therefore, in everything you do, because you are his dear children. [2]Live a life filled with love, following the example of Christ. He loved us* and offered himself as a sacrifice for us, a pleasing aroma to God.

[3]Let there be no sexual immorality, impurity, or greed among you. Such sins have no place among God's people. [4]Obscene stories, foolish talk, and coarse jokes—these are not for you. Instead, let there be thankfulness to God. [5]You can be sure that no immoral, impure, or greedy person will inherit the Kingdom of Christ and of God. For a greedy person is an idolater, worshiping the things of this world.

[6]Don't be fooled by those who try to excuse these sins, for the anger of God will fall on all who disobey him. [7]Don't participate in the things these people do. [8]For once you were full of darkness, but now you have light from the Lord. So live as people of light! [9]For this light within you produces only what is good and right and true.

[10]Carefully determine what pleases the Lord. [11]Take no part in the worthless deeds of evil and darkness; instead, expose them. [12]It is shameful even to talk about the things that ungodly people do in secret. [13]But their evil intentions will be exposed when the light shines on them, [14]for the light makes everything visible. This is why it is said,

"Awake, O sleeper,
    rise up from the dead,
    and Christ will give you light."

[15]So be careful how you live. Don't live like fools, but like those who are wise. [16]Make the most of every opportunity in these evil days. [17]Don't act thoughtlessly, but understand what the Lord wants you to do. [18]Don't be drunk with wine, because that will ruin your life. Instead, be filled with the Holy Spirit, [19]singing psalms and hymns and spiritual songs among yourselves, and making music to the Lord in your hearts. [20]And give thanks for everything to God the Father in the name of our Lord Jesus Christ.

[21]And further, submit to one another out of reverence for Christ.

[22]For wives, this means submit to your husbands as to the Lord. [23]For a husband is the head of his wife as Christ is the head of the church. He is the Savior of his body, the church. [24]As the church submits to Christ, so you wives should submit to your husbands in everything.

[25]For husbands, this means love your wives, just as Christ loved the church. He gave up his life for her [26]to make her holy and clean, washed by the cleansing of God's word.* [27]He did this to present her to himself as a glorious church without a spot or wrinkle or any other blemish. Instead, she will be holy and without fault. [28]In the same way, husbands ought to love their wives as they love their own bodies. For a man who loves his wife actually shows love for himself. [29]No one hates his own body but feeds and cares for it, just as Christ cares for the church. [30]And we are members of his body.

[31]As the Scriptures say, "A man leaves his father and mother and is joined to his wife, and the two are united into one."* [32]This is a great mystery, but it is an illustration of the way Christ and the church are one. [33]So again I say, each man must love his wife as he loves himself, and the wife must respect her husband.

5:2 Some manuscripts read *loved you.* 5:26 Greek *washed by water with the word.* 5:31 Gen 2:24.

PSALM 69:19-36

You [LORD] know of my shame, scorn,
        and disgrace.
    You see all that my enemies are
        doing.
[20] Their insults have broken my heart,
        and I am in despair.
    If only one person would show some
        pity;
    if only one would turn and comfort
        me.
[21] But instead, they give me poison*
        for food;
    they offer me sour wine for
        my thirst.

[22] Let the bountiful table set before them
        become a snare
    and their prosperity become
        a trap.*
[23] Let their eyes go blind so they
        cannot see,

and make their bodies shake
continually.*

24 Pour out your fury on them;
consume them with your
burning anger.

25 Let their homes become desolate
and their tents be deserted.

26 To the one you have punished, they
add insult to injury;
they add to the pain of those you
have hurt.

27 Pile their sins up high,
and don't let them go free.

28 Erase their names from the Book
of Life;
don't let them be counted among
the righteous.

29 I am suffering and in pain.
Rescue me, O God, by your saving
power.

30 Then I will praise God's name with
singing,
and I will honor him with
thanksgiving.

31 For this will please the LORD more
than sacrificing cattle,
more than presenting a bull with its
horns and hooves.

32 The humble will see their God at work
and be glad.
Let all who seek God's help be
encouraged.

33 For the LORD hears the cries of
the needy;
he does not despise his imprisoned
people.

34 Praise him, O heaven and earth,
the seas and all that move
in them.

35 For God will save Jerusalem*
and rebuild the towns of Judah.
His people will live there
and settle in their own land.

36 The descendants of those who obey
him will inherit the land,
and those who love him will live
there in safety.

69:21 Or *gall.* **69:22** Greek version reads *Let their bountiful table set before them become a snare, / a trap that makes them think all is well. / Let their blessings cause them to stumble, / and let them get what they deserve.* Compare Rom 11:9. **69:23** Greek version reads *and let their backs be bent forever.* Compare Rom 11:10. **69:35** Hebrew *Zion.*

PROVERBS 24:7

Wisdom is too lofty for fools. Among leaders at the city gate, they have nothing to say.

SEPTEMBER**28**

ISAIAH 54:1–57:14

The book of Acts in the New Testament reveals what a shock it was to early Jewish Christians that salvation was for everyone, including the Gentiles. This shouldn't have been news. Isaiah prophesied that anyone who was willing to place their faith in God was welcome into his Kingdom.

Sing, O childless woman,
you who have never given birth!
Break into loud and joyful song,
O Jerusalem,
you who have never been in labor.
For the desolate woman now has more
children
than the woman who lives with her
husband,"
says the LORD.

2 "Enlarge your house; build an
addition.
Spread out your home, and spare no
expense!

3 For you will soon be bursting at the
seams.
Your descendants will occupy other
nations
and resettle the ruined cities.

4 "Fear not; you will no longer live in
shame.
Don't be afraid; there is no more
disgrace for you.
You will no longer remember the
shame of your youth
and the sorrows of widowhood.

5 For your Creator will be your husband;
   the LORD of Heaven's Armies is his
   name!
   He is your Redeemer, the Holy One
   of Israel,
   the God of all the earth.
6 For the LORD has called you back from
   your grief—
   as though you were a young wife
   abandoned by her husband,"
   says your God.
7 "For a brief moment I abandoned you,
   but with great compassion I will
   take you back.
8 In a burst of anger I turned my face
   away for a little while.
   But with everlasting love I will have
   compassion on you,"
   says the LORD, your Redeemer.

9 "Just as I swore in the time of Noah
   that I would never again let a flood
   cover the earth,
   so now I swear
   that I will never again be angry and
   punish you.
10 For the mountains may move
   and the hills disappear,
   but even then my faithful love for you
   will remain.
   My covenant of blessing will never
   be broken,"
   says the LORD, who has mercy
   on you.

11 "O storm-battered city,
   troubled and desolate!
   I will rebuild you with precious jewels
   and make your foundations from
   lapis lazuli.
12 I will make your towers of sparkling
   rubies,
   your gates of shining gems,
   and your walls of precious stones.
13 I will teach all your children,
   and they will enjoy great peace.
14 You will be secure under a
   government that is just and fair.
   Your enemies will stay far away.
   You will live in peace,
   and terror will not come near.
15 If any nation comes to fight you,
   it is not because I sent them.
   Whoever attacks you will go down
   in defeat.

16 "I have created the blacksmith
   who fans the coals beneath the
   forge
   and makes the weapons of destruction.
   And I have created the armies that
   destroy.
17 But in that coming day
   no weapon turned against you will
   succeed.
   You will silence every voice
   raised up to accuse you.
   These benefits are enjoyed by the
   servants of the LORD;
   their vindication will come
   from me.
   I, the LORD, have spoken!

55:1 "Is anyone thirsty?
   Come and drink—
   even if you have no money!
   Come, take your choice of wine
   or milk—
   it's all free!
2 Why spend your money on food that
   does not give you strength?
   Why pay for food that does you
   no good?
   Listen to me, and you will eat what is
   good.
   You will enjoy the finest food.

3 "Come to me with your ears wide
   open.
   Listen, and you will find life.
   I will make an everlasting covenant
   with you.
   I will give you all the unfailing love I
   promised to David.
4 See how I used him to display my
   power among the peoples.
   I made him a leader among the
   nations.
5 You also will command nations you do
   not know,
   and peoples unknown to you will
   come running to obey,
   because I, the LORD your God,
   the Holy One of Israel, have made
   you glorious."

6 Seek the LORD while you can find him.
   Call on him now while he is near.
7 Let the wicked change their ways
   and banish the very thought of
   doing wrong.

Let them turn to the LORD that he may
    have mercy on them.
Yes, turn to our God, for he will
    forgive generously.

8 "My thoughts are nothing like your
    thoughts," says the LORD.
"And my ways are far beyond
    anything you could imagine.
9 For just as the heavens are higher than
    the earth,
    so my ways are higher than your
        ways
    and my thoughts higher than your
        thoughts.
10 "The rain and snow come down from
    the heavens
    and stay on the ground to water the
        earth.
They cause the grain to grow,
    producing seed for the farmer
    and bread for the hungry.
11 It is the same with my word.
    I send it out, and it always produces
        fruit.
    It will accomplish all I want it to,
    and it will prosper everywhere I
        send it.
12 You will live in joy and peace.
    The mountains and hills will burst
        into song,
    and the trees of the field will clap
        their hands!
13 Where once there were thorns,
    cypress trees will grow.
Where nettles grew, myrtles will
    sprout up.
These events will bring great honor to
    the LORD's name;
    they will be an everlasting sign of
        his power and love."

56:1 THIS is what the LORD says:

"Be just and fair to all.
    Do what is right and good,
for I am coming soon to rescue you
    and to display my righteousness
        among you.
2 Blessed are all those
    who are careful to do this.
Blessed are those who honor my
    Sabbath days of rest
    and keep themselves from doing
        wrong.

3 "Don't let foreigners who commit
    themselves to the LORD say,
    'The LORD will never let me be part
        of his people.'
And don't let the eunuchs say,
    'I'm a dried-up tree with no
        children and no future.'
4 For this is what the LORD says:
I will bless those eunuchs
    who keep my Sabbath days holy
and who choose to do what pleases me
    and commit their lives to me.
5 I will give them—within the walls of
    my house—
    a memorial and a name
    far greater than sons and daughters
        could give.
For the name I give them is an
    everlasting one.
    It will never disappear!

6 "I will also bless the foreigners who
    commit themselves to the LORD,
    who serve him and love his name,
who worship him and do not
    desecrate the Sabbath day of rest,
    and who hold fast to my covenant.
7 I will bring them to my holy mountain
    of Jerusalem
    and will fill them with joy in my
        house of prayer.
I will accept their burnt offerings and
    sacrifices,
    because my Temple will be called a
        house of prayer for all nations.
8 For the Sovereign LORD,
    who brings back the outcasts of
        Israel, says:
I will bring others, too,
    besides my people Israel."

9 Come, wild animals of the field!
    Come, wild animals of the forest!
    Come and devour my people!
10 For the leaders of my people—
    the LORD's watchmen, his
        shepherds—
    are blind and ignorant.
They are like silent watchdogs
    that give no warning when danger
        comes.
They love to lie around, sleeping and
    dreaming.
11 Like greedy dogs, they are never
    satisfied.

They are ignorant shepherds,
  all following their own path
  and intent on personal gain.
¹² "Come," they say, "let's get some wine
    and have a party.
  Let's all get drunk.
  Then tomorrow we'll do it again
    and have an even bigger party!"

⁵⁷:¹ Good people pass away;
    the godly often die before their time.
  But no one seems to care or
    wonder why.
  No one seems to understand
    that God is protecting them from
    the evil to come.
² For those who follow godly paths
    will rest in peace when they die.

³ "But you—come here, you witches'
    children,
  you offspring of adulterers and
    prostitutes!
⁴ Whom do you mock,
    making faces and sticking out your
    tongues?
  You children of sinners and liars!
⁵ You worship your idols with great
    passion
  beneath the oaks and under every
    green tree.
  You sacrifice your children down in
    the valleys,

among the jagged rocks in
    the cliffs.
⁶ Your gods are the smooth stones in
    the valleys.
  You worship them with liquid
    offerings and grain offerings.
  They, not I, are your inheritance.
  Do you think all this makes me
    happy?
⁷ You have committed adultery on every
    high mountain.
  There you have worshiped idols
    and have been unfaithful to me.
⁸ You have put pagan symbols
    on your doorposts and behind
    your doors.
  You have left me
    and climbed into bed with these
    detestable gods.
  You have committed yourselves to
    them.
  You love to look at their naked
    bodies.
⁹ You have given olive oil to Molech*
    with many gifts of perfume.
  You have traveled far,
    even into the world of the dead,*
    to find new gods to love.
¹⁰ You grew weary in your search,
    but you never gave up.
  Desire gave you renewed strength,
    and you did not grow weary.

WHAT THE BIBLE SAYS

Spiritual warfare

EPHESIANS 6:10-17 There exists a world outside of our own—a world we cannot see, a spirit world where real battles are fought. When you became a Christian, you took a side against evil in this cosmic struggle—and you became a part of it. • The battle is not against enemies of flesh and blood. Instead, we battle the demons over whom Satan has control, the fallen angels who joined Satan in his rebellion and thus became perverted and evil. These are real and powerful beings, not mere fantasies, and believers must not underestimate them. What are their tactics? Demons can at times cause physical, psychological, and emotional turmoil. More often they seek ways to keep nonbelievers in unbelief and render believers ineffective through moral failings. • God does not leave us without protection and weapons, however. With this host of spiritual forces arrayed against us, we need God's full armor. Our enemy is powerful, but he is also a defeated foe. As you prepare to engage him in spiritual warfare, don't be intimidated by his influence. Use the full armor of God and stand together with other believers.

11 "Are you afraid of these idols?
　Do they terrify you?
Is that why you have lied to me
　and forgotten me and my words?
Is it because of my long silence
　that you no longer fear me?
12 Now I will expose your so-called good
　　deeds.
　None of them will help you.
13 Let's see if your idols can save you
　when you cry to them for help.
Why, a puff of wind can knock them
　　down!
If you just breathe on them, they fall
　　over!
But whoever trusts in me will inherit
　　the land
　and possess my holy mountain."

14 God says, "Rebuild the road!
　Clear away the rocks and stones
　so my people can return from
　　captivity."

57:9a Or *to the king.*　**57:9b** Hebrew *into Sheol.*

EPHESIANS 6:1-24
Our faith must affect how we treat people, especially those who are closest to us. Living to please God is a battle, but God provides us with armor for the fight.

Children, obey your parents because you belong to the Lord,* for this is the right thing to do. 2"Honor your father and mother." This is the first commandment with a promise: 3If you honor your father and mother, "things will go well for you, and you will have a long life on the earth."*

4Fathers, do not provoke your children to anger by the way you treat them. Rather, bring them up with the discipline and instruction that comes from the Lord.

5Slaves, obey your earthly masters with deep respect and fear. Serve them sincerely as you would serve Christ. 6Try to please them all the time, not just when they are watching you. As slaves of Christ, do the will of God with all your heart. 7Work with enthusiasm, as though you were working for the Lord rather than for people. 8Remember that the Lord will reward each one of us for the good we do, whether we are slaves or free.

9Masters, treat your slaves in the same way. Don't threaten them; remember, you both have the same Master in heaven, and he has no favorites.

10A final word: Be strong in the Lord and in his mighty power. 11Put on all of God's armor so that you will be able to stand firm against all strategies of the devil. 12For we* are not fighting against flesh-and-blood enemies, but against evil rulers and authorities of the unseen world, against mighty powers in this dark world, and against evil spirits in the heavenly places.

13Therefore, put on every piece of God's armor so you will be able to resist the enemy in the time of evil. Then after the battle you will still be standing firm. 14Stand your ground, putting on the belt of truth and the body armor of God's righteousness. 15For shoes, put on the peace that comes from the Good News so that you will be fully prepared.* 16In addition to all of these, hold up the shield of faith to stop the fiery arrows of the devil.* 17Put on salvation as your helmet, and take the sword of the Spirit, which is the word of God.

18Pray in the Spirit at all times and on every occasion. Stay alert and be persistent in your prayers for all believers everywhere.*

19And pray for me, too. Ask God to give me the right words so I can boldly explain God's mysterious plan that the Good News is for Jews and Gentiles alike.* 20I am in chains now, still preaching this message as God's ambassador. So pray that I will keep on speaking boldly for him, as I should.

21To bring you up to date, Tychicus will give you a full report about what I am doing and how I am getting along. He is a beloved brother and faithful helper in the Lord's work. 22I have sent him to you for this very purpose—to let you know how we are doing and to encourage you.

23Peace be with you, dear brothers and sisters,* and may God the Father and the Lord Jesus Christ give you love with faithfulness. 24May God's grace be eternally upon all who love our Lord Jesus Christ.

6:1 Or *Children, obey your parents who belong to the Lord;* some manuscripts read simply *Children, obey your parents.*

6:2-3 Exod 20:12; Deut 5:16.   **6:12** Some manuscripts read *you.*   **6:15** Or *For shoes, put on the readiness to preach the Good News of peace with God.*   **6:16** Greek *the evil one.* **6:18** Greek *all of God's holy people.*   **6:19** Greek *explain the mystery of the Good News;* some manuscripts read simply *explain the mystery.*   **6:23** Greek *brothers.*

PSALM 70:1-5

For the choir director: A psalm of David, asking God to remember him.

¹ **P**lease, God, rescue me!
    Come quickly, LORD, and help me.
² May those who try to kill me
    be humiliated and put to shame.
May those who take delight in my
        trouble
    be turned back in disgrace.

³ Let them be horrified by their shame,
    for they said, "Aha! We've got
        him now!"
⁴ But may all who search for you
    be filled with joy and gladness
        in you.
May those who love your salvation
    repeatedly shout, "God is great!"
⁵ But as for me, I am poor and needy;
    please hurry to my aid, O God.
You are my helper and my savior;
    O LORD, do not delay.

PROVERBS 24:8

A person who plans evil will get a reputa-tion as a troublemaker.

ISAIAH 57:15–59:21

The cold, hard truth is that sin separates humanity from God. The Israelites had allowed idolatry and spiritual indifference to distance them from God.

The high and lofty one who lives
    in eternity,
    the Holy One, says this:
"I live in the high and holy place
    with those whose spirits are
        contrite and humble.
I restore the crushed spirit of
        the humble
    and revive the courage of those with
        repentant hearts.
¹⁶ For I will not fight against you forever;
    I will not always be angry.
If I were, all people would pass away—
    all the souls I have made.
¹⁷ I was angry,
    so I punished these greedy people.
I withdrew from them,
    but they kept going on their own
        stubborn way.
¹⁸ I have seen what they do,
    but I will heal them anyway!
    I will lead them.
I will comfort those who mourn,
¹⁹   bringing words of praise to
        their lips.

May they have abundant peace, both
        near and far,"
    says the LORD, who heals them.
²⁰ "But those who still reject me are like
        the restless sea,
    which is never still
    but continually churns up mud
        and dirt.
²¹ There is no peace for the wicked,"
    says my God.

⁵⁸:¹ "**S**HOUT with the voice of a trumpet
        blast.
    Shout aloud! Don't be timid.
Tell my people Israel* of their sins!
²   Yet they act so pious!
They come to the Temple every day
    and seem delighted to learn all
        about me.
They act like a righteous nation
    that would never abandon the laws
        of its God.
They ask me to take action on their
        behalf,
    pretending they want to be near me.
³ 'We have fasted before you!' they say.
    'Why aren't you impressed?
We have been very hard on ourselves,
    and you don't even notice it!'

"I will tell you why!" I respond.
"It's because you are fasting to
please yourselves.
Even while you fast,
you keep oppressing your workers.
4 What good is fasting
when you keep on fighting and
quarreling?
This kind of fasting
will never get you anywhere
with me.
5 You humble yourselves
by going through the motions of
penance,
bowing your heads
like reeds bending in the wind.
You dress in burlap
and cover yourselves with ashes.
Is this what you call fasting?
Do you really think this will please
the LORD?

6 "No, this is the kind of fasting I want:
Free those who are wrongly
imprisoned;
lighten the burden of those who
work for you.
Let the oppressed go free,
and remove the chains that bind
people.
7 Share your food with the hungry,
and give shelter to the homeless.
Give clothes to those who need them,
and do not hide from relatives who
need your help.

8 "Then your salvation will come like
the dawn,
and your wounds will quickly heal.
Your godliness will lead you forward,
and the glory of the LORD will
protect you from behind.
9 Then when you call, the LORD will
answer.
'Yes, I am here,' he will quickly reply.

"Remove the heavy yoke of
oppression.
Stop pointing your finger and
spreading vicious rumors!
10 Feed the hungry,
and help those in trouble.
Then your light will shine out from
the darkness,

and the darkness around you will be
as bright as noon.
11 The LORD will guide you continually,
giving you water when you are dry
and restoring your strength.
You will be like a well-watered garden,
like an ever-flowing spring.
12 Some of you will rebuild the deserted
ruins of your cities.
Then you will be known as a
rebuilder of walls
and a restorer of homes.

13 "Keep the Sabbath day holy.
Don't pursue your own interests on
that day,
but enjoy the Sabbath
and speak of it with delight as the
LORD's holy day.
Honor the Sabbath in everything you
do on that day,
and don't follow your own desires
or talk idly.
14 Then the LORD will be your delight.
I will give you great honor
and satisfy you with the inheritance I
promised to your ancestor Jacob.
I, the LORD, have spoken!"

59:1 LISTEN! The LORD's arm is not too
weak to save you,
nor is his ear too deaf to hear you
call.
2 It's your sins that have cut you off
from God.
Because of your sins, he has turned
away
and will not listen anymore.
3 Your hands are the hands of
murderers,
and your fingers are filthy with sin.
Your lips are full of lies,
and your mouth spews corruption.

4 No one cares about being fair
and honest.
The people's lawsuits are based
on lies.
They conceive evil deeds
and then give birth to sin.
5 They hatch deadly snakes
and weave spiders' webs.
Whoever falls into their webs will die,
and there's danger even in getting
near them.

⁶ Their webs can't be made into
    clothing,
  and nothing they do is productive.
All their activity is filled with sin,
  and violence is their trademark.
⁷ Their feet run to do evil,
  and they rush to commit murder.
They think only about sinning.
  Misery and destruction always
    follow them.
⁸ They don't know where to find peace
  or what it means to be just and
    good.
They have mapped out crooked roads,
  and no one who follows them
    knows a moment's peace.

⁹ So there is no justice among us,
  and we know nothing about
    right living.
We look for light but find only
    darkness.
  We look for bright skies but walk in
    gloom.
¹⁰ We grope like the blind along a wall,
  feeling our way like people
    without eyes.
Even at brightest noontime,
  we stumble as though it were dark.
Among the living,
  we are like the dead.
¹¹ We growl like hungry bears;
  we moan like mournful doves.

We look for justice, but it
    never comes.
  We look for rescue, but it is far away
    from us.
¹² For our sins are piled up before God
  and testify against us.
Yes, we know what sinners we are.
¹³ We know we have rebelled and have
    denied the LORD.
  We have turned our backs on our
    God.
We know how unfair and oppressive
    we have been,
  carefully planning our deceitful
    lies.
¹⁴ Our courts oppose the righteous,
  and justice is nowhere to be found.
Truth stumbles in the streets,
  and honesty has been outlawed.
¹⁵ Yes, truth is gone,
  and anyone who renounces evil
    is attacked.

The LORD looked and was displeased
  to find there was no justice.
¹⁶ He was amazed to see that no one
    intervened
  to help the oppressed.
So he himself stepped in to save them
    with his strong arm,
  and his justice sustained him.
¹⁷ He put on righteousness as his
    body armor

Confessing our sins

ISAIAH 59:1-2 God hates sin so much that when Jesus took the sins of the world upon him as he hung on the cross, God the Father had to turn away. God is holy, the complete opposite of sinful mankind, and he will not tolerate our excuses, rationalizations, or attempts to justify our sins. • Sin separates you from God. Not the kind of separation that means you can't be saved—you've been promised salvation because of your acceptance of Jesus' sacrifice on your behalf. Sin causes the kind of separation that occurs between you and a friend if one of you hurts the other. There's tension; there's a breakdown of communication; there's simmering frustration. When you sin against God, you know it and God knows it. You can try to rationalize and excuse it, but the results are inevitable. If you persist in your sin, you will slowly put up a wall between yourself and God. Then you'll begin to wonder why he seems so far away. • Confession is always the antidote. When you stay pure before God on a daily basis, you won't find yourself trying to pound on a brick wall of your own making.

HOW WE LIVE

and placed the helmet of salvation
on his head.
He clothed himself with a robe
of vengeance
and wrapped himself in a cloak
of divine passion.
[18] He will repay his enemies for their
evil deeds.
His fury will fall on his foes.
He will pay them back even to the
ends of the earth.
[19] In the west, people will respect the
name of the LORD;
in the east, they will glorify him.
For he will come like a raging
flood tide
driven by the breath of the LORD.*

[20] "The Redeemer will come to
Jerusalem
to buy back those in Israel
who have turned from their sins,"*
says the LORD.

[21]"And this is my covenant with them,"
says the LORD. "My Spirit will not leave
them, and neither will these words I have
given you. They will be on your lips and on
the lips of your children and your children's children forever. I, the LORD, have
spoken!"

58:1 Hebrew *Jacob.* See note on 14:1.   **59:19** Or *When the
enemy comes like a raging flood tide, / the Spirit of the LORD
will drive him back.*   **59:20** Hebrew *The Redeemer will
come to Zion / to buy back those in Jacob / who have turned
from their sins.* Greek version reads *The one who rescues will
come on behalf of Zion, / and he will turn Jacob away from
ungodliness.* Compare Rom 11:26.

PHILIPPIANS 1:1-26

Paul's letter to the Philippian church is a letter of
joy written from a man who sat in prison as he
wrote. It is a letter of gratitude from a man who
wanted to thank his children in the faith for the
help they had provided.

This letter is from Paul and Timothy,
slaves of Christ Jesus.

I am writing to all of God's holy people
in Philippi who belong to Christ Jesus, including the elders* and deacons.

[2]May God our Father and the Lord Jesus
Christ give you grace and peace.

[3]Every time I think of you, I give thanks
to my God. [4]Whenever I pray, I make my
requests for all of you with joy, [5]for you
have been my partners in spreading the

Good News about Christ from the time
you first heard it until now. [6]And I am certain that God, who began the good work
within you, will continue his work until it
is finally finished on the day when Christ
Jesus returns.

[7]So it is right that I should feel as I do
about all of you, for you have a special
place in my heart. You share with me the
special favor of God, both in my imprisonment and in defending and confirming
the truth of the Good News. [8]God knows
how much I love you and long for you with
the tender compassion of Christ Jesus.

[9]I pray that your love will overflow
more and more, and that you will keep
on growing in knowledge and understanding. [10]For I want you to understand
what really matters, so that you may live
pure and blameless lives until the day of
Christ's return. [11]May you always be filled
with the fruit of your salvation—the righteous character produced in your life by
Jesus Christ*—for this will bring much
glory and praise to God.

[12]And I want you to know, my dear
brothers and sisters,* that everything that
has happened to me here has helped to
spread the Good News. [13]For everyone
here, including the whole palace guard,*
knows that I am in chains because of
Christ. [14]And because of my imprisonment, most of the believers* here have
gained confidence and boldly speak
God's message* without fear.

[15]It's true that some are preaching out
of jealousy and rivalry. But others preach
about Christ with pure motives. [16]They
preach because they love me, for they
know I have been appointed to defend
the Good News. [17]Those others do not
have pure motives as they preach about
Christ. They preach with selfish ambition,
not sincerely, intending to make my
chains more painful to me. [18]But that
doesn't matter. Whether their motives are
false or genuine, the message about
Christ is being preached either way, so I
rejoice. And I will continue to rejoice.
[19]For I know that as you pray for me and
the Spirit of Jesus Christ helps me, this
will lead to my deliverance.

[20]For I fully expect and hope that I will
never be ashamed, but that I will continue

to be bold for Christ, as I have been in the past. And I trust that my life will bring honor to Christ, whether I live or die. [21]For to me, living means living for Christ, and dying is even better. [22]But if I live, I can do more fruitful work for Christ. So I really don't know which is better. [23]I'm torn between two desires: I long to go and be with Christ, which would be far better for me. [24]But for your sakes, it is better that I continue to live.

[25]Knowing this, I am convinced that I will remain alive so I can continue to help all of you grow and experience the joy of your faith. [26]And when I come to you again, you will have even more reason to take pride in Christ Jesus because of what he is doing through me.

1:1 Or *overseers; or bishops.* 1:11 Greek *with the fruit of righteousness through Jesus Christ.* 1:12 Greek *brothers.* 1:13 Greek *including all the Praetorium.* 1:14a Greek *brothers in the Lord.* 1:14b Some manuscripts read *speak the message.*

PSALM 71:1-24

O LORD, I have come to you for protection;
 don't let me be disgraced.
[2] Save me and rescue me,
 for you do what is right.
 Turn your ear to listen to me,
 and set me free.
[3] Be my rock of safety
 where I can always hide.
 Give the order to save me,
 for you are my rock and my fortress.
[4] My God, rescue me from the power of the wicked,
 from the clutches of cruel oppressors.
[5] O Lord, you alone are my hope.
 I've trusted you, O LORD, from childhood.
[6] Yes, you have been with me from birth;
 from my mother's womb you have cared for me.
 No wonder I am always praising you!

[7] My life is an example to many,
 because you have been my strength and protection.
[8] That is why I can never stop praising you;
 I declare your glory all day long.

[9] And now, in my old age, don't set me aside.
 Don't abandon me when my strength is failing.
[10] For my enemies are whispering against me.
 They are plotting together to kill me.
[11] They say, "God has abandoned him.
 Let's go and get him,
 for no one will help him now."

[12] O God, don't stay away.
 My God, please hurry to help me.
[13] Bring disgrace and destruction on my accusers.
 Humiliate and shame those who want to harm me.
[14] But I will keep on hoping for your help;
 I will praise you more and more.
[15] I will tell everyone about your righteousness.
 All day long I will proclaim your saving power,
 though I am not skilled with words.*
[16] I will praise your mighty deeds,
 O Sovereign LORD.
 I will tell everyone that you alone are just.
[17] O God, you have taught me from my earliest childhood,
 and I constantly tell others about the wonderful things you do.
[18] Now that I am old and gray,
 do not abandon me, O God.
 Let me proclaim your power to this new generation,
 your mighty miracles to all who come after me.
[19] Your righteousness, O God, reaches to the highest heavens.
 You have done such wonderful things.
 Who can compare with you, O God?
[20] You have allowed me to suffer much hardship,
 but you will restore me to life again
 and lift me up from the depths of the earth.
[21] You will restore me to even greater honor
 and comfort me once again.
[22] Then I will praise you with music on the harp,

because you are faithful to your
promises, O my God.
I will sing praises to you with a lyre,
O Holy One of Israel.
²³ I will shout for joy and sing your praises,
for you have ransomed me.
²⁴ I will tell about your righteous deeds
all day long,

for everyone who tried to hurt me
has been shamed and humiliated.

71:15 Or *though I cannot count it.*

PROVERBS 24:9-10

The schemes of a fool are sinful; everyone
detests a mocker. □ If you fail under pressure, your strength is too small.

SEPTEMBER**30**

ISAIAH 60:1–62:5

Like most Old Testament prophets, Isaiah had
messages of mercy and hope for a better future
along with warnings about sin and judgment. The
hope of that future was based on the faithfulness of
God rather than the faithfulness of his people.

"Arise, Jerusalem! Let your light shine
for all to see.
For the glory of the LORD rises to
shine on you.
² Darkness as black as night covers all
the nations of the earth,
but the glory of the LORD rises and
appears over you.
³ All nations will come to your light;
mighty kings will come to see your
radiance.

⁴ "Look and see, for everyone is coming
home!
Your sons are coming from distant
lands;
your little daughters will be carried
home.
⁵ Your eyes will shine,
and your heart will thrill with joy,
for merchants from around the world
will come to you.
They will bring you the wealth of
many lands.
⁶ Vast caravans of camels will converge
on you,
the camels of Midian and Ephah.
The people of Sheba will bring gold
and frankincense
and will come worshiping the LORD.
⁷ The flocks of Kedar will be given
to you,

and the rams of Nebaioth will be
brought for my altars.
I will accept their offerings,
and I will make my Temple glorious.

⁸ "And what do I see flying like clouds to
Israel,
like doves to their nests?
⁹ They are ships from the ends of the
earth,
from lands that trust in me,
led by the great ships of Tarshish.
They are bringing the people of Israel
home from far away,
carrying their silver and gold.
They will honor the LORD your God,
the Holy One of Israel,
for he has filled you with splendor.

¹⁰ "Foreigners will come to rebuild your
towns,
and their kings will serve you.
For though I have destroyed you in my
anger,
I will now have mercy on you
through my grace.
¹¹ Your gates will stay open around the
clock
to receive the wealth of many lands.
The kings of the world will be led as
captives
in a victory procession.
¹² For the nations that refuse to serve you
will be destroyed.

¹³ "The glory of Lebanon will be yours—
the forests of cypress, fir, and pine—
to beautify my sanctuary.
My Temple will be glorious!

¹⁴ The descendants of your tormentors
    will come and bow before you.
Those who despised you
    will kiss your feet.
They will call you the City of the LORD,
    and Zion of the Holy One of Israel.

¹⁵ "Though you were once despised
     and hated,
    with no one traveling through you,
I will make you beautiful forever,
    a joy to all generations.
¹⁶ Powerful kings and mighty nations
    will satisfy your every need,
as though you were a child
    nursing at the breast of a queen.
You will know at last that I, the LORD,
    am your Savior and your Redeemer,
    the Mighty One of Israel.*
¹⁷ I will exchange your bronze for gold,
    your iron for silver,
your wood for bronze,
    and your stones for iron.
I will make peace your leader
    and righteousness your ruler.
¹⁸ Violence will disappear from your
     land;
    the desolation and destruction of
     war will end.
Salvation will surround you like city
     walls,
    and praise will be on the lips of all
     who enter there.

¹⁹ "No longer will you need the sun to
     shine by day,
    nor the moon to give its light by
     night,
for the LORD your God will be your
     everlasting light,
    and your God will be your glory.
²⁰ Your sun will never set;
    your moon will not go down.
For the LORD will be your everlasting
     light.
    Your days of mourning will come to
     an end.
²¹ All your people will be righteous.
    They will possess their land forever,
for I will plant them there with my
     own hands
    in order to bring myself glory.
²² The smallest family will become a
     thousand people,

and the tiniest group will become
    a mighty nation.
At the right time, I, the LORD, will
    make it happen."

⁶¹:¹ THE Spirit of the Sovereign LORD is
     upon me,
    for the LORD has anointed me
    to bring good news to the poor.
He has sent me to comfort the
     brokenhearted
    and to proclaim that captives will
     be released
    and prisoners will be freed.*
² He has sent me to tell those who
     mourn
    that the time of the LORD's favor has
     come,*
    and with it, the day of God's anger
     against their enemies.
³ To all who mourn in Israel,*
    he will give a crown of beauty for
     ashes,
a joyous blessing instead of mourning,
    festive praise instead of despair.
In their righteousness, they will be like
     great oaks
    that the LORD has planted for his
     own glory.

⁴ They will rebuild the ancient ruins,
    repairing cities destroyed long ago.
They will revive them,
    though they have been deserted for
     many generations.
⁵ Foreigners will be your servants.
    They will feed your flocks
and plow your fields
    and tend your vineyards.
⁶ You will be called priests of the LORD,
    ministers of our God.
You will feed on the treasures of
     the nations
    and boast in their riches.
⁷ Instead of shame and dishonor,
    you will enjoy a double share
     of honor.
You will possess a double portion of
     prosperity in your land,
    and everlasting joy will be yours.

⁸ "For I, the LORD, love justice.
    I hate robbery and wrongdoing.
I will faithfully reward my people for
     their suffering

and make an everlasting covenant
with them.
⁹ Their descendants will be recognized
and honored among the nations.
Everyone will realize that they are
a people
the LORD has blessed."

¹⁰ I am overwhelmed with joy in the
LORD my God!
For he has dressed me with the
clothing of salvation
and draped me in a robe of
righteousness.
I am like a bridegroom in his
wedding suit
or a bride with her jewels.
¹¹ The Sovereign LORD will show his
justice to the nations of the
world.
Everyone will praise him!
His righteousness will be like a garden
in early spring,
with plants springing up everywhere.

62:1 BECAUSE I love Zion,
I will not keep still.
Because my heart yearns for
Jerusalem,
I cannot remain silent.
I will not stop praying for her
until her righteousness shines like
the dawn,
and her salvation blazes like
a burning torch.
² The nations will see your
righteousness.
World leaders will be blinded by
your glory.
And you will be given a new name
by the LORD's own mouth.
³ The LORD will hold you in his hand for
all to see—
a splendid crown in the hand
of God.
⁴ Never again will you be called "The
Forsaken City"*
or "The Desolate Land."*
Your new name will be "The City of
God's Delight"*
and "The Bride of God,"*
for the LORD delights in you
and will claim you as his bride.
⁵ Your children will commit themselves
to you, O Jerusalem,

just as a young man commits
himself to his bride.
Then God will rejoice over you
as a bridegroom rejoices over
his bride.

60:16 Hebrew *of Jacob.* See note on 14:1. **61:1** Greek
version reads *and the blind will see.* Compare Luke 4:18.
61:2 Or *to proclaim the acceptable year of the LORD.*
61:3 Hebrew *in Zion.* **62:4a** Hebrew *Azubah,* which means
"forsaken." **62:4b** Hebrew *Shemamah,* which means
"desolate." **62:4c** Hebrew *Hephzibah,* which means "my
delight is in her." **62:4d** Hebrew *Beulah,* which means
"married."

PHILIPPIANS 1:27–2:18

Knowing where you belong gives you perspective in
life. Paul wrote to the Philippian Christians about
belonging to heaven and to each other.

Above all, you must live as citizens of
heaven, conducting yourselves in a manner worthy of the Good News about
Christ. Then, whether I come and see you
again or only hear about you, I will know
that you are standing together with one
spirit and one purpose, fighting together
for the faith, which is the Good News.
²⁸Don't be intimidated in any way by your
enemies. This will be a sign to them that
they are going to be destroyed, but that
you are going to be saved, even by God
himself. ²⁹For you have been given not
only the privilege of trusting in Christ but
also the privilege of suffering for him.
³⁰We are in this struggle together. You
have seen my struggle in the past, and you
know that I am still in the midst of it.

²:¹Is there any encouragement from belonging to Christ? Any comfort from his
love? Any fellowship together in the
Spirit? Are your hearts tender and compassionate? ²Then make me truly happy
by agreeing wholeheartedly with each
other, loving one another, and working together with one mind and purpose.

³Don't be selfish; don't try to impress
others. Be humble, thinking of others as
better than yourselves. ⁴Don't look out
only for your own interests, but take an interest in others, too.

⁵You must have the same attitude that
Christ Jesus had.

⁶ Though he was God,*
he did not think of equality with God
as something to cling to.

⁷ Instead, he gave up his divine
    privileges*;
he took the humble position of
    a slave*
and was born as a human being.
When he appeared in human form,*
⁸ he humbled himself in obedience
    to God
and died a criminal's death
    on a cross.

⁹ Therefore, God elevated him to the
    place of highest honor
and gave him the name above all
    other names,
¹⁰ that at the name of Jesus every knee
    should bow,
in heaven and on earth and under
    the earth,
¹¹ and every tongue confess that Jesus
    Christ is Lord,
to the glory of God the Father.

¹²Dear friends, you always followed my instructions when I was with you. And now that I am away, it is even more important. Work hard to show the results of your salvation, obeying God with deep reverence and fear. ¹³For God is working in you, giving you the desire and the power to do what pleases him.

¹⁴Do everything without complaining and arguing, ¹⁵so that no one can criticize you. Live clean, innocent lives as children of God, shining like bright lights in a world full of crooked and perverse people. ¹⁶Hold firmly to the word of life; then, on the day of Christ's return, I will be proud that I did not run the race in vain and that my work was not useless. ¹⁷But I will rejoice even if I lose my life, pouring it out like a liquid offering to God,* just like your faithful service is an offering to God. And I want all of you to share that joy. ¹⁸Yes, you should rejoice, and I will share your joy.

2:6 Or *Being in the form of God.*   **2:7a** Greek *he emptied himself.*   **2:7b** Or *the form of a slave.*   **2:7c** Some English translations put this phrase in verse 8.   **2:17** Greek *I will rejoice even if I am to be poured out as a liquid offering.*

PSALM 72:1-20
A psalm of Solomon.

¹ **G**ive your love of justice to the king,
    O God,
and righteousness to the king's son.
² Help him judge your people in the
    right way;
let the poor always be treated fairly.
³ May the mountains yield prosperity
    for all,
and may the hills be fruitful.

WHO GOD IS   Jesus humbled himself

PHILIPPIANS 2:7-8 The Christians at Philippi must have been a boisterous bunch. Paul takes some time in his short letter to remind them to get along, to work together, to love each other, and better yet . . . to have the same attitude that Jesus had.   • Jesus had a way of turning things upside down. You want to be great? Then be the least of all. You want to be a leader? Then be a servant. You want to live? Then you must die to yourself. And what do all of these actions have in common? An attitude of humility.   • Notice these aspects of Jesus' humility: (1) He knew who he was, but he was not proud. He did not need to cling to his divine nature in order to lord it over people (2:6). (2) He was secure. He was God, but gave up his divine privileges and lowered himself to become human (2:7). (3) He was obedient. He knew and trusted his Father, submitting to his Father's will, even when it meant unbelievable pain and death (2:8).   • The ultimate motivation for Jesus' attitude was his great love. This kind of amazing love brings out the best in us. Show your love for Jesus by cultivating the same attitude of humility in your life. Give up your pride. Submit to God's will in your life, and he will use you and bless you beyond measure.

4 Help him to defend the poor,
   to rescue the children of the needy,
   and to crush their oppressors.
5 May they fear you as long as the
   sun shines,
   as long as the moon remains in
   the sky.
   Yes, forever!

6 May the king's rule be refreshing like
   spring rain on freshly cut grass,
   like the showers that water
   the earth.
7 May all the godly flourish during
   his reign.
   May there be abundant prosperity
   until the moon is no more.
8 May he reign from sea to sea,
   and from the Euphrates River* to
   the ends of the earth.
9 Desert nomads will bow before him;
   his enemies will fall before him in
   the dust.
10 The western kings of Tarshish and
   other distant lands
   will bring him tribute.
   The eastern kings of Sheba and Seba
   will bring him gifts.
11 All kings will bow before him,
   and all nations will serve him.

12 He will rescue the poor when they cry
   to him;
   he will help the oppressed, who
   have no one to defend them.
13 He feels pity for the weak and
   the needy,
   and he will rescue them.
14 He will redeem them from oppression
   and violence,
   for their lives are precious to him.

15 Long live the king!
   May the gold of Sheba be given
   to him.
   May the people always pray for him
   and bless him all day long.
16 May there be abundant grain
   throughout the land,
   flourishing even on the hilltops.
   May the fruit trees flourish like the
   trees of Lebanon,
   and may the people thrive like grass
   in a field.
17 May the king's name endure forever;
   may it continue as long as the sun
   shines.
   May all nations be blessed through
   him
   and bring him praise.

18 Praise the LORD God, the God of Israel,
   who alone does such wonderful
   things.
19 Praise his glorious name forever!
   Let the whole earth be filled with
   his glory.
   Amen and amen!

20 (This ends the prayers of David son
   of Jesse.)

72:8 Hebrew *the river.*

PROVERBS 24:11-12

Rescue those who are unjustly sentenced to die; save them as they stagger to their death. Don't excuse yourself by saying, "Look, we didn't know." For God understands all hearts, and he sees you. He who guards your soul knows you knew. He will repay all people as their actions deserve.

ISAIAH 62:6–65:25

Isaiah had a passion for his people and their spiritual and geographical center—Jerusalem. Today's reading includes some of his most fervent prayers. As with those of other Old Testament prophets, Isaiah's messages contained a mix of warnings of judgment and promises of deliverance.

O Jerusalem, I have posted watchmen
on your walls;
they will pray day and night,
continually.
Take no rest, all you who pray
to the LORD.
⁷ Give the LORD no rest until he
completes his work,
until he makes Jerusalem the pride
of the earth.
⁸ The LORD has sworn to Jerusalem
by his own strength:
"I will never again hand you over
to your enemies.
Never again will foreign warriors
come
and take away your grain and new
wine.
⁹ You raised the grain, and you will eat it,
praising the LORD.
Within the courtyards of the Temple,
you yourselves will drink the wine
you have pressed."

¹⁰ Go out through the gates!
Prepare the highway for my people
to return!
Smooth out the road; pull out the
boulders;
raise a flag for all the nations to see.
¹¹ The LORD has sent this message to
every land:
"Tell the people of Israel,*
'Look, your Savior is coming.
See, he brings his reward with him
as he comes.'"
¹² They will be called "The Holy People"
and "The People Redeemed by the
LORD."

And Jerusalem will be known as
"The Desirable Place"
and "The City No Longer Forsaken."

⁶³:¹ WHO is this who comes from Edom,
from the city of Bozrah,
with his clothing stained red?
Who is this in royal robes,
marching in his great strength?

"It is I, the LORD, announcing your
salvation!
It is I, the LORD, who has the power
to save!"

² Why are your clothes so red,
as if you have been treading out
grapes?

³ "I have been treading the winepress
alone;
no one was there to help me.
In my anger I have trampled
my enemies
as if they were grapes.
In my fury I have trampled my foes.
Their blood has stained my clothes.
⁴ For the time has come for me to
avenge my people,
to ransom them from their
oppressors.
⁵ I was amazed to see that no one
intervened
to help the oppressed.
So I myself stepped in to save them
with my strong arm,
and my wrath sustained me.
⁶ I crushed the nations in my anger
and made them stagger and fall
to the ground,
spilling their blood upon the earth."

⁷ I will tell of the LORD's unfailing love.
I will praise the LORD for all he
has done.
I will rejoice in his great goodness
to Israel,

which he has granted according
to his mercy and love.
⁸ He said, "They are my very
own people.
Surely they will not betray me
again."
And he became their Savior.
⁹ In all their suffering he also suffered,
and he personally* rescued them.
In his love and mercy he redeemed
them.
He lifted them up and carried them
through all the years.
¹⁰ But they rebelled against him
and grieved his Holy Spirit.
So he became their enemy
and fought against them.

¹¹ Then they remembered those days
of old
when Moses led his people out
of Egypt.
They cried out, "Where is the one who
brought Israel through the sea,
with Moses as their shepherd?
Where is the one who sent his Holy
Spirit
to be among his people?
¹² Where is the one whose power was
displayed
when Moses lifted up his hand—
the one who divided the sea before
them,
making himself famous forever?
¹³ Where is the one who led them
through the bottom of the sea?
They were like fine stallions
racing through the desert, never
stumbling.
¹⁴ As with cattle going down into
a peaceful valley,
the Spirit of the LORD gave
them rest.
You led your people, LORD,
and gained a magnificent
reputation."

¹⁵ LORD, look down from heaven;
look from your holy, glorious home,
and see us.
Where is the passion and the might
you used to show on our behalf?
Where are your mercy and
compassion now?
¹⁶ Surely you are still our Father!

Even if Abraham and Jacob* would
disown us,
LORD, you would still be our Father.
You are our Redeemer from ages
past.
¹⁷ LORD, why have you allowed us to turn
from your path?
Why have you given us stubborn
hearts so we no longer fear you?
Return and help us, for we are your
servants,
the tribes that are your special
possession.
¹⁸ How briefly your holy people
possessed your holy place,
and now our enemies have
destroyed it.
¹⁹ Sometimes it seems as though we
never belonged to you,
as though we had never been
known as your people.

⁶⁴:¹*OH, that you would burst from
the heavens and come down!
How the mountains would quake
in your presence!
²*As fire causes wood to burn
and water to boil,
your coming would make the nations
tremble.
Then your enemies would learn the
reason for your fame!
³ When you came down long ago,
you did awesome deeds beyond our
highest expectations.
And oh, how the mountains quaked!
⁴ For since the world began,
no ear has heard,
and no eye has seen a God like you,
who works for those who wait
for him!
⁵ You welcome those who gladly
do good,
who follow godly ways.
But you have been very angry with us,
for we are not godly.
We are constant sinners;
how can people like us be saved?
⁶ We are all infected and impure
with sin.
When we display our righteous
deeds,
they are nothing but filthy rags.
Like autumn leaves, we wither and fall,

and our sins sweep us away like
the wind.
7 Yet no one calls on your name
or pleads with you for mercy.
Therefore, you have turned away
from us
and turned us over* to our sins.

8 And yet, O Lord, you are our Father.
We are the clay, and you are the
potter.
We all are formed by your hand.
9 Don't be so angry with us, Lord.
Please don't remember our sins
forever.
Look at us, we pray,
and see that we are all your people.
10 Your holy cities are destroyed.
Zion is a wilderness;
yes, Jerusalem is a desolate ruin.
11 The holy and beautiful Temple
where our ancestors praised you
has been burned down,
and all the things of beauty are
destroyed.
12 After all this, Lord, must you still
refuse to help us?
Will you continue to be silent and
punish us?

65:1 The Lord says,

"I was ready to respond, but no one
asked for help.

I was ready to be found, but no one
was looking for me.
I said, 'Here I am, here I am!'
to a nation that did not call on
my name.*
2 All day long I opened my arms to
a rebellious people.*
But they follow their own evil
paths
and their own crooked schemes.
3 All day long they insult me to my face
by worshiping idols in their sacred
gardens.
They burn incense on pagan altars.
4 At night they go out among
the graves,
worshiping the dead.
They eat the flesh of pigs
and make stews with other
forbidden foods.
5 Yet they say to each other,
'Don't come too close or you will
defile me!
I am holier than you!'
These people are a stench
in my nostrils,
an acrid smell that never goes away.

6 "Look, my decree is written out*
in front of me:
I will not stand silent;
I will repay them in full!
Yes, I will repay them—

WHAT THE BIBLE SAYS

The future

ISAIAH 65:17-25 In the future God will create new heavens and a new earth for his people. Not only will we have new bodies prepared for heaven (see the devotional thought on August 24), God will also create a new heaven and earth for his people to enjoy. What we know now will not last forever. As our bodies need to be recreated for eternity, so will earth and heaven.
• The new heaven and earth will be so wonderful, "no one will even think about the old ones anymore" (Isaiah 65:17). They will be full of peace and joy, there will be no tears or death, there will be no lack of food, clothing, or lodging, and best of all, we will have constant access to God.
• Although many of Isaiah's prophecies have already come true, many of his prophecies are still in the distant future. These words about the new heaven and earth are yet to be fulfilled; in fact, you'll later read similar words in Ezekiel, Daniel, and Revelation that describe this future time. This promise of the future is as true as all of God's other promises. The prophecies against the nations of the distant past came true; so will these promises of the future.

7 both for their own sins
  and for those of their ancestors,"
  says the LORD.
"For they also burned incense on
  the mountains
  and insulted me on the hills.
  I will pay them back in full!

8 "But I will not destroy them all,"
  says the LORD.
"For just as good grapes are found
  among a cluster of bad ones
  (and someone will say, 'Don't throw
  them all away—
  some of those grapes are good!'),
  so I will not destroy all Israel.
  For I still have true servants there.

9 I will preserve a remnant of the people
  of Israel*
  and of Judah to possess my land.
  Those I choose will inherit it,
  and my servants will live there.

10 The plain of Sharon will again be filled
  with flocks
  for my people who have searched
  for me,
  and the valley of Achor will be
  a place to pasture herds.

11 "But because the rest of you have
  forsaken the LORD
  and have forgotten his Temple,
  and because you have prepared feasts
  to honor the god of Fate
  and have offered mixed wine to the
  god of Destiny,

12 now I will 'destine' you for the sword.
  All of you will bow down before the
  executioner.
  For when I called, you did not answer.
  When I spoke, you did not listen.
  You deliberately sinned—before my
  very eyes—
  and chose to do what you know
  I despise."

13 Therefore, this is what the Sovereign
  LORD says:
"My servants will eat,
  but you will starve.
  My servants will drink,
  but you will be thirsty.
  My servants will rejoice,
  but you will be sad and ashamed.

14 My servants will sing for joy,

but you will cry in sorrow and
  despair.

15 Your name will be a curse word among
  my people,
  for the Sovereign LORD will destroy
  you
  and will call his true servants by
  another name.

16 All who invoke a blessing or take an
  oath
  will do so by the God of truth.
  For I will put aside my anger
  and forget the evil of earlier days.

17 "Look! I am creating new heavens and
  a new earth,
  and no one will even think about
  the old ones anymore.

18 Be glad; rejoice forever in my creation!
  And look! I will create Jerusalem as
  a place of happiness.
  Her people will be a source of joy.

19 I will rejoice over Jerusalem
  and delight in my people.
  And the sound of weeping and crying
  will be heard in it no more.

20 "No longer will babies die when only
  a few days old.
  No longer will adults die before
  they have lived a full life.
  No longer will people be considered
  old at one hundred!
  Only the cursed will die that young!

21 In those days people will live in the
  houses they build
  and eat the fruit of their own
  vineyards.

22 Unlike the past, invaders will not take
  their houses
  and confiscate their vineyards.
  For my people will live as long as trees,
  and my chosen ones will have time
  to enjoy their hard-won gains.

23 They will not work in vain,
  and their children will not be
  doomed to misfortune.
  For they are people blessed by the
  LORD,
  and their children, too, will be
  blessed.

24 I will answer them before they even
  call to me.
  While they are still talking about
  their needs,

I will go ahead and answer their
    prayers!
25 The wolf and the lamb will feed
    together.
  The lion will eat hay like a cow.
  But the snakes will eat dust.
In those days no one will be hurt
    or destroyed on my holy
    mountain.
I, the LORD, have spoken!"

62:11 Hebrew *Tell the daughter of Zion.*   **63:9** Hebrew *and
the angel of his presence.*   **63:16** Hebrew *Israel.* See note on
14:1.   **64:1** Verse 64:1 is numbered 63:20 in Hebrew text.
64:2 Verses 64:2-12 are numbered 64:1-11 in Hebrew text.
64:7 As in Greek, Syriac, and Aramaic versions; Hebrew reads
melted us.   **65:1** Or *to a nation that did not bear my name.*
65:1-2 Greek version reads *I was found by people who were
not looking for me. / I showed myself to those who were not
asking for me. / All day long I opened my arms to them, / but
they were disobedient and rebellious.* Compare Rom 10:20.
65:6 Or *their sins are written out;* Hebrew reads *it stands
written.*   **65:9** Hebrew *remnant of Jacob.* See note on 14:1.

PHILIPPIANS 2:19–3:4

Faithful, trustworthy companions aided Paul's
ministry. Men like Timothy and Epaphroditus could
be trusted to teach the truth. Unfortunately, there
were others who sought to corrupt the churches
with false teaching. Paul warned against them.

If the Lord Jesus is willing, I [Paul] hope to
send Timothy to you [Philippians] soon
for a visit. Then he can cheer me up by
telling me how you are getting along. 20I
have no one else like Timothy, who genuinely cares about your welfare. 21All the
others care only for themselves and not
for what matters to Jesus Christ. 22But you
know how Timothy has proved himself.
Like a son with his father, he has served
with me in preaching the Good News. 23I
hope to send him to you just as soon as I
find out what is going to happen to me
here. 24And I have confidence from the
Lord that I myself will come to see you
soon.

25Meanwhile, I thought I should send
Epaphroditus back to you. He is a true
brother, co-worker, and fellow soldier.
And he was your messenger to help me in
my need. 26I am sending him because he
has been longing to see you, and he was
very distressed that you heard he was ill.
27And he certainly was ill; in fact, he almost died. But God had mercy on him—
and also on me, so that I would not have
one sorrow after another.

28So I am all the more anxious to send
him back to you, for I know you will be
glad to see him, and then I will not be so
worried about you. 29Welcome him with
Christian love* and with great joy, and
give him the honor that people like him
deserve. 30For he risked his life for the
work of Christ, and he was at the point of
death while doing for me what you
couldn't do from far away.

3:1WHATEVER happens, my dear brothers
and sisters,* rejoice in the Lord. I never
get tired of telling you these things, and I
do it to safeguard your faith.

2Watch out for those dogs, those people who do evil, those mutilators who say
you must be circumcised to be saved. 3For
we who worship by the Spirit of God* are
the ones who are truly circumcised. We
rely on what Christ Jesus has done for us.
We put no confidence in human effort,
4though I could have confidence in my
own effort if anyone could. Indeed, if others have reason for confidence in their
own efforts, I have even more!

2:29 Greek *in the Lord.*   **3:1** Greek *brothers;* also in 3:13, 17.
3:3 Some manuscripts read *worship God in spirit;* one early
manuscript reads *worship in spirit.*

PSALM 73:1-28
A psalm of Asaph.

1 Truly God is good to Israel,
    to those whose hearts are pure.
2 But as for me, I almost lost my footing.
    My feet were slipping, and I was
      almost gone.
3 For I envied the proud
    when I saw them prosper despite
      their wickedness.
4 They seem to live such painless lives;
    their bodies are so healthy and
      strong.
5 They don't have troubles like other
    people;
    they're not plagued with problems
      like everyone else.
6 They wear pride like a jeweled
    necklace
    and clothe themselves with cruelty.
7 These fat cats have everything
    their hearts could ever wish for!
8 They scoff and speak only evil;
    in their pride they seek to crush
      others.

9 They boast against the very heavens,
and their words strut throughout
the earth.
10 And so the people are dismayed and
confused,
drinking in all their words.
11 "What does God know?" they ask.
"Does the Most High even know
what's happening?"
12 Look at these wicked people—
enjoying a life of ease while their
riches multiply.

13 Did I keep my heart pure for nothing?
Did I keep myself innocent for
no reason?
14 I get nothing but trouble all day long;
every morning brings me pain.

15 If I had really spoken this way to others,
I would have been a traitor to
your people.
16 So I tried to understand why the
wicked prosper.
But what a difficult task it is!
17 Then I went into your sanctuary, O God,
and I finally understood the destiny
of the wicked.
18 Truly, you put them on a slippery path
and send them sliding over the cliff
to destruction.
19 In an instant they are destroyed,
completely swept away by terrors.
20 When you arise, O Lord,
you will laugh at their silly ideas
as a person laughs at dreams
in the morning.

21 Then I realized that my heart
was bitter,
and I was all torn up inside.
22 I was so foolish and ignorant—
I must have seemed like a senseless
animal to you.
23 Yet I still belong to you;
you hold my right hand.
24 You guide me with your counsel,
leading me to a glorious destiny.
25 Whom have I in heaven but you?
I desire you more than anything
on earth.
26 My health may fail, and my spirit may
grow weak,
but God remains the strength
of my heart;
he is mine forever.

27 Those who desert him will perish,
for you destroy those who abandon
you.
28 But as for me, how good it is to be
near God!
I have made the Sovereign LORD
my shelter,
and I will tell everyone about the
wonderful things you do.

PROVERBS 24:13-14

My child,* eat honey, for it is good, and the
honeycomb is sweet to the taste. In the
same way, wisdom is sweet to your soul. If
you find it, you will have a bright future,
and your hopes will not be cut short.

24:13 Hebrew *My son;* also in 24:21.

OCTOBER**2**

ISAIAH 66:1-24

The book of Isaiah, like the book of Revelation, closes
with a vivid description of the new heaven and earth.

This is what the LORD says:

"Heaven is my throne,
and the earth is my footstool.
Could you build me a temple as good
as that?
Could you build me such a resting
place?

2 My hands have made both heaven
and earth;
they and everything in them
are mine.*
I, the LORD, have spoken!

"I will bless those who have humble
and contrite hearts,
who tremble at my word.
3 But those who choose their own ways—

delighting in their detestable sins—
will not have their offerings
accepted.
When such people sacrifice a bull,
it is no more acceptable than
a human sacrifice.
When they sacrifice a lamb,
it's as though they had sacrificed
a dog!
When they bring an offering of grain,
they might as well offer the blood
of a pig.
When they burn frankincense,
it's as if they had blessed an idol.
⁴ I will send them great trouble—
all the things they feared.
For when I called, they did not answer.
When I spoke, they did not listen.
They deliberately sinned before my
very eyes
and chose to do what they know
I despise."

⁵ Hear this message from the LORD,
all you who tremble at his words:
"Your own people hate you
and throw you out for being loyal
to my name.
'Let the LORD be honored!' they scoff.
'Be joyful in him!'
But they will be put to shame.
⁶ What is all the commotion in the city?
What is that terrible noise from the
Temple?
It is the voice of the LORD
taking vengeance against his
enemies.

⁷ "Before the birth pains even begin,
Jerusalem gives birth to a son.
⁸ Who has ever seen anything as strange
as this?
Who ever heard of such a thing?
Has a nation ever been born in a
single day?
Has a country ever come forth
in a mere moment?
But by the time Jerusalem's* birth
pains begin,
her children will be born.
⁹ Would I ever bring this nation to the
point of birth
and then not deliver it?" asks
the LORD.

"No! I would never keep this nation
from being born,"
says your God.

¹⁰ "Rejoice with Jerusalem!
Be glad with her, all you who love her
and all you who mourn for her.
¹¹ Drink deeply of her glory
even as an infant drinks at its
mother's comforting breasts."

¹² This is what the LORD says:
"I will give Jerusalem a river of peace
and prosperity.
The wealth of the nations will flow
to her.
Her children will be nursed at
her breasts,
carried in her arms, and held
on her lap.
¹³ I will comfort you there in Jerusalem
as a mother comforts her child."

¹⁴ When you see these things, your heart
will rejoice.
You will flourish like the grass!
Everyone will see the LORD's hand of
blessing on his servants—
and his anger against his enemies.
¹⁵ See, the LORD is coming with fire,
and his swift chariots roar like
a whirlwind.
He will bring punishment with the
fury of his anger
and the flaming fire of his hot
rebuke.
¹⁶ The LORD will punish the world by fire
and by his sword.
He will judge the earth,
and many will be killed by him.

¹⁷"Those who 'consecrate' and 'purify'
themselves in a sacred garden with its idol
in the center—feasting on pork and rats
and other detestable meats—will come to
a terrible end," says the LORD.

¹⁸"I can see what they are doing, and I
know what they are thinking. So I will
gather all nations and peoples together,
and they will see my glory. ¹⁹I will perform
a sign among them. And I will send those
who survive to be messengers to the nations—to Tarshish, to the Libyans* and
Lydians* (who are famous as archers), to
Tubal and Greece,* and to all the lands
beyond the sea that have not heard of my

fame or seen my glory. There they will declare my glory to the nations. [20]They will bring the remnant of your people back from every nation. They will bring them to my holy mountain in Jerusalem as an offering to the LORD. They will ride on horses, in chariots and wagons, and on mules and camels," says the LORD. [21]"And I will appoint some of them to be my priests and Levites. I, the LORD, have spoken!

[22] "As surely as my new heavens and
earth will remain,
so will you always be my people,
with a name that will never disappear,"
says the LORD.
[23] "All humanity will come to worship me
from week to week
and from month to month.
[24] And as they go out, they will see
the dead bodies of those who have
rebelled against me.
For the worms that devour them will
never die,
and the fire that burns them will
never go out.
All who pass by
will view them with utter horror."

66:2 As in Greek, Latin, and Syriac versions; Hebrew reads *these things are.* 66:8 Hebrew *Zion's.* 66:19a As in some Greek manuscripts, which read *Put* (that is, *Libya*); Hebrew reads *Pul.* 66:19b Hebrew *Lud.* 66:19c Hebrew *Javan.*

PHILIPPIANS 3:5-21

What is really important? What are the things that rightfully claim our greatest loyalties and our strongest passions? For Paul, the answers to these questions centered on Christ and Christ alone.

I [Paul] was circumcised when I was eight days old. I am a pure-blooded citizen of Israel and a member of the tribe of Benjamin—a real Hebrew if there ever was one! I was a member of the Pharisees, who demand the strictest obedience to the Jewish law. [6]I was so zealous that I harshly persecuted the church. And as for righteousness, I obeyed the law without fault.

[7]I once thought these things were valuable, but now I consider them worthless because of what Christ has done. [8]Yes, everything else is worthless when compared with the infinite value of knowing Christ Jesus my Lord. For his sake I have discarded everything else, counting it all

as garbage, so that I could gain Christ [9]and become one with him. I no longer count on my own righteousness through obeying the law; rather, I become righteous through faith in Christ.* For God's way of making us right with himself depends on faith. [10]I want to know Christ and experience the mighty power that raised him from the dead. I want to suffer with him, sharing in his death, [11]so that one way or another I will experience the resurrection from the dead!

[12]I don't mean to say that I have already achieved these things or that I have already reached perfection. But I press on to possess that perfection for which Christ Jesus first possessed me. [13]No, dear brothers and sisters, I have not achieved it,* but I focus on this one thing: Forgetting the past and looking forward to what lies ahead, [14]I press on to reach the end of the race and receive the heavenly prize for which God, through Christ Jesus, is calling us.

[15]Let all who are spiritually mature agree on these things. If you disagree on some point, I believe God will make it plain to you. [16]But we must hold on to the progress we have already made.

[17]Dear brothers and sisters, pattern your lives after mine, and learn from those who follow our example. [18]For I have told you often before, and I say it again with tears in my eyes, that there are many whose conduct shows they are really enemies of the cross of Christ. [19]They are headed for destruction. Their god is their appetite, they brag about shameful things, and they think only about this life here on earth. [20]But we are citizens of heaven, where the Lord Jesus Christ lives. And we are eagerly waiting for him to return as our Savior. [21]He will take our weak mortal bodies and change them into glorious bodies like his own, using the same power with which he will bring everything under his control.

3:9 Or *through the faithfulness of Christ.* 3:13 Some manuscripts read *not yet achieved it.*

PSALM 74:1-23
A psalm of Asaph.

[1] **O** God, why have you rejected us so
long?

Why is your anger so intense
against the sheep of your own
pasture?
² Remember that we are the people you
chose long ago,
the tribe you redeemed as your own
special possession!
And remember Jerusalem,* your
home here on earth.
³ Walk through the awful ruins
of the city;
see how the enemy has destroyed
your sanctuary.

⁴ There your enemies shouted their
victorious battle cries;
there they set up their battle
standards.
⁵ They swung their axes
like woodcutters in a forest.
⁶ With axes and picks,
they smashed the carved paneling.
⁷ They burned your sanctuary to the
ground.
They defiled the place that bears
your name.
⁸ Then they thought, "Let's destroy
everything!"
So they burned down all the places
where God was worshiped.
⁹ We no longer see your miraculous
signs.

All the prophets are gone,
and no one can tell us when
it will end.
¹⁰ How long, O God, will you allow our
enemies to insult you?
Will you let them dishonor your
name forever?
¹¹ Why do you hold back your strong
right hand?
Unleash your powerful fist and
destroy them.

¹² You, O God, are my king from ages
past,
bringing salvation to the earth.
¹³ You split the sea by your strength
and smashed the heads of the sea
monsters.
¹⁴ You crushed the heads of Leviathan*
and let the desert animals eat him.
¹⁵ You caused the springs and streams
to gush forth,
and you dried up rivers that never
run dry.
¹⁶ Both day and night belong to you;
you made the starlight* and the
sun.
¹⁷ You set the boundaries of the earth,
and you made both summer and
winter.

¹⁸ See how these enemies insult
you, LORD.

HOW WE LIVE

Setting priorities

PHILIPPIANS 3:5-11 Paul had an impeccable pedigree. He was from the Jewish tribe of Benjamin (the tribe named for Jacob's youngest son; the tribe of Saul, Israel's first king). Paul had been circumcised and educated in the Old Testament and in rabbinic traditions. He excelled as a Pharisee. His credentials were impressive, and the first part of today's reading sounds as if he is boasting. • In fact, any Jewish listeners in Paul's day would have held him in high esteem because of his background. But Paul considered everything he had accomplished on his own as nothing. None of it compared with knowing Christ. • As a believer you have been made right with God by receiving salvation through faith in Jesus Christ. Paul's words here should not be taken to mean that everything you are and do is "garbage." God can use all your training, your experiences (good and bad), your interests, and your abilities—just as he used Paul's. Just remember that your salvation is not based on any good works, degrees, fame, or wealth you might attain. Jesus alone is the source of your salvation.

A foolish nation has dishonored
your name.
19 Don't let these wild beasts destroy
your turtledoves.
Don't forget your suffering people
forever.

20 Remember your covenant
promises,
for the land is full of darkness
and violence!

21 Don't let the downtrodden be
humiliated again.
Instead, let the poor and needy
praise your name.

22 Arise, O God, and defend your cause.

Remember how these fools insult
you all day long.
23 Don't overlook what your enemies
have said
or their growing uproar.

74:TITLE Hebrew *maskil*. This may be a literary or musical
term.   74:2 Hebrew *Mount Zion*.   74:14 The identification
of Leviathan is disputed, ranging from an earthly creature to a
mythical sea monster in ancient literature.   74:16 Or *moon*;
Hebrew reads *light*.

PROVERBS 24:15-16

Don't wait in ambush at the home of the
godly, and don't raid the house where the
godly live. The godly may trip seven times,
but they will get up again. But one disaster
is enough to overthrow the wicked.

OCTOBER**3**

JEREMIAH 1:1–2:30

Jeremiah not only lived through Judah's fall to the
Babylonians, he saw it coming. He spent years warning the people to turn from their evil ways or face
catastrophe. Amid the doom and gloom, however,
Jeremiah gave glimpses of hope, indicating that
restoration would follow 70 years of captivity.

These are the words of Jeremiah son of Hilkiah, one of the priests from the town of
Anathoth in the land of Benjamin. 2 The
LORD first gave messages to Jeremiah during the thirteenth year of the reign of Josiah son of Amon, king of Judah.* 3 The
LORD's messages continued throughout
the reign of King Jehoiakim, Josiah's son,
until the eleventh year of the reign of King
Zedekiah, another of Josiah's sons. In August* of that eleventh year the people of Jerusalem were taken away as captives.

4 The LORD gave me this message:

5 "I knew you before I formed you in
your mother's womb.
Before you were born I set you apart
and appointed you as my prophet to
the nations."

6 "O Sovereign LORD," I said, "I can't
speak for you! I'm too young!"

7 The LORD replied, "Don't say, 'I'm too
young,' for you must go wherever I send
you and say whatever I tell you. 8 And don't
be afraid of the people, for I will be with
you and will protect you. I, the LORD, have
spoken!" 9 Then the LORD reached out and
touched my mouth and said,

"Look, I have put my words in your
mouth!
10 Today I appoint you to stand up
against nations and kingdoms.
Some you must uproot and tear down,
destroy and overthrow.
Others you must build up and plant."

11 Then the LORD said to me, "Look, Jeremiah! What do you see?"
And I replied, "I see a branch from an
almond tree."
12 And the LORD said, "That's right, and
it means that I am watching,* and I will
certainly carry out all my plans."
13 Then the LORD spoke to me again
and asked, "What do you see now?"
And I replied, "I see a pot of boiling water, spilling from the north."
14 "Yes," the LORD said, "for terror from
the north will boil out on the people of

this land. ¹⁵Listen! I am calling the armies of the kingdoms of the north to come to Jerusalem. I, the LORD, have spoken!

"They will set their thrones
at the gates of the city.
They will attack its walls
and all the other towns of Judah.
¹⁶ I will pronounce judgment
on my people for all their evil—
for deserting me and burning incense
to other gods.
Yes, they worship idols made with
their own hands!

¹⁷ "Get up and prepare for action.
Go out and tell them everything
I tell you to say.
Do not be afraid of them,
or I will make you look foolish
in front of them.
¹⁸ For see, today I have made you strong
like a fortified city that cannot be
captured,
like an iron pillar or a bronze wall.
You will stand against the whole
land—
the kings, officials, priests, and
people of Judah.
¹⁹ They will fight you, but they will fail.
For I am with you, and I will take
care of you.
I, the LORD, have spoken!"

^{2:1}THE LORD gave me another message. He said, ²"Go and shout this message to Jerusalem. This is what the LORD says:

"I remember how eager you were
to please me
as a young bride long ago,
how you loved me and followed me
even through the barren
wilderness.
³ In those days Israel was holy to
the LORD,
the first of his children.*
All who harmed his people were
declared guilty,
and disaster fell on them.
I, the LORD, have spoken!"

⁴Listen to the word of the LORD, people of Jacob—all you families of Israel! ⁵This is what the LORD says:

"What did your ancestors find wrong
with me
that led them to stray so far from
me?
They worshiped worthless idols,
only to become worthless
themselves.
⁶ They did not ask, 'Where is the LORD
who brought us safely out of Egypt
and led us through the barren
wilderness—
a land of deserts and pits,
a land of drought and death,
where no one lives or even travels?'

⁷ "And when I brought you into a fruitful
land
to enjoy its bounty and goodness,
you defiled my land and
corrupted the possession I had
promised you.
⁸ The priests did not ask,
'Where is the LORD?'
Those who taught my word ignored
me,
the rulers turned against me,
and the prophets spoke in the name
of Baal,
wasting their time on worthless
idols.
⁹ Therefore, I will bring my case against
you,"
says the LORD.
"I will even bring charges against your
children's children
in the years to come.

¹⁰ "Go west and look in the land
of Cyprus*;
go east and search through the land
of Kedar.
Has anyone ever heard of anything
as strange as this?
¹¹ Has any nation ever traded its gods for
new ones,
even though they are not gods
at all?
Yet my people have exchanged their
glorious God*
for worthless idols!
¹² The heavens are shocked at such
a thing
and shrink back in horror and
dismay,"
says the LORD.

¹³ "For my people have done two evil
things:
They have abandoned me—
the fountain of living water.
And they have dug for themselves
cracked cisterns
that can hold no water at all!

¹⁴ "Why has Israel become a slave?
Why has he been carried away
as plunder?
¹⁵ Strong lions have roared against him,
and the land has been destroyed.
The towns are now in ruins,
and no one lives in them anymore.
¹⁶ Egyptians, marching from their cities
of Memphis* and Tahpanhes,
have destroyed Israel's glory and
power.
¹⁷ And you have brought this upon
yourselves
by rebelling against the LORD your
God,
even though he was leading you on
the way!

¹⁸ "What have you gained by your
alliances with Egypt
and your covenants with Assyria?
What good to you are the streams of
the Nile*
or the waters of the Euphrates
River?*
¹⁹ Your wickedness will bring its own
punishment.
Your turning from me will shame
you.
You will see what an evil, bitter thing
it is
to abandon the LORD your God and
not to fear him.
I, the Lord, the LORD of Heaven's
Armies, have spoken!

²⁰ "Long ago I broke the yoke that
oppressed you
and tore away the chains of your
slavery,
but still you said,
'I will not serve you.'
On every hill and under every green
tree,
you have prostituted yourselves by
bowing down to idols.
²¹ But I was the one who planted you,

choosing a vine of the purest
stock—the very best.
How did you grow into this corrupt
wild vine?
²² No amount of soap or lye can make
you clean.
I still see the stain of your guilt.
I, the Sovereign LORD, have spoken!

²³ "You say, 'That's not true!
I haven't worshiped the images
of Baal!'
But how can you say that?
Go and look in any valley in
the land!
Face the awful sins you have done.
You are like a restless female camel
desperately searching for a mate.
²⁴ You are like a wild donkey,
sniffing the wind at mating time.
Who can restrain her lust?
Those who desire her don't need
to search,
for she goes running to them!
²⁵ When will you stop running?
When will you stop panting after
other gods?
But you say, 'Save your breath.
I'm in love with these foreign gods,
and I can't stop loving them now!'

²⁶ "Israel is like a thief
who feels shame only when he gets
caught.
They, their kings, officials, priests, and
prophets—
all are alike in this.
²⁷ To an image carved from a piece
of wood they say,
'You are my father.'
To an idol chiseled from a block
of stone they say,
'You are my mother.'
They turn their backs on me,
but in times of trouble they cry out
to me,
'Come and save us!'
²⁸ But why not call on these gods you
have made?
When trouble comes, let them save
you if they can!
For you have as many gods
as there are towns in Judah.
²⁹ Why do you accuse me of doing
wrong?

You are the ones who have
rebelled,"
says the LORD.
30 "I have punished your children,
but they did not respond to my
discipline.
You yourselves have killed your
prophets
as a lion kills its prey."

1:2 The thirteenth year of Josiah's reign was 627 B.C.
1:3 Hebrew *In the fifth month*, of the ancient Hebrew lunar
calendar. A number of events in Jeremiah can be cross-
checked with dates in surviving Babylonian records and
related accurately to our modern calendar. The fifth month
in the eleventh year of Zedekiah's reign occurred within the
months of August and September 586 B.C. Also see 52:12 and
the note there.   1:12 The Hebrew word for "watching"
(*shoqed*) sounds like the word for "almond tree" (*shaqed*).
2:3 Hebrew *the firstfruits of his harvest.*   2:10 Hebrew
Kittim.   2:11 Hebrew *their glory.*   2:16 Hebrew *Noph.*
2:18a Hebrew *of Shihor*, a branch of the Nile River.
2:18b Hebrew *the river?*

PHILIPPIANS 4:1-23
Paul's letter to the Philippians is, among other
things, a thank-you note. This church had gathered
support for Paul. His gratitude is more than obvious
in his closing words.

Therefore, my [Paul] dear brothers and
sisters,* stay true to the Lord. I love you
and long to see you, dear friends, for you
are my joy and the crown I receive for my
work.
²Now I appeal to Euodia and Syntyche.
Please, because you belong to the Lord,
settle your disagreement. ³And I ask you,
my true partner,* to help these two
women, for they worked hard with me in
telling others the Good News. They
worked along with Clement and the rest
of my co-workers, whose names are written in the Book of Life.
⁴Always be full of joy in the Lord. I say it
again—rejoice! ⁵Let everyone see that you
are considerate in all you do. Remember,
the Lord is coming soon.
⁶Don't worry about anything; instead,
pray about everything. Tell God what you
need, and thank him for all he has done.
⁷Then you will experience God's peace,
which exceeds anything we can understand. His peace will guard your hearts
and minds as you live in Christ Jesus.
⁸And now, dear brothers and sisters,
one final thing. Fix your thoughts on what
is true, and honorable, and right, and pure,
and lovely, and admirable. Think about
things that are excellent and worthy of
praise. ⁹Keep putting into practice all you
learned and received from me—everything you heard from me and saw me doing. Then the God of peace will be with
you.
¹⁰How I praise the Lord that you are concerned about me again. I know you have always been concerned for me, but you
didn't have the chance to help me. ¹¹Not

HOW WE LIVE — Prayer
PHILIPPIANS 4:6-7 What worries do you have? Do they center on family,
friends, money, education, or illness? Maybe you have a big decision to
make and you don't know what to do. You're worried about making the
wrong choice. • Before you became a believer, what did you do when you
faced such situations? You fretted, you vacillated, you figured that you'd
just have to hope for the best. You talked to all your friends. You probably
also worried. Now that you're a believer, you face all those same situations—and you probably also still feel worried because you just can't
help it. Worry is a natural human reaction. Paul says to change your
worries into prayers. How can you do that? (1) Talk to God about whatever is troubling you. Nothing is too small for his care. (2) Keep on praying. It doesn't matter if he's heard it before. Whenever you feel worried,
pray. (3) Watch and listen for God. Just because you pray doesn't mean
everything will immediately work out. But God *does* promise to hear and
answer. When you trust him, you will gain the peace of knowing that he'll
guide your choices and help you make the right ones.

that I was ever in need, for I have learned how to be content with whatever I have. [12]I know how to live on almost nothing or with everything. I have learned the secret of living in every situation, whether it is with a full stomach or empty, with plenty or little. [13]For I can do everything through Christ,* who gives me strength. [14]Even so, you have done well to share with me in my present difficulty.

[15]As you know, you Philippians were the only ones who gave me financial help when I first brought you the Good News and then traveled on from Macedonia. No other church did this. [16]Even when I was in Thessalonica you sent help more than once. [17]I don't say this because I want a gift from you. Rather, I want you to receive a reward for your kindness.

[18]At the moment I have all I need—and more! I am generously supplied with the gifts you sent me with Epaphroditus. They are a sweet-smelling sacrifice that is acceptable and pleasing to God. [19]And this same God who takes care of me will supply all your needs from his glorious riches, which have been given to us in Christ Jesus.

[20]Now all glory to God our Father forever and ever! Amen.

[21]Give my greetings to each of God's holy people—all who belong to Christ Jesus. The brothers who are with me send you their greetings. [22]And all the rest of God's people send you greetings, too, especially those in Caesar's household.

[23]May the grace of the Lord Jesus Christ be with your spirit.

4:1 Greek *brothers;* also in 4:8.   **4:3** Or *loyal Syzygus.*
4:13 Greek *through the one.*

PSALM 75:1-10
For the choir director: A psalm of Asaph.
A song to be sung to the tune "Do Not Destroy!"

1 **W**e thank you, O God!
     We give thanks because you
        are near.

People everywhere tell of your
   wonderful deeds.

2 God says, "At the time I have planned,
     I will bring justice against the
        wicked.
3 When the earth quakes and its people
     live in turmoil,
   I am the one who keeps its
     foundations firm.   *Interlude*

4 "I warned the proud, 'Stop your
        boasting!'
   I told the wicked, 'Don't raise your
        fists!
5 Don't raise your fists in defiance
     at the heavens
   or speak with such arrogance.'"

6 For no one on earth—from east or west,
     or even from the wilderness—
   should raise a defiant fist.*
7 It is God alone who judges;
     he decides who will rise and who
        will fall.
8 For the LORD holds a cup in his hand
     that is full of foaming wine mixed
        with spices.
   He pours out the wine in judgment,
     and all the wicked must drink it,
        draining it to the dregs.

9 But as for me, I will always proclaim
     what God has done;
   I will sing praises to the God
        of Jacob.
10 For God says, "I will break the strength
     of the wicked,
   but I will increase the power
        of the godly."

75:6 Hebrew *should lift.*

PROVERBS 24:17-20
Don't rejoice when your enemies fall; don't be happy when they stumble. For the LORD will be displeased with you and will turn his anger away from them. □Don't fret because of evildoers; don't envy the wicked. For evil people have no future; the light of the wicked will be snuffed out.

OCTOBER4

JEREMIAH 2:31–4:18

Jeremiah uttered these early messages during a time when Judah (the southern kingdom) was sliding into the same spiritual peril that led to the destruction of Israel (the northern kingdom) over a hundred years earlier.

"**O** my people, listen to the words of
the LORD!
Have I been like a desert to Israel?
Have I been to them a land
of darkness?
Why then do my people say, 'At last we
are free from God!
We don't need him anymore!'
³² Does a young woman forget her
jewelry?
Does a bride hide her wedding dress?
Yet for years on end
my people have forgotten me.

³³ "How you plot and scheme to win your
lovers.
Even an experienced prostitute
could learn from you!
³⁴ Your clothing is stained with the
blood of the innocent and
the poor,
though you didn't catch them
breaking into your houses!
³⁵ And yet you say,
'I have done nothing wrong.
Surely God isn't angry with me!'
But now I will punish you severely
because you claim you have
not sinned.
³⁶ First here, then there—
you flit from one ally to another
asking for help.
But your new friends in Egypt will let
you down,
just as Assyria did before.
³⁷ In despair, you will be led into exile
with your hands on your heads,
for the LORD has rejected the nations
you trust.
They will not help you at all.

^{3:1} "If a man divorces a woman
and she goes and marries someone
else,
he will not take her back again,

for that would surely corrupt
the land.
But you have prostituted yourself with
many lovers,
so why are you trying to come back
to me?"
says the LORD.
² "Look at the shrines on every hilltop.
Is there any place you have not been
defiled
by your adultery with other gods?
You sit like a prostitute beside the
road waiting for a customer.
You sit alone like a nomad in
the desert.
You have polluted the land with your
prostitution
and your wickedness.
³ That's why even the spring rains have
failed.
For you are a brazen prostitute and
completely shameless.
⁴ Yet you say to me,
'Father, you have been my guide
since my youth.
⁵ Surely you won't be angry forever!
Surely you can forget about it!'
So you talk,
but you keep on doing all the evil
you can."

⁶During the reign of King Josiah, the LORD said to me, "Have you seen what fickle Israel has done? Like a wife who commits adultery, Israel has worshiped other gods on every hill and under every green tree. ⁷I thought, 'After she has done all this, she will return to me.' But she did not return, and her faithless sister Judah saw this. ⁸She saw that I divorced faithless Israel because of her adultery. But that treacherous sister Judah had no fear, and now she, too, has left me and given herself to prostitution. ⁹Israel treated it all so lightly—she thought nothing of committing adultery by worshiping idols made of wood and stone. So now the land has been polluted. ¹⁰But despite all this, her faithless sister Judah has never sincerely

returned to me. She has only pretended to be sorry. I, the LORD, have spoken!"

¹¹Then the LORD said to me, "Even faithless Israel is less guilty than treacherous Judah! ¹²Therefore, go and give this message to Israel.* This is what the LORD says:

"O Israel, my faithless people,
come home to me again,
for I am merciful.
I will not be angry with you forever.
¹³ Only acknowledge your guilt.
Admit that you rebelled against the
LORD your God
and committed adultery against him
by worshiping idols under every
green tree.
Confess that you refused to listen to
my voice.
I, the LORD, have spoken!

¹⁴ "Return home, you wayward children,"
says the LORD,
"for I am your master.
I will bring you back to the land of
Israel*—
one from this town and two from
that family—
from wherever you are scattered.
¹⁵ And I will give you shepherds after my
own heart,
who will guide you with knowledge
and understanding.

¹⁶"And when your land is once more filled with people," says the LORD, "you will no longer wish for 'the good old days' when you possessed the Ark of the LORD's Covenant. You will not miss those days or even remember them, and there will be no need to rebuild the Ark. ¹⁷In that day Jerusalem will be known as 'The Throne of the LORD.' All nations will come there to honor the LORD. They will no longer stubbornly follow their own evil desires. ¹⁸In those days the people of Judah and Israel will return together from exile in the north. They will return to the land I gave their ancestors as an inheritance forever.

¹⁹ "I thought to myself,
'I would love to treat you as my own
children!'
I wanted nothing more than to give
you this beautiful land—
the finest possession in the world.
I looked forward to your calling
me 'Father,'
and I wanted you never to turn
from me.
²⁰ But you have been unfaithful to me,
you people of Israel!
You have been like a faithless wife
who leaves her husband.
I, the LORD, have spoken."

²¹ Voices are heard high on the
windswept mountains,
the weeping and pleading of Israel's
people.
For they have chosen crooked paths
and have forgotten the LORD their
God.

²² "My wayward children," says the LORD,
"come back to me, and I will heal
your wayward hearts."

"Yes, we're coming," the people reply,
"for you are the LORD our God.
²³ Our worship of idols on the hills
and our religious orgies on the
mountains
are a delusion.
Only in the LORD our God
will Israel ever find salvation.
²⁴ From childhood we have watched
as everything our ancestors worked
for—
their flocks and herds, their sons and
daughters—
was squandered on a delusion.
²⁵ Let us now lie down in shame
and cover ourselves with dishonor,
for we and our ancestors have sinned
against the LORD our God.
From our childhood to this day
we have never obeyed him."

⁴:¹ "O ISRAEL," says the LORD,
"if you wanted to return to me, you
could.
You could throw away your detestable
idols
and stray away no more.
² Then when you swear by my name,
saying,
'As surely as the LORD lives,'
you could do so
with truth, justice, and
righteousness.

Then you would be a blessing to the
    nations of the world,
and all people would come and
    praise my name."

[3] This is what the LORD says to the people of Judah and Jerusalem:

"Plow up the hard ground of your
    hearts!
Do not waste your good seed among
    thorns.
[4] O people of Judah and Jerusalem,
    surrender your pride and power.
Change your hearts before the LORD,*
    or my anger will burn like an
      unquenchable fire
because of all your sins.

[5] "Shout to Judah, and broadcast
    to Jerusalem!
Tell them to sound the alarm
    throughout the land:
'Run for your lives!
    Flee to the fortified cities!'
[6] Raise a signal flag as a warning
    for Jerusalem*:
'Flee now! Do not delay!'
For I am bringing terrible destruction
    upon you
    from the north."

[7] A lion stalks from its den,
    a destroyer of nations.

It has left its lair and is headed
    your way.
It's going to devastate your land!
Your towns will lie in ruins,
    with no one living in them anymore.
[8] So put on clothes of mourning
    and weep with broken hearts,
for the fierce anger of the LORD
    is still upon us.

[9] "In that day," says the LORD,
    "the king and the officials will
      tremble in fear.
The priests will be struck with
    horror,
    and the prophets will be appalled."

[10] Then I said, "O Sovereign LORD,
    the people have been deceived by
      what you said,
for you promised peace for Jerusalem.
    But the sword is held at their
      throats!"

[11] The time is coming when the LORD
    will say
to the people of Jerusalem,
"My dear people, a burning wind
    is blowing in from the desert,
and it's not a gentle breeze useful
    for winnowing grain.
[12] It is a roaring blast sent by me!
Now I will pronounce your
    destruction!"

HOW WE LIVE | Responding to God

JEREMIAH 3:22 Jeremiah was a prophet of Israel who confronted everyone from kings to the common people with their sins. He urged them to turn back to God and be restored. As a prophet, his words came directly from God. Yet hardly anyone listened. As a result, God sent the promised punishment, resulting in the destruction of Jerusalem (Jeremiah 39, October 22). • As you read the words of the prophets, at times you may feel as though they could have been written today. Just as in Jeremiah's time, our society glorifies sin—the worship of wealth, sexual infidelity and its aberrations, and the murder of unborn children, to name just a few. The world can look pretty awful. "Where is God?" you may wonder. • He's here; he's among us; he's in us. Through his people, he continues to call out to a sin-sick world, "My wayward children . . . come back to me, and I will heal your wayward hearts" (3:22). You responded; you came; your heart has been healed. Now let your light shine in the darkness. Perhaps God will call other wayward children to himself through you.

¹³ Our enemy rushes down on us like
  storm clouds!
  His chariots are like whirlwinds.
  His horses are swifter than eagles.
  How terrible it will be, for we are
  doomed!
¹⁴ O Jerusalem, cleanse your heart
  that you may be saved.
  How long will you harbor
  your evil thoughts?
¹⁵ Your destruction has been announced
  from Dan and the hill country
  of Ephraim.

¹⁶ "Warn the surrounding nations
  and announce this to Jerusalem:
  The enemy is coming from a distant
  land,
  raising a battle cry against the
  towns of Judah.
¹⁷ They surround Jerusalem like
  watchmen around a field,
  for my people have rebelled against
  me,"
  says the LORD.
¹⁸ "Your own actions have brought this
  upon you.
  This punishment is bitter, piercing
  you to the heart!"

3:12 Hebrew *toward the north.*   **3:14** Hebrew *to Zion.*
4:4 Hebrew *Circumcise yourselves to the LORD, and take
away the foreskins of your heart.*   **4:6** Hebrew *Zion.*

COLOSSIANS 1:1-17

It appears that Epaphras and other converts from
Paul's missionary travels started the church at
Colosse. Paul himself had not visited Colosse, but
he wrote this letter to correct certain wrong
doctrines that were threatening the church there.

This letter is from Paul, chosen by the will
of God to be an apostle of Christ Jesus,
and from our brother Timothy.

² We are writing to God's holy people in
the city of Colosse, who are faithful brothers and sisters* in Christ.

May God our Father give you grace and
peace.

³ We always pray for you, and we give
thanks to God, the Father of our Lord
Jesus Christ. ⁴ For we have heard of your
faith in Christ Jesus and your love for all of
God's people, ⁵ which come from your
confident hope of what God has reserved
for you in heaven. You have had this ex-

pectation ever since you first heard the
truth of the Good News.

⁶ This same Good News that came to
you is going out all over the world. It is
bearing fruit everywhere by changing
lives, just as it changed your lives from the
day you first heard and understood the
truth about God's wonderful grace.

⁷ You learned about the Good News
from Epaphras, our beloved co-worker.
He is Christ's faithful servant, and he is
helping us on your behalf.* ⁸ He has told
us about the love for others that the Holy
Spirit has given you.

⁹ So we have not stopped praying for
you since we first heard about you. We ask
God to give you complete knowledge of
his will and to give you spiritual wisdom
and understanding. ¹⁰ Then the way you
live will always honor and please the Lord,
and your lives will produce every kind of
good fruit. All the while, you will grow as
you learn to know God better and better.

¹¹ We also pray that you will be strengthened with all his glorious power so you
will have all the endurance and patience
you need. May you be filled with joy,* ¹² always thanking the Father. He has enabled
you to share in the inheritance that belongs to his people, who live in the light.
¹³ For he has rescued us from the kingdom
of darkness and transferred us into the
Kingdom of his dear Son, ¹⁴ who purchased our freedom* and forgave our sins.

¹⁵ Christ is the visible image of the
  invisible God.
  He existed before anything was
  created and is supreme over all
  creation,*
¹⁶ for through him God created
  everything
  in the heavenly realms and on earth.
  He made the things we can see
  and the things we can't see—
  such as thrones, kingdoms, rulers, and
  authorities in the unseen world.
  Everything was created through
  him and for him.
¹⁷ He existed before anything else,
  and he holds all creation together.

1:2 Greek *faithful brothers.*   **1:7** Or *he is ministering on
your behalf;* some manuscripts read *he is ministering on our
behalf.*   **1:11** Or *all the patience and endurance you need
with joy.*   **1:14** Some manuscripts add *with his blood.*
1:15 Or *He is the firstborn of all creation.*

PSALM 76:1-12

For the choir director: A psalm of Asaph.
A song to be accompanied by stringed
instruments.

1 **G**od is honored in Judah;
   his name is great in Israel.
2 Jerusalem* is where he lives;
   Mount Zion is his home.
3 There he has broken the fiery arrows
     of the enemy,
   the shields and swords and weapons
     of war.   *Interlude*

4 You are glorious and more majestic
   than the everlasting mountains.*
5 Our boldest enemies have been
     plundered.
   They lie before us in the sleep
     of death.
   No warrior could lift a hand
     against us.
6 At the blast of your breath, O God
     of Jacob,
   their horses and chariots lay still.

7 No wonder you are greatly feared!
   Who can stand before you when
     your anger explodes?

8 From heaven you sentenced your
     enemies;
   the earth trembled and stood silent
     before you.
9 You stand up to judge those who do
     evil, O God,
   and to rescue the oppressed
     of the earth.   *Interlude*
10 Human defiance only enhances your
     glory,
   for you use it as a weapon.*

11 Make vows to the LORD your God, and
     keep them.
   Let everyone bring tribute to the
     Awesome One.
12 For he breaks the pride of princes,
   and the kings of the earth fear him.

76:2 Hebrew *Salem*, another name for Jerusalem. 76:4 As
in Greek version; Hebrew reads *than mountains filled with
beasts of prey.* 76:10 The meaning of the Hebrew is
uncertain.

PROVERBS 24:21-22

My child, fear the LORD and the king.
Don't associate with rebels, for disaster
will hit them suddenly. Who knows what
punishment will come from the LORD and
the king?

OCTOBER**5**

JEREMIAH 4:19–6:15

Jeremiah is sometimes called the weeping prophet.
Today's reading sheds light on that nickname—he
was a man who grieved over his people. Jeremiah
also wrote Lamentations, a funeral dirge about the
people of Judah.

My heart, my heart—I writhe in pain!
   My heart pounds within me! I
     cannot be still.
   For I have heard the blast of enemy
     trumpets
   and the roar of their battle cries.
20 Waves of destruction roll over the
     land,
   until it lies in complete desolation.
   Suddenly my tents are destroyed;
   in a moment my shelters are
     crushed.

21 How long must I see the battle flags
   and hear the trumpets of war?

22 "My people are foolish
   and do not know me," says the
     LORD.
   "They are stupid children
   who have no understanding.
   They are clever enough at doing
     wrong,
   but they have no idea how to do
     right!"

23 I looked at the earth, and it was empty
   and formless.
   I looked at the heavens, and there
     was no light.
24 I looked at the mountains and hills,
   and they trembled and shook.

25 I looked, and all the people were gone.
All the birds of the sky had flown
away.
26 I looked, and the fertile fields had
become a wilderness.
The towns lay in ruins,
crushed by the LORD's fierce anger.

27 This is what the LORD says:
"The whole land will be ruined,
but I will not destroy it completely.
28 The earth will mourn
and the heavens will be draped in
black
because of my decree against my
people.
I have made up my mind and will
not change it."

29 At the noise of charioteers and
archers,
the people flee in terror.
They hide in the bushes
and run for the mountains.
All the towns have been abandoned—
not a person remains!
30 What are you doing,
you who have been plundered?
Why do you dress up in beautiful
clothing
and put on gold jewelry?
Why do you brighten your eyes with
mascara?
Your primping will do you no good!
The allies who were your lovers
despise you and seek to kill you.

31 I hear a cry, like that of a woman
in labor,
the groans of a woman giving birth
to her first child.
It is beautiful Jerusalem*
gasping for breath and crying out,
"Help! I'm being murdered!"

5:1 "RUN up and down every street in
Jerusalem," says the LORD.
"Look high and low; search
throughout the city!
If you can find even one just and
honest person,
I will not destroy the city.
2 But even when they are under oath,
saying, 'As surely as the LORD lives,'
they are still telling lies!"

3 LORD, you are searching for honesty.
You struck your people,
but they paid no attention.
You crushed them,
but they refused to be corrected.
They are determined, with faces set
like stone;
they have refused to repent.

4 Then I said, "But what can we expect
from the poor?
They are ignorant.
They don't know the ways
of the LORD.
They don't understand God's laws.
5 So I will go and speak to their leaders.
Surely they know the ways
of the LORD
and understand God's laws."
But the leaders, too, as one man,
had thrown off God's yoke
and broken his chains.
6 So now a lion from the forest will
attack them;
a wolf from the desert will pounce
on them.
A leopard will lurk near their towns,
tearing apart any who dare to
venture out.
For their rebellion is great,
and their sins are many.

7 "How can I pardon you?
For even your children have turned
from me.
They have sworn by gods that are not
gods at all!
I fed my people until they were full.
But they thanked me by committing
adultery
and lining up at the brothels.
8 They are well-fed, lusty stallions,
each neighing for his neighbor's
wife.
9 Should I not punish them for this?"
says the LORD.
"Should I not avenge myself against
such a nation?

10 "Go down the rows of the vineyards
and destroy the grapevines,
leaving a scattered few alive.
Strip the branches from the vines,
for these people do not belong to
the LORD.

¹¹ The people of Israel and Judah
   are full of treachery against me,"
says the LORD.
¹² "They have lied about the LORD
   and said, 'He won't bother us!
No disasters will come upon us.
There will be no war or famine.
¹³ God's prophets are all windbags
   who don't really speak for him.
Let their predictions of disaster fall
   on themselves!'"

¹⁴Therefore, this is what the LORD God of
Heaven's Armies says:

"Because the people are talking like this,
   my messages will flame out of your
      mouth
   and burn the people like kindling
      wood.
¹⁵ O Israel, I will bring a distant nation
   against you,"
says the LORD.
"It is a mighty nation,
   an ancient nation,
a people whose language you do
   not know,
   whose speech you cannot
      understand.
¹⁶ Their weapons are deadly;
   their warriors are mighty.
¹⁷ They will devour the food of your
   harvest;

they will devour your sons
   and daughters.
They will devour your flocks
   and herds;
   they will devour your grapes
      and figs.
And they will destroy your fortified
   towns,
   which you think are so safe.

¹⁸"Yet even in those days I will not blot
you out completely," says the LORD. ¹⁹"And
when your people ask, 'Why did the LORD
our God do all this to us?' you must reply,
'You rejected him and gave yourselves to
foreign gods in your own land. Now you
will serve foreigners in a land that is not
your own.'

²⁰ "Make this announcement to
      Israel,*
   and say this to Judah:
²¹ Listen, you foolish and senseless
      people,
   with eyes that do not see
   and ears that do not hear.
²² Have you no respect for me?
   Why don't you tremble in my
      presence?
I, the LORD, define the ocean's sandy
      shoreline
   as an everlasting boundary that the
      waters cannot cross.

HOW WE LIVE

Overcoming doubt

PSALM 77:1-9 Have you ever been so distraught that you felt as if no one,
not even God, could understand your distress? Have you prayed, only to
doubt that God even heard you? Doubt is sometimes difficult to overcome. What can you do when troubles come and doubts darken your
mind? Consider how Asaph, the writer of this psalm, handled his doubts.
• For the first ten verses, he expressed his heart to God—no holding
back. He had cried out and received no comfort. He was riddled with
doubt about God's care in his current situation. Then he turned a corner
in verse 11 with the little words, "But then." He began to recall all that
God had done for him and for his people in ages past. Those memories
brought him back to reality. • God cares. If circumstances in your life
cause you to doubt God, follow Asaph's example. Pour out your heart to
God, and then consider all he has done in saving you. You may not yet
have a lot of personal stories of experiences with God, but you can
consider the stories of other believers. When doubts creep in, you'll
remember, as Asaph did, that God cares.

The waves may toss and roar,
but they can never pass the
boundaries I set.
23 But my people have stubborn and
rebellious hearts.
They have turned away and
abandoned me.
24 They do not say from the heart,
'Let us live in awe of the LORD
our God,
for he gives us rain each spring and fall,
assuring us of a harvest when the
time is right.'
25 Your wickedness has deprived you of
these wonderful blessings.
Your sin has robbed you of all these
good things.

26 "Among my people are wicked men
who lie in wait for victims like a
hunter hiding in a blind.
They continually set traps
to catch people.
27 Like a cage filled with birds,
their homes are filled with evil plots.
And now they are great and rich.
28 They are fat and sleek,
and there is no limit to their wicked
deeds.
They refuse to provide justice
to orphans
and deny the rights of the poor.
29 Should I not punish them for this?"
says the LORD.
"Should I not avenge myself against
such a nation?
30 A horrible and shocking thing
has happened in this land—
31 the prophets give false prophecies,
and the priests rule with an iron
hand.
Worse yet, my people like it that way!
But what will you do when the end
comes?

6:1 "RUN for your lives, you people
of Benjamin!
Get out of Jerusalem!
Sound the alarm in Tekoa!
Send up a signal at Beth-hakkerem!
A powerful army is coming from the
north,
coming with disaster and
destruction.

2 O Jerusalem,* you are my beautiful
and delicate daughter—
but I will destroy you!
3 Enemies will surround you, like
shepherds camped around the
city.
Each chooses a place for his troops
to devour.
4 They shout, 'Prepare for battle!
Attack at noon!'
'No, it's too late; the day is fading,
and the evening shadows are
falling.'
5 'Well then, let's attack at night
and destroy her palaces!'"

6 This is what the LORD of Heaven's
Armies says:
"Cut down the trees for battering
rams.
Build siege ramps against the walls
of Jerusalem.
This is the city to be punished,
for she is wicked through and
through.
7 She spouts evil like a fountain.
Her streets echo with the sounds
of violence and destruction.
I always see her sickness and sores.
8 Listen to this warning, Jerusalem,
or I will turn from you in disgust.
Listen, or I will turn you into a heap
of ruins,
a land where no one lives."

9 This is what the LORD of Heaven's
Armies says:
"Even the few who remain in Israel
will be picked over again,
as when a harvester checks each vine
a second time
to pick the grapes that were
missed."

10 To whom can I give warning?
Who will listen when I speak?
Their ears are closed,
and they cannot hear.
They scorn the word of the LORD.
They don't want to listen at all.
11 So now I am filled with the LORD's fury.
Yes, I am tired of holding it in!

"I will pour out my fury on children
playing in the streets
and on gatherings of young men,

on husbands and wives
and on those who are old and gray.
¹² Their homes will be turned over to
their enemies,
as will their fields and their wives.
For I will raise my powerful fist
against the people of this land,"
says the LORD.
¹³ "From the least to the greatest,
their lives are ruled by greed.
From prophets to priests,
they are all frauds.
¹⁴ They offer superficial treatments
for my people's mortal wound.
They give assurances of peace
when there is no peace.
¹⁵ Are they ashamed of their disgusting
actions?
Not at all—they don't even know
how to blush!
Therefore, they will lie among the
slaughtered.
They will be brought down when
I punish them,"
says the LORD.

4:31 Hebrew *the daughter of Zion.*   **5:20** Hebrew *to the house of Jacob.* The names "Jacob" and "Israel" are often interchanged throughout the Old Testament, referring sometimes to the individual patriarch and sometimes to the nation.   **6:2** Hebrew *Daughter of Zion.*

COLOSSIANS 1:18–2:7
A proper understanding of Christ's identity is crucial for healthy faith. That is as true today as it was back in Paul's day. To understand Christ is to understand one who is truly worthy of our worship and devotion.

Christ is also the head of the church,
which is his body.
He is the beginning,
supreme over all who rise from
the dead.*
So he is first in everything.
¹⁹ For God in all his fullness
was pleased to live in Christ,
²⁰ and through him God reconciled
everything to himself.
He made peace with everything
in heaven and on earth
by means of Christ's blood on
the cross.

²¹This includes you who were once far away from God. You were his enemies, separated from him by your evil thoughts and actions. ²²Yet now he has reconciled you to himself through the death of Christ in his physical body. As a result, he has brought you into his own presence, and you are holy and blameless as you stand before him without a single fault.

²³But you must continue to believe this truth and stand firmly in it. Don't drift away from the assurance you received when you heard the Good News. The Good News has been preached all over the world, and I, Paul, have been appointed as God's servant to proclaim it.

²⁴I am glad when I suffer for you in my body, for I am participating in the sufferings of Christ that continue for his body, the church. ²⁵God has given me the responsibility of serving his church by proclaiming his entire message to you. ²⁶This message was kept secret for centuries and generations past, but now it has been revealed to God's people. ²⁷For God wanted them to know that the riches and glory of Christ are for you Gentiles, too. And this is the secret: Christ lives in you. This gives you the assurance of sharing his glory.

²⁸So we tell others about Christ, warning everyone and teaching everyone with all the wisdom God has given us. We want to present them to God, perfect* in their relationship to Christ. ²⁹That's why I work and struggle so hard, depending on Christ's mighty power that works within me.

^{2:1}I WANT you to know how much I have agonized for you and for the church at Laodicea, and for many other believers who have never met me personally. ²I want them to be encouraged and knit together by strong ties of love. I want them to have complete confidence that they understand God's mysterious plan, which is Christ himself. ³In him lie hidden all the treasures of wisdom and knowledge.

⁴I am telling you this so no one will deceive you with well-crafted arguments. ⁵For though I am far away from you, my heart is with you. And I rejoice that you are living as you should and that your faith in Christ is strong.

⁶And now, just as you accepted Christ Jesus as your Lord, you must continue to follow him. ⁷Let your roots grow down into him, and let your lives be built on him. Then your faith will grow strong in

the truth you were taught, and you will overflow with thankfulness.

1:18 Or *the firstborn from the dead.*   **1:28** Or *mature.*

PSALM 77:1-20
For Jeduthun, the choir director: A psalm of Asaph.

1 I cry out to God; yes, I shout.
　　Oh, that God would listen to me!
2 When I was in deep trouble,
　　I searched for the Lord.
　All night long I prayed, with hands
　　　lifted toward heaven,
　　but my soul was not comforted.
3 I think of God, and I moan,
　　overwhelmed with longing for
　　　his help.   *Interlude*

4 You don't let me sleep.
　　I am too distressed even to pray!
5 I think of the good old days,
　　long since ended,
6 when my nights were filled with joyful
　　songs.
　I search my soul and ponder the
　　difference now.
7 Has the Lord rejected me forever?
　　Will he never again be kind to me?
8 Is his unfailing love gone forever?
　　Have his promises permanently
　　　failed?
9 Has God forgotten to be gracious?
　　Has he slammed the door on his
　　　compassion?   *Interlude*

10 And I said, "This is my fate;
　　the Most High has turned his hand
　　　against me."
11 But then I recall all you have done,
　　O LORD;
　　I remember your wonderful deeds
　　　of long ago.
12 They are constantly in my thoughts.

I cannot stop thinking about your
　mighty works.

13 O God, your ways are holy.
　　Is there any god as mighty as you?
14 You are the God of great wonders!
　　You demonstrate your awesome
　　　power among the nations.
15 By your strong arm, you redeemed
　　your people,
　　the descendants of Jacob and
　　　Joseph.   *Interlude*

16 When the Red Sea* saw you, O God,
　　its waters looked and trembled!
　　The sea quaked to its very depths.
17 The clouds poured down rain;
　　the thunder rumbled in the sky.
　　Your arrows of lightning flashed.
18 Your thunder roared from the
　　whirlwind;
　　the lightning lit up the world!
　　The earth trembled and shook.
19 Your road led through the sea,
　　your pathway through the mighty
　　　waters—
　　a pathway no one knew was there!
20 You led your people along that road
　　like a flock of sheep,
　　with Moses and Aaron as their
　　shepherds.

77:16 Hebrew *the waters.*

PROVERBS 24:23-25
Here are some further sayings of the wise:
☐ It is wrong to show favoritism when passing judgment. A judge who says to the wicked, "You are innocent," will be cursed by many people and denounced by the nations. But it will go well for those who convict the guilty; rich blessings will be showered on them.

OCTOBER**6**

JEREMIAH 6:16–8:7
Judah was guilty of the very worst form of idol worship. God warned his people not to worship Molech, a Canaanite god. One of the worship rituals for Molech was the sacrifice of children—and God's people were doing it! No wonder God was angry.

This is what the LORD says:
"Stop at the crossroads and look around.
　Ask for the old, godly way, and walk in it.

Travel its path, and you will find rest
for your souls.
But you reply, 'No, that's not the road
we want!'
¹⁷ I posted watchmen over you who said,
'Listen for the sound of the alarm.'
But you replied,
'No! We won't pay attention!'

¹⁸ "Therefore, listen to this, all you
nations.
Take note of my people's situation.
¹⁹ Listen, all the earth!
I will bring disaster on my people.
It is the fruit of their own schemes,
because they refuse to listen to me.
They have rejected my word.
²⁰ There's no use offering me sweet
frankincense from Sheba.
Keep your fragrant calamus
imported from distant lands!
I will not accept your burnt offerings.
Your sacrifices have no pleasing
aroma for me."

²¹ Therefore, this is what the LORD says:
"I will put obstacles in my people's
path.
Fathers and sons will both fall over
them.
Neighbors and friends will die
together."

²² This is what the LORD says:
"Look! A great army coming from the
north!
A great nation is rising against you
from far-off lands.
²³ They are armed with bows and spears.
They are cruel and show no mercy.
They sound like a roaring sea
as they ride forward on horses.
They are coming in battle formation,
planning to destroy you, beautiful
Jerusalem.*"

²⁴ We have heard reports about the
enemy,
and we wring our hands in fright.
Pangs of anguish have gripped us,
like those of a woman in labor.
²⁵ Don't go out to the fields!
Don't travel on the roads!
The enemy's sword is everywhere
and terrorizes us at every turn!

²⁶ Oh, my people, dress yourselves in
burlap
and sit among the ashes.
Mourn and weep bitterly, as for the
loss of an only son.
For suddenly the destroying armies
will be upon you!

²⁷ "Jeremiah, I have made you a tester
of metals,*
that you may determine the quality
of my people.
²⁸ They are the worst kind of rebel,
full of slander.
They are as hard as bronze and iron,
and they lead others into
corruption.
²⁹ The bellows fiercely fan the flames
to burn out the corruption.
But it does not purify them,
for the wickedness remains.
³⁰ I will label them 'Rejected Silver,'
for I, the LORD, am discarding
them."

^{7:1}THE LORD gave another message to Jeremiah. He said, ²"Go to the entrance of the
LORD's Temple, and give this message to
the people: 'O Judah, listen to this message from the LORD! Listen to it, all of you
who worship here! ³This is what the LORD
of Heaven's Armies, the God of Israel, says:

"'Even now, if you quit your evil ways, I
will let you stay in your own land. ⁴But
don't be fooled by those who promise you
safety simply because the LORD's Temple
is here. They chant, "The LORD's Temple is
here! The LORD's Temple is here!" ⁵But I
will be merciful only if you stop your evil
thoughts and deeds and start treating
each other with justice; ⁶only if you stop
exploiting foreigners, orphans, and widows; only if you stop your murdering; and
only if you stop harming yourselves by
worshiping idols. ⁷Then I will let you stay
in this land that I gave to your ancestors to
keep forever.

⁸ "'Don't be fooled into thinking that
you will never suffer because the Temple
is here. It's a lie! ⁹Do you really think you
can steal, murder, commit adultery, lie,
and burn incense to Baal and all those
other new gods of yours, ¹⁰and then come
here and stand before me in my Temple
and chant, "We are safe!"—only to go right

back to all those evils again? [11]Don't you yourselves admit that this Temple, which bears my name, has become a den of thieves? Surely I see all the evil going on there. I, the LORD, have spoken!

[12]"'Go now to the place at Shiloh where I once put the Tabernacle that bore my name. See what I did there because of all the wickedness of my people, the Israelites. [13]While you were doing these wicked things, says the LORD, I spoke to you about it repeatedly, but you would not listen. I called out to you, but you refused to answer. [14]So just as I destroyed Shiloh, I will now destroy this Temple that bears my name, this Temple that you trust in for help, this place that I gave to you and your ancestors. [15]And I will send you out of my sight into exile, just as I did your relatives, the people of Israel.*'

[16]"Pray no more for these people, Jeremiah. Do not weep or pray for them, and don't beg me to help them, for I will not listen to you. [17]Don't you see what they are doing throughout the towns of Judah and in the streets of Jerusalem? [18]No wonder I am so angry! Watch how the children gather wood and the fathers build sacrificial fires. See how the women knead dough and make cakes to offer to the Queen of Heaven. And they pour out liquid offerings to their other idol gods! [19]Am I the one they are hurting?" asks the LORD. "Most of all, they hurt themselves, to their own shame."

[20]So this is what the Sovereign LORD says: "I will pour out my terrible fury on this place. Its people, animals, trees, and crops will be consumed by the unquenchable fire of my anger."

[21]This is what the LORD of Heaven's Armies, the God of Israel, says: "Take your burnt offerings and your other sacrifices and eat them yourselves! [22]When I led your ancestors out of Egypt, it was not burnt offerings and sacrifices I wanted from them. [23]This is what I told them: 'Obey me, and I will be your God, and you will be my people. Do everything as I say, and all will be well!' [24]"But my people would not listen to me. They kept doing whatever they wanted, following the stubborn desires of their evil hearts. They went backward in-

stead of forward. [25]From the day your ancestors left Egypt until now, I have continued to send my servants, the prophets—day in and day out. [26]But my people have not listened to me or even tried to hear. They have been stubborn and sinful—even worse than their ancestors.

[27]"Tell them all this, but do not expect them to listen. Shout out your warnings, but do not expect them to respond. [28]Say to them, 'This is the nation whose people will not obey the LORD their God and who refuse to be taught. Truth has vanished from among them; it is no longer heard on their lips. [29]Shave your head in mourning, and weep alone on the mountains. For the LORD has rejected and forsaken this generation that has provoked his fury.'

[30]"The people of Judah have sinned before my very eyes," says the LORD. "They have set up their abominable idols right in the Temple that bears my name, defiling it. [31]They have built pagan shrines at Topheth, the garbage dump in the valley of Ben-Hinnom, and there they burn their sons and daughters in the fire. I have never commanded such a horrible deed; it never even crossed my mind to command such a thing! [32]So beware, for the time is coming," says the LORD, "when that garbage dump will no longer be called Topheth or the valley of Ben-Hinnom, but the Valley of Slaughter. They will bury the bodies in Topheth until there is no more room for them. [33]The bodies of my people will be food for the vultures and wild animals, and no one will be left to scare them away. [34]I will put an end to the happy singing and laughter in the streets of Jerusalem. The joyful voices of bridegrooms and brides will no longer be heard in the towns of Judah. The land will lie in complete desolation.

8:1"IN that day," says the LORD, "the enemy will break open the graves of the kings and officials of Judah, and the graves of the priests, prophets, and common people of Jerusalem. [2]They will spread out their bones on the ground before the sun, moon, and stars—the gods my people have loved, served, and worshiped. Their bones will not be gathered up again or buried but will be scattered on the ground like manure. ³And the people of this evil nation who survive will wish to die rather than live where I will send them. I, the LORD of Heaven's Armies, have spoken!

⁴"Jeremiah, say to the people, 'This is what the LORD says:

"'When people fall down, don't they get up again?
When they discover they're on the wrong road, don't they turn back?
⁵ Then why do these people stay on their self-destructive path?
Why do the people of Jerusalem refuse to turn back?
They cling tightly to their lies and will not turn around.
⁶ I listen to their conversations and don't hear a word of truth.
Is anyone sorry for doing wrong?
Does anyone say, "What a terrible thing I have done"?
No! All are running down the path of sin
as swiftly as a horse galloping into battle!
⁷ Even the stork that flies across the sky knows the time of her migration,
as do the turtledove, the swallow, and the crane.*
They all return at the proper time each year.

But not my people!
They do not know the LORD's laws.'"

6:23 Hebrew *daughter of Zion.*   6:27 As in Greek version; Hebrew reads *of metals in my people a fortress.* 7:15 Hebrew *of Ephraim,* referring to the northern kingdom of Israel.   8:7 The identification of some of these birds is uncertain.

COLOSSIANS 2:8-23

Focus. In this world there are many competing philosophies that vie for our attention. Believers are to keep their focus on Christ who is sufficient for all of life.

Don't let anyone capture you [Colossians] with empty philosophies and high-sounding nonsense that come from human thinking and from the spiritual powers* of this world, rather than from Christ. ⁹For in Christ lives all the fullness of God in a human body.* ¹⁰So you also are complete through your union with Christ, who is the head over every ruler and authority.

¹¹When you came to Christ, you were "circumcised," but not by a physical procedure. Christ performed a spiritual circumcision—the cutting away of your sinful nature.* ¹²For you were buried with Christ when you were baptized. And with him you were raised to new life because you trusted the mighty power of God, who raised Christ from the dead.

¹³You were dead because of your sins and because your sinful nature was not

HOW WE LIVE

Following Jesus

JEREMIAH 6:16 You have chosen to follow Jesus. You have chosen an "old, godly way" by which to live your life. Sound old-fashioned? Many people would think so. "How stupid to base your life on a dusty old book!" some might say. Many people today think if something isn't new it can't be worth much. • Following Jesus on this "old, godly way" is the only way to heaven. Jesus called himself "the way" (John 14:6, May 24) and said no one gets to the Father except through him. The way doesn't change with time; it isn't different for us than it was for the ancient believers. The way doesn't change with the latest research or the newest thoughts of today's scholarly minds. It doesn't change because some author or some movie script tries to make it different. The old way is the way that has worked for centuries bringing life, peace, and joy to all who walked the path. • You're new on the path, but look at how well trod it is. Consider in whose footsteps you're following. Consider the many who will come behind you. Keep to that old, godly way—for it is the only way to Jesus.

yet cut away. Then God made you alive with Christ, for he forgave all our sins. [14]He canceled the record of the charges against us and took it away by nailing it to the cross. [15]In this way, he disarmed* the spiritual rulers and authorities. He shamed them publicly by his victory over them on the cross.

[16]So don't let anyone condemn you for what you eat or drink, or for not celebrating certain holy days or new moon ceremonies or Sabbaths. [17]For these rules are only shadows of the reality yet to come. And Christ himself is that reality. [18]Don't let anyone condemn you by insisting on pious self-denial or the worship of angels,* saying they have had visions about these things. Their sinful minds have made them proud, [19]and they are not connected to Christ, the head of the body. For he holds the whole body together with its joints and ligaments, and it grows as God nourishes it.

[20]You have died with Christ, and he has set you free from the spiritual powers of this world. So why do you keep on following the rules of the world, such as, [21]"Don't handle! Don't taste! Don't touch!"? [22]Such rules are mere human teachings about things that deteriorate as we use them. [23]These rules may seem wise because they require strong devotion, pious self-denial, and severe bodily discipline. But they provide no help in conquering a person's evil desires.

2:8 Or *the spiritual principles;* also in 2:20.   2:9 Or *in him dwells all the completeness of the Godhead bodily.*
2:11 Greek *the cutting away of the body of the flesh.*
2:15 Or *he stripped off.*   2:18 Or *or worshiping with angels.*

PSALM 78:1-31
A psalm of Asaph.

[1] **O** my people, listen to my instructions.
    Open your ears to what I am saying,
[2]   for I will speak to you in a parable.
    I will teach you hidden lessons from
        our past—
[3]   stories we have heard and known,
        stories our ancestors handed down
        to us.
[4] We will not hide these truths from our
        children;
    we will tell the next generation
    about the glorious deeds of the LORD,

about his power and his mighty
    wonders.
[5] For he issued his laws to Jacob;
    he gave his instructions to Israel.
He commanded our ancestors
    to teach them to their children,
[6] so the next generation might know
        them—
    even the children not yet born—
    and they in turn will teach their
        own children.
[7] So each generation should set its hope
        anew on God,
    not forgetting his glorious miracles
    and obeying his commands.
[8] Then they will not be like their
        ancestors—
    stubborn, rebellious, and unfaithful,
    refusing to give their hearts to God.

[9] The warriors of Ephraim, though
        armed with bows,
    turned their backs and fled on the
        day of battle.
[10] They did not keep God's covenant
    and refused to live by his
        instructions.
[11] They forgot what he had done—
    the great wonders he had shown
        them,
[12] the miracles he did for their ancestors
    on the plain of Zoan in the land of
        Egypt.
[13] For he divided the sea and led them
        through,
    making the water stand up like
        walls!
[14] In the daytime he led them by a cloud,
    and all night by a pillar of fire.
[15] He split open the rocks in the
        wilderness
    to give them water, as from a
        gushing spring.
[16] He made streams pour from the rock,
    making the waters flow down like a
        river!
[17] Yet they kept on sinning against him,
    rebelling against the Most High in
        the desert.
[18] They stubbornly tested God in their
        hearts,
    demanding the foods they craved.
[19] They even spoke against God himself,
        saying,

"God can't give us food in the
wilderness.
[20] Yes, he can strike a rock so water
gushes out,
but he can't give his people bread
and meat."
[21] When the LORD heard them, he was
furious.
The fire of his wrath burned against
Jacob.
Yes, his anger rose against Israel,
[22] for they did not believe God
or trust him to care for them.
[23] But he commanded the skies
to open;
he opened the doors of heaven.
[24] He rained down manna for them
to eat;
he gave them bread from heaven.
[25] They ate the food of angels!
God gave them all they could hold.
[26] He released the east wind in the
heavens

and guided the south wind by his
mighty power.
[27] He rained down meat as thick as dust—
birds as plentiful as the sand on the
seashore!
[28] He caused the birds to fall within
their camp
and all around their tents.
[29] The people ate their fill.
He gave them what they craved.
[30] But before they satisfied their craving,
while the meat was yet in their
mouths,
[31] the anger of God rose against them,
and he killed their strongest men.
He struck down the finest of Israel's
young men.

78:TITLE Hebrew *maskil.* This may be a literary or musical
term.

PROVERBS 24:26

An honest answer is like a kiss of friendship.

OCTOBER7

JEREMIAH 8:8–9:26

From the days of Abraham, the Jews circumcised
their male children as a sign of their covenant relationship with God. The Israelites in Jeremiah's day
had forgotten the spiritual reality that circumcision
was meant to signify. Outward ritual means nothing
without the inner reality.

"How can you say, "We are wise because
we have the word of the LORD,"
when your teachers have twisted it
by writing lies?
[9] These wise teachers will fall
into the trap of their own
foolishness,
for they have rejected the word
of the LORD.
Are they so wise after all?
[10] I will give their wives to others
and their farms to strangers.
From the least to the greatest,
their lives are ruled by greed.

Yes, even my prophets and priests
are like that.
They are all frauds.
[11] They offer superficial treatments
for my people's mortal wound.
They give assurances of peace
when there is no peace.
[12] Are they ashamed of these disgusting
actions?
Not at all—they don't even know
how to blush!
Therefore, they will lie among the
slaughtered.
They will be brought down when
I punish them,
says the LORD.
[13] I will surely consume them.
There will be no more harvests
of figs and grapes.
Their fruit trees will all die.

Whatever I gave them will soon
    be gone.
I, the LORD, have spoken!'

14 "Then the people will say,
    'Why should we wait here to die?
Come, let's go to the fortified towns
    and die there.
For the LORD our God has decreed
    our destruction
and has given us a cup of poison
    to drink
    because we sinned against the
        LORD.
15 We hoped for peace, but no peace
        came.
    We hoped for a time of healing,
        but found only terror.'

16 "The snorting of the enemies'
        warhorses can be heard
    all the way from the land of Dan in
        the north!
The neighing of their stallions makes
    the whole land tremble.
    They are coming to devour the land
        and everything in it—
    cities and people alike.
17 I will send these enemy troops
        among you
    like poisonous snakes you cannot
        charm.
They will bite you, and you will die.
    I, the Lord, have spoken!"

18 My grief is beyond healing;
    my heart is broken.
19 Listen to the weeping of my people;
    it can be heard all across the land.
"Has the LORD abandoned
    Jerusalem?*" the people ask.
    "Is her King no longer there?"

"Oh, why have they provoked my anger
    with their carved idols
    and their worthless foreign gods?"
    says the LORD.

20 "The harvest is finished,
    and the summer is gone," the
        people cry,
    "yet we are not saved!"

21 I hurt with the hurt of my people.
    I mourn and am overcome
        with grief.

22 Is there no medicine in Gilead?
    Is there no physician there?
Why is there no healing
    for the wounds of my people?

9:1* IF only my head were a pool of water
    and my eyes a fountain of tears,
I would weep day and night
    for all my people who have been
        slaughtered.
2* Oh, that I could go away and forget
        my people
    and live in a travelers' shack
        in the desert.
For they are all adulterers—
    a pack of treacherous liars.

3 "My people bend their tongues like
        bows
    to shoot out lies.
They refuse to stand up for the truth.
    They only go from bad to worse.
They do not know me,"
    says the LORD.

4 "Beware of your neighbor!
    Don't even trust your brother!
For brother takes advantage of
        brother,
    and friend slanders friend.
5 They all fool and defraud each other;
    no one tells the truth.
With practiced tongues they tell lies;
    they wear themselves out with all
        their sinning.
6 They pile lie upon lie
    and utterly refuse to acknowledge
        me,"
    says the LORD.

7 Therefore, this is what the LORD of
        Heaven's Armies says:
"See, I will melt them down in
        a crucible
    and test them like metal.
What else can I do with my people?*
8   For their tongues shoot lies like
        poisoned arrows.
    They speak friendly words to their
        neighbors
    while scheming in their heart to
        kill them.
9 Should I not punish them for this?"
    says the LORD.
"Should I not avenge myself against
    such a nation?"

¹⁰ I will weep for the mountains
    and wail for the wilderness pastures.
For they are desolate and empty of life;
    the lowing of cattle is heard no more;
    the birds and wild animals have
        all fled.

¹¹ "I will make Jerusalem into a heap of
    ruins," says the LORD.
  "It will be a place haunted by
    jackals.
The towns of Judah will be ghost
    towns,
    with no one living in them."

¹² Who is wise enough to understand all this? Who has been instructed by the LORD and can explain it to others? Why has the land been so ruined that no one dares to travel through it?

¹³ The LORD replies, "This has happened because my people have abandoned my instructions; they have refused to obey what I said. ¹⁴Instead, they have stubbornly followed their own desires and worshiped the images of Baal, as their ancestors taught them. ¹⁵So now, this is what the LORD of Heaven's Armies, the God of Israel, says: Look! I will feed them with bitterness and give them poison to drink. ¹⁶I will scatter them around the world, in places they and their ancestors never heard of, and even there I will chase them with the sword until I have destroyed them completely."

¹⁷ This is what the LORD of Heaven's
    Armies says:
"Consider all this, and call for the
    mourners.
  Send for the women who mourn at
    funerals.
¹⁸ Quick! Begin your weeping!
    Let the tears flow from your eyes.
¹⁹ Hear the people of Jerusalem* crying
    in despair,
  'We are ruined! We are completely
    humiliated!
We must leave our land,
    because our homes have been torn
    down.'"

²⁰ Listen, you women, to the words of the
    LORD;
  open your ears to what he has
    to say.
Teach your daughters to wail;
    teach one another how to lament.
²¹ For death has crept in through our
    windows
    and has entered our mansions.
It has killed off the flower of our
    youth:
  Children no longer play in the
    streets,
  and young men no longer gather
    in the squares.

²² This is what the LORD says:
"Bodies will be scattered across the
    fields like clumps of manure,

HOW WE LIVE

Obeying God

COLOSSIANS 3:1-17 Do Paul's words here seem a bit strange? How can you die to this life and still be alive? How can you put sin to death when it is a constant temptation? How can you put on a new nature? • Paul uses these word pictures to describe a reality that is virtually indescribable. You *are* a new person because of what Christ has done and because of the Holy Spirit in you. You put the sinful things of your old nature to death by walking in obedience. The next time you have the chance to lie, kill it! The next time a sexual temptation comes your way, resist. This is how you put sin to death in your life. • But Christianity is not just about what you *don't* do. Paul gives a strategy to help you live out your faith each day. Be compassionate, kind, humble, gentle, and patient; let the Holy Spirit produce these virtues in you. Forgive others; after all, the Lord has forgiven you. Let the words of Christ dwell in your heart; internalizing the truths of the Bible will help you to put the sin in your life to death.

like bundles of grain after the
harvest.
No one will be left to bury them."

23 This is what the LORD says:
"Don't let the wise boast in their
wisdom,
or the powerful boast in their
power,
or the rich boast in their riches.
24 But those who wish to boast
should boast in this alone:
that they truly know me and
understand that I am the LORD
who demonstrates unfailing love
and who brings justice and
righteousness to the earth,
and that I delight in these things.
I, the LORD, have spoken!

25"A time is coming," says the LORD,
"when I will punish all those who are circumcised in body but not in spirit—26the
Egyptians, Edomites, Ammonites, Moabites, the people who live in the desert in
remote places,* and yes, even the people
of Judah. And like all these pagan nations,
the people of Israel also have uncircumcised hearts."

8:19 Hebrew *Zion?* 9:1 Verse 9:1 is numbered 8:23 in
Hebrew text. 9:2 Verses 9:2-26 are numbered 9:1-25 in
Hebrew text. 9:7 Hebrew *with the daughter of my people?*
Greek version reads *with the evil daughter of my people?*
9:19 Hebrew *Zion.* 9:26 Or *in the desert and clip the
corners of their hair.*

COLOSSIANS 3:1-17

What does it mean to be alive in Christ? What does
it mean to be holy before God? Paul explains true
Christian behavior to these new believers.

Since you have been raised to new life
with Christ, set your sights on the realities
of heaven, where Christ sits in the place of
honor at God's right hand. 2Think about
the things of heaven, not the things of
earth. 3For you died to this life, and your
real life is hidden with Christ in God. 4And
when Christ, who is your* life, is revealed
to the whole world, you will share in all his
glory.

5So put to death the sinful, earthly
things lurking within you. Have nothing to
do with sexual immorality, impurity, lust,
and evil desires. Don't be greedy, for a
greedy person is an idolater, worshiping

the things of this world. 6Because of these
sins, the anger of God is coming.* 7You
used to do these things when your life was
still part of this world. 8But now is the time
to get rid of anger, rage, malicious behavior, slander, and dirty language. 9Don't lie
to each other, for you have stripped off
your old sinful nature and all its wicked
deeds. 10Put on your new nature, and be
renewed as you learn to know your Creator and become like him. 11In this new
life, it doesn't matter if you are a Jew or a
Gentile,* circumcised or uncircumcised,
barbaric, uncivilized,* slave, or free. Christ
is all that matters, and he lives in all of us.

12Since God chose you to be the holy
people he loves, you must clothe yourselves with tenderhearted mercy, kindness, humility, gentleness, and patience.
13Make allowance for each other's faults,
and forgive anyone who offends you. Remember, the Lord forgave you, so you
must forgive others. 14Above all, clothe
yourselves with love, which binds us all
together in perfect harmony. 15And let the
peace that comes from Christ rule in your
hearts. For as members of one body you
are called to live in peace. And always be
thankful.

16Let the message about Christ, in all its
richness, fill your lives. Teach and counsel
each other with all the wisdom he gives.
Sing psalms and hymns and spiritual
songs to God with thankful hearts. 17And
whatever you do or say, do it as a representative of the Lord Jesus, giving thanks
through him to God the Father.

3:4 Some manuscripts read *our.* 3:6 Some manuscripts
read *is coming on all who disobey him.* 3:11a Greek *a
Greek.* 3:11b Greek *Barbarian, Scythian.*

PSALM 78:32-55

But in spite of this, the people kept
sinning.
Despite his [God's] wonders, they
refused to trust him.
33 So he ended their lives in failure,
their years in terror.
34 When God began killing them,
they finally sought him.
They repented and took God
seriously.
35 Then they remembered that God was
their rock,

that God Most High* was their
   redeemer.
[36] But all they gave him was lip service;
   they lied to him with their tongues.
[37] Their hearts were not loyal to him.
   They did not keep his covenant.
[38] Yet he was merciful and forgave
   their sins
   and did not destroy them all.
   Many times he held back his anger
   and did not unleash his fury!
[39] For he remembered that they were
   merely mortal,
   gone like a breath of wind that
   never returns.

[40] Oh, how often they rebelled against
   him in the wilderness
   and grieved his heart in that dry
   wasteland.
[41] Again and again they tested God's
   patience
   and provoked the Holy One of
   Israel.
[42] They did not remember his power
   and how he rescued them from
   their enemies.
[43] They did not remember his
   miraculous signs in Egypt,
   his wonders on the plain of Zoan.
[44] For he turned their rivers into blood,
   so no one could drink from the
   streams.
[45] He sent vast swarms of flies to
   consume them
   and hordes of frogs to ruin them.
[46] He gave their crops to caterpillars;
   their harvest was consumed by
   locusts.

[47] He destroyed their grapevines
   with hail
   and shattered their sycamore-figs
   with sleet.
[48] He abandoned their cattle to the hail,
   their livestock to bolts of lightning.
[49] He loosed on them his fierce anger—
   all his fury, rage, and hostility.
   He dispatched against them
   a band of destroying angels.
[50] He turned his anger against them;
   he did not spare the Egyptians' lives
   but ravaged them with the plague.
[51] He killed the oldest son in each
   Egyptian family,
   the flower of youth throughout the
   land of Egypt.*
[52] But he led his own people like a flock
   of sheep,
   guiding them safely through
   the wilderness.
[53] He kept them safe so they were
   not afraid;
   but the sea covered their enemies.
[54] He brought them to the border of his
   holy land,
   to this land of hills he had won for
   them.
[55] He drove out the nations before them;
   he gave them their inheritance by
   lot.
   He settled the tribes of Israel into
   their homes.

78:35 Hebrew *El-Elyon.*   **78:51** Hebrew *in the tents of Ham.*

PROVERBS 24:27
Do your planning and prepare your fields
before building your house.

OCTOBER**8**

JEREMIAH 10:1-11:23
Judah was all that was left of what had once been
called the nation of Israel. That nation was based
on the covenant between Abraham and God. But
the people had broken their part of that covenant.

Hear the word that the LORD speaks to
you, O Israel! [2] This is what the LORD says:

"Do not act like the other nations,
   who try to read their future in the
   stars.
Do not be afraid of their predictions,
   even though other nations are
   terrified by them.
[3] Their ways are futile and foolish.

They cut down a tree, and a craftsman carves an idol.
⁴ They decorate it with gold and silver
and then fasten it securely with hammer and nails
so it won't fall over.
⁵ Their gods are like
helpless scarecrows in a cucumber field!
They cannot speak,
and they need to be carried because they cannot walk.
Do not be afraid of such gods,
for they can neither harm you nor do you any good."

⁶ LORD, there is no one like you!
For you are great, and your name is full of power.
⁷ Who would not fear you, O King of nations?
That title belongs to you alone!
Among all the wise people of the earth
and in all the kingdoms of the world,
there is no one like you.

⁸ People who worship idols are stupid and foolish.
The things they worship are made of wood!
⁹ They bring beaten sheets of silver from Tarshish
and gold from Uphaz,
and they give these materials to skillful craftsmen
who make their idols.
Then they dress these gods in royal blue and purple robes
made by expert tailors.
¹⁰ But the LORD is the only true God.
He is the living God and the everlasting King!
The whole earth trembles at his anger.
The nations cannot stand up to his wrath.

¹¹Say this to those who worship other gods: "Your so-called gods, who did not make the heavens and earth, will vanish from the earth and from under the heavens."*

¹² But God made the earth by his power,
and he preserves it by his wisdom.
With his own understanding
he stretched out the heavens.

¹³ When he speaks in the thunder,
the heavens roar with rain.
He causes the clouds to rise over the earth.
He sends the lightning with the rain
and releases the wind from his storehouses.
¹⁴ The whole human race is foolish and has no knowledge!
The craftsmen are disgraced by the idols they make,
for their carefully shaped works are a fraud.
These idols have no breath or power.
¹⁵ Idols are worthless; they are ridiculous lies!
On the day of reckoning they will all be destroyed.
¹⁶ But the God of Israel* is no idol!
He is the Creator of everything that exists,
including Israel, his own special possession.
The LORD of Heaven's Armies is his name!

¹⁷ Pack your bags and prepare to leave;
the siege is about to begin.
¹⁸ For this is what the LORD says:
"Suddenly, I will fling out
all you who live in this land.
I will pour great troubles upon you,
and at last you will feel my anger."

¹⁹ My wound is severe,
and my grief is great.
My sickness is incurable,
but I must bear it.
²⁰ My home is gone,
and no one is left to help me rebuild it.
My children have been taken away,
and I will never see them again.
²¹ The shepherds of my people have lost their senses.
They no longer seek wisdom from the LORD.
Therefore, they fail completely,
and their flocks are scattered.
²² Listen! Hear the terrifying roar of great armies
as they roll down from the north.
The towns of Judah will be destroyed
and become a haunt for jackals.

23 I know, LORD, that our lives are not
   our own.
   We are not able to plan our own
      course.
24 So correct me, LORD, but please be
   gentle.
   Do not correct me in anger, for
   I would die.
25 Pour out your wrath on the nations
      that refuse to acknowledge you—
   on the peoples that do not call upon
      your name.
   For they have devoured your people
      Israel*;
   they have devoured and consumed
      them,
   making the land a desolate
      wilderness.

11:1 THE LORD gave another message to
Jeremiah. He said, 2"Remind the people of
Judah and Jerusalem about the terms of
my covenant with them. 3 Say to them,
'This is what the LORD, the God of Israel,
says: Cursed is anyone who does not obey
the terms of my covenant! 4 For I said to
your ancestors when I brought them out
of the iron-smelting furnace of Egypt, "If
you obey me and do whatever I command
you, then you will be my people, and I will
be your God." 5 I said this so I could keep
my promise to your ancestors to give you
a land flowing with milk and honey—the
land you live in today.'"

Then I replied, "Amen, LORD! May it be
so."

6 Then the LORD said, "Broadcast this
message in the streets of Jerusalem. Go
from town to town throughout the land
and say, 'Remember the ancient covenant,
and do everything it requires. 7 For I solemnly warned your ancestors when I
brought them out of Egypt, "Obey me!" I
have repeated this warning over and over
to this day, 8 but your ancestors did not listen or even pay attention. Instead, they
stubbornly followed their own evil desires. And because they refused to obey, I
brought upon them all the curses described in this covenant.'"

9 Again the LORD spoke to me and said,
"I have discovered a conspiracy against
me among the people of Judah and Jerusalem. 10 They have returned to the sins of
their forefathers. They have refused to
listen to me and are worshiping other
gods. Israel and Judah have both broken
the covenant I made with their ancestors.
11 Therefore, this is what the LORD says: I
am going to bring calamity upon them,
and they will not escape. Though they
beg for mercy, I will not listen to their
cries. 12 Then the people of Judah and Jerusalem will pray to their idols and burn
incense before them. But the idols will
not save them when disaster strikes!
13 Look now, people of Judah; you have as

HOW WE LIVE

Our work

COLOSSIANS 3:23 Since the creation of man, God has given us work to do.
Adam was to "tend and watch over" the Garden of Eden (Genesis 2:15,
January 1). Only after sin entered the world did work become drudgery.
Today most of us work because we have to, not necessarily because we
want to. We are blessed indeed if we enjoy our jobs. • However, Paul
doesn't tell us to do our jobs to the best of our ability only if we like the
job, enjoy our coworkers, or have a good relationship with the boss. Paul
says to "work willingly at whatever you do" (3:23). This all comes back to
true Christian behavior—how we should represent Jesus to the world.
• No matter what your job is, you should do it as though you are working
for the Lord rather than other people. When you see your work as a
service to God, you will be able to exemplify such Christian values as a
strong work ethic, honesty, integrity, respect, and even love, and you will
be content. Your day will be better, and you might just brighten someone
else's day, too! And best of all, God, your ultimate Boss, will be pleased.

many gods as you have towns. You have as many altars of shame—altars for burning incense to your god Baal—as there are streets in Jerusalem.

¹⁴"Pray no more for these people, Jeremiah. Do not weep or pray for them, for I will not listen to them when they cry out to me in distress.

¹⁵ "What right do my beloved people
    have to come to my Temple,
  when they have done so many
    immoral things?
Can their vows and sacrifices prevent
    their destruction?
They actually rejoice in doing evil!
¹⁶ I, the LORD, once called them a
    thriving olive tree,
  beautiful to see and full of good
    fruit.
But now I have sent the fury of their
    enemies
to burn them with fire,
  leaving them charred and broken.

¹⁷"I, the LORD of Heaven's Armies, who planted this olive tree, have ordered it destroyed. For the people of Israel and Judah have done evil, arousing my anger by burning incense to Baal."

¹⁸Then the LORD told me about the plots my enemies were making against me. ¹⁹I was like a lamb being led to the slaughter. I had no idea that they were planning to kill me! "Let's destroy this man and all his words," they said. "Let's cut him down, so his name will be forgotten forever."

²⁰ O LORD of Heaven's Armies,
  you make righteous judgments,
  and you examine the deepest
    thoughts and secrets.
Let me see your vengeance against
    them,
  for I have committed my cause to you.

²¹This is what the LORD says about the men of Anathoth who wanted me dead. They had said, "We will kill you if you do not stop prophesying in the LORD's name." ²²So this is what the LORD of Heaven's Armies says about them: "I will punish them! Their young men will die in battle, and their boys and girls will starve to death. ²³Not one of these plotters from

Anathoth will survive, for I will bring disaster upon them when their time of punishment comes."

11:11 The original text of this verse is in Aramaic.
11:16 Hebrew *the Portion of Jacob.* See note on 5:20.
11:25 Hebrew *devoured Jacob.* See note on 5:20.

COLOSSIANS 3:18–4:18

None of us, ancient or modern, lives in a vacuum. When we accept God's redemption, what does that look like within our families and our work relationships? Paul answers that here.

Wives, submit to your husbands, as is fitting for those who belong to the Lord.

¹⁹Husbands, love your wives and never treat them harshly.

²⁰Children, always obey your parents, for this pleases the Lord. ²¹Fathers, do not aggravate your children, or they will become discouraged.

²²Slaves, obey your earthly masters in everything you do. Try to please them all the time, not just when they are watching you. Serve them sincerely because of your reverent fear of the Lord. ²³Work willingly at whatever you do, as though you were working for the Lord rather than for people. ²⁴Remember that the Lord will give you an inheritance as your reward, and that the Master you are serving is Christ.* ²⁵But if you do what is wrong, you will be paid back for the wrong you have done. For God has no favorites.

⁴:¹MASTERS, be just and fair to your slaves. Remember that you also have a Master—in heaven.

²Devote yourselves to prayer with an alert mind and a thankful heart. ³Pray for us, too, that God will give us many opportunities to speak about his mysterious plan concerning Christ. That is why I am here in chains. ⁴Pray that I will proclaim this message as clearly as I should.

⁵Live wisely among those who are not believers, and make the most of every opportunity. ⁶Let your conversation be gracious and attractive* so that you will have the right response for everyone.

⁷Tychicus will give you a full report about how I am getting along. He is a beloved brother and faithful helper who serves with me in the Lord's work. ⁸I have sent him to you for this very purpose—to

let you know how we are doing and to encourage you. [9]I am also sending Onesimus, a faithful and beloved brother, one of your own people. He and Tychicus will tell you everything that's happening here.

[10]Aristarchus, who is in prison with me, sends you his greetings, and so does Mark, Barnabas's cousin. As you were instructed before, make Mark welcome if he comes your way. [11]Jesus (the one we call Justus) also sends his greetings. These are the only Jewish believers among my co-workers; they are working with me here for the Kingdom of God. And what a comfort they have been!

[12]Epaphras, a member of your own fellowship and a servant of Christ Jesus, sends you his greetings. He always prays earnestly for you, asking God to make you strong and perfect, fully confident that you are following the whole will of God. [13]I can assure you that he prays hard for you and also for the believers in Laodicea and Hierapolis.

[14]Luke, the beloved doctor, sends his greetings, and so does Demas. [15]Please give my greetings to our brothers and sisters* at Laodicea, and to Nympha and the church that meets in her house.

[16]After you have read this letter, pass it on to the church at Laodicea so they can read it, too. And you should read the letter I wrote to them.

[17]And say to Archippus, "Be sure to carry out the ministry the Lord gave you."

[18]HERE IS MY GREETING IN MY OWN HANDWRITING—PAUL.

Remember my chains.

May God's grace be with you.

3:24 Or *and serve Christ as your Master.* 4:6 Greek *and seasoned with salt.* 4:15 Greek *brothers.*

PSALM 78:56-72

But they kept testing and rebelling against God Most High.
They did not obey his laws.
[57] They turned back and were as faithless as their parents.
They were as undependable as a crooked bow.
[58] They angered God by building shrines to other gods;
they made him jealous with their idols.

[59] When God heard them, he was very angry,
and he completely rejected Israel.
[60] Then he abandoned his dwelling at Shiloh,
the Tabernacle where he had lived among the people.
[61] He allowed the Ark of his might to be captured;
he surrendered his glory into enemy hands.
[62] He gave his people over to be butchered by the sword,
because he was so angry with his own people—his special possession.
[63] Their young men were killed by fire;
their young women died before singing their wedding songs.
[64] Their priests were slaughtered,
and their widows could not mourn their deaths.
[65] Then the Lord rose up as though waking from sleep,
like a warrior aroused from a drunken stupor.
[66] He routed his enemies
and sent them to eternal shame.
[67] But he rejected Joseph's descendants;
he did not choose the tribe of Ephraim.
[68] He chose instead the tribe of Judah,
and Mount Zion, which he loved.
[69] There he built his sanctuary as high as the heavens,
as solid and enduring as the earth.
[70] He chose his servant David,
calling him from the sheep pens.
[71] He took David from tending the ewes and lambs
and made him the shepherd of Jacob's descendants—
God's own people, Israel.
[72] He cared for them with a true heart
and led them with skillful hands.

PROVERBS 24:28-29

Don't testify against your neighbors without cause; don't lie about them. And don't say, "Now I can pay them back for what they've done to me! I'll get even with them!"

OCTOBER 9

JEREMIAH 12:1–14:10

Jeremiah knew God and could bare his soul to him. God did not pull punches in his responses. Jeremiah's close communion with God is what gave him strength to carry out his often-difficult ministry.

LORD, you always give me justice
when I bring a case before you.
So let me bring you this complaint:
Why are the wicked so prosperous?
Why are evil people so happy?
² You have planted them,
and they have taken root and
prospered.
Your name is on their lips,
but you are far from their hearts.
³ But as for me, LORD, you know
my heart.
You see me and test my thoughts.
Drag these people away like sheep to
be butchered!
Set them aside to be slaughtered!

⁴ How long must this land mourn?
Even the grass in the fields has
withered.
The wild animals and birds have
disappeared
because of the evil in the land.
For the people have said,
"The LORD doesn't see what's ahead
for us!"

⁵ "If racing against mere men makes
you tired,
how will you race against horses?
If you stumble and fall on open
ground,
what will you do in the thickets near
the Jordan?
⁶ Even your brothers, members of your
own family,
have turned against you.
They plot and raise complaints
against you.
Do not trust them,
no matter how pleasantly they speak.

⁷ "I have abandoned my people, my
special possession.
I have surrendered my dearest ones
to their enemies.

⁸ My chosen people have roared at me
like a lion of the forest,
so I have treated them with
contempt.
⁹ My chosen people act like speckled
vultures,*
but they themselves are surrounded
by vultures.
Bring on the wild animals to pick
their corpses clean!

¹⁰ "Many rulers have ravaged
my vineyard,
trampling down the vines
and turning all its beauty into a
barren wilderness.
¹¹ They have made it an empty
wasteland;
I hear its mournful cry.
The whole land is desolate,
and no one even cares.
¹² On all the bare hilltops,
destroying armies can be seen.
The sword of the LORD devours people
from one end of the nation to
the other.
No one will escape!
¹³ My people have planted wheat
but are harvesting thorns.
They have worn themselves out,
but it has done them no good.
They will harvest a crop of shame
because of the fierce anger of
the LORD."

¹⁴Now this is what the LORD says: "I will uproot from their land all the evil nations reaching out for the possession I gave my people Israel. And I will uproot Judah from among them. ¹⁵But afterward I will return and have compassion on all of them. I will bring them home to their own lands again, each nation to its own possession. ¹⁶And if these nations truly learn the ways of my people, and if they learn to swear by my name, saying, 'As surely as the LORD lives' (just as they taught my people to swear by the name of Baal), then they will be given a place among my people. ¹⁷But any nation who refuses to obey me

will be uprooted and destroyed. I, the LORD, have spoken!"

13:1THIS is what the LORD said to me: "Go and buy a linen loincloth and put it on, but do not wash it." 2So I bought the loincloth as the LORD directed me, and I put it on.

3Then the LORD gave me another message: 4"Take the linen loincloth you are wearing, and go to the Euphrates River.* Hide it there in a hole in the rocks." 5So I went and hid it by the Euphrates as the LORD had instructed me.

6A long time afterward the LORD said to me, "Go back to the Euphrates and get the loincloth I told you to hide there." 7So I went to the Euphrates and dug it out of the hole where I had hidden it. But now it was rotting and falling apart. The loincloth was good for nothing.

8Then I received this message from the LORD: 9"This is what the LORD says: This shows how I will rot away the pride of Judah and Jerusalem. 10These wicked people refuse to listen to me. They stubbornly follow their own desires and worship other gods. Therefore, they will become like this loincloth—good for nothing! 11As a loincloth clings to a man's waist, so I created Judah and Israel to cling to me, says the LORD. They were to be my people, my pride, my glory—an honor to my name. But they would not listen to me.

12"So tell them, 'This is what the LORD, the God of Israel, says: May all your jars be filled with wine.' And they will reply, 'Of course! Jars are made to be filled with wine!'

13"Then tell them, 'No, this is what the LORD means: I will fill everyone in this land with drunkenness—from the king sitting on David's throne to the priests and the prophets, right down to the common people of Jerusalem. 14I will smash them against each other, even parents against children, says the LORD. I will not let my pity or mercy or compassion keep me from destroying them.'"

15 Listen and pay attention!
   Do not be arrogant, for the LORD
      has spoken.
16 Give glory to the LORD your God
   before it is too late.

Acknowledge him before he brings
   darkness upon you,
   causing you to stumble and fall on
      the darkening mountains.
For then, when you look for light,
   you will find only terrible darkness
      and gloom.
17 And if you still refuse to listen,
   I will weep alone because of your
      pride.
My eyes will overflow with tears,
   because the LORD's flock will be led
      away into exile.

18 Say to the king and his mother,
   "Come down from your thrones
      and sit in the dust,
for your glorious crowns
   will soon be snatched from your
      heads."
19 The towns of the Negev will close
      their gates,
   and no one will be able to open
      them.
The people of Judah will be taken
      away as captives.
   All will be carried into exile.

20 Open up your eyes and see
      the armies marching down from
         the north!
Where is your flock—
   your beautiful flock—
      that he gave you to care for?
21 What will you say when the LORD
      takes the allies you have
         cultivated
   and appoints them as your rulers?
Pangs of anguish will grip you,
   like those of a woman in labor!
22 You may ask yourself,
   "Why is all this happening to me?"
It is because of your many sins!
   That is why you have been stripped
      and raped by invading armies.
23 Can an Ethiopian* change the color
      of his skin?
   Can a leopard take away its spots?
Neither can you start doing good,
   for you have always done evil.

24 "I will scatter you like chaff
      that is blown away by the desert
         winds.
25 This is your allotment,

the portion I have assigned to you,"
says the LORD,

"for you have forgotten me,
    putting your trust in false gods.
26 I myself will strip you
    and expose you to shame.
27 I have seen your adultery and lust,
    and your disgusting idol worship
        out in the fields and on the hills.
    What sorrow awaits you, Jerusalem!
        How long before you are pure?"

14:1 THIS message came to Jeremiah from the LORD, explaining why he was holding back the rain:

2 "Judah wilts;
    commerce at the city gates grinds to
        a halt.
    All the people sit on the ground in
        mourning,
    and a great cry rises from
        Jerusalem.
3 The nobles send servants to get water,
    but all the wells are dry.
    The servants return with empty
        pitchers,
    confused and desperate,
        covering their heads in grief.
4 The ground is parched
    and cracked for lack of rain.
    The farmers are deeply troubled;
        they, too, cover their heads.
5 Even the doe abandons her newborn
        fawn
    because there is no grass in
        the field.
6 The wild donkeys stand on the
        bare hills
    panting like thirsty jackals.
    They strain their eyes looking for grass,
        but there is none to be found."

7 The people say, "Our wickedness has
        caught up with us, LORD,
    but help us for the sake of your own
        reputation.
    We have turned away from you
    and sinned against you again and
        again.
8 O Hope of Israel, our Savior in times
        of trouble,
    why are you like a stranger to us?
    Why are you like a traveler passing
        through the land,

stopping only for the night?
9 Are you also confused?
    Is our champion helpless to save us?
    You are right here among us, LORD.
    We are known as your people.
    Please don't abandon us now!"

10 So this is what the LORD says to his
        people:
"You love to wander far from me
    and do not restrain yourselves.
    Therefore, I will no longer accept you
        as my people.
    Now I will remember all your
        wickedness
    and will punish you for your sins."

12:9 Or *speckled hyenas.*   13:4 Hebrew *Perath;* also in 13:5, 6, 7.   13:23 Hebrew *a Cushite.*

1 THESSALONIANS 1:1–2:8

Paul founded the church in Thessalonica on his second missionary journey. The Thessalonian believers suffered for their faith right off the bat, yet Paul rejoiced because their faith remained strong.

This letter is from Paul, Silas,* and Timothy.

We are writing to the church in Thessalonica, to you who belong to God the Father and the Lord Jesus Christ.

May God give you grace and peace.

2 We always thank God for all of you and pray for you constantly. 3 As we pray to our God and Father about you, we think of your faithful work, your loving deeds, and the enduring hope you have because of our Lord Jesus Christ.

4 We know, dear brothers and sisters,* that God loves you and has chosen you to be his own people. 5 For when we brought you the Good News, it was not only with words but also with power, for the Holy Spirit gave you full assurance* that what we said was true. And you know of our concern for you from the way we lived when we were with you. 6 So you received the message with joy from the Holy Spirit in spite of the severe suffering it brought you. In this way, you imitated both us and the Lord. 7 As a result, you have become an example to all the believers in Greece— throughout both Macedonia and Achaia.*

8 And now the word of the Lord is ringing out from you to people everywhere, even beyond Macedonia and Achaia, for wherever we go we find people telling us

about your faith in God. We don't need to tell them about it, ⁹for they keep talking about the wonderful welcome you gave us and how you turned away from idols to serve the living and true God. ¹⁰And they speak of how you are looking forward to the coming of God's Son from heaven—Jesus, whom God raised from the dead. He is the one who has rescued us from the terrors of the coming judgment.

²:¹You yourselves know, dear brothers and sisters,* that our visit to you was not a failure. ²You know how badly we had been treated at Philippi just before we came to you and how much we suffered there. Yet our God gave us the courage to declare his Good News to you boldly, in spite of great opposition. ³So you can see we were not preaching with any deceit or impure motives or trickery.

⁴For we speak as messengers approved by God to be entrusted with the Good News. Our purpose is to please God, not people. He alone examines the motives of our hearts. ⁵Never once did we try to win you with flattery, as you well know. And God is our witness that we were not pretending to be your friends just to get your money! ⁶As for human praise, we have never sought it from you or anyone else.

⁷As apostles of Christ we certainly had a right to make some demands of you, but instead we were like children* among you. Or we were like a mother feeding and caring for her own children. ⁸We loved you so much that we shared with you not only God's Good News but our own lives, too.

1:1 Greek *Silvanus,* the Greek form of the name.   1:4 Greek *brothers.*   1:5 Or *with the power of the Holy Spirit, so you can have full assurance.*   1:7 *Macedonia* and *Achaia* were the northern and southern regions of Greece.   2:1 Greek *brothers;* also in 2:9, 14, 17.   2:7 Some manuscripts read *we were gentle.*

PSALM 79:1-13
A psalm of Asaph.

¹ **O** God, pagan nations have conquered
    your land,
    your special possession.
  They have defiled your holy Temple
    and made Jerusalem a heap of
      ruins.
² They have left the bodies of your
    servants
    as food for the birds of heaven.
  The flesh of your godly ones
    has become food for the wild
      animals.
³ Blood has flowed like water all around
    Jerusalem;
    no one is left to bury the dead.

HOW WE LIVE   Faith and works

1 THESSALONIANS 1:2-3 What do you remember most about people who are no longer with you? Maybe you've moved away and don't see them any longer. Maybe they passed away. When you think of them, what do you remember? Most likely, you remember character traits. To describe a particular person, you probably use examples of how those character traits worked themselves out in the person's life. People are defined by their actions. • That's what Paul wrote about the Thessalonian Christians. He described their faith as it was played out in their faithful work, loving deeds, and enduring hope as they faithfully anticipated Jesus' return. He described what these people *believed* in terms of how they *lived.* • There's no getting around it—we show what we believe by how we live. When the two don't agree, there's a problem. In fact, the people whom we would describe as having the most authentic faith are the people who have the most agreement between what they say and what they do. Are you learning to live what you tell people you believe? Do you need any course correction? What might be a next step in living a life that exemplifies what you believe?

4 We are mocked by our neighbors,
    an object of scorn and derision to
    those around us.

5 O LORD, how long will you be angry
    with us? Forever?
  How long will your jealousy burn
    like fire?
6 Pour out your wrath on the nations
    that refuse to acknowledge you—
  on kingdoms that do not call upon
    your name.
7 For they have devoured your people
    Israel,*
  making the land a desolate
    wilderness.
8 Do not hold us guilty for the sins of
    our ancestors!
  Let your compassion quickly meet
    our needs,
  for we are on the brink of despair.

9 Help us, O God of our salvation!
    Help us for the glory of your name.
  Save us and forgive our sins
    for the honor of your name.
10 Why should pagan nations be allowed
    to scoff,
  asking, "Where is their God?"
  Show us your vengeance against
    the nations,

for they have spilled the blood of
    your servants.
11 Listen to the moaning of the
    prisoners.
  Demonstrate your great power by
    saving those condemned to die.

12 O Lord, pay back our neighbors seven
    times
  for the scorn they have hurled at
    you.
13 Then we your people, the sheep of
    your pasture,
  will thank you forever and ever,
  praising your greatness from
    generation to generation.

79:7 Hebrew *devoured Jacob.* See note on 44:4.

PROVERBS 24:30-34

I walked by the field of a lazy person, the vineyard of one with no common sense. I saw that it was overgrown with nettles. It was covered with weeds, and its walls were broken down. Then, as I looked and thought about it, I learned this lesson: A little extra sleep, a little more slumber, a little folding of the hands to rest—then poverty will pounce on you like a bandit; scarcity will attack you like an armed robber.

OCTOBER**10**

JEREMIAH 14:11-16:15

Circumstances for Judah went from bad to worse. While God had promised eventual deliverance, in Jeremiah's day the nation was going downhill fast.

Then the LORD said to me [Jeremiah], "Do not pray for these people anymore. 12 When they fast, I will pay no attention. When they present their burnt offerings and grain offerings to me, I will not accept them. Instead, I will devour them with war, famine, and disease."

13 Then I said, "O Sovereign LORD, their prophets are telling them, 'All is well—no war or famine will come. The LORD will surely send you peace.'"

14 Then the LORD said, "These prophets are telling lies in my name. I did not send them or tell them to speak. I did not give them any messages. They prophesy of visions and revelations they have never seen or heard. They speak foolishness made up in their own lying hearts. 15 Therefore, this is what the LORD says: I will punish these lying prophets, for they have spoken in my name even though I never sent them. They say that no war or famine will come, but they themselves will die by war and famine! 16 As for the people to whom they prophesy—their bodies will be thrown out into the streets of Jerusalem, victims of famine and war.

There will be no one left to bury them. Husbands, wives, sons, and daughters—all will be gone. For I will pour out their own wickedness on them. [17]Now, Jeremiah, say this to them:

"Night and day my eyes overflow with
    tears.
I cannot stop weeping,
for my virgin daughter—my precious
    people—
has been struck down
and lies mortally wounded.
[18] If I go out into the fields,
    I see the bodies of people
        slaughtered by the enemy.
If I walk the city streets,
    I see people who have died of
        starvation.
The prophets and priests continue
    with their work,
    but they don't know what they're
        doing."

[19] LORD, have you completely rejected
    Judah?
    Do you really hate Jerusalem?*
Why have you wounded us past all
    hope of healing?
    We hoped for peace, but no peace
        came.
    We hoped for a time of healing, but
        found only terror.
[20] LORD, we confess our wickedness
    and that of our ancestors, too.
    We all have sinned against you.
[21] For the sake of your reputation, LORD,
    do not abandon us.
    Do not disgrace your own glorious
        throne.
    Please remember us,
        and do not break your covenant
            with us.
[22] Can any of the worthless foreign gods
    send us rain?
    Does it fall from the sky by itself?
No, you are the one, O LORD our God!
    Only you can do such things.
    So we will wait for you to help us.

[15:1]THEN the LORD said to me, "Even if Moses and Samuel stood before me pleading for these people, I wouldn't help them. Away with them! Get them out of my sight! [2]And if they say to you, 'But where can we go?' tell them, 'This is what the LORD says:

"'Those who are destined for death,
    to death;
those who are destined for war,
    to war;
those who are destined for famine,
    to famine;
those who are destined for captivity,
    to captivity.'

[3]"I will send four kinds of destroyers against them," says the LORD. "I will send the sword to kill, the dogs to drag away, the vultures to devour, and the wild animals to finish up what is left. [4]Because of the wicked things Manasseh son of Hezekiah, king of Judah, did in Jerusalem, I will make my people an object of horror to all the kingdoms of the earth.

[5] "Who will feel sorry for you,
    Jerusalem?
Who will weep for you?
Who will even bother to ask how
    you are?
[6] You have abandoned me
    and turned your back on me,"
        says the LORD.
"Therefore, I will raise my fist to
    destroy you.
    I am tired of always giving you
        another chance.
[7] I will winnow you like grain at the
    gates of your cities
    and take away the children you hold
        dear.
I will destroy my own people,
    because they refuse to change their
        evil ways.
[8] There will be more widows
    than the grains of sand on the
        seashore.
At noontime I will bring a destroyer
    against the mothers of young men.
I will cause anguish and terror
    to come upon them suddenly.
[9] The mother of seven grows faint and
    gasps for breath;
    her sun has gone down while it is
        still day.
She sits childless now,
    disgraced and humiliated.
And I will hand over those who are left

to be killed by the enemy.
I, the LORD, have spoken!"

¹⁰Then I said,

"What sorrow is mine, my mother.
Oh, that I had died at birth!
I am hated everywhere I go.
I am neither a lender who threatens
to foreclose
nor a borrower who refuses to pay—
yet they all curse me."

¹¹The LORD replied,

"I will take care of you, Jeremiah.
Your enemies will ask you to plead
on their behalf
in times of trouble and distress.
¹² Can a man break a bar of iron from
the north,
or a bar of bronze?
¹³ At no cost to them,
I will hand over your wealth and
treasures
as plunder to your enemies,
for sin runs rampant in your land.
¹⁴ I will tell your enemies to take you
as captives to a foreign land.
For my anger blazes like a fire
that will burn forever.*"

¹⁵Then I said,

"LORD, you know what's happening
to me.
Please step in and help me. Punish
my persecutors!
Please give me time; don't let me die
young.
It's for your sake that I am suffering.
¹⁶ When I discovered your words,
I devoured them.
They are my joy and my heart's
delight,
for I bear your name,
O LORD God of Heaven's Armies.
¹⁷ I never joined the people in their
merry feasts.
I sat alone because your hand was
on me.
I was filled with indignation at
their sins.
¹⁸ Why then does my suffering
continue?
Why is my wound so incurable?

Your help seems as uncertain as
a seasonal brook,
like a spring that has gone dry."

¹⁹This is how the LORD responds:

"If you return to me, I will
restore you
so you can continue to serve me.
If you speak good words rather than
worthless ones,
you will be my spokesman.
You must influence them;
do not let them influence you!
²⁰ They will fight against you like an
attacking army,
but I will make you as secure as
a fortified wall of bronze.
They will not conquer you,
for I am with you to protect and
rescue you.
I, the LORD, have spoken!
²¹ Yes, I will certainly keep you safe from
these wicked men.
I will rescue you from their cruel
hands."

¹⁶:¹THE LORD gave me another message.
He said, ²"Do not get married or have children in this place. ³For this is what the
LORD says about the children born here in
this city and about their mothers and fathers: ⁴They will die from terrible diseases. No one will mourn for them or bury
them, and they will lie scattered on the
ground like manure. They will die from
war and famine, and their bodies will be
food for the vultures and wild animals."

⁵This is what the LORD says: "Do not go
to funerals to mourn and show sympathy
for these people, for I have removed my
protection and peace from them. I have
taken away my unfailing love and my
mercy. ⁶Both the great and the lowly will
die in this land. No one will bury them or
mourn for them. Their friends will not cut
themselves in sorrow or shave their heads
in sadness. ⁷No one will offer a meal to
comfort those who mourn for the dead—
not even at the death of a mother or father. No one will send a cup of wine to
console them.

⁸"And do not go to their feasts and parties. Do not eat and drink with them at all.
⁹For this is what the LORD of Heaven's Ar-

mies, the God of Israel, says: In your own lifetime, before your very eyes, I will put an end to the happy singing and laughter in this land. The joyful voices of bridegrooms and brides will no longer be heard.

¹⁰"When you tell the people all these things, they will ask, 'Why has the LORD decreed such terrible things against us? What have we done to deserve such treatment? What is our sin against the LORD our God?'

¹¹"Then you will give them the LORD's reply: 'It is because your ancestors were unfaithful to me. They worshiped other gods and served them. They abandoned me and did not obey my word. ¹²And you are even worse than your ancestors! You stubbornly follow your own evil desires and refuse to listen to me. ¹³So I will throw you out of this land and send you into a foreign land where you and your ancestors have never been. There you can worship idols day and night—and I will grant you no favors!'

¹⁴"But the time is coming," says the LORD, "when people who are taking an oath will no longer say, 'As surely as the LORD lives, who rescued the people of Israel from the land of Egypt.' ¹⁵Instead, they will say, 'As surely as the LORD lives, who brought the people of Israel back to their own land from the land of the north

and from all the countries to which he had exiled them.' For I will bring them back to this land that I gave their ancestors."

14:19 Hebrew *Zion?* **15:14** As in some Hebrew manuscripts (see also 17:4); most Hebrew manuscripts read *will burn against you.*

1 THESSALONIANS 2:9–3:13
Timothy was like a son to Paul. He was also a ministry assistant. Paul sent Timothy to work with many of his churches, including the church in Thessalonica.

Don't you remember, dear brothers and sisters, how hard we [Paul and his co-workers] worked among you? Night and day we toiled to earn a living so that we would not be a burden to any of you as we preached God's Good News to you. ¹⁰You yourselves are our witnesses—and so is God—that we were devout and honest and faultless toward all of you believers. ¹¹And you know that we treated each of you as a father treats his own children. ¹²We pleaded with you, encouraged you, and urged you to live your lives in a way that God would consider worthy. For he called you to share in his Kingdom and glory.

¹³Therefore, we never stop thanking God that when you received his message from us, you didn't think of our words as mere human ideas. You accepted what we said as the very word of God—which, of

HOW WE LIVE

Raising our children

1 THESSALONIANS 2:11-12 In this passage Paul reviews his relationship with the Thessalonians. He speaks as a father to his children, as he tries to strengthen their faith and assure them of Christ's eventual return. Just as no loving father would neglect the safety of his children, Paul was not about to neglect the new believers in the church at Thessalonica. • The responsibility of bringing up children to know and love God belongs first and foremost to parents. By word and example, parents should live in a way worthy of being emulated by their children. Kids are very perceptive, and the "do as I say, not as I do" mindset of many parents often results in a complete breakdown of children's respect for authority figures and the Christian faith. • Parents must encourage and urge their children to live their lives in a way God considers worthy; then those parents must exemplify this lifestyle. Mistakes will be made, for sure. But God forgives us when we fail, and he helps us get back on our feet again. When Mom and Dad have an authentic relationship with God, children have a compelling example to follow.

course, it is. And this word continues to work in you who believe.

[14]And then, dear brothers and sisters, you suffered persecution from your own countrymen. In this way, you imitated the believers in God's churches in Judea who, because of their belief in Christ Jesus, suffered from their own people, the Jews. [15]For some of the Jews killed the prophets, and some even killed the Lord Jesus. Now they have persecuted us, too. They fail to please God and work against all humanity [16]as they try to keep us from preaching the Good News of salvation to the Gentiles. By doing this, they continue to pile up their sins. But the anger of God has caught up with them at last.

[17]Dear brothers and sisters, after we were separated from you for a little while (though our hearts never left you), we tried very hard to come back because of our intense longing to see you again. [18]We wanted very much to come to you, and I, Paul, tried again and again, but Satan prevented us. [19]After all, what gives us hope and joy, and what will be our proud reward and crown as we stand before our Lord Jesus when he returns? It is you! [20]Yes, you are our pride and joy.

[3:1]FINALLY, when we could stand it no longer, we decided to stay alone in Athens, [2]and we sent Timothy to visit you. He is our brother and God's co-worker* in proclaiming the Good News of Christ. We sent him to strengthen you, to encourage you in your faith, [3]and to keep you from being shaken by the troubles you were going through. But you know that we are destined for such troubles. [4]Even while we were with you, we warned you that troubles would soon come—and they did, as you well know. [5]That is why, when I could bear it no longer, I sent Timothy to find out whether your faith was still strong. I was afraid that the tempter had gotten the best of you and that our work had been useless.

[6]But now Timothy has just returned, bringing us good news about your faith and love. He reports that you always remember our visit with joy and that you want to see us as much as we want to see you. [7]So we have been greatly encouraged in the midst of our troubles and suffering, dear brothers and sisters,* because you have remained strong in your faith. [8]It gives us new life to know that you are standing firm in the Lord.

[9]How we thank God for you! Because of you we have great joy as we enter God's presence. [10]Night and day we pray earnestly for you, asking God to let us see you again to fill the gaps in your faith.

[11]May God our Father and our Lord Jesus bring us to you very soon. [12]And may the Lord make your love for one another and for all people grow and overflow, just as our love for you overflows. [13]May he, as a result, make your hearts strong, blameless, and holy as you stand before God our Father when our Lord Jesus comes again with all his holy people. Amen.

3:2 Other manuscripts read *and God's servant;* still others read *and a co-worker,* or *and a servant and co-worker for God,* or *and God's servant and our co-worker.*   **3:7** Greek *brothers.*

PSALM 80:1-19

For the choir director: A psalm of Asaph, to be sung to the tune "Lilies of the Covenant."

[1] Please listen, O Shepherd of Israel,
     you who lead Joseph's descendants
       like a flock.
   O God, enthroned above the cherubim,
     display your radiant glory
[2]   to Ephraim, Benjamin, and
       Manasseh.
   Show us your mighty power.
     Come to rescue us!

[3] Turn us again to yourself, O God.
     Make your face shine down
       upon us.
   Only then will we be saved.
[4] O LORD God of Heaven's Armies,
     how long will you be angry with our
       prayers?
[5] You have fed us with sorrow
     and made us drink tears by the
       bucketful.
[6] You have made us the scorn* of
       neighboring nations.
   Our enemies treat us as a joke.

[7] Turn us again to yourself, O God of
       Heaven's Armies.
   Make your face shine down upon us.
     Only then will we be saved.

8 You brought us from Egypt like
    a grapevine;
  you drove away the pagan nations
    and transplanted us into your
    land.
9 You cleared the ground for us,
  and we took root and filled
    the land.
10 Our shade covered the mountains;
  our branches covered the mighty
    cedars.
11 We spread our branches west to the
    Mediterranean Sea;
  our shoots spread east to the
    Euphrates River.*
12 But now, why have you broken down
    our walls
  so that all who pass by may steal our
    fruit?
13 The wild boar from the forest devours
    it,
  and the wild animals feed on it.

14 Come back, we beg you, O God of
    Heaven's Armies.
  Look down from heaven and see
    our plight.
  Take care of this grapevine
15   that you yourself have planted,
    this son you have raised for yourself.

16 For we are chopped up and burned
    by our enemies.
  May they perish at the sight of your
    frown.
17 Strengthen the man you love,
  the son of your choice.
18 Then we will never abandon you again.
  Revive us so we can call on your
    name once more.

19 Turn us again to yourself, O LORD God
    of Heaven's Armies.
  Make your face shine down upon us.
  Only then will we be saved.

80:6 As in Syriac version; Hebrew reads *the strife.*
80:11 Hebrew *west to the sea, . . . east to the river.*

PROVERBS 25:1-5

These are more proverbs of Solomon, collected by the advisers of King Hezekiah of Judah. □It is God's privilege to conceal things and the king's privilege to discover them. □No one can comprehend the height of heaven, the depth of the earth, or all that goes on in the king's mind! □Remove the impurities from silver, and the sterling will be ready for the silversmith. Remove the wicked from the king's court, and his reign will be made secure by justice.

OCTOBER**11**

JEREMIAH 16:16–18:23

In the midst of Jeremiah's declaration of judgment on his nation's sin are some beautiful thoughts on what it means to trust God. One of Jeremiah's most famous illustrations is also in today's reading: the potter and the clay.

"**B**ut now I am sending for many fishermen who will catch them," says the LORD. "I am sending for hunters who will hunt them down in the mountains, hills, and caves. 17 I am watching them closely, and I see every sin. They cannot hope to hide from me. 18 I will double their punishment for all their sins, because they have defiled my land with lifeless images of their detestable gods and have filled my territory with their evil deeds."

19 LORD, you are my strength and fortress,
    my refuge in the day of trouble!
  Nations from around the world
    will come to you and say,
  "Our ancestors left us a foolish
    heritage,
  for they worshiped worthless idols.
20 Can people make their own gods?
  These are not real gods at all!"

21 The LORD says,
  "Now I will show them my power;
    now I will show them my might.

At last they will know and understand
that I am the LORD.

17:1 "THE sin of Judah
is inscribed with an iron chisel—
engraved with a diamond point on
their stony hearts
and on the corners of their altars.
2 Even their children go to worship
at their pagan altars and Asherah
poles,
beneath every green tree
and on every high hill.
3 So I will hand over my holy
mountain—
along with all your wealth and
treasures
and your pagan shrines—
as plunder to your enemies,
for sin runs rampant in your land.
4 The wonderful possession I have
reserved for you
will slip from your hands.
I will tell your enemies to take you
as captives to a foreign land.
For my anger blazes like a fire
that will burn forever."

5 This is what the LORD says:
"Cursed are those who put their trust
in mere humans,
who rely on human strength
and turn their hearts away from
the LORD.
6 They are like stunted shrubs in the
desert,
with no hope for the future.
They will live in the barren wilderness,
in an uninhabited salty land.

7 "But blessed are those who trust in the
LORD
and have made the LORD their hope
and confidence.
8 They are like trees planted along a
riverbank,
with roots that reach deep into
the water.
Such trees are not bothered by the
heat
or worried by long months of
drought.
Their leaves stay green,
and they never stop producing fruit.

9 "The human heart is the most
deceitful of all things,
and desperately wicked.
Who really knows how bad it is?
10 But I, the LORD, search all hearts
and examine secret motives.
I give all people their due rewards,
according to what their actions
deserve."

11 Like a partridge that hatches eggs she
has not laid,
so are those who get their wealth by
unjust means.
At midlife they will lose their riches;
in the end, they will become poor
old fools.
12 But we worship at your throne—
eternal, high, and glorious!
13 O LORD, the hope of Israel,
all who turn away from you will
be disgraced.
They will be buried in the dust of the
earth,
for they have abandoned the LORD,
the fountain of living water.

14 O LORD, if you heal me, I will be truly
healed;
if you save me, I will be truly saved.
My praises are for you alone!
15 People scoff at me and say,
"What is this 'message from the LORD'
you talk about?
Why don't your predictions come
true?"

16 LORD, I have not abandoned my job
as a shepherd for your people.
I have not urged you to send disaster.
You have heard everything
I've said.
17 LORD, don't terrorize me!
You alone are my hope in the day
of disaster.
18 Bring shame and dismay on all who
persecute me,
but don't let me experience shame
and dismay.
Bring a day of terror on them.
Yes, bring double destruction upon
them!

19 This is what the LORD said to me: "Go
and stand in the gates of Jerusalem, first in
the gate where the king goes in and out,

and then in each of the other gates. ²⁰Say to all the people, 'Listen to this message from the LORD, you kings of Judah and all you people of Judah and everyone living in Jerusalem. ²¹This is what the LORD says: Listen to my warning! Stop carrying on your trade at Jerusalem's gates on the Sabbath day. ²²Do not do your work on the Sabbath, but make it a holy day. I gave this command to your ancestors, ²³but they did not listen or obey. They stubbornly refused to pay attention or accept my discipline.

²⁴" 'But if you obey me, says the LORD, and do not carry on your trade at the gates or work on the Sabbath day, and if you keep it holy, ²⁵then kings and their officials will go in and out of these gates forever. There will always be a descendant of David sitting on the throne here in Jerusalem. Kings and their officials will always ride in and out among the people of Judah in chariots and on horses, and this city will remain forever. ²⁶And from all around Jerusalem, from the towns of Judah and Benjamin, from the western foothills* and the hill country and the Negev, the people will come with their burnt offerings and sacrifices. They will bring their grain offerings, frankincense, and thanksgiving offerings to the LORD's Temple.

²⁷" 'But if you do not listen to me and refuse to keep the Sabbath holy, and if on the Sabbath day you bring loads of merchandise through the gates of Jerusalem just as on other days, then I will set fire to these gates. The fire will spread to the palaces, and no one will be able to put out the roaring flames.'"

18:1THE LORD gave another message to Jeremiah. He said, ²"Go down to the potter's shop, and I will speak to you there." ³So I did as he told me and found the potter working at his wheel. ⁴But the jar he was making did not turn out as he had hoped, so he crushed it into a lump of clay again and started over.

⁵Then the LORD gave me this message: ⁶"O Israel, can I not do to you as this potter has done to his clay? As the clay is in the potter's hand, so are you in my hand. ⁷If I announce that a certain nation or kingdom is to be uprooted, torn down, and destroyed, ⁸but then that nation renounces its evil ways, I will not destroy it as I had planned. ⁹And if I announce that I will plant and build up a certain nation or kingdom, ¹⁰but then that nation turns to evil and refuses to obey me, I will not bless it as I said I would.

¹¹"Therefore, Jeremiah, go and warn all Judah and Jerusalem. Say to them, 'This is what the LORD says: I am planning disaster for you instead of good. So turn from

---

WHAT THE BIBLE SAYS

Sin and its consequences

JEREMIAH 17:9 When God created human beings in his own image (Genesis 1:27, January 1), there was no sin in the human heart. However, God made humans free to choose whether to obey or disobey. When Adam and Eve disobeyed (Genesis 3, January 2), sin entered the heart of the human race. As the first humans fell into sin, they condemned all those yet to be born to come into this world with a stubborn, sinful nature. • Humanity has fallen a long way from the perfection of the Garden of Eden—so far that God considers the human heart to be "deceitful" and "desperately wicked." Even those who are saved and made new in Christ have hearts that are still inclined toward sinning. Thankfully, believers are no longer in complete bondage to sin. We can choose not to sin, and when we fall we can count on God's forgiveness and the arms of Jesus to lift us up once again. • You have been saved, but don't be surprised at the strong pull of sin. The battle with sin will continue until your death—or until Jesus comes back. If you fall, however, confess your sin and let Christ help you get up, dust off, and keep going.

your evil ways, each of you, and do what is right.'"

¹²But the people replied, "Don't waste your breath. We will continue to live as we want to, stubbornly following our own evil desires."

¹³So this is what the LORD says:

"Has anyone ever heard of such a thing,
    even among the pagan nations?
My virgin daughter Israel
    has done something terrible!
¹⁴ Does the snow ever disappear from
        the mountaintops of Lebanon?
    Do the cold streams flowing from
        those distant mountains ever
        run dry?
¹⁵ But my people are not so reliable,
        for they have deserted me;
    they burn incense to worthless idols.
    They have stumbled off the ancient
        highways
    and walk in muddy paths.
¹⁶ Therefore, their land will become
        desolate,
    a monument to their stupidity.
    All who pass by will be astonished
    and will shake their heads in
        amazement.
¹⁷ I will scatter my people before their
        enemies
    as the east wind scatters dust.
    And in all their trouble I will turn my
        back on them
    and refuse to notice their distress."

¹⁸Then the people said, "Come on, let's plot a way to stop Jeremiah. We have plenty of priests and wise men and prophets. We don't need him to teach the word and give us advice and prophecies. Let's spread rumors about him and ignore what he says."

¹⁹ LORD, hear me and help me!
    Listen to what my enemies are
        saying.
²⁰ Should they repay evil for good?
    They have dug a pit to kill me,
        though I pleaded for them
    and tried to protect them from
        your anger.
²¹ So let their children starve!
    Let them die by the sword!
    Let their wives become childless
        widows.

Let their old men die in a plague,
    and let their young men be killed
        in battle!
²² Let screaming be heard from their
        homes
    as warriors come suddenly upon
        them.
For they have dug a pit for me
    and have hidden traps along
        my path.
²³ LORD, you know all about their
        murderous plots against me.
    Don't forgive their crimes and blot
        out their sins.
    Let them die before you.
    Deal with them in your anger.

17:26 Hebrew *the Shephelah*.

1 THESSALONIANS 4:1–5:3

Paul's letters to the Thessalonians include some of the most notable New Testament passages about Jesus' second coming. Living in preparation for that event really means living the Christian life.

Finally, dear brothers and sisters,* we [Paul and his coworkers] urge you in the name of the Lord Jesus to live in a way that pleases God, as we have taught you. You live this way already, and we encourage you to do so even more. ²For you remember what we taught you by the authority of the Lord Jesus.

³God's will is for you to be holy, so stay away from all sexual sin. ⁴Then each of you will control his own body* and live in holiness and honor—⁵not in lustful passion like the pagans who do not know God and his ways. ⁶Never harm or cheat a Christian brother in this matter by violating his wife,* for the Lord avenges all such sins, as we have solemnly warned you before. ⁷God has called us to live holy lives, not impure lives. ⁸Therefore, anyone who refuses to live by these rules is not disobeying human teaching but is rejecting God, who gives his Holy Spirit to you.

⁹But we don't need to write to you about the importance of loving each other,* for God himself has taught you to love one another. ¹⁰Indeed, you already show your love for all the believers* throughout Macedonia. Even so, dear brothers and sisters, we urge you to love them even more.

¹¹Make it your goal to live a quiet life,

minding your own business and working with your hands, just as we instructed you before. [12]Then people who are not Christians will respect the way you live, and you will not need to depend on others.

[13]And now, dear brothers and sisters, we want you to know what will happen to the believers who have died* so you will not grieve like people who have no hope. [14]For since we believe that Jesus died and was raised to life again, we also believe that when Jesus returns, God will bring back with him the believers who have died.

[15]We tell you this directly from the Lord: We who are still living when the Lord returns will not meet him ahead of those who have died.* [16]For the Lord himself will come down from heaven with a commanding shout, with the voice of the archangel, and with the trumpet call of God. First, the Christians who have died* will rise from their graves. [17]Then, together with them, we who are still alive and remain on the earth will be caught up in the clouds to meet the Lord in the air. Then we will be with the Lord forever. [18]So encourage each other with these words.

[5:1]Now concerning how and when all this will happen, dear brothers and sisters,* we don't really need to write you. [2]For you know quite well that the day of the Lord's return will come unexpectedly, like a thief in the night. [3]When people are saying, "Everything is peaceful and secure," then disaster will fall on them as suddenly as a pregnant woman's labor pains begin. And there will be no escape.

4:1 Greek *brothers;* also in 4:10, 13. **4:4** Or *will know how to take a wife for himself;* or *will learn to live with his own wife;* Greek reads *will know how to possess his own vessel.* **4:6** Greek *Never harm or cheat a brother in this matter.* **4:9** Greek *about brotherly love.* **4:10** Greek *the brothers.* **4:13** Greek *those who have fallen asleep;* also in 4:14. **4:15** Greek *those who have fallen asleep.* **4:16** Greek *the dead in Christ.* **5:1** Greek *brothers;* also in 5:4, 12, 14, 25, 26, 27.

PSALM 81:1-16
*For the choir director: A psalm of Asaph, to be accompanied by a stringed instrument.**

[1] **S**ing praises to God, our strength.
    Sing to the God of Jacob.
[2] Sing! Beat the tambourine.
    Play the sweet lyre and the harp.
[3] Blow the ram's horn at new moon,

and again at full moon to call
    a festival!
[4] For this is required by the decrees
    of Israel;
    it is a regulation of the God of Jacob.
[5] He made it a law for Israel*
    when he attacked Egypt to set
    us free.

I heard an unknown voice say,
[6] "Now I will take the load from your
    shoulders;
    I will free your hands from their
    heavy tasks.
[7] You cried to me in trouble, and
    I saved you;
    I answered out of the thundercloud
    and tested your faith when there
    was no water at Meribah.
                                        Interlude

[8] "Listen to me, O my people, while
    I give you stern warnings.
    O Israel, if you would only listen
    to me!
[9] You must never have a foreign god;
    you must not bow down before
    a false god.
[10] For it was I, the LORD your God,
    who rescued you from the land
    of Egypt.
    Open your mouth wide, and I will
    fill it with good things.

[11] "But no, my people wouldn't listen.
    Israel did not want me around.
[12] So I let them follow their own
    stubborn desires,
    living according to their own ideas.
[13] Oh, that my people would listen to me!
    Oh, that Israel would follow me,
    walking in my paths!
[14] How quickly I would then subdue
    their enemies!
    How soon my hands would be upon
    their foes!
[15] Those who hate the LORD would
    cringe before him;
    they would be doomed forever.
[16] But I would feed you with the finest
    wheat.
    I would satisfy you with wild honey
    from the rock."

81:TITLE Hebrew *according to the gittith.* **81:5** Hebrew *for Joseph.*

PROVERBS 25:6-8

Don't demand an audience with the king or push for a place among the great. It's better to wait for an invitation to the head table than to be sent away in public disgrace. □ Just because you've seen something, don't be in a hurry to go to court. For what will you do in the end if your neighbor deals you a shameful defeat?

OCTOBER**12**

JEREMIAH 19:1–21:14

Jeremiah used a pottery jar to show his people the destruction that comes to a life that refuses God's guidance. If the people continued to choose their own way instead of God's, they would be broken to pieces by foreign invaders.

This is what the LORD said to me [Jeremiah]: "Go and buy a clay jar. Then ask some of the leaders of the people and of the priests to follow you. ²Go out through the Gate of Broken Pots to the garbage dump in the valley of Ben-Hinnom, and give them this message. ³Say to them, 'Listen to this message from the LORD, you kings of Judah and citizens of Jerusalem! This is what the LORD of Heaven's Armies, the God of Israel, says: I will bring a terrible disaster on this place, and the ears of those who hear about it will ring!

⁴" 'For Israel has forsaken me and turned this valley into a place of wickedness. The people burn incense to foreign gods—idols never before acknowledged by this generation, by their ancestors, or by the kings of Judah. And they have filled this place with the blood of innocent children. ⁵They have built pagan shrines to Baal, and there they burn their sons as sacrifices to Baal. I have never commanded such a horrible deed; it never even crossed my mind to command such a thing! ⁶So beware, for the time is coming, says the LORD, when this garbage dump will no longer be called Topheth or the valley of Ben-Hinnom, but the Valley of Slaughter.

⁷" 'For I will upset the careful plans of Judah and Jerusalem. I will allow the people to be slaughtered by invading armies, and I will leave their dead bodies as food for the vultures and wild animals. ⁸I will reduce Jerusalem to ruins, making it a monument to their stupidity. All who pass by will be astonished and will gasp at the destruction they see there. ⁹I will see to it that your enemies lay siege to the city until all the food is gone. Then those trapped inside will eat their own sons and daughters and friends. They will be driven to utter despair.'

¹⁰"As these men watch you, Jeremiah, smash the jar you brought. ¹¹Then say to them, 'This is what the LORD of Heaven's Armies says: As this jar lies shattered, so I will shatter the people of Judah and Jerusalem beyond all hope of repair. They will bury the bodies here in Topheth, the garbage dump, until there is no more room for them. ¹²This is what I will do to this place and its people, says the LORD. I will cause this city to become defiled like Topheth. ¹³Yes, all the houses in Jerusalem, including the palace of Judah's kings, will become like Topheth—all the houses where you burned incense on the rooftops to your star gods, and where liquid offerings were poured out to your idols.'"

¹⁴Then Jeremiah returned from Topheth, the garbage dump where he had delivered this message, and he stopped in front of the Temple of the LORD. He said to the people there, ¹⁵"This is what the LORD of Heaven's Armies, the God of Israel, says: 'I will bring disaster upon this city and its surrounding towns as I promised,

because you have stubbornly refused to listen to me.'"

20:1Now Pashhur son of Immer, the priest in charge of the Temple of the LORD, heard what Jeremiah was prophesying. 2So he arrested Jeremiah the prophet and had him whipped and put in stocks at the Benjamin Gate of the LORD's Temple.

3The next day, when Pashhur finally released him, Jeremiah said, "Pashhur, the LORD has changed your name. From now on you are to be called 'The Man Who Lives in Terror.'* 4For this is what the LORD says: 'I will send terror upon you and all your friends, and you will watch as they are slaughtered by the swords of the enemy. I will hand the people of Judah over to the king of Babylon. He will take them captive to Babylon or run them through with the sword. 5And I will let your enemies plunder Jerusalem. All the famed treasures of the city—the precious jewels and gold and silver of your kings— will be carried off to Babylon. 6As for you, Pashhur, you and all your household will go as captives to Babylon. There you will die and be buried, you and all your friends to whom you prophesied that everything would be all right.'"

7 O LORD, you misled me,
    and I allowed myself to be misled.
 You are stronger than I am,
    and you overpowered me.
 Now I am mocked every day;
    everyone laughs at me.
8 When I speak, the words burst out.
    "Violence and destruction!" I shout.
 So these messages from the LORD
    have made me a household joke.
9 But if I say I'll never mention the LORD
    or speak in his name,
 his word burns in my heart like a fire.
    It's like a fire in my bones!
 I am worn out trying to hold it in!
    I can't do it!
10 I have heard the many rumors
    about me.
    They call me "The Man Who Lives
       in Terror."
    They threaten, "If you say anything,
       we will report it."

 Even my old friends are
    watching me,
    waiting for a fatal slip.
 "He will trap himself," they say,
    "and then we will get our revenge
       on him."

11 But the LORD stands beside me like
    a great warrior.
 Before him my persecutors will
    stumble.
    They cannot defeat me.
 They will fail and be thoroughly
    humiliated.
    Their dishonor will never be
       forgotten.
12 O LORD of Heaven's Armies,
 you test those who are righteous,
    and you examine the deepest
       thoughts and secrets.
 Let me see your vengeance against
    them,
    for I have committed my cause
       to you.
13 Sing to the LORD!
    Praise the LORD!
 For though I was poor and needy,
    he rescued me from my
       oppressors.

14 Yet I curse the day I was born!
    May no one celebrate the day of
       my birth.
15 I curse the messenger who told my
    father,
    "Good news—you have a son!"
16 Let him be destroyed like the cities
    of old
    that the LORD overthrew without
       mercy.
 Terrify him all day long with battle
    shouts,
17   because he did not kill me
       at birth.
 Oh, that I had died in my mother's
    womb,
    that her body had been my grave!
18 Why was I ever born?
    My entire life has been filled
       with trouble, sorrow, and shame.

21:1THE LORD spoke through Jeremiah when King Zedekiah sent Pashhur son of Malkijah and Zephaniah son of Maaseiah, the priest, to speak with him. They begged

Jeremiah, [2]"Please speak to the LORD for us and ask him to help us. King Nebuchadnezzar* of Babylon is attacking Judah. Perhaps the LORD will be gracious and do a mighty miracle as he has done in the past. Perhaps he will force Nebuchadnezzar to withdraw his armies."

[3]Jeremiah replied, "Go back to King Zedekiah and tell him, [4]'This is what the LORD, the God of Israel, says: I will make your weapons useless against the king of Babylon and the Babylonians* who are outside your walls attacking you. In fact, I will bring your enemies right into the heart of this city. [5]I myself will fight against you with a strong hand and a powerful arm, for I am very angry. You have made me furious! [6]I will send a terrible plague upon this city, and both people and animals will die. [7]And after all that, says the LORD, I will hand over King Zedekiah, his staff, and everyone else in the city who survives the disease, war, and famine. I will hand them over to King Nebuchadnezzar of Babylon and to their other enemies. He will slaughter them and show them no mercy, pity, or compassion.'

[8]"Tell all the people, 'This is what the LORD says: Take your choice of life or death! [9]Everyone who stays in Jerusalem will die from war, famine, or disease, but those who go out and surrender to the Babylonians will live. Their reward will be life! [10]For I have decided to bring disaster and not good upon this city, says the LORD. It will be handed over to the king of Babylon, and he will reduce it to ashes.'

[11]"Say to the royal family of Judah, 'Listen to this message from the LORD! [12]This is what the LORD says to the dynasty of David:

"'Give justice each morning to the
    people you judge!
  Help those who have been
    robbed;
  rescue them from their
    oppressors.
Otherwise, my anger will burn like
    an unquenchable fire
  because of all your sins.
[13] I will personally fight against the
    people in Jerusalem,
  that mighty fortress—

the people who boast, "No one can
    touch us here.
  No one can break in here."
[14] And I myself will punish you for your
    sinfulness,
  says the LORD.
I will light a fire in your forests
  that will burn up everything
    around you.'"

20:3 Hebrew *Magor-missabib*, which means "surrounded by terror"; also in 20:10.   21:2 Hebrew *Nebuchadrezzar*, a variant spelling of Nebuchadnezzar; also in 21:7.   21:4 Or *Chaldeans;* also in 21:9.

1 THESSALONIANS 5:4-28

The advice Paul gives at the end of his letters often contains powerful information about living the Christian life. As he closes this first letter to the Thessalonians, Paul reminds them (and us) how to relate to each other in faith and love.

But you aren't in the dark about these things, dear brothers and sisters, and you won't be surprised when the day of the Lord comes like a thief.* [5]For you are all children of the light and of the day; we don't belong to darkness and night. [6]So be on your guard, not asleep like the others. Stay alert and be clearheaded. [7]Night is the time when people sleep and drinkers get drunk. [8]But let us who live in the light be clearheaded, protected by the armor of faith and love, and wearing as our helmet the confidence of our salvation.

[9]For God chose to save us through our Lord Jesus Christ, not to pour out his anger on us. [10]Christ died for us so that, whether we are dead or alive when he returns, we can live with him forever. [11]So encourage each other and build each other up, just as you are already doing.

[12]Dear brothers and sisters, honor those who are your leaders in the Lord's work. They work hard among you and give you spiritual guidance. [13]Show them great respect and wholehearted love because of their work. And live peacefully with each other.

[14]Brothers and sisters, we urge you to warn those who are lazy. Encourage those who are timid. Take tender care of those who are weak. Be patient with everyone.

[15]See that no one pays back evil for evil, but always try to do good to each other and to all people.

[16]Always be joyful. [17]Never stop praying. [18]Be thankful in all circumstances, for this is God's will for you who belong to Christ Jesus.

[19]Do not stifle the Holy Spirit. [20]Do not scoff at prophecies, [21]but test everything that is said. Hold on to what is good. [22]Stay away from every kind of evil.

[23]Now may the God of peace make you holy in every way, and may your whole spirit and soul and body be kept blameless until our Lord Jesus Christ comes again. [24]God will make this happen, for he who calls you is faithful.

[25]Dear brothers and sisters, pray for us.

[26]Greet all the brothers and sisters with Christian love.*

[27]I command you in the name of the Lord to read this letter to all the brothers and sisters.

[28]May the grace of our Lord Jesus Christ be with you.

5:4 Some manuscripts read *comes upon you as if you were thieves.*   5:26 Greek *with a holy kiss.*

PSALM 82:1-8
A psalm of Asaph.

[1] **G**od presides over heaven's court;
he pronounces judgment on the heavenly beings:

[2] "How long will you hand down unjust decisions
by favoring the wicked?   *Interlude*

[3] "Give justice to the poor and the orphan;
uphold the rights of the oppressed and the destitute.

[4] Rescue the poor and helpless;
deliver them from the grasp of evil people.

[5] But these oppressors know nothing;
they are so ignorant!
They wander about in darkness,
while the whole world is shaken to the core.

[6] I say, 'You are gods;
you are all children of the Most High.

[7] But you will die like mere mortals
and fall like every other ruler.'"

[8] Rise up, O God, and judge the earth,
for all the nations belong to you.

PROVERBS 25:9-10
When arguing with your neighbor, don't betray another person's secret. Others may accuse you of gossip, and you will never regain your good reputation.

HOW WE LIVE

Our speech

1 THESSALONIANS 5:11 "Good job." "Awesome work on that project." "Wow, you did just great on that." "We so appreciate your help." Isn't it a great encouragement to be thanked and appreciated for your hard work? Paul instructed believers to be encouragers of one another in the life of faith. The believers in Thessalonica had experienced persecution and sorrow, so Paul told them to encourage one another about the certainty of their future and the promise of eternal life through Jesus Christ. They ought also to "build each other up" in the faith.   •Believers will never stop needing encouragement. Just as one believer receives encouragement, he or she at another time will be in a position to offer it. The mutual giving and receiving in the body of Christ keep the church strong against the forces that attack it. Look around. Who could use a word of encouragement from you today?

OCTOBER**13**

JEREMIAH 22:1–23:20

The kings of Israel and Judah wielded much spiritual influence over the people. As the king's heart went toward or away from God, so went the nation. Here, Jeremiah has stern words for the king of Judah.

This is what the LORD said to me [Jeremiah]: "Go over and speak directly to the king of Judah. Say to him, ²'Listen to this message from the LORD, you king of Judah, sitting on David's throne. Let your attendants and your people listen, too. ³This is what the LORD says: Be fair-minded and just. Do what is right! Help those who have been robbed; rescue them from their oppressors. Quit your evil deeds! Do not mistreat foreigners, orphans, and widows. Stop murdering the innocent! ⁴If you obey me, there will always be a descendant of David sitting on the throne here in Jerusalem. The king will ride through the palace gates in chariots and on horses, with his parade of attendants and subjects. ⁵But if you refuse to pay attention to this warning, I swear by my own name, says the LORD, that this palace will become a pile of rubble.'"

⁶Now this is what the LORD says concerning Judah's royal palace:

"I love you as much as fruitful Gilead
and the green forests of Lebanon.
But I will turn you into a desert,
with no one living within your walls.
⁷ I will call for wreckers,
who will bring out their tools to
dismantle you.
They will tear out all your fine cedar
beams
and throw them on the fire.

⁸"People from many nations will pass by the ruins of this city and say to one another, 'Why did the LORD destroy such a great city?' ⁹And the answer will be, 'Because they violated their covenant with the LORD their God by worshiping other gods.'"

¹⁰ Do not weep for the dead king or
mourn his loss.
Instead, weep for the captive king
being led away!

For he will never return to see his
native land again.

¹¹For this is what the LORD says about Jehoahaz,* who succeeded his father, King Josiah, and was taken away as a captive: "He will never return. ¹²He will die in a distant land and will never again see his own country."

¹³ And the LORD says, "What sorrow
awaits Jehoiakim,*
who builds his palace with forced
labor.*
He builds injustice into its walls,
for he makes his neighbors work
for nothing.
He does not pay them for their labor.
¹⁴ He says, 'I will build a magnificent
palace
with huge rooms and many windows.
I will panel it throughout with fragrant
cedar
and paint it a lovely red.'
¹⁵ But a beautiful cedar palace does not
make a great king!
Your father, Josiah, also had plenty
to eat and drink.
But he was just and right in all his
dealings.
That is why God blessed him.
¹⁶ He gave justice and help to the poor
and needy,
and everything went well for him.
Isn't that what it means to know me?"
says the LORD.
¹⁷ "But you! You have eyes only for greed
and dishonesty!
You murder the innocent,
oppress the poor, and reign
ruthlessly."

¹⁸Therefore, this is what the LORD says about Jehoiakim, son of King Josiah:

"The people will not mourn for him,
crying to one another,
'Alas, my brother! Alas, my sister!'
His subjects will not mourn for him,
crying,
'Alas, our master is dead! Alas, his
splendor is gone!'

¹⁹ He will be buried like a dead donkey—
   dragged out of Jerusalem and
     dumped outside the gates!
²⁰ Weep for your allies in Lebanon.
   Shout for them in Bashan.
   Search for them in the regions east
     of the river.*
   See, they are all destroyed.
   Not one is left to help you.
²¹ I warned you when you were
     prosperous,
   but you replied, 'Don't bother me.'
   You have been that way since
     childhood—
   you simply will not obey me!
²² And now the wind will blow away
     your allies.
   All your friends will be taken away
     as captives.
   Surely then you will see your
     wickedness and be ashamed.
²³ It may be nice to live in a beautiful
     palace
   paneled with wood from the cedars
     of Lebanon,
   but soon you will groan with pangs
     of anguish—
   anguish like that of a woman
     in labor.

²⁴"As surely as I live," says the LORD, "I will abandon you, Jehoiachin* son of Jehoiakim, king of Judah. Even if you were the signet ring on my right hand, I would pull you off. ²⁵I will hand you over to those who seek to kill you, those you so desperately fear—to King Nebuchadnezzar* of Babylon and the mighty Babylonian* army. ²⁶I will expel you and your mother from this land, and you will die in a foreign country, not in your native land. ²⁷You will never again return to the land you yearn for.

²⁸ "Why is this man Jehoiachin like
     a discarded, broken jar?
   Why are he and his children to be
     exiled to a foreign land?
²⁹ O earth, earth, earth!
   Listen to this message from
     the LORD!
³⁰ This is what the LORD says:
   'Let the record show that this man
     Jehoiachin was childless.
   He is a failure,

for none of his children will succeed
     him on the throne of David
   to rule over Judah.'

^{23:1}"WHAT sorrow awaits the leaders of my people—the shepherds of my sheep—for they have destroyed and scattered the very ones they were expected to care for," says the LORD.

²Therefore, this is what the LORD, the God of Israel, says to these shepherds: "Instead of caring for my flock and leading them to safety, you have deserted them and driven them to destruction. Now I will pour out judgment on you for the evil you have done to them. ³But I will gather together the remnant of my flock from the countries where I have driven them. I will bring them back to their own sheepfold, and they will be fruitful and increase in number. ⁴Then I will appoint responsible shepherds who will care for them, and they will never be afraid again. Not a single one will be lost or missing. I, the LORD, have spoken!

⁵ "For the time is coming,"
     says the LORD,
   "when I will raise up a righteous
     descendant*
   from King David's line.
   He will be a King who rules with
     wisdom.
   He will do what is just and right
     throughout the land.
⁶ And this will be his name:
   'The LORD Is Our Righteousness.'*
   In that day Judah will be saved,
   and Israel will live in safety.

⁷"In that day," says the LORD, "when people are taking an oath, they will no longer say, 'As surely as the LORD lives, who rescued the people of Israel from the land of Egypt.' ⁸Instead, they will say, 'As surely as the LORD lives, who brought the people of Israel back to their own land from the land of the north and from all the countries to which he had exiled them.' Then they will live in their own land."

⁹ My heart is broken because of the
     false prophets,
   and my bones tremble.
   I stagger like a drunkard,
     like someone overcome by wine,

because of the holy words
  the LORD has spoken against them.
¹⁰ For the land is full of adultery,
  and it lies under a curse.
The land itself is in mourning—
  its wilderness pastures are dried up.
For they all do evil
  and abuse what power they have.

¹¹ "Even the priests and prophets
  are ungodly, wicked men.
I have seen their despicable acts
  right here in my own Temple,"
  says the LORD.
¹² "Therefore, the paths they take
  will become slippery.
They will be chased through the dark,
  and there they will fall.
For I will bring disaster upon them
  at the time fixed for their
  punishment.
I, the LORD, have spoken!

¹³ "I saw that the prophets of Samaria
  were terribly evil,
for they prophesied in the name
  of Baal
and led my people of Israel into sin.
¹⁴ But now I see that the prophets of
  Jerusalem are even worse!
They commit adultery and love
  dishonesty.
They encourage those who are doing
  evil
so that no one turns away from
  their sins.
These prophets are as wicked
  as the people of Sodom and
  Gomorrah once were."

¹⁵ Therefore, this is what the LORD of
Heaven's Armies says concerning the
prophets:

"I will feed them with bitterness
  and give them poison to drink.
For it is because of Jerusalem's
  prophets
  that wickedness has filled this land."

¹⁶ This is what the LORD of Heaven's Ar-
mies says to his people:

"Do not listen to these prophets when
  they prophesy to you,
  filling you with futile hopes.

They are making up everything
  they say.
They do not speak for the LORD!
¹⁷ They keep saying to those who despise
  my word,
'Don't worry! The LORD says you will
  have peace!'
And to those who stubbornly follow
  their own desires,
  they say, 'No harm will come your
  way!'

¹⁸ "Have any of these prophets been in
  the LORD's presence
to hear what he is really saying?
Has even one of them cared enough
  to listen?
¹⁹ Look! The LORD's anger bursts out like
  a storm,
a whirlwind that swirls down on the
  heads of the wicked.
²⁰ The anger of the LORD will not
  diminish
until it has finished all he has
  planned.
In the days to come
  you will understand all this very
  clearly."

22:11 Hebrew *Shallum*, another name for Jehoahaz.
22:13a The brother and successor of the exiled Jehoahaz. See
22:18.   22:13b Hebrew *by unrighteousness*.   22:20 Or *in
Abarim*.   22:24 Hebrew *Coniah*, a variant spelling of
Jehoiachin; also 22:28.   22:25a Hebrew *Nebuchadrezzar*,
a variant spelling of Nebuchadnezzar.   22:25b Or *Chaldean*.
23:5 Hebrew *a righteous branch*.   23:6 Hebrew *Yahweh
Tsidqenu*.

2 THESSALONIANS 1:1-12

Paul's second letter to the Thessalonian church was
a letter of clarification. Some members of the
community had misunderstood Paul's teaching
about Jesus' second coming. Paul took pains to
clarify his teaching here.

This letter is from Paul, Silas,* and Timothy.
  We are writing to the church in Thessalonica, to you who belong to God our Father and the Lord Jesus Christ.

² May God our Father* and the Lord
Jesus Christ give you grace and peace.

³ Dear brothers and sisters,* we can't
help but thank God for you, because your
faith is flourishing and your love for one
another is growing. ⁴ We proudly tell
God's other churches about your endurance and faithfulness in all the persecu-

tions and hardships you are suffering. [5]And God will use this persecution to show his justice and to make you worthy of his Kingdom, for which you are suffering. [6]In his justice he will pay back those who persecute you.

[7]And God will provide rest for you who are being persecuted and also for us when the Lord Jesus appears from heaven. He will come with his mighty angels, [8]in flaming fire, bringing judgment on those who don't know God and on those who refuse to obey the Good News of our Lord Jesus. [9]They will be punished with eternal destruction, forever separated from the Lord and from his glorious power. [10]When he comes on that day, he will receive glory from his holy people—praise from all who believe. And this includes you, for you believed what we told you about him.

[11]So we keep on praying for you, asking our God to enable you to live a life worthy of his call. May he give you the power to accomplish all the good things your faith prompts you to do. [12]Then the name of our Lord Jesus will be honored because of the way you live, and you will be honored along with him. This is all made possible because of the grace of our God and Lord, Jesus Christ.*

1:1 Greek *Silvanus*, the Greek form of the name.   1:2 Some manuscripts read *God the Father.*   1:3 Greek *Brothers.*
1:12 Or *of our God and our Lord Jesus Christ.*

PSALM 83:1-18
A song. A psalm of Asaph.

[1] **O** God, do not be silent!
Do not be deaf.
Do not be quiet, O God.

[2] Don't you hear the uproar of your
enemies?
Don't you see that your arrogant
enemies are rising up?

[3] They devise crafty schemes against
your people;
they conspire against your precious
ones.

[4] "Come," they say, "let us wipe out Israel
as a nation.
We will destroy the very memory
of its existence."

[5] Yes, this was their unanimous
decision.
They signed a treaty as allies against
you—

[6] these Edomites and Ishmaelites;
Moabites and Hagrites;

[7] Gebalites, Ammonites, and
Amalekites;
and people from Philistia and Tyre.

[8] Assyria has joined them, too,
and is allied with the descendants
of Lot.   *Interlude*

[9] Do to them as you did to the
Midianites

WHAT THE BIBLE SAYS

The reality of hell

2 THESSALONIANS 1:7-10 Each of today's passages discusses an aspect of accountability. Jeremiah called his people to be accountable for their lives. The psalmist asked for accountability for his enemies. The proverbs describe accountability among friends.   • The most final form of accountability is hell, one of the two eternal destinations for the souls of humanity. From Paul's words here, we gain three insights into hell: (1) *It is a place for those who don't know God.* To know God, to be his child, means to live with him eternally. To not know God—eternally—is hell. (2) *It is a place of unending destruction.* It is the opposite of God's goodness and redemption. It is the reaping of sin's eternal consequences. (3) *It is a place of separation from God.* Those who choose not to connect with God alienate themselves from the source of life and light. They are left with darkness and death.   • You have chosen an eternal relationship with God. Many around you have not. (If you wonder how a loving God could send anyone to hell, see the note for October 31.) As a believer, pray for the unbelievers around you, and share your faith whenever you can.

and as you did to Sisera and Jabin at
the Kishon River.
¹⁰ They were destroyed at Endor,
and their decaying corpses
fertilized the soil.
¹¹ Let their mighty nobles die as Oreb
and Zeeb did.
Let all their princes die like Zebah
and Zalmunna,
¹² for they said, "Let us seize for our own
use
these pasturelands of God!"
¹³ O my God, scatter them like
tumbleweed,
like chaff before the wind!
¹⁴ As a fire burns a forest
and as a flame sets mountains
ablaze,
¹⁵ chase them with your fierce storm;
terrify them with your tempest.

OCTOBER**14**

JEREMIAH 23:21–25:38
Jeremiah warned against false prophets and
explained that no matter what happy picture those
prophets may have been painting for the future, the
nation was going to go into captivity for seventy
years as punishment for persistent sin.

"**I** [the LORD] have not sent these
prophets,
yet they run around claiming to
speak for me.
I have given them no message,
yet they go on prophesying.
²² If they had stood before me and
listened to me,
they would have spoken my words,
and they would have turned my people
from their evil ways and deeds.
²³ Am I a God who is only close at hand?"
says the LORD.
"No, I am far away at the same time.
²⁴ Can anyone hide from me in a secret
place?
Am I not everywhere in all the
heavens and earth?"
says the LORD.

¹⁶ Utterly disgrace them
until they submit to your name,
O LORD.
¹⁷ Let them be ashamed and terrified
forever.
Let them die in disgrace.
¹⁸ Then they will learn that you alone are
called the LORD,
that you alone are the Most High,
supreme over all the earth.

PROVERBS 25:11-14
Timely advice is lovely, like golden apples in
a silver basket. □ To one who listens, valid
criticism is like a gold earring or other gold
jewelry. □ Trustworthy messengers refresh
like snow in summer. They revive the spirit
of their employer. □ A person who promises a gift but doesn't give it is like clouds
and wind that bring no rain.

²⁵"I have heard these prophets say, 'Listen to the dream I had from God last night.'
And then they proceed to tell lies in my
name. ²⁶How long will this go on? If they
are prophets, they are prophets of deceit,
inventing everything they say. ²⁷By telling
these false dreams, they are trying to get
my people to forget me, just as their ancestors did by worshiping the idols of Baal.

²⁸ "Let these false prophets tell their
dreams,
but let my true messengers
faithfully proclaim my every
word.
There is a difference between straw
and grain!
²⁹ Does not my word burn like fire?"
says the LORD.
"Is it not like a mighty hammer
that smashes a rock to pieces?

³⁰"Therefore," says the LORD, "I am
against these prophets who steal messages from each other and claim they are
from me. ³¹I am against these smooth-

tongued prophets who say, 'This prophecy is from the LORD!' [32]I am against these false prophets. Their imaginary dreams are flagrant lies that lead my people into sin. I did not send or appoint them, and they have no message at all for my people. I, the LORD have spoken!

[33]"Suppose one of the people or one of the prophets or priests asks you, 'What prophecy has the LORD burdened you with now?' You must reply, 'You are the burden!* The LORD says he will abandon you!'

[34]"If any prophet, priest, or anyone else says, 'I have a prophecy from the LORD,' I will punish that person along with his entire family. [35]You should keep asking each other, 'What is the LORD's answer?' or 'What is the LORD saying?' [36]But stop using this phrase, 'prophecy from the LORD.' For people are using it to give authority to their own ideas, turning upside down the words of our God, the living God, the LORD of Heaven's Armies.

[37]"This is what you should say to the prophets: 'What is the LORD's answer?' or 'What is the LORD saying?' [38]But suppose they respond, 'This is a prophecy from the LORD!' Then you should say, 'This is what the LORD says: Because you have used this phrase, "prophecy from the LORD," even though I warned you not to use it, [39]I will forget you completely. I will expel you from my presence, along with this city that I gave to you and your ancestors. [40]And I will make you an object of ridicule, and your name will be infamous throughout the ages.'"

[24:1]AFTER King Nebuchadnezzar* of Babylon exiled Jehoiachin* son of Jehoiakim, king of Judah, to Babylon along with the officials of Judah and all the craftsmen and artisans, the LORD gave me this vision. I saw two baskets of figs placed in front of the LORD's Temple in Jerusalem. [2]One basket was filled with fresh, ripe figs, while the other was filled with bad figs that were too rotten to eat.

[3]Then the LORD said to me, "What do you see, Jeremiah?"

I replied, "Figs, some very good and some very bad, too rotten to eat."

[4]Then the LORD gave me this message:
[5]"This is what the LORD, the God of Israel, says: The good figs represent the exiles I sent from Judah to the land of the Babylonians.* [6]I will watch over and care for them, and I will bring them back here again. I will build them up and not tear them down. I will plant them and not uproot them. [7]I will give them hearts that recognize me as the LORD. They will be my people, and I will be their God, for they will return to me wholeheartedly.

[8]"But the bad figs," the LORD said, "represent King Zedekiah of Judah, his officials, all the people left in Jerusalem, and those who live in Egypt. I will treat them like bad figs, too rotten to eat. [9]I will make them an object of horror and a symbol of evil to every nation on earth. They will be disgraced and mocked, taunted and cursed, wherever I scatter them. [10]And I will send war, famine, and disease until they have vanished from the land of Israel, which I gave to them and their ancestors."

[25:1]THIS message for all the people of Judah came to Jeremiah from the LORD during the fourth year of Jehoiakim's reign over Judah.* This was the year when King Nebuchadnezzar* of Babylon began his reign.

[2]Jeremiah the prophet said to all the people in Judah and Jerusalem, [3]"For the past twenty-three years—from the thirteenth year of the reign of Josiah son of Amon,* king of Judah, until now—the LORD has been giving me his messages. I have faithfully passed them on to you, but you have not listened.

[4]"Again and again the LORD has sent you his servants, the prophets, but you have not listened or even paid attention. [5]Each time the message was this: 'Turn from the evil road you are traveling and from the evil things you are doing. Only then will I let you live in this land that the LORD gave to you and your ancestors forever. [6]Do not provoke my anger by worshiping idols you made with your own hands. Then I will not harm you.'

[7]"But you would not listen to me," says the LORD. "You made me furious by worshiping idols you made with your own hands, bringing on yourselves all the disasters you now suffer. [8]And now the LORD of Heaven's Armies says: Because

you have not listened to me, [9]I will gather together all the armies of the north under King Nebuchadnezzar of Babylon, whom I have appointed as my deputy. I will bring them all against this land and its people and against the surrounding nations. I will completely destroy* you and make you an object of horror and contempt and a ruin forever. [10]I will take away your happy singing and laughter. The joyful voices of bridegrooms and brides will no longer be heard. Your millstones will fall silent, and the lights in your homes will go out. [11]This entire land will become a desolate wasteland. Israel and her neighboring lands will serve the king of Babylon for seventy years.

[12]"Then, after the seventy years of captivity are over, I will punish the king of Babylon and his people for their sins," says the LORD. "I will make the country of the Babylonians* a wasteland forever. [13]I will bring upon them all the terrors I have promised in this book—all the penalties announced by Jeremiah against the nations. [14]Many nations and great kings will enslave the Babylonians, just as they enslaved my people. I will punish them in proportion to the suffering they cause my people."

[15]This is what the LORD, the God of Israel, said to me: "Take from my hand this cup filled to the brim with my anger, and make all the nations to whom I send you drink from it. [16]When they drink from it, they will stagger, crazed by the warfare I will send against them."

[17]So I took the cup of anger from the LORD and made all the nations drink from it—every nation to which the LORD sent me. [18]I went to Jerusalem and the other towns of Judah, and their kings and officials drank from the cup. From that day until this, they have been a desolate ruin, an object of horror, contempt, and cursing. [19]I gave the cup to Pharaoh, king of Egypt, his attendants, his officials, and all his people, [20]along with all the foreigners living in that land. I also gave it to all the kings of the land of Uz and the kings of the Philistine cities of Ashkelon, Gaza, Ekron, and what remains of Ashdod. [21]Then I gave the cup to the nations of Edom, Moab, and Ammon, [22]and the kings of Tyre and Sidon,

and the kings of the regions across the sea. [23]I gave it to Dedan, Tema, and Buz, and to the people who live in distant places.* [24]I gave it to the kings of Arabia, the kings of the nomadic tribes of the desert, [25]and to the kings of Zimri, Elam, and Media. [26]And I gave it to the kings of the northern countries, far and near, one after the other—all the kingdoms of the world. And finally, the king of Babylon* himself drank from the cup of the LORD's anger.

[27]Then the LORD said to me, "Now tell them, 'This is what the LORD of Heaven's Armies, the God of Israel, says: Drink from this cup of my anger. Get drunk and vomit; fall to rise no more, for I am sending terrible wars against you.' [28]And if they refuse to accept the cup, tell them, 'The LORD of Heaven's Armies says: You have no choice but to drink from it. [29]I have begun to punish Jerusalem, the city that bears my name. Now should I let you go unpunished? No, you will not escape disaster. I will call for war against all the nations of the earth. I, the LORD of Heaven's Armies, have spoken!'

[30]"Now prophesy all these things, and say to them,

"'The LORD will roar against his own land
    from his holy dwelling in heaven.
He will shout like those who tread grapes;
    he will shout against everyone on earth.
[31] His cry of judgment will reach the ends of the earth,
    for the LORD will bring his case against all the nations.
He will judge all the people of the earth,
    slaughtering the wicked with the sword.
I, the LORD, have spoken!'"

[32] This is what the LORD of Heaven's Armies says:

"Look! Disaster will fall upon nation after nation!
A great whirlwind of fury is rising
    from the most distant corners of the earth!"

[33]In that day those the LORD has slaughtered will fill the earth from one end to

the other. No one will mourn for them or gather up their bodies to bury them. They will be scattered on the ground like manure.

[34] Weep and moan, you evil shepherds!
Roll in the dust, you leaders of the flock!
The time of your slaughter has arrived;
you will fall and shatter like a fragile vase.
[35] You will find no place to hide;
there will be no way to escape.
[36] Listen to the frantic cries of the shepherds.
The leaders of the flock are wailing in despair,
for the LORD is ruining their pastures.
[37] Peaceful meadows will be turned into a wasteland
by the LORD's fierce anger.
[38] He has left his den like a strong lion seeking its prey,
and their land will be made desolate
by the sword of the enemy
and the LORD's fierce anger.

23:33 As in Greek version and Latin Vulgate; Hebrew reads *What burden?* 24:1a Hebrew *Nebuchadrezzar*, a variant spelling of Nebuchadnezzar. 24:1b Hebrew *Jeconiah*, a variant spelling of Jehoiachin. 24:5 Or *Chaldeans.* 25:1a The fourth year of Jehoiakim's reign and the accession year of Nebuchadnezzar's reign was 605 B.C. 25:1b Hebrew *Nebuchadrezzar*, a variant spelling of Nebuchadnezzar; also

in 25:9. 25:3 The thirteenth year of Josiah's reign was 627 B.C. 25:9 The Hebrew term used here refers to the complete consecration of things or people to the LORD, either by destroying them or by giving them as an offering. 25:12 Or *Chaldeans.* 25:23 Or *who clip the corners of their hair.* 25:26 Hebrew *of Sheshach*, a code name for Babylon.

2 THESSALONIANS 2:1-17

One of the purposes for Paul's second letter to the Thessalonians was to warn them not to be so involved in preparing for Jesus' return that they didn't live the life they'd been given here and now.

Now, dear brothers and sisters,* let us [Paul and his coworkers] clarify some things about the coming of our Lord Jesus Christ and how we will be gathered to meet him. [2]Don't be so easily shaken or alarmed by those who say that the day of the Lord has already begun. Don't believe them, even if they claim to have had a spiritual vision, a revelation, or a letter supposedly from us. [3]Don't be fooled by what they say. For that day will not come until there is a great rebellion against God and the man of lawlessness* is revealed—the one who brings destruction.* [4]He will exalt himself and defy everything that people call god and every object of worship. He will even sit in the temple of God, claiming that he himself is God.

[5]Don't you remember that I told you about all this when I was with you? [6]And you know what is holding him back, for he can be revealed only when his time

WHAT THE BIBLE SAYS

The future

2 THESSALONIANS 2:1-17 The Bible has numerous passages dealing with the end times. Some of these passages are difficult to understand, and Christians interpret them differently. Don't feel discouraged if you don't understand it all. What you need to know from this passage is that Jesus *will* return, but before he comes back there will be a time of great rebellion—sort of a last-ditch effort by Satan and his demons. You also need to know that no matter what happens, you will be saved. • In the meantime, don't spend your time worrying about how and when all of this will happen. No one can predict when these events will occur. There are many circumstances that must come together before the Second Coming, and because God controls all events in the world, you need not be fearful of what lies ahead. • Instead, prepare for Christ's second coming by living a life pleasing to God. Share the gospel. Stand firm and hold to the truth. After all, you already know the end—you win!

comes. [7] For this lawlessness is already at work secretly, and it will remain secret until the one who is holding it back steps out of the way. [8] Then the man of lawlessness will be revealed, but the Lord Jesus will kill him with the breath of his mouth and destroy him by the splendor of his coming.

[9] This man will come to do the work of Satan with counterfeit power and signs and miracles. [10] He will use every kind of evil deception to fool those on their way to destruction, because they refuse to love and accept the truth that would save them. [11] So God will cause them to be greatly deceived, and they will believe these lies. [12] Then they will be condemned for enjoying evil rather than believing the truth.

[13] As for us, we can't help but thank God for you, dear brothers and sisters loved by the Lord. We are always thankful that God chose you to be among the first* to experience salvation—a salvation that came through the Spirit who makes you holy and through your belief in the truth. [14] He called you to salvation when we told you the Good News; now you can share in the glory of our Lord Jesus Christ.

[15] With all these things in mind, dear brothers and sisters, stand firm and keep a strong grip on the teaching we passed on to you both in person and by letter.

[16] Now may our Lord Jesus Christ himself and God our Father, who loved us and by his grace gave us eternal comfort and a wonderful hope, [17] comfort you and strengthen you in every good thing you do and say.

2:1 Greek *brothers;* also in 2:13, 15. 2:3a Some manuscripts read *the man of sin.* 2:3b Greek *the son of destruction.* 2:13 Some manuscripts read *chose you from the very beginning.*

PSALM 84:1-12
*For the choir director: A psalm of the descendants of Korah, to be accompanied by a stringed instrument.**

[1] **H**ow lovely is your dwelling place,
    O Lord of Heaven's Armies.
[2] I long, yes, I faint with longing
    to enter the courts of the Lord.
    With my whole being, body and soul,
    I will shout joyfully to the living
    God.

[3] Even the sparrow finds a home,
    and the swallow builds her nest and
    raises her young
    at a place near your altar,
    O Lord of Heaven's Armies, my
    King and my God!
[4] What joy for those who can live in
    your house,
    always singing your praises.
                        Interlude

[5] What joy for those whose strength
    comes from the Lord,
    who have set their minds on a
    pilgrimage to Jerusalem.
[6] When they walk through the Valley of
    Weeping,*
    it will become a place of refreshing
    springs.
    The autumn rains will clothe it with
    blessings.
[7] They will continue to grow stronger,
    and each of them will appear before
    God in Jerusalem.*

[8] O Lord God of Heaven's Armies, hear
    my prayer.
    Listen, O God of Jacob.   *Interlude*

[9] O God, look with favor upon the king,
    our shield!
    Show favor to the one you have
    anointed.

[10] A single day in your courts
    is better than a thousand anywhere
    else!
    I would rather be a gatekeeper in the
    house of my God
    than live the good life in the homes
    of the wicked.
[11] For the Lord God is our sun and our
    shield.
    He gives us grace and glory.
    The Lord will withhold no good thing
    from those who do what is right.
[12] O Lord of Heaven's Armies,
    what joy for those who trust in you.

84:TITLE Hebrew *according to the gittith.* 84:6 Or *Valley of Poplars;* Hebrew reads *valley of Baca.* 84:7 Hebrew *Zion.*

PROVERBS 25:15
Patience can persuade a prince, and soft speech can break bones.

JEREMIAH 26:1–27:22

Like many Old Testament prophets, Jeremiah confronted people who did not want to be confronted. Consequently, Jeremiah's messages were often unwelcome. But instead of crafting a new message to build popularity, he stuck to the message God gave him.

This message came to Jeremiah from the LORD early in the reign of Jehoiakim son of Josiah,* king of Judah. ²"This is what the LORD says: Stand in the courtyard in front of the Temple of the LORD, and make an announcement to the people who have come there to worship from all over Judah. Give them my entire message; include every word. ³Perhaps they will listen and turn from their evil ways. Then I will change my mind about the disaster I am ready to pour out on them because of their sins.

⁴"Say to them, 'This is what the LORD says: If you will not listen to me and obey my word I have given you, ⁵and if you will not listen to my servants, the prophets— for I sent them again and again to warn you, but you would not listen to them— ⁶then I will destroy this Temple as I destroyed Shiloh, the place where the Tabernacle was located. And I will make Jerusalem an object of cursing in every nation on earth.'"

⁷The priests, the prophets, and all the people listened to Jeremiah as he spoke in front of the LORD's Temple. ⁸But when Jeremiah had finished his message, saying everything the LORD had told him to say, the priests and prophets and all the people at the Temple mobbed him. "Kill him!" they shouted. ⁹"What right do you have to prophesy in the LORD's name that this Temple will be destroyed like Shiloh? What do you mean, saying that Jerusalem will be destroyed and left with no inhabitants?" And all the people threatened him as he stood in front of the Temple.

¹⁰When the officials of Judah heard what was happening, they rushed over from the palace and sat down at the New Gate of the Temple to hold court. ¹¹The priests and prophets presented their accusations to the officials and the people. "This man should die!" they said. "You have heard with your own ears what a traitor he is, for he has prophesied against this city."

¹²Then Jeremiah spoke to the officials and the people in his own defense. "The LORD sent me to prophesy against this Temple and this city," he said. "The LORD gave me every word that I have spoken. ¹³But if you stop your sinning and begin to obey the LORD your God, he will change his mind about this disaster that he has announced against you. ¹⁴As for me, I am in your hands—do with me as you think best. ¹⁵But if you kill me, rest assured that you will be killing an innocent man! The responsibility for such a deed will lie on you, on this city, and on every person living in it. For it is absolutely true that the LORD sent me to speak every word you have heard."

¹⁶Then the officials and the people said to the priests and prophets, "This man does not deserve the death sentence, for he has spoken to us in the name of the LORD our God."

¹⁷Then some of the wise old men stood and spoke to all the people assembled there. ¹⁸They said, "Remember when Micah of Moresheth prophesied during the reign of King Hezekiah of Judah. He told the people of Judah,

'This is what the LORD of Heaven's
　　Armies says:
Mount Zion will be plowed like an
　　open field;
Jerusalem will be reduced to ruins!
A thicket will grow on the heights
　　where the Temple now stands.'*

¹⁹But did King Hezekiah and the people kill him for saying this? No, they turned from their sins and worshiped the LORD. They begged him for mercy. Then the LORD changed his mind about the terrible disaster he had pronounced against them. So we are about to do ourselves great harm."

²⁰At this time Uriah son of Shemaiah

from Kiriath-jearim was also prophesying for the LORD. And he predicted the same terrible disaster against the city and nation as Jeremiah did. [21]When King Jehoiakim and the army officers and officials heard what he was saying, the king sent someone to kill him. But Uriah heard about the plan and escaped in fear to Egypt. [22]Then King Jehoiakim sent Elnathan son of Acbor to Egypt along with several other men to capture Uriah. [23]They took him prisoner and brought him back to King Jehoiakim. The king then killed Uriah with a sword and had him buried in an unmarked grave.

[24]Nevertheless, Ahikam son of Shaphan stood up for Jeremiah and persuaded the court not to turn him over to the mob to be killed.

[27:1]THIS message came to Jeremiah from the LORD early in the reign of Zedekiah* son of Josiah, king of Judah.

[2]This is what the LORD said to me: "Make a yoke, and fasten it on your neck with leather thongs. [3]Then send messages to the kings of Edom, Moab, Ammon, Tyre, and Sidon through their ambassadors who have come to see King Zedekiah in Jerusalem. [4]Give them this message for their masters: 'This is what the LORD of Heaven's Armies, the God of Israel, says: [5]With my great strength and powerful arm I made the earth and all its people and every animal. I can give these things of mine to anyone I choose. [6]Now I will give your countries to King Nebuchadnezzar of Babylon, who is my servant. I have put everything, even the wild animals, under his control. [7]All the nations will serve him, his son, and his grandson until his time is up. Then many nations and great kings will conquer and rule over Babylon. [8]So you must submit to Babylon's king and serve him; put your neck under Babylon's yoke! I will punish any nation that refuses to be his slave, says the LORD. I will send war, famine, and disease upon that nation until Babylon has conquered it.

[9]"'Do not listen to your false prophets, fortune-tellers, interpreters of dreams, mediums, and sorcerers who say, "The king of Babylon will not conquer you." [10]They are all liars, and their lies will lead

to your being driven out of your land. I will drive you out and send you far away to die. [11]But the people of any nation that submits to the king of Babylon will be allowed to stay in their own country to farm the land as usual. I, the LORD, have spoken!'"

[12]Then I repeated this same message to King Zedekiah of Judah. "If you want to live, submit to the yoke of the king of Babylon and his people. [13]Why do you insist on dying—you and your people? Why should you choose war, famine, and disease, which the LORD will bring against every nation that refuses to submit to Babylon's king? [14]Do not listen to the false prophets who keep telling you, 'The king of Babylon will not conquer you.' They are liars. [15]This is what the LORD says: 'I have not sent these prophets! They are telling you lies in my name, so I will drive you from this land. You will all die—you and all these prophets, too.'"

[16]Then I spoke to the priests and the people and said, "This is what the LORD says: 'Do not listen to your prophets who claim that soon the gold articles taken from my Temple will be returned from Babylon. It is all a lie! [17]Do not listen to them. Surrender to the king of Babylon, and you will live. Why should this whole city be destroyed? [18]If they really are prophets and speak the LORD's messages, let them pray to the LORD of Heaven's Armies. Let them pray that the articles remaining in the LORD's Temple and in the king's palace and in the palaces of Jerusalem will not be carried away to Babylon!'

[19]"For the LORD of Heaven's Armies has spoken about the pillars in front of the Temple, the great bronze basin called the Sea, the water carts, and all the other ceremonial articles. [20]King Nebuchadnezzar of Babylon left them here when he exiled Jehoiachin* son of Jehoiakim, king of Judah, to Babylon, along with all the other nobles of Judah and Jerusalem. [21]Yes, this is what the LORD of Heaven's Armies, the God of Israel, says about the precious things still in the Temple and in the palace of Judah's king: [22]'They will all be carried away to Babylon and will stay there until I send for them,' says the LORD. 'Then I will bring them back to Jerusalem again.'"

26:1 The first year of Jehoiakim's reign was 608 B.C.
26:18 Mic 3:12.   **27:1** As in some Hebrew manuscripts and Syriac version (see also 27:3, 12); most Hebrew manuscripts read *Jehoiakim.*   **27:20** Hebrew *Jeconiah,* a variant spelling of Jehoiachin.

2 THESSALONIANS 3:1-18

It is one thing to be prepared for Christ's return. It is another thing to fail to take responsibility for your life as you wait. Paul addressed this temptation as he closed this second letter to the Thessalonians.

Finally, dear brothers and sisters,* we [Paul and his coworkers] ask you to pray for us. Pray that the Lord's message will spread rapidly and be honored wherever it goes, just as when it came to you. ²Pray, too, that we will be rescued from wicked and evil people, for not everyone is a believer. ³But the Lord is faithful; he will strengthen you and guard you from the evil one.* ⁴And we are confident in the Lord that you are doing and will continue to do the things we commanded you. ⁵May the Lord lead your hearts into a full understanding and expression of the love of God and the patient endurance that comes from Christ.

⁶And now, dear brothers and sisters, we give you this command in the name of our Lord Jesus Christ: Stay away from all believers* who live idle lives and don't follow the tradition they received* from us. ⁷For you know that you ought to imitate us. We were not idle when we were with you. ⁸We never accepted food from anyone without paying for it. We worked hard day and night so we would not be a burden to any of you. ⁹We certainly had the right to ask you to feed us, but we wanted to give you an example to follow. ¹⁰Even while we were with you, we gave you this command: "Those unwilling to work will not get to eat."

¹¹Yet we hear that some of you are living idle lives, refusing to work and meddling in other people's business. ¹²We command such people and urge them in the name of the Lord Jesus Christ to settle down and work to earn their own living. ¹³As for the rest of you, dear brothers and sisters, never get tired of doing good.

¹⁴Take note of those who refuse to obey what we say in this letter. Stay away from them so they will be ashamed. ¹⁵Don't think of them as enemies, but warn them as you would a brother or sister.*

¹⁶Now may the Lord of peace himself give you his peace at all times and in every situation. The Lord be with you all.

¹⁷HERE IS MY GREETING IN MY OWN HANDWRITING—PAUL. I DO THIS IN ALL MY LETTERS TO PROVE THEY ARE FROM ME.

¹⁸May the grace of our Lord Jesus Christ be with you all.

3:1 Greek *brothers;* also in 3:6, 13.   **3:3** Or *from evil.*
3:6a Greek *from every brother.*   **3:6b** Some manuscripts read *you received.*   **3:15** Greek *as a brother.*

HOW WE LIVE

Following Jesus

JEREMIAH 26:7-11 Following God put Jeremiah in a difficult situation. God had told Jeremiah that he wanted his entire message given: "Include every word" (Jeremiah 26:2). So Jeremiah did as he was told—predicting the destruction of the glorious Temple—and a riot ensued. Next thing you know, the religious leaders in Judah were calling him a traitor and saying he should die because he had "prophesied against this city" (Jeremiah 26:11). • Jeremiah may have been tempted to leave out the parts that would turn his audience against him or would sound too harsh. After all, prophesying the defeat of his own nation would indeed make him sound like a traitor. But by God's command, he did not delete parts of God's message to suit himself, his audience, or the circumstances in which he found himself. He spoke the truth even when it made him unpopular. • Clearly, following Jesus is not always easy. God doesn't always lay the easiest path before us. You will find that at times obedience brings difficulty. Don't make circumstances or the opinion of others the source of your joy. Keep focused on pleasing God, the source of unending joy.

PSALM 85:1-13

For the choir director: A psalm of the descendants of Korah.

1 LORD, you poured out blessings on
    your land!
    You restored the fortunes
       of Israel.*
2 You forgave the guilt of your people—
    yes, you covered all their sins.
                              Interlude
3 You held back your fury.
    You kept back your blazing anger.
4 Now restore us again, O God of our
    salvation.
    Put aside your anger against us once
       more.
5 Will you be angry with us always?
    Will you prolong your wrath to all
       generations?
6 Won't you revive us again,
    so your people can rejoice in you?
7 Show us your unfailing love,
    O LORD,
    and grant us your salvation.

8 I listen carefully to what God the LORD
    is saying,

for he speaks peace to his faithful
    people.
    But let them not return to their
       foolish ways.
9 Surely his salvation is near to those
    who fear him,
    so our land will be filled with his
       glory.

10 Unfailing love and truth have met
    together.
    Righteousness and peace have
       kissed!
11 Truth springs up from the earth,
    and righteousness smiles down
       from heaven.
12 Yes, the LORD pours down his
    blessings.
    Our land will yield its bountiful
       harvest.
13 Righteousness goes as a herald
    before him,
    preparing the way for his steps.

85:1 Hebrew *of Jacob.* See note on 44:4.

PROVERBS 25:16

Do you like honey? Don't eat too much, or
it will make you sick!

OCTOBER**16**

JEREMIAH 28:1–29:32

Did ancient prophets ever disagree? Only if one
was a true prophet of God and the other was a
false prophet. Hananiah told the people what they
wanted to hear. Unfortunately, none of it was true.

One day in late summer* of that same
year—the fourth year of the reign of Zedekiah, king of Judah—Hananiah son of Azzur, a prophet from Gibeon, addressed me
publicly in the Temple while all the priests
and people listened. He said, 2"This is
what the LORD of Heaven's Armies, the
God of Israel, says: 'I will remove the yoke
of the king of Babylon from your necks.
3 Within two years I will bring back all the
Temple treasures that King Nebuchadnezzar carried off to Babylon. 4And I will

bring back Jehoiachin* son of Jehoiakim,
king of Judah, and all the other captives
that were taken to Babylon. I will surely
break the yoke that the king of Babylon
has put on your necks. I, the LORD, have
spoken!'"

5Jeremiah responded to Hananiah as
they stood in front of all the priests and
people at the Temple. 6He said, "Amen!
May your prophecies come true! I hope
the LORD does everything you say. I hope
he does bring back from Babylon the treasures of this Temple and all the captives.
7But listen now to the solemn words I
speak to you in the presence of all these
people. 8The ancient prophets who preceded you and me spoke against many na-

tions, always warning of war, disaster, and disease. [9]So a prophet who predicts peace must show he is right. Only when his predictions come true can we know that he is really from the LORD."

[10]Then Hananiah the prophet took the yoke off Jeremiah's neck and broke it in pieces. [11]And Hananiah said again to the crowd that had gathered, "This is what the LORD says: 'Just as this yoke has been broken, within two years I will break the yoke of oppression from all the nations now subject to King Nebuchadnezzar of Babylon.'" With that, Jeremiah left the Temple area.

[12]Soon after this confrontation with Hananiah, the LORD gave this message to Jeremiah: [13]"Go and tell Hananiah, 'This is what the LORD says: You have broken a wooden yoke, but you have replaced it with a yoke of iron. [14]The LORD of Heaven's Armies, the God of Israel, says: I have put a yoke of iron on the necks of all these nations, forcing them into slavery under King Nebuchadnezzar of Babylon. I have put everything, even the wild animals, under his control.'"

[15]Then Jeremiah the prophet said to Hananiah, "Listen, Hananiah! The LORD has not sent you, but the people believe your lies. [16]Therefore, this is what the LORD says: 'You must die. Your life will end this very year because you have rebelled against the LORD.'"

[17]Two months later* the prophet Hananiah died.

29:1 JEREMIAH wrote a letter from Jerusalem to the elders, priests, prophets, and all the people who had been exiled to Babylon by King Nebuchadnezzar. [2]This was after King Jehoiachin,* the queen mother, the court officials, the other officials of Judah, and all the craftsmen and artisans had been deported from Jerusalem. [3]He sent the letter with Elasah son of Shaphan and Gemariah son of Hilkiah when they went to Babylon as King Zedekiah's ambassadors to Nebuchadnezzar. This is what Jeremiah's letter said:

[4]This is what the LORD of Heaven's Armies, the God of Israel, says to all the captives he has exiled to Babylon from Jerusalem: [5]"Build homes, and plan to stay. Plant gardens, and eat the food they produce. [6]Marry and have children. Then find spouses for them so that you may have many grandchildren. Multiply! Do not dwindle away! [7]And work for the peace and prosperity of the city where I sent you into exile. Pray to the LORD for it, for its welfare will determine your welfare."

[8]This is what the LORD of Heaven's Armies, the God of Israel, says: "Do not let your prophets and fortune-tellers who are with you in the land of Babylon trick you. Do not listen to their dreams, [9]because they are telling you lies in my name. I have not sent them," says the LORD.

[10]This is what the LORD says: "You will be in Babylon for seventy years. But then I will come and do for you all the good things I have promised, and I will bring you home again. [11]For I know the plans I have for you," says the LORD. "They are plans for good and not for disaster, to give you a future and a hope. [12]In those days when you pray, I will listen. [13]If you look for me wholeheartedly, you will find me. [14]I will be found by you," says the LORD. "I will end your captivity and restore your fortunes. I will gather you out of the nations where I sent you and will bring you home again to your own land."

[15]You claim that the LORD has raised up prophets for you in Babylon. [16]But this is what the LORD says about the king who sits on David's throne and all those still living here in Jerusalem—your relatives who were not exiled to Babylon. [17]This is what the LORD of Heaven's Armies says: "I will send war, famine, and disease upon them and make them like bad figs, too rotten to eat. [18]Yes, I will pursue them with war, famine, and disease, and I will scatter them around the world. In every nation where I send them, I will make them an object of damnation, horror, contempt, and mockery. [19]For they refuse to listen to me, though I have spoken to them repeatedly through the prophets

I sent. And you who are in exile have not listened either," says the LORD.

²⁰Therefore, listen to this message from the LORD, all you captives there in Babylon. ²¹This is what the LORD of Heaven's Armies, the God of Israel, says about your prophets—Ahab son of Kolaiah and Zedekiah son of Maaseiah—who are telling you lies in my name: "I will turn them over to Nebuchadnezzar* for execution before your eyes. ²²Their terrible fate will become proverbial, so that the Judean exiles will curse someone by saying, 'May the LORD make you like Zedekiah and Ahab, whom the king of Babylon burned alive!' ²³For these men have done terrible things among my people. They have committed adultery with their neighbors' wives and have lied in my name, saying things I did not command. I am a witness to this. I, the LORD, have spoken."

²⁴The LORD sent this message to Shemaiah the Nehelamite in Babylon: ²⁵"This is what the LORD of Heaven's Armies, the God of Israel, says: You wrote a letter on your own authority to Zephaniah son of Maaseiah, the priest, and you sent copies to the other priests and people in Jerusalem. You wrote to Zephaniah,

²⁶"The LORD has appointed you to replace Jehoiada as the priest in charge of the house of the LORD. You are responsible to put into stocks and neck irons any crazy man who claims to be a prophet. ²⁷So why have you done nothing to stop Jeremiah from Anathoth, who pretends to be a prophet among you? ²⁸Jeremiah sent a letter here to Babylon, predicting that our captivity will be a long one. He said, 'Build homes, and plan to stay. Plant gardens, and eat the food they produce.'"

²⁹But when Zephaniah the priest received Shemaiah's letter, he took it to Jeremiah and read it to him. ³⁰Then the LORD gave this message to Jeremiah: ³¹"Send an open letter to all the exiles in Babylon. Tell them, 'This is what the LORD says concerning Shemaiah the Nehelamite: Since he has prophesied to you

when I did not send him and has tricked you into believing his lies, ³²I will punish him and his family. None of his descendants will see the good things I will do for my people, for he has incited you to rebel against me. I, the LORD, have spoken!'"

29:1 Hebrew *In the fifth month,* of the ancient Hebrew lunar calendar. The fifth month in the fourth year of Zedekiah's reign occurred within the months of August and September 593 B.C. Also see note on 1:3.   28:4 Hebrew *Jeconiah,* a variant spelling of Jehoiachin.   28:17 Hebrew *In the seventh month of that same year.* See 28:1 and the note there. 29:2 Hebrew *Jeconiah,* a variant spelling of Jehoiachin. 29:21 Hebrew *Nebuchadrezzar,* a variant spelling of Nebuchadnezzar.

1 TIMOTHY 1:1-20

Timothy was Paul's protégé, his "son" in the faith. Paul wisely understood that he needed to prepare leaders who could carry on his ministry when he was gone. Timothy was one of those young men to whom Paul gave great responsibility.

This letter is from Paul, an apostle of Christ Jesus, appointed by the command of God our Savior and Christ Jesus, who gives us hope.

²I am writing to Timothy, my true son in the faith.

May God the Father and Christ Jesus our Lord give you grace, mercy, and peace.

³When I left for Macedonia, I urged you to stay there in Ephesus and stop those whose teaching is contrary to the truth. ⁴Don't let them waste their time in endless discussion of myths and spiritual pedigrees. These things only lead to meaningless speculations,* which don't help people live a life of faith in God.*

⁵The purpose of my instruction is that all believers would be filled with love that comes from a pure heart, a clear conscience, and genuine faith. ⁶But some people have missed this whole point. They have turned away from these things and spend their time in meaningless discussions. ⁷They want to be known as teachers of the law of Moses, but they don't know what they are talking about, even though they speak so confidently.

⁸We know that the law is good when used correctly. ⁹For the law was not intended for people who do what is right. It is for people who are lawless and rebellious, who are ungodly and sinful, who consider nothing sacred and defile what

is holy, who kill their father or mother or commit other murders. ¹⁰The law is for people who are sexually immoral, or who practice homosexuality, or are slave traders,* liars, promise breakers, or who do anything else that contradicts the wholesome teaching ¹¹ that comes from the glorious Good News entrusted to me by our blessed God.

¹²I thank Christ Jesus our Lord, who has given me strength to do his work. He considered me trustworthy and appointed me to serve him, ¹³even though I used to blaspheme the name of Christ. In my insolence, I persecuted his people. But God had mercy on me because I did it in ignorance and unbelief. ¹⁴Oh, how generous and gracious our Lord was! He filled me with the faith and love that come from Christ Jesus.

¹⁵This is a trustworthy saying, and everyone should accept it: "Christ Jesus came into the world to save sinners"—and I am the worst of them all. ¹⁶But God had mercy on me so that Christ Jesus could use me as a prime example of his great patience with even the worst sinners. Then others will realize that they, too, can believe in him and receive eternal life. ¹⁷All honor and glory to God forever and ever! He is the eternal King, the unseen one who never dies; he alone is God. Amen.

¹⁸Timothy, my son, here are my instructions for you, based on the prophetic words spoken about you earlier. May they help you fight well in the Lord's battles. ¹⁹Cling to your faith in Christ, and keep your conscience clear. For some people have deliberately violated their consciences; as a result, their faith has been shipwrecked. ²⁰Hymenaeus and Alexander are two examples. I threw them out and handed them over to Satan so they might learn not to blaspheme God.

1:4a Greek *in myths and endless genealogies, which cause speculation.* 1:4b Greek *a stewardship of God in faith.* 1:10 Or *kidnappers.*

PSALM 86:1-17
A prayer of David.

¹ **B**end down, O Lord, and hear my prayer;
     answer me, for I need your help.
² Protect me, for I am devoted to you.
     Save me, for I serve you and trust you.
     You are my God.
³ Be merciful to me, O Lord,
     for I am calling on you constantly.
⁴ Give me happiness, O Lord,
     for I give myself to you.
⁵ O Lord, you are so good, so ready to forgive,
     so full of unfailing love for all who ask for your help.

HOW WE LIVE

Seeking God's will

JEREMIAH 29:11 When Jeremiah uttered these words, he was reminding the people of Judah about a key principle behind God's dealings with his people in any era. It is a principle still very much at work today: God wants to bless us, not harm us. • Whatever the circumstances of your life, whatever important and life-changing decisions face you, remember that God is in control of your future. He knows the plans he has for you, and they are for your good. When you come to the crossroads and you have your heart set on turning right, he may want you to turn left instead. You must be open to God's leading in whatever direction he sees is best for you. If you follow his leading, you will be in the center of his will, fulfilling the purpose he has in mind. When you find yourself in the midst of suffering and hardship, don't think his plans for you have changed. God uses all things for the ultimate good of those who love him. You might not understand his purpose in all things, but he promises to be working for your good (Romans 8:28, July 24). You can be confident that God will keep that promise.

6 Listen closely to my prayer, O LORD;
  hear my urgent cry.
7 I will call to you whenever I'm in
   trouble,
   and you will answer me.
8 No pagan god is like you, O Lord.
  None can do what you do!
9 All the nations you made
   will come and bow before
     you, Lord;
   they will praise your holy name.
10 For you are great and perform
    wonderful deeds.
   You alone are God.

11 Teach me your ways, O LORD,
    that I may live according to your
      truth!
   Grant me purity of heart,
     so that I may honor you.
12 With all my heart I will praise you,
     O Lord my God.
   I will give glory to your name
     forever,
13 for your love for me is very great.

You have rescued me from the
  depths of death.*
14 O God, insolent people rise up
    against me;
   a violent gang is trying to kill me.
   You mean nothing to them.
15 But you, O Lord,
    are a God of compassion and mercy,
   slow to get angry
     and filled with unfailing love and
       faithfulness.
16 Look down and have mercy on me.
    Give your strength to your servant;
    save me, the son of your servant.
17 Send me a sign of your favor.
    Then those who hate me will be put
      to shame,
    for you, O LORD, help and
      comfort me.

86:13 Hebrew *of Sheol.*

PROVERBS 25:17
Don't visit your neighbors too often, or
you will wear out your welcome.

OCTOBER**17**

JEREMIAH 30:1–31:26
Jeremiah's duty was to preach God's message,
never wavering from that message whether it
contained good news or bad. In today's passage,
Jeremiah spoke of the future restoration of the
nation.

The LORD gave another message to Jeremiah. He said, [2]"This is what the LORD, the God of Israel, says: Write down for the record everything I have said to you, Jeremiah. [3]For the time is coming when I will restore the fortunes of my people of Israel and Judah. I will bring them home to this land that I gave to their ancestors, and they will possess it again. I, the LORD, have spoken!"

[4]This is the message the LORD gave concerning Israel and Judah. [5]This is what the LORD says:

"I hear cries of fear;
  there is terror and no peace.
6 Now let me ask you a question:
  Do men give birth to babies?
Then why do they stand there, ashen-
    faced,
  hands pressed against their sides
    like a woman in labor?
7 In all history there has never been
    such a time of terror.
  It will be a time of trouble for my
    people Israel.*
  Yet in the end they will be saved!
8 For in that day,"
    says the LORD of Heaven's Armies,
  "I will break the yoke from their necks
    and snap their chains.
  Foreigners will no longer be their
    masters.

⁹   For my people will serve the LORD
          their God
and their king descended from David—
    the king I will raise up for them.

¹⁰ "So do not be afraid, Jacob, my servant;
      do not be dismayed, Israel,"
    says the LORD.
    "For I will bring you home again from
          distant lands,
      and your children will return from
          their exile.
    Israel will return to a life of peace
          and quiet,
      and no one will terrorize them.
¹¹ For I am with you and will save you,"
      says the LORD.
    "I will completely destroy the nations
          where I have scattered you,
      but I will not completely destroy you.
    I will discipline you, but with justice;
      I cannot let you go unpunished."

¹² This is what the LORD says:
    "Your injury is incurable—
      a terrible wound.
¹³ There is no one to help you
      or to bind up your injury.
    No medicine can heal you.
¹⁴ All your lovers—your allies—have
          left you
      and do not care about you anymore.
    I have wounded you cruelly,
      as though I were your enemy.
    For your sins are many,
      and your guilt is great.
¹⁵ Why do you protest your punishment—
      this wound that has no cure?
    I have had to punish you
      because your sins are many
      and your guilt is great.

¹⁶ "But all who devour you will be
          devoured,
      and all your enemies will be sent
          into exile.
    All who plunder you will be
          plundered,
      and all who attack you will be
          attacked.
¹⁷ I will give you back your health
      and heal your wounds," says the
          LORD.
    "For you are called an outcast—
      'Jerusalem* for whom no one cares.'"

¹⁸ This is what the LORD says:
    "When I bring Israel home again from
          captivity
      and restore their fortunes,
    Jerusalem will be rebuilt on its ruins,
      and the palace reconstructed as
          before.
¹⁹ There will be joy and songs of
          thanksgiving,
      and I will multiply my people, not
          diminish them;
    I will honor them, not despise them.
²⁰   Their children will prosper as they
          did long ago.
    I will establish them as a nation
          before me,
      and I will punish anyone who hurts
          them.
²¹ They will have their own ruler again,
      and he will come from their own
          people.
    I will invite him to approach me," says
          the LORD,
    "for who would dare to come unless
          invited?
²² You will be my people,
      and I will be your God."

²³ Look! The LORD's anger bursts out
          like a storm,
    a driving wind that swirls down
          on the heads of the wicked.
²⁴ The fierce anger of the LORD will not
          diminish
      until it has finished all he has
          planned.
    In the days to come
      you will understand all this.

31:1"IN that day," says the LORD, "I will be
the God of all the families of Israel, and
they will be my people. ²This is what the
LORD says:

    "Those who survive the coming
          destruction
      will find blessings even in the
          barren land,
    for I will give rest to the people
          of Israel."

³ Long ago the LORD said to Israel:
    "I have loved you, my people, with an
          everlasting love.
    With unfailing love I have drawn
      you to myself.

⁴ I will rebuild you, my virgin Israel.
    You will again be happy
    and dance merrily with your
        tambourines.
⁵ Again you will plant your vineyards on
        the mountains of Samaria
    and eat from your own gardens
        there.
⁶ The day will come when watchmen
        will shout
    from the hill country of Ephraim,
    'Come, let us go up to Jerusalem*
        to worship the LORD our God.'"

⁷ Now this is what the LORD says:
    "Sing with joy for Israel.*
    Shout for the greatest of nations!
    Shout out with praise and joy:
    'Save your people, O LORD,
        the remnant of Israel!'
⁸ For I will bring them from the north
        and from the distant corners of
        the earth.
    I will not forget the blind and lame,
        the expectant mothers and women
        in labor.
    A great company will return!
⁹ Tears of joy will stream down their
        faces,
    and I will lead them home with
        great care.
    They will walk beside quiet streams
        and on smooth paths where they
        will not stumble.
    For I am Israel's father,
        and Ephraim is my oldest child.

¹⁰ "Listen to this message from
        the LORD,
    you nations of the world;
    proclaim it in distant coastlands:
    The LORD, who scattered his people,
        will gather them and watch over
        them
    as a shepherd does his flock.
¹¹ For the LORD has redeemed Israel
    from those too strong for them.
¹² They will come home and sing songs
        of joy on the heights of
        Jerusalem.
    They will be radiant because of the
        LORD's good gifts—
    the abundant crops of grain, new wine,
        and olive oil,
    and the healthy flocks and herds.

    Their life will be like a watered
        garden,
    and all their sorrows will be gone.
¹³ The young women will dance for joy,
    and the men—old and young—will
        join in the celebration.
    I will turn their mourning into joy.
    I will comfort them and exchange
        their sorrow for rejoicing.
¹⁴ The priests will enjoy abundance,
    and my people will feast on my
        good gifts.
    I, the LORD, have spoken!"

¹⁵ This is what the LORD says:

    "A cry is heard in Ramah—
        deep anguish and bitter weeping.
    Rachel weeps for her children,
        refusing to be comforted—
    for her children are gone."

¹⁶ But now this is what the LORD says:
    "Do not weep any longer,
        for I will reward you," says the
        LORD.
    "Your children will come back to you
        from the distant land of the enemy.
¹⁷ There is hope for your future," says the
        LORD.
    "Your children will come again to
        their own land.
¹⁸ I have heard Israel* saying,
    'You disciplined me severely,
        like a calf that needs training for the
        yoke.
    Turn me again to you and restore me,
        for you alone are the LORD my God.
¹⁹ I turned away from God,
        but then I was sorry.
    I kicked myself for my stupidity!
        I was thoroughly ashamed of all I
        did in my younger days.'

²⁰ "Is not Israel still my son,
        my darling child?" says the LORD.
    "I often have to punish him,
        but I still love him.
    That's why I long for him
        and surely will have mercy on him.
²¹ Set up road signs;
        put up guideposts.
    Mark well the path
        by which you came.
    Come back again, my virgin Israel;
        return to your towns here.

²² How long will you wander,
    my wayward daughter?
For the LORD will cause something
    new to happen—
    Israel will embrace her God.*"

²³ This is what the LORD of Heaven's Armies, the God of Israel, says: "When I bring them back from captivity, the people of Judah and its towns will again say, 'The LORD bless you, O righteous home, O holy mountain!' ²⁴Townspeople and farmers and shepherds alike will live together in peace and happiness. ²⁵For I have given rest to the weary and joy to the sorrowing."

²⁶ At this, I woke up and looked around. My sleep had been very sweet.

30:7 Hebrew *Jacob;* also in 30:10b, 18. See note on 5:20.
30:17 Hebrew *Zion.*   31:6 Hebrew *Zion;* also in 31:12.
31:7 Hebrew *Jacob;* also in 31:11. See note on 5:20.
31:18 Hebrew *Ephraim,* referring to the northern kingdom of Israel; also in 31:20.   31:22 Hebrew *a woman will court a suitor.*

---

1 TIMOTHY 2:1-15
One of Timothy's main tasks in Ephesus was to guard the truth on which the people's faith was based. In today's reading, Paul instructs Timothy on how to lead the church in faithful adherence to the truth.

1 [Paul] urge you [Timothy], first of all, to pray for all people. Ask God to help them; intercede on their behalf, and give thanks for them. ²Pray this way for kings and all who are in authority so that we can live peaceful and quiet lives marked by godliness and dignity. ³This is good and pleases God our Savior, ⁴who wants everyone to be saved and to understand the truth. ⁵For there is only one God and one Mediator who can reconcile God and humanity—the man Christ Jesus. ⁶He gave his life to purchase freedom for everyone. This is the message God gave to the world at just the right time. ⁷And I have been chosen as a preacher and apostle to teach the Gentiles this message about faith and truth. I'm not exaggerating—just telling the truth.

⁸In every place of worship, I want men to pray with holy hands lifted up to God, free from anger and controversy.

⁹And I want women to be modest in their appearance.* They should wear decent and appropriate clothing and not draw attention to themselves by the way they fix their hair or by wearing gold or pearls or expensive clothes. ¹⁰For women

---

HOW WE LIVE

Church involvement

1 TIMOTHY 2:1-15 In Paul's day, the culture prescribed relatively clear boundaries for the roles men and women could play. Paul's instructions here fall closely in line with those distinctions. In today's world, the cultural expectations (at least in North America and Europe) are different. Men's and women's roles are not as distinctly defined. How should this affect the involvement of women in church ministry? How should this passage be applied today? • First, remember that Paul had great respect for women of the church, as evidenced by his coworkers in the faith: Priscilla (Acts 18:26, June 28), Phoebe and Mary (Romans 16, August 2), and Euodia and Syntyche (Philippians 4:2, October 3). Women have the dignifying responsibility to work toward furthering God's kingdom.
• At the same time, believers must be careful never to set aside the Bible in the interest of accommodating current cultural preferences. In this passage, Paul bases the appropriateness of keeping certain roles distinct for men and women on the Bible, not culture. You will soon discover that different churches and organizations interpret these distinctions differently. It is a challenging issue. Seek out a church that is committed to basing its policies and practices on Scripture. Such is the kind of church in which men and women can serve God in the roles to which God has genuinely called them.

who claim to be devoted to God should make themselves attractive by the good things they do. ¹¹Women should learn quietly and submissively. ¹²I do not let women teach men or have authority over them.* Let them listen quietly. ¹³For God made Adam first, and afterward he made Eve. ¹⁴And it was not Adam who was deceived by Satan. The woman was deceived, and sin was the result. ¹⁵But women will be saved through childbearing,* assuming they continue to live in faith, love, holiness, and modesty.

2:9 Or *to pray in modest apparel.* **2:12** Or *teach men or usurp their authority.* **2:15** Or *will be saved by accepting their role as mothers,* or *will be saved by the birth of the Child.*

PSALM 87:1-7

A song. A psalm of the descendants of Korah.

¹ **O**n the holy mountain
   stands the city founded by the LORD.
² He loves the city of Jerusalem
   more than any other city in Israel.*
³ O city of God,
   what glorious things are said of you!
                                        Interlude

⁴ I will count Egypt* and Babylon
   among those who know me—

also Philistia and Tyre, and even
   distant Ethiopia.*
They have all become citizens of
   Jerusalem!
⁵ Regarding Jerusalem* it will be said,
   "Everyone enjoys the rights of
   citizenship there."
And the Most High will personally
   bless this city.
⁶ When the LORD registers the nations,
   he will say,
   "They have all become citizens of
   Jerusalem,"   *Interlude*

⁷ The people will play flutes* and sing,
   "The source of my life springs from
   Jerusalem!"

87:2 Hebrew *He loves the gates of Zion more than all the dwellings of Jacob.* See note on 44:4.   **87:4a** Hebrew *Rahab,* the name of a mythical sea monster that represents chaos in ancient literature. The name is used here as a poetic name for Egypt.   **87:4b** Hebrew *Cush.*   **87:5** Hebrew *Zion.*   **87:7** Or *will dance.*

PROVERBS 25:18-19

Telling lies about others is as harmful as hitting them with an ax, wounding them with a sword, or shooting them with a sharp arrow. ☐ Putting confidence in an unreliable person in times of trouble is like chewing with a broken tooth or walking on a lame foot.

OCTOBER**18**

JEREMIAH 31:27–32:44

Per the Lord's instructions, Jeremiah bought a small piece of the land as a sign that even though his nation was about to lose everything, they would come home again someday.

"**T**he day is coming," says the LORD, "when I will greatly increase the human population and the number of animals here in Israel and Judah. ²⁸In the past I deliberately uprooted and tore down this nation. I overthrew it, destroyed it, and brought disaster upon it. But in the future I will just as deliberately plant it and build it up. I, the LORD, have spoken!

²⁹"The people will no longer quote this proverb:

   'The parents have eaten sour grapes,
     but their children's mouths pucker
     at the taste.'

³⁰All people will die for their own sins— those who eat the sour grapes will be the ones whose mouths will pucker. ³¹"The day is coming," says the LORD, "when I will make a new covenant with the people of Israel and Judah. ³²This covenant will not be like the one I made with their ancestors when I took them by the

hand and brought them out of the land of Egypt. They broke that covenant, though I loved them as a husband loves his wife," says the LORD.

[33]"But this is the new covenant I will make with the people of Israel on that day," says the LORD. "I will put my instructions deep within them, and I will write them on their hearts. I will be their God, and they will be my people. [34]And they will not need to teach their neighbors, nor will they need to teach their relatives, saying, 'You should know the LORD.' For everyone, from the least to the greatest, will know me already," says the LORD. "And I will forgive their wickedness, and I will never again remember their sins."

[35] It is the LORD who provides the sun
           to light the day
       and the moon and stars to light
           the night,
       and who stirs the sea into roaring
           waves.
   His name is the LORD of Heaven's
           Armies,
       and this is what he says:
[36] "I am as likely to reject my people
           Israel
       as I am to abolish the laws
           of nature!"
[37] This is what the LORD says:
   "Just as the heavens cannot be
           measured
       and the foundations of the earth
           cannot be explored,
   so I will not consider casting
           them away
       for the evil they have done.
       I, the LORD, have spoken!

[38]"The day is coming," says the LORD, "when all Jerusalem will be rebuilt for me, from the Tower of Hananel to the Corner Gate. [39]A measuring line will be stretched out over the hill of Gareb and across to Goah. [40]And the entire area—including the graveyard and ash dump in the valley, and all the fields out to the Kidron Valley on the east as far as to the Horse Gate—will be holy to the LORD. The city will never again be captured or destroyed."

32:1THE following message came to Jeremiah from the LORD in the tenth year of the reign of Zedekiah,* king of Judah. This was also the eighteenth year of the reign of King Nebuchadnezzar.* [2]Jerusalem was then under siege from the Babylonian army, and Jeremiah was imprisoned in the courtyard of the guard in the royal palace. [3]King Zedekiah had put him there, asking why he kept giving this prophecy: "This is what the LORD says: 'I am about to hand this city over to the king of Babylon, and he will take it. [4]King Zedekiah will be captured by the Babylonians* and taken to meet the king of Babylon face to face. [5]He will take Zedekiah to Babylon, and I will deal with him there,' says the LORD. 'If you fight against the Babylonians, you will never succeed.'"

[6]At that time the LORD sent me a message. He said, [7]"Your cousin Hanamel son of Shallum will come and say to you, 'Buy my field at Anathoth. By law you have the right to buy it before it is offered to anyone else.'"

[8]Then, just as the LORD had said he would, my cousin Hanamel came and visited me in the prison. He said, "Please buy my field at Anathoth in the land of Benjamin. By law you have the right to buy it before it is offered to anyone else, so buy it for yourself." Then I knew that the message I had heard was from the LORD.

[9]So I bought the field at Anathoth, paying Hanamel seventeen pieces* of silver for it. [10]I signed and sealed the deed of purchase before witnesses, weighed out the silver, and paid him. [11]Then I took the sealed deed and an unsealed copy of the deed, which contained the terms and conditions of the purchase, [12]and I handed them to Baruch son of Neriah and grandson of Mahseiah. I did all this in the presence of my cousin Hanamel, the witnesses who had signed the deed, and all the men of Judah who were there in the courtyard of the guardhouse.

[13]Then I said to Baruch as they all listened, [14]"This is what the LORD of Heaven's Armies, the God of Israel, says: 'Take both this sealed deed and the unsealed copy, and put them into a pottery jar to preserve them for a long time.' [15]For this is what the LORD of Heaven's Armies, the God of Israel, says: 'Someday people will again own property here in this land

and will buy and sell houses and vineyards and fields.'"

16Then after I had given the papers to Baruch, I prayed to the LORD:

17"O Sovereign LORD! You made the heavens and earth by your strong hand and powerful arm. Nothing is too hard for you! 18You show unfailing love to thousands, but you also bring the consequences of one generation's sin upon the next. You are the great and powerful God, the LORD of Heaven's Armies. 19You have all wisdom and do great and mighty miracles. You see the conduct of all people, and you give them what they deserve. 20You performed miraculous signs and wonders in the land of Egypt—things still remembered to this day! And you have continued to do great miracles in Israel and all around the world. You have made your name famous to this day.

21"You brought Israel out of Egypt with mighty signs and wonders, with a strong hand and powerful arm, and with overwhelming terror. 22You gave the people of Israel this land that you had promised their ancestors long before—a land flowing with milk and honey. 23Our ancestors came and conquered it and lived in it, but they refused to obey you or follow your word. They have not done anything you commanded. That is why you have sent this terrible disaster upon them.

24"See how the siege ramps have been built against the city walls! Through war, famine, and disease, the city will be handed over to the Babylonians, who will conquer it. Everything has happened just as you said. 25And yet, O Sovereign LORD, you have told me to buy the field—paying good money for it before these witnesses—even though the city will soon be handed over to the Babylonians."

26Then this message came to Jeremiah from the LORD: 27"I am the LORD, the God of all the peoples of the world. Is anything too hard for me? 28Therefore, this is what the LORD says: I will hand this city over to the Babylonians and to Nebuchadnezzar, king of Babylon, and he will capture it. 29The Babylonians outside the walls will come in and set fire to the city. They will burn down all these houses where the people provoked my anger by burning incense to Baal on the rooftops and by pouring out liquid offerings to other gods. 30Israel and Judah have done nothing but wrong since their earliest days. They have infuriated me with all their evil deeds," says the LORD. 31"From the time this city was built until now, it has done nothing but anger me, so I am determined to get rid of it.

32"The sins of Israel and Judah—the sins of the people of Jerusalem, the kings, the officials, the priests, and the prophets—have stirred up my anger. 33My people have turned their backs on me and have refused to return. Even though I diligently taught them, they would not receive instruction or obey. 34They have set up their abominable idols right in my own Temple, defiling it. 35They have built pagan shrines to Baal in the valley of Ben-Hinnom, and there they sacrifice their sons and daughters to Molech. I have never commanded such a horrible deed; it never even crossed my mind to command such a thing. What an incredible evil, causing Judah to sin so greatly!

36"Now I want to say something more about this city. You have been saying, 'It will fall to the king of Babylon through war, famine, and disease.' But this is what the LORD, the God of Israel, says: 37I will certainly bring my people back again from all the countries where I will scatter them in my fury. I will bring them back to this very city and let them live in peace and safety. 38They will be my people, and I will be their God. 39And I will give them one heart and one purpose: to worship me forever, for their own good and for the good of all their descendants. 40And I will make an everlasting covenant with them: I will never stop doing good for them. I will put a desire in their hearts to worship me, and they will never leave me. 41I will find joy doing good for them and will faithfully and wholeheartedly replant them in this land.

42"This is what the LORD says: Just as I

have brought all these calamities on them, so I will do all the good I have promised them. ⁴³Fields will again be bought and sold in this land about which you now say, 'It has been ravaged by the Babylonians, a desolate land where people and animals have all disappeared.' ⁴⁴Yes, fields will once again be bought and sold—deeds signed and sealed and witnessed—in the land of Benjamin and here in Jerusalem, in the towns of Judah and in the hill country, in the foothills of Judah* and in the Negev, too. For someday I will restore prosperity to them. I, the LORD, have spoken!"

32:1a The tenth year of Zedekiah's reign and the eighteenth year of Nebuchadnezzar's reign was 587 B.C. 32:1b Hebrew *Nebuchadrezzar*, a variant spelling of Nebuchadnezzar; also in 32:28. 32:4 Or *Chaldeans;* also in 32:5, 24, 25, 28, 29, 43. 32:9 Hebrew *17 shekels*, about 7 ounces or 194 grams in weight. 32:44 Hebrew *the Shephelah*.

1 TIMOTHY 3:1-16
Paul wrote about what leadership qualities to look for in elders and deacons. While our culture is different from this first century culture in many ways, the values we need in the people who lead us are very much the same.

This is a trustworthy saying: "If someone aspires to be an elder,* he desires an honorable position." ²So an elder must be a man whose life is above reproach. He must be faithful to his wife.* He must exercise self-control, live wisely, and have a good reputation. He must enjoy having guests in his home, and he must be able to teach. ³He must not be a heavy drinker* or be violent. He must be gentle, not quarrelsome, and not love money. ⁴He must manage his own family well, having children who respect and obey him. ⁵For if a man cannot manage his own household, how can he take care of God's church?

⁶An elder must not be a new believer, because he might become proud, and the devil would cause him to fall.* ⁷Also, people outside the church must speak well of him so that he will not be disgraced and fall into the devil's trap.

⁸In the same way, deacons must be well respected and have integrity. They must not be heavy drinkers or dishonest with money. ⁹They must be committed to the mystery of the faith now revealed and must live with a clear conscience. ¹⁰Before they are appointed as deacons, let them be closely examined. If they pass the test, then let them serve as deacons.

¹¹In the same way, their wives* must be respected and must not slander others. They must exercise self-control and be faithful in everything they do.

¹²A deacon must be faithful to his wife, and he must manage his children and household well. ¹³Those who do well as

HOW WE LIVE

Accountability to others

JEREMIAH 31:29-30 Popular culture tells us that we are never at fault for our own failings; rather, society, parents, and our environment are to blame. While it is true that circumstances can affect us in ways that are beyond our control, too many people believe that they are never accountable for any of their own actions—it's always someone else's fault. • In this passage, the Lord affirms the principle of personal accountability. The people had no business blaming their situation on the sins of their ancestors; God had sent messengers—including the prophet Jeremiah—to speak directly to *them. They* were responsible for how *they* responded to Jeremiah's message. • Are you blaming other people for your mistakes? God says that each person is responsible to deal with the sin in his or her own life; fortunately, he provided a way to be forgiven and renewed through Christ. As a believer, your life *can* change for the better through God's grace. Don't look for someone to blame. Own up to your mistakes. Only then can God get to work deep in your life and make you all he wants you to be.

deacons will be rewarded with respect from others and will have increased confidence in their faith in Christ Jesus.

[14]I am writing these things to you now, even though I hope to be with you soon, [15]so that if I am delayed, you will know how people must conduct themselves in the household of God. This is the church of the living God, which is the pillar and foundation of the truth.

[16]Without question, this is the great mystery of our faith*:

Christ* was revealed in a human body
and vindicated by the Spirit.*
He was seen by angels
and announced to the nations.
He was believed in throughout the
world
and taken to heaven in glory.

3:1 Or *an overseer,* or *a bishop;* also in 3:2, 6. **3:2** Or *must have only one wife,* or *must be married only once;* Greek reads *must be the husband of one wife;* also in 3:12. **3:3** Greek *must not drink too much wine;* similarly in 3:8. **3:6** Or *he might fall into the same judgment as the devil.* **3:11** Or *the women deacons.* The Greek word can be translated *women* or *wives.* **3:16a** Or *of godliness.* **3:16b** Greek *He who;* other manuscripts read *God.* **3:16c** Or *in his spirit.*

PSALM 88:1-18
For the choir director: A psalm of the descendants of Korah. A song to be sung to the tune "The Suffering of Affliction." A psalm of Heman the Ezrahite.*

[1] **O** LORD, God of my salvation,
I cry out to you by day.
I come to you at night.
[2] Now hear my prayer;
listen to my cry.
[3] For my life is full of troubles,
and death* draws near.
[4] I am as good as dead,
like a strong man with no strength
left.
[5] They have left me among the dead,
and I lie like a corpse in a grave.
I am forgotten,
cut off from your care.
[6] You have thrown me into the lowest
pit,
into the darkest depths.
[7] Your anger weighs me down;
with wave after wave you have
engulfed me. *Interlude*

[8] You have driven my friends away
by making me repulsive to them.
I am in a trap with no way of escape.
[9] My eyes are blinded by my tears.
Each day I beg for your help, O LORD;
I lift my hands to you for mercy.
[10] Are your wonderful deeds of any use
to the dead?
Do the dead rise up and praise you?
Interlude

[11] Can those in the grave declare your
unfailing love?
Can they proclaim your
faithfulness in the place of
destruction?*
[12] Can the darkness speak of your
wonderful deeds?
Can anyone in the land of
forgetfulness talk about your
righteousness?
[13] O LORD, I cry out to you.
I will keep on pleading day by day.
[14] O LORD, why do you reject me?
Why do you turn your face from
me?
[15] I have been sick and close to death
since my youth.
I stand helpless and desperate
before your terrors.
[16] Your fierce anger has overwhelmed
me.
Your terrors have paralyzed me.
[17] They swirl around me like floodwaters
all day long.
They have engulfed me completely.
[18] You have taken away my companions
and loved ones.
Darkness is my closest friend.

88:TITLE Hebrew *maskil.* This may be a literary or musical term. **88:3** Hebrew *Sheol.* **88:11** Hebrew *in Abaddon?*

PROVERBS 25:20-22
Singing cheerful songs to a person with a heavy heart is like taking someone's coat in cold weather or pouring vinegar in a wound.* □If your enemies are hungry, give them food to eat. If they are thirsty, give them water to drink. You will heap burning coals of shame on their heads, and the LORD will reward you.

25:20 As in Greek version; Hebrew reads *pouring vinegar on soda.*

JEREMIAH 33:1–34:22

The restoration spoken of in this passage was only partially fulfilled when the Jews returned from captivity in Babylon. The fulfillment awaited the coming of God's Messiah, Jesus Christ.

While Jeremiah was still confined in the courtyard of the guard, the LORD gave him this second message: 2"This is what the LORD says—the LORD who made the earth, who formed and established it, whose name is the LORD: 3Ask me and I will tell you remarkable secrets you do not know about things to come. 4For this is what the LORD, the God of Israel, says: You have torn down the houses of this city and even the king's palace to get materials to strengthen the walls against the siege ramps and swords of the enemy. 5You expect to fight the Babylonians,* but the men of this city are already as good as dead, for I have determined to destroy them in my terrible anger. I have abandoned them because of all their wickedness.

6"Nevertheless, the time will come when I will heal Jerusalem's wounds and give it prosperity and true peace. 7I will restore the fortunes of Judah and Israel and rebuild their towns. 8I will cleanse them of their sins against me and forgive all their sins of rebellion. 9Then this city will bring me joy, glory, and honor before all the nations of the earth! The people of the world will see all the good I do for my people, and they will tremble with awe at the peace and prosperity I provide for them.

10"This is what the LORD says: You have said, 'This is a desolate land where people and animals have all disappeared.' Yet in the empty streets of Jerusalem and Judah's other towns, there will be heard once more 11the sounds of joy and laughter. The joyful voices of bridegrooms and brides will be heard again, along with the joyous songs of people bringing thanksgiving offerings to the LORD. They will sing,

'Give thanks to the LORD of Heaven's
  Armies,
  for the LORD is good.
  His faithful love endures forever!'

For I will restore the prosperity of this land to what it was in the past, says the LORD.

12"This is what the LORD of Heaven's Armies says: This land—though it is now desolate and has no people and animals—will once more have pastures where shepherds can lead their flocks. 13Once again shepherds will count their flocks in the towns of the hill country, the foothills of Judah,* the Negev, the land of Benjamin, the vicinity of Jerusalem, and all the towns of Judah. I, the LORD, have spoken!

14"The day will come, says the LORD, when I will do for Israel and Judah all the good things I have promised them.

15 "In those days and at that time
  I will raise up a righteous
    descendant* from King David's
    line.
  He will do what is just and right
    throughout the land.
16 In that day Judah will be saved,
    and Jerusalem will live in safety.
  And this will be its name:
  'The LORD Is Our Righteousness.'*

17For this is what the LORD says: David will have a descendant sitting on the throne of Israel forever. 18And there will always be Levitical priests to offer burnt offerings and grain offerings and sacrifices to me."

19Then this message came to Jeremiah from the LORD: 20"This is what the LORD says: If you can break my covenant with the day and the night so that one does not follow the other, 21only then will my covenant with my servant David be broken. Only then will he no longer have a descendant to reign on his throne. The same is true for my covenant with the Levitical priests who minister before me. 22And as the stars of the sky cannot be counted and the sand on the seashore cannot be measured, so I will multiply the descendants of my servant David and the Levites who minister before me."

23The LORD gave another message to Jeremiah. He said, 24"Have you noticed what people are saying?—'The LORD chose Judah and Israel and then abandoned them!' They are sneering and saying that Israel is not worthy to be counted as a nation. ²⁵ But this is what the LORD says: I would no more reject my people than I would change my laws that govern night and day, earth and sky. ²⁶ I will never abandon the descendants of Jacob or David, my servant, or change the plan that David's descendants will rule the descendants of Abraham, Isaac, and Jacob. Instead, I will restore them to their land and have mercy on them."

34:1 KING Nebuchadnezzar of Babylon came with all the armies from the kingdoms he ruled, and he fought against Jerusalem and the towns of Judah. At that time this message came to Jeremiah from the LORD: ² "Go to King Zedekiah of Judah, and tell him, 'This is what the LORD, the God of Israel, says: I am about to hand this city over to the king of Babylon, and he will burn it down. ³ You will not escape his grasp but will be captured and taken to meet the king of Babylon face to face. Then you will be exiled to Babylon.

⁴ "'But listen to this promise from the LORD, O Zedekiah, king of Judah. This is what the LORD says: You will not be killed in war ⁵ but will die peacefully. People will burn incense in your memory, just as they did for your ancestors, the kings who preceded you. They will mourn for you, crying, "Alas, our master is dead!" This I have decreed, says the LORD.'"

⁶ So Jeremiah the prophet delivered the message to King Zedekiah of Judah. ⁷ At this time the Babylonian army was besieging Jerusalem, Lachish, and Azekah—the only fortified cities of Judah not yet captured.

⁸ This message came to Jeremiah from the LORD after King Zedekiah made a covenant with the people, proclaiming freedom for the slaves. ⁹ He had ordered all the people to free their Hebrew slaves—both men and women. No one was to keep a fellow Judean in bondage. ¹⁰ The officials and all the people had obeyed the king's command, ¹¹ but later they changed their minds. They took back the men and women they had freed, forcing them to be slaves again.

¹² So the LORD gave them this message through Jeremiah: ¹³ "This is what the LORD, the God of Israel, says: I made a covenant with your ancestors long ago when I rescued them from their slavery in Egypt. ¹⁴ I told them that every Hebrew slave must be freed after serving six years. But your ancestors paid no attention to me. ¹⁵ Recently you repented and did what was right, following my command. You freed your slaves and made a solemn covenant with me in the Temple that bears my name. ¹⁶ But now you have shrugged off your oath and defiled my name by taking back the men and women you had freed, forcing them to be slaves once again.

¹⁷ "Therefore, this is what the LORD says: Since you have not obeyed me by setting your countrymen free, I will set you free to be destroyed by war, disease, and famine. You will be an object of horror to all the nations of the earth. ¹⁸ Because you have broken the terms of our covenant, I will cut you apart just as you cut apart the calf when you walked between its halves to solemnize your vows. ¹⁹ Yes, I will cut you apart, whether you are officials of Judah or Jerusalem, court officials, priests, or common people—for you have broken your oath. ²⁰ I will give you to your enemies, and they will kill you. Your bodies will be food for the vultures and wild animals.

²¹ "I will hand over King Zedekiah of Judah and his officials to the army of the king of Babylon. And although Babylon's king has left Jerusalem for a while, ²² I will call the Babylonian armies back again. They will fight against this city and will capture it and burn it down. I will see to it that all the towns of Judah are destroyed, with no one living there."

33:5 Or *Chaldeans.* **33:13** Hebrew *the Shephelah.* **33:15** Hebrew *a righteous branch.* **33:16** Hebrew *Yahweh Tsidqenu.*

---

1 TIMOTHY 4:1-16
Remember that one of the reasons that Timothy was sent to Ephesus was to combat the false teachings that were infiltrating the church there. Here, Paul addressed that very issue head-on, encouraging Timothy to stand strong.

Now the Holy Spirit tells us clearly that in the last times some will turn away from the true faith; they will follow deceptive spirits and teachings that come from demons. ²These people are hypocrites and liars, and their consciences are dead.*

³They will say it is wrong to be married and wrong to eat certain foods. But God created those foods to be eaten with thanks by faithful people who know the truth. ⁴Since everything God created is good, we should not reject any of it but receive it with thanks. ⁵For we know it is made acceptable* by the word of God and prayer.

⁶If you explain these things to the brothers and sisters,* Timothy, you will be a worthy servant of Christ Jesus, one who is nourished by the message of faith and the good teaching you have followed. ⁷Do not waste time arguing over godless ideas and old wives' tales. Instead, train yourself to be godly. ⁸"Physical training is good, but training for godliness is much better, promising benefits in this life and in the life to come." ⁹This is a trustworthy saying, and everyone should accept it. ¹⁰This is why we work hard and continue to struggle,* for our hope is in the living God, who is the Savior of all people and particularly of all believers.

¹¹Teach these things and insist that everyone learn them. ¹²Don't let anyone think less of you because you are young.

Be an example to all believers in what you say, in the way you live, in your love, your faith, and your purity. ¹³Until I get there, focus on reading the Scriptures to the church, encouraging the believers, and teaching them.

¹⁴Do not neglect the spiritual gift you received through the prophecy spoken over you when the elders of the church laid their hands on you. ¹⁵Give your complete attention to these matters. Throw yourself into your tasks so that everyone will see your progress. ¹⁶Keep a close watch on how you live and on your teaching. Stay true to what is right for the sake of your own salvation and the salvation of those who hear you.

4:2 Greek *are seared.* 4:5 Or *made holy.* 4:6 Greek *brothers.* 4:10 Some manuscripts read *continue to suffer.*

PSALM 89:1-13
A psalm of Ethan the Ezrahite.*

¹ I will sing of the LORD's unfailing love
    forever!
  Young and old will hear of your
    faithfulness.
² Your unfailing love will last forever.
  Your faithfulness is as enduring as
    the heavens.

³ The LORD said, "I have made a
    covenant with David, my chosen
    servant.
  I have sworn this oath to him:

HOW WE LIVE

Prayer

JEREMIAH 33:3 If God already knows everything, doesn't he know what we need? What good does it really do to pray? In this verse the Lord instructs Jeremiah to "ask." In many other places in Scripture, God similarly instructs his people to pray. Why? • While it's true that God knows our needs and even knows before we ask what we're going to ask for, he wants us to pray because of the effect it will have on *us*. When we go to God in prayer with our requests, we grow in our trust in him. We acknowledge our need for God, and we express and build our confidence in God's ability and willingness to meet our needs. • Prayer is not a way for us to control God, as if he is some cosmic grandfather, ready to give us whatever we want. Instead, prayer puts us under God's control when we humbly submit our concerns and requests to him. Prayer is a gift from God giving us the opportunity to draw close to him as we rely on him to do and provide what's best for us.

⁴ 'I will establish your descendants as
     kings forever;
  they will sit on your throne from
     now until eternity.'"   *Interlude*
⁵ All heaven will praise your great
     wonders, LORD;
  myriads of angels will praise you for
     your faithfulness.
⁶ For who in all of heaven can compare
     with the LORD?
  What mightiest angel is anything
     like the LORD?
⁷ The highest angelic powers stand in
     awe of God.
  He is far more awesome than all
     who surround his throne.
⁸ O LORD God of Heaven's Armies!
  Where is there anyone as mighty as
     you, O LORD?
  You are entirely faithful.

⁹ You rule the oceans.
  You subdue their storm-tossed
     waves.

¹⁰ You crushed the great sea monster.*
  You scattered your enemies with
     your mighty arm.
¹¹ The heavens are yours, and the earth is
     yours;
  everything in the world is yours—
     you created it all.
¹² You created north and south.
  Mount Tabor and Mount Hermon
     praise your name.
¹³ Powerful is your arm!
  Strong is your hand!
  Your right hand is lifted high in
     glorious strength.

89:TITLE Hebrew *maskil*. This may be a literary or musical
term.   89:10 Hebrew *Rahab*, the name of a mythical sea
monster that represents chaos in ancient literature.

PROVERBS 25:23-24

As surely as a north wind brings rain, so a gossiping tongue causes anger! □ It's better to live alone in the corner of an attic than with a quarrelsome wife in a lovely home.

OCTOBER**20**

JEREMIAH 35:1–36:32

The Recabites had a reputation for living a simple life with a strict moral code. Jonadab and others helped a man named Jehu in his revolt against an evil regime and the subsequent national reform. While Jehu's reform was not hugely successful, the Recabites were still remembered and blessed here by Jeremiah.

This is the message the LORD gave Jeremiah when Jehoiakim son of Josiah was king of Judah: ²"Go to the settlement where the families of the Recabites live, and invite them to the LORD's Temple. Take them into one of the inner rooms, and offer them some wine."

³So I went to see Jaazaniah son of Jeremiah and grandson of Habazziniah and all his brothers and sons—representing all the Recabite families. ⁴I took them to the Temple, and we went into the room assigned to the sons of Hanan son of Igdaliah, a man of God. This room was located next to the one used by the Temple officials, directly above the room of Maaseiah son of Shallum, the Temple gatekeeper.

⁵I set cups and jugs of wine before them and invited them to have a drink, ⁶but they refused. "No," they said, "we don't drink wine, because our ancestor Jehonadab* son of Recab gave us this command: 'You and your descendants must never drink wine. ⁷And do not build houses or plant crops or vineyards, but always live in tents. If you follow these commands, you will live long, good lives in the land.' ⁸So we have obeyed him in all these things. We have never had a drink of wine to this day, nor have our wives, our sons, or our daughters. ⁹We haven't built houses or owned vineyards or farms or planted crops. ¹⁰We have

lived in tents and have fully obeyed all the commands of Jehonadab, our ancestor. [11]But when King Nebuchadnezzar* of Babylon attacked this country, we were afraid of the Babylonian and Syrian* armies. So we decided to move to Jerusalem. That is why we are here."

[12]Then the LORD gave this message to Jeremiah: [13]"This is what the LORD of Heaven's Armies, the God of Israel, says: Go and say to the people in Judah and Jerusalem, 'Come and learn a lesson about how to obey me. [14]The Recabites do not drink wine to this day because their ancestor Jehonadab told them not to. But I have spoken to you again and again, and you refuse to obey me. [15]Time after time I sent you prophets, who told you, "Turn from your wicked ways, and start doing things right. Stop worshiping other gods so that you might live in peace here in the land I have given to you and your ancestors." But you would not listen to me or obey me. [16]The descendants of Jehonadab son of Recab have obeyed their ancestor completely, but you have refused to listen to me.'

[17]"Therefore, this is what the LORD God of Heaven's Armies, the God of Israel, says: 'Because you refuse to listen or answer when I call, I will send upon Judah and Jerusalem all the disasters I have threatened.'"

[18]Then Jeremiah turned to the Recabites and said, "This is what the LORD of Heaven's Armies, the God of Israel, says: 'You have obeyed your ancestor Jehonadab in every respect, following all his instructions.' [19]Therefore, this is what the LORD of Heaven's Armies, the God of Israel, says: 'Jehonadab son of Recab will always have descendants who serve me.'"

[36:1]DURING the fourth year that Jehoiakim son of Josiah was king in Judah,* the LORD gave this message to Jeremiah: [2]"Get a scroll, and write down all my messages against Israel, Judah, and the other nations. Begin with the first message back in the days of Josiah, and write down every message, right up to the present time. [3]Perhaps the people of Judah will repent when they hear again all the terrible things I have planned for them. Then I will be able to forgive their sins and wrongdoings."

[4]So Jeremiah sent for Baruch son of Neriah, and as Jeremiah dictated all the prophecies that the LORD had given him, Baruch wrote them on a scroll. [5]Then Jeremiah said to Baruch, "I am a prisoner here and unable to go to the Temple. [6]So you go to the Temple on the next day of fasting, and read the messages from the LORD that I have had you write on this scroll. Read them so the people who are there from all over Judah will hear them. [7]Perhaps even yet they will turn from their evil ways and ask the LORD's forgiveness before it is too late. For the LORD has threatened them with his terrible anger."

[8]Baruch did as Jeremiah told him and read these messages from the LORD to the people at the Temple. [9]He did this on a day of sacred fasting held in late autumn,* during the fifth year of the reign of Jehoiakim son of Josiah. People from all over Judah had come to Jerusalem to attend the services at the Temple on that day. [10]Baruch read Jeremiah's words on the scroll to all the people. He stood in front of the Temple room of Gemariah, son of Shaphan the secretary. This room was just off the upper courtyard of the Temple, near the New Gate entrance.

[11]When Micaiah son of Gemariah and grandson of Shaphan heard the messages from the LORD, [12]he went down to the secretary's room in the palace where the administrative officials were meeting. Elishama the secretary was there, along with Delaiah son of Shemaiah, Elnathan son of Acbor, Gemariah son of Shaphan, Zedekiah son of Hananiah, and all the other officials. [13]When Micaiah told them about the messages Baruch was reading to the people, [14]the officials sent Jehudi son of Nethaniah, grandson of Shelemiah and great-grandson of Cushi, to ask Baruch to come and read the messages to them, too. So Baruch took the scroll and went to them. [15]"Sit down and read the scroll to us," the officials said, and Baruch did as they requested.

[16]When they heard all the messages, they looked at one another in alarm. "We must tell the king what we have heard," they said to Baruch. [17]"But first, tell us

how you got these messages. Did they come directly from Jeremiah?"

¹⁸So Baruch explained, "Jeremiah dictated them, and I wrote them down in ink, word for word, on this scroll."

¹⁹"You and Jeremiah should both hide," the officials told Baruch. "Don't tell anyone where you are!" ²⁰Then the officials left the scroll for safekeeping in the room of Elishama the secretary and went to tell the king what had happened.

²¹The king sent Jehudi to get the scroll. Jehudi brought it from Elishama's room and read it to the king as all his officials stood by. ²²It was late autumn, and the king was in a winterized part of the palace, sitting in front of a fire to keep warm. ²³Each time Jehudi finished reading three or four columns, the king took a knife and cut off that section of the scroll. He then threw it into the fire, section by section, until the whole scroll was burned up. ²⁴Neither the king nor his attendants showed any signs of fear or repentance at what they heard. ²⁵Even when Elnathan, Delaiah, and Gemariah begged the king not to burn the scroll, he wouldn't listen.

²⁶Then the king commanded his son Jerahmeel, Seraiah son of Azriel, and Shelemiah son of Abdeel to arrest Baruch and Jeremiah. But the LORD had hidden them.

²⁷After the king had burned the scroll on which Baruch had written Jeremiah's words, the LORD gave Jeremiah another message. He said, ²⁸"Get another scroll, and write everything again just as you did on the scroll King Jehoiakim burned. ²⁹Then say to the king, 'This is what the LORD says: You burned the scroll because it said the king of Babylon would destroy this land and empty it of people and animals. ³⁰Now this is what the LORD says about King Jehoiakim of Judah: He will have no heirs to sit on the throne of David. His dead body will be thrown out to lie unburied—exposed to the heat of the day and the frost of the night. ³¹I will punish him and his family and his attendants for their sins. I will pour out on them and on all the people of Jerusalem and Judah all the disasters I promised, for they would not listen to my warnings.'"

³²So Jeremiah took another scroll and dictated again to his secretary, Baruch. He wrote everything that had been on the scroll King Jehoiakim had burned in the fire. Only this time he added much more!

35:6 Hebrew *Jonadab,* a variant spelling of Jehonadab; also in 35:10, 14, 16, 18, 19. See 2 Kgs 10:15.   35:11a Hebrew *Nebuchadrezzar,* a variant spelling of Nebuchadnezzar.   35:11b Or *Chaldean and Aramean.*   36:1 The fourth year of Jehoiakim's reign was 605 B.C.   36:9 Hebrew *in the ninth month,* of the ancient Hebrew lunar calendar (also in 36:22). The ninth month in the fifth year of Jehoiakim's reign occurred within the months of November and December 604 B.C. Also see note on 1:3.

1 TIMOTHY 5:1-25

Pastors have the challenging task of ministering to people of every age and from all walks of life. The same was true in Timothy's day. Here Paul gives helpful advice on how to do that.

Never speak harshly to an older man,* but appeal to him respectfully as you would to your own father. Talk to younger men as you would to your own brothers. ²Treat older women as you would your mother, and treat younger women with all purity as you would your own sisters.

³Take care of* any widow who has no one else to care for her. ⁴But if she has children or grandchildren, their first responsibility is to show godliness at home and repay their parents by taking care of them. This is something that pleases God.

⁵Now a true widow, a woman who is truly alone in this world, has placed her hope in God. She prays night and day, asking God for his help. ⁶But the widow who lives only for pleasure is spiritually dead even while she lives. ⁷Give these instructions to the church so that no one will be open to criticism.

⁸But those who won't care for their relatives, especially those in their own household, have denied the true faith. Such people are worse than unbelievers.

⁹A widow who is put on the list for support must be a woman who is at least sixty years old and was faithful to her husband.* ¹⁰She must be well respected by everyone because of the good she has done. Has she brought up her children well? Has she been kind to strangers and served other believers humbly?* Has she helped those who are in trouble? Has she always been ready to do good?

¹¹The younger widows should not be

on the list, because their physical desires will overpower their devotion to Christ and they will want to remarry. [12]Then they would be guilty of breaking their previous pledge. [13]And if they are on the list, they will learn to be lazy and will spend their time gossiping from house to house, meddling in other people's business and talking about things they shouldn't. [14]So I advise these younger widows to marry again, have children, and take care of their own homes. Then the enemy will not be able to say anything against them. [15]For I am afraid that some of them have already gone astray and now follow Satan.

[16]If a woman who is a believer has relatives who are widows, she must take care of them and not put the responsibility on the church. Then the church can care for the widows who are truly alone.

[17]Elders who do their work well should be respected and paid well,* especially those who work hard at both preaching and teaching. [18]For the Scripture says, "You must not muzzle an ox to keep it from eating as it treads out the grain." And in another place, "Those who work deserve their pay!"*

[19]Do not listen to an accusation against an elder unless it is confirmed by two or three witnesses. [20]Those who sin should be reprimanded in front of the whole church; this will serve as a strong warning to others.

[21]I solemnly command you in the presence of God and Christ Jesus and the holy angels to obey these instructions without taking sides or showing favoritism to anyone.

[22]Never be in a hurry about appointing a church leader.* Do not share in the sins of others. Keep yourself pure.

[23]Don't drink only water. You ought to drink a little wine for the sake of your stomach because you are sick so often.

[24]Remember, the sins of some people are obvious, leading them to certain judgment. But there are others whose sins will not be revealed until later. [25]In the same way, the good deeds of some people are obvious. And the good deeds done in secret will someday come to light.

5:1 Or *an elder.*   5:3 Or *Honor.*   5:9 Greek *was the wife of one husband.*   5:10 Greek *and washed the feet of God's holy people?*   5:17 Greek *should be worthy of double honor.*   5:18 Deut 25:4; Luke 10:7.   5:22 Greek *about the laying on of hands.*

PSALM 89:14-37

Righteousness and justice are the
    foundation of your throne.
Unfailing love and truth walk
    before you as attendants.
[15] Happy are those who hear the joyful
    call to worship,

HOW WE LIVE

Courageous in trials

JEREMIAH 36:26-28 Sometimes being a believer takes courage. Jeremiah and Baruch's lives were put in danger by the message the Lord gave them. Jehoiakim was a hard-hearted, evil king. When he heard what was written on the scroll, he burned it and sought to have Jeremiah and Baruch arrested. • God protected Jeremiah and Baruch by allowing them to hide from the king's henchmen. But even though they were safe by the Lord's protection, they still had a task to do that required courage and faith. God told them to write the scroll again! In the ancient world, to speak negatively of the king was dangerous. To rewrite a message the king had already destroyed would have been considered brazen rebellion. But Jeremiah was serving a higher King. He was loyal first and foremost to the Lord, serving as his messenger no matter what the cost to himself might be. • There will be times when you need to take a stand for God when doing so isn't popular or advantageous (in earthly terms). During those times, courage is needed—courage to keep going; courage not to waver; courage to trust God.

for they will walk in the light of
your presence, LORD.
[16] They rejoice all day long in your
wonderful reputation.
They exult in your righteousness.
[17] You are their glorious strength.
It pleases you to make us strong.
[18] Yes, our protection comes from
the LORD,
and he, the Holy One of Israel, has
given us our king.

[19] Long ago you spoke in a vision to your
faithful people.
You said, "I have raised up a warrior.
I have selected him from the
common people to be king.
[20] I have found my servant David.
I have anointed him with my
holy oil.
[21] I will steady him with my hand;
with my powerful arm I will make
him strong.
[22] His enemies will not defeat him,
nor will the wicked overpower him.
[23] I will beat down his adversaries
before him
and destroy those who hate him.
[24] My faithfulness and unfailing love will
be with him,
and by my authority he will grow
in power.
[25] I will extend his rule over the sea,
his dominion over the rivers.
[26] And he will call out to me, 'You are
my Father,
my God, and the Rock of my
salvation.'

[27] I will make him my firstborn son,
the mightiest king on earth.
[28] I will love him and be kind to him
forever;
my covenant with him will never end.
[29] I will preserve an heir for him;
his throne will be as endless as the
days of heaven.
[30] But if his descendants forsake
my instructions
and fail to obey my regulations,
[31] if they do not obey my decrees
and fail to keep my commands,
[32] then I will punish their sin with
the rod,
and their disobedience with
beating.
[33] But I will never stop loving him
nor fail to keep my promise to him.
[34] No, I will not break my covenant;
I will not take back a single word
I said.
[35] I have sworn an oath to David,
and in my holiness I cannot lie:
[36] His dynasty will go on forever;
his kingdom will endure as the sun.
[37] It will be as eternal as the moon,
my faithful witness in the sky!"
Interlude

PROVERBS 25:25-27
Good news from far away is like cold water to the thirsty. ☐ If the godly give in to the wicked, it's like polluting a fountain or muddying a spring. ☐ It's not good to eat too much honey, and it's not good to seek honors for yourself.

OCTOBER**21**

JEREMIAH 37:1–38:28
Jeremiah went from a citizen of a land under siege, to a prisoner in that land, to a condemned man in a cistern. After being rescued from the well, he returned to Jerusalem to face the last days of the kingdom. If only the king would listen. . . .

Zedekiah son of Josiah succeeded Jehoiachin* son of Jehoiakim as the king of Judah. He was appointed by King Nebuchadnezzar* of Babylon. [2]But neither King Zedekiah nor his attendants nor the people who were left in the land listened to what the LORD said through Jeremiah.

3Nevertheless, King Zedekiah sent Jehucal son of Shelemiah, and Zephaniah the priest, son of Maaseiah, to ask Jeremiah, "Please pray to the LORD our God for us." 4Jeremiah had not yet been imprisoned, so he could come and go among the people as he pleased.

5At this time the army of Pharaoh Hophra* of Egypt appeared at the southern border of Judah. When the Babylonian* army heard about it, they withdrew from their siege of Jerusalem.

6Then the LORD gave this message to Jeremiah: 7"This is what the LORD, the God of Israel, says: The king of Judah sent you to ask me what is going to happen. Tell him, 'Pharaoh's army is about to return to Egypt, though he came here to help you. 8Then the Babylonians* will come back and capture this city and burn it to the ground.'

9"This is what the LORD says: Do not fool yourselves into thinking that the Babylonians are gone for good. They aren't! 10Even if you were to destroy the entire Babylonian army, leaving only a handful of wounded survivors, they would still stagger from their tents and burn this city to the ground!"

11When the Babylonian army left Jerusalem because of Pharaoh's approaching army, 12Jeremiah started to leave the city on his way to the territory of Benjamin, to claim his share of the property among his relatives there.* 13But as he was walking through the Benjamin Gate, a sentry arrested him and said, "You are defecting to the Babylonians!" The sentry making the arrest was Irijah son of Shelemiah, grandson of Hananiah.

14"That's not true!" Jeremiah protested. "I had no intention of doing any such thing." But Irijah wouldn't listen, and he took Jeremiah before the officials. 15They were furious with Jeremiah and had him flogged and imprisoned in the house of Jonathan the secretary. Jonathan's house had been converted into a prison. 16Jeremiah was put into a dungeon cell, where he remained for many days.

17Later King Zedekiah secretly requested that Jeremiah come to the palace, where the king asked him, "Do you have any messages from the LORD?"

"Yes, I do!" said Jeremiah. "You will be defeated by the king of Babylon."

18Then Jeremiah asked the king, "What crime have I committed? What have I done against you, your attendants, or the people that I should be imprisoned like this? 19Where are your prophets now who told you the king of Babylon would not attack you or this land? 20Listen, my lord the king, I beg you. Don't send me back to the dungeon in the house of Jonathan the secretary, for I will die there."

21So King Zedekiah commanded that Jeremiah not be returned to the dungeon. Instead, he was imprisoned in the courtyard of the guard in the royal palace. The king also commanded that Jeremiah be given a loaf of fresh bread every day as long as there was any left in the city. So Jeremiah was put in the palace prison.

38:1Now Shephatiah son of Mattan, Gedaliah son of Pashhur, Jehucal* son of Shelemiah, and Pashhur son of Malkijah heard what Jeremiah had been telling the people. He had been saying, 2"This is what the LORD says: 'Everyone who stays in Jerusalem will die from war, famine, or disease, but those who surrender to the Babylonians* will live. Their reward will be life. They will live!' 3The LORD also says: 'The city of Jerusalem will certainly be handed over to the army of the king of Babylon, who will capture it.'"

4So these officials went to the king and said, "Sir, this man must die! That kind of talk will undermine the morale of the few fighting men we have left, as well as that of all the people. This man is a traitor!"

5King Zedekiah agreed. "All right," he said. "Do as you like. I can't stop you."

6So the officials took Jeremiah from his cell and lowered him by ropes into an empty cistern in the prison yard. It belonged to Malkijah, a member of the royal family. There was no water in the cistern, but there was a thick layer of mud at the bottom, and Jeremiah sank down into it.

7But Ebed-melech the Ethiopian,* an important court official, heard that Jeremiah was in the cistern. At that time the king was holding court at the Benjamin

Gate, [8]so Ebed-melech rushed from the palace to speak with him. [9]"My lord the king," he said, "these men have done a very evil thing in putting Jeremiah the prophet into the cistern. He will soon die of hunger, for almost all the bread in the city is gone."

[10]So the king told Ebed-melech, "Take thirty of my men with you, and pull Jeremiah out of the cistern before he dies."

[11]So Ebed-melech took the men with him and went to a room in the palace beneath the treasury, where he found some old rags and discarded clothing. He carried these to the cistern and lowered them to Jeremiah on a rope. [12]Ebed-melech called down to Jeremiah, "Put these rags under your armpits to protect you from the ropes." Then when Jeremiah was ready, [13]they pulled him out. So Jeremiah was returned to the courtyard of the guard—the palace prison—where he remained.

[14]One day King Zedekiah sent for Jeremiah and had him brought to the third entrance of the LORD's Temple. "I want to ask you something," the king said. "And don't try to hide the truth."

[15]Jeremiah said, "If I tell you the truth, you will kill me. And if I give you advice, you won't listen to me anyway."

[16]So King Zedekiah secretly promised him, "As surely as the LORD our Creator lives, I will not kill you or hand you over to the men who want you dead."

[17]Then Jeremiah said to Zedekiah, "This is what the LORD God of Heaven's Armies, the God of Israel, says: 'If you surrender to the Babylonian officers, you and your family will live, and the city will not be burned down. [18]But if you refuse to surrender, you will not escape! This city will be handed over to the Babylonians, and they will burn it to the ground.'"

[19]"But I am afraid to surrender," the king said, "for the Babylonians may hand me over to the Judeans who have defected to them. And who knows what they will do to me!"

[20]Jeremiah replied, "You won't be handed over to them if you choose to obey the LORD. Your life will be spared, and all will go well for you. [21]But if you refuse to surrender, this is what the LORD has revealed to me: [22]All the women left in

your palace will be brought out and given to the officers of the Babylonian army. Then the women will taunt you, saying,

'What fine friends you have!
 They have betrayed and misled you.
When your feet sank in the mud,
 they left you to your fate!'

[23]All your wives and children will be led out to the Babylonians, and you will not escape. You will be seized by the king of Babylon, and this city will be burned down."

[24]Then Zedekiah said to Jeremiah, "Don't tell anyone you told me this, or you will die! [25]My officials may hear that I spoke to you, and they may say, 'Tell us what you and the king were talking about. If you don't tell us, we will kill you.' [26]If this happens, just tell them you begged me not to send you back to Jonathan's dungeon, for fear you would die there."

[27]Sure enough, it wasn't long before the king's officials came to Jeremiah and asked him why the king had called for him. But Jeremiah followed the king's instructions, and they left without finding out the truth. No one had overheard the conversation between Jeremiah and the king. [28]And Jeremiah remained a prisoner in the courtyard of the guard until the day Jerusalem was captured.

37:1a Hebrew *Coniah,* a variant spelling of Jehoiachin. **37:1b** Hebrew *Nebuchadrezzar,* a variant spelling of Nebuchadnezzar. **37:5a** Hebrew *army of Pharaoh;* see 44:30. **37:5b** Or *Chaldean;* also in 37:10, 11. **37:8** Or *Chaldeans;* also in 37:9, 13. **37:12** Hebrew *to separate from there in the midst of the people.* **38:1** Hebrew *Jucal,* a variant spelling of Jehucal; see 37:3. **38:2** Or *Chaldeans;* also in 38:18, 19, 23. **38:7** Hebrew *the Cushite.*

1 TIMOTHY 6:1-21

Paul's closing words to Timothy in this letter are rich with wisdom that serves leaders and ordinary believers alike today. Each of us is called to "fight the good fight for the true faith" (6:12).

All slaves should show full respect for their masters so they will not bring shame on the name of God and his teaching. [2]If the masters are believers, that is no excuse for being disrespectful. Those slaves should work all the harder because their efforts are helping other believers* who are well loved.

Teach these things, Timothy, and encourage everyone to obey them. [3] Some people may contradict our teaching, but these are the wholesome teachings of the Lord Jesus Christ. These teachings promote a godly life. [4] Anyone who teaches something different is arrogant and lacks understanding. Such a person has an unhealthy desire to quibble over the meaning of words. This stirs up arguments ending in jealousy, division, slander, and evil suspicions. [5] These people always cause trouble. Their minds are corrupt, and they have turned their backs on the truth. To them, a show of godliness is just a way to become wealthy.

[6] Yet true godliness with contentment is itself great wealth. [7] After all, we brought nothing with us when we came into the world, and we can't take anything with us when we leave it. [8] So if we have enough food and clothing, let us be content.

[9] But people who long to be rich fall into temptation and are trapped by many foolish and harmful desires that plunge them into ruin and destruction. [10] For the love of money is the root of all kinds of evil. And some people, craving money, have wandered from the true faith and pierced themselves with many sorrows.

[11] But you, Timothy, are a man of God; so run from all these evil things. Pursue righteousness and a godly life, along with faith, love, perseverance, and gentleness.

[12] Fight the good fight for the true faith. Hold tightly to the eternal life to which God has called you, which you have confessed so well before many witnesses. [13] And I charge you before God, who gives life to all, and before Christ Jesus, who gave a good testimony before Pontius Pilate, [14] that you obey this command without wavering. Then no one can find fault with you from now until our Lord Jesus Christ comes again. [15] For at just the right time Christ will be revealed from heaven by the blessed and only almighty God, the King of all kings and Lord of all lords. [16] He alone can never die, and he lives in light so brilliant that no human can approach him. No human eye has ever seen him, nor ever will. All honor and power to him forever! Amen.

[17] Teach those who are rich in this world not to be proud and not to trust in their money, which is so unreliable. Their trust should be in God, who richly gives us all we need for our enjoyment. [18] Tell them to use their money to do good. They should be rich in good works and generous to those in need, always being ready to share with others. [19] By doing this they will be storing up their treasure as a good foundation for the future so that they may experience true life.

[20] Timothy, guard what God has entrusted to you. Avoid godless, foolish

---

HOW WE LIVE | Our giving

1 TIMOTHY 6:17-19 How much time do you spend dealing with money—earning it, spending it, thinking about it, worrying about it? There is nothing wrong with money—money in itself is not evil. "The *love of money* is the root of all kinds of evil" (1 Timothy 6:10; italics added). When we love money—when we let it become the central focus of our lives—we have a problem. Soon we're scheming, worrying, refusing to share, looking down on those with less, and yet never having enough. Money is a cruel master. • Christians need to be wise about wealth. It is so easy to slide into foolishness and trust in worldly wealth rather than God. Only God is a reliable source of security. The rich need not be ashamed of their riches; money is a gift from God, given to be enjoyed. But it is also a test. God is looking to see whether those to whom he has entrusted wealth will use it to honor him and further his kingdom. God doesn't *need* our money, but he does need willing hearts that are glad to give. He lets us in on the joy of giving—and that itself is a gift!

discussions with those who oppose you with their so-called knowledge. [21]Some people have wandered from the faith by following such foolishness.

May God's grace be with you all.

6:2 Greek brothers.

PSALM 89:38-52

But now you [the LORD] have rejected him [David] and cast him off.
    You are angry with your anointed king.
[39] You have renounced your covenant with him;
    you have thrown his crown in the dust.
[40] You have broken down the walls protecting him
    and ruined every fort defending him.
[41] Everyone who comes along has robbed him,
    and he has become a joke to his neighbors.
[42] You have strengthened his enemies and made them all rejoice.
[43] You have made his sword useless and refused to help him
    in battle.
[44] You have ended his splendor and overturned his throne.

[45] You have made him old before his time
    and publicly disgraced him.
                                                    Interlude

[46] O LORD, how long will this go on?
    Will you hide yourself forever?
    How long will your anger burn
        like fire?
[47] Remember how short my life is,
    how empty and futile this human existence!
[48] No one can live forever; all will die.
    No one can escape the power of the grave.*   Interlude

[49] Lord, where is your unfailing love?
    You promised it to David with a faithful pledge.
[50] Consider, Lord, how your servants are disgraced!
    I carry in my heart the insults of so many people.
[51] Your enemies have mocked me, O LORD;
    they mock your anointed king wherever he goes.

[52] Praise the LORD forever!
    Amen and amen!

89:48 Hebrew of Sheol.

PROVERBS 25:28
A person without self-control is like a city with broken-down walls.

OCTOBER22

JEREMIAH 39:1–41:18
Finally, Jerusalem fell. King David had named Jerusalem the capital of Judah and had made it the spiritual epicenter. Solomon built the Temple there. But, from this point on, Jerusalem would for many years be the property of another empire.

In January* of the ninth year of King Zedekiah's reign, King Nebuchadnezzar* came with his army to besiege Jerusalem. [2]Two and a half years later, on July 18* in the eleventh year of Zedekiah's reign, the Babylonians broke through the wall, and the city fell. [3]All the officers of the Babylonian army came in and sat in triumph at the Middle Gate: Nergal-sharezer of Sam-

gar, and Nebo-sarsekim,* a chief officer, and Nergal-sharezer, the king's adviser, and all the other officers.

[4]When King Zedekiah and all the soldiers saw that the Babylonians had broken into the city, they fled. They waited for nightfall and then slipped through the gate between the two walls behind the king's garden and headed toward the Jordan Valley.*

[5]But the Babylonian* troops chased the king and caught him on the plains of Jericho. They took him to King Nebuchadnezzar of Babylon, who was at Riblah in the land of Hamath. There the king of

Babylon pronounced judgment upon Zedekiah. [6]He made Zedekiah watch as they slaughtered his sons and all the nobles of Judah. [7]Then they gouged out Zedekiah's eyes, bound him in bronze chains, and led him away to Babylon.

[8]Meanwhile, the Babylonians burned Jerusalem, including the palace, and tore down the walls of the city. [9]Then Nebuzaradan, the captain of the guard, sent to Babylon the rest of the people who remained in the city as well as those who had defected to him. [10]But Nebuzaradan left a few of the poorest people in Judah, and he assigned them vineyards and fields to care for.

[11]King Nebuchadnezzar had told Nebuzaradan, the captain of the guard, to find Jeremiah. [12]"See that he isn't hurt," he said. "Look after him well, and give him anything he wants." [13]So Nebuzaradan, the captain of the guard; Nebushazban, a chief officer; Nergal-sharezer, the king's adviser; and the other officers of Babylon's king [14]sent messengers to bring Jeremiah out of the prison. They put him under the care of Gedaliah son of Ahikam and grandson of Shaphan, who took him back to his home. So Jeremiah stayed in Judah among his own people.

[15]The LORD had given the following message to Jeremiah while he was still in prison: [16]"Say to Ebed-melech the Ethiopian,* 'This is what the LORD of Heaven's Armies, the God of Israel, says: I will do to this city everything I have threatened. I will send disaster, not prosperity. You will see its destruction, [17]but I will rescue you from those you fear so much. [18]Because you trusted me, I will give you your life as a reward. I will rescue you and keep you safe. I, the LORD, have spoken!'"

[40:1]THE LORD gave a message to Jeremiah after Nebuzaradan, the captain of the guard, had released him at Ramah. He had found Jeremiah bound in chains among all the other captives of Jerusalem and Judah who were being sent to exile in Babylon.

[2]The captain of the guard called for Jeremiah and said, "The LORD your God has brought this disaster on this land, [3]just as he said he would. For these people have sinned against the LORD and disobeyed him. That is why it happened. [4]But I am going to take off your chains and let you go. If you want to come with me to Babylon, you are welcome. I will see that you are well cared for. But if you don't want to come, you may stay here. The whole land is before you—go wherever you like. [5]If you decide to stay, then return to Gedaliah son of Ahikam and grandson of Shaphan. He has been appointed governor of Judah by the king of Babylon. Stay there with the people he rules. But it's up to you; go wherever you like."

Then Nebuzaradan, the captain of the guard, gave Jeremiah some food and money and let him go. [6]So Jeremiah returned to Gedaliah son of Ahikam at Mizpah, and he lived in Judah with the few who were still left in the land.

[7]The leaders of the Judean guerrilla bands in the countryside heard that the king of Babylon had appointed Gedaliah son of Ahikam as governor over the poor people who were left behind in Judah—the men, women, and children who hadn't been exiled to Babylon. [8]So they went to see Gedaliah at Mizpah. These included: Ishmael son of Nethaniah, Johanan and Jonathan sons of Kareah, Seraiah son of Tanhumeth, the sons of Ephai the Netophathite, Jezaniah son of the Maacathite, and all their men.

[9]Gedaliah vowed to them that the Babylonians* meant them no harm. "Don't be afraid to serve them. Live in the land and serve the king of Babylon, and all will go well for you," he promised. [10]"As for me, I will stay at Mizpah to represent you before the Babylonians who come to meet with us. Settle in the towns you have taken, and live off the land. Harvest the grapes and summer fruits and olives, and store them away."

[11]When the Judeans in Moab, Ammon, Edom, and the other nearby countries heard that the king of Babylon had left a few people in Judah and that Gedaliah was the governor, [12]they began to return to Judah from the places to which they had fled. They stopped at Mizpah to meet with Gedaliah and then went into the Judean countryside to gather a great harvest of grapes and other crops.

[13] Soon after this, Johanan son of Kareah and the other guerrilla leaders came to Gedaliah at Mizpah. [14] They said to him, "Did you know that Baalis, king of Ammon, has sent Ishmael son of Nethaniah to assassinate you?" But Gedaliah refused to believe them.

[15] Later Johanan had a private conference with Gedaliah and volunteered to kill Ishmael secretly. "Why should we let him come and murder you?" Johanan asked. "What will happen then to the Judeans who have returned? Why should the few of us who are still left be scattered and lost?"

[16] But Gedaliah said to Johanan, "I forbid you to do any such thing, for you are lying about Ishmael."

41:1 But in midautumn,* Ishmael son of Nethaniah and grandson of Elishama, who was a member of the royal family and had been one of the king's high officials, went to Mizpah with ten men to meet Gedaliah. While they were eating together, [2] Ishmael and his ten men suddenly jumped up, drew their swords, and killed Gedaliah, whom the king of Babylon had appointed governor. [3] Ishmael also killed all the Judeans and the Babylonian* soldiers who were with Gedaliah at Mizpah.

[4] The next day, before anyone had heard about Gedaliah's murder, [5] eighty men arrived from Shechem, Shiloh, and Samaria to worship at the Temple of the LORD. They had shaved off their beards, torn their clothes, and cut themselves, and had brought along grain offerings and frankincense. [6] Ishmael left Mizpah to meet them, weeping as he went. When he reached them, he said, "Oh, come and see what has happened to Gedaliah!"

[7] But as soon as they were all inside the town, Ishmael and his men killed all but ten of them and threw their bodies into a cistern. [8] The other ten had talked Ishmael into letting them go by promising to bring him their stores of wheat, barley, olive oil, and honey that they had hidden away. [9] The cistern where Ishmael dumped the bodies of the men he murdered was the large one dug by King Asa when he fortified Mizpah to protect himself against King Baasha of Israel. Ishmael son of Nethaniah filled it with corpses.

[10] Then Ishmael made captives of the king's daughters and the other people who had been left under Gedaliah's care in Mizpah by Nebuzaradan, the captain of the guard. Taking them with him, he started back toward the land of Ammon.

[11] But when Johanan son of Kareah and the other guerrilla leaders heard about Ishmael's crimes, [12] they took all their men and set out to stop him. They caught up with him at the large pool near Gibeon. [13] The people Ishmael had captured shouted for joy when they saw Johanan and the other guerrilla leaders. [14] And all the captives from Mizpah escaped and began to help Johanan. [15] Meanwhile, Ishmael and eight of his men escaped from Johanan into the land of Ammon.

[16] Then Johanan son of Kareah and the other guerrilla leaders took all the people they had rescued in Gibeon—the soldiers, women, children, and court officials* whom Ishmael had captured after he killed Gedaliah. [17] They took them all to the village of Geruth-kimham near Bethlehem, where they prepared to leave for Egypt. [18] They were afraid of what the Babylonians* would do when they heard that Ishmael had killed Gedaliah, the governor appointed by the Babylonian king.

39:1a Hebrew *in the tenth month*, of the ancient Hebrew lunar calendar. A number of events in Jeremiah can be cross-checked with dates in surviving Babylonian records and related accurately to our modern calendar. This event occurred on January 15, 588 B.C.; see 52:4a and the note there.   **39:1b** Hebrew *Nebuchadrezzar*, a variant spelling of Nebuchadnezzar; also in 39:11.   **39:2** Hebrew *On the ninth day of the fourth month.* This day was July 18, 586 B.C.; also see note on 39:1a.   **39:3** Or *Nergal-sharezer, Samgar-nebo, Sarsekim.*   **39:4** Hebrew *the Arabah.*   **39:5** Or *Chaldean;* similarly in 39:8.   **39:16** Hebrew *the Cushite.*   **40:9** Or *Chaldeans;* also in 40:10.   **41:1** Hebrew *in the seventh month,* of the ancient Hebrew lunar calendar. This month occurred within the months of October and November 586 B.C; also see note on 39:1a.   **41:3** Or *Chaldean.*   **41:16** Or *eunuchs.*   **41:18** Or *Chaldeans.*

2 TIMOTHY 1:1-18

Paul's second letter to Timothy was written while he was in prison in Rome. It was probably the last letter Paul wrote. These are the famous apostle's last recorded words.

This letter is from Paul, chosen by the will of God to be an apostle of Christ Jesus. I have been sent out to tell others about the life he has promised through faith in Christ Jesus.

²I am writing to Timothy, my dear son.

May God the Father and Christ Jesus our Lord give you grace, mercy, and peace.

³Timothy, I thank God for you—the God I serve with a clear conscience, just as my ancestors did. Night and day I constantly remember you in my prayers. ⁴I long to see you again, for I remember your tears as we parted. And I will be filled with joy when we are together again.

⁵I remember your genuine faith, for you share the faith that first filled your grandmother Lois and your mother, Eunice. And I know that same faith continues strong in you. ⁶This is why I remind you to fan into flames the spiritual gift God gave you when I laid my hands on you. ⁷For God has not given us a spirit of fear and timidity, but of power, love, and self-discipline.

⁸So never be ashamed to tell others about our Lord. And don't be ashamed of me, either, even though I'm in prison for him. With the strength God gives you, be ready to suffer with me for the sake of the Good News. ⁹For God saved us and called us to live a holy life. He did this, not because we deserved it, but because that was his plan from before the beginning of time—to show us his grace through Christ Jesus. ¹⁰And now he has made all of this

plain to us by the appearing of Christ Jesus, our Savior. He broke the power of death and illuminated the way to life and immortality through the Good News. ¹¹And God chose me to be a preacher, an apostle, and a teacher of this Good News.

¹²That is why I am suffering here in prison. But I am not ashamed of it, for I know the one in whom I trust, and I am sure that he is able to guard what I have entrusted to him* until the day of his return.

¹³Hold on to the pattern of wholesome teaching you learned from me—a pattern shaped by the faith and love that you have in Christ Jesus. ¹⁴Through the power of the Holy Spirit who lives within us, carefully guard the precious truth that has been entrusted to you.

¹⁵As you know, everyone from the province of Asia has deserted me—even Phygelus and Hermogenes.

¹⁶May the Lord show special kindness to Onesiphorus and all his family because he often visited and encouraged me. He was never ashamed of me because I was in chains. ¹⁷When he came to Rome, he searched everywhere until he found me. ¹⁸May the Lord show him special kindness on the day of Christ's return. And you know very well how helpful he was in Ephesus.

1:12 Or *what has been entrusted to me.*

WHAT THE BIBLE SAYS

Angels

PSALM 91:11-12 Satan quoted these verses when he tempted Jesus to jump off of the highest point of the Temple (Matthew 4:5-6, January 3). "After all," Satan basically said, "The angels will catch you." Jesus didn't argue that point; rather, he pointed to a deeper error in Satan's suggestion—namely, that one ought not tempt God. • In Scripture there are examples of angels helping and protecting believers. However, there is no indication that each believer has his or her own personal guardian angel—an angel whose entire job is to watch over and protect one specific individual. Believers are never outside the realm of God's protective care, and sometimes he sends angels to help and protect us. At times God may allow you to deal with a difficult situation so that you can learn and grow from it. At other times, however, God may command his angels to shield you. • The point is not to trust in a guardian angel to take care of you. The point is to marvel in the reality of unseen beings around you who will, at times, step in just when God wills it.

PSALM 90:1–91:16
A prayer of Moses, the man of God.

¹ Lord, through all the generations
you have been our home!
² Before the mountains were born,
before you gave birth to the earth
and the world,
from beginning to end, you are God.

³ You turn people back to dust, saying,
"Return to dust, you mortals!"
⁴ For you, a thousand years are as a
passing day,
as brief as a few night hours.
⁵ You sweep people away like dreams
that disappear.
They are like grass that springs
up in the morning.
⁶ In the morning it blooms and
flourishes,
but by evening it is dry and withered.
⁷ We wither beneath your anger;
we are overwhelmed by your fury.
⁸ You spread out our sins before you—
our secret sins—and you see
them all.
⁹ We live our lives beneath your wrath,
ending our years with a groan.
¹⁰ Seventy years are given to us!
Some even live to eighty.
But even the best years are filled with
pain and trouble;
soon they disappear, and we fly
away.
¹¹ Who can comprehend the power
of your anger?
Your wrath is as awesome as the
fear you deserve.
¹² Teach us to realize the brevity of life,
so that we may grow in wisdom.
¹³ O Lord, come back to us!
How long will you delay?
Take pity on your servants!
¹⁴ Satisfy us each morning with your
unfailing love,
so we may sing for joy to the end
of our lives.
¹⁵ Give us gladness in proportion to our
former misery!
Replace the evil years with good.
¹⁶ Let us, your servants, see you work
again;
let our children see your glory.

¹⁷ And may the Lord our God show
us his approval
and make our efforts successful.
Yes, make our efforts successful!

91:1 THOSE who live in the shelter of the
Most High
will find rest in the shadow of
the Almighty.
² This I declare about the LORD:
He alone is my refuge, my place of
safety;
he is my God, and I trust him.
³ For he will rescue you from every trap
and protect you from deadly
disease.
⁴ He will cover you with his feathers.
He will shelter you with his wings.
His faithful promises are your
armor and protection.
⁵ Do not be afraid of the terrors of the
night,
nor the arrow that flies in the day.
⁶ Do not dread the disease that stalks in
darkness,
nor the disaster that strikes at
midday.
⁷ Though a thousand fall at your side,
though ten thousand are dying
around you,
these evils will not touch you.
⁸ Just open your eyes,
and see how the wicked are
punished.

⁹ If you make the LORD your refuge,
if you make the Most High your
shelter,
¹⁰ no evil will conquer you;
no plague will come near your
home.
¹¹ For he will order his angels
to protect you wherever you go.
¹² They will hold you up with their hands
so you won't even hurt your foot on
a stone.
¹³ You will trample upon lions and
cobras;
you will crush fierce lions and
serpents under your feet!
¹⁴ The LORD says, "I will rescue those
who love me.
I will protect those who trust
in my name.

15 When they call on me,
　　I will answer;
　　I will be with them in trouble.
　　I will rescue and honor them.
16 I will reward them with a long life
　　and give them my salvation."

JEREMIAH 42:1–44:23

Jeremiah could not have been clearer, and his nation could not have been more stubborn. Such was the life of God's prophets.

Then all the guerrilla leaders, including Johanan son of Kareah and Jezaniah* son of Hoshaiah, and all the people, from the least to the greatest, approached ²Jeremiah the prophet. They said, "Please pray to the LORD your God for us. As you can see, we are only a tiny remnant compared to what we were before. ³Pray that the LORD your God will show us what to do and where to go."

⁴"All right," Jeremiah replied. "I will pray to the LORD your God, as you have asked, and I will tell you everything he says. I will hide nothing from you."

⁵Then they said to Jeremiah, "May the LORD your God be a faithful witness against us if we refuse to obey whatever he tells us to do! ⁶Whether we like it or not, we will obey the LORD our God to whom we are sending you with our plea. For if we obey him, everything will turn out well for us."

⁷Ten days later the LORD gave his reply to Jeremiah. ⁸So he called for Johanan son of Kareah and the other guerrilla leaders, and for all the people, from the least to the greatest. ⁹He said to them, "You sent me to the LORD, the God of Israel, with your request, and this is his reply: ¹⁰'Stay here in this land. If you do, I will build you up and not tear you down; I will plant you and not uproot you. For I am sorry about all the punishment I have had to bring upon you. ¹¹Do not fear the king of Babylon anymore,' says the LORD. 'For I am with you

PROVERBS 26:1-2

Honor is no more associated with fools than snow with summer or rain with harvest. □ Like a fluttering sparrow or a darting swallow, an undeserved curse will not land on its intended victim.

OCTOBER23

and will save you and rescue you from his power. ¹²I will be merciful to you by making him kind, so he will let you stay here in your land.'

¹³"But if you refuse to obey the LORD your God, and if you say, 'We will not stay here; ¹⁴instead, we will go to Egypt where we will be free from war, the call to arms, and hunger,' ¹⁵then hear the LORD's message to the remnant of Judah. This is what the LORD of Heaven's Armies, the God of Israel, says: 'If you are determined to go to Egypt and live there, ¹⁶the very war and famine you fear will catch up to you, and you will die there. ¹⁷That is the fate awaiting every one of you who insists on going to live in Egypt. Yes, you will die from war, famine, and disease. None of you will escape the disaster I will bring upon you there.'

¹⁸"This is what the LORD of Heaven's Armies, the God of Israel, says: 'Just as my anger and fury have been poured out on the people of Jerusalem, so they will be poured out on you when you enter Egypt. You will be an object of damnation, horror, cursing, and mockery. And you will never see your homeland again.'

¹⁹"Listen, you remnant of Judah. The LORD has told you: 'Do not go to Egypt!' Don't forget this warning I have given you today. ²⁰For you were not being honest when you sent me to pray to the LORD your God for you. You said, 'Just tell us what the LORD our God says, and we will do it!' ²¹And today I have told you exactly what he said, but you will not obey the LORD your God any better now than you have in the past. ²²So you can be sure that

you will die from war, famine, and disease in Egypt, where you insist on going."

43:1 WHEN Jeremiah had finished giving this message from the LORD their God to all the people, 2 Azariah son of Hoshaiah and Johanan son of Kareah and all the other proud men said to Jeremiah, "You lie! The LORD our God hasn't forbidden us to go to Egypt! 3 Baruch son of Neriah has convinced you to say this, because he wants us to stay here and be killed by the Babylonians* or be carried off into exile."

4 So Johanan and the other guerrilla leaders and all the people refused to obey the LORD's command to stay in Judah. 5 Johanan and the other leaders took with them all the people who had returned from the nearby countries to which they had fled. 6 In the crowd were men, women, and children, the king's daughters, and all those whom Nebuzaradan, the captain of the guard, had left with Gedaliah. The prophet Jeremiah and Baruch were also included. 7 The people refused to obey the voice of the LORD and went to Egypt, going as far as the city of Tahpanhes.

8 Then at Tahpanhes, the LORD gave another message to Jeremiah. He said, 9 "While the people of Judah are watching, take some large rocks and bury them under the pavement stones at the entrance of Pharaoh's palace here in Tahpanhes. 10 Then say to the people of Judah, 'This is what the LORD of Heaven's Armies, the God of Israel, says: I will certainly bring my servant Nebuchadnezzar,* king of Babylon, here to Egypt. I will set his throne over these stones that I have hidden. He will spread his royal canopy over them. 11 And when he comes, he will destroy the land of Egypt. He will bring death to those destined for death, captivity to those destined for captivity, and war to those destined for war. 12 He will set fire to the temples of Egypt's gods; he will burn the temples and carry the idols away as plunder. He will pick clean the land of Egypt as a shepherd picks fleas from his cloak. And he himself will leave unharmed. 13 He will break down the sacred pillars standing in the temple of the sun* in Egypt, and he will burn down the temples of Egypt's gods.'"

44:1 THIS is the message Jeremiah received concerning the Judeans living in northern Egypt in the cities of Migdol, Tahpanhes, and Memphis,* and in southern Egypt* as well: 2 "This is what the LORD of Heaven's Armies, the God of Israel, says: You saw the calamity I brought on Jerusalem and all the towns of Judah. They now lie deserted and in ruins. 3 They provoked my anger with all their wickedness. They burned incense and worshiped other gods—gods that neither they nor you nor any of your ancestors had ever even known.

4 "Again and again I sent my servants, the prophets, to plead with them, 'Don't do these horrible things that I hate so much.' 5 But my people would not listen or turn back from their wicked ways. They kept on burning incense to these gods. 6 And so my fury boiled over and fell like fire on the towns of Judah and into the streets of Jerusalem, and they are still a desolate ruin today.

7 "And now the LORD God of Heaven's Armies, the God of Israel, asks you: Why are you destroying yourselves? For not one of you will survive—not a man, woman, or child among you who has come here from Judah, not even the babies in your arms. 8 Why provoke my anger by burning incense to the idols you have made here in Egypt? You will only destroy yourselves and make yourselves an object of cursing and mockery for all the nations of the earth. 9 Have you forgotten the sins of your ancestors, the sins of the kings and queens of Judah, and the sins you and your wives committed in Judah and Jerusalem? 10 To this very hour you have shown no remorse or reverence. No one has chosen to follow my word and the decrees I gave to you and your ancestors before you.

11 "Therefore, this is what the LORD of Heaven's Armies, the God of Israel, says: I am determined to destroy every one of you! 12 I will take this remnant of Judah—those who were determined to come here and live in Egypt—and I will consume them. They will fall here in Egypt, killed by war and famine. All will die, from the least to the greatest. They will be an object of damnation, horror, cursing, and mock-

ery. [13]I will punish them in Egypt just as I punished them in Jerusalem, by war, famine, and disease. [14]Of that remnant who fled to Egypt, hoping someday to return to Judah, there will be no survivors. Even though they long to return home, only a handful will do so."

[15]Then all the women present and all the men who knew that their wives had burned incense to idols—a great crowd of all the Judeans living in northern Egypt and southern Egypt*—answered Jeremiah, [16]"We will not listen to your messages from the LORD! [17]We will do whatever we want. We will burn incense and pour out liquid offerings to the Queen of Heaven just as much as we like—just as we, and our ancestors, and our kings and officials have always done in the towns of Judah and in the streets of Jerusalem. For in those days we had plenty to eat, and we were well off and had no troubles! [18]But ever since we quit burning incense to the Queen of Heaven and stopped worshiping her with liquid offerings, we have been in great trouble and have been dying from war and famine."

[19]"Besides," the women added, "do you suppose that we were burning incense and pouring out liquid offerings to the Queen of Heaven, and making cakes marked with her image, without our husbands knowing it and helping us? Of course not!"

[20]Then Jeremiah said to all of them, men and women alike, who had given him that answer, [21]"Do you think the LORD did not know that you and your ancestors, your kings and officials, and all the people were burning incense to idols in the towns of Judah and in the streets of Jerusalem? [22]It was because the LORD could no longer bear all the disgusting things you were doing that he made your land an object of cursing—a desolate ruin without inhabitants—as it is today. [23]All these terrible things happened to you because you have burned incense to idols and sinned against the LORD. You have refused to obey him and have not followed his instructions, his decrees, and his laws."

42:1 Greek version reads *Azariah;* compare 43:2.   **43:3** Or *Chaldeans.*   **43:10** Hebrew *Nebuchadrezzar,* a variant spelling of Nebuchadnezzar.   **43:13** Or in *Heliopolis.*   **44:1a** Hebrew *Noph.*   **44:1b** Hebrew in *Pathros.*   **44:15** Hebrew in *Egypt, in Pathros.*

2 TIMOTHY 2:1-21

We are soldiers of faith. We are workers in God's Kingdom. How, then, should we live, fight, work, and love?

Timothy, my dear son, be strong through the grace that God gives you in Christ Jesus. [2]You have heard me teach things that have been confirmed by many reliable witnesses. Now teach these truths to other trustworthy people who will be able to pass them on to others.

HOW WE LIVE

Studying God's Word

2 TIMOTHY 2:15 It can be pretty intimidating, this big book called the Bible. If you have made it this far in the year, you are probably feeling a bit overwhelmed at everything that you *didn't* understand, and you probably have a lot of questions. Don't worry. No one expects you to understand everything. In fact, many trained theologians will be the first to tell you that they don't understand all that the Bible has to say. However, don't let that discourage you from continuing to study. The truth is, the Bible is a book you will keep reading for the rest of your life, and yet it will continue to be fresh, yielding new insights even from old, familiar passages. • Knowing the Bible and, more importantly, applying it to your life, is crucial. It will also enable you to make disciples and to stand against false teaching. So keep reading, studying, and learning. Learn the basics about your faith, and then press on to greater depth. Find a Bible study group that can continue to challenge you to grow. Listen to your pastor's sermons. Take notes. Be a student of God's Word.

³Endure suffering along with me, as a good soldier of Christ Jesus. ⁴Soldiers don't get tied up in the affairs of civilian life, for then they cannot please the officer who enlisted them. ⁵And athletes cannot win the prize unless they follow the rules. ⁶And hardworking farmers should be the first to enjoy the fruit of their labor. ⁷Think about what I am saying. The Lord will help you understand all these things.

⁸Always remember that Jesus Christ, a descendant of King David, was raised from the dead. This is the Good News I preach. ⁹And because I preach this Good News, I am suffering and have been chained like a criminal. But the word of God cannot be chained. ¹⁰So I am willing to endure anything if it will bring salvation and eternal glory in Christ Jesus to those God has chosen.

¹¹This is a trustworthy saying:

If we die with him,
    we will also live with him.
¹² If we endure hardship,
    we will reign with him.
If we deny him,
    he will deny us.
¹³ If we are unfaithful,
    he remains faithful,
    for he cannot deny who he is.

¹⁴Remind everyone about these things, and command them in God's presence to stop fighting over words. Such arguments are useless, and they can ruin those who hear them.

¹⁵Work hard so you can present yourself to God and receive his approval. Be a good worker, one who does not need to be ashamed and who correctly explains the word of truth. ¹⁶Avoid worthless, foolish talk that only leads to more godless behavior. ¹⁷This kind of talk spreads like cancer, as in the case of Hymenaeus and Philetus. ¹⁸They have left the path of truth, claiming that the resurrection of the dead has already occurred; in this way, they have turned some people away from the faith.

¹⁹But God's truth stands firm like a foundation stone with this inscription: "The LORD knows those who are his,"* and "All who belong to the LORD must turn away from evil."*

²⁰In a wealthy home some utensils are made of gold and silver, and some are made of wood and clay. The expensive utensils are used for special occasions, and the cheap ones are for everyday use. ²¹If you keep yourself pure, you will be a special utensil for honorable use. Your life will be clean, and you will be ready for the Master to use you for every good work.

2:19a Num 16:5.   2:19b See Isa 52:11.

PSALM 92:1–93:5
A psalm. A song to be sung on the Sabbath Day.

¹ It is good to give thanks to the LORD,
    to sing praises to the Most High.
² It is good to proclaim your unfailing
        love in the morning,
    your faithfulness in the evening,
³ accompanied by the ten-stringed harp
    and the melody of the lyre.

⁴ You thrill me, LORD, with all you have
        done for me!
    I sing for joy because of what you
        have done.
⁵ O LORD, what great works you do!
    And how deep are your thoughts.
⁶ Only a simpleton would not know,
    and only a fool would not
        understand this:
⁷ Though the wicked sprout like weeds
    and evildoers flourish,
    they will be destroyed forever.

⁸ But you, O LORD, will be exalted
        forever.
⁹ Your enemies, LORD, will surely perish;
    all evildoers will be scattered.
¹⁰ But you have made me as strong as a
        wild ox.
    You have anointed me with the
        finest oil.
¹¹ My eyes have seen the downfall of
        my enemies;
    my ears have heard the defeat
        of my wicked opponents.
¹² But the godly will flourish like palm
        trees
    and grow strong like the cedars
        of Lebanon.
¹³ For they are transplanted to the LORD's
        own house.
    They flourish in the courts of
        our God.

¹⁴ Even in old age they will still produce
          fruit;
     they will remain vital and green.
¹⁵ They will declare, "The LORD is just!
          He is my rock!
     There is no evil in him!"

⁹³:¹THE LORD is king! He is robed in
          majesty.
     Indeed, the LORD is robed in
          majesty and armed with strength.
     The world stands firm
          and cannot be shaken.

² Your throne, O LORD, has stood from
          time immemorial.
     You yourself are from the
          everlasting past.
³ The floods have risen up, O LORD.
     The floods have roared
          like thunder;

the floods have lifted their
     pounding waves.
⁴ But mightier than the violent raging
     of the seas,
     mightier than the breakers on the
          shore—
     the LORD above is mightier than
          these!
⁵ Your royal laws cannot be changed.
     Your reign, O LORD, is holy forever
          and ever.

PROVERBS 26:3-5

Guide a horse with a whip, a donkey with
a bridle, and a fool with a rod to his back!
□ Don't answer the foolish arguments of
fools, or you will become as foolish as
they are. □ Be sure to answer the foolish
arguments of fools, or they will become
wise in their own estimation.

OCTOBER24

JEREMIAH 44:24-47:7

Baruch was Jeremiah's secretary. He recorded Jeremiah's messages and even read them aloud at times to the people. In today's reading Baruch receives a special message from Jeremiah.

Then Jeremiah said to them all, including
the women, "Listen to this message from
the LORD, all you citizens of Judah who
live in Egypt. ²⁵ This is what the LORD of
Heaven's Armies, the God of Israel, says:
'You and your wives have said, "We will
keep our promises to burn incense and
pour out liquid offerings to the Queen of
Heaven," and you have proved by your actions
that you meant it. So go ahead and
carry out your promises and vows to her!'

²⁶"But listen to this message from the
LORD, all you Judeans now living in Egypt:
'I have sworn by my great name,' says the
LORD, 'that my name will no longer be
spoken by any of the Judeans in the land
of Egypt. None of you may invoke my
name or use this oath: "As surely as the
Sovereign LORD lives." ²⁷ For I will watch
over you to bring you disaster and not

good. Everyone from Judah who is now
living in Egypt will suffer war and famine
until all of you are dead. ²⁸ Only a small
number will escape death and return to
Judah from Egypt. Then all those who
came to Egypt will find out whose words
are true—mine or theirs!

²⁹"'And this is the proof I give you,' says
the LORD, 'that all I have threatened will
happen to you and that I will punish you
here.' ³⁰ This is what the LORD says: 'I will
turn Pharaoh Hophra, king of Egypt, over
to his enemies who want to kill him, just
as I turned King Zedekiah of Judah over
to King Nebuchadnezzar* of Babylon.'"

⁴⁵:¹THE prophet Jeremiah gave a message
to Baruch son of Neriah in the fourth year
of the reign of Jehoiakim son of Josiah,*
after Baruch had written down everything
Jeremiah had dictated to him. He
said, ²"This is what the LORD, the God of
Israel, says to you, Baruch: ³ You have said,
'I am overwhelmed with trouble! Haven't
I had enough pain already? And now the

LORD has added more! I am worn out from sighing and can find no rest.'

⁴"Baruch, this is what the LORD says: 'I will destroy this nation that I built. I will uproot what I planted. ⁵Are you seeking great things for yourself? Don't do it! I will bring great disaster upon all these people; but I will give you your life as a reward wherever you go. I, the LORD, have spoken!'"

⁴⁶:¹THE following messages were given to Jeremiah the prophet from the LORD concerning foreign nations.

²This message concerning Egypt was given in the fourth year of the reign of Jehoiakim son of Josiah, the king of Judah, on the occasion of the battle of Carchemish* when Pharaoh Neco, king of Egypt, and his army were defeated beside the Euphrates River by King Nebuchadnezzar* of Babylon.

³ "Prepare your shields,
    and advance into battle!
⁴ Harness the horses,
    and mount the stallions.
Take your positions.
    Put on your helmets.
Sharpen your spears,
    and prepare your armor.
⁵ But what do I see?
    The Egyptian army flees in terror.
The bravest of its fighting men run
    without a backward glance.
They are terrorized at every turn,"
    says the LORD.
⁶ "The swiftest runners cannot flee;
    the mightiest warriors cannot
        escape.
By the Euphrates River to the north,
    they stumble and fall.

⁷ "Who is this, rising like the Nile at
        floodtime,
    overflowing all the land?
⁸ It is the Egyptian army,
    overflowing all the land,
boasting that it will cover the earth
        like a flood,
    destroying cities and their people.
⁹ Charge, you horses and chariots;
    attack, you mighty warriors
        of Egypt!

Come, all you allies from Ethiopia,
        Libya, and Lydia*
    who are skilled with the shield and
        bow!
¹⁰ For this is the day of the Lord, the
        LORD of Heaven's Armies,
    a day of vengeance on his enemies.
The sword will devour until it is
        satisfied,
    yes, until it is drunk with your
        blood!
The Lord, the LORD of Heaven's
        Armies, will receive a sacrifice
        today
    in the north country beside the
        Euphrates River.

¹¹ "Go up to Gilead to get medicine,
        O virgin daughter of Egypt!
But your many treatments
    will bring you no healing.
¹² The nations have heard of your shame.
    The earth is filled with your cries of
        despair.
Your mightiest warriors will run into
        each other
    and fall down together."

¹³Then the LORD gave the prophet Jeremiah this message about King Nebuchadnezzar's plans to attack Egypt.

¹⁴ "Shout it out in Egypt!
    Publish it in the cities of Migdol,
        Memphis,* and Tahpanhes!
Mobilize for battle,
    for the sword will devour everyone
        around you.
¹⁵ Why have your warriors fallen?
    They cannot stand, for the LORD has
        knocked them down.
¹⁶ They stumble and fall over each other
        and say among themselves,
'Come, let's go back to our people,
        to the land of our birth.
    Let's get away from the sword of the
        enemy!'
¹⁷ There they will say,
    'Pharaoh, the king of Egypt, is a
        loudmouth
    who missed his opportunity!'

¹⁸ "As surely as I live," says the King,
    whose name is the LORD of
        Heaven's Armies,
    "one is coming against Egypt

who is as tall as Mount Tabor,
　or as Mount Carmel by the sea!
19 Pack up! Get ready to leave for exile,
　you citizens of Egypt!
The city of Memphis will be destroyed,
　without a single inhabitant.
20 Egypt is as sleek as a beautiful young
　cow,
　but a horsefly from the north is on
　its way!
21 Egypt's mercenaries have become like
　fattened calves.
They, too, will turn and run,
　for it is a day of great disaster for
　Egypt,
　a time of great punishment.
22 Egypt flees, silent as a serpent gliding
　away.
The invading army marches in;
　they come against her with axes like
　woodsmen.
23 They will cut down her people like
　trees," says the LORD,
　"for they are more numerous than
　locusts.
24 Egypt will be humiliated;
　she will be handed over to people
　from the north."

25 The LORD of Heaven's Armies, the
God of Israel, says: "I will punish Amon,
the god of Thebes,* and all the other gods
of Egypt. I will punish its rulers and Pharaoh, too, and all who trust in him. 26 I will
hand them over to those who want them
killed—to King Nebuchadnezzar of Babylon and his army. But afterward the land
will recover from the ravages of war. I, the
LORD, have spoken!

27 "But do not be afraid, Jacob, my
　servant;
　do not be dismayed, Israel.
For I will bring you home again from
　distant lands,
　and your children will return from
　their exile.
Israel* will return to a life of peace
　and quiet,
　and no one will terrorize them.
28 Do not be afraid, Jacob, my servant,
　for I am with you," says the LORD.
"I will completely destroy the nations
　to which I have exiled you,
　but I will not completely destroy
　you.
I will discipline you, but with justice;
　I cannot let you go unpunished."

47:1 THIS is the LORD's message to the
prophet Jeremiah concerning the Philistines of Gaza, before it was captured by
the Egyptian army. 2 This is what the LORD
says:

"A flood is coming from the north
　to overflow the land.

HOW WE LIVE

Remaining pure

2 TIMOTHY 2:21-22 "Keep yourself pure," said Paul. Why? Because purity
matters. Even though it might be difficult to remain pure in a sin-stained
world, God requires it. He wants to use you to further his kingdom, but
you need to remain pure if you are to be useful to him.　• One of the keys
to remaining pure is to keep your relationship with God a priority so that
you will desire to stay within his parameters for life. You will be hit with
temptation from all sides, but believers are not hopelessly enslaved to
sin and impurity. You can resist temptation. You can avoid falling into
impurity. Another key to remaining pure is to be practical. Paul gives Timothy some valuable practical advice: *Run* from anything that stimulates
youthful lusts. Some temptations are too strong to confront head-on.
You will need to avoid those situations that put you face-to-face with difficult temptations. Paul did not stop at mere avoidance. He gave Timothy
further practical advice for pursuing righteous living. One such way is to
choose friends who will be a positive, purifying influence on you.

It will destroy the land and everything
in it—
cities and people alike.
People will scream in terror,
and everyone in the land will wail.
³ Hear the clatter of stallions' hooves
and the rumble of wheels as the
chariots rush by.
Terrified fathers run madly,
without a backward glance at their
helpless children.

⁴ "The time has come for the Philistines
to be destroyed,
along with their allies from Tyre
and Sidon.
Yes, the LORD is destroying the
remnant of the Philistines,
those colonists from the island of
Crete.*
⁵ Gaza will be humiliated, its head
shaved bald;
Ashkelon will lie silent.
You remnant from the Mediterranean
coast,*
how long will you lament and
mourn?

⁶ "Now, O sword of the LORD,
when will you be at rest again?
Go back into your sheath;
rest and be still.

⁷ "But how can it be still
when the LORD has sent it on a
mission?
For the city of Ashkelon
and the people living along the sea
must be destroyed."

44:30 Hebrew *Nebuchadrezzar*, a variant spelling of
Nebuchadnezzar. 45:1 The fourth year of Jehoiakim's reign
was 605 B.C. 46:2a This event occurred in 605 B.C., during
the fourth year of Jehoiakim's reign (according to the
calendar system in which the new year begins in the spring).
46:2b Hebrew *Nebuchadrezzar*, a variant spelling of
Nebuchadnezzar; also in 46:13, 26. 46:9 Hebrew *from
Cush, Put, and Lud.* 46:14 Hebrew *Noph;* also in 46:19.
46:25 Hebrew *of No.* 46:27 Hebrew *Jacob.* See note on
5:20. 47:4 Hebrew *from Caphtor.* 47:5 Hebrew *the plain.*

2 TIMOTHY 2:22–3:17
Paul warned Timothy about the last days. What kind
of world will precede Jesus' return? More importantly, how can believers stay true to their beliefs in
the midst of such a world?

Run from anything that stimulates youthful lusts. Instead, pursue righteous living,
faithfulness, love, and peace. Enjoy the
companionship of those who call on the
Lord with pure hearts.

²³Again I say, don't get involved in foolish, ignorant arguments that only start
fights. ²⁴A servant of the Lord must not
quarrel but must be kind to everyone, be
able to teach, and be patient with difficult
people. ²⁵Gently instruct those who oppose the truth. Perhaps God will change
those people's hearts, and they will learn
the truth. ²⁶Then they will come to their
senses and escape from the devil's trap.
For they have been held captive by him to
do whatever he wants.

³:¹You should know this, Timothy, that in
the last days there will be very difficult
times. ²For people will love only themselves and their money. They will be
boastful and proud, scoffing at God, disobedient to their parents, and ungrateful.
They will consider nothing sacred. ³They
will be unloving and unforgiving; they will
slander others and have no self-control.
They will be cruel and hate what is good.
⁴They will betray their friends, be reckless, be puffed up with pride, and love
pleasure rather than God. ⁵They will act
religious, but they will reject the power
that could make them godly. Stay away
from people like that!

⁶They are the kind who work their way
into people's homes and win the confidence of* vulnerable women who are
burdened with the guilt of sin and controlled by various desires. ⁷(Such women
are forever following new teachings, but
they are never able to understand the
truth.) ⁸These teachers oppose the truth
just as Jannes and Jambres opposed
Moses. They have depraved minds and a
counterfeit faith. ⁹But they won't get away
with this for long. Someday everyone will
recognize what fools they are, just as with
Jannes and Jambres.

¹⁰But you, Timothy, certainly know what
I teach, and how I live, and what my purpose in life is. You know my faith, my patience, my love, and my endurance. ¹¹You
know how much persecution and suffering I have endured. You know all about
how I was persecuted in Antioch, Iconium,
and Lystra—but the Lord rescued me from

all of it. [12]Yes, and everyone who wants to live a godly life in Christ Jesus will suffer persecution. [13]But evil people and impostors will flourish. They will deceive others and will themselves be deceived.

[14]But you must remain faithful to the things you have been taught. You know they are true, for you know you can trust those who taught you. [15]You have been taught the holy Scriptures from childhood, and they have given you the wisdom to receive the salvation that comes by trusting in Christ Jesus. [16]All Scripture is inspired by God and is useful to teach us what is true and to make us realize what is wrong in our lives. It corrects us when we are wrong and teaches us to do what is right. [17]God uses it to prepare and equip his people to do every good work.

3:6 Greek *and take captive.*

PSALM 94:1-23

O LORD, the God of vengeance,
    O God of vengeance, let your
        glorious justice shine forth!
[2] Arise, O judge of the earth.
    Give the proud what they deserve.
[3] How long, O LORD?
    How long will the wicked be
        allowed to gloat?
[4] How long will they speak with
        arrogance?
    How long will these evil people
        boast?
[5] They crush your people, LORD,
    hurting those you claim as your
        own.
[6] They kill widows and foreigners
    and murder orphans.
[7] "The LORD isn't looking," they say,
    "and besides, the God of Israel*
        doesn't care."

[8] Think again, you fools!
    When will you finally catch on?
[9] Is he deaf—the one who made your
        ears?
    Is he blind—the one who formed
        your eyes?
[10] He punishes the nations—won't he
        also punish you?
    He knows everything—doesn't he
        also know what you are doing?

[11] The LORD knows people's thoughts;
    he knows they are worthless!

[12] Joyful are those you discipline, LORD,
    those you teach with your
        instructions.
[13] You give them relief from troubled
        times
    until a pit is dug to capture the
        wicked.
[14] The LORD will not reject his people;
    he will not abandon his special
        possession.
[15] Judgment will again be founded on
        justice,
    and those with virtuous hearts will
        pursue it.

[16] Who will protect me from the wicked?
    Who will stand up for me against
        evildoers?
[17] Unless the LORD had helped me,
    I would soon have settled in the
        silence of the grave.
[18] I cried out, "I am slipping!"
    but your unfailing love, O LORD,
        supported me.
[19] When doubts filled my mind,
    your comfort gave me renewed
        hope and cheer.

[20] Can unjust leaders claim that God is
        on their side—
    leaders whose decrees permit
        injustice?
[21] They gang up against the righteous
    and condemn the innocent to
        death.
[22] But the LORD is my fortress;
    my God is the mighty rock where I
        hide.
[23] God will turn the sins of evil people
        back on them.
    He will destroy them for their sins.
    The LORD our God will destroy
        them.

94:7 Hebrew *of Jacob.* See note on 44:4.

PROVERBS 26:6-8

Trusting a fool to convey a message is like cutting off one's feet or drinking poison! ◻A proverb in the mouth of a fool is as useless as a paralyzed leg. ◻Honoring a fool is as foolish as tying a stone to a slingshot.

OCTOBER 25

Jeremiah continues his words of warning to the nations surrounding Judah. The Moabites, the Ammonites, and the Edomites were all distant relatives of Jeremiah's people.

This message was given concerning Moab. This is what the LORD of Heaven's Armies, the God of Israel, says:

"What sorrow awaits the city of Nebo;
    it will soon lie in ruins.
The city of Kiriathaim will be
    humiliated and captured;
    the fortress will be humiliated and
        broken down.
2 No one will ever brag about Moab
        again,
    for in Heshbon there is a plot to
        destroy her.
'Come,' they say, 'we will cut her off
    from being a nation.'
    The town of Madmen,* too, will be
        silenced;
    the sword will follow you there.
3 Listen to the cries from Horonaim,
    cries of devastation and great
        destruction.
4 All Moab is destroyed.
    Her little ones will cry out.*
5 Her refugees weep bitterly,
    climbing the slope to Luhith.
They cry out in terror,
    descending the slope to Horonaim.
6 Flee for your lives!
    Hide* in the wilderness!
7 Because you have trusted in your
        wealth and skill,
    you will be taken captive.
Your god Chemosh, with his priests
        and officials,
    will be hauled off to distant lands!

8 "All the towns will be destroyed,
    and no one will escape—
either on the plateaus or in the valleys,
    for the LORD has spoken.
9 Oh, that Moab had wings
    so she could fly away,*
for her towns will be left empty,
    with no one living in them.

10 Cursed are those who refuse to do the
        LORD's work,
    who hold back their swords from
        shedding blood!

11 "From his earliest history, Moab has
        lived in peace,
    never going into exile.
He is like wine that has been allowed
        to settle.
He has not been poured from flask
        to flask,
    and he is now fragrant and smooth.
12 But the time is coming soon," says
        the LORD,
    "when I will send men to pour him
        from his jar.
They will pour him out,
    then shatter the jar!
13 At last Moab will be ashamed of his
        idol Chemosh,
    as the people of Israel were
        ashamed of their gold calf at
        Bethel.*

14 "You used to boast, 'We are heroes,
        mighty men of war.'
15 But now Moab and his towns will be
        destroyed.
    His most promising youth are
        doomed to slaughter,"
    says the King, whose name is the
        LORD of Heaven's Armies.
16 "Destruction is coming fast for Moab;
    calamity threatens ominously.
17 You friends of Moab,
    weep for him and cry!
See how the strong scepter is broken,
    how the beautiful staff is
        shattered!

18 "Come down from your glory
    and sit in the dust, you people
        of Dibon,
for those who destroy Moab will
    shatter Dibon, too.
    They will tear down all your towers.
19 You people of Aroer,
    stand beside the road and watch.
Shout to those who flee from Moab,
    'What has happened there?'

²⁰ "And the reply comes back,
  'Moab lies in ruins, disgraced;
    weep and wail!
  Tell it by the banks of the Arnon River:
    Moab has been destroyed!'
²¹ Judgment has been poured out on the
    towns of the plateau—
  on Holon and Jahaz* and
    Mephaath,
²² on Dibon and Nebo and Beth-
    diblathaim,
²³   on Kiriathaim and Beth-gamul and
    Beth-meon,
²⁴ on Kerioth and Bozrah—
  all the towns of Moab, far and near.

²⁵ "The strength of Moab has ended.
  His arm has been broken," says the
    LORD.
²⁶ "Let him stagger and fall like a
    drunkard,
  for he has rebelled against the
    LORD.
  Moab will wallow in his own vomit,
    ridiculed by all.
²⁷ Did you not ridicule the people of
    Israel?
  Were they caught in the company of
    thieves
    that you should despise them as you
      do?

²⁸ "You people of Moab,
  flee from your towns and live
    in the caves.
  Hide like doves that nest
    in the clefts of the rocks.
²⁹ We have all heard of the pride of
    Moab,
  for his pride is very great.
  We know of his lofty pride,
    his arrogance, and his haughty
      heart.
³⁰ I know about his insolence,"
    says the LORD,
  "but his boasts are empty—
    as empty as his deeds.
³¹ So now I wail for Moab;
  yes, I will mourn for Moab.
  My heart is broken for the men
    of Kir-hareseth.*

³² "You people of Sibmah, rich in
    vineyards,

  I will weep for you even more than
    I did for Jazer.
  Your spreading vines once reached as
    far as the Dead Sea,*
  but the destroyer has stripped
    you bare!
  He has harvested your grapes and
    summer fruits.
³³ Joy and gladness are gone from
    fruitful Moab.
  The presses yield no wine.
  No one treads the grapes with shouts
    of joy.
  There is shouting, yes, but not of joy.

³⁴"Instead, their awful cries of terror
can be heard from Heshbon clear across
to Elealeh and Jahaz; from Zoar all the way
to Horonaim and Eglath-shelishiyah. Even
the waters of Nimrim are dried up now.

³⁵"I will put an end to Moab," says the
LORD, "for the people offer sacrifices at the
pagan shrines and burn incense to their
false gods. ³⁶My heart moans like a flute
for Moab and Kir-hareseth, for all their
wealth has disappeared. ³⁷The people
shave their heads and beards in mourning.
They slash their hands and put on clothes
made of burlap. ³⁸There is crying and sorrow in every Moabite home and on every
street. For I have smashed Moab like an
old, unwanted jar. ³⁹How it is shattered!
Hear the wailing! See the shame of Moab!
It has become an object of ridicule, an example of ruin to all its neighbors."

⁴⁰This is what the LORD says:

  "Look! The enemy swoops down like
    an eagle,
  spreading his wings over Moab.
⁴¹ Its cities will fall,
  and its strongholds will be seized.
  Even the mightiest warriors will be
    in anguish
    like a woman in labor.
⁴² Moab will no longer be a nation,
  for it has boasted against the LORD.

⁴³ "Terror and traps and snares will be
    your lot,
  O Moab," says the LORD.
⁴⁴ "Those who flee in terror will fall into
    a trap,
  and those who escape the trap will
    step into a snare.

I will see to it that you do not get away,
 for the time of your judgment has
 come,"
 says the LORD.
45 "The people flee as far as Heshbon
 but are unable to go on.
For a fire comes from Heshbon,
 King Sihon's ancient home,
to devour the entire land
 with all its rebellious people.

46 "O Moab, they weep for you!
 The people of the god Chemosh are
 destroyed!
Your sons and your daughters
 have been taken away as captives.
47 But I will restore the fortunes of Moab
 in days to come.
 I, the LORD, have spoken!"

This is the end of Jeremiah's prophecy
concerning Moab.

49:1THIS message was given concerning the
Ammonites. This is what the LORD says:

"Are there no descendants of Israel
 to inherit the land of Gad?
Why are you, who worship Molech,*
 living in its towns?
2 In the days to come," says the LORD,
 "I will sound the battle cry against
 your city of Rabbah.
It will become a desolate heap of ruins,
 and the neighboring towns will be
 burned.
Then Israel will take back the land
 you took from her," says the LORD.

3 "Cry out, O Heshbon,
 for the town of Ai is destroyed.
Weep, O people of Rabbah!
 Put on your clothes of mourning.
Weep and wail, hiding in the hedges,
 for your god Molech, with his
 priests and officials,
 will be hauled off to distant lands.
4 You are proud of your fertile valleys,
 but they will soon be ruined.
You trusted in your wealth,
 you rebellious daughter,
 and thought no one could ever
 harm you.
5 But look! I will bring terror upon you,"
 says the Lord, the LORD of Heaven's
 Armies.

"Your neighbors will chase you from
 your land,
 and no one will help your exiles as
 they flee.
6 But I will restore the fortunes of the
 Ammonites
 in days to come.
 I, the LORD, have spoken."

7 This message was given concerning
Edom. This is what the LORD of Heaven's
Armies says:

"Is there no wisdom in Teman?
 Is no one left to give wise counsel?
8 Turn and flee!
 Hide in deep caves, you people of
 Dedan!
For when I bring disaster on Edom,*
 I will punish you, too!
9 Those who harvest grapes
 always leave a few for the poor.
If thieves came at night,
 they would not take everything.
10 But I will strip bare the land of Edom,
 and there will be no place left to hide.
Its children, its brothers, and its
 neighbors
 will all be destroyed,
 and Edom itself will be no more.
11 But I will protect the orphans who
 remain among you.
 Your widows, too, can depend on
 me for help."

12And this is what the LORD says: "If the
innocent must suffer, how much more
must you! You will not go unpunished!
You must drink this cup of judgment!
13For I have sworn by my own name," says
the LORD, "that Bozrah will become an object of horror and a heap of ruins; it will be
mocked and cursed. All its towns and villages will be desolate forever."

14 I have heard a message from the LORD
 that an ambassador was sent to the
 nations to say,
"Form a coalition against Edom,
 and prepare for battle!"
15 The LORD says to Edom,
 "I will cut you down to size among
 the nations.
 You will be despised by all.
16 You have been deceived

by the fear you inspire in others
and by your own pride.
You live in a rock fortress
and control the mountain heights.
But even if you make your nest among
the peaks with the eagles,
I will bring you crashing down,"
says the LORD.

17 "Edom will be an object of horror.
All who pass by will be appalled
and will gasp at the destruction they
see there.
18 It will be like the destruction of
Sodom and Gomorrah
and their neighboring towns," says
the LORD.
"No one will live there;
no one will inhabit it.
19 I will come like a lion from the
thickets of the Jordan,
leaping on the sheep in the pasture.
I will chase Edom from its land,
and I will appoint the leader of my
choice.
For who is like me, and who can
challenge me?
What ruler can oppose my will?"

20 Listen to the LORD's plans against Edom
and the people of Teman.
Even the little children will be dragged
off like sheep,

and their homes will
be destroyed.
21 The earth will shake with the noise of
Edom's fall,
and its cry of despair will be heard
all the way to the Red Sea.*
22 Look! The enemy swoops down like
an eagle,
spreading his wings over Bozrah.
Even the mightiest warriors will be
in anguish
like a woman in labor.

48:2 *Madmen* sounds like the Hebrew word for "silence";
it should not be confused with the English word *madmen*.
48:4 Greek version reads *Her cries are heard as far away as
Zoar.*   48:6 Or *Hide like a wild donkey;* or *Hide like a
juniper shrub;* or *Be like* [the town of] *Aroer.* The meaning of
the Hebrew is uncertain.   48:9 Or *Put salt on Moab,* / *for she
will be laid waste.*   48:13 Hebrew *ashamed when they
trusted in Bethel.*   48:21 Hebrew *Jahzah,* a variant spelling
of Jahaz.   48:31 Hebrew *Kir-heres,* a variant spelling of Kir-
hareseth; also in 48:36.   48:32 Hebrew *the sea of Jazer.*
49:1 Hebrew *Malcam,* a variant spelling of Molech; also in
49:3.   49:8 Hebrew *Esau;* also in 49:10.   49:21 Hebrew
sea of reeds.

2 TIMOTHY 4:1-22

This is the apostle Paul's goodbye. He talks about
his life being poured out as an offering, a reference
to an ancient ritual involving wine poured on the
altar as a sacrificial gift for God. That's how Paul
saw his life, and his approaching death.

1 [Paul] solemnly urge you [Timothy] in
the presence of God and Christ Jesus, who
will someday judge the living and the

HOW WE LIVE

In the world, not of it

2 TIMOTHY 4:3-4 Sounds a lot like our world, doesn't it? People listening
only to what they want to hear, following their own desires, rejecting
the truth, chasing after myths. Paul would advise us just as he advised
Timothy: (1) *"Be prepared, whether the time is favorable or not. Patiently
correct, rebuke, and encourage" (4:2).* As you grow in knowledge and
faith, you will grow in your ability to correct wrong thinking and help
people see the truth. (2) *"Keep a clear mind in every situation" (4:5).*
Your best attempts to represent Christ will at times be misunderstood by
others. They will object and ask hard questions. The ability to "keep a
clear mind" in those moments gives credibility to your faith. (3) *"Don't be
afraid of suffering" (4:5).* If you succumb to fear of rejection or persecution, your witness will be ineffective. Don't be arrogant or obnoxious, but
don't be fearful either. • It is normal for a believer to feel at odds with
the world. You are now a stranger in a strange land. Always remember
that you are acting as an ambassador for your heavenly Father. His Kingdom is your true and eternal home.

dead when he appears to set up his Kingdom: [2]Preach the word of God. Be prepared, whether the time is favorable or not. Patiently correct, rebuke, and encourage your people with good teaching.

[3]For a time is coming when people will no longer listen to sound and wholesome teaching. They will follow their own desires and will look for teachers who will tell them whatever their itching ears want to hear. [4]They will reject the truth and chase after myths.

[5]But you should keep a clear mind in every situation. Don't be afraid of suffering for the Lord. Work at telling others the Good News, and fully carry out the ministry God has given you.

[6]As for me, my life has already been poured out as an offering to God. The time of my death is near. [7]I have fought the good fight, I have finished the race, and I have remained faithful. [8]And now the prize awaits me—the crown of righteousness, which the Lord, the righteous Judge, will give me on the day of his return. And the prize is not just for me but for all who eagerly look forward to his appearing.

[9]Timothy, please come as soon as you can. [10]Demas has deserted me because he loves the things of this life and has gone to Thessalonica. Crescens has gone to Galatia, and Titus has gone to Dalmatia. [11]Only Luke is with me. Bring Mark with you when you come, for he will be helpful to me in my ministry. [12]I sent Tychicus to Ephesus. [13]When you come, be sure to bring the coat I left with Carpus at Troas. Also bring my books, and especially my papers.*

[14]Alexander the coppersmith did me much harm, but the Lord will judge him for what he has done. [15]Be careful of him, for he fought against everything we said.

[16]The first time I was brought before the judge, no one came with me. Everyone abandoned them. May it not be counted against them. [17]But the Lord stood with me and gave me strength so that I might preach the Good News in its entirety for all the Gentiles to hear. And he rescued me from certain death.* [18]Yes, and the Lord will deliver me from every evil attack and will bring me safely into his heavenly Kingdom. All glory to God forever and ever! Amen.

[19]Give my greetings to Priscilla and Aq-uila and those living in the household of Onesiphorus. [20]Erastus stayed at Corinth, and I left Trophimus sick at Miletus.

[21]Do your best to get here before winter. Eubulus sends you greetings, and so do Pudens, Linus, Claudia, and all the brothers and sisters.*

[22]May the Lord be with your spirit. And may his grace be with all of you.

4:13 Greek *especially the parchments.*   **4:17** Greek *from the mouth of a lion.*   **4:21** Greek *brothers.*

PSALM 95:1–96:13

Come, let us sing to the LORD!
    Let us shout joyfully to the Rock
        of our salvation.
[2] Let us come to him with thanksgiving.
    Let us sing psalms of praise to him.
[3] For the LORD is a great God,
    a great King above all gods.
[4] He holds in his hands the depths of
        the earth
    and the mightiest mountains.
[5] The sea belongs to him, for he made it.
    His hands formed the dry land, too.

[6] Come, let us worship and bow down.
    Let us kneel before the LORD our
        maker,
[7]   for he is our God.
We are the people he watches over,
    the flock under his care.

If only you would listen to his voice
        today!
[8] The LORD says, "Don't harden your
        hearts as Israel did at Meribah,
    as they did at Massah in the
        wilderness.
[9] For there your ancestors tested and
        tried my patience,
    even though they saw everything
        I did.
[10] For forty years I was angry with them,
        and I said,
    'They are a people whose hearts turn
        away from me.
    They refuse to do what I tell them.'
[11] So in my anger I took an oath:
    'They will never enter my place
        of rest.'"

[96:1] SING a new song to the LORD!
    Let the whole earth sing to the
        LORD!

2 Sing to the LORD; praise his name.
    Each day proclaim the good news
        that he saves.
3 Publish his glorious deeds among the
        nations.
    Tell everyone about the amazing
        things he does.
4 Great is the LORD! He is most worthy
        of praise!
    He is to be feared above all gods.
5 The gods of other nations are mere
        idols,
    but the LORD made the heavens!
6 Honor and majesty surround him;
    strength and beauty fill his
        sanctuary.

7 O nations of the world, recognize the
        LORD;
    recognize that the LORD is glorious
        and strong.
8 Give to the LORD the glory he
        deserves!
    Bring your offering and come into
        his courts.
9 Worship the LORD in all his holy
        splendor.
    Let all the earth tremble before him.

10 Tell all the nations, "The LORD
        reigns!"
    The world stands firm and cannot
        be shaken.
    He will judge all peoples fairly.
11 Let the heavens be glad, and the earth
        rejoice!
    Let the sea and everything in it
        shout his praise!
12 Let the fields and their crops burst out
        with joy!
    Let the trees of the forest rustle
        with praise
13 before the LORD, for he is coming!
    He is coming to judge the earth.
    He will judge the world with justice,
        and the nations with his truth.

PROVERBS 26:9-12

A proverb in the mouth of a fool is like a thorny branch brandished by a drunk. □ An employer who hires a fool or a bystander is like an archer who shoots at random. □ As a dog returns to its vomit, so a fool repeats his foolishness. □ There is more hope for fools than for people who think they are wise.

OCTOBER**26**

JEREMIAH 49:23–50:46

Jeremiah's prophecies included Babylon. Led by Nebuchadnezzar, the nation of Babylon defeated Jerusalem and took the people captive. Babylon was powerful, but God's judgment would come upon them just as it had on Judah's other enemies.

This message was given concerning Damascus. This is what the LORD says:

    "The towns of Hamath and Arpad are
        struck with fear,
    for they have heard the news of
        their destruction.
    Their hearts are troubled
        like a wild sea in a raging storm.
24 Damascus has become feeble,
    and all her people turn to flee.
    Fear, anguish, and pain have
        gripped her
    as they grip a woman in labor.

25 That famous city, a city of joy,
        will be forsaken!
26 Her young men will fall in the streets
        and die.
    Her soldiers will all be killed,
        says the LORD of Heaven's Armies.
27 "And I will set fire to the walls of
        Damascus
    that will burn up the palaces of
        Ben-hadad."

28 This message was given concerning Kedar and the kingdoms of Hazor, which were attacked by King Nebuchadnezzar* of Babylon. This is what the LORD says:

    "Advance against Kedar!
        Destroy the warriors from the East!
29 Their flocks and tents will be
        captured,

and their household goods and
camels will be taken away.
Everywhere shouts of panic will be
heard:
'We are terrorized at every turn!'
30 Run for your lives," says the LORD.
"Hide yourselves in deep caves, you
people of Hazor,
for King Nebuchadnezzar of Babylon
has plotted against you
and is preparing to destroy you.

31 "Go up and attack that complacent
nation,"
says the LORD.
"Its people live alone in the desert
without walls or gates.
32 Their camels and other livestock will
all be yours.
I will scatter to the winds these
people
who live in remote places.*
I will bring calamity upon them
from every direction," says the
LORD.
33 "Hazor will be inhabited by jackals,
and it will be desolate forever.
No one will live there;
no one will inhabit it."

34This message concerning Elam came
to the prophet Jeremiah from the LORD at
the beginning of the reign of King Zedekiah of Judah. 35This is what the LORD of
Heaven's Armies says:

"I will destroy the archers of Elam—
the best of their forces.
36 I will bring enemies from all
directions,
and I will scatter the people of Elam
to the four winds.
They will be exiled to countries
around the world.
37 I myself will go with Elam's enemies to
shatter it.
In my fierce anger, I will bring great
disaster
upon the people of Elam," says the
LORD.
"Their enemies will chase them with
the sword
until I have destroyed them
completely.

38 I will set my throne in Elam," says
the LORD,
"and I will destroy its king and
officials.
39 But I will restore the fortunes of Elam
in days to come.
I, the LORD, have spoken!"

50:1THE LORD gave Jeremiah the prophet
this message concerning Babylon and the
land of the Babylonians.* 2This is what
the LORD says:

"Tell the whole world,
and keep nothing back.
Raise a signal flag
to tell everyone that Babylon will
fall!
Her images and idols* will be
shattered.
Her gods Bel and Marduk will be
utterly disgraced.
3 For a nation will attack her from the
north
and bring such destruction that no
one will live there again.
Everything will be gone;
both people and animals will flee.

4 "In those coming days,"
says the LORD,
"the people of Israel will return home
together with the people of Judah.
They will come weeping
and seeking the LORD their God.
5 They will ask the way to Jerusalem*
and will start back home again.
They will bind themselves to the LORD
with an eternal covenant that will
never be forgotten.

6 "My people have been lost sheep.
Their shepherds have led them
astray
and turned them loose in the
mountains.
They have lost their way
and can't remember how to get
back to the sheepfold.
7 All who found them devoured them.
Their enemies said,
'We did nothing wrong in attacking
them,
for they sinned against the LORD,
their true place of rest,
and the hope of their ancestors.'

8 "But now, flee from Babylon!
　　Leave the land of the Babylonians.
　　Like male goats at the head of the
　　　flock,
　　lead my people home again.
9 For I am raising up an army
　　of great nations from the north.
　　They will join forces to attack Babylon,
　　and she will be captured.
　　The enemies' arrows will go straight
　　　to the mark;
　　they will not miss!
10 Babylonia* will be looted
　　until the attackers are glutted with
　　　loot.
　　I, the LORD, have spoken!

11 "You rejoice and are glad,
　　you who plundered my chosen
　　　people.
　　You frisk about like a calf in a meadow
　　and neigh like a stallion.
12 But your homeland* will be
　　　overwhelmed
　　with shame and disgrace.
　　You will become the least of nations—
　　a wilderness, a dry and desolate
　　　land.
13 Because of the LORD's anger,
　　Babylon will become a deserted
　　　wasteland.
　　All who pass by will be horrified
　　and will gasp at the destruction they
　　　see there.

14 "Yes, prepare to attack Babylon,
　　all you surrounding nations.

Let your archers shoot at her; spare
　　no arrows.
　　For she has sinned against the LORD.
15 Shout war cries against her from every
　　　side.
　　Look! She surrenders!
　　Her walls have fallen.
　　It is the LORD's vengeance,
　　so take vengeance on her.
　　Do to her as she has done to others!
16 Take from Babylon all those who plant
　　　crops;
　　send all the harvesters away.
　　Because of the sword of the enemy,
　　everyone will run away and rush
　　　back to their own lands.

17 "The Israelites are like sheep
　　that have been scattered by lions.
　　First the king of Assyria ate them up.
　　Then King Nebuchadnezzar* of
　　　Babylon cracked their bones."
18 Therefore, this is what the LORD of
　　　Heaven's Armies,
　　the God of Israel, says:
"Now I will punish the king of Babylon
　　and his land,
　　just as I punished the king of
　　　Assyria.
19 And I will bring Israel home again
　　to its own land,
　　to feed in the fields of Carmel and
　　　Bashan,
　　and to be satisfied once more
　　in the hill country of Ephraim
　　　and Gilead.

WHO GOD IS

God is all-knowing

JEREMIAH 50:35-38 The Babylonians had grown arrogantly confident not only in their military power but also in the supposed insight of their false prophets. People today still try to discern the future through false methods. They sit in darkened rooms with tarot cards and crystal balls, or use other occult methods. Such activity is playing with demonic powers—a dangerous, sinful thing to do. It is also futile—the only one capable of telling what the future holds with 100-percent accuracy is God himself.

• Seeking knowledge of the future through the occult is evidence of a lack of trust in God. Believers should have nothing to do with such practices. You can be sure that God will wisely and lovingly direct history according to his plans. You cannot know your future, but you can entrust yourself to the One who knows all things. He is Lord and will bring all things to pass according to his timetable.

20 In those days," says the LORD,
    "no sin will be found in Israel or in
      Judah,
    for I will forgive the remnant
      I preserve.

21 "Go up, my warriors, against the land
      of Merathaim
    and against the people of Pekod.
    Pursue, kill, and completely destroy*
      them,
    as I have commanded you," says the
      LORD.

22 "Let the battle cry be heard in the
      land,
    a shout of great destruction.

23 Babylon, the mightiest hammer in all
      the earth,
    lies broken and shattered.
    Babylon is desolate among the
      nations!

24 Listen, Babylon, for I have set a trap for
      you.
    You are caught, for you have fought
      against the LORD.

25 The LORD has opened his armory
    and brought out weapons to vent
      his fury.
    The terror that falls upon the
      Babylonians
    will be the work of the Sovereign
      LORD of Heaven's Armies.

26 Yes, come against her from distant
      lands.
    Break open her granaries.
    Crush her walls and houses into heaps
      of rubble.
    Destroy her completely, and leave
      nothing!

27 Destroy even her young bulls—
    it will be terrible for them, too!
    Slaughter them all!
    For Babylon's day of reckoning has
      come.

28 Listen to the people who have escaped
      from Babylon,
    as they tell in Jerusalem
    how the LORD our God has taken
      vengeance
    against those who destroyed his
      Temple.

29 "Send out a call for archers to come to
      Babylon.

    Surround the city so none can
      escape.
    Do to her as she has done to others,
    for she has defied the LORD, the
      Holy One of Israel.

30 Her young men will fall in the streets
      and die.
    Her soldiers will all be killed,"
    says the LORD.

31 "See, I am your enemy, you arrogant
      people,"
    says the Lord, the LORD of Heaven's
      Armies.
    "Your day of reckoning has arrived—
      the day when I will punish you.

32 O land of arrogance, you will stumble
      and fall,
    and no one will raise you up.
    For I will light a fire in the cities of
      Babylon
    that will burn up everything around
      them."

33 This is what the LORD of Heaven's
      Armies says:
    "The people of Israel and Judah have
      been wronged.
    Their captors hold them and refuse
      to let them go.

34 But the one who redeems them is
      strong.
    His name is the LORD of Heaven's
      Armies.
    He will defend them
      and give them rest again in Israel.
    But for the people of Babylon
      there will be no rest!

35 "The sword of destruction will strike
      the Babylonians,"
    says the LORD.
    "It will strike the people of Babylon—
      her officials and wise men, too.

36 The sword will strike her wise
      counselors,
    and they will become fools.
    The sword will strike her mightiest
      warriors,
    and panic will seize them.

37 The sword will strike her horses and
      chariots
    and her allies from other lands,
    and they will all become like
      women.

The sword will strike her treasures,
and they all will be plundered.
³⁸ The sword will even strike her water
supply,
causing it to dry up.
And why? Because the whole land is
filled with idols,
and the people are madly in love
with them.

³⁹ "Soon Babylon will be inhabited by
desert animals and hyenas.
It will be a home for owls.
Never again will people live there;
it will lie desolate forever.
⁴⁰ I will destroy it as I* destroyed Sodom
and Gomorrah
and their neighboring towns," says
the LORD.
"No one will live there;
no one will inhabit it.

⁴¹ "Look! A great army is coming from
the north.
A great nation and many kings
are rising against you from far-off
lands.
⁴² They are armed with bows and spears.
They are cruel and show no mercy.
As they ride forward on horses,
they sound like a roaring sea.
They are coming in battle formation,
planning to destroy you, Babylon.
⁴³ The king of Babylon has heard reports
about the enemy,
and he is weak with fright.
Pangs of anguish have gripped him,
like those of a woman in labor.

⁴⁴ "I will come like a lion from the
thickets of the Jordan,
leaping on the sheep in the pasture.
I will chase Babylon from its land,
and I will appoint the leader of my
choice.
For who is like me, and who can
challenge me?
What ruler can oppose my will?"

⁴⁵ Listen to the LORD's plans against
Babylon
and the land of the Babylonians.
Even the little children will be dragged
off like sheep,
and their homes will be destroyed.

⁴⁶ The earth will shake with the shout,
"Babylon has been taken!"
and its cry of despair will be heard
around the world.

49:28 Hebrew *Nebuchadrezzar,* a variant spelling of Nebuchadnezzar; also in 49:30. **49:32** Or *who clip the corners of their hair.* **50:1** Or *Chaldeans;* also in 50:8, 25, 35, 45. **50:2** The Hebrew term (literally *round things*) probably alludes to dung. **50:5** Hebrew *Zion;* also in 50:28. **50:10** Or *Chaldea.* **50:12** Hebrew *your mother.* **50:17** Hebrew *Nebuchadrezzar,* a variant spelling of Nebuchadnezzar. **50:21** The Hebrew term used here refers to the complete consecration of things or people to the LORD, either by destroying them or by giving them as an offering. **50:40** Hebrew *as God.*

TITUS 1:1-16
Titus was a young pastor on the island of Crete. Paul wrote to Titus and Timothy at about the same time. He gave them both instructions for leading their congregations.

This letter is from Paul, a slave of God and an apostle of Jesus Christ. I have been sent to proclaim faith to* those God has chosen and to teach them to know the truth that shows them how to live godly lives. ²This truth gives them confidence that they have eternal life, which God—who does not lie—promised them before the world began. ³And now at just the right time he has revealed this message, which we announce to everyone. It is by the command of God our Savior that I have been entrusted with this work for him.

⁴I am writing to Titus, my true son in the faith that we share.

May God the Father and Christ Jesus our Savior give you grace and peace.

⁵I left you on the island of Crete so you could complete our work there and appoint elders in each town as I instructed you. ⁶An elder must live a blameless life. He must be faithful to his wife,* and his children must be believers who don't have a reputation for being wild or rebellious. ⁷For an elder* must live a blameless life. He must not be arrogant or quick-tempered; he must not be a heavy drinker,* violent, or dishonest with money.

⁸Rather, he must enjoy having guests in his home, and he must love what is good. He must live wisely and be just. He must live a devout and disciplined life. ⁹He must have a strong belief in the trustworthy message he was taught; then he will be able to encourage others with wholesome

teaching and show those who oppose it where they are wrong.

¹⁰For there are many rebellious people who engage in useless talk and deceive others. This is especially true of those who insist on circumcision for salvation. ¹¹They must be silenced, because they are turning whole families away from the truth by their false teaching. And they do it only for money. ¹²Even one of their own men, a prophet from Crete, has said about them, "The people of Crete are all liars, cruel animals, and lazy gluttons."* ¹³This is true. So reprimand them sternly to make them strong in the faith. ¹⁴They must stop listening to Jewish myths and the commands of people who have turned away from the truth.

¹⁵Everything is pure to those whose hearts are pure. But nothing is pure to those who are corrupt and unbelieving, because their minds and consciences are corrupted. ¹⁶Such people claim they know God, but they deny him by the way they live. They are detestable and disobedient, worthless for doing anything good.

1:1 Or *to strengthen the faith of.*   1:6 Or *must have only one wife,* or *must be married only once;* Greek reads *must be the husband of one wife.*   1:7a Or *an overseer,* or *a bishop.* 1:7b Greek *must not drink too much wine.*   1:12 This quotation is from Epimenides of Knossos.

PSALM 97:1–98:9

The LORD is king!
Let the earth rejoice!
Let the farthest coastlands be glad.
² Dark clouds surround him.
Righteousness and justice are the foundation of his throne.
³ Fire spreads ahead of him
and burns up all his foes.
⁴ His lightning flashes out across the world.
The earth sees and trembles.
⁵ The mountains melt like wax before the LORD,
before the Lord of all the earth.
⁶ The heavens proclaim his righteousness;
every nation sees his glory.
⁷ Those who worship idols are disgraced—
all who brag about their worthless gods—
for every god must bow to him.

⁸ Jerusalem* has heard and rejoiced,
and all the towns of Judah are glad
because of your justice, O LORD!
⁹ For you, O LORD, are supreme over all the earth;
you are exalted far above all gods.

¹⁰ You who love the LORD, hate evil!
He protects the lives of his godly people
and rescues them from the power of the wicked.
¹¹ Light shines on the godly,
and joy on those whose hearts are right.
¹² May all who are godly rejoice in the LORD
and praise his holy name!

98:1 SING a new song to the LORD,
for he has done wonderful deeds.
His right hand has won a mighty victory;
his holy arm has shown his saving power!
² The LORD has announced his victory
and has revealed his righteousness to every nation!
³ He has remembered his promise to love and be faithful to Israel.
The ends of the earth have seen the victory of our God.

⁴ Shout to the LORD, all the earth;
break out in praise and sing for joy!
⁵ Sing your praise to the LORD with the harp,
with the harp and melodious song,
⁶ with trumpets and the sound of the ram's horn.
Make a joyful symphony before the LORD, the King!

⁷ Let the sea and everything in it shout his praise!
Let the earth and all living things join in.
⁸ Let the rivers clap their hands in glee!
Let the hills sing out their songs of joy
⁹ before the LORD.
For the LORD is coming to judge the earth.
He will judge the world with justice,
and the nations with fairness.

97:8 Hebrew *Zion.*

PROVERBS 26:13-16

The lazy person claims, "There's a lion on the road! Yes, I'm sure there's a lion out there!" ▢ As a door swings back and forth on its hinges, so the lazy person turns over in bed. ▢ Lazy people take food in their hand but don't even lift it to their mouth. ▢ Lazy people consider themselves smarter than seven wise counselors.

OCTOBER**27**

JEREMIAH 51:1-53

The apostle John, in the book of Revelation, quoted Jeremiah, "Babylon is fallen!" (Revelation 18:2, December 27). Because of Babylon's role in the history of Israel, it became a symbol of all powers that stand against the work of God.

This is what the LORD says:
"I will stir up a destroyer against
    Babylon
    and the people of Babylonia.*
² Foreigners will come and winnow her,
    blowing her away as chaff.
They will come from every side
    to rise against her in her day of
    trouble.
³ Don't let the archers put on their
    armor
    or draw their bows.
Don't spare even her best soldiers!
    Let her army be completely
    destroyed.*
⁴ They will fall dead in the land of the
    Babylonians,*
    slashed to death in her streets.
⁵ For the LORD of Heaven's Armies
    has not abandoned Israel and
    Judah.
He is still their God,
    even though their land was filled
    with sin
    against the Holy One of Israel."

⁶ Flee from Babylon! Save yourselves!
    Don't get trapped in her
    punishment!
It is the LORD's time for vengeance;
    he will repay her in full.
⁷ Babylon has been a gold cup in the
    LORD's hands,
    a cup that made the whole earth
    drunk.

The nations drank Babylon's wine,
    and it drove them all mad.
⁸ But suddenly Babylon, too, has fallen.
    Weep for her.
Give her medicine.
    Perhaps she can yet be healed.
⁹ We would have helped her if we could,
    but nothing can save her now.
Let her go; abandon her.
    Return now to your own land.
For her punishment reaches to the
    heavens;
    it is so great it cannot be measured.
¹⁰ The LORD has vindicated us.
    Come, let us announce in
    Jerusalem*
    everything the LORD our God has
    done.

¹¹ Sharpen the arrows!
    Lift up the shields!*
For the LORD has inspired the kings of
    the Medes
    to march against Babylon and
    destroy her.
This is his vengeance against those
    who desecrated his Temple.
¹² Raise the battle flag against Babylon!
    Reinforce the guard and station the
    watchmen.
Prepare an ambush,
    for the LORD will fulfill all his plans
    against Babylon.
¹³ You are a city by a great river,
    a great center of commerce,
but your end has come.
    The thread of your life is cut.
¹⁴ The LORD of Heaven's Armies has
    taken this vow

and has sworn to it by his own
  name:
"Your cities will be filled with
    enemies,
  like fields swarming with locusts,
  and they will shout in triumph
    over you."

15 The LORD made the earth by his power,
  and he preserves it by his wisdom.
With his own understanding
  he stretched out the heavens.
16 When he speaks in the thunder,
  the heavens are filled with water.
He causes the clouds to rise over the
    earth.
  He sends the lightning with the rain
    and releases the wind from his
      storehouses.

17 The whole human race is foolish and
    has no knowledge!
  The craftsmen are disgraced by the
    idols they make,
  for their carefully shaped works are a
    fraud.
  These idols have no breath or
    power.
18 Idols are worthless; they are ridiculous
    lies!
  On the day of reckoning they will all
    be destroyed.
19 But the God of Israel* is no idol!
  He is the Creator of everything that
    exists,
  including his people, his own special
    possession.
  The LORD of Heaven's Armies is his
    name!

20 "You* are my battle-ax and sword,"
    says the LORD.
  "With you I will shatter nations
    and destroy many kingdoms.
21 With you I will shatter armies—
    destroying the horse and rider,
    the chariot and charioteer.
22 With you I will shatter men and
    women,
    old people and children,
    young men and maidens.
23 With you I will shatter shepherds and
    flocks,
    farmers and oxen,
    captains and officers.

24 "I will repay Babylon
    and the people of Babylonia*
  for all the wrong they have done
    to my people in Jerusalem," says
      the LORD.

25 "Look, O mighty mountain, destroyer
    of the earth!
  I am your enemy," says the LORD.
  "I will raise my fist against you,
    to knock you down from the
      heights.
  When I am finished,
    you will be nothing but a heap of
      burnt rubble.
26 You will be desolate forever.
  Even your stones will never again be
    used for building.
  You will be completely wiped out,"
    says the LORD.

27 Raise a signal flag to the nations.
    Sound the battle cry!
  Mobilize them all against Babylon.
    Prepare them to fight against her!
  Bring out the armies of Ararat, Minni,
    and Ashkenaz.
  Appoint a commander,
    and bring a multitude of horses like
      swarming locusts!
28 Bring against her the armies of the
    nations—
  led by the kings of the Medes
    and all their captains and officers.

29 The earth trembles and writhes in
    pain,
  for everything the LORD has
    planned against Babylon stands
      unchanged.
  Babylon will be left desolate without
    a single inhabitant.
30   Her mightiest warriors no longer
    fight.
  They stay in their barracks, their
    courage gone.
  They have become like women.
  The invaders have burned the houses
    and broken down the city gates.
31 The news is passed from one runner
    to the next
  as the messengers hurry to tell
    the king
  that his city has been captured.
32 All the escape routes are blocked.

The marshes have been set aflame,
and the army is in a panic.

[33] This is what the LORD of Heaven's
Armies,
the God of Israel, says:
"Babylon is like wheat on a threshing
floor,
about to be trampled.
In just a little while
her harvest will begin."

[34] "King Nebuchadnezzar* of Babylon
has eaten and crushed us
and drained us of strength.
He has swallowed us like a great
monster
and filled his belly with our riches.
He has thrown us out of our own
country.
[35] Make Babylon suffer as she made us
suffer,"
say the people of Zion.
"Make the people of Babylonia pay for
spilling our blood,"
says Jerusalem.

[36] This is what the LORD says to Jerusalem:

"I will be your lawyer to plead your
case,
and I will avenge you.

I will dry up her river,
as well as her springs,
[37] and Babylon will become a heap of
ruins,
haunted by jackals.
She will be an object of horror and
contempt,
a place where no one lives.
[38] Her people will roar together like
strong lions.
They will growl like lion cubs.
[39] And while they lie inflamed with all
their wine,
I will prepare a different kind of
feast for them.
I will make them drink until they fall
asleep,
and they will never wake up again,"
says the LORD.
[40] "I will bring them down
like lambs to the slaughter,
like rams and goats to be sacrificed.

[41] "How Babylon* is fallen—
great Babylon, praised throughout
the earth!
Now she has become an object
of horror
among the nations.
[42] The sea has risen over Babylon;
she is covered by its crashing waves.
[43] Her cities now lie in ruins;

HOW WE LIVE

Our work

TITUS 2:9-10 Paul did not condemn outright the practice of slavery that was
common in his day. However, neither did he encourage it. By urging both
slaves and masters to treat each other with respect, Paul was laying
down principles that undermined the cultural practice. • Being a follower
of Jesus Christ means living in newness of life no matter what our
outward circumstances might be. For slaves who were believers, this
meant they had to exemplify the Christian lifestyle to their masters.
Plenty of people have jobs they don't like today. Even those jobs,
however, are a far cry from the injustice of slavery. Still, Paul's admonition to slaves in this passage is applicable to the attitude we have toward
our work. God wants you to give witness to your faith in Jesus to your
employer, no matter how good or bad you consider your job to be. How
can you do this best? By being industrious, honest, loyal, trustworthy,
and dependable. Then, when your faith is recognized, you will have made
"the teaching about God our Savior attractive in every way" (Titus 2:10).
And that's a great start! Who knows what effect your faith can have on
your workplace?

she is a dry wasteland
where no one lives or even passes by.

⁴⁴ And I will punish Bel, the god of Babylon,
and make him vomit up all he has eaten.
The nations will no longer come and worship him.
The wall of Babylon has fallen!

⁴⁵ "Come out, my people, flee from Babylon.
Save yourselves! Run from the LORD's fierce anger.

⁴⁶ But do not panic; don't be afraid
when you hear the first rumor of approaching forces.
For rumors will keep coming year by year.
Violence will erupt in the land
as the leaders fight against each other.

⁴⁷ For the time is surely coming
when I will punish this great city and all her idols.
Her whole land will be disgraced,
and her dead will lie in the streets.

⁴⁸ Then the heavens and earth will rejoice,
for out of the north will come destroying armies
against Babylon," says the LORD.

⁴⁹ "Just as Babylon killed the people of Israel
and others throughout the world,
so must her people be killed.

⁵⁰ Get out, all you who have escaped the sword!
Do not stand and watch—flee while you can!
Remember the LORD, though you are in a far-off land,
and think about your home in Jerusalem."

⁵¹ "We are ashamed," the people say.
"We are insulted and disgraced
because the LORD's Temple
has been defiled by foreigners."

⁵² "Yes," says the LORD, "but the time is coming
when I will destroy Babylon's idols.
The groans of her wounded people
will be heard throughout the land.

⁵³ Though Babylon reaches as high as the heavens
and makes her fortifications incredibly strong,
I will still send enemies to plunder her.
I, the LORD, have spoken!"

51:1 Hebrew *of Leb-kamai*, a code name for Babylonia.
51:3 The Hebrew term used here refers to the complete consecration of things or people to the LORD, either by destroying them or by giving them as an offering. 51:4 Or *Chaldeans;* also in 51:54. 51:10 Hebrew *Zion;* also in 51:24. 51:11 Greek version reads *Fill up the quivers.* 51:19 Hebrew *the Portion of Jacob.* See note on 5:20. 51:20 Possibly Cyrus, whom God used to conquer Babylon. Compare Isa 44:28; 45:1. 51:24 Or *Chaldea;* also in 51:35. 51:34 Hebrew *Nebuchadrezzar,* a variant spelling of Nebuchadnezzar. 51:41 Hebrew *Sheshach,* a code name for Babylon.

TITUS 2:1-15

Christian leaders spend much of their energy defining the truth, guarding the truth, and teaching the truth. Paul gives Titus instructions about this very thing and more—once we know the truth, then how do we apply it to our lives?

As for you, Titus, promote the kind of living that reflects wholesome teaching. ²Teach the older men to exercise self-control, to be worthy of respect, and to live wisely. They must have sound faith and be filled with love and patience.

³Similarly, teach the older women to live in a way that honors God. They must not slander others or be heavy drinkers.* Instead, they should teach others what is good. ⁴These older women must train the younger women to love their husbands and their children, ⁵to live wisely and be pure, to work in their homes,* to do good, and to be submissive to their husbands. Then they will not bring shame on the word of God.

⁶In the same way, encourage the young men to live wisely. ⁷And you yourself must be an example to them by doing good works of every kind. Let everything you do reflect the integrity and seriousness of your teaching. ⁸Teach the truth so that your teaching can't be criticized. Then those who oppose us will be ashamed and have nothing bad to say about us.

⁹Slaves must always obey their masters and do their best to please them. They must not talk back ¹⁰or steal, but must show themselves to be entirely trust-

worthy and good. Then they will make the teaching about God our Savior attractive in every way.

[11]For the grace of God has been revealed, bringing salvation to all people. [12]And we are instructed to turn from godless living and sinful pleasures. We should live in this evil world with wisdom, righteousness, and devotion to God, [13]while we look forward with hope to that wonderful day when the glory of our great God and Savior, Jesus Christ, will be revealed. [14]He gave his life to free us from every kind of sin, to cleanse us, and to make us his very own people, totally committed to doing good deeds.

[15]You must teach these things and encourage the believers to do them. You have the authority to correct them when necessary, so don't let anyone disregard what you say.

2:3 Greek *be enslaved to much wine.* **2:5** Some manuscripts read *to care for their homes.*

PSALM 99:1-9

[T]he LORD is king!
Let the nations tremble!
He sits on his throne between the cherubim.
Let the whole earth quake!
[2] The LORD sits in majesty in Jerusalem,*
exalted above all the nations.

[3] Let them praise your great and awesome name.
Your name is holy!
[4] Mighty King, lover of justice,
you have established fairness.
You have acted with justice
and righteousness throughout Israel.*
[5] Exalt the LORD our God!
Bow low before his feet, for he is holy!

[6] Moses and Aaron were among his priests;
Samuel also called on his name.
They cried to the LORD for help,
and he answered them.
[7] He spoke to Israel from the pillar of cloud,
and they followed the laws and decrees he gave them.
[8] O LORD our God, you answered them.
You were a forgiving God to them,
but you punished them when they went wrong.

[9] Exalt the LORD our God,
and worship at his holy mountain in Jerusalem,
for the LORD our God is holy!

99:2 Hebrew *Zion.* **99:4** Hebrew *Jacob.* See note on 44:4.

PROVERBS 26:17

[I]nterfering in someone else's argument is as foolish as yanking a dog's ears.

OCTOBER**28**

JEREMIAH 51:54–52:34

Jeremiah's collection of prophecies ends with the destruction of the Temple. This seemed like the final devastating blow to the people of Judah. But in Jeremiah's closing words he offered some hope for the nation.

"[L]isten! Hear the cry of Babylon,
the sound of great destruction from the land of the Babylonians.
[55] For the LORD is destroying Babylon.
He will silence her loud voice.
Waves of enemies pound against her;

the noise of battle rings through the city.
[56] Destroying armies come against Babylon.
Her mighty men are captured,
and their weapons break in their hands.
For the LORD is a God who gives just punishment;
he always repays in full.
[57] I will make her officials and wise men drunk,

along with her captains, officers,
and warriors.
They will fall asleep
and never wake up again!"
says the King, whose name is
the LORD of Heaven's Armies.

⁵⁸ This is what the LORD of Heaven's
Armies says:
"The thick walls of Babylon will be
leveled to the ground,
and her massive gates will be
burned.
The builders from many lands have
worked in vain,
for their work will be destroyed
by fire!"

⁵⁹ The prophet Jeremiah gave this message to Seraiah son of Neriah and grandson of Mahseiah, a staff officer, when Seraiah went to Babylon with King Zedekiah of Judah. This was during the fourth year of Zedekiah's reign.* ⁶⁰ Jeremiah had recorded on a scroll all the terrible disasters that would soon come upon Babylon—all the words written here. ⁶¹ He said to Seraiah, "When you get to Babylon, read aloud everything on this scroll. ⁶² Then say, 'LORD, you have said that you will destroy Babylon so that neither people nor animals will remain here. She will lie empty and abandoned forever.' ⁶³ When you have finished reading the scroll, tie it to a stone and throw it into the Euphrates River. ⁶⁴ Then say, 'In this same way Babylon and her people will sink, never again to rise, because of the disasters I will bring upon her.'"
This is the end of Jeremiah's messages.

⁵²:¹ ZEDEKIAH was twenty-one years old when he became king, and he reigned in Jerusalem eleven years. His mother was Hamutal, the daughter of Jeremiah from Libnah. ² But Zedekiah did what was evil in the LORD's sight, just as Jehoiakim had done. ³ These things happened because of the LORD's anger against the people of Jerusalem and Judah, until he finally banished them from his presence and sent them into exile.

Zedekiah rebelled against the king of Babylon. ⁴ So on January 15,* during the ninth year of Zedekiah's reign, King Neb-

uchadnezzar* of Babylon led his entire army against Jerusalem. They surrounded the city and built siege ramps against its walls. ⁵ Jerusalem was kept under siege until the eleventh year of King Zedekiah's reign.

⁶ By July 18 in the eleventh year of Zedekiah's reign,* the famine in the city had become very severe, and the last of the food was entirely gone. ⁷ Then a section of the city wall was broken down, and all the soldiers fled. Since the city was surrounded by the Babylonians,* they waited for nightfall. Then they slipped through the gate between the two walls behind the king's garden and headed toward the Jordan Valley.*

⁸ But the Babylonian troops chased King Zedekiah and caught him on the plains of Jericho, for his men had all deserted him and scattered. ⁹ They took him to the king of Babylon at Riblah in the land of Hamath. There the king of Babylon pronounced judgment upon Zedekiah. ¹⁰ He made Zedekiah watch as they slaughtered his sons and all the other officials of Judah. ¹¹ Then they gouged out Zedekiah's eyes, bound him in bronze chains, and led him away to Babylon. Zedekiah remained there in prison until the day of his death.

¹² On August 17 of that year,* which was the nineteenth year of King Nebuchadnezzar's reign, Nebuzaradan, the captain of the guard and an official of the Babylonian king, arrived in Jerusalem. ¹³ He burned down the Temple of the LORD, the royal palace, and all the houses of Jerusalem. He destroyed all the important buildings* in the city. ¹⁴ Then he supervised the entire Babylonian* army as they tore down the walls of Jerusalem on every side. ¹⁵ Nebuzaradan, the captain of the guard, then took as exiles some of the poorest of the people, the rest of the people who remained in the city, the defectors who had declared their allegiance to the king of Babylon, and the rest of the craftsmen. ¹⁶ But Nebuzaradan allowed some of the poorest people to stay behind in Judah to care for the vineyards and fields.

¹⁷ The Babylonians broke up the bronze pillars in front of the LORD's Temple, the

bronze water carts, and the great bronze basin called the Sea, and they carried all the bronze away to Babylon. [18]They also took all the ash buckets, shovels, lamp snuffers, basins, dishes, and all the other bronze articles used for making sacrifices at the Temple. [19]Nebuzaradan, the captain of the guard, also took the small bowls, incense burners, basins, pots, lampstands, dishes, bowls used for liquid offerings, and all the other articles made of pure gold or silver.

[20]The weight of the bronze from the two pillars, the Sea with the twelve bronze oxen beneath it, and the water carts was too great to be measured. These things had been made for the LORD's Temple in the days of King Solomon. [21]Each of the pillars was 27 feet tall and 18 feet in circumference.* They were hollow, with walls 3 inches thick.* [22]The bronze capital on top of each pillar was 7½ feet* high and was decorated with a network of bronze pomegranates all the way around. [23]There were 96 pomegranates on the sides, and a total of 100 on the network around the top.

[24]Nebuzaradan, the captain of the guard, took with him as prisoners Seraiah the high priest, Zephaniah the priest of the second rank, and the three chief gatekeepers. [25]And from among the people still hiding in the city, he took an officer who had been in charge of the Judean army; seven of the king's personal advisers; the army commander's chief secretary, who was in charge of recruitment; and sixty other citizens. [26]Nebuzaradan, the captain of the guard, took them all to the king of Babylon at Riblah. [27]And there at Riblah, in the land of Hamath, the king of Babylon had them all put to death. So the people of Judah were sent into exile from their land.

[28]The number of captives taken to Babylon in the seventh year of Nebuchadnezzar's reign* was 3,023. [29]Then in Nebuchadnezzar's eighteenth year* he took 832 more. [30]In Nebuchadnezzar's twenty-third year* he sent Nebuzaradan, the captain of the guard, who took 745 more—a total of 4,600 captives in all.

[31]In the thirty-seventh year of the exile of King Jehoiachin of Judah, Evil-merodach ascended to the Babylonian throne. He was kind to* Jehoiachin and released him from prison on March 31 of that year.* [32]He spoke kindly to Jehoiachin and gave him a higher place than all the other exiled kings in Babylon. [33]He supplied Jehoiachin with new clothes to replace his prison garb and allowed him to dine in the king's presence for the rest of his life. [34]So the Babylonian king gave him a regular

HOW WE LIVE

Praise and thanksgiving

PSALM 100 Whoever said religion is stiff and boring never read the book of Psalms. They literally overflow with joy. Similarly, your love for God should overflow into praise. Praising God and thanking him for his goodness takes your mind off your problems and shortcomings, causes you to consider and appreciate God's character, and lifts your perspective from the earthly to the heavenly. • Don't let feelings of self-consciousness interfere with your praise and thanksgiving. You're doing it for God, not for others. Praise the Lord enthusiastically, whether in public or private. Hold your hands up in the air, fall to your knees, sit still with your eyes closed—whatever form your praise takes, keep your focus on God and keep it genuine. Thank him for all his blessings. Acknowledge that he is God and that you are dependent on him. Rejoice in the fact that he is perfect, holy, and awesome, and yet he draws near to you in your frail condition; rejoice that he is your Father; rejoice that he provides for your every need. Don't miss out on the joy and excitement of a life that is full of praise.

food allowance as long as he lived. This continued until the day of his death.

51:59 The fourth year of Zedekiah's reign was 593 B.C. **52:4a** Hebrew *on the tenth day of the tenth month,* of the ancient Hebrew lunar calendar. A number of events in Jeremiah can be cross-checked with dates in surviving Babylonian records and related accurately to our modern calendar. This day was January 15, 588 B.C. **52:4b** Hebrew *Nebuchadrezzar,* a variant spelling of Nebuchadnezzar; also in 52:12, 28, 29, 30. **52:6** Hebrew *By the ninth day of the fourth month* [in the eleventh year of Zedekiah's reign]. This day was July 18, 586 B.C.; also see note on 52:4a. **52:7a** Or *the Chaldeans;* similarly in 52:8, 17. **52:7b** Hebrew *the Arabah.* **52:12** Hebrew *On the tenth day of the fifth month,* of the ancient Hebrew lunar calendar. This day was August 17, 586 B.C.; also see note on 52:4a. **52:13** Or *destroyed the houses of all the important people.* **52:14** Or *Chaldean.* **52:21a** Hebrew *18 cubits* [8.1 meters] *tall and 12 cubits* [5.4 meters] *in circumference.* **52:21b** Hebrew *4 fingers thick* [8 centimeters]. **52:22** Hebrew *5 cubits* [2.3 meters]. **52:28** This exile in the seventh year of Nebuchadnezzar's reign occurred in 597 B.C. **52:29** This exile in the eighteenth year of Nebuchadnezzar's reign occurred in 586 B.C. **52:30** This exile in the twenty-third year of Nebuchadnezzar's reign occurred in 581 B.C. **52:31a** Hebrew *He raised the head of.* **52:31b** Hebrew *on the twenty-fifth day of the twelfth month,* of the ancient lunar Hebrew calendar. This day was March 31, 561 B.C.; also see note on 52:4a.

TITUS 3:1-15

Paul ended his letter with an exhortation to live an upright life in society. We are able to live this way because of what God has done to save us and transform us into new people.

Remind the believers to submit to the government and its officers. They should be obedient, always ready to do what is good. [2] They must not slander anyone and must avoid quarreling. Instead, they should be gentle and show true humility to everyone.

[3] Once we, too, were foolish and disobedient. We were misled and became slaves to many lusts and pleasures. Our lives were full of evil and envy, and we hated each other.

[4] But—"When God our Savior revealed his kindness and love, [5] he saved us, not because of the righteous things we had done, but because of his mercy. He washed away our sins, giving us a new birth and new life through the Holy Spirit.* [6] He generously poured out the Spirit upon us through Jesus Christ our Savior. [7] Because of his grace he declared us righteous and gave us confidence that we will inherit eternal life." [8] This is a trustworthy saying, and I want you to insist on these teachings so that all who trust in God will devote themselves to do-

ing good. These teachings are good and beneficial for everyone.

[9] Do not get involved in foolish discussions about spiritual pedigrees* or in quarrels and fights about obedience to Jewish laws. These things are useless and a waste of time. [10] If people are causing divisions among you, give a first and second warning. After that, have nothing more to do with them. [11] For people like that have turned away from the truth, and their own sins condemn them.

[12] I am planning to send either Artemas or Tychicus to you. As soon as one of them arrives, do your best to meet me at Nicopolis, for I have decided to stay there for the winter. [13] Do everything you can to help Zenas the lawyer and Apollos with their trip. See that they are given everything they need. [14] Our people must learn to do good by meeting the urgent needs of others; then they will not be unproductive.

[15] Everybody here sends greetings. Please give my greetings to the believers—all who love us.

May God's grace be with you all.

3:5 Greek *He saved us through the washing of regeneration and renewing of the Holy Spirit.* **3:9** Or *spiritual genealogies.*

PSALM 100:1-5

A psalm of thanksgiving.

[1] **S**hout with joy to the LORD, all the
    earth!
[2]   Worship the LORD with gladness.
    Come before him, singing with joy.
[3] Acknowledge that the LORD is God!
    He made us, and we are his.
    We are his people, the sheep of his
    pasture.
[4] Enter his gates with thanksgiving;
    go into his courts with praise.
    Give thanks to him and praise his
    name.
[5] For the LORD is good.
    His unfailing love continues forever,
    and his faithfulness continues to
    each generation.

PROVERBS 26:18-19

Just as damaging as a madman shooting a deadly weapon is someone who lies to a friend and then says, "I was only joking."

LAMENTATIONS 1:1–2:22

When Jeremiah wrote the funeral dirges that we call Lamentations, the city of Jerusalem—along with its Temple—was in ruins. These are his thoughts as he waded through the consequences of his people's disobedience.

*Jerusalem, once so full of people,
  is now deserted.
She who was once great among the
    nations
  now sits alone like a widow.
Once the queen of all the earth,
  she is now a slave.

2 She sobs through the night;
  tears stream down her cheeks.
Among all her lovers,
  there is no one left to comfort her.
All her friends have betrayed her
  and become her enemies.

3 Judah has been led away into
    captivity,
  oppressed with cruel slavery.
She lives among foreign nations
  and has no place of rest.
Her enemies have chased her down,
  and she has nowhere to turn.

4 The roads to Jerusalem* are in
    mourning,
  for crowds no longer come to
    celebrate the festivals.
The city gates are silent,
  her priests groan,
her young women are crying—
  how bitter is her fate!

5 Her oppressors have become her
    masters,
  and her enemies prosper,
for the LORD has punished Jerusalem
  for her many sins.
Her children have been captured
  and taken away to distant lands.

6 All the majesty of beautiful
    Jerusalem*
  has been stripped away.
Her princes are like starving deer
  searching for pasture.
They are too weak to run
  from the pursuing enemy.

7 In the midst of her sadness and
    wandering,
  Jerusalem remembers her ancient
    splendor.
But now she has fallen to her enemy,
  and there is no one to help her.
Her enemy struck her down
  and laughed as she fell.

8 Jerusalem has sinned greatly,
  so she has been tossed away like
    a filthy rag.
All who once honored her now
    despise her,
  for they have seen her stripped
    naked and humiliated.
All she can do is groan
  and hide her face.

9 She defiled herself with immorality
  and gave no thought to her future.
Now she lies in the gutter
  with no one to lift her out.
"LORD, see my misery," she cries.
  "The enemy has triumphed."

10 The enemy has plundered her
    completely,
  taking every precious thing she
    owns.
She has seen foreigners violate her
    sacred Temple,
  the place the LORD had forbidden
    them to enter.

11 Her people groan as they search for
    bread.
  They have sold their treasures for
    food to stay alive.
"O LORD, look," she mourns,
  "and see how I am despised.

12 "Does it mean nothing to you, all you
    who pass by?
  Look around and see if there is any
    suffering like mine,
which the LORD brought on me
  when he erupted in fierce anger.

13 "He has sent fire from heaven that
    burns in my bones.
  He has placed a trap in my path and
    turned me back.

He has left me devastated,
  racked with sickness all day long.

14 "He wove my sins into ropes
  to hitch me to a yoke of captivity.
The Lord sapped my strength and
    turned me over to my enemies;
  I am helpless in their hands.

15 "The Lord has treated my mighty men
    with contempt.
At his command a great army has
    come
  to crush my young warriors.
The Lord has trampled his beloved
    city*
  like grapes are trampled in a
    winepress.

16 "For all these things I weep;
  tears flow down my cheeks.
No one is here to comfort me;
  any who might encourage me are
    far away.
My children have no future,
  for the enemy has conquered us."

17 Jerusalem reaches out for help,
  but no one comforts her.
Regarding his people Israel,*
  the LORD has said,
"Let their neighbors be their enemies!
  Let them be thrown away like a
    filthy rag!"

18 "The LORD is right," Jerusalem says,
  "for I rebelled against him.
Listen, people everywhere;
  look upon my anguish and despair,
for my sons and daughters
  have been taken captive to distant
    lands.

19 "I begged my allies for help,
  but they betrayed me.
My priests and leaders
  starved to death in the city,
even as they searched for food
  to save their lives.

20 "LORD, see my anguish!
  My heart is broken
and my soul despairs,
  for I have rebelled against you.
In the streets the sword kills,
  and at home there is only death.

21 "Others heard my groans,
  but no one turned to comfort me.
When my enemies heard about my
    troubles,
  they were happy to see what you
    had done.
Oh, bring the day you promised,
  when they will suffer as I have
    suffered.

22 "Look at all their evil deeds, LORD.
  Punish them,
as you have punished me
  for all my sins.
My groans are many,
  and I am sick at heart."

2:1 THE Lord in his anger
  has cast a dark shadow over
    beautiful Jerusalem.*
The fairest of Israel's cities lies in the
    dust,
  thrown down from the heights of
    heaven.
In his day of great anger,
  the Lord has shown no mercy even
    to his Temple.*

2 Without mercy the Lord has destroyed
    every home in Israel.*
In his anger he has broken down
  the fortress walls of beautiful
    Jerusalem.*
He has brought them to the ground,
  dishonoring the kingdom and its
    rulers.

3 All the strength of Israel
  vanishes beneath his fierce anger.
The Lord has withdrawn his
    protection
  as the enemy attacks.
He consumes the whole land of Israel
  like a raging fire.

4 He bends his bow against his people,
  as though he were their enemy.
His strength is used against them
  to kill their finest youth.
His fury is poured out like fire
  on beautiful Jerusalem.*

5 Yes, the Lord has vanquished Israel
  like an enemy.
He has destroyed her palaces
  and demolished her fortresses.

He has brought unending sorrow and
  tears
    upon beautiful Jerusalem.

6 He has broken down his Temple
    as though it were merely a garden
    shelter.
  The LORD has blotted out all memory
    of the holy festivals and Sabbath
    days.
  Kings and priests fall together
    before his fierce anger.

7 The Lord has rejected his own altar;
    he despises his own sanctuary.
  He has given Jerusalem's palaces
    to her enemies.
  They shout in the LORD's Temple
    as though it were a day of
    celebration.

8 The LORD was determined
    to destroy the walls of beautiful
    Jerusalem.
  He made careful plans for their
    destruction,
    then did what he had planned.
  Therefore, the ramparts and walls
    have fallen down before him.

9 Jerusalem's gates have sunk into the
    ground.
  He has smashed their locks and
    bars.

Her kings and princes have been
    exiled to distant lands;
    her law has ceased to exist.
  Her prophets receive
    no more visions from the LORD.

10 The leaders of beautiful Jerusalem
    sit on the ground in silence.
  They are clothed in burlap
    and throw dust on their heads.
  The young women of Jerusalem
    hang their heads in shame.

11 I have cried until the tears no longer
    come;
    my heart is broken.
  My spirit is poured out in agony
    as I see the desperate plight of my
    people.
  Little children and tiny babies
    are fainting and dying in the streets.

12 They cry out to their mothers,
    "We need food and drink!"
  Their lives ebb away in the streets
    like the life of a warrior wounded in
    battle.
  They gasp for life
    as they collapse in their mothers'
    arms.

13 What can I say about you?
    Who has ever seen such sorrow?
  O daughter of Jerusalem,

WHAT THE BIBLE SAYS

Salvation and forgiveness

PHILEMON 1:17 Paul's letter to Philemon highlights the ways in which this new Christian faith changed business as usual in the Greco-Roman world. As the slave owner, Philemon had complete power over Onesimus. It is possible that under Roman law he could have had Onesimus put to death for running away. While on the run, Onesimus ran straight into Paul and soon came to faith in Christ. Now both slave and master were brothers in Christ. Onesimus had to go back, and he was probably shaking in his sandals, but Paul wrote this letter asking Philemon to forgive. Why? On the basis of his own salvation and forgiveness in Christ. All three men had been forgiven and saved; all three had freely received grace from God. Now they had to show it. • The fact of salvation and forgiveness is not for you alone. You've been forgiven, so you must forgive. You've been saved, and this opens wide the doors of your life so you can look at other believers as fellow sinners saved by grace. Show patience to others. After all, it is likely that tomorrow someone will need to be patient with you.

to what can I compare your
anguish?
O virgin daughter of Zion,
how can I comfort you?
For your wound is as deep as the sea.
Who can heal you?

¹⁴ Your prophets have said
so many foolish things, false to the
core.
They did not save you from exile
by pointing out your sins.
Instead, they painted false pictures,
filling you with false hope.

¹⁵ All who pass by jeer at you.
They scoff and insult beautiful
Jerusalem,* saying,
"Is this the city called 'Most Beautiful
in All the World'
and 'Joy of All the Earth'?"

¹⁶ All your enemies mock you.
They scoff and snarl and say,
"We have destroyed her at last!
We have long waited for this day,
and it is finally here!"

¹⁷ But it is the LORD who did just as he
planned.
He has fulfilled the promises of
disaster
he made long ago.
He has destroyed Jerusalem without
mercy.
He has caused her enemies to gloat
over her
and has given them power over her.

¹⁸ Cry aloud* before the Lord,
O walls of beautiful Jerusalem!
Let your tears flow like a river
day and night.
Give yourselves no rest;
give your eyes no relief.

¹⁹ Rise during the night and cry out.
Pour out your hearts like water to
the Lord.
Lift up your hands to him in prayer,
pleading for your children,
for in every street
they are faint with hunger.

²⁰ "O LORD, think about this!
Should you treat your own people
this way?

Should mothers eat their own
children,
those they once bounced on their
knees?
Should priests and prophets be killed
within the Lord's Temple?

²¹ "See them lying in the streets—
young and old,
boys and girls,
killed by the swords of the enemy.
You have killed them in your anger,
slaughtering them without mercy.

²² "You have invited terrors from all
around,
as though you were calling them to
a day of feasting.
In the day of the LORD's anger,
no one has escaped or survived.
The enemy has killed all the children
whom I carried and raised."

1 Each of the first four chapters of this book is an acrostic,
laid out in the order of the Hebrew alphabet. The first word
of each verse begins with a successive Hebrew letter.
Chapters 1, 2, and 4 have one verse for each of the 22 Hebrew
letters. Chapter 3 contains 22 stanzas of three verses each.
Though chapter 5 has 22 verses, it is not an acrostic.
1:4 Hebrew *Zion;* also in 1:17.   1:6 Hebrew *of the daughter
of Zion.*   1:15 Hebrew *the virgin daughter of Judah.*
1:17 Hebrew *Jacob.* The names "Jacob" and "Israel" are often
interchanged throughout the Old Testament, referring
sometimes to the individual patriarch and sometimes to the
nation.   2:1a Hebrew *the daughter of Zion;* also in 2:8, 10,
18.   2:1b Hebrew *his footstool.*   2:2a Hebrew *Jacob;* also in
2:3b. See note on 1:17.   2:2b Hebrew *the daughter of Judah;*
also in 2:5.   2:4 Hebrew *on the tent of the daughter of Zion.*
2:15 Hebrew *the daughter of Jerusalem.*   2:18 Hebrew
Their heart cried.

PHILEMON 1:1-25
Philemon was a friend of Paul's whose slave Onesimus had run away. Onesimus met Paul and came to
faith. Paul then sent him back home with a letter
asking Philemon to receive Onesimus as a new
brother in Christ.

This letter is from Paul, a prisoner for
preaching the Good News about Christ
Jesus, and from our brother Timothy.
I am writing to Philemon, our beloved
co-worker, ² and to our sister Apphia, and
to our fellow soldier Archippus, and to the
church that meets in your* house.
³ May God our Father and the Lord Jesus
Christ give you grace and peace.
⁴ I always thank my God when I pray for
you, Philemon, ⁵ because I keep hearing
about your faith in the Lord Jesus and
your love for all of God's people. ⁶ And I

am praying that you will put into action the generosity that comes from your faith as you understand and experience all the good things we have in Christ. [7]Your love has given me much joy and comfort, my brother, for your kindness has often refreshed the hearts of God's people.

[8]That is why I am boldly asking a favor of you. I could demand it in the name of Christ because it is the right thing for you to do. [9]But because of our love, I prefer simply to ask you. Consider this as a request from me—Paul, an old man and now also a prisoner for the sake of Christ Jesus.*

[10]I appeal to you to show kindness to my child, Onesimus. I became his father in the faith while here in prison. [11]Onesimus* hasn't been of much use to you in the past, but now he is very useful to both of us. [12]I am sending him back to you, and with him comes my own heart.

[13]I wanted to keep him here with me while I am in these chains for preaching the Good News, and he would have helped me on your behalf. [14]But I didn't want to do anything without your consent. I wanted you to help because you were willing, not because you were forced. [15]It seems you lost Onesimus for a little while so that you could have him back forever. [16]He is no longer like a slave to you. He is more than a slave, for he is a beloved brother, especially to me. Now he will mean much more to you, both as a man and as a brother in the Lord.

[17]So if you consider me your partner, welcome him as you would welcome me. [18]If he has wronged you in any way or owes you anything, charge it to me. [19]I, PAUL, WRITE THIS WITH MY OWN HAND: I WILL REPAY IT. AND I WON'T MENTION THAT YOU OWE ME YOUR VERY SOUL!

[20]Yes, my brother, please do me this favor* for the Lord's sake. Give me this encouragement in Christ.

[21]I am confident as I write this letter that you will do what I ask and even more! [22]One more thing—please prepare a guest room for me, for I am hoping that God will answer your prayers and let me return to you soon.

[23]Epaphras, my fellow prisoner in Christ Jesus, sends you his greetings. [24]So do Mark, Aristarchus, Demas, and Luke, my co-workers.

[25]May the grace of the Lord Jesus Christ be with your spirit.

2 Throughout this letter, *you* and *your* are singular except in verses 3, 22, and 25.   9 Or *a prisoner of Christ Jesus.*   11 *Onesimus means "useful."*   20 Greek *onaimen,* a play on the name Onesimus.

PSALM 101:1-8
A psalm of David.

[1] I will sing of your love and justice,
    LORD.
  I will praise you with songs.
[2] I will be careful to live a blameless
    life—
  when will you come to help me?
  I will lead a life of integrity
    in my own home.
[3] I will refuse to look at
    anything vile and vulgar.
  I hate all who deal crookedly;
    I will have nothing to do with them.
[4] I will reject perverse ideas
    and stay away from every evil.
[5] I will not tolerate people who slander
    their neighbors.
  I will not endure conceit and pride.

[6] I will search for faithful people
    to be my companions.
  Only those who are above reproach
    will be allowed to serve me.
[7] I will not allow deceivers to serve in
    my house,
  and liars will not stay in my
    presence.
[8] My daily task will be to ferret out the
    wicked
  and free the city of the LORD from
    their grip.

PROVERBS 26:20
Fire goes out without wood, and quarrels disappear when gossip stops.

LAMENTATIONS 3:1-66
The third of Jeremiah's funeral songs has an element of hope. It's a very personal lyric with a well-known reminder of God's faithfulness.

I am the one who has seen the afflictions
that come from the rod of the
LORD's anger.

2 He has led me into darkness,
shutting out all light.

3 He has turned his hand against me
again and again, all day long.

4 He has made my skin and flesh grow
old.
He has broken my bones.

5 He has besieged and surrounded me
with anguish and distress.

6 He has buried me in a dark place,
like those long dead.

7 He has walled me in, and I cannot
escape.
He has bound me in heavy chains.

8 And though I cry and shout,
he has shut out my prayers.

9 He has blocked my way with a high
stone wall;
he has made my road crooked.

10 He has hidden like a bear or a lion,
waiting to attack me.

11 He has dragged me off the path and
torn me in pieces,
leaving me helpless and devastated.

12 He has drawn his bow
and made me the target for his
arrows.

13 He shot his arrows
deep into my heart.

14 My own people laugh at me.
All day long they sing their mocking
songs.

15 He has filled me with bitterness
and given me a bitter cup of sorrow
to drink.

16 He has made me chew on gravel.
He has rolled me in the dust.

17 Peace has been stripped away,
and I have forgotten what
prosperity is.

18 I cry out, "My splendor is gone!
Everything I had hoped for from the
LORD is lost!"

19 The thought of my suffering and
homelessness
is bitter beyond words.*

20 I will never forget this awful time,
as I grieve over my loss.

21 Yet I still dare to hope
when I remember this:

22 The faithful love of the LORD never
ends!*
His mercies never cease.

23 Great is his faithfulness;
his mercies begin afresh each
morning.

24 I say to myself, "The LORD is my
inheritance;
therefore, I will hope in him!"

25 The LORD is good to those who
depend on him,
to those who search for him.

26 So it is good to wait quietly
for salvation from the LORD.

27 And it is good for people to submit
at an early age
to the yoke of his discipline:

28 Let them sit alone in silence
beneath the LORD's demands.

29 Let them lie face down in the dust,
for there may be hope at last.

30 Let them turn the other cheek to those
who strike them
and accept the insults of their
enemies.

31 For no one is abandoned
by the Lord forever.

32 Though he brings grief, he also shows
compassion
because of the greatness of his
unfailing love.

33 For he does not enjoy hurting people
or causing them sorrow.

34 If people crush underfoot
all the prisoners of the land,

35 if they deprive others of their rights
in defiance of the Most High,

³⁶ if they twist justice in the courts—
doesn't the Lord see all these
things?

³⁷ Who can command things to happen
without the Lord's permission?
³⁸ Does not the Most High
send both calamity and good?
³⁹ Then why should we, mere humans,
complain
when we are punished for our sins?

⁴⁰ Instead, let us test and examine our
ways.
Let us turn back to the LORD.
⁴¹ Let us lift our hearts and hands
to God in heaven and say,
⁴² "We have sinned and rebelled,
and you have not forgiven us.

⁴³ "You have engulfed us with your anger,
chased us down,
and slaughtered us without mercy.
⁴⁴ You have hidden yourself in a cloud
so our prayers cannot reach you.
⁴⁵ You have discarded us as refuse and
garbage
among the nations.

⁴⁶ "All our enemies
have spoken out against us.
⁴⁷ We are filled with fear,
for we are trapped, devastated, and
ruined."
⁴⁸ Tears stream from my eyes
because of the destruction of my
people!

⁴⁹ My tears flow endlessly;
they will not stop
⁵⁰ until the LORD looks down
from heaven and sees.
⁵¹ My heart is breaking
over the fate of all the women of
Jerusalem.

⁵² My enemies, whom I have never
harmed,
hunted me down like a bird.
⁵³ They threw me into a pit
and dropped stones on me.
⁵⁴ The water rose over my head,
and I cried out, "This is the end!"

⁵⁵ But I called on your name, LORD,
from deep within the pit.

⁵⁶ You heard me when I cried, "Listen to
my pleading!
Hear my cry for help!"
⁵⁷ Yes, you came when I called;
you told me, "Do not fear."

⁵⁸ Lord, you are my lawyer! Plead my
case!
For you have redeemed my life.
⁵⁹ You have seen the wrong they have
done to me, LORD.
Be my judge, and prove me right.
⁶⁰ You have seen the vengeful plots
my enemies have laid against me.

⁶¹ LORD, you have heard the vile names
they call me.
You know all about the plans they
have made.
⁶² My enemies whisper and mutter
as they plot against me all day long.
⁶³ Look at them! Whether they sit or
stand,
I am the object of their mocking
songs.

⁶⁴ Pay them back, LORD,
for all the evil they have done.
⁶⁵ Give them hard and stubborn hearts,
and then let your curse fall on them!
⁶⁶ Chase them down in your anger,
destroying them beneath the LORD's
heavens.

3:19 Or *is wormwood and gall.*   **3:22** As in Syriac version;
Hebrew reads *of the LORD keeps us from destruction.*

HEBREWS 1:1-14
Christianity was a belief system that emerged out
of Judaism. Jewish expectations for the promised
Messiah provided the backdrop for Jesus. The writer
of this letter to the Hebrews wanted to cement that
connection.

Long ago God spoke many times and in
many ways to our ancestors through the
prophets. ²And now in these final days, he
has spoken to us through his Son. God
promised everything to the Son as an inheritance, and through the Son he created
the universe. ³The Son radiates God's own
glory and expresses the very character of
God, and he sustains everything by the
mighty power of his command. When he
had cleansed us from our sins, he sat
down in the place of honor at the right
hand of the majestic God in heaven. ⁴This

shows that the Son is far greater than the angels, just as the name God gave him is greater than their names.

[5]For God never said to any angel what he said to Jesus:

"You are my Son.
   Today I have become your Father.*"

God also said,

"I will be his Father,
   and he will be my Son."*

[6]And when he brought his firstborn Son into the world, God said,*

"Let all of God's angels worship him."*

[7]Regarding the angels, he says,

"He sends his angels like the winds,
   his servants like flames of fire."*

[8]But to the Son he says,

"Your throne, O God, endures forever
      and ever.
   You rule with a scepter of justice.
[9] You love justice and hate evil.
      Therefore, O God, your God has
         anointed you,
      pouring out the oil of joy on you
         more than on anyone else."*

[10]He also says to the Son,

"In the beginning, Lord, you laid the
      foundation of the earth
   and made the heavens with your
      hands.
[11] They will perish, but you remain
      forever.
   They will wear out like old clothing.
[12] You will fold them up like a cloak
   and discard them like old clothing.
But you are always the same;
   you will live forever."*

[13]And God never said to any of the angels,

"Sit in the place of honor at my right
      hand
   until I humble your enemies,
      making them a footstool under
         your feet."*

[14]Therefore, angels are only servants—spirits sent to care for people who will inherit salvation.

1:5a Or *Today I reveal you as my Son.* Ps 2:7.   **1:5b** 2 Sam 7:14.   **1:6a** Or *when he again brings his firstborn son into the world, God will say.*   **1:6b** Deut 32:43.   **1:7** Ps 104:4 (Greek version).   **1:8-9** Ps 45:6-7.   **1:10-12** Ps 102:25-27.   **1:13** Ps 110:1.

PSALM 102:1-28
A prayer of one overwhelmed with trouble, pouring out problems before the LORD.

[1] L ORD, hear my prayer!
      Listen to my plea!
[2] Don't turn away from me
      in my time of distress.
   Bend down to listen,
      and answer me quickly when I call
         to you.
[3] For my days disappear like smoke,
      and my bones burn like red-hot
         coals.
[4] My heart is sick, withered like grass,
      and I have lost my appetite.
[5] Because of my groaning,
      I am reduced to skin and bones.
[6] I am like an owl in the desert,
      like a little owl in a far-off
         wilderness.
[7] I lie awake,
      lonely as a solitary bird on the roof.
[8] My enemies taunt me day after day.
      They mock and curse me.
[9] I eat ashes for food.
      My tears run down into my drink
[10] because of your anger and wrath.
      For you have picked me up and
         thrown me out.
[11] My life passes as swiftly as the evening
         shadows.
      I am withering away like grass.

[12] But you, O L ORD, will sit on your
         throne forever.
      Your fame will endure to every
         generation.
[13] You will arise and have mercy on
         Jerusalem*—
      and now is the time to pity her,
      now is the time you promised to
         help.
[14] For your people love every stone in her
         walls
      and cherish even the dust in her
         streets.
[15] Then the nations will tremble before
         the L ORD.

The kings of the earth will tremble
  before his glory.
16 For the LORD will rebuild Jerusalem.
  He will appear in his glory.
17 He will listen to the prayers of the
    destitute.
  He will not reject their pleas.

18 Let this be recorded for future
    generations,
  so that a people not yet born will
    praise the LORD.
19 Tell them the LORD looked down
    from his heavenly sanctuary.
  He looked down to earth from heaven
20 to hear the groans of the prisoners,
    to release those condemned to die.
21 And so the LORD's fame will be
    celebrated in Zion,
  his praises in Jerusalem,
22 when multitudes gather together
    and kingdoms come to worship
    the LORD.

23 He broke my strength in midlife,
    cutting short my days.

24 But I cried to him, "O my God, who
    lives forever,
  don't take my life while I am
    so young!
25 Long ago you laid the foundation of
    the earth
  and made the heavens with your
    hands.
26 They will perish, but you remain forever;
    they will wear out like old clothing.
  You will change them like a garment
    and discard them.
27 But you are always the same;
    you will live forever.
28 The children of your people
    will live in security.
  Their children's children
    will thrive in your presence."

102:13 Hebrew *Zion*; also in 102:16.

PROVERBS 26:21-22
A quarrelsome person starts fights as easily as hot embers light charcoal or fire lights wood. □ Rumors are dainty morsels that sink deep into one's heart.

WHAT THE BIBLE SAYS

Angels

HEBREWS 1:5-14 The book of Hebrews gives many examples of how Jesus fulfilled the Old Testament prophecies concerning the Messiah. Because of the difficulty many Jews had, and still have, in accepting Jesus as Messiah, the author of the book of Hebrews explains not only Jesus' fulfillment of prophecy, but also his superiority to angels (God's messengers), the high priests, and even Moses. • The Old Testament is quoted repeatedly in demonstrating Christ's greatness in comparison to the angels: (1) Christ is called "Son of God," a title never given to an angel (1:5-6). (2) Angels are important, but are still only servants under God (1:7, 14). (3) Christ's Kingdom is forever, and the angels are servants within that Kingdom (1:8-9). (4) Christ is the Creator of everything in the world, including the angels (1:10). (5) God gives Christ a unique honor, seating him at his right hand (1:13). • God greatly values his angelic messengers for the role they played in creation. Yet we must remember that they are not to be the focus of our worship. Only God is worthy of our worship.

LAMENTATIONS 4:1–5:22
Jeremiah addressed the fact that while the judgment Judah received was tough, it was deserved. He closed his final song with a prayer for restoration.

How the gold has lost its luster!
  Even the finest gold has become
    dull.
The sacred gemstones
  lie scattered in the streets!

2 See how the precious children of
    Jerusalem,*
  worth their weight in fine gold,
are now treated like pots of clay
  made by a common potter.

3 Even the jackals feed their young,
  but not my people Israel.
They ignore their children's cries,
  like ostriches in the desert.

4 The parched tongues of their little
    ones
  stick to the roofs of their mouths in
    thirst.
The children cry for bread,
  but no one has any to give them.

5 The people who once ate the richest
    foods
  now beg in the streets for anything
    they can get.
Those who once wore the finest
    clothes
  now search the garbage dumps for
    food.

6 The guilt* of my people
  is greater than that of Sodom,
where utter disaster struck in a
    moment
  and no hand offered help.

7 Our princes once glowed with
    health—
  brighter than snow, whiter than
    milk.
Their faces were as ruddy as rubies,
  their appearance like fine jewels.*

8 But now their faces are blacker than
    soot.
  No one recognizes them in the
    streets.

Their skin sticks to their bones;
  it is as dry and hard as wood.

9 Those killed by the sword are better off
  than those who die of hunger.
Starving, they waste away
  for lack of food from the fields.

10 Tenderhearted women
  have cooked their own children.
They have eaten them
  to survive the siege.

11 But now the anger of the LORD is
    satisfied.
  His fierce anger has been poured out.
He started a fire in Jerusalem*
  that burned the city to its
    foundations.

12 Not a king in all the earth—
  no one in all the world—
would have believed that an enemy
  could march through the gates of
    Jerusalem.

13 Yet it happened because of the sins of
    her prophets
  and the sins of her priests,
who defiled the city
  by shedding innocent blood.

14 They wandered blindly
  through the streets,
so defiled by blood
  that no one dared touch them.

15 "Get away!" the people shouted at
    them.
  "You're defiled! Don't touch us!"
So they fled to distant lands
  and wandered among foreign
    nations,
but none would let them stay.

16 The LORD himself has scattered them,
  and he no longer helps them.
People show no respect for the priests
  and no longer honor the leaders.

17 We looked in vain for our allies
  to come and save us,
but we were looking to nations
  that could not help us.

¹⁸ We couldn't go into the streets
    without danger to our lives.
Our end was near; our days were
    numbered.
    We were doomed!

¹⁹ Our enemies were swifter than eagles
    in flight.
If we fled to the mountains, they
    found us.
If we hid in the wilderness,
    they were waiting for us there.

²⁰ Our king—the LORD's anointed, the
    very life of our nation—
was caught in their snares.
We had thought that his shadow
    would protect us against any nation
    on earth!

²¹ Are you rejoicing in the land of Uz,
    O people of Edom?
But you, too, must drink from the cup
    of the LORD's anger.
You, too, will be stripped naked in
    your drunkenness.

²² O beautiful Jerusalem,* your
    punishment will end;
    you will soon return from exile.
But Edom, your punishment is just
    beginning;
    soon your many sins will be exposed.

⁵:¹ LORD, remember what has happened
    to us.
    See how we have been disgraced!

² Our inheritance has been turned over
    to strangers,
    our homes to foreigners.

³ We are orphaned and fatherless.
    Our mothers are widowed.

⁴ We have to pay for water to drink,
    and even firewood is expensive.

⁵ Those who pursue us are at our heels;
    we are exhausted but are given
    no rest.

⁶ We submitted to Egypt and Assyria
    to get enough food to survive.

⁷ Our ancestors sinned, but they have
    died—
and we are suffering the
    punishment they deserved!

⁸ Slaves have now become our masters;
    there is no one left to rescue us.

⁹ We hunt for food at the risk of our lives,
    for violence rules the countryside.

¹⁰ The famine has blackened our skin
    as though baked in an oven.

¹¹ Our enemies rape the women in
    Jerusalem*
    and the young girls in all the towns
    of Judah.

¹² Our princes are being hanged by their
    thumbs,
    and our elders are treated with
    contempt.

¹³ Young men are led away to work at
    millstones,
    and boys stagger under heavy loads
    of wood.

¹⁴ The elders no longer sit in the city
    gates;
    the young men no longer dance and
    sing.

¹⁵ Joy has left our hearts;
    our dancing has turned to
    mourning.

¹⁶ The garlands have* fallen from our
    heads.
    Weep for us because we have sinned.

¹⁷ Our hearts are sick and weary,
    and our eyes grow dim with tears.

¹⁸ For Jerusalem* is empty and desolate,
    a place haunted by jackals.

¹⁹ But LORD, you remain the same
    forever!
    Your throne continues from
    generation to generation.

²⁰ Why do you continue to forget us?
    Why have you abandoned us for
    so long?

²¹ Restore us, O LORD, and bring us back
    to you again!
    Give us back the joys we once had!

²² Or have you utterly rejected us?
    Are you angry with us still?

4:2 Hebrew *precious sons of Zion.*   4:6 Or *punishment.*
4:7 Hebrew *like lapis lazuli.*   4:11 Hebrew *in Zion.*
4:22 Hebrew *O daughter of Zion.*   5:11 Hebrew *in Zion.*
5:16 Or *The crown has.*   5:18 Hebrew *Mount Zion.*

HEBREWS 2:1-18

The book of Hebrews describes Jesus from many
different perspectives. In today's reading Jesus is
presented as someone who understands the human
experience because though he was God, he was
fully human.

So we must listen very carefully to the truth we have heard, or we may drift away from it. ²For the message God delivered through angels has always stood firm, and every violation of the law and every act of disobedience was punished. ³So what makes us think we can escape if we ignore this great salvation that was first announced by the Lord Jesus himself and then delivered to us by those who heard him speak? ⁴And God confirmed the message by giving signs and wonders and various miracles and gifts of the Holy Spirit whenever he chose.

⁵And furthermore, it is not angels who will control the future world we are talking about. ⁶For in one place the Scriptures say,

"What are mere mortals that you
    should think about them,
or a son of man* that you should
    care for him?
⁷ Yet you made them only a little lower
    than the angels
and crowned them with glory and
    honor.*
⁸ You gave them authority over all
    things."*

Now when it says "all things," it means nothing is left out. But we have not yet seen all things put under their authority. ⁹What we do see is Jesus, who was given a position "a little lower than the angels"; and because he suffered death for us, he is now "crowned with glory and honor." Yes, by God's grace, Jesus tasted death for everyone. ¹⁰God, for whom and through whom everything was made, chose to bring many children into glory. And it was only right that he should make Jesus, through his suffering, a perfect leader, fit to bring them into their salvation.

¹¹So now Jesus and the ones he makes holy have the same Father. That is why Jesus is not ashamed to call them his brothers and sisters.* ¹²For he said to God,

"I will proclaim your name to my
    brothers and sisters.
I will praise you among your
    assembled people."*

¹³He also said,

"I will put my trust in him,"

that is, "I and the children God has given me."*

¹⁴Because God's children are human beings—made of flesh and blood—the Son also became flesh and blood. For only as a human being could he die, and only by dying could he break the power of the devil, who had* the power of death. ¹⁵Only in this way could he set free all who have lived their lives as slaves to the fear of dying.

¹⁶We also know that the Son did not come to help angels; he came to help the descendants of Abraham. ¹⁷Therefore, it was necessary for him to be made in every respect like us, his brothers and sisters,* so that he could be our merciful and faithful High Priest before God. Then he could offer a sacrifice that would take away the sins of the people. ¹⁸Since he himself has gone through suffering and testing, he is able to help us when we are being tested.

2:6 Or *the Son of Man.*   2:7 Some manuscripts add *You gave them charge of everything you made.*   2:6-8 Ps 8:4-6 (Greek version).   2:11 Greek *brothers;* also in 2:12.
2:12 Ps 22:22.   2:13 Isa 8:17-18.   2:14 Or *has.*
2:17 Greek *like the brothers.*

PSALM 103:1-22
A psalm of David.

¹ **L**et all that I am praise the LORD;
    with my whole heart, I will praise
        his holy name.
² Let all that I am praise the LORD;
    may I never forget the good things
        he does for me.
³ He forgives all my sins
    and heals all my diseases.
⁴ He redeems me from death
    and crowns me with love and
        tender mercies.
⁵ He fills my life with good things.
    My youth is renewed like the eagle's!

⁶ The LORD gives righteousness
    and justice to all who are treated
        unfairly.
⁷ He revealed his character to Moses
    and his deeds to the people of Israel.
⁸ The LORD is compassionate and
        merciful,
    slow to get angry and filled with
        unfailing love.
⁹ He will not constantly accuse us,

nor remain angry forever.
¹⁰ He does not punish us for all our sins;
    he does not deal harshly with us, as
        we deserve.
¹¹ For his unfailing love toward those
        who fear him
    is as great as the height of the
        heavens above the earth.
¹² He has removed our sins as far
        from us
    as the east is from the west.
¹³ The LORD is like a father to his children,
    tender and compassionate to those
        who fear him.
¹⁴ For he knows how weak we are;
    he remembers we are only dust.
¹⁵ Our days on earth are like grass;
    like wildflowers, we bloom and die.
¹⁶ The wind blows, and we are gone—
    as though we had never been here.
¹⁷ But the love of the LORD remains
        forever
    with those who fear him.
    His salvation extends to the children's
        children

¹⁸   of those who are faithful to his
            covenant,
    of those who obey his
        commandments!

¹⁹ The LORD has made the heavens his
        throne;
    from there he rules over everything.

²⁰ Praise the LORD, you angels,
    you mighty ones who carry out his
        plans,
    listening for each of his commands.
²¹ Yes, praise the LORD, you armies of
        angels
    who serve him and do his will!
²² Praise the LORD, everything he has
        created,
    everything in all his kingdom.

Let all that I am praise the LORD.

PROVERBS 26:23
Smooth* words may hide a wicked heart,
just as a pretty glaze covers a clay pot.

26:23 As in Greek version; Hebrew reads *Burning*.

WHAT THE BIBLE SAYS

The reality of hell

HEBREWS 2:2-3 How could a loving God send anyone to hell? It's a question you're sure to hear, especially from those cynical about your faith. No doubt about it, hell is a difficult topic, and the facts are no less difficult. • First, understand that hell was prepared for the devil and his demons (Matthew 25:41; February 8); it was not intended for humanity. However, humanity rebelled against God, as had the devil and his demons. In the parable in Matthew 25:31-46, God separates those who have rebelled from those who believe. The faithful go to heaven because they have chosen faith; the unbelievers go to hell—a place of eternal separation from God—because that too is what they have chosen. • Second, consider that God does not desire anyone to go to hell, but eventually the opportunities to be saved will run out. The message of salvation can be shared countless times, and yet the person who is hearing it might continue to resist. God is patient with people who turn away from his offer of salvation, but eventually those who persist in their failure to embrace true saving faith will find that his patience has run out. • Hell is real; it is the destiny of those who refuse to believe. But heaven is likewise a reality; and those who trust in God will never regret their decision.

EZEKIEL 1:1–3:15

Ezekiel was born into a priestly family. He prophesied to the people of Judah both before and after they were exiled to Babylon.

On July 31* of my thirtieth year,* while I [Ezekiel] was with the Judean exiles beside the Kebar River in Babylon, the heavens were opened and I saw visions of God. ²This happened during the fifth year of King Jehoiachin's captivity. ³(The LORD gave this message to Ezekiel son of Buzi, a priest, beside the Kebar River in the land of the Babylonians,* and he felt the hand of the LORD take hold of him.)

⁴As I looked, I saw a great storm coming from the north, driving before it a huge cloud that flashed with lightning and shone with brilliant light. There was fire inside the cloud, and in the middle of the fire glowed something like gleaming amber.* ⁵From the center of the cloud came four living beings that looked human, ⁶except that each had four faces and four wings. ⁷Their legs were straight, and their feet had hooves like those of a calf and shone like burnished bronze. ⁸Under each of their four wings I could see human hands. So each of the four beings had four faces and four wings. ⁹The wings of each living being touched the wings of the beings beside it. Each one moved straight forward in any direction without turning around.

¹⁰Each had a human face in the front, the face of a lion on the right side, the face of an ox on the left side, and the face of an eagle at the back. ¹¹Each had two pairs of outstretched wings—one pair stretched out to touch the wings of the living beings on either side of it, and the other pair covered its body. ¹²They went in whatever direction the spirit chose, and they moved straight forward in any direction without turning around.

¹³The living beings looked like bright coals of fire or brilliant torches, and light-

ning seemed to flash back and forth among them. ¹⁴And the living beings darted to and fro like flashes of lightning.

¹⁵As I looked at these beings, I saw four wheels touching the ground beside them, one wheel belonging to each. ¹⁶The wheels sparkled as if made of beryl. All four wheels looked alike and were made the same; each wheel had a second wheel turning crosswise within it. ¹⁷The beings could move in any of the four directions they faced, without turning as they moved. ¹⁸The rims of the four wheels were tall and frightening, and they were covered with eyes all around.

¹⁹When the living beings moved, the wheels moved with them. When they flew upward, the wheels went up, too. ²⁰The spirit of the living beings was in the wheels. So wherever the spirit went, the wheels and the living beings also went. ²¹When the beings moved, the wheels moved. When the beings stopped, the wheels stopped. When the beings flew upward, the wheels rose up, for the spirit of the living beings was in the wheels.

²²Spread out above them was a surface like the sky, glittering like crystal. ²³Beneath this surface the wings of each living being stretched out to touch the others' wings, and each had two wings covering its body. ²⁴As they flew, their wings sounded to me like waves crashing against the shore or like the voice of the Almighty* or like the shouting of a mighty army. When they stopped, they let down their wings. ²⁵As they stood with wings lowered, a voice spoke from beyond the crystal surface above them.

²⁶Above this surface was something that looked like a throne made of blue lapis lazuli. And on this throne high above was a figure whose appearance resembled a man. ²⁷From what appeared to be his waist up, he looked like gleaming amber,

flickering like a fire. And from his waist down, he looked like a burning flame, shining with splendor. ²⁸All around him was a glowing halo, like a rainbow shining in the clouds on a rainy day. This is what the glory of the LORD looked like to me. When I saw it, I fell face down on the ground, and I heard someone's voice speaking to me.

^{2:1}"STAND up, son of man," said the voice. "I want to speak with you." ²The Spirit came into me as he spoke, and he set me on my feet. I listened carefully to his words. ³"Son of man," he said, "I am sending you to the nation of Israel, a rebellious nation that has rebelled against me. They and their ancestors have been rebelling against me to this very day. ⁴They are a stubborn and hard-hearted people. But I am sending you to say to them, 'This is what the Sovereign LORD says!' ⁵And whether they listen or refuse to listen—for remember, they are rebels—at least they will know they have had a prophet among them.

⁶"Son of man, do not fear them or their words. Don't be afraid even though their threats surround you like nettles and briers and stinging scorpions. Do not be dismayed by their dark scowls, even though they are rebels. ⁷You must give them my messages whether they listen or not. But they won't listen, for they are completely rebellious! ⁸Son of man, listen to what I say to you. Do not join them in their rebellion. Open your mouth, and eat what I give you."

⁹Then I looked and saw a hand reaching out to me. It held a scroll, ¹⁰which he unrolled. And I saw that both sides were covered with funeral songs, words of sorrow, and pronouncements of doom.

^{3:1}THE voice said to me, "Son of man, eat what I am giving you—eat this scroll! Then go and give its message to the people of Israel." ²So I opened my mouth, and he fed me the scroll. ³"Fill your stomach with this," he said. And when I ate it, it tasted as sweet as honey in my mouth.

⁴Then he said, "Son of man, go to the people of Israel and give them my messages. ⁵I am not sending you to a foreign people whose language you cannot understand. ⁶No, I am not sending you to people with strange and difficult speech. If I did,

they would listen! ⁷But the people of Israel won't listen to you any more than they listen to me! For the whole lot of them are hard-hearted and stubborn. ⁸But look, I have made you as obstinate and hard-hearted as they are. ⁹I have made your forehead as hard as the hardest rock! So don't be afraid of them or fear their angry looks, even though they are rebels."

¹⁰Then he added, "Son of man, let all my words sink deep into your own heart first. Listen to them carefully for yourself. ¹¹Then go to your people in exile and say to them, 'This is what the Sovereign LORD says!' Do this whether they listen to you or not."

¹²Then the Spirit lifted me up, and I heard a loud rumbling sound behind me. (May the glory of the LORD be praised in his place!)* ¹³It was the sound of the wings of the living beings as they brushed against each other and the rumbling of their wheels beneath them.

¹⁴The Spirit lifted me up and took me away. I went in bitterness and turmoil, but the LORD's hold on me was strong. ¹⁵Then I came to the colony of Judean exiles in Tel-abib, beside the Kebar River. I was overwhelmed and sat among them for seven days.

1:1a Hebrew *On the fifth day of the fourth month,* of the ancient Hebrew lunar calendar. A number of dates in Ezekiel can be cross-checked with dates in surviving Babylonian records and related accurately to our modern calendar. This event occurred on July 31, 593 B.C. **1:1b** Or *in the thirtieth year.* **1:3** Or *Chaldeans.* **1:4** Or *like burnished metal;* also in 1:27. **1:24** Hebrew *Shaddai.* **3:12** A possible reading for this verse is *Then the Spirit lifted me up, and as the glory of the LORD rose from its place, I heard a loud rumbling sound behind me.*

HEBREWS 3:1-19

On a list of the most important players in Old Testament history, Moses would definitely be near the top. Here, the writer of Hebrews compares Jesus to Moses, explaining to his Jewish audience that Jesus was far greater than even Moses.

And so, dear brothers and sisters who belong to God and* are partners with those called to heaven, think carefully about this Jesus whom we declare to be God's messenger* and High Priest. ²For he was faithful to God, who appointed him, just as Moses served faithfully when he was entrusted with God's entire* house.

NOVEMBER1

³But Jesus deserves far more glory than Moses, just as a person who builds a house deserves more praise than the house itself. ⁴For every house has a builder, but the one who built everything is God.

⁵Moses was certainly faithful in God's house as a servant. His work was an illustration of the truths God would reveal later. ⁶But Christ, as the Son, is in charge of God's entire house. And we are God's house, if we keep our courage and remain confident in our hope in Christ.*

⁷That is why the Holy Spirit says,

"Today when you hear his voice,
⁸   don't harden your hearts
as Israel did when they rebelled,
   when they tested me in the
      wilderness.
⁹ There your ancestors tested and tried
      my patience,
   even though they saw my miracles
      for forty years.
¹⁰ So I was angry with them, and I said,
   'Their hearts always turn away from me.
   They refuse to do what I tell them.'
¹¹ So in my anger I took an oath:
   'They will never enter my place
      of rest.'"*

¹²Be careful then, dear brothers and sisters.* Make sure that your own hearts are not evil and unbelieving, turning you away from the living God. ¹³You must warn each other every day, while it is still "today," so that none of you will be deceived by sin and hardened against God. ¹⁴For if we are faithful to the end, trusting God just as firmly as when we first believed, we will share in all that belongs to Christ. ¹⁵Remember what it says:

"Today when you hear his voice,
   don't harden your hearts
   as Israel did when they rebelled."*

¹⁶And who was it who rebelled against God, even though they heard his voice? Wasn't it the people Moses led out of Egypt? ¹⁷And who made God angry for forty years? Wasn't it the people who sinned, whose corpses lay in the wilderness? ¹⁸And to whom was God speaking when he took an oath that they would never enter his rest? Wasn't it the people who disobeyed him? ¹⁹So we see that because of their unbelief they were not able to enter his rest.

3:1a Greek *And so, holy brothers who.*   3:1b Greek *God's apostle.*   3:2 Some manuscripts omit *entire.*   3:6 Some manuscripts add *faithful to the end.*   3:7-11 Ps 95:7-11.
3:12 Greek *brothers.*   3:15 Ps 95:7-8.

PSALM 104:1-23
Let all that I am praise the LORD.

O LORD my God, how great you are!
   You are robed with honor and
      majesty.

Following Jesus

EZEKIEL 2:3-8 Following Jesus means listening for what he has to say—in your times of prayer, in your Bible reading, in your listening to sermons, and in your times of quiet reflection. That's exactly what the Israelites were *not* doing and why God was sending Ezekiel to them. But Ezekiel had the unenviable task of bringing a message to people who weren't going to listen to him. • Actions begin in the thoughts and heart. If our thoughts and hearts are with God, listening to him, then we can follow as we should. If we rebel, refuse to hear God's message, or are simply too busy to spend any time listening to God, then we will find ourselves straying off in the wrong direction. Listening is therefore an act of discipleship. • How can you "hear" God speak? You might feel a "prompting." You might sense God speaking directly to you from words in Scripture or from the words in a sermon. Often, you will pray about an issue and sense a calm that clears your thoughts. The guidance toward a decision brings peace to your heart.

2   You are dressed in a robe of light.
You stretch out the starry curtain of
the heavens;
3   you lay out the rafters of your home
in the rain clouds.
You make the clouds your chariot;
you ride upon the wings of the
wind.
4 The winds are your messengers;
flames of fire are your servants.*

5 You placed the world on its foundation
so it would never be moved.
6 You clothed the earth with floods
of water,
water that covered even the
mountains.
7 At your command, the water fled;
at the sound of your thunder,
it hurried away.
8 Mountains rose and valleys sank
to the levels you decreed.
9 Then you set a firm boundary for
the seas,
so they would never again cover
the earth.

10 You make springs pour water into
the ravines,
so streams gush down from the
mountains.
11 They provide water for all the animals,
and the wild donkeys quench their
thirst.
12 The birds nest beside the streams
and sing among the branches of
the trees.
13 You send rain on the mountains from
your heavenly home,
and you fill the earth with the fruit
of your labor.
14 You cause grass to grow for the livestock
and plants for people to use.

You allow them to produce food from
the earth—
15   wine to make them glad,
olive oil to soothe their skin,
and bread to give them strength.
16 The trees of the LORD are well cared
for—
the cedars of Lebanon that he
planted.
17 There the birds make their nests,
and the storks make their homes
in the cypresses.
18 High in the mountains live the wild
goats,
and the rocks form a refuge for
the hyraxes.*

19 You made the moon to mark the
seasons,
and the sun knows when to set.
20 You send the darkness, and it becomes
night,
when all the forest animals prowl
about.
21 Then the young lions roar for their prey,
stalking the food provided by God.
22 At dawn they slink back
into their dens to rest.
23 Then people go off to their work,
where they labor until evening.

104:4 Greek version reads *He sends his angels like the winds,
/ his servants like flames of fire.* Compare Heb 1:7.
104:18 Or *coneys*, or *rock badgers*.

PROVERBS 26:24-26

People may cover their hatred with
pleasant words, but they're deceiving
you. They pretend to be kind, but don't
believe them. Their hearts are full of
many evils.* While their hatred may be
concealed by trickery, their wrongdoing
will be exposed in public.

26:25 Hebrew *seven evils.*

NOVEMBER**2**

EZEKIEL 3:16–6:14

When Ezekiel was born, a good king—Josiah—ruled
Judah. Despite Josiah's significant reforms and the
preaching of prophets like Jeremiah and Ezekiel,
the nation was so entrenched in sin that judgment
and exile became unavoidable.

After seven days the LORD gave me [Ezek-
iel] a message. He said, [17]"Son of man, I
have appointed you as a watchman for Israel. Whenever you receive a message
from me, warn people immediately. [18]If I

warn the wicked, saying, 'You are under the penalty of death,' but you fail to deliver the warning, they will die in their sins. And I will hold you responsible for their deaths. [19]If you warn them and they refuse to repent and keep on sinning, they will die in their sins. But you will have saved yourself because you obeyed me.

[20]"If righteous people turn away from their righteous behavior and ignore the obstacles I put in their way, they will die. And if you do not warn them, they will die in their sins. None of their righteous acts will be remembered, and I will hold you responsible for their deaths. [21]But if you warn righteous people not to sin and they listen to you and do not sin, they will live, and you will have saved yourself, too."

[22]Then the LORD took hold of me and said, "Get up and go out into the valley, and I will speak to you there." [23]So I got up and went, and there I saw the glory of the LORD, just as I had seen in my first vision by the Kebar River. And I fell face down on the ground.

[24]Then the Spirit came into me and set me on my feet. He spoke to me and said, "Go to your house and shut yourself in. [25]There, son of man, you will be tied with ropes so you cannot go out among the people. [26]And I will make your tongue stick to the roof of your mouth so that you will be speechless and unable to rebuke them, for they are rebels. [27]But when I give you a message, I will loosen your tongue and let you speak. Then you will say to them, 'This is what the Sovereign LORD says!' Those who choose to listen will listen, but those who refuse will refuse, for they are rebels.

4:1"AND now, son of man, take a large clay brick and set it down in front of you. Then draw a map of the city of Jerusalem on it. [2]Show the city under siege. Build a wall around it so no one can escape. Set up the enemy camp, and surround the city with siege ramps and battering rams. [3]Then take an iron griddle and place it between you and the city. Turn toward the city and demonstrate how harsh the siege will be against Jerusalem. This will be a warning to the people of Israel.

[4]"Now lie on your left side and place the sins of Israel on yourself. You are to bear their sins for the number of days you lie there on your side. [5]I am requiring you to bear Israel's sins for 390 days—one day for each year of their sin. [6]After that, turn over and lie on your right side for 40 days—one day for each year of Judah's sin.

[7]"Meanwhile, keep staring at the siege of Jerusalem. Lie there with your arm bared and prophesy her destruction. [8]I will tie you up with ropes so you won't be able to turn from side to side until the days of your siege have been completed.

[9]"Now go and get some wheat, barley, beans, lentils, millet, and emmer wheat, and mix them together in a storage jar. Use them to make bread for yourself during the 390 days you will be lying on your side. [10]Ration this out to yourself, eight ounces* of food for each day, and eat it at set times. [11]Then measure out a jar* of water for each day, and drink it at set times. [12]Prepare and eat this food as you would barley cakes. While all the people are watching, bake it over a fire using dried human dung as fuel and then eat the bread." [13]Then the LORD said, "This is how Israel will eat defiled bread in the Gentile lands to which I will banish them!"

[14]Then I said, "O Sovereign LORD, must I be defiled by using human dung? For I have never been defiled before. From the time I was a child until now I have never eaten any animal that died of sickness or was killed by other animals. I have never eaten any meat forbidden by the law."

[15]"All right," the LORD said. "You may bake your bread with cow dung instead of human dung." [16]Then he told me, "Son of man, I will make food very scarce in Jerusalem. It will be weighed out with great care and eaten fearfully. The water will be rationed out drop by drop, and the people will drink it with dismay. [17]Lacking food and water, people will look at one another in terror, and they will waste away under their punishment.

5:1"SON of man, take a sharp sword and use it as a razor to shave your head and beard. Use a scale to weigh the hair into three equal parts. [2]Place a third of it at the center of your map of Jerusalem. After acting out the siege, burn it there. Scatter another third across your map and chop it with a sword. Scatter the last third to the wind, for I will scatter my people with the sword. ³Keep just a bit of the hair and tie it up in your robe. ⁴Then take some of these hairs out and throw them into the fire, burning them up. A fire will then spread from this remnant and destroy all of Israel.

⁵"This is what the Sovereign LORD says: This is an illustration of what will happen to Jerusalem. I placed her at the center of the nations, ⁶but she has rebelled against my regulations and decrees and has been even more wicked than the surrounding nations. She has refused to obey the regulations and decrees I gave her to follow.

⁷"Therefore, this is what the Sovereign LORD says: You people have behaved worse than your neighbors and have refused to obey my decrees and regulations. You have not even lived up to the standards of the nations around you. ⁸Therefore, I myself, the Sovereign LORD, am now your enemy. I will punish you publicly while all the nations watch. ⁹Because of your detestable idols, I will punish you like I have never punished anyone before or ever will again. ¹⁰Parents will eat their own children, and children will eat their parents. I will punish you and scatter to the winds the few who survive.

¹¹"As surely as I live, says the Sovereign LORD, I will cut you off completely. I will show you no pity at all because you have defiled my Temple with your vile images and detestable sins. ¹²A third of your people will die in the city from disease and famine. A third of them will be slaughtered by the enemy outside the city walls. And I will scatter a third to the winds, chasing them with my sword. ¹³Then at last my anger will be spent, and I will be satisfied. And when my fury against them has subsided, all Israel will know that I, the LORD, have spoken to them in my jealous anger.

¹⁴"So I will turn you into a ruin, a mockery in the eyes of the surrounding nations and to all who pass by. ¹⁵You will become an object of mockery and taunting and horror. You will be a warning to all the nations around you. They will see what happens when the LORD punishes a nation in anger and rebukes it, says the LORD.

¹⁶"I will shower you with the deadly arrows of famine to destroy you. The famine will become more and more severe until every crumb of food is gone. ¹⁷And along with the famine, wild animals will attack you and rob you of your children. Disease and war will stalk your land, and I will bring the sword of the enemy against you. I, the LORD, have spoken!"

6:1AGAIN a message came to me from the LORD: ²"Son of man, turn and face the mountains of Israel and prophesy against them. ³Proclaim this message from the Sovereign LORD against the mountains of Israel. This is what the Sovereign LORD says to the mountains and hills and to the ravines and valleys: I am about to bring war upon you, and I will smash your pagan shrines. ⁴All your altars will be demolished, and your places of worship will be destroyed. I will kill your people in front of your idols.* ⁵I will lay your corpses in front of your idols and scatter your bones around your altars. ⁶Wherever you live there will be desolation, and I will destroy your pagan shrines. Your altars will be demolished, your idols will be smashed, your places of worship will be torn down, and all the religious objects you have made will be destroyed. ⁷The place will be littered with corpses, and you will know that I alone am the LORD.

⁸"But I will let a few of my people escape destruction, and they will be scattered among the nations of the world. ⁹Then when they are exiled among the nations, they will remember me. They will recognize how hurt I am by their unfaithful hearts and lustful eyes that long for their idols. Then at last they will hate themselves for all their detestable sins. ¹⁰They will know that I alone am the LORD and that I was serious when I said I would bring this calamity on them.

¹¹"This is what the Sovereign LORD says: Clap your hands in horror, and stamp your feet. Cry out because of all the detestable sins the people of Israel have committed. Now they are going to die from war and famine and disease. ¹²Disease will strike down those who are far away in exile. War will destroy those who are nearby. And anyone who survives will

be killed by famine. So at last I will spend my fury on them. [13]They will know that I am the LORD when their dead lie scattered among their idols and altars on every hill and mountain and under every green tree and every great shade tree—the places where they offered sacrifices to their idols. [14]I will crush them and make their cities desolate from the wilderness in the south to Riblah* in the north. Then they will know that I am the LORD."

4:10 Hebrew *20 shekels* [228 grams].   4:11 Hebrew *⅙ of a hin* [about 1 pint or 0.6 liters].   6:4 The Hebrew term (literally *round things*) probably alludes to dung; also in 6:5, 6, 9, 13.   6:14 As in some Hebrew manuscripts; most Hebrew manuscripts read *Diblah*.

HEBREWS 4:1-16

The Sabbath rest is one of the most basic Jewish traditions. Here the writer talks about the eternal rest enjoyed by those who believe in Jesus. It is rest from the futility of living in rebellion toward God.

God's promise of entering his rest still stands, so we ought to tremble with fear that some of you might fail to experience it. [2]For this good news—that God has prepared this rest—has been announced to us just as it was to them. But it did them no good because they didn't share the faith of those who listened to God.* [3]For only we who believe can enter his rest. As for the others, God said,

> "In my anger I took an oath:
> 'They will never enter my place
>   of rest,'"*

even though this rest has been ready since he made the world. [4]We know it is ready because of the place in the Scriptures where it mentions the seventh day: "On the seventh day God rested from all his work."* [5]But in the other passage God said, "They will never enter my place of rest."*

[6]So God's rest is there for people to enter, but those who first heard this good news failed to enter because they disobeyed God. [7]So God set another time for entering his rest, and that time is today. God announced this through David much later in the words already quoted:

> "Today when you hear his voice,
>   don't harden your hearts."*

[8]Now if Joshua had succeeded in giving them this rest, God would not have spoken about another day of rest still to come. [9]So there is a special rest* still waiting for the people of God. [10]For all who have entered into God's rest have rested from their labors, just as God did after creating the world. [11]So let us do our best to enter that

HOW WE LIVE

Dealing with problems

HEBREWS 4:16 Sometimes our problems are such a tangle that solving them seems too far out of our grasp. That's when we have to get back to the basics—do the right thing one step at a time. We need to boldly approach God's throne, admit our utter confusion, and ask him to show us the next step. • Ask God, "What do I do today?" Then walk in obedience, doing what is right for today. "What about tomorrow?" you ask. God responds, "Don't worry about tomorrow. Today is all you can handle. I've got tomorrow taken care of. Tomorrow we'll talk about tomorrow." And so it goes, one step at a time. Suddenly, we've walked through the problem and out the other side. We've learned a thing or two about ourselves. We've learned a thing or two about God. We've grown. And we've gotten rather used to visiting God's throne on a daily basis—and liking it there. That's what those utterly confusing problems do; they drive us to God. • Confused? Out of options? Go boldly to the throne of your gracious God. Get used to being there. He'll show you the next obedient step.

rest. But if we disobey God, as the people of Israel did, we will fall.

¹²For the word of God is alive and powerful. It is sharper than the sharpest two-edged sword, cutting between soul and spirit, between joint and marrow. It exposes our innermost thoughts and desires. ¹³Nothing in all creation is hidden from God. Everything is naked and exposed before his eyes, and he is the one to whom we are accountable.

¹⁴So then, since we have a great High Priest who has entered heaven, Jesus the Son of God, let us hold firmly to what we believe. ¹⁵This High Priest of ours understands our weaknesses, for he faced all of the same testings we do, yet he did not sin. ¹⁶So let us come boldly to the throne of our gracious God. There we will receive his mercy, and we will find grace to help us when we need it most.

4:2 Some manuscripts read *they didn't combine what they heard with faith.* 4:3 Ps 95:11. 4:4 Gen 2:2.
4:5 Ps 95:11. 4:7 Ps 95:7-8. 4:9 Or *a Sabbath rest.*

PSALM 104:24-35

O LORD, what a variety of things you
        have made!
    In wisdom you have made them all.
    The earth is full of your creatures.
²⁵ Here is the ocean, vast and wide,
        teeming with life of every kind,
        both large and small.
²⁶ See the ships sailing along,
        and Leviathan,* which you made
        to play in the sea.

²⁷ They all depend on you
        to give them food as they need it.

²⁸ When you supply it, they gather it.
    You open your hand to feed them,
        and they are richly satisfied.
²⁹ But if you turn away from them,
            they panic.
    When you take away their breath,
        they die and turn again to dust.
³⁰ When you give them your breath,* life
        is created,
    and you renew the face of
        the earth.

³¹ May the glory of the LORD continue
        forever!
    The LORD takes pleasure in all
        he has made!
³² The earth trembles at his glance;
    the mountains smoke at his touch.

³³ I will sing to the LORD as long as I live.
    I will praise my God to my last
        breath!
³⁴ May all my thoughts be pleasing
        to him,
    for I rejoice in the LORD.
³⁵ Let all sinners vanish from the face
        of the earth;
    let the wicked disappear forever.

    Let all that I am praise the LORD.

    Praise the LORD!

104:26 The identification of Leviathan is disputed, ranging from an earthly creature to a mythical sea monster in ancient literature. 104:30 Or *When you send your Spirit.*

PROVERBS 26:27

If you set a trap for others, you will get caught in it yourself. If you roll a boulder down on others, it will crush you instead.

NOVEMBER**3**

EZEKIEL 7:1–9:11

Throughout their history, the Israelites had fluctuated between all-out rebellion and half-hearted dedication. Then, as now, God wanted whole-hearted dedication from his people.

Then this message came to me [Ezekiel] from the LORD: ²"Son of man, this is what the Sovereign LORD says to Israel:

"The end is here!
    Wherever you look—
east, west, north, or south—
    your land is finished.
³ No hope remains,
    for I will unleash my anger against
        you.

I will call you to account
  for all your detestable sins.
[4] I will turn my eyes away and show
    no pity.
  I will repay you for all your
    detestable sins.
  Then you will know that I am the LORD.

[5] "This is what the Sovereign LORD says:
  Disaster after disaster
    is coming your way!
[6] The end has come.
    It has finally arrived.
    Your final doom is waiting!
[7] O people of Israel, the day of your
      destruction is dawning.
    The time has come; the day
      of trouble is near.
  Shouts of anguish will be heard
    on the mountains,
    not shouts of joy.
[8] Soon I will pour out my fury on you
    and unleash my anger against you.
  I will call you to account
    for all your detestable sins.
[9] I will turn my eyes away and show
    no pity.
  I will repay you for all your
    detestable sins.
  Then you will know that it is I, the LORD,
    who is striking the blow.

[10] "The day of judgment is here;
    your destruction awaits!
  The people's wickedness and pride
    have blossomed to full flower.
[11] Their violence has grown into a rod
      that will beat them for their
      wickedness.
  None of these proud and wicked
    people will survive.
  All their wealth and prestige will
    be swept away.
[12] Yes, the time has come;
    the day is here!
  Buyers should not rejoice over bargains,
    nor sellers grieve over losses,
  for all of them will fall
    under my terrible anger.
[13] Even if the merchants survive,
    they will never return to their
    business.
  For what God has said applies
    to everyone—
    it will not be changed!

Not one person whose life is twisted
    by sin
  will ever recover.

[14] "The trumpet calls Israel's army
    to mobilize,
  but no one listens,
    for my fury is against them all.
[15] There is war outside the city
    and disease and famine within.
  Those outside the city walls
    will be killed by enemy swords.
  Those inside the city
    will die of famine and disease.
[16] The survivors who escape to the
      mountains
  will moan like doves, weeping
    for their sins.
[17] Their hands will hang limp,
    their knees will be weak as water.
[18] They will dress themselves in burlap;
    horror and shame will cover them.
  They will shave their heads
    in sorrow and remorse.

[19] "They will throw their money
      in the streets,
  tossing it out like worthless trash.
  Their silver and gold won't save them
    on that day of the LORD's anger.
  It will neither satisfy nor feed them,
    for their greed can only trip them up.
[20] They were proud of their beautiful
      jewelry
  and used it to make detestable idols
    and vile images.
  Therefore, I will make all their wealth
    disgusting to them.
[21] I will give it as plunder to foreigners,
    to the most wicked of nations,
    and they will defile it.
[22] I will turn my eyes from them
    as these robbers invade and defile
    my treasured land.

[23] "Prepare chains for my people,
    for the land is bloodied by terrible
    crimes.
  Jerusalem is filled with violence.
[24] I will bring the most ruthless of nations
    to occupy their homes.
  I will break down their proud fortresses
    and defile their sanctuaries.
[25] Terror and trembling will overcome
    my people.

They will look for peace but not
find it.

26 Calamity will follow calamity;
rumor will follow rumor.
They will look in vain
for a vision from the prophets.
They will receive no teaching from
the priests
and no counsel from the leaders.

27 The king and the prince will stand
helpless,
weeping in despair,
and the people's hands
will tremble with fear.
I will bring on them
the evil they have done to others,
and they will receive the punishment
they so richly deserve.
Then they will know that I am
the LORD."

8:1THEN on September 17,* during the sixth year of King Jehoiachin's captivity, while the leaders of Judah were in my home, the Sovereign LORD took hold of me. ²I saw a figure that appeared to be a man. From what appeared to be his waist down, he looked like a burning flame. From the waist up he looked like gleaming amber.* ³He reached out what seemed to be a hand and took me by the hair. Then the Spirit lifted me up into the sky and transported me to Jerusalem in a vision from God. I was taken to the north gate of the inner courtyard of the Temple, where there is a large idol that has made the LORD very jealous. ⁴Suddenly, the glory of the God of Israel was there, just as I had seen it before in the valley.

⁵Then the LORD said to me, "Son of man, look toward the north." So I looked, and there to the north, beside the entrance to the gate near the altar, stood the idol that had made the LORD so jealous.

⁶"Son of man," he said, "do you see what they are doing? Do you see the detestable sins the people of Israel are committing to drive me from my Temple? But come, and you will see even more detestable sins than these!" ⁷Then he brought me to the door of the Temple courtyard, where I could see a hole in the wall. ⁸He said to me, "Now, son of man, dig into the wall." So I dug into the wall and found a hidden doorway.

⁹"Go in," he said, "and see the wicked and detestable sins they are committing in there!" ¹⁰So I went in and saw the walls engraved with all kinds of crawling animals and detestable creatures. I also saw the various idols* worshiped by the people of Israel. ¹¹Seventy leaders of Israel were standing there with Jaazaniah son of Shaphan in the center. Each of them held an incense burner, from which a cloud of incense rose above their heads.

¹²Then the LORD said to me, "Son of man, have you seen what the leaders of Israel are doing with their idols in dark rooms? They are saying, 'The LORD doesn't see us; he has deserted our land!'" ¹³Then the LORD added, "Come, and I will show you even more detestable sins than these!"

¹⁴He brought me to the north gate of the LORD's Temple, and some women were sitting there, weeping for the god Tammuz. ¹⁵"Have you seen this?" he asked. "But I will show you even more detestable sins than these!"

¹⁶Then he brought me into the inner courtyard of the LORD's Temple. At the entrance to the sanctuary, between the entry room and the bronze altar, there were about twenty-five men with their backs to the sanctuary of the LORD. They were facing east, bowing low to the ground, worshiping the sun!

¹⁷"Have you seen this, son of man?" he asked. "Is it nothing to the people of Judah that they commit these detestable sins, leading the whole nation into violence, thumbing their noses at me, and provoking my anger? ¹⁸Therefore, I will respond in fury. I will neither pity nor spare them. And though they cry for mercy, I will not listen."

9:1THEN the LORD thundered, "Bring on the men appointed to punish the city! Tell them to bring their weapons with them!" ²Six men soon appeared from the upper gate that faces north, each carrying a deadly weapon in his hand. With them was a man dressed in linen, who carried a writer's case at his side. They all went into the Temple courtyard and stood beside the bronze altar.

³Then the glory of the God of Israel rose up from between the cherubim, where it

had rested, and moved to the entrance of the Temple. And the LORD called to the man dressed in linen who was carrying the writer's case. ⁴He said to him, "Walk through the streets of Jerusalem and put a mark on the foreheads of all who weep and sigh because of the detestable sins being committed in their city."

⁵Then I heard the LORD say to the other men, "Follow him through the city and kill everyone whose forehead is not marked. Show no mercy; have no pity! ⁶Kill them all—old and young, girls and women and little children. But do not touch anyone with the mark. Begin right here at the Temple." So they began by killing the seventy leaders.

⁷"Defile the Temple!" the LORD commanded. "Fill its courtyards with corpses. Go!" So they went and began killing throughout the city.

⁸While they were out killing, I was all alone. I fell face down on the ground and cried out, "O Sovereign LORD! Will your fury against Jerusalem wipe out everyone left in Israel?"

⁹Then he said to me, "The sins of the people of Israel and Judah are very, very great. The entire land is full of murder; the city is filled with injustice. They are saying, 'The LORD doesn't see it! The LORD has abandoned the land!' ¹⁰So I will not spare them or have any pity on them.

I will fully repay them for all they have done."

¹¹Then the man in linen clothing, who carried the writer's case, reported back and said, "I have done as you commanded."

8:1 Hebrew *on the fifth day of the sixth month,* of the ancient Hebrew lunar calendar. This event occurred on September 17, 592 B.C.; also see note on 1:1.   8:2 Or *like burnished metal.*   8:10 The Hebrew term (literally *round things*) probably alludes to dung.

HEBREWS 5:1-14
Many Old Testament images point to Christ. The high priest functioned as a middleman between God and his people. Jesus came as the perfect high priest, permanently bridging the gap between us and God.

Every high priest is a man chosen to represent other people in their dealings with God. He presents their gifts to God and offers sacrifices for their sins. ²And he is able to deal gently with ignorant and wayward people because he himself is subject to the same weaknesses. ³That is why he must offer sacrifices for his own sins as well as theirs.

⁴And no one can become a high priest simply because he wants such an honor. He must be called by God for this work, just as Aaron was. ⁵That is why Christ did not honor himself by assuming he could become High Priest. No, he was chosen by God, who said to him,

"You are my Son.
Today I have become your Father.*"

HOW WE LIVE: Growing in faith

HEBREWS 5:12-14 As a new believer, you're still on a "milk diet," as you should be. We don't feed babies steak and potatoes; we feed them a diet they are able to take in and digest, with all the right nutrients and ingredients to help them grow. This "milk diet," part of which is included in the notes in this Bible, is meant to give you that basic nutrition. As you read these notes, you're learning the basics of the Christian faith. Admittedly, there's a lot of material here and at times you may feel a bit overwhelmed. But keep chewing, keep swallowing, keep taking in the nutrition. You're growing. • Eventually, these basics will be second nature. You won't need to be on a "milk diet" anymore; you'll move on to solid food. In other words, you'll keep growing and your capacity to feast on deeper knowledge of God will also grow. Don't be worried if you don't understand everything. Some parts of God's banquet may be too difficult to digest right now. As you grow in the Lord, your capacity to understand will also grow.

[6]And in another passage God said to him,

"You are a priest forever in the order
of Melchizedek."*

[7]While Jesus was here on earth, he offered prayers and pleadings, with a loud cry and tears, to the one who could rescue him from death. And God heard his prayers because of his deep reverence for God. [8]Even though Jesus was God's Son, he learned obedience from the things he suffered. [9]In this way, God qualified him as a perfect High Priest, and he became the source of eternal salvation for all those who obey him. [10]And God designated him to be a High Priest in the order of Melchizedek.

[11]There is much more we would like to say about this, but it is difficult to explain, especially since you are spiritually dull and don't seem to listen. [12]You have been believers so long now that you ought to be teaching others. Instead, you need someone to teach you again the basic things about God's word.* You are like babies who need milk and cannot eat solid food. [13]For someone who lives on milk is still an infant and doesn't know how to do what is right. [14]Solid food is for those who are mature, who through training have the skill to recognize the difference between right and wrong.

5:5 Or *Today I reveal you as my Son.* Ps 2:7.   5:6 Ps 110:4.
5:12 Or *about the oracles of God.*

PSALM 105:1-15

Give thanks to the LORD and proclaim
his greatness.
Let the whole world know what
he has done.
[2] Sing to him; yes, sing his praises.
Tell everyone about his wonderful
deeds.

[3] Exult in his holy name;
rejoice, you who worship the LORD.
[4] Search for the LORD and for his
strength;
continually seek him.
[5] Remember the wonders he has
performed,
his miracles, and the rulings
he has given,
[6] you children of his servant Abraham,
you descendants of Jacob, his
chosen ones.

[7] He is the LORD our God.
His justice is seen throughout
the land.
[8] He always stands by his covenant—
the commitment he made to
a thousand generations.
[9] This is the covenant he made with
Abraham
and the oath he swore to Isaac.
[10] He confirmed it to Jacob as a decree,
and to the people of Israel as
a never-ending covenant:
[11] "I will give you the land of Canaan
as your special possession."

[12] He said this when they were few
in number,
a tiny group of strangers in Canaan.
[13] They wandered from nation to nation,
from one kingdom to another.
[14] Yet he did not let anyone oppress
them.
He warned kings on their behalf:
[15] "Do not touch my chosen people,
and do not hurt my prophets."

PROVERBS 26:28

A lying tongue hates its victims, and flattering words cause ruin.

EZEKIEL 10:1–11:25
God's glory filled the Tabernacle initially and later the Temple. However, by Ezekiel's day the people had been so rebellious that God's glory left the Temple and the city.

In my [Ezekiel's] vision I saw what appeared to be a throne of blue lapis lazuli above the crystal surface over the heads of the cherubim. [2]Then the LORD spoke to the man in linen clothing and said, "Go between the whirling wheels beneath the cherubim, and take a handful of burning coals and scatter them over the city." He did this as I watched.

³The cherubim were standing at the south end of the Temple when the man went in, and the cloud of glory filled the inner courtyard. ⁴Then the glory of the LORD rose up from above the cherubim and went over to the door of the Temple. The Temple was filled with this cloud of glory, and the courtyard glowed brightly with the glory of the LORD. ⁵The moving wings of the cherubim sounded like the voice of God Almighty* and could be heard even in the outer courtyard.

⁶The LORD said to the man in linen clothing, "Go between the cherubim and take some burning coals from between the wheels." So the man went in and stood beside one of the wheels. ⁷Then one of the cherubim reached out his hand and took some live coals from the fire burning among them. He put the coals into the hands of the man in linen clothing, and the man took them and went out. ⁸(All the cherubim had what looked like human hands under their wings.)

⁹I looked, and each of the four cherubim had a wheel beside him, and the wheels sparkled like beryl. ¹⁰All four wheels looked alike and were made the same; each wheel had a second wheel turning crosswise within it. ¹¹The cherubim could move in any of the four directions they faced, without turning as they moved. They went straight in the direction they faced, never turning aside. ¹²Both the cherubim and the wheels were covered with eyes. The cherubim had eyes all over their bodies, including their hands, their backs, and their wings. ¹³I heard someone refer to the wheels as "the whirling wheels." ¹⁴Each of the four cherubim had four faces: the first was the face of an ox,* the second was a human face, the third was the face of a lion, and the fourth was the face of an eagle.

¹⁵Then the cherubim rose upward. These were the same living beings I had seen beside the Kebar River. ¹⁶When the cherubim moved, the wheels moved with them. When they lifted their wings to fly, the wheels stayed beside them. ¹⁷When the cherubim stopped, the wheels stopped. When they flew upward, the wheels rose up, for the spirit of the living beings was in the wheels.

¹⁸Then the glory of the LORD moved out from the door of the Temple and hovered above the cherubim. ¹⁹And as I watched, the cherubim flew with their wheels to the east gate of the LORD's Temple. And the glory of the God of Israel hovered above them.

²⁰These were the same living beings I had seen beneath the God of Israel when I was by the Kebar River. I knew they were cherubim, ²¹for each had four faces and four wings and what looked like human hands under their wings. ²²And their faces were just like the faces of the beings I had seen at the Kebar, and they traveled straight ahead, just as the others had.

11:1THEN the Spirit lifted me and brought me to the east gateway of the LORD's Temple, where I saw twenty-five prominent men of the city. Among them were Jaazaniah son of Azzur and Pelatiah son of Benaiah, who were leaders among the people.

²The Spirit said to me, "Son of man, these are the men who are planning evil and giving wicked counsel in this city. ³They say to the people, 'Is it not a good time to build houses? This city is like an iron pot. We are safe inside it like meat in a pot.*' ⁴Therefore, son of man, prophesy against them loudly and clearly."

⁵Then the Spirit of the LORD came upon me, and he told me to say, "This is what the LORD says to the people of Israel: I know what you are saying, for I know every thought that comes into your minds. ⁶You have murdered many in this city and filled its streets with the dead.

⁷"Therefore, this is what the Sovereign LORD says: This city is an iron pot all right, but the pieces of meat are the victims of your injustice. As for you, I will soon drag you from this pot. ⁸I will bring on you the sword of war you so greatly fear, says the Sovereign LORD. ⁹I will drive you out of Jerusalem and hand you over to foreigners, who will carry out my judgments against you. ¹⁰You will be slaughtered all the way

to the borders of Israel. I will execute judgment on you, and you will know that I am the LORD. [11]No, this city will not be an iron pot for you, and you will not be like meat safe inside it. I will judge you even to the borders of Israel, [12]and you will know that I am the LORD. For you have refused to obey my decrees and regulations; instead, you have copied the standards of the nations around you."

[13]While I was still prophesying, Pelatiah son of Benaiah suddenly died. Then I fell face down on the ground and cried out, "O Sovereign LORD, are you going to kill everyone in Israel?"

[14]Then this message came to me from the LORD: [15]"Son of man, the people still left in Jerusalem are talking about you and your relatives and all the people of Israel who are in exile. They are saying, 'Those people are far away from the LORD, so now he has given their land to us!'

[16]"Therefore, tell the exiles, 'This is what the Sovereign LORD says: Although I have scattered you in the countries of the world, I will be a sanctuary to you during your time in exile. [17]I, the Sovereign LORD, will gather you back from the nations where you have been scattered, and I will give you the land of Israel once again.'

[18]"When the people return to their homeland, they will remove every trace of their vile images and detestable idols. [19]And I will give them singleness of heart and put a new spirit within them. I will take away their stony, stubborn heart and give them a tender, responsive heart,* [20]so they will obey my decrees and regulations. Then they will truly be my people, and I will be their God. [21]But as for those who long for vile images and detestable idols, I will repay them fully for their sins. I, the Sovereign LORD, have spoken!"

[22]Then the cherubim lifted their wings and rose into the air with their wheels beside them, and the glory of the God of Israel hovered above them. [23]Then the glory of the LORD went up from the city and stopped above the mountain to the east.

[24]Afterward the Spirit of God carried me back again to Babylonia,* to the people in exile there. And so ended the vision of my visit to Jerusalem. [25]And I told the exiles everything the LORD had shown me.

10:5 Hebrew *El-Shaddai.*   **10:14** Hebrew *the face of a cherub;* compare 1:10.   **11:3** Hebrew *This city is the pot, and we are the meat.*   **11:19** Hebrew *a heart of flesh.*   **11:24** Or *Chaldea.*

HEBREWS 6:1-20

True saving faith perseveres through thick and thin. Persevering faith is possible because we can utterly count on God's faithfulness to his promises and Christ's work on our behalf.

So let us stop going over the basic teachings about Christ again and again. Let us go on instead and become mature in our understanding. Surely we don't need to start again with the fundamental importance of repenting from evil deeds and placing our faith in God. [2]You don't need further instruction about baptisms, the laying on of hands, the resurrection of the dead, and eternal judgment. [3]And so, God willing, we will move forward to further understanding.

[4]For it is impossible to bring back to repentance those who were once enlightened—those who have experienced the good things of heaven and shared in the Holy Spirit, [5]who have tasted the goodness of the word of God and the power of the age to come—[6]and who then turn away from God. It is impossible to bring such people back to repentance; by rejecting the Son of God, they themselves are nailing him to the cross once again and holding him up to public shame.

[7]When the ground soaks up the falling rain and bears a good crop for the farmer, it has God's blessing. [8]But if a field bears thorns and thistles, it is useless. The farmer will soon condemn that field and burn it.

[9]Dear friends, even though we are talking this way, we really don't believe it applies to you. We are confident that you are meant for better things, things that come with salvation. [10]For God is not unjust. He will not forget how hard you have worked for him and how you have shown your love to him by caring for other believers,* as you still do. [11]Our great desire is that you will keep on loving others as long as life lasts, in order to make certain that what you hope for will come true. [12]Then

you will not become spiritually dull and indifferent. Instead, you will follow the example of those who are going to inherit God's promises because of their faith and endurance.

¹³For example, there was God's promise to Abraham. Since there was no one greater to swear by, God took an oath in his own name, saying:

¹⁴ "I will certainly bless you,
    and I will multiply your
        descendants beyond number."*

¹⁵Then Abraham waited patiently, and he received what God had promised.

¹⁶Now when people take an oath, they call on someone greater than themselves to hold them to it. And without any question that oath is binding. ¹⁷God also bound himself with an oath, so that those who received the promise could be perfectly sure that he would never change his mind. ¹⁸So God has given both his promise and his oath. These two things are unchangeable because it is impossible for God to lie. Therefore, we who have fled to him for refuge can have great confidence as we hold to the hope that lies before us. ¹⁹This hope is a strong and trustworthy anchor for our souls. It leads us through the curtain into God's inner sanctuary. ²⁰Jesus has already gone in there for us. He has be-

come our eternal High Priest in the order of Melchizedek.

6:10 Greek *for God's holy people.*   6:14 Gen 22:17.

PSALM 105:16-36

    He [the LORD] called for a famine on
        the land of Canaan,
            cutting off its food supply.
¹⁷ Then he sent someone to Egypt ahead
        of them—
    Joseph, who was sold as a slave.
¹⁸ They bruised his feet with fetters
        and placed his neck in an iron
            collar.
¹⁹ Until the time came to fulfill his
        dreams,*
    the LORD tested Joseph's character.
²⁰ Then Pharaoh sent for him and set
        him free;
    the ruler of the nation opened his
        prison door.
²¹ Joseph was put in charge of all the
        king's household;
    he became ruler over all the king's
        possessions.
²² He could instruct the king's aides
        as he pleased
    and teach the king's advisers.

²³ Then Israel arrived in Egypt;
    Jacob lived as a foreigner in the land
        of Ham.

WHO GOD IS · God is loving

EZEKIEL 11:18-21 In the face of judgment, promise; in the face of sorrow, joy; in the face of rebellion, love: That's the kind of God we serve. • These chapters in Ezekiel contain desperate sadness. God had finally had enough. He had sent prophets to his people, pleading with them to turn from their wicked ways, but they refused. Ezekiel 11:22-23 describes God's glory leaving the Temple and the city. You'd think it was over. You'd think God had given up. However, God had made a promise and he had a big plan. God had promised to Abraham that he would bless the world through him (Genesis 12:3, January 5); to David he had promised an heir who would reign over his people forever (2 Samuel 7:16, May 25). God would not give up on his people. So in the face of certain judgment shines a glorious promise of restoration. • When you became a believer, God took out your stony heart and gave you a tender, responsive heart. He has made you his child. What awesome love is this, that God would call you his own! He will never give up on you.

24 And the LORD multiplied the people
of Israel
until they became too mighty for
their enemies.
25 Then he turned the Egyptians against
the Israelites,
and they plotted against the LORD's
servants.

26 But the LORD sent his servant Moses,
along with Aaron, whom he had
chosen.
27 They performed miraculous signs
among the Egyptians,
and wonders in the land of Ham.
28 The LORD blanketed Egypt in
darkness,
for they had defied his commands
to let his people go.
29 He turned their water into blood,
poisoning all the fish.
30 Then frogs overran the land
and even invaded the king's
bedrooms.

31 When the LORD spoke, flies
descended on the Egyptians,
and gnats swarmed across Egypt.
32 He sent them hail instead of rain,
and lightning flashed over the land.
33 He ruined their grapevines and fig
trees
and shattered all the trees.
34 He spoke, and hordes of locusts came—
young locusts beyond number.
35 They ate up everything green in the
land,
destroying all the crops in their
fields.
36 Then he killed the oldest son in each
Egyptian home,
the pride and joy of each family.

105:19 Hebrew *his word.*

PROVERBS 27:1-2

Don't brag about tomorrow, since you
don't know what the day will bring. □ Let
someone else praise you, not your own
mouth—a stranger, not your own lips.

NOVEMBER**5**

EZEKIEL 12:1–14:11

While Ezekiel was warning of destruction and
exile, false prophets were promising sunshine
on the horizon.

Again a message came to me [Ezekiel]
from the LORD: 2"Son of man, you live
among rebels who have eyes but refuse to
see. They have ears but refuse to hear. For
they are a rebellious people.

3"So now, son of man, pretend you are
being sent into exile. Pack the few items
an exile could carry, and leave your home
to go somewhere else. Do this right in
front of the people so they can see you.
For perhaps they will pay attention to this,
even though they are such rebels. 4Bring
your baggage outside during the day so
they can watch you. Then in the evening,
as they are watching, leave your house as
captives do when they begin a long march

to distant lands. 5Dig a hole through the
wall while they are watching and go out
through it. 6As they watch, lift your pack
to your shoulders and walk away into the
night. Cover your face so you cannot see
the land you are leaving. For I have made
you a sign for the people of Israel."

7So I did as I was told. In broad daylight
I brought my pack outside, filled with the
things I might carry into exile. Then in the
evening while the people looked on, I dug
through the wall with my hands and went
out into the night with my pack on my
shoulder.

8The next morning this message came
to me from the LORD: 9"Son of man, these
rebels, the people of Israel, have asked
you what all this means. 10Say to them,
'This is what the Sovereign LORD says:
These actions contain a message for King

Zedekiah in Jerusalem* and for all the people of Israel.' ¹¹Explain that your actions are a sign to show what will soon happen to them, for they will be driven into exile as captives.

¹²"Even Zedekiah will leave Jerusalem at night through a hole in the wall, taking only what he can carry with him. He will cover his face, and his eyes will not see the land he is leaving. ¹³Then I will throw my net over him and capture him in my snare. I will bring him to Babylon, the land of the Babylonians,* though he will never see it, and he will die there. ¹⁴I will scatter his servants and warriors to the four winds and send the sword after them. ¹⁵And when I scatter them among the nations, they will know that I am the LORD. ¹⁶But I will spare a few of them from death by war, famine, or disease, so they can confess all their detestable sins to their captors. Then they will know that I am the LORD."

¹⁷Then this message came to me from the LORD: ¹⁸"Son of man, tremble as you eat your food. Shake with fear as you drink your water. ¹⁹Tell the people, 'This is what the Sovereign LORD says concerning those living in Israel and Jerusalem: They will eat their food with trembling and sip their water in despair, for their land will be stripped bare because of their violence. ²⁰The cities will be destroyed and the farmland made desolate. Then you will know that I am the LORD.'"

²¹Again a message came to me from the LORD: ²²"Son of man, you've heard that proverb they quote in Israel: 'Time passes, and prophecies come to nothing.' ²³Tell the people, 'This is what the Sovereign LORD says: I will put an end to this proverb, and you will soon stop quoting it.' Now give them this new proverb to replace the old one: 'The time has come for every prophecy to be fulfilled!'

²⁴"There will be no more false visions and flattering predictions in Israel. ²⁵For I am the LORD! If I say it, it will happen. There will be no more delays, you rebels of Israel. I will fulfill my threat of destruction in your own lifetime. I, the Sovereign LORD, have spoken!"

²⁶Then this message came to me from the LORD: ²⁷"Son of man, the people of Israel are saying, 'He's talking about the distant future. His visions won't come true for a long, long time.' ²⁸Therefore, tell them, 'This is what the Sovereign LORD says: No more delay! I will now do everything I have threatened. I, the Sovereign LORD, have spoken!'"

¹³:¹THEN this message came to me from the LORD: ²"Son of man, prophesy against the false prophets of Israel who are inventing their own prophecies. Say to them, 'Listen to the word of the LORD. ³This is what the Sovereign LORD says: What sorrow awaits the false prophets who are following their own imaginations and have seen nothing at all!'

⁴"O people of Israel, these prophets of yours are like jackals digging in the ruins. ⁵They have done nothing to repair the breaks in the walls around the nation. They have not helped it to stand firm in battle on the day of the LORD. ⁶Instead, they have told lies and made false predictions. They say, 'This message is from the LORD,' even though the LORD never sent them. And yet they expect him to fulfill their prophecies! ⁷Can your visions be anything but false if you claim, 'This message is from the LORD,' when I have not even spoken to you?

⁸"Therefore, this is what the Sovereign LORD says: Because what you say is false and your visions are a lie, I will stand against you, says the Sovereign LORD. ⁹I will raise my fist against all the prophets who see false visions and make lying predictions, and they will be banished from the community of Israel. I will blot their names from Israel's record books, and they will never again set foot in their own land. Then you will know that I am the Sovereign LORD.

¹⁰"This will happen because these evil prophets deceive my people by saying, 'All is peaceful' when there is no peace at all! It's as if the people have built a flimsy wall, and these prophets are trying to reinforce it by covering it with whitewash! ¹¹Tell these whitewashers that their wall will soon fall down. A heavy rainstorm will undermine it; great hailstones and mighty winds will knock it down. ¹²And when the wall falls, the people will cry out, 'What happened to your whitewash?'

¹³"Therefore, this is what the Sovereign LORD says: I will sweep away your whitewashed wall with a storm of indignation, with a great flood of anger, and with hailstones of fury. ¹⁴I will break down your wall right to its foundation, and when it falls, it will crush you. Then you will know that I am the LORD. ¹⁵At last my anger against the wall and those who covered it with whitewash will be satisfied. Then I will say to you: 'The wall and those who whitewashed it are both gone. ¹⁶They were lying prophets who claimed peace would come to Jerusalem when there was no peace. I, the Sovereign LORD, have spoken!'

¹⁷"Now, son of man, speak out against the women who prophesy from their own imaginations. ¹⁸This is what the Sovereign LORD says: What sorrow awaits you women who are ensnaring the souls of my people, young and old alike. You tie magic charms on their wrists and furnish them with magic veils. Do you think you can trap others without bringing destruction on yourselves? ¹⁹You bring shame on me among my people for a few handfuls of barley or a piece of bread. By lying to my people who love to listen to lies, you kill those who should not die, and you promise life to those who should not live.

²⁰"This is what the Sovereign LORD says: I am against all your magic charms, which you use to ensnare my people like birds. I will tear them from your arms, setting my people free like birds set free from a cage. ²¹I will tear off the magic veils and save my people from your grasp. They will no longer be your victims. Then you will know that I am the LORD. ²²You have discouraged the righteous with your lies, but I didn't want them to be sad. And you have encouraged the wicked by promising them life, even though they continue in their sins. ²³Because of all this, you will no longer talk of seeing visions that you never saw, nor will you make predictions. For I will rescue my people from your grasp. Then you will know that I am the LORD."

¹⁴:¹THEN some of the leaders of Israel visited me, and while they were sitting with me, ²this message came to me from the LORD: ³"Son of man, these leaders have set up idols* in their hearts. They have embraced things that will make them fall into sin. Why should I listen to their requests? ⁴Tell them, 'This is what the Sovereign LORD says: The people of Israel have set up idols in their hearts and fallen into sin, and then they go to a prophet asking for a message. So I, the LORD, will give them the kind of answer their great idolatry deserves. ⁵I will do this to capture the minds and hearts of all my people who have turned from me to worship their detestable idols.'

⁶"Therefore, tell the people of Israel, 'This is what the Sovereign LORD says: Repent and turn away from your idols, and stop all your detestable sins. ⁷I, the LORD, will answer all those, both Israelites and foreigners, who reject me and set up idols in their hearts and so fall into sin, and who then come to a prophet asking for my advice. ⁸I will turn against such people and make a terrible example of them, eliminating them from among my people. Then you will know that I am the LORD.

⁹"'And if a prophet is deceived into giving a message, it is because I, the LORD, have deceived that prophet. I will lift my fist against such prophets and cut them off from the community of Israel. ¹⁰False prophets and those who seek their guidance will all be punished for their sins. ¹¹In this way, the people of Israel will learn not to stray from me, polluting themselves with sin. They will be my people, and I will be their God. I, the Sovereign LORD, have spoken!'"

12:10 Hebrew *the prince in Jerusalem;* similarly in 12:12.
12:13 Or *Chaldeans.*   14:3 The Hebrew term (literally *round things*) probably alludes to dung; also in 14:4, 5, 6, 7.

HEBREWS 7:1-17
The writer uses this story from Genesis 14:18-20 (January 6) to show that Christ is greater even than Abraham, the father of the Jewish nation.

This Melchizedek was king of the city of Salem and also a priest of God Most High. When Abraham was returning home after winning a great battle against the kings, Melchizedek met him and blessed him. ²Then Abraham took a tenth of all he had captured in battle and gave it to Melchizedek. The name Melchizedek means "king of justice," and king of Salem means "king of peace." [3]There is no record of his father or mother or any of his ancestors—no beginning or end to his life. He remains a priest forever, resembling the Son of God.

[4]Consider then how great this Melchizedek was. Even Abraham, the great patriarch of Israel, recognized this by giving him a tenth of what he had taken in battle. [5]Now the law of Moses required that the priests, who are descendants of Levi, must collect a tithe from the rest of the people of Israel,* who are also descendants of Abraham. [6]But Melchizedek, who was not a descendant of Levi, collected a tenth from Abraham. And Melchizedek placed a blessing upon Abraham, the one who had already received the promises of God. [7]And without question, the person who has the power to give a blessing is greater than the one who is blessed.

[8]The priests who collect tithes are men who die, so Melchizedek is greater than they are, because we are told that he lives on. [9]In addition, we might even say that these Levites—the ones who collect the tithe—paid a tithe to Melchizedek when their ancestor Abraham paid a tithe to him. [10]For although Levi wasn't born yet, the seed from which he came was in Abraham's body when Melchizedek collected the tithe from him.

[11]So if the priesthood of Levi, on which the law was based, could have achieved the perfection God intended, why did God need to establish a different priesthood, with a priest in the order of Melchizedek instead of the order of Levi and Aaron?*

[12]And if the priesthood is changed, the law must also be changed to permit it. [13]For the priest we are talking about belongs to a different tribe, whose members have never served at the altar as priests. [14]What I mean is, our Lord came from the tribe of Judah, and Moses never mentioned priests coming from that tribe.

[15]This change has been made very clear since a different priest, who is like Melchizedek, has appeared. [16]Jesus became a priest, not by meeting the physical requirement of belonging to the tribe of Levi, but by the power of a life that cannot be destroyed. [17]And the psalmist pointed this out when he prophesied,

"You are a priest forever in the order of Melchizedek."*

7:5 Greek *from their brothers.*   7:11 Greek *the order of Aaron?*   7:17 Ps 110:4.

False prophets

WHAT THE BIBLE SAYS

EZEKIEL 12:10-16 You saved every last penny for a down payment. After looking at dozens of homes, you finally found a place. Because buying a home is such an important investment, you paid to have the house inspected by a professional, who took one look at the place from the road and told you with a grin that all was well. Confidently, you signed the deal. Then the first rain comes and the roof and the basement leak. You discover shoddy construction and neglect. The foundation needs repairs. Lots of expensive work will need to be done. Imagine the heartbreak and disappointment, all because you acted out of false confidence. • The Israelites in Ezekiel's day were in a similar situation. False prophets were telling the people not to worry about anything. Jerusalem's future was bright. God wasn't angry at their sin. They didn't need to change. Ezekiel warned the people not to trust such false assurances. • Still today there are people who "look for teachers who will tell them whatever their itching ears want to hear" (2 Timothy 4:3, October 25). Don't be like that. Base your confidence only on teaching that conforms to the Bible, and steer clear of those who contradict it.

PSALM 105:37-45

The LORD brought his people out of
    Egypt, loaded with silver and gold;
    and not one among the tribes of
    Israel even stumbled.
[38] Egypt was glad when they were gone,
    for they feared them greatly.
[39] The LORD spread a cloud above them
    as a covering
    and gave them a great fire to light
    the darkness.
[40] They asked for meat, and he sent them
    quail;
    he satisfied their hunger with
    manna—bread from heaven.
[41] He split open a rock, and water
    gushed out
    to form a river through the dry
    wasteland.

[42] For he remembered his sacred
    promise
    to his servant Abraham.
[43] So he brought his people out of Egypt
    with joy,
    his chosen ones with rejoicing.
[44] He gave his people the lands of pagan
    nations,
    and they harvested crops that others
    had planted.
[45] All this happened so they would follow
    his decrees
    and obey his instructions.

Praise the LORD!

PROVERBS 27:3

A stone is heavy and sand is weighty, but
the resentment caused by a fool is even
heavier.

NOVEMBER6

EZEKIEL 14:12–16:41

Israel's disobedience is frequently compared to the
unfaithfulness of an adulterous spouse. God chose
the Israelites and required them to choose him
(and only him) also. Israel's ongoing choice to
ignore God provided the backdrop for most Old
Testament prophecy.

Then this message came to me [Ezekiel]
from the LORD: [13]"Son of man, suppose the
people of a country were to sin against me,
and I lifted my fist to crush them, cutting
off their food supply and sending a famine
to destroy both people and animals. [14]Even
if Noah, Daniel, and Job were there, their
righteousness would save no one but
themselves, says the Sovereign LORD.

[15]"Or suppose I were to send wild animals to invade the country, kill the people,
and make the land too desolate and dangerous to pass through. [16]As surely as I
live, says the Sovereign LORD, even if those
three men were there, they wouldn't be
able to save their own sons or daughters.
They alone would be saved, but the land
would be made desolate.

[17]"Or suppose I were to bring war
against the land, and I sent enemy armies
to destroy both people and animals. [18]As
surely as I live, says the Sovereign LORD,
even if those three men were there, they
wouldn't be able to save their own sons or
daughters. They alone would be saved.

[19]"Or suppose I were to pour out my
fury by sending an epidemic into the land,
and the disease killed people and animals
alike. [20]As surely as I live, says the Sovereign LORD, even if Noah, Daniel, and Job
were there, they wouldn't be able to save
their own sons or daughters. They alone
would be saved by their righteousness.

[21]"Now this is what the Sovereign
LORD says: How terrible it will be when
all four of these dreadful punishments
fall upon Jerusalem—war, famine, wild
animals, and disease—destroying all her
people and animals. [22]Yet there will be
survivors, and they will come here to join
you as exiles in Babylon. You will see with
your own eyes how wicked they are, and
then you will feel better about what I have

done to Jerusalem. ²³When you meet them and see their behavior, you will understand that these things are not being done to Israel without cause. I, the Sovereign LORD, have spoken!"

¹⁵:¹THEN this message came to me from the LORD: ²"Son of man, how does a grapevine compare to a tree? Is a vine's wood as useful as the wood of a tree? ³Can its wood be used for making things, like pegs to hang up pots and pans? ⁴No, it can only be used for fuel, and even as fuel, it burns too quickly. ⁵Vines are useless both before and after being put into the fire!

⁶"And this is what the Sovereign LORD says: The people of Jerusalem are like grapevines growing among the trees of the forest. Since they are useless, I have thrown them on the fire to be burned. ⁷And I will see to it that if they escape from one fire, they will fall into another. When I turn against them, you will know that I am the LORD. ⁸And I will make the land desolate because my people have been unfaithful to me. I, the Sovereign LORD, have spoken!"

¹⁶:¹THEN another message came to me from the LORD: ²"Son of man, confront Jerusalem with her detestable sins. ³Give her this message from the Sovereign LORD: You are nothing but a Canaanite! Your father was an Amorite and your mother a Hittite. ⁴On the day you were born, no one cared about you. Your umbilical cord was not cut, and you were never washed, rubbed with salt, and wrapped in cloth. ⁵No one had the slightest interest in you; no one pitied you or cared for you. On the day you were born, you were unwanted, dumped in a field and left to die.

⁶"But I came by and saw you there, helplessly kicking about in your own blood. As you lay there, I said, 'Live!' ⁷And I helped you to thrive like a plant in the field. You grew up and became a beautiful jewel. Your breasts became full, and your body hair grew, but you were still naked. ⁸And when I passed by again, I saw that you were old enough for love. So I wrapped my cloak around you to cover your nakedness and declared my marriage vows. I made a covenant with you, says the Sovereign LORD, and you became mine.

⁹"Then I bathed you and washed off your blood, and I rubbed fragrant oils into your skin. ¹⁰I gave you expensive clothing of fine linen and silk, beautifully embroidered, and sandals made of fine goatskin leather. ¹¹I gave you lovely jewelry, bracelets, beautiful necklaces, ¹²a ring for your nose, earrings for your ears, and a lovely crown for your head. ¹³And so you were adorned with gold and silver. Your clothes were made of fine linen and were beautifully embroidered. You ate the finest foods—choice flour, honey, and olive oil— and became more beautiful than ever. You looked like a queen, and so you were! ¹⁴Your fame soon spread throughout the world because of your beauty. I dressed you in my splendor and perfected your beauty, says the Sovereign LORD.

¹⁵"But you thought your fame and beauty were your own. So you gave yourself as a prostitute to every man who came along. Your beauty was theirs for the asking. ¹⁶You used the lovely things I gave you to make shrines for idols, where you played the prostitute. Unbelievable! How could such a thing ever happen? ¹⁷You took the very jewels and gold and silver ornaments I had given you and made statues of men and worshiped them. This is adultery against me! ¹⁸You used the beautifully embroidered clothes I gave you to dress your idols. Then you used my special oil and my incense to worship them. ¹⁹Imagine it! You set before them as a sacrifice the choice flour, olive oil, and honey I had given you, says the Sovereign LORD.

²⁰"Then you took your sons and daughters—the children you had borne to me— and sacrificed them to your gods. Was your prostitution not enough? ²¹Must you also slaughter my children by sacrificing them to idols? ²²In all your years of adultery and detestable sin, you have not once remembered the days long ago when you lay naked in a field, kicking about in your own blood.

²³"What sorrow awaits you, says the Sovereign LORD. In addition to all your other wickedness, ²⁴you built a pagan shrine and put altars to idols in every town square. ²⁵On every street corner you defiled your beauty, offering your body to

every passerby in an endless stream of prostitution. ²⁶Then you added lustful Egypt to your lovers, provoking my anger with your increasing promiscuity. ²⁷That is why I struck you with my fist and reduced your boundaries. I handed you over to your enemies, the Philistines, and even they were shocked by your lewd conduct. ²⁸You have prostituted yourself with the Assyrians, too. It seems you can never find enough new lovers! And after your prostitution there, you still were not satisfied. ²⁹You added to your lovers by embracing Babylonia,* the land of merchants, but you still weren't satisfied.

³⁰"What a sick heart you have, says the Sovereign LORD, to do such things as these, acting like a shameless prostitute. ³¹You build your pagan shrines on every street corner and your altars to idols in every square. In fact, you have been worse than a prostitute, so eager for sin that you have not even demanded payment. ³²Yes, you are an adulterous wife who takes in strangers instead of her own husband. ³³Prostitutes charge for their services—but not you! You give gifts to your lovers, bribing them to come and have sex with you. ³⁴So you are the opposite of other prostitutes. You pay your lovers instead of their paying you!

³⁵"Therefore, you prostitute, listen to this message from the LORD! ³⁶This is what the Sovereign LORD says: Because you have poured out your lust and exposed yourself in prostitution to all your lovers, and because you have worshiped detestable idols,* and because you have slaughtered your children as sacrifices to your gods, ³⁷this is what I am going to do. I will gather together all your allies—the lovers with whom you have sinned, both those you loved and those you hated—and I will strip you naked in front of them so they can stare at you. ³⁸I will punish you for your murder and adultery. I will cover you with blood in my jealous fury. ³⁹Then I will give you to these many nations who are your lovers, and they will destroy you. They will knock down your pagan shrines and the altars to your idols. They will strip you and take your beautiful jewels, leaving you stark naked. ⁴⁰They will band together in a mob to

stone you and cut you up with swords. ⁴¹They will burn your homes and punish you in front of many women. I will stop your prostitution and end your payments to your many lovers."

16:29 Or *Chaldea.*   16:36 The Hebrew term (literally *round things*) probably alludes to dung.

HEBREWS 7:18-28

Christ not only took away the penalty for our sin; he also opened the way for us to go directly to God without the mediation of a human priest.

Yes, the old requirement about the priesthood was set aside because it was weak and useless. ¹⁹For the law never made anything perfect. But now we have confidence in a better hope, through which we draw near to God.

²⁰This new system was established with a solemn oath. Aaron's descendants became priests without such an oath, ²¹but there was an oath regarding Jesus. For God said to him,

"The LORD has taken an oath and will
    not break his vow:
'You are a priest forever.'"*

²²Because of this oath, Jesus is the one who guarantees this better covenant with God.

²³There were many priests under the old system, for death prevented them from remaining in office. ²⁴But because Jesus lives forever, his priesthood lasts forever. ²⁵Therefore he is able, once and forever, to save* those who come to God through him. He lives forever to intercede with God on their behalf.

²⁶He is the kind of high priest we need because he is holy and blameless, unstained by sin. He has been set apart from sinners and has been given the highest place of honor in heaven.* ²⁷Unlike those other high priests, he does not need to offer sacrifices every day. They did this for their own sins first and then for the sins of the people. But Jesus did this once for all when he offered himself as the sacrifice for the people's sins. ²⁸The law appointed high priests who were limited by human weakness. But after the law was given, God appointed his Son with an

oath, and his Son has been made the perfect High Priest forever.

7:21 Ps 110:4.   7:25 Or *is able to save completely.*
7:26 Or *has been exalted higher than the heavens.*

PSALM 106:1-12

Praise the LORD!

Give thanks to the LORD, for he
     is good!
   His faithful love endures
     forever.
2 Who can list the glorious miracles
     of the LORD?
   Who can ever praise him enough?
3 There is joy for those who deal justly
     with others
   and always do what is right.

4 Remember me, LORD, when you show
     favor to your people;
   come near and rescue me.
5 Let me share in the prosperity of your
     chosen ones.
   Let me rejoice in the joy of your
     people;
   let me praise you with those who
     are your heritage.

6 Like our ancestors, we have sinned.
   We have done wrong! We have
     acted wickedly!

7 Our ancestors in Egypt
     were not impressed by the LORD's
     miraculous deeds.
   They soon forgot his many acts
     of kindness to them.
   Instead, they rebelled against him
     at the Red Sea.*
8 Even so, he saved them—
   to defend the honor of his name
   and to demonstrate his mighty
     power.
9 He commanded the Red Sea* to dry up.
   He led Israel across the sea as if it
     were a desert.
10 So he rescued them from their
     enemies
   and redeemed them from their foes.
11 Then the water returned and covered
     their enemies;
   not one of them survived.
12 Then his people believed his promises.
   Then they sang his praise.

106:7 Hebrew *at the sea, the sea of reeds.*   106:9 Hebrew
sea of reeds; also in 106:22.

PROVERBS 27:4-6

Anger is cruel, and wrath is like a flood,
but jealousy is even more dangerous. □ An
open rebuke is better than hidden love!
□ Wounds from a sincere friend are better
than many kisses from an enemy.

WHO GOD IS

Jesus is our advocate

HEBREWS 7:25 You were caught committing a crime. The trial date has arrived. The judge is known to be a no-nonsense kind of guy. The evidence is clear. You're guilty. Then your lawyer stands up. He is your advocate in this courtroom. He doesn't lie. He doesn't spin the story. The first thing he says is, "This person is guilty." Now you know it's over. But the next thing he says takes you by surprise. "But remember, Judge, that this person's guilt has already been taken. This person doesn't need to be punished because I took the punishment myself." Your jaw would drop, to say the least. • Your sin had to be punished. God sent his Son to pay the penalty for you, but his work on your behalf didn't stop there. Jesus is in heaven right now serving as your advocate, one who "lives forever to intercede with God" on your behalf. Don't wallow in guilt. Don't be overwhelmed by fear. The Judge is on your side. He has dealt with your sin, and he has provided an advocate for you. You've been set free, so live like it!

EZEKIEL 16:42–17:24

Sodom was an ancient city whose wickedness was world-renowned. Samaria was the capital of the northern kingdom, which was destroyed because of persistent sin. The Lord found Judah (the southern kingdom) more sinful than both.

"Then at last my [LORD'S] fury against you will be spent, and my jealous anger will subside. I will be calm and will not be angry with you anymore. ⁴³But first, because you have not remembered your youth but have angered me by doing all these evil things, I will fully repay you for all of your sins, says the Sovereign LORD. For you have added lewd acts to all your detestable sins. ⁴⁴Everyone who makes up proverbs will say of you, 'Like mother, like daughter.' ⁴⁵For your mother loathed her husband and her children, and so do you. And you are exactly like your sisters, for they despised their husbands and their children. Truly your mother was a Hittite and your father an Amorite.

⁴⁶"Your older sister was Samaria, who lived with her daughters in the north. Your younger sister was Sodom, who lived with her daughters in the south. ⁴⁷But you have not merely sinned as they did. You quickly surpassed them in corruption. ⁴⁸As surely as I live, says the Sovereign LORD, Sodom and her daughters were never as wicked as you and your daughters. ⁴⁹Sodom's sins were pride, gluttony, and laziness, while the poor and needy suffered outside her door. ⁵⁰She was proud and committed detestable sins, so I wiped her out, as you have seen.*

⁵¹"Even Samaria did not commit half your sins. You have done far more detestable things than your sisters ever did. They seem righteous compared to you. ⁵²Shame on you! Your sins are so terrible that you make your sisters seem righteous, even virtuous.

⁵³"But someday I will restore the fortunes of Sodom and Samaria, and I will restore you, too. ⁵⁴Then you will be truly ashamed of everything you have done, for your sins make them feel good in compar-

ison. ⁵⁵Yes, your sisters, Sodom and Samaria, and all their people will be restored, and at that time you also will be restored. ⁵⁶In your proud days you held Sodom in contempt. ⁵⁷But now your greater wickedness has been exposed to all the world, and you are the one who is scorned—by Edom* and all her neighbors and by Philistia. ⁵⁸This is your punishment for all your lewdness and detestable sins, says the LORD.

⁵⁹"Now this is what the Sovereign LORD says: I will give you what you deserve, for you have taken your solemn vows lightly by breaking your covenant. ⁶⁰Yet I will remember the covenant I made with you when you were young, and I will establish an everlasting covenant with you. ⁶¹Then you will remember with shame all the evil you have done. I will make your sisters, Samaria and Sodom, to be your daughters, even though they are not part of our covenant. ⁶²And I will reaffirm my covenant with you, and you will know that I am the LORD. ⁶³You will remember your sins and cover your mouth in silent shame when I forgive you of all that you have done. I, the Sovereign LORD, have spoken!"

17:1Then this message came to me from the LORD: ²"Son of man, give this riddle, and tell this story to the people of Israel. ³Give them this message from the Sovereign LORD:

"A great eagle with broad wings and
　　long feathers,
　　covered with many-colored
　　　plumage, came to Lebanon.
He seized the top of a cedar tree
⁴ 　and plucked off its highest
　　　branch.
He carried it away to a city filled with
　　merchants.
　　He planted it in a city of traders.
⁵ He also took a seedling from the land
　　and planted it in fertile soil.
He placed it beside a broad river,
　　where it could grow like a willow
　　　tree.

6 It took root there and
    grew into a low, spreading vine.
Its branches turned up toward
    the eagle,
and its roots grew down into
    the ground.
It produced strong branches
    and put out shoots.
7 But then another great eagle came
    with broad wings and full
    plumage.
So the vine now sent its roots and
    branches
    toward him for water,
8 even though it was already planted
    in good soil
    and had plenty of water
so it could grow into a splendid vine
    and produce rich leaves and
    luscious fruit.
9 "So now the Sovereign LORD asks:
Will this vine grow and prosper?
    No! I will pull it up, roots and all!
I will cut off its fruit
    and let its leaves wither and die.
I will pull it up easily
    without a strong arm or a large
    army.
10 But when the vine is transplanted,
    will it thrive?
No, it will wither away
    when the east wind blows against it.

It will die in the same good soil
    where it had grown so well."

11 Then this message came to me from
the LORD: 12 "Say to these rebels of Israel:
Don't you understand the meaning of this
riddle of the eagles? The king of Babylon
came to Jerusalem, took away her king
and princes, and brought them to Babylon. 13 He made a treaty with a member of
the royal family and forced him to take an
oath of loyalty. He also exiled Israel's most
influential leaders, 14 so Israel would not
become strong again and revolt. Only by
keeping her treaty with Babylon could Israel survive.

15 "Nevertheless, this man of Israel's
royal family rebelled against Babylon,
sending ambassadors to Egypt to request
a great army and many horses. Can Israel
break her sworn treaties like that and get
away with it? 16 No! For as surely as I live,
says the Sovereign LORD, the king of Israel
will die in Babylon, the land of the king
who put him in power and whose treaty
he disregarded and broke. 17 Pharaoh and
all his mighty army will fail to help Israel
when the king of Babylon lays siege to Jerusalem again and destroys many lives.
18 For the king of Israel disregarded his
treaty and broke it after swearing to obey;
therefore, he will not escape.

19 "So this is what the Sovereign LORD

WHAT THE BIBLE SAYS | The old and new covenants

HEBREWS 8:7-12 This passage is a quotation of Jeremiah 31:31-34 (October 18), which compares the new covenant with the old covenant. The old
covenant was a covenant of law between God and Israel. The new covenant is a covenant of grace between God and all who believe. • In Old
Testament times, animals were sacrificed because blood was demanded
as atonement for sins (Leviticus 17:11, February 25). The old covenant
was a shadow of the new, pointing forward to the day when Jesus himself
would be the final and ultimate sacrifice for sin. Jesus instituted a new
covenant between humans and God. Rather than an unblemished lamb
slain on the altar, the perfect Lamb of God was slain on the cross, a
sinless sacrifice so that our sins could be forgiven once and for all. All
those who believe in Christ receive that forgiveness. • Under this new
covenant, Jesus died in the place of sinners. Unlike the blood of animals,
his blood (because he is God) truly removes the sins of all who put their
faith in him. Because Jesus died *once for all*, he brought the sacrificial
system to an end. He forgave all sins—past, present, and future.

says: As surely as I live, I will punish him for breaking my covenant and disregarding the solemn oath he made in my name. [20]I will throw my net over him and capture him in my snare. I will bring him to Babylon and put him on trial for this treason against me. [21]And all his best warriors* will be killed in battle, and those who survive will be scattered to the four winds. Then you will know that I, the LORD, have spoken.

[22]"This is what the Sovereign LORD says: I will take a branch from the top of a tall cedar, and I will plant it on the top of Israel's highest mountain. [23]It will become a majestic cedar, sending forth its branches and producing seed. Birds of every sort will nest in it, finding shelter in the shade of its branches. [24]And all the trees will know that it is I, the LORD, who cuts the tall tree down and makes the short tree grow tall. It is I who makes the green tree wither and gives the dead tree new life. I, the LORD, have spoken, and I will do what I said!"

16:50 As in a few Hebrew manuscripts and Greek version; Masoretic Text reads *as I have seen.*   16:57 Many ancient manuscripts read *Aram.*   17:21 Or *his fleeing warriors.* The meaning of the Hebrew is uncertain.

HEBREWS 8:1-13

The death of a sacrificial animal represented the deserved punishment for a person's sin. Christ's work on our behalf did away with the sacrificial system. His sacrifice paid the price once and for all for our sin.

Here is the main point: We have a High Priest who sat down in the place of honor beside the throne of the majestic God in heaven. [2]There he ministers in the heavenly Tabernacle,* the true place of worship that was built by the Lord and not by human hands.

[3]And since every high priest is required to offer gifts and sacrifices, our High Priest must make an offering, too. [4]If he were here on earth, he would not even be a priest, since there already are priests who offer the gifts required by the law. [5]They serve in a system of worship that is only a copy, a shadow of the real one in heaven. For when Moses was getting ready to build the Tabernacle, God gave him this warning: "Be sure that you make everything according to the pattern I have shown you here on the mountain."*

[6]But now Jesus, our High Priest, has been given a ministry that is far superior to the old priesthood, for he is the one who mediates for us a far better covenant with God, based on better promises.

[7]If the first covenant had been faultless, there would have been no need for a second covenant to replace it. [8]But when God found fault with the people, he said:

"The day is coming, says the LORD,
  when I will make a new covenant
  with the people of Israel and
    Judah.
[9] This covenant will not be like
    the one
  I made with their ancestors
when I took them by the hand
  and led them out of the land of
    Egypt.
They did not remain faithful to my
    covenant,
  so I turned my back on them, says
    the LORD.
[10] But this is the new covenant I will
    make
  with the people of Israel on that
    day,* says the LORD:
I will put my laws in their minds,
  and I will write them on their
    hearts.
I will be their God,
  and they will be my people.
[11] And they will not need to teach their
    neighbors,
  nor will they need to teach their
    relatives,*
  saying, 'You should know the
    LORD.'
For everyone, from the least to the
    greatest,
  will know me already.
[12] And I will forgive their wickedness,
  and I will never again remember
    their sins."*

[13]When God speaks of a "new" covenant, it means he has made the first one obsolete. It is now out of date and will soon disappear.

8:2 Or *tent;* also in 8:5.   8:5 Exod 25:40; 26:30.   8:10 Greek *after those days.*   8:11 Greek *their brother.*   8:8-12 Jer 31:31-34.

PSALM 106:13-31

Yet how quickly they [the Israelites]
        forgot what he had done!
    They wouldn't wait for his
        counsel!
¹⁴ In the wilderness their desires ran
        wild,
    testing God's patience in that dry
        wasteland.
¹⁵ So he gave them what they asked for,
    but he sent a plague along with it.
¹⁶ The people in the camp were jealous
        of Moses
    and envious of Aaron, the LORD's
        holy priest.
¹⁷ Because of this, the earth opened up;
    it swallowed Dathan
    and buried Abiram and the other
        rebels.
¹⁸ Fire fell upon their followers;
    a flame consumed the wicked.

¹⁹ The people made a calf at Mount
        Sinai*;
    they bowed before an image made
        of gold.
²⁰ They traded their glorious God
    for a statue of a grass-eating bull.
²¹ They forgot God, their savior,
    who had done such great things
        in Egypt—
²² such wonderful things in the land
        of Ham,
    such awesome deeds at the
        Red Sea.
²³ So he declared he would destroy them.
    But Moses, his chosen one, stepped
        between the LORD and the people.

He begged him to turn from his
    anger and not destroy them.

²⁴ The people refused to enter the
        pleasant land,
    for they wouldn't believe his
        promise to care for them.
²⁵ Instead, they grumbled in their tents
    and refused to obey the LORD.
²⁶ Therefore, he solemnly swore
    that he would kill them in the
        wilderness,
²⁷ that he would scatter their
        descendants among the nations,
    exiling them to distant lands.

²⁸ Then our ancestors joined in the
        worship of Baal at Peor;
    they even ate sacrifices offered
        to the dead!
²⁹ They angered the LORD with all these
        things,
    so a plague broke out among them.
³⁰ But Phinehas had the courage
        to intervene,
    and the plague was stopped.
³¹ So he has been regarded as a righteous
        man
    ever since that time.

106:19 Hebrew *at Horeb,* another name for Sinai.

PROVERBS 27:7-9

A person who is full refuses honey, but
even bitter food tastes sweet to the hungry. □A person who strays from home
is like a bird that strays from its nest.
□The heartfelt counsel of a friend is as
sweet as perfume and incense.

NOVEMBER**8**

EZEKIEL 18:1–19:14

God is just. He holds each individual accountable
for his or her own sin. He likewise extends mercy
to anyone who turns to him in repentance!

Then another message came to me [Ezek-
iel] from the LORD: ²"Why do you quote
this proverb concerning the land of Israel:
'The parents have eaten sour grapes, but
their children's mouths pucker at the

taste'? ³As surely as I live, says the Sovereign LORD, you will not quote this proverb
anymore in Israel. ⁴For all people are mine
to judge—both parents and children alike.
And this is my rule: The person who sins
is the one who will die.

⁵"Suppose a certain man is righteous
and does what is just and right. ⁶He does
not feast in the mountains before Israel's

idols* or worship them. He does not commit adultery or have intercourse with a woman during her menstrual period. ⁷He is a merciful creditor, not keeping the items given as security by poor debtors. He does not rob the poor but instead gives food to the hungry and provides clothes for the needy. ⁸He grants loans without interest, stays away from injustice, is honest and fair when judging others, ⁹and faithfully obeys my decrees and regulations. Anyone who does these things is just and will surely live, says the Sovereign LORD.

¹⁰"But suppose that man has a son who grows up to be a robber or murderer and refuses to do what is right. ¹¹And that son does all the evil things his father would never do—he worships idols on the mountains, commits adultery, ¹²oppresses the poor and helpless, steals from debtors by refusing to let them redeem their security, worships idols, commits detestable sins, ¹³and lends money at excessive interest. Should such a sinful person live? No! He must die and must take full blame.

¹⁴"But suppose that sinful son, in turn, has a son who sees his father's wickedness and decides against that kind of life. ¹⁵This son refuses to worship idols on the mountains and does not commit adultery. ¹⁶He does not exploit the poor, but instead is fair to debtors and does not rob them. He gives food to the hungry and provides clothes for the needy. ¹⁷He helps the poor, does not lend money at interest, and obeys all my regulations and decrees. Such a person will not die because of his father's sins; he will surely live. ¹⁸But the father will die for his many sins—for being cruel, robbing people, and doing what was clearly wrong among his people.

¹⁹"'What?' you ask. 'Doesn't the child pay for the parent's sins?' No! For if the child does what is just and right and keeps my decrees, that child will surely live. ²⁰The person who sins is the one who will die. The child will not be punished for the parent's sins, and the parent will not be punished for the child's sins. Righteous people will be rewarded for their own righteous behavior, and wicked people will be punished for their own wickedness. ²¹But if wicked people turn away from all their sins and begin to obey my decrees and do what is just and right, they will surely live and not die. ²²All their past sins will be forgotten, and they will live because of the righteous things they have done.

²³"Do you think that I like to see wicked people die? says the Sovereign LORD. Of course not! I want them to turn from their wicked ways and live. ²⁴However, if righteous people turn from their righteous behavior and start doing sinful things and act like other sinners, should they be allowed to live? No, of course not! All their righteous acts will be forgotten, and they will die for their sins.

²⁵"Yet you say, 'The Lord isn't doing what's right!' Listen to me, O people of Israel. Am I the one not doing what's right, or is it you? ²⁶When righteous people turn from their righteous behavior and start doing sinful things, they will die for it. Yes, they will die because of their sinful deeds. ²⁷And if wicked people turn from their wickedness, obey the law, and do what is just and right, they will save their lives. ²⁸They will live because they thought it over and decided to turn from their sins. Such people will not die. ²⁹And yet the people of Israel keep saying, 'The Lord isn't doing what's right!' O people of Israel, it is you who are not doing what's right, not I.

³⁰"Therefore, I will judge each of you, O people of Israel, according to your actions, says the Sovereign LORD. Repent, and turn from your sins. Don't let them destroy you! ³¹Put all your rebellion behind you, and find yourselves a new heart and a new spirit. For why should you die, O people of Israel? ³²I don't want you to die, says the Sovereign LORD. Turn back and live!

19:1"SING this funeral song for the princes of Israel:

² "What is your mother?
    A lioness among lions!
  She lay down among the young lions
    and reared her cubs.
³ She raised one of her cubs
    to become a strong young lion.
  He learned to hunt and devour prey,
    and he became a man-eater.

4 Then the nations heard about him,
   and he was trapped in their pit.
They led him away with hooks
   to the land of Egypt.

5 "When the lioness saw
   that her hopes for him were gone,
she took another of her cubs
   and taught him to be a strong
      young lion.
6 He prowled among the other lions
   and stood out among them in his
      strength.
He learned to hunt and devour prey,
   and he, too, became a man-eater.
7 He demolished fortresses*
   and destroyed their towns
      and cities.
Their farms were desolated,
   and their crops were destroyed.
The land and its people trembled
      in fear
   when they heard him roar.
8 Then the armies of the nations
      attacked him,
   surrounding him from every
      direction.
They threw a net over him
   and captured him in their pit.
9 With hooks, they dragged him into
      a cage
   and brought him before the king
      of Babylon.

They held him in captivity,
   so his voice could never again
      be heard
   on the mountains of Israel.

10 "Your mother was like a vine
   planted by the water's edge.
It had lush, green foliage
   because of the abundant water.
11 Its branches became strong—
   strong enough to be a ruler's scepter.
It grew very tall,
   towering above all others.
It stood out because of its height
   and its many lush branches.
12 But the vine was uprooted in fury
   and thrown down to the ground.
The desert wind dried up its fruit
   and tore off its strong branches,
so that it withered
   and was destroyed by fire.
13 Now the vine is transplanted
   to the wilderness,
   where the ground is hard and dry.
14 A fire has burst out from its branches
   and devoured its fruit.
Its remaining limbs are not
   strong enough to be a ruler's scepter.

"This is a funeral song, and it will be used
in a funeral."

18:6 The Hebrew term (literally *round things*) probably
alludes to dung; also in 18:12, 15.   **19:7** As in Greek version;
Hebrew reads *He knew widows.*

WHAT THE BIBLE SAYS

Sin and its consequences

EZEKIEL 18:1-4, 20 Ezekiel brought a prophecy from the Lord that clearly
stated, "The person who sins is the one who will die" (18:4). While that
seems logical to us, it wasn't that clear to the people of Judah. They had
gone into exile away from their homeland, and many of them believed
they were being punished for the sins of their ancestors, not their own.
Thus, they did not honestly look at themselves and their own sinfulness,
preferring instead to cast the blame elsewhere. • God judges each
person individually. Although we often suffer from the effects of sins
committed by those who came before us, God does not punish us
for someone else's sins, and we can't use their mistakes as an excuse
for our sins. • God is a God of love, but he is also a God of perfect
justice. His perfect love causes him to be merciful to those who recognize their sin and turn to him, but he cannot ignore those who willfully
sin. He would prefer that they turn to him and have eternal life. Likewise,
we should not rejoice in the misfortunes of nonbelievers. Instead, we
should do all in our power to bring them to faith.

HEBREWS 9:1-10

The Tabernacle and the Old Testament rituals of worship were object lessons, physical markers that pointed to the spiritual truth that was fulfilled in Jesus Christ.

That first covenant between God and Israel had regulations for worship and a place of worship here on earth. [2]There were two rooms in that Tabernacle.* In the first room were a lampstand, a table, and sacred loaves of bread on the table. This room was called the Holy Place. [3]Then there was a curtain, and behind the curtain was the second room* called the Most Holy Place. [4]In that room were a gold incense altar and a wooden chest called the Ark of the Covenant, which was covered with gold on all sides. Inside the Ark were a gold jar containing manna, Aaron's staff that sprouted leaves, and the stone tablets of the covenant. [5]Above the Ark were the cherubim of divine glory, whose wings stretched out over the Ark's cover, the place of atonement. But we cannot explain these things in detail now.

[6]When these things were all in place, the priests regularly entered the first room* as they performed their religious duties. [7]But only the high priest ever entered the Most Holy Place, and only once a year. And he always offered blood for his own sins and for the sins the people had committed in ignorance. [8]By these regulations the Holy Spirit revealed that the entrance to the Most Holy Place was not freely open as long as the Tabernacle* and the system it represented were still in use.

[9]This is an illustration pointing to the present time. For the gifts and sacrifices that the priests offer are not able to cleanse the consciences of the people who bring them. [10]For that old system deals only with food and drink and various cleansing ceremonies—physical regulations that were in effect only until a better system could be established.

9:2 Or *tent;* also in 9:11, 21.   9:3 Greek *second tent.*
9:6 Greek *first tent.*   9:8 Or *the first room;* Greek reads *the first tent.*

PSALM 106:32-48

At Meribah, too, they [the Israelites]
    angered the LORD,
    causing Moses serious trouble.

[33] They made Moses angry,*
    and he spoke foolishly.

[34] Israel failed to destroy the nations
        in the land,
    as the LORD had commanded
        them.

[35] Instead, they mingled among
        the pagans
    and adopted their evil customs.

[36] They worshiped their idols,
    which led to their downfall.

[37] They even sacrificed their sons
    and their daughters to the demons.

[38] They shed innocent blood,
    the blood of their sons and
        daughters.
By sacrificing them to the idols
        of Canaan,
    they polluted the land with murder.

[39] They defiled themselves by their evil
        deeds,
    and their love of idols was adultery
        in the LORD's sight.

[40] That is why the LORD's anger burned
        against his people,
    and he abhorred his own special
        possession.

[41] He handed them over to pagan
        nations,
    and they were ruled by those who
        hated them.

[42] Their enemies crushed them
    and brought them under their cruel
        power.

[43] Again and again he rescued them,
    but they chose to rebel against him,
    and they were finally destroyed by
        their sin.

[44] Even so, he pitied them in their
        distress
    and listened to their cries.

[45] He remembered his covenant
        with them
    and relented because of his
        unfailing love.

[46] He even caused their captors
    to treat them with kindness.

[47] Save us, O LORD our God!
    Gather us back from among
        the nations,
    so we can thank your holy name
    and rejoice and praise you.

⁴⁸ Praise the LORD, the God of Israel,
who lives from everlasting
to everlasting!
Let all the people say, "Amen!"
Praise the LORD!

106:33 Hebrew *They embittered his spirit.*

PROVERBS 27:10

Never abandon a friend—either yours or your father's. When disaster strikes, you won't have to ask your brother for assistance. It's better to go to a neighbor than to a brother who lives far away.

NOVEMBER**9**

EZEKIEL 20:1-49

When Jehoiachin came to the throne at the age of eighteen, Judah was already under the control of Babylon and, unfortunately for Jehoiachin, already in rebellion against Babylon. Jehoiachin was taken captive and replaced with a king of Nebuchadnezzar's choosing.

On August 14,* during the seventh year of King Jehoiachin's captivity, some of the leaders of Israel came to request a message from the LORD. They sat down in front of me to wait for his reply. ² Then this message came to me from the LORD: ³"Son of man, tell the leaders of Israel, 'This is what the Sovereign LORD says: How dare you come to ask me for a message? As surely as I live, says the Sovereign LORD, I will tell you nothing!'

⁴"Son of man, bring charges against them and condemn them. Make them realize how detestable the sins of their ancestors really were. ⁵Give them this message from the Sovereign LORD: When I chose Israel—when I revealed myself to the descendants of Jacob in Egypt—I took a solemn oath that I, the LORD, would be their God. ⁶I took a solemn oath that day that I would bring them out of Egypt to a land I had discovered and explored for them—a good land, a land flowing with milk and honey, the best of all lands anywhere. ⁷Then I said to them, 'Each of you, get rid of the vile images you are so obsessed with. Do not defile yourselves with the idols* of Egypt, for I am the LORD your God.'

⁸"But they rebelled against me and would not listen. They did not get rid of the vile images they were obsessed with,

or forsake the idols of Egypt. Then I threatened to pour out my fury on them to satisfy my anger while they were still in Egypt. ⁹But I didn't do it, for I acted to protect the honor of my name. I would not allow shame to be brought on my name among the surrounding nations who saw me reveal myself by bringing the Israelites out of Egypt. ¹⁰So I brought them out of Egypt and led them into the wilderness. ¹¹There I gave them my decrees and regulations so they could find life by keeping them. ¹²And I gave them my Sabbath days of rest as a sign between them and me. It was to remind them that I am the LORD, who had set them apart to be holy.

¹³"But the people of Israel rebelled against me, and they refused to obey my decrees there in the wilderness. They wouldn't obey my regulations even though obedience would have given them life. They also violated my Sabbath days. So I threatened to pour out my fury on them, and I made plans to utterly consume them in the wilderness. ¹⁴But again I held back in order to protect the honor of my name before the nations who had seen my power in bringing Israel out of Egypt. ¹⁵But I took a solemn oath against them in the wilderness. I swore I would not bring them into the land I had given them, a land flowing with milk and honey, the most beautiful place on earth. ¹⁶For they had rejected my regulations, refused to follow my decrees, and violated my Sabbath days. Their hearts were given to their idols. ¹⁷Nevertheless, I took pity on them and held back from destroying them in the wilderness.

¹⁸"Then I warned their children not to follow in their parents' footsteps, defiling themselves with their idols. ¹⁹'I am the LORD your God,' I told them. 'Follow my decrees, pay attention to my regulations, ²⁰and keep my Sabbath days holy, for they are a sign to remind you that I am the LORD your God.'

²¹"But their children, too, rebelled against me. They refused to keep my decrees and follow my regulations, even though obedience would have given them life. And they also violated my Sabbath days. So again I threatened to pour out my fury on them in the wilderness. ²²Nevertheless, I withdrew my judgment against them to protect the honor of my name before the nations that had seen my power in bringing them out of Egypt. ²³But I took a solemn oath against them in the wilderness. I swore I would scatter them among all the nations ²⁴because they did not obey my regulations. They scorned my decrees by violating my Sabbath days and longing for the idols of their ancestors. ²⁵I gave them over to worthless decrees and regulations that would not lead to life. ²⁶I let them pollute themselves* with the very gifts I had given them, and I allowed them to give their firstborn children as offerings to their gods—so I might devastate them and remind them that I alone am the LORD.

²⁷"Therefore, son of man, give the people of Israel this message from the Sovereign LORD: Your ancestors continued to blaspheme and betray me, ²⁸for when I brought them into the land I had promised them, they offered sacrifices on every high hill and under every green tree they saw! They roused my fury as they offered up sacrifices to their gods. They brought their perfumes and incense and poured out their liquid offerings to them. ²⁹I said to them, 'What is this high place where you are going?' (This kind of pagan shrine has been called Bamah—'high place'—ever since.)

³⁰"Therefore, give the people of Israel this message from the Sovereign LORD: Do you plan to pollute yourselves just as your ancestors did? Do you intend to keep prostituting yourselves by worshiping vile images? ³¹For when you offer gifts to them and give your little children to be burned as sacrifices,* you continue to pollute yourselves with idols to this day. Should I allow you to ask for a message from me, O people of Israel? As surely as I live, says the Sovereign LORD, I will tell you nothing.

³²"You say, 'We want to be like the nations all around us, who serve idols of wood and stone.' But what you have in mind will never happen. ³³As surely as I live, says the Sovereign LORD, I will rule over you with an iron fist in great anger and with awesome power. ³⁴And in anger I will reach out with my strong hand and powerful arm, and I will bring you back* from the lands where you are scattered. ³⁵I will bring you into the wilderness of the nations, and there I will judge you face to face. ³⁶I will judge you there just as I did your ancestors in the wilderness after bringing them out of Egypt, says the Sovereign LORD. ³⁷I will examine you carefully and hold you to the terms of the covenant. ³⁸I will purge you of all those who rebel and revolt against me. I will bring them out of the countries where they are in exile, but they will never enter the land of Israel. Then you will know that I am the LORD.

³⁹"As for you, O people of Israel, this is what the Sovereign LORD says: Go right ahead and worship your idols, but sooner or later you will obey me and will stop bringing shame on my holy name by worshiping idols. ⁴⁰For on my holy mountain, the great mountain of Israel, says the Sovereign LORD, the people of Israel will someday worship me, and I will accept them. There I will require that you bring me all your offerings and choice gifts and sacrifices. ⁴¹When I bring you home from exile, you will be like a pleasing sacrifice to me. And I will display my holiness through you as all the nations watch. ⁴²Then when I have brought you home to the land I promised with a solemn oath to give to your ancestors, you will know that I am the LORD. ⁴³You will look back on all the ways you defiled yourselves and will hate yourselves because of the evil you have done. ⁴⁴You will know that I am the LORD, O people of Israel, when I have honored my name by treating you mercifully

in spite of your wickedness. I, the Sovereign LORD, have spoken!"

45*Then this message came to me from the LORD: 46"Son of man, turn and face the south* and speak out against it; prophesy against the brushlands of the Negev. 47Tell the southern wilderness, 'This is what the Sovereign LORD says: Hear the word of the LORD! I will set you on fire, and every tree, both green and dry, will be burned. The terrible flames will not be quenched and will scorch everything from south to north. 48And everyone in the world will see that I, the LORD, have set this fire. It will not be put out.'"

49Then I said, "O Sovereign LORD, they are saying of me, 'He only talks in riddles!'"

20:1 Hebrew *In the fifth month, on the tenth day,* of the ancient Hebrew lunar calendar. This day was August 14, 591 B.C.; also see note on 1:1.   **20:7** The Hebrew term (literally *round things*) probably alludes to dung; also in 20:8, 16, 18, 24, 31, 39.   **20:25-26** Or *I gave them worthless decrees and regulations.... I polluted them.*   **20:31** Or *and make your little children pass through the fire.*   **20:34** Greek version reads *I will welcome you.* Compare 2 Cor 6:17.   **20:45** Verses 20:45-49 are numbered 21:1-5 in Hebrew text.   **20:46** Hebrew *toward Teman.*

HEBREWS 9:11-28

Today's reading contains a truth that many today would like to ignore—that each of us must face judgment after we die. Fortunately, Jesus died on the cross to take the penalty of our sins.

So Christ has now become the High Priest over all the good things that have come.*

He has entered that greater, more perfect Tabernacle in heaven, which was not made by human hands and is not part of this created world. 12With his own blood—not the blood of goats and calves—he entered the Most Holy Place once for all time and secured our redemption forever.

13Under the old system, the blood of goats and bulls and the ashes of a young cow could cleanse people's bodies from ceremonial impurity. 14Just think how much more the blood of Christ will purify our consciences from sinful deeds* so that we can worship the living God. For by the power of the eternal Spirit, Christ offered himself to God as a perfect sacrifice for our sins. 15That is why he is the one who mediates a new covenant between God and people, so that all who are called can receive the eternal inheritance God has promised them. For Christ died to set them free from the penalty of the sins they had committed under that first covenant.

16Now when someone leaves a will,* it is necessary to prove that the person who made it is dead.* 17The will goes into effect only after the person's death. While the person who made it is still alive, the will cannot be put into effect.

18That is why even the first covenant was put into effect with the blood of an animal. 19For after Moses had read each

WHO GOD IS

Jesus is our sacrifice

HEBREWS 9:26-28 As you read this chapter, some of it may sound familiar because you've read the portions of the Old Testament from which these rituals originated. You read in Leviticus about the sacrifices. At the end of Exodus, you read about how the Most Holy Place was where God himself dwelt among his people. The author is explaining how that system foreshadowed what God would do about sin through his Son. • In the Old Testament method of cleansing from sin, the people were not allowed to approach God themselves. They had to rely upon the priest to offer an animal sacrifice. Once a year, the high priest would enter the Most Holy Place in the Temple and sprinkle the blood that would atone for the sins of the nation as a whole. Now, however, we can approach God at any time. We don't have to bring an animal to be sacrificed because Jesus was the final and perfect sacrifice for all sin. By the sacrifice of God's Son, we are free from the power of sin and death. He "died once for all time as a sacrifice to take away the sins of many people"—including you.

of God's commandments to all the people, he took the blood of calves and goats,* along with water, and sprinkled both the book of God's law and all the people, using hyssop branches and scarlet wool. ²⁰Then he said, "This blood confirms the covenant God has made with you."* ²¹And in the same way, he sprinkled blood on the Tabernacle and on everything used for worship. ²²In fact, according to the law of Moses, nearly everything was purified with blood. For without the shedding of blood, there is no forgiveness.

²³That is why the Tabernacle and everything in it, which were copies of things in heaven, had to be purified by the blood of animals. But the real things in heaven had to be purified with far better sacrifices than the blood of animals.

²⁴For Christ did not enter into a holy place made with human hands, which was only a copy of the true one in heaven. He entered into heaven itself to appear now before God on our behalf. ²⁵And he did not enter heaven to offer himself again and again, like the high priest here on earth who enters the Most Holy Place year after year with the blood of an animal. ²⁶If that had been necessary, Christ would have had to die again and again, ever since the world began. But now, once for all time, he has appeared at the end of the age* to remove sin by his own death as a sacrifice.

²⁷And just as each person is destined to die once and after that comes judgment, ²⁸so also Christ died once for all time as a sacrifice to take away the sins of many people. He will come again, not to deal with our sins, but to bring salvation to all who are eagerly waiting for him.

9:11 Some manuscripts read *that are about to come.*
9:14 Greek *from dead works.*   **9:16a** Or *covenant;* also in 9:17.   **9:16b** Or *Now when someone makes a covenant, it is necessary to ratify it with the death of a sacrifice.*
9:19 Some manuscripts omit *and goats.*   **9:20** Exod 24:8.
9:26 Greek *the ages.*

PSALM 107:1-43

Give thanks to the LORD, for he is good!
    His faithful love endures forever.
² Has the LORD redeemed you? Then speak out!

Tell others he has redeemed you
    from your enemies.
³ For he has gathered the exiles from many lands,
    from east and west,
    from north and south.

⁴ Some wandered in the wilderness,
    lost and homeless.
⁵ Hungry and thirsty,
    they nearly died.
⁶ "LORD, help!" they cried in their trouble,
    and he rescued them from their distress.
⁷ He led them straight to safety,
    to a city where they could live.
⁸ Let them praise the LORD for his great love
    and for the wonderful things he has done for them.
⁹ For he satisfies the thirsty
    and fills the hungry with good things.

¹⁰ Some sat in darkness and deepest gloom,
    imprisoned in iron chains of misery.
¹¹ They rebelled against the words of God,
    scorning the counsel of the Most High.
¹² That is why he broke them with hard labor;
    they fell, and no one was there to help them.
¹³ "LORD, help!" they cried in their trouble,
    and he saved them from their distress.
¹⁴ He led them from the darkness and deepest gloom;
    he snapped their chains.
¹⁵ Let them praise the LORD for his great love
    and for the wonderful things he has done for them.
¹⁶ For he broke down their prison gates of bronze;
    he cut apart their bars of iron.

¹⁷ Some were fools; they rebelled
    and suffered for their sins.
¹⁸ They couldn't stand the thought of food,

and they were knocking on death's door.

¹⁹ "LORD, help!" they cried in their trouble,
　and he saved them from their distress.
²⁰ He sent out his word and healed them,
　snatching them from the door of death.
²¹ Let them praise the LORD for his great love
　and for the wonderful things he has done for them.
²² Let them offer sacrifices of thanksgiving
　and sing joyfully about his glorious acts.

²³ Some went off to sea in ships,
　plying the trade routes of the world.
²⁴ They, too, observed the LORD's power in action,
　his impressive works on the deepest seas.
²⁵ He spoke, and the winds rose,
　stirring up the waves.
²⁶ Their ships were tossed to the heavens
　and plunged again to the depths;
　the sailors cringed in terror.
²⁷ They reeled and staggered like drunkards
　and were at their wits' end.
²⁸ "LORD, help!" they cried in their trouble,
　and he saved them from their distress.
²⁹ He calmed the storm to a whisper
　and stilled the waves.
³⁰ What a blessing was that stillness
　as he brought them safely into harbor!
³¹ Let them praise the LORD for his great love
　and for the wonderful things he has done for them.
³² Let them exalt him publicly before the congregation

and before the leaders of the nation.

³³ He changes rivers into deserts,
　and springs of water into dry, thirsty land.
³⁴ He turns the fruitful land into salty wastelands,
　because of the wickedness of those who live there.
³⁵ But he also turns deserts into pools of water,
　the dry land into springs of water.
³⁶ He brings the hungry to settle there
　and to build their cities.
³⁷ They sow their fields, plant their vineyards,
　and harvest their bumper crops.
³⁸ How he blesses them!
　They raise large families there,
　and their herds of livestock increase.

³⁹ When they decrease in number and become impoverished
　through oppression, trouble, and sorrow,
⁴⁰ the LORD pours contempt on their princes,
　causing them to wander in trackless wastelands.
⁴¹ But he rescues the poor from trouble
　and increases their families like flocks of sheep.
⁴² The godly will see these things and be glad,
　while the wicked are struck silent.
⁴³ Those who are wise will take all this to heart;
　they will see in our history the faithful love of the LORD.

PROVERBS 27:11

Be wise, my child,* and make my heart glad. Then I will be able to answer my critics.

27:11 Hebrew *my son.*

EZEKIEL 21:1-22:31

Today's reading includes a prophecy against the Ammonites, who were distant relatives and enemies of the Israelites.

¹*Then this message came to me [Ezekiel] from the LORD: ²"Son of man, turn and face Jerusalem and prophesy against Israel and her sanctuaries. ³Tell her, 'This is what the LORD says: I am your enemy, O Israel, and I am about to unsheath my sword to destroy your people—the righteous and the wicked alike. ⁴Yes, I will cut off both the righteous and the wicked! I will draw my sword against everyone in the land from south to north. ⁵Everyone in the world will know that I am the LORD. My sword is in my hand, and it will not return to its sheath until its work is finished.'

⁶"Son of man, groan before the people! Groan before them with bitter anguish and a broken heart. ⁷When they ask why you are groaning, tell them, 'I groan because of the terrifying news I have heard. When it comes true, the boldest heart will melt with fear; all strength will disappear. Every spirit will faint; strong knees will become as weak as water. And the Sovereign LORD says: It is coming! It's on its way!'"

⁸Then the LORD said to me, ⁹"Son of man, give the people this message from the LORD:

"A sword, a sword
    is being sharpened and polished.
¹⁰ It is sharpened for terrible slaughter
    and polished to flash like lightning!
Now will you laugh?
    Those far stronger than you have
        fallen beneath its power!*
¹¹ Yes, the sword is now being sharpened
        and polished;
    it is being prepared for the
        executioner.

¹² "Son of man, cry out and wail;
    pound your thighs in anguish,
for that sword will slaughter my
        people and their leaders—
    everyone will die!

¹³ It will put them all to the test.
    What chance do they have?*
    says the Sovereign LORD.

¹⁴ "Son of man, prophesy to them
    and clap your hands.
Then take the sword and brandish
        it twice,
    even three times,
to symbolize the great massacre,
    the great massacre facing them
        on every side.
¹⁵ Let their hearts melt with terror,
    for the sword glitters at every gate.
It flashes like lightning
    and is polished for slaughter!
¹⁶ O sword, slash to the right,
    then slash to the left,
wherever you will,
    wherever you want.
¹⁷ I, too, will clap my hands,
    and I will satisfy my fury.
    I, the LORD, have spoken!"

¹⁸Then this message came to me from the LORD: ¹⁹"Son of man, make a map and trace two routes on it for the sword of Babylon's king to follow. Put a signpost on the road that comes out of Babylon where the road forks into two—²⁰one road going to Ammon and its capital, Rabbah, and the other to Judah and fortified Jerusalem. ²¹The king of Babylon now stands at the fork, uncertain whether to attack Jerusalem or Rabbah. He calls his magicians to look for omens. They cast lots by shaking arrows from the quiver. They inspect the livers of animal sacrifices. ²²The omen in his right hand says, 'Jerusalem!' With battering rams his soldiers will go against the gates, shouting for the kill. They will put up siege towers and build ramps against the walls. ²³The people of Jerusalem will think it is a false omen, because of their treaty with the Babylonians. But the king of Babylon will remind the people of their rebellion. Then he will attack and capture them.

²⁴"Therefore, this is what the Sovereign LORD says: Again and again you remind me of your sin and your guilt. You don't

even try to hide it! In everything you do, your sins are obvious for all to see. So now the time of your punishment has come!

²⁵"O you corrupt and wicked prince of Israel, your final day of reckoning is here! ²⁶This is what the Sovereign LORD says:

"Take off your jeweled crown,
for the old order changes.
Now the lowly will be exalted,
and the mighty will be brought
down.
²⁷ Destruction! Destruction!
I will surely destroy the kingdom.
And it will not be restored until the
one appears
who has the right to judge it.
Then I will hand it over to him.

²⁸"And now, son of man, prophesy concerning the Ammonites and their mockery. Give them this message from the Sovereign LORD:

"A sword, a sword
is drawn for your slaughter.
It is polished to destroy,
flashing like lightning!
²⁹ Your prophets have given false visions,
and your fortune-tellers have told lies.
The sword will fall on the necks of the
wicked
for whom the day of final reckoning
has come.

³⁰ "Now return the sword to its sheath,
for in your own country,
the land of your birth,
I will pass judgment upon you.
³¹ I will pour out my fury on you
and blow on you with the fire
of my anger.
I will hand you over to cruel men
who are skilled in destruction.
³² You will be fuel for the fire,
and your blood will be spilled
in your own land.
You will be utterly wiped out,
your memory lost to history,
for I, the LORD, have spoken!"

²²:¹Now this message came to me from the LORD: ²"Son of man, are you ready to judge Jerusalem? Are you ready to judge this city of murderers? Publicly denounce her detestable sins, ³and give her this message from the Sovereign LORD: O city of murderers, doomed and damned—city of idols,* filthy and foul—⁴you are guilty because of the blood you have shed. You are defiled because of the idols you have made. Your day of destruction has come! You have reached the end of your years. I will make you an object of mockery throughout the world. ⁵O infamous city, filled with confusion, you will be mocked by people far and near.

⁶"Every leader in Israel who lives within your walls is bent on murder. ⁷Fathers and mothers are treated with contempt. Foreigners are forced to pay for protection. Orphans and widows are wronged and oppressed among you. ⁸You despise my holy things and violate my Sabbath days of rest. ⁹People accuse others falsely and send them to their death. You are filled with idol worshipers and people who do obscene things. ¹⁰Men sleep with their fathers' wives and have intercourse with women who are menstruating. ¹¹Within your walls live men who commit adultery with their neighbors' wives, who defile their daughters-in-law, or who rape their own sisters. ¹²There are hired murderers, loan racketeers, and extortioners everywhere. They never even think of me and my commands, says the Sovereign LORD.

¹³"But now I clap my hands in indignation over your dishonest gain and bloodshed. ¹⁴How strong and courageous will you be in my day of reckoning? I, the LORD, have spoken, and I will do what I said. ¹⁵I will scatter you among the nations and purge you of your wickedness. ¹⁶And when I have been dishonored among the nations because of you,* you will know that I am the LORD."

¹⁷Then this message came to me from the LORD: ¹⁸"Son of man, the people of Israel are the worthless slag that remains after silver is smelted. They are the dross that is left over—a useless mixture of copper, tin, iron, and lead. ¹⁹So tell them, 'This is what the Sovereign LORD says: Because you are all worthless slag, I will bring you to my crucible in Jerusalem. ²⁰Just as copper, iron, lead, and tin are melted down in a furnace, I will melt you down in the heat of my fury. ²¹I will gather you together and blow the fire of my anger upon you, ²²and

you will melt like silver in fierce heat. Then you will know that I, the LORD, have poured out my fury on you.'"

²³Again a message came to me from the LORD: ²⁴"Son of man, give the people of Israel this message: In the day of my indignation, you will be like a polluted land, a land without rain. ²⁵Your princes* plot conspiracies just as lions stalk their prey. They devour innocent people, seizing treasures and extorting wealth. They make many widows in the land. ²⁶Your priests have violated my instructions and defiled my holy things. They make no distinction between what is holy and what is not. And they do not teach my people the difference between what is ceremonially clean and unclean. They disregard my Sabbath days so that I am dishonored among them. ²⁷Your leaders are like wolves who tear apart their victims. They actually destroy people's lives for money! ²⁸And your prophets cover up for them by announcing false visions and making lying predictions. They say, 'My message is from the Sovereign LORD,' when the LORD hasn't spoken a single word to them. ²⁹Even common people oppress the poor, rob the needy, and deprive foreigners of justice.

³⁰"I looked for someone who might rebuild the wall of righteousness that guards the land. I searched for someone to stand in the gap in the wall so I wouldn't have to destroy the land, but I found no one. ³¹So now I will pour out my fury on them, consuming them with the fire of my anger. I will heap on their heads the full penalty for all their sins. I, the Sovereign LORD, have spoken!"

21:1 Verses 21:1-32 are numbered 21:6-37 in Hebrew text. 21:10 The meaning of the Hebrew is uncertain. 21:13 The meaning of the Hebrew is uncertain. 22:3 The Hebrew term (literally *round things*) probably alludes to dung; also in 22:4. 22:16 Or *when you have been dishonored among the nations.* 22:25 As in Greek version; Hebrew reads *prophets.*

HEBREWS 10:1-17
God is the same throughout the entire Bible. In the Old Testament, the prophets told Israel over and over, "God wants your hearts, not just your rituals." Jesus came to prove that fact.

The old system under the law of Moses was only a shadow, a dim preview of the good things to come, not the good things themselves. The sacrifices under that system were repeated again and again, year after year, but they were never able to provide perfect cleansing for those who came to worship. ²If they could have provided perfect cleansing, the sacrifices would have stopped, for the worshipers would have been purified once for all time, and their feelings of guilt would have disappeared. ³But instead, those sacrifices actually reminded them of their sins year after year. ⁴For it is not possible for the blood of bulls and goats to take away sins. ⁵That is why, when Christ* came into the world, he said to God,

"You did not want animal sacrifices
   or sin offerings.
But you have given me a body
   to offer.
⁶ You were not pleased with burnt
   offerings
   or other offerings for sin.
⁷ Then I said, 'Look, I have come to do
   your will, O God—
   as is written about me in the
   Scriptures.'"*

⁸First, Christ said, "You did not want animal sacrifices or sin offerings or burnt offerings or other offerings for sin, nor were you pleased with them" (though they are required by the law of Moses). ⁹Then he said, "Look, I have come to do your will." He cancels the first covenant in order to put the second into effect. ¹⁰For God's will was for us to be made holy by the sacrifice of the body of Jesus Christ, once for all time.

¹¹Under the old covenant, the priest stands and ministers before the altar day after day, offering the same sacrifices again and again, which can never take away sins. ¹²But our High Priest offered himself to God as a single sacrifice for sins, good for all time. Then he sat down in the place of honor at God's right hand. ¹³There he waits until his enemies are humbled and made a footstool under his feet. ¹⁴For by that one offering he forever made perfect those who are being made holy.

¹⁵And the Holy Spirit also testifies that this is so. For he says,

¹⁶ "This is the new covenant I will make
   with my people on that day,* says
   the LORD:

I will put my laws in their hearts,
and I will write them on their
minds."*

[17] Then he says,

"I will never again remember
their sins and lawless deeds."*

10:5 Greek *he;* also in 10:8.   10:5-7 Ps 40:6-8 (Greek version).   10:16a Greek *after those days.*   10:16b Jer 31:33a.   10:17 Jer 31:34b.

PSALM 108:1-13

A song. A psalm of David.

[1] My heart is confident in you, O God;
no wonder I can sing your praises
with all my heart!
[2] Wake up, lyre and harp!
I will wake the dawn with my song.
[3] I will thank you, LORD, among all
the people.
I will sing your praises among
the nations.
[4] For your unfailing love is higher than
the heavens.
Your faithfulness reaches to the
clouds.
[5] Be exalted, O God, above the highest
heavens.
May your glory shine over all the
earth.
[6] Now rescue your beloved people.
Answer and save us by your power.
[7] God has promised this by his
holiness*:

"I will divide up Shechem with joy.
I will measure out the valley
of Succoth.
[8] Gilead is mine,
and Manasseh, too.
Ephraim, my helmet, will produce
my warriors,
and Judah, my scepter, will produce
my kings.
[9] But Moab, my washbasin, will become
my servant,
and I will wipe my feet on Edom
and shout in triumph over
Philistia."

[10] Who will bring me into the fortified
city?
Who will bring me victory over
Edom?
[11] Have you rejected us, O God?
Will you no longer march with
our armies?
[12] Oh, please help us against our
enemies,
for all human help is useless.
[13] With God's help we will do mighty
things,
for he will trample down our foes.

108:7 Or *in his sanctuary.*

PROVERBS 27:12

A prudent person foresees danger and takes precautions. The simpleton goes blindly on and suffers the consequences.

HOW WE LIVE

Growing in faith

EZEKIEL 22:30 Have you ever heard the story of the little Dutch boy who saved his city? The story is about a boy who was passing one of the many dykes that held back the sea. Water trickled through a small hole. The boy stopped and placed his finger in the hole. Eventually, an adult came along who got help and the dyke was repaired. The story is meant to teach that even a small trickle of water can become a torrent that might have eventually taken down the dyke and the town with it. The boy, with just his pudgy little finger in a hole, had saved the city. In Israel, God was looking for someone to put his finger in the dyke—someone to stand in the gap. The wall spoken of here is not made of stones, but of faithful people united in their efforts to resist evil. • Being a believer means making a stand. Sometimes you'll be alone. But stand in the gap and hold back the water. It only takes one person to stem the tide of evil and make a difference in the world. Maybe that one person is you.

EZEKIEL 23:1-49

When the Israelites settled into the Promised Land, they were a united kingdom. As time passed, the nation divided into the northern and southern kingdoms of Israel and Judah respectively. Ezekiel described these kingdoms as two sisters.

This message came to me [Ezekiel] from the LORD: ²"Son of man, once there were two sisters who were daughters of the same mother. ³They became prostitutes in Egypt. Even as young girls, they allowed men to fondle their breasts. ⁴The older girl was named Oholah, and her sister was Oholibah. I married them, and they bore me sons and daughters. I am speaking of Samaria and Jerusalem, for Oholah is Samaria and Oholibah is Jerusalem.

⁵"Then Oholah lusted after other lovers instead of me, and she gave her love to the Assyrian officers. ⁶They were all attractive young men, captains and commanders dressed in handsome blue, charioteers driving their horses. ⁷And so she prostituted herself with the most desirable men of Assyria, worshiping their idols* and defiling herself. ⁸For when she left Egypt, she did not leave her spirit of prostitution behind. She was still as lewd as in her youth, when the Egyptians slept with her, fondled her breasts, and used her as a prostitute.

⁹"And so I handed her over to her Assyrian lovers, whom she desired so much. ¹⁰They stripped her, took away her children as their slaves, and then killed her. After she received her punishment, her reputation was known to every woman in the land.

¹¹"Yet even though Oholibah saw what had happened to Oholah, her sister, she followed right in her footsteps. And she was even more depraved, abandoning herself to her lust and prostitution. ¹²She fawned over all the Assyrian officers—those captains and commanders in handsome uniforms, those charioteers driving their horses—all of them attractive young men. ¹³I saw the way she was going, defiling herself just like her older sister.

¹⁴"Then she carried her prostitution even further. She fell in love with pictures that were painted on a wall—pictures of Babylonian* military officers, outfitted in striking red uniforms. ¹⁵Handsome belts encircled their waists, and flowing turbans crowned their heads. They were dressed like chariot officers from the land of Babylonia.* ¹⁶When she saw these paintings, she longed to give herself to them, so she sent messengers to Babylonia to invite them to come to her. ¹⁷So they came and committed adultery with her, defiling her in the bed of love. After being defiled, however, she rejected them in disgust.

¹⁸"In the same way, I became disgusted with Oholibah and rejected her, just as I had rejected her sister, because she flaunted herself before them and gave herself to satisfy their lusts. ¹⁹Yet she turned to even greater prostitution, remembering her youth when she was a prostitute in Egypt. ²⁰She lusted after lovers with genitals as large as a donkey's and emissions like those of a horse. ²¹And so, Oholibah, you relived your former days as a young girl in Egypt, when you first allowed your breasts to be fondled.

²²"Therefore, Oholibah, this is what the Sovereign LORD says: I will send your lovers against you from every direction—those very nations from which you turned away in disgust. ²³For the Babylonians will come with all the Chaldeans from Pekod and Shoa and Koa. And all the Assyrians will come with them—handsome young captains, commanders, chariot officers, and other high-ranking officers, all riding their horses. ²⁴They will all come against you from the north* with chariots, wagons, and a great army prepared for attack. They will take up positions on every side, surrounding you with men armed with shields and helmets. And I will hand you over to them for punishment so they can do with you as they please. ²⁵I will turn my jealous anger against you, and they will deal harshly with you. They will cut off your nose and ears, and any survivors will then be slaughtered by the sword. Your

children will be taken away as captives, and everything that is left will be burned. ²⁶They will strip you of your beautiful clothes and jewels. ²⁷In this way, I will put a stop to the lewdness and prostitution you brought from Egypt. You will never again cast longing eyes on those things or fondly remember your time in Egypt.

²⁸"For this is what the Sovereign LORD says: I will surely hand you over to your enemies, to those you loathe, those you rejected. ²⁹They will treat you with hatred and rob you of all you own, leaving you stark naked. The shame of your prostitution will be exposed to all the world. ³⁰You brought all this on yourself by prostituting yourself to other nations, defiling yourself with all their idols. ³¹Because you have followed in your sister's footsteps, I will force you to drink the same cup of terror she drank.

³²"Yes, this is what the Sovereign LORD says:

"You will drink from your sister's cup
        of terror,
    a cup that is large and deep.
It is filled to the brim
    with scorn and derision,
³³ Drunkenness and anguish will fill you,
    for your cup is filled to the brim
        with distress and desolation,
    the same cup your sister Samaria
        drank.
³⁴ You will drain that cup of terror
    to the very bottom.
Then you will smash it to pieces
    and beat your breast in anguish.
    I, the Sovereign LORD, have spoken!

³⁵"And because you have forgotten me and turned your back on me, this is what the Sovereign LORD says: You must bear the consequences of all your lewdness and prostitution."

³⁶The LORD said to me, "Son of man, you must accuse Oholah and Oholibah of all their detestable sins. ³⁷They have committed both adultery and murder—adultery by worshiping idols and murder by burning as sacrifices the children they bore to me. ³⁸Furthermore, they have defiled my Temple and violated my Sabbath day! ³⁹On the very day that they sacrificed their children to their idols, they boldly came into my Temple to worship! They came in and defiled my house.

⁴⁰"You sisters sent messengers to distant lands to get men. Then when they arrived, you bathed yourselves, painted your eyelids, and put on your finest jewels for them. ⁴¹You sat with them on a beautifully embroidered couch and put my incense and my special oil on a table that was spread before you. ⁴²From your room came the sound of many men carousing. They were lustful men and drunkards* from the wilderness, who put bracelets on your wrists and beautiful crowns on your heads. ⁴³Then I said, 'If they really want to have sex with old worn-out prostitutes like these, let them!' ⁴⁴And that is what they did. They had sex with Oholah and Oholibah, these shameless prostitutes. ⁴⁵But righteous people will judge these sister cities for what they really are— adulterers and murderers.

⁴⁶"Now this is what the Sovereign LORD says: Bring an army against them and hand them over to be terrorized and plundered. ⁴⁷For their enemies will stone them and kill them with swords. They will butcher their sons and daughters and burn their homes. ⁴⁸In this way, I will put an end to lewdness and idolatry in the land, and my judgment will be a warning to others not to follow their wicked example. ⁴⁹You will be fully repaid for all your prostitution—your worship of idols. Yes, you will suffer the full penalty. Then you will know that I am the Sovereign LORD."

23:7 The Hebrew term (literally *round things*) probably alludes to dung; also in 23:30, 37, 39, 49.   **23:14** Or *Chaldean.*   **23:15** Or *Chaldea;* also in 23:16.   **23:24** As in Greek version; the meaning of the Hebrew is uncertain. **23:42** Or *Sabeans.*

HEBREWS 10:18-39

Sin is serious. There's no getting around that fact. But sins can be forgiven because of Christ's once-and-for-all sacrifice. God has made a way for us to be holy.

And when sins have been forgiven, there is no need to offer any more sacrifices.

¹⁹And so, dear brothers and sisters,* we can boldly enter heaven's Most Holy Place because of the blood of Jesus. ²⁰By his death,* Jesus opened a new and life-giving way through the curtain into the Most

Holy Place. ²¹And since we have a great High Priest who rules over God's house, ²²let us go right into the presence of God with sincere hearts fully trusting him. For our guilty consciences have been sprinkled with Christ's blood to make us clean, and our bodies have been washed with pure water.

²³Let us hold tightly without wavering to the hope we affirm, for God can be trusted to keep his promise. ²⁴Let us think of ways to motivate one another to acts of love and good works. ²⁵And let us not neglect our meeting together, as some people do, but encourage one another, especially now that the day of his return is drawing near.

²⁶Dear friends, if we deliberately continue sinning after we have received knowledge of the truth, there is no longer any sacrifice that will cover these sins. ²⁷There is only the terrible expectation of God's judgment and the raging fire that will consume his enemies. ²⁸For anyone who refused to obey the law of Moses was put to death without mercy on the testimony of two or three witnesses. ²⁹Just think how much worse the punishment will be for those who have trampled on the Son of God, and have treated the blood of the covenant, which made us holy, as if it were common and unholy, and have insulted and disdained the Holy Spirit who brings God's mercy to us. ³⁰For we know the one who said,

"I will take revenge.
I will pay them back."*

He also said,

"The LORD will judge his own people."*

³¹It is a terrible thing to fall into the hands of the living God.

³²Think back on those early days when you first learned about Christ.* Remember how you remained faithful even though it meant terrible suffering. ³³Sometimes you were exposed to public ridicule and were beaten, and sometimes you helped others who were suffering the same things. ³⁴You suffered along with those who were thrown into jail, and when all you owned was taken from you, you accepted it with joy. You knew there were better things waiting for you that will last forever.

³⁵So do not throw away this confident trust in the Lord. Remember the great reward it brings you! ³⁶Patient endurance is what you need now, so that you will continue to do God's will. Then you will receive all that he has promised.

³⁷ "For in just a little while,
　　the Coming One will come and not
　　　delay.
³⁸ And my righteous ones will live
　　　by faith.*
　　But I will take no pleasure in anyone
　　　who turns away."*

³⁹But we are not like those who turn away from God to their own destruction. We are the faithful ones, whose souls will be saved.

10:19 Greek *brothers.*　10:20 Greek *Through his flesh.* 10:30a Deut 32:35.　10:30b Deut 32:36.　10:32 Greek *when you were first enlightened.*　10:38 Or *my righteous ones will live by their faithfulness;* Greek reads *my righteous one will live by faith.*　10:37-38 Hab 2:3-4.

PSALM 109:1-31
For the choir director: A psalm of David.

¹ **O** God, whom I praise,
　　don't stand silent and aloof
² while the wicked slander me
　　and tell lies about me.
³ They surround me with hateful words
　　and fight against me for no reason.
⁴ I love them, but they try to destroy me
　　with accusations
　　even as I am praying for them!
⁵ They repay evil for good,
　　and hatred for my love.

⁶ They say,* "Get an evil person to turn
　　　against him.
　　Send an accuser to bring him
　　　to trial.
⁷ When his case comes up for
　　　judgment,
　　let him be pronounced guilty.
　　Count his prayers as sins.
⁸ Let his years be few;
　　let someone else take his position.
⁹ May his children become fatherless,
　　and his wife a widow.
¹⁰ May his children wander as beggars
　　and be driven from their ruined
　　　homes.
¹¹ May creditors seize his entire estate,
　　and strangers take all he has earned.

¹² Let no one be kind to him;
  let no one pity his fatherless children.
¹³ May all his offspring die.
  May his family name be blotted out
    in a single generation.
¹⁴ May the LORD never forget the sins
    of his fathers;
  may his mother's sins never
    be erased from the record.
¹⁵ May the LORD always remember these
    sins,
  and may his name disappear from
    human memory.
¹⁶ For he refused all kindness to others;
  he persecuted the poor and needy,
  and he hounded the brokenhearted
    to death.
¹⁷ He loved to curse others;
  now you curse him.
  He never blessed others;
  now don't you bless him.
¹⁸ Cursing is as natural to him
    as his clothing,
  or the water he drinks,
  or the rich food he eats.
¹⁹ Now may his curses return and cling
    to him like clothing;
  may they be tied around him like
    a belt."
²⁰ May those curses become the LORD's
    punishment
  for my accusers who speak evil
    of me.

²¹ But deal well with me, O Sovereign
    LORD,
  for the sake of your own reputation!
Rescue me
  because you are so faithful and good.
²² For I am poor and needy,
  and my heart is full of pain.
²³ I am fading like a shadow at dusk;
  I am brushed off like a locust.
²⁴ My knees are weak from fasting,
  and I am skin and bones.
²⁵ I am a joke to people everywhere;
  when they see me, they shake their
    heads in scorn.

²⁶ Help me, O LORD my God!
  Save me because of your unfailing
    love.
²⁷ Let them see that this is your doing,
  that you yourself have done it,
    LORD.
²⁸ Then let them curse me if they like,
    but you will bless me!
  When they attack me, they will
    be disgraced!
  But I, your servant, will go right
    on rejoicing!
²⁹ May my accusers be clothed with
    disgrace;
  may their humiliation cover them
    like a cloak.
³⁰ But I will give repeated thanks
    to the LORD,
  praising him to everyone.

HOW WE LIVE

Church involvement

HEBREWS 10:25 Have you found a local church to attend yet? As a new believer, you may wonder what all the fuss is about. Maybe you'd prefer to just stay home and read your Bible. Maybe you visited a couple of churches and just couldn't get the hang of it. Is it really so important? • The Bible is clear that believers should not neglect meeting together. The reason? Believers gather together to strengthen and encourage each other. You need to be a part of this group. The story is told of a pastor who visited a member who had stopped coming to church. The pastor didn't say a word, but sat beside the glowing embers in the fireplace. As the two sat in silence, the pastor took the tongs and pulled one glowing coal from the fire and laid it on the hearth. Together, they watched as that lone ember slowly lost its glow. Minutes later, it was cold and black. The pastor got up and left. The man was back in church on Sunday. • Don't neglect meeting together. Ask the Lord to guide you to a church where you can grow, serve, love, and worship.

³¹ For he stands beside the
needy,
ready to save them from those
who condemn them.

109:6 Hebrew lacks *They say*.

NOVEMBER**12**

EZEKIEL 24:1–26:21

The city of Jerusalem was like a pot so encrusted with sin that it would not come clean. God wanted to cleanse the people—but punishment came instead, because the people would not repent.

On January 15,* during the ninth year of King Jehoiachin's captivity, this message came to me [Ezekiel] from the LORD: ²"Son of man, write down today's date, because on this very day the king of Babylon is beginning his attack against Jerusalem. ³Then give these rebels an illustration with this message from the Sovereign LORD:

"Put a pot on the fire,
and pour in some water.
⁴ Fill it with choice pieces of meat—
the rump and the shoulder
and all the most tender cuts.
⁵ Use only the best sheep from the flock,
and heap fuel on the fire beneath
the pot.
Bring the pot to a boil,
and cook the bones along with
the meat.

⁶ "Now this is what the Sovereign LORD
says:

What sorrow awaits Jerusalem,
the city of murderers!
She is a cooking pot
whose corruption can't be cleaned
out.
Take the meat out in random order,
for no piece is better than another.
⁷ For the blood of her murders
is splashed on the rocks.
It isn't even spilled on the ground,
where the dust could cover it!

PROVERBS 27:13

Get security from someone who guarantees a stranger's debt. Get a deposit if he does it for foreigners.*

27:13 As in Greek and Latin versions (see also 20:16); Hebrew reads *for a promiscuous woman*.

⁸ So I will splash her blood on a rock
for all to see,
an expression of my anger
and vengeance against her.

⁹ "This is what the Sovereign LORD says:
What sorrow awaits Jerusalem,
the city of murderers!
I myself will pile up the fuel
beneath her.
¹⁰ Yes, heap on the wood!
Let the fire roar to make the pot
boil.
Cook the meat with many spices,
and afterward burn the bones.
¹¹ Now set the empty pot on the coals.
Heat it red hot!
Burn away the filth and corruption.
¹² But it's hopeless;
the corruption can't be cleaned out.
So throw it into the fire.
¹³ Your impurity is your lewdness
and the corruption of your idolatry.
I tried to cleanse you,
but you refused.
So now you will remain in your filth
until my fury against you has been
satisfied.

¹⁴"I, the LORD, have spoken! The time has come, and I won't hold back. I will not change my mind, and I will have no pity on you. You will be judged on the basis of all your wicked actions, says the Sovereign LORD."

¹⁵Then this message came to me from the LORD: ¹⁶"Son of man, with one blow I will take away your dearest treasure. Yet you must not show any sorrow at her death. Do not weep; let there be no tears.

¹⁷Groan silently, but let there be no wailing at her grave. Do not uncover your head or take off your sandals. Do not perform the usual rituals of mourning or accept any food brought to you by consoling friends."

¹⁸So I proclaimed this to the people the next morning, and in the evening my wife died. The next morning I did everything I had been told to do. ¹⁹Then the people asked, "What does all this mean? What are you trying to tell us?"

²⁰So I said to them, "A message came to me from the LORD, ²¹and I was told to give this message to the people of Israel. This is what the Sovereign LORD says: I will defile my Temple, the source of your security and pride, the place your heart delights in. Your sons and daughters whom you left behind in Judea will be slaughtered by the sword. ²²Then you will do as Ezekiel has done. You will not mourn in public or console yourselves by eating the food brought by friends. ²³Your heads will remain covered, and your sandals will not be taken off. You will not mourn or weep, but you will waste away because of your sins. You will mourn privately for all the evil you have done. ²⁴Ezekiel is an example for you; you will do just as he has done. And when that time comes, you will know that I am the LORD."

²⁵Then the LORD said to me, "Son of man, on the day I take away their stronghold—their joy and glory, their heart's desire, their dearest treasure—I will also take away their sons and daughters. ²⁶And on that day a survivor from Jerusalem will come to you in Babylon and tell you what has happened. ²⁷And when he arrives, your voice will suddenly return so you can talk to him, and you will be a symbol for these people. Then they will know that I am the LORD."

²⁵:¹THEN this message came to me from the LORD: ²"Son of man, turn and face the land of Ammon and prophesy against its people. ³Give the Ammonites this message from the Sovereign LORD: Hear the word of the Sovereign LORD! Because you cheered when my Temple was defiled, mocked Israel in her desolation, and laughed at Judah as she went away into exile, ⁴I will allow nomads from the eastern

deserts to overrun your country. They will set up their camps among you and pitch their tents on your land. They will harvest all your fruit and drink the milk from your livestock. ⁵And I will turn the city of Rabbah into a pasture for camels, and all the land of the Ammonites into a resting place for sheep and goats. Then you will know that I am the LORD.

⁶"This is what the Sovereign LORD says: Because you clapped and danced and cheered with glee at the destruction of my people, ⁷I will raise my fist of judgment against you. I will give you as plunder to many nations. I will cut you off from being a nation and destroy you completely. Then you will know that I am the LORD.

⁸"This is what the Sovereign LORD says: Because the people of Moab have said that Judah is just like all the other nations, ⁹I will open up their eastern flank and wipe out their glorious frontier towns—Beth-jeshimoth, Baal-meon, and Kiriathaim. ¹⁰And I will hand Moab over to nomads from the eastern deserts, just as I handed over Ammon. Yes, the Ammonites will no longer be counted among the nations. ¹¹In the same way, I will bring my judgment down on the Moabites. Then they will know that I am the LORD.

¹²"This is what the Sovereign LORD says: The people of Edom have sinned greatly by avenging themselves against the people of Judah. ¹³Therefore, says the Sovereign LORD, I will raise my fist of judgment against Edom. I will wipe out its people and animals with the sword. I will make a wasteland of everything from Teman to Dedan. ¹⁴I will accomplish this by the hand of my people of Israel. They will carry out my vengeance with anger, and Edom will know that this vengeance is from me. I, the Sovereign LORD, have spoken!

¹⁵"This is what the Sovereign LORD says: The people of Philistia have acted against Judah out of bitter revenge and long-standing contempt. ¹⁶Therefore, this is what the Sovereign LORD says: I will raise my fist of judgment against the land of the Philistines. I will wipe out the Kerethites and utterly destroy the people who live by the sea. ¹⁷I will execute terrible vengeance against them to punish

them for what they have done. And when I have inflicted my revenge, they will know that I am the LORD."

26:1ON February 3, during the twelfth year of King Jehoiachin's captivity,* this message came to me from the LORD: ²"Son of man, Tyre has rejoiced over the fall of Jerusalem, saying, 'Ha! She who was the gateway to the rich trade routes to the east has been broken, and I am the heir! Because she has been made desolate, I will become wealthy!'

³"Therefore, this is what the Sovereign LORD says: I am your enemy, O Tyre, and I will bring many nations against you, like the waves of the sea crashing against your shoreline. ⁴They will destroy the walls of Tyre and tear down its towers. I will scrape away its soil and make it a bare rock! ⁵It will be just a rock in the sea, a place for fishermen to spread their nets, for I have spoken, says the Sovereign LORD. Tyre will become the prey of many nations, ⁶and its mainland villages will be destroyed by the sword. Then they will know that I am the LORD.

⁷"This is what the Sovereign LORD says: From the north I will bring King Nebuchadnezzar* of Babylon against Tyre. He is king of kings and brings his horses, chariots, charioteers, and great army. ⁸First he will destroy your mainland villages. Then he will attack you by building a siege wall, constructing a ramp, and raising a roof of shields against you. ⁹He will pound your walls with battering rams and demolish your towers with sledgehammers. ¹⁰The hooves of his horses will choke the city with dust, and the noise of the charioteers and chariot wheels will shake your walls as they storm through your broken gates. ¹¹His horsemen will trample through every street in the city. They will butcher your people, and your strong pillars will topple.

¹²"They will plunder all your riches and merchandise and break down your walls. They will destroy your lovely homes and dump your stones and timbers and even your dust into the sea. ¹³I will stop the music of your songs. No more will the sound of harps be heard among your people. ¹⁴I will make your island a bare rock, a place

for fishermen to spread their nets. You will never be rebuilt, for I, the LORD, have spoken. Yes, the Sovereign LORD has spoken!

¹⁵"This is what the Sovereign LORD says to Tyre: The whole coastline will tremble at the sound of your fall, as the screams of the wounded echo in the continuing slaughter. ¹⁶All the seaport rulers will step down from their thrones and take off their royal robes and beautiful clothing. They will sit on the ground trembling with horror at your destruction. ¹⁷Then they will wail for you, singing this funeral song:

"O famous island city,
    once ruler of the sea,
    how you have been destroyed!
Your people, with their naval power,
    once spread fear around the world.
¹⁸ Now the coastlands tremble at
    your fall.
    The islands are dismayed as you
    disappear.

¹⁹"This is what the Sovereign LORD says: I will make Tyre an uninhabited ruin, like many others. I will bury you beneath the terrible waves of enemy attack. Great seas will swallow you. ²⁰I will send you to the pit to join those who descended there long ago. Your city will lie in ruins, buried beneath the earth, like those in the pit who have entered the world of the dead. You will have no place of respect here in the land of the living. ²¹I will bring you to a terrible end, and you will exist no more. You will be looked for, but you will never again be found. I, the Sovereign LORD, have spoken!"

24:1 Hebrew *On the tenth day of the tenth month,* of the ancient Hebrew lunar calendar. This event occurred on January 15, 588 B.C.; also see note on 1:1.   **26:1** Hebrew *In the eleventh year, on the first day of the month,* of the ancient Hebrew lunar calendar year. Since an element is missing in the date formula here, scholars have reconstructed this probable reading: *In the eleventh [month of the twelfth] year, on the first day of the month.* This reading would put this message on February 3, 585 B.C.; also see note on 1:1.   **26:7** Hebrew *Nebuchadrezzar,* a variant spelling of Nebuchadnezzar.

HEBREWS 11:1-16

This chapter is sometimes called the "Hall of Faith" chapter because it lists great heroes of faith from throughout biblical history.

Faith is the confidence that what we hope for will actually happen; it gives us assurance about things we cannot see. ²Through their faith, the people in days of old earned a good reputation.

³By faith we understand that the entire universe was formed at God's command, that what we now see did not come from anything that can be seen.

⁴It was by faith that Abel brought a more acceptable offering to God than Cain did. Abel's offering gave evidence that he was a righteous man, and God showed his approval of his gifts. Although Abel is long dead, he still speaks to us by his example of faith.

⁵It was by faith that Enoch was taken up to heaven without dying—"he disappeared, because God took him."* For before he was taken up, he was known as a person who pleased God. ⁶And it is impossible to please God without faith. Anyone who wants to come to him must believe that God exists and that he rewards those who sincerely seek him.

⁷It was by faith that Noah built a large boat to save his family from the flood. He obeyed God, who warned him about things that had never happened before. By his faith Noah condemned the rest of the world, and he received the righteousness that comes by faith.

⁸It was by faith that Abraham obeyed when God called him to leave home and go to another land that God would give him as his inheritance. He went without knowing where he was going. ⁹And even when he reached the land God promised him, he lived there by faith—for he was like a foreigner, living in tents. And so did Isaac and Jacob, who inherited the same promise. ¹⁰Abraham was confidently looking forward to a city with eternal foundations, a city designed and built by God.

¹¹It was by faith that even Sarah was able to have a child, though she was barren and was too old. She believed* that God would keep his promise. ¹²And so a whole nation came from this one man who was as good as dead—a nation with so many people that, like the stars in the sky and the sand on the seashore, there is no way to count them.

¹³All these people died still believing what God had promised them. They did not receive what was promised, but they saw it all from a distance and welcomed it. They agreed that they were foreigners and nomads here on earth. ¹⁴Obviously people who say such things are looking forward to a country they can call their own. ¹⁵If they had longed for the country

HOW WE LIVE: Growing in faith

HEBREWS 11:1 Three words describe faith: confidence, hope, and assurance. Faith involves believing in God's character, that he is who he says he is; it involves believing in God's promises, that he will do what he says he will do. When we believe that God will fulfill his promises even though we don't yet see any evidence, we demonstrate true faith. • "Confidence that what we hope for will actually happen" means to have complete confidence that God will fulfill his promises. We often think of the word "hope" in terms of uncertain desire—"I hope it doesn't rain on Saturday." For believers, however, "hope" is an assured desire based on their confidence in God's character and promises. "Assurance about things we cannot see" means to believe in the reality of something that we cannot see, taste, hear, or touch—such as eternal life, future rewards, heaven, and so forth. • Faith allows Christians to make God-honoring decisions based on unseen realities. You have faith now, as a new believer. Your faith, like a muscle, will grow the more you exercise it. Trust God today and every day. Your faith will grow stronger and you will gain confidence the more you experience life with God.

they came from, they could have gone back. [16]But they were looking for a better place, a heavenly homeland. That is why God is not ashamed to be called their God, for he has prepared a city for them.

11:5 Gen 5:24.   11:11 Or *It was by faith that he [Abraham] was able to have a child, even though Sarah was barren and he was too old. He believed.*

PSALM 110:1-7
A psalm of David.

[1] The LORD said to my Lord,
"Sit in the place of honor
at my right hand
until I humble your enemies,
making them a footstool under
your feet."

[2] The LORD will extend your
powerful kingdom from
Jerusalem*;
you will rule over your enemies.
[3] When you go to war,
your people will serve you
willingly.

You are arrayed in holy garments,
and your strength will be renewed
each day like the morning dew.

[4] The LORD has taken an oath and will
not break his vow:
"You are a priest forever in the
order of Melchizedek."

[5] The Lord stands at your right hand
to protect you.
He will strike down many kings
when his anger erupts.
[6] He will punish the nations
and fill their lands with corpses;
he will shatter heads over the whole
earth.
[7] But he himself will be refreshed from
brooks along the way.
He will be victorious.

110:2 Hebrew *Zion.*

PROVERBS 27:14
A loud and cheerful greeting early in the morning will be taken as a curse!

NOVEMBER**13**

EZEKIEL 27:1-28:26
The cities of Tyre and Sidon were centers of commerce and industry located north of the Holy Land. Old Testament prophets such as Isaiah, Jeremiah, and Ezekiel spoke against the arrogance of Tyre and Sidon.

Then this message came to me [Ezekiel] from the LORD: [2]"Son of man, sing a funeral song for Tyre, [3]that mighty gateway to the sea, the trading center of the world. Give Tyre this message from the Sovereign LORD:

"You boasted, O Tyre,
'My beauty is perfect!'
[4] You extended your boundaries into
the sea.
Your builders made your beauty
perfect.
[5] You were like a great ship
built of the finest cypress from
Senir.*

They took a cedar from Lebanon
to make a mast for you.
[6] They carved your oars
from the oaks of Bashan.
Your deck of pine from the coasts
of Cyprus*
was inlaid with ivory.
[7] Your sails were made of Egypt's finest
linen,
and they flew as a banner above
you.
You stood beneath blue and purple
awnings
made bright with dyes from the
coasts of Elishah.
[8] Your oarsmen came from Sidon
and Arvad;
your helmsmen were skilled men
from Tyre itself.
[9] Wise old craftsmen from Gebal did
the caulking.

Ships from every land came with
goods to barter for your trade.

[10]"Men from distant Persia, Lydia, and
Libya* served in your great army. They
hung their shields and helmets on your
walls, giving you great honor. [11]Men from
Arvad and Helech stood on your walls.
Your towers were manned by men from
Gammad. Their shields hung on your
walls, completing your beauty.

[12]"Tarshish sent merchants to buy your
wares in exchange for silver, iron, tin, and
lead. [13]Merchants from Greece,* Tubal,
and Meshech brought slaves and articles
of bronze to trade with you.

[14]"From Togarmah came riding horses,
chariot horses, and mules, all in exchange
for your goods. [15]Merchants came to you
from Dedan.* Numerous coastlands were
your captive markets; they brought payment in ivory tusks and ebony wood.

[16]"Syria* sent merchants to buy your
rich variety of goods. They traded turquoise, purple dyes, embroidery, fine
linen, and jewelry of coral and rubies.
[17]Judah and Israel traded for your wares,
offering wheat from Minnith, figs,* honey, olive oil, and balm.

[18]"Damascus sent merchants to buy
your rich variety of goods, bringing wine
from Helbon and white wool from Zahar.
[19]Greeks from Uzal* came to trade for
your merchandise. Wrought iron, cassia,
and fragrant calamus were bartered for
your wares.

[20]"Dedan sent merchants to trade their
expensive saddle blankets with you.
[21]The Arabians and the princes of Kedar
sent merchants to trade lambs and rams
and male goats in exchange for your
goods. [22]The merchants of Sheba and Raamah came with all kinds of spices, jewels, and gold in exchange for your wares.

[23]"Haran, Canneh, Eden, Sheba, Asshur,
and Kilmad came with their merchandise,
too. [24]They brought choice fabrics to
trade—blue cloth, embroidery, and multi-
colored carpets rolled up and bound with
cords. [25]The ships of Tarshish were your
ocean caravans. Your island warehouse
was filled to the brim!

[26] "But look! Your oarsmen
have taken you into stormy seas!
A mighty eastern gale
has wrecked you in the heart
of the sea!
[27] Everything is lost—
your riches and wares,
your sailors and pilots,
your ship builders, merchants,
and warriors.
On the day of your ruin,
everyone on board sinks into the
depths of the sea.
[28] Your cities by the sea tremble
as your pilots cry out in terror.
[29] All the oarsmen abandon their ships;
the sailors and pilots on shore come
to stand on the beach.
[30] They cry aloud over you
and weep bitterly.
They throw dust on their heads
and roll in ashes.
[31] They shave their heads in grief for you
and dress themselves in burlap.
They weep for you with bitter anguish
and deep mourning.
[32] As they wail and mourn over you,
they sing this sad funeral song:
'Was there ever such a city as Tyre,
now silent at the bottom of the sea?
[33] The merchandise you traded
satisfied the desires of many nations.
Kings at the ends of the earth
were enriched by your trade.
[34] Now you are a wrecked ship,
broken at the bottom of the sea.
All your merchandise and crew
have gone down with you.
[35] All who live along the coastlands
are appalled at your terrible fate.
Their kings are filled with horror
and look on with twisted faces.
[36] The merchants among the nations
shake their heads at the sight
of you,*
for you have come to a horrible end
and will exist no more.'"

28:1THEN this message came to me from
the LORD: [2]"Son of man, give the prince of
Tyre this message from the Sovereign
LORD:

"In your great pride you claim, 'I am
a god!
I sit on a divine throne in the heart
of the sea.'

But you are only a man and not a god,
though you boast that you are a god.

3 You regard yourself as wiser than
Daniel
and think no secret is hidden
from you.

4 With your wisdom and understanding
you have amassed great wealth—
gold and silver for your treasuries.

5 Yes, your wisdom has made you very
rich,
and your riches have made you very
proud.

6 "Therefore, this is what the Sovereign
LORD says:
Because you think you are as wise
as a god,

7 I will now bring against you
a foreign army,
the terror of the nations.
They will draw their swords against
your marvelous wisdom
and defile your splendor!

8 They will bring you down to the pit,
and you will die in the heart of
the sea,
pierced with many wounds.

9 Will you then boast, 'I am a god!'
to those who kill you?
To them you will be no god
but merely a man!

10 You will die like an outcast*
at the hands of foreigners.
I, the Sovereign LORD, have spoken!"

11 Then this further message came to me
from the LORD: 12"Son of man, sing this funeral song for the king of Tyre. Give him
this message from the Sovereign LORD:

"You were the model of perfection,
full of wisdom and exquisite
in beauty.

13 You were in Eden,
the garden of God.
Your clothing was adorned with every
precious stone*—
red carnelian, pale-green peridot,
white moonstone,
blue-green beryl, onyx, green jasper,
blue lapis lazuli, turquoise, and
emerald—
all beautifully crafted for you
and set in the finest gold.

They were given to you
on the day you were created.

14 I ordained and anointed you
as the mighty angelic guardian.*
You had access to the holy mountain
of God
and walked among the stones of fire.

15 "You were blameless in all you did
from the day you were created
until the day evil was found in you.

16 Your rich commerce led you to
violence,
and you sinned.
So I banished you in disgrace
from the mountain of God.
I expelled you, O mighty guardian,
from your place among the stones
of fire.

17 Your heart was filled with pride
because of all your beauty.
Your wisdom was corrupted
by your love of splendor.
So I threw you to the ground
and exposed you to the curious
gaze of kings.

18 You defiled your sanctuaries
with your many sins and your
dishonest trade.
So I brought fire out from within you,
and it consumed you.
I reduced you to ashes on the ground
in the sight of all who were
watching.

19 All who knew you are appalled
at your fate.
You have come to a terrible end,
and you will exist no more."

20 Then another message came to me
from the LORD: 21"Son of man, turn and
face the city of Sidon and prophesy
against it. 22Give the people of Sidon this
message from the Sovereign LORD:

"I am your enemy, O Sidon,
and I will reveal my glory by what
I do to you.
When I bring judgment against you
and reveal my holiness among you,
everyone watching will know
that I am the LORD.

23 I will send a plague against you,
and blood will be spilled in your
streets.

The attack will come from every
    direction,
    and your people will lie slaughtered
        within your walls.
Then everyone will know
    that I am the LORD.
24 No longer will Israel's scornful
    neighbors
    prick and tear at her like briers
        and thorns.
For then they will know
    that I am the Sovereign LORD.

25"This is what the Sovereign LORD says: The people of Israel will again live in their own land, the land I gave my servant Jacob. For I will gather them from the distant lands where I have scattered them. I will reveal to the nations of the world my holiness among my people. 26They will live safely in Israel and build homes and plant vineyards. And when I punish the neighboring nations that treated them with contempt, they will know that I am the LORD their God."

27:5 Or *Hermon.*   27:6 Hebrew *Kittim.*   27:10 Hebrew *Paras, Lud, and Put.*   27:13 Hebrew *Javan.*   27:15 Greek version reads *Rhodes.*   27:16 Hebrew *Aram;* some manuscripts read *Edom.*   27:17 The meaning of the Hebrew is uncertain. 27:19 Hebrew *Vedan and Javan from Uzal.* The meaning of the Hebrew is uncertain.   27:36 Hebrew *hiss at you.* 28:10 Hebrew *will die the death of the uncircumcised.* 28:13 The identification of some of these gemstones is uncertain.   28:14 Hebrew *guardian cherub;* similarly in 28:16.

HEBREWS 11:17-31
The continuing list in this "Hall of Faith" includes the chief patriarch of the Jews and a prostitute. God calls all kinds to his service.

It was by faith that Abraham offered Isaac as a sacrifice when God was testing him. Abraham, who had received God's promises, was ready to sacrifice his only son, Isaac, 18even though God had told him, "Isaac is the son through whom your descendants will be counted."* 19Abraham reasoned that if Isaac died, God was able to bring him back to life again. And in a sense, Abraham did receive his son back from the dead.

20It was by faith that Isaac promised blessings for the future to his sons, Jacob and Esau.

21It was by faith that Jacob, when he was old and dying, blessed each of Joseph's sons and bowed in worship as he leaned on his staff.

22It was by faith that Joseph, when he was about to die, said confidently that the people of Israel would leave Egypt. He even commanded them to take his bones with them when they left.

23It was by faith that Moses' parents hid him for three months when he was born. They saw that God had given them an

WHAT THE BIBLE SAYS

The devil

EZEKIEL 28:12-19 In today's reading you find what many believe to be the description of Satan's fall from heaven. Although it is Ezekiel's prophecy against the king of Tyre, some of the terms used could not apply to a mere human. Much of what we believe about the devil is based on this description combined with other statements throughout Scripture. Satan was once good, a mighty angelic guardian with access to God (28:14). He had been good, but succumbed to evil (28:15). He was created by God but fell from grace when he was blinded by pride and so was cast out of heaven (28:17). • You don't have to live the Christian life very long to discover that the devil is present today. His presence makes it essential that we stay close to God so we are not easily deceived. Even though God permits the devil to do his work in this world, God is still in control. And Jesus has complete power over Satan—he defeated Satan when he died and rose again for the sins of humanity. One day Satan will be bound forever, never again to do his evil work.

unusual child, and they were not afraid to disobey the king's command.

²⁴It was by faith that Moses, when he grew up, refused to be called the son of Pharaoh's daughter. ²⁵He chose to share the oppression of God's people instead of enjoying the fleeting pleasures of sin. ²⁶He thought it was better to suffer for the sake of Christ than to own the treasures of Egypt, for he was looking ahead to his great reward. ²⁷It was by faith that Moses left the land of Egypt, not fearing the king's anger. He kept right on going because he kept his eyes on the one who is invisible. ²⁸It was by faith that Moses commanded the people of Israel to keep the Passover and to sprinkle blood on the doorposts so that the angel of death would not kill their firstborn sons.

²⁹It was by faith that the people of Israel went right through the Red Sea as though they were on dry ground. But when the Egyptians tried to follow, they were all drowned.

³⁰It was by faith that the people of Israel marched around Jericho for seven days, and the walls came crashing down.

³¹It was by faith that Rahab the prostitute was not destroyed with the people in her city who refused to obey God. For she had given a friendly welcome to the spies.

11:18 Gen 21:12.

PSALM 111:1-10*

Praise the LORD!

I will thank the LORD with all my heart
    as I meet with his godly people.
² How amazing are the deeds
        of the LORD!
    All who delight in him should
        ponder them.
³ Everything he does reveals his glory
        and majesty.
    His righteousness never fails.
⁴ He causes us to remember his
        wonderful works.
    How gracious and merciful is our
        LORD!
⁵ He gives food to those who fear him;
    he always remembers his
        covenant.
⁶ He has shown his great power to his
        people
    by giving them the lands of other
        nations.
⁷ All he does is just and good,
    and all his commandments are
        trustworthy.
⁸ They are forever true,
    to be obeyed faithfully and with
        integrity.
⁹ He has paid a full ransom for his
        people.
    He has guaranteed his covenant
        with them forever.
    What a holy, awe-inspiring name
        he has!
¹⁰ Fear of the LORD is the foundation
        of true wisdom.
    All who obey his commandments
        will grow in wisdom.

    Praise him forever!

111 This psalm is a Hebrew acrostic poem; after the introductory note of praise, each line begins with a successive letter of the Hebrew alphabet.

PROVERBS 27:15-16

A quarrelsome wife is as annoying as constant dripping on a rainy day. Stopping her complaints is like trying to stop the wind or trying to hold something with greased hands.

NOVEMBER**14**

EZEKIEL 29:1–30:26
The Jews had a long history with Egypt. It was there that Jacob's family had grown from twelve sons to a nation. At times, Israel's kings made alliances with Egypt. Many of the Old Testament prophets spoke out against Egypt, as Ezekiel does in today's reading.

On January 7,* during the tenth year of King Jehoiachin's captivity, this message came to me [Ezekiel] from the LORD: ²"Son of man, turn and face Egypt and prophesy against Pharaoh the king and all the people of Egypt. ³Give them this message from the Sovereign LORD:

"I am your enemy, O Pharaoh, king
      of Egypt—
   you great monster, lurking in the
      streams of the Nile.
For you have said, 'The Nile River
      is mine;
   I made it for myself.'
⁴ I will put hooks in your jaws
   and drag you out on the land
      with fish sticking to your scales.
⁵ I will leave you and all your fish
      stranded in the wilderness to die.
   You will lie unburied on the open
      ground,
   for I have given you as food to the
      wild animals and birds.
⁶ All the people of Egypt will know that
      I am the LORD,
   for to Israel you were just a staff
      made of reeds.
⁷ When Israel leaned on you,
   you splintered and broke
      and stabbed her in the armpit.
When she put her weight on you,
      you gave way,
   and her back was thrown out
      of joint.

⁸"Therefore, this is what the Sovereign LORD says: I will bring an army against you, O Egypt, and destroy both people and animals. ⁹The land of Egypt will become a desolate wasteland, and the Egyptians will know that I am the LORD.

"Because you said, 'The Nile River is mine; I made it,' ¹⁰I am now the enemy of both you and your river. I will make the land of Egypt a totally desolate wasteland, from Migdol to Aswan, as far south as the border of Ethiopia.* ¹¹For forty years not a soul will pass that way, neither people nor animals. It will be completely uninhabited. ¹²I will make Egypt desolate, and it will be surrounded by other desolate nations. Its cities will be empty and desolate for forty years, surrounded by other ruined cities. I will scatter the Egyptians to distant lands.

¹³"But this is what the Sovereign LORD also says: At the end of the forty years I will bring the Egyptians home again from the nations to which they have been scattered.

¹⁴I will restore the prosperity of Egypt and bring its people back to the land of Pathros in southern Egypt from which they came. But Egypt will remain an unimportant, minor kingdom. ¹⁵It will be the lowliest of all the nations, never again great enough to rise above its neighbors.

¹⁶"Then Israel will no longer be tempted to trust in Egypt for help. Egypt's shattered condition will remind Israel of how sinful she was to trust Egypt in earlier days. Then Israel will know that I am the Sovereign LORD."

¹⁷On April 26, the first day of the new year,* during the twenty-seventh year of King Jehoiachin's captivity, this message came to me from the LORD: ¹⁸"Son of man, the army of King Nebuchadnezzar* of Babylon fought so hard against Tyre that the warriors' heads were rubbed bare and their shoulders were raw and blistered. Yet Nebuchadnezzar and his army won no plunder to compensate them for all their work. ¹⁹Therefore, this is what the Sovereign LORD says: I will give the land of Egypt to Nebuchadnezzar, king of Babylon. He will carry off its wealth, plundering everything it has so he can pay his army. ²⁰Yes, I have given him the land of Egypt as a reward for his work, says the Sovereign LORD, because he was working for me when he destroyed Tyre.

²¹"And the day will come when I will cause the ancient glory of Israel to revive,* and then, Ezekiel, your words will be respected. Then they will know that I am the LORD."

30:1THIS is another message that came to me from the LORD: ²"Son of man, prophesy and give this message from the Sovereign LORD:

"Weep and wail
      for that day,
³ for the terrible day is almost here—
      the day of the LORD!
It is a day of clouds and gloom,
      a day of despair for the nations.
⁴ A sword will come against Egypt,
   and those who are slaughtered will
      cover the ground.
Its wealth will be carried away
      and its foundations destroyed.
The land of Ethiopia* will be ravished.

5   Ethiopia, Libya, Lydia, all Arabia,*
and all their other allies
    will be destroyed in that war.

6 "For this is what the LORD says:
All of Egypt's allies will fall,
    and the pride of her power will end.
From Migdol to Aswan*
    they will be slaughtered by the
        sword,
    says the Sovereign LORD.

7 Egypt will be desolate,
    surrounded by desolate nations,
and its cities will be in ruins,
    surrounded by other ruined cities.

8 And the people of Egypt will know
        that I am the LORD
    when I have set Egypt on fire
    and destroyed all their allies.

9 At that time I will send swift
        messengers in ships
    to terrify the complacent
        Ethiopians.
Great panic will come upon them
    on that day of Egypt's certain
        destruction.
Watch for it!
    It is sure to come!

10 "For this is what the Sovereign LORD
        says:
By the power of King
        Nebuchadnezzar* of Babylon,
    I will destroy the hordes of Egypt.

11 He and his armies—the most ruthless
        of all—
    will be sent to demolish the land.
They will make war against Egypt
    until slaughtered Egyptians cover
        the ground.

12 I will dry up the Nile River
    and sell the land to wicked men.
I will destroy the land of Egypt and
        everything in it
    by the hands of foreigners.
    I, the LORD, have spoken!

13 "This is what the Sovereign LORD says:
I will smash the idols* of Egypt
    and the images at Memphis.*
There will be no rulers left in Egypt;
    terror will sweep the land.

14 I will destroy southern Egypt,*
    set fire to Zoan,
    and bring judgment against Thebes.*

15 I will pour out my fury on Pelusium,*
    the strongest fortress of Egypt,
and I will stamp out
    the hordes of Thebes.

16 Yes, I will set fire to all Egypt!
    Pelusium will be racked with pain;
Thebes will be torn apart;
    Memphis will live in constant terror.

17 The young men of Heliopolis and
        Bubastis* will die in battle,
    and the women* will be taken away
        as slaves.

18 When I come to break the proud
        strength of Egypt,
    it will be a dark day for Tahpanhes,
        too.
A dark cloud will cover Tahpanhes,
    and its daughters will be led away
        as captives.

19 And so I will greatly punish Egypt,
    and they will know that I am the
        LORD."

20On April 29,* during the eleventh year
of King Jehoiachin's captivity, this message
came to me from the LORD: 21"Son of man,
I have broken the arm of Pharaoh, the king
of Egypt. His arm has not been put in a cast
so that it may heal. Neither has it been
bound up with a splint to make it strong
enough to hold a sword. 22Therefore, this
is what the Sovereign LORD says: I am the
enemy of Pharaoh, the king of Egypt! I will
break both of his arms—the good arm
along with the broken one—and I will
make his sword clatter to the ground. 23I
will scatter the Egyptians to many lands
throughout the world. 24I will strengthen
the arms of Babylon's king and put my
sword in his hand. But I will break the
arms of Pharaoh, king of Egypt, and he will
lie there mortally wounded, groaning in
pain. 25I will strengthen the arms of the
king of Babylon, while the arms of Pharaoh
fall useless to his sides. And when I put my
sword in the hand of Babylon's king and he
brings it against the land of Egypt, Egypt
will know that I am the LORD. 26I will scatter the Egyptians among the nations, dis-
persing them throughout the earth. Then
they will know that I am the LORD."

29:1 Hebrew *On the twelfth day of the tenth month,* of the
ancient Hebrew lunar calendar. This event occurred on
January 7, 587 B.C.; also see note on 1:1. 29:10 Hebrew *from*

Migdol to Syene as far as the border of Cush. **29:17** Hebrew On the first day of the first month, of the ancient Hebrew lunar calendar. This event occurred on April 26, 571 B.C.; also see note on 1:1. **29:18** Hebrew Nebuchadrezzar, a variant spelling of Nebuchadnezzar; also in 29:19. **29:21** Hebrew I will cause a horn to sprout for the house of Israel. **30:4** Hebrew Cush; similarly in 30:9. **30:5** Hebrew Cush, Put, Lud, all Arabia, Cub. Cub is otherwise unknown and may be another spelling for Lub (Libya). **30:6** Hebrew to Syene. **30:10** Hebrew Nebuchadrezzar, a variant spelling of Nebuchadnezzar. **30:13a** The Hebrew term (literally round things) probably alludes to dung. **30:13b** Hebrew Noph; also in 30:16. **30:14a** Hebrew Pathros. **30:14b** Hebrew No; also in 30:15, 16. **30:15** Hebrew Sin; also in 30:16. **30:17a** Hebrew of Awen and Pi-beseth. **30:17b** Or and her cities. **30:20** Hebrew On the seventh day of the first month, of the ancient Hebrew lunar calendar. This event occurred on April 29, 587 B.C.; also see note on 1:1.

HEBREWS 11:32–12:13

So, what do we learn from this continuing list of people who lived lives of faith? We learn that having faith doesn't make life easy. Difficult times still come, but they serve a purpose—they mature our faith.

How much more do I need to say? It would take too long to recount the stories of the faith of Gideon, Barak, Samson, Jephthah, David, Samuel, and all the prophets. ³³By faith these people overthrew kingdoms, ruled with justice, and received what God had promised them. They shut the mouths of lions, ³⁴quenched the flames of fire, and escaped death by the edge of the sword. Their weakness was turned to strength. They became strong in battle and put whole armies to flight. ³⁵Women received their loved ones back again from death.

But others were tortured, refusing to turn from God in order to be set free. They placed their hope in a better life after the resurrection. ³⁶Some were jeered at, and their backs were cut open with whips. Others were chained in prisons. ³⁷Some died by stoning, some were sawed in half,* and others were killed with the sword. Some went about wearing skins of sheep and goats, destitute and oppressed and mistreated. ³⁸They were too good for this world, wandering over deserts and mountains, hiding in caves and holes in the ground.

³⁹All these people earned a good reputation because of their faith, yet none of them received all that God had promised. ⁴⁰For God had something better in mind for us, so that they would not reach perfection without us.

12:1THEREFORE, since we are surrounded by such a huge crowd of witnesses to the life of faith, let us strip off every weight that slows us down, especially the sin that so easily trips us up. And let us run with endurance the race God has set before us. ²We do this by keeping our eyes on Jesus, the champion who initiates and perfects our faith.* Because of the joy* awaiting him, he endured the cross, disregarding

Persevering in faith

HOW WE LIVE

HEBREWS 12:1-3 The last few New Testament readings took you through a famous Bible chapter—Hebrews 11, sometimes called the "Hall of Faith." For the original readers of Hebrews, hearing all of those familiar names must have been an inspiring reminder of their heritage and of the many faithful followers of God who had gone before. Apparently those original readers were weary from persecution and struggling to stay true to their faith in an increasingly hostile environment. After hearing the names of faithful believers throughout the centuries, the readers were challenged to also persevere in their faith. These faithful people from the past are a "huge crowd of witnesses," witnessing to those first-century believers and to us today through the historical record of their faithfulness. They encourage us to keep going, for the reward is well worth it! • You run your own race, but you don't run alone. You have the example of those who have gone before you, you have fellow believers alive today to encourage you, and you have Jesus to empower you. When you're sweating and your legs ache, your lungs burn and you don't know if you can keep going—look to Jesus. Remember what he did for you. Keep going. The finish line is just ahead.

its shame. Now he is seated in the place of honor beside God's throne. ³Think of all the hostility he endured from sinful people;* then you won't become weary and give up. ⁴After all, you have not yet given your lives in your struggle against sin.

⁵And have you forgotten the encouraging words God spoke to you as his children?* He said,

"My child,* don't make light of the LORD's discipline,
and don't give up when he corrects you.
⁶ For the LORD disciplines those he loves,
and he punishes each one he accepts as his child."*

⁷As you endure this divine discipline, remember that God is treating you as his own children. Who ever heard of a child who is never disciplined by its father? ⁸If God doesn't discipline you as he does all of his children, it means that you are illegitimate and are not really his children at all. ⁹Since we respected our earthly fathers who disciplined us, shouldn't we submit even more to the discipline of the Father of our spirits, and live forever?*

¹⁰For our earthly fathers disciplined us for a few years, doing the best they knew how. But God's discipline is always good for us, so that we might share in his holiness. ¹¹No discipline is enjoyable while it is happening—it's painful! But afterward there will be a peaceful harvest of right living for those who are trained in this way.

¹²So take a new grip with your tired hands and strengthen your weak knees. ¹³Mark out a straight path for your feet so that those who are weak and lame will not fall but become strong.

11:37 Some manuscripts add *some were tested.*   12:2a Or *Jesus, the originator and perfecter of our faith.*   12:2b Or *Instead of the joy.*   12:3 Some manuscripts read *Think of how people hurt themselves by opposing him.*   12:5a Greek *sons;* also in 12:7, 8.   12:5b Greek *son;* also in 12:6, 7.   12:5-6 Prov 3:11-12 (Greek version).   12:9 Or *and really live?*

PSALM 112:1-10*
Praise the LORD!

How joyful are those who fear the LORD
and delight in obeying his commands.
² Their children will be successful everywhere;
an entire generation of godly people will be blessed.
³ They themselves will be wealthy,
and their good deeds will last forever.
⁴ Light shines in the darkness for the godly.
They are generous, compassionate, and righteous.
⁵ Good comes to those who lend money generously
and conduct their business fairly.
⁶ Such people will not be overcome by evil.
Those who are righteous will be long remembered.
⁷ They do not fear bad news;
they confidently trust the LORD to care for them.
⁸ They are confident and fearless
and can face their foes triumphantly.
⁹ They share freely and give generously to those in need.
Their good deeds will be remembered forever.
They will have influence and honor.
¹⁰ The wicked will see this and be infuriated.
They will grind their teeth in anger;
they will slink away, their hopes thwarted.

112 This psalm is a Hebrew acrostic poem; after the introductory note of praise, each line begins with a successive letter of the Hebrew alphabet.

PROVERBS 27:17
As iron sharpens iron, so a friend sharpens a friend.

EZEKIEL 31:1-32:32

Assyria was northeast of Judah. Egypt was to the southwest. Babylon was to the east. The boundaries of these nations were only as strong as their armies. They protected themselves from each other, but from God's judgment they had no defense.

On June 21,* during the eleventh year of King Jehoiachin's captivity, this message came to me [Ezekiel] from the LORD: ²"Son of man, give this message to Pharaoh, king of Egypt, and all his hordes:

"To whom would you compare your
    greatness?
³ You are like mighty Assyria,
    which was once like a cedar
        of Lebanon,
    with beautiful branches that cast deep
        forest shade
    and with its top high among
        the clouds.
⁴ Deep springs watered it
    and helped it to grow tall and
        luxuriant.
    The water flowed around it like a river,
        streaming to all the trees nearby.
⁵ This great tree towered high,
    higher than all the other trees
        around it.
    It prospered and grew long thick
        branches
    because of all the water at its roots.
⁶ The birds nested in its branches,
    and in its shade all the wild animals
        gave birth.
    All the great nations of the world
        lived in its shadow.
⁷ It was strong and beautiful,
    with wide-spreading branches,
    for its roots went deep
        into abundant water.
⁸ No other cedar in the garden of God
    could rival it.
    No cypress had branches to equal it;
        no plane tree had boughs to
            compare.
    No tree in the garden of God
        came close to it in beauty.
⁹ Because I made this tree so beautiful,
    and gave it such magnificent foliage,

it was the envy of all the other trees
    of Eden,
    the garden of God.

¹⁰"Therefore, this is what the Sovereign LORD says: Because Egypt* became proud and arrogant, and because it set itself so high above the others, with its top reaching to the clouds, ¹¹I will hand it over to a mighty nation that will destroy it as its wickedness deserves. I have already discarded it. ¹²A foreign army—the terror of the nations—has cut it down and left it fallen on the ground. Its branches are scattered across the mountains and valleys and ravines of the land. All those who lived in its shadow have gone away and left it lying there.

¹³ "The birds roost on its fallen trunk,
    and the wild animals lie among its
        branches.
¹⁴ Let the tree of no other nation
    proudly exult in its own prosperity,
    though it be higher than the clouds
        and it be watered from the depths.
    For all are doomed to die,
        to go down to the depths of the earth.
    They will land in the pit
        along with everyone else on earth.

¹⁵"This is what the Sovereign LORD says: When Assyria went down to the grave,* I made the deep springs mourn. I stopped its rivers and dried up its abundant water. I clothed Lebanon in black and caused the trees of the field to wilt. ¹⁶I made the nations shake with fear at the sound of its fall, for I sent it down to the grave with all the others who descend to the pit. And all the other proud trees of Eden, the most beautiful and the best of Lebanon, the ones whose roots went deep into the water, took comfort to find it there with them in the depths of the earth. ¹⁷Its allies, too, were all destroyed and had passed away. They had gone down to the grave—all those nations that had lived in its shade.

¹⁸"O Egypt, to which of the trees of Eden will you compare your strength and glory? You, too, will be brought down to

the depths with all these other nations. You will lie there among the outcasts* who have died by the sword. This will be the fate of Pharaoh and all his hordes. I, the Sovereign LORD, have spoken!"

32:1ON March 3,* during the twelfth year of King Jehoiachin's captivity, this message came to me from the LORD: 2"Son of man, mourn for Pharaoh, king of Egypt, and give him this message:

"You think of yourself as a strong
  young lion among the nations,
but you are really just a sea monster,
heaving around in your own rivers,
  stirring up mud with your feet.
3 Therefore, this is what the Sovereign
  LORD says:
I will send many people
  to catch you in my net
  and haul you out of the water.
4 I will leave you stranded on the land
  to die.
All the birds of the heavens will
  land on you,
and the wild animals of the whole
  earth
  will gorge themselves on you.
5 I will scatter your flesh on the hills
  and fill the valleys with your bones.
6 I will drench the earth with your
  gushing blood
all the way to the mountains,
  filling the ravines to the brim.
7 When I blot you out,
I will veil the heavens and darken
  the stars.
I will cover the sun with a cloud,
  and the moon will not give you
  its light.
8 I will darken the bright stars overhead
  and cover your land in darkness.
  I, the Sovereign LORD, have spoken!

9"I will disturb many hearts when I bring news of your downfall to distant nations you have never seen. 10Yes, I will shock many lands, and their kings will be terrified at your fate. They will shudder in fear for their lives as I brandish my sword before them on the day of your fall. 11For this is what the Sovereign LORD says:

"The sword of the king of Babylon
  will come against you.

12 I will destroy your hordes with the
  swords of mighty warriors—
  the terror of the nations.
They will shatter the pride of Egypt,
  and all its hordes will be destroyed.
13 I will destroy all your flocks and herds
  that graze beside the streams.
Never again will people or animals
  muddy those waters with their feet.
14 Then I will let the waters of Egypt
  become calm again,
  and they will flow as smoothly
  as olive oil,
  says the Sovereign LORD.
15 And when I destroy Egypt
  and strip you of everything you own
  and strike down all your people,
  then you will know that I am the
  LORD.
16 Yes, this is the funeral song
  they will sing for Egypt.
Let all the nations mourn.
  Let them mourn for Egypt and its
  hordes.
  I, the Sovereign LORD, have spoken!"

17On March 17,* during the twelfth year, another message came to me from the LORD: 18"Son of man, weep for the hordes of Egypt and for the other mighty nations.* For I will send them down to the world below in company with those who descend to the pit. 19Say to them,

'O Egypt, are you lovelier than the
  other nations?
No! So go down to the pit and lie
  there among the outcasts.*'

20The Egyptians will fall with the many who have died by the sword, for the sword is drawn against them. Egypt and its hordes will be dragged away to their judgment. 21Down in the grave* mighty leaders will mockingly welcome Egypt and its allies, saying, 'They have come down; they lie among the outcasts, hordes slaughtered by the sword.'

22"Assyria lies there surrounded by the graves of its army, those who were slaughtered by the sword. 23 Their graves are in the depths of the pit, and they are surrounded by their allies. They struck terror in the hearts of people everywhere, but now they have been slaughtered by the sword.

²⁴"Elam lies there surrounded by the graves of all its hordes, those who were slaughtered by the sword. They struck terror in the hearts of people everywhere, but now they have descended as outcasts to the world below. Now they lie in the pit and share the shame of those who have gone before them. ²⁵They have a resting place among the slaughtered, surrounded by the graves of all their hordes. Yes, they terrorized the nations while they lived, but now they lie in shame with others in the pit, all of them outcasts, slaughtered by the sword.

²⁶"Meshech and Tubal are there, surrounded by the graves of all their hordes. They once struck terror in the hearts of people everywhere. But now they are outcasts, all slaughtered by the sword. ²⁷They are not buried in honor like their fallen heroes, who went down to the grave* with their weapons—their shields covering their bodies* and their swords beneath their heads. Their guilt rests upon them because they brought terror to everyone while they were still alive.

²⁸"You too, Egypt, will lie crushed and broken among the outcasts, all slaughtered by the sword.

²⁹"Edom is there with its kings and princes. Mighty as they were, they also lie among those slaughtered by the sword, with the outcasts who have gone down to the pit.

³⁰"All the princes of the north and the Sidonians are there with others who have died. Once a terror, they have been put to shame. They lie there as outcasts with others who were slaughtered by the sword. They share the shame of all who have descended to the pit.

³¹"When Pharaoh and his entire army arrive, he will take comfort that he is not alone in having his hordes killed, says the Sovereign LORD. ³²Although I have caused his terror to fall upon all the living, Pharaoh and his hordes will lie there among the outcasts who were slaughtered by the sword. I, the Sovereign LORD, have spoken!"

31:1 Hebrew *On the first day of the third month,* of the ancient Hebrew lunar calendar. This event occurred on June 21, 587 B.C.; also see note on 1:1.   31:10 Hebrew *you.*   31:15 Hebrew *to Sheol;* also in 31:16, 17.   31:18 Hebrew *among the uncircumcised.*   32:1 Hebrew *On the first day of the twelfth month,* of the ancient Hebrew lunar calendar. This event occurred on March 3, 585 B.C.; also see note on 1:1.   32:17 Hebrew *On the fifteenth day of the month,* presumably in the twelfth month of the ancient Hebrew lunar calendar (see 32:1). This would put this message at the end of King Jehoiachin's twelfth year of captivity, on March 17, 585 B.C.; also see note on 1:1. Greek version reads *On the fifteenth day of the first month,* which would put this message on April 27, 586 B.C., at the beginning of Jehoiachin's twelfth year.   32:18 The meaning of the Hebrew is uncertain.   32:19 Hebrew *the uncircumcised;* also in 32:21, 24, 25, 26, 28, 29, 30, 32.   32:21 Hebrew *in Sheol.*   32:27a Hebrew *to Sheol.*   32:27b The meaning of the Hebrew is uncertain.

HOW WE LIVE

Revering God

HEBREWS 12:28 Our God is an awesome God, and his heavenly kingdom is unshakable. Eventually, the entire world will crumble; everything that you know of this universe will disappear forever. But no matter what happens here, your future is built upon the solid foundation of Jesus Christ which can never be shaken or destroyed. • How can you show your reverence for your amazing God? The writer of Hebrews shares some advice in verses 14-17: (1) *Work at living at peace with everyone.* A right relationship with God will lead to right relationships with others. You may not always feel loving toward others, but you should pursue a peaceful coexistence. (2) *Work at living a holy life.* Show reverence for God by renouncing sin and obeying God's commands. (3) *Look after others so that no one misses out on God's grace.* Share the good news of the gospel. (4) *Do not allow bitterness to take root in you.* If allowed to grow, bitterness gives root to jealousy, dissension, and anger. (5) *Do not live an immoral life.* Keep your purity a priority. • When you show reverence for God by the life you live, you will be able to rejoice when that unshakeable kingdom arrives!

HEBREWS 12:14-29
Because of what Christ did to establish the new covenant, we can come into God's awesome presence not only with reverence and awe but also with confidence and joy.

Work at living in peace with everyone, and work at living a holy life, for those who are not holy will not see the Lord. ¹⁵Look after each other so that none of you fails to receive the grace of God. Watch out that no poisonous root of bitterness grows up to trouble you, corrupting many. ¹⁶Make sure that no one is immoral or godless like Esau, who traded his birthright as the firstborn son for a single meal. ¹⁷You know that afterward, when he wanted his father's blessing, he was rejected. It was too late for repentance, even though he begged with bitter tears.

¹⁸You have not come to a physical mountain,* to a place of flaming fire, darkness, gloom, and whirlwind, as the Israelites did at Mount Sinai. ¹⁹For they heard an awesome trumpet blast and a voice so terrible that they begged God to stop speaking. ²⁰They staggered back under God's command: "If even an animal touches the mountain, it must be stoned to death."* ²¹Moses himself was so frightened at the sight that he said, "I am terrified and trembling."*

²²No, you have come to Mount Zion, to the city of the living God, the heavenly Jerusalem, and to countless thousands of angels in a joyful gathering. ²³You have come to the assembly of God's firstborn children, whose names are written in heaven. You have come to God himself, who is the judge over all things. You have come to the spirits of the righteous ones in heaven who have now been made perfect. ²⁴You have come to Jesus, the one who mediates the new covenant between God and people, and to the sprinkled blood, which speaks of forgiveness instead of crying out for vengeance like the blood of Abel.

²⁵Be careful that you do not refuse to listen to the One who is speaking. For if the people of Israel did not escape when they refused to listen to Moses, the earthly messenger, we will certainly not escape if we reject the One who speaks to us from heaven! ²⁶When God spoke from Mount Sinai his voice shook the earth, but now he makes another promise: "Once again I will shake not only the earth but the heavens also."* ²⁷This means that all of creation will be shaken and removed, so that only unshakable things will remain.

²⁸Since we are receiving a Kingdom that is unshakable, let us be thankful and please God by worshiping him with holy fear and awe. ²⁹For our God is a devouring fire.

12:18 Greek *to something that can be touched.*
12:20 Exod 19:13.   12:21 Deut 9:19.   12:26 Hag 2:6.

PSALM 113:1–114:8
Praise the LORD!

Yes, give praise, O servants of the LORD.
   Praise the name of the LORD!
² Blessed be the name of the LORD
   now and forever.
³ Everywhere—from east to west—
   praise the name of the LORD.
⁴ For the LORD is high above the nations;
   his glory is higher than the heavens.

⁵ Who can be compared with the LORD
      our God,
   who is enthroned on high?
⁶ He stoops to look down
   on heaven and on earth.
⁷ He lifts the poor from the dust
   and the needy from the garbage
      dump.
⁸ He sets them among princes,
   even the princes of his own people!
⁹ He gives the childless woman a family,
   making her a happy mother.

Praise the LORD!

114:1WHEN the Israelites escaped from
      Egypt—
   when the family of Jacob left that
      foreign land—
² the land of Judah became God's
      sanctuary,
   and Israel became his kingdom.

³ The Red Sea* saw them coming and
      hurried out of their way!
   The water of the Jordan River
      turned away.
⁴ The mountains skipped like rams,
   the hills like lambs!

⁵ What's wrong, Red Sea, that made you
   hurry out of their way?
   What happened, Jordan River, that
   you turned away?
⁶ Why, mountains, did you skip like
   rams?
   Why, hills, like lambs?

⁷ Tremble, O earth, at the presence
   of the Lord,
   at the presence of the God of Jacob.
⁸ He turned the rock into a pool of
   water;

EZEKIEL 33:1–34:31

Ezekiel's prophecy continues to be full of images,
metaphors, and object lessons. He explains his own
role as "watchman." He rebukes the "shepherds" of
Israel. He draws a picture of oppression by describing fat shepherds and scrawny sheep.

Once again a message came to me [Ezek-
iel] from the LORD: ²"Son of man, give
your people this message: 'When I bring
an army against a country, the people of
that land choose one of their own to be a
watchman. ³When the watchman sees the
enemy coming, he sounds the alarm
to warn the people. ⁴Then if those who
hear the alarm refuse to take action, it is
their own fault if they die. ⁵They heard
the alarm but ignored it, so the responsibility is theirs. If they had listened to the
warning, they could have saved their lives.
⁶But if the watchman sees the enemy
coming and doesn't sound the alarm to
warn the people, he is responsible for
their captivity. They will die in their sins,
but I will hold the watchman responsible
for their deaths.'

⁷"Now, son of man, I am making you a
watchman for the people of Israel. Therefore, listen to what I say and warn them
for me. ⁸If I announce that some wicked
people are sure to die and you fail to tell
them to change their ways, then they will
die in their sins, and I will hold you responsible for their deaths. ⁹But if you

yes, a spring of water flowed from
   solid rock.

114:3 Hebrew *the sea;* also in 114:5.

PROVERBS 27:18-20

As workers who tend a fig tree are allowed
to eat the fruit, so workers who protect
their employer's interests will be rewarded. □As a face is reflected in water,
so the heart reflects the real person. □Just
as Death and Destruction* are never satisfied, so human desire is never satisfied.
27:20 Hebrew *Sheol and Abaddon.*

NOVEMBER**16**

warn them to repent and they don't repent, they will die in their sins, but you
will have saved yourself.

¹⁰"Son of man, give the people of Israel
this message: You are saying, 'Our sins are
heavy upon us; we are wasting away! How
can we survive?' ¹¹As surely as I live, says
the Sovereign LORD, I take no pleasure in
the death of wicked people. I only want
them to turn from their wicked ways so
they can live. Turn! Turn from your wickedness, O people of Israel! Why should
you die?

¹²"Son of man, give your people this
message: The righteous behavior of righteous people will not save them if they
turn to sin, nor will the wicked behavior
of wicked people destroy them if they repent and turn from their sins. ¹³When I
tell righteous people that they will live,
but then they sin, expecting their past
righteousness to save them, then none of
their righteous acts will be remembered.
I will destroy them for their sins. ¹⁴And
suppose I tell some wicked people that
they will surely die, but then they turn
from their sins and do what is just and
right. ¹⁵For instance, they might give back
a debtor's security, return what they have
stolen, and obey my life-giving laws, no
longer doing what is evil. If they do this,
then they will surely live and not die.

[16]None of their past sins will be brought up again, for they have done what is just and right, and they will surely live.

[17]"Your people are saying, 'The Lord isn't doing what's right,' but it is they who are not doing what's right. [18]For again I say, when righteous people turn away from their righteous behavior and turn to evil, they will die. [19]But if wicked people turn from their wickedness and do what is just and right, they will live. [20]O people of Israel, you are saying, 'The Lord isn't doing what's right.' But I judge each of you according to your deeds."

[21]On January 8,* during the twelfth year of our captivity, a survivor from Jerusalem came to me and said, "The city has fallen!" [22]The previous evening the LORD had taken hold of me and given me back my voice. So I was able to speak when this man arrived the next morning.

[23]Then this message came to me from the LORD: [24]"Son of man, the scattered remnants of Judah living among the ruined cities keep saying, 'Abraham was only one man, yet he gained possession of the entire land. We are many; surely the land has been given to us as a possession.' [25]So tell these people, 'This is what the Sovereign LORD says: You eat meat with blood in it, you worship idols,* and you murder the innocent. Do you really think the land should be yours? [26]Murderers! Idolaters! Adulterers! Should the land belong to you?'

[27]"Say to them, 'This is what the Sovereign LORD says: As surely as I live, those living in the ruins will die by the sword. And I will send wild animals to eat those living in the open fields. Those hiding in the forts and caves will die of disease. [28]I will completely destroy the land and demolish her pride. Her arrogant power will come to an end. The mountains of Israel will be so desolate that no one will even travel through them. [29]When I have completely destroyed the land because of their detestable sins, then they will know that I am the LORD.'

[30]"Son of man, your people talk about you in their houses and whisper about you at the doors. They say to each other, 'Come on, let's go hear the prophet tell us what the LORD is saying!' [31]So my people come pretending to be sincere and sit before you. They listen to your words, but they have no intention of doing what you say. Their mouths are full of lustful words, and their hearts seek only after money. [32]You are very entertaining to them, like someone who sings love songs with a beautiful voice or plays fine music on an instrument. They hear what you say, but they don't act on it! [33]But when all these terrible things happen to them—as they certainly will—then they will know a prophet has been among them."

[34:1]THEN this message came to me from the LORD: [2]"Son of man, prophesy against the shepherds, the leaders of Israel. Give them this message from the Sovereign LORD: What sorrow awaits you shepherds who feed yourselves instead of your flocks. Shouldn't shepherds feed their sheep? [3]You drink the milk, wear the wool, and butcher the best animals, but you let your flocks starve. [4]You have not taken care of the weak. You have not tended the sick or bound up the injured. You have not gone looking for those who have wandered away and are lost. Instead, you have ruled them with harshness and cruelty. [5]So my sheep have been scattered without a shepherd, and they are easy prey for any wild animal. [6]They have wandered through all the mountains and all the hills, across the face of the earth, yet no one has gone to search for them.

[7]"Therefore, you shepherds, hear the word of the LORD: [8]As surely as I live, says the Sovereign LORD, you abandoned my flock and left them to be attacked by every wild animal. And though you were my shepherds, you didn't search for my sheep when they were lost. You took care of yourselves and left the sheep to starve. [9]Therefore, you shepherds, hear the word of the LORD. [10]This is what the Sovereign LORD says: I now consider these shepherds my enemies, and I will hold them responsible for what has happened to my flock. I will take away their right to feed the flock, and I will stop them from feeding themselves. I will rescue my flock from their mouths; the sheep will no longer be their prey.

[11]"For this is what the Sovereign LORD says: I myself will search and find my

sheep. [12]I will be like a shepherd looking for his scattered flock. I will find my sheep and rescue them from all the places where they were scattered on that dark and cloudy day. [13]I will bring them back home to their own land of Israel from among the peoples and nations. I will feed them on the mountains of Israel and by the rivers and in all the places where people live. [14]Yes, I will give them good pastureland on the high hills of Israel. There they will lie down in pleasant places and feed in the lush pastures of the hills. [15]I myself will tend my sheep and give them a place to lie down in peace, says the Sovereign LORD. [16]I will search for my lost ones who strayed away, and I will bring them safely home again. I will bandage the injured and strengthen the weak. But I will destroy those who are fat and powerful. I will feed them, yes—feed them justice!

[17]"And as for you, my flock, this is what the Sovereign LORD says to his people: I will judge between one animal of the flock and another, separating the sheep from the goats. [18]Isn't it enough for you to keep the best of the pastures for yourselves? Must you also trample down the rest? Isn't it enough for you to drink clear water for yourselves? Must you also muddy the rest

with your feet? [19]Why must my flock eat what you have trampled down and drink water you have fouled?

[20]"Therefore, this is what the Sovereign LORD says: I will surely judge between the fat sheep and the scrawny sheep. [21]For you fat sheep pushed and butted and crowded my sick and hungry flock until you scattered them to distant lands. [22]So I will rescue my flock, and they will no longer be abused. I will judge between one animal of the flock and another. [23]And I will set over them one shepherd, my servant David. He will feed them and be a shepherd to them. [24]And I, the LORD, will be their God, and my servant David will be a prince among my people. I, the LORD, have spoken!

[25]"I will make a covenant of peace with my people and drive away the dangerous animals from the land. Then they will be able to camp safely in the wildest places and sleep in the woods without fear. [26]I will bless my people and their homes around my holy hill. And in the proper season I will send the showers they need. There will be showers of blessing. [27]The orchards and fields of my people will yield bumper crops, and everyone will live in safety. When I have broken their chains of slavery and rescued them from those who

HOW WE LIVE

Our marriages

HEBREWS 13:4 Just think how many marriages could be improved (or saved) if marriage partners would follow the very basic guidelines of this verse: Honor your marriage and remain faithful. Giving honor to your marriage means praying for your spouse, putting his or her needs before your own, seeking to be a servant, and loving with the kind of love described in 1 Corinthians 13 (August 20)—patient, kind, never giving up, never losing faith, always hopeful, enduring through every circumstance. Remaining faithful means staying away from immoral behavior and adultery. Immorality and adultery have split marriages for thousands of years. God's commands against such actions have been in place for just as long. • Christians are to maintain high standards—in their lives and in their marriages. This is important not just for the marriages and families, but also for the church. Honesty, moral purity, and faithfulness are essential to the proper worship of God. Because the marriage relationship often illustrates the relationship of God with his people, a relationship on earth with one's spouse ought to illustrate the love, trust, and devotion available with the Creator. This pleases God.

enslaved them, then they will know that I am the LORD. ²⁸They will no longer be prey for other nations, and wild animals will no longer devour them. They will live in safety, and no one will frighten them.

²⁹"And I will make their land famous for its crops, so my people will never again suffer from famines or the insults of foreign nations. ³⁰In this way, they will know that I, the LORD their God, am with them. And they will know that they, the people of Israel, are my people, says the Sovereign LORD. ³¹You are my flock, the sheep of my pasture. You are my people, and I am your God. I, the Sovereign LORD, have spoken!"

33:21 Hebrew *On the fifth day of the tenth month,* of the ancient Hebrew lunar calendar. This event occurred on January 8, 585 B.C.; also see note on 1:1. 33:25 The Hebrew term (literally *round things*) probably alludes to dung.

HEBREWS 13:1-25

Obeying God, who was described in yesterday's reading as a "devouring fire" (Hebrews 12:29) affects every part of our lives—relationships, associations, marriages, and our community. As the writer of Hebrews closes his letter, he touches on many of the ways that our faith is to make a difference in our lives.

Keep on loving each other as brothers and sisters.* ²Don't forget to show hospitality to strangers, for some who have done this have entertained angels without realizing it! ³Remember those in prison, as if you were there yourself. Remember also those being mistreated, as if you felt their pain in your own bodies.

⁴Give honor to marriage, and remain faithful to one another in marriage. God will surely judge people who are immoral and those who commit adultery.

⁵Don't love money; be satisfied with what you have. For God has said,

"I will never fail you.
I will never abandon you."*

⁶So we can say with confidence,

"The LORD is my helper,
so I will have no fear.
What can mere people do to me?"*

⁷Remember your leaders who taught you the word of God. Think of all the good that has come from their lives, and follow the example of their faith.

⁸Jesus Christ is the same yesterday, today, and forever. ⁹So do not be attracted by strange, new ideas. Your strength comes from God's grace, not from rules about food, which don't help those who follow them.

¹⁰We have an altar from which the priests in the Tabernacle* have no right to eat. ¹¹Under the old system, the high priest brought the blood of animals into the Holy Place as a sacrifice for sin, and the bodies of the animals were burned outside the camp. ¹²So also Jesus suffered and died outside the city gates to make his people holy by means of his own blood. ¹³So let us go out to him, outside the camp, and bear the disgrace he bore. ¹⁴For this world is not our permanent home; we are looking forward to a home yet to come.

¹⁵Therefore, let us offer through Jesus a continual sacrifice of praise to God, proclaiming our allegiance to his name. ¹⁶And don't forget to do good and to share with those in need. These are the sacrifices that please God.

¹⁷Obey your spiritual leaders, and do what they say. Their work is to watch over your souls, and they are accountable to God. Give them reason to do this with joy and not with sorrow. That would certainly not be for your benefit.

¹⁸Pray for us, for our conscience is clear and we want to live honorably in everything we do. ¹⁹And especially pray that I will be able to come back to you soon.

²⁰ Now may the God of peace—
who brought up from the dead our
Lord Jesus,
the great Shepherd of the sheep,
and ratified an eternal covenant
with his blood—
²¹ may he equip you with all you need
for doing his will.
May he produce in you,*
through the power of Jesus Christ,
every good thing that is pleasing
to him.
All glory to him forever and ever!
Amen.

²²I urge you, dear brothers and sisters,* to pay attention to what I have written in this brief exhortation. ²³I want you to know that our brother

Timothy has been released from jail. If he comes here soon, I will bring him with me to see you.

²⁴Greet all your leaders and all the believers there.* The believers from Italy send you their greetings.

²⁵May God's grace be with you all.

13:1 Greek *Continue in brotherly love.*   13:5 Deut 31:6, 8.
13:6 Ps 118:6.   13:10 Or *tent.*   13:21 Some manuscripts read *in us.*   13:22 Greek *brothers.*   13:24 Greek *all of God's people.*

PSALM 115:1-18

Not to us, O Lᴏʀᴅ, not to us,
 but to your name goes all the glory
 for your unfailing love and
  faithfulness.
² Why let the nations say,
 "Where is their God?"
³ Our God is in the heavens,
 and he does as he wishes.
⁴ Their idols are merely things of silver
  and gold,
 shaped by human hands.
⁵ They have mouths but cannot speak,
 and eyes but cannot see.
⁶ They have ears but cannot hear,
 and noses but cannot smell.
⁷ They have hands but cannot feel,
 and feet but cannot walk,
 and throats but cannot make
  a sound.
⁸ And those who make idols are just like
  them,
 as are all who trust in them.

⁹ O Israel, trust the Lᴏʀᴅ!
 He is your helper and your shield.

¹⁰ O priests, descendants of Aaron, trust
  the Lᴏʀᴅ!
 He is your helper and your shield.
¹¹ All you who fear the Lᴏʀᴅ, trust the
  Lᴏʀᴅ!
 He is your helper and your shield.

¹² The Lᴏʀᴅ remembers us and will
  bless us.
 He will bless the people of Israel
 and bless the priests,
  descendants of Aaron.
¹³ He will bless those who fear the Lᴏʀᴅ,
 both great and lowly.

¹⁴ May the Lᴏʀᴅ richly bless
 both you and your children.
¹⁵ May you be blessed by the Lᴏʀᴅ,
 who made heaven and earth.
¹⁶ The heavens belong to the Lᴏʀᴅ,
 but he has given the earth to all
  humanity.
¹⁷ The dead cannot sing praises to the
  Lᴏʀᴅ,
 for they have gone into the silence
  of the grave.
¹⁸ But we can praise the Lᴏʀᴅ
 both now and forever!

 Praise the Lᴏʀᴅ!

PROVERBS 27:21-22

Fire tests the purity of silver and gold, but a person is tested by being praised.* □ You cannot separate fools from their foolishness, even though you grind them like grain with mortar and pestle.
27:21 Or *by flattery.*

NOVEMBER**17**

EZEKIEL 35:1–36:38

The nations of Israel and Edom descended from twin brothers—Jacob and Esau. Unfortunately, the conflict that originated with the brothers extended down through the generations. Prophets such as Isaiah, Joel, Amos, Obadiah, and Malachi spoke against Edom, as Ezekiel does here.

Again a message came to me [Ezekiel] from the Lᴏʀᴅ: ²"Son of man, turn and face Mount Seir, and prophesy against its

people. ³Give them this message from the Sovereign Lᴏʀᴅ:

 "I am your enemy, O Mount Seir,
  and I will raise my fist against you
  to destroy you completely.
⁴ I will demolish your cities
  and make you desolate.
 Then you will know that I am
  the Lᴏʀᴅ.

[5]"Your eternal hatred for the people of Israel led you to butcher them when they were helpless, when I had already punished them for all their sins. [6]As surely as I live, says the Sovereign LORD, since you show no distaste for blood, I will give you a bloodbath of your own. Your turn has come! [7]I will make Mount Seir utterly desolate, killing off all who try to escape and any who return. [8]I will fill your mountains with the dead. Your hills, your valleys, and your ravines will be filled with people slaughtered by the sword. [9]I will make you desolate forever. Your cities will never be rebuilt. Then you will know that I am the LORD.

[10]"For you said, 'The lands of Israel and Judah will be ours. We will take possession of them. What do we care that the LORD is there!' [11]Therefore, as surely as I live, says the Sovereign LORD, I will pay back your angry deeds with my own. I will punish you for all your acts of anger, envy, and hatred. And I will make myself known to Israel* by what I do to you. [12]Then you will know that I, the LORD, have heard every contemptuous word you spoke against the mountains of Israel. For you said, 'They are desolate; they have been given to us as food to eat!' [13]In saying that, you boasted proudly against me, and I have heard it all!

[14]"This is what the Sovereign LORD says: The whole world will rejoice when I make you desolate. [15]You rejoiced at the desolation of Israel's territory. Now I will rejoice at yours! You will be wiped out, you people of Mount Seir and all who live in Edom! Then you will know that I am the LORD.

36:1"SON of man, prophesy to Israel's mountains. Give them this message: O mountains of Israel, hear the word of the LORD! [2]This is what the Sovereign LORD says: Your enemies have taunted you, saying, 'Aha! Now the ancient heights belong to us!' [3]Therefore, son of man, give the mountains of Israel this message from the Sovereign LORD: Your enemies have attacked you from all directions, making you the property of many nations and the object of much mocking and slander. [4]Therefore, O mountains of Israel, hear the word of the Sovereign LORD. He speaks to the hills and mountains, ravines and valleys, and to ruined wastes and long-deserted cities that have been destroyed and mocked by the surrounding nations. [5]This is what the Sovereign LORD says: My jealous anger burns against these nations, especially Edom, because they have shown utter contempt for me by gleefully taking my land for themselves as plunder.

[6]"Therefore, prophesy to the hills and mountains, the ravines and valleys of Israel. This is what the Sovereign LORD says: I am furious that you have suffered shame before the surrounding nations. [7]Therefore, this is what the Sovereign LORD says: I have taken a solemn oath that those nations will soon have their own shame to endure.

[8]"But the mountains of Israel will produce heavy crops of fruit for my people—for they will be coming home again soon! [9]See, I care about you, and I will pay attention to you. Your ground will be plowed and your crops planted. [10]I will greatly increase the population of Israel, and the ruined cities will be rebuilt and filled with people. [11]I will increase not only the people, but also your animals. O mountains of Israel, I will bring people to live on you once again. I will make you even more prosperous than you were before. Then you will know that I am the LORD. [12]I will cause my people to walk on you once again, and you will be their territory. You will never again rob them of their children.

[13]"This is what the Sovereign LORD says: The other nations taunt you, saying, 'Israel is a land that devours its own people and robs them of their children!' [14]But you will never again devour your people or rob them of their children, says the Sovereign LORD. [15]I will not let you hear those other nations insult you, and you will no longer be mocked by them. You will not be a land that causes its nation to fall, says the Sovereign LORD."

[16]Then this further message came to me from the LORD: [17]"Son of man, when the people of Israel were living in their own land, they defiled it by the evil way they lived. To me their conduct was as unclean as a woman's menstrual cloth.

¹⁸They polluted the land with murder and the worship of idols,* so I poured out my fury on them. ¹⁹I scattered them to many lands to punish them for the evil way they had lived. ²⁰But when they were scattered among the nations, they brought shame on my holy name. For the nations said, 'These are the people of the LORD, but he couldn't keep them safe in his own land!' ²¹Then I was concerned for my holy name, on which my people brought shame among the nations.

²²"Therefore, give the people of Israel this message from the Sovereign LORD: I am bringing you back, but not because you deserve it. I am doing it to protect my holy name, on which you brought shame while you were scattered among the nations. ²³I will show how holy my great name is—the name on which you brought shame among the nations. And when I reveal my holiness through you before their very eyes, says the Sovereign LORD, then the nations will know that I am the LORD. ²⁴For I will gather you up from all the nations and bring you home again to your land.

²⁵"Then I will sprinkle clean water on you, and you will be clean. Your filth will be washed away, and you will no longer worship idols. ²⁶And I will give you a new heart, and I will put a new spirit in you. I will take out your stony, stubborn heart and give you a tender, responsive heart.*

²⁷And I will put my Spirit in you so that you will follow my decrees and be careful to obey my regulations.

²⁸"And you will live in Israel, the land I gave your ancestors long ago. You will be my people, and I will be your God. ²⁹I will cleanse you of your filthy behavior. I will give you good crops of grain, and I will send no more famines on the land. ³⁰I will give you great harvests from your fruit trees and fields, and never again will the surrounding nations be able to scoff at your land for its famines. ³¹Then you will remember your past sins and despise yourselves for all the detestable things you did. ³²But remember, says the Sovereign LORD, I am not doing this because you deserve it. O my people of Israel, you should be utterly ashamed of all you have done!

³³"This is what the Sovereign LORD says: When I cleanse you from your sins, I will repopulate your cities, and the ruins will be rebuilt. ³⁴The fields that used to lie empty and desolate in plain view of everyone will again be farmed. ³⁵And when I bring you back, people will say, 'This former wasteland is now like the Garden of Eden! The abandoned and ruined cities now have strong walls and are filled with people!' ³⁶Then the surrounding nations that survive will know that I, the LORD, have rebuilt the ruins and replanted the

---

HOW WE LIVE

Relying on God's power

EZEKIEL 36:26-27 Who are we as believers? All four of today's readings give a slice of that answer. Ezekiel says we are people with new, obedient hearts. James says we will face trouble in this life, but we are to focus on God's presence. According to the psalmist, we are God's servants. The proverbs say we are responsible to manage our lives well. Pretty tall orders, wouldn't you say? • We find the strength to rise to the challenge in the very one who defines the challenge. Ezekiel wrote that God will "take out your stony, stubborn heart and give you a tender, responsive heart" (Ezekiel 36:26). You received a heart transplant when you became a believer. You had to, because you can't live the Christian life in your own strength. God never expected that. Instead, he wants to live the Christian life through you. When you realize that, you begin to catch a glimpse of the awesome love of a God who wants to keep your personality, your character traits, your gifts, your likes and dislikes, and yet make you holy through his presence in you.

wasteland. For I, the LORD, have spoken, and I will do what I say.

³⁷"This is what the Sovereign LORD says: I am ready to hear Israel's prayers and to increase their numbers like a flock. ³⁸They will be as numerous as the sacred flocks that fill Jerusalem's streets at the time of her festivals. The ruined cities will be crowded with people once more, and everyone will know that I am the LORD."

35:11 Hebrew *to them;* Greek version reads *to you.*
36:18 The Hebrew term (literally *round things*) probably alludes to dung; also in 36:25.   **36:26** Hebrew *a heart of flesh.*

JAMES 1:1-18

Wouldn't you like to read a book written by one of Jesus' family members? James was Jesus' younger brother. Many believe this letter was the earliest New Testament letter written.

This letter is from James, a slave of God and of the Lord Jesus Christ.

I am writing to the "twelve tribes"—Jewish believers scattered abroad.

Greetings!

²Dear brothers and sisters,* when troubles come your way, consider it an opportunity for great joy. ³For you know that when your faith is tested, your endurance has a chance to grow. ⁴So let it grow, for when your endurance is fully developed, you will be perfect and complete, needing nothing.

⁵If you need wisdom, ask our generous God, and he will give it to you. He will not rebuke you for asking. ⁶But when you ask him, be sure that your faith is in God alone. Do not waver, for a person with divided loyalty is as unsettled as a wave of the sea that is blown and tossed by the wind. ⁷Such people should not expect to receive anything from the Lord. ⁸Their loyalty is divided between God and the world, and they are unstable in everything they do.

⁹Believers who are* poor have something to boast about, for God has honored them. ¹⁰And those who are rich should boast that God has humbled them. They will fade away like a little flower in the field. ¹¹The hot sun rises and the grass withers; the little flower droops and falls, and its beauty fades away. In the same way, the rich will fade away with all of their achievements.

¹²God blesses those who patiently endure testing and temptation. Afterward they will receive the crown of life that God has promised to those who love him. ¹³And remember, when you are being tempted, do not say, "God is tempting me." God is never tempted to do wrong,* and he never tempts anyone else. ¹⁴Temptation comes from our own desires, which entice us and drag us away. ¹⁵These desires give birth to sinful actions. And when sin is allowed to grow, it gives birth to death.

¹⁶So don't be misled, my dear brothers and sisters. ¹⁷Whatever is good and perfect comes down to us from God our Father, who created all the lights in the heavens.* He never changes or casts a shifting shadow.* ¹⁸He chose to give birth to us by giving us his true word. And we, out of all creation, became his prized possession.*

1:2 Greek *brothers;* also in 1:16, 19.   **1:9** Greek *The brother who is.*   **1:13** Or *God should not be put to a test by evil people.*   **1:17a** Greek *from above, from the Father of lights.*
1:17b Some manuscripts read *He never changes, as a shifting shadow does.*   **1:18** Greek *we became a kind of firstfruit of his creatures.*

PSALM 116:1-19

I love the LORD because he hears my
   voice
   and my prayer for mercy.
² Because he bends down to listen,
   I will pray as long as I have breath!
³ Death wrapped its ropes around me;
   the terrors of the grave* overtook me.
   I saw only trouble and sorrow.
⁴ Then I called on the name of the LORD:
   "Please, LORD, save me!"
⁵ How kind the LORD is! How good he is!
   So merciful, this God of ours!
⁶ The LORD protects those of childlike
   faith;
   I was facing death, and he saved me.
⁷ Let my soul be at rest again,
   for the LORD has been good to me.
⁸ He has saved me from death,
   my eyes from tears,
   my feet from stumbling.
⁹ And so I walk in the LORD's presence
   as I live here on earth!
¹⁰ I believed in you, so I said,
   "I am deeply troubled, LORD."
¹¹ In my anxiety I cried out to you,
   "These people are all liars!"

¹² What can I offer the LORD
    for all he has done for me?
¹³ I will lift up the cup of salvation
    and praise the LORD's name for
      saving me.
¹⁴ I will keep my promises to the LORD
    in the presence of all his people.

¹⁵ The LORD cares deeply
    when his loved ones die.
¹⁶ O LORD, I am your servant;
    yes, I am your servant, born into
      your household;
    you have freed me from my chains.
¹⁷ I will offer you a sacrifice of
      thanksgiving
    and call on the name of the LORD.
¹⁸ I will fulfill my vows to the LORD
    in the presence of all his people—

¹⁹ in the house of the LORD
    in the heart of Jerusalem.

    Praise the LORD!

116:3 Hebrew *of Sheol.*

PROVERBS 27:23-27

Know the state of your flocks, and put your heart into caring for your herds, for riches don't last forever, and the crown might not be passed to the next generation. After the hay is harvested and the new crop appears and the mountain grasses are gathered in, your sheep will provide wool for clothing, and your goats will provide the price of a field. And you will have enough goats' milk for yourself, your family, and your servant girls.

NOVEMBER **18**

EZEKIEL 37:1-38:23

Ezekiel's vision in the valley of dry bones is a story of new life, offered to God's people even though they had failed and fallen many times over.

The LORD took hold of me [Ezekiel], and I was carried away by the Spirit of the LORD to a valley filled with bones. ²He led me all around among the bones that covered the valley floor. They were scattered everywhere across the ground and were completely dried out. ³Then he asked me, "Son of man, can these bones become living people again?"

"O Sovereign LORD," I replied, "you alone know the answer to that."

⁴Then he said to me, "Speak a prophetic message to these bones and say, 'Dry bones, listen to the word of the LORD! ⁵This is what the Sovereign LORD says: Look! I am going to put breath into you and make you live again! ⁶I will put flesh and muscles on you and cover you with skin. I will put breath into you, and you will come to life. Then you will know that I am the LORD.'"

⁷So I spoke this message, just as he told me. Suddenly as I spoke, there was a rattling noise all across the valley. The bones of each body came together and attached themselves as complete skeletons. ⁸Then as I watched, muscles and flesh formed over the bones. Then skin formed to cover their bodies, but they still had no breath in them.

⁹Then he said to me, "Speak a prophetic message to the winds, son of man. Speak a prophetic message and say, 'This is what the Sovereign LORD says: Come, O breath, from the four winds! Breathe into these dead bodies so they may live again.'"

¹⁰So I spoke the message as he commanded me, and breath came into their bodies. They all came to life and stood up on their feet—a great army.

¹¹Then he said to me, "Son of man, these bones represent the people of Israel. They are saying, 'We have become old, dry bones—all hope is gone. Our nation is finished.' ¹²Therefore, prophesy to them and say, 'This is what the Sovereign LORD says: O my people, I will open your graves of exile and cause you to rise again. Then I will bring you back to the land of Israel. ¹³When this happens, O my people, you will know that I am the LORD. ¹⁴I will put

my Spirit in you, and you will live again and return home to your own land. Then you will know that I, the Lᴏʀᴅ, have spoken, and I have done what I said. Yes, the Lᴏʀᴅ has spoken!'"

¹⁵Again a message came to me from the Lᴏʀᴅ: ¹⁶"Son of man, take a piece of wood and carve on it these words: 'This represents Judah and its allied tribes.' Then take another piece and carve these words on it: 'This represents Ephraim and the northern tribes of Israel.'* ¹⁷Now hold them together in your hand as if they were one piece of wood. ¹⁸When your people ask you what your actions mean, ¹⁹say to them, 'This is what the Sovereign Lᴏʀᴅ says: I will take Ephraim and the northern tribes and join them to Judah. I will make them one piece of wood in my hand.'

²⁰"Then hold out the pieces of wood you have inscribed, so the people can see them. ²¹And give them this message from the Sovereign Lᴏʀᴅ: I will gather the people of Israel from among the nations. I will bring them home to their own land from the places where they have been scattered. ²²I will unify them into one nation on the mountains of Israel. One king will rule them all; no longer will they be divided into two nations or into two kingdoms. ²³They will never again pollute themselves with their idols* and vile images and rebellion, for I will save them from their sinful backsliding. I will cleanse them. Then they will truly be my people, and I will be their God.

²⁴"My servant David will be their king, and they will have only one shepherd. They will obey my regulations and be careful to keep my decrees. ²⁵They will live in the land I gave my servant Jacob, the land where their ancestors lived. They and their children and their grandchildren after them will live there forever, generation after generation. And my servant David will be their prince forever. ²⁶And I will make a covenant of peace with them, an everlasting covenant. I will give them their land and increase their numbers,* and I will put my Temple among them forever. ²⁷I will make my home among them. I will be their God, and they will be my people. ²⁸And when my Temple is among them forever, the nations will know that I am the Lᴏʀᴅ, who makes Israel holy."

38:1 This is another message that came to me from the Lᴏʀᴅ: ²"Son of man, turn and face Gog of the land of Magog, the prince who rules over the nations of Meshech and Tubal, and prophesy against him. ³Give him this message from the Sovereign Lᴏʀᴅ: Gog, I am your enemy! ⁴I will turn you around and put hooks in your jaws to lead you out with your whole army—your horses and charioteers in full armor and a great horde armed with shields and swords. ⁵Persia, Ethiopia, and Libya* will join you, too, with all their weapons. ⁶Gomer and all its armies will also join you, along with the armies of Beth-togarmah from the distant north, and many others.

⁷"Get ready; be prepared! Keep all the armies around you mobilized, and take command of them. ⁸A long time from now you will be called into action. In the distant future you will swoop down on the land of Israel, which will be enjoying peace after recovering from war and after its people have returned from many lands to the mountains of Israel. ⁹You and all your allies—a vast and awesome army—will roll down on them like a storm and cover the land like a cloud.

¹⁰"This is what the Sovereign Lᴏʀᴅ says: At that time evil thoughts will come to your mind, and you will devise a wicked scheme. ¹¹You will say, 'Israel is an unprotected land filled with unwalled villages! I will march against her and destroy these people who live in such confidence! ¹²I will go to those formerly desolate cities that are now filled with people who have returned from exile in many nations. I will capture vast amounts of plunder, for the people are rich with livestock and other possessions now. They think the whole world revolves around them!' ¹³But Sheba and Dedan and the merchants of Tarshish will ask, 'Do you really think the armies you have gathered can rob them of silver and gold? Do you think you can drive away their livestock and seize their goods and carry off plunder?'

¹⁴"Therefore, son of man, prophesy against Gog. Give him this message from the Sovereign Lᴏʀᴅ: When my people are

living in peace in their land, then you will rouse yourself.* [15] You will come from your homeland in the distant north with your vast cavalry and your mighty army, [16] and you will attack my people Israel, covering their land like a cloud. At that time in the distant future, I will bring you against my land as everyone watches, and my holiness will be displayed by what happens to you, Gog. Then all the nations will know that I am the LORD.

[17] "This is what the Sovereign LORD asks: Are you the one I was talking about long ago, when I announced through Israel's prophets that in the future I would bring you against my people? [18] But this is what the Sovereign LORD says: When Gog invades the land of Israel, my fury will boil over! [19] In my jealousy and blazing anger, I promise a mighty shaking in the land of Israel on that day. [20] All living things—the fish in the sea, the birds of the sky, the animals of the field, the small animals that scurry along the ground, and all the people on earth—will quake in terror at my presence. Mountains will be thrown down; cliffs will crumble; walls will fall to the earth. [21] I will summon the sword against you on all the hills of Israel, says the Sovereign LORD. Your men will turn their swords against each other. [22] I will punish you and your armies with disease and bloodshed; I will send torrential rain, hailstones, fire, and burning sulfur! [23] In this way, I will show my greatness and holiness, and I will make myself known to all the nations of the world. Then they will know that I am the LORD."

37:16 Hebrew *This is Ephraim's wood, representing Joseph and all the house of Israel.*   37:23 The Hebrew term (literally *round things*) probably alludes to dung.
37:26 Hebrew reads *I will give them and increase their numbers;* Greek version omits the entire phrase.
38:5 Hebrew *Paras, Cush, and Put.*   38:14 As in Greek version; Hebrew reads *then you will know.*

JAMES 1:19–2:17

There's a theme that runs through James—walking your talk. He emphasizes the connection that must exist between what a person believes and how a person lives.

Understand this, my dear brothers and sisters: You must all be quick to listen, slow to speak, and slow to get angry. [20] Human anger* does not produce the righteousness* God desires. [21] So get rid of all the filth and evil in your lives, and humbly accept the word God has planted in your hearts, for it has the power to save your souls.

[22] But don't just listen to God's word. You must do what it says. Otherwise, you are only fooling yourselves. [23] For if you listen to the word and don't obey, it is like glancing at your face in a mirror. [24] You see yourself, walk away, and forget what you look like. [25] But if you look carefully into the perfect law that sets you free, and if you do

HOW WE LIVE

Faith and works

JAMES 2:14-24 As you read these verses, you may become a bit confused. "I thought all I needed was faith to be saved. Now I'm reading that faith alone *doesn't* save me?" As you study the Bible, remember that God never contradicts himself. Don't take a verse out of context; instead, examine it in the context of the passage and the entire Bible. • Paul wrote: "We are made right with God through faith and not by obeying the law" (Romans 3:28, July 16). James says we are "shown to be right with God by what we do, not by faith alone" (James 2:24, November 19). The two are not contradictory. True saving faith will manifest itself in a life of good works. Faith is what is required to get into God's kingdom. But true faith never stands alone. It always produces a changed life. Now, your life will not change to perfection overnight. In fact, this side of heaven, you'll never attain perfection. But now that Christ has given you new life in him, you will continue to grow in your desire to please him more and your sinful nature less. Good works will flow naturally from your life in Christ.

what it says and don't forget what you heard, then God will bless you for doing it.

²⁶If you claim to be religious but don't control your tongue, you are fooling yourself, and your religion is worthless. ²⁷Pure and genuine religion in the sight of God the Father means caring for orphans and widows in their distress and refusing to let the world corrupt you.

2:1 My dear brothers and sisters,* how can you claim to have faith in our glorious Lord Jesus Christ if you favor some people over others?

²For example, suppose someone comes into your meeting* dressed in fancy clothes and expensive jewelry, and another comes in who is poor and dressed in dirty clothes. ³If you give special attention and a good seat to the rich person, but you say to the poor one, "You can stand over there, or else sit on the floor"—well, ⁴doesn't this discrimination show that your judgments are guided by evil motives?

⁵Listen to me, dear brothers and sisters. Hasn't God chosen the poor in this world to be rich in faith? Aren't they the ones who will inherit the Kingdom he promised to those who love him? ⁶But you dishonor the poor! Isn't it the rich who oppress you and drag you into court? ⁷Aren't they the ones who slander Jesus Christ, whose noble name* you bear?

⁸Yes indeed, it is good when you obey the royal law as found in the Scriptures: "Love your neighbor as yourself."* ⁹But if you favor some people over others, you are committing a sin. You are guilty of breaking the law.

¹⁰For the person who keeps all of the laws except one is as guilty as a person who has broken all of God's laws. ¹¹For the same God who said, "You must not commit adultery," also said, "You must not murder."* So if you murder someone but do not commit adultery, you have still broken the law.

¹²So whatever you say or whatever you do, remember that you will be judged by the law that sets you free. ¹³There will be no mercy for those who have not shown mercy to others. But if you have been merciful, God will be merciful when he judges you.

¹⁴What good is it, dear brothers and sisters, if you say you have faith but don't show it by your actions? Can that kind of faith save anyone? ¹⁵Suppose you see a brother or sister who has no food or clothing, ¹⁶and you say, "Good-bye and have a good day; stay warm and eat well"—but then you don't give that person any food or clothing. What good does that do?

¹⁷So you see, faith by itself isn't enough. Unless it produces good deeds, it is dead and useless.

1:20a Greek *A man's anger.*   **1:20b** Or *the justice.*
2:1 Greek *brothers;* also in 2:5, 14.   **2:2** Greek *your synagogue.*   **2:7** Greek *slander the noble name.*   **2:8** Lev 19:18.   **2:11** Exod 20:13-14; Deut 5:17-18.

PSALM 117:1-2

Praise the LORD, all you nations.
    Praise him, all you people of the earth.
² For he loves us with unfailing love;
    the LORD's faithfulness endures forever.

Praise the LORD!

PROVERBS 28:1

The wicked run away when no one is chasing them, but the godly are as bold as lions.

NOVEMBER**19**

EZEKIEL 39:1–40:27

Gog may be a name for an actual ruler who was going to attack God's people, or it could be a name for evil in general. Gog is also referred to in Revelation (Revelation 20:8; December 29). There it seems to represent the nations of the earth who will stand against God.

"**S**on of man, prophesy against Gog. Give him this message from the Sovereign LORD: I am your enemy, O Gog, ruler of the nations of Meshech and Tubal. ²I will turn you around and drive you toward the mountains of Israel, bringing you from the distant north. ³I will knock the bow from your left hand and the arrows from your right hand, and I will leave you helpless. ⁴You and your army and your allies will all die on the mountains. I will feed you to the vultures and wild animals. ⁵You will fall in the open fields, for I have spoken, says the Sovereign LORD. ⁶And I will rain down fire on Magog and on all your allies who live safely on the coasts. Then they will know that I am the LORD.

⁷"In this way, I will make known my holy name among my people of Israel. I will not let anyone bring shame on it. And the nations, too, will know that I am the LORD, the Holy One of Israel. ⁸That day of judgment will come, says the Sovereign LORD. Everything will happen just as I have declared it.

⁹"Then the people in the towns of Israel will go out and pick up your small and large shields, bows and arrows, javelins and spears, and they will use them for fuel. There will be enough to last them seven years! ¹⁰They won't need to cut wood from the fields or forests, for these weapons will give them all the fuel they need. They will plunder those who planned to plunder them, and they will rob those who planned to rob them, says the Sovereign LORD.

¹¹"And I will make a vast graveyard for Gog and his hordes in the Valley of the Travelers, east of the Dead Sea.* It will block the way of those who travel there, and they will change the name of the place to the Valley of Gog's Hordes. ¹²It will take seven months for the people of Israel to bury the bodies and cleanse the land. ¹³Everyone in Israel will help, for it will be a glorious victory for Israel when I demonstrate my glory on that day, says the Sovereign LORD.

¹⁴"After seven months, teams of men will be appointed to search the land for skeletons to bury, so the land will be made clean again. ¹⁵Whenever bones are found, a marker will be set up so the burial crews will take them to be buried in the Valley of Gog's Hordes. ¹⁶(There will be a town there named Hamonah, which means 'horde.') And so the land will finally be cleansed.

¹⁷"And now, son of man, this is what the Sovereign LORD says: Call all the birds and wild animals. Say to them: Gather together for my great sacrificial feast. Come from far and near to the mountains of Israel, and there eat flesh and drink blood! ¹⁸Eat the flesh of mighty men and drink the blood of princes as though they were rams, lambs, goats, and bulls—all fattened animals from Bashan! ¹⁹Gorge yourselves with flesh until you are glutted; drink blood until you are drunk. This is the sacrificial feast I have prepared for you. ²⁰Feast at my banquet table—feast on horses and charioteers, on mighty men and all kinds of valiant warriors, says the Sovereign LORD.

²¹"In this way, I will demonstrate my glory to the nations. Everyone will see the punishment I have inflicted on them and the power of my fist when I strike. ²²And from that time on the people of Israel will know that I am the LORD their God. ²³The nations will then know why Israel was sent away to exile—it was punishment for sin, for they were unfaithful to their God. Therefore, I turned away from them and let their enemies destroy them. ²⁴I turned my face away and punished them because of their defilement and their sins.

²⁵"So now, this is what the Sovereign LORD says: I will end the captivity of my people*; I will have mercy on all Israel, for I jealously guard my holy reputation! ²⁶They will accept responsibility for their past shame and unfaithfulness after they come home to live in peace in their own land, with no one to bother them. ²⁷When I bring them home from the lands of their enemies, I will display my holiness among them for all the nations to see. ²⁸Then my people will know that I am the LORD their God, because I sent them away to exile and brought them home again. I will leave none of my people behind. ²⁹And I will never again turn my face from them, for I will pour out my Spirit upon the people of Israel. I, the Sovereign LORD, have spoken!"

⁴⁰:¹On April 28,* during the twenty-fifth year of our captivity—fourteen years after the fall of Jerusalem—the LORD took hold of me. ²In a vision from God he took me to the land of Israel and set me down on a very high mountain. From there I could see toward the south what appeared to be

a city. [3]As he brought me nearer, I saw a man whose face shone like bronze standing beside a gateway entrance. He was holding in his hand a linen measuring cord and a measuring rod.

[4]He said to me, "Son of man, watch and listen. Pay close attention to everything I show you. You have been brought here so I can show you many things. Then you will return to the people of Israel and tell them everything you have seen."

[5]I could see a wall completely surrounding the Temple area. The man took a measuring rod that was 10½ feet* long and measured the wall, and the wall was 10½ feet* thick and 10½ feet high.

[6]Then he went over to the eastern gateway. He climbed the steps and measured the threshold of the gateway; it was 10½ feet front to back.* [7]There were guard alcoves on each side built into the gateway passage. Each of these alcoves was 10½ feet square, with a distance between them of 8¾ feet* along the passage wall. The gateway's inner threshold, which led to the entry room at the inner end of the gateway passage, was 10½ feet front to back. [8]He also measured the entry room of the gateway.* [9]It was 14 feet* across, with supporting columns 3½ feet* thick. This entry room was at the inner end of the gateway structure, facing toward the Temple.

[10]There were three guard alcoves on each side of the gateway passage. Each had the same measurements, and the dividing walls separating them were also identical. [11]The man measured the gateway entrance, which was 17½ feet* wide at the opening and 22¾ feet* wide in the gateway passage. [12]In front of each of the guard alcoves was a 21-inch* curb. The alcoves themselves were 10½ feet* on each side.

[13]Then he measured the entire width of the gateway, measuring the distance between the back walls of facing guard alcoves; this distance was 43¾ feet.* [14]He measured the dividing walls all along the inside of the gateway up to the entry room of the gateway; this distance was 105 feet.* [15]The full length of the gateway passage was 87½ feet* from one end to the other. [16]There were recessed windows that narrowed inward through the walls of the guard alcoves and their dividing walls. There were also windows in the entry room. The surfaces of the dividing walls were decorated with carved palm trees.

[17]Then the man brought me through the gateway into the outer courtyard of the Temple. A stone pavement ran along the walls of the courtyard, and thirty rooms were built against the walls, opening onto the pavement. [18]This pavement flanked the gates and extended out from the walls into the courtyard the same distance as the gateway entrance. This was the lower pavement. [19]Then the man measured across the Temple's outer courtyard between the outer and inner gateways; the distance was 175 feet.*

[20]The man measured the gateway on the north just like the one on the east. [21]Here, too, there were three guard alcoves on each side, with dividing walls and an entry room. All the measurements matched those of the east gateway. The gateway passage was 87½ feet long and 43¾ feet wide between the back walls of facing guard alcoves. [22]The windows, the entry room, and the palm tree decorations were identical to those in the east gateway. There were seven steps leading up to the gateway entrance, and the entry room was at the inner end of the gateway passage. [23]Here on the north side, just as on the east, there was another gateway leading to the Temple's inner courtyard directly opposite this outer gateway. The distance between the two gateways was 175 feet.

[24]Then the man took me around to the south gateway and measured its various parts, and they were exactly the same as in the others. [25]It had windows along the walls as the others did, and there was an entry room where the gateway passage opened into the outer courtyard. And like the others, the gateway passage was 87½ feet long and 43¾ feet wide between the back walls of facing guard alcoves. [26]This gateway also had a stairway of seven steps leading up to it, and an entry room at the inner end, and palm tree decorations along the dividing walls. [27]And here again, directly opposite the outer gateway, was

another gateway that led into the inner courtyard. The distance between the two gateways was 175 feet.

39:11 Hebrew *the sea.*   **39:25** Hebrew *of Jacob.*
40:1 Hebrew *At the beginning of the year, on the tenth day of the month,* of the ancient Hebrew lunar calendar. This event occurred on April 28, 573 B.C.; also see note on 1:1.
40:5a Hebrew *6 long cubits* [3.2 meters], *each being a cubit* [18 inches or 45 centimeters] *and a handbreadth* [3 inches or 8 centimeters] *in length.*   **40:5b** Hebrew *1 rod* [3.2 meters]; also in 40:5c, 7.   **40:6** As in Greek version, which reads *1 rod* [3.2 meters] *deep;* Hebrew reads *1 rod deep, and 1 threshold, 1 rod deep.*   **40:7** Hebrew *5 cubits* [2.7 meters]; also in 40:48.   **40:8** Many Hebrew manuscripts add *which faced inward toward the Temple; it was 1 rod* [10.5 feet or 3.2 meters] *deep. 'Then he measured the entry room of the gateway.*   **40:9a** Hebrew *8 cubits* [4.2 meters].
40:9b Hebrew *2 cubits* [1.1 meters].   **40:11a** Hebrew *10 cubits* [5.3 meters].   **40:11b** Hebrew *13 cubits* [6.9 meters].   **40:12a** Hebrew *1 cubit* [53 centimeters].
40:12b Hebrew *6 cubits* [3.2 meters].   **40:13** Hebrew *25 cubits* [13.3 meters]; also in 40:21, 25, 29, 30, 33, 36.
40:14 Hebrew *60 cubits* [31.8 meters]. The meaning of the Hebrew in this verse is uncertain.   **40:15** Hebrew *50 cubits* [26.5 meters]; also in 40:21, 25, 29, 33, 36.   **40:19** Hebrew *100 cubits* [53 meters]; also in 40:23, 27, 47.

JAMES 2:18-3:18

Words are a powerful force for good or evil. Unfortunately, our tongues are often a servant of evil. Only God's wisdom can bring peace into a world where humans—including believers—try to destroy one another with their words.

Now someone may argue, "Some people have faith; others have good deeds." But I [James] say, "How can you show me your faith if you don't have good deeds? I will show you my faith by my good deeds."

¹⁹You say you have faith, for you believe that there is one God.* Good for you! Even the demons believe this, and they tremble in terror. ²⁰How foolish! Can't you see that faith without good deeds is useless?

²¹Don't you remember that our ancestor Abraham was shown to be right with God by his actions when he offered his son Isaac on the altar? ²²You see, his faith and his actions worked together. His actions made his faith complete. ²³And so it happened just as the Scriptures say: "Abraham believed God, and God counted him as righteous because of his faith."* He was even called the friend of God.* ²⁴So you see, we are shown to be right with God by what we do, not by faith alone.

²⁵Rahab the prostitute is another example. She was shown to be right with God by her actions when she hid those messengers and sent them safely away by a different road. ²⁶Just as the body is dead without breath,* so also faith is dead without good works.

³:¹DEAR brothers and sisters,* not many of you should become teachers in the church, for we who teach will be judged more strictly. ²Indeed, we all make many mistakes. For if we could control our tongues, we would be perfect and could also control ourselves in every other way.

³We can make a large horse go wherever we want by means of a small bit in its

HOW WE LIVE

Our speech

JAMES 3:2-12 Ever said something you regretted? Ever let slip a word or two that caused great hurt to someone? Then you know firsthand the power of the tongue. Like the bit in the horse's mouth, the rudder on the ship, the tiny spark—small things can have enormous power. The tongue is proportionately a small part of a body, but it can do great damage if it's not under control! • We need help from God to speak wisely. All types of speech, both out in the world and in our own homes, need to be brought under Christ's control. Why? Because the tongue is "a whole world of wickedness, corrupting your entire body." It is "restless and evil, full of deadly poison." Sounds pretty bad, doesn't it? • So what can you do? Think before you speak. Consider if what you're going to say is loving or helpful in any way. If not, keep your mouth shut—or find another way to say it. Ask God to help you speak carefully and wisely. Remember to count your blessings. Trust in God's care for you. When you do those things, you will be less likely to lash out at others.

mouth. ⁴And a small rudder makes a huge ship turn wherever the pilot chooses to go, even though the winds are strong. ⁵In the same way, the tongue is a small thing that makes grand speeches.

But a tiny spark can set a great forest on fire. ⁶And the tongue is a flame of fire. It is a whole world of wickedness, corrupting your entire body. It can set your whole life on fire, for it is set on fire by hell itself.*

⁷People can tame all kinds of animals, birds, reptiles, and fish, ⁸but no one can tame the tongue. It is restless and evil, full of deadly poison. ⁹Sometimes it praises our Lord and Father, and sometimes it curses those who have been made in the image of God. ¹⁰And so blessing and cursing come pouring out of the same mouth. Surely, my brothers and sisters, this is not right! ¹¹Does a spring of water bubble out with both fresh water and bitter water? ¹²Does a fig tree produce olives, or a grapevine produce figs? No, and you can't draw fresh water from a salty spring.*

¹³If you are wise and understand God's ways, prove it by living an honorable life, doing good works with the humility that comes from wisdom. ¹⁴But if you are bitterly jealous and there is selfish ambition in your heart, don't cover up the truth with boasting and lying. ¹⁵For jealousy and selfishness are not God's kind of wisdom. Such things are earthly, unspiritual, and demonic. ¹⁶For wherever there is jealousy and selfish ambition, there you will find disorder and evil of every kind.

¹⁷But the wisdom from above is first of all pure. It is also peace loving, gentle at all times, and willing to yield to others. It is full of mercy and good deeds. It shows no favoritism and is always sincere. ¹⁸And those who are peacemakers will plant seeds of peace and reap a harvest of righteousness.*

2:19 Some manuscripts read *that God is one;* see Deut 6:4. 2:23a Gen 15:6. 2:23b See Isa 41:8. 2:26 Or *without spirit.* 3:1 Greek *brothers;* also in 3:10. 3:6 Or *for it will burn in hell* (Greek *Gehenna*). 3:12 Greek *from salt.* 3:18 Or *of good things,* or *of justice.*

PSALM 118:1-18

Give thanks to the LORD, for he is good!
 His faithful love endures forever.

² Let all Israel repeat:
 "His faithful love endures forever."

³ Let Aaron's descendants, the priests, repeat:
 "His faithful love endures forever."

⁴ Let all who fear the LORD repeat:
 "His faithful love endures forever."

⁵ In my distress I prayed to the LORD,
 and the LORD answered me and set me free.

⁶ The LORD is for me, so I will have no fear.
 What can mere people do to me?

⁷ Yes, the LORD is for me; he will help me.
 I will look in triumph at those who hate me.

⁸ It is better to take refuge in the LORD
 than to trust in people.

⁹ It is better to take refuge in the LORD
 than to trust in princes.

¹⁰ Though hostile nations surrounded me,
 I destroyed them all with the authority of the LORD.

¹¹ Yes, they surrounded and attacked me,
 but I destroyed them all with the authority of the LORD.

¹² They swarmed around me like bees;
 they blazed against me like a crackling fire.
 But I destroyed them all with the authority of the LORD.

¹³ My enemies did their best to kill me,
 but the LORD rescued me.

¹⁴ The LORD is my strength and my song;
 he has given me victory.

¹⁵ Songs of joy and victory are sung in the camp of the godly.
 The strong right arm of the LORD has done glorious things!

¹⁶ The strong right arm of the LORD is raised in triumph.
 The strong right arm of the LORD has done glorious things!

¹⁷ I will not die; instead, I will live to tell what the LORD has done.

¹⁸ The LORD has punished me severely,
 but he did not let me die.

PROVERBS 28:2

When there is moral rot within a nation, its government topples easily. But wise and knowledgeable leaders bring stability.

EZEKIEL 40:28–41:26
The Temple was central to Judah's national identity. God's glory earlier left the Temple (Ezekiel 10, November 4), and later the invading Babylonians destroyed it. To envision the Temple being restored was the same as envisioning the nation's political and spiritual restoration.

Then the man took me [Ezekiel] to the south gateway leading into the inner courtyard. He measured it, and it had the same measurements as the other gateways. ²⁹Its guard alcoves, dividing walls, and entry room were the same size as those in the others. It also had windows along its walls and in the entry room. And like the others, the gateway passage was 87½ feet long and 43¾ feet wide. ³⁰(The entry rooms of the gateways leading into the inner courtyard were 14 feet* across and 43¾ feet wide.) ³¹The entry room to the south gateway faced into the outer courtyard. It had palm tree decorations on its columns, and there were eight steps leading to its entrance.

³²Then he took me to the east gateway leading to the inner courtyard. He measured it, and it had the same measurements as the other gateways. ³³Its guard alcoves, dividing walls, and entry room were the same size as those of the others, and there were windows along the walls and in the entry room. The gateway passage measured 87½ feet long and 43¾ feet wide. ³⁴Its entry room faced into the outer courtyard. It had palm tree decorations on its columns, and there were eight steps leading to its entrance.

³⁵Then he took me around to the north gateway leading to the inner courtyard. He measured it, and it had the same measurements as the other gateways. ³⁶The guard alcoves, dividing walls, and entry room of this gateway had the same measurements as in the others and the same window arrangements. The gateway passage measured 87½ feet long and 43¾ feet wide. ³⁷Its entry room faced into the outer courtyard, and it had palm tree decorations on the columns. There were eight steps leading to its entrance.

³⁸A door led from the entry room of one of the inner gateways into a side room, where the meat for sacrifices was washed. ³⁹On each side of this entry room were two tables, where the sacrificial animals were slaughtered for the burnt offerings, sin offerings, and guilt offerings. ⁴⁰Outside the entry room, on each side of the stairs going up to the north entrance, were two more tables. ⁴¹So there were eight tables in all—four inside and four outside—where the sacrifices were cut up and prepared. ⁴²There were also four tables of finished stone for preparation of the burnt offerings, each 31½ inches square and 21 inches high.* On these tables were placed the butchering knives and other implements for slaughtering the sacrificial animals. ⁴³There were hooks, each 3 inches* long, fastened to the foyer walls. The sacrificial meat was laid on the tables.

⁴⁴Inside the inner courtyard were two rooms,* one beside the north gateway, facing south, and the other beside the south* gateway, facing north. ⁴⁵And the man said to me, "The room beside the north inner gate is for the priests who supervise the Temple maintenance. ⁴⁶The room beside the south inner gate is for the priests in charge of the altar—the descendants of Zadok—for they alone of all the Levites may approach the LORD to minister to him."

⁴⁷Then the man measured the inner courtyard, and it was a square, 175 feet wide and 175 feet across. The altar stood in the courtyard in front of the Temple. ⁴⁸Then he brought me to the entry room of the Temple. He measured the walls on either side of the opening to the entry room, and they were 8¾ feet thick. The entrance itself was 24½ feet* wide, and the walls on each side of the entrance were an additional 5¼ feet* long. ⁴⁹The entry room was 35 feet* wide and 21 feet* deep. There were ten steps leading up to it, with a column on each side.

41:1AFTER that, the man brought me into the sanctuary of the Temple. He measured the walls on either side of its doorway, and they were 10½ feet* thick. ²The doorway was 17½ feet* wide, and the walls on each side of it were 8¾ feet* long. The sanctuary itself was 70 feet long and 35 feet wide.*

³Then he went beyond the sanctuary into the inner room. He measured the walls on either side of its entrance, and they were 3½ feet* thick. The entrance was 10½ feet wide, and the walls on each side of the entrance were 12¼ feet* long. ⁴The inner room of the sanctuary was 35 feet* long and 35 feet wide. "This," he told me, "is the Most Holy Place."

⁵Then he measured the wall of the Temple, and it was 10½ feet thick. There was a row of rooms along the outside wall; each room was 7 feet* wide. ⁶These side rooms were built in three levels, one above the other, with thirty rooms on each level. The supports for these side rooms rested on exterior ledges on the Temple wall; they did not extend into the wall. ⁷Each level was wider than the one below it, corresponding to the narrowing of the Temple wall as it rose higher. A stairway led up from the bottom level through the middle level to the top level.

⁸I saw that the Temple was built on a terrace, which provided a foundation for the side rooms. This terrace was 10½ feet* high. ⁹The outer wall of the Temple's side rooms was 8¾ feet thick. This left an open area between these side rooms ¹⁰and the row of rooms along the outer wall of the inner courtyard. This open area was 35 feet wide, and it went all the way around the Temple. ¹¹Two doors opened from the side rooms into the terrace yard, which was 8¾ feet wide. One door faced north and the other south.

¹²A large building stood on the west, facing the Temple courtyard. It was 122½ feet wide and 157½ feet long, and its walls were 8¾ feet* thick. ¹³Then the man measured the Temple, and it was 175 feet* long. The courtyard around the building, including its walls, was an additional 175 feet in length. ¹⁴The inner courtyard to the east of the Temple was also 175 feet wide. ¹⁵The building to the west, including its two walls, was also 175 feet wide.

The sanctuary, the inner room, and the entry room of the Temple ¹⁶were all pan-

eled with wood, as were the frames of the recessed windows. The inner walls of the Temple were paneled with wood above and below the windows. ¹⁷The space above the door leading into the inner room, and its walls inside and out, were also paneled. ¹⁸All the walls were decorated with carvings of cherubim, each with two faces, and there was a carving of a palm tree between each of the cherubim. ¹⁹One face—that of a man—looked toward the palm tree on one side. The other face—that of a young lion—looked toward the palm tree on the other side. The figures were carved all along the inside of the Temple, ²⁰from the floor to the top of the walls, including the outer wall of the sanctuary.

²¹There were square columns at the entrance to the sanctuary, and the ones at the entrance of the Most Holy Place were similar. ²²There was an altar made of wood, 5¼ feet high and 3½ feet across.* Its corners, base, and sides were all made of wood. "This," the man told me, "is the table that stands in the LORD's presence."

²³Both the sanctuary and the Most Holy Place had double doorways, ²⁴each with two swinging doors. ²⁵The doors leading into the sanctuary were decorated with carved cherubim and palm trees, just as on the walls. And there was a wooden roof at the front of the entry room to the Temple. ²⁶On both sides of the entry room were recessed windows decorated with carved palm trees. The side rooms along the outside wall also had roofs.

40:30 As in 40:9, which reads 8 cubits [14 feet or 4.2 meters]; here the Hebrew reads 5 cubits [8¾ feet or 2.7 meters]. Some Hebrew manuscripts and the Greek version omit this entire verse.   40:42 Hebrew 1½ cubits [80 centimeters] long and 1½ cubits wide and 1 cubit [53 centimeters] high.   40:43 Hebrew a handbreadth [8 centimeters].   40:44a As in Greek version; Hebrew reads rooms for singers.   40:44b As in Greek version; Hebrew reads east.   40:48a Hebrew 14 cubits [7.4 meters].   40:48b Hebrew 3 cubits [1.6 meters].   40:49a Hebrew 20 cubits [10.6 meters].   40:49b As in Greek version, which reads 12 cubits [21 feet or 6.4 meters]; Hebrew reads 11 cubits [19¼ feet or 5.8 meters].   41:1 Hebrew 6 cubits [3.2 meters]; also in 41:3, 5.   41:2a Hebrew 10 cubits [5.3 meters].   41:2b Hebrew 5 cubits [2.7 meters]; also in 41:9, 11.   41:2c Hebrew 40 cubits [21.2 meters] long and 20 cubits [10.6 meters] wide.   41:3a Hebrew 2 cubits [1.1 meters].   41:3b Hebrew 7 cubits [3.7 meters].   41:4 Hebrew 20 cubits [10.6 meters]; also in 41:4b, 10.   41:5 Hebrew 4 cubits [2.1 meters].   41:8 Hebrew 1 rod, 6 cubits [3.2 meters].   41:12 Hebrew 70 cubits [37.1 meters] wide and 90 cubits [47.7 meters] long, and its walls were 5 cubits [2.7 meters] thick.   41:13 Hebrew 100 cubits [53 meters]; also in 41:13b, 14, 15.   41:22 Hebrew 3 cubits [1.6 meters] high and 2 cubits [1.1 meters] across.

JAMES 4:1-17

So much of what James wrote has to do with living wisely and carefully. We should never be so foolish that we forget how much is out of our control or so careless that we forget how much is within our control.

What is causing the quarrels and fights among you? Don't they come from the evil desires at war within you? [2] You want what you don't have, so you scheme and kill to get it. You are jealous of what others have, but you can't get it, so you fight and wage war to take it away from them. Yet you don't have what you want because you don't ask God for it. [3] And even when you ask, you don't get it because your motives are all wrong—you want only what will give you pleasure.

[4] You adulterers!* Don't you realize that friendship with the world makes you an enemy of God? I say it again: If you want to be a friend of the world, you make yourself an enemy of God. [5] What do you think the Scriptures mean when they say that the spirit God has placed within us is filled with envy?* [6] But he gives us even more grace to stand against such evil desires. As the Scriptures say,

"God opposes the proud
    but favors the humble."*

[7] So humble yourselves before God. Resist the devil, and he will flee from you. [8] Come close to God, and God will come close to you. Wash your hands, you sinners; purify your hearts, for your loyalty is divided between God and the world. [9] Let there be tears for what you have done. Let there be sorrow and deep grief. Let there be sadness instead of laughter, and gloom instead of joy. [10] Humble yourselves before the Lord, and he will lift you up in honor.

[11] Don't speak evil against each other, dear brothers and sisters.* If you criticize and judge each other, then you are criticizing and judging God's law. But your job is to obey the law, not to judge whether it applies to you. [12] God alone, who gave the law, is the Judge. He alone has the power to save or to destroy. So what right do you have to judge your neighbor?

[13] Look here, you who say, "Today or tomorrow we are going to a certain town and will stay there a year. We will do business there and make a profit." [14] How do you know what your life will be like tomorrow? Your life is like the morning fog—it's here a little while, then it's gone. [15] What you ought to say is, "If the Lord wants us to, we will live and do this or that." [16] Otherwise you are boasting about your own plans, and all such boasting is evil.

[17] Remember, it is sin to know what you ought to do and then not do it.

4:4 Greek *You adulteresses!*   4:5 Or *that God longs jealously for the human spirit he has placed within us?* or *that the Holy Spirit, whom God has placed within us, opposes our envy?*   4:6 Prov 3:34 (Greek version).   4:11 Greek *brothers.*

HOW WE LIVE

Resisting temptation

JAMES 4:7-8 Who doesn't know the moment of temptation well? We feel torn. We wonder what to do. We feel pulled between *should* and *shouldn't*. • James gives some practical advice for facing temptation. (1) *"Humble yourselves before God."* Take a moment and acknowledge that there is a power greater than yourself and that he has claimed you for his own. (2) *"Resist the devil, and he will flee from you."* Usually, the reason we *shouldn't* do something is that it is bad for us or for someone around us. Usually the reason we *want* to do it is because it feels good. Set your focus on what is destructive about the choice you're struggling with. You can trace that back to evil. Resist the bully and watch him run. (3) *"Come close to God, and God will come close to you."* It's hard to step away from something that is desirable without something to step toward. Focus on your relationship with God. Ask for his help and his presence. • Temptation is a part of our lives—no getting around it. But the last thing we should feel when we are tempted is powerless.

PSALM 118:19-29

Open for me the gates where the
righteous enter,
and I will go in and thank the LORD.
20 These gates lead to the presence of the
LORD,
and the godly enter there.

21 I thank you for answering my prayer
and giving me victory!

22 The stone that the builders rejected
has now become the cornerstone.
23 This is the LORD's doing,
and it is wonderful to see.
24 This is the day the LORD has made.
We will rejoice and be glad in it.
25 Please, LORD, please save us.
Please, LORD, please give us success.
26 Bless the one who comes in the name
of the LORD.

We bless you from the house
of the LORD.
27 The LORD is God, shining upon us.
Take the sacrifice and bind it with
cords on the altar.
28 You are my God, and I will praise you!
You are my God, and I will exalt you!

29 Give thanks to the LORD, for he
is good!
His faithful love endures forever.

PROVERBS 28:3-5

A poor person who oppresses the poor is
like a pounding rain that destroys the
crops. □ To reject the law is to praise the
wicked; to obey the law is to fight them.
□ Evil people don't understand justice,
but those who follow the LORD understand completely.

NOVEMBER**21**

EZEKIEL 42:1–43:27
Earlier Ezekiel lamented the departure of God's
glory from the Temple. In today's reading he
describes the return of God's glory.

Then the man led me [Ezekiel] out of the
Temple courtyard by way of the north
gateway. We entered the outer courtyard
and came to a group of rooms against the
north wall of the inner courtyard. 2 This
structure, whose entrance opened toward
the north, was 175 feet long and 87½ feet
wide.* 3 One block of rooms overlooked
the 35-foot* width of the inner courtyard.
Another block of rooms looked out onto
the pavement of the outer courtyard. The
two blocks were built three levels high and
stood across from each other. 4 Between
the two blocks of rooms ran a walkway
17½ feet* wide. It extended the entire
175 feet* of the complex, and all the
doors faced north. 5 Each of the two upper
levels of rooms was narrower than the one
beneath it because the upper levels had to
allow space for walkways in front of them.
6 Since there were three levels and they did
not have supporting columns as in the

courtyards, each of the upper levels was
set back from the level beneath it. 7 There
was an outer wall that separated the
rooms from the outer courtyard; it was
87½ feet* long. 8 This wall added length to
the outer block of rooms, which extended
for only 87½ feet, while the inner block—
the rooms toward the Temple—extended
for 175 feet. 9 There was an eastern entrance from the outer courtyard to these
rooms.

10 On the south* side of the Temple
there were two blocks of rooms just south
of the inner courtyard between the Temple and the outer courtyard. These rooms
were arranged just like the rooms on the
north. 11 There was a walkway between the
two blocks of rooms just like the complex
on the north side of the Temple. This complex of rooms was the same length and
width as the other one, and it had the same
entrances and doors. The dimensions of
each were identical. 12 So there was an entrance in the wall facing the doors of the
inner block of rooms, and another on the
east at the end of the interior walkway.

¹³Then the man told me, "These rooms that overlook the Temple from the north and south are holy. Here the priests who offer sacrifices to the LORD will eat the most holy offerings. And because these rooms are holy, they will be used to store the sacred offerings—the grain offerings, sin offerings, and guilt offerings. ¹⁴When the priests leave the sanctuary, they must not go directly to the outer courtyard. They must first take off the clothes they wore while ministering, because these clothes are holy. They must put on other clothes before entering the parts of the building complex open to the public."

¹⁵When the man had finished measuring the inside of the Temple area, he led me out through the east gateway to measure the entire perimeter. ¹⁶He measured the east side with his measuring rod, and it was 875 feet long.* ¹⁷Then he measured the north side, and it was also 875 feet. ¹⁸The south side was also 875 feet, ¹⁹and the west side was also 875 feet. ²⁰So the area was 875 feet on each side with a wall all around it to separate what was holy from what was common.

43:1AFTER this, the man brought me back around to the east gateway. ²Suddenly, the glory of the God of Israel appeared from the east. The sound of his coming was like the roar of rushing waters, and the whole landscape shone with his glory. ³This vision was just like the others I had seen, first by the Kebar River and then when he came to destroy Jerusalem. I fell face down on the ground. ⁴And the glory of the LORD came into the Temple through the east gateway.

⁵Then the Spirit took me up and brought me into the inner courtyard, and the glory of the LORD filled the Temple. ⁶And I heard someone speaking to me from within the Temple, while the man who had been measuring stood beside me. ⁷The LORD said to me, "Son of man, this is the place of my throne and the place where I will rest my feet. I will live here forever among the people of Israel. They and their kings will not defile my holy name any longer by their adulterous worship of other gods or by honoring the relics of their kings who have died. ⁸They put their

idol altars right next to mine with only a wall between them and me. They defiled my holy name by such detestable sin, so I consumed them in my anger. ⁹Now let them stop worshiping other gods and honoring the relics of their kings, and I will live among them forever.

¹⁰"Son of man, describe to the people of Israel the Temple I have shown you, so they will be ashamed of all their sins. Let them study its plan, ¹¹and they will be ashamed* of what they have done. Describe to them all the specifications of the Temple—including its entrances and exits—and everything else about it. Tell them about its decrees and laws. Write down all these specifications and decrees as they watch so they will be sure to remember and follow them. ¹²And this is the basic law of the Temple: absolute holiness! The entire top of the mountain where the Temple is built is holy. Yes, this is the basic law of the Temple.

¹³"These are the measurements of the altar*: There is a gutter all around the altar 21 inches deep and 21 inches wide,* with a curb 9 inches* wide around its edge. And this is the height* of the altar: ¹⁴From the gutter the altar rises 3½ feet* to a lower ledge that surrounds the altar and is 21 inches* wide. From the lower ledge the altar rises 7 feet* to the upper ledge that is also 21 inches wide. ¹⁵The top of the altar, the hearth, rises another 7 feet higher, with a horn rising up from each of the four corners. ¹⁶The top of the altar is square, measuring 21 feet by 21 feet.* ¹⁷The upper ledge also forms a square, measuring 24½ feet by 24½ feet,* with a 21-inch gutter and a 10½-inch curb* all around the edge. There are steps going up the east side of the altar."

¹⁸Then he said to me, "Son of man, this is what the Sovereign LORD says: These will be the regulations for the burning of offerings and the sprinkling of blood when the altar is built. ¹⁹At that time, the Levitical priests of the family of Zadok, who minister before me, are to be given a young bull for a sin offering, says the Sovereign LORD. ²⁰You will take some of its blood and smear it on the four horns of the altar, the four corners of the upper ledge, and the curb that runs around that

ledge. This will cleanse and make atonement for the altar. ²¹Then take the young bull for the sin offering and burn it at the appointed place outside the Temple area.

²²"On the second day, sacrifice as a sin offering a young male goat that has no physical defects. Then cleanse and make atonement for the altar again, just as you did with the young bull. ²³When you have finished the cleansing ceremony, offer another young bull that has no defects and a perfect ram from the flock. ²⁴You are to present them to the LORD, and the priests are to sprinkle salt on them and offer them as a burnt offering to the LORD.

²⁵"Every day for seven days a male goat, a young bull, and a ram from the flock will be sacrificed as a sin offering. None of these animals may have physical defects of any kind. ²⁶Do this each day for seven days to cleanse and make atonement for the altar, thus setting it apart for holy use. ²⁷On the eighth day, and on each day afterward, the priests will sacrifice on the altar the burnt offerings and peace offerings of the people. Then I will accept you. I, the Sovereign LORD, have spoken!"

42:2 Hebrew *100 cubits* [53 meters] *long and 50 cubits* [26.5 meters] *wide.*   42:3 Hebrew *20 cubits* [10.6 meters].
42:4a Hebrew *10 cubits* [5.3 meters].   42:4b Hebrew *100 cubits* [53 meters]; also in 42:8.   42:7 Hebrew *50 cubits* [26.5 meters]; also in 42:8.   42:10 As in Greek version; Hebrew reads *east.*   42:16 As in 45:2 and in Greek version at 42:17, which reads *500 cubits* [265 meters]; Hebrew reads *500 rods* [5,250 feet or 1,590 meters]; similarly in 42:17, 18, 19, 20.   43:11 As in Greek version; Hebrew reads *if they are ashamed.*   43:13a Hebrew *measurements of the altar in long cubits, each being a cubit* [18 inches or 45 centimeters] *and a handbreadth* [3 inches or 8 centimeters] *in length.*   43:13b Hebrew *a cubit* [53 centimeters] *deep and a cubit wide.*   43:13c Hebrew *1 span* [23 centimeters].   43:13d As in Greek version; Hebrew reads *base.*   43:14a Hebrew *2 cubits* [1.1 meters].
43:14b Hebrew *1 cubit* [53 centimeters]; also in 43:14d.
43:14c Hebrew *4 cubits* [2.1 meters]; also in 43:15.
43:16 Hebrew *12 cubits* [6.4 meters] *long and 12 cubits wide.*
43:17a Hebrew *14 cubits* [7.4 meters] *long and 14 cubits wide.*   43:17b Hebrew *a gutter of 1 cubit* [53 centimeters] *and a curb of ½ a cubit* [27 centimeters].

JAMES 5:1-20
James's letter closes with an important reminder about prayer. As a community of believers, we should uphold one another in prayer, and we can expect God to hear and answer our prayers.

Look here, you rich people: Weep and groan with anguish because of all the terrible troubles ahead of you. ²Your wealth is rotting away, and your fine clothes are moth-eaten rags. ³Your gold and silver have become worthless. The very wealth you were counting on will eat away your flesh like fire. This treasure you have accumulated will stand as evidence against you on the day of judgment. ⁴For listen! Hear the cries of the field workers whom you have cheated of their pay. The wages you held back cry out against you. The cries of those who harvest your fields have reached the ears of the LORD of Heaven's Armies.

⁵You have spent your years on earth in luxury, satisfying your every desire. You have fattened yourselves for the day of slaughter. ⁶You have condemned and killed innocent people,* who do not resist you.*

⁷Dear brothers and sisters,* be patient as you wait for the Lord's return. Consider the farmers who patiently wait for the rains in the fall and in the spring. They eagerly look for the valuable harvest to ripen. ⁸You, too, must be patient. Take courage, for the coming of the Lord is near.

⁹Don't grumble about each other, brothers and sisters, or you will be judged. For look—the Judge is standing at the door!

¹⁰For examples of patience in suffering, dear brothers and sisters, look at the prophets who spoke in the name of the Lord. ¹¹We give great honor to those who endure under suffering. For instance, you know about Job, a man of great endurance. You can see how the Lord was kind to him at the end, for the Lord is full of tenderness and mercy.

¹²But most of all, my brothers and sisters, never take an oath, by heaven or earth or anything else. Just say a simple yes or no, so that you will not sin and be condemned.

¹³Are any of you suffering hardships? You should pray. Are any of you happy? You should sing praises. ¹⁴Are any of you sick? You should call for the elders of the church to come and pray over you, anointing you with oil in the name of the Lord. ¹⁵Such a prayer offered in faith will heal the sick, and the Lord will make you well. And if you have committed any sins, you will be forgiven.

¹⁶Confess your sins to each other and pray for each other so that you may be healed. The earnest prayer of a righteous person has great power and produces

wonderful results. ¹⁷Elijah was as human as we are, and yet when he prayed earnestly that no rain would fall, none fell for three and a half years! ¹⁸Then, when he prayed again, the sky sent down rain and the earth began to yield its crops.

¹⁹My dear brothers and sisters, if someone among you wanders away from the truth and is brought back, ²⁰you can be sure that whoever brings the sinner back will save that person from death and bring about the forgiveness of many sins.

5:6a Or *killed the Righteous One.*   5:6b Or *Don't they resist you?* or *Doesn't God oppose you?* or *Aren't they now accusing you before God?*   5:7 Greek *brothers;* also in 5:9, 10, 12, 19.

PSALM 119:1-16
Aleph*
¹ **J**oyful are people of integrity,
who follow the instructions
of the LORD.
² Joyful are those who obey his laws
and search for him with all their
hearts.
³ They do not compromise with evil,
and they walk only in his paths.
⁴ You have charged us
to keep your commandments
carefully.
⁵ Oh, that my actions would consistently
reflect your decrees!
⁶ Then I will not be ashamed
when I compare my life with your
commands.

⁷ As I learn your righteous regulations,
I will thank you by living as
I should!
⁸ I will obey your decrees.
Please don't give up on me!

Beth
⁹ How can a young person stay pure?
By obeying your word.
¹⁰ I have tried hard to find you—
don't let me wander from your
commands.
¹¹ I have hidden your word in my heart,
that I might not sin against you.
¹² I praise you, O LORD;
teach me your decrees.
¹³ I have recited aloud
all the regulations you have given us.
¹⁴ I have rejoiced in your laws
as much as in riches.
¹⁵ I will study your commandments
and reflect on your ways.
¹⁶ I will delight in your decrees
and not forget your word.

119 This psalm is a Hebrew acrostic poem; there are twenty-two stanzas, one for each successive letter of the Hebrew alphabet. Each of the eight verses within each stanza begins with the Hebrew letter named in its heading.

PROVERBS 28:6-7
Better to be poor and honest than to be dishonest and rich. □ Young people who obey the law are wise; those with wild friends bring shame to their parents.*

28:7 Hebrew *their father.*

HOW WE LIVE

Our money

JAMES 5:1-6 James was not condemning all people who have money; rather, he condemned those whose greed for money led them to do evil. You may not feel rich, but compared to people in other parts of the world, you probably are. The dollar amount is not as important as how we view it. Greedy people find themselves literally torn apart by the money they so desire. They can never have enough. It becomes their god. • Money can easily become a snare. However, it is necessary to deal with money if we are to live in this world. Believers need to learn how to care for their needs without becoming greedy or making money an idol. God wants his followers to be responsible stewards. You must provide for your family. It's wise to save for a rainy day, to invest, and to have money set aside that can help others. God wants you to be fair and honest—if you borrow, repay. If you employ people, pay fairly and on time. If you are employed, don't cheat your employer. • The best way to strike the balance is simply to remember that all you have is a gracious gift from God. Ask him to show you how to use it wisely.

EZEKIEL 44:1–45:12

Because of their role in leading people astray and into idolatry, some of the Levites were demoted from their role as priests. Some of the priests—the descendants of Zadok (himself a descendant of Aaron, the first high priest)—had remained faithful, however, and were given the privilege of entering God's presence.

Then the man brought me [Ezekiel] back to the east gateway in the outer wall of the Temple area, but it was closed. ²And the LORD said to me, "This gate must remain closed; it will never again be opened. No one will ever open it and pass through, for the LORD, the God of Israel, has entered here. Therefore, it must always remain shut. ³Only the prince himself may sit inside this gateway to feast in the LORD's presence. But he may come and go only through the entry room of the gateway."

⁴Then the man brought me through the north gateway to the front of the Temple. I looked and saw that the glory of the LORD filled the Temple of the LORD, and I fell face down on the ground.

⁵And the LORD said to me, "Son of man, take careful notice. Use your eyes and ears, and listen to everything I tell you about the regulations concerning the LORD's Temple. Take careful note of the procedures for using the Temple's entrances and exits. ⁶And give these rebels, the people of Israel, this message from the Sovereign LORD: O people of Israel, enough of your detestable sins! ⁷You have brought uncircumcised foreigners into my sanctuary—people who have no heart for God. In this way, you defiled my Temple even as you offered me my food, the fat and blood of sacrifices. In addition to all your other detestable sins, you have broken my covenant. ⁸Instead of safeguarding my sacred rituals, you have hired foreigners to take charge of my sanctuary.

⁹"So this is what the Sovereign LORD says: No foreigners, including those who live among the people of Israel, will enter my sanctuary if they have not been circumcised and have not surrendered themselves to the LORD. ¹⁰And the men of the tribe of Levi who abandoned me when Israel strayed away from me to worship idols* must bear the consequences for their unfaithfulness. ¹¹They may still be Temple guards and gatekeepers, and they may slaughter the animals brought for burnt offerings and be present to help the people. ¹²But they encouraged my people to worship idols, causing Israel to fall into deep sin. So I have taken a solemn oath that they must bear the consequences for their sins, says the Sovereign LORD. ¹³They may not approach me to minister as priests. They may not touch any of my holy things or the holy offerings, for they must bear the shame of all the detestable sins they have committed. ¹⁴They are to serve as the Temple caretakers, taking charge of the maintenance work and performing general duties.

¹⁵"However, the Levitical priests of the family of Zadok continued to minister faithfully in the Temple when Israel abandoned me for idols. These men will serve as my ministers. They will stand in my presence and offer the fat and blood of the sacrifices, says the Sovereign LORD. ¹⁶They alone will enter my sanctuary and approach my table to serve me. They will fulfill all my requirements.

¹⁷"When they enter the gateway to the inner courtyard, they must wear only linen clothing. They must wear no wool while on duty in the inner courtyard or in the Temple itself. ¹⁸They must wear linen turbans and linen undergarments. They must not wear anything that would cause them to perspire. ¹⁹When they return to the outer courtyard where the people are, they must take off the clothes they wear while ministering to me. They must leave them in the sacred rooms and put on other clothes so they do not endanger anyone by transmitting holiness to them through this clothing.

²⁰"They must neither shave their heads nor let their hair grow too long. Instead, they must trim it regularly. ²¹The priests must not drink wine before entering the inner courtyard. ²²They may choose their

wives only from among the virgins of Israel or the widows of the priests. They may not marry other widows or divorced women. [23] They will teach my people the difference between what is holy and what is common, what is ceremonially clean and unclean.

[24] "They will serve as judges to resolve any disagreements among my people. Their decisions must be based on my regulations. And the priests themselves must obey my instructions and decrees at all the sacred festivals, and see to it that the Sabbaths are set apart as holy days.

[25] "A priest must not defile himself by being in the presence of a dead person unless it is his father, mother, child, brother, or unmarried sister. In such cases it is permitted. [26] Even then, he can return to his Temple duties only after being ceremonially cleansed and then waiting for seven days. [27] The first day he returns to work and enters the inner courtyard and the sanctuary, he must offer a sin offering for himself, says the Sovereign LORD.

[28] "The priests will not have any property or possession of land, for I alone am their special possession. [29] Their food will come from the gifts and sacrifices brought to the Temple by the people—the grain offerings, the sin offerings, and the guilt offerings. Whatever anyone sets apart* for the LORD will belong to the priests. [30] The first of the ripe fruits and all the gifts brought to the LORD will go to the priests. The first samples of each grain harvest and the first of your flour must also be given to the priests so the LORD will bless your homes. [31] The priests may not eat meat from any bird or animal that dies a natural death or that dies after being attacked by another animal.

[45:1] "WHEN you divide the land among the tribes of Israel, you must set aside a section for the LORD as his holy portion. This piece of land will be 8⅓ miles long and 6⅔ miles wide.* The entire area will be holy. [2] A section of this land, measuring 875 feet by 875 feet,* will be set aside for the Temple. An additional strip of land 87½ feet* wide is to be left empty all around it. [3] Within the larger sacred area, measure out a portion of land 8⅓ miles long and 3⅓ miles wide.* Within it the sanctuary of the Most Holy Place will be located. [4] This area will be holy, set aside for the priests who minister to the LORD in the sanctuary. They will use it for their homes, and my Temple will be located within it. [5] The strip of sacred land next to it, also 8⅓ miles long and 3⅓ miles wide, will be a living area for the Levites who work at the Temple. It will be their possession and a place for their towns.*

HOW WE LIVE

Courageous in trials

1 PETER 1:3-7 Crushed, devastated, demoralized, beaten down—these and other feelings of despondency wash over all who suffer, threatening to drown all feelings of hope. Suffering has many sources: social, physical, economic, even persecution for your spiritual beliefs. Sometimes the suffering becomes so great that you are tempted to give in and give up hope. •Peter had been threatened, beaten, jailed, had seen fellow Christians killed for their faith, and eventually he would become a martyr for Christ. But he knew Jesus Christ, and nothing would shake his faith in the risen Lord. •Do you need courage? As a believer, you have the living hope of eternal life. God has provided an everlasting inheritance for you that will never change nor decay. Although trials are not pleasant, they teach patience, strengthen your faith, and allow you to grow to be the kind of person God wants. But no matter what pain or suffering you face in this life, you know that this is not your final experience. God will help you remain true to him, and you will live an everlasting life free from trials. This is your promise for a living hope as a child of God.

⁶"Adjacent to the larger sacred area will be a section of land 8⅓ miles long and 1⅔ miles wide.* This will be set aside for a city where anyone in Israel can live.

⁷"Two special sections of land will be set apart for the prince. One section will share a border with the east side of the sacred lands and city, and the second section will share a border on the west side. Then the far eastern and western borders of the prince's lands will line up with the eastern and western boundaries of the tribal areas. ⁸These sections of land will be the prince's allotment. Then my princes will no longer oppress and rob my people; they will assign the rest of the land to the people, giving an allotment to each tribe.

⁹"For this is what the Sovereign LORD says: Enough, you princes of Israel! Stop your violence and oppression and do what is just and right. Quit robbing and cheating my people out of their land. Stop expelling them from their homes, says the Sovereign LORD. ¹⁰Use only honest weights and scales and honest measures, both dry and liquid.* ¹¹The homer* will be your standard unit for measuring volume. The ephah and the bath* will each measure one-tenth of a homer. ¹²The standard unit for weight will be the silver shekel.* One shekel will consist of twenty gerahs, and sixty shekels will be equal to one mina.*"

44:10 The Hebrew term (literally *round things*) probably alludes to dung; also in 44:12.   **44:29** The Hebrew term used here refers to the complete consecration of things or people to the LORD, either by destroying them or by giving them as an offering.   **45:1** Reflecting the Greek version, which reads *25,000 cubits* [13.3 kilometers] *long and 20,000 cubits* [10.6 kilometers] *wide*; Hebrew reads *25,000 cubits long and 10,000 cubits* [3⅓ miles or 5.3 kilometers] *wide*. Compare 45:3; 48:9.   **45:2a** Hebrew *500 cubits* [265 meters] *by 500 cubits, a square.*   **45:2b** Hebrew *50 cubits* [26.5 meters].   **45:3** Hebrew *25,000 cubits* [13.3 kilometers] *long and 10,000 cubits* [5.3 kilometers] *wide;* also in 45:5.   **45:5** As in Greek version; Hebrew reads *They will have as their possession 20 rooms.*   **45:6** Hebrew *25,000 cubits* [13.3 kilometers] *long and 5,000 cubits* [2.65 kilometers] *wide.*   **45:10** Hebrew *use honest scales, an honest ephah, and an honest bath.*   **45:11a** The *homer* measures about 40 gallons or 182 liters.   **45:11b** The *ephah* is a dry measure; the *bath* is a liquid measure.   **45:12a** The *shekel* weighs about 0.4 ounces or 11 grams.   **45:12b** Elsewhere the *mina* is equated to 50 shekels.

1 PETER 1:1-12
First and Second Peter were written by the apostle Peter toward the end of his life. Here we see the pastoral care and concern of one who knew Jesus

personally and who had followed him faithfully (though not always perfectly) in his role as leader of the apostles.

This letter is from Peter, an apostle of Jesus Christ.

I am writing to God's chosen people who are living as foreigners in the provinces of Pontus, Galatia, Cappadocia, Asia, and Bithynia.* ²God the Father knew you and chose you long ago, and his Spirit has made you holy. As a result, you have obeyed him and have been cleansed by the blood of Jesus Christ.

May God give you more and more grace and peace.

³All praise to God, the Father of our Lord Jesus Christ. It is by his great mercy that we have been born again, because God raised Jesus Christ from the dead. Now we live with great expectation, ⁴and we have a priceless inheritance—an inheritance that is kept in heaven for you, pure and undefiled, beyond the reach of change and decay. ⁵And through your faith, God is protecting you by his power until you receive this salvation, which is ready to be revealed on the last day for all to see.

⁶So be truly glad.* There is wonderful joy ahead, even though you have to endure many trials for a little while. ⁷These trials will show that your faith is genuine. It is being tested as fire tests and purifies gold—though your faith is far more precious than mere gold. So when your faith remains strong through many trials, it will bring you much praise and glory and honor on the day when Jesus Christ is revealed to the whole world.

⁸You love him even though you have never seen him. Though you do not see him now, you trust him; and you rejoice with a glorious, inexpressible joy. ⁹The reward for trusting him will be the salvation of your souls.

¹⁰This salvation was something even the prophets wanted to know more about when they prophesied about this gracious salvation prepared for you. ¹¹They wondered what time or situation the Spirit of Christ within them was talking about when he told them in advance about Christ's suffering and his great glory afterward.

¹²They were told that their messages were not for themselves, but for you. And now this Good News has been announced to you by those who preached in the power of the Holy Spirit sent from heaven. It is all so wonderful that even the angels are eagerly watching these things happen.

1:1 *Pontus, Galatia, Cappadocia, Asia,* and *Bithynia* were Roman provinces in what is now Turkey. 1:6 Or *So you are truly glad.*

PSALM 119:17-32

Gimel

¹⁷ **B**e good to your servant,
　　that I may live and obey your word.
¹⁸ Open my eyes to see
　　the wonderful truths in your
　　　instructions.
¹⁹ I am only a foreigner in the land.
　　Don't hide your commands from me!
²⁰ I am always overwhelmed
　　with a desire for your regulations.
²¹ You rebuke the arrogant;
　　those who wander from your
　　　commands are cursed.
²² Don't let them scorn and insult me,
　　for I have obeyed your laws.
²³ Even princes sit and speak against me,
　　but I will meditate on your decrees.
²⁴ Your laws please me;
　　they give me wise advice.

EZEKIEL 45:13–46:24

Ezekiel described the reinstitutionalization of the Jewish feasts, Passover being the most significant. The Passover reminded the nation of their original deliverance from slavery in Egypt. Likewise, it served as a fitting image of restoration from exile.

"**Y**ou must give this tax to the prince: one bushel of wheat or barley for every 60* you harvest, ¹⁴one percent of your olive oil,* ¹⁵and one sheep or goat for every 200 in your flocks in Israel. These will be the grain offerings, burnt offerings, and peace offerings that will make atonement for the people who bring them, says the Sovereign LORD. ¹⁶All the people of Israel

Daleth

²⁵ I lie in the dust;
　　revive me by your word.
²⁶ I told you my plans, and you
　　answered.
　　Now teach me your decrees.
²⁷ Help me understand the meaning
　　of your commandments,
　　and I will meditate on your
　　　wonderful deeds.
²⁸ I weep with sorrow;
　　encourage me by your word.
²⁹ Keep me from lying to myself;
　　give me the privilege of knowing
　　　your instructions.
³⁰ I have chosen to be faithful;
　　I have determined to live by your
　　　regulations.
³¹ I cling to your laws.
　　LORD, don't let me be put to shame!
³² I will pursue your commands,
　　for you expand my understanding.

PROVERBS 28:8-10

Income from charging high interest rates will end up in the pocket of someone who is kind to the poor. □ God detests the prayers of a person who ignores the law. □ Those who lead good people along an evil path will fall into their own trap, but the honest will inherit good things.

NOVEMBER**23**

must join in bringing these offerings to the prince. ¹⁷The prince will be required to provide offerings that are given at the religious festivals, the new moon celebrations, the Sabbath days, and all other similar occasions. He will provide the sin offerings, burnt offerings, grain offerings, liquid offerings, and peace offerings to purify the people of Israel, making them right with the LORD.*

¹⁸"This is what the Sovereign LORD says: In early spring, on the first day of each new year,* sacrifice a young bull with no defects to purify the Temple.

¹⁹The priest will take blood from this sin offering and put it on the doorposts of the Temple, the four corners of the upper ledge of the altar, and the gateposts at the entrance to the inner courtyard. ²⁰Do this also on the seventh day of the new year for anyone who has sinned through error or ignorance. In this way, you will purify* the Temple.

²¹"On the fourteenth day of the first month,* you must celebrate the Passover. This festival will last for seven days. The bread you eat during that time must be made without yeast. ²²On the day of Passover the prince will provide a young bull as a sin offering for himself and the people of Israel. ²³On each of the seven days of the feast he will prepare a burnt offering to the LORD, consisting of seven young bulls and seven rams without defects. A male goat will also be given each day for a sin offering. ²⁴The prince will provide a basket of flour as a grain offering and a gallon of olive oil* with each young bull and ram.

²⁵"During the seven days of the Festival of Shelters, which occurs every year in early autumn,* the prince will provide these same sacrifices for the sin offering, the burnt offering, and the grain offering, along with the required olive oil.

46:1"THIS is what the Sovereign LORD says: The east gateway of the inner courtyard will be closed during the six workdays each week, but it will be open on Sabbath days and the days of new moon celebrations. ²The prince will enter the entry room of the gateway from the outside. Then he will stand by the gatepost while the priest offers his burnt offering and peace offering. He will bow down in worship inside the gateway passage and then go back out the way he came. The gateway will not be closed until evening. ³The common people will bow down and worship the LORD in front of this gateway on Sabbath days and the days of new moon celebrations.

⁴"Each Sabbath day the prince will present to the LORD a burnt offering of six lambs and one ram, all with no defects. ⁵He will present a grain offering of a basket of choice flour to go with the ram and

whatever amount of flour he chooses to go with each lamb, and he is to offer one gallon of olive oil* for each basket of flour. ⁶At the new moon celebrations, he will bring one young bull, six lambs, and one ram, all with no defects. ⁷With the young bull he must bring a basket of choice flour for a grain offering. With the ram he must bring another basket of flour. And with each lamb he is to bring whatever amount of flour he chooses to give. With each basket of flour he must offer one gallon of olive oil.

⁸"The prince must enter the gateway through the entry room, and he must leave the same way. ⁹But when the people come in through the north gateway to worship the LORD during the religious festivals, they must leave by the south gateway. And those who entered through the south gateway must leave by the north gateway. They must never leave by the same gateway they came in, but must always use the opposite gateway. ¹⁰The prince will enter and leave with the people on these occasions.

¹¹"So at the special feasts and sacred festivals, the grain offering will be a basket of choice flour with each young bull, another basket of flour with each ram, and as much flour as the prince chooses to give with each lamb. Give one gallon of olive oil with each basket of flour. ¹²When the prince offers a voluntary burnt offering or peace offering to the LORD, the east gateway to the inner courtyard will be opened for him, and he will offer his sacrifices as he does on Sabbath days. Then he will leave, and the gateway will be shut behind him.

¹³"Each morning you must sacrifice a one-year-old lamb with no defects as a burnt offering to the LORD. ¹⁴With the lamb, a grain offering must also be given to the LORD—about three quarts of flour with a third of a gallon of olive oil* to moisten the choice flour. This will be a permanent law for you. ¹⁵The lamb, the grain offering, and the olive oil must be given as a daily sacrifice every morning without fail.

¹⁶"This is what the Sovereign LORD says: If the prince gives a gift of land to one of his sons as his inheritance, it will belong to

him and his descendants forever. ¹⁷But if the prince gives a gift of land from his inheritance to one of his servants, the servant may keep it only until the Year of Jubilee, which comes every fiftieth year.* At that time the land will return to the prince. But when the prince gives gifts to his sons, those gifts will be permanent. ¹⁸And the prince may never take anyone's property by force. If he gives property to his sons, it must be from his own land, for I do not want any of my people unjustly evicted from their property."

¹⁹In my vision, the man brought me through the entrance beside the gateway and led me to the sacred rooms assigned to the priests, which faced toward the north. He showed me a place at the extreme west end of these rooms. ²⁰He explained, "This is where the priests will cook the meat from the guilt offerings and sin offerings and bake the flour from the grain offerings into bread. They will do it here to avoid carrying the sacrifices through the outer courtyard and endangering the people by transmitting holiness to them."

²¹Then he brought me back to the outer courtyard and led me to each of its four corners. In each corner I saw an enclosure. ²²Each of these enclosures was 70 feet long and 52½ feet wide,* surrounded by walls. ²³Along the inside of these walls was a ledge of stone with fireplaces under the ledge all the way around. ²⁴The man said to me, "These are the kitchens to be used by the Temple assistants to boil the sacrifices offered by the people."

45:13 Hebrew ⅙ of an ephah from each homer of wheat and ⅙ of an ephah from each homer of barley.   **45:14** Hebrew the portion of oil, measured by the bath, is ¹⁄₁₀ of a bath from each cor, which consists of 10 baths or 1 homer, for 10 baths are equivalent to a homer.   **45:17** Or to make atonement for the people of Israel.   **45:18** Hebrew On the first day of the first month, of the Hebrew calendar. This day in the ancient Hebrew lunar calendar occurred in March or April. **45:20** Or will make atonement for.   **45:21** This day in the ancient Hebrew lunar calendar occurred in late March, April, or early May.   **45:24** Hebrew an ephah [20 quarts or 22 liters] of flour . . . and a hin [3.8 liters] of olive oil. **45:25** Hebrew the festival which begins on the fifteenth day of the seventh month (see Lev 23:33). This day in the ancient Hebrew lunar calendar occurred in late September, October, or early November.   **46:5** Hebrew an ephah [20 quarts or 22 liters] of choice flour . . . a hin [3.8 liters] of olive oil; similarly in 46:7, 11.   **46:14** Hebrew ⅙ of an ephah [3.7 liters] of flour with ⅓ of a hin [1.3 liters] of olive oil. **46:17** Hebrew until the Year of Release; see Lev 25:8-17. **46:22** Hebrew 40 cubits [21.2 meters] long and 30 cubits [15.9 meters] wide.

1 PETER 1:13–2:10

Peter's first letter opens by reminding us who the child of God is. What is this new life? What have we each become a part of when we commit to the Christian faith? As a community, what is our role in the world?

So think clearly and exercise self-control. Look forward to the gracious salvation that will come to you when Jesus Christ is

HOW WE LIVE

Having integrity

1 PETER 2:9-10 Christians should be above reproach, imitating Christ in all their social roles—family member, friend, neighbor, coworker, spouse, and church member. Why? Because we are a chosen people, God's royal priests, a holy nation, God's very own possession. Our role in this world is to show God's goodness because he called us out of the darkness into his wonderful light. • In tomorrow's reading, Peter elaborates further, "Be careful to live properly among your unbelieving neighbors. Then even if they accuse you of doing wrong, they will see your honorable behavior, and they will give honor to God" (1 Peter 2:12, November 24). As a Christian in an unbelieving world, you must give extra attention to how you live. Your neighbors, coworkers, and others are watching to see if you remain calm or lose your temper; if you use kind words or curses; if you are respectful or arrogant; if you are honest or dishonest. When you announced that you became a believer, you were immediately held to a higher standard. Because of your status as God's child, you must be different in the way you live—like light in the darkness.

revealed to the world. [14]So you must live as God's obedient children. Don't slip back into your old ways of living to satisfy your own desires. You didn't know any better then. [15]But now you must be holy in everything you do, just as God who chose you is holy. [16]For the Scriptures say, "You must be holy because I am holy."*

[17]And remember that the heavenly Father to whom you pray has no favorites. He will judge or reward you according to what you do. So you must live in reverent fear of him during your time as "foreigners in the land." [18]For you know that God paid a ransom to save you from the empty life you inherited from your ancestors. And the ransom he paid was not mere gold or silver. [19]It was the precious blood of Christ, the sinless, spotless Lamb of God. [20]God chose him as your ransom long before the world began, but he has now revealed him to you in these last days.

[21]Through Christ you have come to trust in God. And you have placed your faith and hope in God because he raised Christ from the dead and gave him great glory.

[22]You were cleansed from your sins when you obeyed the truth, so now you must show sincere love to each other as brothers and sisters.* Love each other deeply with all your heart.*

[23]For you have been born again, but not to a life that will quickly end. Your new life will last forever because it comes from the eternal, living word of God. [24]As the Scriptures say,

"People are like grass;
   their beauty is like a flower
      in the field.
The grass withers and the flower
   fades.
[25]   But the word of the Lord remains
      forever."*

And that word is the Good News that was preached to you.

2:1 So get rid of all evil behavior. Be done with all deceit, hypocrisy, jealousy, and all unkind speech. [2]Like newborn babies, you must crave pure spiritual milk so that you will grow into a full experience of salvation. Cry out for this nourishment, [3]now that you have had a taste of the Lord's kindness.

[4]You are coming to Christ, who is the living cornerstone of God's temple. He was rejected by people, but he was chosen by God for great honor.

[5]And you are living stones that God is building into his spiritual temple. What's more, you are his holy priests.* Through the mediation of Jesus Christ, you offer spiritual sacrifices that please God. [6]As the Scriptures say,

"I am placing a cornerstone
      in Jerusalem,*
   chosen for great honor,
and anyone who trusts in him
   will never be disgraced."*

[7]Yes, you who trust him recognize the honor God has given him. But for those who reject him,

"The stone that the builders rejected
   has now become the cornerstone."*

[8]And,

"He is the stone that makes people
      stumble,
   the rock that makes them fall."*

They stumble because they do not obey God's word, and so they meet the fate that was planned for them.

[9]But you are not like that, for you are a chosen people. You are royal priests,* a holy nation, God's very own possession. As a result, you can show others the goodness of God, for he called you out of the darkness into his wonderful light.

[10] "Once you had no identity as a people;
   now you are God's people.
Once you received no mercy;
   now you have received God's
      mercy."*

1:16 Lev 11:44-45; 19:2; 20:7.   **1:22a** Greek *must have brotherly love.*   **1:22b** Some manuscripts read *with a pure heart.*   **1:24-25** Isa 40:6-8.   **2:5** Greek *holy priesthood.*   **2:6a** Greek *in Zion.*   **2:6b** Isa 28:16 (Greek version).   **2:7** Ps 118:22.   **2:8** Isa 8:14.   **2:9** Greek *a royal priesthood.*   **2:10** Hos 1:6, 9; 2:23.

PSALM 119:33-48

He
[33] **T**each me your decrees, O LORD;
   I will keep them to the end.
[34] Give me understanding and I will obey
   your instructions;

I will put them into practice with all
 my heart.

³⁵ Make me walk along the path of your
 commands,
 for that is where my happiness is
 found.

³⁶ Give me an eagerness for your laws
 rather than a love for money!

³⁷ Turn my eyes from worthless things,
 and give me life through your
 word.*

³⁸ Reassure me of your promise,
 made to those who fear you.

³⁹ Help me abandon my shameful ways;
 for your regulations are good.

⁴⁰ I long to obey your commandments!
 Renew my life with your goodness.

Waw

⁴¹ LORD, give me your unfailing love,
 the salvation that you promised me.

⁴² Then I can answer those who taunt me,
 for I trust in your word.

⁴³ Do not snatch your word of truth
 from me,
 for your regulations are my only
 hope.

⁴⁴ I will keep on obeying your
 instructions
 forever and ever.

⁴⁵ I will walk in freedom,
 for I have devoted myself to your
 commandments.

⁴⁶ I will speak to kings about your laws,
 and I will not be ashamed.

⁴⁷ How I delight in your commands!
 How I love them!

⁴⁸ I honor and love your commands.
 I meditate on your decrees.

119:37 Some manuscripts read *in your ways.*

PROVERBS 28:11

Rich people may think they are wise, but a poor person with discernment can see right through them.

NOVEMBER**24**

EZEKIEL 47:1–48:35

Ezekiel's prophecy closes with a description not only of a new Temple, but also of the land and of Jerusalem. His final description of the gates of the city implies complete restoration of the spiritual center of the nation.

In my vision, the man brought me [Ezekiel] back to the entrance of the Temple. There I saw a stream flowing east from beneath the door of the Temple and passing to the right of the altar on its south side. ²The man brought me outside the wall through the north gateway and led me around to the eastern entrance. There I could see the water flowing out through the south side of the east gateway.

³Measuring as he went, he took me along the stream for 1,750 feet* and then led me across. The water was up to my ankles. ⁴He measured off another 1,750 feet and led me across again. This time the water was up to my knees. After another 1,750 feet, it was up to my waist. ⁵Then he measured another 1,750 feet, and the river was too deep to walk across. It was deep enough to swim in, but too deep to walk through.

⁶He asked me, "Have you been watching, son of man?" Then he led me back along the riverbank. ⁷When I returned, I was surprised by the sight of many trees growing on both sides of the river. ⁸Then he said to me, "This river flows east through the desert into the valley of the Dead Sea.* The waters of this stream will make the salty waters of the Dead Sea fresh and pure. ⁹There will be swarms of living things wherever the water of this river flows. Fish will abound in the Dead Sea, for its waters will become fresh. Life will flourish wherever this water flows. ¹⁰Fishermen will stand along the shores of the Dead Sea. All the way from En-gedi to En-eglaim, the shores will be covered with nets drying in the sun. Fish of every kind will fill the Dead Sea, just as they fill the Mediterranean.* ¹¹But the marshes and swamps will not be purified; they will

still be salty. ¹²Fruit trees of all kinds will grow along both sides of the river. The leaves of these trees will never turn brown and fall, and there will always be fruit on their branches. There will be a new crop every month, for they are watered by the river flowing from the Temple. The fruit will be for food and the leaves for healing."

¹³This is what the Sovereign LORD says: "Divide the land in this way for the twelve tribes of Israel: The descendants of Joseph will be given two shares of land.* ¹⁴Otherwise each tribe will receive an equal share. I took a solemn oath and swore that I would give this land to your ancestors, and it will now come to you as your possession.

¹⁵"These are the boundaries of the land: The northern border will run from the Mediterranean toward Hethlon, then on through Lebo-hamath to Zedad; ¹⁶then it will run to Berothah and Sibraim, which are on the border between Damascus and Hamath, and finally to Hazer-hatticon, on the border of Hauran. ¹⁷So the northern border will run from the Mediterranean to Hazar-enan, on the border between Hamath to the north and Damascus to the south.

¹⁸"The eastern border starts at a point between Hauran and Damascus and runs south along the Jordan River between Israel and Gilead, past the Dead Sea* and as far south as Tamar.* This will be the eastern border.

¹⁹"The southern border will go west from Tamar to the waters of Meribah at Kadesh* and then follow the course of the Brook of Egypt to the Mediterranean. This will be the southern border.

²⁰"On the west side, the Mediterranean itself will be your border from the southern border to the point where the northern border begins, opposite Lebo-hamath.

²¹"Divide the land within these boundaries among the tribes of Israel. ²²Distribute the land as an allotment for yourselves and for the foreigners who have joined you and are raising their families among

you. They will be like native-born Israelites to you and will receive an allotment among the tribes. ²³These foreigners are to be given land within the territory of the tribe with whom they now live. I, the Sovereign LORD, have spoken!

48:1"HERE is the list of the tribes of Israel and the territory each is to receive. The territory of Dan is in the extreme north. Its boundary line follows the Hethlon road to Lebo-hamath and then runs on to Hazar-enan on the border of Damascus, with Hamath to the north. Dan's territory extends all the way across the land of Israel from east to west.

²"Asher's territory lies south of Dan's and also extends from east to west. ³Naphtali's land lies south of Asher's, also extending from east to west. ⁴Then comes Manasseh south of Naphtali, and its territory also extends from east to west. ⁵South of Manasseh is Ephraim, ⁶and then Reuben, ⁷and then Judah, all of whose boundaries extend from east to west.

⁸"South of Judah is the land set aside for a special purpose. It will be 8⅓ miles* wide and will extend as far east and west as the tribal territories, with the Temple at the center.

⁹"The area set aside for the LORD's Temple will be 8⅓ miles long and 6⅔ miles wide.* ¹⁰For the priests there will be a strip of land measuring 8⅓ miles long by 3⅓ miles wide,* with the LORD's Temple at the center. ¹¹This area is set aside for the ordained priests, the descendants of Zadok who served me faithfully and did not go astray with the people of Israel and the rest of the Levites. ¹²It will be their special portion when the land is distributed, the most sacred land of all. Next to the priests' territory will lie the land where the other Levites will live.

¹³"The land allotted to the Levites will be the same size and shape as that belonging to the priests—8⅓ miles long and 3⅓ miles wide. Together these portions of land will measure 8⅓ miles long by 6⅔ miles wide.* ¹⁴None of this special land may ever be sold or traded or used by others, for it belongs to the LORD; it is set apart as holy.

¹⁵"An additional strip of land 8⅓ miles

long by 1⅔ miles wide,* south of the sacred Temple area, will be allotted for public use—homes, pasturelands, and common lands, with a city at the center. ¹⁶The city will measure 1½ miles* on each side—north, south, east, and west. ¹⁷Open lands will surround the city for 150 yards* in every direction. ¹⁸Outside the city there will be a farming area that stretches 3⅓ miles to the east and 3⅓ miles to the west* along the border of the sacred area. This farmland will produce food for the people working in the city. ¹⁹Those who come from the various tribes to work in the city may farm it. ²⁰This entire area—including the sacred lands and the city—is a square that measures 8⅓ miles* on each side.

²¹"The areas that remain, to the east and to the west of the sacred lands and the city, will belong to the prince. Each of these areas will be 8⅓ miles wide, extending in opposite directions to the eastern and western borders of Israel, with the sacred lands and the sanctuary of the Temple in the center. ²²So the prince's land will include everything between the territories allotted to Judah and Benjamin, except for the areas set aside for the sacred lands and the city.

²³"These are the territories allotted to the rest of the tribes. Benjamin's territory lies just south of the prince's lands, and it extends across the entire land of Israel from east to west. ²⁴South of Benjamin's territory lies that of Simeon, also extending across the land from east to west. ²⁵Next is the territory of Issachar with the same eastern and western boundaries.

²⁶"Then comes the territory of Zebulun, which also extends across the land from east to west. ²⁷The territory of Gad is just south of Zebulun with the same borders to the east and west. ²⁸The southern border of Gad runs from Tamar to the waters of Meribah at Kadesh* and then follows the Brook of Egypt to the Mediterranean.*

²⁹"These are the allotments that will be set aside for each tribe's exclusive possession. I, the Sovereign LORD, have spoken!

³⁰"These will be the exits to the city: On the north wall, which is 1½ miles long, ³¹there will be three gates, each one named after a tribe of Israel. The first will be named for Reuben, the second for Judah, and the third for Levi. ³²On the east wall, also 1½ miles long, the gates will be named for Joseph, Benjamin, and Dan. ³³The south wall, also 1½ miles long, will have gates named for Simeon, Issachar, and Zebulun. ³⁴And on the west wall, also

HOW WE LIVE | Persevering in faith

1 PETER 2:21 People follow after any number of things—they might try to emulate a successful business person or an athletic hero; they might take up a cause like trying to save the environment or find a cure for cancer; they might be dedicated followers of a certain diet and exercise regimen. The possibilities are endless. Few, however, will follow something that leads into pain and difficulty. • That the believers are to "follow in [Christ's] steps" does not mean we must all die by crucifixion (although some first-century believers may have been crucified). Instead, we're to follow Jesus' example of willingness to sacrifice and face persecution with peaceful trust in God. Jesus himself followed the lead of his Father, no matter where it took him, no matter how difficult it might have been. Jesus said, "If any of you wants to be my follower, you must turn from your selfish ways, take up your cross, and follow me" (Mark 8:34, February 26). • Christ has given us an example of how we are to face injustice and persecution. His example greatly comforted these believers, who were persecuted for their faith—and it comforts us in our daily difficulties. We should face tough times with perseverance and supreme dignity, trusting God's control.

1½ miles long, the gates will be named for Gad, Asher, and Naphtali.

³⁵"The distance around the entire city will be 6 miles.* And from that day the name of the city will be 'The LORD Is There.'*"

47:3 Hebrew *1,000 cubits* [530 meters]; also in 47:4, 5.
47:8 Hebrew *the sea.* 47:10 Hebrew *the great sea;* also in 47:15, 17, 19, 20. 47:13 It was important to retain twelve portions of land. Since Levi had no portion, the descendants of Joseph's sons, Ephraim and Manasseh, received land as two tribes. 47:18a Hebrew *the eastern sea.* 47:18b As in Greek version; Hebrew reads *you will measure.* 47:19 Hebrew *waters of Meribath-kadesh.* 48:8 Hebrew *25,000 cubits* [13.3 kilometers]. 48:9 Reflecting one Greek manuscript and the Greek reading in 45:1: *25,000 cubits* [13.3 kilometers] *long and 20,000 cubits* [10.6 kilometers] *wide;* Hebrew reads *25,000 cubits long and 10,000 cubits* [3½ miles or 5.3 kilometers] *wide.* Similarly in 48:13b. Compare 45:1-5; 48:10-13. 48:10 Hebrew *25,000 cubits* [13.3 kilometers] *long by 10,000 cubits* [5.3 kilometers] *wide;* also in 48:13a. 48:13 See note on 48:9. 48:15 Hebrew *25,000 cubits* [13.3 kilometers] *long by 5,000 cubits* [2.65 kilometers] *wide.* 48:16 Hebrew *4,500 cubits* [2.4 kilometers]; also in 48:30, 32, 33, 34. 48:17 Hebrew *250 cubits* [133 meters]. 48:18 Hebrew *10,000 cubits* [5.3 kilometers] *to the east and 10,000 cubits to the west.* 48:20 Hebrew *25,000 cubits* [13.3 kilometers]; also in 48:21. 48:28a Hebrew *waters of Meribath-kadesh.* 48:28b Hebrew *the great sea.* 48:35a Hebrew *18,000 cubits* [9.6 kilometers]. 48:35b Hebrew *Yahweh Shammah.*

1 PETER 2:11–3:7

Peter addresses human relationships of all kinds: those who have power over us, those who serve us, and those who are bound to us by law and by love. Since our faith is to permeate our lives, it should affect all of these relationships.

Dear friends, I warn you as "temporary residents and foreigners" to keep away from worldly desires that wage war against your very souls. ¹²Be careful to live properly among your unbelieving neighbors. Then even if they accuse you of doing wrong, they will see your honorable behavior, and they will give honor to God when he judges the world.*

¹³For the Lord's sake, respect all human authority—whether the king as head of state, ¹⁴or the officials he has appointed. For the king has sent them to punish those who do wrong and to honor those who do right.

¹⁵It is God's will that your honorable lives should silence those ignorant people who make foolish accusations against you. ¹⁶For you are free, yet you are God's slaves, so don't use your freedom as an excuse to do evil. ¹⁷Respect everyone, and love your Christian brothers and sisters.* Fear God, and respect the king.

¹⁸You who are slaves must accept the authority of your masters with all respect.* Do what they tell you—not only if they are kind and reasonable, but even if they are cruel. ¹⁹For God is pleased with you when you do what you know is right and patiently endure unfair treatment. ²⁰Of course, you get no credit for being patient if you are beaten for doing wrong. But if you suffer for doing good and endure it patiently, God is pleased with you.

²¹For God called you to do good, even if it means suffering, just as Christ suffered* for you. He is your example, and you must follow in his steps.

²² He never sinned,
   nor ever deceived anyone.*
²³ He did not retaliate when he was
      insulted,
   nor threaten revenge when he
      suffered.
He left his case in the hands of God,
   who always judges fairly.
²⁴ He personally carried our sins
   in his body on the cross
so that we can be dead to sin
   and live for what is right.
By his wounds
   you are healed.
²⁵ Once you were like sheep
   who wandered away.
But now you have turned to your
      Shepherd,
   the Guardian of your souls.

³:¹IN the same way, you wives must accept the authority of your husbands. Then, even if some refuse to obey the Good News, your godly lives will speak to them without any words. They will be won over ²by observing your pure and reverent lives.

³Don't be concerned about the outward beauty of fancy hairstyles, expensive jewelry, or beautiful clothes. ⁴You should clothe yourselves instead with the beauty that comes from within, the unfading beauty of a gentle and quiet spirit, which is so precious to God. ⁵This is how the holy women of old made themselves beautiful. They trusted God and accepted the authority of their husbands. ⁶For instance,

Sarah obeyed her husband, Abraham, and called him her master. You are her daughters when you do what is right without fear of what your husbands might do.

⁷In the same way, you husbands must give honor to your wives. Treat your wife with understanding as you live together. She may be weaker than you are, but she is your equal partner in God's gift of new life. Treat her as you should so your prayers will not be hindered.

2:12 Or *on the day of visitation.*   2:17 Greek *love the brotherhood.*   2:18 Or *because you fear God.*   2:21 Some manuscripts read *died.*   2:22 Isa 53:9.

PSALM 119:49-64

Zayin

⁴⁹ **R**emember your promise to me;
    it is my only hope.
⁵⁰ Your promise revives me;
    it comforts me in all my troubles.
⁵¹ The proud hold me in utter contempt,
    but I do not turn away from your
        instructions.
⁵² I meditate on your age-old regulations;
    O LORD, they comfort me.
⁵³ I become furious with the wicked,
    because they reject your
        instructions.
⁵⁴ Your decrees have been the theme
        of my songs
    wherever I have lived.
⁵⁵ I reflect at night on who you are,
    O LORD;

therefore, I obey your instructions.
⁵⁶ This is how I spend my life:
    obeying your commandments.

Heth

⁵⁷ LORD, you are mine!
    I promise to obey your words!
⁵⁸ With all my heart I want your blessings.
    Be merciful as you promised.
⁵⁹ I pondered the direction of my life,
    and I turned to follow your laws.
⁶⁰ I will hurry, without delay,
    to obey your commands.
⁶¹ Evil people try to drag me into sin,
    but I am firmly anchored to your
        instructions.
⁶² I rise at midnight to thank you
    for your just regulations.
⁶³ I am a friend to anyone who fears you—
    anyone who obeys your
        commandments.
⁶⁴ O LORD, your unfailing love fills the
        earth;
    teach me your decrees.

PROVERBS 28:12-13

When the godly succeed, everyone is glad. When the wicked take charge, people go into hiding. □ People who conceal their sins will not prosper, but if they confess and turn from them, they will receive mercy.

DANIEL 1:1-2:23

Daniel was one of the Jews taken into exile when Babylon conquered the southern kingdom. Taken to Babylon as a young man, he rose to great prominence there. This book is both the story of Daniel and the prophecies of Daniel—some of which predict the Messiah, Jesus.

During the third year of King Jehoiakim's reign in Judah,* King Nebuchadnezzar of Babylon came to Jerusalem and besieged it. ²The LORD gave him victory over King

NOVEMBER**25**

Jehoiakim of Judah and permitted him to take some of the sacred objects from the Temple of God. So Nebuchadnezzar took them back to the land of Babylonia* and placed them in the treasure-house of his god.

³Then the king ordered Ashpenaz, his chief of staff, to bring to the palace some of the young men of Judah's royal family and other noble families, who had been brought to Babylon as captives. ⁴"Select

only strong, healthy, and good-looking young men," he said. "Make sure they are well versed in every branch of learning, are gifted with knowledge and good judgment, and are suited to serve in the royal palace. Train these young men in the language and literature of Babylon.*" ⁵The king assigned them a daily ration of food and wine from his own kitchens. They were to be trained for three years, and then they would enter the royal service.

⁶Daniel, Hananiah, Mishael, and Azariah were four of the young men chosen, all from the tribe of Judah. ⁷The chief of staff renamed them with these Babylonian names:

Daniel was called Belteshazzar.
Hananiah was called Shadrach.
Mishael was called Meshach.
Azariah was called Abednego.

⁸But Daniel was determined not to defile himself by eating the food and wine given to them by the king. He asked the chief of staff for permission not to eat these unacceptable foods. ⁹Now God had given the chief of staff both respect and affection for Daniel. ¹⁰But he responded, "I am afraid of my lord the king, who has ordered that you eat this food and wine. If you become pale and thin compared to the other youths your age, I am afraid the king will have me beheaded."

¹¹Daniel spoke with the attendant who had been appointed by the chief of staff to look after Daniel, Hananiah, Mishael, and Azariah. ¹²"Please test us for ten days on a diet of vegetables and water," Daniel said. ¹³"At the end of the ten days, see how we look compared to the other young men who are eating the king's food. Then make your decision in light of what you see." ¹⁴The attendant agreed to Daniel's suggestion and tested them for ten days.

¹⁵At the end of the ten days, Daniel and his three friends looked healthier and better nourished than the young men who had been eating the food assigned by the king. ¹⁶So after that, the attendant fed them only vegetables instead of the food and wine provided for the others.

¹⁷God gave these four young men an unusual aptitude for understanding every aspect of literature and wisdom. And God gave Daniel the special ability to interpret the meanings of visions and dreams.

¹⁸When the training period ordered by the king was completed, the chief of staff brought all the young men to King Nebuchadnezzar. ¹⁹The king talked with them, and no one impressed him as much as Daniel, Hananiah, Mishael, and Azariah. So they entered the royal service. ²⁰Whenever the king consulted them in any matter requiring wisdom and balanced judgment, he found them ten times more capable than any of the magicians and enchanters in his entire kingdom.

²¹Daniel remained in the royal service until the first year of the reign of King Cyrus.*

2:¹ONE night during the second year of his reign,* Nebuchadnezzar had such disturbing dreams that he couldn't sleep. ²He called in his magicians, enchanters, sorcerers, and astrologers,* and he demanded that they tell him what he had dreamed. As they stood before the king, ³he said, "I have had a dream that deeply troubles me, and I must know what it means."

⁴Then the astrologers answered the king in Aramaic,* "Long live the king! Tell us the dream, and we will tell you what it means."

⁵But the king said to the astrologers, "I am serious about this. If you don't tell me what my dream was and what it means, you will be torn limb from limb, and your houses will be turned into heaps of rubble! ⁶But if you tell me what I dreamed and what the dream means, I will give you many wonderful gifts and honors. Just tell me the dream and what it means!"

⁷They said again, "Please, Your Majesty. Tell us the dream, and we will tell you what it means."

⁸The king replied, "I know what you are doing! You're stalling for time because you know I am serious when I say, ⁹'If you don't tell me the dream, you are doomed.' So you have conspired to tell me lies, hoping I will change my mind. But tell me the dream, and then I'll know that you can tell me what it means."

¹⁰The astrologers replied to the king, "No one on earth can tell the king his dream! And no king, however great and powerful,

has ever asked such a thing of any magician, enchanter, or astrologer! ¹¹The king's demand is impossible. No one except the gods can tell you your dream, and they do not live here among people."

¹²The king was furious when he heard this, and he ordered that all the wise men of Babylon be executed. ¹³And because of the king's decree, men were sent to find and kill Daniel and his friends.

¹⁴When Arioch, the commander of the king's guard, came to kill them, Daniel handled the situation with wisdom and discretion. ¹⁵He asked Arioch, "Why has the king issued such a harsh decree?" So Arioch told him all that had happened. ¹⁶Daniel went at once to see the king and requested more time to tell the king what the dream meant.

¹⁷Then Daniel went home and told his friends Hananiah, Mishael, and Azariah what had happened. ¹⁸He urged them to ask the God of heaven to show them his mercy by telling them the secret, so they would not be executed along with the other wise men of Babylon. ¹⁹That night the secret was revealed to Daniel in a vision. Then Daniel praised the God of heaven. ²⁰He said,

"Praise the name of God forever and ever,
for he has all wisdom and power.

²¹ He controls the course of world events;
he removes kings and sets up other kings.
He gives wisdom to the wise
and knowledge to the scholars.
²² He reveals deep and mysterious things
and knows what lies hidden in darkness,
though he is surrounded by light.
²³ I thank and praise you, God of my ancestors,
for you have given me wisdom and strength.
You have told me what we asked of you
and revealed to us what the king demanded."

1:1 This event occurred in 605 B.C., during the third year of Jehoiakim's reign (according to the calendar system in which the new year begins in the spring). 1:2 Hebrew *the land of Shinar.* 1:4 Or *of the Chaldeans.* 1:21 Cyrus began his reign (over Babylon) in 539 B.C. 2:1 The second year of Nebuchadnezzar's reign was 603 B.C. 2:2 Or *Chaldeans;* also in 2:4, 5, 10. 2:4 The original text from this point through chapter 7 is in Aramaic.

1 PETER 3:8-4:6

We often wonder why there has to be suffering in the world. As Peter addressed this issue, he reminded his readers that God will judge evil in the end. Our responsibility is to live a godly life here and now despite our circumstances.

Finally, all of you should be of one mind. Sympathize with each other. Love each

HOW WE LIVE: Sharing our faith

1 PETER 3:15-16 Think back to when and where you first heard about Jesus Christ and his salvation. Was it a good experience or one that drove you further away from Christianity for a long period of time? What made the difference? • If you haven't yet begun to share your faith, take Peter's advice: Always be ready to explain your faith, but do so in a gentle and respectful manner. Telling your unbelieving neighbor that she's going to hell or shouting from a street corner that non-Christians are doomed for eternity is neither gentle nor respectful. Recognize that people are intelligent and capable of thinking on their own, making their own determinations about your testimony. If you lovingly share why you believe in Jesus, you will be giving someone the opportunity to accept—or reject—salvation, or you'll be planting a seed that may sprout later. • God expects all Christians to spread the good news to anyone willing to listen. Be eager to obey this command, but don't let your manner of sharing your faith be a stumbling block to those seeking the truth of salvation.

other as brothers and sisters.* Be tender-hearted, and keep a humble attitude. ⁹Don't repay evil for evil. Don't retaliate with insults when people insult you. Instead, pay them back with a blessing. That is what God has called you to do, and he will bless you for it. ¹⁰For the Scriptures say,

"If you want to enjoy life
    and see many happy days,
keep your tongue from speaking evil
    and your lips from telling lies.
¹¹ Turn away from evil and do good.
    Search for peace, and work to
        maintain it.
¹² The eyes of the Lord watch over those
        who do right,
    and his ears are open to their
        prayers.
But the Lord turns his face
    against those who do evil."*

¹³Now, who will want to harm you if you are eager to do good? ¹⁴But even if you suffer for doing what is right, God will reward you for it. So don't worry or be afraid of their threats. ¹⁵Instead, you must worship Christ as Lord of your life. And if someone asks about your Christian hope, always be ready to explain it. ¹⁶But do this in a gentle and respectful way.* Keep your conscience clear. Then if people speak against you, they will be ashamed when they see what a good life you live because you belong to Christ. ¹⁷Remember, it is better to suffer for doing good, if that is what God wants, than to suffer for doing wrong!

¹⁸Christ suffered* for our sins once for all time. He never sinned, but he died for sinners to bring you safely home to God. He suffered physical death, but he was raised to life in the Spirit.*

¹⁹So he went and preached to the spirits in prison—²⁰those who disobeyed God long ago when God waited patiently while Noah was building his boat. Only eight people were saved from drowning in that terrible flood.* ²¹And that water is a picture of baptism, which now saves you, not by removing dirt from your body, but as a response to God from* a clean conscience. It is effective because of the resurrection of Jesus Christ.

²²Now Christ has gone to heaven. He is seated in the place of honor next to God, and all the angels and authorities and powers accept his authority.

⁴:¹So then, since Christ suffered physical pain, you must arm yourselves with the same attitude he had, and be ready to suffer, too. For if you have suffered physically for Christ, you have finished with sin.* ²You won't spend the rest of your lives chasing your own desires, but you will be anxious to do the will of God. ³You have had enough in the past of the evil things that godless people enjoy—their immorality and lust, their feasting and drunkenness and wild parties, and their terrible worship of idols.

⁴Of course, your former friends are surprised when you no longer plunge into the flood of wild and destructive things they do. So they slander you. ⁵But remember that they will have to face God, who will judge everyone, both the living and the dead. ⁶That is why the Good News was preached to those who are now dead*—so although they were destined to die like all people,* they now live forever with God in the Spirit.*

3:8 Greek *Show brotherly love.*   3:10-12 Ps 34:12-16.
3:16 Some English translations put this sentence in verse 15.
3:18a Some manuscripts read *died.*   3:18b Or *in spirit.*
3:20 Greek *saved through water.*   3:21 Or *as an appeal to God for.*   4:1 Or *For the one* [or *One*] *who has suffered physically has finished with sin.*   4:6a Greek *preached even to the dead.*   4:6b Or *so although people had judged them worthy of death.*   4:6c Or *in spirit.*

PSALM 119:65-80

Teth

⁶⁵ **Y**ou have done many good things for
        me, LORD,
    just as you promised.
⁶⁶ I believe in your commands;
    now teach me good judgment and
        knowledge.
⁶⁷ I used to wander off until you
        disciplined me;
    but now I closely follow your word.
⁶⁸ You are good and do only good;
    teach me your decrees.
⁶⁹ Arrogant people smear me with lies,
    but in truth I obey your
        commandments with all my heart.
⁷⁰ Their hearts are dull and stupid,
    but I delight in your instructions.

[71] My suffering was good for me,
   for it taught me to pay attention to
   your decrees.
[72] Your instructions are more valuable
   to me
   than millions in gold and silver.

Yodh

[73] You made me; you created me.
   Now give me the sense to follow
   your commands.
[74] May all who fear you find in me
   a cause for joy,
   for I have put my hope in your
   word.
[75] I know, O LORD, that your regulations
   are fair;
   you disciplined me because
   I needed it.
[76] Now let your unfailing love comfort
   me,

just as you promised me, your
   servant.
[77] Surround me with your tender
   mercies so I may live,
   for your instructions are my delight.
[78] Bring disgrace upon the arrogant
   people who lied about me;
   meanwhile, I will concentrate on
   your commandments.
[79] Let me be united with all who fear you,
   with those who know your laws.
[80] May I be blameless in keeping your
   decrees;
   then I will never be ashamed.

PROVERBS 28:14

Blessed are those who fear to do wrong,*
but the stubborn are headed for serious
trouble.

28:14 Or *those who fear the LORD;* Hebrew reads *those
who fear.*

DANIEL 2:24–3:30

Daniel found himself to be the only one who could
advise the king. It's an amazing thing to consider,
but God often gives you the very gifts that the most
significant moment in your life requires. Ask God for
the wisdom to live those moments well.

Then Daniel went in to see Arioch, whom
the king had ordered to execute the wise
men of Babylon. Daniel said to him,
"Don't kill the wise men. Take me to the
king, and I will tell him the meaning of his
dream."

[25] Arioch quickly took Daniel to the
king and said, "I have found one of the
captives from Judah who will tell the king
the meaning of his dream!"

[26] The king said to Daniel (also known
as Belteshazzar), "Is this true? Can you tell
me what my dream was and what it
means?"

[27] Daniel replied, "There are no wise
men, enchanters, magicians, or fortune-
tellers who can reveal the king's secret.
[28] But there is a God in heaven who reveals

NOVEMBER**26**

secrets, and he has shown King Nebuchadnezzar what will happen in the future.
Now I will tell you your dream and the visions you saw as you lay on your bed.

[29] "While Your Majesty was sleeping,
you dreamed about coming events. He
who reveals secrets has shown you what is
going to happen. [30] And it is not because I
am wiser than anyone else that I know the
secret of your dream, but because God
wants you to understand what was in your
heart.

[31] "In your vision, Your Majesty, you saw
standing before you a huge, shining statue
of a man. It was a frightening sight. [32] The
head of the statue was made of fine gold.
Its chest and arms were silver, its belly and
thighs were bronze, [33] its legs were iron,
and its feet were a combination of iron
and baked clay. [34] As you watched, a rock
was cut from a mountain, but not by human hands. It struck the feet of iron and
clay, smashing them to bits. [35] The whole
statue was crushed into small pieces of

iron, clay, bronze, silver, and gold. Then the wind blew them away without a trace, like chaff on a threshing floor. But the rock that knocked the statue down became a great mountain that covered the whole earth.

36"That was the dream. Now we will tell the king what it means. 37Your Majesty, you are the greatest of kings. The God of heaven has given you sovereignty, power, strength, and honor. 38He has made you the ruler over all the inhabited world and has put even the wild animals and birds under your control. You are the head of gold.

39"But after your kingdom comes to an end, another kingdom, inferior to yours, will rise to take your place. After that kingdom has fallen, yet a third kingdom, represented by bronze, will rise to rule the world. 40Following that kingdom, there will be a fourth one, as strong as iron. That kingdom will smash and crush all previous empires, just as iron smashes and crushes everything it strikes. 41The feet and toes you saw were a combination of iron and baked clay, showing that this kingdom will be divided. Like iron mixed with clay, it will have some of the strength of iron. 42But while some parts of it will be as strong as iron, other parts will be as weak as clay. 43This mixture of iron and clay also shows that these kingdoms will try to strengthen themselves by forming alliances with each other through intermarriage. But they will not hold together, just as iron and clay do not mix.

44"During the reigns of those kings, the God of heaven will set up a kingdom that will never be destroyed or conquered. It will crush all these kingdoms into nothingness, and it will stand forever. 45That is the meaning of the rock cut from the mountain, though not by human hands, that crushed to pieces the statue of iron, bronze, clay, silver, and gold. The great God was showing the king what will happen in the future. The dream is true, and its meaning is certain."

46Then King Nebuchadnezzar threw himself down before Daniel and worshiped him, and he commanded his people to offer sacrifices and burn sweet incense before him. 47The king said to Daniel, "Truly, your God is the greatest of gods, the Lord over kings, a revealer of mysteries, for you have been able to reveal this secret."

48Then the king appointed Daniel to a high position and gave him many valuable gifts. He made Daniel ruler over the whole province of Babylon, as well as chief over all his wise men. 49At Daniel's request, the king appointed Shadrach, Meshach, and Abednego to be in charge of all the affairs of the province of Babylon, while Daniel remained in the king's court.

3:1King Nebuchadnezzar made a gold statue ninety feet tall and nine feet wide* and set it up on the plain of Dura in the province of Babylon. 2Then he sent messages to the high officers, officials, governors, advisers, treasurers, judges, magistrates, and all the provincial officials to come to the dedication of the statue he had set up. 3So all these officials* came and stood before the statue King Nebuchadnezzar had set up.

4Then a herald shouted out, "People of all races and nations and languages, listen to the king's command! 5When you hear the sound of the horn, flute, zither, lyre, harp, pipes, and other musical instruments,* bow to the ground to worship King Nebuchadnezzar's gold statue. 6Anyone who refuses to obey will immediately be thrown into a blazing furnace."

7So at the sound of the musical instruments,* all the people, whatever their race or nation or language, bowed to the ground and worshiped the gold statue that King Nebuchadnezzar had set up.

8But some of the astrologers* went to the king and informed on the Jews. 9They said to King Nebuchadnezzar, "Long live the king! 10You issued a decree requiring all the people to bow down and worship the gold statue when they hear the sound of the horn, flute, zither, lyre, harp, pipes, and other musical instruments. 11That decree also states that those who refuse to obey must be thrown into a blazing furnace. 12But there are some Jews—Shadrach, Meshach, and Abednego—whom you have put in charge of the province of Babylon. They pay no attention to you,

Your Majesty. They refuse to serve your gods and do not worship the gold statue you have set up."

[13]Then Nebuchadnezzar flew into a rage and ordered that Shadrach, Meshach, and Abednego be brought before him. When they were brought in, [14]Nebuchadnezzar said to them, "Is it true, Shadrach, Meshach, and Abednego, that you refuse to serve my gods or to worship the gold statue I have set up? [15]I will give you one more chance to bow down and worship the statue I have made when you hear the sound of the musical instruments.* But if you refuse, you will be thrown immediately into the blazing furnace. And then what god will be able to rescue you from my power?"

[16]Shadrach, Meshach, and Abednego replied, "O Nebuchadnezzar, we do not need to defend ourselves before you. [17]If we are thrown into the blazing furnace, the God whom we serve is able to save us. He will rescue us from your power, Your Majesty. [18]But even if he doesn't, we want to make it clear to you, Your Majesty, that we will never serve your gods or worship the gold statue you have set up."

[19]Nebuchadnezzar was so furious with Shadrach, Meshach, and Abednego that his face became distorted with rage. He commanded that the furnace be heated seven times hotter than usual. [20]Then he ordered some of the strongest men of his army to bind Shadrach, Meshach, and Abednego and throw them into the blazing furnace. [21]So they tied them up and threw them into the furnace, fully dressed in their pants, turbans, robes, and other garments. [22]And because the king, in his anger, had demanded such a hot fire in the furnace, the flames killed the soldiers as they threw the three men in. [23]So Shadrach, Meshach, and Abednego, securely tied, fell into the roaring flames.

[24]But suddenly, Nebuchadnezzar jumped up in amazement and exclaimed to his advisers, "Didn't we tie up three men and throw them into the furnace?"

"Yes, Your Majesty, we certainly did," they replied.

[25]"Look!" Nebuchadnezzar shouted. "I see four men, unbound, walking around in the fire unharmed! And the fourth looks like a god*!"

[26]Then Nebuchadnezzar came as close as he could to the door of the flaming furnace and shouted: "Shadrach, Meshach, and Abednego, servants of the Most High God, come out! Come here!"

So Shadrach, Meshach, and Abednego stepped out of the fire. [27]Then the high officers, officials, governors, and advisers crowded around them and saw that the fire had not touched them. Not a hair on their heads was singed, and their clothing

HOW WE LIVE: Dealing with problems

DANIEL 3:16-18 As stressful as life is, few of us face situations as stressful as being thrown into a blazing fire. Daniel's three friends faced certain and horrific death because they refused to disobey God and bow down to the idol. They dealt with this deadly problem head on: "Because we love God, we will be obedient. Because we trust him, we know he will do what is best." • What difference would it make in the day-to-day problems you face if you believed God was with you and able to deliver you—maybe not the way you expect, but that he will indeed do so? Think about the stress points you endure during a week. Think about the fears and worries about what *might* happen or what *has* happened. You can face them with clear-headedness, faith, and courage when you believe God's goodness waits for you at the other side of whatever fire you're facing. • Look past the fire to what is deep within—that "fourth man"—that unexpected lesson, that unseen rescue, that unknown comfort. Let your problems be an opportunity for you to see God and experience what he can do!

was not scorched. They didn't even smell of smoke!

²⁸Then Nebuchadnezzar said, "Praise to the God of Shadrach, Meshach, and Abednego! He sent his angel to rescue his servants who trusted in him. They defied the king's command and were willing to die rather than serve or worship any god except their own God. ²⁹Therefore, I make this decree: If any people, whatever their race or nation or language, speak a word against the God of Shadrach, Meshach, and Abednego, they will be torn limb from limb, and their houses will be turned into heaps of rubble. There is no other god who can rescue like this!"

³⁰Then the king promoted Shadrach, Meshach, and Abednego to even higher positions in the province of Babylon.

3:1 Aramaic *60 cubits* [27 meters] *tall and 6 cubits* [2.7 meters] *wide.*   3:3 Aramaic *the high officers, officials, governors, advisers, treasurers, judges, magistrates, and all the provincial officials.*   3:5 The identification of some of these musical instruments is uncertain.   3:7 Aramaic *the horn, flute, zither, lyre, harp, and other musical instruments.*   3:8 Aramaic *Chaldeans.*   3:15 Aramaic *the horn, flute, zither, lyre, harp, pipes, and other musical instruments.*   3:25 Aramaic *like a son of the gods.*

1 PETER 4:7–5:14

Have you ever been persecuted for your faith? Ignored? Slighted? Passed over? What was the end product? How did it change your perspective? Your character? Peter knew what it was to fear for one's life because of one's beliefs.

But the end of all things is at hand
→The end of the world is coming soon. Therefore, be earnest and disciplined in your prayers. ⁸Most important of all, continue to show deep love for each other, for love covers a multitude of sins. ⁹Cheerfully share your home with those who need a meal or a place to stay.

¹⁰God has given each of you a gift from his great variety of spiritual gifts. Use them well to serve one another. ¹¹Do you have the gift of speaking? Then speak as though God himself were speaking through you. Do you have the gift of helping others? Do it with all the strength and energy that God supplies. Then everything you do will bring glory to God through Jesus Christ. All glory and power to him forever and ever! Amen.

¹²Dear friends, don't be surprised at the fiery trials you are going through, as if something strange were happening to you. ¹³Instead, be very glad—for these trials make you partners with Christ in his suffering, so that you will have the wonderful joy of seeing his glory when it is revealed to all the world.

¹⁴So be happy when you are insulted for being a Christian,* for then the glorious Spirit of God* rests upon you.* ¹⁵If you suffer, however, it must not be for murder, stealing, making trouble, or prying into other people's affairs. ¹⁶But it is no shame to suffer for being a Christian. Praise God for the privilege of being called by his name! ¹⁷For the time has come for judgment, and it must begin with God's household. And if judgment begins with us, what terrible fate awaits those who have never obeyed God's Good News? ¹⁸And also,

"If the righteous are barely saved,
    what will happen to godless
        sinners?"*

¹⁹So if you are suffering in a manner that pleases God, keep on doing what is right, and trust your lives to the God who created you, for he will never fail you.

⁵:¹And now, a word to you who are elders in the churches. I, too, am an elder and a witness to the sufferings of Christ. And I, too, will share in his glory when he is revealed to the whole world. As a fellow elder, I appeal to you: ²Care for the flock that God has entrusted to you. Watch over it willingly, not grudgingly—not for what you will get out of it, but because you are eager to serve God. ³Don't lord it over the people assigned to your care, but lead them by your own good example. ⁴And when the Great Shepherd appears, you will receive a crown of never-ending glory and honor.

⁵In the same way, you younger men must accept the authority of the elders. And all of you, serve each other in humility, for

"God opposes the proud
    but favors the humble."*

⁶So humble yourselves under the mighty power of God, and at the right time he will

lift you up in honor. [7]Give all your worries and cares to God, for he cares about you.

[8]Stay alert! Watch out for your great enemy, the devil. He prowls around like a roaring lion, looking for someone to devour. [9]Stand firm against him, and be strong in your faith. Remember that your Christian brothers and sisters* all over the world are going through the same kind of suffering you are.

[10]In his kindness God called you to share in his eternal glory by means of Christ Jesus. So after you have suffered a little while, he will restore, support, and strengthen you, and he will place you on a firm foundation. [11]All power to him forever! Amen.

[12]I have written and sent this short letter to you with the help of Silas,* whom I commend to you as a faithful brother. My purpose in writing is to encourage you and assure you that what you are experiencing is truly part of God's grace for you. Stand firm in this grace.

[13]Your sister church here in Babylon* sends you greetings, and so does my son Mark. [14]Greet each other with Christian love.*

Peace be with all of you who are in Christ.

4:14a Greek *for the name of Christ.* 4:14b Or *for the glory of God, which is his Spirit.* 4:14c Some manuscripts add *On their part he is blasphemed, but on your part he is glorified.* 4:18 Prov 11:31 (Greek version). 5:5 Prov 3:34 (Greek version). 5:9 Greek *your brothers.* 5:12 Greek *Silvanus.* 5:13 Greek *The elect one in Babylon.* Babylon was probably symbolic for Rome. 5:14 Greek *with a kiss of love.*

PSALM 119:81-96

Kaph

[81] I am worn out waiting for your [the LORD's] rescue,
   but I have put my hope in your word.
[82] My eyes are straining to see your promises come true.
   When will you comfort me?
[83] I am shriveled like a wineskin in the smoke,
   but I have not forgotten to obey your decrees.

[84] How long must I wait?
   When will you punish those who persecute me?
[85] These arrogant people who hate your instructions
   have dug deep pits to trap me.
[86] All your commands are trustworthy.
   Protect me from those who hunt me down without cause.
[87] They almost finished me off,
   but I refused to abandon your commandments.
[88] In your unfailing love, spare my life;
   then I can continue to obey your laws.

Lamedh

[89] Your eternal word, O LORD,
   stands firm in heaven.
[90] Your faithfulness extends to every generation,
   as enduring as the earth you created.
[91] Your regulations remain true to this day,
   for everything serves your plans.
[92] If your instructions hadn't sustained me with joy,
   I would have died in my misery.
[93] I will never forget your commandments,
   for by them you give me life.
[94] I am yours; rescue me!
   For I have worked hard at obeying your commandments.
[95] Though the wicked hide along the way to kill me,
   I will quietly keep my mind on your laws.
[96] Even perfection has its limits,
   but your commands have no limit.

PROVERBS 28:15-16

A wicked ruler is as dangerous to the poor as a roaring lion or an attacking bear. □ A ruler with no understanding will oppress his people, but one who hates corruption will have a long life.

DANIEL 4:1-37

Daniel was given an audience with the king and the abilities to be impressively wise, and then got sandbagged for being the bearer of bad fortune. It makes you wonder if it didn't cross his mind to sweeten the interpretation a little. But his integrity shined through.

¹***K**ing Nebuchadnezzar sent this message to the people of every race and nation and language throughout the world:

"Peace and prosperity to you!

²"I want you all to know about the miraculous signs and wonders the Most High God has performed for me.

³ How great are his signs,
how powerful his wonders!
His kingdom will last forever,
his rule through all generations.

⁴*"I, Nebuchadnezzar, was living in my palace in comfort and prosperity. ⁵But one night I had a dream that frightened me; I saw visions that terrified me as I lay in my bed. ⁶So I issued an order calling in all the wise men of Babylon, so they could tell me what my dream meant. ⁷When all the magicians, enchanters, astrologers,* and fortune-tellers came in, I told them the dream, but they could not tell me what it meant. ⁸At last Daniel came in before me, and I told him the dream. (He was named Belteshazzar after my god, and the spirit of the holy gods is in him.)

⁹"I said to him, 'Belteshazzar, chief of the magicians, I know that the spirit of the holy gods is in you and that no mystery is too great for you to solve. Now tell me what my dream means.

¹⁰"'While I was lying in my bed, this is what I dreamed. I saw a large tree in the middle of the earth. ¹¹The tree grew very tall and strong, reaching high into the heavens for all the world to see. ¹²It had fresh green leaves, and it was loaded with fruit for all to eat. Wild animals lived in its shade, and birds nested in its branches. All the world was fed from this tree.

¹³"'Then as I lay there dreaming, I saw a messenger,* a holy one, coming down from heaven. ¹⁴The messenger shouted,

"Cut down the tree and lop off
its branches!
Shake off its leaves and scatter
its fruit!
Chase the wild animals from
its shade
and the birds from its branches.
¹⁵ But leave the stump and the roots
in the ground,
bound with a band of iron and
bronze
and surrounded by tender grass.
Now let him be drenched with the
dew of heaven,
and let him live with the wild
animals among the plants
of the field.
¹⁶ For seven periods of time,
let him have the mind of a wild
animal
instead of the mind of a human.
¹⁷ For this has been decreed by the
messengers*;
it is commanded by the holy ones,
so that everyone may know
that the Most High rules over the
kingdoms of the world.
He gives them to anyone he
chooses—
even to the lowliest of people."

¹⁸"'Belteshazzar, that was the dream that I, King Nebuchadnezzar, had. Now tell me what it means, for none of the wise men of my kingdom can do so. But you can tell me because the spirit of the holy gods is in you.'

¹⁹"Upon hearing this, Daniel (also known as Belteshazzar) was overcome for a time, frightened by the meaning of the dream. Then the king said to him, 'Belteshazzar, don't be alarmed by the dream and what it means.'

"Belteshazzar replied, 'I wish the events foreshadowed in this dream would happen to your enemies, my lord, and not to you! ²⁰The tree you saw was growing very tall and strong, reaching high into the heavens for all the world to see. ²¹It had fresh green leaves and was loaded with fruit for all to eat. Wild animals lived in its shade, and birds nested in its branches. ²²That tree, Your Majesty, is you. For you have grown strong and great; your greatness reaches up to heaven, and your rule to the ends of the earth.

²³"'Then you saw a messenger, a holy one, coming down from heaven and saying, "Cut down the tree and destroy it. But leave the stump and the roots in the ground, bound with a band of iron and bronze and surrounded by tender grass. Let him be drenched with the dew of heaven. Let him live with the animals of the field for seven periods of time."

²⁴"'This is what the dream means, Your Majesty, and what the Most High has declared will happen to my lord the king. ²⁵You will be driven from human society, and you will live in the fields with the wild animals. You will eat grass like a cow, and you will be drenched with the dew of heaven. Seven periods of time will pass while you live this way, until you learn that

the Most High rules over the kingdoms of the world and gives them to anyone he chooses. ²⁶But the stump and roots of the tree were left in the ground. This means that you will receive your kingdom back again when you have learned that heaven rules.

²⁷"'King Nebuchadnezzar, please accept my advice. Stop sinning and do what is right. Break from your wicked past and be merciful to the poor. Perhaps then you will continue to prosper.'

²⁸"But all these things did happen to King Nebuchadnezzar. ²⁹Twelve months later he was taking a walk on the flat roof of the royal palace in Babylon. ³⁰As he looked out across the city, he said, 'Look at this great city of Babylon! By my own mighty power, I have built this beautiful city as my royal residence to display my majestic splendor.'

³¹"While these words were still in his mouth, a voice called down from heaven, 'O King Nebuchadnezzar, this message is for you! You are no longer ruler of this kingdom. ³²You will be driven from human society. You will live in the fields with the wild animals,

---

HOW WE LIVE

Persevering in faith

2 PETER 1:5-7 Faith changed your life; faith makes you different from much of the world around you. But you cannot stop at faith alone. You have work to do. To your faith, you must add a lifestyle that mirrors Christ's. Why? The shining moral quality of Christ's life compels you to be your very best. • Faith must be more than belief in certain facts; it must result in action. Peter lists several of faith's actions: Supplement your faith with moral excellence, knowledge, self-control, patient endurance, godliness, brotherly affection, and love for everyone. These actions do not come automatically; they require hard work. They are not optional; all of them must be a continual part of the Christian life. • Patient endurance is the ability to steadfastly endure suffering or evil without giving up your faith. Patient endurance is not a stoic indifference to whatever fate allows; rather, it springs from faith in God's goodness and control over all that happens in your life. Patient endurance allows you to go through the darkest times with the light of Christ. Patient endurance trusts that God, in his wisdom and love, will do what's best.

and you will eat grass like a cow. Seven periods of time will pass while you live this way, until you learn that the Most High rules over the kingdoms of the world and gives them to anyone he chooses.'

³³"That same hour the judgment was fulfilled, and Nebuchadnezzar was driven from human society. He ate grass like a cow, and he was drenched with the dew of heaven. He lived this way until his hair was as long as eagles' feathers and his nails were like birds' claws.

³⁴"After this time had passed, I, Nebuchadnezzar, looked up to heaven. My sanity returned, and I praised and worshiped the Most High and honored the one who lives forever.

His rule is everlasting,
    and his kingdom is eternal.
³⁵ All the people of the earth
    are nothing compared to him.
He does as he pleases
    among the angels of heaven
    and among the people of the
        earth.
No one can stop him or say to him,
    'What do you mean by doing
        these things?'

³⁶"When my sanity returned to me, so did my honor and glory and kingdom. My advisers and nobles sought me out, and I was restored as head of my kingdom, with even greater honor than before. ³⁷Now I, Nebuchadnezzar, praise and glorify and honor the King of heaven. All his acts are just and true, and he is able to humble the proud."

4:1 Verses 4:1-3 are numbered 3:31-33 in Aramaic text.
4:4 Verses 4:4-37 are numbered 4:1-34 in Aramaic text.
4:7 Or *Chaldeans.*   4:13 Aramaic *a watcher;* also in 4:23.
4:17 Aramaic *the watchers.*

2 PETER 1:1-21

In Peter's second letter he focused his attention on false teachers and their destructive teachings. It was fitting, then, that he opened his letter with a reminder of the importance of Scripture, the final authority in matters of doctrine and practical living.

This letter is from Simon* Peter, a slave and apostle of Jesus Christ.

I am writing to you who share the same precious faith we have. This faith was given to you because of the justice and fairness* of Jesus Christ, our God and Savior.

²May God give you more and more grace and peace as you grow in your knowledge of God and Jesus our Lord.

³By his divine power, God has given us everything we need for living a godly life. We have received all of this by coming to know him, the one who called us to himself by means of his marvelous glory and excellence. ⁴And because of his glory and excellence, he has given us great and precious promises. These are the promises that enable you to share his divine nature and escape the world's corruption caused by human desires.

⁵In view of all this, make every effort to respond to God's promises. Supplement your faith with a generous provision of moral excellence, and moral excellence with knowledge, ⁶and knowledge with self-control, and self-control with patient endurance, and patient endurance with godliness, ⁷and godliness with brotherly affection, and brotherly affection with love for everyone.

⁸The more you grow like this, the more productive and useful you will be in your knowledge of our Lord Jesus Christ. ⁹But those who fail to develop in this way are shortsighted or blind, forgetting that they have been cleansed from their old sins.

¹⁰So, dear brothers and sisters,* work hard to prove that you really are among those God has called and chosen. Do these things, and you will never fall away. ¹¹Then God will give you a grand entrance into the eternal Kingdom of our Lord and Savior Jesus Christ.

¹²Therefore, I will always remind you about these things—even though you already know them and are standing firm in the truth you have been taught. ¹³And it is only right that I should keep on reminding you as long as I live.* ¹⁴For our Lord Jesus Christ has shown me that I must soon leave this earthly life,* ¹⁵so I will work hard to make sure you always remember these things after I am gone.

¹⁶For we were not making up clever stories when we told you about the powerful coming of our Lord Jesus Christ. We

saw his majestic splendor with our own eyes [17] when he received honor and glory from God the Father. The voice from the majestic glory of God said to him, "This is my dearly loved Son, who brings me great joy."* [18] We ourselves heard that voice from heaven when we were with him on the holy mountain.

[19] Because of that experience, we have even greater confidence in the message proclaimed by the prophets. You must pay close attention to what they wrote, for their words are like a lamp shining in a dark place—until the Day dawns, and Christ the Morning Star shines* in your hearts. [20] Above all, you must realize that no prophecy in Scripture ever came from the prophet's own understanding,* [21] or from human initiative. No, those prophets were moved by the Holy Spirit, and they spoke from God.

1:1a Greek *Symeon.*   1:1b Or *to you in the righteousness.*
1:10 Greek *brothers.*   1:13 Greek *as long as I am in this tent* [or *tabernacle*].   1:14 Greek *I must soon put off my tent* [or *tabernacle*].   1:17 Matt 17:5; Mark 9:7; Luke 9:35.   1:19 Or *rises.*   1:20 Or *is a matter of one's own interpretation.*

PSALM 119:97-112

Mem

[97] **O**h, how I love your [the LORD's] instructions!
    I think about them all day long.
[98] Your commands make me wiser than my enemies,
    for they are my constant guide.
[99] Yes, I have more insight than my teachers,
    for I am always thinking of your laws.
[100] I am even wiser than my elders,
    for I have kept your commandments.
[101] I have refused to walk on any evil path,

so that I may remain obedient to your word.
[102] I haven't turned away from your regulations,
    for you have taught me well.
[103] How sweet your words taste to me;
    they are sweeter than honey.
[104] Your commandments give me understanding;
    no wonder I hate every false way of life.

Nun

[105] Your word is a lamp to guide my feet
    and a light for my path.
[106] I've promised it once, and I'll promise it again:
    I will obey your righteous regulations.
[107] I have suffered much, O LORD;
    restore my life again as you promised.
[108] LORD, accept my offering of praise,
    and teach me your regulations.
[109] My life constantly hangs in the balance,
    but I will not stop obeying your instructions.
[110] The wicked have set their traps for me,
    but I will not turn from your commandments.
[111] Your laws are my treasure;
    they are my heart's delight.
[112] I am determined to keep your decrees to the very end.

PROVERBS 28:17-18

A murderer's tormented conscience will drive him into the grave. Don't protect him! □ The blameless will be rescued from harm, but the crooked will be suddenly destroyed.

DANIEL 5:1-31
Ever heard the saying, "He saw the handwriting on the wall"? That phrase comes from today's reading. It's a way of saying that the inevitable is about to occur.

NOVEMBER**28**

Many years later King Belshazzar gave a great feast for 1,000 of his nobles, and he drank wine with them. [2] While Belshazzar was drinking the wine, he gave orders to bring in the gold and silver cups that his predecessor,* Nebuchadnezzar, had taken from the Temple in Jerusalem. He wanted to drink from them with his nobles, his wives, and his concubines. ³So they brought these gold cups taken from the Temple, the house of God in Jerusalem, and the king and his nobles, his wives, and his concubines drank from them. ⁴While they drank from them they praised their idols made of gold, silver, bronze, iron, wood, and stone.

⁵Suddenly, they saw the fingers of a human hand writing on the plaster wall of the king's palace, near the lampstand. The king himself saw the hand as it wrote, ⁶and his face turned pale with fright. His knees knocked together in fear and his legs gave way beneath him.

⁷The king shouted for the enchanters, astrologers,* and fortune-tellers to be brought before him. He said to these wise men of Babylon, "Whoever can read this writing and tell me what it means will be dressed in purple robes of royal honor and will have a gold chain placed around his neck. He will become the third highest ruler in the kingdom!"

⁸But when all the king's wise men had come in, none of them could read the writing or tell him what it meant. ⁹So the king grew even more alarmed, and his face turned pale. His nobles, too, were shaken.

¹⁰But when the queen mother heard what was happening, she hurried to the banquet hall. She said to Belshazzar, "Long live the king! Don't be so pale and frightened. ¹¹There is a man in your kingdom who has within him the spirit of the holy gods. During Nebuchadnezzar's reign, this man was found to have insight, understanding, and wisdom like that of the gods. Your predecessor, the king—your predecessor King Nebuchadnezzar—made him chief over all the magicians, enchanters, astrologers, and fortune-tellers of Babylon. ¹²This man Daniel, whom the king named Belteshazzar, has exceptional ability and is filled with divine knowledge and understanding. He can interpret dreams, explain riddles, and solve difficult problems. Call for Daniel, and he will tell you what the writing means."

¹³So Daniel was brought in before the king. The king asked him, "Are you Daniel, one of the exiles brought from Judah by my predecessor, King Nebuchadnezzar? ¹⁴I have heard that you have the spirit of the gods within you and that you are filled with insight, understanding, and wisdom. ¹⁵My wise men and enchanters have tried to read the words on the wall and tell me their meaning, but they cannot do it. ¹⁶I am told that you can give interpretations and solve difficult problems. If you can read these words and tell me their meaning, you will be clothed in purple robes of royal honor, and you will have a gold chain placed around your neck. You will become the third highest ruler in the kingdom."

¹⁷Daniel answered the king, "Keep your gifts or give them to someone else, but I will tell you what the writing means. ¹⁸Your Majesty, the Most High God gave sovereignty, majesty, glory, and honor to your predecessor, Nebuchadnezzar. ¹⁹He made him so great that people of all races and nations and languages trembled before him in fear. He killed those he wanted to kill and spared those he wanted to spare. He honored those he wanted to honor and disgraced those he wanted to disgrace. ²⁰But when his heart and mind were puffed up with arrogance, he was brought down from his royal throne and stripped of his glory. ²¹He was driven from human society. He was given the mind of a wild animal, and he lived among the wild donkeys. He ate grass like a cow, and he was drenched with the dew of heaven, until he learned that the Most High God rules over the kingdoms of the world and appoints anyone he desires to rule over them.

²²"You are his successor,* O Belshazzar, and you knew all this, yet you have not humbled yourself. ²³For you have proudly defied the Lord of heaven and have had these cups from his Temple brought before you. You and your nobles and your wives and concubines have been drinking wine from them while praising gods of silver, gold, bronze, iron, wood, and stone—gods that neither see nor hear nor know anything at all. But you have not honored the God who gives you the breath of life and controls your destiny! ²⁴So God has sent this hand to write this message.

²⁵"This is the message that was written:
MENE, MENE, TEKEL, and PARSIN. ²⁶This is
what these words mean:

Mene means 'numbered'—God has
numbered the days of your reign
and has brought it to an end.

²⁷ Tekel means 'weighed'—you have been
weighed on the balances and have
not measured up.

²⁸ Parsin* means 'divided'—your
kingdom has been divided and
given to the Medes and Persians."

²⁹Then at Belshazzar's command, Daniel was dressed in purple robes, a gold chain was hung around his neck, and he was proclaimed the third highest ruler in the kingdom.

³⁰That very night Belshazzar, the Babylonian* king, was killed.*

³¹*And Darius the Mede took over the kingdom at the age of sixty-two.

5:2 Aramaic *father;* also in 5:11, 13, 18.   5:7 Or *Chaldeans;* also in 5:11.   5:22 Aramaic *son.*   5:28 Aramaic *Peres,* the singular of *Parsin.*   5:30a Or *Chaldean.*   5:30b The Persians and Medes conquered Babylon in October 539 B.C.   5:31 Verse 5:31 is numbered 6:1 in Aramaic text.

2 PETER 2:1-22
The first century was filled with differing interpretations, theologies, and basic opinions about Christianity. False teachers will be severely judged because of the damage they cause to the church.

But there were also false prophets in Israel, just as there will be false teachers among you. They will cleverly teach destructive heresies and even deny the Master who bought them. In this way, they will bring sudden destruction on themselves. ²Many will follow their evil teaching and shameful immorality. And because of these teachers, the way of truth will be slandered. ³In their greed they will make up clever lies to get hold of your money. But God condemned them long ago, and their destruction will not be delayed.

⁴For God did not spare even the angels who sinned. He threw them into hell,* in gloomy pits of darkness,* where they are being held until the day of judgment. ⁵And God did not spare the ancient world—except for Noah and the seven others in his family. Noah warned the world of God's righteous judgment. So God protected Noah when he destroyed the world of ungodly people with a vast flood. ⁶Later, God condemned the cities of Sodom and Gomorrah and turned them into heaps of ashes. He made them an example of what will happen to ungodly people. ⁷But God also rescued Lot out of Sodom because he was a righteous man who was sick of the shameful immorality of the wicked people around him. ⁸Yes, Lot was a righteous man who was tormented in his soul by the

WHAT THE BIBLE SAYS

How to discern truth

2 PETER 2:1-22 Discernment is the ability to grasp the obscure; to distinguish and select what is true, appropriate, or excellent. In Peter's letter in the New Testament, he describes discernment as a necessity for living the Christian life. It's the way we find the truth in the midst of many voices shouting at us to believe in them. It is the way that we can live our lives in wisdom, honoring God. • The people to whom Peter wrote were being deceived. They believed they were doing the right thing, but they were committing evil acts. They thought they spoke for God, while all along they had turned against him. Peter's descriptions are enough to make a person a little queasy. It is terrifying to think that we could be so blind as to think we are serving God, when we are actually fighting against him. That's why discernment—the ability to distinguish light from shadow, truth from fiction—is an essential element of walking in faith. And how do you gain it? "Be on guard. . . . Grow in the grace and knowledge of our Lord and Savior Jesus Christ" (2 Peter 3:17-18, November 29).

wickedness he saw and heard day after day. ⁹So you see, the Lord knows how to rescue godly people from their trials, even while keeping the wicked under punishment until the day of final judgment. ¹⁰He is especially hard on those who follow their own twisted sexual desire, and who despise authority.

These people are proud and arrogant, daring even to scoff at supernatural beings* without so much as trembling. ¹¹But the angels, who are far greater in power and strength, do not dare to bring from the Lord* a charge of blasphemy against those supernatural beings.

¹²These false teachers are like unthinking animals, creatures of instinct, born to be caught and destroyed. They scoff at things they do not understand, and like animals, they will be destroyed. ¹³Their destruction is their reward for the harm they have done. They love to indulge in evil pleasures in broad daylight. They are a disgrace and a stain among you. They delight in deception* even as they eat with you in your fellowship meals. ¹⁴They commit adultery with their eyes, and their desire for sin is never satisfied. They lure unstable people into sin, and they are well trained in greed. They live under God's curse. ¹⁵They have wandered off the right road and followed the footsteps of Balaam son of Beor,* who loved to earn money by doing wrong. ¹⁶But Balaam was stopped from his mad course when his donkey rebuked him with a human voice.

¹⁷These people are as useless as dried-up springs or as mist blown away by the wind. They are doomed to blackest darkness. ¹⁸They brag about themselves with empty, foolish boasting. With an appeal to twisted sexual desires, they lure back into sin those who have barely escaped from a lifestyle of deception. ¹⁹They promise freedom, but they themselves are slaves of sin and corruption. For you are a slave to whatever controls you. ²⁰And when people escape from the wickedness of the world by knowing our Lord and Savior Jesus Christ and then get tangled up and enslaved by sin again, they are worse off than before. ²¹It would be better if they had never known the way to righteousness than to know it and then reject the command they were given to live a holy life. ²²They prove the truth of this proverb: "A dog returns to its vomit."* And another says, "A washed pig returns to the mud."

2:4a Greek *Tartarus.*   **2:4b** Some manuscripts read *in chains of gloom.*   **2:10** Greek *at glorious ones,* which are probably evil angels.   **2:11** Other manuscripts read *to the Lord;* still others omit this phrase.   **2:13** Some manuscripts read *in fellowship meals.*   **2:15** Some manuscripts read *Bosor.*   **2:22** Prov 26:11.

PSALM 119:113-128

Samekh

¹¹³I [the LORD] hate those with divided loyalties,
    but I love your instructions.
¹¹⁴You are my refuge and my shield;
    your word is my source of hope.
¹¹⁵Get out of my life, you evil-minded people,
    for I intend to obey the commands of my God.
¹¹⁶LORD, sustain me as you promised, that I may live!
    Do not let my hope be crushed.
¹¹⁷Sustain me, and I will be rescued;
    then I will meditate continually on your decrees.
¹¹⁸But you have rejected all who stray from your decrees.
    They are only fooling themselves.
¹¹⁹You skim off the wicked of the earth like scum;
    no wonder I love to obey your laws!
¹²⁰I tremble in fear of you;
    I stand in awe of your regulations.

Ayin

¹²¹Don't leave me to the mercy of my enemies,
    for I have done what is just and right.
¹²²Please guarantee a blessing for me.
    Don't let the arrogant oppress me!
¹²³My eyes strain to see your rescue,
    to see the truth of your promise fulfilled.
¹²⁴I am your servant; deal with me in unfailing love,
    and teach me your decrees.
¹²⁵Give discernment to me, your servant;
    then I will understand your laws.
¹²⁶LORD, it is time for you to act,
    for these evil people have violated your instructions.

¹²⁷ Truly, I love your commands
more than gold, even the finest
gold.
¹²⁸ Each of your commandments
is right.
That is why I hate every false way.

DANIEL 6:1-28

The story could be in our newspapers: sneaky politi-
cians get a bill signed just to get back at someone
who has showed them up. Daniel stood courageously
for his convictions and prospered in the end.

¹*Darius the Mede decided to divide the
kingdom into 120 provinces, and he appointed a high officer to rule over each
province. ² The king also chose Daniel and
two others as administrators to supervise
the high officers and protect the king's
interests. ³Daniel soon proved himself
more capable than all the other administrators and high officers. Because of Daniel's great ability, the king made plans to
place him over the entire empire.

⁴Then the other administrators and
high officers began searching for some
fault in the way Daniel was handling government affairs, but they couldn't find
anything to criticize or condemn. He was
faithful, always responsible, and completely trustworthy. ⁵So they concluded,
"Our only chance of finding grounds for
accusing Daniel will be in connection
with the rules of his religion."

⁶So the administrators and high officers
went to the king and said, "Long live King
Darius! ⁷We are all in agreement—we administrators, officials, high officers, advisers, and governors—that the king should
make a law that will be strictly enforced.
Give orders that for the next thirty days any
person who prays to anyone, divine or human—except to you, Your Majesty—will be
thrown into the den of lions. ⁸And now,
Your Majesty, issue and sign this law so it
cannot be changed, an official law of the
Medes and Persians that cannot be revoked." ⁹So King Darius signed the law.

PROVERBS 28:19-20

A hard worker has plenty of food, but
a person who chases fantasies ends up in
poverty. □ The trustworthy person will get
a rich reward, but a person who wants
quick riches will get into trouble.

NOVEMBER**29**

¹⁰But when Daniel learned that the law
had been signed, he went home and knelt
down as usual in his upstairs room, with its
windows open toward Jerusalem. He
prayed three times a day, just as he had always done, giving thanks to his God.
¹¹Then the officials went together to Dan-
iel's house and found him praying and asking for God's help. ¹²So they went straight
to the king and reminded him about his
law. "Did you not sign a law that for the
next thirty days any person who prays to
anyone, divine or human—except to you,
Your Majesty—will be thrown into the den
of lions?"

"Yes," the king replied, "that decision
stands; it is an official law of the Medes
and Persians that cannot be revoked."
¹³Then they told the king, "That man
Daniel, one of the captives from Judah, is
ignoring you and your law. He still prays to
his God three times a day."

¹⁴Hearing this, the king was deeply
troubled, and he tried to think of a way to
save Daniel. He spent the rest of the day
looking for a way to get Daniel out of this
predicament.

¹⁵In the evening the men went together
to the king and said, "Your Majesty, you
know that according to the law of the
Medes and the Persians, no law that the
king signs can be changed."

¹⁶So at last the king gave orders for
Daniel to be arrested and thrown into the
den of lions. The king said to him, "May
your God, whom you serve so faithfully,
rescue you."

¹⁷A stone was brought and placed over
the mouth of the den. The king sealed the

stone with his own royal seal and the seals of his nobles, so that no one could rescue Daniel. [18]Then the king returned to his palace and spent the night fasting. He refused his usual entertainment and couldn't sleep at all that night.

[19]Very early the next morning, the king got up and hurried out to the lions' den. [20]When he got there, he called out in anguish, "Daniel, servant of the living God! Was your God, whom you serve so faithfully, able to rescue you from the lions?"

[21]Daniel answered, "Long live the king! [22]My God sent his angel to shut the lions' mouths so that they would not hurt me, for I have been found innocent in his sight. And I have not wronged you, Your Majesty."

[23]The king was overjoyed and ordered that Daniel be lifted from the den. Not a scratch was found on him, for he had trusted in his God.

[24]Then the king gave orders to arrest the men who had maliciously accused Daniel. He had them thrown into the lions' den, along with their wives and children. The lions leaped on them and tore them apart before they even hit the floor of the den.

[25]Then King Darius sent this message to the people of every race and nation and language throughout the world:

"Peace and prosperity to you!

[26]"I decree that everyone throughout my kingdom should tremble with fear before the God of Daniel.

For he is the living God,
    and he will endure forever.
His kingdom will never be
    destroyed,
    and his rule will never end.
[27] He rescues and saves his people;
    he performs miraculous signs
        and wonders
    in the heavens and on earth.
He has rescued Daniel
    from the power of the lions."

[28]So Daniel prospered during the reign of Darius and the reign of Cyrus the Persian.*

6:1 Verses 6:1-28 are numbered 6:2-29 in Aramaic text.
6:28 Or *of Darius, that is, the reign of Cyrus the Persian.*

2 PETER 3:1-18
Christ will one day return to set up his kingdom on earth. That is a fact. Believers in every generation are to remain vigilant—that is, live a godly life of obedience—as they wait for that glorious event.

This is my second letter to you, dear friends, and in both of them I [Peter] have tried to stimulate your wholesome thinking and refresh your memory. [2]I want you to remember what the holy prophets said long ago and what our Lord and Savior commanded through your apostles.

[3]Most importantly, I want to remind you that in the last days scoffers will come, mocking the truth and following their own desires. [4]They will say, "What happened to the promise that Jesus is coming again? From before the times of our ancestors, everything has remained the same since the world was first created."

[5]They deliberately forget that God made the heavens by the word of his command, and he brought the earth out from the water and surrounded it with water. [6]Then he used the water to destroy the ancient world with a mighty flood. [7]And by the same word, the present heavens and earth have been stored up for fire. They are being kept for the day of judgment, when ungodly people will be destroyed.

[8]But you must not forget this one thing, dear friends: A day is like a thousand years to the Lord, and a thousand years is like a day. [9]The Lord isn't really being slow about his promise, as some people think. No, he is being patient for your sake. He does not want anyone to be destroyed, but wants everyone to repent. [10]But the day of the Lord will come as unexpectedly as a thief. Then the heavens will pass away with a terrible noise, and the very elements themselves will disappear in fire, and the earth and everything on it will be found to deserve judgment.*

[11]Since everything around us is going to be destroyed like this, what holy and godly lives you should live, [12]looking forward to the day of God and hurrying it along. On that day, he will set the heavens on fire, and the elements will melt away in the flames. [13]But we are looking forward to the new heavens and new earth he has promised, a world filled with God's righteousness.

¹⁴And so, dear friends, while you are waiting for these things to happen, make every effort to be found living peaceful lives that are pure and blameless in his sight. ¹⁵And remember, the Lord's patience gives people time to be saved. This is what our beloved brother Paul also wrote to you with the wisdom God gave him— ¹⁶speaking of these things in all of his letters. Some of his comments are hard to understand, and those who are ignorant and unstable have twisted his letters to mean something quite different, just as they do with other parts of Scripture. And this will result in their destruction.

¹⁷I am warning you ahead of time, dear friends. Be on guard so that you will not be carried away by the errors of these wicked people and lose your own secure footing. ¹⁸Rather, you must grow in the grace and knowledge of our Lord and Savior Jesus Christ.

All glory to him, both now and forever! Amen.

3:10 Other manuscripts read *will be burned up;* still others read *will be found destroyed.*

PSALM 119:129-152

Pe

¹²⁹**Y**our [the LORD's] laws are wonderful.
　　No wonder I obey them!

¹³⁰The teaching of your word gives light,
　　so even the simple can understand.
¹³¹I pant with expectation,
　　longing for your commands.
¹³²Come and show me your mercy,
　　as you do for all who love your name.
¹³³Guide my steps by your word,
　　so I will not be overcome by evil.
¹³⁴Ransom me from the oppression of
　　evil people;
　　then I can obey your
　　commandments.
¹³⁵Look upon me with love;
　　teach me your decrees.
¹³⁶Rivers of tears gush from my eyes
　　because people disobey your
　　instructions.

Tsadhe

¹³⁷O LORD, you are righteous,
　　and your regulations are fair.
¹³⁸Your laws are perfect
　　and completely trustworthy.
¹³⁹I am overwhelmed with indignation,
　　for my enemies have disregarded
　　your words.
¹⁴⁰Your promises have been thoroughly
　　tested;
　　that is why I love them so much.
¹⁴¹I am insignificant and despised,
　　but I don't forget your
　　commandments.

HOW WE LIVE

Our work

DANIEL 6:1-28 Daniel made enemies among his peers all because he did his job well. At the time of this story, Daniel was more than eighty years old and one of King Darius' top officials. He had received this position of authority because he worked efficiently, diligently, and responsibly. Yet Daniel was not in "full-time ministry"—he was in as secular a place as could be imagined—the court of King Darius (having already served under two other kings). He had been placed in that position for a reason. He served well, he was honored for his abilities, the kings promoted him, and all the while he remained true to his principles—but not without incident, as this story illustrates. He had excelled, and some jealous coworkers schemed to get him killed. He stayed faithful, and as happened with King Nebuchadnezzar, Daniel's faith once again had an impact on a world leader. • So what's your job like? Tough boss? Tough coworkers? Think of Daniel. Work hard, work well, and stay true to your faith. God has you right where you are for a reason. You never know who might be impacted by the way you do your job.

142 Your justice is eternal,
   and your instructions are perfectly
   true.
143 As pressure and stress bear down
   on me,
   I find joy in your commands.
144 Your laws are always right;
   help me to understand them so
   I may live.

Qoph

145 I pray with all my heart; answer me,
   LORD!
   I will obey your decrees.
146 I cry out to you; rescue me,
   that I may obey your laws.
147 I rise early, before the sun is up;
   I cry out for help and put my hope
   in your words.

148 I stay awake through the night,
   thinking about your promise.
149 In your faithful love, O LORD, hear
   my cry;
   let me be revived by following your
   regulations.
150 Lawless people are coming to attack
   me;
   they live far from your instructions.
151 But you are near, O LORD,
   and all your commands are true.
152 I have known from my earliest days
   that your laws will last forever.

PROVERBS 28:21-22

Showing partiality is never good, yet some
will do wrong for a mere piece of bread.
□ Greedy people try to get rich quick but
don't realize they're headed for poverty.

NOVEMBER**30**

DANIEL 7:1-28

Daniel was a trustworthy individual. The king of
Babylon entrusted him with significant responsibilities in his kingdom. God trusted him to record revelations about the future.

Earlier, during the first year of King Belshazzar's reign in Babylon,* Daniel had a
dream and saw visions as he lay in his bed.
He wrote down the dream, and this is
what he saw.

2 In my vision that night, I, Daniel, saw a
great storm churning the surface of a
great sea, with strong winds blowing from
every direction. 3 Then four huge beasts
came up out of the water, each different
from the others.

4 The first beast was like a lion with eagles' wings. As I watched, its wings were
pulled off, and it was left standing with its
two hind feet on the ground, like a human
being. And it was given a human mind.

5 Then I saw a second beast, and it looked
like a bear. It was rearing up on one side,
and it had three ribs in its mouth between
its teeth. And I heard a voice saying to it,
"Get up! Devour the flesh of many people!"

6 Then the third of these strange beasts
appeared, and it looked like a leopard. It
had four bird's wings on its back, and it
had four heads. Great authority was given
to this beast.

7 Then in my vision that night, I saw a
fourth beast—terrifying, dreadful, and
very strong. It devoured and crushed its
victims with huge iron teeth and trampled their remains beneath its feet. It was
different from any of the other beasts,
and it had ten horns.

8 As I was looking at the horns, suddenly
another small horn appeared among
them. Three of the first horns were torn
out by the roots to make room for it. This
little horn had eyes like human eyes and a
mouth that was boasting arrogantly.

9 I watched as thrones were put in place
   and the Ancient One* sat down
   to judge.
His clothing was as white as snow,
   his hair like purest wool.
He sat on a fiery throne
   with wheels of blazing fire,

¹⁰ and a river of fire was pouring out,
   flowing from his presence.
Millions of angels ministered to him;
   many millions stood to attend him.
Then the court began its session,
   and the books were opened.

¹¹I continued to watch because I could hear the little horn's boastful speech. I kept watching until the fourth beast was killed and its body was destroyed by fire. ¹²The other three beasts had their authority taken from them, but they were allowed to live a while longer.*

¹³As my vision continued that night, I saw someone like a son of man* coming with the clouds of heaven. He approached the Ancient One and was led into his presence. ¹⁴He was given authority, honor, and sovereignty over all the nations of the world, so that people of every race and nation and language would obey him. His rule is eternal—it will never end. His kingdom will never be destroyed.

¹⁵I, Daniel, was troubled by all I had seen, and my visions terrified me. ¹⁶So I approached one of those standing beside the throne and asked him what it all meant. He explained it to me like this: ¹⁷"These four huge beasts represent four kingdoms that will arise from the earth. ¹⁸But in the end, the holy people of the Most High will be given the kingdom, and they will rule forever and ever."

¹⁹Then I wanted to know the true meaning of the fourth beast, the one so different from the others and so terrifying. It had devoured and crushed its victims with iron teeth and bronze claws, trampling their remains beneath its feet. ²⁰I also asked about the ten horns on the fourth beast's head and the little horn that came up afterward and destroyed three of the other horns. This horn had seemed greater than the others, and it had human eyes and a mouth that was boasting arrogantly. ²¹As I watched, this horn was waging war against God's holy people and was defeating them, ²²until the Ancient One—the Most High—came and judged in favor of his holy people. Then the time arrived for the holy people to take over the kingdom.

²³Then he said to me, "This fourth beast is the fourth world power that will rule the earth. It will be different from all the others. It will devour the whole world, trampling and crushing everything in its path. ²⁴Its ten horns are ten kings who will rule that empire. Then another king will arise, different from the other ten, who will subdue three of them. ²⁵He will defy the Most High and oppress the holy people of the Most High. He will try to change their sacred festivals and laws, and they will be placed under his control for a time, times, and half a time.

²⁶But then the court will pass judgment, and all his power will be taken away and completely destroyed. ²⁷Then the sovereignty, power, and greatness of all

HOW WE LIVE

Confessing our sins

1 JOHN 1:9 When you were born again, God forgave all of your sins and your salvation was secured. However, because you will keep sinning (you're human), sin that isn't dealt with can drive a wedge between you and God. • Some people are so guilt-ridden over sins from their past that they feel the need to confess the same sins over and over. Others are fearful that if they don't name each individual sin, they might forget one and not receive forgiveness. Neither approach is correct. Instead, you need to come to God on a daily basis, pray, and ask God to show you any areas of sin that you need to confess (unless you already know!). Then tell God you're sorry and ask him to forgive you. When we confess, he assures us of forgiveness and cleansing! With your sin forgiven and out of the picture, your conscience is clear and you are free to enjoy fellowship with Christ.

the kingdoms under heaven will be given to the holy people of the Most High. His kingdom will last forever, and all rulers will serve and obey him."

²⁸That was the end of the vision. I, Daniel, was terrified by my thoughts and my face was pale with fear, but I kept these things to myself.

7:1 The first year of Belshazzar's reign (who was co-regent with his father, Nabonidus) was 556 B.C. (or perhaps as late as 553 B.C.).   7:9 Aramaic *an Ancient of Days;* also in 7:13, 22.   7:12 Aramaic *for a season and a time.*   7:13 Or *like a Son of Man.*

1 JOHN 1:1-10

The apostle John wrote the next three letters in addition to the Gospel of John and the book of Revelation. First John is packed with practical advice concerning what it means to follow Jesus.

We proclaim to you the one who existed from the beginning,* whom we have heard and seen. We saw him with our own eyes and touched him with our own hands. He is the Word of life. ²This one who is life itself was revealed to us, and we have seen him. And now we testify and proclaim to you that he is the one who is eternal life. He was with the Father, and then he was revealed to us. ³We proclaim to you what we ourselves have actually seen and heard so that you may have fellowship with us. And our fellowship is with the Father and with his Son, Jesus Christ. ⁴We are writing these things so that you may fully share our joy.*

⁵This is the message we heard from Jesus* and now declare to you: God is light, and there is no darkness in him at all. ⁶So we are lying if we say we have fellowship with God but go on living in spiritual darkness; we are not practicing the truth. ⁷But if we are living in the light, as God is in the light, then we have fellowship with each other, and the blood of Jesus, his Son, cleanses us from all sin.

⁸If we claim we have no sin, we are only fooling ourselves and not living in the truth. ⁹But if we confess our sins to him, he is faithful and just to forgive us our sins and to cleanse us from all wickedness. ¹⁰If we claim we have not sinned, we are calling God a liar and showing that his word has no place in our hearts.

1:1 Greek *What was from the beginning.*   1:4 Or *so that our joy may be complete;* some manuscripts read *your joy.*   1:5 Greek *from him.*

PSALM 119:153-176

Resh

¹⁵³ Look upon my suffering and rescue me,
    for I have not forgotten your
    [the LORD's] instructions.
¹⁵⁴ Argue my case; take my side!
    Protect my life as you promised.
¹⁵⁵ The wicked are far from rescue,
    for they do not bother with your
    decrees.
¹⁵⁶ LORD, how great is your mercy;
    let me be revived by following your
    regulations.
¹⁵⁷ Many persecute and trouble me,
    yet I have not swerved from
    your laws.
¹⁵⁸ Seeing these traitors makes me sick
    at heart,
    because they care nothing for
    your word.
¹⁵⁹ See how I love your commandments,
    LORD.
    Give back my life because of your
    unfailing love.
¹⁶⁰ The very essence of your words
    is truth;
    all your just regulations will stand
    forever.

Shin

¹⁶¹ Powerful people harass me without
    cause,
    but my heart trembles only at
    your word.
¹⁶² I rejoice in your word
    like one who discovers a great
    treasure.
¹⁶³ I hate and abhor all falsehood,
    but I love your instructions.
¹⁶⁴ I will praise you seven times a day
    because all your regulations
    are just.
¹⁶⁵ Those who love your instructions
    have great peace
    and do not stumble.
¹⁶⁶ I long for your rescue, LORD,
    so I have obeyed your commands.
¹⁶⁷ I have obeyed your laws,
    for I love them very much.

168 Yes, I obey your commandments
and laws
because you know everything I do.

Taw

169 O LORD, listen to my cry;
give me the discerning mind you
promised.
170 Listen to my prayer;
rescue me as you promised.
171 Let praise flow from my lips,
for you have taught me your
decrees.
172 Let my tongue sing about your word,
for all your commands are right.
173 Give me a helping hand,
for I have chosen to follow your
commandments.

174 O LORD, I have longed for your rescue,
and your instructions are my
delight.
175 Let me live so I can praise you,
and may your regulations help me.
176 I have wandered away like a lost
sheep;
come and find me,
for I have not forgotten your
commands.

PROVERBS 28:23-24

In the end, people appreciate honest criticism far more than flattery. □ Anyone who steals from his father and mother and says, "What's wrong with that?" is no better than a murderer.

168Yes, I obey your commandments
and laws
because you know everything I do.

Tav

169O LORD, listen to my cry;
give me the discerning mind you
promised.
170Listen to my prayer;
rescue me as you promised.
171Let praise flow from my lips,
for you have taught me your
decrees.
172Let my tongue sing about your word
for all your commands are right
173Give me a helping hand,
for I have chosen to follow your
commandments.

174O LORD, I have longed for your rescue
and your instructions are my
delight.
175Let me live so I can praise you,
and may your regulations help me.
176I have wandered away like a lost
sheep;
come and find me,
for I have not forgotten your
commands.

PROVERBS 28:23-24
In the end, people appreciate honest criticism far more than flattery. Anyone
who steals from his father and mother
and says, "What's wrong with that?" is no
better than a murderer.

DANIEL 8:1-27

Have you ever had a troubling dream or a *what if?* thought that left you feeling unsettled? The vision described in today's reading left Daniel distraught and exhausted.

¹***D**uring the third year of King Belshazzar's reign, I, Daniel, saw another vision, following the one that had already appeared to me. ²In this vision I was at the fortress of Susa, in the province of Elam, standing beside the Ulai River.*

³As I looked up, I saw a ram with two long horns standing beside the river.* One of the horns was longer than the other, even though it had grown later than the other one. ⁴The ram butted everything out of his way to the west, to the north, and to the south, and no one could stand against him or help his victims. He did as he pleased and became very great.

⁵While I was watching, suddenly a male goat appeared from the west, crossing the land so swiftly that he didn't even touch the ground. This goat, which had one very large horn between its eyes, ⁶headed toward the two-horned ram that I had seen standing beside the river, rushing at him in a rage. ⁷The goat charged furiously at the ram and struck him, breaking off both his horns. Now the ram was helpless, and the goat knocked him down and trampled him. No one could rescue the ram from the goat's power.

⁸The goat became very powerful. But at the height of his power, his large horn was broken off. In the large horn's place grew four prominent horns pointing in the four directions of the earth. ⁹Then from one of the prominent horns came a small horn whose power grew very great. It extended toward the south and the east and toward the glorious land of Israel. ¹⁰Its power reached to the heavens, where it attacked the heavenly army, throwing some of the heavenly beings and some of the stars to the ground and trampling them. ¹¹It even challenged the Commander of heaven's army by canceling the daily sacrifices offered to him and by destroying his Temple. ¹²The army of heaven was restrained from responding to this rebellion. So the daily sacrifice was halted, and truth was overthrown. The horn succeeded in everything it did.*

HOW WE LIVE

Following Jesus

1 JOHN 2:3-6 Following Jesus means living as Jesus did. How do we do that? John was pretty clear. For him, it came down to obedience. If we love God, then we obey him. While that can sound a little cut and dried, there is something wonderful in knowing that each act of obedience has meaning. Even the most unnoticed act—the honest claim on our tax return, the extra twenty dollars we return to the bank teller who mistakenly gave us too much cash, the act of kindness that no one saw, the forgiveness we find in our heart for someone who absentmindedly wounded us—can be a meaningful expression of love for God. • Obeying God isn't about keeping rules; it's about honoring your relationship with him. It's about understanding that God is the source of any light and life in your existence. When you show your love for God by your obedience, you are following Jesus—living as he lived.

¹³Then I heard two holy ones talking to each other. One of them asked, "How long will the events of this vision last? How long will the rebellion that causes desecration stop the daily sacrifices? How long will the Temple and heaven's army be trampled on?"

¹⁴The other replied, "It will take 2,300 evenings and mornings; then the Temple will be made right again."

¹⁵As I, Daniel, was trying to understand the meaning of this vision, someone who looked like a man stood in front of me. ¹⁶And I heard a human voice calling out from the Ulai River, "Gabriel, tell this man the meaning of his vision."

¹⁷As Gabriel approached the place where I was standing, I became so terrified that I fell with my face to the ground. "Son of man," he said, "you must understand that the events you have seen in your vision relate to the time of the end."

¹⁸While he was speaking, I fainted and lay there with my face to the ground. But Gabriel roused me with a touch and helped me to my feet.

¹⁹Then he said, "I am here to tell you what will happen later in the time of wrath. What you have seen pertains to the very end of time. ²⁰The two-horned ram represents the kings of Media and Persia. ²¹The shaggy male goat represents the king of Greece,* and the large horn between his eyes represents the first king of the Greek Empire. ²²The four prominent horns that replaced the one large horn show that the Greek Empire will break into four kingdoms, but none as great as the first.

²³"At the end of their rule, when their sin is at its height, a fierce king, a master of intrigue, will rise to power. ²⁴He will become very strong, but not by his own power. He will cause a shocking amount of destruction and succeed in everything he does. He will destroy powerful leaders and devastate the holy people. ²⁵He will be a master of deception and will become arrogant; he will destroy many without warning. He will even take on the Prince of princes in battle, but he will be broken, though not by human power.

²⁶"This vision about the 2,300 evenings and mornings* is true. But none of

these things will happen for a long time, so keep this vision a secret."

²⁷Then I, Daniel, was overcome and lay sick for several days. Afterward I got up and performed my duties for the king, but I was greatly troubled by the vision and could not understand it.

8:1 The original text from this point through chapter 12 is in Hebrew. See note at 2:4.   **8:2** Or *the Ulai Gate;* also in 8:16.   **8:3** Or *the gate;* also in 8:6.   **8:11-12** The meaning of the Hebrew for these verses is uncertain.   **8:21** Hebrew *of Javan.*   **8:26** Hebrew *about the evenings and mornings;* compare 8:14.

1 JOHN 2:1-17

The apostle John used a fatherly tone, calling his audience "my dear children." This was appropriate because John was a wise, experienced pastor addressing his spiritual children.

My dear children, I [John] am writing this to you so that you will not sin. But if anyone does sin, we have an advocate who pleads our case before the Father. He is Jesus Christ, the one who is truly righteous. ²He himself is the sacrifice that atones for our sins—and not only our sins but the sins of all the world.

³And we can be sure that we know him if we obey his commandments. ⁴If someone claims, "I know God," but doesn't obey God's commandments, that person is a liar and is not living in the truth. ⁵But those who obey God's word truly show how completely they love him. That is how we know we are living in him. ⁶Those who say they live in God should live their lives as Jesus did.

⁷Dear friends, I am not writing a new commandment for you; rather it is an old one you have had from the very beginning. This old commandment—to love one another—is the same message you heard before. ⁸Yet it is also new. Jesus lived the truth of this commandment, and you also are living it. For the darkness is disappearing, and the true light is already shining.

⁹If anyone claims, "I am living in the light," but hates a Christian brother or sister,* that person is still living in darkness. ¹⁰Anyone who loves another brother or sister* is living in the light and does not cause others to stumble. ¹¹But anyone who hates another brother or sister is still living and walking in darkness. Such a

person does not know the way to go, having been blinded by the darkness.

12 I am writing to you who are God's children
   because your sins have been forgiven through Jesus.*
13 I am writing to you who are mature in the faith*
   because you know Christ, who existed from the beginning.
I am writing to you who are young in the faith
   because you have won your battle with the evil one.
14 I have written to you who are God's children
   because you know the Father.
I have written to you who are mature in the faith
   because you know Christ, who existed from the beginning.
I have written to you who are young in the faith
   because you are strong.
God's word lives in your hearts,
   and you have won your battle with the evil one.

15Do not love this world nor the things it offers you, for when you love the world, you do not have the love of the Father in you. 16For the world offers only a craving for physical pleasure, a craving for everything we see, and pride in our achievements and possessions. These are not from the Father, but are from this world. 17And this world is fading away, along with everything that people crave. But anyone who does what pleases God will live forever.

2:9 Greek *hates his brother;* similarly in 2:11.   **2:10** Greek *loves his brother.*   **2:12** Greek *through his name.*   **2:13** Or *to you fathers;* also in 2:14.

PSALM 120:1-7
A song for pilgrims ascending to Jerusalem.

1 I took my troubles to the LORD;
   I cried out to him, and he answered my prayer.
2 Rescue me, O LORD, from liars
   and from all deceitful people.
3 O deceptive tongue, what will God do to you?
   How will he increase your punishment?
4 You will be pierced with sharp arrows
   and burned with glowing coals.

5 How I suffer in far-off Meshech.
   It pains me to live in distant Kedar.
6 I am tired of living
   among people who hate peace.
7 I search for peace;
   but when I speak of peace, they want war!

PROVERBS 28:25-26
Greed causes fighting; trusting the LORD leads to prosperity. □ Those who trust their own insight are foolish, but anyone who walks in wisdom is safe.

DECEMBER**2**

DANIEL 9:1-11:1
This is Daniel's final vision, giving further insight into the great spiritual battle between God's people and those who want to destroy them. Daniel was frightened by the vision, but the heavenly messenger reassured him.

It was the first year of the reign of Darius the Mede, the son of Ahasuerus, who became king of the Babylonians.* 2During the first year of his reign, I, Daniel, learned from reading the word of the LORD, as revealed to Jeremiah the prophet, that Jerusalem must lie desolate for seventy years.* 3So I turned to the LORD God and pleaded with him in prayer and fasting. I also wore rough burlap and sprinkled myself with ashes.

4I prayed to the LORD my God and confessed:

"O Lord, you are a great and awesome God! You always fulfill your covenant and keep your promises of unfailing love to those who love you and obey your commands. ⁵But we have sinned and done wrong. We have rebelled against you and scorned your commands and regulations. ⁶We have refused to listen to your servants the prophets, who spoke on your authority to our kings and princes and ancestors and to all the people of the land.

⁷"Lord, you are in the right; but as you see, our faces are covered with shame. This is true of all of us, including the people of Judah and Jerusalem and all Israel, scattered near and far, wherever you have driven us because of our disloyalty to you. ⁸O LORD, we and our kings, princes, and ancestors are covered with shame because we have sinned against you. ⁹But the Lord our God is merciful and forgiving, even though we have rebelled against him. ¹⁰We have not obeyed the LORD our God, for we have not followed the instructions he gave us through his servants the prophets. ¹¹All Israel has disobeyed your instruction and turned away, refusing to listen to your voice.

"So now the solemn curses and judgments written in the Law of Moses, the servant of God, have been poured down on us because of our sin. ¹²You have kept your word and done to us and our rulers exactly as you warned. Never has there been such a disaster as happened in Jerusalem. ¹³Every curse written against us in the Law of Moses has come true. Yet we have refused to seek mercy from the LORD our God by turning from our sins and recognizing his truth. ¹⁴Therefore, the LORD has brought upon us the disaster he prepared. The LORD our God was right to do all of these things, for we did not obey him.

¹⁵"O Lord our God, you brought lasting honor to your name by rescuing your people from Egypt in a great display of power. But we have sinned and are full of wickedness. ¹⁶In view of all your faithful mercies, Lord, please turn your furious anger away from your city Jerusalem, your holy mountain. All the neighboring nations mock Jerusalem and your people because of our sins and the sins of our ancestors.

¹⁷"O our God, hear your servant's prayer! Listen as I plead. For your own sake, Lord, smile again on your desolate sanctuary.

¹⁸"O my God, lean down and listen to me. Open your eyes and see our despair. See how your city—the city that bears your name—lies in ruins. We make this plea, not because we deserve help, but because of your mercy.

¹⁹"O Lord, hear. O Lord, forgive. O Lord, listen and act! For your own sake, do not delay, O my God, for your people and your city bear your name."

²⁰I went on praying and confessing my sin and the sin of my people, pleading with the LORD my God for Jerusalem, his holy mountain. ²¹As I was praying, Gabriel, whom I had seen in the earlier vision, came swiftly to me at the time of the evening sacrifice. ²²He explained to me, "Daniel, I have come here to give you insight and understanding. ²³The moment you began praying, a command was given. And now I am here to tell you what it was, for you are very precious to God. Listen carefully so that you can understand the meaning of your vision.

²⁴"A period of seventy sets of seven* has been decreed for your people and your holy city to finish their rebellion, to put an end to their sin, to atone for their guilt, to bring in everlasting righteousness, to confirm the prophetic vision, and to anoint the Most Holy Place.* ²⁵Now listen and understand! Seven sets of seven plus sixty-two sets of seven* will pass from the time the command is given to rebuild Jerusalem until a ruler—the Anointed One*—comes. Jerusalem will be rebuilt with streets and strong defenses,* despite the perilous times.

²⁶"After this period of sixty-two sets of seven,* the Anointed One will be killed, appearing to have accomplished nothing, and a ruler will arise whose armies will destroy the city and the Temple. The end

will come with a flood, and war and its miseries are decreed from that time to the very end. [27] The ruler will make a treaty with the people for a period of one set of seven,* but after half this time, he will put an end to the sacrifices and offerings. And as a climax to all his terrible deeds,* he will set up a sacrilegious object that causes desecration,* until the fate decreed for this defiler is finally poured out on him."

[10:1] In the third year of the reign of King Cyrus of Persia,* Daniel (also known as Belteshazzar) had another vision. He understood that the vision concerned events certain to happen in the future—times of war and great hardship.

[2] When this vision came to me, I, Daniel, had been in mourning for three whole weeks. [3] All that time I had eaten no rich food. No meat or wine crossed my lips, and I used no fragrant lotions until those three weeks had passed.

[4] On April 23,* as I was standing on the bank of the great Tigris River, [5] I looked up and saw a man dressed in linen clothing, with a belt of pure gold around his waist. [6] His body looked like a precious gem. His face flashed like lightning, and his eyes flamed like torches. His arms and feet shone like polished bronze, and his voice roared like a vast multitude of people.

[7] Only I, Daniel, saw this vision. The men with me saw nothing, but they were suddenly terrified and ran away to hide. [8] So I was left there all alone to see this amazing vision. My strength left me, my face grew deathly pale, and I felt very weak. [9] Then I heard the man speak, and when I heard the sound of his voice, I fainted and lay there with my face to the ground.

[10] Just then a hand touched me and lifted me, still trembling, to my hands and knees. [11] And the man said to me, "Daniel, you are very precious to God, so listen carefully to what I have to say to you. Stand up, for I have been sent to you." When he said this to me, I stood up, still trembling.

[12] Then he said, "Don't be afraid, Daniel. Since the first day you began to pray for understanding and to humble yourself before your God, your request has been heard in heaven. I have come in answer to your prayer. [13] But for twenty-one days the spirit prince* of the kingdom of Persia blocked my way. Then Michael, one of the archangels,* came to help me, and I left him there with the spirit prince of the kingdom of Persia.* [14] Now I am here to explain what will happen to your people in the future, for this vision concerns a time yet to come."

[15] While he was speaking to me, I looked down at the ground, unable to say a

WHAT THE BIBLE SAYS

Angels

DANIEL 10:12-14 Daniel saw the spiritual battle between God's chosen people and the empires of the world that want to destroy them. He saw a man, but not an ordinary man. With a body like a precious stone, a face as bright as lightning, eyes like fire, and a voice with a deep roar—this was a powerful angel, sent to answer Daniel's prayer. These verses pull back the curtain on the spiritual world, giving us insight into the battles that go on between the forces of good and evil. This angel had been dispatched to bring an answer to Daniel, but had been blocked by a "spirit prince" (a powerful evil being) and had been unable to come for 21 days. When reinforcements arrived (in the form of the archangel Michael), the angel finally reached Daniel. • From this glimpse into the other world, we learn that angels are God's messengers. We also learn that they are involved in battles with the forces of evil. Hebrews 1:14 (October 30) reminds us that angels are carrying out their duties as a ministry to believers.

word. ¹⁶Then the one who looked like a man* touched my lips, and I opened my mouth and began to speak. I said to the one standing in front of me, "I am filled with anguish because of the vision I have seen, my lord, and I am very weak. ¹⁷How can someone like me, your servant, talk to you, my lord? My strength is gone, and I can hardly breathe."

¹⁸Then the one who looked like a man touched me again, and I felt my strength returning. ¹⁹"Don't be afraid," he said, "for you are very precious to God. Peace! Be encouraged! Be strong!"

As he spoke these words to me, I suddenly felt stronger and said to him, "Please speak to me, my lord, for you have strengthened me."

²⁰He replied, "Do you know why I have come? Soon I must return to fight against the spirit prince of the kingdom of Persia, and after that the spirit prince of the kingdom of Greece* will come. ²¹Meanwhile, I will tell you what is written in the Book of Truth. (No one helps me against these spirit princes except Michael, your spirit prince.* ^{11:1}I have been standing beside Michael* to support and strengthen him since the first year of the reign of Darius the Mede.)"

9:1 Or *the Chaldeans.* 9:2 See Jer 25:11-12; 29:10. 9:24a Hebrew *seventy sevens.* 9:24b Or *the Most Holy One.* 9:25a Hebrew *Seven sevens plus sixty-two sevens.* 9:25b Or *an anointed one;* similarly in 9:26. Hebrew reads *a messiah.* 9:25c Or *and a moat,* or *and trenches.* 9:26 Hebrew *After sixty-two sevens.* 9:27a Hebrew *for one seven.* 9:27b Hebrew *And on the wing of abominations;* the meaning of the Hebrew is uncertain. 9:27c Hebrew *an abomination of desolation.* 10:1 The third year of Cyrus's reign was 536 B.C. 10:4 Hebrew *On the twenty-fourth day of the first month,* of the ancient Hebrew lunar calendar. This date in the book of Daniel can be cross-checked with dates in surviving Persian records and can be related accurately to our modern calendar. This event occurred on April 23, 536 B.C. 10:13a Hebrew *the prince;* also in 10:13c, 20. 10:13b Hebrew *the chief princes.* 10:13c As in one Greek version; Hebrew reads *and I was left there with the kings of Persia.* The meaning of the Hebrew is uncertain. 10:16 As in most manuscripts of the Masoretic Text; one manuscript of the Masoretic Text and one Greek version read *Then something that looked like a human hand.* 10:20 Hebrew *of Javan.* 10:21 Hebrew *against these except Michael, your prince.* 11:1 Hebrew *him.*

1 JOHN 2:18–3:6
Like other New Testament writers, John had to contend for the truth of the Christian faith in light of false teachers.

Dear children, the last hour is here. You have heard that the Antichrist is coming,

and already many such antichrists have appeared. From this we know that the last hour has come. ¹⁹These people left our churches, but they never really belonged with us; otherwise they would have stayed with us. When they left, it proved that they did not belong with us.

²⁰But you are not like that, for the Holy One has given you his Spirit,* and all of you know the truth. ²¹So I am writing to you not because you don't know the truth but because you know the difference between truth and lies. ²²And who is a liar? Anyone who says that Jesus is not the Christ.* Anyone who denies the Father and the Son is an antichrist.* ²³Anyone who denies the Son doesn't have the Father, either. But anyone who acknowledges the Son has the Father also.

²⁴So you must remain faithful to what you have been taught from the beginning. If you do, you will remain in fellowship with the Son and with the Father. ²⁵And in this fellowship we enjoy the eternal life he promised us.

²⁶I am writing these things to warn you about those who want to lead you astray. ²⁷But you have received the Holy Spirit,* and he lives within you, so you don't need anyone to teach you what is true. For the Spirit* teaches you everything you need to know, and what he teaches is true—it is not a lie. So just as he has taught you, remain in fellowship with Christ.

²⁸And now, dear children, remain in fellowship with Christ so that when he returns, you will be full of courage and not shrink back from him in shame.

²⁹Since we know that Christ is righteous, we also know that all who do what is right are God's children.

^{3:1}SEE how very much our Father loves us, for he calls us his children, and that is what we are! But the people who belong to this world don't recognize that we are God's children because they don't know him. ²Dear friends, we are already God's children, but he has not yet shown us what we will be like when Christ appears. But we do know that we will be like him, for we will see him as he really is. ³And all who have this eager expectation will keep themselves pure, just as he is pure.

⁴Everyone who sins is breaking God's law, for all sin is contrary to the law of God. ⁵And you know that Jesus came to take away our sins, and there is no sin in him. ⁶Anyone who continues to live in him will not sin. But anyone who keeps on sinning does not know him or understand who he is.

2:20 Greek *But you have an anointing from the Holy One.* **2:22a** Or *not the Messiah.* **2:22b** Or *the antichrist.* **2:27a** Greek *the anointing from him.* **2:27b** Greek *the anointing.*

PSALM 121:1-8
A song for pilgrims ascending to Jerusalem.

¹ I look up to the mountains—
    does my help come from there?
² My help comes from the LORD,
    who made heaven and earth!

³ He will not let you stumble;
    the one who watches over you will
    not slumber.

⁴ Indeed, he who watches over
        Israel
    never slumbers or sleeps.

⁵ The LORD himself watches over you!
    The LORD stands beside you as your
        protective shade.
⁶ The sun will not harm you by day,
    nor the moon at night.

⁷ The LORD keeps you from all harm
    and watches over your life.
⁸ The LORD keeps watch over you as you
        come and go,
    both now and forever.

PROVERBS 28:27-28
Whoever gives to the poor will lack nothing, but those who close their eyes to poverty will be cursed. □ When the wicked take charge, people go into hiding. When the wicked meet disaster, the godly flourish.

DECEMBER**3**

DANIEL 11:2-35
Part of what makes apocalyptic literature challenging is the blending of actual events with symbolic descriptions of events. These visions could be interpreted many ways. The bottom line is that no matter the strength of evil, God will prevail.

"Now then, I will reveal the truth to you. Three more Persian kings will reign, to be succeeded by a fourth, far richer than the others. He will use his wealth to stir up everyone to fight against the kingdom of Greece.*

³"Then a mighty king will rise to power who will rule with great authority and accomplish everything he sets out to do. ⁴But at the height of his power, his kingdom will be broken apart and divided into four parts. It will not be ruled by the king's descendants, nor will the kingdom hold the authority it once had. For his empire will be uprooted and given to others.

⁵"The king of the south will increase in power, but one of his own officials will become more powerful than he and will rule his kingdom with great strength.

⁶"Some years later an alliance will be formed between the king of the north and the king of the south. The daughter of the king of the south will be given in marriage to the king of the north to secure the alliance, but she will lose her influence over him, and so will her father. She will be abandoned along with her supporters. ⁷But when one of her relatives* becomes king of the south, he will raise an army and enter the fortress of the king of the north and defeat him. ⁸When he returns to Egypt, he will carry back their idols with him, along with priceless articles of gold and silver. For some years afterward he will leave the king of the north alone.

⁹"Later the king of the north will invade the realm of the king of the south but will soon return to his own land. ¹⁰However,

the sons of the king of the north will assemble a mighty army that will advance like a flood and carry the battle as far as the enemy's fortress.

11"Then, in a rage, the king of the south will rally against the vast forces assembled by the king of the north and will defeat them. 12After the enemy army is swept away, the king of the south will be filled with pride and will execute many thousands of his enemies. But his success will be short lived.

13"A few years later the king of the north will return with a fully equipped army far greater than before. 14At that time there will be a general uprising against the king of the south. Violent men among your own people will join them in fulfillment of this vision, but they will not succeed. 15Then the king of the north will come and lay siege to a fortified city and capture it. The best troops of the south will not be able to stand in the face of the onslaught.

16"The king of the north will march onward unopposed; none will be able to stop him. He will pause in the glorious land of Israel,* intent on destroying it. 17He will make plans to come with the might of his entire kingdom and will form an alliance with the king of the south. He will give him a daughter in marriage in order to overthrow the kingdom from within, but his plan will fail.

18"After this, he will turn his attention to the coastland and conquer many cities. But a commander from another land will put an end to his insolence and cause him to retreat in shame. 19He will take refuge in his own fortresses but will stumble and fall and be seen no more.

20"His successor will send out a tax collector to maintain the royal splendor. But after a very brief reign, he will die, though not from anger or in battle.

21"The next to come to power will be a despicable man who is not in line for royal succession. He will slip in when least expected and take over the kingdom by flattery and intrigue. 22Before him great armies will be swept away, including a covenant prince. 23With deceitful promises, he will make various alliances. He will become strong despite having only a handful of followers. 24Without

warning he will enter the richest areas of the land. Then he will distribute among his followers the plunder and wealth of the rich—something his predecessors had never done. He will plot the overthrow of strongholds, but this will last for only a short while.

25"Then he will stir up his courage and raise a great army against the king of the south. The king of the south will go to battle with a mighty army, but to no avail, for there will be plots against him. 26His own household will cause his downfall. His army will be swept away, and many will be killed. 27Seeking nothing but each other's harm, these kings will plot against each other at the conference table, attempting to deceive each other. But it will make no difference, for the end will come at the appointed time.

28"The king of the north will then return home with great riches. On the way he will set himself against the people of the holy covenant, doing much damage before continuing his journey.

29"Then at the appointed time he will once again invade the south, but this time the result will be different. 30For warships from western coastlands* will scare him off, and he will withdraw and return home. But he will vent his anger against the people of the holy covenant and reward those who forsake the covenant.

31"His army will take over the Temple fortress, pollute the sanctuary, put a stop to the daily sacrifices, and set up the sacrilegious object that causes desecration.* 32He will flatter and win over those who have violated the covenant. But the people who know their God will be strong and will resist him.

33"Wise leaders will give instruction to many, but these teachers will die by fire and sword, or they will be jailed and robbed. 34During these persecutions, little help will arrive, and many who join them will not be sincere. 35And some of the wise will fall victim to persecution. In this way, they will be refined and cleansed and made pure until the time of the end, for the appointed time is still to come."

11:2 Hebrew *of Javan.* 11:7 Hebrew *a branch from her roots.* 11:16 Hebrew *the glorious land.* 11:30 Hebrew *from Kittim.* 11:31 Hebrew *the abomination of desolation.*

1 JOHN 3:7-24
In today's reading John points out a profound truth: our love for others and our love for God are directly related.

Dear children, don't let anyone deceive you about this: When people do what is right, it shows that they are righteous, even as Christ is righteous. [8]But when people keep on sinning, it shows that they belong to the devil, who has been sinning since the beginning. But the Son of God came to destroy the works of the devil. [9]Those who have been born into God's family do not make a practice of sinning, because God's life* is in them. So they can't keep on sinning, because they are children of God. [10]So now we can tell who are children of God and who are children of the devil. Anyone who does not live righteously and does not love other believers* does not belong to God.

[11]This is the message you have heard from the beginning: We should love one another. [12]We must not be like Cain, who belonged to the evil one and killed his brother. And why did he kill him? Because Cain had been doing what was evil, and his brother had been doing what was righteous. [13]So don't be surprised, dear brothers and sisters,* if the world hates you.

[14]If we love our Christian brothers and sisters,* it proves that we have passed from death to life. But a person who has no love is still dead. [15]Anyone who hates another brother or sister* is really a murderer at heart. And you know that murderers don't have eternal life within them.

[16]We know what real love is because Jesus gave up his life for us. So we also ought to give up our lives for our brothers and sisters. [17]If someone has enough money to live well and sees a brother or sister* in need but shows no compassion— how can God's love be in that person?

[18]Dear children, let's not merely say that we love each other; let us show the truth by our actions. [19]Our actions will show that we belong to the truth, so we will be confident when we stand before God. [20]Even if we feel guilty, God is greater than our feelings, and he knows everything.

[21]Dear friends, if we don't feel guilty, we can come to God with bold confidence. [22]And we will receive from him whatever we ask because we obey him and do the things that please him.

[23]And this is his commandment: We must believe in the name of his Son, Jesus Christ, and love one another, just as he commanded us. [24]Those who obey God's commandments remain in fellowship with him, and he with them. And we know he lives in us because the Spirit he gave us lives in us.

HOW WE LIVE

Obeying God

1 JOHN 3:9 At first reading you may wonder how to interpret this verse because you know that you sin every day. And you will continue to battle sin, as does every believer. So what does this verse mean? The key is in the phrases "practice of sinning" and "keep on sinning." John is telling all Christians that, because they have the Spirit of God within them, they should not make a habit of sinful actions or thoughts or become indifferent to God's moral law. All believers sin, but they are working to gain victory over sin by overcoming temptation and becoming more like Christ. They shouldn't continue to fall into the same temptations over and over if they are truly new creations in Christ. • When you became a Christian, God forgave and accepted you into his family, and the Holy Spirit began to help you become more like Christ. When a difficult situation arises, ask yourself, "What would Jesus do?" Using the knowledge you have gained from reading the Bible and listening to your pastor, you should have an insight into how best to obey God.

3:9 Greek *because his seed.*   3:10 Greek *does not love his brother.*   3:13 Greek *brothers.*   3:14 Greek *the brothers;* similarly in 3:16.   3:15 Greek *hates his brother.* 3:17 Greek *sees his brother.*

PSALM 122:1-9
A song for pilgrims ascending to Jerusalem. A psalm of David.

¹ **I** was glad when they said to me,
    "Let us go to the house of the
    LORD."
² And now here we are,
    standing inside your gates,
    O Jerusalem.
³ Jerusalem is a well-built city;
    its seamless walls cannot
    be breached.
⁴ All the tribes of Israel—the LORD's
    people—
    make their pilgrimage here.
    They come to give thanks to the name
    of the LORD,
    as the law requires of Israel.

⁵ Here stand the thrones where
    judgment is given,
    the thrones of the dynasty
    of David.
⁶ Pray for peace in Jerusalem.
    May all who love this city
    prosper.
⁷ O Jerusalem, may there be peace
    within your walls
    and prosperity in your palaces.
⁸ For the sake of my family and friends,
    I will say,
    "May you have peace."
⁹ For the sake of the house of the LORD
    our God,
    I will seek what is best for you,
    O Jerusalem.

PROVERBS 29:1
Whoever stubbornly refuses to accept criticism will suddenly be destroyed beyond recovery.

DECEMBER**4**

DANIEL 11:36–12:13
The book of Daniel closes with the somber reality that while God's goodness will triumph in the end, God's people will face adversity along the way. While Daniel's prophecies give us insight into end times, the life he lived gives us insight into how to follow God each day.

"**T**he king will do as he pleases, exalting himself and claiming to be greater than every god, even blaspheming the God of gods. He will succeed, but only until the time of wrath is completed. For what has been determined will surely take place. ³⁷He will have no respect for the gods of his ancestors, or for the god loved by women, or for any other god, for he will boast that he is greater than them all. ³⁸Instead of these, he will worship the god of fortresses—a god his ancestors never knew—and lavish on him gold, silver, precious stones, and expensive gifts. ³⁹Claiming this foreign god's help, he will attack the strongest fortresses. He will honor those who submit to him, appointing them to positions of authority and dividing the land among them as their reward.*

⁴⁰"Then at the time of the end, the king of the south will attack the king of the north. The king of the north will storm out with chariots, charioteers, and a vast navy. He will invade various lands and sweep through them like a flood. ⁴¹He will enter the glorious land of Israel,* and many nations will fall, but Moab, Edom, and the best part of Ammon will escape. ⁴²He will conquer many countries, and even Egypt will not escape. ⁴³He will gain control over the gold, silver, and treasures of Egypt, and the Libyans and Ethiopians* will be his servants.

⁴⁴"But then news from the east and the north will alarm him, and he will set out in great anger to destroy and obliterate many. ⁴⁵He will stop between the glorious holy mountain and the sea and will pitch his royal tents. But while he is there, his time will suddenly run out, and no one will help him.

12:1"AT that time Michael, the archangel* who stands guard over your nation, will arise. Then there will be a time of anguish greater than any since nations first came into existence. But at that time every one of your people whose name is written in the book will be rescued. ²Many of those whose bodies lie dead and buried will rise up, some to everlasting life and some to shame and everlasting disgrace. ³Those who are wise will shine as bright as the sky, and those who lead many to righteousness will shine like the stars forever. ⁴But you, Daniel, keep this prophecy a secret; seal up the book until the time of the end, when many will rush here and there, and knowledge will increase."

⁵Then I, Daniel, looked and saw two others standing on opposite banks of the river. ⁶One of them asked the man dressed in linen, who was now standing above the river, "How long will it be until these shocking events are over?"

⁷The man dressed in linen, who was standing above the river, raised both his hands toward heaven and took a solemn oath by the One who lives forever, saying, "It will go on for a time, times, and half a time. When the shattering of the holy people has finally come to an end, all these things will have happened."

⁸I heard what he said, but I did not understand what he meant. So I asked, "How will all this finally end, my lord?"

⁹But he said, "Go now, Daniel, for what I have said is kept secret and sealed until the time of the end. ¹⁰Many will be purified, cleansed, and refined by these trials. But the wicked will continue in their wickedness, and none of them will understand. Only those who are wise will know what it means.

¹¹"From the time the daily sacrifice is stopped and the sacrilegious object that causes desecration* is set up to be worshiped, there will be 1,290 days. ¹²And blessed are those who wait and remain until the end of the 1,335 days!

¹³"As for you, go your way until the end. You will rest, and then at the end of the days, you will rise again to receive the inheritance set aside for you."

11:39 Or *at a price*.   **11:41** Hebrew *the glorious land*.
11:43 Hebrew *Cushites*.   **12:1** Hebrew *the great prince*.
12:11 Hebrew *the abomination of desolation*.

1 JOHN 4:1-21

Love is to be at the center of our relationship with God and with others. When love is at the center of your relationship with God, fear of judgment fades.

Dear friends, do not believe everyone who claims to speak by the Spirit. You must test them to see if the spirit they have comes from God. For there are many

How to discern truth

1 JOHN 4:1-3 Some people believe everything they read or hear. They hear something on the news, or read it on the Internet, or hear about it from a friend and, deciding that it's true, they react without verifying the information. How much more informed many of us would be if we just checked the facts. When it comes to knowing what to believe about Jesus, you are holding in your hands the sourcebook. The Bible is the true authority on what to believe. If you encounter a teacher who contradicts the Bible, stear clear. • False teachers tend to contradict the Bible in more ways than just their teachings. You can see if teachers are trustworthy by looking at their commitment to the body of believers (1 John 2:19, December 2), their lifestyle (1 John 3:23-24, December 3), and the fruit of their ministry (1 John 4:6). The most important test of all is what they believe about Christ. • Our world is filled with voices claiming to speak for God. Give them these tests to see if they are indeed speaking God's truth.

false prophets in the world. ²This is how we know if they have the Spirit of God: If a person claiming to be a prophet* acknowledges that Jesus Christ came in a real body, that person has the Spirit of God. ³But if someone claims to be a prophet and does not acknowledge the truth about Jesus, that person is not from God. Such a person has the spirit of the Antichrist, which you heard is coming into the world and indeed is already here.

⁴But you belong to God, my dear children. You have already won a victory over those people, because the Spirit who lives in you is greater than the spirit who lives in the world. ⁵Those people belong to this world, so they speak from the world's viewpoint, and the world listens to them. ⁶But we belong to God, and those who know God listen to us. If they do not belong to God, they do not listen to us. That is how we know if someone has the Spirit of truth or the spirit of deception.

⁷Dear friends, let us continue to love one another, for love comes from God. Anyone who loves is a child of God and knows God. ⁸But anyone who does not love does not know God, for God is love.

⁹God showed how much he loved us by sending his one and only Son into the world so that we might have eternal life through him. ¹⁰This is real love—not that we loved God, but that he loved us and sent his Son as a sacrifice to take away our sins.

¹¹Dear friends, since God loved us that much, we surely ought to love each other. ¹²No one has ever seen God. But if we love each other, God lives in us, and his love is brought to full expression in us.

¹³And God has given us his Spirit as proof that we live in him and he in us. ¹⁴Furthermore, we have seen with our own eyes and now testify that the Father sent his Son to be the Savior of the world. ¹⁵All who confess that Jesus is the Son of God have God living in them, and they live in God. ¹⁶We know how much God loves us, and we have put our trust in his love.

God is love, and all who live in love live in God, and God lives in them. ¹⁷And as we live in God, our love grows more perfect. So we will not be afraid on the day of judgment, but we can face him with confidence because we live like Jesus here in this world.

¹⁸Such love has no fear, because perfect love expels all fear. If we are afraid, it is for fear of punishment, and this shows that we have not fully experienced his perfect love. ¹⁹We love each other* because he loved us first.

²⁰If someone says, "I love God," but hates a Christian brother or sister,* that person is a liar; for if we don't love people we can see, how can we love God, whom we cannot see? ²¹And he has given us this command: Those who love God must also love their Christian brothers and sisters.*

4:2 Greek *If a spirit;* similarly in 4:3. **4:19** Greek *We love.* Other manuscripts read *We love God;* still others read *We love him.* **4:20** Greek *hates his brother.* **4:21** Greek *The one who loves God must also love his brother.*

PSALM 123:1-4
A song for pilgrims ascending to Jerusalem.

¹ I lift my eyes to you,
O God, enthroned in heaven.
² We keep looking to the LORD our God
for his mercy,
just as servants keep their eyes on
their master,
as a slave girl watches her mistress
for the slightest signal.
³ Have mercy on us, LORD, have mercy,
for we have had our fill of
contempt.
⁴ We have had more than our fill of the
scoffing of the proud
and the contempt of the arrogant.

PROVERBS 29:2-4
When the godly are in authority, the people rejoice. But when the wicked are in power, they groan. □ The man who loves wisdom brings joy to his father, but if he hangs around with prostitutes, his wealth is wasted. □ A just king gives stability to his nation, but one who demands bribes destroys it.

HOSEA 1:1–3:5

Hosea did something few people would have done. He married a woman with very little hope of her being faithful. He lived the reality that God wanted Israel to see: the people had been spiritually unfaithful to the very One who had supplied their needs. Hosea's faithfulness revealed God's character.

The LORD gave this message to Hosea son of Beeri during the years when Uzziah, Jotham, Ahaz, and Hezekiah were kings of Judah, and Jeroboam son of Jehoash* was king of Israel.

²When the LORD first began speaking to Israel through Hosea, he said to him, "Go and marry a prostitute,* so that some of her children will be conceived in prostitution. This will illustrate how Israel has acted like a prostitute by turning against the LORD and worshiping other gods."

³So Hosea married Gomer, the daughter of Diblaim, and she became pregnant and gave Hosea a son. ⁴And the LORD said, "Name the child Jezreel, for I am about to punish King Jehu's dynasty to avenge the murders he committed at Jezreel. In fact, I will bring an end to Israel's independence. ⁵I will break its military power in the Jezreel Valley."

⁶Soon Gomer became pregnant again and gave birth to a daughter. And the LORD said to Hosea, "Name your daughter Lo-ruhamah—'Not loved'—for I will no longer show love to the people of Israel or forgive them. ⁷But I will show love to the people of Judah. I will free them from their enemies—not with weapons and armies or horses and charioteers, but by my power as the LORD their God."

⁸After Gomer had weaned Lo-ruhamah, she again became pregnant and gave birth to a second son. ⁹And the LORD said, "Name him Lo-ammi—'Not my people'—for Israel is not my people, and I am not their God.

¹⁰*"Yet the time will come when Israel's people will be like the sands of the seashore—too many to count! Then, at the place where they were told, 'You are not my people,' it will be said, 'You are chil-

dren of the living God.' ¹¹Then the people of Judah and Israel will unite together. They will choose one leader for themselves, and they will return from exile together. What a day that will be—the day of Jezreel*—when God will again plant his people in his land.

²:¹*"In that day you will call your brothers Ammi—'My people.' And you will call your sisters Ruhamah—'The ones I love.'

²:² "BUT now bring charges against
    Israel—your mother—
  for she is no longer my wife,
    and I am no longer her husband.
Tell her to remove the prostitute's
    makeup from her face
  and the clothing that exposes her
    breasts.
³ Otherwise, I will strip her as naked
    as she was on the day she was born.
I will leave her to die of thirst,
    as in a dry and barren wilderness.
⁴ And I will not love her children,
    for they were conceived in
      prostitution.
⁵ Their mother is a shameless prostitute
  and became pregnant in a shameful
    way.
She said, 'I'll run after other lovers
  and sell myself to them for food and
    water,
for clothing of wool and linen,
    and for olive oil and drinks.'

⁶ "For this reason I will fence her in with
    thornbushes.
I will block her path with a wall
    to make her lose her way.
⁷ When she runs after her lovers,
    she won't be able to catch them.
She will search for them
    but not find them.
Then she will think,
'I might as well return to my husband,
  for I was better off with him than
    I am now.'
⁸ She doesn't realize it was I who gave
    her everything she has—

the grain, the new wine,
the olive oil;
I even gave her silver and gold.
But she gave all my gifts to Baal.

9 "But now I will take back the ripened
grain and new wine
I generously provided each harvest
season.
I will take away the wool and linen
clothing
I gave her to cover her nakedness.
10 I will strip her naked in public,
while all her lovers look on.
No one will be able
to rescue her from my hands.
11 I will put an end to her annual
festivals,
her new moon celebrations,
and her Sabbath days—
all her appointed festivals.
12 I will destroy her grapevines and fig
trees,
things she claims her lovers gave
her.
I will let them grow into tangled
thickets,
where only wild animals will eat
the fruit.
13 I will punish her for all those times
when she burned incense to her
images of Baal,
when she put on her earrings and
jewels
and went out to look for her lovers
but forgot all about me,"
says the LORD.

14 "But then I will win her back once
again.
I will lead her into the desert
and speak tenderly to her there.
15 I will return her vineyards to her
and transform the Valley of
Trouble* into a gateway of hope.
She will give herself to me there,
as she did long ago when she was
young,
when I freed her from her captivity
in Egypt.
16 When that day comes," says the LORD,
"you will call me 'my husband'
instead of 'my master.'*
17 O Israel, I will wipe the many names
of Baal from your lips,

and you will never mention them
again.
18 On that day I will make a covenant
with all the wild animals and the
birds of the sky
and the animals that scurry along
the ground
so they will not harm you.
I will remove all weapons of war from
the land,
all swords and bows,
so you can live unafraid
in peace and safety.
19 I will make you my wife forever,
showing you righteousness and
justice,
unfailing love and compassion.
20 I will be faithful to you and make
you mine,
and you will finally know me
as the LORD.

21 "In that day, I will answer,"
says the LORD.
"I will answer the sky as it pleads
for clouds.
And the sky will answer the earth
with rain.
22 Then the earth will answer the thirsty
cries
of the grain, the grapevines,
and the olive trees.
And they in turn will answer,
'Jezreel'—'God plants!'
23 At that time I will plant a crop
of Israelites
and raise them for myself.
I will show love
to those I called 'Not loved.'*
And to those I called 'Not my people,'*
I will say, 'Now you are my people.'
And they will reply, 'You are our God!'"

3:1 THEN the LORD said to me, "Go and love
your wife again, even though she* commits adultery with another lover. This will
illustrate that the LORD still loves Israel,
even though the people have turned to
other gods and love to worship them.*"

2 So I bought her back for fifteen pieces
of silver* and five bushels of barley and a
measure of wine.* 3 Then I said to her,
"You must live in my house for many days
and stop your prostitution. During this

time, you will not have sexual relations with anyone, not even with me.*"

⁴This shows that Israel will go a long time without a king or prince, and without sacrifices, sacred pillars, priests,* or even idols! ⁵But afterward the people will return and devote themselves to the LORD their God and to David's descendant, their king.* In the last days, they will tremble in awe of the LORD and of his goodness.

1:1 Hebrew *Joash*, a variant spelling of Jehoash.   1:2 Or *a promiscuous woman.*   2:1-2 in Hebrew text.   1:11 *Jezreel* means "God plants."   2:1 Verses 2:1-23 are numbered 2:3-25 in Hebrew text.   2:15 Hebrew *valley of Achor.*   2:16 Hebrew *'my baal.'*   2:23a Hebrew *Lo-ruhamah;* see 1:6.   2:23b Hebrew *Lo-ammi;* see 1:9.   3:1a Or *Go and love a woman who.*   3:1b Hebrew *love their raisin cakes.*   3:2a Hebrew *15 shekels of silver,* about 6 ounces or 171 grams in weight.   3:2b As in Greek version, which reads *a homer of barley and a measure of wine;* Hebrew reads *a homer* [5 bushels or 182 liters] *of barley and a lethech* [2.5 bushels or 91 liters] *of barley.*   3:3 Or *and I will live with you.*   3:4 Hebrew *ephod,* the vest worn by the priest.   3:5 Hebrew *to David their king.*

1 JOHN 5:1-21

John closed his first letter by reflecting on the person of Jesus Christ. Understanding Jesus' nature is a vital part of growth as a new believer: he is the one through whom God extends to us his life and love.

Everyone who believes that Jesus is the Christ* has become a child of God. And everyone who loves the Father loves his children, too. ²We know we love God's children if we love God and obey his commandments. ³Loving God means keeping his commandments, and his commandments are not burdensome. ⁴For every child of God defeats this evil world, and we achieve this victory through our faith. ⁵And who can win this battle against the world? Only those who believe that Jesus is the Son of God.

⁶And Jesus Christ was revealed as God's Son by his baptism in water and by shedding his blood on the cross*—not by water only, but by water and blood. And the Spirit, who is truth, confirms it with his testimony. ⁷So we have these three witnesses*—⁸the Spirit, the water, and the blood—and all three agree. ⁹Since we believe human testimony, surely we can believe the greater testimony that comes from God. And God has testified about his Son. ¹⁰All who believe in the Son of God know in their hearts that this testimony is true. Those who don't believe this are actually calling God a liar because they don't believe what God has testified about his Son.

¹¹And this is what God has testified: He has given us eternal life, and this life is in his Son. ¹²Whoever has the Son has life; whoever does not have God's Son does not have life.

WHAT THE BIBLE SAYS

Hosea and Gomer

HOSEA 1:2 Why would God tell one of his own followers to marry a prostitute? Why would God put Hosea through such difficulty? Hosea was a prophet, called by God to bring important messages to the people. The Hebrew people had fallen away from the worship of God and were worshiping idols. Hosea's book highlights the parallels between his relationship with Gomer and God's relationship with the nation of Israel. Although Israel had made a covenant with the one true God, the nation had gone after other false gods. In the same way, Hosea had married Gomer, knowing ahead of time that she would go after other men.

• The struggles Hosea lived out in front of the people were an undeniable picture of the pain God experienced because the nation rejected him and went after other gods. Those who listened to Hosea would come to understand that they were just like Gomer—unfaithful, unthankful, and full of sin. Even more, Hosea tenderly dealt with his wife in spite of her sin, a further picture of God's willingness to bring his people back and forgive them.

[13]I have written this to you who believe in the name of the Son of God, so that you may know you have eternal life. [14]And we are confident that he hears us whenever we ask for anything that pleases him. [15]And since we know he hears us when we make our requests, we also know that he will give us what we ask for.

[16]If you see a Christian brother or sister* sinning in a way that does not lead to death, you should pray, and God will give that person life. But there is a sin that leads to death, and I am not saying you should pray for those who commit it. [17]All wicked actions are sin, but not every sin leads to death.

[18]We know that God's children do not make a practice of sinning, for God's Son holds them securely, and the evil one cannot touch them. [19]We know that we are children of God and that the world around us is under the control of the evil one.

[20]And we know that the Son of God has come, and he has given us understanding so that we can know the true God.* And now we live in fellowship with the true God because we live in fellowship with his Son, Jesus Christ. He is the only true God, and he is eternal life.

[21]Dear children, keep away from anything that might take God's place in your hearts.*

5:1 Or the Messiah.   5:6 Greek This is he who came by water and blood.   5:7 A few very late manuscripts add in heaven—the Father, the Word, and the Holy Spirit, and these three are one. And we have three witnesses on earth.
5:16 Greek a brother.   5:20 Greek the one who is true.
5:21 Greek keep yourselves from idols.

PSALM 124:1-8
A song for pilgrims ascending to Jerusalem. A psalm of David.

[1] **W**hat if the LORD had not been
on our side?
Let all Israel repeat:
[2] What if the LORD had not been
on our side
when people attacked us?
[3] They would have swallowed us alive
in their burning anger.
[4] The waters would have engulfed us;
a torrent would have overwhelmed
us.
[5] Yes, the raging waters of their fury
would have overwhelmed our
very lives.

[6] Praise the LORD,
who did not let their teeth tear us
apart!
[7] We escaped like a bird from a hunter's
trap.
The trap is broken, and we are
free!
[8] Our help is from the LORD,
who made heaven and earth.

PROVERBS 29:5-8
To flatter friends is to lay a trap for their feet. □ Evil people are trapped by sin, but the righteous escape, shouting for joy. □ The godly care about the rights of the poor; the wicked don't care at all. □ Mockers can get a whole town agitated, but the wise will calm anger.

DECEMBER**6**

HOSEA 4:1–5:15
God was filing a lawsuit against his people. They were in breach of contract. They had promised to be faithful to the Lord but were persistently unfaithful to him instead.

Hear the word of the LORD, O people
of Israel!

The LORD has brought charges
against you, saying:
"There is no faithfulness, no kindness,
no knowledge of God in your land.
[2] You make vows and break them;
you kill and steal and commit
adultery.

There is violence everywhere—
one murder after another.
³ That is why your land is in mourning,
and everyone is wasting away.
Even the wild animals, the birds
of the sky,
and the fish of the sea are
disappearing.

⁴ "Don't point your finger at someone
else
and try to pass the blame!
My complaint, you priests,
is with you.*
⁵ So you will stumble in broad daylight,
and your false prophets will fall
with you in the night.
And I will destroy Israel, your
mother.
⁶ My people are being destroyed
because they don't know me.
Since you priests refuse to know me,
I refuse to recognize you as my
priests.
Since you have forgotten the laws of
your God,
I will forget to bless your children.
⁷ The more priests there are,
the more they sin against me.
They have exchanged the glory of God
for the shame of idols.*

⁸ "When the people bring their sin
offerings, the priests get fed.
So the priests are glad when the
people sin!
⁹ 'And what the priests do, the people
also do.'
So now I will punish both priests
and people
for their wicked deeds.
¹⁰ They will eat and still be hungry.
They will play the prostitute and
gain nothing from it,
for they have deserted the LORD
¹¹ to worship other gods.

"Wine has robbed my people
of their understanding.
¹² They ask a piece of wood for advice!
They think a stick can tell them the
future!
Longing after idols
has made them foolish.
They have played the prostitute,

serving other gods and deserting
their God.
¹³ They offer sacrifices to idols on the
mountaintops.
They go up into the hills to burn
incense
in the pleasant shade of oaks,
poplars, and terebinth trees.

"That is why your daughters turn
to prostitution,
and your daughters-in-law commit
adultery.
¹⁴ But why should I punish them
for their prostitution and adultery?
For your men are doing the same
thing,
sinning with whores and shrine
prostitutes.
O foolish people! You refuse
to understand,
so you will be destroyed.

¹⁵ "Though you, Israel, are a prostitute,
may Judah avoid such guilt.
Do not join the false worship at Gilgal
or Beth-aven,*
even though they take oaths there
in the LORD's name.
¹⁶ Israel is stubborn,
like a stubborn heifer.
So should the LORD feed her
like a lamb in a lush pasture?
¹⁷ Leave Israel* alone,
because she is married to idolatry.
¹⁸ When the rulers of Israel finish their
drinking,
off they go to find some prostitutes.
They love shame more than honor.*
¹⁹ So a mighty wind will sweep them
away.
Their sacrifices to idols will bring
them shame.

5:1 "HEAR this, you priests.
Pay attention, you leaders of Israel.
Listen, you members of the royal
family.
Judgment has been handed down
against you.
For you have led the people into
a snare
by worshiping the idols at Mizpah
and Tabor.

2 You have dug a deep pit to trap them
at Acacia Grove.*
But I will settle with you for what
you have done.
3 I know what you are like, O Ephraim.
You cannot hide yourself from me,
O Israel.
You have left me as a prostitute leaves
her husband;
you are utterly defiled.
4 Your deeds won't let you return to
your God.
You are a prostitute through and
through,
and you do not know the LORD.

5 "The arrogance of Israel testifies
against her;
Israel and Ephraim will stumble
under their load of guilt.
Judah, too, will fall with them.
6 When they come with their flocks and
herds
to offer sacrifices to the LORD,
they will not find him,
because he has withdrawn from
them.
7 They have betrayed the honor
of the LORD,
bearing children that are not his.
Now their false religion will devour
them
along with their wealth.*

8 "Sound the alarm in Gibeah!
Blow the trumpet in Ramah!
Raise the battle cry in Beth-aven*!
Lead on into battle, O warriors of
Benjamin!
9 One thing is certain, Israel*:
On your day of punishment,
you will become a heap of rubble.

10 "The leaders of Judah have become
like thieves.*
So I will pour my anger on them like
a waterfall.
11 The people of Israel will be crushed
and broken by my judgment
because they are determined
to worship idols.*
12 I will destroy Israel as a moth
consumes wool.
I will make Judah as weak as rotten
wood.

13 "When Israel and Judah saw how sick
they were,
Israel turned to Assyria—
to the great king there—
but he could neither help nor cure
them.
14 I will be like a lion to Israel,
like a strong young lion to Judah.
I will tear them to pieces!
I will carry them off,
and no one will be left to rescue
them.
15 Then I will return to my place
until they admit their guilt and turn
to me.
For as soon as trouble comes,
they will earnestly search
for me."

4:4 Hebrew *Your people are like those with a complaint
against the priests.*   **4:7** As in Syriac version and an ancient
Hebrew tradition; Masoretic Text reads *I will turn their glory
into shame.*   **4:15** *Beth-aven* means "house of wickedness";
it is being used as another name for Bethel, which means
"house of God."   **4:17** Hebrew *Ephraim,* referring to the
northern kingdom of Israel.   **4:18** As in Greek version; the
meaning of the Hebrew is uncertain.   **5:2** Hebrew *at
Shittim.* The meaning of the Hebrew for this sentence is
uncertain.   **5:7** The meaning of the Hebrew is uncertain.
5:8 *Beth-aven* means "house of wickedness"; it is being used
as another name for Bethel, which means "house of God."
5:9 Hebrew *Ephraim,* referring to the northern kingdom of
Israel; also in 5:11, 12, 13, 14.   **5:10** Hebrew *like those
who move a boundary marker.*   **5:11** Or *determined to
follow human commands.* The meaning of the Hebrew is
uncertain.

2 JOHN 1:1-13

John's second letter is a note to "the chosen lady"
and her children. The content of the letter suggests
John was referring figuratively to a church. He
included a warning about false teachers.

This letter is from John, the elder.*
I am writing to the chosen lady and to
her children,* whom I love in the truth—
as does everyone else who knows the
truth—²because the truth lives in us and
will be with us forever.

³Grace, mercy, and peace, which come
from God the Father and from Jesus
Christ—the Son of the Father—will continue to be with us who live in truth and
love.

⁴How happy I was to meet some of your
children and find them living according to
the truth, just as the Father commanded.

⁵I am writing to remind you, dear
friends,* that we should love one another.
This is not a new commandment, but one

we have had from the beginning. [6]Love means doing what God has commanded us, and he has commanded us to love one another, just as you heard from the beginning.

[7]I say this because many deceivers have gone out into the world. They deny that Jesus Christ came* in a real body. Such a person is a deceiver and an antichrist. [8]Watch out that you do not lose what we* have worked so hard to achieve. Be diligent so that you receive your full reward. [9]Anyone who wanders away from this teaching has no relationship with God. But anyone who remains in the teaching of Christ has a relationship with both the Father and the Son.

[10]If anyone comes to your meeting and does not teach the truth about Christ, don't invite that person into your home or give any kind of encouragement. [11]Anyone who encourages such people becomes a partner in their evil work.

[12]I have much more to say to you, but I don't want to do it with paper and ink. For I hope to visit you soon and talk with you face to face. Then our joy will be complete.

[13]Greetings from the children of your sister,* chosen by God.

1a Greek *From the elder.*   **1b** Or *the church God has chosen and its members.*   **5** Greek *I urge you, lady.*   **7** Or *will come.*   **8** Some manuscripts read *you.*   **13** Or *from the members of your sister church.*

PSALM 125:1-5
A song for pilgrims ascending to Jerusalem.

[1] Those who trust in the LORD are as
      secure as Mount Zion;
   they will not be defeated but will
      endure forever.
[2] Just as the mountains surround
      Jerusalem,
   so the LORD surrounds his people,
      both now and forever.
[3] The wicked will not rule the land
      of the godly,
   for then the godly might be
      tempted to do wrong.
[4] O LORD, do good to those who are good,
      whose hearts are in tune with you.
[5] But banish those who turn to crooked
      ways, O LORD.
   Take them away with those who
      do evil.

   May Israel have peace!

PROVERBS 29:9-11
If a wise person takes a fool to court, there will be ranting and ridicule but no satisfaction. ▢The bloodthirsty hate blameless people, but the upright seek to help them.* ▢Fools vent their anger, but the wise quietly hold it back.

29:10 Or *The bloodthirsty hate blameless people, / and they seek to kill the upright;* Hebrew reads *The bloodthirsty hate blameless people; / as for the upright, they seek their life.*

WHAT THE BIBLE SAYS

How to discern truth

2 JOHN 1:10-11 Being loving is not separate from being discerning. John constantly urged believers to love one another, but when it came to false teachers, it was time for that love to get tough. John made it very clear that the believers were not to show any kind of hospitality to those who didn't teach the truth about Christ.   •When traveling preachers came through town, the litmus test for whether they should be listened to or "run out of town" was whether they acknowledged that Christ came in a real body (a common false teaching at the time was that Jesus wasn't really human). If they taught something different, they were not to be encouraged in any way. The believers needed to be discerning and then act on that discernment.   •You can go to any religion section in your local bookstore and find shelves of books—all with varied opinions about who Jesus really was. John advises you not to listen to their nonsense. Sure, you'll be labeled "closed-minded," but take comfort in the fact that you are obeying what one of Jesus' closest disciples commanded. Keep God's Word the authority for discerning truth and error.

DECEMBER7

Hosea addressed his listeners as Israel and Samaria. At first, Israel was the whole nation. After the nation divided, Israel became the northern kingdom. Its capital city was Samaria.

"Come, let us return to the LORD.
He has torn us to pieces;
   now he will heal us.
He has injured us;
   now he will bandage our wounds.
2 In just a short time he will restore us,
   so that we may live in his presence.
3 Oh, that we might know the LORD!
   Let us press on to know him.
He will respond to us as surely as the
      arrival of dawn
   or the coming of rains in early
      spring."

4 "O Israel* and Judah,
   what should I do with you?" asks
      the LORD.
"For your love vanishes like
      the morning mist
   and disappears like dew in
      the sunlight.
5 I sent my prophets to cut you
      to pieces—
   to slaughter you with my words,
   with judgments as inescapable as
      light.
6 I want you to show love,*
   not offer sacrifices.
I want you to know me*
   more than I want burnt offerings.
7 But like Adam,* you broke my
      covenant
   and betrayed my trust.
8 "Gilead is a city of sinners,
   tracked with footprints of blood.
9 Priests form bands of robbers,
   waiting in ambush for their victims.
They murder travelers along the road
      to Shechem
   and practice every kind of sin.
10 Yes, I have seen something horrible
      in Ephraim and Israel:
My people are defiled by
      prostituting themselves with
      other gods!

11 "O Judah, a harvest of punishment
      is also waiting for you,
   though I wanted to restore the
      fortunes of my people.

7:1 "I WANT to heal Israel,* but its sins are
      too great.
Samaria is filled with liars.
Thieves are on the inside
   and bandits on the outside!
2 Its people don't realize
   that I am watching them.
Their sinful deeds are all around them,
   and I see them all.

3 "The people entertain the king with
      their wickedness,
   and the princes laugh at their lies.
4 They are all adulterers,
   always aflame with lust.
They are like an oven that is kept hot
   while the baker is kneading the
      dough.
5 On royal holidays, the princes get
      drunk with wine,
   carousing with those who mock
      them.
6 Their hearts are like an oven
      blazing with intrigue.
Their plot smolders* through the night,
   and in the morning it breaks out
      like a raging fire.
7 Burning like an oven,
   they consume their leaders.
They kill their kings one after another,
   and no one cries to me for help.

8 "The people of Israel mingle with
      godless foreigners,
   making themselves as worthless
      as a half-baked cake!
9 Worshiping foreign gods has sapped
      their strength,
   but they don't even know it.
Their hair is gray,
   but they don't realize they're old
      and weak.
10 Their arrogance testifies against them,
   yet they don't return to the LORD
      their God
   or even try to find him.

[11] "The people of Israel have become like
        silly, witless doves,
   first calling to Egypt, then flying
        to Assyria for help.
[12] But as they fly about,
   I will throw my net over them
   and bring them down like a bird from
        the sky.
   I will punish them for all the evil
        they do.*

[13] "What sorrow awaits those who have
        deserted me!
   Let them die, for they have rebelled
        against me.
   I wanted to redeem them,
        but they have told lies about me.
[14] They do not cry out to me with sincere
        hearts.
   Instead, they sit on their couches
        and wail.
   They cut themselves,* begging foreign
        gods for grain and new wine,
        and they turn away from me.
[15] I trained them and made them strong,
        yet now they plot evil against me.
[16] They look everywhere except to the
        Most High.
   They are as useless as a crooked
        bow.
   Their leaders will be killed by their
        enemies
   because of their insolence toward
        me.
   Then the people of Egypt
        will laugh at them.

[8:1] "SOUND the alarm!
   The enemy descends like an eagle
        on the people of the LORD,
   for they have broken my covenant
        and revolted against my law.
[2] Now Israel pleads with me,
        'Help us, for you are our God!'
[3] But it is too late.
   The people of Israel have rejected
        what is good,
        and now their enemies will chase
        after them.
[4] The people have appointed kings
        without my consent,
        and princes without my knowledge.
   By making idols for themselves from
        their silver and gold,

they have brought about their own
        destruction.
[5] "O Samaria, I reject this calf—
        this idol you have made.
   My fury burns against you.
   How long will you be incapable
        of innocence?
[6] This calf you worship, O Israel,
        was crafted by your own hands!
   It is not God!
   Therefore, it must be smashed
        to bits.

[7] "They have planted the wind
        and will harvest the whirlwind.
   The stalks of grain wither
        and produce nothing to eat.
   And even if there is any grain,
        foreigners will eat it.
[8] The people of Israel have been
        swallowed up;
   they lie among the nations like an
        old discarded pot.
[9] Like a wild donkey looking for a mate,
        they have gone up to Assyria.
   The people of Israel* have sold
        themselves—
   sold themselves to many lovers.
[10] But though they have sold themselves
        to many allies,
   I will now gather them together
        for judgment.
   Then they will writhe
        under the burden of the great king.

[11] "Israel has built many altars to take
        away sin,
   but these very altars became places
        for sinning!
[12] Even though I gave them all my laws,
        they act as if those laws don't apply
        to them.
[13] The people of Israel love their rituals
        of sacrifice,
        but to me their sacrifices are all
        meaningless.
   I will hold my people accountable
        for their sins,
        and I will punish them.
   They will return to Egypt.
[14] Israel has forgotten its Maker and
        built great palaces,
        and Judah has fortified its cities.

Therefore, I will send down fire on
their cities
and will burn up their fortresses."

9:1 O PEOPLE of Israel,
do not rejoice as other nations do.
For you have been unfaithful to your
God,
hiring yourselves out like
prostitutes,
worshiping other gods on every
threshing floor.
2 So now your harvests will be too small
to feed you.
There will be no grapes for making
new wine.
3 You may no longer stay here in the
LORD's land.
Instead, you will return to Egypt,
and in Assyria you will eat food
that is ceremonially unclean.
4 There you will make no offerings
of wine to the LORD.
None of your sacrifices there will
please him.
They will be unclean, like food
touched by a person in
mourning.
All who present such sacrifices
will be defiled.
They may eat this food themselves,
but they may not offer it to the
LORD.
5 What then will you do on festival
days?
How will you observe the LORD's
festivals?
6 Even if you escape destruction from
Assyria,
Egypt will conquer you, and
Memphis* will bury you.
Nettles will take over your treasures
of silver;
thistles will invade your ruined
homes.
7 The time of Israel's punishment
has come;
the day of payment is here.
Soon Israel will know this all too
well.
Because of your great sin and hostility,
you say, "The prophets are crazy
and the inspired men are fools!"

8 The prophet is a watchman over
Israel* for my God,
yet traps are laid for him wherever
he goes.
He faces hostility even in the house
of God.
9 The things my people do are as
depraved
as what they did in Gibeah long ago.
God will not forget.
He will surely punish them for
their sins.

10 The LORD says, "O Israel, when I first
found you,
it was like finding fresh grapes
in the desert.
When I saw your ancestors,
it was like seeing the first ripe figs
of the season.
But then they deserted me for Baal-
peor,
giving themselves to that shameful
idol.
Soon they became vile,
as vile as the god they worshiped.
11 The glory of Israel will fly away like
a bird,
for your children will not be born
or grow in the womb
or even be conceived.
12 Even if you do have children
who grow up,
I will take them from you.
It will be a terrible day when I turn
away
and leave you alone.
13 I have watched Israel become as
beautiful as Tyre.
But now Israel will bring out her
children for slaughter."

14 O LORD, what should I request for your
people?
I will ask for wombs that don't give
birth
and breasts that give no milk.

15 The LORD says, "All their wickedness
began at Gilgal;
there I began to hate them.
I will drive them from my land
because of their evil actions.
I will love them no more
because all their leaders are rebels.

16 The people of Israel are struck down.
  Their roots are dried up,
  and they will bear no more fruit.
  And if they give birth,
  I will slaughter their beloved
    children."

17 My God will reject the people of Israel
  because they will not listen or obey.
  They will be wanderers,
  homeless among the nations.

6:4 Hebrew *Ephraim*, referring to the northern kingdom of
Israel. 6:6a Greek version reads *to show mercy.* Compare
Matt 9:13; 12:7. 6:6b Hebrew *to know God.* 6:7 Or *But
at Adam.* 7:1 Hebrew *Ephraim*, referring to the northern
kingdom of Israel; also in 7:8, 11. 7:6 Hebrew *Their baker
sleeps.* 7:12 Hebrew *I will punish them because of what
was reported against them in the assembly.* 7:14 As in
Greek version; Hebrew reads *They gather together.*
8:9 Hebrew *Ephraim*, referring to the northern kingdom
of Israel; also in 8:11. 9:6 Memphis was the capital of
northern Egypt. 9:8 Hebrew *Ephraim*, referring to the
northern kingdom of Israel; also in 9:11, 13, 16.

3 JOHN 1:1-15
As 2 John told the believers to withhold hospitality
from false teachers, this letter from John expresses
appreciation to a man named Gaius for his willingness to open his home to those who legitimately
taught the Christian faith.

This letter is from John, the elder.*

I am writing to Gaius, my dear friend,
whom I love in the truth.

2Dear friend, I hope all is well with you
and that you are as healthy in body as you
are strong in spirit. 3Some of the traveling
teachers* recently returned and made me
very happy by telling me about your faithfulness and that you are living according
to the truth. 4I could have no greater joy
than to hear that my children are following the truth.

5Dear friend, you are being faithful to
God when you care for the traveling
teachers who pass through, even though
they are strangers to you. 6They have told
the church here of your loving friendship.
Please continue providing for such teachers in a manner that pleases God. 7For
they are traveling for the Lord,* and they
accept nothing from people who are not
believers.* 8So we ourselves should support them so that we can be their partners
as they teach the truth.

9I wrote to the church about this, but
Diotrephes, who loves to be the leader, refuses to have anything to do with us.
10When I come, I will report some of the
things he is doing and the evil accusations
he is making against us. Not only does he
refuse to welcome the traveling teachers,
he also tells others not to help them. And
when they do help, he puts them out of
the church.

11Dear friend, don't let this bad example influence you. Follow only what is
good. Remember that those who do good

HOW WE LIVE

Experiencing joy

PSALM 126:1-6 The series of psalms from 120–134 were special songs
sung by Jews who came from all over the world to Jerusalem to celebrate
the festivals. Each psalm is a "step" along the journey. Psalm 120 begins
the journey in a distant land; Psalm 122 pictures the arrival in Jerusalem;
the rest of the psalms move toward the Temple, praising and worshiping
God. • Here in Psalm 126 is a joyous reminder that God blesses his
people, here bringing them back from exile and restoring them. The
people celebrating would sing this psalm, remembering that at times the
nation had "plant[ed] in tears" but was now able to "harvest with shouts
of joy." That's why these people were singing songs of praise. • That's
the God we worship. He can take our times of tears and sadness and
bring about a harvest of joy. And that's what happens when we look past
whatever circumstance is before us and choose to praise God. When we
praise him for what he has done, even through our tears, we know that
our tears will one day be turned to joy. And the joy God gives is unquenchable and eternal.

prove that they are God's children, and those who do evil prove that they do not know God.*

12Everyone speaks highly of Demetrius, as does the truth itself. We ourselves can say the same for him, and you know we speak the truth.

13I have much more to say to you, but I don't want to write it with pen and ink. 14For I hope to see you soon, and then we will talk face to face.

15*Peace be with you.

Your friends here send you their greetings. Please give my personal greetings to each of our friends there.

1 Greek *From the elder.*   3 Greek *the brothers;* also in verses 5 and 10.   7a Greek *They went out on behalf of the Name.*   7b Greek *from Gentiles.*   11 Greek *they have not seen God.*   15 Some English translations combine verses 14 and 15 into verse 14.

PSALM 126:1-6
A song for pilgrims ascending to Jerusalem.

1 When the LORD brought back his
    exiles to Jerusalem,*
    it was like a dream!

2 We were filled with laughter,
    and we sang for joy.
And the other nations said,
    "What amazing things the LORD
      has done for them."
3 Yes, the LORD has done amazing
    things for us!
    What joy!

4 Restore our fortunes, LORD,
    as streams renew the desert.
5 Those who plant in tears
    will harvest with shouts of joy.
6 They weep as they go to plant their
    seed,
    but they sing as they return with
      the harvest.

126:1 Hebrew *Zion.*

PROVERBS 29:12-14
If a ruler pays attention to liars, all his advisers will be wicked. □ The poor and the oppressor have this in common—the LORD gives sight to the eyes of both. □ If a king judges the poor fairly, his throne will last forever.

DECEMBER**8**

HOSEA 10:1–14:9
Hosea closed his prophecy with yet a third lawsuit. In this case, however, there was an element of restoration. Throughout the Old Testament, God expressed his anger and disappointment with the people of Israel, yet their redemption was always his goal.

How prosperous Israel is—
    a luxuriant vine loaded with fruit.
But the richer the people get,
    the more pagan altars they build.
The more bountiful their harvests,
    the more beautiful their sacred
      pillars.
2 The hearts of the people are fickle;
    they are guilty and must be
      punished.
The LORD will break down their altars
    and smash their sacred pillars.
3 Then they will say, "We have no king

because we didn't fear the
    LORD.
But even if we had a king,
    what could he do for us anyway?"
4 They spout empty words
    and make covenants they don't
      intend to keep.
So injustice springs up among them
    like poisonous weeds in a farmer's
      field.
5 The people of Samaria tremble in fear
    for what might happen to their calf
      idol at Beth-aven.*
The people mourn and the priests wail,
    because its glory will be stripped
      away.*
6 This idol will be carted away
    to Assyria,
    a gift to the great king there.

Ephraim will be ridiculed and Israel
　　will be shamed,
　　because its people have trusted in
　　　this idol.
7 Samaria and its king will be cut off;
　　they will float away like driftwood
　　　on an ocean wave.
8 And the pagan shrines of Aven,* the
　　place of Israel's sin, will crumble.
　　Thorns and thistles will grow up
　　　around their altars.
They will beg the mountains,
　　"Bury us!"
and plead with the hills, "Fall on us!"

9 The LORD says, "O Israel, ever since
　　Gibeah,
　　there has been only sin and more
　　　sin!
You have made no progress
　　whatsoever.
Was it not right that the wicked
　　men of Gibeah were attacked?
10 Now whenever it fits my plan,
　　I will attack you, too.
I will call out the armies of the nations
　　to punish you for your multiplied
　　　sins.

11 "Israel* is like a trained heifer
　　treading out the grain—
　　an easy job she loves.
But I will put a heavy yoke on her
　　tender neck.
I will force Judah to pull the plow
　　and Israel* to break up the hard
　　　ground.
12 I said, 'Plant the good seeds of
　　righteousness,
　　and you will harvest a crop of love.
Plow up the hard ground of your hearts,
　　for now is the time to seek the LORD,
that he may come
　　and shower righteousness upon
　　　you.'

13 "But you have cultivated wickedness
　　and harvested a thriving crop
　　　of sins.
You have eaten the fruit of lies—
　　trusting in your military might,
believing that great armies
　　could make your nation safe.
14 Now the terrors of war
　　will rise among your people.

All your fortifications will fall,
　　just as when Shalman destroyed
　　　Beth-arbel.
Even mothers and children
　　were dashed to death there.
15 You will share that fate, Bethel,
　　because of your great wickedness.
When the day of judgment dawns,
　　the king of Israel will be completely
　　　destroyed.

11:1"WHEN Israel was a child, I loved him,
　　and I called my son out of Egypt.
2 But the more I* called to him,
　　the farther he moved from me,
offering sacrifices to the images
　　　of Baal
　　and burning incense to idols.
3 I myself taught Israel* how to walk,
　　leading him along by the hand.
But he doesn't know or even care
　　that it was I who took care of him.
4 I led Israel along
　　with my ropes of kindness and love.
I lifted the yoke from his neck,
　　and I myself stooped to feed him.

5 "But since my people refuse to return
　　to me,
　　they will return to Egypt
　　and will be forced to serve Assyria.
6 War will swirl through their cities;
　　their enemies will crash through
　　　their gates.
They will destroy them,
　　trapping them in their own evil
　　　plans.
7 For my people are determined
　　to desert me.
They call me the Most High,
　　but they don't truly honor me.

8 "Oh, how can I give you up, Israel?
　　How can I let you go?
How can I destroy you like Admah
　　or demolish you like Zeboiim?
My heart is torn within me,
　　and my compassion overflows.
9 No, I will not unleash my fierce anger.
　　I will not completely destroy Israel,
for I am God and not a mere mortal.
　　I am the Holy One living among you,
　　and I will not come to destroy.
10 For someday the people will follow me.
　　I, the LORD, will roar like a lion.

And when I roar,
my people will return trembling
from the west.
¹¹ Like a flock of birds, they will come
from Egypt.
Trembling like doves, they will
return from Assyria.
And I will bring them home again,"
says the LORD.

¹²*Israel surrounds me with lies and
deceit,
but Judah still obeys God
and is faithful to the Holy One.*

^{12:1}*THE people of Israel* feed on
the wind;
they chase after the east wind all
day long.
They pile up lies and violence;
they are making an alliance with
Assyria
while sending olive oil to buy
support from Egypt.

² Now the LORD is bringing charges
against Judah.
He is about to punish Jacob* for all
his deceitful ways,
and pay him back for all he has
done.
³ Even in the womb,
Jacob struggled with his brother;
when he became a man,
he even fought with God.
⁴ Yes, he wrestled with the angel
and won.
He wept and pleaded for a blessing
from him.
There at Bethel he met God face
to face,
and God spoke to him*—
⁵ the LORD God of Heaven's Armies,
the LORD is his name!
⁶ So now, come back to your God.
Act with love and justice,
and always depend on him.

⁷ But no, the people are like crafty
merchants
selling from dishonest scales—
they love to cheat.
⁸ Israel boasts, "I am rich!
I've made a fortune all by myself!
No one has caught me cheating!
My record is spotless!"

⁹ "But I am the LORD your God,
who rescued you from slavery
in Egypt.
And I will make you live in tents again,
as you do each year at the Festival
of Shelters.*
¹⁰ I sent my prophets to warn you
with many visions and parables."

¹¹ But the people of Gilead are worthless
because of their idol worship.
And in Gilgal, too, they sacrifice bulls;
their altars are lined up like the
heaps of stone
along the edges of a plowed field.
¹² Jacob fled to the land of Aram,
and there he* earned a wife by
tending sheep.
¹³ Then by a prophet
the LORD brought Jacob's
descendants* out of Egypt;
and by that prophet
they were protected.
¹⁴ But the people of Israel
have bitterly provoked the LORD,
so their Lord will now sentence them
to death
in payment for their sins.

^{13:1}WHEN the tribe of Ephraim spoke,
the people shook with fear,
for that tribe was important
in Israel.
But the people of Ephraim sinned by
worshiping Baal
and thus sealed their destruction.
² Now they continue to sin by making
silver idols,
images shaped skillfully with
human hands.
"Sacrifice to these," they cry,
"and kiss the calf idols!"
³ Therefore, they will disappear like
the morning mist,
like dew in the morning sun,
like chaff blown by the wind,
like smoke from a chimney.

⁴ "I have been the LORD your God
ever since I brought you out
of Egypt.
You must acknowledge no God but me,
for there is no other savior.
⁵ I took care of you in the wilderness,
in that dry and thirsty land.

6 But when you had eaten and were
    satisfied,
  you became proud and forgot me.
7 So now I will attack you like a lion,
    like a leopard that lurks along
    the road.
8 Like a bear whose cubs have been
    taken away,
  I will tear out your heart.
  I will devour you like a hungry
    lioness
  and mangle you like a wild animal.

9 "You are about to be destroyed,
    O Israel—
  yes, by me, your only helper.
10 Now where is* your king?
  Let him save you!
  Where are all the leaders of the land,
    the king and the officials you
    demanded of me?
11 In my anger I gave you kings,
  and in my fury I took them away.

12 "Ephraim's guilt has been collected,
  and his sin has been stored up for
    punishment.
13 Pain has come to the people
  like the pain of childbirth,
  but they are like a child
    who resists being born.
  The moment of birth has arrived,
    but they stay in the womb!

14 "Should I ransom them from
    the grave*?
  Should I redeem them from death?
  O death, bring on your terrors!
  O grave, bring on your plagues!*
  For I will not take pity on them.
15 Ephraim was the most fruitful of all
    his brothers,
  but the east wind—a blast from
    the LORD—
  will arise in the desert.
  All their flowing springs will run dry,
    and all their wells will disappear.
  Every precious thing they own
    will be plundered and carried away.
16 The people of Samaria
    must bear the consequences
    of their guilt
  because they rebelled against their
    God.
  They will be killed by an invading
    army,
    their little ones dashed to death
    against the ground,
    their pregnant women ripped open
    by swords."

14:1 RETURN, O Israel, to the LORD your
    God,
  for your sins have brought you down.
2 Bring your confessions, and return
    to the LORD.
  Say to him,

HOW WE LIVE: Prayer

HOSEA 14:1-2 Prayer is sometimes the most difficult thing to do, especially when you know you've blown it (maybe for the umpteenth time) and you just don't want to bother God again. "He must be really tired of me now," you think. "I'm hopeless." But God says, "Return . . . to the Lord your God." You know from experience that "your sins have brought you down." Israel knew it, too. Hosea's entire prophecy (and life) was about God's love for an unfaithful people. Yet here God calls them to return, bring their confessions, and ask for his forgiveness. • So pray—even when it's difficult. You will find forgiveness and power over that sin when you recognize its destructive power and that you need God to help you fight it. Say to him, "I cannot get past this on my own. I don't want to keep falling into this sin. I need your forgiveness, and I ask for your strength and power to help me overcome." What will God say? "I will heal you of your faithlessness; my love will know no bounds" (14:4). Now that's a welcome answer to a difficult prayer!

"Forgive all our sins and graciously
receive us,
so that we may offer you our
praises.
³ Assyria cannot save us,
nor can our warhorses.
Never again will we say to the idols
we have made,
'You are our gods.'
No, in you alone
do the orphans find mercy."

⁴ The LORD says,
"Then I will heal you of your
faithlessness;
my love will know no bounds,
for my anger will be gone forever.
⁵ I will be to Israel
like a refreshing dew from heaven.
Israel will blossom like the lily;
it will send roots deep into the soil
like the cedars in Lebanon.
⁶ Its branches will spread out like
beautiful olive trees,
as fragrant as the cedars
of Lebanon.
⁷ My people will again live under my
shade.
They will flourish like grain and
blossom like grapevines.
They will be as fragrant as the wines
of Lebanon.

⁸ "O Israel,* stay away from idols!
I am the one who answers your
prayers and cares for you.
I am like a tree that is always green;
all your fruit comes from me."

⁹ Let those who are wise understand
these things.
Let those with discernment listen
carefully.
The paths of the LORD are true and
right,
and righteous people live by
walking in them.
But in those paths sinners stumble
and fall.

10:5a *Beth-aven* means "house of wickedness"; it is being
used as another name for Bethel, which means "house of
God." 10:5b Or *because it will be taken away into exile.*
10:8 *Aven* is a reference to Beth-aven; see 10:5a and the note
there. 10:11a Hebrew *Ephraim*, referring to the northern
kingdom of Israel. 10:11b Hebrew *Jacob.* The names
"Jacob" and "Israel" are often interchanged throughout
the Old Testament, referring sometimes to the individual

patriarch and sometimes to the nation. 11:2 As in Greek
version; Hebrew reads *they.* 11:3 Hebrew *Ephraim*,
referring to the northern kingdom of Israel; also in 11:8, 9,
12. 11:12a Verse 11:12 is numbered 12:1 in Hebrew text.
11:12b Or *and Judah is unruly against God, the faithful
Holy One.* The meaning of the Hebrew is uncertain.
12:1a Verses 12:1-14 are numbered 12:2-15 in Hebrew text.
12:1b Hebrew *Ephraim*, referring to the northern kingdom
of Israel; also in 12:8, 14. 12:2 *Jacob* sounds like the
Hebrew word for "deceiver." 12:4 As in Greek and Syriac
versions; Hebrew reads *to us.* 12:9 Hebrew *as in the days
of your appointed feast.* 12:12 Hebrew *Israel.* See note on
10:11b. 12:13 Hebrew *brought Israel.* See note on 10:11b.
13:10 As in Greek and Syriac versions and Latin Vulgate;
Hebrew reads *Sheol*; also in 13:14b. 13:14a Hebrew *Sheol*; also in
13:14b. 13:14b Greek version reads *O death, where is
your punishment? / O grave [Hades], where is your sting?*
Compare 1 Cor 15:55. 14:8 Hebrew *Ephraim*, referring to
the northern kingdom of Israel.

JUDE 1:1-25

Jude, along with James, was one of Jesus' half-
brothers. You might remember that during Jesus'
lifetime, his family didn't fully comprehend his identity and mission. Jude evidently didn't come to faith
until after the resurrection. In this letter, he reminds
his readers to be on guard against false teachers.

This letter is from Jude, a slave of Jesus
Christ and a brother of James.

I am writing to all who have been called
by God the Father, who loves you and
keeps you safe in the care of Jesus Christ.*
²May God give you more and more
mercy, peace, and love.

³Dear friends, I had been eagerly planning to write to you about the salvation we
all share. But now I find that I must write
about something else, urging you to defend the faith that God has entrusted
once for all time to his holy people. ⁴I say
this because some ungodly people have
wormed their way into your churches,
saying that God's marvelous grace allows
us to live immoral lives. The condemnation of such people was recorded long
ago, for they have denied our only Master
and Lord, Jesus Christ.

⁵So I want to remind you, though you already know these things, that Jesus* first
rescued the nation of Israel from Egypt,
but later he destroyed those who did not
remain faithful. ⁶And I remind you of the
angels who did not stay within the limits of
authority God gave them but left the place
where they belonged. God has kept them
securely chained in prisons of darkness,
waiting for the great day of judgment.
⁷And don't forget Sodom and Gomorrah
and their neighboring towns, which were

filled with immorality and every kind of sexual perversion. Those cities were destroyed by fire and serve as a warning of the eternal fire of God's judgment.

[8]In the same way, these people—who claim authority from their dreams—live immoral lives, defy authority, and scoff at supernatural beings.* [9]But even Michael, one of the mightiest of the angels,* did not dare accuse the devil of blasphemy, but simply said, "The Lord rebuke you!" (This took place when Michael was arguing with the devil about Moses' body.) [10]But these people scoff at things they do not understand. Like unthinking animals, they do whatever their instincts tell them, and so they bring about their own destruction. [11]What sorrow awaits them! For they follow in the footsteps of Cain, who killed his brother. Like Balaam, they deceive people for money. And like Korah, they perish in their rebellion.

[12]When these people eat with you in your fellowship meals commemorating the Lord's love, they are like dangerous reefs that can shipwreck you.* They are like shameless shepherds who care only for themselves. They are like clouds blowing over the land without giving any rain. They are like trees in autumn that are doubly dead, for they bear no fruit and have been pulled up by the roots. [13]They are like wild waves of the sea, churning up the foam of their shameful deeds. They are like wandering stars, doomed forever to blackest darkness.

[14]Enoch, who lived in the seventh generation after Adam, prophesied about these people. He said, "Listen! The Lord is coming with countless thousands of his holy ones [15]to execute judgment on the people of the world. He will convict every person of all the ungodly things they have done and for all the insults that ungodly sinners have spoken against him."*

[16]These people are grumblers and complainers, living only to satisfy their desires. They brag loudly about themselves, and they flatter others to get what they want.

[17]But you, my dear friends, must remember what the apostles of our Lord Jesus Christ said. [18]They told you that in the last times there would be scoffers whose purpose in life is to satisfy their ungodly desires. [19]These people are the ones who are creating divisions among you. They follow their natural instincts because they do not have God's Spirit in them.

[20]But you, dear friends, must build each other up in your most holy faith, pray in the power of the Holy Spirit,* [21]and await the mercy of our Lord Jesus Christ, who will bring you eternal life. In this way, you will keep yourselves safe in God's love.

[22]And you must show mercy to those whose faith is wavering. [23]Rescue others by snatching them from the flames of judgment. Show mercy to still others,* but do so with great caution, hating the sins that contaminate their lives.*

[24]Now all glory to God, who is able to keep you from falling away and will bring you with great joy into his glorious presence without a single fault. [25]All glory to him who alone is God, our Savior through Jesus Christ our Lord. All glory, majesty, power, and authority are his before all time, and in the present, and beyond all time! Amen.

1 Or *keeps you for Jesus Christ.*   **5** As in the best manuscripts; various other manuscripts read *[the] Lord,* or *God,* or *Christ;* one reads *God Christ.*   **8** Greek *at glorious ones,* which are probably evil angels.   **9** Greek *Michael, the archangel.*   **12** Or *they are contaminants among you;* or *they are stains.*   **14-15** The quotation comes from intertestamental literature: Enoch 1:9.   **20** Greek *pray in the Holy Spirit.*   **22-23a** Some manuscripts have only two categories of people: (1) those whose faith is wavering and therefore need to be snatched from the flames of judgment, and (2) those who need to be shown mercy.   **23b** Greek *with fear, hating even the clothing stained by the flesh.*

PSALM 127:1-5

A song for pilgrims ascending to Jerusalem. A psalm of Solomon.

[1] Unless the LORD builds a house,
      the work of the builders is wasted.
   Unless the LORD protects a city,
      guarding it with sentries will
         do no good.
[2] It is useless for you to work so hard
      from early morning until late
         at night,
   anxiously working for food to eat;
      for God gives rest to his loved ones.

[3] Children are a gift from the LORD;
      they are a reward from him.

4 Children born to a young man
are like arrows in a warrior's
hands.
5 How joyful is the man whose quiver
is full of them!
He will not be put to shame when
he confronts his accusers at the
city gates.

DECEMBER**9**

JOEL 1:1–3:21

Joel ministered as the nation of Judah struggled
with good and bad kings (and a terrible queen).
Joel's prophecy opens with a plague of locusts—
swarming insects that migrate en masse causing
horrible destruction to vegetation. The locusts
served as an image of invading armies.

The LORD gave this message to Joel son of
Pethuel.

2 Hear this, you leaders of the people.
Listen, all who live in the land.
In all your history,
has anything like this happened
before?
3 Tell your children about it in the years
to come,
and let your children tell their
children.
Pass the story down from
generation to generation.
4 After the cutting locusts finished
eating the crops,
the swarming locusts took what
was left!
After them came the hopping locusts,
and then the stripping locusts,* too!

5 Wake up, you drunkards, and weep!
Wail, all you wine-drinkers!
All the grapes are ruined,
and all your sweet wine is gone.
6 A vast army of locusts* has invaded
my land,
a terrible army too numerous
to count.
Its teeth are like lions' teeth,
its fangs like those of a lioness.

PROVERBS 29:15-17

To discipline a child produces wisdom,
but a mother is disgraced by an undisci-
plined child. □ When the wicked are in
authority, sin flourishes, but the godly will
live to see their downfall. □ Discipline
your children, and they will give you peace
of mind and will make your heart glad.

7 It has destroyed my grapevines
and ruined my fig trees,
stripping their bark and destroying it,
leaving the branches white and
bare.
8 Weep like a bride dressed in black,
mourning the death of her
husband.
9 For there is no grain or wine
to offer at the Temple of the LORD.
So the priests are in mourning.
The ministers of the LORD are
weeping.
10 The fields are ruined,
the land is stripped bare.
The grain is destroyed,
the grapes have shriveled,
and the olive oil is gone.

11 Despair, all you farmers!
Wail, all you vine growers!
Weep, because the wheat and barley—
all the crops of the field—
are ruined.
12 The grapevines have dried up,
and the fig trees have withered.
The pomegranate trees, palm trees,
and apple trees—
all the fruit trees—have dried up.
And the people's joy has dried up
with them.

13 Dress yourselves in burlap and weep,
you priests!
Wail, you who serve before the altar!
Come, spend the night in burlap,
you ministers of my God.

For there is no grain or wine
   to offer at the Temple of your God.
14 Announce a time of fasting;
   call the people together for
      a solemn meeting.
   Bring the leaders
      and all the people of the land
   into the Temple of the LORD your God,
      and cry out to him there.
15 The day of the LORD is near,
   the day when destruction comes
      from the Almighty.
   How terrible that day will be!

16 Our food disappears before our very
      eyes.
   No joyful celebrations are held
      in the house of our God.
17 The seeds die in the parched ground,
      and the grain crops fail.
   The barns stand empty,
      and granaries are abandoned.
18 How the animals moan with hunger!
   The herds of cattle wander about
      confused,
   because they have no pasture.
   The flocks of sheep and goats bleat
      in misery.

19 LORD, help us!
   The fire has consumed the wilderness
      pastures,
   and flames have burned up all the
      trees.
20 Even the wild animals cry out to you
   because the streams have dried up,
   and fire has consumed the
      wilderness pastures.

2:1 SOUND the alarm in Jerusalem*!
   Raise the battle cry on my holy
      mountain!
   Let everyone tremble in fear
   because the day of the LORD is upon
      us.
2 It is a day of darkness and gloom,
   a day of thick clouds and deep
      blackness.
   Suddenly, like dawn spreading across
      the mountains,
   a great and mighty army appears.
   Nothing like it has been seen before
      or will ever be seen again.

3 Fire burns in front of them,
   and flames follow after them.

Ahead of them the land lies
   as beautiful as the Garden of Eden.
Behind them is nothing but desolation;
   not one thing escapes.
4 They look like horses;
   they charge forward like
      warhorses.*
5 Look at them as they leap along the
      mountaintops.
   Listen to the noise they make—
      like the rumbling of chariots,
   like the roar of fire sweeping across
      a field of stubble,
   or like a mighty army moving
      into battle.

6 Fear grips all the people;
   every face grows pale with terror.
7 The attackers march like warriors
   and scale city walls like soldiers.
   Straight forward they march,
      never breaking rank.
8 They never jostle each other;
   each moves in exactly the right
      position.
   They break through defenses
      without missing a step.
9 They swarm over the city
   and run along its walls.
   They enter all the houses,
      climbing like thieves through
      the windows.
10 The earth quakes as they advance,
      and the heavens tremble.
   The sun and moon grow dark,
      and the stars no longer shine.

11 The LORD is at the head of the column.
   He leads them with a shout.
   This is his mighty army,
      and they follow his orders.
   The day of the LORD is an awesome,
      terrible thing.
   Who can possibly survive?

12 That is why the LORD says,
   "Turn to me now, while there
      is time.
   Give me your hearts.
   Come with fasting, weeping, and
      mourning.
13 Don't tear your clothing in your grief,
      but tear your hearts instead."
   Return to the LORD your God,
      for he is merciful and
      compassionate,

slow to get angry and filled with
unfailing love.
He is eager to relent and not punish.
¹⁴ Who knows? Perhaps he will give you
a reprieve,
sending you a blessing instead
of this curse.
Perhaps you will be able to offer grain
and wine
to the LORD your God as before.

¹⁵ Blow the ram's horn in Jerusalem!
Announce a time of fasting;
call the people together
for a solemn meeting.
¹⁶ Gather all the people—
the elders, the children, and even
the babies.
Call the bridegroom from his quarters
and the bride from her private
room.
¹⁷ Let the priests, who minister in the
LORD's presence,
stand and weep between the entry
room to the Temple and the altar.
Let them pray, "Spare your people,
LORD!
Don't let your special possession
become an object of mockery.
Don't let them become a joke for
unbelieving foreigners who say,
'Has the God of Israel left them?'"

¹⁸ Then the LORD will pity his people
and jealously guard the honor
of his land.
¹⁹ The LORD will reply,
"Look! I am sending you grain and
new wine and olive oil,
enough to satisfy your needs.
You will no longer be an object
of mockery
among the surrounding nations.
²⁰ I will drive away these armies from
the north.
I will send them into the parched
wastelands.
Those in the front will be driven into
the Dead Sea,
and those at the rear into the
Mediterranean.*
The stench of their rotting bodies will
rise over the land."

Surely the LORD has done great things!

²¹ Don't be afraid, my people.
Be glad now and rejoice,
for the LORD has done great things.
²² Don't be afraid, you animals of the
field,
for the wilderness pastures will
soon be green.
The trees will again be filled with fruit;
fig trees and grapevines will be
loaded down once more.
²³ Rejoice, you people of Jerusalem!
Rejoice in the LORD your God!
For the rain he sends demonstrates
his faithfulness.
Once more the autumn rains will
come,
as well as the rains of spring.
²⁴ The threshing floors will again be
piled high with grain,
and the presses will overflow with
new wine and olive oil.

²⁵ The LORD says, "I will give you back
what you lost
to the swarming locusts, the
hopping locusts,
the stripping locusts, and the cutting
locusts.*
It was I who sent this great
destroying army against you.
²⁶ Once again you will have all the food
you want,
and you will praise the LORD your
God,
who does these miracles for you.
Never again will my people be
disgraced.
²⁷ Then you will know that I am among
my people Israel,
that I am the LORD your God,
and there is no other.
Never again will my people be
disgraced.

²⁸*"Then, after doing all those things,
I will pour out my Spirit upon all
people.
Your sons and daughters will
prophesy.
Your old men will dream dreams,
and your young men will see visions.
²⁹ In those days I will pour out my Spirit
even on servants—men and women
alike.

30 And I will cause wonders in the
　　heavens and on the earth—
　　blood and fire and columns
　　　of smoke.
31 The sun will become dark,
　　and the moon will turn blood red
　　before that great and terrible* day
　　　of the LORD arrives.
32 But everyone who calls on the name
　　　of the LORD
　　will be saved,
　for some on Mount Zion in Jerusalem
　　will escape,
　　just as the LORD has said.
　These will be among the survivors
　　whom the LORD has called.

3:1* "AT the time of those events," says
　　　the LORD,
　　"when I restore the prosperity
　　　of Judah and Jerusalem,
2 I will gather the armies of the world
　　into the valley of Jehoshaphat.*
　There I will judge them
　　for harming my people, my special
　　　possession,
　for scattering my people among
　　　the nations,
　　and for dividing up my land.
3 They threw dice* to decide which
　　　of my people
　　would be their slaves.

They traded boys to obtain prostitutes
　　and sold girls for enough wine to
　　　get drunk.

4 "What do you have against me, Tyre
and Sidon and you cities of Philistia? Are
you trying to take revenge on me? If you
are, then watch out! I will strike swiftly
and pay you back for everything you have
done. 5 You have taken my silver and gold
and all my precious treasures, and have
carried them off to your pagan temples.
6 You have sold the people of Judah and Jerusalem to the Greeks,* so they could take
them far from their homeland.

7 "But I will bring them back from all
the places to which you sold them, and I
will pay you back for everything you have
done. 8 I will sell your sons and daughters
to the people of Judah, and they will sell
them to the people of Arabia,* a nation far
away. I, the LORD, have spoken!"

9 　Say to the nations far and wide:
　　"Get ready for war!
　Call out your best warriors.
　　Let all your fighting men advance
　　　for the attack.
10 Hammer your plowshares into swords
　　and your pruning hooks into
　　　spears.
　Train even your weaklings to
　　be warriors.

HOW WE LIVE

Confessing our sins

JOEL 2:12-13 As much as people don't like to think about it, there will be
an end to all this, and a judgment to follow. Many people scoff at any
kind of accountability for how their lives were lived on earth. Throughout
this book, Joel repeatedly refers to "the day of the LORD." On this day,
judgment will come. For those who have accepted Christ's sacrifice on
their behalf (as you have), the Judge will find that the penalty for their
sins has already been paid. Eternal life is theirs (and yours!). We believers will also receive rewards in heaven according to how we've lived.
That's why you stay close to God, live as you should, and keep short
accounts with him by confessing your sins. • For unbelievers, however,
it's a different story—judgment is something to be feared. The day of the
Lord will be a time of punishment. That's why God says, "Turn to me now,
while there is time," because one day, the time will run out. • Confession brings unbelievers to God and keeps believers close to him. As you
confess your sins to God, remember to pray for those who have yet to
understand that their time will one day run out. Pray that they will turn
to God while there is still time.

¹¹ Come quickly, all you nations
everywhere.
Gather together in the valley."

And now, O LORD, call out your
warriors!

¹² "Let the nations be called to arms.
Let them march to the valley of
Jehoshaphat.
There I, the LORD, will sit
to pronounce judgment on them all.
¹³ Swing the sickle,
for the harvest is ripe.*
Come, tread the grapes,
for the winepress is full.
The storage vats are overflowing
with the wickedness of these
people."

¹⁴ Thousands upon thousands are
waiting in the valley of decision.
There the day of the LORD will soon
arrive.
¹⁵ The sun and moon will grow dark,
and the stars will no longer shine.
¹⁶ The LORD's voice will roar from Zion
and thunder from Jerusalem,
and the heavens and the earth
will shake.
But the LORD will be a refuge for
his people,
a strong fortress for the people
of Israel.

¹⁷ "Then you will know that I, the LORD
your God,
live in Zion, my holy mountain.
Jerusalem will be holy forever,
and foreign armies will never
conquer her again.
¹⁸ In that day the mountains will drip
with sweet wine,
and the hills will flow with milk.
Water will fill the streambeds
of Judah,
and a fountain will burst forth from
the LORD's Temple,
watering the arid valley of acacias.*
¹⁹ But Egypt will become a wasteland
and Edom will become a
wilderness,
because they attacked the people
of Judah
and killed innocent people
in their land.

²⁰ "But Judah will be filled with people
forever,
and Jerusalem will endure through
all generations.
²¹ I will pardon my people's crimes,
which I have not yet pardoned;
and I, the LORD, will make my home
in Jerusalem* with my people."

1:4 The precise identification of the four kinds of locusts
mentioned here is uncertain.   1:6 Hebrew *A nation.*
2:1 Hebrew *Zion;* also in 2:15, 23.   2:4 Or *like charioteers.*
2:20 Hebrew *into the eastern sea, . . . into the western sea.*
2:25 The precise identification of the four kinds of locusts
mentioned here is uncertain.   2:28 Verses 2:28-32 are
numbered 3:1-5 in Hebrew text.   2:31 Greek version reads
glorious.   3:1 Verses 3:1-21 are numbered 4:1-21 in
Hebrew text.   3:2 *Jehoshaphat* means "the LORD judges."
3:3 Hebrew *They cast lots.*   3:6 Hebrew *to the peoples of
Javan.*   3:8 Hebrew *to the Sabeans.*   3:13 Greek version
reads *for the harvest time has come.* Compare Mark 4:29.
3:18 Hebrew *valley of Shittim.*   3:21 Hebrew *Zion.*

REVELATION 1:1-20

John was an apostle of Jesus, author of the Gospel
of John, the three letters that bear his name, and
Revelation. John was given this vision of the end
of the world while exiled to the island of Patmos,
which was his punishment for preaching the
Good News.

This is a revelation from* Jesus Christ,
which God gave him to show his servants
the events that must soon* take place. He
sent an angel to present this revelation to
his servant John, ²who faithfully reported
everything he saw. This is his report of the
word of God and the testimony of Jesus
Christ.

³God blesses the one who reads the
words of this prophecy to the church, and
he blesses all who listen to its message
and obey what it says, for the time is near.

⁴This letter is from John to the seven
churches in the province of Asia.*

Grace and peace to you from the one
who is, who always was, and who is still to
come; from the sevenfold Spirit* before
his throne; ⁵and from Jesus Christ. He is
the faithful witness to these things, the
first to rise from the dead, and the ruler of
all the kings of the world.

All glory to him who loves us and has
freed us from our sins by shedding his
blood for us. ⁶He has made us a Kingdom
of priests for God his Father. All glory and
power to him forever and ever! Amen.

[7] Look! He comes with the clouds
of heaven.
And everyone will see him—
even those who pierced him.
And all the nations of the world
will mourn for him.
Yes! Amen!

[8]"I am the Alpha and the Omega—the
beginning and the end,"* says the Lord
God. "I am the one who is, who always was,
and who is still to come—the Almighty
One."

[9]I, John, am your brother and your partner in suffering and in God's Kingdom
and in the patient endurance to which
Jesus calls us. I was exiled to the island of
Patmos for preaching the word of God
and for my testimony about Jesus. [10]It was
the Lord's Day, and I was worshiping in
the Spirit.* Suddenly, I heard behind me a
loud voice like a trumpet blast. [11]It said,
"Write in a book* everything you see, and
send it to the seven churches in the cities
of Ephesus, Smyrna, Pergamum, Thyatira,
Sardis, Philadelphia, and Laodicea."

[12]When I turned to see who was speaking to me, I saw seven gold lampstands.
[13]And standing in the middle of the lampstands was someone like the Son of Man.*
He was wearing a long robe with a gold
sash across his chest. [14]His head and his
hair were white like wool, as white as
snow. And his eyes were like flames of
fire. [15]His feet were like polished bronze
refined in a furnace, and his voice thundered like mighty ocean waves. [16]He held
seven stars in his right hand, and a sharp
two-edged sword came from his mouth.
And his face was like the sun in all its bril-
liance.

[17]When I saw him, I fell at his feet as if I
were dead. But he laid his right hand on me
and said, "Don't be afraid! I am the First
and the Last. [18]I am the living one. I died,
but look—I am alive forever and ever! And I
hold the keys of death and the grave.*

[19]"Write down what you have seen—
both the things that are now happening
and the things that will happen.* [20]This is
the meaning of the mystery of the seven
stars you saw in my right hand and the
seven gold lampstands: The seven stars
are the angels* of the seven churches,
and the seven lampstands are the seven
churches."

1:1a Or *of.*   1:1b Or *suddenly,* or *quickly.*   1:4a *Asia* was a
Roman province in what is now western Turkey.   1:4b Greek
the seven spirits.   1:8 Greek *I am Alpha and the Omega,*
referring to the first and last letters of the Greek alphabet.
1:10 Or *in spirit.*   1:11 Or *on a scroll.*   1:13 Or *like a son
of man.* See Dan 7:13. "Son of Man" is a title Jesus used for
himself.   1:18 Greek *and Hades.*   1:19 Or *what you have
seen and what they mean—the things that have already
begun to happen.*   1:20 Or *the messengers.*

PSALM 128:1-6
A song for pilgrims ascending to Jerusalem.

[1] **H**ow joyful are those who fear
the LORD—
all who follow his ways!
[2] You will enjoy the fruit of your labor.
How joyful and prosperous you
will be!
[3] Your wife will be like a fruitful
grapevine,
flourishing within your home.
Your children will be like vigorous
young olive trees
as they sit around your table.
[4] That is the LORD's blessing
for those who fear him.

[5] May the LORD continually bless you
from Zion.
May you see Jerusalem prosper
as long as you live.
[6] May you live to enjoy your
grandchildren.
May Israel have peace!

PROVERBS 29:18
When people do not accept divine guidance, they run wild. But whoever obeys
the law is joyful.

DECEMBER**10**

The first part of Amos's prophecy was against the nations. He spoke first against the nations surrounding the northern kingdom of Israel. Then he turned his attention to Israel itself.

This message was given to Amos, a shepherd from the town of Tekoa in Judah. He received this message in visions two years before the earthquake, when Uzziah was king of Judah and Jeroboam II, the son of Jehoash,* was king of Israel.

² This is what he saw and heard:

"The LORD's voice will roar from Zion
and thunder from Jerusalem!
The lush pastures of the shepherds
will dry up;
the grass on Mount Carmel will
wither and die."

³ This is what the LORD says:

"The people of Damascus have sinned
again and again,*
and I will not let them go
unpunished!
They beat down my people in Gilead
as grain is threshed with iron
sledges.
⁴ So I will send down fire on King
Hazael's palace,
and the fortresses of King Ben-
hadad will be destroyed.
⁵ I will break down the gates of
Damascus
and slaughter the people in the
valley of Aven.
I will destroy the ruler in Beth-eden,
and the people of Aram will go as
captives to Kir,"
says the LORD.

⁶ This is what the LORD says:

"The people of Gaza have sinned again
and again,
and I will not let them go
unpunished!
They sent whole villages into exile,
selling them as slaves to Edom.
⁷ So I will send down fire on the walls
of Gaza,

and all its fortresses will
be destroyed.
⁸ I will slaughter the people of Ashdod
and destroy the king of Ashkelon.
Then I will turn to attack Ekron,
and the few Philistines still left will
be killed,"
says the Sovereign LORD.

⁹ This is what the LORD says:

"The people of Tyre have sinned again
and again,
and I will not let them go
unpunished!
They broke their treaty of
brotherhood with Israel,
selling whole villages as slaves
to Edom.
¹⁰ So I will send down fire on the walls
of Tyre,
and all its fortresses will be
destroyed."

¹¹ This is what the LORD says:

"The people of Edom have sinned
again and again,
and I will not let them go
unpunished!
They chased down their relatives,
the Israelites, with swords,
showing them no mercy.
In their rage, they slashed them
continually
and were unrelenting in their anger.
¹² So I will send down fire on Teman,
and the fortresses of Bozrah will
be destroyed."

¹³ This is what the LORD says:

"The people of Ammon have sinned
again and again,
and I will not let them go
unpunished!
When they attacked Gilead to extend
their borders,
they ripped open pregnant women
with their swords.
¹⁴ So I will send down fire on the walls
of Rabbah,

and all its fortresses will
   be destroyed.
The battle will be upon them with
      shouts,
   like a whirlwind in a mighty storm.
¹⁵ And their king* and his princes will
      go into exile together,"
   says the LORD.

²:¹THIS is what the LORD says:

"The people of Moab have sinned
      again and again,*
   and I will not let them go
      unpunished!
They desecrated the bones of Edom's
      king,
   burning them to ashes.
² So I will send down fire on the land
      of Moab,
   and all the fortresses in Kerioth will
      be destroyed.
The people will fall in the noise
      of battle,
   as the warriors shout and the ram's
      horn sounds.
³ And I will destroy their king
   and slaughter all their princes,"
   says the LORD.

⁴This is what the LORD says:

"The people of Judah have sinned
      again and again,
   and I will not let them go
      unpunished!
They have rejected the instruction
      of the LORD,
   refusing to obey his decrees.
They have been led astray by the same
      lies
   that deceived their ancestors.
⁵ So I will send down fire on Judah,
   and all the fortresses of Jerusalem
      will be destroyed."

⁶This is what the LORD says:

"The people of Israel have sinned
      again and again,
   and I will not let them go
      unpunished!
They sell honorable people for silver
   and poor people for a pair
      of sandals.

⁷ They trample helpless people
      in the dust
   and shove the oppressed out
      of the way.
Both father and son sleep with
      the same woman,
   corrupting my holy name.
⁸ At their religious festivals,
      they lounge in clothing their
      debtors put up as security.
In the house of their god,
   they drink wine bought with unjust
      fines.

⁹ "But as my people watched,
   I destroyed the Amorites,
though they were as tall as cedars
   and as strong as oaks.
I destroyed the fruit on their branches
   and dug out their roots.
¹⁰ It was I who rescued you from Egypt
   and led you through the desert for
      forty years,
so you could possess the land
   of the Amorites.
¹¹ I chose some of your sons to be
      prophets
   and others to be Nazirites.
Can you deny this, my people
   of Israel?"
   asks the LORD.
¹² "But you caused the Nazirites to sin
      by making them drink wine,
   and you commanded the prophets,
      'Shut up!'

¹³ "So I will make you groan
   like a wagon loaded down with
      sheaves of grain.
¹⁴ Your fastest runners will not get away.
   The strongest among you will
      become weak.
Even mighty warriors will be unable
   to save themselves.
¹⁵   The archers will not stand their
         ground.
The swiftest runners won't be fast
      enough to escape.
   Even those riding horses won't
      be able to save themselves.
¹⁶ On that day the most courageous
      of your fighting men
   will drop their weapons and run
      for their lives,"
   says the LORD.

3:1LISTEN to this message that the LORD has spoken against you, O people of Israel and Judah—against the entire family I rescued from Egypt:

2 "From among all the families
    on the earth,
  I have been intimate with you alone.
  That is why I must punish you
    for all your sins."

3 Can two people walk together
    without agreeing on the direction?
4 Does a lion ever roar in a thicket
    without first finding a victim?
  Does a young lion growl in its den
    without first catching its prey?
5 Does a bird ever get caught in a trap
    that has no bait?
  Does a trap spring shut
    when there's nothing to catch?
6 When the ram's horn blows a warning,
    shouldn't the people be alarmed?
  Does disaster come to a city
    unless the LORD has planned it?
7 Indeed, the Sovereign LORD never
    does anything
  until he reveals his plans to his
    servants the prophets.

8 The lion has roared—
    so who isn't frightened?
  The Sovereign LORD has spoken—
    so who can refuse to proclaim his
    message?
9 Announce this to the leaders
    of Philistia*
  and to the great ones of Egypt:
  "Take your seats now on the hills
    around Samaria,
  and witness the chaos and
    oppression in Israel."

10 "My people have forgotten how
    to do right,"
  says the LORD.
  "Their fortresses are filled with wealth
    taken by theft and violence.
11 Therefore," says the Sovereign LORD,
  "an enemy is coming!
  He will surround them and shatter
    their defenses.
  Then he will plunder all their
    fortresses."

12 This is what the LORD says:

"A shepherd who tries to rescue
    a sheep from a lion's mouth
  will recover only two legs or a piece
    of an ear.
So it will be for the Israelites in
    Samaria lying on luxurious beds,
  and for the people of Damascus
    reclining on couches.*

13"Now listen to this, and announce it throughout all Israel,*" says the Lord, the LORD God of Heaven's Armies.

14 "On the very day I punish Israel
    for its sins,
  I will destroy the pagan altars
    at Bethel.
  The horns of the altar will be cut off
    and fall to the ground.
15 And I will destroy the beautiful homes
    of the wealthy—
  their winter mansions and their
    summer houses, too—
  all their palaces filled with ivory,"
    says the LORD.

1:1 Hebrew *Joash,* a variant spelling of Jehoash.   1:3 Hebrew *have committed three sins, even four;* also in 1:6, 9, 11, 13.   1:15 Hebrew *malcam,* possibly referring to their god Molech.   2:1 Hebrew *have committed three sins, even four;* also in 2:4, 6.   3:9 Hebrew *Ashdod.*   3:12 Or *So it will be when the Israelites in Samaria are rescued / with only a broken bed and a tattered pillow.*   3:13 Hebrew *the house of Jacob.* The names "Jacob" and "Israel" are often interchanged throughout the Old Testament, referring sometimes to the individual patriarch and sometimes to the nation.

REVELATION 2:1-17
John's vision opens with a series of messages for seven first-century churches. Each message includes an assessment of the spiritual state of the congregation. The churches are listed in geographical order, starting at Ephesus (on the western coast of Asia Minor), circling north, east, and then south to Laodicea.

"**W**rite this letter to the angel* of the church in Ephesus. This is the message from the one who holds the seven stars in his right hand, the one who walks among the seven gold lampstands:

2"I know all the things you do. I have seen your hard work and your patient endurance. I know you don't tolerate evil people. You have examined the claims of those who say they are apostles but are not. You have discovered they are liars. [3]You have patiently suffered for me without quitting.

[4]"But I have this complaint against you. You don't love me or each other as you did at first!* [5]Look how far you have fallen! Turn back to me and do the works you did at first. If you don't repent, I will come and remove your lampstand from its place among the churches. [6]But this is in your favor: You hate the evil deeds of the Nicolaitans, just as I do.

[7]"Anyone with ears to hear must listen to the Spirit and understand what he is saying to the churches. To everyone who is victorious I will give fruit from the tree of life in the paradise of God.

[8]"Write this letter to the angel of the church in Smyrna. This is the message from the one who is the First and the Last, who was dead but is now alive:

[9]"I know about your suffering and your poverty—but you are rich! I know the blasphemy of those opposing you. They say they are Jews, but they are not, because their synagogue belongs to Satan. [10]Don't be afraid of what you are about to suffer. The devil will throw some of you into prison to test

you. You will suffer for ten days. But if you remain faithful even when facing death, I will give you the crown of life.

[11]"Anyone with ears to hear must listen to the Spirit and understand what he is saying to the churches. Whoever is victorious will not be harmed by the second death.

[12]"Write this letter to the angel of the church in Pergamum. This is the message from the one with the sharp two-edged sword:

[13]"I know that you live in the city where Satan has his throne, yet you have remained loyal to me. You refused to deny me even when Antipas, my faithful witness, was martyred among you there in Satan's city.

[14]"But I have a few complaints against you. You tolerate some among you whose teaching is like that of Balaam, who showed Balak how to trip up the people of Israel. He taught them to sin by eating food offered to idols and by committing sexual sin. [15]In a similar way, you have some Nicolaitans among you who follow the same teaching. [16]Repent of your sin, or I will come to you suddenly and fight against them with the sword of my mouth.

[17]"Anyone with ears to hear must listen to the Spirit and understand

WHO GOD IS — God is personal

REVELATION 2:17 As the Israelites had traveled toward the Promised Land, God had provided manna from heaven for their physical nourishment (Exodus 16:13-18, February 2). "The manna that has been hidden away in heaven" in today's reading likely refers to the eternal-life-giving spiritual nourishment that Jesus gives to faithful believers. The "white stone" might symbolize an "entry ticket" of sorts to heaven. In heaven we will be given a new name. • In these strange words is an amazing picture of our very personal God. He not only will make sure to provide for your spiritual nourishment, but he also will one day give you a name that is completely yours alone, a new name that only you and he will understand. In this life, you may feel like one in a very crowded world—or even one in a very large group of worldwide believers. But in the end, God will take you to be with him forever, and he won't forget one single person who is his own. The little white stones will be proof of something already true: he knows you by name.

what he is saying to the churches. To everyone who is victorious I will give some of the manna that has been hidden away in heaven. And I will give to each one a white stone, and on the stone will be engraved a new name that no one understands except the one who receives it.

2:1 Or *the messenger;* also in 2:8, 12, 18. **2:4** Greek *You have lost your first love.*

PSALM 129:1-8
A song for pilgrims ascending to Jerusalem.

1 From my earliest youth my enemies
    have persecuted me.
    Let all Israel repeat this:
2 From my earliest youth my enemies
    have persecuted me,
    but they have never defeated me.
3 My back is covered with cuts,
    as if a farmer had plowed long
    furrows.
4 But the LORD is good;

he has cut me free from the ropes
    of the ungodly.
5 May all who hate Jerusalem*
    be turned back in shameful
    defeat.
6 May they be as useless as grass
    on a rooftop,
    turning yellow when only half
    grown,
7 ignored by the harvester,
    despised by the binder.
8 And may those who pass by
    refuse to give them this blessing:
    "The LORD bless you;
    we bless you in the LORD's name."

129:5 Hebrew *Zion.*

PROVERBS 29:19-20
Words alone will not discipline a servant; the words may be understood, but they are not heeded. □ There is more hope for a fool than for someone who speaks without thinking.

DECEMBER**11**

AMOS 4:1-6:14
Amos railed against his people's pride and complacency. He warned his people of the sure judgment they would face on their actions and attitudes, especially toward the poor.

    Listen to me, you fat cows*
    living in Samaria,
you women who oppress the poor
    and crush the needy,
and who are always calling to your
    husbands,
    "Bring us another drink!"
2 The Sovereign LORD has sworn this
    by his holiness:
"The time will come when you will
    be led away
    with hooks in your noses.
Every last one of you will be dragged
    away
    like a fish on a hook!
3 You will be led out through the ruins
    of the wall;

you will be thrown from your
    fortresses,*"
    says the LORD.

4 "Go ahead and offer sacrifices to the
    idols at Bethel.
    Keep on disobeying at Gilgal.
Offer sacrifices each morning,
    and bring your tithes every three
    days.
5 Present your bread made with yeast
    as an offering of thanksgiving.
Then give your extra voluntary
    offerings
    so you can brag about it everywhere!
This is the kind of thing you Israelites
    love to do,"
    says the Sovereign LORD.

6 "I brought hunger to every city
    and famine to every town.
But still you would not return to me,"
    says the LORD.

⁷ "I kept the rain from falling
      when your crops needed it the most.
I sent rain on one town
      but withheld it from another.
Rain fell on one field,
      while another field withered away.
⁸ People staggered from town to town
      looking for water,
      but there was never enough.
But still you would not return to me,"
      says the LORD.

⁹ "I struck your farms and vineyards
      with blight and mildew.
Locusts devoured all your fig and
      olive trees.
But still you would not return to me,"
      says the LORD.

¹⁰ "I sent plagues on you
      like the plagues I sent on Egypt
      long ago.
I killed your young men in war
      and led all your horses away.*
      The stench of death filled the air!
But still you would not return to me,"
      says the LORD.

¹¹ "I destroyed some of your cities,
      as I destroyed* Sodom and
      Gomorrah.
Those of you who survived
      were like charred sticks pulled from
      a fire.
But still you would not return to me,"
      says the LORD.

¹² "Therefore, I will bring upon you all
      the disasters I have announced.
Prepare to meet your God in
      judgment, you people of Israel!"

¹³ For the LORD is the one who shaped
      the mountains,
stirs up the winds, and reveals his
      thoughts to mankind.
He turns the light of dawn into darkness
      and treads on the heights
      of the earth.
The LORD God of Heaven's Armies
      is his name!

5:1 LISTEN, you people of Israel! Listen to
this funeral song I am singing:

² "The virgin Israel has fallen,
      never to rise again!
She lies abandoned on the ground,
      with no one to help her up."

³ The Sovereign LORD says:

"When a city sends a thousand men
      to battle,
      only a hundred will return.
When a town sends a hundred,
      only ten will come back alive."

⁴ Now this is what the LORD says to the
family of Israel:

"Come back to me and live!
⁵ Don't worship at the pagan altars
      at Bethel;
      don't go to the shrines at Gilgal
      or Beersheba.
For the people of Gilgal will be
      dragged off into exile,
      and the people of Bethel will be
      reduced to nothing."
⁶ Come back to the LORD and live!
Otherwise, he will roar through Israel*
      like a fire,
devouring you completely.
Your gods in Bethel
      won't be able to quench the flames.
⁷ You twist justice, making it a bitter pill
      for the oppressed.
You treat the righteous like dirt.

⁸ It is the LORD who created the stars,
      the Pleiades and Orion.
He turns darkness into morning
      and day into night.
He draws up water from the oceans
      and pours it down as rain
      on the land.
The LORD is his name!
⁹ With blinding speed and power
      he destroys the strong,
      crushing all their defenses.

¹⁰ How you hate honest judges!
      How you despise people who tell
      the truth!
¹¹ You trample the poor,
      stealing their grain through taxes
      and unfair rent.
Therefore, though you build beautiful
      stone houses,
      you will never live in them.
Though you plant lush vineyards,
      you will never drink wine from
      them.

¹² For I know the vast number of your sins
    and the depth of your rebellions.
  You oppress good people by taking
      bribes
    and deprive the poor of justice
      in the courts.
¹³ So those who are smart keep their
      mouths shut,
    for it is an evil time.

¹⁴ Do what is good and run from evil
    so that you may live!
  Then the LORD God of Heaven's
      Armies will be your helper,
    just as you have claimed.
¹⁵ Hate evil and love what is good;
    turn your courts into true halls
      of justice.
  Perhaps even yet the LORD God
      of Heaven's Armies
    will have mercy on the remnant
      of his people.*

¹⁶Therefore, this is what the Lord, the
LORD God of Heaven's Armies, says:

  "There will be crying in all the public
      squares
    and mourning in every street.
  Call for the farmers to weep with you,
    and summon professional
      mourners to wail.
¹⁷ There will be wailing in every vineyard,
    for I will destroy them all,"
    says the LORD.

¹⁸ What sorrow awaits you who say,
    "If only the day of the LORD were
      here!"
  You have no idea what you are wishing
      for.
    That day will bring darkness,
      not light.
¹⁹ In that day you will be like a man who
      runs from a lion—
    only to meet a bear.
  Escaping from the bear, he leans his
      hand against a wall in his house—
    and he's bitten by a snake.
²⁰ Yes, the day of the LORD will be dark
      and hopeless,
    without a ray of joy or hope.

²¹ "I hate all your show and pretense—
    the hypocrisy of your religious
      festivals and solemn assemblies.

²² I will not accept your burnt offerings
    and grain offerings.
  I won't even notice all your choice
      peace offerings.
²³ Away with your noisy hymns of praise!
    I will not listen to the music of your
      harps.
²⁴ Instead, I want to see a mighty flood
      of justice,
    an endless river of righteous living.

²⁵"Was it to me you were bringing sacrifices and offerings during the forty
years in the wilderness, Israel? ²⁶No, you
served your pagan gods—Sakkuth your
king god and Kaiwan your star god—the
images you made for yourselves. ²⁷So I
will send you into exile, to a land east of
Damascus,*" says the LORD, whose name
is the God of Heaven's Armies.

6:1 WHAT sorrow awaits you who lounge
      in luxury in Jerusalem,*
    and you who feel secure in Samaria!
  You are famous and popular in Israel,
    and people go to you for help.
² But go over to Calneh
    and see what happened there.
  Then go to the great city of Hamath
    and down to the Philistine city of
      Gath.
  You are no better than they were,
    and look at how they were destroyed.
³ You push away every thought
      of coming disaster,
    but your actions only bring the day
      of judgment closer.
⁴ How terrible for you who sprawl
      on ivory beds
    and lounge on your couches,
  eating the meat of tender lambs from
      the flock
    and of choice calves fattened in the
      stall.
⁵ You sing trivial songs to the sound
      of the harp
    and fancy yourselves to be great
      musicians like David.
⁶ You drink wine by the bowlful
    and perfume yourselves with
      fragrant lotions.
  You care nothing about the ruin
      of your nation.*
⁷ Therefore, you will be the first to be
      led away as captives.

Suddenly, all your parties
will end.

⁸The Sovereign LORD has sworn by his own name, and this is what he, the LORD God of Heaven's Armies, says:

"I despise the arrogance of Israel,*
and I hate their fortresses.
I will give this city
and everything in it to their enemies."

(⁹If there are ten men left in one house, they will all die. ¹⁰And when a relative who is responsible to dispose of the dead* goes into the house to carry out the bodies, he will ask the last survivor, "Is anyone else with you?" When the person begins to swear, "No, by . . . ," he will interrupt and say, "Stop! Don't even mention the name of the LORD.")

¹¹ When the LORD gives the command, homes both great and small will be smashed to pieces.

¹² Can horses gallop over boulders?
Can oxen be used to plow them?
But that's how foolish you are when you turn justice into poison
and the sweet fruit of righteousness into bitterness.
¹³ And you brag about your conquest of Lo-debar.*

You boast, "Didn't we take Karnaim* by our own strength?"

¹⁴ "O people of Israel, I am about to bring an enemy nation against you,"
says the LORD God of Heaven's Armies.
"They will oppress you throughout your land—
from Lebo-hamath in the north
to the Arabah Valley in the south."

4:1 Hebrew *you cows of Bashan.*   4:3 Or *thrown out toward Harmon,* possibly a reference to Mount Hermon.   4:10 Or *and slaughtered your captured horses.*   4:11 Hebrew *as when God destroyed.*   5:6 Hebrew *the house of Joseph.*   5:15 Hebrew *the remnant of Joseph.*   5:26-27 Greek version reads *No, you carried your pagan gods—the shrine of Molech, the star of your god Rephan, and the images you made for yourselves. So I will send you into exile, to a land east of Damascus.* Compare Acts 7:43.   6:1 Hebrew *in Zion.*   6:6 Hebrew *of Joseph.*   6:8 Hebrew *Jacob.* See note on 3:13.   6:10 Or *to burn the dead.* The meaning of the Hebrew is uncertain.   6:13a *Lo-debar* means "nothing."   6:13b *Karnaim* means "horns," a term that symbolizes strength.

REVELATION 2:18–3:6
John continues the messages to the churches of Thyatira and Sardis. The truth for these churches is still true today. Thyatira was too tolerant of sin, and Sardis was infected by sin and spiritually dead. God calls us to abundant life. These churches were missing that mark.

"**W**rite this letter to the angel of the church in Thyatira. This is the message from the

WHAT THE BIBLE SAYS — The letters of Revelation

REVELATION 2-3 The Book of Revelation was originally meant to be circulated and read in seven churches in Asia Minor. The positives and negatives of each church were meant to be object lessons to all of them. As the messages applied to them individually and corporately, so do they apply to the church through the ages. That's why these letters are so important: Taken together, they give us a good picture of what Jesus expects from his church—gatherings of believers who don't tolerate sin or lukewarm faith, who refuse to compromise or be superficial—but instead are able to overcome, love joyously, remain true to the faith, and work hard for the Kingdom. • This is how much God cares about every individual church that dots the landscape across the world—the megachurch, the storefront church, and the secret gathering in a land that persecutes believers. He knows what's going on; he knows the faithfulness (or lack thereof) of the members. He wants to make the church strong. He wants it to reach its greatest potential. The group of believers with whom you worship and serve is God's vehicle for changing the world. Take it seriously—God does.

Son of God, whose eyes are like flames of fire, whose feet are like polished bronze:

[19]"I know all the things you do. I have seen your love, your faith, your service, and your patient endurance. And I can see your constant improvement in all these things.

[20]"But I have this complaint against you. You are permitting that woman—that Jezebel who calls herself a prophet—to lead my servants astray. She teaches them to commit sexual sin and to eat food offered to idols. [21]I gave her time to repent, but she does not want to turn away from her immorality.

[22]"Therefore, I will throw her on a bed of suffering,* and those who commit adultery with her will suffer greatly unless they repent and turn away from her evil deeds. [23]I will strike her children dead. Then all the churches will know that I am the one who searches out the thoughts and intentions of every person. And I will give to each of you whatever you deserve.

[24]"But I also have a message for the rest of you in Thyatira who have not followed this false teaching ('deeper truths,' as they call them—depths of Satan, actually). I will ask nothing more of you [25]except that you hold tightly to what you have until I come. [26]To all who are victorious, who obey me to the very end,

> To them I will give authority over all the nations.
>
> [27] They will rule the nations with an iron rod
> and smash them like clay pots.*

[28]They will have the same authority I received from my Father, and I will also give them the morning star! [29]"Anyone with ears to hear must listen to the Spirit and understand what he is saying to the churches.

[3:1]"WRITE this letter to the angel* of the church in Sardis. This is the message from the one who has the sevenfold Spirit* of God and the seven stars:

"I know all the things you do, and that you have a reputation for being alive—but you are dead. [2]Wake up! Strengthen what little remains, for even what is left is almost dead. I find that your actions do not meet the requirements of my God. [3]Go back to what you heard and believed at first; hold to it firmly. Repent and turn to me again. If you don't wake up, I will come to you suddenly, as unexpected as a thief.

[4]"Yet there are some in the church in Sardis who have not soiled their clothes with evil. They will walk with me in white, for they are worthy. [5]All who are victorious will be clothed in white. I will never erase their names from the Book of Life, but I will announce before my Father and his angels that they are mine.

[6]"Anyone with ears to hear must listen to the Spirit and understand what he is saying to the churches."

2:22 Greek *a bed.* 2:26-27 Ps 2:8-9 (Greek Version). 3:1a Or *the messenger;* also in 3:7, 14. 3:1b Greek *the seven spirits.*

PSALM 130:1-8
A song for pilgrims ascending to Jerusalem.

[1] **F**rom the depths of despair, O LORD,
 I call for your help.
[2] Hear my cry, O Lord.
 Pay attention to my prayer.

[3] LORD, if you kept a record of our sins,
 who, O Lord, could ever survive?
[4] But you offer forgiveness,
 that we might learn to fear you.

[5] I am counting on the LORD;
 yes, I am counting on him.
 I have put my hope in his word.
[6] I long for the Lord
 more than sentries long for the dawn,
 yes, more than sentries long for the dawn.

[7] O Israel, hope in the LORD;
 for with the LORD there is unfailing love.
 His redemption overflows.
[8] He himself will redeem Israel
 from every kind of sin.

PROVERBS 29:21-22
A servant pampered from childhood will become a rebel. □ An angry person starts fights; a hot-tempered person commits all kinds of sin.

AMOS 7:1–9:15

Amos's prophecy closes with five visions of accountability—a harvest, a fire, a plumb line, ripened fruit, and an altar. Then he added, as many prophets did, a reminder of hope.

The Sovereign LORD showed me [Amos] a vision. I saw him preparing to send a vast swarm of locusts over the land. This was after the king's share had been harvested from the fields and as the main crop was coming up. ²In my vision the locusts ate every green plant in sight. Then I said, "O Sovereign LORD, please forgive us or we will not survive, for Israel* is so small."

³ So the LORD relented from this plan. "I will not do it," he said.

⁴Then the Sovereign LORD showed me another vision. I saw him preparing to punish his people with a great fire. The fire had burned up the depths of the sea and was devouring the entire land. ⁵Then I said, "O Sovereign LORD, please stop or we will not survive, for Israel is so small."

⁶Then the LORD relented from this plan, too. "I will not do that either," said the Sovereign LORD.

⁷Then he showed me another vision. I saw the Lord standing beside a wall that had been built using a plumb line. He was using a plumb line to see if it was still straight. ⁸And the LORD said to me, "Amos, what do you see?"

I answered, "A plumb line."

And the Lord replied, "I will test my people with this plumb line. I will no longer ignore all their sins. ⁹The pagan shrines of your ancestors* will be ruined, and the temples of Israel will be destroyed; I will bring the dynasty of King Jeroboam to a sudden end."

¹⁰Then Amaziah, the priest of Bethel, sent a message to Jeroboam, king of Israel: "Amos is hatching a plot against you right here on your very doorstep! What he is saying is intolerable. ¹¹He is saying, 'Jeroboam will soon be killed, and the people of Israel will be sent away into exile.'"

¹²Then Amaziah sent orders to Amos: "Get out of here, you prophet! Go on back to the land of Judah, and earn your living by prophesying there! ¹³Don't bother us with your prophecies here in Bethel. This is the king's sanctuary and the national place of worship!"

¹⁴But Amos replied, "I'm not a professional prophet, and I was never trained to be one.* I'm just a shepherd, and I take care of sycamore-fig trees. ¹⁵But the LORD called me away from my flock and told me, 'Go and prophesy to my people in Israel.' ¹⁶Now then, listen to this message from the LORD:

"You say,
'Don't prophesy against Israel.
    Stop preaching against my people.*'
¹⁷ But this is what the LORD says:
'Your wife will become a prostitute in
        this city,
    and your sons and daughters will be
        killed.
Your land will be divided up,
    and you yourself will die in a
        foreign land.
And the people of Israel will certainly
        become captives in exile,
    far from their homeland.'"

8:1THEN the Sovereign LORD showed me another vision. In it I saw a basket filled with ripe fruit. ²"What do you see, Amos?" he asked.

I replied, "A basket full of ripe fruit."

Then the LORD said, "Like this fruit, Israel is ripe for punishment! I will not delay their punishment again. ³In that day the singing in the Temple will turn to wailing. Dead bodies will be scattered everywhere. They will be carried out of the city in silence. I, the Sovereign LORD, have spoken!"

⁴ Listen to this, you who rob the poor
    and trample down the needy!
⁵ You can't wait for the Sabbath day
        to be over
    and the religious festivals to end
    so you can get back to cheating
        the helpless.
You measure out grain with dishonest
        measures

and cheat the buyer with dishonest scales.*

6 And you mix the grain you sell
with chaff swept from the floor.
Then you enslave poor people
for one piece of silver or a pair
of sandals.

7 Now the LORD has sworn this oath
by his own name, the Pride of
Israel*:
"I will never forget
the wicked things you have done!
8 The earth will tremble for your deeds,
and everyone will mourn.
The ground will rise like the Nile River
at floodtime;
it will heave up, then sink again.

9 "In that day," says the Sovereign LORD,
"I will make the sun go down at noon
and darken the earth while it is still
day.
10 I will turn your celebrations into times
of mourning
and your singing into weeping.
You will wear funeral clothes
and shave your heads to show your
sorrow—
as if your only son had died.
How very bitter that day will be!

11 "The time is surely coming," says the
Sovereign LORD,
"when I will send a famine on the
land—
not a famine of bread or water
but of hearing the words of the
LORD.
12 People will stagger from sea to sea
and wander from border to border*
searching for the word of the LORD,
but they will not find it.
13 Beautiful girls and strong young men
will grow faint in that day,
thirsting for the LORD's word.
14 And those who swear by the shameful
idols of Samaria—
who take oaths in the name of the
god of Dan
and make vows in the name of the
god of Beersheba*—
they will all fall down,
never to rise again."

9:1 THEN I saw a vision of the Lord standing
beside the altar. He said,

"Strike the tops of the Temple
columns,
so that the foundation will shake.
Bring down the roof
on the heads of the people below.
I will kill with the sword those who
survive.
No one will escape!
2 "Even if they dig down to the place
of the dead,*
I will reach down and pull them up.
Even if they climb up into the heavens,
I will bring them down.
3 Even if they hide at the very top
of Mount Carmel,
I will search them out and capture
them.
Even if they hide at the bottom of the
ocean,
I will send the sea serpent after
them to bite them.
4 Even if their enemies drive them
into exile,
I will command the sword to kill
them there.
I am determined to bring disaster
upon them
and not to help them."

5 The Lord, the LORD of Heaven's
Armies,
touches the land and it melts,
and all its people mourn.
The ground rises like the Nile River at
floodtime,
and then it sinks again.
6 The LORD's home reaches up to the
heavens,
while its foundation is on the earth.
He draws up water from the oceans
and pours it down as rain on the
land.
The LORD is his name!

7 "Are you Israelites more important
to me
than the Ethiopians?*" asks the
LORD.
"I brought Israel out of Egypt,
but I also brought the Philistines
from Crete*
and led the Arameans out of Kir.

8 "I, the Sovereign LORD,
    am watching this sinful nation
        of Israel.
I will destroy it
    from the face of the earth.
But I will never completely destroy the
        family of Israel,*"
    says the LORD.
9 "For I will give the command
    and will shake Israel along with
        the other nations
as grain is shaken in a sieve,
    yet not one true kernel will be lost.
10 But all the sinners will die by the
        sword—
    all those who say, 'Nothing bad will
        happen to us.'

11 "In that day I will restore the fallen
        house* of David.
I will repair its damaged walls.
From the ruins I will rebuild it
    and restore its former glory.
12 And Israel will possess what is left
        of Edom
    and all the nations I have called
        to be mine.*"
The LORD has spoken,
    and he will do these things.

13 "The time will come," says the LORD,
    "when the grain and grapes will grow
        faster
    than they can be harvested.

Then the terraced vineyards
    on the hills of Israel
    will drip with sweet wine!
14 I will bring my exiled people
        of Israel
    back from distant lands,
and they will rebuild their ruined
        cities
    and live in them again.
They will plant vineyards and gardens;
    they will eat their crops and drink
        their wine.
15 I will firmly plant them there
    in their own land.
They will never again be uprooted
    from the land I have given them,"
    says the LORD your God.

7:2 Hebrew *Jacob;* also in 7:5. See note on 3:13. **7:9** Hebrew *of Isaac.* **7:14** Or *I'm not a prophet nor the son of a prophet.* **7:16** Hebrew *against the house of Isaac.* **8:5** Hebrew *You make the ephah* [a unit for measuring grain] *small and the shekel* [a unit of weight] *great, and you deal falsely by using deceitful balances.* **8:7** Hebrew *the pride of Jacob.* See note on 3:13. **8:12** Hebrew *from north to east.* **8:14** Hebrew *the way of Beersheba.* **9:2** Hebrew to *Sheol.* **9:7a** Hebrew *the Cushites?* **9:7b** Hebrew *Caphtor.* **9:8** Hebrew *the house of Jacob.* See note on 3:13. **9:11a** Or *kingdom;* Hebrew reads *tent.* **9:11b-12** Greek version reads *and restore its former glory, / so that the rest of humanity, including the Gentiles— / all those I have called to be mine—might seek me.* Compare Acts 15:16-17.

REVELATION 3:7-22
John finishes the messages to the last two churches—Philadelphia and Laodicea. Philadelphia fared well in its assessment, but Laodicea was sickeningly mediocre.

HOW WE LIVE

Confessing our sins

REVELATION 3:19 When you were a kid, you probably remember being disciplined. You may have stood in the corner, been "grounded," or been required to pay for something you damaged. Your parents wanted you to grow up into a respectable adult, and so they punished you to teach you a lesson. When you became a believer, you joined the family of God and he became your Father. Like any good father, God also must discipline his children at times. "I correct and discipline everyone I love," he says. God's purpose in discipline is not to punish, but to teach. • As you walk through your Christian life, you may find at times that God is acting the part of your heavenly Father and disciplining you. When that happens, know that it is only because he loves you. He warns you away from something that will hurt you; he asks you to face the consequences of a sinful act; he causes you to feel quite alone for awhile—as though "grounded" and left to think about what you've done. In those times, don't despair. Rather, be glad that God cares enough to mold you into the person he wants you to be.

"**W**rite this letter to the angel of the church in Philadelphia.

This is the message from the one who is holy and true,
the one who has the key of David.
What he opens, no one can close;
and what he closes, no one can open.*

⁸"I know all the things you do, and I have opened a door for you that no one can close. You have little strength, yet you obeyed my word and did not deny me. ⁹Look, I will force those who belong to Satan's synagogue—those liars who say they are Jews but are not—to come and bow down at your feet. They will acknowledge that you are the ones I love.

¹⁰"Because you have obeyed my command to persevere, I will protect you from the great time of testing that will come upon the whole world to test those who belong to this world. ¹¹I am coming soon.* Hold on to what you have, so that no one will take away your crown. ¹²All who are victorious will become pillars in the Temple of my God, and they will never have to leave it. And I will write on them the name of my God, and they will be citizens in the city of my God—the new Jerusalem that comes down from heaven from my God. And I will also write on them my new name.

¹³"Anyone with ears to hear must listen to the Spirit and understand what he is saying to the churches.

¹⁴"Write this letter to the angel of the church in Laodicea. This is the message from the one who is the Amen—the faithful and true witness, the beginning* of God's new creation:

¹⁵"I know all the things you do, that you are neither hot nor cold. I wish that you were one or the other! ¹⁶But since you are like lukewarm water, neither hot nor cold, I will spit you

out of my mouth! ¹⁷You say, 'I am rich. I have everything I want. I don't need a thing!' And you don't realize that you are wretched and miserable and poor and blind and naked. ¹⁸So I advise you to buy gold from me—gold that has been purified by fire. Then you will be rich. Also buy white garments from me so you will not be shamed by your nakedness, and ointment for your eyes so you will be able to see. ¹⁹I correct and discipline everyone I love. So be diligent and turn from your indifference.

²⁰"Look! I stand at the door and knock. If you hear my voice and open the door, I will come in, and we will share a meal together as friends. ²¹Those who are victorious will sit with me on my throne, just as I was victorious and sat with my Father on his throne.

²²"Anyone with ears to hear must listen to the Spirit and understand what he is saying to the churches."

3:7 Isa 22:22.   3:11 Or *suddenly*, or *quickly*.   3:14 Or *the ruler*, or *the source*.

PSALM 131:1-3
A song for pilgrims ascending to Jerusalem. A psalm of David.

¹ LORD, my heart is not proud;
   my eyes are not haughty.
I don't concern myself with matters too great
   or too awesome for me to grasp.
² Instead, I have calmed and quieted myself,
   like a weaned child who no longer cries for its mother's milk.
   Yes, like a weaned child is my soul within me.

³ O Israel, put your hope in the LORD—
   now and always.

PROVERBS 29:23
Pride ends in humiliation, while humility brings honor.

OBADIAH 1:1-21

Obadiah's prophecy is the shortest book in the Old Testament. He opens with a judgment against Edom, a nation of distant relatives of Israel. He closes with God's promise to one day restore Israel.

This is the vision that the Sovereign LORD revealed to Obadiah concerning the land of Edom.

We have heard a message from the
LORD
that an ambassador was sent
to the nations to say,
"Get ready, everyone!
Let's assemble our armies and
attack Edom!"
² The LORD says to Edom,
"I will cut you down to size among
the nations;
you will be greatly despised.
³ You have been deceived by your own
pride
because you live in a rock fortress
and make your home high in the
mountains.
'Who can ever reach us way up here?'
you ask boastfully.
⁴ But even if you soar as high as eagles
and build your nest among the stars,
I will bring you crashing down,"
says the LORD.
⁵ "If thieves came at night and robbed
you
(what a disaster awaits you!),
they would not take everything.
Those who harvest grapes
always leave a few for the poor.
But your enemies will wipe you out
completely!
⁶ Every nook and cranny of Edom*
will be searched and looted.
Every treasure will be found and
taken.
⁷ "All your allies will turn against you.
They will help to chase you from
your land.
They will promise you peace
while plotting to deceive and
destroy you.

Your trusted friends will set traps
for you,
and you won't even know about it.
⁸ At that time not a single wise person
will be left in the whole land
of Edom,"
says the LORD.
"For on the mountains of Edom
I will destroy everyone who has
understanding.
⁹ The mightiest warriors of Teman
will be terrified,
and everyone on the mountains of Edom
will be cut down in the slaughter.

¹⁰ "Because of the violence you did
to your close relatives in Israel,*
you will be filled with shame
and destroyed forever.
¹¹ When they were invaded,
you stood aloof, refusing to help
them.
Foreign invaders carried off their
wealth
and cast lots to divide up Jerusalem,
but you acted like one of Israel's
enemies.

¹² "You should not have gloated
when they exiled your relatives
to distant lands.
You should not have rejoiced
when the people of Judah suffered
such misfortune.
You should not have spoken arrogantly
in that terrible time of trouble.
¹³ You should not have plundered the
land of Israel
when they were suffering such
calamity.
You should not have gloated over their
destruction
when they were suffering such
calamity.
You should not have seized their wealth
when they were suffering such
calamity.
¹⁴ You should not have stood at the
crossroads,
killing those who tried to escape.

You should not have captured the
   survivors
      and handed them over in their
      terrible time of trouble.

15 "The day is near when I, the LORD,
      will judge all godless nations!
   As you have done to Israel,
      so it will be done to you.
   All your evil deeds
      will fall back on your own heads.
16 Just as you swallowed up my people
      on my holy mountain,
   so you and the surrounding nations
      will swallow the punishment I pour
      out on you.
   Yes, all you nations will drink and
      stagger
      and disappear from history.

17 "But Jerusalem* will become a refuge
      for those who escape;
      it will be a holy place.
   And the people of Israel* will come
      back
      to reclaim their inheritance.
18 The people of Israel will be a raging fire,
   and Edom a field of dry stubble.
   The descendants of Jospeh will be
      a flame
      roaring across the field, devouring
      everything.
   There will be no survivors in Edom.
   I, the LORD, have spoken!

19 "Then my people living in the Negev
      will occupy the mountains of Edom.
   Those living in the foothills of Judah*
      will possess the Philistine plains
   and take over the fields of Ephraim
      and Samaria.
   And the people of Benjamin
      will occupy the land of Gilead.
20 The exiles of Israel will return to their
      land
   and occupy the Phoenician coast
      as far north as Zarephath.
   The captives from Jerusalem exiled
      in the north*
   will return home and resettle the
      towns of the Negev.
21 Those who have been rescued* will go
      up to* Mount Zion in Jerusalem
      to rule over the mountains of Edom.
   And the LORD himself will be king!"

6 Hebrew *Esau;* also in 8b, 9, 18, 19, 21.   10 Hebrew *your brother Jacob.* The names "Jacob" and "Israel" are often interchanged throughout the Old Testament, referring sometimes to the individual patriarch and sometimes to the nation.   17a Hebrew *Mount Zion.*   17b Hebrew *house of Jacob;* also in 18. See note on 10.   19 Hebrew *the Shephelah.*   20 Hebrew *in Sepharad.*   21a As in Greek and Syriac versions; Hebrew reads *Rescuers.*   21b Or *from.*

REVELATION 4:1-11

John describes a throne room in which most of the rest of Revelation will take place. Many sermons and many songs have been written based on this image of a holy God surrounded by mysterious beings and millions of angels.

Then as I [John] looked, I saw a door standing open in heaven, and the same voice I had heard before spoke to me like a trumpet blast. The voice said, "Come up here, and I will show you what must happen after this." 2And instantly I was in the Spirit,* and I saw a throne in heaven and someone sitting on it. 3The one sitting on the throne was as brilliant as gemstones—like jasper and carnelian. And the glow of an emerald circled his throne like a rainbow. 4Twenty-four thrones surrounded him, and twenty-four elders sat on them. They were all clothed in white and had gold crowns on their heads. 5From the throne came flashes of lightning and the rumble of thunder. And in front of the throne were seven torches with burning flames. This is the sevenfold Spirit* of God. 6In front of the throne was a shiny sea of glass, sparkling like crystal.

In the center and around the throne were four living beings, each covered with eyes, front and back. 7The first of these living beings was like a lion; the second was like an ox; the third had a human face; and the fourth was like an eagle in flight. 8Each of these living beings had six wings, and their wings were covered all over with eyes, inside and out. Day after day and night after night they keep on saying,

   "Holy, holy, holy is the Lord God, the
      Almighty—
      the one who always was, who is,
      and who is still to come."

9Whenever the living beings give glory and honor and thanks to the one sitting on the throne (the one who lives forever and ever), 10the twenty-four elders fall down and worship the one sitting on the throne (the one who lives forever and ever). And they lay their crowns before the throne and say,

11 "You are worthy, O Lord our God,
    to receive glory and honor and
       power.
  For you created all things,
    and they exist because you created
       what you pleased."

4:2 Or *in spirit.*   4:5 Greek *They are the seven spirits.*

PSALM 132:1-18
A song for pilgrims ascending to Jerusalem.

1 LORD, remember David
    and all that he suffered.
2 He made a solemn promise to the
    LORD.
  He vowed to the Mighty One
    of Israel,*
3 "I will not go home;
    I will not let myself rest.
4 I will not let my eyes sleep
    nor close my eyelids in slumber
5 until I find a place to build a house
    for the LORD,
  a sanctuary for the Mighty One
    of Israel."

6 We heard that the Ark was in
    Ephrathah;

then we found it in the distant
    countryside of Jaar.
7 Let us go to the sanctuary of the LORD;
    let us worship at the footstool of his
       throne.
8 Arise, O LORD, and enter your resting
       place,
  along with the Ark, the symbol
    of your power.
9 May your priests be clothed in
       godliness;
  may your loyal servants sing for joy.
10 For the sake of your servant David,
    do not reject the king you have
       anointed.

11 The LORD swore an oath to David
    with a promise he will never take
       back:
  "I will place one of your descendants
    on your throne.
12 If your descendants obey the terms
    of my covenant
  and the laws that I teach them,
then your royal line
    will continue forever and ever."

13 For the LORD has chosen Jerusalem*;
    he has desired it for his home.
14 "This is my resting place forever,"
    he said.
  "I will live here, for this is the home
    I desired.

WHAT THE BIBLE SAYS

Understanding John's vision

REVELATION 4:1-11 John sees a vision of God on the throne, orchestrating the events that will occur on the earth at the time of its end. The glory seen in heaven depicts God's complete power and holiness. The twenty-four thrones and twenty-four elders may refer to the twelve tribes of Israel and the twelve apostles—thereby representing all of the saved people across all time (both before and after Jesus). The four living beings are a high order of angels who lead all of heaven in worship and praise of God. The appearance of these creatures symbolizes God's attributes. The animal-like appearances of the four creatures include majesty and power (the lion), faithfulness (the ox), intelligence (the human), and sovereignty (the eagle). • So what is the point of all this? John's vision will be frightening, for it will show the end of the world and the coming judgment of evil. First, however, John shows us a glimpse of heaven. No matter what is yet to happen, we know who is in control—he who is on the throne, "the one who always was, who is, and who is still to come."

¹⁵ I will bless this city and make
it prosperous;
I will satisfy its poor with food.
¹⁶ I will clothe its priests with godliness;
its faithful servants will sing for joy.
¹⁷ Here I will increase the power of
David;
my anointed one will be a light for
my people.
¹⁸ I will clothe his enemies with
shame,

but he will be a glorious
king."

132:2 Hebrew *of Jacob;* also in 132:5. See note on 44:4.
132:13 Hebrew *Zion.*

PROVERBS 29:24-25

If you assist a thief, you only hurt yourself.
You are sworn to tell the truth, but you
dare not testify. □ Fearing people is a dangerous
trap, but trusting the LORD means
safety.

DECEMBER**14**

JONAH 1:1-4:11
Jonah was the famous prophet who was swallowed
by a big fish. He had run away because God asked
him to go to Nineveh, a key city in Assyria. Would
you want to offer redemption to the people who
could easily destroy you? Jonah didn't. Read what
happened.

The LORD gave this message to Jonah son
of Amittai: ²"Get up and go to the great
city of Nineveh. Announce my judgment
against it because I have seen how wicked
its people are."

³But Jonah got up and went in the opposite
direction to get away from the
LORD. He went down to the port of Joppa,
where he found a ship leaving for Tarshish.
He bought a ticket and went on
board, hoping to escape from the LORD by
sailing to Tarshish.

⁴But the LORD hurled a powerful wind
over the sea, causing a violent storm that
threatened to break the ship apart. ⁵Fearing
for their lives, the desperate sailors
shouted to their gods for help and threw
the cargo overboard to lighten the ship.

But all this time Jonah was sound
asleep down in the hold. ⁶So the captain
went down after him. "How can you sleep
at a time like this?" he shouted. "Get up
and pray to your god! Maybe he will pay
attention to us and spare our lives."

⁷Then the crew cast lots to see which of
them had offended the gods and caused
the terrible storm. When they did this,
the lots identified Jonah as the culprit.
⁸"Why has this awful storm come down

on us?" they demanded. "Who are you?
What is your line of work? What country
are you from? What is your nationality?"

⁹Jonah answered, "I am a Hebrew, and I
worship the LORD, the God of heaven, who
made the sea and the land."

¹⁰The sailors were terrified when they
heard this, for he had already told them
he was running away from the LORD. "Oh,
why did you do it?" they groaned. ¹¹And
since the storm was getting worse all the
time, they asked him, "What should we do
to you to stop this storm?"

¹²"Throw me into the sea," Jonah said,
"and it will become calm again. I know
that this terrible storm is all my fault."

¹³Instead, the sailors rowed even harder
to get the ship to the land. But the stormy
sea was too violent for them, and they
couldn't make it. ¹⁴Then they cried out to
the LORD, Jonah's God. "O LORD," they
pleaded, "don't make us die for this man's
sin. And don't hold us responsible for his
death. O LORD, you have sent this storm
upon him for your own good reasons."

¹⁵Then the sailors picked Jonah up and
threw him into the raging sea, and the
storm stopped at once! ¹⁶The sailors were
awestruck by the LORD's great power, and
they offered him a sacrifice and vowed to
serve him.

¹⁷*Now the LORD had arranged for a
great fish to swallow Jonah. And Jonah
was inside the fish for three days and
three nights.

2:1*Then Jonah prayed to the Lord his God from inside the fish. ²He said,

"I cried out to the Lord in my great
trouble,
   and he answered me.
I called to you from the land
   of the dead,*
   and Lord, you heard me!
³ You threw me into the ocean depths,
   and I sank down to the heart
   of the sea.
The mighty waters engulfed me;
   I was buried beneath your wild and
   stormy waves.
⁴ Then I said, 'O Lord, you have driven
   me from your presence.
   Yet I will look once more toward
   your holy Temple.'

⁵ "I sank beneath the waves,
   and the waters closed over me.
   Seaweed wrapped itself around
   my head.
⁶ I sank down to the very roots of the
   mountains.
   I was imprisoned in the earth,
   whose gates lock shut forever.
But you, O Lord my God,
   snatched me from the jaws of death!
⁷ As my life was slipping away,
   I remembered the Lord.
And my earnest prayer went out to you
   in your holy Temple.
⁸ Those who worship false gods
   turn their backs on all God's mercies.

⁹ But I will offer sacrifices to you with
   songs of praise,
   and I will fulfill all my vows.
   For my salvation comes from
   the Lord alone."

¹⁰Then the Lord ordered the fish to spit Jonah out onto the beach.

3:1 Then the Lord spoke to Jonah a second time: ²"Get up and go to the great city of Nineveh, and deliver the message I have given you."

³This time Jonah obeyed the Lord's command and went to Nineveh, a city so large that it took three days to see it all.* ⁴On the day Jonah entered the city, he shouted to the crowds: "Forty days from now Nineveh will be destroyed!" ⁵The people of Nineveh believed God's message, and from the greatest to the least, they declared a fast and put on burlap to show their sorrow.

⁶When the king of Nineveh heard what Jonah was saying, he stepped down from his throne and took off his royal robes. He dressed himself in burlap and sat on a heap of ashes. ⁷Then the king and his nobles sent this decree throughout the city:

"No one, not even the animals from your herds and flocks, may eat or drink anything at all. ⁸People and animals alike must wear garments of mourning, and everyone must pray earnestly to God. They must turn from their evil ways and stop

---

Seeking God's will

HOW WE LIVE

JONAH 1:1-3 Jonah was a believing Israelite who worshiped God (1:9) and who probably wanted to be obedient. But when God sent him to Nineveh, Jonah bought a ticket on a ship going the opposite direction, "hoping to escape from the Lord." Bad idea. • Why would Jonah do such a thing? Nineveh was the capital of the Assyrian empire—a nation known for its cruelty, a rising power with its sights set on world dominance. Jonah didn't want those people saved; he wanted them destroyed! • We live in a world where wickedness abounds. You may wish that judgment and destruction would rain down upon those who spread evil. But until that happens, God called us to bring the Good News to such people. Will you follow God's will or run the other way? Learn from the story of this reluctant prophet that it's a good thing to obey God's leading and go where he wants you to go. Following God's will is always the best idea.

all their violence. ⁹Who can tell? Perhaps even yet God will change his mind and hold back his fierce anger from destroying us."

¹⁰When God saw what they had done and how they had put a stop to their evil ways, he changed his mind and did not carry out the destruction he had threatened.

4:1THIS change of plans greatly upset Jonah, and he became very angry. ²So he complained to the LORD about it: "Didn't I say before I left home that you would do this, LORD? That is why I ran away to Tarshish! I knew that you are a merciful and compassionate God, slow to get angry and filled with unfailing love. You are eager to turn back from destroying people. ³Just kill me now, LORD! I'd rather be dead than alive if what I predicted will not happen."

⁴The LORD replied, "Is it right for you to be angry about this?"

⁵Then Jonah went out to the east side of the city and made a shelter to sit under as he waited to see what would happen to the city. ⁶And the LORD God arranged for a leafy plant to grow there, and soon it spread its broad leaves over Jonah's head, shading him from the sun. This eased his discomfort, and Jonah was very grateful for the plant.

⁷But God also arranged for a worm! The next morning at dawn the worm ate through the stem of the plant so that it withered away. ⁸And as the sun grew hot, God arranged for a scorching east wind to blow on Jonah. The sun beat down on his head until he grew faint and wished to die. "Death is certainly better than living like this!" he exclaimed.

⁹Then God said to Jonah, "Is it right for you to be angry because the plant died?"

"Yes," Jonah retorted, "even angry enough to die!"

¹⁰Then the LORD said, "You feel sorry about the plant, though you did nothing to put it there. It came quickly and died quickly. ¹¹But Nineveh has more than 120,000 people living in spiritual darkness,* not to mention all the animals. Shouldn't I feel sorry for such a great city?"

1:17 Verse 1:17 is numbered 2:1 in Hebrew text.
2:1 Verses 2:1-10 are numbered 2:2-11 in Hebrew text.

2:2 Hebrew *from Sheol.* **3:3** Hebrew *a great city to God, of three days' journey.* **4:11** Hebrew *people who don't know their right hand from their left.*

REVELATION 5:1-14

John's next series of images surround a scroll with seven seals. In that day, scrolls were sealed to ensure that the message written on it stayed secure until it reached the hands of the one for whom it was intended.

Then I [John] saw a scroll* in the right hand of the one who was sitting on the throne. There was writing on the inside and the outside of the scroll, and it was sealed with seven seals. ²And I saw a strong angel, who shouted with a loud voice: "Who is worthy to break the seals on this scroll and open it?" ³But no one in heaven or on earth or under the earth was able to open the scroll and read it.

⁴Then I began to weep bitterly because no one was found worthy to open the scroll and read it. ⁵But one of the twenty-four elders said to me, "Stop weeping! Look, the Lion of the tribe of Judah, the heir to David's throne,* has won the victory. He is worthy to open the scroll and its seven seals."

⁶Then I saw a Lamb that looked as if it had been slaughtered, but it was now standing between the throne and the four living beings and among the twenty-four elders. He had seven horns and seven eyes, which represent the sevenfold Spirit* of God that is sent out into every part of the earth. ⁷He stepped forward and took the scroll from the right hand of the one sitting on the throne. ⁸And when he took the scroll, the four living beings and the twenty-four elders fell down before the Lamb. Each one had a harp, and they held gold bowls filled with incense, which are the prayers of God's people. ⁹And they sang a new song with these words:

"You are worthy to take the scroll
and break its seals and open it.
For you were slaughtered, and your
blood has ransomed people
for God
from every tribe and language
and people and nation.
¹⁰ And you have caused them
to become

a Kingdom of priests for our God.
And they will reign* on the earth."

[11]Then I looked again, and I heard the voices of thousands and millions of angels around the throne and of the living beings and the elders. [12]And they sang in a mighty chorus:

"Worthy is the Lamb who was
        slaughtered—
    to receive power and riches
and wisdom and strength
    and honor and glory and
        blessing."

[13]And then I heard every creature in heaven and on earth and under the earth and in the sea. They sang:

"Blessing and honor and glory
        and power
    belong to the one sitting on the
        throne
    and to the Lamb forever and ever."

[14]And the four living beings said, "Amen!" And the twenty-four elders fell down and worshiped the Lamb.

MICAH 1:1–4:13
Micah's prophecy was a mixture of messages to Israel, Judah, and the surrounding nations; it was also a mixture of judgment and hope.

The LORD gave this message to Micah of Moresheth during the years when Jotham, Ahaz, and Hezekiah were kings of Judah. The visions he saw concerned both Samaria and Jerusalem.

[2] Attention! Let all the people of the
        world listen!
    Let the earth and everything
        in it hear.
    The Sovereign LORD is making
        accusations against you;
        the LORD speaks from his holy
            Temple.

5:1 Or *book;* also in 5:2, 3, 4, 5, 7, 8, 9.   **5:5** Greek *the root of David.* See Isa 11:10.   **5:6** Greek *which are the seven spirits.*   **5:10** Some manuscripts read *they are reigning.*

PSALM 133:1-3
*A song for pilgrims ascending to Jerusalem.
A psalm of David.*

[1] **H**ow wonderful and pleasant it is
        when brothers live together
            in harmony!
[2] For harmony is as precious as the
        anointing oil
        that was poured over Aaron's head,
        that ran down his beard
        and onto the border of his robe.
[3] Harmony is as refreshing as the dew
        from Mount Hermon
        that falls on the mountains of Zion.
    And there the LORD has pronounced
        his blessing,
        even life everlasting.

PROVERBS 29:26-27
Many seek the ruler's favor, but justice comes from the LORD. □ The righteous despise the unjust; the wicked despise the godly.

DECEMBER**15**

[3] Look! The LORD is coming!
        He leaves his throne in heaven
        and tramples the heights of the earth.
[4] The mountains melt beneath his feet
        and flow into the valleys
    like wax in a fire,
        like water pouring down a hill.
[5] And why is this happening?
        Because of the rebellion of Israel*—
        yes, the sins of the whole nation.
    Who is to blame for Israel's rebellion?
        Samaria, its capital city!
    Where is the center of idolatry in Judah?
        In Jerusalem, its capital!
[6] "So I, the LORD, will make the city
        of Samaria
        a heap of ruins.

Her streets will be plowed up
for planting vineyards.
I will roll the stones of her walls into
the valley below,
exposing her foundations.
⁷ All her carved images will be smashed.
All her sacred treasures will be
burned.
These things were bought with
the money
earned by her prostitution,
and they will now be carried away
to pay prostitutes elsewhere."

⁸ Therefore, I will mourn and lament.
I will walk around barefoot and
naked.
I will howl like a jackal
and moan like an owl.
⁹ For my people's wound
is too deep to heal.
It has reached into Judah,
even to the gates of Jerusalem.

¹⁰ Don't tell our enemies in Gath*;
don't weep at all.
You people in Beth-leaphrah,*
roll in the dust to show your
despair.
¹¹ You people in Shaphir,*
go as captives into exile—naked
and ashamed.
The people of Zaanan*
dare not come outside their walls.
The people of Beth-ezel* mourn,
for their house has no support.
¹² The people of Maroth* anxiously wait
for relief,
but only bitterness awaits them
as the LORD's judgment reaches
even to the gates of Jerusalem.

¹³ Harness your chariot horses and flee,
you people of Lachish.*
You were the first city in Judah
to follow Israel in her rebellion,
and you led Jerusalem* into sin.
¹⁴ Send farewell gifts to Moresheth-
gath*;
there is no hope of saving it.
The town of Aczib*
has deceived the kings of Israel.
¹⁵ O people of Mareshah,*
I will bring a conqueror to capture
your town.

And the leaders* of Israel
will go to Adullam.

¹⁶ Oh, people of Judah, shave your heads
in sorrow,
for the children you love will be
snatched away.
Make yourselves as bald as a vulture,
for your little ones will be exiled
to distant lands.

²:¹ WHAT sorrow awaits you who lie
awake at night,
thinking up evil plans.
You rise at dawn and hurry to carry
them out,
simply because you have the power
to do so.
² When you want a piece of land,
you find a way to seize it.
When you want someone's house,
you take it by fraud and violence.
You cheat a man of his property,
stealing his family's inheritance.

³ But this is what the LORD says:
"I will reward your evil with evil;
you won't be able to pull your neck
out of the noose.
You will no longer walk around
proudly,
for it will be a terrible time."

⁴ In that day your enemies will make
fun of you
by singing this song of despair
about you:
"We are finished,
completely ruined!
God has confiscated our land,
taking it from us.
He has given our fields
to those who betrayed us.*"
⁵ Others will set your boundaries then,
and the LORD's people will have
no say
in how the land is divided.

⁶ "Don't say such things,"
the people respond.*
"Don't prophesy like that.
Such disasters will never come our
way!"

⁷ Should you talk that way, O family
of Israel?*

Will the LORD's Spirit have
    patience with such behavior?
If you would do what is right,
    you would find my words
    comforting.
⁸ Yet to this very hour
    my people rise against me like
    an enemy!
You steal the shirts right off the backs
    of those who trusted you,
making them as ragged as men
    returning from battle.
⁹ You have evicted women from their
    pleasant homes
and forever stripped their children
    of all that God would give them.
¹⁰ Up! Begone!
    This is no longer your land and
    home,
for you have filled it with sin
    and ruined it completely.
¹¹ Suppose a prophet full of lies would
    say to you,
    "I'll preach to you the joys of wine
    and alcohol!"
That's just the kind of prophet you
    would like!
¹² "Someday, O Israel, I will gather you;
    I will gather the remnant who are left.
I will bring you together again like
    sheep in a pen,
    like a flock in its pasture.

Yes, your land will again
    be filled with noisy crowds!
¹³ Your leader will break out
    and lead you out of exile,
out through the gates of the enemy
    cities,
    back to your own land.
Your king will lead you;
    the LORD himself will guide you."

³:¹ I SAID, "Listen, you leaders of Israel!
    You are supposed to know right
        from wrong,
² but you are the very ones
    who hate good and love evil.
You skin my people alive
    and tear the flesh from their
    bones.
³ Yes, you eat my people's flesh,
    strip off their skin,
    and break their bones.
You chop them up
    like meat for the cooking pot.
⁴ Then you beg the LORD for help
    in times of trouble!
Do you really expect him to answer?
After all the evil you have done,
    he won't even look at you!"
⁵ This is what the LORD says:
    "You false prophets are leading
    my people astray!
You promise peace for those who give
    you food,

HOW WE LIVE

Knowing God's peace

MICAH 4:4 When you know you have a hopeful, joyous, and peaceful future, enduring today is easier. If you face a difficult situation—debt, tragedy, conflict, loss, the kind of situations that chase hope away—it's much easier to get through it if you know God is with you. Things will get better; you will eventually be victorious. There is a peace to be found in that knowledge, isn't there? That's what a lot of the prophecies in the Bible are all about. No matter what we face today, we read in the writings of men like Micah and John that we have a hopeful future, protected by God himself. That knowledge gives us peace and resilience. • How connected are you to God's vision of the future? What does the word *future* even conjure in your mind? Do you have peace about the future? Does your peace easily fade away during difficult times? Take a moment and let God make the connection for you between this moment and the future Micah described in which, "everyone will live in peace." Let that truth sink in. Let that peace begin today.

but you declare war on those who
refue to feed you.
⁶ Now the night will close around you,
cutting off all your visions.
Darkness will cover you,
putting an end to your predictions.
The sun will set for you prophets,
and your day will come to an end.
⁷ Then you seers will be put to shame,
and you fortune-tellers will be
disgraced.
And you will cover your faces
because there is no answer
from God."

⁸ But as for me, I am filled with
power—
with the Spirit of the LORD.
I am filled with justice and strength
to boldly declare Israel's sin and
rebellion.
⁹ Listen to me, you leaders of Israel!
You hate justice and twist all that
is right.
¹⁰ You are building Jerusalem
on a foundation of murder and
corruption.
¹¹ You rulers make decisions based
on bribes;
you priests teach God's laws only
for a price;
you prophets won't prophesy unless
you are paid.
Yet all of you claim to depend
on the LORD.
"No harm can come to us," you say,
"for the LORD is here among us."
¹² Because of you, Mount Zion will be
plowed like an open field;
Jerusalem will be reduced to ruins!
A thicket will grow on the heights
where the Temple now stands.

⁴:¹ IN the last days, the mountain of the
LORD's house
will be the highest of all—
the most important place on earth.
It will be raised above the other hills,
and people from all over the world
will stream there to worship.
² People from many nations will come
and say,
"Come, let us go up to the mountain
of the LORD,
to the house of Jacob's God.

There he will teach us his ways,
and we will walk in his paths."
For the LORD's teaching will go out
from Zion;
his word will go out from
Jerusalem.
³ The LORD will mediate between
peoples
and will settle disputes between
strong nations far away.
They will hammer their swords into
plowshares
and their spears into pruning
hooks.
Nation will no longer fight against
nation,
nor train for war anymore.
⁴ Everyone will live in peace and
prosperity,
enjoying their own grapevines and
fig trees,
for there will be nothing to fear.
The LORD of Heaven's Armies
has made this promise!
⁵ Though the nations around us follow
their idols,
we will follow the LORD our God
forever and ever.

⁶ "In that coming day," says the LORD,
"I will gather together those who are
lame,
those who have been exiles,
and those whom I have filled with
grief.
⁷ Those who are weak will survive
as a remnant;
those who were exiles will become
a strong nation.
Then I, the LORD, will rule from
Jerusalem*
as their king forever."
⁸ As for you, Jerusalem,
the citadel of God's people,*
your royal might and power
will come back to you again.
The kingship will be restored
to my precious Jerusalem.

⁹ But why are you now screaming
in terror?
Have you no king to lead you?
Have your wise people all died?
Pain has gripped you like a woman
in childbirth.

¹⁰ Writhe and groan like a woman
　　in labor,
　　you people of Jerusalem,*
for now you must leave this city
　　to live in the open country.
You will soon be sent in exile
　　to distant Babylon.
But the LORD will rescue you there;
　　he will redeem you from the grip
　　of your enemies.

¹¹ Now many nations have gathered
　　against you.
　　"Let her be desecrated," they say.
　　"Let us see the destruction of
　　Jerusalem.*"
¹² But they do not know the LORD's
　　thoughts
　　or understand his plan.
These nations don't know
　　that he is gathering them together
to be beaten and trampled
　　like sheaves of grain on a threshing
　　floor.
¹³ "Rise up and crush the nations,
　　O Jerusalem!"*
　　says the LORD.
"For I will give you iron horns and
　　bronze hooves,
　　so you can trample many nations
　　to pieces.
You will present their stolen riches
　　to the LORD,
　　their wealth to the LORD of all the
　　earth."

1:5 Hebrew *Jacob;* also in 1:5b. The names "Jacob" and "Israel" are often interchanged throughout the Old Testament, referring sometimes to the individual patriarch and sometimes to the nation.　1:10a *Gath* sounds like the Hebrew term for "tell."　1:10b *Beth-leaphrah* means "house of dust."　1:11a *Shaphir* means "pleasant."　1:11b *Zaanan* sounds like the Hebrew term for "come out."　1:11c *Beth-ezel* means "adjoining house."　1:12 *Maroth* sounds like the Hebrew term for "bitter."　1:13a *Lachish* sounds like the Hebrew term for "team of horses."　1:13b Hebrew *the daughter of Zion.*　1:14a *Moresheth* sounds like the Hebrew term for "gift" or "dowry."　1:14b *Aczib* means "deception."　1:15a *Mareshah* sounds like the Hebrew term for "conqueror."　1:15b Hebrew *the glory.*　2:4 Or *to those who took us captive.*　2:6 Or *the prophets respond;* Hebrew reads *they prophesy.*　2:7 Hebrew *O house of Jacob?* See note on 1:5a.　4:7 Hebrew *Mount Zion.*　4:8 Hebrew *As for you, Migdal-eder, / the Ophel of the daughter of Zion.*　4:10 Hebrew *O daughter of Zion.*　4:11 Hebrew *of Zion.*　4:13 Hebrew "Rise up and thresh, O daughter of Zion."

REVELATION 6:1-17
Today's reading switches perspectives between what was happening in heaven to what was happening on earth. John's description of the first six seals may seem a bit familiar. It is similar to Jesus' description of the end times when he preached from the Mount of Olives (Mark 13:1-37, March 6–7).

As I [John] watched, the Lamb broke the first of the seven seals on the scroll.* Then I heard one of the four living beings say with a voice like thunder, "Come!" ²I looked up and saw a white horse standing there. Its rider carried a bow, and a crown was placed on his head. He rode out to win many battles and gain the victory.

³ When the Lamb broke the second seal, I heard the second living being say, "Come!" ⁴Then another horse appeared, a red one. Its rider was given a mighty sword and the authority to take peace from the earth. And there was war and slaughter everywhere.

⁵ When the Lamb broke the third seal, I heard the third living being say, "Come!" I looked up and saw a black horse, and its rider was holding a pair of scales in his hand. ⁶And I heard a voice from among the four living beings say, "A loaf of wheat bread or three loaves of barley will cost a day's pay.* And don't waste* the olive oil and wine."

⁷ When the Lamb broke the fourth seal, I heard the fourth living being say, "Come!" ⁸I looked up and saw a horse whose color was pale green. Its rider was named Death, and his companion was the Grave.* These two were given authority over one-fourth of the earth, to kill with the sword and famine and disease* and wild animals.

⁹ When the Lamb broke the fifth seal, I saw under the altar the souls of all who had been martyred for the word of God and for being faithful in their testimony. ¹⁰They shouted to the Lord and said, "O Sovereign Lord, holy and true, how long before you judge the people who belong to this world and avenge our blood for what they have done to us?" ¹¹Then a white robe was given to each of them. And they were told to rest a little longer until the full number of their brothers and sisters*—their fellow servants of Jesus who were to be martyred—had joined them.

¹² I watched as the Lamb broke the sixth seal, and there was a great earthquake. The sun became as dark as black cloth, and the moon became as red as blood.

[13]Then the stars of the sky fell to the earth like green figs falling from a tree shaken by a strong wind. [14]The sky was rolled up like a scroll, and all of the mountains and islands were moved from their places.

[15]Then everyone—the kings of the earth, the rulers, the generals, the wealthy, the powerful, and every slave and free person—all hid themselves in the caves and among the rocks of the mountains. [16]And they cried to the mountains and the rocks, "Fall on us and hide us from the face of the one who sits on the throne and from the wrath of the Lamb. [17]For the great day of their wrath has come, and who is able to survive?"

6:1 Or *book.*   **6:6a** Greek *A choinix* [1 quart or 1 liter] *of wheat for a denarius, and 3 choinix of barley for a denarius.* A denarius was equivalent to a laborer's full day's wage. **6:6b** Or *harm.*   **6:8a** Greek *was Hades.*   **6:8b** Greek *death.* **6:11** Greek *their brothers.*

PSALM 134:1-3

A song for pilgrims ascending to Jerusalem.

[1] **O**h, praise the Lord, all you servants
        of the Lord,

you who serve at night in the house
        of the Lord.
[2] Lift up holy hands in prayer,
        and praise the Lord.

[3] May the Lord, who made heaven
        and earth,
        bless you from Jerusalem.*

134:3 Hebrew *Zion.*

PROVERBS 30:1-4

The sayings of Agur son of Jakeh contain this message.* □I am weary, O God; I am weary and worn out, O God.* I am too stupid to be human, and I lack common sense. I have not mastered human wisdom, nor do I know the Holy One. □Who but God goes up to heaven and comes back down? Who holds the wind in his fists? Who wraps up the oceans in his cloak? Who has created the whole wide world? What is his name—and his son's name? Tell me if you know!

30:1a Or *son of Jakeh from Massa;* or *son of Jakeh, an oracle.* **30:1b** The Hebrew can also be translated *The man declares this to Ithiel, / to Ithiel and to Ucal.*

DECEMBER**16**

MICAH 5:1-7:20
The second half of Micah has some well-known passages. In 5:2, Micah names Bethlehem as the village from which a ruler of Israel would be born (as Jesus was). In 6:8, Micah boils the godly life down to three directives: do right, love mercy, and walk humbly with God.

[1]* **M**obilize! Marshal your troops!
        The enemy is laying siege to
        Jerusalem.
        They will strike Israel's leader
        in the face with a rod.
[2]* But you, O Bethlehem Ephrathah,
        are only a small village among all
        the people of Judah.
        Yet a ruler of Israel will come from you,
        one whose origins are from the
        distant past.

[3] The people of Israel will be
        abandoned to their enemies
        until the woman in labor gives
        birth.
    Then at last his fellow countrymen
        will return from exile to their own
        land.
[4] And he will stand to lead his flock
        with the Lord's strength,
        in the majesty of the name of the
        Lord his God.
    Then his people will live there
        undisturbed,
        for he will be highly honored
        around the world.
[5]   And he will be the source of peace.

    When the Assyrians invade our land
        and break through our defenses,

we will appoint seven rulers to watch
over us,
eight princes to lead us.
⁶ They will rule Assyria with drawn
swords
and enter the gates of the land
of Nimrod.
He will rescue us from the Assyrians
when they pour over the borders
to invade our land.

⁷ Then the remnant left in Israel*
will take their place among the
nations.
They will be like dew sent by the LORD
or like rain falling on the grass,
which no one can hold back
and no one can restrain.
⁸ The remnant left in Israel
will take their place among the
nations.
They will be like a lion among the
animals of the forest,
like a strong young lion among
flocks of sheep and goats,
pouncing and tearing as they go
with no rescuer in sight.
⁹ The people of Israel will stand up
to their foes,
and all their enemies will be
wiped out.

¹⁰ "In that day," says the LORD,
"I will slaughter your horses
and destroy your chariots.
¹¹ I will tear down your walls
and demolish your defenses.
¹² I will put an end to all witchcraft,
and there will be no more fortune-
tellers.
¹³ I will destroy all your idols and sacred
pillars,
so you will never again worship the
work of your own hands.
¹⁴ I will abolish your idol shrines with
their Asherah poles
and destroy your pagan cities.
¹⁵ I will pour out my vengeance
on all the nations that refuse
to obey me."

⁶:¹LISTEN to what the LORD is saying:

"Stand up and state your case
against me.
Let the mountains and hills be
called to witness your
complaints.
² And now, O mountains,
listen to the LORD's complaint!
He has a case against his people.
He will bring charges against Israel.

³ "O my people, what have I done to you?
What have I done to make you tired
of me?
Answer me!
⁴ For I brought you out of Egypt
and redeemed you from slavery.
I sent Moses, Aaron, and Miriam
to help you.
⁵ Don't you remember, my people,
how King Balak of Moab tried
to have you cursed
and how Balaam son of Beor
blessed you instead?
And remember your journey from
Acacia Grove* to Gilgal,
when I, the LORD, did everything
I could
to teach you about my faithfulness."

⁶ What can we bring to the LORD?
What kind of offerings should
we give him?
Should we bow before God
with offerings of yearling calves?
⁷ Should we offer him thousands
of rams
and ten thousand rivers of olive oil?
Should we sacrifice our firstborn
children
to pay for our sins?

⁸ No, O people, the LORD has told you
what is good,
and this is what he requires of you:
to do what is right, to love mercy,
and to walk humbly with your God.

⁹ Fear the LORD if you are wise!
His voice calls to everyone
in Jerusalem:
"The armies of destruction are
coming;
the LORD is sending them.*
¹⁰ What shall I say about the homes
of the wicked
filled with treasures gained
by cheating?
What about the disgusting
practice

of measuring out grain with
dishonest measures?*

¹¹ How can I tolerate your merchants
who use dishonest scales and
weights?

¹² The rich among you have become
wealthy
through extortion and violence.
Your citizens are so used to lying
that their tongues can no longer tell
the truth.

¹³ "Therefore, I will wound you!
I will bring you to ruin for all
your sins.

¹⁴ You will eat but never have enough.
Your hunger pangs and emptiness
will remain.
And though you try to save your
money,
it will come to nothing in the end.
You will save a little,
but I will give it to those who
conquer you.

¹⁵ You will plant crops
but not harvest them.
You will press your olives
but not get enough oil to anoint
yourselves.
You will trample the grapes
but get no juice to make your wine.

¹⁶ You keep only the laws of evil King
Omri;
you follow only the example
of wicked King Ahab!
Therefore, I will make an example
of you,
bringing you to complete ruin.
You will be treated with contempt,
mocked by all who see you."

⁷:¹ How miserable I am!
I feel like the fruit picker after the
harvest
who can find nothing to eat.
Not a cluster of grapes or a single early
fig
can be found to satisfy my hunger.

² The godly people have all disappeared;
not one honest person is left on the
earth.
They are all murderers,
setting traps even for their own
brothers.

³ Both their hands are equally skilled
at doing evil!
Officials and judges alike demand
bribes.
The people with influence get what
they want,
and together they scheme to twist
justice.

⁴ Even the best of them is like a brier;
the most honest is as dangerous
as a hedge of thorns.
But your judgment day is coming
swiftly now.
Your time of punishment is here,
a time of confusion.

⁵ Don't trust anyone—
not your best friend or even your
wife!

⁶ For the son despises his father.
The daughter defies her mother.
The daughter-in-law defies her
mother-in-law.
Your enemies are right in your own
household!

⁷ As for me, I look to the LORD for help.
I wait confidently for God to save
me,
and my God will certainly hear me.

⁸ Do not gloat over me, my enemies!
For though I fall, I will rise again.
Though I sit in darkness,
the LORD will be my light.

⁹ I will be patient as the LORD punishes
me,
for I have sinned against him.
But after that, he will take up my case
and give me justice for all I have
suffered from my enemies.
The LORD will bring me into the light,
and I will see his righteousness.

¹⁰ Then my enemies will see that the
LORD is on my side.
They will be ashamed that they
taunted me, saying,
"So where is the LORD—
that God of yours?"
With my own eyes I will see their
downfall;
they will be trampled like mud
in the streets.

¹¹ In that day, Israel, your cities will be
rebuilt,
and your borders will be extended.

12 People from many lands will come and
    honor you—
    from Assyria all the way to the
      towns of Egypt,
from Egypt all the way to the
    Euphrates River,*
and from distant seas and
    mountains.
13 But the land* will become empty and
    desolate
    because of the wickedness of those
      who live there.

14 O LORD, protect your people with your
    shepherd's staff;
    lead your flock, your special
      possession.
Though they live alone in a thicket
    on the heights of Mount Carmel,*
let them graze in the fertile pastures
    of Bashan and Gilead
    as they did long ago.

15 "Yes," says the LORD,
    "I will do mighty miracles for you,
like those I did when I rescued you
    from slavery in Egypt."

16 All the nations of the world will stand
    amazed
    at what the LORD will do for you.
They will be embarrassed
    at their feeble power.

They will cover their mouths in silent
    awe,
    deaf to everything around them.
17 Like snakes crawling from their holes,
    they will come out to meet the
      LORD our God.
They will fear him greatly,
    trembling in terror at his presence.

18 Where is another God like you,
    who pardons the guilt of the remnant,
    overlooking the sins of his special
      people?
You will not stay angry with your
    people forever,
    because you delight in showing
      unfailing love.
19 Once again you will have compassion
    on us.
    You will trample our sins under
      your feet
    and throw them into the depths
      of the ocean!
20 You will show us your faithfulness
    and unfailing love
    as you promised to our ancestors
      Abraham and Jacob long ago.

5:1 Verse 5:1 is numbered 4:14 in Hebrew text.   **5:2** Verses
5:2-15 are numbered 5:1-14 in Hebrew text.   **5:7** Hebrew
in Jacob; also in 5:8. See note on 1:5a.   **6:5** Hebrew *Shittim.*
6:9 Hebrew *"Listen to the rod. / Who appointed it?"*
6:10 Hebrew *of using the short ephah?* The ephah was
a unit for measuring grain.   **7:12** Hebrew *the river.*
7:13 Or *earth.*   **7:14** Or *surrounded by a fruitful land.*

WHAT THE BIBLE SAYS

The reality of heaven

REVELATION 7:13-17 Heaven will be a place with no tears—no tears of pain,
sorrow, regret, wounds, loss, hurt feelings, unmet desires, unrequited
love—not even of hay fever or colds. Have you ever really thought about
what a world with no tears would be like? We are so used to tears, even
those who don't cry much themselves. Tears come when we've been
physically hurt—like the child with the skinned knee. Tears come when
we're emotionally spent, when we're grieving, or when we're completely
overwhelmed. Tears come when we say good-bye. Tears come with
sadness. Tears indicate sickness of the body or the heart. They can
reveal a loss of hope. But in heaven there will be no sickness of the
heart or body, no regrets, no pain, no sorrow, no unmet desires, no grief.
The world will be perfect, everything in its place and everyone with what
they need. No tears. •Imagine it. Have faith in it. Envision the hand of
God wiping from your face the last tear you'll ever cry and sending you
out to live in the sunshine. "God will wipe every tear from their eyes."

REVELATION 7:1-17

Revelation 7 is a break between the six seals described in chapter 6 and the seventh seal being opened in chapter 8. Here John envisions the 144,000 who were marked with the seal of God—the number symbolizes completeness.

Then I [John] saw four angels standing at the four corners of the earth, holding back the four winds so they did not blow on the earth or the sea, or even on any tree. ²And I saw another angel coming up from the east, carrying the seal of the living God. And he shouted to those four angels, who had been given power to harm land and sea, ³"Wait! Don't harm the land or the sea or the trees until we have placed the seal of God on the foreheads of his servants."

⁴And I heard how many were marked with the seal of God—144,000 were sealed from all the tribes of Israel:

5	from Judah.	12,000
	from Reuben	12,000
	from Gad	12,000
6	from Asher	12,000
	from Naphtali	12,000
	from Manasseh	12,000
7	from Simeon	12,000
	from Levi	12,000
	from Issachar	12,000
8	from Zebulun	12,000
	from Joseph	12,000
	from Benjamin	12,000

⁹After this I saw a vast crowd, too great to count, from every nation and tribe and people and language, standing in front of the throne and before the Lamb. They were clothed in white robes and held palm branches in their hands. ¹⁰And they were shouting with a mighty shout,

"Salvation comes from our God who
  sits on the throne
and from the Lamb!"

¹¹And all the angels were standing around the throne and around the elders and the four living beings. And they fell with their faces to the ground before the throne and worshiped God. ¹²They sang,

"Amen! Blessing and glory and wisdom
  and thanksgiving and honor

and power and strength belong
  to our God
forever and ever! Amen."

¹³Then one of the twenty-four elders asked me, "Who are these who are clothed in white? Where did they come from?"

¹⁴And I said to him, "Sir, you are the one who knows."

Then he said to me, "These are the ones who died in* the great tribulation.* They have washed their robes in the blood of the Lamb and made them white.

¹⁵ "That is why they stand in front
  of God's throne
and serve him day and night in his
  Temple.
And he who sits on the throne
  will give them shelter.
¹⁶ They will never again be hungry
  or thirsty;
  they will never be scorched by
    the heat of the sun.
¹⁷ For the Lamb on the throne*
  will be their Shepherd.
He will lead them to springs of life-
  giving water.
And God will wipe every tear from
  their eyes."

7:14a Greek *who came out of.* 7:14b Or *the great suffering.*
7:17 Greek *on the center of the throne.*

PSALM 135:1-21

Praise the LORD!

Praise the name of the LORD!
  Praise him, you who serve the LORD,
² you who serve in the house of the LORD,
  in the courts of the house of our
    God.

³ Praise the LORD, for the LORD is good;
  celebrate his lovely name with
    music.
⁴ For the LORD has chosen Jacob for
  himself,
  Israel for his own special treasure.

⁵ I know the greatness of the LORD—
  that our Lord is greater than any
    other god.
⁶ The LORD does whatever pleases him
  throughout all heaven and earth,
  and on the seas and in their depths.

7 He causes the clouds to rise over
the whole earth.
He sends the lightning with the rain
and releases the wind from his
storehouses.

8 He destroyed the firstborn in each
Egyptian home,
both people and animals.
9 He performed miraculous signs and
wonders in Egypt
against Pharaoh and all his people.
10 He struck down great nations
and slaughtered mighty kings—
11 Sihon king of the Amorites,
Og king of Bashan,
and all the kings of Canaan.
12 He gave their land as an inheritance,
a special possession to his people
Israel.

13 Your name, O LORD, endures forever;
your fame, O LORD, is known
to every generation.
14 For the LORD will give justice to his
people
and have compassion on his servants.

15 The idols of the nations are merely
things of silver and gold,
shaped by human hands.
16 They have mouths but cannot speak,
and eyes but cannot see.
17 They have ears but cannot hear,
and noses but cannot smell.
18 And those who make idols are just like
them,
as are all who trust in them.

19 O Israel, praise the LORD!
O priests—descendants of Aaron—
praise the LORD!
20 O Levites, praise the LORD!
All you who fear the LORD, praise
the LORD!
21 The LORD be praised from Zion,
for he lives here in Jerusalem.

Praise the LORD!

PROVERBS 30:5-6
Every word of God proves true. He is a
shield to all who come to him for protection. Do not add to his words, or he may
rebuke you and expose you as a liar.

DECEMBER**17**

NAHUM 1:1–3:19
The book of Nahum deals with the destruction of
Nineveh, which was, during Nahum's day, the capital
of Assyria, Israel's fierce foe to the east. When Jonah
had traveled to Nineveh, the city had repented and
was given another chance. Unfortunately, that repentance didn't continue. The city fell in 512 BC.

This message concerning Nineveh came
as a vision to Nahum, who lived in Elkosh.

2 The LORD is a jealous God,
filled with vengeance and rage.
He takes revenge on all who oppose
him
and continues to rage against his
enemies!
3 The LORD is slow to get angry, but his
power is great,
and he never lets the guilty
go unpunished.

He displays his power in the
whirlwind and the storm.
The billowing clouds are the dust
beneath his feet.
4 At his command the oceans dry up,
and the rivers disappear.
The lush pastures of Bashan and
Carmel fade,
and the green forests of Lebanon
wither.
5 In his presence the mountains quake,
and the hills melt away;
the earth trembles,
and its people are destroyed.
6 Who can stand before his fierce anger?
Who can survive his burning fury?
His rage blazes forth like fire,
and the mountains crumble to dust
in his presence.

7 The LORD is good,
a strong refuge when trouble
comes.
He is close to those who trust
in him.
8 But he will sweep away his enemies
in an overwhelming flood.
He will pursue his foes
into the darkness of night.

9 Why are you scheming against
the LORD?
He will destroy you with one blow;
he won't need to strike twice!
10 His enemies, tangled like thornbushes
and staggering like drunks,
will be burned up like dry stubble
in a field.
11 Who is this wicked counselor of yours
who plots evil against the LORD?

12 This is what the LORD says:
"Though the Assyrians have many
allies,
they will be destroyed and
disappear.
O my people, I have punished you
before,
but I will not punish you again.
13 Now I will break the yoke of bondage
from your neck
and tear off the chains of Assyrian
oppression."

14 And this is what the LORD says
concerning the Assyrians
in Nineveh:
"You will have no more children
to carry on your name.
I will destroy all the idols in the
temples of your gods.
I am preparing a grave for you
because you are despicable!"

15*Look! A messenger is coming over the
mountains with good news!
He is bringing a message of peace.
Celebrate your festivals, O people
of Judah,
and fulfill all your vows,
for your wicked enemies will never
invade your land again.
They will be completely destroyed!

2:1*YOUR enemy is coming to crush you,
Nineveh.

Man the ramparts! Watch the roads!
Prepare your defenses! Call out your
forces!

2 Even though the destroyer has
destroyed Judah,
the LORD will restore its honor.
Israel's vine has been stripped
of branches,
but he will restore its splendor.

3 Shields flash red in the sunlight!
See the scarlet uniforms of the
valiant troops!
Watch as their glittering chariots
move into position,
with a forest of spears waving above
them.
4 The chariots race recklessly along
the streets
and rush wildly through the
squares.
They flash like firelight
and move as swiftly as lightning.
5 The king shouts to his officers;
they stumble in their haste,
rushing to the walls to set up their
defenses.
6 The river gates have been torn open!
The palace is about to collapse!
7 Nineveh's exile has been decreed,
and all the servant girls mourn its
capture.
They moan like doves
and beat their breasts in sorrow.
8 Nineveh is like a leaking water
reservoir!
The people are slipping away.
"Stop, stop!" someone shouts,
but no one even looks back.
9 Loot the silver!
Plunder the gold!
There's no end to Nineveh's treasures—
its vast, uncounted wealth.
10 Soon the city is plundered, empty,
and ruined.
Hearts melt and knees shake.
The people stand aghast,
their faces pale and trembling.

11 Where now is that great Nineveh,
that den filled with young lions?
It was a place where people—like lions
and their cubs—
walked freely and without fear.

¹² The lion tore up meat for his cubs
 and strangled prey for his mate.
He filled his den with prey,
 his caverns with his plunder.

¹³ "I am your enemy!"
 says the LORD of Heaven's Armies.
"Your chariots will soon go up in
 smoke.
Your young men* will be killed in
 battle.
Never again will you plunder
 conquered nations.
The voices of your proud
 messengers will be heard
 no more."

³:¹ WHAT sorrow awaits Nineveh,
 the city of murder and lies!
She is crammed with wealth
 and is never without victims.
² Hear the crack of whips,
 the rumble of wheels!
Horses' hooves pound,
 and chariots clatter wildly.
³ See the flashing swords and glittering
 spears
 as the charioteers charge past!
There are countless casualties,
 heaps of bodies—
so many bodies that
 people stumble over them.
⁴ All this because Nineveh,
 the beautiful and faithless city,

mistress of deadly charms,
 enticed the nations with her beauty.
She taught them all her magic,
 enchanting people everywhere.

⁵ "I am your enemy!"
 says the LORD of Heaven's Armies.
"And now I will lift your skirts
 and show all the earth your
 nakedness and shame.
⁶ I will cover you with filth
 and show the world how vile you
 really are.
⁷ All who see you will shrink back
 and say,
 'Nineveh lies in ruins.
 Where are the mourners?'
 Does anyone regret your
 destruction?"

⁸ Are you any better than the city
 of Thebes,*
 situated on the Nile River,
 surrounded by water?
She was protected by the river
 on all sides,
 walled in by water.
⁹ Ethiopia* and the land of Egypt
 gave unlimited assistance.
The nations of Put and Libya
 were among her allies.
¹⁰ Yet Thebes fell,
 and her people were led away
 as captives.

Praise and thanksgiving

HOW WE LIVE

PSALM 136:1-26 The refrain continues over and over: "Give thanks to" him who did something, because "his faithful love endures forever." Each refrain also includes a particular example of God's unfailing love in action. The Israelites sang this glorious song as they praised God for his creation, for rescuing them from Egypt, for helping them conquer and inhabit the Promised Land, for remembering them in their weakness, for saving them from their enemies, and for giving them food and supplying their needs.   • Rewrite this psalm with your own words. Thank God for his glorious creation—what you see right outside your window, and what you can't see deep within the atoms or out in the universe. Give thanks to God for saving you, for the various sins for which you've been forgiven, and for the blessings you've been given. Then, when you feel low, read your psalm. Nothing helps to get life back into perspective than express- ing your praise to God for what he has done—and continues to do— in your life.

Her babies were dashed to death
against the stones of the streets.
Soldiers threw dice* to get Egyptian
officers as servants.
All their leaders were bound
in chains.

¹¹ And you, Nineveh, will also stagger like
a drunkard.
You will hide for fear of the
attacking enemy.
¹² All your fortresses will fall.
They will be devoured like
the ripe figs
that fall into the mouths
of those who shake the trees.
¹³ Your troops will be as weak
and helpless as women.
The gates of your land will be opened
wide to the enemy
and set on fire and burned.
¹⁴ Get ready for the siege!
Store up water!
Strengthen the defenses!
Go into the pits to trample clay,
and pack it into molds, making
bricks to repair the walls.
¹⁵ But the fire will devour you;
the sword will cut you down.
The enemy will consume you like
locusts,
devouring everything they see.
There will be no escape,
even if you multiply like swarming
locusts.
¹⁶ Your merchants have multiplied
until they outnumber the stars.
But like a swarm of locusts,
they strip the land and fly away.
¹⁷ Your guards* and officials are also like
swarming locusts
that crowd together in the hedges
on a cold day.
But like locusts that fly away when
the sun comes up,
all of them will fly away and
disappear.
¹⁸ Your shepherds are asleep, O Assyrian
king;
your princes lie dead in the dust.
Your people are scattered across the
mountains

with no one to gather them
together.
¹⁹ There is no healing for your wound;
your injury is fatal.
All who hear of your destruction
will clap their hands for joy.
Where can anyone be found
who has not suffered from your
continual cruelty?

1:15 Verse 1:15 is numbered 2:1 in Hebrew text.
2:1 Verses 2:1-13 are numbered 2:2-14 in Hebrew text.
2:13 Hebrew *young lions.* **3:8** Hebrew *No-amon;* also
in 3:10. **3:9** Hebrew *Cush.* **3:10** Hebrew *They cast lots.*
3:17 Or *princes.*

REVELATION 8:1-13

As the final seal on the scroll is broken, John's next
series of images begins—trumpets. Each trumpet
heralds judgment. The first four include plagues
similar to the plagues described in Exodus. The last
three (described in upcoming chapters) are called
"terrors" for the earth.

When the Lamb broke the seventh seal on
the scroll,* there was silence throughout
heaven for about half an hour. ²I [John]
saw the seven angels who stand before
God, and they were given seven trumpets.

³ Then another angel with a gold incense burner came and stood at the altar.
And a great amount of incense was given
to him to mix with the prayers of God's
holy people as an offering on the gold altar before the throne. ⁴The smoke of the
incense, mixed with the prayers of God's
people, ascended up to God from the altar
where the angel had poured them out.
⁵ Then the angel filled the incense burner
with fire from the altar and threw it down
upon the earth; and thunder crashed,
lightning flashed, and there was a terrible
earthquake.

⁶ Then the seven angels with the seven
trumpets prepared to blow their mighty
blasts.

⁷ The first angel blew his trumpet, and
hail and fire mixed with blood were
thrown down on the earth. One-third of
the earth was set on fire, one-third of the
trees were burned, and all the green grass
was burned.

⁸ Then the second angel blew his trumpet, and a great mountain of fire was
thrown into the sea. One-third of the water in the sea became blood, ⁹one-third

of all things living in the sea died, and one-third of all the ships on the sea were destroyed.

¹⁰Then the third angel blew his trumpet, and a great star fell from the sky, burning like a torch. It fell on one-third of the rivers and on the springs of water. ¹¹The name of the star was Bitterness.* It made one-third of the water bitter, and many people died from drinking the bitter water.

¹²Then the fourth angel blew his trumpet, and one-third of the sun was struck, and one-third of the moon, and one-third of the stars, and they became dark. And one-third of the day was dark, and also one-third of the night.

¹³Then I looked, and I heard a single eagle crying loudly as it flew through the air, "Terror, terror, terror to all who belong to this world because of what will happen when the last three angels blow their trumpets."

8:1 Or *book.*   **8:11** Greek *Wormwood.*

PSALM 136:1-26

Give thanks to the LORD, for he is good!
  His faithful love endures forever.
² Give thanks to the God of gods.
  His faithful love endures forever.
³ Give thanks to the Lord of lords.
  His faithful love endures forever.
⁴ Give thanks to him who alone does
    mighty miracles.
  His faithful love endures forever.
⁵ Give thanks to him who made the
    heavens so skillfully.
  His faithful love endures forever.
⁶ Give thanks to him who placed the
    earth among the waters.
  His faithful love endures forever.
⁷ Give thanks to him who made the
    heavenly lights—
  His faithful love endures forever.
⁸ the sun to rule the day,
  His faithful love endures forever.
⁹ and the moon and stars to rule the
    night.
  His faithful love endures forever.
¹⁰ Give thanks to him who killed the
    firstborn of Egypt.
  His faithful love endures forever.

¹¹ He brought Israel out of Egypt.
  His faithful love endures forever.
¹² He acted with a strong hand and
    powerful arm.
  His faithful love endures forever.
¹³ Give thanks to him who parted the
    Red Sea.*
  His faithful love endures forever.
¹⁴ He led Israel safely through,
  His faithful love endures forever.
¹⁵ but he hurled Pharaoh and his army
    into the Red Sea.
  His faithful love endures forever.
¹⁶ Give thanks to him who led his people
    through the wilderness.
  His faithful love endures forever.
¹⁷ Give thanks to him who struck down
    mighty kings.
  His faithful love endures forever.
¹⁸ He killed powerful kings—
  His faithful love endures forever.
¹⁹ Sihon king of the Amorites,
  His faithful love endures forever.
²⁰ and Og king of Bashan.
  His faithful love endures forever.
²¹ God gave the land of these kings as
    an inheritance—
  His faithful love endures forever.
²² a special possession to his servant
    Israel.
  His faithful love endures forever.
²³ He remembered us in our weakness.
  His faithful love endures forever.
²⁴ He saved us from our enemies.
  His faithful love endures forever.
²⁵ He gives food to every living thing.
  His faithful love endures forever.
²⁶ Give thanks to the God of heaven.
  His faithful love endures forever.

136:13 Hebrew *sea of reeds;* also in 136:15.

PROVERBS 30:7-9

O God, I beg two favors from you; let me have them before I die. First, help me never to tell a lie. Second, give me neither poverty nor riches! Give me just enough to satisfy my needs. For if I grow rich, I may deny you and say, "Who is the LORD?" And if I am too poor, I may steal and thus insult God's holy name.

DECEMBER **18**

Habakkuk's prophecy is organized around questions about what a child of God should think and do regarding evil in the world. Habakkuk asks the same questions that we often struggle with today. How do we make sense of evil? Why does God allow it to exist?

This is the message that the prophet Habakkuk received in a vision.

2 How long, O LORD, must I call for help?
　　But you do not listen!
"Violence is everywhere!" I cry,
　　but you do not come to save.
3 Must I forever see these evil deeds?
　　Why must I watch all this misery?
Wherever I look,
　　I see destruction and violence.
I am surrounded by people
　　who love to argue and fight.
4 The law has become paralyzed,
　　and there is no justice in the courts.
The wicked far outnumber the
　　righteous,
　　so that justice has become
　　perverted.

5 The LORD replied,

"Look around at the nations;
　　look and be amazed!*
For I am doing something in your own
　　day,
　　something you wouldn't believe
　　even if someone told you about it.
6 I am raising up the Babylonians,*
　　a cruel and violent people.
They will march across the world
　　and conquer other lands.
7 They are notorious for their cruelty
　　and do whatever they like.
8 Their horses are swifter than
　　cheetahs*
　　and fiercer than wolves at dusk.
Their charioteers charge from far
　　away.
　　Like eagles, they swoop down
　　to devour their prey.
9 "On they come, all bent on violence.
　　Their hordes advance like a desert
　　wind,

sweeping captives ahead of them
　　like sand.
10 They scoff at kings and princes
　　and scorn all their fortresses.
They simply pile ramps of earth
　　against their walls and capture them!
11 They sweep past like the wind
　　and are gone.
But they are deeply guilty,
　　for their own strength is their god."

12 O LORD my God, my Holy One, you
　　who are eternal—
　　surely you do not plan to wipe us out?
O LORD, our Rock, you have sent these
　　Babylonians to correct us,
　　to punish us for our many sins.
13 But you are pure and cannot stand the
　　sight of evil.
　　Will you wink at their treachery?
Should you be silent while the wicked
　　swallow up people more righteous
　　than they?
14 Are we only fish to be caught and
　　killed?
　　Are we only sea creatures that have
　　no leader?
15 Must we be strung up on their hooks
　　and caught in their nets while they
　　rejoice and celebrate?
16 Then they will worship their nets
　　and burn incense in front of them.
"These nets are the gods who have
　　made us rich!"
　　they will claim.
17 Will you let them get away with this
　　forever?
　　Will they succeed forever in their
　　heartless conquests?

2:1 I WILL climb up to my watchtower
　　and stand at my guardpost.
There I will wait to see what the LORD
　　says
　　and how he* will answer my
　　complaint.

2 Then the LORD said to me,

"Write my answer plainly on tablets,
　　so that a runner can carry the
　　correct message to others.

3 This vision is for a future time.
   It describes the end, and it will
     be fulfilled.
  If it seems slow in coming, wait
     patiently,
  for it will surely take place.
     It will not be delayed.

4 "Look at the proud!
   They trust in themselves, and their
     lives are crooked.
  But the righteous will live by their
     faithfulness to God.*
5 Wealth* is treacherous,
   and the arrogant are never at rest.
  They open their mouths as wide as the
     grave,*
   and like death, they are never
     satisfied.
  In their greed they have gathered
     up many nations
   and swallowed many peoples.

6 "But soon their captives will taunt them.
   They will mock them, saying,
  'What sorrow awaits you thieves!
   Now you will get what you deserve!
  You've become rich by extortion,
   but how much longer can this go on?'
7 Suddenly, your debtors will take
     action.
  They will turn on you and take
     all you have,
  while you stand trembling
     and helpless.
8 Because you have plundered many
     nations;
  now all the survivors will plunder
     you.
  You committed murder throughout
     the countryside
   and filled the towns with violence.

9 "What sorrow awaits you who build
     big houses
  with money gained dishonestly!
  You believe your wealth will buy
     security,
  putting your family's nest beyond
     the reach of danger.
10 But by the murders you committed,
   you have shamed your name and
     forfeited your lives.
11 The very stones in the walls cry out
     against you,

and the beams in the ceilings echo
   the complaint.

12 "What sorrow awaits you who build
     cities
  with money gained through murder
     and corruption!
13 Has not the LORD of Heaven's Armies
     promised
  that the wealth of nations will turn
     to ashes?
  They work so hard,
   but all in vain!
14 For as the waters fill the sea,
   the earth will be filled with
     an awareness
   of the glory of the LORD.

15 "What sorrow awaits you who make
     your neighbors drunk!
  You force your cup on them
   so you can gloat over their shameful
     nakedness.
16 But soon it will be your turn
     to be disgraced.
  Come, drink and be exposed!
  Drink from the cup of the LORD's
     judgment,
   and all your glory will be turned
     to shame.
17 You cut down the forests of Lebanon.
   Now you will be cut down.
  You destroyed the wild animals,
   so now their terror will be yours.
  You committed murder throughout
     the countryside
   and filled the towns with violence.

18 "What good is an idol carved by man,
   or a cast image that deceives you?
  How foolish to trust in your own
     creation—
   a god that can't even talk!
19 What sorrow awaits you who say
     to wooden idols,
  'Wake up and save us!'
  To speechless stone images you say,
   'Rise up and teach us!'
  Can an idol tell you what to do?
  They may be overlaid with gold
     and silver,
   but they are lifeless inside.
20 But the LORD is in his holy Temple.
   Let all the earth be silent before
     him."

3:1THIS prayer was sung by the prophet Habakkuk*:

2   I have heard all about you, LORD.
    I am filled with awe by your
        amazing works.
    In this time of our deep need,
        help us again as you did in years
        gone by.
    And in your anger,
        remember your mercy.

3   I see God moving across the deserts
        from Edom,*
        the Holy One coming from Mount
        Paran.*
    His brilliant splendor fills the heavens,
        and the earth is filled with his
        praise.
4   His coming is as brilliant as the
        sunrise.
    Rays of light flash from his hands,
        where his awesome power is
        hidden.
5   Pestilence marches before him;
        plague follows close behind.
6   When he stops, the earth shakes.
    When he looks, the nations
        tremble.
    He shatters the everlasting mountains
        and levels the eternal hills.
    He is the Eternal One!
7   I see the people of Cushan in distress,
        and the nation of Midian trembling
        in terror.

8   Was it in anger, LORD, that you struck
        the rivers
        and parted the sea?
    Were you displeased with them?
        No, you were sending your chariots
        of salvation!
9   You brandished your bow
        and your quiver of arrows.
    You split open the earth with
        flowing rivers.
10 The mountains watched and
        trembled.
    Onward swept the raging waters.
    The mighty deep cried out,
        lifting its hands to the LORD.
11 The sun and moon stood still
        in the sky
    as your brilliant arrows flew
        and your glittering spear flashed.

12 You marched across the land in anger
        and trampled the nations in your
        fury.
13 You went out to rescue your chosen
        people,
        to save your anointed ones.
    You crushed the heads of the wicked
        and stripped their bones from head
        to toe.
14 With his own weapons,
        you destroyed the chief of those
    who rushed out like a whirlwind,
        thinking Israel would be easy prey.
15 You trampled the sea with your
        horses,
        and the mighty waters piled high.

16 I trembled inside when I heard this;
        my lips quivered with fear.
    My legs gave way beneath me,*
        and I shook in terror.
    I will wait quietly for the coming day
        when disaster will strike the people
        who invade us.
17 Even though the fig trees have
        no blossoms,
    and there are no grapes on the
        vines;
    even though the olive crop fails,
        and the fields lie empty and barren;
    even though the flocks die in the
        fields,
        and the cattle barns are empty,
18 yet I will rejoice in the LORD!
    I will be joyful in the God
        of my salvation!
19 The Sovereign LORD is my strength!
    He makes me as surefooted as
        a deer,*
        able to tread upon the heights.

(For the choir director: This prayer is to be accompanied by stringed instruments.)

1:5 Greek version reads *Look you mockers; / look and be amazed and die.* Compare Acts 13:41.   **1:6** Or *Chaldeans.*   **1:8** Or *leopards.*   **2:1** As in Syriac version; Hebrew reads *I.*   **2:3b-4** Greek version reads *If the vision is delayed, wait patiently, / for it will surely come and not delay. / "I will take no pleasure in anyone who turns away. / But the righteous person will live by my faith.* Compare Rom 1:17; Gal 3:11; Heb 10:37-38.   **2:5a** As in Dead Sea Scroll 1QpHab; other Hebrew manuscripts read *Wine.*   **2:5b** Hebrew *as Sheol.*   **3:1** Hebrew adds *according to shigionoth,* probably indicating the musical setting for the prayer.   **3:3a** Hebrew *Teman.*   **3:3b** Hebrew adds *selah;* also in 3:9, 13. The meaning of this Hebrew term is uncertain; it is probably a musical or literary term.   **3:16** Hebrew *Decay entered my bones.*   **3:19** Or *He gives me the speed of a deer.*

REVELATION 9:1-21
In today's reading, the final trumpets are blown, yet people still refuse to turn to God. In their pain and agony, they long to die—but they don't long for God.

Then the fifth angel blew his trumpet, and I [John] saw a star that had fallen to earth from the sky, and he was given the key to the shaft of the bottomless pit.* ²When he opened it, smoke poured out as though from a huge furnace, and the sunlight and air turned dark from the smoke.

³Then locusts came from the smoke and descended on the earth, and they were given power to sting like scorpions. ⁴They were told not to harm the grass or plants or trees, but only the people who did not have the seal of God on their foreheads. ⁵They were told not to kill them but to torture them for five months with pain like the pain of a scorpion sting. ⁶In those days people will seek death but will not find it. They will long to die, but death will flee from them!

⁷The locusts looked like horses prepared for battle. They had what looked like gold crowns on their heads, and their faces looked like human faces. ⁸They had hair like women's hair and teeth like the teeth of a lion. ⁹They wore armor made of iron, and their wings roared like an army of chariots rushing into battle. ¹⁰They had tails that stung like scorpions, and for five months they had the power to torment people. ¹¹Their king is the angel from the bottomless pit; his name in Hebrew is *Abaddon,* and in Greek, *Apollyon*—the Destroyer.

¹²The first terror is past, but look, two more terrors are coming!

¹³Then the sixth angel blew his trumpet, and I heard a voice speaking from the four horns of the gold altar that stands in the presence of God. ¹⁴And the voice said to the sixth angel who held the trumpet, "Release the four angels who are bound at the great Euphrates River." ¹⁵Then the four angels who had been prepared for this hour and day and month and year were turned loose to kill one-third of all the people on earth. ¹⁶I heard the size of their army, which was 200 million mounted troops.

¹⁷And in my vision, I saw the horses and the riders sitting on them. The riders wore armor that was fiery red and dark blue and yellow. The horses had heads like lions, and fire and smoke and burning sulfur billowed from their mouths. ¹⁸One-third of all the people on earth were killed by these three plagues—by the fire and smoke and burning sulfur that came from the mouths of the horses. ¹⁹Their power was in their mouths and in

WHO GOD IS God is in control

HABAKKUK 3:3-17 Habakkuk's questions were valid; he was saddened by the violence and injustice that was prevalent in his time. You might feel the same as this prophet, wondering why the world is plagued with wars and famine, why governments are riddled with corruption, and why violence against the weakest members of society continues unobstructed. You may wonder why God doesn't put an end to the madness and immediately hold accountable all who deserve judgment. • Take heart: God is in control. Evil will not triumph forever. God will punish evil and vindicate those who are faithful to him and have accepted Christ as their Savior. Be thankful that he has delayed his return, allowing you to have the opportunity to come to know Christ. In the meantime, don't be afraid to ask God your questions, yet be willing to continue to trust him. When nothing makes sense and the troubles of this world seem unbearable, say, along with Habakkuk, that no matter what happens, "yet I will rejoice in the LORD! I will be joyful in the God of my salvation!" (Habakkuk 3:18). You can trust that God will do what is best in his way, in his time.

their tails. For their tails had heads like snakes, with the power to injure people. [20]But the people who did not die in these plagues still refused to repent of their evil deeds and turn to God. They continued to worship demons and idols made of gold, silver, bronze, stone, and wood—idols that can neither see nor hear nor walk! [21]And they did not repent of their murders or their witchcraft or their sexual immorality or their thefts.

9:1 Or *the abyss,* or *the underworld;* also in 9:11.

PSALM 137:1-9

Beside the rivers of Babylon, we sat and wept
as we thought of Jerusalem.*
[2] We put away our harps,
hanging them on the branches
of poplar trees.
[3] For our captors demanded a song
from us.
Our tormentors insisted on a joyful
hymn:
"Sing us one of those songs
of Jerusalem!"
[4] But how can we sing the songs
of the LORD
while in a pagan land?

[5] If I forget you, O Jerusalem,
let my right hand forget how to play
the harp.
[6] May my tongue stick to the roof
of my mouth
if I fail to remember you,
if I don't make Jerusalem
my greatest joy.

[7] O LORD, remember what the Edomites
did
on the day the armies of Babylon
captured Jerusalem.
"Destroy it!" they yelled.
"Level it to the ground!"
[8] O Babylon, you will be destroyed.
Happy is the one who pays
you back
for what you have done to us.
[9] Happy is the one who takes your
babies
and smashes them against the
rocks!

137:1 Hebrew *Zion;* also in 137:3.

PROVERBS 30:10

Never slander a worker to the employer, or the person will curse you, and you will pay for it.

DECEMBER**19**

ZEPHANIAH 1:1–3:20

Like other prophets, Zephaniah spoke of the "day of the LORD," a day when God will judge all nations. Zephaniah wrote to remind his people of what they already knew but often refused to live out: disobeying God has grim consequences.

The LORD gave this message to Zephaniah when Josiah son of Amon was king of Judah. Zephaniah was the son of Cushi, son of Gedaliah, son of Amariah, son of Hezekiah.

[2] "I will sweep away everything
from the face of the earth,"
says the LORD.
[3] "I will sweep away people and animals
alike.

I will sweep away the birds
of the sky and the fish in
the sea.
I will reduce the wicked to heaps
of rubble,*
and I will wipe humanity from
the face of the earth," says the
LORD.
[4] "I will crush Judah and Jerusalem with
my fist
and destroy every last trace of their
Baal worship.
I will put an end to all the idolatrous
priests,
so that even the memory of them
will disappear.

5 For they go up to their roofs
    and bow down to the sun, moon,
      and stars.
  They claim to follow the LORD,
    but then they worship Molech,* too.
6 And I will destroy those who used
    to worship me
  but now no longer do.
  They no longer ask for the LORD's
    guidance
  or seek my blessings."

7 Stand in silence in the presence of the
    Sovereign LORD,
  for the awesome day of the LORD's
    judgment is near.
  The LORD has prepared his people for
    a great slaughter
  and has chosen their executioners.*
8 "On that day of judgment,"
    says the LORD,
  "I will punish the leaders and princes
    of Judah
  and all those following pagan
    customs.
9 Yes, I will punish those who participate
    in pagan worship ceremonies,
  and those who fill their masters'
    houses with violence and deceit.

10 "On that day," says the LORD,
    "a cry of alarm will come from the
      Fish Gate
  and echo throughout the New Quarter
    of the city.*
    And a great crash will sound from
      the hills.
11 Wail in sorrow, all you who live in the
    market area,
  for all the merchants and traders
    will be destroyed.

12 "I will search with lanterns in
    Jerusalem's darkest corners
  to punish those who sit complacent
    in their sins.
  They think the LORD will do nothing
    to them,
  either good or bad.
13 So their property will be plundered,
    their homes will be ransacked.
  They will build new homes
    but never live in them.
  They will plant vineyards
    but never drink wine from them.

14 "That terrible day of the LORD is near.
  Swiftly it comes—
  a day of bitter tears,
    a day when even strong men will
      cry out.
15 It will be a day when the LORD's anger
    is poured out—
  a day of terrible distress and
    anguish,
  a day of ruin and desolation,
    a day of darkness and gloom,
  a day of clouds and blackness,
16   a day of trumpet calls and battle
      cries.
  Down go the walled cities
    and the strongest battlements!

17 "Because you have sinned against
    the LORD,
  I will make you grope around like
    the blind.
  Your blood will be poured into
    the dust,
    and your bodies will lie rotting
      on the ground."

18 Your silver and gold will not save you
    on that day of the LORD's anger.
  For the whole land will be devoured
    by the fire of his jealousy.
  He will make a terrifying end
    of all the people on earth.*

2:1 GATHER together—yes, gather
    together,
  you shameless nation.
2 Gather before judgment begins,
    before your time to repent is blown
      away like chaff.
  Act now, before the fierce fury of the
    LORD falls
  and the terrible day of the LORD's
    anger begins.
3 Seek the LORD, all who are humble,
    and follow his commands.
  Seek to do what is right
    and to live humbly.
  Perhaps even yet the LORD will protect
    you—
  protect you from his anger on that
    day of destruction.

4 Gaza and Ashkelon will be abandoned,
    Ashdod and Ekron torn down.
5 And what sorrow awaits you
    Philistines*

who live along the coast and in the
    land of Canaan,
  for this judgment is against you,
    too!
The LORD will destroy you
  until not one of you is left.
6 The Philistine coast will become
    a wilderness pasture,
  a place of shepherd camps
    and enclosures for sheep and goats.
7 The remnant of the tribe of Judah will
    pasture there.
  They will rest at night in the
    abandoned houses in Ashkelon.
  For the LORD their God will visit his
    people in kindness
    and restore their prosperity again.

8 "I have heard the taunts of the
    Moabites
  and the insults of the Ammonites,
  mocking my people
    and invading their borders.
9 Now, as surely as I live,"
    says the LORD of Heaven's Armies,
    the God of Israel,
  "Moab and Ammon will be
    destroyed—
  destroyed as completely as Sodom
    and Gomorrah.
  Their land will become a place
    of stinging nettles,
  salt pits, and eternal desolation.
  The remnant of my people will
    plunder them
    and take their land."

10 They will receive the wages of their
    pride,
  for they have scoffed at the people
    of the LORD of Heaven's Armies.
11 The LORD will terrify them
  as he destroys all the gods in the
    land.
  Then nations around the world will
    worship the LORD,
    each in their own land.

12 "You Ethiopians* will also
    be slaughtered
  by my sword," says the LORD.

13 And the LORD will strike the lands
    of the north with his fist,
    destroying the land of Assyria.

He will make its great capital, Nineveh,
    a desolate wasteland,
    parched like a desert.
14 The proud city will become a pasture
    for flocks and herds,
  and all sorts of wild animals will
    settle there.
  The desert owl and screech owl will
    roost on its ruined columns,
  their calls echoing through the
    gaping windows.
  Rubble will block all the doorways,
  and the cedar paneling will be
    exposed to the weather.
15 This is the boisterous city,
    once so secure.
  "I am the greatest!" it boasted.
    "No other city can compare with me!"
  But now, look how it has become an
    utter ruin,
    a haven for wild animals.
  Everyone passing by will laugh
    in derision
    and shake a defiant fist.

3:1 WHAT sorrow awaits rebellious,
    polluted Jerusalem,
    the city of violence and crime!
2 No one can tell it anything;
    it refuses all correction.
  It does not trust in the LORD
    or draw near to its God.
3 Its leaders are like roaring lions
    hunting for their victims.
  Its judges are like ravenous wolves
    at evening time,
  who by dawn have left no trace
    of their prey.
4 Its prophets are arrogant liars seeking
    their own gain.
  Its priests defile the Temple by
    disobeying God's instructions.
5 But the LORD is still there in the city,
    and he does no wrong.
  Day by day he hands down justice,
    and he does not fail.
  But the wicked know no shame.

6 "I have wiped out many nations,
    devastating their fortress walls and
    towers.
  Their streets are now deserted;
    their cities lie in silent ruin.
  There are no survivors—
    none at all.

7 I thought, 'Surely they will have
    reverence for me now!
Surely they will listen to my
    warnings.
Then I won't need to strike again,
    destroying their homes.'
But no, they get up early
    to continue their evil deeds.
8 Therefore, be patient," says the LORD.
    "Soon I will stand and accuse these
    evil nations.
For I have decided to gather the
    kingdoms of the earth
    and pour out my fiercest anger and
    fury on them.
All the earth will be devoured
    by the fire of my jealousy.

9 "Then I will purify the speech of all
    people,
so that everyone can worship the
    LORD together.
10 My scattered people who live beyond
    the rivers of Ethiopia*
will come to present their offerings.
11 On that day you will no longer need
    to be ashamed,
for you will no longer be rebels
    against me.
I will remove all proud and arrogant
    people from among you.
There will be no more haughtiness
    on my holy mountain.

12 Those who are left will be the lowly
    and humble,
for it is they who trust in the name
    of the LORD.
13 The remnant of Israel will do no
    wrong;
they will never tell lies or deceive
    one another.
They will eat and sleep in safety,
    and no one will make them afraid."

14 Sing, O daughter of Zion;
    shout aloud, O Israel!
Be glad and rejoice with all your heart,
    O daughter of Jerusalem!
15 For the LORD will remove his hand
    of judgment
    and will disperse the armies of your
    enemy.
And the LORD himself, the King of
    Israel,
    will live among you!
At last your troubles will be over,
    and you will never again fear
    disaster.
16 On that day the announcement
    to Jerusalem will be,
"Cheer up, Zion! Don't be afraid!
17 For the LORD your God is living among
    you.
He is a mighty savior.
He will take delight in you with
    gladness.

WHO GOD IS

The final judge

ZEPHANIAH 1:14 While we often talk about God's love and take comfort in his promises of blessing and faithfulness, we must never forget the equally true part of his character—that he is a Judge and, in the end, will judge and punish all who have rejected him. It's not a picture most of us like to paint, but that doesn't make it any less true. • God is perfectly loving and perfectly just. In fact it was that perfect justice that put Jesus on the cross. Because he is holy, God couldn't decide that he just wouldn't punish sin or that he would go ahead and save a few people anyway. No, the penalty had to be paid in order for sin and Satan to be defeated. And Jesus paid the price so that we wouldn't have to. God is perfect love. He is also perfect justice. • A day will come when God will judge all people. He will defeat all evil and injustice once and for all. The unrepentant will perish. As a believer, you don't need to fear that day. You can love God, the Judge, because he has already declared you "Not guilty." Your future is safe in his hands.

With his love, he will calm all your
fears.*
He will rejoice over you with joyful
songs."

18 "I will gather you who mourn for the
appointed festivals;
you will be disgraced no more.*
19 And I will deal severely with all who
have oppressed you.
I will save the weak and helpless
ones;
I will bring together
those who were chased away.
I will give glory and fame to my former
exiles,
wherever they have been mocked
and shamed.
20 On that day I will gather you together
and bring you home again.
I will give you a good name, a name
of distinction,
among all the nations of the earth,
as I restore your fortunes before their
very eyes.
I, the LORD, have spoken!"

1:3 The meaning of the Hebrew is uncertain.   1:5 Hebrew
Malcam, a variant spelling of Molech; or it could possibly
mean *their king*.   1:7 Hebrew *has prepared a sacrifice and
sanctified his guests*.   1:10 Or *the Second Quarter*, a newer
section of Jerusalem. Hebrew reads *the Mishneh*.   1:18 Or
the people living in the land.   2:5 Hebrew *Kerethites*.
2:12 Hebrew *Cushites*.   3:10 Hebrew *Cush*.   3:17 Or *He
will be silent in his love*. Greek and Syriac versions read *He
will renew you with his love*.   3:18 The meaning of the
Hebrew for this verse is uncertain.

REVELATION 10:1-11

Today's reading begins a break before the last
trumpet sounds, just as Revelation 7 functioned as
a break before the last seal was broken. It paints a
picture of John's call to speak the truth—though the
truth was not all pleasant.

Then I [John] saw another mighty angel
coming down from heaven, surrounded by
a cloud, with a rainbow over his head. His
face shone like the sun, and his feet were
like pillars of fire. 2And in his hand was a
small scroll* that had been opened. He
stood with his right foot on the sea and his
left foot on the land. 3And he gave a great
shout like the roar of a lion. And when he
shouted, the seven thunders answered.

4When the seven thunders spoke, I was
about to write. But I heard a voice from
heaven saying, "Keep secret* what the
seven thunders said, and do not write it
down."

5Then the angel I saw standing on the
sea and on the land raised his right hand
toward heaven. 6He swore an oath in the
name of the one who lives forever and
ever, who created the heavens and everything in them, the earth and everything in
it, and the sea and everything in it. He
said, "There will be no more delay. 7When
the seventh angel blows his trumpet,
God's mysterious plan will be fulfilled. It
will happen just as he announced it to his
servants the prophets."

8Then the voice from heaven spoke to
me again: "Go and take the open scroll
from the hand of the angel who is standing on the sea and on the land."

9So I went to the angel and told him to
give me the small scroll. "Yes, take it and
eat it," he said. "It will be sweet as honey
in your mouth, but it will turn sour in your
stomach!" 10So I took the small scroll
from the hand of the angel, and I ate it! It
was sweet in my mouth, but when I swallowed it, it turned sour in my stomach.

11Then I was told, "You must prophesy
again about many peoples, nations, languages, and kings."

10:2 Or *book;* also in 10:8, 9, 10.   10:4 Greek *Seal up.*

PSALM 138:1-8
A psalm of David.

1 I give you thanks, O LORD, with all
my heart;
I will sing your praises before the
gods.
2 I bow before your holy Temple as
I worship.
I praise your name for your
unfailing love and faithfulness;
for your promises are backed
by all the honor of your name.
3 As soon as I pray, you answer me;
you encourage me by giving me
strength.

4 Every king in all the earth will thank
you, LORD,
for all of them will hear your words.
5 Yes, they will sing about the LORD's
ways,
for the glory of the LORD is very
great.

⁶ Though the Lᴏʀᴅ is great, he cares
    for the humble,
  but he keeps his distance from
    the proud.
⁷ Though I am surrounded by
    troubles,
  you will protect me from the anger
    of my enemies.
  You reach out your hand,
    and the power of your right hand
      saves me.
⁸ The Lᴏʀᴅ will work out his plans for
    my life—

for your faithful love, O Lᴏʀᴅ,
    endures forever.
  Don't abandon me, for you made me.

PROVERBS 30:11-14

Some people curse their father and do
not thank their mother. They are pure in
their own eyes, but they are filthy and unwashed. They look proudly around, casting disdainful glances. They have teeth
like swords and fangs like knives. They
devour the poor from the earth and the
needy from among humanity.

DECEMBER**20**

HAGGAI 1:1–2:23

Haggai's main message was this: Consider your
ways. Haggai lived among the Jewish people after
they had returned from a long exile to what was left
of Jerusalem. They had begun to rebuild but already
their priorities were getting misaligned.

On August 29* of the second year of King
Darius's reign, the Lᴏʀᴅ gave a message
through the prophet Haggai to Zerubbabel son of Shealtiel, governor of Judah,
and to Jeshua* son of Jehozadak, the high
priest.

²"This is what the Lᴏʀᴅ of Heaven's Armies says: The people are saying, 'The
time has not yet come to rebuild the
house of the Lᴏʀᴅ.'"

³Then the Lᴏʀᴅ sent this message
through the prophet Haggai: ⁴"Why are
you living in luxurious houses while my
house lies in ruins? ⁵This is what the
Lᴏʀᴅ of Heaven's Armies says: Look at
what's happening to you! ⁶You have
planted much but harvest little. You eat
but are not satisfied. You drink but are
still thirsty. You put on clothes but cannot
keep warm. Your wages disappear as
though you were putting them in pockets
filled with holes!

⁷"This is what the Lᴏʀᴅ of Heaven's Armies says: Look at what's happening to
you! ⁸Now go up into the hills, bring down
timber, and rebuild my house. Then I will

take pleasure in it and be honored, says
the Lᴏʀᴅ. ⁹You hoped for rich harvests,
but they were poor. And when you
brought your harvest home, I blew it away.
Why? Because my house lies in ruins, says
the Lᴏʀᴅ of Heaven's Armies, while all of
you are busy building your own fine
houses. ¹⁰It's because of you that the
heavens withhold the dew and the earth
produces no crops. ¹¹I have called for a
drought on your fields and hills—a
drought to wither the grain and grapes
and olive trees and all your other crops, a
drought to starve you and your livestock
and to ruin everything you have worked
so hard to get."

¹²Then Zerubbabel son of Shealtiel,
and Jeshua son of Jehozadak, the high
priest, and the whole remnant of God's
people began to obey the message
from the Lᴏʀᴅ their God. When they
heard the words of the prophet Haggai,
whom the Lᴏʀᴅ their God had sent, the
people feared the Lᴏʀᴅ. ¹³Then Haggai,
the Lᴏʀᴅ's messenger, gave the people
this message from the Lᴏʀᴅ: "I am with
you, says the Lᴏʀᴅ!"

¹⁴So the Lᴏʀᴅ sparked the enthusiasm
of Zerubbabel son of Shealtiel, governor
of Judah, and the enthusiasm of Jeshua
son of Jehozadak, the high priest, and the
enthusiasm of the whole remnant of

God's people. They began to work on the house of their God, the LORD of Heaven's Armies, ¹⁵on September 21* of the second year of King Darius's reign.

2:1THEN on October 17 of that same year,* the LORD sent another message through the prophet Haggai. ²"Say this to Zerubbabel son of Shealtiel, governor of Judah, and to Jeshua* son of Jehozadak, the high priest, and to the remnant of God's people there in the land: ³'Does anyone remember—this Temple—in its former splendor? How, in comparison, does it look to you now? It must seem like nothing at all! ⁴But now the LORD says: Be strong, Zerubbabel. Be strong, Jeshua son of Jehozadak, the high priest. Be strong, all you people still left in the land. And now get to work, for I am with you, says the LORD of Heaven's Armies. ⁵My Spirit remains among you, just as I promised when you came out of Egypt. So do not be afraid.'

⁶"For this is what the LORD of Heaven's Armies says: In just a little while I will again shake the heavens and the earth, the oceans and the dry land. ⁷I will shake all the nations, and the treasures of all the nations will be brought to this Temple. I will fill this place with glory, says the LORD of Heaven's Armies. ⁸The silver is mine, and the gold is mine, says the LORD of Heaven's Armies. ⁹The future glory of this Temple will be greater than its past glory, says the LORD of Heaven's Armies. And in this place I will bring peace. I, the LORD of Heaven's Armies, have spoken!"

¹⁰On December 18* of the second year of King Darius's reign, the LORD sent this message to the prophet Haggai: ¹¹"This is what the LORD of Heaven's Armies says. Ask the priests this question about the law: ¹²'If one of you is carrying some meat from a holy sacrifice in his robes and his robe happens to brush against some bread or stew, wine or olive oil, or any other kind of food, will it also become holy?'"

The priests replied, "No."

¹³Then Haggai asked, "If someone becomes ceremonially unclean by touching a dead person and then touches any of these foods, will the food be defiled?"

And the priests answered, "Yes."

¹⁴Then Haggai responded, "That is how it is with this people and this nation, says the LORD. Everything they do and everything they offer is defiled by their sin. ¹⁵Look at what was happening to you before you began to lay the foundation of the LORD's Temple. ¹⁶When you hoped for a twenty-bushel crop, you harvested only ten. When you expected to draw fifty gallons from the winepress, you found only twenty. ¹⁷I sent blight and mildew and hail to destroy everything you worked so hard to produce. Even so, you refused to return to me, says the LORD.

¹⁸"Think about this eighteenth day of December, the day* when the foundation of the LORD's Temple was laid. Think carefully. ¹⁹I am giving you a promise now while the seed is still in the barn.* You have not yet harvested your grain, and your grapevines, fig trees, pomegranates, and olive trees have not yet produced their crops. But from this day onward I will bless you."

²⁰On that same day, December 18,* the LORD sent this second message to Haggai: ²¹"Tell Zerubbabel, the governor of Judah, that I am about to shake the heavens and the earth. ²²I will overthrow royal thrones and destroy the power of foreign kingdoms. I will overturn their chariots and riders. The horses will fall, and their riders will kill each other.

²³"But when this happens, says the LORD of Heaven's Armies, I will honor you, Zerubbabel son of Shealtiel, my servant. I will make you like a signet ring on my finger, says the LORD, for I have chosen you. I, the LORD of Heaven's Armies, have spoken!"

1:1a Hebrew *On the first day of the sixth month,* of the ancient Hebrew lunar calendar. A number of dates in Haggai can be cross-checked with dates in surviving Persian records and related accurately to our modern calendar. This event occurred on August 29, 520 B.C.   1:1b Hebrew *Joshua,* a variant spelling of Jeshua; also in 1:12, 14.   1:15 Hebrew *on the twenty-fourth day of the sixth month,* of the ancient Hebrew lunar calendar. This event occurred on September 21, 520 B.C.; also see note on 1:1a.   2:1 Hebrew *on the twenty-first day of the seventh month,* of the ancient Hebrew lunar calendar. This event (in the second year of Darius's reign) occurred on October 17, 520 B.C.; also see note on 1:1a.   2:2 Hebrew *Joshua,* a variant spelling of Jeshua; also in 2:4.   2:10 Hebrew *On the twenty-fourth day of the ninth month,* of the ancient Hebrew lunar calendar (similarly in 2:18). This event occurred on December 18, 520 B.C.; also see note on 1:1a.   2:18 Or *On this eighteenth day of December, think about the day.*   2:19 Hebrew *Is the seed yet in the barn?*   2:20 Hebrew *On the twenty-fourth day of the (ninth) month;* see note on 2:10.

REVELATION 11:1-19

This chapter includes many images that are interpreted a variety of ways. It's easy to get bogged down in Revelation, trying to figure out each vision as you go. Keep the big picture in mind. God is bringing his people through turmoil and into triumph.

Then I [John] was given a measuring stick, and I was told, "Go and measure the Temple of God and the altar, and count the number of worshipers. ²But do not measure the outer courtyard, for it has been turned over to the nations. They will trample the holy city for 42 months. ³And I will give power to my two witnesses, and they will be clothed in burlap and will prophesy during those 1,260 days."

⁴These two prophets are the two olive trees and the two lampstands that stand before the Lord of all the earth. ⁵If anyone tries to harm them, fire flashes from their mouths and consumes their enemies. This is how anyone who tries to harm them must die. ⁶They have power to shut the sky so that no rain will fall for as long as they prophesy. And they have the power to turn the rivers and oceans into blood, and to strike the earth with every kind of plague as often as they wish.

⁷When they complete their testimony, the beast that comes up out of the bottomless pit* will declare war against them, and he will conquer them and kill them. ⁸And their bodies will lie in the main street of Jerusalem,* the city that is figuratively called "Sodom" and "Egypt," the city where their Lord was crucified. ⁹And for three and a half days, all peoples, tribes, languages, and nations will stare at their bodies. No one will be allowed to bury them. ¹⁰All the people who belong to this world will gloat over them and give presents to each other to celebrate the death of the two prophets who had tormented them.

¹¹But after three and a half days, God breathed life into them, and they stood up! Terror struck all who were staring at them. ¹²Then a loud voice from heaven called to the two prophets, "Come up here!" And they rose to heaven in a cloud as their enemies watched.

¹³At the same time there was a terrible earthquake that destroyed a tenth of the city. Seven thousand people died in that earthquake, and everyone else was terrified and gave glory to the God of heaven.

¹⁴The second terror is past, but look, the third terror is coming quickly.

¹⁵Then the seventh angel blew his trumpet, and there were loud voices shouting in heaven:

"The world has now become the
    Kingdom of our Lord and of his
    Christ,*
and he will reign forever and ever."

HOW WE LIVE

Knowing God's peace

PSALM 139:1 There is an old saying about people having "skeletons" in their closets—things they want to keep hidden. There are probably things about your own past that you would prefer to keep hidden as well. But as David says in this psalm, God knows everything about you. He knows about all those "skeletons" and loves you anyway! • When you became a believer, God didn't take away your past or the memories of things you did or things that were done to you. You might wish he would do that. However, God wants to redeem every part of your life—even the difficult parts—for his glory. So those skeletons remain a part of your life and who you are. Perhaps a painful past will be used to open the door to help others facing the same pain and bring them to the Savior. Perhaps the lessons you've learned will be just what someone else needs to hear. So don't spend an ounce of time regretting the past. The past has been forgiven. God will use every experience to shape you and use you in the bright future he has for you! You can count on it.

16The twenty-four elders sitting on their thrones before God fell with their faces to the ground and worshiped him. 17And they said,

"We give thanks to you, Lord God,
    the Almighty,
    the one who is and who always
        was,
for now you have assumed your great
        power
    and have begun to reign.
18 The nations were filled with wrath,
    but now the time of your wrath
        has come.
It is time to judge the dead
    and reward your servants
        the prophets,
    as well as your holy people,
    and all who fear your name,
        from the least to the greatest.
It is time to destroy
    all who have caused destruction
        on the earth."

19Then, in heaven, the Temple of God was opened and the Ark of his covenant could be seen inside the Temple. Lightning flashed, thunder crashed and roared, and there was an earthquake and a terrible hailstorm.

11:7 Or *the abyss,* or *the underworld.* 11:8 Greek *the great city.* 11:15 Or *his Messiah.*

PSALM 139:1-24
For the choir director: A psalm of David.

1 **O** LORD, you have examined my heart
    and know everything about me.
2 You know when I sit down or stand up.
    You know my thoughts even when
        I'm far away.
3 You see me when I travel
    and when I rest at home.
    You know everything I do.
4 You know what I am going to say
    even before I say it, LORD.
5 You go before me and follow me.
    You place your hand of blessing
        on my head.
6 Such knowledge is too wonderful
        for me,
    too great for me to understand!

7 I can never escape from your
        Spirit!
    I can never get away from your
        presence!
8 If I go up to heaven, you are there;
    if I go down to the grave,* you are
        there.
9 If I ride the wings of the morning,
    if I dwell by the farthest oceans,
10 even there your hand will guide me,
    and your strength will support me.
11 I could ask the darkness to hide me
    and the light around me to become
        night—
12 but even in darkness I cannot hide
        from you.
    To you the night shines as bright as day.
    Darkness and light are the same
        to you.

13 You made all the delicate, inner parts
        of my body
    and knit me together in my
        mother's womb.
14 Thank you for making me so
        wonderfully complex!
    Your workmanship is marvelous—
        how well I know it.
15 You watched me as I was being
        formed in utter seclusion,
    as I was woven together in the dark
        of the womb.
16 You saw me before I was born.
    Every day of my life was recorded
        in your book.
Every moment was laid out
    before a single day had passed.

17 How precious are your thoughts about
        me,* O God.
    They cannot be numbered!
18 I can't even count them;
    they outnumber the grains of sand!
And when I wake up,
    you are still with me!

19 O God, if only you would destroy
        the wicked!
    Get out of my life, you murderers!
20 They blaspheme you;
    your enemies misuse your name.
21 O LORD, shouldn't I hate those who
        hate you?
    Shouldn't I despise those who
        oppose you?
22 Yes, I hate them with total hatred,
    for your enemies are my enemies.

23 Search me, O God, and know my heart;
　　test me and know my anxious
　　　thoughts.
24 Point out anything in me that offends
　　you,
　　and lead me along the path of
　　　everlasting life.

139:8 Hebrew *to Sheol.*　**139:17** Or *How precious to me are your thoughts.*

PROVERBS 30:15-16

The leech has two suckers that cry out, "More, more!"* □ There are three things that are never satisfied—no, four that never say, "Enough!": the grave,* the barren womb, the thirsty desert, the blazing fire.

30:15 Hebrew *two daughters who cry out, "Give, give!"*
30:16 Hebrew *Sheol.*

DECEMBER**21**

ZECHARIAH 1:1-21

Like Haggai, Zechariah ministered after the Jews returned from exile in Babylon and had a part in motivating them to rebuild the Temple.

In November* of the second year of King Darius's reign, the LORD gave this message to the prophet Zechariah son of Berekiah and grandson of Iddo:

2"I, the LORD, was very angry with your ancestors. 3 Therefore, say to the people, 'This is what the LORD of Heaven's Armies says: Return to me, and I will return to you, says the LORD of Heaven's Armies.' 4 Don't be like your ancestors who would not listen or pay attention when the earlier prophets said to them, 'This is what the LORD of Heaven's Armies says: Turn from your evil ways, and stop all your evil practices.'

5"Where are your ancestors now? They and the prophets are long dead. 6 But everything I said through my servants the prophets happened to your ancestors, just as I said. As a result, they repented and said, 'We have received what we deserved from the LORD of Heaven's Armies. He has done what he said he would do.'"

7 Three months later, on February 15,* the LORD sent another message to the prophet Zechariah son of Berekiah and grandson of Iddo.

8 In a vision during the night, I saw a man sitting on a red horse that was standing among some myrtle trees in a small valley. Behind him were riders on red, brown, and white horses. 9 I asked the angel who was talking with me, "My lord, what do these horses mean?"

"I will show you," the angel replied.

10 The rider standing among the myrtle trees then explained, "They are the ones the LORD has sent out to patrol the earth."

11 Then the other riders reported to the angel of the LORD, who was standing among the myrtle trees, "We have been patrolling the earth, and the whole earth is at peace."

12 Upon hearing this, the angel of the LORD prayed this prayer: "O LORD of Heaven's Armies, for seventy years now you have been angry with Jerusalem and the towns of Judah. How long until you again show mercy to them?" 13 And the LORD spoke kind and comforting words to the angel who talked with me.

14 Then the angel said to me, "Shout this message for all to hear: 'This is what the LORD of Heaven's Armies says: My love for Jerusalem and Mount Zion is passionate and strong. 15 But I am very angry with the other nations that are now enjoying peace and security. I was only a little angry with my people, but the nations inflicted harm on them far beyond my intentions.

16 " 'Therefore, this is what the LORD says: I have returned to show mercy to Jerusalem. My Temple will be rebuilt, says the LORD of Heaven's Armies, and measurements will be taken for the reconstruction of Jerusalem.*'

17 "Say this also: 'This is what the LORD of Heaven's Armies says: The towns of

Israel will again overflow with prosperity, and the LORD will again comfort Zion and choose Jerusalem as his own.'"

¹⁸*Then I looked up and saw four animal horns. ¹⁹"What are these?" I asked the angel who was talking with me.

He replied, "These horns represent the nations that scattered Judah, Israel, and Jerusalem."

²⁰Then the LORD showed me four blacksmiths. ²¹"What are these men coming to do?" I asked.

The angel replied, "These four horns—these nations—scattered and humbled Judah. Now these blacksmiths have come to terrify those nations and throw them down and destroy them."

1:1 Hebrew *In the eighth month.* A number of dates in Zechariah can be cross-checked with dates in surviving Persian records and related accurately to our modern calendar. This month of the ancient Hebrew lunar calendar occurred within the months of October and November 520 B.C.   1:7 Hebrew *On the twenty-fourth day of the eleventh month, the month of Shebat, in the second year of Darius.* This event occurred on February 15, 519 B.C.; also see note on 1:1.   1:16 Hebrew *and the measuring line will be stretched out over Jerusalem.*   1:18 Verses 1:18-21 are numbered 2:1-4 in Hebrew text.

REVELATION 12:1-17

Three characters appear in this part of John's vision: a woman, a child, and a dragon. Many believe the woman's suffering represents the suffering of God's people; the child from the woman represents Jesus, born of the Jews; the dragon represents Satan.

Then I [John] witnessed in heaven an event of great significance. I saw a woman clothed with the sun, with the moon beneath her feet, and a crown of twelve stars on her head. ²She was pregnant, and she cried out because of her labor pains and the agony of giving birth.

³Then I witnessed in heaven another significant event. I saw a large red dragon with seven heads and ten horns, with seven crowns on his heads. ⁴His tail swept away one-third of the stars in the sky, and he threw them to the earth. He stood in front of the woman as she was about to give birth, ready to devour her baby as soon as it was born.

⁵She gave birth to a son who was to rule all nations with an iron rod. And her child was snatched away from the dragon and was caught up to God and to his throne.

⁶And the woman fled into the wilderness, where God had prepared a place to care for her for 1,260 days.

⁷Then there was war in heaven. Michael and his angels fought against the dragon and his angels. ⁸And the dragon lost the battle, and he and his angels were forced out of heaven. ⁹This great dragon—the ancient serpent called the devil, or Satan, the one deceiving the whole world—was thrown down to the earth with all his angels.

¹⁰Then I heard a loud voice shouting across the heavens,

"It has come at last—
    salvation and power
and the Kingdom of our God,
    and the authority of his Christ.*
For the accuser of our brothers and
    sisters*
has been thrown down to earth—
the one who accuses them
    before our God day and night.
¹¹ And they have defeated him by the
        blood of the Lamb
    and by their testimony.
And they did not love their lives
        so much
    that they were afraid to die.
¹² Therefore, rejoice, O heavens!
    And you who live in the heavens,
        rejoice!
But terror will come on the earth
        and the sea,
    for the devil has come down to
        you in great anger,
    knowing that he has little time."

¹³When the dragon realized that he had been thrown down to the earth, he pursued the woman who had given birth to the male child. ¹⁴But she was given two wings like those of a great eagle so she could fly to the place prepared for her in the wilderness. There she would be cared for and protected from the dragon* for a time, times, and half a time.

¹⁵Then the dragon tried to drown the woman with a flood of water that flowed from his mouth. ¹⁶But the earth helped her by opening its mouth and swallowing the river that gushed out from the mouth of the dragon. ¹⁷And the dragon was angry at the woman and declared war

against the rest of her children—all who keep God's commandments and maintain their testimony for Jesus.

12:10a Or *his Messiah.*   12:10b Greek *brothers.*
12:14 Greek *the serpent;* also in 12:15. See 12:9.

PSALM 140:1-13
For the choir director: A psalm of David.

1 **O** LORD, rescue me from evil people.
  Protect me from those who are violent,
2 those who plot evil in their hearts
  and stir up trouble all day long.
3 Their tongues sting like a snake;
  the venom of a viper drips
    from their lips.   *Interlude*

4 O LORD, keep me out of the hands
  of the wicked.
  Protect me from those who are violent,
  for they are plotting against me.
5 The proud have set a trap to catch me;
  they have stretched out a net;
  they have placed traps all along
    the way.   *Interlude*

6 I said to the LORD, "You are my God!"
  Listen, O LORD, to my cries
    for mercy!
7 O Sovereign LORD, the strong one who
  rescued me,

you protected me on the day
  of battle.
8 LORD, do not let evil people have their way.
  Do not let their evil schemes succeed,
  or they will become proud.
                              Interlude

9 Let my enemies be destroyed
  by the very evil they have planned
    for me.
10 Let burning coals fall down on their heads.
  Let them be thrown into the fire
  or into watery pits from which they
    can't escape.
11 Don't let liars prosper here in our land.
  Cause great disasters to fall on the violent.

12 But I know the LORD will help those
  they persecute;
  he will give justice to the poor.
13 Surely righteous people are praising
  your name;
  the godly will live in your presence.

PROVERBS 30:17
The eye that mocks a father and despises a mother's instructions will be plucked out by ravens of the valley and eaten by vultures.

WHAT THE BIBLE SAYS
The devil

REVELATION 12:10-12 The devil knows the truth; he knows his fate; he knows he can't win. He may be able to blind much of the world to that truth, but he ought not to be able to blind believers. When Jesus confronted a man possessed by many demons, the demons asked if Jesus had come to torture them "before God's appointed time" (Matthew 8:29, January 11), and then begged Jesus to cast them into the pigs and not into the "bottomless pit" (Luke 8:31, March 29). These spirits clearly understood their fate. John's prophecy in Revelation confirms that Satan knows his fate: "The devil has come down to you in great anger, knowing that he has little time" (12:12). • Understanding this about the devil should give us confidence. When we face spiritual opposition, we can know that our opponent understands he's not going to win. This means he has nothing to lose, which explains the anger and desperation of evil. In the end, the love and life of God will win.

DECEMBER 22

Zechariah calls the people out of Babylon and back to their homeland. They don't belong in Babylon, even though they had made a life there. He reminds them that they were meant for something else.

¹*When I [Zechariah] looked again, I saw a man with a measuring line in his hand. ²"Where are you going?" I asked.

He replied, "I am going to measure Jerusalem, to see how wide and how long it is."

³Then the angel who was with me went to meet a second angel who was coming toward him. ⁴The other angel said, "Hurry, and say to that young man, 'Jerusalem will someday be so full of people and livestock that there won't be room enough for everyone! Many will live outside the city walls. ⁵Then I, myself, will be a protective wall of fire around Jerusalem, says the LORD. And I will be the glory inside the city!'"

⁶The LORD says, "Come away! Flee from Babylon in the land of the north, for I have scattered you to the four winds. ⁷Come away, people of Zion, you who are exiled in Babylon!"

⁸After a period of glory, the LORD of Heaven's Armies sent me* against the nations who plundered you. For he said, "Anyone who harms you harms my most precious possession.* ⁹I will raise my fist to crush them, and their own slaves will plunder them." Then you will know that the LORD of Heaven's Armies has sent me.

¹⁰The LORD says, "Shout and rejoice, O beautiful Jerusalem,* for I am coming to live among you. ¹¹Many nations will join themselves to the LORD on that day, and they, too, will be my people. I will live among you, and you will know that the LORD of Heaven's Armies sent me to you. ¹²The land of Judah will be the LORD's special possession in the holy land, and he will once again choose Jerusalem to be his own city. ¹³Be silent before the LORD, all humanity, for he is springing into action from his holy dwelling."

3:1THEN the angel showed me Jeshua* the high priest standing before the angel of the LORD. The Accuser, Satan,* was there at the angel's right hand, making accusations against Jeshua. ²And the LORD said to Satan, "I, the LORD, reject your accusations, Satan. Yes, the LORD, who has chosen Jerusalem, rebukes you. This man is like a burning stick that has been snatched from the fire."

³Jeshua's clothing was filthy as he stood there before the angel. ⁴So the angel said to the others standing there, "Take off his filthy clothes." And turning to Jeshua he said, "See, I have taken away your sins, and now I am giving you these fine new clothes."

⁵Then I said, "They should also place a clean turban on his head." So they put a clean priestly turban on his head and dressed him in new clothes while the angel of the LORD stood by.

⁶Then the angel of the LORD spoke very solemnly to Jeshua and said, ⁷"This is what the LORD of Heaven's Armies says: If you follow my ways and carefully serve me, then you will be given authority over my Temple and its courtyards. I will let you walk among these others standing here.

⁸"Listen to me, O Jeshua the high priest, and all you other priests. You are symbols of things to come. Soon I am going to bring my servant, the Branch. ⁹Now look at the jewel I have set before Jeshua, a single stone with seven facets.* I will engrave an inscription on it, says the LORD of Heaven's Armies, and I will remove the sins of this land in a single day.

¹⁰"And on that day, says the LORD of Heaven's Armies, each of you will invite your neighbor to sit with you peacefully under your own grapevine and fig tree."

2:1 Verses 2:1-13 are numbered 2:5-17 in Hebrew text. **2:8a** The meaning of the Hebrew is uncertain. **2:8b** Hebrew *Anyone who touches you touches the pupil of his eye.* **2:10** Hebrew *O daughter of Zion.* **3:1a** Hebrew *Joshua,* a variant spelling of Jeshua; also in 3:3, 4, 6, 8, 9. **3:1b** Hebrew *The satan;* similarly in 3:2. **3:9** Hebrew *seven eyes.*

REVELATION 12:18–13:18

Although scholars debate the identity of the two "beasts" in this passage, what is clear is that they represent a concentration of Satanic evil in the world. God will triumph over all of Satan's evil schemes.

Then the dragon took his stand* on the shore beside the sea.

13:1**T**HEN I saw a beast rising up out of the sea. It had seven heads and ten horns, with ten crowns on its horns. And written on each head were names that blasphemed God. 2This beast looked like a leopard, but it had the feet of a bear and the mouth of a lion! And the dragon gave the beast his own power and throne and great authority.

3I saw that one of the heads of the beast seemed wounded beyond recovery—but the fatal wound was healed! The whole world marveled at this miracle and gave allegiance to the beast. 4They worshiped the dragon for giving the beast such power, and they also worshiped the beast. "Who is as great as the beast?" they exclaimed. "Who is able to fight against him?"

5Then the beast was allowed to speak great blasphemies against God. And he was given authority to do whatever he wanted for forty-two months. 6And he spoke terrible words of blasphemy against God, slandering his name and his dwelling— that is, those who dwell in heaven.* 7And the beast was allowed to wage war against God's holy people and to conquer them. And he was given authority to rule over every tribe and people and language and nation. 8And all the people who belong to this world worshiped the beast. They are the ones whose names were not written in the Book of Life before the world was made—the Book that belongs to the Lamb who was slaughtered.*

9 Anyone with ears to hear
    should listen and understand.
10 Anyone who is destined for prison
    will be taken to prison.
  Anyone destined to die by the sword
    will die by the sword.

This means that God's holy people must endure persecution patiently and remain faithful.

11Then I saw another beast come up out of the earth. He had two horns like those of a lamb, but he spoke with the voice of a dragon. 12He exercised all the authority of the first beast. And he required all the earth and its people to worship the first beast, whose fatal wound had been healed. 13He did astounding miracles, even making fire flash down to earth from the sky while everyone was watching. 14And with all the miracles he

WHAT THE BIBLE SAYS

Understanding John's vision

REVELATION 13:9 "Anyone with ears to hear should listen and understand," wrote John, but what happens if you don't understand? Don't be alarmed. Revelation is a difficult book and even theologians disagree on how to interpret every point. If we could completely understand it or if its images were clearly identifiable, we might be tempted to think that we can pinpoint when Jesus will return or that we can have an inside scoop on who the players are. Instead, God leaves us with lots of questions, because, in the end, only he knows when and exactly how all of this will occur. • As you read this prophecy, remember the following: (1) We don't know the day or the hour when Jesus will come back. (2) We need to be vigilant as we await Jesus' return, remaining faithful in the face of temptation and persecution. (3) History is winding down to a God-determined ending. Even when it seems like events of history are spiraling out of control, it is important to remember that God is working all things according to his plan. (4) God will one day triumph fully and finally over evil. • Don't let Revelation's difficult imagery distract you from these clear points, which are meant to encourage you.

was allowed to perform on behalf of the first beast, he deceived all the people who belong to this world. He ordered the people to make a great statue of the first beast, who was fatally wounded and then came back to life. [15]He was then permitted to give life to this statue so that it could speak. Then the statue of the beast commanded that anyone refusing to worship it must die.

[16]He required everyone—small and great, rich and poor, free and slave—to be given a mark on the right hand or on the forehead. [17]And no one could buy or sell anything without that mark, which was either the name of the beast or the number representing his name. [18]Wisdom is needed here. Let the one with understanding solve the meaning of the number of the beast, for it is the number of a man.* His number is 666.*

12:18 Greek *Then he took his stand;* some manuscripts read *Then I took my stand.* Some translations put this entire sentence into 13:1.   13:6 Some manuscripts read *and his dwelling and all who dwell in heaven.*   13:8 Or *not written in the Book of Life that belongs to the Lamb who was slaughtered before the world was made.*   13:18a Or *of humanity.*   13:18b Some manuscripts read *616.*

PSALM 141:1-10
A psalm of David.

[1] O LORD, I am calling to you.
  Please hurry!
Listen when I cry to you
  for help!
[2] Accept my prayer as incense offered
    to you,
  and my upraised hands as an
    evening offering.

[3] Take control of what I say, O LORD,
  and guard my lips.

[4] Don't let me drift toward evil
  or take part in acts of wickedness.
Don't let me share in the delicacies
  of those who do wrong.

[5] Let the godly strike me!
  It will be a kindness!
If they correct me, it is soothing
    medicine.
  Don't let me refuse it.

But I pray constantly
  against the wicked and their deeds.
[6] When their leaders are thrown down
    from a cliff,
  the wicked will listen to my words
    and find them true.
[7] Like rocks brought up by a plow,
  the bones of the wicked will lie
    scattered without burial.*

[8] I look to you for help, O Sovereign
  LORD.
  You are my refuge; don't let them
    kill me.
[9] Keep me from the traps they have set
    for me,
  from the snares of those who
    do wrong.
[10] Let the wicked fall into their own nets,
  but let me escape.

141:7 Hebrew *scattered at the mouth of Sheol.*

PROVERBS 30:18-20
There are three things that amaze me—no, four things that I don't understand: how an eagle glides through the sky, how a snake slithers on a rock, how a ship navigates the ocean, how a man loves a woman. □ An adulterous woman consumes a man, then wipes her mouth and says, "What's wrong with that?"

DECEMBER**23**

ZECHARIAH 4:1-5:11
Zerubbabel was the governor of Jerusalem while the exiles were returning from Babylon and rebuilding the Temple. Because of his significant role in their history, he is greatly honored in Jewish tradition.

Then the angel who had been talking with me [Zechariah] returned and woke me, as though I had been asleep. [2]"What do you see now?" he asked.

I answered, "I see a solid gold lampstand

with a bowl of oil on top of it. Around the bowl are seven lamps, each having seven spouts with wicks. ³And I see two olive trees, one on each side of the bowl." ⁴Then I asked the angel, "What are these, my lord? What do they mean?"

⁵"Don't you know?" the angel asked.

"No, my lord," I replied.

⁶Then he said to me, "This is what the LORD says to Zerubbabel: It is not by force nor by strength, but by my Spirit, says the LORD of Heaven's Armies. ⁷Nothing, not even a mighty mountain, will stand in Zerubbabel's way; it will become a level plain before him! And when Zerubbabel sets the final stone of the Temple in place, the people will shout: 'May God bless it! May God bless it!'*"

⁸Then another message came to me from the LORD: ⁹"Zerubbabel is the one who laid the foundation of this Temple, and he will complete it. Then you will know that the LORD of Heaven's Armies has sent me. ¹⁰Do not despise these small beginnings, for the LORD rejoices to see the work begin, to see the plumb line in Zerubbabel's hand."

(The seven lamps* represent the eyes of the LORD that search all around the world.)

¹¹Then I asked the angel, "What are these two olive trees on each side of the lampstand, ¹²and what are the two olive branches that pour out golden oil through two gold tubes?"

¹³"Don't you know?" he asked.

"No, my lord," I replied.

¹⁴Then he said to me, "They represent the two heavenly beings who stand in the court of the Lord of all the earth."

⁵:¹I LOOKED up again and saw a scroll flying through the air.

²"What do you see?" the angel asked.

"I see a flying scroll," I replied. "It appears to be about 30 feet long and 15 feet wide.*"

³Then he said to me, "This scroll contains the curse that is going out over the entire land. One side of the scroll says that those who steal will be banished from the land; the other side says that those who swear falsely will be banished from the land. ⁴And this is what the LORD of Heaven's Armies says: I am sending this curse into the house of every thief and into the house of everyone who swears falsely using my name. And my curse will remain in that house and completely destroy it—even its timbers and stones."

⁵Then the angel who was talking with me came forward and said, "Look up and see what's coming."

⁶"What is it?" I asked.

He replied, "It is a basket for measuring

WHAT THE BIBLE SAYS

Angels

REVELATION 14:6-11 The first time Jesus came to earth, the angels announced his arrival to a group of shepherds in the hills outside of Bethlehem. In this passage, angels once again bring messages—this time they proclaim salvation and judgment, and they bring warnings. One delivers the news that "the time has come"—perhaps as a final opportunity for earth's people to repent, perhaps as an announcement that time has run out. Another angel announces the fall of "Babylon," referring to the end of evil and to God's judgment. A third angel warns against receiving the mark of the beast. • While this passage may seem frightening, you have the assurance of salvation because you have placed your faith in Jesus Christ. You have nothing to fear from God's judgment because the Judge is your Savior. God's special messengers, the angels, have been at work for God since the beginning of time—guarding his people, passing on God's messages to his prophets, announcing good and bad news—and they will continue to work for their Creator throughout the future of our time and on into eternity.

grain,* and it's filled with the sins* of everyone throughout the land."

⁷Then the heavy lead cover was lifted off the basket, and there was a woman sitting inside it. ⁸The angel said, "The woman's name is Wickedness," and he pushed her back into the basket and closed the heavy lid again.

⁹Then I looked up and saw two women flying toward us, gliding on the wind. They had wings like a stork, and they picked up the basket and flew into the sky.

¹⁰"Where are they taking the basket?" I asked the angel.

¹¹He replied, "To the land of Babylonia,* where they will build a temple for the basket. And when the temple is ready, they will set the basket there on its pedestal."

4:7 Hebrew 'Grace, grace to it.'   4:10 Or The seven facets (see 3:9); Hebrew reads These seven.   5:2 Hebrew 20 cubits [9 meters] long and 10 cubits [4.5 meters] wide.   5:6a Hebrew an ephah [20 quarts or 22 liters]; also in 5:7, 8, 9, 10, 11.   5:6b As in Greek version; Hebrew reads the appearance.   5:11 Hebrew the land of Shinar.

REVELATION 14:1-20
This Scripture once again highlights the 144,000, God's chosen, mentioned early in Revelation 7. In that chapter, God's people were promised deliverance, but since then John only described suffering. In today's reading you begin to see the deliverance of God's people.

Then I [John] saw the Lamb standing on Mount Zion, and with him were 144,000 who had his name and his Father's name written on their foreheads. ²And I heard a sound from heaven like the roar of mighty ocean waves or the rolling of loud thunder. It was like the sound of many harpists playing together.

³This great choir sang a wonderful new song in front of the throne of God and before the four living beings and the twenty-four elders. No one could learn this song except the 144,000 who had been redeemed from the earth. ⁴They have kept themselves as pure as virgins,* following the Lamb wherever he goes. They have been purchased from among the people on the earth as a special offering* to God and to the Lamb. ⁵They have told no lies; they are without blame.

⁶And I saw another angel flying through the sky, carrying the eternal Good News to proclaim to the people who belong to this world—to every nation, tribe, language, and people. ⁷"Fear God," he shouted. "Give glory to him. For the time has come when he will sit as judge. Worship him who made the heavens, the earth, the sea, and all the springs of water."

⁸Then another angel followed him through the sky, shouting, "Babylon is fallen—that great city is fallen—because she made all the nations of the world drink the wine of her passionate immorality."

⁹Then a third angel followed them, shouting, "Anyone who worships the beast and his statue or who accepts his mark on the forehead or on the hand ¹⁰must drink the wine of God's anger. It has been poured full strength into God's cup of wrath. And they will be tormented with fire and burning sulfur in the presence of the holy angels and the Lamb. ¹¹The smoke of their torment will rise forever and ever, and they will have no relief day or night, for they have worshiped the beast and his statue and have accepted the mark of his name."

¹²This means that God's holy people must endure persecution patiently, obeying his commands and maintaining their faith in Jesus.

¹³And I heard a voice from heaven saying, "Write this down: Blessed are those who die in the Lord from now on. Yes, says the Spirit, they are blessed indeed, for they will rest from their hard work; for their good deeds follow them!"

¹⁴Then I saw a white cloud, and seated on the cloud was someone like the Son of Man.* He had a gold crown on his head and a sharp sickle in his hand.

¹⁵Then another angel came from the Temple and shouted to the one sitting on the cloud, "Swing the sickle, for the time of harvest has come; the crop on earth is ripe." ¹⁶So the one sitting on the cloud swung his sickle over the earth, and the whole earth was harvested.

¹⁷After that, another angel came from the Temple in heaven, and he also had a sharp sickle. ¹⁸Then another angel, who had power to destroy with fire, came from the altar. He shouted to the angel with the sharp sickle, "Swing your sickle now to gather the clusters of grapes from the

vines of the earth, for they are ripe for judgment." [19] So the angel swung his sickle over the earth and loaded the grapes into the great winepress of God's wrath. [20] The grapes were trampled in the winepress outside the city, and blood flowed from the winepress in a stream about 180 miles* long and as high as a horse's bridle.

14:4a Greek *They are virgins who have not defiled themselves with women.*   14:4b Greek *as firstfruits.*
14:14 Or *like a son of man.* See Dan 7:13. "Son of Man" is a title Jesus used for himself.   14:20 Greek *1,600 stadia* [296 kilometers].

PSALM 142:1-7
A psalm of David, regarding his experience in the cave. A prayer.*

[1] **I** cry out to the LORD;
    I plead for the LORD's mercy.
[2] I pour out my complaints before him
    and tell him all my troubles.
[3] When I am overwhelmed,
    you alone know the way I should turn.
    Wherever I go,
    my enemies have set traps for me.
[4] I look for someone to come and
        help me,

but no one gives me a passing
        thought!
No one will help me;
    no one cares a bit what happens
        to me.
[5] Then I pray to you, O LORD.
    I say, "You are my place of refuge.
    You are all I really want in life.
[6] Hear my cry,
    for I am very low.
Rescue me from my persecutors,
    for they are too strong for me.
[7] Bring me out of prison
    so I can thank you.
The godly will crowd around me,
    for you are good to me."

142:TITLE Hebrew *maskil.* This may be a literary or musical term.

PROVERBS 30:21-23

There are three things that make the earth tremble—no, four it cannot endure: a slave who becomes a king, an overbearing fool who prospers, a bitter woman who finally gets a husband, a servant girl who supplants her mistress.

DECEMBER**24**

ZECHARIAH 6:1–7:14
Zechariah had to remind the returning exiles of the same point that so many of the Old Testament prophets declared: God wants your hearts more than your rituals. Obedience starts from the inside.

Then I [Zechariah] looked up again and saw four chariots coming from between two bronze mountains. [2] The first chariot was pulled by red horses, the second by black horses, [3] the third by white horses, and the fourth by powerful dappled-gray horses. [4] "And what are these, my lord?" I asked the angel who was talking with me.

[5] The angel replied, "These are the four spirits* of heaven who stand before the Lord of all the earth. They are going out to do his work. [6] The chariot with black horses is going north, the chariot with white horses is going west,* and the char-

iot with dappled-gray horses is going south."

[7] The powerful horses were eager to set out to patrol the earth. And the LORD said, "Go and patrol the earth!" So they left at once on their patrol.

[8] Then the LORD summoned me and said, "Look, those who went north have vented the anger of my Spirit* there in the land of the north."

[9] Then I received another message from the LORD: [10] "Heldai, Tobijah, and Jedaiah will bring gifts of silver and gold from the Jews exiled in Babylon. As soon as they arrive, meet them at the home of Josiah son of Zephaniah. [11] Accept their gifts, and make a crown* from the silver and gold. Then put the crown on the head

of Jeshua* son of Jehozadak, the high priest. [12]Tell him, 'This is what the LORD of Heaven's Armies says: Here is the man called the Branch. He will branch out from where he is and build the Temple of the LORD. [13]Yes, he will build the Temple of the LORD. Then he will receive royal honor and will rule as king from his throne. He will also serve as priest from his throne,* and there will be perfect harmony between his two roles.'

[14]"The crown will be a memorial in the Temple of the LORD to honor those who gave it—Heldai,* Tobijah, Jedaiah, and Josiah* son of Zephaniah."

[15]People will come from distant lands to rebuild the Temple of the LORD. And when this happens, you will know that my messages have been from the LORD of Heaven's Armies. All this will happen if you carefully obey what the LORD your God says.

[7:1]ON December 7* of the fourth year of King Darius's reign, another message came to Zechariah from the LORD. [2]The people of Bethel had sent Sharezer and Regemmelech,* along with their attendants, to seek the LORD's favor. [3]They were to ask this question of the prophets and the priests at the Temple of the LORD of Heaven's Armies: "Should we continue to mourn and fast each summer on the anniversary of the Temple's destruction,* as we have done for so many years?"

[4]The LORD of Heaven's Armies sent me this message in reply: [5]"Say to all your people and your priests, 'During these seventy years of exile, when you fasted and mourned in the summer and in early autumn,* was it really for me that you were fasting? [6]And even now in your holy festivals, aren't you eating and drinking just to please yourselves? [7]Isn't this the same message the LORD proclaimed through the prophets in years past when Jerusalem and the towns of Judah were bustling with people, and the Negev and the foothills of Judah* were well populated?'"

[8]Then this message came to Zechariah from the LORD: [9]"This is what the LORD of Heaven's Armies says: Judge fairly, and show mercy and kindness to one another.

[10]Do not oppress widows, orphans, foreigners, and the poor. And do not scheme against each other.

[11]"Your ancestors refused to listen to this message. They stubbornly turned away and put their fingers in their ears to keep from hearing. [12]They made their hearts as hard as stone, so they could not hear the instructions or the messages that the LORD of Heaven's Armies had sent them by his Spirit through the earlier prophets. That is why the LORD of Heaven's Armies was so angry with them.

[13]"Since they refused to listen when I called to them, I would not listen when they called to me, says the LORD of Heaven's Armies. [14]As with a whirlwind, I scattered them among the distant nations, where they lived as strangers. Their land became so desolate that no one even traveled through it. They turned their pleasant land into a desert."

6:5 Or *the four winds.*   **6:6** Hebrew *is going after them.*
6:8 Hebrew *have given my Spirit rest.*   **6:11a** As in Greek and Syriac versions; Hebrew reads *crowns.*   **6:11b** Hebrew *Joshua,* a variant spelling of Jeshua.   **6:13** Or *There will be a priest by his throne.*   **6:14a** As in Syriac version (compare 6:10); Hebrew reads *Helem.*   **6:14b** As in Syriac version (compare 6:10); Hebrew reads *Hen.*   **7:1** Hebrew *On the fourth day of the ninth month, the month of Kislev,* of the ancient Hebrew lunar calendar. This event occurred on December 7, 518 B.C.; also see note on 1:1.   **7:2** Or *Bethel-sharezer had sent Regemmelech.*   **7:3** Hebrew *mourn and fast in the fifth month.* The Temple had been destroyed in the fifth month of the ancient Hebrew lunar calendar (August 586 B.C.); see 2 Kgs 25:8.   **7:5** Hebrew *fasted and mourned in the fifth and seventh months.* The fifth month of the ancient Hebrew lunar calendar usually occurs within the months of July and August. The seventh month usually occurs within the months of September and October; both the Day of Atonement and the Festival of Shelters were celebrated in the seventh month.   **7:7** Hebrew *the Shephelah.*

REVELATION 15:1-8
The seven last plagues will actually begin in chapter 16. Unlike the previous plagues, these will be universal and will end in the destruction of all evil and the end of the world.

Then I [John] saw in heaven another marvelous event of great significance. Seven angels were holding the seven last plagues, which would bring God's wrath to completion. [2]I saw before me what seemed to be a glass sea mixed with fire. And on it stood all the people who had been victorious over the beast and his statue and the number representing his name. They were all holding harps that God had given them. [3]And they were singing the song of Moses, the servant of God, and the song of the Lamb:

"Great and marvelous are your
    works,
    O Lord God, the Almighty.
Just and true are your ways,
    O King of the nations.*
⁴ Who will not fear you, Lord,
    and glorify your name?
For you alone are holy.
All nations will come and worship
        before you,
    for your righteous deeds have
        been revealed."

⁵ Then I looked and saw that the Temple in heaven, God's Tabernacle, was thrown wide open. ⁶ The seven angels who were holding the seven plagues came out of the Temple. They were clothed in spotless white linen* with gold sashes across their chests. ⁷ Then one of the four living beings handed each of the seven angels a gold bowl filled with the wrath of God, who lives forever and ever. ⁸ The Temple was filled with smoke from God's glory and power. No one could enter the Temple until the seven angels had completed pouring out the seven plagues.

15:3 Some manuscripts read *King of the ages.*   15:6 Other manuscripts read *white stone;* still others read *white [garments] made of linen.*

PSALM 143:1-12
A psalm of David.

¹ **H**ear my prayer, O LORD;
    listen to my plea!
    Answer me because you are faithful
        and righteous.
² Don't put your servant on trial,
    for no one is innocent before you.
³ My enemy has chased me.
    He has knocked me to the ground
        and forces me to live in darkness
        like those in the grave.
⁴ I am losing all hope;
    I am paralyzed with fear.
⁵ I remember the days of old.
    I ponder all your great works
        and think about what you have
        done.
⁶ I lift my hands to you in prayer.
    I thirst for you as parched land
        thirsts for rain.   *Interlude*

⁷ Come quickly, LORD, and answer me,
    for my depression deepens.
Don't turn away from me,
    or I will die.
⁸ Let me hear of your unfailing love
        each morning,
    for I am trusting you.
Show me where to walk,
    for I give myself to you.

HOW WE LIVE

Worshiping God

REVELATION 15:1-8 This "song of Moses," sung by "all the people who had been victorious over the beast and his statue" remembers Israel's deliverance from Egypt (Exodus 15, February 1–2). This is "the song of the Lamb," celebrating the ultimate deliverance of God's people from the power of Satan. The song glorifies God and his ultimate victory over the entire world. A great crowd in heaven worships God for his great and marvelous works, for his just and true character, for his holiness, for his righteousness, and for the fact that one day he will receive the worship of all his people. • Chills ought to run up your spine as you watch the events of Revelation unfold. The end will come, but God's people are safe. We know that because we trust God's character. And because we trust him completely, we ought to be on our knees in grateful worship; for through all this, God draws us close, protects us, and loves us. As you worship, picture your God in heaven receiving your worship along with all believers across the world and all the angels of heaven.

⁹ Rescue me from my enemies,
   LORD;
   I run to you to hide me.
¹⁰ Teach me to do your will,
   for you are my God.
   May your gracious Spirit lead me
      forward
   on a firm footing.
¹¹ For the glory of your name, O LORD,
   preserve my life.
   Because of your faithfulness, bring
   me out of this distress.
¹² In your unfailing love, silence all
   my enemies

PROVERBS 30:24-28
There are four things on earth that are small but unusually wise: Ants—they aren't strong, but they store up food all summer. Hyraxes*—they aren't powerful, but they make their homes among the rocks. Locusts—they have no king, but they march in formation. Lizards—they are easy to catch, but they are found even in kings' palaces.
30:26 Or *Coneys,* or *Rock badgers.*

DECEMBER**25**

ZECHARIAH 8:1-23
Just as Jerusalem had been destroyed by the will of the Lord, so it would be restored by his hand. He would see to it that it would again be a place in which his name was honored.

Then another message came to me [Zechariah] from the LORD of Heaven's Armies: ²"This is what the LORD of Heaven's Armies says: My love for Mount Zion is passionate and strong; I am consumed with passion for Jerusalem!

³"And now the LORD says: I am returning to Mount Zion, and I will live in Jerusalem. Then Jerusalem will be called the Faithful City; the mountain of the LORD of Heaven's Armies will be called the Holy Mountain.

⁴"This is what the LORD of Heaven's Armies says: Once again old men and women will walk Jerusalem's streets with their canes and will sit together in the city squares. ⁵And the streets of the city will be filled with boys and girls at play.

⁶"This is what the LORD of Heaven's Armies says: All this may seem impossible to you now, a small remnant of God's people. But is it impossible for me? says the LORD of Heaven's Armies.

⁷"This is what the LORD of Heaven's Armies says: You can be sure that I will rescue my people from the east and from the west. ⁸I will bring them home again to live safely in Jerusalem. They will be my people, and I will be faithful and just toward them as their God.

⁹"This is what the LORD of Heaven's Armies says: Be strong and finish the task! Ever since the laying of the foundation of the Temple of the LORD of Heaven's Armies, you have heard what the prophets have been saying about completing the building. ¹⁰Before the work on the Temple began, there were no jobs and no money to hire people or animals. No traveler was safe from the enemy, for there were enemies on all sides. I had turned everyone against each other.

¹¹"But now I will not treat the remnant of my people as I treated them before, says the LORD of Heaven's Armies. ¹²For I am planting seeds of peace and prosperity among you. The grapevines will be heavy with fruit. The earth will produce its crops, and the heavens will release the dew. Once more I will cause the remnant in Judah and Israel to inherit these blessings. ¹³Among the other nations, Judah and Israel became symbols of a cursed nation. But no longer! Now I will rescue you and make you both a symbol and a source of blessing. So don't be afraid. Be strong, and get on with rebuilding the Temple!

¹⁴"For this is what the LORD of Heaven's Armies says: I was determined to punish you when your ancestors angered me, and I did not change my mind, says the LORD of Heaven's Armies. ¹⁵But now I am determined to bless Jerusalem and the people of Judah. So don't be afraid. ¹⁶But this is what you must do: Tell the truth to each other. Render verdicts in your courts that are just and that lead to peace. ¹⁷Don't scheme against each other. Stop your love of telling lies that you swear are the truth. I hate all these things, says the LORD."

¹⁸Here is another message that came to me from the LORD of Heaven's Armies. ¹⁹"This is what the LORD of Heaven's Armies says: The traditional fasts and times of mourning you have kept in early summer, midsummer, autumn, and winter* are now ended. They will become festivals of joy and celebration for the people of Judah. So love truth and peace.

²⁰"This is what the LORD of Heaven's Armies says: People from nations and cities around the world will travel to Jerusalem. ²¹The people of one city will say to the people of another, 'Come with us to Jerusalem to ask the LORD to bless us. Let's worship the LORD of Heaven's Armies. I'm determined to go.' ²²Many peoples and powerful nations will come to Jerusalem to seek the LORD of Heaven's Armies and to ask for his blessing.

²³"This is what the LORD of Heaven's Armies says: In those days ten men from different nations and languages of the world will clutch at the sleeve of one Jew. And they will say, 'Please let us walk with you, for we have heard that God is with you.'"

8:19 Hebrew *in the fourth, fifth, seventh, and tenth months.* The fourth month of the ancient Hebrew lunar calendar usually occurs within the months of June and July. The fifth month usually occurs within the months of July and August. The seventh month usually occurs within the months of September and October. The tenth month usually occurs within the months of December and January.

REVELATION 16:1-21

First there were seven seals, then seven trumpets. Now there are seven bowls. Unlike the seals and trumpets, the bowls of judgment are poured out without much interruption. Babylon, the recipient of the last judgment, was an ancient enemy of Israel, so it represents all the enemies of God.

Then I [John] heard a mighty voice from the Temple say to the seven angels, "Go your ways and pour out on the earth the seven bowls containing God's wrath."

²So the first angel left the Temple and poured out his bowl on the earth, and horrible, malignant sores broke out on everyone who had the mark of the beast and who worshiped his statue.

WHAT THE BIBLE SAYS

The future

ZECHARIAH 8:6 Zechariah's visions provided hope for his people, the Jews who had returned from exile to rebuild the Temple and their nation. Written 500 years before the birth of Christ, this book contains Messianic prophecies that were fulfilled by Christ. We have the advantage of looking back and seeing these prophecies fulfilled, but the people of Zechariah's time could only look ahead to the future with hopeful anticipation. And the people needed encouragement and hope. They had sinned greatly. They had been away in exile. They were now trying, brick by brick, to rebuild their nation. Along came Zechariah with God's promises that he would live in Jerusalem and that the streets would be filled with happy people. "'All this may seem impossible to you now, a small remnant of God's people. But is it impossible for me?' says the LORD of Heaven's Armies." • Maybe it all seems impossible to you. *A future of hope—for me? A future in heaven, for eternity—for me?* At times, especially times of discouragement and failure, it all seems impossible. But God says to you what he said to that tired remnant: "Look at the future and be encouraged! Nothing is impossible with me!"

³Then the second angel poured out his bowl on the sea, and it became like the blood of a corpse. And everything in the sea died. ⁴Then the third angel poured out his bowl on the rivers and springs, and they became blood. ⁵And I heard the angel who had authority over all water saying,

"You are just, O Holy One, who is and
    who always was,
  because you have sent these
    judgments.
⁶ Since they shed the blood
  of your holy people and your
    prophets,
you have given them blood to drink.
  It is their just reward."

⁷And I heard a voice from the altar,* saying,

"Yes, O Lord God, the Almighty,
  your judgments are true and just."

⁸Then the fourth angel poured out his bowl on the sun, causing it to scorch everyone with its fire. ⁹Everyone was burned by this blast of heat, and they cursed the name of God, who had control over all these plagues. They did not repent of their sins and turn to God and give him glory.

¹⁰Then the fifth angel poured out his bowl on the throne of the beast, and his kingdom was plunged into darkness. His subjects ground their teeth in anguish, ¹¹and they cursed the God of heaven for their pains and sores. But they did not repent of their evil deeds and turn to God.

¹²Then the sixth angel poured out his bowl on the great Euphrates River, and it dried up so that the kings from the east could march their armies toward the west without hindrance. ¹³And I saw three evil* spirits that looked like frogs leap from the mouths of the dragon, the beast, and the false prophet. ¹⁴They are demonic spirits who work miracles and go out to all the rulers of the world to gather them for battle against the Lord on that great judgment day of God the Almighty.

¹⁵"Look, I will come as unexpectedly as a thief! Blessed are all who are watching for me, who keep their clothing ready so they will not have to walk around naked and ashamed."

¹⁶And the demonic spirits gathered all the rulers and their armies to a place with the Hebrew name *Armageddon.**

¹⁷Then the seventh angel poured out his bowl into the air. And a mighty shout came from the throne in the Temple, saying, "It is finished!" ¹⁸Then the thunder crashed and rolled, and lightning flashed. And a great earthquake struck—the worst since people were placed on the earth. ¹⁹The great city of Babylon split into three sections, and the cities of many nations fell into heaps of rubble. So God remembered all of Babylon's sins, and he made her drink the cup that was filled with the wine of his fierce wrath. ²⁰And every island disappeared, and all the mountains were leveled. ²¹There was a terrible hailstorm, and hailstones weighing seventy-five pounds* fell from the sky onto the people below. They cursed God because of the terrible plague of the hailstorm.

16:7 Greek *I heard the altar.*   16:13 Greek *unclean.*
16:16 Or *Harmagedon.*   16:21 Greek *1 talent* [34 kilograms].

PSALM 144:1-15
A psalm of David.

¹ **P**raise the LORD, who is my rock.
  He trains my hands for war
    and gives my fingers skill for battle.
² He is my loving ally and my fortress,
    my tower of safety, my rescuer.
  He is my shield, and I take refuge
    in him.
  He makes the nations* submit to me.

³ O LORD, what are human beings that
    you should notice them,
  mere mortals that you should think
    about them?
⁴ For they are like a breath of air;
    their days are like a passing shadow.

⁵ Open the heavens, LORD, and come
    down.
  Touch the mountains so they billow
    smoke.
⁶ Hurl your lightning bolts and scatter
    your enemies!
  Shoot your arrows and confuse them!
⁷ Reach down from heaven and
    rescue me;

rescue me from deep waters,
from the power of my enemies.
⁸ Their mouths are full of lies;
they swear to tell the truth, but they
lie instead.

⁹ I will sing a new song to you, O God!
I will sing your praises with a ten-
stringed harp.
¹⁰ For you grant victory to kings!
You rescued your servant David
from the fatal sword.
¹¹ Save me!
Rescue me from the power
of my enemies.
Their mouths are full of lies;
they swear to tell the truth, but they
lie instead.

¹² May our sons flourish in their youth
like well-nurtured plants.
May our daughters be like graceful
pillars,
carved to beautify a palace.

¹³ May our barns be filled
with crops of every kind.
May the flocks in our fields multiply
by the thousands,
even tens of thousands,
¹⁴   and may our oxen be loaded down
with produce.
May there be no enemy breaking
through our walls,
no going into captivity,
no cries of alarm in our town
squares.
¹⁵ Yes, joyful are those who live like this!
Joyful indeed are those whose God
is the LORD.

144:2 Some manuscripts read *my people.*

PROVERBS 30:29-31

There are three things that walk with
stately stride—no, four that strut about:
the lion, king of animals, who won't turn
aside for anything, the strutting rooster,
the male goat, a king as he leads his army.

DECEMBER**26**

ZECHARIAH 9:1-17

Chapter 9 begins the second part of Zechariah's
prophecy. The focus shifts to a future salvation.
Zechariah describes the coming King who would
ride into Jerusalem on a donkey. Jesus fulfilled this
prophecy when he sent his disciples to find a colt
for him to ride into Jerusalem (Matthew 21:5,
January 31).

This is the message* from the LORD
against the land of Aram* and the city of
Damascus, for the eyes of humanity, including all the tribes of Israel, are on the
LORD.

² Doom is certain for Hamath,
near Damascus,
and for the cities of Tyre and Sidon,
though they are so clever.
³ Tyre has built a strong fortress
and has made silver and gold
as plentiful as dust in the streets!

⁴ But now the Lord will strip away Tyre's
possessions
and hurl its fortifications into
the sea,
and it will be burned to the
ground.
⁵ The city of Ashkelon will see Tyre fall
and will be filled with fear.
Gaza will shake with terror,
as will Ekron, for their hopes will
be dashed.
Gaza's king will be killed,
and Ashkelon will be deserted.
⁶ Foreigners will occupy the city
of Ashdod.
I will destroy the pride of the
Philistines.
⁷ I will grab the bloody meat from
their mouths
and snatch the detestable sacrifices
from their teeth.

Then the surviving Philistines will
worship our God
and become like a clan in Judah.*
The Philistines of Ekron will join
my people,
as the ancient Jebusites once did.
8 I will guard my Temple
and protect it from invading armies.
I am watching closely to ensure
that no more foreign oppressors
overrun my people's land.

9 Rejoice, O people of Zion!*
Shout in triumph, O people of
Jerusalem!
Look, your king is coming to you.
He is righteous and victorious,*
yet he is humble, riding on a donkey—
riding on a donkey's colt.
10 I will remove the battle chariots from
Israel*
and the warhorses from Jerusalem.
I will destroy all the weapons used in
battle,
and your king will bring peace
to the nations.
His realm will stretch from sea to sea
and from the Euphrates River*
to the ends of the earth.*
11 Because of the covenant I made with
you,
sealed with blood,
I will free your prisoners
from death in a waterless dungeon.
12 Come back to the place of safety,
all you prisoners who still have
hope!
I promise this very day
that I will repay two blessings for
each of your troubles.
13 Judah is my bow,
and Israel is my arrow.
Jerusalem* is my sword,
and like a warrior, I will brandish
it against the Greeks.*

14 The LORD will appear above his
people;
his arrows will fly like lightning!
The Sovereign LORD will sound the
ram's horn
and attack like a whirlwind from
the southern desert.
15 The LORD of Heaven's Armies will
protect his people,

and they will defeat their enemies
by hurling great stones.
They will shout in battle as though
drunk with wine.
They will be filled with blood like
a bowl,
drenched with blood like the
corners of the altar.
16 On that day the LORD their God will
rescue his people,
just as a shepherd rescues his
sheep.
They will sparkle in his land
like jewels in a crown.
17 How wonderful and beautiful
they will be!
The young men will thrive on
abundant grain,
and the young women will flourish
on new wine.

9:1a Hebrew *An Oracle: The message.* **9:1b** Hebrew *land of
Hadrach.* **9:7** Hebrew *and will become a leader in Judah.*
9:9a Hebrew *O daughter of Zion!* **9:9b** Hebrew *and is
being vindicated.* **9:10a** Hebrew *Ephraim,* referring to the
northern kingdom of Israel; also in 9:13. **9:10b** Hebrew *the
river.* **9:10c** Or *the end of the land.* **9:13a** Hebrew *Zion.*
9:13b Hebrew *the sons of Javan.*

REVELATION 17:1-18
The destruction of Babylon mentioned in 16:17-21
is described here in greater detail. This "great prostitute" represents the seductiveness of this government system that uses any means for its own power
and pleasure.

One of the seven angels who had poured
out the seven bowls came over and spoke
to me [John]. "Come with me," he said,
"and I will show you the judgment that is
going to come on the great prostitute,
who rules over many waters. 2 The kings
of the world have committed adultery
with her, and the people who belong to
this world have been made drunk by the
wine of her immorality."

3 So the angel took me in the Spirit* into
the wilderness. There I saw a woman sitting on a scarlet beast that had seven
heads and ten horns, and blasphemies
against God were written all over it. 4 The
woman wore purple and scarlet clothing
and beautiful jewelry made of gold and
precious gems and pearls. In her hand she
held a gold goblet full of obscenities and
the impurities of her immorality. 5 A mysterious name was written on her forehead:

"Babylon the Great, Mother of All Prostitutes and Obscenities in the World." ⁶I could see that she was drunk—drunk with the blood of God's holy people who were witnesses for Jesus. I stared at her in complete amazement.

⁷"Why are you so amazed?" the angel asked. "I will tell you the mystery of this woman and of the beast with seven heads and ten horns on which she sits. ⁸The beast you saw was once alive but isn't now. And yet he will soon come up out of the bottomless pit* and go to eternal destruction. And the people who belong to this world, whose names were not written in the Book of Life before the world was made, will be amazed at the reappearance of this beast who had died.

⁹"This calls for a mind with understanding: The seven heads of the beast represent the seven hills where the woman rules. They also represent seven kings. ¹⁰Five kings have already fallen, the sixth now reigns, and the seventh is yet to come, but his reign will be brief. ¹¹"The scarlet beast that was, but is no longer, is the eighth king. He is like the other seven, and he, too, is headed for destruction. ¹²The ten horns of the beast are ten kings who have not yet risen to power. They will be appointed to their kingdoms for one brief moment to reign with the beast. ¹³They will all agree to give him their power and authority. ¹⁴Together they will go to war against the Lamb, but the Lamb will defeat them because he is Lord of all lords and King of all kings. And his called and chosen and faithful ones will be with him."

¹⁵Then the angel said to me, "The waters where the prostitute is ruling represent masses of people of every nation and language. ¹⁶The scarlet beast and his ten horns all hate the prostitute. They will strip her naked, eat her flesh, and burn her remains with fire. ¹⁷For God has put a plan into their minds, a plan that will carry out his purposes. They will agree to give their authority to the scarlet beast, and so the words of God will be fulfilled. ¹⁸And this woman you saw in your vision represents the great city that rules over the kings of the world."

17:3 Or *in spirit.*   17:8 Or *the abyss,* or *the underworld.*

PSALM 145:1-21*
A psalm of praise of David.

¹ I will exalt you, my God and King,
    and praise your name forever and
    ever.
² I will praise you every day;
    yes, I will praise you forever.
³ Great is the LORD! He is most worthy
    of praise!
    No one can measure his greatness.

WHAT THE BIBLE SAYS

The future

REVELATION 17:15-18 The book of Revelation gives an amazing look into the future. Rich with images, John's account of his vision allows us to see the way the world will end. For those who walk the earth during this time of the tribulation, life will be saturated with evil. The blood of Christian martyrs will flow, and the nations of the world will turn their power over to the beast. In the midst of this nightmarish scene, God has a plan.
• Because God is omniscient (all-knowing), no matter what happens in life you can be confident that God is in control and in charge of your future. He will overcome any evil plan of Satan. You have no need to fear the prophecies in this passage because you are assured of salvation through Jesus. Although we still see evil permeating the world, the new earth will never see the sin of the old earth. And thanks to your faith in Christ, you will be there to enjoy it. Your name is written in the Book of Life and it will not be erased.

⁴ Let each generation tell its children
of your mighty acts;
let them proclaim your power.
⁵ I will meditate* on your majestic,
glorious splendor
and your wonderful miracles.
⁶ Your awe-inspiring deeds will be
on every tongue;
I will proclaim your greatness.
⁷ Everyone will share the story of your
wonderful goodness;
they will sing with joy about your
righteousness.

⁸ The LORD is merciful and
compassionate,
slow to get angry and filled with
unfailing love.
⁹ The LORD is good to everyone.
He showers compassion on all his
creation.
¹⁰ All of your works will thank you, LORD,
and your faithful followers will
praise you.
¹¹ They will speak of the glory of your
kingdom;
they will give examples of your
power.
¹² They will tell about your mighty deeds
and about the majesty and glory
of your reign.
¹³ For your kingdom is an everlasting
kingdom.
You rule throughout all generations.

The LORD always keeps his promises;
he is gracious in all he does.*

¹⁴ The LORD helps the fallen
and lifts those bent beneath their
loads.
¹⁵ The eyes of all look to you in hope;
you give them their food as they
need it.
¹⁶ When you open your hand,
you satisfy the hunger and thirst
of every living thing.
¹⁷ The LORD is righteous in everything
he does;
he is filled with kindness.
¹⁸ The LORD is close to all who call
on him,
yes, to all who call on him
in truth.
¹⁹ He grants the desires of those who
fear him;
he hears their cries for help and
rescues them.
²⁰ The LORD protects all those who love
him,
but he destroys the wicked.

²¹ I will praise the LORD,
and may everyone on earth bless his
holy name
forever and ever.

145 This psalm is a Hebrew acrostic poem; each verse (including 13b) begins with a successive letter of the Hebrew alphabet.   **145:5** Some manuscripts read *They will speak.*   **145:13** The last two lines of 145:13 are not found in many of the ancient manuscripts.

PROVERBS 30:32
If you have been a fool by being proud or plotting evil, cover your mouth in shame.

DECEMBER**27**

ZECHARIAH 10:1–11:17
Chapters 10 and 11 contain some familiar imagery. Watch the role of the shepherd and remember that Jesus, the Good Shepherd, was rejected by his own. Watch the thirty pieces of silver thrown to the potters, and remember Judas's fateful betrayal for thirty pieces of silver.

Ask the LORD for rain in the spring,
for he makes the storm clouds.
And he will send showers of rain

so every field becomes a lush
pasture.
² Household gods give worthless advice,
fortune-tellers predict only lies,
and interpreters of dreams pronounce
falsehoods that give no comfort.
So my people are wandering like lost
sheep;
they are attacked because they have
no shepherd.

³ "My anger burns against your
 shepherds,
   and I will punish these leaders.*
For the LORD of Heaven's Armies has
 arrived
   to look after Judah, his flock.
He will make them strong and
 glorious,
   like a proud warhorse in battle.
⁴ From Judah will come the
 cornerstone,
   the tent peg,
the bow for battle,
   and all the rulers.
⁵ They will be like mighty warriors
 in battle,
   trampling their enemies in the mud
   under their feet.
Since the LORD is with them as they
 fight,
   they will overthrow even the
   enemy's horsemen.
⁶ "I will strengthen Judah and save
 Israel*;
   I will restore them because of my
   compassion.
It will be as though I had never
 rejected them,
   for I am the LORD their God, who
   will hear their cries.
⁷ The people of Israel* will become like
 mighty warriors,
   and their hearts will be made happy
   as if by wine.
Their children, too, will see it and
 be glad;
   their hearts will rejoice in the LORD.
⁸ When I whistle to them, they will
 come running,
   for I have redeemed them.
From the few who are left,
   they will grow as numerous as they
   were before.
⁹ Though I have scattered them like
 seeds among the nations,
   they will still remember me in
   distant lands.
They and their children will survive
   and return again to Israel.
¹⁰ I will bring them back from Egypt
 and gather them from Assyria.
I will resettle them in Gilead and
 Lebanon

until there is no more room
 for them all.
¹¹ They will pass safely through the sea
 of distress,*
   for the waves of the sea will be held
   back,
   and the waters of the Nile will dry
   up.
The pride of Assyria will be crushed,
   and the rule of Egypt will end.
¹² By my power* I will make my people
 strong,
   and by my authority they will go
   wherever they wish.
   I, the LORD, have spoken!"

¹¹:¹ OPEN your doors, Lebanon,
   so that fire may devour your cedar
   forests.
² Weep, you cypress trees, for all the
 ruined cedars;
   the most majestic ones have fallen.
Weep, you oaks of Bashan,
   for the thick forests have been cut
   down.
³ Listen to the wailing of the shepherds,
   for their rich pastures are
   destroyed.
Hear the young lions roaring,
   for their thickets in the Jordan
   Valley are ruined.

⁴This is what the LORD my God says: "Go
and care for the flock that is intended for
slaughter. ⁵The buyers slaughter their
sheep without remorse. The sellers say,
'Praise the LORD! Now I'm rich!' Even the
shepherds have no compassion for them.
⁶Likewise, I will no longer have pity on the
people of the land," says the LORD. "I will
let them fall into each other's hands and
into the hands of their king. They will turn
the land into a wilderness, and I will not
rescue them."

⁷So I cared for the flock intended for
slaughter—the flock that was oppressed.
Then I took two shepherd's staffs and
named one Favor and the other Union. ⁸I
got rid of their three evil shepherds in a
single month.

But I became impatient with these sheep,
and they hated me, too. ⁹So I told them, "I
won't be your shepherd any longer. If you die,
you die. If you are killed, you are killed. And
let those who remain devour each other!"

[10]Then I took my staff called Favor and cut it in two, showing that I had revoked the covenant I had made with all the nations. [11]That was the end of my covenant with them. The suffering flock was watching me, and they knew that the LORD was speaking through my actions.

[12]And I said to them, "If you like, give me my wages, whatever I am worth; but only if you want to." So they counted out for my wages thirty pieces of silver.

[13]And the LORD said to me, "Throw it to the potter*"—this magnificent sum at which they valued me! So I took the thirty coins and threw them to the potter in the Temple of the LORD.

[14]Then I took my other staff, Union, and cut it in two, showing that the bond of unity between Judah and Israel was broken.

[15]Then the LORD said to me, "Go again and play the part of a worthless shepherd. [16]This illustrates how I will give this nation a shepherd who will not care for those who are dying, nor look after the young,* nor heal the injured, nor feed the healthy. Instead, this shepherd will eat the meat of the fattest sheep and tear off their hooves.

[17] "What sorrow awaits this worthless shepherd
    who abandons the flock!
The sword will cut his arm
    and pierce his right eye.
His arm will become useless,
    and his right eye completely blind."

10:3 Or *these male goats.*   10:6 Hebrew *save the house of Joseph.*   10:7 Hebrew *of Ephraim.*   10:11 Or *the sea of Egypt,* referring to the Red Sea.   10:12 Hebrew *In the LORD.*   11:13 Syriac version reads *into the treasury;* also in 11:13b. Compare Matt 27:6-10.   11:16 Or *the scattered.*

REVELATION 18:1-24

John continues his description of the destruction of Babylon. For John's Jewish readers, the meaning of Babylon's description would be clearly spiritual. Babylon symbolized all who opposed God and his people.

After all this I [John] saw another angel come down from heaven with great authority, and the earth grew bright with his splendor. [2]He gave a mighty shout:

"Babylon is fallen—that great city
    is fallen!
She has become a home for
    demons.
She is a hideout for every foul* spirit,
    a hideout for every foul vulture
    and every foul and dreadful animal.*
[3] For all the nations have fallen*
    because of the wine of her
        passionate immorality.
The kings of the world
    have committed adultery with her.
Because of her desires for extravagant
        luxury,
    the merchants of the world have
        grown rich."

[4]Then I heard another voice calling from heaven,

"Come away from her, my people.
    Do not take part in her sins,
    or you will be punished with her.
[5] For her sins are piled as high as heaven,
    and God remembers her evil deeds.
[6] Do to her as she has done to others.
    Double her penalty* for all her evil
        deeds.
She brewed a cup of terror for others,
    so brew twice as much* for her.
[7] She glorified herself and lived
        in luxury,
    so match it now with torment
        and sorrow.
She boasted in her heart,
    'I am queen on my throne.
I am no helpless widow,
    and I have no reason to mourn.'
[8] Therefore, these plagues will overtake
        her in a single day—
    death and mourning and famine.
She will be completely consumed
        by fire,
    for the Lord God who judges her
        is mighty."

[9]And the kings of the world who committed adultery with her and enjoyed her great luxury will mourn for her as they see the smoke rising from her charred remains. [10]They will stand at a distance, terrified by her great torment. They will cry out,

"How terrible, how terrible for you,
    O Babylon, you great city!
In a single moment
    God's judgment came on you."

¹¹The merchants of the world will weep and mourn for her, for there is no one left to buy their goods. ¹²She bought great quantities of gold, silver, jewels, and pearls; fine linen, purple, silk, and scarlet cloth; things made of fragrant thyine wood, ivory goods, and objects made of expensive wood; and bronze, iron, and marble. ¹³She also bought cinnamon, spice, incense, myrrh, frankincense, wine, olive oil, fine flour, wheat, cattle, sheep, horses, chariots, and bodies—that is, human slaves.

¹⁴ "The fancy things you loved so
        much
        are gone," they cry.
"All your luxuries and splendor
        are gone forever,
        never to be yours again."

¹⁵The merchants who became wealthy by selling her these things will stand at a distance, terrified by her great torment. They will weep and cry out,

¹⁶ "How terrible, how terrible for that
        great city!
        She was clothed in finest purple
        and scarlet linens,
        decked out with gold and precious
        stones and pearls!
¹⁷ In a single moment
        all the wealth of the city is gone!"

And all the captains of the merchant ships and their passengers and sailors and crews will stand at a distance. ¹⁸They will cry out as they watch the smoke ascend, and they will say, "Where is there another city as great as this?" ¹⁹And they will weep and throw dust on their heads to show their grief. And they will cry out,

"How terrible, how terrible for that
        great city!
        The shipowners became wealthy
        by transporting her great wealth on
        the seas.
In a single moment it is all gone."

²⁰ Rejoice over her fate, O heaven
        and people of God and apostles and
        prophets!
For at last God has judged her
        for your sakes.

²¹Then a mighty angel picked up a boulder the size of a huge millstone. He threw it into the ocean and shouted,

"Just like this, the great city Babylon
        will be thrown down with violence
        and will never be found again.
²² The sound of harps, singers, flutes,
        and trumpets
        will never be heard in you again.
No craftsmen and no trades
        will ever be found in you again.

The future

REVELATION 18 Babylon was the name of both an immoral city and an evil empire. In the Old Testament, Babylon ransacked the Temple and carried the people of Judah into captivity (2 Kings 25, July 4). In John's vision, the evil of this ancient city of Babylon represents the mighty enemy of God's people—as a world power that will come to a violent end. • Those who put their faith in the world will lose everything when the world's economy falls. No one will remain unaffected—possessions will be destroyed, trade and commerce will cease, wealth will disintegrate. Those who worked only for material gain will lose it all and have nothing to show for their lifetime of labor. However, those who worked for God's Kingdom, sharing the Good News and bringing others to salvation, will enter the new heaven and earth with much greater wealth. The relationships they built, the people they led to Christ, and their character and integrity— these matter far more than power, prestige, or wealth. • Consider what you're working for, what matters most in your life. Are your priorities in line with what matters most to God? In the end, all that matters is him.

WHAT THE BIBLE SAYS

The sound of the mill
will never be heard in you again.
23 The light of a lamp
will never shine in you again.
The happy voices of brides and
grooms
will never be heard in you again.
For your merchants were the greatest
in the world,
and you deceived the nations with
your sorceries.
24 In your* streets flowed the blood of the
prophets and of God's holy people
and the blood of people slaughtered
all over the world."

18:2a Greek *unclean*; also in each of the two following phrases.
18:2b Some manuscripts condense the last two lines to read
a hideout for every foul and dreadful vulture. 18:3 Some
manuscripts read *have drunk.* 18:6a Or *Give her an equal
penalty.* 18:6b Or *brew just as much.* 18:24 Greek *her.*

PSALM 146:1-10

Praise the LORD!

Let all that I am praise the LORD.
2 I will praise the LORD as long as I live.
I will sing praises to my God with
my dying breath.

3 Don't put your confidence in powerful
people;
there is no help for you there.
4 When they breathe their last, they
return to the earth,
and all their plans die with them.

5 But joyful are those who have the God
of Israel* as their helper,
whose hope is in the LORD their
God.
6 He made heaven and earth,
the sea, and everything in them.
He keeps every promise forever.
7 He gives justice to the oppressed
and food to the hungry.
The LORD frees the prisoners.
8 The LORD opens the eyes
of the blind.
The LORD lifts up those who are
weighed down.
The LORD loves the godly.
9 The LORD protects the foreigners
among us.
He cares for the orphans and
widows,
but he frustrates the plans
of the wicked.

10 The LORD will reign forever.
He will be your God, O Jerusalem,*
throughout the generations.

Praise the LORD!

146:5 Hebrew *of Jacob.* See note on 44:4. 146:10 Hebrew
Zion.

PROVERBS 30:33

As the beating of cream yields butter and
striking the nose causes bleeding, so stirring up anger causes quarrels.

DECEMBER**28**

ZECHARIAH 12:1–13:9

What happens when God pours out his Spirit on his
people? Their eyes are opened to the truth. When
that happens, there is mourning because of the lies
that the people had believed, and joy because of
the hope that is restored. In these chapters, Zechariah describes such a time.

This* message concerning the fate of Israel came from the LORD: "This message
is from the LORD, who stretched out the
heavens, laid the foundations of the earth,
and formed the human spirit. 2I will make

Jerusalem like an intoxicating drink that
makes the nearby nations stagger when
they send their armies to besiege Jerusalem and Judah. 3On that day I will make
Jerusalem an immovable rock. All the nations will gather against it to try to move
it, but they will only hurt themselves.

4"On that day," says the LORD, "I will
cause every horse to panic and every
rider to lose his nerve. I will watch over
the people of Judah, but I will blind all
the horses of their enemies. 5And the

clans of Judah will say to themselves, 'The people of Jerusalem have found strength in the LORD of Heaven's Armies, their God.'

⁶"On that day I will make the clans of Judah like a flame that sets a woodpile ablaze or like a burning torch among sheaves of grain. They will burn up all the neighboring nations right and left, while the people living in Jerusalem remain secure.

⁷"The LORD will give victory to the rest of Judah first, before Jerusalem, so that the people of Jerusalem and the royal line of David will not have greater honor than the rest of Judah. ⁸On that day the LORD will defend the people of Jerusalem; the weakest among them will be as mighty as King David! And the royal descendants will be like God, like the angel of the LORD who goes before them! ⁹For on that day I will begin to destroy all the nations that come against Jerusalem.

¹⁰"Then I will pour out a spirit* of grace and prayer on the family of David and on the people of Jerusalem. They will look on me whom they have pierced and mourn for him as for an only son. They will grieve bitterly for him as for a firstborn son who has died. ¹¹The sorrow and mourning in Jerusalem on that day will be like the great mourning for Hadad-rimmon in the valley of Megiddo.

¹²"All Israel will mourn, each clan by itself, and with the husbands separate from their wives. The clan of David will mourn alone, as will the clan of Nathan, ¹³the clan of Levi, and the clan of Shimei. ¹⁴Each of the surviving clans from Judah will mourn separately, and with the husbands separate from their wives.

¹³:¹"ON that day a fountain will be opened for the dynasty of David and for the people of Jerusalem, a fountain to cleanse them from all their sins and impurity.

²"And on that day," says the LORD of Heaven's Armies, "I will erase idol worship throughout the land, so that even the names of the idols will be forgotten. I will remove from the land both the false prophets and the spirit of impurity that came with them. ³If anyone continues to prophesy, his own father and mother will tell him, 'You must die, for you have

prophesied lies in the name of the LORD.' And as he prophesies, his own father and mother will stab him.

⁴"On that day people will be ashamed to claim the prophetic gift. No one will pretend to be a prophet by wearing prophet's clothes. ⁵He will say, 'I'm no prophet; I'm a farmer. I began working for a farmer as a boy.' ⁶And if someone asks, 'Then what about those wounds on your chest?*' he will say, 'I was wounded at my friends' house!'

⁷ "Awake, O sword, against my shepherd,
       the man who is my partner,"
    says the LORD of Heaven's Armies.
   "Strike down the shepherd,
       and the sheep will be scattered,
       and I will turn against the lambs.
⁸ Two-thirds of the people in the land
       will be cut off and die," says the LORD.
    "But one-third will be left in the
       land.
⁹ I will bring that group through the fire
       and make them pure.
    I will refine them like silver
       and purify them like gold.
    They will call on my name,
       and I will answer them.
    I will say, 'These are my people,'
       and they will say, 'The LORD is
          our God.'"

12:1 Hebrew *An Oracle: This.*   12:10 Or *the Spirit.*
13:6 Hebrew *wounds between your hands?*

REVELATION 19:1-21

Going from chapter 18 to chapter 19 is like going from darkness to light. The destruction of evil was the topic of the last few readings. Here, God's victory over evil is celebrated.

After this, I [John] heard what sounded like a vast crowd in heaven shouting,

   "Praise the LORD!*
       Salvation and glory and power
          belong to our God.
² His judgments are true and just.
       He has punished the great
          prostitute
    who corrupted the earth with her
       immorality.
    He has avenged the murder
       of his servants."

³And again their voices rang out:

"Praise the LORD!
The smoke from that city ascends
forever and ever!"

⁴Then the twenty-four elders and the four living beings fell down and worshiped God, who was sitting on the throne. They cried out, "Amen! Praise the LORD!"

⁵And from the throne came a voice that said,

"Praise our God,
all his servants,
all who fear him,
from the least to the greatest."

⁶Then I heard again what sounded like the shout of a vast crowd or the roar of mighty ocean waves or the crash of loud thunder:

"Praise the LORD!
For the Lord our God,* the
Almighty, reigns.
⁷ Let us be glad and rejoice,
and let us give honor to him.
For the time has come for the wedding
feast of the Lamb,
and his bride has prepared herself.
⁸ She has been given the finest of pure
white linen to wear."
For the fine linen represents the
good deeds of God's holy people.

⁹And the angel said to me, "Write this: Blessed are those who are invited to the wedding feast of the Lamb." And he added, "These are true words that come from God."

¹⁰Then I fell down at his feet to worship him, but he said, "No, don't worship me. I am a servant of God, just like you and your brothers and sisters* who testify about their faith in Jesus. Worship only God. For the essence of prophecy is to give a clear witness for Jesus.*"

¹¹Then I saw heaven opened, and a white horse was standing there. Its rider was named Faithful and True, for he judges fairly and wages a righteous war. ¹²His eyes were like flames of fire, and on his head were many crowns. A name was written on him that no one understood except himself. ¹³He wore a robe dipped in blood, and his title was the Word of God. ¹⁴The armies of heaven, dressed in the finest of pure white linen, followed him on white horses. ¹⁵From his mouth came a sharp sword to strike down the nations. He will rule them with an iron rod. He will release the fierce wrath of God, the Almighty, like juice flowing from a winepress. ¹⁶On his robe at his thigh* was written this title: King of all kings and Lord of all lords.

¹⁷Then I saw an angel standing in the sun, shouting to the vultures flying high in the sky: "Come! Gather together for the great banquet God has prepared. ¹⁸Come and eat the flesh of kings, generals, and strong warriors; of horses and their riders; and of all humanity, both free and slave, small and great."

¹⁹Then I saw the beast and the kings of the world and their armies gathered together to fight against the one sitting on the horse and his army. ²⁰And the beast was captured, and with him the false prophet who did mighty miracles on behalf of the beast—miracles that deceived all who had accepted the mark of the beast and who worshiped his statue. Both the beast and his false prophet were thrown alive into the fiery lake of burning sulfur. ²¹Their entire army was killed by the sharp sword that came from the mouth of the one riding the white horse. And the vultures all gorged themselves on the dead bodies.

19:1 Greek *Hallelujah;* also in 19:3, 4, 6. *Hallelujah* is the transliteration of a Hebrew term that means "Praise the LORD." **19:6** Some manuscripts read *the Lord God.* **19:10a** Greek *brothers.* **19:10b** Or *is the message confirmed by Jesus.* **19:16** Or *On his robe and thigh.*

PSALM 147:1-20

Praise the LORD!

How good to sing praises to our God!
How delightful and how fitting!
² The LORD is rebuilding Jerusalem
and bringing the exiles back to
Israel.
³ He heals the brokenhearted
and bandages their wounds.
⁴ He counts the stars
and calls them all by name.
⁵ How great is our Lord! His power
is absolute!
His understanding is beyond
comprehension!
⁶ The LORD supports the humble,

but he brings the wicked down
  into the dust.

7 Sing out your thanks to the LORD;
  sing praises to our God with
    a harp.
8 He covers the heavens with clouds,
  provides rain for the earth,
  and makes the grass grow in
    mountain pastures.
9 He gives food to the wild animals
  and feeds the young ravens when
    they cry.
10 He takes no pleasure in the strength
    of a horse
  or in human might.
11 No, the LORD's delight is in those who
    fear him,
  those who put their hope in his
    unfailing love.

12 Glorify the LORD, O Jerusalem!
  Praise your God, O Zion!
13 For he has strengthened the bars
    of your gates
  and blessed your children within
    your walls.
14 He sends peace across your nation
  and satisfies your hunger with
    the finest wheat.
15 He sends his orders to the world—
  how swiftly his word flies!
16 He sends the snow like white wool;

he scatters frost upon the ground
  like ashes.
17 He hurls the hail like stones.*
  Who can stand against his freezing
    cold?
18 Then, at his command, it all melts.
  He sends his winds, and the ice
    thaws.
19 He has revealed his words
    to Jacob,
  his decrees and regulations
    to Israel.
20 He has not done this for any other
    nation;
  they do not know his regulations.

Praise the LORD!

147:17 Hebrew *like bread crumbs.*

PROVERBS 31:1-7

The sayings of King Lemuel contain this message,* which his mother taught him. □O my son, O son of my womb, O son of my vows, do not waste your strength on women, on those who ruin kings. □It is not for kings, O Lemuel, to guzzle wine. Rulers should not crave alcohol. For if they drink, they may forget the law and not give justice to the oppressed. Alcohol is for the dying, and wine for those in bitter distress. Let them drink to forget their poverty and remember their troubles no more.

31:1 Or *of Lemuel, king of Massa;* or *of King Lemuel, an oracle.*

WHO GOD IS

Jesus is King

REVELATION 19:11-16 Most of the world will be worshiping the Beast, the Antichrist, whom they believe has all power and authority. Then suddenly out of heaven Christ and his army will appear. On his robe his name is inscribed—"King of all kings and Lord of all lords" (19:16). This verse describes the second coming of Christ—the moment God's people are waiting for. Jesus had said, "You will see the Son of Man . . . coming on the clouds of heaven" (Mark 14:62, March 10), and as the disciples had stared into the sky during Jesus' ascension, an angel said, "Jesus has been taken from you into heaven, but someday he will return from heaven in the same way you saw him go!" (Acts 1:11, June 3). • Christ's return will be unmistakable. This rider, called Faithful and True, contrasts with the faithless and deceitful Babylon described in chapter 18. Christ will come to bring judgment against all evil and to inaugurate his reign. "He will rule with fairness and justice . . . for all eternity" (Isaiah 9:7, September 11), and "his Kingdom will never end" (Luke 1:33, March 14).

DECEMBER **29**

1433

ZECHARIAH 14:1-21

Consider the fact that Zechariah's people had been through years of trouble (though some of it was of their own making). Imagine the jubilation they must have felt as Zechariah described a Messiah who would plant his feet on the Mount of Olives. The Messiah would bring their ultimate restoration.

Watch, for the day of the LORD is coming when your possessions will be plundered right in front of you [the people of Jerusalem]! ²I will gather all the nations to fight against Jerusalem. The city will be taken, the houses looted, and the women raped. Half the population will be taken into captivity, and the rest will be left among the ruins of the city.

³Then the LORD will go out to fight against those nations, as he has fought in times past. ⁴On that day his feet will stand on the Mount of Olives, east of Jerusalem. And the Mount of Olives will split apart, making a wide valley running from east to west. Half the mountain will move toward the north and half toward the south. ⁵You will flee through this valley, for it will reach across to Azal.* Yes, you will flee as you did from the earthquake in the days of King Uzziah of Judah. Then the LORD my God will come, and all his holy ones with him.*

⁶On that day the sources of light will no longer shine,* ⁷yet there will be continuous day! Only the LORD knows how this could happen. There will be no normal day and night, for at evening time it will still be light.

⁸On that day life-giving waters will flow out from Jerusalem, half toward the Dead Sea and half toward the Mediterranean,* flowing continuously in both summer and winter.

⁹And the LORD will be king over all the earth. On that day there will be one LORD— his name alone will be worshiped.

¹⁰All the land from Geba, north of Judah, to Rimmon, south of Jerusalem, will become one vast plain. But Jerusalem will be raised up in its original place and will be inhabited all the way from the Benjamin Gate over to the site of the old gate, then to the Corner Gate, and from the Tower of Hananel to the king's winepresses. ¹¹And Jerusalem will be filled, safe at last, never again to be cursed and destroyed.

¹²And the LORD will send a plague on all the nations that fought against Jerusalem. Their people will become like walking corpses, their flesh rotting away. Their eyes will rot in their sockets, and their tongues will rot in their mouths. ¹³On that day they will be terrified, stricken by the LORD with great panic. They will fight their neighbors hand to hand. ¹⁴Judah, too, will be fighting at Jerusalem. The wealth of all the neighboring nations will be captured—great quantities of gold and silver and fine clothing. ¹⁵This same plague will strike the horses, mules, camels, donkeys, and all the other animals in the enemy camps.

¹⁶In the end, the enemies of Jerusalem who survive the plague will go up to Jerusalem each year to worship the King, the LORD of Heaven's Armies, and to celebrate the Festival of Shelters. ¹⁷Any nation in the world that refuses to come to Jerusalem to worship the King, the LORD of Heaven's Armies, will have no rain. ¹⁸If the people of Egypt refuse to attend the festival, the LORD will punish them with the same plague that he sends on the other nations who refuse to go. ¹⁹Egypt and the other nations will all be punished if they don't go to celebrate the Festival of Shelters.

²⁰On that day even the harness bells of the horses will be inscribed with these words: HOLY TO THE LORD. And the cooking pots in the Temple of the LORD will be as sacred as the basins used beside the altar. ²¹In fact, every cooking pot in Jerusalem and Judah will be holy to the LORD of Heaven's Armies. All who come to worship will be free to use any of these pots to boil their sacrifices. And on that day there will no longer be traders* in the Temple of the LORD of Heaven's Armies.

14:5a The meaning of the Hebrew is uncertain.   **14:5b** As in Greek version; Hebrew reads *with you.*   **14:6** Hebrew *there will be no light, no cold or frost.* The meaning of the Hebrew is uncertain.   **14:8** Hebrew *half toward the eastern sea and half toward the western sea.*   **14:21** Hebrew *Canaanites.*

REVELATION 20:1-15
In this passage, you have the sense of sweeping up the details after the deal is done. Satan is put in his place, and God gathers his people to make a final accounting. It is time for a new order of things.

Then I [John] saw an angel coming down from heaven with the key to the bottomless pit* and a heavy chain in his hand. ²He seized the dragon—that old serpent, who is the devil, Satan—and bound him in chains for a thousand years. ³The angel threw him into the bottomless pit, which he then shut and locked so Satan could not deceive the nations anymore until the thousand years were finished. Afterward he must be released for a little while.

⁴Then I saw thrones, and the people sitting on them had been given the authority to judge. And I saw the souls of those who had been beheaded for their testimony about Jesus and for proclaiming the word of God. They had not worshiped the beast or his statue, nor accepted his mark on their forehead or their hands. They all came to life again, and they reigned with Christ for a thousand years.

⁵This is the first resurrection. (The rest of the dead did not come back to life until the thousand years had ended.) ⁶Blessed and holy are those who share in the first resurrection. For them the second death holds no power, but they will be priests of

God and of Christ and will reign with him a thousand years.

⁷When the thousand years come to an end, Satan will be let out of his prison. ⁸He will go out to deceive the nations—called Gog and Magog—in every corner of the earth. He will gather them together for battle—a mighty army, as numberless as sand along the seashore. ⁹And I saw them as they went up on the broad plain of the earth and surrounded God's people and the beloved city. But fire from heaven came down on the attacking armies and consumed them.

¹⁰Then the devil, who had deceived them, was thrown into the fiery lake of burning sulfur, joining the beast and the false prophet. There they will be tormented day and night forever and ever.

¹¹And I saw a great white throne and the one sitting on it. The earth and sky fled from his presence, but they found no place to hide. ¹²I saw the dead, both great and small, standing before God's throne. And the books were opened, including the Book of Life. And the dead were judged according to what they had done, as recorded in the books. ¹³The sea gave up its dead, and death and the grave* gave up their dead. And all were judged according to their deeds. ¹⁴Then death and the grave were thrown into the lake of fire. This lake of fire is the second death. ¹⁵And anyone whose

HOW WE LIVE

Worshiping God

ZECHARIAH 14:9, 20-21 Worship doesn't have to occur only on Sunday mornings at church; worship can be a part of everyday life. Zechariah pictures a day when God alone will be worshiped—obviously that's a prophecy yet to be fulfilled. On that day, every item in the city will be holy because God will fill everything with his presence. • The true fulfillment is future, but with God's Spirit residing in your life, you have been made holy. That means, as you walk through life, you can experience what it means to worship God at all times. You can worship God as you change a baby's diaper. You can worship God as you wash your dishes. You can worship God as you answer those e-mails or prepare that assignment. You can worship God as you wait in the airport for that next business trip. • Get the picture? You show your love for God by your worship—and every part of your life can be an act of worship to him by your attitudes, your actions, and your focus. Ask God to infuse your life with worship. Imagine what a joy each moment can be!

name was not found recorded in the Book of Life was thrown into the lake of fire.

20:1 Or *the abyss,* or *the underworld;* also in 20:3.
20:13 Greek *and Hades;* also in 20:14.

PSALM 148:1-14

Praise the LORD!

Praise the LORD from the heavens!
Praise him from the skies!
[2] Praise him, all his angels!
Praise him, all the armies of heaven!
[3] Praise him, sun and moon!
Praise him, all you twinkling stars!
[4] Praise him, skies above!
Praise him, vapors high above
the clouds!
[5] Let every created thing give praise
to the LORD,
for he issued his command,
and they came into being.
[6] He set them in place forever and ever.
His decree will never be revoked.

[7] Praise the LORD from the earth,
you creatures of the ocean depths,
[8] fire and hail, snow and clouds,*
wind and weather that obey him,

[9] mountains and all hills,
fruit trees and all cedars,
[10] wild animals and all livestock,
small scurrying animals and
birds,
[11] kings of the earth and all people,
rulers and judges of the earth,
[12] young men and young women,
old men and children.

[13] Let them all praise the name
of the LORD.
For his name is very great;
his glory towers over the earth and
heaven!
[14] He has made his people strong,
honoring his faithful ones—
the people of Israel who are close
to him.

Praise the LORD!

148:8 Or *mist,* or *smoke.*

PROVERBS 31:8-9

Speak up for those who cannot speak for themselves; ensure justice for those being crushed. Yes, speak up for the poor and helpless, and see that they get justice.

DECEMBER**30**

MALACHI 1:1–2:17

Malachi ministered to his people after they returned from their exile and during the rebuilding of Jerusalem. He confronted them about neglecting the Temple and worshiping with mere ritual and no heart.

This is the message* that the LORD gave to Israel through the prophet Malachi.*

[2]"I have always loved you," says the LORD.
But you retort, "Really? How have you loved us?"

And the LORD replies, "This is how I showed my love for you: I loved your ancestor Jacob, [3] but I rejected his brother, Esau, and devastated his hill country. I turned Esau's inheritance into a desert for jackals."

[4]Esau's descendants in Edom may say, "We have been shattered, but we will rebuild the ruins."

But the LORD of Heaven's Armies replies,

"They may try to rebuild, but I will demolish them again. Their country will be known as 'The Land of Wickedness,' and their people will be called 'The People with Whom the LORD Is Forever Angry.' [5] When you see the destruction for yourselves, you will say, 'Truly, the LORD's greatness reaches far beyond Israel's borders!'"

[6]The LORD of Heaven's Armies says to the priests: "A son honors his father, and a servant respects his master. If I am your father and master, where are the honor and respect I deserve? You have shown contempt for my name!

"But you ask, 'How have we ever shown contempt for your name?'

[7]"You have shown contempt by offering defiled sacrifices on my altar.

"Then you ask, 'How have we defiled the sacrifices?*'

"You defile them by saying the altar of the LORD deserves no respect. [8]When you give blind animals as sacrifices, isn't that wrong? And isn't it wrong to offer animals that are crippled and diseased? Try giving gifts like that to your governor, and see how pleased he is!" says the LORD of Heaven's Armies.

[9]"Go ahead, beg God to be merciful to you! But when you bring that kind of offering, why should he show you any favor at all?" asks the LORD of Heaven's Armies.

[10]"How I wish one of you would shut the Temple doors so that these worthless sacrifices could not be offered! I am not pleased with you," says the LORD of Heaven's Armies, "and I will not accept your offerings. [11]But my name is honored* by people of other nations from morning till night. All around the world they offer* sweet incense and pure offerings in honor of my name. For my name is great among the nations," says the LORD of Heaven's Armies.

[12]"But you dishonor my name with your actions. By bringing contemptible food, you are saying it's all right to defile the Lord's table. [13]You say, 'It's too hard to serve the LORD,' and you turn up your noses at my commands," says the LORD of Heaven's Armies. "Think of it! Animals that are stolen and crippled and sick are being presented as offerings! Should I accept from you such offerings as these?" asks the LORD.

[14]"Cursed is the cheat who promises to give a fine ram from his flock but then sacrifices a defective one to the Lord. For I am a great king," says the LORD of Heaven's Armies, "and my name is feared among the nations!

[2:1]"LISTEN, you priests—this command is for you! [2]Listen to me and make up your minds to honor my name," says the LORD of Heaven's Armies, "or I will bring a terrible curse against you. I will curse even the blessings you receive. Indeed, I have already cursed them, because you have not taken my warning to heart. [3]I will punish your descendants and splatter your faces with the manure from your festival sacrifices, and I will throw you on the manure pile. [4]Then at last you will know it was I who sent you this warning so that my covenant with the Levites can continue," says the LORD of Heaven's Armies.

[5]"The purpose of my covenant with the Levites was to bring life and peace, and that is what I gave them. This required reverence from them, and they greatly revered me and stood in awe of my name. [6]They passed on to the people the truth of the instructions they received from me. They did not lie or cheat; they walked with me, living good and righteous lives, and they turned many from lives of sin.

[7]"The words of a priest's lips should preserve knowledge of God, and people should go to him for instruction, for the priest is the messenger of the LORD of Heaven's Armies. [8]But you priests have left God's paths. Your instructions have caused many to stumble into sin. You have corrupted the covenant I made with the Levites," says the LORD of Heaven's Armies. [9]"So I have made you despised and humiliated in the eyes of all the people. For you have not obeyed me but have shown favoritism in the way you carry out my instructions."

[10]Are we not all children of the same Father? Are we not all created by the same God? Then why do we betray each other, violating the covenant of our ancestors?

[11]Judah has been unfaithful, and a detestable thing has been done in Israel and in Jerusalem. The men of Judah have defiled the LORD's beloved sanctuary by marrying women who worship idols. [12]May the LORD cut off from the nation of Israel* every last man who has done this and yet brings an offering to the LORD of Heaven's Armies.

[13]Here is another thing you do. You cover the LORD's altar with tears, weeping and groaning because he pays no attention to your offerings and doesn't accept them with pleasure. [14]You cry out, "Why doesn't the LORD accept my worship?" I'll tell you why! Because the LORD witnessed the vows you and your wife made when you were young. But you have been unfaithful to her, though she remained your faithful partner, the wife of your marriage vows.

[15]Didn't the LORD make you one with your wife? In body and spirit you are his.* And what does he want? Godly children

from your union. So guard your heart; remain loyal to the wife of your youth. [16]"For I hate divorce!" says the LORD, the God of Israel. "To divorce your wife is to overwhelm her with cruelty,*" says the LORD of Heaven's Armies. "So guard your heart; do not be unfaithful to your wife."

[17]You have wearied the LORD with your words.

"How have we wearied him?" you ask.

You have wearied him by saying that all who do evil are good in the LORD's sight, and he is pleased with them. You have wearied him by asking, "Where is the God of justice?"

1:1a Hebrew *An Oracle: The message.*   1:1b *Malachi* means "my messenger."   1:7 As in Greek version; Hebrew reads *defiled you?*   1:11a Or *will be honored.*   1:11b Or *will offer.*   2:12 Hebrew *from the tents of Jacob.* The names "Jacob" and "Israel" are often interchanged throughout the Old Testament, referring sometimes to the individual patriarch and sometimes to the nation.   2:15 Or *Didn't the one LORD make us and preserve our life and breath?* or *Didn't the one LORD make her, both flesh and spirit?* The meaning of the Hebrew is uncertain.   2:16 Hebrew *to cover one's garment with violence.*

REVELATION 21:1-27
John is given access to a new and better world. It is a world completely filled with God's presence.

Then I [John] saw a new heaven and a new earth, for the old heaven and the old earth had disappeared. And the sea was also gone. [2]And I saw the holy city, the new Jerusalem, coming down from God out of heaven like a bride beautifully dressed for her husband.

[3]I heard a loud shout from the throne, saying, "Look, God's home is now among his people! He will live with them, and they will be his people. God himself will be with them.* [4]He will wipe every tear from their eyes, and there will be no more death or sorrow or crying or pain. All these things are gone forever."

[5]And the one sitting on the throne said, "Look, I am making everything new!" And then he said to me, "Write this down, for what I tell you is trustworthy and true." [6]And he also said, "It is finished! I am the Alpha and the Omega—the Beginning and the End. To all who are thirsty I will give freely from the springs of the water of life. [7]All who are victorious will inherit all these blessings, and I will be their God, and they will be my children.

[8]"But cowards, unbelievers, the cor-rupt, murderers, the immoral, those who practice witchcraft, idol worshipers, and all liars—their fate is in the fiery lake of burning sulfur. This is the second death."

[9]Then one of the seven angels who held the seven bowls containing the seven last plagues came and said to me, "Come with me! I will show you the bride, the wife of the Lamb."

[10]So he took me in the Spirit* to a great, high mountain, and he showed me the holy city, Jerusalem, descending out of heaven from God. [11]It shone with the glory of God and sparkled like a precious stone—like jasper as clear as crystal. [12]The city wall was broad and high, with twelve gates guarded by twelve angels. And the names of the twelve tribes of Israel were written on the gates. [13]There were three gates on each side—east, north, south, and west. [14]The wall of the city had twelve foundation stones, and on them were written the names of the twelve apostles of the Lamb.

[15]The angel who talked to me held in his hand a gold measuring stick to measure the city, its gates, and its wall. [16]When he measured it, he found it was a square, as wide as it was long. In fact, its length and width and height were each 1,400 miles.* [17]Then he measured the walls and found them to be 216 feet thick* (according to the human standard used by the angel).

[18]The wall was made of jasper, and the city was pure gold, as clear as glass. [19]The wall of the city was built on foundation stones inlaid with twelve precious stones:* the first was jasper, the second sapphire, the third agate, the fourth emerald, [20]the fifth onyx, the sixth carnelian, the seventh chrysolite, the eighth beryl, the ninth topaz, the tenth chrysoprase, the eleventh jacinth, the twelfth amethyst.

[21]The twelve gates were made of pearls—each gate from a single pearl! And the main street was pure gold, as clear as glass.

[22]I saw no temple in the city, for the Lord God Almighty and the Lamb are its temple. [23]And the city has no need of sun or moon, for the glory of God illuminates the city, and the Lamb is its light. [24]The nations will walk in its light, and the kings of the world will enter the city in all their glory. [25]Its gates will never be closed at the end of day because there is no night there.

²⁶And all the nations will bring their glory and honor into the city. ²⁷Nothing evil* will be allowed to enter, nor anyone who practices shameful idolatry and dishonesty—but only those whose names are written in the Lamb's Book of Life.

21:3 Some manuscripts read *God himself will be with them, their God.*   21:10 Or *in spirit.*   21:16 Greek *12,000 stadia* [2,220 kilometers].   21:17 Greek *144 cubits* [65 meters].   21:19 The identification of some of these gemstones is uncertain.   21:27 Or *ceremonially unclean.*

PSALM 149:1-9

Praise the LORD!

Sing to the LORD a new song.
Sing his praises in the assembly
of the faithful.
² O Israel, rejoice in your Maker.
O people of Jerusalem,* exult
in your King.
³ Praise his name with dancing,
accompanied by tambourine
and harp.
⁴ For the LORD delights in his people;
he crowns the humble with victory.
⁵ Let the faithful rejoice that he honors
them.
Let them sing for joy as they lie
on their beds.
⁶ Let the praises of God be in their
mouths,
and a sharp sword in their hands—

⁷ to execute vengeance on the nations
and punishment on the peoples,
⁸ to bind their kings with shackles
and their leaders with iron chains,
⁹ to execute the judgment written
against them.
This is the glorious privilege of his
faithful ones.

Praise the LORD!

149:2 Hebrew *Zion.*

PROVERBS 31:10-24

*Who can find a virtuous and capable wife? She is more precious than rubies. Her husband can trust her, and she will greatly enrich his life. She brings him good, not harm, all the days of her life. ▫She finds wool and flax and busily spins it. She is like a merchant's ship, bringing her food from afar. She gets up before dawn to prepare breakfast for her household and plan the day's work for her servant girls. ▫She goes to inspect a field and buys it; with her earnings she plants a vineyard. She is energetic and strong, a hard worker. She makes sure her dealings are profitable; her lamp burns late into the night. ▫Her hands are busy spinning thread, her fingers twisting fiber. She extends a helping hand to the poor and opens her arms to the needy. She has no fear of winter for her household, for

HOW WE LIVE Our marriages

MALACHI 2:16 God flat-out states, "I hate divorce!" The people of Israel were much like people today—divorcing for no other reason than a desire for a change or because of rampant infidelity. They didn't want to follow God's plan then, and people continue to ignore his plan for marriage today. • God made a commitment to us by offering his Son as a sacrifice for our sin. What would we do if he suddenly decided to break his commitment? The union we have with God is unbreakable because he promised to be faithful to us. He will never go back on his word. • Your home should be a place where unconditional love is practiced as an example to your spouse and to your children. Although it may not always be easy, forgiveness is an essential part of marriage. Holding a grudge or nagging about mistakes long past does nothing to foster a spirit of unity. Treat your spouse and children in the same way God has treated you—with dignity, respect, honor, and love. When you decide that divorce is not an option, and when you make your marriage a place of stability, you are honoring God in your marriage.

everyone has warm* clothes. □ She makes her own bedspreads. She dresses in fine linen and purple gowns. Her husband is well known at the city gates, where he sits with the other civic leaders. She makes

belted linen garments and sashes to sell to the merchants.

31:10 Verses 10-31 comprise a Hebrew acrostic poem; each verse begins with a successive letter of the Hebrew alphabet.　**31:21** As in Greek and Latin versions; Hebrew reads *scarlet*.

DECEMBER**31**

MALACHI 3:1–4:6

Malachi gives two key messages in this section. First is the command to give to God from our income; not to do so amounts to stealing. Second is the prophecy that Elijah would come (4:5). Jesus said this prophecy was fulfilled in John the Baptist (Mark 9:12-13, February 27).

"**L**ook! I [the LORD] am sending my messenger, and he will prepare the way before me. Then the Lord you are seeking will suddenly come to his Temple. The messenger of the covenant, whom you look for so eagerly, is surely coming," says the LORD of Heaven's Armies.

²"But who will be able to endure it when he comes? Who will be able to stand and face him when he appears? For he will be like a blazing fire that refines metal, or like a strong soap that bleaches clothes. ³He will sit like a refiner of silver, burning away the dross. He will purify the Levites, refining them like gold and silver, so that they may once again offer acceptable sacrifices to the LORD. ⁴Then once more the LORD will accept the offerings brought to him by the people of Judah and Jerusalem, as he did in the past.

⁵"At that time I will put you on trial. I am eager to witness against all sorcerers and adulterers and liars. I will speak against those who cheat employees of their wages, who oppress widows and orphans, or who deprive the foreigners living among you of justice, for these people do not fear me," says the LORD of Heaven's Armies.

⁶"I am the LORD, and I do not change. That is why you descendants of Jacob are not already destroyed. ⁷Ever since the days of your ancestors, you have scorned my decrees and failed to obey them. Now

return to me, and I will return to you," says the LORD of Heaven's Armies.

"But you ask, 'How can we return when we have never gone away?'

⁸"Should people cheat God? Yet you have cheated me!

"But you ask, 'What do you mean? When did we ever cheat you?'

"You have cheated me of the tithes and offerings due to me. ⁹You are under a curse, for your whole nation has been cheating me. ¹⁰Bring all the tithes into the storehouse so there will be enough food in my Temple. If you do," says the LORD of Heaven's Armies, "I will open the windows of heaven for you. I will pour out a blessing so great you won't have enough room to take it in! Try it! Put me to the test! ¹¹Your crops will be abundant, for I will guard them from insects and disease.* Your grapes will not fall from the vine before they are ripe," says the LORD of Heaven's Armies. ¹²"Then all nations will call you blessed, for your land will be such a delight," says the LORD of Heaven's Armies.

¹³"You have said terrible things about me," says the LORD.

"But you say, 'What do you mean? What have we said against you?'

¹⁴"You have said, 'What's the use of serving God? What have we gained by obeying his commands or by trying to show the LORD of Heaven's Armies that we are sorry for our sins? ¹⁵From now on we will call the arrogant blessed. For those who do evil get rich, and those who dare God to punish them suffer no harm.'"

¹⁶Then those who feared the LORD spoke with each other, and the LORD listened to what they said. In his presence, a scroll of remembrance was written to re-

cord the names of those who feared him and always thought about the honor of his name.

[17]"They will be my people," says the LORD of Heaven's Armies. "On the day when I act in judgment, they will be my own special treasure. I will spare them as a father spares an obedient child. [18]Then you will again see the difference between the righteous and the wicked, between those who serve God and those who do not."

[4:1]*THE LORD of Heaven's Armies says, "The day of judgment is coming, burning like a furnace. On that day the arrogant and the wicked will be burned up like straw. They will be consumed—roots, branches, and all.

[2]"But for you who fear my name, the Sun of Righteousness will rise with healing in his wings.* And you will go free, leaping with joy like calves let out to pasture. [3]On the day when I act, you will tread upon the wicked as if they were dust under your feet," says the LORD of Heaven's Armies.

[4]"Remember to obey the Law of Moses, my servant—all the decrees and regulations that I gave him on Mount Sinai* for all Israel.

[5]"Look, I am sending you the prophet Elijah before the great and dreadful day

of the LORD arrives. [6]His preaching will turn the hearts of fathers to their children, and the hearts of children to their fathers. Otherwise I will come and strike the land with a curse."

3:11 Hebrew *from the devourer.*   **4:1** Verses 4:1-6 are numbered 3:19-24 in Hebrew text.   **4:2** Or *the sun of righteousness will rise with healing in its wings.*   **4:4** Hebrew *Horeb,* another name for Sinai.

REVELATION 22:1-21
John's prophecy closes with an invitation and a warning. The time is coming when God will judge the world. Those who follow Jesus have the hope of eternal life in God's presence. The consequences of rejecting Jesus are grave.

Then the angel showed me a river with the water of life, clear as crystal, flowing from the throne of God and of the Lamb. [2]It flowed down the center of the main street. On each side of the river grew a tree of life, bearing twelve crops of fruit,* with a fresh crop each month. The leaves were used for medicine to heal the nations.

[3]No longer will there be a curse upon anything. For the throne of God and of the Lamb will be there, and his servants will worship him. [4]And they will see his face, and his name will be written on their foreheads. [5]And there will be no night there—no need for lamps or sun—for the Lord

WHAT THE BIBLE SAYS

The reality of heaven

REVELATION 22:1-6 Today's readings are all the "lasts" for the year—the last proverbs, the last psalm, the last prophecies. It's a good day to think about heaven because heaven is a grand mix of lasts and firsts. Revelation 22 describes many things about heaven, but most of it can be summed up in verse 3: "No longer will there be a curse upon anything." Remember the curses from the Garden of Eden? The serpent, the woman Eve, and the man Adam all received the consequences of the great falling out of innocence (Genesis 3:14-19, January 2). When this world is over and God's redemption is complete, nothing will be cursed. • Heaven is unimaginable to us at this time because we are so used to the process of death and destruction. We've come to expect it, to incorporate it into our existence. Everything around us is in a state of decay, including ourselves. Heaven will not have that element. Everything will be shiny and new—not decaying, but flourishing; not cursed, but redeemed; not temporary, but eternal. And there we "will reign forever and ever" in the presence of our glorious God, whose majesty will consume our hearts and minds for eternity.

God will shine on them. And they will reign forever and ever.

[6]Then the angel said to me, "Everything you have heard and seen is trustworthy and true. The Lord God, who inspires his prophets,* has sent his angel to tell his servants what will happen soon.*"

[7]"Look, I am coming soon! Blessed are those who obey the words of prophecy written in this book.*"

[8]I, John, am the one who heard and saw all these things. And when I heard and saw them, I fell down to worship at the feet of the angel who showed them to me. [9]But he said, "No, don't worship me. I am a servant of God, just like you and your brothers the prophets, as well as all who obey what is written in this book. Worship only God!"

[10]Then he instructed me, "Do not seal up the prophetic words in this book, for the time is near. [11]Let the one who is doing harm continue to do harm; let the one who is vile continue to be vile; let the one who is righteous continue to live righteously; let the one who is holy continue to be holy."

[12]"Look, I am coming soon, bringing my reward with me to repay all people according to their deeds. [13]I am the Alpha and the Omega, the First and the Last, the Beginning and the End."

[14]Blessed are those who wash their robes. They will be permitted to enter through the gates of the city and eat the fruit from the tree of life. [15]Outside the city are the dogs—the sorcerers, the sexually immoral, the murderers, the idol worshipers, and all who love to live a lie.

[16]"I, Jesus, have sent my angel to give you this message for the churches. I am both the source of David and the heir to his throne.* I am the bright morning star."

[17]The Spirit and the bride say, "Come." Let anyone who hears this say, "Come." Let anyone who is thirsty come. Let anyone who desires drink freely from the water of life. [18]And I solemnly declare to everyone who hears the words of prophecy

written in this book: If anyone adds anything to what is written here, God will add to that person the plagues described in this book. [19]And if anyone removes any of the words from this book of prophecy, God will remove that person's share in the tree of life and in the holy city that are described in this book.

[20]He who is the faithful witness to all these things says, "Yes, I am coming soon!" Amen! Come, Lord Jesus!

[21]May the grace of the Lord Jesus be with God's holy people.*

22:2 Or *twelve kinds of fruit.* **22:6a** Or *The Lord, the God of the spirits of the prophets.* **22:6b** Or *suddenly,* or *quickly;* also in 22:7, 12, 20. **22:7** Or *scroll;* also in 22:9, 10, 18, 19. **22:16** Greek *I am the root and offspring of David.* **22:21** Other manuscripts read *be with all;* still others read *be with all of God's holy people.* Some manuscripts add *Amen.*

PSALM 150:1-6

Praise the LORD!

Praise God in his sanctuary;
　　praise him in his mighty heaven!
[2] Praise him for his mighty works;
　　praise his unequaled greatness!
[3] Praise him with a blast of the ram's horn;
　　praise him with the lyre and harp!
[4] Praise him with the tambourine and dancing;
　　praise him with strings and flutes!
[5] Praise him with a clash of cymbals;
　　praise him with loud clanging cymbals.
[6] Let everything that breathes sing praises to the LORD!

Praise the LORD!

PROVERBS 31:25-31

She is clothed with strength and dignity, and she laughs without fear of the future. When she speaks, her words are wise, and she gives instructions with kindness. She carefully watches everything in her household and suffers nothing from laziness. ☐ Her children stand and bless her. Her husband praises her: "There are many virtuous and capable women in the world, but you surpass them all!" ☐ Charm is deceptive, and beauty does not last; but a woman who fears the LORD will be greatly praised. Reward her for all she has done. Let her deeds publicly declare her praise.